HARRAP'S

Spanish–English
Inglés–Español

MINI
Dictionary/Diccionario

HARRAP'S

MINI

Spanish

DICTIONARY

HARRAP

Distributed in the United States by
Macmillan ∎ **USA**

First published in Great Britain 1992 by HARRAP BOOKS Ltd
43–45 Annandale Street, Edinburgh EH7 4AZ, Scotland

This dictionary is a shortened version of *Harrap's Concise Spanish and English Dictionary*. The project management was carried out by LEXUS LTD.

El presente diccionario es una versión abreviada del *Harrap's Concise Spanish and English Dictionary*. La direcciòn del proyecto corrió a cargo de LEXUS LTD.

Editors/Redactores:
Joaquín Blasco   Fernando León Solis   Hugh O'Donnell

In the United States, ISBN 0-13-381005-4

Library of Congress Cataloging-in-Publication Data

Harrap's mini Spanish dictionary.

p.   cm.

1. Spanish Language — Dictionaries — English.
2. English Language — Dictionaries — Spanish.

PC4640.H34   1992   92-8271
463'.21—dc20   CIP

MACMILLAN is a trademark of Macmillan, Inc. registered

Preface

This dictionary is a shortened version of *Harrap's Concise Spanish and English Dictionary*. The selection of headwords and phrases - over 57,000 in total - is aimed at providing a broad coverage of modern English and Spanish, including a considerable number of important Latin American and North American terms.

The new system for Spanish alphabetical order has been adopted. In this system 'ch' and 'll' are no longer considered as separate letters of the alphabet, but are each incorporated at their respective alphabetical positions under 'c' and 'l' - 'ñ', however, is treated as a separate letter.

Entries are divided into grammatical categories by Roman numerals (I, II etc) and into sense categories by Arabic numerals (1, 2 etc). A lozenge ◆ has been used i) to highlight adverbs which have been placed directly after their related adjective (for example: happily/happy) and which are not always therefore in strict alphabetical order and ii) to identify phrasal verbs (give up, come out, send back etc).

A major feature of this introductory dictionary is the systematic use of signposting to guide users and to enable them to identify the translation they require quickly and accurately. There are two main types of signpost: **field labels** (of which a complete list is given on pages vii-x) identify the area of usage of a word, for example: *Ftb* is for football, *Comput* is for computers. **Indicators** show, for example, what might be the typical subject or object of a verb or what might be the typical noun used with a certain adjective. These help the user to identify the correct translation for a particular word by showing the context in which a certain translation is appropriate.

Gender markers for Spanish translations are not given where the presence of an adjective makes the gender of a noun self-evident. For example 'centro deportivo' has no gender marker whereas 'centro *m* comercial' does.

Spanish verbs with irregular conjugations are coded ([12], [24] etc). By looking at the information in the introductory section on pages xii-xxi it is possible to work out the form of an irregular Spanish verb in any required tense or person. A list of irregular English verbs is given on pages (ii)-(iv) of the English-Spanish section.

Full IPA (International Phonetic Alphabet) pronunciation is given for English headwords in the English-Spanish part of the dictionary with a guide to IPA on pages (v)-(vi) of the introduction. There is also an introduction to Spanish pronunciation on pages xxii-xxiii of the Spanish-English part of the dictionary.

Prólogo

El presente diccionario es una versión abreviada del *Harrap's Concise Spanish and English Dictionary*. La selección de las entradas y frases idiomáticas - más de 57000 en total - tiene como objetivo ofrecer una amplia cobertura del inglés y del español actuales, incluído un número importante de términos usados en Latinoamérica y Norteamérica.

Se ha adoptado la nueva ordenación alfabética del español. Según ésta, los dígrafos "ch" y "ll" no se consideran letras independientes, sino que ocupan el lugar que les corresponde alfabéticamente dentro de la "c" y "l", respectivamente. La "ñ", sin embargo, se considera letra independiente.

Las diferentes categorías gramaticales de una misma entrada se señalan mediante números romanos (I, II, etc), mientras que la numeración árabe (1, 2, etc) indica las diferentes categorías semánticas. Se utilizan los rombos ◆ para i) resaltar los adverbios colocados justo después del adjetivo del que derivan (por ejemplo: justo/justamente) y que no siguen, por tanto, un riguroso orden alfabético y ii) para identificar los "phrasal verbs" (give up, come out, send back etc).

Una característica relevante de esta obra es el uso sistemático de señales indicadoras que orientan al usuario y le permiten identificar la traducción adecuada con rapidez y precisión. Hay dos tipos de señales indicadoras: las **abreviaturas de campo semántico** (de las que aparece una lista completa en las páginas vii-x) identifican el área de uso de una palabra, por ejemplo: *Ftb* es fútbol, *Inform* es informática. Los **indicadores** muestran, por ejemplo, un sujeto o un objeto típicos de un verbo, o un sustantivo que frecuentemente acompaña a determinado adjetivo. Estos ayudan al usuario a identificar la traducción correcta de una determinada palabra al mostrar el contexto adecuado para cada traducción.

Los indicadores de género de las traducciones españolas no aparecerán cuando la presencia de un adjetivo deje claro el género del sustantivo. Por ejemplo "centro deportivo" no lleva indicador de género, mientras que, por el contrario, sí aparece en "centro m comercial".

Los verbos españoles de conjugación irregular vienen seguidos de un número de referencia ([12], [24] etc). En la sección introductoria, en las páginas xii-xxi, viene dada la información necesaria para poder conjugar los verbos irregulares en español. Una lista de verbos irregulares del inglés aparece en las páginas (ii)-(iv) de la sección Inglés-Español.

Las entradas inglesas de la sección Inglés-Español del diccionario van acompañadas de una transcripción fonética basada en el Alfabeto Fonético Internacional (AFI). En la página (v)-(vi) de la introducción de la sección Inglés-Español aparece una guía explicativa de dicho alfabeto. También viene dada una guía introductoria de pronunciación española en las páginas xxii-xxiii de la sección Español-Inglés.

Abbreviations used in this dictionary
Abreviaturas usadas en este diccionario

abbreviation	*abbr, abr*	abreviatura
adjective	*adj*	adjetivo
adverb	*adv*	adverbio
agriculture	*Agr*	agricultura
chess	*Ajedrez*	
somebody, someone	*algn*	alguien
Latin American	*Am*	hispanoamericano
anatomy	*Anat*	anatomía
approximately	*approx, aprox*	aproximadamente
archaic	*arc, arch*	arcaico
architecture	*Archit*	arquitectura
slang	*arg*	argot
architecture	*Arquit*	arquitectura
article	*art*	artículo
art	*Art, Arte*	bellas artes
astronomy	*Astron*	astronomía
	Astronaut,	
space travel	*Astronáut*	astronáutica
Australian	*Austral*	australiano
motoring	*Aut*	automóviles
auxiliary	*aux*	auxiliar
aviation	*Av*	aviación
biology	*Biol*	biología
bowling	*Bolos*	
botany	*Bot*	botánica
	Bowling	bolos
boxing	*Box*	boxeo
Canary Islands	*Can*	Canarias
	Cards	naipes
chemistry	*Chem*	químico
	Chess	ajedrez
cycling	*Cicl*	ciclismo
cinema	*Cin*	cine
commerce	*Com*	comercio
comparative	*comp*	comparativo
computers	*Comput*	informática
conditional	*cond*	condicional
conjunction	*conj*	conjunción
building industry	*Constr*	construcción
sewing	*Cost*	costura
cookery	*Culin*	cocina
cycling	*Cycl*	ciclismo
definite	*def*	definido
defective	*defect*	defectivo
demonstrative	*dem*	demostrativo
sport	*Dep*	deporte
ecology	*Ecol*	ecología
economics	*Econ*	economía
education	*Educ*	educación
electricity	*Elec*	electricidad
entomology	*Ent*	entomología
especially	*esp*	especialmente
only in Spain	*Esp*	solo en España
etcetera	*etc*	etcétera

English	Abbreviation	Spanish
euphemism	*euf, euph*	eufemismo
exclamatory	*exclam*	exclamativo
feminine	*f*	femenino
familiar	*fam*	familiar
pharmacy	*Farm*	farmacia
railways	*Ferroc*	ferrocarriles
figurative use	*fig*	uso figurado
finance	*Fin*	finanzas
physics	*Fís*	física
	Fishing	pesca
formal use	*fml*	uso formal
photography	*Fot*	fotografía
feminine plural	*fpl*	plural femenino
football	*Ftb*	fútbol
future	*fut*	futuro
British	*GB*	británico
geography	*Geog*	geografía
geology	*Geol*	geología
geometry	*Geom*	geometría
present participle	*ger*	gerundio
gymnastics	*Gimn, Gym*	gimnasia
history	*Hist*	historia
humorous	*hum*	humorístico
imperative	*imperat*	imperativo
imperfect	*imperf*	imperfecto
impersonal	*impers*	impersonal
printing	*Impr*	imprenta
industry	*Ind*	industria
indefinite	*indef*	indefinido
indeterminate	*indet*	indeterminado
indicative	*indic*	indicativo
infinitive	*infin*	infinitivo
computers	*Inform*	informática
insurance	*Ins*	seguros
interjection	*interj*	interjección
interrogative	*interr*	interrogativo
invariable	*inv*	invariable
ironic	*iron*	irónico
irregular	*irreg*	irregular
law	*Jur*	derecho
linguistics	*Ling*	lingüística
literary	*lit*	literario
literature	*Lit*	literatura
phrase	*loc*	locución
masculine	*m*	masculino
mathematics	*Mat, Math*	matemáticas
medicine	*Med*	medicina
meteorology	*Meteor*	meteorología
military	*Mil*	militar
mining	*Min*	minas
masculine plural	*mpl*	plural masculino
music	*Mus, Mús*	música
noun	*n*	nombre
cards	*Naipes*	
swimming	*Natación*	
nautical	*Naut, Náut*	náutica
negative	*neg*	negativo

neuter	*neut*	neutro
feminine noun	*nf*	nombre femenino
plural feminine noun	*nfpl*	nombre femenino plural
masculine noun	*nm*	nombre masculino
masculine and feminine noun	*nmflnm,f*	nombre masculino y femenino
plural masculine noun	*nmpl*	nombre masculino plural
plural noun	*npl*	nombre plural
obsolete	*obs*	obsoleto
offensive	*ofens, offens*	ofensivo
optics	*Opt*	óptica
ornithology	*Orn*	ornitología
Parliament	*Parl*	parlamento
pejorative	*pej*	peyorativo
personal	*pers*	personal
fishing	*Pesca*	
petroleum industry	*Petrol, Petról*	industria petrolera
pejorative	*pey*	peyorativo
pharmacy	*Pharm*	farmacia
photography	*Phot*	fotografía
physics	*Phys*	física
plural	*pl*	plural
politics	*Pol*	política
possessive	*pos, poss*	posesivo
past participle	*pp*	participio pasado
prefix	*pref*	prefijo
press	*Prensa*	
preposition	*prep*	preposición
present	*pres*	presente
present participle	*pres p*	gerundio
	Press	prensa
preterite	*pret*	pretérito
printing	*Print*	imprenta
pronoun	*pron*	pronombre
psychology	*Psic, Psych*	psicología
past tense	*pt*	pretérito
chemistry	*Quím*	químico
radio	*Rad*	radio
railways	*Rail*	ferrocarriles
relative	*rel*	relativo
religion	*Rel*	religión
somebody, someone	*sb*	alguien
Scottish	*Scot*	escocés
insurance	*Seg*	seguros
sewing	*Sew*	costura
singular	*sing*	singular
slang	*sl*	argot
Spanish	*Span*	español
something	*sth*	algo
subjunctive	*subj*	subjuntivo
suffix	*suf, suff*	sufijo
superlative	*superl*	superlativo
	Swimming	natación
also	*tamb*	también
bullfighting	*Taur*	tauromaquia

theatre	*Teat*	teatro
technical	*Téc, Tech*	técnica
telephones	*Tel*	teléfonos
telecommunications	*Telec*	telecomunicaciones
tennis	*Ten*	tenis
textiles	*Tex*	textiles
theatre	*Theat*	teatro
typography	*Tip*	tipografía
television	*TV*	televisión
typography	*Typ*	tipografía
university	*Univ*	universidad
United States	*US*	Estados Unidos
usually	*usu*	usualmente
verb	*v*	verbo
auxiliary verb	*v aux*	verbo auxiliar
veterinary medicine	*Vet*	veterinaria
intransitive verb	*vi*	verbo intransitivo
impersonal verb	*v impers*	verbo impersonal
reflexive verb	*vr*	verbo reflexivo
transitive verb	*vtr*	verbo transitivo
vulgar	*vulg*	vulgar
zoology	*Zool*	zoología
see	→	véase
cultural equivalent	≈	equivalencia cultural
registered trade mark	®	marca registrada

Spanish - English
Español - Inglés

SPANISH VERBS

Regular Spelling Changes

The rules of spelling in Spanish cause a number of verbs to have regular spelling changes. These are listed below.

Spanish verbs fall into three groups depending on whether their infinitive ends in **-ar**, **-er** or **-ir**. The stem of the verb is the part which is left when the **-ar**, **-er** or **-ir** is removed from the infinitive. For example, the stem of **tomar** is **tom**, the stem of **beber** is **beb**, and the stem of **salir** is **sal**.

In the lists given below, the following indicators are used:

> **(1)** = first person singular present indicative
> **(2)** = present subjunctive, all persons
> **(3)** = first person singular preterite

Verbs ending in -ar

Verbs with a stem ending in **c**, for example **buscar**

The **c** changes to **qu** in:

> **(2)** busque, busques, busque, busquemos, busquéis, busquen
> **(3)** busqué

Verbs with a stem ending in **g**, for example **cargar**

The **g** changes to **gu** in:

> **(2)** cargue, cargues, cargue, carguemos, carguéis, carguen
> **(3)** cargué

Verbs with a stem ending in **gu**, for example **averiguar**

The **gu** changes to **gü** in:

> **(2)** averigüe, averigües, averigüe, averigüemos, averigüéis, averigüen
> **(3)** averigüé

Verbs with a stem ending in **z**, for example **realizar**

The **z** changes to **c** in:

> **(2)** realice, realices, realice, realicemos, realicéis, realicen
> **(3)** realicé

Verbs ending in -er *or* -ir

Verbs with a stem ending in c, for example **esparcir**

The c changes to z in:

> (1) esparzo
> (2) esparza, esparzas, esparza, esparzamos, esparzáis, esparzan

Verbs with a stem ending in g, for example **coger**

The g changes to j in:

> (1) cojo
> (2) coja, cojas, coja, cojamos, cojáis, cojan

Verbs with a stem ending in qu, for example **delinquir**

The qu changes to c in:

> (1) delinco
> (2) delinca, delincas, delinca, delincamos, delincáis, delincan

Verbs with a stem ending in gu, for example **distinguir**

The gu changes to g in:

> (1) distingo
> (2) distinga, distingas, distinga, distingamos, distingáis, distingan

Models for regular conjugation

TOMAR to take

INDICATIVE

PRESENT	**FUTURE**	**CONDITIONAL**
1. tomo	tomaré	tomaría
2. tomas	tomarás	tomarías
3. toma	tomará	tomaría
1. tomamos	tomaremos	tomaríamos
2. tomáis	tomaréis	tomaríais
3. toman	tomarán	tomarían

IMPERFECT	**PRETERITE**	**PERFECT**
1. tomaba	tomé	he tomado
2. tomabas	tomaste	has tomado
3. tomaba	tomó	ha tomado
1. tomábamos	tomamos	hemos tomado
2. tomabais	tomasteis	habéis tomado
3. tomaban	tomaron	han tomado

FUTURE PERFECT	**CONDITIONAL PERFECT**	**PLUPERFECT**
1. habré tomado	habría tomado	había tomado
2. habrás tomado	habrías tomado	habías tomado
3. habrá tomado	habría tomado	había tomado
1. habremos tomado	habríamos tomado	habíamos tomado
2. habréis tomado	habríais tomado	habíais tomado
3. habrán tomado	habrían tomado	habían tomado

SUBJUNCTIVE

PRESENT	**IMPERFECT**	**PERFECT/PLUPERFECT**
1. tome	tom-ara/ase	haya/hubiera* tomado
2. tomes	tom-aras/ases	hayas/hubieras tomado
3. tome	tom-ara/ase	haya/hubiera tomado
1. tomemos	tom-áramos/ásemos	hayamos/hubiéramos tomado
2. toméis	tom-arais/aseis	hayáis/hubierais tomado
3. tomen	tom-aran/asen	hayan/hubieran tomado

IMPERATIVE	*INFINITIVE*	*PARTICIPLE*
(tú) toma	**PRESENT**	**PRESENT**
(Vd) tome	tomar	tomando
(nosotros) tomemos		
(vosotros) tomad	**PERFECT**	**PAST**
(Vds) tomen	haber tomado	tomado

* the alternative form 'hubiese' etc is also possible

xiv

COMER to eat

INDICATIVE

PRESENT	FUTURE	CONDITIONAL
1. como	comeré	comería
2. comes	comerás	comerías
3. come	comerá	comería
1. comemos	comeremos	comeríamos
2. coméis	comeréis	comeríais
3. comen	comerán	comerían

IMPERFECT	PRETERITE	PERFECT
1. comía	comí	he comido
2. comías	comiste	has comido
3. comía	comió	ha comido
1. comíamos	comimos	hemos comido
2. comíais	comisteis	habéis comido
3. comían	comieron	han comido

FUTURE PERFECT	CONDITIONAL PERFECT	PLUPERFECT
1. habré comido	habría comido	había comido
2. habrás comido	habrías comido	habías comido
3. habrá comido	habría comido	había comido
1. habremos comido	habríamos comido	habíamos comido
2. habréis comido	habríais comido	habíais comido
3. habrán comido	habrían comido	habían comido

SUBJUNCTIVE

PRESENT	IMPERFECT	PERFECT/PLUPERFECT
1. coma	com-iera/iese	haya/hubiera* comido
2. comas	com-ieras/ieses	hayas/hubieras comido
3. coma	com-iera/iese	haya/hubiera comido
1. comamos	com-iéramos/iésemos	hayamos/hubiéramos comido
2. comáis	com-ierais/ieseis	hayáis/hubierais comido
3. coman	com-ieran/iesen	hayan/hubieran comido

IMPERATIVE	*INFINITIVE*	*PARTICIPLE*
(tú) come	**PRESENT**	**PRESENT**
(Vd) coma	comer	comiendo
(nosotros) comamos		
(vosotros) comed	**PERFECT**	**PAST**
(Vds) coman	haber comido	comido

* the alternative form 'hubiese' etc is also possible

xv

PARTIR to leave

INDICATIVE

PRESENT	**FUTURE**	**CONDITIONAL**
1. parto	partiré	partiría
2. partes	partirás	partirías
3. parte	partirá	partiría
1. partimos	partiremos	partiríamos
2. partís	partiréis	partiríais
3. parten	partirán	partirían

IMPERFECT	**PRETERITE**	**PERFECT**
1. partía	partí	he partido
2. partías	partiste	has partido
3. partía	partió	ha partido
1. partíamos	partimos	hemos partido
2. partíais	partisteis	habéis partido
3. partían	partieron	han partido

FUTURE PERFECT	**CONDITIONAL PERFECT**	**PLUPERFECT**
1. habré partido	habría partido	había partido
2. habrás partido	habrías partido	habías partido
3. habrá partido	habría partido	había partido
1. habremos partido	habríamos partido	habíamos partido
2. habréis partido	habríais partido	habíais partido
3. habrán partido	habrían partido	habían partido

SUBJUNCTIVE

PRESENT	**IMPERFECT**	**PERFECT/PLUPERFECT**
parta	parti-era/ese	haya/hubiera* partido
partas	parti-eras/eses	hayas/hubieras partido
parta	parti-era/ese	haya/hubiera partido
partamos	parti-éramos/ésemos	hayamos/hubiéramos partido
partáis	parti-erais/eseis	hayáis/hubierais partido
partan	parti-eran/esen	hayan/hubieran partido

IMPERATIVE	*INFINITIVE*	*PARTICIPLE*
(tú) parte	**PRESENT**	**PRESENT**
(Vd) parta	partir	partiendo
(nosotros) partamos		
(vosotros) partid	**PERFECT**	**PAST**
(Vds) partan	haber partido	partido

* the alternative form 'hubiese' etc is also possible

Models for irregular conjugation

[1] **pensar** *PRES* pienso, piensas, piensa, pensamos, pensáis, piensan; *PRES SUBJ* piense, pienses, piense, pensemos, penséis, piensen; *IMPERAT* piensa, piense, pensemos, pensad, piensen

[2] **contar** *PRES* cuento, cuentas, cuenta, contamos, contáis, cuentan; *PRES SUBJ* cuente, cuentes, cuente, contemos, contéis, cuenten; *IMPERAT* cuenta, cuente, contemos, contad, cuenten

[3] **perder** *PRES* pierdo, pierdes, pierde, perdemos, perdéis, pierden; *PRES SUBJ* pierda, pierdas, pierda, perdamos, perdáis, pierdan; *IMPERAT* pierde, pierda, perdamos, perded, pierdan

[4] **morder** *PRES* muerdo, muerdes, muerde, mordemos, mordéis, muerden; *PRES SUBJ* muerda, muerdas, muerda, mordamos, mordáis, muerdan; *IMPERAT* muerde, muerda, mordamos, morded, muerdan

[5] **sentir** *PRES* siento, sientes, siente, sentimos, sentís, sienten; *PRES SUBJ* sienta, sientas, sienta, sintamos, sintáis, sientan; *PRES P* sintiendo; *IMPERAT* siente, sienta, sintamos, sentid, sientan

[6] **vestir** *PRES* visto, vistes, viste, vestimos, vestís, visten; *PRES SUBJ* vista, vistas, vista, vistamos, vistáis, vistan; *PRES P* vistiendo; *IMPERAT* viste, vista, vistamos, vestid, vistan

[7] **dormir** *PRES* duermo, duermes, duerme, dormimos, dormís, duermen; *PRES SUBJ* duerma, duermas, duerma, durmamos, durmáis, duerman; *PRES P* durmiendo; *IMPERAT* duerme, duerma, durmamos, dormid, duerman

[8] **andar** *PRET* anduve, anduviste, anduvo, anduvimos, anduvisteis, anduvieron; *IMPERF SUBJ* anduviera/anduviese

[9] **caber** *PRES* quepo, cabes, cabe, cabemos, cabéis, caben; *PRES SUBJ* quepa, quepas, quepa, quepamos, quepáis, quepan; *FUT* cabré; *COND* cabría; *PRET* cupe, cupiste, cupo, cupimos, cupisteis, cupieron; *IMPERF SUBJ* cupiera/cupiese; *IMPERAT* cabe, quepa, quepamos, cabed, quepan

[10] **conducir** *PRES* conduzco, conduces, conduce, conducimos, conducís, conducen; *PRES SUBJ* conduzca, conduzcas, conduzca, conduzcamos, conduzcáis, conduzcan; *PRET* conduje, condujiste, condujo, condujimos, condujisteis, condujeron; *IMPERF SUBJ* condujera/condujese; *IMPERAT* conduce, conduzca, conduzcamos, conducid, conduzcan

[11] **dar** *PRES* doy, das, da, damos, dais, dan; *PRES SUBJ* dé, des, dé, demos, deis, den; *PRET* di, diste, dio, dimos, disteis, dieron; *IMPERF SUBJ* diera/diese; *IMPERAT* da, dé, demos, dad, den

[12] **decir** *PRES* digo, dices, dice, decimos, decís, dicen; *PRES SUBJ* diga, digas, diga, digamos, digáis, digan; *FUT* diré; *COND* diría; *PRET* dije, dijiste, dijo, dijimos, dijisteis, dijeron; *IMPERF SUBJ* dijera/dijese; *PRES P* diciendo; *PP* dicho; *IMPERAT* di, diga, digamos, decid, digan

[13] **ESTAR** to be

INDICATIVE

PRESENT	FUTURE	CONDITIONAL
1. estoy	estaré	estaría
2. estás	estarás	estarías
3. está	estará	estaría
1. estamos	estaremos	estaríamos
2. estáis	estaréis	estaríais
3. están	estarán	estarían

IMPERFECT	PRETERITE	PERFECT
1. estaba	estuve	he estado
2. estabas	estuviste	has estado
3. estaba	estuvo	ha estado
1. estábamos	estuvimos	hemos estado
2. estabais	estuvisteis	habéis estado
3. estaban	estuvieron	han estado

FUTURE PERFECT	CONDITIONAL PERFECT	PLUPERFECT
1. habré estado	habría estado	había estado
2. habrás estado	habrías estado	habías estado
3. habrá estado	habría estado	había estado
1. habremos estado	habríamos estado	habíamos estado
2. habréis estado	habríais estado	habíais estado
3. habrán estado	habrían estado	habían estado

SUBJUNCTIVE

PRESENT	IMPERFECT	PERFECT/PLUPERFECT
1. esté	estuv-iera/iese	haya/hubiera* estado
2. estés	estuv-ieras/ieses	hayas/hubieras estado
3. esté	estuv-iera/iese	haya/hubiera estado
1. estemos	estuv-iéramos/iésemos	hayamos/hubiéramos estado
2. estéis	estuv-ierais/ieseis	hayáis/hubierais estado
3. estén	estuv-ieran/iesen	hayan/hubieran estado

IMPERATIVE	*INFINITIVE*	*PARTICIPLE*
(tú) está	**PRESENT**	**PRESENT**
(Vd) esté	estar	estando
(nosotros) estemos		
(vosotros) estad	**PERFECT**	**PAST**
(Vds) estén	haber estado	estado

* the alternative form 'hubiese' etc is also possible

xviii

[14] **HABER** to have *(auxiliary)*

INDICATIVE

PRESENT	**FUTURE**	**CONDITIONAL**
1. he	habré	habría
2. has	habrás	habrías
3. ha/hay*	habrá	habría
1. hemos	habremos	habríamos
2. habéis	habréis	habríais
3. han	habrán	habrían

IMPERFECT	**PRETERITE**	**PERFECT**
1. había	hube	
2. habías	hubiste	
3. había	hubo	ha habido*
1. habíamos	hubimos	
2. habíais	hubisteis	
3. habían	hubieron	

FUTURE PERFECT	**CONDITIONAL PERFECT**	**PLUPERFECT**
1.		
2.		
3. habrá habido*	habría habido*	había habido*
1.		
2.		
3.		

SUBJUNCTIVE

PRESENT	**IMPERFECT**	**PERFECT/PLUPERFECT**
1. haya	hub-iera/iese	
2. hayas	hub-ieras/ieses	
3. haya	hub-iera/iese	haya/hubiera** habido*
1. hayamos	hub-iéramos/iésemos	
2. hayáis	hub-ierais/ieseis	
3. hayan	hub-ieran/iesen	

INFINITIVE   *PARTICIPLE*

PRESENT	**PRESENT**
haber	habiendo
PERFECT	**PAST**
haber habido*	habido

* 'haber' is an auxiliary verb used with the participle of another verb to form compound tenses (eg he bebido - I have drunk). 'hay' means 'there is/are' and all third person singular forms in their respective tenses have this meaning. The forms highlighted with an asterisk are used only for this latter construction.

** the alternative form 'hubiese' is also possible

[15] **hacer** *PRES* hago, haces, hace, hacemos, hacéis, hacen; *PRES SUBJ* haga, hagas, haga, hagamos, hagáis, hagan; *FUT* haré; *COND* haría; *PRET* hice, hiciste, hizo, hicimos, hicisteis, hicieron; *IMPERF SUBJ* hiciera/hiciese; *PP* hecho; *IMPERAT* haz, haga, hagamos, haced, hagan

[16] **ir** *PRES* voy, vas, va, vamos, vais, van; *PRES SUBJ* vaya, vayas, vaya, vayamos, vayáis, vayan; *IMPERF* iba, ibas, iba, íbamos, ibais, iban; *PRET* fui, fuiste, fue, fuimos, fuisteis, fueron; *IMPERF SUBJ* fuera/fuese; *PRES P* yendo; *IMPERAT* ve, vaya, vamos, id, vayan

[17] **oír** *PRES* oigo, oyes, oye, oímos, oís, oyen; *PRES SUBJ* oiga, oigas, oiga, oigamos, oigáis, oigan; *PRET* oí, oíste, oyó, oímos, oísteis, oyeron; *IMPERF SUBJ* oyera/oyese; *PRES P* oyendo; *PP* oído; *IMPERAT* oye, oiga, oigamos, oíd, oigan

[18] **poder** *PRES* puedo, puedes, puede, podemos, podéis, pueden; *PRES SUBJ* pueda, puedas, pueda, podamos, podáis, puedan; *FUT* podré; *COND* podría; *PRET* pude, pudiste, pudo, pudimos, pudisteis, pudieron; *IMPERF SUBJ* pudiera/pudiese; *PRES P* pudiendo; *IMPERAT* puede, pueda, podamos, poded, puedan

[19] **poner** *PRES* pongo, pones, pone, ponemos, ponéis, ponen; *PRES SUBJ* ponga, pongas, ponga, pongamos, pongáis, pongan; *FUT* pondré; *COND* pondría; *PRET* puse, pusiste, puso, pusimos, pusisteis, pusieron; *IMPERF SUBJ* pusiera/pusiese; *PP* puesto; *IMPERAT* pon, ponga, pongamos, poned, pongan

[20] **querer** *PRES* quiero, quieres, quiere, queremos, queréis, quieren; *PRES SUBJ* quiera, quieras, quiera, queramos, queráis, quieran; *FUT* querré; *COND* querría; *PRET* quise, quisiste, quiso, quisimos, quisisteis, quisieron; *IMPERF SUBJ* quisiera/quisiese; *IMPERAT* quiere, quiera, queramos, quered, quieran

[21] **saber** *PRES* sé, sabes, sabe, sabemos, sabéis, saben; *PRES SUBJ* sepa, sepas, sepa, sepamos, sepáis, sepan; *FUT* sabré; *COND* sabría; *PRET* supe, supiste, supo, supimos, supisteis, supieron; *IMPERF SUBJ* supiera/supiese; *IMPERAT* sabe, sepa, sepamos, sabed, sepan

[22] **salir** *PRES* salgo, sales, sale, salimos, salís, salen; *PRES SUBJ* salga, salgas, salga, salgamos, salgáis, salgan; *FUT* saldré; *COND* saldría; *IMPERAT* sal, salga, salgamos, salid, salgan

[23] **ser** *PRES* soy, eres, es, somos, sois, son; *PRES SUBJ* sea, seas, sea, seamos, seáis, sean; *IMPERF* era, eras, era, éramos, erais, eran; *PRET* fui, fuiste, fue, fuimos, fuisteis, fueron; *IMPERF SUBJ* fuera/fuese; *IMPERAT* sé, sea, seamos, sed, sean

[24] **tener** *PRES* tengo, tienes, tiene, tenemos, tenéis, tienen; *PRES SUBJ* tenga, tengas, tenga, tengamos, tengáis, tengan; *FUT* tendré; *COND* tendría; *PRET* tuve, tuviste, tuvo, tuvimos, tuvisteis, tuvieron; *IMPERF SUBJ* tuviera/tuviese; *IMPERAT* ten, tenga, tengamos, tened, tengan

[25] **traer** *PRES* traigo, traes, trae, traemos, traéis, traen; *PRES SUBJ* traiga, traigas, traiga, traigamos, traigáis, traigan; *PRET* traje, trajiste, trajo, trajimos, trajisteis, trajeron; *IMPERF SUBJ* trajera/trajese; *IMPERAT* trae, traiga, traigamos, traed, traigan

[26] **valer** *PRES* valgo, vales, vale, valemos, valéis, valen; *PRES SUBJ* valga, valgas, valga, valgamos, valgáis, valgan; *FUT* valdré; *COND* valdría; *IMPERAT* vale, valga, valgamos, valed, valgan

[27] **venir** *PRES* vengo, vienes, viene, venimos, venís, vienen; *PRES SUBJ* venga, vengas, venga, vengamos, vengáis, vengan; *FUT* vendré; *COND* vendría; *PRET* vine, viniste, vino, vinimos, vinisteis, vinieron; *IMPERF SUBJ* viniera/viniese; *PRES P* viniendo; *IMPERAT* ven, venga, vengamos, venid, vengan

[28] **ver** *PRES* veo, ves, ve, vemos, veis, ven; *PRES SUBJ* vea, veas, vea, veamos, veáis, vean; *IMPERF* veía, veías, veía, veíamos, veíais, veían; *PRET* vi, viste, vio, vimos, visteis, vieron; *IMPERF SUBJ* viera/viese; *IMPERAT* ve, vea, veamos, ved, vean

[29] **desviar** *PRES* desvío, desvías, desvía, desviamos, desviáis, desvían; *PRES SUBJ* desvíe, desvíes, desvíe, desviemos, desviéis, desvíen; *IMPERAT* desvía, desvíe, desviemos, desviéis, desvíen

[30] **continuar** *PRES* continúo, continúas, continúa, continuamos, continuáis, continúan; *PRES SUBJ* continúe, continúes, continúe, continuemos, continuéis, continúen; *IMPERAT* continúa, continúe, continuemos, continuad, continúen

[31] **adquirir** *PRES* adquiero, adquieres, adquiere, adquirimos, adquirís, adquieren; *PRES SUBJ* adquiera, adquieras, adquiera, adquiramos, adquiráis, adquieran; *IMPERAT* adquiere, adquiera, adquiramos, adquirid, adquieran

[32] **jugar** *PRES* juego, juegas, juega, jugamos, jugáis, juegan; *PRES SUBJ* juegue, juegues, juegue, juguemos, juguéis, jueguen; *IMPERAT* juega, juegue, juguemos, jugad, jueguen

[33] **agradecer** *PRES* agradezco, agradeces, agradece, agradecemos, agradecéis, agradecen; *PRES SUBJ* agradezca, agradezcas, agradezca, agradezcamos, agradezcáis, agradezcan; *IMPERAT* agradece, agradezca, agradezcamos, agradeced, agradezcan

[34] **conocer** *PRES* conozco, conoces, conoce, conocemos, conocéis, conocen; *PRES SUBJ* conozca, conozcas, conozca, conozcamos, conozcáis, conozcan; *IMPERAT* conoce, conozca, conozcamos, conoced, conozcan

[35] **lucir** *PRES* luzco, luces, luce, lucimos, lucís, lucen; *PRES SUBJ* luzca, luzcas, luzca, luzcamos, luzcáis, luzcan; *IMPERAT* luce, luzca, luzcamos, lucid, luzcan

[36] **leer** *PRET* leí, leíste, leyó, leimos, leísteis, leyeron; *IMPERF SUBJ* leyera/leyese; *PRES P* leyendo; *PP* leido; *IMPERAT* lee, lea, leamos, leed, lean

[37] **huir** *PRES* huyo, huyes, huye, huimos, huís, huyen; *PRES SUBJ* huya, huyas, huya, huyamos, huyáis, huyan; *PRET* huí, huiste, huyó, huimos, huisteis, huyeron; *IMPERF SUBJ* huyera/huyese; *PRES P* huyendo; *PP* huido; *IMPERAT* huye, huya, huyamos, huid, huyan

[38] **roer** *PRES* roo/roigo/royo, roes, roe, roemos, roéis, roen; *PRES SUBJ* roa/roiga/roya, roas, roa, roamos, roáis, roan; *PRET* roí, roíste, royó, roímos, roísteis, royeron; *IMPERF SUBJ* royera/royese; *PRES P* royendo; *PP* roído; *IMPERAT* roe, roa, roamos, roed, roan

[39] **caer** *PRES* caigo, caes, cae, caemos, caéis, caen; *PRES SUBJ* caiga, caigas, caiga, caigamos, caigáis, caigan; *PRES P* cayendo; *PP* caído; *IMPERAT* cae, caiga, caigamos, caed, caigan

Guide to the Pronunciation of Spanish

The following table is based on IPA (the International Phonetic Alphabet) with certain modifications and attempts to give an approximate idea of the Spanish sound system as compared with the British English one.

Letter	Phonetic symbol	Examples	Approximate British English equivalent
Vowels:			
a	[a]	gato, amar, mesa	as in father, but shorter
e	[e]	estrella, vez, firme	as in labour
i	[i]	inicuo, iris	as in see, but shorter
o	[o]	bolo, cómodo, oso	between lot and taught
u	[u]	turuta, puro, tribu	as in food, but shorter, but u in -que- or -qui- and -gue- or -gui- is silent (unless -güe- or -güe-)
y	[i]	y	as in see, but shorter
Diphthongs:			
ai, ay	[ai]	baile, hay	as in life, aisle
au	[au]	fauna	as in fowl, house
ei, ey	[ei]	peine, ley	as in hate, feign
eu	[eu]	feudo	pronounce each vowel separately
oi, oy	[oi]	boina, hoy	as in boy
Semi-consonants:			
u	[w]	buey, cuando, fuiste	as in twait
i	[j]	viernes, vicio, ciudad, ciar	as in yes
y	[i]	yermo, ayer, rey	as in yes
Consonants:			
b	[b]	boda, burro, ambos	as in be
	[β]	haba, traba	a very light b
c	[k]	cabeza, cuco, acoso, frac	as in car, keep
	[θ]	cecina, cielo	as in thing, but in Andalusia and all of Latin America as s in silly
ch	[tʃ]	chepa, ocho	as in chamber
d	[d]	dedo, andar	as in day
	[ð]	dedo, ánade, abad	as in this (often omitted in spoken Spanish when at the end of a word)
f	[f]	fiesta, afición	as in for
g	[g]	gas, rango, gula	as in get
	[ɣ]	agua, agosto, lagar	a very light g
	[x]	genio, legión	similar to Scottish [x] in loch
h	-	hambre, ahíto	Spanish h is silent
j	[x]	jabón, ajo, carcaj	similar to Scottish [x] in loch
k	[k]	kilo, kimono	as in car, keep
l	[l]	labio, hábil, elegante	as in law
ll	[ʎ]	lluvia, calle	similar to the sound in million
m	[m]	mano, amigo, hambre	as in man
n	[n]	nata, ratón, antes, enemigo	as in night

ñ	[ɲ]	año, ñoño	similar to the sound in on*ion*
p	[p]	**p**ipa, **p**elo	as in *p*oint
q	[k]	**q**uiosco, quer**e**r, alambi**q**ue	as in *c*ar
r(r)	[r]	pe**r**o, cor**r**er, pad**r**e	always pronounced, rolled as in Scots
	[rr]	reír, honrado, perro	**rr** is a lengthened r sound
s	[s]	**s**auna, a**s**ado, corté**s**	similar to the **s** in hi**s**sing
t	[t]	**t**eja, es**t**én, a**t**raco	as in *t*ime
v	[b]	**v**erbena, **v**ena	as in *b*e
	[β]	a**v**e, vi**v**o	a very light **b**
w	[b]	**w**agón, **w**aterpolo	as in *b*e
x	[ks]	é**x**ito, e**x**amen	as in e**x**ercise
	[s]	e**x**tensión	as in e**s**tate
z	[θ]	**z**orro, a**z**ul, ca**z**a, soe**z**	as in *th*ing, but in Andalusia and in all of Latin America as **s** in si**ll**y

Stress rules

If a word ends in a vowel, **-n** or **-s**, the stress should fall on the second last syllable, for example:

mano, examen, bocadillos

If a word has any other ending, the stress falls on the last syllable, for example:

hablar, Madrid, ayer

Exceptions to these rules carry a written accent on the stressed syllable, for example:

cómodo, legión, hábil

A

A, a |a| *nf (la letra)* A, a.

a *abr de* área, area.

a *prep* → **al. 1** *(dirección)* to; **ir a Colombia**, to go to Colombia; **llegar a Valencia**, to arrive in Valencia; **subir al tren**, to get on the train; **ir al cine**, to go to the cinema; **vete a casa**, go home. **2** *(lugar)* at, on; **a la derecha**, on the right; **a la entrada**, at the entrance; **a lo lejos**, in the distance; **a mi lado**, at *o* by my side, next to me; **al sol**, in the sun; **a la mesa**, at (the) table. **3** *(tiempo)* at; **a las doce**, at twelve o'clock; **a los sesenta años**, at the age of sixty; **a los tres meses/la media hora**, three months/half an hour later; **al final**, in the end; **al principio**, at first. **4** *(distancia)* away; **a cien kilómetros de aquí**, a hundred kilometres from here. **5** *(manera)* **a la inglesa**, (in) the English fashion *o* manner *o* style; **escrito a máquina**, typed, typewritten; **a mano**, by hand. **6** *(proporción)* **a 90 kilómetros por hora**, at 90 kilometres an hour; **a 300 pesetas el kilo**, three hundred pesetas a kilo; **tres veces a la semana**, three times a week. **7** *Dep* **ganar cuatro a dos**, to win four (to) two. **8** *(complemento indirecto)* to; *(procedencia)* from; **díselo a Javier**, tell Javier; **te lo di a ti**, I gave it to you; **comprarle algo a algn**, to buy sth from sb; *(para algn)* to buy sth for sb; *(complemento directo de persona)* **saludé a tu tía**, I said hello to your aunt. **9** *[am ir a por algn/algo]*, to go and fetch sb/sth. **10** *(verbo + a + infin)* to; **aprender a nadar**, to learn (how) to swim; **fueron a ayudarle**, they went to help him. **11** *(nombre + a + infin)* **distancia a recorrer**, distance to be covered. **12** *a decir verdad*, to tell (you) the truth; **a no ser por ...**, if it were not for ...; **a no ser que**, unless; **a ver**, let's see; **¡a comer!**, lunch/dinner *etc* is ready!; **¡a dormir!**, bedtime!; **¿a que no lo haces?**, *(desafío)* I bet you don't do it!

abad *nm* abbot.

abadía *nf* abbey.

abajeño,-a *nm,f Am* lowlander, coastal dweller.

abajo I *adv* **1** *(en una casa)* downstairs; **el piso de a.**, the flat downstairs. **2** *(dirección)* down, downwards; **ahí/aquí a.**, down there/here; **la parte de a.**, the bottom (part); **más a.**, further down; **hacia a.**, down, downwards; **calle a.**, down the street; **echar algo a.**, to knock sth down; **venirse a.**, *(edificio)* to fall down; *fig (proyecto)* to fall through. **II** *interj* **¡a. la censura!**, down with censorship!

abalanzarse |4| *vr* **a. sobre/contra**, to

rush towards.

abalear *vtr Am* to shoot *o* fire at.

abalorio *nm* **1** *(cuenta)* glass bead. **2** *(baratija)* trinket.

abanderado,-a *nm,f* standard bearer.

abandonado,-a *adj* **1** abandoned; **tiene a su familia muy abandonada**, he takes absolutely no interest in his family. **2** *(desaseado)* untidy, unkempt.

abandonar I *vtr* **1** *(lugar)* to leave, quit; *(persona, cosa)* to abandon; *(proyecto, plan)* to give up. **2** *Dep (carrera)* to drop out of. **II abandonarse** *vr* to let oneself go.

abandono *nm (acción)* abandoning, desertion. **2** *(de proyecto, idea)* giving up. **3** *(descuido)* neglect.

abanicarse *vr* to fan oneself.

abanico *nm* **1** fan. **2** *(gama)* range; **un amplio a. de posibilidades**, a wide range of possibilities.

abaratar I *vtr* to cut *o* reduce the price of. **II abaratarse** *vr (artículos)* to become cheaper, come down in price; *(precios)* to come down.

abarcar |1| *vtr* **1** to embrace. **2** *Am (acaparar)* to monopolize.

abarrotado,-a *adj* packed (**de**, with), crammed (**de**, with).

abarrotar *vtr* to pack, cram (**de**, with); **el público abarrotaba la sala**, the room was packed (with people).

abarrotes *nmpl Am* groceries.

abastecedor,-a *nm,f* supplier.

abastecer |33| **I** *vtr* to supply. **II abastecerse** *vr* **a. de**, to be supplied with.

abastecimiento *nm* supplying; **a. de agua**, water supply.

abasto *nm* **1** *fam* **no doy a.**, I can't cope, I can't keep up. **2** **mercado de abastos**, wholesale food market.

abatible *adj* folding, collapsible; **asiento a.**, reclining seat.

abatido,-a *adj* downcast.

abatir I *vtr* **1** *(derribar)* to knock down, pull down. **2** *(matar)* to kill; **a. a tiros**, to shoot down. **3** *(desanimar)* to depress, dishearten. **II abatirse** *vr (desanimarse)* to lose heart, become depressed.

abdicación *nf* abdication.

abdicar |1| *vtr & vi* to abdicate.

abdomen *nm* abdomen.

abdominales *nmpl* sit-ups.

abecedario *nm* alphabet.

abedul *nm* birch.

abeja *nf* bee; **a. reina**, queen bee.

abejorro *nm* bumblebee.

aberración *nf* aberration.

aberrante *adj* deviant.

abertura *nf (hueco)* opening, gap; *(grieta)*

crack, slit.

abertzale *adj & nm,f* Basque nationalist.

abeto *nm Bot* fir (tree); *a.* rojo, spruce.

abierto,-a *adj* **1** open; *(grifo)* (turned) on; **a. de par en par**, wide open. **2** *(persona)* open-minded.

abigarrado,-a *adj (mezclado)* jumbled, mixed up.

abismal *adj* abysmal; *fig* **una diferencia a.**, a world of a difference.

abismo *nm* abyss; *fig* **al borde del a.**, on the brink of ruin; *fig* **entre ellos media un a.**, they are worlds apart.

ablandar **I** *vtr* to soften. **II ablandarse** *vr* **1** to soften, go soft *o* softer. **2** *fig (persona)* to mellow.

abnegación *nf* abnegation, self-denial.

abnegado,-a *adj* selfless, self-sacrificing.

abocado,-a *adj* **1** **está a. al fracaso**, it is doomed to failure. **2** *(vino)* medium dry.

abochornar *vtr* to shame, embarrass.

abofetear *vtr* to slap.

abogacía *nf* legal profession.

abogado,-a *nm,f* lawyer, solicitor; *(en tribunal supremo)* barrister; **a. de oficio**, legal aid lawyer; **a. defensor**, counsel for the defense; **a. del diablo**, devil's advocate; **a. laboralista**, union lawyer.

abogar [7] *vtr* to plead; **a. a favor de**, to plead for, defend; **a. por algo**, to advocate *o* champion sth.

abolengo *nm* ancestry, lineage.

abolición *nf* abolition.

abolir *vtr defect* to abolish.

abolladura *nf* dent.

abollar *vtr* to dent.

abominable *adj* abominable.

abominar *vi* **a. (de)**, to abominate, loathe.

abonado,-a **I** *nm,f* subscriber. **II** *adj Fin (pagado)* paid; **a. en cuenta**, credited.

abonar **I** *Agr* to fertilize. **2** *(pagar)* to pay (for). **3** *(subscribir)* to subscribe. **II abonarse** *vr* to subscribe (a, to).

abono *nm* **1** *Agr (producto)* fertilizer; *(estiércol)* manure. **2** *(pago)* payment. **3** *(a revista etc)* subscription; *(billete)* season ticket.

abordar *vtr (persona)* to approach; *(barco)* to board; **a. un asunto**, to tackle a subject.

aborigen *(pl* **aborígenes)** **I** *adj* native, indigenous; *esp Austral* aboriginal. **II** *nmf* native; *esp Austral* aborigine.

aborrecer [33] *vtr* to detest, loathe.

abortar **I** *vi (involuntariamente)* to miscarry, have a miscarriage; *(intencionadamente)* to abort, have an abortion. **II** *vtr* to abort.

abortista *nmf* abortionist.

aborto *nm* miscarriage; *(provocado)* abortion.

abotargado,-a *adj* swollen.

abotonar *vtr (ropa)* to button (up).

abovedado,-a *adj* vaulted, arched.

abracadabra *nm* abracadabra.

abrasador,-a *adj* scorching.

abrasar **I** *vtr & vi* to scorch. **II abrasarse** *vr* to burn.

abrazadera *nf* clamp.

abrazar [4] **I** *vtr* to embrace, hug; *fig (doctrina)* to embrace. **II abrazarse** *vr* **a. a algn**, to embrace sb; **se abrazaron**, they embraced each other.

abrazo *nm* embrace, hug; **un a., abrazos**, *(en carta)* best wishes.

abrecartas *nm inv* letter-opener, paper-knife.

abrefácil *nm Com* **caja con a.**, easy-open carton.

abrelatas *nm inv* tin-opener, *US* can opener.

abreviar [12] **1** *vtr* to shorten; *(texto)* to abridge; *(palabra)* to abbreviate. **II** *vi* to be quick *o* brief; **para a.**, to cut a long story short.

abreviatura *nf* abbreviation.

abridor *nm (de latas, botellas)* opener.

abrigado,-a *adj* wrapped up; **ir muy a.**, to be well wrapped-up.

abrigar [7] *vtr* **1** to keep warm; **esta chaqueta abriga mucho**, this cardigan is very warm. **2** *(proteger)* to protect, shelter. **3** *(esperanza)* to cherish; *(duda)* to have, harbour, *US* harbor.

abrigo *nm* **1** *(prenda)* coat, overcoat; **ropa de a.**, warm clothes *pl.* **2** **al a. de**, protected *o* sheltered from.

abril *nm* April.

abrillantador *nm* polish.

abrillantar *vtr* to polish.

abrir[1] *nm* **en un a. y cerrar de ojos**, in the twinkling of an eye.

abrir[2] *(pp* **abierto)** **I** *vtr* to open. **II** *vtr* **1** to open; *(cremallera)* to undo. **2** *(gas, grifo)* to turn on. **3** *Jur* **a. (un) expediente**, to start proceedings. **III abrirse** *vr* **1** to open; *fig* **a. paso**, to make one's way. **2** *arg* **¡me abro!**, I'm off!

abrochar *vtr*, **abrocharse** *vr (botones)* to do up; *(camisa)* to button (up); *(cinturón)* to fasten; *(zapatos)* to tie up; *(cremallera)* to do up.

abrumado,-a *adj* overwhelmed.

abrumador,-a *adj* overwhelming.

abrumar *vtr* to overwhelm, crush; **tantos problemas me abruman**, all these problems are getting on top of me.

abrupto,-a *adj* **1** *(terreno)* steep, abrupt. **2** *fig* abrupt, sudden.

absceso *nm* abscess.

absentismo *nm* absenteeism; **a. laboral**, absenteeism from work.

absolución *nf* **1** *Rel* absolution. **2** *Jur* acquittal.

absoluto,-a *adj* absolute; **en a.**, not at all, by no means. ◆**absolutamente** *adv* absolutely, completely; **a. nada**, nothing at all.

absolutorio,-a *adj Jur* **sentencia absolutoria,** verdict of not guilty.

absolver [4] (*pp* **absuelto**) *vtr* **1** *Rel* to absolve. **2** *Jur* to acquit.

absorbente *adj* **1** (*papel*) absorbent. **2** *fig* absorbing, engrossing.

absorber *vtr* to absorb.

absorción *nf* absorption.

absorto,-a *adj* absorbed, engrossed (**en**, in).

abstemio,-a I *adj* teetotal, abstemious. **II** *nm,f* teetotaller.

abstención *nf* abstention.

abstenerse [24] *vr* to abstain (**de**, from); (*privarse*) to refrain (**de**, from).

abstinencia *nf* abstinence; **síndrome de a.,** withdrawal symptoms *pl*.

abstracción *nf* abstraction.

abstracto,-a *adj* abstract.

abstraer [25] **I** *vtr* to abstract. **II abstraerse** *vr* to become lost in thought.

abstraído,-a *adj* (*ensimismado*) absorbed, engrossed (**en**, in); (*distraído*) absentminded.

absuelto,-a *pp* → **absolver**.

absurdo,-a I *adj* absurd. **II** *nm* absurdity, absurd thing.

abuchear *vt* to boo, jeer at.

abucheo *nm* booing, jeering.

abuela *nf* grandmother; *fam* grandma, granny; *fig* old woman.

abuelo *nm* **1** grandfather; *fam* grandad, grandpa; *fig* old man. **2 abuelos,** grandparents.

abulense I *adj* of *o* from Avila. **II** *nmf* native *o* inhabitant of Avila.

abulia *nf* apathy, lack of willpower.

abultado,-a *adj* bulky, big.

abultar I *vi* to be bulky; **abulta mucho,** it takes up a lot of space. **II** *vtr* to exaggerate.

abundancia *nf* abundance, plenty; *fig* **nadar en la a.,** to be rolling in money.

abundante *adj* abundant, plentiful.

abundar *vi* to abound, be plentiful.

abur *interj fam* cheerio!, see you!

aburrido,-a *adj* **1 ser a.,** to be boring. **2 estar a.,** to be bored; (*harto*) to be tired (**de**, of).

aburrimiento *nm* boredom; **¡qué a.!,** how boring!, what a bore!

aburrir I *vtr* to bore. **II aburrirse** *vr* to get bored; **a. como una ostra,** to be bored stiff.

abusar *vi* **1** (*propasarse*) to go too far. **2 a. de,** (*situación, persona*) to take (unfair) advantage of; (*poder, amabilidad*) to abuse; **a. de la bebida/del tabaco,** to drink/smoke too much *o* to excess; *Jur* **a. de un niño/una mujer,** to abuse a child/woman.

abusivo,-a *adj* (*precio*) exorbitant.

abuso *nm* abuse.

abyecto,-a *adj* abject.

a. C. *abr de* **antes de Cristo,** before Christ, BC.

a/c *Com abr de* **a cuenta,** on account.

acá *adv* **1** (*lugar*) here, over here; **más a.,** nearer; **¡ven a.!,** come here! **2** (*de entonces a*), since then.

acabado,-a I *adj* **1** (*terminado*) finished. **2** *fig* (*persona*) worn-out, spent. **II** *nm* finish.

acabar I *vtr* to finish (off); (*completar*) to complete. **II** *vi* **1** to finish, end; **a. bien,** to have a happy ending; **a. con algo,** (*terminarlo*) to finish sth; (*romperlo*) to break sth. **2 a. de ...,** to have just ...; **acaba de entrar,** he has just come in; **no acaba de convencerme,** I'm not quite convinced. **3 acabaron casándose** *o* **por casarse,** they ended up getting married; **acabó en la cárcel,** he ended up in jail. **III acabarse** *vr* to finish, come to an end; **se nos acabó la gasolina,** we ran out of petrol; *fam* **¡se acabó!,** that's that!

acabóse *nm fam* **esto es el a.,** this is the end.

acacia *nf* acacia.

academia *nf* academy.

académico,-a *adj & nm,f* academic.

acaecer [33] *v impers* to happen, occur.

acallar *vtr* to silence.

acalorado,-a *adj* **1** hot. **2** *fig* (*excitado*) worked up, excited; (*debate etc*) heated, angry.

acalorarse *vr* to get warm *o* hot. **2** *fig* to get excited *o* worked up.

acampada *nf* camping; **ir de a.,** to go camping; **zona de a.,** camp site.

acampanado,-a *adj* bell-shaped; (*prendas*) flared.

acampar *vi* to camp.

acantilado *nm* cliff.

acantonar *vtr* (*tropas*) to billet, quarter (**en**, in).

acaparar *vtr* **1** (*productos*) to hoard; (*el mercado*) to corner. **2** *fig* to monopolize.

acaramelado,-a *adj* **1** (*color*) caramelcoloured, *US* caramel-colored. **2** (*pareja*) lovey-dovey, starry-eyed.

acariciar [12] *vtr* to caress; (*pelo, animal*) to stroke; (*esperanza*) to cherish.

acarrear *vtr* **1** (*transportar*) to carry, transport. **2** *fig* (*conllevar*) to entail.

acaso *adv* perhaps, maybe; **¿a. no te lo dije?,** did I not tell you, by any chance?; **por si a.,** just in case; **si a. viene ...,** if he should come ...

acatamiento *nm* respect; (*de la ley*) observance.

acatar *vtr* to observe, comply with.

acatarrado,-a *adj* **estar a.,** to have a cold.

acatarrarse *vr* to catch a cold.

acaudalado,-a *adj* rich, wealthy.

acaudalar *vtr* to accumulate, amass.

acaudillar *vtr* to lead.

acceder *vi* **a. a,** *(consentir)* to accede to, consent to; *(tener acceso)* to gain admittance to; *Inform* to access.

accesible *adj* accessible; *(persona)* approachable.

acceso *nm* **1** *(entrada)* access, entry; *Inform* **a. al azar, a. directo,** random access; *Univ* **prueba de a.,** entrance examination. **2** *(carretera)* approach, access. **3** *Med & fig* fit.

accesorio,-a *adj & nm* accessory.

accidentado,-a I *adj (terreno)* uneven, hilly; *(viaje, vida)* eventful. **II** *nm,f* casualty, accident victim.

accidental *adj* accidental; **un encuentro a.,** a chance meeting.

accidente *nm* **1** accident; **por a.,** by chance; **a. laboral,** industrial accident. **2** *Geog* **accidentes geográficos,** geographical features.

acción *nf* **1** action; *(acto)* act; **poner en a.,** to put in action; **ponerse en a.,** to go into action; **campo de a.,** field of action; **película de a.,** adventure film. **2** *Fin* share.

accionar *vtr* to drive.

accionista *nmf* shareholder.

acebo *nm (hoja)* holly; *(árbol)* holly tree.

acechar *vtr* to lie in wait for; **un grave peligro nos acecha,** great danger awaits us.

acecho *nm* **estar al a. de,** *(esperar)* to lie in wait for.

acedía *nf (pez)* dab.

aceite *nm* oil; **a. de girasol/maíz/oliva,** sunflower/corn/olive oil.

aceitera *nf* **1** *Culin* oil bottle; **aceiteras,** oil and vinegar set *sing.* **2** *Aut* oil can.

aceitero,-a I *adj* oil. **II** *nm,f* oil merchant.

aceitoso,-a *adj* oily.

aceituna *nf* olive; **a. rellena,** stuffed olive.

aceitunado,-a *adj* olive, olive-coloured.

aceitunero,-a *nm,f* **1** *(recolector)* olive picker *o* harvester. **2** *(vendedor)* olive seller.

acelerado,-a *adj* accelerated, fast.

acelerador *nm* *Aut* accelerator.

acelerar *vtr* to accelerate.

acento *nm* **1** accent; *(de palabra)* stress. **2** *(énfasis)* stress, emphasis.

acentuar [30] **I** *vtr* **1** to stress. **2** *fig* to emphasize, stress. **II acentuarse** *vr fig* to become more pronounced *o* noticeable.

aceña *nf* watermill.

acepción *nf* meaning, sense.

aceptable *adj* acceptable.

aceptación *nf* **1** acceptance. **2 tener poca a.,** to have little success, not to be popular.

aceptar *vtr* to accept.

acequia *nf* irrigation ditch *o* channel.

acera *nf* pavement, *US* sidewalk; *fam pey* **ser de la a. de enfrente,** to be gay *o* queer.

acerado *nm* pavement.

acerbo,-a *adj* harsh, bitter.

acerca *adv* **a. de,** about.

acercamiento *nm* bringing together, coming together; *Pol* rapprochement.

acercar [1] **I** *vtr* to bring near *o* nearer, bring (over); *fig* to bring together; **¿te acerco a casa?,** can I give you a lift home? **II acercarse** *vr* **1** to approach (**a,** -). **2** *(ir)* to go; *(venir)* to come.

acerico *nm* pincushion.

acero *nm* steel; **a. inoxidable,** stainless steel.

acérrimo,-a *adj (partidario)* staunch; *(enemigo)* bitter.

acertado,-a *adj* **1** *(solución)* right, correct; *(decisión)* wise. **2 no estuviste muy a. al decir eso,** it wasn't very wise of you to say that.

acertante I *nmf* winner. **II** *adj* winning.

acertar [1] **I** *vtr (pregunta)* to get right; *(adivinar)* to guess correctly; **a. las quinielas,** to win the pools. **II** *vi* to be right; **acertó con la calle que buscaba,** she found the street she was looking for.

acertijo *nm* riddle.

acervo *nm* **a. cultural,** cultural tradition *o* heritage.

acetona *nf* acetone.

achacar [1] *vtr (atribuir)* to attribute.

achacoso,-a *adj* ailing, unwell.

achaque *nm* ailment, complaint.

achicar [1] **I** *vtr* **1** *(amilanar)* to intimidate. **2** *(encoger)* to reduce, make smaller. **3** *(barco)* to bale out. **II achicarse** *vr* **1** *(amilanarse)* to lose heart. **2** *(encogerse)* to get smaller.

achicharrar *vtr* to burn to a crisp.

achicoria *nf* chicory.

achinado,-a *adj* **1** *(ojos)* slanting. **2** *Am* with mestizo features.

acholado,-a *adj Am* half-caste.

achuchar *vtr (empujar)* to shove.

achuchón *nm (empujón)* push, shove.

aciago,-a *adj* ill-fated, fateful.

acicalado,-a *adj* well-dressed, smart.

acicalarse *vr* to dress up, smarten up.

acicate *nm fig (aliciente)* spur, incentive.

acidez *nf (de sabor)* sharpness, sourness; *Quím* acidity; *Med* **a. de estómago,** heartburn.

ácido,-a I *adj (sabor)* sharp, tart; *Quím* acidic; *fig (tono)* harsh. **II** *nm Quím* acid.

acierto *nm (buena decisión)* good choice *o* idea; **con gran a.,** very wisely.

aclamación *nf* acclamation, acclaim.

aclamar *vtr* to acclaim.

aclaración *nf* explanation.

aclarado *nm* rinsing, rinse.

aclarar I *vtr* **1** *(explicar)* to clarify, explain; *(color)* to lighten, make lighter. **2** *(enjuagar)* to rinse. **II** *v impers Meteor* to clear (up). **III aclararse** vr 1 (decidirse) to make up one's mind; (entender) to understand. 2 Meteor to clear (up).

aclaratorio,-a adj explanatory.

aclimatación nf acclimatization, US acclimation.

aclimatar I vr to acclimatize, US acclimate (a, to). **II aclimatarse** vr fig **a algo**, to get used to sth.

acné nf acne.

acobardar I vtr to frighten. **II acobardarse** vr to become frightened, lose one's nerve, shrink back (**ante**, from).

acodarse vr to lean (**en**, on).

acogedor,-a adj cosy, warm.

acoger |5| **I** vr 1 (recibir) to receive; (a invitado) to welcome. 2 (persona desvalida) to take in. **II acogerse** vr fig **a. a**, to take refuge in; (amnistía) to avail oneself of; **a. a la ley**, to have recourse to the law.

acogida nf reception, welcome.

acojonado,-a adj vulg shit-scared.

acojonante adj vulg bloody great o terrific.

acojonarse vr vulg (acobardarse) to shit oneself, be shit-scared.

acolchar vr (rellenar) to pad; (prenda) to quilt.

acometer vtr 1 (emprender) to undertake. 2 (atacar) to attack.

acometida nf (ataque) attack; (de gas etc) connection.

acomodado,-a adj well-off, well-to-do.

acomodador,-a nm,f (hombre) usher; (mujer) usherette.

acomodar I vr 1 (alojar) to lodge, accommodate. 2 (en cine etc) to find a place for. **II acomodarse** vr 1 to make oneself comfortable. 2 (adaptarse) to adapt.

acomodaticio,-a adj 1 accommodating, easy-going. 2 pey pliable.

acompañante I nmf companion. **II** adj accompanying.

acompañar vtr 1 to accompany; **le acompañó hasta la puerta**, she saw him to the door; **me acompañó al médico**, he came with me to see the doctor; **¿te acompaño a casa?**, can I walk you home?; fml **le acompaño en el sentimiento**, my condolences. 2 (adjuntar) to enclose.

acompasado,-a adj (rítmico) rhythmic.

acomplejado,-a adj estar **a**, to have a complex (**por**, about).

acomplejar I vtr to give a complex. **II acomplejarse** vr **a. por**, to develop a complex about.

acondicionado,-a adj aire **a.**, air conditioning.

acondicionador nm conditioner.

acondicionar vtr to prepare, set up; (mejorar) to improve; (cabello) to condition.

acongojar vtr to distress.

aconsejable adj advisable.

aconsejar vr to advise.

acontecer [33] v impers to happen, take place.

acontecimiento nm event.

acopio nm store, stock; **hacer a. de**, to store.

acoplar vr 1 to fit (together), join. 2 Téc to couple, connect. **II acoplarse** vr (nave espacial) to dock.

acorazado,-a I adj armoured, US armored, armour-plated, US armor-plated. **II** nm battleship.

acordado,-a adj agreed; **según lo a.**, as agreed.

acordar [2] **I** vtr to agree; (decidir) to decide. **II acordarse** vr to remember; **no me acuerdo (de Silvia)**, I can't remember (Silvia).

acorde I adj in agreement. **II** nm Mús chord.

acordeón nm accordion.

acordonado,-a adj cordoned off, sealed off.

acordonar vtr 1 (zona) to cordon off, seal off. 2 (atar) to lace up.

acorralar vtr to corner.

acortar vtr to shorten; **a. distancias**, to cut down the distance.

acosar vtr to harass; fig **a. a algn a preguntas**, to bombard sb with questions.

acoso nm harassment; **a. sexual**, sexual harassment.

acostar |2| **I** vtr to put to bed. **II acostarse** vr 1 to go to bed. 2 fam **a. con algn**, to sleep with sb, go to bed with sb.

acostumbrado,-a adj 1 usual, customary; **es lo a.**, it is the custom. 2 adj **a. al frío/calor**, used to the cold/heat.

acostumbrar I vi **a.**, (soler) to be in the habit of. **II** vtr **a. a algn a algo**, (habituar) to get sb used to sth. **III acostumbrarse** vr (habituarse) to become accustomed (**a**, to), get used (**a**, to).

acotación nf 1 (en escrito) (marginal) note; Teat stage direction. 2 (en mapa) elevation mark.

acotar vtr 1 (área) to enclose; fig (tema) to delimit. 2 (texto) to annotate. 3 (mapa) to mark with elevations.

acotejar vtr Am to arrange.

ácrata adj & nmf anarchist.

acre¹ adj 1 (sabor) sour, bitter; (olor) acrid. 2 fig (palabras) bitter, harsh; (crítica) biting.

acre² nm (medida) acre.

acrecentar |1| vtr to increase.

acreditar vtr 1 to be a credit to. 2 (probar) to prove. 3 (embajador) to accredit. 4 Fin to credit.

acreditativo,-a adj which proves, which gives proof.

acreedor,-a nm,f Com creditor.

acribillar *vtr* (*moneda*) to riddle, pepper; **a. a algn a balazos,** to riddle sb with bullets.

acrílico,-a *adj* acrylic.

acriollarse *vr Am* to adopt local customs.

acritud *nf* (*mordacidad*) acrimony.

acrobacia *nf* acrobatics *sing.*

acróbata *nmf* acrobat.

acta *nf* 1 (*de reunión*) minutes *pl*, record. 2 (*certificado*) certificate, official document; **a. notarial,** affidavit.

actitud *nf* attitude.

activar *vtr* 1 to activate. 2 (*avivar*) to liven up.

actividad *nf* activity.

activista *nmf* activist.

activo,-a I *adj* active; **en a.,** on active service. II *nm Fin* assets *pl.*

acto *nm* 1 act, action; **a. sexual,** sexual intercourse; **en el a.,** at once; **a. seguido,** immediately afterwards; **Mil en a. de servicio,** in action; **hacer a. de presencia,** to put in an appearance. 2 (*ceremonia*) ceremony. 3 *Teat* act.

actor *nm* actor.

actriz *nf* actress.

actuación *nf* 1 performance. 2 (*intervención*) intervention, action.

actual *adj* current, present; (*al día*) up-to-date; **un tema muy a.,** a very topical subject. ♦ **actualmente** *adv* (*hoy en día*) nowadays, these days; (*ahora*) at the moment, at present.

actualidad *nf* 1 present time; **en la a.,** at present; **estar de a.,** to be fashionable; **temas de a.,** topical subjects. 2 (*hechos*) current affairs *pl.*

actualizar [4] *vtr* to update, bring up to date.

actuar [30] *vi* 1 to act; **a. como** *o* **de,** to act as. 2 *Cin Teat* to perform, act.

acuarela *nf* watercolour, *US* watercolor.

Acuario *nm* Aquarius.

acuario *nm* aquarium.

acuartelar *vtr* to confine to barracks.

acuático,-a *adj* aquatic; **esquí a.,** water skiing.

acuchillar *vtr* to knife, stab.

acuciante *adj* urgent, pressing.

acuciar [12] *vtr* to urge on.

acudir *vi* (*ir*) to go; (*venir*) to come, arrive; **nadie acudió en su ayuda,** nobody came to help him; **no sé dónde a.,** I don't know where to turn.

acueducto *nm* aqueduct.

acuerdo *nm* agreement; **¡de a.!,** all right!, O.K.!; **de a. con,** in accordance with; **de común a.,** by common consent; **estar de a. en algo,** to agree on sth; **ponerse de a.,** to agree; **a. marco,** framework agreement.

acumular I *vtr* to accumulate. II **acumularse** *vr* 1 to accumulate, build up. 2 (*gente*) to crowd.

acunar *vtr* to rock.

acuñar *vtr* (*moneda*) to mint; (*frase*) to coin.

acuoso,-a *adj* watery; (*jugoso*) juicy.

acupuntura *nf* acupuncture.

acurrucarse [1] *vr* to curl up, snuggle up.

acusación *nf* 1 accusation. 2 *Jur* charge.

acusado,-a I *nm,f* accused, defendant. II *adj* (*marcado*) marked, noticeable.

acusar I *vtr* 1 to accuse (**de,** of); *Jur* to charge (**de,** with). 2 (*golpe etc*) to feel; *fig* **su cara acusaba el cansancio,** his face showed his exhaustion. 3 *Com* **a. recibo,** to acknowledge receipt. II **acusarse** *vr* 1 (*acentuarse*) to become more pronounced. 2 *fig* (*notarse*) to show.

acuse *nm* **a. de recibo,** acknowledgment of receipt.

acusica *adj & nmf fam* telltale.

acústica *nf* acoustics *sing.*

acústico,-a *adj* acoustic.

adán *nm fam* untidy *o* slovenly person.

adaptable *adj* adaptable.

adaptación *nf* adaptation.

adaptador *nm* adapter.

adaptar I *vtr* 1 to adapt. 2 (*ajustar*) to adjust. II **adaptarse** *vr* to adapt oneself (**a,** to).

adecentar *vtr* to tidy (up), clean (up).

adecuado,-a *adj* appropriate, suitable.

adecuar [10] *vtr* to adapt.

adefesio *nm* (*persona*) freak; (*cosa*) monstrosity.

a. de J.C. *abr de* **antes de Jesucristo,** before Christ, BC.

adelantado,-a *adj* 1 advanced; (*desarrollado*) developed; (*precoz*) precocious. 2 (*reloj*) fast. 3 **pagar por a.,** to pay in advance.

adelantamiento *nm* overtaking; **hacer un a.,** to overtake.

adelantar I *vtr* 1 to move *o* bring forward; (*reloj*) to put forward; *fig* to advance. 2 *Aut* to overtake. 3 (*fecha*) to bring forward; *fig* **a. (los) acontecimientos,** to get ahead of oneself. II *vi* 1 to advance. 2 (*progresar*) to make progress. 3 (*reloj*) to be fast. III **adelantarse** *vr* 1 (*ir delante*) to go ahead. 2 (*reloj*) to gain, be fast. 3 **el verano se ha adelantado,** we are having an early summer.

adelante I *adv* forward; **más a.,** (*lugar*) further on; (*tiempo*) later; **seguir a.,** to keep going, carry on; **llevar a. un plan,** to carry out a plan. II *interj* **¡a!,** come in!

adelanto *nm* 1 advance; (*progreso*) progress. 2 **el reloj lleva diez minutos de a.,** the watch is ten minutes fast. 3 (*de dinero*) advance payment.

adelfa *nf* oleander, rosebay.

adelgazamiento *nm* slimming.

adelgazar [4] *vi* to slim, lose weight.

ademán *nm* 1 gesture. 2 **ademanes,** manners.

además *adv* moreover, furthermore; **a., no lo he visto nunca**, what's more, I've never seen him; **a. de él**, besides him.

adentrarse *vr* **a. en**, *(bosque)* to go deep into; *(asunto)* to study thoroughly.

adentro I *adv* *(dentro)* inside; **mar a.**, out to sea; **tierra a.**, inland. II *nmpl* **decir algo para sus adentros**, to say sth to oneself.

adepto,-a *nm,f* follower, supporter.

aderezar [4] *vtr* *(comida)* to season; *(ensalada)* to dress.

aderezo *nm* *(de comida)* seasoning; *(de ensalada)* dressing.

adeudar I *vtr* to owe. II **adeudarse** *vr* to get into debt.

adherencia *nf* adherence; *Aut* roadholding.

adherir [5] I *vtr* to stick on. II **adherirse** *vr* **a. a**, to adhere to; *(partido)* to join.

adhesión *nf* adhesion; *(a partido)* joining; *(a teoría)* adherence.

adhesivo,-a *adj & nm* adhesive.

adicción *nf* addiction; **crear a.**, to be addictive.

adición *nf* addition.

adicional *adj* additional.

adicto,-a I *nm,f* addict. II *adj* addicted (**a**, to).

adiestrar *vtr* to train.

adinerado,-a I *adj* wealthy, rich. II *nm,f* rich person.

adiós *(pl* **adioses)** I *interj* goodbye; *(am* bye-bye); *(al cruzarse)* hello. II *nm* goodbye.

aditivo,-a *adj & nm* additive.

adivinanza *nf* riddle, puzzle.

adivinar *vtr* to guess; **a. el pensamiento de algn**, to read sb's mind.

adivino,-a *nm,f* fortune-teller.

adjetivo,-a I *nm* I adjective. II *adj* adjectival.

adjudicación *nf* award; *(en subasta)* sale.

adjudicar [15] I *vtr* 1 *(premio, contrato)* to award. 2 *(en subasta)* to sell. II **adjudicarse** *vr* to appropriate, take over.

adjuntar *vtr* to enclose.

adjunto,-a I *adj* 1 enclosed, attached. 2 *Educ* assistant. II *nm,f* *Educ* assistant teacher.

adm., admón., *abr de* **administración,** administration.

administración *nf* 1 *(gobierno)* administration, authorities *pl*; *Pol* **a. central,** central government; **a. pública,** civil service. 2 *(de empresa)* administration, management. 3 *(oficina)* (branch) office.

administrador,-a I *nm,f* administrator. II *adj* administrating.

administrar I *vtr* to administer. 2 *(dirigir)* to run, manage. II **administrarse** *vr* to manage one's own money.

administrativo,-a I *adj* administrative. II *nm,f* *(funcionario)* official.

admirable *adj* admirable.

admiración *nf* 1 admiration; **causar a.,** to impress. 2 *Ling* exclamation mark.

admirador,-a *nm,f* admirer.

admirar I *vtr* 1 to admire. 2 *(sorprender)* to amaze, astonish. II **admirarse** *vr* to be amazed, be astonished.

admisible *adj* admissible, acceptable.

admisión *nf* admission; **'reservado el derecho de a.',** 'the management reserves the right to refuse admission'.

admitir *vtr* 1 to admit, let in. 2 *(aceptar)* to accept; **'no se admiten cheques',** 'no cheques accepted'. 3 *(tolerar)* to allow. 4 *(reconocer)* to admit, acknowledge; **admito que mentí,** I admit that I lied.

admonición *nf* warning.

ADN *nm abr de* **ácido desoxirribonucleico,** desoxyribonucleic acid, DNA.

adobar *vtr Culin* to marinate.

adobe *nm* adobe.

adobo *nm* marinade.

adoctrinar *vtr* to indoctrinate.

adolecer [33] *vi* **a. de,** *(carecer de)* to lack; *fig fml* to suffer from.

adolescencia *nf* adolescence.

adolescente *adj & nmf* adolescent.

adónde *adv inter* where (to)?

adonde *adv* where.

adondequiera *adv* wherever.

adopción *nf* adoption.

adoptar *vtr* to adopt.

adoptivo,-a *adj* *(hijo)* adopted; *(padres)* adoptive; *fig* **país a.,** country of adoption.

adoquín *nm* cobble, paving stone.

adorable *adj* adorable.

adorar *vtr* 1 *Rel* to worship. 2 *fig* to adore.

adormecer [33] I *vtr* to send to sleep, make sleepy. II **adormecerse** *vr* 1 *(dormirse)* to doze off. 2 *(brazo etc)* to go to sleep, go numb.

adormecido,-a *adj* sleepy, drowsy.

adormilarse *vr* to doze, drowse.

adornar *vtr* to adorn, decorate.

adorno *nm* decoration, adornment; **de a.,** decorative.

adosado,-a *adj* adjacent; *(casa)* semidetached.

adquirir [31] *vtr* to acquire; *(comprar)* to purchase.

adquisición *nf* acquisition; *(compra)* buy, purchase.

adquisitivo,-a *adj* **poder a.,** purchasing power.

adrede *adv* deliberately, on purpose.

adrenalina *nf* adrenalin.

adriático,-a *nm* **el (Mar) A.,** the Adriatic (Sea).

adscribir *(pp* **adscrito)** I *vtr* 1 *(atribuir)* to ascribe to. 2 *(a un trabajo)* to appoint to. II **adscribirse** *vr* to affiliate (**a**, to).

adscrito,-a *pp de* **adscribir.**

aduana *nf* customs *pl*.

aduanero,-a I *adj* customs. II *nm,f* customs officer.

aducir [10] *vtr* to adduce, allege.

adueñarse *vr* a. de, to take over; *(pánico etc)* to take hold of.

aduje *pt indef* → aducir.

adulación *nf* adulation.

adular *vtr* to adulate.

adulterar *vtr* to adulterate.

adulterio *nm* adultery.

adúltero,-a I *adj* adulterous. II *nm,f (hombre)* adulterer; *(mujer)* adulteress.

adulto,-a *adj & adj* adult.

adusto,-a *adj* harsh, severe.

aduzco *indic pres* → aducir.

advenedizo,-a *adj & nm,f* upstart.

advenimiento *nm* advent, coming.

adverbio *nm* adverb.

adversario,-a I *nm,f* adversary, opponent. II *adj* opposing.

adversidad *nf* adversity; *(revés)* setback.

adverso,-a *adj* adverse.

advertencia *nf* warning.

advertido,-a *adj* warned; *(informado)* informed; **estás o quedas a.**, you've been warned.

advertir [5] *vtr* 1 to warn; *(informar)* to inform, advise; *fam* **te advierto que yo tampoco lo vi**, mind you, I didn't see it either. 2 *(notar)* to realize, notice.

adviento *nm* Advent.

adyacente *adj* adjacent.

aéreo,-a *adj* 1 aerial. 2 *Av* air; **tráfico a.**, air traffic; *Com* **por vía aerea**, by air.

aero- *pref* aero-.

aeróbic *nm* aerobics *sing*.

aerodinámico,-a *adj* aerodynamic; **de línea aerodinámica**, streamlined.

aeródromo *nm* aerodrome.

aeromodelismo *nm* aeroplane modelling *o US* modeling.

aeromoza *nf Am* air hostess.

aeronáutica *nf* aeronautics *sing*.

aeronáutico,-a *adj* **la industria aeronáutica**, the aeronautics industry.

aeronave *nf* airship.

aeroplano *nm* light aeroplane.

aeropuerto *nm* airport.

aerosol *nm* aerosol.

aerostático,-a *adj* **globo a.**, hot-air balloon.

a/f *abr de* a favor, in favour *o US* favor.

afable *adj* affable.

afamado,-a *adj* famous, well-known.

afán *nm (pl* afanes) 1 *(esfuerzo)* effort. 2 *(celo)* zeal.

afanar I *vtr (robar)* to nick, pinch. II **afanarse** *vr* a. por conseguir algo, to do one's best to achieve sth.

afanoso,-a *adj* 1 *(persona)* keen, eager. 2 *(tarea)* hard, tough.

afección *nf* disease.

afectación *nf* affectation.

afectado,-a *adj* affected.

afectar *vtr* a. a, to affect; **le afectó mucho**, she was deeply affected; **nos afecta a todos**, it concerns all of us.

afecto,-a *nm* affection; **tomarle a. a algn**, to become fond of sb.

afectuoso,-a *adj* affectionate.

afeitado *nm* shave.

afeitar *vtr*, **afeitarse** *vr* to shave.

afeminado,-a *adj* effeminate.

aferrado,-a *adj* a. a, clinging to.

aferrar I *vtr Náut* to anchor, moor. II **aferrarse** *vr* to clutch, cling; *fig* a. a una creencia, to cling to a belief.

Afganistán *n* Afghanistan.

afgano,-a *adj & nm,f* Afghan.

afianzamiento *nm* strengthening, reinforcement.

afianzar [4] I *vtr* to strengthen, reinforce. II **afianzarse** *vr (persona)* to become established.

afición *nf* 1 liking; **tiene a. por la música**, he is fond of music. 2 *Dep* **la a.**, the fans *pl*.

aficionado,-a I *nm,f* 1 enthusiast; **un a. a la música**, a music lover. 2 *(no profesional)* amateur. I *adj* 1 keen, fond; **ser a. a algo**, to be fond of sth. 2 *(no profesional)* amateur.

aficionarse *vr* to become fond (a, of), take a liking (a, to).

afilado,-a *adj* sharp.

afilar *vtr* to sharpen.

afiliación *nf* affiliation.

afiliado,-a *nm,f* member.

afiliarse [12] *vr* to become a member.

afín *adj (semejante)* kindred, similar; *(relacionado)* related.

afinar *vtr* 1 *(puntería)* to sharpen. 2 *(instrumento)* to tune.

afincarse [1] *vr* to settle down.

afinidad *nf* affinity.

afirmación *nf* affirmation; **afirmaciones**, *(declaracion)* statement.

afirmar I *vtr (aseverar)* to state, declare. 2 *(afianzar)* to strengthen, reinforce.

afirmativo,-a *adj* affirmative; **en caso a. ...**, if the answer is yes ...

aflicción *nf* affliction.

afligir [6] I *vtr* to afflict. II **afligirse** *vr* to grieve, be distressed.

aflojar I *vtr* to loosen. II *vi (viento etc)* to weaken, grow weak. III **aflojarse** *vr* to come *o* work loose; *(rueda)* to go down.

aflorar *vi* to come to the surface, appear.

afluencia *nf* inflow, influx; **gran a. de público**, great numbers of people.

afluente *nm* tributary.

afluir [37] *vi* to flow (a, into).

afónico,-a *adj* **estar a.**, to have lost one's voice.

aforismo *nm* aphorism.

aforo *nm (capacidad)* seating capacity.

afortunado,-a *adj* fortunate; **las Islas Afortunadas**, the Canaries.

afrenta *nf fml* affront.

África *n* África.

africano,-a *adj & nm,f* African.

afrodisíaco,-a *adj & nm* aphrodisiac.

afrontar *vtr* to confront, face; **a. las consecuencias**, to face the consequences.

afuera I *adv* outside; **la parte de a.**, the outside; **más a.**, further out; **salir a.**, to come *o* go out. II *nfpl* **afueras**, outskirts.

agachar I *vtr* to lower. II **agacharse** *vr* to duck.

agalla *nf* 1 (*de pez*) gill. 2 **tiene agallas**, she's got guts.

agarraderas *nfpl fam* **tener buenas a.**, to be well connected.

agarrado,-a *adj* 1 *fam* stingy, tight. 2 **baile a.**, cheek-to-cheek dancing.

agarrar I *vtr* 1 to grasp, seize; **agárralo fuerte**, hold it tight. 2 *Am* to take. 3 *fam* (*pillar*) to catch; **a. una borrachera**, to get drunk *o* pissed. II **agarrarse** *vr* to hold on; **agarraos bien**, hold tight.

agarrotarse *vr* 1 (*músculo*) to stiffen. 2 (*máquina*) to seize up.

agasajar *vtr* to smother with attentions.

ágata *nf* agate.

agazaparse *vr* to crouch (down).

agencia *nf* agency; (*sucursal*) branch; **a. de viajes**, travel agency; **a. de seguros**, insurance agency; **a. inmobiliaria**, estate agency.

agenciarse [12] *vr* 1 to get oneself; **se agenció una moto**, he got himself a motorbike. 2 **agenciárselas**, to manage.

agenda *nf* diary.

agente *nmf* agent; **a. de policía**, (*hombre*) policeman; (*mujer*) policewoman; **a. de bolsa**, stockbroker; **a. de seguros**, insurance broker.

agigantado,-a *adj* **a pasos agigantados**, by leaps and bounds.

ágil *adj* agile.

agilidad *nf* agility.

agilización *nf* speeding up.

agilizar [4] *vtr* (*trámites*) to speed up.

agitación *nf* (*intranquilidad*) restlessness; (*social, político*) unrest.

agitado,-a *adj* agitated; (*persona*) anxious; (*mar*) rough; **una vida muy agitada**, a very hectic life.

agitar I *vtr* (*botella*) to shake; (*multitud*) to agitate. II **agitarse** *vr* (*persona*) to become agitated; (*mar*) to become rough.

aglomeración *nf* agglomeration; (*de gente*) crowd.

aglomerar *vtr*, **aglomerarse** *vr* 1 (*agruparse*) to agglomerate, amass. 2 (*gente*) to crowd, form a crowd.

agnóstico,-a *adj & nm,f* agnostic.

agobiado,-a *adj* **a. de problemas**, snowed under with problems; *fig* **a. de trabajo**, up to one's eyes in work.

agobiante *adj* (*trabajo*) overwhelming; (*lugar*) claustrophobic; (*calor*) oppressive;

(*persona*) tiresome, tiring.

agobiar [12] I *vtr* to overwhelm. II **agobiarse** *vr* (*con problemas*) to be over-anxious; (*por el calor*) to suffocate.

agobio *nm* 1 (*angustia*) anxiety. 2 (*sofoco*) suffocation.

agolpamiento *nm* crowd, crush.

agolparse *vr* to crowd, throng.

agonía *nf* dying breath, last gasp.

agonizante *adj* dying.

agonizar [4] *vi* to be dying.

agosto *nm* August; *fam* **hacer su a.**, to make a packet.

agotado,-a *adj* 1 (*cansado*) exhausted, worn out. 2 *Com* sold out; (*existencias*) exhausted; (*libro*) out of print.

agotador,-a *adj* exhausting.

agotamiento *nm* exhaustion.

agotar I *vtr* 1 (*cansar*) to exhaust, wear out. 2 (*acabar*) to exhaust, use up (completely). II **agotarse** *vr* 1 (*acabarse*) to run out, be used up; *Com* to be sold out. 2 (*persona*) to become exhausted *o* tired out.

agraciado,-a *adj* 1 (*hermoso*) pretty. 2 (*ganador*) winning; **ser a. con**, to win.

agradable *adj* pleasant.

agradar *vi* to please; **no me agrada, I** don't like it.

agradecer [33] *vtr* 1 (*dar las gracias*) to thank for; **les agradezco su atención**, (I) thank you for your attention; **te lo agradezco mucho**, thank you very much. 2 (*estar agradecido*) to be grateful to; **te agradecería que vinieras**, I'd be grateful if you'd come. 3 (*uso impers*) **siempre se agradece un descanso**, a rest is always welcome.

agradecido,-a *adj* grateful; **le estoy muy a.**, I am very grateful to you.

agradecimiento *nm* gratitude.

agrado *nm* pleasure; **no es de su a.**, it isn't to his liking.

agrandar I *vtr* to enlarge, make larger. II **agrandarse** *vr* to enlarge, become larger.

agrario,-a *adj* agrarian; **política agraria**, agricultural policy.

agravamiento *nm* aggravation.

agravante I *adj Jur* aggravating. II *nm Jur* aggravating circumstance.

agravar I *vtr* to aggravate. II **agravarse** *vr* to worsen, get worse.

agraviar [12] *vtr* to offend, insult.

agravio *nm* offense, insult.

agredir *vtr* defect to assault.

agregación *nf* aggregation.

agregado,-a I *adj Educ* **profesor a.**, (*escuela*) secondary school teacher; *Univ* assistant teacher. II *nm,f Pol* attaché.

agregar [7] I *vtr* 1 (*añadir*) to add. 2 (*destinar*) to appoint. II **agregarse** *vr* **a. a**, to join.

agresión *nf* aggression.

agresividad *nf* aggressiveness.

agresivo,-a adj aggressive.

agresor,-a I nm,f aggressor, attacker. **II** adj attacking.

agriarse vr to turn sour.

agrícola adj agricultural.

agricultor,-a nm,f farmer.

agricultura nf agriculture.

agridulce adj bittersweet.

agrietar I vtr to crack; (piel, labios) to chap. **II agrietarse** vr to crack; (piel) to get chapped.

agringarse [7] vr Am to behave like a gringo.

agrio,-a I adj sour. **II** nmpl agrios, citrus fruits.

agrónomo,-a nm,f (ingeniero) a., agronomist.

agropecuario,-a adj farming, agricultural.

agrupación nf association.

agrupar I vtr to group. **II agruparse** vr I (congregarse) to group together, form a group. 2 (asociarse) to associate.

agua nf water; a. **potable**, drinking water; a. **corriente/del grifo**, running/tap water; a. **dulce/salada**, fresh/salt water; a. **mineral sin/con gas**, still/fizzy or sparkling mineral water; a. **de colonia**, (eau de) cologne; fig **estar con el a. al cuello**, to be up to one's neck in it; **aguas jurisdiccionales**, territorial waters; **aguas residuales**, sewage sing.

aguacate nm (árbol) avocado; (fruto) avocado (pear).

aguacero nm shower, downpour.

aguado,-a adj watered down.

aguafiestas nmf inv spoilsport, wet blanket.

aguafuerte nf 1 Arte etching. 2 Quím nitric acid.

aguamarina nf aquamarine.

aguanieve nf sleet.

aguantar I vtr (soportar) to tolerate; **no lo aguanto más**, I can't stand it any longer. 2 (sostener) to support, hold; **aguanta esto**, hold this. 3 **aguanta la respiración**, hold your breath. **II aguantarse** vr 1 (contenerse) to keep back; (lágrimas) to hold back; **no pude aguantarme la risa**, I couldn't help laughing. 2 (resignarse) to resign oneself.

aguante nm endurance; **tener mucho a.**, (ser paciente) to be very patient; (tener resistencia) to be strong, have a lot of stamina.

aguar [22] vtr to water down; fig **a. la fiesta a algn**, to spoil sb's fun.

aguardar I vtr to await. **II** vi to wait.

aguardiente nm liquor, brandy.

aguarrás nm turpentine.

aguatero,-a nm,f Am water carrier o seller.

agudeza nf 1 sharpness; (del dolor) acuteness. 2 fig (ingenio) witticism, witty say-

ing.

agudización nf 1 sharpening. 2 (empeoramiento) worsening.

agudizar [4] I vtr to intensify, make more acute. **II agudizarse** vr to intensify, become more acute.

agudo,-a adj (dolor) acute; (voz) high-pitched; (sonido) treble, high; fig (ingenioso) witty; fig (sentido) sharp, keen.

agüero nm omen.

aguijón nm sting; fig (estímulo) spur.

águila nf eagle; á. **real**, golden eagle.

aguileño,-a adj aquiline; **nariz aguileña**, aquiline nose.

aguinaldo nm Christmas box; **pedir el a.**, to go carol singing.

aguja nf 1 needle; (de reloj) hand; (de tocadiscos) stylus. 2 Arquit spire. 3 Ferroc point, US switch.

agujerear vtr to make holes in.

agujero nm 1 hole; a. **negro**, black hole. 2 Econ deficit, shortfall.

agujetas nfpl stiffness sing; **tener a.**, to be stiff.

agur interj fam bye!, see you!

aguzar [4] vtr 1 (afilar) to sharpen. 2 fig **a. el oído**, to prick up one's ears; **a. la vista**, to look attentively; **aguzar el ingenio**, to sharpen one's wits.

ahí adv there; a. **está**, there he o she o it is; **ve por a.**, go that way; **está por a.**, it's over there; **setenta o por a.**, seventy or thereabouts; **de a.**, hence.

ahijado,-a nm,f godchild; (niño) godson; (niña) goddaughter; **ahijados**, godchildren.

ahínco nm eagerness; **con a.**, eagerly.

ahíto,-a adj (de comida) full, stuffed; (harto) fed up.

ahogado,-a adj 1 (en líquido) drowned; **morir a.**, to drown. 2 (asfixiado) suffocated. **II** nm,f drowned person.

ahogar [7] I vtr 1 (en líquido) to drown. 2 (asfixiar) to suffocate. **II ahogarse** vr 1 (en líquido) to drown, be drowned; fig **a. en un vaso de agua**, to make a mountain out of a molehill. 2 (asfixiarse) to suffocate. 3 (motor) to be flooded.

ahondar I vtr to deepen. 2 **II** vi to go deep; fig **a. en un problema**, to go into a problem in depth.

ahora I adv 1 (en este momento) now; a. **mismo**, right now; **de a. en adelante**, from now on; **por a.**, for the time being. 2 a. **voy**, I'm coming; a. **vuelvo**, I'll be back in a minute. 3 **hasta a.**, (hasta el momento) until now, so far; (hasta luego) see you later. **II** conj a. **bien**, (sin embargo) however; (y bueno) well then.

ahorcado,-a I nm,f hanged person. **II** adj hanged.

ahorcar [1] I vtr to hang. **II ahorcarse** vr to hang oneself.

ahorita adv Am right now.

ahorrador,-a *adj* thrifty.

ahorrar I *vtr* to save. II **ahorrarse** *vr* **ahórrate los comentarios**, keep your comments to yourself.

ahorrativo,-a *adj* thrifty.

ahorro *nm* 1 saving; **a. energético**, energy saving. 2 **ahorros**, savings; *Fin* **caja de a.**, savings bank.

ahuecar |1| *vtr* 1 to hollow out; *fam* **a. el ala**, to clear off, beat it. 2 (*voz*) to deepen.

ahuevado *adj Am* stupid.

ahumado,-a *adj* (*cristal, jamón*) smoked; (*bacon*) smoky; **salmón a.**, smoked salmon.

ahumar |16| I *vtr* to smoke. II *vi* (*echar humo*) to smoke, give off smoke.

ahuyentar *vtr* to scare away.

aindiado,-a *adj Am* Indian-like.

airado,-a *adj* angry.

airar |15| I *vtr* to anger. II **airarse** *vr* to get angry.

aire *nm* 1 air; **a. acondicionado**, air conditioning; **al a.**, (*hacia arriba*) into the air; (*al descubierto*) uncovered; **al a. libre**, in the open air; **en el a.**, (*pendiente*) in the air; *Rad* on the air; **hacerse a.**, to fan oneself; **saltar por los aires**, to blow up; **tomar el a.**, to get some fresh air; **necesito un cambio de aires**, I need a change of scene. 2 *Aut* choke. 3 (*viento*) wind; **hace a.**, it's windy. 4 (*aspecto*) air, appearance. 5 **él va a su a.**, he goes his own sweet way. 6 **darse aires**, to put on airs.

airear *vtr* (*ropa, lugar*) to air; *fig* (*asunto*) to publicize.

airoso,-a *adj* graceful, elegant; *fig* **salir a. de una situación**, to come out of a situation with flying colours.

aislacionismo *nm* isolationism.

aislado,-a *adj* 1 isolated. 2 *Téc* insulated.

aislamiento *nm* 1 isolation. 2 *Téc* insulation.

aislante I *adj* **cinta a.**, insulating tape. II *nm* insulator.

aislar |15| *vtr* 1 to isolate. 2 *Téc* to insulate.

ajar *vtr* to wear out.

ajedrez *nm* 1 (*juego*) chess. 2 (*piezas y tablero*) chess set.

ajeno,-a *adj* belonging to other people; **los bienes ajenos**, other peoples' goods; **por causas ajenas a nuestra voluntad**, for reasons beyond our control.

ajetreado,-a *adj* (*very*) busy, hectic.

ajetreo *nm* activity, hard work, bustle.

ajillo *nm Culin* **al a.**, fried with garlic.

ajo *nm* garlic; **cabeza/diente de a.**, head/clove of garlic; *fam* **estar en el a.**, to be in on it.

ajonjolí *nm* sesame.

ajorca *nf* bracelet; (*en el tobillo*) anklet.

ajuar *nm* (*de novia*) trousseau.

ajustado,-a *adj* tight.

ajustador,-a *nm,f* fitter.

ajustar *vtr* 1 to adjust. 2 (*apretar*) to tighten. 3 *Fin* (*cuenta*) to settle; *fig* **ajustarle las cuentas a algn**, to settle a score with sb.

ajuste *nm* 1 adjustment; *Téc* assembly; *TV* **carta de a.**, test card. 2 (*de precio*) fixing; (*de cuenta*) settlement; *fig* **a. de cuentas**, settling of scores.

ajusticiar |12| *vtr* to execute.

al (*contracción de a & el*) 1 → **a**. 2 (**al** + *infin*) **al salir**, on leaving; **está al caer**, it's about to happen; **al parecer**, apparently.

ala 1 *nf* 1 wing; *fig* **cortarle las alas a algn**, to clip sb's wings. 2 (*de sombrero*) brim. II *nmf Dep* winger.

alabanza *nf* praise.

alabar *vtr* to praise.

alabastro *nm* alabaster.

alacena *nf* (*food*) cupboard.

alacrán *nm* scorpion.

alambicado,-a *adj* intricate.

alambique *nm* still.

alambrada *nf*, **alambrado** *nm* wire fence.

alambrar *vtr* to fence with wire.

alambre *nm* wire; **a. de púas**, barbed wire.

alambrista *nmf* tightrope walker.

alameda *nf* 1 poplar grove. 2 (*paseo*) avenue, boulevard.

álamo *nm* poplar.

alano,-a *nm,f* (*perro*) a., mastiff.

alarde *nm* (*ostentación*) bragging, boasting; **hacer a. de**, to show off.

alardear *vi* to brag, boast; **a. de rico o de riqueza**, to flaunt one's wealth.

alargadera *nf Elec* extension.

alargado,-a *adj* elongated.

alargar |7| I *vtr* 1 to lengthen; (*estirar*) to stretch; **ella alargó la mano para cogerlo**, she stretched out her hand to get it. 2 (*prolongar*) to prolong, extend. 3 (*dar*) to pass, hand over; **alárgame ese jersey**, can you pass me that jumper? II **alargarse** *vr* 1 to get longer. 2 (*prolongarse*) to go on. 3 **¿puedes a. a casa?**, can you give me a lift home?

alarido *nm* screech, shriek; **dar un a.**, to howl.

alarma *nf* alarm; **la a. saltó**, the alarm went off; **falsa a.**, a false alarm; **señal de a.**, alarm (signal).

alarmado,-a *adj* alarmed.

alarmante *adj* alarming.

alarmar I *vtr* to alarm. II **alarmarse** *vr* to be alarmed.

alazán,-ana *adj & nm,f* (*caballo*) a., chestnut.

alba *nf* dawn, daybreak.

albacea *nmf* (*hombre*) executor; (*mujer*) executrix.

albahaca *nf* basil.
albanés,-esa *adj & nm,f* Albanian.
Albania *n* Albania.
albañal *nm* sewer, drain.
albañil *nm* bricklayer.
albañilería *nf* bricklaying; **pared de a.**, (*obra*) brick wall.
albarán *nm* Com delivery note, despatch note.
albaricoque *nm* (*fruta*) apricot; (*árbol*) apricot tree.
albatros *nm inv* albatross.
albedrío *nm* will; **libre a.**, free will.
alberca *nf* (small) reservoir.
albergar [7] **I** *vtr* (*alojar*) to house, accommodate; *fig* (*sentimientos*) to cherish, harbour, US harbor. **II albergarse** *vtr* to stay.
albergue *nm* hostel; **a. juvenil**, youth hostel.
albino,-a *adj & nm,f* albino.
albóndiga *nf* meatball.
albores *nmpl* beginning *sing*; **en los a. de ...**, at the beginning of ...
albornoz *nm* bathrobe.
alborotado,-a *adj* 1 worked up, agitated. 2 (*desordenado*) untidy, messy. 3 (*mar*) rough; (*tiempo*) stormy.
alborotar I *vtr* (*agitar*) to agitate, work up. 2 (*desordenar*) to make untidy, turn upside down. **II** *vi* to kick up a racket. **III alborotarse** *vr* 1 to get excited *o* worked up. 2 (*mar*) to get rough; (*tiempo*) to get stormy.
alboroto *nm* 1 (*jaleo*) din, racket. 2 (*desorden*) disturbance, uproar.
alborozo *nm* merriment, gaiety.
albufera *nf* lagoon.
álbum *nm* album.
alcachofa *nf* 1 *Bot* artichoke. 2 (*de tubo, regadera*) rose, sprinkler.
alcalde *nm* mayor.
alcaldesa *nf* mayoress.
alcaldía *nf* 1 (*cargo*) mayorship. 2 (*oficina*) mayor's office.
alcalino,-a *adj* alkaline.
alcance *nm* 1 reach; **al a. de cualquiera**, within everybody's reach; **dar a. a**, to catch up with; **fuera del a. de los niños**, out of the reach of children. 2 *fig* scope; (*de noticia*) importance.
alcancía *nf* money box; (*cerdito*) piggy bank.
alcanfor *nm* camphor.
alcantarilla *nf* sewer; (*boca*) drain.
alcantarillado *nm* sewer system.
alcanzar [4] **I** *vtr* 1 to reach; (*persona*) to catch up with; **la producción alcanza dos mil unidades**, production is up to two thousand units. 2 **alcánzame la sal**, (*pasar*) pass me the salt. 3 (*conseguir*) to attain, achieve. **II** *vi* (*ser suficiente*) to be sufficient; **con un kilo no alcanza para todos**, one kilo won't be enough for all

of us.
alcaparra *nf* (*fruto*) caper; (*planta*) caper bush.
alcatraz *nm* Orn gannet.
alcayata *nf* hook.
alcazaba *nf* fortress, citadel.
alcázar *nm* 1 (*fortaleza*) fortress, citadel. 2 (*castillo*) castle, palace.
alcista I *adj* (*bolsa*) rising, bullish; **tendencia a.**, upward tendency. **II** *nmf* (*bolsa*) bull.
alcoba *nf* bedroom.
alcohol *nm* alcohol.
alcoholemia *nf* blood alcohol level; **prueba de a.**, breath test.
alcohólico,-a *adj & nm,f* alcoholic.
alcoholímetro *nm* Breathalyzer®.
alcoholismo *nm* alcoholism.
alcoholizado,-a *adj & nm,f* alcoholic.
alcornoque *nm* cork oak.
alcurnia *nf* lineage, ancestry; **de alta a.**, of noble lineage.
alcuzcuz *nm* couscous.
aldaba *nf* (*llamador*) door knocker.
aldabonazo *nm* 1 loud knock. 2 (*advertencia*) warning.
aldea *nf* village.
aldeano,-a I *adj* village. **II** *nm,f* villager.
aleación *nf* alloy.
aleatorio,-a *adj* random.
aleccionador,-a *adj* (*instructivo*) instructive; (*ejemplar*) exemplary.
aleccionar *vtr* (*instruir*) to teach, instruct; (*adiestrar*) to train.
aledaño,-a I *adj* adjoining, adjacent. **II** *nmpl* aledaños, outskirts.
alegar [7] *vtr* 1 (*aducir*) to claim; *Jur* to allege. 2 (*presentar*) to put forward.
alegato *nm* argument.
alegoría *nf* allegory.
alegrar I *vtr* 1 (*complacer*) to make happy *o* glad; **me alegra que se lo hayas dicho**, I am glad you told her. 2 *fig* (*avivar*) to enliven, brighten up. **II alegrarse** *vr* to be glad, be happy; **me alegro de verte**, I am pleased to see you; **me alegro por ti**, I am happy for you.
alegre I *adj* 1 (*contento*) happy, glad. 2 (*color*) bright; (*música*) lively; (*lugar*) pleasant, cheerful. 3 *fig* (*borracho*) tipsy, merry.
alegría *nf* joy, happiness.
alejado,-a *adj* far away, remote.
alejar I *vtr* to move further away. **II alejarse** *vr* to go away, move away; **no te alejes de mí**, keep close to me.
aleluya *nm & f* hallelujah, alleluia.
alemán,-ana I *adj & nm,f* German. **II** *nm* (*idioma*) German.
Alemania *n* Germany; **A. del Este/Oeste**, East/West Germany; **A. Occidental/Oriental**, West/East Germany.
alentador,-a *adj* encouraging; **un panorama poco a.**, a rather bleak outlook.

alentar |1| *vtr fig* to encourage.
alergia *nf* allergy.
alérgico,-a *adj* allergic.
alero *nm* eaves *pl*.
alerón *nm Av* aileron.
alerta *nf & adj* alert; **estar en estado de a.**, to be (on the) alert.
alertar *vtr* to alert (**de**, to); **nos alertó del peligro**, he alerted us to the danger.
aleta *nf (de pez)* fin; *(de foca, de nadador)* flipper.
aletargado,-a *adj* lethargic.
aletargar |7| *I vtr* to make lethargic. **II aletargarse** *vr* to become lethargic.
aletear *vi* to flutter *o* flap its wings.
alevín *(pescado)* young fish; *fig (principiante)* beginner.
alevosía *nf (traición)* treachery; *(premeditación)* premeditation.
alevoso,-a *adj (persona)* treacherous; *(acto)* premeditated.
alfabético,-a *adj* alphabetic.
alfabetización *nf* teaching to read and write; **campaña de a.**, literacy campaign.
alfabeto *nm* alphabet.
alfalfa *nf* lucerne, alfalfa.
alfarería *nf* **1** *(arte)* pottery. **2** *(taller)* potter's workshop; *(tienda)* pottery shop.
alfarero,-a *nm,f* potter.
alféizar *nm* sill, windowsill.
alférez *nm* second lieutenant.
alfil *nm Ajedrez* bishop.
alfiler *nm* pin; *(broche)* pin, brooch; *(de corbata)* tiepin; *(para tender)* peg.
alfiletero *nm* pin box, pin case.
alfombra *nf (moqueta)* carpet.
alfombrar *vtr* to carpet.
alfombrilla *nf* rug, mat.
alforja *nf (para caballos)* saddlebag; *(para hombro)* knapsack.
alga *nf* alga, *(marina)* seaweed.
algarabía *nf* hubbub, hullabaloo.
algarrobo *nm* carob tree.
algazara *nf* din, row.
álgebra *nf* algebra.
álgido,-a *adj* culminating, critical; **el punto a.**, the climax.
algo I *pron indef* **1** *(afirmativo)* something; *(interrogativo)* anything; **a. así**, something like that; **¿a. más?**, anything else? por **a. será**, there must be a reason for it; **fam a. es a.**, it's better than nothing. **2** *(cantidad indeterminada)* some; **¿queda a. de pastel?**, is there any cake left? **II** *adv* *(un poco)* quite, somewhat; **se siente a. mejor**, she's feeling a bit better.
algodón *nm* cotton; **a. (hidrófilo)**, cotton wool; **a. de azúcar**, candy floss.
algodonero,-a I *nm,f* cotton grower. **II** *adj* cotton.
alguacil *nm* bailiff.
alguien *pron* **1** *(afirmativo)* somebody, someone; *(interrogativo)* anybody, anyone.
algún *adj (delante de nombres masculinos)*

→ **alguno,-a**.
alguno,-a I *adj* **1** *(delante de nombre)* *(afirmativo)* some; *(interrogativo)* any; **algunos días**, some days; **algunas veces**, sometimes; **alguna que otra vez**, now and then; **¿has tomado alguna medicina?**, have you taken any medicine?; **¿le has visto alguna vez?**, have you ever seen him? **2** *(después de nombre)* not at all; **no vino persona alguna**, nobody came. **II** *pron indef* **1** someone, somebody; **a. dirá que ...**, someone might say that ...; **a. que otro**, some. **2** **algunos,-as**, some (people).
alhaja *nf* jewel.
alhelí *nm (pl alhelíes)* wallflower, stock.
aliado,-a I *adj* allied. **II** *nm,f* **los Aliados**, the Allies.
alianza *nf* **1** *(pacto)* alliance. **2** *(anillo)* wedding ring.
aliarse |29| *vr* to become allies, form an alliance.
alias *adv & nm inv* alias.
alicaído,-a *adj* **1** *fig (débil)* weak, feeble. **2** *fig (deprimido)* down, depressed.
alicatar *vtr* to tile.
alicates *nmpl* pliers.
aliciente *nm* **1** *(atractivo)* lure, charm. **2** *(incentivo)* incentive.
alienación *nf* alienation.
alienado,-a *adj* insane, deranged.
alienar *vtr* to alienate.
alienígena *adj & nmf* alien.
aliento *nm* **1** breath; **sin a.**, breathless. **2** *(ánimo)* encouragement.
aligerar I *vtr (acelerar)* to speed up; **a. el paso**, to quicken one's pace. **II** *vi fam* **¡aligera!**, hurry up!
alijo *nm* haul; **un a. de drogas**, a consignment of drugs.
alimaña *nf* vermin.
alimentación *nf (comida)* food; *(acción)* feeding; *Téc* supply.
alimentar I *vtr* **1** *(dar alimento)* to feed; *(ser nutritivo)* to be nutritious. **2** *fig (sentimientos)* to nourish. **3** *Inform* to feed; *Téc* to supply. **II alimentarse** *vr* **a. con** *o* **de**, to live on.
alimentario,-a *adj* food.
alimenticio,-a *adj* nutritious; **productos alimenticios**, food products, foodstuffs; **valor a.**, nutritional value.
alimento *nm* **1** *(comida)* food. **2** *fig* **tiene poco a.**, it is not very nourishing.
alimón *adv* **al a.**, together.
alineación *nf* **1** alignment. **2** *Dep (equipo)* line-up.
alineado,-a *adj* aligned, lined-up; **países no alineados**, non-aligned countries.
alineamiento *nm* alignment.
alinear I *vtr* to align, line up. **II alinearse** *vr* to line up.
aliñar *vtr* to season, flavour, *US* flavor; *(ensalada)* to dress.

aliño *nm* seasoning, dressing.

alioli *nm* garlic mayonnaise.

alisar *vtr*, **alisarse** *vr* to smooth.

alistar I *vtr* *Mil* to recruit, enlist. **II alistarse** *vr* *Mil* to enlist, enrol, *US* enroll.

aliviar [12] **I** *vtr* (*dolor*) to soothe, relieve; (*carga*) to lighten, make lighter. **II aliviarse** *vr* (*dolor*) to diminish, get better.

alivio *nm* relief.

aljibe *nm* cistern, tank.

allá *adv* 1 (*lugar alejado*) there, over there; **a. abajo/arriba**, down/up there; **¡a. voy!**, here I go!; **más a.**, further on; **más a. de**, beyond; **el más a.**, the beyond. 2 (*tiempo*) **a. por los años veinte**, back in the twenties. 3 **a. tú**, that's your problem.

allanamiento *nm* *Jur* **a. de morada**, unlawful entry.

allanar *vtr* 1 (*terreno*) to level, flatten; *fig* (*camino*) to smooth. 2 *Jur* to break into.

allegado,-a I *adj* close. **II** *nm,f* close friend.

allende *adv* *fml* beyond; **a. los mares**, overseas.

allí *adv* there, over there; **a. abajo/arriba**, down/up there; **de a. para acá**, back and forth; **por a.**, (*movimiento*) that way; (*posición*) over there.

alma *nf* soul; **no había ni un a.**, there was not a soul.

almacén *nm* 1 (*local*) warehouse; (*habitación*) storeroom. 2 *Com* (**grandes**) **almacenes**, department store *sing*.

almacenaje *nm* storage, warehousing.

almacenamiento *nm* storage, warehousing; *Inform* storage.

almacenar *vtr* to store.

almacenista *nmf* (*vendedor*) wholesaler; (*propietario*) warehouse owner.

almanaque *nm* calendar.

almeja *nf* clam; *vulg* cunt.

almena *nf* merlon.

almendra *nf* almond; **a. garapiñada**, sugared almond.

almendro *nm* almond tree.

almiar *nm* haystack.

almíbar *nm* syrup.

almidón *nm* starch.

almidonar *vtr* to starch.

alminar *nm* minaret.

almirante *nm* admiral.

almizcle *nm* musk.

almohada *nf* pillow; *fam* **consultarlo con la a.**, to sleep on it.

almohadilla *nf* (small) cushion.

almohadón *nm* large pillow, cushion.

almorrana *nf* *fam* pile.

almorzar [2] **I** *vi* to have lunch. **II** *vtr* to have for lunch.

almuerzo *nm* lunch.

alocado,-a *adj* thoughtless, rash.

alocución *nf* speech, address.

alojamiento *nm* accommodation; **dar a.**, to accommodate.

alojar I *vtr* to accommodate. **II alojarse** *vr* to stay.

aló *interj* *Am* *Tel* hello.

alondra *nf* lark; **a. común**, skylark.

alpaca *nf* alpaca.

alpargata *nf* canvas sandal, espadrille.

Alpes *npl* **los A.**, the Alps.

alpinismo *nm* mountaineering, climbing.

alpinista *nmf* mountaineer, climber.

alpino,-a *adj* Alpine; **esquí a.**, downhill skiing.

alquilar *vtr* to hire; (*pisos, casas*) to rent; **'se alquila'**, 'to let'.

alquiler *nm* 1 (*de pisos, casas*) renting, letting; **a. de coches**, car hire; **de a.**, (*pisos, casas*) to let, rented; (*coche*) for hire; (*televisión*) for rent. 2 (*precio*) hire, rental; (*de pisos, casas*) rent.

alquimia *nf* alchemy.

alquitrán *nm* tar.

alrededor I *adv* (*lugar*) round, around; **mira a.**, look around; **a. de la mesa**, round the table; **a. de las dos**, around two o'clock; **a. de quince**, about fifteen; **II** *nmpl* **alrededores**, surrounding area *sing*; **en los alrededores de Murcia**, in the area round Murcia.

alta *nf* **dar de** *o* **el a.**, (*a un enfermo*) to discharge from hospital.

altanería *nf* arrogance.

altanero,-a *adj* arrogant.

altar *nm* altar.

altavoz *nm* loudspeaker.

alterable *adj* changeable.

alteración *nf* 1 (*cambio*) alteration. 2 (*alboroto*) quarrel, row; **a. del orden público**, disturbance of the peace. 3 (*excitación*) agitation.

alterar I *vtr* to alter, change; **a. el orden público**, to disturb the peace. **II alterarse** *vr* 1 (*cambiar*) to change. 2 (*inquietarse*) to be upset.

altercado *nm* quarrel, argument.

alternar I *vtr* to alternate. **II** *vi* (*relacionarse*) to meet people, socialize. **III alternarse** *vr* to alternate.

alternativa *nf* alternative.

alternativo,-a *adj* alternative.

alterno,-a *adj* alternate; **días alternos**, alternate days.

alteza *nf* Highness; **Su A. Real**, His *o* Her Royal Highness.

altibajos *nmpl* *fig* ups and downs.

altiplano *nm* high plateau.

altísimo *-a* *nm* **el A.**, the Almighty.

altisonante *adj* grandiloquent.

altitud *nf* altitude.

altivez *nf* arrogance, haughtiness.

altivo,-a *adj* arrogant, haughty.

alto¹ *nm* 1 (*interrupción*) stop, break. 2 *Mil* halt; **dar el a.**, to order to halt; **un a. el fuego**, a cease-fire.

alto,-a² I *adj* 1 (*persona, árbol, edificio*) tall; (*montaña, techo, presión*) high; (*sonido*) loud; *fig* (*precio, tecnología*) high; (*tono*) high-pitched; **los pisos altos**, the top floors; **en lo a.**, at the top; **alta sociedad**, high society; **clase alta**, upper class; **en voz alta**, aloud, in a loud voice; **a altas horas de la noche**, late at night. II *adv* 1 high, high up. 2 (*sonar, hablar etc*) loud, loudly; **pon la radio más alta**, turn the radio up; **¡habla más a.!**, speak up. III *nm* 1 (*altura*) height; **¿cuánto tiene de a.?**, how tall/high is it?; *fig* **por todo lo a.**, in a grand way. 2 (*elevación*) hill.
◆**altamente** *adv* highly, extremely.

altoparlante *nm Am* loudspeaker.

altozano *nm* hillock, hill.

altramuz *nm* lupin.

altruista I *adj* altruistic. II *nmf* altruist.

altura *nf* 1 height; **de diez metros de a.**, ten metres high. 2 (*nivel*) level; **a la misma a.**, on the same level; *Geog* on the same latitude; **a la a. del cine**, by the cinema; *fig* **estar a la a. de las circunstancias**, to meet the challenge; *fig* **no está a su a.**, he does not measure up to him; *fig* **a estas alturas**, at this stage. 3 *Rel* **alturas**, heaven *sing*.

alubia *nf* bean.

alucinación *nf* hallucination.

alucinado,-a *adj arg* amazed.

alucinante *adj arg* brilliant, mind-blowing.

alucinar I *vtr* to hallucinate; *fig* (*encantar*) to fascinate. II *vi arg* to be amazed, be spaced out.

alucinógeno,-a I *adj* hallucinogenic. II *nm* hallucinogen.

alud *nm* avalanche.

aludido,-a *adj fig* **darse por a.**, to take it personally.

aludir *vi* to allude to, mention.

alumbrado,-a I *adj* lit. II *nm Elec* lighting; **a. público**, street lighting.

alumbrar I *vtr* (*iluminar*) to light, illuminate. II *vi* (*parir*) to give birth.

aluminio *nm* aluminium, *US* aluminum.

alumnado *nm* (*de colegio*) pupils *pl*; *Univ* student body.

alumno,-a *nm,f* 1 (*de colegio*) pupil; **a. externo**, day pupil; **a. interno**, boarder. 2 *Univ* student.

alusión *nf* allusion, mention.

aluvión *nm* downpour; *fig* **un a. de preguntas**, a barrage of questions.

alverja, alverjana *nf Am* pea.

alza *nf* 1 rise, rising; **en a.**, rising; **jugar al a.**, (*bolsa*) to bull the market. 2 *Mil* sight.

alzado,-a I *adj* raised, lifted; **votación a mano alzada**, vote by a show of hands. II *nm Arquit* elevation.

alzamiento *nm* (*rebelión*) uprising.

alzar [4] I *vtr* to raise, lift; **a. el vuelo**, to take off; **a. los ojos/la vista**, to look up;

álzate el cuello, turn your collar up. II **alzarse** *vr* 1 (*levantarse*) to get up, rise. 2 (*rebelarse*) to rise, rebel. 3 **a. con la victoria**, to win, be victorious.

ama *nf* (*señora*) lady of the house; (*dueña*) owner; **a. de casa**, housewife; **a. de llaves**, housekeeper.

amabilidad *nf* kindness; *fml* **tenga la a. de esperar**, would you be so kind as to wait?

amable *adj* kind, nice; *fml* **¿sería usted tan a. de ayudarme?**, would you be so kind as to help me?

a.m. *adv a.m.*

amado,-a I *adj* loved, beloved. II *nm,f* sweetheart.

amaestrar *vtr* to train; (*domar*) to tame.

amagar [7] *vtr* (*amenazar*) to threaten; **amaga tormenta**, a storm is threatening.

amago *nm* 1 (*indicio*) first sign; **a. de infarto**, onset of a heart attack. 2 (*intento*) attempt. 3 *fig* (*amenaza*) threat.

amainar *vi* (*viento etc*) to drop, die down.

amalgama *nf* amalgam.

amalgamar *vtr* to amalgamate.

amamantar *vtr* to breast-feed; *Zool* to suckle.

amancay *nm Am* amaryllis.

amancebarse *vr* to cohabit.

amanecer [33] I *v impers* to dawn; **¿a qué hora amanece?**, when does it get light?; **amaneció lluvioso**, it was rainy at daybreak. II *vi* **amanecimos en Finlandia**, we were in Finland at daybreak; **amaneció muy enfermo**, he woke up feeling very ill. III *nm* dawn, daybreak; **al a.**, at dawn.

amanerado,-a *adj* mannered, affected.

amansar *vtr* 1 to tame. 2 *fig* (*apaciguar*) to tame, calm.

amante *nmf* lover; **a. del arte**, art lover.

amañar *vtr* to fix, fiddle; (*elecciones*) to rig.

amapola *nf* poppy.

amar I *vtr* to love. II **amarse** *vr* to love each other.

amaraje *nm Av* landing at sea.

amargado,-a I *adj* (*rencoroso*) embittered, bitter; *fam* (*agobiado*) pissed off; **estoy a. con los exámenes**, I'm pissed off with the exams. II *nm,f* bitter person.

amargar [7] I *vtr* to make bitter; *fig* to embitter, sour. II **amargarse** *vr fig* to become embittered *o* bitter; **no te amargues por eso**, don't let that make you bitter.

amargo,-a *adj* bitter.

amargor *nm*, **amargura** *nf* bitterness.

amarillento,-a *adj* yellowish.

amarillo,-a *adj & nm* yellow; **prensa amarilla**, gutter press.

amarilloso,-a *adj Am* yellowish.

amarra *nf* mooring rope; **soltar amarras**, to cast off, let go.

amarradero *nm* mooring.

amarrar *vtr Náut* to moor, tie up; *(atar)* to tie (up), bind.

amasar *vtr* 1 *Culin* to knead. 2 *fig (fortuna)* to amass.

amasijo *nm fam* hotchpotch, jumble.

amateur *adj & nmf* amateur.

amatista *nf* amethyst.

amazona *nf* 1 *(jinete)* horsewoman. 2 *(en mitología)* Amazon.

Amazonas *n* el A., the Amazon.

amazónico,-a *adj* Amazonian.

ambages *nmpl* **hablar sin a.**, to go straight to the point.

ámbar *nm* amber.

Amberes *n* Antwerp.

ambición *nf* ambition.

ambicionar *vtr* to have as an ambition; **ambiciona ser presidente**, his ambition is to become president.

ambicioso,-a I *adj* ambitious. II *nm,f* ambitious person.

ambidextro,-a *nm,f* ambidextrous person.

ambientación *nf Cin Teat* setting.

ambientado,-a *adj (bar etc)* lively.

ambiental *adj* environmental.

ambientar I *vtr* 1 *(bar etc)* to liven up. 2 *Cin Teat* to set. II **ambientarse** *vr (a-daptarse)* to get used to.

ambiente I *nm* environment; *fig (medio)* environment, milieu. II *adj* environmental; **temperatura a.**, room temperature.

ambigüedad *nf* ambiguity.

ambiguo,-a *adj* ambiguous.

ámbito *nm* field; **empresa de a. nacional**, nationwide company.

ambos,-as *adj pl fml* both; **por a. lados**, on both sides.

ambulancia *nf* ambulance.

ambulante *adj* travelling, *US* traveling, mobile; **biblioteca a.**, a mobile library.

ambulatorio *nm* surgery, clinic.

amedrentar *vtr* to frighten, scare.

amén[1] *nm* amen.

amén[2] *adv* **a. de**, in addition to.

amenaza *nf* threat.

amenazador,-a, amenazante *adj* threatening, menacing.

amenazar [4] *vtr* to threaten; **a. de muerte a algn**, to threaten to kill sb.

amenizar [4] *vtr* to liven up.

ameno,-a *adj* entertaining.

América *n* America; **A. Central/del Norte/del Sur**, Central/North/South America.

americana *nf (prenda)* jacket.

americano,-a *adj & nm,f* American.

amerindio,-a *adj & nm,f* Amerindian, American Indian.

amerizar [4] *vi* → **amarar**.

ametralladora *nf* machine gun.

ametrallar *vtr* to machine-gun.

amianto *nm* asbestos *sing*.

amigable *adj* friendly.

amígdala *nf* tonsil.

amigdalitis *nf* tonsillitis.

amigo,-a I *nm,f* friend; **hacerse a. de**, to make friends with; **hacerse amigos**, to become friends; **son muy amigos**, they are very good friends. II *adj (aficionado)* fond (de, of).

amilanar I *vtr* to frighten, scare. II **amilanarse** *vr* to be frightened.

aminorar *vtr* to reduce; **a. el paso**, to slow down.

amistad *nf* 1 friendship. 2 **amistades**, friends.

amistoso,-a *adj* friendly.

amnesia *nf* amnesia.

amnistía *nf* amnesty.

amo *nm* 1 *(dueño)* owner. 2 *(señor)* master.

amodorrarse *vr* to become sleepy *o* drowsy.

amoldar I *vtr* to adapt, adjust. II **amoldarse** *vr* to adapt oneself.

amonestación *nf* 1 rebuke, reprimand; *Dep* warning. 2 *Rel* **amonestaciones**, banns.

amonestar *vtr* 1 *(advertir)* to rebuke, reprimand; *Dep* to warn. 2 *Rel* to publish the banns of.

amoníaco, amoniaco *nm* ammonia.

amontonar I *vtr* to pile up, heap up. II **amontonarse** *vr* to pile up, heap up; *(gente)* to crowd together.

amor *nm* love; **hacer el a.**, to make love; **a. propio**, self-esteem; **¡por el a. de Dios!**, for God's sake!

amoral *adj* amoral.

amoratado,-a *adj (de frío)* blue with cold; *(de un golpe)* black and blue.

amordazar [4] *vtr (perro)* to muzzle; *(persona)* to gag.

amorfo,-a *adj* amorphous.

amorío *nm* love affair, flirtation.

amoroso,-a *adj* loving, affectionate.

amortajar *vtr* to shroud, wrap in a shroud.

amortiguador *nm Aut* shock absorber.

amortiguar [22] *vtr (golpe)* to cushion; *(ruido)* to muffle; *(luz)* to subdue.

amortización *nf* payment.

amortizar [4] *vtr* to pay off.

amotinado,-a *nm,f* rioter; *Mil* mutineer.

amotinamiento *nm* riot, rioting; *Mil* mutiny.

amotinar I *vtr* to incite to riot; *Mil* to incite to mutiny. II **amotinarse** *vr* to rise up; *Mil* to mutiny.

amparar I *vtr* to protect. II **ampararse** *vr* to seek refuge.

amparo *nm* protection, shelter; **al a. de la ley**, under the protection of the law.

amperio *nm* ampère, amp.

ampliación *nf* enlargement; *(de plazo, casa)* extension.

ampliar [29] *vtr* to enlarge; *(casa, plazo)*

to extend.

amplificador *nm* amplifier.

amplificar [1] *vtr* to amplify.

amplio,-a *adj* large, roomy; *(ancho)* wide, broad; **en el sentido más a. de la palabra,** in the broadest sense of the word.

amplitud *nf* 1 spaciousness; a. **de miras,** broad-mindedness. 2 *(de espacio)* room, space. 3 *Fís* amplitude.

ampolla *nf* 1 *Med* blister; *fig* **levantar ampollas,** to raise people's hackles. 2 *(de medicina)* ampoule.

ampuloso,-a *adj* pompous, bombastic.

amputar *vtr Med* to amputate; *fig* to cut out.

amueblar *vtr* to furnish.

amuermar *vtr fam* 1 *(atontar)* to make feel dopey *o* groggy. 2 *(aburrir)* to bore.

amuleto *nm* amulet; a. **de la suerte,** lucky charm.

amurallar *vtr* to wall, fortify.

anacronismo *nm* anachronism.

ánade *nm* duck; á. **real,** mallard.

anales *nmpl* annals.

analfabetismo *nm* illiteracy.

analfabeto,-a *adj & nm,f* illiterate.

analgésico,-a *adj & nm* analgesic.

análisis *nm inv* analysis; a. **de sangre,** blood test.

analista *nmf* analyst.

analizar [4] *vtr* to analyze.

analogía *nf* analogy.

analógico,-a *adj* analog.

análogo,-a *adj* analogous, similar.

ananá *nm (pl ananaes),* **ananás** *nm (pl ananases)* pineapple.

anaquel *nm* shelf.

anaranjado,-a *adj & nm* orange.

anarquía *nf* anarchy.

anarquismo *nm* anarchism.

anarquista *adj & nmf* anarchist.

anatomía *nf* anatomy.

anatómico,-a *adj* anatomical.

anca *nf* haunch; **ancas de rana,** frogs' legs.

ancestral *adj* ancestral.

ancho,-a I *adj* wide, broad; a **lo a.,** breadthwise; **te está muy a.,** it's too big for you. II *nm* 1 *(anchura)* width, breadth; **dos metros de a.,** two metres wide; **¿qué a. tiene?,** how wide is it? 2 *Cost* width. III *nfpl fam* a **mis o tus anchas,** at ease, comfortable.

anchoa *nf* anchovy.

anchura *nf* width, breadth.

anciano,-a I *adj* very old. II *nm,f* old person; **los ancianos,** old people.

ancla *nf* anchor.

anclar *vtr & vi* to anchor.

andadas *nfpl* **volver a las a.,** to go back to one's old tricks.

andaderas *nfpl* baby-walker *sing.*

andadura *nf* walking.

Andalucía *n* Andalusia.

andaluz,-a *adj & nm,f* Andalusian.

andamiaje, andamio *nm* scaffolding.

andanza *nf* adventure, happening.

andar *nm, andares nmpl* walk *sing,* gait *sing.*

andar [8] I *vi* 1 to walk. 2 *(coche etc)* to move; **este coche anda despacio,** this car goes very slowly. 3 *(funcionar)* to work; **esto no anda,** this doesn't work. 4 *fam* **anda por los cuarenta,** he's about forty; **anda siempre diciendo que ...,** he's always saying that ...; **¿cómo andamos de tiempo?,** how are we off for time?; **tu bolso debe a. por ahí,** your bag must be over there somewhere. II *vtr (recorrer)* to walk.

andariego,-a *adj* fond of walking.

andén *nm* platform.

Andes *npl* Andes.

andinismo *nm Am* mountaineering.

andino,-a *adj & nm,f* Andean.

andrajo *nm* rag, tatter.

andrajoso,-a *adj* ragged, tattered.

androide *nm* android.

andurriales *nmpl fam* out-of-the way place *sing.*

anécdota *nf* anecdote.

anecdótico,-a *adj* anecdotal.

anegar *vtr,* **anegarse** *vr* [7] to flood.

anejo a I *adj* attached, joined (a, to). II *nm* appendix.

anemia *nf* anaemia, *US* anemia.

anestesia *nf* anaesthesia, *US* anesthesia.

anestésico,-a *adj & nm* anaesthetic, *US* anesthetic.

anexar *vtr* to annex.

anexión *nf* annexation.

anexionar *vtr* to annex.

anexo a I *adj* attached, joined (a, to). II *nm* appendix.

anfetamina *nf* amphetamine.

anfibio,-a I *adj* amphibious. II *nm* amphibian.

anfiteatro *nm* 1 amphitheatre, *US* amphitheater. 2 *Cin Teat* gallery.

anfitrión,-ona I *nm* host. II *nf* hostess.

ángel *nm* 1 angel; á. **de la guarda,** guardian angel. 2 *Am (micrófono)* hand microphone.

angelical, angélico,-a *adj* angelic.

angina *nf* angina; **tener anginas,** to have tonsilitis; *Med* a. **de pecho,** angina pectoris.

anglófono,-a I *adj* English speaking. II *nm,f* English speaker.

anglosajón,-ona *adj & nm,f* Anglo-Saxon.

angosto,-a *adj fml* narrow.

anguila *nf* eel; a. **de mar,** conger eel.

angula *nf* elver.

angular *adj* angular; *Fot (objetivo)* **gran a.,** wide-angle lens; **piedra a.,** cornerstone.

ángulo *nm* angle; *(rincón)* corner.

angustia *nf* anguish.

angustiar [12] *vtr* to distress.

angustioso,-a *adj* distressing.

anhelar *vtr* to long for, yearn for.

anhelo *nm* longing, yearning.

anhídrido *nm* a. carbónico, carbon dioxide.

anidar *vi* to nest.

anilla *nf* ring; **carpeta de anillas,** ring-binder.

anillo *nm* ring; **a. de boda,** wedding ring.

ánima *nf* soul.

animación *nf* (*diversión*) entertainment.

animado,-a *adj* (*fiesta etc*) lively.

animador,-a *nm,f* 1 entertainer; *TV* presenter; **a. cultural,** cultural organiser. 2 *Dep* cheerleader.

animadversión *nf* ill feeling, animosity.

animal I *nm* animal; *fig* (*basto*) brute; (*necio*) dunce. II *adj* animal.

animar I *vtr* 1 (*alentar*) to encourage. 2 (*alegrar*) (*persona*) to cheer up; (*fiesta, bar*) to liven up, brighten up. II **animarse** *vr* 1 (*persona*) to cheer up; (*fiesta, reunión*) to brighten up. 2 **¿te animas a venir?**, do you fancy coming along?

anímico,-a *adj* **estado a.,** frame *o* state of mind.

ánimo *nm* 1 (*espíritu*) spirit; **estado de á.,** frame *o* state of mind. 2 **con á. de,** (*intención*) with the intention of. 3 (*valor, coraje*) courage; **dar ánimos a,** to encourage; **¡a.!,** cheer up!.

animosidad *nf* animosity.

animoso,-a *adj* cheerful.

aniñado,-a *adj* childlike; *pey* childish.

aniquilación *nf* annihilation.

aniquilar *vtr* to annihilate.

anís *nm* 1 (*bebida*) anisette. 2 (*grano*) aniseed.

anisete *nm* anisette.

aniversario *nm* anniversary.

ano *nm* anus.

anoche *adv* last night; (*por la tarde*) yesterday evening; **antes de a.,** the night before last.

anochecer [33] I *v impers* to get dark; **cuando anochece,** at nightfall, at dusk. II *vi* to be somewhere at dusk; **anochecimos en Cuenca,** we were in Cuenca at dusk. III *nm* nightfall, dusk.

anodino,-a *adj* (*insustancial*) insubstantial; (*soso*) insipid, dull.

anomalía *nf* anomaly.

anómalo,-a *adj* anomalous.

anonadado,-a *adj* **me quedé/dejó a.,** I was astonished.

anonimato *nm* anonimity; **permanecer en el a.,** to remain anonymous *o* nameless.

anónimo,-a I *adj* 1 (*desconocido*) anonymous. 2 *Com* **sociedad anónima,** public liability company, *US* corporation. II *nm* (*carta*) anonymous letter.

anorak *nm* (*pl* **anoraks**) anorak.

anorexia *nf* anorexia.

anormal I *adj* 1 abnormal. 2 (*inhabitual*) unusual; **una situación a.,** an irregular situation. 3 *Med* subnormal. II *nmf Med* subnormal person.

anotación *nf* 1 annotation. 2 (*apunte*) note.

anotar *vtr* 1 to annotate. 2 (*apuntar*) to take down, make a note of.

anquilosado,-a *adj fig* fossilized; **a. en el pasado,** locked in the past.

anquilosarse *vr fig* to stagnate.

ansia *nf* 1 (*deseo*) longing, yearning. 2 (*ansiedad*) anxiety. 3 *Med* sick feeling.

ansiar [29] *vtr* to long for, yearn for.

ansiedad *nf* anxiety; **con a.,** anxiously.

ansioso,-a *adj* 1 (*deseoso*) eager (**por,** for). 2 (*avaricioso*) greedy.

antagónico,-a *adj* antagonistic.

antagonismo *nm* antagonism.

antagonista I *adj* antagonistic. II *nmf* antagonist.

antaño *adv* in the past, formerly.

antártico,-a I *adj* Antarctic. II *nm* **el A.,** the Antarctic.

Antártida *n* Antarctica.

ante¹ *nm* 1 *Zool* elk, moose. 2 (*piel*) suede.

ante² *prep* 1 before, in the presence of; *Jur* **a. notario,** in the presence of a notary; **a. todo,** most of all. 2 (*en vista de*) faced with, in view of; **a. la crisis energética,** faced with the energy crisis.

anteanoche *adv* the night before last.

anteayer *adv* the day before yesterday.

antecedente I *adj* previous. II *nm* antecedent. III *nmpl* 1 **antecedentes,** (*historial*) record *sing*; *Jur* **antecedentes penales,** criminal record *sing*. 2 *fig* **poner en antecedentes,** to put in the picture.

anteceder *vtr* to precede, go before.

antecesor,-a *nm,f* 1 (*en un cargo*) predecessor. 2 (*antepasado*) ancestor.

antedicho,-a *adj* abovementioned.

antelación *nf* notice; **con poca a.,** at short notice; **con un mes de a.,** a month beforehand, with a month's notice.

antemano *adv* **de a.,** beforehand, in advance.

antena *nf* 1 *Rad TV* aerial; **a. parabólica,** dish aerial; **en a.,** on the air. 2 *Zool* antenna, feeler.

anteojo *nm* 1 telescope. 2 **anteojos,** (*binoculares*) binoculars, field glasses; *Am* (*gafas*) glasses, spectacles.

antepasado,-a *nm,f* ancestor.

antepecho *nm* (*de ventana*) sill; (*pretil*) parapet, guardrail.

antepenúltimo,-a *adj* antepenultimate; **el capítulo a.,** the last chapter but two.

anteponer [19] (*pp* **antepuesto**) *vtr fig* to give preference to.

anteproyecto *nm* preliminary plan, draft;

Pol a. de ley, draft bill.

antepuesto,-a *pp* → **anteponer**.

antepuse *pt indef* → **anteponer**.

anterior *adj* 1 previous; **el día a.**, the day before. 2 *(delantero)* front; **parte a.**, front part. ◆**anteriormente** *adv* previously, before.

anterioridad *nf* **con a.**, before; **con a. a**, prior to, before.

antes *adv* 1 *(tiempo)* before; **a. de las tres**, before three o'clock; **mucho a.**, long before; **la noche a.**, the night before; **cuanto a.**, as soon as possible. 2 *(antaño)* in the past; **a. llovía más**, it used to rain more in the past. 3 *(lugar)* before; **a. del semáforo**, before the traffic lights. 4 **a. prefiero hacerlo yo**, I'd rather do it myself; **a. (bien)**, on the contrary.

antesala *nf* antechamber, anteroom; *fig* **en la a. de**, on the eve of.

anti- *pref* anti-.

antiadherente *adj* nonstick.

antiaéreo,-a *adj* anti-aircraft.

antibiótico,-a *adj & nm* antibiotic.

anticaspa *adj* anti-dandruff.

anticición *nm* anticyclone, high pressure area.

anticipación *nf* bringing forward; **con a.**, in advance.

anticipado,-a *adj* brought forward; **elecciones anticipadas**, early elections; **gracias anticipadas**, thanks in advance; *Com* **por a.**, in advance. ◆**anticipadamente** *adv* in advance.

anticipar I *vtr (acontecimiento)* to bring forward; *(dinero)* to pay in advance; **no anticipemos acontecimientos**, we'll cross that bridge when we come to it. II **anticiparse** *vr* 1 *(adelantarse)* to beat to it; **iba a decírtelo, pero él se me anticipó**, I was going to tell you, but he beat me to it. 2 *(llegar pronto)* to arrive early; *fig* **a. a su tiempo**, to be ahead of one's time.

anticipo *nm (adelanto)* advance; **pedir un a.**, to ask for an advance (on one's wages).

anticonceptivo,-a *adj & nm* contraceptive.

anticongelante *adj & nm (de radiador)* antifreeze; *(de parabrisas)* de-icer.

anticonstitucional *adj* unconstitutional.

anticuado,-a *adj* antiquated.

anticuario,-a *nm,f* antique dealer.

anticuerpo *nm* antibody.

antídoto *nm* antidote.

antier *adv* the day before yesterday.

antiestético,-a *adj* ugly, unsightly.

antifaz *nm* mask.

antigás *adj inv* **careta/mascarilla a.**, gas mask.

antigualla *nf* old-fashioned thing.

antigüedad *nf* 1 *(período histórico)* antiquity; **en la a.**, in olden days, in for-

mer times. 2 *(en cargo)* seniority. 3 **tienda de antigüedades**, antique shop.

antiguo,-a *adj* 1 old, ancient. 2 *(pasado de moda)* old-fashioned. 3 *(en cargo)* senior. 4 *(anterior)* former.

antihigiénico,-a *adj* unhygienic, unhealthy.

antihistamínico,-a *adj & nm* antihistamine.

Antillas *npl* **las A.**, the West Indies, the Antilles.

antinatural *adj* unnatural, contrary to nature.

antiniebla *adj inv* **luces a.**, foglamps, *US* foglights.

antipatía *nf* antipathy, dislike; **tener a. a**, to dislike.

antipático,-a *adj* unpleasant; **Pedro me es a.**, I don't like Pedro.

antípodas *npl* **las A.**, the Antipodes.

antiquísimo,-a *adj (superl de antiguo)* very old, ancient.

antirrobo I *adj inv* antitheft; **alarma a.**, burglar alarm; *(para coche)* car alarm. II *nm (para coche)* car alarm; *(para casa)* burglar alarm.

antisemita I *adj* anti-Semitic. II *nmf* anti-Semite.

antiséptico,-a *adj & nm* antiseptic.

antítesis *nf inv* antithesis.

antojadizo,-a *adj* capricious, unpredictable.

antojarse *vr* 1 **cuando se me antoja**, when I feel like it; **se le antojó un helado**, he fancied an ice-cream. 2 *(suponer)* **se me antoja que no lo sabe**, I have the feeling that he doesn't know.

antojo *nm* 1 *(capricho)* whim, caprice; *(de embarazada)* craving; **a su a.**, in one's own way, as one pleases. 2 *(en la piel)* birthmark.

antología *nf* anthology.

antonomasia *nf* **por a.**, par excellence.

antorcha *nf* torch.

antro *nm* dump, hole; *fig* **a. de perdición**, den of vice.

antropología *nf* anthropology.

antropólogo,-a *nm,f* anthropologist.

anual *adj* annual; **ingresos anuales**, yearly income.

anualidad *nf* annual payment, annuity.

anuario *nm* yearbook.

anudar *vtr* 1 *(atar)* to knot, tie. 2 *fig (unir)* to join, bring together.

anulación *nf* cancellation; *(de matrimonio)* annulment; *(de ley)* repeal.

anular[1] *nm* ring finger.

anular[2] *vtr* 1 *Com (pedido)* to cancel; *Dep (gol)* to disallow; *(matrimonio)* to annul; *(ley)* to repeal. 2 *Inform* to delete.

anunciador,-a *adj* **empresa anunciadora**, advertising company.

anunciante *nmf* advertiser.

anunciar [12] I *vtr* 1 *(producto etc)* to

advertise. 2 *(avisar)* to announce. II **anunciarse** *vr* to advertise oneself; **a. en un periódico**, to put an advert in a newspaper.

anuncio *nm* 1 *(comercial)* advertisment, advert, ad. 2 *(aviso)* announcement. 3 *(cartel)* notice, poster.

anzuelo *nm* (fish) hook.

añadidura *nf* addition; **por a.**, besides, on top of everything else.

añadir *vtr* to add (a, to).

añejo,-a *adj* 1 *(vino, queso)* mature. 2 *(estropeado)* stale.

añicos *nmpl* smithereens; **hacer a.**, to smash to smithereens.

añil I *adj* indigo, blue. II *nm* 1 *Bot* indigo plant. 2 *(color)* indigo.

año *nm* 1 year; **el a. pasado**, last year; **el a. que viene**, next year; **hace años**, a long time ago, years ago; **los años noventa**, the nineties; **todo el a.**, all the year (round); **a. luz**, light year. 2 **¿cuántos años tienes?**, how old are you?; **tiene seis años**, he's six years old; **entrado en años**, getting on.

añoranza *nf* longing, yearning.

añorar *vtr (pasado)* to long for, yearn for; *(país)* to feel homesick for, miss.

apabullar *vtr* to bewilder.

apacentar [1] *vtr* to put out to pasture, graze.

apacible *adj* mild, calm.

apaciguar I *vtr (calmar)* to pacify, appease. II **apaciguarse** *vr (persona)* to calm down; *(tormenta)* to abate.

apadrinar *vtr* 1 *(en bautizo)* to act as godfather to; *(en boda)* to be best man for. 2 *(artista)* to sponsor.

apagado,-a *adj* 1 *(luz, cigarro)* out. 2 *(color)* dull; *(voz)* sad; *(mirada)* expressionless, lifeless; *(carácter, persona)* spiritless.

apagar [7] *vtr (fuego)* to put out; *(luz, tele etc)* to turn off, switch off; *(color)* to soften; *(sed)* to quench.

apagón *nm* power cut, blackout.

apaisado,-a *adj* 1 oblong. 2 *(papel)* landscape.

apalabrar *vtr (concertar)* to make a verbal agreement on.

apalancar [1] I *vtr* to lever up. II **apalancarse** *vr arg* to ensconce oneself, settle down.

apalear¹ *vtr* to beat, thrash.

apalear² *vtr Agr (grano)* to winnow.

apañar I *vtr* to mend, fix. II **apañarse** *vr fam* **apañárselas**, to manage.

apaño *nm* mend, repair.

aparador *nm (mueble)* sideboard; *(de tienda)* shop window.

aparato *nm* 1 (piece of) apparatus; *(dispositivo)* device; *(instrumento)* instrument; **a. de radio/televisión**, radio/television set; **a. digestivo**, digestive system; **a. eléctrico**, thunder and lightning. 2 *Tel* **¿quién**

está al a.?, who's speaking? 3 *(ostentación)* display.

aparatoso,-a *adj* 1 *(pomposo)* ostentatious, showy. 2 *(espectacular)* spectacular. 3 *(grande)* bulky.

aparcamiento *nm (en la calle)* parking place; *(parking)* car park, *US* parking lot.

aparcar [1] *vtr* to park.

aparcería *nf Agr* sharecropping.

apareamiento *nm* 1 *(de cosas)* pairing off. 2 *(de animales)* mating.

aparear *vtr*, **aparearse** *vr* to mate.

aparecer [33] I *vi* 1 to appear; **no aparece en mi lista**, he is not on my list. 2 to turn up, show up; **¿apareció el dinero?**, did the money turn up?; **no apareció nadie**, nobody turned up. II **aparecerse** *vr* to appear.

aparejado,-a *adj* **llevar** *o* **traer a.**, to entail.

aparejador,-a *nm,f* quantity surveyor.

aparejar *vtr* 1 *(caballo)* to harness. 2 *(emparejar)* to pair off.

aparejo *nm* 1 *(equipo)* equipment. 2 *(de caballo)* harness.

aparentar *vtr* 1 *(fingir)* to affect. 2 *(tener aspecto)* to look; **no aparenta esa edad**, she doesn't look that age. II *vi* to show off.

aparente *adj* 1 apparent; **sin motivo a.**, for no apparent reason. 2 *fam (conveniente)* suitable.

aparición *nf* 1 appearance. 2 *(visión)* apparition.

apariencia *nf* appearance; **en a.**, apparently; *fig* **guardar las apariencias**, to keep up appearances.

apartado,-a I *adj (lugar)* remote, isolated; **mantente a. de él**, keep away from him. II *nm* 1 *(párrafo)* section, paragraph. 2 **a. de correos**, Post Office Box.

apartamento *nm* (small) flat, apartment.

apartar I *vtr* 1 *(alejar)* to move away, remove; **a. la mirada**, to look away. 2 *(guardar)* to put aside. II *vi* **¡aparta!**, move out of the way! III **apartarse** *vr (alejarse)* to move over, move away; **apártate de en medio**, move out of the way.

aparte I *adv* 1 aside; **ponlo a.**, put it aside; **modestia/bromas a.**, modesty/joking apart. 2 **eso hay que pagarlo a.**, *(separadamente)* you have to pay for that separately. 3 **a. de eso**, *(además)* besides that; *(excepto)* apart from that. 4 **eso es caso a.**, that's completely different. II *nm* 1 *Teat* aside. 2 *Ling* **punto y a.**, full stop, new paragraph.

apasionado,-a I *adj* passionate; **a. de la música**, very fond of music. II *nm,f* enthusiast.

apasionante *adj* exciting.

apasionar *vtr* to excite, thrill; **le apasiona el jazz**, he is mad about jazz.

apatía *nf* apathy.

apático,-a I *adj* apathetic. II *nm,f* apathetic person.

apátrida I *adj* stateless. II *nmf* stateless person.

apdo. *abr de* **apartado**, Post Office Box, P.O.B.

apeadero *nm* halt.

apearse *vi* (*de un autobús, tren*) to get off, alight; (*de un coche*) to get out; **se apeó en Jerez**, he got off in Jerez.

apechugar [7] *vi* **a. con**, to shoulder.

apedrear *vtr* to throw stones at.

apegado *adj* devoted, attached (**a**, to).

apegarse [7] *vr* to become devoted *o* attached (**a**, to).

apego *nm* love, affection; **tener a. a**, to be attached to.

apelación *nf* appeal; **interponer una a.**, to lodge and appeal.

apelar *vi* 1 *Jur* to appeal. 2 (*recurrir*) to resort (**a**, to).

apellidarse *vr* to have as a surname, be called.

apellido *nm* surname; **a. de soltera**, maiden name.

apelmazado,-a *adj* stodgy.

apelotonar I *vtr* to pile up, put into a pile. II **apelotonarse** *vr* (*gente*) to crowd together.

apenar I *vtr* to grieve. II **apenarse** *vr* 1 to be grieved. 2 *Am* (*avergonzarse*) to be ashamed.

apenas *adv* 1 (*casi no*) hardly, scarcely; **a. come**, he hardly eats anything; **a. (si) hay nieve**, there is hardly any snow. 2 (*tan pronto como*) scarcely; **a. llegó, sonó el teléfono**, no sooner had he arrived than the phone rang.

apéndice *nm* appendix.

apendicitis *nf* appendicitis.

apercibir I *vtr* to warn. II **apercibirse** *vr* to notice (**de**, -).

aperitivo *nm* (*bebida*) apéritif; (*comida*) appetizer.

apero *nm* (*usu pl*) equipment, tools *pl*; **aperos de labranza**, farming implements.

apertura *nf* 1 (*comienzo*) opening. 2 *Pol* liberalization.

apestar I *vi* to stink (**a**, of). II *vtr* to infect with the plague.

apetecer [33] *vi* to appeal to; **¿qué te apetece para cenar?**, what would you like for supper?; **¿te apetece ir al cine?**, do you fancy going to the cinema?

apetecible *adj* tempting, inviting.

apetito *nm* appetite; **tengo mucho a.**, I'm really hungry.

apetitoso,-a *adj* appetizing; tempting; (*comida*) delicious, tasty.

apiadarse *vr* to take pity (**de**, on).

ápice *nm* 1 (*punta*) apex. 2 *fig* **ni un á.**, not a bit.

apicultura *nf* beekeeping, apiculture.

apilar *vtr*, **apilarse** *vr* to pile up, heap up.

apiñarse *vr* to crowd together.

apio *nm* celery.

apisonadora *nf* roadroller, steamroller.

apisonar *vtr* to roll.

aplacar [1] I *vtr* to placate, calm. II **aplacarse** *vr* to calm down.

aplanar *vtr* to level.

aplastante *adj* crushing; *Pol* **victoria a.**, landslide victory.

aplastar *vtr* 1 to flatten, squash. 2 *fig* (*vencer*) to crush.

aplatanarse *vr fam* to become lethargic.

aplaudir *vtr* 1 to clap, applaud. 2 *fig* to applaud.

aplauso *nm* applause.

aplazamiento *nm* postponement, adjournment; (*de un pago*) deferment.

aplazar [4] *vtr* to postpone, adjourn; *Fin* (*pago*) to defer.

aplicación *nf* application.

aplicado,-a *adj* hard-working.

aplicar [1] I *vtr* to apply. II **aplicarse** *vr* 1 (*esforzarse*) to apply oneself, work hard. 2 (*norma, ley*) to apply, be applicable.

aplique *nm* wall light, wall lamp.

aplomo *nm* aplomb.

apocado,-a *adj* shy, timid.

apocamiento *nm* timidity, lack of self-confidence.

apocarse [1] *vr* to become frightened.

apodar *vtr* to nickname.

apoderado,-a *nm,f* 1 agent, representative. 2 (*de torero, deportista*) manager.

apoderarse *vr* to take possession (**de**, of), seize; *fig* **el miedo se apoderó de ella**, she was seized by fear.

apodo *nm* nickname.

apogeo *nm* height; **estar en pleno a.**, (*fama etc*) to be at its height.

apolillarse *vr* to get moth-eaten.

apolítico,-a *adj* apolitical.

apología *nf* apology, defence, *US* defense.

apoltronarse *vr fam* to vegetate.

apoplejía *nf* apoplexy.

apoquinar *vtr fam* to cough up, fork out.

aporrear *vtr* to beat, hit, thrash; (*puerta*) to bang; *fam* **a. el piano**, to bang (away) on the piano.

aportación *nf* contribution.

aportar I *vtr* to contribute. II *vi Náut* to reach port.

aposentarse *vr* to stay, lodge.

aposento *nm* room.

aposta *adv* on purpose, intentionally.

apostar[1] [2] I *vtr* to bet; **te apuesto una cena a que no viene**, I bet you a dinner that he won't come. II *vi* to bet (**por**, on); **a. a los caballos**, to bet on horses; **apuesto a que sí viene**, I bet she will come. III **apostarse** *vr* to bet; **me apuesto lo que quieras**, I bet you anything.

apostar² *vtr* (*situar*) to post, station.

apostilla *nf* note.

apóstol *nm* apostle.

apóstrofo *nm* apostrophe.

apostura *nf* good bearing.

apoteósico,-a *adj* enormous, tremendous.

apoyacabezas *nm* *Aut* headrest.

apoyar I *vtr* 1 to lean. 2 (*causa*) to support. II **apoyarse** *vr* 1 a. **en**, to lean on; **apóyate en mi brazo**, take my arm. 2 a. **en**, (*opinión*) to be based on, rest on.

apoyo *nm* support.

apreciable *adj* appreciable, noticeable.

apreciación *nf* appreciation.

apreciar [12] *vtr* 1 to appreciate. 2 (*percibir*) to notice, see. II **apreciarse** *vr* to be noticeable.

aprecio *nm* regard, esteem; **tener a. a algn**, to be fond of sb.

aprehender *vtr* (*alijo, botín*) to apprehend, seize.

aprehensión *nf* seizure.

apremiante *adj* urgent, pressing.

apremiar [12] *vtr* to be urgent; **el tiempo apremia**, time is at a premium.

aprender *vtr* to learn; **así aprenderás**, that'll teach you.

aprendiz,-a *nm,f* apprentice, trainee.

aprendizaje *nm* 1 learning. 2 (*instrucción*) apprenticeship, traineeship.

aprensión *nf* apprehension.

aprensivo,-a *adj* apprehensive.

apresar *vtr* to seize, capture.

aprestar I *vtr* to prepare, get ready. II **aprestarse** *vr* to get ready.

apresurado,-a *adj* (*persona*) in a hurry; (*cosa*) hurried.

apresuramiento *nm* haste, hurry.

apresurar I *vtr* (*paso etc*) to speed up. II **apresurarse** *vr* to hurry up.

apretado,-a *adj* 1 (*ropa, cordón*) tight; **íbamos todos apretados en el coche**, we were all squashed together in the car. 2 (*día, agenda*) busy.

apretar [1] I *vtr* (*botón*) to press; (*nudo, tornillo*) to tighten; **a. el gatillo**, to pull the trigger; **me aprietan las botas**, these boots are too tight for me. II *vi* **apretaba el calor**, it was really hot. III **apretarse** *vr* to squeeze together, cram together; *fig* **a. el cinturón**, to tighten one's belt.

apretón *nm* squeeze; **a. de manos**, handshake.

apretujar I *vtr* to squeeze, crush. II **apretujarse** *vr* to squeeze together, cram together.

aprieto *nm* tight spot, fix, jam; **poner a algn en un a.**, to put sb in an awkward position.

aprisa *adv* quickly.

aprisionar *vtr* (*atrapar*) to trap.

aprobación *nf* approval.

aprobado *nm* *Educ* pass.

aprobar [2] *vtr* 1 (*autorizar*) to approve. 2 (*estar de acuerdo con*) to approve of. 3 *Educ* to pass. 4 *Pol* (*ley*) to pass.

apropiado,-a *adj* suitable, appropriate.

apropiarse [12] *vr* to appropriate.

aprovechado,-a *adj* 1 **mal a.**, (*recurso, tiempo*) wasted; **bien a.**, put to good use. 2 (*espacio*) well-planned. 3 *pey* (*egoísta*) self-seeking.

aprovechamiento *nm* use.

aprovechar I *vtr* 1 to make good use of, make the most of; **aprovechamos bien la tarde**, we've done lots of things this afternoon. 2 (*recursos etc*) to take advantage of; **a. la ocasión**, to seize the opportunity. II *vi* **¡que aproveche!**, enjoy your meal!, bon appétit!. III **aprovecharse** *vr* to use to one's advantage, take advantage; **a. de algn**, to take advantage of sb; **a. de algo**, to make the most of sth.

aprovisionar *vtr* to supply, provide; **a. las tropas**, to give supplies to the troops.

aproximación *nf* 1 approximation. 2 (*en lotería*) consolation prize.

aproximado,-a *adj* approximate; **un cálculo a.**, a rough estimate. ◆**aproximadamente** approximately, roughly.

aproximar I *vtr* to bring *o* put nearer. II **aproximarse** *vr* to approach (a, -).

aproximativo,-a *adj* approximate, rough.

aptitud *nf* aptitude; **prueba de a.**, aptitude test.

apto,-a *adj* 1 (*apropiado*) suitable, appropriate; *Cin* **a. para todos los públicos**, U-certificate film, *US* rated 'G'. 2 (*capacitado*) capable, able. 3 *Educ* passed.

apuesta *nf* bet, wager.

apuesto,-a *adj* good-looking; (*hombre*) handsome.

apuntador,-a *nm,f* *Teat* prompter.

apuntalar *vtr* to prop up, shore up, underpin.

apuntar I *vtr* (*con arma*) to aim. 2 (*señalar*) to point out. 3 (*anotar*) to note down, make a note of. 4 (*indicar*) to indicate, suggest; **todo parece a. a ...**, everything seems to point to .... II *vi* **cuando apunta el día**, when day breaks. III **apuntarse** *vr* 1 (*en una lista*) to put one's name down. 2 *fam* **¿te apuntas?**, are you game?; **me apunto**, count me in.

apunte *nm* (*usu pl*) note; **tomar apuntes**, to take notes.

apuñalar *vtr* to stab.

apurado,-a I *adj* 1 (*necesitado*) in need; **a. de dinero**, hard up for money; **a. de tiempo**, in a hurry. 2 (*preocupado*) worried; (*avergonzado*) embarrassed. 3 (*situación*) awkward, difficult. 4 (*afeitado*) close, II *nm* (*afeitado*) close shave.

apurar I *vtr* 1 (*terminar*) to finish off, end. 2 (*preocupar*) to worry. II **apurarse** *vr* 1 *(preocuparse)* to worry, get worried; **no te apures,** don't worry. **2** *(darse prisa)* to rush, hurry, pester; **apúrate,** get a move on.

apuro *nm* **1** *(situación difícil)* tight spot, fix, jam; **estar en un a.,** to be in a tight spot. **2** *(escasez de dinero)* hardship; **pasar apuros,** to be hard up. **3** *(vergüenza)* embarrassment; **¡qué a.!,** how embarrassing!

aquejado,-a suffering *(de,* from).

aquel,-ella *adj dem* **1** that; **a. niño,** that boy. **2 aquellos,-as,** those; **aquellas niñas,** those girls.

aquél,-élla *pron dem* **1** that one; *(el anterior)* the former; **aquél/-élla ... éste/ ésta,** the former ... the latter. **2 todo a. que,** anyone who, whoever. **3 aquéllos, -as,** those; *(los anteriores)* the former.

aquella *adj dem* f → **aquel.**

aquélla *pron dem* f → **aquél.**

aquello *pron dem neut* that, it.

aquellos,-as *adj dem pl* → **aquel,-ella.**

aquéllos,-as *pron dem m,fpl* → **aquél, -élla.**

aquí *adv* **1** *(lugar)* here; **a. arriba/fuera,** up/out here; **a. está,** here it is; **a. mismo,** right here; **de a. para allá,** up and down, to and fro; **hasta a.,** this far; **por a., por favor,** this way please; **está por a.,** it's around here somewhere. **2** *(tiempo)* **de a. en adelante,** from now on; **de aquí a junio,** between now and June; **hasta a.,** up till now.

aquietar *vtr* to pacify, calm down.

ara *nf fml* **en aras de,** for the sake of.

árabe 1 *adj (de Arabia)* Arab. **II** *nmf (persona)* Arab. **III** *nm (idioma)* Arabic.

Arabia *n* Arabia; **A. Saudita,** Saudi Arabia.

arado *nm* plough, *US* plow.

Aragón *n* Aragon.

aragonés,-esa *adj & nm,f* Aragonese.

arancel *nm* tariff, customs duty.

arancelario,-a *adj* tariff, duty; **derechos arancelarios,** duties; **barreras arancelarias,** customs barriers.

arandela *nf Téc* washer; *(anilla)* ring.

araña *nf* **1** spider. **2** *(lámpara)* chandelier.

arañar *vtr* to scratch.

arañazo *nm* scratch.

arar *vtr* to plough, *US* plow.

araucaria *nf* araucaria, monkey puzzle tree.

arbitraje *nm* **1** arbitration. **2** *Dep* refereeing; *Ten* umpiring.

arbitrar *vtr* **1** to arbitrate. **2** *Dep* to referee; *Ten* umpire.

arbitrariedad *nf* **1** arbitrariness. **2** *(acto)* arbitrary action.

arbitrario,-a *adj* arbitrary.

arbitrio *nm* *(voluntad)* will; *(juicio)* judgement.

árbitro,-a *nm,f* **1** *Dep* referee; *(de tenis)*

umpire. **2** *(mediador)* arbitrator.

árbol *nm* **1** *Bot* tree. **2** *Téc* shaft. **3** *Náut* mast. **4** *(gráfico)* tree (diagram); **á. genealógico,** family o genealogical tree.

arbolado,-a I *adj* wooded. **II** *nm* woodland.

arboleda *nf* grove.

arbusto *nm* bush, shrub.

arca *nf* **1** chest. **2** *(para caudales)* strongbox, safe; **arcas públicas,** Treasury *sing.*

arcada *nf* **1** arcade; *(de puente)* arch. **2** *(náusea)* retching.

arcaico,-a *adj* archaic.

arcén *nm* verge; *(de autopista)* hard shoulder.

archi- *pref* super-.

archiconocido,-a *adj* extremely well-known.

archipiélago *nm* archipelago.

archivador *nm* filing cabinet.

archivar *vtr* **1** *(documento etc)* to file (away). **2** *(caso, asunto)* to shelve. **3** *Inform* to save.

archivo *nm* **1** file. **2** *(archivador)* filing cabinet. **3 archivos,** archives.

arcilla *nf* clay.

arco *nm* **1** *Arquit* arch. **2** *Mat Elec* arc. **3** *(de violín)* bow. **4** *Dep* bow; **tiro con a.,** archery. **5 a. iris,** rainbow.

arder *vi* to burn; *fam* **la conversación está que arde,** the conversation is really heating up; **Juan está que arde,** Juan is really fuming.

ardid *nm* scheme, plot.

ardiente *adj* **1** *(encendido)* burning; **capilla a.,** chapel of rest. **2** *fig (fervoroso)* eager.

ardilla *nf* squirrel.

ardor *nm* **1** heat; *Med* **a. de estómago,** heartburn. **2** *fig* ardour, *US* ardor, fervour, *US* fervor.

ardoroso,-a *adj fig* ardent, passionate.

arduo,-a *adj* arduous.

área *nf* **1** area; *Dep* penalty area. **2** *(medida)* are (100 square metres).

arena *nf* **1** sand; **playa de a.,** sandy beach. **2** *Taur* bullring.

arengar [7] *vtr* to harangue.

arenisca *nf* sandstone.

arenoso,-a *adj* sandy.

arenque *nm* herring; *Culin* **a. ahumado,** kipper.

arete *nm* earring.

argamasa *nf* mortar.

Argel *n* Algiers.

Argelia *n* Algeria.

argelino,-a *adj & nm,f* Algerian.

Argentina *n* Argentina.

argentino,-a *adj & nm,f* Argentinean, Argentine.

argolla *nf* **1** *(large)* ring. **2** *Am (alianza)* wedding ring.

argot *nm (popular)* slang; *(técnico)* jargon.

argucia *nf* ruse.

argüir [37] *vtr* **1** *(deducir)* to deduce, conclude. 2 (*argumentar*) to argue.

argumentación nf argument.

argumentar vtr → **argüir**.

argumento nm 1 *Lit Teat* (*trama*) plot. 2 (*razonamiento*) argument.

arguyo *indic pres* → **argüir**.

aridez nf aridity; *fig* dryness.

árido,-a adj arid; *fig* dry.

Aries nm Aries.

ariete nm *Mil* battering ram.

ario,-a adj & nm,f Aryan.

arisco,-a adj (*persona*) unfriendly, standoffish; (*animal*) unfriendly.

arista nf edge.

aristocracia nf aristocracy.

aristócrata nmf aristocrat.

aristocrático,-a adj aristocratic.

aritmética nf arithmetic.

arma nf weapon; **a. blanca**, knife; **a. de fuego**, firearm; **a. homicida**, murder weapon; **a. nuclear**, nuclear weapon; *fig* **a. de doble filo**, double-edged sword.

armada nf navy.

armado,-a adj armed; **ir a.**, to be armed; **lucha armada**, armed struggle.

armador,-a nm,f shipowner.

armadura nf 1 (*armazón*) frame. 2 *Hist* suit of armour o *US* armor.

armamentista adj arms; **la carrera a.**, the arms race.

armamento nm armaments pl; **a. nuclear**, nuclear weapons.

armar I vtr 1 (*tropa, soldado*) to arm. 2 (*piezas*) to fit o put together, assemble. 3 *fam* **armaron un escándalo**, they created a scandal. II **armarse** vr to arm oneself; *fig* **a. de paciencia**, to summon up one's patience; *fig* **a. de valor**, to pluck up courage; *fam* **se armó la gorda**, all hell broke loose.

armario nm (*para ropa*) wardrobe; (*de cocina*) cupboard; **a. empotrado**, built-in wardrobe o cupboard.

armatoste nm (*cosa*) monstrosity.

armazón nm frame; (*de madera*) timberwork; *Arquit* shell.

armería nf gunsmith's (shop).

armiño nm ermine.

armisticio nm armistice.

armonía nf harmony.

armonioso,-a adj harmonious.

armonizar [4] vtr & vi to harmonize.

aro nm hoop; (*servilletero*) serviette ring; *fam* **pasar por el a.**, to knuckle under.

aroma nm aroma; (*de vino*) bouquet.

aromático,-a adj aromatic.

arpa nf harp.

arpía nf (*en mitología*) harpy; *fig* harpy, old witch.

arpón nm harpoon.

arquear vtr, **arquearse** vr to bend, curve.

arqueología nf archaeology, *US* archeology.

arqueólogo,-a nm,f archaeologist, *US* archeologist.

arquero,-a nm,f archer.

arquetipo nm archetype.

arquitecto,-a nm,f architect.

arquitectónico,-a adj architectural.

arquitectura nf architecture.

arrabales nmpl slums.

arrabalero,-a adj pey coarse.

arraigado,-a adj deeply rooted.

arraigar [7] vi to take root.

arraigo nm *fig* roots pl; **una tradición con mucho a.**, a deeply-rooted tradition.

arrancar [1] I vtr 1 (*planta*) to uproot, pull up; **a. de raíz**, to uproot. 2 (*extraer*) to pull o tear off o out; (*diente, pelo*) to pull out; *fig* (*confesión etc*) to extract; **arranca una hoja del cuaderno**, tear a page out of the notebook. 3 (*coche, motor*) to start. II vi 1 *Aut Téc* to start. 2 (*empezar*) to begin; **a. a llorar**, to burst out crying.

arranque nm 1 *Aut Téc* starting. 2 (*comienzo*) start. 3 *fam* (*arrebato*) outburst, fit.

arrasar I vtr to devastate, destroy. II vi (*en elecciones etc*) to win by a landslide.

arrastrado,-a *fam* I adj wretched. II nm,f bad egg.

arrastrar I vtr to pull (along), drag (along); **vas arrastrando el vestido**, your dress is trailing on the ground; **lo arrastró la corriente**, he was swept away by the current. II **arrastrarse** vr to drag oneself; *fig* (*humillarse*) to crawl.

arrastre nm 1 pulling, dragging; *fam* **para el a.**, (*persona*) on one's last legs; (*cosa*) done for. 2 (*pesca de*) **a.**, trawling.

arrayán nm myrtle.

arre interj gee up!, giddy up!

arrear *fam* vtr 1 to spur on; (*caballos*) to urge on. 2 *fam* (*bofetada*) to give.

arrebatador,-a adj *fig* captivating, fascinating.

arrebatar I vtr (*coger*) to snatch, seize; (*cautivar*) to captivate, fascinate. II **arrebatarse** vr (*enfurecerse*) to become furious; (*exaltarse*) to get carried away.

arrebato nm outburst, fit.

arreciar [12] vi (*viento, tormenta*) to get worse.

arrecife nm reef.

arreglado,-a adj 1 (*reparado*) repaired, fixed. 2 (*solucionado*) settled. 3 (*habitación*) tidy, neat. 4 (*persona*) well-dressed, smart.

arreglar I vtr 1 to arrange; (*problema*) to sort out; (*habitación*) to tidy; (*papeles*) to put in order. 2 (*reparar*) to repair, fix. 3 (*vestir*) to get ready. II **arreglarse** vr 1 (*vestirse*) to get ready. 2 *fam* **arreglárselas**, to manage. 3 (*reconciliarse*) to make up.

arreglo nm 1 arrangement; (*acuerdo*) compromise. **2** (*reparación*) repair; **no tiene a.**, it is beyond repair; *fam* **¡no tienes a.!**, you're hopeless! **3** *fml* **con a. a**, in accordance with.

arrellanarse *vr* to sit back.

arremangarse [7] *vr* to roll one's sleeves *o* trousers up.

arremeter *vi* to attack.

arremolinarse *vr* to whirl about; *fig* (*gente*) to crowd together, cram together.

arrendamiento *nm* **1** (*alquiler*) renting. **2** (*precio*) rent.

arrendar [1] *vtr* (*piso*) to rent; (*dar en arriendo*) to let on lease; (*tomar en arriendo*) to take on lease.

arrendatario,-a *nm,f* leaseholder, lessee; (*inquilino*) tenant.

arreos *nmpl* **1** (*de caballería*) harness *sing*, trappings. **2** (*adorno*) adornment.

arrepentido,-a *adj* regretful.

arrepentimiento *nm* regret.

arrepentirse [5] *vr* **a. de**, to regret; *Rel* to repent.

arrestar *vtr* to arrest, detain; (*encarcelar*) to put in prison.

arresto *nm* arrest; *Jur* **a. domiciliario**, house arrest.

arriar [29] *vtr* (*bandera*) to strike; (*velas*) to lower.

arriba I *adv* up; (*encima*) on the top; **ahí a.**, up there; **de a. abajo**, from top to bottom; *fam* **mirar a algn de a. abajo**, to look sb up and down; **desde a.**, from above; **hacia a.**, upwards; **de un millón para a.**, from one million upwards; **más a.**, higher up, further up; **a. del todo**, right on *o* at the top; **la parte de a.**, the top (part); **vive a.**, he lives upstairs; **véase más a.**, see above. II *interj* get up!; **¡a. la República!**, long live the Republic!; **¡a. las manos!**, hands up! III *prep Am* on top of.

arribar *vi* to reach port, arrive.

arribeño,-a *Am* I *adj* highland. II *nm,f* highlander.

arribista *nmf* parvenu, social climber.

arriendo *nm* lease; (*de un piso*) renting; **dar en a.**, to let out on lease; **tomar en a.**, to take on lease.

arriesgado,-a *adj* **1** (*peligroso*) risky. **2** (*temerario*) fearless, daring.

arriesgar [7] I *vtr* to risk. II **arriesgarse** *vr* to risk; **se arriesga demasiado**, he's taking too many risks.

arrimar I *vtr* to move closer, bring near *o* nearer; *fam* **a. el hombro**, to lend a hand. II **arrimarse** *vr* to move *o* get close, come near *o* nearer.

arrinconar *vtr* **1** (*poner en un rincón*) to put in a corner. **2** (*abandonar*) to put away, lay aside. **3** (*acorralar*) to corner.

arrobo *nm* rapture, enthralment, *US* enthrallment.

arrocero,-a *adj* **la industria arrocera**, the

rice industry.

arrodillarse *vr* to kneel down.

arrogancia *nf* arrogance.

arrogante *adj* arrogant.

arrojadizo,-a *adj* **arma arrojadiza**, missile.

arrojado,-a *adj* (*osado*) bold, daring.

arrojar I *vtr* **1** (*tirar*) to throw, fling. **2** *Com* (*saldo*) to show. II **arrojarse** *vr* to throw oneself, fling oneself.

arrojo *nm* daring, courage.

arrollador,-a *adj fig* overwhelming; (*éxito*) resounding; (*personalidad*) captivating.

arrollar *vtr* **1** (*atropellar*) to run over, knock down. II *vi Dep Pol* to win easily.

arropar I *vtr* to wrap up; (*en la cama*) to tuck in. II **arroparse** *vr* to wrap oneself up.

arrostrar *vtr* to face.

arroyo *nm* brook, stream.

arroz *nm* rice; **a. con leche**, rice pudding.

arruga *nf* (*en la piel*) wrinkle; (*en la ropa*) crease.

arrugar [7] I *vtr* (*piel*) to wrinkle; (*ropa*) to crease; (*papel*) to crumple (up). II **arrugarse** *vr* (*piel*) to wrinkle; (*ropa*) to crease.

arruinado,-a *adj* bankrupt, ruined.

arruinar I *vtr* to ruin. II **arruinarse** *vr* to be ruined.

arrullar I *vtr* (*bebé*) to lull. II *vi* (*paloma*) to coo.

arrullo *nm* **1** (*de paloma*) cooing. **2** (*nana*) lullaby.

arrumaco *nm fam* kissing and hugging; (*halago*) flattery.

arsenal *nm* arsenal.

arsénico *nm* arsenic.

arte *nm* & *f* **1** art; **bellas artes**, fine arts; *fam* **por amor al a.**, for the love of it. **2** (*habilidad*) skill.

artefacto *nm* device; **a. explosivo**, explosive device.

arteria *nf* artery; (*carretera*) highway.

artesanal *adj* handmade.

artesanía *nf* **1** (*cualidad*) craftsmanship. **2** (*objetos*) crafts *pl*, handicrafts *pl*.

artesano,-a I *nm,f* (*hombre*) craftsman; (*mujer*) craftswoman. II *adj* handmade.

ártico,-a I *adj* arctic; **el océano A.**, the Arctic Ocean. II *nm* **el Á.**, the Arctic.

articulación *nf* **1** *Anat* joint, articulation. **2** *Téc* joint.

articulado,-a *adj* (*tren etc*) articulated.

articular *vtr* to articulate.

artículo *nm* article; **a. de fondo**, leader (article).

artífice *nmf* author; *fig* **el a. del acuerdo**, the architect of the agreement.

artificial *adj* artificial; *Tex* man-made *o* synthetic.

artificio *nm* **1** artifice; **fuego de a.**, firework. **2** (*artimaña*) ruse.

artillería *nf* artillery; **a. antiaérea**, anti-aircraft guns *pl.*

artillero *nm* artilleryman.

artilugio *nm* gadget, device.

artimaña *nf* trick, ruse.

artista *nmf* artist; **a. de cine**, film star.

artístico,-a *adj* artistic.

artritis *nf* arthritis.

arveja *nf Am* pea.

arzobispo *nm* archbishop.

as *nm* ace.

asa *nf* handle.

asado,-a I *adj Culin* roast; **pollo a.**, roast chicken; *fig* **a. de calor**, roasting, boiling hot. **II** *nm Culin* roast.

asaduras *nfpl* offal *sing*; *(de ave)* giblets.

asalariado,-a I *adj* salaried. **II** *nm,f* wage earner, salaried worker.

asaltador,-a *nm,f,* **asaltante** *nmf* attacker; *(en un robo)* robber.

asaltar *vtr* to assault, attack; *(banco)* to rob; *fig* to assail.

asalto *nm* 1 assault, attack; **a. a un banco**, bank robbery. 2 *Box* round.

asamblea *nf* meeting; **a. general**, general meeting.

asar I *vtr* to roast. **II asarse** *vr fig* to be roasting, be boiling hot.

ascendencia *nf* ancestry, ancestors *pl*; **de a. escocesa**, of Scottish descent.

ascender [3] **I** *vtr (en un cargo)* to promote. **II** *vi* 1 move upward; *(temperatura)* to rise; **la factura asciende a ...**, the bill adds up to ... 2 *(al trono)* to ascend. 3 *(de categoría)* to be promoted.

ascendiente *nmf* ancestor.

ascensión *nf* 1 climb. 2 *(al trono)* accession.

ascenso *nm* promotion; *(subida)* rise.

ascensor *nm* lift, *US* elevator.

asco *nm* disgust, repugnance; **me da a.**, it makes me (feel) sick; **¡qué a.!**, how disgusting *o* revolting!

ascua *nf* ember; *fig* **en ascuas**, on tenterhooks.

aseado,-a *adj* tidy, neat.

asear I *vtr* to clean, tidy up. **II asearse** *vr* to wash, get washed.

asediar [12] *vtr* to besiege.

asedio *nm* siege.

asegurado,-a *adj* 1 insured. 2 *(indudable)* secure.

asegurador,-a I *adj* insurance. **II** *nm,f* insurer.

asegurar I *vtr* 1 to insure. 2 *(garantizar)* **me aseguró que ...**, he assured me that ...; **a. el éxito de un proyecto**, to ensure the success of a project. 3 *(cuerda)* to fasten. **II asegurarse** *vr* 1 to make sure; **a. de que ...**, to make sure that .... 2 *Seg* to insure onself.

asemejarse *vr* **a. a**, to look like.

asentado,-a *adj (establecido)* established, settled.

asentamiento *nm* settlement.

asentar [1] **I** *vtr* **a. la cabeza**, to settle down. **II asentarse** *vr* 1 *(establecerse)* to settle down, establish oneself. 2 *(té, polvo)* to settle.

asentimiento *nm* assent, consent.

asentir [5] *vi* to assent, agree; **a. con la cabeza**, to nod.

aseo *nm* 1 cleanliness, tidiness. 2 **aseos** *o* **(cuarto de) a.**, bathroom; *(retrete)* toilet.

asequible *adj* affordable; *(comprensible)* easy to understand; *(alcanzable)* attainable.

aserrín *nm* sawdust.

asesinar *vtr* to murder; *(rey, ministro)* to assassinate.

asesinato *nm* murder; *(de rey, ministro)* assassination.

asesino,-a I *adj* murderous. **II** *nm,f* killer; *(hombre)* murderer; *(mujer)* murderess; *Pol* assassin.

asesor,-a I *nm,f* adviser; **a. fiscal**, tax advisor. **II** *adj* advisory.

asesoramiento *nm* 1 *(acción)* advising. 2 *(consejo)* advice.

asesorar I *vtr* 1 to advise, give (professional) advice to. 2 *Com* to act as consultant to. **II asesorarse** *vr* to consult.

asesoría *nf* consultant's office.

asestar *vtr* to deal; **a. un golpe a algn**, to deal sb a blow.

aseverar *vtr* to assert.

asfalto *nm* asphalt.

asfixia *nf* asphyxiation, suffocation.

asfixiante *adj* asphyxiating, suffocating; *fam* **hace un calor a.**, it's stifling.

asfixiar [12] *vtr,* **asfixiarse** *vr* to asphyxiate, suffocate.

así I *adv* 1 *(de esta manera)* like this *o* that, this way, thus; **ponlo a.**, put it this way; **a. de grande/alto**, this big/tall; **algo a.**, something like this *o* that; **¿no es a.?**, isn't that so *o* right?; **a. es la vida**, such is life; **a. a.**, so-so. 2 **a las seis o a.**, around six *o*'clock; **diez años o a.**, ten years more or less. 3 **a. como**, as well as. 4 **a. tenga que ...**, *(aunque)* even if I have to .... 5 **aun a.**, and despite that. 6 **a. pues**, so; **a. que ...**, so .... 7 **a. que lleguen**, as soon as.

Asia *n* Asia; **A. Menor**, Asia Minor.

asiático,-a I *adj & nm,f* Asian.

asidero *nm (asa)* handle; *fig* pretext, excuse.

asiduidad *nf* assiduity; **con a.**, frequently, regularly.

asiduo,-a I *adj* assiduous. **II** *nm,f* regular customer.

asiento *nm* 1 seat; **a. trasero/delantero**, front/back seat; **tome a.**, take a seat. 2 *(poso)* sediment. 3 **Fin** entry.

asignación *nf* 1 *(de dinero)* assignment, allocation. 2 *(de puesto)* appointment. 3 *(paga)* allowance.

asignar *vtr* 1 to assign, allocate. 2 *(nom-*

brar) to appoint.
asignatura *nf* subject; **a. pendiente**, failed subject.
asilado,-a *nm,f* refugee.
asilar *vtr* to grant *o* give political asylum to.
asilo *nm* asylum. **a. de ancianos**, old people's home; *Pol* **a. político**, political asylum.
asimilación *nf* assimilation.
asimilar *vtr* to assimilate.
asimismo *adv* also, as well.
asir [22] *vtr* to grasp, seize.
asistencia *nf* 1 (*presencia*) attendance; **falta de a.**, absence. 2 **a. médica/técnica**, medical/technical assistance. 3 (*público*) audience, public.
asistenta *nf* charlady, cleaning lady.
asistente I *adj* attending, el público a., the audience. II *nmf* 1 (*ayudante*) assistant; **a. social**, social worker. 2 los asistentes, the public *sing*.
asistido,-a *adj* assisted; **a. por ordenador**, computer-assisted; *Aut* **dirección asistida**, power steering.
asistir I *vtr* to assist, help. II *vi* to attend (**a, -**),.be present (**a, at**).
asma *nf* asthma.
asno *nm* donkey, ass.
asociación *nf* association.
asociado,-a *adj* associated. III *nm,f* associate, partner.
asociar [12] I *vtr* to associate. II **asociarse** *vr* 1 to be associated. 2 *Com* to become partners.
asolar [2] *vtr* to devastate, destroy.
asomar I *vtr* to put out, stick out; **asomó la cabeza por la ventana**, he put his head out the window. II *vi* to appear. III **asomarse** *vr* 1 to lean out; **a. a la ventana**, to lean out of the window. 2 (*entrar*) to pop in; (*salir*) to pop out.
asombrar I *vtr* to amaze, astonish. II **asombrarse** *vr* to be astonished; **a. de algo**, to be amazed at sth.
asombro *nm* amazement, astonishment.
asombroso,-a *adj* amazing, astonishing.
asomo *nm* trace, hint.
asonada *nf* putsch.
asorocharse *vr Am* to suffer from altitude sickness.
aspa *nf* 1 (*de molino*) arm; (*de ventilador*) blade. 2 (*cruz*) cross.
aspaviento *nm* **hacer aspavientos**, to wave one's arms about.
aspecto *nm* 1 look, appearance. 2 (*de un asunto*) aspect.
aspereza *nf* roughness; *fig* **limar asperezas**, to smooth things over.
áspero,-a *adj* rough; *fig* (*carácter*) surly.
aspersión *nf* sprinkling.
aspersor *nm* sprinkler.
aspiración *nf* 1 inhalation, breathing in. 2 (*pretensión*) aspiration.

aspiradora *nf* vacuum cleaner.
aspirante *nmf* candidate, applicant.
aspirar I *vtr* 1 (*respirar*) to inhale, breath in. 2 *Téc* (*absorber*) to suck in, draw in. II *vi fig* **a. a algo**, to aspire after sth.
aspirina *nf* aspirin.
asquear *vtr* to disgust.
asquerosidad *nf* filthy *o* revolting thing; **¡que a.!**, how revolting!
asqueroso,-a I *adj* (*sucio*) filthy; (*desagradable*) revolting, disgusting. II *nm,f* filthy *o* revolting person.
asta *nf* 1 (*de bandera*) staff, pole; **a media a.**, at half-mast. 2 *Zool* (*cuerno*) horn.
asterisco *nm* asterisk.
astilla *nf* splinter.
astillero *nm* shipyard.
astral *adj* astral; **carta a.**, birth chart
astringente *adj* & *nm* astringent.
astro *nm* star.
astrología *nf* astrology.
astrólogo,-a *nm,f* astrologer.
astronauta *nmf* astronaut.
astronave *nf* spaceship.
astronomía *nf* astronomy.
astronómico,-a *adj* astronomical.
astrónomo,-a *nm,f* astronomer.
astucia *nf* shrewdness; (*artimaña*) ruse.
asturiano,-a *adj* & *nm,f* Asturian.
Asturias *n* Asturias.
astuto,-a *adj* astute, shrewd.
asumir *vtr* to assume.
asunción *nf* assumption.
asunto *nm* 1 subject; **no es a. tuyo**, it's none of your business. 2 Asuntos Exteriores, Foreign Affairs.
asustar I *vtr* to frighten, scare. II **asustarse** *vr* to be frightened, be scared.
atacante *nmf* attacker, assailant.
atacar [1] *vtr* to attack, assault; *fig* **me ataca los nervios**, he gets on my nerves.
atado *adj* tied; (*ocupado*) tied up.
atadura *nf fig* hindrance.
atajar *vi* to take a shortcut (**por**, across *o* through).
atajo *nm* 1 shortcut. 2 (*grupo*) bunch.
atalaya *nf* watchtower.
atañer [38] *v impers* to concern, have to do with; **eso no te atañe**, that has nothing to do with you.
ataque *nm* 1 attack, assault; **a. aéreo**, air raid. 2 *Med* fit; **a. cardíaco** *o* **al corazón**, heart attack; **a. de nervios/tos**, fit of hysterics/coughing.
atar I *vtr* to tie; *fig* **a. cabos**, to put two and two together; *fam* **loco de a.**, as mad as a hatter. 2 *fig* to tie down. II **atarse** *vr fig* to get tied up; **átate los zapatos**, do your shoes up.
atardecer [33] I *v impers* to get *o* grow dark. II *nm* evening, dusk.
atareado,-a *adj* busy.
atascado,-a *adj* stuck.
atascar [1] I *vtr* (*bloquear*) to block, ob-

struct. II **atascarse** vr 1 (bloquearse) to become obstructed, become blocked. 2 fig (estancarse) to get bogged down.

atasco nm traffic jam.

ataúd nm coffin.

ataviarse [29] vr to dress oneself up.

atavío nm dress, attire.

atemorizar [4] vtr to frighten, scare.

atemperar vtr to moderate, temper.

Atenas n Athens.

atención I nf attention; **llamar la a.**, to attract attention; **prestar/poner a.**, to pay attention (**a**, to). II interj attention!

atender [3] I vtr to attend to; (petición) to agree to. II vi (alumno) to pay attention (**a**, to).

atenerse [24] vr 1 (a reglas etc) to abide (**a**, by); **a. a las consecuencias**, to bear the consequences. 2 (remitirse) to go by; **me atengo a sus palabras**, I'm going by what he said; **no saber a qué a.**, not to know what to expect.

atentado nm attack; **a. terrorista**, terrorist attack.

atentar vi. **a. a** o **contra**, to commit a crime against; **a. contra la vida de algn**, to make an attempt on sb's life.

atento,-a adj 1 attentive; **estar a. a**, to be mindful o aware of. 2 (amable) thoughtful, considerate; **atentos saludos de**, (en carta) yours faithfully. ◆**atentamente** adv **le saluda a.**, (en carta) yours sincerely o faithfully.

atenuante I adj attenuating. II nm Jur extenuating circumstance.

atenuar [30] vtr 1 to attenuate; Jur to extenuate. 2 (importancia) to lessen, diminish.

ateo,-a I adj atheistic. II nm,f atheist.

aterciopelado,-a adj velvety; (vino) smooth.

aterido,-a adj. **a. de frío**, stiff with cold, numb.

aterrador,-a adj terrifying.

aterrar I vtr to terrify. II **aterrarse** vr to be terrified.

aterrizaje nm Av landing; **a. forzoso**, forced landing.

aterrizar [4] vi to land.

aterrorizar [4] I vtr to terrify; Mil Pol to terrorize. II **aterrorizarse** vr to be terrified.

atesorar vtr to accumulate; (dinero) to hoard.

atestado[1] nm Jur affidavit, statement; **atestados**, testimonials.

atestado,-a[2] adj packed, crammed; **estaba a. de gente**, it was full of people.

atestar[1] vtr Jur to testify.

atestar[2] [1] vtr (abarrotar) to pack, cram (**de**, with).

atestiguar [22] vtr 1 Jur to testify to. 2 fig to vouch for.

atiborrar I vtr to pack, stuff (**de**, with). II

atiborrarse vr fam to stuff oneself (**de**, with).

ático nm attic.

atinado,-a adj (juicioso) sensible; (pertinente) pertinent.

atinar vi to get it right; **a. a hacer algo**, to succeed in doing sth; **a. al blanco**, to hit the target; **atinó con la solución**, he found the solution.

atingencia nf Am connection, relation.

atípico,-a adj atypical.

atisbar vtr to make out.

atisbo nm fig slight sign, inkling.

atizar [4] vtr 1 (fuego) to poke, stoke. 2 fig (rebelión) to stir up; (pasión) to rouse, excite.

atlántico,-a I adj Atlantic. II nm **el** (océano) **A.**, the Atlantic (Ocean).

atlas nm inv atlas.

atleta nmf athlete.

atlético,-a adj athletic.

atletismo nm athletics sing.

atmósfera nf atmosphere.

atmosférico,-a adj atmospheric.

atolladero nm fix, jam; **estar en un a.**, to be in a jam.

atolondrado,-a adj stunned, bewildered; (atontado) stupid.

atolondrar I vtr to confuse, bewilder. II **atolondrarse** vr to be confused, bewildered.

atómico,-a adj atomic.

átomo nm atom.

atónito,-a adj amazed, astonished.

atontado,-a adj 1 (tonto) silly, foolish. 2 (aturdido) bewildered, amazed.

atontar I vtr to confuse, bewilder. II **atontarse** vr to be o get confused, bewildered.

atorarse vr Am to get stuck.

atormentar I vtr to torment. II **atormentarse** vr to torment oneself, suffer agonies.

atornillar vtr to screw on.

atosigar [7] vtr to harass.

atracador,-a nm,f (de banco) (bank) robber; (en la calle) attacker, mugger.

atracar [1] I vtr to hold up; (persona) to rob. II vi Náut to come alongside, tie up. III **atracarse** vr (de comida) to stuff oneself (**de**, with), gorge oneself (**de**, on).

atracción nf attraction; **parque de atracciones**, funfair.

atraco nm hold-up, robbery; **a. a mano armada**, armed robbery.

atracón nm fam binge, blowout; **darse un a. de comer**, to make a pig of oneself.

atractivo,-a I adj attractive, appealing. II nm attraction, appeal.

atraer [25] vtr to attract.

atragantarse vr to choke (**con**, on), swallow the wrong way; fig **esa chica se me ha atragantado**, I can't stand that girl.

atraigo *indic pres* → **atraer**.

ataje *pt indef* → **atraer**.

atrancar |1| **I** *vtr (puerta)* to bolt. **II atrancarse** *vr* to get stuck; *(al hablar, leer)* to get bogged down.

atrapar *vtr* to catch.

atrás **I** *adv* 1 *(lugar)* at the back, behind; **hacia/para a.**, backwards; **puerta de a.**, back *o* rear door; *fig* **echarse a.**, to back out. 2 *(tiempo)* previously, in the past, ago; **un año a.**, a year ago; **venir de muy a.**, to go *o* date back a long time.

atrasado,-a *adj* late, slow; *(pago)* overdue; *(reloj)* slow; *(país)* backward; *Prensa* **número a.**, back number.

atrasar **I** *vtr* to put back. **II** *vi (reloj)* to be slow. **III atrasarse** *vr* 1 to remain *o* stay behind, lag behind. 2 *(tren)* to be late.

atraso *nm* 1 delay. 2 *(de país)* backwardness. 3 *Fin* **atrasos**, arrears.

atravesado,-a *adj (cruzado)* lying crosswise; *(persona)* difficult; **lo tengo a.**, I can't stand him.

atravesar |1| **I** *vtr* 1 *(calle)* to cross. 2 *(muro)* to pierce, go through. 3 *(poner a través)* to lay across, put across, put crosswise. **II atravesarse** *vr* to get in the way; *fig* **se me ha atravesado Luis**, I can't stand Luis.

atrayente *adj* attractive.

atreverse *vr* to dare; **a. a hacer algo**, to dare to do sth.

atrevido,-a *adj* 1 *(osado)* daring, bold. 2 *(insolente)* insolent, impudent. 3 *(ropa etc)* daring, risqué.

atrevimiento *nm* 1 *(osadía)* daring, audacity. 2 *(insolencia)* insolence, impudence.

atribuir |37| **I** *vtr* to attribute, ascribe. **II atribuirse** *vr* to assume.

atribular *vtr* to afflict.

atributo *nm* attribute.

atril *nm* music stand.

atrochar *vi* to take a short cut.

atrocidad *nf* atrocity.

atrofiar |12| *vtr*, **atrofiarse** *vr* to atrophy.

atropellado,-a *adj* hasty, impetuous.

atropellar *vtr* to knock down, run over.

atropello *nm* 1 *Aut* knocking down, running over. 2 *(abuso)* abuse.

atroz *adj* 1 *(bárbaro)* atrocious. 2 *fam (hambre, frío)* enormous, tremendous.

ATS *nmf abr de* **ayudante técnico sanitario**.

atta. *abr de* **atenta**.

atto. *abr de* **atento**.

atuendo *nm* dress, attire.

atún *nm* tuna, tunny.

aturdido,-a *adj* stunned, dazed.

aturdimiento *nm* confusion, bewilderment.

aturdir *vtr* 1 *(con un golpe)* to stun, daze. 2 *(confundir)* to bewilder, confuse.

aturrullar *vtr* to confuse, bewilder.

atuve *pt indef* → **atenerse**.

audacia *nf* audacity.

audaz *adj* audacious, bold.

audible *adj* audible.

audición *nf* 1 hearing. 2 *Teat* audition.

audiencia *nf* 1 *(público)* audience; *TV Rad* **horas de máxima a.**, prime time; **índice de a.**, viewing figures, ratings. 2 *(entrevista)* audience. 3 *Jur* high court.

audiovisual *adj* audio-visual.

auditivo,-a I *adj* auditory; **comprensión auditiva**, listening comprehension. **II** *nm* receiver.

auditor *nm Fin* auditor.

auditorio *nm* 1 *(público)* audience. 2 *(sala)* auditorium, hall.

auge *nm* peak; *Econ* boom; *fig* **estar en a.**, to be thriving *o* booming.

augurar *vtr* to augur.

augurio *nm* omen.

aula *nf (en colegio)* classroom; *Univ* lecture room; **a. magna**, amphitheatre.

aulaga *nf* gorse.

aullar |16| *vtr* to howl, yell.

aullido *nm* howl, yell.

aumentar I *vtr* to increase; *(precios)* to put up; *(producción)* to step up; *Fot* to enlarge; *Opt* to magnify. **II** *vi (precios)* to go up, rise; *(valor)* to appreciate. **III aumentarse** *vr* to increase, be on the increase.

aumento *nm* increase; *Opt* magnification; **a. de precios**, rise in prices; **ir en a.**, to be on the increase.

aun *adv* even; **a. así**, even so, even then; **a. más**, even more.

aún *adv* still; *(en negativas)* yet; **a. está aquí**, he's still here; **ella no ha venido a.**, she hasn't come yet.

aunar |16| *vtr* to unite, join.

aunque *conj* although, though; *(enfático)* even if, even though; **a. no vengas**, even if you don't come.

aúpa *interj* up!; get up!

aura *nf* aura.

aureola *nf* halo.

auricular *nm* 1 *Tel* receiver. 2 **auriculares**, earphones, headphones.

aurora *nf* daybreak, dawn.

auscultar *vtr* to sound (with a stethoscope).

ausencia *nf* absence.

ausentarse *vr* to leave.

ausente I *adj* absent. **II** *nmf* absentee.

austeridad *nf* austerity.

austero,-a *adj* austere.

austral I *adj* southern. **II** *nm Fin* standard monetary unit of Argentina.

Australia *n* Australia.

australiano,-a *adj & nm,f* Australian.

Austria *n* Austria.

austríaco,-a *adj & nm,f* Austrian.

autenticidad *nf* authenticity.

auténtico,-a *adj* authentic.

autentificar |1| *vtr* to authenticate.

autismo *nm* autism.

autista *adj* autistic.

auto¹ *nm* TV car.

auto² *nm* Jur decree, writ; **autos**, *(pleito)* papers, documents.

autoadhesivo,-a *adj* self-adhesive.

autobiografía *nf* autobiography.

autobiográfico,-a *adj* autobiographical.

autobombo *nm fam* self-praise, blowing one's own trumpet.

autobús *nm* bus.

autocar *nm* coach.

autocrítica *nf* self-criticism.

autóctono,-a *adj* indigenous, autochthonous.

autodefensa *nf* self-defence, US self-defense.

autodisciplina *nf* self-discipline.

autoescuela *nf* driving school, school of motoring.

autogobierno *nm* self-government.

autógrafo *nm* autograph.

autómata *nm* automaton.

automático,-a *adj* automatic.

automatización *nf* automation.

automatizar |4| *vtr* to automate.

automotor,-a I *adj* self-propelled. II *nm* Ferroc diesel train.

automóvil *nm* car.

automovilismo *nm* motoring.

automovilista *nmf* motorist.

automovilístico,-a *adj* car; **accidente a.**, car accident.

autonomía *nf* 1 autonomy. 2 *(región)* autonomous region.

autonómico,-a *adj* autonomous, self-governing; **elecciones autonómicas**, elections for the autonomous parliament; **televisión autonómica**, regional television.

autónomo,-a *adj* autonomous.

autopista *nf* motorway.

autopsia *nf* autopsy, post mortem.

autor,-a *nm,f (hombre)* author; *(mujer)* authoress; *(de crimen)* perpetrator.

autoridad *nf* authority.

autoritario,-a *adj* authoritarian.

autorizado,-a *adj* authoritative, official.

autorizar |4| *vtr* to authorize.

autorretrato *nm* self-portrait.

autoservicio *nm* self-service; *(supermercado)* supermarket.

autostop *nm* hitch-hiking; **hacer a.**, to hitch-hike.

autostopista *nmf* hitch-hiker.

autosuficiencia *nf* self-sufficiency.

autosuficiente *adj* self-sufficient.

auxiliar |14| I *adj & nmf* auxiliary, assistant. II *vtr* to help, assist.

auxilio *nm* help, assistance; **primeros auxilios**, first aid *sing*.

Av., Avda. *abr de* **Avenida**, Avenue, Ave.

aval *nm* Com Fin endorsement.

avalancha *nf* avalanche.

avalar *vtr* to guarantee, endorse.

avance *nm* 1 advance. 2 Fin advance payment. 3 TV **a. informativo**, headlines, US news brief.

avanzado,-a *adj* advanced; **de avanzada edad**, advanced in years.

avanzar |4| *vtr* to advance.

avaricia *nf* avarice.

avaricioso,-a *adj* greedy.

avaro,-a I *adj* avaricious, miserly. II *nm,f* miser.

avasallar *vtr* to subdue.

avatares *nmpl* quirks.

ave *nf* bird; **aves de corral**, poultry.

AVE *nf abr de* **Alta Velocidad Española**, High Speed Train.

avecinarse *vr* to approach, come near.

avellana *nf* hazelnut.

avellano *nm* hazelnut tree.

avena *nf* oats *pl*.

avendré *indic fut → avenir*.

avenencia *nf* compromise.

avengo *indic pres → avenir*.

avenida *nf* avenue.

avenido,-a *adj* **bien/mal avenidos**, on good/bad terms.

avenir [27] I *vtr* to reconcile. II **avenirse** *vr* to be on good terms; *(consentir)* to agree (**en**, to).

aventajado,-a *adj (destacado)* outstanding, exceptional; *(en cabeza)* in the lead.

aventajar *vtr* 1 to be ahead *o* in front (**a**, of). 2 *(superar)* to surpass, outdo.

aventar |1| *vtr* 1 Agr to winnow. 2 *(el fuego)* to blow (on), fan.

aventura *nf* 1 adventure. 2 *(amorosa)* (love) affair.

aventurado,-a *adj* risky.

aventurarse *vr* to venture.

aventurero,-a *adj* adventurous.

avergonzado,-a *adj* ashamed.

avergonzar [2] I *vtr* to shame. II **avergonzarse** *vr* to be ashamed (**de**, of).

avería *nf* breakdown.

averiado,-a *adj* out of order; *(coche)* broken down.

averiar [29] I *vtr* to break. II **averiarse** *vr (estropearse)* to malfunction, go wrong; *(coche)* to break down.

averiguación *nf* enquiry.

averiguar [22] *vtr* to ascertain.

aversión *nf* aversion.

avestruz *nm* ostrich.

aviación *nf* 1 aviation; **accidente de a.**, plane crash; **a. civil**, civil aviation. 2 Mil air force.

aviador,-a *nm,f* aviator, flier; Mil *(piloto)* air force pilot.

aviar [29] *vtr (preparar)* to prepare, get ready.

avícola *adj* poultry.

avicultura *nf* aviculture; *(de aves de corral)* poultry keeping.

avidez *nf* avidity, eagerness.

ávido,-a adj avid; **a. de,** eager for.

avinagrado,-a adj vinegary, sour; fig sour.

avinagrarse vr to turn sour; fig to become sour o bitter.

avión[1] nm aeroplane, US airplane, plane, aircraft; **viajar en a.,** to fly, go by plane; **por a.,** (en carta) airmail.

avión[2] nm Orn martin.

avioneta nf light aircraft o plane.

avíos nmpl Culin ingredients.

avisar vtr 1 (informar) to inform; **avísame cuando hayas acabado,** let me know when you finish. 2 (advertir) to warn; **ya te avisé,** I warned you. 3 (llamar) to call for; **a. a la policía,** to notify the police; **a. al médico,** to send for the doctor.

aviso nm 1 notice; (advertencia) warning; (nota) note; **hasta nuevo a.,** until further notice; **sin previo a.,** without notice. 2 **estar sobre a.,** to know what's going on, be in on it.

avispa nf wasp.

avispado,-a adj fam quick-witted.

avispero nm (nido) wasps' nest.

avistar vtr to see, sight.

avituallamiento nm provisioning.

avivar vtr (fuego) to stoke (up); (pasión) to intensify; (paso) to quicken.

avizor,-a adj **estar ojo a.,** to be on the alert o on the lookout.

axila nf armpit, axilla.

axioma nm axiom.

ay interj (dolor) ouch!

aya nf arc (niñera) nanny.

ayer I adv yesterday; **a. por la mañana/ por la tarde,** yesterday morning/ afternoon; **a. por la noche,** last night; **antes de a.,** the day before yesterday. II nm **el a.,** yesteryear.

ayuda nf help, assistance; **ir en a. de algn,** to come to sb's assistance.

ayudante nmf assistant; Med **a. técnicosanitario,** nurse.

ayudar I vtr to help; **¿en qué puedo ayudarle?,** (how) can I help you? II ayu-

darse vr 1 (unos a otros) to help. 2 **a. de,** to use, make use of.

ayunar vi to fast.

ayunas nfpl **en a.,** without having eaten breakfast.

ayuno nm fasting; **guardar/hacer a.,** to fast.

ayuntamiento nm (institución) town council; (edificio) town hall.

azabache nm jet; **negro a.,** jet black.

azada nf hoe.

azafata nf 1 Av air hostess. 2 (de congresos) stewardess; (de concurso) hostess.

azafrán nm saffron.

azahar nm (del naranjo) orange blossom; (del limonero) lemon blossom.

azar nm chance; **por a.** by chance; **al a.,** at random; **juegos de a.,** games of chance; **los azares de la vida,** the ups and downs of life.

azaroso,-a adj hazardous, dangerous.

azogue nm mercury, quicksilver.

azorado,-a adj embarrassed.

azorar I vtr to embarrass. II azorarse vr to be embarrassed.

Azores nfpl **las (Islas) A.,** the Azores.

azotar vtr to beat; (con látigo) to whip, flog; fig to scourge.

azote nm 1 (golpe) smacking; (latigazo) lash, stroke (of the whip). 2 fig scourge.

azotea nf flat roof.

azteca adj & nmf Aztec.

azúcar nm & f sugar; **a. blanco,** refined sugar; **a. moreno,** brown sugar.

azucarado,-a adj sweetened.

azucarero,-a I nm & f sugar bowl. II adj sugar.

azucena nf white lily.

azufre nm sulphur, US sulfur.

azul adj & nm blue; **a. celeste,** sky blue; **a. marino,** navy blue; **a. turquesa,** turquoise; **sangre a.,** blue blood.

azulado,-a adj bluish.

azulejo nm (glazed) tile.

azuzar [4] vtr **a. los perros a algn,** to set the dogs on sb.

B

B, b [be] nf (la letra) B, b.

baba nf dribble; fig **se le caía la b.,** he was delighted.

babear vi (niño) to dribble; (adulto, animal) to slobber.

babel nm & f bedlam.

babero nm bib.

Babia n fig **estar en B.,** to be daydreaming.

babor nm Náut port, port side.

babosa nf slug.

baboso,-a adj fam slimy; Am fool, idiot.

babucha nf slipper.

baca nf Aut roof rack.

bacalao nm (pez) cod.

bache nm 1 (en carretera) pot hole. 2 Av air pocket. 3 fig bad patch; **pasar un b.,** to go through a bad patch.

bachillerato nm ≈ General Certificate of Secondary Education, US high school degree.

bacilo nm bacillus.

bacon nm bacon.

bacteria nf bacterium; **bacterias,** bacteria.

bacteriológico,-a adj bacteriological;

guerra bacteriológica, germ warfare.

báculo nm walking stick; (de obispo) crosier.

badén nm Aut bump.

bádminton nm badminton.

bafle nm loudspeaker.

bagaje nm baggage.

bagatela nf (baratija) knick-knack; fig trifle.

Bagdad n Baghdad.

Bahamas npl las (Islas) B., the Bahamas.

bahía nf bay.

baila(d)or,-a nm,f flamenco dancer.

bailar [15] vtr & vi to dance; fig b. al son que le tocan, to toe the line; fam ¡que me quiten lo baila(d)o!, but at least I had a good time!

bailarín,-ina nm,f dancer; (clásico) ballet dancer.

baile nm 1 (danza) dance. 2 (fiesta popular) dance; (formal) ball; **b. de disfraces,** fancy dress ball.

baja nf 1 drop, fall; Fin jugar a la b., to bear. 2 Mil loss, casualty. 3 dar de b. a algn, (despedir) to lay sb off; darse de b., (por enfermedad) to take sick leave; (de un club) to resign (de, from), drop out (de, of).

bajada nf 1 (descenso) descent. 2 (cuesta) slope. 3 b. de bandera, (de taxi) minimum fare.

bajamar nf low tide.

bajar I vtr 1 to come o go down; b. la escalera, to come o go downstairs. 2 (descender) to bring o get o take down; (volumen) to turn down; (voz, telón) to lower; (precios etc) to reduce, cut; (persiana) to let down; (cabeza) to bow o lower. II vi 1 to go o come down. 2 (apearse) to get off; (de un coche) to get out (de, of). 3 (disminuir) to fall, drop. III bajarse vr 1 to come o go down. 2 (apearse) to get off; (de un coche) to get out (de, of).

bajeza nf despicable action.

bajinis (por lo) loc adv fam on the sly.

bajío nm 1 sandbank. 2 Am lowland.

bajista I adj Fin bearish; **tendencia b.,** downward trend. II nmf 1 Fin bear. 2 Mús bass guitarist.

bajo,-a I adj 1 low; (persona) short; (sonido) faint, soft; **en voz baja,** in a low voice; **planta baja,** ground floor; **de baja calidad,** of poor quality; **la clase baja,** the lower class. 2 fig (vil) base, contemptible. II nm 1 Mús bass. 2 (planta baja) ground floor. III adv low; **hablar b.,** to speak quietly; fig por lo b., on the sly. IV prep 1 (lugar) under, underneath; **b. tierra,** underground; **b. la lluvia,** in the rain. 2 Pol Hist under; **b. la República,** under the Republic. 3 **b. cero,** (temperatura) below zero. 4 Jur under; **b. juramento,** under oath; **b. pena de muerte,**

on pain of death; **b. fianza,** on bail.

bajón nm 1 (bajada) sharp fall, decline. 2 Com slump. 3 (de salud) relapse, deterioration.

bajorrelieve nm bas-relief.

bajura nf pesca de b., coastal fishing.

bala nf bullet; fig como una b., like a shot.

balada nf ballad.

baladí adj (pl baladíes) trivial.

balance nm 1 Fin balance; (declaración) balance sheet; fig hacer b. de una situación, to take stock of a situation. 2 (resultado) outcome.

balancear I vtr to rock. II balancearse vr (en mecedora) to rock; (en columpio) to swing.

balanceo nm rocking, swinging.

balanza nf scales pl; fig estar en la b., to be in the balance o in danger; **b. comercial,** balance of trade; **b. de pagos,** balance of payments.

balar vi to bleat.

balaustrada nf balustrade, railing.

balazo nm 1 (disparo) shot; **matar a algn de un b.,** to shoot sb dead. 2 (herida) bullet wound.

balboa nf Fin standard monetary unit of Panama.

balbucear vi (adulto) to stutter, stammer; (niño) to babble.

balbuceo nm (de adulto) stuttering, stammering; (de niño) babbling.

balbucir vi defect → balbucear.

Balcanes npl los B., the Balkans.

balcón nm balcony.

baldado,-a adj fam shattered.

baldar vtr to cripple, maim.

balde[1] nm pail, bucket.

balde[2] loc adv 1 de b., (gratis) free. 2 en b., (en vano) in vain.

baldío,-a adj (terreno) uncultivated, waste; (esfuerzo) vain, useless.

baldosa nf (ceramic) floor tile; (para pavimentar) flagstone, paving stone.

balear I adj Balearic. II nmf native o inhabitant of the Balearic Islands.

Baleares npl las (Islas) B., the Balearic Islands.

balido nm bleating, bleat.

balística nf ballistics sing.

balístico,-a adj ballistic.

baliza nf 1 Náut buoy. 2 Av beacon.

ballena nf whale.

ballet nm ballet.

balneario nm spa, health resort.

balompié nm football.

balón nm ball, football; fig **b. de oxígeno,** boost.

baloncesto nm basketball.

balonmano nm handball.

balonvolea nm volleyball.

balsa nf 1 Náut raft. 2 fig como una b. de aceite, very quiet.

bálsamo nm balsam, balm.

Báltico nm **el (Mar) B.**, the Baltic (Sea).

baluarte nm fig stronghold.

bambas® nfpl trainers.

bambolear vi, **bambolearse** vr to swing; (persona, árbol) to sway; (mesa, silla) to wobble.

bambú nm (pl **bambúes**) bamboo.

banal adj banal, trivial.

banalidad nf triviality, banality.

banana nf banana.

banano nm (fruto) banana; (árbol) banana tree.

banca nf 1 (asiento) bench. 2 Com Fin (the) banks; (actividad) banking. 3 (en juegos) bank.

bancario,-a adj banking.

bancarrota nf Fin bankruptcy; **estar en b.**, to be bankrupt.

banco nm 1 bench. 2 Com Fin bank. 3 **b. de arena**, sandbank. 4 (de peces) shoal, school. 5 Geol layer.

banda nf 1 Mús band. 2 Cin **b. sonora**, sound track. 3 (de pájaros) flock. 4 (cinta) sash. 5 (lado) side; Ftb **línea de b.**, touchline; **saque de b.**, throw-in.

bandada nf flock.

bandazo nm **dar bandazos**, to lurch.

bandeja nf tray; fig **servir algo a algn en b.**, to hand sth to sb on a plate.

bandera nf flag.

banderín nm pennant, small flag.

bandido,-a nm,f bandit, outlaw.

bando[1] nm 1 Jur (edicto) edict, proclamation. 2 bandos, banns.

bando[2] nm faction, side; **pasarse al otro b.**, to go over to the other side, change allegiances.

bandolero,-a nm,f bandit, outlaw.

banquero,-a nm,f banker.

banqueta nf stool.

banquete nm banquet, feast; **b. de bodas**, wedding reception.

banquillo nm 1 Jur dock. 2 Dep bench.

bañador nm (de mujer) bathing o swimming costume; (de hombre) swimming trunks pl.

bañar I vtr 1 to bath. 2 (cubrir) to coat, cover; **b. en oro**, to goldplate. II **bañarse** vr (en baño) to have o take a bath; (en mar, piscina) to go for a swim.

bañera nf bath, bathtub.

bañista nmf bather, swimmer.

baño nm 1 bath; **tomar un b.**, to have o take a bath; fig **darse un b. de sol**, to sunbathe; **b. de sangre**, bloodbath. 2 (de oro etc) coat; (de chocolate etc) coating, covering. 3 (cuarto de baño) bathroom; (lavabo) toilet.

bar nm bar, pub.

barahúnda nf din, uproar.

baraja nf pack, deck.

barajar vtr (cartas) to shuffle; fig (nombres, cifras) to juggle with.

baranda, barandilla nf (de escalera) handrail, banister; (de balcón) handrail.

baratija nf trinket, knick-knack.

baratillo nm flea market.

barato,-a adj I cheap. II adv cheaply.

baraúnda nf din, uproar.

barba nf 1 Anat chin. 2 (pelo) beard; fig **cien pesetas por b.**, a hundred pesetas a head.

barbacoa nf barbecue.

barbaridad nf 1 atrocity. 2 (disparate) piece of nonsense; **no digas barbaridades**, don't talk nonsense. 3 **una b.**, a lot; **costar una b.**, to cost a fortune.

barbarie nf savagery, cruelty.

bárbaro,-a adj 1 Hist barbarian. 2 (cruel) barbaric, barbarous. 3 fam (enorme) massive. 4 fam (estupendo) tremendous, terrific. II nm,f Hist barbarian.

barbecho nm fallow land; **dejar en b.**, to leave fallow.

barbería nf barber's (shop).

barbero nm barber.

barbilla nf chin.

barbitúrico nm barbiturate.

barbudo,-a adj with a heavy beard.

barca nf small boat.

barcaza nf lighter.

barcelonés,-esa I adj de o from Barcelona. II nm,f native o inhabitant of Barcelona.

barco nm boat, ship; **b. de pasajeros**, liner; **b. de vapor**, steamer.

baremo nm scale.

barítono nm baritone.

barlovento nm windward.

barman nm barman.

barniz nm 1 (en madera) varnish; (en cerámica) glaze. 2 fig veneer.

barnizar [4] vtr (madera) to varnish; (cerámica) to glaze.

barómetro nm barometer.

barón nm baron.

baronesa nf baroness.

barquero,-a nm,f (hombre) boatman; (mujer) boatwoman.

barquillo nm wafer.

barra nf 1 bar; **b. de pan**, French loaf, baguette; **b. de labios**, lipstick. 2 (mostrador) bar. 3 Gimn **b. fija**, horizontal bar.

barraca nf 1 (caseta) shack, hut. 2 (en Valencia y Murcia) thatched farmhouse.

barracón nm Mil prefabricated hut.

barranco nm (despeñadero) cliff, precipice; (torrentera) gully, ravine.

barrena nf twist drill.

barrenar vtr Téc to drill.

barrendero,-a nm,f sweeper, street sweeper.

barreno nm 1 (taladro) large drill. 2 Min charge.

barreño nm tub.

barrer I vtr to sweep. II vi (en elecciones)

to win by landslide.

barrera *nf* barrier.

barricada *nf* barricade.

barrida *nf* landslide victory.

barriga *nf* belly; *fam* tummy.

barrigón,-ona, **barrigudo,-a** *adj* potbellied.

barril *nm* barrel; **cerveza de b.,** draught beer.

barrillo *nm* pimple, spot.

barrio *nm* area, district; **del b.,** local; **el B. Gótico,** the Gothic Quarter; **b. chino,** red-light district; **barrios bajos,** slums.

barrizal *nm* mire, quagmire.

barro *nm* 1 (*lodo*) mud. 2 (*arcilla*) clay; **objetos de b.,** earthenware *sing*.

barroco,-a *adj* baroque.

barruntar *vtr* (*sospechar*) to suspect; (*presentir*) to have a feeling.

barrunto *nm* (*presentimiento*) feeling, presentiment; (*sospecha*) suspicion.

bartola (a la) *loc adv fam* **tenderse** *o* **tumbarse a la b.,** to laze around, idle away one's time.

bártulos *nmpl fam* things, bits and pieces.

barullo *nm* (*alboroto*) row, din; (*confusión*) confusion.

basar *vt* to base (**en,** on). II **basarse** *vr* (*teoría, película*) to be based (**en,** on); ¿en qué te basas para decir eso?, what grounds do you have for saying that?

basca *nf arg* people, crowd.

báscula *nf* scales *pl*; (*para camiones*) weighbridge.

bascular *vi* to tilt.

base *nf* 1 base; **sueldo b.,** minimum wage; *Inform* **b. de datos,** data base. 2 (*de argumento, teoría*) basis; **en b. a,** on the basis of; **a b. de estudiar,** by studying; **a b. de productos naturales,** using natural products. 3 (*de partido*) grass roots; **miembro de b.,** rank and file member. 4 (*nociones*) grounding.

básico,-a *adj* basic.

basílica *nf* basilica.

básquet *nm* basketball.

bastante I *adj* 1 (*suficiente*) enough; **b. tiempo/comida,** enough time/food; **bastantes platos,** enough plates. 2 (*abundante*) quite a lot of; **hace b. calor/frío,** it's quite hot/cold; **bastantes amigos,** quite a lot of friends. II *adv* 1 (*suficiente*) enough; **con esto hay b.,** that is enough; **no soy lo b. rico (como) para ...,** I am not rich enough to .... 2 (*considerablemente*) fairly, quite; **me gusta b.,** I quite like it; **vamos b. al cine,** we go to the cinema quite *o* fairly often.

bastar I *vi* to be sufficient *o* enough, suffice; **basta con tres,** three will be enough; **¡basta de tonterías!,** enough of this nonsense!; **basta con tocarlo para que se abra,** you only have to touch it and it opens; **¡basta (ya)!,** that's

enough!, that will do! II **bastarse** *vr* **b. a sí mismo,** to be self-sufficient, rely only on oneself.

bastardilla *nf Impr* italics *pl*.

bastardo,-a *adj & nm,f* bastard.

bastidor *nm* 1 frame. 2 *Teat* **bastidores,** wings; *fig* **entre b.,** behind the scenes.

bastión *nm* bastion.

basto,-a *adj* (*cosa*) rough, coarse; (*persona*) coarse, uncouth.

bastos *nm Naipes* ≈ clubs.

bastón *nm* stick, walking stick.

basura *nf* rubbish, *US* trash, garbage.

basurero *nm* 1 (*persona*) dustman, refuse collector, *US* garbage collector. 2 (*lugar*) rubbish dump, *US* garbage dump.

bata *nf* (*para casa*) dressing gown; (*de médico etc*) white coat; (*de científico*) lab coat.

batacazo *nm* 1 crash, bang. 2 *Am* fluke, stroke of luck.

batalla *nf* battle; **librar b.,** to do *o* join battle; **b. campal,** pitched battle.

batallar *vi* to fight, quarrel.

batallón *nm* battalion.

batata *nf* sweet potato.

batatazo *nm Am* → **batacazo.**

bate *nm Dep* bat.

batear I *vi* to bat. II *vtr* to hit.

batería I *nf* 1 battery. 2 *Mús* drums *pl.* 3 **b. de cocina,** pots and pans, set of pans. II *nmf* drummer.

batiburrillo *nm* jumble, mess.

batida *nf* 1 (*de la policía*) raid. 2 (*en caza*) beat.

batido,-a I *adj* 1 *Culin* whipped. 2 *Dep* **tierra batida,** clay. II *nm* milk shake.

batidora *nf Culin* beater, whisk.

batiente *adj* reírse a **mandíbula b.,** to laugh one's head off.

batín *nm* short dressing gown.

batir I *vtr* 1 to beat. 2 (*huevo*) to beat; (*nata*) to whip, whisk. 3 (*récord*) to break. 4 (*en caza*) to beat. II **batirse** *vr* to fight.

batuta *nf Mús* baton; *fig* **llevar la b.,** to be in charge.

baúl *nm* 1 trunk. 2 *Am Aut* boot, *US* trunk.

bautismo *nm* baptism, christening.

bautizar [4] *vtr* to baptize, christen; (*vino*) to water down.

bautizo *nm* baptism, christening.

Baviera *n* Bavaria.

baya *nf* berry.

bayeta *nf* floorcloth.

bayo,-a *adj* whitish yellow.

bayoneta *nf* bayonet.

baza *nf* trick; *fig* **meter b.,** to butt in.

bazar *nm* bazaar.

bazo *nm* spleen.

bazofia *nf pey* rubbish.

beatería *nf* sanctimoniousness.

beato,-a *adj* (*piadoso*) devout; *pey* prudish, sanctimonious.

bebé *nm* baby; **b. probeta**, test-tube baby.

bebedero *nm* drinking trough, water trough.

bebedor,-a *nm,f* (hard *o* heavy) drinker.

beber *vtr* & *vi* to drink.

bebible *adj* drinkable.

bebida *nf* drink; **darse a la b.**, to take to drink.

bebido,-a *adj* drunk.

beca *nf* grant.

becar [1] *vtr* to award a grant to.

becario,-a *nm,f* grant holder.

becerro *nm* calf.

bechamel *nf* bechamel; **salsa b.**, bechamel sauce, white sauce.

becuadro *nm Mús* natural sign.

bedel *nm* beadle.

begonia *nf* begonia.

beige *adj* & *nm inv* beige.

béisbol *nm* baseball.

Belén *n* Bethlehem.

belén *nm* nativity scene, crib.

belga *adj* & *nmf* Belgian.

Bélgica *n* Belgium.

Belgrado *n* Belgrade.

Belice *n* Belize.

bélico,-a *adj* warlike, bellicose; (*preparativos etc*) war; **material b.**, armaments *pl*.

belicoso,-a *adj* warlike, bellicose; (*agresivo*) aggressive.

beligerancia *nf* belligerence.

beligerante *adj* belligerent; **los países beligerantes**, the countries at war.

bellaco,-a I *adj* wicked, roguish. **II** *nm,f* scoundrel, rogue.

belleza *nf* beauty.

bello,-a *adj* beautiful.

bellota *nf Bot* acorn; *fig* **animal de b.**, blockhead.

bemol I *adj Mús* flat. **II** *nm* **esto tiene bemoles**, this is a tough one.

bencina *nf Am* petrol.

bendecir [12] *vtr* to bless; **b. la mesa**, to say grace; **¡Dios te bendiga!**, God bless you!

bendición *nf* blessing.

bendito,-a I *adj* blessed; (*maldito*) damned. **II** *nm,f* (*bonachón*) good sort, kind soul; (*tontorrón*) simple soul.

beneficencia *nf* beneficence, charity.

beneficiado,-a *adj* favoured, *US* favored; **salir b. de algo**, to do well out of sth.

beneficiar [12] **I** *vtr* to benefit. **II beneficiarse** *vr* **b. de** *o* **con algo**, to profit from *o* by sth.

beneficiario,-a *nm,f* beneficiary; **margen b.**, profit margin.

beneficio *nm* **1** *Com Fin* profit. **2** (*bien*) benefit; **en b. propio**, in one's own interest; **un concierto a b. de ...**, a concert in aid of ....

beneficioso,-a *adj* beneficial.

benéfico,-a *adj* charitable.

benemérita *nf* **la B.**, the Spanish Civil Guard.

beneplácito *nm fml* approval, consent.

benevolencia *nf* benevolence.

benevolente, benévolo,-a *adj* benevolent.

bengala *nf* flare.

benigno,-a *adj* (*persona*) gentle, benign; (*clima*) mild; (*tumor*) benign.

benjamín,-ina *nm,f* youngest child.

beodo,-a *adj* drunk.

berberecho *nm* (common) cockle.

berbiquí *nm Téc* drill.

berenjena *nf* aubergine, *US* eggplant.

Berlín *n* Berlin.

berlina *nf* (*coche*) saloon; (*carruaje*) sedan.

berlinés,-esa I *adj* of *o* from Berlin. **II** *nm,f* Berliner.

bermejo,-a *adj* reddish.

bermellón *nm* vermilion.

Bermudas I *nfpl* **las (Islas) B.**, Bermuda *sing*. **II** *nmpl* **bermudas**, (*prenda*) Bermuda shorts.

Berna *n* Bern.

berrear *vi* to bellow, low.

berrido *nm* bellowing, lowing.

berrinche *nm fam* rage, tantrum.

berro *nm* cress, watercress.

berza *nf* cabbage.

besar I *vtr* to kiss. **II besarse** *vr* to kiss.

beso *nm* kiss.

best-seller *nm* best-seller.

bestia I *nf* beast, animal; **b. de carga**, beast of burden. **II** *nmf fam fig* brute, beast. **III** *adj fig* brutish, boorish; **a lo b.**, rudely.

bestial *adj* bestial; *fam* (*enorme*) huge, tremendous; (*extraordinario*) fantastic, terrific.

bestialidad *nf* **1** *fam* (*estupidez*) stupidity. **2** (*crueldad*) act of cruelty. **3** *fam* **una b. de**, tons of, stacks of.

besugo *nm* **1** (*pez*) sea bream. **2** (*persona*) idiot, half-wit.

besuquear *fam* **I** *vtr* to kiss, cover with kisses. **II besuquearse** *vr* to smooch.

betún *nm* (*para el calzado*) shoe polish; *Quím* bitumen.

biberón *nm* baby's bottle, feeding bottle.

Biblia *nf* Bible.

bíblico,-a *adj* biblical.

bibliografía *nf* bibliography.

biblioteca *nf* library; **b. ambulante**, mobile library.

bibliotecario,-a *nm,f* librarian.

BIC *nf abr de* **Brigada de Investigación Criminal**, ≈ Criminal Investigation Department, CID.

bicameral *adj Pol* bicameral, two-chamber.

bicarbonato *nm* bicarbonate; **b. sódico**, bicarbonate of soda.

bicentenario *nm* bicentenary, *US* bicentennial.

bíceps nm inv biceps.

bicha nf snake.

bicho nm 1 bug, insect; ¿qué b. te ha picado?, what's bugging you? 2 Taur bull. 3 fam todo b. viviente, every living soul; un b. raro, a weirdo, an oddball.

bici nf fam bike.

bicicleta nf bicycle; montar en b., to ride a bicycle.

bicolor adj two-coloured; Pol gobierno b., two-party government.

bidé nm bidet.

bidón nm drum.

biela nf Aut connecting rod.

bien¹ I adv 1 (correctamente) well; habla b. (el) inglés, she speaks English well; responder b., to answer correctly; hiciste b. en decírmelo, you were right to tell me; las cosas le van b., things are going well for him; ¡b.!, good!, great!; ¡muy b.!, excellent, first class!; ¡qué b.!, great!, fantastic! 2 (de salud) well; sentirse/encontrarse/estar b., to feel well. 3 vivir b., to be comfortably off; ¡está b.!, (¡de acuerdo!) all right!; ¡ya está b.!, that's (quite) enough!; aquí se está muy b., it's really nice here; esta falda te sienta b., this skirt suits you; fam ese libro está muy b., that book is very good; fam su novia está muy b., his girlfriend is very nice. 4 (intensificador) very, quite; b. temprano, very early, nice and early; b. caliente, pretty hot; b. es verdad que ..., it's quite clear that .... 5 más b., rather, a little. 6 b. podía haberme avisado, she might have let me know. 7 (de buena gana) willingly, gladly; b. me tomaría una cerveza, I'd really love a beer.

II conj ahora b., now, now then; o b., or, or else; b. ... o b. ..., either ... or ...; no b., as soon as; no b. llegó ..., no sooner had she arrived than ...; si b., although, even if.

III adj la gente b., the wealthy, the upper classes.

bien² nm 1 (bondad) good; el b. y el mal, good and evil; un hombre/familia de b., a good man/family. 2 (bienestar) por el b. de, for the good of; lo hace por tu b., he does it for your sake. 3 bienes, goods; bienes de equipo, capital goods; bienes gananciales, communal property; bienes inmuebles, real estate; bienes de consumo, consumer goods.

bienal nf biennial exhibition.

bienestar nm (personal) well-being, contentment; (comodidad) ease, comfort; la sociedad del b., the affluent society.

bienhechor,-a nm,f (hombre) benefactor; (mujer) benefactress.

bienintencionado,-a adj well-meaning, well-intentioned.

bienio nm biennium, two-year period.

bienvenida nf welcome; dar la b. a algn, to welcome sb.

bienvenido,-a adj welcome.

bife nm steak.

bifocal adj bifocal; gafas bifocales, bifocals.

bifurcación nf bifurcation; (de la carretera) fork.

bifurcarse [1] vr to fork, branch off.

bigamia nf bigamy.

bígamo,-a I adj bigamous. II nm,f bigamist.

bigote nm (de persona) moustache, US mustache; (de animal) (usu pl) whiskers pl.

bilateral adj bilateral; acuerdo b., bilateral agreement.

bilbaíno,-a I adj of o from Bilbao. II nm,f native o inhabitant of Bilbao.

bilingüe adj bilingual.

bilis nf bile.

billar nm 1 (juego) billiards sing; b. americano, pool; b. ruso, snooker. 2 (mesa) billiard table.

billete nm 1 ticket; b. de ida y vuelta, return (ticket), US round-trip ticket; b. sencillo o de ida, single (ticket). 2 (de banco) note, US bill; un b. de mil pesetas, a thousand peseta note.

billetera nf, **billetero** nm wallet, US billfold.

billón nm billion, US trillion.

bimensual adj twice-monthly, bi-monthly.

bimotor I adj twin-engined. II nm twin-engined plane.

binario,-a adj binary.

bingo nm 1 (juego) bingo. 2 (sala) bingo hall.

binomio nm binomial.

biodegradable adj biodegradable.

biofísica nf biophysics.

biografía nf biography.

biográfico,-a adj biographical.

biógrafo,-a nm,f biographer.

biología nf biology.

biológico,-a adj biological.

biólogo,-a nm,f biologist.

biombo nm (folding) screen.

biomasa nf bio-mass.

biopsia nf biopsy.

bioquímica nf biochemistry.

bioquímico,-a I adj biochemical. II nm,f biochemist.

bióxido nm dioxide; b. de carbono, carbon dioxide.

bipartidismo nm two-party system.

biquini nm bikini.

birlar vtr fam to pinch, nick.

Birmania n Burma.

birmano,-a adj & nm,f Burmese.

birrete nm cap, beret; Rel biretta; Univ mortar-board.

birria nf fam rubbish.

bis I nm encore. II adv twice.

bisabuela nf great-grandmother.

bisabuelo nm great-grandfather; **bisabuelos**, great-grandparents.

bisagra nf hinge; **partido b.**, party holding the balance of power.

bisbisar, bisbisear vtr to whisper.

bisexual adj & nmf bisexual.

bisiesto adj **año b.**, leap year.

bisnieto,-a nm,f (niño) great-grandson; (niña) great-granddaughter; **mis bisnietos**, my great-grandchildren.

bisonte nm bison, American buffalo.

bisoño,-a adj inexperienced.

bisté, bistec nm steak.

bisturí nm scalpel.

bisutería nf imitation jewellery o US jewelry.

bit nm Inform bit.

bíter nm bitters pl.

bizantino,-a adj fig **discusiones bizantinas**, hair-splitting arguments.

bizco,-a I adj cross-eyed. II nm,f cross-eyed person.

bizcocho nm sponge cake.

biznieto,-a nm,f → bisnieto,-a.

blanca nf fam **estar sin b.**, to be flat broke.

blanco,-a[1] I adj white; (tez) fair. II nm,f (hombre) white man; (mujer) white woman; **los blancos**, whites.

blanco[2] nm 1 (color) white. 2 (hueco) blank; **dejó la hoja en b.**, he left the page blank; **votos en b.**, blank votes; fig **pasar la noche en b.**, to have a sleepless night; **me quedé en b.**, my mind went blank. 3 (diana) target; **dar en el b.**, to hit the target; fig **ser el b. de todas las miradas**, to be the centre of attention.

blancura nf whiteness.

blandengue adj pey weak, soft.

blandir vtr to brandish.

blando,-a adj soft.

blanquear vtr 1 to whiten. 2 (encalar) to whitewash. 3 (dinero) to launder.

blanquecino,-a adj whitish.

blanqueo nm 1 whitening. 2 (encalado) whitewashing. 3 (de dinero) laundering.

blasfemar vi to blaspheme (**contra**, against).

blasfemia nf blasphemy.

blasón nm coat of arms.

bledo nm fam **me importa un b.**, I couldn't give a damn.

blindado,-a adj Mil armoured, US armored, armour-plated, US armor-plated; (antibalas) bullet-proof; **coche b.**, bulletproof car; **puerta blindada**, reinforced door, security door.

blindaje nm armour, US armor; (vehículo) armour o US armor plating.

bloc nm pad; b. de notas, notepad.

bloque nm 1 block; **en b.**, en bloc; **b. de pisos**, (block of) flats. 2 Pol bloc; **el b.**

comunista, the Communist Bloc.

bloquear vtr 1 to block. 2 Mil to blockade.

bloqueo nm blockade; Dep block.

blues nm blues pl.

blusa nf blouse.

blusón nm loose blouse, smock.

boato nm show, ostentation.

bobada nf nonsense; **decir bobadas**, to talk nonsense.

bobalicón,-ona fam I adj simple, stupid. II nmf simpleton, idiot.

bobería nf → bobada.

bobo,-a I adj (tonto) stupid, silly; (ingenuo) naïve. II nm,f fool.

boca nf 1 mouth; **b. abajo**, face downwards; b. arriba, face upward; fig a **pedir de b.**, in accordance with one's wishes; fig **andar de b. en b.**, to be the talk of the town; fam **¡cierra la b!**, shut up!; fam **con la b. abierta**, open-mouthed; fam **se le hizo la b. agua**, his mouth watered; **el b. a b.**, kiss of life, mouth-to-mouth respiration. 2 **la b. del metro**, the entrance to the tube o underground station; **b. de riego**, hydrant.

bocacalle nf entrance to a street.

bocadillo nm 1 sandwich; **un b. de jamón/tortilla**, a ham/omelette sandwich. 2 (de cómic) balloon.

bocado nm 1 (mordedura) bite. 2 (de caballo) bit.

bocajarro (a) loc adv point-blank.

bocanada nf 1 (de vino) mouthful. 2 (de humo) puff; **una b. de viento**, a gust of wind.

bocata nm sandwich.

bocazas nmf inv fam bigmouth, blabbermouth.

boceto nm Arte sketch, outline; (esquema) outline, plan.

bochinche nm fam uproar; **armar un b.**, to kick up a row.

bochorno nm 1 (tiempo) sultry o close weather; (calor sofocante) stifling heat. 2 fig (vergüenza) shame, embarrassment.

bochornoso,-a adj 1 (tiempo) sultry, close, muggy; (calor) stifling. 2 fig (vergonzoso) shameful, embarrassing.

bocina nf horn; **tocar la b.**, to blow o sound one's horn.

bocinazo nm hoot, toot.

boda nf wedding, marriage; **bodas de plata**, silver wedding sing.

bodega nf 1 wine cellar; (tienda) wine shop. 2 Náut hold. 3 (almacén) warehouse. 4 Am grocery store, grocer's.

bodegón nm still-life.

bodrio nm fam rubbish, trash.

body nm bodystocking, leotard.

BOE nm abr de **Boletín Oficial del Estado**, Official Gazette.

bofetada nf, **bofetón** nm slap on the

face; **dar una b./un b. a algn**, to slap sb's face.

boga *nf fig* **estar en b.**, to be in vogue.

bogar [7] *vi* 1 (*remar*) to row. 2 (*navegar*) to sail.

bogavante *nm* lobster.

bogotano,-a I *adj* of *o* from Bogotá. II *n m,f* native of Bogotá.

bohío *nm Am* hut, cabin.

boicot *nm* (*pl* **boicots**) boycott.

boicotear *vtr* to boycott.

boicoteo *nm* boycott.

boina *nf* beret.

bol *nm* bowl.

bola *nf* 1 ball; (*canica*) marble; **b. de nieve**, snowball; **no dar pie con b.**, to be unable to do anything right. 2 *fam* (*mentira*) fib, lie; **meter bolas**, to tell fibs. 3 *Am* (*rumor*) rumour.

bolchevique *adj & nmf* Bolshevik.

bolear *vtr* to throw.

bolera *nf* bowling alley.

boletería *nf Am Dep Ferroc* ticket office, *GB* booking office; *Teat* ticket office, box office.

boletín *nm* bulletin; **B. Oficial del Estado**, Official Gazette.

boleto *nm* ticket.

boli *nm fam* ball-point pen, biro®.

boliche *nm* 1 (*juego*) bowling, skittles. 2 (*bola*) jack. 3 (*lugar*) bowling alley.

bólido *nm Aut* racing car.

bolígrafo *nm* ballpoint (pen), biro®.

bolívar *nm Fin* standard monetary unit of Venezuela.

Bolivia *n* Bolivia.

boliviano,-a I *adj & nm,f* Bolivian.

bollar *vtr* to dent.

bollo *nm* 1 *Culin* bun, bread roll. 2 (*abolladura*) dent.

bolo *nm* 1 skittle, ninepin. 2 **bolos**, (*juego*) skittles.

bolsa[1] *nf* bag; *Av* **b. de aire**, air pocket; **b. de deportes**, sports bag; **b. de la compra**, shopping bag; **b. de viaje**, travel bag.

bolsa[2] *nf Fin* Stock Exchange; **jugar a la b.**, to play the market.

bolsillo *nm* (*en prenda*) pocket; **de b.**, pocket, pocket-size; **libro de b.**, paperback; **lo pagó de su b.**, he paid for it out of his own pocket.

bolso *nm* handbag, bag, *US* purse.

bomba[1] *nf* pump; **b. de aire**, air pump; **b. de incendios**, fire engine.

bomba[2] *nf* bomb; **b. atómica/de hidrógeno/de neutrones**, atomic/ hydrogen/neutron bomb; **b. de relojería**, time bomb; **b. fétida**, stink bomb; *fam* **noticia b.**, shattering piece of news; *fam* **pasarlo b.**, to have a whale of a time.

bombardear *vtr* to bomb, shell; **b. a algn a preguntas**, to bombard sb with questions.

bombardeo *nm* bombing, bombardment.

bombardero *nm Av* bomber.

bombazo *nm* bomb blast.

bombear *vtr* 1 (*agua etc*) to pump. 2 (*pelota*) to blow up.

bombeo *nm* (*de líquido*) pumping; **estación de b.**, pumping station.

bombero,-a *nm,f* (*hombre*) fireman; (*mujer*) firewoman; *US* (*ambos sexos*) firefighter; **cuerpo de bomberos**, fire brigade; **parque de bomberos**, fire station.

bombilla *nf* (light) bulb.

bombín *nm* bowler hat.

bombo *nm* 1 *Mús* bass drum; *fig* **a b. y platillo(s)**, with a great song and dance; *fam* **darse b.**, to blow one's own trumpet. 2 (*de sorteo*) lottery drum.

bombón *nm* chocolate.

bombona *nf* cylinder; **b. de butano**, butane gas cylinder.

bombonera *nf* chocolate box.

bonachón,-ona *adj* good-natured, easygoing.

bonaerense I *adj* of *o* from Buenos Aires. II *nmf* native *o* inhabitant of Buenos Aires.

bonanza *nf* 1 *Náut* (*tiempo*) fair weather; (*mar*) calm at sea. 2 *fig* (*prosperidad*) prosperity.

bondad *nf* goodness; *fml* **tenga la b. de esperar**, please be so kind as to wait.

bondadoso,-a *adj* kind, good-natured.

bonete *nm Rel* cap, biretta; *Univ* mortar-board.

boniato *nm* sweet potato.

bonificación *nf* bonus.

bonificar [1] *vtr Com* to give a bonus to.

bonito,-a[1] *adj* pretty, nice.

bonito[2] *nm* tuna.

bono *nm* 1 (*vale*) voucher. 2 *Fin* bond, debenture; **bonos del tesoro** *o* **del Estado**, Treasury bonds.

bono-bus *nm* bus pass.

boom *nm* boom.

boomerang *nm* boomerang.

boquerón *nm* anchovy.

boquete *nm* hole.

boquiabierto,-a *adj* open-mouthed; **se quedó b.**, he was flabbergasted.

boquilla *nf* 1 (*de cigarro*) tip; (*de pipa*) mouthpiece; **decir algo de b.**, to pay lip service to sth. 2 *Mús* mouthpiece. 3 (*orificio*) opening.

borbotar, borbotear *vi* to bubble.

borbotón *nm* bubbling; *fig* **salir a borbotones**, to gush forth.

borda *nf Náut* gunwale; **arrojar** *o* **echar por la b.**, to throw overboard; **fuera b.**, (*motor*) outboard motor.

bordado,-a I *adj* embroidered; **el examen me salió b.**, I made a good job of that exam. II *nm* embroidery.

bordar *vtr* 1 to embroider. 2 *fig* to do excellently.

borde[1] *nm* (*de mesa, camino*) edge; *Cost* hem, edge; (*de vasija*) rim, brim; **al b. de**, on the brink of; **al b. del mar**, at the seaside.

borde[2] *fam* **I** *adj* stroppy. **II** *nmf* stroppy person.

bordear *vtr* to go round the edge of, skirt.

bordillo *nm* kerb, *US* curb.

bordo *nm* **a b.**, on board; **subir a b.**, to go on board.

borla *nf* tassel.

borne *nm* *Elec* terminal.

borra *nf* **1** (*pelusa*) fluff. **2** (*poso*) sediment, dregs *pl*.

borrachera *nf* (*embriaguez*) drunkenness; (*curda*) binge; **coger** *o* **pillar una b.**, to get drunk.

borracho,-a *adj* **1** (*bebido*) drunk; **estar b.**, to be drunk. **2** (*bizcocho*) with rum. **II** *nm,f* drunkard, drunk.

borrador *nm* **1** (*escrito*) rough copy, *US* first draft. **2** (*croquis*) rough *o* preliminary sketch. **3** (*de pizarra*) duster.

borraja *nf* **quedar en agua de borrajas**, to come to nothing, fizzle *o* peter out.

borrar **I** *vtr* **1** (*con goma*) to erase, rub out; (*pizarra*) to clean. **2** *Inform* to delete. **II borrarse** *vr* (*de un club etc*) to drop out, withdraw.

borrasca *nf* area of low pressure.

borrascoso,-a *adj* stormy.

borrego,-a *nm,f* **1** yearling lamb. **2** *fam* (*persona*) sheep.

borrico *nm* ass, donkey; *fam* *fig* ass, dimwit.

borrón *nm* blot, smudge.

borroso,-a *adj* blurred; **veo b.**, I can't see clearly, everything's blurred.

bosque *nm* wood.

bosquejar *vtr* (*dibujo*) to sketch, outline; (*plan*) to draft, outline.

bosquejo *nm* (*de dibujo*) sketch, study; (*de plan*) draft.

bostezar [4] *vi* to yawn.

bostezo *nm* yawn.

bota *nf* **1** boot; *fig* **ponerse las botas**, to make a killing. **2** (*de vino*) wineskin.

botana *nf* *Am* snack.

botánica *nf* botany.

botánico,-a **I** *adj* botanic; **jardín b.**, botanic gardens. **II** *nm,f* botanist.

botar **I** *vi* **1** (*saltar*) to jump. **2** (*pelota*) to bounce. **II** *vtr* **1** (*barco*) to launch. **2** (*pelota*) to bounce. **3** *Am* (*arrojar*) to throw *o* chuck out.

botarate *nmf* madcap, fool.

bote[1] *nm* **1** jump, bound; **dar botes**, to jump up and down; **de un b.**, with one leap. **2** (*de pelota*) bounce, rebound.

bote[2] *nm* (*lata*) can, tin; (*para propinas*) jar *o* box for tips; (*en lotería*) jackpot; *fam* **chupar del b.**, to scrounge.

bote[3] *nm* (*lancha*) boat; **b. salvavidas**,

lifeboat.

bote *nm* **de b. en b.**, packed, full to bursting.

botella *nf* bottle.

botellín *nm* small bottle.

botepronto *nm* *fam* **a b.**, all of a sudden.

botica *nf* (*chemist's* (*shop*)) pharmacy, *US* drugstore; *fam* **hay de todo como en b.**, there's everything under the sun.

boticario,-a *nm,f* chemist, pharmacist, *US* druggist.

botijo *nm* earthenware pitcher (with spout and handle).

botín[1] *nm* (*de un robo*) loot, booty.

botín[2] *nm* (*calzado*) ankle boot.

botiquín *nm* **1** medicine chest *o* cabinet; (*portátil*) first aid kit. **2** (*enfermería*) first aid post.

botón *nm* button; **pulsar el b.**, to press the button; **b. de muestra**, sample.

botones *nm* *inv* (*en hotel*) bellboy, *US* bellhop; (*recadero*) messenger, errand boy.

boutique *nf* boutique.

bóveda *nf* vault.

bovino,-a *adj* bovine; **ganado b.**, cattle.

boxeador *nm* boxer.

boxear *vi* to box.

boxeo *nm* boxing.

boya *nf* **1** *Náut* buoy. **2** (*corcho*) float.

boyante *adj* buoyant.

boy-scout *nm* boy scout.

bozal *nm* muzzle.

bracero *nm* (*day*) labourer.

bragas *nfpl* panties *pl*, knickers *pl*.

bragueta *nf* (*de pantalón etc*) fly, flies *pl*.

braguetazo *nm* *vulg* **dar el b.**, to marry for money.

braille *nm* braille.

bramar *vi* to low, bellow.

bramido *nm* lowing, bellowing.

brandy *nm* brandy.

branquia *nf* gill.

brasa *nf* ember, red-hot coal; **chuletas a la b.**, barbecued chops.

brasero *nm* brazier.

Brasil *n* Brazil.

brasileño,-a, **brasilero,-a** *adj* & *nm,f* Brazilian.

bravata *nf* piece *o* act of bravado.

bravo,-a **I** *adj* **1** (*valiente*) brave, courageous. **2** (*feroz*) fierce, ferocious; **un toro b.**, a fighting bull. **3** (*mar*) rough, stormy. **II** *interj* ¡**b.**!, well done!, bravo!

bravucón,-ona *nm,f* boaster, braggart.

bravura *nf* **1** (*de animal*) ferocity, fierceness. **2** (*de persona*) courage, bravery. **3** (*de toro*) fighting spirit.

braza *nf* **1** *Náut* fathom. **2** *Natación* breast stroke; **nadar a b.**, to do the breast stroke.

brazada *nf* *Natación* stroke.

brazalete *nm* **1** (*insignia*) armband. **2** (*pulsera*) bracelet.

brazo *nm* arm; *(de animal)* foreleg; *(de sillón, tocadiscos)* arm; **en brazos,** in one's arms; **ir del b.,** to walk arm in arm; **fig con los brazos abiertos,** with open arms; **fig no dar su b. a torcer,** not to give in, stand firm; **b. de gitano,** type of Swiss roll containing cream.

brea *nf* tar, pitch.

brebaje *nm* concoction, brew.

brecha *nf (en muro)* opening, gap; *Mil & fig* breach; **fig estar siempre en la b.,** to be always in the thick of things.

brécol *nm* broccoli.

bregar [7] *vi* to fight.

Bretaña *nf* 1 Brittany. 2 **Gran B.,** Great Britain.

brete *nm fig* poner a algn en un b., to put sb in a tight spot.

breva *nf* early fig; *fam* de higos a brevas, once in a blue moon; *fam* ¡no caerá esa b.!, no such luck!

breve *adj* brief; **en b., en breves momentos,** shortly, soon; **en breves palabras,** in short.

brevedad *nf* briefness; *(concision)* brevity; **con la mayor b. posible,** as soon as possible.

brezo *nm* heather.

bribón,-ona I *adj* roguish, dishonest. II *nm,f* rogue, rascal.

bricolaje *nm* do-it-yourself, DIY.

brida *nf* 1 *(rienda)* rein, bridle. 2 *Téc* flange.

bridge *nm Naipes* bridge.

brigada I *nf* 1 *Mil* brigade. 2 *(de policías)* squad; **b. antiterrorista,** anti-terrorist squad. II *nm Mil* sergeant major.

brigadier *nm* brigadier.

brillante I *adj* brilliant. II *nm* diamond.

brillantez *nf* brilliance.

brillantina *nf* brilliantine.

brillar *vi (resplandecer)* to shine; *(ojos, joyas)* to sparkle; *(lentejuelas etc)* to glitter; **b. por su ausencia,** to be conspicuous by one's absence.

brillo *nm (resplandor)* shine; *(del sol, de la luna)* brightness; *(de lentejuelas etc)* glittering; *(del cabello, tela)* sheen; *(de color)* brilliance; *(de pantalla)* brightness; *(de zapatos)* shine; **sacar b. a,** to shine, polish.

brincar [1] *vi* to skip.

brinco *nm* skip.

brindar I *vi* to drink a toast; **b. por algn/algo,** to drink to sb/sth. II *vtr* 1 *(oportunidad)* to offer, provide. 2 *Taur* to dedicate the bull **(a,** to). III **brindarse** *vr* to offer **(a,** to), volunteer **(a,** to).

brindis *nm* 1 toast. 2 *Taur* dedication (of the bull).

brío *nm* energy.

brioso,-a *adj* energetic, vigorous.

brisa *nf* breeze; **b. marina,** sea breeze.

británico,-a I *adj* British; **las Islas Britá-**

nicas, the British Isles. II *nm,f* Briton; **los británicos,** the British.

brizna *nf (de hierba)* blade; *(de carne)* string.

broca *nf Téc* bit.

brocha *nf (para pintar)* paintbrush; **b. de afeitar,** shaving brush.

broche *nm* 1 *(joya)* brooch; *fig* poner el b. de oro, to finish with a flourish. 2 *(de vestido)* fastener.

bróculi *nm* broccoli.

broma *nf (chiste)* joke; **bromas aparte,** joking apart; **en b.,** as a joke; **¡ni en b.!,** not on your life!; **b. pesada,** practical joke; **gastar una b.,** to play a joke.

bromear *vi* to joke.

bromista I *adj* fond of joking o playing jokes. II *nmf* joker, prankster.

bronca *nf (riña)* quarrel, row. 2 **echar una b. a algn,** to bawl sb out.

bronce *nm* bronze.

bronceado,-a I *adj* suntanned, tanned. II *nm* suntan, tan.

bronceador,-a I *adj* **leche bronceadora,** suntan cream. II *nm* suntan cream o lotion.

broncearse *vr* to get a tan o a suntan.

bronco,-a *adj* rough, coarse.

bronquitis *nf inv* bronchitis.

brotar *vi (planta)* to sprout; *(agua)* to spring, gush; *(lágrimas)* to well up; *(epidemia)* to break out.

brote *nm* 1 *Bot (renuevo)* bud, shoot; *(de agua)* gushing. 2 *(de epidemia, violencia)* outbreak.

bruces *(de)* *loc adv* face downwards; **se cayó de b.,** he fell flat on his face.

bruja *nf* witch, sorceress.

brujería *nf* witchcraft, sorcery.

brújula *nf* compass.

bruma *nf* mist.

brumoso,-a *adj* misty.

bruñir *vtr* to polish.

brusco,-a *adj* 1 *(persona)* brusque, abrupt. 2 *(repentino)* sudden, sharp.

Bruselas *n* Brussels; **coles de B.,** Brussels sprouts.

brusquedad *nf* brusqueness, abruptness.

brutal *adj* brutal.

brutalidad *nf* brutality.

bruto,-a *adj* 1 *(necio)* stupid, thick; *(grosero)* coarse, uncouth. 2 *Fin* gross; **peso b.,** gross weight. 3 **un diamante en b.,** an uncut diamond. II *nm,f* blockhead, brute.

búcaro *nm* earthenware jug.

bucear *vi* to swim under water.

buche *nm* maw; *(de ave)* craw; *fam (estómago)* belly, stomach.

bucle *nm* curl, ringlet.

budín *nm* pudding.

budismo *nm* Buddhism.

budista *adj* Buddhist.

buen *adj (delante de un nombre masculino)*

singular) good; **¡b. viaje!**, have a good trip!; → **bueno,-a**.

buenaventura *nf* good fortune, good luck; **echar la b. a algn**, to tell sb's fortune.

bueno,-a *adj* 1 good; **un alumno muy b.**, a very good pupil; **una buena película**, a good film; **lo b.**, the good thing. 2 (*amable*) (*con ser*) good, kind; **el b. de Carlos**, good old Carlos; **es muy buena persona**, he's a very kind soul. 3 (*sano*) (*con estar*) well, in good health. 4 (*tiempo*) good; **hoy hace buen tiempo**, it's fine today; **mañana hará b.**, it will be fine *o* a nice day tomorrow. 5 (*conveniente*) good; **no es b. comer tanto**, it's not good for you to eat so much; **sería b. que vinieras**, it would be a good idea if you came. 6 (*considerable*) considerable; **un buen número de**, a good number of; **una buena cantidad**, a considerable amount. 7 (*grande*) good, big; **un buen trozo de pastel**, a nice *o* good big piece of cake. 8 *fam* (*atractivo*) gorgeous, sexy; **Rosa está muy buena**, Rosa's a bit of all right!; **una tía buena**, a good-looking girl. 9 *irón* fine, real, proper; **¡en buen lío te has metido!**, that's a fine mess you've got yourself into! 10 **¡buenas!**, (*saludos*) hello!; **buenas tardes**, (*desde mediodía hasta las cinco*) good afternoon; (*desde las cinco*) good evening; **buenas noches**, (*al llegar*) good evening; (*al irse*) good night; **buenos días**, good morning. 11 (*locuciones*) **de buenas a primeras**, suddenly, all at once; **estar de buenas**, to be in a good mood; **los buenos tiempos**, the good old days; **por las buenas**, willingly; **por las buenas o por las malas**, willy-nilly; *irón* **¡buena la has hecho!**, that's done it!; **un susto de los buenos**, a real fright; *irón* **¡estaría b.!**, I should jolly well hope not!; *irón* **librarse de una buena**, to get off scot free.
II *interj* **¡b.!**, (*vale*) all right, OK.
◆ **buenamente** *adv* **haz lo que b. puedas**, just do what you can; **si b. puedes**, if you possibly can.

buey *nm* ox, bullock.

búfalo,-a *nm,f* buffalo.

bufanda *nf* scarf.

bufar *vi* 1 (*toro*) to snort; (*caballo*) to neigh. 2 (*persona*) to be fuming.

bufé *nm* buffet; **b. libre**, self-service buffet meal.

bufete *nm* (*despacho de abogado*) lawyer's office.

buffet *nm* (*pl* **buffets**) → **bufé**.

bufido *nm* (*de toro*) snort; (*de caballo*) neigh.

bufón,-ona *nm,f* clown, buffoon.

buhardilla *nf* attic, garret.

búho *nm* owl; **b. real**, eagle owl.

buhonero,-a *nm,f* pedlar, hawker.

buitre *nm* vulture.

bujía *nf* 1 *Aut* spark plug. 2 *Fís* candle-power.

bulbo *nm* bulb.

buldog *nm* bulldog.

bulevar *nm* boulevard.

Bulgaria *n* Bulgaria.

búlgaro,-a *adj & nm,f* Bulgarian.

bulla *nf* 1 (*muchedumbre*) crowd, mob. 2 (*ruido*) din; **armar b.**, to kick up a din.

bullicio *nm* din, hubbub.

bullir *vi* 1 (*hervir*) to boil, bubble (up). 2 **b. de gente**, to be teeming with people.

bulto *nm* 1 (*cosa indistinta*) shape, form. 2 (*maleta, caja*) piece of luggage. 3 *Med* lump. 4 **hacer mucho b.**, to be very bulky; *fam* **escurrir el b.**, to pass the buck.

bumerán ~~**humerang**~~ *nm* ~~boomerang~~.

bungalow *nm* bungalow.

búnker *nm* bunker.

buñuelo *nm* doughnut.

BUP *nm abr de* **Bachillerato Unificado Polivalente**, ≈ GCSE studies.

buque *nm* ship; **b. de guerra**, warship; **b. de pasajeros**, liner, passenger ship; **b. insignia**, flagship.

burbuja *nf* bubble; **hacer burbujas**, to bubble, make bubbles.

burbujear *vi* to bubble.

burdel *nm* brothel.

Burdeos *n* Bordeaux.

burdo,-a *adj* coarse, rough.

burgalés,-a I *adj* of *o* from Burgos. II *nm,f* native *o* inhabitant of Burgos.

burgués,-a *adj & nm,f* bourgeois.

burguesía *nf* bourgeoisie.

burla *nf* gibe, jeer; **hacer b. de algo *o* algn**, to make fun of sth *o* sb; **hacer b. a algn**, to stick one's tongue out at sb.

burladero *nm Taur* refuge in bullring.

burlar I *vtr* 1 (*engañar*) to deceive. 2 (*eludir*) to dodge, evade. II **burlarse** *vr* to make fun (**de**, of), laugh (**de**, at).

burlón,-ona *adj* mocking.

buró *nm* 1 *Pol* executive committee. 2 (*escritorio*) bureau, desk.

burocracia *nf* bureaucracy.

burócrata *nmf* bureaucrat.

burocrático,-a *adj* bureaucratic.

buromática *nf* office automation.

burrada *nf* (*comentario*) stupid *o* foolish remark; (*hecho*) stupid *o* foolish act.

burro,-a I *nm,f* 1 donkey, ass; *fam fig* **bajarse del b.**, to climb *o* back down. 2 *fam* (*estúpido*) dimwit, blockhead. 3 **b. de carga**, dogsbody, drudge. II *adj* 1 *fam* (*necio*) stupid, dumb. 2 *fam* (*obstinado*) stubborn.

bursátil *adj* stock-market.

bus *nm* bus.

busca *nf* search; **ir en b. de**, to go in search of.

buscapersonas *nm* pager.

buscapleitos *nmf inv* troublemaker.

buscar [1] I *vtr* 1 to look *o* search for; **b. una palabra en el diccionario**, to look up a word in the dictionary. 2 **ir a b. algo**, to go and get sth, fetch sth; **fue a buscarme a la estación**, she picked me up at the station. II **buscarse** *vr fam* **b. la vida**, to try and earn one's living; *fam* **te la estás buscando**, you're asking for it; **se busca**, wanted.

búsqueda *nf* search, quest; *Inform* search.

busto *nm* bust.

butaca *nf* 1 (*sillón*) armchair, easy chair. 2 *Cin Teat* seat; **b. de platea** *o* **patio**, seat in the stalls.

butano *nm* butane; (**gas**) **b.**, butane gas.

butifarra *nf* sausage.

buzo *nm* diver.

buzón *nm* letter box, *US* mailbox; **echar una carta al b.**, to post a letter.

byte *nm Inform* byte.

C

C, c [θe] *nf* (*la letra*) C, c.

C 1 *abr de* **Celsius**, Celsius, C. 2 *abr de* **centígrado**, centigrade, C.

c/ 1 *abr de* **calle**, Street, St; Road, Rd. 2 *abr de* **cargo**, cargo, freight. 3 *abr de* **cuenta**, account, a/c.

C., Cª *abr de* **compañía**, Company, Co.

cabal I *adj* 1 (*exacto*) exact, precise. 2 (*honesto*) honest, upright. II *nmpl fam* **estar algn en sus cabales**, to be in full possession of one's faculties.

cábala *nf fig* **hacer cábalas sobre algo**, to speculate about sth.

cabalgadura *nf* mount.

cabalgar [7] *vtr & vi* to ride.

cabalgata *nf* cavalcade; **la c. de los Reyes Magos**, the procession of the Three Wise Men.

caballa *nf* mackerel.

caballar *adj* **ganado c.**, horses *pl*.

caballería *nf* 1 (*cabalgadura*) mount, steed. 2 *Mil* cavalry.

caballeriza *nf* stable.

caballero *nm* 1 gentleman; **¿qué desea, c.?**, can I help you, sir?; **ropa de c.**, menswear. 2 *Hist* knight. 3 **caballeros**, (*en letrero*) gents.

caballeroso,-a *adj* gentlemanly, chivalrous.

caballete *nm* 1 (*de pintor*) easel. 2 *Téc* trestle. 3 (*de nariz*) bridge.

caballito *nm* 1 **c. de mar**, sea-horse. 2 **caballitos**, merry-go-round *sing, US* carousel *sing*.

caballo *nm* 1 horse; **a c.**, on horseback; **montar a c.**, to ride; *fig* **a c. entre ...**, halfway between .... 2 *Téc* **c. de vapor**, horse power. 3 *Ajedrez* knight. 4 *Naipes* queen. 5 *arg* (*heroína*) horse, smack.

cabaña *nf* cabin.

cabaret *nm* (*pl* **cabarets**) cabaret.

cabecear I *vi* to nod. II *vtr Dep* to head.

cabecera *nf* 1 top, head. 2 *Tip* headline.

cabecilla *nmf* leader.

cabellera *nf* head of hair.

cabello *nm* 1 hair. 2 *Culin* **c. de ángel**, sweet made of gourd and syrup.

cabelludo,-a *adj* **cuero c.**, scalp.

caber [9] *vi* 1 to fit, be (able to be) contained; **cabe en el maletero**, it fits in the boot; **¿cabemos todos?**, is there room for all of us?; **en este coche/jarro caben ...**, this car/jug holds ...; **no cabe por la puerta**, it won't go through the door; **no c. en sí de gozo**, to be beside oneself with joy; **no me cabe en la cabeza**, I can't understand it; **no cabe duda**, there is no doubt; **cabe la posibilidad de que ...**, there is a possibility *o* chance that ...; **no está mal dentro de lo que cabe**, it isn't bad, under the circumstances. 2 **cabe señalar que ...**, we should point out that .... 3 *Mat* **doce entre cuatro caben a tres**, four into twelve goes three (times).

cabestrillo *nm* sling.

cabestro *nm* halter.

cabeza I *nf* head; **en c.**, in the lead; **por c.**, a head, per person; *fig* **a la c. de**, at the front *o* top of; *fig* **estar mal de la c.**, to be a mental case; **c. de turco**, scapegoat; **c. de familia**, the head of the family. II *nm* **c. rapada**, skinhead.

cabezada *nf* 1 (*golpe*) butt, blow on the head. 2 *fam* **echar una c.**, to have a snooze; **dar cabezadas**, to nod.

cabezal *nm Téc* head; (*de tocadiscos*) pick-up.

cabezota *fam* I *adj* pigheaded. II *nmf* pigheaded person.

cabezudo *nm* carnival figure with a huge head.

cabida *nf* capacity; **dar c. a**, to leave room for.

cabildo *nm Rel* chapter.

cabina *nf* cabin; **c. telefónica**, telephone box, *US* telephone booth.

cabizbajo,-a *adj* crestfallen.

cable *nm* cable; *arg* **echarle un c. a algn**, to give sb a hand.

cabo *nm* 1 (*extremo*) end; **al c. de**, after; **de c. a rabo**, from start to finish. 2 *Mil* corporal; (*policía*) sergeant. 3 *Náut* rope, cable; *fig* **atar cabos**, to put two and two together; *fig* **no dejar ningún c. suelto**, to leave no loose ends. 4 *Geog* cape; **Ciudad del C.**, Cape Town; **C. Verde**, Cape

Verde.

cabra nf goat; fam **estar como una c.**, to be off one's head.

cabré indic fut → **caber.**

cabreado,-a adj vulg pissed-off.

cabrear I vtr vulg to make angry. **II cabrearse** vr to get worked up.

cabreo nm vulg anger.

cabrío,-a adj **macho c.**, billy goat; **ganado c.**, goats pl.

cabriola nf skip.

cabrito nm Zool kid.

cabrón,-ona nm,f ofens (hombre) bastard; (woman) bitch.

cabronada nf vulg dirty trick.

cabuya nf Am agave, pita.

caca nf fam poopoo.

cacahuete nm peanut.

cacao nm 1 Bot cacao. 2 (polvo, bebida) cocoa. 3 fam (lío) mess, cockup.

cacarear I vi (gallina) to cluck. **II** vtr fig to boast about.

cacareo nm 1 (de gallina) clucking. 2 fig boasting, bragging.

cacatúa nf cockatoo.

cacereño,-a I adj of o from Cáceres. **II** nm,f native o inhabitant of Cáceres.

cacería nf 1 (actividad) hunting, shooting. 2 (partida) hunt, shoot.

cacerola nf saucepan.

cacha nf fam (muslo) thigh; **estar cachas**, to be really muscular.

cachalote nm sperm whale.

cacharro nm 1 earthenware pot o jar. 2 fam (cosa) thing, piece of junk. 3 **cacharros**, (de cocina) pots and pans.

cachear vtr to frisk, search.

cachemir nm, **cachemira** nf cashmere.

cacheo nm frisk, frisking.

cachetada nf Am slap.

cachete nm 1 (bofetada) slap. 2 Am (mejilla) cheek.

cachimba nf Am pipe.

cachiporra nf club, truncheon.

cachivache nm fam thing, knick-knack.

cacho¹ nm fam (pedazo) bit, piece; fig **¡qué c. de animal!**, what a nasty piece of work!

cacho² nm Am (cuerno) horn.

cachondearse vr fam **c. de**, to take the mickey out of.

cachondeo nm fam laugh; **tomar algo a c.**, to take sth as a joke.

cachondo,-a adj fam 1 (sexualmente) randy. 2 (divertido) funny.

cachorro,-a nm,f (de perro) pup, puppy; (de gato) kitten; (de otros animales) cub, baby.

cacique nm (jefe) local boss.

caco nm fam thief.

cacofonía nf cacophony.

cacto nm, **cactus** nm inv Bot cactus inv.

cada adj (de dos) each; (de varios) each, every; **c. día**, every day; **c. dos días**

every second day; **c. vez más**, more and more; **¿c. cuánto?**, how often?; **c. dos por tres**, every other minute; **cuatro de c. diez**, four out of (every) ten; **¡tienes c. cosa!**, you come up with some fine ideas!

cadalso nm scaffold.

cadáver nm (de persona) corpse, (dead) body; (de animal) body, carcass; **ingresar c.**, to be dead on arrival.

cadena nf 1 chain; (correa de perro) lead, leash. 2 TV channel. 3 Ind line; **c. de montaje**, assembly line; **trabajo en c.**, assembly line work. 4 Geog **c. montañosa**, mountain range. 5 Jur **c. perpetua**, life imprisonment. 6 Aut **cadenas**, tyre o US tire chains.

cadencia nf rhythm; Mús cadenza.

cadera nf hip.

cadete nm cadet.

caducar [1] vi to expire.

caducidad nf expiry; **fecha de c.**, (en alimentos) ≈ sell-by date; (en medicinas) to be used before.

caduco,-a adj Bot deciduous. 2 pey (anticuado) out-of-date.

caer [39] **I** vi 1 to fall; **dejar c.**, to drop; fig **está al c.**, (llegar) he'll arrive any minute now; (ocurrir) it's on the way. 2 (fecha) to be; **su cumpleaños cae en sábado**, his birthday falls on a Saturday. 3 (entender) to understand, see; **ya caigo**, I get it; **no caí**, I didn't twig. 4 (hallarse) to be; **cae por Granada**, it is somewhere near Granada. 5 **me cae bien/mal**, I like/don't like her. 6 **al c. del día**, in the evening; **al c. la noche**, at nightfall. **II caerse** vr to fall (down); **me caí de la moto**, I fell off the motorbike; **se le ha caído el pañuelo**, she dropped her handkerchief.

café nm 1 coffee; **c. solo/con leche**, black/white coffee. 2 (cafetería) café.

cafeína nf caffeine.

cafetal nm coffee plantation.

cafetera nf coffee-maker.

cafetería nf snack bar, coffee bar; Ferroc buffet car.

cafetero,-a adj 1 coffee. 2 fam **es muy c.**, (persona) he loves coffee.

cafre nm,f savage, beast.

cagado,-a adj vulg (cobarde) coward; **estar c. de miedo**, to be shit-scared.

cagar [7] vulg **I** vi 1 to (have a) shit. 2 (estropear) to ruin, spoil; **cagarla**, to cock it up. **II cagarse** vr to shit oneself; **c. de miedo**, to be shit-scared; **¡me cago en diez!**, damn it!

caída nf 1 fall; (de pelo, diente) loss. 2 (de precios) drop. 3 Pol downfall, collapse.

caído,-a adj fallen. **II** nmpl **los caídos**, the fallen pl.

caigo indic pres → **caer.**

caimán nm alligator.

Cairo n El C., Cairo.

caja *nf* 1 box; **c. fuerte**, safe; *fam* **TV la c. tonta**, the idiot box. 2 *(de leche etc)* carton. 3 *(de embalaje)* crate, case; **una c. de cerveza**, a crate of beer. 4 *Fin (en tienda)* cash desk; *(en banco)* cashier's desk. 5 *Aut* **c. de cambios**, gearbox. 6 *Com* **c. de ahorros** *o* **de pensiones**, savings bank. 7 *(féretro)* coffin, *US* casket.

cajero,-a *nm,f* cashier; **c. automático**, cash point, dispenser.

cajetilla *nf* packet, *US* pack.

cajón *nm* 1 *(en un mueble)* drawer; *fig* **c. de sastre**, jumble; *fam* **de c.**, obvious, self-evident. 2 *(caja grande)* crate, chest.

cal¹ *nf* lime; *fig* **a c. y canto**, hermetically; *fam* **una de c. y otra de arena**, six of one and half a dozen of the other.

cal² *abr* **de caloría(s)**, calorie(s), cal.

cala *nf* 1 *Geog* creek, cove. 2 *Náut* hold.

calabacín *nm Bot* 1 *(pequeño)* courgette, *US* zucchini. 2 *(grande)* marrow, *US* squash.

calabaza *nf* pumpkin, gourd.

calabobos *nm inv fam* drizzle.

calabozo *nm* 1 *(prisión)* jail, prison. 2 *(celda)* cell.

calada *nf fam (de cigarrillo)* drag, puff.

calado,-a **I** *adj* soaked. **II** *nm Náut* draught, *US* draft.

calamar *nm* squid *inv*; *Culin* **calamares a la romana**, squid fried in batter.

calambre *nm* 1 *Elec (descarga)* electric shock; **ese cable da c.**, that wire is live. 2 *(en músculo)* cramp.

calamidad *nf* calamity.

calaña *nf pey* kind, sort; **una persona de mala c.**, a bad sort.

calar **I** *vtr* 1 *(mojar)* to soak, drench. 2 *(agujerear)* to pierce, penetrate. 3 *fam (a alguien)* to rumble; **¡te hemos calado!**, we've got your number!. **II** *vi* 1 *(prenda)* to let in water. 2 *Náut* to draw. **III calarse** *vr* 1 *(prenda, techo)* to let in water; *(mojarse)* to get soaked. 2 *(el sombrero)* to pull down. 3 *Aut* to stall.

calavera **I** *nf* skull. **II** *nm* tearaway, madcap.

calcar [1] *vtr* 1 *(un dibujo)* to trace. 2 *fig (imitar)* to copy, imitate.

calceta *nf* 1 *(prenda)* stocking. 2 **hacer c.**, to knit.

calcetín *nm* sock.

calcinar *vtr* to burn.

calcio *nm* calcium.

calco *nm* tracing; **papel de c.**, carbon paper.

calcomanía *nf* transfer.

calculadora *nf* calculator.

calcular *vtr* 1 *Mat* to calculate. 2 *(evaluar)* to (make) an estimate. 3 *(suponer)* to figure, guess.

cálculo *nm* 1 calculation; **según mis cálculos**, by my reckoning. 2 *Med* gallstone. 3 *Mat* calculus.

caldear *vtr* to heat up.

caldera *nf* boiler.

caldereta *nf* stew.

calderilla *nf* small change.

caldo *nm* stock, broth; **c. de cultivo**, culture medium; *fig* breeding ground.

calé *adj* & *nm* gypsy.

calefacción *nf* heating; **c. central**, central heating.

calefactor *nm* heater.

caleidoscopio *nm* kaleidoscope.

calendario *nm* calendar.

calentador *nm* heater.

calentamiento *nm Dep* warm up.

calentar [1] **I** *vtr* 1 *(agua, horno)* to heat; *(comida, habitación)* to warm up; *fig* **no me calientes la cabeza**, don't bug me. 2 *fam (pegar)* to smack. 3 *fam (excitar)* to arouse (sexually), turn on. **II calentarse** *vr* 1 to get hot *o* warm, heat up. 2 *fig* **se calientan los ánimos**, people became very excited.

calentón,-ona, **calentorro,-a** *adj* randy.

calentura *nf* fever, temperature.

calibrar *vtr* to gauge, bore.

calibre *nm* 1 *(de arma)* calibre. 2 *fig (importancia)* importance.

calidad *nf* 1 quality; **de primera c.**, first-class; **un vino de c.**, good-quality wine. 2 **en c. de**, as.

cálido,-a *adj* warm; **una cálida acogida**, a warm welcome.

caliente *adj* 1 hot. 2 *fig (debate)* heated; **en c.**, in the heat of the moment. 3 *fam (cachondo)* hot, randy.

calificación *nf* 1 qualification. 2 *Educ* mark.

calificar [1] *vtr* 1 to describe *(de, as)*; **le calificó de inmoral**, he called him immoral. 2 *(examen)* to mark, grade.

calificativo *nm* epithet.

caligrafía *nf* calligraphy; *(modo de escribir)* handwriting.

calima *nf* haze, mist.

calimocho *nm* drink made with wine and Coca-Cola.

calina *nf* → **calima**.

cáliz *nm* chalice.

caliza *nf* limestone.

calizo,-a *adj* lime.

callado,-a *adj* quiet; **te lo tenías muy c.**, you were keeping that quiet.

callar **I** *vi* 1 *(dejar de hablar)* to stop talking; **¡calla!**, be quiet!; *fam* **¡calla!** shut up! 2 *(no hablar)* to keep quiet, say nothing. **II** *vtr (noticia)* not to mention, keep to oneself. **III callarse** *vr* to stop talking, be quiet; **¡cállate!**, shut up!

calle *nf* 1 street, road; **c. de dirección única**, one-way street; **c. mayor**, high street, *US* main street; **el hombre de la c.**, the man in the street. 2 *Dep* lane.

calleja nf narrow street.

callejero,-a I nm (mapa) street directory. **II** adj street; **gato c.**, alley cat.

callejón nm back alley o street; **c. sin salida**, cul-de-sac, dead end.

callejuela nf narrow street, lane.

callista nmf chiropodist.

callo nm 1 Med callus, corn; fam **dar el c.**, to slog. 2 Culin **callos**, tripe sing.

calma nf 1 calm; **¡c.!**, calm down!; **con c.**, calm; **tómatelo con c.**, take it easy. 2 Meteor calm weather; **c. chicha**, dead calm.

calmante nm painkiller.

calmar I vtr (persona) to calm (down); (dolor) to soothe, relieve. **II calmarse** vr 1 (persona) to calm down. 2 (dolor, viento) to ease off.

caló nm gypsy dialect

calor nm 1 heat; **hace c.**, it's hot; **tengo c.**, I'm hot; **entrar en c.**, to warm up. 2 fig (afecto) warmth.

caloría nf calorie.

calumnia nf 1 calumny. 2 Jur slander.

calumniar [12] vtr 1 to calumniate. 2 Jur to slander.

caluroso,-a adj hot; (acogida etc) warm.

calva nf bald patch.

calvicie nf baldness.

calvinismo nm Calvinism.

calvo,-a I adj bald; **ni tanto ni tan c.**, neither one extreme nor the other. **II** nm bald man.

calza nf wedge.

calzada nf road, carriageway.

calzado nm shoes pl, footwear.

calzador nm shoehorn.

calzar [4] **I** vtr 1 (poner calzado) to put shoes on; **¿qué número calzas?**, what size do you take? 2 (mueble) to wedge. **II calzarse** vr **c. los zapatos**, to put on one's shoes.

calzones nmpl trousers.

calzonazos nm inv fam henpecked husband.

calzoncillos nmpl underpants, pants.

cama nf bed; **estar en** o **guardar c.**, to be confined to bed; **hacer la c.**, to make the bed; **irse a la c.**, to go to bed; **c. doble/sencilla**, double/single bed; **c. turca**, couch.

camada nf litter; (de pájaros) brood.

camafeo nm cameo.

camaleón nm chameleon.

cámara I nf 1 (aparato) camera; **a c. lenta**, in slow motion. 2 Pol Chamber, House; **C. Alta/Baja**, Lower/Upper House. 3 Aut inner tube. 4 (habitación) room, chamber; **c. de gas**, gas chamber; **c. frigorífica**, cold-storage room; **música de c.**, chamber music. **II** nmf (hombre) cameraman; (mujer) camerawoman.

camarada nmf comrade.

camaradería nf camaraderie.

camarera nf (de hotel) chambermaid.

camarero,-a nm,f 1 (de restaurante) (hombre) waiter; (mujer) waitress; (tras la barra) (hombre) barman; (mujer) barmaid. 2 (de avión) (hombre) steward; (mujer) stewardess.

camarilla nf clique.

camarón nm (common) prawn.

camarote nm cabin.

cambiante adj changing; (carácter) changeable.

cambiar [12] **I** vtr 1 to change; **c. algo de sitio**, to move sth. 2 (intercambiar) to swap, exchange. 3 (dinero) to change. **II** vi to change; **c. de casa**, to move (house); **c. de idea**, to change one's mind; **c. de trabajo**, to get another job; **c. de velocidad**, to change gear. **III** cambiarse o **I** (de ropa) to change (clothes). 2 (de casa) to move (house).

cambiazo nm switch.

cambio nm 1 change; (de impresiones) exchange; **c. de planes**, change of plans; **un c. en la opinión pública**, a shift in public opinion; fig **a c. de**, in exchange for; **en c.**, on the other hand. 2 (dinero) change; **¿tienes c. de mil pesetas?**, have you got change for a thousand pesetas? 3 Fin (de divisas) exchange; (de acciones) price. 4 Aut gear change; **c. automático**, automatic transmission.

cambista nmf moneychanger.

Camboya n Cambodia.

camelar vtr, **camelarse** vr fam 1 to cajole. 2 (galantear) to win over.

camelia nf camellia.

camello,-a I nm,f camel. **II** nm arg (traficante de drogas) (drug) pusher.

camelo nm fam (engaño) hoax. 2 (trola) cock-and-bull story.

camerino nm dressing room.

Camerún n Cameroon.

camilla nf 1 stretcher. 2 **mesa c.**, small round table under which a heater is placed.

caminante nmf walker.

caminar I vi to walk. **II** vtr to cover, travel; **caminaron diez kilómetros**, they walked for ten kilometres.

caminata nf long walk.

camino nm 1 (ruta) route, way; **ir c. de**, to be going to; **ponerse en c.**, to set off; fig **ir por buen/mal c.**, to be on the right/wrong track; **abrirse c.**, to break through; **a medio c.**, half-way; **en el c.**, **a** o **de c.**, on the way to; **estar en c.**, to be on the way; **nos coge** o **pilla de c.**, it is on the way. 2 (vía) path, track. 3 (modo) way.

camión nm lorry, US truck; **c. cisterna**, tanker; **c. de la basura**, refuse lorry, US garbage truck; **c. frigorífico**, refrigerator lorry.

camionero,-a nm,f lorry o US truck

driver.
camioneta nf van.
camisa nf shirt; **en mangas de c.**, in one's shirtsleeves; *fig* **cambiar de c.**, to change sides; **c. de fuerza**, straightjacket.
camiseta nf 1 (*de uso interior*) vest, *US* undershirt. 2 (*de uso exterior*) T-shirt. 3 *Dep* shirt; **sudar la c.**, to run oneself into the ground.
camisón nm nightdress, *fam* nightie.
camomila nf camomile.
camorra nf *fam* trouble.
camorrista I adj quarrelsome, rowdy. II nmf troublemaker.
camote nm *Am* sweet potato.
campal adj **batalla c.**, pitched battle.
campamento nm camp.
campana nf bell; **pantalones de campana**, bell-bottom trousers.
campanada nf peal o ring of a bell.
campanario nm belfry, bell tower.
campanilla nf 1 small bell. 2 *Anat* uvula. 3 *Bot* bell flower.
campante adj *fam* **se quedó tan c.**, he didn't bat an eyelid.
campaña nf 1 campaign; **c. electoral**, election campaign; **c. publicitaria**, advertising campaign. 2 *Mil* expedition; **de c.**, field.
campar vi *fam* **c. por sus respetos**, to do as one pleases.
campechano,-a adj unpretentious.
campeón,-ona nm,f champion; **c. mundial**, world champion.
campeonato nm championship; **un tonto de c.**, an utter idiot.
campero,-a adj country, rural; (*botas*) **camperas**, leather boots.
campesino,-a nm,f (*hombre*) countryman; (*mujer*) countrywoman.
campestre adj rural.
camping nm campsite; **hacer** o **ir de c.**, to go camping.
campista nmf camper.
campiña nf open country.
campo nm 1 country, countryside; **a c. traviesa** o **través**, cross-country; **trabaja (en) el c.**, he works (on) the land; **trabajo de c.**, fieldwork. 2 (*parcela*) field. 3 *Fís Fot* field. 4 (*ámbito*) field; **c. de acción**, field of action; *Mil* **c. de batalla**, battlefield; **c. de concentración**, concentration camp; **c. de trabajo**, work camp. 5 *Dep* field; (*de fútbol*) pitch; (*de golf*) course.
camposanto nm cemetery.
camuflaje nm camouflage.
camuflar vtr to camouflage.
cana nf (*gris*) grey hair; (*blanco*) white hair; **tener canas**, to have grey hair; *fam* **echar una c. al aire**, to let one's hair down.
Canadá n Canada.
canadiense adj & nmf Canadian.

canal nf 1 (*artificial*) canal; (*natural*) channel; **C. de la Mancha**, English Channel. 2 *TV Elec Inform* channel.
canalizar [4] vtr to channel.
canalla pey I nm swine, rotter. II nf riffraff, mob.
canallesco,-a adj pey rotten, despicable.
canalón nm gutter.
canalones nmpl *Culin* cannelloni.
canapé nm 1 *Culin* canapé. 2 (*sofá*) couch, sofa.
canario,-a I adj & nm,f Canarian; **Islas Canarias**, Canary Islands, Canaries. II nm *Orn* canary.
canasta nf basket.
canastilla nf small basket; (*de un bebé*) layette.
canasto nm big basket, hamper.
cancán nm frilly petticoat.
cancela nf wrought-iron gate.
cancelación nf cancellation.
cancelar vtr 1 (*acto etc*) to cancel. 2 (*deuda*) to pay off.
cáncer nm cancer; **c. de pulmón/mama**, lung/breast cancer.
cancerbero,-a nm,f *Ftb* goalkeeper.
cancerígeno,-a adj carcinogenic.
canceroso,-a adj cancerous.
cancha nf (*ground*; *Ten*) court.
canciller nm chancellor.
canción nf song.
candado nm padlock.
candela nf fire.
candelabro nm candelabrum.
candelero nm candlestick; *fig* **en el c.**, at the top.
candente adj red-hot; *fig* **tema c.**, topical issue.
candidato,-a nm,f candidate; (*a un puesto*) applicant.
candidatura nf 1 (*lista*) list of candidates. 2 **presentar su c.**, to submit one's application.
candidez nf candour, *US* candor.
cándido,-a adj candid.
candil nm oil lamp.
candilejas nfpl *Teat* footlights.
candor nm candour, *US* candor.
candoroso,-a adj innocent, pure.
canela nf cinnamon.
cangrejo nm (*de mar*) crab; (*de río*) freshwater crayfish.
canguro I nm kangaroo. II nmf *fam* baby-sitter.
caníbal adj & nmf cannibal.
canica nf marble.
canícula nf dog days, midsummer heat.
caniche nm poodle.
canijo,-a adj *fam* puny, weak.
canilla nf *Am* (*cobardía*) cowardice; (*miedo*) fear.
canillita nm *Am* newspaper boy.
canino,-a I adj canine; *fam* **tener un hambre canina**, to be starving. II nm

(colmillo) canine.

canjear *vtr* to exchange.

cano,-a *adj (blanco)* white; *(gris)* grey.

canoa *nf* canoe.

canódromo *nm* dog *o* greyhound track.

canon *nm* 1 canon, norm. 2 *Mús Rel* canon. 3 *Com* royalty.

canónigo *nm* canon.

canonizar |4| *vtr* to canonize.

canoso,-a *adj (pelo blanco)* white-haired; *(de pelo gris)* grey-haired; *(pelo)* white, grey.

cansado,-a *adj* 1 *(agotado)* tired, weary; **estar c.**, to be tired. 2 **ser c.**, *(pesado)* to be boring *o* tiresome.

cansancio *nm* tiredness, weariness; **fam estoy muerto de c.**, I'm on my last legs.

cansar I *vtr* to tire. II *vi* to be tiring. III **cansarse** *vr* to get tired; **se cansó de esperar**, he got fed up (with) waiting.

Cantabria *n* Cantabria.

cantábrico,-a *adj* Cantabrian; **Mar C.**, Bay of Biscay.

cántabro,-a *adj & nm,f* Cantabrian.

cantante I *nmf* singer. II *adj* singing; **llevar la voz c.**, to rule the roost.

cantaor,-a *nm,f* flamenco singer.

cantar[1] *vtr & vi* 1 *Mús* to sing; *fig* **en menos que canta un gallo**, in a flash. 2 *arg (confesar)* to sing, spill the beans. 3 *arg (oler mal)* to hum.

cantar[2] *nm* lit song; *fam* **¡eso es otro c.!**, that's a totally different thing!

cantarín,-ina *adj (voz)* sing-song.

cántaro *nm* pitcher; *fig* **llover a cántaros**, to rain cats and dogs.

cante *nm* 1 *(canto)* singing; *Esp* **c. hondo**, **c. jondo**, flamenco. 2 *arg* **dar el c.**, to attract attention.

cantera *nf* 1 *(de piedra)* quarry. 2 *fig Ftb* young players.

cantero *nm* stonemason.

cantidad I *nf* quantity; *(de dinero)* amount, sum; **en c.**, a lot; *fam* **c. de gente**, thousands of people. II *adv fam* a lot; **me gusta c.**, I love it.

cantimplora *nf* water bottle.

cantina *nf* canteen.

cantinero,-a *nm,f* bar attendant.

canto[1] *nm* 1 *(arte)* singing. 2 *(canción)* song.

canto[2] *nm (borde)* edge; **de c.**, on its side.

canto[3] *nm (guijarro)* pebble, stone; **c. rodado**, *(grande)* boulder; *(pequeño)* pebble.

cantor,-a I *adj* singing; **pájaro c.**, songbird. II *nm,f* singer.

canturrear *vi* to hum, croon.

canutas *nfpl fam* **pasarlas c.**, to have a hard time.

canuto *nm* 1 *(tubo)* tube. 2 *arg (porro)* joint.

caña *nf* 1 *(vaso)* glass; *(de cerveza)* glass of draught *o* US draft beer. 2 *Bot* reed; *(tallo)* cane, stem; **c. de azúcar**, sugar cane.

3 *(de pescar)* rod. 4 *fam* **darle c. al coche**, to go at full speed.

cañada *nf* gully, ravine.

cáñamo *nm* hemp.

cañería *nf (piece) of* piping; **cañerías**, plumbing.

cañí *adj & nmf (pl cañís) fam* gypsy.

cañón *nm* 1 cannon; *fig* **estar siempre al pie del c.**, to be always ready for a fight. 2 *(de fusil)* barrel. 3 *Geog* canyon.

cañonazo *nm* gunshot.

caoba *nf* mahogany.

caos *nm* chaos.

caótico,-a *adj* chaotic.

cap. *abr de* **capítulo**, chapter, ch.

capa *nf* 1 *(prenda)* cloak, cape; **de c. caída**, low-spirited. 2 *(de pintura)* layer, coat; *Culin* coating. 3 *Geol* stratum, layer.

capacidad *nf* 1 *(cabida)* capacity. 2 *(aptitud)* capacity, ability.

capacitación *nf* qualification.

capacitar *vtr (autorizar)* to authorize.

capar *vtr* to castrate.

caparazón *nm* shell.

capataz *nm,f (hombre)* foreman; *(mujer)* forewoman.

capaz *adj* 1 capable, able; **ser c. de hacer algo**, *(tener la habilidad de)* to be able to do sth; *(atreverse a)* to dare to do sth; **si se entera es c. de despedirle**, if he finds out he could quite easily sack me. 2 *Am* **es c. que**, it is likely that.

capcioso,-a *adj* captious; **pregunta capciosa**, catch question.

capea *nf* amateur bullfight.

capear *vtr (dificultad etc)* to dodge, shirk; *fig* **c. el temporal**, to weather the storm.

capellán *nm* chaplain.

caperuza *nf* hood.

capicúa *adj* **número c.**, reversible number; **palabra c.**, palindrome.

capilar *adj* hair; **loción c.**, hair lotion.

capilla *nf* chapel; **c. ardiente**, chapel of rest.

capirote *nm fam* **tonto de c.**, silly idiot.

capital I *nf* capital. II *nm Fin* capital; **c. activo** *o* **social**, working *o* share capital. III *adj* capital, main; **de importancia c.**, of capital importance; **pena c.**, capital punishment.

capitalismo *nm* capitalism.

capitalista *adj & nmf* capitalist.

capitalizar |4| *vtr* to capitalize.

capitán,-ana *nm,f* captain; **c. general**, field marshal, US general of the army.

capitanear *vtr* 1 *Mil Náut* to captain, command. 2 *(dirigir)* to lead; *Dep* to captain.

capitulación *nf* agreement; *Mil* capitulation; **capitulaciones matrimoniales**, marriage settlement.

capitular *vi* 1 *Mil* to capitulate,

surrender. 2 *(convenir)* to reach an agreement.

capítulo *nm* 1 *(de libro)* chapter. 2 *fig* **dentro del c. de ...**, *(tema)* under the heading of ....

capó *nm* Aut bonnet, US hood.

capón *nm* rap on the head with the knuckles.

capota *nf* Aut folding hood *o* top.

capote *nm* 1 Taur cape. 2 Mil greatcoat.

capricho *nm* 1 *(antojo)* whim, caprice. 2 Mús caprice, capriccio.

caprichoso,-a *adj* whimsical.

Capricornio *nm* Capricorn.

cápsula *nf* capsule.

captar *vtr* 1 *(ondas)* to receive, pick up. 2 *(comprender)* to understand, grasp. 3 *(interés etc)* to attract.

captura *nf* capture.

capturar *vtr* *(criminal)* to capture; *(cazar, pescar)* to catch; Mil to seize.

capucha *nf* hood.

capuchino *nm (café)* capuccino.

capullo *nm* 1 *(de insecto)* cocoon. 2 Bot bud. 3 *vulg (prepucio)* foreskin. 4 *ofens (persona)* silly bugger.

caqui I *adj (color)* khaki. II *nm (fruto)* persimmon.

cara *nf* 1 face; **c. a c.**, face to face; **c. a la pared**, facing the wall; **poner mala c.**, to pull a long face; **tener buena/mala c.**, to look good/bad; *fig* **c. de circunstancias**, serious look; *fig* **dar la c.**, to face the consequences (of one's acts); *fig* **dar la c. por algn**, to stand up for sb; *fig* **(de) c. a**, with a view to; *fig* **echarle a algn algo en c.**, to reproach sb for sth; *fig* **plantar c. a algn**, to face up to sb. 2 *(lado)* side; *(de moneda)* right side; **¿c. o cruz?**, heads or tails?; **echar algo a c. o cruz**, to toss (a coin) for sth. 3 *fam (desfachatez)* cheek, nerve; **¡qué c. (más dura) tienes!**, what a cheek you've got! II *nm fam (desvergonzado)* cheeky person.

carabela *nf* caravel.

carabina *nf* 1 *(arma)* carbine, rifle. 2 *(persona)* chaperon.

caracense I *adj* of *o* from Guadalajara. II *nmf* native *o* inhabitant of Guadalajara.

caracol I *nm* 1 *(de tierra)* snail; Am shell. 2 *(rizo)* kiss-curl. II *interj* **¡caracoles!**, good heavens!

caracola *nf* conch.

carácter *nm* (*pl* **caracteres**) 1 *(temperamento)* character; **de mucho c.**, with a strong character; **tener buen/mal c.**, to be good-natured/bad-tempered. 2 *fig (índole)* nature; **con c. de invitado**, as a guest. 3 Impr character.

característica *nf* characteristic.

característico,-a *adj* characteristic.

caracterizar [4] *vtr* to characterize.

caradura *nmf fam* cheeky devil; **¡qué c. eres!**, you're so cheeky!

carajillo *nm fam* coffee with a dash of brandy.

carajo *interj vulg* shit!; **¡vete al c.!**, go to hell!

caramba *interj fam (sorpresa)* good grief!; *(enfado)* damn it!

carámbano *nm* icicle.

carambola *nf* cannon, US carom.

caramelo *nm* 1 *(dulce)* sweet, US candy. 2 *(azúcar quemado)* caramel; Culin **a punto de c.**, syrupy.

carantoña *nf* caress.

caraqueño,-a I *adj* of *o* from Caracas. II *nm,f* native *o* inhabitant of Caracas.

carátula *nf* 1 *(cubierta)* cover. 2 *(máscara)* mask.

caravana *nf* 1 *(vehículo)* caravan. 2 *(de tráfico)* tailback.

caray *interj* God!; good heavens!

carbón *nm* coal; **c. vegetal**, charcoal; **c. mineral**, coal.

carboncillo *nm* charcoal.

carbonero *nm* coal merchant.

carbónico,-a *adj* carbonic; **agua carbónica**, mineral water.

carbonilla *nf* coal dust.

carbonizar [4] I *vtr* to carbonize, char; **morir carbonizado**, to be burnt to death. II **carbonizarse** *vr* to carbonize, char.

carbono *nm* carbon.

carburador *nm* carburettor, US carburetor.

carburante *nm* fuel.

carburar *vi fam (funcionar)* to work properly.

carca *adj & nmf fam* old fogey; Pol reactionary.

carcaj *nm* quiver.

carcajada *nf* guffaw.

carcamal *nm fam* old fogey.

cárcel *nf* prison, jail.

carcelario,-a *adj* prison, jail.

carcelero,-a *nm,f* jailer, warder, US warden.

carcoma *nf* woodworm.

carcomer I *vtr* to eat away. II **carcomerse** *vr* to be consumed (**de**, with).

cardar *vtr* 1 *(lana, algodón)* to card. 2 *(pelo)* to backcomb.

cardenal *nm* 1 Rel cardinal. 2 Med bruise.

cárdeno,-a *adj* purple.

cardiaco,-a, cardíaco,-a I *adj* cardiac, heart; **ataque c.**, heart attack. II *nm,f* person with a heart condition.

cardinal *adj* cardinal; **punto/número c.**, cardinal point/number.

cardiólogo,-a *nm,f* cardiologist.

cardo *nm (con espinas)* thistle.

carear *vtr* 1 Jur to bring two people face to face. 2 *(cotejar)* to compare.

carecer [33] *vi* **c. de**, to lack.

carencia *nf* lack (**de**, of).

carente *adj* lacking; **c. de interés**, lacking

interest.
careo nm Jur confrontation.
carestía nf 1 (falta) lack, shortage. 2 Fin high price o cost.
careta nf mask; c. **antigás**, gas mask.
carey nm tortoiseshell.
carezco indic pres → carecer.
carga nf 1 (acción) loading. 2 (cosa cargada) load; (de avión, barco) cargo, freight; fig c. **afectiva**, emotional content. 3 Fin (gasto) debit; c. **fiscal**, tax charge. 4 fig (obligación) burden. 5 Mil Elec charge.
cargado,-a adj 1 loaded. 2 (bebida) strong; **un café c.**, a strong coffee. 3 (ambiente) heavy; **atmósfera cargada**, stuffy atmosphere. 4 fig burdened; c. **de deudas**, up to one's eyes in debt. 5 Elec charged.
cargamento nm 1 (carga) load. 2 (mercancías) cargo, freight.
cargante adj fam annoying.
cargar [7] I vtr 1 to load; (mechero, pluma) to fill; (batería) to charge; fig c. **las culpas a algn**, to put the blame on sb. 2 Com to charge; **cárguelo a mi cuenta**, charge it to my account; fam Educ **me han cargado las matemáticas**, I failed maths. II vi 1 c. **con**, (llevar) to carry; fig c. **con la responsabilidad**, to take the responsibility; fig c. **con las consecuencias**, to suffer the consequences. 2 Mil c. **contra**, to charge. III cargarse vr 1 fam **te la vas a c.**, you're asking for trouble and you're going to get it. 2 fam (estropear) to smash, ruin. 3 fam (matar) to kill, bump off.
cargo nm 1 (puesto) post, position; **alto c.**, (puesto) top job, high ranking position; (persona) top person. 2 **estar al c. de**, to be in charge of; **correr a c. de**, (gastos) to be met by; **hacerse c. de**, to take charge of; **hazte c. de mi situación**, please try to understand my situation; c. **de conciencia**, weight on one's conscience. 3 Fin charge, debit; **con c. a mi cuenta**, charged to my account. 4 Jur charge, accusation.
carguero nm 1 (avión) transport plane. 2 (barco) freighter.
cariarse vr to decay.
caribe nm (idioma) Carib; **el (mar) C.**, the Caribbean Sea.
caricatura nf caricature.
caricaturizar [4] vtr to caricature.
caricia nf caress, stroke.
caridad nf charity.
caries nf inv decay, caries.
carilla nf page, side of a piece of paper.
cariño nm 1 (amor) affection; **coger/tener c. a algo/algn**, to grow/to be fond of sth/sb; **con c.**, (en carta) love. 2 (querido) darling. 3 (abrazo) cuddle.
cariñoso,-a adj loving, affectionate.
carisma nm charisma.

carismático,-a adj charismatic.
caritativo,-a adj charitable.
cariz nm look.
carmesí adj & nm crimson.
carmín nm (de color) c., carmine; c. (de labios), lipstick.
carnal adj 1 (de carne) carnal. 2 (pariente) first; **primo c.**, first cousin.
carnaval nm carnival.
carne nf 1 flesh; fam **ser de c. y hueso**, to be only human; fig c. **de cañón**, cannon fodder; c. **de gallina**, goosepimples; c. **viva**, raw flesh. 2 (alimento) meat; c. **de cerdo/cordero/ternera/vaca**, pork/lamb/veal/beef. 3 (de fruta) pulp.
carné, carnet nm card; c. **de conducir**, driving licence; c. **de identidad**, identity card.
carnero nm ram; Culin mutton.
carnicería nf 1 butcher's (shop). 2 fig (masacre) slaughter.
carnicero,-a nm,f butcher.
cárnico,-a adj **productos cárnicos**, meat products.
carnívoro,-a I adj carnivorous. II nm,f carnivore.
carnoso,-a adj fleshy.
caro,-a I adj expensive, dear. II adv **salir c.**, to cost a lot; **te costará c.**, (amenaza) you'll pay dearly for this.
carpa nf 1 (pez) carp. 2 (de circo) big top, marquee. 3 Am (de camping) tent.
carpeta nf folder.
carpetazo nm **dar c. a un asunto**, to shelve a matter.
Cárpatos npl Carpathians.
carpintería nf 1 (oficio) carpentry; c. **metálica**, metalwork. 2 (taller) carpenter's (shop).
carpintero,-a nm,f carpenter.
carraca nf rattle.
carraspear vi to clear one's throat.
carraspeo nm clearing of the throat.
carraspera nf hoarseness.
carrera nf 1 run; (de malas) run, ladder; **a la c.**, in a hurry. 2 (competición) race; c. **contra reloj**, race against the clock; c. **de coches**, rally, meeting; **echar una c. a algn**, to race sb; c. **de armamentos**, arms race. 3 (estudios) degree. 4 (profesión) career, profession.
carrerilla nf run; **tomar c.**, to take a run; **de c.**, parrot fashion.
carreta nf cart.
carrete nm (de hilo) reel; (de película) spool; (de cable) coil.
carretera nf road; c. **comarcal/nacional**, B/A road; c. **de circunvalación**, ring road; c. **de acceso**, access road; (en autopista) slip road.
carretilla nf wheelbarrow.
carricoche nm caravan.
carril nm 1 Ferroc rail. 2 Aut lane.
carrillo nm cheek; fam **comer a dos carri-**

llos, to devour, gobble up.
carro nm 1 (*carreta*) cart; *fam* ¡para el c.!, hold your horses! 2 *Mil* c. de combate, tank. 3 (*de máquina de escribir*) carriage. 4 *Am* car.
carrocería nf *Aut* bodywork.
carroña nf carrion.
carroza nf 1 (*coche de caballos*) coach, carriage. 2 (*de carnaval*) float. II nmf *fam* old fogey.
carruaje nm carriage, coach.
carta nf 1 letter; c. certificada/urgente, registered/express letter. 2 (*menú*) menu; a la c., à la carte; c. de vinos, wine list. 3 *Naipes* card; echar las cartas a algn, to tell sb's fortune; *fig* poner las cartas sobre la mesa, to put o lay one's cards on the table, come clean. 4 *Geog* (*mapa*) chart. 5 *fig* adquirir c. de naturaleza, to become widely accepted; tomar cartas en un asunto, to take part in an affair.
cartabón nm set square.
cartearse vr to correspond (con, with), exchange letters (con, with).
cartel nm poster; pegar/fijar carteles, to put o stick up bills.
cartel nm *Com* cartel.
cartelera nf hoarding; *US* billboard; *Prensa* c. de espectáculos, entertainments section o page.
cartera nf 1 (*de bolsillo*) wallet. 2 (*de mano*) handbag; (*para documentos etc*) briefcase; (*de colegial*) satchel, schoolbag. 3 *Pol* (*ministerio*) portfolio. 4 *Com* portfolio; c. de pedidos, order book. 5 *Am* (*bolso*) handbag, *US* purse.
carterista nmf pickpocket.
cartero,-a nm,f (*hombre*) postman; (*mujer*) postwoman.
cartilla nf 1 (*libreta*) book; c. de ahorros, savings book. 2 (*libro*) first reader; *fam* leerle la c. a algn, to tell sb off.
cartografía nf cartography.
cartón nm 1 (*material*) card, cardboard; c. piedra, papier mâché. 2 (*de cigarrillos*) carton.
cartucho nm 1 (*de balas*) cartridge. 2 (*de papel*) cone.
cartulina nf card.
casa nf 1 (*edificio*) house; c. de huéspedes, boarding house; c. de socorro, first aid post. 2 (*hogar*) home; vete a c., go home; en c. de Daniel, at Daniel's; de andar por c., everyday. 3 (*empresa*) company, firm; c. matriz/principal, head/central office.
casación nf *Jur* cassation, annulment.
casadero,-a adj of marrying age.
casado,-a I adj married. II nm,f married person; los recién casados, the newlyweds.
casamiento nm marriage; (*boda*) wedding.
casar[1] I vtr to marry. II vi to match, go o

fit together. III casarse vr to marry, get married; c. por la iglesia/por lo civil, to get married in church/in a registry office.
casar[2] vtr *Jur* to annul, quash.
cascabel nm bell.
cascada nf waterfall, cascade.
cascanueces nm inv nutcracker.
cascar[1] I vtr 1 to crack. 2 *fam* cascarla, to kick the bucket, snuff it. II vi *fam* (*charlar*) to chat away. III cascarse vr to crack.
cáscara nf shell; (*de fruta*) skin, peel; (*de grano*) husk.
cascarón nm eggshell.
cascarrabias nmf inv *fam* short-tempered person.
casco nm 1 (*para la cabeza*) helmet. 2 (*de caballo*) hoof. 3 (*envase*) empty bottle. 4 c. urbano, city centre. 5 (*de barco*) hull. 6 cascos, (*auriculares*) headphones.
cascote nm piece of rubble o debris.
caserío nm country house.
casero,-a I adj 1 (*hecho en casa*) homemade. 2 (*persona*) home-loving. II nm,f (*dueño*) landlord; (*mujer*) landlady.
caseta nf hut, booth; (*de feria, exposición*) stand, stall.
casete nm 1 (*magnetófono*) cassette player o recorder. II nf (*cinta*) cassette (tape).
casi adv almost, nearly; c. mil personas, almost one thousand people; c. ni me acuerdo, I can hardly remember it; c. nunca, hardly ever; c. nadie, hardly anyone; c. me caigo, I almost fell.
casilla nf 1 (*de casillero*) pigeonhole. 2 (*recuadro*) box. 3 *Am* P.O. Box. 4 *fig* sacar a algn de sus casillas, to drive sb mad.
casillero nm pigeonholes pl.
casino nm casino.
caso nm case; el c. es que ..., the fact o thing is that ...; el c. Mattei, the Mattei affair; (en) c. contrario, otherwise; en c. de necesidad, if need be; en cualquier c., in any case; en el mejor/peor de los casos, at best/worst; en ese c., in such a case; en todo c., in any case; en el peor extremo, en último c., as a last resort; hacer c. a o de algn, to pay attention to sb; hacer c. omiso de, to take no notice of; no venir al c., to be beside the point; pongamos por c., let's say.
caspa nf dandruff.
casquete nm 1 (*de bala*) case, shell. 2 *Geog* c. polar, polar cap.
casquillo nm (*de bala*) case.
cassette nm & f → **casete**.
casta nf 1 (*linaje*) lineage, descent. 2 (*animales*) breed; de c., thoroughbred, purebred. 3 (*división social*) caste.
castaña nf chestnut; *fig* sacarle a algn las castañas del fuego, to save sb's bacon.
castañetear vi (*dientes*) to chatter.
castaño,-a I adj chestnut-brown; (*pelo,*

ojos) brown, dark. **II** *nm Bot* chestnut.
castañuela *nf* castanet.
castellano,-a I *adj* Castilian. **II** *nm,f (persona)* Castilian. **III** *nm (idioma)* Spanish, Castilian.
castidad *nf* chastity.
castigar [7] *vtr* **1** to punish. **2** *(dañar)* to harm, ruin. **3** *Jur Dep* to penalize.
castigo *nm* punishment; *Jur* penalty; *Dep* **área de c.**, penalty area.
Castilla *n* Castile.
castillo *nm* castle.
castizo,-a *adj* pure, authentic.
casto,-a *adj* chaste.
castor *nm* beaver.
castrar *vtr* to castrate.
castrense *adj* military.
casual I *adj* accidental, chance. **II** *nm fam* chance. ◆**casualmente** *adv* by chance.
casualidad *nf* chance, coincidence; **de o por c.**, by chance; **dió t. que ...**, it so happened that ...; **¿tienes un lápiz, por c.?**, do you happen to have a pencil?; **¡que c.!**, what a coincidence!
cata *nf* tasting.
cataclismo *nm* cataclysm.
catador,-a *nm,f* taster.
catalán,-ana I *adj & nm,f* Catalan. **II** *nm (idioma)* Catalan.
catalejo *nm* telescope.
catalepsia *nf* catalepsy.
catalizador *nm* catalyst; *Aut* catalytic converter.
catalizar [4] *vtr fig* to act as a catalyst for.
catalogar [7] *vtr* **1** to catalogue, *US* catalog. **2** *(clasificar)* to classify.
catálogo *nm* catalogue, *US* catalog.
Cataluña *n* Catalonia.
cataplasma *nf* **1** *Farm* cataplasm, poultice. **2** *fam (pelmazo)* bore.
catapulta *nf* catapult; *fig* springboard.
catapultar *vtr* to catapult.
catar *vtr* to taste.
catarata *nf* **1** waterfall. **2** *Med* cataract.
catarro *nm* (common) cold.
catastral *adj* **valor c.**, rateable value.
catastro *nm* cadastre, cadaster.
catástrofe *nf* catastrophe.
catastrófico,-a *adj* catastrophic.
catear *vtr fam Educ* to fail, *US* flunk.
catecismo *nm* catechism.
cátedra *nf* (professorial) chair; **le han dado la c.**, they have appointed him professor.
catedral *nf* cathedral.
catedrático,-a *nm,f Educ* **1** *Univ* professor. **2** *(de instituto)* head of department.
categoría *nf* category; *fig* class; **de c.**, *(persona)* important; *(vino etc)* quality.
categórico,-a *adj* categoric; **un no c.**, a flat refusal.
cateto,-a *nm,f pey* yokel, bumpkin.
catolicismo *nm* Catholicism.

católico,-a *adj & nm,f* Catholic.
catorce *adj & nm inv* fourteen.
catre *nm fam* bed.
Cáucaso *n* Caucasus.
cauce *nm* **1** *(de un río)* bed. **2** *fig (canal)* channel; **cauces oficiales**, official channels.
caucho *nm* **1** rubber. **2** *Am (cubierta)* tyre, *US* tire.
caudal *nm* **1** *(de un río)* flow. **2** *(riqueza)* wealth, riches *pl.*
caudaloso,-a *adj (río)* plentiful.
caudillo *nm* leader, head.
causa *nf* **1** cause; **a o por c. de**, because of. **2** *(ideal)* cause. **3** *Jur (caso)* case; *(juicio)* trial.
causante I *adj* causal, causing. **II** *nm,f* **el c. del incendio**, the person who caused the fire.
causar *vtr* to cause, bring about; **me causa un gran placer**, it gives me great pleasure; **c. buena/mala impresión**, to make a good/bad impression.
cáustico,-a *adj* caustic.
cautela *nf* caution.
cautivar *vtr* **1** to capture, take prisoner. **2** *fig (fascinar)* to captivate.
cautiverio *nm,* **cautividad** *nf* captivity.
cautivo,-a *adj & nm,f* captive.
cauto,-a *adj* cautious, wary.
cava I *nf (bodega)* wine cellar. **II** *nm (vino espumoso)* cava, champagne.
cavar *vtr* to dig.
caverna *nf* cave; **hombre de las cavernas**, caveman.
cavernícola *nm,f* cave dweller.
caviar *nm* caviar.
cavidad *nf* cavity.
cavilar *vtr* to ponder.
cayado *nm* **1** *(de pastor)* crook. **2** *(de obispo)* crosier, crozier.
cayuco *nm Am* small flat-bottomed canoe.
caza I *nf* **1** hunting; **ir de c.**, to go hunting; **c. furtiva**, poaching. **2** *(animales)* game; **c. mayor/menor**, big/small game. **3** *fig (persecución)* hunt; **c. de brujas**, witch hunt. **II** *nm Av* fighter, fighter plane.
cazabombardero *nm Av* fighter bomber.
cazador,-a *nm,f* hunter; **c. furtivo**, poacher.
cazadora *nf* (waist-length) jacket.
cazar [4] *vtr* to hunt; *fam* **cazarlas al vuelo**, to be quick on the uptake.
cazatalentos *nmf inv* head-hunter.
cazo *nm* **1** *(cacerola)* saucepan. **2** *(cucharón)* ladle.
cazuela *nf* saucepan; *(guiso)* casserole, stew; **a la c.**, stewed.
c/c *abr de* **cuenta corriente**, current account, c/a.
CCOO *nfpl abr de* **Comisiones Obreras**.
CDS *nm Pol abr de* **Centro Democrático y Social**.

cebada *nf* barley.

cebar I *vtr* **1** *(animal)* to fatten; *fam (persona)* to feed up. **2** *(anzuelo)* to bait. **II cebarse** *vr* **c. con,** *(ensañarse)* to delight in tormenting.

cebo *nm* bait.

cebolla *nf* onion.

cebolleta *nf* **1** *(especie)* chives *pl.* **2** *(cebolla tierna)* spring onion.

cebra *nf* zebra; **paso de c.,** zebra crossing, *US* crosswalk.

cecear *vi* to lisp.

ceceo *nm* lisp.

cedazo *nm* sieve.

ceder I *vtr* to give, hand over; *Aut* **c. el paso,** to give way. **II** *vi* **1** *(cuerda, cable)* to give way. **2** *(lluvia, calor)* to diminish, slacken. **3** *(consentir)* to give in.

cedro *nm* cedar.

cédula *nf* **1** document, certificate; *Am* **c. de identidad,** identity card. **2** *Com Fin* bond, certificate, warrant.

C(E)E *nf abr de* **Comunidad (Económica) Europea,** European (Economic) Community, E(E)C.

cegador,-a *adj* blinding.

cegar [1] *vtr* **1** to blind. **2** *(puerta, ventana)* to wall up.

ceguera *nf* blindness.

CEI *abr de* **Comunidad de Estados Independientes,** Commonwealth of Independent States, CIS.

Ceilán *n* Ceylon.

ceja *nf* eyebrow.

cejar *vi* **c. en el empeño,** to give up.

celada *nf* trap, ambush.

celador,-a *nm,f* attendant; *(de una cárcel)* warder.

celda *nf* cell. **c. de castigo,** punishment cell.

celebración *nf* **1** *(festejo)* celebration. **2** *(de juicio etc)* holding.

celebrar I *vtr* **1** to celebrate; **celebro que todo saliera bien,** I'm glad everything went well. **2** *(reunión, juicio, elecciones)* to hold. **3** *(triunfo)* to laud. **II celebrarse** *vr* to take place, be held.

célebre *adj* famous, well-known.

celebridad *nf* **1** celebrity, fame. **2** *(persona)* celebrity.

celeste I *adj* **1** *(de cielo)* celestial. **2** *(color)* sky-blue. **II** *nm* sky blue.

celestial *adj* celestial, heavenly.

celibato *nm* celibacy.

célibe *adj & nmf* celibate.

celo *nm* **1** zeal. **2 en c.,** *(macho)* in rut; *(hembra)* on *o* in heat. **3 celos,** jealousy *sing;* **tener celos (de algn),** to be jealous (of sb).

celo® *nm fam* sellotape®, *US* Scotch tape®.

celofán *nm* cellophane.

celosía *nf* lattice.

celoso,-a *adj* **1** jealous. **2** *(cumplidor)* con-

scientious.

celta I *adj* Celtic. **II** *nm,f* Celt. **III** *nm* *(idioma)* Celtic.

célula *nf* cell.

celular *adj* **1** cellular. **2 coche c.,** Black Maria.

celulitis *nf inv* cellulitis.

celuloide *nm* celluloid.

celulosa *nf* cellulose.

cementerio *nm* cemetery, graveyard; **c. de coches,** scrapyard.

cemento *nm* cement; **c. armado,** reinforced cement.

cena *nf* evening meal; *(antes de acostarse)* supper; **la Ultima C.,** the Last Supper.

cenagal *nm* marsh, swamp.

cenar I *vi* to have supper *o* dinner. **II** *vtr* to have for supper *o* dinner.

cencerro *nm* cowbell.

cenefa *nf (de ropa)* edging, trimming; *(de suelo, techo)* ornamental border, frieze.

cenetista I *adj* of *o* related to the CNT (Confederación Nacional del Trabajo). **II** *nmf* member of the CNT.

cenicero *nm* ashtray.

cenit *nm* zenith.

ceniza *nf* ash.

cenizo *nm fam (gafe)* jinx.

censo *nm* census; **c. electoral,** electoral roll.

censor *nm* censor.

censura *nf* **1** censorship. **2** *Pol* **moción de c.,** vote of no confidence.

censurar *vtr* **1** *(libro, película)* to censor. **2** *(criticar)* to censure, criticize.

centavo *nm Am Fin* cent, centavo.

centella *nf* spark.

centellear *vi* to flash, sparkle.

centelleo *nm* flashing, sparkling.

centena *nf,* **centenar** *nm* hundred; **a centenares,** in hundreds.

centenario *nm* centenary, hundredth anniversary.

centeno *nm* rye.

centésimo,-a *adj & nm,f* hundredth.

centigrado,-a *adj* centigrade.

centilitro *nm* centilitre, *US* centiliter.

centímetro *nm* centimetre, *US* centimeter.

céntimo *nm* cent.

centinela *nm* sentry.

centollo *nm* spider crab.

centrado,-a *adj* **1** centred, *US* centered. **2** *(equilibrado)* balanced.

central I *adj* central. **II** *nf* **1** *Elec* **c. nuclear/térmica,** nuclear/coal-fired power station. **2** *(oficina principal)* head office.

centralismo *nm* centralism.

centralita *nf Tel* switchboard.

centralizar [4] *vtr* to centralize.

centrar I *vtr* **1** to centre *o US* center. **2** *(esfuerzos, atención)* to concentrate, centre, *US* center. **II centrarse** *vr* **1** to be centred *o US* based. **2**

(concentrarse) to concentrate (**en**, on).

céntrico,-a *adj* centrally situated; **zona céntrica**, centrally situated area.

centrifugar [7] *vtr* to centrifuge; *(ropa)* to spin-dry.

centrista *Pol* **I** *adj* centre, *US* center; **partido c.**, centre party. **II** *nmf* centrist.

centro *nm* **1** middle, centre, *US* center; **c. de la ciudad**, town *o* city centre. **2** *(establecimiento)* institution, centre, *US* center; **c. comercial**, shopping centre.

Centroamérica *n* Central America.

centroamericano,-a *adj & nm,f* Central American.

centrocampista *nmf Ftb* midfield player.

centuria *nf* century.

ceñido,-a *adj* tight-fitting, clinging.

ceñirse [6] *vr* **1** *(atenerse, limitarse)* to limit oneself, stick (**a**, to); **c. al tema**, to keep to the subject; **ciñéndonos a este caso en concreto**, coming down to this particular case. **2** *(prenda)* to cling (**a**, to).

ceño *nm* scowl, frown; **con el c. fruncido**, frowning.

CEOE *nf abr de* **Confederación Española de Organizaciones Empresariales**, ≈ Confederation of British Industry, CBI.

cepa *nf* **1** *(de vid)* vine. **2 fig vasco de pura c.**, *(origen)* Basque through and through.

cepillar I *vtr* **1** to brush. **2** *(en carpintería)* to plane (down). **3 fam** *(robar)* to pinch. **II cepillarse** *vr* **1** *(con cepillo)* to brush. **2 fam** *(matar)* to do in. **3 vulg** to lay.

cepillo *nm* brush; *(en carpintería)* plane; **c. de dientes**, toothbrush; **c. del pelo**, hairbrush.

cepo *nm* **1** *Caza* trap. **2** *Aut* clamp.

cera *nf* wax; *(de abeja)* beeswax.

cerámica *nf* ceramics *sing*.

cerca¹ *adv* **1** near, close; **ven más c.**, come closer; **ya estamos c.**, we are almost there. **2 c. de**, *(al lado de)* near, close; **el colegio está c. de mi casa**, the school is near my house. **3 c. de**, *(casi)* nearly, around; **c. de cien personas**, about one hundred people. **4 de c.**, closely; **lo vi muy de c.**, I saw it close up.

cerca² *nf* fence, wall.

cercado *nm* **1** *(lugar cerrado)* enclosure. **2** *(valla)* fence, wall.

cercanía *nf* **1** proximity, nearness. **2 cercanías**, outskirts, suburbs; **(tren de) c.**, suburban train.

cercano,-a *adj* nearby; **el C. Oriente**, the Near East.

cercar [1] *vtr* **1** *(tapiar)* to fence, enclose. **2** *(rodear)* to surround.

cercenar *vtr* to cut off, amputate.

cerciorar I *vtr* to assure. **II cerciorarse** *vr* to make sure.

cerco *nm* **1** circle, ring. **2** *Mil* *(sitio)* siege; **poner c. (a una ciudad)**, to besiege (a town).

cerda *nf* **1** *Zool* sow. **2** *(pelo)* bristle; **cepillo de c.**, bristle brush.

Cerdeña *n* Sardinia.

cerdo *nm* **1** pig. **2** *(carne)* pork. **3 fam pey** pig, arsehole.

cereal *nm* cereal.

cerebral *adj* **1** cerebral. **2** *(frío)* calculating.

cerebro *nm* brain; *fig* *(inteligencia)* brains *pl*.

ceremonia *nf* ceremony.

ceremonioso,-a *adj* ceremonious, formal; *pey* pompous, stiff.

cereza *nf* cherry.

cerezo *nm* cherry tree.

cerilla *nf* match.

cernerse [3] *fig* to loom (**sobre**, above).

cernícalo *nm* kestrel.

cernir [5] *vtr & vr* → **cerner**.

cero *nm* zero; *Dep* nil; *fig* **partir de c.**, to start from scratch; *fig* **ser un c. a la izquierda**, to be useless *o* a good-for-nothing.

cerrado,-a *adj* **1** closed, shut; **a puerta cerrada**, behind closed doors. **2** *(reservado)* reserved; *(intransigente)* uncompromising, unyielding; *fam* *(torpe)* thick; *(acento)* broad; *(curva)* tight, sharp. **3** *(barba)* bushy.

cerradura *nf* lock.

cerrajero,-a *nm,f* locksmith.

cerrar I *vtr* **1** to shut, close; *(grifo, gas)* to turn off; *(luz)* to turn off, switch off; *(cremallera)* to do up; *(negocio)* to close down; *(cuenta)* to close; *(carta)* to seal; *(puños)* to clench; **c. con llave**, to lock; **c. el paso a algn**, to block sb's way; *fam* **c. el pico**, to shut one's trap. **II** *vi* to close, shut. **III cerrarse** *vr* to close, shut; *fam* **c. en banda**, to stick to one's guns.

cerro *nm* hill; *fig* **irse por los cerros de Úbeda**, to beat around the bush.

cerrojo *nm* bolt; **echar el c. (de una puerta)**, to bolt (a door).

certamen *nm* competition, contest.

certero,-a *adj* accurate.

certeza, certidumbre *nf* certainty; **saber (algo) con c.**, to be certain (of sth); **tener la c. de que ...**, to be sure *o* certain that ....

certificado,-a I *adj* **1** certified. **2** *(correo)* registered. **II** *nm* certificate.

certificar [1] *vtr* **1** to certify. **2** *(carta)* to register.

cervatillo *nm* fawn.

cervecería *nf* **1** *(bar)* pub, bar. **2** *(fábrica)* brewery.

cerveza *nf* beer; **c. de barril**, draught beer; **c. dorada o ligera**, lager; **c. negra**, stout.

cervical *adj* cervical.

cesar I *vi* to stop, cease (**de**, -); **sin c.**, incessantly. **II** *vtr* *(empleado)* to dismiss.

cesárea *nf* Caesarean (section), *US* Cesarean (section).

cese *nm* 1 cessation, suspension. 2 *(despido)* dismissal.

CESID *nm Mil abr de* **Centro Superior de Información de la Defensa.**

césped *nm* lawn, grass.

cesta *nf* basket; **c. de Navidad,** Christmas hamper.

cesto *nm* basket.

cetáceo *nm* cetacean, whale.

cetrino,-a *adj* sallow.

cetro *nm* sceptre, *US* scepter.

Ceuta *n* Ceuta.

ceutí I *adj* of *o* from Ceuta. II *nmf* native *o* inhabitant of Ceuta.

chabacano,-a *adj* cheap.

chabola *nf* shack; **barrio de chabolas,** shanty town.

chacal *nm* jackal.

chacha *nf* maid.

cháchara *nf fam* small talk, chinwag; **estar de c.,** to have a yap.

chachi *adj* smashing.

chacinería *nf* pork bucher's shop.

chacra *nf Am* small farm *o* holding.

chafar *vtr* 1 *fam (plan etc)* to ruin, spoil. 2 *(aplastar)* to squash, flatten.

chal *nm* shawl.

chalado,-a *adj fam* crazy, nuts (**por,** about).

chalé *nm (pl* **chalés)** → **chalet.**

chaleco *nm* waistcoat, *US* vest; *(de punto)* sleeveless pullover; **c. antibalas,** bulletproof vest; **c. salvavidas,** life jacket.

chalet *nm* villa.

chalupa *nf* boat, launch.

chamarra *nf* sheepskin jacket.

chambelán *nm* chamberlain.

chambergo *nm* heavy coat.

chamizo *nm* thatched hut.

champán, champaña *nm* champagne.

champiñón *nm* mushroom.

champú *nm* shampoo.

chamuscar [1] *vtr* to singe, scorch.

chamusquina *nf* singeing, scorching; *fam* **esto me huele a c.,** there's something fishy going on here.

chancaca *nf Am* syrup cake.

chance *nm Am* opportunity.

chancear *vi Am* to joke, horse around.

chanchada *nf Am fam* dirty trick.

chancho,-a *nm,f Am* pig, hog.

chanchullo *nm fam* fiddle, wangle.

chancla *nf* flipflop.

chanclo *nm (zueco)* clog; *(de goma)* overshoe, galosh.

chándal *nm* track *o* jogging suit.

chantaje *nm* blackmail; **hacer c. a algn,** to blackmail sb.

chantajear *vtr* to blackmail.

chantajista *nmf* blackmailer.

chanza *nf* joke.

chapa *nf* 1 *(de metal)* sheet; *(de madera)* panel-board. 3 *(tapón)* bottle top, cap. 4

(de adorno) badge. 5 *Am* lock.

chapado,-a *adj (metal)* plated; **c. en oro,** gold-plated; *fig* **c. a la antigua,** old-fashioned.

chaparro *nm Bot* holm oak.

chaparrón *nm* downpour, heavy shower.

chapotear *vi* to splash about, paddle.

chapucero,-a *adj (trabajo)* slapdash, shoddy; *(persona)* bungling.

chapurrear *vtr* to speak badly *o* with difficulty; **sólo chapurreaba el francés,** he spoke only a few words of French.

chapuza *nf* 1 *(trabajo mal hecho)* shoddy piece of work. 2 *(trabajo ocasional)* odd job.

chapuzón *nm (baño corto)* dip; **darse un c.,** to have a dip.

chaqué *nm* morning coat.

chaqueta *nf* jacket; *Pol* **cambiar de c.,** to change sides.

chaquetero,-a *nm,f fam Pol* turncoat.

chaquetilla *nf* short jacket.

charanga *nf Mús* brass band.

charca *nf* pond, pool.

charco *nm* puddle.

charcutería *nf* delicatessen.

charla *nf (conversación)* talk, chat; *(conferencia)* informal lecture *o* address.

charlar *vi* to talk, chat.

charlatán,-ana I *adj (parlanchín)* talkative; *(chismoso)* gossipy. II *nm,f* 1 *(parlanchín)* chatterbox; *(chismoso)* gossip; *(bocazas)* bigmouth. 2 *(embaucador)* trickster, charmer.

charol *nm* patent leather; **zapatos de c.,** patent leather shoes.

charqui *nm Am (carne)* dried beef, cured meat; *(fruta)* dried fruit.

chárter *adj inv (vuelo)* **c.,** charter (flight).

chasca *nf Am* mop of hair, tangled hair.

chascar [1] *vtr (lengua)* to click; *(dedos)* to snap; *(látigo)* to crack.

chascarrillo *nm* shaggy dog story.

chasco *nm fam* disappointment; **llevarse un c.,** to be disappointed.

chasis *nm inv* chassis.

chasquear *vtr (lengua)* to click; *(dedos)* to snap; *(látigo)* to crack.

chasqui *nm Am* messenger, courier.

chasquido *nm (de la lengua)* click; *(de los dedos)* snap; *(de látigo, madera)* crack.

chatarra *nf* scrap (metal), scrap iron; *fam* junk.

chato,-a I *adj* 1 *(nariz)* snub; *(persona)* snub-nosed. 2 *(objeto)* flat, flattened. II *nm (small)* glass of wine.

chauvinista *adj & nmf* chauvinist.

chaval,-a *nm,f fam (chico)* boy, lad; *(chica)* girl.

checo,-a *adj* Czech.

checoslovaco,-a I *adj* Czechoslovakian, Czech. II *nm,f (persona)* Czechoslovakian, Czechoslovak, Czech.

Checoslovaquia *n* Czechoslovakia.

chelín nm shilling.

chepa nf fam hump.

cheque nm cheque, US check; **c. al portador**, cheque payable to bearer; **c. de viaje** o **(de) viajero**, traveller's cheque, US traveler's check.

chequeo nm Med checkup; Aut service.

chévere adj Am fam great, terrific, fantastic.

chic adj inv chic, elegant.

chicano,-a adj & nm,f chicano.

chicha[1] nf Am chicha, maize liquor.

chicha[2] adj inv Náut **calma c.**, dead calm.

chícharo nm Am pea.

chicharra nf cicada.

chichón nm bump, lump.

~~**chichonera** nf helmet.~~

chicle nm chewing gum.

chico,-a I nm,f (muchacho) boy, lad; (muchacha) girl. II adj small, little.

chicoria nf chicory.

chicote nm Am whip.

chiflado,-a adj fam mad, crazy (por, about).

chiflar vtr 1 (silbar) to hiss (at), boo (at). 2 fam **le chiflan las motos**, he's really into motorbikes.

chiflido nm whistle, whistling.

chiita adj & nmf Shiite.

chile nm chili (pepper).

Chile n Chile.

chileno,-a adj & nm,f Chilean.

chillar vi (persona) to scream, shriek; (ratón) to squeak; (frenos) to screech, squeal; (puerta) to creak, squeak.

chillido nm (de persona) scream, shriek; (de ratón) squeak; (de frenos) screech, squeal; (de puerta) creaking, sweaking.

chillón,-ona adj (voz) shrill, high-pitched; (sonido) harsh, strident. 2 (color) loud, gaudy.

chimenea nf 1 (hogar abierto) fireplace, hearth. 2 (conducto) chimney; (de barco) funnel, stack.

China n China.

china[1] nf 1 (piedra) pebble, small stone; fam **tocarle a uno la c.**, to get the short straw. 2 arg (droga) deal.

chinche I nf bug, bedbug; fam **caer como chinches**, to fall like flies. II nm,f fam nuisance, pest.

chincheta nf drawing pin, US thumbtack.

chinchín interj **¡c.!**, cheers!, (to) your (good) health!

chinescos,-a adj **sombras chinescas**, shadow theatre sing.

chingana nf Am bar.

chingar [7] vtr 1 (fastidiar) to annoy. 2 vulg (estropear) to fuck up. 3 vulg (joder) to fuck, screw.

chino[1] nm (piedrecita) pebble, stone.

chino,-a[2] adj (de la China) Chinese; fam **eso me suena a c.**, it's all Greek to me.

chip nm (pl **chips**) Inform chip.

chipirón nm baby squid.

Chipre n Cyprus.

chipriota adj & nmf Cypriot.

chiquillo,-a nm,f kid, youngster.

chiquito,-a adj tiny.

chirimiri nm drizzle, fine misty rain.

chirimoya nf custard apple.

chiringuito nm (en playa etc) refreshment stall; (en carretera) roadside snack bar.

chiripa nf fam fluke, lucky stroke; fam **fig de o por c.**, by a fluke, by chance; **cogió el tren por c.**, it was sheer luck that he caught the train.

chirla nf small clam.

chirona nf arg clink, nick.

chirriar [29] vi 1 (puerta etc) to creak; (frenos) to screech, squeal.

chirrido nm (de puerta etc) crack, cracking; (de frenos) screech, squeal.

chisme nm 1 (habladuría) piece of gossip. 2 fam (trasto) knick-knack; (cosa) thing.

chismorrear vi fam to gossip.

chismorreo nm fam gossip, gossiping.

chismoso,-a I adj gossipy. II nm,f fam gossip.

chispa nf 1 spark; **echar chispas**, to fume. 2 fam (un poco) bit, tiny amount. 3 fam (agudeza) wit, sparkle; (viveza) liveliness.

chispear vi 1 to spark, throw out sparks. 2 (lloviznar) to spit.

chiste nm joke; **contar un c.**, to tell a joke; **c. verde**, blue joke, dirty joke.

chistera nf top hat.

chistoso,-a adj (persona) funny, witty; (anécdota) funny, amusing.

chivarse vr fam to tell tales.

chivatazo nm fam tip-off; **dar el c.**, to squeal.

chivato,-a nm,f fam (delator) squealer, grass; (acusica) telltale.

chivo,-a nm,f Zool kid, young goat; fig **c. expiatorio**, scapegoat.

chocante adj 1 (persona) off-putting. 2 (sorprendente) surprising, startling; (raro) strange.

chocar [1] I vi 1 (topar) to crash, collide; **c. con** o **contra**, to run into, collide with. 2 (en discusión) to clash. II vtr 1 to knock; (la mano) to shake; fam **¡chócala!**, **¡choca esos cinco!**, shake (on it)!, put it there! 2 (sorprender) to surprise.

chochear vi 1 to be senile o in one's dotage. 2 **c. con algn**, to dote on sb.

chocho,-a I adj (senil) senile; **viejo c.**, old dodderer. II nm 1 (altramuz) lupin. 2 vulg cunt.

chocolate nm 1 chocolate; **c. con leche**, milk chocolate. 2 arg (droga) dope.

chocolatina nf bar of chocolate, chocolate bar.

chófer nm (pl **chóferes**) Am, **chofer** nm (pl **choferes**) driver; (particular) chauffeur.

chollo nm fam (ganga) bargain, snip.

chomba nf Am jumper, pullover.

chonta nf Am palm tree.

chopo nm poplar.

choque nm 1 impact; (de coches etc) crash, collision; **c. frontal**, head-on collision; **c. múltiple**, pile-up. 2 fig (contienda) clash.

choricear, chorizar vtr fam to pinch.

chorizo I nm 1 chorizo, highly-seasoned pork sausage. 2 fam (ratero) thief, pickpocket.

chorlito nm Orn plover; fam fig **cabeza de c.**, scatterbrain.

chorra I nmf vulg (tonto) idiot, fool. II nf fam (suerte) luck.

chorrada nf fam piece of nonsense.

chorrear vi to drip, trickle; fam **c. de sudor**, to pour with sweat; fam **tengo el abrigo chorreando**, my coat is dripping wet.

chorro nm 1 (de agua etc) spurt; (muy fino) trickle; **salir a chorros**, to gush forth. 2 Téc jet. 3 fig stream, flood.

chovinismo nm chauvinism.

chovinista I adj chauvinistic. II nmf chauvinist.

choza nf hut, shack.

christmas nm Christmas card.

chubasco nm heavy shower, downpour.

chubasquero nm raincoat.

chuchería nf fam sweet, US candy.

chufa nf groundnut.

chulear fam vi to strut around; **c. de**, to go on about.

chuleta nf 1 chop, cutlet; **c. de cerdo**, pork chop. 2 Educ fam (note), US trot.

chulo,-a fam I nm,f show off. II nm (proxeneta) pimp. III adj (bonito) smashing.

chungo,-a adj fam dodgy.

chupa nf arg short jacket.

chupachup® nm lollipop.

chupado,-a adj fam 1 (flaco) skinny, thin. 2 fam **está c.**, it's dead easy.

chupar I vtr 1 to suck. 2 (lamer) to lick. 3 (absorber) to soak up, absorb. II vi to suck. III **chuparse** vr 1 **está para c. los dedos**, it's really mouthwatering. 2 fam **nos chupamos toda la película**, we sat through the whole film.

chupatintas nm inv pey penpusher.

chupete nm dummy, US pacifier.

chupi adj fam great, terrific, fantastic.

chupón nm 1 lollipop. 2 (desatrancador) plunger.

churrasco nm barbecued meat.

churrería nf fritter shop.

churrete nm dirty mark, grease spot.

churro nm 1 fritter, US cruller. 2 fam (chapuza) mess.

chusco nm chunk of stale bread; Mil fam ration bread.

chusma nf rabble, mob.

chutar I vi 1 Dep (a gol) to shoot. 2 fam **¡y vas que chutas!**, and then you're well away! II **chutarse** vr arg (drogas) to shoot up.

chute nm 1 Dep shot. 2 arg (drogas) fix.

CI nm abr de **coeficiente intelectual**, intelligence quotient, IQ.

Cía., cía abr de **compañía**, Company, Co.

cianuro nm cyanide.

cibernética nf cybernetics sing.

cicatear vi fam to be stingy.

cicatero,-a I adj stingy, mean. II nm,f miser.

cicatriz nf scar.

cicatrizar [4] vtr & vi Med to heal.

cíclico,-a adj cyclical.

ciclismo nm cycling.

ciclista I adj cycling. II nmf cyclist.

ciclo nm cycle; (de conferencias etc) course, series.

ciclocrós nm cyclo-cross.

ciclomotor nm moped.

ciclón nm cyclone.

ciego,-a I adj (persona) blind; fam (borracho) blind drunk; (de droga) stoned; **a ciegas**, blindly. II nm,f blind person; **los ciegos**, the blind pl.

cielo nm 1 sky. 2 Rel heaven; fig **caído del c.**, (oportuno) heaven-sent; (inesperado) out of the blue; **¡c. santo!**, good heavens! 3 Arquit **c. raso**, ceiling. 4 **c. de la boca**, roof of the mouth.

ciempiés nm inv centipede.

cien adj & nm inv hundred; **c. libras**, a o one hundred pounds; **c. por c.**, one hundred per cent.

ciénaga nf marsh, bog.

ciencia nf 1 science; fig **saber algo a c. cierta**, to know something for certain; **c. ficción**, science fiction; **c. infusa**, intuition; **ciencias ocultas**, the occult sing. 2 (conocimiento) knowledge.

cieno nm mud, mire.

científico,-a I adj scientific. II nm,f scientist.

ciento adj hundred; **c. tres**, one hundred and three; **por c.**, per cent.

cierne nm fig **en ciernes**, budding.

cierre nm 1 (acción) closing, shutting; (de fábrica) shutdown; TV close-down; **c. patronal**, lockout. 2 (de bolso) clasp; (de puerta) catch; (prenda) fastener; **c. de seguridad**, safety lock; **c. centralizado**, central locking.

cierto,-a adj 1 (verdadero) true; (seguro) certain; **estar en lo c.**, to be right; **lo c. es que ...**, the fact is that ...; **por c.**, by the way. 2 (algún) certain; **ciertas personas**, certain o some people. II adv certainly.

ciervo,-a nm,f deer; (macho) stag; (hembra) doe, hind.

cifra nf 1 (número) figure, number. 2 (código) cipher, code.

cifrar vtr to express in figures.

cigala nf Norway lobster.

cigarra nf cicada.

cigarrillo nm cigarette.

cigarro nm 1 (puro) cigar. 2 (cigarrillo) cigarette.

cigüeña nf 1 Orn stork. 2 Téc crank.

cigüeñal nm crankshaft.

cilindrada nf Aut cylinder capacity.

cilíndrico,-a adj cylindrical.

cilindro nm cylinder.

cima nf summit.

cimbrearse vr to sway.

cimentar vtr to lay the foundations of; fig (amistad) to strengthen.

cimientos nmpl foundations; **echar o poner los c.**, to lay the foundations.

cinc nm zinc.

cincel nm chisel.

cincelar vtr to chisel.

cinco adj & nm inv five.

cincuenta adj & nm inv fifty.

cine nm 1 (local) cinema, US movie theater. 2 (arte) cinema; **c. mudo/sonoro**, silent/talking films pl.

cineasta nmf film director, film maker.

cinéfilo,-a nm,f film lover, US moviegoer.

cinematográfico,-a adj cinematographic; **la industria cinematográfica**, the film o US movie industry.

cíngaro,-a adj & nm,f gypsy.

cínico,-a I adj cynical. **II** nm,f cynic.

cinismo nm cynicism.

cinta nf 1 (tira) band, strip; (para adornar) ribbon; Cost braid, edging. 2 Téc Mús tape; **c. adhesiva/aislante**, adhesive/insulating tape; **c. de video**, video tape; **c. transportadora**, conveyor belt. 3 Cin film.

cinto nm belt.

cintura nf waist.

cinturón nm belt; fig **apretarse el c.**, to tighten one's belt; **c. de seguridad**, safety belt.

ciprés nm cypress.

circense adj circus.

circo nm circus.

circuito nm circuit.

circulación nf 1 circulation. 2 Aut (tráfico) traffic.

circular I adj & nf circular. **II** vi (moverse) to circulate; (líquido) to flow; (tren, autobús) to run; fig (rumor) to go round; **circule por la izquierda**, (en letrero) keep to the left.

circulatorio,-a adj circulatory; Aut **un caos c.**, traffic chaos.

círculo nm circle; fig **c. vicioso**, vicious circle.

circuncisión nf circumcision.

circundante adj surrounding.

circundar vtr to surround, encircle.

circunferencia nf circumference.

circunloquio nm circumlocution.

circunscribirse (pp **circunscrito**) vr to

confine o limit oneself (**a**, to).

circunscripción nf district; **c. electoral**, constituency.

circunscrito,-a adj circumscribed.

circunspecto,-a adj circumspect.

circunstancia nf circumstance; **en estas circunstancias ...**, under the circumstances ....

circunstancial adj circumstancial.

cirio nm wax candle.

cirrosis nf cirrhosis.

ciruela nf plum; **c. claudia**, greengage; **c. pasa**, prune.

ciruelo nm plum tree.

cirugía nf surgery; **c. estética** o **plástica**, plastic surgery.

cirujano,-a nm,f surgeon.

cisma nm 1 Rel schism. 2 Pol split.

cisne nm swan.

cisterna nf cistern, tank.

cistitis nf inv cystitis.

cita nf 1 appointment; **darse c.**, to come together. 2 (amorosa) date. 3 (mención) quotation.

citación nf Jur citation, summons sing.

citado,-a adj aforementioned.

citar I vtr 1 (dar cita) to arrange to meet, make an appointment with. 2 (mencionar) to quote. 3 Jur to summon. **II citarse** vr to arrange to meet, make a date (**con**, with).

cítrico,-a I adj citric, citrus. **II** nmpl **cítricos**, citrus fruits.

ciudad nf town; (capital) city.

ciudadanía nf citizenship.

ciudadano,-a I nm,f citizen; **c. de a pie**, the man in the street. **II** adj civic.

cívico,-a adj civic.

civil I adj 1 civil; **matrimonio c.**, civil marriage. 2 Mil civilian. **II** nm member of the Guardia Civil.

civilización nf civilization.

civilizado,-a adj civilized.

civilizar [4] vtr to civilize.

civismo nm civility.

cizaña nf Bot bearded darnel; fig **sembrar c.**, to sow discord.

cl abr de centilitro(s), centilitre(s), US centiliter(s), cl.

clamar vtr to cry out for, clamour o US clamor for.

clamor nm clamour, US clamor.

clamoroso,-a adj resounding.

clan nm clan.

clandestinidad nf **en la c.**, underground.

clandestino,-a adj clandestine, underground; **aborto c.**, backstreet abortion.

clara nf (de huevo) white.

claraboya nf skylight.

clarear vi 1 (amanecer) to dawn. 2 (despejar) to clear up. 3 (transparentar) to wear thin, become transparent.

clarete adj & nm claret.

claridad nf 1 (luz) light, brightness. 2

(inteligibilidad) clarity; **con c.**, clearly.
clarificador,-a *adj* clarifying.
clarificar [1] *vtr* to clarify.
clarín *nm* bugle.
clarinete *nm* clarinet.
clarividente **I** *adj* **1** *(lúcido)* far-sighted. **2** *(lúcido)* lucid. **II** *nmf (persona)* clairvoyant.
claro,-a **I** *adj* **1** clear; **dejar algo c.**, to make sth clear. **2** *(líquido, salsa)* thin. **3** *(color)* light. **II** *interj* of course!; **¡c. que no!**, of course not!; **¡c. que sí!**, certainly!. **III** *nm* **1** *(espacio)* gap, space; *(en un bosque)* clearing. **2** *Meteor* bright spell. **IV** *adv* clearly.
clase *nf* **1** *(grupo)* class; **c. alta/media**, upper/middle class; **clases pasivas**, pensioners; **primera/segunda c.**, first/second class. **2** *(tipo)* kind, sort; **toda c. de ...**, all kinds of .... **3** *Educ (curso)* class; *(aula)* classroom; **c. particular**, private class *o* lesson. **4** *(estilo)* class; **tener c.**, to have class.
clásico,-a **I** *adj* classical; *(típico)* classic; *(en el vestir)* classic. **II** *nm* classic.
clasificación *nf* **1** classification; *Dep* league table. **2** *(para campeonato, concurso)* qualification.
clasificar [1] **I** *vtr* to classify, class. **II clasificarse** *vr Dep* to qualify.
claudicar [1] *vi* to give in.
claustro *nm* **1** *Arquit* cloister. **2** *(reunión)* staff meeting.
claustrofobia *nf* claustrophobia.
cláusula *nf* clause.
clausura *nf* **1** *(cierre)* closure; **ceremonia de c.**, closing ceremony. **2** *Rel* enclosure.
clausurar *vtr* to close.
clavar **I** *vtr* **1** to nail; *(clavo)* to bang *o* hammer in; *(estaca)* to drive in. **2** *fam (timar)* to sting *o* fleece. **II clavarse** *vr* **c. una astilla**, to get a splinter.
clave **I** *nf* key; **la palabra c.**, the key word. **II** *nm* harpsichord.
clavel *nm* carnation.
clavícula *nf* collarbone.
clavija *nf Téc* jack.
clavo *nm* **1** nail; *fig* **dar en el c.**, to hit the nail on the head. **2** *Bot* clove.
claxon *nm (pl* **cláxones)** horn; **tocar el c.**, to sound the horn.
clemencia *nf* mercy, clemency.
clementina *nf* clementine.
cleptómano,-a *adj & nm,f* kleptomaniac.
clerical *adj* clerical.
clérigo *nm* priest.
clero *nm* clergy.
cliché *nm* **1** *fig (tópico)* cliché. **2** *Fot* negative. **3** *Impr* plate.
cliente *nmf* customer, client.
clientela *nf* clientele.
clima *nm* climate.
climatizado,-a *adj* air-conditioned.
climatizar [4] *vtr* to air-condition.
clímax *nm inv* climax.

clínica *nf* clinic.
clínico,-a *adj* clinical.
clip *nm* clip.
clitoris *nm inv* clitoris.
cloaca *nf* sewer, drain.
clorhídrico,-a *adj* hydrochloric.
cloro *nm* chlorine.
cloroformo *nm* chloroform.
cloruro *nm* chloride; **c. sódico**, sodium chloride.
club *nm (pl* **clubs** *o* **clubes)** club; **c. náutico**, yacht club.
cm *abr de* **centímetro(s)**, centimetre(s), *US* centimeter(s), cm.
CNT *nf abr de* **Confederación Nacional de Trabajadores**.
coacción *nf* coercion.
coaccionar *vtr* to coerce.
coactivo,-a *adj* coercive.
coadyuvar *vtr* to assist.
coagular *vtr & vi*, **coagularse** *vr* to coagulate; *(sangre)* to clot; *(leche)* to curdle.
coágulo *nm* coagulum, clot.
coalición *nf* coalition.
coartada *nf* alibi.
coartar *vtr* to restrict.
coba *nf fam* **dar c. a algn**, to soft-soap sb.
cobalto *nm* cobalt.
cobarde **I** *adj* cowardly. **II** *nmf* coward.
cobardía *nf* cowardice.
cobaya *nf* guinea pig.
cobertizo *nm* shed, shack.
cobertor *nm* bedspread.
cobertura *nf* cover; *(de noticia)* coverage.
cobija *nf Am* blanket.
cobijar **I** *vtr* to shelter. **II cobijarse** *vr* to take shelter.
cobijo *nm* shelter; *fig (protección)* protection.
cobra *nf* cobra.
cobrador,-a *nm,f* **1** *(de autobús) (hombre)* conductor; *(mujer)* conductress. **2** *(de luz, agua etc)* collector.
cobrar **I** *vtr* **1** *(dinero)* to charge; *(cheque)* to cash; *(salario)* to earn. **2** *fig (fuerza)* to gain, get; **c. ánimos**, to take courage *o* heart; **c. importancia**, to become important. **II** *vi fam* to catch it. **III cobrarse** *vr* **¿se cobra?**, *(al pagar)* take it out of this, please.
cobre *nm* **1** copper. **2** *Am (moneda)* copper cent.
cobrizo,-a *adj* copper, copper-coloured, *US* copper-colored.
cobro *nm (pago)* collecting; *(de cheque)* cashing; *Tel* **llamada a c. revertido**, reverse-charge, *US* collect call.
coca *nf* **1** *Bot* coca. **2** *arg (droga)* cocaine, coke.
cocaína *nf* cocaine.
cocainómano,-a *nm,f* cocaine addict.
cocción *nf* cooking; *(en agua)* boiling; *(en horno)* baking.
cocer [4] *vtr* to cook; *(hervir)* to boil;

(*hornear*) to bake. **II** *vi* (*hervir*) to boil. **III** **cocerse** *vr* **1** (*comida*) to cook; (*hervir*) to boil; (*hornear*) to bake. **2** (*tramarse*) to be going on.

cochambroso,-a *adj* squalid.

coche *nm* **1** car; **en c.,** by car; **c. de carreras,** racing car; **c. de bomberos,** fire engine; **c. fúnebre,** hearse. **2** *Ferroc* carriage, coach; **c. cama,** sleeping car, *US* sleeper. **3** (*de caballos*) carriage, coach.

cochecito *nm* (*de niño*) pram, *US* baby carriage.

cochera *nf* **1** garage. **2** (*de autobuses*) depot.

cochinillo *nm* suckling pig.

cochino,-a *nm,f* **1** (*macho*) pig; (*hembra*) sow. **2** *fam* (*persona*) filthy person, pig. **II** *adj* (*sucio*) filthy, disgusting.

cocido *nm* stew.

cociente *nm* quotient.

cocina *nf* **1** kitchen. **2** (*aparato*) cooker, *US* stove; **c. eléctrica/de gas,** electric/gas cooker. **3** (*arte*) cooking; **c. casera,** home cooking; **c. española,** Spanish cooking *o* cuisine.

cocinar *vtr & vi* to cook.

cocinero,-a *nm,f* cook.

cocktail → **cóctel.**

coco[1] *nm* coconut; *arg* (*cabeza*) nut; **comerle el c. a algn,** to brainwash sb; **comerse el c.,** to get obsessed.

coco[2] *nm fam* (*fantasma*) bogeyman.

cocodrilo *nm* crocodile.

cocotero *nm* coconut palm.

cóctel *nm* cocktail; **c. Molotov,** Molotov cocktail.

coctelera *nf* cocktail shaker.

codazo *nm* **1** (*señal*) nudge with one's elbow. **2** (*golpe*) blow with one's elbow.

codearse *vr* to rub shoulders (**con,** with), hobnob (**con,** with).

codeína *nf* codeine.

codicia *nf* greed.

codiciar[12] *vtr* to covet.

codicioso,-a *adj* covetous, greedy.

codificar[1] *vtr* (*ley*) to codify; (*mensajes*) to encode.

código *nm* code; **c. de circulación,** highway code.

codo *nm* elbow; *fig* **c. con c.,** side by side; *fam* **hablar por los codos,** to talk nonstop.

codorniz *nf* quail.

coeficiente *nm* **1** coefficient. **2** (*grado*) rate; **c. intelectual,** intelligence quotient.

coercitivo,-a *adj* coercive.

coetáneo,-a *adj & nm,f* contemporary.

coexistencia *nf* coexistence.

coexistir *vi* to coexist.

cofia *nf* bonnet.

cofradía *nf* (*hermandad*) brotherhood; (*asociación*) association.

cofre *nm* (*arca*) trunk, chest; (*para joyas*) box, casket.

coger [5] **I** *vtr* **1** to take; (*del suelo*) to pick (up); (*fruta, flores*) to pick; (*asir*) to seize, take hold of; (*bus, tren*) to take, catch; (*pelota, ladrón, resfriado*) to catch; (*entender*) to grasp; (*costumbre*) to pick up; (*velocidad, fuerza*) to gather; (*atropellar*) to run over, knock down. **2** *Am vulg* to fuck. **II** *vi fam* **cogió y se fue,** he upped and left. **III** **cogerse** *vr* (*agarrarse*) to hold on.

cogida *nf* goring.

cogollo *nm* (*de lechuga*) heart.

cogotazo *nm fam* blow on the back of the neck.

cogote *nm* nape *o* back of the neck.

cohabitación *nf* cohabitation.

cohabitar *vi* to live together, cohabit.

cohecho *nm Jur* bribery.

coherencia *nf* coherence.

coherente *adj* coherent.

cohesión *nf* cohesion.

cohete *nm* rocket; **c. espacial,** space rocket.

cohibido,-a *adj* inhibited.

cohibir [21] **I** *vtr* to inhibit. **II** **cohibirse** *vr* to feel inhibited.

COI *nm Dep abr de* **Comité Olímpico Internacional,** International Olympic Committee, IOC.

coincidencia *nf* coincidence.

coincidir *vi* **1** to coincide. **2** (*concordar*) to agree; **todos coincidieron en señalar que,** everyone agreed that. **3** (*encontrarse*) to meet by chance.

coito *nm* coitus, intercourse.

cojear *vi* (*persona*) to limp, hobble; (*mueble*) to wobble.

cojera *nf* limp.

cojín *nm* cushion.

cojinete *nm Téc* bearing; **c. de agujas/bolas,** needle/ball bearing.

cojo,-a **I** *adj* (*persona*) lame; (*mueble*) rickety. **II** *nm,f* lame person.

cojón *nm vulg* ball; **de cojones,** (*estupendo*) fucking brilliant *o* good; (*pésimo*) fucking awful *o* bad.

cojonudo,-a *adj vulg* fucking great.

col *nf* cabbage; **c. de Bruselas,** Brussels sprout.

cola[1] *nf* **1** (*de animal*) tail; (*de vestido*) train; (*de pelo*) ponytail; **a la c.,** at the back *o* rear; *fam* **traer c.,** to have consequences. **2** (*fila*) queue, *US* line; **hacer c.,** to queue (up), *US* stand in line.

cola[2] *nf* (*pegamento*) glue.

colaboración *nf* **1** collaboration. **2** *Prensa* contribution.

colaboracionismo *nm Pol* collaboration.

colaborador,-a **I** *nm,f* **1** collaborator. **2** *Prensa* contributor. **II** *adj* collaborating.

colaborar *vi* to collaborate, cooperate.

colación *nf* **sacar** *o* **traer (algo) a c.,** to bring (sth) up.

colada *nf* wash, laundry; **hacer la c.**, to do the washing *o* laundry.

colador *nm* colander, sieve; (*de té, café*) strainer.

colapsar I *vtr* to bring to a standstill. II **colapsarse** *vr* to come to a standstill.

colapso *nm* 1 *Med* collapse. 2 *Aut* **c. circulatorio**, traffic jam, hold-up.

colar [2] I *vtr* 1 (*líquido*) to strain, filter. 2 (*por agujero*) to slip. II *vi fam* **esa mentira no cuela**, that lie won't wash. III **colarse** *vr* 1 to slip in; (*a fiesta*) to gate-crash; (*en una cola*) to jump the queue. 2 *fam* (*pasarse*) to go too far.

colateral *adj* collateral.

colcha *nf* bedspread.

colchón *nm* mattress.

colchoneta *nf* air bed.

colear *vi* 1 to wag its tail; *fam* **vivito y coleando**, alive and kicking. 2 *fam* **el asunto aún colea**, we haven't heard the last of it yet.

colección *nf* collection.

coleccionable *adj & nm* collectable.

coleccionar *vtr* to collect.

coleccionista *nmf* collector.

colecta *nf* collection.

colectividad *nf* community.

colectivo,-a I *adj* collective. II *nm* 1 (*asociación*) association. 2 *Am* long-distance taxi.

colega *nmf* 1 colleague. 2 *arg* (*amigo*) buddy, mate.

colegiado,-a *nm* *Dep* referee.

colegial I *adj* (*escolar*) school. II *nmf* (*alumno*) schoolboy; (*alumna*) schoolgirl; **los colegiales**, the schoolchildren.

colegio *nm* 1 (*escuela*) school; **c. privado**, *GB* public *o* independent school. 2 (*profesional*) association, college; **c. de abogados**, the Bar; *Pol* **c. electoral**, electoral college. 3 *Univ* **c. mayor** *o* **universitario**, hall of residence.

colegir [6] *vtr* to infer, deduce.

cólera¹ *nf* anger, rage.

cólera² *nm* *Med* cholera.

colérico,-a *adj* furious.

colesterol *nm* cholesterol.

coleta *nf* pigtail, ponytail; *fig* **cortarse la c.**, to retire.

coletazo *nm* **dar los últimos coletazos**, to be on one's last legs.

coletilla *nf* postcript.

colgado,-a *adj* 1 *arg* **dejar (a algn) c.**, to leave (sb) in the lurch. 2 *arg* weird; (*drogado*) high.

colgante I *nm* (*joya*) pendant. II *adj* hanging.

colgar [2] I *vtr* 1 to hang (up); (*colada*) to hang (out). 2 (*ahorcar*) to hang. II *vi* 1 to hang (**de**, from); *fig* **c. de un hilo**, to hang by a thread. 2 *Tel* to hang up. III **colgarse** *vr* (*ahorcarse*) to hang oneself.

colibrí *nm* humming bird.

cólico *nm* colic.

coliflor *nf* cauliflower.

colijo *indic pres* → **colegir**.

colilla *nf* (*cigarette*) end *o* butt.

colina *nf* hill.

colindante *adj* adjoining, adjacent.

colindar *vi* to be adjacent (**con**, to).

colirio *nm* eyedrops.

colisión *nf* collision, crash; (*de ideas*) clash.

colisionar *vi* to collide, crash.

colitis *nf* colitis.

collage *nm* collage.

collar *nm* 1 (*adorno*) necklace. 2 (*de perro*) collar.

colmado,-a *adj* full, filled; (*cucharada*) heaped.

colmar *vtr* 1 to fill (right up); (*vaso, copa*) to fill to the brim; *fig* to shower (**de**, with). 2 (*ambiciones*) to fulfil, satisfy.

colmena *nf* beehive.

colmillo *nm* eye *o* canine tooth; *Zool* (*de carnívoro*) fang; (*de jabalí, elefante*) tusk.

colmo *nm* height; **el c. de**, the height of; **¡eso es el c.!**, that's the last straw!; **para c.**, to top it all.

colocación *nf* 1 (*acto*) positioning. 2 (*disposición*) lay-out. 3 (*empleo*) job, employment.

colocado,-a *adj* 1 (*empleado*) employed. 2 *arg* (*drogado*) high.

colocar [1] I *vtr* 1 to place, put. 2 *Fin* (*invertir*) to invest. 3 (*emplear*) to give work to. 4 *arg* (*droga*) to stone. II **colocarse** *vr* 1 (*situarse*) to put oneself. 2 (*emplearse*) to take a job (**de**, as). 3 *arg* (*drogarse*) to get high.

colofón *nm* 1 (*apéndice*) colophon. 2 *fig* climax.

Colombia *nf* Colombia.

colombiano,-a *adj & nm,f* Colombian.

colón *nm* *Fin* standard monetary unit of Costa Rica and El Salvador.

Colón *n* Columbus.

colonia¹ *nf* 1 colony; (*campamento*) summer camp.

colonia² *nf* (*perfume*) cologne.

colonial *adj* colonial.

colonialismo *nm* colonialism.

colonización *nf* colonization.

colonizar [4] *vtr* to colonize.

coloquial *adj* colloquial.

coloquio *nm* discussion, colloquium.

color *nm* colour, *US* color; *Cin* **Fot en c.**, in colour; **de colores**, multicoloured; **persona de c.**, coloured person.

colorado,-a *adj* red; **ponerse c.**, to blush. II *nm* red.

colorante *nm* colouring, *US* coloring.

colorear *vtr* to colour, *US* color.

colorete *nm* rouge.

colorido *nm* colour, *US* color.

colorín *nm* goldfinch.

colosal *adj* colossal.

columna *nf* column; *Anat* **c. vertebral**, vertebral column, spinal column.

columpiar [12] **I** *vtr* to swing. **II columpiarse** *vr* to swing.

columpio *nm* swing.

coma¹ *nf* **1** *Ling Mús* comma. **2** *Mat* point; **tres c. cinco**, three point five.

coma² *nm Med* coma.

comadre *nf* godmother.

comadreja *nf* weasel.

comadreo *nm* gossip, gossiping.

comadrona *nf* midwife.

comandancia *nf* command.

comandante *nm* **1** *Mil* commander, commanding officer. **2** *Av* captain.

comandar *vtr* to command.

comando *nm* **1** *Mil* commando. **2** *Inform* command.

comarca *nf* region.

comarcal *adj* regional.

comba *nf* **1** *(curvatura)* curve, bend. **2** *(cuerda)* skipping rope; **saltar a la c.**, to skip.

combar *vtr* to bend.

combate *nm* combat; *Box* fight; *Mil* battle; **fuera de c.**, out for the count; *(eliminado)* out of action.

combatiente I *adj* fighting. **II** *nmf* combatant.

combatir I *vtr* to combat. **II** *vi* to fight *(contra,* against).

combativo,-a *adj* spirited, aggressive.

combinación *nf* **1** combination. **2** *(prenda)* slip.

combinado,-a I *adj* combined. **III** *nm* **1** *(cóctel)* cocktail. **2** *Dep* line-up.

combinar *vtr*, **combinarse** *vr* to combine.

combustible I *nm* fuel. **II** *adj* combustible.

combustión *nf* combustion.

comedia *nf* comedy.

comediante,-a *nm,f (hombre)* actor; *(mujer)* actress.

comedido,-a *adj* self-restrained, reserved.

comedor *nm* dining room.

comensal *nmf* companion at table.

comentar *vtr* **c. algo con algn**, to talk sth over with sb; **me han comentado que ...**, I've been told that ....

comentario *nm* **1** comment, remark; *(crítica)* commentary; **sin c.**, no comment. **2** **comentarios**, *(cotilleos)* gossip.

comentarista *nmf* commentator.

comenzar [1] *vtr & vi* to begin, start; **comenzó a llover**, it started raining *o* to rain; **comenzó diciendo que ...**, he started by saying that ....

comer I *vtr* **1** to eat. **2** *(en juegos)* to take, capture. **II** *vi* to eat; **dar de c. a algn**, to feed sb. **III comerse** *vr* **1** to eat. **2** *fig (saltarse)* to omit.

comercial *adj* commercial.

comercialización *nf* marketing.

comercializar [4] *vtr* to market.

comerciante *nmf* merchant.

comerciar [12] *vi* to trade; **comercia con oro**, he trades in gold.

comercio *nm* **1** commerce, trade; **c. exterior**, foreign trade. **2** *(tienda)* shop.

comestible I *adj* edible. **II** *nmpl* **comestibles**, food *sing*, foodstuff(s); **tienda de comestibles**, grocer's shop, *US* grocery store.

cometa I *nm Astron* comet. **II** *nf (juguete)* kite.

cometer *vtr (error, falta)* to make; *(delito, crimen)* to commit.

cometido *nm* **1** *(tarea)* task, assignment. **2** *(deber)* duty; **cumplir su c.**, to do one's duty.

comezón *nm* itch.

cómic *nm* comic.

comicios *nmpl* elections.

cómico,-a I *adj* **1** comical, funny. **2** *Teat* **actor c.**, comedian. **II** *nm,f* comic; *(hombre)* comedian; *(mujer)* comedienne.

comida *nf* **1** *(alimento)* food. **2** *(almuerzo, cena)* meal.

comidilla *nf fam* **la c. del pueblo**, the talk of the town.

comienzo *nm* beginning, start; **a comienzos de**, at the beginning of; **dar c.** **(a algo)**, to begin *o* start (sth).

comilón,-ona I *adj* greedy, gluttonous. **II** *nm,f* big eater, glutton.

comilona *nf fam* big meal, feast.

comillas *nfpl* inverted commas; **entre c.**, in inverted commas.

comino *nm* cumin, cummin; *fam* **me importa un c.**, I don't give a damn (about it).

comisaría *nf* police station.

comisario *nm* **1** *(de policía)* police inspector. **2** *(delegado)* commissioner.

comisión *nf* **1** *Com (retribución)* commission; **a** *o* **con c.**, on a commission basis. **2** *(comité)* committee.

comité *nm* committee.

comitiva *nf* suite, retinue.

como I *adv* **1** *(manera)* how; **me gusta c. cantas**, I like the way you sing; **dilo c. quieras**, say it however you like. **2** *(comparación)* as; **blanco c. la nieve**, as white as snow; **habla c. su padre**, he talks like his father. **3** *(según)* as; **c. decíamos ayer**, as we were saying yesterday. **4** *(en calidad de)* as; **c. presidente**, as president; **lo compré c. recuerdo**, I bought it as a souvenir. **5** *(aproximadamente)* about; **c. a la mitad de camino**, halfway; **c. unos diez**, about ten.

II *conj* **1** **c. + subj, (si)** if; **c. no estudies vas a suspender**, if you don't study hard, you'll fail. **2** *(porque)* as, since; **c. no venías me marché**, as you didn't come I left. **3 c. si**, as if; **c. si nada** *o* **tal cosa**, as if nothing had happened; *fam* **c.**

si lo viera, I can imagine perfectly well.

cómo I *adv* **1** *¿c.?*, *(¿perdón?)* what? **2** *(interrogativo)* how; *¿c. estás?*, how are you?; *¿c. lo sabes?*, how do you know?; *¿c. es de grande/ancho?*, how big/wide is it?; *¿a c. están los tomates?*, how much are the tomatoes?; *¿c. es que no viniste a la fiesta?*, *(por qué)* how come you didn't come to the party?; *fam ¡c. es eso?*, how come? **3** *(exclamativo)* how; *¡c. has crecido!*, you've really grown a lot!; *¡c. no!*, but of course!. II *nm* **el c. y el porqué,** the whys and wherefores.

cómoda *nf* chest of drawers.

comodidad *nf* **1** comfort. **2** *(conveniencia)* convenience.

comodín *nm Naipes* joker.

cómodo,-a *adj* **1** comfortable; **ponerse c.,** to make oneself comfortable. **2** *(útil)* handy, convenient.

comoquiera *adv* **1** however, whatever way; **c. que sea,** one way or another. **2** **c. que no estaba enterado,** *(puesto que)* as he didn't know.

compacto,-a *adj* compact; **disco c.,** compact disc.

compadecer [33] I *vtr* to feel sorry for, pity. II **compadecerse** *vr* to have *o* take pity *(de,* on).

compadre *nm* **1** *(padrino)* godfather. **2** *Am fam (amigo)* friend, mate.

compaginar *vtr* to combine.

compañerismo *nm* companionship, comradeship.

compañero,-a *nm,f* companion; **c. de colegio,** school friend; **c. de piso,** flatmate.

compañía *nf* company; **hacer c. (a algn),** to keep (sb) company; **c. de seguros/de teatro,** insurance/theatre company.

comparable *adj* comparable.

comparación *nf* comparison; **en c.,** comparatively; **en c. con,** compared to; **sin c.,** beyond compare.

comparar *vtr* to compare *(con,* with).

comparativo,-a *adj & nm* comparative.

comparecencia *nf* appearance.

comparecer [33] *vi Jur* to appear *(ante,* before).

comparsa *nf* band of revellers.

compartimento, compartimiento *nm* compartment; **c. de primera/segunda clase,** first-/second-class compartment.

compartir *vtr* to share.

compás *nm* **1** *Téc* (pair of) compasses. **2** *Náut* compass. **3** *Mús (división)* time; *(intervalo)* beat; *(ritmo)* rhythm; **c. de espera,** *Mús* bar rest; *fig (pausa)* delay; **al c. de,** in time to.

compasión *nf* compassion, pity; **tener c. (de algn),** to feel sorry for (sb).

compasivo,-a *adj* compassionate.

compatible *adj* compatible.

compatriota *nmf* compatriot; *(hombre)*

fellow countryman; *(mujer)* fellow countrywoman.

compendiar [12] *vtr* to abridge, summarize.

compendio *nm* compendium.

compenetrarse *vr* to understand each other *o* one another.

compensación *nf* compensation.

compensar I *vtr (pérdida, error)* to make up for; *(indemnizar)* to compensate (for). II *vi* to be worthwhile; **este trabajo no compensa,** this job's not worth my time.

competencia *nf* **1** *(rivalidad, empresas rivales)* competition. **2** *(capacidad)* competence. **3** *(incumbencia)* field, province; **no es de mi c.,** it's not up to me.

competente *adj* competent.

competición *nf* competition, contest.

competido,-a *adj* hard-fought.

competidor,-a I *nm,f* **1** *Com Dep* competitor. **2** *(participante)* contestant. II *adj* competing.

competir [6] *vi* to compete **(con,** with *o* against; **en,** in; **por,** for).

competitividad *nf* competitivity.

competitivo,-a *adj* competitive.

compilar *vtr* to compile.

compinche *nmf* **1** *(compañero)* chum, pal. **2** *pey (cómplice)* accomplice.

complacencia *nf* **1** *(satisfacción)* satisfaction. **2** *(indulgencia)* indulgence.

complacer [33] I *vtr* to please; *fml* **me complace presentarles a ...,** it gives me great pleasure to introduce to you .... II **complacerse** *vr* to delight **(en,** in), take pleasure **(en,** in).

complaciente *adj* obliging.

complejidad *nf* complexity.

complejo,-a *adj & nm* complex.

complementar I *vtr* to complement. II **complementarse** *vr* to complement (each other), be complementary to (each other).

complementario,-a *adj* complementary.

complemento *nm* complement; *Ling* object.

completar *vtr* to complete.

completo,-a *adj* **1** *(terminado)* complete; **por c.,** completely. **2** *(lleno)* full; **al c.,** full up, to capacity. ◆**completamente** *adv* completely.

complexión *nf* build; **de c. fuerte,** well-built.

complicación *nf* complication.

complicado,-a *adj* **1** *(complejo)* complicated. **2** *(implicado)* involved.

complicar [1] I *vtr* **1** to complicate. **2** *(involucrar)* to involve **(en,** in). II **complicarse** *vr* to get complicated; **c. la vida,** to make life difficult for oneself.

cómplice *nmf* accomplice.

complot *nm (pl* **complots)** conspiracy, plot.

componente I *adj* component. II *nm* **1**

(pieza) component; *(ingrediente)* ingredient. 2 *(persona)* member.

componer [19] *(pp* **compuesto)** I *vtr* 1 *(formar)* to compose, make up. 2 *Mús Lit* to compose. 3 *(reparar)* to mend, repair. II **componerse** *vr* 1 *(consistir)* to be made up **(de,** of), consist **(de,** of). 2 *(arreglarse)* to dress up. 3 *fam* **componérselas,** to manage.

comportamiento *nm* behaviour, *US* behavior.

comportar I *vtr* to entail, involve. II **comportarse** *vr* to behave; **c. mal,** to misbehave.

composición *nf* composition.

compositor,-a *nm,f* composer.

compostelano,-a *adj* from Santiago de Compostela.

compostura *nf* composure.

compota *nf* compote.

compra *nf (acción)* buying; *(cosa comprada)* purchase, buy; **ir de c.,** to go shopping.

comprador,-a *nm,f* purchaser, buyer.

comprar *vtr* 1 to buy. 2 *fig (sobornar)* to bribe, buy off.

compraventa *nf* buying and selling; **contrato de c.,** contract of sale.

comprender *vtr* 1 *(entender)* to understand; **se comprende,** it's understandable. 2 *(contener)* to comprise, include.

comprensible *adj* understandable.

comprensión *nf* understanding.

comprensivo,-a *adj* understanding.

compresa *nf* 1 *(para mujer)* sanitary towel. 2 *Med* compress.

comprimido,-a I *nm Farm* tablet. II *adj* compressed; **escopeta de aire c.,** air rifle.

comprimir *vtr* to compress.

comprobante *nm (de compra etc)* voucher, receipt.

comprobar [2] *vtr* to check.

comprometer I *vtr* 1 *(arriesgar)* to compromise, jeopardize. 2 *(obligar)* to compel, force. II **comprometerse** *vr* 1 **c. a hacer algo,** to undertake to do sth. 2 *(novios)* to become engaged.

comprometido,-a *adj* 1 *(situación)* difficult. 2 *(para casarse)* engaged.

compromiso *nm* 1 *(obligación)* obligation, commitment; **sin c.,** without obligation; **por c.,** out of a sense of duty. 2 **poner (a algn) en un c.,** to put (sb) in a difficult *o* embarrassing situation. 3 *(acuerdo)* agreement; *fml* **c. matrimonial,** engagement; **soltero y sin c.,** single and unattached.

compuesto,-a I *adj* 1 compound. 2 **c. de,** composed of. II *nm* compound.

compulsar *vtr* to make a certified true copy of.

compungido,-a *adj (arrepentido)* remorseful; *(triste)* sorrowful, sad.

compuse *pt indef* → **componer.**

computadora *nf* computer.

cómputo *nm* calculation.

comulgar [7] *vi* 1 to receive Holy Communion. 2 *fig* **no comulgo con sus ideas,** I don't share his ideas.

común I *adj* 1 common; **de c. acuerdo,** by common consent; **hacer algo en c.,** to do sth jointly; **poco c.,** unusual; **por lo c.,** generally. 2 *(compartido)* shared, communal; **amigos comunes,** mutual friends. II *nm GB Pol* **los Comunes,** the Commons.

comunal *adj* communal.

comunicación *nf* 1 communication; **ponerse en c. (con algn),** to get in touch (with sb). 2 *(comunicado)* communication; **c. oficial,** communiqué. 3 *Tel* connection; **se nos cortó la c.,** we were cut off. 4 *(unión)* link, connection.

comunicado,-a I *adj* **una zona bien comunicada,** a well-served zone; **dos ciudades bien comunicadas,** two towns with good connections (between them). II *nm* communiqué; **c. de prensa,** press release.

comunicar [1] I *vtr* 1 to communicate; **comuníquenoslo lo antes posible,** let us know as soon as possible. II *vi* 1 to communicate. 2 *Tel* to be engaged; **está comunicando,** it's engaged. III **comunicarse** *vr* to communicate.

comunicativo,-a *adj* communicative.

comunidad *nf* community; **C. Europea,** European Community; **C. de Estados Independientes,** Commonwealth of Independent States.

comunión *nf* communion.

comunismo *nm* communism.

comunista *adj & nmf* communist.

comunitario,-a *adj* 1 of *o* relating to the community. 2 *(de CE)* of *o* relating to the EC; **la política agraria comunitaria,** the common agricultural policy.

con *prep* 1 with; **córtalo c. las tijeras,** cut it with the scissors; **voy cómodo c. este jersey,** I'm comfortable in this sweater. 2 *(compañía)* with; **vine c. mi hermana,** I came with my sister. 3 **c. ese frío/niebla,** in that cold/fog; **estar c. (la) gripe,** to have the flu. 4 *(contenido)* with; **una bolsa c. dinero,** a bag (full) of money. 5 *(a)* to; **habló c. todos,** he spoke to everybody; **sé amable c. ella,** be nice to her. 6 *(con infinitivo)* **c. llamar será suficiente,** it will be enough just to phone; *(+ que + subjuntivo)* **bastará c. que lo esboces,** a general idea will do. 7 **c. tal (de) que ...,** provided that ...; **c. todo (y eso),** even so.

conato *nm* attempt; **c. de asesinato,** attempted murder.

concebible *adj* conceivable, imaginable.

concebir [6] I *vtr* 1 *(plan, hijo)* to conceive. 2 *(entender)* to understand. II *vi*

(mujer) to become pregnant, conceive.
conceder *vtr* to grant; *(premio)* to award.
concejal,-a *nm,f* town councillor.
concejo *nm* council.
concentración *nf* concentration; *(de manifestantes)* gathering; *(de coches, motos)* rally; *(de equipo)* base.
concentrado *nm* concentrate.
concentrar I *vtr* to concentrate. **II concentrarse** *vr* 1 to concentrate (en, on). 2 *(reunirse)* to gather.
concepción *nf* conception.
concepto *nm* 1 *(idea)* concept; **tener buen/mal c. de,** to have a good/a bad opinion of; **bajo/por ningún c.,** under no circumstances. 2 **en c. de,** under the heading of. 3 *(en factura)* item.
concerniente *adj* concerning, regarding (a, -); *fml* **en lo c. a,** with regard to.
concernir [5] *v impers* 1 *(afectar)* to concern; **en lo que a mí concierne,** as far as I am concerned; **en lo que concierne a,** with regard/respect to. 2 *(corresponder)* to be up to.
concertación *nf* compromise.
concertar [1] **I** *vtr* 1 *(cita)* to arrange; *(precio)* to agree on; *(acuerdo)* to reach. 2 *(una acción etc)* to plan, co-ordinate. **II** *vi* to agree, tally.
concesión *nf* 1 concession. 2 *(de un premio, contrato)* awarding.
concesionario,-a *nm,f* dealer.
concha *nf* 1 *Zool (caparazón)* shell; *(carey)* tortoiseshell. 2 *Am vulg* cunt.
conchabarse *vr* to gang up.
conciencia *nf* 1 conscience; **tener la c. tranquila,** with a clear conscience. 2 *(conocimiento)* consciousness, awareness; **a c.,** conscientiously; **tener/tomar c. (de algo),** to be/become aware (of sth).
concienciar [12] I *vtr* to make aware (de, of). **II concienciarse** *vr* to become aware (de, of).
concienzudo,-a *adj* conscientious.
concierto *nm* 1 *Mús* concert; *(composición)* concerto. 2 *(acuerdo)* agreement.
conciliar [12] *vtr* to reconcile; **c. el sueño,** to get to sleep.
concilio *nm* council.
conciso,-a *adj* concise.
conciudadano,-a *nm,f* fellow citizen.
concluir [37] *vtr* to conclude.
conclusión *nf* conclusion; **sacar una c.,** to draw a conclusion.
concluyente *adj* conclusive.
concomerse *vr* to be consumed; **c. de envidia,** to be green with envy.
concordar [2] **I** *vi* to agree; **esto no concuerda con lo que dije ayer,** this doesn't fit in with what he said yesterday. **II** *vtr* to bring into agreement.
concordia *nf* concord.
concretar *vtr* *(precisar)* to specify, state explicitly; *(fecha, hora)* to fix.

concreto,-a I *adj* 1 *(preciso, real)* concrete. 2 *(particular)* specific; **en c.,** specifically; **en el caso de ...,** in the specific case of .... **II** *nm Am* concrete.
◆concretamente *adv* specifically.
concurrencia *nf* 1 *(de dos cosas)* concurrence. 2 *(público)* audience.
concurrido,-a *adj* crowded, busy.
concurrir *vi* 1 *(gente)* to converge (en, on), meet (en, in). 2 *(coincidir)* to concur, coincide. 3 *(participar)* to compete; *(en elecciones)* to be a candidate.
concursante *nmf* 1 contestant, competitor. 2 *(para un empleo)* candidate.
concursar *vi* to compete, take part.
concurso *nm* 1 *(competición)* competition; *(de belleza etc)* contest; *TV* quiz show; **presentar (una obra) a c.,** to invite tenders (for a piece of work). 2 *fml (ayuda)* help.
condal *adj* of o relating to a count; **la Ciudad C.,** Barcelona.
conde *nm* count.
condecoración *nf* decoration.
condecorar *vtr* to decorate.
condena *nf* 1 *Jur* sentence. 2 *(desaprobación)* condemnation, disapproval.
condenado,-a I *adj* 1 *Jur* convicted; **c. a muerte,** condemned to death. 2 *Rel & fam* damned; **c. al fracaso,** doomed to failure. **II** *nm,f* 1 *Jur* convicted person; *(a muerte)* condemned person. 2 *Rel* damned.
condenar I *vtr* 1 *Jur* to convict, find guilty; **c. a algn a muerte,** to condemn sb to death. 2 *(desaprobar)* to condemn. **II condenarse** *vr Rel* to be damned.
condensado,-a *adj* condensed; **leche condensada,** condensed milk.
condensador *nm* condenser.
condensar *vtr,* **condensarse** *vr* to condense.
condesa *nf* countess.
condescender [3] *vi* 1 to condescend. 2 *(ceder)* to comply (with), consent (to).
condescendiente *adj* 1 *(displicente)* condescending. 2 *(complaciente)* complacent.
condición *nf* 1 condition; **en buenas/ malas condiciones,** in good/bad condition; **condiciones de trabajo,** working conditions; **con la c. de que ...,** on the condition that .... 2 *(manera de ser)* nature, character. 3 **en su c. de director,** *(calidad)* in his capacity as director.
condicional *adj* conditional.
condicionar *vtr* 1 to condition. 2 **una cosa condiciona la otra,** one thing determines the other.
condimentar *vtr* to season, flavour, *US* flavor.
condimento *nm* seasoning, flavouring, *US* flavoring.
condolerse [4] *vr* **c. de,** to sympathize with.

condón *nm* condom.
condonar *vtr (ofensa)* to condone; *(deuda)* to cancel.
cóndor *nm* condor.
conducir [10] I *vtr (coche)* to drive; *(electricidad)* to conduct. II *vi* 1 *Aut* to drive; **permiso de c.**, driving licence, *US* driver's license. 2 *(camino, actitud)* to lead; **eso no conduce a nada**, this leads nowhere.
conducta *nf* behaviour, *US* behavior, conduct; **mala c.**, misbehaviour, misconduct.
conducto *nm* 1 *(tubería)* pipe; *fig* **por conductos oficiales**, through official channels. 2 *Anat* duct, canal.
conductor,-a I *nm,f* *Aut* driver. II *Elec* conductor.
conectar *vtr* 1 to connect up. 2 *Elec* to plug in, switch on.
coneja *nf* doe rabbit.
conejillo *nm* **c. de Indias**, guinea pig.
conejo *nm* rabbit.
conexión *nf* connection.
confabularse *vr* to conspire, plot.
confección *nf* 1 *Cost* dressmaking, tailoring; **la i. de la c.**, the rag trade. 2 *(de un plan etc)* making, making up.
confeccionar *vtr* to make (up).
confederación *nf* confederation.
conferencia *nf* 1 lecture; **dar una c. (sobre algo)**, to give a lecture (on sth.). 2 **c. de prensa**, press conference. 3 *Tel* long-distance call.
conferenciante *nmf* lecturer.
conferir [5] *vtr* *fml (honor, privilegio)* to confer.
confesar [1] I *vtr* to confess, admit; *(crimen)* to own up to; *Rel (pecados)* to confess. II *vi* *Jur* to own up. III **confesarse** *vr* to confess; **c. culpable**, to admit one's guilt; *Rel* to go to confession.
confesión *nf* confession, admission; *Rel* confession.
confesionario *nm* *Rel* confessional.
confeti *nm* *(pl confetis)* confetti.
confiado,-a *adj* 1 *(seguro)* self-confident. 2 *(crédulo)* gullible, unsuspecting.
confianza *nf* 1 *(seguridad)* confidence; **tener c. en uno mismo**, to be self-confident. 2 *(fe)* reliability, trust. 3 **tener c. con algn**, to be on intimate terms with sb; **con toda c.**, in all confidence; **tomarse (demasiadas) confianzas**, to take liberties.
confiar [29] I *vtr (entregar)* to entrust; *(información, secreto)* to confide. II *vi* **c. en**, to trust; **confío en ella**, I trust her; **no confíes en su ayuda**, don't count on his help. III **confiarse** *vr* to confide (**en** *o* **a**, in); **c. demasiado**, to be over-confident.
confidencia *nf* confidence.
confidencial *adj* confidential.

confidente,-a *nm,f* 1 *(hombre)* confidant; *(mujer)* confidante. 2 *(de la policía)* informer.
configuración *nf* configuration; *Inform* configuration.
configurar *vtr* to shape, form.
confín *nm* limit, boundary.
confinar *vtr* *Jur* to confine.
confirmación *nf* confirmation.
confirmar *vtr* to confirm; *prov* **la excepción confirma la regla**, the exception proves the rule.
confiscar [1] *vtr* to confiscate.
confite *nm* sweet, *US* candy.
confitería *nf* 1 confectioner's (shop), *US* candy store. 2 *Am* café.
confitura *nf* preserve, jam.
conflagración *nf* *fig* **c. mundial**, world war.
conflictividad *nf* **c. laboral**, industrial unrest.
conflictivo,-a *adj* *(asunto)* controversial; *(época)* unsettled; **niño c.**, problem child.
conflicto *nm* conflict; **c. laboral**, industrial dispute.
confluencia *nf* confluence.
confluir [37] *vi* to converge; *(caminos, ríos)* to meet, come together.
conformar I *vtr* to shape. II **conformarse** *vr* to resign oneself, be content.
conforme I *adj* 1 *(satisfecho)* satisfied; **c.**, agreed, all right; **no estoy c.**, I don't agree. 2 **c. a**, in accordance *o* keeping with. II *conj* 1 *(según, como)* as; **c. lo vi/lo oí**, as I saw/heard it. 2 *(a medida que)* as; **la policía los detenía c. iban saliendo**, the police were arresting them as they came out.
conformidad *nf* approval, consent. 2 **en c.**, in conformity (**con**, with).
conformismo *nm* conformity.
conformista *adj & nmf* conformist.
confort *nm* *(pl conforts)* comfort; **'todo c.'**, 'all mod cons'.
confortable *adj* comfortable.
confortar *vtr* to comfort.
confraternizar [4] *vi* to fraternize.
confrontación *nf* 1 *(enfrentamiento)* confrontation. 2 *(comparación)* contrast.
confrontar *vtr* 1 to confront. 2 *(cotejar)* to compare, collate.
confundir I *vtr* to confuse (**con**, with); **c. a una persona con otra**, to mistake somebody for somebody else. 2 *(persona)* to mislead. 3 *(turbar)* to confound. II **confundirse** *vr* 1 *(equivocarse)* to be mistaken; *Tel* **se ha confundido**, you've got the wrong number. 2 *(mezclarse)* to mingle; **se confundió entre el gentío**, he disappeared into the crowd.
confusión *nf* confusion.
confuso,-a *adj* 1 confused; *(formas, recuerdo)* blurred, vague. 2 *(mezclado)* mixed up.

congelación nf 1 freezing. 2 Fin freeze. 3 Med frostbite.

congelado,-a I adj frozen; Med frostbitten. II nmpl **congelados**, frozen food sing.

congelador nm freezer.

congelar I vtr to freeze. II **congelarse** vr 1 to freeze; fam **me estoy congelando**, I'm freezing. 2 Med to get o become frostbitten.

congeniar [12] vi to get on (con, with).

congénito,-a adj congenital.

congestión nf congestion; Med **c. cerebral**, stroke.

congestionar vtr to congest.

conglomerado nm conglomerate.

conglomerar vtr, **conglomerarse** vr to conglomerate.

congoja nf sorrow, grief.

congraciarse [12] vr to ingratiate oneself (con, with).

congratular vtr fml to congratulate (por, on).

congregación nf congregation.

congregar [7] vtr, **congregarse** vr to congregate, assemble.

congresista nmf member of a congress.

congreso nm congress, conference; Pol **c. de los Diputados**, ≈ Parliament, US Congress.

congrio nm conger (eel).

congruente adj coherent, suitable.

conjetura nf conjecture; **por c.**, by guesswork.

conjeturar vtr to conjecture.

conjugación nf conjugation.

conjugar [7] vtr to conjugate; fig (planes, opiniones) to combine.

conjunción nf conjunction.

conjuntar vtr to co-ordinate.

conjuntivitis nf conjunctivitis.

conjunto,-a I nm 1 (grupo) collection, group. 2 (todo) whole; **de c.**, overall; **en c.**, on the whole. 3 Mús (pop) group, band. 4 (prenda) outfit, ensemble. 5 Mat set. 6 Dep team. II adj joint.

conjurar I vtr 1 to exorcise; (peligro) to ward off. II **conjurarse** vr to conspire, plot.

conjuro nm 1 (exorcismo) exorcism. 2 (encantamiento) spell, incantation.

conllevar vtr to entail.

conmemoración nf commemoration.

conmemorar vtr to commemorate.

conmigo pron pers with me; **vino c.**, he came with me; **él habló c.**, he talked to me.

conminar vtr to threaten, menace.

conmoción nf commotion, shock; **c. cerebral**, concussion.

conmocionar vtr to shock; to concuss.

conmovedor,-a adj touching; **una película conmovedora**, a moving film.

conmover [4] vtr to touch, move.

conmutador nm 1 Elec switch. 2 Am Tel switchboard.

conmutar vtr to exchange; Jur to commute; Elec to commutate.

connivencia nf connivance, collusion.

connotación nf connotation.

cono nm cone; **C. Sur**, South America.

conocedor,-a adj & nm,f expert; (de vino, arte etc) connoisseur.

conocer [34] I vtr 1 to know; **dar (algo/algn) a c.**, to make (sth/sb) known. 2 (a una persona) to meet. 2 (reconocer) to recognize; **te conocí por la voz**, I recognized you by your voice. II **conocerse** vr (dos personas) to know each other; (por primera vez) to meet.

conocido,-a I adj known; (famoso) well-known. II nm,f acquaintance.

conocimiento nm 1 knowledge; **con c. de causa**, with full knowledge of the facts. 2 (conciencia) consciousness; **perder/recobrar el c.**, to lose/regain consciousness. 3 **conocimientos**, knowledge.

conque conj so.

conquense I adj of o from Cuenca. II nmf native o inhabitant of Cuenca.

conquista nf conquest.

conquistador,-a nm,f conqueror.

conquistar vtr (país, ciudad) to conquer; fig (puesto, título) to win; (a una persona) to win over.

consabido,-a adj 1 (bien conocido) well-known. 2 (usual) familiar, usual.

consagración nf 1 Rel consecration. 2 (de un artista) recognition.

consagrar I vtr 1 Rel to consecrate. 2 (artista) to confirm. 3 (tiempo, vida) to devote. II **consagrarse** vr 1 (dedicarse) to devote oneself (a, to), dedicate oneself (a, to). 2 (lograr fama) to establish oneself.

consciente adj 1 conscious, aware; **ser c. de algo**, to be aware of sth. 2 Med conscious.

consecución nf 1 (de un objetivo) achievement. 2 (obtención) obtaining.

consecuencia nf 1 consequence; **a o como c. de**, as a consequence o result of; **en c.**, therefore; **tener o traer (malas) consecuencias**, to have (ill) effects; **sacar como o en c.**, to come to a conclusion. 2 (coherencia) consistency; **actuar en c.**, to be consistent.

consecuente adj consistent.

consecutivo,-a adj consecutive; **tres días consecutivos**, three days in a row.

conseguir [6] vtr 1 to get, obtain; (objetivo) to achieve. 2 **conseguí terminar**, I managed to finish.

consejero,-a nm,f 1 (asesor) adviser. 2 Pol councillor. 3 Com **c. delegado**, managing director.

consejo nm 1 (recomendación) advice; **un**

c., a piece of advice. **2** (*junta*) council; **c. de ministros**, cabinet; (*reunión*) cabinet meeting; **c. de administración**, board of directors; **c. de guerra**, court martial.

consenso *nm* consensus.

consensuar *vtr* to approve by consensus.

consentido,-a *adj* spoiled.

consentimiento *nm* consent.

consentir [5] **I** *vtr* **1** (*tolerar*) to allow, permit; **no consientas que haga eso**, don't allow him to do that. **2** (*mimar*) to spoil. **II** *vi* to consent; **c. en**, to agree to.

conserje *nm* commissionaire; (*en escuela etc*) janitor.

conserva *nf* tinned *o* canned food.

conservación *nf* **1** preservation. **2** (*mantenimiento*) maintenance, upkeep.

conservador,-a **I** *adj & nm,f* conservative; *Pol* Conservative. **II** *nm* (*de museo*) curator.

conservadurismo *nm* conservatism.

conservante *nm* preservative.

conservar **I** *vtr* to conserve, preserve; (*mantener*) to keep up, maintain; (*alimentos*) to preserve. **II conservarse** *vr* **1** (*tradición etc*) to survive. **2 c. bien**, (*persona*) to age well.

conservatorio *nm* conservatory.

considerable *adj* considerable.

consideración *nf* **1** consideration; **tomar algo en c.**, to take sth into account. **2** (*respeto*) regard. **3 de c.**, important, considerable; **herido de c.**, seriously injured.

considerado,-a *adj* (*atento*) considerate, thoughtful. **2 estar bien/mal c.**, to well/badly thought of.

considerar *vtr* to consider; **lo considero imposible**, I think it's impossible.

consigna *nf* **1** (*para maletas*) left-luggage office, *US* check-room. **2** *Mil* orders, instructions.

consignar *vtr* **1** (*puesto*) to allocate; (*cantidad*) to assign. **2** (*mercancía*) to ship, dispatch.

consigo[1] *pron pers* **1** (*tercera persona*) (*hombre*) with him; (*mujer*) with her; (*cosa, animal*) with it; (*plural*) with them; (*usted*) with you. **2 hablar c. mismo**, to speak to oneself.

consigo[2] *indic pres* → **conseguir**.

consiguiente *adj* resulting, consequent; **por c.**, therefore, consequently.

consistencia *nf* **1** consistency. **2** (*de argumento*) soundness.

consistente *adj* **1** (*firme*) firm, solid. **2** (*teoría*) sound. **3 c. en**, consisting of.

consistir *vi* to consist (**en**, of); **el secreto consiste en tener paciencia**, the secret lies in being patient.

consistorial *adj* **casa c.**, town hall.

consola *nf* console table; *Inform* console.

consolación *nf* consolation; **premio de c.**, consolation prize.

consolador,-a **I** *adj* consoling, comfort-

ing. **II** *nm* dildo.

consolar [2] **I** *vtr* to console, comfort. **II consolarse** *vr* to console oneself, take comfort (**con**, from).

consolidar *vtr*, **consolidarse** *vr* to consolidate.

consomé *nm* clear soup, consommé.

consonancia *nf* **en c. con**, in keeping with.

consonante *adj & nf* consonant.

consorcio *nm* consortium.

consorte **I** *adj* **príncipe c.**, prince consort. **II** *nmf* (*cónyuge*) partner, spouse.

conspicuo,-a *adj* prominent, outstanding.

conspiración *nf* conspiracy, plot.

conspirar *vi* to conspire, plot.

constancia *nf* **1** constancy, perseverance. **2** (*testimonio*) proof, evidence; **dejar c. de algo**, to put sth on record.

constante **I** *adj* constant; (*persona*) steadfast. **II** *nf* constant feature; *Mat* constant.
  ◆**constantemente** *adv* constantly.

constar *vi* **1** (*figurar*) to figure in, be included (**en**); **c. en acta**, to be on record. **2 me consta que …**, I am absolutely certain that …. **3 c. de**, to be made up of, consist of.

constatar *vtr* to state; (*comprobar*) to check.

constelación *nf* constellation.

consternación *nf* consternation.

consternar *vtr* to dismay.

constipado,-a **I** *adj* **estar c.**, to have a cold *o* a chill. **II** *nm* cold, chill.

constiparse *vr* to catch a cold *o* a chill.

constitución *nf* constitution.

constitucional *adj* constitutional.

constituir [37] **I** *vtr* **1** (*formar*) to constitute; **estar constituido por**, to consist of. **2** (*suponer*) to represent. **3** (*fundar*) to constitute, set up. **II constituirse** *vr* to set oneself up (**en**, as).

constituyente *adj & nmf* constituent.

constreñir [6] *vtr* **1** (*forzar*) to compel, force. **2** (*oprimir*) to restrict. **3** *Med* to constrict.

construcción *nf* **1** construction; (*sector*) the building industry; **en c.**, under construction. **2** (*edificio*) building.

constructivo,-a *adj* constructive.

constructor,-a **I** *nm,f* builder. **II** *adj* **empresa constructora**, builders *pl*, construction company.

construir [37] *vtr* to construct, build.

consuelo *nm* consolation.

cónsul *nmf* consul.

consulado *nm* consulate.

consulta *nf* **1** consultation; **obra de c.**, reference book. **2** *Med* surgery; (*despacho*) consulting room; **horas de c.**, surgery hours.

consultar *vtr* to consult, seek advice (**con**, from); (*libro*) to look up.

consultivo,-a *adj* consultative, advisory.

consultorio *nm* 1 *Med* medical center. 2 *Prensa* problem page, advice column.

consumado,-a *adj* 1 consummated; **hecho c.**, fait accompli, accomplished fact. 2 *fig* (*artista*) consummate.

consumar *vtr* to complete, carry out; (*crimen*) to commit.

consumición *nf* 1 consumption. 2 (*bebida*) drink.

consumidor,-a I *nm,f* consumer. II *adj* consuming.

consumir I *vtr* to consume. II **consumirse** *vr* (*al hervir*) to boil away; *fig* (*persona*) to waste away.

consumismo *nm* consumerism.

consumo *nm* consumption; **bienes de c.**, consumer goods; **sociedad de c.**, consumer society.

contabilidad *nf* *Com* 1 (*profesión*) accountancy. 2 (*de empresa, sociedad*) accounting, book-keeping.

contabilizar [4] *vtr* *Com* to enter in the books; *Dep* to score.

contable *nmf* accountant.

contactar *vi* **c. con**, to contact, get in touch with.

contacto *nm* contact; *Aut* ignition; **perder el c.**, to lose touch; **ponerse en c.**, to get in touch.

contado,-a I *adj* few and far between; **contadas veces**, very seldom; **tiene los días contados**, his days are numbered. II *nm* **pagar al c.**, to pay cash.

contador *nm* meter; **c. de agua**, water meter.

contagiar [12] I *vtr* *Med* to pass on. II **contagiarse** *vr* 1 (*persona*) to get infected. 2 (*enfermedad*) to be contagious.

contagio *nm* contagion.

contagioso,-a *adj* contagious; *fam* (*risa*) infectious.

contaminación *nf* contamination; (*del aire*) pollution.

contaminar *vtr* to contaminate; (*aire, agua*) to pollute.

contante *adj* **dinero c. (y sonante)**, hard o ready cash.

contar [2] I *vtr* 1 (*sumar*) to count. 2 (*narrar*) to tell. II *vi* 1 to count. 2 **c. con**, (*confiar en*) to count on; (*tener*) to have. III **contarse** *vr* *fam* **¿qué te cuentas?**, how's it going?

contemplación *nf* contemplation; *fam* **no andarse con contemplaciones**, to make no bones about it.

contemplar *vtr* to contemplate; (*considerar*) to consider; (*estipular*) to stipulate.

contemporáneo,-a *adj* & *nm,f* contemporary.

contención *nf* **muro de c.**, retaining wall; **c. salarial**, wage restraint.

contencioso,-a I *adj* contentious; *Jur* litigious. II *nm* *Jur* legal dispute.

contendiente *nmf* contender, contestant.

contenedor *nm* container.

contener [24] I *vtr* to contain. 2 (*pasiones etc*) to restrain, hold back. II **contenerse** *vr* to control oneself, hold (oneself) back.

contenido *nm* content, contents *pl*.

contentar I *vtr* 1 (*satisfacer*) to please. 2 (*alegrar*) to cheer up. II **contentarse** *vr* 1 (*conformarse*) to make do (**con**, with), be satisfied (**con**, with). 2 (*alegrarse*) to cheer up.

contento,-a *adj* happy, pleased (**con**, with).

contestador *nm* **c. automático**, answering machine.

contestación *nf* answer; **dar c.**, to answer.

contestar *vtr* 1 to answer. 2 *fam* (*replicar*) to answer back.

contestatario,-a *adj* anti-establishment.

contexto *nm* context.

contienda *nf* struggle.

contigo *pron pers* with you.

contiguo,-a *adj* contiguous (**a**, to), adjoining.

continente *nm* 1 *Geog* continent. 2 (*compostura*) countenance.

contingencia *nf* limit, restriction.

contingente *nm* contingent.

continuación *nf* continuation; **a c.**, next.

continuar [30] *vtr* & *vi* to continue, carry on (with); **continúa en Francia**, he's still in France; **continuará**, to be continued.

continuidad *nf* continuity.

continuo,-a I *adj* 1 continuous; *Aut* **línea continua**, solid white line. 2 (*reiterado*) continual, constant. II *nm* continuum. **◆continuamente** *adv* continuously.

contonearse *vr* to swing one's hips.

contorno *nm* 1 outline. 2 **contornos**, surroundings *pl*, environment.

contorsión *nf* contortion.

contorsionarse *vr* to contort o twist oneself.

contra I *prep* against; **en c. de**, against. II *nm* **los pros y los contras**, the pros and cons.

contraataque *nm* counterattack.

contrabajo *nm* double bass.

contrabandista *nmf* smuggler; **c. de armas**, gunrunner.

contrabando *nm* smuggling; **c. de armas**, gunrunning; **pasar algo de c.**, to smuggle sth in.

contracción *nf* contraction.

contracepción *nf* contraception.

contrachapado *nm* plywood.

contracorriente I *nf* crosscurrent. II *adv* **ir (a) c.**, to go against the tide.

contradecir [12] (*pp* **contradicho**) *vtr* to contradict.

contradicción *nf* contradiction.

contradictorio,-a *adj* contradictory.

contraer [25] I *vtr* to contract; **c. matri-**

monio con algn, to marry sb. **II contraerse** *vr* to contract.

contraigo *indic pres* → **contraer.**

contraindicación *nf* contraindication.

contraje *pt indef* → **contraer.**

contraluz *nm* view against the light; **a c.,** against the light.

contramaestre *nm* foreman.

contramano (a) *loc adv* the wrong way *o* direction.

contrapartida *nf* **en c.,** in return.

contrapelo (a) *loc adv* the wrong way; *fig* against the grain.

contrapesar *vtr* **1** to counterbalance, counterpoise. **2** *fig* (*compensar*) to offset, balance.

contrapeso *nm* counterweight.

contraportada *nf* back page.

contraposición *nf* contrast.

contraproducente *adj* counterproductive.

contrapunto *nm* counterpoint.

contrariar [29] *vtr* **1** (*oponerse a*) to oppose, go against. **2** (*disgustar*) to upset.

contrariedad *nf* **1** (*contratiempo*) setback. **2** (*disgusto*) annoyance.

contrario,-a I *adj* **1** opposite; **lo c. de,** the opposite of; **en el lado/sentido c.,** on the other side/in the other direction; **al c., por el c.,** on the contrary; **de lo c.,** otherwise; **todo lo c.,** quite the opposite. **2** (*perjudicial*) contrary (**a,** to). **II** *nm,f* opponent, rival. **III** *nf* **llevar la contraria,** to be contrary. ◆**contrariamente** *adv* **c. a ...,** contrary to ....

contrarrestar *vtr* to offset, counteract.

contrasentido *nm* contradiction.

contraseña *nf* password.

contrastar *vtr* to contrast (**con,** with).

contraste *nm* **1** contrast. **2** (*en oro, plata*) hallmark.

contrata *nf* contract.

contratar *vtr* to hire, engage.

contratiempo *nm* setback, hitch.

contratista *nmf* contractor.

contrato *nm* contract; **c. de trabajo,** work contract; **c. de alquiler,** lease, leasing agreement.

contravenir [27] *vtr* to contravene, infringe.

contraventana *nf* shutter.

contribución *nf* **1** contribution. **2** (*impuesto*) tax.

contribuir [37] **I** *vtr* to contribute (**a,** to). **II** *vi* **1** to contribute. **2** (*pagar impuestos*) to pay taxes.

contribuyente *nmf* taxpayer.

contrincante *nmf* rival, opponent.

control *nm* **1** control; **c. a distancia,** remote control. **2** (*inspección*) check; (*de policía etc*) checkpoint.

controlador,-a *nm,f* **c. (aéreo),** air traffic controller.

controlar I *vtr* **1** to control. **2** (*comprobar*)

to check. **II controlarse** *vr* to control oneself.

controversia *nf* controversy.

controvertido,-a *adj* controversial.

contumaz *adj* obstinate.

contundente *adj* **1** (*arma*) blunt. **2** (*argumento*) forceful, convincing.

contusión *nf* contusion, bruise.

convalecencia *nf* convalescence.

convaleciente *adj & nmf* convalescent.

convalidar *vtr* to validate; (*documento*) to ratify.

convencer [2] *vtr* to convince; **c. a algn de algo,** to convince sb about sth.

convencimiento *nm* conviction; **tener el c. de que ...,** to be convinced that ....

convención *nf* convention.

convencional *adj* conventional.

convenido,-a *adj* agreed; **según lo c.,** as agreed.

conveniencia *nf* **1** (*provecho*) convenience. **2 conveniencias sociales,** social proprieties.

conveniente *adj* **1** (*oportuno*) convenient; (*aconsejable*) advisable. **2** (*precio*) good, fair.

convenio *nm* agreement; **c. laboral,** agreement on salary and conditions.

convenir [27] *vtr & vi* **1** (*acordar*) to agree; **c. una fecha,** to agree on a date; **sueldo a c.,** salary negotiable; **c. en,** to agree on. **2** (*ser oportuno*) to suit, be good for; **conviene recordar que ...,** it's as well to remember that ....

convento *nm* (*de monjas*) convent; (*de monjes*) monastery.

convergente *adj* convergent.

converger [5] *vi* to converge.

conversación *nf* conversation.

conversar *vi* to converse, talk.

conversión *nf* conversion.

converso,-a *nm,f* convert.

convertible *adj* convertible.

convertir [5] **I** *vtr* to change, convert. **II convertirse** *vr* **1 c. en,** to turn into, become. **2** *Rel* to be converted (**a,** to).

convexo,-a *adj* convex.

convicción *nf* conviction; **tengo la c. de que ...,** I am convinced that ...

convicto,-a *adj* convicted.

convidado,-a *adj & nm,f* guest.

convidar *vtr* to invite.

convincente *adj* convincing.

convite *nm* reception.

convivencia *nf* life together; *fig* coexistence.

convivir *vi* to live together; *fig* to coexist (**con,** with).

convocar [1] *vtr* to summon; (*reunión, elecciones*) to call.

convocatoria *nf* **1** (*a huelga etc*) call. **2** *Educ* diet.

convulsión *nf* *Med* convulsion; (*agitación social*) upheaval.

convulsivo,-a *adj* convulsive.
conyugal *adj* conjugal; **vida c.,** married life.
cónyuge *nmf* spouse; **cónyuges,** married couple *sing,* husband and wife.
coña *nf vulg* **estar de c.,** to be joking.
coñac *nm* brandy, cognac.
coñazo *nm vulg* pain, drag; **dar el c.,** to be a real pain.
coño I *nm vulg* cunt. II *interj vulg* for fuck's sake!
cooperación *nf* co-operation.
cooperador,-a *nm,f* collaborator, co-operator.
cooperar *vi* to co-operate (**a, en,** in; **con,** with).
cooperativa *nf* co-operative.
coordenada *nf* co-ordinate.
coordinación *nf* co-ordination.
coordinadora *nf* coordinating committee; **c. general,** joint committee.
coordinador,-a *nm,f* co-ordinator.
coordinar *vtr* to co-ordinate.
copa *nf* 1 glass; **tomar una c.,** to have a drink. 2 (*de árbol*) top. 3 *Dep* cup. 4 *Naipes* **copas,** hearts.
copar *vtr* to take up.
copartícipe *adj & nmf* (*socio*) partner; (*colaborador*) collaborator; (*copropietario*) joint owner, co-owner.
Copenhague *n* Copenhagen.
copia *nf* copy.
copiar [12] *vtr* to copy.
copiloto *nm Av* copilot; *Aut* co-driver.
copioso,-a *adj* abundant, copious.
copistería *nf* photocopying service.
copla *nf* verse, couplet.
copo *nm* flake; (*de nieve*) snowflake; **copos de maíz,** cornflakes.
coproducción *nf* co-production, joint production.
cópula *nf* 1 (*coito*) copulation, intercourse. 2 *Ling* conjunction.
copular *vtr* to copulate (**con,** with).
COPYME *nm abr de* **Confederación de la Pequeña y Mediana Empresa.**
coquetear *vi* to flirt (**con,** with).
coqueta *nf* dressing table.
coqueto,-a I *adj* coquettish. II *nm,f* flirt.
coraje *nm* 1 (*valor*) courage. 2 (*ira*) anger, annoyance; *fig* **dar c.** a algn, to infuriate sb; **¡qué c.!,** how maddening!
coral[1] *nm Zool* coral.
coral[2] *nf Mús* choral, chorale.
Corán *nm* Koran.
coraza *nf* armour, *US* armor; *fig* protection.
corazón *nm* 1 heart; *fig* **de (todo) c.,** in all sincerity; *fig* **tener buen c.,** to be kind-hearted. 2 (*parte central*) heart; (*de fruta*) core. 3 *Naipes* **corazones,** hearts.
corazonada *nf* hunch, feeling.
corbata *nf* tie, *US* necktie; **con c.,** wearing a tie.

Córcega *n* Corsica.
corchete *nm* 1 *Impr* square bracket. 2 *Cost* hook and eye, snap fastener.
corcho *nm* cork; (*de pesca*) float.
cordel *nm* rope, cord.
cordero,-a *nm,f* lamb.
cordial *adj* cordial, warm.
cordialidad *nf* cordiality, warmth.
cordillera *nf* mountain chain *o* range.
córdoba *nm Fin* monetary unit of Nicaragua.
cordón *nm* string; (*de zapatos*) shoelace; *Anat* **c. umbilical,** umbilical cord; **c. policial,** police cordon.
cordura *nf* common sense.
Corea *n* Korea.
coreano,-a *adj & nm,f* Korean.
corear *vtr* 1 (*cantar a coro*) to sing in chorus. 2 (*aclamar*) to applaud.
coreografía *nf* choreography.
cornada *nf Taur* goring.
corneja *nf* crow.
córner *nm Ftb* corner (kick); **sacar un c.,** to take a corner.
corneta *nf* bugle; **c. de llaves,** cornet.
cornisa *nf* cornice.
cornudo,-a *nm ofens* cuckold.
coro *nm Mús* choir; *Teat* chorus; *fig* **a c.,** all together.
corona *nf* 1 crown. 2 (*de flores etc*) wreath, garland; **c. funeraria,** funeral wreath.
coronación *nf* 1 coronation. 2 *fig* (*culminación*) crowning point.
coronar *vtr* to crown.
coronel *nm* colonel.
coronilla *nf* crown of the head; *fam* **estar hasta la c.,** to be fed up (**de,** with).
corpiño *nm* bodice.
corporación *nf* corporation.
corporal *adj* corporal; **castigo c.,** corporal punishment; **olor c.,** body odour, BO.
corporativo,-a *adj* corporative.
corpulento,-a *adj* corpulent, stout.
corpus *nm* corpus.
corral *nm* farmyard, *US* corral; (*de casa*) courtyard.
correa *nf* 1 (*tira*) strap; (*de reloj*) watchstrap; (*de pantalón*) belt; (*de perro*) lead, *US* leash. 2 *Téc* belt.
corrección *nf* 1 (*rectificación*) correction. 2 (*urbanidad*) courtesy, politeness.
correcto,-a *adj* 1 (*sin errores*) correct. 2 (*educado*) polite, courteous (**con,** to); (*conducta*) proper.
corredera *nf* **puerta/ventana de c.,** sliding door/window.
corredizo,-a *adj* sliding; **nudo c.,** slipknot; **techo c.,** sunroof.
corredor,-a *nm,f* 1 *Dep* runner. 2 *Fin* **c. de bolsa,** stockbroker.
corregir [6] I *vtr* to correct. II **corregirse** *vr* to mend one's ways.
correo *nm* 1 post, *US* mail; **echar al c.,** to post; **por c.,** by post; **c. aéreo,** air-

mail; **c. certificado**, registered post; **(tren) c.**, mail train. **2 correos**, (*edificio*) post office *sing*.

correr I *vi* **1** to run; (*coche*) to go fast; (*conductor*) to drive fast; (*viento*) to blow; *fig* **no corras, habla más despacio**, don't rush, speak slower; **c. prisa**, to be urgent. **2 c. con los gastos**, to foot the bill; **corre a mi cargo**, I'll take care of it. **II** *vtr* **1** (*cortina*) to draw; (*cerrojo*) to close; (*aventura etc*) to have; **c. el riesgo o peligro**, to run the risk. **2** (*mover*) to pull up, draw up. **III correrse** *vr* **1** (*moverse*) to move over. **2** *fam* **c. una juerga**, to go on a spree. **3** *arg* (*tener orgasmo*) to come.

correspondencia *nf* **1** correspondence. **2** *Ferroc* connection.

corresponder I *vi* **1** to correspond (a, to; con, with). **2** (*incumbir*) to concern, be incumbent upon; **esta tarea te corresponde a ti**, it's your job to do this. **3** (*pertenecer*) to belong; **me dieron lo que me correspondía**, they gave me my share. **II corresponderse** *vr* **1** (*ajustarse*) to correspond. **2** (*dos cosas*) to tally; **no se corresponde con la descripción**, it does not match the description. **3** (*dos personas*) to love each other.

correspondiente *adj* corresponding (a, to).

corresponsal *nmf* correspondent.

corrida *nf* **c.** (**de toros**), bullfight.

corrido,-a *adj* **1** (*avergonzado*) abashed. **2 de c.**, without stopping.

corriente I *adj* **1** (*común*) common. **2** (*agua*) running. **3** (*mes, año*) current, present; **el diez del c.**, the tenth of this month. **4** *Fin* (*cuenta*) current. **5 estar al c.**, to be up to date. **II** *nf* **1** current, stream; *fig* **ir o navegar contra c.**, to go against the tide; *fam* **seguirle o llevarle la c. a algn**, to humour sb; *Elec* **c. eléctrica**, (electric) current. **2** (*de aire*) draught, *US* draft. **3** (*tendencia*) trend, current.

corrijo *indic pres* → **corregir**.

corrillo *nm* small group of people talking; *fig* clique.

corro *nm* **1** circle, ring. **2** (*juego*) ring-a-ring-a-roses.

corroborar *vtr* to corroborate.

corroer [38] *vtr* to corrode; *fig* **la envidia le corroe**, envy eats away at him.

corromper I *vtr* **1** (*pudrir*) to turn bad, rot. **2** (*pervertir*) to corrupt, pervert. **II corromperse** *vr* **1** (*pudrirse*) to go bad, rot. **2** (*pervertirse*) to become corrupted.

corrosivo,-a *adj* corrosive; *fig* (*mordaz*) caustic.

corrupción *nf* **1** (*putrefacción*) rot, decay. **2** *fig* corruption; *Jur* **c. de menores**, corruption of minors.

corrupto,-a *adj* corrupt.

corsé *nm* corset.

cortacésped *nm* & *f* lawnmower.

cortado,-a I *adj* **1** cut (up). **2** (*leche*) sour. **3** (*labios*) chapped. **4** *fam* (*tímido*) shy. **II** *nm* small coffee with a dash of milk.

cortafuego *nm* firebreak.

cortapisa *nf* *fig* restriction, limitation.

cortar I *vtr* **1** to cut; (*carne*) to carve; (*árbol*) to cut down; *fam* **c. por lo sano**, to take drastic measures; **fam cortó con su novio**, she split up with her boyfriend. **2** (*piel*) to chap, crack. **3** (*luz, teléfono*) to cut off. **4** (*paso, carretera*) to block. **II cortarse** *vr* **1** (*herirse*) to cut oneself. **2 c. el pelo**, to have one's hair cut. **3** (*leche etc*) to curdle. **4 Tel se cortó la comunicación**, we were cut off. **5** *fam* (*aturdirse*) to become all shy.

cortaúñas *nm inv nail clippers pl.*

corte¹ *nm* **1** cut; **c. de pelo**, haircut; *TV* **c. publicitario**, commercial break; **c. de mangas**, ≈ V-sign. **2** (*sección*) section; **c. transversal**, cross section. **3** *fam* rebuff; **dar un c. a algn**, to cut sb dead.

corte² *nf* **1** (*real*) court. **2 Las Cortes**, (Spanish) Parliament *sing*.

cortejar *vtr* to court.

cortejo *nm* **1** (*galanteo*) courting. **2** (*comitiva*) entourage, retinue; **c. fúnebre**, funeral cortège.

cortés *adj* courteous, polite.

cortesía *nf* courtesy, politeness.

corteza *nf* (*de árbol*) bark; (*de queso*) rind; (*de pan*) crust.

cortijo *nm* Andalusian farm *o* farmhouse.

cortina *nf* curtain; **c. de humo**, smoke screen.

corto,-a I *adj* **1** (*distancia, tiempo*) short; *fam* **c. de luces**, dim-witted; **c. de vista**, short-sighted; *Aut* **luz corta**, dipped headlights *pl*. **2** *fam* **quedarse c.**, (*calcular mal*) to underestimate. **3** (*apocado*) timid, shy. **II** *nm* *Cin* short (film).

cortocircuito *nm* short circuit.

cortometraje *nm* short (film).

corvo,-a *adj* curved, bent.

cosa *nf* **1** thing; **no he visto c. igual**, I've never seen anything like it; **no ser gran c.**, not to be up to much. **2** (*asunto*) matter, business; **eso es c. tuya**, that's your business *o* affair; **eso es otra c.**, that's different. **3 hace c. de una hora**, about an hour ago.

coscorrón *nm* knock *o* blow on the head.

cosecha *nf* **1** *Agr* harvest, crop. **2** (*año del vino*) vintage.

cosechadora *nf* combine harvester.

cosechar *vtr* to harvest, gather (in).

coser *vtr* **1** to sew; *fam* **es c. y cantar**, it's a piece of cake. **2** *Med* to stitch up.

cosmético,-a *adj* & *nm* cosmetic.

cósmico,-a *adj* cosmic.

cosmonauta *n* *mf* cosmonaut.

cosmopolita *adj* & *nmf* cosmopolitan.

cosmos *nm inv* cosmos.

coso *nm Taur* bullring.

cosquillas *nfpl* tickling *sing*; **hacer c. a algn**, to tickle sb; **tener c.**, to be ticklish.

cosquilleo *nm* tickling.

costa¹ *nf* coast; *(litoral)* coastline; *(playa)* beach, seaside, *US* shore.

costa² *nf* **a c. de**, at the expense of; **a toda c.**, at all costs, at any price; **vive a c. mía**, he lives off me.

costado *nm* side; **de c.**, sideways; **es catalana por los cuatro costados**, she's Catalan through and through.

costal *nm* sack.

costar [2] *vi* 1 to cost; **¿cuánto cuesta?**, how much is it?; **c. barato/caro**, to be cheap/expensive. 2 *fig* **te va a c. caro**, you'll pay dearly for this; **c. trabajo** *o* **mucho**, to be hard; **me cuesta hablar francés**, I find it difficult to speak French; **cueste lo que cueste**, at any cost.

costarricense, costarriqueño,-a *adj & nm,f* Costa Rican.

coste *nm* cost; **a precio de c.**, (at) cost price; **c. de la vida**, cost of living.

costear I *vtr* to afford, pay for; **c. los gastos**, to foot the bill. II **costearse** *vr* to pay for.

costero,-a *adj* coastal; **ciudad costera**, seaside town.

costilla *nf* 1 *Anat* rib. 2 *Culin* cutlet.

costo¹ *nm* cost.

costo² *nm arg (hachís)* dope, shit, stuff.

costoso,-a *adj* costly, expensive.

costra *nf* crust; *Med* scab.

costumbre *nf* 1 *(hábito)* habit; **como de c.**, as usual; **tengo la c. de levantarme temprano**, I usually get up early; **tenía la c. de ...**, he used to .... 2 *(tradición)* custom.

costura *nf* 1 sewing. 2 *(confección)* dressmaking; **alta c.**, haute couture. 3 *(línea de puntadas)* seam.

costurera *nf* seamstress.

costurero *nm* sewing basket.

cota *nf Geog* height above sea level; *fig* rating.

cotejar *vtr* to compare.

cotidiano,-a *adj* daily; **vida cotidiana**, everyday life.

cotilla *nmf fam* busybody, gossip.

cotillear *vi fam* to gossip (de, about).

cotilleo *nm fam* gossip.

cotización *nf* 1 *Fin* (market) price, quotation. 2 *(cuota)* membership fees *pl*, subscription.

cotizar [4] I *vtr Fin* to quote. II *vi* to pay national insurance. III **cotizarse** *vr Fin* **c. a**, to sell at.

coto *nm* 1 enclosure, reserve; **c. de caza**, game reserve. 2 **poner c. a**, to put a stop to.

cotorra *nf* parrot; *fig (persona)* chatterbox.

COU *nm Educ abr de* **Curso de Orientación Universitaria**, ≈ GCE A-level studies, sixth-form studies.

coyote *nm* coyote, prairie wolf.

coyuntura *nf Anat* articulation, joint. 2 *fig (circunstancia)* juncture; **la c. económica**, the economic situation.

coz *nf* kick; **dar una c.**, to kick.

C.P. *abr de* **código postal**, postcode.

crac(k) *nm* 1 *Fin* crash. 2 *(droga)* crack.

cráneo *nm* cranium, skull.

cráter *nm* crater.

creación *nf* creation.

creador,-a *nm,f* creator.

crear *vtr* to create.

creatividad *nf* creativity.

creativo,-a *adj* creative.

crecer [33] *vi* 1 to grow; **c. en importancia**, to become more important. 2 *(al tricotar)* to increase.

creces *nfpl* **con c.**, fully, in full; **devolver con c.**, to return with interest.

crecido,-a *adj (persona)* grown-up.

creciente *adj* growing, increasing; **cuarto c.**, crescent.

crecimiento *nm* growth.

credencial *adj* credential; **(cartas) credenciales**, credentials.

credibilidad *nf* credibility.

crédito *nm* 1 *Com Fin* credit. 2 *(confianza)* belief; **dar c. a**, to believe.

credo *nm* creed.

crédulo,-a *adj* credulous, gullible.

creencia *nf* belief.

creer [36] I *vtr* 1 to believe. 2 *(pensar)* to think; **creo que no**, I don't think so; **creo que sí**, I think so; **ya lo creo**, I should think so. II *vi* to believe; **c. en**, to believe in. III **creerse** *vr* 1 to consider oneself to be; **¿qué te has creído?**, what *o* who do you think you are? 2 **no me lo creo**, I can't believe it.

creíble *adj* credible, believable.

creído,-a I *adj* arrogant, vain. II *nm,f* big head.

crema *nf* cream.

cremallera *nf* zip (fastener), *US* zipper.

crematorio,-a *nm* **(horno) c.**, crematorium.

cremoso,-a *adj* creamy.

crepe *nf* crêpe, pancake.

crepería *nf* creperie.

crepitar *vi* to crackle.

crepúsculo *nm* twilight.

crespo,-a *adj* frizzy.

crespón *nm* crepe.

cresta *nf* 1 crest; *(de gallo)* comb. 2 *(de punk)* mohican.

Creta *n* Crete.

cretino,-a I *adj* stupid, cretinous. II *nm,f* cretin.

creyente *nmf* believer.

crezco *indic pres* → **crecer**.

cría *nf* 1 *(cachorro)* young. 2 *(crianza)*

breeding, raising.
criada *nf* maid.
criadero *nm* nursery.
criadilla *nf* Culin bull's testicle.
criado,-a I *adj* **mal c.**, spoilt. II *nm,f* servant.
crianza *nf* (*de animales*) breeding; *fig* vinos de c., vintage wines.
criar [29] *vtr* 1 (*animales*) to breed, raise; (*niños*) to bring up, rear. 2 (*producir*) to have, grow.
criatura *nf* 1 (living) creature. 2 (*crío*) baby, child.
criba *nf* sieve.
cribar *vtr* to sieve, sift.
crimen *nm* (*pl* **crímenes**) murder.
criminal *nmf & adj* criminal.
crin *nf*, **crines** *nfpl* mane *sing*.
crío,-a I *nm fam* kid. II *adj* babyish.
criollo,-a *adj & nm,f* Creole.
críquet *nm* cricket.
crisantemo *nm* chrysanthemum.
crisis *nf inv* 1 crisis. 2 (*ataque*) attack; **c. nerviosa**, nervous breakdown.
crispación *nf* tension.
crispar *vtr* to make tense; *fig* eso me crispa los nervios, that sets my nerves on edge.
cristal *nm* 1 crystal; **c. de roca**, rock crystal. 2 (*vidrio*) glass; (*de gafas*) lense; (*de ventana*) (window) pane.
cristalera *nf* window.
cristalería *nf* (*conjunto*) glassware; (*vasos*) glasses *pl*.
cristalino,-a *adj* crystal clear.
cristalizar [4] *vi* to crystallize.
cristiandad *nf* Christendom.
cristianismo *nm* Christianity.
cristiano,-a *adj & nm,f* Christian.
Cristo *nm* Christ.
criterio *nm* 1 (*pauta*) criterion. 2 (*opinión*) opinion. 3 (*discernimiento*) discretion; **lo dejo a tu c.**, I'll leave it up to you.
crítica *nf* 1 criticism. 2 Prensa review; **tener buena c.**, to get good reviews. 3 (*conjunto de críticos*) critics.
criticar [1] I *vtr* to criticize. II *vi* (*murmurar*) to gossip.
crítico,-a I *adj* critical. II *nm,f* critic.
criticón,-ona *nm,f fam* fault-finder.
croar *vi* to croak.
croché *nm* crochet.
croissant *nm* croissant.
crol *nm* Natación crawl.
cromo *nm* 1 (*metal*) chromium, chrome. 2 (*estampa*) picture card.
cromosoma *nm* chromosome.
crónica *nf* 1 account, chronicle. 2 Prensa feature, article.
crónico,-a *adj* chronic.
cronista *nmf* Prensa feature writer.
cronología *nf* chronology.
cronológico,-a *adj* chronological.
cronometrar *vtr* to time.

cronómetro *nm* stopwatch.
croqueta *nf* croquette.
croquis *nm inv* sketch.
cruce *nm* 1 crossing; (*de carreteras*) crossroads; (*de razas*) crossbreeding. 2 Tel crossed line.
crucero *nm* Náut cruise; (*barco*) cruiser.
crucial *adj* crucial.
crucificar [1] *vtr* to crucify.
crucifijo *nm* crucifix.
crucigrama *nm* crossword (puzzle).
crudeza *nf* crudeness, coarseness.
crudo,-a I *adj* 1 raw; (*comida*) underdone; *fam fig* lo veo muy c., it doesn't look too good. 2 (*clima*) harsh. 3 (*color*) cream. II *nm* (*petróleo*) crude.
cruel *adj* cruel.
crueldad *nf* cruelty; *fig* (*del clima*) severity.
cruento,-a *adj* bloody.
crujido *nm* (*de puerta*) creak, creaking; (*de dientes*) grinding.
crujiente *adj* crunchy.
crujir *vi* (*madera*) to creak; (*comida*) to crunch; (*dientes*) to grind.
cruz *nf* 1 cross; **C. Roja**, Red Cross; **c. gamada**, swastika. 2 ¿cara o c.?, ≈ heads or tails?
cruzada *nf* crusade.
cruzado,-a I *adj* 1 crossed; **con los brazos cruzados**, arms folded. 2 Cost double-breasted. 3 (*atravesado*) lying across. 4 (*animal*) crossbred. II *nm* Hist crusader.
cruzar [4] I *vtr* 1 to cross. 2 (*palabras, miradas*) to exchange. 3 (*animal, planta*) to cross, crossbreed. II *vi* (*atravesar*) to cross. III **cruzarse** *vr* to cross; **c. con algn**, to pass sb.
cta. Com *abr de* **cuenta**, account, a/c.
cta. cte. Com *abr de* **cuenta corriente**, current account, c/a.
CTNE *nf abr de* **Compañía Telefónica Nacional de España**, ≈ British Telecom.
c/u *abr de* **cada uno**, each, ea.
cuaderno *nm* notebook.
cuadra *nf* 1 (*establo*) stable. 2 Am block (of houses).
cuadrado,-a I *adj* 1 Geom square. 2 (*complexión física*) broad, stocky. 3 *fig* (*mente*) rigid. II *nm* 1 Geom square. 2 Mat square; **elevar (un número) al c.**, to square (a number).
cuadrar I *vtr* Mat to square. II *vi* (*coincidir*) to square, agree (**con**, with); (*sumas, cifras*) to tally. III **cuadrarse** *vr* (*soldado*) to stand to attention.
cuadriculado,-a *adj* papel c., square paper.
cuadrilátero,-a I *adj* quadrilateral. II *nm* Box ring.
cuadrilla *nf* (*equipo*) gang, team; Mil squad; Taur bullfighter's team.
cuadro *nm* 1 Geom square; **tela a cua-**

dros, checked cloth. **2** *Arte* painting, picture. **3** *Teat* scene. **4** *Elec Téc* panel; **c. de mandos,** control panel. **5** *(gráfico)* chart, graph.

cuádruple *adj* quadruple, fourfold.

cuajada *nf* curd.

cuajar I *vtr (leche)* to curdle; *(sangre)* to clot. **II** *vi* **1** *(nieve)* to lie. **2** *(moda)* to catch on; *(plan, esfuerzo)* to get off the ground.

cual I *pron rel (precedido de artículo)* **1** *(persona) (sujeto)* who; *(objeto)* whom. **2** *(cosa)* which. **II** *pron* **1** *tal* **c.,** exactly as. **2** *arc (comparativo)* such as, like.

cuál I *pron interr* which (one)?, what?; **¿c. quieres?,** which one do you want? **II** *adj interr* which 1. **III** *loc adv* **a c. más tonto,** each more stupid than the other.

cualidad *nf* quality.

cualificado,-a *adj* qualified.

cualquier *adj indef* any; **c. cosa,** anything; **en c. momento,** at any moment o time.

cualquiera (*pl* **cualesquiera**) **I** *adj indef* **1** *(indefinido)* any; **un profesor c.,** any teacher. **2** *(corriente)* ordinary. **II** *pron indef* **1** *(persona)* anybody; **c. te lo puede decir,** anybody can tell you. **2** *(cosa, animal)* anyone. **3** **c. que sea,** whatever it is. **III** *nmf fig pey* **ser un c.,** to be a nobody; **es una c.,** she's a tart.

cuando I *adv (de tiempo)* when; **c. más,** at the most; **c. menos,** at least; **de c. en c., de vez en c.,** from time to time. **II** *conj* **1** *(temporal)* when; **c. quieras,** whenever you want; **c. vengas,** when you come. **2** *(condicional) (si)* if. **3** *(concesiva) (aunque)* **(aun)** even if. **III** *prep* during, at the time of; **c. la guerra,** during the war; **c. niño,** as a child.

cuándo *adv interr* when?; **¿desde c.?,** since when; **¿para c. lo quieres?,** when do you want it for?

cuantía *nf* quantity, amount.

cuantioso,-a *adj* substantial, considerable.

cuanto,-a I *adj* all; **gasta c. dinero gana,** he spends all the money o as much as he earns; **unas cuantas niñas,** a few girls. **II** *pron rel* as much as; **coma c. quiera,** eat as much as you want; **regala todo c. tiene,** he gives away everything he's got. **III** *pron indef pl* **unos cuantos,** a few. **IV** *adv* **1** *(tiempo)* **c. antes,** as soon as possible; **en c.,** as soon as. **2** *(cantidad)* **c. más ... más,** the more ... the more; **c. más lo miro, más me gusta,** the more I look at it the more I like it; **cuantas más personas (haya) mejor,** the more the merrier. **3** **en c. a,** with respect to, regarding; **en c. a Juan,** as for Juan, as far as Juan is concerned.

cuánto,-a I *adj & pron interr (sing)* how much?; *(pl)* how many?; **¿cuántas ve-**

ces?, how many times?; **¿c. es?,** how much is it? **II** *adv* how, how much; **¡cuánta gente hay!,** what a lot of people there are!

cuarenta *adj & nm inv* forty; *fam* **cantarle a algn las c.,** to give sb a piece of one's mind.

cuarentena *nf Med* quarantine.

cuarentón,-ona *nm,f* forty-year old.

cuaresma *nf* Lent.

cuartear *vtr* to quarter.

cuartel *nm Mil* barracks *pl*; **c. general,** headquarters; *fig* **no dar c.,** to give no quarter.

cuartelada *nf,* **cuartelazo** *nm* putsch, military uprising.

cuartelillo *nm Mil* post, station.

cuarteto *nm* quartet.

cuartilla *nf* sheet of paper.

cuarto,-a I *nm* **1** *(habitación)* room; **c. de baño,** bathroom; **c. de estar,** living room. **2** *(cuarta parte)* quarter; **c. de hora,** quarter of an hour; *Dep* **cuartos de final,** quarter finals. **3** *fam* **cuartos,** *(dinero)* dough, money. **II** *adj & nm,f* fourth.

cuarzo *nm* quartz.

cuatro I *adj & nm inv* four. **II** *nm fam* a few; **cayeron c. gotas,** it rained a little bit.

cuatrocientos,-as *adj & nm,f* four hundred.

Cuba *nf* Cuba.

cuba *nf* cask, barrel; *fam* **como una c.,** (as) drunk as a lord.

cubalibre *nm* rum o gin and coke.

cubano,-a *adj & nm,f* Cuban.

cubata *nm fam* → **cubalibre.**

cubertería *nf* cutlery.

cúbico,-a *adj* cubic; *Mat* **raíz cúbica,** cube root.

cubierta *nf* **1** cover. **2** *(de rueda)* tyre, *US* tire. **3** *Náut* deck. **4** *(techo)* roof.

cubierto,-a I *adj* **1** covered; *(piscina)* indoors; *(cielo)* overcast. **2** *(trabajo, plaza)* filled. **II** *nm* **1** *(en la mesa)* place setting. **2** cubiertos, cutlery *sing.*

cubil *nm* lair.

cubismo *nm* cubism.

cubito *nm* little cube; **c. de hielo,** ice cube.

cubo *nm* **1** bucket; **c. de la basura,** rubbish bin. **2** *Mat* cube. **3** *(de rueda)* hub.

cubrecama *nf* bedspread.

cubrir (*pp* **cubierto**) **I** *vtr* to cover. **II** **cubrirse** *v r (cielo)* to become overcast.

cucaracha *nf* cockroach.

cuchara *nf* spoon.

cucharada *nf* spoonful; **c. rasa/colmada,** level/heaped spoonful.

cucharilla *nf* teaspoon; **c. de café,** coffee spoon.

cucharón *nm* ladle.

cuchichear *vi* to whisper.

cuchicheo *nm* whispering.

cuchilla *nf* blade; **c. de afeitar**, razor blade.

cuchillada *nf*, **cuchillazo** *nm* stab.

cuchillo *nm* knife.

cuchitril *nm fam* hovel, hole.

cuclillas *loc adv* **en c.**, crouching; **ponerse en c.**, to crouch down.

cuco,-a I *nm* cuckoo. II *adj fam (astuto)* shrewd, crafty.

cucurucho *nm* 1 *(para helado)* cornet. 2 *(de papel)* paper cone.

cuello *nm* 1 neck. 2 *(de camisa etc)* collar.

cuenca *nf* 1 *Geog* basin. 2 *(de los ojos)* socket.

cuenco *nm* earthenware bowl.

cuenta *nf* 1 *(factura)* bill. 2 *Fin (de banco)* account; **c. corriente**, current account. 3 *(cálculo) soum* **hacer cuentas**, tu dó sums; **c. atrás**, countdown. 4 *(de collar)* bead. 5 *(locuciones)* **caer en la c.**, to realize; **dar c.**, to report; **tener en c.**, to take into account; **traer c.**, to be worthwhile; **más sillas de la c.**, too many chairs; **en resumidas cuentas**, in short; **pedir cuentas**, to ask for an explanation; **trabajar por c. propia**, to be self-employed.

cuentagotas *nm inv* dropper.

cuentakilómetros *nm inv (distancia)* milometer; *(velocidad)* speedometer.

cuento *nm* 1 story; *Lit* short story; **contar un c.**, to tell a story; **fig eso no viene a c.**, that's beside the point; **c. chino**, tall story; **c. de hadas**, fairy story.

cuerda *nf* 1 *(cordel)* rope; *fig* **bajo c.**, dishonestly; **c. floja**, tightrope; **cuerdas vocales**, vocal chords. 2 *(de instrumento)* string. 3 *(del reloj)* spring; **dar c. al reloj**, to wind up a watch.

cuerdo,-a *adj* sane.

cuerno *nm* horn; *(de ciervo)* antler; *fam* **¡vete al c.!**, get lost!; *fam* **ponerle cuernos a algn**, to be unfaithful to sb.

cuero *nm* leather; **chaqueta de c.**, leather jacket. 2 **c. cabelludo**, scalp; *fam* **en cueros (vivos)**, (stark) naked.

cuerpo *nm* 1 body; **c. entero**, full-length; *fig* **tomar c.**, to take shape. 2 *(cadáver)* corpse; **de c. presente**, lying in state. 3 *(parte)* section, part. 4 *(grupo)* corps, force; **c. de bomberos**, fire brigade; **c. diplomático**, diplomatic corps.

cuervo *nm* raven.

cuesta I *nf* slope; **c. abajo**, downhill; **c. arriba**, uphill. II *loc adv* **a cuestas**, on one's back o shoulders.

cuestión *nf* 1 *(asunto)* matter, question; **es c. de vida o muerte**, it's a matter of life or death; **en c. de unas horas**, in just a few hours. 2 *(pregunta)* question.

cuestionario *nm* questionnaire.

cueva *nf* cave.

cuezo *indic pres* → **cocer.**

cuidado,-a I *nm* 1 care; **con c.**, carefully; **tener c.**, to be careful; **estar al c. de**, *(cosa)* to be in charge of; *(persona)* to look after; **me trae sin c.**, I couldn't care less. 2 *Med* **cuidados intensivos**, intensive care *sing*. II *interj* **¡c.!**, look out!, watch out!; **¡c. con lo que dices!**, watch what you say!; **¡c. con el escalón!**, mind the step!

cuidadoso,-a *adj* careful.

cuidar I *vtr* to care for, look after; **c. de que todo salga bien**, to make sure that everything goes alright; **c. los detalles**, to pay attention to details. II **cuidarse** *vr* **cuídate**, look after yourself.

culata *nf* 1 *(de arma)* butt. 2 *Aut* cylinder head.

culebra *nf* snake.

culebrilla *nf Med* ringworm.

culebrón *nm* soap opera.

culinario,-a *adj* culinary.

culminación *nf* culmination.

culminante *adj (punto)* highest; *(momento)* culminating.

culminar *vi* to culminate.

culo *nm* 1 *fam (trasero)* backside; *ofens* **¡vete a tomar por c.!**, fuck off! 2 *(de recipiente)* bottom.

culpa *nf* 1 blame; **echar la c. a algn**, to put the blame on sb; **fue c. mía**, it was my fault; **por tu c.**, because of you. 2 *(culpabilidad)* guilt.

culpabilidad *nf* guilt, culpability.

culpable I *nmf* offender, culprit. II *adj* guilty; *Jur* **declararse c.**, to plead guilty.

culpar *vtr* to blame; **c. a algn de un delito**, to accuse sb of an offence.

cultivado,-a *adj* 1 *Agr* cultivated. 2 *(con cultura)* cultured, refined.

cultivar *vtr* 1 to cultivate. 2 *Biol* to culture.

cultivo *nm* 1 cultivation; *(planta)* crop. 2 *Biol* culture.

culto,-a I *adj* educated; *(palabra)* learned. II *nm* cult; *Rel* worship.

cultura *nf* culture.

cultural *adj* cultural.

culturismo *nm* body building.

culturista *nmf* body builder.

cumbre *nf* 1 *(de montaña)* summit, top; *(conferencia)* **c.**, summit conference. 2 *fig (culminación)* pinnacle.

cumple *nm fam* birthday.

cumpleaños *nm inv* birthday; **¡feliz c.!**, happy birthday!

cumplido,-a I *adj* 1 completed; *(plazo)* expired; **misión cumplida**, mission accomplished. 2 *(cortés)* polite. II *nm* compliment.

cumplidor,-a *adj* reliable, dependable.

cumplimiento *nm* fulfilment, *US* fulfillment; **c. de la ley**, observance of the law.

cumplir I *vtr* 1 to carry out, fulfil, *US*

fulfill; (deseo) to fulfil; (promesa) to keep; (sentencia) to serve. **2 ayer cumplí veinte años**, I was twenty (years old) yesterday. **II** vi **1** (plazo) to expire, end. **2 c. con el deber**, to do one's duty. **III cumplirse** vr **1** (deseo, sueño) to be fulfilled, come true. **2** (plazo) to expire.

cúmulo nm pile, load.

cuna nf **1** cot. **2** fig (origen) cradle.

cundir vi **1 me cunde mucho el trabajo o el tiempo**, I seem to get a lot done. **2** (extenderse) to spread; **cundió el pánico**, panic spread; **cundió la voz de que ...**, rumour had it that ....

cuneta nf (de la carretera) gutter; **quedarse en la c.**, to be left behind.

cuña nf wedge; **c. publicitaria**, commercial break.

cuñado,-a nm,f (hombre) brother-in-law; (mujer) sister-in-law.

cuño de nuevo c., newly-coined.

cuota nf **1** (de club etc) membership fees pl, dues pl. **2** (porción) quota, share. **3** Am **carretera de c.**, toll road.

cupe pt indef → **caber**.

cupiera subj imperf → **caber**.

cupo nm ceiling; **Mil excedente de c.**, exempt from military service.

cupón nm coupon, voucher.

cúpula nf dome, cupola; (líderes) leadership.

cura I nm Rel priest. **II** nf Med cure; fig **no tiene c.**, there's no remedy.

curación nf cure, treatment.

curandero,-a nm,f quack.

curar I vtr **1** (sanar) to cure; (herida) to dress; (enfermedad) to treat. **2** (carne, pescado) to cure. **II** vi & vr **curar(se)** (sanar) to recover, get well; (herida) to heal up; **c. en salud**, to make sure.

curiosear vi to pry.

curiosidad nf curiosity; **tener c. de**, to be curious about.

curioso,-a I adj **1** (indiscreto) curious, in-

quisitive. **2** (extraño) strange, odd; **lo c. es que ...**, the strange thing is that .... **3** (limpio) neat, tidy. **II** nm,f **1** (mirón) onlooker. **2** pey (chismoso) nosey-parker, busybody.

currante nmf arg worker.

currar, currelar vi arg to graft, grind.

currículum nm (pl **currícula**) **c. vitae**, curriculum vitae.

curro nm arg job, meal ticket.

cursar vtr (estudiar) to study; (enviar) to send.

cursi adj pey vulgar.

cursillo nm short course; **c. de reciclaje**, refresher course.

cursivo,-a adj **letra cursiva**, italics.

curso nm **1** (año académico) year; (clase) class. **2** fig **año o mes en c.**, current year o month; **en el c. de**, during. **3** (de acontecimientos, río) course. **4** Fin **moneda de c. legal**, legal tender.

cursor nm cursor.

curtido,-a adj **1** (piel) weatherbeaten; (cuero) tanned. **2** fig (persona) hardened.

curtir vtr **1** (cuero) to tan. **2** fig (avezar) to harden, toughen.

curva nf **1** curve. **2** (en carretera) bend; **c. cerrada**, sharp bend.

curvilíneo,-a adj curvaceous.

curvo,-a adj curved.

cuscús nm couscous.

cúspide nf summit, peak; fig peak.

custodia nf custody.

custodiar [12] vtr to watch over.

cutáneo,-a adj cutaneous, skin; Med **erupción cutánea**, rash.

cutícula nf cuticle.

cutis nm complexion.

cuyo,-a pron rel & pos (de persona) whose; (de cosa) of which; **en c. caso**, in which case.

cv abr de **caballos de vapor**, horse power, hp.

D

D, d [de] nf (la letra) D, d.

D. abr de **don**, Mister, Mr.

D.ª abr de **doña**, Mrs, Miss.

dactilar adj **huellas dactilares**, fingerprints.

dádiva nf (regalo) gift, present; (donativo) donation.

dadivoso,-a adj generous.

dado,-a¹ adj **1** given; **en un momento d.**, at a certain point. **2 ser d. a**, to be given to. **3 d. que**, since, given that.

dado² nm die, dice pl.

daga nf dagger.

dalia nf dahlia.

dálmata nm Dalmatian (dog).

daltónico,-a adj colour-blind o US colorblind.

dama nf **1** (señora) lady. **2** (en damas) king. **3 damas**, (juego) draughts, US checkers.

damasco nm damask.

damnificado,-a nm,f victim, injured person.

danés,-esa I adj Danish. **II** nm,f (persona) Dane. **III** nm **1** (idioma) Danish. **2 gran d.**, (perro) Great Dane.

Danubio nm **el D.**, the Danube.

danza nf dancing; (baile) dance.

danzar [4] vtr & vi to dance.

dañar vtr (cosa) to damage; (persona) to

hurt, harm.

dañino,-a *adj* harmful, damaging (para, to).

daño *nm* (*a cosa*) damage; (*a persona*) (*físico*) hurt; (*perjuicio*) harm; **se hizo d. en la pierna**, he hurt his leg; *Jur* **daños y perjuicios**, (legal) damages.

dar [30] **I** *vtr* **1** to give; (*recado, recuerdos*) to pass on, give; (*noticia*) to tell. **2** (*mano de pintura, cera*) to apply, put on. **3** (*película*) to show, screen; (*fiesta*) to throw, give. **4** (*cosecha*) to produce, yield; (*fruto, flores*) to bear; (*beneficio, interés*) to give, yield. **5** (*bofetada etc*) to deal; **d. a algn en la cabeza**, to hit sb on the head. **6** **dale a la luz**, switch the light on; **d. la mano a algn**, to shake hands with sb; **d. los buenos días/las buenas noches a algn**, to say good morning/good evening to sb; **me da lo mismo, me da igual**, it's all the same to me; **¿qué más da?**, what difference does it make? **7** (*hora*) to strike; **ya han dado las nueve**, it's gone nine (o'clock). **8** **d. de comer a**, to feed. **9** **d. a conocer**, (*noticia*) to release; **d. a entender a algn que ...**, to give sb to understand that .... **10** **d. por**, (*considerar*) to assume, consider; **lo dieron por muerto**, he was assumed dead, he was given up for dead; **d. por descontado/sabido**, to take for granted, to assume.
II *vi* **1** **me dio un ataque de tos/risa**, I had a coughing fit/an attack of the giggles. **2** **d. a**, (*ventana, habitación*) to look out onto, overlook; (*puerta*) to open onto, lead to. **3** **d. con**, (*persona*) to come across; **d. con la solución**, to hit upon the solution. **4** **d. de sí**, (*ropa*) to stretch, give. **5** **d. en**, to hit; **el sol me daba en los ojos**, the sun was (shining) in my eyes. **6** **d. para**, to be enough o sufficient for; **el presupuesto no da para más**, the budget will not stretch any further. **7** **le dio por nadar**, he took it into his head to go swimming. **8** **d. que hablar**, to set people talking; **el suceso dio que pensar**, the incident gave people food for thought.
III darse *vr* **1** **se dio un caso extraño**, something strange happened. **2** (*hallarse*) to be found, exist. **3** **d. a**, to take to; **se dio a la bebida**, he took to drink. **4** **d. con o contra**, to bump o crash into. **5** **dárselas de**, to consider oneself. **6** **d. por satisfecho**, to feel satisfied; **d. por vencido**, to give in. **7** **se le da bien/mal el francés**, she's good/bad at French.

dardo *nm* dart.

dársena *nf* dock.

datar I *vtr* to date. **II** *vi* **d. de**, to date back to o from.

dátil *nm* date.

dato *nm* **1** piece of information; **datos personales**, personal details. **2** *Inform* **da-**

tos, data.

d.C. *abr de* **después de Cristo**, Anno Domini, AD.

dcha. *abr de* **derecha**, right.

de *prep* **1** (*pertenencia*) of; **el título de la novela**, the title of the novel; **el coche/hermano de Sofía**, Sofía's car/brother; **las bicicletas de los niños**, the boys' bicycles. **2** (*procedencia*) from; **de Madrid a Valencia**, from Madrid to Valencia; **soy de Palencia**, I'm from o I come from Palencia. **3** (*descripción*) **el niño de ojos azules**, the boy with blue eyes; **el señor de la chaqueta**, the man in the jacket; **el bobo del niño**, the silly boy; **un reloj de oro**, a gold watch; **un joven de veinte años**, a young man of twenty. **4** (*contenido*) of; **un saco de patatas**, a sack of potatoes. **5 gafas de sol**, sunglasses; **goma de borrar**, rubber, *US* eraser. **6** (*oficio*) by as; **es arquitecto de profesión**, he's an architect by profession; **trabaja de secretaria**, she's working as a secretary. **7** (*acerca de*) about; **curso de informática**, computer course. **8** (*tiempo*) **a las tres de la tarde**, at three in the afternoon; **de día**, by day; **de noche**, at night; **de lunes a jueves**, from Monday to Thursday; **de pequeño**, as a child; **de año en año**, year in year out. **9** (*precio*) **patatas de treinta pesetas el kilo**, potatoes at thirty pesetas a kilo. **10 una avenida de quince kilómetros**, an avenue fifteen kilometres long; **una botella de litro**, a litre bottle. **11** (*con superlativo*) in; **el más largo de España**, the longest in Spain. **12** (*causa*) with, because of; **llorar de alegría**, to cry with joy; **morir de hambre**, to die of hunger. **13** (*condicional*) **de haber llegado antes**, if he had arrived before; **de no ser así**, if that wasn't o weren't the case; **de ser cierto**, if it was o were true. **14 lo mismo de siempre**, the usual thing. **15 de cuatro en cuatro**, in fours, four at a time.

deambular *vi* to saunter, stroll.

debajo *adv* underneath, below; **el mío es el de d.**, mine is the one below; **está d. de la mesa**, it's under the table; **por d. de lo normal**, below normal; **salió por d. del coche**, he came out from under the car.

debate *nm* debate.

debatir I *vtr* to debate. **II debatirse** *vr* to struggle; **d. entre la vida y la muerte**, to fight for one's life.

debe *nm* *Com* debit, debit side.

deber¹ *nm* **1** duty; **cumplir con su d.**, to do one's duty. **2** *Educ* **deberes**, homework *sing*.

deber² **I** *vtr* (*dinero, explicación*) to owe. **II** *vi* **1 debe (de) comer**, he must eat; **debe (de) irse ahora**, she has to leave now; **la factura debe pagarse mañana**, the bill must be paid tomorrow; **el tren debe llegar a las dos**, the train is expected to arrive at two. 2 *(consejo)* **deberías visitar a tus padres**, you ought to visit your parents; **debería haber ido ayer**, I should have gone yesterday; **no debiste hacerlo**, you shouldn't have done it. 3 *(suposición)* **deben de estar fuera**, they must be out. III **deberse** *vr* **d. a**, to be due to; **esto se debe a la falta de agua**, this is due to lack of water.

debido,-a *adj* 1 due; **a su d. tiempo**, in due course; **con el d. respeto**, with due respect. 2 *(adecuado)* proper; **más de lo d.**, too much; **tomaron las debidas precauciones**, they took the proper precautions; **como es d.**, properly. 3 **d. a**, because of, due to; **d. a que**, because of the fact that.

debidamente *adv* duly, properly.

débil *adj* weak; *(luz)* dim; **punto d.**, weak spot.

debilidad *nf* weakness; *fig* **tener d. por**, *(persona)* to have a soft spot for; *(cosa)* to have a weakness for.

debilitamiento *nm* weakening.

debilitar I *vtr* to weaken, debilitate. II **debilitarse** *vr* to weaken, grow weak.

débito *nm* 1 *(deuda)* debt. 2 *(debe)* debit.

debut *nm* début, debut.

debutar *vi* to make one's début *o* debut.

década *nf* decade; **en la d. de los noventa**, during the nineties.

decadencia *nf* decadence.

decadente *adj & nmf* decadent.

decaer [39] *vi* to deteriorate.

decaído,-a *adj* down.

decaimiento *nm* 1 *(debilidad)* weakness. 2 *(desaliento)* low spirits *pl*.

decano,-a *nm,f Univ* dean.

decantarse *vr* to lean towards; **d. por**, to come down on the side of.

decapitar *vtr* to behead, decapitate.

decena *nf* *(about)* ten; **una d. de veces**, *(about)* ten times; **por decenas**, in tens.

decencia *nf* 1 *(decoro)* decency. 2 *(honradez)* honesty.

decenio *nm* decade.

decente *adj* decent; *(decoroso)* modest.

decepción *nf* disappointment.

decepcionante *adj* disappointing.

decepcionar *vtr* to disappoint.

decidido,-a *adj* determined, resolute.

decididamente *adv* 1 *(resueltamente)* resolutely. 2 *(definitivamente)* definitely.

decidir I *vtr & vi* to decide. II **decidirse** *vr* to make up one's mind. **d. a hacer algo**, to make up one's mind to do sth; **d. por algo**, to decide on sth.

décima *nf* tenth.

decimal *adj & nm* decimal; **el sistema métrico d.**, the decimal system.

décimo,-a I *adj & nm,f* tenth. II *nm* 1 *(parte)* tenth. 2 *(billete de lotería)* tenth

part of a lottery ticket.

decir[1] *nm* saying.

decir[2] [12] *(pp* **dicho)** I *vtr* 1 to say; **dice que no quiere venir**, he says he doesn't want to come. 2 **d. una mentira/la verdad**, to tell a lie/the truth. 3 *Tel Esp* **dígame**, hello. 4 **¿qué me dices del nuevo jefe?**, what do you think of the new boss? 5 *(mostrar)* to tell, show; **su cara dice que está mintiendo**, you can tell from his face that he's lying. 6 *(sugerir)* to mean; **esta película no me dice nada**, this film doesn't appeal to me; **¿qué te dice el cuadro?**, what does the picture mean to you? 7 **querer d.**, to mean. 8 *(locuciones)* **es d.**, that is (to say); **por así decirlo**, so to speak, so to speak; **digo yo**, in my opinion; **el qué dirán**, what people say; **ni que d. tiene**, needless to say; **¡no me digas!**, really!; **¡y que lo digas!**, you bet!
II **decirse** *vr* **¿cómo se dice 'mesa' en inglés?**, how do you say 'mesa' in English?; **se dice que ...**, they say that ...; **sé lo que me digo**, I know what I am saying.

decisión *nf* 1 decision; **tomar una d.**, to take *o* make a decision. 2 *(resolución)* determination; **con d.**, decisively.

decisivo,-a *adj* decisive.

decisorio *adj* decision-making.

declamar *vtr & vi* to declaim, recite.

declaración *nf* 1 declaration; **d. de (la) renta**, tax declaration *o* return. 2 *(afirmación)* statement; **hacer declaraciones**, to comment. 3 *Jur* **prestar d.**, to give evidence.

declarante *nmf Jur* witness.

declarar I *vtr* 1 to declare; **d. la guerra a**, to declare war on. 2 *(afirmar)* to state. 2 *Jur* **d. culpable/inocente a algn**, to find sb guilty/not guilty. II *vi* 1 to declare. 2 *Jur* to testify. III **declararse** *vr* 1 **d. a favor/en contra de**, to declare oneself in favour of/against; **d. en huelga**, to go on strike; **d. a algn**, to declare one's love for sb. 2 *(guerra, incendio)* to start, break out. 3 *Jur* **d. culpable**, to plead guilty.

declinar *vi & vtr* to decline.

declive *nm* 1 *(del terreno)* incline, slope. 2 *(de imperio etc)* decline.

decolorante *nm* bleaching agent.

decolorar I *vtr* to fade; *(pelo)* to bleach. II **decolorarse** *vr* to fade.

decomisar *vtr* to confiscate, seize.

decoración *nf* decoration.

decorado *nm* scenery, set.

decorador,-a *nm,f* 1 decorator. 2 *Teat* set designer.

decorar *vtr* to decorate.

decorativo,-a *adj* decorative.

decoro *nm* 1 *(respeto)* dignity, decorum. 2 *(pudor)* modesty, decency.

decoroso,-a *adj* 1 *(correcto)* seemly, de-

corous. 2 (*decente*) decent, modest.
decrecer [33] *vi* to decrease, diminish.
decrépito,-a *adj* decrepit.
decretar *vtr* to decree.
decreto *nm* decree; **d.-ley,** decree.
dedal *nm* thimble.
dedicación *nf* dedication.
dedicar [1] **I** *vtr* to dedicate; (*tiempo, esfuerzos*) to devote (**a,** to). **II dedicarse** *vr* ¿a qué se dedica Vd.? what do you do for a living?; **los fines de semana ella se dedica a pescar,** at weekends she spends her time fishing.
dedicatoria *nf* dedication.
dedillo **nm saber algo al d.,** to have sth at one's fingertips, know sth very well.
dedo *nm* (*de la mano*) finger; (*del pie*) toe; **d. anular/ corazón/índice/meñique, ring/middle/index/little finger; d. pulgar, d. gordo,** thumb; **hacer d.,** to hitchhike; *fig* **elegir a algn a d.,** to hand-pick sb.
deducción *nf* deduction.
deducible *adj Com* deductible.
deducir [10] **I** *vtr* **1** to deduce, infer. **2** *Com* to deduct. **II deducirse** *vr* **de aquí se deduce que ...,** from this it follows that ....
deductivo,-a *adj* deductive.
defecar [1] *vi* to defecate.
defecto *nm* defect, fault; **d. físico,** physical defect.
defectuoso,-a *adj* defective, faulty.
defender [3] **I** *vtr* to defend (**contra,** against; **de,** from); **d. del frío/viento,** to shelter from the cold/wind. **II defenderse** *vr* **1** to defend oneself. **2** *fam* **se defiende en francés,** he can get by in French.
defendido,-a *adj Jur* defended.
defensa **I** *nf* defence, *US* defense; **en d. propia, en legítima d.,** in self-defence; **salir en d. de algn,** to come out in defence of sb. **II** *nm Dep* defender, back.
defensiva *nf* defensive; **estar/ponerse a la d.,** to be/go on the defensive.
defensivo,-a *adj* defensive.
defensor,-a *nm,f* defender; **abogado d.,** counsel for the defence; **el defensor del pueblo,** the ombudsman.
deferencia *nf* deference; **en *o* por d. a,** out of deference to.
deficiencia *nf* deficiency, shortcoming; **d. mental,** mental deficiency; **d. renal,** kidney failure.
deficiente **I** *adj* deficient. **II** *nmf* **d. mental,** mentally retarded person. **III** *nm Educ* fail.
déficit *nm* (*pl* **déficits**) deficit; (*carencia*) shortage.
deficitario,-a *adj* showing a deficit.
definición *nf* definition; **por d.,** by definition.
definido,-a *adj* clear; *Ling* definite.
definir *vtr* to define.
definitivo,-a *adj* definitive; **en definitiva,**

in short. ◆**definitivamente** *adv* **1** (*para siempre*) for good, once and for all. **2** (*con toda seguridad*) definitely.
deflación *nf Econ* deflation.
deflacionista *adj Econ* deflationary.
deformación *nf* deformation.
deformar **I** *vtr* to deform, put out of shape; (*cara*) to disfigure; *fig* (*la verdad, una imagen*) to distort. **II deformarse** *vr* to go out of shape, become distorted.
deforme *adj* deformed; (*objeto*) misshapen.
defraudación *nf* fraud; **d. fiscal,** tax evasion.
defraudar *vtr* **1** (*decepcionar*) to disappoint. **2** (*al fisco*) to defraud, cheat; **d. a Hacienda,** to evade taxes.
defunción *nf Jur* decease, demise.
degeneración *nf* degeneration.
degenerado,-a *adj & nm,f* degenerate.
degenerar *vi* to degenerate.
degollar [2] *vtr* to behead.
degradación *nf* degradation.
degradante *adj* degrading.
degradar *vtr* to degrade.
degustación *nf* tasting.
degustar *vtr* to taste, sample.
dehesa *nf* pasture, meadow.
deificar [1] *vtr* to deify.
dejadez *nf* slovenliness.
dejado,-a *adj* **1** (*descuidado*) untidy, slovenly. **2** (*negligente*) negligent, careless. **3** *fam* **de la mano de Dios,** godforsaken.
dejar **I** *vtr* **1** to leave; **déjame en paz,** leave me alone; **d. dicho,** to leave word *o* a message. **2** (*prestar*) to lend. **3** (*abandonar*) to give up; **d. algo por imposible,** to give sth up; **dejé el tabaco y la bebida,** I gave up smoking and drinking. **4** (*permitir*) to let, allow; **d. caer,** to drop; **d. entrar/salir,** to let in/out. **5** (*omitir*) to leave out, omit. **6** (*ganancias*) to produce. **7** (+ *adj*) to make; **d. triste,** to make sad; **d. preocupado/sorprendido,** to worry/surprise. **8** (*posponer*) **dejaron el viaje para el verano,** they put the trip off until the summer.
II *v aux* **d. de** + *inf,* to stop, give up; **dejó de fumar el año pasado,** he gave up smoking last year; **no deja de llamarme,** she's always phoning me up.
III dejarse *vr* **1 me he dejado las llaves dentro,** I've left the keys inside. **2** (*locuciones*) **d. barba,** to grow a beard; **d. caer,** to flop down; **d. llevar por,** to be influenced by.
del (*contracción de* **de** + **el**) → **de.**
delantal *nm* apron.
delante *adv* **1** in front; **la entrada de d.,** the front entrance. **2 d. de,** in front of; (*en serie*) ahead of. **3 por d.,** in front; **se lo lleva todo por d.,** he destroys everything in his path; **tiene toda la vida por**

d., he has his whole life ahead of him.

delantera *nf* 1 (*ventaja*) lead; **tomar la d.,** take the lead. 2 *Ftb* forward line, the forwards *pl*.

delantero,-a I *adj* front. II *nm Ftb* forward; **d. centro,** centre forward.

delatar *vtr* 1 to inform against. 2 *fig* to give away.

delator,-a *nm,f* informer.

delegación *nf* 1 (*acto, delegados*) delegation. 2 (*oficina*) local office, branch; **D. de Hacienda,** Tax Office.

delegado,-a *nm,f* 1 delegate; **d. de Hacienda,** chief tax inspector. 2 *Com* representative.

delegar [7] *vtr* to delegate (**en,** to).

deleitar I *vtr* to delight. II **deleitarse** *vr* to delight in, take delight in.

deleite *nm* delight.

deletrear *vtr* to spell (out).

deleznable *adj* brittle.

delfín *nm* dolphin.

delgadez *nf* slimness.

delgado,-a *adj* 1 slim; (*capa*) fine.

deliberación *nf* deliberation.

deliberado,-a *adj* deliberate.

deliberar *vi* to deliberate (**on,** consider.

delicadeza *nf* 1 (*finura*) delicacy, daintiness. 2 (*tacto*) tactfulness; **falta de d.,** tactlessness.

delicado,-a *adj* 1 delicate. 2 (*exigente*) fussy, hard to please. 3 (*sensible*) hypersensitive.

delicia *nf* delight; **hacer las delicias de algn,** to delight sb.

delicioso,-a *adj* (*comida*) delicious; (*agradable*) delightful.

delictivo,-a *adj* criminal, punishable.

delimitar *vtr* to delimit.

delincuencia *nf* delinquency.

delincuente *nmf* delinquent; **d. juvenil,** juvenile delinquent.

delineante *nmf* (*hombre*) draughtsman; (*mujer*) draughtswoman.

delinear *vtr* to delineate, outline.

delinquir [9] *vi* to break the law, commit an offence *o US* offense.

delirante *adj* delirious.

delirar *vi* to be delirious.

delirio *nm* delirium; **delirios de grandeza,** delusions of grandeur.

delito *nm* crime, offence, *US* offense.

delta *nm* delta; **ala d.,** hang-glider.

demacrado,-a *adj* emaciated.

demagogia *nf* demagogy.

demagogo,-a *nm,f* demagogue.

demanda *nf* 1 *Jur* lawsuit. 2 *Com* demand.

demandado,-a I *nm,f* defendant. II *adj* in demand.

demandante *nmf* claimant.

demandar *vtr* to sue.

demarcar [1] *vtr* to demarcate.

demás I *adj* **los/las d.,** the rest of the; **la d.**

gente, the rest of the people. II *pron* **lo/los/las d.,** the rest; **por lo d.,** otherwise, apart from that; **y d.,** etcetera.

demasía *nf* **en d.,** excessively.

demasiado,-a I *adj* (*singular*) too much; (*plural*) too many; **hay demasiada comida,** there is too much food; **quieres demasiadas cosas,** you want too many things. II *adv* too (much); **es d. grande/caro,** it is too big/dear; **fumas/trabajas d.,** you smoke/work too much.

demencia *nf* dementia, insanity.

demente I *adj* insane, mad. II *nmf* mental patient.

democracia *nf* democracy.

demócrata I *adj* democratic. II *nmf* democrat.

democrático,-a *adj* democratic.

democratizar [4] *vtr* to democratize.

demografía *nf* demography.

demográfico,-a *adj* demographic; **crecimiento d.,** population growth.

demoledor,-a *adj fig* devastating.

demoler [4] *vtr* to demolish.

demonio *nm* devil, demon; *fam* ¿**cómo/dónde demonios ...?,** how/where the hell ...?; *fam* ¡**demonio(s)!,** hell!, damn!; *fam* ¡**d. de niño!,** you little devil!

demora *nf* delay.

demorar I *vtr* to delay, hold up. II **demorarse** *vr* 1 (*retrasarse*) to be delayed, be held up. 2 (*detenerse*) to dally.

demostrable *adj* demonstrable.

demostración *nf* demonstration; **una d. de fuerza/afecto,** a show of strength.

demostrar [2] *vtr* 1 (*mostrar*) to show, demonstrate. 2 (*evidenciar*) to prove.

demudado,-a *adj* pale.

denegar [1] *vtr* to refuse; *Jur* **d. una demanda,** to dismiss a claim.

denigrante *adj* humiliating.

denigrar *vtr* to humiliate.

denominación *nf* denomination; '**d. de origen',** (*vinos*) ≈ 'appellation d'origine'.

denominado,-a *adj* so-called.

denominador *nm* denominator.

denominar *vtr* to name, designate.

denotar *vtr* to denote.

densidad *nf* density; **d. de población,** population density.

denso,-a *adj* dense.

dentadura *nf* teeth, set of teeth; **d. postiza,** false teeth *pl*, dentures *pl*.

dental *adj* dental.

dentera *nf* **me da d.,** it sets my teeth on edge.

dentífrico,-a I *adj* **pasta/crema dentífrica,** toothpaste. II *nm* toothpaste.

dentista *nmf* dentist.

dentro *adv* 1 (*en el interior*) inside; **aquí d.,** in here; **por d.,** (on the) inside; **por d. está triste,** deep down (inside) he feels sad. 2 **d. de,** (*lugar*) inside. 3 **d. de poco,** shortly; soon; **d. de un mes,** in a month's time; **d. de lo que cabe**, all things considered.

denuncia *nf* 1 *Jur* report. 2 *(crítica)* denunciation.

denunciar [12] *vtr* 1 *(delito)* to report (**a**, to). 2 *(criticar)* to denounce.

deparar *vtr* to give; **no sabemos qué nos depara el destino**, we don't know what fate has in store for us.

departamento *nm* 1 department. 2 *Ferroc* compartment. 3 *(territorial)* province, district. 4 *Am (piso)* flat.

dependencia *nf* 1 dependence (**de**, on). 2 **dependencias**, premises.

depender *vi* to depend (**de**, on); *(económicamente)* to be dependent (**de**, on).

dependienta *nf* shop assistant.

dependiente I *adj* dependent (**de**, on). II *nm* shop assistant.

depilación *nf* depilation; **d. a la cera**, waxing.

depilar *vtr* to remove the hair from; *(cejas)* to pluck.

depilatorio,-a *adj & nm* depilatory; **crema depilatoria**, hair-remover, hair-removing cream.

deplorable *adj* deplorable.

deplorar *vtr* to deplore.

deponer [19] *(pp* **depuesto)** *vtr* 1 *(destituir)* to remove from office; *(líder)* to depose. 2 *(actitud)* to abandon.

deportado,-a *nm,f* deportee, deported person.

deportar *vtr* to deport.

deporte *nm* sport; **hacer d.**, to practise sports.

deportista I *nmf (hombre)* sportsman; *(mujer)* sportswoman. II *adj* sporty.

deportividad *nf* sportsmanship.

deportivo,-a I *adj* sports; **club/chaqueta d.**, sports club/jacket. II *nm Aut* sports car.

deposición *nf* removal from office; *(de un líder)* deposition.

depositar I *vtr* 1 *Fin* to deposit. 2 *(colocar)* to place, put. II **depositarse** *vr* to settle.

depósito *nm* 1 *Fin* deposit; **en d.**, on deposit. 2 *(de agua, gasolina)* tank. 3 **d. de basuras**, rubbish tip *o* dump; **d. de cadáveres**, mortuary, *US* morgue.

depravación *nf* depravity.

depravar *vtr* to deprave.

depre *nf fam* downer, depression.

depreciación *nf* depreciation.

depreciar [12] I *vtr* to reduce the value of. II **depreciarse** *vr* to depreciate, lose value.

depredador,-a I *adj* predatory. II *nm,f* predator.

depresión *nf* depression; **d. nerviosa**, nervous breakdown.

depresivo,-a *adj* depressive.

deprimente *adj* depressing.

deprimido,-a *adj* depressed.

deprimir I *vtr* to depress. II **deprimirse** *vr* to get depressed.

deprisa *adv* quickly.

depuesto,-a *pp → deponer.

depuración *nf* 1 *(del agua)* purification. 2 *(purga)* purge.

depurador,-a *adj* **planta depuradora**, purification plant.

depuradora *nf* purifier.

depurar *vtr* 1 *(agua)* to purify. 2 *(partido)* to purge. 3 *(estilo)* to refine.

derecha *nf* 1 *(mano)* right hand. 2 *(lugar)* right, right-hand side; **a la d.**, to *o* on the right, on the right-hand side. 3 *Pol* **a la d.**, the right; **de derechas**, right-wing.

derechista *nmf* right winger.

derecho,-a I *adj* 1 *(de la derecha)* right. 2 *(recto)* upright, straight. II *nm* 1 *(privilegio)* right; **derechos civiles/humanos**, civil/human rights; **tener d. a**, to be entitled to, have the right to; **estar en su d.**, to be within one's rights; **no hay d.**, it's not fair; **d. de admisión**, right to refuse admission. 2 *Jur* law; **d. penal/político**, criminal/constitutional law. 3 *Com* **derechos**, duties; **d. de autor**, royalties; **d. de matrícula**, enrolment fees. III *adv* **siga todo d.**, go straight ahead.

deriva *nf* drift; **ir a la d.**, to drift.

derivado *nm (producto)* derivative, by-product.

derivar I *vtr* 1 to divert; *(conversación)* to steer. II *vi* 1 to drift. 2 **d. de**, to derive from. III **derivarse** *vr* 1 *(proceder)* to result *o* stem (**de**, from). 2 *Ling* to be derived (**de**, from).

dermatitis *nf inv* dermatitis.

dermatólogo,-a *nm,f* dermatologist.

derogar [7] *vtr* to repeal.

derramamiento *nm* spilling; **d. de sangre**, bloodshed.

derramar I *vtr* to spill; *(lágrimas)* to shed. II **derramarse** *vr* to spill.

derrame *nm Med* discharge; **d. cerebral**, brain haemorrhage.

derrapar *vi* to skid.

derredor *nm* **en d. de**, round, around.

derretir [6] *vtr*, **derretirse** *vr* to melt; *(hielo, nieve)* to thaw.

derribar *vtr* 1 *(edificio)* to pull down, knock down. 2 *(avión)* to shoot down. 3 *(gobierno)* to bring down.

derrocar [1] *vtr* to bring down; *(violentamente)* to overthrow.

derrochador,-a I *adj* wasteful. II *nm,f* wasteful person, squanderer.

derrochar *vtr* to waste, squander.

derroche *nm* 1 *(de dinero, energía)* waste, squandering. 2 *(abundancia)* profusion, abundance.

derrota *nf* 1 defeat. 2 *Náut* (ship's) course.

derrotar *vtr* to defeat, beat.

derrotero *nm* **1** *fig* path, course *o* plan of action. **2** *Náut* sailing directions *pl.*

derrotista *adj & nmf* defeatist.

derruido,-a *adj* in ruins.

derruir [37] *vtr* to demolish.

derrumbar I *vtr* (*edificio*) to knock down, pull down. **II derrumbarse** *vr* to collapse, fall down; (*techo*) to fall in, cave in.

desabastecido,-a *adj* d. de, out of.

desaborido,-a I *adj* **1** (*comida*) tasteless. **2** *fig* (*persona*) dull. **II** *nm,f fig* dull person.

desabrido,-a *adj* **1** (*comida*) tasteless. **2** (*tiempo*) unpleasant. **3** *fig* (*tono*) harsh; (*persona*) moody, irritable.

desabrigado,-a *adj* ir/estar d., to be lightly dressed.

desabrochar I *vtr* to undo. **II desabrocharse** *vr* **1** desabróchate la camisa, undo your shirt. **2** (*prenda*) to come undone.

desacatar *vtr* to disobey.

desacato *nm* lack of respect, disrespect (a, for); *Jur* d. al tribunal, contempt of court.

desacertado,-a *adj* unwise.

desacierto *nm* mistake, error.

desaconsejar *vtr* to advise against.

desacorde *adj* estar d. con, to be in disagreement with.

desacreditar I *vtr* (*desprestigiar*) to discredit, bring into discredit. **2** (*criticar*) to disparage.

desactivador,-a *nm,f* bomb disposal expert.

desactivar *vtr* (*bomba*) to defuse.

desacuerdo *nm* disagreement.

desafiante *adj* defiant.

desafiar [29] *vtr* to challenge.

desafinado,-a *adj* out of tune.

desafinar I *vi* to sing out of tune; (*instrumento*) to play out of tune. **II** *vtr* to put out of tune. **III desafinarse** *vr* to go out of tune.

desafío *nm* challenge.

desaforado,-a *adj* wild.

desafortunado,-a *adj* unlucky, unfortunate.

desagradable *adj* unpleasant, disagreeable.

desagradar *vi* to displease.

desagradecido,-a I *adj* ungrateful. **II** *nm,f* ungrateful person.

desagrado *nm* displeasure.

desagraviar [12] *vtr* to make amends for.

desaguar [22] *vtr* to drain.

desagüe *nm* (*vaciado*) drain; (*cañería*) waste pipe, drainpipe.

desaguisado *nm* mess.

desahogado,-a *adj* **1** (*acomodado*) well-off, well-to-do. **2** (*espacioso*) spacious, roomy.

desahogarse [7] *vr* to let off steam; **se**

desahogó de su depresión, he got his depression out of his system.

desahogo *nm* **1** (*alivio*) relief. **2** vivir con d., to live comfortably.

desahuciado,-a *adj* **1** (*enfermo*) hopeless. **2** (*inquilino*) evicted.

desahuciar [12] *vtr* **1** (*desalojar*) to evict. **2** (*enfermo*) to deprive of all hope.

desahucio *nm* eviction.

desairado,-a *adj* **1** (*humillado*) spurned. **2** (*sin gracia*) awkward.

desairar *vtr* to slight, snub.

desaire *nm* slight, rebuff.

desajustar I *vtr* to upset. **II desajustarse** *vr* (*piezas*) to come apart.

desajuste *nm* upset; **d. económico,** economic imbalance; **un d. de horarios,** clashing timetables.

desalentador,-a *adj* discouraging, disheartening.

desalentar [1] **I** *vtr* to discourage, dishearten. **II desalentarse** *vr* to get discouraged, lose heart.

desaliento *nm* discouragement.

desaliñado,-a *adj* scruffy, untidy.

desaliño *nm* scruffiness, untidiness.

desalmado,-a *adj* cruel, heartless.

desalojamiento *nm* (*de inquilino*) eviction; (*de público*) removal; (*de lugar*) evacuation.

desalojar *vtr* **1** (*inquilino*) to evict; (*público*) to move on; (*lugar*) to evacuate. **2** (*abandonar*) to move out of, abandon.

desalojo *nm* → desalojamiento.

desamor *nm* lack of affection.

desamortizar [4] *vtr* to alienate, disentail.

desamparado,-a I *adj* (*persona*) helpless, unprotected; (*lugar*) abandoned, forsaken. **II** *nm,f* helpless *o* abandoned person.

desamparar *vtr* **1** to abandon, desert. **2** *Jur* to renounce, relinquish.

desamparo *nm* helplessness.

desamueblado,-a *adj* unfurnished.

desandar [8] *vtr* d. lo andado, to retrace one's steps.

desangrarse *vr* to lose (a lot of) blood.

desanimado,-a *adj* **1** (*persona*) downhearted, dejected. **2** (*fiesta etc*) dull, lifeless.

desanimar I *vtr* to discourage, dishearten. **II desanimarse** *vr* to lose heart, get discouraged.

desánimo *nm* discouragement, dejection.

desapacible *adj* unpleasant.

desaparecer [33] *vi* to disappear.

desaparecido,-a I *adj* missing. **II** *nm,f* missing person.

desaparición *nf* disappearance.

desapego *nm* indifference, lack of affection.

desapercibido,-a *adj* **1** (*inadvertido*) unnoticed; **pasar d.,** to go unnoticed. **2** (*desprevenido*) unprepared.

desaprensivo,-a *adj* unscrupulous **II** *nm,f* unscrupulous person.

desaprobar [2] *vtr* 1 (*no aprobar*) to disapprove of. 2 (*rechazar*) to reject.

desaprovechar *vtr* (*dinero, tiempo*) to waste; **d. una ocasión**, to fail to make the most of an opportunity.

desarmable *adj* that can be taken to pieces.

desarmar *vtr* 1 (*desmontar*) to dismantle, take to pieces. 2 *Mil* to disarm.

desarme *nm* disarmament; **d. nuclear**, nuclear disarmament.

desarraigado,-a *adj* rootless, without roots.

desarraigar [7] *vtr* to uproot.

desarraigo *nm* rootlessness.

desarreglado, a *adj* 1 (*lugar*) untidy. 2 (*persona*) untidy, slovenly.

desarreglar *vtr* 1 (*desordenar*) to make untidy, mess up. 2 (*planes etc*) to spoil, upset.

desarreglo *nm* difference of opinion.

desarrollado,-a *adj* developed; **país d.**, developed country.

desarrollar I *vtr* to develop. II **desarrollarse** *vr* 1 (*persona, enfermedad*) to develop. 2 (*tener lugar*) to take place.

desarrollo *nm* development; **países en vías de d.**, developing countries.

desarticular *vtr* to dismantle; **d. un complot**, to foil a plot.

desaseado,-a *adj* unkempt.

desasir [22] I *vtr* to release. II **desasirse** *vr* to get loose; **d. de**, to free *o* rid oneself of.

desasosegar [1] *vtr* to make restless *o* uneasy.

desasosiego *nm* restlessness, uneasiness.

desastrado,-a I *adj* untidy, scruffy. II *nm,f* scruffy person.

desastre *nm* disaster; **eres un d.**, you're just hopeless.

desastroso,-a *adj* disastrous.

desatar I *vtr* to untie, undo; (*provocar*) to unleash. II **desatarse** *vr* 1 (*zapato, cordón*) to come undone. 2 (*tormenta*) to break; (*pasión*) to run wild.

desatascar [1] *vtr* to unblock, clear.

desatender [3] *vtr* to neglect, not pay attention to.

desatento,-a *adj* inattentive; (*descortés*) impolite, discourteous.

desatinado,-a *adj* unwise.

desatino *nm* blunder.

desatornillar *vtr* to unscrew.

desatrancar [1] *vtr* to unblock; (*puerta*) to unbolt.

desautorizar [4] *vtr* 1 to disallow. 2 (*huelga etc*) to ban, forbid. 3 (*desmentir*) to deny.

desavenencia *nf* disagreement.

desaventajado,-a *adj* at a disadvantage.

desayunar I *vi* to have breakfast; *fml* to

breakfast. II *vtr* to have for breakfast.

desayuno *nm* breakfast.

desazón *nf* malaise.

desazonar *vtr* to cause malaise.

desbancar [1] *vtr* to oust.

desbandada *nf* scattering; **hubo una d. general**, everyone scattered.

desbandarse *vr* to scatter, disperse.

desbarajuste *nm* confusion, disorder.

desbaratar *vtr* to ruin, wreck; (*jersey*) to unravel.

desbloquear *vtr* 1 (*negociaciones*) to get going again. 2 (*créditos, precios*) to unfreeze.

desbocado,-a *adj* (*caballo*) runaway.

desbocarse *vr* (*caballo*) to bolt, run away.

desbordante *adj* overflowing, bursting.

desbordar I *vtr* to overflow; *fig* to overwhelm. II *vi* to overflow (**de**, with). II **desbordarse** *vr* to overflow, flood.

descabalgar [7] *vi* to dismount.

descabellado,-a *adj* crazy, wild.

descafeinado,-a *adj* 1 (*café*) decaffeinated. 2 *fig* watered-down, diluted.

descalabrar *vtr* 1 to wound in the head. 2 *fig* to damage, harm.

descalabro *nm* setback, misfortune.

descalificar [1] *vtr* to disqualify.

descalzarse [4] *vr* to take one's shoes off.

descalzo,-a *adj* barefoot.

descambiar [12] *vtr* to exchange.

descaminado,-a *adj* *fig* **ir d.**, to be on the wrong track.

descampado *nm* waste ground.

descansado,-a *adj* 1 (*persona*) rested. 2 (*vida, trabajo*) restful.

descansar *vi* 1 to rest, have a rest; (*corto tiempo*) to take a break. 2 *euf* **que en paz descanse**, may he *o* she rest in peace.

descansillo *nm* landing.

descanso *nm* 1 rest, break; **un día de d.**, a day off. 2 *Cin Teat* interval; *Dep* half-time, interval. 3 (*alivio*) relief. 4 (*rellano*) landing.

descapotable *adj & nm* convertible.

descarado,-a I *adj* 1 (*insolente*) cheeky, insolent; (*desvergonzado*) shameless. 2 *fam* **d. que sí/no**, (*por supuesto*) of course/course not. II *nm,f* cheeky person.

descarga *nf* 1 unloading. 2 *Elec Mil* discharge.

descargar [7] I *vtr* 1 to unload. 2 *Elec* to discharge. 3 (*disparar*) to fire; (*golpe*) to deal. II *vi* (*tormenta*) to burst. III **descargarse** *vr* (*batería*) to go flat.

descargo *nm* *Jur* discharge; **testigo de d.**, witness for the defence.

descarnado,-a *adj* crude.

descaro *nm* cheek, nerve; **¡qué d.!**, what a cheek!

descarriar *vtr* 1 to lead astray, put on the wrong road. II **descarriarse** *vr* to go astray, lose one's way.

descarrilar *vi* to go off the rails, be derailed.

descartar I *vtr* to rule out. II **descartarse** *vr Naipes* to discard, throw away.

descascarillarse *vr* to chip, peel.

descendencia *nf* descendants *pl;* **morir sin d.,** to die without issue.

descendente *adj* descending, downward.

descender [3] I *vi* 1 *(temperatura, nivel)* to fall, drop. **2 d. de,** to descend from. II *vtr* to lower.

descendiente *nmf* descendant.

descenso *nm* 1 descent; *(de temperatura)* fall, drop. 2 *Dep* relegation.

descentrado,-a *adj* off-centre.

descentralizar [4] *vtr* to decentralize.

descifrar *vtr* to decipher; *(mensaje)* decode; *(misterio)* to solve; *(motivos, causas)* to figure out.

descojonarse *vr vulg (reírse)* to piss oneself laughing.

descolgar [2] I *vtr (el teléfono)* to pick up; *(cuadro, cortinas)* to take down. II **descolgarse** *vr* to let oneself down, slide down.

descolorido,-a *adj* faded.

descombros *nmpl* rubble, debris.

descompasado,-a *adj* inconsistent.

descomponer [19] *(pp descompuesto)* I *vtr* 1 to break down. 2 *(corromper)* to rot, decompose. II **descomponerse** *vi (corromperse)* to rot, decompose; *(ponerse nervioso)* to lose one's cool.

descomposición *nf* 1 *(de carne)* decomposition, rotting; *(de país)* disintegration. 2 *Quim* breakdown.

descompuesto,-a *adj* 1 *(podrido)* rotten, decomposed. 2 *(furioso)* furious.

descompuse *pt indef* → **descomponer.**

descomunal *adj* huge, massive.

desconcertante *adj* disconcerting.

desconcertar [1] I *vtr* to disconcert. II **desconcertarse** *vr* to be bewildered, be puzzled.

desconchón *nm* bare patch.

desconcierto *nm* chaos, confusion.

desconectar *vtr* to disconnect.

desconexión *nf* disconnection.

desconfiado,-a *adj* distrustful, wary.

desconfianza *nf* distrust, mistrust.

desconfiar [29] *vi* to distrust **(de,** -), mistrust **(de,** -).

descongelar *vtr (nevera)* to defrost; *(créditos)* to unfreeze.

descongestionar *vtr* to clear.

desconocer [34] *vtr* not to know, be unaware of.

desconocido,-a I *adj* unknown; *(irreconocible)* unrecognizable. II *nm* lo d., the unknown. III *nm,f* stranger.

desconsiderado,-a I *adj* inconsiderate, thoughtless. II *nm,f* inconsiderate *o* thoughtless person.

desconsolado,-a *adj* disconsolate, grief-stricken.

desconsuelo *nm* grief, sorrow.

descontado,-a *adj fam* **dar por d.,** to take for granted; **por d.,** needless to say, of course.

descontar [2] *vtr* 1 to deduct. 2 *Dep (tiempo)* to add on.

descontento,-a I *adj* unhappy. II *nm* dissatisfaction.

descontrol *nm fam* lack of control; **había un d. total,** it was absolute chaos.

descontrolarse *vr* to lose control.

desconvocar *vtr* to call off.

descorchar *vtr* to uncork.

descornarse [2] *vr fam (trabajar)* to slave (away).

descorrer *vtr* to draw back.

descortés *adj* impolite, discourteous.

descortesía *nf* discourtesy, impoliteness.

descoser *vtr* to unstitch, unpick.

descosido *nm (en camisa etc)* open seam; *fam* **como un d.,** like mad, wildly.

descoyuntar *vtr* to dislocate.

descrédito *nm* disrepute, discredit.

descremado,-a *adj* skimmed.

describir *(pp descrito) vtr* to describe.

descripción *nf* description.

descriptivo,-a *adj* descriptive.

descrito,-a *pp* → **describir.**

descuajaringar [7] *vtr fam* to pull *o* take to pieces.

descuartizar [4] *vtr* to cut up, cut into pieces.

descubierto,-a I *adj* open, uncovered; **a cielo d.,** in the open. II *nm* 1 *Fin* overdraft. 2 **al d.,** in the open; **poner al d.,** to uncover, bring out into the open.

descubridor,-a *nm,f* discoverer.

descubrimiento *nm* discovery.

descubrir *(pp descubierto) vtr* to discover; *(conspiración)* to uncover; *(placa)* to unveil.

descuento *nm* discount.

descuidado,-a *adj* 1 *(desaseado)* untidy, neglected. 2 *(negligente)* careless, negligent. 3 *(desprevenido)* off one's guard.

descuidar I *vtr* to neglect, overlook. II *vi* descuida, **voy yo,** don't worry, I'll go. III **descuidarse** *vr (despistarse)* to be careless; **como te descuides, llegarás tarde,** if you don't watch out, you'll be late.

descuido *nm* 1 oversight, mistake; **por d.,** inadvertently, by mistake. 2 *(negligencia)* negligence, carelessness.

desde *adv* 1 *(tiempo)* since; **d. ahora,** from now on; **d. el lunes/entonces,** since Monday/then; **espero d. hace media hora,** I've been waiting for half an hour; **no lo he visto d. hace un año,** I haven't seen him for a year; **¿d. cuándo?,** since when?; **d. siempre,** always. 2 *(lugar)* from; **d. aquí,** from here; **d. arriba/abajo,** from above/below. 3 **d. luego,** of course. 4 **d. que,** ever since; **d. que lo**

conozco, ever since I've known him.
desdecir [12] (*pp* **desdicho**) I *vi* not to
live up (**de**, to). II **desdecirse** *vr* to go
back on one's word.
desdén *nm* disdain.
desdentado,-a *adj* toothless.
desdeñar *vtr* to disdain.
desdeñoso,-a *adj* disdainful.
desdibujarse *vr* to become blurred *o*
faint.
desdicha *nf* misfortune; **por d.**, unfortunately.
desdichado,-a I *adj* unfortunate. II *nm,f*
poor devil, wretch.
desdigo *indic pres* → **desdecir**.
desdiré *indic fut* → **desdecir**.
desdoblar *vtr* to unfold.
deseable *adj* desirable.
desear *vtr* **1** to desire; **deja mucho que
d.**, it leaves a lot to be desired. **2** (*querer*)
to want; **¿qué desea?**, can I help you?;
estoy deseando que vengas, I'm looking
forward to your coming. **3 te deseo buena suerte/feliz Navidad**, I wish you good
luck/a merry Christmas.
desecar [1] *vtr* to dry up.
desechable *adj* disposable, throw-away.
desechar *vtr* **1** (*tirar*) to discard, throw
out *o* away. **2** (*oferta*) to turn down, refuse; (*idea, proyecto*) to drop, discard.
desechos *nmpl* waste *sing*.
desembalar *vtr* to unpack.
desembarcar [1] I *vtr* (*mercancías*) to unload; (*personas*) to disembark. II *vi* to disembark.
desembarco, desembarque *nm* (*de
mercancías*) unloading; (*de personas*) dis-
embarkation.
desembocadura *nf* mouth.
desembocar [1] *vi* (*río*) to flow (**en**, into);
(*calle, situación*) to lead (**en**, to).
desembolsar *vtr* to pay out.
desembolso *nm* expenditure.
desembragar [7] *vtr* *Aut* to declutch.
desembrollar *vtr* *fam* **1** (*aclarar*) to clarify, clear up. **2** (*desenredar*) to disentangle.
desembuchar *vtr* *fig* to blurt out; *fam*
¡desembucha!, out with it!
desempañar *vtr* to wipe the condensation
from; *Aut* to demist.
desempaquetar *vtr* to unpack, unwrap.
desempatar *vi* *Dep* to break the deadlock.
desempate *nm* play-off; **partido de d.**,
play-off, deciding match.
desempeñar *vtr* **1** (*cargo*) to hold, occupy; (*función*) to fulfil; (*papel*) to play. **2**
(*recuperar*) to redeem.
desempleado,-a I *adj* unemployed, out
of work. II *nm,f* unemployed person; **los
desempleados**, the unemployed.
desempleo *nm* unemployment; **cobrar el
d.**, to be on the dole.
desempolvar *vtr* **1** to dust. **2** *fig* (*pasado*)

to revive.
desencadenar I *vtr* **1** to unchain. **2** (*provocar*) to unleash. II **desencadenarse** *vr* **1**
(*prisionero*) to break loose; (*viento, pasión*)
to rage. **2** (*conflicto*) to start, break out.
desencajar I *vtr* (*pieza*) to knock out;
(*hueso*) to dislocate. II **desencajarse** *vr* **1**
(*pieza*) to come out; (*hueso*) to become
dislocated. **2** (*cara*) to become distorted.
desencaminado,-a *adj* →
descaminado,-a.
desencanto *nm* disenchantment.
desenchufar *vtr* to unplug.
desenfadado,-a *adj* carefree, free and
easy.
desenfado *nm* ease.
desenfocado,-a *adj* out of focus.
desenfoque *nm* incorrect focusing; *fig* (*de
asunto*) wrong approach.
desenfrenado,-a *adj* frantic, uncontrolled; (*vicio, pasión*) unbridled.
desenfreno *nm* debauchery.
desenganchar *vtr* to unhook; (*vagón*) to
uncouple.
desengañar I *vtr* **d. a algn**, to open sb's
eyes. II **desengañarse** *vr* **1** to be disappointed. **2** *fam* **¡desengáñate!**, get real!
desengaño *nm* disappointment; **llevarse
o sufrir un d. con algo**, to be disappointed in sth.
desengrasar *vtr* to degrease, remove the
grease from.
desenlace *nm* **1** result, outcome; **un feliz
d.**, a happy end. **2** *Cin Teat* ending, dé-
nouement.
desenmarañar *vtr* (*pelo*) to untangle;
(*problema*) to unravel; (*asunto*) to sort
out.
desenmascarar *vtr* to unmask.
desenredar *vtr* to untangle, disentangle.
desenrollar *vtr* to unroll; (*cable*) to unwind.
desenroscar [1] *vtr* to unscrew.
desentenderse [3] *vr* *Aut* **se desentendió de
mi problema**, he didn't want to have
anything to do with my problem.
desenterrar [1] *vtr* **1** (*cadáver*) to exhume,
disinter; (*tesoro etc*) to dig up. **2** (*recuerdo*)
to revive.
desentonar *vi* **1** *Mús* to sing out of tune,
be out of tune. **2** (*colores etc*) not to
match. **3** (*persona, comentario*) to be out
of place.
desentrañar *vtr* (*misterio*) to unravel, get
to the bottom of.
desentrenado,-a *adj* out of training *o*
shape.
desentumecer [33] *vtr* to put the feeling
back into.
desenvoltura *nf* ease.
desenvolver [4] (*pp* **desenvuelto**) I *vtr* to
unwrap. II **desenvolverse** *vr* **1** (*persona*)
to manage, cope. **2** (*hecho*) to develop.
desenvuelto,-a *adj* relaxed.

deseo *nm* wish; (*sexual*) desire; **formular un d.**, to make a wish.

deseoso,-a *adj* eager; **estar d. de**, be eager to.

desequilibrado,-a I *adj* unbalanced. **II** *nm,f* unbalanced person.

desequilibrar I *vtr* to unbalance, throw off balance. **II desequilibrarse** *vr* to become mentally disturbed.

desequilibrio *nm* imbalance; **d. mental**, mental disorder.

deserción *nf* desertion.

desertar *vi* to desert.

desértico,-a *adj* desert.

desertización *nf* desertification.

desertor,-a *nm,f* deserter.

desesperación *nf* (*desesperanza*) despair; (*exasperación*) desperation.

desesperado,-a *adj* **1** (*sin esperanza*) desperate, hopeless. **2** (*exasperado*) exasperated, infuriated.

desesperante *adj* exasperating.

desesperar I *vtr* to drive to despair; (*exasperar*) to exasperate. **II desesperarse** *vr* to despair.

desestabilizar [4] *vtr* to destabilize.

desestimar *vtr* to reject.

desfachatez *nf* cheek, nerve.

desfalco *nm* embezzlement, misappropriation.

desfallecer [33] *vi* **1** (*debilitarse*) to feel faint; (*desmayarse*) to faint. **2** (*desanimarse*) to lose heart.

desfasado,-a *adj* **1** outdated. **2** (*persona*) old-fashioned, behind the times. **3** *Téc* out of phase.

desfase *nm* gap; **d. horario**, time lag.

desfavorable *adj* unfavourable, *US* unfavorable.

desfigurar *vtr* (*cara*) to disfigure; (*verdad*) to distort.

desfiladero *nm* narrow pass.

desfilar *vi* **1** to march in single file. **2** *Mil* to march past, parade.

desfile *nm* *Mil* parade, march past; **d. de modas**, fashion show.

desfogar [7] **I** *vtr* to give vent to. **II desfogarse** *vr* to let off steam.

desgajar I *vtr* (*arrancar*) to rip o tear out; (*rama*) to tear off. **II desgajarse** *vr* to come off.

desgana *nf* **1** (*inapetencia*) lack of appetite. **2** (*apatía*) apathy, indifference; **con d.**, reluctantly, unwillingly.

desganado,-a *adj* **I estar d.**, (*inapetente*) to have no appetite. **2** (*apático*) apathetic.

desgañitarse *vr fam* to shout oneself hoarse.

desgarbado,-a *adj* ungraceful, ungainly.

desgarrador,-a *adj* bloodcurdling.

desgarrar *vtr* to tear.

desgarrón *nm* big tear, rip.

desgastar I *vtr* to wear out. **II desgastarse** *vr* (*consumirse*) to wear out; (*per-*

sona) to wear oneself out.

desgaste *nm* wear; **d. del poder**, wear and tear of power.

desgracia *nf* **1** misfortune; **por d.**, unfortunately. **2** (*deshonor*) disgrace. **3 desgracias personales**, loss of life.

desgraciado,-a I *adj* unfortunate; (*infeliz*) unhappy. **II** *nm,f* unfortunate person; **un pobre d.**, a poor devil. ◆**desgraciadamente** *adv* unfortunately.

desgravable *adj* tax-deductible.

desgravación *nf* deduction; **d. fiscal**, tax deduction.

desgravar *vtr* to deduct.

desguazar [4] *vtr* (*un barco*) to break up; *Aut* to scrap.

deshabitado,-a *adj* uninhabited, unoccupied.

deshabitar *vtr* to abandon, vacate.

deshacer [15] (*pp* **deshecho**) **I** *vtr* **1** (*paquete*) to undo; (*maleta*) to unpack. **2** (*plan*) to destroy, ruin. **3** (*acuerdo*) to break off. **4** (*disolver*) to dissolve; (*derretir*) to melt. **II deshacerse** *vr* **1** to come undone o untied. **2 d. de algn/algo**, to get rid of sb/sth. **3** (*afligirse*) to go to pieces; **d. en lágrimas**, to cry one's eyes out. **4** (*disolverse*) to dissolve; (*derretirse*) to melt. **5** (*niebla*) to fade away, disappear.

deshecho,-a *adj* **1** (*cama*) unmade; (*maleta*) unpacked; (*paquete*) unwrapped. **2** (*roto*) broken, smashed. **3** (*disuelto*) dissolved; (*derretido*) melted. **4** (*abatido*) devasted, shattered. **5** (*cansado*) exhausted, tired out.

desheredar *vtr* to disinherit.

deshidratar *vtr* to dehydrate.

deshielo *nm* thaw.

deshilachar *vtr* to fray.

deshilvanado,-a *adj fig* (*inconexo*) disjointed.

deshonesto,-a *adj* **1** dishonest. **2** (*indecente*) indecent, improper.

deshonor *nm*, **deshonra** *nf* dishonour, *US* dishonor.

deshonrar *vtr* **1** to dishonour, *US* dishonor. **2** (*a la familia etc*) to bring disgrace on.

deshora (a) *loc adv* at an inconvenient time; **comer a d.**, to eat at odd times.

deshuesar *vtr* (*carne*) to bone; (*fruta*) to stone.

deshumanizar [4] *vtr* to dehumanize.

desidia *nf* apathy.

desierto I *nm* desert. **II** *adj* **1** (*deshabitado*) uninhabited. **2** (*vacío*) empty, deserted. **3** (*premio*) void.

designación *nf* designation.

designar *vtr* **1** to designate. **2** (*fecha, lugar*) to fix.

designio *nm* intention, plan.

desigual *adj* **1** uneven. **2** (*lucha*) unequal.

3 (*carácter*) changeable.

desigualdad *nf* 1 inequality. 2 (*del terreno*) unevenness.

desilusión *nf* disappointment, disillusionment.

desilusionar *vtr* to disappoint, disillusion.

desinfectante *adj* & *nm* disinfectant.

desinfectar *vtr* to disinfect.

desinflar I *vtr* to deflate; (*rueda*) to let down. II **desinflarse** *vr* to go flat.

desintegración *nf* disintegration.

desintegrar *vtr*, **desintegrarse** *vr* to disintegrate.

desinterés *nm* 1 (*indiferencia*) lack of interest, apathy. 2 (*generosidad*) unselfishness.

desinteresado,-a *adj* selfless, unselfish.

desintoxicar [1] I *vtr* to detoxicate; (*de alcohol*) to dry out. II **desintoxicarse** *vr* *Med* to detoxicate oneself; (*de alcohol*) to dry out.

desistir *vi* to desist.

deslavazado,-a *adj* disjointed.

desleal *adj* disloyal; (*competencia*) unfair.

deslealtad *nf* disloyalty.

deslenguado,-a *adj* (*insolente*) insolent, cheeky; (*grosero*) coarse, foul-mouthed.

desliar [29] *vtr* to unwrap.

desligar [7] I *vtr* 1 (*separar*) to separate. 2 (*desatar*) to untie, unfasten. II **desligarse** *vr* **d. de**, to disassociate oneself from.

desliz *nm* mistake, slip; **cometer** *o* **tener un d.**, to slip up.

deslizar [4] I *vi* to slide. II **deslizarse** *vr* 1 (*patinar*) to slide. 2 (*fluir*) to flow.

deslucir [35] *vtr* 1 (*espectáculo*) to spoil. 2 (*metal*) to make dull.

deslumbrador,-a, **deslumbrante** *adj* dazzling; *fig* stunning.

deslumbrar *vtr* to dazzle.

desmadrarse *vr* *fam* to go wild.

desmadre *nm* *fam* hullabaloo.

desmandarse *vr* to get out of hand, run wild; (*caballo*) to bolt.

desmano (a) *loc adv* out of the way; **me coge a d.**, it is out of my way.

desmantelar *vtr* 1 to dismantle. 2 *Náut* to dismast, unrig.

desmaquillador,-a I *nm* make-up remover. II *adj* **leche desmaquilladora**, cleansing cream.

desmaquillarse *vr* to remove one's make-up.

desmarcarse [1] *vr* *Dep* to lose one's marker.

desmayado,-a *adj* unconscious; **caer d.**, to faint.

desmayarse *vr* to faint.

desmayo *nm* faint, fainting fit; **tener un d.**, to faint.

desmedido,-a *adj* disproportionate, out of all proportion; (*ambición*) unbounded.

desmejorar(se) *vi* & *vr* to deteriorate, go downhill.

desmelenarse *vr* *fam* to let one's hair down.

desmembración *nf*, **desmembramiento** *nm* dismemberment.

desmemoriado,-a *adj* forgetful, absent-minded.

desmentir [5] *vtr* to deny.

desmenuzar [4] *vtr* 1 (*deshacer*) to break into little pieces, crumble; (*carne*) to cut into little pieces. 2 (*asunto*) to examine in detail.

desmerecer [33] *vi* 1 to be unworthy (**de**, of). 2 (*deteriorarse*) to deteriorate.

desmesura *nf* excess.

desmesurado,-a *adj* excessive.

desmilitarizar [4] *vtr* to demilitarize.

desmontable *adj* that can be taken to pieces.

desmontar I *vtr* 1 (*desarmar*) to take to pieces, dismantle. 2 (*allanar*) to level. II *vi* to dismount (**de**, -), get off (**de**, -).

desmoralizar [4] *vtr* to demoralize.

desmoronarse *vr* to crumble, fall to pieces.

desnatado,-a *adj* (*leche*) skimmed.

desnivel *nm* (*en el terreno*) drop, difference in height.

desnivelar *vtr* to throw out of balance.

desnucarse [1] *vr* to break one's neck.

desnuclearizar *vtr* to denuclearize.

desnudar I *vtr* to undress. II **desnudarse** *vr* to get undressed.

desnudismo *nm* nudism.

desnudista *adj* & *nmf* nudist.

desnudo,-a I *adj* naked, nude. II *nm* *Arte* nude.

desnutrición *nf* malnutrition.

desnutrido,-a *adj* undernourished.

desobedecer [33] *vtr* to disobey.

desobediencia *nf* disobedience.

desobediente I *adj* disobedient. II *nmf* disobedient person.

desocupado,-a *adj* 1 (*vacío*) empty, vacant. 2 (*ocioso*) free, not busy. 3 (*sin empleo*) unemployed.

desocupar *vtr* to empty, vacate.

desodorante *adj* & *nm* deodorant.

desolación *nf* desolation.

desolar [2] *vtr* to devastate.

desollar [2] I *vtr* to skin. II **desollarse** *vr* to scrape; **me desollé el brazo**, I scraped my arm.

desorbitado,-a *adj* (*precio*) exhorbitant.

desorden *nm* untidiness, mess; **¡qué d.!**, what a mess!; **d. público**, civil disorder.

desordenado,-a *adj* messy, untidy.

desordenar *vtr* to make untidy, mess up.

desorganizar [4] *vtr* to disorganize, disrupt.

desorientación *nf* disorientation.

desorientar I *vtr* to disorientate. II **desorientarse** *vr* to lose one's sense of direction, lose one's bearings; *fig* to become disorientated.

despabilado,-a *adj* 1 (*sin sueño*) wide awake. 2 (*listo*) quick, smart.

despachar *vtr* 1 (*asunto*) to get through. 2 (*correo*) to send, dispatch. 3 (*en tienda*) to serve. 4 *fam* (*despedir*) to send packing, sack.

despacho *nm* 1 (*oficina*) office; (*en casa*) study. 2 (*venta*) sale. 3 (*comunicación*) dispatch.

despachurrar *vtr fam* to squash, flatten.

despacio *adv* 1 (*lentamente*) slowly. 2 (*en voz baja*) quietly.

despampanante *adj fam* stunning.

desparpajo *nm* self-assurance; **con d.**, in a carefree manner.

desparramar *vtr*, **desparramarse** *vr* to spread, scatter; (*líquido*) to spill.

despavorido,-a *adj* terrified.

despecho *nm* spite; **por d.**, out of spite.

despectivo,-a *adj* derogatory, disparaging.

despedazar [4] *vtr* to cut o tear to pieces.

despedida *nf* farewell, goodbye; **d. de soltera/soltero**, hen/stag party.

despedido,-a *adj* **salir d.**, to be off like a shot.

despedir [6] I *vtr* 1 (*empleado*) to sack, fire. 2 (*decir adiós*) to see off, say goodbye to. 3 (*olor, humo etc*) to give off. II **despedirse** *vr* 1 (*decir adiós*) to say goodbye (**de**, to). 2 *fig* to forget, give up; **ya puedes despedirte del coche**, you can say goodbye to the car.

despegado,-a *adj* 1 unstuck. 2 (*persona*) couldn't-care-less.

despegar [7] I *vtr* to take off, detach. II *vi* *Av* to take off. III **despegarse** *vr* to come unstuck.

despego *nm* detachment.

despegue *nm* takeoff.

despeinado,-a *adj* dishevelled, with untidy hair.

despejado,-a *adj* clear; (*cielo*) cloudless.

despejar I *vtr* to clear; (*misterio, dudas*) to clear up. II **despejarse** *vr* 1 (*cielo*) to clear. 2 (*persona*) to clear one's head.

despeje *nm* *Dep* clearance.

despellejar *vtr* to skin.

despelotarse *vr* *vulg* 1 (*desnudarse*) to strip. 2 **d. de risa**, to laugh one's head off.

despensa *nf* pantry, larder.

despeñadero *nm* cliff, precipice.

despeñarse *vr* to go over a cliff.

desperdiciar [12] *vtr* to waste; (*oportunidad*) to throw away.

desperdicio *nm* 1 (*acto*) waste. 2 **desperdicios**, (*basura*) rubbish *sing*; (*desechos*) scraps, leftovers.

desperdigar [7] *vtr*, **desperdigarse** *vr* to scatter, separate.

desperezarse [4] *vr* to stretch (oneself).

desperfecto *nm* 1 (*defecto*) flaw, imperfection. 2 (*daño*) damage.

despertador *nm* alarm clock; **reloj d.**, alarm watch.

despertar [1] I *vtr* to wake (up), awaken; *fig* (*sentimiento etc*) to arouse. II **despertarse** *vr* to wake (up).

despiadado,-a *adj* merciless.

despido *nm* dismissal, sacking.

despierto,-a *adj* 1 (*desvelado*) awake. 2 (*vivo*) quick, sharp.

despilfarrar *vtr* to waste, squander.

despilfarro *nm* wasting, squandering.

despintar *vi*, **despintarse** *vr* (*ropa*) to fade.

despistado,-a I *adj* 1 (*olvidadizo*) scatterbrained. 2 (*confuso*) confused. II *nm,f* scatterbrain.

despistar I *vtr* 1 (*hacer perder la pista a*) to lose, throw off one's scent. 2 *fig* to mislead. II **despistarse** *vr* (*perderse*) to get lost. 2 (*distraerse*) to switch off.

despiste *nm* 1 (*cualidad*) absent-mindedness. 2 (*error*) slip-up.

desplazamiento *nm* (*viaje*) trip, journey; **dietas de d.**, travelling expenses.

desplazar [4] I *vtr* to displace. II **desplazarse** *vr* to travel.

desplegar [1] I *vtr* 1 to open (out), spread (out). 2 (*energías etc*) to use, deploy. II **desplegarse** *vr* (*abrirse*) to open (out), spread (out). 2 *Mil* to deploy.

despliegue *nm* 1 *Mil* deployment. 2 (*de medios etc*) display.

desplomarse *vr* to collapse; (*precios*) to slump, fall sharply.

desplumar *vtr* to pluck.

despoblar [2] *vtr* to depopulate.

despojar *vtr* to strip (**de**, of). 2 *fig* to divest, deprive (**de**, of).

despojo *nm* 1 stripping. 2 **despojos**, leftovers, scraps.

desposado,-a *adj fml* newly-wed.

desposar *vtr fml* to marry.

desposeer [36] *vtr* **d. de**, to dispossess of; (*autoridad*) to strip of.

desposeído *nm* **los desposeídos**, the have-nots.

déspota *nmf* despot.

despótico,-a *adj* despotic.

despotismo *nm* despotism.

despotricar [1] *vi* to rant and rave (**contra**, about).

despreciable *adj* despicable, contemptible; (*cantidad*) negligible.

despreciar [12] *vtr* 1 (*desdeñar*) to scorn, despise. 2 (*rechazar*) to reject, spurn.

desprecio *nm* 1 (*desdén*) scorn, disdain. 2 (*desaire*) slight, snub.

desprender I *vtr* 1 (*separar*) to remove, detach. 2 (*olor, humo etc*) to give off. II **desprenderse** *vr* 1 (*soltarse*) to come off o away. 2 **d. de**, to rid oneself (**de**, of), free oneself (**de**, from). 3 **de aquí se desprende que ...**, it can be deduced from this that ....

desprendido,-a adj fig generous, un-selfish.

desprendimiento nm 1 loosening, detachment; **d. de tierras**, landslide. 2 fig (generosidad) generosity, unselfishness.

despreocupado,-a adj 1 (tranquilo) unconcerned. 2 (descuidado) careless; (estilo) casual.

despreocuparse vr 1 (tranquilizarse) to stop worrying. 2 (desentenderse) to be unconcerned, be indifferent (**de**, to).

desprestigiar [12] vtr to discredit, run down.

desprestigio nm discredit, loss of reputation; **campaña de d.**, smear campaign.

desprevenido,-a adj unprepared; **coger** o **pillar a algn d.**, to catch sb unawares.

desproporción nf disproportion, lack of proportion.

desproporcionado,-a adj disproportionate.

desprovisto,-a adj lacking (**de**, -), without (**de**, -), devoid (**de**, of).

después adv 1 afterwards; later; (entonces) then; (seguidamente) next; **una semana d.**, a week later; **poco d.**, soon after. 2 (lugar) next. 3 **d. de**, after; **d. de la gerra**, after the war; **mi calle está d. de la tuya**, my street is the one after yours; **d. de cenar**, after eating; **d. de todo**, after all. 4 **d. de que**, after; **d. de que viniera**, after he came.

despuntar I vtr to blunt, make blunt. II vi 1 (día) to dawn. 2 (destacar) to excel, stand out.

desquiciar [12] I vtr (persona) to unhinge. II **desquiciarse** vr (persona) to go crazy.

desquitarse vr to take revenge (**de**, for).

desquite nm revenge.

destacado,-a adj outstanding.

destacamento nm detachment.

destacar [1] I vtr fig to emphasize, stress. II **destacar(se)** vi & vr to stand out.

destajo nm piecework; **trabajar a d.**, to do piecework.

destapar I vtr to take the lid off; (botella) to open; fig (asunto) to uncover. II **destaparse** vr to get uncovered.

destartalado,-a adj rambling; (desvencijado) ramshackle.

destello nm flash, sparkle.

destemplado,-a adj 1 (voz, gesto) sharp, snappy; **con cajas destempladas**, rudely, brusquely. 2 (tiempo) unpleasant. 3 (enfermo) indisposed, out of sorts. 4 Mús out of tune, discordant.

desteñir [6] I vi & vtr to discolour, US discolor. II **desteñirse** vr to lose colour o US color, fade.

desternillarse vi **d. (de risa)**, to split one's sides laughing.

desterrar [1] vtr to exile.

destiempo (a) loc adv at the wrong time o moment.

destierro nm exile.

destilado,-a adj distilled; **agua destilada**, distilled water.

destilar vtr to distil.

destilería nf distillery.

destinado,-a adj destined, bound; fig **d. al fracaso**, doomed to failure.

destinar vtr 1 (dinero etc) to set aside, assign. 2 (empleado) to appoint.

destinatario,-a nm,f (de carta) addressee. 2 (de mercancías) consignee.

destino nm (rumbo) destination; **el avión con d. a Bilbao**, the plane to Bilbao. 2 (sino) fate, fortune. 3 (empleo) post.

destitución nf dismissal from office.

destituir [37] vtr to dismiss o remove from office.

destornillador nm screwdriver.

destornillar vtr to unscrew.

destreza nf skill.

destrozado,-a adj 1 (roto) torn-up, smashed. 2 (cansado) worn-out, exhausted. 3 (abatido) shattered.

destrozar [4] vtr 1 (destruir) to destroy; (rasgar) to tear to shreds o pieces. 2 (afligir) to shatter; (vida, reputación) to ruin.

destrozo nm 1 destruction. 2 **destrozos** damage sing.

destrucción nf destruction.

destructivo,-a adj destructive.

destructor,-a I adj destructive. II nm Náut destroyer.

destruir [37] vtr to destroy.

desusado,-a adj old-fashioned, outdated.

desuso nm disuse; **caer en d.**, to fall into disuse; **en d.**, obsolete, outdated.

desvalido,-a adj defenceless.

desvalijar vtr (robar) to clean out, rob; (casa, tienda) to burgle.

desvalorizar [4] vtr to devalue.

desván nm attic, loft.

desvanecerse [33] vr 1 (disiparse) to vanish, fade away. 2 (desmayarse) to faint.

desvariar [29] vi to talk nonsense.

desvarío nm 1 (delirio) raving, delirium. 2 (disparate) nonsense.

desvelado,-a adj awake, wide awake.

desvelar I vtr to keep awake. II **desvelarse** vr 1 (despabilarse) to stay awake. 2 (desvivirse) to devote oneself (**por**, to).

desvencijar I vtr to take apart. II **desvencijarse** vr to fall apart.

desventaja nf 1 disadvantage; **estar en d.**, to be at a disadvantage. 2 (inconveniente) drawback.

desventura nf misfortune, bad luck.

desvergonzado,-a I adj 1 (indecente) shameless. 2 (descarado) insolent. II nm,f 1 (sinvergüenza) shameless person. 2 (fresco) insolent o cheeky person.

desvergüenza nf 1 (indecencia) shamelessness. 2 (atrevimiento) insolence; **tuvo la d. de negarlo**, he had the cheek to deny it.

3 (*impertinencia*) insolent o rude remark.

desvestir [6] I *vtr* to undress. II **desvestirse** *vr* to undress, get undressed.

desviación *nf* deviation; (*de carretera*) diversion, detour; *Med* d. de columna, slipped disc.

desviar [29] I *vtr* (*río, carretera*) to divert; (*golpe, conversación*) to deflect; d. la mirada, to look away. II **desviarse** *vr* to go off course; (*coche*) to turn off; *fig* d. del tema, to digress.

desvincular I *vtr* to separate. II **desvincularse** *vr* to separate, cut oneself off.

desvío *nm* diversion, detour.

desvirgar [7] *vtr* to deflower.

desvirtuar [30] *vtr* to distort.

desvivirse *vr* to bend over backwards.

detallado,-a *adj* detailed, thorough.
◆**detalladamente** *adv* in (great) detail.

detallar *vtr* to give the details of.

detalle *nm* 1 detail; **entrar en detalles**, to go into details. 2 (*delicadeza*) nice thought, nicety; **¡qué d.!**, how nice!, how sweet! 3 (*toque decorativo*) touch, ornament.

detallista I *adj* perfectionist. II *nmf Com* retailer.

detectar *vtr* to detect.

detective *nmf* detective; **d. privado**, private detective o eye.

detector,-a *nm,f* detector; **d. de incendios**, fire detector.

detención *nf* 1 *Jur* detention, arrest. 2 **con d.**, carefully, thoroughly.

detener [24] I *vtr* 1 to stop, halt. 2 *Jur* (*arrestar*) to arrest, detain. II **detenerse** *vr* to stop.

detenido,-a I *adj* 1 (*parado*) standing still, stopped. 2 (*arrestado*) detained. 3 (*minucioso*) detailed, thorough. II *nm,f* detainee, person under arrest.
◆**detenidamente** *adv* carefully, thoroughly.

detenimiento *nm* **con d.**, carefully, thoroughly.

detentar *vtr* to hold.

detergente *adj & nm* detergent.

deteriorar I *vtr* to spoil, damage. II **deteriorarse** *vr* 1 (*estropearse*) to get damaged. 2 (*empeorar*) to get worse.

deterioro *nm* 1 (*empeoramiento*) deterioration, worsening. 2 (*daño*) damage; **ir en d. de**, to be to the detriment of.

determinación *nf* 1 determination; **con d.**, determinedly. 2 (*decisión*) decision.

determinado,-a *adj* 1 (*preciso*) definite, precise. 2 (*resuelto*) decisive, resolute. 3 *Ling* definite.

determinante *adj* decisive.

determinar I *vtr* 1 (*fecha etc*) to fix, set. 2 (*decidir*) to decide on. 3 (*condicionar*) to determine. 4 (*ocasionar*) to bring about. II **determinarse** *vr* to make up one's mind to.

detestable *adj* detestable, repulsive.

detestar *vtr* to detest, hate.

detonante *nm* detonator; *fig* trigger.

detonar *vtr* to detonate.

detractor,-a *nm,f* detractor.

detrás *adv* 1 behind, on o at the back (**de, of**). 2 **d. de**, behind.

detrimento *nm* detriment; **en d. de**, to the detriment of.

detuve *pt indef* → **detener**.

deuda *nf* debt; **estoy en d. contigo**, (*monetaria*) I am in debt to you; (*moral*) I am indebted to you; **d. del Estado**, public debt; **d. pública**, national debt.

deudor,-a I *adj* indebted. II *nm,f* debtor.

devaluación *nf* devaluation.

devaluar [30] *vtr* to devalue.

devanar I *vtr* (*hilo*) to wind; (*alambre*) to coil. II **devanarse** *vr fam* d. los sesos, to rack one's brains.

devaneo *nm* dabbling.

devastador,-a *adj* devastating.

devastar *vtr* to devastate, ravage.

devengar [7] *vtr Com* to earn, accrue.

devenir [27] *vi* to become.

devoción *nf* 1 *Rel* devoutness. 2 (*al trabajo etc*) devotion; *fam* **Juan no es santo de mi d.**, Juan isn't really my cup of tea.

devolución *nf* 1 giving back, return; *Com* refund, repayment. 2 *Jur* devolution.

devolver [4] I *vtr* (*pp* **devuelto**) 1 to give back, return; (*dinero*) to refund. II *vi* (*vomitar*) to vomit, throw o bring up. II **devolverse** *vr Am* to go o come back, return.

devorar *vtr* to devour.

devoto,-a I *adj* pious, devout. II *nm,f* 1 *Rel* pious person. 2 (*seguidor*) devotee.

devuelto,-a *pp de* → **devolver**.

DF *nm abr de* **Distrito Federal**, Federal District.

DGS *nf* 1 *abr de* **Dirección General de Seguridad**, government department responsible for National Security. 2 *abr de* **Dirección General de Sanidad**, government department responsible for Public Health.

DGT *nf abr de* **Dirección General de Tráfico**, government department responsible for Traffic.

di 1 *pt indef* → **dar**. 2 *imperat* → **decir**.

día *nm* day; **¿qué d. es hoy?**, what's the date today?; **d. a d.**, day by day; **de d.**, by day; **durante el d.**, during the daytime; **de un d. para otro**, overnight; **un d. sí y otro no**, every other day; **pan del d.**, fresh bread; **hoy (en) d.**, nowadays; **el d. de mañana**, in the future; *fig* **estar al d.**, to be up to date; *fig* **poner al d.**, to bring up to date; **d. festivo**, holiday; **d. laborable**, working day; **d. libre**, free day, day off; **es de d.**, it is daylight; **hace buen/mal d.**, it's a nice/bad day, the weather is nice/bad today.

diabetes nf diabetes.
diabético,-a adj & nm,f diabetic.
diablo nm devil; fam ¡**al d. con ...!**, to hell with ...!; fam **vete al d.**, get lost; fam ¿**qué/cómo diablos ...?**, what/how the hell ...?
diablura nf mischief.
diácono nm deacon.
diadema nf tiara.
diáfano,-a adj clear.
diafragma nm diaphragm; Fot aperture; Med cap.
diagnosis nf inv diagnosis.
diagnosticar [1] vtr to diagnose.
diagnóstico nm diagnosis.
diagonal adj & nf diagonal; **en d.**, diagonally.
diagrama nm diagram; Inform d. de flujo, flowchart.
dial nm dial.
dialecto nm dialect.
dialogar [7] vi to have a conversation; (para negociar) to talk.
diálogo nm dialogue.
diamante nm diamond.
diámetro nm diameter.
diana nf 1 Mil reveille. 2 (blanco) bull's eye.
diapositiva nf slide.
diario,-a I nm 1 Prensa (daily) newspaper. 2 (memorias) diary; Náut **d. de a bordo**, **d. de navegación**, logbook. II adj daily; **a d.**, daily, every day. ◆**diariamente** adv daily, every day.
diarrea nf diarrhoea, US diarrhea.
diatriba nf diatribe.
dibujante nmf 1 drawer. 2 (de cómic) cartoonist. 3 Téc (hombre) draughtsman, US draftsman; (mujer) draughtswoman, US draftswoman.
dibujar vtr to draw.
dibujo nm 1 drawing; **dibujos animados**, cartoons. 2 (arte) drawing; **d. artístico**, artistic drawing; **d. lineal**, draughtsmanship.
diccionario nm dictionary; **buscar/mirar una palabra en el d.**, to look up a word in the dictionary.
dicha nf happiness.
dicharachero,-a adj talkative and witty.
dicho,-a adj 1 said; **mejor d.**, or rather; **d. de otro modo**, to put it another way; **d. sea de paso**, let it be said in passing; **d. y hecho**, no sooner said than done. 2 **dicha persona**, (mencionado) the above mentioned person.
dichoso,-a adj 1 (feliz) happy. 2 fam damned; ¡**este d. trabajo!**, this damned job!
diciembre nm December.
dictado nm dictation fig **dictados**, dictates.
dictador,-a nm,f dictator.
dictadura nf dictatorship.

dictáfono® nm Dictaphone®.
dictamen nm (juicio) ruling; (informe) report.
dictaminar vi to rule (sobre, on).
dictar vtr 1 to dictate. 2 (ley) to enact; (sentencia) to pass.
dictatorial adj dictatorial.
didáctica,-a adj didactic.
diecinueve adj & nm inv nineteen.
dieciocho adj & nm inv eighteen.
dieciséis adj & nm inv sixteen.
diecisiete adj & nm inv* seventeen.
diente nm tooth; Téc cog; (de ajo) clove; **d. de leche**, milk tooth; **dientes postizos**, false teeth; fig **hablar entre dientes**, to mumble; fig **poner los dientes largos a algn**, to make sb green with envy.
diéresis nf inv diaeresis.
diesel adj & nm diesel.
diestra nf right hand.
diestro,-a adj 1 (hábil) skilful, US skillful, clever. 2 **a d. y siniestro**, right, left and centre. II nm Taur bullfighter, matador.
dieta nf 1 diet; **estar a d.**, to be on a diet. 2 **dietas**, expenses o subsistence allowance.
dietética nf dietetics sing.
dietista nmf dietician.
diez adj & nm inv ten.
difamación nf defamation, slander; (escrita) libel.
difamar vtr to defame, slander; (por escrito) to libel.
diferencia nf difference; **a d. de**, unlike.
diferencial I adj distinguishing. II nm differential.
diferenciar [12] I vtr to differentiate, distinguish (entre, between). II **diferenciarse** vr to differ (de, from), be different (de, from).
diferente I adj different (de, from, US than). II adv differently.
diferido,-a adj TV **en d.**, recorded.
difícil adj difficult, hard; **d. de creer/hacer**, difficult to believe/do; **es d. que venga**, it is unlikely that she'll come.
dificultad nf difficulty; (aprieto) trouble, problem.
dificultar vtr to make difficult.
dificultoso,-a adj difficult, hard.
difuminar vtr to blur.
difundir vtr, **difundirse** vr to spread.
difunto,-a I adj late, deceased. II nm,f deceased.
difusión nf 1 (de noticia) spreading; **tener gran d.**, to be widely broadcast. 2 Rad TV broadcasting.
difuso,-a adj diffuse.
digerir [5] vtr to digest; fig to assimilate.
digestión nf digestion; **corte de d.**, sudden indigestion.
digestivo,-a adj easy to digest.

digital *adj* digital; **huellas digitales,** fingerprints; **tocadiscos d.,** CD player.

digitalizar *vtr* digitize.

dígito *nm* digit.

dignarse *vr* to deign (**a,** to), condescend (**a,** to).

dignidad *nf* dignity.

digno,-a *adj* 1 *(merecedor)* worthy; **d. de admiración,** worthy of admiration; **d. de mención/verse,** worth mentioning/seeing. 2 *(decoroso)* decent, good.

digo *indic pres* → **decir.**

dije *pt indef* → **decir.**

dilación *nf* delay, hold-up; **sin d.,** without delay.

dilatado,-a *adj* 1 *(agrandado)* dilated. 2 *(vasto)* vast, extensive.

dilatar I *vtr* 1 *(agrandar)* to expand. 2 *(pupila)* to dilate. II **dilatarse** *vr* 1 *(agrandarse)* to expand. 2 *(pupila)* to dilate.

dilema *nm* dilemma.

diligencia *nf* 1 diligence; **con d.,** diligently. 2 **diligencias,** formalities.

diligente *adj* diligent.

dilucidar *vtr* to elucidate, clarify.

diluir [37] I *vtr* to dilute. II **diluirse** *vr* to dilute.

diluviar [12] *v impers* to pour with rain.

diluvio *nm* flood; **el D. (Universal),** the Flood.

diluyo *indic pres* → **diluir.**

dimensión *nf* 1 dimension, size; **de gran d.,** very large. 2 *fig (importancia)* importance.

diminutivo,-a *adj & nm* diminutive.

diminuto,-a *adj* minute, tiny.

dimisión *nm* resignation; **presentar la d.,** to hand in one's resignation.

dimitir *vi* to resign (**de,** from); **d. de un cargo,** to give in *o* tender one's resignation.

Dinamarca *n* Denmark.

dinámica *nf* dynamics *sing.*

dinámico,-a *adj* dynamic.

dinamita *nf* dynamite.

dinamitar *vtr* to dynamite.

dinamo, dínamo *nf* dynamo.

dinar *nm Fin* dinar.

dinastía *nf* dynasty.

dineral *nm fam* fortune.

dinero *nm* money; **d. contante (y sonante),** cash; **d. efectivo** *o* **en metálico,** cash; **gente de d.,** wealthy people.

dinosaurio *nm* dinosaur.

diócesis *nf inv* diocese.

dios *nm* god; **¡D. mío!,** my God!; **¡por D.!,** for goodness sake!; **a la buena de D.,** any old how; **hacer algo como D. manda,** to do sth properly; *arg* **ni d.,** nobody; *arg* **todo d.,** everybody.

diosa *nf* goddess.

diploma *nm* diploma.

diplomacia *nf* diplomacy.

diplomarse *vr* to graduate.

diplomático,-a I *adj* diplomatic; **cuerpo d.,** diplomatic corps. II *nm,f* diplomat.

diptongo *nm* diphthong.

diputación *nf* **d. provincial,** ≈ county council.

diputado,-a *nm,f* ≈ Member of Parliament, M.P.; *US (hombre)* Congressman; *(mujer)* Congresswoman; **Congreso de Diputados,** ≈ House of Commons, *US* Congress; **d. provincial,** ≈ county councillor.

dique *nm* dike.

diré *fut* → **decir.**

dirección *nf* 1 direction; **d. prohibida,** no entry; **calle de d. única,** one-way street. 2 *(señas)* address. 3 *Cin Teat* direction. 4 *(destino)* destination. 5 *Aut Téc* steering. 6 *(dirigentes)* management; *(cargo)* directorship; *(de un partido)* leadership; *(de un colegio)* headship.

directa *nf Aut* top gear.

directiva *nf* board of directors, management.

directivo,-a *adj* directive; **junta directiva,** board of directors.

directo,-a *adj* direct; *TV Rad* **en d.,** live. ◆**directamente** *adv* directly, straight away.

director,-a *nm,f* director; *(de colegio) (hombre)* headmaster; *(mujer)* headmistress; *(de periódico)* editor; **d. de cine,** (film) director; **d. de orquesta,** conductor; **d. gerente,** managing director.

directorio *nm Inform* directory.

directriz *nf* directive; *Mat* directrix.

dirigente I *adj* leading; **clase d.,** ruling class. II *nmf* leader.

dirigir [6] I *vtr* to direct; *(empresa)* to manage; *(negocio, colegio)* to run; *(orquesta)* to conduct; *(partido)* to lead; *(periódico)* to edit; *(coche, barco)* to steer; **d. la palabra a algn,** to speak to sb. II **dirigirse** *vr* 1 **d. a** *o* **hacia,** to go to, make one's way towards. 2 *(escribir)* to write; **diríjase al apartado de correos 42,** write to P.O. Box 42. 3 *(hablar)* to speak.

discapacidad *nf* disability.

discernir [5] *vtr* to discern.

disciplina *nf* discipline.

disciplinado,-a *adj* disciplined.

discípulo,-a *nm,f* disciple.

disco *nm* 1 disc, *US* disk; **d. de freno,** brake disc. 2 *Mús* record; **d. compacto,** compact disc. 3 *Inform* disk; **d. duro** *o* **fijo/flexible,** hard/floppy disk. 4 *Dep* discus. 5 *Tel* dial.

discográfico,-a *adj* **casa/compañía discográfica,** record company.

disconforme *adj* **estar d. con,** to disagree with.

discontinuo,-a *adj* discontinuous; *Aut* **línea discontinua,** broken line.

discordante adj discordant; **ser la nota d.**, to be the odd man out.

discordia nf discord; **la manzana de la d.**, the bone of contention; **sembrar d.**, to sow discord.

discoteca nf 1 (lugar) discotheque. 2 (colección) record collection.

discreción nf 1 discretion. 2 **a d.**, at will.

discrecional adj optional; **servicio d.**, special service.

discrepancia nf (desacuerdo) disagreement; (diferencia) discrepancy.

discrepar vi (disentir) to disagree (**de**, with; **en**, on); (diferenciarse) to be different (**en**, from).

discreto,-a adj 1 discreet. 2 (mediocre) average.

discriminación nf discrimination.

discriminar vtr 1 to discriminate against. 2 fml (diferenciar) to discriminate between, distinguish.

disculpa nf excuse; **dar disculpas**, to make excuses; **pedir disculpas a algn**, to apologize to sb.

disculpar I vtr to excuse. II **disculparse** vr to apologize (**por**, for).

discurrir vi 1 (reflexionar) to think. 2 fig (transcurrir) to pass, go by. 3 fml (río) to wander.

discurso nm speech; **dar o pronunciar un d.**, to make a speech.

discusión nf argument.

discutir I vi to argue (**de**, about). II vtr to discuss, talk about.

disecar [1] vtr 1 (animal) to stuff. 2 (planta) to dry.

diseminar vtr to disseminate, spread.

disentir [5] vi to dissent, disagree (**de**, with).

diseñar vtr to design.

diseño nm design; **d. de interiores**, interior design.

disertar vi to expound (**sobre**, on, upon).

disfraz nm disguise; (para fiesta) fancy dress; **fiesta de disfraces**, fancy dress party.

disfrazar [4] I vtr to disguise. II **disfrazarse** vr to disguise oneself; **d. de pirata**, to dress up as a pirate.

disfrutar I vi 1 (gozar) to enjoy oneself. 2 (poseer) to enjoy (**de**, -). II vtr to enjoy.

disgregar [7] vtr 1 to disintegrate, break up. 2 (dispersar) to disperse.

disgustado,-a adj upset, displeased.

disgustar I vtr to upset. II **disgustarse** vr 1 (molestarse) to get upset, be annoyed. 2 (dos amigos) to quarrel.

disgusto nm 1 (preocupación) upset; **llevarse un d.**, to get upset; **dar un d. a algn**, to upset sb. 2 (desgracia) trouble; a **d.**, unwillingly; **sentirse o estar a d.**, to feel ill at ease. 3 (desavenencia) fall-out.

disidente adj & nmf dissident.

disimulado,-a adj 1 (persona) sly, crafty.

2 (oculto) hidden, concealed.

◆**disimuladamente** adv surreptitiously.

disimular vtr to conceal, hide.

disimulo nm pretence.

disipar I vtr (niebla) to drive away; (temor, duda) to dispel. II **disiparse** vr (gaseosa) to go flat; (niebla, temor etc) to disappear.

disketera nf Inform disk drive.

dislexia nf dyslexia.

dislocar [1] vtr to dislocate.

disminución nf decrease.

disminuir [37] I vtr to reduce. II vi to diminish.

disolución nf dissolution.

disolvente adj & nm solvent.

disolver [4] (pp **disuelto**) vtr to dissolve.

disparar I vtr (pistola etc) to fire, (flecha, balón) to shoot; **d. a algn**, to shoot at sb. II **dispararse** vr 1 (arma) to go off, fire. 2 (precios) to rocket.

disparatado,-a adj absurd.

disparate nm 1 (dicho) nonsense; **decir disparates**, to talk nonsense. 2 (acto) foolish act.

disparidad nf disparity.

disparo nm shot; Dep **d. a puerta**, shot.

dispensar vtr 1 (disculpar) to pardon, forgive. 2 (eximir) to exempt.

dispersar I vtr to disperse; (esparcir) to scatter. II **dispersarse** vr to disperse.

disperso,-a adj (separado) dispersed; (esparcido) scattered.

displicencia nf condescension.

displicente adj condescending.

disponer [19] (pp **dispuesto**) I vtr 1 (arreglar) to arrange, set out. 2 (ordenar) to order. II vi **d. de**, to have at one's disposal. III **disponerse** vr to prepare, get ready.

disponible adj available.

disposición nf 1 (uso) disposal; **a su d.**, at your disposal o service. 2 (colocación) arrangement, layout. 3 **no estar en d. de**, not to be prepared to. 4 (orden) order, law.

dispositivo nm device.

dispuesto,-a adj 1 (ordenado) arranged. 2 (a punto) ready. 3 (decidido) determined; **no estar d.**, a, not to be prepared to. 4 **según lo d. por la ley**, in accordance with what the law stipulates.

disputa nf (discusión) argument; (contienda) contest.

disputar I vtr (premio) to compete for. 2 Dep (partido) to play. II **disputarse** vr (premio) to compete for.

disquete nm Inform diskette, floppy disk.

disquetera nf Inform disk drive.

distancia nf distance; **a d.**, from a distance.

distanciamiento nm distancing.

distanciar [12] I vtr to separate. II **distanciarse** vr to become separated; (de

otra persona) to distance oneself.
distante *adj* distant, far-off.
distar *vi* to be distant *o* away; *fig* to be far from; **dista mucho de ser perfecto,** it's far from (being) perfect.
distender [3] *vtr fig* to ease, relax.
distensión *nf Pol* détente.
distinción *nf* distinction; **a d. de,** unlike; **sin d. de,** irrespective of.
distinguido,-a *adj* distinguished.
distinguir [8] I *vtr* 1 *(diferenciar)* to distinguish. 2 *(reconocer)* to recognize. 3 *(honrar)* to honour, *US* honor. II *vi (diferenciar)* to discriminate. III **distinguirse** *vr* to distinguish oneself.
distintivo,-a I *adj* distinctive, distinguishing. II *nm* distinctive sign *o* mark.
distinto,-a *adj* different.
distorsión *nf* 1 distortion. 2 *Med* sprain.
distracción *nf* 1 entertainment; *(pasatiempo)* pastime, hobby. 2 *(descuido)* distraction, absent-mindedness.
distraer [25] I *vtr* 1 *(atención)* to distract. 2 *(divertir)* to amuse. II **distraerse** *vr* 1 *(divertirse)* to amuse oneself. 2 *(abstraerse)* to let one's mind wander.
distraído,-a *adj* 1 *(divertido)* entertaining. 2 *(abstraído)* absent-minded.
distribución *nf* 1 distribution. 2 *(disposición)* layout.
distribuidor,-a I *adj* distributing. II *nm,f* 1 distributor. 2 *Com* wholesaler.
distribuir [37] *vtr* to distribute; *(trabajo)* to share out.
distrito *nm* district; **d. postal,** postal district.
disturbio *nm* riot, disturbance.
disuadir *vtr* to dissuade.
disuasión *nf* dissuasion.
disuelto,-a *pp* → **disolver**.
DIU *nm abr de* **dispositivo intrauterino,** intrauterine device, IUD.
diurético,-a *adj & nm* diuretic.
diurno,-a *adj* daytime.
divagar [7] *vi* to digress, wander.
diván *nm* divan, couch.
divergencia *nf* divergence.
divergente *adj* diverging.
diversidad *nf* diversity.
diversificar [1] I *vtr* to diversify. II **diversificarse** *vr* to be diversified *o* varied; *(empresa)* to diversify.
diversión *nf* fun.
diverso,-a *adj* different; **diversos,** several, various.
divertido,-a *adj* amusing, funny.
divertir [5] I *vtr* to amuse, entertain. II **divertirse** *vr* to enjoy oneself, have a good time; **¡que te diviertas!,** enjoy yourself!, have fun!
dividendo *nm* dividend.
dividir I *vtr* to divide (**en,** into); *Mat* 15 **dividido entre 3,** 15 divided by 3. II **dividirse** *vr* to divide, split up.

divinidad *nf* divinity.
divino,-a *adj* divine.
divisa *nf* 1 *(emblema)* symbol, emblem. 2 *Com* **divisas,** foreign currency *sing*.
divisar *vtr* to make out, discern.
división *nf* division.
divisorio,-a *adj* dividing.
divorciado,-a I *adj* divorced. II *nm,f (hombre)* divorcé; *(mujer)* divorcée.
divorciar [12] I *vtr* to divorce. II **divorciarse** *vr* to get divorced; **se divorció de él,** she divorced him, she got a divorce from him.
divorcio *nm* divorce.
divulgación *nf* disclosure.
divulgar [7] *vtr* to disclose; *Rad TV* to broadcast.
DNI *nm abr de* **Documento Nacional de Identidad,** Identity Card, ID card.
do *nm* **Mús** *(de solfa)* doh, do; *(de escala diatónica)* C; **do de pecho,** high C.
doberman *nm* Doberman (pinscher).
dobladillo *nm* hem.
doblaje *nm Cin* dubbing.
doblar I *vtr* 1 to double; **me dobla la edad,** he is twice as old as I am. 2 *(plegar)* to fold *o* turn up. 3 *(torcer)* to bend. 4 *(la esquina)* to go round. 5 *(película)* to dub. II *vi* 1 *(girar)* to turn; **d. a la derecha/izquierda,** to turn right/left. 2 *(campanas)* to toll. III **doblarse** *vr* 1 *(plegarse)* to fold up. 2 *(torcerse)* to bend.
doble I *adj* double; **arma de d. filo,** double-edged weapon. II *nm* 1 double; **gana el d. que tú,** she earns twice as much as you do. 2 *Dep* **dobles,** doubles.
doblegar [7] I *vtr* to bend. II **doblegarse** *vr* to give in.
doblez [1] *nm (pliegue)* fold. II *nm & f fig* two-facedness, hypocrisy.
doce *adj & nm inv* twelve.
docena *nf* dozen.
docencia *nf* teaching.
docente *adj* teaching; **centro d.,** educational centre.
dócil *adj* docile.
doctor,-a *nm,f* doctor.
doctorado *nm Univ* doctorate, PhD.
doctrina *nf* doctrine.
documentación *nf* documentation; *(DNI, de conducir etc)* papers *pl*.
documental *adj & nm* documentary.
documentar I *vtr* to document. II **documentarse** *vr* to research (**sobre, -**), get information (**sobre,** about *o* on).
documento *nm* document; **d. nacional de identidad,** identity card.
dogma *nm* dogma.
dogmático,-a *adj & nm,f* dogmatic.
dogo *nm* bulldog.
dólar *nm* dollar.
dolencia *nf* ailment.
doler [4] I *vi* 1 to hurt, ache; **me duele la cabeza,** I've got toothache/a headache;

me duele la mano, my hand is sore. II **dolerse** *vr* to be sorry o sad.

dolido,-a *adj* estar **d.**, to be hurt.

dolor *nm* 1 *Med* pain; **d. de cabeza**, headache; **d. de muelas**, toothache. 2 *(pena)* grief, sorrow.

dolorido,-a *adj* 1 *(dañado)* sore, aching. 2 *(apenado)* hurt.

doloroso,-a *adj* painful.

domar *vtr* to tame; *(caballo)* to break in.

domesticar [1] *vtr* to domesticate; *(animal)* to tame.

doméstico,-a *adj* domestic; **animal d.**, pet.

domiciliación *nf* payment by standing order.

domiciliar [12] *vtr* 1 to house. 2 *Fin* to pay by standing order.

domiciliario,-a *adj* arresto **d.**, house arrest.

domicilio *nm* home, residence; *(señas)* address; **sin d. fijo**, of no fixed abode; **d. fiscal**, registered office.

dominación *nf* domination.

dominante *adj* 1 dominant. 2 *(déspota)* domineering.

dominar I *vtr* 1 to dominate, rule. 2 *(situación)* to control; *(idioma)* to speak very well; *(asunto)* to master; *(paisaje etc)* to overlook. II *vi* 1 to dominate. 2 *(resaltar)* to stand out. III **dominarse** *vr* to control oneself.

domingo *nm inv* Sunday; **D. de Resurrección** o **Pascua**, Easter Sunday.

dominguero,-a *nm,f fam (excursionista)* weekend tripper; *(conductor)* weekend driver.

dominical I *adj* Sunday. II *nm (suplemento)* Sunday supplement.

dominicano,-a *adj* & *nm,f* Dominican; **República Dominicana**, Dominican Republic.

dominio *nm* 1 *(poder)* control; *(de un idioma)* command; **d. de sí mismo**, self-control. 2 *(ámbito)* scope, sphere; **ser del d. público**, to be public knowledge. 3 *(territorio)* dominion.

dominó, dómino *nm* dominoes *pl*.

don[1] *nm* 1 *(habilidad)* gift, talent; **tener el d. de**, to have a knack for; **tener d. de gentes**, to get on well with people. 2 *(regalo)* present, gift.

don[2] *nm* Señor **D. José García**, Mr José García; **D. Fulano de Tal**, Mr So-and-So; **d. nadie**, a nobody.

donaire *nm* grace, elegance.

donante *nmf* donor; *Med* **d. de sangre**, blood donor.

donar *vtr fml* to donate; *(sangre)* to give.

donativo *nm* donation.

doncella *nf arc* 1 *(joven)* maid, maiden. 2 *(criada)* maid, housemaid.

dónde *adv interr* where; **¿de d. eres?**, where are you from?; **¿por d. se va a la playa?**, which way is it to the beach?

donde *adv rel* where; **a** o **en d.**, where; **de** o **desde d.**, from where; **está d. lo dejaste**, it is where you left it; *fam* **está d. su tía**, he's at his aunt's.

dondequiera *adv* everywhere; **d. que vaya**, wherever I go.

donostiarra I *adj* of o from San Sebastián. II *nmf* native of San Sebastián.

doña *nf* (Señora) **D. Leonor Benítez**, Mrs Leonor Benítez.

dopaje *nm Dep* drug taking.

dopar I *vtr (caballo etc)* to dope. II **doparse** *vr* to take drugs.

doping *nm Dep* drug taking.

doquier, doquiera *adv lit* por **d.**, everywhere.

dorada *nf (pez)* gilthead bream.

dorado,-a I *adj* golden. II *nm Téc* gilding.

dorar *vtr* 1 to gild. 2 *Culin* to brown.

dormido,-a *adj* 1 asleep; **quedarse d.**, to fall asleep; *(no despertarse)* to oversleep, sleep in. 2 *(pierna, brazo)* numb.

dormilón,-ona I *adj fam* sleepyheaded. II *nm,f* sleepyhead.

dormir [7] I *vi* to sleep; **tener ganas de d.**, to feel sleepy; II *vtr* **d. la siesta**, to have an afternoon nap. III **dormirse** *vr* to fall asleep; **se me ha dormido el brazo**, my arm has gone to sleep.

dormitar *vi* to doze, snooze.

dormitorio *nm* 1 *(de una casa)* bedroom. 2 *(de colegio, residencia)* dormitory; **ciudad d.**, dormitory town.

dorsal I *adj* espina **d.**, spine. II *nm Dep* number.

dorso *nm* back; **instrucciones al d.**, instructions over; **véase al d.**, see overleaf.

dos *adj* & *nm inv* two; **los d.**, both; **nosotros/vosotros d.**, both of us/you; *fam* **cada d. por tres**, every other minute; *fam* **en d. por tres**, in a flash.

doscientos,-as *adj* & *nm,f* two hundred.

dosel *nm* canopy.

dosificación *nf* dosage.

dosificar [1] *vtr* 1 to dose. 2 *(esfuerzos, energías)* to measure.

dosis *nf inv* dose.

dossier *nm* dossier.

dotación *nf (dinero)* grant; *(personal)* personnel, staff; *(de barco)* crew.

dotado,-a *adj* 1 *(persona)* gifted. 2 *(equipado)* equipped; **d. de**, provided with.

dotar *vtr* **d. de**, to provide with.

dote *nf* 1 *(de novia)* dowry. 2 **dotes**, *(talento)* gift *sing*, talent *sing*.

doy *indic prec* → **dar**.

DP *nm abr de* **distrito postal**, postal district, PD.

dpt. *abr de* **departamento**, department, Dept.

Dr. *abr de* **doctor**, doctor, Dr.

Dra. *abr de* **doctora**, doctor, Dr.

dragar [7] *vtr* to dredge.

dragón nm dragon.

drama nm drama.

dramático,-a adj dramatic.

dramatismo nm drama.

dramaturgo,-a nm,f playwright, dramatist.

drástico,-a adj drastic.

drenar vtr to drain.

driblar vtr to dribble.

droga nf drug; **d. blanda/dura**, soft/hard drug.

drogadicto,-a nm,f drug addict.

drogar [7] I vtr to drug. II **drogarse** vr to drug oneself, take drugs.

droguería nf hardware and household goods shop.

dto. abr de descuento, discount.

dual adj dual.

dualidad nf duality.

dubitativo,-a adj doubtful.

Dublín n Dublin.

dublinés,-esa I adj de o from Dublin. II nm,f Dubliner.

ducha nf shower; **darse/tomar una d.**, to take/have a shower.

ducharse vr to shower, have o take a shower.

ducho,-a adj expert; **ser d. en**, to be well versed in.

duda nf doubt; **sin d.**, without a doubt; **no cabe d.**, (there is) no doubt; **poner algo en d.**, to question sth; **sacar a algn de dudas**, to dispel sb's doubts.

dudar I vi 1 to doubt. 2 (vacilar) to hesitate (en, to); **dudaba entre ir o quedarme**, I hesitated whether to go o to stay. 3 **d. de algn**, (desconfiar) to suspect sb. II vtr to doubt.

dudoso,-a adj 1 **ser d.**, (incierto) to be uncertain o doubtful. 2 (indeciso) to be undecided. 3 (poco honrado) dubious.

duelo¹ nm (combate) duel.

duelo² nm (luto) mourning.

duende nm 1 (espíritu) goblin, elf. 2 (encanto) magic, charm.

dueña nf owner; (de pensión) landlady.

dueño nm owner; (de casa etc) landlord; fig **ser d. de sí mismo**, to be self-possessed.

Duero n el D., the Douro.

dulce I adj 1 (sabor) sweet. 2 (carácter, voz) gentle. 3 (metal) soft. 4 **agua d.**, fresh water. II nm 1 Culin (pastel) cake. 2 (caramelo) sweet, US candy.

dulzura nf 1 sweetness. 2 fig gentleness, softness.

duna nf dune.

dúo nm duet.

duodécimo,-a adj & nm,f twelfth.

dúplex nm 1 (piso) duplex, duplex apartment. 2 Telec linkup.

duplicado,-a I adj **por d.**, in duplicate. II nm duplicate, copy.

duplicar [1] I vtr to duplicate; (cifras) to double. II **duplicarse** vr to double.

duplo,-a adj & nm,f double.

duque nm duke.

duquesa nf duchess.

duración nf duration, length; **disco de larga d.**, long-playing record.

duradero,-a adj durable, lasting.

durante prep during; **d. el día**, during the day; **d. todo el día**, all day long; **viví en La Coruña d. un año**, I lived in La Coruña for a year.

durar vi 1 to last. 2 (ropa, calzado) to wear well, last.

durazno nm (fruto) peach; (árbol) peach tree.

dureza nf 1 hardness; (severidad) harshness, severity. 2 (callosidad) corn.

duro,-a I adj 1 hard; Dep **juego d.**, rough play. 2 (resistente) tough; (severo) hard. 3 (clima) harsh. 4 (moneda) five-peseta coin. III adv hard; **trabajar d.**, to work hard.

E

E, e [e] nf (la letra) E, e.

E abr de Este, East, E.

e conj (delante de palabras que empiecen por i o hi) and; **verano e invierno**, summer and winter.

ebanista nm cabinet-maker.

ébano nm ebony.

ebrio,-a adj inebriated; **e. de dicha**, drunk with joy.

ebullición nf boiling; **punto de e.**, boiling point.

eccema nm eczema.

echar I vtr 1 (lanzar) to throw; fig **e. una mano**, to give a hand; fig **e. una mirada/una ojeada**, to have a look/a quick look o

glance. 2 (carta) to post; (vino, agua) to pour; **e. sal al estofado**, to put salt in the stew; **e. gasolina al coche**, to put petrol in the car. 3 (expulsar) to throw out; (despedir) to sack, fire. 4 (humo, olor etc) to give off. 5 fam (película) to show. 6 **le echó 37 años**, he reckoned she was about 37. 7 **e. de menos o en falta**, to miss. 8 **e. abajo**, (edificio) to demolish. II vi (+ a + infin) (empezar) to begin to; **echó a correr**, he ran off.

III **echarse** vr 1 (tumbarse) to lie down; (lanzarse) to throw oneself; fig **la noche se nos echó encima**, it was night before we knew it. 2 **échate a un lado**, stand aside; *fig* **e. atrás**, to get cold feet. **3** *fam* **e. novio/novia**, to get a boyfriend/girlfriend. **4** (+ **a** + *infin*) (*empezar*) to begin to; **e. a llorar**, to burst into tears; **e. a reír**, to burst out laughing; **e. a perder**, (*comida*) to go bad.

ecléctico,-a *adj & nm,f* eclectic.

eclesiástico,-a I *adj* ecclesiastical. **II** *nm* clergyman.

eclipsar *vtr* to eclipse.

eclipse *nm* eclipse.

eco *nm* echo; *fig* **hacerse e. de una noticia**, to publish an item of news; **tener e.**, to arouse interest.

ecografía *nf* scan.

ecología *nf* ecology.

ecológico,-a *adj* ecological.

ecologista I *adj* ecological; *Pol* **partido e.**, ecology party. **II** *nmf* ecologist.

economía *nf* **1** economy; **con e.**, economically. **2** (*ciencia*) economics.

económico,-a *adj* **1** economic. **2** (*barato*) economical, inexpensive. **3** (*persona*) thrifty.

economista *nmf* economist.

economizar [4] *vtr & vi* to economize.

ecosistema *nm* ecosystem.

ecuación *nf* equation.

Ecuador *n* Ecuador.

ecuador *nm Geog* equator.

ecualizador *nm* graphic equalizer.

ecuánime *adj* **1** (*temperamento*) equable, even-tempered. **2** (*juicio*) impartial.

ecuatorial *adj* equatorial; **Guinea E.**, Ecuatorial Guinea.

ecuatoriano,-a *adj & nm,f* Ecuadorian.

ecuestre *adj* equestrian.

ecuménico,-a *adj* ecumenical.

eczema *nm* eczema.

edad *nf* age; **¿qué e. tienes?**, how old are you?; **la tercera e.**, senior citizens *pl*; **E. Media**, Middle Ages *pl*.

edición *nf* **1** (*publicación*) publication; (*de sellos*) issue. **2** (*conjunto de ejemplares*) edition.

edicto *nm* edict, proclamation.

edificante *adj* edifying.

edificar [1] *vtr* to build.

edificio *nm* building.

edil,-a *nm,f* town councillor.

Edimburgo *n* Edinburgh.

editar *vtr* **1** (*libro, periódico*) to publish; (*disco*) to release. **2** *Inform* to edit.

editor,-a I *adj* publishing. **II** *nm,f* publisher.

editorial I *adj* publishing. **II** *nf* publishers, publishing house. **III** *nm Prensa* editorial, leader article.

edredón *nm* continental quilt, duvet, *US* comforter.

educación *nf* **1** education. **2** (*formación*) upbringing. **3** **buena/mala e.**, (*modales*) good/bad manners; **falta de e.**, bad manners.

educado,-a *adj* polite.

educador,-a I *adj* educating. **II** *nm,f* educationalist.

educar [1] *vtr* (*hijos*) to raise; (*alumnos*) to educate; (*la voz*) to train.

educativo,-a *adj* educational; **sistema e.**, education system.

edulcorante *nm* sweetener.

EE.UU. *abr de* **Estados Unidos**, United States of America, USA.

efectista *adj* spectacular.

efectividad *nf* effectiveness.

efectivo,-a I *adj* effective; **hacer algo e.**, to carry sth out; *Fin* **hacer e. un cheque**, to cash a cheque. **II** *nm* **1** *Fin* **en e.**, in cash. **2 efectivos,** *Mil* forces. ◆**efectivamente** *adv* quite!, yes indeed!

efecto *nm* **1** (*resultado*) effect; **efectos especiales/sonoros**, special/sound effects; **efectos personales**, personal belongings *o* effects; **a efectos de ...**, for the purposes of ...; **en e.**, quite!, yes indeed! **2** (*impresión*) impression; **causar** *o* **hacer e.**, to make an impression. **3** *Dep* spin.

efectuar [30] *vtr* to carry out; (*viaje*) to make; *Com* (*pedido*) to place.

efeméride *nf* event.

efervescente *adj* effervescent; **aspirina e.**, soluble aspirin.

eficacia *nf* (*de persona*) efficiency; (*de remedio etc*) effectiveness.

eficaz *adj* (*persona*) efficient; (*remedio, medida etc*) effective.

eficiencia *nf* efficiency.

eficiente *adj* efficient.

efigie *nf* effigy.

efímero,-a *adj* ephemeral.

efusivo,-a *adj* effusive.

EGB *nf Educ abr de* **Enseñanza General Básica**, ≃ Primary School Education.

Egeo *n* el (**Mar**) **E.**, the Aegean Sea.

egipcio,-a *adj & nm,f* Egyptian.

Egipto *n* Egypt.

egocéntrico,-a *adj* egocentric, self-centred.

egoísmo *nm* egoism, selfishness.

egoísta I *adj* ego(t)istic, selfish. **II** *nmf* ego(t)ist, selfish person.

egregio,-a *adj* eminent, illustrious.

egresar *vi Am* to leave school, *US* graduate.

Eire *n* Eire, Republic of Ireland.

ej. *abr de* **ejemplo**, example.

eje *nm* **1** *Téc* (*de rueda*) axle; (*de máquina*) shaft. **2** *Mat* axis. **3** *Hist* **El E.**, the Axis.

ejecución *nf* **1** (*de orden*) carrying out. **2** (*ajusticiamiento*) execution. **3** *Mús* performance.

ejecutar *vtr* **1** (*orden*) to carry out. **2** (*ajusticiar*) to execute. **3** *Mús* to perform, play. **4** *Inform* to run.

ejecutiva *nf Pol* executive.

ejecutivo,-a I adj executive; Pol el poder e., the government. II nm executive.

ejecutor,-a nm,f 1 Jur executor. 2 (verdugo) executioner.

ejemplar I nm 1 (de libro) copy; (de revista, periódico) number, issue. 2 (especimen) specimen. II adj exemplary, model.

ejemplificar [1] vtr to exemplify.

ejemplo nm example; **por e.**, for example; **dar e.**, to set an example.

ejercer [2] I vtr 1 (profesión etc) to practise. 2 (influencia) to exert. 3 **e. el derecho de/a ...**, to exercise one's right to .... II vi to practise (**de, as**).

ejercicio nm 1 exercise; (de profesión) practice; **hacer e.**, to take o do exercise. 2 Fin tax year; **e. económico**, financial o fiscal year.

ejercitar vtr to practise.

ejército nm army.

el I art def m 1 the. 2 (no se traduce) **el Sr. García**, Mr. Garcia; **el hambre/destino**, hunger/fate. 3 (con partes del cuerpo, prendas de vestir) **me he cortado el dedo**, I've cut my finger; **métetelo en el bolsillo**, put it in your pocket. 4 (con días de la semana) **el lunes**, on Monday. II pron 1 the one; **el de las once**, the eleven o'clock one; **el que tienes en la mano**, the one you've got in your hand; **el que quieras**, whichever one you want. 2 (no se traduce) **el de tu amigo**, your friend's.

él pron pers 1 (sujeto) (persona) he; (animal, cosa) it. 2 (complemento) (persona) him; (animal, cosa) it.

elaboración nf 1 (de un producto) manufacture, production. 2 (de una idea) working out, development.

elaborar vtr 1 (producto) to manufacture, produce. 2 (teoría) to develop.

elasticidad nf elasticity; fig flexibility.

elástico,-a adj & nm elastic.

elección nf choice; Pol election.

elector,-a nm,f elector.

electorado nm electorate pl.

electoral adj electoral; **campaña e.**, election campaign; **colegio e.**, polling station.

electoralismo nm electioneering.

electricidad nf electricity.

electricista nmf electrician.

eléctrico,-a adj electric.

electrificar [1] vtr to electrify.

electrizar [4] vtr to electrify.

electrochoque nm electric shock therapy.

electrocutar vtr to electrocute.

electrodo nm electrode.

electrodoméstico nm (domestic) electrical appliance.

electroimán nm electromagnet.

electromagnético,-a adj electromagnetic.

electrón nm electron.

electrónica nf electronics sing.

electrónico,-a adj electronic.

elefante nm elephant.

elegancia nf elegance.

elegante adj elegant.

elegía nf elegy.

elegir [6] vtr 1 to choose. 2 Pol to elect.

elemental adj 1 (fundamental) basic, fundamental. 2 (simple) elementary.

elemento nm 1 element. 2 (componente) component, part. 3 (individuo) type, individual. 4 **elementos**, elements; (fundamentos) rudiments.

elepé nm LP (record).

elevación nf elevation; **e. de precios**, rise in prices; **e. del terreno**, rise in the ground.

elevado,-a adj 1 high; (edificio) tall. 2 (pensamiento etc) lofty, noble.

elevalunas nm inv Aut **e. eléctrico**, electric windows.

elevar I vtr to raise. II **elevarse** vr 1 (subir) to rise; (edificio) to stand. 2 **e. a**, (cantidad) to amount o come to.

elijo etc pres → **elegir**.

eliminación nf elimination.

eliminar vtr to eliminate.

eliminatoria nf Dep heat, qualifying round.

eliminatorio,-a adj qualifying, eliminatory.

élite nf elite, élite.

elitista adj elitist.

elixir nm (enjuague bucal) mouthwash; Lit elixir.

ella pron pers f 1 (sujeto) she; (animal, cosa) it, she. 2 (complemento) her; (animal, cosa) it, her.

ellas pron pers fpl → **ellos**.

ello pron pers neut it; **por e.**, for that reason.

ellos pron pers mpl 1 (sujeto) they. 2 (complemento) them.

elocuencia nf eloquence.

elocuente adj eloquent; **los hechos son elocuentes**, the facts speak for themselves.

elogiar [12] vtr to praise.

elogio nm praise.

elote nm Am tender corncob.

El Salvador n El Salvador.

elucidar vtr to elucidate.

eludir vtr to avoid.

emanar vtr to emanate; fig (derivar) to derive o come (**de**, from).

emancipar I vtr to emancipate. II **emanciparse** vr to become emancipated.

embadurnar vtr to daub, smear (**de**, with).

embajada nf embassy.

embajador,-a nm,f ambassador.

embalaje nm packing, packaging.

embalar vtr to pack.

embalarse vr to speed up; fig **no te embales**, hold your horses.

embalsamar vtr to embalm.

embalsar I *vtr* to dam; *(problema)* to contain. **II embalsarse** *vr* to form a pool.

embalse *nm* dam, reservoir.

embarazada I *adj* pregnant; **dejar e.,** to get pregnant. **II** *nf* pregnant woman, expectant mother.

embarazar [4] *vtr fig* to hinder.

embarazo *nm* **1** *(preñez)* pregnancy. **2** *(obstáculo)* obstacle. **3** *(turbación)* embarrassment.

embarazoso,-a *adj* awkward, embarrassing.

embarcación *nf* **1** *(nave)* boat, craft. **2** *(embarco)* embarkation.

embarcadero *nm* quay.

embarcar [1] **I** *vtr* to ship. **II** *vi* to embark, go on board. **III embarcarse** *vr* **1** *Náut* to go on board **(en,** -); *Av* to board **(en,** -). **2 e. en un proyecto,** to embark on a project.

embarco *nm* embarkation.

embargar [7] *vtr* **1** *Jur* to seize, impound. **2** *fig* **le embarga la emoción,** he's overwhelmed with joy.

embargo *nm* **1** *Jur* seizure of property. **2** *Com Pol* embargo. **3 sin e.,** however, nevertheless.

embarque *nm* *(de persona)* boarding; *(de mercancías)* loading; **tarjeta de e.,** boarding card.

embarrancar(se) [1] *vi & vr Náut* to run aground.

embaucador,-a I *adj* deceitful. **II** *nm,f* swindler, cheat.

embaucar [1] *vtr* to swindle, cheat.

embeber I *vtr* to soak up. **II embeberse** *vr* to become absorbed *o* engrossed.

embelesar *vtr* to fascinate.

embellecer [33] *vtr* to embellish.

embestida *nf* **1** onslaught. **2** *Taur* charge.

embestir [6] *vtr* **1** *Taur* to charge. **2** *(atacar)* to attack.

emblandecer [33] **I** *vtr* to soften. **II emblandecerse** *vr fig* to relent.

emblema *nm* emblem.

embobado,-a *adj* fascinated.

embobarse *vr* to be fascinated *o* besotted **(con, de,** by).

embolia *nf* embolism.

émbolo *nm* piston.

embolsar, embolsarse *vr* to pocket.

emborrachar *vtr,* **emborracharse** *vr* to get drunk.

emboscada *nf* ambush; **tender una e.,** to lay an ambush.

embotar *vtr* to blunt; *fig (sentidos)* to dull; *(mente)* to befuddle.

embotellado *nm* bottling.

embotellamiento *nm Aut* traffic jam.

embotellar *vtr* **1** to bottle. **2** *(tráfico)* to block.

embragar [7] *vi Aut* to engage the clutch.

embrague *nm* clutch.

embravecerse [33] *vr* **1** *(enfadarse)* to become enraged. **2** *(mar)* to become rough.

embriagador,-a *adj* intoxicating.

embriagar [7] **I** *vtr* to intoxicate; *fig* to enrapture. **II embriagarse** *vr* to get drunk; *fig* to be enraptured.

embriaguez *nf* intoxication.

embridar *vtr* to bridle.

embrión *nm* embryo.

embrollar I *vtr* to confuse, muddle. **II embrollarse** *vr* to get muddled *o* confused.

embrollo *nm* **1** *(lío)* muddle, confusion. **2** *(aprieto)* fix, jam.

embrujado,-a *adj* *(persona)* bewitched; *(sitio)* haunted.

embrujo *nm* spell, charm; *fig* attraction, fascination.

embrutecer [33] *vtr* to stultify.

embuchar *vtr* to stuff.

embudo *nm* funnel.

embuste *nm* lie, trick.

embustero,-a *nm,f* cheater, liar.

embutido *nm* sausage.

embutir I *vtr* **1** *(carne)* to stuff. **2** *(meter)* to stuff *o* cram **(en,** into). **3** *(incrustar)* to inlay.

emergencia *nf* emergency; **salida de e.,** emergency exit; **en caso de e.,** in an emergency.

emerger [5] *vi* to emerge.

emigración *nf* emigration; *(de pájaros)* migration.

emigrado,-a *nm,f* emigrant; *Pol* émigré.

emigrante *adj & nmf* emigrant.

emigrar *vi* to emigrate; *(pájaros)* to migrate.

eminencia *nf* eminence; *(genio)* genius.

eminente *adj* eminent.

emirato *nm* emirate.

emisario,-a *nm,f* emissary.

emisión *nf* **1** emission. **2** *(de bonos, sellos)* issue. **3** *Rad TV* broadcasting.

emisora *nf* radio *o* television station.

emitir *vtr* **1** to emit; *(luz, calor)* to give off. **2** *(opinión, juicio)* to express. **3** *Rad TV* to transmit. **4** *(bonos, sellos)* to issue.

emoción *nf* **1** emotion. **2** *(excitación)* excitement; **¡qué e.!,** how exciting!

emocionado,-a *adj* deeply moved *o* touched.

emocionante *adj* **1** *(conmovedor)* moving, touching. **2** *(excitante)* exciting, thrilling.

emocionar I *vtr* **1** *(conmover)* to move, touch. **2** *(excitar)* to thrill. **II emocionarse** *vr* **1** *(conmoverse)* to be moved. **2** *(excitarse)* to get excited.

emotivo,-a *adj* emotional.

empacar [1] *vtr* **1** *(mercancías)* to pack. **2** *Am* to annoy.

empachar *vtr* to give indigestion to.

empacho *nm* *(de comida)* indigestion, upset stomach; *fig* surfeit.

empadronar, empadronarse *vr* to register.

empalagar [7] *vi* to pall.
empalagoso,-a *adj* 1 (*dulce*) sickly sweet.
2 *fig* (*persona*) smarmy.
empalizada *nf* fence.
empalmar I *vtr* 1 (*unir*) to join; (*cuerdas, cables*) to splice. 2 *Ftb* to volley. II *vi* to converge; *Ferroc* to connect. III **empalmarse** *vr vulg* to get a hard-on.
empalme *nm* 1 connection. 2 *Ferroc* junction; (*en carretera*) intersection, T-junction.
empanada *nf* pie.
empanadilla *nf* pasty.
empanado,-a *adj* (*filete etc*) breaded, in breadcrumbs.
empantanarse *vr* 1 (*inundarse*) to become flooded. 2 *fig* to be bogged down.
empañar *vtr*, **empañarse** *vr* (*cristales*) to steam up.
empapado,-a *adj* soaked.
empapar I *vtr* 1 (*mojar*) to soak. 2 (*absorber*) to soak up. II **emparparse** *vr* 1 (*persona*) to get soaked. 3 *fam fig* to take in (**de,** -).
empapelar *vtr* to wallpaper.
empaque *nm* bearing, presence.
empaquetar *vtr* to pack.
emparedado *nm* sandwich.
emparejar *vtr* 1 (*cosas*) to match; (*personas*) to pair off.
empastar *vtr* (*diente*) to fill.
empaste *nm* (*de diente*) filling.
empatado,-a *adj* drawn; **estar/ir empatados,** to be drawing.
empatar I *vi Dep* to tie, draw. II *vtr* 1 *Dep* **e. el partido,** to equalize. 2 *Am* (*unir*) to join.
empate *nm Dep* draw, tie.
empecinarse *vr* to dig one's heels in.
empedernido,-a *adj* (*fumador, bebedor*) hardened.
empedrado,-a I *adj* cobbled. III *nm* 1 (*adoquines*) cobblestones *pl.* 2 (*acción*) paving.
empeine *nm* instep.
empellón *nm* push, shove.
empeñar I *vtr* to pawn, *US* hock. II **empeñarse** *vr* 1 (*insistir*) to insist (**en,** on), be determined (**en,** to). 2 (*endeudarse*) to get into debt.
empeño *nm* 1 (*insistencia*) insistence; **poner e. en algo,** to put a lot of effort into sth. 2 (*deuda*) pledge; **casa de empeños,** pawnshop.
empeoramiento *nm* deterioration, worsening.
empeorar I *vi* to deteriorate, worsen. II *vtr* to make worse. III **empeorarse** *vr* to deteriorate, worsen.
empequeñecer [33] *vtr fig* to belittle.
emperador *nm* emperor.
emperatriz *nf* empress.
emperifollarse *vr fam* to get dolled up.
emperrarse *vr* to dig one's heels in, be-

come stubborn.
empezar [1] *vtr & vi* (a hacer algo) to begin; (*algo*) to start, commence.
empinado,-a *adj* (*cuesta*) steep.
empinar I *vtr* to raise; *fam* **e. el codo,** to drink. II **empinarse** *vr* (*persona*) to stand on tiptoe.
empírico,-a *adj* empirical.
emplasto *nm* poultice.
emplazamiento *nm* 1 (*colocación*) site, location. 2 *Jur* summons *sing.*
emplazar¹ [4] *vtr* to locate, situate.
emplazar² [4] *vtr* 1 *Jur* to summons. 2 (*a una reunión etc*) to call.
empleado,-a *nm,f* employee; (*de oficina, banco*) clerk; **empleada del hogar,** servant, maid.
emplear I *vtr* 1 (*usar*) to use; (*contratar*) to employ. 2 (*dinero, tiempo*) to spend.
empleo *nm* 1 (*oficio*) job; *Pol* employment. 2 (*uso*) use; **modo de e.,** instructions for use.
emplomar *vtr Am* (*diente*) to fill.
empobrecer [33] I *vi* to impoverish. II **empobrecerse** *vr* to become impoverished *o* poor.
empobrecimiento *nm* impoverishment.
empollar *vtr* 1 (*huevos*) to sit on. 2 *fam* (*estudiar*) to swot (up), *US* bone up on.
empollón,-ona *fam* I *adj* swotty. II *nm,f* swot.
empolvar I *vtr* to cover in dust. II **empolvarse** *vr* (*la cara*) to powder.
emponzoñar *vtr* to poison.
emporcar [1] *vtr* to foul, dirty.
emporio *nm* 1 *Com* emporium, trading *o* commercial centre. 2 *Am* department store.
emporrarse *vr arg* to get high.
empotrado,-a *adj* fitted.
emprendedor,-a *adj* enterprising.
emprender *vtr* to undertake; *fam* **emprenderla con algn,** to pick on sb.
empresa *nf* 1 *Com Ind* firm, company. 2 *Pol* **la libre e.,** free enterprise. 3 (*tarea*) undertaking.
empresariado *nm* employers *pl.*
empresarial *adj* 1 (*de empresa*) business; (*ciencias*) **empresariales,** business studies. 2 (*espíritu*) entrepreneurial; **organización e.,** employers' organization.
empresario,-a *nm,f* 1 (*hombre*) businessman; (*mujer*) businesswoman. 2 (*patrón*) employer.
empréstito *nm Fin* debenture loan.
empujar *vtr* to push, shove.
empuje *nm* push; *fig* (*brío*) verve, get-up-and-go.
empujón *nm* push, shove; **dar empujones,** to push and shove.
empuñadura *nf* (*de espada*) hilt.
empuñar *vtr* to grasp, seize.
emular *vtr* to emulate.
emulsión *nf* emulsion.

en *prep* **1** (*posición*) in, on, at; **en Madrid/ Bolivia,** in Madrid/Bolivia; **en la mesa,** on the table; **en el bolso,** in the bag; **en casa/el trabajo,** at home/work. **2** (*movimiento*) into; **entró en el cuarto,** he went into the room. **3** (*tiempo*) in, on, at; **en 1940,** in 1940; **en verano,** in summer; *Am* **en la mañana,** in the morning; **cae en martes,** it falls on a Tuesday; **en ese momento,** at that moment. **3** (*transporte*) by, in; **en coche/tren,** by car/train; **en avión,** by air. **4** (*modo*) **en español,** in Spanish; **en broma,** jokingly; **en serio,** seriously. **5** (*reducción, aumento*) by; **los precios aumentaron en un diez por ciento,** the prices went up by ten percent. **6** (*tema, materia*) at, in; **bueno en deportes,** good at sports; **experto en política,** expert in politics. **7** (*división, separación*) in; **lo dividió en tres partes,** he divided it in three. **8** (*con infinitivo*) **fue rápido en responder,** he was quick to answer; **la conocí en el andar,** I recognized her by her walk; **ser sobrio en el vestir,** to dress simply.

enaguas *nfpl* underskirt *sing*, petticoat *sing*.

enajenación *nf*, **enajenamiento** *nm* alienation; **e. mental,** mental derangement, insanity.

enajenar I *vtr* **1** (*alienar*) *Jur* to alienate. **2** (*turbar*) to drive insane. II **enajenarse** *vr* (*enloquecer*) to go insane.

enaltecer [33] *vtr* **1** (*alabar*) to praise, extol. **2** (*ennoblecer*) to do credit to.

enamorado,-a I *adj* in love. II *nm,f* person in love.

enamorar I *vtr* to win the heart of. II **enamorarse** *vr* to fall in love (**de,** with).

enano,-a *adj & nm,f* dwarf.

enardecer [33] I *vtr* (*sentimientos*) to rouse, stir up; (*persona*) to fill with enthusiasm. II **enardecerse** *vr* fig to become excited.

encabezamiento *nm* (*de carta*) heading; (*de periódico*) headline; (*preámbulo*) foreword, preamble.

encabezar [4] *vtr* **1** (*carta, lista*) to head; (*periódico*) to lead. **2** (*rebelión, carrera, movimiento*) to lead.

encabritarse *vr* **1** (*caballo*) to rear (up). **2** *fig* (*persona*) to get cross.

encadenar *vtr* to chain.

encajar I *vtr* **1** (*ajustar*) to insert; **e. la puerta,** to push the door to. **2** *fam* (*asimilar*) to take. **3** (*comentario*) to get in; **e. un golpe a algn,** to land sb a blow. II I (*ajustarse*) to fit. **2** *fig* **e. con,** to fit (in) with, square with.

encaje *nm* lace.

encalar *vtr* to whitewash.

encallar *vi* **1** *Náut* to run aground. **2** *fig* to flounder, fail.

encaminado,-a *adj* estar **bien/mal e.,** to be on the right/wrong track.

encaminar I *vtr* to direct. II **encaminarse** *vr* to head (**a, for;** *hacia,* towards).

encandilar *vtr* to dazzle.

encantado,-a *adj* **1** (*contento*) delighted; **e. de conocerle,** pleased to meet you. **2** (*embrujado*) enchanted.

encantador,-a I *adj* charming, delightful. II *nm,f* magician.

encantamiento *nm* spell.

encantar *vtr* (*hechizar*) to bewitch, cast a spell on; *fig* **me encanta nadar,** I love swimming.

encanto *nm* **1** (*atractivo*) charm; **ser un e.,** to be charming. **2** (*hechizo*) spell.

encapricharse *vr* to set one's mind (**con,** on); (*encariñarse*) to take a fancy (**con,** to); (*enamorarse*) to get a crush (**con,** on).

encapuchado,-a *adj* hooded.

encaramarse *vr* to climb up.

encarar I *vtr* to face, confront. II **encararse** *vr* **e. con,** to face up to.

encarcelar *vtr* to imprison, jail.

encarecer [33] I *vtr* to put up the price of. II **encarecerse** *vr* to go up (in price).

encarecidamente *adv* earnestly, insistently; **le rogamos e. que ...,** we would earnestly request you to ....

encarecimiento *nm* increase *o* rise in price.

encargado,-a I *nm,f* Com (*hombre*) manager; (*mujer*) manager, manageress; (*responsable*) person in charge. II *adj* in charge.

encargar [7] I *vtr* **1** to put in charge of, entrust with. **2** Com (*mercancías*) to order, place an order for; (*encuesta*) to commission. II **encargarse** *vr* **e. de,** to see to, deal with.

encargo *nm* **1** Com order; **hecho de e.,** (*a petición*) made to order. **2** (*recado*) errand. **3** (*tarea*) job, assignment.

encariñarse *vr* to become fond (**con,** of), get attached (**con,** to).

encarnación *nf* incarnation, embodiment.

encarnado,-a *adj* (*rojo*) red.

encarnar *vtr* to personify, embody.

encarnizado,-a *adj* fierce.

encarrilar *vtr* (*coche, tren*) to put on the road *o* rails; *fig* to put on the right track.

encasillar *vtr* to pigeonhole.

encausar *vtr* to prosecute.

encauzar [4] *vtr* to channel.

encenagarse [7] *vr* to get covered in mud.

encendedor *nm* lighter.

encender [3] I *vtr* **1** (*luz, radio, tele*) to switch on, put on; (*cigarro, vela, fuego*) to light; (*cerilla*) to strike, light. **2** *fig* to inflame, stir up. II **encenderse** *vr* **1** (*fuego*) to catch; (*luz*) to go *o* come on. **2** (*cara*) to blush, go red.

encendido *nm* ignition.

encerado *nm* (*pizarra*) blackboard.

encerar *vtr* to wax, polish.

encerrar [1] I *vtr* 1 to shut in; (*con llave*) to lock in. 2 *fig* (*contener*) to contain, include. II **encerrarse** *vr* to shut oneself up *o* in; (*con llave*) to lock oneself in.

encestar *vi Dep* to score (a basket).

enchaquetado,-a *adj* smartly dressed.

encharcar [1] I *vtr* to flood, swamp. II **encharcarse** *vr* to get flooded.

enchilada *nf Culin* stuffed corn pancake seasoned with chili.

enchironar *vtr arg* to put away.

enchufado,-a I *adj fam* **estar e.**, to have good connections *o* contacts. III *nm,f fam* (*favorito*) pet.

enchufar *vtr* 1 *Elec* to plug in. 2 (*unir*) to join, connect. 3 *fam* (*para un trabajo*) to pull strings for.

enchufe *nm* 1 *Elec* (*hembra*) socket; (*macho*) plug. 2 *fam* contact.

enchufismo *nm fam* string-pulling.

encía *nf* gum.

enciclopedia *nf* encyclopaedia, encyclopedia.

encierro *nm Pol* (*protesta*) sit-in.

encima *adv* 1 on top; (*arriba*) above; (*en el aire*) overhead; **déjalo e.**, put it on top; **¿llevas cambio e.?**, do you have any change on you?; *fig* **quitarse algo de e.**, to get rid of sth; **ahí e.**, up there. 2 (*además*) besides. 3 **e. de**, (*sobre*) on; (*en el aire*) above; *fig* (*además*) besides; **e. de la mesa**, on the table. 4 **por e.**, above; *fig* **por e. de sus posibilidades**, beyond his abilities; **leer un libro por e.**, to skip through a book.

encimera *nf* (*de cocina*) worktop.

encina *nf* holm *o* evergreen oak, ilex.

encinta *adj* pregnant.

enclaustrarse *vr* to shut oneself up.

enclave *nm* enclave.

enclenque *adj* (*débil*) puny; (*enfermizo*) sickly.

encoger [5] I *vi* (*contraerse*) to contract; (*prenda*) to shrink. II *vtr* to contract; (*prenda*) to shrink. III **encogerse** *vr* (*contraerse*) to contract; (*prenda*) to shrink; **e. de hombros**, to shrug (one's shoulders).

encolar *vtr* (*papel*) to paste; (*madera*) to glue.

encolerizar [4] I *vtr* to infuriate, anger. II **encolerizarse** *vr* to become furious.

encomendar [1] I *vtr* to entrust with, put in charge of. II **encomendarse** *vr* to entrust oneself (**a**, to).

encomienda 1 *nf* assignment, mission. 2 (*paquete postal*) parcel.

encomio *nm* praise.

enconado,-a *adj* 1 (*discusión*) bitter, fierce. 2 *Med* inflamed, sore.

enconarse *vr* 1 (*exasperarse*) to get angry *o* irritated. 2 *Med* (*herida*) to become inflamed *o* sore.

encono *nm* spitefulness, ill feeling.

encontrado,-a *adj* (*contrario*) conflicting.

encontrar [2] I *vtr* 1 (*hallar*) to find; **no lo encuentro**, I can't find it; **lo encuentro muy agradable**, I find it very pleasant. 2 (*dar con*) to meet; (*problema*) to run into, come up against. II **encontrarse** *vr* 1 (*persona*) to meet. 2 (*sentirse*) to feel, be; **e. a gusto**, to feel comfortable. 3 (*estar*) to be.

encontronazo *nm* 1 (*choque*) collision, crash. 2 *fig* (*de ideas etc*) clash.

encorvar I *vtr* to bend. II **encorvarse** *vr* to stoop *o* bend (over).

encrespar I *vtr* 1 (*pelo*) to curl. 2 (*mar*) to make choppy *o* rough. 3 *fig* (*enfurecer*) to infuriate. II **encresparse** *vr* 1 (*mar*) to get rough. 2 *fig* (*enfurecerse*) to get cross *o* irritated.

encrucijada *nf* crossroads.

encrudecer [33] *vi*, **encrudecerse** *vr* to get worse.

encuadernación *nf* 1 (*oficio*) bookbinding. 2 (*cubierta*) binding.

encuadernador,-a *nm,f* bookbinder.

encuadernar *vtr* to bind.

encuadrar I *vtr* 1 (*imagen etc*) to frame. 2 *fig* (*encajar*) to fit, insert.

encuadre *nm Cin TV* framing.

encubierto,-a *adj* (*secreto*) hidden; (*operación*) covert.

encubridor,-a *nm,f Jur* accessory (after the fact), abettor.

encubrir *vtr* to conceal.

encuentro *nm* 1 encounter, meeting. 2 *Dep* meeting, match; **e. amistoso**, friendly match.

encuesta *nf* 1 (*sondeo*) (opinion) poll, survey. 2 (*investigación*) investigation, inquiry.

encuestador,-a *nm,f* pollster.

encuestar *vtr* to poll.

encumbrar I *vtr* to exalt. II **encumbrarse** *vr* to rise to a high (social) position.

ende (por) *loc adv* therefore.

endeble *adj* weak, feeble.

endeblez *nf* weakness, feebleness.

endémico,-a *adj Med* endemic; *fig* chronic.

endemoniado,-a *adj* 1 (*poseso*) possessed. 2 *fig* (*travieso*) mischievous.

enderezar [4] I *vtr* (*poner derecho*) to straighten out; (*poner vertical*) to set upright. II **enderezarse** *vr* to straighten up.

endeudarse *vr* to get *o* fall into debt.

endiablado,-a *adj* 1 (*poseso*) possessed. 2 (*travieso*) mischievous, devilish.

endibia *nf* endive.

endiosar *vtr* to deify.

endomingarse [7] *vr fam* to put on one's Sunday best.

endosar *vtr* 1 (*cheque*) to endorse. 2 *fam* (*tarea*) to lumber with.

endrina *nf Bot* sloe.

endrogarse [7] *vr Am* to take drugs, use drugs.

endulzar [4] *vtr* to sweeten.

endurecer [33] I *vtr* to harden. II **endurecerse** *vr* to harden, become hard.

enebro *nm* juniper.

enema *nm* enema.

enemigo,-a I *adj* enemy; **soy e. de la bebida**, I'm against drink. II *nm,f* enemy.

enemistad *nf* hostility, enmity.

enemistar I *vtr* to set at odds, cause a rift between. II **enemistarse** *vr* to become enemies; **e. con algn**, to fall out with sb.

energético,-a *adj* energy.

energía *nf* energy; **e. hidráulica/nuclear**, hydro-electric/nuclear power; *fig* **e. vital**, vitality.

enérgico,-a *adj* energetic; *(decisión)* firm; *(tono)* emphatic.

energúmeno,-a *nm,f fam (hombre)* madman; *(mujer)* mad woman; **ponerse como un e.**, to go up the wall.

enero *nm* January.

enervante *adj* enervating.

enervar *vtr* to enervate.

enésimo,-a *adj* 1 *Mat* nth. 2 *fam* umpteenth; **por enésima vez**, for the umpteenth time.

enfadado,-a *adj* angry, annoyed, *US* mad; **estamos enfadados**, we've fallen out with each other.

enfadar I *vtr* to make angry *o* annoyed. II **enfadarse** *vr* 1 to get angry (**con**, with). 2 *(dos personas)* to fall out.

enfado *nm* anger; *(desavenencia)* fall-out.

enfangarse [7] *vr* to get muddy; *fig* to get involved in (dirty business).

énfasis *nm inv* emphasis, stress; **poner e. en algo**, to lay stress on sth.

enfático,-a *adj* emphatic.

enfatizar [4] *vtr* to emphasize, stress.

enfermar *vi*, **enfermarse** *vr* to become *o* fall ill, be taken ill.

enfermedad *nf* illness; *(contagiosa)* disease.

enfermería *nf* infirmary.

enfermero,-a *nm,f (mujer)* nurse; *(hombre)* male nurse.

enfermizo,-a *adj* unhealthy, sickly.

enfermo,-a I *adj* ill; **caer e.**, to be taken ill; *fam* **esa gente me pone e.**, those people make me sick. II *nm,f* ill person; *(paciente)* patient.

enfervorizar [4] *vtr* to enthuse.

enfilar *vi* **e. hacia**, to make for.

enflaquecer [33] *vtr (adelgazar)* to make thin; *(debilitar)* to weaken.

enfocado,-a *adj Fot* **bien/mal enfocado**, in/out of focus.

enfocar [1] *vtr* 1 *(imagen)* to focus; *(persona)* to focus on. 2 *(tema)* to approach. 3 *(con linterna)* to shine a light on.

enfoque *nm* 1 focus; *(acción)* focusing. 2 *(de un tema)* approach.

enfrentamiento *nm* clash.

enfrentar I *vtr* 1 *(situación, peligro)* to confront. 2 *(enemistar)* to set at odds. II **enfrentarse** *vr* 1 **e. con** *o* **a**, to face up to, confront. 2 *Dep (rival)* to face (**a**, -), meet (**a**, -).

enfrente *adv* 1 opposite, facing; **la casa de e.**, the house opposite *o* across the road. 2 **e. de.**, opposite (to); facing; **e. del colegio**, opposite the school.

enfriamiento *nm* 1 *(proceso)* cooling. 2 *Med (catarro)* cold, chill.

enfriar [29] I *vtr* to cool (down), chill. II *vi* to cool down. III **enfriarse** *vr* 1 to get *o* go cold. 2 *(resfriarse)* to catch *o* catch a cold. 3 *fig (pasión)* to cool down.

enfurecer [33] I *vtr* to enrage, enfuriate. II **enfurecerse** *vr* to get furious, lose one's temper.

enfurruñarse *vr fam* to sulk.

engalanar I *vtr* to deck out, adorn. II **engalanarse** *vr* to dress up, get dressed up.

enganchado,-a *adj arg* **estar e. (a la droga)**, to be hooked (on drugs).

enganchar I *vtr* 1 to hook; *Ferroc* to couple. 2 *fam (pillar)* to nab. II **engancharse** *vr* to get caught *o* hooked; *arg (a la droga)* to get hooked.

enganche *nm (gancho)* hook; *Ferroc* coupling.

engañabobos *nm inv (persona)* con man, confidence trickster; *(truco)* con trick.

engañar I *vtr* to deceive, mislead; *(estafar)* to cheat, trick; *(mentir a)* to lie to; *(al marido, mujer)* to be unfaithful to. II **engañarse** *vr* to deceive oneself.

engañifa *nf fam* swindle.

engaño *nm* 1 deceit; *(estafa)* fraud, swindle; *(mentira)* lie. 2 *(error)* mistake, misunderstanding.

engañoso,-a *adj (palabras)* deceitful; *(apariencias)* deceptive; *(consejo)* misleading.

engarzar [4] *vtr* 1 *(unir)* to link. 2 *(engastar)* to mount, set.

engastar *vtr* to set, mount.

engatusar *vtr fam* to coax; **e. a algn para que haga algo**, to coax sb into doing sth.

engendrar *vtr* 1 *Biol* to engender. 2 *fig* to give rise to, cause.

engendro *nm* freak.

englobar *vtr* to include.

engomar *vtr* to gum, glue.

engordar I *vtr* to fatten (up), make fat. II *vi* 1 to put on weight, get fat; **he engordado tres kilos**, I've put on three kilos. 2 *(comida, bebida)* to be fattening.

engorro *nm fam* bother, nuisance.

engorroso,-a *adj fam* bothersome, tiresome.

engranaje *nm* 1 *Téc* gearing. 2 *fig* machinery.

engranar *vtr Téc* to engage.

engrandecer [33] *vtr* to exalt.
engrasar *vtr* 1 (*lubricar*) to lubricate, oil. 2 (*manchar*) to make greasy, stain with grease.
engrase *nm* lubrication.
engreído,-a *adj* vain, conceited.
engreírse [6] *vr* to become vain *o* conceited.
engrosar [2] *vtr* (*incrementar*) to enlarge; (*cantidad*) to increase, swell.
engrudo *nm* paste.
enguatar *vtr* to pad.
engullir *vtr* to gobble up.
enharinar *vtr* to cover with flour.
enhebrar *vtr* to thread.
enhorabuena *nf* congratulations *pl*; **dar la e. a algn**, to congratulate sb.
enigma *nm* enigma.
enigmático,-a *adj* enigmatic.
enjabonar *vtr* to soap.
enjalbegar [7] *vtr* to whitewash.
enjambre *nm* swarm.
enjaular *vtr* 1 (*animal*) to cage. 2 *fam* to put inside, put in jail.
enjuagar [7] *vtr* to rinse.
enjuague *nm* rinse; **e. bucal**, mouthwash.
enjugar [7] *vtr*, **enjugarse** *vr* 1 (*secar*) to mop up; (*lágrimas*) to wipe away. 2 (*deuda, déficit*) to clear, wipe out.
enjuiciamiento *nm* 1 (*opinión*) judgement. 2 *Jur* (*civil*) lawsuit; (*criminal*) trial, prosecution.
enjuiciar [12] *vtr* 1 (*juzgar*) to judge, examine. 2 *Jur* (*criminal*) to indict, prosecute.
enjundia *nf fig* (*sustancia*) substance; (*importancia*) importance.
enjuto,-a *adj* lean, skinny.
enlace *nm* 1 (*unión*) link, connection; **e. químico**, chemical bond. 2 *Ferroc* connection. 3 (*casamiento*) marriage. 4 (*persona*) liaison officer; **e. sindical**, shop steward, *US* union delegate.
enlatado,-a *adj* canned, tinned.
enlatar *vtr* to can, tin.
enlazar [4] *vtr* & *vi* to link, connect (**con**, with).
enlodar *vtr* 1 (*enfangar*) to muddy, cover with mud. 2 *fig* (*reputación*) to stain, besmirch.
enloquecedor,-a *adj* maddening.
enloquecer [33] **I** *vi* to go mad. **II** *vtr* 1 (*volver loco*) to drive mad. 2 *fam* **me enloquecen las motos**, I'm mad about motorbikes. **III** **enloquecerse** *vr* to go mad, go out of one's mind.
enlosar *vtr* to tile.
enlucir [35] *vtr* (*pared*) to plaster; (*plata, oro*) to polish.
enlutado,-a *adj* in mourning.
enmadrado,-a *adj* **estar e.**, to be tied to one's mother's apron strings.
enmarañar **I** *vtr* 1 (*pelo*) to tangle. 2 *fig* (*complicar*) to complicate, confuse. **II**

enmarañarse *vr* 1 (*pelo*) to get tangled. 2 *fig* (*situación*) to get confused, get into a mess *o* a muddle.
enmarcar [1] *vtr* to frame.
enmascarar **I** *vtr* 1 to mask. 2 (*problema, la verdad*) to mask, disguise. **II** **enmascararse** *vr* to put on a mask.
enmendar [1] **I** *vtr* (*corregir*) to correct, put right; *Jur* to amend. **II** **enmendarse** *vr* (*persona*) to reform, mend one's ways.
enmienda *nf* correction; *Jur Pol* amendment.
enmohecerse [33] *vr* (*metal*) to rust, get rusty; *Bot* to go mouldy *o US* moldy.
enmoquetar *vtr* to carpet.
enmudecer [33] *vi* (*callar*) to fall silent; *fig* to be dumbstruck.
ennegrecer [33] *vtr*, **ennegrecerse** *vr* to blacken, turn black.
ennoblecer [33] *vtr* to ennoble.
enojado,-a *adj* angry, cross.
enojadizo *adj* irritable, touchy.
enojar **I** *vtr* to anger, annoy. **II** **enojarse** *vr* to get angry, lose one's temper.
enojo *nm* anger, annoyance.
enorgullecer [33] **I** *vtr* to fill with pride. **II** **enorgullecerse** *vtr* to be *o* feel proud (**de**, of).
enorme *adj* enormous.
enormidad *nf* enormity; *fam* **una e.**, loads.
enraizado,-a *adj* rooted.
enraizar [24] *vi*, **enraizarse** *vr* (*persona*) to put down roots; (*planta, costumbre*) to take root.
enrarecerse [33] *vr* (*aire*) to become rarefied.
enredadera *nf* climbing plant, creeper.
enredar **I** *vtr* 1 (*pelo*) to entangle, tangle up. 2 *fig* (*asunto*) to confuse, complicate. 3 *fig* (*implicar*) to involve (**en**, in). 4 (*confundir*) to mix up. **II** **enredarse** *vr* 1 (*pelo*) to get entangled, get tangled (up) *o* in a tangle. 2 *fig* (*asunto*) to get complicated *o* confused. 3 *fig* (*involucrarse*) to get involved (**con**, with). 4 (*confundirse*) to get mixed up.
enredo *nm* 1 (*maraña*) tangle. 2 *fig* (*lío*) muddle, mess.
enrejado *nm* (*de ventana*) lattice.
enrevesado,-a *adj* complicated, difficult.
enriquecer [33] *vtr* to make rich; *fig* to enrich. **II** **enriquecerse** *vr* to get *o* become rich, prosper; *fig* to become enriched.
enrocar [1] *vi Ajedrez* to castle.
enrojecer [33] **I** *vtr* to redden, turn red. **II** **enrojecer(se)** *vi* & *vr* (*ruborizarse*) to blush.
enrolarse *vr* to enrol, *US* enroll, sign on; *Mil* to enlist, join up.
enrollado,-a *adj* 1 rolled up. 2 (*persona*) great. 3 *fam* **estar e. con algn**, (*estar saliendo con*) to go out with sb.

enrollar I *vtr* to roll up; (*cable*) to coil; (*hilo*) to wind up. **II enrollarse** *vr* 1 *fam* (*hablar*) to chatter, go on and on. 2 *fam* **e. con algn**, (*tener relaciones*) to have an affair with sb.

enroque *nm Ajedrez* castling.

enroscar [1] **I** *vtr* 1 to coil (round), wind. 2 (*tornillo, tapón*) to screw in *o* on. **II enroscarse** *vr* to coil, wind.

ensaimada *nf* kind of spiral pastry from Majorca.

ensalada *nf* salad.

ensaladera *nf* salad bowl.

ensaladilla I e. rusa, Russian salad.

ensalzar [4] *vtr* (*enaltecer*) to exalt; (*elogiar*) to praise, extol, US extoll.

ensamblador *nm Inform* assembler.

ensamblaje *nm 1 e.* assembly.

ensamblar *vtr* to assemble.

ensanchar I *vtr* to enlarge, widen; *Cost* to let out. **II ensancharse** *vr* to get wider.

ensanche *nm* enlargement, widening; (*de ciudad*) urban development.

ensangrentado,-a *adj* bloodstained, covered in blood.

ensangrentar [1] *vtr* to stain with blood, cover in blood.

ensañarse *vr* to be brutal (**con**, with); (*cebarse*) to delight in tormenting (**con**, -).

ensartar *vtr* 1 (*perlas etc*) to string together. 2 (*mentiras etc*) to reel off, rattle off.

ensayar *vtr* to test, try out; *Teat* to rehearse; *Mús* to practise.

ensayista *nmf* essayist.

ensayo *nm* 1 (*prueba*) test, trial. 2 *Teat* rehearsal; **e. general**, dress rehearsal. 3 (*escrito*) essay.

enseguida, en seguida *adv* (*inmediatamente*) at once, straight away; (*poco después*) in a minute, soon; **e. voy**, I'll be right there.

ensenada *nf* inlet, cove.

enseña *nf* ensign, standard.

enseñanza *nf* 1 (*educación*) education. 2 (*de idioma etc*) teaching. 3 **enseñanzas**, teachings.

enseñar *vtr* 1 to teach; **e. a algn a hacer algo**, to teach sb how to do sth. 2 (*mostrar*) to show; (*señalar*) to point out.

enseres *nmpl* (*bártulos*) belongings, goods; (*de trabajo*) tools.

ensillar *vtr* to saddle (up).

ensimismado,-a *adj* (*en la lectura etc*) engrossed; (*abstraído*) lost in thought.

ensimismarse *vr* (*en la lectura etc*) to become engrossed; (*abstraerse*) to be lost in thought.

ensombrecer [33] **I** *vtr* to cast a shadow over. **II ensombrecerse** *vr* to darken.

ensopar *vtr Am* to soak.

ensordecedor,-a *adj* deafening.

ensordecer [33] **I** *vtr* to deafen. **II** *vi* to

go deaf.

ensortijado,-a *adj* curly.

ensuciar [12] **I** *vtr* 1 to get dirty. 2 *fig* (*reputación*) to harm, damage. **II ensuciarse** *vr* to get dirty.

ensueño *nm* dream; **una casa de e.**, a dream house.

entablado *nm* 1 (*entarimado*) planking, planks *pl*. 2 (*suelo*) wooden floor.

entablar *vtr* 1 (*conversación*) to open, begin; (*amistad*) to strike up; (*negocios*) to start. 2 *Ajedrez* to set up. 3 (*pleito*) to initiate.

entablillar [1] *vtr Med* to splint.

entallado,-a *adj* (*vestido*) close-fitting; (*camisa*) fitted.

entallar I *vtr* to take in at the waist. **II** *vi* to fit at the waist.

entarimado *nm* parquet floor.

entarimar *vtr* to cover with parquet.

ente *nm* 1 (*institución*) organization, body; **e. público**, public service organization. 2 (*ser*) being.

entendederas *nfpl fam* brains; **ser duro de e.**, to be slow on the uptake.

entender [3] **I** *vtr* (*comprender*) to understand; **a mi e.**, to my way of thinking; **dar a algn a e. que ...**, to give sb to understand that .... **II** *vi* 1 (*comprender*) to understand. 2 **e. de**, (*saber*) to know about. **III entenderse** *vr* 1 (*comprenderse*) to be understood, be meant. 2 *fam* **e. (bien) con**, to get on (well) with.

entendido,-a I *nm,f* expert. **II** *adj* **tengo entendido que ...**, I understand that ....

entendimiento *nm* understanding.

enterado,-a I *adj* knowledgeable, well-informed; **estar e.**, to be in the know; **estar e. de ...**, to be aware of .... **II** *nm,f* (*listillo*) know-all.

enterar I *vtr* to inform (**de**, about, of). **II enterarse** *vr* to find out; **me he enterado de que ...**, I understand ...; **ni me enteré**, I didn't even realize it.

entereza *nf* strength of character.

enternecedor,-a *adj* moving, touching.

enternecer [33] **I** *vtr* to move, touch. **II enternecerse** *vr* to be moved *o* touched.

entero,-a I *adj* 1 (*completo*) entire, whole; **por e.**, completely. 2 *fig* (*íntegro*) honest, upright. 3 *fig* (*firme*) strong. **II** *nm* 1 *Mat* whole number. 2 *Fin* point. ◆**enteramente** *adv* entirely, completely.

enterrador *nm* gravedigger.

enterramiento *nm* burial.

enterrar [1] *vtr* to bury.

entidad *nf* organization; **e. comercial**, company, firm.

entierro *nm* 1 burial. 2 (*ceremonia*) funeral.

entomología *nf* entomology.

entonación *nf* intonation.

entonar I *vtr* 1 (*canto*) to sing. 2 *Med* to

tone up. **II** *vi* to be in harmony, be in tune (**con**, with).

entonces *adv* then; **por aquel e.**, at that time; **el e. ministro**, the then minister.

entornar *vtr* (*ojos etc*) to half-close; (*puerta*) to leave ajar.

entorno *nm* environment.

entorpecer [33] *vtr* (*obstaculizar*) to hinder, impede.

entrada *nf* **1** entrance. **2** (*billete*) ticket; (*recaudación*) takings *pl*. **3 de e.**, for a start. **4** *Culin* entrée. **5** *Com* entry; (*pago inicial*) down payment, deposit; **e. de capital**, capital inflow. **6** *Com* **entradas**, (*ingresos*) receipts, takings. **7** (*en la frente*) receding hairline.

entrado,-a *adj* **e. en años**, advanced in years; **hasta bien entrada la noche**, well into the night.

entramado *nm* framework; (*de sistema etc*) network.

entramparse *vr fam* to get into debt.

entrante I *adj* coming; **el mes e.**, next month; **el ministro e.**, the incoming minister. **II** *Culin* starter.

entrañable *adj* **1** (*lugar*) intimate, close. **2** (*persona*) affectionate, warm-hearted.

entrañar *vtr* to entail.

entrañas *nfpl* bowels.

entrar I *vi* **1** to come in, go in, enter; *fig* **no me entran las matemáticas**, I can't get the hang of maths. **2** (*encajar*) to fit. **3 el año que entra**, next year, the coming year. **4** (*venir*) to come over; **me entró dolor de cabeza**, I got a headache; **me entraron ganas de reír**, I felt like laughing. **II** *vtr* **1** to introduce. **2** *Inform* to enter.

entre *prep* **1** (*dos*) between. **2** (*más de dos*) among(st).

entreabierto,-a *adj* (*ojos etc*) half-open; (*puerta*) ajar.

entreacto *nm* interval, intermission.

entrecejo *nm* space between the eyebrows; **fruncir el e.**, to frown, knit one's brow.

entrecortado,-a *adj* (*voz*) faltering, hesitant.

entrecot *nm* fillet steak.

entrecruzar *vtr*, **entrecruzarse** [4] *vr* to entwine.

entredicho *nm* **1** *Jur* injunction. **2 estar en e.**, to be suspect; **poner algo en e.**, to bring sth into question.

entrega *nf* **1** (*de productos*) delivery; (*de premios*) presentation. **2** (*fascículo*) part, instalment, *US* installment. **3** (*devoción*) selflessness.

entregar [7] **I** *vtr* (*deberes etc*) to hand over; (*deberes etc*) to give in, hand in; *Com* to deliver. **II entregarse** *vr* **1** (*rendirse*) to give in, surrender. **2 e. a**, to devote oneself to; *pey* to indulge in.

entreguismo *nm* *Pol* appeasement.

entrelazar [4] *vtr*, **entrelazarse** *vr* to entwine.

entremedias *adv* in between; (*mientras tanto*) meanwhile, in the meantime.

entremés *nm* *Culin* hors d'oeuvres.

entremeterse *vr* → **entrometerse**

entremezclarse *vr* to mix, mingle.

entrenador,-a *nm,f* trainer, coach.

entrenamiento *nm* training.

entrenar *vi*, **entrenarse** *vr* to train.

entrepierna *nf* crotch, crutch.

entresacar [1] *vtr* to pick out, select.

entresijos *nmpl* nooks and crannies.

entresuelo *nm* mezzanine.

entretanto I *adv* meanwhile. **II** *nm* **en el e.**, in the meantime.

entretejer *vtr* to interweave.

entretención *nf* *Am* amusement, entertainment.

entretener [24] **I** *vtr* **1** (*divertir*) to entertain, amuse. **2** (*retrasar*) to delay; (*detener*) to hold up, detain. **II entretenerse** *vr* **1** (*distraerse*) to amuse oneself, while away the time. **2** (*retrasarse*) to be delayed, be held up.

entretenido,-a *adj* enjoyable, entertaining.

entretenimiento *nm* entertainment, amusement.

entretiempo *adj* **ropa de e.**, lightweight clothing.

entrever [28] *vtr* **1** to glimpse, catch sight of; *fig* **dejó e. que ...**, she hinted that ....

entrevista *nf* interview.

entrevistador,-a *nm,f* interviewer.

entrevistar I *vtr* to interview. **II entrevistarse** *vr* **e. con algn**, to have an interview with sb.

entristecer [33] **I** *vtr* to sadden, make sad. **II entristecerse** *vr* to be sad (**por**, about).

entrometerse *vr* to meddle, interfere (**en**, in).

entrometido,-a I *nm,f* meddler, busybody. **II** *adj* interfering.

entroncar *vi* to connect.

entumecer [33] **I** *vtr* to numb. **II entumecerse** *vr* to go numb.

entumecido,-a *adj* numb.

enturbiar [12] **I** *vtr* **1** (*agua*) to make cloudy. **2** *fig* (*asunto*) to cloud, obscure. **II enturbiarse** *vr* to become cloudy.

entusiasmar I *vtr* to fill with enthusiasm. **II entusiasmarse** *vr* to get excited *o* enthusiastic (**con**, about).

entusiasmo *nm* enthusiasm; **con e.**, enthusiastically.

entusiasta I *adj* enthusiastic, keen (**de**, on). **II** *nmf* enthusiast.

enumerar *vtr* to enumerate.

enunciado *nm* (*de teoría, problema*) wording.

envainar *vtr* to sheathe.

envanecer [33] **I** *vtr* to make proud *o*

vain. **II envanecerse** *vr* to become conceited *o* proud, give oneself airs.

envasado,-a I *nm* (*en botella*) bottling; (*en paquete*) packing; (*en lata*) canning. **II** *adj* **e. al vacío**, vacuum-packed.

envasar *vtr* (*embotellar*) to bottle; (*empaquetar*) to pack; (*enlatar*) to can, tin.

envase *nm* 1 (*acto*) packing; (*de botella*) bottling; (*de lata*) canning. 2 (*recipiente*) container. 3 (*botella vacía*) empty.

envejecer [33] I *vi* to grow old. **II** *vtr* to age.

envejecimiento *nm* ageing.

envenenar *vtr* to poison.

envergadura *nf* 1 (*importancia*) importance, scope; **de gran e.**, large-scale. 2 (*de pájaro, avión*) span, wingspan; *Náut* breadth (*of sail*)

envés *nm* other side.

envestidura *nf* investiture.

enviado *nm,f* envoy; *Prensa* **e. especial**, special correspondent.

enviar [29] *vtr* to send.

enviciarse [12] *vr* to become addicted (**con**, to).

envidia *nf* envy; **tener e. de algn**, to envy sb.

envidiable *adj* enviable.

envidiar [12] *vtr* to envy; **no tener nada que e.**, to be in no way inferior (**a**, to).

envidioso,-a *adj* envious.

envilecer [33] *vtr* to degrade, debase.

envío *nm* sending; (*remesa*) consignment; (*paquete*) parcel; **gastos de e.**, postage and packing; **e. contra reembolso**, cash on delivery.

enviudar *vi* (*hombre*) to become a widower, lose one's wife; (*mujer*) to become a widow, lose one's husband.

envoltorio *nm*, **envoltura** *nf* wrapper, wrapping.

envolver [4] (*pp* **envuelto**) I *vtr* 1 (*con papel*) to wrap. 2 (*cubrir*) to envelope. 3 (*en complot etc*) to involve (**en**, in). **II envolverse** *vr* 1 to wrap oneself up (**en**, in). 2 (*implicarse*) to become involved (**en**, in).

enyesar *vtr* to plaster; *Med* to put in plaster.

enzima *nf* enzyme.

épica *nf* epic poetry.

epicentro *nm* epicentre, *US* epicenter.

épico,-a *adj* epic.

epidemia *nf* epidemic.

epilepsia *nf* epilepsy.

epílogo *nm* epilogue, *US* epilog.

episcopal *adj* episcopal.

episodio *nm* episode.

epístola *nf* epistle.

epitafio *nm* epitaph.

epíteto *nm* epithet.

época *nf* time; *Hist* period, epoch; *Agr* season; **en esta é. del año**, at this time of the year; **hacer é.**, to be a landmark;

mueble de é., period furniture.

equidad *nf* equity.

equilátero *adj* equilateral.

equilibrar *vtr* to balance.

equilibrio *nm* balance.

equilibrismo *nm* balancing act.

equilibrista *nmf* 1 tightrope walker. 2 *Am Pol* opportunist.

equipaje *nm* luggage; **hacer el e.**, to pack, do the packing.

equipar *vtr* to equip, furnish (**con, de**, with).

equiparable *adj* comparable (**a**, to; **con**, with).

equiparar *vtr* to compare (**con**, with), liken (**con**, to).

equipo *nm* 1 (*de expertos, jugadores*) team. 2 (*aparatos*) equipment; **e. de alta fidelidad**, hi-fi stereo system. 3 (*ropas*) outfit.

equis *nf* name of the letter X in Spanish.

equitación *nf* horse *o* *US* horseback riding.

equitativo,-a *adj* equitable, fair.

equivalente *adj* equivalent.

equivaler [26] *vi* to be equivalent (**to**, a).

equivocación *nf* error, mistake.

equivocado,-a *adj* mistaken, wrong.

equivocar [1] I *vtr* to mix up. **II equivocarse** *vr* to make a mistake; *Tel* **se equivocó de número**, he dialled the wrong number; **se equivocó de fecha**, he got the wrong date.

equívoco,-a I *adj* equivocal, misleading. **II** *nm* misunderstanding.

era¹ *nf* (*época*) era, age.

era² *nf* *Agr* threshing floor.

era³ *pt indef* → **ser**.

erario *nm* exchequer, treasury.

eras *pt indef* → **ser**.

erección *nf* erection.

erecto,-a *adj* upright; (*pene*) erect.

eres *indic pres* → **ser**.

erguir [5] I *vtr* to erect. **II erguirse** *vr* to straighten up, stand *o* sit up straight.

erial *nm* uncultivated land.

erigir [6] I *vtr* to erect. **II erigirse** *vr* **e. en algo**, to set oneself up in sth.

erizado,-a *adj* bristly, prickly.

erizarse [4] *vr* to bristle, stand on end.

erizo *nm* hedgehog; **e. de mar** *o* **marino**, sea urchin.

ermita *nf* hermitage, shrine.

ermitaño,-a *nm,f* hermit.

erosión *nf* erosion.

erosionar *vtr* to erode.

erótico,-a *adj* erotic.

erotismo *nm* eroticism.

erradicar [1] *vtr* to eradicate.

errante *adj* wandering.

errar [1] I *vtr* to miss, get wrong. **II** *vi* 1 (*vagar*) to wander, roam. 2 (*fallar*) to err.

errata *nf* erratum, misprint; **fe de erratas**, errata.

erre *nf* **e. que e.**, stubbornly, pigheadededly.

erróneo,-a adj erroneous, wrong.

error nm error, mistake; *Inform* bug; **por e.**, by mistake, in error; *Impr* **e. de imprenta**, misprint; **caer en un e.**, to make a mistake.

Ertzaintza nf Basque police force.

eructar vi to belch, burp.

eructo nm belch, burp.

erudición nf erudition.

erudito,-a I adj erudite, learned. **II** nm,f scholar.

erupción nf 1 (de volcán) eruption. 2 (en la piel) rash.

es indic pres → **ser**.

esa adj dem → **ese**.

ésa adj dem → **ése**.

esbelto,-a adj slender.

esbirro nm henchman.

esbozar [4] vt to sketch, outline.

esbozo nm sketch, outline, rough draft.

escabeche nm brine.

escabechina nf massacre.

escabroso,-a adj 1 (espinoso) tricky. 2 (indecente) crude.

escabullirse vr to slip away, scuttle o scurry off.

escacharrar vtr fam to break.

escafandra nf diving helmet or suit; **e. espacial**, spacesuit.

escala nf 1 scale; (de colores) range; **e. musical**, scale; **en gran e.**, on a large scale. 2 (parada) *Náut* port of call; *Av* stopover; **hacer e. en**, to call in at, stop over in. 3 (escalera) ladder, stepladder.

escalada nf 1 climb. 2 fig (de violencia) escalation; (de precios) rise.

escalador,-a nm,f climber, mountaineer.

escalafón nm (graduación) rank; (de salarios) salary o wage scale.

escalar vtr to climb, scale.

escaldar vtr to scald.

escalera nf 1 stair; **e. de incendios**, fire escape; **e. mecánica**, escalator; **e. de caracol**, spiral staircase. 2 (escala) ladder. 3 *Naipes* run.

escalerilla nf (de piscina) steps pl; *Náut* gangway; *Av* (boarding) ramp.

escalfar vtr to poach.

escalinata nf stoop.

escalofriante adj hair-raising, bloodcurdling.

escalofrío nm shiver; **me dió un e.**, it made me shiver.

escalón nm step; **e. lateral** (en letrero) ramp.

escalonar vtr to place at intervals, space out.

escalope nm escalope.

escalpelo nm scalpel.

escama nf *Zool* scale; (de jabón) flake.

escamarse vr to smell a rat, become suspicious.

escamotear vtr fam to diddle out of, do

out of.

escampar vi to stop raining, clear up.

escanciar [12] vtr (vino) to pour out, serve.

escandalizar [4] **I** vtr to scandalize, shock. **II escandalizarse** vr to be shocked (de, at, by).

escándalo nm 1 (alboroto) racket, din; **armar un e.**, to kick up a fuss. 2 (desvergüenza) scandal.

escandaloso,-a adj 1 (ruidoso) noisy, rowdy. 2 (ofensivo) scandalous.

Escandinavia nf Scandinavia.

escandinavo,-a adj & nm,f Scandinavian.

escáner nm scanner.

escaño nm *Parl* seat.

escapada nf 1 (de prisión) escape; *Dep* breakaway. 2 (viaje rápido) flying visit, quick trip.

escapar I vi to escape, run away. **II escaparse** vr 1 to escape, run away; **se me escapó de las manos**, it slipped out of my hands; **se me escapó el tren**, I missed the train. 2 (gas etc) to leak, escape.

escaparate nm shop window.

escapatoria nf escape; **no tener e.**, to have no way out.

escape nm 1 (de gas etc) leak, escape. 2 *Téc* exhaust; **tubo de e.**, exhaust (pipe). 3 (huida) escape; (escapatoria) way out.

escaquearse vr fam to shirk, skive off.

escarabajo nm beetle.

escaramuza nf *Mil* skirmish; fig (riña) squabble, brush.

escarceo nm attempt.

escarbar vtr 1 (suelo) to scratch; (fuego) to poke. 2 fig to inquire into, investigate.

escarcha nf hoarfrost, frost.

escarchado,-a adj (fruta) crystallized, candied.

escardar vtr to hoe.

escardillo nm weeding hoe.

escarlata adj scarlet.

escarlatina nf scarlet fever.

escarmentar [1] vi to learn one's lesson.

escarmiento nm punishment, lesson.

escarnio nm derision, mockery.

escarola nf curly endive, *US* escarole.

escarpado,-a adj (paisaje) craggy; (pendiente) steep.

escasear vi to be scarce.

escasez nf scarcity.

escaso,-a adj scarce; (dinero) tight; (conocimientos) scant; **e. de dinero**, short of money.

escatimar vtr to skimp on; **no escatimó esfuerzos para ...**, he spared no efforts to ....

escayola nf 1 plaster of Paris, stucco. 2 *Med* plaster.

escayolar vtr *Med* to put in plaster.

escena nf 1 scene. 2 (escenario) stage; **poner en e.**, to stage.

escenario *nm* 1 *Teat* stage. 2 *(entorno)* scenario; *(de crimen)* scene; *(de película)* setting.

escénico,-a *adj* scenic.

escenografía *nf Cin* set design; *Teat* stage design.

escepticismo *nm* scepticism, US skepticism.

escéptico,-a *adj & nm,f* sceptic, US skeptic.

escindirse *vr* to split (off) (**en**, into).

escisión *nf* split.

esclarecer [33] *vtr* to shed light on.

esclavitud *nf* slavery.

esclavizar [4] *vtr* to enslave.

esclava *nf* bangle.

esclavo,-a *adj & nm,f* slave.

esclusa *nf* lock, sluicegate.

escoba *nf* brush, broom.

escocer [4] I *vi* to sting, smart. II **escocerse** *vr (piel)* to chafe.

escocés,-a I *adj* Scottish, Scots; *falda escocesa*, kilt. II *nm,f (hombre)* Scotsman; *(mujer)* Scotswoman.

Escocia *n* Scotland.

escoger [5] *vtr* to choose.

escogido,-a *adj* chosen, selected; *(producto)* choice, select; *Lit obras escogidas*, selected works.

escolar I *adj (curso, año)* school. II *nm,f (niño)* schoolboy; *(niña)* schoolgirl.

escolaridad *nf* schooling.

escollo *nm* reef; *fig* pitfall.

escolta *nf* escort.

escoltar *vtr* to escort.

escombros *nmpl* rubbish *sing*, debris *sing*.

esconder I *vtr* to hide (**de**, from), conceal (**de**, from). II **esconderse** *vr* to hide (**de**, from).

escondidas *adv* **a e.**, secretly.

escondite *nm* 1 *(lugar)* hiding place, hide-out. 2 *(juego)* hide-and-seek.

escondrijo *nm* hiding place, hide-out.

escopeta *nf* shotgun; **e. de aire comprimido**, air gun; **e. de cañones recortados**, sawn-off shotgun.

escopetazo *nm* gunshot.

escorbuto *nm* scurvy.

escoria *nf* 1 *(de metal)* slag. 2 *fig pey* scum, dregs *pl*.

Escorpio *nm* Scorpio.

escorpión *nm* scorpion.

escotado,-a *adj* low-cut.

escote *nm* low neckline.

escotilla *nf* hatch, hatchway.

escozor *nm* stinging, smarting.

escribano,-a *nm,f Jur* court clerk.

escribiente *nmf* clerk.

escribir *(pp escrito)* I *vtr* to write; **e. a mano**, to write in longhand; **e. a máquina**, to type. II **escribirse** *vr* 1 *(dos personas)* to write to each other, correspond. 2 **se escribe con h**, it is spelt with an h.

escrito,-a I *adj* written; **e. a mano**, handwritten, in longhand; **por e.**, in writing. II *nm* writing.

escritor,-a *nm,f* writer.

escritorio *nm (mueble)* writing desk, bureau; *(oficina)* office.

escritura *nf* 1 *Jur* deed, document; **e. de propiedad**, title deed. 2 *Rel* **Sagradas Escrituras**, Holy Scriptures.

escrúpulo *nm* 1 scruple; **una persona sin escrúpulos**, an unscrupulous person. 2 *(esmero)* care. 3 **me da e.**, *(asco)* it makes me feel squeamish.

escrupuloso,-a *adj* 1 *(honesto)* scrupulous. 2 *(meticuloso)* painstaking. 3 *(delicado)* squeamish.

escrutar *vtr* 1 to scrutinize. 2 *(votos)* to count.

escrutinio *nm* 1 scrutiny. 2 *(de votos)* count.

escuadra *nf* 1 *(instrumento)* square. 2 *Mil* squad; *Naut* squadron; *Dep* team; *(de coches)* fleet.

escuadrilla *nf* squadron.

escuadrón *nm* squadron.

escuálido,-a *adj* emaciated.

escucha *nf* listening; **escuchas telefónicas**, phone tapping *sing*; **estar a la e.**, to be listening out (**de**, for).

escuchar I *vtr* to listen to; *(oír)* to hear. II *vi* to listen; *(oír)* to hear.

escudarse *vr fig* **e. en algo**, to hide behind sth.

escudería *nf Aut* racing team.

escudilla *nf* bowl.

escudo *nm* 1 *(arma defensiva)* shield. 2 *(blasón)* coat of arms.

escudriñar *vtr* to scrutinize.

escuela *nf* school; **e. de Bellas Artes**, Art School; **e. de conducir/de idiomas**, driving/language school.

escueto,-a *adj* plain, unadorned.

escuezo *indic pres* → **escocer**.

escular [1] *vtr Am* to search.

esculpir *vtr* to sculpt; *(madera)* to carve; *(metal)* to engrave.

escultor,-a *nm,f (hombre)* sculptor; *(mujer)* sculptress; *(de madera)* woodcarver; *(de metales)* engraver.

escultura *nf* sculpture.

escultural *adj* sculptural; *(persona)* statuesque.

escupidera *nf* 1 *(recipiente)* spittoon, US cuspidor. 2 *(orinal)* chamberpot.

escupir I *vi* to spit. II *vtr* to spit out.

escupitajo *nm vulg* spit.

escurreplatos *nm inv* dish rack.

escurridizo,-a *adj* 1 *(resbaladizo)* slippery. 2 *fig (huidizo)* elusive, slippery.

escurridor *nm (colador)* colander; *(escurreplatos)* dish rack.

escurrir I *vtr (plato, vaso)* to drain; *(ropa)* to wring out; **e. el bulto**, to wriggle out. II **escurrirse** *vr* 1 *(platos etc)* to drip. 2

(escaparse) to run *o* slip away. **3** *(resbalarse)* to slip.

escúter nm (motor) scooter.

ese,-a adj dem **I** that. **2** esos,-as, those.

ése,-a pron dem m,f **1** that one. **2** ésos,-as, those (ones); fam **¡ni por ésas!**, no way!; fam **¡no me vengas con ésas!**, come off it!

esencia nf essence.

esencial adj essential; **lo e.**, the main thing. ◆**esencialmente** adv essentially.

esfera nf **1** sphere; fig sphere, field. **2** *(de reloj de pulsera)* dial; *(de reloj de pared)* face.

esférico,-a adj **I** spherical. **II** nm Ftb ball.

esfinge nf sphinx.

esforzarse [2] vr to endeavour (**por**, to).

esfuerzo nm effort.

esfumarse vr fam to beat it.

esgrima nf Dep fencing.

esgrimir vtr to wield.

esguince nm sprain.

eslabón nm link.

eslavo,-a **I** adj Slav, Slavonic. **II** nm,f *(persona)* Slav. **III** nm *(idioma)* Slavonic.

eslip nm (pl **eslips**) men's briefs pl, underpants pl.

eslogan nm (pl **eslóganes**) slogan; **e. publicitario**, advertising slogan.

eslora nf Náut length.

esmaltar vtr to enamel.

esmalte nm enamel; *(de uñas)* nail polish *o* varnish.

esmerado,-a adj painstaking, careful.

esmeralda nf emerald.

esmerarse vr to be careful; *(esforzarse)* to go to great lengths.

esmero nm great care.

esmoquin nm (pl **esmóquines**) dinner jacket, US tuxedo.

esnifar vtr arg *(drogas)* to sniff.

esnob (pl **esnobs**) **I** adj *(persona)* snobbish; *(restaurante etc)* posh. **II** nmf snob.

esnobismo nm snobbery, snobbishness.

eso pron dem neut that; **¡e. es!**, that's it!; **por e.**, that's why; fam **a e. de las diez**, around ten; fam **e. de las Navidades sale muy caro**, this whole Christmas thing costs a fortune.

esófago nm oesophagus, US esophagus.

esos,-as adj dem pl → **ese,-a**.

ésos,-as pron dem m,fpl → **ése,-a**.

esotérico,-a adj esoteric.

espabilado,-a adj **1** *(despierto)* wide awake. **2** *(niño)* bright.

espabilar **I** vtr to wake up. **II** espabilarse vr to wake up, make up.

espachurrar vtr to squash.

espacial adj spatial, space; **nave e.**, space ship.

espaciar [12] vtr to space out.

espacio nm **1** space; *(de tiempo)* length; **a doble e.**, double-spaced. **2** Rad TV programme, US program.

espacioso,-a adj spacious, roomy.

espada **I** nf **1** sword; **estar entre la e. y la pared**, to be between the devil and the deep blue sea; **pez e.**, swordfish. **2** Naipes spade. **II** nm Taur matador.

espadaña nf belfry.

espaguetis nmpl spaghetti sing.

espalda nf **1** Anat back; **espaldas**, back sing; **a espaldas de algn**, behind sb's back; **por la e.**, from behind; **volver la e. a algn**, to turn one's back on sb; fam **e. mojada**, US wetback. **2** Natación backstroke.

espaldar nm *(de silla)* back.

espaldilla nf shoulder blade.

espantapájaros nm inv scarecrow.

espantar **I** vtr **1** *(asustar)* to frighten, scare. **2** *(ahuyentar)* to frighten away. **II** espantarse vr to get *o* feel frightened (**de**, of), get *o* feel scared (**de**, of).

espanto nm fright; fam **de e.**, dreadful, shocking.

espantoso,-a adj dreadful.

España nf Spain.

español,-a **I** adj Spanish. **II** nm,f Spaniard; **los españoles**, the Spanish. **III** nm *(idioma)* Spanish.

esparadrapo nm sticking plaster.

esparcimiento nm *(relajación)* relaxation.

esparcir [3] **I** vtr *(papeles, semillas)* to scatter; fig *(rumor)* to spread. **II** esparcirse vr **1** to be scattered. **2** *(relajarse)* to relax.

espárrago nm asparagus.

espartano,-a adj fig spartan.

espasmo nm spasm.

espástico,-a adj spastic.

espátula nf Culin spatula; Art palette knife; Téc stripping knife; *(de albañil)* trowel.

especia nf spice.

especial adj special; **en e.**, especially; **e. para ...**, suitable for .... ◆**especialmente** adv *(exclusivamente)* specially; *(muy)* especially.

especialidad nf speciality, US specialty; Educ main subject.

especialista nmf specialist.

especializarse [4] vr to specialize (**en**, in).

especie nf **1** Biol species inv. **2** *(clase)* kind; **una e. de salsa**, a kind of sauce. **3** Com **en e.**, in kind.

especificar [1] vtr to specify.

específico,-a adj specific; **peso e.**, specific gravity. ◆**específicamente** adv specifically.

espécimen nm (pl **especímenes**) specimen.

espectacular adj spectacular.

espectacularidad nf **de gran e.**, really spectacular.

espectáculo nm **1** *(escena)* spectacle,

sight; *fam* **dar un e.**, to make a spectacle of oneself. **2** *Teat Cin* TV show; **montar un e.**, to put on a show.

espectador,-a *nm,f Dep* spectator; *(de accidente)* onlooker; *Teat Cin* member of the audience; **los espectadores**, the audience *sing*; TV viewers.

espectro *nm* **1** *Fís* spectrum. **2** *(fantasma)* spectre, US specter. **3** *(gama)* range.

especulación *nf* speculation; **e. del suelo**, land speculation.

especulador,-a *nm,f Fin* speculator.

especular *vi* to speculate.

especulativo,-a *adj* speculative.

espejismo *nm* mirage.

espejo *nm* mirror; *Aut* **e. retrovisor**, rear-view mirror.

espeleología *nf* potholing, speleology.

espeluznante *adj* hair-raising, horrifying.

espera *nf* wait; **en e. de ...**, waiting for ...; **a la e. de**, expecting; **sala de e.**, waiting room.

esperanza *nf* hope; **tener la e. puesta en algo**, to have one's hopes pinned on sth; **e. de vida**, life expectancy; **en estado de buena e.**, expecting, pregnant.

esperanzador,-a *adj* encouraging.

esperanzar *vtr* to give hope to.

esperar **I** *vi* **1** *(aguardar)* to wait. **2** *(tener esperanza de)* to hope. **II** *vtr* **1** *(aguardar)* to wait for; **espero a mi hermano**, I'm waiting for my brother. **2** *(tener esperanza de)* to hope for; **espero que sí**, I hope so; **espero que vengas**, I hope you'll come. **3** *(estar a la espera de)* to expect; **te esperábamos ayer**, we were expecting you yesterday. **4** *fig (bebé)* to expect.

esperma **1** *nm Biol* sperm. **2** *Am (vela)* candle.

espermaticida *nm* spermicide.

espermatozoide *nm* spermatozoid.

esperpéntico,-a *adj fam* grotesque.

espesar **I** *vtr* to thicken. **II** **espesarse** *vr* to thicken, get thicker.

espeso,-a *adj (bosque, niebla)* dense; *(líquido)* thick; *(masa)* stiff.

espesor *nm* thickness; **tres metros de e.**, three metres thick.

espesura *nf* denseness.

espetar *vtr fig* to spit out.

espía *nmf* spy.

espiar [29] **I** *vi* to spy. **II** *vtr* to spy on.

espichar *vi vulg (morir)* to snuff it; **espicharla**, to kick the bucket.

espiga *nf* **1** *(de trigo)* ear. **2** *Téc* pin.

espigado,-a *adj* slender.

espina *nf* **1** *Bot* thorn. **2** *(de pescado)* bone. **3** *Anat* **e. dorsal**, spinal column, spine. **4** *fig* **ése me da mala e.**, there's something fishy about that one.

espinaca *nf* spinach.

espinal *adj* spinal; **médula e.**, spinal marrow.

espinazo *nm* spine, backbone.

espinilla *nf* **1** *Anat* shin. **2** *(en la piel)* spot.

espinillera *nf Dep* shin pad.

espino *nm* hawthorn; **alambre de e.**, barbed wire.

espionaje *nm* spying, espionage; **novela de e.**, spy story.

espiral *adj & nf* spiral.

espirar *vi* to breathe out, exhale.

espiritismo *nm* spiritualism.

espíritu *nm* **1** spirit; **e. deportivo**, sportsmanship. **2** *Rel (alma)* soul; **el E. Santo**, the Holy Ghost.

espiritual *adj* spiritual.

espléndido,-a *adj* **1** *(magnífico)* splendid. **2** *(generoso)* lavish, generous.

esplendor *nm* splendour, US splendor.

esplendoroso,-a *adj* magnificent.

espliego *nm* lavender.

espolear *vtr* to spur on.

espolio *nm → expolio*.

espolvorear *vtr* to sprinkle (**de**, with).

esponja *nf* sponge.

esponjoso,-a *adj* spongy; *(bizcocho)* light.

esponsales *nmpl* betrothal *sing*, engagement *sing*.

espontaneidad *nf* spontaneity; **con e.**, naturally.

espontáneo,-a **I** *adj* spontaneous. **II** *nm Taur* spectator who spontaneously joins in the bullfight.

esporádico,-a *adj* sporadic.

esposado,-a *adj* **1** *(recién casado)* newly married. **2** *(con esposas)* handcuffed.

esposar *vtr* to handcuff.

esposas *nfpl* handcuffs.

esposo,-a *nm,f* spouse; *(hombre)* husband; *(mujer)* wife.

esprint *nm* sprint.

esprintar *vi* to sprint.

espuela *nf* spur.

espuerta *nf* hod.

espuma *nf* foam; *(de olas)* surf; *(de cerveza)* froth, head; *(de jabón)* lather; **e. de afeitar**, shaving foam.

espumoso,-a *adj* frothy; *(vino)* sparkling.

esputo *nm* spit.

esquela *nf* notice, announcement; **e. mortuoria**, announcement of a death.

esquelético,-a *adj* **1** *Anat* skeletal. **2** *(flaco)* skinny.

esqueleto *nm* **1** skeleton. **2** *Constr* framework.

esquema *nm* diagram.

esquemático,-a *adj (escueto)* schematic; *(con diagramas)* diagrammatic.

esquí *nm* **1** *(objeto)* ski. **2** *(deporte)* skiing; **e. acuático**, water-skiing.

esquiador,-a *nm,f* skier.

esquiar [29] *vi* to ski.

esquilar *vtr* to shear.

esquimal *adj & nmf* Eskimo.

esquina *nf* corner; *Dep* **saque de e.**, corner kick.

esquinazo nm **dar e. a algn**, to give sb the slip.

esquirla nf splinter.

esquirol nm Ind blackleg, scab.

esquivar vtr (a una persona) to avoid; (un golpe) to dodge.

esquivo,-a adj cold, aloof.

esquizofrenia nf schizophrenia.

esquizofrénico,-a adj & nm,f schizophrenic.

esta adj dem → **este,-a.**

está indic pres → **estar.**

ésta pron dem f → **éste.**

estabilidad nf stability.

estabilizar [4] vtr to stabilize.

estable adj stable.

establecer [33] I vtr to establish; (fundar) to set up, found; (récord) to set. II **establecerse** vr to settle.

establecimiento nm establishment.

establo nm cow shed.

estaca nf stake, post; (de tienda de campaña) peg.

estacada nf fence; fig **dejar a algn en la e.**, to leave sb in the lurch.

estacazo nm blow with a stick.

estación nf 1 station; **e. de servicio**, service station; **e. de esquí**, ski resort. 2 (del año) season.

estacional adj seasonal.

estacionamiento nm Aut (acción) parking; (lugar) car park, US parking lot.

estacionar vtr, **estacionarse** vr Aut to park.

estacionario,-a adj stationary.

estada nf, **estadía** nf Am stay.

estadio nm 1 Dep stadium. 2 (fase) stage, phase.

estadista nmf Pol (hombre) statesman; (mujer) stateswoman.

estadística nf statistics sing; **una e.**, a statistic.

estado nm 1 Pol state. 2 (situación) state, condition; **en buen e.**, in good condition; **e. de salud**, condition, state of health; **e. de excepción**, state of emergency; **estar en e.**, to be pregnant; **e. civil**, marital status; **Com e. de cuentas**, statement of accounts. 3 Mil **e. mayor**, general staff.

Estados Unidos npl the United States.

estadounidense I adj United States, American. II nmf United States citizen.

estafa nf swindle.

estafador,-a nm,f swindler.

estafar vtr to swindle.

estafeta nf **e. de Correos**, sub post office.

estalactita nf stalactite.

estalagmita nf stalagmite.

estallar vi 1 to burst; (bomba) to explode, go off; (guerra) to break out. 2 fig (de cólera etc) to explode; **en sollozos**, to burst into tears.

estallido nm explosion; (de guerra) out-

estambre nm Bot stamen.

Estambul n Istanbul.

estamento nm Hist estate; fig (grupo) group.

estampa nf illustration.

estampado,-a I adj (tela) printed. II nm 1 (tela) print. 2 (proceso) printing.

estampar vtr 1 (tela) to print. 2 (dejar impreso) to imprint. 3 fig (bofetada, beso) to plant, place.

estampida nf 1 (estampido) bang. 2 (carrera rápida) stampede; **de e.**, suddenly.

estampido nm bang.

estampilla nf Am (postage) stamp.

estancado,-a adj (agua) stagnant; fig static, at a standstill; **quedarse e.**, to get stuck o bogged down.

estancar [1] I vtr 1 (agua) to hold back. 2 fig (asunto) to block; (negociaciones) to bring to a standstill. II **estancarse** vr to stagnate; fig to get bogged down.

estancia nf 1 (permanencia) stay. 2 (habitación) room. 3 Am (hacienda) ranch, farm.

estanco,-a I nm tobacconist's. II adj watertight.

estándar (pl **estándares**) adj & nm standard.

estandarizar [4] vtr to standardize.

estandarte nm standard, banner.

estanque nm pool, pond.

estanquero,-a nm,f tobacconist.

estante nm shelf; (para libros) bookcase.

estantería nf shelves pl, shelving.

estaño nm tin.

estar [13] I vi 1 to be; **está en la playa**, he is at the beach; **e. en casa**, to be in, be at home; **estamos en Caracas**, we are in Caracas; **¿está tu madre?**, is your mother in?; **¿cómo estás?** how are you?; **los precios están bajos**, prices are low; **el problema está en el dinero**, the problem is money; **e. en lo cierto**, to be right; **e. en todo**, not to miss a trick. 2 (+ adj) to be; **está cansado/enfermo**, he's tired/ill; **está vacío**, it's empty. 3 (+ adv) to be; **está bien/mal**, it's all right/ wrong; **e. mal de dinero**, he's short of money; **estará enseguida**, it'll be ready in a minute. 4 (+ ger) to be; **está escribiendo**, she is writing; **estaba comiendo**, he was eating. 5 (+ a + fecha) to be; **¿a cuántos estamos?**, what's the date (today)?; **estamos a 2 de Noviembre**, it is the 2nd of November. 6 (+ precio) to be at; **están a 100 pesetas el kilo**, they're at 100 pesetas a kilo. 7 (locuciones) **e. al caer**, to be just round the corner; **¿estamos?**, OK? 8 (+ de) **e. de más**, not to be needed; **e. de paseo**, to be out for a walk; **e. de vacaciones/viaje**, to be (away) on holiday/a trip; **estoy de jefe hoy**, I'm the boss today. 9 (+ para) **esta-**

rá para las seis, it will be finished by six; **hoy no estoy para bromas**, I'm in no mood for jokes today; **el tren está para salir**, the train is just about to leave. **10** (+ **por**) **está por hacer**, it has still to be done; **eso está por ver**, it remains to be seen; **estoy por esperar**, (*a favor de*) I'm for waiting. **11** (+ **con**) to have; **e. con la gripe**, to have the flu, be down with flu; **estoy con Jaime**, (*de acuerdo con*) I agree with Jaime. **12** (+ **sin**) to have no; **e. sin luz/agua**, to have no light/water. **13** (+ **que**) **está que se duerme**, he is nearly asleep; *fam* **está que rabia**, (*de empresa etc*) rules sake. **II estarse** *vr* **¡éstate quieto!**, keep still!, stop fidgeting!

estatal *adj* state; **enseñanza e.**, state education.

estático,-a *adj* static.

estatua *nf* statue.

estatura *nf* **1** height; **¿cuál es tu e.?**, how tall are you? **2** (*renombre*) stature.

estatus *nm* status; **e. quo**, status quo.

estatutario *adj* statutory.

estatuto *nm* *Jur* statute; (*de ciudad*) by-law; (*de empresa etc*) rules.

este I *adj* eastern; (*dirección*) easterly. **II** *nm* east; **al e. de**, to the east of.

esté *subj pres* → **estar**.

este,-a *adj dem* **1** this. **2** *estos,-as*, these.

éste,-a *pron dem* *m,f* **1** this one; **aquél ... é.**, the former ... the latter. **2** *éstos,-as*, these (ones); **aquéllos ... é.**, the former ... the latter.

estela *nf* (*de barco*) wake; (*de avión*) vapour trail; (*de cometa*) tail.

estelar *adj* **1** *Astron* stellar. **2** *fig Cin Teat* star.

estentóreo,-a *adj* stentorian, thundering.

estepa *nf* steppe.

estera *nf* rush mat.

estercolero *nm* dunghill; *fig* pigsty.

estéreo *nm* & *adj* stereo.

estereofónico,-a *adj* stereophonic, stereo.

estereotipar *vtr* to stereotype.

estereotipo *nm* stereotype.

estéril *adj* **1** sterile. **2** *fig* (*esfuerzo*) futile.

esterilidad *nf* **1** sterility. **2** *fig* futility, uselessness.

esterilizar [4] *vtr* to sterilize.

esterilla *nf* small mat.

esterlina *adj* & *nf* sterling; **libra e.**, pound (sterling).

esternón *nm* sternum, breastbone.

estero *nm* *Am* marsh, swamp.

estertor *nm* death rattle.

estética *nf* aesthetics, *US* esthetics *sing*.

esteticienne, esteticista *nf* beautician.

estético,-a *adj* aesthetic, *US* esthetic; **cirugía estética**, plastic surgery.

estibador *nm* docker, stevedore.

estiércol *nm* manure, dung.

estigma *nm* stigma; *Rel* stigmata.

estilarse *vr* to be in vogue, be fashionable.

estilete *nm* (*punzón*) stylus; (*puñal*) stiletto.

estilístico,-a *adj* stylistic.

estilizar [4] *vtr* to stylize.

estilo *nm* **1** style; (*modo*) manner, fashion; **algo por el e.**, something like that; **e. de vida**, way of life. **2** *Natación* stroke. **3** *Ling* **e. directo/indirecto**, direct/indirect speech.

estilográfica *nf* (**pluma**) **e.**, fountain pen.

estima *nf* esteem, respect.

estimación *nf* **1** (*estima*) esteem, respect. **2** (*valoración*) evaluation; (*cálculo aproximado*) estimate.

estimado,-a *adj* esteemed, respected; **E. Señor**, (*en carta*) Dear Sir.

estimar *vtr* **1** (*apreciar*) to esteem. **2** (*considerar*) to consider, think; **lo estimo conveniente**, I think it appropriate. **3** (*valorar*) to value.

estimativo,-a *adj* approximate, estimated.

estimulante I *adj* stimulating. **II** *nm* stimulant.

estimular *vtr* **1** to stimulate. **2** *fig* to encourage.

estímulo *nm* *Biol Fís* stimulus; *fig* encouragement.

estío *nm* summer.

estipendio *nm* stipend, fee.

estipular *vtr* to stipulate.

estirado,-a *adj* *fig* stiff.

estirar I *vtr* to stretch; *fig* (*dinero*) to spin out; *fig* **e. la pata**, to kick the bucket. **II estirarse** *vr* to stretch.

estirón *nm* pull, jerk, tug; **fam dar o pegar un e.**, to shoot up o grow quickly.

estirpe *nf* stock, pedigree.

estival *adj* summer; **época e.**, summertime.

esto *pron dem neut*, this, this thing, this matter; *fam* **e. de la fiesta**, this business about the party.

estocada *nf* *Taur* stab.

Estocolmo *n* Stockholm.

estofado *nm* stew.

estoico,-a I *adj* stoical. **II** *nm,f* stoic.

estómago *nm* stomach; **dolor de e.**, stomach ache.

estoque *nm* *Taur* sword.

estorbar *vtr* **1** (*dificultar*) to hinder, get in the way of. **2** (*molestar*) to disturb. **II** *vi* to be in the way.

estorbo *nm* **1** (*obstáculo*) obstruction, obstacle. **2** (*molestia*) nuisance.

estornino *nm* starling.

estornudar *vi* to sneeze.

estornudo *nm* sneeze.

estos,-as *adj dem pl* → **este,-a**.

éstos,-as *pron dem m,fpl* → **éste,-a**.

estoy *indic pres* → **estar**.

estrabismo *nm* squint.

estrado *nm* platform; *Mús* bandstand; *Jur*

stand.

estrafalario,-a *adj fam* outlandish.

estragos *nmpl* **hacer e. en,** to wreak havoc with *o* on.

estrambótico,-a *adj fam* outlandish, eccentric.

estrangulador,-a *nm,f* strangler.

estrangular *vtr* to strangle; *Med* to strangulate.

estraperlo *nm* black market; **tabaco de e.,** black market cigarettes.

Estrasburgo *n* Strasbourg.

estratagema *nf Mil* stratagem; *fam* trick, ruse.

estratega *nmf* strategist.

estrategia *nf* strategy.

estratégico,-a *adj* strategic.

estratificar [1] *vtr* to stratify.

estrato *nm* stratum.

estraza *nf* **papel de e.,** brown paper.

estrechamiento *nm* 1 narrowing; **'e. de calzada',** (*en letrero*) 'road narrows'. 2 (*de amistad etc*) tightening.

estrechar I *vtr* 1 to make narrow. 2 (*mano*) to shake; (*lazos de amistad*) to tighten; **me estrechó entre sus brazos,** he hugged me. II **estrecharse** *vr* to narrow, become narrower.

estrechez *nf* 1 narrowness; *fig* **e. de miras,** narrow-mindedness. 2 *fig* (*dificultad económica*) want, need; **pasar estrecheces,** to be hard up.

estrecho,-a I *adj* 1 narrow; (*ropa, zapato*) tight; (*amistad, relación*) close, intimate; *fig* **e. de miras,** narrow-minded. II *nm Geog* strait, straits *pl.* ◆**estrechamente** *adv* (*íntimamente*) closely, intimately; **e. relacionados,** closely related.

estregar *vtr* to scrub.

estrella *nf* star; *fig* **e. de cine,** film star; *Zool* **e. de mar,** starfish; **e. fugaz,** shooting star.

estrellado,-a *adj* 1 (*en forma de estrella*) star-shaped. 2 (*cielo*) starry. 3 (*huevos*) scrambled.

estrellar I *vtr fam* to smash. II **estrellarse** *vr Aut Av* (*chocar*) to crash (**contra,** into); (*morir*) to die in a car crash.

estrellato *nm* stardom.

estremecedor,-a *adj* bloodcurdling.

estremecer [33] *vtr,* **estremecerse** *vr* to shake.

estrenar *vtr* 1 to use for the first time; (*ropa*) to wear for the first time. 2 *Teat Cin* to premiere.

estreno *nm Teat* first performance; *Cin* premiere.

estreñido,-a *adj* constipated.

estreñimiento *nm* constipation.

estrépito *nm* din, racket.

estrepitoso,-a *adj* deafening; *fig* (*fracaso*) spectacular.

estrés *nm* stress.

estresante *adj* stressful.

estría *nf* 1 (*en la piel*) stretch mark. 2 *Arquit* flute, fluting.

estribar *vi* **e. en,** to lie in, be based on.

estribillo *nm* (*en canción*) chorus; (*en poema*) refrain.

estribo *nm* 1 stirrup; *fig* **perder los estribos,** to lose one's temper, lose one's head. 2 *Arquit* buttress; (*de puente*) pier, support.

estribor *nm* starboard.

estricto,-a *adj* strict.

estridente *adj* strident.

estrofa *nf* verse.

estropajo *nm* scourer.

estropear I *vtr* (*máquina, cosecha*) to damage; (*fiesta, plan*) to spoil, ruin; (*pelo, manos*) to ruin. II **estropearse** *vr* to be ruined; (*máquina*) to break down.

estropicio *nm fam* (*destrozo*) damage; (*ruido*) crash, clatter.

estructura *nf* structure; (*armazón*) frame, framework.

estructurar *vtr* to structure.

estruendo *nm* roar.

estrujar I *vtr* (*limón etc*) to squeeze; (*ropa*) to wring; (*apretar*) to crush. II **estrujarse** *vr fam* **e. los sesos** *o* **el cerebro,** to rack one's brains.

estrujón *nm* tight squeeze, big hug.

estuche *nm* case; (*para lápices*) pencil case.

estuco *nm* stucco.

estudiante *nmf* student.

estudiantil *adj* student.

estudiar [12] *vtr & vi* to study.

estudio *nm* 1 study; (*encuesta*) survey; *Com* **e. de mercado,** market research. 2 (*sala*) studio; **e. cinematográfico/de grabación,** film/recording studio. 3 (*apartamento*) studio (flat). 4 **estudios,** studies.

estudioso,-a I *adj* studious. II *nm,f* specialist.

estufa *nf* (*calentador*) heater; (*de leña*) stove.

estupefaciente *nm* drug, narcotic.

estupefacto,-a *adj* astounded, flabbergasted.

estupendo,-a *adj* super, marvellous, US marvelous; **¡e.!,** great! ◆**estupendamente** *adv* marvellously, US marvelously, wonderfully.

estupidez *nf* stupidity.

estúpido,-a I *adj* stupid. II *nm,f* berk, idiot.

estupor *nm* amazement, astonishment.

estupro *nm Jur* rape (of a minor).

estuve *pt indef* → **estar.**

esvástica *nf* swastika.

ETA *nf abr de* **Euzkadi Ta Askatasuna** (*Patria Vasca y Libertad*), ETA.

etapa *nf* stage; **por etapas,** in stages.

etarra *nmf* member of ETA.

etc. *abr de* **etcétera,** etcetera, etc.

etcétera *adv* etcetera.

éter nm ether.

etéreo,-a adj ethereal.

eternidad nf eternity; fam **una e.**, ages.

eterno,-a adj eternal.

ética nf ethic; (ciencia) ethics sing.

ético,-a adj ethical.

etílico,-a adj ethylic; **alcohol e.**, ethyl alcohol; **en estado e.**, intoxicated; **intoxicación etílica**, alcohol poisoning.

etimología nf etymology.

etimológico,-a adj etymological.

etiope, etíope adj & nmf Ethiopian.

Etiopía nf Ethiopia.

etiqueta nf 1 (de producto) label. 2 (ceremonia) etiquette; **de e.**, formal.

etiquetar vtr to label.

etnia nf ethnic group.

étnico,-a adj ethnic.

eucalipto nm eucalyptus.

eucaristía nf eucharist.

eufemismo nm euphemism.

euforia nf euphoria.

eufórico,-a adj euphoric.

eureka interj eureka!

eurocomunismo nm Eurocommunism.

eurodiputado,-a nm,f Euro MP.

euromisil nm Euromissile.

Europa n Europe.

europeísmo nm Europeanism.

europeizar [26] vtr to europeanize.

europeo,-a adj & nm,f European.

euscalduna I adj Basque; (que habla vasco) Basque-speaking. **II** nmf Basque speaker.

euskera adj & nm Basque.

eutanasia nf euthanasia.

evacuación nf evacuation.

evacuar [10] vtr to evacuate.

evadir I vtr (respuesta, peligro, impuestos) to avoid; (responsabilidad) to shirk. **II evadirse** vr to escape.

evaluación nf evaluation; Educ assessment; **e. continua**, continuous assessment.

evaluar [30] vtr to evaluate, assess.

evangélico,-a adj evangelical.

evangelio nm gospel.

evangelista nm evangelist.

evaporación nf evaporation.

evaporar I vtr to evaporate. **II evaporarse** vr to evaporate; fig to vanish.

evasión nf (fuga) escape; fig evasion; **e. fiscal o de impuestos**, tax evasion.

evasiva nf evasive answer.

evasivo,-a adj evasive.

evento nm 1 (acontecimiento) event. 2 (incidente) contingency, unforeseen event.

eventual I adj 1 (posible) possible; (gastos) incidental. 2 (trabajo, obrero) casual, temporary. ◆**eventualmente** adv by chance; **los problemas que e. surjan**, such problems as may arise.

eventualidad nf contingency.

evidencia nf obviousness; **poner a algn en e.**, to show sb up.

evidenciar [12] vtr to show, demonstrate.

evidente adj obvious. ◆**evidentemente** adv obviously.

evitar vtr to avoid; (prevenir) to prevent; (desastre) to avert.

evocador,-a adj evocative.

evocar [1] vtr (traer a la memoria) to evoke; (acordarse de) to recall.

evolución nf evolution; (desarrollo) development.

evolucionar vi to develop; Biol to evolve; **el enfermo evoluciona favorablemente**, the patient is improving.

ex pref former, ex-; **ex alumno**, former pupil, ex-student; **ex combatiente**, ex-serviceman, US veteran; **ex marido**, ex-husband; fam **mi ex**, my ex.

exabrupto nm sharp comment.

exacerbar I vtr 1 (agravar) to exacerbate, aggravate. 2 (irritar) to exasperate, irritate. **II exacerbarse** vr (irritarse) to feel exasperated.

exactitud nf accuracy; **con e.**, precisely.

exacto,-a adj exact; ¡e.!, precisely!; **para ser e.**, to be precise. ◆**exactamente** adv exactly, precisely.

exageración nf exaggeration.

exagerado,-a adj exaggerated; (excesivo) excessive.

exagerar I vtr to exaggerate. **II** vi to overdo it.

exaltado,-a adj (persona) excitable, hotheaded. **II** nm,f fam fanatic.

exaltar I vtr 1 to praise, extol. **II exaltarse** vr (acalorarse) to get overexcited, get carried away.

examen nm examination, exam; **e. de conducir**, driving test; Med **e. médico**, checkup.

examinador,-a nm,f examiner.

examinar I vtr to examine. **II examinarse** vr to take o sit an examination.

exasperante adj exasperating.

exasperar I vtr to exasperate. **II exasperarse** vr to become exasperated.

Exc., Exca., Exc.ª abr de **Excelencia**, Excellency.

excavación nf excavation; (en arqueología) dig.

excavadora nf digger.

excavar vtr to excavate, dig.

excedencia nf leave (of absence).

excedente adj & nm excess, surplus.

exceder I vtr to exceed, surpass. **II excederse** vr to go too far.

excelencia nf 1 excellence; **por e.**, par excellence. 2 (título) **Su E.**, His o Her Excellency.

excelente adj excellent.

excelso,-a adj sublime, lofty.

excentricidad nf eccentricity.

excéntrico,-a adj eccentric.

excepción nf exception; **a e. de**, with the

exception of, except for; **de e.**, exceptional; *Pol* **estado de e.**, state of emergency.

excepcional *adj* exceptional.

excepto *adv* except (for), apart from.

exceptuar [30] *vtr* to except, exclude.

excesivo,-a *adj* excessive.

exceso *nm* excess; **en e.**, in excess, excessively; **e. de equipaje**, excess baggage; **e. de velocidad**, speeding.

excitable *adj* excitable.

excitación *nf* (*sentimiento*) excitement.

excitante I *adj* exciting; *Med* stimulating. II *nm* stimulant.

excitar I *vtr* to excite. II **excitarse** *vr* to get excited.

exclamación *nf* exclamation.

exclamar *vtr & vi* to exclaim, cry out.

excluir [37] *vtr* to exclude; (*rechazar*) to reject.

exclusión *nf* exclusion.

exclusiva *nf Prensa* exclusive; *Com* sole right.

exclusive *adv* (*en fechas*) exclusive.

exclusivo,-a *adj* exclusive.

Excma. *abr de* **Excelentísima**, Most Excellent.

Excmo. *abr de* **Excelentísimo**, Most Excellent.

excomulgar [7] *vtr Rel* to excommunicate.

excomunión *nf* excommunication.

excremento *nm* excrement.

exculpar *vtr* to exonerate.

excursión *nf* excursion.

excursionista *nmf* tripper; (*a pie*) hiker.

excusa *nf* (*pretexto*) excuse; (*disculpa*) apology.

excusado *nm* (*retrete*) toilet.

excusar I *vtr* 1 (*justificar*) to excuse. 2 (*eximir*) to exempt (**de**, from). II **excusarse** *vr* (*disculparse*) to apologize.

execrar *vtr* to execrate, abhor.

exención *nf* exemption; **e. de impuestos**, tax exemption.

exento,-a *adj* exempt, free (**de**, from).

exequias *nfpl* funeral rites.

exhalar *vtr* to exhale, breathe out; (*gas*) to give off, emit; (*suspiro*) to heave.

exhaustivo,-a *adj* exhaustive.

exhausto,-a *adj* exhausted.

exhibición *nf* exhibition.

exhibicionista *nmf* exhibitionist.

exhibir I *vtr* 1 (*mostrar*) to exhibit, display. 2 (*lucir*) to show off. II **exhibirse** *vr* to show off, make an exhibition of oneself.

exhortar *vtr* to exhort.

exhumar *vtr* to exhume.

exigencia *nf* 1 demand. 2 (*requisito*) requirement.

exigente *adj* demanding, exacting.

exigir [6] *vtr* to demand.

exiguo,-a *adj* minute.

exilado,-a I *adj* exiled, in exile. II *nm,f* exile.

exilar I *vtr* to exile, send into exile. II **exilarse** *vr* to go into exile.

exiliado,-a *adj & nm,f → **exilado,-a**.

exiliar [12] *vtr*, **exiliarse** *vr → **exilar**.

exilio *nm* exile.

eximio,-a *adj* distinguished, eminent.

eximir *vtr* to exempt (**de**, from).

existencia *nf* 1 (*vida*) existence. 2 *Com* **existencias**, stock *sing*, stocks.

existente *adj* existing; *Com* in stock.

existir *vi* to exist, be (in existence).

éxito *nm* success; **con é.**, successfully; **tener é.**, to be successful.

exitoso,-a *adj* successful.

éxodo *nm* exodus.

exonerar *vtr* to exonerate.

exorbitante *adj* exorbitant, excessive.

exorcista *nmf* exorcist.

exorcizar [4] *vtr* to exorcize.

exótico,-a *adj* exotic.

expandir I *vtr* to expand. II **expandirse** (*gas etc*) to expand; (*noticia*) to spread.

expansión *nf* 1 expansion; (*de noticia*) spreading. 2 (*diversión*) relaxation, recreation.

expansionarse *vr fig* (*divertirse*) to relax, let one's hair down.

expatriado,-a *adj & nm,f* expatriate.

expatriar [19] I *vtr* to exile, banish. II **expatriarse** *vr* to leave one's country.

expectación *nf* excitement.

expectativa *nf* expectancy; **estar a la e. de**, to be on the lookout for.

expectorante *nm* expectorant.

expedición *nf* expedition.

expedientar *vtr* to place under enquiry.

expediente *nm* 1 (*informe*) dossier, record; (*ficha*) file; *Educ* **e. académico**, student's record; **abrirle e. a algn**, to place sb under enquiry. 2 *Jur* proceedings *pl*, action.

expedir [6] *vtr* 1 (*carta*) to send, dispatch. 2 (*pasaporte etc*) to issue.

expedito,-a *adj* free, clear.

expendedor,-a I *nm,f* seller. II *nm* **e. automático**, vending machine.

expendeduría *nf* tobacconist's.

expensas *nfpl* **a e. de**, at the expense of.

experiencia *nf* 1 experience; **por e.**, from experience. 2 (*experimento*) experiment.

experimentado,-a *adj* experienced.

experimental *adj* experimental.

experimentar I *vi* to experiment. II *vtr* to undergo; (*aumento*) to show; (*pérdida*) to suffer; (*sensación*) to experience, feel; *Med* **e. una mejoría**, to improve, make progress.

experimento *nm* experiment.

experto,-a *nm,f* expert.

expiar [29] *vtr* to expiate, atone for.

expirar *vi* to expire.

explanada *nf* esplanade.

explayarse *vr* to talk at length (about).

explicación *nf* explanation.

explicar [1] I *vtr* to explain. II **explicarse** *vr* (*persona*) to explain (oneself); **no me lo explico,** I can't understand it.

explicativo,-a *adj* explanatory.

explícito,-a *adj* explicit.

exploración *nf* exploration; *Téc* scanning; *Med* probe; *Mil* reconnaissance.

explorador,-a *nm,f* **1** (*persona*) explorer. **2** *Med* probe; *Téc* scanner.

explorar *vtr* to explore; *Med* to probe; *Téc* to scan; *Mil* to reconnoitre.

explosión *nf* explosion, blast; **hacer e.,** to explode; **motor de e.,** internal combustion engine; **e. demográfica,** population explosion.

explosionar *vtr & vi* to explode, blow up.

explosivo,-a *adj & nm* explosive.

explotación *nf* **1** (*abuso*) exploitation. **2** (*uso*) exploitation, working; *Agr* cultivation (of land); **granja e.** farm.

explotador,-a *nm,f* **pey** exploiter.

explotar I *vi* (*bomba*) to explode, go off. II *vtr* **1** (*aprovechar*) to exploit; (*recursos*) to tap; (*tierra*) to cultivate. **2** (*abusar de*) to exploit.

expoliar [12] *vtr* to plunder, pillage.

exponente *nmf* exponent.

exponer [19] (*pp* **expuesto**) I *vtr* **1** (*mostrar*) to exhibit, display. **2** (*explicar*) to expound, put forward. **3** (*arriesgar*) to expose. II **exponerse** *vr* to expose oneself (**a,** to); **te expones a perder el trabajo,** you run the risk of losing your job.

exportación *nf* export.

exportador,-a I *adj* exporting. II *nm,f* exporter.

exportar *vtr* to export.

exposición *nf* **1** *Arte* exhibition; **e. universal,** world fair; **sala de exposiciones,** gallery. **2** (*de hechos, ideas*) exposé. **3** *Fot* exposure.

exprés *adj* express; (*olla*) **e.,** pressure cooker; (*café*) **e.,** espresso (coffee).

expresar I *vtr* to express; (*manifestar*) to state. II **expresarse** *vr* to express oneself.

expresión *nf* expression; **la mínima e.,** the bare minimum.

expresivo,-a *adj* expressive.

expreso,-a I *adj* express; **con el fin e. de,** with the express purpose of. II *nm Ferroc* express (train). III *adv* on purpose, deliberately. ◆**expresamente** *adv* specifically, expressly.

exprimidor *nm* squeezer, *US* juicer.

exprimir *vtr* (*limón*) to squeeze; (*zumo*) to squeeze out; *fig* (*persona*) to exploit, bleed dry.

expropiar [12] *vtr* to expropriate.

expuesto,-a *adj* **1** (*sin protección*) exposed; **estar e. a,** to be exposed to. **2** (*peligroso*) risky, dangerous. **3** (*exhibido*) on display,

on show.

expulsar *vtr* **1** to expel, throw out; *Dep* (*jugador*) to send off. **2** (*gas etc*) to belch out.

expulsión *nf* expulsion; *Dep* sending off.

expurgar [7] *vtr* to expurgate; *fig* to purge.

expuse *pt indef* → **exponer**.

exquisito,-a *adj* exquisite; (*comida*) delicious; (*gusto*) refined.

extasiado,-a *adj* ecstatic; **quedarse e.,** to go into ecstasies *o* raptures.

extasiarse [29] *vr* to go into ecstasies *o* raptures.

éxtasis *nm inv* ecstasy.

extender [3] I *vtr* **1** to extend; (*agrandar*) to enlarge. **2** (*mantel, mapa*) to spread (out), open (out); (*mano, brazo*) to stretch (out). **3** (*crema, mantequilla*) to spread. **3** (*cheque*) to make out; (*documento*) to draw up; (*certificado*) to issue. II **extenderse** *vr* **1** (*en el tiempo*) to extend, last. **2** (*en el espacio*) to spread out, stretch. **3** (*rumor, noticia*) to spread, extend. **4** *fig* (*hablar demasiado*) to go on.

extendido,-a *adj* **1** extended; (*mapa, plano*) spread out, open; (*mano, brazo*) outstretched. **2** (*costumbre, rumor*) widespread.

extensible *adj* extending.

extensión *nf* (*de libro etc*) length; (*de cuerpo*) size; (*de terreno*) area, expanse; (*edificio anexo*) extension; **en toda la e. de la palabra,** in every sense of the word; **por e.,** by extension.

extensivo,-a *adj* **hacer e.,** to extend; **ser e. a,** to cover.

extenso,-a *adj* (*terreno*) extensive; (*libro, película*) long.

extenuar [30] I *vtr* to exhaust. II **extenuarse** *vr* to exhaust oneself.

exterior I *adj* **1** (*de fuera*) outer; (*puerta*) outside. **2** (*política, deuda*) foreign; *Pol* **Ministerio de Asuntos Exteriores,** Ministry of Foreign Affairs, *GB* Foreign Office, *US* State Department. II *nm* **1** (*parte de fuera*) exterior, outside. **2** (*extranjero*) abroad. **3** **exteriores,** *Cin* location *sing*. ◆**exteriormente** *adv* outwardly.

exteriorizar [4] *vtr* to show.

exterminar *vtr* to exterminate.

exterminio *nm* extermination.

externo,-a I *adj* external; *Farm* **de uso e.,** for external use only. II *nm,f Educ* day pupil.

extinción *nf* extinction.

extinguir [8] I *vtr* (*fuego*) to extinguish, put out; (*raza*) to wipe out. II **extinguirse** *vr* (*fuego*) to go out; (*especie*) to become extinct, die out.

extinto,-a *adj* extinct.

extintor *nm* fire extinguisher.

extirpar *vtr* **1** *Med* to remove. **2** *fig* to

eradicate, stamp out.
extorsión *nf* extortion.
extorsionar *vtr* to extort.
extra¹ I *adj* 1 (*suplementario*) extra; **horas e.**, overtime; **paga e.**, bonus. 2 (*superior*) top quality. II *nm* extra. III *nm,f* *Cin Teat* extra.
extra² *pref* extra; **extramatrimonial**, extramarital.
extracción *nf* 1 extraction. 2 (*en lotería*) draw.
extracto *nm* 1 extract; **e. de fresa**, strawberry extract; **e. de regaliz**, liquorice; **Fin e. de cuenta**, statement of account. 2 (*resumen*) summary.
extractor *nm* extractor.
extradición *nf* extradition.
extraer [25] *vtr* to extract, take out.
extraescolar *adj* (*actividad etc*) extra-curricular.
extrafino,-a *adj* superfine.
extralimitarse *vr* to overstep the mark.
extranjería *nf* ley de e., law on aliens.
extranjero,-a I *adj* foreign. II *nm,f* foreigner. III *nm* abroad; **en el e.**, abroad.
extrañar I *vtr* 1 (*sorprender*) to surprise; **no es de e.**, it's hardly surprising. 2 *Am* (*echar de menos*) to miss. II **extrañarse** *vr* **e. de**, to be surprised at.
extrañeza *nf* 1 (*sorpresa*) surprise, astonishment. 2 (*singularidad*) strangeness.
extraño,-a I *adj* strange; *Med* **cuerpo e.**, foreign body. II *nm,f* stranger.
extraoficial *adj* unofficial.
extraordinaria *nf* (*paga*) bonus.

extraordinario,-a *adj* extraordinary; *Prensa* **edición extraordinaria**, special edition.
extrarradio *nm* outskirts *pl*, suburbs *pl*.
extraterrestre *nmf* alien.
extravagancia *nf* extravagance.
extravagante *adj* odd, outlandish.
extravertido,-a *adj* → extrovertido,-a.
extraviado,-a *adj* lost, missing.
extraviar [29] I *vtr* to mislay, lose. II **extraviarse** *vr* to be missing, get mislaid.
extremado,-a *adj* extreme.
◆**extremadamente** *adv* extremely.
Extremadura *n* Estremadura.
extremar I *vtr* **e. la prudencia**, to be extremely careful. II **extremarse** *vr* to take great pains, do one's utmost.
extremaunción *nf* extreme unction.
extremeño,-a I *adj* of o from Estremadura. II *nm,f* native of Estremadura.
extremidad *nf* 1 (*extremo*) end, tip. 2 *Anat* (*miembro*) limb, extremity.
extremista *adj & nmf* extremist.
extremo,-a I *nm* (*de calle, cable*) end; (*máximo*) extreme; **en e.**, very much; **en último e.**, as a last resort. II *nm,f* *Dep* winger; *Ftb* **e. derecha/izquierda**, outside-right/-left. III *adj* extreme; **E. Oriente**, Far East.
extrovertido,-a *adj & nm,f* extrovert.
exuberante *adj* exuberant; (*vegetación*) lush, abundant.
eyaculación *nf* ejaculation; **e. precoz**, premature ejaculation.
eyacular *vt* to ejaculate.
eyectable *adj* asiento e., ejector seat.

F

F, f [ˈefe] *nf* (*la letra*) F, f.
F *abr de* **Fahrenheit**, Fahrenheit, F.
fa *nm* Mús F.
fabada *nf* stew of beans, pork sausage and bacon.
fábrica *nf* factory; **marca de f.**, trademark; **precio de f.**, factory o ex-works price.
fabricación *nf* manufacture; **de f. casera**, home-made; **de f. propia**, our own make; **f. en cadena**, mass production.
fabricante *nmf* manufacturer.
fabricar [1] *vtr* 1 *Ind* to manufacture. 2 *fig* (*mentiras etc*) to fabricate.
fabril *adj* manufacturing.
fábula *nf* fable.
fabuloso,-a *adj* fabulous.
faca *nf* large curved knife.
facción *nf* 1 *Pol* faction. 2 **facciones**, (*rasgos*) features.
faccioso,-a I *adj* seditious. II *nm,f* rebel.
faceta *nf* facet.
facha¹ *nf fam* appearance, look.

facha² *nmf pey* fascist.
fachada *nf* façade.
facial *adj* facial.
fácil *adj* 1 easy; **f. de comprender**, easy to understand. 2 (*probable*) likely, probable; **es f. que ...**, it's (quite) likely that ....
◆**fácilmente** *adv* easily.
facilidad *nf* 1 (*sencillez*) easiness. 2 (*soltura*) ease. 3 (*servicio*) facility; **dar facilidades**, to make things easy; *Com* **facilidades de pago**, easy terms. 4 **f. para los idiomas**, gift for languages.
facilitar *vtr* (*proporcionar*) to provide, supply (a, with).
facineroso,-a *adj* criminal.
facsímil, facsímile *nm* facsimile.
factible *adj* feasible.
fáctico,-a *adj* **poderes fácticos**, vested interests.
factor *nm* 1 factor. 2 *Ferroc* luggage clerk.
factoría *nf* (*fábrica*) factory.
factura *nf Com* invoice.
facturación *nf* 1 *Com* invoicing. 2 (*de*

equipajes) (*en aeropuerto*) check-in; (*en estación*) registration.

facturar *vtr* 1 *Com* to invoice. 2 (*en aeropuerto*) to check in; (*en estación*) to register.

facultad *nf* faculty; **facultades mentales**, faculties.

facultativo,-a I *adj* optional. II *nm,f* doctor.

faena *nf* 1 (*tarea*) task. 2 *fam* (*mala pasada*) dirty trick. 3 *Taur* performance.

faenar *vi* to fish.

fagot *nm Mús* bassoon.

faisán *nm* pheasant.

faja *nf* 1 (*corsé*) girdle, corset. 2 (*banda*) sash. 3 (*de terreno*) strip.

fajo *nm* (*de ropa etc*) bundle; (*de billetes*) wad.

falacia *nf* fallacy.

falaz *adj* 1 (*erróneo*) fallacious. 2 (*engañoso*) deceitful.

falda *nf* 1 (*prenda*) skirt; **f. pantalón**, culottes *pl*. 2 (*de montaña*) slope, hillside. 3 (*de mesa*) cover. 4 (*regazo*) lap.

faldero,-a *adj* **perro f.**, lapdog.

falla[1] *nf Am* (*defecto*) defect, fault.

falla[2] *nf Geol* fault.

fallar[1] I *vi Jur* to rule. II *vtr* (*premio*) to award.

fallar[2] I *vi* to fail; **le falló la puntería**, he missed his aim; **fig no me falles**, don't let me down. II *vtr* to miss.

fallecer [33] *vi fml* to pass away, die.

fallecido,-a *adj* deceased.

fallecimiento *nm* demise.

fallido,-a *adj* unsuccessful, vain.

fallo[1] *nm* 1 (*error*) mistake; **f. humano**, human error. 2 (*del corazón, de los frenos*) failure.

fallo[2] *nm Jur* judgement, sentence. 2 (*en concurso*) awarding.

falo *nm* phallus.

falsear *vtr* 1 (*informe etc*) to falsify; (*hechos, la verdad*) to distort. 2 (*moneda*) to forge.

falsedad *nf* 1 falseness, (*doblez*) hypocrisy. 2 (*mentira*) falsehood.

falsificar [1] *vtr* to falsify; (*cuadro, firma, moneda*) to forge.

falso,-a *adj* false; **dar un paso en f.**, (*tropezar*) to trip, stumble; *fig* to make a blunder; **jurar en f.**, to commit perjury. 2 (*persona*) insincere.

falta *nf* 1 (*carencia*) lack; **por f. de**, for want *o* lack of; **sin f.**, without fail; **f. de educación**, bad manners. 2 (*escasez*) shortage. 3 (*ausencia*) absence; **echar algo/a algn en f.**, to miss sth/sb. 4 (*error*) mistake; (*defecto*) fault, defect; **f. de ortografía**, spelling mistake; **sacar faltas a algo/a algn**, to find fault with sth/sb. 5 *Jur* misdemeanour. 6 *Dep* (*fútbol*) foul; (*tenis*) fault. 7 **hacer f.**, to be necessary; (**nos**) **hace f. una escalera**, we need a

ladder; **harán f. dos personas para mover el piano**, it'll take two people to move the piano; **no hace f. que …**, there is no need for ….

faltar *vi* 1 (*no estar*) to be missing; **¿quién falta?**, who is missing? 2 (*escasear*) to be lacking *o* needed; **le falta confianza en sí mismo**, he lacks confidence in himself; **¡lo que me faltaba!**, that's all I needed!; **¡no faltaría o faltaba más!**, (*por supuesto*) (but) of course! 3 (*quedar*) to be left; **¿cuántos kilómetros faltan para Managua?**, how many kilometres is it to Managua?; **ya falta poco para las vacaciones**, it won't be long now till the holidays; **faltó poco para que me cayera**, I very nearly fell. 4 **f. a la verdad**, not to tell the truth; **f. al deber**, to fail in one's duty; **f. a su palabra/promesa**, to break one's word/promise; **f. al respeto a algn**, to treat sb with disrespect.

falto,-a *adj* **f. de**, lacking in.

fama *nf* 1 fame, renown; **de f. mundial**, world-famous. 2 (*reputación*) reputation.

famélico,-a *adj* starving, famished.

familia *nf* family; **estar en f.**, to be among friends; **f. numerosa**, large family.

familiar I *adj* 1 (*de la familia*) family; **empresa f.**, family business. 2 (*conocido*) familiar. II *nmf* relation, relative.

familiaridad *nf* familiarity.

familiarizarse [4] *vr* to familiarize oneself (**con**, with).

famoso,-a I *adj* famous. II *nm,f* famous person.

fan *nmf* fan.

fanático,-a I *adj* fanatical. II *nm,f* fanatic.

fanatismo *nm* fanaticism.

fanfarrón,-ona *fam* I *adj* boastful. II *nm,f* show-off.

fanfarronear *vi fam* (*chulear*) to show off; (*bravear*) to brag, boast.

fango *nm* 1 (*barro*) mud. 2 *fig* degradation.

fantasear *vi* to daydream, dream.

fantasía *nf* fantasy; **joya de f.**, imitation jewellery.

fantasioso,-a *adj* imaginative.

fantasma *nm* 1 (*espectro*) ghost. 2 *fam* (*fanfarrón*) braggart, show-off.

fantasmal *adj* ghostly.

fantástico,-a *adj* fantastic.

fantoche *nm pey* nincompoop, ninny.

faraón *nm* Pharaoh.

fardar *vi arg* to show off.

fardo *nm* bundle.

farfullar *vtr* to jabber.

faringe *nf* pharynx.

faringitis *nf* pharyngitis.

fariseo,-a *nm,f* (*falso*) hypocrite.

farmacéutico,-a I *adj* pharmaceutical. II *nm,f* pharmacist.

farmacia *nf* 1 (*tienda*) chemist's (shop),

US pharmacy. 2 (*ciencia*) pharmacology.

fármaco nm medicine, medication.

faro nm 1 (*torre*) lighthouse. 2 (*de coche*) headlight, headlamp.

farol nm 1 lantern; (*en la calle*) streetlight, streetlamp. 2 arg (*fanfarronada*) bragging; **tirarse un f.**, to brag. 3 (*en naipes*) bluff.

farola nf streetlight, streetlamp.

farolear vi arg to brag.

farolillo nm fig ser el f. rojo, to bring up the rear.

farragoso,-a adj confused, rambling.

farruco,-a adj fam cocky.

farsa nf farce.

farsante nmf fake, impostor.

fascículo nm Impr instalment, US instalment.

fascinador,-a, fascinante adj fascinating.

fascinar vtr to fascinate.

fascismo nm fascism.

fascista adj & nmf fascist.

fase nf 1 (*etapa*) phase, stage. 2 Elec Fís phase.

fastidiado,-a adj fam 1 (*roto*) broken. 2 (*enfermo*) sick; **tiene el estómago f.**, he's got a bad stomach.

fastidiar [12] I vtr 1 (*molestar*) to annoy, bother; (*dañar*) to hurt; fam **¡no fastidies!**, you're kidding! 2 fam (*estropear*) to damage, ruin; (*planes*) to spoil. II **fastidiarse** vr 1 (*aguantarse*) to put up with it, resign oneself; **que se fastidie**, that's his tough luck. 2 fam (*estropearse*) to get damaged, break down. 3 **me he fastidiado el tobillo**, I've hurt my ankle.

fastidio nm nuisance.

fastuoso,-a adj 1 (*acto*) splendid, lavish. 2 (*persona*) lavish, ostentatious.

fatal adj 1 fam (*muy malo*) awful, dreadful. 2 (*mortal*) deadly, fatal. 3 (*inexorable*) fateful, inevitable. II adv fam awfully, terribly; **lo pasó f.**, he had a rotten time.

fatalidad nf 1 (*destino*) fate. 2 (*desgracia*) misfortune.

fatalista I adj fatalistic. II nmf fatalist.

fatiga nf 1 (*cansancio*) fatigue. 2 **fatigas**, (*dificultades*) troubles, difficulties.

fatigar [7] I vtr to tire, weary. II **fatigarse** vr to tire, become tired.

fatigoso,-a adj tiring, exhausting.

fatuo,-a adj 1 (*envanecido*) vain, conceited. 2 (*necio*) fatuous, foolish.

fauces nfpl fig jaws.

fauna nf fauna.

favor nm favour, US favor; **por f.**, please; **¿puedes hacerme un f.?**, can you do me a favour?; **estar a f. de**, to be in favour of; **haga el f. de sentarse**, please sit down.

favorable adj favourable, US favorable; **f. a**, in favour of.

favorecedor,-a adj flattering.

favorecer [33] vtr 1 to favour, US favor. 2 (*sentar bien*) to flatter.

favoritismo nm favouritism, US favoritism.

favorito,-a adj & nm,f favourite, US favorite.

faz nf (pl **faces**) lit (*cara*) face.

fe nf 1 faith; **de buena/mala fe**, with good/dishonest intentions. 2 (*certificado*) certificate; **fe de bautismo/matrimonio**, baptism/marriage certificate. 3 Impr **fe de erratas**, list of errata.

fealdad nf ugliness.

febrero nm February.

febril adj 1 Med feverish. 2 (*actividad*) hectic.

fecha nf 1 date; **f. límite** o **tope**, deadline; **f. de caducidad**, sell-by date; **hasta la f.**, so far; **en f. próxima**, at an early date. 2 **fechas**, (*época*) time sing; **el año pasado por estas fechas**, this time last year.

fechar vtr to date.

fechoría nf (*de niños*) mischief; arc misdeed.

fécula nf starch.

fecundación nf fertilization; **f. in vitro**, in vitro fertilization.

fecundar vtr to fertilize.

fecundo,-a adj fertile.

federación nf federation.

federal adj & nmf federal.

fehaciente adj 1 fml authentic, reliable. 2 Jur irrefutable; **documento** o **prueba f.**, irrefutable proof.

felicidad nf happiness; **(muchas) felicidades**, (*en cumpleaños*) many happy returns.

felicitación nf **tarjeta de f.** greetings card.

felicitar vtr to congratulate (**por**, on); **¡te felicito!**, congratulations!

feligrés,-a nm,f parishioner.

felino,-a adj & nm feline.

feliz adj 1 (*contento*) happy; **¡felices Navidades!**, Happy o Merry Christmas! 2 (*decisión etc*) fortunate.

felonía nf treachery.

felpa nf 1 Tex plush; **oso** o **osito de f.**, teddy bear. 2 (*para el pelo*) hairband.

felpudo nm mat, doormat.

femenino,-a adj feminine; (*equipo, ropa*) women's; **sexo f.**, female sex.

feminismo nm feminism.

feminista adj & nmf feminist.

fémur nm femur.

fenecer [33] vi euf to pass away, die.

fenomenal I adj 1 phenomenal. 2 fam (*fantástico*) great, terrific. II adv fam wonderfully, marvellously; **lo pasamos f.**, we had a fantastic time.

fenómeno,-a I nm 1 phenomenon. 2 (*prodigio*) genius. 3 (*monstruo*) freak. II adj fam fantastic, terrific. III interj fantastic!, terrific!

feo,-a I adj ugly; (*asunto etc*) nasty. II nm fam **hacerle un f. a algn**, to offend sb.

féretro nm coffin.

feria nf fair; **f. de muestras/del libro**, trade/book fair.

feriado,-a adj **día f.**, holiday.

ferial adj **recinto f.**, (de exposiciones) exhibition centre; (de fiestas) fairground.

ferina adj **tos f.**, whooping cough.

fermentar vi to ferment.

fermento nm ferment.

ferocidad nf ferocity, fierceness.

feroz adj fierce, ferocious; **el lobo f.**, the big bad wolf.

férreo,-a adj ferreous; fig iron.

ferretería nf ironmonger's (shop), hardware store.

ferrocarril nm railway, US railroad.

ferroviario,-a adj railway, rail.

ferry nm ferry.

fértil adj fertile.

fertilidad nf fertility.

fertilizante I adj fertilizing. II nm fertilizer.

fertilizar [4] vtr to fertilize.

ferviente adj fervent.

fervor nm fervour, US fervor.

fervoroso,-a adj fervent.

festejar vtr to celebrate.

festejos nmpl festivities.

festín nm feast, banquet.

festival nm festival.

festividad nf festivity.

festivo,-a I adj 1 (ambiente etc) festive. 2 **día f.**, holiday. II nm holiday.

fetal adj foetal, US fetal.

fetiche nm fetish.

fétido,-a adj stinking, fetid.

feto nm foetus, US fetus.

feudalismo nm feudalism.

feudo nm fief; Pol stronghold.

FEVE nmpl abr de Ferrocarriles Españoles de Vía Estrecha.

FF.AA. nfpl abr de Fuerzas Armadas, Armed Forces.

FF.CC. nmpl abr de ferrocarriles, railways.

fiabilidad nf reliability, trustworthiness.

fiable adj reliable, trustworthy.

fiador,-a nm,f guarantor; **salir** o **ser f. de algn**, (pagar fianza) to stand bail for sb; (avalar) to vouch for sb.

fiambre nm 1 Culin cold meat. 2 fam (cadáver) stiff, corpse.

fiambrera nf lunch box.

fianza nf (depósito) deposit; Jur bail; **en libertad bajo f.**, on bail.

fiar [29] I vtr 1 (avalar) to guarantee. 2 (vender sin cobrar) to sell on credit. II **fiarse** vr to trust (**de**, -).

fiasco nm fiasco.

fibra nf fibre, US fiber; (de madera) grain; **f. de vidrio**, fibreglass.

ficción nf fiction.

ficha nf 1 (tarjeta) filing card; **f. técnica**, specifications pl, technical data; Cin credits pl. 2 (en juegos) counter; (de ajedrez) piece, man; (de dominó) domino.

fichado,-a **está f. por la policía**, he has a police record.

fichaje nm Dep signing.

fichar I vtr 1 to put on file. 2 Dep to sign up. II vi 1 (en el trabajo) (al entrar) to clock in; (al salir) to clock out. 2 Dep to sign.

fichero nm card index.

ficticio,-a adj fictitious.

fidedigno,-a adj reliable, trustworthy; **fuentes fidedignas**, reliable sources.

fidelidad nf faithfulness; **alta f.**, high fidelity, hi-fi.

fideo nm noodle.

fiebre nf fever; **tener f.**, to have a temperature.

fiel I adj 1 (leal) faithful, loyal. 2 (exacto) accurate, exact. II nm 1 (de balanza) needle, pointer. 2 Rel **los fieles**, the congregation.

fieltro nm felt.

fiera nf 1 wild animal; fam **estaba hecho una f.**, he was hopping mad. 2 Taur bull.

fiero,-a adj (salvaje) wild; (feroz) fierce, ferocious.

fierro nm Am 1 (hierro) iron. 2 (navaja) knife.

fiesta nf 1 (entre amigos) party. 2 **día de f.**, holiday. 3 Rel feast; **f. de guardar**, holy day of obligation. 4 (festividad) celebration, festivity.

figura nf figure.

figurado,-a adj figurative; **en sentido f.**, figuratively.

figurar I vi (en lista) to figure. II **figurarse** vr 1 to imagine, suppose; **ya me lo figuraba**, I thought as much. 2 **¡figúrate!**, **¡figúrese!**, just imagine!

figurinista nmf Teat Cin costume designer.

fijador nm (gomina) gel. 2 Fot fixative.

fijar I vtr to fix; **prohibido f. carteles**, (en letrero) post no bills. II **fijarse** vr 1 (darse cuenta) to notice. 2 (poner atención) to pay attention, watch.

fijo,-a adj 1 fixed; **sin domicilio f.**, of no fixed abode. 2 (trabajo) steady.
◆**fijamente** adv **mirar f.**, to stare.

fila nf 1 file; **en f. india**, in single file; **poner en f.**, to line up. 2 (de cine, teatro) row. 3 Mil **filas**, ranks; **llamar a algn a f.**, to call sb up; **¡rompan f.!**, fall out!, dismiss!

filamento nm filament.

filantropía nf philanthropy.

filántropo,-a nm,f philanthropist.

filarmónico,-a adj philharmonic.

filatelia nf philately, stamp collecting.

filete nm (de carne, pescado) fillet.

filiación nf Pol affiliation.

filial I adj 1 (de hijo) filial. 2 Com subsidiary. II nf subsidiary.

filigrana nf 1 filigree. 2 fig **filigranas**, intricacy sing, intricate work sing.

Filipinas npl (las) F., (the) Philippines.

filipino,-a adj & nm,f Philippine, Filipino.

filmar vtr to film, shoot.

film(e) nm film.

fílmico,-a adj film.

filmoteca nf (archivo) film library.

filo nm (cutting) edge; **al f. de la medianoche,** on the stroke of midnight; fig **de doble f.,** double-edged.

filón nm 1 Min seam, vein. 2 fig (buen negocio) gold mine.

filoso,-a adj Am sharp-edged.

filosofal adj piedra f., philosopher's stone.

filosofía nf philosophy; fig **con f.,** philosophically.

filosófico,-a adj philosophical.

filósofo,-a nm,f philosopher.

filtración nf filtration; (de información) leak.

filtrar I vtr 1 to filter. 2 (información) to leak. II **filtrarse** vr 1 (líquido) seep. 2 (información) to leak out.

filtro nm filter.

fin nm 1 (final) end; **dar** o **poner f. a,** to put an end to; **llegar** o **tocar a su f.,** to come to an end; **en f.,** anyway; **¡por** o **al f.!,** at last!; **f. de semana,** weekend; **al f. y al cabo,** when all's said and done; **noche de F. de Año,** New Year's Eve. 2 (objetivo) purpose, aim; **a f. de,** in order to, so as to; **a f. de que,** in order that, so that; **con el f. de,** with the intention of.

final I adj final. II nm end; **al f.,** in the end; **f. de línea,** terminal; **f. feliz,** happy ending; **a finales de octubre,** at the end of October. III nf Dep final.
◆**finalmente** adv finally.

finalidad nf purpose, aim.

finalista nmf finalist. II adj in the final.

finalizar [4] vtr & vi to end, finish.

financiación nf financing.

financiar [12] vtr to finance.

financiero,-a I adj financial. II nm,f financier.

financista nmf Am financier, financial expert.

finanzas nfpl finances.

finca nf (inmueble) property; (de campo) country house.

finés,-a adj & nm,f → **finlandés,-esa.**

fingido nf adj feigned, false; **nombre f.,** assumed name.

fingir [6] I vtr to feign. II **fingirse** vr to pretend to be.

finlandés,-a I adj Finnish. II nm,f (persona) Finn. III nm (idioma) Finnish.

Finlandia nf Finland.

fino,-a I adj 1 (hilo, capa) fine. 2 (flaco) thin. 3 (educado) refined, polite. 4 (oído) sharp, acute; (olfato) keen. 5 (humor, ironía) subtle. II nm (vino) type of dry sherry.

finta nf (en boxeo) feint; (en fútbol) dummy.

finura nf 1 (refinamiento) refinement, politeness. 2 (sutileza) subtlety.

firma nf 1 signature. 2 (empresa) firm, company.

firmamento nm firmament.

firmante adj & nmf signatory; **el** o **la abajo f.,** the undersigned.

firmar vtr to sign.

firme I adj 1 firm; fig **mantenerse f.,** to hold one's ground; **tierra f.,** terra firma. 2 Mil **¡firmes!,** attention!. II nm (de carretera) road surface. III adv hard.
◆**firmemente** adv firmly.

firmeza nf firmness.

fiscal I adj fiscal, tax. II nmf Jur public prosecutor, US district attorney.

fisco nm treasury, exchequer.

fisgar [7] vi fam to snoop, pry.

fisgón,-ona nm,f snooper.

fisgonear vi to snoop, pry.

física nf physics sing.

físico,-a I adj physical. II nm,f (profesión) physicist. III nm physique.

fisión nf fission.

fisioterapeuta nmf physiotherapist.

fisioterapia nf Med physiotherapy.

fisonomía nf physiognomy.

fisonomista nmf fam ser buen/mal f., to be good/no good at remembering faces.

fisura nf fissure.

flácido,-a adj flaccid, flabby.

flaco,-a adj 1 (delgado) skinny. 2 fig **punto f.,** weak spot.

flagelar vtr to flagellate.

flagelo nm (látigo) whip; fig scourge.

flagrante adj flagrant; **en f. delito,** red-handed.

flamante adj 1 nuevecito f., (nuevo) brand-new. 2 (vistoso) splendid, brilliant.

flamenco,-a I adj 1 Mús flamenco. 2 (de Flandes) Flemish. II nm 1 Mús flamenco. 2 Orn flamingo. 3 (idioma) Flemish.

flan nm caramel custard.

flanco nm flank, side.

flanquear vtr to flank.

flaquear vi (fuerzas, piernas) to weaken, give way.

flaqueza nf weakness.

flash nm Fot flash.

flato nm wind, flatulence.

flatulencia nf flatulence.

flauta nf flute; f. dulce, recorder.

flautín nm (instrumento) piccolo.

flautista nmf Mús flautist, US flutist, flute player.

flecha nf arrow.

flechazo nm fig (enamoramiento) love at first sight.

fleco nm fringe.

flema nf phlegm.

flemático,-a adj phlegmatic.

flemón nm gumboil, abscess.

flequillo nm fringe, US bangs.
fletar vtr to charter.
flete nm 1 (alquiler) charter. 2 (carga) freight.
flexibilidad nf flexibility.
flexible adj flexible.
flexión nf 1 flexion. 2 Ling inflection. 3 Gimn flexiones, press-ups, US push-ups.
flexionar vtr to bend; (músculo) to flex.
flexo nm reading lamp.
flipante adj fam great, cool.
flipar vtr fam le flipan las motos, he's crazy about motorbikes.
flirtear vi to flirt.
flirteo nm flirting.
flojear vi (ventas etc) to fall off, go down; (piernas) to weaken, grow weak; (memoria) to fail.
flojedad nf weakness.
flojera nf fam weakness, faintness.
flojo,-a adj 1 (tornillo, cuerda etc) loose, slack. 2 (perezoso) lazy, idle; (examen, trabajo, resultado) poor.
flor nf 1 flower; **en f.**, in blossom; fig **en la f. de la vida**, in the prime of life; fig **la f. y nata**, the cream (of society). 2 **a f. de piel**, skin-deep.
flora nf flora.
floreado,-a adj flowery.
florecer [33] vi 1 (plantas) to flower. 2 fig (negocio) to flourish, thrive.
floreciente adj fig flourishing, prosperous.
Florencia n Florence.
florero nm vase.
floricultura nf flower growing, floriculture.
florido,-a adj 1 (con flores) flowery. 2 (estilo) florid.
floripondio nm pey (adorno) heavy ornamentation.
florista nmf florist.
floristería nf florist's (shop).
flota nf fleet.
flotador nm 1 (de pesca) float. 2 (para nadar) rubber ring.
flotar vi to float.
flote nm floating; **a f.**, afloat; **sacar a f. un negocio**, to put a business on a sound footing.
flotilla nf flotilla.
fluctuación nf fluctuation.
fluctuar [30] vi to fluctuate.
fluidez nf fluency.
fluido,-a I adj fluid; (estilo etc) fluent. II nm fluid; **f. eléctrico**, current.
fluir [37] vi to flow.
flujo nm 1 flow. 2 rising tide; **f. y reflujo**, ebb and flow. 3 Fís flux. 4 Med discharge. 5 Inform stream.
flúor nm fluorine.
fluorescente adj fluorescent.
fluvial adj river.
FM nf abr de **Frecuencia Modulada**, frequency modulation, FM.

FMI nm abr de **Fondo Monetario Internacional**, International Monetary Fund, IMF.
fobia nf phobia (a, about).
foca nf seal.
foco nm 1 Elec spotlight, floodlight. 2 (de ideas, revolución etc) centre, US center, focal point. 2 Am (bombilla) (electric light) bulb; (de coche) (car) headlight; (farola) street light.
fofo,-a adj soft; (persona) flabby.
fogata nf bonfire.
fogón nm (de cocina) ring.
fogonazo nm flash.
fogosidad nf ardour, US ardor, fire.
fogoso,-a adj fiery, spirited.
fogueo nm cartucho de f., blank cartridge.
folio nm sheet of paper.
folklore nm folklore.
folklórico,-a adj m. **folklórica**, folk music.
follaje nm foliage.
follar vulg I vi to fuck, screw. II vtr (suspender) to fail. III follarse vr f. a algn, to fuck sb, screw sb.
folletín nm (relato) newspaper serial. 2 fig melodrama.
folleto nm leaflet; (turístico) brochure.
follón nm fam 1 (alboroto) rumpus, shindy; **armar un f.**, to kick up a rumpus. 2 (enredo, confusión) mess, trouble; **meterse en un f.**, to get into a mess. 3 **un f. de**, (montón) a load of.
follonero,-a nm,f troublemaker.
fomentar vtr to promote.
fomento nm promotion.
fonda nf inn.
fondear vi to anchor.
fondista nmf Dep long-distance runner.
fondo¹ nm 1 (parte más baja) bottom; **a f.**, thoroughly; **al f. de la calle**, at the bottom of the street; **tocar f.**, Náut to touch bottom; fig to reach rock bottom; fig **en el f. es bueno**, deep down he's kind; **bajos fondos**, dregs of society; **doble f.**, false bottom. 2 (de habitación) back; (de pasillo) end. 3 (segundo término) background; **música de f.**, background music. 4 Prensa **artículo de f.**, leading article. 5 Dep **corredor de f.**, long-distance runner; **esquí de f.**, cross-country skiing.
fondo² nm Fin fund; **cheque sin fondos**, bad cheque; fam **f. común**, kitty.
fonendoscopio nm stethoscope.
fonética nf phonetics sing.
fonético,-a adj phonetic.
fontanería nf plumbing.
fontanero,-a nm,f plumber.
footing nm jogging; **hacer f.**, to go jogging.
forajido nm,f outlaw.
foral adj Comunidad F., Navarre.

foráneo,-a *adj* foreign.

forastero,-a *nm,f* outsider, stranger.

forcejear *vi* to wrestle, struggle.

forcejeo *nm* struggle.

fórceps *nm inv* forceps *pl.*

forense I *adj* forensic. **II** *nmf* (*médico*) f., forensic surgeon.

forestal *adj* forest; **repoblación** f., re-afforestation.

forjado,-a *adj* wrought.

forjar *vtr* (*metal*) to forge; *fig* to create, make.

forma *nf* 1 form, shape; **en f. de L,** L-shaped; **¿qué f. tiene?,** what shape is it? 2 (*manera*) way; **de esta f.,** in this way; **de f. que,** so that; **de todas formas,** anyway, in any case; **no hubo f. de convencerla,** there was no way we could convince her; **f. de pago,** method of payment. 3 *Dep* form; **estar en f.,** to be on form; **estar en baja f.,** to be off form. 4 *Rel* Sagrada F., Host. 5 formas, (*modales*) manners.

formación *nf* 1 formation. 2 (*educación*) upbringing. 3 (*enseñanza*) training; **f. profesional,** vocational training.

formal *adj* formal; (*serio*) serious, serious-minded; (*fiable*) reliable, dependable.

formalidad *nf* 1 formality. 2 (*seriedad*) seriousness. 3 (*fiabilidad*) reliability. 4 **formalidades,** (*trámites*) formalities.

formalizar [4] **I** *vtr* to formalize. **II formalizarse** *vr* to settle down.

formar I *vtr* 1 to form; **f. parte de algo,** to be a part of sth. 2 (*educar*) to bring up; (*enseñar*) to educate, train. **II formarse** *vr* 1 to be formed, form; **se formó un charco,** a puddle formed; **f. una impresión de algo,** to get an impression of sth. 2 (*educarse*) to be educated *o* trained.

formato *nm* format; (*del papel*) size.

formica® *nf* Formica®.

formidable *adj* 1 (*estupendo*) wonderful, terrific. 2 (*espantoso*) formidable.

fórmula *nf* formula; *Aut* f. uno, formula one.

formular *vtr* (*quejas, peticiones*) to make; (*deseo*) to express; (*pregunta*) to ask; (*una teoría*) to formulate.

formulario *nm* form.

fornicación *nf* fornication.

fornicar [1] *vi* to fornicate.

fornido,-a *adj* strapping, hefty.

foro *nm* 1 forum. 2 (*mesa redonda*) round table. 3 *Teat* back (of the stage). 4 *Jur* law court, court of justice.

forofo,-a *nm,f fam* fan, supporter.

forrado,-a *adj* lined; *fam* **estar f.,** to be well-heeled, be well-off.

forraje *nm* fodder.

forrar I *vtr* (*por dentro*) to line; (*por fuera*) to cover. **II forrarse** *vr fam* (*de dinero*) to make a packet.

forro *nm* (*por dentro*) lining; (*por fuera*) cover, case.

fortalecer [33] *vtr* to fortify, strengthen.

fortaleza *nf* 1 strength; (*de espíritu*) fortitude. 2 *Mil* fortress, stronghold.

fortificante I *adj* fortifying. **II** *nm* tonic.

fortificar [1] *vtr* to fortify.

fortísimo,-a *adj* very strong.

fortuito,-a *adj* fortuitous.

fortuna *nf* 1 (*destino*) fortune, fate. 2 (*suerte*) luck; **por f.,** fortunately. 3 (*capital*) fortune.

forzado,-a *adj* forced; **a marchas forzadas,** at a brisk pace; **trabajos forzados,** hard labour *sing.*

forzar [2] *vtr* 1 (*obligar*) to force; **f. a algn a hacer algo,** to force sb to do sth. 2 (*puerta, candado*) to force, break open.

forzoso,-a *adj* obligatory, compulsory; *Av* aterrizaje f., forced landing.

◆**forzosamente** *adv* necessarily.

fosa *nf* 1 (*sepultura*) grave. 2 (*hoyo*) pit. 3 *Anat* fosas nasales, nostrils.

fosforescente *adj* phosphorescent.

fósforo *nm* (*cerilla*) match.

fósil *adj & nm* fossil.

fosilizarse [4] *vr* to fossilize, become fossilized.

foso *nm* 1 (*hoyo*) pit. 2 (*de fortificación*) moat. 3 (*en garaje*) inspection pit.

foto *nf fam* photo; **sacar/echar una f.,** to take a photo.

fotocopia *nf* photocopy.

fotocopiadora *nf* photocopier.

fotocopiar [12] *vtr* to photocopy.

fotogénico,-a *adj* photogenic.

fotografía *nf* 1 photograph; **echar** *o* **hacer** *o* **sacar fotografías,** to take photographs. 2 (*arte*) photography.

fotografiar [29] *vtr* to photograph, take a photograph of.

fotográfico,-a *adj* photographic.

fotógrafo,-a *nm,f* photographer.

fotograma *nm* still, shot.

fotomatón *nm* automatic coin-operated photo machine.

fotómetro *nm* light meter, exposure meter.

FP *nf Educ abr de* **Formación Profesional,** vocational training.

frac *nm* (*pl* fracs *o* fraques) (*prenda*) dress coat, tails *pl.*

fracasado,-a I *adj* unsuccessful. **II** *nm,f* (*persona*) failure.

fracasar *vi* to fail.

fracaso *nm* failure.

fracción *nf* 1 fraction. 2 *Pol* faction.

fraccionar *vtr*, **fraccionarse** *vr* to break up, split up.

fraccionario,-a *adj* fractional; **moneda fraccionaria,** small change.

fractura *nf* fracture.

fracturar *vtr*, **fracturarse** *vr* to fracture, break.

fragancia nf fragrance.

fragata nf frigate.

frágil adj 1 (quebradizo) fragile. 2 (débil) frail.

fragmentar vtr to fragment. II **fragmentarse** vr to break up.

fragmento nm fragment; (de novela etc) passage.

fragor nm din.

fragua nf forge.

fraguar [22] vtr 1 (metal) to forge. 2 (plan) to think up, fabricate; (conspiración) to hatch.

fraile nm friar, monk.

frailecillo nm puffin.

frambuesa nf raspberry.

francés,-a I adj French; Culin **tortilla francesa**, plain omelette. II nm,f (hombre) Frenchman; (mujer) Frenchwoman. III nm (idioma) French.

Francfort, Francfurt n Frankfurt; Culin **salchicha estilo f.**, frankfurter.

Francia n France.

francmasón,-ona nm,f freemason.

franco,-a¹ adj 1 (persona) frank. 2 Com **f. a bordo**, free on board; **f. fábrica**, ex-works; **puerto f.**, free port. ◆**francamente** adv frankly.

franco² nm Fin (moneda) franc.

francotirador,-a nm,f sniper.

franela nf flannel.

franja nf (de terreno) strip; (de bandera) stripe; Cost fringe, border.

franquear vtr 1 (atravesar) to cross; fig (dificultad, obstáculo) to overcome. 2 (carta) to frank. 3 (camino, paso) to free, clear.

franqueo nm postage.

franqueza nf frankness.

franquicia nf exemption; Com franchise.

franquismo nm Hist 1 (ideología) Francoism. 2 (régimen) the Franco regime.

franquista adj & nmf Francoist.

frasco nm small bottle, flask.

frase nf (oración) sentence; (expresión) phrase; **f. hecha**, set phrase o expression.

fraternidad nf brotherhood, fraternity.

fraternizar [4] vi to fraternize.

fraterno,-a adj fraternal, brotherly.

fraude nm fraud; **f. fiscal**, tax evasion.

fraudulento,-a adj fraudulent.

fray nm Rel brother.

frecuencia nf frequency; **con f.**, frequently, often.

frecuentar vtr to frequent.

frecuente adj frequent. ◆**frecuentemente** adv frequently, often.

fregadero nm (kitchen) sink.

fregado¹ nm 1 (lavado) washing. 2 fam (follón) racket.

fregado²,-a² adj Am tiresome, annoying.

fregar [1] vtr 1 (lavar) to wash; (suelo) to mop. 2 Am vulg to annoy, irritate.

fregona nf mop.

fregón,-ona adj Am annoying.

freidora nf (deep) fryer.

freír [5] (pp **frito**) I vtr to fry. II **freírse** vr to fry; fig **f. de calor**, to be roasting.

frenar vtr to brake; fig (inflación etc) to slow down; (impulsos) to restrain.

frenazo nm sudden braking; **dar un f.**, to jam on the brakes.

frenesí nm frenzy.

frenético,-a adj frantic.

freno nm 1 brake; **pisar/soltar el f.**, to press/release the brake; **f. de disco/tambor**, disc/drum brake; **f. de mano**, handbrake. 2 (de caballería) bit. 3 fig curb, check; **poner f. a algo**, to curb sth.

frente I nm 1 front; **al f. de**, at the head of; **chocar de f.**, to crash head on; **hacer f. a algo**, to face sth, stand up to sth. II nf Anat forehead; **f. a f.**, face to face. III adv **f. a**, in front of, opposite.

fresa nf fam strawberry. 2 Téc milling cutter.

fresco,-a I adj 1 (frío) cool. 2 (comida, fruta) fresh. 3 (reciente) fresh, new. 4 (descarado) cheeky, shameless; **se quedó tan f.**, he didn't bat an eyelid; **¡qué f.!**, what a nerve!. II nm 1 (frescor) fresh air, cool air; **al f.**, in the cool; **hace f.**, it's chilly. 2 Arte fresco.

frescor nm freshness.

frescura nf 1 freshness. 2 (desvergüenza) cheek, nerve.

fresno nm ash tree.

fresón nm (large) strawberry.

frialdad nf coldness.

fricción nf 1 friction. 2 (masaje) massage.

friega nf rub.

friegaplatos nmf inv (persona) dishwasher.

frígido,-a adj frigid.

frigorífico,-a I nm refrigerator, fridge. II adj **cámara frigorífica**, coldstorage room.

frijol, frijol nm kidney bean.

frío,-a I adj 1 cold. 2 (indiferente) cold, cool, indifferent. 3 **su comentario me dejó f.**, I was stunned by his remark. II nm cold; **hace f.**, it's cold. ◆**fríamente** adv coolly.

friolera nf fam **la f. de diez mil pesetas/dos horas**, a mere ten thousand pesetas/two hours.

friolero,-a adj sensitive to the cold.

fritanga nf Am fried food. 2 Esp greasy food.

frito,-a I adj 1 Culin fried. 2 fam exasperated, fed up; **me tienes f.**, I'm sick to death of you. II nm fry, piece of fried food.

frívolo,-a adj frivolous.

frondoso,-a adj leafy, luxuriant.

frontera nf frontier.

fronterizo,-a adj frontier, border; **países fronterizos**, neighbouring countries.

frontón nm Dep pelota.
frotar I vtr to rub. II **frotarse** vr to rub; f. **las manos**, to rub one's hands together.
fructífero,-a adj (árbol) fruit-bearing; (esfuerzo) fruitful.
frugal adj frugal.
fruncir [3] vtr 1 Cost to gather. 2 (labios) to purse, pucker; f. **el ceño**, to frown, knit one's brow.
frustración nf frustration.
frustrado,-a adj frustrated; **intento f.**, unsuccessful attempt.
frustrante adj frustrating.
frustrar I vtr to frustrate; (defraudar) to disappoint. II **frustrarse** vr 1 (esperanza) to fail, go awry. 2 (persona) to be frustrated o disappointed.
fruta nf fruit; f. **del tiempo**, fresh fruit.
frutería nf fruit shop.
frutero,-a I nm,f fruiterer. II nm fruit dish o bowl.
frutilla nf Am (large) strawberry.
fruto nm 1 fire; **frutos secos**, nuts; **dar f.**, to bear fruit; fig (dar buen resultado) to be fruitful; **sacar f. de algo**, to profit from sth.
fu interj **ni fu ni fa**, so-so.
fucsia nf fuchsia.
fuego nm 1 fire; **fuegos artificiales**, fireworks. 2 (lumbre) light; ¿**me da f., por favor?**, have you got a light, please? 3 Culin **a f. lento**, on a low flame; (al horno) in a slow oven.
fuel, fuel-oil nm diesel.
fuente nf 1 fountain. 2 (recipiente) dish, serving dish. 3 (de información) source.
fuera¹ adv 1 outside, out; **quédate f.**, stay outside; **sal f.**, go out; **desde f.**, from (the) outside; **por f.**, on the outside; **la puerta de f.**, the outer door. 2 f. **de**, out of; f. **de serie**, extraordinary; fig **estar f. de sí**, to be beside oneself. 3 Dep **el equipo de f.**, the away team; **jugar f.**, to play away; f. **de juego**, offside.
fuera² I subj imperf → **ir**. II subj imperf → **ser**.
fuero nm 1 Hist code of laws. 2 fig **en tu f. interno**, deep down, in your heart of hearts.
fuerte I adj 1 strong; (dolor) severe; (sonido) loud; (comida) heavy; **el plato f.**, the main course; fig the most important event. II nm 1 (fortaleza) fort. 2 (punto fuerte) forte, strong point. III adv ¡**abrázame f.!**, hold me tight!; **comer f.**, to eat a lot; ¡**habla más f.!**, speak up!; ¡**pégale f.!**, hit him hard!
fuerza I nf 1 (fortaleza) strength; fig **a f. de**, by dint of. 2 (violencia) force; **a la f.**, (por obligación) of necessity; (con violencia) by force; **por f.**, of necessity; f. **mayor**, force majeure. 3 Fís force. 4 (cuerpo) force; **las fuerzas del orden**, the forces of law and order; **Fuerzas Aéreas**,

≈ GB Royal Air Force; **Fuerzas Armadas**, Armed Forces.
fuese I subj imperf → **ir**. II subj imperf → **ser**.
fuete nm Am whip.
fuga nf 1 (huida) escape; **darse a la f.**, to take flight. 2 (de gas etc) leak.
fugarse [7] vr to escape; f. **de casa**, to run away from home.
fugaz adj fleeting, brief.
fugitivo,-a adj & nm,f fugitive.
fui I pt indef → **ir**. II pt indef → **ser**.
fulana nf pey whore, tart.
fulano,-a nm,f so-and-so; (hombre) what's his name; (mujer) what's her name; **Doña Fulana de tal**, Mrs So-and-so. II nf fam pey tart, slag.
fular nm foulard, scarf.
fulgor nm lit brilliance, glow.
fullería nf cheating; **hacer fullerías**, to cheat.
fullero,-a I adj cheating. II nm,f cheat.
fulminante adj (cese) summary; (muerte, enfermedad) sudden; (mirada) withering.
fulminar vtr fig to strike dead; f. **a algn con la mirada**, to look daggers at sb.
fumada nf Am (calada) pull, drag.
fumado,-a adj arg (colocado) stoned.
fumador,-a nm,f smoker; **los no fumadores**, nonsmokers.
fumar I vtr & vi to smoke; **no f.**, (en letrero) no smoking. II **fumarse** vr to smoke; f. **un cigarro**, to smoke a cigarette.
fumigar [7] vtr to fumigate.
funambulista nmf, **funámbulo,-a** nm,f tightrope walker.
función nf 1 function; **en f. de**, according to. 2 (cargo) duties pl; **entrar en funciones**, to take up one's duties; **presidente en funciones**, acting president. 3 Cin Teat performance.
funcionamiento nm operation; **poner/ entrar en f.**, to put/come into operation.
funcionar vi to work; **no funciona**, (en letrero) out of order.
funcionario,-a nm,f civil servant; f. **público**, public official.
funda nf cover; (de gafas etc) case; (de espada) sheath; f. **de almohada**, pillowcase.
fundación nf foundation.
fundador,-a nm,f founder.
fundamental adj fundamental.
fundamentar vtr to base (en, on).
fundamento nm basis, grounds; **sin f.**, unfounded.
fundar I vtr 1 (empresa) to found. 2 (teoría) to base, found. II **fundarse** vr 1 (empresa) to be founded. 2 (teoría) to be based; (persona) to base oneself.
fundición nf 1 (de metales) smelting. 2 (fábrica) foundry.
fundir I vtr 1 to melt; (bombilla, plomos) to blow. 2 (unir) to unite, join. II

fundirse *vr* **1** (*derretirse*) to melt. **2** (*bombilla, plomos*) to blow. **3** (*unirse*) to merge.

fúnebre *adj* **1** (*mortuorio*) funeral; **coche f.**, hearse. **2** (*lúgubre*) mournful, lugubrious.

funeral *nm* funeral.

funeraria *nf* undertaker's, *US* funeral parlor.

funesto,-a *adj* ill-fated, fatal; (*consecuencias*) disastrous.

fungir *vi Am* to act (**de**, as).

funicular *nm* funicular (railway).

furcia *nf ofens* whore, tart.

furgón *nm Aut* van.

furgoneta *nf* van.

furia *nf* fury; **ponerse hecho una f.**, to become furious, fly into a rage.

furibundo,-a *adj* furious, enraged.

furioso,-a *adj* furious; **ponerse f.**, to get furious.

furor *nm* fury, rage; *fig* **hacer f.**, to be all the rage.

furtivo,-a *adj* furtive, stealthy; **caza/pesca furtiva**, poaching; **cazador/pescador f.**, poacher.

furúnculo *nm Med* boil.

fuselaje *nm* fuselage.

fusible *nm* fuse.

fusil *nm* gun, rifle.

fusilamiento *nm* shooting, execution.

fusilar *vtr* to shoot, execute.

fusión *nf* **1** (*de metales*) fusion; (*del hielo*) thawing, melting; **punto de f.**, melting point. **2** *Com* merger.

fusionar *vtr*, **fusionarse** *vr* **1** *Fís* to fuse. **2** *Com* to merge.

fútbol *nm* football, soccer.

futbolín *nm* table football.

futbolista *nmf* footballer, football o soccer player.

fútil *adj* futile, trivial.

futilidad *nf* futility, triviality.

futurista *adj* futuristic.

futuro,-a I *adj* future. **II** *nm* future; **en un f. próximo**, in the near future.

G

G, g |xe| *nf* (*la letra*) G, g.

gabán *nm* overcoat.

gabardina *nf* (*prenda*) raincoat.

gabinete *nm* **1** (*despacho*) study; **g. de abogados**, lawyers' office. **2** *Pol* cabinet.

gaceta *nf* gazette.

gachas *nfpl* porridge *sing*.

gacho,-a *adj* **con la cabeza gacha**, hanging one's head.

gaditano,-a I *adj* of *o* from Cadiz. **II** *nm,f* inhabitant *o* native of Cadiz.

gafas *nfpl* glasses, spectacles; **g. de sol**, sunglasses.

gafar *vtr fam* to put a jinx on, bring bad luck to.

gafe *adj* & *nm fam* **ser g.**, to be a jinx.

gaita *nf* bagpipes *pl*.

gajes *nmpl fam irón* **g. del oficio**, occupational hazards.

gajo *nm* **1** (*de naranja, pomelo etc*) segment. **2** (*rama desprendida*) torn-off branch.

gala *nf* **1** (*vestido*) full dress; **de g.**, dressed up; (*ciudad*) decked out. **2** (*espectáculo*) gala; **hacer g. de**, to glory in. **3 galas**, finery *sing*.

galán *nm* **1** handsome young man; *hum* ladies' man. **2** *Teat* leading man.

galante *adj* gallant.

galantear *vtr* to court.

galanteo *nm* courtship.

galantería *nf* gallantry.

galápago *nm* turtle.

galardón *nm* prize.

galardonado,-a *nm,f* prizewinner.

galardonar *vtr* to award a prize to.

galaxia *nf* galaxy.

galeón *nm* galleon.

galeote *nm* galley slave.

galera *nf* **1** *Náut* galley. **2** (*carro*) covered wagon. **3** *Impr* galley.

galería *nf* **1** *Arquit* covered balcony. **2** (*museo*) art gallery. **3** *Teat* gallery, gods *pl*.

Gales *n* (*el país de*) **G.**, Wales.

galés,-esa I *adj* Welsh. **II** *nm,f* (*hombre*) Welshman; (*mujer*) Welshwoman; **los galeses**, the Welsh. **III** *adj* (*idioma*) Welsh.

galgo *nm* greyhound.

Galicia *n* Galicia.

galimatías *nm inv fam* gibberish.

gallardo,-a *adj* **1** (*apuesto*) smart. **2** (*valeroso*) brave.

gallego,-a I *adj* **1** Galician. **2** *Am pey* Spanish. **II** *nm,f* **1** Galician, native of Galicia. **2** *Am pey* Spaniard. **III** *nm* (*idioma*) Galician.

galleta *nf* **1** *Culin* biscuit. **2** *fam* (*cachete*) slap.

gallina I *nf* hen. **II** *nmf fam* coward, chicken.

gallinero *nm* **1** hen run. **2** *Teat* **el g.**, the gods *pl*.

gallito *nm fam* (*peleón*) bully.

gallo *nm* **1** cock, rooster; *fam fig* **en menos que un canto de g.**, before you could say Jack Robinson. **2** *Mús fam* off-key note.

galón¹ *nm Mil* stripe.

galón² *nm* (*medida*) gallon; *GB* 4.55 litres, *US* 3.79 litres.

galopante *adj fig* (*inflación etc*) galloping.

galopar *vi* to gallop.
galope *nm* gallop; **a g. tendido,** flat out.
gama *nf* range; *Mús* scale.
gamba *nf* prawn.
gamberrismo *nm* hooliganism.
gamberro,-a I *nm,f* hooligan. **II** *adj* uncouth.
gamo *nm* fallow deer.
gamuza *nf* **1** *Zool* chamois. **2** *(trapo)* chamois *o* shammy leather.
gana *nf* **1** *(deseo)* wish (**de,** for); **de buena g.,** willingly; **de mala g.,** reluctantly; *fam* **no me da la g.,** I don't feel like it. **2 tener ganas de (hacer) algo,** to feel like (doing) sth; **quedarse con las ganas,** not to manage. **3** *(apetito)* appetite; **comer con ganas,** to eat heartily.
ganadería *nf* **1** *(crianza)* livestock farming. **2** *(conjunto de ganado)* livestock.
ganadero,-a *nm,f* livestock farmer.
ganado *nm* **1** livestock. **2** *fam fig (gente)* crowd.
ganador,-a I *adj* winning. **II** *nm,f* winner.
ganancia *nf* profit.
ganar I *vtr* **1** *(sueldo)* to earn. **2** *(victoria)* to win. **3** *(aventajar)* to beat. **4** *(alcanzar)* to reach. **II ganarse** *vr* **1** to earn; **g. el pan,** to earn one's daily bread. **2** *(merecer)* to deserve; **se lo ha ganado,** he deserves it.
ganchillo *nm* crochet work.
gancho *nm* **1** hook. **2** *fam fig (gracia, atractivo)* charm. **3** *Am (horquilla)* hairpin.
gandul,-a *nm,f* loafer.
ganga *nf* bargain.
gangoso,-a *adj* nasal.
gangrena *nf* gangrene.
gansada *nf fam* silly thing to say *o* do.
ganso,-a I *nm,f* **1** goose; *(macho)* gander. **2** *fam* dolt. **II** *adj fam* ginormous; **pasta gansa,** bread, dough.
ganzúa *nf* picklock.
gañán *nm* *(obrero)* farmhand; *fam (bribón)* cheat.
garabatear *vtr & vi* to scribble.
garabato *nm* scrawl.
garaje *nm* garage.
garante *nmf Fin* guarantor.
garantía *nf* **1** guarantee. **2** *Jur (fianza)* bond, security.
garantizar [4] *vtr* to guarantee.
garbanzo *nm* chickpea.
garbeo *nm arg (paseo)* stroll; **darse un g.,** to go for a stroll.
garbo *nm* grace.
garfio *nm* hook, grappling iron.
gargajo *nm* spit.
garganta *nf* **1** throat. **2** *(desfiladero)* narrow pass.
gargantilla *nf* short necklace.
gárgaras *nfpl* **1** gargling *sing*; *fam* **¡vete a hacer g.!,** get lost! **2** *Am (licor)* gargling solution *sing*.

gárgola *nf* gargoyle.
garita *nf* *(caseta)* hut; *Mil* sentry box.
garito *nm* gaming joint.
garra *nf* **1** *Zool* claw; *(de ave)* talon. **2** *fig (fuerza)* force; **tener g.,** to be compelling.
garrafa *nf* carafe.
garrafal *adj* monumental.
garrapata *nf Ent* tick.
garrote *nm* **1** *(porra)* club. **2** *Jur* garrotte.
garrucha *nf* pulley.
gárrulo,-a *adj fig* garrulous.
garza *nf* heron.
gas *nm* **1** gas; **g. ciudad,** town gas; **gases (nocivos),** fumes; **g. de escape,** exhaust fumes. **2** *(en bebida)* fizz; **agua con g.,** fizzy water. **3** *Med* **gases,** flatulence *sing*.
gasa *nf* gauze.
gaseosa *nf* lemonade.
gasoducto *nm* gas pipeline.
gasoil, gasóleo *nm* diesel oil.
gasolina *nf* petrol, *US* gasoline.
gasolinera *nf* petrol *o US* gas station.
gastado,-a *adj (zapatos etc)* worn-out; *fig (frase)* hackneyed.
gastar I *vtr* **1** *(consumir) (dinero, tiempo)* to spend; *(gasolina, electricidad)* to consume. **2** *fig (malgastar)* to waste. **3** *(ropa)* to wear; **¿qué número gastas?,** what size do you take? **4 g. una broma a algn,** to play a practical joke on sb. **II gastarse** *vr* **1** *(zapatos etc)* to wear out. **2** *(gasolina etc)* to run out.
gasto *nm* expenditure; **gastos,** expenses; **gastos de viaje,** travelling expenses.
gatas (a) *loc adv* on all fours.
gatear *vi* **1** to crawl. **2** *(trepar)* to climb.
gatillo *nm* *(de armas)* trigger; **apretar el g.,** to pull the trigger.
gato *nm* **1** cat. **2** *Aut Téc* jack.
gaveta *nf* **1** *(cajón)* drawer. **2** *Am Aut (guantera)* glove compartment.
gavilán *nm Orn* sparrowhawk.
gavilla *nf (de ramillas etc)* sheaf.
gaviota *nf* seagull.
gay *adj inv & nm (pl* **gays)** homosexual, gay.
gazapo *nm* **1** *(error)* misprint. **2** *Zool* young rabbit.
gaznate *nm* gullet.
gazpacho *nm Culin* gazpacho.
gel *nm* gel; **g. (de ducha),** shower gel.
gelatina *nf (ingrediente)* gelatin; *Culin* jelly.
gema *nf Min* gem.
gemelo,-a I *adj & nm,f (identical)* twin. **II** *nmpl* **gemelos 1** *(de camisa)* cufflinks. **2** *(anteojos)* binoculars.
gemido *nm* groan.
Géminis *nm* Gemini.
gemir [6] *vi* to groan.
generación *nf* generation.
general I *adj* general; **por lo** *o* **en g.,** in general, generally; **II** *nm Mil Rel* general.
◆ **generalmente** *adv* generally.

Generalitat nf Catalan/Valencian/Balearic parliament.
generalización nf 1 generalization. 2 (extensión) spread.
generalizar [4] I vtr 1 to generalize. 2 (extender) to spread. II **generalizarse** vr to become widespread o common.
generar vtr to generate.
género nm 1 (clase) kind, sort. 2 Arte Lit genre. 3 (mercancía) article. 4 Ling gender. 5 Biol genus; **el g. humano**, mankind.
generosidad nf generosity.
generoso,-a adj 1 generous (con, para, to). 2 (vino) full-bodied.
Génesis nm Rel Genesis.
genética nf genetics sing.
genético,-a adj genetic.
genial adj brilliant; fam terrific.
genio nm 1 (carácter) temperament; (mal carácter) temper; **estar de mal g.**, to be in a bad mood. 2 (facultad) genius.
genocidio nm genocide.
Génova n Genoa.
gente nf 1 people pl. 2 (familia) folks pl. 3 Am respectable people.
gentil adj 1 (amable) kind. 2 (pagano) pagan.
gentileza nf kindness; fml **por g. de**, by courtesy of.
gentío nm crowd.
gentuza nf pey riffraff.
genuino,-a adj (puro) genuine; (verdadero) authentic.
geografía nf geography.
geología nf geology.
geometría nf geometry.
geranio nm geranium.
gerencia nf management.
gerente nmf manager.
germano,-a I adj German, Germanic. II nm,f German.
germen nm 1 Biol germ. 2 fig (inicio) germ; (fuente) origin.
germinar vi to germinate.
gerundio nm gerund.
gesta nf arc heroic exploit.
gestación nf gestation.
gestar vtr to gestate.
gesticular vi to gesticulate.
gestión nf 1 (administración) management. 2 **gestiones**, (negociaciones) negotiations; (trámites) formalities.
gestionar vtr to take steps to acquire o obtain; (negociar) to negotiate.
gesto nm 1 (mueca) face. 2 (con las manos) gesture.
gestor,-a nm,f ≈ solicitor.
giba nf hump.
gibar vtr fam to annoy.
Gibraltar n Gibraltar; **el peñón de G.**, the Rock of Gibraltar.
gibraltareño,-a I adj of o from Gibraltar. II nm,f Gibraltarian.

gigante,-a I nm,f giant. II adj giant, enormous.
gigantesco,-a adj gigantic.
gigoló nm gigolo.
gili, gili nm arg ofens → **gilipollas**.
gilipollas nmf ofens bloody fool o idiot.
gimnasia nf gymnastics pl.
gimnasio nm gymnasium.
gimotear vi to whine.
Ginebra n Geneva.
ginebra nf (bebida) gin.
ginecología nf gynaecology, US gynecology.
ginecólogo,-a nm,f gynaecologist, US gynecologist.
gira nf Teat Mus tour.
girar I vi 1 (dar vueltas) to spin. 2 **g. a la derecha/izquierda**, to turn right/left. 3 Fin (expedir) to draw. II vtr Fin (dinero) to send by giro.
girasol nm sunflower.
giratorio,-a adj revolving.
giro nm 1 (vuelta) turn. 2 (de acontecimientos) direction. 3 (frase) turn of phrase. 4 Fin draft; **g. telegráfico**, giro o money order; **g. postal**, postal o money order.
gitano,-a adj & nm,f gypsy, gipsy.
glacial adj icy.
glaciar nm glacier.
glándula nf gland.
glasear vtr Culin to glaze.
global adj comprehensive; **precio g.**, all-inclusive price. ◆**globalmente** adv as a whole.
globo nm 1 balloon. 2 (esfera) globe. 3 (lámpara) globe, glass lampshade.
glóbulo nm globule.
gloria nf 1 (fama) glory. 2 Rel heaven; fam fig **estar en la g.**, to be in seventh heaven. 3 fam (delicia) delight.
glorieta nf 1 (plazoleta) small square. 2 (encrucijada de calles) roundabout, US traffic circle. 3 (en un jardín) arbour, US arbor.
glorificar [1] vtr to glorify.
glorioso,-a adj glorious.
glosa nf 1 gloss. 2 Lit (comentario) notes pl, commentary.
glosar vtr 1 (explicar) to gloss; (texto) to interpret. 2 (comentar) to comment on.
glosario nm glossary.
glotón,-ona I adj greedy. II nm,f glutton.
glotonería nf gluttony.
glucosa nf Quím glucose.
gobernación nf government; Pol Hist **Ministerio de la G.**, ≈ GB Home Office, US Department of the Interior.
gobernador,-a nm,f governor.
gobernante adj ruling.
gobernar [1] I vtr to govern; (un país) to rule. II vi Náut to steer.
gobierno nm 1 Pol government. 2 (mando) running. 3 Náut steering. 4 Náut

(timón) rudder.

goce nm enjoyment.

gofio nm Am Can roasted maize meal.

gol nm goal.

goleada nf lots of goals; **ganar por g.,** to win by a barrowload.

golear vtr to hammer.

golf nm golf; **palo de g.,** golf club.

golfista nmf golfer.

golfo,-a¹ I nm,f good-for-nothing. II nf fam pey tart.

golfo² nm Geog gulf; **el g. Pérsico,** the Persian Gulf.

golondrina nf swallow.

golosina nf sweet, US candy.

goloso,-a adj sweet-toothed.

golpe nm 1 blow; (llamada) knock; (puñetazo) punch; **de g.,** all of a sudden; **g. de estado,** coup d'état; **g. de suerte,** stroke of luck; **no dar ni g.,** not to lift a finger. 2 Aut bump. 3 (desgracia) blow; **un duro g.,** a great blow. 4 (de humor) witticism.

golpear vtr to hit; (con el puño) to punch; (puerta, cabeza) to bang.

goma nf 1 rubber; **g. de pegar,** glue; **g. de borrar,** rubber, US eraser. 2 (elástica) rubber band. 3 arg (preservativo) condom.

gomaespuma nf foam rubber.

gomal nm Am Agr rubber plantation.

gomero nm Am 1 Bot gum tree. 2 (recolector) rubber collector.

gomina nf hair cream.

góndola nf gondola.

gordo,-a I adj 1 (carnoso) fat. 2 (grueso) thick. 3 (importante) big; **me cae g.,** I can't stand him; **de g.,** in a big way. II nm,f fat person; fam fatty. III nm **el g.,** (de lotería) the jackpot.

gordura nf fatness.

gorgorito nm trill.

gorila nm 1 gorilla. 2 fig (en discoteca etc) bouncer.

gorjear I vi to chirp. II **gorjearse** vr Am **g. de algn,** to laugh at sb's expense.

gorjeo nm chirping.

gorra nf cap; (con visera) peaked cap; fam **de g.,** free.

gorrión nm sparrow.

gorro nm 1 cap. 2 fam **estar hasta el g.,** to be up to here (**de,** with).

gorrón,-ona nm,f sponger.

gota nf 1 drop; (de sudor) bead; **g. a g.,** drop by drop; **ni g.,** not a bit. 2 Med gout.

gotear v impers to drip; **el techo gotea,** there's a leak in the ceiling.

gotera nf leak.

gótico,-a adj Gothic.

gozar [4] I vtr to enjoy. II vi (disfrutar) to enjoy (**de,** -).

gozne nm hinge.

gozo nm pleasure.

grabación nf recording.

grabado,-a nm 1 (arte) engraving. 2 (dibujo) drawing.

grabadora nf tape recorder.

grabar vtr 1 (sonidos, imágenes) to record. 2 Inform to save. 3 Arte to engrave.

gracia nf 1 (atractivo) grace. 2 (chiste) joke; **hacer o tener g.,** to be funny. 3 (indulto) pardon.

gracias nfpl (agradecimiento) thanks; **g. a Dios,** thank God, thank goodness; **g. a,** thanks to; **muchas o muchísimas g.,** thank you very much.

gracioso,-a I adj 1 (divertido) funny. 2 (garboso) graceful. II nm,f Teat comic character.

grada nf 1 (peldaño) step. 2 **gradas,** flight sing of steps, US forecourt sing; (en estadio) terracing.

gradación nf 1 gradation. 2 Mús scale.

graderío nm tiers pl of seats; Dep terracing, US bleachers pl.

gradiente I nm gradient, US grade. II nf Am slope.

grado nm 1 degree. 2 Mil rank. 3 **de buen g.,** willingly, gladly.

graduable adj adjustable.

graduación nf 1 gradation. 2 Mil rank.

graduado,-a nmf graduate.

gradual adj gradual. ◆**gradualmente** adv gradually.

graduar [30] I vtr 1 Educ Mil to confer a degree o a rank on. 2 (regular) to regulate. II **graduarse** vr 1 Educ Mil to graduate. 2 **g. la vista,** to have one's eyes tested.

gráfico,-a I adj graphic; **diseño g.,** graphic design. II nm,f graph.

grafista nmf graphic designer.

gragea nf Med pill.

grajo,-a I nm,f Orn rook. II nm Am body odour.

gral. abr de **General,** General, gen.

gramática nf grammar.

gramo nm gram, gramme.

gran adj → **grande.**

grana adj scarlet.

granada nf 1 (fruto) pomegranate. 2 Mil grenade.

granate I adj inv (color) maroon. II nm (color) maroon.

Gran Bretaña n Great Britain.

grande adj (before singular noun gran is used) 1 (tamaño) big, large; fig (persona) great. 2 (cantidad) large; **vivir a lo g.,** to live in style; fig **pasarlo en g.,** to have a great time.

grandeza nf 1 (importancia) greatness. 2 (grandiosidad) grandeur; **delirios de g.,** delusions of grandeur.

grandioso,-a adj grandiose.

granel (a) loc adv (sin medir exactamente) loose.

granero nm Agr granary.

granito nm granite.

granizada nf, **granizado** nm iced drink.

granizar |4| v impers to hail.

granizo nm hail.

granja nf farm.

granjear(se) vtr & vr to gain.

granjero,-a nm,f farmer.

grano nm **1** grain; (de café) bean; **ir al g.**, to get to the point. **2** (espinilla) spot.

granuja nm **1** (pilluelo) ragamuffin. **2** (estafador) con-man.

grapa nf **1** staple. **2** Constr cramp.

grapadora nf stapler.

grapar vtr to staple.

grasa nf grease.

grasiento adj greasy.

graso,-a adj (pelo) greasy; (materia) fatty.

gratificar |1| vtr **1** (satisfacer) to gratify. **2** (recompensar) to reward.

gratinar vtr Culin to cook in a sauce until golden brown.

gratis adv inv free.

gratitud nf gratitude.

grato,-a adj pleasant.

gratuito,-a adj **1** (de balde) free (of charge). **2** (arbitrario) gratuitous.

grava nf (guijas) gravel; (en carretera) chippings.

gravamen nm Jur **1** (carga) burden. **2** (impuesto) tax.

gravar vtr Jur **1** (cargar) to burden. **2** (impuestos) to tax.

grave adj **1** (importante) serious. **2** (muy enfermo) seriously ill. **3** (voz, nota) low.

gravedad nf **1** (seriedad, importancia) seriousness. **2** Fís gravity.

gravilla nf chippings.

gravitar vi **1** Fís to gravitate. **2 g. sobre**, to rest on.

gravoso,-a adj **1** (costoso) costly. **2** (molesto) burdensome.

graznar vi to squawk; (de pato) to quack; (de cuervo) to caw.

graznido nm (un sonido) squawk; (varios) squawking; (de pato) quack; (de cuervo) caw.

Grecia n Greece.

gregario,-a adj gregarious; **instinto g.**, herd instinct.

gremio nm **1** Hist guild. **2** (profesión) profession.

greña nf lock of entangled hair; fam **andar a la g.**, to squabble.

gres nm artículos de g., stoneware.

gresca nf **1** (bulla) racket. **2** (riña) row.

griego,-a adj & nm,f Greek.

grieta nf crack; (en la piel) chap.

grifo nm tap, US faucet.

grillete nm shackle.

grillo nm Ent cricket.

gringo,-a pey I adj foreign; Am yankee. II nm,f foreigner; Am yankee, gringo.

gripe nf flu.

gris adj & nm grey, US gray.

grisáceo,-a adj greyish.

gritar vtr & vi to shout.

grito nm shout; **a v. en g.**, at the top of one's voice.

grosella nf (fruto) redcurrant; **g. negra**, blackcurrant; **g. silvestre**, gooseberry.

grosería nf **1** (ordinariez) rude word or expression. **2** (rusticidad) rudeness.

grosero,-a adj (tosco) coarse; (maleducado) rude.

grosor nm thickness.

grotesco,-a adj grotesque.

grúa nf **1** Constr crane. **2** Aut breakdown van, US tow truck.

grueso,-a adj **1** thick; (persona) stout. II nm (parte principal) bulk.

grulla nf Orn crane.

grumo nm lump; (de leche) curd.

gruñido nm grunt.

gruñir vi to grunt.

gruñón,-ona adj grumpy.

grupa nf hindquarters.

grupo nm **1** group. **2** Téc unit, set.

gruta nf cave.

guacamayo,-a nm,f Orn macaw.

guacamol, guacamole nm Am Culin guacamole, avocado sauce.

guachafita nf Am uproar.

guacho,-a adj & nm,f Am orphan.

guadaña nf scythe.

guagua¹ nf **1** (perro) bow-wow. **2** Can Cuba bus.

guagua² nf Am baby.

guantazo nm slap.

guante nm glove.

guantera nf Aut glove compartment.

guapo,-a I adj **1** good-looking, US cute; (mujer) beautiful, pretty; (hombre) handsome. **2** Am (matón) bully.

guaraca nf Am sling.

guarango,-a adj Am rude.

guarda nm,f guard; **g. jurado**, security guard.

guardabarros nm inv Aut mudguard, US fender.

guardabosque nmf gamekeeper.

guardacoches nmf inv parking attendant.

guardacostas nm inv (persona) coastguard; (embarcación) coastguard vessel.

guardaespaldas nmf inv bodyguard.

guardameta nmf Dep goalkeeper.

guardapolvo nm inv overalls pl.

guardar I vtr **1** (conservar) to keep. **2** (un secreto) to keep; **g. silencio**, to remain silent; **g. cama**, to stay in bed. **3** (poner en un sitio) to put away. **4** (reservar) to keep. **5** Inform to save. II **guardarse** vr **g. de hacer algo**, (abstenerse) to be careful not to do sth; **guardársela a algn**, to have it in for sb.

guardarropa nm **1** (cuarto) cloakroom. **2** (armario) wardrobe.

guardería nf **g. infantil**, nursery (school).

guardia nf **1** (vigilancia) watch. **2 la G. Civil**, the civil guard. **3** (turno de servicio) duty; Mil guard duty; **de g.**, on duty;

farmacia de g., duty chemist. II *nmf* policeman; (*mujer*) policewoman.
guardián,-ana *nm,f* watchman.
guarecer [33] I *vtr* to shelter. II **guarecerse** *vr* to take shelter *o* refuge (**de**, from).
guarida *nf* (*de animal*) lair; (*refugio*) hide-out.
guarismo *nm* digit.
guarnecer [33] *vtr* 1 *Culin* to garnish. 2 (*dotar*) to provide (**de**, with). 3 *Mil* to garrison.
guarnición *nf* 1 *Culin* garnish. 2 *Mil* garrison.
guarro,-a I *adj* filthy. II *nm,f* pig.
guasa *nf* mockery.
guasearse *vr fam* **g. de**, to make fun of.
guaso,-a *adj Am* peasant.
guasón,-ona I *adj* humorous. II *nm,f* joker.
guata *nf* 1 (*relleno*) padding. 2 *Am* (*barriga*) paunch.
guay *adj inv fam* brilliant, terrific.
guayabera *nf* short jacket.
guayabo,-a *nm,f Am fig* (*chica bonita*) pretty young girl; (*chico guapo*) good-looking boy.
guepardo *nm* cheetah.
guerra *nf* war; **en g.**, at war; **g. bacteriológica**, germ warfare; **g. civil/fría/mundial/nuclear**, civil/cold/world/nuclear war; *fam* **dar g.**, to be a real nuisance.
guerrero,-a I *nm,f* warrior. II *adj* warlike.
guerrilla *nf* 1 (*partida armada*) guerrilla force *o* band. 2 (*lucha*) guerrilla warfare.
guía I *nmf* (*persona*) guide. II *nf* 1 (*norma*) guideline. 2 (*libro*) guide; (*lista*) directory; **g. de teléfonos**, telephone directory.
guiar [29] I *vtr* 1 (*indicar el camino*) to guide. 2 *Aut* to drive; *Náut* to steer; (*caballo, bici*) to ride. II **guiarse** *vr* to be guided, to go (**por**, by).
guija *nf* pebble.
guijarro *nm* pebble.

guinda *nf* (*fruto*) morello (cherry).
guindilla *nf* chilli.
guiñapo *nm* 1 (*andrajo*) rag. 2 *fig* (*persona*) wreck; **poner a algn como un g.**, to tear sb to pieces.
guiñar *vtr* to wink.
guiño *nm* wink.
guión *nm* 1 *Cin TV* script. 2 *Ling* hyphen, dash. 3 (*esquema*) sketch.
guionista *nmf* scriptwriter.
guiri *nmf arg* foreigner.
guirigay *nm* hubbub.
guirnalda *nf* garland.
guisa *nf* way, manner; **a g. de**, as, by way of.
guisado *nm Culin* stew.
guisante *nm* pea.
guisar *vtr* to cook.
guiso *nm* dish; (*guisado*) stew.
guita *nf* 1 (*cuerda*) rope. 2 *arg* dough.
guitarra I *nf* guitar. II *nmf* guitarist.
guitarrista *nmf* guitarist.
gula *nf* gluttony.
gusano *nm* worm; (*oruga*) caterpillar; **g. de seda**, silkworm.
gustar I *vtr* 1 **me gusta el vino**, I like wine; **me gustaban los caramelos**, I used to like sweets; **me gusta nadar**, I like swimming; **me gustaría ir**, I would like to go. 2 *fml* **¿gustas?**, would you like some?; **cuando gustes**, whenever you like. II *vi* **g. de**, to enjoy.
gusto *nm* 1 (*sentido*) taste. 2 (*en fórmulas de cortesía*) pleasure; **con (mucho) g.**, with (great) pleasure; **tanto g.**, pleased to meet you. 3 **estar a g.**, to feel comfortable *o* at ease; **por g.**, for the sake of it; **ser de buen/mal g.**, to be in good/bad taste; **tener buen/mal g.**, to have good/bad taste; **tenemos el gusto de comunicarle que ...**, we are pleased to inform you that ....
gutural *adj* guttural.

H

H, h [atʃe] *nf* (*la letra*) H,h; **bomba H**, H-bomb.
ha *indic pres* → **haber**.
haba *nf* broad bean.
Habana *nf* **La H.**, Havana.
habano *nm* Havana cigar.
haber [14] I *v aux* 1 (*en tiempos compuestos*) to have; **lo he visto**, I have seen it; **ya lo había hecho**, he had already done it. 2 **h. de** + *infin*, (*obligación*) to have to; **has de ser bueno**, you must be good.
II *v impers* (*special form of present tense:* **hay**) 1 (*existir, estar*) (*singular used also with plural nouns*) **hay**, there is *o* are; **había**, there was *o* were; **había un gato en**

el tejado, there was a cat on the roof; **había muchos libros**, there were a lot of books; **hay 500 kilómetros entre Madrid y Granada**, it's 500 kilometers from Madrid to Granada. 2 **h. que** + *infin*, it is necessary to; **hay que trabajar**, you've got to *o* you must work; **habrá que comprobarlo**, I/you/we *etc* will have to check it. 3 (*tener lugar*) **habrá una fiesta**, there will be a party; **hoy hay partido**, there's a match today; **los accidentes habidos en esta carretera**, the accidents which have happened on this road. 4 **había una vez ...**, once upon a time ...; **no hay de qué**, you're welcome, don't mention it; **¿qué hay?**, how are things?

III *nm* **1** *Fin* credit; **haberes**, assets. **2 en su h.**, in his possession.

habichuela *nf* kidney bean.

hábil *adj* **1** *(diestro)* skilful, *US* skillful. **2** *(astuto)* smart. **3 días hábiles**, working days.

habilidad *nf* **1** *(destreza)* skill. **2** *(astucia)* cleverness.

habilitar *vtr* **1** *(espacio)* to fit out. **2** *(persona)* to entitle. **3** *Fin* *(financiar)* to finance.

habitación *nf* *(cuarto)* room; *(dormitorio)* bedroom; **h. individual/doble**, single/double room.

habitante *nmf* inhabitant.

habitar **I** *vtr* to live in, inhabit. **II** *vi* to live.

hábitat *nm* *(pl hábitats)* habitat.

hábito *nm* **1** *(costumbre)* habit. **2** *Rel* habit.

habitual *adj* usual, habitual; *(cliente, lector)* regular.

habituar [30] **I** *vtr* to accustom (a, to). **II habituarse** *vr* to get used (a, to), become accustomed (a, to).

habla *nf* **1** *(idioma)* language; **países de h. española**, Spanish-speaking countries. **2** *(facultad de hablar)* speech; **quedarse sin h.**, to be left speechless. **3** *Tel* **¡al h.!**, speaking!

hablado,-a *adj* spoken; **el inglés h.**, spoken English; **mal h.**, coarse, foulmouthed.

hablador,-a *adj* *(parlanchín)* talkative; *pey* *(chismoso)* gossipy.

habladuría *nf* *(rumor)* rumour, *US* rumor; *(chisme)* piece of gossip.

hablante *nmf* speaker.

hablar **I** *vi* **1** to speak, talk; **h. con algn**, to speak to sb. **2** **¡ni h.!**, certainly not!; *fam* **¡quién fue a h.!**, look who's talking!. **II** *vtr* **1** *(idioma)* to speak; **habla alemán**, he speaks German. **2** *(tratar un asunto)* to talk over, discuss. **III hablarse** *vr* **1** to speak *o* talk to one another. **2 'se habla español'**, *(en letrero)* 'Spanish spoken'.

habré *indic fut* → **haber**.

hacendoso,-a *adj* hardworking.

hacer [15] **I** *vtr* **1** *(crear, producir, fabricar)* to make; **h. una casa**, to build a house. **2** *(obrar, ejecutar)* to do; **eso no se hace**, it isn't done; **hazme un favor**, do me a favour; **¿qué haces?**, *(en este momento)* what are you doing?; *(para vivir)* what do you do *(for a living)?*; **tengo mucho que h.**, I have a lot to do; **h. deporte**, to do sports; **h. una carrera/medicina**, to do a degree/medicine. **3** *(conseguir)* *(amigos, dinero)* to make. **4** *(obligar)* to make; **hazle callar/trabajar**, make him shut up/work. **5** *(arreglar)* to make; **h. la cama**, to make the bed. **6** *Mat* *(sumar)* to make; **y con éste hacen cien**, and that makes a hundred. **7** *(dar aspecto)* to make look; **el negro le hace más delgado**, black makes

him look slimmer. **8** *(sustituyendo a otro verbo)* to do; **ya no puedo leer como solía hacerlo**, I can't read as well as I used to. **9** *(representar)* to play; **h. el bueno**, to play the *(part of the)* baddy. **10 ¡bien hecho!**, well done!

II *vi* **1** *(actuar)* to play; **hizo de Desdémona**, she played Desdemona. **2 h. por** *o* **para** + *infin*, to try to; **hice por venir**, I tried to come. **3** *(fingir)* to pretend; **h. como si**, to act as if. **4** *(convenir)* to be suitable; **a las ocho si te hace**, will eight o'clock be all right for you?

III *v impers* **1** *hace* **calor/frío**, it's hot/cold. **2** *(tiempo transcurrido)* ago; **hace mucho (tiempo)**, a long time ago; **hace dos días que no te he visto**, I haven't seen him for two days; **hace dos años que vivo en Glasgow**, I've been living in Glasgow for two years.

IV hacerse *vr* **1** *(volverse)* to become, grow; **h. viejo**, to grow old. **2** *(simular)* to pretend; **h. el dormido**, to pretend to be sleeping. **3 h. con**, *(apropiarse)* to get hold of. **4** *(habituarse)* to get used (a, to); **enseguida me hago a todo**, I soon get used to anything.

hacha *nf* **1** *(herramienta)* axe, *US* ax. **2** *fam* **ser una h. en algo**, to be an ace *o* a wizard at sth.

hachís *nm* hashish.

hacia *prep* **1** *(dirección)* towards, to; **h. abajo**, down, downwards; **h. adelante**, forwards; **h. arriba**, up, upwards; **h. atrás**, back, backwards. **2** *(tiempo)* at about, at around; **h. las tres**, at about three o'clock.

hacienda *nf* **1** *(finca agrícola)* estate, *US* ranch. **2** *Fin* Treasury; **h. pública**, public funds *o* finances *pl*; **Ministerio de H.**, = Exchequer, Treasury.

hacinamiento *nm* **1** *Agr* stacking; *fig* *(montón)* piling. **2** *(de gente)* overcrowding.

hacinar **I** *vtr* *Agr* to stack; *fig* *(amontonar)* to pile up, heap up. **II hacinarse** *vr* *(gente)* to be packed (en, into).

hada *nf* fairy; **cuento de hadas**, fairy tale; **h. madrina**, fairy godmother.

hado *nm* destiny.

hago *indic pres* → **hacer**.

halagar [7] *vtr* to flatter.

halago *nm* flattery.

halagüeño,-a *adj* *(noticia, impresión)* promising.

halcón *nm* falcon; **h. peregrino**, peregrine (falcon).

hálito *nm* **1** *(aliento)* breath. **2** *(vapor)* vapour, *US* vapor.

hallar **I** *vtr* *(encontrar)* to find; *(averiguar)* to find out; *(descubrir)* to discover. **II hallarse** *vr* *(estar)* to be, find oneself; *(estar situado)* to be situated.

hallazgo *nm* **1** *(descubrimiento)* discovery.

2 (cosa encontrada) find.
hamaca nf hammock; (mecedora) rocking chair.
hambre nf (apetito) hunger; (inanición) starvation; (catástrofe) famine; **tener h.**, to be hungry.
hambriento,-a adj starving.
hamburguesa nf hamburger.
hampa nf underworld.
han indic pres → **haber**.
harapo nm rag; **hecho un h.**, in tatters.
haré indic fut → **hacer**.
harén nm (pl harenes) harem.
harina nf flour.
hartar I vtr 1 (cansar, fastidiar) to annoy. 2 (atiborrar) to satiate; **el dulce harta enseguida**, sweet things soon fill you up. II **hartarse** vr 1 (saciar el apetito) to eat one's fill. 2 (cansarse) to get fed up (**de**, with), grow tired (**de**, of).
harto,-a adj 1 (de comida) full. 2 (cansado) fed up; **¡me tienes h.!**, I'm fed up with you!; **estoy h. de trabajar**, I'm fed up working. ◆**harto** adv (muy) very.
hartura nf bellyful; **¡qué h.!**, what a drag!
has indic pres → **haber**.
hasta I prep 1 (lugar) up to, as far as, down to. 2 (tiempo) until, till, up to; **h. el domingo**, until Sunday; **h. la fecha**, right to the end; **h. la fecha**, up to now; **h. luego**, see you later. 3 (con cantidad) up to, as many as. 4 (incluso) even. II conj **h. que**, until.
hastiado,-a adj sick, tired (**de**, of).
hastiar [29] vtr to sicken.
hastío nm weariness.
hato nm bundle.
hay indic pres → **haber**.
Haya (La) nf The Hague.
haya¹ nf 1 Bot (árbol) beech. 2 (madera) beech (wood).
haya² subj pres → **haber**.
haz¹ nm 1 Agr sheaf. 2 (de luz) shaft.
haz² nf (de hoja) top side.
haz³ imperat → **hacer**.
hazaña nf deed, exploit.
hazmerreír nm laughing stock.
he¹ adv **he ahí/aquí ...**, there/here you have ....
he² indic pres → **haber**.
hebilla nf buckle.
hebra nf thread; (de carne) sinew; (de madera) grain; **pegar la h.**, to chat.
hebreo,-a I adj Hebrew. II nm,f Hebrew.
hecatombe nf disaster.
hechicería nf witchcraft.
hechicero,-a I adj bewitching. II nm,f (hombre) wizard, sorcerer; (mujer) witch, sorceress.
hechizar [4] vtr 1 (embrujar) to cast a spell on. 2 fig (fascinar) to bewitch, charm.
hechizo nm 1 (embrujo) spell. 2 fig (fascinación) fascination, charm.
hecho,-a I adj 1 made, done; **¡bien h.!**,

well done! 2 (carne) done. 3 (persona) mature. 4 (frase) set; (ropa) ready-made. II nm 1 (realidad) fact; **de h.**, in fact; **el h. es que ...**, the fact is that .... 2 (acto) act, deed. 3 (suceso) event, incident.
hechura nf (forma) shape; Cost cut.
hectárea nf hectare.
hectolitro nm hectolitre, US hectoliter.
heder [3] vi to stink, smell foul.
hediondo,-a adj foul-smelling.
hedor nm stink, stench.
hegemonía nf hegemony.
helada nf frost.
heladería nf ice-cream parlour.
helado,-a I nm ice cream. II adj 1 (muy frío) frozen, freezing cold; **estoy h. (de frío)**, I'm frozen. 2 fig **quedarse h.**, (atónito) to be flabbergasted.
helar [1] I vtr (congelar) to freeze. II vi impers to freeze; **anoche heló**, there was a frost last night. III **helarse** vr (congelarse) to freeze.
helecho nm Bot fern.
hélice nf 1 Av Náut propeller. 2 Anat Arquit Mat helix.
helicóptero nm Av helicopter.
helipuerto nm Av heliport.
hematoma nm Med haematoma, US hematoma.
hembra nf 1 Bot Zool female. 2 (mujer) woman. 3 Téc female; (de tornillo) nut; (de enchufe) socket.
hemiciclo nm fam (Spanish) parliament.
hemisferio nm hemisphere.
hemorragia nf Med haemorrhage, US hemorrhage.
hemos indic pres → **haber**.
henchir [6] vtr to stuff.
hender [3] vtr (resquebrajar) to crack, split; fig (olas) to cut.
hendidura nf crack.
hendir [5] vtr → **hender**.
heno nm hay.
heráldica nf heraldry.
herbicida nm weedkiller, herbicide.
herbívoro,-a I adj herbivorous, grass-eating. II nm,f Zool herbivore.
herbolario nm herbalist's (shop).
herboso,-a adj grassy.
hercio nm Herz.
heredad nf 1 (finca) country estate. 2 (conjunto de bienes) private estate.
heredar vtr 1 Jur to inherit. 2 **ha heredado la sonrisa de su madre**, she's got her mother's smile.
heredero,-a nm (hombre) heir; (mujer) heiress; **príncipe h.**, crown prince.
hereditario,-a adj hereditary.
hereje nmf Rel heretic.
herejía nf Rel heresy.
herencia nf 1 Jur inheritance, legacy. 2 Biol heredity.
herida nf (lesión) injury; (corte) wound.
herido,-a n injured person; **no hubo heri-**

dos, there were no casualties.

herir [5] I *vtr* **1** *(físicamente) (lesionar)* to injure; *(cortar)* to wound. **2** *(emocionalmente)* to hurt, wound. **3** *(vista)* to offend. **II herirse** *vr* to injure o hurt oneself.

hermana *nf* **1** sister. **2** *Rel (monja)* sister (→ **hermano**).

hermanado,-a *adj* twinned; **ciudad hermanada,** twin town.

hermanar I *vtr* **1** *(personas)* to unite spiritually. **2** *(ciudades)* to twin. **3** *(unir)* to unite, combine. **II hermanarse** *vr* **1** *(ciudades)* to twin. **2** *(combinar)* to combine.

hermanastro,-a *nm,f (hombre)* stepbrother; *(mujer)* stepsister.

hermandad *nf* **1** *(grupo)* fraternity, brotherhood, sisterhood. **2** *(relación)* brotherhood, sisterhood.

hermano *nm* **1** brother; **h. político,** brother-in-law; **primo h.,** first cousin. **2** *Rel (fraile)* brother. **3 hermanos,** brothers and sisters.

hermético,-a *adj* **1** *(cierre)* hermetic, airtight. **2** *fig (abstruso)* secretive. ◆**herméticamente** *adv* **h. cerrado,** hermetically sealed.

hermetismo *nm* hermeticism; *fig* impenetrability.

hermoso,-a *adj* beautiful, lovely; *(grande)* fine.

hermosura *nf* beauty.

héroe *nm* hero.

heroico,-a *adj* heroic.

heroína *nf* **1** *(mujer)* heroine. **2** *(droga)* heroin.

heroinómano,-a *nm,f* heroin addict.

heroísmo *nm* heroism.

herrador *nm* blacksmith.

herradura *nf* horseshoe.

herramienta *nf* *Téc* tool; **caja de herramientas,** toolbox.

herrar [1] *vtr* **1** *(caballo)* to shoe. **2** *(ganado)* to brand.

herrería *nf* forge, smithy.

herrero *nm* blacksmith, smith.

herrumbre *nf* rust.

hervidero *nm fig (lugar)* hotbed.

hervir [5] I *vtr (hacer bullir)* to boil. **II** *vi* **1** *Culin* to boil; **romper a h.,** to come to the boil. **2** *(abundar)* to swarm, seethe (**de,** with).

heterodoxo,-a *adj* unorthodox.

heterogéneo,-a *adj* heterogeneous.

hez *nf* **1** *(usu pl) (poso)* sediment, dregs *pl.* **2 heces,** faeces.

hiato *nm Ling* hiatus.

híbrido,-a *adj & nm,f* hybrid.

hice *pt indef* → **hacer**.

hiciste *pt indef* → **hacer**.

hidalgo *nm Hist* nobleman, gentleman.

hidalguía *nf* nobility; *fig* chivalry, gentlemanliness.

hidratación *nf* **1** *Quím* hydration. **2** *(de la*

piel) moisturizing.

hidratante *adj* moisturizing; **crema/leche h.,** moisturizing cream/lotion.

hidráulico,-a *adj* hydraulic; **energía hidráulica,** hydro-electric energy.

hidroavión *nm* seaplane, *US* hydroplane.

hidrocarburo *nm* hydrocarbon.

hidrófilo,-a *adj* absorbent; **algodón h.,** cotton wool.

hidrógeno *nm Quím* hydrogen.

hidroterapia *nf Med* hydrotherapy.

hiedra *nf* ivy.

hiel *nf* **1** *Anat* bile. **2** *fig* bitterness, gall.

hielo *nm* ice; *fig* **romper el h.,** to break the ice.

hiena *nf* hyena.

hierba *nf* **1** grass; **mala h.,** *Bot* weed; *fig (persona)* bad lot; *fam* **hum ... y otras hierbas,** ... among others. **2** *Culin* herb; **h. luisa,** lemon verbena. **3** *sl (marihuana)* grass.

hierbabuena *nf* mint.

hierro *nm* **1** *(metal)* iron; **h. forjado,** wrought iron. **2** *(punta de arma)* head, point. **3** *(marca en el ganado)* brand.

hígado *nm* **1** *Anat* liver. **2** *euf* guts *pl.*

higiene *nf* hygiene.

higiénico,-a *adj* hygienic; **papel h.,** toilet paper.

higo *nm Bot* fig; *fig* **hecho un h.,** wizened, crumpled.

higuera *nf Bot* fig tree.

hija *nf* daughter (→ **hijo**).

hijastro,-a *nm,f (hombre)* stepson; *(mujer)* stepdaughter.

hijo *nm* **1** son, child; *pey* **h. de papá,** daddy's boy; *vulg ofens* **h. de puta,** bastard, son of a bitch. **2 hijos,** children.

hijoputa *nm vulg ofens* bastard.

hilacha *nf,* **hilacho** *nm* loose o hanging thread.

hilandería *nf* mill; *(de algodón)* cotton mill.

hilandero,-a *nm,f* spinner.

hilar *vtr & vi* **1** to spin. **2** *fig (idea, plan)* to work out; **h. muy fino,** to split hairs.

hilaridad *nf* hilarity, mirth.

hilera *nf* line, row.

hilo *nm* **1** *Cost* thread; *(grueso)* yarn. **2** *fig (de historia, discurso)* thread; *(de pensamiento)* train; **perder el h.,** to lose the thread; **h. musical,** background music. **3** *Tex* linen.

hilvanar *vtr* **1** *Cost* to tack, baste. **2** *fig (ideas etc)* to outline.

himno *nm* hymn; **h. nacional,** national anthem.

hincapié *nm* **hacer h. en,** *(insistir)* to insist on; *(subrayar)* to emphasize, stress.

hincar [1] I *vtr (clavar)* to drive (in); **h. el diente a,** to sink one's teeth into. **II hincarse** *vr* **h. de rodillas,** to kneel (down).

hincha *fam* I *nmf Ftb* fan, supporter. **II** *nf*

(*antipatía*) grudge, dislike; **me tiene h.,** he's got it in for me.

hinchada *nf Ftb fam* fans *pl,* supporters *pl.*

hinchado,-a *adj* 1 inflated, blown up. 2 *Med* (*cara etc*) swollen, puffed up; (*estómago*) bloated. 3 *fig* (*estilo*) bombastic, pompous.

hinchar I *vtr* 1 (*inflar*) to inflate, blow up. 2 *fig* (*exagerar*) to inflate, exaggerate. II **hincharse** *vr* 1 *Med* to swell (up). 2 *fam* **me hinché de comida,** I stuffed myself; **me hinché de llorar,** I cried for all I was worth.

hinchazón *nf Med* swelling.

hindú *adj & nmf* Hindu.

hipermercado *nm* hypermarket.

hipertensión *nf* high blood pressure.

hípica *nf* (horse) riding.

hípico,-a *adj* horse; **club h.,** riding club.

hipnotizar [4] *vtr* to hypnotize.

hipo *nm* hiccup, hiccough; **me ha dado h.,** it's given me the hiccups.

hipocondríaco,-a *adj & nm,f* hypochondriac.

hipocresía *nf* hypocrisy.

hipócrita I *adj* hypocritical. II *nmf* hypocrite.

hipódromo *nm* racetrack, racecourse.

hipopótamo *nm* hippopotamus.

hipoteca *nf Fin* mortgage.

hipotecar [1] *vtr* 1 *Fin* to mortgage. 2 *fig* to jeopardize.

hipótesis *nf inv* hypothesis.

hipotético,-a *adj* hypothetical.

hiriente *adj* offensive, wounding; (*palabras*) cutting.

hirsuto,-a *adj* 1 hirsute, hairy; (*cerdoso*) bristly.

hispánico,-a *adj* Hispanic, Spanish.

hispanidad *nf* **el Día de la H.,** Columbus Day (12 October).

hispano- I *adj* (*español*) Spanish; (*español y sudamericano*) Hispanic; (*sudamericano*) Spanish American. II *nm,f* Spanish American, *US* Hispanic.

Hispanoamérica *nf* Latin America.

hispanoamericano,-a *adj & nm,f* Latin American.

hispanohablante I *adj* Spanish-speaking. II *nmf* Spanish speaker.

histeria *nf* hysteria; **un ataque de h.,** hysterics *pl.*

histérico,-a *adj* hysterical; *fam fig* **me pones h.,** you're driving me mad.

historia *nf* 1 history; **esto pasará a la h.,** this will go down in history. 2 (*narración*) story, tale; *fam* **¡déjate de historias!,** don't give me that!

historiador,-a *nm,f* historian.

historial *nm* 1 *Med* medical record, case history. 2 (*curriculum*) curriculum vitae. 3 (*antecedentes*) background.

historiar [29] *vtr* to recount.

histórico,-a *adj* 1 historical. 2 (*auténtico*) factual, true; **hechos históricos,** true facts. 3 (*de gran importancia*) historic, memorable.

historieta *nf* 1 (*cuento*) short story, tale. 2 (*tira cómica*) comic strip.

hito *nm* milestone; **mirar de h. en h.,** to stare at.

hizo *indic indef* → **hacer.**

hnos. *abr de* **Hermanos,** Brothers, Bros.

hocico *nm* 1 (*de animal*) snout. 2 *pey* (*de persona*) mug, snout; *fam* **meter los hocicos en algo,** to stick *o* poke one's nose into sth.

hogar *nm* 1 (*casa*) home. 2 (*de la chimenea*) hearth, fireplace. 3 *fig* **formar *o* crear un h.,** (*familia*) to start a family.

hogareño,-a *adj* (*vida*) home, family; (*persona*) home-loving, stay-at-home.

hoguera *nf* bonfire.

hoja *nf* 1 *Bot* leaf. 2 (*pétalo*) petal. 3 (*de papel*) sheet, leaf; **h. de cálculo,** spreadsheet. 4 (*de libro*) leaf, page. 5 (*de metal*) sheet. 6 (*de cuchillo, espada*) blade. 7 (*impreso*) hand-out, printed sheet. 8 (*de puerta o ventana*) leaf.

hojalata *nf* tin, tin plate.

hojaldre *nm Culin* puff pastry.

hojarasca *nf* fallen *o* dead leaves *pl.*

hojear *vtr* to leaf through, flick through.

hola *interj* hello!, hullo!, hi!

Holanda *n* Holland.

holandés,-esa I *adj* Dutch. II *nm,f* (*hombre*) Dutchman; (*mujer*) Dutchwoman. III *nm* (*idioma*) Dutch.

holding *nm Fin* holding company.

holgado,-a *adj* 1 (*ropa*) loose, baggy. 2 (*económicamente*) comfortable. 3 (*espacio*) roomy; **andar h. de tiempo,** to have plenty of time.

holgar [2] *vi* 1 (*no trabajar*) to be idle. 2 (*sobrar*) **huelga decir que ...,** it goes without saying that ....

holgazán,-ana I *adj* lazy, idle. II *nm,f* lazybones *inv,* layabout.

holgura *nf* 1 (*ropa*) looseness. 2 (*espacio*) space, roominess. 3 *Téc* play, give. 3 (*bienestar económico*) affluence, comfort; **vivir con h.,** to be comfortably off, be well-off.

hollar [2] *vtr fig* to walk on; **terrenos jamás hollados,** uncharted territory.

hollín *nm* soot.

hombre I *nm* 1 man; **de h. a h.,** man-to-man; **¡pobre h.!,** poor chap!; **ser muy h.,** to be every inch a man; **h. de estado,** statesman; **h. de negocios,** businessman. 2 (*especie*) mankind, man. II *interj* 1 (*saludo*) hey!, hey there!; **¡h., Juan!,** hey, Juan! 2 **¡sí h.!, ¡h. claro!,** (*enfático*) sure!, you bet!; **¡anda, h.!,** (*incredulidad*) oh come on!

hombrera *nf* shoulder pad.

hombría *nf* manliness, virility.

hombro *nm* shoulder; **a hombros,** on one's shoulders; **encogerse de hombros,** to shrug one's shoulders; **mirar a algn por encima del h.,** to look down one's nose at sb.

hombruno,-a *adj* mannish, butch.

homenaje *nm* homage, tribute; **rendir h. a algn,** to pay homage o tribute to sb.

homenajear *vtr* to pay tribute to.

homicida I *nmf (hombre)* murderer; *(mujer)* murderess. **II** *adj* homicidal; **el arma h.,** the murder weapon.

homicidio *nm* homicide.

homogéneo,-a *adj* homogeneous, uniform.

homologable *adj* comparable (**con,** with).

homologar [7] *vtr* to give official approval o recognition to.

homólogo,-a I *adj (equiparable)* comparable. **II** *nm,f (persona con mismas condiciones)* counterpart.

homosexual *adj & nmf* homosexual.

homosexualidad *nf* homosexuality.

honda *nf (arma)* sling.

hondo,-a *adj* 1 *(profundo)* deep; **plato h.,** soup dish. 2 *fig (pesar)* profound, deep.

hondonada *nf Geog* hollow, depression.

hondura *nf* depth; *fig* **meterse en honduras,** *(profundizar)* to go into too much detail.

Honduras *n* Honduras.

hondureño,-a *adj & nm,f* Honduran.

honestidad *nf* 1 *(honradez)* honesty, uprightness. 2 *(decencia)* modesty.

honesto,-a *adj* 1 *(honrado)* honest, upright. 2 *(decente)* modest.

hongo *nm* 1 *Bot* fungus; **h. venenoso,** toadstool. 2 *(sombrero)* bowler, bowler hat.

honor *nm* 1 *(virtud)* honour, *US* honor; **palabra de h.,** word of honour. 2 **en h. a la verdad ...,** to be fair ...; **es un h. para mí,** it's an honour for me. 3 **hacer h. a,** to live up to.

honorable *adj* honourable, *US* honorable; *Pol* **el h.,** head of the Catalan government.

honorario,-a I *adj* honorary. **II** *nmpl* **honorarios,** fees, fee *sing.*

honorífico,-a *adj* honorary.

honra *nf* 1 *(dignidad)* dignity, self-esteem. 2 *(fama)* reputation, good name. 3 *(honor)* honour, *US* honor; **me cabe la h. de ...,** I have the honour of ...; **¡a mucha h.!,** and proud of it!

honradez *nf* honesty, integrity.

honrado,-a *adj* 1 *(de fiar)* honest. 2 *(decente)* upright, respectable.

honrar *vtr* 1 *(respetar)* to honour, *US* honor. 2 *(enaltecer)* to be a credit to.

honrilla *nf* self-respect, pride.

honroso,-a *adj (loable)* honourable, *US* honorable.

hora *nf* 1 hour; **media h.,** half an hour; **a altas horas de la madrugada,** in the small hours; **dar la h.,** to strike the hour; **(trabajo) por horas,** (work) paid by the hour; **h. punta,** rush hour; **horas extra,** overtime (hours). 2 *fig* time; **¿qué h. es?,** what time is it?; **a su h.,** at the proper time; **a última h.,** at the last moment; **la h. de la verdad,** the moment of truth. 3 *(cita)* appointment; **pedir h.,** *(al médico etc)* to ask for an appointment.

horadar *vtr (perforar)* to drill o bore a hole in.

horario-a I *nm* timetable, *US* schedule. **II** *adj* time; *Rad* **señal horaria,** pips.

horca *nf* gallows *pl.*

horcajadas *a h* **horcajadas,** astride.

horchata *nf Culin* sweet milky drink made from chufa nuts or almonds.

horda *nf* horde, mob.

horizonte *nm* horizon.

horma *nf (de zapato)* last.

hormiga *nf* ant.

hormigón *nm Constr* concrete; **h. armado,** reinforced concrete.

hormiguear *vi* to itch, tingle; **me hormigueaba la pierna,** I had pins and needles in my leg.

hormigueo *nm* 1 pins and needles *pl,* tingling o itching sensation. 2 *fig* anxiety.

hormiguero *nm* 1 anthill. 2 *fig* **ser un h.,** *(lugar)* to be swarming (with people).

hormona *nf* hormone.

hornada *nf (pan)* batch. 2 *fig* set, batch.

hornillo *nm (de cocinar)* stove; *(placa)* hotplate.

horno *nm (cocina)* oven; *Téc* furnace; *(para cerámica, ladrillos)* kiln; *Culin* **pescado al h.,** baked fish; *fam fig* **esta habitación es un h.,** this room is boiling hot.

Hornos *n* Cabo de H., Cape Horn.

horóscopo *nm* horoscope.

horquilla *nf* 1 *(del pelo)* hair-grip, hairpin, *US* bobby pin. 2 *(estadística)* chart. 3 **h. de precios,** price range.

horrendo,-a *adj* horrifying, horrible.

hórreo *nm Agr* granary.

horrible *adj* horrible, dreadful, awful.

horripilante *adj* hair-raising, scary.

horror *nm* 1 horror, terror; **¡qué h.!,** how awful!; *fam* **tengo h. a las motos,** I hate motorbikes. 2 *fam fig* **me gusta horrores,** *(muchísimo)* I like it an awful lot.

horrorizar [4] *vtr* to horrify, terrify.

horroroso,-a *adj* 1 *(que da miedo)* horrifying, terrifying. 2 *fam (muy feo)* hideous, ghastly. 3 *fam (malísimo)* awful, dreadful.

hortaliza *nf* vegetable.

hortelano *nm,f* market gardener, *US* truck farmer.

hortensia *nf Bot* hydrangea.

hortera *adj arg (persona)* flashy; *(cosa)* tacky, kitsch.

horterada *nf arg* tacky thing *o* act.

hosco,-a *adj* 1 *(poco sociable)* surly, sullen. 2 *(tenebroso)* dark, gloomy. 3 *(difícil)* tough.

hospedaje *nm* lodgings *pl,* accommodation, *US* accommodations.

hospedar I *vtr* to put up, lodge. II **hospedarse** *vr* to stay *(en,* at).

hospicio *nm* orphanage.

hospital *nm* hospital.

hospitalario,-a *adj* 1 *(acogedor)* hospitable. 2 *Med* hospital; **instalaciones hospitalarias,** hospital facilities.

hospitalidad *nf* hospitality.

hospitalizar .4] *vtr* to take *o* send into hospital, hospitalize.

hostal *nm* guest house.

hostelería *nf (negocio)* catering business; *(estudios)* hotel management.

hostelero,-a *nm,f (hombre)* landlord; *(mujer)* landlady.

hostería *nf Am* inn, lodging house.

hostia I *nf* 1 *Rel* host. 2 *vulg (tortazo)* bash. ● **estar de mala h.,** to be in a foul mood; **ser la h.,** *(fantástico)* to be bloody amazing *o* fantastic; *(penoso)* to be bloody useless. II *interj* damn! bloody hell!

hostiar *vtr vulg* to bash, sock.

hostigar [7] *vtr* 1 to harass. 2 *(caballerías)* to whip.

hostil *adj* hostile.

hostilidad *nf* hostility.

hotel *nm* hotel.

hotelero,-a I *adj* hotel; **el sector h.,** the hotel sector. II *nm,f* hotel-keeper, hotelier.

hoy *adv* 1 *(día)* today. 2 *fig (presente)* now; **h. (en) día,** nowadays; **h. por h.,** at the present time.

hoya *nf Geog* dale, valley.

hoyo *nm* 1 *(agujero)* hole, pit. 2 *(sepultura)* grave. 3 *Golf* hole.

hoyuelo *nm* dimple.

hoz *nf Agr* sickle; **la h. y el martillo,** the hammer and sickle.

HR *nm abr de* **Hostal Residencia.**

hube *pt indef →* **haber.**

hubiera *subj imperf →* **haber.**

hucha *nf* piggy bank.

hueco,-a I *adj* 1 *(vacío)* empty, hollow. 2 *(sonido)* resonant. II *nm* 1 *(cavidad)* hollow, hole. 2 *(sitio no ocupado)* empty space. 3 *(rato libre)* free time.

huele *indic pres →* **oler.**

huelga *nf* strike; **estar en** *o* **de h.,** to be on strike; **h. de brazos caídos,** go-slow; **h. de celo,** work- to-rule.

huelguista *nmf* striker.

huella *nf* 1 *(del pie)* footprint; *(coche)* track; **h. dactilar,** fingerprint. 2 *fig (vestigio)* trace, sign; **dejar h.,** to leave one's mark.

huérfano,-a *nmf* orphan.

huero,-a *adj fig* empty.

huerta *nf Agr* 1 *(parcela)* market *o US* truck garden. 2 *(región)* irrigated area used for cultivation.

huerto *nm (de verduras)* vegetable garden, kitchen garden; *(de frutales)* orchard.

hueso *nm* 1 *Anat* bone; **estar en los huesos,** to be all skin and bone. 2 *(de fruto)* stone, *US* pit. 3 *fig (difícil)* hard work; *(profesor)* hard nut. 4 *Am (enchufe)* contact.

huésped,-a *nm,f (invitado)* guest; *(en hotel etc)* lodger, boarder; **casa de huéspedes,** guesthouse.

hueste *nf Mil* army, host.

huesudo,-a *adj* bony.

huevera *nf* 1 *(caja)* egg box. 2 *vulg (suspensorio)* jockstrap.

huevo *nm* 1 egg; **h. duro,** hard-boiled egg; **h. escalfado,** poached egg; **h. frito,** fried egg; **h. pasado por agua,** *Am* **h. tibio,** soft-boiled egg; **huevos revueltos,** scrambled eggs. 2 *vulg (usu pl)* balls *pl;* **hacer algo por huevos,** to do sth even if it kills you; **tener huevos,** to have guts.

huida *nf* flight, escape.

huidizo,-a *adj* elusive.

huir [37] *vtr* 1 to run away *(de,* from), flee; **h. de la cárcel,** to escape from prison; **h. de algn,** to avoid sb.

hule *nm* 1 *(tela impermeable)* oilcloth, oilskin. 2 *(de mesa)* tablecloth. 3 *Am* rubber.

hulla *nf Min* coal.

humanidad *nf* 1 *(género humano)* humanity, mankind. 2 *(cualidad)* humanity, humaneness. 3 *(bondad)* compassion, kindness.

humanitario,-a *adj* humanitarian.

humano,-a I *adj* 1 *(relativo al hombre)* human. 2 *(compasivo)* humane. II *nm* human *(being);* **ser h.,** human being.

humareda *nf (de humo)* smoke; *(arrojar vapor)* to steam, be steaming hot.

humear *vi (echar humo)* to smoke; *(arrojar vapor)* to steam, be steaming hot.

humedad *nf (atmosférica)* humidity; *(de lugar)* dampness; **a prueba de h.,** dampproof.

humedecer [33] I *vtr* to moisten, dampen. II **humedecerse** *vr* to become damp *o* wet *o* moist.

húmedo,-a *adj (casa, ropa)* damp; *(clima)* humid, damp, moist.

humildad *nf* humility; *(pobreza)* humbleness.

humilde *adj* humble, modest; *(pobre)* poor.

humillación *nf* humiliation.

humillante *adj* humiliating, humbling.

humillar I *vtr (rebajar)* to humiliate, humble. II **humillarse** *vr* **h. ante algn,** to humble oneself before sb.

humo *nm* 1 smoke; *(gas)* fumes *pl; (vapor)* vapour, *US* vapor, steam. 2 **¡qué humos tiene!,** she thinks a lot of herself.

humor *nm* 1 *(genio)* mood; **estar de buen**

o **mal h.,** to be in a good *o* bad mood. **2** (*carácter*) temper; **es persona de mal h.,** he's bad tempered. **3** (*gracia*) humour, *US* humor; **sentido del h.,** sense of humour.

humorismo *nm* humour, *US* humor.

humorista *nmf* humorist; **h. gráfico,** cartoonist.

humorístico *adj* humorous, funny.

hundido,-a *adj* **1** (*barco*) sunken; (*ojos*) deep- set. **2** *fig* (*abatido*) down, demoralized.

hundimiento *nm* **1** (*de edificio*) collapse. **2** (*de barco*) sinking. **3** (*de tierra*) subsidence. **4** *fig* *Fin* crash, slump; (*ruina*) downfall.

hundir I *vtr* **1** (*barco*) to sink. **2** (*edificio*) to bring *o* knock down. **3** *fig* (*desmoralizar*) to demoralize. II **hundirse** *vr* **1** (*barco*) to sink. **2** (*edificio*) to collapse. **3** *fig* (*empresa*) to collapse, crash.

húngaro,-a I *adj* Hungarian. II *nm,f* (*persona*) Hungarian. III *nm* (*idioma*) Hungarian.

Hungría *n* Hungary.

huracán *nm* hurricane.

huraño,-a *adj pey* unsociable.

hurgar [7] I *vi* (*fisgar*) to poke one's nose in. II *vtr* (*fuego etc*) to poke, rake. III **hurgarse** *vr* **h. las narices,** to pick one's nose.

hurón,-ona I *nm* Zool ferret. II *nm,f fam fig* (*fisgón*) busybody, nosey-parker.

hurraca *nf Orn* → **urraca.**

hurtadillas *adv* **a h.,** stealthily, on the sly.

hurtar *vtr* to steal, pilfer.

hurto *nm* petty theft, pilfering.

husmear I *vtr* (*olfatear*) to sniff out, scent. II *vi* (*curiosear*) to snoop, pry.

huyo *indic pres* → **huir.**

I

I, i [i] *nf* (*la letra*) I, i; **i griega,** Y, y.

ib. *abr de* **ibídem,** ibidem, ibid., ib.

IB *nm Educ abr de* **Instituto de Bachillerato,** ≈ state secondary school.

ibérico,-a *adj* Iberian.

Iberoamérica *n* Latin America.

iberoamericano,-a *adj* & *nm,f* Latin American.

iceberg *nm* (*pl* **icebergs**) iceberg.

ICONA *nm abr de* **Instituto para la Conservación de la Naturaleza.**

icono *nm* icon; *Inform* icon.

iconoclasta I *adj* iconoclastic. II *nmf* iconoclast.

iconografía *nf* iconography.

ictericia *nf Med* jaundice.

íd. *abr de* **ídem,** idem, id.

I+D *abr de* **Investigación más Desarrollo,** Research and Development, R&D.

ida *nf* **billete de i. y vuelta,** return ticket; **idas y venidas,** comings and goings.

idea *nf* **1** idea; **i. fija,** fixed idea. **2** (*noción*) idea; **hacerse a la i. de,** to get used to the idea of; *fam* **ni i.,** no idea, not a clue. **3** (*opinión*) opinion; **cambiar de i.,** to change one's mind. **4** (*intención*) intention; **a mala i.,** on purpose.

ideal *adj* & *nm* ideal.

idealismo *nm* idealism.

idealista I *adj* idealistic. II *nmf* idealist.

idealizar [4] *vtr* to idealize, glorify.

idear *vtr* **1** (*inventar*) to devise, invent. **2** (*concebir*) to think up, conceive.

ídem *adv* idem, ditto; *fam* **í. de í.,** exactly the same.

idéntico,-a *adj* identical.

identidad *nf* **1** identity; **carnet de i.,** identity card. **2** (*semejanza*) identity, sameness.

identificación *nf* identification.

identificar [1] I *vtr* to identify. II **identificarse** *vr* to identify oneself; *fig* **i. con,** to identify with.

ideología *nf* ideology.

ideológico,-a *adj* ideological.

idílico,-a *adj* idyllic.

idilio *nm* **1** *Lit* idyll. **2** *fig* (*romance*) romance, love affair.

idioma *nm* language.

idiomático,-a *adj* idiomatic.

idiosincrasia *nf* idiosyncrasy.

idiota I *adj* idiotic, stupid. II *nmf* idiot, fool.

idiotez *nf* idiocy, stupidity.

ido,-a *adj* **1** (*distraído*) absent-minded. **2** *fam* (*chiflado*) crazy, nuts.

idólatra I *adj* idolatrous. II *nmf* (*hombre*) idolater; (*mujer*) idolatress.

idolatrar *vtr* to worship; *fig* to idolize.

idolatría *nf* idolatry.

ídolo *nm* idol.

idóneo,-a *adj* suitable, fit.

iglesia *nf* **1** (*edificio*) church. **2 la I.,** (*institución*) the Church.

ignominia *nf* ignominy.

ignominioso,-a *adj* ignominious, shameful.

ignorancia *nf* ignorance.

ignorante I *adj* **1** (*sin instrucción*) ignorant. **2** (*no informado*) ignorant, unaware (**de,** of). II *nmf* ignoramus.

ignorar I *vtr* **1** (*algo*) not to know. **2** (*a algn*) to ignore. II **ignorarse** *vr* to be unknown.

ignoto,-a *adj* unknown.

igual I *adj* **1** (*idéntico*) the same, alike;

son todos iguales, they're all the same; **es i.,** it doesn't matter; **i. que,** the same as. 2 *(equivalente)* equal; **a partes iguales,** fifty-fifty. 3 *Dep (empatados)* even; **treinta iguales,** thirty all. 4 *Mat* equal; **tres más tres i. a seis,** three plus three equals six. 5 **al i. que,** just like. **6 por i.,** equally. II *nm* equal; **de i. a i.,** on an equal footing; **sin i.,** unique, unrivalled. III *adv* 1 **lo haces i. que yo,** you do it the same way I do. 2 *(probablemente)* probably; **i. vengo,** I'll probably come. ◆**igualmente** *adv* equally; *(también)* also, likewise; *fam* **¡gracias!** - **¡i.!,** thank you! - the same to you!

igualar I *vtr* 1 to make equal. 2 *(nivelar)* to level; 3 *Dep* **i. el partido,** to equalize, square the match. II **igualarse** *vr* 1 to be equal. 2 **i. con algn,** to place oneself on an equal footing with sb.

igualdad *nf* 1 equality; **i. ante la ley,** equality before the law. 2 *(identidad)* sameness; **en i. de condiciones,** on equal terms.

igualitario,-a *adj* egalitarian.

ijada *nf,* **ijar** *nm* *Anat* flank.

ikastola *nf* Basque language school.

ikurriña *nf* Basque flag.

ilegal *adj* illegal. ◆**ilegalmente** *adv* illegally.

ilegalidad *nf* illegality.

ilegible *adj* illegible, unreadable.

ilegítimo,-a *adj* illegitimate.

ileso,-a *adj* unhurt, unharmed.

ilícito,-a *adj* illicit, unlawful.

ilimitado,-a *adj* unlimited, limitless.

Ilmo. *abr de* **Ilustrísimo,** His Excellence *o* Excellency.

ilógico,-a *adj* illogical.

iluminación *nf* *(alumbrado)* illumination, lighting.

iluminar *vtr* 1 to illuminate, light (up). 2 *fig (a persona)* to enlighten; *(tema)* to throw light upon.

ilusión *nf* 1 *(esperanza)* hope; *(esperanza vana)* illusion, delusion; **hacerse ilusiones,** to build up one's hopes. 2 *(sueño)* dream. 3 *(emoción)* excitement, thrill; **me hace i. verla,** I'm looking forward to seeing her; **¡qué i.!,** how exciting!

ilusionar I *vtr* 1 *(esperanzar)* to build up sb's hopes. 2 *(entusiasmar)* to excite, thrill. II **ilusionarse** *vr* 1 *(esperanzarse)* to build up one's hopes. 2 *(entusiasmarse)* to be excited *o* thrilled *(con,* about).

iluso,-a *adj* easily deceived, gullible.

ilusorio,-a *adj* illusory, unreal.

ilustración *nf* 1 *(grabado)* illustration, picture; *(ejemplo)* illustration. 2 *(erudición)* learning, erudition; **la I.,** the Enlightenment.

ilustrado,-a *adj* 1 *(con dibujos, ejemplos)* illustrated. 2 *(erudito)* learned, erudite.

ilustrar I *vtr* 1 to illustrate. 2 *(aclarar)* to

explain, make clear. II **ilustrarse** *vr* to acquire knowledge *(sobre,* of), learn.

ilustrativo,-a *adj* illustrative.

ilustre *adj* illustrious, distinguished.

imagen *nf* 1 image; **ser la viva i. de algn,** to be the spitting image of sb; **tener buena i.,** to have a good image. 2 *Rel* image, statue. 3 *TV* picture.

imaginación *nf* imagination; **eso son imaginaciones tuyas,** you're imagining things.

imaginar I *vtr* to imagine. II **imaginarse** *vr* to imagine; **me imagino que sí,** I suppose so.

imaginario,-a *adj* imaginary.

imaginativo,-a *adj* imaginative.

imán *nm* magnet.

imbatible *adj* unbeatable.

imbatido,-a *adj* unbeaten, undefeated.

imbécil I *adj* stupid, silly. II *nmf* idiot, imbecile.

imbecilidad *nf* stupidity, imbecility.

imborrable *adj* indelible.

imbuir [37] *vtr fml* to imbue.

imitación *nf* imitation.

imitar *vtr* to imitate; *(gestos)* to mimic; **este collar imita al oro,** this necklace is of imitation gold.

impaciencia *nf* impatience.

impacientar I *vtr* **i. a algn,** to make sb lose patience, exasperate sb. II **impacientarse** *vr* to get *o* grow impatient *(por,* at).

impaciente *adj* *(deseoso)* impatient; *(intranquilo)* anxious.

impactar *vtr* to shock, stun.

impacto *nm* impact; *Mil* hit.

impactante *adj* **una noticia i.,** a sensational piece of news.

impar *adj* *Mat* odd; **número i.,** odd number.

imparable *adj* *Dep* unstoppable.

imparcial *adj* impartial, unbiased.

imparcialidad *nf* impartiality.

impartir *vtr* *(clases)* to give.

impasible *adj* impassive.

impávido,-a *adj* fearless.

impecable *adj* impeccable.

impedido,-a I *adj* disabled, handicapped. II *nm,f* disabled *o* handicapped person.

impedimento *nm* impediment; *(obstáculo)* hindrance, obstacle.

impedir [6] *vtr* *(obstaculizar)* to impede, hinder; *(imposibilitar)* to prevent, stop; **i. el paso,** to block the way.

impeler *vtr* *Téc* to drive, propel; *fig* to drive, impel.

impenetrable *adj* impenetrable.

impenitente *adj* *Rel* impenitent, unrepentant.

impensable *adj* unthinkable.

impepinable *adj* *fam* dead sure, certain.

imperante *adj* *(gobernante)* ruling; *(predominante)* prevailing.

imperar *vi* (*gobernar*) to rule; (*predominar*) to prevail.

imperativo,-a I *adj* imperative. **II** *nm* *Ling* imperative.

imperceptible *adj* imperceptible.

imperdible *nm* safety pin.

imperdonable *adj* unforgivable, inexcusable.

imperecedero,-a *adj* imperishable; *fig* enduring.

imperfección *nf* **1** imperfection. **2** (*defecto*) defect, fault.

imperfecto,-a *adj* **1** imperfect, fallible. **2** (*defectuoso*) defective, faulty. **3** *Ling* imperfect.

imperial *adj* imperial.

imperialismo *nm* imperialism.

impericia *nf* incompetence.

imperio *nm* impire; el i. de la ley, the rule of law.

imperioso,-a *adj* **1** (*autoritario*) imperious. **2** (*ineludible*) urgent, imperative; **una necesidad imperiosa**, a pressing need.

impermeable I *adj* impermeable, impervious; (*ropa*) waterproof. **II** *nm* raincoat, mac.

impersonal *adj* impersonal.

impertérrito,-a *adj* undaunted, fearless.

impertinencia *nf* impertinence.

impertinente I *adj* (*insolente*) impertinent; (*inoportuno*) irrelevant. **II** *nmpl* **impertinentes**, lorgnette *sing*.

imperturbable *adj* imperturbable, unruffled.

impetu *nm* **1** (*impulso*) impetus, momentum. **2** (*violencia*) violence. **3** (*energía*) energy.

impetuosidad *nf* **1** (*violencia*) violence. **2** (*fogosidad*) impetuosity, impulsiveness.

impetuoso,-a *adj* **1** (*violento*) violent. **2** (*fogoso*) impetuous, impulsive.

impío,-a *adj* ungodly, irreligious.

implacable *adj* relentless, implacable.

implantar *vtr* (*costumbres*) to implant, instil; (*reformas*) to introduce; *Med* to implant.

implicación *nf* (*participación*) involvement; (*significado*) implication.

implicar [1] *vtr* **1** (*involucrar*) to involve, implicate (**en**, in). **2** (*conllevar*) to imply.

implícito,-a *adj* implicit, implied.

implorar *vtr* to implore, beg.

impoluto,-a *adj* pure, spotless.

imponente *adj* **1** (*impresionante*) imposing, impressive. **2** (*sobrecogedor*) stunning. **2** *fam* (*atractivo*) terrific, tremendous, smashing.

imponer [19] (*pp* **impuesto**) **I** *vtr* **1** to impose. **2** (*impresionar*) to be impressive; (*respeto*) to inspire respect. **3** (*depósito*) to deposit. **II imponerse** *vr* **1** (*infundir respeto*) to command respect. **2** (*prevalecer*) to prevail. **3** (*ser necesario*) to be necessary.

imponible *adj* *Fin* taxable.

impopular *adj* unpopular, disliked.

importación *nf* (*mercancía*) import; (*acción*) importing; **artículos de i.**, imported goods.

importancia *nf* importance, significance; **dar i. a**, to attach importance to; **sin i.**, unimportant.

importante *adj* important, significant; **una suma i.**, a considerable sum.

importar¹ I *vi* **1** (*atañer*) **eso no te importa a tí**, that doesn't concern you, that's none of your business. **2** (*tener importancia*) to be important; **no importa**, it doesn't matter, *fam* **me importa un bledo** *o* **un pito**, I couldn't care less. **3** (*molestar*) **¿te importaría repetirlo?**, would you mind repeating it?; **¿te importa si fumo?**, do you mind if I smoke? **II** *vtr* (*valer*) to amount to; **los libros importan dos mil pesetas**, the books come to two thousand pesetas.

importar² *vtr* to import.

importe *nm* *Com Fin* amount, total.

importunar *vtr* to bother, pester.

imposibilidad *nf* impossibility.

imposibilitar *vtr* **1** (*impedir*) to make impossible, prevent. **2** (*incapacitar*) to disable, cripple.

imposible *adj* impossible; **me es i. hacerlo**, I can't (possibly) do it.

imposición *nf* **1** (*disciplina, condiciones*) imposing. **2** *Fin* deposit; (*impuesto*) taxation.

impostor,-a *nm,f* (*farsante*) impostor.

impotencia *nf* powerlessness, helplessness; *Med* impotence.

impotente *adj* powerless, helpless; *Med* impotent.

impracticable *adj* **1** (*inviable*) impracticable, unviable. **2** (*camino*) impassable.

imprecar [1] *vtr* to imprecate, curse.

imprecisión *nf* imprecision, vagueness.

impreciso,-a *adj* imprecise, vague.

impregnar I *vtr* to impregnate (**en**, **de**, with). **II impregnarse** *vr* to become impregnated.

imprenta *nf* (*taller*) printer's, (*tint* works. **2** (*aparato*) printing press. **3** **libertad de i.**, freedom of the press.

imprescindible *adj* essential, indispensable.

impresentable *adj* unpresentable.

impresión *nf* **1** *fig* (*efecto*) impression; **causar i.**, to make an impression. **2** *fig* (*opinión*) impression; **cambiar impresiones**, to exchange impressions. **3** *Impr* (*acto*) printing; (*edición*) edition. **4** (*huella*) impression, imprint.

impresionable *adj* impressionable.

impresionante *adj* impressive, striking; *fam* **un error i.**, (*tremendo*) a terrible mistake.

impresionar *vtr* **1** (*causar admiración*) to impress; (*sorprender*) to stun, shock. **2** *Fot* to expose.

impresionismo *nm Arte* impressionism.

impresionista *adj & nmf* impressionist.

impreso,-a I *adj* printed. **II** *nm* **1** *(papel, folleto)* printed matter. **2** *(formulario)* form; **i. de solicitud,** application form. **3** **impresos,** *(de correos)* printed matter *sing.*

impresora *nf Inform* printer; **i. láser,** laser printer.

imprevisible *adj* unforeseeable, unpredictable.

imprevisión *nf* lack of foresight.

imprevisto,-a I *adj* unforeseen, unexpected. **II** *nm (incidente)* unforeseen event.

imprimir *vtr (pp* **impreso) 1** *Impr Inform* to print. **2** *(marcar)* to stamp.

improbable *adj* improbable, unlikely.

ímprobo,-a *adj (inmoral)* dishonest, corrupt.

improcedente *adj* **1** inappropriate, unsuitable. **2** *Jur* inadmissible.

improductivo,-a *adj* unproductive.

improperio *nm* insult, offensive remark.

impropio,-a *adj (inadecuado)* inappropriate, unsuitable; **i. de,** uncharacteristic of.

improvisación *nf* improvisation; *Mús* extemporization.

improvisado,-a *adj (espontáneo)* improvised, impromptu, ad lib; *(provisional)* makeshift; **discurso i.,** impromptu speech.

improvisar *vtr* to improvise; *Mús* to extemporize.

improviso *adj* **de i.,** unexpectedly, suddenly; *fam* **coger** *o* **pillar a algn de i.,** to catch sb unawares.

imprudencia *nf* imprudence, rashness; *(indiscreción)* indiscretion.

imprudente *adj* imprudent, unwise; *(indiscreto)* indiscreet.

impudicia *nf (falta de pudor)* immodesty; *(desvergüenza)* shamelessness.

impudor *nm* immodesty; *(desvergüenza)* shamelessness.

impuesto,-a I *nm* **1** *Fin* tax; **i. sobre la renta,** income tax; **libre de impuestos,** tax-free; **i. sobre el valor añadido,** value added tax. **II** *adj* imposed.

impugnar *vtr (teoría)* to refute, disprove; *(decisión)* to challenge, contest.

impulsar *vtr* to impel, drive.

impulsivo,-a *adj* impulsive.

impulso *nm* impulse, thrust; *Dep* **tomar i.,** to take a run up.

impune *adj* unpunished.

♦**impunemente** *adv* with impunity.

impunidad *nf* impunity.

impureza *nf* impurity.

impuro,-a *adj* impure.

impuse *pt indef* → **imponer.**

imputar *vtr* to impute, attribute.

inabarcable *adj* unfathomable.

inabordable *adj* unapproachable, inaccessible.

inacabable *adj* interminable, endless.

inaccesible *adj* inaccessible.

inaceptable *adj* unacceptable.

inactividad *nf* inactivity; *Fin* lull, stagnation.

inactivo,-a *adj* inactive.

inadaptación *nf* maladjustment.

inadaptado,-a I *adj* maladjusted. **II** *nm,f* misfit.

inadecuado,-a *adj* unsuitable, inappropriate.

inadmisible *adj* inadmissible.

inadvertido,-a *adj (desapercibido)* unnoticed, unseen; **pasar i.,** to escape notice, pass unnoticed.

inagotable *adj* **1** *(recursos etc)* inexhaustible. **2** *(persona)* tireless, indefatigable.

inaguantable *adj* unbearable, intolerable.

inalámbrico,-a I *adj* cordless. **II** *nm* cordless telephone.

inalcanzable *adj* unattainable, unachievable.

inalterable *adj* **1** unalterable. **2** *(persona)* impassive, imperturbable.

inamovible *adj* immovable, fixed.

inanición *nf* starvation; *Med* inanition.

inanimado,-a *adj* inanimate.

inapreciable *adj* **1** *(valioso)* invaluable, inestimable. **2** *(insignificante)* insignificant, trivial.

inasequible *adj* **1** *(producto)* unaffordable. **2** *(meta)* unattainable, unachievable. **3** *(persona)* unapproachable, inaccessible. **4** *(cuestión)* incomprehensible.

inaudito,-a *adj* **1** *(sin precedente)* unprecedented. **2** *fig (escandaloso)* outrageous.

inauguración *nf* inauguration, opening.

inaugural *adj* inaugural, opening; **ceremonia i.,** inaugural ceremony.

inaugurar *vtr* to inaugurate, open.

inca *adj & nmf* Inca.

incalculable *adj* incalculable, indeterminate.

incandescente *adj* white hot, incandescent.

incansable *adj* tireless, indefatigable.

incapacidad *nf* **1** incapacity, inability; **i. física,** physical disability. **2** *(incompetencia)* incompetence, inefficiency.

incapacitado,-a *adj (imposibilitado)* incapacitated, disabled; *(desautorizado)* incapacitated.

incapacitar *vtr* **1** to incapacitate, disable. **2** *(inhabilitar)* to disqualify, make unfit **(para,** for).

incapaz *adj* **1** unable **(de,** to), incapable **(de,** of); **soy i. de continuar,** I can't go on. **2** *Jur* unfit.

incautación *nf Jur* seizure, confiscation.

incautarse *vr Jur* **i. de,** to seize, confiscate.

incauto,-a *adj* **1** *(imprudente)* incautious, unwary. **2** *(crédulo)* gullible.

incendiar [12] **I** *vtr* to set fire to, set alight. **II incendiarse** *vr* to catch fire.

incendiario,-a I *adj* incendiary; *fig (discurso etc)* inflammatory. **II** *nm,f (persona)* arsonist, fire-raiser.

incendio *nm* fire; **i. forestal**, forest fire.

incentivar *vtr* to give an incentive to.

incentivo *nm* incentive.

incertidumbre *nf* uncertainty, doubt.

incesante *adj* incessant, never-ending.

incesto *nm* incest.

incestuoso,-a *adj* incestuous.

incidencia *nf* 1 *(repercusión)* impact, effect; **la huelga tuvo escasa i.**, the strike had little effect. 2 *(hecho)* incident. 3 *Fís* incidence.

incidente *nm* incident.

incidir *vi* 1 *(incurrir)* to fall (**en**, into). 2 **i. en**, *(afectar)* to affect, influence.

incienso *nm* incense.

incierto,-a *adj (inseguro)* uncertain.

incineración *nf (de basuras)* incineration; *(de cadáveres)* cremation.

incinerar *vtr (basura)* to incinerate; *(cadáveres)* to cremate.

incipiente *adj* incipient, budding.

incisión *nf* incision, cut.

incisivo,-a I *adj (mordaz)* incisive, cutting; *(cortante)* sharp. **II** *nm Anat* incisor.

inciso *nm (paréntesis)* digression; **a modo de i.**, in passing, incidentally.

incitación *nf* incitement.

incitante *adj* 1 *(instigador)* inciting. 2 *(provocativo)* provocative.

incitar *vtr* to incite, urge.

incivil *adj* uncivil, rude.

inclemencia *nf* inclemency, harshness.

inclemente *adj* inclement, harsh.

inclinación *nf* 1 *(de terreno)* slope, incline; *(del cuerpo)* stoop. 2 *(reverencia)* bow. 3 *fig (tendencia)* tendency, inclination, penchant.

inclinado,-a *adj* inclined, slanting; *fig* **me siento i. a creerle**, I feel inclined to believe him.

inclinar I *vtr* 1 to incline, bend; *(cabeza)* to nod. 2 *fig (persuadir)* to persuade, induce. **II inclinarse** *vr* 1 to lean, slope, incline. 2 *(al saludar)* to bow; **i. ante**, to bow down to. 3 *fig (optar)* **i. a**, to feel inclined to; **me inclino por éste**, I'd rather have this one, I prefer this one.

incluido,-a *adj* 1 *(después del sustantivo)* included; *(antes del sustantivo)* including; **servicio no i.**, service not included; **i. I.V.A.**, including VAT; **todos pagan, incluidos los niños**, everyone has to pay, including children. 2 *(adjunto)* enclosed.

incluir [37] *vtr* 1 to include. 2 *(contener)* to contain, comprise. 3 *(adjuntar)* to enclose.

inclusión *nf* inclusion.

inclusive *adv* 1 *(incluido)* inclusive; de

martes a viernes i., from Tuesday to Friday inclusive; **hasta la lección ocho i.**, up to and including lesson eight. 2 *(incluso)* even.

incluso *adv & prep* even; **i. mi madre**, even my mother.

incoar *vtr defect Jur* to initiate.

incógnita *nf* 1 *Mat* unknown quantity, unknown. 2 *(misterio)* mystery.

incógnito *nm* **de i.**, incognito.

incoherencia *nf* incoherence.

incoherente *adj* incoherent.

incoloro,-a *adj* colourless.

incólume *adj fml* unharmed; **salir i.**, to escape unharmed.

incombustible *adj* incombustible, fireproof.

incomodar I *vtr* 1 *(causar molestia)* to inconvenience, put out. 2 *(fastidiar)* to bother, annoy. **II incomodarse** *vr* 1 *(tomarse molestias)* to put oneself out, go out of one's way. 2 *(disgustarse)* to get annoyed o angry.

incomodidad *nf (falta de comodidad)* discomfort; *(molestia)* inconvenience.

incómodo,-a *adj* uncomfortable; **sentirse i.**, to feel uncomfortable o awkward.

incompatibilidad *nf* incompatibility; *Jur* **i. de caracteres**, mutual incompatibility.

incompatible *adj* incompatible.

incompetencia *nf* incompetence.

incompetente *adj & nmf* incompetent.

incompleto,-a *adj* incomplete; *(inacabado)* unfinished.

incomprensible *adj* incomprehensible.

incomprensión *nf* lack of understanding, failure to understand; *(indiferencia)* lack of sympathy.

incomunicado,-a *adj* 1 *(aislado)* isolated; **el pueblo se quedó i.**, the town was cut off. 2 *(en la cárcel)* in solitary confinement.

incomunicar [1] *vtr* 1 *(ciudad)* to isolate, cut off. 2 *(recluso)* to place in solitary confinement.

inconcebible *adj* inconceivable, unthinkable.

inconcluso,-a *adj* unfinished.

incondicional I *adj* unconditional; *(apoyo)* wholehearted; *(amigo)* faithful; *(partidario)* staunch. **II** *nmf* diehard.

inconexo,-a *adj (incoherente)* incoherent, confused.

inconformismo *nm* nonconformity.

inconformista *adj & nmf* nonconformist.

inconfundible *adj* unmistakable, obvious.

incongruencia *nf* incongruity.

incongruente *adj* incongruous.

inconmensurable *adj* immeasurable, vast.

inconsciencia *nf Med* unconsciousness; *fig (irreflexión)* thoughtlessness; *(irresponsabilidad)* irresponsibility.

inconsciente I *adj* 1 *(con estar)* *(desmaya-*

do) unconscious. 2 *(con ser) (despreocupa-do)* unaware **(de,** of); *fig (irreflexivo)* thoughtless, irresponsible.

inconsecuente *adj* inconsistent.

inconsistente *adj* flimsy; *(argumento)* weak.

inconstancia *nf* inconstancy, fickleness.

inconstante *adj* inconstant, fickle.

incontable *adj* countless, innumerable.

incontenible *adj* uncontrollable, irrepressible.

incontestable *adj* indisputable, unquestionable.

incontinencia *nf* incontinence.

incontrolable *adj* uncontrollable.

incontrolado,-a I *adj* uncontrolled. **II** *nmf* troublemaker.

inconveniencia *nf* 1 inconvenience. 2 *(impropiedad)* unsuitability.

inconveniente I *adj* 1 inconvenient. 2 *(inapropiado)* unsuitable. **II** *nm* 1 *(objeción)* objection; **poner inconvenientes,** to raise objections. 2 *(desventaja)* disadvantage, drawback; *(problema)* difficulty; **¿tienes i. en acompañarme?,** would you mind coming with me?

incordiar [12] *vtr fam* to bother, pester.

incordio *nm fam* nuisance, pain.

incorporación *nf* incorporation.

incorporar I *vtr* 1 to incorporate **(en,** into). 2 *(levantar)* to help to sit up. **II incorporarse** *vr* 1 **i. a,** *(sociedad)* to join; *(trabajo)* to start; **Mil i. a filas,** to join up. 2 *(en la cama)* to sit up.

incorrección *nf* 1 *(falta)* incorrectness, inaccuracy; *(gramatical)* mistake. 2 *(descortesía)* discourtesy, impropriety.

incorrecto,-a *adj* 1 *(equivocado)* incorrect, inaccurate. 2 *(grosero)* impolite, discourteous.

incorregible *adj* incorrigible.

incrédulo,-a I *adj* 1 incredulous, disbelieving. 2 *Rel* unbelieving. **II** *nm,f* 1 disbeliever. 2 *Rel* unbeliever.

increíble *adj* incredible, unbelievable.

incrementar I *vtr* to increase. **II incrementarse** *vr* to increase.

incremento *nm* *(aumento)* increase; *(crecimiento)* growth; **i. de la temperatura,** rise in temperature.

increpar *vtr fml* to rebuke, reprimand.

incruento,-a *adj* bloodless.

incrustar *vtr* 1 *(insertar)* to encrust o incrust. 2 *(embutir)* to inlay; **incrustado con perlas,** inlaid with pearls.

incubadora *nf* incubator.

incubar *vtr* to incubate.

incuestionable *adj* unquestionable, indisputable.

inculcar [1] *vtr (principios, ideas)* to instil **(en,** into).

inculpado,-a *nm,f* the accused.

inculpar *vtr* to accuse **(de,** of), blame **(de,** for); *Jur* to charge **(de,** with).

inculto,-a I *adj (ignorante)* uneducated, uncouth. **II** *nm,f* ignoramus.

incultura *nf (ignorancia)* ignorance, lack of culture.

incumbencia *nf* **no es de mi i.,** it doesn't come within my province, it isn't my concern.

incumbir *vi* be incumbent **(a,** upon); **esto no te incumbe,** this is none of your business.

incumplimiento *nm (de un deber)* nonfulfilment; *(de una orden)* failure to execute; **i. de contrato,** breach of contract.

incumplir *vtr* not to fulfil; *(deber)* fail to fulfil; *(promesa, contrato)* to break; *(orden)* to fail to carry out.

incurrir *vi (cometer)* to fall **(en, into);** **i. en delito,** to commit a crime; **i. en (un) error,** to fall into error.

incursión *nf* raid, incursion.

indagar [7] *vtr* to investigate, inquire into.

indebido,-a *adj* 1 *(desconsiderado)* improper, undue. 2 *(ilegal)* unlawful, illegal.

indecencia *nf* indecency, obscenity.

indecente *adj* 1 *(impúdico)* indecent. 2 *(impresentable)* dreadful.

indecible *adj* unspeakable; *(inefable)* indescribable; **sufrir lo i.,** to suffer agonies.

indecisión *nf* indecision, hesitation.

indeciso,-a *adj* 1 *(vacilante)* hesitant, irresolute. 2 *(resultados etc)* inconclusive.

indefenso,-a *adj* defenceless, helpless.

indefinido,-a *adj* 1 *(indeterminado)* indefinite; *(impreciso)* undefined, vague. 2 *Ling* indefinite. ◆**indefinidamente** *adv* indefinitely.

indeleble *adj* indelible.

indemne *adj (persona)* unharmed, unhurt; *(cosa)* undamaged.

indemnización *nf* 1 *(acto)* indemnification. 2 *Fin (compensación)* indemnity, compensation; **i. por despido,** redundancy payment.

indemnizar [4] *vtr* to indemnify, compensate **(de, por,** for).

independencia *nf* independence.

independiente *adj (libre)* independent; *(individualista)* self-reliant. ◆**independientemente** *adv* 1 independently **(de,** of). 2 *(aparte de)* regardless, irrespective **(de,** of).

independizar [4] **I** *vtr* to make independent, grant independence to. **II independizarse** *vr* to become independent.

indescifrable *adj* indecipherable.

indescriptible *adj* indescribable.

indeseable *adj & nmf* undesirable.

indeterminación *nf* indecision, irresolution.

indeterminado,-a *adj* 1 indefinite; *(impreciso)* vague. 2 *(persona)* irresolute. 3 *Ling* indefinite.

India *nf* **(la)** I., India.

Indias *nfpl* (**las**) I., the Indies; **las I. Orientales/Occidentales**, the East/West Indies.

indicación *nf* 1 (*señal*) indication, sign. 2 (*instrucción*) instruction, direction; **por i. de algn**, at sb's suggestion.

indicado,-a *adj* right, suitable; **a la hora indicada**, at the specified time; **en el momento menos i.**, at the worst possible moment.

indicador,-a *nm* 1 *Téc* gauge, dial, meter; *Aut* i. **del nivel de aceite**, (oil) dipstick; *Aut* i. **de velocidad**, speedometer.

indicar [1] *vtr* (*señalar*) to indicate, show, point out; **¿me podría i. el camino?**, could you show me the way?

indicativo,-a *adj* 1 indicative (**de**, of). 2 *Ling* (*modo*) i., indicative (mode).

índice *nm* 1 (*de libro*) index, table of contents. 2 (*relación*) rate. **í. de natalidad/mortalidad**, birth/death rate; *Fin* **í. de precios**, price index. 3 *Anat* (*dedo*) í., index finger, forefinger.

indicio *nm* 1 (*señal*) indication, sign, token (**de**, of). 2 *Jur* **indicios**, (*prueba*) evidence *sing*.

índico,-a *adj* Indian; **Océano I.**, Indian Ocean.

indiferencia *nf* indifference, apathy.

indiferente *adj* 1 (*no importante*) unimportant; **me es i.**, it makes no difference to me. 2 (*apático*) indifferent.

indígena I *adj* indigenous, native (**de**, to). II *nmf* native (**de**, of).

indigencia *nf fml* poverty, indigence.

indigente *fml adj* needy, poverty-stricken.

indigestarse *vr* 1 **se le indigestó la comida**, the meal gave her indigestion. 2 (*sufrir indigestión*) to get indigestion.

indigestión *nf* indigestion.

indigesto,-a *adj* (*comida*) indigestible, difficult to digest; **me siento i.**, I've got indigestion.

indignación *nf* indignation.

indignado,-a *adj* indignant (**por**, at, about).

indignante *adj* outrageous, infuriating.

indignar I *vtr* to infuriate, make angry. II **indignarse** *vr* to be o feel indignant (**por**, at, about).

indigno,-a *adj* 1 unworthy (**de**, of). 2 (*despreciable*) wretched, dreadful.

indio,-a *adj & nm,f* Indian; **en fila india**, in single file; *fam* **hacer el i.**, to act the fool.

indirecta *nf fam* (*insinuación*) hint, insinuation; **tirar** o **lanzar una i.**, to drop a hint; **coger la i.**, to get the message.

indirecto,-a *adj* indirect; *Ling* **estilo i.**, indirect o reported speech.

indisciplinado,-a *adj* undisciplined, unruly.

indiscreción *nf* indiscretion; (*comentario*) tactless remark.

indiscreto,-a *adj* indiscreet, tactless.

indiscutible *adj* indisputable, unquestionable.

indispensable *adj* indispensable, essential.

indisponer [19] (*pp* **indispuesto**) I *vtr* to upset, make unwell. II **indisponerse** *vr* 1 to fall ill, become unwell. 2 *fig* i. **con algn**, to fall out with sb.

indispuesto,-a *adj* indisposed, unwell.

indispuse *pt indef* → **indisponer**.

indistinto,-a *adj* (*indiferente*) immaterial, inconsequential; ◆**indistintamente** *adv* **pueden escribir en inglés o en español i.**, you can write in English or Spanish, it doesn't matter which.

individual I *adj* individual; **habitación i.**, single room. II *nmpl Dep* **individuales**, singles.

individualismo *nm* individualism.

individualista I *adj* individualistic. II *nmf* individualist.

individuo *nm* 1 individual. 2 (*tío*) bloke, guy.

índole *nf* 1 (*carácter*) character, nature. 2 (*clase, tipo*) kind, sort.

indolencia *nf* indolence, laziness.

indolente I *adj* indolent, lazy. II *nmf* idler.

indomable *adj* 1 (*animal*) untameable. 2 (*pueblo*) ungovernable, unruly; (*niño*) uncontrollable; (*pasión*) indomitable.

indómito,-a *adj* 1 (*no domado*) untamed; (*indomable*) untameable. 2 (*pueblo*) unruly; (*persona*) uncontrollable.

inducir [10] *vtr* 1 (*incitar, mover*) to lead, induce; **i. a error**, to lead into error, mislead. 2 *Elec* (*corriente*) to induce.

inductivo,-a *adj* inductive.

indudable *adj* indubitable, unquestionable; **es i. que**, there is no doubt that.

induje *pt indef* → **inducir**.

indulgencia *nf* indulgence, leniency.

indulgente *adj* indulgent (**con**, towards), lenient (**con**, with).

indultar *vtr Jur* to pardon.

indulto *nm Jur* pardon, amnesty.

indumentaria *nf* clothing, clothes *pl*.

industria *nf* industry.

industrial I *adj* industrial. II *nmf* industrialist.

industrialización *nf* industrialization.

industrializar [4] *vtr* to industrialize.

induzco *indic pres* → **inducir**.

INE *nm abr de* **Instituto Nacional de Estadística**.

inédito,-a *adj* 1 (*libro, texto*) unpublished. 2 (*nuevo*) completely new; (*desconocido*) unknown.

inefable *adj* ineffable, indescribable.

ineficacia *nf* (*ineptitud*) inefficiency; (*inutilidad*) ineffectiveness.

ineficaz adj (inepto) inefficient; (inefectivo) ineffective.

ineludible adj inescapable, unavoidable.

INEM nm abr de **Instituto Nacional de Empleo**.

ineptitud nf ineptitude, incompetence.

inepto,-a I adj inept, incompetent. II nm,f incompetent person.

inequívoco,-a adj unmistakable, unequivocal.

inercia nf 1 Fís inertia. 2 fig (pasividad) inertia, passivity; **hacer algo por i.**, to do sth out of habit.

inerte adj (inanimado) inert; (inmóvil) motionless.

inesperado,-a adj (fortuito) unexpected, unforeseen; (imprevisto) sudden.

inestabilidad nf instability.

inestable adj unstable, unsteady.

inestimable adj inestimable, invaluable.

inevitable adj inevitable, unavoidable.

inexistente adj non-existent.

inexorable adj inexorable.

inexperiencia nf lack of experience.

inexperto,-a adj (inexperto) inexpert; (sin experiencia) inexperienced.

inexplicable adj inexplicable.

inexpugnable adj Mil impregnable.

infalible adj infallible.

infamar vtr to defame, slander.

infame adj (vil) infamous, vile; (despreciable) dreadful, awful.

infamia nf disgrace, infamy.

infancia nf childhood, infancy.

infanta nf infanta, princess.

infante nm 1 infante, prince. 2 Mil infantryman.

infantería nf Mil infantry; **la i. de marina**, the marines.

infantil adj 1 literatura i., (para niños) children's literature. 2 (aniñado) childlike; pey childish, infantile.

infarto nm Med infarction, infarct; **i. (de miocardio)**, heart attack, coronary thrombosis; fam de i., thrilling, stunning.

infatigable adj indefatigable, tireless.

infección nf infection.

infeccioso,-a adj infectious.

infectar I vtr to infect. II infectarse vr to become infected (de, with).

infeliz I adj unhappy; (desdichado) unfortunate. II nmf fam simpleton; **es un pobre i.**, he is a poor devil.

inferior I adj 1 (más bajo) lower. 2 (calidad) inferior; **de calidad i.**, of inferior quality. 3 (cantidad) lower, less; **i. a la media**, below average. II nmf (persona) subordinate, inferior.

inferioridad nf inferiority; **estar en i. de condiciones**, to be at a disadvantage; **complejo de i.**, inferiority complex.

inferir [5] vtr lit (deducir) to infer, deduce (de, from).

infernal adj infernal, hellish; fig **había un ruido i.**, there was a hell of a noise.

infestar vtr 1 **infestado de**, (parásitos) infested with; (plantas) overgrown with. 2 fig (llenar) to overrun, invade; **infestado de turistas**, swarming with tourists. 3 (infectar) to infect.

infidelidad nf infidelity, unfaithfulness.

infiel I adj (desleal) unfaithful. II nmf Rel infidel.

infierno nm 1 Rel hell. 2 fig (tormento) hell; **su vida es un i.**, his life is sheer hell. 3 (horno) inferno; **en verano esto es un i.**, in summer it's like an inferno here; fam **¡vete al i.!**, go to hell!, get lost!

infiltración nf (de agua) infiltration; (de noticia) leak.

infiltrado,-a nm,f infiltrator.

infiltrar I vtr to infiltrate; (noticia) to leak. II infiltrarse vr to infiltrate (en, into).

ínfimo,-a adj fml (mínimo) extremely low; **detalle i.**, smallest detail; **ínfima calidad**, very poor quality.

infinidad nf 1 infinity; 2 (sinfín) great number; **en i. de ocasiones**, on countless occasions.

infinitivo,-a adj & nm Ling infinitive.

infinito,-a I adj infinite, endless. II nm infinity. ◆**infinito** adv fam (muchísimo) infinitely, immensely.

inflación nf Econ inflation.

inflacionario,-a, inflacionista adj Econ inflationary.

inflamable adj flammable.

inflamación nf Med inflammation.

inflamar I vtr 1 Med to inflame. 2 (encender) to set on fire, ignite. II inflamarse vr 1 Med to become inflamed. 2 (incendiarse) to catch fire.

inflar I vtr 1 (hinchar) to inflate, blow up; Náut (vela) to swell. 2 fig (exagerar) to exaggerate. II inflarse vr 1 to inflate; Náut (vela) to swell. 2 fam i. de, to overdo; **se inflaron de macarrones**, they stuffed themselves with macaroni.

inflexible adj inflexible.

infligir [6] vtr to inflict.

influencia nf influence; **ejercer o tener i. sobre algn**, to have an influence on o upon sb; **tener influencias**, to be influential; **tráfico de influencias**, old boy network.

influenciar [12] vtr to influence.

influir [37] I vtr to influence. II vi 1 to have influence. 2 **i. en o sobre**, to influence, have an influence on.

influjo nm influence.

influyente adj influential.

información nf 1 information; **oficina de i.**, information bureau. 2 **una i.**, (noticia) a piece of news, news sing. 3 Tel directory enquiries pl. 4 (referencias) references pl.

informado,-a adj informed; **de fuentes bien informadas,** from well-informed sources.

informal adj 1 (reunión, cena) informal. 2 (comportamiento) casual. 3 (persona) unreliable, untrustworthy.

informalidad nf (incumplimiento) unreliability; (desenfado) informality.

informar I vtr to inform (de, of); (dar informes) to report. II **informarse** vr (procurarse noticias) to find out (de, about); (enterarse) to enquire (de, about).

informática nf information technology, IT; **ley de i.,** data protection act.

informático,-a I adj computer, computing. II nm,f (computer) technician.

informativo,-a I adj 1 Rad TV news; **boletín i.,** news (broadcast). 2 (explicativo) informative, explanatory. II nm Rad TV news bulletin.

informe nm 1 report. 2 **informes,** references; **pedir i. sobre algn,** to make enquiries about sb.

infracción nf (de ley) infringement, breach (de, of).

infractor,-a nm,f offender.

infraestructura nf infrastructure.

in fraganti loc adv in the act; **coger** o **pillar a algn in f.,** to catch sb red-handed.

infrahumano-o adj subhuman.

infranqueable adj impassable; fig insurmountable.

infrarrojo-a adj infra-red.

infrautilizar vtr to under-utilise.

infringir [6] vtr to infringe, contravene; **i. una ley,** to break a law.

infructuoso,-a adj fruitless, unsuccessful.

infundado,-a adj unfounded, groundless.

infundir vtr to infuse; fig to instil; **i. dudas,** to give rise to doubt; **i. respeto,** to command respect.

infusión nf infusion.

infuso,-a adj fam irón **ciencia infusa,** sheer genius.

ingeniar [12] I vtr to invent, devise. II **ingeniarse** vr **ingeniárselas para hacer algo,** to manage to do sth.

ingeniería nf engineering.

ingeniero,-a nm,f engineer; **i. agrónomo,** agricultural engineer; **i. de caminos,** civil engineer; **i. de minas/montes,** mining/forestry engineer; **i. de telecomunicaciones,** telecommunications engineer; **i. técnico,** technician.

ingenio nm 1 (talento) talent; (inventiva) inventiveness, creativeness; (agudeza) wit. 2 (aparato) device.

ingenioso,-a adj ingenious, clever; (vivaz) witty.

ingente adj huge, enormous.

ingenuidad nf ingenuousness, naiveté.

ingenuo,-a I adj ingenuous, naive. II nm,f naïve person.

ingerir [5] vtr (comida) to ingest, consume; (líquidos, alcohol) to drink, consume.

Inglaterra n England.

ingle nf Anat groin.

inglés,-esa I adj English. II nm,f (hombre) Englishman; (mujer) Englishwoman; **los ingleses,** the English. III nm (idioma) English.

ingratitud nf ingratitude, ungratefulness.

ingrato,-a I adj 1 (persona) ungrateful. 2 (noticia) unpleasant. 3 (trabajo) thankless, unrewarding. 4 (tierra) unproductive. II nm,f ungrateful person.

ingrediente nm ingredient.

ingresar I vtr 1 Fin to deposit, pay in. 2 Med to admit; **la ingresaron en el hospital,** she was admitted to hospital. II vi 1 to enter; **i. en el ejército,** to enlist in the army, join the army; **i. en un club,** to join a club. 2 **i. cadáver,** to be dead on arrival.

ingreso nm 1 Fin deposit; **hacer un i. en una cuenta,** to pay money into an account. 2 (entrada) entry (en, into); (admisión) admission (en, to). 3 **ingresos,** (sueldo, renta) income sing; (beneficios) revenue sing.

inhábil adj 1 (incapaz) unfit; **i. para el trabajo,** unfit for work. 2 **día i.,** nonworking day.

inhabilitación nf 1 fml (incapacidad) disablement. 2 Jur disqualification.

inhabilitar vtr 1 fml (incapacitar) to disable; **inhabilitado para el trabajo,** unfit for work. 2 Jur to disqualify.

inhabitable adj uninhabitable.

inhalación nf inhalation.

inhalador nm Med inhaler.

inhalar vtr to inhale.

inherente adj inherent (a, in).

inhibición nf inhibition.

inhibir I vtr to inhibit. II **inhibirse** vr 1 (cohibirse) to be o feel inhibited. 2 (abstenerse) to refrain (de, from).

inhóspito,-a adj inhospitable.

inhumación nf burial.

inhumano,-a adj inhumane; (cruel) inhuman.

inhumar vtr to bury.

INI nm abr de **Instituto Nacional de Industria.**

inicial adj & nf initial; **punto i.,** starting point.

iniciar [12] I vtr 1 (empezar) to begin, start; (discusión) to initiate; (una cosa nueva) to pioneer. 2 (introducir) to initiate. II **iniciarse** vr 1 **i. en algo,** (aprender) to start to study sth. 2 (empezar) to begin, start.

iniciativa nf initiative; **i. privada,** private enterprise; **por i. propia,** on one's own initiative.

inicio nm beginning, start; **a inicios de,** at the beginning of.

inimitable adj inimitable.
ininterrumpido,-a adj uninterrupted, continuous.
iniquidad nf iniquity.
injerencia nf interference, meddling (**en**, in).
injerirse vr to interfere, meddle (**en**, in).
injertar vtr Agr Med to graft.
injerto nm graft.
injuria nf (insulto) insult, affront; (agravio) outrage.
injuriar [12] vtr (insultar) to insult; (ultrajar) to outrage.
injusticia nf injustice, unfairness.
injustificado,-a adj unjustified.
injusto,-a adj unjust, unfair.
inmaculado,-a adj immaculate.
inmadurez nf immaturity.
inmaduro,-a adj immature.
inmediaciones nfpl neighbourhood sing.
inmediato,-a adj 1 (en el tiempo) immediate; **de i.**, at once. 2 (en el espacio) next (**a**, to), adjoining. ◆**inmediatamente** adv immediately, at once.
inmejorable adj (trabajo) excellent; (precio) unbeatable.
inmemorial adj immemorial; **desde tiempos inmemoriales**, since time immemorial.
inmensidad nf immensity, enormity.
inmenso,-a adj immense, vast.
inmerecido,-a adj undeserved, unmerited.
inmersión nf immersion; (de submarino) dive.
inmerso,-a adj immersed (**en**, in).
inmigración nf immigration.
inmigrante adj & nm,f immigrant.
inmigrar vi to immigrate.
inminente adj imminent, impending.
inmiscuirse [37] vr to interfere, meddle (**en**, in).
inmobiliaria nf estate agency, US real estate company.
inmobiliario,-a adj property, real-estate; **agente i.**, estate agent, US realtor.
inmolar vtr fml to immolate, sacrifice.
inmoral adj immoral.
inmoralidad nf immorality.
inmortal adj & nmf immortal.
inmortalidad nf immortality.
inmortalizar [4] vtr to immortalize.
inmóvil adj motionless, immobile.
inmovilista adj ultra-conservative.
inmovilizar [4] vtr 1 (persona, cosa) to immobilize. 2 Fin (capital) to immobilize, tie up.
inmueble I adj **bienes inmuebles**, real estate. II nm building.
inmundicia nf 1 (suciedad) dirt, filth; fig dirtiness. 2 (basura) rubbish, refuse.
inmundo,-a adj dirty, filthy; fig nasty.
inmune adj immune (**a**, to), exempt (**de**, from).

inmunidad nf immunity (**contra**, against); **i. diplomática/parlamentaria**, diplomatic/parliamentary immunity.
inmunizar [4] vtr to immunize (**contra**, against).
inmutarse vr to change countenance; **ni se inmutó**, he didn't turn a hair.
innato,-a adj innate, inborn.
innecesario,-a adj unnecessary.
innegable adj undeniable.
innovación nf innovation.
innovar vtr & vi to innovate.
innumerable adj innumerable, countless.
inocencia nf 1 innocence. 2 (ingenuidad) naïveté.
inocentada nf fam ≈ April Fool's joke; **hacer una i. a algn**, to play an April Fool's joke on sb.
inocente I adj innocent. II nmf innocent; **día de los Inocentes**, Holy Innocents' Day, 28th December, ≈ April Fools' Day.
inocuo,-a adj innocuous.
inodoro,-a I adj odourless. II nm toilet, lavatory.
inofensivo,-a adj harmless.
inolvidable adj unforgettable.
inoperante adj ineffective.
inopia nf fig **estar en la i.**, to be in the clouds, be miles away.
inopinado,-a adj unexpected.
inoportuno,-a adj inappropriate; **llegó en un momento muy i.**, he turned up at a very awkward moment.
inorgánico,-a adj inorganic.
inoxidable adj **acero i.**, stainless steel.
INP nm abr de **Instituto Nacional de Previsión**.
inquebrantable adj fig unshakeable; (persona) unyielding.
inquietante adj worrying.
inquietar I vtr to worry. II **inquietarse** vr to worry (**por**, about).
inquieto,-a adj 1 (preocupado) worried, (**por**, about). 2 (intranquilo) restless. 3 (emprendedor) eager.
inquietud nf 1 (preocupación) worry. 2 (agitación) restlessness. 3 (anhelo) eagerness.
inquilino,-a nm,f tenant.
inquirir [31] vtr to investigate.
inquisitivo,-a adj inquisitive.
inri nm fam insult; **para más o mayor i.**, to make matters worse.
insaciable adj insatiable.
insalubre adj unhealthy.
insano,-a adj 1 (loco) insane, mad. 2 (insalubre) unhealthy.
insatisfecho,-a adj dissatisfied.
inscribir (pp **inscrito**) I vtr 1 (registrar) to register; **i. a un niño en el registro civil**, to register a child's birth. 2 (matricular) to enrol, US enroll. 3 (grabar) to inscribe. II **inscribirse** vr 1 (registrarse) to

register; (*hacerse miembro*) to join. 2 (*matricularse*) to enrol, US enroll.

inscripción nf 1 (*matriculación*) enrolment, US enrollment, registration. 2 (*escrito etc*) inscription.

insecticida nm insecticide.

insecto nm insect.

inseguridad nf 1 (*falta de confianza*) insecurity. 2 (*duda*) uncertainty. 3 (*peligro*) lack of safety; **la i. ciudadana**, the breakdown of law and order.

inseguro,-a adj 1 (*poco confiado*) insecure. 2 (*dubitativo*) uncertain. 3 (*peligroso*) unsafe.

inseminar vtr to inseminate.

insensatez nf foolishness.

insensato,-a I adj foolish. **II** nm,f fool.

insensibilidad nf insensitivity.

insensible adj 1 (*indiferente*) insensitive (**a**, to), unfeeling. 2 (*imperceptible*) imperceptible. 3 Med numb.

inseparable adj inseparable.

insertar vtr to insert.

inservible adj useless.

insidia nf 1 (*trampa*) malicious ploy. 2 (*malicia*) maliciousness.

insidioso,-a adj insidious.

insigne adj distinguished.

insignia nf 1 (*emblema*) badge. 2 (*bandera*) flag.

insignificancia nf 1 (*intrascendencia*) insignificance. 2 (*nadería*) trifle.

insignificante adj insignificant.

insinuación nf insinuation.

insinuante adj insinuating; (*atrevido*) forward.

insinuar [30] **I** vtr to insinuate. **II insinuarse** vr **i. a algn**, to make advances to sb.

insípido,-a adj insipid; fig dull, flat.

insistencia nf insistence; **con i.**, insistently.

insistente adj insistent.

insistir vi to insist (**en**, on); **insistió en ese punto**, he stressed that point.

insociable adj unsociable.

insolación nf Med sunstroke; **coger una i.**, to get sunstroke.

insolencia nf insolence.

insolente adj insolent.

insolidaridad nf unsupportive stance.

insólito,-a adj (*poco usual*) unusual; (*extraño*) strange, odd.

insoluble adj insoluble.

insolvencia nf Fin insolvency.

insolvente adj Fin insolvent.

insomnio nm insomnia; **noche de i.**, sleepless night.

insondable adj unfathomable.

insonorizado,-a adj soundproof.

insonorizar [4] vtr to soundproof.

insoportable adj unbearable.

insospechado,-a adj unsuspected.

insostenible adj untenable.

inspección nf inspection.

inspeccionar vtr to inspect.

inspector,-a nm,f inspector; **i. de Hacienda**, tax inspector.

inspiración nf 1 inspiration. 2 (*inhalación*) inhalation.

inspirado,-a adj inspired.

inspirar I vtr 1 to inspire. 2 (*inhalar*) to inhale, breathe in. **II inspirarse** vr **i. en**, to be inspired by.

instalación nf installation; **instalaciones deportivas**, sports facilities.

instalar I vtr 1 to instal, US install. 2 (*puesto, tienda*) to set up. **II instalarse** vr (*persona*) to settle (down).

instancia nf 1 (*solicitud*) request; **a instancia(s) de**, at the request of. 2 (*escrito*) application form. 3 Jur **tribunal de primera i.**, court of first instance. 4 **en primera i.**, first of all; **en última i.**, as a last resort.

instantánea nf snapshot.

instantáneo,-a adj instantaneous; **café i.**, instant coffee. ◆**instantáneamente** adv instantly.

instante nm instant, moment; **a cada i.**, constantly; **al i.**, immediately; right away; **por instantes**, with every second; **¡un i.!**, just a moment!

instar vtr to urge.

instauración nf founding.

instaurar vtr to found.

instigador,-a nm,f instigator.

instigar [7] vtr to instigate; **i. a la rebelión**, to incite a rebellion.

instintivo,-a adj instinctive.

instinto nm instinct; **por i.**, instinctively; **i. de conservación**, instinct of self-preservation.

institución nf institution.

instituir [37] vtr to institute.

instituto nm 1 institute. 2 Educ state secondary school, US high school.

institutriz nf governess.

instruyo indic pres → **instruir**.

instrucción nf 1 (*educación*) education. 2 (*usu pl*) (*indicación*) instruction; **instrucciones para el o de uso**, directions for use. 3 Jur preliminary investigation; **la i. del sumario**, proceedings pl; **juez de i.**, examining magistrate. 4 Mil drill.

instructivo,-a adj instructive.

instruido,-a adj educated, well-educated.

instruir [37] vtr 1 to instruct. 2 (*enseñar*) to educate. 3 Mil to drill. 4 Jur to investigate.

instrumental adj instrumental.

instrumento nm instrument.

insubordinación nf insubordination.

insubordinado,-a adj insubordinate.

insubordinarse vr (*sublevarse*) to rebel (**contra**, against).

insuficiencia nf insufficiency.

insuficiente I adj insufficient. **II** nm Educ

(nota) fail.

insufrible *adj* insufferable.

insular I *adj* insular, island. II *nmf* islander.

insulso,-a *adj* insipid.

insultante *adj* insulting.

insultar *vtr* to insult.

insulto *nm* insult.

insumisión *nf* refusal to do military service.

insumiso,-a I *adj* unsubmissive. II *nm* person who refuses to do military service.

insuperable *adj* 1 *(inmejorable)* unsurpassable. 2 *(problema)* insurmountable.

insurgente *adj & nmf* insurgent.

insurrección *nf* insurrection.

intacto,-a *adj* intact.

intachable *adj* irreproachable; **conducta i.**, impeccable behaviour.

integral I *adj* integral; *Culin* **pan i.**, wholemeal bread; **arroz i.**, brown rice. II *nf Mat* integral.

integrante I *adj* integral; **ser parte i. de**, to be an integral part of. II *nmf* member.

integrar I *vtr (formar)* to compose, make up; **el equipo lo integran once jugadores**, there are eleven players in the team. II **integrarse** *vr* to integrate (**en**, with).

integridad *nf* integrity.

íntegro,-a *adj* 1 *(entero)* whole, entire; *Cin Lit* **versión íntegra**, unabridged version. 2 *(honrado)* upright.

intelecto *nm* intellect.

intelectual *adj & nmf* intellectual.

inteligencia *nf (intelecto)* intelligence; **cociente de i.**, intelligence quotient, IQ.

inteligente *adj* intelligent.

inteligible *adj* intelligible.

intemperie *nf* bad weather; **a la i.**, in the open (air).

intempestivo,-a *adj* untimely.

intención *nf* intention; **con i.**, deliberately, on purpose; **con segunda/doble i.**, with an ulterior motive; **tener la i. de hacer algo**, to intend to do sth.

intencionado,-a *adj* deliberate.

intencional *adj* intentional.

   ◆**intencionadamente** *adv* on purpose.

intensidad *nf* intensity; *(del viento)* force.

intensificar [1] *vtr*, **intensificarse** *vr* to intensify; *(amistad)* to strengthen.

intensivo,-a *adj* intensive; *Agr* **cultivo i.**, intensive farming; *Educ* **curso i.**, crash course.

intenso,-a *adj* intense.

intentar *vtr* to try, attempt; *fam* **¡inténtalo!**, give it a go!.

intento *nm* attempt; **i. de suicidio**, attempted suicide.

intentona *nf* putsch.

inter- *pref* inter-.

intercalar *vtr* to insert.

intercambiar [12] *vtr* to exchange.

intercambio *nm* exchange; **i. comercial**, trade.

interceder *vi* to intercede.

interceptar *vtr* 1 *(detener)* to intercept. 2 *(carretera)* to block; *(tráfico)* to hold up.

intercesión *nf* intercession.

intercontinental *adj* intercontinental.

interdicto *nm* prohibition.

interés *nm* 1 interest; **poner i. en**, to take an interest in; **tener i. en** *o* **por**, to be interested in. 2 *(provecho personal)* self-interest; **hacer algo (sólo) por i.**, to do sth out of self-interest; **intereses creados**, vested interests. 3 *Fin* interest; **con un i. del 11%**, at an interest of 11%; **tipos de i.**, interest rates.

interesado,-a I *adj* 1 interested (**en**, in); **las partes interesadas**, the interested parties. 2 *(egoísta)* selfish. II *nm,f* interested person; **los interesados**, those interested *o* concerned.

interesante *adj* interesting.

interesar I *vtr* 1 *(tener interés)* to interest; **la poesía no me interesa nada**, poetry doesn't interest me at all. 2 *(concernir)* to concern. II *vi (ser importante)* to be of interest, to be important; **interesaría llegar pronto**, it is important to get there early. III **interesarse** *vr* **i. por** *o* **en**, to be interested in; **se interesó por ti**, he asked about *o* after you.

interferencia *nf* interference; *Rad TV* jamming.

interferir [5] *vtr* 1 to interfere with; *(plan)* to upset. 2 *Rad TV* to jam.

interfono *nm Tel* intercom.

interinidad *nf* 1 *(temporalidad)* temporariness. 2 *(empleo)* temporary employment.

interino,-a I *adj (persona)* acting. II *nm,f (trabajador temporal)* temporary worker.

interior I *adj* 1 inner, inside, interior; **habitación i.**, inner room; **ropa i.**, underwear. 2 *Pol* domestic, internal. 3 *Geog* inland. II *nm* 1 inside, interior; *fig* **en su i. no estaba de acuerdo**, deep down she disagreed. 2 *Geog* interior; *Pol* **Ministerio del I.**, Home Office, *US* Department of the Interior.

interiorizar [4] *vtr* to internalize.

interjección *nf Ling* interjection.

interlocutor,-a *nm,f* speaker; *(negociador)* negotiator.

intermediario,-a *nm Com* middleman.

intermedio,-a I *adj* intermediate. II *nm TV (intervalo)* break.

interminable *adj* endless.

intermitente I *adj* intermittent. II *nm Aut* indicator.

internacional *adj* international.

internado,-a I *nm,f* inmate. II *(colegio)* boarding school.

internar I *vtr (en hospital)* to confine. II **internarse** *vr* 1 *(penetrar)* to advance (**en**, into). 2 *Dep* to break through.

interno,-a I *adj* 1 internal; **por vía**

interna, internally. 2 *Pol* domestic. II *nm,f* (*alumno*) boarder; *Med* (*enfermo*) patient; (*preso*) inmate.

interponer [19] (*pp* **interpuesto**) I *vtr* to insert; *Jur* **i. un recurso**, to give notice of appeal. II **interponerse** *vr* to intervene.

interpretación *nf* 1 interpretation. 2 *Mús Teat* performance.

interpretar *vtr* 1 to interpret. 2 *Teat* (*papel*) to play; (*obra*) to perform; *Mús* (*concierto*) to play, perform; (*canción*) to sing.

intérprete *nmf* 1 (*traductor*) interpreter. 2 *Teat* performer; *Mús* (*cantante*) singer; (*músico*) performer.

interpuse *pt indef* → **interponer**.

interrogación *nf* interrogation; *Ling* (**signo de**) **i.**, question *o* interrogation mark.

interrogante *nf fig* question mark.

interrogar [7] *vtr* to question; (*testigo etc*) to interrogate.

interrogatorio *nm* interrogation.

interrumpir *vtr* to interrupt; (*tráfico*) to block.

interrupción *nf* interruption; **i. del embarazo**, termination of pregnancy.

interruptor *nm Elec* switch.

intersección *nf* intersection.

interurbano,-a *adj* intercity; *Tel* **conferencia interurbana**, long-distance call.

intervalo *nm* interval; **habrá intervalos de lluvia**, there will be periods of rain.

intervención *nf* 1 (*participación*) intervention, participation (**en**, in); (*aportación*) contribution (**en**, to). 2 *Med* intervention.

intervenir [27] I *vi* (*mediar*) to intervene (**en**, in); (*participar*) to take part (**en**, in); (*contribuir*) to contribute (**en**, to). II *vtr* 1 (*confiscar*) to confiscate, seize. 2 *Tel* (*teléfono*) to tap. 3 *Med* to operate on.

interventor,-a *nm,f* (*supervisor*) inspector; *Fin* **i.** (**de cuentas**), auditor.

interviú *nm* (*pl* **interviús**) interview.

intestino,-a I *adj* (*luchas*) internal. II *nm Anat* intestine.

intimar *vi* to become close (**con**, to).

intimidad *nf* (*amistad*) intimacy; (*vida privada*) private life; (*privacidad*) privacy; **en la i.**, privately, in private.

intimidar *vtr* to intimidate.

íntimo,-a I *adj* 1 intimate. 2 (*vida*) private; **una boda íntima**, a quiet wedding. 3 (*amistad*) close. II *nm,f* close friend, intimate.

intolerable *adj* intolerable.

intolerancia *nf* intolerance.

intolerante I *adj* intolerant. II *nmf* intolerant person.

intoxicación *nf* poisoning; **i. alimentaria**, food poisoning.

intoxicar [1] *vtr* to poison.

intra- *pref* intra-.

intranquilidad *nf* worry.

intranquilizarse *vr* to get worried.

intranquilo,-a *adj* (*preocupado*) worried; (*agitado*) restless.

intransigente *adj* intransigent.

intransitable *adj* impassable.

intransitivo,-a *adj Ling* intransitive.

intratable *adj* 1 (*problema*) intractable. 2 (*persona*) unsociable.

intrépido,-a *adj* intrepid.

intriga *nf* intrigue; *Cin Teat* plot.

intrigante I *adj* 1 (*interesante*) intriguing, interesting. 2 *pey* (*maquinador*) scheming. II *nmf* (*persona*) schemer.

intrigar [7] I *vtr* (*interesar*) to intrigue, interest. II *vi* (*maquinar*) to plot.

intrincado,-a *adj* 1 (*cuestión, problema*) intricate. 2 (*bosque*) dense.

intrínseco,-a *adj* intrinsic.

introducción *nf* introduction.

introducir [10] I *vtr* 1 to introduce. 2 (*meter*) to insert, put in.

intromisión *nf* (*injerencia*) meddling; **perdón por la i.**, forgive the intrusion.

introspectivo,-a *adj* introspective.

introvertido,-a *adj* introverted. II *nm,f* introvert.

intruso,-a I *adj* intrusive. II *nm,f* intruder; *Jur* trespasser.

intuición *nf* intuition.

intuir [37] *vtr* to know by intuition.

intuitivo,-a *adj* intuitive.

inundación *nf* flood.

inundar *vtr* to flood; *fig* (*de trabajo etc*) to swamp.

inusitado,-a *adj* unusual.

inútil I *adj* 1 useless; (*esfuerzo, intento*) vain, pointless. 2 *Mil* unfit (for service). II *nmf fam* good-for-nothing.

inutilidad *nf* uselessness.

inutilizar [4] *vtr* to make *o* render useless; (*máquina etc*) to put out of action.

invadir *vtr* to invade; *fig* **los estudiantes invadieron la calle**, students poured out onto the street.

invalidar *vtr* to invalidate.

invalidez *nf* 1 *Jur* (*nulidad*) invalidity. 2 *Med* (*minusvalía*) disability.

inválido,-a I *adj* 1 *Jur* (*nulo*) invalid. 2 *Med* (*minusválido*) disabled, handicapped. II *nm,f Med* disabled *o* handicapped person.

invariable *adj* invariable.

invasión *nf* invasion.

invasor,-a I *adj* invading. II *nm,f* invader.

invencible *adj* 1 (*enemigo*) invincible. 2 (*obstáculo*) insurmountable.

invención *nf* (*invento*) invention; (*mentira*) fabrication.

inventar *vtr* to invent; (*excusa, mentira*) to make up, concoct.

inventario *nm* inventory.

inventiva *nf* inventiveness; (*imaginación*) imagination.

invento *nm* invention.
inventor,-a *nm,f* inventor.
invernadero *nm* greenhouse; **efecto i.**, greenhouse effect.
invernal *adj* winter, wintry.
invernar [1] *vi* to hibernate.
inverosímil *adj* unlikely, improbable.
inversión *nf* 1 inversion. 2 *Fin* investment.
inverso,-a *adj* opposite; **en sentido i.**, in the opposite direction; **en orden i.**, in reverse order.
inversor,-a *nm,f Fin* investor.
invertebrado,-a *adj & nm Zool* invertebrate.
invertido,-a I *adj* inverted, reversed. II *nm,f* homosexual.
invertir [5] *vtr* 1 (*orden*) to invert, reverse. 2 (*dinero*) to invest (**en**, in); (*tiempo*) to spend (**en**, on).
investidura *nf* investiture; *Pol* vote of confidence.
investigación *nf* 1 (*policial etc*) investigation. 2 (*científica*) research.
investigador,-a *nm,f* 1 (*detective*) investigator. 2 (*científico*) researcher, research worker.
investigar [7] *vtr* to research; (*indagar*) to investigate.
investir [6] *vtr* to invest.
invidente I *adj* unsighted. II *nmf* unsighted person.
invierno *nm* winter.
invisible *adj* invisible.
invitación *nf* invitation.
invitado,-a I *adj* invited; **artista i.**, guest artist. II *nm,f* guest.
invitar *vtr* to invite; **hoy invito yo**, it's on me today; **me invitó a una copa**, he treated me to a drink.
invocar [1] *vtr* to invoke.
involucrar I *vtr* to involve (**en**, in). II **involucrarse** *vr* to get involved (**en**, in).
involuntario,-a *adj* involuntary; (*impremeditado*) unintentional.
invulnerable *adj* invulnerable.
inyección *nf* injection; **poner una i.**, to give an injection.
inyectar *vtr* to inject (**en**, into); **i. algo a algn**, to inject sb with sth.
IPC *abr de* **Índice de Precios al Consumo**, Retail Price Index, RPI.
ir [16] I *vi* 1 to go; **¡vamos!**, let's go!; **voy a Lima**, I'm going to Lima; **¡ya voy!**, (I'm) coming! 2 (*río, camino*) to lead; **esta carretera va a la frontera**, this road leads to the border. 3 (*funcionar*) to work (properly); **el ascensor no va**, the lift is out of order. 4 (*desenvolverse*) **¿cómo le va el nuevo trabajo?**, how is he getting on in his new job?; **¿cómo te va?**, how are things?, how are you doing? 5 (*sentar bien*) to suit; **el verde te va mucho**, green really suits you. 6 (*combinar*) to

match; **el rojo no va con el verde**, red doesn't go with green. 7 (*vestir*) to wear; **ir con falda**, to wear a skirt; **ir de blanco/de uniforme**, to be dressed in white/in uniform. 8 *fam* (*importar, concernir*) to concern; **eso va por ti también**, and the same goes for you; **ni me va ni me viene**, I don't care one way or the other. 9 *fam* (*comportarse*) to act; **ir de guapo por la vida**, to be a flash Harry. 10 **va para abogado**, he's studying to be a lawyer. 11 (*ir + por*) **ir por la derecha**, to keep (to the) right; (*ir a buscar*) **ve (a) por agua**, go and fetch some water; (*haber llegado*) **voy por la página noventa**, I've got as far as page ninety. 12 (*locuciones*) **a eso iba**, I was coming to that; **¡ahí va!**, catch!; **en lo que va de año**, so far this year; **ir a parar**, to end up; **¡qué va!**, of course not!, nothing of the sort!; **va a lo suyo**, he looks after his own interests; **¡vamos a ver!**, let's see!; **¡vaya!**, fancy that; **¡vaya moto!**, what a bike!
II *v aux* 1 (*ir + gerundio*) **ir andando**, to go on foot; **va mejorando**, she's improving. 2 (*ir + pp*) **ya van rotos tres**, three (of them) have already been broken. 3 (*ir a + inf*) **iba a decir que**, I was going to say that; **va a llover**, it's going to rain; **vas a caerte**, you'll fall.
III **irse** *vr* 1 (*marcharse*) to go away, leave; **me voy**, I'm off; **¡vámonos!**, let's go!; **¡vete!**, go away!; **vete a casa**, go home. 2 (*líquido, gas*) (*escaparse*) to leak. 3 (*direcciones*) **¿por dónde se va a …?** which is the way to …? **por aquí se va al río**, this is the way to the river.
ira *nf* wrath, rage, anger.
iracundo,-a *adj* 1 (*irascible*) irascible. 2 (*enfadado*) irate, angry.
Irak *n* Irak.
Irán *n* Iran.
iraní *adj & nmf* (*pl* **iraníes**) Iranian.
Iraq *n* → **Irak**.
iraquí *adj & nmf* (*pl* **iraquíes**) Iraqi.
irascible *adj* irascible, irritable.
iris *nm inv Anat* iris; **arco i.**, rainbow.
Irlanda *n* Ireland; **I. del Norte**, Northern Ireland.
irlandés,-esa I *adj* Irish. II *nm,f* (*hombre*) Irishman; (*mujer*) Irishwoman; **los irlandeses**, the Irish. III *nm* (*idioma*) Irish.
ironía *nf* irony.
irónico,-a *adj* ironic.
IRPF *nm Econ abr de* **impuesto sobre la renta de las personas físicas**, income tax.
irracional *adj* irrational.
irradiar [12] *vtr* 1 (*emitir*) to radiate. 2 *Am fig* (*expulsar*) to expel.
irreal *adj* unreal.
irrealizable *adj* unattainable, unfeasible;

fig unreachable.

irreconocible *adj* unrecognizable.
irregular *adj* irregular.
irregularidad *nf* irregularity.
irremediable *adj* irremediable, incurable.
irremplazable *adj* irreplaceable.
irreparable *adj* irreparable.
irreprochable *adj* irreproachable, blameless.
irresistible *adj* 1 (*impulso, persona*) irresistible. 2 (*insoportable*) unbearable.
irresoluto,-a *adj* irresolute.
irresponsable *adj* irresponsible.
irreverente *adj* irreverent.
irrigación *nf* irrigation.
irrigar [7] *vtr* to irrigate, water.
irrisorio,-a *adj* derisory, ridiculous.
irritación *nf* irritation.
irritante *adj* irritating.
irritar *vtr* 1 (*enfadar*) to irritate, exasperate. 2 *Med* to irritate. II **irritarse** *vr* 1 (*enfadarse*) to lose one's temper, get angry. 2 *Med* to become irritated.
irrompible *adj* unbreakable.
irrumpir *vi* to burst (**en**, into).
isla *nf* island, isle.
islam *nm Rel* Islam.
islámico,-a *adj* Islamic.
islandés,-esa I *adj* Icelandic. II *nm,f* (*persona*) Icelander. III *nm* (*idioma*) Icelandic.

Islandia *n* Iceland.
isleño,-a I *adj* island. II *nm,f* islander.
islote *nm* small *o* rocky island.
ismo *nm fam* ism.
Israel *n* Israel.
israelí *adj & nmf* (*pl* **israelíes**) Israeli.
istmo *nm Geog* isthmus.
Italia *n* Italy.
italiano,-a I *adj* Italian. II *nm,f* (*persona*) Italian. III *nm* (*idioma*) Italian.
itinerante *adj* itinerant, itinerating.
itinerario *nm* itinerary, route.
IVA *nm Econ abr de* **impuesto sobre el valor añadido**, value-added tax, VAT.
izar [4] *vtr* to hoist, raise.
izda, izdª *abr de* **izquierda**, left.
izdo., izdºª *abr de* **izquierdo**, left.
izquierda *nf* 1 left; **a la i.**, on the left; **girar a la i.**, to turn left. 2 (*mano*) left hand. 3 *Pol* **la i.**, the left; **de izquierdas**, left-wing.
izquierdista *Pol* I *adj* leftist, left-wing. II *nmf* leftist, left-winger.
izquierdo,-a *adj* 1 left; **brazo i.**, left arm. 2 (*zurdo*) left-handed.
izquierdoso,-a *adj fam* leftish.

J

J, j ['xota] *nf* (*la letra*) J,j.
jabalí *nm* (*pl* **jabalíes**) wild boar.
jabalina *nf Dep* javelin.
jabón *nm* soap; **j. de afeitar/tocador**, shaving/toilet soap.
jabonera *nf* soapdish.
jaca *nf* gelding.
jacaré *nm Am Zool* caiman.
jacinto *nm Bot* hyacinth.
jactancia *nf* boastfulness.
jactancioso,-a I *adj* boastful. II *nm,f* braggart.
jactarse *vr* to boast, brag (**de**, about).
jadeante *adj* panting, breathless.
jadear *vi* to pant, gasp.
jadeo *nm* panting, gasping.
jaez *nm pey* (*ralea*) kind, sort.
jalar I *vtr fam* (*comer*) to wolf down. II **jalarse** *vr fam* (*comerse*) to wolf down, scoff.
jalbegar [7] *vtr* to whitewash.
jalea *nf* jelly; **j. real**, royal jelly.
jalear *vtr* (*animar*) to cheer (on).
jaleo *nm* (*alboroto*) din, racket; (*riña*) row; (*confusión*) muddle; **armar j.**, to make a racket.
jalón¹ *nm* (*estaca*) stake; *fig* (*hito*) milestone.
jalón² *nm* 1 (*tirón*) pull, tug. 2 *Am Aut* lift.

jamaicano,-a *adj & nm,f* Jamaican.
jamar *vtr fam* to scoff, eat.
jamás *adv* 1 never; **j. he estado allí**, I have never been there. 2 ever; **el mejor libro que j. se ha escrito**, the best book ever written. 3 **nunca j.**, never again; **por siempre j.**, for ever (and ever).
jamba *nf Arquit* jamb.
jamón *nm* ham; **j. de York/serrano**, boiled/cured ham.
jamona *nf fam adj* buxom.
Japón *n* (**el**) **J.**, Japan.
japonés,-esa I *adj* Japanese. II *nm,f* (*persona*) Japanese; **los japoneses**, the Japanese. III *nm* (*idioma*) Japanese.
japuta *nf* (*pez*) Ray's bream.
jaque *nm Ajedrez* check; **dar j. a**, to check; **j. mate**, checkmate; **j. al rey**, check; *fig* **estar en j.**, to be stymied.
jaqueca *nf* migraine.
jara *nf Bot* rockrose.
jarabe *nm* syrup; **j. para la tos**, cough mixture.
jarana *nf fam* 1 (*juerga*) wild party, spree; **ir de j.**, to go on a spree *o* a binge. 2 (*jaleo*) racket, din.
jaranero,-a I *adj* fun-loving, party-loving. II *nm,f* pleasure seeker, party-lover.
jardín *nm* garden; **j. botánico**, botanical garden; **j. de infancia**, nursery school,

kindergarten.

jardinería *nf* gardening.

jardinero *nm* gardener.

jarra *nf* pitcher; **j. de cerveza**, beer mug; *fig* **de o en jarras**, arms akimbo, hands on hips.

jarro *nm* (*recipiente*) jug; (*contenido*) jugful; *fig* **echar un j. de agua fría a**, to pour cold water on.

jarrón *nm* vase; (*en arqueología*) urn.

jaspe *nm* *Min* jasper; **como el j.**, spotless, like a new pin.

Jauja *nf* *fig* promised land; **¡esto es J.!**, this is the life!

jaula *nf* (*para animales*) cage.

jauría *nf* pack of hounds.

jazmín *nm* *Bot* jasmine.

J.C. *abr de* **Jesucristo**, Jesus Christ, J.C.

jeep *nm* *Aut* jeep.

jefa *nf* female boss, manageress.

jefatura *nf* 1 (*cargo, dirección*) leadership. 2 (*sede*) central office; **j. de policía**, police headquarters.

jefe *nm* 1 head, chief, boss; *Com* manager; **j. de estación**, stationmaster; **j. de redacción**, editor-in-chief; **j. de ventas**, sales manager. 2 *Pol* leader; **J. de Estado**, Head of State. 3 *Mil* officer in command; **comandante en j.**, commander-in-chief.

Jehová *nm* Jehovah; **testigos de J.**, Jehovah's Witnesses.

jején *nm* *Am Ent* black fly.

jengibre *nm* *Bot* ginger.

jeque *nm* sheik, sheikh.

jerarquía *nf* 1 hierarchy. 2 (*categoría*) rank.

jerárquico,-a *adj* hierarchical.

jeremías *nmf inv* whiner, whinger.

jerez *nm* sherry.

jerga *nf* (*argot*) (*técnica*) jargon; (*vulgar*) slang; **la j. legal**, legal jargon.

jerigonza *nf* 1 (*extravagancia*) oddness. 2 (*galimatías*) gibberish.

jeringa *nf* *Med* syringe; *Aut* **j. de engrase**, grease gun.

jeringar [7] *vtr fam* 1 (*molestar*) to pester, annoy. 2 (*romper*) to break.

jeringuilla *nf* (*hypodermic*) syringe.

jeroglífico,-a I *adj* hieroglyphic. II *nm* 1 *Ling* hieroglyph, hieroglyphic. 2 (*juego*) rebus.

jersey *nm* (*pl* **jerseis**) sweater, pullover, jumper.

Jerusalén *n* Jerusalem.

Jesucristo *nm* Jesus Christ.

jesuita *adj & nmf* Jesuit.

Jesús I *nm* Jesus. II *interj* 1 (*expresa sorpresa*) good heavens! 2 (*al estornudar*) bless you!

jet *nf* jet set.

jet-set *nf* jet set.

jíbaro,-a *nm,f Am* peasant.

jícara *nf* (*bol*) small cup; *Am* gourd.

jilguero,-a *nm,f Orn* goldfinch.

jilipollas *nmf inv fam ofens* → **gilipollas**.

jinete *nm* rider, horseman.

jiñar *vi vulg* to shit.

jirafa *nf* 1 giraffe. 2 (*de micrófono*) boom.

jirón *nm* (*trozo desgarrado*) shred, strip; (*pedazo suelto*) bit, scrap; **hecho jirones**, in shreds o tatters.

JJOO *nmpl abr de* **Juegos Olímpicos**, Olympic Games.

jocoso,-a *adj* funny, humorous.

joder *vulg ofens* I *interj* bloody hell!, shit! II *vtr* 1 (*fastidiar*) to piss off; **¡no me jodas!**, come on, don't give me that! 2 (*copular*) to fuck. 3 (*echar a perder*) to screw up; **¡la jodiste!**, you screwed it up! 4 (*romper*) to bugger. II *joderse vr* 1 (*aguantarse*) to put up with it; **¡hay que j.!**, you'll just have to grin and bear it. 2 (*echarse a perder*) to get screwed up; **¡se jodió el invento!**, that's really screwed things up. **¡que se joda!**, to hell with him! 3 (*romperse*) to go bust.

jodido,-a *adj vulg ofens* 1 (*maldito*) bloody, damned. 2 (*molesto*) annoying. 3 (*enfermo*) in a bad way; (*cansado*) knackered, exhausted. 4 (*estropeado, roto*) bust, kaput, buggered. 5 (*difícil*) shitty.

jodienda *nf vulg ofens* 1 (*coito*) fuck. 2 (*molestia*) pain in the arse.

jofaina *nf* washbasin.

jolgorio *nm fam* (*juerga*) binge; (*algazara*) fun.

jolín, jolines *interj fam* (*sorpresa*) gosh!, good grief!; (*enfado*) blast!, damn!

Jordania *n* Jordan.

jornada *nf* 1 **j. (laboral)**, (*día de trabajo*) working day; **j. intensiva**, continuous working day; **j. partida**, working day with a lunch break; **trabajo de media j./ j. completa**, part-time/full-time work. 2 **jornadas**, conference *sing*.

jornal *nm* (*paga*) day's wage; **trabajar a j.**, to be paid by the day.

jornalero,-a *nm,f* day labourer *o US* labourer.

joroba I *nf* (*jiba*) hump. II *interj* drat!

jorobado,-a I *adj* hunchbacked. II *nm,f* hunchback.

jorobar *fam* I *vtr* 1 (*fastidiar*) to annoy, bother; **me joroba**, it really gets up my nose; **¡no jorobes!**, (*incredulidad*) pull the other one! 2 (*estropear*) to ruin, wreck. II *jorobarse vr* 1 (*fastidiarse*) to grin and bear it. 2 (*estropearse*) to break.

jota¹ *nf* 1 name of the letter J in Spanish. 2 (*cantidad mínima*) iot, scrap; **ni j.**, not an iota; **no entiendo ni j.**, I don't understand a thing.

jota² *nf Mús* Spanish dance and music.

joven I *adj* young; **de aspecto j.**, young-looking. II *nmf* (*hombre*) youth, young man; (*mujer*) girl, young woman; **de j.**, as a young man *o* woman; **los jóvenes**, young people, youth.

jovial *adj* jovial, good-humoured.

joya *nf* 1 jewel, piece of jewellery; **joyas de imitación**, imitation jewellery *sing.* 2 *fig* **ser una j.**, (*persona*) to be a real treasure *o* gem.

joyería *nf* (*tienda*) jewellery shop, jeweller's (shop).

joyero,-a I *nm,f* jeweller. II *nm* jewel case *o* box.

juanete *nm* (*en el pie*) bunion.

jubilación *nf* 1 (*acción*) retirement; **j. anticipada**, early retirement. 2 (*pensión*) pension.

jubilado,-a I *adj* retired. II *nm,f* retired person, pensioner; **los jubilados**, retired people.

jubilar I *vtr* (*retirar*) to retire, pension off; *fam fig* to get rid of, ditch. II **jubilarse** *vr* (*retirarse*) to retire, go into retirement.

júbilo *nm* jubilation, joy.

jubón *nm* doublet, jerkin.

judería *nf* (*barrio*) Jewish quarter.

judía *nf* bean; **j. verde**, French bean, green bean.

judicial *adj* judicial; **vía j.**, legal channels.

judío,-a I *adj* Jewish. II *nm,f* Jew.

judo *nm Dep* judo.

juego *nm* 1 game; **j. de azar**, game of chance; **j. de cartas**, card game; *fig* **j. de manos**, sleight of hand; *fig* **j. de palabras**, play on words, pun; *fig* **j. limpio/sucio**, fair/foul play; 2 *Dep* game; **Juegos Olímpicos**, Olympic Games; **terreno de j.**, *Ten* court; *Ftb* field; **fuera de j.**, offside. 3 (*apuestas*) gambling; *fig* **poner algo en j.**, to put sth at stake. 4 (*conjunto de piezas*) set; **j. de café/té**, coffee/tea service; *fig* **ir a j. con**, to match.

juerga *nf fam* binge, rave-up; **ir de j.**, to go on a binge.

juerguista I *adj* fun-loving. II *nmf* fun-loving person, raver.

jueves *nm inv* Thursday; **J. Santo**, Maundy Thursday.

juez *nmf* judge; **j. de instrucción**, examining magistrate; **j. de paz**, justice of the peace; *Dep* **j. de salida**, starter; **j. de línea**, linesman.

jugada *nf* 1 move; (*en billar*) shot. 2 *fam* dirty trick.

jugador,-a player; (*apostador*) gambler.

jugar [32] I *vi* 1 to play; **j. a(l) fútbol/tenis**, to play football/tennis; *fig* **j. sucio**, to play dirty. 2 **j. con**, (*no tomar en serio*) to toy with. II *vtr* 1 to play. 2 (*apostar*) to bet, stake. II **jugarse** *vr* 1 (*arriesgar*) to risk; *fam* **j. el pellejo**, to risk one's neck. 2 to take (*apuesta*).

jugarreta *nf fam* dirty trick.

jugo *nm* juice; *fig* **sacar el j. a**, (*aprove-*

char) to make the most of; (*explotar*) to squeeze dry.

jugoso,-a *adj* 1 juicy; **un filete j.**, a juicy steak. 2 *fig* (*sustancioso*) substantial, meaty; **un tema j.**, a meaty topic.

juguete *nm* toy; **pistola de j.**, toy gun; *fig* **ser el j. de algn**, to be sb's plaything.

juguetear *vi* to play.

juguetón,-ona *adj* playful.

juicio *nm* 1 (*facultad mental*) judgement, discernment; (*opinión*) opinion, judgement; **a j. de**, in the opinion of; **a mi j.**, in my opinion. 2 (*sensatez*) reason, common sense; **en su sano j.**, in one's right mind; **perder el j.**, to go mad *o* insane. 3 *Jur* trial, lawsuit; **llevar a algn a j.**, to take legal action against sb, sue sb.

juicioso,-a *adj* judicious, wise.

julio *nm* July.

junco *nm Bot* rush.

jungla *nf* jungle.

junio *nm* June.

júnior *adj Dep* junior; **campeonato j. de golf**, junior golf championship.

junta *nf* 1 (*reunión*) meeting, assembly; *Pol* **j. de gobierno**, cabinet meeting. 2 (*dirección*) board, committee; **j. directiva**, board of directors. 3 *Mil* junta; **j. militar**, military junta. 4 (*parlamento regional*) regional parliament. 5 *Téc* joint.

juntar I *vtr* 1 (*unir*) to join, put together; (*piezas*) to assemble. 2 (*reunir*) (*sellos*) to collect; (*dinero*) to raise. II **juntarse** *vr* 1 (*unirse*) to join; (*ríos, caminos*) to meet; (*personas*) to gather. 2 (*amancebarse*) to live together.

junto,-a *adj* together; **dos mesas juntas**, two tables side by side; **todos juntos**, all together. II **junto** *adv* **j. con**, together with; **j. a**, next to.

juntura *nf Téc* joint, seam. *Anat* joint.

jura *nf* (*acción*) (*ceremonia*) swearing in; **j. de bandera**, oath of allegiance to the flag.

jurado *nm* 1 (*tribunal*) jury; (*en un concurso*) panel of judges, jury. 2 (*miembro del tribunal*) juror, member of the jury.

juramento *nm* 1 *Jur* oath; **bajo j.**, under oath. 2 (*blasfemia*) swearword, curse.

jurar I *vi Jur Rel* to swear, take an oath. II *vtr* to swear; **j. el cargo**, to take the oath of office; **j. por Dios**, to swear to God. III **jurarse** *vr fam* **jurársela(s) a algn**, to have it in for sb.

jurel *nm* (*pez*) scad, horse mackerel.

jurídico,-a *adj* legal.

jurisdicción *nf* jurisdiction.

jurisdiccional *adj* jurisdictional; **aguas jurisdiccionales**, territorial waters.

jurista *nmf* lawyer.

justicia *nf* justice; **tomarse la j. por su mano**, to take the law into one's own hands.

justiciero,-a adj severe.
justificable adj justifiable.
justificación nf justification.
justificado,-a adj justified, well-grounded.
justificante nm written proof; **j. de pago,** proof of payment.
justificar [1] I vtr to justify. II **justificarse** vr to clear oneself, justify oneself.
justo,-a I adj 1 just, fair, right; **un trato j.,** a fair deal. 2 (apretado) (ropa) tight; **estamos justos de tiempo,** we're pressed for time. 3 (exacto) right, accurate; **la palabra justa,** the right word. 4 (preciso) **llegamos en el momento j. en que salían,** we arrived just as they were leav-

ing. 5 **lo** j., just enough. II nm,f just o righteous person; **los justos,** the just, the righteous. III **justo** adv (exactamente) exactly, precisely; **j. al lado,** right beside. ◆**justamente** adv ¡j.!, precisely!; **j. detrás de,** right behind.
juvenil I adj (aspecto) youthful, young; **ropa j.,** young people's clothes; **delincuencia j.,** juvenile delinquency. II nmf **los juveniles,** the juveniles.
juventud nf 1 (edad) youth. 2 (jóvenes) young people.
juzgado nm court, tribunal; **j. de guardia,** police court.
juzgar [7] vtr to judge; **a j. por ...,** judging by ....

K

K, k [ka] nf (la letra) K, k.
ka nf name of the letter K in Spanish.
kárate nm Dep karate.
karateka nmf Dep person who does karate.
Kg, kg abr de **kilogramo(s),** kilograms, kilogrammes, kg.
kilo nm 1 (medida) kilo; fam **pesa un k.,** it weighs a ton. 2 arg (millón) a million pesetas.
kilogramo nm kilogram, kilogramme.
kilolitro nm kilolitre, US kiloliter.
kilometraje nm ≈ mileage.

kilométrico,-a adj kilometric, kilometrical; **billete k.,** multiple-journey ticket.
kilómetro nm kilometre, US kilometer.
kilovatio nm kilowatt; **k. hora,** kilowatt-hour.
kiosco nm → quiosco.
kiwi nm 1 Orn kiwi. 2 (fruto) kiwi (fruit), Chinese gooseberry.
Kleenex® nm Kleenex®, tissue.
Km, km abr de **kilómetro(s),** kilometre, kilometres, km, kms.
Kw, kw abr de **kilovatio(s),** kilowatt, kilowatts, kW, kw.

L

L, l ['ele] nf (la letra) L, l.
l abr de **litro(s),** litre, litres, US liter, liters, l.
la¹ art def f I the; **la mesa,** the table. II pron dem the one; **la del vestido azul,** the one in the blue dress; **la que vino ayer,** the one who came yesterday; → **el.**
la² pron pers f (persona) her; (usted) you; (cosa) it; **la invitaré,** I'll invite her along; **no la dejes abierta,** don't leave it open; **ya la avisaremos, señora,** we'll let you know, madam; → **le.**
la³ nm Mús la, A.
laberinto nm labyrinth.
labia nf fam loquacity; pey glibness; **tener mucha l.,** to have the gift of the gab.
labio nm lip.
labor nf 1 job, task; **l. de equipo,** teamwork; (de profesión) **sus labores,** housewife. 2 Agr farmwork. 3 (de costura) needlework, sewing.
laborable adj 1 **día l.,** (no festivo) working day. 2 Agr arable.
laboral adj industrial; **accidente l.,** industrial accident; **conflictividad l.,** in-

dustrial unrest; **jornada l.,** working day; **Universidad L.,** technical training college.
laboratorio nm laboratory.
laborioso,-a adj 1 (persona) hardworking. 2 (tarea) laborious.
laborista Pol I adj Labour; **partido l.,** Labour Party. II nmf Labour (Party) member o supporter.
labrado,-a adj Arte carved.
labrador,-a nm,f (granjero) farmer; (trabajador) farm worker.
labranza nf farming.
labrar I vtr 1 Agr to till. 2 (madera) to carve; (piedra) to cut; (metal) to work. II **labrarse** vr fig **l. un porvenir,** to build a future for oneself.
laca nf 1 hair lacquer, hairspray; **l. de uñas,** nail polish o varnish. 2 Arte lacquer.
lacio,-a adj 1 (pelo) lank, limp. 2 **qué l.!,** (soso) what a weed!
lacónico,-a adj laconic, (conciso) terse.
lacra nf evil, curse; **una l. social,** a scourge of society.

lacrar *vtr* to seal with wax.

lacre *nm* sealing wax.

lacrimógeno,-a *adj* **1** *gas* l., tear gas. **2** *fig* **una película lacrimógena**, a tearjerker.

lactar *vi* to breastfeed.

lácteo,-a *adj* **productos lácteos**, milk *o* dairy products; *Astron* **Vía Láctea**, Milky Way.

ladear **I** *vtr* (*inclinar*) to tilt; (*cabeza*) to lean. **II ladearse** *vr* **1** (*inclinarse*) to lean, tilt. **2** (*desviarse*) to go off to one side.

ladera *nf* slope.

ladino,-a *adj* (*astuto*) cunning, crafty.

lado *nm* **1** side; **a un l.**, aside; **al l.**, close by, nearby; **al l. de**, next to, beside; **ponte de l.**, stand sideways. **2** (*en direcciones*) direction; **por todos lados**, on *o* from all sides. **3** *fig* **dar de l. a algn**, to cold-shoulder sb; **por otro l.**, (*además*) moreover; **por un l. ...**, **por otro l. ...**, on the one hand ..., on the other hand ....

ladrar *vi* to bark.

ladrillo *nm* *Constr* brick. **2** *fam* (*pesado*) bore, drag.

ladrón,-ona *I* *nm,f* thief, robber; **¡al l.!**, stop thief! **II** *nm* *Elec* multiple socket.

lagartija *nf* small lizard.

lagarto *nm* lizard.

lago *nm* lake.

lágrima *nf* **1** tear; **llorar a l. viva**, to cry one's eyes out. **2** (*en lámpara*) teardrop.

lagrimoso,-a *adj* tearful.

laguna *nf* **1** small lake. **2** *fig* (*hueco*) gap.

La Haya *nf* The Hague.

laico,-a *I* *adj* lay. **II** *nm,f* lay person; (*hombre*) layman; (*mujer*) laywoman.

lameculos *nmf* *inv* *ofens* bootlicker, arselicker.

lamentable *adj* regrettable; (*infame*) lamentable.

lamentar *I* *vtr* to regret; **lo lamento**, I'm sorry. **II lamentarse** *vr* to complain.

lamento *nm* moan, wail.

lamer *vtr* to lick.

lámina *nf* **1** sheet, plate; **l. de acero**, steel sheet. **2** *Impr* plate.

laminado,-a *I* *adj* **1** laminated. **2** (*metales*) rolled; **acero l.**, rolled steel. **II** *nm* lamination.

laminar *vtr* (*metal*) to roll.

lámpara *nf* **1** lamp; **l. de pie**, standard lamp. **2** *Elec* (*bombilla*) bulb. **3** *Rad* valve.

lamparón *nm* *fam* oil *o* grease stain.

lana *nf* wool; **pura l. virgen**, pure new wool.

lanar *adj* **ganado l.**, sheep.

lance *nm* *lit* (*episodio*) incident.

lancha *nf* **1** motorboat, launch; **l. motora**, speedboat; **l. neumática**, rubber dinghy; **l. salvavidas**, lifeboat.

langosta *nf* **1** lobster. **2** (*insecto*) locust.

langostino *nm* king prawn.

languidecer [33] *vi* to languish.

lánguido,-a *adj* languid; (*sin vigor*) listless.

lanudo,-a *adj* woolly, fleecy; (*peludo*) furry.

lanza *nf* spear, lance; **punta de l.**, spearhead; *fig* **romper una l. en favor de algn/de algo**, to defend sb/sth.

lanzadera *nf* shuttle; **l. espacial**, space shuttle.

lanzado,-a *adj* *fam* reckless; **ir l.**, to tear along.

lanzagranadas *nm* *inv* *Mil* grenade launcher.

lanzamiento *nm* **1** throwing, hurling. **2** *Dep* (*de disco, jabalina*) throw; (*de peso*) put. **3** *Mil* (*de cohete etc*) launching. **4** *Com* launch; **precio de l.**, launch price. **5** *Náut* launch.

lanzar [4] **I** *vtr* **1** (*arrojar*) to throw, fling. **2** *fig* (*grito*) to let out. **3** *Náut Com Mil* to launch. **II lanzarse** *vr* **1** (*arrojarse*) to throw *o* hurl oneself; **l. al suelo**, to throw oneself to the ground. **2** (*emprender*) to embark on; **l. a los negocios**, to go into business. **3** (*irse, largarse*) *fam* to scram.

lapa *nf* **1** *Zool* limpet. **2** *pey* **es una verdadera l.**, he/she sticks to you like glue.

lapicero *nm* pencil-case.

lápida *nf* headstone.

lapidario,-a *adj* lapidary.

lápiz *nm* pencil; **l. labial** *o* **de labios**, lipstick; **l. de ojos**, eyeliner.

lapso *nm* **1** (*periodo de tiempo*) period. **2** (*error*) lapse, slip.

lapsus *nm* slip; **l. linguae**, slip of the tongue.

largas *nfpl* **dar l. a un asunto**, to put a matter off.

largar [7] **I** *vtr* **1** *fam* (*golpe, discurso, dinero*) to give. **2** *Náut* **l. amarras**, to cast off. **II largarse** *vr* *fam* to clear off, split; **¡lárgate!**, beat it!

largo,-a *I* *adj* **1** (*espacio*) long; (*tiempo*) long, lengthy; **pasamos un mes l. allí**, we spent a good month there; **a lo l. de**, (*espacio*) along; (*tiempo*) through; **a la larga**, in the long run. **2** (*excesivo*) too long; **se hizo l. el día**, the day dragged on. **3 largos años**, many years. **II** *nm* **1** (*longitud*) length; **¿cuánto tiene de l.?**, how long is it? **2** *Mús* largo. **III largo** *adv* **l. y tendido**, at length; *fam* **¡l. (de aquí)!**, clear off!; **esto va para l.**, this is going to last a long time.

largometraje *nm* feature film, full-length film.

laringe *nf* larynx.

laringitis *nf* laryngitis.

las¹ *art def fpl* **1** the; **l. sillas**, the chairs; **lávate l. manos**, wash your hands; (*no se traduce*) **me gustan l. flores**, I like flowers. 2 l. que, (personas) the ones who, those who; (objetos) the ones that, those that; toma l. que quieras, take whichever ones you want; → la y los.

las² pron pers fpl (ellas) them; (ustedes) you; **l. llamaré mañana** (a ustedes), I'll call you tomorrow; **no l. rompas,** don't break them; **Pepa es de l. mías,** Pepa thinks the way I do; → **los**.

lasaña nf lasagna, lasagne.

lascivo,-a adj lewd, lecherous.

láser nm inv laser; **impresora l.,** laser printer.

lástima nf pity; **¡qué l.!,** what a pity!, what a shame!; **es una l. que ...,** it's a pity (that) ...; **estar hecho una l.,** to be a sorry sight; **tener l. a algn,** to feel sorry for sb.

lastimar vtr to hurt, injure.

lastre nm 1 (peso) ballast. 2 fig dead weight.

lata¹ nf 1 (envase) tin, US can; **en l.,** tinned o US canned. 2 (hojalata) tin(plate); **hecho de l.,** made of tin.

lata² nf fam nuisance, drag; **dar la l.,** to be a nuisance o a pest.

latente adj latent.

lateral I adj side, lateral; **salió por la puerta l.,** he went out by the side door; **escalón l.,** (en letrero) ramp. II side passage; Aut (carril) l., side lane.

latido nm (del corazón) beat.

latifundio nm large landed estate.

latigazo nm 1 lash. 2 arg (trago) drink, swig.

látigo nm whip.

latín nm Latin.

latino,-a I adj Latin; **América Latina,** Latin America. II nm,f Latin American.

Latinoamérica nf Latin America.

latinomericano,-a adj & nm,f Latin American.

latir vi to beat.

latitud nf 1 Geog latitude. 2 latitudes, region sing, area sing.

latón nm brass.

latoso,-a adj fam annoying.

laucha nf Am mouse.

laúd nm lute.

laurel nm Bot laurel, (sweet) bay; Culin bay leaf; fig **dormirse en los laureles,** to rest on one's laurels.

lava nf lava.

lavable adj washable.

lavabo nm 1 (pila) washbasin. 2 (cuarto de aseo) washroom. 3 (retrete) lavatory, toilet.

lavadero nm (de coches) carwash.

lavado nm wash, washing; fig **l. de cerebro,** brainwashing; **l. en seco,** dry-cleaning.

lavadora nf washing machine.

lavanda nf lavender.

lavandería nf 1 (automática) launderette,

US laundromat. 2 (atendida por personal) laundry.

lavaplatos nm inv dishwasher.

lavar vtr to wash; **l. en seco,** to dry-clean.

lavativa nf enema.

lavavajillas nm inv dishwasher.

laxante adj & nm laxative.

laxar vtr (vientre) to loosen.

laxitud nf laxity, laxness.

lazada nf (nudo) bow.

lazarillo nm perro l., guide dog, US Seeing Eye dog.

lazo nm 1 (adorno) bow. 2 (nudo) knot; **l. corredizo,** slipknot. 3 (para reses) lasso. 4 fig (usu pl) (vínculo) tie, bond.

le I pron pers mf (objeto indirecto) (a él) (to o for) him; (a ella) (to o for) her; (a cosa) (to o for) it; (a usted) (to o for) you; **lávale la cara,** wash his face; **le compraré uno,** I'll buy one for her; **¿qué le pasa (usted)?,** what's the matter with you? II pron pers m (objeto directo) (él) him; (usted) you; **no le oigo,** I can't hear him; **no quiero molestarle,** I don't wish to disturb you.

leal I adj loyal, faithful. II nmf loyalist.

lealtad nf loyalty, faithfulness.

lebrel nm greyhound.

lección nf lesson; fig **dar una l. a algn,** to teach sb a lesson; fig **te servirá de l.,** let that be a lesson to you.

leche nf 1 milk; Anat **dientes de l.,** milk teeth; **l. descremada** o **desnatada,** skim o skimmed milk. 2 fam **mala l.,** badness. 3 **l.!,** damn! 4 arg (golpe) knock; **dar** o **pegar una l. a algn,** to clobber sb. 5 vulg semen.

lechera nf 1 (vasija) churn. 2 arg police car.

lechería nf dairy, creamery.

lechero,-a I adj milk, dairy; **central lechera,** dairy co-operative; **vaca lechera,** milk cow. II nm milkman.

lecho nm Lit bed; **l. del río,** river-bed; **l. mortuorio,** deathbed.

lechón nm sucking pig.

lechoso,-a adj milky.

lechuga nf lettuce.

lechuza nf owl.

lectivo,-a adj school; **horas lectivas,** teaching hours.

lector,-a I nm,f 1 (persona) reader. 2 Univ lector, (language) assistant. II nm **l. de microfichas,** (aparato) microfile reader.

lectura nf reading.

leer [36] vtr to read; **léenos el menú,** read out the menu for us; fig **l. entre líneas,** to read between the lines.

legado nm (herencia) legacy.

legajo nm bundle (of papers).

legal adj 1 Jur legal, lawful; **requisitos legales,** legal formalities. 2 fam (persona) honest, trustworthy.

legalidad nf legality, lawfulness.

legalizar [4] *vtr* to legalize; (*documento*) to authenticate.

legaña *nf* sleep.

legar [7] *vtr* (*propiedad etc*) to bequeath; *fig* (*tradiciones etc*) to hand down, pass on.

legendario,-a *adj* legendary.

legión *nf* legion.

legionela *nf* legionnaire's disease.

legislación *nf* legislation.

legislar *vi* to legislate.

legislativo,-a *adj* legislative; **el poder l.**, parliament.

legislatura *nf* legislature.

legitimar *vtr* to legitimize; (*legalizar*) to legalize.

legitimidad *nf* *Jur* legitimacy; (*licitud*) justice.

legítimo,-a *adj* *Jur* legitimate; **en legítima defensa**, in self-defence. 2 (*auténtico*) authentic, real; **oro l.**, pure gold.

lego,-a I *adj* *Rel* lay. II *nm* 1 layman; **ser l. en la materia**, to be a layman in the subject. 2 *Rel* lay brother.

legua *nf* (*medida*) league; **fig se nota a la l.**, it stands out a mile.

legumbres *nfpl* pulses.

lejanía *nf* distance.

lejano,-a *adj* distant, far-off; **parientes lejanos**, distant relatives; **el L. Oriente**, the Far East.

lejía *nf* bleach.

lejos *adv* far (away); **a lo l.**, in the distance; **de l.**, from a distance; *fig* **ir demasiado l.**, to go too far; *fig* **llegar l.**, to go a long way; *fig* **sin ir más l.**, to take an obvious example.

lelo,-a *fam* I *adj* stupid, silly. II *nm,f* ninny.

lema *nm* 1 (*divisa*) motto, slogan. 2 (*contraseña*) code name.

lencería *nf* 1 (*prendas*) lingerie. 2 (*ropa blanca*) linen (*goods pl*).

lendakari *nm* head of the Basque government.

lengua *nf* 1 tongue; *fig* **malas lenguas**, gossips; *fam* **fig irse de la l.**, to spill the beans; *fam* **fig tirarle a algn de la l.**, to try to draw sth out of sb. 2 *Ling* language; **l. materna**, native *o* mother tongue.

lenguado *nm* (*pez*) sole.

lenguaje *nm* language; *Inform* language; **l. corporal**, body language.

lengüeta *nf* 1 (*de zapato*) tongue. 2 *Mús* reed.

lente *nmf* lens; *Opt* **l. de contacto**, contact lenses.

lenteja *nf* lentil.

lentejuela *nf* sequin, spangle.

lentilla *nf* contact lens.

lentitud *nf* slowness; **con l.**, slowly.

lento,-a *adj* slow; **a fuego l.**, on a low heat.

leña *nf* 1 firewood; *fig* **echar l. al fuego**,
to add fuel to the fire. 2 *fam* (*golpes*) knocks *pl*.

leñazo *nm* *arg* (*golpe*) blow, smash.

leñe *interj* damn it!

leño *nm* 1 log. 2 *fam* (*persona*) blockhead, half-wit.

león *nm* lion.

leona *nf* lioness.

leonera *nf* lion's den; *fig* (*habitación*) den.

leopardo *nm* leopard.

leotardos *nmpl* thick tights.

lepra *nf* leprosy.

leproso,-a I *adj* leprous. II *nm,f* leper.

les I *pron pers mfpl* (*objeto indirecto*) (*a ellos,-as*) them; (*a ustedes*) you; **dales el dinero**, give them the money; **les he comprado un regalo**, I've bought you a present. II *pron pers mpl* (*objeto directo*) (*ellos*) them; (*ustedes*) you; **l. esperaré**, I shall wait for you; **no quiero molestarles**, I don't wish to disturb you.

lesbiana *nf* lesbian.

lesbiano *adj* lesbian.

lesión *nf* 1 (*corporal*) injury. 2 *Jur* (*perjuicio*) damage.

lesionar *vtr* to injure.

leso,-a *adj* *Jur* **crimen de lesa humanidad**, crime against humanity.

letal *adj* lethal, deadly.

letanía *nf* litany.

letargo *nm* lethargy.

letón,-ona I *adj* Latvian. II *nm,f* Latvian. III *nm* (*idioma*) Latvian, Lettish.

Letonia *n* Latvia.

letra *nf* 1 letter; **l. de imprenta**, block capitals; **l. mayúscula** capital letter; **l. minúscula** small letter; **l. pequeña**, small print. 2 (*escritura*) (hand)writing. 3 *Mús* (*texto*) lyrics *pl*, words *pl*. 4 *Fin* **l. (de cambio)**, bill of exchange, draft. 5 *Univ* **letras**, arts.

letrado,-a *nm,f* lawyer.

letrero *nm* (*aviso*) notice, sign; (*cartel*) poster; **l. luminoso**, neon sign.

leucemia *nf* leukaemia, *US* leukemia.

levadizo,-a *adj* **puente l.**, drawbridge.

levadura *nf* yeast; **l. en polvo**, baking powder.

levantamiento *nm* 1 raising, lifting; *Dep* **l. de pesos**, weightlifting. 2 (*insurrección*) uprising, insurrection.

levantar I *vtr* 1 to raise, lift; (*mano, voz*) to raise; (*edificio*) to erect; *fig* (*ánimos*) to raise; **l. los ojos**, to look up. 2 (*castigo*) to suspend. II *vr* 1 (*ponerse de pie*) to stand up, rise. 2 (*salir de la cama*) to get up. 3 (*concluir*) to finish; **se levanta la sesión**, the meeting is closed. 4 *Pol* to rise, revolt; **l. en armas**, to rise up in arms. 5 (*viento*) to come up; (*tormenta*) to gather.

levante *nm* 1 (**el) L.**, Levante, the regions of Valencia and Murcia. 2 (*viento*) east wind, Levanter.

levar *vtr* **l. ancla**, to weigh anchor.

leve *adj* (*ligero*) light; *fig* (*de poca importancia*) slight. ◆**levemente** *adv* slightly.

levedad *nf* (*ligereza*) lightness; *fig* slightness; *fig* (*de ánimo*) levity; **heridas de l.**, minor injuries.

levitar *vi* to levitate.

léxico Ling I *nm* (*diccionario*) lexicon; (*vocabulario*) vocabulary, word list. II *adj* lexical.

ley [29] I *nf* 1 law; *Parl* bill, act; **aprobar una l.**, to pass a bill. **2 oro de l.**, pure gold; **plata de l.**, sterling silver.

leyenda *nf* 1 (*relato*) legend. 2 (*en un mapa*) legend; (*en una moneda*) inscription; (*bajo ilustración*) caption.

liar [29] I *vtr* 1 (*envolver*) to wrap up; (*un cigarrillo*) to roll. 2 (*enredar*) to muddle up; (*confundir*) to confuse. II **liarse** *vr* 1 (*embarullarse*) to get muddled up. 2 *fam* (*salir con*) to get involved; (*besarse*) to neck. 3 **l. a bofetadas**, to come to blows.

libanés,-esa *adj & nm,f* Lebanese.

Líbano *n* el L., the Lebanon.

libelo *nm* (*difamación*) lampoon, satire.

libélula *nf* dragonfly.

liberación *nf* (*de país*) liberation; (*de rehén*) release, freeing.

liberal I *adj* 1 liberal; (*carácter*) open-minded; *Pol* **Partido L.**, Liberal Party; **profesión l.**, profession. 2 (*generoso*) generous, liberal. II *nmf* liberal.

liberalizar [4] *vtr* to liberalize.

liberar *vtr* (*país*) to liberate; (*prisionero*) to free, release.

líbero *nm* Ftb sweeper.

libertad *nf* freedom, liberty; **en l.**, free; *Jur* (**en**) **l. bajo palabra/fianza**, (on) parole/bail; *Jur* (**en**) **l. condicional**, (on) parole; **l. de comercio**, free trade; **l. de expresión**, freedom of speech.

libertador,-a *nm,f* liberator.

libertar *vtr* to set free, release.

libertinaje *nm* licentiousness.

libertino,-a *adj & nm,f* libertine.

Libia *n* Libya.

libio,-a *adj & nm,f* Libyan.

libra *nf* (*moneda, peso*) pound; **l. esterlina**, pound sterling.

librador,-a *nm,f* Fin drawer.

librar I *vtr* 1 to free; *Jur* to free, release. 2 *Com* (*una letra*) to draw. 3 **l. batalla**, to do *o* join battle. II *vi* **libro los martes**, (*no ir a trabajar*) I have Tuesdays off. III **librarse** *vr* to escape; **l. de algn**, to get rid of sb.

libre *adj* free; **entrada l.**, (*gratis*) admission free; (*sin restricción*) open to the public; **l. cambio**, free trade; **l. de impuestos**, tax-free.

librecambio, librecambismo *nm* free trade.

librería *nf* 1 (*tienda*) bookshop, US bookstore. 2 (*estante*) bookcase.

librero,-a *nm,f* bookseller.

libreta *nf* notebook; **l. (de ahorro)**, savings book.

libro *nm* book; **l. de texto**, textbook; *Com* **l. de caja**, cashbook; *Fin* **l. mayor**, ledger.

licencia *nf* 1 (*permiso*) permission; (*documentos*) permit, licence, US license; **l. de armas/caza**, gun/hunting licence. 2 (*libertad abusiva*) licence, US license, licentiousness. 3 *Am Aut* driving licence, US driver's license.

licenciado,-a *nm,f* 1 *Univ* graduate; **l. en Ciencias**, Bachelor of Science. 2 *Am* lawyer.

licenciar [12] I *vtr* 1 *Mil* to discharge. 2 *Univ* to confer a degree on. II **licenciarse** *vr Univ* to graduate.

licenciatura *nf Univ* (*título*) (bachelor's) degree (course); (*carrera*) degree (course).

liceo *nm* 1 (*sociedad literaria*) literary society. 2 (*escuela*) secondary school.

licitar *vtr Com* (*pujar*) to bid for.

lícito,-a *adj* (*permisible*) allowed; *Jur* lawful.

licor *nm* liquor, spirits *pl*, US licor.

licuadora *nf* liquidizer.

licuar [10] *vtr* to liquidize.

lid *nf* (*combate*) contest.

líder *nmf* leader.

liderar *vtr* to lead, head.

liderato, liderazgo *nm* leadership; *Dep* top *o* first position.

lidia *nf* bullfight, bullfighting.

lidiador,-a *nm,f* bullfighter.

lidiar [12] I *vtr Taur* to fight. II *vi* to fight; **l. con**, to contend with, fight against.

liebre *nf* 1 hare. 2 *Dep* pacemaker.

liendre *nf* nit.

lienzo *nm* 1 *Tex* linen. 2 *Arte* canvas.

lifting *nm* facelift.

liga *nf* 1 *Dep Pol* league; **hacer buena l.**, to get on well together. 2 (*prenda*) garter.

ligamento *nm* ligament.

ligar [7] I *vtr* 1 to join; *fig* (*dos personas*) to unite. 2 *fam* (*coger*) to get. II *vi fam* (*seducir*) to get off with sb. III **ligarse** *vr* (*vincularse*) to become attached (**a**, to).

ligazón *nf* bond, tie.

ligereza *nf* 1 lightness; (*de tela, argumento*) flimsiness. 2 (*frivolidad*) flippancy; (*acto*) indiscretion; (*dicho*) indiscreet remark. 3 (*rapidez*) speed.

ligero,-a *adj* 1 (*peso*) light, lightweight; **l. de ropa**, lightly clad. 2 (*ágil*) light on one's feet; (*veloz*) swift, quick. 3 (*leve*) slight; **brisa/comida ligera**, light breeze/meal. 4 **a la ligera**, lightly. II *adv* **ligero** (*rápido*) fast, swiftly. ◆**ligeramente** *adv* 1 (*levemente*) lightly. 2 (*un poco*) slightly.

light *adj inv* (*tabaco*) mild; *fig* (*persona*) lightweight.

ligón,-ona *adj & nm,f fam* (*hombre*) ladies' man; **es muy ligona**, she's hot stuff.

ligue *nm* pick-up.

liguero,-a I *adj Dep* league; **partido l.**, league match. II *nm* suspenders *pl*, *US* garter belt.

lija *nf* sandpaper; **papel de l.**, sandpaper.

lijar *vtr* to sand *o* sandpaper (down).

lila¹ *adj inv & nf* lilac.

lila² I *adj* (*tonto*) dumb, stupid. II *nmf* (*tonto*) twit.

lima¹ *nf* (*fruto*) lime.

lima² *nf* (*herramienta*) file; **l. de uñas**, nailfile.

limar *vtr* to file; *fig* **l. asperezas**, to smooth things over.

limbo *nm* limbo.

limitación *nf* limitation; **l. de velocidad**, speed limit.

limitar I *vtr* to limit, restrict. II *vi* to border; **l. con**, to border on.

límite *nm* limit; *Geog Pol* boundary, border; **caso l.**, borderline case; **fecha l.**, deadline; **velocidad l.**, maximum speed.

limítrofe *adj* neighbouring, *US* neighboring.

limo *nm* slime.

limón *nm* lemon.

limonada *nf* lemon squash.

limonero *nm* lemon tree.

limosna *nf* alms; **pedir l.**, to beg.

limpiabotas *nm inv* bootblack, shoeshine.

limpiacristales *nm inv* window cleaner.

limpiador,-a I *adj* cleansing. II *nm,f* (*persona*) cleaner. III *nm* (*producto*) cleaner.

limpiaparabrisas *nm inv* windscreen *o US* windshield wiper.

limpiar [12] *vtr* I to clean; (*con un trapo*) to wipe; (*zapatos*) to polish; *fig* to cleanse. 2 *fam* (*hurtar*) to pinch, nick.

limpieza *nf* (*calidad*) cleanliness; (*acción*) cleaning; *fig* (*integridad*) integrity; **con l.**, cleanly.

limpio,-a I *adj* 1 (*aseado*) clean. 2 *Dep* **juego l.**, fair play. 3 *Fin* (*neto*) net; **beneficios en l.**, net profit. 4 *fam* **pasar algo a l.**, to produce a fair copy of sth. II *adv* **jugar l.**, to play fair.

linaje *nm* lineage.

linaza *nf* **aceite de l.**, linseed oil.

lince *nm* lynx; **tiene ojos de l.**, he's eagle-eyed.

linchar *vtr* to lynch; *fam* (*pegar*) to beat up.

lindante *adj* bordering.

lindar *vi* **l. con**, to border on.

linde *nmf* boundary, limit.

lindero,-a I *adj* bordering, adjoining. II *nm* boundary, limit.

lindo,-a I *adj* (*bonito*) pretty, lovely; **de lo l.**, a great deal. II *adv Am* (*bien*) nicely.

línea *nf* 1 line; **l. aérea**, airline; **en líneas generales**, roughly speaking; *Inform* **fuera de l.**, off-line; **en l.**, on-line. 2

guardar la l., to watch one's figure.

lineal *adj* linear; **dibujo l.**, line drawing.

lingote *nm* ingot; (*de oro, plata*) bar.

lingüista *nmf* linguist.

lino *nm* 1 *Bot* flax. 2 *Tex* linen.

linterna *nf* torch.

lío *nm* 1 (*paquete*) bundle. 2 *fam* (*embrollo*) mess, muddle; **hacerse un l.**, to get mixed up; **meterse en líos**, to get into trouble; **armar un l.**, to kick up a fuss. 3 *fam* (*relación amorosa*) affair.

lioso,-a *adj fam* (*asunto*) confusing.

lipotimia *nf* fainting fit.

liquidación *nf* 1 *Com* (*saldo*) clearance sale. 2 *Fin* liquidation.

liquidar I *vtr Com* (*deuda, cuenta*) to settle; (*mercancías*) to sell off. 2 *Fin* (*gastar*) to spend. 2 *fam* **l. a algn**, (*matar*) to bump sb off.

liquidez *nf Fin* liquidity.

líquido,-a I *adj* 1 liquid. 2 *Fin* net. II *nm* 1 (*fluido*) liquid. 2 *Fin* liquid assets *pl*; **l. imponible**, taxable income.

lira *nf* (*moneda*) lira.

lírico,-a *adj* lyrical.

lirio *nm* iris.

lirismo *nm* lyricism.

lirón *nm* dormouse; *fig* **dormir como un l.**, to sleep like a log.

Lisboa *n* Lisbon.

lisiado,-a I *adj* crippled. II *nm,f* cripple.

lisiar [12] *vtr* to maim, cripple.

liso,-a *adj* 1 (*superficie*) smooth, even; *Dep* **los cien metros lisos**, the one hundred metres sprint. 2 (*pelo, falda*) straight. 3 (*tela*) self-coloured. 4 *Am* (*desvergonzado*) rude. II *adv* **lisa y llanamente**, purely and simply.

lisonjero,-a I *adj* flattering. II *nm,f* flatterer.

lista *nf* 1 (*relación*) list; **l. de espera**, waiting list; (*en avión*) standby; **pasar l.**, to call the register *o* the roll. 2 (*franja*) stripe; **de/a listas**, striped.

listado,-a I *adj* striped. II *nm* list; *Inform* listing.

listín *nm* **l. telefónico**, telephone directory.

listo,-a *adj* 1 *ser l.*, (*inteligente*) to be clever, smart. 2 *estar l.*, (*a punto*) to be ready.

listón *nm Dep* bar; *fig* **subir el l.**, to raise the requirements level.

litera *nf* (*cama*) bunk bed; (*en tren*) couchette.

literal *adj* literal.

literario,-a *adj* literary.

literato,-a *nm,f* writer, man *o* woman of letters.

literatura *nf* literature.

litigar [7] *vi Jur* to litigate.

litigio *nm Jur* lawsuit; *fig* dispute; **en l.**, in dispute.

litografía *nf* 1 (*técnica*) lithography. 2

(imagen) lithograph.

litoral I *nm* coast, seaboard. **II** *adj* coastal.

litro *nm* litre, *US* liter.

liturgia *nf* liturgy.

liviano,-a *adj (de poco peso)* lightweight.

lívido,-a *adj* livid.

liza *nf* contest.

llaga *nf* sore; *(herida)* wound.

llama I *nf* flame; **en llamas**, in flames, ablaze.

llamada *nf* call; *Tel* **l. interurbana**, long-distance call; **señal de l.**, ringing tone.

llamado,-a *adj* so-called.

llamamiento *nm* appeal.

llamar I *vtr* **1** to call; **l. (por teléfono)**, to ring up, call. **2** *(atraer)* to draw, attract; **l. la atención**, to attract attention. **4** *vi (a la puerta)* to knock. **III llamarse** *vr* to be called; **¿cómo te llamas?**, what's your name?

llamarada *nf* blaze.

llamativo,-a *adj* **1** *(color, ropa)* loud, flashy. **2** *(persona)* striking.

llaneza *nf (sencillez)* simplicity.

llano,-a I *adj* **1** *(superficie)* flat, level. **2** *(claro)* clear. **3** *(sencillo)* simple; **el pueblo l.**, the common people. **II** *nm* plain.

llanta *nf* **1** *(de rueda)* wheel rim. **2** *Am (neumático)* tyre, *US* tire.

llanto *nm* crying, weeping.

llanura *nf* plain.

llave *nf* key; **cerrar con l.**, to lock; **llaves en mano**, *(en anuncio)* available for immediate occupation; *Aut* **l. de contacto**, ignition key. **2** *Téc* spanner; **l. inglesa**, adjustable spanner. **3** *(interruptor)* switch; **l. de paso**, stopcock. **4** *(en lucha)* lock. **5** *Tip* brace.

llavero *nm* key ring.

llegada *nf* arrival; *Dep* finish.

llegar [7] **I** *vi* **1** to arrive; **l. a Madrid**, to arrive in Madrid. **2** *(ser bastante)* to be enough. **3** *(alcanzar)* to reach; **¿llegas al techo?**, can you reach the ceiling? **4** *fig* **1. a las manos**, to come to blows; **l. a presidente.**, to become president. **5 l. a** + *inf.*, to go so far as to. **6 l. a ser**, to become. **II llegarse** *vr* to stop by.

llenar I *vtr* **1** to fill; *(cubrir)* to cover. **2** *(satisfacer)* to satisfy. **II** *vi (comida)* to be filling. **III llenarse** *vr* to fill (up), become full.

lleno,-a I *adj* full (up); *fig* **de l.**, fully. **II** *nm Teat* full house.

llevadero,-a *adj* bearable, tolerable.

llevar I *vtr* **1** to take; *(hacia el oyente)* to bring; **adónde llevas eso?**, where are you taking that?; **te llevaré un regalo**, I'll bring you a present. **2** *(transportar)* to carry; **dejarse l.**, to get carried away. **3** *(prenda)* to wear; **llevaba falda**, she was wearing a skirt. **4** *(soportar)* to bear; **¿cómo lleva lo de su enfermedad?**, how's he bearing up? **5** *(tiempo)* **llevo dos años aquí**, I've been here for two years; **esto lleva mucho tiempo**, this takes a long time. **6** *(negocio)* to be in charge of. **II** *v aux* **1 l.** + *gerundio*, to have been + *present participle*; **llevo dos años estudiando español**, I've been studying Spanish for two years. **2 l.** + *participio pasado*, to have + *past participle*; **llevaba escritas seis cartas**, I had written six letters. **III llevarse** *vr* **1** to take away; *(premio)* to win; *(recibir)* to get. **2** *(arrastrar)* to carry away. **3** *(estar de moda)* to be fashionable. **4 l. bien con algn**, to get on well with sb.

llorar *vi* to cry; *Lit* weep.

llorica *nmf fam* crybaby.

lloriquear *vi* to whimper, snivel.

llorón,-ona *adj* **un bebé l.**, a baby which cries a lot.

lloroso,-a *adj* tearful.

llover [4] *v impers* to rain.

llovizna *nf* drizzle.

lloviznar *v impers* to drizzle.

lluvia *nf* rain; **una l. de**, lots of; **l. radiactiva**, fallout; **l. ácida**, acid rain.

lluvioso,-a *adj* rainy.

lo¹ *art det neut* **lo mejor**, the best (part); **lo mismo**, the same thing; **lo mío**, mine; **lo tuyo**, yours.

lo² *pron pers m & neut* **1** *(cosa)* it; **debes hacerlo**, you must do it; **no lo creo**, I don't think so; *(no se traduce)* **no se lo dije**, I didn't tell her; → **le**. **2 lo que ...**, what ...; **no sé lo que pasa**, I don't know what's going on. **3 lo cual ...**, which ... **4 lo de ...**, the business of ...; **cuéntame lo del juicio**, tell me about the trial.

loable *adj* praiseworthy, laudable.

loar *vtr* to praise.

lobo *nm* wolf; **como boca de l.**, pitch-dark; *fam* **¡menos lobos!**, pull the other one!

lóbrego,-a *adj* gloomy.

lóbulo *nm* lobe.

local I *adj* local. **II** *nm (recinto)* premises *pl*, site.

localidad *nf* **1** *(pueblo)* locality; *(en impreso)* place of residence. **2** *Cin Teat (asiento)* seat; *(entrada)* ticket.

localizar [4] *vtr* **1** *(encontrar)* to find. **2** *(fuego, dolor)* to localize.

loción *nf* lotion.

loco,-a I *adj* mad, crazy; **a lo l.**, crazily; **l. por**, crazy about; **volverse l.**, to go mad; *fam* **¡ni l.!**, I'd sooner die! **II** *nm,f* madman, madwoman; **hacerse el l.**, to act the fool.

locomotora *nf* locomotive.

locomotriz *adj* locomotive.

locuaz *adj* loquacious, talkative.

locución *nf* phrase.

locura *nf (enfermedad)* madness, insanity; **con l.**, madly; *fam* **esto es una l.**, this is crazy.

locutor,-a *nm,f TV Rad* presenter.

locutorio *nm* telephone booth.

lodo *nm* mud.

logaritmo *nm* logarithm.

lógica *nf* logic; **no tiene l.**, there's no logic to it.

lógico,-a *adj* logical; **era l. que ocurriera**, it was bound to happen.

logística *nf* logistics *sing o pl*.

logotipo *nm* logo.

lograr *vtr* 1 to get, obtain; *(premio)* to win; *(ambición)* to achieve. 2 **l. hacer algo**, to manage to do something.

logro *nm* achievement.

loma *nf* hillock, rise.

lombriz *nf* worm, earthworm.

lomo *nm* 1 *back;* a lomo(s), on the back, 2 *Culin* loin. 3 *(de libro)* spine.

lona *nf* canvas.

loncha *nf* slice; **l. de bacon**, rasher.

lonchería *nf Am* snack bar.

londinense I *adj* of *o* from London. II *nmf* native *o* inhabitant of London.

Londres *n* London.

longaniza *nf* spicy (pork) sausage.

longevo,-a *adj* long lived.

longitud *nf* 1 length; **dos metros de l.**, two metres long; **l. de onda**, wavelength; *Dep* **salto de l.**, long jump. 2 *Geog* longitude.

lonja¹ *nf (loncha)* slice; **l. de bacon**, rasher.

lonja² *nf* **l. de pescado**, fish market.

loquería *nf Am* mental asylum, mental hospital.

lord *nm (pl* **lores)** lord; *GB Parl* **Cámara de los Lores**, House of Lords.

loro *nm* parrot.

los¹ I *art def mpl* the; **l. libros**, the books; **cierra l. ojos**, close your eyes; **l. García**, the Garcías, **→ el, las y lo**. II *pron* **l. que**, *(personas)* those who; *(cosas)* the ones (that); **toma l. que quieras**, take whichever ones you want; **esos son l. míos/tuyos**, these are mine/yours; **→ las**.

los² *pron pers mpl* them; **¿l. has visto?**, have you seen them?

losa *nf (stone)* slab, flagstone.

lote *nm* 1 set. 2 *Com* lot. 3 *Inform* batch. 4 *fam* **darse el l.**, to pet.

lotería *nf* lottery; **me tocó la l.**, I won a prize in the lottery.

loto *nf* 1 *Bot* lotus. 2 *(lotería)* lottery.

loza *nf* 1 *(material)* earthenware. 2 *(de cocina)* crockery.

lozano,-a *adj* 1 *(persona)* healthy looking. 2 *(plantas)* lush, luxuriant.

Ltda. *abr de* **Limitada**, Limited, Ltd.

lubricante *nm* lubricant.

lubricar [1] *vtr* to lubricate.

lucero *nm* (bright) star.

lucidez *nf* lucidity.

lúcido,-a *adj* lucid, clear.

luciérnaga *nf* glow-worm.

lucir [35] I *vi* 1 *(brillar)* to shine. 2 *fam (compensar)* **no le luce lo que estudia**, his studies don't get him anywhere. II *vtr (ropas)* to sport; *(talento)* to display. III **lucirse** *vr* 1 *(hacer buen papel)* to do very well. 2 *(pavonearse)* to show off.

lucrativo,-a *adj* lucrative, profitable.

lucro *nm* profit, gain; **afán de l.**, greed for money.

lucha *nf* 1 fight, struggle; **l. de clases**, class struggle. 2 *Dep* wrestling; **l. libre**, free-style wrestling.

luchador,-a *nm,f* 1 fighter. 2 *Dep* wrestler.

luchar *vi* 1 to fight, struggle. 2 *Dep* to wrestle.

lúdico,-a *adj* relating to games, recreational.

luego I *adv* 1 *(después)* then, next, afterwards. 2 *(más tarde)* later (on); **¡hasta l.!**, so long!; *Am* **l. de**, after. 3 **desde l.**, of course. II *conj* therefore.

lugar *nm* 1 place; **en primer l.**, in the first place; **en l. de**, instead of; **sin l. a dudas**, without a doubt; **tener l.**, to take place. 2 **dar l. a**, to cause, give rise to.

lugareño,-a *adj & nm,f* local.

lugarteniente *nm* lieutenant.

lúgubre *adj* gloomy, lugubrious.

lujo *nm* luxury; **productos de l.**, luxury products; **no puedo permitirme ese l.**, I can't afford that.

lujoso,-a *adj* luxurious.

lujuria *nf* lechery, lust.

lujurioso,-a *adj* lecherous, lustful.

lumbre *nf* fire.

lumbrera *nf* luminary.

luminoso,-a *adj* luminous; *fig* bright.

luna *nf* 1 moon; *fig* **estar en la l.**, to have one's head in the clouds; **l. creciente/llena**, crescent/full moon; *fig* **l. de miel**, honeymoon. 2 *(de escaparate)* pane; *(espejo)* mirror.

lunar *nm (redondel)* dot; *(en la piel)* mole, beauty spot; **vestido de lunares**, spotted dress.

lunar *adj* lunar.

lunático,-a *nm,f* lunatic.

lunes *nm inv* Monday; **vendré el l.**, I'll come on Monday.

lupa *nf* magnifying glass.

luso,-a *adj & nm,f* Portuguese.

lustrar *vtr* to polish; *(zapatos)* to shine.

lustre *nm (brillo)* shine, lustre, *US* luster; *fig (esplendor)* splendour, *US* splendor, glory; **dar o sacar l. a algo**, to polish sth.

lustro *nm* five-year period.

lustroso,-a *adj* shiny, glossy.

luto *nm* mourning.

Luxemburgo *n* Luxembourg.

luz *nf* 1 light; **apagar la l.**, to put out the light; **a la l. de**, in the light of; **a todas luces**, obviously; *fig* **dar a l.**, *(parir)* to give birth to; *fig* **dar l. verde a**, to give the green light to. **2** *Aut* **light; luces de cruce**, dipped headlights; **luces de posición**, sidelights; **l. larga**, headlights *pl*. **3**

luces, *(inteligencia)* intelligence *sing*; **corto de l.**, dim-witted. **4 traje de luces**, bullfighter's costume.

luzco *indic pres* → **lucir**.

M

M, m ['eme] *nf (la letra)* M, m.

m 1 *abr de* **metro(s)**, metre, metres, *US* meter, meters, m. **2** *abr de* **minuto(s)**, minute, minutes, min. **3** *abr de* **milla(s)**, mile, miles.

macabro,-a *adj* macabre.

macana *nf* **1** *Am (palo)* club. **2** *(trasto)* rubbish.

macanear *vtr Am (paparruchas)* to make up.

macanudo,-a *adj fam* great, terrific.

macarra *nm arg* yob.

macarrón *nm* **1** macaroon. **2** *Elec* sheath.

macarrones *nmpl* macaroni *sing*.

macedonia *nf* fruit salad.

macerar *vtr* to macerate.

maceta *nf (tiesto)* plant pot, flowerpot.

machacar [1] **I** *vtr* **1** to crush; *Dep* to smash. **2** *fam (estudiar con ahínco)* to swot up on, *US* grind away at. **3** *fam (insistir en)* to harp on about, go on about. **II** *vi* **1** *fam (insistir mucho)* to harp on, go on. **2** *fam (estudiar con ahínco)* to swot, cram, *US* grind. **3** *(en baloncesto)* to smash.

machacón,-ona *fam* **I** *adj (repetitivo)* repetitious; *(pesado)* boring, tiresome. **II** *nm,f (muy estudioso)* swot, *US* grind.

machamartillo (a) *loc adv (con firmeza)* firmly; *(con obstinación)* obstinately.

machete *nm* machete.

machismo *nm* machismo, male chauvinism.

machista *adj & nm* male chauvinist.

macho 1 *adj* **1** *(animal, planta)* male. **2** *fam (viril)* manly, virile, macho. **II** *nm* **1** *(animal, planta)* male. **2** *Téc (pieza)* male piece *o* part; *(de enchufe)* plug. **3** *fam (hombre viril)* macho, he-man, tough guy.

machote *nm Am (borrador)* rough draft.

macilento,-a *adj* gaunt.

macizo,-a I *adj* **1** *(sólido)* solid; **de oro m.**, of solid gold. **2** *(robusto)* solid, robust; *fam (atractivo)* well built. **II** *nm (masa sólida)* mass.

macramé *nm* macramé.

macro- *pref* macro-.

macro *nf Inform* macro.

macroeconomía *nf* macroeconomics *sing*.

macuto *nm (morral)* knapsack, haversack.

madeja *nf (de lana etc)* hank, skein.

madera *nf* **1** wood; *(de construcción)* timber, wood. **2** *US* lumber; **de m.**, wood, wooden. **2** *fig* **tiene m. de líder**, he has all the makings of a leader.

madero *nm* **1** *(de construcción)* timber; *(le-*

ño) log. **2** *arg (policía)* cop; **los maderos**, the fuzz *pl*.

madrastra *nf* stepmother.

madre I *nf* **1** mother; **es m. de tres hijos**, she is a mother of three (children); **m. adoptiva**, adoptive mother; **m. alquilada**, surrogate mother; **m. de familia**, mother, housewife; **m. política**, mother-in-law; **m. soltera**, unmarried mother; *fig* **la m. patria**, one's motherland. **2** *(de río)* bed. **II** *interj* **¡m. de Dios!**, **¡m. mía!**, good heavens!

madreperla *nf (nácar)* mother-of-pearl.

madreselva *nf* honeysuckle.

Madrid *n* Madrid.

madriguera *nf* burrow, hole.

madrileño,-a I *adj o* from Madrid. **II** *nm,f* native *o* inhabitant of Madrid.

madrina *nf* **1** *(de bautizo)* godmother. **2** *(de boda)* ≈ bridesmaid. **3** *fig (protectora)* protectress.

madrugada *nf* **1** dawn; **de m.**, in the wee small hours. **2** early morning; **las tres de la m.**, three o'clock in the morning.

madrugador,-a I *adj* early rising. **II** *nm,f* early riser.

madrugar [7] *vi* to get up early.

madurar I *vtr fig (un plan)* to think out. **II** *vi* **1** *(persona)* to mature. **2** *(fruta)* to ripen.

madurez *nf* **1** maturity. **2** *(de la fruta)* ripeness.

maduro,-a *adj* **1** mature; **de edad madura**, middle-aged. **2** *(fruta)* ripe.

maestría *nf* mastery; **con m.**, masterfully.

maestro,-a I *nm,f* **1** *Educ* teacher; **m. de escuela**, schoolteacher. **2** *(especialista)* master; **m. de obras**, foreman. **3** *Mús* maestro. **II** *adj* **obra maestra**, masterpiece; **llave maestra**, master key.

mafia *nf* mafia.

mafioso,-a I *adj o* relating to the mafia. **II** *nm,f* member of the mafia, mafioso.

magdalena *nf* bun, cake.

magia *nf* magic; **por arte de m.**, as if by magic.

mágico,-a *adj* **1** magic. **2** *fig (maravilloso)* magical, wonderful.

magisterio *nm* teaching.

magistrado,-a *nm,f* judge; *Am* **primer m.**, prime minister.

magistral *adj (excelente)* masterly; **una jugada m.**, a master stroke.

magistratura *nf* magistracy.

magnánimo,-a *adj* magnanimous.

magnate *nm* magnate, tycoon.

magnesio *nm* magnesium.

magnético,-a *adj* magnetic.

magnetizar [4] *vtr* **1** (*imantar*) to magnetize. **2** *fig* (*hipnotizar*) to hypnotize.

magnetofón, magnetófono *nm* tape recorder.

magnetofónico,-a *adj* magnetic.

magnífico,-a *adj* magnificent, splendid.

magnitud *nf* magnitude, dimension; **de primera m.**, of the first order.

magno,-a *adj lit* great; **aula magna**, main amphitheatre.

mago,-a *nm,f* wizard, magician; **los tres Reyes Magos**, the Three Wise Men, the Three Kings.

magrear *vtr vulg* to grope.

magro,-a **I** *nm* (*de cerdo*) lean meat. **II** *adj* (*sin grasa*) lean.

magullar *I vtr* to bruise, damage. **II magullarse** *vr* to get bruised, get damaged.

mahometano,-a *adj & nm,f Rel* Mohammedan, Muslim.

mahonesa *nf* mayonnaise.

maillot *nm* (*malla*) leotard; *Dep* shirt.

maíz *nm* maize, *US* corn.

maizal *nm* field of maize *o US* corn.

majadería *nf* silly thing, absurdity.

majadero,-a *nm,f* fool, idiot.

majara, majareta *adj fam* loony, nutty.

majestad *nf* majesty.

majestuosidad *nf* majesty.

majestuoso,-a *adj* majestic, stately.

majo,-a *adj* (*bonito*) pretty, nice; *fam* (*simpático*) nice; **tiene un hijo muy m.**, she's got a lovely little boy; *fam* **ven aquí, m.**, come here, dear.

mal *I nm* **1** evil, wrong. **2** (*daño*) harm; **no le deseo ningún m.**, I don't wish him any harm. **3** (*enfermedad*) illness, disease. **II** *adj* **un m. año**, a bad year; → **malo,-a**. **III** *adv* badly, wrong; **lo hizo muy m.**, he did it very badly; **menos m. que ...**, it's a good job (that) ...; **no está (nada) m.**, it is not bad (at all); **te oigo/veo (muy) m.**, I can hardly hear/see you; **tomar a m.**, (*enfadarse*) to take badly.

malabar *adj* (*juegos*) **malabares**, juggling *sing*.

malabarista *nmf* juggler.

malapata *nf fam* (*mala suerte*) bad luck.

malaria *nf* malaria.

malcriado,-a **I** *adj* ill-mannered, ill-bred. **II** *nm,f* ill-mannered *o* uncivil person.

malcriar [29] *vtr* to spoil.

maldad *nf* **1** badness, evil. **2** (*acción perversa*) evil *o* wicked thing.

maldecir [12] **I** *vtr* to curse. **II** *vi* **1** (*blasfemar*) to curse. **2** (*criticar*) to speak ill (**de**, of).

maldición **I** *nf* curse. **II** *interj* damnation!

maldito,-a *adj* **1** *fam* (*molesto*) damned, bloody. **2** (*endemoniado*) damned, cursed;

¡maldita sea!, damn it!

maleante *adj & nmf* delinquent, criminal.

malear **I** *vtr fig* to corrupt, pervert. **II malearse** *vr* to go bad.

maleducado,-a **I** *adj* bad-mannered. **II** *nm,f* bad-mannered person.

maleficio *nm* (*hechizo*) curse, spell.

maléfico,-a *adj* evil, harmful.

malentendido *nm* misunderstanding.

malestar *nm* **1** (*molestia*) discomfort. **2** *fig* (*inquietud*) uneasiness; **tengo m.**, I feel uneasy.

maleta **I** *nf* suitcase, case; **hacer la m.**, to pack one's things *o* case. **II** *nm fam* (*persona*) bungler.

maletero *nm Aut* boot, *US* trunk.

maletín *nm* briefcase.

malévolo,-a *adj* malevolent.

maleza *nf* **1** (*arbustos*) thicket, undergrowth. **2** (*malas hierbas*) weeds *pl*.

malgastar *vtr & vi* to waste, squander.

malhablado,-a **I** *adj* foul-mouthed. **II** *nm,f* foulmouthed person.

malhechor,-a *nm,f* wrongdoer, criminal.

malhumor *nm* bad temper *o* mood; **de m.**, in a bad temper *o* mood.

malicia *nf* **1** (*mala intención*) malice, maliciousness. **2** (*astucia*) cunning, slyness. **3** (*maldad*) badness, evil.

malicioso,-a **I** *adj* malicious, spiteful. **II** *nm,f* malicious *o* spiteful person.

maligno,-a *adj* malignant.

malintencionado,-a **I** *adj* ill-intentioned. **II** *nm,f* ill-intentioned person.

malla *nf* **1** (*prenda*) leotard. **2** (*red*) mesh. **3** *Am* (*bañador*) swimsuit, swimming costume.

Mallorca *n* Majorca.

mallorquín,-ina *adj & nm,f* Majorcan.

malo,-a *adj* → **mal**. **1** bad; **un año m.**, a bad year; **estar a malas**, to be on bad terms; **por las malas**, by force. **2** (*persona*) (*malvado*) wicked, bad; (*travieso*) naughty. **3** (*de poca calidad*) bad, poor; **una mala canción/comida**, a poor song/ meal. **4** (*perjudicial*) harmful; **el tabaco es m.**, tobacco is harmful. **5** **lo m. es que ...**, the problem is that .... **6** (*enfermo*) ill, sick. **II** *nm,f fam* **el m.**, the baddy *o* villain.

malograr **I** *vtr* to upset. **II malograrse** *vr* to fail, fall through.

maloliente *adj* foul-smelling.

malparado,-a *adj* **salir m.**, to end up in a sorry state.

malpensado,-a **I** *adj* nasty-minded. **II** *nm,f* nasty-minded person.

malsonante *adj* (*grosero*) rude, offensive; **palabras malsonantes**, foul language.

malta *nf* (*cebada*) malt.

maltratado,-a *adj* battered.

maltratar *vtr* to ill-treat, mistreat.

maltrecho,-a *adj* in a sorry state, wrecked.

malva I *adj inv* mauve. II *nm* (*color*) mauve. III *nf Bot* mallow.

malvado,-a I *adj* evil, wicked. II *nm,f* villain, evil person.

malvender *vtr* to sell at a loss.

malversar *vtr* to misappropriate, embezzle.

Malvinas *npl* las (Islas M.), the Falkland Islands.

malvivir *vi* to live very badly.

mamá *nf fam* mum, mummy.

mama *nf* 1 (*de mujer*) breast; (*de animal*) teat. 2 *fam* (*mamá*) mum, mummy.

mamada *nf* (*bebé*) feed. 2 *vulg* (*felatio*) blow job.

mamadera *nf Am* feeding bottle.

mamar *vtr* (*leche*) to suck; *fig* (*adquirir*) to absorb.

mamarracho,-a *nm,f* (*persona*) ridiculous-looking person, mess, sight; (*cosa*) mess.

mameluco *nm fig* 1 fool, idiot, dim-wit. 2 *Am* boiler-suit.

mamífero,-a *nm,f* mammal.

mamón *nm vulg ofens* prick.

mampara *nf* screen.

mamporro *nm fam* wallop.

mampostería *nf* masonry.

mamut *nm* mammoth.

manada *nf* 1 *Zool* (*de vacas, elefantes*) herd; (*de ovejas*) flock; (*de lobos, perros*) pack; (*de leones*) pride. 2 *fam* (*multitud*) crowd, mob; **en manada(s)**, in crowds.

manager *nmf Dep Mús* manager.

manantial *nm* spring.

manar I *vi* to flow, run (**de**, from). II *vtr* to run with, flow with; **la herida manaba sangre**, blood flowed from his wound.

manazas *nmf inv* fam ham-fisted person.

mancebo *nm* 1 (*de farmacia*) assistant. 2 *arc* (*muchacho*) young man.

Mancha (La) *n* La Mancha.

Mancha[2] *n* el Canal de la M., the English Channel.

mancha *nf* stain, spot; mark, sunspot; **m. de tinta/vino**, ink/wine stain.

manchado,-a *adj* dirty, stained; **leche manchada**, milky coffee.

manchar I *vtr* to stain, dirty; *fig* to stain, blemish. II **mancharse** *vtr* to get dirty.

manchego,-a *adj* o *n* from La Mancha.

manco,-a I *adj* 1 (*de un brazo*) one-armed; (*sin brazos*) armless. 2 (*de una mano*) one-handed; (*sin manos*) handless. II *nm,f* 1 (*de brazos*) one-armed o armless person. 2 (*de manos*) one-handed o handless person.

mancomunidad *nf* community, association.

mancornas *nfpl Am* cufflinks.

mandado *nm* (*recado*) order, errand; **hacer un m.**, to run an errand.

mandamás *nmf* (*pl* **mandamases**) *fam* bigwig, boss.

mandamiento *nm* 1 (*orden*) order, command. 2 **los Diez Mandamientos**, the Ten Commandments.

mandar *vtr* 1 to order; *fam* ¿**mande**?, pardon? 2 (*grupo*) to lead, be in charge o command of; *Mil* to command. 3 (*enviar*) to send; **m. (a) por**, to send for; **m. algo por correo**, to post sth, send sth by the post; **m. recuerdos**, to send regards.

mandarina *nf* mandarin (orange), tangerine.

mandatario,-a *nm,f Pol* president.

mandato *nm* 1 (*orden*) order, command. 2 *Jur* writ, warrant. 3 *Pol* (*legislatura*) mandate, term of office.

mandíbula *nf* jaw; *fam* reír a m. batiente, to laugh one's head off.

mandil *nm* apron.

mando *nm* 1 (*autoridad*) command, control. 2 **los altos mandos del ejército**, high-ranking army officers. 3 *Téc* (*control*) controls *pl*; *Aut* **cuadro** o **tablero de mandos**, dashboard; **m. a distancia**, remote control; **palanca de m.**, *Téc* control lever; (*de avión, videojuego*) joystick.

mandón,-ona I *adj fam* bossy, domineering. II *nm,f fam* bossy o domineering person. III *nm Am* (mine) foreman.

manecilla *nf* (*de reloj*) hand.

manejable *adj* manageable; (*herramienta*) easy-to-use; (*coche*) manoeuvrable, *US* maneuvrable.

manejar I *vtr* 1 (*máquina*) to handle, operate; *fig* (*situación*) to handle. 2 (*negocio*) to run, manage. 3 *fig* (*a otra persona*) to domineer, boss about. 4 (*coche*) to drive. II **manejarse** *vtr* to manage.

manejo *nm* 1 (*uso*) handling, use; **de fácil m.**, easy-to-use. 2 *fig* (*de un negocio*) management; (*de un coche*) driving. 3 *fig* tricks *pl*.

manera *nf* 1 way, manner; **a mi/tu m.**, (in) my/your way; **de cualquier m.**, (*mal*) carelessly, any old how; (*en cualquier caso*) in any case; **de esta m.**, in this way; **de ninguna m.**, in no way, certainly not; **de todas maneras**, anyway, at any rate, in any case; **es mi m. de ser**, that's the way I am; **no hay m.**, it's impossible. 2 **de m. que**, so; **de tal m. que**, in such a way that. 3 **maneras**, manners; **de buenas maneras**, politely.

manga *nf* 1 sleeve; **de m. corta/larga**, short-/long-sleeved; **sin mangas**, sleeveless; *fig* hacer un corte de mangas a algn., ≈ to give sb the fingers; *fig* **m. por hombro**, messy and untidy; *fig* sacarse algo de la m., to pull sth out of one's hat. 2 (*de riego*) hose. 3 (*del mar*) arm. 4 *Dep* leg, round; *Ten* set.

mangante *arg nmf* thief.

mangar [7] *vtr arg* to pinch, nick, swipe.

mango *nm* handle.

mangonear *vi* 1 *fam* (*entrometerse*) to

meddle. 2 *fam* (*dar órdenes*) to throw one's weight around.

manguera nf hose.

mangui nmf *arg* thief.

manguito nm 1 (*para las mangas*) oversleeve; (*para flotar*) armband. 2 *Téc* sleeve.

maní nm (*pl* **manises**) peanut.

manía nf 1 dislike, ill will; **me tiene m.**, he has it in for me. 2 (*costumbre*) habit; **tiene la m. de llegar tarde**, he's always arriving late. 3 (*afición exagerada*) craze; **la m. de las motos**, the motorbike craze. 4 *Med* mania.

maníaco,-a, maniaco,-a adj & nm,f *Psic* manic; *fam* (*obseso*) maniac.

maniatar vtr to tie the hands of.

maniático,-a I adj fussy. II nm,f fusspot.

manicomio nm mental hospital.

manicura nf manicure.

manido,-a adj 1 (*comida*) off. 2 (*asunto*) trite, hackneyed.

manifestación nf 1 demonstration. 2 (*expresión*) manifestation, expression.

manifestante nmf demonstrator.

manifestar [1] I vtr 1 (*declarar*) to state, declare. 2 (*mostrar*) to show, display. II **manifestarse** vr 1 (*por la calle*) to demonstrate. 2 (*declararse*) to declare oneself; **se manifestó contrario a …**, he spoke out against …

manifiesto,-a I adj clear, obvious; **poner de m.**, (*revelar*) to reveal, show; (*hacer patente*) to make clear. II nm manifesto.

manigua nf *Am Geog* scrubland.

manilla nf 1 (*de reloj*) hand. 2 *Am* (*palanca*) lever.

manillar nm handlebar.

maniobra nf manoeuvre, *US* maneuver.

maniobrar vi to manoeuvre, *US* maneuver.

manipulación nf manipulation.

manipular vtr to manipulate; (*máquina*) to handle.

maniquí nm (*muñeco*) dummy.

manitas nmf inv *fam* 1 **ser un m.**, to be handy, be very good with one's hands. 2 **hacer m.**, to hold hands.

manivela nf *Téc* crank.

manjar nm dish, food.

mano nf 1 hand; **a m.**, (*sin máquina*) by hand; (*asequible*) at hand; **escrito a m.**, hand-written; **hecho a m.**, hand-made; **a m. armada**, armed; **estrechar la m. a algn**, to shake hands with sb; **de segunda m.**, second-hand; **echar una m. a algn**, to give sb a hand; **¡manos a la obra!**, shoulders to the wheel!; **meter m.**, (*a un problema*) to tackle; *vulg* to touch up; **traerse algo entre manos**, to be up to sth; **equipaje de m.**, hand luggage. 2 (*lado*) side; **a m. derecha/izquierda**, on the right/left(-hand side.) 3 **m. de pintura**, coat of paint. 4 **m. de obra**, labour (force).

manojo nm bunch; **ser un m. de nervios**, to be a bundle of nerves.

manopla nf mitten.

manoseado,-a adj (*objeto*) worn(-out); (*tema*) hackneyed.

manosear vtr to touch repeatedly, finger; *fam* to paw.

manotazo nm cuff, slap.

mansalva (a) loc adv (*en gran cantidad*) galore.

mansedumbre nf 1 (*de persona*) meekness, gentleness. 2 (*de animal*) tameness, docility.

manso,-a adj 1 (*persona*) gentle, meek. 2 (*animal*) tame, docile.

manta I nf 1 blanket; **m. eléctrica**, electric blanket. 2 (*zurra*) beating, hiding. II nmf *fam* lazy person, idler.

manteca nf (*de animal*) fat; **m. de cacao/cacahuete**, cocoa/peanut butter; **m. de cerdo**, lard.

mantecado nm shortcake.

mantel nm tablecloth.

mantener [24] I vtr 1 (*conservar*) to keep; **mantén el fuego encendido**, keep the fire burning; **m. la línea**, to keep in trim. 2 (*entrevista, reunión*) to have; **m. correspondencia con algn**, to correspond with sb. 3 (*ideas, opiniones*) to defend, maintain. 4 (*familia*) to support, feed. 5 (*peso*) to support, hold up. II **mantenerse** vr 1 (*sostenerse*) to stand. 2 **m. firme**, (*perseverar*) to hold one's ground. 3 (*sustentarse*) to live (**de**, on).

mantenimiento nm 1 *Téc* maintenance, upkeep; **servicio de m.**, maintenance service. 2 (*alimento*) sustenance, support. 3 **gimnasia y m.**, keep-fit.

mantequilla nf butter.

manto nm cloak.

mantón nm shawl.

mantuve pt indef → **mantener**.

manual I adj manual; **trabajo m.**, manual labour; *Educ* **trabajos manuales**, handicrafts. II nm manual, handbook.

manufactura nf 1 (*fabricación*) manufacture. 2 (*fábrica*) factory.

manufacturar vtr to manufacture.

manuscrito,-a nm manuscript.

manutención nf maintenance.

manzana nf 1 apple. 2 (*de edificios*) block.

manzanilla nf 1 *Bot* camomile. 2 (*infusión*) camomile tea. 3 (*vino*) manzanilla.

maña nf 1 (*astucia*) cunning. 2 (*habilidad*) skill.

mañana I nf morning; **a las dos de la m.**, at two in the morning; **de m.**, early in the morning; **por la m.**, in the morning. II nm tomorrow, the future. III adv tomorrow; **¡hasta m.!**, see you tomorrow! **m. por la m.**, tomorrow morning; **pasado m.**, the day after tomorrow.

mañoso,-a adj skilful, *US* skillful.

mapa *nm* map; **m. mudo**, blank map; *fam* **borrar del m.**, to wipe out. **2** *fam* demo (tape).

maqueta *nf* **1** *(miniatura)* scale model, maquette. **2** *Mús* demo (tape).

maquiavélico,-a *adj* Machiavellian.

maquillaje *nm* make-up.

maquillar I *vtr* to make up. **II maquillarse** *vr* **1** *(ponerse maquillaje)* to put one's make-up on, make (oneself) up. **2** *(usar maquillaje)* to wear make-up.

máquina *nf* **1** machine; **escrito a m.**, typewritten; **hecho a m.**, machine-made; *fam* **a toda m.**, at full speed. **m. de afeitar (eléctrica)**, (electric) razor *o* shaver; **m. de coser**, sewing machine; **m. de escribir**, typewriter; **m. fotográfica** *o* **de fotos**, camera; **m. tragaperras**, slot machine, one-armed bandit. **2** *fam (coche)* car.

maquinar *vtr* to machinate, plot.

maquinaria *nf* **1** machinery, machines *pl.* **2** *(de reloj etc) (mecanismo)* mechanism, works *pl.*

maquinilla *nf* **m. de afeitar**, safety razor.

maquinista *nmf (de tren)* engine driver.

mar *nm & f* **1** sea; **en alta m.**, on the high seas; **m. adentro**, out to sea; **por m.**, by sea; **m. gruesa**, heavy sea; **m. picada**, rough sea. **2** *fam* **está la m. de guapa**, she's looking really beautiful; **llover a mares**, to rain cats and dogs. **II** *nm* sea. **M. del Norte**, North Sea; **M. Muerto/Negro**, Dead/Black Sea.

maraña *nf* tangle.

maratón *nm* marathon.

maratoniano,-a *adj* marathon.

maravilla *nf* marvel, wonder; **de m.**, wonderfully; **¡qué m. de película!**, what a wonderful film!; *fam* **a las mil maravillas**, marvellously.

maravillar I *vtr* to amaze, astonish. **II maravillarse** *vr* to marvel *(con,* at), wonder *(con,* at).

maravilloso,-a *adj* wonderful, marvellous, *US* marvelous.

marca *nf* **1** mark, sign. **2** *Com* brand, make; **ropa de m.**, brand-name clothes; **m. de fábrica**, trademark; **m. registrada**, registered trademark. **3** *Dep (récord)* record; **batir la m. mundial**, to break the world record.

marcador,-a *nm* **1** marker. **2** *Dep (tablero)* scoreboard; *(persona)* scorer.

marcaje *nm* *Dep* marking.

marcapasos *nm inv Med* pacemaker.

marcar [1] **I** *vtr* **1** to mark. **2** *Tel* to dial. **3** *(indicar)* to indicate, show; **el contador marca 1.327**, the meter reads 1,327. **4** *Dep (gol, puntos)* to score; *(a jugador)* to mark. **5** *(cabello)* to set. **II marcarse** *vr* *fam* **m. un farol**, to show off, boast.

marcha *nf* **1** march; **hacer algo sobre la m.**, to do sth as one goes along; **a marchas forzadas**, against the clock. **2 estar**

en m., *(vehículo)* to be in motion; *(máquina)* to be working; *(proyecto etc)* to be under way; **poner en m.**, to start. **3** *Aut* gear; **m. atrás**, reverse (gear). **4** *Mús* march. **5** *fam (juerga)* **hay mucha m.**, there's lots going on; **ella tiene mucha m.**, she likes a good time.

marchar I *vi* **1** *(ir)* to go, walk; *fam* **¡marchando!**, on your way!; **¡una cerveza! - ¡marchando!**, a beer, please! - coming right up! **2** *(aparato)* to be on; **m. bien**, *(negocio)* to be going well. **3** *Mil* to march. **II marcharse** *or (irse)* to leave, go away.

marchitar *vtr*, **marchitarse** *vr* to shrivel, wither.

marchito,-a *adj* shrivelled, *US* shriveled, withered.

marchoso,-a *fam* **I** *adj (persona)* fun-loving, wild. **II** *nm,f* raver, fun lover.

marcial *adj* martial; **artes marciales**, martial arts.

marcianitos *nmpl (juego)* space invaders.

marciano,-a *adj & nm,f* Martian.

marco *nm* **1** *(de cuadro etc)* frame. **2** *fig (ámbito)* framework; **acuerdo m.**, framework agreement. **3** *Fin (moneda)* mark.

marea *nf* **1** tide; **m. alta/baja**, high/low tide; **m. negra**, oil slick. **2** *fig (multitud)* crowd, mob.

mareado,-a *adj* **1** sick; *(en un avión)* airsick; *(en un coche)* carsick, travel-sick; *(en el mar)* seasick. **2** *euf (bebido)* tipsy. **3** *(aturdido)* dizzy.

marear I *vtr* **1** to make sick; *(en el mar)* to make seasick; *(en un avión)* to make airsick; *(en un coche)* to make carsick *o* travel-sick. **2** *(aturdir)* to make dizzy. **3** *fam (fastidiar)* to annoy, pester. **4** *Culin* to stir. **II marearse** *vr* **1** to get sick/ seasick/airsick/carsick *o* travel-sick. **2** *(quedar aturdido)* to get dizzy. **3** *euf (emborracharse)* to get tipsy.

mareo *nm* **1** *(náusea)* sickness; *(en el mar)* seasickness; *(en un avión)* airsickness; *(en un coche)* carsickness, travel-sickness. **2** *(aturdimiento)* dizziness, lightheadedness.

marfil *nm* ivory.

margarina *nf* margarine.

margarita *nf* daisy.

margen *nm* **1** border, edge; *(de río)* bank; *fig* **dejar algn/algo al m.**, to leave sb/sth out; *fig* **mantenerse al m.**, not to get involved; **al margen de**, leaving aside. **2** *(del papel)* margin. **3** *Com* **m. beneficiario**, profit margin.

marginación *nf (exclusión)* exclusion.

marginado,-a I *adj* excluded. **II** *nm,f* dropout.

marginal *adj* **1** marginal. **2** *Pol* fringe.

marginar *vtr (de un grupo, sociedad)* to leave out, exclude.

maría *nf arg* **1** *(droga)* marijuana, pot. **2** *Educ arg (asignatura fácil)* easy subject. **3**

fam (ama de casa) housewife.

marica *nm vulg ofens* queer, poof.

maricón *nm vulg ofens* queer, poof.

marido *nm* husband.

mariguana, marihuana, marijuana *nf* marijuana.

marimacho *nm vulg* mannish woman, butch woman.

marimandón,-ona *nm,f fam* domineering person.

marimorena *nf fam* row, fuss; *fam* **armar(se) la m.,** to kick up a racket.

marina *nf* 1 *Náut* seamanship. 2 *Mil* navy; **m. de guerra,** navy; **m. mercante,** merchant navy. 3 *Geog (zona costera)* seacoast.

marinero,-a I *nm* sailor, seaman. II *adj* seafaring.

marino,-a I *adj* marine, brisa marina, sea breeze. II *nm* sailor.

marioneta *nf* marionette, puppet.

mariposa *nf* 1 *Ent* butterfly. 2 *(lamparilla)* oil lamp. 3 *Natación* butterfly.

mariposear *vi fig (flirtear)* to flirt. 2 *(ser inconstante)* to be fickle.

mariposón *nm* 1 *(galanteador)* flirt. 2 *ofens (marica)* queer, pansy, poof.

mariquita I *nf Ent* ladybird. II *nm fam ofens (marica)* queer, pansy, poof.

mariscal *nm Mil* marshal; **m. de campo,** field marshal.

marisco *nm* shellfish; **mariscos,** seafood.

marisma *nf* marsh.

marisquería *nf* seafood restaurant, shellfish bar.

marítimo,-a *adj* maritime, sea; **ciudad marítima,** coastal town; **paseo m.,** promenade.

mármol *nm* marble.

marmóreo,-a *adj* marble.

maroma *nf* 1 *Náut* cable. 2 *(cuerda)* thick rope.

marqués *nm* marquis.

marquesa *nf* marchioness.

marquesina *nf* canopy; **m. (del autobús),** bus shelter.

marquetería *nf* marquetry, inlaid work.

marrano,-a I *adj (sucio)* filthy, dirty. II *nm,f fam (persona)* dirty pig, slob. 2 *(animal)* pig.

marras (de) *loc adv* **el individuo de m.,** the man in question.

marrón I *adj (color)* brown. II *nm* 1 *(color)* brown. 2 *arg (condena)* sentence.

marroquí *adj & nmf* Moroccan.

marroquinería *nf* leather goods.

Marruecos *n* Morocco.

marrullero,-a I *adj* cajoling, wheedling. II *nm,f* cajoler, wheedler.

Marte *n* Mars.

martes *nm inv* Tuesday; **m. y trece,** ≈ Friday the thirteenth.

martillo *nm* hammer.

mártir *nmf* martyr.

martirio *nm* 1 martyrdom. 2 *fig (fastidio)* torment.

martirizar [4] *vtr* 1 to martyr. 2 *fig (fastidiar)* to torture, torment.

marxista *adj & nmf* Marxist.

marzo *nm* March.

mas *conj* lit but.

más I *adv* 1 *(adicional)* more; **no tengo m.,** I haven't got any more. 2 *(comparativo)* more; **es m. alta/inteligente que yo,** she's taller/more intelligent than me; **tengo más dinero que tú,** I've more money than you; **más gente de la que esperas,** more people than you're expecting; **m. de,** *(con numerales, cantidad)* more than, over. 3 *(superlativo)* most; **es el m. bonito/caro,** it's the prettiest/most expensive. 4 *exclam* so ..., what a ...; **¡qué casa m. bonita!,** what a lovely house! **¡está m. guapa!,** she looks so beautiful! 5 *(después de pron interr e indef)* else; **¿algo m.?,** anything else?; **no, nada m.,** no, nothing else; **¿quién m.?,** who else?; **nadie/alguien m.,** nobody/somebody else. 7 **cada día o vez m.,** more and more; **estar de m.,** to be unnecessary; **traje uno de m.,** I brought a spare one; **es m.,** what's more, furthermore; **lo m. posible,** as much as possible; **m. bien,** rather; **m. o menos,** more or less; **m. aún,** even more; **¿qué m. da?,** what's the difference?; **todo lo m.,** at the most. 8 **por m. + (adj/adv +) que + subj,** however (much), no matter how (much); **por m. fuerte que sea,** however strong he may be; **por m. que grites no te oirá nadie,** no matter how much you shout nobody will hear you.

II *nm inv* **los/las m.,** the majority, most people; **sus m. y sus menos,** its pros and cons.

III *prep Mat* plus; **dos m. dos,** two plus o and two.

masa *nf* 1 mass. 2 *(de cosas)* bulk, volume; **m. salarial,** total wage bill. 3 *(gente)* mass; **en m.,** en masse; **medios de comunicación de masas,** mass media. 4 *Culin* dough. 5 *Constr* mortar.

masacrar *vtr* to massacre.

masacre *nf* massacre.

masaje *nm* massage; **dar masaje(s) (a),** to massage.

masajista *nmf (hombre)* masseur; *(mujer)* masseuse.

mascar [1] *vtr & vi* to chew, masticate.

máscara *nf* mask; **m. de gas,** gas mask; **traje de m.,** fancy dress.

mascarilla *nf* 1 mask; **m. de oxígeno,** oxygen mask. 2 *Med* face mask. 3 *(cosmética)* face pack.

mascota *nf* mascot.

masculino,-a *adj* 1 *Zool Bot* male. 2 *(de hombre)* male, manly; **una voz masculina,** a manly voice. 3 *(para hombre)* men's; **ropa masculina**, men's clothes, menswear. **4** *Ling* masculine.

mascullar *vtr* to mumble.

masificación *nf* overcrowding.

masificado,-a *adj* overcrowded.

masilla *nf* putty.

masivo,-a *adj* massive.

masón *nm* freemason, mason.

masonería *nf* freemasonry, masonry.

masoquista **I** *adj* masochistic. **II** *nmf* masochist.

máster *nm* master's degree.

masticar [1] *vt* to chew.

mástil *nm* **1** (*asta*) mast, pole. **2** *Náut* mast. **3** (*de guitarra*) neck.

mastín *nm* mastiff.

masturbación *nf* masturbation.

masturbar *vtr*, **masturbarse** *vr* to masturbate.

mata *nf* **1** (*matorral*) bush, shrub; **m. de pelo**, head of hair. **2** (*ramita*) sprig.

matadero *nm* slaughterhouse, abattoir.

matador *nm* matador, bullfighter.

matadura *nf* sore.

matamoscas *nm inv* (*pala*) fly swat.

matanza *nf* slaughter.

matar *vtr* **1** to kill; *fam* **m. el hambre/el tiempo**, to kill one's hunger/the time; *fam* **que me maten si ...**, I'll be damned if .... **2** (*cigarro, bebida*) to finish off. **3** (*sello*) to frank.

matasellos *nm inv* postmark.

matasuegras *nm inv* party blower.

mate[1] *adj* (*sin brillo*) matt.

mate[2] *nm Ajedrez* mate; **jaque m.**, checkmate.

matemática *nf*, **matemáticas** *nfpl* mathematics *sing*.

matemático,-a **I** *adj* mathematical. **II** *nm,f* mathematician.

materia *nf* **1** matter; **m. prima**, raw material. **2** (*tema*) matter, question; **índice de materias**, table of contents. **3** *Educ* (*asignatura*) subject.

material **I** *adj* material, physical; **daños materiales**, damage to property. **II** *nm* **1** material; **m. escolar/de construcción**, teaching/building material *o* materials *pl*. **2** (*equipo*) equipment; **m. de oficina**, office equipment. ◆**materialmente** *adv* physically.

materialista *adj* & *nmf* materialist.

maternal *adj* maternal, motherly.

maternidad *nf* maternity, motherhood.

materno,-a *adj* maternal; **abuelo m.**, maternal grandfather; **lengua materna**, native *o* mother tongue.

mates *nfpl fam* maths *sing*, *US* math *sing*.

matinal *adj* morning; **televisión m.**, breakfast television.

matiz *nm* **1** (*de color*) shade. **2** (*de palabra*) shade of meaning, nuance; **un m. irónico**, a touch of irony.

matización *nf* **hacer una m.**, to add a

rider.

matizar [1] *vtr* **1** *fig* (*precisar*) to be more precise *o* explicit about. **2** *Arte* to blend, harmonize. **3** *fig* (*palabras, discurso*) to tinge; (*voz*) to vary, modulate.

matón,-ona *nm,f fam* thug, bully.

matorral *nm* brushwood, thicket.

matraca *nf* (*ruido*) rattle; *fam* **dar la m. a algn**, to pester *o* bother sb.

matrero,-a *nm,f Am* (*bandolero*) bandit, brigand.

matriarcado *nm* matriarchy.

matrícula *nf* **1** registration; **derechos de m.**, registration fee; **m. de honor**, distinction; **plazo de m.**, registration period. **2** *Aut* (*número*) registration number; (*placa*) number *o US* license plate.

matriculación *nf* registration.

matricular *vtr*, **matricularse** *vr* to register.

matrimonial *adj* matrimonial; **agencia m.**, marriage bureau; **enlace m.**, wedding; **vida m.**, married life.

matrimonio *nm* **1** marriage; **m. civil/religioso**, registry office/church wedding; **contraer m.**, to marry; **cama de m.**, double bed. **2** (*pareja casada*) married couple; **el m. y los niños**, the couple and their children; **el m. Romero**, Mr and Mrs Romero, the Romeros.

matriz *nf* **1** *Anat* womb, uterus. **2** *Mat* matrix. **3** (*de documento*) (*original*) original, master copy. **4** *Téc* mould, *US* mold. **5** **casa m.**, parent company.

matrona *nf* midwife.

matutino,-a *adj* morning; **prensa matutina**, morning papers.

maullar [16] *vi* to miaow.

maullido *nm* miaowing, miaow.

maxilar *nm* jaw, jawbone.

máxima *nf* **1** *nf Meteor* maximum temperature. **2** (*aforismo*) maxim.

máxime *adv* especially, all the more so.

máximo,-a **I** *adj* maximum, highest; **la máxima puntuación**, the highest score. **II** *nm* maximum; **al m.**, to the utmost; **como m.**, (*como mucho*) at the most; (*lo más tarde*) at the latest.

mayo *nm* May.

mayonesa *nf* mayonnaise.

mayor **I** *adj* **1** (*comparativo*) (*tamaño*) larger, bigger (**que**, than); (*edad*) older, elder; **m. que yo**, older than me. **2** (*superlativo*) (*tamaño*) largest, biggest; (*edad*) oldest, eldest; **la m. parte**, the majority; **la m. parte de las veces**, most often. **3** (*adulto*) grown-up; **ser m. de edad**, to be of age. **4** (*maduro*) elderly, mature. **5** (*principal*) major, main; *Educ* **colegio m.**, hall of residence. **6** *Mús* major. **7** *Com* **al por m.**, wholesale; *fig* (*en abundancia*) by the score, galore. **II** *nm* **1** *Mil* major. **2** **mayores**, (*adultos*) grown-

ups, adults.
mayordomo *nm* butler.
mayoría *nf* majority; **en su m.**, in the main; **la m. de los niños**, most children; **m. absoluta/relativa**, absolute/relative majority; **m. de edad**, majority.
mayorista I *adj* wholesale. II *nmf* wholesaler; **precios de m.**, wholesale prices.
mayoritario,-a *adj* majority; **un gobierno m.**, a majority government.
mayúscula *nf* capital letter.
mayúsculo,-a *adj* 1 *Ling (letra)* capital. 2 *(error)* very big, enormous.
mazacote *nm* 1 *Culin* solid mass, stodge. 2 *(mezcla confusa)* hotch-potch.
mazapán *nm* marzipan.
mazmorra *nf* dungeon.
mazo *nm* mallet.
mazorca *nf Agr* cob.
me *pron pers* 1 *(objeto directo)* me; **no me mires**, don't look at me. 2 *(objeto indirecto)* me, to me, for me; **¿me das un caramelo?**, will you give me a sweet?; **me lo dio**, he gave it to me; **me es difícil hacerlo**, it is difficult for me to do it. 3 *(pron reflexivo)* myself; **me he cortado**, I've cut myself; **me voy/muero**, *(no se traduce)* I'm off/dying.
meada *nf vulg* piss; **echar una m.**, to have a piss.
meadero *nm vulg* bog.
meandro *nm* meander.
mear I *vi vulg* to have (a) piss. II **mearse** *vr* to wet oneself; *fig* **m. de risa**, to piss oneself (laughing).
MEC *nm abr de* **Ministerio de Educación y Ciencia**, Department of Education and Science.
mecachis *fam interj* darn it!, damn it!
mecánica *nf* 1 *(ciencia)* mechanics *sing*. 2 *(mecanismo)* mechanism, works *pl*.
mecánico,-a I *adj* mechanical. II *nm,f* mechanic.
mecanismo *nm* mechanism.
mecanizar [4] *vtr* to mechanize.
mecanografía *nf* typewriting, typing.
mecanografiar [29] *vtr* to type.
mecanógrafo,-a *nm,f* typist.
mecedora *nf* rocking chair.
mecenas *nmf inv* patron.
mecer [2] I *vtr* to rock. II **mecerse** *vr* to swing, rock.
mecha *nf* 1 *(de vela)* wick. 2 *Mil Min* fuse; *fam* **aguantar m.**, to grin and bear it. 3 *(de pelo)* streak; **hacerse mechas**, to have one's hair streaked.
mechar *vtr (carne)* to lard.
mechero,-a *nm* (cigarette) lighter.
mechón *nm* 1 *(de pelo)* lock. 2 *(de lana)* tuft.
medalla I *nf* medal. II *nmf Dep (campeón)* medallist, *US* medalist.
medallón *nm* medallion.

(promedio) average; *Mat* mean; **m. aritmética/geométrica**, arithmetic/geometric mean. 3 **a medias**, *(incompleto)* unfinished; *(entre dos)* half and half; **ir a medias**, to go halves.
mediación *nf* mediation, intervention; **por m. de un amigo**, through a friend.
mediado,-a *adj* half-full, half-empty; **a mediados de mes/semana**, about the middle of the month/week.
mediador,-a *nm,f* mediator.
medialuna *nf* 1 *(símbolo musulmán)* crescent. 2 *Am Culin (pasta)* croissant.
mediano,-a *adj* 1 *(calidad)* middling, average. 2 *(tamaño)* medium-sized.
medianoche *nf* midnight.
mediante *prep* by means of, with the help of, using; **Dios m.**, God willing.
mediar [12] *vi* 1 *(intervenir)* to mediate, intervene; **m. en favor de** o **por algn**, to intercede on behalf of sb. 2 *(tiempo)* to pass; **mediaron tres semanas**, three weeks passed.
mediático,-a *adj* media.
medicación *nf* medication, medical treatment.
medicamento *nm* medicine, medicament.
medicina *nf* medicine; **estudiante de m.**, medical student, medic.
médico,-a I *nm,f* doctor; **m. de cabecera**, family doctor, general practitioner, GP. II *adj* medical.
medida *nf* 1 measure; **a (la) m.**, *(ropa)* made-to-measure; **a m. que avanzaba**, as he advanced; **en gran m.**, to a great extent. 2 *(dimensión)* measurement. 3 *(disposición)* measure; **adoptar** o **tomar medidas**, to take steps; **m. represiva**, deterrent.
medieval *adj* medieval.
medievo *nm* Middle Ages *pl*.
medio,-a I *adj* 1 half; **a m. camino**, half-way; **m. kilo**, half a kilo; **una hora y media**, one and a half hours, an hour and a half. 2 *(intermedio)* middle; **a media mañana/tarde**, in the middle of the morning/afternoon; **clase media**, middle class; **punto m.**, middle ground. 3 *(normal)* average; **salario m.**, average wage. II *adv* half; **está m. muerta**, she is half dead. III *nm* 1 *(mitad)* half. 2 *(centro)* middle; **en m. (de)**, *(en el centro)* in the middle (of); *(entre dos)* in between. 3 **medios de transporte**, means of transport; **por m. de ...**, by means of ...; **medios económicos**, means; **medios de comunicación**, (mass) media. 4 **m. ambiente**, environment. 5 *Dep (jugador)* halfback.
medioambiental *adj* environmental.
medioambientalista *nmf* environmentalist.
mediocre *adj* mediocre.
mediocridad *nf* mediocrity.
mediodía *nm* 1 *(hora exacta)* midday,

noon. 2 *(período aproximado)* early afternoon, lunchtime. 3 *(sur)* south.

medir [6] I *vtr* 1 *(distancia, superficie, temperatura)* to measure. 2 *(moderar)* to weigh; **mide tus palabras**, weigh your words. II *vi* to measure, be; **¿cuánto mides?**, how tall are you?; **mide dos metros**, he is two metres tall; **mide dos metros de alto/ancho/largo**, it is two metres high/wide/long.

meditar *vtr & vi* to meditate, ponder; **m. sobre algo**, to ponder over sth.

mediterráneo,-a I *adj* Mediterranean. II *nm* **el M.**, the Mediterranean.

medrar *vi* to climb the social ladder.

medroso,-a *adj* 1 *(temeroso)* fearful, fainthearted. 2 *(que causa miedo)* frightening.

médula *nf* 1 marrow; **m. ósea**, bone marrow. 2 *fig (lo más profundo)* marrow, pith; **hasta la m.**, to the marrow.

medusa *nf* jellyfish.

megafonía *nf* public-address system, PA system.

megáfono *nm* megaphone.

megalito *nm* megalith.

megalómano,-a *nm,f* megalomaniac.

mejicano,-a *adj & nm,f* Mexican.

Méjico *n* Mexico; **ciudad de M.**, Mexico City; **Nuevo M.**, New Mexico.

mejilla *nf* cheek.

mejillón *nm* mussel.

mejor I *adj* 1 *(comparativo)* better **(que**, than); **el m. de los dos**, the better of the two; **es m. no decírselo**, it's better not to tell her; **es m. que vayas**, you'd better go. 2 *(superlativo)* best; **el m. de los tres**, the best of the three; **tu m. amiga**, your best friend; **lo m.**, the best thing. II *adv* 1 *(comparativo)* better **(que**, than); **cada vez m.**, better and better; **ella conduce m.**, she drives better; **m. dicho**, or rather; **¡mucho o tanto m.!**, so much the better! 2 *(superlativo)* best; **es él que m. canta**, he is the one who sings the best; **a lo m.**, *(quizás)* perhaps; *(ojalá)* hopefully.

mejora *nf* improvement.

mejorar I *vtr* to improve; **m. la red vial**, to improve the road system; **m. una marca o un récord**, to break a record. II *vi* to improve, get better. III **mejorarse** *vr* to get better; **¡que te mejores!**, get well soon!

mejoría *nf* improvement.

melancolía *nf* melancholy.

melancólico,-a *adj* melancholic, melancholy.

melé *nf Dep* scrum.

melena *nf* (head of) hair; *(de león)* mane.

Melilla *n* Melilla.

melindroso,-a I *adj* affected, fussy, finicky. II *nm,f* affected o finicky person.

mella *nf* 1 *(hendedura)* nick, notch; *(en plato, taza etc)* chip. 2 *(en dentadura)* gap.

3 *fig* impression; **hacer m. en algn**, to make an impression on sb.

mellado,-a *adj (sin dientes)* gap-toothed.

mellizo,-a *adj & nm,f* twin.

melocotón *nm* peach.

melodía *nf* melody, tune.

melodrama *nm* melodrama.

melón *nm* 1 *(fruto)* melon. 2 *fam (tonto)* ninny. 3 *vulg* **melones**, *(tetas)* boobs.

melopea *nf fam* **coger o agarrar/llevar una m.**, to get/be drunk o pissed.

meloso,-a *adj* sweet, honeyed.

membrana *nf* membrane.

membrete *nm* letterhead.

membrillo *nm* 1 *Bot* quince; *(árbol)* quince tree; *(dulce)* quince preserve o jelly. 2 *fam (tonto)* dimwit.

memo,-a *fam* I *adj* silly, stupid. II *nm,f* nincompoop, ninny.

memorable *adj* memorable.

memorándum *nm (pl* **memorándums)** memorandum.

memoria *nf* 1 memory; **aprender/saber algo de m.**, to learn/know sth by heart; **irse de la m.**, to slip one's mind. 2 *(informe)* report, statement; **m. anual**, annual report. 3 *(recuerdo)* memory, recollection. 4 **memorias**, *(biografía)* memoirs.

memorístico *adj* acquired by memory.

memorizar [4] *vtr* to memorize.

menaje *nm* furniture and furnishing *pl*; **m. de cocina**, kitchen equipment o utensils.

mención *nf* mention; **m. honorífica**, honourable mention.

mencionar *vtr* to mention.

mendicidad *nf* begging.

mendigar [7] *vtr & vi* to beg.

mendigo,-a *nm,f* beggar.

mendrugo *nm* 1 crust o chunk (of stale bread). 2 *(tonto)* dimwit.

menear I *vtr* to shake, move; *(cola)* to wag, waggle; *fam (culo)* to wiggle. II **menearse** *vr* to move, shake; *fam* **una tormenta de no te menees**, a hell of a storm; *vulg* **meneársela**, to wank.

meneo *nm* shake; *(de cola)* wag, waggle; *(de culo)* wiggle.

menester *nm* 1 **es m.**, it is necessary. 2 **menesteres**, *(deberes)* jobs.

menestra *nf* vegetable stew.

mengano,-a *nm,f* so-and-so, what's-his o her-name.

menguante *adj* waning, on the wane; **cuarto m.**, last quarter.

menguar [22] I *vtr* 1 to diminish, reduce. 2 *(en labor de punto)* to decrease. II *vi* 1 to diminish, decrease. 2 *(la luna)* to wane.

meñique *adj & nm* **(dedo) m.**, little finger.

menopausia *nf Med* menopause.

menor I *adj* 1 *(comparativo)* *(de tamaño)*

smaller (que, than); (de edad) younger (que, than); **mal m.**, the lesser of two evils; **el m. de los dos**, the smaller of the two; **ser m. de edad**, to be a minor o under age. 2 (superlativo) (de tamaño) smallest; (de intensidad) least, slightest; **al m. ruido**, at the slightest noise; (de edad) youngest; **el m. de los tres**, the youngest of the three; **es la m.**, she's the youngest child. 3 Mús minor. 4 Com **al por m.**, retail. II nmf minor; Jur **tribunal de menores**, juvenile court.

menos adj 1 (comparativo) (con singular) less; (con plural) fewer; **m. dinero/leche/tiempo que**, less money/milk/time than; **m. libros/pisos que**, fewer books/flats than; (con cláusula) **tiene m. años de lo que parece**, he's younger than he looks. 2 (superlativo) **fui el que perdí m. dinero**, I lost the least money. II adv 1 **m. de**, (con singular) less than; **m. de media hora**, less than a half hour; (con plural) fewer than, less than. 2 (superlativo) (con singular) least; (con plural) the fewest; **el m. inteligente de la clase**, the least intelligent boy in the class; **ayer fue cuando vinieron m. personas**, yesterday was when the fewest people came; (con cantidad) the least. III (locuciones) **a m. que** + subj, unless; **al o por lo m.**, at least; **echar a algo m. de**, to miss sb; **eso es lo de m.**, that's the least of it; **¡m. mal!**, just as well!; **nada m. que**, no less o no fewer than; **ni mucho m.**, far from it. IV prep 1 but, except; **todo m. eso**, anything but that. 2 Mat minus; **tres m. uno**, three minus one.

menoscabar vtr 1 (perjudicar) to damage. 2 fig (desacreditar) to discredit.

menoscabo nm harm, damage; **ir en m. de algo**, to be to the detriment of sth.

menospreciar [12] vtr to scorn, disdain.

menosprecio nm contempt, scorn, disdain.

mensáfono nm ansaphone.

mensaje nm message.

mensajero,-a nm,f messenger, courier.

menstruación nf menstruation.

mensual adj monthly; **dos visitas mensuales**, two visits a month.

mensualidad nf (pago) monthly payment; (sueldo) monthly salary o wage.

menta nf 1 Bot mint. 2 (licor) crème de menthe.

mental adj mental.

mentalidad nf mentality; **de m. abierta/cerrada**, open-/narrow-minded.

mentalizar [4] I vtr (concienciar) to make aware. II **mentalizarse** vr 1 (concienciarse) to become aware. 2 (hacerse a la idea) to come to terms (a, with).

mentar [1] vtr to mention.

mente nf mind; **se me quedó la m. en blanco**, my mind went blank; **m.**

abierta/tolerante/cerrada, open/broad/closed mind.

mentecato,-a nm,f fool, idiot.

mentir [5] vi to lie, tell lies.

mentira nf lie; **aunque parezca m.**, strange as it may seem; **parece m.**, it is unbelievable.

mentiroso,-a I adj lying. II nm,f liar.

mentis nm denial.

mentón nm Anat chin.

menú nm menu.

menudillos nmpl giblets.

menudo,-a I adj minute, tiny; (irónico) tremendous; **la gente menuda**, the little ones pl; **¡m. lío/susto!**, what a mess/fright! II adv **a m.**, often.

meollo nm 1 fig (quid) essence. 2 (miga) crumb.

mercado nm market; **M. Común**, Common Market; **m. negro**, black market; **sacar algo al m.**, to put sth on the market.

mercadotecnia nf marketing.

mercancía nf commodity, goods pl.

mercante adj merchant; **barco/marina m.**, merchant ship/navy.

mercantil adj mercantile, commercial.

merced nf fml favour, US favor, grace; **a m. de**, at the mercy of.

mercenario,-a adj & nm,f mercenary.

mercería nf haberdasher's (shop), US notions store.

mercurio nm 1 Quím mercury, quicksilver. 2 M., Mercury.

merecer [33] I vtr 1 to deserve. 2 (uso impers) **no merece la pena hacerlo**, it's not worth while doing it. II **merecerse** vr to deserve.

merecido,-a I adj deserved; **ella lo tiene m.**, (recompensa) she deserves it; (castigo) it serves her right. II nm just deserts pl.

merendar [1] I vtr to have as an afternoon snack, have for tea. II vi to have an afternoon snack, have tea.

merendero nm (establecimiento) tearoom, snack bar; (en el campo) picnic spot.

merengue nm Culin meringue.

merezco indic pres → **merecer**.

meridiano,-a nm meridian.

meridional I adj southern. II nmf southerner.

merienda nf afternoon snack, tea.

mérito nm merit, worth; **hacer méritos para algo**, to strive to deserve sth.

merluza nf (pez) hake.

merma nf decrease, reduction.

mermar I vtr to cause to decrease o diminish. II vi to decrease, diminish. III **mermarse** vr to decrease, diminish.

mermelada nf 1 jam; **m. de fresa**, strawberry jam. 2 (de agrios) marmalade; **m. de naranja**, orange marmalade.

mero,-a adj mere, pure; **por el m. hecho de**, through the mere fact of.

merodear vi to prowl.

mes nm 1 month; **el m. pasado/que viene**, last/next month. 2 (cobro) monthly salary o wages pl; (pago) monthly payment. 3 fam (menstruación) period.

mesa nf 1 table; **poner/recoger la m.**, to set/clear the table; (de despacho etc) desk; **m. redonda**, round table. 2 (junta directiva) board, executive; **el presidente de la m.**, the chairman; **m. electoral**, electoral college.

meseta nf plateau, tableland, meseta; **la M.**, the plateau of Castile.

mesilla nf **m. de noche**, bedside table.

mesón nm old-style tavern.

mesonero,-a nm,f innkeeper.

mestizo,-a adj & nm,f half-breed, half-caste, mestizo.

mesura nf fml moderation, restraint.

meta nf 1 (objetivo) goal, aim, objective. 2 (de carrera) finish, finishing line. 3 Ftb (portería) goal.

metafísica nf metaphysics.

metáfora nf metaphor.

metal nm 1 metal; **metales preciosos**, precious metals. 2 (timbre de la voz) timbre. 3 Mús brass.

metálico,-a I adj metallic. II nm cash; **pagar en m.**, to pay (in) cash.

metalizado-a adj metallic.

metalúrgico,-a I adj metallurgical. II nm,f metallurgist.

metedura nf fam **m. de pata**, blunder.

meteorito nm meteorite.

meteorología nf meteorology.

meteorológico,-a adj meteorological; **parte m.**, weather report.

meter I vtr 1 (poner) to put (en, in); fig **m. las narices en algo**, to poke one's nose into sth. 2 (comprometer) to involve (en, in), to get mixed up (en, in). 3 fam fig (dar) to give; **m. un rollo**, to go on and on; **m. prisa a algn**, to hurry sb up. 4 (hacer) to make; **m. ruido**, to make a noise. II **meterse** vr 1 (entrar) to go o come in, get into. 2 (estar) to be; **¿dónde te habías metido?**, where have you been (all this time)? 3 (entrometerse) to meddle. 4 **m. con algn**, (en broma) to get at sb.

meticuloso,-a adj meticulous.

metido,-a adj fam **estar muy m. en algo**, to be deeply involved in sth; **m. en años**, getting on (in years).

metódico,-a adj methodical.

método nm 1 method. 2 Educ course.

metodología nf methodology.

metomentodo nmf inv fam busybody.

metralleta nf sub machine-gun.

métrico,-a adj metric; **sistema m.**, metric system.

metro nm 1 (medida) metre, US meter. 2 (tren) underground, tube, US subway.

metrópoli nf metropolis.

metropolitano,-a I adj metropolitan. II

nm fml underground, tube, US subway.

mexicano,-a adj & nm,f Mexican.

México nm Mexico.

mezcla nf 1 (acción) mixing, blending; Rad Cin mixing. 2 (producto) mixture, blend.

mezclar I vtr 1 (dos o más cosas) to mix, blend. 2 (desordenar) to mix up. 3 (involucrar) to involve, mix up. II **mezclarse** vr 1 (cosas) to get mixed up; (gente) to mingle. 2 (relacionarse) to get involved (con, with).

mezcolanza nf fml strange mixture, hotch-potch.

mezquino,-a adj 1 (persona) mean, stingy. 2 (sueldo) miserable.

mezquita nf mosque.

m/g abr de **miligramo**, milligramme, milligram, mg.

mi¹ adj my; **mi casa/trabajo**, my house/job; **mis cosas/libros**, my things/books.

mi² nm Mús E; **mi menor**, E minor.

mí pron pers me; **a mí me dio tres**, he gave me three; **compra otro para mí**, buy one for me too; **por mí mismo**, by myself.

mía adj & pron pos f ⟶ **mío**.

miaja nf crumb; fig bit.

michelín nm fam spare tyre.

mico,-a nm 1 Zool long-tailed monkey. 2 fam (pequeñajo) little kid.

micra nf (medida) micron.

micro nm fam mike, microphone.

microbio nm microbe.

microbús nm minibus.

microchip nm (pl **microchips**) Inform microchip.

microficha nf microfiche.

micrófono nm microphone.

microonda nf un (horno) **microondas**, a microwave (oven).

microscopio nm microscope.

miedica nmf fam scaredy-cat.

miedo nm (pavor) fear; (temor) apprehension; **una película de m.**, a horror film; **tener m. de algo/algn**, to be afraid of sth/sb; fam **lo pasamos de m.**, we had a fantastic time; **un calor de m.**, sizzling heat.

miedoso,-a adj fearful.

miel nf honey; **luna de m.**, honeymoon.

miembro nm 1 (socio) member; **estado m.**, member state. 2 Anat limb; **m. viril**, penis.

mientras I conj 1 (al mismo tiempo que) while. 2 (durante el tiempo que) when, while; **m. viví en Barcelona**, when I lived in Barcelona. 3 **m. que**, (por el contrario) whereas. 4 fam (cuanto más) **más/menos …**, the more/less … II adv **m. (tanto)**, meanwhile, in the meantime.

miércoles nm inv Wednesday; **M. de Ceniza**, Ash Wednesday.

mierda nf vulg 1 shit; **ese libro es una**

m., that book is crap; **¡vete a la m.!**, piss off! 2 *fig (porquería)* dirt, filth. 3 *(borrachera)* bender.

miga *nf (de pan etc)* crumb; *fig* **hacer buenas migas con algn**, to get on well with sb.

migaja *nf* 1 *(de pan)* crumb. 2 *fig* bit, scrap. 3 **migajas**, *(del pan)* crumbs; *fig* leftovers.

migraña *nf Med* migraine.

mil *adj & nm* thousand; **m. pesetas**, a *o* one thousand pesetas.

milagro *nm* miracle.

milagroso,-a *adj* miraculous.

milano *nm Orn* kite; **m. real**, red kite.

milenario,-a I *adj* millenarian, millenial. **II** *nm* millennium.

milenio *nm* millennium.

milésimo,-a *adj & nm,f* thousandth.

mili *nf fam* military *o* national service; **hacer la m.**, to do one's military service.

milicia *nf (ejército)* militia; *(servicio militar)* military service.

milímetro *nm* millimetre, *US* millimeter.

militar I *adj* military. **II** *nm* military man, soldier. **III** *vi Pol (en un partido)* to be a member.

milla *nf* mile.

millar *nm* thousand.

millón *nm* million.

millonario,-a *adj & nm,f* millionaire.

mimar *vtr* to spoil, pamper.

mimbre *nm* wicker.

mimetismo *nm* mimicry.

mímica *nf* mimicry.

mimo *nm* 1 *(delicadeza)* care. 2 *fig (zalamería)* pampering. 3 *Teat (actor)* mime.

mina *nf* 1 mine; **ingeniero de minas**, mining engineer. 2 *(explosivo)* mine; **campo de minas**, minefield. 3 *(de lápiz)* lead; **lápiz de m.**, propelling pencil. 4 *fig (ganga)* gold mine.

minar *vtr* 1 *Mil Min* to mine. 2 *fig (desgastar)* to undermine.

mineral I *adj* mineral. **II** *nm* ore.

minería *nf* 1 *Min* mining. 2 *Ind* mining industry.

minero,-a I *nm,f* miner. **II** *adj* mining.

miniatura *nf* miniature.

minifalda *nf* miniskirt.

minifundio *nm* smallholding.

mínima *nf* minimum temperature.

minimizar *vtr* to minimize.

mínimo,-a I *adj* 1 *(muy pequeño)* minute, tiny. 2 *Mat Téc* minimum, lowest; **m. común múltiplo**, lowest common denominator. **II** *nm* minimum; **como m.**, at least; **ni lo más m.**, not in the least.

minipímer® *nm o f* liquidizer, blender.

ministerio *nm* 1 *Pol* ministry, *US* department. 2 *Rel* ministry.

ministro,-a *nm,f* 1 *Pol* minister; **primer m.**, Prime Minister. 2 *Rel* minister.

minoría *nf* minority; *Jur* **m. de edad**, minority.

minoritario,-a *adj* minority.

minucioso,-a *adj* 1 *(persona)* meticulous. 2 *(informe, trabajo etc)* minute, detailed.

minúsculo,-a *adj* miniscule, minute; **letra minúscula**, lower-case *o* small letter.

minusválido,-a I *adj* handicapped, disabled. **II** *nm,f* handicapped person, disabled person.

minuta *nf* 1 *(cuenta)* lawyer's bill. 2 *(menú)* menu.

minutero *nm* minute hand.

minuto *nm* minute.

mío,-a I *adj pos* of mine; **un amigo m.**, a friend of mine; **no es asunto m.**, it is none of my business. **II** *pron* mine; **ese libro es m.**, that book is mine; **lo m. es el tenis**, tennis is my strong point; *fam los míos, my people o folks.*

miope *nmf* myopic *o* short-sighted person.

miopía *nf* myopia, short-sightedness.

mira *nf* 1 *Téc* sight. 2 *fig (objetivo)* aim, target; **con miras a**, with a view to; **amplitud de miras**, broad-mindedness.

mirada *nf* look; **lanzar** *o* **echar una m.**, to glance at; **levantar la m.**, to raise one's eyes; **m. fija**, stare.

mirador *nm* 1 *(lugar con vista)* viewpoint. 2 *(balcón)* bay window, windowed balcony.

mirar *vtr* 1 to look at. 2 *(observar)* to watch. 3 **m. por algn/algo**, *(cuidar)* to look after sb/sth. 4 *(procurar)* to see; **mira que no le pase nada**, see that nothing happens to him. 5 *(dar a)* to look, face; **la casa mira al sur**, the house faces south.

mirilla *nf* spyhole, peephole.

mirlo *nm* blackbird.

misa *nf* mass.

misántropo,-a I *adj* misanthropic. **II** *nm,f* misanthrope, misanthropist.

miserable I *adj* 1 *(mezquino) (persona)* despicable; *(sueldo etc)* miserable. 2 *(pobre)* wretched, poor; **una vida m.**, a wretched life. **II** *nmf* 1 *(mezquino)* miser. 2 *(canalla)* wretch.

miseria *nf* 1 *(pobreza extrema)* extreme poverty. 2 *(insignificancia)* pittance; **ganar una m.**, to earn next to nothing. 3 *(tacañería)* miserliness, meanness.

misericordia *nf* mercy, compassion.

mísero,-a *adj* miserable, wretched.

misil *nm* missile; **m. tierra-aire**, surface-to-air missile.

misión *nf* mission; **m. cumplida**, mission accomplished.

misionero,-a *nm,f* missionary.

mismísimo,-a *adj superl fam* 1 *(preciso)* very; **en el m. centro**, right in the centre. 2 *(en persona)* in person.

mismo,-a I *adj* 1 same. 2 *(uso enfático)* **yo m.**, I myself; **aquí m.**, right here. **II** *pron* same; **es el m. de ayer**, it's the same one as yesterday; **estamos en las mismas**, we're back to square one; **lo m.**, the same (thing); **dar** o **ser lo m.**, to make no difference; **por eso m.**, that is why; **por uno** o **sí m.**, by oneself. II **1** (*por ejemplo*) for instance; **que venga algn, Juan m.**, ask one of them to come, Juan, for instance. **2 así m.**, likewise.

misógino,-a I *adj* misogynous. II *nm,f* misogynist.

miss *nf* beauty queen.

míster *nm Ftb* coach, trainer.

misterio *nm* mystery.

misterioso,-a *adj* mysterious.

MIT *nm abr de Ministerio de Información y Turismo*.

mitad *nf* **1** half; **a m. de camino**, halfway there; **a m. de precio**, half price. **2** (*centro*) middle; **en la m. del primer acto**, half way through the first act; *fam* **eso me parte por la m.**, that really screws things up for me.

mítico,-a *adj* mythical.

mitigar [7] *vtr fml* to mitigate, palliate; (*luz*) to reduce.

mitin *nm Pol* meeting, rally.

mito *nm* myth.

mitología *nf* mythology.

mitote *nm Am* (*bulla*) uproar.

mixto *adj* mixed.

mobiliario *nm* furniture.

moca *nm* mocha, coffee.

mochila *nf* rucksack, backpack.

mochuelo *nm Zool* little owl.

moción *nf* motion; **m. de censura**, vote of censure.

moco *nm* snot; **sonarse los mocos**, to blow one's nose.

mocoso,-a *nm,f fam* brat.

moda *nf* **1** fashion; **a la m., de m.**, in fashion; **pasado de m.**, old-fashioned. **2** (*furor pasajero*) craze.

modales *nmpl* manners.

modalidad *nf* form, category; *Com* **m. de pago**, method of payment; *Dep* **m. deportiva**, sport.

modelar *vtr* to model, shape.

modélico,-a *adj* model.

modelo I *adj inv & nm* model. II *nmf* (*fashion*) model; **desfile de modelos**, fashion show.

modem *nm Inform Tel* modem.

moderación *nf* moderation.

moderado,-a *adj* moderate; **un m. aumento de temperatura**, a mild increase in temperature.

moderador,-a *nm,f* chairperson; (*hombre*) chairman; (*mujer*) chairwoman.

moderar I *vtr* **1** to moderate; (*velocidad*) to reduce. **2** (*debate*) to chair. II **moderarse** *vr* to be moderate.

modernizar [4] *vtr*, **modernizarse** *vr* to modernize.

moderno,-a *adj* modern.

modestia *nf* modesty; **m. aparte**, without wishing to be immodest.

modesto,-a *adj* modest.

módico,-a *adj* moderate; **una módica suma**, a modest o small sum.

modificar [1] *vtr* to modify.

modismo *nm* idiom.

modisto,-a *nm,f* **1** (*diseñador*) fashion designer. **2** (*sastre*) (*hombre*) couturier; (*mujer*) couturière.

modo *nm* **1** (*manera*) way, manner; **m. de empleo**, instructions for use; → **manera**. **2 modos**, manners. **3** *Ling* mood.

modorra *nf* (*somnolencia*) drowsiness.

modoso,-a *adj* **1** (*educado*) well-behaved. **2** (*recatado*) modest.

modulación *nf* modulation.

modular *vtr* to modulate.

módulo *nm* module.

mofa *nf* mockery; **en tono de m.**, in a gibing tone.

mofarse *vr* to laugh (**de**, at), make fun (**de**, of).

moflete *nm* chubby cheek.

mogollón *nm arg* **1 m. de**, loads of; **me gusta un m.**, I like it loads. **2** (*confusión*) commotion; (*ruido*) racket.

moho *nm* **1** *Bot* mould, *US* mold. **2** (*de metales*) rust.

mohoso,-a *adj* **1** mouldy, *US* moldy. **2** (*oxidado*) rusty.

mojado,-a *adj* (*empapado*) wet; (*húmedo*) damp.

mojar I *vtr* **1** to wet; (*humedecer*) to damp; **m. pan en la leche**, to dip o dunk bread in one's milk. **2** *arg* **mojarla** to have it off. II **mojarse** *vr* to get wet.

mojón *nm* **1** kilométrico, ≈ milestone. **2** *arg* (*mierda*) shit.

moka *nm* mocha.

molar I *vi fam* **me mola cantidad**, I really love it, it's brilliant. II *adj & nm Anat* molar.

molde *nm* mould, *US* mold; **letras de m.**, printed letters; **pan de m.**, ≈ sliced bread.

moldeador *nm* (*del pelo*) wave.

moldear *vtr* to mould, *US* mold.

mole *nf* mass, bulk.

molécula *nf* molecule.

moler [4] *vtr* **1** (*triturar*) to grind. **2 m. a algn a golpes**, to beat sb up.

molestar I *vtr* **1** (*incomodar*) to disturb, bother. **2** *fml* to bother; **le molestaría esperar fuera?**, would you mind waiting outside? **3** (*causar malestar*) to hurt. II **molestarse** *vr* **1** (*tomarse la molestia*) to bother. **2** (*ofenderse*) to take offence o *US* offense, get upset.

molestia *nf* **1** bother; **no es ninguna m.**, it is no trouble at all; **perdone las molestias**, forgive the inconvenience. **2** *Med* (*dolor*) trouble, slight pain.

molesto,-a *adj* **1** (*irritante*) annoying,

upsetting. 2 **estar m. con algn**, *(enfadado)* to be annoyed *o* upset with sb.

molinillo nm grinder.

molino nm mill; **m. de agua**, watermill; **m. de viento**, windmill.

mollera nf fam brains pl; **duro de m.**, *(tonto)* dense, thick; *(testarudo)* pigheaded.

molón,-ona adj arg flashy, showy.

momentáneo,-a adj momentary.

momento nm 1 *(instante)* moment; **al m.**, at once; **por momentos**, by the minute. 2 *(período)* time; **de m.**, for the time being; **en cualquier m.**, at any time.

momia nf mummy.

mona nf fam **coger una m.**, to get drunk; **dormir la m.**, to sleep it off.

monada nf fam **¡qué m.!**, how cute!

monaguillo nm Rel altar boy.

monarca nmf monarch.

monarquía nf monarchy.

monasterio nm Rel monastery.

monda nf 1 *(piel)* peel, skin. 2 fam **ser la m.**, *(divertido)* to be a scream.

mondadientes nm inv toothpick.

mondar I vtr to peel. II **mondarse** vr fam **m. (de risa)**, to laugh one's head off.

moneda nf 1 *(pieza)* coin; **m. suelta**, small change; **acuñar m.**, to mint money. 2 Fin currency.

monedero nm purse.

monería nf → **monada**.

monetario,-a adj monetary.

mongol I adj Mongolian. II nmf *(persona)* Mongolian. III nm *(idioma)* Mongolian.

mongólico,-a adj Med I adj Down's syndrome. II nm,f **ser m.**, to have Down's syndrome.

monigote nm 1 pey *(persona)* wimp. 2 *(dibujo)* rough drawing *o* sketch (of a person).

monitor,-a nm,f monitor; *(profesor)* instructor.

monja nf nun.

monje nm monk.

mono,-a I nm 1 monkey. 2 *(prenda)* *(de trabajo)* boiler suit, overalls pl; *(de vestir)* catsuit. 3 arg *(droga)* cold turkey. II adj fam *(bonito)* pretty, cute.

monográfico,-a I adj monographic. II nm monograph.

monólogo nm monologue.

monopolio nm monopoly.

monopolizar [4] vtr to monopolize.

monótono,-a adj monotonous.

monserga nf fam drag.

monstruo nm 1 monster. 2 *(genio)* genius.

monstruoso,-a adj 1 *(repugnante)* monstrous. 2 *(enorme)* massive, huge.

monta nf fig **de poca m.**, of little importance.

montacargas nm inv service lift, US freight elevator.

montado,-a I adj *(nata)* whipped. II nm

sandwich.

montador,-a nm,f 1 *(operario)* fitter. 2 Cin TV film editor. 3 Teat producer.

montaje nm 1 Téc *(instalación)* fitting; *(ensamblaje)* assembling; **cadena de m.**, assembly line. 2 Cin editing and mounting. 3 Teat staging. 4 Fot montage. 5 fam *(farsa)* farce.

montaña nf mountain; **m. rusa**, big dipper.

montañismo nm mountaineering.

montañoso,-a adj mountainous.

montante nm 1 Fin amount. 2 *(de puerta)* post.

montar I vi 1 *(subirse)* to get in; *(en bici, a caballo)* to ride. 2 Fin *(ascender)* **m. a**, to amount to, come to. II vtr 1 *(colocar)* to put on. 2 *(máquina etc)* to assemble, *(negocio)* to set up, start. 3 Culin to whip. 4 Cin Fot *(película)* to edit, mount; *(fotografía)* to mount. 5 Teat *(obra)* to stage, mount. 6 Zool *(cubrir)* to mount. III **montarse** vr 1 *(subirse)* to get on; *(en coche)* to get in (en, to). 2 fam *(armarse)* to break out. 3 arg **montárselo bien**, to have things (nicely) worked out *o* set up.

monte nm 1 *(montaña)* mountain; *(con nombre propio)* mount; **de m.**, wild. 2 **el m.**, *(zona)* the hills.

montés,-a adj *(animal)* wild.

monto nm total.

montón nm heap, pile; **un m. de**, a load of; arg **me gusta un m.**, I really love it; fam **del m.**, run-of-the-mill, nothing special.

montura nf 1 *(cabalgadura)* mount. 2 *(de gafas)* frame.

monumento nm monument.

monzón nm monsoon.

moño nm *(de pelo)* bun.

MOPU nm abr de **Ministerio de Obras Públicas y Urbanismo**, ≈ Ministry of Public Works.

moquear vi to have a runny nose.

moqueta nf fitted carpet.

mora nf *(zarzamora)* blackberry.

morado,-a I adj purple; fam **pasarlas moradas**, to have a tough time; **ponerse m.**, to stuff oneself. II adj purple.

moral I adj moral. II nf 1 *(ética)* morals pl. 2 *(ánimo)* morale, spirits pl; **levantar la m. a algn**, raise sb's spirits.

moraleja nf moral.

moralista I adj moralistic. II nmf moralist.

moratoria nf moratorium.

morbo nm fam *(interés malsano)* morbid curiosity.

morboso,-a adj fam morbid.

morcilla nf black pudding; fam **que le den m.**, he can drop dead for all I care.

mordaz adj biting.

mordaza nf gag.

mordedura nf bite.

morder [4] vtr to bite; **me ha mordido**, it

has bitten me; *fig* **m. el anzuelo,** to take the bait.
mordida *nf Am* (*soborno*) bribe.
mordisco *nm* bite.
mordisquear *vtr* to nibble (at).
moreno,-a I *adj* **1** (*pelo*) dark-haired; (*piel*) dark-skinned. **2** (*bronceado*) tanned; **ponerse m.,** to get a suntan; **pan/azúcar m.,** brown bread/sugar. **II** *nm,f* (*persona*) (*de pelo*) dark-haired person; (*de piel*) dark-skinned person.
morera *nf Bot* white mulberry.
moretón *nm fam* bruise.
morfina *nf* morphine.
morfinómano,-a I *nm,f* morphine addict. **II** *adj* addicted to morphine.
morgue *nf Am* morgue.
moribundo,-a *adj & nm,f* moribund.
morir [7] **1** *vi* **1** to die; **m. de frío/ hambre/cáncer,** to die of cold/hunger/ cancer; **m. de amor o pena,** to die from a broken heart. **II morirse** *vr* to die; **m. de hambre,** to starve to death; *fig* to be starving; **m. de aburrimiento,** to be bored to death; **m. de ganas (de hacer algo),** to be dying (to do sth); **m. de risa,** to die laughing.
mormón,-ona *adj & nm,f* Mormon.
moro,-a *adj nm,f* **1** *Hist* Moor; *fam* **no hay moros en la costa,** the coast is clear. **2** *pey* (*musulmán*) Muslim; (*árabe*) Arab.
morocho,-a *adj Am* (*moreno*) swarthy.
moroso,-a *nm,f* bad debtor.
morral *nm* **1** (*para pienso*) nosebag. **2** *Mil* haversack; (*de cazador*) gamebag.
morralla *nf* **1** (*cosas sin valor*) rubbish, junk. **2** (*chusma*) scum.
morrear *vtr,* **morrearse** *vr vulg* to snog.
morreo *nm vulg* snog.
morro *nm* **1** (*de animal*) (*hocico*) snout. **2** *fam* (*de persona*) mouth, (thick) lips; **caerse de m.,** to fall flat on one's face; **por los morros,** without so much as a by your leave; *fam* **¡vaya m.!,** what a cheek! **3** (*de coche*) nose.
morrón *adj* **pimiento m.,** (fleshy) red pepper.
morsa *nf* walrus.
morse *nm* morse.
mortadela *nf* mortadella.
mortaja *nf* shroud.
mortal I *adj* **1** mortal. **2** (*mortífero*) fatal; **un accidente m.,** a fatal accident. **II** *nmf* mortal.
mortalidad *nf* mortality; **índice de m.,** death rate.
mortandad *nf* death toll.
mortecino,-a *adj* colourless, *US* colorless.
mortero *nm Culin Mil* mortar.
mortífero,-a *adj* deadly, lethal.
mortificar [1] *vtr* to mortify.
mortuorio,-a *adj* death; **lecho m.,** deathbed.

moruno,-a *adj* Moorish; *Culin* **pincho m.,** ≈ kebab.
mosaico *nm* mosaic.
mosca I *nf* fly; **peso m.,** flyweight; *fam* **estar m.,** (*suspicaz*) to be suspicious; (*borracho*) to be pissed; *fam* **por si las moscas,** just in case; *fam* **¿qué m. te ha picado?,** what's biting you?
moscada *adj* **nuez m.,** nutmeg.
moscardón *nm* **1** *Ent* blowfly. **2** *fam* (*pesado*) pest.
moscovita *adj & nmf* Muscovite.
Moscú *n* Moscow.
mosquearse *vr fam* **1** (*enfadarse*) to get cross. **2** (*sospechar*) to smell a rat.
mosquetero *nm Hist* musketeer.
mosquitero *nm* (*red*) mosquito net.
mosquito *nm* mosquito.
mostaza *nf Bot Culin* mustard.
mosto *nm* (*bebida*) grape juice; (*del vino*) must.
mostrador *nm* **1** (*de tienda*) counter. **2** (*de bar*) bar.
mostrar [2] *vtr* to show; **muéstramelo,** show it to me. **II mostrarse** *vr* to be; **se mostró muy comprensiva,** she was very understanding.
mostrenco,-a I *nm,f* **1** (*ignorante*) blockhead. **2** (*gordo*) very fat person. **II** *adj* (*sin dueño*) ownerless; **bienes mostrencos,** ownerless property.
mota *nf* speck.
mote¹ *nm* (*apodo*) nickname; **poner m. a algn,** to give sb a nickname.
mote² *nm Am* boiled salted maize *o US* corn.
moteado,-a *adj* dotted.
motín *nm* (*amotinamiento*) mutiny; (*disturbio*) riot.
motivación *nf* motivation.
motivar *vtr* **1** (*causar*) to cause, give rise to. **2** (*inducir*) to motivate.
motivo *nm* **1** (*causa*) reason; (*usu pl*) grounds (*pl*); **con este o tal m.,** for this reason; **con m. de,** on the occasion of; **sin m.,** for no reason at all; **bajo ningún m.,** under no circumstances. **2** *Art Mús* motif, leitmotif.
moto *nf Aut* motorbike.
motocicleta *nf* motorcycle.
motociclismo *nm* motorcycling.
motociclista *nmf* motorcyclist.
motocross *nm* motocross.
motor,-a I *nm* (*grande*) engine; (*pequeño*) motor; **m. de reacción,** jet engine; **m. de explosión,** internal combustion engine; **m. eléctrico,** electric motor. **II** *adj Téc* motive.
motora *nf* motorboat.
motorista *nmf* motorcyclist.
motorizar [4] **I** *vtr* to motorize. **II motorizarse** *vr fam* to get oneself a car *o* motorbike.
motosierra *nf* power saw.

motriz adj **fuerza m.**, motive power.
movedizo,-a adj **arenas movedizas,** quicksand sing.
mover [4] I vtr 1 to move; **m. algo de su sitio,** to move sth out of its place. 2 (hacer funcionar) to drive; **el motor mueve el coche,** the engine drives the car. II **moverse** vr 1 to move. 2 fam (gestionar) to do everything possible. 3 (darse prisa) to hurry up; **¡muévete!,** get a move on!
movida nf arg **hay mucha m.,** there's a lot going on.
movido,-a adj 1 Fot blurred. 2 (ocupado) busy.
móvil I adj mobile; TV Rad **unidad m.,** outside broadcast unit. II nm (de delito) motive.
movilización nf mobilization.
movilizar [4] vtr to mobilize.
movimiento nm 1 gen movement; Fís Téc motion; (poner algo) **en m.,** (to set sth) in motion; **(m. sísmico,** earth tremor. 2 (actividad) activity. 3 Com Fin (entradas y salidas) operations. 4 Esp Hist **el M.,** the Falangist Movement.
moviola nf Cin TV 1 (cámara) editing projector. 2 (repetición) action replay.
moza nf lass, young girl.
mozo nm 1 lad, boy. 2 (de estación) porter; (de hotel) bellboy, US bellhop. 3 Mil conscript.
mucamo,-a nm,f Am servant.
muchacha nf girl.
muchacho nm boy.
muchedumbre nf (de gente) crowd.
mucho,-a I adj 1 sing (usu en frases afirmativas) a lot of, lots of; (usu en frases neg) much; **m. tiempo,** a long time; **tengo m. sueño/mucha sed,** I am very sleepy/thirsty; **hay m. tonto suelto,** there are lots of idiots around; **¿bebes m. café? - no, no m.,** do you drink a lot of coffee?; - no, not much. 2 (demasiado) **es m. coche para mí,** this car is a bit too much for me. 3 **muchos,-as,** (usu en frases afirmativas) a lot of, lots of; (usu en frases neg) many; **tiene m. años,** he is very old. II pron 1 a lot, a great deal; **¿cuánta leche queda? - mucha,** how much milk is there left? - a lot. 2 **muchos,-as,** a lot, lots, many; **¿cuántos libros tienes? - muchos,** how many books have you got? - lots o a lot; **muchos creemos que ...,** many of us believe that ...
III adv a lot, very much; **lo siento m.,** I'm very sorry; **como m.,** at the most; **con m.,** by far; **m. antes/después,** long before/after; **¡ni m. menos!,** no way!; **por m. (que) + subj,** however much. 2 (tiempo) **hace m. que no viene por aquí,** he has not been to see us for a long time. 3 (a menudo) often; **vamos m. al cine,** we go to the cinema quite often.
muda nf (de ropa) change of clothes.

mudanza nf move; **estar de m.,** to be moving; **camión de m.,** removal van.
mudar I vtr 1 (ropa) to change. 2 (plumas, pelo) to moult, US molt; (piel) to shed, slough. II **mudarse** vr **m. de casa/ropa** to move house/to change one's clothes.
mudo,-a I adj 1 (que no habla) dumb; **cine m.,** silent films pl. 2 fig (callado) speechless. II nm,f mute.
mueble I nm piece of furniture; **muebles,** furniture sing; **con/sin muebles,** furnished/unfurnished; **m. bar,** cocktail cabinet. II adj movable.
mueca nf 1 (de burla) mocking face; **hacer muecas,** to pull faces. 2 (de dolor, asco) grimace.
muela nf 1 Anat molar; **dolor de muelas,** toothache; **m. del juicio,** wisdom tooth. 2 Téc (de molino) millstone.
muelle¹ nm spring.
muelle² nm Náut dock.
muermo nm fam (tedio) boredom; (rollo) drag.
muerte nf death; **m. natural,** natural death; **dar m. a algn,** to kill sb; **odiar a algn a m.,** to loathe sb; fam **de mala m.,** lousy, rotten; fam **un susto de m.,** the fright of one's life.
muerto,-a I adj 1 dead; **caer m.,** to drop dead; **m. de hambre,** starving; **m. de frío,** frozen to death; **m. de miedo,** scared stiff; **m. de risa,** laughing one's head off; **horas muertas,** spare time; Aut **(en) punto m.,** (in) neutral. II nm,f 1 (difunto) dead person; **hacerse el m.,** to pretend to be dead; fam **cargar con el m.,** to do the dirty work. 2 (víctima) fatality; **hubo dos muertos,** two (people) died.
muesca nf notch.
muestra nf 1 (espécimen) sample, specimen. 2 (modelo a copiar) model. 3 (prueba, señal) sign; **dar muestras de,** to show signs of; **m. de cariño/respeto,** token of affection/respect; **una m. más de ...,** yet another example of ...
muestral adj **error m.,** margin of error.
muestreo nm sampling.
mugido nm (de vaca) moo; (de toro) bellow.
mugir [6] vi (vaca) to moo, low; (toro) to bellow.
mugre nf filth.
mugriento,-a adj filthy.
mujer nf 1 woman; **dos mujeres,** two women; **m. de la limpieza,** cleaner; **m. de su casa,** houseproud woman. 2 (esposa) wife; **su futura m.,** his bride-to-be.
mujeriego I adj woman-chasing. II nm womanizer, woman chaser.
muleta nf 1 (prótesis) crutch. 2 Taur muleta.
muletilla nf pet word o phrase.
mullido,-a adj soft.

mulo nm mule.

multa nf fine; Aut ticket.

multar vtr to fine.

multi- pref multi-.

multicolor adj multicoloured, US multicolored.

multicopista nf duplicator.

multilateral adj multilateral.

multinacional adj & nf multinational.

múltiple adj 1 multiple; accidente m., pile up. 2 **múltiples**, (muchos) many.

multiplicación nf Mat multiplication.

multiplicar [1] I vtr & vi to multiply (por), by). II **multiplicarse** vr (reproducirse, aumentar) to multiply.

múltiplo,-a adj & nm multiple.

multirriesgo adj inv póliza m., multiple risk policy.

multitud nf 1 (de personas) crowd. 2 (de cosas) multitude.

mundano,-a adj mundane.

mundial I adj worldwide; campeón m., world champion; de fama m., world-famous. II nm world championship.
◆**mundialmente** adv m. famoso, world-famous, famous worldwide.

mundo nm world; todo el m., everyone; correr o ver m., to travel widely; nada del otro m., nothing special; el otro m., the hereafter.

muñeca nf 1 wrist. 2 (juguete, muchacha) doll.

muñeco nm (juguete) (little) boy doll; m. de trapo, rag doll; m. de nieve, snowman.

muñequera nf wristband.

munición nf ammunition.

municipal I adj municipal. II nm (municipal) policeman.

municipio nm 1 (territorio) municipality. 2 (ayuntamiento) town council.

muñón nm Anat stump.

muralla nf wall.

Murcia nf Murcia.

murciélago nm Zool bat.

murmullo nm murmur.

murmuración nf gossip.

murmurar vi 1 (criticar) to gossip. 2 (susurrar) to whisper; (refunfuñar) to grumble. 3 fig (río) to murmur.

muro nm wall.

murrio,-a adj fam sad, blue.

musa nf muse.

musaraña nf fam estar mirando a o pensando en las musarañas, to be daydreaming o in the clouds.

musculatura nf musculature; desarrollar la m., to develop one's muscles.

músculo nm muscle.

musculoso,-a adj muscular.

museo nm museum; m. de arte o pintura, art gallery.

musgo nm moss.

música nf music; m. clásica, classical music; m. de fondo, background music.

musical I adj musical. II nm musical.

músico,-a I adj musical. II nm,f musician.

muslo nm thigh.

mustio,-a adj 1 (plantas) wilted, withered. 2 (persona) sad, gloomy.

musulmán,-ana adj & nm,f Muslim, Moslem.

mutación nf Biol mutation.

mutilación nf mutilation.

mutilado,-a nm,f disabled person; m. de guerra, disabled serviceman.

mutilar vtr to mutilate.

mutis nm Teat exit.

mutua nf mutual benefit society.

mutualidad nf 1 (reciprocidad) mutuality. 2 (asociación) mutual benefit society.

mutuo,-a adj mutual.

muy adv very; m. bueno/malo, very good/bad; jes m. bien!, very good!; fam m. mucho, very much; M. señor mío, Dear Sir; m. de los andaluces, typically Andalusian; m. de mañana/noche, very early/late.

N

N, n ['ene] nf (la letra) N, n.

N abr de Norte, North, N.

n/ abr de nuestro,-a, our.

nabo nm 1 Bot turnip. 2 vulg (pene) prick.

nácar nm mother-of-pearl.

nacer [33] vi 1 to be born; al n., at birth; nací en Montoro, I was born in Montoro; fam fig n. de pie, to be born under a lucky star. 2 (pájaro) to hatch (out). 3 (pelo) to begin to grow. 4 (río) to rise.

nacido,-a adj born; n. de padre español, born of a Spanish father; recién n., newborn; fig mal n., despicable, mean.

naciente adj (nuevo) new, recent; (sol)

rising.

nacimiento nm 1 birth; sordo de n., deaf from birth; lugar de n., birthplace, place of birth. 2 fig (principio) origin, beginning; (de río) source. 3 (belén) Nativity scene, crib.

nación nf nation; las Naciones Unidas, the United Nations.

nacional I adj 1 national. 2 (producto, mercado) domestic; vuelos nacionales, domestic flights. II nmf national; Hist los nacionales, the Francoist forces.

nacionalidad nf nationality.

nacionalismo nm nationalism.

nacionalista *adj & nmf* nationalist.

nacionalizar [4] **I** *vtr 1 Econ (banca, industria)* to nationalize. *(naturalizar)* to naturalize. **II nacionalizarse** *vr* to become naturalized; **n. español,** to take up Spanish citizenship.

nada I *pron 1 (como respuesta)* nothing; **qué quieres? - n.,** what do you want? - nothing. **2** *(con verbo)* not ... anything; *(enfático)* nothing; **no sé n.,** I don't know anything; **yo no digo n.,** I'm saying nothing. **3** *(con otro negativo)* anything; **no hace nunca n.,** he never does anything. **4** *(en ciertas construcciones)* anything; **más que n.,** more than anything; **sin decir n.,** without saying anything; **casi n.,** hardly anything. **5 gracias, - de n.,** thanks, - don't mention it; *fam* **para n.,** not at all; **casi n.,** almost nothing; **como si n.,** just like that; **un rasguño de n.,** an insignificant little scratch; **n. de eso,** nothing of the sort; **n. de n.,** nothing at all; **n. más verla,** as soon as he saw her. **II** *adv* not at all; **no me gusta n.,** I don't like it at all; **no lo encuentro n. interesante,** I don't find it remotely interesting. **III** *nf* nothingness; **salir de la n.,** to come out of nowhere.

nadar *vi 1 Dep* to swim; **n. a braza,** to do the breaststroke. **2** *(flotar)* to float.

nadador,-a *nmf* swimmer.

nadie I *pron 1 (como respuesta)* no-one, nobody; **quién vino? - n.,** who came? - no-one. **2** *(con verbo)* not ... anyone, anybody; *(enfático)* no-one, nobody; **no conozco a n.,** I don't know anyone *o* anybody; **no vi a n.,** I saw no-one. **3** *(con otro negativo)* anyone, anybody; **nunca habla con n.,** he never speaks to anybody. **4** *(en ciertas construcciones)* anybody, anyone; **más que n.,** more than anyone; **sin decírselo a n.,** without telling anyone; **casi n.,** hardly anyone. **II** *pron* nobody; **ser un don n.,** to be a nobody.

nado (a) *loc adv* swimming; **cruzar** *o* **pasar a n.,** to swim across.

nafta *nf Am (gasolina)* petrol, *US* gasoline.

nailon *nm* nylon; **medias de n.,** nylons *pl*.

naipe *nm* playing card.

nalga *nf* buttock; **nalgas,** bottom *sing*, buttocks.

nana *nf* lullaby.

napalm *nm* napalm.

napias *nfpl fam* snout *sing*.

Nápoles *n* Naples.

napolitano,-a *adj & nmf* Neapolitan.

naranja I *nf* orange; *fig* **mi media n.,** my better half. **II** *adj & nm (color)* orange.

naranjada *nf* orangeade.

naranjo *nm* orange tree.

narciso *nm 1 (blanco)* narcissus; *(amarillo)* daffodil. **2** *fig (hombre)* narcissist.

narcótico *nm* narcotic; *(droga)* drug.

narcotizar [4] *vtr (drogar)* to drug.

narcotraficante *nmf* drug trafficker.

narcotráfico *nm* drug trafficking.

nariz *nf 1* nose; *fam* **me da en la n. que ...,** I've got this feeling that .... **2** *fam* **narices,** nose *sing*; *fam* **en mis (propias) narices,** right under my very nose; *fam* **estar hasta las narices de,** to be totally fed up with; *fam* **meter las narices en algo,** to poke one's nose into sth; *fam* **por narices,** because I say so; *fam* **tocarle a algn las narices,** to get on sb's wick.

narración *nf* narration.

narrar *vtr* to narrate, tell.

narrativo,-a *adj & nf* narrative.

nata *nf 1* cream; **n. batida/montada,** whipped cream. **2** *(de leche hervida)* skin. **3** *fig* cream, best.

natación *nf Dep* swimming.

natal *adj* **mi país n.,** my native country; **su pueblo n.,** his home town.

natalicio *nm fml* birthday.

natalidad *nf* birth rate; **control de n.,** birth control.

natillas *nfpl Culin* custard *sing*.

natividad *nf* Nativity.

nativo,-a *adj & nm,f* native.

nato,-a *adj* born.

natura *nf lit* nature; **contra n.,** against nature.

natural I *adj* natural; *(fruta, flor)* fresh; **de tamaño n.,** life-size; **en estado n.,** in its natural state; *Jur* **hijo n.,** illegitimate child. **II** *nmf* native.

naturaleza *nf 1* nature; **en plena n.,** in the wild, in unspoilt countryside; *Arte* **n. muerta,** still life. **2** *(complexión)* physical constitution.

naturalidad *nf (sencillez)* naturalness; **con n.,** naturally, straightforwardly.

naturalismo *nm* naturalism.

naturalista I *adj* naturalistic. **II** *nmf* naturalist.

naturalización *nf* naturalization.

naturalizar [4] **I** *vtr* to naturalize. **II naturalizarse** *vr* to become naturalized.

naturalmente *adv* naturally; **¡n.!,** of course!

naturismo *nm* naturism.

naturista *nmf* naturist.

naufragar [7] *vi (barco)* to sink, be wrecked; *(persona)* to be shipwrecked.

naufragio *nm Náut* shipwreck.

náufrago,-a *nmf* shipwrecked person, castaway.

náusea *nf (usu pl)* nausea, sickness; **me da n.,** it makes me sick; **sentir náuseas,** to feel sick.

nauseabundo,-a *adj* nauseating, sickening.

náutico,-a *adj* nautical.

navaja *nf 1 (cuchillo)* penknife, pocket-

knife; **n. de afeitar**, razor. 2 *(molusco)* razor-shell.
navajada *nf*, **navajazo** *nm* stab, gash.
navajero *nm fam* thug.
naval *adj* naval.
Navarra *n* Navarre.
navarro,-a I *adj* Navarrese, of *o* from Navarre. II *nm,f* native *o* inhabitant of Navarre.
nave *nf* 1 ship; **n. (espacial)**, spaceship, spacecraft. 2 *Ind* plant, building. 3 *(de iglesia)* nave; **n. lateral**, aisle.
navegable *adj* navigable.
navegación *nf* navigation; **n. costera**, coastal shipping.
navegar [7] *vi* 1 to navigate, sail. 2 *Av* to navigate, fly.
Navidad(es) *nf(pl)* Christmas; **árbol de Navidad**, Christmas tree; **Feliz Navidad/Felices Navidades**, Merry Christmas.
navideño,-a *adj* Christmas.
navío *nm* ship.
nazi *adj & nmf* Nazi.
nazismo *nm* Nazism.
n/c., **n/cta.** *abr de* **nuestra cuenta**, our account, our acct.
neblina *nf* mist, thin fog.
nebulosa *nf Astron* nebula.
nebuloso,-a *adj* 1 *Meteor* cloudy, hazy. 2 *fig* nebulous, vague.
necedad *nf* 1 *(estupidez)* stupidity, foolishness. 2 *(tontería)* stupid thing to say *o* to do.
necesario,-a *adj* necessary; **es n. hacerlo**, it has to be done; **es n. que vayas**, you must go; **no es n. que vayas**, there is no need for you to go; **si fuera n.**, if need be.
neceser *nm (de aseo)* toilet bag; *(de maquillaje)* make-up bag.
necesidad *nf* 1 necessity, need; **artículos de primera n.**, essentials; **por n.**, of necessity; **tener n. de**, to need. 2 *(pobreza)* poverty, hardship. 3 **hacer sus necesidades**, to relieve oneself.
necesitado,-a I *adj (pobre)* needy, poor; **n. de**, in need of. II *npl* **los necesitados**, the needy.
necesitar *vtr* to need; **'se necesita chico'**, *(en anuncios)* 'boy wanted'.
necio,-a I *adj* silly, stupid. II *nm,f* fool, idiot.
necrología *nf* obituary.
néctar *nm* nectar.
nectarina *nf* nectarine.
neerlandés,-esa I *adj* Dutch, of *o* from the Netherlands. II *nm,f (persona) (hombre)* Dutchman; *(mujer)* Dutchwoman; **los neerlandeses**, the Dutch. III *nm (idioma)* Dutch.
nefasto,-a *adj* 1 *(perjudicial)* harmful. 2 *(funesto)* unlucky, ill-fated. 3 *(inútil)* hopeless.

negación *nf* 1 negation. 2 *(negativa)* denial; *(rechazo)* refusal. 3 *Ling* negative.
negado,-a I *adj* **ser n. para algo**, to be hopeless *o* useless at sth. II *nm,f* nohoper.
negar [1] I *vtr* 1 to deny; **negó haberlo robado**, he denied stealing it. 2 *(rechazar)* to refuse, deny; **le negaron la beca**, they refused him the grant. II **negarse** *vr* to refuse (**a**, to).
negativa *nf* denial.
negativo,-a *adj & nm* negative.
negligencia *nf* negligence.
negociación *nf* negotiation.
negociador,-a *adj* negotiating; **comité n.**, negotiating commitee.
negociante *nmf* dealer; *(hombre)* businessman; *(mujer)* businesswoman.
negociar [12] I *vtr Fin Pol* to negotiate. II *vi (comerciar)* to do business, deal.
negocio *nm Com Fin* business; *(transacción)* deal, transaction; *(asunto)* affair; **hombre de negocios**, businessman; **mujer de negocios**, businesswoman.
negra *nf* 1 *fig (mala suerte)* bad luck; **tener la n.**, to be very unlucky. 2 *Mús* crotchet, *US* quarter note.
negrilla, **negrita** *adj & nf Impr* bold (face).
negro,-a I *adj* 1 black; **estar n.**, *(bronceado)* to be suntanned. 2 *fig (suerte)* awful; *(desesperado)* desperate; *(furioso)* furious; **verlo todo n.**, to be very pessimistic; **vérselas negras para hacer algo**, to have a tough time doing sth. II *nm,f (hombre)* black; *(mujer)* black (woman). III *nm (color)* black.
nene,-a *nm,f (niño)* baby boy; *(niña)* baby girl.
nenúfar *nm Bot* water lily.
neocelandés,-esa I *adj* of *o* from New Zealand. II *nm,f* New Zealander.
neoclásico,-a *adj Arte Lit* neoclassic, neoclassical.
neologismo *nm* neologism.
neón *nm* neon.
neoyorkino,-a I *adj* of *o* from New York. II *nm,f* New Yorker.
neozelandés,-esa *adj & nm,f* → **neocelandés,-esa**.
nepotismo *nm* nepotism.
Neptuno *n* Neptune.
nervio *nm* 1 *Anat Bot* nerve; *(de la carne)* sinew. 2 *fig (fuerza, vigor)* nerve, courage. 3 **nervios**, nerves; **ataque de n.**, a fit of hysterics; **ser un manojo de n.**, to be a bundle of nerves; **tener los nervios de acero**, to have nerves of steel.
nerviosismo *nm* nerves *pl*.
nervioso,-a *adj* 1 nervous; **poner n. a algn**, to get on sb's nerves. 2 *(inquieto)* fidgety.
neto,-a *adj* 1 *(peso, cantidad)* net. 2 *(nítido)* neat, clear.

neumático,-a I adj pneumatic. **II** nm tyre, US tire; **n. de recambio,** spare tyre.

neumonía nf pneumonia.

neurálgico,-a adj neuralgic; fig **punto n.,** nerve centre.

neurólogo,-a nm,f neurologist.

neurosis nf neurosis.

neurótico,-a adj & nm,f neurotic.

neutral adj neutral.

neutralidad nf neutrality.

neutralizar [4] vtr to neutralize.

neutro,-a adj **1** (imparcial) neutral. **2** Ling neuter.

neutrón nm Fís neutron; **bomba de neutrones,** neutron bomb.

nevada nf snowfall.

~~nevau~~ [1] ~~o impaiu vi unow~~

nevera nf **1** (frigorífico) refrigerator, fam fridge. **2** (portátil) cool box.

nexo nm connection, link.

ni conj **1 no ... ni, ni ... ni,** neither ... nor, not ... or; **no tengo tiempo ni dinero,** I have got neither time nor money; **ni ha venido ni ha llamado,** he hasn't come o phoned; **no vengas ni hoy ni mañana,** don't come today or tomorrow. **2** (ni siquiera) not even; **ni por dinero,** not even for money; **ni se te ocurra,** don't even think about it; **¡ni hablar!,** no way!

Nicaragua nf Nicaragua.

nicaragüense, nicaragüeño,-a adj & nm,f Nicaraguan.

nicho nm niche.

nicotina nf nicotine.

nido nm nest.

niebla nf fog; **hay mucha n.,** it is very foggy.

nieto,-a nm,f (niño) grandson; (niña) granddaughter; **mis nietos,** my grandchildren.

nieve nf **1** Meteor snow; Culin **a punto de n.,** (beaten) stiff. **2** arg (cocaína) snow.

nigeriano,-a adj & nm,f Nigerian.

nigerino,-a adj & nm,f Nigerien.

Nilo n el N., the Nile.

nilón nm Tex nylon.

nimio,-a adj (insignificante) insignificant, petty.

ninfómana nf nymphomaniac.

ningún adj (delante de nm sing) → **ninguno,-a.**

ninguno,-a I adj **1** (con verbo) not ... any; **no leí ninguna revista,** I didn't read any magazines; **no tiene ninguna gracia,** it is not funny at all. **2** (enfático) none, not a; **en ninguna parte,** nowhere; **de ningún modo,** no way. **II** pron **1** (persona) nobody, no one; **n. lo vio,** no one saw it; **n. de los dos,** neither of the two; **n. de ellos,** none of them. **2** (cosa) not ... any of them; (enfático) none of them; **me gusta n.,** I don't like any of them; **no vi n.,** I saw none of them.

niña nf **1** girl; → **niño,-a. 2** Anat pupil;

fig **es la n. de sus ojos,** she's the apple of his eye.

niñera nf nursemaid, nanny.

niñez nf infancy; (a partir de los cuatro años) childhood.

niño,-a nm,f **1** child; (muchacho) (small) boy; (muchacha) (little) girl; **de n.,** as a child; **n. prodigio,** child prodigy; pey **bien** o **de papá,** rich boy, rich kid; pey **n. bonito** o **mimado,** mummy's o daddy's boy. **2** (bebé) baby. **3** niños, children; fig **juego de niños,** child's play.

nipón,-ona adj & nm,f Japanese; **los nipones,** the Japanese.

níquel nm nickel.

niqui nm T-shirt.

níspero nm (fruto) medlar; (árbol) medlar tree.

nítido,-a adj (claro) clear; (imagen) sharp.

nitrógeno nm nitrogen.

nitroglicerina nf nitroglycerine.

nivel nm **1** (altura) level; **a n. del mar,** at sea level. **2** (categoría) standard; **n. de vida,** standard of living. **3** (instrumento) level; **n. de aire,** spirit level. **4** Ferroc **paso a n.,** level crossing, US grade crossing.

nivelar vtr **1** to level out o off. **2** (equilibrar) to balance out.

nº abr de **número,** number, n.

no I adv **1** (como respuesta) no; **¿te gusta? - no.,** do you like it? - no. **2** (en otros contextos) not; **n. vi a nadie,** I didn't see anyone; **aún no,** not yet; **ya no,** no longer, not any more. **no sin antes ...,** not without first ...; **¿por qué no?,** why not? **3 no fumar/aparcar,** (en letrero) no smoking/parking. **4 no sea que + subj,** in case. **5 es rubia, ¿no?,** she's blonde, isn't she? **llegaron anoche, no?,** they arrived yesterday, didn't they? **6** (como prefijo negativo) non; **la no violencia,** non-violence. **II** nm no; **un no rotundo,** a definite no.

noble I adj noble. **II** nmf (hombre) nobleman; (mujer) noblewoman; **los nobles,** the nobility sing.

nobleza nf nobility.

noche nf evening; (después de las diez) night, night-time; **de n.,** by night, at night; **esta n.,** tonight; **mañana por la n.,** tomorrow night o evening; **buenas noches,** (saludo) good evening; (despedida) good night; **son las nueve de la noche,** it's nine p.m.

nochebuena nf Christmas Eve.

nochevieja nf New Year's Eve.

noción nf **1** notion, idea. **2 nociones,** smattering sing, basic knowledge sing; **n. de español,** a smattering of Spanish.

nocivo,-a adj noxious, harmful.

noctámbulo,-a nm,f sleepwalker; fam night-bird.

nocturno,-a adj **1** night; **vida nocturna,**

night life; **clases nocturnas,** evening classes. 2 *Bot Zool* nocturnal.

nodriza *nf* 1 (*ama*) wet nurse. 2 **buque n.,** supply ship.

nogal *nm Bot* walnut (tree).

nómada I *adj* nomadic. II *nmf* nomad.

nombrado,-a *adj* (*célebre*) famous, well-known.

nombramiento *nm* appointment.

nombrar *vtr* 1 (*designar*) to name, appoint; **n. a algn director,** to appoint sb director. 2 (*mencionar*) to name, mention.

nombre *nm* 1 name; **n. de pila,** Christian name; **n. y apellidos,** full name; **a n. de,** addressed to; **en n. de,** on behalf of. 2 *Ling* noun; **n. propio,** proper noun.

nómina *nf* 1 (*de sueldo*) pay slip. 2 (*plantilla*) payroll.

nominar *vtr* to nominate.

nominativo,-a *adj* **cheque n. a,** cheque made out to.

non *nm* 1 *Mat* odd number; **pares y nones,** odds and evens. 2 *fam* **nones,** (*negación*) no; **decir (que) nones,** to refuse.

nono,-a *adj* → **noveno,-a.**

norcoreano,-a *adj & nm,f* North Korean.

nordeste *nm* → **noreste**

nórdico,-a I *adj* 1 (*del norte*) northern. 2 (*escandinavo*) Nordic. II *nm,f* Nordic person.

noreste *nm* northeast.

noria *nf* 1 (*de feria*) big wheel. 2 (*para agua*) water-wheel.

norirlandés,-esa I *adj* Northern Irish. II *nm,f* (*persona*) (*hombre*) Northern Irishman; (*mujer*) Northern Irishwoman; **los norirlandeses,** the Northern Irish.

norma *nf* norm; **n. de seguridad,** safety standard.

normal *adj* normal, usual; **lo n.,** the normal thing, what usually happens.

normalidad *nf* normality; **volver a la n.,** to return to normal.

normalizar [4] I *vtr* to normalize, restore to normal. II **normalizarse** *vr* to return to normal.

normativa *nf* rules *pl.*

noroeste *nm* northwest.

norte *nm* 1 north; **al n. de,** to the north of. 2 *fig* aim, goal.

norteafricano,-a *adj & nm,f* North African.

Norteamérica *n* North America.

norteamericano,-a *adj & nm,f* North American.

norteño,-a I *adj* northern. II *nm,f* Northerner.

Noruega *n* Norway.

noruego,-a I *adj* Norwegian. II *nm,f* Norwegian. III *nm* (*idioma*) Norwegian.

nos I *pron pers* (*directo*) us; (*indirecto*) us; **n. ha visto,** he has seen us; **n. trajo un regalo,** he brought us a present; **n. lo dio,** he gave it to us. II *pron* (*reflexivo*)

ourselves; (*recíproco*) each other; **n. hemos divertido mucho,** we enjoyed ourselves a lot; **n. queremos mucho,** we love each other very much.

nosotros,-as *pron pers pl* 1 (*sujeto*) we; **n. lo vimos,** we saw it; **somos n.,** it is us. 2 (*complemento*) us; **con n.,** with us.

nostalgia *nf* nostalgia; (*morriña*) homesickness.

nostálgico,-a *adj* nostalgic; (*con morriña*) homesick.

nota *nf* 1 (*anotación*) note. 2 *Educ* mark, grade; **sacar buenas notas,** to get good marks. 3 *fig* (*detalle*) element, quality; **la n. dominante,** the prevailing quality. 4 *Mús* note; *fam* **dar la n.,** to make oneself noticed.

notable I *adj* (*apreciable*) noticeable; (*destacado*) outstanding, remarkable. II *nm* (*nota*) very good.

notar I *vtr* (*percibir*) to notice, note. II **notarse** *vr* 1 to be noticeable *o* evident, show; **no se nota,** it doesn't show; **se nota que ...,** one can see that ....

notaría *nf* (*despacho*) notary's office.

notarial *adj* notarial; **acta n.,** affidavit.

notario,-a *nm,f* notary (public), solicitor.

noticia *nf* news *sing;* **una n.,** a piece of news; **una buena n.,** good news; **no tengo n. de esto,** I don't know anything about it.

notificación *nf* notification; **sin n. previa,** without (previous) notice; *Jur* **n. judicial,** summons *sing.*

notificar [1] *vtr* to notify.

notorio,-a *adj* 1 (*evidente*) noticeable, evident. 2 (*famoso*) famous, well-known.

novatada *nf* (*broma*) rough joke, rag. 2 **pagar la n.,** to learn the hard way.

novato,-a I *adj* (*persona*) inexperienced; *fam* green. II *nm,f* 1 (*principiante*) novice, beginner. 2 *Univ* fresher.

novecientos,-as *adj & nm,f* nine hundred.

novedad *nf* 1 (*cosa nueva*) novelty; **últimas novedades,** latest arrivals. 2 (*cambio*) change, development. 3 (*cualidad*) newness.

novedoso,-a *adj* 1 (*nuevo*) new, full of novelties. 2 (*innovador*) innovative.

novel *adj* new, inexperienced. II *nmf* beginner, novice.

novela *nf Lit* novel; **n. corta,** short story; **n. policíaca,** detective story.

novelero,-a *adj* 1 fond of new things. 2 (*fantasioso*) highly imaginative.

novelesco,-a *adj* 1 (*de novela*) novelistic, fictional. 2 (*extraordinario*) bizarre, fantastic.

novelista *nmf* novelist.

noveno,-a *adj & nm* ninth; **novena parte,** ninth.

noventa *adj & nm inv* ninety.

novia *nf* 1 (*amiga*) girlfriend. 2 (*prometida*)

fiancée. 3 (*en boda*) bride.

noviazgo *nm* engagement.

noviembre *nm* November.

novillada *nf* *Taur* bullfight with young bulls.

novillero,-a *nm,f* *Taur* apprentice matador.

novillo,-a *nm,f* 1 (*toro*) young bull; (*vaca*) young cow. 2 *fam* **hacer novillos**, to play truant *o* US hooky.

novio,-a *nm* 1 (*amigo*) boyfriend. 2 (*prometido*) fiancé. 3 (*en boda*) bridegroom; **los novios**, the bride and groom.

nubarrón *nm fam* storm cloud.

nube *nf* cloud; *fig* **vivir en las nubes**, to have one's head in the clouds; *fig* **poner a algn por las nubes**, to praise sb to the skies.

nublado,-a *adj* cloudy, overcast.

nublarse *vr* to become cloudy, cloud over; *fig* **se le nubló la vista**, his eyes clouded over.

nuboso,-a *adj* cloudy.

nuca *nf* nape, back of the neck.

nuclear *adj* nuclear; **central n.**, nuclear power station.

núcleo *nm* nucleus; (*parte central*) core; **n. urbano**, city centre.

nudillo *nm* (*usu pl*) knuckle.

nudista *adj & nmf* nudist.

nudo *nm* 1 knot; **hacer un n.**, to tie a knot; *fig* **se me hizo un n. en la garganta**, I got a lump in my throat. 2 (*punto principal*) crux, core. 3 (*de comunicaciones*) centre, US center.

nuera *nf* daughter-in-law.

nuestro,-a I *adj pos* 1 our; **nuestra familia**, our family. 2 (*después del sustantivo*) of ours; **un amigo n.**, a friend of ours. II *pron pos* ours; **este libro es n.**, this book is ours.

nueve *adj & nm inv* nine.

nuevo,-I *adj* 1 new; *fam* **¿qué hay de n.?**, what's new?; **de n.**, again; **N. York**, New York; **N. Zelanda**, New Zealand. 2

(*adicional*) further. II *nm,f* newcomer; (*principiante*) beginner. ◆**nuevamente** *adv* again.

nuez *nf* 1 walnut; **n. moscada**, nutmeg. 2 *Anat* **n. (de Adán)**, Adam's apple.

nulidad *nf* 1 (*ineptitud*) incompetence. 2 *Jur* nullity.

nulo,-a *adj* 1 (*inepto*) useless, totally incapable. 2 (*sin valor*) null and void, invalid; **voto n.**, invalid vote. 3 **crecimiento n.**, zero growth.

núm. *abr de* **número**, number, n.

numeral *adj & nm* numeral.

numerar *vtr* to number.

numerario,-a I *adj* **profesor no n.**, teacher on a temporary contract. II *nm* 1 (*miembro*) full member. 2 (*dinero*) cash.

numérico,-a *adj* numerical.

número *nm* 1 number; **n. de matrícula**, registration number, US license number; **n. de serie**, serial number; *fig* **sin n.**, countless. 2 *Prensa* number, issue; **n. atrasado**, back number. 3 (*de zapatos*) size. 4 (*en espectáculo*) sketch, act; *fam* **montar un n.**, to make a scene.

numeroso,-a *adj* numerous.

nunca *adv* 1 (*como respuesta*) never; **cuándo volverás? - n.**, when will you come back? - never. 2 (*con verbo*) never; (*enfático*) not ... ever; **no he estado n. en España**, I've never been to Spain; **yo no haría n. eso**, I wouldn't ever do that. 3 (*en ciertas construcciones*) ever; **casi n.**, hardly ever; **más que n.**, more than ever. 4 **n. jamás**, never ever; (*futuro*) never ever.

nupcial *adj* wedding, nuptial; **marcha n.**, wedding march.

nupcias *nfpl fml* wedding *sing*, nuptials; **casarse en segundas n.**, to marry again.

nutrición *nf* nutrition.

nutrir I *vtr* to nourish, feed. II **nutrirse** *vr* to feed (**de, con**, on).

nutritivo,-a *adj* nutritious, nourishing; **valor n.**, nutritional value.

Ñ

Ñ, ñ [ˈeɲe] *nf* (*la letra*) Ñ, ñ.

ñam *interj fam* |ñ., ñ.!, yum-yum!, yummy!

ñame *nm* Am yarn.

ñapa *nf* Am bonus, little extra.

ñato,-a *adj* Am snub-nosed.

ñiquiñaque *nm fam* 1 (*objeto*) junk,

rubbish. 2 (*persona*) good-for-nothing.

ñoñería, ñoñez *nf* 1 (*sosería*) insipidness, bore. 2 (*melindrería*) fussiness.

ñoño,-a I *adj* 1 (*soso*) insipid, dull. 2 (*melindroso*) fussy. II *nm,f* dull *or* spineless person.

ñu *nm* gnu.

O

O, o |o| *nf (la letra)* O, o.

o *conj* or; **jueves o viernes,** Thursday or Friday; **o ... o,** either ... or; **o sea,** that is (to say), in other words.

O. *abr de* **Oeste,** West, W.

oasis *nm inv* oasis.

obcecado,-a *adj fig* stubborn.

obcecar [1] I *vtr fig* to blind; **la ira lo obceca,** he is blinded by anger. II **obcecarse** *vr fig* to refuse to budge; *(obsesionarse)* to become obsessed.

obedecer [33] I *vtr* to obey. II *vi* **o. a,** *(provenir)* to be due to; **¿a qué obedece esa actitud?,** what's the reason behind this attitude?

obediencia *nf* obedience.

obediente *adj* obedient.

obertura *nf* overture.

obesidad *nf* obesity.

obeso,-a *adj* obese.

óbice *nm* obstacle; **eso no es ó. para que yo no ...,** it won't prevent me from ....

obispo *nm* bishop.

objeción *nf* objection; **poner una o.,** to raise an objection, object.

objetar I *vtr* **no tengo nada que o.,** I've got no objections. II *vi* Mil to be a conscientious objector.

objetividad *nf* objectivity.

objetivo,-a I *nm* 1 *(fin, meta)* objective, aim. 2 *Mil* target. II *nm Cin Fot* lens; **o. zoom,** zoom lens. II *adj* objective.

objeto *nm* 1 object; **objetos perdidos,** lost property *sing;* **mujer o.,** sex object. 2 *(fin)* aim, purpose; **con o. de ...,** in order to ...; **tiene por o. ...,** it is designed to .... 3 *Ling* object.

objetor,-a I *nm,f* objector; **o. de conciencia,** conscientious objector. II *adj* objecting, dissenting.

obligación *nf* 1 *(deber)* obligation; **por o.,** out of a sense of duty; **tengo o. de ...,** I have to .... 2 *Fin* bond, debenture.

obligado,-a *adj* obliged; **verse** *o* **estar o. a,** to be obliged to.

obligar [7] *vtr* to compel, force.

obligatorio,-a *adj* compulsory, obligatory.

obra *nf* 1 *(trabajo)* (piece of) work; **por o. de,** thanks to. 2 *Arte* work; **o. maestra,** masterpiece. 3 *(acto)* deed. 4 *Constr* building site. 5 **obras,** *(arreglos)* repairs; **'carretera en o.,'** 'roadworks'; **'cerrado por o.,'** 'closed for repairs'.

obrar I *vi* 1 *(proceder)* to act, behave; **o. bien/mal,** to do the right/wrong thing. 2 *fml* **obra en nuestro poder ...,** we are in receipt of .... II *vtr (milagro)* to work.

obrero,-a I *nm,f* worker, labourer, *US* laborer. II *adj* working; **clase obrera,**

working class; **movimiento o.,** labour movement.

obscenidad *nf* obscenity.

obsceno,-a *adj* obscene.

obscurecer [33] I *vi impers* to get dark. II *vtr* to darken. III **obscurecerse** *vr (nublarse)* to become cloudy.

obscuridad *nf* darkness; *fig* obscurity.

obscuro,-a *adj* 1 dark. 2 *fig (origen, idea)* obscure; *(futuro)* uncertain, gloomy; *(asunto)* shady; *(nublado)* overcast.

obsequiar [12] *vtr* to give away.

obsequio *nm* gift, present.

observación *nf* observation.

observador,-a I *nm,f* observer. II *adj* observant.

observancia *nf* observance.

observar *vtr* 1 *(mirar)* to observe, watch. 2 *(notar)* to notice. 3 *(cumplir)* to observe.

observatorio *nm* observatory.

obsesión *nf* obsession.

obsesionar *vtr* to obsess; **estoy obsesionado con eso,** I can't get it out of my mind. II **obsesionarse** *vr* to get obsessed.

obsesivo,-a *adj* obsessive.

obseso,-a *nm,f* obsessed person; **un o. sexual,** a sex maniac.

obsoleto,-a *adj* obsolete.

obstaculizar [4] *vtr* to obstruct, get in the way of.

obstáculo *nm* obstacle.

obstante (no) *loc adv* nevertheless; *prep* notwithstanding.

obstetricia *nf* obstetrics *sing.*

obstinación *nf* obstinacy.

obstinado,-a *adj* obstinate.

obstinarse *vr* to persist **(en,** in).

obstrucción *nf* obstruction; *Med* blockage.

obstruir [37] I *vtr* 1 *(salida, paso)* to block, obstruct. 2 *(progreso)* to impede, block. II **obstruirse** *vr* to get blocked up.

obtención *nf* obtaining.

obtener [24] I *vtr (alcanzar)* to obtain, get. II **obtenerse** *vr* **o. de,** *(provenir)* to come from.

obturador *nm Fot* shutter.

obtuso,-a *adj* obtuse.

obús *nm* shell.

obviar [12] *vtr (problema)* to get round.

obvio,-a *adj* obvious.

oca *nf* goose.

ocasión *nf* 1 *(momento)* occasion; **con o. de ...,** on the occasion of ...; **en cierta o.,** once. 2 *(oportunidad)* opportunity, chance; **aprovechar la o.,** to make the most of an opportunity. 3 *Com* bargain; **de o.,** cheap; **precios de o.,** bargain prices.

ocasional *adj* 1 *(eventual)* occasional; **tra-**

bajo o., casual work; **de forma o.**, occasionally. 2 (*fortuito*) accidental, chance.

ocasionar *vtr* to cause, bring about.

ocaso *nm* (*anochecer*) sunset; *fig* (*declive*) fall, decline.

occidental *adj* western, occidental.

occidente *nm* west; **el O.**, the West.

OCDE *nf abr de* **Organización para la Cooperación y el Desarrollo Económico**, Organization for Economic Cooperation and Development, OECD.

Oceanía *n* Oceania.

oceánico,-a *adj* oceanic.

océano *nm* ocean.

ochenta *adj & nm inv* eighty.

ocho *adj & nm inv* eight.

ochocientos,-as *adj & nm,f* eight hundred.

odio nm leisure; **en mis ratos de o.**, in my spare *o* leisure time.

ocioso,-a *adj* 1 (*inactivo*) idle. 2 (*inútil*) pointless.

ocre *nm* ochre, *US* ocher.

octavilla *nf* (*panfleto*) hand-out, leaflet.

octavo,-a *adj & nm,f* eighth.

octogenario,-a *adj & nm,f* octogenarian.

octogésimo,-a *adj & nm,f* eightieth.

octubre *nm* October.

ocular *adj* **testigo o.**, eye witness.

oculista *nmf* ophthalmologist.

ocultar I *vtr* to conceal, hide; **o. algo a algn**, to hide sth from sb. II **ocultarse** *vr* to hide.

oculto,-a *adj* concealed, hidden.

ocupación *nf* occupation.

ocupado,-a *adj* (*persona*) busy; (*asiento*) taken; (*aseos, teléfono*) engaged; (*puesto de trabajo*) filled.

ocupante *nmf* (*de casa*) occupant, occupier; (*ilegal*) squatter; (*de vehículo*) occupant.

ocupar I *vtr* 1 to occupy. 2 (*espacio, tiempo*) to take up; (*cargo*) to hold, fill. II **ocuparse** *vr* 1 **o. de**, (*cuidar*) to look after; (*encargarse*) to see to.

ocurrencia *nf* (*agudeza*) witty remark, wisecrack; (*idea*) idea.

ocurrente *adj* witty.

ocurrir I *v impers* to happen, occur; **¿qué ocurre?**, what's going on?; **¿qué te ocurre?**, what's the matter with you? II **ocurrirse** *vr* **no se me ocurre nada**, I can't think of anything; **se me ocurre que ...**, it occurs to me that ....

odiar [12] *vtr* to detest, hate; **odio tener que ...**, I hate having to ....

odio *nm* hatred, loathing; **mirada de o.**, hateful look.

odioso,-a *adj* hateful.

odontología *nf* dentistry, odontology.

odontólogo,-a *nm,f* dental surgeon, odontologist.

odre *nm* wineskin.

OEA *nf abr de* **Organización de Estados Americanos**, Organization of American States, OAS.

oeste *nm* west.

ofender I *vtr* to offend. II **ofenderse** *vr* to get offended (**con, por**, by), take offence *o US* offense (**con, por**, at).

ofensa *nf* offence, *US* offense.

ofensiva *nf* offensive.

ofensivo,-a *adj* offensive.

oferta *nf* offer; *Fin Ind* bid, tender, proposal; **Com de/en o.**, on (special) offer; **o. y demanda**, supply and demand.

ofertar *vtr* to offer.

off *adj* **voz en o.**, *Cin TV* voice-over; *Teat* voice offstage.

offset *nm Impr* offset.

oficial,-a I *adj* official. II *nm* 1 *Mil Náut* officer. 2 (*empleado*) clerk. 3 (*obrero*) skilled worker.

oficialismo *nm Am* (*gobierno*) government.

oficina *nf* office; **o. de empleo**, job centre, *US* job office; **o. de turismo**, tourist office; **o. de correos**, post office; **horas/horario de o.**, business hours.

oficinista *nmf* office worker, clerk.

oficio *nm* 1 (*ocupación*) job, occupation; (*profesión*) trade; **ser del o.**, to be in the trade. 2 (*comunicación oficial*) official letter *o* note; **de o.**, ex-officio; **abogado de o.**, state-appointed lawyer. 3 *Rel* service.

oficioso,-a *adj* (*noticia, fuente*) unofficial.

ofimática *nf* office automation.

ofimático,-a *adj Inform* **paquete o.**, business package.

ofrecer [33] I *vtr* 1 to offer. 2 (*aspecto*) to present. II **ofrecerse** *vr* 1 (*prestarse*) to offer, volunteer. 2 (*situación*) to present itself. 3 *fml* **¿qué se le ofrece?**, what can I do for you?

ofrecimiento *nm* offering.

ofrendar *vtr Rel* to make offerings *o* an offering.

ofrezco *indic pres* → **ofrecer**.

oftalmología *nf* ophthalmology.

oftalmólogo,-a *nm,f* ophthalmologist.

ofuscación *nf*, **ofuscamiento** *nm* blinding, dazzling.

ofuscar [1] *vtr* 1 *fig* (*confundir*) to blind. 2 (*deslumbrar*) to dazzle.

oídas (de) *loc adv* by hearsay.

oído *nm* 1 (*sentido*) hearing. 2 (*órgano*) ear; **aprender de o.**, to learn by ear; *fig* **hacer oídos sordos**, to turn a deaf ear.

oír [17] *vtr* to hear; **¡oye!, hey!; ¡oiga!**, excuse me!; *fam* **como lo oyes**, believe it or not.

OIT *nf abr de* **Organización Internacional del Trabajo**, International Labour Organization, ILO.

ojal *nm* buttonhole.

ojalá I *interj* let's hope so!, I hope so! II *conj* (+ *subj*) **¡o. sea cierto!**, I hope it's true!

ojeada *nf* echar una o., to have a quick look.

ojeras *nfpl* rings o bags under the eyes.

ojeriza *nf* dislike.

ojo I *nm* 1 eye; o. morado black eye; ojos saltones, buiging eyes; a ojos vista, clearly, openly; *fig* calcular a o., to guess; *fam* no pegué o., I didn't sleep a wink. 2 *(de aguja)* eye; *(de cerradura)* keyhole. 3 *(de un puente)* span. II *interj* careful!, look out!

ojota *nf Am* sandal.

okupa *nmf* squatter.

ola *nf* wave; o. de calor, heatwave.

ole, olé *interj* bravo!

oleada *nf* wave; *fig* o. de turistas, influx of tourists.

oleaje *nm* swell.

óleo *nm Arte* oil; pintura o cuadro al ó., oil painting.

oleoducto *nm* pipeline.

oler [4] I *vtr* 1 *(percibir olor)* to smell. 2 *fig (adivinar)* to smell, feel. II *vi* 1 *(exhalar)* to smell; o. a, to smell of; o. bien/mal, to smell good/bad. 2 *fig (parecer)* to smack (a, of). III olerse *vr fig (adivinar)* to feel, sense; me lo olía, I thought as much.

olfatear *vtr 1 (oler)* to sniff. 2 *fig (indagar)* to pry into.

olfato *nm* sense of smell; *fig* good nose, instinct.

oligarquía *nf* oligarchy.

olimpiada *nf Dep* Olympiad, Olympic Games *pl*; las olimpiadas, the Olympic Games.

olímpico,-a *adj* Olympic; Juegos Olímpicos, Olympic Games.

olímpicamente *adv* paso o. de estudiar, I couldn't give a damn about studying.

oliva *nf* olive; aceite de o., olive oil.

olivar *nm* olive grove.

olivo *nm* olive (tree).

olmo *nm* smooth-leaved elm.

olor *nm* smell; o. corporal, body odour.

oloroso,-a *adj* fragrant, sweet-smelling.

OLP *nf abr de* Organización para la Liberación de Palestina, Palestine Liberation Organization, PLO.

olvidadizo,-a *adj* forgetful.

olvidar I *vtr* 1 to forget; *fam* ¡olvídame!, leave me alone! 2 olvidé el paraguas allí, I left my umbrella there. II olvidarse *vr* to forget; se me ha olvidado hacerlo, I forgot to do it.

olvido *nm* 1 *(desmemoria)* oblivion. 2 *(lapsus)* oversight.

olla *nf* saucepan, pot; o. exprés o a presión, pressure cooker.

ombligo *nm* navel.

ominoso,-a *adj* shameful.

omisión *nf* omission.

omiso,-a *adj* hacer caso o. de, to take no

notice of.

omitir *vtr* to omit, leave out.

omnipotente *adj* omnipotent, almighty.

omnipresente *adj* omnipresent.

omnisciente *adj* omniscient, all-knowing.

omnívoro,-a I *adj* omnivorous. II *nm,f* omnivore.

omóplato, omoplato *nm* shoulder blade.

OMS *nf abr de* Organización Mundial de la Salud, World Health Organization, WHO.

once I *adj inv* eleven. II *nm inv* eleven; *Ftb* eleven, team.

ONCE *nf abr de* Organización Nacional de Ciegos Españoles, ≈ Royal National Institute for the Blind, RNIB.

onda *nf* 1 *Fís* wave; *fam fig* estar en la o., to be with it; o. expansiva, shock wave; *Rad* o. larga/media/corta, long/medium/ short wave. 2 *(en el agua)* ripple. 3 *(de pelo)* wave.

ondear *vi* 1 *(bandera)* to flutter. 2 *(de agua)* to ripple.

ondulación *nf* undulation; *(de agua)* ripple.

ondulado,-a *adj (pelo)* wavy; *(paisaje)* rolling.

ondulante *adj* undulating.

ondular I *vtr (el pelo)* to wave. II *vi (moverse)* to undulate.

oneroso,-a *adj (impuesto)* heavy.

onomástica *nf* saint's day.

onomatopeya *nf* onomatopoeia.

ONU *nf abr de* Organización de las Naciones Unidas, United Nations (Organization), UN(O).

onubense I *adj* o. from Huelva. II *nmf* native o inhabitant of Huelva.

onza *nf (medida)* ounce.

OPA *nf abr de* Oferta Pública de Adquisición, takeover bid.

opaco,-a *adj* opaque.

ópalo *nm* opal.

opción *nf* 1 *(elección)* option, choice; *(alternativa)* alternative. 2 *(posibilidad)* opportunity, chance.

opcional *adj* optional.

open *nm Golf* open.

OPEP *nf abr de* Organización de los Países Exportadores de Petróleo, Organization of Petroleum Exporting Countries, OPEC.

ópera *nf Mús* opera.

operación *nf* 1 *Med* operation; o. quirúrgica, surgical operation. 2 *Fin* transaction, deal; operaciones bursátiles, stock exchange transactions. 3 *Mat* operation.

operador,-a *nm,f* 1 *(técnico)* operator. 2 *Cin (de cámara) (hombre)* cameraman; *(mujer)* camerawoman; *(del proyector)* projectionist. 3 *Tel* operator.

operante *adj* operating.

operar I *vtr* 1 *Med* to operate (a, on). 2 *(cambio etc)* to bring about. II *vi Fin* to

deal, do business (**con**, with). **III ope-
rarse** *vr* **1** *Med* to have an operation (**de**,
for). **2** (*producirse*) to occur, come about.

operario,-a *nm,f* operator; (*obrero*) worker.

operativo,-a *adj* operative.

opereta *nf* operetta.

opinar *vi* **1** (*pensar*) to think. **2** (*declarar*)
to give one's opinion, be of the opinion.

opinión *nf* **1** (*juicio*) opinion; **cambiar de
o.**, to change one's mind.

opio *nm* opium.

oponente *nmf* opponent.

oponer [19] (*pp* **opuesto**) **I** *vtr* (*resistencia*)
to offer. **II oponerse** *vr* (*estar en contra*)
to be opposed, be against; **se opone a
aceptarlo**, he refuses to accept it.

oporto *nm* (*vino*) port.

oportunidad *nf* opportunity, chance.

oportunista *adj & nmf* opportunist.

oportuno,-a *adj* **1** (*adecuado*) timely; **¡qué
o.!**, what good timing! **2** (*conveniente*) appropriate; **si te parece o.**, if you think it
appropriate.

oposición *nf* **1** opposition. **2** (*examen*)
competitive examination.

opositar *vi* to sit a competitive examination.

opositor,-a *nm,f* **1** (*candidato*) candidate
for a competitive examination. **2** *Am Pol*
opponent.

opresión *nf* oppression; **o. en el pecho**,
tightness of the chest.

opresivo,-a *adj* oppressive.

opresor,-a *nm,f* oppressor. **II** *adj* oppressive, oppressing.

oprimir *vtr* **1** (*pulsar*) to press. **2** (*subyugar*) to oppress.

oprobio *nm* ignominy, opprobrium.

optar *vi* **1** (*elegir*) to choose (**entre**,
between); **opté por yo mismo**, I de-
cided to go myself. **2** (*aspirar*) to apply
(**a**, for); **puede o. a medalla**, he's in with
a chance of winning a medal.

optativo,-a *adj* optional.

óptica *nf* **1** (*tienda*) optician's (shop). **2**
(*punto de vista*) angle.

óptico,-a I *adj* optical. **II** *nm,f* optician.

optimismo *nm* optimism.

optimista I *adj* optimistic. **II** *nmf* optimist.

óptimo,-a *adj* optimum, excellent.

opuesto,-a *adj* **1** (*contrario*) contrary; **en
direcciones opuestas**, in opposite directions; **gustos opuestos**, conflicting tastes.
2 (*de enfrente*) opposite; **el extremo o.**,
the other end.

opulencia *nf* opulence.

opulento,-a *adj* opulent.

opuse *pt indef* → **oponer**.

oración *nf* **1** *Rel* prayer. **2** *Ling* clause,
sentence.

oráculo *nm* oracle.

orador,-a *nm,f* speaker, orator.

oral *adj* oral; *Med* **por vía o.**, to be taken
orally.

orangután *nm* orang-outang, orang-utan.

orar *vi* *Rel* to pray.

oratoria *nf* oratory.

órbita *nf* **1** orbit. **2** *Anat* eye socket.

orden I *nm* order; **o. público**, law and
order; **por o. alfabético**, in alphabetical
order; **de primer o.**, first-rate; **o. del día**,
agenda; **del o. de**, approximately. **II** *nf* **1**
(*mandato*) order; **Mil ¡a la o.!**, sir! **2** *Jur*
warrant, order; **o. de registro**, search
warrant; **o. judicial**, court order.

ordenado,-a *adj* tidy.

ordenador,-a *nm* computer; **o. personal**,
personal computer.

ordenamiento *nm* ordering.

ordenanza I *nm* (*empleado*) office boy. **II**
nf regulations; **o. municipal**, by-laws.

ordenar I *vtr* **1** (*organizar*) to put in
order; (*habitación*) to tidy up. **2** (*mandar*)
to order. **II ordenarse** *vr* *Rel* to be
ordained (**de**, as), take holy orders.

ordeñar *vtr* to milk.

ordinario,-a *adj* **1** (*corriente*) ordinary,
common. **2** (*grosero*) vulgar, common.

orégano *nm* oregano, marjoram.

oreja *nf* ear; (*de sillón*) wing.

orejero,-a *adj* *Am* (*soplón*) grass.

orfanato *nm* orphanage.

orfebre *nm* (*del oro*) goldsmith; (*de la plata*) silversmith.

orfebrería *nf* gold o silver work.

orfelinato *nm* orphanage.

orgánico,-a *adj* organic.

organigrama *nm* organization chart;
Inform flow chart.

organismo *nm* **1** (*ser vivo*) organism. **2**
(*institución*) organization, body.

organista *nmf* organist.

organización *nf* organization.

organizado,-a *adj* organized; **viaje o.**,
package tour.

organizador,-a I *adj* organizing. **II** *nm,f*
organizer.

organizar [4] **I** *vtr* to organize. **II organi-
zarse** *vr* fig (*armarse*) to happen.

órgano *nm* organ.

orgasmo *nm* orgasm.

orgía *nf* orgy.

orgullo *nm* **1** (*propia estima*) pride. **2** (*arrogancia*) arrogance.

orgulloso,-a *adj* **1 estar o.**, (*satisfecho*) to
be proud. **2 ser o.**, (*arrogante*) to be arrogant, haughty.

orientación *nf* **1** (*dirección*) orientation,
direction. **2** (*guía*) guidance; **curso de o.**,
induction course.

oriental I *adj* eastern, oriental. **II** *nmf* Oriental.

orientar I *vtr* **1** (*enfocar*) to aim (**a**, at), intend (**a**, for); **orientado al consumo**, intended for consumption. **2** (*indicar camino*) to give directions to; fig (*aconsejar*) to

advise. **3** *una casa orientada al sur*, a house facing south. **4** (*esfuerzo*) to direct. **II orientarse** *vr* (*encontrar el camino*) to get one's bearings, find one's way about.

oriente *nm* East, Orient; **el Extremo o Lejano/Medio/Próximo O.**, the Far/Middle/Near East.

orificio *nm* hole, opening; *Anat Téc* orifice; **o. de entrada**, inlet; **o. de salida**, outlet.

origen *nm* origin; **país de o.**, country of origin; **dar o. a**, to give rise to.

original *adj & nmf* original.

originalidad *nf* originality.

originar *I vtr* to cause, give rise to. **II originarse** *vr* to originate.

originario,-a *adj* native.

◆**originariamente** *adv* originally.

orilla *nf* (*borde*) edge; (*del río*) bank; (*del mar*) shore.

orillero,-a *adj Am* (*persona*) suburban.

orín¹ *nm* (*herrumbre*) rust.

orín² *nm* (*usu pl*) (*orina*) urine.

orina *nf* urine.

orinal *nm* chamberpot; *fam* potty.

orinar *I vi* to urinate. **II orinarse** *vr* to wet oneself.

oriundo,-a *adj* native of; **ser o. de**, to come from.

orla *nf Univ* graduation photograph.

ornamentar *vtr* to adorn, embellish.

ornamento *nm* ornament.

ornar *vtr* to adorn, embellish.

ornato *nm* (*atavío*) finery; (*adorno*) decoration.

ornitología *nf* ornithology.

ornitólogo,-a *nm,f* ornithologist.

oro *nm* **1** gold; **de o.**, gold, golden; **o. de ley**, fine gold. **2** *Naipes* oros, (*baraja española*) ≈ diamonds.

orquesta *nf* orchestra; (*de verbena*) dance band.

orquestar *vtr* to orchestrate.

orquídea *nf* orchid.

ortiga *nf* (*stinging*) nettle.

ortodoxia *nf* orthodoxy.

ortodoxo,-a *adj & nm,f* orthodox.

ortografía *nf* orthography, spelling; **faltas de o.**, spelling mistakes.

ortográfico,-a *adj* orthographic, orthografical; **signos ortográficos**, punctuation *sing*.

ortopédico,-a *adj* orthopaedic, *US* orthopedic; **pierna ortopédica**, artificial leg.

oruga *nf* caterpillar.

orzuelo *nm Med* sty, stye.

os *pron pers pl* **1** (*complemento directo*) you; **os veo mañana**, I'll see you tomorrow. **2** (*complemento indirecto*) you, to you; **os daré el dinero**, I'll give you the money; **os escribiré**, I'll write to you. **3** (*con verbo reflexivo*) yourselves. **4** (*con verbo recíproco*) each other; **os queréis mucho**, you love each other very much.

osa *nf* **O. Mayor**, Great Bear, *US* Big Dipper; **O. Menor**, Little Bear, *US* Little Dipper.

osadía *nf* **1** (*audacia*) daring. **2** (*desvergüenza*) impudence.

osado,-a *adj* **1** (*audaz*) daring. **2** (*desvergonzado*) shameless.

osar *vi* to dare.

osario *nm* ossuary.

oscilación *nf* **1** oscillation. **2** (*de precios*) fluctuation.

oscilante *adj* **1** oscillating. **2** (*precios*) fluctuating.

oscilar *vi* **1** *Fís* to oscillate. **2** (*variar*) to vary, fluctuate.

oscuras (a) *loc adv* in the dark; **nos quedamos a o.**, we were left in darkness.

oscurecer [33] *vi impers & vtr & vr* → **obscurecer**.

oscuridad *nf* → **obscuridad**.

oscuro,-a *adj* → **obscuro,-a**.

óseo,-a *adj* osseous, bony; **tejido ó.**, bone tissue.

osito *nm fam* **o. (de peluche)**, teddy bear.

ósmosis, osmosis *nf inv* osmosis.

oso *nm* bear; **o. polar**, polar bear; **o. hormiguero**, anteater; **o. marino**, fur seal; *fam* *fig* **hacer el o.**, to play the fool.

ostensible *adj* ostensible.

ostentación *nf* ostentation; **hacer o. de algo**, to show off.

ostentar *vtr* **1** (*lucir*) to flaunt. **2** (*cargo*) to hold.

ostentoso,-a *adj* ostentatious.

osteópata *nmf* osteopath.

osteopatía *nf* osteopathy.

ostra *nf* oyster; *fig* **aburrirse como una o.**, to be bored stiff; *fam* **¡ostras!**, crikey!, *US* gee!

ostracismo *nm* ostracism.

OTAN *nf abr de* **Organización del Tratado del Atlántico Norte**, North Atlantic Treaty Organization, NATO.

otear *vtr* (*horizonte*) to scan, search.

OTI *nf abr de* **Organización de la Televisión Iberoamericana**.

otitis *nf inv* infection and inflammation of the ear, otitis.

otoñal *adj* autumnal, autumn, *US* fall.

otoño *nm* autumn, *US* fall.

otorgamiento *nm* (*concesión*) granting; (*de un premio*) award.

otorgar [7] *vtr* **1** (*premio*) to award (**a**, to); **o. un indulto**, to grant pardon. **2** (*permiso*) to grant (**a**, to).

otorrinolaringólogo,-a *nm,f* ear, nose and throat specialist.

otro,-a *adj indef* **1** (*sin artículo*) (*sing*) another; (*pl*) other; **o. coche**, another car; **otras personas**, other people. **2** (*con artículo definido*) other; **el o. coche**, the other car. **3** **otra cosa**, something else; **otra vez**, again. **II** *pron* **1** (*sin artículo*) (*sing*) another (one); (*pl*) (*personas*) others; (cosas) other ones; **dame o.,** give me another (one); **no es mío, es de o.,** it's not mine, it's somebody else's. **2** (con artículo definido) (sing) the other (one); (pl) (personas) the others; (cosas) the other ones. **3 hacer o. tanto,** to do likewise.

ovación nf ovation.

ovacionar vtr to give an ovation to, applaud.

oval, ovalado,-a adj oval.

óvalo nm oval.

ovario nm ovary.

oveja nf **1** sheep; (hembra) ewe; fig **la o. negra,** the black sheep.

overol nm Am overalls pl.

ovillo nm ball (of wool); fig **hacerse un o.,** to curl up into a ball.

ovino,-a adj ovine; **ganado o.,** sheep pl.

OVNI nm abr de **objeto volador no identificado,** unidentified flying object,

UFO.

ovular I adj ovular. **II** vi to ovulate.

óvulo nm ovule.

oxidación nf (metal) rusting.

oxidado,-a adj (metal) rusty; fig **su inglés está un poco o.,** her English is a bit rusty.

oxidar I vtr Quím to oxidize; (metales) to rust. **II oxidarse** vr Quím to oxidize; (metales) to rust, go rusty.

óxido nm **1** oxide; **ó. de carbono,** carbon monoxide. **2** (orín) rust.

oxigenado,-a adj oxygenated; **agua oxigenada,** (hydrogen) peroxide.

oxígeno nm oxygen; **bomba de o.,** oxygen cylinder o tank.

oye indic pres & imperat → oír.

oyente nmf **1** Rad listener. **2** Univ occasional student.

ozono nm ozone; **capa de o.,** ozone layer.

P

P, p [pe] nf (la letra) P, p.

pabellón nm **1 p. de deportes,** sports centre. **2** (en feria) stand. **3** (bloque) wing. **4** (bandera) flag.

pábulo nm fml fig fuel; **dar p. a,** to encourage.

pacer [33] vtr & vi to graze, pasture.

pachá nm fam fig **vivir como un p.,** to live like a king.

pachanguero,-a adj fam pey (música) catchy.

pachón,-ona nm,f (perro) pointer.

pachorra nf fam sluggishness; **tener p.,** to be phlegmatic.

paciencia nf patience; **armarse de p.,** to grin and bear it.

paciente adj & nmf patient.

pacificación nf pacification.

pacificador,-a I adj pacifying. **II** nm,f peacemaker.

pacificar [1] **I** vtr to pacify; fig (apaciguar) to appease, calm. **II pacificarse** vr to calm down.

pacífico,-a adj peaceful.

Pacífico nm **el (océano) P.,** the Pacific (Ocean).

pacifismo nm pacifism.

pacifista adj & nmf pacifist.

paco nm Am fam (policía) policeman.

pacotilla nf fam **de p.,** second-rate.

pactar vtr to agree.

pacto nm pact; **el P. de Varsovia,** the Warsaw Pact; **p. de caballeros,** gentlemen's agreement.

padecer [33] vtr & vi to suffer; **padece del corazón,** he suffers from heart trouble.

padecimiento nm suffering.

padrastro nm **1** stepfather. **2** (pellejo)

hangnail.

padrazo nm easy-going o indulgent father.

padre I nm **1** father; **p. de familia,** family man. **2 padres,** parents. **II** adj fam huge; **pegarse la vida p.,** to live like a king.

padrenuestro nm Lord's Prayer.

padrino nm **1** (de bautizo) godfather; (de boda) best man; **padrinos,** godparents. **2** (espónsor) sponsor.

padrón nm census.

paella nf paella (rice dish made with vegetables, meat and/or seafood).

paellera nf paella pan.

pág abr de **página,** page, p.

paga nf (salario) wages; (de niños) pocket money; **p. extra,** bonus.

pagadero,-a adj payable; Fin **cheque p. al portador,** cheque payable to bearer.

pagador,-a nm,f payer.

pagano,-a adj & nm,f pagan, heathen.

pagar [7] vtr **1** to pay; **en metálico** o **al contado,** to pay cash; **p. por,** (producto, mala acción) to pay for; fig (ella) **lo ha pagado caro,** she's paid dearly for it. **2** (recompensar) repay.

pagaré nm Fin promissory note, IOU; **p. del tesoro,** treasury note.

página nf page; **en la p. 3,** on page 3; fig **una p. importante de la historia,** an important chapter in history.

pago nm payment; **p. adelantado** o **anticipado,** advance payment; **p. contra reembolso,** cash on delivery; **p. inicial,** down payment.

paila nf Am (frying) pan.

paipái, paipay nm (pl **paipáis**) large palm fan.

país nm country, land; **vino del p.,** local wine; **P. Vasco,** Basque Country; **P. Va-**

lenciano, Valencia.

paisaje *nm* landscape, scenery.

paisano,-a I *adj* of the same country. **II** *nm,f (compatriota)* fellow countryman *o* countrywoman, compatriot; **en traje de p.,** in plain clothes.

Países Bajos *npl* (los) P. B., the Netherlands, the Low Countries.

paja *nf* 1 straw. 2 *fam (de bazofia)* padding, waffle. 3 *vulg* **hacerse una p.,** to wank.

pajar *nm (almacén)* straw loft; *(en el exterior)* straw rick.

pajarita *nf* 1 bow tie. 2 *(de papel)* paper bird.

pájaro *nm* 1 bird; **Madrid a vista de p.,** a bird's-eye view of Madrid; **p. carpintero,** woodpecker. 2 *fam* **tener pájaros,** to have daft ideas.

Pakistán *n* Pakistan.

pakistaní *adj & nmf* Pakistani.

pala *nf* 1 shovel; *(de jardinero)* spade; *(de cocina)* slice. 2 *Dep (de ping-pong, frontón)* bat; *(de remo)* blade.

palabra *nf* 1 word; **de p.,** by word of mouth; **dirigir la p. a algn,** to address sb; **juego de palabras,** pun. 2 *(promesa)* word; **p. de honor,** word of honour. 3 *(turno para hablar)* right to speak; **tener la p.,** to have the floor.

palabrería *nf* palaver.

palabrota *nf* swearword.

palacio *nm (grande)* palace; *(pequeño)* mansion; **P. de Justicia,** Law Courts.

paladar *nm* 1 palate. 2 *(sabor)* taste.

paladear *vtr* to savour, *US* savor, relish.

palanca *nf* 1 lever. 2 *(manecilla)* handle, stick; *Aut* **p. de cambio,** gearstick, *US* gearshift; **p. de mando,** control lever. 3 *Dep (trampolín)* diving board.

palangana *nf* washbasin.

palco *nm* box.

paleolítico,-a *adj* palaeolithic, paleolithic.

paleontología *nf* palaeontology, paleontology.

Palestina *n* Palestine.

palestino,-a *adj & nmf* Palestinian.

palestra *nf* arena; **fig salir** *o* **saltar a la p.,** to enter the fray, take the field.

paleta *nf* 1 *(espátula)* slice. 2 *(de pintor)* palette; *(de albañil)* trowel. 3 *Dep (de cricket, pingpong)* bat.

paletilla *nf* 1 shoulder blade. 2 *Culin* shoulder.

paleto,-a I *adj fam pey* unsophisticated, boorish. **II** *nm,f fam pey* country bumpkin, yokel.

paliar [12] *vtr* to alleviate, palliate.

paliativo,-a *adj & nm* palliative.

palidecer [33] *vi* 1 *(persona)* to turn pale. 2 *fig (disminuir)* to diminish, be on the wane.

palidez *nf* paleness, pallor.

pálido,-a *adj* pale.

palillero *nm* toothpick case.

palillo *nm* 1 *(mondadientes)* toothpick; **palillos chinos,** chopsticks. 2 *Mús* drumstick.

palio *nm* 1 canopy. 2 *Rel* pallium.

palique *nm fam* chat, small talk.

paliza *nf* 1 *(zurra)* thrashing, beating; **darle a algn una p.,** to beat sb up. 2 *(derrota)* beating. 3 *fam (pesadez)* bore, pain (in the neck).

palma *nf* 1 *Anat* palm. 2 *Bot* palm tree. 3 **hacer palmas,** to applaud.

palmada *nf* 1 *(golpe)* slap. 2 **palmadas,** applause, clapping.

palmar *vtr fam* **palmarla,** to snuff it, kick the bucket.

palmarés *nm* 1 *(historial)* service record. 2 *(vencedores)* list of winners.

palmatoria *nf* candlestick.

palmera *nf* palm tree.

palmo *nm (medida)* span; *fig* **p. a p.,** inch by inch.

palo *nm* 1 stick; *(vara)* rod; *(de escoba)* broomstick; *fig* **a p. seco,** on its own. 2 *(golpe)* blow; *fig* **dar un p. a algn,** to let sb down. 3 **p.** **de,** wooden. 4 *Dep (de portería)* woodwork. 5 *Golf* club. 6 *Naipes* suit.

paloma *nf* pigeon; *Lit* dove; **p. mensajera,** homing *o* carrier pigeon.

palomar *nm* pigeon house, dovecote.

palomilla *nf* 1 grain moth. 2 *(tuerca)* wing *o* butterfly nut.

palomitas *(de maíz)* *nfpl* popcorn sing.

palpable *adj* palpable.

palpar *vtr* to touch, feel; *Med* to palpate.

palpitación *nf* palpitation, throbbing.

palpitante *adj* palpitating, throbbing; *(asunto)* burning.

palpitar *vi* to palpitate, throb.

palúdico,-a *adj* malarial.

paludismo *nm* malaria.

palurdo,-a *adj* uncouth, boorish.

pamela *nf* broad-brimmed hat.

pampa *nf* pampa, pampas *pl.*

pamplina *nf fam* nonsense.

pan *nm* bread; **p. de molde,** loaf of bread; **p. integral,** wholemeal *o* wholewheat bread; **p. rallado,** breadcrumbs *pl*; *fam fig* **más bueno que el p.,** as good as gold; *fam fig* **es p. comido,** it's a piece of cake.

pana *nf* corduroy.

panacea *nf* panacea.

panadería *nf* baker's (shop), bakery.

panadero,-a *nm,f* baker.

panal *nm* honeycomb.

Panamá *n* Panama.

panamá *nm (sombrero)* Panama hat.

panameño,-a *adj & nmf* Panamanian.

pancarta *nf* placard; *(en manifestación)* banner.

páncreas *nm inv* pancreas.

panda¹ *nm* panda.

panda² *nf* gang.

pandereta *nf* tambourine.
pandilla *nf fam* gang.
panecillo *nm* bread roll.
panel *nm* panel.
panera *nf* breadbasket.
pánfilo,-a *adj fam (bobo)* silly, stupid; *(crédulo)* gullible.
panfleto *nm* lampoon, political pamphlet.
pánico *nm* panic; **sembrar el p.**, to cause panic.
panocha *nf Bot* corncob; *(de trigo etc)* ear.
panoli *nmf fam* idiot.
panorama *nm (vista)* panorama, view; *fig* panorama.
panorámico,-a *adj* panoramic.
pantaletas *nfpl Am* panties.
pantalón *nm (usu pl)* trousers *pl;* **p. vaquero**, jeans *pl.*
pantalla *nf* 1 *Cin TV Inform* screen. 2 *(de lámpara)* shade. 3 *fig* **servir de p.**, to act as a decoy.
pantano *nm Geog* 1 *(natural)* marsh, bog. 2 *(artificial)* reservoir.
panteón *nm* pantheon, mausoleum; **p. familiar**, family vault.
pantera *nf* panther.
pantomima *nf Teat* pantomime, mime; *pey (farsa)* farce.
pantorrilla *nf Anat* calf.
pantufla *nf* slipper.
panty *nm* (pair of) tights *pl.*
panza *nf fam* belly, paunch.
panzada *nf fam* bellyful.
panzudo,-a, panzón,-ona, *adj* potbellied, paunchy.
pañal *nm* nappy, *US* diaper; *fig* **estar en pañales**, to be in one's infancy.
paño *nm* 1 cloth material; *(de lana)* woollen *o US* woolen cloth; *(para polvo)* duster, rag; *(de cocina)* dishcloth; *fig* **paños calientes**, half measures. 2 **paños**, *(ropa)* clothes; **en p. menores**, in one's underclothes.
pañoleta *nf* 1 shawl. 2 *Taur* bullfighter's tie.
pañuelo *nm* handkerchief; *(pañoleta)* shawl.
papa *nf* potato; *fam* **no saber ni p.** *(de algo)*, not to have the faintest idea (about sth).
Papa *nm* **el P.**, the Pope.
papá *nm fam* dad, daddy.
papada *nf* double chin.
papagayo *nm* parrot.
papamoscas *nm inv* flycatcher.
papanatas *nmf inv* sucker, twit.
paparrucha(da) *nf (piece) of* nonsense.
papaya *nf* papaya *o* pawpaw fruit.
papear *vi arg* to eat.
papel *nm* 1 paper; *(hoja)* piece *o* sheet of paper; **papeles**, *(documentos)* documents, identification papers; **p. higiénico**, toilet paper; **p. carbón**, carbon paper; **p. de carta**, writing paper; **p. de**

aluminio/de estraza, aluminium foil/brown paper; **p. de fumar**, cigarette paper; **p. de lija**, sandpaper; *Fin* **p. moneda**, paper money, banknotes *pl;* **p. pintado**, wallpaper; **p. secante**, blotting paper. 2 *Cin Teat* role, part.
papeleo *nm fam* paperwork.
papelera *nf (en despacho)* wastepaper basket; *(en calle)* litter bin.
papelería *nf (tienda)* stationer's.
papeleta *nf* 1 *(de rifa)* ticket; *(de votación)* ballot paper; *(de resultados)* report. 2 *fam (dificultad)* tricky problem, difficult job.
papeo *nm arg* grub.
paperas *nfpl Med* mumps.
papilla *nf* pap, mush; *(de niños)* baby food.
papista *nmf* papist.
Papúa Nueva Guinea *n* Papua New Guinea.
paquete *nm* 1 *(de cigarrillos etc)* packet; *(postal)* parcel, package. 2 *(conjunto)* set, package; *Fin* **p. de acciones**, share package. 3 *Inform* software package. 4 *arg (castigo)* punishment. 5 *arg (pene)* prick.
Paquistán *n* Pakistan.
paquistaní *adj & nmf* Pakistani.
par I *adj Mat* even. **II** *nm* 1 *(pareja)* pair; *(dos)* couple. 2 *Mat* even number; **pares y nones**, odds and evens. 3 *(noble)* peer. 4 *(locuciones)* **a la p.**, *(a la vez)* at the same time; **de p. en p.**, wide open; *fig* **sin p.**, matchless.
para *prep* 1 for; **bueno p. la salud**, good for your health; **¿p. qué?**, what for?; **p. ser inglés habla muy bien español**, for an Englishman he speaks very good Spanish. 2 *(finalidad)* to, in order to; **p. terminar antes**, to *o* in order to finish earlier; **p. que lo disfrutes**, for you to enjoy. 3 *(tiempo)* by; **p. entonces**, by then. 4 *(a punto de)* **está p. salir**, it's about to leave. 5 *(locuciones)* **decir p. sí**, to say to oneself; **ir p. viejo**, to be getting old; **no es p. tanto**, it's not as bad as all that; **p. mí**, in my opinion.
parábola *nf* 1 *Geom* parabola. 2 *Rel* parable.
parabólico,-a *adj* parabolic; *TV* **antena parabólica**, satellite dish.
parabrisas *nm inv Aut* windscreen, *US* windshield.
paraca *nm fam* para(chutist).
paracaídas *nm inv* parachute.
paracaidista *nmf Dep* parachutist; *Mil* paratrooper.
parachoques *nm inv* bumper, *US* fender.
parada *nf* 1 stop; **p. de autobús**, bus stop; **p. de taxis**, taxi stand *o* rank. 2 *Ftb* save, stop.
paradero *nm* 1 *(lugar)* whereabouts *pl.* 2 *Am (apeadero)* stop.
parado,-a a I *adj* 1 stopped, stationary; *(quieto)* still; *(fábrica)* at a standstill; *fig*

salir bien/mal p., to come off well/badly. 2 *(desempleado)* unemployed, out of work. 3 *fig (lento)* slow. 4 *Am (de pie)* standing. II *nm,f* unemployed person.

paradoja *nf* paradox.

paradójico,-a *adj* paradoxical.

parador *nm* roadside inn; **p. nacional** *o* **de turismo,** state-run hotel.

parafernalia *nf* paraphernalia *pl.*

parafrasear *vtr* to paraphrase.

paráfrasis *nf inv* paraphrase.

paraguas *nm inv* umbrella.

Paraguay *n* Paraguay.

paragüero *nm* umbrella stand.

paraíso *nm* 1 paradise; **p. terrenal,** heaven on earth; *Fin* **p. fiscal,** tax haven. 2 *Teat* gods *pl,* gallery.

paraje *nm* spot, place.

paralelo,-a *adj & nm* parallel.

parálisis *nm inv* paralysis; **p. infantil,** poliomyelitis.

paralítico,-a *adj & nm,f* paralytic.

paralización *nf* 1 *Med* paralysis. 2 *(detención)* halting, stopping.

paralizar [1] I *vtr* to paralyse; *(circulación)* to stop. II **paralizarse** *vr fig* to come to a standstill.

parámetro *nm* parameter.

paramilitar *adj* paramilitary.

páramo *nm* bleak plain *o* plateau, moor.

parangón *nm fml* comparison; **sin p.,** incomparable.

paranoia *nf* paranoia.

paranoico,-a *adj & nm,f* paranoiac, paranoid.

parapeto *nm* 1 parapet. 2 *(de defensa)* barricade.

parapléjico,-a *adj & nm,f* paraplegic.

parar I *vtr* 1 to stop. 2 *Dep* to save. II *vi* 1 to stop; **p. de hacer algo,** to stop doing sth; **sin p.,** nonstop, without stopping; *fam* **no p.,** to be always on the go 2 *(alojarse)* to stay. 3 *(acabar)* **fue a p. a la cárcel,** he ended up in jail. III **pararse** *vtr* 1 to stop; **p. a pensar,** to stop to think. 2 *Am (ponerse en pie)* to stand up.

pararrayos *nm inv* lightning conductor, *US* lightning rod.

parásito,-a *adj* parasite.

parasol *nm* sunshade, parasol.

parcela *nf* plot.

parche *nm* 1 patch. 2 *(emplasto)* plaster. 3 *pey (chapuza)* botched up *o* slapdash job.

parchís *nm* ludo.

parcial I *adj* 1 *(partidario)* biased. 2 *(no completo)* partial; **a tiempo p.,** part-time. II *adj & nm* **(examen) p.,** class examination.

parcialmente *adv* partially, partly.

parco,-a *adj (moderado)* sparing; *(frugal)* scant.

pardillo,-a I *nm,f pey* yokel, bumpkin. II *nm Orn* linnet.

pardo,-a *adj (marrón)* brown; *(gris)* dark grey.

parecer¹ *nm* 1 *(opinión)* opinion. 2 *(aspecto)* appearance.

parecer² [33] I *vi* to seem, look (like); **parece difícil,** it seems *o* looks difficult; **parecía (de) cera,** it looked like wax; *(uso impers)* **parece que no arranca,** it looks as if it won't start; **como te parezca,** whatever you like; **¿te parece?,** is that okay with you?; **parece que sí/no,** I think/don't think so; **¿qué te parece?,** what do you think of it? II **parecerse** 1 *vr* to be alike; **no se parecen,** they're not alike. 2 **p. a,** to look like, resemble; **se parecen a su madre,** they look like their mother.

parecido,-a *adj* 1 alike, similar. 2 **bien p.,** good-looking. II *nm* likeness, resemblance; **tener p. con algn,** to bear a resemblance to sb.

pared *nf* wall.

paredón *nm* 1 thick wall. 2 *fam* **le llevaron al p.,** he was shot by firing squad.

pareja *nf* 1 pair; **por parejas,** in pairs. 2 *(hombre y mujer)* couple; *(hijo e hija)* boy and girl; **hacen buena p.,** they make a nice couple, they're well matched. 3 *(en naipes)* pair; **doble p.,** two pairs. 4 *(de baile, juego)* partner.

parejo,-a *adj* 1 *(parecido)* similar, alike. 2 **ir parejos,** to be neck and neck.

parentela *nf fam* relations *pl,* relatives *pl.*

parentesco *nm* relationship, kinship.

paréntesis *nm inv* 1 parenthesis, bracket; **entre p.,** in parentheses *o* brackets. 2 *(descanso)* break, interruption; *(digresión)* digression.

parezco *indic pres* → **parecer.**

paria *nmf* pariah.

parida *nf fam* silly thing.

pariente *nmf* relative, relation.

parir *vtr & vi* to give birth (to).

París *n* Paris.

parking *nm* car park, *US* parking lot.

parlamentario,-a I *adj* parliamentary. II *nm,f* member of parliament, MP, *US* congressman.

parlamento *nm* parliament.

parlanchín,-ina *adj fam* talkative, chatty.

parné *nm arg* dough, cash.

paro *nm* 1 *(huelga)* strike, stoppage. 2 *(desempleo)* unemployment; **estar en p.,** to be unemployed; **cobrar el p.,** to be on the dole.

parodia *nf* parody.

parodiar [12] *vtr* to parody.

parpadear *vi (ojos)* to blink; *fig (luz)* to flicker.

parpadeo *nm (de ojos)* blinking; *fig (de luz)* flickering.

párpado *nm* eyelid.

parque *nm* 1 park; **p. de atracciones,** funfair; **p. zoológico,** zoo; **p. nacional/ natural,** national park/nature reserve. 2

(de niños) playpen. **3 p. móvil,** total number of cars.

parqué nm parquet.

parquear vtr Am to park.

parquet nm → **parqué.**

parquímetro nm Aut parking meter.

parra nf grapevine.

párrafo nm paragraph.

parranda nf fam spree.

parricidio nm parricide.

parrilla nf **1** Culin grill; **pescado a la p.,** grilled fish. **2** Téc grate. **3** Aut Dep starting grid.

párroco nm parish priest.

parroquia nf parish; *(iglesia)* parish church.

parroquiano,-a nm,f *(regular)* customer.

parsimonia nf phlegm, calmness.

parte I nf **1** *(sección)* part. **2** *(en una repartición)* share. **3** *(lugar)* place, spot; **en o por todas partes,** everywhere; **se fue por otra p.,** he went another way. **4** Jur party. **5** *(bando)* side; **estoy de tu p.** I'm on your side. **6** euf **partes,** *(genitales)* private parts. **7** *(locuciones)* **por mi p.,** as far as I am concerned; **de p. de ...,** on behalf of ...; **¿de p. de quién?,** who's calling?; **en gran p.,** to a large extent; **en p.,** partly; **la mayor p.,** the majority; **por otra p.,** on the other hand; **tomar p. en,** to take part in. **II** nm *(informe)* report.

partición nf *(reparto)* division, sharing out; *(de herencia)* partition; *(de territorio)* partition.

participación nf **1** participation. **2** Fin *(acción)* share, US stock; **p. en los beneficios,** profit-sharing. **3** *(en lotería)* part of a lottery ticket. **4** *(notificación)* notice, notification.

participante I adj participating. **II** nmf participant.

participar I vi **1** to take part, participate *(en, in)*. **2** Fin to have shares in. **3** fig **p. de,** to share. **II** vtr *(notificar)* to notify.

participio nm Ling participle.

partícula nf particle.

particular I adj **1** *(concreto)* particular. **2** *(privado)* private, personal. **3** *(raro)* peculiar. **II** nmf *(individuo)* private individual. **III** nm *(asunto)* subject, matter.

particularidad nf special feature.

partida nf **1** *(salida)* departure. **2** Com *(remesa)* batch, consignment. **3** *(juego)* game. **4** Fin *(entrada)* item. **5** Jur *(certificado)* certificate; **p. de nacimiento,** birth certificate.

partidario,-a I adj ser/no ser **p. de algo,** to be for/against sth. **II** nm,f supporter, follower; **es p. del aborto,** he is in favour of abortion.

partidista adj biased, partisan.

partido,-a nm **1** Pol party. **2** Dep match, game; **p. amistoso,** friendly game; **p. de vuelta,** return match. **3** *(provecho)* advantage; **sacar p. de,** to profit from. **4** Jur *(distrito)* district. **5** **tomar p. por,** to side with. **6** **ser un buen p.,** to be a good catch.

partir I vtr **1** to break; *(dividir)* to split, divide; *(cortar)* to cut; **p. a algn por la mitad,** to mess things up for sb. **II** vi **1** *(marcharse)* to leave, set out o off. **2** **a p. de,** from. **III partirse** vr to split *(up)*, break *(up)*; fam **p. de risa,** to split one's sides laughing.

partisano,-a nm,f partian.

partitura nf Mús score.

parto nm childbirth, labour, US labor; **estar de p.,** to be in labour.

parvulario nm nursery school, kindergarten.

párvulo,-a nm,f infant.

pasa nf raisin; **p. de Corinto,** currant.

pasable adj passable, tolerable.

pasada nf **1** de **p.,** in passing. **2** *(jugarreta)* dirty trick. **3** fam **eso es una p.,** it's too much!

pasadizo nm corridor, passage.

pasado,-a I adj **1** *(último)* last; **el año/lunes p.,** last year/Monday. **2** *(anticuado)* dated, old-fashioned; **p. (de moda),** out of date o fashion. **3** *(alimento)* bad. **4** Culin cooked; **lo quiero muy p.,** I want it well done. **5 p. mañana,** the day after tomorrow. **II** nm past.

pasador nm **1** *(prenda)* pin, clasp; *(para el pelo)* (hair) slide, hairpin. **2** *(pestillo)* bolt, fastener.

pasaje nm **1** passage. **2** *(calle)* alley. **3** *(pasajeros)* passengers pl. **4** *(billete)* ticket.

pasajero,-a I adj passing, temporary; **aventura pasajera,** fling. **II** nm,f passenger.

pasamanos nm inv *(barra)* handrail; *(de escalera)* banister, bannister.

pasamontañas nm inv balaclava.

pasaporte nm passport.

pasapurés nm inv Culin potato masher.

pasar I vtr **1** to pass; *(objeto)* to pass, give; *(mensaje)* to give; *(página)* to turn; *(trasladar)* to move; **p. algo a limpio,** to make a clean copy of sth. **2** *(tiempo)* to spend, pass; **p. el rato,** to kill time. **3** *(padecer)* to suffer, endure; **p. hambre,** to go hungry. **4** *(río, calle)* to cross; *(barrera)* to pass through o over; *(límite)* to go beyond. **5** *(perdonar)* to forgive, tolerate; **p. algo (por alto),** to overlook sth. **6** *(introducir)* to insert, put through. **7** *(examen)* to pass. **8** Cin to run, show.

II vi **1** to pass; **¿ha pasado el autobús?,** has the bus gone by?; **ha pasado un hombre,** a man has gone past; **p. de largo,** to go by *(without stopping)*; **el tren pasa por Burgos,** the train goes via

Burgos; **pasa por casa mañana**, come round to my house tomorrow. **2 p. a**, (*continuar*) to go on to; **p. a ser**, to become. **3** (*entrar*) to come in. **4** (*tiempo*) to pass, go by. **5 p. sin**, to do without; **ya no paso de tí**, I couldn't care less about you; *fam* **yo paso**, count me out.

III *v impers* (*suceder*) to happen; *¿qué pasa aquí?*, what's going on here?; *¿qué te pasa?*, what's the matter?; *fam ¿qué pasa?*, (*saludo*) how are you?; **pase lo que pase**, whatever happens, come what may.

IV pasarse *vr* **1** se me pasó la ocasión, I missed my chance; **se le pasó llamarme**, he forgot to phone me. **2** (*gastar tiempo*) to spend *o* pass time; **pasárselo bien/mal**, to have a good/bad time. **3** (*comida*) to go off. **4** *fam* (*excederse*) to go too far; **no te pases**, don't overdo it. **5 pásate por mi casa**, call round to my place.

pasarela *nf* (*puente*) footbridge; (*de barco*) gangway; (*de moda*) catwalk.

pasatiempo *nm* pastime, hobby.

pascua *nf* **1** Easter. **2 pascuas**, (*Navidad*) Christmas *sing*; **¡felices Pascuas!**, Merry Christmas!

pase *nm* **1** pass, permit. **2** *Cin* showing.

pasear I *vi* to go for a walk, take a walk. **II** *vt* **1** (*persona*) to take for a walk; (*perro*) to walk. **2** *fig* (*exhibir*) to show off. **III** pasearse *vr* to go for a walk.

paseíllo *nm Taur* opening parade.

paseo *nm* **1** walk; (*en bicicleta, caballo*) ride; (*en coche*) drive; **dar un p.**, to go for a walk *o* a ride. **2** (*avenida*) avenue.

pasillo *nm* corridor; *Av* **p. aéreo**, air corridor.

pasión *nf* passion.

pasional *adj* passionate; **crimen p.**, crime of passion.

pasividad *nf* passivity, passiveness.

pasivo,-a I *adj* passive; (*inactivo*) inactive. **II** *nm Com* liabilities *pl*.

pasmado,-a *adj* (*asombrado*) astounded, amazed; (*atontado*) flabbergasted; **dejar p.**, to astonish; **quedarse p.**, to be amazed.

pasmo *nm* astonishment, amazement.

paso,-a¹ *adj* ciruela pasa, prune; **uva pasa**, raisin.

paso² *nm* **1** step; (*modo de andar*) gait, walk; (*ruido al andar*) footstep; **Mil llevar el p.**, to keep in step; *fig* **a dos pasos**, a short distance away; *fig* **seguir los pasos de algn**, to follow in sb's footsteps. **2** (*camino*) passage, way; **abrirse p.**, to force one's way through; *Aut* **'ceda el p.'**, 'give way'; **'prohibido el p.'**, 'no entry'; **a nivel**, level *o US* grade crossing; **p. de cebra**, zebra crossing; **p. de peatones**, pedestrian crossing, *US* crosswalk; **p. elevado**, flyover, *US* overpass; **p. subterráneo**, (*para peatones*) subway; (*para co-*

ches) underpass. **3** (*acción*) passage, passing; **a su p.**, when he was in town; **el p. del tiempo**, the passage of time; **estar de p.**, to be just passing through. **4 p. de montaña**, mountain pass.

pasodoble *nm* paso doble.

pasota *nmf fam* waster.

pasta *nf* **1** paste; **p. de dientes** *o* **dentífrica**, toothpaste. **2** (*de pan, pasteles*) dough; (*italiana*) pasta. **3** (*galleta*) biscuit. **4** *fam* (*dinero*) dough, bread.

pastar *vtr & vi* to graze, pasture.

pastel *nm* **1** cake; (*de carne, fruta*) pie. **2** *Arte* pastel. **3** *fam* **descubrir el p.**, to spill the beans.

pastelería *nf* **1** (*tienda*) confectioner's (snop). **2** (*dulces*) confectionery.

pastelero,-a *nm,f* pastrycook, confectioner.

pastiche *nm* **1** pastiche. **2** *fam* (*chapuza*) botch(-up).

pastilla *nf* **1** tablet, pill; **pastillas para la tos**, cough drops. **2** (*de jabón*) bar. **3** *fam* **a toda p.**, at full speed.

pastizal *nm* grazing land, pasture.

pasto *nm* **1** (*hierba*) grass. **2** (*alimento*) fodder; **ser p. de**, to fall prey to.

pastor,-a I *nm,f* (*mujer*) shepherd; (*mujer*) shepherdess; **perro p.**, sheepdog; **p. alemán**, Alsatian. **II** *nm Rel* pastor, minister.

pastoreo *nm* shepherding.

pastoso,-a *adj* pasty; (*lengua*) furry.

pata *nf* leg; *fig* **patas arriba**, upside down; **estirar la p.**, to kick the bucket; **mala p.**, bad luck; **meter la p.**, to put one's foot in it; **p. de gallo**, crow's foot.

patada *nf* (*puntapié*) kick, stamp.

patalear *vi* to stamp one's feet (with rage).

pataleo *nm* kicking; (*de rabia*) stamping.

patán *nm* bumpkin, yokel.

patata *nf* potato; **patatas fritas**, chips, *US* French fries; (*de bolsa*) crisps, *US* potato chips.

patatús *nm inv fam* dizzy spell, queer turn.

paté *nm* pâté.

patear I *vtr* (*pelota*) to kick; (*pisotear*) to stamp on. **II** *vi* (*patalear*) to stamp (one's foot with rage).

patentar *vtr* to patent.

patente I *nf* (*autorización*) licence, *US* license; (*de invención*) patent. **II** *adj* (*evidente*) patent, obvious.

pateo *nm* stamping; (*abucheo*) boo(ing), jeer(ing).

paternal *adj* paternal, fatherly.

paternalista *adj* paternalistic.

paternidad *nf* paternity, fatherhood.

paterno,-a *adj* paternal.

patético,-a *adj* moving.

patíbulo *nm* scaffold, gallows *pl*.

patidifuso,-a adj fam dumbfounded, flabbergasted.

patilla nf **1** (de gafas) leg. **2 patillas,** (pelo) sideboards, US sideburns.

patín nm **1** skate; (patinete) scooter; **p. de ruedas/de hielo,** roller/ice skate. **2** Náut pedal boat.

patinaje nm skating; **p. artístico,** figure skating; **p. sobre hielo/ruedas,** ice-/roller skating.

patinar vi **1** to skate; (sobre ruedas) to roller-skate; (sobre hielo) to ice-skate. **2** (deslizarse) to slide; (resbalar) to slip; (vehículo) to skid. **3** fam (equivocarse) to put one's foot in it, slip up.

patinazo nm **1** skid. **2** fam (equivocación) blunder, boob.

patinete nm scooter.

patio nm **1** (de una casa) yard, patio; (de recreo) playground. **2** Teat Cin **p. de butacas,** stalls.

pato nm duck; fam **pagar el p.,** to carry the can.

patochada nf blunder, boob.

patógeno,-a adj pathogenic.

patología nf pathology.

patológico,-a adj pathological.

patoso,-a adj clumsy, awkward.

patraña nf nonsense.

patria nf fatherland, native country; **madre p.,** motherland; **p. chica,** one's home town o region.

patriarca nm patriarch.

patrimonio nm (bienes) wealth; (herencia) inheritance.

patriota nmf patriot.

patriótico,-a adj patriotic.

patriotismo nm patriotism.

patrocinador,-a I adj sponsoring. **II** nmf sponsor.

patrocinar vtr to sponsor.

patrocinio nm sponsorship, patronage.

patrón,-ona I nm,f (jefe) boss. **2** (de pensión) (hombre) landlord; (mujer) landlady. **3** Rel patron saint. **II** nm **1** pattern. **2** (medida) standard.

patronal I adj employers'; **cierre p.,** lock-out; **clase p.,** managerial class. **II** nf (dirección) management.

patronato, patronazgo nm **1** (institución benéfica) foundation. **2** (protección) patronage.

patrono,-a nm,f **1** boss; (empresario) employer. **2** Rel patron saint.

patrulla nf **1** patrol; **estar de p.,** to be on patrol; **coche p.,** patrol car. **2** (grupo) group, band; **p. de rescate,** rescue party; **p. ciudadana,** vigilante group.

patrullar I vtr to patrol. **II** vi to patrol.

paulatino,-a adj gradual.

paupérrimo,-a (adj superl de **pobre**) extremely poor, poverty-stricken.

pausa nf pause, break; Mús rest.

pausado,-a adj unhurried, calm.

pauta nf guidelines pl.

pava nf fam **pelar la p.,** to chat.

pavesa nf ash.

pavimentar vtr to pave.

pavimento nm (de calle) paving; (de habitación) flooring.

pavo nm **1** turkey; fam **no ser moco de p.,** to be nothing to scoff at. **2** fam (tonto) twit; fam **estar en la edad del p.,** to be growing up.

pavonearse vr fam to show off, strut.

pavoneo nm fam showing off, strutting.

pavor nm terror, dread.

payaso nm clown; **hacer el p.,** to act the clown.

payés,-a nm,f Catalan o Balearic peasant.

payo,-a nm,f non-Gipsy person.

paz nf peace; (sosiego) peacefulness; fam **¡déjame en p.!,** leave me alone!, **hacer las paces,** to make (it) up.

pazguato,-a adj **1** (estúpido) silly, stupid. **2** (mojigato) prudish.

PCE nm Pol abr de **Partido Comunista de España,** Spanish Communist party.

pe nf fam de **pe a pa,** from A to Z.

peaje nm toll; **autopista de p.,** toll motorway, US turnpike.

peatón nm pedestrian.

peca nf freckle.

pecado nm Rel sin; **p. capital o mortal,** deadly sin.

pecador,-a nm,f sinner.

pecaminoso,-a adj sinful.

pecar [1] vi to sin; fig **p. por defecto,** to fall short of the mark.

pecera nf fishbowl, fishtank.

pecho nm chest; (de mujer) breast, bust; (de animal) breast; **dar el p. (a un bebé),** to breast-feed (a baby); fig **tomar(se) (algo) a p.,** to take (sth) to heart.

pechuga nf **1** (de ave) breast. **2** fam pey (de mujer) boob.

pectoral adj pectoral, chest.

peculiar adj (raro) peculiar; (característico) characteristic.

peculiaridad nf peculiarity.

pedagogía nf pedagogy.

pedagógico,-a adj pedagogical.

pedal nm pedal.

pedalear vi to pedal.

pedante I adj pedantic. **II** nmf pedant.

pedantería nf pedantry.

pedazo nm piece, bit; **a pedazos,** in pieces; **caerse a pedazos,** to fall apart o to pieces; **hacer pedazos,** to break o tear to pieces, smash (up); fam **¡qué p. de coche!,** what a terrific car!

pederasta nm pederast.

pedernal nm flint.

pedestal nm pedestal.

pediatra nmf paediatrician, US pediatrician.

pediatría nf paediatrics sing, US pediatrics *sing.*

pedicuro,-a *nm,f* chiropodist.

pedido *nm* 1 *Com* order; **hacer un p. a,** to place an order with. 2 *(petición)* request.

pedigrí *nm* pedigree.

pedir [6] *vtr* 1 to ask (for); **p. algo a algn,** to ask sb for sth; **te pido que te quedes,** I'm asking you to stay; **p. prestado,** to borrow; **fig p. cuentas,** to ask for an explanation. 2 *Com & (en bar etc)* to order. 3 *(mendigar)* to beg.

pedo *nm vulg* 1 fart; **tirarse un p.,** to fart. 2 *(borrachera)* bender.

pedrada *nf (golpe)* blow from a stone; *(lanzamiento)* throw of a stone.

pedrea *nf (en lotería)* small prize *pl.*

pedregoso,-a *adj* stony, rocky.

pedrería *nf* precious stones *pl,* gems *pl.*

pedrisco *nm* hailstorm.

pega *nf* 1 *(objeción)* objection; **poner pegas,** to find fault. 2 **de p.,** *(falso)* sham.

pegadizo,-a *adj* catchy.

pegado,-a *adj* 1 *(adherido)* stuck. 2 *(quemado)* burnt.

pegajoso,-a *adj (pegadizo)* sticky; *fig (persona)* tiresome, hard to get rid of.

pegamento *nm* glue.

pegar [7] *I vtr* 1 *(adherir)* to stick; *(con pegamento)* to glue; *(coser)* to sew on; **fam no pegó ojo,** he didn't sleep a wink; **p. fuego a,** to set fire to. 2 *(golpear)* to hit. 3 **p. un grito,** to shout; **p. un salto,** to jump. 4 *fam (contagiar)* to give; **me ha pegado sus manías,** I've caught his bad habits. 5 *(arrimar)* to put against, lean against. *II vi* 1 *(adherirse)* to stick. 2 *(armonizar)* to match, go; **el azul no pega con el verde,** blue and green don't go together *o* don't match; *fig* **ella no pegaría aquí,** she wouldn't fit in here. 3 *(sol)* to beat down. *III* **pegarse** *vr* 1 *(adherirse)* to stick; *(pelearse)* to fight. 2 *fam (darse)* to have, get; **p. un tiro,** to shoot oneself. 3 *(comida)* to get burnt; **se me ha pegado el sol,** I've got a touch of the sun. 4 *fam* **pegársela a algn,** to trick *o* deceive sb. 5 *(arrimarse)* to get close. 6 *fam fig* to stick. 7 *Med (enfermedad)* to be catching *o* contagious; *fig (melodía)* to be catchy.

pegatina *nf* sticker.

peinado,-a *nm* hairstyle, *fam* hairdo.

peinar I *vtr* 1 *(pelo)* to comb. 2 *(registrar)* to comb. II **peinarse** *vr* to comb one's hair.

peine *nm* comb.

peineta *nf* ornamental comb.

pela *nf fam* peseta.

pelado,-a I *adj* 1 *(cabeza)* shorn; *(piel, fruta)* peeled; *(terreno)* bare. 2 *fam* **saqué un cinco p., (en escuela)** I just scraped a pass; **a grito p.,** shouting and bawling. 3 *fam (arruinado)* broke, penniless. 4 *(des-*

vergonzado) impudent, insolent. II *nm fam* haircut.

peladura *nf* peeling.

pelagatos *nmf inv fam* poor devil, nobody.

pelaje *nm* 1 fur, hair. 2 *pey (apariencia)* looks *pl,* appearance.

pelambrera *nf fam* mop (of hair), long *o* thick hair.

pelapatatas *nm inv* potato peeler.

pelar I *vtr (cortar el pelo a)* to cut the hair of; *(fruta, patata)* to peel; *fam* **hace un frío que pela,** it's brass monkey weather. II *vi (despellejar)* to peel. II **pelarse** *vr* 1 *(cortarse el pelo)* to have a hair cut. 2 *fam* **pelárselas,** to do sth fast.

peldaño *nm* step; *(de escalera de mano)* rung.

pelea *nf* fight; *(riña)* row, quarrel; **buscar p.,** to look for trouble.

peleado,-a *adj* estar **p. (con algn),** not to be on speaking terms (with sb).

pelear I *vi* to fight; *(reñir)* to quarrel. II **pelearse** *vr* 1 to fight; *(reñir)* to quarrel. 2 *(enemistarse)* to fall out.

pelele *nm (muñeco)* straw puppet; *fig* puppet.

peleón,-ona *adj* 1 quarrelsome, aggressive. 2 *(vino)* cheap.

peletería *nf* furrier's; *(tienda)* fur shop.

peletero,-a *nm,f* furrier.

peliagudo,-a *adj* difficult, tricky.

pelícano *nm* pelican.

película *nf* 1 *Cin* film, picture, *US* movie; **p. de miedo** *o* **terror,** horror film; **p. del Oeste,** Western; *fam* **de p.,** fabulous. 2 *Fot* film.

peligrar *vi* to be in danger, be threatened; **hacer p.,** to endanger, jeopardize.

peligro *nm* danger; *(riesgo)* risk; **con p. de ...,** at the risk of ...; **correr (el) p. de ...,** to run the risk of ...; **poner en p.,** to endanger.

peligroso,-a *adj* dangerous, risky.

pelirrojo,-a I *adj* red-haired; *(anaranjado)* ginger-haired. II *nm,f* redhead.

pellejo *nm* 1 *(piel)* skin. 2 *(odre)* wineskin. 3 *fam* **arriesgar** *o* **jugarse el p.,** to risk one's neck.

pelliza *nf* fur jacket.

pellizcar [1] *vtr* to pinch, nip.

pellizco *nm* pinch, nip.

pelma *nmf,* **pelmazo,-a** *nm,f (persona)* bore, drag.

pelo *nm* 1 hair; **cortarse el p., (uno mismo)** to cut one's hair; *(en la peluquería)* to have one's hair cut; *fig* **no tiene ni un p. de tonto,** he's no fool; *fig* **no tener pelos en la lengua,** to be very outspoken; *fig* **tomar el p. a algn,** to pull sb's leg, take the mickey out of sb; *fam* **con pelos y señales,** in full detail; *fam* **por los pelos,** by the skin of one's teeth; **me puso el p. de punta,** it gave me the creeps. **2** (de animal) fur, coat, hair. **3** Tex (de una tela) nap, pile. **4** (cerda) bristle.

pelón,-ona adj (sin pelo) bald.

pelota I nf **1** ball; fam **devolver la p.**, to give tit for tat. **2** Dep pelota. **3** fam (cabeza) nut. **4 hacer la p. a algn**, to toady to sb, butter sb up. **5** vulg **pelotas**, (testículos) balls; **en p.**, starkers. **II** nmf fam (pelotillero) crawler.

pelotari nm pelota player.

pelotear vi Dep to kick a ball around; **Ten** to knock up.

peloteo nm Ten knock-up.

pelotilla nf fam **hacer la p. (a algn)**, to fawn on (sb).

pelotillero,-a nm,f fam crawler.

pelotón nm **1** Mil squad. **2** fam (grupo) small crowd, bunch; (en ciclismo) pack. **3** (amasijo) bundle.

pelotudo,-a adj Am slack, sloppy.

peluca nf wig.

peluche nf osito de p., teddy bear.

peludo,-a adj hairy, furry.

peluquería nf hairdresser's (shop).

peluquero,-a nm,f hairdresser.

pelusa nf toupee.

pelusa, pelusilla nf fluff; (de planta) down. **2** fam jealousy (among children).

pelvis nf inv pelvis.

pena nf **1** (tristeza) grief, sorrow; fig **me da p. de ella**, I feel sorry for her; **¡qué p.!**, what a pity! **2** (dificultad) hardships pl, trouble; **no merece** o **vale la p. (ir)**, it's not worth while (going); **a duras penas**, with great difficulty. **3** (castigo) punishment, penalty; **p. de muerte** o **capital**, death penalty.

penacho nm **1** (de ave) crest, tuft. **2** Mil (de plumas) plume.

penal I adj penal; Jur **código p.**, penal code. **II** nm prison, jail.

penalidad nf (usu pl) hardships pl, troubles pl.

penalización nf penalization; Dep penalty.

penalizar [4] vtr to penalize.

penalti nm (pl **penaltis**) Dep penalty; fam **casarse de p.**, to have a shotgun wedding.

penar I vtr to punish. **II** vi to be in torment, suffer.

pendejo nm Am (tonto) jerk, dummy.

pendenciero,-a adj quarrelsome, argumentative.

pendiente I adj **1** (por resolver) pending; Educ **asignatura p.**, failed subject; Com **p. de pago**, unpaid. **2 estar p. de**, (esperar) to be waiting for; (vigilar) to be on the lookout for. **3** (colgante) hanging (de, from). **II** nm (joya) earring. **III** nf slope; (de tejado) pitch.

pendón nm **1** (bandera) banner. **2** pey (mujer) slut, whore; (hombre) playboy.

péndulo nm pendulum.

pene nm penis.

penetración nf penetration; (perspicacia) insight, perception.

penetrante adj penetrating; (frío, voz, mirada) piercing; fig (inteligencia) sharp, acute.

penetrar I vtr to penetrate; **p. un misterio**, to get to the bottom of a mystery. **II** vi (entrar) to go o get (**en**, in).

penicilina nf penicillin.

península nf peninsula.

penique nm penny, pl **pence**.

penitencia nf penance.

penitenciaria nf prison.

penitenciario,-a adj penitentiary, prison.

penoso,-a adj **1** (lamentable) sorry, distressing. **2** (laborioso) laborious, difficult.

pensado,-a adj **1** thought out; **bien p.**, ... on reflection, ...; **en el momento menos p.**, when least expected; **mal p.**, twisted; **tener algo p.**, to have sth planned, have sth in mind; **p. p. ir**, I intend to go. **2** (concebido) designed.

pensamiento nm **1** thought. **2** (máxima) saying, motto. **3** Bot pansy.

pensar [1] **1** vi to think (**en**, of, about; **sobre**, about, over); fig **sin p.**, (con precipitación) without thinking; (involuntariamente) involuntarily. **II** vtr **1** to think (**de**, of); (considerar) to think over o about; **piénsalo bien**, think it over; fam **¡ni pensarlo!**, not on your life! **2** (proponerse) to intend; **pienso quedarme**, I plan to stay. **3** (concebir) to make; **p. un plan**, to make a plan; **p. una solución**, to find a solution.

pensativo,-a adj pensive, thoughtful.

pensión nf **1** (residencia) boarding house; (hotel) guesthouse; **media p.**, half board; **p. completa**, full board. **2** (paga) pension, allowance; **p. vitalicia**, life annuity.

pensionista nmf pensioner.

pentágono nm pentagon.

pentagrama nm staff, stave.

penúltimo,-a adj & nm,f next to the last, penultimate.

penumbra nf penumbra, half-light.

penuria nf scarcity, shortage.

peña nf **1** rock, crag. **2** (de amigos) club. **3** fam (gente) people.

peñasco nm rock, crag.

peñón nm rock; **el P. de Gibraltar**, the Rock of Gibraltar.

peón nm **1** unskilled labourer o US laborer; **p. agrícola**, farmhand. **2** Ajedrez pawn.

peonada nf day's work.

peonza nf (spinning) top.

peor I adj **1** (comparativo) worse. **2** (superlativo) worst; **en el p. de los casos**, if the worst comes to the worst; **lo p. es que**, the worst of it is that. **II** adv **1** (comparativo) worse; **¡p. para mí o ti!**, too

bad! 2 (*superlativo*) worst.
pepinillo *nm* gherkin.
pepino *nm* cucumber; *fam* **me importa un p.**, I don't give a hoot.
pepita *nf* (*de fruta*) pip, seed; (*de metal*) nugget.
pepitoria *nf* fricassee; **pollo en p.**, fricassee of chicken.
peque *nm fam* (*niño*) kid.
pequeño,-a I *adj* small, little; (*bajo*) short. II *nm,f* child; **de p.**, as a child.
Pequín *n* Peking.
pera *nf* 1 *Bot* pear; **p. de agua**, juicy pear. 2 *vulg* (*pene*) prick.
peral *nm* pear tree.
percance *nm* mishap, setback.
percatarse *vr* **p. de**, to realise.
percepción *nf* perception.
perceptible *adj* 1 perceptible. 2 *Fin* receivable, payable.
percha *nf* (*colgador*) (coat) hanger; (*de gallina*) perch.
perchero *nm* clothes rack.
percibir *vtr* 1 (*notar*) to perceive, notice. 2 (*cobrar*) to receive.
percusión *nf* percussion.
perdedor,-a I *nf* losing. II *nm,f* loser.
perder [3] I *vtr* 1 to lose. 2 (*tren, autobús*) to miss; (*tiempo*) to waste; (*oportunidad*) to miss. 3 (*pervertir*) to be the ruin o downfall of. II *vi* to lose; **echar (algo) a p.**, to spoil (sth); **echarse a p.**, to be spoilt; **salir perdiendo**, to come off worst. III **perderse** *vr* 1 (*extraviarse*) (*persona*) to get lost; **se me ha perdido la llave**, I've lost my key; **no te lo pierdas**, don't miss it. 2 (*pervertirse*) to go to rack and ruin.
perdición *nf* undoing, downfall.
pérdida *nf* 1 loss; **no tiene p.**, you can't miss it. 2 (*de tiempo, esfuerzos*) waste. 3 *Mil* **pérdidas**, losses.
perdido,-a *adj* 1 (*extraviado*) lost. 2 ´ *nm* (*sucio*) filthy. 3 *fam* (*loco*) mad as a hatter. 4 **estar p. por algn**, (*enamorado*) to be crazy about sb. 5 (*acabado*) finished; **¡estoy p.!**, I'm a goner!
perdigón *nm* pellet.
perdiguero,-a *adj* partidge-hunting; **perro p.**, setter.
perdiz *nf* partridge.
perdón *nm* pardon, forgiveness; **¡p.!**, sorry!; **pedir p.**, to apologize.
perdonar *vtr* 1 (*remitir*) to forgive. 2 **perdone!**, sorry!; **perdone que le moleste**, sorry for bothering you. 3 (*eximir*) to pardon; **perdonarle la vida a algn**, to spare sb's life; **p. una deuda**, to write off a debt.
perdurable *adj* 1 (*eterno*) everlasting. 2 (*duradero*) durable, long-lasting.
perdurar *vi* 1 (*durar*) to endure, last. 2 (*persistir*) to persist, continue to exist.
perecedero,-a *adj* perishable; **artículos**

perecederos, perishables.
perecer [33] *vi* to perish, die.
peregrinación *nf*, **peregrinaje** *nm* pilgrimage.
peregrino,-a I *nm,f* pilgrim. II *adj* **ideas peregrinas**, crazy ideas.
perejil *nm* parsley.
perenne *adj* perennial, everlasting.
perentorio,-a *adj* peremptory, urgent.
pereza *nf* laziness, idleness.
perezoso,-a *adj* (*vago*) lazy, idle.
perfección *nf* perfection; **a la p.**, to perfection.
perfeccionamiento *nm* 1 (*acción*) perfecting. 2 (*mejora*) improvement.
perfeccionar *vtr* to perfect; (*mejorar*) improve, make better.
perfeccionista *adj & nmf* perfectionist.
perfecto,-a *adj* perfect.
◆perfectamente *adv* perfectly; **¡p.!**, (*de acuerdo*) agreed!, all right!
perfidia *nf* perfidy, treachery.
perfil *nm* 1 profile; (*contorno*) outline, contour; **de p.**, in profile. 2 *Geom* cross section.
perfilar I *vtr* (*dar forma*) to shape, outline. II **perfilarse** *vr* (*tomar forma*) to take shape.
perforación, perforado *nm* perforation; *Min* drilling, boring; *Inform* (*de tarjetas*) punching.
perforadora punch; *Min* drill; *Inform* **p. de teclado**, keypunch.
perforar *vtr* to perforate; *Min* to drill, bore; *Inform* to punch.
perfumar I *vtr & vi* to perfume. II **perfumarse** *vr* to put on perfume.
perfume *nm* perfume, scent.
pergamino *nm* parchment.
pericia *nf* expertise, skill.
periferia *nf* periphery; (*alrededores*) outskirts *pl*.
periférico,-a *adj & nm* peripheral.
perífrasis *nf inv* periphrasis, long-winded explanation.
perilla *nf* (*barba*) goatee; *fam* **de perilla(s)**, (*oportuno*) at the right moment; (*útil*) very handy.
perímetro *nm* perimeter.
periódico,-a I *nm* newspaper. II *adj* periodic; *Quím* **tabla periódica**, periodic table.
periodismo *nm* journalism.
periodista *nmf* journalist, reporter.
periodo, período *nm* period.
peripecia *nf* sudden change, vicissitude.
periplo *nm* voyage, tour.
periquete *nm fam* **en un p.**, in a jiffy.
periquito *nm* budgerigar, *fam* budgie.
periscopio *nm* periscope.
peritaje *nm* (*estudios*) technical studies *pl*.
perito,-a *nm,f* technician, expert; **p. industrial/agrónomo**, ≈ industrial/ agricultural expert.

peritonitis *nf* peritonitis.
perjudicar [1] *vtr* to harm, injure; *(intereses)* to prejudice.
perjudicial *adj* prejudicial, harmful.
perjuicio *nm* harm, damage; **en p. de,** to the detriment of; **sin p. de,** without prejudice to.
perjurar *vi* to commit perjury.
perjurio *nm* perjury.
perla *nf* pearl; *fig (persona)* gem, jewel; *fam* **me viene de perlas,** it's just the ticket.
permanecer [33] *vi* to remain, stay.
permanencia *nf* 1 *(inmutabilidad)* permanence. 2 *(estancia)* stay.
permanente I *adj* permanent. II *nf (de pelo)* permanent wave, perm; **hacerse la p.,** to have one's hair permed.
permisivo,-a *adj* permissive.
permiso *nm* 1 *(autorización)* permission. 2 *(licencia)* licence, *US* license, permit; **p. de conducir,** driving licence, *US* driver's license; **p. de residencia/trabajo,** residence/work permit. 3 *Mil* leave; **estar de p.,** to be on leave.
permitir I *vtr* to permit, allow; **¿me permite?,** may I? II **permitirse** *vr* 1 to permit o allow oneself; **me permito recordarle que,** let me remind you that. 2 **'no se permite fumar',** 'no smoking'.
permutar *vtr* to exchange.
pernicioso,-a *adj* pernicious.
pernil *nm (de pantalón)* leg; *(jamón)* leg of pork.
pernocta *nf Mil (pase de) p.,** overnight pass.
pero I *conj* but; **p., ¿qué pasa aquí?,** now, what's going on here? II *nm* objection.
perogrullada *nf* truism, platitude.
perol *nm* large saucepan, pot.
perorata *nf* boring speech.
perpendicular *adj & nf* perpendicular.
perpetrar *vtr* to perpetrate, commit.
perpetuar [30] *vtr* to perpetuate.
perpetuo,-a *adj* perpetual, everlasting; *Jur* **cadena perpetua,** life imprisonment.
perplejidad *nf* perplexity, bewilderment.
perplejo,-a *adj* perplexed, bewildered.
perra *nf* 1 bitch. 2 *fam (moneda)* penny; **estar sin una p.,** to be broke.
perrera *nf* kennel, kennels *pl.*
perrería *nf fam* dirty trick.
perro,-a I *nm* dog; *fam* **un día de perros,** a lousy day; *fam* **vida de perros,** dog's life; *Culin* **p. caliente,** hot dog. II *adj fam (vago)* lazy.
persecución *nf* 1 pursuit. 2 *Pol (represión)* persecution.
perseguir [6] *vtr* 1 to pursue, chase; *(correr tras)* to run after, follow. 2 *(reprimir)* to persecute.
perseverante *adj* persevering.
perseverar *vi* 1 to persevere, persist. 2

(durar) to last.
persiana *nf* blinds *pl.*
pérsico,-a *adj* Persian; **golfo P.,** Persian Gulf.
persignarse *vr* to cross oneself.
persistencia *nf* persistence.
persistente *adj* persistent.
persistir *vi* to persist.
persona *nf* person; **algunas personas,** some people; *fam* **p. mayor,** grown-up.
personaje *nm* 1 *Cin Lit Teat* character. 2 *(celebridad)* celebrity, important person.
personal I *adj* personal, private. II *nm* 1 *(plantilla)* staff, personnel. 2 *fam (gente)* people.
personalidad *nf* personality.
personarse *vr* to present oneself, appear in person.
personificar [1] *vtr* to personify.
perspectiva *nf* 1 perspective. 2 *(futuro)* prospect.
perspicacia *nf* insight, perspicacity.
perspicaz *adj* sharp, perspicacious.
persuadir *vtr* to persuade; **estar persuadido de que,** to be convinced that.
persuasión *nf* persuasion.
persuasivo,-a *adj* persuasive, convincing.
pertenecer [33] *vi* to belong (**a,** to).
perteneciente *adj* belonging.
pertenencia *nf* 1 possessions *pl,* property. 2 *(a un partido etc)* affiliation, membership.
pértiga *nf* pole; *Dep* **salto con p.,** pole vault.
pertinaz *adj* 1 persistent. 2 *(obstinado)* obstinate, stubborn.
pertinente *adj* 1 pertinent, relevant. 2 *(apropiado)* appropriate.
perturbación *nf* disturbance; **p. del orden público,** breach of the peace; *Med* **p. mental,** mental disorder.
perturbado,-a *adj* (mentally) deranged o unbalanced.
perturbador,-a I *adj* disturbing. II *nm,f* unruly person.
perturbar *vtr (el orden)* to disturb.
Perú (el) *n* Peru.
peruano,-a *adj & nm,f* Peruvian.
perversión *nf* perversion.
perverso,-a *adj* perverse, evil.
pervertir [5] *vtr* to pervert, corrupt.
pervivir *vi* to survive.
pesa *nf* weight; **levantamiento de pesas,** weightlifting.
pesadez *nf* 1 heaviness; *(de estómago)* fullness. 2 *fam (fastidio)* drag, nuisance.
pesadilla *nf* nightmare; **de p.,** nightmarish.
pesado,-a I *adj* 1 heavy. 2 *(aburrido)* tedious, dull; **¡qué p.!,** what a drag!. II *nm,f* bore.
pesadumbre *nf* grief, affliction.
pésame *nm* condolence, sympathy; **dar el p.,** to offer one's condolences; **mi más**

sentido p., my deepest sympathy.

pesar I vtr to weigh; fig (entristecer) to grieve. **II** vi 1 to weigh; ¿cuánto pesas?, how much do you weigh? 2 (ser pesado) to be heavy. 3 fig (tener importancia) este factor pesa mucho, this is a very important factor. **III** nm 1 (pena) sorrow, grief. 2 (arrepentimiento) regret; **a su p.**, to his regret. 3 **a p. de**, in spite of.

pesaroso,-a adj 1 (triste) sorrowful, sad. 2 (arrepentido) regretful, sorry.

pesca nf fishing; fam **y toda la p.**, and all that.

pescadería nf fish shop, fishmonger's (shop).

pescadero,-a nm,f fishmonger.

pescadilla nf young hake.

pescado nm fish.

pescador,-a I adj fishing. **II** nm,f (hombre) fisherman; (mujer) fisherwoman.

pescante nm 1 (de carruaje) coachman's seat. 2 Constr jib, boom. 3 Náut davit.

pescar [1] **I** vi to fish. **II** vtr 1 to fish. 2 fam (coger) to catch.

pescozada nf, **pescozón** nm slap on the neck o head.

pescuezo nm fam neck.

pese a (que) loc adv in spite of (the fact that).

pesebre nm manger, stall.

peseta nf peseta; fam **hacer la p. a algn**, to give sb the fingers.

pesetero,-a nm,f skinflint.

pesimismo nm pessimism.

pesimista I adj pessimistic. **II** nmf pessimist.

pésimo,-a adj very bad, awful, terrible.

peso nm 1 weight; **al p.**, by weight; **p. bruto/neto**, gross/net weight; fig **me quité un p. de encima**, it took a load off my mind; Box **p. mosca/pesado**, flyweight/heavyweight. 2 (importancia) importance; **de p.**, (persona) influential; (razón) convincing.

pespunte nm backstitch.

pesquero,-a I adj fishing. **II** nm fishing boat.

pesquisa nf inquiry.

pestaña nf 1 eyelash, lash. 2 Téc flange; (de neumático) rim.

pestañear vi to blink; **sin p.**, without batting an eyelid.

peste nf 1 (hedor) stench, stink. 2 Med plague; Hist **la p. negra**, the Black Death. 3 **decir o echar pestes**, to curse.

pesticida nm pesticide.

pestilencia nf stench, stink.

pestilente adj stinking, foul.

pestillo nm bolt, latch.

petaca nf 1 (para cigarrillos) cigarette case; (para bebidas) flask. 2 Am (maleta) suitcase.

petaco nm (de juego) flipper; **máquina de petacos**, pinball machine.

pétalo nm petal.

petardo nm 1 firecracker, firework; Mil petard. 2 fam (persona aburrida) bore. 3 (droga) joint.

petate nm Mil luggage.

petición nf request; Jur petition, plea.

peto nm pantalón de p., dungarees pl.

petrificar [1] vtr, **petrificarse** vr to petrify.

petróleo nm petroleum, oil.

petrolero nm oil tanker.

petulante adj arrogant, vain.

petunia nf petunia.

peyorativo,-a adj pejorative, derogatory.

pez¹ nm fish; **ella está como p. en el agua**, she's in her element; **p. gordo**, big shot.

pez² nf pitch, tar.

pezón nm nipple.

pezuña nf hoof.

piadoso,-a adj 1 (devoto) pious. 2 (compasivo) compassionate; **mentira piadosa**, white lie.

pianista nmf pianist, piano player.

piano nm piano.

piar [29] vi to chirp, tweet.

piara nf herd of pigs.

PIB nm Fin abr de **producto interior bruto**, gross domestic product, GDP.

pibe,-a nm,f Am (niño) kid.

picadero nm riding school.

picadillo nm (de carne) minced meat; (de verduras) vegetable salad.

picado,-a I adj 1 (carne) minced. 2 (fruta) bad; (diente) decayed. 3 (mar) choppy. 4 fam (enfadado) narked. 5 **estar p. con**, (en competición) to be at loggerheads with. **II** nm Av dive; **caer en p.**, to plummet.

picador nm Taur mounted bullfighter, picador.

picadora nf mincer.

picadura nf 1 (mordedura) bite; (de avispa, abeja) sting. 2 (en fruta) spot; Med (de viruela) pockmark; (en diente) decay, caries sing; (en metalurgia) pitting.

picajoso,-a I adj touchy. **II** nm,f touchy person.

picante adj 1 Culin hot, spicy. 2 fig (chiste etc) risqué, spicy.

picapica nf polvos p., itching powder sing.

picaporte nm (aldaba) door knocker; (pomo) door handle.

picar [1] **I** vtr 1 (de insecto, serpiente) to bite; (de avispas, abejas) to sting; (barba) to prick. 2 (comer) (aves) to peck (at); (persona) to nibble, pick at. 3 Pesca to bite. 4 (perforar) to pick, puncture. 5 Culin (carne) to mince. 6 (incitar) to incite, goad; **p. la curiosidad (de algn)**, to arouse (sb's) curiosity. **II** vi 1 (escocer) to itch; (herida) to smart; (el sol) to burn. 2 Culin to be hot. 3 Pesca to bite. 4 fig (dejarse engañar) to swallow it. **III** picarse vr

1 (*hacerse rivales*) to be at loggerheads. 2 (*fruta*) to spot, rot; (*ropa*) to become moth-eaten; (*dientes*) to decay. 3 (*enfadarse*) to get cross. 4 (*drogadicto*) to shoot up.

picardía *nf* 1 (*astucia*) craftiness. 2 (*palabrota*) swear word. 3 (*prenda*) baby-doll pyjamas.

pícaro,-a I *adj* 1 (*travieso*) naughty, mischievous; (*astuto*) sly, crafty. 2 (*procaz*) risqué. II *nm,f* rascal, rogue.

picatoste *nm* crouton.

pichi *nm* pinafore dress.

pichón *nm* young pigeon; **tiro al** *o* **de p.**, pigeon shooting.

pico *nm* 1 (*de ave*) beak, bill; *fam* (*boca*) mouth; **tener un p. de oro**, to have the gift of the gab. 2 (*punta*) corner. 3 *Geog* peak. 4 (*herramienta*) pick, pickaxe, US pickax. 5 (*cantidad*) odd amount; **cincuenta y p.**, fifty odd; **las dos y p.**, just after two. 6 (*drogas*) fix.

picoleto *nm fam* civil guard.

picor *nm* itch, tingling.

picotazo *nm* peck.

picotear *vtr & vi* 1 (*pájaro*) to peck. 2 (*comer*) to nibble.

pictórico,-a *adj* pictorial.

pídola *nf* leapfrog.

pie *nm* 1 foot; **pies**, feet; **a p.**, on foot; **de p.**, standing up; **de pies a cabeza**, from head to foot; **en p.**, standing; **el acuerdo sigue en p.**, the agreement still stands; **hacer p.**, to touch the bottom; **perder p.**, to get out of one's depth; *fig* **a p. o pies juntillas**, blindly; *fig* **al p. de la letra**, to the letter, word for word; *fig* **con buen/mal p.**, on the right/wrong footing; *fig* **con pies de plomo**, gingerly, cautiously; *fig* **dar p. a**, to give cause for. 2 (*de instrumento*) stand; (*de copa*) stem. 3 foot; (*de una ilustración*) caption; **p. de página**, foot of the page. 4 (*medida*) foot. 5 *Teat* cue. 6 *Lit* foot.

piedad *nf* 1 devoutness, piety. 2 (*compasión*) compassion, pity.

piedra *nf* stone; (*de mechero*) flint; **poner la primera p.**, to lay the foundation stone; *fam fig* **me dejó o quedé de p.**, I was flabbergasted.

piel *nf* 1 skin; **p. de gallina**, goose pimples *pl*. 2 (*de fruta, de patata*) skin, peel. 3 (*cuero*) leather; (*con pelo*) fur.

pienso *nm* fodder, feed; **piensos compuestos**, mixed feed *sing*.

pierna *nf* leg.

pieza *nf* 1 piece, part; **p. de recambio**, spare part; *fig* **me dejó o me quedé de una p.**, I was speechless *o* dumbfounded *o* flabbergasted. 2 (*habitación*) room. 3 *Teat* play.

pigmento *nm* pigment.

pigmeo,-a I *adj* pigmy; *fig* pygman. II *nm,f* Pygmy, Pigmy; *fig* pygmy, pigmy.

pijama *nm* pyjamas *pl*.

pijo,-a *fam* I *adj* posh; **un barrio p.**, a posh area. II *nm,f* (*chico*) poor little rich boy; (*chica*) poor little rich girl. III *nm* (*pene*) willy.

pila *nf* 1 *Elec* battery. 2 (*montón*) pile, heap; *fig* (*muchos*) piles *pl*, heaps *pl*, loads *pl*. 3 (*lavadero*) basin. 4 *fig* **nombre de p.**, Christian name.

pilar *nm* 1 *Arquit* pillar. 2 (*fuente*) waterhole.

píldora *nf* pill; **p. abortiva**, morning-after pill; *fig* **dorar la p. a algn**, to butter sb up.

pileta *nf* 1 (*pila*) sink. 2 *Am* (*piscina*) swimming pool.

pilila *nf fam* willy.

pillaje *nm* looting, pillage.

pillar I *vtr* 1 (*robar*) to plunder, loot. 2 (*coger*) to catch; (*alcanzar*) to catch up with; **lo pilló un coche**, he was run over by a car. 3 *fam* to be; **me pilla un poco lejos**, it's a bit far for *o* from me. II **pillarse** *vr* to catch; **p. una dedo/una mano**, to catch one's finger/hand.

pillo,-a I *adj* 1 (*travieso*) naughty. 2 (*astuto*) sly, cunning. II *nm,f* rogue.

pilotar *vtr Av* to pilot, fly; *Aut* to drive; *Náut* to pilot, steer.

piloto *nm* 1 *Av Náut* pilot; *Aut* driver; **piso p.**, show flat; **programa p.**, pilot programme. 2 (*luz*) pilot lamp, light.

piltrafa *nf* 1 (*persona*) weakling; **estar hecho una p.**, to be on one's last legs. 2 (*desecho*) scraps.

pimentón *nm* paprika, red pepper.

pimienta *nf* pepper.

pimiento *nm* (*fruto*) pepper; (*planta*) pimiento; **p. morrón**, sweet pepper; *fam* **me importa un p.**, I don't give a damn, I couldn't care less.

pimpollo *nm* 1 *Bot* shoot. 2 *fam* (*hombre*) handsome young man; (*mujer*) elegant young woman.

pinacoteca *nf* art gallery.

pináculo *nm* pinnacle.

pinar *nm* pine grove, pine wood.

pincel *nm* brush, paintbrush.

pincelada *nf* brushstroke, stroke of a brush.

pinchadiscos *nmf inv fam* disc jockey, DJ.

pinchar I *vtr* 1 (*punzar*) to jag; (*balón, globo*) to burst; (*rueda*) to puncture. 2 *fam* (*incitar*) to prod; (*molestar*) to get at, nag. 3 *Med* to inject, give an injection to. 4 *Tel* to bug. II *vi* 1 *Aut* to get a puncture. 2 *fam* **ni pincha ni corta**, he cuts no ice.

pinchazo *nm* 1 (*punzadura*) prick; *Aut* puncture, blowout. 2 (*de dolor*) sudden *o* sharp pain.

pinche *nm* 1 **p. de cocina**, kitchen assistant. 2 *Am* (*bribón*) rogue.

pinchito *nm* (*de carne*) type of kebab.

pincho nm 1 (*púa*) barb. 2 **p. moruno**, shish kebab; **p. de tortilla**, small portion of omelette.

ping-pong® nm table tennis, ping-pong.

pingüe adj abundant, plentiful; **pingües beneficios**, fat profits.

pingüino nm penguin.

pino nm pine; *fig* **hacer el p.**, to do a handstand; *fam* **en el quinto p.**, in the back of beyond.

pinole nm Am maize drink.

pinta I nf 1 *fam* (*aspecto*) look; **tiene p. de ser interesante**, it looks interesting. 2 (*mota*) dot; (*lunar*) spot. 3 (*medida*) pint. **II** nmf fam shameless person.

pintada nf graffiti.

pintado,-a adj 'recién p.', 'wet paint'; *fam fig* **nos viene que ni p.**, it is just the ticket; *fam fig* **te está que ni p.**, it suits you to a tee.

pintar I vtr 1 (*dar color*) to paint. 2 (*dibujar*) to draw, sketch. **II** vi (*importar*) to count; *fig* **yo aquí no pinto nada**, I am out of place here. **III** pintarse vr 1 (*maquillarse*) to put make-up on. 2 *fam* **pintárselas**, to manage.

pintarraj(e)ar vtr to daub.

pintor,-a nm,f painter.

pintoresco,-a adj 1 (*lugar*) picturesque. 2 (*raro*) eccentric, bizarre.

pintura nf 1 painting; **p. rupestre**, cave painting; *fam fig* **no la puedo ver ni en p.**, I can't stand the sight of her. 2 (*materia*) paint.

pinza nf (*para depilar*) tweezers pl; (*para tender*) clothes peg; (*de animal*) pincer, nipper; *Téc* tongs pl.

piña nf 1 (*de pino*) pine cone; (*ananás*) pineapple. 2 *fig* (*grupo*) clan, clique. 3 *fam* (*golpe*) thump.

piñón nm 1 pine seed o nut. 2 *Téc* pinion.

pío[1] nm fam **no dijo ni p.**, there wasn't a cheep out of him.

pío,-a[2] adj pious.

piojo nm louse.

pionero,-a nm,f pioneer.

pipa nf 1 (*de fumar*) pipe; **fumar en p.**, to smoke a pipe. 2 (*de fruta*) pip; (*de girasol*) sunflower seed.

pipí nm fam pee, wee-wee; **hacer p.**, to pee, wee-wee.

pique nm 1 resentment. 2 (*rivalidad*) needle. 3 **a p. de**, on the point of. 4 **irse a p.**, Náut to sink; (*un plan*) to fall through; (*un negocio*) to go bust.

piqueta nf pickaxe, US pickax.

piquete nm 1 (*de huelga*) picket. 2 *Mil* **p. de ejecución**, firing squad.

pira nf pyre.

pirado,-a adj arg crazy.

piragua nf canoe.

piragüismo nm canoeing.

piragüista nmf canoeist.

pirámide nf pyramid.

piraña nf piranha.

pirarse, pirárselas vr arg to clear off, hop it.

pirata adj & nmf pirate.

piratear vtr fig to pirate.

Pirineo(s) nmpl Pyrenees.

pirita nf pyrite.

pirómano,-a nm,f Med pyromaniac; *Jur* arsonist.

piropo nm echar un p., to pay a compliment.

pirueta nf pirouette; *fig Pol* **hacer una p.**, to do a U-turn.

pirulí nm lollipop; *TV* television tower.

pis nm fam wee-wee, pee; **hacer p.**, to wee-wee, have a pee.

pisada nf step, footstep; (*huella*) footprint.

pisapapeles nm inv paperweight.

pisar vtr to tread on, step on.

piscifactoría nf fish farm.

piscina nf swimming pool.

piscolabis nm inv fam snack.

piso nm 1 flat, apartment; *Pol* **p. franco**, safe house. 2 (*planta*) floor; (*de carretera*) surface.

pisotear vtr (*aplastar*) to stamp on; (*pisar*) to trample on.

pisotón nm **me dio un p.**, he stood on my foot.

pista nf 1 track; **p. de baile**, dance floor; *Dep* **p. de esquí**, ski run o slope; *Dep* **p. de patinaje**, ice rink; *Dep* **p. de tenis**, tennis court; **p. de aterrizaje**, landing strip; **p. de despegue**, runway. 2 (*rastro*) trail, track. 3 **dame una p.**, give me a clue.

pistacho nm pistachio nut.

pisto nm Culin ≈ ratatouille.

pistola nf 1 gun, pistol. 2 (*para pintar*) spray gun.

pistolero nm gunman, gangster.

pistón nm 1 *Téc* (*émbolo*) piston. 2 (*de arma*) cartridge cap. 3 *Mús* key.

pita nf agave.

pitada nf booing, hissing.

pitar I vtr 1 (*silbato*) to blow. 2 *Dep* **el árbitro pitó un penalti**, the referee awarded a penalty. **II** vi 1 to whistle. 2 *Aut* to toot one's horn. 3 *Dep* to referee. 4 *fam* **salir pitando**, to fly off.

pitido nm whistle.

pitillera nf cigarette case.

pitillo nm cigarette, fag.

pito nm 1 whistle; *Aut* horn; *fam* **me importa un p.**, I don't give a hoot. 2 *fam* (*cigarrillo*) fag. 3 *fam* (*pene*) prick, willie.

pitón nm 1 (*serpiente*) python. 2 (*de toro*) horn.

pitorreo nm fam scoffing, teasing; **hacer algo a p.**, to do sth for a laugh.

pivot, pivote nmf pivot.

pizarra nf 1 (*encerado*) blackboard. 2 *Min* slate.

pizca *nf* little bit, tiny piece; **ni p.**, not a bit; **una p. de sal**, a pinch of salt.

placa *nf* 1 plate. 2 *(conmemorativa)* plaque.

placaje *nm Dep* tackle.

placentero,-a *adj* pleasant, agreeable.

placer *nm* pleasure; **ha sido un p.** *(conocerle)*, it's been a pleasure (meeting you); **fml tengo el p. de**, it gives me great pleasure to; **un viaje de p.**, a holiday trip.

placer [33] *vtr* to please.

placidez *nf* placidity.

plácido,-a *adj* placid, easy-going.

plaga *nf* 1 plague. 2 *Agr* pest, blight.

plagar [7] *vtr* to cover, fill.

plagiar [12] *vtr* 1 *(copiar)* to plagiarize. 2 *Am (secuestrar)* to kidnap.

plagiario,-a *nm,f Am (secuestrador)* kidnapper.

plagio *nm* plagiarism.

plan *nm* 1 *(proyecto)* plan. 2 *(programa)* scheme, programme; *Educ* **p. de estudios**, syllabus; **estar a p.** to be on a diet. 3 *fam* **en p. de broma**, for a laugh; **si te pones en ese p.**, if you're going to be like that (about it); **en p. barato**, cheaply. 4 *fam (cita)* date.

plana *nf* 1 page; **a toda p.**, full page; **primera p.**, front page. 2 *Impr* **p. mayor**, staff.

plancha *nf* 1 iron; *(de metal)* plate. 2 *Culin* hotplate; **sardinas a la p.**, grilled sardines. 3 *Impr* plate.

planchado *nm* ironing.

planchar *vtr* to iron.

planchazo *nm fam* blunder, boob.

planeador *nm* glider.

planear I *vtr* to plan. II *vi* to glide.

planeta *nm* planet.

planetario,-a I *adj* planetary. II *nm* planetarium.

planicie *nf* plain.

planificación *nf* planning; **p. familiar**, family planning.

planificar [1] *vtr* to plan.

planilla *nf Am* application form.

plano,-a I *nm* 1 *(de ciudad)* map; *Arquit* plan, draft. 2 *Cin* shot; **un primer p.**, a close-up; *fig* **estar en primer/segundo p.**, to be in the limelight/in the background. 3 *Mat* plane. II *adj* flat, even.

planta *nf* 1 plant. 2 *(del pie)* sole. 3 *(piso)* floor, storey; **p. baja**, ground floor.

plantación *nf* 1 plantation. 2 *(acción)* planting.

plantado,-a *fam* **dejar a algn p.**, to stand sb up.

plantar I *vtr* 1 *(árboles, campo)* to plant. 2 *(poner)* to put, place; **p. cara a algn**, to stand up to sb. 3 *fam* **p. a algn en la calle**, to throw sb out; **le ha plantado su novia**, his girlfriend has ditched him. II **plantarse** *vr* 1 to stand. 2 *(llegar)* to

arrive; **en cinco minutos se plantó aquí**, he got here in five minutes flat.

planteamiento *nm (enfoque)* approach.

plantear I *vtr* 1 *(problema)* to pose, raise. 2 *(planear)* to plan. 3 *(proponer)* to put forward. 4 *(exponer)* to present. II **plantearse** *vr* 1 *(considerar)* to consider. 2 *(problema)* to arise.

plantel *nm fig* cadre, clique.

plantilla *nf* 1 *(personal)* staff, personnel. 2 *(de zapato)* insole. 3 *(patrón)* model, pattern.

plantón *nm* **dar un p. a algn**, to stand sb up.

plañir *vi* to mourn.

plasmar I *vtr* 1 *(reproducir)* to capture. 2 *(expresar)* to express. II **plasmarse** *vr* **p. en**, to take the shape of.

plasta *nmf fam* bore.

plástico,-a I *adj* plastic. II *nm* 1 plastic. 2 *(disco)* record.

plastificar [1] *vtr* to coat *o* cover with plastic.

plastilina® *nf* Plasticine®.

plata *nf* 1 silver; *(objetos de plata)* silverware; *fam* **hablar en p.**, to lay (it) on the line; **p. de ley**, sterling silver. 2 *Am* money.

plataforma *nm* platform.

plátano *nm* 1 *(fruta)* banana. 2 *(árbol)* plane tree; **falso p.**, sycamore.

platea *nf Cin Teat* stalls *pl*, *US* ground floor.

platear *vtr* to silver-plate.

platense I *adj* of *o* from the River Plate. II *nmf* native *o* inhabitant of the River Plate.

plática *nf* chat, talk.

platicar [1] *vi* to chat, talk.

platillo *nm* 1 saucer; **p. volante**, flying saucer. 2 *Mús* cymbal.

platina *nf (de tocadiscos)* deck; **doble p.**, double deck.

platino *nm* 1 platinum. 2 *Aut* **platinos**, contact breaker *sing*, points.

plato *nm* 1 plate, dish. 2 *(parte de una comida)* course; **de primer p.**, for starters; **p. fuerte**, main course; **p. combinado**, one-course meal. 3 *(guiso)* dish. 4 *(de balanza)* pan, tray. 5 *(de tocadiscos)* turntable.

plató *nm Cin TV* (film) set.

plausible *adj* 1 *(admisible)* plausible, acceptable. 2 *(loable)* commendable.

playa *nf* 1 beach; *(costa)* seaside. 2 *Am* **p. de estacionamiento**, car park, *US* parking lot.

playera *nf* 1 *(zapatilla)* sandshoe, *US* sneaker. 2 *Am (camiseta)* teeshirt.

plaza *nf* 1 square. 2 *(mercado)* market, marketplace. 3 *Aut* seat. 4 *(laboral)* post, position. 5 **p. de toros**, bullring.

plazo *nm* 1 *(periodo)* time, period; *(término)* deadline; **a corto/largo p.**, in the

short term/in the long run; **el p. termina el viernes**, Friday is the deadline. 2 *Fin* **comprar a plazos**, to buy on hire purchase, *US* buy on an installment plan; **en seis plazos**, in six instalments.
pleamar *nf* high tide.
plebe *nf* masses *pl*, plebs *pl*.
plebeyo,-a I *adj* plebeian. II *nm,f* plebeian, pleb.
plebiscito *nm* plebiscite.
plegable *adj* folding, collapsible.
plegar [1] I *vtr* to fold. II **plegarse** *vr* to give way, bow.
plegaria *nf* prayer.
pleitear *vi* to conduct a lawsuit, plead.
pleito *nm* 1 *Jur* lawsuit, litigation; **poner un p. (a algn)**, to sue (sb).
plenilunio *nm* full moon.
plenitud *nf* plenitude, fullness; **en la p. de la vida**, in the prime of life.
pleno,-a I *adj* full; **en plena noche**, in the middle of the night; **los empleados en p.**, the entire staff. II *nm* plenary meeting.
pletórico,-a *adj* abundant.
plexiglás® *nm* (*plástico*) Perspex®, *US* Plexiglass®.
pliego *nm* 1 (*hoja*) sheet *o* piece of paper; **p. de condiciones**, bidding specifications. 2 (*carta*) sealed letter.
pliegue *nm* 1 fold. 2 (*de vestido*) pleat.
plinto *nm* Gimn horse.
plisar *vtr* to pleat.
plomero *nm* Am plumber.
plomizo,-a *adj* lead, leaden; (*color*) lead-colored, *US* lead-colored.
plomo *nm* 1 (*en metalurgia*) lead. 2 *Elec* (*fusible*) fuse. 3 (*bala*) slug, pellet.
pluma *nf* 1 feather. 2 (*de escribir*) fountain pen.
plumaje *nm* plumage.
plumazo *nm* **de un p.**, at a stroke.
plumero *nm* 1 (*para el polvo*) feather duster. 2 *fam* **se te ve el p.**, I can see through you.
plumier *nm* pencil box.
plural *adj & nm* plural.
pluralismo *nm* pluralism.
pluriempleo *nm* moonlighting.
plus *nm* bonus, bonus payment.
plusmarca *nf* record.
plusmarquista *nmf* record breaker.
plusvalía *nf* capital gain.
población *nf* 1 (*ciudad*) town; (*pueblo*) village. 2 (*habitantes*) population.
poblado,-a I *adj* 1 populated; *fig* **p. de**, full of. 2 (*barba*) bushy, thick.
poblador,-a *nm,f* settler.
poblar [2] *vtr* 1 (*con gente*) to settle, people; (*con plantas*) to plant. 2 (*vivir*) to inhabit.
pobre I *adj* poor; **¡p.!**, poor thing!; **un hombre p.**, a poor man; **un p. hombre**, a poor devil. II *nmf* poor person; **los po-**

bres, the poor.
pobreza *nf* poverty; *fig* (*de medios, recursos*) lack.
pocilga *nf* pigsty.
pocillo *nm* Am cup.
pócima, poción *nf* potion; *pey* concoction, brew.
poco,-a I *nm* 1 un **p.**, (*con adj o adv*) a little; **un p. tarde/frío**, a little late/cold. 2 **un p.**, (*con sustantivo*) a little; **un p. de azúcar**, a little sugar. II *adj* 1 not much, little; **p. sitio/tiempo**, not much *o* little space/time; **poca cosa**, not much. 2 **pocos,-as**, not many, few; **pocas personas**, not many *o* few people. 3 **unos-as pocos-as**, a few. III *pron* 1 not much; **queda p.**, there isn't much left. 2 **pocos,-as**, (*cosas*) few, not many; **tengo muy pocos**, I have very few, I don't have very many. 3 **pocos,-as**, (*personas*) few people, not many people; **vinieron pocos**, few people came, not many people came. IV *adv* 1 (*con verbo*) not (very) much, little; **ella come p.**, she doesn't eat much, she eats little. 2 (*con adj*) not very; **es p. probable**, it's not very likely. V (*locuciones*) **a p. de**, shortly *o* a little after; **dentro de p.**, soon; **p. a p.**, little by little, gradually; **p. antes/después**, shortly *o* a little before/afterwards; **por p.**, almost.
pocho,-a *adj* 1 (*fruta*) bad, overripe. 2 *fig* (*persona*) (*débil*) off-colour, *US* off-color; (*triste*) depressed, down.
podar *vtr* to prune.
poder¹ *nm* power; *Econ* **p. adquisitivo**, purchasing power.
poder² [18] I *vtr* 1 (*capacidad*) to be able to; **no puede hablar**, she can't speak; **no podré llamarte**, I won't be able to phone; **no puedo más**, I can't take anymore; **guapa a más no p.**, unbelievably pretty. 2 (*permiso*) may, might; **¿puedo pasar?**, can *o* may I (come in)?; **¿se puede (entrar)?**, may I (come in)?; **aquí no se puede fumar**, you can't smoke here. 3 (*uso impers*) (*posibilidad*) may, might; **puede que no lo sepan**, they may *o* might not know; **no puede ser**, that's impossible; **puede (ser)** (que sí), maybe, perhaps. 4 (*deber*) **podrías haberme advertido**, you might have warned me. II *vi* 1 to cope (*con*, with); **no puede con tanto trabajo**, he can't cope with so much work. 2 (*batir*) to be stronger than; **les puede a todos**, he can take on anybody.
poderoso,-a *adj* powerful.
podio, pódium *nm* Dep podium.
podré *indic fut* → **poder**.
podrido,-a *adj* 1 (*putrefacto*) rotten, putrid. 2 (*corrupto*) corrupt; *fam* **p. de dinero**, stinking rich.
podrir *vtr defect* → **pudrir**.

poema nm poem.
poesía nf 1 (género) poetry. 2 (poema) poem.
poeta nmf poet.
poético,-a adj poetic.
póker nm poker.
polaco,-a I adj Polish. II nm,f Pole. III nm (idioma) Polish.
polaridad nf polarity.
polarizar [4] vtr 1 Fís to polarize. 2 fig (ánimo, atención) to concentrate.
polea nf pulley.
polémica nf controversy.
polémico,-a adj controversial.
polemizar [4] vi to argue, debate.
polen nm pollen.
poli- pref poly-.
poli fam I nmf cop. II nf la p., the fuzz pl.
policía I nf police (force). II nmf (hombre) policeman; (mujer) policewoman.
policíaco,-a, policiaco,-a, policial adj police; **novela/película policíaca**, detective story/film.
polideportivo nm sports centre o US center o complex.
poliéster nm polyester.
polietileno nm polythene, US polyethylene.
polifacético,-a adj versatile, many-sided; **es un hombre muy p.**, he's a man of many talents.
poligamia nf polygamy.
políglota adj & nm,f polyglot.
polígono nm polygon; **p. industrial**, industrial estate.
polilla nf moth.
poliomielitis nf polio, poliomyelitis.
politécnico,-a adj & nm polytechnic.
política nf 1 politics sing. 2 (estrategia) policy.
político,-a I adj 1 political. 2 (pariente) in-law; **hermano p.**, brother-in-law; **su familia política**, her in-laws. II nm,f politician.
póliza nf 1 (sello) stamp. 2 **p. de seguros**, insurance policy.
polizón nm stowaway.
polo nm 1 Elec Geog pole; **P. Norte/Sur**, North/South Pole. 2 (selado) ice lolly, US Popsicle®. 2 (prenda) sports shirt, polo neck (sweater). 3 Dep polo.
Polonia n Poland.
polución nf pollution.
poltrona nf easy chair.
polvareda nf cloud of dust.
polvera nf powder compact.
polvo nm 1 dust; **limpiar o quitar el p.**, to dust; **en p.**, powdered; **polvo(s) de talco**, talcum powder. 2 fam **estar hecho p.**, (cansado) to be knackered; (deprimido) to be depressed. 3 vulg **echar un p.**, to have a screw.
pólvora nf gunpowder.

polvoriento,-a adj dusty.
polvorín nm gunpowder arsenal; fig powder keg.
polvorón nm sweet pastry.
polla nf 1 vulg (pene) prick. 2 Orn **p. de agua**, moorhen.
pollo nm 1 chicken. 2 fam (joven) lad.
pomada nf ointment.
pomelo nm (fruto) grapefruit; (árbol) grapefruit tree.
pómez adj inv **piedra p.**, pumice (stone).
pomo nm (de puerta) knob.
pompa nf 1 bubble. 2 (ostentación) pomp.
pompis nm inv fam botty.
pomposo,-a adj pompous.
pómulo nm cheekbone.
ponche nm punch.
poncho nm poncho.
ponderar vtr 1 (asunto) to weigh up o consider. 2 (alabar) to praise.
pondré indic fut → **poner**.
ponencia nf paper.
poner [19] (pp **puesto**) I vtr 1 to put; (mesa, huevo) to lay; (gesto) to make; (multa) to impose; (telegrama) to send; (negocio) to set up. 2 (tele, radio etc) to turn o switch on. 3 (+ adj) to make; **p. triste a algn**, to make sb sad; **p. colorado a algn**, to make sb blush. 4 **¿qué te llevaba puesto?**, what was he wearing? 5 (decir) **¿qué pone aquí?**, what does it say here? 6 (suponer) to suppose; **pongamos que Ana no viene**, supposing Ana doesn't turn up. 7 TV Cin to put on, show; **¿qué ponen en la tele?**, what's on the telly? 8 Tel **ponme con Manuel**, put me through to Manuel. 9 (nombrar) **le pondremos (de nombre) Pilar**, we are going to call her Pilar.
II **ponerse** vi 1 to put oneself; **ponte en mi lugar**, put yourself in my place; **ponte más cerca**, come closer. 2 (vestirse) to put on; **ella se puso el jersey**, she put her jumper on. 3 (+ adj) to become; **p. furioso/malo**, to become furious/ill. 4 (sol) to set. 5 Tel **p. al teléfono**, to answer the phone. 6 **p. a**, to start to; **p. a trabajar**, to get down to work.
poney nm pony.
pongo indic pres → **poner**.
poniente nm 1 (occidente) West. 2 (viento) westerly (wind).
pontífice nm Pontiff; **el Sumo P.**, His Holiness the Pope.
ponzoña nf 1 venom, poison. 2 **tener p.**, (tristeza) to be down in the dumps.
ponzoñoso,-a adj 1 venomous, poisonous. 2 (triste) down in the dumps.
popa nf stern; fig **ir viento en p.**, to go full speed ahead.
populacho nm pey plebs pl, masses pl.
popular adj 1 folk; **arte/música p.**, folk art/music. 2 (medida) popular. 3 (actor) well-known.

popularidad *nf* popularity.

popularizar [4] *vtr* to popularize.

populoso,-a *adj* densely populated.

popurri *nm* Mús medley.

póquer *nm* poker.

por *prep* 1 *(agente)* by; **pintado p. Picasso**, painted by Picasso. 2 *p. qué,* why. 3 *(causa)* because of; **p. sus ideas,** because of her ideas; **p. necesidad/amor,** out of need/love; **suspendió p. no estudiar,** he failed because he didn't study. 4 *(tiempo)* **p. la mañana/noche,** in the morning/at night; **p. ahora,** for the time being; **p. entonces,** at that time. 5 *(en favor de)* for; **lo hago p. mi hermano,** I'm doing it for my brother('s sake). 6 *(lugar)* **pasamos p. Córdoba,** we went through Córdoba; **p. ahí,** over there; **¿p. dónde vamos?,** which way are we taking?; **p. la calle,** in the street; **mirar p. la ventana,** to look out the window; **entrar p. la ventana,** to get in through the window. 7 *(medio)* by; **p. avión/correo,** by plane/post. 8 *(a cambio de)* for; **cambiar algo p. otra cosa,** to exchange sth for sth else. 9 *(distributivo)* **p. cabeza,** a head, per person; **p. hora/mes,** per hour/month. 10 Mat **dos p. tres, seis,** two times three is six; **un diez p. ciento,** ten per cent. 11 *(con infinitivo)* in order to, so as to; **hablar p. hablar,** to talk for the sake of it. 12 *(locuciones)* **p. así decirlo,** so to speak; **p. más/muy ... que sea,** no matter how ... he o she is; **p. mí,** as far as I'm concerned.

porcelana *nf* porcelain.

porcentaje *nm* percentage.

porcino,-a *adj* **ganado p.,** pigs.

porción *nf* portion, part.

porche *nm* porch.

pordiosero,-a *nm,f* tramp.

porfía *nf* *(obstinación)* obstinacy, stubbornness.

porfolio *nm* portfolio.

pormenor *nm* detail; **venta al p.,** retail.

porno *adj inv fam* porn.

pornografía *nf* pornography.

pornográfico,-a *adj* pornographic.

poro *nm* pore.

poroso,-a *adj* porous.

porque *conj* 1 *(causal)* because; **¡p. no!,** just because. 2 *(final)* *(+ subj)* so that, in order that.

porqué *nm* reason.

porquería *nf* 1 *(suciedad)* dirt, filth. 2 *(birria)* rubbish. 3 *fam (chuchería)* rubbish, US junk food.

porra *nf* 1 *(de policía)* truncheon, baton. 2 *fam (locuciones)* **¡una p.!,** rubbish!; **¡vete a la p.!,** get lost!

porrazo *nm* thump.

porro *nm arg* joint.

porrón *nm* glass bottle with a spout coming out of its base, used for drinking wine.

porta(a)viones *nm inv* aircraft carrier.

portada *nf* 1 *(de libro etc)* cover; *(de periódico)* front page; *(de disco)* sleeve. 2 *(fachada)* front, facade.

portador,-a *nm,f* Com bearer; Med carrier.

portaequipajes *nm inv* 1 Aut *(maletero)* boot, US trunk; *(baca)* roof rack. 2 *(carrito)* luggage trolley.

portafolios *nm inv* briefcase.

portal *nm* 1 *(zaguán)* porch, entrance hall. 2 *(puerta de la calle)* main door. 3 **p. de Belén,** Nativity scene.

portamaletas *nm inv* → **portaequipajes.**

portaminas *nm inv* propelling pencil.

portamonedas *nm inv* purse.

portarse *vr* to behave; **p. mal,** to misbehave.

portátil *adj* portable.

portavoz *nmf* spokesperson; *(hombre)* spokesman; *(mujer)* spokeswoman.

portazo *nm* slam of a door; **dar un p.,** to slam the door.

porte *nm* 1 *(aspecto)* bearing. 2 *(transporte)* carriage.

portento *nm* 1 *(cosa)* wonder, marvel. 2 *(persona)* genius.

portentoso,-a *adj* extraordinary, prodigious.

porteño,-a I *adj o* of *o* from Buenos Aires. II *nm,f* native *o* inhabitant of Buenos Aires.

portería *nf* 1 porter's lodge. 2 Dep goal.

portero,-a *nm,f* 1 *(de vivienda)* porter, caretaker; *(de edificio público)* doorman; **p. automático,** entryphone. 2 Dep goalkeeper.

pórtico *nm* 1 *(portal)* portico, porch. 2 *(con arcadas)* arcade.

portorriqueño,-a *adj & nm,f* Puerto Rican.

portuario,-a *adj* harbour, US harbor, port.

Portugal *n* Portugal.

portugués,-a I *adj* Portuguese. II *nm (idioma)* Portuguese.

porvenir *nm* future; **sin p.,** with no prospects.

pos- *pref* post-.

pos *adv* **en p. de,** after.

posada *nf* inn.

posaderas *nfpl fam* buttocks.

posadero,-a *nm,f* innkeeper.

posar I *vi (para retrato etc)* to pose. II *vtr* to put *o* lay down. III **posarse** *vr* to settle, alight.

posdata *nf* postscript.

pose *nf* 1 *(postura)* pose. 2 *(afectación)* posing.

poseedor,-a *nm,f* possessor.

poseer [36] *vtr* to possess, own.

poseído,-a *adj* possessed.

posesión *nf* possession; **estar en p. de,** to

have; **tomar p.,** *(de un cargo)* to take up (a post).
posesivo,-a *adj* possessive.
poseso,-a *adj & nm,f* possessed.
posguerra *nf* postwar period.
posibilidad *nf* possibility; *(oportunidad)* chance.
posibilitar *vtr* to make possible.
posible I *adj* possible; **de ser p.,** if possible; **en (la medida de) lo p.,** as far as possible; **haré todo lo p.,** I'll do everything I can; **lo antes p.,** as soon as possible; **es p. que venga,** he might come. **II** *nmpl* **posibles,** means.
posición *nf* position.
positivo,-a *adj* positive.
posmoderno,-a *adj* postmodern.
poso *nm* dregs *pl*, sediment.
posponer [19] *vtr* **1** *(aplazar)* to postpone, put off. **2** *(relegar)* to put in second place *o* behind, relegate.
post- *pref* post-.
posta *nf* **a p.,** on purpose.
postal I *adj* postal. **II** *nf* postcard.
poste *nm* pole; *Dep (de portería)* post.
póster *nm* poster.
postergar [7] *vtr* **1** *(relegar)* to relegate. **2** *(retrasar)* to delay; *(aplazar)* to postpone.
posteridad *nf* posterity; **pasar a la p.,** to go down in history.
posterior *adj* **1** *(lugar)* posterior, rear. **2** *(tiempo)* later (**a,** than), subsequent (**a,** to). ◆**posteriormente** *adv* subsequently, later.
posterioridad *nf* posteriority; **con p.,** later.
postgraduado,-a *adj & nm,f* postgraduate.
postigo *nm (de puerta)* wicket; *(de ventana)* shutter.
postín *nm fam* boasting, showing-off; **darse p.,** to show off, swank; **de p.,** posh, swanky.
postizo,-a I *adj* false, artificial; **dentadura postiza,** false teeth, dentures. **II** *nm* hairpiece.
postor *nm* bidder.
postrarse *vr* to prostrate oneself, kneel down.
postre *nm* dessert, sweet.
postrero,-a *adj (delante de nm sing, postrer)* last.
postrimería *nf (usu pl)* last part *o* period.
postular *vtr* to collect.
póstumo,-a *adj* posthumous.
postura *nf* **1** position, posture. **2** *fig (actitud)* attitude.
pos(t)venta *adj* **servicio p.,** after-sales service.
potable *adj* drinkable; **agua p./no p.,** drinking water/not drinking water.
potaje *nm* hotpot, stew.
pote *nm* pot; *(jarra)* jug.
potencia *nf* power; **en p.,** potential.

potencial I *adj* potential. **II** *nm* **1** potential; **p. eléctrico,** voltage; **p. humano,** manpower. **2** *Ling* conditional (tense).
potenciar [12] *vtr* to promote, strengthen.
potente *adj* powerful, strong.
potestad *nf* power, authority.
potingue *nm fam pey* **1** *(bebida)* concoction. **2** *(maquillaje)* make-up, face cream *o* lotion.
potra *nf fam* luck.
potro *nm Zool* colt; *(de gimnasia)* horse.
poyo *nm* stone bench.
pozo *nm* well; *Min* shaft, pit.
PP *nm Pol abr de* **Partido Popular.**
práctica *nf* **1** practice; **en la p.,** in practice. **2** *(formación)* placement; **período de prácticas,** practical training period.
practicante I *adj Rel* practising, *US* practicing. **II** *nmf Med* medical assistant.
practicar [1] **I** *vtr* to practise, *US* practice; *(operación)* to carry out. **II** *vi* to practise, *US* practice.
práctico,-a *adj* practical; *(útil)* handy, useful.
pradera *nf* meadow.
prado *nm* meadow, field.
Praga *n* Prague.
pragmático,-a I *adj* pragmatic. **II** *nm,f* pragmatist.
pre- *pref* pre-.
preámbulo *nm* **1** *(introducción)* preamble. **2** *(rodeo)* circumlocution.
preaviso *nm* previous warning, notice.
precalentamiento *nm* warm-up.
precalentar [1] *vtr* to preheat.
precario,-a *adj* precarious.
precaución *nf* **1** *(cautela)* caution; **con p.,** cautiously. **2** *(medida)* precaution.
precaver **I** *vtr* to guard against. **II** **precaverse** *vr* to take precautions (**de, contra,** against).
precavido,-a *adj* cautious, prudent.
precedencia *nf* precedence, priority.
precedente I *adj* preceding. **II** *nmf* predecessor. **III** *nm* precedent; **sin p.,** unprecedented.
preceder *vtr* to precede.
precepto *nm* precept.
preciarse [12] *vtr* to fancy oneself (**de, as**).
precintar *vtr* to seal.
precinto *nm* seal.
precio *nm* price; **p. de coste,** cost price; **a cualquier p.,** at any price.
preciosidad *nf* **1** *(hermosura) (cosa)* lovely thing; *(persona)* darling. **2** *fml (cualidad)* preciousness.
precioso,-a I *adj* **1** *(hermoso)* lovely, beautiful. **2** *(valioso)* precious, valuable.
precipicio *nm* precipice.
precipitación *nf* **1** *(prisa)* haste. **2** *(lluvia)* rainfall.
precipitado,-a *adj (apresurado)* hasty, hurried; *(irreflexivo)* rash.

precipitar I *vtr* **1** (*acelerar*) to hurry, rush. **2** (*arrojar*) to throw, hurl down. **II precipitarse** *vr* **1** (*persona*) to hurl oneself; (*acontecimientos*) to gather speed. **2** (*actuar irreflexivamente*) to hurry, rush.

precisar *vtr* **1** (*determinar*) to determine, give full details of; (*especificar*) to specify. **2** (*necesitar*) to require, need.

precisión *nm* **1** (*exactitud*) precision, accuracy; **con p.**, precisely, accurately. **2** (*aclaración*) clarification.

preciso,-a *adj* **1** (*necesario*) necessary, essential. **2** (*exacto*) accurate, exact; **en este p. momento**, at this very moment. **3** (*claro*) concise, clear. ◆**precisamente** *adv* (*con precisión*) precisely; (*exactamente*) exactly; **p. por eso**, for that very reason.

preconizar [4] *vtr* to advocate.

precoz *adj* **1** (*persona*) precocious. **2** (*fruta*) early.

precursor,-a *nm,f* precursor.

predecesor,-a *nm,f* predecessor.

predecir [12] (*pp* **predicho**) *vtr* to foretell, predict.

predestinado,-a *adj* predestined.

predeterminar *vtr* to predetermine.

predicado *nm* predicate.

predicador,-a *nm,f* preacher.

predicar [1] *vtr* to preach.

predicción *nf* prediction, forecast.

predice *indic pres* → **predecir**.

predije *pt indef* → **predecir**.

predilección *nf* predilection.

predilecto,-a *adj* favourite, *US* favorite, preferred.

predisponer [19] (*pp* **predispuesto**) *vtr* to predispose.

predisposición *nf* predisposition.

predominante *adj* predominant.

predominar *vi* to predominate.

predominio *nm* predominance.

preescolar *adj* preschool; **en p.**, in the nursery school.

prefabricado,-a *adj* prefabricated.

prefacio *nm* preface.

preferencia *nf* preference.

preferente *adj* preferable, preferential.

preferible *adj* preferable; **es p. que no vengas**, you'd better not come.

preferido,-a *nm,f* favourite, *US* favorite.

preferir [5] *vtr* to prefer.

prefijo *nm* **1** *Tel* code, *US* area code. **2** *Ling* prefix.

pregonar *vtr* (*anunciar*) to announce publicly; *fig* (*divulgar*) to reveal, disclose.

pregunta *nf* question; **hacer una p.** to ask a question.

preguntar I *vtr* to ask; **p. algo a algn**, to ask sb sth; **p. por algn**, to ask after o about sb. **II preguntarse** *vr* to wonder; **me pregunto si ....**, I wonder whether ....

preguntón,-ona *nm,f fam* busybody.

prehistoria *nf* prehistory.

prehistórico,-a *adj* prehistoric.

prejuicio *nm* prejudice; **tener prejuicios**, to be prejudiced, be biased.

preliminar *adj & nm* preliminary.

preludio *nm* prelude.

prematrimonial *adj* premarital.

prematuro,-a *adj* premature.

premeditación *nf* premeditation; **con p.**, deliberately.

premeditado,-a *adj* premeditated, deliberate.

premiado,-a *adj* prize-winning.

premiar [12] *vtr* **1** to award a prize (**a**, to). **2** (*recompensar*) to reward.

premio *nm* prize, award; (*recompensa*) reward.

premisa *nf* premise.

premonición *nf* premonition.

premura *nf* (*urgencia*) urgency; **p. de tiempo**, haste.

prenatal *adj* antenatal, prenatal.

prenda *nf* **1** (*prenda*) garment; (*garantía*) token, pledge.

prendar I *vtr* to captivate, delight. **II prendarse** *vr* (*enamorarse*) to fall in love (**de**, with).

prendedor *nm* brooch, pin.

prender I *vtr* **1** (*sujetar*) to fasten, attach; (*con alfileres*) to pin. **2 p. fuego a**, to set fire to. **3** (*arrestar*) to arrest. **II** *vi* (*fuego*) to catch; (*madera*) to catch fire; (*planta*) to take root. **III prenderse** *vr* to catch fire.

prensa *nf* press; *fig* **tener buena/mala p.**, to have a good/bad press.

prensar *vtr* to press.

preñado,-a *adj* **1** pregnant. **2** *fig* (*lleno*) pregnant (**de**, with), full (**de**, of).

preñar *vtr* (*mujer*) to make pregnant; (*animal*) to impregnate.

preocupación *nf* worry, concern.

preocupado,-a *adj* worried, concerned.

preocupar I *vtr* to worry; **me preocupa que llegue tan tarde**, I'm worried about him arriving so late. **II preocuparse** *vr* to worry, get worried (**por**, about); **no te preocupes**, don't worry; **p. de algn/algo**, to look after sb/to see to sth.

preparación *nf* preparation; (*formación*) training.

preparado,-a I *adj* **1** (*dispuesto*) ready, prepared; **comidas preparadas**, ready-cooked meals. **2** (*capacitado*) trained, qualified. **II** *nm Farm* preparation.

preparador,-a *nm,f* coach, trainer.

preparar I *vtr* **1** to prepare, get ready; **p. un examen**, to prepare for an exam. **2** *Dep* (*entrenar*) to train, coach. **II prepararse** *vr* **1** to prepare oneself, get ready. **2** *Dep* (*entrenarse*) to train.

preparativo *nm* preparation.

preparatorio,-a *adj* preparatory.

preponderante *adj* preponderant.

preposición *nf Ling* preposition.

prepotente *adj* domineering; (*arrogante*)

overbearing.

prerrogativa *nf* prerogative.

presa *nf* 1 prey; *fig* **ser p. de**, to be a victim of; **p. del pánico**, panic-stricken. 2 (*embalse*) dam.

presagiar [12] *vtr* to predict, foretell.

presagio *nm* 1 (*señal*) omen; **buen/mal p.**, good/bad omen. 2 (*premonición*) premonition.

presbiteriano,-a *adj & nm,f* Presbyterian.

presbítero *nm* priest.

prescindir *vi* **p. de**, to do without.

prescribir (*pp* **prescrito**) *vtr* to prescribe.

prescripción *nf* prescription; **p. facultativa**, medical prescription.

presencia *nf* presence; **hacer acto de p.**, to put in an appearance; **p. de ánimo**, presence of mind.

presencial *adj* **testigo p.**, eyewitness.

presenciar [12] *vtr* (*ver*) to witness.

presentable *adj* presentable; **no estoy p.**, I'm not dressed for the occasion.

presentación *nf* presentation; (*aspecto*) appearance; (*de personas*) introduction.

presentador,-a *nm,f* Rad TV presenter, host, hostess.

presentar I *vtr* 1 to present; (*mostrar*) to show, display; (*ofrecer*) to offer. 2 (*una persona a otra*) to introduce; **le presento al doctor Ruiz**, may I introduce you to Dr Ruiz. **II presentarse** *vr* 1 (*comparecer*) to present oneself; (*inesperadamente*) to turn o come up. 2 (*ocasión, oportunidad*) to present itself, arise. 3 (*candidato*) to stand; **p. a unas elecciones**, to stand for election, *US* run for office; **p. a un examen**, to sit an examination. 4 (*darse a conocer*) to introduce oneself (**a**, to).

presente I *adj* present; **la p.** (*carta*), this letter; **hacer p.**, to declare, state; **tener p.**, (*tener en cuenta*) to bear in mind; (*recordar*) to remember. **II** *nm* present.

presentimiento *nm* premonition, premonition; **tengo el p. de que ...**, I have the feeling that ....

presentir [5] *vtr* to have a presentiment o premonition (**de**, of); **presiento que lloverá**, I've got the feeling that it's going to rain.

preservación *nf* preservation, protection.

preservar *vtr* to preserve, protect (**de**, from; **contra**, against).

preservativo,-a *nm* sheath, condom.

presidencia *nf* 1 Pol presidency. 2 (*de una reunión*) (*hombre*) chairmanship; (*mujer*) chairwomanship.

presidencial *adj* presidential.

presidente,-a *nm,f* Pol president; **p. del gobierno**, Prime Minister, Premier. 2 (*de una reunión*) chairperson.

presidiario,-a *nm,f* prisoner, convict.

presidio *nm* prison, penitentiary.

presidir *vtr* 1 Pol to rule, head. 2 (*reunión*) to chair, preside over.

presión *nf* pressure; **a o bajo p.**, under pressure; **grupo de p.**, pressure group, lobby; **p. arterial o sanguínea**, blood pressure; **p. atmosférica**, atmospheric pressure.

presionar *vtr* to press; *fig* to pressurize, put pressure on.

preso,-a I *adj* imprisoned. **II** *nm,f* prisoner.

prestación *nf* 1 service. 2 **prestaciones**, (*de coche etc*) performance.

prestado,-a *adj* **dejar p.**, to lend; **pedir p.**, to borrow; **vivir de p.**, to scrounge.

prestamista *nmf* moneylender.

préstamo *nm* loan.

prestar I *vtr* 1 to lend, loan; **¿me prestas tu pluma?**, can I borrow your pen? 2 (*atención*) to pay; (*ayuda*) to give; (*servicio*) to do. **II prestarse** *vr* 1 (*ofrecerse*) to offer oneself (**a**, to); **p. a**, (*dar motivo*) to cause; **se presta a (crear) malentendidos**, it makes for misunderstandings.

presteza *nf* promptness; **con p.**, promptly.

prestidigitador,-a *nm,f* conjuror, magician.

prestigiar [12] *vtr* to give prestige to.

prestigio *nm* prestige.

prestigioso,-a *adj* prestigious.

presto,-a *adj* *fml* 1 (*dispuesto*) ready, prepared. 2 (*rápido*) swift, prompt.

presumible *adj* probable, likely.

presumido,-a I *adj* vain, conceited. **II** *nm,f* vain person.

presumir I *vtr* (*suponer*) to presume, suppose. **II** *vi* 1 (*ser vanidoso*) to show off. 2 **presume de guapo**, he thinks he's good-looking.

presunción *nf* 1 (*suposición*) presumption, supposition. 2 (*vanidad*) vanity, conceit.

presunto,-a *adj* supposed; *Jur* alleged.

presuntuoso,-a *adj* 1 (*vanidoso*) vain, conceited. 2 (*pretencioso*) pretentious, showy.

presuponer [19] (*pp* **presupuesto**) *vtr* to presuppose.

presupuestar *vtr* to budget for; (*importe*) to estimate for.

presupuestario,-a *adj* budgetary.

presupuesto,-a *nm* 1 Fin budget; (*cálculo*) estimate. 2 (*supuesto*) supposition, assumption.

presuroso,-a *adj* (*rápido*) quick; (*con prisa*) in a hurry.

pretencioso,-a *adj* pretentious.

pretender *vtr* 1 (*intentar*) to try; **¿qué pretendes insinuar?**, what are you getting at? 2 (*afirmar*) to claim. 3 (*aspirar a*) to try for. 4 (*cortejar*) to court, woo.

pretendiente,-a *nm,f* 1 (*al trono*) pretender. 2 (*a un cargo*) applicant, candidate. 3 (*amante*) suitor.

pretensión *nf* 1 (*aspiración*) aim, aspiration. 2 (*presunción*) pretentiousness.

pretérito,-a I *adj* past, former. **II** *nm* Ling

preterite, simple past tense.
pretextar *vtr* to plead, allege.
pretexto *nm* pretext, excuse.
pretil *nm* parapet.
prevalecer [33] *vi* to prevail.
prevaler [26] *vi* → prevalecer.
prevención *nf* 1 (*precaución*) prevention; **en p. de**, as a prevention against. 2 (*medida*) precaution.
prevenir [27] *vtr* 1 (*preparar*) to prepare, get ready. 2 (*prever*) to prevent, forestall; (*evitar*) to avoid; **para p. la gripe**, to prevent flu; *prov* **más vale p. que curar**, prevention is better than cure. 3 (*advertir*) to warn.
preventivo,-a *adj* preventive; (*medidas*) precautionary; *Jur* **detención** *o* **prisión preventiva**, remand in custody.
prever [28] (*pp* **previsto**) *vtr* 1 (*prevenir*) to foresee, forecast. 2 (*preparar de antemano*) to cater for.
previo,-a *adj* previous, prior; **p. pago de su importe**, only on payment; **sin p. aviso**, without prior notice.
previsible *adj* predictable.
previsión *nf* 1 (*predicción*) forecast; **p. del tiempo**, weather forecast. 2 (*precaución*) precaution; **en p. de**, as a precaution against.
previsor,-a *adj* careful, far-sighted.
previsto,-a *adj* foreseen, forecast; **según lo p.**, as expected.
prima *nf* 1 (*gratificación*) bonus; **p. de seguro**, insurance premium. 2 (*persona*) → **primo,-a**.
primacía *nf* primacy.
primar I *vi* to have priority, prevail. II *vtr* to give a bonus to.
primario,-a *adj* primary.
primavera *nf* spring.
primer (*delante de nm*) → **primero,-a**.
primera *nf* 1 (*en tren*) first class. 2 *Aut* (*marcha*) first gear. 3 **a la p.**, at the first attempt; **tener de p.**, great, first class.
primero,-a I *adj* first; **a primera hora de la mañana**, first thing in the morning; **primera página/plana**, front page; **de primera necesidad**, basic. II *nm,f* first; **a primero(s) de mes**, at the beginning of the month. III *adv* 1 first. 2 (*más bien*) rather, sooner; → **primera**.
primicia *nf* novelty; **p. informativa**, scoop; **p. mundial**, world premiere.
primitivo,-a *adj* 1 primitive. 2 (*tosco*) coarse, rough.
primo,-a I *nm,f* 1 cousin; **p. hermano**, first cousin. 2 *fam* (*tonto*) fool, drip, dunce. II *adj* 1 **materia prima**, raw material. 2 (*número*) prime.
primogénito,-a *adj & nmf* first-born.
primor *nm* 1 (*delicadeza*) delicacy. 2 (*belleza*) beauty.
primordial *adj* essential, fundamental.
primoroso,-a *adj* delicate, exquisite.

princesa *nf* princess.
principado *nm* principality.
principal *adj* main, principal; **lo p. es que ...**, the main thing is that ...; **puerta p.**, front door.
príncipe *nm* prince.
principiante I *adj* novice. II *nmf* beginner, novice.
principio *nm* 1 beginning, start; **a principio(s) de**, at the beginning of; **al p., en un p.**, at first, in the beginning. 2 (*fundamento*) principle; **en p.**, in principle. 3 **principios**, rudiments, basics.
pringar [7] I *vtr* (*ensuciar*) to make greasy *o* dirty. II *vi* (*trabajar*) to work hard. III **pringarse** *vr* 1 (*ensuciarse*) to get greasy *o* dirty. 2 *fam* (*meterse de lleno*) to get involved.
pringoso,-a *adj* (*grasiento*) greasy; (*sucio*) dirty.
pringue *nm* (*grasa*) grease.
prior,-a *nm,f* (*hombre*) prior; (*mujer*) prioress.
priori (a) *adv* a priori.
prioridad *nf* priority.
prioritario,-a *adj* priority.
prisa *nf* 1 (*rapidez*) hurry; **date p.**, hurry up; **tener p.**, to be in a hurry; **de/a p.**, in a hurry. 2 **correr p.**, to be urgent; **me corre mucha p.**, I need it right away.
prisión *nf* prison, jail.
prisionero,-a *nm,f* prisoner.
prisma *nm* prism.
prismáticos *nmpl* binoculars, field glasses.
priva *nf arg* booze.
privación *nf* deprivation.
privado,-a *adj* private.
privar I *vtr* (*despojar*) to deprive (**de**, of). II *vi* 1 *arg* (*gustar*) to like; (*estar de moda*) to be fashionable *o* popular. 2 *fam* (*beber*) to booze. III **privarse** *vr* (*abstenerse*) to deprive oneself (**de**, of), go without.
privativo,-a *adj* exclusive (**de**, of).
privilegiado,-a I *adj* privileged. II *nm,f* privileged person.
privilegio *nm* privilege.
pro I *nm* advantage; **los pros y los contras**, the pros and cons; **en p. de**, in favour of. II *prep* in favour *o US* favor of; **campaña p. desarme**, campaign for disarmament, disarmament campaign.
pro- *pref* pro-.
proa *nf* prow, bows *pl*.
probabilidad *nf* probability, likelihood; **tiene pocas probabilidades**, he stands little chance.
probable *adj* probable, likely; **es p. que llueva**, it'll probably rain.
probador *nm* fitting room.
probar [2] I *vtr* 1 (*comida, bebida*) to try. 2 (*comprobar*) to test, check. 3 (*intentar*) to try. 4 (*demostrar*) to prove, show. II *vi* to try; **p. a**, to attempt *o* try to. III **pro-**

barse *vr (ropa)* to try on.

probeta *nf* test tube; **niño p.**, test-tube baby.

problema *nm* problem.

problemático,-a *adj* problematic.

procedencia *nf* origin, source.

procedente *adj* 1 *(originario)* coming *(de, from)*. 2 *(adecuado)* appropriate; *Jur* proper.

proceder I *vi* 1 **p. de**, *(provenir)* to come from. 2 *(actuar)* to act. 3 *(ser oportuno)* to be advisable *o* appropriate; *Jur* **la protesta no procede**, objection overruled. 4 **p. a**, *(continuar)* to go on to. II *nm (comportamiento)* behaviour, *US* behavior.

procedimiento *nm* 1 *(método)* procedure. 2 *Jur (trámites)* proceedings *pl*.

procesado,-a I *nm,f* accused. II *nm Inform* processing.

procesador *nm* processor; **p. de textos**, word processor.

procesamiento *nm* 1 *Jur* prosecution. 2 *Inform* **p. de datos/textos**, data/word processing.

procesar *vtr* 1 *Jur* to prosecute. 2 *(elaborar, transformar)* to process; *Inform* to process.

procesión *nf* procession.

proceso *nm* 1 process; *Inform* **p. de datos**, data processing. 2 *Jur* trial.

proclamación *nf* proclamation.

proclamar *vtr* to proclaim.

proclive *adj* prone, inclined.

procreación *nf* procreation.

procrear *vtr* to procreate.

procurador,-a *nm,f Jur* attorney.

procurar *vtr* 1 *(intentar)* to try, attempt; **procura que no te vean**, make sure they don't see you. 2 *(proporcionar)* (to manage) to get.

prodigar [7] *fml* I *vtr (dar generosamente)* to lavish. II **prodigarse** *vr* **p. en**, to be lavish in.

prodigio *nm* prodigy, miracle; **hacer prodigios**, to work wonders; **niño p.**, child prodigy.

prodigioso,-a *adj (sobrenatural)* prodigious; *(maravilloso)* wonderful, marvellous, *US* marvelous.

pródigo,-a *adj* generous, lavish; **ella es pródiga en regalos**, she's very generous with presents.

producción *nf (acción)* production; *(producto)* product; *Cin* production; **p. en cadena/serie**, assembly-line/mass production.

producir [10] I *vtr* 1 to produce; *(fruto, cosecha)* to yield, bear; *(ganancias)* to yield. 2 *fig (originar)* to cause, bring about. II **producirse** *vr* to take place, happen.

productividad *nf* productivity.

productivo,-a *adj* productive; *(beneficioso)* profitable.

producto *nm* product; *Agr (producción)* produce.

productor,-a I *adj* producing. II *nm,f* producer.

proeza *nf* heroic deed, exploit.

profanación *nf* desecration, profanation.

profanar *vtr* to desecrate, profane.

profano,-a I *adj* profane, secular. II *nm,f (hombre)* layman; *(mujer)* laywoman.

profecía *nf* prophecy.

proferir [5] *vtr* to utter; **p. insultos**, to hurl insults.

profesar *vtr* to profess.

profesión *nf* profession; **de p.**, by profession.

profesional *adj & nmf* professional.

profeso *adv* **ex p.**, intentionally.

profesor,-a *nm,f* teacher; *Univ* lecturer.

profesorado *nm (profesión)* teaching; *(grupo de profesores)* staff.

profeta *nm* prophet.

profetizar [4] *vtr* to prophesy, foretell.

profiláctico,-a I *adj* prophylactic. II *nm* condom, *US* prophylactic.

prófugo,-a I *adj & nm,f* fugitive. II *nm Mil* deserter.

profundidad *nf* depth; **un metro de p.**, one metre deep *o* in depth; *fig (de ideas etc)* profundity, depth.

profundizar [4] *vtr & vi (cavar)* to deepen; *fig (examinar)* to study in depth.

profundo,-a *adj* deep; *fig (idea, sentimiento)* profound.

profusión *nf* profusion.

progenitor,-a *nm,f (antepasado)* ancestor, progenitor; **progenitores**, *(padres)* parents.

programa *nm* programme, *US* program; *Inform* program; *Educ* syllabus.

programación *nf Rad TV* programme planning.

programador,-a *nm,f Inform* programmer.

programar *vtr* to programme, *US* to program; *Inform* to program.

progre *adj & nmf fam* trendy, lefty.

progresar *vi* to progress, make progress.

progresista *adj & nmf* progressive.

progresivo,-a *adj* progressive.

progreso *nm* progress; **hace grandes progresos**, he's making great progress.

prohibición *nf* prohibition, ban.

prohibido,-a *adj* forbidden, prohibited; 'prohibida la entrada', 'no admittance'; **p. aparcar/fumar**, no parking/smoking.

prohibir [21] *vtr* to forbid, prohibit; 'se prohíbe pasar', 'no admittance *o* entry'.

prohibitivo,-a, prohibitorio,-a *adj* prohibitive.

prójimo,-a *nm,f* one's fellow man, one's neighbour *o US* neighbor.

proletariado *nm* proletariat.

proletario,-a *adj & nm,f* proletarian.

proliferar *vi* to proliferate.

prolífico,-a *adj* prolific.

prolijo,-a *adj* verbose, long-winded.

prólogo *nm* prologue, *US* prolog.

prolongación *nf* prolonging, extension, prolongation.

prolongado,-a *adj* long.

prolongar [7] I *vtr* (*alargar*) to prolong, extend. II **prolongarse** *vr* (*continuar*) to carry on.

promedio *nm* average; **como p.**, on average.

promesa *nf* promise; *fig* **la joven p. de la música**, the promising young musician.

prometedor,-a *adj* promising.

prometer I *vtr* to promise; **te lo prometo**, I promise. II *vi* to be promising. III **prometerse** *vr* (*pareja*) to get engaged.

prometido,-a I *adj* promised. II *nm,f* (*hombre*) fiancé; (*mujer*) fiancée.

prominente *adj* (*elevado*) protruding, projecting; (*importante*) prominent.

promiscuo,-a *adj* promiscuous.

promoción *nf* promotion; *Educ* **p. universitaria**, class *o* year.

promocionar *vtr* (*cosas*) to promote; (*personas*) to give promotion to.

promotor,-a I *adj* promoting. II *nm,f* promoter.

promover [4] *vtr* 1 (*cosas, personas*) to promote; (*juicio, querella*) to initiate. 2 (*causar*) to cause, give rise to.

promulgar [7] *vtr* to promulgate.

pronombre *nm* pronoun.

pronosticar [1] *vtr* to predict, forecast; *Med* to make a prognosis of.

pronóstico *nm* (*del tiempo*) forecast; *Med* prognosis.

pronto,-a I *adj* quick, prompt; *fml* (*dispuesto*) prepared. II *nm* (*impulso*) sudden impulse. III *adv* 1 (*deprisa*) quickly, rapidly; **al p.**, at first; **de p.**, suddenly; **por de o lo p.**, (*para empezar*) to start with. 2 (*temprano*) soon, early; **hasta p.**, see you soon!

pronunciación *nf* pronunciation.

pronunciamiento *nm* 1 *Mil* uprising, insurrection. 2 *Jur* pronouncement.

pronunciar [12] I *vtr* to pronounce; (*discurso*) to deliver. II **pronunciarse** *vr* 1 (*opinar*) to declare oneself. 2 (*sublevarse*) to rise up.

propagación *nf* propagation, spreading.

propagador,-a *nm,f* propagator.

propaganda *nf* (*política*) propaganda; (*comercial*) advertising, publicity.

propagar [7] I *vtr* to propagate, spread. II **propagarse** *vr* to spread.

propano *nm* propane.

propasarse *vr* to go too far.

propensión *nf* tendency, inclination.

propenso,-a *adj* 1 (*inclinado*) prone, inclined. 2 *Med* susceptible.

propiciar [12] *vtr* 1 (*causar*) to cause. 2 *Am* (*patrocinar*) to sponsor.

propicio,-a *adj* propitious, suitable; **ser p. a**, to be inclined to.

propiedad *nf* 1 (*posesión*) ownership; (*cosa poseída*) property. 2 (*cualidad*) property, quality; **con p.**, properly, appropriately.

propietario,-a *nm,f* owner.

propina *nf* tip; **dar p. (a algn)**, to tip (sb).

propinar *vtr* to give.

propio,-a *adj* 1 (*de uno*) own; **en su propia casa**, in his own house. 2 (*correcto*) suitable, appropriate; **juegos propios para su edad**, games suitable for their age. 3 (*característico*) typical, peculiar. 4 (*mismo*) (*hombre*) himself; (*mujer*) herself; (*animal, cosa*) itself; **el p. autor**, the author himself. 5 **propios,-as**, themselves; **los propios inquilinos**, the tenants themselves. 6 *Ling* proper.
◆**propiamente** *adv* **p. dicho**, strictly speaking.

proponer [19] (*pp* **propuesto**) I *vtr* to propose, suggest. II **proponerse** *vr* to intend.

proporción *nf* 1 proportion; **en p. con**, in proportion to. 2 **proporciones**, (*tamaño*) size *sing*.

proporcionado,-a *adj* (*mesurado*) proportionate, in proportion.

proporcional *adj* proportional.

proporcionar *vtr* (*dar*) to give; to supply *o* provide.

proposición *nf* 1 (*propuesta*) proposal. 2 (*oración*) clause.

propósito *nm* 1 (*intención*) intention. 2 **a p.**, (*por cierto*) by the way; (*adrede*) on purpose, intentionally; **a p. de viajes ...**, speaking of travelling ....

propuesta *nf* suggestion, proposal.

propuesto,-a *pp* → **proponer**.

propugnar *vtr* to advocate.

propulsar *vtr* (*vehículo*) to drive; *fig* (*idea*) to promote.

propulsión *nf* propulsion.

propulsor,-a *nm,f fig* (*persona*) promoter.

propuse *pt indef* → **proponer**.

prórroga *nf* 1 (*prolongación*) extension; *Dep* extra time, *US* overtime. 2 (*aplazamiento*) postponement; *Mil* deferment.

prorrogar [7] *vtr* 1 (*prolongar*) to extend. 2 (*aplazar*) to postpone; *Mil* to defer.

prorrumpir *vi* to burst (**en**, into).

prosa *nf* prose.

proscrito,-a I *adj* 1 (*persona*) exiled, banished; (*cosa*) banned. II *nm,f* exile, outlaw.

proseguir [6] *vtr* & *vi* to carry on, continue.

prospección *nf* 1 *Min* prospect. 2 *Com* survey.

prospecto *nm* leaflet, prospectus.

prosperar *vi* (*negocio, país*) to prosper, thrive; (*propuesta*) to be accepted.

prosperidad *nf* prosperity.

próspero,-a *adj* prosperous, thriving; **p. año nuevo,** Happy New Year.

prostíbulo *nm* brothel.

prostitución *nf* prostitution.

prostituir [37] **I** *vtr* to prostitute. **II prostituirse** *vr* to prostitute oneself.

prostituta *nf* prostitute.

protagonista *nmf* **1** main character, leading role; ¿quién es el p.?, who plays the lead? **2** *fig (centro)* centre *o* US center of attraction.

protagonizar [4] *vtr* to play the lead in, star in.

protección *nf* protection.

proteccionismo *nm* protectionism.

protector,-a I *adj* protecting, protective. **II** *nm,f* protector.

proteger [5] *vtr* to protect, defend.

protegido,-a *nm,f (hombre)* protégé; *(mujer)* protégée.

proteína *nf* protein.

prótesis *nf inv* prosthesis.

protesta *nf* protest; *Jur* objection.

protestante *adj & nmf Rel* Protestant.

protestar *vi* **1** to protest; *Jur* to object. **2** *fam (quejarse)* to complain.

protestón,-ona *nm,f* moaner, grumbler.

protocolo *nm* protocol.

protón *nm* proton.

prototipo *nm* prototype.

protuberancia *nf* protuberance.

protuberante *adj* protuberant, bulging.

prov. *abr de* **provincia,** province, prov.

provecho *nm* profit, benefit; **¡buen p.!,** enjoy your meal!; **sacar p. de algo,** to benefit from sth.

provechoso,-a *adj* beneficial.

proveedor,-a *nm,f* supplier, purveyor.

proveer [36] *(pp* **provisto)** *vtr* to supply, provide.

proveniente *adj (procedente)* coming; *(resultante)* arising, resulting.

provenir [27] *vi* **p. de,** to come from.

proverbio *nm* proverb.

providencia *nf* providence.

provincia *nf* province.

provincial *adj* provincial.

provinciano,-a *adj & nm,f pey* provincial.

provisión *nf* provision.

provisional *adj* provisional.

provisto,-a *adj* **p. de,** equipped with.

provocación *nf* provocation.

provocado,-a *adj* provoked, caused; **incendio p.,** arson.

provocador,-a I *nm,f* instigator, agent provocateur. **II** *adj* provocative.

provocar [1] *vtr* **1** *(causar)* to cause; **p. un incendio,** to start a fire. **2** *(instigar)* to provoke. **3** *Am* **si no le provoca,** if he doesn't feel like it.

provocativo,-a *adj* provocative.

proxeneta *nmf* procurer, pimp.

proximidad *nf* proximity, closeness; **en las proximidades de,** close to, in the vicinity of.

próximo,-a *adj* **1** *(cercano)* near, close. **2** *(siguiente)* next. ◆**próximamente** *adv (pronto)* soon; *Cin Teat* 'coming soon'.

proyección *nf* **1** projection. **2** *Cin* showing.

proyectar *vtr* **1** *(luz)* to project. **2** *(planear)* to plan. **3** *Cin* to show.

proyectil *nm* projectile.

proyecto *nm (plan)* project, plan; **tener algo en p.,** to be planning sth; **p. de ley,** bill.

proyector *nm Cin* projector.

prudencia *nf* prudence, discretion; *(moderación)* care.

prudente *adj* prudent, sensible; *(conductor)* careful; **a una hora p.,** at a reasonable time.

prueba *nf* **1** proof; **en p. de,** as a sign of. **2** *(examen etc)* test; **a p.,** on trial; **a p. de agua/balas,** waterproof/bullet-proof; **haz la p.,** try it. **3** *Dep* event.

pseudo *adj* pseud, pseudo.

psicoanálisis *nm inv* psychoanalysis.

psicodélico,-a *adj* psychedelic.

psicología *nf* psychology.

psicológico,-a *adj* psychological.

psicólogo,-a *nm,f* psychologist.

psicópata *nmf* psychopath.

psicosis *nf inv* psychosis.

psicotécnico,-a *adj* psychometric.

psicoterapia *nf* psychotherapy.

psique *nf* psyche.

psiquiatra *nmf* psychiatrist.

psiquiatría *nf* psychiatry.

psiquiátrico,-a I *adj* psychiatric; **hospital p.,** psychiatric hospital. **II** *nm* psychiatric hospital.

psíquico,-a *adj* psychic.

PSOE *nm Pol abr de* **Partido Socialista Obrero Español,** Socialist Workers' Party.

pta(s). *abr de* **peseta(s),** peseta(s).

pts *abr de* pesetas.

púa *nf* **1** *(de planta)* thorn; *(de animal)* quill, spine; *(de peine)* tooth; **alambre de púas,** barbed wire. **2** *Mús* plectrum.

pub *nm (pl* **pubs, pubes)** pub.

pubertad *nf* puberty.

publicación *nf* publication.

publicar [1] *vtr* **1** *(libro etc)* to publish. **2** *(secreto)* to publicize.

publicidad *nf* **1** *Com* advertising. **2** *(conocimiento público)* publicity.

publicitario,-a *adj* advertising.

público,-a I *adj* public. **II** *nm* public; *Teat* audience; *Dep* spectators *pl*.

pucherazo *nm* rigging of an election.

puchero *nm* **1** *(olla)* cooking pot; *(cocido)* stew. **2** **hacer pucheros,** to pout.

pucho *nm Am* dog-end.

pude *pt indef* → **poder.**

pudendo,-a *adj* **partes pudendas,** private

parts.

púdico,-a *adj* modest.

pudiente *adj* rich, wealthy.

pudor *nm* modesty.

pudoroso,-a *adj* modest.

pudrir *vtr* defect, **pudrirse** *vr* to rot, decay.

pueblerino,-a *adj* pey *(provinciano)* countrified, provincial.

pueblo *nm* 1 village; (small) town. 2 *(gente)* people; **el p. español**, the Spanish people.

puente *nm* 1 bridge; *Av* **p. aéreo**, *(civil)* air shuttle service; *Mil* airlift; **p. colgante**, suspension bridge; **p. levadizo**, drawbridge. 2 *(entre dos fiestas)* long weekend.

puerco,-a I *adj* filthy. **II** *nm,f* pig; **p. espín**, porcupine.

puericultura *nf* paediatrics *sing*, *US* pediatrics *sing*.

pueril *adj* childish, puerile.

puerro *nm* leek.

puerta *nf* door; *(verja, en aeropuerto)* gate; *Dep* goal; **p. corredera/giratoria**, sliding/revolving door; *fig* **a las puertas, en puertas**, imminent; *fig* **a p. cerrada**, behind closed doors.

puerto *nm* 1 *(de mar)* port, harbour, *US* harbor; **p. deportivo**, marina. 2 *(de montaña)* (mountain) pass.

Puerto Rico *n* Puerto Rico.

puertorriqueño,-a *adj & nm,f* Puerto Rican.

pues *conj* 1 *(puesto que)* as, since. 2 *(por lo tanto)* therefore. 3 *(entonces)* so. 4 *(para reforzar)* **¡p. claro que sí!**, but of course!; **p. como iba diciendo**, well, as I was saying; **¡p. mejor!**, so much the better!; **¡p. no!**, certainly not! 5 *(como pregunta)* **¿p.?**, why?

puesta *nf* 1 **p. de sol**, sunset. 2 *fig* **p. a punto**, tuning, adjusting; *fig* **p. al día**, updating; *Teat* **p. en escena**, staging; **p. en marcha**, starting-up, start-up; → **puesto,-a**.

puestero,-a *nm,f Am* stallholder.

puesto,-a I *conj* **p. que**, since, as. **II** *nm* 1 *(lugar)* place; *(asiento)* seat. 2 *(empleo)* position, post, job; **p. de trabajo**, job. 3 *(tienda)* stall. 4 *Mil* post. **III** *adj* 1 *(colocado)* set, put. 2 **llevar p.**, *(ropa)* to have on; *fam* **ir muy p.**, to be all dressed up. 3 *fam (borracho)* drunk. 4 *fam* **estar p. en una materia**, to be well up in a subject.

púgil *nm* boxer.

pugilato *nm* boxing.

pugna *nf* battle, fight.

pugnar *vi* to fight, struggle *(por, for)*.

puja *nf (acción)* bidding; *(cantidad)* bid.

pujante *adj* thriving, prosperous.

pujanza *nf* strength, vigour, *US* vigor.

pujar *vtr* 1 *(pugnar)* to struggle. 2 *(en una subasta)* to bid higher.

pulcro,-a *adj* (extremely) neat.

pulga *nf* flea; *fam* **tener malas pulgas**, to be nasty, have a nasty streak.

pulgada *nf* inch.

pulgar *nm* thumb.

pulimentar *vtr* to polish.

pulir *vtr* 1 *(metal, madera)* to polish. 2 *(mejorar)* to polish up.

pulmón *nm* lung.

pulmonía *nf* pneumonia.

pulpa *nf* pulp.

pulpería *nf Am* store.

púlpito *nm* pulpit.

pulpo *nm* octopus.

pulsación *nf* pulsation; *(en mecanografía)* stroke, tap; **pulsaciones por minuto**, ≈ keystrokes per minute.

pulsar *vtr (timbre, botón)* to press; *(tecla)* to hit, strike.

pulsera *nf (aro)* bracelet; *(de reloj)* watchstrap; **reloj de p.**, wristwatch.

pulso *nm* 1 pulse; *fig* **tomar el p. a la opinión pública**, to sound out opinion. 2 *(mano firme)* steady hand; **a p.**, freehand; **ganarse algo a p.**, to deserve sth. 3 *fig* trial of strength; **echarse un p.**, to arm-wrestle.

pulverizador,-a *nm* spray, atomizer.

pulverizar [4] *vtr (sólidos)* to pulverize; *(líquidos)* to spray; *(un récord)* to smash.

pulla *nf* dig.

puma *nm* puma.

puna *nf Am* 1 high moor. 2 *(mal)* mountain *o* altitude sickness.

pundonor *nm* self-respect, self-esteem.

punta *nf* 1 *(extremo)* tip; *(extremo afilado)* point; *(de cabello)* end; **sacar p. a un lápiz**, to sharpen a pencil; **tecnología p.**, state-of-the-art technology; **me pone los nervios de p.**, he makes me very nervous. 2 *(período)* peak; **hora p.**, rush hour. 3 *(pequeña cantidad)* bit; **una p. de sal**, a pinch of salt. 4 *(clavo)* nail.

puntal *nm* prop; *(travesaño)* beam; *fig (soporte)* pillar, support.

puntapié *nm* kick.

puntear *vtr* 1 *(dibujar)* to dot. 2 *Mús (guitarra)* to pluck.

punteo *nm* plucking.

puntería *nf* aim; **tener buena/mala p.**, to be a good/bad shot.

puntero,-a *adj* leading.

puntiagudo,-a *adj* pointed, sharp.

puntilla *nf 1 (encaje)* lace. 2 *(toro)*, *Taur* to finish (the bull) off; *fig (liquidar)* to finish off. 3 **de puntillas**, on tiptoe.

puntilloso,-a *adj* touchy.

punto *nm* 1 point; **a p.**, ready; *Culin* **en su p.**, just right; **a p. de**, on the point of; **hasta cierto p.**, to a certain *o* some extent; **p. muerto**, *Aut* neutral; *fig (impasse)* deadlock; **p. de vista**, point of view. 2 *(marca)* dot; **línea de puntos**, dotted line. 3 *(lugar)* place, point. 4 **p. y seguido**, full stop; **p. y coma**, semicolon; **dos puntos**, colon; **p. y aparte**, full stop, new paragraph. 5 *(tiempo)* **en p.**, sharp, on the dot. 6 *Dep (tanto)* point. 7 *Cost Med* stitch; **hacer p.**, to knit.

puntuable *adj Dep* **una prueba p. para**, a race counting towards.

puntuación *nf* 1 *Ling* punctuation. 2 *Dep* score. 3 *Educ* mark.

puntual I *adj* 1 punctual. 2 *(exacto)* accurate, precise. 3 *(caso)* specific. II *adv* punctually.

puntualidad *nf* punctuality.

puntualizar [4] *vtr* to make it clear.

puntuar [30] I *vtr* 1 *(al escribir)* to punctuate. 2 *Educ (calificar)* to mark. II *vi Dep* 1 *(marcar)* to score. 2 *(ser puntuable)* to count.

punzada *nf (de dolor)* sudden sharp pain.

punzante *adj (objeto)* sharp; *(dolor)* acute, piercing.

punzar [4] *vtr Téc* to punch.

puñado *nm* handful; *fam* **a puñados**, by the score, galore.

puñal *nm* dagger.

puñalada *nf* stab; *fig* **p. trapera**, stab in the back.

puñeta *nf fam* **hacer la p. a algn**, to pester sb, annoy sb; **¡puñetas!**, damn!; **¡vete a hacer puñetas!**, go to hell!

puñetazo *nm* punch.

puño *nm* 1 fist. 2 *(de camisa etc)* cuff. 3 *(de herramienta)* handle.

pupa *nf* 1 *(herida)* cold sore. 2 *fam (daño)* pain.

pupila *nf* pupil.

pupilo,-a *nm,f* pupil.

pupitre *nm* desk.

purasangre *adj & nm* thoroughbred.

puré *nm* purée; **p. de patata**, mashed potatoes; **p. de verduras**, thick vegetable soup.

pureta *nmf* old fogey.

pureza *nf* 1 purity. 2 *(castidad)* chastity.

purga *nf Med* purgative; *fig* purge.

purgante *adj & nm* purgative.

purgar [7] *vtr Med & fig* to purge.

purgatorio *nm* purgatory.

purificación *nf* purification.

purificar [1] *vtr* to purify.

purista *nmf* purist.

puritano,-a I *adj* puritanical. II *nm,f* puritan, Puritan.

puro,-a I *adj* 1 *(sin mezclas)* pure; **aire p.**, fresh air; **la pura verdad**, the plain truth; *Pol* **p. y duro**, hardline. 2 *(mero)* sheer, mere; **por pura curiosidad**, out of sheer curiosity. 3 *(casto)* chaste, pure. II *nm (cigarro)* cigar.

púrpura *adj inv* purple.

purpúreo,-a *adj* purple.

pus *nm* pus.

puse *pt indef* → **poner**.

pusilánime *adj* faint-hearted.

pústula *nf* sore, pustule.

puta *nf ofens* whore; **de p. madre**, great, terrific; **de p. pena**, bloody awful; **no tengo ni p. idea**, I haven't (got) a bloody clue; **pasarlas putas**, to go through hell, have a rotten time.

putada *nf vulg* dirty trick.

putear *vtr* to fuck o piss around.

puticlub *nm fam* brothel.

puto,-a I *adj ofens* bloody. II *nm* male prostitute, stud.

putrefacto,-a, **pútrido,-a** *adj* putrefied, rotten.

puzzle *nm* jigsaw puzzle.

P.V.P. *nm abr de* **precio de venta al público**, recommended retail price, RRP.

Pza., Plza. *abr de* **plaza**, square, Sq.

Q

Q, q [ku] *nf (la letra)* Q, q.

que[1] *pron rel* 1 *(sujeto) (persona)* who; *(cosa)* that, which; **el hombre q. vino**, the man who came; **la bomba q. estalló**, the bomb that o which went off. 2 *(complemento) (persona) no se traduce o* that *o* who *o* that whom; *(cosa) no se traduce o* that; which; **la chica q. conocí**, the girl (that o whom) I met; **el coche q. compré**, the car (that o which) I bought. 3 **lo q.**, what; **lo q. más me gusta**, what I like best. 4 *(con infinitivo) no se traduce o* that; **hay mucho q. hacer**, there's a lot to do.

que[2] *conj* 1 *no se traduce o* that; **dijo que llamaría**, he said (that) he would call; **quiero q. vengas**, I want you to come. 2 *(consecutivo) no se traduce o* that; *(en comparativas)* than; **habla tan bajo q. no**

se le oye, he speaks so quietly (that) he can't be heard; **más alto q. yo**, taller than me. 3 *(causal) no se traduce* **date deprisa q. no tenemos mucho tiempo**, hurry up, we haven't got much time. 4 *(enfático) no se traduce* **¡q. no!**, no!; **¡q. te calles!**, I said be quiet! 5 *(deseo, mandato) (+ subj) no se traduce* **¡q. te diviertas!**, enjoy yourself! 6 *(final)* so that; **ven q. te dé un beso**, come and let me give you a kiss. 7 *(disyuntivo)* whether; **me da igual que suba o no**, I couldn't care less whether he comes up or not. 8 *(locuciones)* **¿a q. no ...?**, I bet you can't ...!; **q. yo sepa**, as far as I know; **yo q. tú**, if I were you.

qué I *pron interr* 1 what; **¿q. quieres?**, what do you want?; *fam* **¡y q.!**, so what? 2 *(exclamativo)* (+ *adj*) how; **¡q. bonito!**, how pretty! **3** (+ *n*) what a; **¡q. lástima!**, what a pity! **4** *fam* **¡q. de ...!**, what a lot of ...!. **II** *adj interr* which; **¿q. libro quieres?**, which book do you want?

quebrada *nf Am* stream.

quebradero *nm fig* **q. de cabeza**, headache.

quebradizo,-a *adj* (*débil*) fragile; (*cabello, hielo*) brittle.

quebrado *nm Mat* fraction.

quebradura *nf* **1** (*grieta*) crack. **2** *Med* hernia, rupture.

quebrantamiento *nm* (*de una ley*) violation, infringement.

quebrantar **I** *vtr* (*promesa, ley*) to break. **II quebrantarse** *vr* to break down.

quebrar [1] **I** *vtr* (*romper*) to break. **II** *vi Fin* to go bankrupt. **III quebrarse** *vr* to break; *Med* to rupture oneself.

queda *nf* **toque de q.**, curfew.

quedar **I** *vi* **1** (*restar*) to be left, remain; **quedan dos**, there are two left. **2** (*en un lugar*) to arrange to meet; **quedamos en el bar**, I'll meet you in the bar. **3 me queda corta**, (*ropa*) it's too short for me; **quedaría muy bien allí**, (*objeto*) it would look very nice there. **4** (*acordar*) to agree (**en**, to); **¿en qué quedamos?**, so what's it to be? **5** (*estar situado*) to be; **¿dónde queda la estación?**, where's the station? **6** (*terminar*) to end; **¿en qué quedó la película?**, how did the film end? **7** (*locuciones*) **q. en ridículo**, to make a fool of oneself; **q. bien/mal**, to make a good/bad impression. **II quedarse** *vr* **1** (*permanecer*) to stay; **se quedó en casa**, they stayed home; **q. sin dinero/pan**, to run out of money/bread; **q. con hambre**, to still be hungry. **2 q.** (**con**), (*retener*) to keep; **quédese** (**con**) **el cambio**, keep the change. **3** *fam* **q. con algn**, to make a fool of sb.

quedo *adv* softly, quietly.

quehacer *nm* task, chore.

queja *nf* complaint; (*de dolor*) groan, moan.

quejarse *vr* to complain (**de**, about).

quejica *fam* **I** *adj* grumpy. **II** *nmf* moaner.

quejido *nm* groan, cry.

quemado,-a **1** burnt, burned; (*del sol*) sunburnt. **2** *fig* (*agotado*) burnt-out.

quemador *nm* (*de cocina etc*) burner.

quemadura *nf* burn.

quemar **I** *vtr* to burn; *fig* (*agotar*) to burn out. **II** *vi* to be burning hot; **este café quema**, this coffee's boiling hot. **III quemarse** *vr fig* to burn oneself out.

quemarropa *loc adv* **a q.**, point-blank.

quemazón *nf* smarting.

quepo *indic pres* → **caber**.

querella *nf Jur* lawsuit.

querer [20] **I** *vtr* **1** (*amar*) to love. **2** (*desear*) to want; **¿cuánto quiere por la casa?**, how much does he want for the

house?; **sin q.**, without meaning to; **queriendo**, on purpose; **¡por lo que más quieras!**, for heaven's sake!; **¿quiere pasarme el pan?**, would you pass me the bread? **3 q. decir**, to mean. **4** *no quiso darme permiso*, he refused me permission. **II quererse** *vr* to love each other. **III** *nm* love, affection.

querido,-a **I** *adj* dear, beloved; **q. amigo**, (*en carta*) dear friend. **II** *nm,f* (*amante*) lover; (*mujer*) mistress.

queroseno *nm* kerosene, kerosine.

querré *indic fut* → **querer**.

queso *nm* cheese; **q. rallado**, grated cheese; **q. de cerdo**, brawn, *US* headcheese.

quetzal *nm* (*moneda*) standard monetary unit of Guatemala.

quicio *nm* **1** (*de puerta*) doorpost. **2** *fig* **fuera de q.**, beside oneself; **sacar de q.**, (*a algn*) to infuriate; (*algo*) to take too far.

quid *nm* crux; **has dado en el q.**, you've hit the nail on the head.

quiebra *nf Fin* (*bancarrota*) bankruptcy; (*crack*) crash.

quiebro *nm* (*con el cuerpo*) dodge; *Ftb* dribbling.

quien *pron rel* **1** (*con prep*) *no se traduce o* *fml* whom; **el hombre con q. vino**, the man she came with; *fml* the man with whom she came. **2** (*indefinido*) whoever, anyone who; **q. quiera venir que venga**, whoever wants to come may come; **hay q. dice lo contrario**, some people say the opposite; *fig* **q. más q. menos**, everybody.

quién *pron interr* **1** (*sujeto*) who? **¿q. es?**, who is it? **2** (*complemento*) who; *fml* whom; **¿para q. es?**, who is it for?; **¿de q. es esa bici?**, whose bike is that?

quienquiera *pron indef* (*pl* **quienesquiera**) whoever.

quieto,-a *adj* still; (*mar*) calm; **¡estáte q.!**, keep still!, don't move!

quietud *nf* stillness; (*calma*) calm.

quijada *nf* jawbone.

quilate *nm* carat.

quilo *nm* → **kilo**.

quilla *nf* keel.

quimera *nf fig* fantasy, pipe dream.

química *nf* chemistry.

químico,-a **I** *adj* chemical. **II** *nm,f* chemist.

quimioterapia *nf* chemotherapy.

quimono *nm* kimono.

quincalla *nf* metal pots and pans *pl*, tinware.

quince *adj & nm inv* fifteen.

quinceañero,-a *adj & nm,f* fifteen-year-old.

quincena *nf* fortnight, two weeks.

quincenal *adj* fortnightly.

quiniela *nf* football pools *pl*.

quinientos,-as *adj & nm,f* five

hundred.

quinina *nf* quinine.

quinqué *nm* oil lamp.

quinquenal *adj* quinquennial, five-year.

quinqui *nm fam* delinquent, petty criminal.

quinta *nf* 1 (*casa*) country house. 2 *Mil* conscription, *US* draft.

quintaesencia *nf* quintessence.

quintal *nm* (*medida*) 46 kg; **q. métrico**, ≈ 100 kg.

quinteto *nm* quintet.

quinto,-a I *adj & nm,f* fifth. **II** *nm Mil* conscript, recruit.

quiosco *nm* kiosk; **q. de periódicos**, newspaper stand.

quirófano *nm* operating theatre.

quiromancia *nf* palmistry.

quirúrgico,-a *adj* surgical.

quise *indic fut* → **querer**.

quisque, quisqui *pron fam* **todo** *o* **cada q.**, everyone, everybody.

quisquilloso,-a I *adj* fussy, finicky. **II** *nm,f* fusspot.

quiste *nm* cyst.

quitaesmalte(s) *nm inv* nail varnish *o* polish remover.

quitamanchas *nm inv* stain remover.

quitanieves *nm* (*máquina*) **q.**, snowplough, *US* snowplow.

quitar I *vtr* 1 to remove; (*ropa*) to take off; (*la mesa*) to clear; (*mancha*) to remove; (*dolor*) to relieve; (*hipo*) to stop; (*sed*) quench; (*hambre*) to take away. 2 (*apartar*) to take away, take off; **fig q. importancia a algo**, to play sth down; **fig q. las ganas a algn**, to put sb off. 3 (*robar*) to steal, take; **fig** (*tiempo*) to take up; (*sitio*) to take. 4 (*descontar*) to take off. 5 *fam* (*apagar*) to turn off. **6 eso no quita para que ...**, that's no reason not to be .... 7 **¡quita!**, go away!. **II quitarse** *vr* 1 (*apartarse*) to move away. 2 (*mancha*) to come out; (*dolor*) to go away; **se me han quitado las ganas**, I don't feel like it any more. 3 (*ropa, gafas*) to take off. 4 **q. de beber/fumar**, to give up drinking/smoking. 5 **q. a algn de encima**, to get rid of sb.

quizá(s) *adv* perhaps, maybe.

R

R, r ['erre] *nf* (*la letra*) R, r.

rábano *nm* radish; *fam* **me importa un r.**, I couldn't care less.

rabia *nf* 1 *fig* (*ira*) fury, rage; **¡qué r.!**, how annoying!; **me da r.**, it gets up my nose; **me tiene r.**, he's got it in for me. 2 *Med* rabies *sing*.

rabiar [12] *vi* 1 *fig* (*sufrir*) to be in great pain. 2 *fig* (*enfadar*) to rage; **hacer r. a algn**, to make sb see red. 3 *Med* to have rabies.

rabieta *nf fam* tantrum; **coger una r.**, to throw a tantrum.

rabillo *nm* (*del ojo*) corner.

rabino *nm* rabbi.

rabioso,-a *adj* 1 *Med* rabid; **perro r.**, rabid dog. 2 *fig* (*enfadado*) furious. 3 **de rabiosa actualidad**, up-to-the-minute.

rabo *nm* tail; (*de fruta etc*) stalk.

racanear *vi fam* (*ser tacaño*) to be stingy.

rácano,-a *adj fam* 1 (*tacaño*) stingy, mean. 2 *pey* (*novato*) fresher.

racha *nf* 1 (*de viento*) gust; (*período*) spell, patch; **a rachas**, in fits and starts.

racial *adj* **discriminación r.**, racial discrimination; **disturbios raciales**, race riots.

racimo *nm* bunch, cluster.

raciocinio *nm* reason.

ración *nf* portion.

racional *adj* rational.

racionalizar [4] *vtr* to rationalize.

racionamiento *nm* rationing; **cartilla de r.**, ration book.

racionar *vtr* (*limitar*) to ration; (*repartir*) to ration out.

racismo *nm* racism.

racista *adj & nmf* racist.

radar *nm* (*pl* **radares**) *Téc* radar.

radiación *nf* radiation.

radiactividad *nf* radioactivity.

radiactivo,-a *adj* radioactive.

radiador *nm* radiator.

radiante *adj* radiant (**de**, with).

radiar [12] *vtr* to broadcast, transmit.

radical *adj* radical.

radicalizar [4] *vtr*, **radicalizarse** *vr* (*conflicto*) to intensify; (*postura*) to harden.

radicar [1] *vi* (*estar*) to be (situated) (**en**, in), be rooted (**en**, in).

radio 1 *nf* radio, wireless; (*aparato*) radio (set). 2 *nm* radius. **2 de acción**, field of action, scope. 2 (*de rueda*) spoke.

radioactividad *nf* radioactivity.

radioactivo,-a *adj* radioactive.

radioaficionado,-a *nm,f* radio ham.

radiocasete *nm* (*pl* **radiocasetes**) radio cassette.

radioescucha *nmf* listener.

radiografía *nf* (*imagen*) X-ray.

radioyente *nmf* listener.

ráfaga *nf* (*de viento*) gust, squall; (*de disparos*) burst.

raído,-a *adj* 1 (*gastado*) worn. 2 *fam* (*desvergonzado*) insolent.

raigambre *nf* roots *pl*.

rail *nm* rail.

raíz *nf* (*pl* **raíces**) root; **r. cuadrada**, square root; *fig* **a r. de**, as a result of.

raja *nf* (*corte*) cut, slit; (*hendidura*) crack, split.

rajar I *vtr* (*hender*) to crack, split; *arg* (*acuchillar*) to cut up. II *vi fam* to backbite. III **rajarse** *vr* 1 (*partirse*) to crack, split. 2 *fam* (*echarse atrás*) to back out. 3 *Am* (*acobardarse*) to chicken out.

rajatabla (a) *loc adv* strictly.

ralea *nf pey* type, sort.

ralentí *nm* neutral; **estar a r.**, to be ticking over.

ralentizar *vtr* to slow down.

rallado,-a *adj* **queso r.**, grated cheese; **pan r.**, breadcrumbs.

rallador *nm* grater.

ralladura *nf* gratings *pl*.

rallar *vtr* to grate.

ralo,-a *adj* sparse, thin.

rama *nf* branch; *fam* **andarse** *o* **irse por las ramas**, to beat about the bush.

ramaje *nm* branches *pl*.

ramalazo *nm fam* (*toque*) touch.

rambla *nf* (*avenida*) boulevard, avenue.

ramera *nf* prostitute, whore.

ramificación *nf* ramification.

ramificarse [1] *vr* to ramify, branch (out).

ramillete *nm* (*de flores*) posy.

ramo *nm* 1 (*de flores*) bunch, bouquet. 2 (*sector*) branch.

rampa *nf* ramp; **r. de lanzamiento**, launch pad.

ramplón,-ona *adj* coarse, vulgar.

rana *nf* frog; *fam* **salir r.**, to be a disappointment.

ranchero,-a *nm,f* (*granjero*) rancher, farmer.

rancho *nm* 1 (*granja*) ranch. 2 *Mil* (*comida*) mess.

rancio,-a *adj* 1 (*comida*) stale. 2 (*antiguo*) ancient.

rango *nm* rank; (*jerarquía elevada*) high social standing.

ranura *nf* slot.

rapar *vtr* (*afeitar*) to shave; (*pelo*) to crop.

rapaz *adj* predatory; **ave r.**, bird of prey. II *nm,f* (*muchacho*) youngster; (*muchacho*) lad; (*muchacha*) lass.

rape *nm* 1 (*pez*) angler fish. 2 *fam* **cortado al r.**, close-cropped.

rapidez *nf* speed, rapidity.

rápido,-a I *adj* quick, fast, rapid. II *adv* quickly. III *nm* 1 (*tren*) fast train. 2 **rápidos**, (*de un río*) rapids.

rapiña *nf* robbery, theft; **ave de r.**, bird of prey.

raptar *vtr* to kidnap, abduct.

rapto *nm* 1 (*secuestro*) kidnapping, abduction. 2 *fig* (*arrebato*) outburst, fit.

raqueta *nf* 1 (*de tenis*) racket; (*de ping-pong*) bat, *US* paddle. 2 (*de nieve*) snow-shoe.

raquítico,-a *adj fam* (*escaso*) small,

meagre, *US* meager; (*delgado*) emaciated.

raquitismo *nm* rickets *pl*.

rareza *nf* 1 rarity, rareness. 2 (*extravagancia*) eccentricity.

raro,-a *adj* 1 rare; **rara vez**, seldom. 2 (*extraño*) odd, strange.

ras *nm* level; **a r. de**, (on a) level with; **a r. de tierra**, at ground level.

rasante I *nf Aut* **cambio de r.**, brow of a hill. II *adj* (*vuelo*) low.

rasar *vtr* (*nivelar*) to level.

rasca *nf fam* (*frío*) cold.

rascacielos *nm inv* skyscraper.

rascar [1] I *vtr* (*con las uñas*) to scratch; (*guitarra*) to strum. II *vi* to chafe.

rasero *nm fig* **medir con el mismo r.**, to treat impartially.

rasgado,-a *adj* (*ojos*) slit, almond-shaped.

rasgar [7] *vtr* to tear, rip.

rasgo *nm* (*característica*) characteristic, feature; (*de la cara*) feature; *fig* **a grandes rasgos**, broadly speaking.

rasgón *nm* tear, rip.

rasguñar *vtr* to scratch, scrape.

rasguño *nm* scratch, scrape.

rasilla *nf* (*ladrillo*) tile.

raso,-a I *adj* (*llano*) flat, level; (*vuelo*) low; (*cielo*) clear, cloudless; **soldado r.**, private. II *nm* satin.

raspa *nf* (*de pescado*) bone, backbone.

raspador *nm* scraper.

raspadura *nf* (*ralladura*) scraping, scrapings *pl*.

raspar I *vtr* (*limar*) to scrape (off). II *vi* (*ropa etc*) to chafe.

rasposo,-a *adj* rough, sharp.

rastra *nf Agr* harrow; **a la r.**, **a rastras**, dragging; *fig* (*de mal grado*) grudgingly.

rastreador *nm* tracker.

rastrear *vtr* (*zona*) to comb.

rastreo *nm* search.

rastrero,-a *adj* creeping; *fig* (*despreciable*) vile, base.

rastrillo *nm* 1 rake. 2 *fam* (*mercadillo*) flea market.

rastro *nm* 1 trace, sign; (*en el suelo*) track, trail. 2 **el R.**, the Madrid flea market.

rastrojo *nm* stubble.

rasurar *vtr*, **rasurarse** *vr* to shave.

rata I *nf* rat. II *nm fam* (*tacaño*) mean *o* stingy person.

ratero,-a *nm,f* pickpocket.

raticida *nm* rat poison.

ratificar [1] *vtr* to ratify.

rato *nm* 1 (*momento*) while, time; **a ratos**, at times; **al poco r.**, shortly after; **hay para r.**, it'll take a while; **pasar un buen/mal r.**, to have a good/bad time; **ratos libres**, free time *sing*. 2 *fam* **un r.**, (*mucho*) very, a lot.

ratón *nm* mouse; *Inform* mouse.

ratonera *nf* mousetrap.

raudal *nm* torrent, flood; *fig* **a raudales**, in abundance.

raya *nf* **1** (*línea*) line; (*del pantalón*) crease; (*del pelo*) parting; **camisa a rayas**, striped shirt. **2** *fig* **tener a r.**, to keep at bay; **pasarse de la r.**, to go over the score. **3** (*de droga*) fix, dose.

rayano,-a *adj* bordering (**en**, on).

rayar **I** *vtr* (*arañar*) to scratch. **II** *vi* **r. en/con**, to border on.

rayo *nm* **1** ray, beam. **2** (*relámpago*) (flash of) lightning; **¡mal r. la parta!**, to hell with her!

rayón *nm* rayon.

rayuela *nf Am* hopscotch.

raza *nf* **1** (*humana*) race. **2** (*de animal*) breed.

razón *nf* **1** (*facultad*) reason; **uso de r.**, power of reasoning. **2** (*motivo*) reason; **r. de más para**, all the more reason to. **3** (*justicia*) rightness, justice; **dar la r. a algn**, to say that sb is right; **tienes r.**, you're right. **4** (*proporción*) ratio, rate; **a r. de**, at the rate of. **5** **'r. aquí'**, 'enquire within', 'apply within'.

razonable *adj* reasonable.

razonado,-a *adj* reasoned, well-reasoned.

razonamiento *nm* reasoning.

razonar **I** *vtr* (*argumentar*) to reason out. **II** *vi* (*discurrir*) to reason.

RDA *nf Hist abr de* **República Democrática Alemana** *o* **Alemania**, GDR.

re- *pref* re-.

reacción *nf* reaction; **avión de r.**, jet (plane); **r. en cadena**, chain reaction.

reaccionar *vi* to react.

reaccionario,-a *adj & nm,f* reactionary.

reacio,-a *adj* reluctant, unwilling.

reactor *nm* reactor; (*avión*) jet (plane).

readaptación *nf* rehabilitation; **r. profesional**, industrial retraining.

reafirmar *vtr* to reaffirm, reassert.

reagrupar *vtr*, **reagruparse** *vr* to regroup.

reajuste *nm* readjustment; **r. ministerial**, cabinet reshuffle.

real[1] *adj* (*efectivo*, *verdadero*) real; **en la vida r.**, in real life. ◆**realmente** *adv* really; (*en realidad*) actually, in fact.

real[2] *adj* (*regio*) royal.

realce *nm* (*relieve*) relief; *fig* (*esplendor*) splendour, *US* splendor.

realeza *nf* royalty.

realidad *nf* reality; **en r.**, in fact, actually; **la r. es que ...**, the fact of the matter is that ....

realismo *nm* realism.

realista **I** *adj* realistic. **II** *nmf* realist.

realizable *adj* feasible.

realización *nf* (*ejecución*) carrying out; *Cin TV* production.

realizador,-a *nm,f Cin TV* producer.

realizar [4] **I** *vtr* **1** (*hacer*) to carry out; (*ambición*) to achieve fulfil, *US* fulfill. **2** *Cin TV* to produce. **3** *Fin* to realize. **II realizarse** *vr* (*persona*) to fulfil *o US*

fulfill oneself; (*sueño*) to come true.

realzar [4] *vtr* (*recalcar*) to highlight; *fig* (*belleza*, *importancia*) to enhance, heighten.

reanimación *nf* revival.

reanimar *vtr*, **reanimarse** *vr* to revive.

reanudación *nf* renewal, resumption, re-establishment; **r. de las clases**, return to school.

reanudar **I** *vtr* to renew, resume; **r. el paso** *o* **la marcha**, to set off again; **r. las clases**, to go back to school. **II reanudarse** *vr* to start again, resume.

reaparición *nf* reappearance, recurrence; (*de artista etc*) comeback.

reapertura *nf* reopening.

rearme *nm* rearmament.

reaseguro *nm* reinsurance.

reavivar *vtr* to revive.

rebaja *nf* (*descuento*) reduction, discount; **rebajas**, sales; **precio de r.**, sale price.

rebajar **I** *vtr* **1** (*precio*) to cut, reduce; (*cantidad*) to take off. **2** (*color*) to tone down, soften; (*intensidad*) to diminish. **3** (*trabajador*) to excuse, exempt (**de**, from). **4** (*humillar*) to humiliate. **II rebajarse** *vr* (*humillarse*) to humble oneself.

rebanada *nf* slice.

rebanar *vtr* to slice, cut into slices.

rebañar *vtr* (*plato etc*) to finish off.

rebaño *nm* (*de ovejas*) flock; (*de otros animales*) herd.

rebasar *vtr* **1** (*exceder*) to exceed, go beyond. **2** *Aut* to overtake.

rebatir *vtr* to refute.

rebeca *nf* cardigan.

rebelarse *vr* to rebel, revolt.

rebelde **I** *nmf* rebel. **II** *adj* rebellious; *fig* **una tos r.**, a persistent cough.

rebeldía *nf* **1** rebelliousness. **2** *Jur* default.

rebelión *nf* rebellion, revolt.

rebenque *nm Am* whip.

reblandecer [33] *vtr* to soften.

rebobinar *vtr* to rewind.

rebosante *adj* overflowing (**de**, with), brimming (**de**, with).

rebosar **I** *vi* to overflow, brim over; *fig* **r. de**, to be overflowing *o* brimming with. **II rebosar** (*irradiar*) to radiate.

rebotar *vi* (*pelota*) to bounce, rebound; (*bala*) to ricochet.

rebote *nm* (*de pelota*) bounce, rebound; (*de bala*) ricochet; **de r.**, on the rebound.

rebozar [4] *vtr* to coat in breadcrumbs *o* batter.

rebullir *vi*, **rebullirse** *vr* to stir.

rebuscado,-a *adj* recherché.

rebuznar *vi* to bray.

recabar *vtr* (*información*) to obtain, manage to get.

recado *nm* (*mandado*) errand; (*mensaje*) message; **dejar un r.**, to leave a message.

recaer [39] *vi* **1** *Med* to relapse. **2** (*culpa*,

responsabilidad) to fall (**sobre**, on).
recaída *nf* relapse.
recalcar [1] *vtr* to stress, emphasize.
recalcitrante *adj* recalcitrant.
recalentar [1] *vtr* (*comida*) to reheat, warm up; (*calentar demasiado*) to overheat.
recámara *nf* 1 (*de rueda*) tube. 2 *Am* (*habitación*) dressing room.
recambiar [12] *vtr* to change (over).
recambio *nm* 1 (*repuesto*) spare (part); **rueda de r.**, spare wheel. 2 (*de pluma etc*) refill.
recapacitar *vi* to think over.
recargable *adj* (*pluma*) refillable; (*mechero*) rechargeable.
recargado,-a *adj* overloaded; *fig* (*estilo*) overelaborate, affected.
recargar [7] *vtr* 1 *Elec* to recharge. 2 (*sobrecargar*) to overload; (*adornar mucho*) to overelaborate. 3 *Fin* to increase.
recargo *nm* extra charge, surcharge.
recatado,-a *adj* (*prudente*) prudent, cautious; (*modesto*) modest, decent.
recato *nm* (*cautela*) caution, prudence; (*pudor*) modesty.
recaudación *nf* (*cobro*) collection; (*cantidad recaudada*) takings *pl*; *Dep* gate.
recaudador,-a *nm,f* tax collector.
recaudar *vtr* to collect.
recaudo *nm* **estar a buen r.**, to be in safekeeping.
recelar *vtr* **r. de**, to distrust.
recelo *nm* suspicion, distrust.
receloso,-a *adj* suspicious, distrustful.
recepción *nf* reception; (*en hotel*) reception (desk).
recepcionista *nmf* receptionist.
receptivo,-a *adj* receptive.
receptor,-a I *nm,f* (*persona*) recipient. II *nm Rad TV* receiver.
recesión *nf* recession.
receta *nf* recipe; *Med* prescription.
recetar *vtr Med* to prescribe.
rechache *nm Dep* rebound.
rechazar [4] *vtr* to reject, turn down; *Mil* to repel, drive back.
rechazo *nm* rejection.
rechiflar *vtr* 1 (*silbar*) to hiss, boo. 2 (*mofarse*) to mock, jeer at.
rechinar *vi* (*madera*) to creak; (*metal*) to squeak, screech; (*dientes*) to chatter.
rechistar *vi sin* **r.**, that's final.
rechoncho,-a *adj fam* chubby, tubby.
rechupete (**de**) *loc fam* **me sé el tema de r.**, I know the subject inside out; **la comida estaba de r.**, the food was mouthwateringly good.
recibidor *nm* entrance hall.
recibimiento *nm* reception, welcome.
recibir I *vtr* to receive; (*en casa*) to welcome; (*en la estación etc*) to meet. II **recibirse** *vr Am* **r. de**, to qualify as.
recibo *nm* 1 (*factura*) invoice; bill;

(*resguardo*) receipt; **r. de la luz**, electricity bill. 2 **acusar r. de**, to acknowledge receipt of.
reciclado,-a I *adj* recycled. II *nm* (*reciclaje*) recycling.
reciclaje *nm* (*de residuos*) recycling; *fig* (*renovación*) retraining; **curso de r.**, refresher course.
reciclar *vtr* (*residuos*) to recycle; *fig* (*profesores etc*) to retrain.
recién *adv* 1 (*recientemente*) (*antes de pp*) recently, newly; **café r. hecho**, freshly-made coffee; **r. casados**, newlyweds; **r. nacido**, newborn baby. 2 *Am* (*hace poco*) recently. **◆recientemente** *adv* recently, lately.
reciente *adj* recent.
recinto *nm* (*cercado*) enclosure; **r. comercial**, shopping precinct.
recio,-a I *adj* (*robusto*) strong, sturdy; (*grueso*) thick; (*voz*) loud. II *adv* hard.
recipiente *nm* receptacle, container.
recíproco,-a *adj* reciprocal.
recital *nm Mús* recital; *Lit* reading.
recitar *vtr* to recite.
reclamación *nf* 1 (*demanda*) claim, demand. 2 (*queja*) complaint.
reclamar I *vtr* to claim, demand. II *vi* 1 to protest (**contra**, against). 2 *Jur* to appeal.
reclamo *nm* 1 (*publicitario*) appeal. 2 (*en caza*) decoy bird, lure; *fig* inducement.
reclinar I *vtr* to lean (**sobre**, on). II **reclinarse** *vr* to lean back, recline.
recluir [37] *vtr* to shut away, lock away; (*encarcelar*) to imprison, intern.
reclusión *nf* seclusion; (*encarcelamiento*) imprisonment, internment.
recluso,-a *nm,f* prisoner, inmate.
recluta *nmf* recruit.
reclutamiento *nm* (*voluntario*) recruitment; (*obligatorio*) conscription.
recobrar I *vtr* to recover, retrieve; (*conocimiento*) to regain; **r. el aliento**, to get one's breath back. II **recobrarse** *vr* to recover, recuperate.
recochineo *nm fam* mockery.
recodo *nm* (*de río*) twist, turn; (*de camino*) bend.
recogedor *nm* dustpan.
recoger [5] I *vtr* 1 (*del suelo etc*) to pick up. 2 (*datos etc*) to gather, collect. 3 (*ordenar, limpiar*) to clear; **r. la mesa**, to clear the table. 4 (*ir a buscar*) to pick up, fetch. 5 (*cosecha*) to gather, pick. II **recogerse** *vr* 1 (*irse a casa*) to go home. 2 (*pelo*) to lift up.
recogida *nf* collection; *Agr* (*cosecha*) harvest, harvesting.
recolección *nf Agr* harvest, harvesting; (*recogida*) collection, gathering.
recomendable *adj* recommendable.
recomendación *nf* recommendation, reference.

recomendar [1] vtr to recommend.

recompensa nf reward.

recompensar vtr to reward.

recomponer [19] (pp **recompuesto**) vtr to repair, mend.

reconciliación nf reconciliation.

reconciliar [12] I vtr to reconcile. II **reconciliarse** vr to be reconciled.

recóndito,-a adj hidden, secret.

reconfortante adj comforting.

reconfortar vtr to comfort.

reconocer [34] vtr 1 to recognize. 2 (admitir) to recognize, admit. 3 Med (paciente) to examine.

reconocimiento nm 1 recognition. 2 Med examination, checkup.

reconquista nf reconquest.

reconstituyente nm tonic.

reconstruir [37] vtr to reconstruct.

reconversión nf reconversion; **r. industrial**, industrial redeployment.

reconvertir [5] vtr to reconvert; Ind to modernize.

recopilación nf 1 (resumen) summary, resumé. 2 (compendio) compilation, collection.

recopilar vtr to compile, collect.

récord nm record.

recordar [2] I vtr 1 (rememorar) to remember. 2 **r. algo a algn**, to remind sb of sth. II vi to remember.

recordatorio nm (aviso) reminder; (de defunción) notice of death.

recordman nmf record holder.

recorrer vtr (distancia) to cover, travel; (país) to tour, travel through o round; (ciudad) to visit, walk round.

recorrido nm (distancia) distance travelled; (trayecto) trip, journey; (itinerario) itinerary, route.

recortable adj & nm cutout.

recortar vtr to cut out.

recorte nm (acción, de periódico) cutting; (de pelo) trim, cut; fig (de salarios etc) cut.

recostado,-a adj reclining, leaning.

recostar [2] I vtr to lean. II **recostarse** vr (tumbarse) to lie down.

recoveco nm (curva) turn, bend; (rincón) nook, corner.

recreación nf recreation.

recrear I vtr 1 (divertir) to amuse, entertain. 2 (crear de nuevo) to recreate. II **recrearse** vr to amuse oneself, enjoy oneself; **r. con**, to take pleasure o delight in.

recreativo,-a adj recreational.

recreo nm 1 (diversión) recreation. 2 (en el colegio) break, recreation.

recriminar vtr to recriminate; (reprochar) to reproach.

recrudecer(se) [33] vtr & vr to worsen.

recrudecimiento nm worsening.

recta nf Geom straight line; (de carretera) straight stretch; Dep **la r. final**, the home straight.

rectangular adj rectangular.

rectángulo nm rectangle.

rectificación nf rectification; (corrección) correction.

rectificar [1] vtr to rectify; (corregir) to correct, remedy.

rectilíneo,-a adj straight.

rectitud nf straightness; fig uprightness, rectitude.

recto,-a I adj 1 (derecho) straight. 2 (honesto) upright, honest. 3 Geom right. II nm Anat rectum. III adv straight (on).

rector,-a I adj (principio) guiding, ruling. II nm,f rector.

recua nf string, series.

recuadro nm Prensa box.

recubrir (pp **recubierto**) vtr to cover.

recuento nm count; **hacer (el) r. de**, to count.

recuerdo nm 1 (memoria) memory. 2 (regalo etc) souvenir. 3 **recuerdos**, regards.

recuperación nf recovery; (examen) resit.

recuperar I vtr (salud) to recover; (conocimiento) to regain; (tiempo, clases) to make up. II **recuperarse** vr to recover.

recurrir vi I Jur to appeal. 2 **r. a**, (a algn) to turn to; (a algo) to make use of, resort to.

recurso nm 1 resource; **recursos naturales**, natural resources; **como último r.**, as a last resort. 2 Jur appeal.

recusar vtr to challenge, object to.

red nf net; (sistema) network; Com (cadena) chain of supermarkets; fig (trampa) trap.

redacción nf (escrito) composition, essay; (acción) writing; Prensa editing; (redactores) editorial staff.

redactar vtr to draft; Prensa to edit.

redactor,-a nm,f Prensa editor.

redada nf **r. policial**, (en un solo sitio) raid; (en varios lugares a la vez) round-up.

redentor,-a nm,f redeemer.

redicho,-a adj fam affected, pretentious.

redil nm fold, sheepfold.

redimir vtr to redeem.

rédito nm yield, interest.

redivivo adj revived.

redoblar I vtr to redouble. II vi (tambor) to roll.

redoble nm roll; (de campanas) peal.

redomado,-a adj utter, out-and-out.

redonda nf **a la r.**, around.

redondear vtr (objeto) to round, make round; (cantidad) to round up.

redondel nm fam (círculo) circle, ring; Taur ring, arena.

redondo,-a adj 1 round; fig **caer r.**, to collapse. 2 (rotundo) categorical; (perfecto) perfect.

reducción nf reduction.

reducido,-a adj (disminuido) reduced, decreased; (pequeño) limited, small.

reducir [10] I vtr (disminuir) to reduce. II

reducirse *vr* 1 (*disminuirse*) to be reduced, diminish. 2 (*limitarse*) to confine oneself.

redundancia *nf* redundancy, superfluousness; **valga la r.**, if I might say so again.

redundante *adj* redundant.

redundar *vi* **r. en**, (*resultar*) to result in, lead to.

reduplicar [1] *vtr* to redouble.

reembolsar *vtr* to reimburse; (*deuda*) to repay; (*importe*) to refund.

reembolso *nm* reimbursement; (*de deuda*) repayment; (*devolución*) refund; **contra r.**, cash on delivery.

reemplazar [4] *vtr* to replace (**con**, with).

reemplazo *nm* replacement; *Mil* call-up.

reestructuración *nf* restructuring.

reestructurar *vtr* to restructure.

ref. *abr de* **referencia**, reference, ref.

refaccionar *vtr Am* to repair, do up.

refectorio *nm* refectory, canteen.

referencia *nf* reference; **con r. a**, with reference to.

referéndum *nm* (*pl* **referéndums**) referendum.

referente *adj* **r. a**, concerning, regarding.

referir [5] I *vtr* to tell, relate. II **referirse** *vr* (*aludir*) to refer (**a**, to); **¿a qué te refieres?**, what do you mean?

refilón (de) *loc adv* (*de pasada*) briefly.

refinado,-a *adj* refined.

refinamiento *nm* refinement.

refinar *vtr* to refine.

refinería *nf* refinery.

reflector,-a I *adj* reflecting. II *nm Elec* spotlight, searchlight.

reflejar I *vtr* to reflect. II **reflejarse** *vr* to be reflected (**en**, in).

reflejo,-a I *nm* 1 (*imagen*) reflection. 2 (*destello*) gleam, glint. 3 *Anat* reflex. 4 **reflejos**, (*en el cabello*) streaks, highlights. II *adj* (*movimiento*) reflex.

reflexión *nf* reflection.

reflexionar *vi* to reflect (**sobre**, on), think (**sobre**, about).

reflexivo,-a *adj* 1 (*persona*) thoughtful. 2 *Ling* reflexive.

reflujo *nm* ebb (tide).

reforma *nf* 1 reform; **r. fiscal**, tax reform. 2 (*reparación*) repair.

reformador,-a *nm,f* reformer.

reformar I *vtr* to reform; (*edificio*) to renovate. II **reformarse** *vr* to reform.

reformatorio *nm* reformatory, reform school.

reforzar [2] *vtr* to reinforce, strengthen.

refractario,-a *adj* 1 *Téc* heat-resistant. 2 (*persona*) unwilling, reluctant.

refrán *nm* proverb, saying.

refregar [1] *vtr* to rub vigorously; *fig* **no me lo refriegues**, don't rub it in.

refrenar I *vtr* (*contener*) to restrain, curb. II **refrenarse** *vr* to restrain oneself.

refrendar *vtr* (*firmar*) to endorse, counter-

sign; (*aprobar*) to approve.

refrescante *adj* refreshing.

refrescar [1] I *vtr* to refresh. II *vi* 1 (*tiempo*) to turn cool. 2 (*bebida*) to be refreshing. III **refrescarse** *vr* to cool down.

refresco *nm* soft drink, refreshments *pl*.

refriega *nf* (*lucha*) scuffle, brawl; (*escaramuza*) skirmish.

refrigeración *nf* (*enfriamento*) refrigeration; (*aire acondicionado*) air conditioning.

refrigerado,-a *adj* air-conditioned.

refrigerador *nm* refrigerator, fridge.

refrigerar *vtr* to refrigerate; (*habitación*) to air-condition.

refrigerio *nm* snack, refreshments *pl*.

refuerzo *nm* reinforcement, strengthening.

refugiado,-a *adj & nm,f* refugee.

refugiarse [12] *vr* to shelter, take refuge.

refugio *nm* refuge.

refulgente *adj* radiant, brilliant.

refulgir [6] *vi* (*brillar*) to shine; (*resplandecer*) to glitter, sparkle.

refunfuñar *vi* to grumble, moan.

refutar *vtr* to refute.

regadera *nf* watering can; *fam* **estar como una r.**, to be as mad as a hatter.

regadío *nm* (*tierra*) irrigated land.

regalado,-a *adj* 1 (*gratis*) free; (*muy barato*) dirt cheap. 2 **una vida regalada**, an easy life.

regalar *vtr* 1 (*dar*) to give (as a present); (*en ofertas etc*) to give away. 2 **r. el oído a algn**, to flatter sb.

regaliz *nm* liquorice, *US* licorice.

regalo *nm* 1 gift, present; **de r.**, as a present. 2 (*comodidad*) pleasure, comfort.

regañadientes (a) *loc adv* reluctantly, unwillingly.

regañar I *vtr fam* to scold, tell off. II *vi* to nag.

regañina *nf* scolding, telling-off.

regañón,-ona *nm,f fam* nag.

regar [1] *vtr* to water.

regata *nf* boat race.

regatear I *vi* 1 to haggle, bargain. 2 *Dep* to dribble. II *vtr* **no r. esfuerzos**, to spare no effort.

regateo *nm* 1 (*de precios*) haggling. 2 *Dep* dribbling.

regazo *nm* lap.

regeneración *nf* regeneration.

regenerar *vtr* to regenerate.

regentar *vtr* to rule, govern; (*cargo*) to hold.

regente I *nmf Pol* regent. II *nm* (*director*) manager.

régimen *nm* (*pl* **regímenes**) 1 *Pol* regime. 2 *Med* diet; **estar a r.**, to be on a diet.

regimiento *nm* regiment.

regio,-a *adj* 1 (*real*) royal, regal. 2 (*suntuoso*) sumptuous, luxurious; *Am* (*magnífico*) splendid, majestic.

región *nf* region.

regional *adj* regional.

regionalista *adj & nmf* regionalist.

regir [6] I *vtr* to govern. II *vi* to be in force. III **regirse** *vr* to be guided, go (**por**, by).

registrado,-a *adj* **marca registrada**, registered trademark.

registrador,-a *adj* **caja registradora**, cash register.

registrar I *vtr* 1 (*examinar*) to inspect; (*cachear*) to frisk. 2 (*inscribir*) to register. 3 (*grabar*) to record. II **registrarse** *vr* 1 (*inscribirse*) to register, enrol. 2 (*detectarse*) to be recorded.

registro *nm* 1 inspection. 2 (*inscripción*) registration, recording; (*oficina*) registry office. 3 *Mús* register.

regla *nf* 1 (*norma*) rule; **en r.**, in order; **por r. general**, as a (general) rule; **r. de oro**, golden rule. 2 (*instrumento*) ruler. 3 *Mat* rule. 4 *Med* (*período*) period.

reglamentación *nf* 1 (*acción*) regulation. 2 (*reglamento*) regulations *pl*, rules *pl*.

reglamentar *vtr* to regulate.

reglamentario,-a *adj* statutory; *Mil* **arma reglamentaria**, regulation gun.

reglamento *nm* regulations *pl*, rules *pl*.

reglar *vtr* to regulate.

regocijar I *vtr* to delight, amuse. II **regocijarse** *vr* to be delighted, rejoice.

regocijo *nm* (*placer*) delight, joy; (*alborozo*) rejoicing, merriment.

regodearse *vr fam* to delight (**con**, in).

regodeo *nm fam* delight.

regordete,-a *adj fam* plump, chubby.

regresar *vi* to return.

regresión *nf* regression; (*decaimiento*) deterioration, decline.

regreso *nm* return.

reguero *nm* (*corriente*) trickle; (*de humo*) trail.

regulable *adj* adjustable.

regular I *vtr* 1 to regulate, control. 2 (*ajustar*) to adjust. II *adj* 1 regular; **por lo r.**, as a rule; **vuelo r.**, scheduled flight. 2 *fam* (*mediano*) average, so-so. III *adv* so-so.

regularidad *nf* regularity; **con r.**, regularly.

regularizar [4] *vtr* to regularize.

regusto *nm* aftertaste.

rehabilitar *vtr* to rehabilitate; (*edificio*) to convert.

rehacer [15] (*pp* **rehecho**) I *vtr* to redo. II **rehacerse** *vr* (*recuperarse*) to recover, recuperate.

rehén *nm* hostage.

rehogar [7] *vtr* to brown.

rehuir [37] *vtr* to shun, avoid.

rehusar [18] *vtr* to refuse.

reina *nf* queen.

reinado *nm* reign.

reinante *adj* (*que reina*) reigning, ruling; (*prevaleciente*) prevailing.

reinar *vi* to reign.

reincidente *nmf Jur* recidivist.

reincidir *vi* to relapse, fall back (**en**, into).

reincorporarse *vr* **r. al trabajo**, to return to work.

reino *nm* kingdom; **el R. Unido**, the United Kingdom.

reinserción *nf* reintegration.

reinsertar(se) *vtr & vr* to reintegrate.

reintegrar *vtr* 1 (*trabajador*) to reinstate. 2 (*dinero*) to reimburse, refund.

reintegro *nm* (*en lotería*) winning of one's stake.

reír [6] I *vi* to laugh. II **reírse** *vr* 1 to laugh. 2 (*mofarse*) to laugh (**de**, at), make fun (**de**, of).

reiterar *vtr* to reiterate, repeat.

reivindicación *nf* claim, demand.

reivindicar [1] *vtr* to claim, demand; **el atentado fue reivindicado por los terroristas**, the terrorists claimed responsibility for the attack.

reivindicativo,-a *adj* protest.

reja *nf* 1 (*de ventana*) grill, grating; *fam* **estar entre rejas**, to be behind bars. 2 *Agr* ploughshare, *US* plowshare.

rejilla *nf* (*de ventana, ventilador, radiador*) grill; (*de horno*) gridiron; (*para equipaje*) luggage rack.

rejoneador,-a *nm,f Taur* bullfighter on horseback.

rejonear *vtr Taur* to fight on horseback.

rejuvenecer [33] *vtr* to rejuvenate.

relación *nf* 1 relationship; (*conexión*) connection, link; **con** *o* **en r. a**, with regard to; **relaciones públicas**, public relations. 2 (*lista*) list. 3 (*relato*) account. 4 *Mat Téc* ratio.

relacionado,-a *adj* related (**con**, to), connected (**con**, with).

relacionar I *vtr* to relate (**con**, to), connect (**con**, with). II **relacionarse** *vr* 1 to be related, be connected. 2 (*alternar*) to mix, get acquainted.

relajación *nf* relaxation.

relajante *adj* relaxing.

relajar I *vtr* to relax. II **relajarse** *vr* to relax; (*moral*) to deteriorate.

relamerse *vr* to lick one's lips.

relamido,-a *adj* (*afectado*) affected; (*pulcro*) prim and proper.

relámpago *nm* flash of lightning; *fig* **pasó como un r.**, he flashed past; *fig* **visita r.**, flying visit.

relampaguear *vi impers* to flash.

relanzar *vtr* to relaunch.

relatar *vtr* to narrate, relate.

relatividad *nf* relativity.

relativo,-a *adj* relative (**a**, to); **en lo r. a**, with regard to, concerning.

relato *nm* (*cuento*) tale, story.

relax *nm fam* relaxation.

relegar [7] *vtr* to relegate.

relente *nm* dew.

relevante adj important.

relevancia nf importance.

relevar I vtr to relieve, take over from; **fue relevado del cargo,** he was relieved of his duties. II **relevarse** vr (turnarse) to relieve one another.

relevo nm relief; Dep relay.

relieve nm Arte relief; fig **poner de r.,** to emphasize.

religión nf religion.

religioso,-a I adj religious. II nm,f (hombre) monk; (mujer) nun.

relinchar vi to neigh, whinny.

relincho nm neigh, whinny.

reliquia nf relic.

rellamada nf Tel redial.

rellano nm landing.

rellenar vtr 1 (impreso etc) to fill in. 2 (un ave) to stuff; (un pastel) to fill.

relleno,-a I nm (de aves) stuffing; (de pasteles) filling. II adj stuffed.

reloj nm clock; (de pulsera) watch; **r. de arena,** hourglass; **r. de sol,** sundial; **r. despertador,** alarm clock.

relojería nf (tienda) watchmaker's, clockmaker's; **bomba de r.,** time bomb.

relojero,-a nm,f watchmaker, clockmaker.

reluciente adj shining, gleaming.

relucir [35] vi (brillar) to shine, gleam; **sacar a r. un tema,** to bring up a subject.

relumbrar vi to shine, gleam.

reluzco indic pres → relucir.

remachar vtr to drive home, hammer home.

remache nm rivet.

remanente nm (restos) remainder; (extra) surplus.

remangar(se) [7] vtr & vr (mangas, pantalones) to roll up; (camisa) to tuck up.

remanso nm pool; (lugar tranquilo) quiet place.

remar vi to row.

remarcar [1] vtr to stress, underline.

rematadamente adv r. loco, as mad as a hatter.

rematar vtr 1 to finish off, put the finishing touches to. 2 Com to sell off cheaply. 3 Dep to shoot.

remate nm 1 (final) end, finish; **para r.,** to crown it all. 2 Dep shot at goal. 3 **de r.,** utter, utterly.

rembolsar vtr → reembolsar.

rembolso nm → reembolso.

remedar vtr to imitate, copy.

remediar [12] vtr 1 to remedy; (enmendar) to repair, make good. 2 (evitar) to avoid, prevent; **no pude remediarlo,** I couldn't help it.

remedio nm (cura) remedy, cure; (solución) solution; **¡qué r.!,** what else can I do!; **no hay más r.,** there's no choice; **sin r.,** without fail; fam **¡no tienes r.!,** you're hopeless!

remedo nm (imitación) imitation, copy; (parodia) parody.

rememorar vtr to remember, recall.

remendar [1] vtr (ropa) to patch.

remero,-a nm,f rower.

remesa nf (de mercancías) consignment, shipment; (de dinero) remittance.

remiendo nm (parche) patch.

remilgado,-a adj (afectado) affected; (melindroso) fussy, finicky; (gazmoño) prudish.

remilgo nm affectation; (gazmoñería) prudishness.

reminiscencia nf reminiscence.

remiso,-a adj reluctant.

remite nm (en carta) sender's name and address.

remitente nmf sender.

remitir I vtr 1 (enviar) to send. 2 (referir) to refer. II vi (fiebre, temporal) to subside. III **remitirse** vr si nos remitimos a los hechos, if we look at the facts; **remítase a la página diez,** see page ten.

remo nm oar; (deporte) rowing.

remodelación nf (modificación) reshaping; (reorganización) reorganization; Pol r. **ministerial** o **del gobierno,** cabinet reshuffle.

remodelar vtr to reshape; (reorganizar) to reorganize.

remojar vtr to soak (en, in).

remojo nm dejar o poner en r., to soak, leave to soak.

remojón nm fam darse un r., to go for a dip.

remolacha nf beetroot.

remolcador nm 1 Náut tug, tugboat. 2 Aut breakdown truck, US tow truck.

remolcar [1] vtr to tow.

remolino nm (de agua) whirlpool, eddy; (de aire) whirlwind.

remolón,-ona adj hacerse el r., to shirk, slack.

remolonear vi to shirk, slack.

remolque nm (acción) towing; (vehículo) trailer; fig **ir a r. de algn,** to trundle along behind sb.

remontar I vtr 1 (subir) to go up. 2 (superar) to overcome. II **remontarse** vr 1 (pájaros, aviones) to soar. 2 (datar) to go back, date back (a, to).

remorder [4] vtr to trouble; **me remuerde la conciencia por ...,** I've got a bad conscience about .....

remordimiento nm remorse.

remoto,-a adj remote, faraway; **no tengo la más remota idea,** I haven't got the faintest idea.

remover [4] vtr 1 (trasladar) to move over. 2 (tierra) to turn over; (líquido) to shake up; (comida etc) to stir; (asunto) to stir up.

remozar [4] vtr to modernize.

remplazar [4] vtr → reemplazar.

remplazo nm → **reemplazo**.

remuneración nf remuneration.

remunerar vtr to remunerate.

renacer [33] vi to be reborn; fig (revivir) to revive, come back to life.

renacentista adj Renaissance.

renacimiento nm el R., the Renaissance.

renacuajo nm tadpole; fam (niño pequeño) shrimp.

renal adj kidney; **insuficiencia** r., kidney failure.

rencilla nf quarrel.

rencor nm rancour, US rancor; (resentimiento) resentment; **guardar r. a algn**, to have a grudge against sb.

rencoroso,-a adj (hostil) rancorous; (resentido) resentful.

rendición nf surrender.

rendido,-a adj (muy cansado) exhausted, worn out.

rendija nf crack, split.

rendimiento nm (producción) yield, output; (de máquina, motor) efficiency, performance.

rendir [6] I vtr 1 (fruto, beneficios) to yield, produce. 2 (cansar) to exhaust, wear out. 3 r. **culto a**, to worship; r. **homenaje a**, to pay homage to. II vi (dar beneficios) to pay, be profitable. III **rendirse** vr 1 to surrender, give in; **¡me rindo!**, I give up! 2 (cansarse) to wear oneself out.

renegado,-a adj & nm,f renegade.

renegar [1] vtr r. **de**, to renounce, disown.

renegrido,-a adj blackened.

RENFE abr de **Red Nacional de los Ferrocarriles Españoles**.

renglón nm line; **a r. seguido**, immediately afterwards.

reno nm reindeer.

renombrado,-a adj renowned, famous.

renombre nm renown, fame.

renovable adj renewable.

renovación nf (de contrato, pasaporte) renewal; (de una casa) renovation.

renovar [2] vtr 1 to renew; (edificio) to renovate.

renta nf 1 Fin (ingresos) income; (beneficio) interest, return; r. **per cápita**, per capita income; r. **fija**, fixed interest security. 2 (alquiler) rent.

rentable adj profitable.

rentar vtr to produce, yield.

renuncia nf 1 renunciation. 2 (dimisión) resignation.

renunciar [12] vi 1 r. **a**, to renounce, give up; (no aceptar) to decline. 2 (dimitir) to resign.

reñido,-a adj (disputado) tough, hardfought.

reñir [6] I vtr (regañar) to scold, tell off. II vi (discutir) to quarrel, argue; (pelear) to fight. r. **con algn**, to fall out with sb.

reo nmf (acusado) defendant, accused;

(culpable) culprit.

reojo (de) loc adv **mirar algo de r.**, to look at sth out of the corner of one's eye.

reparación nf repair; (compensación) reparation, amends pl.

reparar I vtr to repair; (ofensa, injuria) to make amends for; (daño) to make good. II vi r. **en**, (darse cuenta de) to notice; (reflexionar sobre) to think about.

reparo nm **no tener reparos en**, not to hesitate to; **me da r.**, I feel embarrassed.

repartidor,-a nm,f distributor.

repartir vtr 1 (dividir) to distribute, share out. 2 (regalo, premio) to give out, hand out; (correo) to deliver; Naipes to deal.

reparto nm 1 distribution, sharing out. 2 (distribución) handing out. 2 (de mercancías) delivery. 3 Cin Teat cast.

repasar vtr 1 to revise, go over. 2 (ropa) to mend.

repaso nm revision.

repatear vtr fam to annoy, turn off.

repatriar [14] vtr to repatriate.

repecho nm short steep slope.

repelente adj repulsive, repellent; fam **niño r.**, little know-all.

repeler vtr (rechazar) to repel, repulse; (repugnar) to disgust.

repente nm fam (arrebato) fit, outburst; **de r.**, suddenly, all of a sudden.

repentino,-a adj sudden.

repercusión nf repercussion.

repercutir vi 1 (sonido) to resound, reverberate; (objeto) to rebound. 2 fig r. **en**, to have repercussions on, affect.

repertorio nm repertoire, repertory.

repesca nf fam second chance; (examen) resit.

repetición nf repetition; r. **de la jugada**, action replay.

repetido,-a adj **repetidas veces**, repeatedly.

repetidor,-a I adj repeating. II nm,f fam Educ student who is repeating a year.

repetir [6] I vtr 1 to repeat. 2 (plato) to have a second helping. II vi Educ to repeat a year. III **repetirse** vr 1 (persona) to repeat oneself. 2 (hecho) to recur. 3 **el pepino se repite**, cucumber repeats (on me/you/him etc).

repicar [1] vtr (las campanas) to peal, ring out.

repipi adj fam **niño r.**, little know-all.

repique nm (de campanas) peal, ringing.

repiquetear vtr & vi (campanas) to ring; (tambor) to beat.

repisa nf shelf, ledge.

replantear vtr, **replantearse** vr to reconsider, rethink.

replegarse [1] vr to fall back, retreat.

repleto,-a adj full (up), jam-packed; r. **de**, packed with, crammed with.

réplica nf 1 answer, reply. 2 (copia) réplica.

replicar [1] I *vtr* to answer back. II *vi* 1 to reply, retort. 2 (*objetar*) to argue. 3 *Jur* to answer.

repliegue *nm Mil* withdrawal, retreat.

repoblación *nf* repopulation; **r. forestal**, reafforestation.

repoblar [2] *vtr* to repopulate; (*bosque*) to reafforest.

repollo *nm* cabbage.

reponer [19] I *vtr* 1 to put back, replace. 2 *Teat* (*obra*) to put on again; *Cin* (*película*) to rerun; *TV* (*programa*) to repeat. II **reponerse** *vr* **r. de**, to recover from, get over.

reportaje *nm Prensa Rad* report; (*noticias*) article, news item.

reportar *vtr* (*beneficios etc*) to bring.

reportero,-a *nm,f* reporter.

reposar I *vtr* to rest (**en**, on). II *vi* (*descansar*) to rest, take a rest; (*té*) to infuse; (*comida*) to stand.

reposición *nf TV* repeat; *Cin* rerun, re-showing.

reposo *nm* rest; **en r.**, at rest.

repostar *vtr* (*provisiones*) to stock up with; *Aut* (*gasolina*) to fill up.

repostería *nf* confectionery; (*tienda*) confectioner's (shop).

repostero,-a *nm,f* confectioner.

reprender *vtr* to reprimand, scold.

represalia *nf* (*usu pl*) reprisals *pl*, retaliation.

representación *nf* 1 representation. 2 *Teat* performance.

representante *nmf* representative.

representar *vtr* 1 to represent. 2 (*significar*) to mean, represent. 3 *Teat* (*obra*) to perform.

representativo,-a *adj* representative.

represión *nf* repression.

represivo,-a *adj* repressive.

reprimenda *nf* reprimand.

reprimir *vtr* to repress.

reprobar [2] *vtr* (*cosa*) to condemn; (*a persona*) to reproach, reprove.

réprobo,-a *adj & nm,f* reprobate.

reprochable *adj* reproachable.

reprochar *vtr* to reproach; **r. algo a algn**, to reproach sb for sth.

reproche *nm* reproach.

reproducción *nf* reproduction.

reproducir [10] I *vtr* to reproduce. II **producirse** *vr* 1 to reproduce, breed. 2 (*repetirse*) to recur, happen again.

reproductor,-a *adj* reproductive.

reptar *vi* to slither.

reptil *nm* reptile.

república *nf* republic.

republicano,-a *adj & nm,f* republican.

repudiar [12] *vtr* to repudiate.

repuesto *nm* (*recambio*) spare part; spare; *Aut* **rueda de r.**, spare wheel.

repugnancia *nf* loathing, disgust.

repugnante *adj* disgusting, revolting.

repugnar *vtr* to disgust, revolt.

repujar *vtr* to emboss.

repulsa *nf* rebuff.

repulsión *nf* repulsion, repugnance.

repulsivo,-a *adj* repulsive, revolting.

repuse *pt indef* → **reponer**.

reputación *nf* reputation.

reputar *vtr* to consider, deem.

requemar *vtr* to scorch.

requerimiento *nm* 1 (*súplica*) request. 2 *Jur* (*aviso*) summons *pl*.

requerir [5] *vtr* 1 to require. 2 (*solicitar*) to request. 3 *Jur* (*avisar*) to summon.

requesón *nm* cottage cheese.

requete- *pref fam* really, very, incredibly; **requetebueno**, brilliant.

réquiem *nm* (*pl* **réquiems**) requiem.

requisa *nf* 1 (*inspección*) inspection. 2 *Mil* requisition.

requisar *vtr* to requisition.

requisito *nm* requirement, requisite.

res *nf* animal.

resabiado,-a *adj pey* pedantic.

resabio *nm* 1 (*mal sabor*) unpleasant *o* bad aftertaste. 2 (*vicio*) bad habit.

resaca *nf* 1 hangover. 2 *Náut* undertow, undercurrent.

resaltar *vi* 1 (*sobresalir*) to project, jut out. 2 *fig* to stand out.

resarcir [3] *vtr* to compensate.

resbaladizo,-a *adj* slippery.

resbalar(se) *vi & vr* to slip; *Aut* to skid.

resbalón *nm* slip.

rescatar *vtr* (*persona*) to rescue; (*objeto*) to recover.

rescate *nm* 1 (*salvamento*) rescue; (*recuperación*) recovery. 2 (*suma*) ransom.

rescindir *vtr* to rescind, annul; (*contrato*) to cancel.

rescisión *nf* rescission, annulment.

rescoldo *nm* 1 embers *pl*. 2 *fig* (*recelo*) lingering doubt.

resecarse [1] *vr* to dry up, become parched.

reseco,-a *adj* very dry, parched.

resentido,-a *adj* resentful.

resentimiento *nm* resentment.

resentirse [5] *vr* 1 **r. de**, to suffer from, feel the effects of. 2 (*ofenderse*) to feel offended; **r. por algo**, to take offence at sth, feel bitter about sth.

reseña *nf* (*review*); *Prensa* write-up.

reserva I *nf* 1 (*de entradas etc*) reservation, booking. 2 (*provisión*) reserve, stock; **un vino de r.**, a vintage wine. 3 *Mil* reserve, reserves *pl*. 4 (*duda*) reservation. II *nmf Dep* reserve, substitute.

reservado,-a I *adj* (*persona*) reserved, quiet. II *nm* private room.

reservar I *vtr* 1 (*billetes etc*) to reserve, book. 2 (*dinero, tiempo etc*) to keep, save. II **reservarse** *vr* 1 to save oneself (**para**, for). 2 (*sentimientos*) to keep to oneself. 3 **r. el derecho de**, to reserve the right to.

resfriado,-a I nm (*catarro*) cold; **coger un r.**, to catch (a) cold. II adj **estar r.**, to have a cold.

resfriarse vr to catch (a) cold.

resguardar vtr (*proteger*) to protect, shelter (**de**, from).

resguardo nm 1 (*recibo*) receipt. 2 (*protección*) protection, shelter.

residencia nf residence; **r. de ancianos**, old people's home.

residencial adj residential.

residente adj & nmf resident.

residir vi to reside, live (**en**, in); fig to lie (**en**, in).

residuo nm 1 residue. 2 **residuos**, waste sing.

resignación nf resignation.

resignado,-a adj resigned.

resignarse vr to resign oneself (**a**, to).

resina nf resin.

resistencia nf 1 resistance. 2 (*aguante*) endurance, stamina. 3 *Elec* element.

resistente adj 1 resistant (**a**, to). 2 (*fuerte*) tough, hardy.

resistir I vi 1 to resist. 2 (*aguantar*) to hold (out). II vtr (*situación, persona*) to put up with; (*tentación*) to resist. III **resistirse** vr (*negarse*); (*oponerse*) to offer resistance; (*negarse*) to refuse.

resolución nf 1 (*solución*) solution. 2 (*decisión*) resolution.

resolver [4] (pp **resuelto**) I vtr (*problema*) to solve; (*asunto*) to settle. II vi (*decidir*) to resolve, decide. III **resolverse** vr 1 (*solucionarse*) to be solved. 2 (*decidirse*) to resolve, make up one's mind (**a**, to).

resollar [7] vi to breathe heavily; (*con silbido*) to wheeze.

resonancia nf 1 (*sonora*) resonance. 2 (*repercusión*) repercussions pl.

resonar [6] vi to resound; (*tener eco*) to echo.

resoplar vi (*respirar*) to breathe heavily; (*de cansancio*) to puff and pant; (*de enfado*) to huff and puff.

resoplido nm (*silbido*) wheezing; (*de cansancio*) panting; (*de enfado*) snort.

resorte nm 1 (*muelle*) spring. 2 fig means pl.

respaldar vtr to support, back (up).

respaldo nm (*de silla etc*) back; fig (*apoyo*) support, backing.

respectar vtr to concern, regard; **por lo que a mí respecta**, as far as I'm concerned.

respectivo,-a adj respective; **en lo r. a**, with regard to, regarding.

respecto nm **al r., a este r.**, in this respect; **con r. a, r. a, r. de**, with regard to; **r. a mí**, as for me, as far as I am concerned.

respetable I adj respectable. II nm fam **el r.**, the audience.

respetar vtr to respect; **hacerse r. de to-**

dos, to command everyone's respect.

respeto nm 1 respect; **por r.**, out of consideration. 2 (*recelo*) fear.

respetuoso,-a adj respectful.

respingar [7] vi to shy.

respingo nm start, jump.

respingón,-ona adj (*nariz*) snub, upturned.

respiración nf (*acción*) breathing, respiration; (*aliento*) breath; **r. artificial**, artificial resuscitation.

respirar vi to breathe; **¡por fin respiro!**, well, that's a relief!

respiratorio,-a adj respiratory.

respiro nm 1 breathing. 2 (*descanso*) breather, break.

resplandecer [33] vi to shine.

resplandeciente adj (*brillante*) shining; (*esplendoroso*) resplendent, radiant.

resplandor nm (*brillo*) brightness; (*muy intenso*) brilliance; (*de fuego*) glow, blaze.

responder I vtr to answer. II vi 1 (*una carta*) to reply. 2 (*reaccionar*) to respond. 3 (*protestar*) to answer back. 4 **r. de algn**, to be responsible for sb; **r. por algn**, to vouch for sb.

respondón,-ona adj fam argumentative, cheeky.

responsabilidad nf responsibility.

responsabilizar [4] I vtr to make o hold responsible (**de**, for). II **responsabilizarse** vr to assume o claim responsibility (**de**, for).

responsable I adj responsible. II nmf **el/la r.**, (*encargado*) the person in charge; (*de robo etc*) the perpetrator.

respuesta nf answer, reply; (*reacción*) response.

resquebrajarse vr to crack.

resquemor nm resentment, ill feeling.

resquicio nm crack, chink.

resta nf subtraction.

restablecer [33] I vtr to re-establish; (*el orden*) to restore. II **restablecerse** vr *Med* to recover.

restablecimiento nm 1 re-establishment; (*del orden etc*) restoration. 2 *Med* recovery.

restante adj remaining; **lo r.**, the rest, the remainder.

restar I vtr 1 *Mat* to subtract, take away. 2 **r. importancia a algo**, to play sth down. II vi (*quedar*) to be left, remain.

restauración nf restoration.

restaurador,-a I nm,f restorer. II adj restoring.

restaurante nm restaurant.

restaurar vtr to restore.

restitución nf restitution.

restituir [37] vtr (*restablecer*) to restore; (*devolver*) to return, give back.

resto nm 1 rest, remainder; *Mat* remainder. 2 **restos**, remains; (*de comida*) leftovers.

restregar [1] *vtr* to rub hard, scrub.

restricción *nf* restriction.

restrictivo,-a *adj* restrictive.

restringir [6] *vtr* to restrict, limit.

resucitar *vtr & vi* to resuscitate.

resuelto,-a *adj (decidido)* resolute, determined.

resuello *nm* breath, gasp.

resultas *nfpl* **a r. de,** as a result of.

resultado *nm* result; *(consecuencia)* outcome; **dar buen r.,** to work, give results.

resultante *adj* resulting.

resultar I *vi* 1 *(ser)* to turn *o* work out; **así resulta más barato,** it works out cheaper this way; **me resultó fácil,** it turned out to be easy for me. 2 *(ocurrir)* **resulta que ...,** the thing is ...; **y ahora resulta que no puede venir,** and now it turns out that she can't come. 3 *(tener éxito)* to be successful; **la fiesta no resultó,** the party wasn't a success.

resumen *nm* summary; **en r.,** in short, to sum up.

resumir I *vtr* to sum up; *(recapitular)* to summarize. II **resumirse** *vr (reducirse)* to be reduced to.

resurgir [6] *vi* to reappear.

resurrección *nf* resurrection.

retablo *nm* altarpiece.

retaguardia *nf* rearguard.

retahíla *nf* series *sing*, string.

retal *nm (pedazo)* scrap.

retar *vtr* to challenge.

retardarse *vr* to be delayed.

retardo *nm* delay.

retazo *nm (pedazo)* scrap; *(fragmento)* fragment, piece.

rete- *pref fam Am* very.

retención *nf* retention; *Fin* withholding; **r. de tráfico,** (traffic) hold-up, traffic jam.

retener [24] *vtr* 1 *(conservar)* to retain. 2 *Fin (descontar)* to deduct. 3 *(detener)* to detain.

reticencia *nf* reticence, reserve.

reticente *adj* reticent, reserved.

retina *nf* retina.

retintín *nm (tono irónico)* innuendo, sarcastic tone.

retirada *nf* retreat, withdrawal.

retirado,-a I *adj* 1 *(alejado)* remote. 2 *(jubilado)* retired. II *nm,f* retired person, *US* retiree.

retirar I *vtr* to take away, remove; *(dinero)* to withdraw; *(ofensa)* to take back. II **retirarse** *vr 1 (apartarse)* to withdraw, draw back; *(irse)* to retire. 2 *(jubilarse)* to retire. 3 *Mil* to retreat, withdraw.

retiro *nm* 1 *(jubilación)* retirement; *(pensión)* pension. 2 *(lugar tranquilo)* retreat. 3 *Rel* retreat.

reto *nm* challenge.

retocar [1] *vtr* to touch up.

retoño *nm (rebrote)* shoot, sprout; *fig (niño)* kid.

retoque *nm* retouching, touching up; **los últimos retoques,** the finishing touches.

retorcer [4] I *vtr (cuerda, hilo)* to twist; *(ropa)* to wring (out). II **retorcerse** *vr* to twist, become twisted; **r. de dolor,** to writhe in pain.

retorcido,-a *adj fig* twisted.

retórica *nf* rhetoric.

retórico,-a *adj* rhetorical.

retornable *adj* returnable; **'envase no r.',** 'nondeposit bottle'.

retornar I *vtr* to return, give back. II *vi* to return, come back, go back.

retorno *nm* return.

retortijón *nm (dolor)* stomach cramp.

retozar [4] *vi* to frolic, romp.

retracción *nf* retraction.

retractar I *vtr* to retract. II **retractarse** *vr* to retract, take back (**de,** -).

retraerse *vr (retirarse)* to withdraw; *(por miedo)* to shy away.

retraído,-a *adj* shy, reserved.

retraimiento *nm (timidez)* shyness.

retransmisión *nf* broadcast, transmission.

retransmitir *vtr* to broadcast.

retrasado,-a I *adj* 1 *(tren)* late; *(reloj)* slow; **voy r.,** I'm behind schedule. 2 *(país)* backward, underdeveloped. 3 *(mental)* retarded, backward. II *nm,f* **r. (mental),** mentally retarded person.

retrasar I *vtr* 1 *(retardar)* to slow down. 2 *(atrasar)* to delay, postpone. 3 *(reloj)* to put back. II **retrasarse** *vr* to be late, be delayed; *(reloj)* to be slow.

retraso *nm* delay; **con r.,** late; **una hora de r.,** an hour behind schedule; **r. mental,** mental deficiency.

retratar I *vtr (pintar)* to paint a portrait of; *Fot* to take a photograph of; *fig (describir)* to describe, depict. II **retratarse** *vr Fot* to have one's photograph taken.

retrato *nm (pintura)* portrait; *Fot* photograph; **r. robot,** identikit picture, photofit picture; **ser el vivo r. de,** to be the spitting image of.

retreta *nf* retreat.

retrete *nm* lavatory, toilet.

retribución *nf (pago)* pay, payment; *(recompensa)* reward.

retribuir *vtr (pagar)* to pay; *(recompensar)* to reward.

retro *adj inv fam (retrógrado)* reactionary; *(antiguo)* old-fashioned.

retroactivo,-a *adj* retroactive; **con efecto r.,** retrospectively.

retroceder *vi* to move back, back away.

retroceso *nm* 1 *(movimiento)* backward movement. 2 *Med* deterioration, worsening. 3 *Econ* recession.

retrógrado,-a *adj & nm,f (reaccionario)* reactionary.

retropropulsión *nf Av* jet propulsion.

retrospectivo,-a *adj & nf* retrospective.

retrovisor *nm Aut* rear-view mirror.
retumbar *vi (resonar)* to resound; echo; *(tronar)* to thunder, boom.
retuve *pt indef* → **retener**.
reúma, reumatismo *nm* rheumatism.
reumático,-a *adj & nmf* rheumatic.
reunión *nf* meeting; *(reencuentro)* reunion.
reunir [19] I *vtr* to gather together; *(dinero)* to raise; *(cualidades)* to have, possess; *(requisitos)* to fulfil. II **reunirse** *vr* to meet, gather; **r. con algn**, to meet sb.
revalidar *vtr* to ratify, confirm; *Dep (título)* to retain.
revalorizar [4] *vtr*, **revalorizarse** *vr (moneda)* to revalue.
revancha *nf* revenge; *Dep* return match.
revanchista *adj* vengeful, vindictive.
revelación *nf* revelation.
revelado *nm Fot* developing.
revelar *vtr* 1 to reveal, disclose. 2 *Fot (película)* to develop.
revender *vtr (entradas)* to tout.
reventa *nf (de entradas)* touting.
reventado,-a *adj fam (cansado)* knackered.
reventar [1] I *vtr* 1 to burst. 2 *(romper)* to break, smash. 3 *(fastidiar)* to annoy, bother. II *vi (estallar)* to burst; **r. de ganas de hacer algo**, to be dying to do sth; **está que revienta**, he's bursting at the seams. III **reventarse** *vr (estallar)* to burst, explode.
reventón *nm (de neumático)* blowout, puncture, flat tyre *o US* tire.
reverberación *nf* reverberation.
reverberar *vi* to reverberate.
reverencia *nf* 1 *(respeto)* reverence. 2 *(inclinación) (de hombre)* bow; *(de mujer)* curtsy.
reverenciar [12] *vtr* to revere, venerate.
reverendo,-a *adj & nmf* reverend.
reversible *adj* reversible.
reverso *nm* reverse, back.
revertido,-a *adj* **llamada a cobro r.**, reverse-charge call, *US* collect call.
revertir [5] *vi* to result *(en, in).*
revés *nm* 1 *(reverso)* reverse; **al o del r.**, *(al contrario)* the other way round; *(la parte interior del exterior)* inside out; *(boca abajo)* upside down; *(la parte de detrás delante)* back to front; **al r. de lo que dicen**, contrary to what they say. 2 *(bofetada)* slap; *Ten* backhand (stroke). 3 *fig (contrariedad)* setback, reverse; **los reveses de la vida**, life's misfortunes; **reveses de fortuna**, setbacks, blows of fate.
revestimiento *nm Téc* covering, coating.
revestir [6] I *vtr* 1 *(recubrir)* to cover (de, with), coat (de, with), line (de, with). 2 *fig* **la herida no reviste importancia**, the wound is not serious.
revisar *vtr (coche)* to service.
revisión *nf* checking; *(de coche)* service, overhaul; **r. médica**, checkup.

revisor,-a *nmf* ticket inspector.
revista *nf* 1 magazine. 2 **pasar r. a**, to inspect, review. 3 *Teat* revue.
revitalizar [4] *vtr* to revitalize.
revivir *vi & vtr* to revive.
revocar [1] *vtr* to revoke, repeal.
revolcar [2] I *vtr fam (oponente)* to floor, crush. II **revolcarse** *vr* to roll about.
revolcón *nm* fall, tumble; *vulg (sexual)* romp.
revolotear *vi* to fly about, flutter about.
revoltijo, revoltillo *nm* mess, jumble.
revoltoso,-a *adj (travieso)* mischievous, naughty.
revolución *nf* revolution.
revolucionar *vtr* to revolutionize.
revolucionario,-a *adj & nmf* revolutionary.
revolver [4] *(pp* **revuelto)** I *vtr (desordenar)* to mess up, disturb; **me revuelve el estómago**, it turns my stomach. II **revolverse** *vr* 1 *(agitarse)* to roll. 2 *fig* **r. contra algn**, to turn against sb. 3 *(el tiempo)* to turn stormy; *(el mar)* to become rough.
revólver *nm (pl* **revólveres)** revolver.
revuelo *nm fig* stir, commotion.
revuelta *nf* 1 *(insurrección)* revolt. 2 *(curva)* bend, turn.
revuelto,-a *adj* 1 *(desordenado)* jumbled, in a mess. 2 *(tiempo)* stormy, unsettled; *(mar)* rough. 3 *(agitado)* excited.
revulsivo,-a *adj nm* revulsive.
rey *nm* king; *Rel* **(el día de los) Reyes**, (the) Epiphany, 6 January.
reyerta *nf* quarrel, dispute.
rezagado,-a *nmf* straggler, latecomer.
rezagarse *vr* to lag *o* fall behind.
rezar [4] I *vi* 1 *(orar)* to pray. 2 *(decir)* to say, read. II *vtr (oración)* to say.
rezo *nm* prayer.
rezumar *vtr* to ooze; *fig* to exude.
RFA *nf Hist abr de* **República Federal de Alemania**, Federal Republic of Germany, FRG.
ría *nf* estuary.
riada *nf* flood.
ribera *nf (de río)* bank; *(zona)* riverside, waterfront.
ribete *nm* edging, border.
ribetear *vtr* to edge, border.
rico,-a I *adj* 1 **ser r.**, *(adinerado)* to be rich, wealthy; *(abundante)* to be rich; *(bonito)* to be lovely *o* adorable; *(fértil)* to be rich *o* fertile. 2 **estar r.**, *(delicioso)* to be delicious. II *nmf* rich person. ◆**ricamente** *adv fam* **tan r.**, very well.
rictus *nm inv* grin.
ridiculez *nf* ridiculous thing; *(cualidad)* ridiculousness.
ridiculizar [4] *vtr* to ridicule.
ridículo,-a I *adj* 1 *nm* ridicule; **hacer el r.**, **quedar en r.**, to make a fool of oneself; **poner a algn en r.**, to make a

fool of sb.

riego nm watering, irrigation; **r. sanguíneo**, blood circulation.

riel nm rail.

rienda nf rein; fig **dar r. suelta a**, to give free rein to; fig **llevar las riendas**, to hold the reins, be in control.

riesgo nm risk; **correr el r. de**, to run the risk of; **seguro a todo r.**, fully-comprehensive insurance.

rifa nf raffle.

rifar vtr to raffle (off).

rifle nm rifle.

rigidez nf rigidity, stiffness; fig (severidad) strictness, inflexibility.

rígido,-a adj rigid, stiff; fig (severo) strict, inflexible.

rigor nm rigour, US rigor; (severidad) severity; **con r.**, rigorously; **de r.**, indispensable.

riguroso,-a adj rigorous; (severo) severe, strict. ◆**rigurosamente** adv rigorously; (meticulosamente) meticulously; (severamente) severely; **r. cierto**, absolutely true.

rijo indic pres → **regir**.

rima nf rhyme.

rimar vtr & vi to rhyme (con, with).

rimbombante adj (lenguaje) pompous, pretentious.

rímel nm mascara.

Rin n el R., the Rhine.

rincón nm corner; fam (lugar remoto) nook.

rinoceronte nm rhinoceros.

riña nf (pelea) fight; (discusión) row, quarrel.

riñón nm kidney; fam **costar un r.**, to cost an arm and a leg; Med **r. artificial**, kidney machine.

río nm river; **r. abajo**, downstream; **r. arriba**, upstream.

Rioja n Rioja.

rioplatense adj from o of Buenos Aires.

ripio nm (palabras de relleno) waffle; fam **no perder r.**, not to miss a trick.

riqueza nf 1 wealth. 2 (cualidad) wealthiness.

risa nf laugh; (carcajadas) laughter; **es (cosa) de r.**, it's laughable; **me da r.**, it makes me laugh; **tomarse algo a r.**, to laugh sth off; fig **morirse o mondarse de r.**, to die o fall about laughing; fam **mi hermano es una r.**, my brother is a laugh; fam fig **tener algo muerto de r.**, to leave sth lying around.

risco nm crag, cliff.

risible adj laughable.

risilla, risita nf giggle, titter; (risa falsa) false laugh.

risotada nf guffaw.

ristra nf string.

ristre nm **en r.**, at the ready.

risueño,-a adj smiling.

rítmico,-a adj rhythmic; **gimnasia rítmi-**ca, eurhythmics sing, US eurythmics sing.

ritmo nm 1 rhythm. 2 (paso) rate; **llevar un buen r. de trabajo**, to work at a good pace.

rito nm 1 rite. 2 (ritual) ritual.

ritual adj & nm ritual.

rival adj & nmf rival.

rivalidad nf rivalry.

rivalizar [4] vi to rival (en, in).

rizado,-a adj 1 (pelo) curly. 2 (mar) choppy.

rizar [4] I vtr (pelo) to curl; (tela, papel) to crease; **r. el rizo**, fig to make things even more complicated. II **rizarse** vr (pelo) to curl, go curly.

rizo nm 1 (de pelo) curl. 2 (en el agua) ripple.

RNE nf abr de **Radio Nacional de España**.

róbalo nm (pez) bass.

robar vtr 1 (objeto) to steal; (banco, persona) to rob; (casa) to burgle; fig **en aquel supermercado te roban**, they really rip you off in that supermarket. 2 Naipes to draw.

roble nm oak (tree).

robledal, robledo nm oak grove o wood.

robo nm robbery, theft; (en casa) burglary; fam (timo) rip-off.

robot nm (pl robots) robot; **r. de cocina**, food processor.

robótica nf robotics sing.

robustecer [33] vtr to strengthen.

robusto,-a adj robust, sturdy.

roca nf rock.

rocalla nf pebbles pl, stone chippings pl.

rocambolesco,-a adj incredible, farfetched.

roce nm 1 (fricción) rubbing; (en la piel) chafing. 2 (marca) (en la pared etc) scuff mark; (en la piel) chafing mark, graze. 3 (contacto ligero) brush, light touch. 4 fam (trato entre personas) contact. 5 fam (discusión) brush.

rociar [29] vtr (salpicar) to spray, sprinkle.

rocín nm nag, hack.

rocío nm dew.

Rocosas npl las R., the Rockies.

rocoso,-a adj rocky, stony.

rodaballo nm (pez) turbot.

rodado,-a adj 1 (piedra) smooth, rounded; **canto r.**, boulder. 2 **tráfico r.**, road traffic, vehicular traffic.

rodaja nf slice; **en rodajas**, sliced.

rodaje nm 1 (filmación) filming, shooting. 2 Aut running in.

Ródano n el R., the Rhone.

rodante adj rolling.

rodar [2] I vtr (película etc) to film, shoot. II vi to roll, turn.

rodear I vtr to surround, encircle. II **rodearse** vr to surround oneself (de, with).

rodeo nm 1 (desvío) detour. 2 (al hablar)

evasiveness; **andarse con rodeos,** to beat about the bush; **no andarse con rodeos,** to get straight to the point. 3 *Am* robe.

rodilla *nf* knee; **de rodillas,** *(arrodillado)* kneeling; **hincarse/ponerse de rodillas,** to kneel down, go down on one's knees.

rodillera *nf (de pantalón)* knee patch; *Dep* knee pad.

rodillo *nm* roller; **r. de cocina,** rolling pin.

rododendro *nm* rhododendron.

roedor *nm* rodent.

roer [38] *vtr (hueso)* to gnaw; *(galleta)* to nibble at; *fig (conciencia)* to gnaw at, nag at; *fig* **un hueso duro de r.,** a hard nut to crack.

rogar [2] *vtr (pedir)* to request, ask; *(implorar)* **to beg; hacerse de r.,** to play hard to get; **'se ruega silencio',** 'silence please'; **rogamos disculpen la molestia,** please forgive the inconvenience.

roído,-a *adj* gnawed, eaten away.

rojizo,-a *adj* reddish.

rojo,-a I *adj* 1 red; *Fin* **estar en números rojos,** to be in the red. 2 *Pol (comunista)* red. **II** *nm (color)* red; **al r. vivo,** *(caliente)* red-hot; *fig (tenso)* very tense. **III** *nm,f Pol (comunista)* red.

rol *nm* role; **juego de r.,** role play.

rollizo,-a *adj* chubby, plump.

rollo *nm* 1 *(de papel etc)* roll. 2 *fam (pesadez)* drag, bore; **es el mismo r. de siempre,** it's the same old story; **un r. de libro,** a boring book. 3 *fam (amorío)* affair.

Roma *n* Rome.

romana *nf* **calamares a la r.,** squid in batter.

romance *nm* 1 *(aventura amorosa)* romance. 2 *(idioma)* Romance; *fig* **hablar en r.,** to speak plainly. 3 *Lit* narrative poem, ballad.

románico,-a *adj* Romanesque.

romanticismo *nm* romanticism.

romántico,-a *adj & nm,f* romantic.

rombo *nm* rhombus.

romería *nf Rel* pilgrimage.

romero *nm Bot* rosemary.

romo,-a *adj* 1 blunt. 2 *(nariz)* snub.

rompecabezas *nm inv (juego)* (jigsaw) puzzle; *fig (problema)* riddle, puzzle.

rompeolas *nm inv* breakwater, jetty.

romper *(pp* **roto) I** *vtr* 1 to break; *(papel, tela)* to tear; *(vajilla, cristal)* to smash, shatter. 2 *(relaciones)* to break off. **II** *vi* 1 *(olas, día)* to break. 2 *(acabar)* to break *(con,* with); **rompió con su novio,** she broke it off with her boyfriend. 3 **r. a llorar,** to burst out crying; **r. en llanto,** to burst into tears. **III romperse** *vr* to break; *(papel, tela)* to tear; **se rompió por la mitad,** it broke *o* split in half; *fig* **r. la cabeza,** to rack one's brains.

ron *nm* rum.

roncar [1] *vi* to snore.

roncha *nf (en la piel)* swelling, lump.

ronco,-a *adj* hoarse; **quedarse r.,** to lose one's voice.

ronda *nf* 1 round; *(patrulla)* patrol. 2 *(carretera)* ring road; *(paseo)* avenue. 3 **pagar una r.,** to pay for a round of drinks.

rondar I *vtr* 1 *(vigilar)* to patrol, do the rounds of. 2 *pey (merodear)* to prowl around, hang about. 3 *(estar cerca de)* to be about *o* approximately; **ronda los cuarenta,** she's around forty. **II** *vi* 1 *(vigilar)* to patrol. 2 *(merodear)* to prowl around, roam around.

ronquera *nf* hoarseness.

ronquido *nm* snore.

ronronear *vi* to purr.

ronroneo *nm* purring.

roña *nf* 1 *(mugre)* filth, dirt. 2 *Vet (sarna)* mange.

roñica *fam* **I** *adj* mean, stingy. **II** *nmf* scrooge, miser.

roñoso,-a *adj* 1 *(mugriento)* filthy, dirty. 2 *Vet (sarnoso)* mangy. 3 *fam (tacaño)* mean, stingy.

ropa *nf* clothes *pl,* clothing; *fig* **a quema r.,** point-blank; **r. blanca,** (household) linen; **r. interior,** underwear.

ropaje *nm* clothes.

ropero *nm (armario)* r., wardrobe, *US* (clothes) closet.

roque *nm* 1 *(en ajedrez)* rook. 2 *fam* **quedarse r.,** to fall fast asleep.

rosa I *adj inv (color)* pink; **novela r.,** romantic novel. **II** *nf Bot* rose; *(en la piel)* birthmark; **r. de los vientos,** compass (rose). **III** *nm (color)* pink.

rosáceo,-a *adj* rose-coloured, rosy.

rosado,-a I *adj (color)* pink, rosy; *(vino)* rosé. **II** *nm (vino)* rosé.

rosal *nm* rosebush.

rosaleda *nf* rose garden.

rosario *nm Rel* rosary; *(sarta)* string, series *sing.*

rosbif *nm* roast beef.

rosca *nf* 1 *(de tornillo)* thread; **tapón de r.,** screw top; *fig* **pasarse de r.,** to go too far. 2 *(espiral)* spiral, coil.

rosco *nm (pastel)* ring-shaped roll *o* pastry; *arg* **no comerse un r.,** not to get one's oats.

rosetón *nm* rose window.

rosquilla *nf* ring-shaped pastry; *fam fig* **venderse como rosquillas,** to sell like hot cakes.

rostro *nm* face; *fam* **tener mucho r.,** to have a lot of nerve; *fam* **¡vaya r.!,** what cheek!

rotación *nf* rotation.

rotativo,-a I *adj* rotary, revolving. **II** *nm* newspaper.

roto,-a I *adj* broken; *(papel)* torn; *(ropa)* in tatters, tattered. **II** *nm (agujero)* hole, tear.

rótula *nf* 1 *Anat* kneecap. 2 *Téc* ball-and-socket joint.

rotulador *nm* felt-tip pen.

rotular *vtr* to letter, label.

rótulo *nm* (*letrero*) sign, notice; (*titular*) title, heading.

rotundo,-a *adj* categorical; **éxito r.**, resounding success; **un no rotundo**, a flat refusal.

rotura *nf* (*ruptura*) breaking; *Med* fracture.

roturar *vtr* to plough, *US* plow.

roulotte *nf* caravan.

rozadura *nf* scratch, abrasion.

rozamiento *nm* rubbing, friction.

rozar [4] I *vtr* to touch, rub against, brush against. II *vi* to rub. III **rozarse** *vr* to rub, brush (**con**, against).

Rte. *abr de* **remite, remitente,** sender.

RTVE *nf abr de* **Radio Televisión Española.**

rubéola *nf* German measles *pl*, rubella.

rubí *nm* (*pl* **rubíes**) ruby.

rubicundo,-a *adj* rosy, reddish.

rubio,-a I *adj* (*pelo, persona*) fair, blond; **r. de bote**, peroxide blonde; **tabaco r.**, Virginia tobacco. II *nm,f* blond.

rublo *nm* rouble.

rubor *nm* blush, flush.

ruborizarse [4] *vr* to blush, go red.

ruboroso,-a *adj* blushing, bashful.

rúbrica *nf* 1 (*de firma*) flourish added to a signature. 2 (*título*) title, heading.

rubricar [1] *vtr* 1 (*firmar*) to sign with a flourish. 2 (*respaldar*) to endorse, ratify.

rudeza *nf* roughness, coarseness.

rudimentario,-a *adj* rudimentary.

rudimento *nm* rudiment.

rudo,-a *adj* rough, coarse.

rueda *nf* 1 wheel; *Aut* **r. de recambio,** spare wheel; *Aut* **r. delantera/trasera,** front/rear wheel; **r. de prensa,** press conference; *fam* **ir sobre ruedas,** to go very smoothly. 2 (*rodaja*) round slice.

ruedo *nm* 1 *Taur* bullring, arena. 2 (*de falda*) hem.

ruego *nm* request.

rufián *nm* villain, scoundrel.

rugby *nm* rugby.

rugido *nm* (*de animal*) roar; (*del viento*) howl; (*de tripas*) rumbling *sing*.

rugir [6] *vi* to roar; (*viento*) to howl.

rugoso,-a *adj* rough.

ruibarbo *nm* rhubarb.

ruido *nm* noise; (*sonido*) sound; (*jaleo*) din, row; *fig* stir, commotion; **hacer r.**, to make a noise.

ruidoso,-a *adj* noisy, loud.

ruin *adj* 1 (*vil*) vile, despicable. 2 (*tacaño*) mean, stingy.

ruina *nf* ruin; (*derrumbamiento*) collapse; (*de persona*) downfall.

ruindad *nf* vileness, meanness; (*acto*) mean act, low trick.

ruinoso,-a *adj* dilapidated, tumbledown.

ruiseñor *nm* nightingale.

ruleta *nf* roulette.

rulo *nm* 1 (*para el pelo*) curler, roller. 2 *Culin* rolling pin.

rulot(a) *nf* (*pl* **rulots**) caravan.

Rumanía *n* Rumania, Romania.

rumba *nf* rhumba, rumba.

rumbo *nm* direction, course; (**con**) **r. a,** bound for, heading for.

rumiante *nm* ruminant.

rumiar [12] I *vtr* 1 (*mascar*) to chew. 2 *fig* (*pensar*) to ruminate, reflect on, chew over. II *vi* to ruminate, chew the cud.

rumor *nm* 1 rumour, *US* rumor. 2 (*murmullo*) murmur.

rumorearse *v impers* to be rumoured, *US* be rumored.

runrún, runruneo *nm* buzz, noise.

rupestre *adj* **pintura r.**, cave painting.

ruptura *nf* breaking; (*de relaciones*) breaking-off.

rural *adj* rural, country.

Rusia *n* Russia.

ruso,-a *adj & nm,f* Russian.

rústico,-a *adj* rustic, rural.

ruta *nf* route, road.

rutilar *vi* to sparkle.

rutina *nf* routine; **por r.,** as a matter of course.

rutinario,-a *adj* routine.

S

S, s ['ese] *nf* (*la letra*) S,s.

S *abr de* **Sur,** South, S.

S. *abr de* **San** *o* **Santo,** Saint, St.

s. *abr de* **siglo,** century, c.

S.A. *abr de* **Sociedad Anónima,** PLC, plc.

sábado *nm* Saturday.

sabana *nf* savannah.

sábana *nf* sheet; *fam* **se me pegaron las sábanas,** I overslept.

sabandija *nf* (*insecto*) creepy-crawly; (*persona*) creep.

sabañón *nm* chilblain.

sabático,-a *adj* sabbatical.

sabelotodo *nmf inv* know-all.

saber¹ *nm* knowledge.

saber² [21] I *vtr* 1 to know; **hacer s.,** to inform; **para que lo sepas,** for your information; **que yo sepa,** as far as I know; **vete tú a s.,** goodness knows; **¡y yo qué sé!,** how should I know!; *fig* **a s.,** namely. 2 (*tener habilidad*) to be able to; **¿sabes cocinar?,** can you cook?; **¿sabes hablar inglés?,** can you speak English? 3 (*enterarse*) to learn, find out; **lo supe**

ayer, I found this out yesterday. II *vi* 1 (*tener sabor a*) to taste (a, of); **sabe a fresa,** it tastes of strawberries; *fig* **me sabe mal,** I feel guilty *o* bad about that. 2 *Am* (*soler*) to be accustomed to.

sabido,-a *adj* known; **como es s.,** as everyone knows.

sabiduría *nf* wisdom.

sabiendas (a) *loc adv* **lo hizo a s.,** he did it in the full knowledge of what he was doing; **s. de que ...,** knowing full well that ....

sabihondo,-a *fam* *nm,f* (*sabelotodo*) know-all; (*pedante*) pedant.

sabio,-a I *adj* (*prudente*) wise. II *nm,f* scholar.

sabiondo,-a *adj* *fam* → **sabihondo,-a.**

sable *nm* sabre, *US* saber.

sabor *nm* (*gusto*) taste, flavour, *US* flavor; **con s. a limón,** lemon-flavoured; **sin s.,** tasteless; **me deja mal s. de boca,** it leaves a bad taste in my mouth.

saborear *vtr* (*degustar*) to taste; *fig* (*apreciar*) to savour, *US* savor.

sabotaje *nm* sabotage.

saboteador,-a *nm,f* saboteur.

sabotear *vtr* to sabotage.

sabré *indic fut* → **saber.**

sabroso,-a *adj* 1 tasty; (*delicioso*) delicious. 2 (*agradable*) delightful.

sabueso *nm* bloodhound.

sacacorchos *nm inv* corkscrew.

sacamuelas *nmf inv* dentist.

sacapuntas *nm inv* pencil sharpener.

sacar [1] *vtr* 1 to take out; (*con más fuerza*) to pull out; **s. dinero del banco,** to withdraw money from the bank; **s. la lengua,** to stick one's tongue out; *fig* **s. faltas a algo,** to find fault with sth; *fig* **s. adelante,** to help to get on; **s. provecho de algo,** to benefit from sth; **s. algo en claro o en limpio,** to make sense of sth. 2 (*obtener*) to get; (*dinero*) to get, make; (*conclusiones*) to draw, reach; (*entrada*) to get, buy. 3 (*producto*) to bring out; (*nueva moda*) to bring in; (*libro, disco*) to bring out. 4 (*fotografía*) to take; (*fotocopia*) to make. 5 *Ten* to serve; *Ftb* to kick off.

sacarina *nf* saccharin.

sacerdotal *adj* priestly.

sacerdote *nm* priest; **sumo s.,** high priest.

saciar [12] *vtr* to satiate; (*sed*) to quench; (*deseos, hambre*) to satisfy; (*ambiciones*) to fulfil, *US* fulfill.

saciedad *nf* satiety; **repetir algo hasta la s.,** to repeat sth ad nauseam.

saco *nm* 1 sack; **s. de dormir,** sleeping bag. 2 *Mil* **entrar a s. en una ciudad,** to pillage a town. 3 *Am* (*chaqueta*) jacket.

sacralizar [4] *vtr* to consecrate.

sacramento *nm* sacrament.

sacrificar [1] I *vtr* to sacrifice. II **sacrificarse** *vr* to make a sacrifice *o* sacrifices.

sacrificio *nm* sacrifice.

sacrilegio *nm* sacrilege.

sacrílego,-a *adj* sacrilegious.

sacristán *nm* verger, sexton.

sacristía *nf* vestry, sacristy.

sacro,-a *adj* sacred.

sacudida *nf* 1 shake; (*espasmo*) jolt, jerk; **s. eléctrica,** electric shock. 2 (*de terremoto*) tremor.

sacudir *vtr* 1 (*agitar*) to shake; (*alfombra, sábana*) to shake out; (*arena, polvo*) to shake off. 2 (*golpear*) to beat. 3 (*conmover*) to shock, stun.

sádico,-a I *adj* sadistic. II *nm,f* sadist.

sadismo *nm* sadism.

sadomasoquista I *adj* sadomasochistic. II *nmf* sadomasochist.

saeta *nf* 1 (*dardo*) dart. 2 (*canción*) popular religious song.

safari *nm* (*cacería*) safari; (*parque*) safari park.

sagacidad *nf* *fml* (*listeza*) cleverness; (*astucia*) astuteness, shrewdness.

sagaz *adj* (*listo*) clever; (*astuto*) astute, shrewd.

Sagitario *nm* Sagittarius.

sagrado,-a *adj* sacred.

sagrario *nm* tabernacle.

Sáhara *n* Sahara.

saharaui *adj & nmf* Saharan.

sahariana *nf* safari jacket.

sainete *nm* *Teat* comic sketch, one-act farce.

sajón,-ona *adj & nm,f* Saxon.

sal *nf* 1 salt; **s. fina,** table salt; **s. gema,** salt crystals; **s. gorda,** cooking salt. 2 *fig* (*gracia*) wit.

sal *imperat* → **salir.**

sala *nf* room; (*en un hospital*) ward; *Jur* courtroom. **s. de estar,** lounge, living room; **s. de espera,** waiting room; **s. de exposiciones,** exhibition hall; **s. de fiestas,** nightclub, discotheque; **s. de lectura,** reading room.

salado,-a *adj* 1 (*con sal*) salted; (*con exceso de sal*) salty; **agua salada,** salt water. 2 *fig* (*encantador*) charming. 3 *Am* (*infortunado*) unlucky.

salamandra *nf* salamander.

salamanquesa *nf* gecko.

salame, salami *nm* salami.

salar *vtr* to salt, add salt to.

salarial *adj* salary, wage.

salario *nm* salary, wage; **s. mínimo,** minimum wage.

salazón *nf* salted meat *o* fish.

salchicha *nf* sausage.

salchichón *nm* (salami-type) sausage.

saldar *vtr* 1 *Fin* (*cuenta*) to settle; (*deuda*) to pay off. 2 *Com* (*vender barato*) to sell off. 3 *fig* (*diferencias*) to settle, resolve.

saldo *nm* 1 saldos, sales; **a precio de s.,** at bargain prices. 2 *Fin* balance. 3 (*de* *una deuda)* liquidation, settlement. **4** *(resto de mercancía)* remainder, leftover.

saldré *indic fut → salir.*

saledizo,-a *adj* projecting.

salero *nm* **1** *(recipiente)* saltcellar. **2** *fig (gracia)* charm.

salgo *indic pres → salir.*

salida *nf* **1** *(partida)* departure; *(puerta etc)* exit, way out; **callejón sin s.,** dead end; **s. de emergencia,** emergency exit. **2** *Dep* start; **línea de s.,** starting line; **s. nula,** false start. **3** **te vi a la s. del cine,** I saw you leaving the cinema. **4** *(de un astro)* rising; **s. del sol,** sunrise. **5** *(profesional)* opening; *Com* outlet. **6** *(recurso)* solution, way out; **no tengo otra s.,** I have no other option. **7** *fam (ocurrencia)* witty remark, witticism. **8** *Inform* output.

salido,-a *adj* **1** prominent, projecting. **2** *vulg (persona)* horny.

saliente *adj* **1** projecting, prominent; *fig* outstanding. **2** *(cesante)* outgoing.

salina *nf* salt mine.

salino,-a *adj* saline.

salir [22] *I vi* **1** *(de un sitio)* to go out, leave; *(venir de dentro)* to come out; **salió de la habitación,** she left the room; **s. de la carretera,** to go off the road. **2** *(tren etc)* to depart. **3** *(novios)* to go out *(con,* with). **4** *(aparecer)* to appear; *(revista, disco)* to come out; *(ley)* to come in; *(trabajo, vacante)* to come up. **5** *(resultar)* to turn out, turn out to be; **el pequeño les ha salido muy listo,** their son has turned out to be very clever; **¿cómo te salió el examen?,** how did your exam go?; **s. ganando,** to come out ahead o on top; **salió presidente,** he was elected president. **6 s. a,** *(precio)* to come to, work out at; **salió barato/caro,** to work out cheap/ expensive. **7 ha salido al abuelo,** she takes after her grandfather. **8** *(problema)* to work out; **esta cuenta no me sale,** I can't work this sum out. **8 ¡con qué cosas sales!,** the things you come out with! **II salirse** *vr* **1** *(líquido, gas)* to leak (out); *fig* **s. de lo normal,** to be out of the ordinary; **se salió de la carretera,** he went off the road. **2** *fam* **s. con la suya,** to get one's own way.

saliva *nf* saliva.

salivar *vi* to salivate.

salivazo *nm* spit.

salmantino,-a *I adj* of o from Salamanca. **II** *nm,f* native o inhabitant of Salamanca.

salmo *nm* psalm.

salmón *I nm (pescado)* salmon. **II** *adj inv (color)* salmon pink, salmon.

salmonete *nm (pescado)* red mullet.

salmorejo *nm (salsa)* sauce made from vinegar, water, pepper and salt.

salmuera *nf* brine.

salobre *adj (agua)* brackish; *(gusto)* salty, briny.

salón *nm* **1** *(en una casa)* lounge, sitting room. **2 s. de actos,** assembly hall; **s. de baile,** dance hall. **3 s. de belleza,** beauty salon; **s. de té,** tearoom, teashop. **4 s. del automóvil,** motor show.

salpicadura *nf* splashing.

salpicar [1] *vtr* **1** *(rociar)* to splash; **me salpicó el abrigo de barro,** he splashed mud on my coat. **2** *fig (esparcir)* to sprinkle.

salpicón *nm* **1** splash. **2** *Culin* cocktail.

salpimentar [1] *vtr* to season.

salpullido *nm* rash.

salsa *nf n* sauce; *(de carne)* gravy; *fig* **en su (propia) s.,** in one's element.

saltador,-a *nm,f Dep* jumper.

saltamontes *nm inv* grasshopper.

saltar **I** *vtr (obstáculo, valla)* to jump (over). **II** *vi* **1** to jump; *fig* **s. a la vista,** to be obvious. **2** *(cristal etc)* to break, shatter; *(plomos)* to go, blow. **3** *(desprenderse)* to come off. **4** *(encolerizarse)* to explode, blow up; **por menos de nada salta,** the smallest thing makes him explode. **III saltarse** *vr* **1** *(omitir)* to skip, miss out; **s. el semáforo/turno,** to jump the lights/the queue. **2** *(botón)* to come off; **se me saltaron las lágrimas,** tears came to my eyes.

salteado,-a *adj* **1** *(espaciado)* spaced out. **2** *Culin* sauté, sautéed.

saltear *vtr Culin* to sauté.

saltimbanqui *nmf* acrobat, tumbler.

salto *nm* **1** *(acción)* jump, leap; *fig (paso adelante)* leap forward; **a saltos,** in leaps and bounds; **dar** *o* **pegar un s.,** to jump, leap; **de un s.,** in a flash; *fig* **a s. de mata,** every now and then; **s. de agua,** waterfall; **s. de cama,** negligée. **2** *Dep* jump; **s. de altura,** high jump; **s. de longitud,** long jump; **s. mortal,** somersault.

saltón,-ona *adj* prominent; **ojos saltones,** bulging eyes.

salubre *adj* salubrious.

salubridad *nf* healthiness; **por razones de s.,** for health reasons.

salud *nf* **1** *(sano)* health; **beber a la s. de algn,** to drink to sb's health; *fam* **¡s.!,** cheers!

saludable *adj* **1** *(sano)* healthy, wholesome. **2** *fig (beneficioso)* good, beneficial.

saludar *vtr* **1** *(decir hola a)* to say hello to, to greet; **saluda de mi parte a,** give my regards to; **le saluda atentamente,** *(en una carta)* yours faithfully. **2** *Mil* to salute.

saludo *nm* **1** greeting; **un s. de,** best wishes from. **2** *Mil* salute.

salva *nf Mil* salvo, volley.

salvación *nf* salvation.

salvado *nm* bran.

salvador,-a I *nm,f* saviour; *(rescatador)* rescuer. **II** *nm* **El S.,** El Salvador.

salvadoreño,-a *adj* & *nm,f* Salvadoran,

Salvadorian.

salvaguarda *nf* → salvaguardia.

salvaguardar *vtr* to safeguard (de, from), protect (de, from).

salvajada *nf* brutal act.

salvaje *adj* 1 *Bot* wild, uncultivated; *Zool* wild; (*pueblo, tribu*) savage, uncivilized. 2 *fam* (*violento*) savage, wild.

salvajismo *nm* savagery.

salvamento *nm*, **salvamiento** *nm* rescue.

salvar I *vtr* 1 to save, rescue (de, from). 2 (*obstáculo*) to clear; (*dificultad*) to get round, overcome. 3 (*exceptuar*) to exclude, except; **salvando ciertos errores**, except for a few mistakes. II **salvarse** *vr* 1 (*sobrevivir*) to survive, come out alive; *fam* (*escaparse*) to escape (de, from); **¡sálvese quien pueda!**, every man for himself!; *fam* **s. por los pelos**, to have a narrow escape. 2 *Rel* to be saved, save one's soul.

salvavidas *nm inv* life belt.

salvedad *nf* 1 (*excepción*) exception. 2 (*reserva*) proviso.

salvia *nf Bot* sage.

salvo,-a I *adj* unharmed, safe; **a s.**, safe. II *adv* (*exceptuando*) except (for); **s. que**, unless.

salvoconducto *nm* safe-conduct.

san *adj inv*; → santo,-a.

sanar I *vtr* (*curar*) to cure, heal. II *vi* 1 (*persona*) to recover, get better. 2 (*herida*) to heal.

sanatorio *nm* sanatorium.

sanción *nf* 1 sanction. 2 (*aprobación*) sanction, approval. 3 *Jur* penalty.

sancionar *vtr* 1 (*castigar*) to penalize. 2 (*aprobar*) to sanction.

sancochar *vtr* to parboil; *Am* to boil meat in water and salt.

sandalia *nf* sandal.

sándalo *nm* sandalwood.

sandez *nf* piece of nonsense.

sandía *nf* watermelon.

sandwich *nm* sandwich.

sandwichera *nf* toasted sandwich maker.

saneamiento *nm* (*de terreno*) drainage, draining; (*de una empresa*) reorganisation.

sanear *vtr* (*terrenos*) to drain; (*empresa*) to reorganise.

sangrar I *vtr* 1 to bleed. 2 *fam* (*sacar dinero*) to bleed dry. II *vi* to bleed.

sangre *nf* blood; **donar s.**, to give blood; **s. fría**, sang-froid; **a s. fría**, in cold blood.

sangría *nf* 1 *Med* bleeding, bloodletting; *fig* drain. 2 (*timo*) rip-off. 3 (*bebida*) sangría.

sangriento,-a *adj* (*guerra etc*) bloody.

sanguijuela *nf* leech, bloodsucker.

sanguinario,-a *adj* bloodthirsty.

sanguíneo,-a *adj* blood; **grupo s.**, blood group.

sanidad *nf* health; **Ministerio de S.**, Department of Health.

sanitario,-a I *adj* health. II *nm* toilet.

sano,-a *adj* 1 (*bien de salud*) healthy; **s. y salvo**, safe and sound. 2 (*comida*) healthy, wholesome. 3 **en su s. juicio**, in one's right mind.

santiamén *nm fam* **en un s.**, in a flash, in no time at all.

santidad *nf* saintliness, holiness.

santificar [1] *vtr* to sanctify.

santiguarse [22] *vr* to cross oneself.

santo,-a I *adj* 1 holy, sacred. 2 (*bueno*) saintly; **un s. varón**, a saint. II *nm,f* 1 saint; *fam* **¡por todos los santos!**, for heaven's sake!; *fig* **se me fue el s. al cielo**, I clean forgot. 2 (*día onomástico*) saint's day; *fig* **¿a s. de qué?**, why on earth?

santuario *nm* sanctuary, shrine.

saña *nf* fury; **con s.**, furiously.

sapo *nm* toad; *fam* **echar sapos y culebras**, to rant and rave.

saque *nm* 1 *Ftb* **s. inicial**, kick-off; **s. de banda**, throw-in; **s. de esquina**, corner kick. 2 *Ten* service.

saquear *vtr* (*ciudad*) to sack, plunder; (*casas, tiendas*) to loot.

saqueo *nm* (*de ciudades*) sacking, plundering; (*de casa, tienda*) looting.

S.A.R. *abr de* **Su Alteza Real**, His *o* Her Royal Highness, H.R.H.

sarampión *nm* measles *pl*.

sarao *nm* knees-up.

sarcasmo *nm* sarcasm.

sarcástico,-a *adj* sarcastic.

sarcófago *nm* sarcophagus.

sardana *nf* sardana (Catalan dance and music).

sardina *nf* sardine.

sardónico,-a *adj* sardonic.

sargento *nm* sergeant.

sarmiento *nm* vine shoot.

sarna *nf Med* scabies *sing*; *Zool* mange.

sarpullido *nm* rash.

sarracina *nf* massacre.

sarro *nm* (*sedimento*) deposit; (*en los dientes*) tartar; (*en la lengua*) fur.

sarta *nf* string.

sartén *nf* frying pan, *US* skillet; *fig* **tener la s. por el mango**, to have the upper hand.

sastre *nm* tailor.

Satanás *nm* Satan.

satánico,-a *adj* satanic.

satélite *nm* satellite; *fig* **país s.**, satellite state; **televisión vía s.**, satellite TV.

satén *nm* satin.

satinar *vtr* to gloss, make glossy.

sátira *nf* satire.

satírico,-a *adj* satirical.

satirizar [4] *vtr* to satirize.

satisfacción *nf* satisfaction; **s. de un deseo**, fulfilment of a desire.

satisfacer [15] (*pp* satisfecho) *vtr* 1 (*de-*

seos, necesidades) to satisfy. **2** (*requisitos*) to meet, satisfy. **3** (*deuda*) to pay.
satisfactorio,-a *adj* satisfactory.
satisfecho,-a *adj* satisfied; **me doy por s.**, that's good enough for me; **s. de sí mismo**, self-satisfied, smug.
saturar *vtr* to saturate.
Saturno *nm* Saturn.
sauce *nm* willow; **s. llorón**, weeping willow.
saudí, saudita *adj & nmf* Saudi; **Arabia Saudita**, Saudi Arabia.
sauna *nf* sauna.
savia *nf* sap.
saxo *nm* Mús fam sax.
saxofón *nm* saxophone.
saxofonista *nmf* saxophonist.
sayo *nm* cassock, smock.
sazonar *vtr* to season, flavour, US flavor.
s/c. *abr de* **su cuenta**, your account.
Sdad. *abr de* **sociedad**, Society, Soc.
se¹ *pron* **1** (*reflexivo*) (*objeto directo*) (*a él mismo*) himself; (*animal*) itself; (*a ella misma*) herself; (*animal*) itself; (*a usted mismo*) yourself; (*a ellos mismos*) themselves; (*a ustedes mismos*) yourselves. **2** (*objeto indirecto*) (*a él mismo*) (*to o for*) himself; (*animal*) (*to o for*) itself; (*a ella misma*) (*to o for*) herself; (*animal*) (*to o for*) itself; (*a usted mismo*) (*to o for*) yourself; (*a ellos mismos*) (*to o for*) themselves; (*a ustedes mismos*) (*to o for*) yourselves; **se compró un nuevo coche**, he bought himself a new car; **todos los días se lava el pelo**, she washes her hair every day. **3** (*recíproco*) one another, each other. **4** (*voz pasiva*) **el vino se guarda en cubas**, wine is kept in casks. **5** (*impersonal*) **nunca se sabe**, you never know; **se habla inglés**, English spoken; **se dice que ...**, it is said that ....
se² *pron pers* (*a él*) (*to o for*) him; (*a ella*) (*to o for*) her; (*a usted o ustedes*) (*to o for*) you; (*a ellos*) (*to o for*) them; **se lo diré en cuanto les vea**, I'll tell them as soon as I see them; **¿se lo explico?**, shall I explain it to you?; **¿se lo has dado ya?**, have you given it to him yet?
sé¹ *indic pres* → **saber**.
sé² *imperat* → **ser**.
S.E. *abr de* **Su Excelencia**, His o Her Excellency, HE.
sea *subj pres* → **ser**.
sebo *nm* (*grasa*) fat.
secado *nm* drying.
secador,-a I *nm* dryer, drier; **s. de pelo**, hairdryer. **II** *nf* tumble dryer.
secano *nm* dry land.
secante *adj* **papel s.**, blotting paper.
secar [1] **I** *vtr* to dry. **II secarse** *vr* **1** to dry; **sécate**, dry yourself; **s. las manos**, to dry one's hands. **2** (*marchitarse*) to dry up, wither.
sección *nf* section.

seco,-a *adj* **1** dry; **frutos secos**, dried fruit; **limpieza en s.**, dry-cleaning; **fig a palo s.**, on its own; *fig* **a secas**, just, only. **2** (*tono*) curt, sharp; (*golpe, ruido*) sharp; *fig* **frenar en s.**, to pull up sharply; *fig* **parar en s.**, to stop dead. **3** (*delgado*) skinny.
secreción *nf* secretion.
secretaría *nf* (*oficina*) secretary's office; **S. de Estado**, State Department.
secretariado *nm* **1** (*oficina*) secretariat. **2** Educ secretarial course.
secretario,-a *nm,f* secretary.
secreto,-a I *adj* secret; **en s.**, in secret, secretly. **II** *nm* secret; **guardar un s.**, to keep a secret; **con mucho s.**, in great secrecy.
secta *nf* sect.
sectario,-a *adj* sectarian.
sector *nm* **1** sector. **2** (*zona*) area; **un s. de la ciudad**, an area of the city.
sectorial *adj* sectoral.
secuela *nf* consequence.
secuencia *nf* sequence.
secuestrador,-a *nm,f* **1** (*de persona*) kidnapper; (*de un avión*) hijacker. **2** Jur sequestrator.
secuestrar *vtr* **1** (*persona*) to kidnap; (*aviones*) to hijack. **2** Jur to confiscate.
secuestro *nm* **1** (*de persona*) kidnapping; (*de un avión*) highjacking. **2** Jur confiscation.
secular *adj* **1** Rel secular, lay. **2** (*antiquísimo*) ancient, age-old.
secundar *vtr* to back.
secundario,-a *adj* secondary.
secuoya *nf* Bot redwood, sequoia; **s. gigante**, giant sequoia.
sed *nf* thirst; **tener s.**, to be thirsty.
seda *nf* silk.
sedal *nm* fishing line.
sedante *adj & nm* sedative.
sede *nf* **1** headquarters, head office; (*de gobierno*) seat. **2 la Santa S.**, the Holy See.
sedentario,-a *adj* sedentary.
sedición *nf* sedition.
sedicioso,-a I *adj* rebellious. **II** rebel.
sediento,-a *adj* thirsty; *fig* **s. de poder**, hungry for power.
sedimentarse *vr* to settle.
sedimentario,-a *adj* sedimentary.
sedimento *nm* sediment, deposit.
sedoso,-a *adj* silky, silken.
seducción *nf* seduction.
seducir [10] *vtr* to seduce; (*persuadir*) to tempt.
seductor,-a I *adj* seductive; (*persuasivo*) tempting. **II** *nm,f* seducer.
segadora *nf* (*máquina*) reaper, harvester.
segar [1] *vtr* to reap, cut.
seglar I *adj* secular, lay. **II** *nmf* lay person; (*hombre*) layman; (*mujer*) laywoman.

segmento *nm* segment.

segregación *nf* 1 (*separación*) segregation. 2 (*secreción*) secretion.

segregar [7] *vtr* 1 (*separar*) to segregate. 2 (*secretar*) to secrete.

seguida *nf* en s., immediately, straight away.

seguido,-a *adj* 1 (*continuo*) continuous. 2 (*consecutivo*) consecutive, successive; **tres veces seguidas**, on three consecutive occasions; **tres lunes seguidos**, three Mondays in a row.

seguido *adv* straight; **todo s.**, straight on, straight ahead.

seguidor,-a *nm,f* follower.

seguimiento *nm* 1 pursuit. 2 *Prensa* in-depth coverage. 3 **estación de s.** (*espacial*), tracking station.

seguir [6] 1 *vtr* 1 to follow. 2 (*camino*) to continue. 3 (*perseguir*) to chase. II *vi* 1 to follow. 2 **s.** + *ger*, (*continuar*) to continue, go on, keep on; **siguió hablando**, he continued o went on o kept on speaking. 3 **s.** + *adj/pp*, to continue to be, be still; **sigo resfriado**, I've still got the cold; **sigue con vida**, he's still alive. III **seguirse** *vtr* to follow, ensue.

según 1 *prep* 1 according to; **s. la Biblia**, according to the Bible. 2 (*en función de*) depending on; **varía s. el tiempo (que haga)**, it varies depending on the weather. II *adv* 1 depending on; **s. están las cosas**, depending on how things stand; **¿vendrás mañana? - s.**, will you come tomorrow? - it depends. 2 (*tal como*) just as; **estaba s. lo dejé**, it was just as I had left it. 3 (*a medida que*) as; **s. iba leyendo ...**, as I read on ....

segundero *nm* second hand.

segundo,-a [1] *adj* second; *fig* **decir algo con segundas (intenciones)**, to say sth with a double meaning. II *nm,f* (*de una serie*) second (one).

segundo [2] *nm* (*tiempo*) second; **sesenta segundos**, sixty seconds.

seguramente *adv* 1 (*seguro*) surely. 2 (*probablemente*) most probably; **s. no lloverá**, it isn't likely to rain.

seguridad *nf* 1 security; **cerradura de s.**, security lock. 2 (*física*) safety; **s. en carretera**, road safety; **para mayor s.**, to be on the safe side. 3 (*confianza*) confidence; **s. en sí mismo**, self-confidence. 4 (*certeza*) sureness; **con toda s.**, most probably; **tener la s. de que ...**, to be certain that .... **S. Social**, ≈ Social Security, *GB* National Health Service. 6 (*fiabilidad*) reliability.

seguro,-a 1 *adj* 1 (*cierto*) sure; **estoy s. de que ...**, I am sure that ...; **dar algo por s.**, to take sth for granted. 2 (*libre de peligro*) safe; *fig* **ir sobre s.**, to play safe. 3 (*protegido*) secure. 4 (*fiable*) reliable. 5 **está segura de ella misma**, she has self-

confidence. 6 (*firme*) steady, firm. II *nm* 1 *Seg* insurance; **s. a todo riesgo**, fully comprehensive insurance; **s. contra terceros**, third party insurance; **s. de vida**, life insurance. 2 (*dispositivo*) safety catch o device. III *adv* for sure, definitely.

seis *adj & nm inv* six.

seiscientos,-as *adj & nm,f* six hundred.

seísmo *nm* (*terremoto*) earthquake; (*temblor de tierra*) earth tremor.

selección *nf* 1 selection. 2 *Dep* team.

seleccionador,-a *nm,f* 1 selector. 2 *Dep* manager.

seleccionar *vtr* to select.

selectividad *nf* selectivity; *Univ* (**prueba de**) s., entrance examination.

selectivo,-a *adj* selective.

selecto,-a *adj* select; **ambiente s.**, exclusive atmosphere.

self-service *nm* self-service cafeteria.

selva *nf* jungle.

sellar *vtr* (*documento*) to seal; (*carta*) to stamp.

sello *nm* 1 (*de correos*) stamp; (*para documentos*) seal. 2 (*precinto*) seal.

semáforo *nm* traffic lights *pl*.

semana *nf* week; **entre s.**, during the week; **S. Santa**, Holy Week.

semanal *adj & nm* weekly.

semanario *nm* weekly magazine.

semblante *nm* 1 (*cara*) face; *fig* (*aspecto*) look.

sembrado *nm* sown field.

sembrar [26] *vtr* 1 *Agr* to sow. 2 *fig* **s. el pánico**, to spread panic.

semejante 1 *adj* 1 (*parecido*) similar; **nunca he visto nada s.**, I've never seen anything like it. 2 *pey* (*comparativo*) such; **s. desvergüenza**, such insolence. II *nm* (*prójimo*) fellow being.

semejanza *nf* similarity, likeness.

semen *nm* semen.

semental *nm* stud.

semestral *adj* half-yearly.

semestre *nm* six-month period, semester.

semicírculo *nm* semicircle.

semifinal *nf* semifinal.

semifinalista *nmf* semifinalist.

semilla *nf* seed.

semillero *nm* seedbed.

seminario *nm* 1 *Educ* seminar. 2 *Rel* seminary.

sémola *nf* semolina.

Sena *n* el S., the Seine.

senado *nm* senate.

senador,-a *nm,f* senator.

sencillez *nf* simplicity.

sencillo,-a *adj* 1 (*fácil*) simple, easy. 2 (*natural*) natural, unaffected. 3 (*billete*) single. 4 (*sin adornos*) simple, plain.

senda *nf*, **sendero** *nm* path.

sendos,-as *adj nm pl* one each; **con sendas carteras**, each carrying a briefcase.

senil *adj* senile.

seno *nm* 1 *(pecho)* breast. 2 *fig* bosom, heart; **en el s. de,** within. 3 *Mat* sine.

sensación *nf* 1 sensation, feeling; **tengo la s. de que ...,** I have a feeling that .... 2 *(impresión)* sensation; **causar s.,** to cause a sensation.

sensacional *adj* sensational.

sensacionalista *adj* sensationalist; **prensa s.,** gutter press.

sensato,-a *adj* sensible.

sensibilizar [4] *vtr* to make aware; **s. a la opinión pública,** to increase public awareness.

sensible *adj* ◆ sensitive. 2 *(perceptible)* perceptible. ◆ **sensiblemente** *adv* noticeably, considerably.

sensiblero,-a *adj* over-sentimental, mawkish.

sensitivo,-a *adj (perceptible)* sensitive. 2 *(relativo a los sentidos)* sensory, sense; **órgano s.,** sense organ.

sensorial, sensorio,-a *adj* sensory.

sensual *adj* sensual.

sensualidad *nf* sensuality.

sentada *nf* 1 sitting. 2 *fam (protesta)* sit-in (demonstration).

sentado,-a *adj (establecido)* established, settled; **dar algo por s.,** to take sth for granted; **dejar s. que ...,** to make it clear that ....

sentar [1] **I** *vtr* 1 to sit. 2 *(establecer)* to establish; **s. las bases,** to lay the foundations. **II** *vi* 1 *(color, ropa etc)* to suit; **el pelo corto le sienta mal,** short hair doesn't suit you. 2 **s. bien/mal a,** *(comida)* to agree/disagree with; **la sopa te sentará bien,** the soup will do you good. 3 **le sentó mal la broma,** she didn't like the joke. **III sentarse** *vr* to sit, sit down.

sentencia *nf* 1 sentence; **visto para s.,** ready for judgement. 2 *(aforismo)* maxim, saying.

sentenciar [12] *vtr Jur* to sentence (a, to).

sentido,-a I *nm* 1 sense; **los cinco sentidos,** the five senses; **s. común,** common sense; **s. del humor,** sense of humour. 2 *(significado)* meaning; **doble s.,** double meaning; **no tiene s.,** it doesn't make sense. 3 *(dirección)* direction; **(de) s. único,** one-way. 4 *(conciencia)* consciousness; **perder el s.,** to faint. **II** *adj* deeply felt; **fml mi más s. pésame,** my deepest sympathy.

sentimental I *adj* sentimental; **vida s.,** love life. **II** *nmf* sentimental person.

sentimiento *nm* 1 feeling. 2 *(pesar)* sorrow, grief; **fml le acompaño en el s.,** my deepest sympathy.

sentir¹ *nm* 1 *(sentimiento)* feeling. 2 *(opinión)* opinion, view.

sentir² [5] **I** *vtr* 1 to feel; **s. hambre/calor,** to feel hungry/hot. 2 *(lamentar)* to regret, be sorry about; **lo siento** *(mu-*

cho), I'm (very) sorry; **siento molestarle,** I'm sorry to bother you. **II sentirse** *vr* to feel; **me siento mal,** I feel ill; **s. con ánimos de hacer algo,** to feel like doing sth.

senyera *nf* Catalan flag.

seña *nf* 1 mark. 2 *(gesto)* sign; **hacer señas a algn,** to signal to sb. 3 *(indicio)* sign. 3 **señas,** *(dirección)* address *sing.*

señal *nf* 1 *(indicio)* sign, indication; **en s. de,** as a sign of, as a token of. 2 *(placa)* sign; **s. de tráfico,** road sign. 3 *(gesto etc)* signal, sign. 4 *(marca)* mark; *(vestigio)* trace. 5 *Tel* tone; **s. de llamada,** dialling *o US* dial tone. 6 *Com* deposit.

señalado,-a *adj (importante)* important; **un día s.,** a red-letter day.

señalar I *vtr* 1 *(indicar)* to mark, indicate; **s. con el dedo,** to point at. 2 *(resaltar)* to point out. 3 *(precio, fecha)* to fix, arrange.

señor *nm* 1 *(hombre)* man; *(caballero)* gentleman. 2 *Rel* **El S.,** the Lord. 3 *(con apellido)* Mr; *(tratamiento de respeto)* sir; **el Sr. Gutiérrez,** Mr Gutiérrez; **muy s. mío,** *(en carta)* Dear Sir. 4 *(con título)* *(no se traduce)* **el s. ministro,** the Minister.

señora *nf* 1 *(mujer)* woman; *fml* lady; **¡señoras y señores!,** ladies and gentlemen! 2 *Rel* **Nuestra S.,** Our Lady. 3 *(con apellido)* Mrs; *(tratamiento de respeto)* madam; **la Sra. Salinas,** Mrs Salinas; **muy s. mía,** *(en carta)* Dear Madam. 4 *(con título)* *(no se traduce)* **la s. ministra,** the Minister. 5 *(esposa)* wife.

señoría *nf* 1 *Jur (hombre)* lordship; *(mujer)* ladyship. 2 *Pol* **sus señorías,** the honourable gentlemen.

señorita *nf* 1 *(joven)* young woman; *fml* young lady. 2 *(tratamiento de respeto)* Miss; **S. Padilla,** Miss Padilla. 3 *Educ* **la s.,** the teacher, Miss.

señuelo *nm (en caza)* decoy.

sepa *subj pres* → **saber.**

separación *nf* 1 separation; *Jur* **s. conyugal,** legal separation. 2 *(espacio)* space, gap.

separado,-a *adj* 1 separate; **por s.,** separately, individually. 2 *(divorciado)* separated.

separar I *vtr* 1 to separate. 2 *(desunir)* to detach, remove. 3 *(dividir)* to divide, separate. 4 *(apartar)* to move away. **II separarse** *vr* 1 to separate, part company. 2 *(matrimonio)* to separate. 3 *(apartarse)* to move away (de, from).

separata *nf* offprint.

separatismo *nm* separatism.

separatista *adj & nmf* separatist.

sepia I *nf (pez)* cuttlefish. **II** *adj & nm (color)* sepia.

septentrional *adj* northern.

septiembre *nm* September; **el 5 de s.,** the 5th of September; **en s.,** in September.

séptimo,-a *adj & nm,f* seventh; **la** *o* **una séptima parte**, a seventh.

sepulcral *adj (silencio)* deathly.

sepulcro *nm* tomb.

sepultura *nf* grave.

sepulturero,-a *nm,f* gravedigger.

sequía *nf* drought.

séquito *nm* entourage, retinue.

SER *nf Rad TV abr de* **Sociedad Española de Radiodifusión**

ser¹ *nm* being; **s. humano**, human being; **s. vivo**, living being.

ser² [23] *vi* 1 (+ *adj*) **es alto y rubio**, he is tall and fair; **el edificio es gris**, the building is grey. 2 (+ *profesión*) to be a(n); **Rafael es músico**, Rafael is a musician. 3 **s. de**, *(procedencia)* to be *o* come from; **¿de dónde eres?**, where are you from?, where do you come from? 4 **s. de**, (+ *material*) to be made of. 5 **s. de**, (+ *poseedor*) to belong to; **el perro es de Miguel**, the dog belongs to Miguel; **¿de quién es este abrigo?**, whose coat is this? 6 **s. para**, *(finalidad)* to be for; **esta agua es para lavar**, this water is for washing. 7 (+ *día, hora*) to be; **hoy es dos de noviembre**, today is the second of November; **son las cinco de la tarde**, it's five o'clock. 8 (+ *cantidad*) **¿cuántos estaremos en la fiesta?** how many of us will there be at the party? 9 *(costar)* to be, cost; **¿cuánto es?**, how much is it? 10 *(tener lugar)* to be; **el estreno será mañana**, tomorrow is the opening night. 11 **¿qué es de Gonzalo?**, what has become of Gonzalo? 12 *(auxiliar en pasiva)* to be; **fue asesinado**, he was murdered. 13 *(locuciones)* **¿cómo es eso?**, **¿cómo puede s.?**, how can that be?; **es más**, furthermore; **es que ...**, it's just that ...; **como sea**, anyhow; **lo que sea**, whatever; **o sea**, that is (to say); **por si fuera poco**, to top it all; **sea como sea**, in any case, be that as it may; **a no s. que**, unless; **de no s. por ...**, had it not been for ...; **eso era de esperar**, it was to be expected.

serenarse *vr* to calm down.

serenidad *nf* serenity.

sereno¹ *nm (vigilante)* night watchman.

sereno,-a² *adj* 1 calm. 2 *fam* **estar s.**, *(sobrio)* to be sober.

serial *nm Rad TV* serial.

serie *nf* 1 series *sing*; **fabricación en s.**, mass production; **lleva ABS de s.**, it has ABS fitted as standard; **fuera de s.**, out of the ordinary. 2 *Rad TV* series *sing*.

seriedad *nf* 1 seriousness. 2 *(formalidad)* reliability, dependability; **falta de s.**, irresponsibility.

serio,-a *adj* 1 *(severo)* serious; **en s.**, seriously. 2 *(formal)* reliable, responsible.

sermón *nm* sermon.

sermonear *vi & vtr fam* to lecture.

seropositivo,-a *adj* HIV-positive.

serpentear *vi (zigzaguear)* to wind one's way, meander.

serpentina *nf (de papel)* streamer.

serpiente *nf* snake; **s. de cascabel**, rattlesnake; **s. pitón**, python.

serranía *nf* mountainous area *o* country.

serrar [1] *vtr* to saw.

serrín *nm* sawdust.

serrucho *nm* handsaw.

servicial *adj* helpful, obliging.

servicio *nm* 1 service; **s. a domicilio**, delivery service. 2 *Mil* service; **s. militar**, military service; **estar de s.**, to be on duty. 3 **servicios**, *(retrete)* toilet *sing*, *US* rest room *sing*.

servidor,-a *nm,f* servant; *fam* **un s.**, yours truly.

servil *adj* servile.

servilleta *nf* serviette, napkin.

servilletero *nm* serviette ring, napkin ring.

servio,-a *adj & nm,f* Serbian.

servir [6] **I** *vtr* to serve; **¿en qué puedo servirle?**, what can I do for you?, may I help you?; **¿te sirvo una copa?**, may I pour you a drink? **II** *vi* 1 to serve. 2 *(valer)* to be useful, be suitable; **no sirve de nada llorar**, it's no use crying; **ya no sirve**, it's no use; **¿para qué sirve esto?**, what is this (used) for? 3 **s. de**, to serve as, act as. **III servirse** *vr* 1 *(comida etc)* to help oneself. 2 *fml* **sírvase comunicarnos su decisión**, please inform us of your decision.

sésamo *nm* sesame.

sesenta *adj & nm inv* sixty.

sesgar [7] *vtr* 1 *(cortar)* to cut diagonally. 2 *(torcer)* to slant.

sesgo *nm fig* slant, turn; **tomar un s. favorable**, to take a turn for the better.

sesión *nf* 1 *(reunión)* meeting, session; *Jur* session, sitting. 2 *Cin* showing.

seso *nm* brain.

set *nm Ten* set.

seta *nf (comestible)* mushroom; **s. venenosa**, toadstool.

setecientos,-as *adj & nm inv* seven hundred.

setenta *adj & nm inv* seventy.

setiembre *nm* September.

seto *nm* hedge.

seudónimo *nm* pseudonym; *(de escritores)* pen name.

severidad *nf* severity.

severo,-a *adj* severe.

Sevilla *n* Seville.

sexismo *nm* sexism.

sexista *adj* sexist.

sexo *nm* 1 sex. 2 *(órgano)* genitals *pl*.

sexólogo,-a *nm,f* sexologist.

sexto,-a *adj & nm,f* sixth.

sexual *adj* sexual; **vida s.**, sex life.

sexualidad *nf* sexuality.

sexy *adj* sexy.

s/f. *abr de* **su favor,** your favour *o US* favor.

shock *nm* shock.

show *nm* show.

si¹ *conj* **1** *(condicional)* if; **como si,** as if; **si no,** if not; **si quieres,** if you like, if you wish. **2** *(pregunta indirecta)* whether, if; **me preguntó si me gustaba,** he asked me if I liked it; **no sé si ir o no,** *(disyuntivo)* I don't know whether to go or not. **3** *(sorpresa)* **¡si está llorando!,** but she's crying!

si² *nm* (*pl* **sis**) *Mús* B; *(en solfeo)* ti.

sí¹ *pron pers* **1** *(singular)* *(él)* himself; *(ella)* herself; *(cosa)* itself; *(plural)* themselves; **de por sí, en sí,** in itself; **hablaban entre sí,** they were talking among themselves *o* to each other; **por sí mismo,** by himself. **2** *(uno mismo)* oneself; **decir para sí,** to say to oneself.

sí² **I** *adv* **1** yes; **dije que sí,** I said yes, I accepted, I agreed; **porque sí,** just because; **¡que sí!,** yes, I tell you!; **un día sí y otro no,** every other day. **2** *(uso enfático)* *(no se traduce)* **sí que me gusta,** of course I like it; **¡eso sí que no!,** certainly not!. **II** *nm* (*pl* **síes**) yes; **los síes,** *(en parlamento)* the ayes.

siamés,-esa *nm,f* Siamese twin.

sibarita *nmf* sybarite.

sicario *nm* hired gunman; *fam* hitman.

Sicilia *n* Sicily.

sico- → **psico-**.

sicómoro *nm* sycamore.

SIDA *nm abr de* **síndrome de inmunodeficiencia adquirida,** acquired immune deficiency syndrome, AIDS.

sidecar *nm* sidecar.

siderurgia *nf* iron and steel industry.

siderúrgico,-a *adj* iron and steel; **la industria siderúrgica,** the iron and steel industry.

sidra *nf* cider.

siempre *adv* always; **s. pasa lo mismo,** it's always the same; **como s.,** as usual; **a la hora de s.,** at the usual time; **eso es así desde s.,** it has always been like that; **para s.,** for ever; **s. que,** *(cada vez que)* whenever; *(a condición de que)* provided, as long as; **s. y cuando,** provided, as long as.

sien *nf* temple.

sierra *nf* **1** saw; **s. mecánica,** power saw. **2** *Geog* mountain range, sierra.

siervo,-a *nm,f* slave.

siesta *nf* siesta, nap; **dormir la s.,** to have a siesta *o* an afternoon nap.

siete *adj* & *nm inv* seven.

sietemesino,-a *nm,f* seven-month baby, premature baby.

sífilis *nf inv* syphilis.

sifón *nm* siphon; **whisky con s.,** whisky and soda.

sig. *abr de* **siguiente,** following.

sigilo *nm* secrecy; **entrar con mucho s.,** to tiptoe in.

sigiloso,-a *adj* secretive.
 ◆**sigilosamente** *adv* *(secretamente)* secretly; **entró s. en la habitación,** she crept *o* slipped into the room.

sigla *nf* acronym.

siglo *nm* century; **el s. veintiuno,** the twenty-first century; *fam* **hace siglos que no le veo,** I haven't seen him for ages.

signatario,-a *adj* & *nm,f* signatory.

significación *nf* **1** *(sentido)* meaning. **2** *(importancia)* significance.

significado *nm* meaning.

significar [1] *vtr* to mean.

significativo,-a *adj* significant; *(expresivo)* meaningful.

signo *nm* **1** sign; **s. del zodiaco,** zodiac sign. **2** *Ling* mark; **s. de interrogación,** question mark.

sigo *indic pres* → **seguir**.

siguiente *adj* following, next; **¡el s.!,** next, please!; **al día s.,** the following day.

sílaba *nf* syllable.

silbar *vi* to whistle; *(abuchear)* to hiss, boo.

silbato *nm* whistle.

silbido *nm* whistle, whistling; *(agudo)* hiss.

silenciador *nm* *(de arma)* silencer; *(de coche, moto)* silencer, *US* muffler.

silenciar [12] *vtr* **1** *(un sonido)* to muffle. **2** *(noticia)* to hush up.

silencio *nm* silence; **imponer s. a algn,** to make sb be quiet.

silencioso,-a *adj* *(persona)* quiet; *(motor etc)* silent.

silicio *nm* silicon.

silicona *nf* silicone.

silla *nf* **1** chair; **s. de ruedas,** wheelchair; **s. giratoria,** swivel chair. **2** *(de montura)* saddle.

sillín *nm* saddle.

sillón *nm* armchair.

silo *nm* silo.

silueta *nf* silhouette; *(de cuerpo)* figure.

silvestre *adj* wild.

simbólico,-a *adj* symbolic; **precio s.,** token price.

simbolizar [4] *vtr* to symbolize.

símbolo *nm* symbol.

simetría *nf* symmetry.

simétrico,-a *adj* symmetrical.

simiente *nf* seed.

similar *adj* similar.

similitud *nf* similarity.

simio *nm* monkey.

simpatía *nf* liking, affection; **le tengo mucha s.,** I am very fond of him.

simpático,-a *adj* *(amable)* nice, likeable; **me cae s.,** I like him.

simpatizante *nmf* sympathizer.

simpatizar [4] *vi* **1** to sympathise (**con**, with). **2** (*llevarse bien*) to hit it off (**con**, with).

simple *adj* **1** simple. **2** (*fácil*) simple, easy. **3** (*mero*) mere. **4** (*persona*) simple, simple-minded. **II** *nm* (*persona*) simpleton.

simpleza *nf* simple-mindedness; (*tontería*) nonsense.

simplificar [1] *vtr* to simplify.

simposio *nm* symposium.

simulacro *nm* sham, pretence; **un s. de ataque**, a mock attack.

simular *vtr* to simulate.

simultanear *vtr* to combine; **simultanea el trabajo y los estudios**, he's working and studying at the same time.

simultáneo,-a *adj* simultaneous.

sin *prep* **1** without; **s. dinero/ti**, without money/you; **estamos s. pan**, we're out of bread; **s. hacer nada**, without doing anything; **cerveza s.**, alcohol-free beer; **s. más ni más**, without further ado. **2** (+ *inf*) **está s. secar**, it hasn't been dried.

sinagoga *nf* synagogue.

sincerarse *vr* to open one's heart (**con**, to).

sinceridad *nf* sincerity; **con toda s.**, in all sincerity.

sincero,-a *adj* sincere.

sincronizar [4] *vtr* to synchronize.

sindical *adj* trade union, union.

sindicalista *nmf* trade unionist.

sindicato *nm* union, trade union.

síndrome *nm* syndrome.

sinfín *nm* endless number; **un s. de**, lots of.

sinfonía *nf* symphony.

single *nm* single, 7-inch.

singular **I** *adj* **1** singular. **2** (*excepcional*) exceptional, unique. **3** (*raro*) peculiar, odd. **II** *nm* *Ling* singular; **en s.**, in the singular.

siniestrado,-a *adj* stricken.

siniestro,-a *adj* sinister, ominous. **II** *nm* disaster, catastrophe.

sino[1] *nm* *fml* fate, destiny.

sino[2] *conj* **1** but; **no fui a Madrid, s. a Barcelona**, I didn't go to Madrid but to Barcelona. **2** (*excepto*) **nadie s. él**, no-one but him; **no quiero s. que me oigan**, I only want them to listen to me.

sinónimo,-a **I** *adj* synonymous. **II** *nm* synonym.

sinóptico,-a *adj* **cuadro s.**, diagram, chart.

sinsabor *nm* (*usu pl*) trouble, worry.

sintético,-a *adj* synthetic.

sintetizador *nm* synthesizer.

sintetizar [4] *vtr* to synthesize.

síntoma *nm* symptom.

sintonía *nf* **1** *Elec Rad* tuning. **2** *Mús Rad* (*de programa*) signature tune. **3** *fig* harmony.

sintonizador *nm* *Rad* tuning knob.

sintonizar [4] *vtr* **1** *Rad* to tune in. **2** (*simpatizar*) to be in tune (**con**, with).

sinuoso,-a *adj* (*camino*) winding.

sinvergüenza **I** *adj* (*desvergonzado*) shameless; (*descarado*) cheeky. **II** *nmf* (*desvergonzado*) rogue; (*caradura*) cheeky devil.

sionismo *nm* Zionism.

siquiera **I** *adv* (*por lo menos*) at least; **ni s.**, not even. **II** *conj* *fml* (*aunque*) although, even though.

sirena *nf* **1** siren, mermaid. **2** (*señal acústica*) siren.

Siria *n* Syria.

sirimiri *nm* fine drizzle.

sirio,-a *adj* & *nm,f* Syrian.

sirviente,-a *nm,f* servant.

sisar *vtr* to pilfer, filch.

sisear *vi* to hiss.

sísmico,-a *adj* seismic.

sismógrafo *nm* seismograph.

sistema *nm* system; **por s.**, as a rule; **s. nervioso**, nervous system; **s. montañoso**, mountain chain.

sistemático,-a *adj* systematic.

sitiar [12] *vtr* to besiege.

sitio[1] *nm* **1** (*lugar*) place; **en cualquier s.**, anywhere; **en todos los sitios**, everywhere; *fig* **quedarse en el s.**, to die. **2** (*espacio*) room; **hacer s.**, to make room.

sitio[2] *nm* siege; **estado de s.**, state of emergency.

sito,-a *adj* *fml* situated, located.

situación *nf* **1** situation; **su s. económica es buena**, his financial position is good. **2** (*ubicación*) situation, location.

situado,-a *adj* situated; *fig* **estar bien s.**, to have a good position.

situar [30] **I** *vtr* to locate. **II** **situarse** *vr* to be situated *o* located.

sketch *nm* *Cin Teat* sketch.

s/l *abr de* **su letra** (**de crédito**).

S.L. *abr de* **Sociedad Limitada**, limited company, Ltd.

slip *nm* underpants *pl*.

slogan *nm* slogan.

S.M. *abr de* **Su Majestad**, (*rey*) His Majesty; (*reina*) Her Majesty.

smoking *nm* dinner jacket, US tuxedo.

s/n. *abr de* **sin número**.

snob *adj* & *nmf* = **esnob**.

snobismo *nm* = **esnobismo**.

so[1] *prep* (*bajo*) under; **so pena de**, under penalty of.

so[2] *nm* *fam* **¡so imbécil!**, you damned idiot!

sobaco *nm* armpit.

sobar *vtr* **1** *fam* (*dormir*) to sleep. **2** *vulg* (*manosear*) to fondle, paw.

soberanía *nf* sovereignty.

soberano,-a **I** *adj* **1** sovereign. **2** *fam* huge, great. **II** *nm,f* (*monarca*) sovereign.

soberbia *nf* pride.

soberbio,-a adj 1 proud. 2 (magnífico) splendid, magnificent.

sobón,-ona nm,f fam **ser un s.**, to be fresh o all hands.

sobornar vtr to bribe.

soborno nm (acción) bribery; (dinero etc) bribe.

sobra nf 1 **de s.**, (no necesario) superfluous; **tener de s.**, to have plenty; **estar de s.**, not to be needed; **saber algo de s.**, to know sth only too well. 2 **sobras**, (restos) leftovers.

sobrado,-a adj (que sobra) abundant, more than enough; **sobradas veces**, repeatedly; **andar s. de tiempo/dinero**, to have plenty of time/money.
◆**sobradamente** adv only too well.

sobrante I adj remaining, spare. II nm surplus, excess.

sobrar vi 1 to be more than enough, (sing) be too much, (pl) to be too many; **sobran tres sillas**, there are three chairs too many; **sobran comentarios**, I've nothing further to add; fam **tú sobras aquí**, you are not wanted here. 2 (quedar) to be left over; **ha sobrado carne**, there's still some meat left.

sobrasada nf sausage spread.

sobre[1] nm 1 (para carta) envelope. 2 (de sopa etc) packet.

sobre[2] prep 1 (encima de) on, upon, on top of. 2 (por encima) over, above. 3 (acerca de) about, on. 4 (aproximadamente) about; **vendré s. las ocho**, I'll come at about eight o'clock. 5 **s. todo**, especially, above all.

sobre- pref super-, over-.

sobrealimentado,-a adj overfed.

sobrecarga nf overload.

sobrecargar [7] vtr to overload.

sobrecogedor,-a adj dramatic, awesome.

sobrecoger [5] vtr (conmover) to shock.

sobredosis nf inv overdose.

sobreentenderse vr **se sobreentiende**, that goes without saying.

sobrehumano,-a adj superhuman.

sobregiro nm overdraft.

sobreimpresión nf Fot Cin superimposing.

sobrellevar vtr to endure, bear.

sobremesa[1] nf afternoon.

sobremesa[2] nf **ordenador de s.**, desktop computer.

sobrenatural adj supernatural.

sobrenombre nm nickname.

sobrepasar I vtr to exceed, surpass; (rival) to beat. II **sobrepasarse** vr to go too far.

sobrepeso nm (de carga) overload, excess weight; (de persona) excess weight.

sobreponerse vr 1 **s. a**, (superar) to overcome; **s. al dolor**, to overcome pain. 2 (animarse) to pull oneself together.

sobreproducción nf overproduction.

sobresaliente I nm (nota) A. II adj (que destaca) outstanding, excellent.

sobresalir [22] vi stick out, protrude; fig (destacar) to stand out, excel.

sobresaltar I vtr to startle. II **sobresaltarse** vr to be startled, start.

sobresalto nm (movimiento) start; (susto) fright.

sobreseer [36] vtr Jur to stay; **s. una causa**, to stay proceedings.

sobretodo nm (abrigo) overcoat; (guardapolvo) overalls pl.

sobrevalorar vtr to overestimate.

sobrevenir [27] vi to happen unexpectedly.

sobreviviente I adj surviving. II nmf survivor.

sobrevivir vi to survive.

sobrevolar [2] vtr to fly over.

sobriedad nf sobriety; (en la bebida) soberness.

sobrina nf niece.

sobrino nm nephew.

sobrio,-a adj sober.

socarrón,-ona adj,nm,f 1 (sarcástico) sarcastic. 2 (astuto) sly, cunning.

socavar vtr fig to undermine.

socavón nm (bache) pothole.

sociable adj sociable, friendly.

social adj social.

socialdemócrata I adj social democratic. II nmf social democrat.

socialismo nm socialism.

socialista adj & nmf socialist.

socializar [4] vtr to socialize.

sociedad nf 1 society; **s. de consumo**, consumer society. 2 (asociación) association, society. 3 Com company; **s. anónima**, public liability company; **s. limitada**, limited company.

socio,-a nm,f 1 (miembro) member; **hacerse s. de un club**, to become a member of a club, join a club. 2 Com (asociado) partner.

sociología nf sociology.

sociológico,-a adj sociological.

sociólogo,-a nm,f sociologist.

socorrer vtr to help, assist.

socorrido,-a adj handy, useful.

socorrista nmf life-saver, lifeguard.

socorro nm help, assistance; **js.!**, help!; **puesto de s.**, first-aid post.

soda nf soda water.

soez adj vulgar, crude.

sofá nm (pl **sofás**) sofa, settee; **s. cama**, sofa bed, studio couch.

Sofía n Sophia.

sofisticado,-a adj sophisticated.

sofocado,-a adj suffocated.

sofocante adj suffocating, stifling; **hacía un calor s.**, it was unbearably hot.

sofocar [1] I vtr 1 (ahogar) to suffocate, smother. 2 (incendio) to extinguish, put out. II **sofocarse** vr 1 (ahogarse) to suffo-

cate, stifle. 2 *fam* (*irritarse*) to get upset.
sofoco *nm fig* (*vergüenza*) embarrassment; **le dio un s.,** (*disgusto*) it gave her quite a turn.
sofocón *nm fam* shock; **llevarse un s.,** to get upset.
sofreír [6] *vtr* to fry lightly, brown.
sofrito *nm* fried tomato and onion sauce.
software *nm* software.
soga *nf* rope; *fig* **estar con la s. al cuello,** to be in dire straits.
soja *nf* soya bean, *US* soybean.
sojuzgar [7] *vtr* to subjugate.
sol[1] *nm* 1 sun. 2 (*luz*) sunlight; (*luz y calor*) sunshine; **hace s.,** it's sunny, the sun is shining; **tomar el s.,** to sunbathe; **al** *o* **bajo el s.,** in the sun; **de s. a s.,** from sunrise to sunset. 3 *Fin* standard monetary unit of Peru.
sol[2] *nm Mús* G; (*solfeo*) so.
solamente *adv* only; **no s.,** not only; **s. con mirarte lo sé,** I know just by looking at you; **s. que ...,** except that ....
solapa *nf* (*de chaqueta*) lapel; (*de sobre, bolsillo, libro*) flap.
solapado,-a *adj* (*persona*) sly. ◆ **solapadamente** *adv* stealthily, in an underhand way.
solapamiento *nm* overlap.
solapar I *vtr fig* to conceal, cover up. II *vi* to overlap.
solar[1] *adj* solar; **luz s.,** sunlight.
solar[2] *nm* (*terreno*) plot; (*en obras*) building site.
solario, solárium *nm* sunbed.
solaz *nm fml* (*descanso*) rest, relaxation; (*esparcimiento*) recreation, entertainment.
solazarse [4] *vr* (*relajar*) to relax; (*divertir*) to entertain oneself, amuse oneself.
soldado *nm* soldier; **s. raso,** private.
soldador,-a I *nm,f* welder. II *nm* soldering iron.
soldar [2] *vtr* (*cable*) to solder; (*chapa*) to weld.
soleado,-a *adj* sunny.
soledad *nf* (*estado*) solitude; (*sentimiento*) loneliness.
solemne *adj* 1 (*majestuoso*) solemn. 2 *pey* downright.
solemnidad *nf* solemnity.
soler [4] *vi defect* 1 (*en presente*) to be in the habit of; **solemos ir en coche,** we usually go by car; **sueles equivocarte,** you are usually wrong. 2 (*en pasado*) to use to; **solía pasear por aquí,** he used to walk round here.
solera *nf fig* tradition; **de s.,** old-established; **vino de s.,** vintage wine.
solfa *nf* 1 *Mús* solfa; *fam* **poner en s.,** to ridicule. 2 *fam* (*paliza*) thrashing, beating.
solicitar *vtr* (*información etc*) to request, ask for; (*trabajo*) to apply for.
solícito,-a *adj* obliging, attentive.

solicitud *nf* (*petición*) request; (*de trabajo*) application.
solidaridad *nf* solidarity.
solidario,-a *adj* 1 supportive; **una sociedad solidaria,** a caring society. 2 *Jur* jointly responsible.
solidarizarse *vr* to show one's solidarity (**con,** with).
solidez *nf* solidity, strength.
sólido,-a *adj* solid, strong.
soliloquio *nm* soliloquy.
solista *nmf* soloist.
solitario,-a I *adj* 1 (*que está solo*) solitary, lone; (*que se siente solo*) lonely. II *nm* 1 (*diamante*) solitaire. 2 *Naipes* solitaire, patience.
soliviantar *vtr* (*irritar*) to irritate.
sollozar [4] *vi* to sob.
sollozo *nm* sob.
solo,-a I *adj* 1 only, single; **ni un s. día,** not a single day; **una sola vez,** only once, just once. 2 (*solitario*) lonely. 3 hablar **s.,** to talk to oneself; **se enciende s.,** it switches itself on automatically; **a solas,** alone, by oneself. II *nm Mús* solo.
sólo *adv* only; **tan s.,** only; **no s. ... sino (también),** not only ... but (also); **con s., (tan) s. con,** just by.
solomillo *nm* sirloin.
soltar [2] I *vtr* 1 (*desasir*) to let go of; **¡suéltame!,** let me go! 2 (*prisionero*) to release. 3 (*humo, olor*) to give off. 4 (*bofetada*) to deal; (*carcajada*) to let out; **me soltó un rollo,** he bored me to tears. II **soltarse** *vr* 1 (*desatarse*) to come loose. 2 (*perro etc*) to get loose, break loose. 3 (*desprenderse*) to come off.
soltero,-a I *adj* single, unmarried. II *nm* (*hombre*) bachelor, single man. III *nf* (*mujer*) single woman, spinster.
solterón,-ona *pey* I *nm* (*hombre*) old bachelor. II *nf* (*mujer*) old maid.
soltura *nf* (*agilidad*) agility; (*seguridad*) confidence, assurance; **habla italiano con s.,** he speaks Italian fluently.
soluble *adj* soluble; **café s.,** instant coffee.
solución *nf* solution.
solucionar *vtr* to solve; (*arreglar*) to settle.
solvencia *nf* 1 *Fin* solvency. 2 (*fiabilidad*) reliability; **fuentes de toda s.,** completely reliable sources.
solventar *vtr* (*problema*) to solve, resolve; (*deuda, asunto*) to settle.
solvente *adj* 1 *Fin* solvent. 2 (*fiable*) reliable.
sombra *nf* 1 shade. 2 (*silueta proyectada*) shadow; **s. de ojos,** eyeshadow; **sin s. de duda,** beyond a shadow of doubt. 3 *fig* **tener buena s.,** (*tener suerte*) to be lucky.
sombrero *nm* hat; **s. de copa,** top hat; **s. hongo,** bowler hat.
sombrilla *nf* parasol, sunshade.
sombrío,-a *adj* (*oscuro*) dark; (*tenebroso*)

sombre, gloomy; *fig (persona)* gloomy, sullen.

somero,-a *adj* superficial, shallow.

someter I *vtr* 1 to subject; **s. a prueba,** to put to the test; **s. algo a votación,** to put sth to the vote. 2 *(rebeldes)* to subdue, put down. **II someterse** *vr* 1 *(subordinarse)* to submit. 2 *(rendirse)* to surrender, yield. 3 **s. a un tratamiento,** to undergo treatment.

somier *nm (pl* **somieres)** spring mattress.

somnífero *nm* sleeping pill.

somnoliento,-a *adj* sleepy, drowsy.

son *nm* sound; **al s. del tambor,** to the sound of the drum; **venir en s. de paz,** to come in peace.

sonado,-a *adj* 1 much talked of. 2 *(trastocado)* mad, crazy.

sonajero *nm* baby's rattle.

sonámbulo,-a *nm,f* somnambulist, sleepwalker.

sonar [2] **I** *vi* 1 to sound; **s. a,** to sound like; **suena bien,** it sounds good. 2 *(timbre, teléfono)* to ring; **sonaron las cinco,** the clock struck five. 3 **tu nombre/cara me suena,** your name/face rings a bell. **II sonarse** *vr* **s. (la nariz),** to blow one's nose.

sonda *nf* 1 *Med* sound, probe. 2 **s. espacial,** space probe.

sondear *vtr* 1 *(opinión)* to test, sound out. 2 *Med* to sound, probe. 3 *Náut* to sound.

sondeo *nm* 1 *(encuesta)* poll. 2 *Med* sounding, probing. 3 *Náut* sounding.

soneto *nm Lit* sonnet.

sonido *nm* sound.

sonoro,-a *adj* 1 *Cin* sound; **banda sonora,** soundtrack. 2 *(resonante)* loud, resounding. 3 *Ling* voiced.

sonreír [6] *vi,* **sonreírse** *vr* to smile; **me sonrió,** he smiled to me.

sonriente *adj* smiling.

sonrisa *nf* smile.

sonrojarse *vr* to blush.

sonrojo *nm* blush.

sonsacar [1] *vtr* to wheedle; *(secreto)* to worm out.

soñador,-a *nm,f* dreamer.

soñar [2] *vtr & vi* 1 to dream; **s. con,** to dream of *o* about; *fig* **¡ni soñarlo!,** not on your life! 2 *(fantasear)* to daydream, dream.

soñoliento,-a *adj* sleepy, drowsy.

sopa *nf* soup; **s. juliana,** spring vegetable soup; *fig* **quedar hecho una s.,** to get soaked to the skin.

sopera *nf* soup tureen.

sopero,-a *adj* **cucharada sopera,** soup spoon.

sopesar *vtr* to try the weight of; *fig* to weigh up.

sopetón *nm fam* slap; **de s.,** all of a sudden.

soplado *nm* glass-blowing.

soplar I *vi (viento)* to blow. **II** *vtr* 1 *(polvo etc)* to blow away; *(para enfriar)* to blow on. 2 *(para apagar)* to blow out. 3 *(para inflar)* to blow up. 4 *(en examen etc)* to whisper *o* tell the answer.

soplete *nm* blowlamp, blowtorch.

soplido *nm* blow, puff.

soplillo *nm* fan; *fam* **orejas de s.,** cauliflower ears.

soplo *nm* 1 *(acción)* blow, puff; *(de viento)* gust. 2 *Med* murmur.

soplón,-ona *nm,f fam (niño)* telltale, sneak; *(delator)* informer, squealer.

soporífero,-a *adj* 1 *(que adormece)* soporific, sleep-inducing. 2 *(aburrido)* boring, dull.

soportable *adj* bearable.

soportal *nm* porch; **soportales,** arcade *sing.*

soportar *vtr* 1 *(peso)* to support, bear. 2 *fig (calor, ruido)* to bear, endure; *(situación)* to put up with; to bear; **no te soporto,** I can't stand you.

soporte *nm* support; **s. publicitario,** advertising medium.

soprano *nmf* soprano.

sorber *vtr* 1 *(beber)* to sip. 2 *(absorber)* to soak up, absorb.

sorbete *nm* sorbet, sherbet.

sorbo *nm* sip; *(trago)* gulp; **de un s.,** in one gulp.

sordera *nf* deafness.

sórdido,-a *adj* squalid, sordid.

sordo,-a I *adj* 1 *(persona)* deaf; **s. como una tapia,** stone-deaf. 2 *(golpe, ruido, dolor)* dull. **II** *nm,f* deaf person; **los sordos,** the deaf *pl; fam fig* **hacerse el s.,** to turn a deaf ear.

sordomudez *nf* deaf-muteness.

sordomudo,-a I *adj* deaf and dumb, deaf-mute. **II** *nm,f* deaf and dumb person, deaf-mute.

sorprendente *adj* surprising.

sorprender *vtr* 1 *(extrañar)* to surprise. 2 *(coger desprevenido)* to catch unawares, take by surprise.

sorpresa *nf* surprise; **coger** *o* **por s.,** to take by surprise.

sorpresivo,-a *adj Am* unexpected, surprising.

sortear *vtr* 1 to draw *o* cast lots for; *(rifar)* to raffle (off). 2 *(evitar)* to avoid, get round.

sorteo *nm* draw; *(rifa)* raffle.

sortija *nf* ring.

sortilegio *nm* spell.

S.O.S. *nm* SOS.

sosa *nf* soda; **s. cáustica,** caustic soda.

sosegado,-a *adj (tranquilo)* calm, quiet; *(pacífico)* peaceful.

sosegar [1] **I** *vtr* to calm, quieten. **II sosegarse** *vr* to calm down.

sosiego *nm (calma)* calmness; *(paz)* peace, tranquility.

soslayo (al, de) *loc adv* mirar de s., to look sideways (at).
soso,-a *adj* lacking in salt; *fig (persona)* insipid, dull.
sospecha *nf* suspicion.
sospechar I *vi (desconfiar)* to suspect; **s. de algn**, to suspect sb. II *vtr (pensar)* to suspect.
sospechoso,-a I *adj* suspicious; **s. de**, suspected of. II *nm,f* suspect.
sostén *nm* 1 *(apoyo)* support. 2 *(sustento)* sustenance. 3 *(prenda)* bra, brassière.
sostener [24] I *vtr* 1 *(sujetar)* to support, hold up. 2 *(con la mano)* to hold. 3 *fig (teoría etc)* to defend, uphold; **s. que ...**, to maintain that .... 4 *(conversación)* to hold, sustain. 5 *(familia)* to support. II **sostenerse** *vr* 1 *(mantenerse)* to support oneself. 2 *(permanecer)* to stay, remain.
sostenido,-a *adj* 1 *(continuado)* sustained. 2 *Mús* sharp.
sostuve *pt indef* → **sostener**.
sota *nf Naipes* jack, knave.
sotana *nf* cassock, soutane.
sótano *nm* basement, cellar.
soto *nm* grove.
soviético,-a *adj & nm,f* Soviet; *Hist* la Unión Soviética, the Soviet Union.
soy *indic pres* → **ser**.
S.P. *abr de* Servicio Público.
sport (de) *loc adj* casual, sports; **chaqueta s.**, sports jacket.
spot *nm (pl* spots*) TV* commercial, advert, ad.
spray *nm (pl* sprays*)* spray.
sprint *nm* sprint.
Sr. *abr de* Señor, Mister, Mr.
Sra. *abr de* Señora, Mrs.
S.R.C., s.r.c. *abr de* se ruega contestación, please reply, R.S.V.P.
Srta. *abr de* Señorita, Miss.
SS *nf abr de* Seguridad Social, ≈ National Health Service, NHS.
SS.AA. *abr de* Sus Altezas, Their Royal Highnesses.
Sta., sta. *abr de* Santa, Saint, St.
stand *nm Com* stand.
standard *adj & nm* standard.
status *nm inv* status.
Sto., sto. *abr de* Santo, Saint, St.
su *adj pos (de él)* his; *(de ella)* her; *(de usted, ustedes)* your; *(de animales o cosas)* its; *(impersonal)* one's; *(de ellos)* their; **su coche**, his *o* her *o* your *o* their car; **su pata**, its leg; **sus libros**, his *o* her *o* your *o* their books; **sus patas**, its legs.
suave *adj* 1 smooth; *(luz, voz etc)* soft. 2 *Meteor (templado)* mild.
suavidad *nf* 1 smoothness; *(dulzura)* softness. 2 *Meteor* mildness.
suavizante *nm (para el pelo)* (hair) conditioner; *(para la ropa)* fabric softener.
suavizar [4] I *vtr* to smooth (out). II **suavizarse** *vr (temperatura)* to get milder;

(persona) to calm down.
subacuático,-a *adj* underwater.
subalimentado,-a *adj* undernourished, underfed.
subalterno,-a *adj & nm,f* subordinate, subaltern.
subarrendar [1] *vtr Com* to sublet, sublease.
subasta *nf* auction.
subastar *vtr* to auction (off), sell at auction.
subcampeón *nm Dep* runner-up.
subconsciente *adj & nm* subconscious.
subdesarrollado,-a *adj* underdeveloped.
subdesarrollo *nm* underdevelopment.
subdirector,-a *nm,f* assistant director *o* manager.
súbdito,-a *nm,f* subject, citizen; **s. francés**, French citizen.
subdividir *vtr* to subdivide.
subestimar *vtr* to underestimate.
subida *nf* 1 *(de temperatura)* rise; *(de precios, salarios)* rise, increase. 2 *(ascenso)* ascent, climb. 3 *(pendiente)* slope, hill. 4 *fam (drogas)* high.
subido,-a *adj* **s. de tono**, daring, risqué.
subir I *vtr* 1 to go up. 2 *(llevar arriba)* to take up, bring up. 3 *(cabeza, mano)* to lift, raise. 4 *(precio, salario)* to raise, put up. 5 *(volumen)* to turn up; *(voz)* to raise. II *vi* 1 *(ir arriba)* to go up, come up. 2 **s. a**, *(un coche)* to get into; *(un autobús)* to get on; *(un barco, avión, tren)* to board, get on. 3 *(aumentar)* to rise, go up. III **subirse** *vr* 1 to climb up; *fig* **el vino se le subió a la cabeza**, the wine went to his head. 2 **s. a**, *(un coche)* to get into; *(un autobús, avión, tren)* to get on; board; *(caballo, bici)* to get on. 3 *(cremallera)* to do up; *(mangas)* to roll up.
súbito,-a *adj* sudden. ◆**súbitamente** *adv* suddenly.
subjetivo,-a *adj* subjective.
sublevación *nf* rising, rebellion.
sublevar I *vtr fig (indignar)* to infuriate, enrage. II **sublevarse** *vr* to rebel, revolt.
sublime *adj* sublime.
submarinismo *nm* skin-diving.
submarino,-a I *adj* submarine, underwater. II *nm* submarine.
subnormal I *adj* mentally handicapped. II *nmf* mentally handicapped person.
suboficial *nm* 1 *Mil* noncommissioned officer. 2 *Náut* petty officer.
subordinado,-a *adj & nm,f* subordinate.
subordinar *vtr* to subordinate.
subproducto *nm* by-product.
subrayar *vtr* to underline; *fig (recalcar)* to emphasize, stress.
subrepticio,-a *adj* surreptitious.
subrutina *nf* subroutine.
subsanar *vtr (error)* to rectify, put right; *(daño)* to make up for.
subscribir *(pp* subscrito*) vtr* → **suscribir**.

subscripción nf subscription.
subscrito,-a adj & nm,f → **suscrito,-a.**
subsecretario,-a nm,f undersecretary.
subsidiario,-a adj subsidiary.
subsidio nm allowance, benefit; **s. de desempleo,** unemployment benefit.
subsistencia nf subsistence.
subsistir vi to subsist, remain; (vivir) to live on, survive.
subsuelo nm subsoil.
subterráneo,-a I adj underground. **II** nm (túnel) tunnel, underground passage.
subtítulo nm subtitle.
suburbano,-a adj suburban.
suburbio nm (barrio pobre) slums pl; (barrio periférico) suburb.
subvención nf subsidy.
subvencionar vtr to subsidize.
subversión nf subversion.
subversivo,-a adj subversive.
subyacente adj underlying.
subyugar [7] vtr to subjugate.
succionar vtr to suck (in).
sucedáneo,-a nm adj & nm,f substitute.
suceder I vi 1 (ocurrir) (uso impers) to happen, occur; ¿qué sucede?, what's going on?, what's the matter? 2 (seguir) to follow, succeed. **II sucederse** vr to follow one another, come after the other.
sucesión nf 1 (serie) series sing, succession. 2 (al trono) succession. 3 (descendencia) issue, heirs pl.
sucesivo,-a adj following, successive; **en lo s.,** from now on. ◆**sucesivamente** adv y así s., and so on.
suceso nm (hecho) event, occurrence; (incidente) incident; Prensa sección de **sucesos,** accident and crime reports.
sucesor,-a nm,f successor.
suciedad nf 1 dirt. 2 (calidad) dirtiness.
sucinto,-a adj concise, succinct.
sucio,-a adj dirty; **en s.,** in rough; fig **juego s.,** foul play; fig **negocio s.,** shady business. **II** adv jugar **s.,** to play dirty.
sucre nm Fin standard monetary unit of Ecuador.
suculento,-a adj succulent, juicy.
sucumbir vi to succumb, yield.
sucursal nf Com Fin branch, branch office.
sudaca nmf pey South American.
sudadera nf sweatshirt.
Sudáfrica n South Africa.
sudafricano,-a adj & nm,f South African.
Sudamérica n South America.
sudamericano,-a adj & nm,f South American.
sudar vtr & vi to sweat; fam fig **s. la gota gorda,** to sweat blood.
sudeste nm southeast.
sudoeste nm southwest.
sudor nm sweat; fig **con el s. de mi frente,** by the sweat of my brow.
sudoroso,-a adj sweaty.

Suecia n Sweden.
sueco,-a I adj Swedish. **II** nm,f (persona) Swede. **III** nm (idioma) Swedish.
suegra nf mother-in-law.
suegro nm father-in-law; **mis suegros,** my in-laws.
suela nf (de zapato) sole.
sueldo nm salary, wages pl.
suelo nm 1 (superficie) ground; (de interior) floor; fig **estar por los suelos,** (precios) to be rock-bottom. 2 (territorio) soil, land. 3 (campo, terreno) land; **s. cultivable,** arable land. 4 (de carretera) surface.
suelto,-a I adj 1 loose; (desatado) undone. 2 fig **dinero s.,** loose change; **hojas sueltas,** loose sheets (of paper); **se venden sueltos,** they are sold singly o separately o loose. 3 (en libertad) free; (huido) at large. 4 (vestido, camisa) loose, loose-fitting. **II** nm (dinero) (loose) change.
sueño nm 1 sleep; (ganas de dormir) sleepiness; **tener s.,** to feel o be sleepy. 2 (cosa soñada) dream.
suero nm Med serum; (de la leche) whey.
suerte nf (fortuna) luck; **por s.,** fortunately; **probar s.,** to try one's luck; **tener s.,** to be lucky; **¡que tengas s.!,** good luck! 2 **echar algo a suertes,** to draw lots for sth. 3 (destino) fate, destiny. 4 fml (género) kind, sort, type.
suéter nm sweater.
suficiencia nf 1 (engreimiento) smugness, complacency. 2 Educ **prueba de s.,** final exam.
suficiente I adj (bastante) sufficient, enough. **II** nm Educ pass. ◆**suficientemente** adv sufficiently; **no es lo s. rico como para ...** he isn't rich enough to ....
sufijo nm suffix.
sufragar [7] **I** vtr (gastos) to pay, defray. **II** vi Am to vote (por, for).
sufragio nm Pol suffrage; (voto) vote.
sufrido,-a adj (persona) long-suffering.
sufrimiento nm suffering.
sufrir I vi to suffer; **s. del corazón,** to have a heart condition. **II** vtr 1 (accidente) to have; (operación) to undergo; (dificultades, cambios) to experience; **s. dolores de cabeza,** to suffer from headaches. 2 (aguantar) to bear, put up with.
sugerencia nf suggestion.
sugerente adj suggestive.
sugerir [5] vtr to suggest.
sugestión nf suggestion.
sugestionar vtr to influence, persuade.
sugestivo,-a adj suggestive; (atractivo) alluring.
suicida I nmf (persona) suicide. **II** adj suicidal.
suicidarse vr to commit suicide, kill oneself.
suicidio nm suicide.
suite nf suite.

Suiza n Switzerland.

suizo,-a I adj Swiss. **II** nm,f (persona) Swiss. **III** nm Culin eclair.

sujetador nm (prenda) bra, brassière.

sujetar I vtr **1** (agarrar) to hold. **2** (fijar) to hold down, hold in place. **3** fig (someter) to restrain. **II sujetarse** vr (agarrarse) to hold on.

sujeto,-a I nm subject; (individuo) fellow, individual. **II** adj (atado) fastened, secure; **s. a,** (sometido) subject to, liable to.

sulfato nm sulphate.

sulfurar I vtr fam (exasperar) to exasperate, infuriate. **II sulfurarse** vr fam to lose one's temper, blow one's top.

sultán nm sultan.

suma nf **1** (cantidad) sum, amount. **2** Mat sum, addition; **s. total,** sum total. **3 en s.,** in short.

sumamente adv extremely, highly.

sumar I vtr Mat to add, add up. **II sumarse** vr **s. a,** (huelga) to join; (propuesta) to support.

sumario,-a I adj summary, brief; Jur juicio **s.,** summary proceedings pl. **II** nm Jur summary.

sumarísimo,-a adj Jur swift, expeditious.

sumergible adj & nm submersible.

sumergir [6] **I** vtr to submerge, submerse; (hundir) to sink, plunge. **II sumergirse** vr to submerge, go underwater; (hundirse) to sink.

sumidero nm drain, sewer.

suministrar vtr to supply, provide; **s. algo a algn,** to supply sb with sth.

suministro nm supply.

sumir vtr (hundir) to sink, plunge; fig to plunge.

sumiso,-a adj submissive, obedient.

sumo,-a adj (supremo) supreme; **con s. cuidado,** with extreme care; **a lo s.,** at (the) most.

suntuoso,-a adj sumptuous, magnificent.

supe pt indef → **saber.**

supeditar vtr to subject (**a,** to).

super- pref super-.

súper fam **I** adj super, great. **II** nm **1** (supermercado) supermarket. **2** (gasolina) **4** star.

superado,-a adj outdated, obsolete.

superar I vtr **1** (obstáculo etc) to overcome, surmount; (prueba) pass. **2** (aventajar) to surpass, excel. **II superarse** vr to improve o better oneself.

superávit nm surplus.

superdotado,-a I adj exceptionally gifted. **II** nm,f genius.

superficial adj superficial.

superficialidad nf superficiality.

superficie nf surface; (área) area; Com **grandes superficies,** hypermarkets.

superfluo,-a adj superfluous.

superhombre nm superman.

superior I adj **1** (posición) top, upper. **2**
(cantidad) greater, higher, larger (**a,** than). **3** (calidad) superior; **calidad s.,** top quality. **4** Educ higher. **II** nm (jefe) superior.

superioridad nf superiority.

supermán nm (pl supermanes) superman.

supermercado nm supermarket.

superpoblación nf overpopulation.

superponer [19] vtr to superimpose.

superpotencia nf superpower.

superproducción nf **1** Ind overproduction. **2** Cin mammoth production.

supersónico,-a adj supersonic.

superstición nf superstition.

supersticioso,-a adj superstitious.

supervisar vtr to supervise.

supervisor,-a nm,f supervisor.

supervivencia nf survival.

supino,-a adj **1** (boca arriba) supine, face up. **2** fig (absoluto) total absolute.

súpito,-a adj Am sudden.

suplantar vtr to supplant, take the place of.

suplementario,-a adj supplementary, additional.

suplemento nm supplement; **sin s.,** without extra charge.

suplente adj & nmf (sustituto) substitute, deputy; Dep substitute.

supletorio,-a adj supplementary, additional; **cama supletoria,** extra bed; **teléfono s.,** extension.

súplica nf entreaty, plea.

suplicar [1] vtr to beseech, beg.

suplicio nm (tortura) torture; fig (tormento) torment.

suplir vtr **1** (reemplazar) to replace, substitute. **2** (compensar) to make up for.

suponer [19] (pp **supuesto**) vtr **1** (significar) to mean. **2** (implicar) to entail. **3** (representar) to account for. **4** (pensar) to suppose; **supongo que sí,** I suppose so; **supongamos que ...,** let's assume that .... **5** (adivinar) to guess; (**me**) **lo suponía,** I guessed as much.

suposición nf supposition.

supositorio nm suppository.

supremacía nf supremacy.

supremo,-a adj supreme.

supresión nf (de una ley etc) abolition; (de restricciones) lifting; (de una palabra) deletion; (de una rebelión) suppression; (omisión) omission.

suprimir vtr **1** (ley, impuesto) to abolish; (restricción) to lift; (palabra) to delete, take o leave out; (rebelión) to suppress. **2** (omitir) to omit.

supuesto,-a I adj **1** (asumido) supposed, assumed; **¡por s.!,** of course!; **dar algo por s.,** to take sth for granted. **2** (presunto) alleged. **II** nm assumption; **en el s. de que,** on the assumption that.

supurar vi to suppurate, fester.

supuse pt indef → **suponer.**

sur nm south.

Suramérica nf South America.

suramericano,-a adj & nm,f South American.

surcar [1] vtr Agr to plough; fig (olas) to cut through.

surco nm Agr furrow; (en un disco) groove.

sureño,-a I adj southern. II nm,f southerner.

sureste adj & nm → **sudeste**.

surf(ing) nm Dep surfing.

surfista nmf surfer.

surgir [6] vi (aparecer) to arise, emerge, appear; (problema, dificultad) to crop up.

suroeste adj & nm → **sudoeste**.

surrealista adj & nmf surrealist.

surtido,-a I adj 1 (variado) assorted. 2 **bien s.**, well stocked. II nm selection, assortment.

surtidor nm spout; **s. de gasolina**, petrol o US gas pump.

surtir vtr 1 to supply, provide. 2 **s. efecto**, to have the desired effect.

susceptible adj susceptible; (quisquilloso) oversensitive, touchy.

suscitar vtr (provocar) to cause, provoke; (rebelión) to stir up, arouse; (interés etc) to arouse.

suscribir (pp suscrito) I vtr 1 to subscribe to, endorse. 2 fml (firmar) to sign. II **suscribirse** vr to subscribe (a, to).

suscripción nf subscription.

susodicho,-a adj above-mentioned, aforesaid.

suspender I vtr 1 (ley) to suspend; (reunión) to adjourn. 2 (examen) to fail; **me han suspendido**, I've failed the exam. 3 (colgar) to hang, suspend. II vi Educ he **suspendido**, I've failed.

suspense nm suspense; **novela/película de s.**, thriller.

suspensión nf 1 hanging (up), suspension. 2 Aut suspension. 3 Fin Jur **s. de pagos**, suspension of payments.

suspensivo,-a adj **puntos suspensivos**, suspension points.

suspenso nm 1 Educ fail. 2 **en s.**, (asunto, trabajo) pending; **estar en s.**, to be pending.

suspicacia nf suspiciousness.

suspicaz adj suspicious; (desconfiado) distrustful.

suspirar vi to sigh.

suspiro nm sigh.

sustancia nf substance.

sustancial adj 1 substantial. 2 (fundamental) essential, fundamental.

sustantivo,-a I adj substantive. II nm Ling noun.

sustentar vtr 1 (peso) to support. 2 (familia) to maintain, support. 3 (teoría) to support, defend.

sustento nm 1 (alimento) sustenance, food. 2 (apoyo) support.

sustitución nf substitution, replacement.

sustituir [37] vtr to substitute, replace.

sustituto,-a nm,f substitute, stand-in.

susto nm fright, scare; **llevarse** o **darse un s.**, to get a fright.

sustraer [25] vtr 1 Mat to subtract. 2 (robar) to steal, remove.

sustrato nm substratum.

susurrar vtr to whisper.

susurro nm whisper.

sutil adj 1 (diferencia, pregunta) subtle. 2 (delgado) thin, fine. 3 (aroma) delicate.

sutileza nf 1 (dicho) subtlety. 2 (finura) fineness.

suyo,-a adj & pron pos (de él) his; (de ella) hers; (de usted, ustedes) yours; (de animal o cosa) its; (de ellos, ellas) theirs; **los zapatos no son suyos**, the shoes aren't hers; **varios amigos suyos**, several friends of his o hers o yours o theirs; fam **es muy s.**, he's very aloof; fam **hacer de las suyas**, to be up to one's tricks; fam **ir (cada uno) a lo s.**, to mind one's own business; fam **salirse con la suya**, to get one's way.

svástica nf swastika.

T

T, t [te] nf (la letra) T, t.

t abr de **tonelada(s)**, ton, tons.

tabacalero,-a I nm,f (vendedor) tobacco trader. II nf **La Tabacalera**, Spanish state tobacco monopoly.

tabaco nm 1 (planta, hoja) tobacco; **t. rubio**, Virginia tobacco. 2 (cigarrillos) cigarettes pl.

tábano nm horsefly.

tabaquismo nm nicotine poisoning.

tabarra nf fam nuisance, bore; **dar la t.**, to go on and on.

tabasco nm tabasco sauce.

taberna nf pub, bar; (antiguamente) tavern.

tabernero,-a nm,f publican; (hombre) landlord; (mujer) landlady.

tabique nm 1 (pared) partition (wall). 2 Anat t. nasal, nasal wall.

tabla nf 1 board; Dep t. de surf, surfboard. II Dep t. de windsurf, sailboard. 2 (de vestido) pleat. 3 Mat table. 4 Ajedrez **tablas**, stalemate sing, draw sing; **quedar en t.**, (juego) to end in a draw. 5 Taur **tablas**, fence sing. 6 Teat **las tablas**, the stage sing; fig **tener (muchas) t.**, to be an old hand.

tablado nm 1 (plataforma) wooden platform. 2 *Teat* stage.

tablao nm fam flamenco bar o show.

tablero nm 1 (*tablón*) panel, board; **t. de mandos**, (*de coche*) dashboard. 2 (*en juegos*) board; **t. de ajedrez**, chessboard.

tableta nf (*de chocolate*) bar.

tablón nm (*plank*); (*en construcción*) beam; **t. de anuncios**, notice o *US* bulletin board.

tabú adj & nm (*pl* **tabúes**) taboo.

tabular vtr to tabulate.

taburete nm stool.

tacaño,-a I adj mean, stingy. II nm,f miser.

tacatá, tacataca nm baby-walker.

tacha nf (*defecto*) flaw, defect; **sin t.**, flawless, without blemish.

tachar vtr 1 to cross out. 2 fig **t. de**, to accuse of.

tacho nm *Am* bucket.

tachón nm (*borrón*) crossing out.

tachuela nf tack, stud.

tácito,-a adj tacit.

taciturno,-a adj 1 (*callado*) taciturn. 2 (*triste*) sullen.

taco nm 1 plug; (*de billetes*) wad; *Culin* (*de jamón, queso*) cube, piece; (*de bota de fútbol*) stud; (*en billar*) cue. 2 *Culin* taco, rolled-up tortilla pancake. 3 fam (*palabrota*) swearword. 4 fam (*lío*) mess, muddle; **armarse o hacerse un t.**, to get all mixed up. 5 **me gusta un t.**, I like it a lot. 6 fam **tacos**, (*años*) years.

tacón nm heel; **zapatos de t.**, high-heeled shoes.

taconeo nm (*pisada*) heel tapping; (*golpe*) stamping with the heels.

táctica nf tactics pl.

táctil adj tactile; **pantalla t.**, touch screen.

táctico,-a adj tactical.

tacto nm 1 (*sentido*) touch. 2 fig (*delicadeza*) tact; **tener t.**, to be tactful.

taekwondo nm tae kwon do.

tafetán nm taffeta.

tahur nm cardsharp.

Tailandia n Thailand.

tailandés,-esa I adj Thai. II nm,f (*persona*) Thai; **los tailandeses**, the Thai o Thais. III nm (*idioma*) Thai.

taimado,-a adj sly, crafty.

tajada nf 1 slice; fig **sacar o llevarse t.**, to take one's share. 2 fam (*borrachera*) drunkenness.

tajante adj incisive.

Tajo n el T., the Tagus.

tal I adj 1 (*semejante*) such; (*más sustantivo singular contable*) such a; **en tales condiciones**, in such conditions; **nunca dije t. cosa**, I never said such a thing. 2 (*indeterminado*) such and such; **t. día y a t. hora**, such and such a day and at such and such a time. 3 (*persona*) person called ...; **te llamó una t. Amelia**, someone called Amelia phoned you. 4 (*locuciones*)

t. vez, perhaps, maybe; **como si t. cosa**, as if nothing had happened. II adv 1 (*así*) just; **t. cual**, just as it is; **t. (y) como**, just as. 2 ¿**qué t.**?, how are things?; ¿**qué t. ese vino?**, how do you find this wine? III conj so; **con t. (de) que + subj**, so long as, provided. IV pron (*cosa*) something; (*persona*) someone, somebody; **t. para cual**, two of a kind; **y t. y cual**, and so on.

tala nf tree felling.

taladradora nf drill.

taladrar vtr to drill; (*pared*) to bore through; (*papeles*) to punch.

taladro nm 1 (*herramienta*) drill. 2 (*agujero*) hole.

talante nm 1 (*carácter*) disposition. 2 (*voluntad*) de buen t., willingly; **de mal t.**, unwillingly, reluctantly.

talar vtr (*árboles*) to fell, cut down.

talco nm talc; **polvos de t.**, talcum powder.

talega nf bag, sack.

talego nm 1 long bag, long sack. 2 arg (*cárcel*) clink, hole. 3 arg (*mil pesetas*) one thousand peseta note.

talento nm talent.

Talgo nm fast passenger train.

talismán nm talisman, lucky charm.

talla nf 1 (*de prenda*) size; ¿**qué t. usas?**, what size are you? 2 (*estatura*) height; fig stature; fig **dar la t.**, to make the grade. 3 (*escultura*) carving, sculpture. 4 (*tallado*) cutting, carving.

tallado,-a nm (*de madera*) carving; (*de piedras preciosas*) cutting; (*de metales*) engraving.

tallar vtr 1 (*madera, piedra*) to carve, shape; (*piedras preciosas*) to cut; (*metales*) to engrave. 2 (*medir*) to measure the height of.

tallarines nmpl tagliatelle sing.

talle nm 1 (*cintura*) waist. 2 (*cuerpo*) (*de hombre*) build, physique; (*de mujer*) figure, shape.

taller nm 1 (*obrador*) workshop; *Aut* **t. de reparaciones**, garage. 2 *Ind* factory, mill.

tallo nm stem, stalk.

talón nm 1 (*del pie*) heel. 2 (*cheque*) cheque, *US* check.

talonario nm (*de cheques*) cheque o *US* check book; (*de billetes*) book of tickets.

tamaño nm size; **de gran t.**, large; **del t. de**, as large as, as big as.

tamaño,-a adj such a big, so big a.

tamarindo nm tamarind.

tambalearse vi (*persona*) to stagger; (*mesa*) to wobble; fig to teeter.

tambero nm *Am* (*mesonero*) innkeeper, landlord.

también adv (*igualmente*) too, also, as well; **tú t. puedes venir**, you can come too; ¿**lo harás?, yo t.**, are you going to do it?, so am I.

tambor nm 1 (*Mús, de lavadora, de freno*) drum. 2 *Anat* eardrum.

Támesis n el T., the Thames.

tamiz nm sieve.

tamizar [1] vtr to sieve.

tampoco adv 1 (*en afirmativas*) nor, neither; **Juan no vendrá y María t.**, Juan won't come and neither will María; **no lo sé, - yo t.**, I don't know, - neither do I. 2 (*en negativas*) either, not ... either; **la Bolsa no sube, pero t. baja**, the stock market isn't going up, but it's not going down either.

tampón nm tampon.

tan adv 1 such; (*más sustantivo singular contable*) such a; **es t. listo**, he's such a clever fellow; **no me gusta t. dulce**, I don't like it so sweet; **¡qué gente t. agradable!**, such nice people!; **¡qué vestido t. bonito!**, what a beautiful dress! 2 (*comparativo*) **t. ... como, as ... as**; **t. alto como tú**, as tall as you (are). 3 (*consecutivo*) so ... (that); **iba t. deprisa que no lo vi**, he was going so fast that I couldn't see him. 4 **t. siquiera**, at least; **t. sólo**, only.

tanda nf (*conjunto*) batch, lot; (*serie*) series sing; **por tandas**, in groups.

tándem nm tandem.

tanga nm tanga.

tangente nf tangent; fig **salirse o escaparse por la t.**, to go off at a tangent.

Tánger n Tangier.

tangible adj tangible.

tango nm tango.

tanque nm tank.

tantear I vtr 1 fig **t. a algn**, to sound sb out; **t. el terreno**, to see how the land lies. 2 (*calcular*) to estimate, guess. II vi *Dep* to (keep) score.

tanteo nm (*cálculo*) estimate, guess. 2 *Dep* score.

tanto,-a I nm 1 (*punto*) point. 2 (*cantidad imprecisa*) so much, a certain amount; **t. por ciento**, percentage. 3 **un t., a bit**; **la casa es un t. pequeña**, the house is rather o somewhat small. 4 **estar al t.**, (*informado*) to be informed; (*pendiente*) to be on the lookout.
II pron 1 (*+ singular*) so much; (*+ plural*) so many; **no le des t. dinero**, don't give him so much money; **¡ha pasado t. tiempo!**, it's been so long!; **no comas tantas manzanas**, don't eat so many apples. 2 **cincuenta y tantas personas**, fifty odd people; **en el año sesenta y tantos**, in nineteen sixty something. 3 **t. como**, as much as; **tantos,-as como**, as many as.
III pron 1 (*+ singular*) so much; **otro t.**, as much again, the same again; **no es o hay para t.**, it's not that bad. 2 (*+ plural*) so many; **otros tantos**, as many again; **uno de tantos**, run-of-the-mill; fam **a las tantas**, very late, at an un-

earthly hour.
IV adv 1 (*cantidad*) so much; **t. mejor/peor**, so much the better/worse; **t. más cuanto que**, all the more so because. 2 (*tiempo*) so long. 3 (*frecuencia*) so often. 4 **t. ... como, both ... and**; **t. tú como yo, both you and I**; **t. si vienes como si no**, whether you come or not. 5 (*locuciones*) **por lo t.**, therefore; **¡y t.!**, oh yes!, and how!

tañer [38] vtr to play.

tapa nf 1 (*cubierta*) lid; (*de botella*) cap, top; (*de libro*) cover; (*de zapato*) heelplate; *Aut* (*de cilindro*) head. 2 (*aperitivo*) appetizer.

tapadera nf (*tapa*) cover, lid; fig cover, front.

tapadillo nm **hacer algo de t.**, to do sth secretly.

tapar I vtr 1 to cover; (*botella etc*) to put the lid o top on; (*con ropas o mantas*) to wrap up. 2 (*ocultar*) to hide; (*vista*) to block. 3 (*encubrir*) to cover up for sb. II **taparse** vr (*cubrirse*) to cover oneself; (*abrigarse*) to wrap up.

taparrabos nm inv loincloth.

tapete nm (table) cover; fig **poner algo sobre el t.**, to table sth.

tapia nf garden wall.

tapiar [12] vtr 1 (*área*) to wall off. 2 (*puerta, ventana etc*) to wall, close up.

tapicería nf 1 tapestry; (*de muebles, coche*) upholstery. 2 (*tienda*) upholsterer's shop o workshop.

tapioca nf tapioca.

tapiz nm tapestry.

tapizar [4] vtr to upholster.

tapón nm 1 (*de lavabo etc*) stopper, plug; (*de botella*) cap, cork; **t. de rosca**, screw-on cap. 2 (*de oídos*) earplug. 3 (*en baloncesto*) block. 4 *Aut* traffic jam.

taponar I vtr 1 (*tubería, hueco*) to plug. 2 *Med* (*herida*) to tampon. II **taponarse** vr **se me han taponado los oídos**, my ears are blocked up.

taquigrafía nf shorthand.

taquígrafo,-a nm,f shorthand writer.

taquilla nf 1 ticket office, booking office; *Cin Teat* box-office; **un éxito de t.**, a box-office success. 2 (*recaudación*) takings pl. 3 (*armario*) locker.

taquillero,-a I adj popular; **película taquillera**, box office hit. II nm,f booking o ticket clerk.

tara nf 1 (*peso*) tare. 2 (*defecto*) defect, fault.

tarántula nf tarantula.

tararear vtr to hum.

tardanza nf delay.

tardar I vtr to take time; **¿cuánto va a t.?**, how long will it take?; **tardé dos horas en venir**, it took me two hours to get here. II vi (*demorar*) to take long; **si tarda mucho me voy**, if it takes much longer, I'm going; **no tardes**, don't be long; **a más t.**, at the latest. **III tardarse** *vr* ¿cuánto se tarda en llegar?, how long does it take to get there?

tarde I *nf* **1** *(hasta las cinco)* afternoon. **2** *(después de las cinco)* evening. **3 la t.- noche**, late evening. **II** *adv* **1** late; **siento llegar t.**, sorry I'm late. **2** *(locuciones)* **de t. en t.**, very rarely, not very often; **(más) t. o (más) temprano**, sooner or later.

tardío,-a *adj* late, belated.

tardo,-a *adj* slow.

tarea *nf* **1** job, task; **tareas**, *(de ama de casa)* housework *sing*; *(de estudiante)* homework *sing*.

tarifa *nf* **1** *(precio)* tariff, rate; *(en transportes)* fare. **2** *(lista de precios)* price list.

tarima *nf* platform, dais.

tarjeta *nf* card; **t. postal**, postcard; **t. de crédito**, credit card; **t. de visita**, visiting *o* US calling card; *Inform* **t. perforada**, punch *o* punched card.

tarraconense I *adj o* **de** *o* from Tarragona. II *nmf* native *o* inhabitant of Tarragona.

tarro *nm* **1** *(vasija)* jar, pot, tub. **2** *fam (cabeza)* bonce. **3** *Am (lata)* tin, can.

tarta *nf* tart, pie.

tartamudear *vi* to stutter, stammer.

tartamudo,-a I *adj* stuttering, stammering. II *nm,f* stutterer, stammerer.

tartana *nf fam (coche viejo)* banger, heap.

tártaro,-a *adj* **salsa tártara**, tartar sauce.

tartera *nf* **1** *(fiambrera)* lunch box. **2** *(cazuela)* baking tin.

tarugo *nm* **1** *(de madera)* lump of wood. **2** *fam (persona)* blockhead.

tarumba *adj fam* crazy, mad; **estar t.**, to be bonkers.

tasa *nf* **1** *(precio)* fee; **tasas académicas**, course fees. **2** *(impuesto)* tax. **3** *(índice)* rate; **t. de natalidad/mortalidad**, birth/ death rate. **4** *(valoración)* valuation, appraisal.

tasación *nf* valuation.

tasador,-a *nm,f* valuer.

tasar *vtr* **1** *(valorar)* to value; **t. una casa en diez millones de pesetas**, to value a house at ten million pesetas. **2** *(poner precio)* to set *o* fix the price of.

tasca *nf fam* bar, pub.

tata *nf fam* nanny.

tatarabuelo,-a *nm,f (hombre)* great-great-grandfather; *(mujer)* great-great-grandmother; **tatarabuelos**, great-great grandparents.

tataranieto,-a *nm,f (hombre)* great-great-grandson; *(mujer)* great-great-granddaughter; **tataranietos**, great-great-grandchildren.

tatuaje *nm* tattoo.

tatuar [10] *vtr* to tattoo.

Tauro *nm* Taurus.

tauromaquia *nf* tauromachy, (art of) bullfighting.

TAV *abr de* **Tren de Alta Velocidad**.

taxativo,-a *adj* categorical.

taxi *nm* taxi.

taxímetro *nm* taximeter, clock.

taxista *nmf* taxi driver.

taza *nf* **1** cup; **una t. de café**, *(recipiente)* coffee cup; *(contenido)* a cup of coffee. **2** *(de retrete)* bowl.

tazón *nm* bowl.

te *pron pers* **1** *(complemento directo)* you; *(complemento indirecto)* (to *o* for) you; **no quiero verte**, I don't want to see you; **te compraré uno**, I'll buy one for you, I'll buy you one; **te lo dije**, I told you so. **2** *(reflexivo)* yourself; **lávate**, wash yourself; *(sin traducción)* **bébetelo todo**, drink it up; **no te vayas**, don't go.

té *nm (pl* **tés)** tea; **t. con limón**, lemon tea.

tea *nf* torch.

teatral *adj* **1 grupo t.**, theatre company; **obra t.**, play. **2** *fig (teatrero)* theatrical.

teatrero,-a *adj* theatrical.

teatro *nm* **1** theatre, US theater; **obra de t.**, play; **autor de t.**, playwright. **2** *Lit* drama.

tebeo *nm* children's comic.

techar *vtr* to roof.

techo *nm (de habitación)* ceiling; *(tejado)* roof; *Aut* **t. corredizo**, sun roof.

tecla *nf* key; *fig* **dar en la t.**, to get it right.

teclado *nm* keyboard; *Inform* **t. expandido**, expanded keyboard.

teclear I *vtr* to key in. II *vi* to drum with one's fingers.

técnica *nf* **1** *(tecnología)* technology. **2** *(método)* technique. **3** *(habilidad)* skill.

técnico,-a I *adj* technical. II *nm,f* technician, technical expert.

tecnicolor *nm* Technicolor.

tecno- pref techno-.

tecnócrata *nmf* technocrat.

tecnología *nf* technology.

tecnológico,-a *adj* technological.

tedio *nm* tedium, boredom.

tedioso,-a *adj* tedious, boring.

teja *nf Constr* tile; *fam fig* **a toca t.**, on the nail.

tejado *nm* roof.

tejanos *nmpl* jeans.

tejemaneje *nm fam* **1** *(actividad)* bustle, fuss. **2** *(maquinación)* intrigue, scheming.

tejer *vtr (en el telar)* to weave; *(hacer punto)* to knit; *(telaraña)* to spin; *fig (plan)* to plot, to scheme.

tejido *nm* **1** fabric; **t. de punto**, knitted fabric. **2** *Anat* tissue.

tejo *nm fam* tirar los tejos a algn, to make a play for sb.

tejón *nm* badger.

tel. *abr de* **teléfono**, telephone, tel.

tela *nf* **1** *Tex* material, fabric, cloth; *(de la*

leche) skin; **t. de araña**, cobweb; **t. metálica**, gauze. 2 *fam (dinero)* dough. 3 *Arte* canvass. 4 *fig* **poner en t. de juicio**, to question; *fig* **tiene mucha t.**, it's not an easy thing.

telar *nm Tex* loom.

telaraña *nf* cobweb, spider's web.

tele *nf fam* telly, TV.

telearrastre *nm* ski lift.

telecabina *nm* cable car.

telecomunicaciones *nfpl* telecommunications.

telediario *nm TV* television news bulletin.

teledirigido,-a *adj* remote-controlled.

telefax *nm* telefax, fax.

teleférico *nm* cable car *o* railway.

telefilm, telefilme *nm* TV film.

telefonazo *nm* **dar un t. (a algn)**, to give (sb) a ring.

telefonear *vt & vi* to telephone, phone.

telefónica *nf* **Compañía T.,** ≈ British Telecom.

telefónico,-a *adj* telephone; **llamada telefónica**, telephone call.

telefonista *nmf* (telephone) operator.

teléfono *nm* telephone, phone; **t. portátil**, portable telephone; **t. móvil**, car phone; **está hablando por t.**, she's on the phone; **te llamó por t.**, she phoned you.

telegrafiar [29] *vtr* to telegraph, wire.

telegráfico,-a *adj* telegraphic; **giro t.**, giro, money order.

telégrafo *nm* 1 telegraph. 2 **telégrafos**, post office *sing.*

telegrama *nm* telegram, cable.

teleimpresor *nm*, **teleimpresora** *nf* teleprinter.

telele *nm fam* **darle a uno un t.**, to have a fit.

telemando *nm* remote control (unit).

telenovela *nf* television serial.

teleobjetivo *nm* telephoto lens *sing.*

telepático,-a *adj* telepathic.

telescopio *nm* telescope.

teleserie *nf* television series.

telesilla *nm* chair lift.

telespectador,-a *nm,f TV* viewer.

telesquí *nm* ski lift.

teletexto *nm* teletext.

teletipo *nm* teleprinter.

televidente *nm,f TV* viewer.

televisar *vtr* to televise.

televisión *nf* 1 *(sistema)* television. 2 *fam (aparato)* television set; **t. en color/en blanco y negro**, colour/black and white television; **ver la t.**, to watch television.

televisivo,-a *adj* television; **espacio t.**, television programme.

televisor *nm* television set.

télex *nm inv* telex.

telón *nm Teat* curtain; *Pol Hist* **t. de acero**, iron curtain; **t. de fondo**, *Teat* backdrop; *fig* background.

telonero,-a *adj (grupo)* **t.**, support band.

tema *nm* 1 *(asunto)* topic, subject; *(de examen)* subject; **temas de actualidad**, current affairs. 2 *Mús* theme.

temario *nm (de examen)* programme.

temática *nf* subject matter.

temático,-a *adj* thematic.

temblar [1] *vi (de frío)* to shiver; *(de miedo)* to tremble (**de**, with); *(voz)* to quiver; *(pulso)* to shake.

tembleque *nm fam* shaking fit.

temblón,-ona *adj fam* trembling, shaky.

temblor *nm* tremor, shudder; **t. de tierra**, earth tremor.

tembloroso,-a, tembloso,-a *adj* shaking; *(voz)* quivering, *(de frío)* shivering; *(de miedo)* trembling; **manos temblorosas**, shaky hands.

temer I *vtr* to fear, be afraid; **temo que esté muerto**, I fear he's dead; **temo que no podrá recibirte**, I'm afraid (that) he won't be able to see you. II *vi* to be afraid. III **temerse** *vr* to fear, be afraid; **¡me lo temía!**, I was afraid this would happen!

temerario,-a *adj* reckless, rash.

temeridad *nf* 1 *(actitud)* temerity, rashness. 2 *(acto temerario)* reckless act.

temeroso,-a *adj* 1 fearful, timid. 2 *(temible)* frightful.

temible *adj* fearful, frightful.

temor *nm* 1 fear. 2 *(recelo)* worry, apprehension.

témpano *nm* ice floe.

temperamental *adj* temperamental.

temperamento *nm* temperament; **tener t.**, to have a strong character.

temperatura *nf* temperature.

tempestad *nf* storm; *fig* turmoil, uproar.

tempestuoso,-a *adj* stormy, tempestuous.

templado,-a *adj* 1 *(agua)* lukewarm; *(clima)* mild, temperate. 2 *Mús (afinado)* tuned.

templanza *nf* moderation, restraint.

templar *vtr* 1 to moderate. 2 *(algo frío)* to warm up; *(algo caliente)* to cool down. 3 *Mús (instrumento)* to tune. 4 *Téc (metal)* to temper.

temple *nm* 1 *(fortaleza)* boldness, courage. 2 *Arte* tempera.

templete *nm* bandstand.

templo *nm* temple.

temporada *nf* 1 season; **t. alta**, high *o* peak season; **t. baja**, low *o* off season. 2 *(período)* period, time; **por temporadas**, on and off.

temporal I *adj* temporary, provisional. II *nm* storm.

temporero,-a *nm,f* seasonal *o* temporary worker.

tempranero,-a *adj* 1 *(persona)* earlyrising. 2 *(cosecha)* early.

temprano,-a *adj & adv* early.

tenacidad *nf* 1 *(perseverancia)* tenacity,

perseverance. **2** *(de metal)* tensile strength.

tenacillas *nfpl (para pelo)* curling tongs.

tenaz *adj* tenacious.

tenaza *nf,* **tenazas** *nfpl (herramienta)* pliers, pincers; *(para el fuego)* tongs.

tendedero *nm* clothesline, drying place.

tendencia *nf* tendency.

tendencioso,-a *adj* tendentious, biased.

tender [3] **I** *vtr* **1** *(mantel etc)* to spread out; *(para secar)* to hang out. **2** *(red)* to cast; *(puente)* to build; *(vía, cable)* to lay; *(trampa)* to lay, set. **3** *(mano)* to stretch o hold out. **4** *(tumbar)* to lay. **II** *vi* to tend **(a,** to), have a tendency **(a,** to). **III tenderse** *vr* to lie down, stretch out.

tenderete *nm (puesto)* market stall.

tendero,-a *nm,f* shopkeeper.

tendido *nm* **1** *(de vía, cable)* laying; *(de puente)* construction; **t.** *eléctrico,* electrical installation. **2** *Taur (asientos)* front tiers *pl* of seats, *US* bleachers *pl.*

tendón *nm* tendon, sinew.

tenebroso,-a *adj (sombrío)* dark, gloomy; *(siniestro)* sinister, shady.

tenedor *nm* fork.

teneduría *nf* **t.** *de libros,* book-keeping.

tenencia *nf* *Jur* **t.** *ilícita de armas,* illegal possession of arms.

tener [24] **I** *vtr* **1** to have, have got; **tenemos un examen,** we've got o we have an exam; **va a t. un niño,** she's going to have a baby, she's expecting; **¡ahí (lo) tienes!,** here you are! **2** *(poseer)* to own, possess. **3** *(sostener)* to hold; **tenme el bolso un momento,** hold my bag a minute; **ten, es para ti,** take this o here you are, it's for you. **4** **t.** *calor/frío,* to be hot/cold; **t.** *cariño a algn,* to be fond of sb; **t.** *miedo,* to be frightened. **5** *(edad)* to be; **tiene dieciocho (años),** he's eighteen (years old). **6** *(medida)* **la casa tiene cien metros cuadrados,** the house is 100 square metres. **7** *(contener)* to hold, contain. **8** *(mantener)* to keep; **me tuvo despierto toda la noche,** he kept me up all night. **9** **t.** *por, (considerar)* to consider, think; **me tienen por estúpido,** they think I'm a fool; **ten por seguro que lloverá,** you can be sure it'll rain. **10** **t. que,** to have (got) to; **tengo que irme,** I must leave; **tienes/tendrías que verlo,** you must/should see it.
II tenerse *vr* **1 t. en pie,** to stand (up). **2 t. por,** *(considerarse)* to think o consider oneself; **se tiene por muy inteligente,** he thinks he's very intelligent.

tenga *subj pres* → **tener.**

tengo *indic pres* → **tener.**

teniente *nm* **1** *Mil* lieutenant. **2 t. (de) alcalde,** deputy mayor.

tenis *nm* tennis.

tenista *nmf* tennis player.

tenor¹ *nm* *Mús* tenor.

tenor² *nm* **a t. de,** according to.

tensar *vtr (cable etc)* to tighten; *(arco)* to draw.

tensión *nf* **1** tension; **en t.,** tense. **2** *Elec* tension, voltage. **3** *Med* **t. arterial,** blood pressure; **t. nerviosa,** nervous strain. **4** *Téc* stress.

tenso,-a *adj* **1** *(cuerda, cable)* tense, taut. **2** *(persona)* tense; *(relaciones)* strained.

tentación *nf* temptation.

tentáculo *nm* tentacle.

tentador,-a *adj* tempting.

tentar [1] *vtr* **1** *(palpar)* to feel, touch. **2** *(incitar)* to tempt.

tentativa *nf* attempt; *Jur* **t. de asesinato,** attempted murder.

tentempié *nm* *fam (pl* **tentempiés)** **1** *(comida)* snack, bite. **2** *(juguete)* tumbler.

tenue *adj* **1** *(luz, sonido)* subdued, faint. **2** *(delgado)* thin, light.

teñir [6] **I** *vtr* **1** *(pelo etc)* to dye. **2** *fig* to tinge with. **II teñirse** *vr* **t. el pelo,** to dye one's hair.

teología *nf* theology.

teorema *nm* theorem.

teoría *nf* theory; **en t.,** theoretically.

teórico,-a *adj* theoretical.

teorizar [4] *vi* to theorize **(sobre,** on).

tequila *nm* tequila.

terapeuta *nmf* therapist.

terapia *nf* therapy.

tercer *adj* third; **el t. mundo,** the third world.

tercermundista *adj* third-world.

tercero,-a **I** *adj* third. **II** *nm,f* **1** *(de una serie)* third. **2 a la tercera va la vencida,** third time lucky. **III** *nm (mediador)* mediator; *Jur* third party.

terceto *nm* *Mús* trio.

terciar [12] **I** *vi* **1** *(mediar)* to mediate, arbitrate. **2** *(participar)* to take part, participate. **II terciarse** *vr* **si se tercia,** should the occasion arise.

terciario,-a *adj* tertiary.

tercio *nm* **1** *(parte)* (one) third. **2** *(de cerveza)* medium-size bottle of beer. **3** *Taur* stage, part (of a bullfight).

terciopelo *nm* velvet.

terco,-a *adj* stubborn, obstinate.

tergiversar *vtr (verdad)* to distort; *(palabras)* to twist.

termal *adj* thermal.

termas *nfpl (baños)* spa *sing,* hot baths o springs *pl.*

térmico,-a *adj* thermal; **central térmica,** coal-fired power station.

terminación *nf* completion.

terminal **I** *adj* terminal. **II** *nf* **1** *(de aeropuerto)* terminal; *(de autobús)* terminus. **2** *Elec Inform* terminal.

terminante *adj* **1** *(categórico)* categorical, final. **2** *(dato, resultado)* conclusive.
◆**terminantemente** *adv* categorically; **t. prohibido,** strictly forbidden.

terminar I vtr (acabar) to finish, complete; (completamente) to finish off. **II** vi **1** (acabarse) to finish, end; **termina en seis**, it ends with a six; **no termina de convencerme**, he still isn't quite convinced. **2** (ir a parar) to end up (en, in); **terminó por comprarlo**, he ended up buying it. **3** t. con, (eliminar) to put an end to. **III terminarse** vr **1** to finish, end, be over. **2** (vino, dinero etc) to run out.

término nm **1** (final) end, finish. **2** (palabra) term, word; **en otros términos**, in other words; **en términos generales**, generally speaking. **3** t. municipal, district. **4** por t. medio, on average. **5** fig **en último t.**, as a last resort.

terminología nf terminology.

termo nm thermos (flask), flask.

termodinámico,-a adj thermodynamic.

termómetro nm thermometer.

termonuclear adj thermonuclear.

termostato nm thermostat.

ternera nf calf; (carne) veal.

ternero nm calf.

ternura nf tenderness.

terquedad nf stubbornness, obstinacy.

terracota nf terracotta.

Terranova n Newfoundland.

terraplén nm embankment.

terráqueo,-a adj globo t., (tierra) (the) earth; (esfera) globe.

terrateniente nmf landowner.

terremoto nm earthquake.

terrenal adj un paraíso t., a heaven on earth.

terreno nm **1** (tierra) (piece of) land, ground; Geol terrain; (campo) field; **ganar/perder t.**, to gain/lose ground. **2** Dep field, ground. **3** fig field, sphere.

terrestre adj **1** (de la tierra) terrestrial, earthly. **2** (por tierra) by land; **por vía t.**, by land.

terrible adj terrible, awful.

terrícola nmf (en ciencia ficción) earthling.

terrier nm terrier.

territorio nm territory.

terrón nm (de azúcar) lump; (de tierra) clod.

terror nm terror; Cin horror.

terrorífico,-a adj terrifying, frightening.

terrorismo nm terrorism.

terrorista adj & nmf terrorist.

terroso,-a adj (color) earth-coloured, US earth-colored.

terruño nm (terreno) piece of land; (patria chica) homeland, native land.

terso,-a adj smooth.

tersura nf smoothness.

tertulia nf get-together; **t. literaria**, literary gathering.

tesina nf first degree dissertation.

tesis nf inv thesis; (opinión) view, theory.

tesón nm tenacity, firmness.

tesorero,-a nm,f treasurer.

tesoro nm **1** treasure. **2** (erario) exchequer; **T. Público**, Treasury.

test nm test.

testaferro nm front man.

testamentario,-a Jur **I** adj testamentary. **II** nm,f executor.

testamento nm **1** Jur will; **hacer o otorgar t.**, to make o draw up one's will. **2** Rel Testament.

testar vi to make o draw up one's will.

testarudo,-a adj stubborn, obstinate.

testículo nm testicle.

testificar [1] vtr to testify.

testigo I nmf witness; Jur **t. de cargo/descargo**, witness for the prosecution/defence; Jur **t. ocular/presencial**, eyewitness; Rel **Testigos de Jehová**, Jehovah's Witnesses. **II** nm Dep baton.

testimoniar [12] vtr **1** (dar testimonio) to testify to, attest to. **2** (mostrar) to show.

testimonio nm Jur testimony; (prueba) evidence, proof.

teta nf fam **1** tit, boob; **niño de t.**, breastfeeding baby. **2** (de vaca) udder.

tétano nm tetanus.

tetera nf teapot.

tetilla nf **1** Anat man's nipple. **2** (de biberón) (rubber) teat.

tetina nf (rubber) teat.

tétrico,-a adj gloomy, dull.

textil adj & nm textile.

texto nm text; **libro de t.**, textbook.

textual adj textual; (exacto) literal; **en palabras textuales**, literally.

textura nf Tex texture; (en minerales) structure.

tez nf complexion.

ti pron pers you; **es para ti**, it's for you; **hazlo por ti**, do it for your own sake; **piensas demasiado en ti mismo**, you think too much about yourself.

tía nf **1** (pariente) aunt. **2** arg (mujer) girl, woman.

tibieza nf tepidity; fig lack of enthusiasm.

tibio,-a adj tepid, lukewarm; fam **ponerse t. de cerveza**, to get pissed.

tiburón nm shark.

tic nm (pl tiques) tic, twitch; **t. nervioso**, nervous tic o twitch.

ticket nm (pl tickets) (billete) ticket; (recibo) receipt.

tictac nm tick-tock, ticking.

tiempo nm **1** time; **a t.**, in time; **a su (debido) t.**, in due course; **a un t.**, **al mismo t.**, at the same time; **al poco t.**, soon afterwards; **antes de t.**, (too) early o soon; **con el t.**, in the course of time, with time; **con t.**, in advance; **¿cuánto t.?**, how long?; **¿cuánto t. hace?**, how long ago?; **demasiado t.**, too long; **estar a t. de**, to still have time to; **hacer t.**, to kill time; **¿nos da t. de llegar?**, have we got (enough) time to get there?; **t. libre**, free time; fig **dar t. al t.**, to let matters take their course. 2 (*meteorológico*) weather; **¿qué t. hace?**, what's the weather like?; **hace buen/mal t.**, the weather is good/bad. 3 (*edad*) age; **¿cuánto o qué t. tiene tu niño?**, how old is your baby o child? 4 *Mús* movement. 5 *Dep* half. 6 *Ling* tense.

tienda *nf* 1 shop, *US* store; **ir de tiendas**, to go shopping. 2 **t. (de campaña)**, tent.

tienta *nf* **a tientas**, by touch; **andar a tientas**, to feel one's way; **buscar (algo) a tientas**, to grope (for sth).

tiento *nm* tact; **con t.**, tactfully.

tierno,-a *adj* 1 (*blando*) tender, soft. 2 (*reciente*) fresh.

tierra *nf* 1 (*planeta*) earth. 2 *Agr* land, soil. 3 (*continente*) land; **tocar t.**, to land. 4 (*país*) country; **t. de nadie**, no-man's-land. 5 (*suelo*) ground; *fig* **echar o tirar por t.**, to spoil. 6 *Elec* earth, *US* ground.

tierral *nm Am* cloud of dust.

tieso,-a *adj* (*rígido*) stiff, rigid; (*erguido*) upright, erect.

tiesto *nm* flowerpot.

tifoidea *nf* (*fiebre*) **t.**, typhoid (fever).

tifón *nm* typhoon.

tifus *nm inv* typhus (fever).

tigre *nm* tiger; *Am* jaguar.

tijeras *nfpl* (pair of) scissors *pl*.

tijereta *nf* 1 (*insecto*) earwig. 2 *Dep* scissors *pl*.

tila *nf* (*flor*) lime o linden blossom; (*infusión*) lime o linden blossom tea.

tildar *vtr* to call, brand; **me tildó de ladrón**, he called me a thief.

tilde *nm & f* written accent.

tilín *nm* (*sonido*) ting-a-ling; *fig* **José le hace t.**, she fancies José.

tilo *nm* lime tree.

timar *vtr* to swindle; **me han timado**, they did me.

timbal *nm* kettledrum.

timbrar *vtr* (*carta*) to stamp; (*documento*) to seal.

timbre *nm* 1 (*de la puerta*) bell. 2 (*sello*) stamp, seal; *Fin* fiscal o revenue stamp. 3 *Mús* (*sonido*) timbre.

timidez *nf* shyness, timidity.

tímido,-a *adj* shy, timid; *fig* (*mejoría*) light; (*intento*) cautious.

timo *nm* swindle, fiddle; **es un t.**, it's a rip-off.

timón *nm* 1 *Náut Av* rudder; **golpe de t.**, U-turn. 2 *Am Aut* steering wheel.

timonel *nm* helmsman.

tímpano *nm Anat* eardrum.

tinaja *nf* large earthenware jar.

tinerfeño,-a I *adj* of o from to Tenerife. II *nm,f* native o inhabitant of Tenerife.

tinglado *nm* 1 (*intriga*) intrigue. 2 (*cobertizo*) shed.

tinieblas *nfpl* darkness *sing*.

tino *nm* 1 (*puntería*) (good) aim; **tener buen t.**, to be a good shot. 2 (*tacto*)

(common) sense, good judgement.

tinta *nf* 1 ink; **t. china**, Indian ink; **t. simpática**, invisible ink. 2 *fig* **medias tintas**, ambiguities, half measures.

tintar *vtr* to dye.

tinte *nm* 1 dye. 2 *fig* (*matiz*) shade, overtone.

tintero *nm* inkpot, inkwell; *fig* **se quedó en el t.**, it wasn't said.

tintinear *vi* (*vidrio*) to clink; (*campana*) to jingle, tinkle.

tintineo *nm* (*de vidrio*) clinking; (*de campana*) jingling.

tinto I *adj* (*vino*) red. II *nm* (*vino*) red wine.

tintorería *nf* dry-cleaner's.

tintura *nf* 1 (*colorante*) dye. 2 *Quím* tincture; **t. de yodo**, iodine.

tío *nm* 1 (*pariente*) uncle; **mis tíos**, my uncle and aunt. 2 *fam* fellow, bloke, *US* guy.

tiovivo *nm* roundabout, merry-go-round.

tipazo *nm fam* good figure.

típico,-a *adj* 1 typical; **eso es t. de Antonio**, that's just like Antonio. 2 (*baile, traje*) traditional.

tipificar [1] *vtr* 1 (*normalizar*) to standardize. 2 (*caracterizar*) to typify.

tipismo *nm* local colour.

tipo *nm* 1 (*clase*) type, kind. 2 *fam* (*persona*) guy, fellow, bloke, *US* guy; **t. raro**, weirdo. 3 *Anat* (*de hombre*) build, physique; (*de mujer*) figure; *fig* **jugarse el t.**, to risk one's neck; **aguantar el t.**, to keep one's cool o head. 4 *Fin* rate; **t. bancario o de descuento**, bank rate; **t. de cambio/interés**, rate of exchange/interest. 5 **el político t. de la izquierda**, the typical left-wing politician.

tipografía *nf* typography.

tipográfico,-a *adj* typographic; **error t.**, printing error.

tipógrafo,-a *nm,f* typographer.

tiquismiquis *fam* I *nmf inv* fusspot. II *nmpl* 1 (*escrúpulos*) silly scruples. 2 (*rencillas*) bickering *sing*.

tira *nf* 1 (*banda, cinta*) strip. 2 (*de dibujos*) comic strip. 3 *fam* **la t. de gente**, a lot o loads of people. 4 **t. y afloja**, tug of war.

tirabuzón *nm* ringlet.

tirachinas *nm inv* catapult, *US* slingshot.

tirada *nf* (*impresión*) printing; (*edición*) edition.

tirado,-a *adj fam* 1 (*precio*) dirt cheap. 2 (*examen*) dead easy. 3 *fam* **dejar t. (a algn)**, to let (sb) down.

tirador *nm* 1 (*persona*) marksman. 2 (*pomo*) knob, handle; (*cordón*) bell pull. 3 (*tirachinas*) catapult, *US* slingshot.

tiralíneas *nm inv* tracer, drawing o ruling pen.

tiranía *nf* tyranny.

tiránico,-a *adj* tyrannical.

tiranizar [4] *vtr* to tyrannize.

tirano,-a nm,f tyrant.
tirante I adj (cable etc) tight, taut; (situación, relación) tense. II nm 1 (de vestido etc) strap; **tirantes**, braces, US suspenders. 2 Téc brace, stay.
tirar I vtr 1 (echar) to throw, fling. 2 (dejar caer) to drop. 3 (desechar) to throw away; fig (dinero) to squander. 4 (derribar) to knock down; **t. la puerta (abajo)**, to smash the door in. 5 (foto) to take. 6 Impr to print. 7 (beso) to blow. II vi 1 **t. de**, (cuerda, puerta) to pull. 2 (chimenea, estufa) to draw. 3 (funcionar) to work, run. 4 **ir tirando**, to get by; 5 **t. a**, to tend towards; **tira a rojo**, it's reddish. 6 **tira a la izquierda**, turn left; **¡venga, tira ya!**, come on, get going! 7 (disparar) to shoot, fire; Ftb **t. a puerta**, to shoot at goal. III **tirarse** vr 1 (lanzarse) to throw o hurl oneself; **t. de cabeza al agua**, to dive into the water. 2 (tumbarse) to lie down. 3 fam (tiempo) to spend; **me tiré una hora esperando**, I waited (for) a good hour. 4 vulg **t. a algn**, to lay sb.
tirita® nf Elastoplast®, Band-aid®, plaster.
tiritar vi to shiver, to shake.
tiro nm 1 (lanzamiento) throw. 2 (disparo, ruido) shot; Ftb **t. a gol**, shot at goal; **t. al blanco**, target shooting; **t. al plato**, clay pigeon shooting; **t. con arco**, archery. 3 (de vestido) shoulder width. 4 (de chimenea) draught, US draft; **animal de t.**, draught animal.
tirón nm pull, tug; (del bolso) snatch; fam **de un t.**, in one go.
tirotear vtr to shoot, snipe.
tiroteo nm shooting, firing to and fro.
tirria nf fam dislike; **le tengo t.**, I dislike him, I can't stand him.
tísico,-a adj tubercular, consumptive.
tisis nf inv tuberculosis, consumption.
tisú nm tissue, paper hankie.
títere nm (marioneta) puppet; **no dejar t. con cabeza**, to spare no-one.
titilar vi (luz) to flicker; (estrella) to twinkle.
titiritero,-a nm,f 1 puppeteer. 2 (acróbata) travelling acrobat.
titubeante adj (indeciso) hesitant; (al hablar) stammering.
titubear vi 1 (dudar) to hesitate, waver. 2 (al hablar) to stammer.
titubeo nm 1 (duda) hesitation. 2 (al hablar) stammering.
titulación nf qualifications pl.
titulado,-a adj (licenciado) graduate; (diplomado) qualified.
titular¹ I nmf (persona) holder. II nm Prensa headline. III adj appointed, official.
titular² I vtr (poner título) to call. II **titularse** vr 1 (película etc) to be called; **¿cómo se titula?**, what is it called? 2 Educ to graduate (en, in).

titulariedad nf Educ tenure.
titulitis I nf obsession with qualifications. II nm fam certificate.
título nm 1 title. 2 Educ degree; (diploma) diploma. 3 Prensa (titular) headline. 4 **a t. de ejemplo**, by way of example.
tiza nf chalk; **una t.**, a piece of chalk.
tiznada nf Am hijo de la t., son of a bitch.
tiznar vtr to blacken (with soot).
tizne nm soot.
tizón nm half-burnt stick, brand.
toalla nf towel; **tirar la t.**, to throw in the towel.
toallero nm towel rack o rail.
tobera nf nozzle.
tobillo nm ankle.
tobogán nm slide, chute.
toca nf (sombrero) headdress; (de monja) wimple.
tocadiscos nm inv record player; **t. digital o compacto**, CD player.
tocado¹ nm 1 (peinado) coiffure, hairdo. 2 (prenda) headdress.
tocado,-a² adj fam crazy, touched.
tocador nm 1 (mueble) dressing table. 2 (habitación) dressing room; **t. de señoras**, powder room.
tocante a loc adv **en lo t. a …**, with reference to ….
tocar [1] I vtr 1 to touch; fam fig **toca madera**, touch wood. 2 (instrumento, canción) to play; (timbre, campana) to ring; (puerta) to knock; (bocina) to blow. 3 (tema, asunto) to touch on. 4 (afectar) to concern; **por lo que a mí me toca**, as far as I am concerned. II vi 1 **¿a quién le toca?**, (en juegos) whose turn is it? 2 **me tocó el gordo**, (en rifa) I won the jackpot. 3 **t. con**, to be next to; fig **t. a su fin**, to be coming to an end. III **tocarse** vr (una cosa con otra) to touch each other; **¿os tocáis algo?**, (ser parientes) are you related?
tocarse vr (cubrirse) to cover one's head.
tocata I nf Mús toccata. II nm fam record player.
tocateja (a) loc adv **pagar a t.**, to pay on the nail.
tocayo,-a nm,f namesake.
tocho nm fam (libro) (grande) tome.
tocino nm lard; **t. ahumado**, smoked bacon; **t. de cielo**, sweet made with egg yolk.
tocólogo,-a nm tocologist, obstetrician.
tocuyo nm Am coarse cotton cloth.
todavía adv 1 (aún) still; (en negativas) yet; **t. la quiere**, he still loves her; **t. no**, not yet; **no mires t.**, don't look yet. 2 (para reforzar) even, still; **t. más/menos**, even more/less.
todo,-a I adj 1 all; **t. el pan**, all the bread; **t. el mundo**, (absolutely) everybody; **t. el día**, all day, the whole o en-

tire day; *fam* t. **quisqui**, every Tom, Dick and Harry. 2 (*cada*) every; t. **ciudadano de más de dieciocho años**, every citizen over eighteen years of age. 3 (*entero*) complete, thorough; **es toda una mujer**, she is every inch a woman. 4 **todos,-as**, all; (*con expresiones de tiempo*) every; **t. los niños**, all the children; **t. los martes**, every Tuesday.

II *nm* (*totalidad*) whole.

III *pron* 1 (*sin excluir nada*) all, everything; **ante t.**, first of all; **con t.**, in spite of everything; **del t.**, completely; **después de t.**, after all; **eso es t.**, that's all, that's it; **estar en t.**, to be really with it; **hay de t.**, there are all sorts; **lo sé t.**, I know all about it; **t. lo contrario**, quite the contrary *o* opposite; **t. lo más**, at the most. 2 (*cualquiera*) anybody; **t. aquél** *o* **el que quiera**, anybody who wants (to). 3 **todos,-as**, (*cada uno*) t. **aprobamos**, we all passed; **t. fueron**, they all went.

IV *adv* completely, totally; **volví t. sucio**, he was all dirty when he got home.

todopoderoso,-a *adj* all-powerful, almighty.

todoterreno *nm* all-terrain vehicle.

toga *nf* 1 gown, robe. 2 *Hist* toga.

Tokio *n* Tokyo.

toldo *nm* 1 (*cubierta*) awning. 2 *Am* (*cabaña*) tent, teepee.

tolerancia *nf* tolerance.

tolerante *adj* tolerant.

tolerar *vtr* to tolerate; (*situación*) to stand; (*gente*) to put up with.

toma *nf* 1 (*acción*) taking; *Elec* t. **de corriente**, plug, socket. 2 *Med* dose. 3 *Mil* capture. 4 *Cin* take, shot. 5 t. **de posesión**, swearing-in. 6 *fam fig* **toma y daca**, give and take.

tomado,-a *adj* 1 (*voz*) hoarse. 2 *Am* (*borracho*) drunk. 3 **tenerla tomada con algn**, to have it in for sb.

tomadura *nf fam* t. **de pelo**, leg-pull; (*timo*) rip-off.

tomar **I** *vtr* 1 (*coger*) to take; (*autobús, tren*) to catch; (*dirección*) to take, take; **toma**, here (you are); **t. el sol**, to sunbathe; *Av* **t. tierra**, to land; *fam* **tomarla con algn**, to have it in for sb. 2 (*comer, beber*) to have. 3 **t. algo a mal**, to take sth badly; **t. en serio/broma**, to take seriously/as a joke. 4 (*confundir*) to take (**por**, for). 5 *Mil* to take. **II tomarse** *vr* 1 (*comer*) to eat; (*beber*) to drink. 2 *fam* **no te lo tomes así**, don't take it like that.

tomate *nm* tomato; **salsa de t.**, (*de lata*) tomato sauce; (*da botella*) ketchup.

tomavistas *nm inv* cine *o* US movie camera.

tómbola *nf* tombola.

tomillo *nm* thyme.

tomo *nm* volume; *fam* **de t. y lomo**, utter, out-and-out.

ton *nm* **sin t. ni son**, without rhyme *o* reason.

tonada *nf* 1 *Mús* tune, song. 2 *Am* (*acento*) accent.

tonalidad *nf* tonality.

tonel *nm* barrel, cask.

tonelada *nf* ton; **t. métrica**, tonne.

tonelaje *nm* tonnage.

tonelero,-a *nm,f* cooper.

tongo *nm* fix.

tónico,-a **I** *nm* *Med* tonic; (*cosméticos*) skin tonic. **II** *nf* 1 (*tendencia*) tendency, trend; **tónica general**, overall trend. 2 (*bebida*) tonic (water). 3 *Mús* tonic. **III** *adj* 1 *Ling* tonic, stressed. 2 *Mús* *Med* tonic.

tonificante *adj* invigorating.

tonificar [1] *vtr* to tone up, invigorate.

tono *nm* tone, a t. **con**, in tune *o* harmony with; **subir de t.** *o* **el t.**, to speak louder; **un t. alto/bajo**, a high/low pitch; *fig* **darse t.**, to put on airs; *fig* **fuera de t.**, inappropriate, out of place; **dar el t.**, to set the tone.

tontear *vi* 1 to act the clown, fool about. 2 (*galantear*) to flirt.

tontería *nf* 1 stupidity, silliness. 2 (*dicho, hecho*) silly *o* stupid thing. 3 (*insignificancia*) trifle.

tonto,-a **I** *adj* silly, dumb. **II** *nm,f* fool, idiot; **t. de remate** *o* **de capirote**, prize idiot.

topacio *nm* topaz.

toparse *vr* **t. con**, to bump into; (*dificultades*) to run up against, encounter; **t. con algo**, to come across sth.

tope **I** *nm* 1 (*límite*) limit, end; *fam* **a t.**, (*al máximo*) flat out; *fig* **estar hasta los topes**, to be full up; **fecha t.**, deadline. 2 *Téc* stop, check. 3 *Ferroc* buffer. **II** *adv fam* incredibly; t. **difícil**, really difficult.

tópico,-a **I** *nm* commonplace, cliché. **II** *adj* *Med* *Farm* for external use.

topo *nm* mole.

topografía *nf* topography.

topónimo *nm* place name.

toque *nm* 1 touch; *fam* **dar un t. a algn**, (*avisar*) to let sb know; (*advertir*) to warn sb. 2 (*de campanas*) peal; *fig* warning; **t. de queda**, curfew.

toquetear *vtr* to fiddle with, finger.

toquilla *nf* (knitted) shawl.

tórax *nm* thorax.

torbellino *nm* 1 (*de viento*) whirlwind. 2 *fig* (*confusión*) whirl, turmoil.

torcedura *nf* (*acción*) twist, twisting; *Med* sprain.

torcer [4] **I** *vtr* 1 (*metal*) to bend; (*cuerda, hilo*) to twist; *Med* to sprain; *fig* (*esquina*) to turn. 2 (*inclinar*) to tilt. **II** *vi* to turn (left *o* right). **III torcerse** *vr* 1 (*doblarse*) to twist, bend. 2 **Me se me torció el tobillo**, I sprained my ankle. 3 (*plan*) to fall through. 4 (*desviarse*) to go off to the side.

torcido,-a adj twisted; (ladeado) slanted, lopsided; (corbata) crooked.

tordo,-a I adj dapple-grey. **II** nm Orn thrush.

torear I vtr to fight; fam **t. a algn,** to tease o confuse sb; fam **t. un asunto,** to tackle a matter skilfully. **II** vi to fight.

toreo nm bullfighting.

torero,-a nm,f bullfighter.

tormenta nf storm.

tormento nm (tortura) torture; (padecimiento) torment.

tormentoso,-a adj stormy.

tornado nm tornado.

tornar fml **I** vtr (convertir) to transform, to turn (en, into). **II** vi (regresar) to return, go back; **t. en sí,** to regain consciousness. **III tornarse** vr to become, turn.

tornasolado,-a adj iridescent.

torneo nm **1** Dep tournament. **2** Hist tourney, joust.

tornillo nm screw.

torniquete nm **1** turnstile. **2** Med tourniquet.

torno nm **1** Téc lathe; (de alfarero) wheel. **2 en t. a,** (alrededor de) around; (acerca de) about.

toro nm bull; **¿te gustan los toros?,** do you like bullfighting?

toronja nf grapefruit.

torpe adj **1** (sin habilidad) clumsy. **2** (tonto) dim, thick. **3** (movimiento) slow, awkward.

torpedear vtr to torpedo.

torpedo nm torpedo.

torpeza nf **1** (física) clumsiness; (mental) dimness, stupidity. **2** (lentitud) slowness, heaviness. **3** (error) blunder.

torre nf **1** tower. **2** Mil Náut turret. **3** Ajedrez rook, castle.

torrefacto,-a adj roasted; **café t.,** high roast coffee.

torrencial adj torrential.

torrente nm **1** (de agua) torrent. **2** fig **t. de voz,** strong o powerful voice.

torrezno nm rasher of fried bacon.

tórrido,-a adj torrid.

torrija nf French toast.

torsión nf **1** (torcedura) twist, twisting. **2** Téc torsion.

torso nm **1** Anat torso. **2** Arte bust.

torta nf **1** Culin cake; **2** fam (golpe) slap, punch.

tortazo nm fam **1** (bofetada) slap, punch. **2** (golpe) whack, thump.

tortícolis nf inv crick in the neck.

tortilla nf **1** (egg) omelette, US omelet; **t. francesa/española,** (plain)/potato omelette. **2** Am tortilla.

tortillera nf vulg dyke, lesbian.

tórtola nf dove.

tortuga nf (de tierra) tortoise, US turtle; (de mar) turtle.

tortuoso,-a adj tortuous.

tortura nf torture.

torturar vtr to torture.

tos nf cough; **t. ferina,** whooping cough.

tosco,-a adj (basto) rustic, rough; (persona) uncouth.

toser vi to cough.

tosquedad nf roughness.

tostada nf (slice of) toast.

tostado,-a adj **1** (pan) toasted. **2** (moreno) tanned, brown.

tostador nm toaster.

tostar [2] vtr (pan) to toast; (café) to roast; (carne, pescado) to brown; fig (la piel) to tan.

tostón nm **1** Culin (pan frito) crouton. **2** fam (tabarra) bore, drag.

total I adj (completo) total. **II** nm **1** (todo) whole; **en t.,** in all. **2** Mat total. **III** adv so, in short; **¿t. para qué?,** what's the point anyhow?; fam **t. que ..., so ...; t., tampoco te hará caso,** he won't listen to you, anyway.

totalidad nf whole, totality; **la t. de,** all of; **en su t.,** as a whole.

totalitario,-a adj totalitarian.

totalizar [4] vtr to total. **II** vi to amount to.

tóxico,-a I adj toxic, poisonous. **II** nm poison.

toxicología nf toxicology.

toxicólogo,-a nm,f toxicologist.

toxicomanía nf drug addiction.

toxicómano,-a Med **I** adj addicted to drugs. **II** nm,f drug addict.

tozudo,-a adj obstinate, stubborn.

traba nf (de rueda) chock; (enlace) bond, tie. **2** fig (obstáculo) hindrance, obstacle.

trabajador,-a I nm,f worker, labourer, US laborer. **II** adj hard-working.

trabajar I vi to work; **trabaja mucho,** he works hard; **t. de camarera,** to work as a waitress. **II** vtr **1** to work (on); (la tierra) to till. **2** (asignatura etc) to work on. **3** fam (convencer) to (try to) persuade.

trabajo nm **1** (ocupación) work; **t. a destajo,** piecework; **t. eventual,** casual labour; **trabajos manuales,** arts and crafts. **2** (empleo) employment, job. **3** (tarea) task, job. **4** Educ (redacción) report, paper. **5** (esfuerzo) effort; **cuesta t. creerlo,** it's hard to believe.

trabajoadicto nm,f workaholic.

trabajoso,-a adj (laborioso) hard, laborious; (difícil) difficult.

trabalenguas nm inv tongue twister.

trabar I vtr **1** (sujetar) to lock, fasten; (un plan) to obstruct. **2** (conversación, amistad) to start, to strike up. **3** Culin to thicken. **II trabarse** vr **1** (cuerdas) to get tangled up. **2** fig **se le trabó la lengua,** he got tongue-tied.

trabazón nf (de ideas) link.

trabilla nf (de pantalón) belt loop.

trabuco nm blunderbuss.

tracción *nf* traction; *Aut* **t. delantera/ trasera,** front-/rear-wheel drive; *Aut* **t. en las cuatro ruedas,** four-wheel drive.

tractor *nm* tractor.

tradición *nf* tradition.

tradicional *adj* traditional.

traducción *nf* translation; **t. directa/ inversa,** translation from/into a foreign language.

traducir [10] I *vtr* to translate (**a,** into). II **traducirse** *vr fig* to result (**en,** in).

traductor,-a *nm,f* translator.

traer [25] I *vtr* 1 to bring; **trae,** give it to me. 2 (*llevar puesto*) to wear. 3 (*llevar consigo*) to carry. 4 (*problemas*) to cause; **traerá como consecuencia ...,** it will result in .... II **traerse** *vr* (*llevar consigo*) to bring along; *fig* **¿qué se trae entre manos?,** what is he up to?

traficante *nmf* (*de drogas etc*) trafficker, pusher.

traficar [1] *vi* (*ilegalmente*) to traffic (**con,** in).

tráfico *nm* 1 *Aut* traffic; **t. rodado,** road traffic. 2 *Com* traffic, trade; **t. de drogas,** drug traffic.

tragaluz *nm* skylight.

tragaperras *nf inv* (*máquina*) **t.,** slot machine.

tragar [7] I *vtr* 1 (*ingerir*) to swallow. 2 *fam* (*engullir*) to gobble up, tuck away. 3 *fig* (*a una persona*) to stand, stomach. 4 *fig* (*creer*) to believe, swallow. II **tragarse** *vr* 1 (*ingerir*) to swallow. 2 *fig* (*creer*) to believe, swallow.

tragedia *nf* tragedy.

trágico,-a *adj* tragic.

trago *nm* 1 (*bebida*) swig; **de un t.,** in one go. 2 **pasar un mal t.,** to have a bad time of it.

tragón,-ona *nm,f* glutton, big eater.

traición *nf* treason, betrayal; **a t.,** treacherously; **alta t.,** high treason.

traicionar *vtr* to betray; (*delatar*) to give away, betray.

traicionero,-a *adj* treacherous.

traidor,-a I *adj* treacherous. II *nm,f* traitor.

traigo *indic pres* → **traer.**

tráiler *nm* (*pl* **tráilers**) 1 *Cin* trailer, US preview. 2 *Aut* articulated lorry, US trailer truck.

traje¹ *nm* 1 (*de hombre*) suit; **t. de baño,** bathing suit *o* costume, swimsuit; **t. de paisano,** civilian clothes *pl*; **t. de luces,** bullfighter's costume. 2 (*de mujer*) dress; **t. de chaqueta,** two-piece suit; **t. de novia,** wedding dress.

traje² *pt indef* → **traer.**

trajeado,-a *adj fam* sharp, dapper.

trajearse *vr* to dress up.

trajín *nm fam* comings and goings *pl*, hustle and bustle.

trajinar *vi* to run *o* bustle about.

trama *nf* 1 *Tex* weft, woof. 2 *Lit* plot.

tramar *vtr* to plot, cook up; **¿qué tramas?,** what are you up to?

tramitar *vtr* 1 (*gestionar*) to take the necessary (legal) steps to obtain. 2 *fml* (*despachar*) to convey, transmit. 3 *Com Jur Fin* to carry out, to process.

trámite *nm* (*paso*) step; (*formalidad*) formality; *Com Jur Fin* procedures *pl*, proceeding.

tramo *nm* (*de carretera*) section, stretch; (*de escalera*) flight.

tramoya *nf* (*maquinaria*) stage machinery; (*trama*) plot, scheme.

trampa *nf* 1 (*de caza*) trap, snare. 2 (*puerta*) trap door. 3 (*engaño*) fiddle; **hacer trampa(s),** to cheat. 4 (*truco*) trick.

trampilla *nf* trap door, hatch.

trampolín *nm* 1 *Natación* diving board. 2 *Esquí* ski jump.

tramposo,-a I *adj* deceitful. II *nm,f* cheat; *Naipes* cardsharp.

tranca *nf* 1 (*garrote*) cudgel; *fam* **a trancas y barrancas,** with great difficulty. 2 (*en puerta, ventana*) bar.

trance *nm* 1 (*coyuntura*) (critical) moment; **estar en t. de ...,** to be on the point of ... 2 (*éxtasis*) trance.

tranquilidad *nf* calmness, tranquillity, US tranquility; **con t.,** calmly; **pídemelo con toda t.,** don't hesitate to ask me.

tranquilizante *nm* tranquillizer, US tranquilizer.

tranquilizar [4] I *vtr* to calm down; **lo dijo para tranquilizarme,** he said it to reassure me. II **tranquilizarse** *vr* (*calmarse*) to calm down.

tranquilo,-a *adj* 1 (*persona, lugar*) calm; (*agua*) still; (*conciencia*) clear; *fam* **tú t.,** don't you worry. 2 (*despreocupado*) placid, easy-going.

tranquillo *nm fig* knack; **coger el t. a algo,** to get the knack of sth.

transacción *nf* transaction, deal.

transatlántico,-a I *nm Náut* (ocean) liner. II *adj* transatlantic.

transbordador *nm* (car) ferry; **t. espacial,** space shuttle.

transbordar I *vtr* to transfer; *Náut* (*mercancías*) to transship. II *vi* *Ferroc* to change trains, US transfer.

transbordo *nm* 1 *Ferroc* change, US transfer; **hacer t.,** to change *o* transfer. 2 *Náut* transshipment.

transcurrir *vi* 1 (*tiempo*) to pass, to go by. 2 (*acontecer*) to take place.

transcurso *nm* (*tiempo*) passing *o* passing (of time); **en el t. de,** in the course of, during.

transeúnte *nmf* 1 (*peatón*) passer-by. 2 (*residente temporal*) temporary resident, US transient.

transferencia *nf* transference; *Fin* transfer; **t. bancaria,** banker's order.

transferible *adj* transferable.

transferir [5] *vtr* to transfer.
transformación *nf* transformation.
transformador *nm* Elec transformer.
transformar I *vtr* to transform, change. **II transformarse** *vr* to change, to turn (**en**, into); *(algo plegable)* to convert.
tránsfuga *nmf* 1 Mil deserter. 2 Pol turn-coat.
transfusión *nf* transfusion.
transgredir *vtr* defect to transgress, break.
transgresor,-a *nm,f* transgressor, law-breaker.
transición *nf* transition.
transido,-a *adj fml* t. **de angustia**, overcome by anxiety; t. **de dolor**, racked with pain.
transigente *adj* tolerant.
transigir [6] *vi* to compromise.
transistor *nm* transistor.
transitable *adj* passable.
transitado,-a *adj (carretera)* busy.
transitar *vi* to pass.
transitivo,-a *adj* transitive.
tránsito *nm* 1 Aut traffic. 2 *(movimiento)* movement, passage; **pasajeros en t.**, passengers in transit.
transitorio,-a *adj* transitory.
traslucir [35] *vtr* → **traslucir**.
transmisión *nf* 1 transmission. 2 Téc drive; t. **delantera/trasera**, front-/rear-wheel drive. 3 Rad TV transmission, broadcast.
transmisor *nm* transmitter.
transmitir *vtr* 1 to transmit, pass on. 2 Rad TV to transmit, broadcast. 3 Jur to transfer, hand down.
transparencia *nf* 1 transparency; Pol openness. 2 Fot slide.
transparentarse *vr* to be transparent; **esta tela se transparenta**, this is see-through material; **se le transparentaban las bragas**, you could see her underpants.
transparente I *adj* transparent; Pol open. **II** *nm* 1 *(visillo)* net curtain. 2 *(pantalla)* shade, blind.
transpiración *nf* perspiration.
transpirar *vi* to perspire.
transplante *nm* transplant; Med t. **de corazón/córnea**, heart/eye transplant.
transponer [19] **I** *vtr (mudar de sitio)* to transpose, move about. **II transponerse** *vr (desmayarse)* to faint.
transportar *vtr* to transport; *(pasajeros)* to carry; *(mercancías)* to ship.
transporte *nm* 1 transport. 2 Com freight; t. **de mercancías**, freight transport; t. **marítimo**, shipment.
transportista *nmf* carrier.
transvase *nm* 1 *(de líquidos)* decanting. 2 *(de ríos)* transfer.
transversal *adj* transverse, cross.
tranvía *nm* tram, tramcar, US streetcar.
trapecio *nm* trapeze.

trapecista *nmf* trapeze artiste.
trapero,-a I *nm* rag-and-bone man, US junkman. **II** *adj* **puñalada trapera**, stab in the back.
trapichear *vi* to be up to something.
trapicheo *nm* jiggery-pokery.
trapo *nm* 1 *(viejo, roto)* rag. 2 *(bayeta)* cloth; t. **de cocina**, dishcloth; t. **del polvo**, duster; *fam* **poner a (algn) como un t.** (**sucio**), to tear sb apart.
tráquea *nf* trachea, windpipe.
traqueteo *nm* rattle, clatter.
tras *prep* 1 *(después de)* after; **uno t. otro**, one after the other. 2 *(detrás)* behind; **sentados uno t. oto**, sitting one behind the other. 3 **andar/ir t.**, to be after; **la policía iba t. ella**, the police were after her.
trasatlántico,-a *adj & nm* → **transatlántico,-a**.
trasbordador *nm* → **transbordador**.
trasbordar *vtr & vi* → **transbordar**.
trasbordo *nm* → **transbordo**.
trascendencia *nf* 1 *(importancia)* importance, significance. 2 *(en filosofía)* transcendence.
trascendental, trascendente *adj* 1 significant, far-reaching. 2 *(en filosofía)* transcendental.
trascender [31] *vtr vi* 1 *(noticia)* to become known, leak out. 2 *(tener consecuencias)* to have far-reaching consequences. 3 t. **de**, to go beyond.
trascribir *vtr* → **transcribir**.
trascripción *nf* → **transcripción**.
trascurrir *vi* → **transcurrir**.
trascurso *nm* → **transcurso**.
trasero,-a I *adj* back, rear; **en la parte trasera**, at the back. **II** *nm euf* bottom, bum.
trasferencia *nf* → **transferencia**.
trasferible *adj* → **transferible**.
trasferir [5] *vtr* → **transferir**.
trasfondo *nm* background.
trasformación *nf* → **transformación**.
trasformador *adj & nm* → **transformador**.
trasformar *vtr* → **transformar**.
trásfuga *nmf* → **tránsfuga**.
trasfusión *nf* → **transfusión**.
trasgredir *vtr* → **transgredir**.
trasgresión *nf* → **transgresión**.
trasgresor,-a *nm,f* → **transgresor,-a**.
trashumancia *nf* seasonal movement of livestock.
trasiego *nm* comings and goings *pl*, hustle and bustle.
trasladar I *vtr (cosa)* to move; *(persona)* to move, transfer. **II trasladarse** *vr* to go, move.
traslado *nm (de casa)* move, removal; *(de personal)* transfer; Educ t. **de expediente**, transfer of student record.
traslucirse *vr* to show (through).

trasluz nm mirar algo al t., to hold sth against the light.

trasmano a t., out of reach; (me) **coge a t.**, it's out of my way.

transmisión nf → **transmisión**.

trasmisor,-a adj & nm → **transmisor,-a**.

trasmitir vtr → **transmitir**.

trasnochado,-a adj (desfasado) old, hackneyed.

trasnochador,-a I adj given to staying up late. II nm,f night bird, nighthawk.

trasnochar vi to stay up (very) late.

traspapelarse vr to get mislaid o misplaced.

transparencia nf → **transparencia**.

transparentar vtr → **transparentar**.

transparente adj & nm → **transparente**.

traspasar vtr 1 (atravesar) to go through; (río) to cross. 2 (negocio, local) to transfer; **'se traspasa'**, 'for sale'. 3 fig (exceder) to exceed, go beyond.

traspaso nm (de propiedad etc) transfer. 2 Com (venta) sale.

traspié nm (pl traspiés) stumble, trip; **dar un t.**, to trip; fig to slip up.

transpiración nf → **transpiración**.

transpirar vi → **transpirar**.

trasplantar vtr → **transplantar**.

trasplante nm → **transplante**.

trasponer [19] vtr → **transponer**.

trasportador,a adj & nm adj → **transportador,-a**.

trasportar vtr → **transportar**.

trasporte nm → **transporte**.

traspuesto,-a adj quedarse t., to faint.

trasquilar vtr (oveja) to shear; (pelo) to crop.

trastabillar vi (tambalearse) to stagger, totter.

trastada nf fam hacer trastadas, to be up to mischief.

trastazo nm fam wallop, thump.

traste[1] nm Mús fret.

traste[2] nm 1 (trasto) piece of junk. 2 fig **dar al t. (con un plan)**, to spoil a plan; **irse al t.**, to fall through.

trastear vi (revolver) to rummage about.

trastero nm (cuarto) t., junk room.

trastienda nf back shop.

trasto nm (objeto cualquiera) thing; (cosa inservible) piece of junk.

trastocar [2] vtr → **trastornar**.

trastornado,-a adj (loco) mad, unhinged.

trastornar I vtr 1 (planes) to disrupt. 2 fig (persona) to unhinge. II **trastornarse** vr (enloquecer) to go out of one's mind, go mad.

trastorno nm (molestia) trouble, inconvenience; **t. mental**, mental disorder o disturbance.

trasvasar vtr → **transvasar**.

trasvase nm → **transvase**.

trasversal adj → **transversal**.

trasverso,-a adj → **transverso,-a**.

trata nf slave trade o traffic; **t. de blancas**, white slave trade.

tratable adj easy to get along with, congenial.

tratado nm 1 (pacto) treaty. 2 (estudio) treatise.

tratamiento nm 1 treatment. 2 Téc processing, treatment. 3 Inform processing.

tratar I vtr 1 (atender) to treat; **t. bien/mal**, to treat well/badly. 2 Med to treat. 3 (asunto) to discuss. 4 Inform Téc to process. 5 **me trata de tú**, he addresses me as 'tu'. II vi 1 t. de, (intentar) to try. 2 t. de o sobre o acerca, to be about; **¿de qué trata?**, what is it about? 3 t. con, (tener tratos) to deal with; (negociar) to negotiate with; (relacionarse) to move among. 4 Com t. en, to deal in III tratarse vr 1 (relacionarse) to be on speaking terms. 2 se trata de, (es cuestión de) it's a question of; **se trata de un caso excepcional**, it's an exceptional case.

trato nm 1 (de personas) manner; (contacto) contact; **malos tratos**, ill-treatment sing. 2 (acuerdo) agreement; **¡t. hecho!**, it's a deal! 3 Com deal.

trauma nm trauma.

traumático,-a adj traumatic.

traumatizar vtr Med to traumatize; fam to shock.

través I prep 1 a t. de, (superficie) across, over; (agujero etc) through; **a t. del río**, across the river; **a t. del agujero**, through the hole. 2 fig a t. de, through; **a t. del periódico**, through the newspaper. II adv de t., (transversalmente) crosswise; (de lado) sideways. III nm (pl traveses) fig (desgracia) misfortune.

travesaño nm Ftb crossbar.

travesía nf (viaje) crossing.

travestí, travestí nmf transvestite.

travesura nf mischief, childish prank.

travieso,-a adj mischievous.

trayecto nm 1 (distancia) distance; (recorrido) route; (trecho) stretch. 2 (viaje) journey.

trayectoria nf 1 (de proyectil, geométrica) trajectory. 2 fig (orientación) line, course.

traza nf 1 (apariencia) looks pl, appearance; **no lleva trazas de curarse**, it doesn't look as if he's going to get better. 2 Arquit plan, design.

trazado,-a nm 1 (plano) layout, plan. 2 (de carretera, ferrocarril) route.

trazar [4] vtr (línea) to draw; (plano) to design; fig (plan) to draw up the broad lines of.

trazo nm 1 (línea) line. 2 (de letra) stroke.

trébol nm 1 trefoil. 2 Naipes club.

trece inv I adj thirteen. II nm thirteen; fig **estar o mantenerse o seguir en sus t.**, to stick to one's guns.

trecho nm distance, way; (tramo) stretch; **de t. en t.**, from time to time.

tregua nf Mil truce; fig respite.
treinta adj & nm inv thirty.
treintena nf **una t. de**, (about) thirty.
treintavo,-a adj & nm thirtieth.
tremendista adj over the top.
tremendo,-a adj 1 (terrible) terrible, dreadful. 2 (muy grande) enormous; fig tremendous.
trementina nf turpentine.
trémulo,-a adj lit (vacilante) quivering, tremulous; (luz) flickering.
tren nm 1 train. 2 Av **t. de aterrizaje**, undercarriage; **t. de lavado**, car wash. 3 **t. de vida**, life style.
trenca nf duffle coat.
trenza nf (de pelo) plait, US braid.
trepador,-a adj climbing.
trepar vtr & vi to climb.
trepidante adj vibrating, shaking; fig **lleva un ritmo de vida t.**, he leads a hectic o frantic life.
trepidar vi to vibrate, shake.
tres I adj inv (cardinal) three; (ordinal) third; fam **de t. al cuarto**, cheap, of little value. II nm (pl **treses**) three; **t. en raya**, noughts and crosses, US tick-tack-toe.
trescientos,-as adj & nm,f three hundred.
tresillo nm 1 (mueble) (three-piece) suite. 2 Mús triplet.
treta nf trick, ruse.
triángulo nm triangle; fig **t. amoroso**, eternal triangle.
tribal adj tribal.
tribu nf tribe.
tribuna nf 1 (plataforma) rostrum, dais; **t. de (la) prensa**, press box. 2 Dep stand.
tribunal nm 1 Jur court; **t. de apelación**, court of appeal; **T. Supremo**, High Court, US Supreme Court; **t. (tutelar) de menores**, juvenile court. 2 (de examen) board of examiners.
tributar vtr to pay.
tributario,-a adj **sistema t.**, tax system.
tributo nm 1 Com tax. 2 **pagar t. a**, (homenaje) to pay tribute to.
triciclo nm tricycle.
tricornio nm three-cornered hat.
tridimensional adj three-dimensional.
trienio nm three year period.
trifásico,-a adj I Elec three-phase. II nm adapter.
trigésimo,-a adj & nm,f thirtieth; **t. primero**, thirty-first.
trigo nm wheat.
trilogía nf trilogy.
trilla nf threshing.
trillado,-a adj fig well-worn.
trilladora nf threshing machine; **t. segadora**, combine harvester.
trillar vtr to thresh.
trimestral adj quarterly, three-monthly.
trimestre nm quarter; Educ term.
trinar vi 1 to warble. 2 fam to rage, fume;

Santiago está que trina, Santiago is really fuming.
trincar¹ [1] vtr fam (capturar) to catch.
trincar² vtr fam to drink.
trinchar vtr (carne) to carve, slice (up).
trinchera nf trench.
trineo nm sledge, sleigh.
trinidad nf **la Santísima T.**, the Holy Trinity.
trino nm 1 warble, trill. 2 Mús trill.
trío nm trio.
tripa nf 1 (intestino) gut, intestine; fam tummy; **dolor de t.**, stomach ache. 2 **tripas**, innards.
triple adj & nm triple.
triplicado,-a adj triplicate; **por t.**, in triplicate.
triplicar [1] vtr to triple, treble.
trípode nm tripod.
tríptico nm 1 (cuadro) triptych. 2 (folleto) leaflet.
tripulación nf crew.
tripulante nmf crew member.
tripular vtr to man.
trip(y) nm arg (droga) trip.
triquiñuela nf fam trick, dodge.
tris nm **estar en un t. de**, to be on the verge of.
triste adj 1 (persona, situación) sad. 2 (lugar) gloomy.
tristeza nf sadness.
triturar vtr (machacar) to grind (up).
triunfador,-a I adj winning. II nm,f winner.
triunfal adj triumphant.
triunfar vi to triumph.
triunfo nm 1 (victoria) triumph, victory; Dep win. 2 (éxito) success.
trivial adj trivial.
trivialidad nf triviality.
trivializar vtr to trivialize, minimize.
triza nf bit, fragment; **hacer trizas**, to tear to shreds.
trocar [2] vtr to barter.
trocear vtr to cut up (into bits o pieces).
trochemoche (a) loc adv fam haphazardly.
trofeo nm trophy.
trola nf fam fib.
trolebús nm trolley bus.
tromba nf **t. de agua**, violent downpour.
trombón nm trombone.
trombosis nf inv thrombosis.
trompa nf 1 Mús horn. 2 (de elefante) trunk. 3 Anat tube. 4 fam **estar t.**, to be sloshed o plastered.
trompazo nm fam bump; **darse o pegarse un t.**, to have a bump.
trompeta nf trumpet.
trompetista nmf trumpet player, trumpeter.
trompicón nm trip, stumble; **hacer algo a trompicones**, to do sth in fits and starts.

trompo *nm* spinning top.

tronar [2] I *vi* to thunder. II *vtr Am* to shoot.

tronchar I *vtr* (*rama, tronco*) to cut down, fell; *fig* (*esperanzas etc*) to destroy. II **troncharse** *vr* **t. de risa**, to split one's sides with laughter.

troncho *nm* stem, stalk.

tronco *nm* 1 *Anat* trunk, torso. 2 *Bot* (*de árbol*) trunk; (*leño*) log; *fam fig* **dormir como un t.**, to sleep like a log.

tronera *nf* 1 (*de billar*) pocket. 2 (*ventana*) small window; (*de fortificación*) loophole; *Náut* porthole.

trono *nm* throne.

tropa *nf* 1 squad. 2 **tropas**, troops *pl*.

tropel *nm* throng, mob; **en t.**, in a mad rush.

tropezar [1] I *vi* 1 to trip, stumble (*con*, on). 2 **t. con algo**, to come across sth; **t. con algn/dificultades**, to run into sb/ difficulties.

tropezón *nm* 1 (*traspié*) trip, stumble; **dar un t.**, to trip. 2 (*error*) slip-up, faux pas. 3 (*de comida*) chunk of meat.

tropical *adj* tropical.

trópico *nm* tropic.

tropiezo I *nm* 1 (*obstáculo*) trip. 2 *fig* (*error*) blunder, faux pas. II *indic pres* → **tropezar**.

trotamundos *nmf inv* globe-trotter.

trotar *vi* to trot.

trote *nm* 1 trot; **al t.**, at a trot. 2 *fam* **ya no está para esos trotes**, he cannot keep up the pace any more.

trovador *nm* troubadour.

trozo *nm* piece.

trucar [1] *vtr* to doctor, alter.

truco *nm* 1 (*ardid*) trick; **aquí hay t.**, there's something fishy going on here. 2 **coger el t. (a algo)**, to get the knack *o* hang (of sth).

truculento,-a *adj* cruel.

trucha *nf* trout.

trueno *nm* thunder; **un t.**, a thunderclap.

trueque *nm* barter.

trufa *nf* truffle.

truhán,-ana *nm,f* rogue, crook.

truncar [1] *vtr* to truncate; *fig* (*vida etc*) to cut short; *fig* (*esperanzas etc*) to shatter.

trust *nm* (*pl* **trusts**) trust, cartel.

tu *adj pos* your; **tu libro**, your book; **tus libros**, your books.

tú *pron* you; **de tú a tú**, on equal terms.

tuba *nf* tuba.

tubérculo *nm* 1 *Bot* tuber. 2 *Med* tubercle.

tuberculosis *nf inv* tuberculosis.

tubería *nf* 1 (*de agua*) piping, pipes *pl*. 2 (*de gas*) piping.

tubo *nm* 1 tube; **t. de ensayo**, test tube. 2 (*tubería*) pipe; *Aut* **t. de escape**, exhaust (pipe).

tucán *nm* toucan.

tuerca *nf* nut.

tuerto,-a I *adj* one-eyed, blind in one eye. II *nm,f* one-eyed person.

tuerzo *indic pres* → **torcer**.

tuétano *nm* marrow; **hasta el t.**, to one's fingertips.

tufo *nm* foul odour *o US* odor *o* smell.

tugurio *nm* hovel.

tul *nm* tulle.

tulipa *nf* small tulip.

tulipán *nm* tulip.

tullido,-a *adj* crippled, disabled.

tullir *vtr* to cripple.

tumba *nf* grave, tomb.

tumbar I *vtr* to knock down *o* over. II **tumbarse** *vr* (*acostarse*) to lie down, to stretch out.

tumbo *nm* **dar tumbos**, to reel.

tumbona *nf* easy chair; (*de lona*) deck chair.

tumor *nm* tumour, *US* tumor.

tumulto *nm* tumult, commotion.

tumultuoso,-a *adj* tumultuous, riotous.

tuna *nf* student folkloric music group.

tunante,-a *nm,f* rogue, crook.

túnel *nm* tunnel; **el t. del Canal de la Mancha**, the Channel Tunnel.

Túnez *n* 1 (*país*) Tunisia. 2 (*ciudad*) Tunis.

túnica *nf* tunic.

tuno,-a I *nm,f* (*bribón*) rogue, crook. II *nm* member of a **tuna**.

tuntún (al) *adv* haphazardly, any old how.

tupé *nm* (*pl* **tupés**) (*flequillo*) quiff.

tupido,-a *adj* thick, dense.

turba[1] *nf* (*combustible*) peat.

turba[2] *nf* (*muchedumbre*) mob, crowd.

turbado,-a *adj* 1 (*alterado*) disturbed. 2 (*preocupado*) worried, anxious. 3 (*desconcertado*) confused.

turbante *nm* turban.

turbar I *vtr* 1 (*alterar*) to unsettle. 2 (*preocupar*) to upset *o* worry. 3 (*desconcertar*) to baffle, put off. II **turbarse** *vr* 1 (*preocuparse*) to be *o* become upset. 2 (*desconcertarse*) to be *o* become confused *o* baffled.

turbina *nf* turbine.

turbio,-a *adj* (*agua*) cloudy; *pey* (*negocio etc*) shady, dubious.

turborreactor *nm* turbojet (engine).

turbulencia *nf* turbulence.

turbulento,-a *adj* turbulent.

turco,-a I *adj* Turkish. II *nm,f* (*persona*) Turk; *fig* **cabeza de t.**, scapegoat. III *nm* (*idioma*) Turkish.

turismo *nm* 1 tourism; **ir de t.**, to go touring. 2 *Aut* car.

turista *nmf* tourist.

turístico,-a *adj* tourist; **de interés t.**, of interest to tourists.

turnarse *vr* to take turns.

turno *nm* 1 (*en juegos etc*) turn, go. 2 (*de trabajo*) shift; **estar de t.**, to be on duty;

t. de día/noche, day/night shift.

turquesa *adj & nf* turquoise.

Turquía *n* Turkey.

turrón *nm* nougat.

tute *nm fam* **darse un t. de algo**, to go to town doing sth.

tutear I *vtr* to address as **tú**. II **tutearse** *vr* to address (each other *o* one another) as **tú**.

tutela *nf* 1 *Jur* guardianship, tutelage. 2 *fig (protección)* protection, guidance.

tuteo *nm* use of the **tú** form of address.

tutor *nm* 1 *Jur* guardian. 2 *Educ* tutor.

tuve *pt indef* → **tener**.

tuyo,-a I *adj pos (con personas)* of yours; *(con objetos)* one of your; **¿es amigo t.?**, is he a friend of yours?; **unas amigas tuyas**, some friends of yours; **un libro t.**, one of your books. II *pron pos* yours; **éste es t.**, this one is yours; *fam* **los tuyos**, *(familiares)* your family.

TV *abr de* **televisión**, television, TV.

TVE *nf abr de* **Televisión Española**.

U

U, u [u] *nf (la letra)* U, u.

u *conj (delante de palabras que empiecen por o o ho)* or; **siete u ocho**, seven or eight; **ayer u hoy**, today or today.

ubicación *nf* location, position.

ubicar [1] I *vtr Am (situar)* to locate, situate. II **ubicarse** *vr* to be situated *o* located.

ubicuo,-a *adj* ubiquitous.

ubre *nf* udder.

Ucrania *n* Ukraine.

ucraniano,-a *adj & nm,f* Ukrainian.

Ud. *abr de* **usted**, you.

Uds. *abr de* **ustedes**, you.

ufanarse *vr* to boast **(de,** of).

ufano,-a *adj* conceited.

UGT *nf abr de* **Unión General de Trabajadores**.

ugetista *adj* relating to the UGT.

ujier *nm* usher.

úlcera *nf* ulcer.

ulcerar *vtr*, **ulcerarse** *vr* to ulcerate.

ulterior *adj (siguiente)* subsequent.

ultimar *vtr* 1 *(terminar)* to finalize. 2 *Am (matar)* to kill, finish off.

ultimátum *nm (pl* **ultimátums)** ultimatum.

último,-a *adj* 1 last; **el u. día**, the last day; **llegar el ú.**, to arrive last; **por ú.**, finally; **a últimos de mes**, at the end of the month; **en las últimas**, on one's last legs. 2 *(más reciente)* latest; **últimas noticias**, latest news; *fam* **a la última**, up to the minute. 3 *(más alto)* top; **el u. piso**, the top flat. 4 *(más bajo)* lowest; **el u. de la lista**, the lowest in the list. 5 *(más lejano)* back, last; **la última fila**, the back row. 6 *(definitivo)* final. **◆últimamente** *adv* lately, recently.

ultra *nmf* extreme right-winger; **los ultras**, the extreme right *sing.*

ultra- *pref* ultra-.

ultraderecha *nf Pol* extreme right.

ultraderechista *Pol* I *adj* extreme right-wing. II *nmf* extreme right-winger.

ultraizquierda *nf* extreme left.

ultrajar *vtr* to outrage, offend.

ultraje *nm* outrage, offence.

ultramar *nm* overseas (countries); **abroad; del** *o* **en u.**, overseas.

ultramarinos *nm* groceries; **tienda de u.**, greengrocer.

ultranza (a) *loc adv* 1 *(a todo trance)* at all costs, at any price; **defender algo a u.**, to defend sth to the death. 2 *(acérrimo)* out-and-out, extreme.

ultrasónico,-a *adj* ultrasonic.

ultratumba *nf* afterlife.

ultravioleta *adj inv* ultraviolet.

ulular *vi (viento)* to howl; *(búho)* to hoot.

umbral *nm* threshold.

umbrío,-a, umbroso,-a *adj* shady.

un,-a *art indef* 1 a; *(antes de vocal)* an; **un coche**, a car; **un huevo**, an egg; **una flor**, a flower. 2 *unos,-as*, some; **unas flores**, some flowers. II *adj (delante de nm sing)* one; **un chico y dos chicas**, one boy and two girls; → *tamb* **uno,-a** I.

unánime *adj* unanimous.

unanimidad *nf* unanimity; **por u.**, unanimously.

unción *nf* unction.

undécimo,-a *adj* eleventh.

UNED *nf abr de* **Universidad Nacional de Educación a Distancia**, ≈ Open University, OU.

ungir [6] *vtr Rel* to anoint.

ungüento *nm* ointment.

único,-a *adj* 1 *(solo)* only; **es el ú. que tengo**, it's the only one I've got; **hijo ú.**, only child; **lo ú. que quiero**, the only thing I want; **el Mercado Ú.**, the Single Market; **el Acta Única**, the Single European Act. 2 *(extraordinario)* unique. **◆únicamente** *adv* only, solely.

unidad *nf* 1 unit. 2 *(cohesión)* unity.

unido,-a *adj* united; **están muy unidos**, they are very attached to one another; **una familia muy unida**, a very close family.

unifamiliar *adj* **vivienda u.**, detached house.

unificación *nf* unification.

unificar [1] *vtr* to unify.

uniformar vtr 1 (igualar) to make uniform, standardize. 2 (poner un uniforme a) to put into uniform, give a uniform to.

uniforme I nm (prenda) uniform. II adj 1 (igual) uniform. 2 (superficie) even.

uniformidad nf 1 (igualdad) uniformity. 2 (de superficie) evenness.

unilateral adj unilateral.

unión nf union.

Unión Soviética n Soviet Union.

unir I vtr (juntar) to unite, join (together); **esta carretera une las dos comarcas**, this road links both districts. II **unirse** vr (juntarse) to unite, join.

unisex adj inv unisex.

unísono,-a adj unison; **al u.**, in unison.

unitario,-a adj unitary; **precio u.**, unit price.

universal adj universal; **historia u.**, world history.

universidad nf university; **u. a distancia**, ≈ Open University; **u. laboral**, technical college.

universitario,-a I adj university. II nm,f university student.

universo nm universe.

uno,-a I nm inv one; **el u.**, (number) one; **el u. de mayo**, the first of May. II nf (hora) **es la una**, it's one o'clock. III adj **unos,-as**, some; **unas cajas**, some boxes; **habrá unos o unas veinte**, there must be around twenty. IV pron 1 one; **u. (de ellos), una (de ellas)**, one of them; **unos cuantos**, a few; **se miraron el u. al otro**, they looked at each other; **de u. en u.**, one by one; **un trás otro**, one after the other; **una de dos**, one of the two. 2 (persona) someone, somebody; **u. que pasaba por allí**, some passer-by; **vive con u.**, she's living with some man. **unos ... otros**, some people ... others. 3 (impers) you, one; **u. tiene que ...**, you have to ....

untar vtr to grease, smear; (mantequilla) to spread.

untura nf ointment.

uña nf 1 nail; **morderse o comerse las uñas** to bite one's fingernails; fig **ser u. y carne**, to be hand in glove. 2 Zool (garra) claw; (pezuña) hoof.

uperizado,-a adj **leche uperizada**, UHT milk.

Urales nmpl **los U.**, the Urals.

uranio nm uranium.

Urano nm Uranus.

urbanidad nf urbanity, politeness.

urbanismo nm town planning.

urbanístico,-a adj town-planning.

urbanización nf 1 (barrio) housing development o estate. 2 (proceso) urbanization.

urbanizar vtr to build up.

urbano,-a adj urban, city; **guardia u.**, (traffic) policeman.

urbe nf large city.

urdimbre nf 1 Tex warp. 2 (trama) intrigue.

urdir vtr 1 Tex to warp. 2 (tramar) to plot, scheme.

urgencia nf 1 urgency. 2 (emergencia) emergency.

urgente adj urgent; **correo u.**, express mail.

urgir [6] vi to be urgent o pressing; **me urge (tenerlo)**, I need it urgently.

urinario nm urinal.

urna nf 1 Pol ballot box. 2 (vasija) urn.

urólogo,-a nm,f Med urologist.

urraca nf magpie.

URSS nf Hist abr de **Unión de Repúblicas Socialistas Soviéticas**, Union of Socialist Soviet Republics, USSR.

urticaria nf Med hives.

Uruguay n (el) U., Uruguay.

uruguayo,-a adj & nm,f Uruguayan.

usado,-a adj (ropa) second-hand, used.

usanza nf lit **a la antigua u.**, in the old style.

usar I vtr 1 to use. 2 (prenda) to wear. II **usarse** vr to be used o in fashion.

usina nf Am (central eléctrica) power station.

USO nf abr de **Unión Sindical Obrera**.

uso nm 1 use; Farm **u. externo/tópico**, external/local application. 2 (de poder, privilegio) exercise. 3 (de prenda) wearing; **haga u. del casco**, wear a helmet. 4 (costumbre) usage, custom; **al u.**, conventional.

usted, pl **ustedes** pron pers fml you; **¿quién es u.?, ¿quiénes son ustedes?**, who are you?

usual adj usual, common.

usuario,-a nm,f user.

usura nf usury.

usurero,-a nm,f usurer.

usurpar vtr to usurp.

utensilio nm utensil; (herramienta) tool.

útero nm uterus, womb.

útil I adj useful; (día) working. II nm (herramienta) tool, instrument.

utilidad nf usefulness, utility; (beneficio) profit.

utilitario,-a I nm (coche) utility vehicle. II adj utilitarian.

utilización nf use, utilization.

utilizar [4] vtr to use, utilize.

utopía nf utopia.

utópico,-a adj & nm,f utopian.

uva nf grape; **u. blanca**, green grape.

UVI nf abr de **unidad de vigilancia intensiva**, intensive care unit, ICU.

úvula nf uvula.

V

V, v ['uβe] *nf (la letra)* V, v.

V *Elec abr de* **voltio(s),** volt, volts, V.

vaca *nf* 1 cow. 2 *(carne)* beef.

vacaciones *nfpl* holidays *pl, US* vacation; *(viaje)* holiday; **durante las v.,** during the holidays; **estar/irse de v.,** to be/go on holiday.

vacante I *adj* vacant. II *nf* vacancy.

vaciar [29] I *vtr* 1 *(recipiente)* to empty; *(contenido)* to empty out. 2 *(terreno)* to hollow out. 3 *Arte* to cast, mould, *US* mold. II **vaciarse** *vr* to empty.

vacilación *nf* hesitation.

vacilante *adj* 1 *(persona)* hesitant, irresolute. 2 *(voz)* hesitant, faltering. 3 *(luz)* flickering.

vacilar *vi* 1 *(dudar)* to hesitate; **sin v.,** without hesitation. 2 *(voz)* to falter. 3 *(luz)* to flicker. 4 *fam (jactarse)* to show off.

vacío,-a I *adj* 1 empty; *(hueco)* hollow. 2 *(sin ocupar)* vacant, unoccupied. II *nm* 1 emptiness, void. 2 *(hueco)* gap; *(espacio)* (empty) space. 3 *Fís* vacuum; **envasado al v.,** vacuum-packed.

vacuna *nf* vaccine; *Vet* cowpox.

vacunación *nf* vaccination.

vacunar I *vtr* to vaccinate **(contra,** against); *fig* to inure. II **vacunarse** *vr* to get oneself vaccinated.

vacuno,-a *adj* bovine; **ganado v.,** cattle.

vacuo,-a *adj* vacuous, empty.

vadear *vtr (río)* to ford; *fig (dificultad)* to overcome.

vado *nm* 1 *(de un río)* ford. 2 *Aut* **'v. permanente',** 'keep clear'.

vagabundear *vi* to wander, roam.

vagabundo,-a I *adj (errante)* wandering; *pey* vagrant; **perro v.,** stray dog. II *nm,f* wanderer; *(sin casa)* tramp, *US* hobo; *pey* vagrant, tramp.

vagancia *nf* idleness, laziness.

vagar [7] *vi* to wander about, roam about.

vagido *nm* cry of a newborn baby.

vagina *nf* vagina.

vago,-a I *adj* 1 *(perezoso)* lazy. 2 *(indefinido)* vague. II *nm,f* 1 *(holgazán)* layabout. 2 *Jur* vagrant.

vagón *nm (para pasajeros)* carriage, coach, *US* car; *(para mercancías)* truck, wagon, *US* freight car, *US* boxcar.

vaguedad *nf* vagueness.

vaho *nm (de aliento)* breath; *(vapor)* vapour, *US* vapor.

vaina I *nf* 1 *(de espada)* sheath, scabbard. 2 *Bot* pod. 3 *Am fam (molestia)* bother, nuisance. II *nmf (persona)* dimwit.

vainilla *nf* vanilla.

vaivén *nm* 1 *(oscilación)* swinging, to-and-fro movement. 2 *(de gente)* coming and go-

ing, bustle; *fig* **vaivenes,** ups and downs.

vajilla *nf* crockery, dishes *pl;* **una v.,** a set of dishes, a dinner service.

valdré *indic fut* → **valer.**

vale¹ *interj* all right, O.K.

vale² *nm* 1 *(comprobante)* voucher. 2 *(pagaré)* promissory note, IOU (I owe you).

valedero,-a *adj* valid.

valenciano,-a *adj* Valencian; **Comunidad Valenciana,** Valencia.

valentía *nf* courage, bravery.

valentón,-ona *pey* I *adj* bragging, boastful. II *nm,f* braggart.

valer [26] I *vtr* 1 to be worth; **no vale nada,** it is worthless; **vale una fortuna,** it is worth a fortune; **no vale la pena** *(ir),* it's not worth while (going). 2 *(costar)* to cost; **¿cuánto vale?,** how much is it? 3 *(proporcionar)* to earn. II *vi* 1 *(servir)* to be useful, be of use. 2 *(ser válido)* to be valid, count; **no vale hacer trampa,** cheating isn't on. 3 **más vale,** it is better; **más vale que te vayas ya,** you had better leave now. III **valerse** *vr* to use, make use **(de,** of); **v. por sí mismo,** to be able to manage on one's own.

valeroso,-a *adj* brave, courageous.

valgo *indic pres* → **valer.**

valía *nf* value, worth.

validez *nf* validity.

válido,-a *adj* valid.

valiente *adj* 1 *(valeroso)* brave, courageous. 2 *irón* **¡v. amigo eres tú!,** a fine friend you are!

valija *nf (de correos)* mailbag; **v. diplomática,** diplomatic bag.

valioso,-a *adj* valuable.

valor *nm* 1 *(valía)* value, worth; *(precio)* price; **objetos de v.,** valuables; **sin v.,** worthless; **v. alimenticio,** food value. 2 *(valentía)* courage. 3 *Fin* **valores,** securities, bonds.

valoración *nf* valuation.

valorar *vtr* to value, calculate the value of.

valorización *nf* 1 *(tasación)* valuation. 2 *(revalorización)* appreciation.

valorizar [4] *vtr* 1 *(tasar)* to value. 2 *(revalorizar)* to raise the value of.

vals *nm* waltz; **bailar el v.,** to waltz.

válvula *nf* valve; **v. de seguridad,** safety valve.

valla *nf* 1 *(cerca)* fence; *(muro)* wall; **v. publicitaria,** hoarding, *US* billboard. 2 *Dep* hurdle; **los 100 metros vallas,** the 100 metres hurdle race.

vallado *nm* fence.

vallar *vtr* to fence (in).

valle *nm* valley.

vallisoletano,-a I *adj* of o from Valladolid. II *nm,f* native *o* inhabitant of Valladolid.

vampiro *nm* vampire.

vanagloriarse [12] *vr* to boast (**de**, of).

vandalismo *nm* vandalism.

vándalo,-a *nm,f* vandal.

vanguardia *nf* 1 avant-garde, vanguard; *fig* **ir a la v. de**, to be at the forefront of. 2 *Mil* vanguard, van.

vanguardista I *adj* avant-garde. II *nm,f* avant-gardist.

vanidad *nf* vanity.

vanidoso,-a *adj* vain, conceited.

vano,-a *adj* 1 (*vanidoso*) vain, conceited. 2 (*esfuerzo, esperanza*) vain, futile; **en v.**, in vain.

vapor *nm* 1 (*de agua hirviendo*) steam; *Culin* **al v.**, steamed. 2 (*gas*) vapour, *US* vapor; **v. de agua**, water vapour.

vaporizador *nm* vaporizer, spray.

vaporizar [4] I *vtr* to vaporize. II **vaporizarse** *vr* to vaporize, become vaporized, evaporate.

vaporoso,-a *adj* vaporous.

vapulear *vtr* (*físicamente*) to shake; (*con palabras*) to slate.

vaqueriza *nf* cowshed.

vaquero,-a I *nm* cowherd, *US* cowboy. II *adj* **pantalón v.**, jeans *pl*, pair *sing* of jeans. III *nmpl* **vaqueros**, (*prenda*) jeans, pair *sing* of jeans.

vara *nf* pole, rod.

varar I *vtr* to beach, dock. II *vi* to run aground.

variable *adj & nf* variable.

variación *nf* variation.

variado,-a *adj* varied; **galletas variadas**, assorted biscuits.

variante *nf* variant; *Aut* detour.

variar [29] I *vtr* to vary, change. II *vi* to vary, change; *irón* **para v.**, as usual, just for a change.

varice, várice *nf* → **variz**.

varicela *nf* chickenpox.

variedad *nf* 1 variety. 2 *Teat* **variedades**, variety show *sing*.

varilla *nf* (*vara*) rod, stick; (*de abanico, paraguas*) rib.

varios,-as *adj* several.

variopinto,-a *adj* diverse, assorted; **un público v.**, a varied audience.

varita *nf* **v. mágica**, magic wand.

variz *nm* varicose vein.

varón *nm* (*hombre*) man; (*chico*) boy; **hijo v.**, male child; **sexo v.**, male sex.

varonil *adj* manly, virile.

Varsovia *n* Warsaw.

vas *indic pres* → **ir**.

vasallo,-a *nm,f Hist* vassal.

vasco,-a *adj* Basque; **el País V.**, the Basque Country.

vascuence *nm* (*idioma*) Basque.

vasectomía *nf* vasectomy.

vaselina *nf* vaseline®.

vasija *nf* pot.

vaso *nm* 1 (*para beber*) glass. 2 (*florero*) vase. 3 *Anat* vessel.

vástago *nm* 1 *Bot* shoot. 2 *fig* (*hijo*) offspring. 3 *Téc* rod, stem.

vasto,-a *adj* vast.

Vaticano *nm* el V., Vatican.

vaticinar *vtr* to prophesy, predict.

vaticinio *nm* prophesy, prediction.

vatio *nm* watt.

vaya¹ *interj* ¡v. lío!, what a mess!

vaya² *subj pres* → **ir**.

Vd. Vds. *abr* **de usted, ustedes**, you.

ve I *imperat* → **ir**. II *indic pres* → **ver**.

vecinal *adj* local.

vecindad *nf*, **vecindario** *nm* 1 (*área*) neighbourhood, *US* neighborhood, vicinity. 2 (*vecinos*) community, residents *pl*.

vecino,-a I *nm,f* 1 (*persona*) neighbour, *US* neighbor; **el v. de al lado**, the next-door neighbour. 2 (*residente*) resident. II *adj* neighbouring, *US* neighboring, nearby.

veda *nf* (*de caza*) close season, *US* closed season; **levantar la v.**, to open the season.

vedado *adj* **coto v. de caza**, private hunting ground.

vedar *vtr* to forbid, prohibit.

vega *nf* fertile plain *o* lowland.

vegetación *nf* 1 *Bot* vegetation. 2 *Med* **vegetaciones**, adenoids.

vegetal *nm* vegetable.

vegetar *vi* *fig* to vegetate.

vegetariano,-a *adj & nm,f* vegetarian.

vehemencia *nf* vehemence.

vehemente *adj* vehement.

vehículo *nm* vehicle.

veinte *adj & nm inv* twenty.

veintena *nf* (*veinte*) twenty; **una v. de**, about twenty.

vejación *nf* humiliation.

vejar *vtr* to humiliate.

vejatorio,-a *adj* humiliating.

vejez *nf* old age.

vejiga *nf* bladder.

vela¹ *nf* 1 candle. 2 *fam* **quedarse a dos velas**, to be in the dark. 3 **pasar la noche en v.**, to have a sleepless night.

vela² *nf Náut* sail.

velada *nf* evening (party).

velado,-a *adj* 1 (*oculto*) veiled, hidden. 2 *Fot* blurred.

velador *nm* 1 (*mesa*) table. 2 *Am* (*mesilla de noche*) bedside table.

velar¹ I *vi* 1 **v. por**, to watch over. 2 (*hacer guardia*) to keep watch.

velar² *Fot* I *vtr* to blur. II **velarse** *vr* to become blurred.

velatorio *nm* vigil, wake.

veleidad *nf* fickleness.

veleidoso,-a *adj* fickle.

velero *nm* sailing boat *o* ship.

veleta I *nf* weather vane, weathercock. II

nmf fam fickle *o* changeable person.
velo *nm* veil.
velocidad *nf* 1 *(rapidez)* speed; *(de proyectil etc)* velocity; *Aut* v. máxima, speed limit; *Inform* v. de transmisión, bit rate; *Inform* v. operativa, operating speed. 2 *Aut (marcha)* gear.
velocímetro *nm* speedometer.
velocista *nmf* sprinter.
velódromo *nm* cycle track, *US* velodrome.
veloz I *adj* swift, rapid. II *adv* quickly, fast.
vello *nm* hair.
vellón *nm* fleece.
velloso,-a, velludo,-a *adj* downy.
vena *nf* vein.
venado *nm* deer, stag; *Culin* venison.
vencedor,-a I *nm,f* winner. II winning.
vencejo *nm Orn* swift.
vencer [2] I *vtr* 1 *(al enemigo)* to defeat; *(al contrincante)* to beat. 2 *(dificultad)* to overcome, surmount. II *vi* 1 *(pago, deuda)* to fall due, be payable. 2 *(plazo)* to expire. III **vencerse** *vr (torcerse)* to warp.
vencido,-a *adj* 1 *Mil (derrotado)* defeated; *Dep* beaten; *fig* darse por v., to give up, accept defeat. 2 *(pago, deuda)* due, payable. 3 *(plazo)* expired. 4 *fam* a la tercera va la vencida, third time lucky.
vencimiento *nm* 1 *Com* maturity. 2 *(de un plazo)* expiry.
venda *nf* bandage.
vendaje *nm* dressing.
vendar *vtr* to bandage; *fig* v. los ojos a algn, to blindfold sb.
vendaval *nm* gale.
vendedor,-a *nm,f* seller; *(hombre)* salesman; *(mujer)* saleswoman.
vender I *vtr* to sell; v. a plazos/al contado, to sell on credit/for cash; v. al por mayor/menor, to (sell) wholesale/retail. II **venderse** *vr* 1 to sell; este disco se vende bien, this record is selling well; for sale. 2 *(claudicar)* to sell out.
vendimia *nf* grape harvest.
vendré *indic fut* → venir.
Venecia *nf* Venice.
veneno *nm* poison; *(de serpiente)* venom.
venenoso,-a *adj* poisonous.
venerable *adj* venerable.
veneración *nf* veneration.
venerar *vtr* to venerate, revere.
venéreo,-a *adj* venereal.
venero *nm* spring.
venezolano,-a *adj & nm,f* Venezuelan.
Venezuela *nf* Venezuela.
venga *subj pres* → venir.
venganza *nf* vengeance, revenge.
vengar [7] I *vtr* to avenge. II **vengarse** *vr* to avenge oneself; v. de algn, to take revenge on sb.
vengativo,-a *adj* vengeful, vindictive.
vengo *indic pres* → venir.

venia *nf* 1 *fml (permiso)* permission. 2 *(perdón)* pardon.
venial *adj* venial.
venida *nf* coming, arrival.
venidero,-a *adj* future, coming.
venir [27] I *vi* 1 to come; *fig* v. a menos, to come down in the world; *fig* v. al mundo, to be born; el año que viene, next year; *fig* v. a la memoria, to remember; *fam* ¡venga ya!, *(vamos)* come on!; *(expresa incredulidad)* come off it! 2 v. grande/pequeño, *(ropa)* to be too big/small; v. mal/bien, to be inconvenient/convenient; el metro me viene muy bien, I find the underground very handy. 3 *(en pasivas)* esto vino provocado por ..., this was brought about by ... . 4 esto viene ocurriendo desde hace mucho tiempo, this has been going on for a long time now. II **venirse** *vr* v. abajo, to collapse.
venta *nf* 1 sale; en v., for sale; a la v., on sale; v. a plazos/al contado, credit/cash sale; v. al por mayor/al por menor, wholesale/retail. 2 *(posada)* country inn.
ventaja *nf* advantage; llevar v. a, to have the advantage over; le sacó dos metros de v. a, he beat him by two metres.
ventajoso,-a *adj* advantageous.
ventana *nf* 1 window. 2 *(de la nariz)* nostril.
ventanal *nm* large window.
ventanilla *nf* 1 window. 2 *(de la nariz)* nostril.
ventanuco *nm* small window.
ventilación *nf* ventilation; sin v., unventilated.
ventilador *nm* ventilator; *(de coche)* fan.
ventilar I *vtr* 1 *(habitación)* to ventilate, air. 2 *fig (opinión)* to air. II **ventilarse** *vr fam (terminar)* to finish off.
ventisca *nf* blizzard; *(de nieve)* snowstorm.
ventosa *nf* sucker; *Med* cupping glass.
ventosear *vi* to break wind.
ventoso,-a *adj* windy.
ventrílocuo,-a *nm,f* ventriloquist.
ventura *nf* 1 *(felicidad)* happiness. 2 *(suerte)* luck; *(casualidad)* chance.
venturoso,-a *adj* lucky, fortunate.
Venus *nm* Venus.
veo-veo *nm fam* el (juego del) v.-v., I-spy.
ver¹ *nm* de buen v., good-looking.
ver² [28] I *vtr* 1 to see; *(televisión)* to watch; a v., let me see, let's see; a v. si escribes, I hope you'll write; *(ya)* veremos, we'll see; *fam* había un jaleo que no veas, you should have seen the fuss that was made; no veo por qué, I can't see why; a mi modo de v., as I see it. 2 no tener nada que v. con, to have nothing to do with. II **verse** *vr* 1 *(imagen etc)* to be seen. 2 *(encontrarse con algn)* to

meet, see each other; ¡nos vemos!, see you later! **3 no se pueden ni v.**, (soportarse) they can't stand (the sight of) each other. **4** Am **te ves divina**, you look divine.

vera nf edge, border; **a la v. de**, beside, next to.

veracidad nf veracity, truthfulness.

veraneante nmf holidaymaker, US (summer) vacationist.

veranear vi to spend one's summer holiday.

veraneo nm summer holiday.

veraniego,-a adj summer.

verano nm summer.

veras nfpl **de v.**, really, seriously.

veraz adj veracious, truthful.

verbal adj verbal.

verbena nf street party.

verbo nm verb.

verborrea nf fam verbosity, verbal diarrhoea.

verdad nf **1** truth; **es v.**, it is true; **a decir v.**, to tell the truth; **¡de v!.**, really, truly; **un amigo de v.**, a real friend. **2** (en frase afirmativa) **está muy bien, ¿(no es) v.?**, it is very good, isn't it?; (en frase negativa) **no te gusta, ¿v.?**, you don't like it, do you?.

verdadero,-a adj true, real.
◆**verdaderamente** adv truly, really.

verde **I** adj **1** green. **2** (fruta) unripe. **3** fam (chiste, película) blue; **viejo v.**, dirty old man. **4** fam fig **poner v. a algn**, to call sb every name under the sun. **II** nm **1** (color) green. **2** Pol **los verdes**, the Greens.

verdear vi to turn green.

verdor nm (color) greenness; (de plantas) verdure.

verdoso,-a adj greenish.

verdugo,-a **I** nm executioner. **II** nmf fig tyrant.

verdulería nf greengrocer's (shop).

verdulero,-a nm,f greengrocer.

verdura nf vegetables pl, greens pl.

vereda nf **1** (camino) path, lane. **2** Am (acera) pavement, US sidewalk.

veredicto nm verdict.

verga nf penis.

vergonzoso,-a adj **1** (penoso) shameful, disgraceful. **2** (tímido) shy, bashful.

vergüenza nf **1** shame; **¿no te da v.?**, aren't you ashamed?, have you no shame?; **es una v.**, it's a disgrace. **2** (timidez) shyness, bashfulness; **tener v.**, to be shy; **me da v.**, I'm too embarrassed.

vericueto nm winding path; fig **los vericuetos**, the ins and outs.

verídico,-a adj truthful, true.

verificar [1] **I** vtr (comprobar) to check. **II** **verificarse** vr to take place, occur.

verja nf (reja) grating; (cerca) railing, railings pl; (puerta) iron gate.

vermut, vermú nm (pl **vermús**) vermouth.

verosímil adj probable, likely; (creíble) credible.

verruga nf wart.

versado,-a adj well-versed (**en**, in).

versar vi **v. sobre**, to be about, deal with.

versátil adj **1** versatile. **2** (voluble) changeable, inconstant.

versatilidad nf **1** versatility. **2** (volubilidad) changeableness, inconstancy.

versículo nm verse.

versión nf version; **película en v. original**, film in the original language.

verso nm **1** (poesía) verse. **2** (línea) line.

vértebra nf vertebra.

vertebrado,-a adj & nm vertebrate.

vertedero nm (de basura) rubbish dump, tip.

verter [3] **I** vtr **1** to pour (out). **2** (basura) to dump. **II** vi (río) to flow, run (**a**, into).

vertical adj vertical.

vértice nm vertex.

vertiente nf **1** (de una montaña, un tejado) slope; fig aspect. **2** Am (manantial) spring.

vertiginoso,-a adj dizzy, giddy; fig (velocidad) breakneck.

vértigo nm vertigo; **me da v.**, it makes me dizzy.

vesícula nf vesicle; **v. biliar**, gall bladder.

vespa® nf (motor) scooter.

vespertino,-a **I** adj evening. **II** nm Prensa evening newspaper.

vespino® nm moped.

vestíbulo nm (de casa) hall; (de edificio público) foyer.

vestido,-a **I** nm (ropa) clothes pl; (de mujer) dress. **II** adj dressed; **policía v. de paisano**, plain clothes policeman.

vestidura nf clothing, clothes pl.

vestigio nm vestige, trace.

vestimenta nf clothes pl, garments pl.

vestir [6] **I** vtr **1** (a alguien) to dress. **2** (llevar puesto) to wear. **II** vi **1** to dress; **ropa de (mucho) v.**, formal dress. **2** fam **la seda viste mucho**, silk always looks very elegant. **III** **vestirse** vr **1** to get dressed, dress. **2 v. de**, to wear, dress in; (disfrazarse) to disguise oneself as, to dress up as.

vestuario nm **1** (conjunto de vestidos) clothes pl, wardrobe; Teat wardrobe, costumes pl. **2** (camerino) dressing room. **3** Dep changing room sing.

veta nf Min vein, seam; (de carne) streak.

vetar vtr to veto.

veterano,-a adj & nm,f veteran.

veterinario,-a **I** nm,f veterinary surgeon, vet, US veterinarian. **II** nf veterinary medicine o science.

veto nm veto; **derecho a v.**, power o right of veto.

vetusto,-a adj fml ancient.

vez *nf* **1** time; **una v.**, once; **dos veces**, twice; **cinco veces**, five times; **a** *o* **algunas veces**, sometimes; **cada v.**, each *o* every time; **cada v. más**, more and more; **de v. en cuando**, now and again, every now and then; **¿le has visto alguna v.?**, have you ever seen him?; **otra v.**, again; **a la v.**, at the same time; **tal v.**, perhaps, maybe; **de una v.**, in one go; **de una v. para siempre**, once and for all; **en v. de**, instead of; **érase** *o* **había una v.**, (*en cuentos etc*) once upon a time. **2** (*turno*) turn. **3** **hacer las veces de**, to do duty as.

v.g(r). *abr de* **verbigracia**, for example, eg.

vía *nf* **1** **Ferroc** track, line. **2** (*camino*) road; **v. pública**, public thoroughfare; **V. Láctea**, Milky Way. **3** **Anat** passage, tract; **Farm (por) v. oral**, to be taken orally. **4** *fig* **por v. oficial**, through official channels; **por v. aérea/marítima**, by air/sea. **5** **en vías de**, in the process of; **países en vías de desarrollo**, developing countries. **II** *prep* (*a través de*, through; **v. París**, via Paris; **transmisión v. satélite**, satellite transmission.

viable *adj* viable.

viaducto *nm* viaduct.

viajante *nmf* commercial traveller, travelling salesman *o* saleswoman.

viajar *vi* to travel.

viaje *nm* (*recorrido*) journey, trip; (*largo, en barco*) voyage; **¡buen v.!**, bon voyage!, have a good trip!; **estar de v.**, to be away (on a trip); **irse** *o* **marcharse de v.**, to go on a journey *o* trip; **v. de negocios**, business trip; **v. de novios**, honeymoon.

viajero,-a **I** *nm,f* **1** traveller. **2** (*en transporte público*) passenger. **II** *adj* **cheque v.**, travellers cheque.

viandante *nmf* passer-by.

viario,-a *adj* road, highway; **red viaria**, road network.

víbora *nf* viper.

vibración *nf* vibration.

vibrador *nm* vibrator.

vibrar *vtr & vi* to vibrate.

vicario,-a *nm,f* vicar.

vicepresidente,-a *nm,f* **1** **Pol** vice president. **2** (*de compañía, comité*) vicechairperson; (*hombre*) vice-chairman; (*mujer*) vice-chairwoman.

vicesecretario,-a *nm,f* assistant secretary.

viceversa *adv* vice versa.

viciado,-a *adj* **1** (*corrompido*) corrupt. **2** (*aire*) foul.

viciar [12] **I** *vtr* **1** (*corromper*) to corrupt. **2** (*estropear*) to waste. **II** **viciarse** *vr* **1** (*deformarse*) to go out of shape. **2** (*corromperse*) to become corrupted.

vicio *nm* **1** vice. **2** (*mala costumbre*) bad habit. **3** *fam* (*destreza*) skill.

vicioso,-a **I** *adj* **1** (*persona*) depraved,

perverted. **2** **círculo v.**, vicious circle. **II** *nm,f* depraved person; **v. del trabajo**, workaholic.

vicisitud *nf* (*usu pl*) vicissitude.

víctima *nf* victim.

victoria *nf* victory.

victorioso,-a *adj* victorious.

vicuña *nf* vicuna.

vid *nf* vine, grapevine.

vida *nf* **1** life; (*período*) lifetime; **de toda la v.**, life-long; **en mi v.**, never in my life; **de por v.**, for life; **ganarse la v.**, to earn one's living; **¿qué es de tu v.?**, how's life?; **estar con/sin v.**, to be alive/dead.

vidente *nmf* clairvoyant.

vídeo *nm* video; **grabar en v.**, to videotape.

videoclub *nm* video club.

videocámara *nf* video camera.

videoconferencia *nf* videoconferencing; (*sesión*) videoconference.

videojuego *nm* video game.

vidriera *nf* **1** stained-glass window. **2** *Am* (*escaparate*) shop window.

vidrio *nm* glass.

viejo,-a **I** *adj* **1** old; **hacerse v.**, to grow old; **un v. amigo**, an old friend. **II** *nm,f* **1** (*hombre, padre*) old man; (*mujer, madre*) old woman; **los viejos**, old people; *fam* **mis viejos**, my parents.

Viena *nf* Vienna.

vienés,-esa *adj & nm,f* Viennese.

viento *nm* wind; **hace** *o* **sopla mucho v.**, it is very windy; *fam* **fig vete a tomar v.**, get lost.

vientre *nm* belly; **hacer de v.**, to have a bowel movement. **2** (*útero*) womb.

viernes *nm inv* Friday; **V. Santo**, Good Friday.

Vietnam *nm* Vietnam.

vietnamita *adj & nmf* Vietnamese.

viga *nf* (*de madera*) beam; (*de hierro*) girder.

vigencia *nf* validity; **entrar en v.**, to come into force *o* effect.

vigente *adj* in force.

vigésimo,-a *adj & nm,f* twentieth.

vigía **I** *nf* watchtower, lookout post. **II** *nmf* lookout; (*hombre*) watchman; (*mujer*) watchwoman.

vigilancia *nf* vigilance, watchfulness; **Med unidad de v. intensiva**, intensive care unit.

vigilante *nm* watchman; (*de banco*) guard.

vigilar **I** *vtr* to watch; (*un lugar*) to guard; **vigila que no entren**, make sure they don't get in. **II** *vi* (*gen*) to keep watch.

vigilia *nf* **1** vigil. **2** (*víspera*) eve. **3** **Rel** (*abstinencia*) abstinence.

vigor *nm* **1** vigour, *US* vigor; (*fuerza*) strength. **2** **en v.**, in force.

vigoroso,-a *adj* vigorous.

VIH *abr de* **Virus de Inmunodeficiencia Humana**, Human Immunodeficiency

Virus, HIV.

vikingo nm Viking.

vil adj fml vile, base.

vileza nf 1 vileness, baseness. 2 (acto) vile act, despicable deed.

vilipendiar [12] vtr fml to vilify, revile.

vilo (en) loc adv (persona) on tenterhooks; (cosa) up in the air.

villa nf 1 (población) town. 2 (casa) villa, country house.

villancico nm (Christmas) carol.

vinagre nm vinegar.

vinagrera nf vinagreras, oil and vinegar cruets, cruet (stand) sing.

vinagreta nf vinaigrette sauce.

vinajeras nfpl cruets.

vincha nf Am headband.

vinculante adj binding.

vincular vtr to link, bind; (relacionar) to relate, connect.

vínculo nm link.

vine pt indef → **venir**.

vinícola adj wine-producing.

vinicultor,-a nm,f wine producer.

vinicultura nf wine production o growing.

vinilo nm vinyl.

vino nm wine; **tomar un v.**, to have a glass of wine; **v. blanco/tinto/dulce/seco**, white/red/sweet/dry wine; **v. rosado**, rosé.

viña nf vineyard.

viñedo nm vineyard.

viñeta nf illustration.

viola nf viola.

violación nf 1 (de una persona) rape. 2 (de ley, derecho) violation, infringement.

violador,-a n rapist.

violar vtr 1 (persona) to rape. 2 (ley, derecho) to violate, infringe.

violencia nf 1 violence; **la no v.**, non-violence. 2 (incomodidad) embarrassment.

violentar vtr 1 (forzar) to force, break open; (sitio) to break into, enter by force. 2 (enojar) to infuriate.

violento,-a adj 1 violent. 2 (situación) embarrassing, awkward. 3 **sentirse v.**, (incómodo) to feel embarrassed o awkward.

violeta adj & nm & nf violet.

violín nm violin; fam fiddle.

violinista nmf violinist.

violón nm double bass.

violoncelista, violonchelista nmf cellist.

violoncelo, violonchelo nm violoncello, cello.

viraje nm 1 turn. 2 fig about-face, U-turn.

virar vi 1 (girar) to turn round. 2 fig to change.

virgen I adj 1 (persona, selva) virgin. 2 (aceite, lana) pure; (cinta) blank. II nmf virgin; fam **ser un viva la v.**, to be a devil-may-care person.

virginidad nf virginity.

virgo nm hymen.

Virgo nm Virgo.

virguería nf arg gem, marvel; **hacer virguerías**, to work wonders, be a dab hand.

virguero,-a adj arg smart, great; **esta camisa es muy virguera**, that shirt is the business.

vírico,-a adj viral.

viril adj virile, manly; **miembro v.**, penis.

virilidad nf virility.

virtual adj virtual.

virtud nf 1 virtue; fig **en v. de**, by virtue of. 2 (propiedad) property, quality.

virtuoso,-a I adj virtuous. II nm,f 1 virtuous person. 2 (músico) virtuoso.

viruela nf smallpox; **viruelas**, pockmarks pl.

virulé (a la) loc adv fam 1 (torcido) crooked, twisted. 2 **un ojo a la v.**, a black eye.

virulencia nf virulence.

virulento,-a adj virulent.

virus nm inv virus.

visa nf Am visa.

visado nm visa.

víscera nf 1 internal organ. 2 **vísceras**, viscera, entrails.

visceral adj 1 Anat visceral. 2 fig profound, deep-rooted.

viscoso,-a adj viscous.

visera nf (de gorra) peak; (de casco) visor.

visibilidad nf visibility; **curva con mala v.**, blind corner.

visible adj visible; (evidente) evident.

visillo nm small lace o net curtain.

visión nf 1 vision. 2 (vista) sight; fig **v. de conjunto**, overall view; **con v. de futuro**, forward-looking. 2 (aparición) vision.

visionario,-a nm,f visionary; (iluso) person who imagines things.

visita nf 1 (acción) visit; **hacer una v.**, to pay a visit; **estar de v.**, to be visiting. 2 (invitado) visitor, guest.

visitador,-a nm,f Farm pharmaceutical salesman o saleswoman.

visitante I nmf visitor. II adj (equipo) away.

visitar vtr to visit.

vislumbrar vtr to glimpse.

viso nm 1 (reflejo) sheen. 2 fig **tener visos de**, to seem, appear.

visón nm mink.

visor nm Fot viewfinder.

víspera nf (día anterior) day before; (de festivo) eve; **en vísperas de**, in the period leading up to.

vista nf 1 sight; **a la v.**, visible; **a primera o simple v.**, at first sight, on the face of it; **con vistas a**, with a view to; **en v. de**, in view of, considering; **corto de v.**, short-sighted; **conocer a algn de v.**, to know sb by sight; **perder de v. a**, to lose sight of; **quitalo de mi v.**, take it away;

fig **tener mucha v. para,** to have a good eye for; *fig* **volver la v. atrás,** to look back; *fam* **¡hasta la v.!,** goodbye!, see you!; *fam* **hacer la v. gorda,** to turn a blind eye. **2** (*panorama*) view; **con vista(s) al mar,** overlooking the sea. **3** *Jur* trial, hearing.

vistazo *nm* glance; **echar un v. a algo,** (*ojear*) to have a (quick) look at sth; (*tener cuidado de*) to keep an eye on sth.

visto,-a I *adj* **1 está v. que ...,** it is obvious that ...; **por lo v.,** evidently, apparently; **v. que,** in view of the fact that, seeing *o* given that. **2 estar bien v.,** to be well looked upon, be considered acceptable; **estar mal v.,** to be frowned upon. **3 estar muy v.,** to be old hat. **II** *nm* **v. bueno,** approval, O.K.

vistoso,-a *adj* eye-catching.

visual *adj* visual; **campo v.,** field of vision.

visualizar [4] *vtr* to visualize; (*película*) to view.

vital *adj* **1** vital. **2** (*persona*) full of vitality.

vitalicio,-a *adj* life, for life; **pensión/cargo v.,** life pension/permanent post.

vitalidad *nf* vitality.

vitamina *nf* vitamin.

vitamínico,-a *adj* vitamin; **complejo v.,** multivitamins.

viticultura *nf* wine growing.

viticultor,-a *nmf* wine grower.

vitorear *vtr* to cheer.

vítreo,-a *adj* vitreous.

vitrina *nf* (*aparador*) glass *o* display cabinet; (*de exposición*) glass case, showcase; *Am* (*escaparate*) shop window.

vituallas *nfpl* provisions.

vituperar *vtr* to condemn.

vituperio *nm* condemnation.

viudo,-a *nm,f* (*hombre*) widower; (*mujer*) widow.

viva *interj* **¡v.!,** hurrah!

vivacidad *nf* vivacity.

vivaracho,-a *adj fam* lively, sprightly.

vivaz *adj* **1** lively, vivacious. **2** (*perspicaz*) sharp, quick-witted.

vivencias *nfpl* personal experience.

víveres *nmpl* provisions, supplies.

vivero *nm* (*de plantas*) nursery; (*de peces*) fish farm *o* hatchery; *fig* breeding ground, hotbed.

viveza *nf* **1** liveliness, vivacity; (*en los ojos*) sparkle. **2** (*agudeza*) sharpness, quick-wittedness.

vividor,-a *nm,f pey* sponger, scrounger.

vivienda *nf* **1** housing. **2** (*casa*) house; (*piso*) flat.

vivir I *vi* to live; **vive de sus ahorros,** she lives off her savings; **viven de la pesca,** they make their living by fishing. **II** *vtr* to live through. **III** *nm* life.

vivito,-a *adj fam* **v. y coleando,** alive and kicking.

vivo,-a I *adj* **1** alive; **de viva voz,** verbally, by word of mouth; **en v.,** (*programa*) live; *fam* **es el v. retrato** *o* **la viva imagen de,** she is the spitting image of. **2 al rojo v.,** red-hot. **3** (*vivaz*) lively, vivacious. **4** (*listo*) sharp, clever. **5** (*color*) vivid, bright. **6** (*descripción*) lively, graphic. **II** *nm* los vivos, the living.

Vizcaya *n* **el golfo de V.,** the Bay of Biscay.

V²B² *abr de* visto bueno.

vocablo *nm* word, term.

vocabulario *nm* vocabulary.

vocación *nf* vocation, calling; **con v. europea,** with leanings towards Europe.

vocacional *adj* vocational.

vocal I *nf Ling* vowel. **II** *nmf* member.

vocalista *nmf Mús* vocalist, singer.

vocalizar [4] *vtr & vi* to vocalize.

voceador,-a *nm,f Am* reporter.

vocerío *nm* shouting.

vocero,-a *nm,f Am* spokesperson; (*hombre*) spokesman; (*mujer*) spokeswoman.

vociferante *adj* vociferous.

vociferar *vtr & vi* to vociferate.

vodka *nm* vodka.

vol. *abr de* volumen, volume, vol.

volado,-a *nm,f fam* **estar v.,** to have a screw loose.

volador,-a *adj* flying.

volandas (en) *loc adv* (*por el aire*) in the air, flying through the air.

volante I *nm* **1** *Aut* steering wheel; **ir al v.,** to be driving; **un as del v.,** a motor-racing champion. **2** *Cost* frill, ruffle. **3** *Med* note. **II** *adj* flying; **platillo v.,** flying saucer.

volantín *nm Am* (*cometa*) small kite.

volar [2] **I** *vi* **1** to fly; *fig* **lo hizo volando,** he did it in a flash. **2** *fam* (*desaparecer*) to disappear, vanish. **II** *vtr* (*edificios*) to blow up; (*caja fuerte*) to blow open; *Min* to blast. **III volarse** *vr* (*papel etc*) to be blown away.

volátil *adj* volatile.

volatinero,-a *nm,f* acrobat.

volcán *nm* volcano.

volcánico,-a *adj* volcanic.

volcar [2] **I** *vtr* **1** (*cubo etc*) to knock over; (*barco, bote*) to capsize. **2** (*vaciar*) to empty out. **3** (*tiempo*) to invest. **II** *vi* (*coche*) to turn over; (*barco*) to capsize. **III volcarse** *vr* **1** (*vaso, jarra*) to fall over, tip over; (*coche*) to turn over; (*barco*) to capsize. **2** *fig* **v. con,** to do one's utmost for.

voleibol *nm* volleyball.

voleo *nm fig* **a(l) v.,** at random, haphazardly.

voltaje *nm* voltage.

voltear **I** *vtr* to turn down. **II** *vi* to turn over, roll over.

voltereta *nf* somersault.

voltio *nm* volt.

voluble *adj* fickle, changeable.
volumen *nm* volume.
voluminoso,-a *adj* voluminous; *(enorme)* massive, bulky.
voluntad *nf* will; **fuerza de v.**, willpower; **tiene mucha v.**, he is very strong-willed; **a v.**, at will.
voluntario,-a I *adj* voluntary; **ofrecerse v.**, to volunteer. **II** *nm,f* volunteer.
voluntarioso,-a *adj* willing.
voluptuoso,-a *adj* voluptuous.
volver [4] *(pp* **vuelto)** **I** *vi* 1 to return; *(venir)* to come back; *(ir)* to go back; **v. en sí**, to come round, recover consciousness. 2 **v. a hacer algo**, to do sth again. **II** *vtr* 1 *(convertir)* to turn, make; **me vas a v. loco**, you are driving me mad. 2 *(dar vuelta a)* to turn; *(boca abajo)* to turn upside down; *(de fuera adentro)* to turn inside out; *(de atrás adelante)* to turn back to front; *(dar la vuelta a)* to turn over; **volverle la espalda a algn**, to turn one's back on sb; *fig* **v. la vista atrás**, to look back; **al v. la esquina**, on turning the corner. **III volverse** *vr* 1 to turn. 2 *(regresar)* *(venir)* to come back; *(ir)* to go back. 3 *(convertirse)* to become; **v. loco -a**, to go mad.
vomitar I *vi* to vomit, be sick; **tengo ganas de v.**, I feel sick, I want to be sick. **II** *vtr* to vomit, bring up.
vómito *nm (lo vomitado)* vomit; *(acción)* vomiting.
vomitona *nf fam* vomit.
voracidad *nf* voracity, voraciousness.
vorágine *nf* whirlpool; *fig* maelstrom.
voraz *adj* voracious; *fig* raging, fierce.
vórtice *nm* vortex.
vos *pron pers* 1 *arc (usted)* ye, you. 2 *Am (tú)* you.
vosotros,-as *pron pers pl* 1 *(sujeto)* you. 2 *(con prep)* you; **entre v.**, among yourselves; **sin vosotras**, without you.
votación *nf* 1 *(voto)* vote, ballot. 2 *(acción)* voting.
votante *nmf* voter.
votar *vi* to vote; **v. a algn**, to vote (for) sb.
voto *nm* 1 vote; **tener v.**, to have the right to vote; **v. secreto**, secret ballot. 2 *Rel* vow.
vox *nf* **esto es v. populi**, this is common knowledge.

voy *indic pres* → **ir**.
voz *nf* 1 voice; **en v. alta**, aloud; **en v. baja**, in a low voice; **a media v.**, in a low voice, softly; **de viva v.**, verbally. 2 *(grito)* shout; **a voces**, shouting; **dar voces**, to shout; *fig* **estar pidiendo algo a voces**, to be crying out for sth; *fig* **secreto a voces**, open secret; **a v. en grito**, at the top of one's voice. 3 **no tener ni v. ni voto**, to have no say in the matter; *fig* **llevar la v. cantante**, to rule the roost. 4 *Gram* **v. pasiva**, passive voice.
vudú *nm* voodoo.
vuelco *nm* upset, tumble; **dar un v.**, *(coche)* to overturn; *fig* **me dio un v. el corazón**, my heart missed a beat.
vuelo *nm* 1 flight; **v. chárter/regular**, charter/scheduled flight; **v. sin motor**, gliding; **v. con cazarlas** *o* **cogerlas al v.**, to be quick on the uptake. 2 *Cost* **una falda de v.**, a full skirt.
vuelta *nf* 1 *(regreso)* return; *(viaje)* return journey; **a v. de correo**, by return post; **estar de v.**, to be back; *Dep* **partido de v.**, return match. 2 *(giro)* turn; *(en carreras)* lap; *(paseo)* tour; **dar media v.**, to turn round; *fig* **la cabeza me da vueltas**, my head is spinning; *fig* **no le des más vueltas**, stop worrying about it; **v. de campana**, somersault. 3 *(dinero)* change. 4 **dar una v.**, *(a pie)* to go for a walk *o* stroll; *(en coche)* to go for a drive *o* a spin (in the car). 5 *fig* **no tiene v. de hoja**, there's no doubt about it.
vuelto,-a I *adj* jersey de cuello v., roll-neck sweater. **II** *nm Am* change.
vuestro,-a I *adj pos (antes del sustantivo)* your; *(después del sustantivo)* of yours; **v. libro**, your book; **un amigo v.**, a friend of yours. **II** *pron pos* yours; **éstos son los vuestros**, these are yours; **lo v.**, what is yours, what belongs to you.
vulgar *adj* 1 vulgar. 2 **el término v.**, the everyday term. ◆**vulgarmente** *adv* **v. llamado**, commonly known as.
vulgaridad *nf* vulgarity.
vulgarizar [4] *vtr (popularizar)* to popularize.
vulgo *nm* **el v.**, the common people *pl*; *pey* the masses.
vulnerable *adj* vulnerable.
vulnerar *vtr (ley, acuerdo)* to violate.
vulva *nf* vulva.

W

W, w [uβe'δoβle] *nf (la letra)* W, w.
W *abr de* vatio**(s)**, Watt, Watts, W.
walkie-talkie *nm* walkie-talkie.
walkman® *nm* walkman®.
wáter *nm (pl* **wáteres)** *fam* toilet.

waterpolo *nm* water polo.
whisky *nm (escocés)* whisky; *(irlandés, US)* whiskey.
windsurf, windsurfing *nm* windsurfing.
windsurfista *nmf* windsurfer.

X

X, x ['ekis] *nf (la letra)* X, x.
xenofobia *nf* xenophobia.
xenófobo,-a I *adj* xenophobic. **II** *nm,f* xe-
nophobe.
xerografía *nf* xerography.
xilófono *nm* xylophone.

Y

Y, y [iɣri'eɣa] *nf (la letra)* Y, y.
y *conj* **1** and; **una chica alta y morena,** a
tall, dark-haired girl; **son las tres y
cuarto,** it's a quarter past three. **2** *¿y
qué?,* so what?; *¿y si no llega a tiempo?,*
what if he doesn't arrive in time?; *¿y tú?,*
what about you?; *¿y eso?,* how come?; **y
eso que,** although, even though; **¡y
tanto!,** you bet!, and how!; → **e.**
ya *adv* **1** already; **ya lo sabía,** I already
knew; **ya en la Edad Media,** as far back
as the Middle Ages. **2** *(ahora mismo)* now;
es preciso actuar ya, it is vital that we
act now; **¡hazlo ya!,** do it at once!; **ya
mismo,** right away. **3** *(en el futuro)* **ya hablaremos luego,** we'll talk about it later;
ya nos veremos, see you!; **ya verás,**
you'll see. **4 ya no,** no longer; **ya no viene por aquí,** he doesn't come round here
any more. **5** *(refuerza el verbo)* **ya era
hora,** about time too; **ya lo creo,** of
course, I should think so; **¡ya voy!,** coming!; **¡ya está!,** that's it! **II** *conj* **ya que,**
since.
yacaré *nm Am* alligator, cayman.
yacer [33] *vi* to lie, be lying.
yacimiento *nm* bed, deposit; **yacimientos
petrolíferos,** oilfields.
yaguar *nm* jaguar.
yanqui *pey* **I** *adj* Yankee. **II** *nmf* Yankee,
Yank.
yarar. á *nm Am* large poisonous snake.
yarda *nf* yard.
yate *nm* yacht.
yaya *nf Am Bot* lancewood; *fam (abuela)*
granny.
yedra *nf* → **hiedra.**
yegua *nf* mare.
yema *nf* **1** *(de huevo)* yolk. **2** *Bot* bud. **3**

y. del dedo, fingertip. **4** *Culin* sweet
made from sugar and egg yolk.
Yemen *n* Yemen.
yen *nm (moneda)* yen.
yendo *ger* → **ir.**
yerba *nf* **1** → **hierba. 2** *Am* maté.
yerbatero,-a *Am* **I** *nm,f (curandero)* witch
doctor who uses herbs. **II** *adj* maté.
yermo,-a *adj* **1** *(baldío)* barren, uncultivated. **2** *(despoblado)* deserted, uninhabited.
yerno *nm* son-in-law.
yerro *indic pres* → **errar.**
yeso *nm* **1** *Geol* gypsum. **2** *Constr* plaster.
Yibuti *n* Djibouti.
yiu-yitsu *nm* jujitsu.
yo *pron pers* I; **entre tú y yo,** between you
and me; **¿quién es? - soy yo,** who is it? -
it's me; **yo no,** not me; **yo que tú,** if I
were you; **yo mismo,** I myself.
yodo *nm* iodine.
yoga *nm* yoga.
yogur *nm* yogurt, yoghurt.
yogurtera *nf* yoghurt maker.
yonqui *nmf arg* junkie, drug addict.
yoyo, yoyó *nm* yo-yo.
yuca *nf* yucca.
Yucatán *n* Yucatan.
yudo *nm* judo.
yudoka *nmf* judoka.
yugo *nm* yoke.
Yugoslavia *n* Yugoslavia.
yugoslavo,-a, yugoeslavo,-a *adj & nm,f*
Yugoslav, Yugoslavian.
yugular *nf* jugular.
yunque *nm* anvil.
yunta *nf* yoke *o* team of oxen.
yuxtaponer [19] *(pp* **yuxtapuesto)** *vtr* to
juxtapose.
yuxtaposición *nf* juxtaposition.

Z

Z, z ['θeta] *nf (la letra)* Z, z.
zafarse *vr (librarse)* to get away (**de,**
from), escape (**de,** from).
zafio,-a *adj* uncouth.
zafiro *nm* sapphire.
zaga *nf* **a la z.,** behind, at the rear.
zaguán *nm* hall, hallway.

zaherir [5] *vtr* to hurt.
zahúrda *nf* pigsty.
zaino,-a *adj (caballo)* chestnut; *(toro)*
black.
Zaire *n* Zaire.
zalamería *nf* flattery.
zalamero,-a I *nm,f* flatterer, fawner. **II**

adj flattering, fawning.

zamarra *nf (prenda)* sheepskin jacket.

Zambia *n* Zambia.

zambo,-a I *adj* 1 *(patizambo)* knock-kneed. 2 *Am (persona)* half Indian and half Negro. II *nm,f Am (persona)* person who is half Indian and half Negro.

zambomba *nf* kind of primitive drum.

zambullida *nf* plunge.

zambullirse *vr* to plunge.

zamparse *vr fam* to gobble down.

zanahoria *nf* carrot.

zancada *nf* stride.

zancadilla *nf* ponerle la z. a algn, to trip sb up.

zanco *nm* stilt.

zancudo,-a I *adj* 1 long-legged. 2 *Orn* wading; **ave zancuda**, wading bird, wader. II *nm Am* mosquito.

zángano,-a I *nm (insecto)* drone. II *nm,f fam (persona)* idler, lazybones *inv*.

zanja *nf* ditch, trench.

zanjar *vtr (asunto)* to settle.

zapallo *nm Am* pumpkin, calabash.

zapata *nf* 1 *(cuña)* wedge. 2 *Téc* shoe.

zapatear *vi* to tap one's feet.

zapatería *nf* shoe shop.

zapatero,-a *nm,f (vendedor)* shoe dealer; *(fabricante)* shoemaker, cobbler.

zapatilla *nf* slipper; **zapatillas de deporte**, trainers.

zapato *nm* shoe; **zapatos de tacón**, high-heeled shoes.

zar *nm* czar, tsar.

Zaragoza *n* Saragossa.

zaragozano,-a I *adj* of *o* from Saragossa. II *nm,f* native *o* inhabitant of Saragossa.

zarandear *vtr* to shake.

zarandeo *nm* shaking.

zarcillo *nm* 1 *(pendiente)* earring. 2 *Bot* tendril.

zarina *nf* czarina, tsarina.

zarpa *nf* claw.

zarpar *vi* to weigh anchor, set sail.

zarpazo *nm* clawing; **dar** *o* **pegar un z. a**, to claw.

zarza *nf* bramble, blackberry bush.

zarzal *nm* bramble patch.

zarzamora *nf (zarza)* blackberry bush; *(fruto)* blackberry.

zarzuela *nf* 1 Spanish operetta. 2 **la Z.**, royal residence in Madrid. 3 *Culin* fish stew.

zenit *nm* zenith.

zigzag *nm (pl zigzags o zigzagues)* zigzag.

zigzaguear *vi* to zigzag.

Zimbabwe *n* Zimbabwe.

zinc *nm* zinc.

zócalo *nm* 1 *(de pared)* skirting board. 2 *(pedestal)* plinth.

zodiaco, zodíaco *nm* zodiac; **signo del z.**, sign of the zodiac.

zona *nf* zone; *(región)* region; **z. verde**, park.

zoo *nm* zoo.

zoología *nf* zoology.

zoológico,-a I *adj* zoological; **parque z.**, zoo. II *nm* zoo.

zoom *nm Cin Fot* zoom.

zopenco,-a *nm,f fam* dope, half-wit.

zopilote *nm Am* buzzard.

zoquete *nmf fam* blockhead.

zorra *nf* 1 vixen. 2 *fam* slut.

zorro,-a I *nm* fox. II *adj fam* 1 *(astuto)* cunning, sly. 2 *vulg* **no tener ni zorra (idea)**, not to have the slightest idea.

zorzal *nm Orn* thrush.

zozobrar *vi* to be in danger of going under.

zueco *nm* clog.

zumbado,-a *adj fam* crazy, mad.

zumbar I *vi* to buzz, hum; **me zumban los oídos**, my ears are buzzing; *fam* **salir zumbando**, to zoom off. II *vtr fam* to thrash.

zumbido *nm* buzzing, humming.

zumo *nm* juice.

zurcir [3] *vtr Cost* to darn; *fam* **¡que te zurzan!**, go to hell!

zurda *nf (mano)* left hand.

zurdo,-a I *nm,f (persona)* left-handed person. II *adj* left-handed.

zurrar *vtr (pegar)* to beat, flog.

zutano,-a *nm,f (persona)* so-and-so; *(hombre)* what's-his-name; *(mujer)* what's-her-name.

English - Spanish
Inglés - Español

TABLA DE VERBOS IRREGULARES INGLESES

American forms have been indicated by *. Unusual, archaic or literary forms are given in brackets.

infinitive	past tense	past participle
abide	abided, (abode)	abided
arise	arose	arisen
be	was, were	been
awake	awoke, awaked	awoken, (awaked)
bear	bore	borne
beat	beat	beaten
become	became	become
befall	befell	befallen
begin	began	begun
behold	beheld	beheld
bend	bent	bent
beseech	besought	besought
bet	bet, betted	bet, betted
bid (offer)	bid	bid
bid (command)	bade	bidden
bind	bound	bound
bite	bit	bitten
bleed	bled	bled
blow	blew	blown
break	broke	broken
breed	bred	bred
bring	brought	brought
broadcast	broadcast	broadcast
build	built	built
burn	burnt, burned	burnt, burned
burst	burst	burst
buy	bought	bought
cast	cast	cast
catch	caught	caught
choose	chose	chosen
cling	clung	clung
clothe	clothed, (clad)	clothed, (clad)
come	came	come
cost	cost	cost
creep	crept	crept
crow	crowed, (crew)	crowed
cut	cut	cut
deal	dealt	dealt
dig	dug	dug
dive	dived, dove*	dived
do	did	done
draw	drew	drawn
dream	dreamt, dreamed	dreamt, dreamed
drink	drank	drunk
drive	drove	driven
dwell	dwelt, dwelled	dwelt, dwelled
eat	ate	eaten
fall	fell	fallen
feed	fed	fed
feel	felt	felt
fight	fought	fought
find	found	found

fit	fit*, fitted	fit*, fitted
flee	fled	fled
fling	flung	flung
fly	flew	flown
forbid	forbad(e)	forbidden
forget	forgot	forgotten
forgive	forgave	forgiven
forsake	forsook	forsaken
freeze	froze	frozen
get	got	got, gotten*
give	gave	given
go	went	gone
grind	ground	ground
grow	grew	grown
hang	hung, hanged	hung, hanged
have	had	had
hear	heard	heard
hide	hid	hidden
hit	hit	hit
hold	held	held
hurt	hurt	hurt
keep	kept	kept
kneel	knelt, kneeled	knelt, kneeled
know	knew	known
lay	laid	laid
lead	led	led
lean	leant, leaned	leant, leaned
leap	leapt, leaped	leapt, leaped
learn	learnt, learned	learnt, learned
leave	left	left
lend	lent	lent
let	let	let
lie	lay	lain
light	lit, lighted	lit, lighted
lose	lost	lost
make	made	made
mean	meant	meant
meet	met	met
mow	mowed	mown, mowed
pay	paid	paid
plead	pled*, pleaded	pled*, pleaded
put	put	put
quit	quit, (quitted)	quit, (quitted)
read	read [red]	read [red]
rend	rent	rent
rid	rid	rid
ride	rode	ridden
ring	rang	rung
rise	rose	risen
run	ran	run
saw	sawed	sawn, sawed
say	said	said
see	saw	seen
seek	sought	sought
sell	sold	sold
send	sent	sent
set	set	set
sew	sewed	sewn, sewed

shake	shook	shaken
shear	sheared	shorn, sheared
shed	shed	shed
shine	shone	shone
shoe	shod, shoed	shod, shoed
shoot	shot	shot
show	showed	shown, showed
shrink	shrank, shrunk	shrunk
shut	shut	shut
sing	sang	sung
sink	sank	sunk
sit	sat	sat
slay	slew	slain
sleep	slept	slept
slide	slid	slid
sling	slung	slung
slink	slunk	slunk
slit	slit	slit
smell	smelt, smelled	smelt, smelled
sneak	snuck*, sneaked	snuck*, sneaked
sow	sowed	sown, sowed
speak	spoke	spoken
speed	sped, speeded	sped, speeded
spell	spelt, spelled	spelt, spelled
spend	spent	spent
spill	spilt, spilled	spilt, spilled
spin	spun	spun
spit	spat, spit*	spat, spit*
split	split	split
spoil	spoilt, spoiled	spoilt, spoiled
spread	spread	spread
spring	sprang	sprung
stand	stood	stood
steal	stole	stolen
stick	stuck	stuck
sting	stung	stung
stink	stank	stunk
strew	strewed	strewn, strewed
stride	strode	stridden
strike	struck	struck
string	strung	strung
strive	strove	striven
swear	swore	sworn
sweat	sweat*, sweated	sweat*, sweated
sweep	swept	swept
swell	swelled	swollen, swelled
swim	swam	swum
swing	swung	swung
take	took	taken
teach	taught	taught
tear	tore	torn
tell	told	told
think	thought	thought
thrive	thrived, (throve)	thrived, (thriven)
throw	threw	thrown
thrust	thrust	thrust
tread	trod	trodden
understand	understood	understood

undertake	undertook	undertaken
wake	woke	woken
wear	wore	worn
weave	wove	woven
weep	wept	wept
wet	wet, wetted	wet, wetted
win	won	won
wind	wound	wound
wring	wrung	wrung
write	wrote	written

Fonética Inglesa

En este diccionario la transcripción fonética de las palabras inglesas se basa en el sistema de la Asociación Fonética Internacional (AFI) con algunas modificaciones. Cada entrada viene seguida de su correspondiente transcripción fonética entre corchetes ([ ]). El acento primario se indica mediante un ' delante de la sílaba acentuada.

Las consonantes

[p]	*p*en
[b]	*b*ill
[t]	*t*ent
[d]	*d*esk
[k]	*c*ar
[g]	*g*oal
[tʃ]	*t*eacher
[dʒ]	*a*ge
[f]	*f*ish
[v]	ha*v*e
[θ]	me*th*od
[ð]	mo*th*er
[s]	i*c*y
[z]	ea*s*y
[ʃ]	*sh*oe
[ʒ]	mea*s*ure
[h]	*h*at
[m]	*m*ilk
[n]	*n*ame
[ŋ]	si*ng*
[l]	*l*ight
[r]	*r*ead
[j]	*y*oghurt
[w]	*w*atch
[x]	lo*ch* (como en legión)
[ʳ]	se llama *'linking r'* y se encuentra únicamente a final de palabra. Se pronuncia sólo cuando la palabra siguiente empieza por una vocal: mo*th*er ['mʌðəʳ]

Las vocales y los diptongos

[iː]	sh*ee*p
[ɪ]	sh*i*p, hous*e*s
[e]	b*e*d
[æ]	c*a*t
[ɑː]	f*a*ther
[ɒ]	d*o*g
[ɔː]	h*o*rse
[ʊ]	w*o*man
[uː]	bl*ue*
[ʌ]	c*u*p
[ɜː]	*ea*rth
[ə]	*a*bout
[ə]	opcional. En algunos casos se pronuncia y en otros se omite: trifle ['traɪfəl]
[eɪ]	t*a*ble
[əʊ]	g*o*
[aɪ]	t*i*me
[aʊ]	h*ou*se
[ɔɪ]	b*oy*
[ɪə]	f*ie*rce
[eə]	c*a*re
[ʊə]	d*u*ring

A

A, a [eɪ] *n* **1** (*the letter*) A, a *f*. **2** *Mus* la *m*.

a [eɪ, *unstressed* ə] *indef art* (*before vowel or silent h* **an**) **1** un, una; **a man/a woman**, un hombre/una mujer; **he has a big nose**, tiene la nariz grande. **2** (*omitted in Span*) half a litre/an hour, medio litro/media hora; **a hundred/thousand people**, cien/mil personas; **let's have a drink**, vamos a beber algo; **he's a teacher**, es profesor; **what a pity**, qué pena. **3** (*each*) 60 pence a kilo, 60 peniques el kilo; **to eat grapes two at a time**, comer las uvas de dos en dos; **three times a week**, tres veces a la semana. **4** (*a certain*) un or una tal; **a Mr Rees phoned**, llamó un tal Sr. Rees.

AA [eɪ'eɪ] **1** *abbr of* **Alcoholics Anonymous**, Alcohólicos Anónimos, AA. **2** *abbr of* **Automobile Association**, ≈ Automóvil Club *m*, AC.

AAA [eɪeɪ'eɪ] **1** *GB abbr of* **Amateur Athletic Association**, Asociación Atlética Amateur, AAA. **2** *US abbr of* **Automobile Association of America**, ≈ Automóvil Club *m*, AC.

aback [ə'bæk] *adv* **to be taken a.**, quedarse de una pieza (**by**, por).

abandon [ə'bændən] **I** *n* desenfreno *m*; **with reckless a.**, desenfrenadamente. **II** *vtr* (*child*) abandonar; (*job*) dejar; (*project*) renunciar a.

abase [ə'beɪs] *vtr* **to a. oneself**, humillarse.

abashed [ə'bæʃt] *adj* desconcertado,-a.

abate [ə'beɪt] *vi* (*anger*) apaciguarse; (*storm*) amainar.

abattoir ['æbətwɑːr] *n* matadero *m*.

abbey ['æbɪ] *n* abadía *f*.

abbot ['æbət] *n* abad *m*.

abbreviate [ə'briːvɪeɪt] *vtr* abreviar.

abbreviation [əbriːvɪ'eɪʃən] *n* abreviatura *f*.

abdicate ['æbdɪkeɪt] *vtr & vi* abdicar.

abdication [æbdɪ'keɪʃən] *n* abdicación *f*.

abdomen ['æbdəmən] *n* abdomen *m*.

abduct [æb'dʌkt] *vtr* raptar, secuestrar.

aberration [æbə'reɪʃən] *n* aberración *f*.

abet [ə'bet] *vtr* **to aid and a. sb**, ser cómplice de algn.

abeyance [ə'beɪəns] *n* **to be in a.**, estar en desuso.

abhor [əb'hɔːr] *vtr* aborrecer.

abhorrent [əb'hɒrənt] *adj* aborrecible.

abide [ə'baɪd] *vtr* aguantar; **I can't a. it**, no lo aguanto. ◆**abide by** *vtr* (*promise*) cumplir con; (*rules*) atenerse a.

ability [ə'bɪlɪtɪ] *n* (*capability*) capacidad *f*, aptitud *f*; (*talent*) talento *m*.

abject ['æbdʒekt] *adj* (*state*) miserable; (*apology*) rastrero,-a.

ablaze [ə'bleɪz] *adj & adv* en llamas, ardiendo.

able ['eɪbəl] *adj* (*capable*) capaz; **will you be a. to come on Tuesday?**, ¿podrás venir el martes?

able-bodied [eɪbəl'bɒdɪd] *adj* sano,-a; **a.-b. seaman**, marinero *m* de primera.

abnormal [æb'nɔːməl] *adj* anormal. ◆**abnormally** *adv* anormalmente; (*large*) extraordinariamente.

aboard [ə'bɔːd] **I** *adv* a bordo; **to go a.**, (*ship*) embarcarse; (*train*) subir. **II** *prep* a bordo de.

abode [ə'bəʊd] *n* *Jur* **of no fixed a.** sin domicilio fijo.

abolish [ə'bɒlɪʃ] *vtr* abolir.

abolition [æbə'lɪʃən] *n* abolición *f*.

abominable [ə'bɒmɪnəbəl] *adj* abominable; (*dreadful*) terrible.

aborigine [æbə'rɪdʒɪnɪ] *n* aborigen *mf* australiano,-a.

abort [ə'bɔːt] **I** *vtr Med* hacer abortar; *fig* (*plan etc*) archivar. **II** *vi Med* abortar.

abortion [ə'bɔːʃən] *n Med* aborto *m*; **a. law**, ley *f* del aborto; **to have an a.**, abortar.

abortive [ə'bɔːtɪv] *adj* (*plan*) fracasado,-a; (*attempt*) frustrado,-a.

abound [ə'baʊnd] *vi* **to a. in** or **with**, abundar en.

about [ə'baʊt] *adv & prep* **1** (*concerning*) acerca de, sobre; **a programme a. Paris**, un programa sobre París; **to be worried a. sth**, estar preocupado,-a por algo; **to speak a. sth**, hablar de algo; **what's it all a.?**, (*what's happening?*) ¿qué pasa?; (*story etc*) ¿de qué se trata?; *fam* **how a. a game of tennis?**, ¿qué te parece un partido de tenis? **2** (*around*) por todas partes; **don't leave things lying a.**, no dejes las cosas por medio; **there's nobody a.**, no hay nadie; **to look a.**, mirar alrededor; **to rush a.**, correr de un lado para otro; **we went for a walk a. the town**, dimos una vuelta por el pueblo. **3** (*approximately*) más o menos; **it's a. 3 o'clock**, son más o menos las 3; **it's a. time you got up**, ya es hora de que te levantes; **it's just a. finished**, está casi terminado; **she's a. 40**, tiene unos 40 años. **4** it's **a. to start**, está a punto de empezar; **not to be a. to do sth**, no estar dispuesto,-a a hacer algo.

about-turn [əbaʊt'tɜːn, əbaʊt'fers], *US* **about-face** *n* media vuelta *f*; **to do an a.-t.**, dar media vuelta; *fig* cambiar de idea por completo.

above [ə'bʌv] *adv & prep* **1** (*higher than*) encima de, sobre, arriba; **100 metres a. sea level**, 100 metros sobre el nivel del mar; **it's a. the door**, está encima de la puerta; **the flat a.**, el piso de arriba. **2** (*greater than*) superior (a); **amounts a. £10**, cantidades superiores a las 10 libras; *fig* **a policy imposed from a.**, una política impuesta desde arriba. **3 a. all**, sobre todo; **he's not a. stealing**, es capaz incluso de robar. **4** (*in book etc*) más arriba.

above-board [ə'bʌvbɔːd] *adj* (*scheme*) legítimo,-a.

above-mentioned [ə'bʌvmenʃənd] *adj* susodicho,-a.

abrasive [ə'breɪsɪv] **I** *adj* (*substance*) abrasivo,-a; *fig* (*voice, wit etc*) cáustico,-a. **II** *n* abrasivo *m*.

abreast [ə'brest] *adv* **to walk 3 a.**, ir de 3 en fondo; *fig* **to keep a. of things**, mantenerse al día.

abridged [ə'brɪdʒd] *adj* (*book*) abreviado,-a.

abroad [ə'brɔːd] *adv* **to be a.**, estar en el extranjero; **to go a.**, irse al extranjero.

abrupt [ə'brʌpt] *adj* (*manner*) brusco,-a; (*tone*) áspero,-a; (*change*) súbito,-a. **◆abruptly** *adv* (*act*) bruscamente; (*speak*) con aspereza; (*change*) repentinamente.

abscess ['æbses] *n* absceso *m*; (*on gum*) flemón *m*.

abscond [əb'skɒnd] *vi* huir.

absence ['æbsəns] *n* (*of person*) ausencia *f*; (*of thing*) falta *f*.

absent ['æbsənt] *adj* ausente; *fig* **an a. look**, una mirada distraída. **◆absently** *adv* distraídamente.

absentee [æbsən'tiː] *n* ausente *mf*.

absenteeism [æbsən'tiːɪzəm] *n* absentismo *m*.

absent-minded [æbsənt'maɪndɪd] *adj* distraído,-a.

absolute ['æbsəluːt] *adj* absoluto,-a; (*failure*) total; (*truth*) puro,-a; **it's an a. disgrace**, es una auténtica vergüenza. **◆absolutely I** *adv* (*completely*) completamente; **a.** (*wrong*), totalmente equivocado,-a; **a. not**, en absoluto; **you're a. right**, tienes toda la razón. **II** *interj* **a.!**, ¡desde luego!

absolve [əb'zɒlv] *vt* absolver (*from*, de).

absorb [əb'zɔːb] *vt* (*liquid*) absorber; (*sound, blow*) amortiguar; *fig* **to be absorbed in sth**, estar absorto,-a en algo.

absorbing [əb'zɔːbɪŋ] *adj* (*book, work*) absorbente.

abstain [əb'steɪn] *vi* abstenerse (*from*, de).

abstemious [əb'stiːmɪəs] *adj* abstemio,-a.

abstention [əb'stenʃən] *n* abstención *f*.

abstinence ['æbstɪnəns] *n* abstinencia *f*.

abstract ['æbstrækt] **I** *adj* abstracto,-a. **II** *n* (*of thesis etc*) resumen *m*.

abstruse [əb'struːs] *adj* abstruso,-a.

absurd [əb'sɜːd] *adj* absurdo,-a.

abundance [ə'bʌndəns] *n* abundancia *f*.

abundant [ə'bʌndənt] *adj* abundante,

rico,-a (**in**, en).

abuse [ə'bjuːs] **I** *n* **1** (*ill-treatment*) malos tratos; (*misuse*) abuso *m*. **2** (*insults*) injurias *fpl*. **II** [ə'bjuːz] *vt* **1** (*ill-treat*) maltratar; (*misuse*) abusar de. **2** (*insult*) injuriar.

abusive [əb'juːsɪv] *adj* (*insulting*) insultante.

abysmal [ə'bɪzməl] *adj* (*conditions*) extremo,-a; *fam* (*very bad*) fatal, pésimo,-a.

abyss [ə'bɪs] *n* abismo *m*; *fig* extremo *m*.

AC ['eɪsiː] *abbr* of **alternating current**, corriente alterna, CA.

academic [ækə'demɪk] **I** *adj* académico, -a; (*career*) universitario,-a; (*discussion*) teórico,-a; **a. year**, año *m* escolar. **II** *n* académico,-a *m,f*.

academy [ə'kædəmɪ] *n* (*society*) academia *f*; *Educ* instituto *m* de enseñanza media; **a. of music**, conservatorio *m*.

accede [æk'siːd] *vi* acceder (**to**, a).

accelerate [æk'seləreɪt] **I** *vtr* (*engine*) acelerar; (*step*) aligerar. **II** *vi* (*car, engine*) acelerar.

acceleration [ækselə'reɪʃən] *n* aceleración *f*.

accelerator [æk'seləreɪtər] *n* acelerador *m*.

accent ['æksənt] *n* acento *m*.

accentuate [æk'sentjʊeɪt] *vtr* subrayar.

accept [ək'sept] *vtr & vi* aceptar; (*theory*) admitir; **do you a. that ...?**, ¿estás de acuerdo en que ...?

acceptable [ək'septəbl] *adj* (*satisfactory*) aceptable; (*tolerable*) admisible.

acceptance [ək'septəns] *n* (*act of accepting*) aceptación *f*; (*good reception*) aprobación *f*.

access ['ækses] *n* acceso *m*; **a. road**, carretera *f* de acceso; **to have a. to sth**, tener libre acceso a algo.

accessible [ək'sesəbl] *adj* (*place, position*) accesible; (*person*) asequible.

accession [ək'seʃən] *n* subida *f* (al trono).

accessory [ək'sesərɪ] *n* **1** *Jur* cómplice *mf*. **2 accessories**, accesorios *mpl*; (*for outfit*) complementos *mpl*.

accident ['æksɪdənt] *n* accidente *m*; (*coincidence*) casualidad *f*; **it was an a. on my part**, lo hice sin querer; **car a.**, accidente *m* de carretera; **by a.**, por casualidad.

accidental [æksɪ'dentəl] *adj* fortuito,-a; (*unintended*) imprevisto,-a. **◆accidentally** *adv* (*by chance*) por casualidad; **he did it a.**, lo hizo sin querer.

accident-prone ['æksɪdəntprəʊn] *adj* propenso,-a a los accidentes.

acclaim [ə'kleɪm] **I** *n* aclamación *f*. **II** *vtr* aclamar.

acclimatize [ə'klaɪmətaɪz] *vtr* aclimatar.

acclimatized [ə'klaɪmətaɪzd] *adj* aclimatado,-a; **to become a.**, aclimatarse.

accolade [ˈækəleɪd] n elogio m.

accommodate [əˈkɒmədeɪt] vtr 1 (guests) alojar. 2 to a. sb's wishes, complacer a algn.

accommodating [əˈkɒmədeɪtɪŋ] adj (obliging) complaciente; (understanding) comprensivo,-a.

accommodation [əkɒməˈdeɪʃən] n (US also **accommodations**) (lodgings) alojamiento m.

accompany [əˈkʌmpənɪ] vtr acompañar.

accomplice [əˈkʌmplɪs] n cómplice mf.

accomplish [əˈkʌmplɪʃ] vtr (aim) conseguir; (task, mission) llevar a cabo.

accomplished [əˈkʌmplɪʃt] adj dotado,-a, experto,-a.

accomplishment [əˈkʌmplɪʃmənt] n 1 (of task) realización f; (of duty) cumplimiento m. 2 **accomplishments**, (talents) dotes fpl.

accord [əˈkɔːd] I n (agreement) acuerdo m; of her or his own a., espontáneamente. II vtr (honour etc) conceder.

accordance [əˈkɔːdəns] n in a. with, de acuerdo con.

according [əˈkɔːdɪŋ] prep a. to, según; everything went a. to plan, todo salió conforme a los planes.

accordingly [əˈkɔːdɪŋlɪ] adv 1 to act a., (appropriately) obrar según y conforme. 2 (therefore) así pues.

accordion [əˈkɔːdɪən] n acordeón m.

account [əˈkaʊnt] n 1 (report) informe m; by all accounts, al decir de todos. 2 I was fearful on her a., sufría por ella; it's of no a., no tiene importancia; on a. of, a causa de; on no a., bajo ningún concepto; to take a. of, to take into a., tener en cuenta. 3 Com cuenta f; to keep the accounts, llevar las cuentas; accounts department, servicio m de contabilidad; to open/close an a., abrir/cancelar una cuenta; current a., cuenta corriente; a. number, número m de cuenta. ◆**account for** vtr (explain) explicar.

accountable [əˈkaʊntəbəl] adj to be a. to sb for sth, ser responsable ante algn de algo.

accountancy [əˈkaʊntənsɪ] n contabilidad f.

accountant [əˈkaʊntənt] n contable mf.

accredited [əˈkredɪtɪd] adj acreditado,-a.

accrue [əˈkruː] vi (interest) acumularse.

accumulate [əˈkjuːmjʊleɪt] I vtr acumular; (fortune) amasar. II vi acumularse.

accuracy [ˈækjʊrəsɪ] n (of number etc) exactitud f; (of shot, criticism) certeza f.

accurate [ˈækjʊrɪt] adj (number) exacto,-a; (shot, criticism) certero,-a; (answer) correcto,-a; (instrument) de precisión; (translation) fiel.

accusation [ækjʊˈzeɪʃən] n acusación f.

accuse [əˈkjuːz] vtr acusar.

accused [əˈkjuːzd] n the a., el/la acusado,-a.

accustom [əˈkʌstəm] vtr acostumbrar; to be accustomed to doing sth, estar acostumbrado,-a a hacer algo.

ace [eɪs] n 1 Cards & fig as m. 2 Ten ace m.

acetate [ˈæsɪteɪt] n acetato m.

acetone [ˈæsɪtəʊn] n acetona f.

ache [eɪk] I n dolor m; **aches and pains**, achaques mpl. II vi doler; **my back aches**, me duele la espalda.

achieve [əˈtʃiːv] vtr (attain) conseguir, alcanzar; (accomplish) llevar a cabo, realizar.

achievement [əˈtʃiːvmənt] n (attainment) logro m; (completion) realización f; (feat) hazaña f.

acid [ˈæsɪd] I adj ácido,-a; (taste) agrio,-a; (remark) mordaz; a. rain, lluvia ácida; fig a. test, prueba decisiva. II n ácido m.

acknowledge [əkˈnɒlɪdʒ] vtr 1 (recognize) reconocer; (claim, defeat) admitir; (present) agradecer; (letter) acusar recibo de. 2 (greet) saludar.

acknowledgement [əkˈnɒlɪdʒmənt] n 1 (recognition) reconocimiento m; (of letter) acuse m de recibo. 2 **acknowledgements**, (in preface) menciones fpl.

acne [ˈæknɪ] n acné m.

acorn [ˈeɪkɔːn] n bellota f.

acoustic [əˈkuːstɪk] I adj acústico,-a. II npl **acoustics**, acústica f sing.

acquaint [əˈkweɪnt] vtr to a. sb with the facts, informar a algn de los detalles; to be acquainted with the procedure, estar al corriente de como se procede; to be acquainted with sb, conocer a algn.

acquaintance [əˈkweɪntəns] n 1 conocimiento m; to make sb's a., conocer a algn. 2 (person) conocido,-a m,f.

acquiesce [ækwɪˈes] vi consentir (in, en).

acquiescent [ækwɪˈesənt] adj conforme.

acquire [əˈkwaɪər] vtr adquirir.

acquisition [ækwɪˈzɪʃən] n adquisición f.

acquisitive [əˈkwɪzɪtɪv] adj codicioso,-a.

acquit [əˈkwɪt] vtr 1 Jur to a. sb of sth, absolver a algn de algo. 2 to a. oneself well, defenderse bien.

acquittal [əˈkwɪtəl] n absolución f.

acre [ˈeɪkər] n acre m (aprox 40,47 áreas).

acrid [ˈækrɪd] adj (smell, taste) acre.

acrimonious [ækrɪˈməʊnɪəs] adj (remark) cáustico,-a; (dispute) enconado,-a.

acrobat [ˈækrəbæt] n acróbata mf.

across [əˈkrɒs] I adv a través; **the river is 30 metres a.**, el río mide 30 metros de ancho; **to go a.**, atravesar; **to run a.**, atravesar corriendo. II prep 1 a través de; **they live a. the road**, viven enfrente; **to go a. the street**, cruzar la calle. 2 (at the other side of) al otro lado de.

acrylic [əˈkrɪlɪk] adj acrílico,-a.

act [ækt] I n 1 (action) acto m, acción f; a.

of God, caso m de fuerza mayor. **2** *Parl* ley f, decreto m. **3** *Theat* acto m; *(turn in show)* número m. **II** *vtr* *Theat* (part) interpretar; *(character)* representar; *fig* to **a. the fool,** hacer el tonto. **III** *vi* **1** *Theat* hacer teatro; *Cin* hacer cine; *fig* (pretend) fingir. **2** *(behave)* comportarse. **3** *(take action)* actuar, obrar; to **a. on sb's advice,** seguir el consejo de algn. **4** *(work)* funcionar; *(drug etc)* actuar; to **a. as a deterrent,** servir de disuasivo. **5** to **a. as director,** hacer de director. ◆**act out** *vtr* exteriorizar. ◆**act up** *vi fam* (machine) funcionar mal; (child) dar guerra.

acting ['æktɪŋ] **I** *adj* interino,-a. **II** *n* (profession) teatro m; **he's done some a.,** ha hecho algo de teatro.

action ['ækʃən] *n* **1** *(deed)* acción f; *Mil* acción de combate; to **be out of a.,** (person) estar fuera de servicio; (machine) estar estropeado,-a; to **take a.,** tomar medidas. **2** *Jur* demanda f. **3** *TV* a. replay, repetición f.

activate ['æktɪveɪt] *vtr* activar.

active ['æktɪv] *adj* activo,-a; *(energetic)* vigoroso,-a; *(interest)* vivo,-a; *Ling* a. voice, voz activa.

activist ['æktɪvɪst] *n* activista mf.

activity [æk'tɪvɪtɪ] *n* (of person) actividad f; (on street etc) bullicio m.

actor ['æktər] *n* actor m.

actress ['æktrɪs] *n* actriz f.

actual ['æktʃʊəl] *adj* real, verdadero,-a.

actually ['æktʃʊəlɪ] *adv* (really) en efecto, realmente; (even) incluso, hasta; (in fact) de hecho.

acumen ['ækjʊmən] *n* perspicacia f.

acupuncture ['ækjʊpʌŋktʃər] *n* acupuntura f.

acute [ə'kjuːt] *adj* agudo,-a; (pain) intenso,-a; (hearing) muy fino,-a; (shortage) grave; (mind) perspicaz.

ad [æd] *n fam* anuncio m.

AD [eɪ'diː] *abbr* de *Anno Domini,* después de Cristo, d.d.C.

adamant ['ædəmənt] *adj* firme, inflexible.

adapt [ə'dæpt] **I** *vtr* adaptar (to, a); to **a. oneself to sth,** adaptarse a algo. **II** *vi* adaptarse.

adaptable [ə'dæptəbəl] *adj* (instrument) ajustable; **he's very a.,** se amolda fácilmente a las circunstancias.

adaptation [ædəp'teɪʃən] *n* adaptación f.

adapter, adaptor [ə'dæptər] *n Elec* ladrón m.

add [æd] **I** *vtr* (numbers) sumar; (one thing to another) añadir. **II** *vi* (count) sumar. ◆**add to** *vtr* aumentar. ◆**add up I** *vtr* sumar. **II** *vi* (numbers) sumar; *fig* it **doesn't a. up,** no tiene sentido; it **doesn't a. up to much,** no es gran cosa.

added ['ædɪd] *adj* adicional.

adder ['ædər] *n* víbora f.

addict ['ædɪkt] *n* adicto,-a m,f; *fam* **television a.,** teleadicto,-a m,f.

addicted [ə'dɪktɪd] *adj* adicto,-a; to **become a. to sth,** enviciarse con algo.

addiction [ə'dɪkʃən] *n* (to gambling etc) vicio m; (to drugs) adicción f.

addictive [ə'dɪktɪv] *adj* que crea adicción.

addition [ə'dɪʃən] *n Math* adición f; (increase) aumento m; **an a. to the family,** un nuevo miembro de la familia; **in a. to,** además de.

additional [ə'dɪʃənəl] *adj* adicional.

additive ['ædɪtɪv] *n* aditivo m.

address [ə'dres] **I** *n* **1** (on letter) dirección f, señas fpl. **2** (speech) discurso m. **II** *vtr* **1** (letter) dirigir. **2** (speak to) dirigirse (to, a); **to a. the floor,** tomar la palabra. **3** (use form of address to) tratar de.

adenoids ['ædɪnɔɪdz] *npl* vegetaciones fpl (adenoideas).

adept [ə'dept] **I** *adj* experto,-a, (at, en). **II** *n* experto,-a.

adequate ['ædɪkwɪt] *adj* (enough) suficiente; (satisfactory) adecuado,-a.

adhere [əd'hɪər] *vi* **1** (stick) pegarse (to, a). ◆**adhere to** *vtr* (policy) adherirse a; (contract) cumplir con.

adherent [əd'hɪərənt] *n* partidario,-a m,f.

adhesive [əd'hiːsɪv] **I** *adj* adhesivo,-a; (sticky) pegajoso,-a; **a. tape,** cinta adhesiva. **II** *n* adhesivo m.

ad hoc [æd'hɒk] *adj* (remark) improvisado,-a; **an ad h. committee,** un comité especial.

ad infinitum [ædɪnfɪ'naɪtəm] *adv* hasta el infinito.

adjacent [ə'dʒeɪsənt] *adj* (building) contiguo,-a; (land) colindante; **a. to,** contiguo,-a a.

adjective ['ædʒɪktɪv] *n* adjetivo m.

adjoining [ə'dʒɔɪnɪŋ] *adj* contiguo,-a; (land) colindante; **the a. room,** la habitación de al lado.

adjourn [ə'dʒɜːn] **I** *vtr* (postpone) aplazar; (court) levantar. **II** *vi* aplazarse (until, hasta).

adjudicate [ə'dʒuːdɪkeɪt] *vtr* juzgar.

adjudicator [ə'dʒuːdɪkeɪtər] *n* juez,-za m,f.

adjust [ə'dʒʌst] **I** *vtr* (machine etc) ajustar; *fig* (methods) variar. **II** *vi* (person) adaptarse (to, a).

adjustable [ə'dʒʌstəbəl] *adj* ajustable.

adjustment [ə'dʒʌstmənt] *n* **1** (to machine etc) ajuste m; (by person) adaptación f. **2** (change) modificación f.

ad lib [æd'lɪb] **I** *adv* (speak) sin preparación; (continue) a voluntad. **II** *adj* (speech) improvisado,-a. **III** **ad-lib** *vi* improvisar.

administer [əd'mɪnɪstər] *vtr* (country) gobernar; (justice) administrar.

administration [ədmɪnɪ'streɪʃən] *n* (of country) gobierno m; (of justice) administración f; (governing body) dirección f.

administrative [əd'mɪnɪstrɪtɪv] *adj*

administrativo,-a.
admirable [ædmərəbəl] *adj* admirable.
admiral [ˈædmərəl] *n* almirante *m*.
admiration [ædməˈreɪʃən] *n* admiración *f*.
admire [ədˈmaɪər] *vtr* admirar.
admirer [ədˈmaɪərər] *n* admirador,-a *m,f*.
admissible [ədˈmɪsəbəl] *adj* admisible.
admission [ədˈmɪʃən] *n* 1 (*to school etc*) ingreso *m*; (*price*) entrada *f*. 2 (*of fact*) reconocimiento *m*; (*confession*) confesión *f*.
admit [ədˈmɪt] *vtr* 1 (*person*) dejar entrar; **to be admitted to hospital**, ser ingresado,-a en el hospital. 2 (*acknowledge*) reconocer; (*crime, guilt*) confesar.
admittance [ədˈmɪtəns] *n* (*entry*) entrada *f*.
admittedly [ədˈmɪtɪdlɪ] *adv* la verdad es que ....
admonish [ədˈmɒnɪʃ] *vtr* amonestar.
ad nauseam [ædˈnɔːzɪæm] *adv* hasta la saciedad.
ado [əˈduː] *n without further a.*, sin más.
adolescence [ædəˈlesəns] *n* adolescencia *f*.
adolescent [ædəˈlesənt] *n* adolescente *mf*.
adopt [əˈdɒpt] *vtr* adoptar; (*suggestion*) aceptar.
adopted [əˈdɒptɪd] *adj a. child*, hijo,-a *m,f* adoptivo,-a.
adoption [əˈdɒpʃən] *n* adopción *f*; *country of a.*, país adoptivo.
adore [əˈdɔːr] *vtr* adorar.
adorn [əˈdɔːn] *vtr* adornar.
adornment [əˈdɔːnmənt] *n* adorno *m*.
adrenalin [əˈdrenəlɪn] *n* adrenalina *f*.
Adriatic [eɪdrɪˈætɪk] *adj the A. (Sea)*, el (Mar) Adriático.
adrift [əˈdrɪft] *adv* **to come a.**, (*boat*) irse a la deriva; (*rope*) soltarse; *fig* to go a., (*plans*) ir a la deriva.
adult [ˈædʌlt] **I** *adj* (*person*) adulto,-a, mayor; (*film, education*) para adultos. **II** *n* adulto,-a *m,f*.
adulterate [əˈdʌltəreɪt] *vtr* adulterar.
adulterer [əˈdʌltərər] *n* adúltero *m*.
adulteress [əˈdʌltrɪs] *n* adúltera *f*.
adultery [əˈdʌltərɪ] *n* adulterio *m*.
advance [ədˈvɑːns] **I** *n* 1 (*movement*) avance *m*; *fig* (*progress*) progreso *m*; **to have sth ready in a.**, tener algo preparado de antemano; **to make advances**, (*to a person*) insinuarse (**to**, a). 2 (*loan*) anticipo *m*. **II** *adj* (*before time*) adelantado,-a; *Cin Theat* a. **bookings**, reservas *fpl* por adelantado. **III** *vtr* 1 (*troops*) avanzar; (*time, date*) adelantar. 2 (*idea*) proponer; (*opinion*) dar. 3 *Fin* (*sum of money*) anticipar. **IV** *vi* (*move forward*) avanzar, adelantarse; (*make progress*) hacer progresos; (*gain promotion*) ascender.
advanced [ədˈvɑːnst] *adj* (*developed*)

avanzado,-a; (*student*) adelantado,-a; (*course*) superior; *Educ* **A. level**, examen *m* superior de segunda enseñanza, ≈ COU *m*.
advancement [ədˈvɑːnsmənt] *n* (*progress*) adelanto *m*; (*promotion*) ascenso *m*.
advantage [ədˈvɑːntɪdʒ] *n* ventaja *f*; *Ten* **a. Velasco**, ventaja para Velasco; **to take a. of sb/sth**, abusar de/aprovechar algo.
advantageous [ædvənˈteɪdʒəs] *adj* ventajoso,-a.
advent [ˈædvent] *n* (*arrival*) llegada *f*; (*of Christ*) advenimiento *m*; **A.**, Adviento *m*.
adventure [ədˈventʃər] *n* aventura *f*.
adventurous [ədˈventʃərəs] *adj* aventurero,-a.
adverb [ˈædvɜːb] *n* adverbio *m*.
adversary [ˈædvəsərɪ] *n* adversario,-a *m,f*.
adverse [ˈædvɜːs] *adj* (*effect*) desfavorable; (*conditions*) adverso,-a; (*winds*) contrario,-a.
adversity [ədˈvɜːsɪtɪ] *n* adversidad *f*.
advert [ˈædvɜːt] *n fam* anuncio *m*.
advertise [ˈædvətaɪz] **I** *vtr* anunciar. **II** *vi* hacer publicidad; (*in newspaper*) poner un anuncio; **to a. for sth/sb**, buscar algo/a algn mediante un anuncio.
advertisement [ədˈvɜːtɪsmənt] *n* anuncio *m*; **advertisements**, publicidad *f sing*.
advertiser [ˈædvətaɪzər] *n* anunciante *mf*.
advertising [ˈædvətaɪzɪŋ] **I** *n* publicidad *f*, propaganda *f*; (*in newspaper*) anuncios *mpl*. **II** *adj* publicitario,-a; **a. agency**, agencia *f* de publicidad.
advice [ədˈvaɪs] *n* consejos *mpl*; **a piece of a.**, un consejo; **to take legal a. on a matter**, consultar el caso con un abogado; **to take sb's a.**, seguir los consejos de algn.
advisable [ədˈvaɪzəbəl] *adj* aconsejable.
advise [ədˈvaɪz] *vtr* aconsejar; (*on business etc*) asesorar; **I a. you to do it**, te aconsejo que lo hagas.
adviser [ədˈvaɪzər] *n* consejero,-a *m,f*; (*in business etc*) asesor,-a *m,f*.
advisory [ədˈvaɪzərɪ] *adj* asesor,-a.
advocate [ˈædvəkɪt] **I** *n Scot Jur* abogado,-a *m,f*; (*supporter*) defensor,-a *m,f*. **II** [ˈædvəkeɪt] *vtr* (*reform*) abogar por; (*plan*) apoyar.
aerial [ˈeərɪəl] **I** *adj* aéreo,-a. **II** *n* antena *f*.
aerobics [eəˈrəʊbɪks] *n* aerobic *m*.
aerodrome [ˈeərədrəʊm] *n GB* aeródromo *m*.
aerodynamics [eərəʊdaɪˈnæmɪks] *n* aerodinámica *f*.
aeroplane [ˈeərəpleɪn] *n* avión *m*.
aerosol [ˈeərəsɒl] *n* aerosol *m*.
aerospace [ˈeərəʊspeɪs] *adj* aeroespacial.
aesthetic [iːsˈθetɪk] *adj* estético,-a.
afar [əˈfɑːr] *adv* lejos; **from a.**, desde lejos.

affair [əˈfeər] *n* (*matter*) asunto *m*; (*event*) acontecimiento *m*; **that's my a.**, eso es asunto mío; **business affairs**, negocios *mpl*; **foreign affairs**, asuntos exteriores; **love a.**, aventura *f* amorosa.

affect [əˈfekt] *vtr* (*person, health*) afectar; (*prices, future*) influir en; (*touch emotionally*) conmover.

affected [əˈfektɪd] *adj* 1 (*unnatural*) afectado,-a. 2 (*influenced*) influido,-a. 3 (*touched emotionally*) conmovido,-a. 4 (*pretended*) fingido,-a.

affection [əˈfekʃən] *n* afecto *m*, cariño *m*.

affectionate [əˈfekʃənɪt] *adj* cariñoso,-a.

affidavit [æfɪˈdeɪvɪt] *n* declaración escrita y jurada.

affiliated [əˈfɪlieɪtɪd] *adj* afiliado,-a; **to be** *or* **become a.**, afiliarse (**to, with**, a).

affinity [əˈfɪnɪtɪ] *n* afinidad *f*; (*liking*) simpatía *f*.

affirm [əˈfɜːm] *vtr* afirmar, sostener.

affirmation [æfəˈmeɪʃən] *n* afirmación *f*.

affirmative [əˈfɜːmətɪv] I *adj* afirmativo,-a. II *n* **he answered in the a.**, contestó que sí.

affix [əˈfɪks] *vtr* (*stamp*) pegar.

afflict [əˈflɪkt] *vtr* afligir.

affluence [ˈæfluəns] *n* opulencia *f*.

affluent [ˈæfluənt] *adj* (*society*) opulento, -a; (*person*) rico,-a.

afford [əˈfɔːd] *vtr* 1 (*be able to buy*) permitirse el lujo de; **I can't a. a new car**, no puedo pagar un coche nuevo. 2 (*be able to do*) permitirse; **you can't a. to miss the opportunity**, no puedes perderte la ocasión.

affront [əˈfrʌnt] I *n* afrenta *f*. II *vtr* afrentar.

afield [əˈfiːld] *adv* **far a.**, muy lejos.

afloat [əˈfləʊt] *adv* **to keep a.**, mantenerse a flote.

afoot [əˈfʊt] *adv* **there's a plan a.**, hay un proyecto en marcha; **there's something strange a.**, se está tramando algo.

aforementioned [əˈfɔːmenʃənd], **aforesaid** [əˈfɔːsed] *adj* susodicho,-a.

afraid [əˈfreɪd] *adj* 1 **to be a.**, tener miedo (**of** sb, a algn; **of** sth, de algo); **I'm a. of it**, me da miedo. 2 **I'm a. not**, me temo que no; **I'm a. so**, me temo que sí; **I'm a. you're wrong**, me temo que estás equivocado,-a.

afresh [əˈfreʃ] *adv* de nuevo.

Africa [ˈæfrɪkə] *n* África.

African [ˈæfrɪkən] *adj* & *n* africano,-a (*m,f*).

Afro [ˈæfrəʊ] *n* & *adj* fam (*hairstyle*) afro (*m*).

aft [ɑːft] *adv* en popa; **to go a.**, ir en popa.

after [ˈɑːftər] I *adv* después; **soon a.**, poco después; **the day a.**, el día siguiente. II *prep* 1 (*later*) después de; *US* **it's ten a. five**, son las cinco y diez; **soon**

a. arriving, al poco rato de llegar; **the day a. tomorrow**, pasado mañana. 2 (*behind*) detrás de, tras; **a. you!**, ¡pase usted!; **they went in one a. the other**, entraron uno tras otro; **the police are a. them**, la policía anda tras ellos. 3 (*about*) por; **they asked a. you**, preguntaron por ti; **what's he a.?**, ¿qué pretende? 4 **he takes a. his uncle**, se parece a su tío; **she was named a. her grandmother**, la llamaron como su abuela. III *conj* después de que; **a. it happened**, después de que ocurriera.

after-effect [ˈɑːftərɪfekt] *n* efecto *m* secundario.

afterlife [ˈɑːftəlaɪf] *n* vida *f* después de la muerte.

aftermath [ˈɑːftəmæθ] *n* secuelas *fpl*.

afternoon [ɑːftəˈnuːn] *n* tarde *f*; **good a.!**, ¡buenas tardes!; **in the a.**, por la tarde.

afters [ˈɑːftəz] *npl fam* postre *m*.

after-sales service [ɑːftəseɪlzˈsɜːvɪs] *n Com* servicio *m* posventa.

aftershave (lotion) [ˈɑːftəʃeɪv(ˈləʊʃən)] *n* loción *f* para después del afeitado.

afterthought [ˈɑːftəθɔːt] *n* ocurrencia *f* tardía.

afterwards [ˈɑːftəwədz] *adv* después, más tarde.

again [əˈgen] *adv* 1 otra vez, de nuevo; **I tried a. and a.**, lo intenté una y otra vez; **to do sth a.**, volver a hacer algo; **never a.!**, ¡nunca más!; **now and a.**, de vez en cuando; **once a.**, otra vez. 2 (*besides*) además; **then a.**, por otra parte.

against [əˈgenst] *prep* 1 (*touching*) contra. 2 (*opposing*) contra, en contra (de); **a. the grain**, a contrapelo; **it's a. the law**, es ilegal. 3 **as a.**, en contraste con, comparado con.

age [eɪdʒ] I *n* 1 edad *f*; **she's 18 years of a.**, tiene 18 años; **to be under a.**, ser menor de edad; **to come of a.**, llegar a la mayoría de edad; **a. limit**, límite *m* de edad; **old a.**, vejez *f*. 2 (*period*) época *f*; **the Iron A.**, la Edad de Hierro. 3 *fam* (*long time*) eternidad *f*; **it's ages since I last saw her**, hace siglos que no la veo. II *vtr* & *vi* envejecer.

aged[1] [eɪdʒd] *adj* de *or* a la edad de.

aged[2] [ˈeɪdʒɪd] *npl* **the a.**, los ancianos.

agency [ˈeɪdʒənsɪ] *n* 1 *Com* agencia *f*. 2 **by the a. of**, por medio de.

agenda [əˈdʒendə] *n* orden *m* del día.

agent [ˈeɪdʒənt] *n* agente *mf*; (*representative*) representante *mf*.

aggravate [ˈægrəveɪt] *vtr* (*worsen*) agravar; (*annoy*) molestar.

aggregate [ˈægrɪgət] *n* conjunto *m*; **on a.**, en conjunto.

aggression [əˈgreʃən] *n* agresión *f*.

aggressive [əˈgresɪv] *adj* (*violent*) agresivo,-a, violento,-a; (*dynamic*) dinámico,-a.

aggrieved [ə'gri:vd] *adj* apenado,-a.

aghast [ə'gɑ:st] *adj* espantado,-a.

agile ['ædʒaɪl] *adj* ágil.

agitate ['ædʒɪteɪt] **I** *vtr* (*shake*) agitar; *fig* (*worry*) perturbar. **II** *vi Pol* **a. against sth,** hacer campaña en contra de algo.

agitator ['ædʒɪteɪtər] *n Pol* agitador,-a *m,f.*

AGM [eɪdʒi:'em] *abbr of* **annual general meeting,** junta *f* general anual.

agnostic [æg'nɒstɪk] *n* agnóstico,-a *m,f.*

ago [ə'gəʊ] *adv* **a long time ago,** hace mucho tiempo; **as long as** as 1910, ya en 1910; **a week** a**,** hace una semana; **how long a.?,** ¿hace cuánto tiempo?

agog [ə'gɒg] *adj* ansioso,-a.

agonizing ['ægənaɪzɪŋ] *adj* (*pain*) atroz; (*decision*) desesperante.

agony ['ægənɪ] *n* dolor *m* muy fuerte; (*anguish*) angustia *f*; **he was in a.** **with his back,** tenía un dolor insoportable de espalda.

agree [ə'gri:] **I** *vi* **1** (*be in agreement*) estar de acuerdo; (*reach agreement*) ponerse de acuerdo; (*consent*) consentir; **to a. to do sth,** consentir en hacer algo; **to a. with sb,** estar de acuerdo con algn. **2** (*harmonize*) (*things*) concordar; (*people*) congeniar; **onions don't a. with me,** la cebolla no me sienta bien. **II** *vtr* acordar.

agreeable [ə'gri:əbəl] *adj* (*pleasant*) agradable; (*person*) simpático,-a; (*in agreement*) de acuerdo.

agreement [ə'gri:mənt] *n* (*arrangement*) acuerdo *m*; *Com* contrato *m*; **to reach an a.,** llegar a un acuerdo.

agricultural [ægrɪ'kʌltʃərəl] *adj* agrícola; (*college*) de agricultura.

agriculture ['ægrɪkʌltʃər] *n* agricultura *f.*

aground [ə'graʊnd] *adv* **to run a.,** encallar, varar.

ahead [ə'hed] *adv* delante; (*early*) antes; **go a.!,** ¡adelante!; **to be a.,** llevar la ventaja; **to go a.,** ir adelante; *fig* **to go a. with sth,** llevar algo adelante; (*start*) comenzar algo; **to get a.,** triunfar; **to look a.,** pensar en el futuro.

aid [eɪd] **I** *n* ayuda *f*; (*rescue*) auxilio *m*; **in a. of,** a beneficio de; **to come to the a. of sb,** acudir en ayuda de algn. **II** *vtr* ayudar; **to a. and abet sb,** ser cómplice de algn.

aide [eɪd] *n* ayudante *mf.*

Aids [eɪdz] *n* (*abbr of* **Acquired Immune Deficiency Syndrome**), SIDA *m* (Síndrome *m* de Inmunodeficiencia Adquirida).

ailing ['eɪlɪŋ] *adj* achacoso,-a.

ailment ['eɪlmənt] *n* enfermedad *f* (leve), achaque *m.*

aim [eɪm] **I** *n* (*with weapon*) puntería *f*; (*target*) propósito *m.* **II** *vtr* (*gun*) apuntar (at, a, hacia); (*attack, action*) dirigir (at, a, hacia). ◆**aim at** *vtr* (*target*) tirar para;

to a. at doing sth, tener pensado hacer algo. ◆**aim to** *vtr* **to a. to do sth,** tener la intención de hacer algo.

aimless ['eɪmlɪs] *adj* sin objeto, sin propósito. ◆**aimlessly** *adv* (*wander*) sin rumbo fijo.

air [eər] **I** *n* **1** aire *m*; (*to travel by a.*, viajar en avión; **to throw sth up in the a.,** lanzar algo al aire; *fig* **it's still in the a.,** todavía por resolver; **a. base,** base aérea; **a. bed,** colchón *m* hinchable; **a. conditioning,** aire acondicionado; A. Force, Fuerzas Aéreas; **a. freshener,** ambientador *m*; **a. gun,** pistola *f* de aire comprimido; **a. hostess,** azafata *f*; **a. letter,** carta aérea; **a. pocket,** bache *m*; **a. pressure,** presión atmosférica; **a. raid,** ataque aéreo; **a. terminal,** terminal aérea; **a. traffic control,** control *m* de tráfico aéreo; **a. traffic controller,** controlador,-a *m,f* aéreo,-a. **2** *Rad TV* **to be on the a.,** (*programme*) estar emitiendo; (*person*) estar transmitiendo. **3** (*appearance*) aspecto *m.* **II** *vtr* (*bed, clothes*) airear; (*room*) ventilar; *fig* (*grievance*) airear; (*knowledge*) hacer alarde de.

airborne ['eəbɔ:n] *adj* (*aircraft*) en vuelo; (*troops*) aerotransportado,-a.

air-conditioned ['eəkɒndɪʃənd] *adj* climatizado,-a.

aircraft ['eəkrɑ:ft] *n inv* avión *m*; **a. carrier,** portaviones *m inv.*

airfield ['eəfi:ld] *n* campo *m* de aviación.

airlift ['eəlɪft] *n* puente aéreo.

airline ['eəlaɪn] *n* línea aérea.

airlock ['eəlɒk] *n* (*in pipe*) bolsa *f* de aire; (*in spacecraft*) esclusa *f* de aire.

airmail ['eəmeɪl] *n* correo *m* aéreo; **by a.,** por avión.

airplane ['eəpleɪn] *n US* avión *m.*

airport ['eəpɔ:t] *n* aeropuerto *m.*

airsick ['eəsɪk] *adj* **to be a.,** marearse en avión.

airstrip ['eəstrɪp] *n* pista *f* de aterrizaje.

airtight ['eətaɪt] *adj* hermético,-a.

airy ['eərɪ] *adj* (*airier, airiest*) (*well-ventilated*) bien ventilado,-a; (*vague, carefree*) ligero,-a.

aisle [aɪl] *n* (*in church*) nave *f*; (*in theatre*) pasillo *m.*

ajar [ə'dʒɑ:r] *adj & adv* entreabierto,-a.

akin [ə'kɪn] *adj* semejante.

alacrity [ə'lækrɪtɪ] *n* **with a.,** con presteza.

alarm [ə'lɑ:m] **I** *n* **1** alarma *f*; **a. clock,** despertador *m.* **2** (*fear*) inquietud *f*; **to cause a.,** provocar temor. **II** *vtr* alarmar.

alas [ə'læs] *interj* ¡ay!; ¡ay de mí!

albatross ['ælbətrɒs] *n* albatros *m.*

albeit [ɔ:l'bi:ɪt] *conj* aunque, no obstante.

album ['ælbəm] *n* álbum *m.*

alcohol ['ælkəhɒl] *n* alcohol *m.*

alcoholic [ælkə'hɒlɪk] *adj & n* alcohólico,-a (*m,f*).

alcove ['ælkəʊv] n hueco m.

ale [eɪl] n cerveza f; **brown/pale a.**, cerveza negra/rubia.

alert [ə'lɜːt] I adj alerta; (lively) despabilado,-a. II n alerta m; **to be on the a.**, estar alerta. III vtr **a. sb to sth**, avisar a algn de algo.

A-level ['eɪlevl] n GB Educ abbr of Advanced Level, ≈ Curso m de Orientación Universitaria, COU m.

algae ['ældʒiː] npl algas fpl.

algebra ['ældʒɪbrə] n álgebra f.

Algeria [æl'dʒɪərɪə] n Argelia.

Algerian [æl'dʒɪərɪən] adj & n argelino,-a (m,f).

Algiers [æl'dʒɪəz] n Argel.

alias ['eɪlɪəs] I n alias m. II adv alias.

alibi ['ælɪbaɪ] n coartada f.

alien ['eɪlɪən] I adj (foreign) extranjero,-a; (from space) extraterrestre; **a. to**, ajeno a. II n (foreigner) extranjero,-a m,f; (from space) extraterrestre mf.

alienate ['eɪlɪəneɪt] vtr 1 **to a. sb**, ofender a algn; **to a. oneself from sb**, alejarse de algn. 2 Fur enajenar.

alight¹ [ə'laɪt] adj (on fire) ardiendo,-a.

alight² [ə'laɪt] vi (get off) apearse (from, de).

align [ə'laɪn] vtr alinear.

alike [ə'laɪk] I adj (similar) parecidos,-as; (the same) iguales. II adv (in the same way) de la misma manera, igualmente; dressed a., vestidos,-as iguales.

alimony ['ælɪmənɪ] n Fur pensión alimenticia.

alive [ə'laɪv] adj vivo,-a; fig (teeming) lleno,-a (with, de); **to be a.**, estar vivo,-a.

alkaline ['ælkəlaɪn] adj alcalino,-a.

all [ɔːl] I adj todo,-a, todos,-as; **a. year**, (durante) todo el año; **a. kinds of things**, todo tipo de cosas; **at a. hours**, a todas horas; **at a. times**, siempre; **she works a. the time**, siempre está trabajando; **all six of us were there**, los seis estábamos allí. II pron todo,-a, todos,-as; **after a.**, al fin y al cabo; **a. of his work**, toda su obra; **a. of us**, todos,-as nosotros,-as; **a. who saw it**, todos los que lo vieron; **a. you can do is wait**, lo único que puedes hacer es esperar; **I don't like it at a.**, no me gusta en absoluto; **is that a.?**, ¿eso es todo?; **most of** or **above a.**, sobre todo; **once and for a.**, de una vez por todas; **thanks - not at a.**, gracias - de nada; **in a.**, en conjunto; **that's a.**, ya está; **the score was one a.**, empataron a uno. III adv **a. by myself**, completamente solo,-a; **a. at once**, (suddenly) de repente; (altogether) de una vez; **a. the better**, tanto mejor; **a. the same**, de todos modos; **he knew a. along**, lo sabía desde el principio; **if it's a. the same to you**, si no te importa; **it's a. but impossible**, es casi imposible; **I'm not a. that tired**, no estoy tan cansado,-a como eso. IV **n to give one's a.**, darse por completo.

Allah ['ælə] n Alá m.

allay [ə'leɪ] vtr (fears, doubts) apaciguar.

allegation [ælɪ'geɪʃən] n alegato m.

allege [ə'ledʒ] vtr sostener, pretender (that, que).

allegedly [ə'ledʒɪdlɪ] adv supuestamente.

allegiance [ə'liːdʒəns] n lealtad f.

allergic [ə'lɜːdʒɪk] adj alérgico,-a (to, a).

allergy ['ælədʒɪ] n alergia f.

alleviate [ə'liːvɪeɪt] vtr (pain) aliviar.

alley ['ælɪ] n callejón m.

alliance [ə'laɪəns] n alianza f.

allied ['ælaɪd] adj aliado,-a.

alligator ['ælɪgeɪtə] n caimán m.

all-in [ɔːl'ɪn] adj (price) todo incluido; Sport **a.-in wrestling**, lucha f libre.

alliteration [əlɪtə'reɪʃən] n aliteración f.

all-night [ɔːl'naɪt] adj (café etc) abierto,-a toda la noche; (vigil) que dura toda la noche.

allocate ['æləkeɪt] vtr destinar (to, para).

allocation [ælə'keɪʃən] n 1 (distribution) asignación f. 2 (amount allocated) cuota f.

allot [ə'lɒt] vtr asignar.

allotment [ə'lɒtmənt] n 1 (distribution) asignación f. 2 (land) parcela f.

all-out ['ɔːlaʊt] I adj (effort) supremo,-a; (attack) concentrado,-a. II **all out** adv **to go a. o. to do sth**, emplearse a fondo para hacer algo.

allow [ə'laʊ] vtr 1 (permit) permitir; (a request) acceder a; **to a. sb to do sth**, permitir que algn haga algo. 2 (allot) (time) dejar; (money) destinar. ◆**allow for** vtr tener en cuenta.

allowance [ə'laʊəns] n (payment) pensión f, subvención f; (discount) descuento m; **to make allowances for sb/sth**, disculpar a algn/tener algo en cuenta; **tax a.**, desgravación f fiscal; **travel a.**, dietas fpl de viaje.

alloy ['ælɔɪ] n aleación f.

all right [ɔːl'raɪt] I adj (okay) bien; **thank you very much - that's a. r.**, muchas gracias - de nada. II adv 1 (well) bien. 2 (definitely) sin duda. 3 (okay) de acuerdo, vale.

all-round [ɔːl'raʊnd] adj (athlete etc) completo,-a.

all-terrain [ɔːltə'reɪn] adj **a.-t. vehicle**, todoterreno m.

all-time ['ɔːltaɪm] adj **an a.-t. low**, una baja sin antecedente; **the a.-t. greats**, los grandes de siempre.

allude [ə'luːd] vi **to a. to**, aludir a.

alluring [ə'ljʊərɪŋ] adj atractivo,-a.

allusion [ə'luːʒən] n alusión f.

ally ['ælaɪ] I n aliado,-a m,f. II vtr **to a. oneself to/with sb**, aliarse a/con algn.

almighty [ɔːl'maɪtɪ] I adj (all-powerful)

todopoderoso,-a. II *n* the A., El Todopoderoso.

almond ['ɑːmənd] *n* almendra *f.*

almost ['ɔːlməʊst] *adv* casi.

alms [ɑːmz] *npl* limosna *f sing.*

aloft [ə'lɒft] *adv* arriba.

alone [ə'ləʊn] I *adj* solo,-a; **can I speak to you a.?**, ¿puedo hablar contigo a solas?; **let a.**, ni mucho menos; **leave it a.!**, ¡no lo toques!; **leave me a.**, déjame en paz; **to be a.**, estar solo,-a. II *adv* solamente, sólo.

along [ə'lɒŋ] I *adv* ¡anda, ven!; **he'll be a. in 10 minutes**, llegará dentro de 10 minutos; **a. with**, junto con. II *prep* (*the length of*) a lo largo de; **to walk a. the street**, andar por la calle; **it's just a. the street**, está un poco más abajo.

alongside [ə'lɒŋsaɪd] I *adv Naut* de costado. II *prep* al lado de.

aloof [ə'luːf] I *adj* (*person*) distante. II *adv* **to keep oneself a.**, mantenerse a distancia (**from**, de).

aloud [ə'laʊd] *adv* en voz alta.

alphabet ['ælfəbet] *n* alfabeto *m.*

alphabetical [ælfə'betɪkəl] *adj* alfabético,-a. ◆**alphabetically** *adv* por orden alfabético.

alpine ['ælpaɪn] *adj* alpino,-a.

Alps [ælps] *npl* the A., los Alpes.

already [ɔːl'redɪ] *adv* ya.

alright [ɔːl'raɪt] *adj & adv → all right.*

Alsatian [æl'seɪʃən] *n* pastor *m* alemán.

also ['ɔːlsəʊ] *adv* también, además.

also-ran ['ɔːlsəʊræn] *n fam* (*person*) segundón,-ona *m,f.*

altar ['ɔːltə'] *n* altar *m.*

alter ['ɔːltə'] I *vtr* (*plan*) cambiar, retocar; (*project*) modificar; (*clothing*) arreglar; (*timetable*) revisar. II *vi* cambiar, cambiarse.

alteration [ɔːltə'reɪʃən] *n* (*to plan*) cambio *m*; (*to project*) modificación *f*; (*to clothing*) arreglo *m*; (*to timetable*) revisión *f*; **alterations**, (*to building*) reformas *fpl.*

alternate [ɔːl'tɜːnɪt] I *adj* alterno,-a; **on a. days**, cada dos días. II [ɔːl'tɜːneɪt] *vtr* alternar. ◆**alternately** *adv* **a. hot and cold**, ahora caliente, ahora frío.

alternative [ɔːl'tɜːnətɪv] I *adj* alternativo,-a. II *n* alternativa *f*; **I have no a. but to accept**, no tengo más remedio que aceptar. ◆**alternatively** *adv* o bien; **a. you could walk**, o bien podrías ir andando.

alternator ['ɔːltəneɪtə'] *n Aut* alternador *m.*

although [ɔːl'ðəʊ] *conj* aunque.

altitude ['æltɪtjuːd] *n* altitud *f.*

alto ['æltəʊ] *adj & n* (*male singer, instrument*) alto (*m*); (*female singer*) contralto (*f*).

altogether [ɔːltə'geðə'] *adv* (*in total*) en conjunto, en total; (*completely*) completamente, del todo.

altruism ['æltruːɪzəm] *n* altruismo *m.*

aluminium [ælju'mɪnɪəm], *US* **aluminum** [ə'luːmɪnəm] *n* aluminio *m.*

always ['ɔːlweɪz] *adv* siempre.

AM [eɪ'em] *Rad abbr of* **amplitude modulation**, AM.

am [æm] *1st person sing pres → be.*

a.m. [eɪ'em] *abbr of* **ante meridiem**, de la mañana.

amalgamate [ə'mælɡəmeɪt] I *vtr* (*metals*) amalgamar. II *vi* (*metals*) amalgamarse; (*companies*) fusionarse.

amalgamation [əmælɡə'meɪʃən] *n* fusión *f.*

amass [ə'mæs] *vtr* (*money*) amontonar; (*information*) acumular.

amateur ['æmətə'] I *n* amateur *mf*, aficionado,-a *m,f*. II *adj* aficionado,-a; (*work etc*) *pej* chapucero,-a.

amateurish ['æmətərɪʃ] *adj* chapucero,-a.

amaze [ə'meɪz] *vtr* asombrar, pasmar; **to be amazed at sth**, quedarse pasmado,-a de algo.

amazement [ə'meɪzmənt] *n* asombro *m*, sorpresa *f.*

amazing [ə'meɪzɪŋ] *adj* asombroso,-a, increíble.

ambassador [æm'bæsədə'] *n* embajador,-a *m,f.*

amber ['æmbə'] I *n* ámbar *m*. II *adj* ambarino,-a; (*traffic light*) amarillo,-a.

ambiguity [æmbɪ'ɡjuːɪtɪ] *n* ambigüedad *f.*

ambiguous [æm'bɪɡjʊəs] *adj* ambiguo,-a.

ambition [æm'bɪʃən] *n* ambición *f.*

ambitious [æm'bɪʃəs] *adj* ambicioso,-a.

ambivalent [æm'bɪvələnt] *adj* ambivalente.

amble ['æmbəl] *vi* deambular.

ambulance ['æmbjʊləns] *n* ambulancia *f*; **a. man**, ambulanciero *m.*

ambush ['æmbʊʃ] I *n* emboscada *f*. II *vtr* tender una emboscada a; *fig* atacar por sorpresa.

amen [ɑː'men] *interj* amén.

amenable [ə'miːnəbəl] *adj* **I'd be quite a. to doing that**, no me importaría nada hacer eso; **a. to reason**, razonable.

amend [ə'mend] *vtr* (*law*) enmendar; (*error*) subsanar.

amendment [ə'mendmənt] *n* enmienda *f.*

amends [ə'mendz] *npl* **to make a. to sb for sth**, compensar a algn por algo.

amenities [ə'miːnɪtɪz] *npl* comodidades *fpl.*

America [ə'merɪkə] *n* (*continent*) América *f*; (*USA*) (los) Estados *mpl* Unidos; **South A.**, América del Sur, Sudamérica *f.*

American [ə'merɪkən] *adj & n* americano,-a (*m,f*); (*of USA*) norteamericano,-a (*m,f*), estadounidense (*mf*).

amiable ['eɪmɪəbəl] *adj* amable, afable.

amicable ['æmɪkəbəl] *adj* amistoso,-a.

amid(st) [ə'mɪd(st)] *prep* entre, en medio de.

amiss [ə'mɪs] *adj & adv* mal; **there's sth a.**, algo anda mal; **to take sth a.**, tomar algo a mal.

ammonia [ə'məʊnɪə] *n* amoníaco *m*.

ammunition [æmjʊ'nɪʃən] *n* municiones *fpl*.

amnesia [æm'niːʒə] *n* amnesia *f*.

amnesty ['æmnɪstɪ] *n* amnistía *f*.

amok [ə'mɒk] *adv fig* **to run a.**, (*child*) desmadrarse; (*inflation etc*) dispararse.

among(st) [ə'mʌŋ(st)] *prep* entre.

amoral [eɪ'mɒrəl] *adj* amoral.

amorous ['æmərəs] *adj* cariñoso,-a.

amorphous [ə'mɔːfəs] *adj* amorfo,-a.

amount [ə'maʊnt] *n* cantidad *f*; (*of money*) suma *f*; (*of bill*) importe *m*.
◆**amount to** *vtr* ascender a; *fig* equivaler a.

amp [æmp], **ampère** ['æmpeər] *n* amperio *m*.

amphetamine [æm'fetəmiːn] *n* anfetamina *f*.

amphibian [æm'fɪbɪən] *adj & n* anfibio,-a (*m*).

amphibious [æm'fɪbɪəs] *adj* anfibio,-a.

amphitheatre ['æmfɪθɪətər] *n* anfiteatro *m*.

ample ['æmpəl] *adj* (*enough*) bastante; (*more than enough*) abundante; (*large*) amplio,-a.

amplifier ['æmplɪfaɪər] *n* amplificador *m*.

amputate ['æmpjʊteɪt] *vtr* amputar.

amuck [ə'mʌk] *adv* → **amok.**

amuse [ə'mjuːz] *vtr* divertir, entretener.

amusement [ə'mjuːzmənt] *n* (*enjoyment*) diversión *f*; (*laughter*) risa *f*; (*pastime*) pasatiempo *m*; **a. arcade**, salón *m* de juegos; **a. park**, parque *m* de atracciones.

amusing [ə'mjuːzɪŋ] *adj* divertido,-a.

an [æn, *unstressed* ən] *indef art* → **a.**

anabolic steroid [ænəbɒlɪk'stɪərɔɪd] *n* esteroide *m* anabolizante.

anaemia [ə'niːmɪə] *n* anemia *f*.

anaemic [ə'niːmɪk] *adj* anémico,-a; *fig (weak)* débil.

anaesthetic [ænɪs'θetɪk] *n* anestesia *f*.

anaesthetist [ə'niːsθɪtɪst] *n* anestesista *mf*.

analog(ue) ['ænəlɒg] *n* análogo *m*; **a. computer**, ordenador analógico; **a. watch**, reloj *m* de agujas.

analogy [ə'nælədʒɪ] *n* analogía *f*.

analyse ['ænəlaɪz] *vtr* analizar.

analysis [ə'nælɪsɪs] *n* (*pl* **analyses** [ə'nælɪsiːz]) análisis *m inv*.

analyst ['ænəlɪst] *n* analista *mf*; (*psychoanalyst*) psicoanalista *mf*.

analyze ['ænəlaɪz] *vtr US* → **analyse.**

analytic(al) [ænə'lɪtɪk(əl)] *adj* analítico,-a.

anarchist ['ænəkɪst] *n* anarquista *mf*.

anarchy ['ænəkɪ] *n* anarquía *f*.

anathema [ə'næθəmə] *n* **the very idea was a. to him**, le repugnaba sólo de pensarlo.

anatomy [ə'nætəmɪ] *n* anatomía *f*.

ancestor ['ænsestər] *n* antepasado *m*.

anchor ['æŋkər] **I** *n Naut* ancla *f*; *fig* áncora *f*; **to drop a.**, echar el ancla; **to weigh a.**, zarpar. **II** *vtr Naut* anclar; *fig (fix securely)* sujetar. **III** *vi* anclar.

anchovy ['æntʃəvɪ] *n* anchoa *f*.

ancient ['eɪnʃənt] *adj* antiguo,-a.

ancillary [æn'sɪlərɪ] *adj & n* auxiliar (*mf*).

and [ænd, *unstressed* ənd, ən] *conj* y; (*before i-, hi-*) e; **a hundred a. one**, ciento uno; **a. so on** etcétera; **Bill a. Pat**, Bill y Pat; **Chinese a. Indian**, chino e indio; **come a. see us**, ven a vernos; **four a. a half**, cuatro y medio; **she cried a. cried**, no paró de llorar; **try a. help me**, trata de ayudarme; **wait a. see**, espera a ver; **worse a. worse**, cada vez peor.

Andalusia [ændə'luːzɪə] *n* Andalucía.

Andalusian [ændə'luːzɪən] *adj* andaluz,-a.

Andes ['ændiːz] *npl* **the A.**, los Andes.

Andorra [æn'dɔːrə] *n* Andorra.

anecdote ['ænɪkdəʊt] *n* anécdota *f*.

anemia [ə'niːmɪə] *n US* → **anaemia.**

anesthetic [ænɪs'θetɪk] *n US* → **anaesthetic.**

angel ['eɪndʒəl] *n* ángel *m*.

anger ['æŋgər] **I** *n* cólera *f*. **II** *vtr* enojar.

angina [æn'dʒaɪnə] *n* angina *f* (de pecho).

angle ['æŋgəl] *n* ángulo *m*; *fig* punto *m* de vista.

angler ['æŋglər] *n* pescador,-a *m,f* de caña.

Anglican ['æŋglɪkən] *adj & n* anglicano,-a (*m,f*).

Anglo-Saxon [æŋgləʊ'sæksən] *adj & n* anglosajón,-ona (*m,f*).

Angola [æŋ'gəʊlə] *n* Angola.

angry ['æŋgrɪ] *adj* (**angrier, angriest**) (*person etc*) enfadado,-a; (*voice*) airado,-a; **to get a. with sb about sth**, enfadarse con algn por algo. ◆**angrily** *adv* furiosamente.

anguish ['æŋgwɪʃ] *n* angustia *f*.

angular ['æŋgjʊlər] *adj* (*shape*) angular; (*face*) anguloso,-a.

animal ['ænɪməl] **I** *adj* animal. **II** *n* animal *m*; *fig* bestia *f*.

animate ['ænɪmɪt] **I** *adj* vivo,-a. **II** ['ænɪmeɪt] *vtr* animar; *fig* estimular.

animated ['ænɪmeɪtɪd] *adj* (*lively*) animado,-a.

animosity [ænɪ'mɒsɪtɪ] *n* animosidad *f*.

aniseed ['ænɪsiːd] *n* anís *m*.

ankle ['æŋkəl] *n* tobillo *m*; **a. boots**, botines *mpl*; **a. socks**, calcetines cortos.

annex [æ'neks] *vtr* (*territory*) anexionar.

annexe, *US* **annex** ['æneks] *n* (*building*) (edificio *m*) anexo *m*.

annihilate [ə'naɪəleɪt] *vtr* aniquilar.

anniversary [æni'vɜːsəri] *n* aniversario *m*; **wedding a.**, aniversario de bodas.

announce [ə'nauns] *vtr* anunciar; (*news*) comunicar; (*fact*) hacer saber.

announcement [ə'naunsmənt] *n* anuncio *m*; (*news*) comunicación *f*; (*statement*) declaración *f*.

announcer [ə'naunsər] *n* TV Rad locutor,-a *m,f*.

annoy [ə'nɔɪ] *vtr* molestar, fastidiar; **to get annoyed**, enfadarse, molestarse.

annoyance [ə'nɔɪəns] *n* (*feeling*) enojo *m*; (*thing*) molestia *f*, fastidio *m*.

annoying [ə'nɔɪɪŋ] *adj* molesto,-a, fastidioso,-a.

annual ['ænjuəl] **I** *adj* anual. **II** *n* (*book*) anuario *m*; (*plant*) anual *m*. ◆**annually** *adv* anualmente.

annul [ə'nʌl] *vtr* anular.

annulment [ə'nʌlmənt] *n* anulación *f*.

anomaly [ə'nɒməlɪ] *n* anomalía *f*.

anonymity [ænə'nɪmɪtɪ] *n* anonimato *m*.

anonymous [ə'nɒnɪməs] *adj* anónimo,-a.

anorak ['ænəræk] *n* anorak *m*.

anorexia [ænə'reksɪə] *n* anorexia *f*.

another [ə'nʌðər] **I** *adj* otro,-a; **a. one**, otro,-a; **without a. word**, sin más. **II** *pron* otro,-a; **have a.**, toma otro,-a; **to love one a.**, quererse el uno al otro.

ansaphone ['ɑːnsəfəun] *n* mensáfono *m*.

answer ['ɑːnsər] **I** *n* (*to letter etc*) contestación *f*; (*to question*) respuesta *f*; (*to problem*) solución *f*; **in a. to your letter**, contestando a su carta; **there's no a.**, (*on telephone*) no contestan; (*at door*) no abren. **II** *vtr* contestar a; (*problem*) resolver; (*door*) abrir; (*phone*) contestar. **III** *vi* contestar, responder. ◆**answer back** *vi* replicar; **don't a. back!**, ¡no seas respondón! ◆**answer for** *vtr* responder de; **he's got a lot to a. for**, es responsable de muchas cosas. ◆**answer to** *vtr* (*name*) responder a; (*description*) corresponder a.

answerable ['ɑːnsərəbl] *adj* **to be a. to sb for sth**, ser responsable ante algo por algo.

answering machine ['ɑːnsərɪŋməʃiːn] *n* contestador automático.

ant [ænt] *n* hormiga *f*; **a. hill**, hormiguero *m*.

antagonism [æn'tægənɪzəm] *n* antagonismo *m* (**between**, entre); hostilidad *f* (**towards**, hacia).

antagonize [æn'tægənaɪz] *vtr* enemistar, malquistar.

Antartic [æn'tɑːktɪk] **I** *adj* antártico,-a; **A. Ocean**, océano Antártico. **II** *n* **the A.**, La Antártica.

Antarctica [æn'tɑːktɪkə] *n* Antártida *f*.

antecedent [æntɪ'siːdənt] *n* antecedente *m*.

antelope ['æntɪləup] *n* antílope *m*.

antenatal [æntɪ'neɪtəl] *adj* antenatal; (*clinic*) prenatal.

antenna [æn'tenə] *n* **1** (*pl* **antennae** [æn'teniː]) (*of animal, insect*) antena *f*. **2** (*pl* **antennas**) TV Rad antena *f*.

anthem ['ænθəm] *n* motete *m*; **national a.**, himno *m* nacional.

anthology [æn'θɒlədʒɪ] *n* antología *f*.

anthracite ['ænθrəsaɪt] *n* antracita *f*.

anthropology [ænθrə'pɒlədʒɪ] *n* antropología *f*.

anti-aircraft [æntɪ'eəkrɑːft] *adj* antiaéreo,-a.

antibiotic [æntɪbaɪ'ɒtɪk] *n* antibiótico *m*.

antibody ['æntɪbɒdɪ] *n* anticuerpo *m*.

anticipate [æn'tɪsɪpeɪt] *vtr* **1** (*expect*) esperar. **2** (*predict*) prever; (*get ahead of*) anticiparse a, adelantarse a.

anticipation [æntɪsɪ'peɪʃən] *n* (*expectation*) esperanza *f*; (*expectancy*) ilusión *f*.

anticlimax [æntɪ'klaɪmæks] *n* (*disappointment*) decepción *f*.

anticlockwise [æntɪ'klɒkwaɪz] *adv* en sentido contrario a las agujas del reloj.

antics ['æntɪks] *npl* payasadas *fpl*; (*naughtiness*) travesuras *fpl*.

anticyclone [æntɪ'saɪkləun] *n* anticiclón *m*.

antidote ['æntɪdəut] *n* antídoto *m*.

antifreeze ['æntɪfriːz] *n* anticongelante *m*.

antihistamine [æntɪ'hɪstəmɪn] *n* antihistamínico *m*.

antinuclear [æntɪ'njuːklɪər] *adj* antinuclear.

antipathy [æn'tɪpəθɪ] *n* antipatía *f* (**to**, a).

antiquated ['æntɪkweɪtɪd] *adj* anticuado,-a.

antique [æn'tiːk] **I** *adj* antiguo,-a. **II** *n* antigüedad *f*; **a. dealer**, anticuario,-a *m,f*; **a. shop**, tienda *f* de antigüedades.

antiquity [æn'tɪkwɪtɪ] *n* antigüedad *f*.

anti-Semitism [æntɪ'semɪtɪzəm] *n* antisemitismo *m*.

antiseptic [æntɪ'septɪk] *adj* & *n* antiséptico,-a *m*.

antisocial [æntɪ'səuʃəl] *adj* (*delinquent*) antisocial; (*unsociable*) insociable.

antithesis [æn'tɪθɪsɪs] *n* antítesis *f*.

antler ['æntlər] *n* cuerna *f*; **antlers**, cornamenta *f*.

Antwerp ['æntwɜːp] *n* Amberes.

anus ['eɪnəs] *n* ano *m*.

anvil ['ænvɪl] *n* yunque *m*.

anxiety [æŋ'zaɪɪtɪ] *n* (*concern*) inquietud *f*; (*worry*) preocupación *f*; (*fear*) angustia *f*; (*eagerness*) ansia *f*.

anxious ['æŋkʃəs] *adj* (*concerned*) inquieto,-a; (*worried*) preocupado,-a; (*fearful*) angustiado,-a; (*eager*) ansioso,-a; **to be a. about sth**, estar preocupado,-a por algo.

any ['enɪ] **I** *adj* (*in questions, conditionals*) algún,-una; (*in negative clauses*) ningún, -una; (*no matter which*) cualquier,-a; (*every*) todo,-a; **a. doctor will say the**

same, cualquier médico te dirá lo mismo; **are there a. seats left?,** ¿quedan plazas?; **at a. moment,** en cualquier momento; **have you a. apples?,** ¿tienes manzanas?; **have you a. money?,** ¿tienes (algo de) dinero?; **I don't want a. time,** no tengo tiempo; **in a. case,** de todas formas. **II** *pron (in questions)* alguno,-a; *(in negative clauses)* ninguno,-a; *(no matter which)* cualquiera; **do they have a.?,** ¿tienen alguno?; **I don't want a.,** no quiero ninguno,-a; **I need some paper, have you a.?,** necesito papel, ¿tienes?; **you can have a. (one),** coge el *or* la que quieras.
III *adv* **is there a. more?,** ¿hay más?; **I used to like it but not a. more/longer,** antes me gustaba pero ya no; **is he a. better?,** ¿está mejor?

anybody ['enɪbɒdɪ] *pron* → **anybody.**

anyhow ['enɪhaʊ] *adv* **1** *(in spite of that)* en todo caso, de todas formas; *(changing the subject)* bueno, pues. **2** *(carelessly)* desordenadamente, de cualquier modo *or* forma.

anyone ['enɪwʌn] *pron* → **anybody.**

anything ['enɪθɪŋ] **I** *pron (in questions, conditionals)* algo, alguna cosa; *(in negative clauses)* nada; *(no matter what)* cualquier cosa; **a. but that,** cualquier cosa menos eso; **a. else?,** ¿algo más?; **can I do a. for you?,** ¿puedo ayudarte en algo?; **hardly a.,** casi nada; **if a., I'd buy the big one,** de comprar uno compraría el grande; **to run/work like a. s.,** correr/trabajar a más no poder. **II** *adv* **is this a. like what you wanted?,** ¿viene a ser éste lo que querías?

anyway ['enɪweɪ] *adv* → **anyhow.**

anywhere ['enɪweər] *adv* **1** *(in questions, conditionals)* *(situation)* en alguna parte; *(movement)* a alguna parte; **could it be a. else?,** ¿podría estar en otro sitio? **2** *(in negative clauses)* *(situation)* en ninguna parte; *(movement)* a ninguna parte; *(no matter where)* dondequiera, en cualquier parte; **go a. you like,** ve a donde quieras; **we aren't a. near finished,** no hemos terminado ni mucho menos.

apart [ə'pɑːt] *adv* **1** aparte; to fall a., deshacerse; **to take sth a.,** desmontar algo. **2** *(distant)* alejado,-a; *(separate)* separado,-a; **to be poles a.,** ser polos opuestos; **you can't tell the twins a.,** no se puede distinguir los mellizos el uno del otro. **3 a. from,** aparte de.

apartheid [ə'pɑːtheɪt] *n* apartheid *m*.

apartment [ə'pɑːtmənt] *n (large room)* salón *m*; *US (flat)* piso *m*, apartamento *m*; **a. block,** bloque *m* de pisos.

apathetic [æpə'θetɪk] *adj* apático,-a.

apathy ['æpəθɪ] *n* apatía *f.*

ape [eɪp] **I** *n* mono *m.* **II** *vtr* imitar, copiar.

aperitif [ə'perɪtɪf] *n* aperitivo *m.*

aperture ['æpətʃər] *n (hole, crack)* resquicio *m,* rendija *f; Phot* abertura *f.*

apex ['eɪpeks] *n (of triangle)* vértice *m; fig* cumbre *f.*

aphrodisiac [æfrə'dɪzɪæk] *n* afrodisíaco *m.*

apiece [ə'piːs] *adv* cada uno,-a.

aplomb [ə'plɒm] *n* aplomo *m.*

apocalypse [ə'pɒkəlɪps] *n* apocalipsis *m inv.*

apolitical [eɪpə'lɪtɪkəl] *adj* apolítico,-a.

apologetic [əpɒlə'dʒetɪk] *adj (remorseful)* de disculpa; **he was very a.,** pidió mil perdones. **◆apologetically** *adv* disculpándose, pidiendo perdón.

apologize [ə'pɒlədʒaɪz] *vi (say sorry)* disculparse; **they apologized to us for the delay,** se disculparon con nosotros por el retraso.

apology [ə'pɒlədʒɪ] *n* disculpa *f,* excusa *f; fam* **what an a. for a meal!,** ¡vaya birria de comida!

apoplectic [æpə'plektɪk] *adj Med* apopléctico,-a; *fam* **to be a. with rage,** estar furioso,-a.

apostle [ə'pɒsəl] *n* apóstol *m.*

apostrophe [ə'pɒstrəfɪ] *n* apóstrofo *m.*

appal, US appall [ə'pɔːl] *vtr* horrorizar; **to be appalled by sth,** quedar horrorizado,-a por algo.

appalling [ə'pɔːlɪŋ] *adj (horrifying)* horroroso,-a; *fam (very bad)* pésimo,-a, fatal.

apparatus [æpə'reɪtəs] *n* aparato *m*; *(equipment)* equipo *m.*

apparent [ə'pærənt] *adj (obvious)* evidente; *(seeming)* aparente; **to become a.,** ponerse de manifiesto. **◆apparently** *adv (seemingly)* por lo visto.

apparition [æpə'rɪʃən] *n* aparición *f.*

appeal [ə'piːl] **I** *n* **1** *(request)* solicitud *f; (plea)* súplica *f.* **2** *(attraction)* atractivo *m; (interest)* interés *m.* **3** *Jur* apelación *f.* **II** *vi* **1** *(plead)* rogar, suplicar (to, a); **to a. for help,** solicitar ayuda. **2** *(attract)* atraer; *(interest)* interesar; **it doesn't a. to me,** no me dice nada. **3** *Jur* apelar.

appealing [ə'piːlɪŋ] *adj (moving)* conmovedor,-a; *(attractive)* atractivo,-a; *(tempting)* atrayente.

appear [ə'pɪər] *vi* **1** *(become visible)* aparecer; *(publicly)* presentarse; *(on stage)* actuar; **to a. before a court,** comparecer ante un tribunal; **to a. on television,** salir en la televisión. **2** *(seem)* parecer; **he**

appears relaxed, parece relajado; **so it appears**, según parece.

appearance [ə'pɪərəns] n 1 (becoming visible) aparición f; (publicly) presentación f; (on stage) actuación f; (before court) comparecencia f; (of book etc) publicación f; **to put in an a.**, hacer acto de presencia. 2 (look) apariencia f, aspecto m; **to all appearances**, al parecer.

appease [ə'piːz] vtr apaciguar; (curiosity) satisfacer.

appeasement [ə'piːzmənt] n Pol entreguismo m.

appendicitis [əpendɪ'saɪtɪs] n apendicitis f.

appendix [ə'pendɪks] n (pl **appendices** [ə'pendɪsiːz]) apéndice m.

appetite ['æpɪtaɪt] n apetito m; fig deseo m.

appetizer ['æpɪtaɪzər] n (drink) aperitivo m; (snack) tapa f, pincho m.

applaud [ə'plɔːd] vtr & vi aplaudir.

applause [ə'plɔːz] n aplausos mpl.

apple ['æpəl] n manzana f; **a. tree**, manzano m.

appliance [ə'plaɪəns] n dispositivo m.

applicable [ə'plɪkəbəl] adj aplicable.

applicant ['æplɪkənt] n (for post) candidato,-a m,f; (to court, for tickets) solicitante mf.

application [æplɪ'keɪʃən] n (for cream) aplicación f. 2 (for post etc) solicitud f; **a. form**, solicitud f; **job a.**, solicitud de empleo. 3 (effort) aplicación f; **she lacks a.**, no se aplica.

applied [ə'plaɪd] adj aplicado,-a.

apply [ə'plaɪ] I vtr aplicar; (brake) echar; (law) recurrir a; (force) usar; **to a. one-self to**, dedicarse a. II vi 1 (refer) aplicarse (to, a). 2 (for job) presentar una solicitud; (for information, to court) presentar una petición. ◆**apply for** vtr (post, information) solicitar; (tickets) pedir.

appoint [ə'pɔɪnt] vtr (person) nombrar; (time, place etc) fijar, señalar.

appointment [ə'pɔɪntmənt] n 1 (to post) nombramiento m; (post) cargo m. 2 (meeting) cita f; **to make an a. with**, citarse con; (at doctor's) pedir hora a.

apportion [ə'pɔːʃən] vtr fig (blame) echar.

appraisal [ə'preɪzəl] n evaluación f.

appreciable [ə'priːʃəbəl] adj (difference) apreciable; (sum) importante.

appreciate [ə'priːʃɪeɪt] I vtr 1 (be thankful for) agradecer. 2 (understand) entender. 3 (value) apreciar, valorar. II vi (increase in value) apreciarse.

appreciation [əpriːʃɪ'eɪʃən] n 1 (of help, advice) agradecimiento m; (of difficulty) comprensión f; (of wine etc) aprecio m; (appraisal) evaluación f. 2 (increase in value) apreciación f.

appreciative [ə'priːʃɪətɪv] adj (thankful) agradecido,-a; (responsive) apreciativo,-a.

apprehend [æprɪ'hend] vtr (arrest) detener.

apprehension [æprɪ'henʃən] n 1 (arrest) detención f. 2 (fear) aprensión f.

apprehensive [æprɪ'hensɪv] adj (fearful) aprensivo,-a.

apprentice [ə'prentɪs] n aprendiz,-a m,f.

apprenticeship [ə'prentɪʃɪp] n aprendizaje m.

approach [ə'prəʊtʃ] I n 1 (coming near) acercamiento m; (to town) acceso m; **a. road**, vía f de acceso. 2 (to problem) enfoque m. II vtr (come near to) acercarse a; (be similar to) aproximarse a; fig (problem) abordar; (person) dirigirse a; **to a. sb about sth**, dirigirse a algn a propósito de algo. III vi acercarse.

approachable [ə'prəʊtʃəbəl] adj (person) accesible.

appropriate[1] [ə'prəʊprɪɪt] adj (suitable) apropiado,-a, adecuado,-a; (convenient) oportuno,-a.

appropriate[2] [ə'prəʊprɪeɪt] vtr (allocate) asignar; (steal) apropiarse de.

approval [ə'pruːvəl] n aprobación f, visto m bueno; Com **to get sth on a.**, adquirir algo sin compromiso de compra.

approve [ə'pruːv] vtr aprobar; **approved school**, reformatorio m. ◆**approve of** vtr aprobar.

approving [ə'pruːvɪŋ] adj (look etc) aprobatorio,-a.

approx [ə'prɒks] abbr of **approximately**, aprox.

approximate [ə'prɒksɪmɪt] I adj aproximado,-a. II [ə'prɒksɪmeɪt] vtr aproximarse a. ◆**approximately** adv aproximadamente.

apricot ['eɪprɪkɒt] n albaricoque m.

April ['eɪprəl] n abril m; **A. Fools' Day**, día m uno de abril, ≈ día de los Inocentes (28 de diciembre).

apron ['eɪprən] n delantal m; (for workman) mandil m.

apt [æpt] adj 1 (suitable) apropiado,-a; (remark) acertado,-a, oportuno,-a; (name) justo,-a, (description) exacto,-a. 2 **to be a. to do sth**, ser propenso,-a a hacer algo. ◆**aptly** adv acertadamente.

aptitude ['æptɪtjuːd] n capacidad f; **a. test**, prueba f de aptitud.

aqualung ['ækwəlʌŋ] n botella f de oxígeno.

aquamarine [ækwəmə'riːn] I n Min aguamarina f. II adj de color de aguamarina.

aquarium [ə'kweərɪəm] n acuario m.

Aquarius [ə'kweərɪəs] n Acuario m.

aquatic [ə'kwætɪk] adj acuático,-a.

aqueduct ['ækwɪdʌkt] n acueducto m.

Arab ['ærəb] adj & n árabe (mf).

Arabian [ə'reɪbɪən] adj árabe.

Arabic ['ærəbɪk] I adj árabe, arábigo,-a; **A. numerals**, numeración f arábiga. II n (language) árabe m.

arable ['ærəbəl] *adj* cultivable.
Aragon ['ærəgən] *n* Aragón.
arbitrary ['ɑːbɪtrərɪ] *adj* arbitrario,-a.
arbitrate ['ɑːbɪtreɪt] *vtr & vi* arbitrar.
arbitration [ɑːbɪ'treɪʃən] *n* arbitraje *m*.
arc [ɑːk] *n* arco *m*; **a. lamp**, arco voltaico.
arcade [ɑː'keɪd] *n* arcada *f*; *(passageway)* pasaje *m*; **shopping a.**, galerías *fpl* (comerciales).
arch [ɑːtʃ] I *n* 1 *Archit* arco *m*; *(vault)* bóveda *f*. 2 *Anat* empeine *m*. II *vtr* (*back*) arquear.
archaeologist [ɑːkɪ'ɒlədʒɪst] *n* arqueólogo,-a *m,f*.
archaeology [ɑːkɪ'ɒlədʒɪ] *n* arqueología *f*.
archaic [ɑː'keɪɪk] *adj* arcaico,-a.
archbishop [ɑːtʃ'bɪʃəp] *n* arzobispo *m*.
arched [ɑːtʃt] *adj* arqueado,-a.
archeology [ɑːkɪ'ɒlədʒɪ] *n US* → **archaeology**.
archer ['ɑːtʃər] *n* arquero,-a *m,f*.
archery ['ɑːtʃərɪ] *n* tiro *m* con arco.
archetypal [ɑːkɪ'taɪpəl] *adj* arquetípico,-a.
archipelago [ɑːkɪ'pelɪgəʊ] *n* archipiélago *m*.
architect ['ɑːkɪtekt] *n* arquitecto,-a *m,f*.
architectural [ɑːkɪ'tektʃərəl] *adj* arquitectónico,-a.
architecture ['ɑːkɪtektʃər] *n* arquitectura *f*.
archives ['ɑːkaɪvz] *npl* archivos *mpl*.
archway ['ɑːtʃweɪ] *n* *(arch)* arco *m*; *(vault)* bóveda *f*; *(in church)* atrio *m*; *(passage)* pasaje *m*.
arctic ['ɑːktɪk] I *adj* ártico,-a; **A. Circle**, círculo *m* polar Ártico. II *n* **the A.**, el Ártico.
ardent ['ɑːdənt] *adj* *(supporter etc)* apasionado,-a; *(desire)* ardiente.
ardour, US ardor ['ɑːdər] *n* pasión *f*, ardor *m*.
arduous ['ɑːdjʊəs] *adj* arduo,-a, penoso,-a.
are [ɑːr] *2nd person sing pres, 1st, 2nd, 3rd person pl pres* → **be**.
area ['eərɪə] *n* *(surface)* área *f*, superficie *f*; *(space)* extensión *f*; *(region)* región *f*; *(of town)* zona *f*; *fig* *(field)* campo *m*; *US Tel* **a. code**, prefijo *m* local.
arena [ə'riːnə] *n* *(stadium)* estadio *m*; *(bullring)* plaza *f*; *(circus)* pista *f*; *fig* *(stage)* campo *m* de batalla.
Argentina [ɑːdʒən'tiːnə] *n* Argentina.
Argentinian [ɑːdʒən'tɪnɪən] *adj & n* argentino,-a *(m,f)*.
arguable [ɑːgjʊəbəl] *adj* discutible.
◆**arguably** *adv* it's **a. the best**, hay quienes dicen que es el mejor.
argue ['ɑːgjuː] I *vtr* *(reason)* discutir; *(point of view)* mantener. II *vi* *(quarrel)* discutir; *(reason)* argumentar, razonar; **to a. for**, abogar por; **to a. against sth**, po-

nerse en contra de algo.
argument ['ɑːgjʊmənt] *n* *(reason)* argumento *m* (**for**, a favor de; **against**, en contra de); *(quarrel)* discusión *f*, disputa *f*; **for the sake of a.**, es un decir.
argumentative [ɑːgjʊ'mentətɪv] *adj* **she's very a.**, le gusta discutir por todo.
aria ['ɑːrɪə] *n* aria *f*.
arid ['ærɪd] *adj* árido,-a.
Aries ['eəriːz] *n* Aries *m*.
arise [ə'raɪz] *vi* *(opportunity)* presentarse; *pp* **arisen** [ə'rɪzən] *(get up)* levantarse; *(happen)* surgir; **should the occasion a.**, si se presenta la ocasión.
aristocracy [ærɪ'stɒkrəsɪ] *n* aristocracia *f*.
aristocrat ['ærɪstəkræt] *n* aristócrata *mf*.
arithmetic [ə'rɪθmətɪk] *n* aritmética *f*.
ark [ɑːk] *n* arca *f*; **Noah's A.**, el arca de Noé.
arm [ɑːm] I *n* 1 brazo *m*; *(of garment)* manga *f*; **to walk a. in a.**, ir cogidos,-as del brazo. 2 *Mil* **arms**, armas *fpl*; **arms race**, carrera armamentística; **coat of arms**, escudo *m*. II *vtr* armar; **to a. oneself against sth**, armarse contra algo.
armaments ['ɑːməmənts] *npl* armamentos *mpl*.
armchair ['ɑːmtʃeər] *n* sillón *m*.
armed [ɑːmd] *adj* armado,-a; **a. forces**, fuerzas armadas; **a. robbery**, robo *m* a mano armada.
armistice ['ɑːmɪstɪs] *n* armisticio *m*.
armour, US armor ['ɑːmər] *n* *(on vehicle)* blindaje *m*; *(suit of)* **a.**, armadura *f*.
armoured car, US armored car [ɑːməd'kɑː] *n* coche *m* blindado.
armour-plated ['ɑːməpleɪtɪd] *adj* acorazado,-a.
armoury, US armory ['ɑːmərɪ] *n* arsenal *m*.
armpit ['ɑːmpɪt] *n* axila *f*, sobaco *m*.
army ['ɑːmɪ] *n* ejército *m*.
aroma [ə'rəʊmə] *n* aroma *m*.
arose [ə'rəʊz] *pt* → **arise**.
around [ə'raʊnd] I *adv* alrededor; **all a.**, por todos los lados; **are the children a.?**, ¿están los niños por aquí?; **he looked a.**, miró (a su) alrededor. II *prep* 1 alrededor de; **a. the corner**, a la vuelta de la esquina; **a. here**, por aquí. 2 *(approximately)* aproximadamente.
arouse [ə'raʊz] *vtr* despertar; *(sexually)* excitar.
arrange [ə'reɪndʒ] I *vtr* 1 *(order)* ordenar; *(hair, flowers)* arreglar; *Mus* adaptar. 2 *(plan)* organizar; *(agree on)* quedar en; **to a. a time**, fijar una hora; **arranged marriage**, boda arreglada. II *vi* **I shall a. for him to be there**, lo arreglaré para que pueda asistir.
arrangement [ə'reɪndʒmənt] *n* 1 *(display)* colocación *f*; *Mus* adaptación *f*. 2 *(agreement)* acuerdo *m*. 3 **arrangements**, *(plans)* planes *mpl*; *(preparations)* preparativos

mpl.

array [ə'reɪ] n colección f; **a great a. of goods,** un gran surtido de productos.

arrears [ə'rɪəz] npl atrasos mpl; **to be in a. with the rent,** estar atrasado,-a con el alquiler; **to be paid in a.,** cobrar con retraso.

arrest [ə'rest] I n detención f; **to be under a.,** estar detenido,-a. II vtr (criminal) detener; fig (progress) frenar.

arresting [ə'restɪŋ] adj llamativo,-a.

arrival [ə'raɪvəl] n llegada f; **a new a.,** un,-a recién llegado,-a.

arrive [ə'raɪv] vi llegar (**at, in, a**).

arrogance ['ærəgəns] n arrogancia f.

arrogant ['ærəgənt] adj arrogante.

arrow ['ærəʊ] n flecha f.

arse [ɑːs] n vulg culo m.

arsenal ['ɑːsənəl] n arsenal m.

arsenic ['ɑːsnɪk] n arsénico m.

arson ['ɑːsən] n incendio m provocado.

art [ɑːt] n 1 arte m; (drawing) dibujo m; **the arts,** las bellas artes; **arts and crafts,** artes fpl y oficios mpl; **a. gallery,** galería f de arte. 2 **arts,** (branch of knowledge) letras fpl.

artefact ['ɑːtɪfækt] n artefacto m; (in archaelogy) objeto m de arte.

artery ['ɑːtərɪ] n arteria f.

artful ['ɑːtfʊl] adj (cunning) ladino,-a.

arthritis [ɑː'θraɪtɪs] n artritis f.

artichoke ['ɑːtɪtʃəʊk] n alcachofa f.

article ['ɑːtɪkəl] n 1 artículo m; Press artículo; **a. of clothing,** prenda f de vestir. 2 Jur **articles,** contrato m sing de aprendizaje.

articulate¹ [ɑː'tɪkjʊlɪt] adj (speech) claro,-a; (person) que se expresa bien.

articulate² [ɑː'tɪkjʊleɪt] vtr & vi articular; (words) pronunciar; **articulated lorry,** camión articulado.

artificial [ɑːtɪ'fɪʃəl] adj artificial; (limb) postizo,-a; **a. intelligence,** inteligencia f artificial.

artillery [ɑː'tɪlərɪ] n artillería f.

artisan ['ɑːtɪzæn] n artesano,-a m,f.

artist ['ɑːtɪst] n artista mf; (painter) pintor,-a m,f.

artistic [ɑː'tɪstɪk] adj artístico,-a.

artistry ['ɑːtɪstrɪ] n arte m, talento artístico.

as [æz, unstressed əz] I adv & conj 1 (comparison) **as ... as ...,** tan ... como ...; **as far as,** hasta; fig **as far as I'm concerned,** por lo que a mí respecta; **as many as,** tantos,-as como; **as much as,** tanto,-a como; **as tall as me,** tan alto,-a como yo; **as opposed to,** a diferencia de; **as little as £5,** tan sólos cinco libras ; **as soon as they arrive,** en cuanto lleguen; **I'll stay as long as I can,** quedaré todo el tiempo que pueda; **just as big,** igual de grande; **three times as fast,** tres veces más rápido; **the same as,** igual que. 2

(manner) como; **as a rule,** por regla general; **as you know,** como ya sabéis; **as you like,** como quieras; **do as I say,** haz lo que yo te digo; **he's working as a doctor,** está trabajando de médico; **I thought as much,** ya me lo suponía; **it serves as a table,** sirve de mesa; **leave it as it is,** déjalo tal como está; **he was dressed as a pirate,** iba vestido de pirata. 3 (while, when) mientras (que); **as a child,** de niño,-a; **as I was eating,** mientras comía; **as we were leaving we saw Pat,** al salir vimos a Pat. 4 (though) aunque; **be that as it may,** por mucho que así sea; **young as he is,** aunque es joven. 5 (because) como, ya que. 6 (and so) igual que; **as do I,** igual que yo; **as well, también.** 7 (purpose) para, **so as to do sth,** para hacer algo. 8 **as for my brother,** en cuanto a mi hermano. 9 **as from, as of,** a partir de. 10 **to act as if,** actuar como si + subj; **it looks as if the concert is off,** parece ser que no habrá concierto. 11 **it's late enough as it is,** ya es muy tarde; **as it were,** por así decirlo. 12 **as long as,** (only if) siempre que, con tal de que. 13 **as regards,** en cuanto a, por lo que se refiere a; **as usual,** como siempre; **as yet,** aún, todavía.

II rel pron such as, tal(es) como.

asbestos [æz'bestəs] n amianto m, asbesto m.

ascend [ə'send] vi subir, ascender.

ascendancy [ə'sendənsɪ] n dominio m, influencia f.

ascendant [ə'sendənt] n **to be in the a.,** estar en auge.

ascent [ə'sent] n subida f.

ascertain [æsə'teɪn] vtr averiguar, enterarse de.

ascribe [ə'skraɪb] vtr **to a. sth to,** imputar algo a.

aseptic [ə'septɪk] adj aséptico,-a.

ash¹ [æʃ] n Bot fresno m.

ash² [æʃ] n ceniza f; **a. bin,** US **a. can,** cubo m de la basura; Rel **A. Wednesday,** miércoles m inv de ceniza.

ashamed [ə'ʃeɪmd] adj avergonzado,-a; **you ought to be a. of yourself!,** ¡te debería dar vergüenza!

ashen ['æʃən] adj (face) pálido,-a.

ashore [ə'ʃɔːr] adv (position) en tierra; **to go a.,** desembarcar; **to swim a.,** nadar hacia tierra.

ashtray ['æʃtreɪ] n cenicero m.

Asia ['eɪʒə] n Asia; **A. Minor,** Asia Menor.

Asian ['eɪʒən] adj & n asiático,-a (m,f).

aside [ə'saɪd] I adv a un lado, aparte; **to cast a.,** echar a un lado; **to stand a.,** apartarse. II prep **a. from,** (apart from) aparte de; (as well as) además de. III n Theat aparte m.

ask [ɑːsk] I vtr 1 preguntar; **to a. sb a**

question, hacer una pregunta a algn. 2 (*request*) pedir, solicitar; **she asked me to post it,** me pidió que lo echara al buzón. 3 (*invite*) invitar. II *vi* (*inquire*) preguntar; (*request*) pedir. ◆**ask after** *vtr* to a. **after sb,** preguntar por algn. ◆**ask for** *vtr* (*help*) pedir, solicitar; (*person*) preguntar por. ◆**ask out** *vtr* to a. **sb out,** invitar a algn a salir.

askance |əˈskæns| *adv* to look a. **at sb,** mirar a algn con recelo.

askew |əˈskjuː| I *adj* ladeado,-a. II *adv* de lado.

asleep |əˈsliːp| *adj* (*person*) dormido,-a; (*limb*) adormecido,-a; **to fall a.,** quedarse dormido,-a.

asparagus |əˈspærəgəs| *n inv* espárragos *mpl.*

aspect |ˈæspekt| *n* 1 (*of question*) aspecto *m.* 2 (*of building*) orientación *f.*

aspersions |əˈspɜːʃənz| *npl* to cast a. **on sb,** difamar a algn.

asphalt |ˈæsfælt| *n* asfalto *m.*

asphyxiation |æsfɪksɪˈeɪʃən| *n* asfixia *f.*

aspiration |æspəˈreɪʃən| *n* aspiración *f.*

aspire |əˈspaɪər| *vi* to a. **to,** aspirar a.

aspirin® |ˈæsprɪn| *n* aspirina® *f.*

ass¹ |æs| *n* *Zool* asno-a *m,f,* burro,-a *m,f; fam fig* burro,-a.

ass² |æs| *n US vulg* culo *m.*

assailant |əˈseɪlənt| *n* agresor,-a *m,f,* atacante *mf.*

assassin |əˈsæsɪn| *n* asesino,-a *m,f.*

assassinate |əˈsæsɪneɪt| *vtr* asesinar.

assassination |əsæsɪˈneɪʃən| *n* asesinato *m.*

assault |əˈsɔːlt| I *n Mil* ataque *m* (**on a,** a); *Jur* agresión *f.* II *vtr Mil* asaltar, atacar; *Jur* agredir; (*sexually*) violar.

assemble |əˈsembəl| I *vtr* (*people*) reunir, juntar; (*furniture*) montar. II *vi* (*people*) reunirse, juntarse.

assembly |əˈsemblɪ| *n* reunión *f,* asamblea *f; Tech* montaje *m; Ind* a. **line,** cadena *f* de montaje; *Educ* **morning a.,** servicio *m* matinal.

assent |əˈsent| I *n* (*agreement*) asentimiento *m;* (*consent*) consentimiento *m;* (*approval*) aprobación *f.* II *vi* asentir, consentir (to, en).

assert |əˈsɜːt| *vtr* afirmar; **to a. oneself,** imponerse; **to a. one's rights,** hacer valer sus derechos.

assertive |əˈsɜːtɪv| *adj* enérgico,-a.

assess |əˈses| *vtr* (*estimate value*) valorar; (*damages, price*) calcular; (*tax*) gravar; *fig* (*effect*) evaluar.

assessment |əˈsesmənt| *n* (*of value*) valoración *f;* (*of damages etc*) cálculo *m;* (*of taxes*) gravamen *m; fig* juicio *m.*

assessor |əˈsesər| *n* asesor,-a *m,f.*

asset |ˈæset| *n* 1 ventaja *f;* **to be an a.,** (*person*) ser de gran valor. 2 *Fin* **assets,** bienes *mpl;* **fixed assets,** bienes raíces.

assiduous |əˈsɪdjʊəs| *adj* asiduo,-a.

assign |əˈsaɪn| *vtr* (*task*) asignar; (*property etc*) ceder; **to a. sb to a job,** designar a algn para un trabajo.

assignment |əˈsaɪnmənt| *n* (*allocation*) asignación *f;* (*task*) tarea *f;* (*mission*) misión *f;* (*appointment*) cita *f.*

assimilate |əˈsɪmɪleɪt| *vtr* asimilar.

assist |əˈsɪst| *vtr* & *vi* ayudar.

assistance |əˈsɪstəns| *n* ayuda *f,* auxilio *m.*

assistant |əˈsɪstənt| *n* ayudante *mf;* a. **manager,** subdirector,-a *m,f;* **shop a.,** dependiente,-a *m,f;* (**language**) a., lector,-a *m,f.*

associate¹ |əˈsəʊʃɪeɪt| I *vtr* (*ideas*) relacionar; (*companies*) asociar; **to be associated with sth,** estar relacionado,-a con algo. II *vi* to a. **with,** tratar con.

associate² |əˈsəʊʃɪɪt| I *adj* asociado,-a. II *n* (*colleague*) colega *mf;* (*partner*) socio,-a *m,f;* (*accomplice*) cómplice *mf.*

association |əsəʊsɪˈeɪʃən| *n* asociación *f;* (*company*) sociedad *f.*

assorted |əˈsɔːtɪd| *adj* surtido,-a, variado,-a.

assortment |əˈsɔːtmənt| *n* surtido *m,* variedad *f.*

assume |əˈsjuːm| I *vtr* (*power*) asumir; (*attitude, name*) adoptar; **an assumed name,** un nombre falso. II *vi* (*suppose*) suponer.

assumption |əˈsʌmpʃən| *n* 1 (*of power*) toma *f;* a. **of office,** toma de posesión. 2 (*supposition*) suposición *f.*

assurance |əˈʃʊərəns| *n* 1 (*guarantee*) garantía *f.* 2 (*confidence*) confianza *f.* 3 (*insurance*) seguro *m.*

assure |əˈʃʊər| *vtr* asegurar.

asterisk |ˈæstərɪsk| *n* asterisco *m.*

astern |əˈstɜːn| *adv* a popa.

asthma |ˈæsmə| *n* asma *f.*

astonish |əˈstɒnɪʃ| *vtr* asombrar, pasmar; **I was astonished,** me quedé pasmado,-a.

astonishing |əˈstɒnɪʃɪŋ| *adj* asombroso, -a, pasmoso,-a.

astonishment |əˈstɒnɪʃmənt| *n* asombro *m;* **to my a.,** para gran sorpresa mía.

astound |əˈstaʊnd| *vtr* asombrar, pasmar.

astray |əˈstreɪ| *adv* to go a., extraviarse; (*fig*) equivocarse; **to lead sb a.,** llevar a algn por mal camino.

astride |əˈstraɪd| *prep* a horcajadas sobre.

astrology |əˈstrɒlədʒɪ| *n* astrología *f.*

astronaut |ˈæstrənɔːt| *n* astronauta *mf.*

astronomer |əˈstrɒnəmər| *n* astrónomo,-a *m,f.*

astronomical |æstrəˈnɒmɪkəl| *adj* astronómico,-a.

astronomy |əˈstrɒnəmɪ| *n* astronomía *f.*

Asturias |æˈstʊərɪəs| *n* Asturias *f.*

astute |əˈstjuːt| *adj* astuto,-a.

asylum |əˈsaɪləm| *n* 1 (*protection*) asilo *m;* **to seek political a.,** pedir asilo político.

2 mental a., manicomio m.

at [æt] prep 1 (position) a, en; **at school/ work**, en el colegio/trabajo; **at the window**, a la ventana; **at the top**, en lo alto. 2 (direction) a; **to be angry at sb/ sth**, enfadarse con algn/por algo; **to laugh at sb**, reírse de algn; **to look at sth/sb**, mirar algo/a algn; **to shout at sb**, gritarle a algn. 3 (time) a; **at Easter/Christmas**, en Semana Santa/Navidad; **at six o'clock**, a las seis; **at first**, al principio; **at last**, por fin; **at once**, enseguida; **at that time**, entonces; **at the moment**, ahora. 4 (manner) a, en; **at best/worst**, en el mejor/peor de los casos; **at hand**, a mano; **at least**, por lo menos; **not at all**, en absoluto; (don't mention it) de nada. 5 (rate) a; **they retail at 100 pesetas each**, se venden a 100 pesetas la unidad; **two at a time**, de dos en dos.

ate [et. eɪt] pt → **eat**.

atheist ['eɪθiːst] n ateo,-a m,f.

Athens ['æθɪnz] n Atenas.

athlete ['æθliːt] n atleta mf.

athletic [æθ'letɪk] I adj atlético,-a; (sporty) deportista. II npl **athletics** atletismo m sing.

Atlantic [ət'læntɪk] adj the A. (Ocean), el (océano) Atlántico.

atlas ['ætləs] n atlas m.

atmosphere ['ætməsfɪəʳ] n atmósfera f; fig (ambience) ambiente m.

atmospheric [ætməs'ferɪk] adj atmosférico,-a.

atom ['ætəm] n átomo m; **a. bomb**, bomba atómica.

atomic [ə'tɒmɪk] adj atómico,-a.

atone [ə'təʊn] vi **to a. for**, expiar.

atrocious [ə'trəʊʃəs] adj atroz.

attach [ə'tætʃ] vtr (stick) pegar; (fasten) sujetar; (document) adjuntar; **to a. importance to sth**, dar importancia a algo; fig **to be attached to**, (be fond of) tener cariño a.

attaché [ə'tæʃeɪ] n agregado,-a m,f; **a. case**, maletín m.

attachment [ə'tætʃmənt] n 1 Tech accesorio m; (action) acoplamiento m. 2 (fondness) apego m (to, por).

attack [ə'tæk] I n 1 (assault) ataque m, asalto m; **an a. on sb's life**, un atentado contra la vida de algn. 2 Med ataque m. II vtr (assault) atacar, asaltar; fig (problem) abordar, (job) emprender; fig (criticize) atacar.

attacker [ə'tækəʳ] n asaltante mf, agresor,-a m,f.

attain [ə'teɪn] vtr (aim) lograr; (rank, age) llegar a.

attainment [ə'teɪnmənt] n (achievement) logro m; (skill) talento m.

attempt [ə'tempt] I n intento m, tentativa f; **at the second a.**, a la segunda; **an a. on sb's life**, un atentado contra la vida

de algn. II vtr intentar; **to a. to do sth**, tratar de or intentar hacer algo; Jur **attempted murder/rape**, intento m de asesinato/violación.

attend [ə'tend] I vtr (be present at) asistir a; (care for, wait on) atender. II vi (be present) asistir; (pay attention) prestar atención. ◆**attend to** vtr (business) ocuparse de; (in shop) atender a.

attendance [ə'tendəns] n asistencia f.

attendant [ə'tendənt] n (in cinema etc) acomodador,-a m,f; (in museum) guía mf; (in car park) vigilante,-a m,f.

attention [ə'tenʃən] n 1 atención f; **for the a. of Miss Jones**, a la atención de la Srta. Jones; **pay a.!**, ¡atiende!; **to pay a. to sb/sth**, prestar atención a algn/algo. 2 Mil **a.!**, ¡firmes!; **to stand to a.**, estar firmes.

attentive [ə'tentɪv] adj (listener) atento,-a; (helpful) solícito,-a.

attest [ə'test] vi **to a. to**, dar testimonio de.

attic ['ætɪk] n ático m.

attire [ə'taɪəʳ] n fml traje m.

attitude ['ætɪtjuːd] n actitud f; (position of body) postura f; **an a. of mind**, un estado de ánimo.

attorney [ə'tɜːnɪ] n 1 US (lawyer) abogado,-a m,f; **A. General**, ≈ Ministro,-a m,f de Justicia; **district a.**, fiscal mf. 2 Jur **power of a.**, poderes mpl.

attract [ə'trækt] vtr atraer; **to a. attention**, llamar la atención; **to a. a waiter's attention**, llamar a un camarero.

attraction [ə'trækʃən] n 1 (power) atracción f. 2 (attractive thing) atractivo m; (charm) encanto m; (amenity) aliciente m; **the main a.**, el número fuerte.

attractive [ə'træktɪv] adj atractivo,-a; (good-looking) guapo,-a; (idea, proposition) atrayente.

attribute¹ ['ætrɪbjuːt] n (quality) atributo m.

attribute² [ə'trɪbjuːt] vtr atribuir.

attrition [ə'trɪʃən] n **war of a.**, guerra f de desgaste.

aubergine ['əʊbəʒiːn] n berenjena f.

auburn ['ɔːbən] adj castaño rojizo inv.

auction ['ɔːkʃən] I n subasta f. II vtr subastar.

auctioneer [ɔːkʃə'nɪəʳ] n subastador,-a m,f.

audacious [ɔː'deɪʃəs] adj (daring) audaz; (bold) atrevido,-a; (impudent) descarado, -a.

audible ['ɔːdɪbəl] adj audible.

audience ['ɔːdɪəns] n 1 (spectators) público m; (at concert, conference) auditorio m; (television) telespectadores mpl. 2 (meeting) audiencia f.

audio-visual [ɔːdɪəʊ'vɪʒʊəl] adj audiovisual; **a.-v. aids**, apoyo m audiovisual.

audit ['ɔːdɪt] I n revisión f de cuentas. II

vtr revisar, intervenir.

audition [ɔːˈdɪʃən] **I** *n* prueba *f*. **II** *vtr* to a. sb for a part, probar a algn para un papel.

auditor [ˈɔːdɪtər] *n* revisor,-a *m,f* de cuentas.

auditorium [ɔːdɪˈtɔːrɪəm] *n* auditorio *m*.

augment [ɔːgˈment] *vtr* aumentar.

augur [ˈɔːgər] *vi* to a. well, ser de buen agüero.

August [ˈɔːgəst] *n* agosto *m*.

aunt [ɑːnt] *n* (*also fam* **auntie, aunty** [ˈɑːntɪ]) tía *f*.

au pair [əʊˈpeər] *n* **au p.** (**girl**), au pair *f*.

aura [ˈɔːrə] *n* aura *f*; *Rel* aureola *f*.

aural [ˈɔːrəl] *adj* auditivo,-a, del oído.

auspices [ˈɔːspɪsɪz] *npl* **under the a. of**, bajo los auspicios de.

auspicious [ɔːˈspɪʃəs] *adj* de buen augurio.

austere [ɒˈstɪər] *adj* austero,-a.

austerity [ɒˈsterɪtɪ] *n* austeridad *f*.

Australia [ɒˈstreɪlɪə] *n* Australia *f*.

Australian [ɒˈstreɪlɪən] *adj & n* australiano,-a (*m,f*).

Austria [ˈɒstrɪə] *n* Austria *f*.

Austrian [ˈɒstrɪən] *adj & n* austríaco,-a (*m,f*).

authentic [ɔːˈθentɪk] *adj* auténtico,-a.

author [ˈɔːθər] *n* autor,-a *m,f*.

authoritarian [ɔːθɒrɪˈteərɪən] *adj* autoritario,-a.

authoritative [ɔːˈθɒrɪtətɪv] *adj* (*reliable*) autorizado,-a; (*authoritarian*) autoritario,-a.

authority [ɔːˈθɒrɪtɪ] *n* autoridad *f*; **local a.**, ayuntamiento *m*.

authorize [ˈɔːθəraɪz] *vtr* autorizar; (*payment etc*) aprobar; **to a. sb to do sth**, autorizar a algn a hacer algo.

auto [ˈɔːtəʊ] *n US* coche *m*, *Am* carro *m*.

autobiography [ɔːtəʊbaɪˈɒgrəfɪ] *n* autobiografía *f*.

autograph [ˈɔːtəgrɑːf] **I** *n* autógrafo *m*. **II** *vtr* (*sign*) firmar; (*book, photo*) dedicar.

automatic [ɔːtəˈmætɪk] **I** *adj* automático,-a. **II** *n* (*car*) coche automático; (*gun*) pistola automática. ◆**automatically** *adv* automáticamente.

automation [ɔːtəˈmeɪʃən] *n* automatización *f*; **office a.**, ofimática *f*.

automaton [ɔːˈtɒmətən] *n* (*pl* **automata** [ɔːˈtɒmətə]) autómata *m*.

automobile [ˈɔːtəməbiːl] *n US* coche *m*, automóvil *m*, *Am* carro *m*.

autonomous [ɔːˈtɒnəməs] *adj* autónomo,-a.

autonomy [ɔːˈtɒnəmɪ] *n* autonomía *f*.

autopsy [ˈɔːtɒpsɪ] *n* autopsia *f*.

autumn [ˈɔːtəm] *n* otoño *m*.

auxiliary [ɔːgˈzɪljərɪ] *adj* auxiliar.

Av., av. *abbr of* **Avenue**, avenida *f*, Av., Avda.

avail [əˈveɪl] **I** *n* **to no a.**, en vano. **II** *vtr*

to a. oneself of sth, aprovecharse de algo.

available [əˈveɪləbəl] *adj* (*thing*) disponible; (*person*) libre.

avalanche [ˈævəlɑːnʃ] *n* avalancha *f*.

avarice [ˈævərɪs] *n* avaricia *f*.

Ave *abbr of* **Avenue**, Avenida *f*, Av., Avda.

avenge [əˈvendʒ] *vtr* vengar.

avenue [ˈævɪnjuː] *n* avenida *f*; *fig* vía *f*.

average [ˈævərɪdʒ] **I** *n* promedio *m*, media *f*; **on a.**, por término medio. **II** *adj* medio,-a; (*condition*) regular. **III** *vtr* sacar la media de; **he averages 8 hours' work a day**, trabaja una media de 8 horas al día. ◆**average out at** *vtr* salir a una media de.

averse [əˈvɜːs] *adj* **to be a. to sth**, ser reacio,-a a algo.

aversion [əˈvɜːʃən] *n* (*feeling*) aversión *f*; (*thing*) bestia negra.

avert [əˈvɜːt] *vtr* (*eyes, thoughts*) apartar (*from*, de); (*accident*) impedir; (*danger*) evitar.

avid [ˈævɪd] *adj* (*reader*) voraz. ◆**avidly** *adv* vorazmente.

avocado [ævəˈkɑːdəʊ] *n* (*also* **avocado pear**) aguacate *m*.

avoid [əˈvɔɪd] *vtr* evitar; (*question*) eludir.

avoidable [əˈvɔɪdəbəl] *adj* evitable.

await [əˈweɪt] *vtr* esperar, aguardar.

awake [əˈweɪk] **I** *adj* despierto,-a; **to be a.**, estar despierto,-a. **II** *vi* (*pt* **awoke, awaked**; *pp* **awoken, awaked**) despertar.

awaken [əˈweɪkən] *vtr & vi* (*pt* **awakened**; *pp* **awoken, awaked**) → **awake II**.

awakening [əˈweɪkənɪŋ] *n* despertar *m*.

award [əˈwɔːd] **I** *n* (*prize*) premio *m*; (*medal*) condecoración *f*; *Jur* indemnización *f*; (*grant*) beca *f*. **II** *vtr* (*prize*) conceder, otorgar; (*medal*) dar; (*damages*) adjudicar.

aware [əˈweər] *adj* (*informed*) enterado,-a; **not that I'm a. of**, que yo sepa no; **to be a. of sth**, ser consciente de algo; **to become a. of sth**, darse cuenta de algo.

awareness [əˈweənɪs] *n* conciencia *f* (**of**, de).

awash [əˈwɒʃ] *adj* inundado,-a (**with**, de).

away [əˈweɪ] *adv* **far a.**, lejos; **go a.!**, ¡lárgate!; **it's 3 miles a.**, está a 3 millas (de distancia); **keep a. from the fire!**, ¡no te acerques al fuego!; **right a.**, en seguida; **to be a.**, (*absent*) estar ausente; (*out*) estar fuera; **to die a.**, desvanecerse; **to give sth a.**, regalar algo; (*secret*) revelar algo; **to go a.**, irse; *Sport* **to play a.**, jugar fuera; **to turn a.**, volver la cara; **to work a.**, trabajar.

awe [ɔː] *n* (*fear*) temor *m*; (*amazement*) asombro *m*; **he was in a. of his father**, le intimidaba su padre.

awe-inspiring [ˈɔːɪnspaɪərɪŋ] *adj* impresionante, imponente.

awesome [ˈɔːsəm] *adj* impresionante.

awful ['ɔːfʊl] *adj* espantoso,-a; **an a. lot of work**, muchísimo trabajo. ◆**awfully** *adv fam* terriblemente.

awkward ['ɔːkwəd] *adj* (clumsy) torpe; (difficult) pesado,-a; (object) incómodo,-a; (moment) inoportuno,-a; (situation) embarazoso,-a; (problem) difícil.

awning ['ɔːnɪŋ] *n* (on ship) toldo *m*; (on shop) marquesina *f*.

awoke [ə'wəʊk] *pt* → **awake**.

awoken [ə'wəʊkən] *pp* → **awake**.

axe, *US* **ax** [æks] **I** *n* hacha *f*. **II** *vtr fig* (jobs) eliminar; (costs) reducir; (plan) cancelar; (person) despedir.

axis ['æksɪs] *n* (*pl* **axes** ['æksɪːz]) eje *m*.

axle ['æksəl] *n* eje *m*; *Tech* árbol *m*.

ayatollah [aɪə'tɒlə] *n* ayatolá *m*.

Aztec ['æztek] *adj & n* azteca (*mf*).

B

B, b [biː] *n* 1 (the letter) B, b *f*; *Aut* **B road,** carretera secundaria. 2 *Mus* si *m*; **B flat,** si *m* bemol.

BA [biː'eɪ] *abbr of* Bachelor of Arts, Licenciado en Filosofía y Letras.

babble ['bæbəl] *vi* (baby) balbucear; (brook) murmurar.

babe [beɪb] *n* 1 (baby) bebé *m*. 2 *US fam* **hi, b.!,** ¡hola, guapa!

baboon [bə'buːn] *n* zambo *m*.

baby ['beɪbɪ] *n* 1 bebé *m*; (young child) niño,-a *m,f*; **b. buggy,** *US* **b. carriage,** cochecito *m* de niño; **b. face,** cara *f* de niño. 2 (animal) cría *f*. 3 *fam* (darling) querido,-a *m,f*.

baby-sit ['beɪbɪsɪt] *vi* hacer de canguro.

baby-sitter ['beɪbɪsɪtə(r)] *n* canguro *mf*.

baby-walker ['beɪbɪwɔːkə(r)] *n* tacataca *m*.

bachelor ['bætʃələr] *n* 1 soltero *m*. 2 *Univ* licenciado,-a *m,f*; **B. of Arts/Science,** licenciado,-a *m,f* en Filosofía y Letras/ Ciencias.

back [bæk] **I** *n* 1 (of person) espalda *f*; (of animal) lomo *m*; **b. to front,** al revés; *fig* **to get sb's b. up,** poner negro a algn; *fig* **to have one's b. to the wall,** estar en un aprieto. 2 (of book) lomo *m*; (of chair) respaldo *m*; (of coin) reverso *m*; (of hand) dorso *m*; (of house, car) parte *f* de atrás; *fig* **he knows Leeds like the b. of his hand,** se conoce Leeds como la palma de la mano. 3 (of stage, cupboard) fondo *m*; *fam* **at the b. of beyond,** en el quinto pino. 4 *Ftb* defensa *m/f*.
II *adj* 1 trasero,-a, de atrás; **b. door,** puerta *f* de atrás; **b. seat,** asiento *m* de detrás; *fig* **to take a b. seat,** pasar al segundo plano; *Aut* **b. wheel,** rueda trasera. 2 **b. rent,** alquiler atrasado; **b. pay,** atrasos *mpl*; *Press* **b. number,** número *m* atrasado.
III *adv* 1 (to the rear) atrás; (towards the rear) hacia atrás; **b. and forth,** de acá para allá. 2 **some years b.,** hace unos años.
IV *vtr* 1 (support) apoyar, respaldar. 2 *Fin* financiar. 3 (bet on) apostar por. 4 (car etc) dar marcha atrás a.
V *vi* 1 (move backwards) retroceder. 2 (car etc) dar marcha atrás.

◆**back away** *vi* retirarse. ◆**back down** *vi* echarse atrás. ◆**back off** *vi* desistir. ◆**back out** *vi* (withdraw) retractarse, volverse atrás. ◆**back up I** *vtr* apoyar. **II** *vi* *Aut* ir marcha atrás.

backache ['bækeɪk] *n* dolor *m* de espalda.

backbencher ['bækbentʃə(r)] *n* diputado,-a *m,f* que no es ministro.

backbiting ['bækbaɪtɪŋ] *n* murmuración *f*.

backbone ['bækbəʊn] *n* *Anat* columna *f*.

backcloth ['bækklɒθ] *n* telón *m* de fondo.

backdate [bæk'deɪt] *vtr* antedatar.

backdated [bæk'deɪtɪd] *adj* con efecto retroactivo.

backdrop ['bækdrɒp] *n* telón *m* de fondo.

backer ['bækər] *n* 1 *Fin* promotor,-a *m,f*. 2 *Pol* partidario, -a *m,f*. 3 (person who bets) apostante *mf*.

backfire [bæk'faɪər] *vi* 1 *Aut* petardear. 2 *fig* **our plan backfired,** nos salió el tiro por la culata.

background ['bækɡraʊnd] *n* 1 fondo *m*; **to stay in the b.,** quedarse en segundo plano; **b. music,** música de fondo. 2 (origin) origen *m*; (past) pasado *m*; (education) formación *f*. 3 (circumstances) antecedentes *mpl*. 4 (atmosphere) ambiente *m*.

backhand ['bækhænd] *n* *Sport* revés *m*.

backhanded ['bæk'hændɪd] *adj* equívoco,-a, ambiguo,-a.

backhander ['bæk'hændər] *n* *sl* (bribe) soborno *m*.

backing ['bækɪŋ] *n* 1 (support) apoyo *m*; *Com Fin* respaldo financiero. 2 *Mus* acompañamiento *m*.

backlash ['bæklæʃ] *n* reacción violenta y repentina.

backlog ['bæklɒɡ] *n* **to have a b. of work,** tener un montón de trabajo atrasado.

backpack ['bækpæk] *n* mochila *f*.

backpedal ['bækpedəl] *vi* *fam* dar marcha atrás.

backside [bæk'saɪd] *n* *fam* trasero *m*, culo *m*.

backstage [bæk'steɪdʒ] *adv* entre bastidores.

backstroke ['bækstrəʊk] *n* espalda *f*.

backtrack ['bæktræk] *vi* *fig* volverse atrás.

backup ['bækʌp] n apoyo m, respaldo m; *Comput* **b. (file)**, fichero m de apoyo.

backward ['bækwəd] I adj 1 (movement) hacia atrás. 2 (country) subdesarrollado, -a; (child) retrasado,-a. II adv esp US hacia atrás.

backwards ['bækwədz] adv hacia atrás; **to walk b.**, andar de espaldas.

backyard [bæk'jɑːd] n patio trasero; US jardín trasero.

bacon ['beɪkən] n tocino m, beicon m.

bacteria [bæk'tɪərɪə] npl bacterias fpl.

bad [bæd] I adj (worse, worst) 1 (poor) malo,-a; **to go from b. to worse**, ir de mal en peor. 2 (decayed) podrido,-a; **to go b.**, echarse a perder. 3 **that's too b.!**, ¡qué pena! 4 (wicked) malo,-a; **to use b. language**, ser mal hablado,-a. 5 (accident) grave; (headache) fuerte. 6 (ill) enfermo, -a. 7 **b. debt**, deuda f incobrable. II n lo malo. ◆**badly** adv 1 mal; **he did b. in the exam**, le salió mal el examen; **to be b. off**, andar mal de dinero. 2 (seriously) gravemente. 3 (very much) mucho; **to miss sb b.**, echar mucho de menos a algn; **we need it b.**, nos hace mucha falta.

bade [beɪd] pt → bid.

badge [bædʒ] n insignia f; (metal disc) chapa f.

badger ['bædʒəʳ] I n tejón m. II vtr acosar.

badminton ['bædmɪntən] n bádminton m.

bad-tempered [bæd'tempəd] adj **to be b.-t.**, (temperament) tener mal genio; (temporarily) estar de mal humor.

baffle ['bæfəl] I vtr desconcertar. II *Tech* pantalla acústica.

baffling ['bæflɪŋ] adj incomprensible, enigmático,-a.

bag [bæg] I n 1 (large) bolsa f; (handbag) bolso m; fam **bags of**, montones de; **travel b.**, bolsa de viaje. 2 (hunting) caza f; fam **it's in the b.**, es cosa hecha. 3 pej **old b.**, (woman) bruja f. 4 **bags**, (under eyes) ojeras fpl. II vtr 1 (put into sacks) meter en sacos. 2 fam coger.

baggage ['bægɪdʒ] n 1 equipaje m. 2 *Mil* bagaje m.

baggy ['bægɪ] adj (baggier, baggiest) holgado,-a; **b. trousers**, pantalones anchos.

bagpipes ['bægpaɪps] npl gaita f sing.

Bahamas [bə'hɑːməz] npl the **B.**, las Bahamas.

bail¹ [beɪl] n *Jur* fianza f; **on b.**, bajo fianza; **to stand b. for sb**, salir fiador por algn. ◆**bail out** vtr fig (person) sacar de un apuro.

bail² [beɪl] vi *Naut* **to b. (out)**, achicar.

bailiff ['beɪlɪf] n 1 *Jur* alguacil m. 2 (steward) administrador m.

bait [beɪt] I n cebo m; **to rise to the b.**, tragar el anzuelo, picar. II vtr 1 *Fishing* cebar. 2 (torment) hostigar.

baize [beɪz] n bayeta f; **green b.**, tapete m verde.

bake [beɪk] I vtr 1 cocer al horno. 2 (harden) endurecer. II vi fam hacer mucho calor.

baked [beɪkt] adj al horno; **b. potato**, patata f al horno.

baker ['beɪkəʳ] n panadero,-a m,f.

bakery ['beɪkərɪ] n panadería f.

baking ['beɪkɪŋ] n cocción f; **b. dish**, fuente f para horno; **b. powder**, levadura f en polvo; **b. tin**, molde m.

balaclava [bælə'klɑːvə] n pasamontañas m inv.

balance ['bæləns] I n 1 (scales) balanza f; fig **to hang in the b.**, estar en juego. 2 (equilibrium) equilibrio m; *Pol* **b. of power**, equilibrio de fuerzas. 3 *Fin* saldo m; **b. of payments**, balanza f de pagos; **b. sheet**, balance m; **credit b.**, saldo acreedor. 4 (remainder) resto m. II vtr 1 poner en equilibrio (**on**, en). 2 (budget) equilibrar; **to b. the books**, hacer el balance. 3 (weigh up) sopesar. III vi guardar el equilibrio. ◆**balance out** vi (figures) corresponderse.

balanced ['bælənst] adj equilibrado,-a.

balcony ['bælkənɪ] n balcón m; *Theat* anfiteatro m.

bald [bɔːld] adj 1 (person) calvo,-a. 2 (tyre) desgastado,-a. 3 (style) escueto,-a.

baldness ['bɔːldnɪs] n 1 (of person) calvicie f. 2 (of tyre) desgaste m. 3 (of style) sencillez f.

bale¹ [beɪl] n 1 fardo m. II vtr embalar.

bale² [beɪl] vtr → bail². ◆**bale out** I vi *Av* saltar en paracaídas de un avión. II vtr fig (person) sacar de apuros.

Balearic [bælɪ'ærɪk] adj the **B. Islands**, las Islas Baleares.

baleful ['beɪlful] adj funesto,-a, siniestro,-a.

Balkan ['bɔːlkən] adj the **Balkans**, los Balcanes.

ball¹ [bɔːl] n 1 (in cricket, tennis etc) pelota f; *Ftb* balón m; (in billiards, golf etc) bola f; fig **the b. is in your court**, ahora te toca a ti; fig **to play b. with sb**, cooperar con algn; fam **to be on the b.**, ser un espabilado; *Tech* **b. bearing**, rodamiento m de bolas. 2 (of paper) bola f; (of wool) ovillo m. 3 US béisbol m; fig **it's a whole new b. game**, es otra historia. 4 vulg offens **balls**, cojones mpl.

ball² [bɔːl] n baile m.

ballad ['bæləd] n balada f.

ballast ['bæləst] n *Naut* lastre m.

ballerina [bælə'riːnə] n bailarina f.

ballet ['bæleɪ] n ballet m; **b. dancer**, bailarín,-ina m,f.

ballistic [bə'lɪstɪk] adj balístico,-a.

ballistics [bə'lɪstɪks] n balística f.

balloon [bə'luːn] I n 1 globo m. 2 (in cartoon) bocadillo m. II vi hincharse; fig aumentar rápidamente.

ballot ['bælət] I n votación f; b. box, urna f; b. paper, papeleta f. II vtr someter a votación.

ballpoint (pen) ['bɔːlpɔɪnt ('pen)] n bolígrafo m.

ballroom ['bɔːlruːm] n salón m de baile.

ballyhoo [bælɪ'huː] n fam (fuss) jaleo m.

balm [bɑːm] n bálsamo m.

balmy ['bɑːmɪ] adj (balmier, balmiest) (weather) suave.

Baltic ['bɔːltɪk] adj báltico,-a; the B. (Sea), el (Mar) Báltico.

balustrade [bæləs'treɪd] n barandilla f.

bamboo [bæm'buː] n bambú m.

bamboozle [bæm'buːzl] vtr fam 1 (puzzle) dejar perplejo. 2 (trick) engañar, embaucar.

ban [bæn] I n prohibición f. II vtr 1 (prohibit) prohibir. 2 (exclude) excluir.

banal [bə'nɑːl] adj banal, trivial.

banana [bə'nɑːnə] n plátano m, Am banana f; fam to go bananas, volverse loco, -a.

band [bænd] I n 1 (strip) tira f; (ribbon) cinta f. 2 (stripe) raya f. 3 Rad banda f. 4 (group) grupo m; (of youths) pandilla f; (of thieves) banda f. II Mus banda f. II vi to b. together, unirse, juntarse.

bandage ['bændɪdʒ] I n venda f. II vtr vendar.

Band-Aid® ['bændeɪd] n US tirita® f.

B & B [biːən'biː] n abbr of bed and breakfast.

bandit ['bændɪt] n bandido m.

bandstand ['bændstænd] n quiosco m de música.

bandwagon ['bændwægən] n fig to jump on the b., subirse al tren.

bandy ['bændɪ] I vtr (words, ideas) intercambiar. II adj (bandier, bandiest) torcido,-a hacia fuera. ◆bandy about vtr (ideas) propagar, difundir.

bandy-legged ['bændɪleg(ɪ)d] adj patizambo,-a.

bang [bæŋ] I n 1 (blow) golpe m. 2 (noise) ruido m; (explosion) estallido m; (of gun) estampido m; to shut the door with a b., dar un portazo. II vtr golpear; to b. sth shut, cerrar algo de golpe. III vi golpear; to b. shut, cerrarse de golpe. IV interj (blow) ¡zas!; b., b.!, (of gun) ¡pum, pum! V adv fam justo.

banger ['bæŋər] n 1 (firework) petardo m. 2 fam (sausage) salchicha f. 3 fam old b., (car) tartana f.

bangle ['bæŋgəl] n brazalete m.

banish ['bænɪʃ] vtr desterrar.

banister ['bænɪstər] n pasamanos m inv.

bank¹ [bæŋk] I n 1 Com Fin banco m; b. account, cuenta bancaria; b. card, tarjeta bancaria; b. clerk, empleado, -a m,f de

banca; b. draft, letra bancaria; b. holiday, fiesta f nacional; b. statement, extracto m de cuenta. 2 (in gambling) banca f. 3 (store) banco m. II vtr Com Fin depositar, ingresar. III vi Com Fin to b. with, tener una cuenta en. ◆bank on vtr contar con.

bank² [bæŋk] I n 1 (mound) loma f; (embankment) terraplén m. 2 (of river) ribera f; (edge) orilla f. II vtr & vi Av ladearse.

bankbook ['bæŋkbʊk] n libreta f de ahorros.

banker ['bæŋkər] n banquero,-a m,f.

banking ['bæŋkɪŋ] n banca f.

banknote ['bæŋknəʊt] n billete m de banco.

bankrupt ['bæŋkrʌpt] I adj en quiebra; to go b., quebrar. II vtr llevar a la bancarrota.

bankruptcy ['bæŋkrʌptsɪ] n quiebra f, bancarrota f.

banner ['bænər] n (in demonstration) pancarta f; (flag) bandera f.

banns [bænz] npl amonestaciones fpl.

banquet ['bæŋkwɪt] n banquete m.

banter ['bæntər] I n bromas fpl. II vi bromear.

bap [bæp] n bollo m, panecillo m.

baptism ['bæptɪzəm] n bautismo m.

baptize [bæp'taɪz] vtr bautizar.

bar [bɑːr] I n 1 (of gold) barra f; (of chocolate) tableta f; (of soap) pastilla f; Com b. code, código m de barras. 2 (of cage) barrote m; fam to be behind bars, estar en la cárcel. 3 (obstacle) obstáculo m. 4 Jur (dock) banquillo m; (court) tribunal m. 5 Jur the B., (profession) abogacía f; (body of lawyers) colegio m de abogados. 6 (pub) bar m; (counter) barra f. 7 Mus compás m. II vtr 1 (door) atrancar; (road) cortar. 2 (exclude) excluir (from, de). 3 (prohibit) prohibir. III prep salvo; b. none, sin excepción.

barbarian [bɑː'beərɪən] adj & n bárbaro,-a (m,f).

barbaric [bɑː'bærɪk] adj bárbaro,-a.

barbecue ['bɑːbɪkjuː] I n barbacoa f. II vtr asar a la parrilla.

barbed [bɑːbd] adj 1 b. wire, alambre m de púas. 2 fig (remark) mordaz.

barber ['bɑːbər] n barbero,-a m,f; b.'s (shop), barbería f.

barbiturate [bɑː'bɪtjʊrɪt] n barbitúrico m.

bare [beər] I adj 1 (naked) desnudo,-a; (head) descubierto,-a; (foot) descalzo,-a; (room) sin muebles; to lay b., poner al descubierto; with his b. hands, sólo con las manos. 2 (basic) mero,-a; the b. minimum, lo mínimo. II vtr desnudar; (uncover) descubrir.

bareback(ed) ['beəbæk(t)] adj & adv to ride b., montar un caballo a pelo.

barefaced ['beəfeɪst] adj desvergonzado,

-a.

barefoot ['beəfut] *adj & adv* descalzo,-a.

barely ['beəlɪ] *adv* apenas.

bargain ['bɑːgɪn] **I** *n* **1** *(agreement)* pacto *m*; *(deal)* negocio *m*; **into the b.**, por añadidura, además; **to drive a hard b.**, imponer condiciones duras; **to strike a b.**, cerrar un trato. **2** *(cheap purchase)* ganga *f*; **b. price**, precio *m* de oferta. **II** *vi* **1** negociar. **2** *(haggle)* regatear. **◆bargain for** *vtr* esperar, contar con.

barge [bɑːdʒ] **I** *n* gabarra *f*. **II** *vtr* **1** tum to **b. into**, *(room)* irrumpir en; *(person)* tropezar con. **◆barge in** *vi fam* **1** *(go in)* entrar sin permiso. **2** *(interfere)* entrometerse.

baritone ['bærɪtəun] *adj & n* barítono *(m)*.

bark[1] [bɑːk] **I** *n* ladrido *m*. **II** *vi* *(dog)* ladrar.

bark[2] [bɑːk] *n Bot* corteza *f*.

barley ['bɑːlɪ] *n* cebada *f*; **b. sugar**, azúcar *m* cande.

barmaid ['bɑːmeɪd] *n* camarera *f*.

barman ['bɑːmən] *n* camarero *m*, barman *m*.

barn [bɑːn] *n* granero *m*; **b. dance**, baile *m* popular.

barnacle ['bɑːnəkəl] *n* percebe *m*.

barometer [bə'rɒmɪtəʳ] *n* barómetro *m*.

baron ['bærən] *n* barón *m*.

baroness ['bærənɪs] *n* baronesa *f*.

baroque [bə'rɒk] *adj* barroco,-a.

barrack ['bærək] *vtr* abuchear.

barracks ['bærəks] *n Mil* cuartel *m sing*.

barrage ['bærɑːʒ] *n* **1** *(dam)* presa *f*. **2** *Mil* barrera *f* de fuego. **3** *fig (of questions)* lluvia *f*.

barrel ['bærəl] *n* **1** *(of wine)* tonel *m*; *(of beer, oil)* barril *m*. **2** *(of firearm)* cañón *m*.

barren ['bærən] *adj* estéril; *(land)* yermo,-a.

barricade [bærɪ'keɪd] **I** *n* barricada *f*. **II** *vtr* levantar barricadas; **to b. oneself in**, parapetarse.

barrier ['bærɪəʳ] *n* barrera *f*.

barrister ['bærɪstəʳ] *n GB* abogado,-a *m,f* (capacitado,-a para ejercer ante tribunales superiores).

barrow ['bærəu] *n* carretilla *f*.

bartender ['bɑːtendəʳ] *n US* camarero *m*, barman *m*.

barter ['bɑːtəʳ] *vtr* trocar (for, por).

base [beɪs] **I** *n* base *f*; *(foot)* pie *m*; *(of column)* base *f*; *Sport (of team)* concentración *f*; **air/naval b.**, base *f* aérea/naval. **II** *vtr* **1** basar, fundar (on, en). **2** *(troops)* estacionar. **III** *adj* **1** *(despicable)* bajo,-a, despreciable. **2** *(metals)* común.

baseball ['beɪsbɔːl] *n* béisbol *m*.

baseline ['beɪslaɪn] *n Ten* línea *f* de saque.

basement ['beɪsmənt] *n* sótano *m*.

bash [bæʃ] **I** *n (heavy blow)* golpetazo *m*;

(dent) bollo *m*; *fam (attempt)* intento *m*. **II** *vtr* golpear.

bashful ['bæʃful] *adj* tímido,-a.

basic ['beɪsɪk] **I** *adj* básico,-a; **b. pay**, sueldo *m* base. **II** *npl* **basics**, lo fundamental. **◆basically** *adv* fundamentalmente.

basil ['bæzɪl] *n* albahaca *f*.

basin ['beɪsən] *n* **1** *(washbowl)* palangana *f*; *(for washing up)* barreño *m*; *(in bathroom)* lavabo *m*; *(dish)* cuenco *m*. **2** *(of river)* cuenca *f*.

basis ['beɪsɪs] *n (pl* **bases** ['beɪsiːz]*)* base *f*; **on the b. of**, en base a.

bask [bɑːsk] *vi* tostarse; **to b. in the sun**, tomar el sol.

basket ['bɑːskɪt] *n* cesta *f*, cesto *m*.

basketball ['bɑːskɪtbɔːl] *n* baloncesto *m*.

Basque [bæsk, bɑːsk] **I** *adj* vasco,-a; **B. Country**, País Vasco, Euskadi; **B. flag**, ikurriña *f*; **B. nationalist**, abertzale *mf*. **II** *n* **1** *(person)* vasco,-a *m,f*. **2** *(language)* vasco *m*, euskera *m*.

bass[1] [bæs] *n inv (seawater)* lubina *f*; *(freshwater)* perca *f*.

bass[2] [beɪs] **I** *n* **1** *(singer)* bajo *m*. **2** *(notes)* graves *mpl*; **b. drum**, bombo *m*; **b. guitar**, bajo *m*. **II** *adj* bajo,-a.

bassoon [bə'suːn] *n* fagot *m*.

bastard ['bɑːstəd, 'bæstəd] **I** *n* **1** bastardo,-a *m,f*. **2** *offens* cabrón *m*, hijo *m* de puta; **poor b.!**, ¡el pobre! **II** *adj* bastardo,-a.

baste [beɪst] *vtr Culin* untar.

bastion ['bæstɪən] *n* baluarte *m*, bastión *m*.

bat[1] [bæt] **I** *n (in cricket, baseball)* bate *m*; *(in table tennis)* pala *f*; *fig* **to do sth off one's own b.**, hacer algo por cuenta propia. **II** *vi (in cricket, baseball)* batear.

bat[2] [bæt] *n Zool* murciélago *m*.

bat[3] [bæt] *vtr fam* **without batting an eyelid**, sin pestañear.

batch [bætʃ] *n (of bread)* hornada *f*; *(of goods)* lote *m*; *Comput* **b. processing**, procesamiento *m* por lotes.

bated ['beɪtɪd] *adj* **with b. breath**, sin respirar.

bath [bɑːθ] **I** *n* **1** baño *m*; **to have a b.**, bañarse; **b. towel**, toalla *f* de baño. **2** *(tub)* bañera *f*. **3** **baths**, piscina *f* municipal. **II** *vtr* bañar.

bathe [beɪð] **I** *vi* bañarse. **II** *vtr* **1** *(wound)* lavar. **2** **he was bathed in sweat**, *(covered)* estaba empapado de sudor.

bather ['beɪðəʳ] *n* bañista *mf*.

bathing ['beɪðɪŋ] *n* baño *m*; **b. cap**, gorro *m* de baño; **b. costume**, traje *m* de baño; **b. trunks**, bañador *m* de hombre.

bathrobe ['bɑːðrəub] *n* albornoz *m*.

bathroom ['bɑːθruːm] *n* cuarto *m* de baño.

bathtub ['bɑːθtʌb] *n* bañera *f*.

baton ['bætən, 'bætɒn] *n* **1** *Mus* batuta *f*.

2 (*truncheon*) porra f. 3 *Sport* testigo m.

battalion [bəˈtæljən] n batallón m.

batter¹ [ˈbætər] vtr aporrear, apalear.

batter² [ˈbætər] n (in cricket, baseball) bateador-a, m,f.

batter³ [ˈbætər] Culin I n pasta f (para rebozar); **fish in b.**, pescado rebozado. II vtr rebozar.

battered [ˈbætəd] adj (car) abollado,-a; (person) maltratado,-a.

battering [ˈbætərɪŋ] n paliza f; **to take a b.**, recibir una paliza; Mil **b. ram**, ariete m.

battery [ˈbætərɪ] n 1 (for torch, radio) pila f; Aut batería f. 2 Jur **assault and b.**, lesiones fpl.

battle [ˈbætəl] I n batalla f; fig lucha f; **to do b.**, librar batalla; fig **b. cry**, lema m. II vi luchar.

battlefield [ˈbætəlfiːld] n campo m de batalla.

battleship [ˈbætəlʃɪp] n acorazado m.

bauble [ˈbɔːbəl] n chuchería f.

bawdy [ˈbɔːdɪ] adj (joke etc) verde.

bawl [bɔːl] vi gritar, chillar.

bay¹ [beɪ] n Geog bahía f; (large) golfo m; **B. of Biscay**, golfo de Vizcaya; **B. of Bengal**, golfo de Bengala.

bay² [beɪ] n 1 (recess) hueco m; **b. window**, ventana salediza. 2 (in factory) nave f; **cargo b.**, bodega f de carga.

bay³ [beɪ] n laurel m.

bay⁴ [beɪ] I vi (dog) aullar. II n ladrido m; fig **at b.**, acorralado,-a; fig **to keep sb at b.**, mantener a algn a raya.

bayonet [ˈbeɪənɪt] n bayoneta f.

bazaar [bəˈzɑːr] n 1 (market) bazar m. 2 (Church) b., (charity sale) rastrillo benéfico.

BBC [biːbiːˈsiː] abbr British Broadcasting Corporation, Compañía británica de radiofusión, BBC f.

BC [biːˈsiː] abbr before Christ, a.d.C.

be [biː, unstressed bɪ] v (pres 1st person sing am; 3rd person sing is; 2nd person sing & all persons pl are; pt 1st & 3rd persons sing was; 2nd person sing & all persons pl were; pp been) I v aux 1 (with pres p) estar; **he is writing a letter**, está escribiendo una carta; **she was singing**, estaba cantando; **they are leaving next week**, se van la semana que viene; **we have been waiting for a long time**, hace mucho que estamos esperando; **he is coming**, (emphatic) es seguro que viene. 2 (passive) ser; **he was murdered**, fue asesinado; **she is allowed to smoke**, se le permite fumar. 3 (obligation) **I am to see him this afternoon**, debo verle esta tarde; **you are not to smoke here**, no puede fumar aquí.
III v impers 1 (with there) haber; **there is, there are, hay; there was, there were**, había; **there will be**, habrá; **there would be**, habría; **there have been a lot of complaints**, ha habido muchas quejas; **there were ten of us**, éramos diez. 2 (with it) **it's late**, es tarde; **it is said that**, se dice que; **who is it?** - ¿quién es? - soy yo; **what is it?**, ¿qué pasa? 3 (weather) **it's foggy**, hay niebla; **it's cold/hot**, hace frío/calor. 4 (time) ser; **it's one o'clock**, es la una; **it's four o'clock**, son las cuatro. 5 (date) **it's the 11th/Tuesday today**, hoy es 11/martes. 6 (tag questions) ¿verdad?, ¿no?; **it's lovely, isn't it?**, es bonito, ¿no?; **you're happy, aren't you?**, estás contento, ¿verdad? **he's not very clever, is he?**, no es muy listo, ¿verdad? 7 (unreal conditions) **if I was/were you …**, yo en tu lugar …; **if you were a millionaire …**, si fueras millionario …. 8 pres & past perfect (visit, go) estar, ir; **I've been to Paris**, he estado en París.

suerte. 6 (location) estar; **Aberdeen is in Scotland**, Aberdeen está en Escocia; **Birmingham is two hundred miles from London**, Birmingham está a doscientas millas de Londres. 7 (age) tener; **she is thirty (years old)**, tiene treinta años.
II v aux 1 (with pres p) estar; **he is writing a letter**, …
III v impers …

beach [biːtʃ] I n playa f. II vtr varar.

beacon [ˈbiːkən] n 1 Av Naut baliza f. 2 (lighthouse) faro m.

bead [biːd] n 1 (of necklace etc) cuenta f; **glass b.**, abalorio m. 2 (of liquid) gota f.

beady [ˈbiːdɪ] adj (beadier, beadiest) (eyes) pequeños y brillantes.

beagle [ˈbiːgəl] n beagle m.

beak [biːk] n 1 (of bird) pico m. 2 fam (nose) nariz ganchuda.

beaker [ˈbiːkər] n (tumbler) taza alta, jarra f.

beam [biːm] I n 1 Archit viga f. 2 (of light) rayo m; Phys haz m. 3 Gymn barra fija. 4 (smile) sonrisa f radiante. II vi 1 (sun) brillar. 2 (smile) sonreír. III vtr 1 (broadcast) difundir, emitir. 2 (transmit) transmitir.

beaming [ˈbiːmɪŋ] adj (smiling) radiante.

bean [biːn] n alubia f, judía f, frijol m; fam **to spill the beans**, descubrir el pastel; **baked beans,** alubias cocidas en salsa de tomate; **broad b.,** haba *f;* **butter b.,** judía; **coffee b.,** grano *m* de café; **green/runner b.,** judía verde; **haricot b.,** alubia; **kidney b.,** frijol.

beansprout ['bi:nspraʊt] *n* brote *m* de soja.

bear¹ [beə^r] *(pt* **bore***; pp* **borne)** I *vtr* 1 *(carry)* llevar. 2 *(support)* sostener. 3 *(endure)* soportar, aguantar; **I can't b. him,** no lo soporto. 4 *(fruit)* dar; *Fin (interest)* devengar. 5 **to b. a resemblance to,** parecerse a. 6 **to b. a grudge against sb,** guardar rencor a algn; **to b. in mind,** tener presente. 7 **to b. witness,** atestiguar. 8 *(pp* **born** *passive only, not followed by* **by***) (give birth to)* dar a luz; **he was born in Wakefield,** nació en Wakefield. II *vi (turn)* girar, torcer; **to b. left,** girar a la izquierda. ◆**bear down** *vi (approach)* correr *(on,* sobre). ◆**bear out** *vtr (confirm)* confirmar. ◆**bear up** *vi (endure)* resistir. ◆**bear with** *vtr* tener paciencia con.

bear² [beə^r] *n* 1 oso *m;* **b. cub,** osezno *m; Astr* **Great B.,** Osa *f* Mayor; **Little B.,** Osa Menor. 2 *Fin* bajista *mf.*

beard [bɪəd] *n* barba *f.*

bearer ['beərə^r] *n* portador,-a *m,f; (of passport, office)* titular *mf.*

bearing ['beərɪŋ] *n* 1 *(posture)* porte *m.* 2 *(relevance)* relación *f;* **to have a b. on,** estar relacionado,-a con. 3 *Tech* cojinete *m.* 4 *Naut* **bearings,** posición *f,* orientación *f;* **to get one's bearings,** orientarse; **to lose one's bearings,** desorientarse.

beast [bi:st] *n* 1 bestia *f;* **b. of burden,** bestia de carga. 2 *fig* bestia *f,* bruto *m.* 3 **beasts,** *(cattle)* reses *fpl.*

beastly ['bi:stlɪ] *adj* **(beastlier, beastliest)** *fam* asqueroso,-a.

beat [bi:t] I *vtr (pt* **beat***; pp* **beaten** ['bi:tən]) 1 *(hit)* pegar, golpear; *(clothes)* sacudir; *(drum)* tocar; **off the beaten track,** en un lugar muy apartado; *sl* **b. it!,** ¡lárgate! 2 *Culin* batir. 3 *(defeat)* batir, vencer; **we b. them 5-2,** los ganamos 5 a 2. 4 **to b. a retreat,** batirse en retirada. 5 *Mus (time)* marcar. 6 **to b. the traffic,** evitar los embotellamientos de tráfico. 7 *sl (puzzle)* extrañar; **it beats me,** no lo entiendo. II *vi* 1 *(heart)* latir. 2 *(strike)* dar golpes; *fig* **to b. about the bush,** andarse por las ramas. III *n* 1 *(of heart)* latido *m.* 2 *Mus* ritmo *m,* compás *m.* 3 *(of policeman)* ronda *f.* IV *adj fam (exhausted)* agotado,-a. ◆**beat down** *vi (sun)* apretar. ◆**beat off** *vtr* rechazar. ◆**beat up** *vtr fam* dar una paliza a.

beating ['bi:tɪŋ] *n* 1 *(thrashing)* paliza *f.* 2 *(defeat)* derrota *f.* 3 *(of drum)* toque *m.* 4 *(of heart)* latido *m.*

beautician [bju:'tɪʃən] *n* esteticista *mf.*

beautiful ['bju:tɪful] *adj* hermoso,-a,

bello,-a; *(delicious)* delicioso,-a; **b. people,** gente *f* guapa.

beauty ['bju:tɪ] *n* belleza *f,* hermosura *f;* **b. contest,** concurso *m* de belleza; **b. queen,** miss *f;* **b. salon,** salón *m* de belleza; **b. spot,** *(on face)* lunar *m; (place)* lugar pintoresco.

beaver ['bi:və^r] I *n* castor *m.* II *vi* **to b. away at sth,** meterse de lleno en algo.

became [bɪ'keɪm] *pt* → **become.**

because [bɪ'kɒz] I *conj* porque. II *prep* **b. of,** a causa de, debido a.

beckon ['bekən] *vtr & vi* llamar *(con la mano);* **to b. to sb,** llamar a algn con señas.

becoming [bɪ'kʌmɪŋ] *adj* 1 *(dress)* favorecedor,-a. 2 *(behaviour)* conveniente, apropiado,-a.

bed [bed] *n* 1 cama *f;* **to get out of b.,** levantarse de la cama; **to go to b.,** acostarse; **to make the b.,** hacer la cama; *GB* **b. and breakfast,** *(service)* cama y desayuno *m; (sign)* 'pensión'; **b. linen,** ropa *f* de cama. 2 *(of river)* lecho *m; (of sea)* fondo *m.* 3 *Geol* capa *f.* 4 *(flower)* **b.,** arriate *m.*

bedbug ['bedbʌg] *n* chinche *mf.*

bedclothes ['bedkləʊðz] *npl,* **bedding** ['bedɪŋ] *n* ropa *f* de cama.

bedlam ['bedləm] *n* algarabía *f,* alboroto *m.*

bedraggled [bɪ'drægəld] *adj (wet)* mojado,-a; *(dirty)* ensuciado,-a.

bedridden ['bedrɪdən] *adj* postrado,-a en cama.

bedroom ['bedru:m] *n* dormitorio *m.*

bedside ['bedsaɪd] *n* **at sb's b.,** junto a la cama de algn; **b. table,** mesilla *f* de noche.

bedsit ['bedsɪt] *n fam,* **bedsitter** ['bed'sɪtə^r] *n* estudio *m.*

bedspread ['bedspred] *n* colcha *f.*

bedtime ['bedtaɪm] *n* hora *f* de acostarse.

bee [bi:] *n* abeja *f.*

beech [bi:tʃ] *n* haya *f.*

beef [bi:f] *n* carne *f* de vaca, *Am* carne de res; **roast b.,** rosbif *m.* ◆**beef up** *vtr fam* reforzar.

beefburger ['bi:fbɜ:gə^r] *n* hamburguesa *f.*

beefsteak ['bi:fsteɪk] *n* bistec *m.*

beehive ['bi:haɪv] *n* colmena *f.*

beeline ['bi:laɪn] *n* **to make a b. for sth,** ir directo hacia algo.

been [bi:n, bɪn] *pp* → **be.**

beep [bi:p] *n (of apparatus)* pitido *m; (of horn)* pito *m.*

beer [bɪə^r] *n* cerveza *f;* **a glass of b.,** una caña.

beet [bi:t] *n* remolacha *f; US* **red b.,** remolacha.

beetle ['bi:təl] *n* escarabajo *m.*

beetroot ['bi:tru:t] *n* remolacha *f.*

befit [bɪ'fɪt] *vtr* convenir a, corresponder a.

before [bɪ'fɔːr] I *conj* 1 (*earlier than*) antes de que (+ *subj*), antes de (+ *infin*); **b. she goes**, antes de que se vaya; **b. leaving**, antes de salir. 2 (*rather than*) antes que (+ *infin*). II *prep* 1 (*place*) delante de; (*in the presence of*) ante. 2 (*order, time*) antes de; **b. Christ**, antes de Cristo; **b. long**, dentro de poco; **b. 1950**, antes de 1950; **I saw it b. you**, lo vi antes que tú. III *adv* 1 (*time*) antes; **I have met him b.**, ya lo conozco; **not long b.**, poco antes; **the night b.**, la noche anterior. 2 (*place*) delante, por delante.

beforehand [bɪ'fɔːhænd] *adv* 1 (*earlier*) antes. 2 (*in advance*) de antemano, con anticipación.

befriend [bɪ'frend] *vtr* trabar amistad con.

beg [beg] I *vtr* 1 (*money etc*) pedir. 2 (*beseech*) rogar, suplicar; **I b. your pardon!**, ¡perdone usted!; **I b. your pardon?**, ¿cómo ha dicho usted? II *vi* 1 (*solicit*) mendigar; (*dog*) pedir; **to b. for money**, pedir limosna. 2 **to b. for help/mercy**, (*beseech*) implorar ayuda/compasión.

began [bɪ'gæn] *pt* → **begin**.

beggar ['begər] *n* 1 mendigo,-a *m,f*. 2 *fam euph* (*chap*) tío *m*.

begin [bɪ'gɪn] *vtr & vi* (*pt began; pp begun*) empezar, comenzar; **to b. again**, volver a empezar; **to b. at the beginning**, empezar por el principio; **to b. doing** or **to do sth**, empezar a hacer algo; **to b. with ...**, (*initially*) para empezar ....

beginner [bɪ'gɪnər] *n* principiante *mf*.

beginning [bɪ'gɪnɪŋ] *n* 1 principio *m*, comienzo *m*; **at the b. of May**, a principios de mayo; **from the b.**, desde el principio; **in the b.**, al principio. 2 (*origin*) origen *m*.

begonia [bɪ'gəʊnjə] *n* begonia *f*.

begrudge [bɪ'grʌdʒ] *vtr* dar de mala gana; (*envy*) envidiar.

beguile [bɪ'gaɪl] *vtr* (*charm*) seducir.

begun [bɪ'gʌn] *pp* → **begin**.

behalf [bɪ'hɑːf] *n* **on b. of**, US **in b. of**, en nombre de, de parte de; **don't worry on my b.**, no te preocupes por mí.

behave [bɪ'heɪv] *vi* 1 (*person*) portarse, comportarse; **b. yourself!**, ¡pórtate bien!; **to b. well/badly**, portarse bien/mal. 2 (*machine*) funcionar.

behaviour, US **behavior** [bɪ'heɪvjər] *n* 1 (*of person*) comportamiento *m*, conducta *f*. 2 (*of machine*) funcionamiento *m*.

behead [bɪ'hed] *vtr* decapitar.

beheld [bɪ'held] *pt & pp* → **behold**.

behind [bɪ'haɪnd] I *prep* 1 detrás de, tras; **sb's back**, a espaldas de algn; **b. the scenes**, entre bastidores; **to be b. sb**, apoyar a algn; **what motive was there b. the crime?**, ¿cuál fue el móvil del crimen? 2 **b. the times**, (*less advanced than*) anticuado,-a. II *adv* 1 (*in the rear*) detrás,

atrás; **I've left my umbrella b.**, se me ha olvidado el paraguas. 2 **to be b. with one's payments**, (*late*) estar atrasado,-a en los pagos. III *n fam* trasero *m*.

behold [bɪ'həʊld] *vtr* (*pt & pp* **beheld**) *arch* contemplar.

beige [beɪʒ] *adj & n* beige (*m*).

being ['biːɪŋ] *n* 1 ser *m*. 2 (*existence*) existencia *f*; **to come into b.**, nacer.

belated [bɪ'leɪtɪd] *adj* tardío,-a.

belch [beltʃ] I *vi* (*person*) eructar. II *vtr* (*smoke, flames*) vomitar, arrojar. III *n* eructo *m*.

beleaguered [bɪ'liːgəd] *adj* asediado,-a.

belfry ['belfrɪ] *n* campanario *m*.

Belgian ['beldʒən] *adj & n* belga (*mf*).

Belgrade [bel'greɪd] *n* Belgrado.

belie [bɪ'laɪ] *vtr* desmentir.

belief [bɪ'liːf] *n* 1 creencia *f*; **beyond b.**, increíble. 2 (*opinion*) opinión *f*. 3 (*faith*) fe *f*. 4 (*confidence*) confianza *f* (**in**, en).

believe [bɪ'liːv] I *vi* 1 (*have faith*) creer. 2 **to b. in**, (*be in favour of*) ser partidario,-a de. 3 (*think*) creer; **I b. so**, creo que sí. II *vtr* creer.

believer [bɪ'liːvər] *n* 1 *Rel* creyente *mf*. 2 partidario,-a *m,f* (**in**, de).

belittle [bɪ'lɪtl] *vtr* (*person*) menospreciar; (*problem*) minimizar.

bell [bel] *n* (*of church*) campana *f*; (*small*) campanilla *f*; (*of school, door, bicycle etc*) timbre *m*; (*on cat*) cascabel *m*; (*on cow*) cencerro *m*; *fig* **that rings a b.**, eso me suena; **b. jar**, campana; **b. tower**, campanario *m*.

bell-bottoms ['belbɒtəmz] *npl* pantalones *mpl* de campana.

belligerent [bɪ'lɪdʒərənt] *adj* agresivo,-a.

bellow ['beləʊ] *vi* (*bull*) bramar; (*person*) rugir.

bellows ['beləʊz] *npl* (*pair of*) **b.**, fuelle *m sing*.

belly ['belɪ] *n* 1 (*of person*) barriga *f*; **b. flop**, panzazo *m*. 2 (*animal*) panza *f*.

bellyache ['belɪeɪk] *n fam* dolor *m* de vientre.

belong [bɪ'lɒŋ] *vi* 1 pertenecer (**to**, a). 2 (*be a member*) ser socio,-a (**to**, de); *Pol* **to b. to a party**, ser miembro de un partido. 3 (*have a proper place*) corresponder; **this chair belongs here**, esta silla va aquí.

belongings [bɪ'lɒŋɪŋz] *npl* efectos *mpl* personales.

beloved [bɪ'lʌvɪd, bɪ'lʌvd] I *adj* amado, -a, querido,-a. II *n* amado,-a *m,f*.

below [bɪ'ləʊ] I *prep* debajo de; **b. average**, por debajo de la media; **ten degrees b. zero**, diez grados bajo cero. II *adv* abajo; **above and b.**, arriba y abajo; **see** *also* **véase más abajo**.

belt [belt] *n* 1 cinturón *m*; **blow below the b.**, golpe *m* bajo. 2 *Tech* correa *f*, cinta f. 3 (area) zona f. II vtr sl pegar una paliza a. ◆belt along vi fam ir a todo gas. ◆belt out vtr fam (song) cantar a voz en grito. ◆belt up vi fam callarse.

bemused [bɪˈmjuːzd] adj perplejo,-a.

bench [bentʃ] n 1 (seat) banco m. 2 Parl escaño m. 3 Jur the b., (judges) la magistratura. 4 Sport banquillo m. 5 b. mark, Geol cota f de referencia; fig punto m de referencia.

bend [bend] I vtr (pt & pp bent) doblar; (back) encorvar; (head) inclinar; fam to b. the rules, hacer una excepción. II vi 1 doblarse; (road) torcerse. 2 to b. (over), inclinarse; fam he bends over backwards to please her, hace lo imposible por complacerla. III n 1 (in river, road) curva f; (in pipe) recodo m; GB sl round the b., loco,-a perdido,-a. ◆bend down vi inclinarse.

beneath [bɪˈniːθ] I prep (below) bajo, debajo de; fig it's b. him, es indigno de él. II adv debajo.

benefactor ['benɪfæktər] n bienhechor,-a m,f.

beneficial [benɪˈfɪʃəl] adj 1 (doing good) benéfico,-a. 2 (advantageous) beneficioso,-a.

beneficiary [benɪˈfɪʃərɪ] n beneficiario,-a m,f.

benefit ['benɪfɪt] I vtr beneficiar. II vi sacar provecho (from or by, de). III n 1 (advantage) beneficio m, provecho m; for the b. of, en beneficio de; I did it for your b., lo hice por tu bien. 2 (allowance) subsidio m; unemployment b., subsidio m de desempleo. 3 (event) función f benéfica.

benevolent [bɪˈnevələnt] adj benévolo,-a.

Bengal [beŋˈɡɔːl] n Bengala.

benign [bɪˈnaɪn] adj benigno,-a.

bent [bent] I adj 1 (curved) curvado,-a. 2 to be b. on doing sth, (determined) estar empeñado,-a en hacer algo. 3 sl (corrupt) deshonesto,-a. 4 sl (homosexual) gay. II n (inclination) inclinación f (towards, hacia).

benzine ['benziːn] n Chem bencina f.

bequeath [bɪˈkwiːð] vtr Jur legar.

bequest [bɪˈkwest] n Jur legado m.

bereaved [bɪˈriːvd] npl the b., los familiares del/de un difunto.

bereavement [bɪˈriːvmənt] n (mourning) duelo m.

bereft [bɪˈreft] adj b. of, privado,-a de.

beret ['bereɪ] n boina f.

Berlin [bɜːˈlɪn] n Berlín.

Bermuda [bəˈmjuːdə] n las (Islas) Bermudas; B. shorts, bermudas fpl.

Bern [bɜːn] n Berna.

berry ['berɪ] n baya f.

berserk [bəˈsɜːk, bəˈzɜːk] adj to go b., volverse loco,-a.

berth [bɜːθ] Naut I n 1 (mooring) amarra-

dero m; fig to give sb a wide b., evitar a algn. 2 (bed) litera f. II vi atracar.

beseech [bɪˈsiːtʃ] vtr suplicar, implorar.

beset [bɪˈset] vtr (pt & pp beset) acosar; it is b. with dangers, está plagado de peligros.

beside [bɪˈsaɪd] prep 1 (next to) al lado de, junto a. 2 (compared with) comparado con. 3 he was b. himself with joy, estaba loco de alegría; that's b. the point, eso no viene al caso; to be b. oneself, estar fuera de sí.

besides [bɪˈsaɪdz] I prep 1 (in addition to) además de. 2 (except) excepto, menos; no one b. me, nadie más que yo. II adv además.

besiege [bɪˈsiːdʒ] vtr (city) sitiar; fig asediar.

besought [bɪˈsɔːt] pt & pp → beseech.

best [best] I adj (superl of good) mejor; b. man, ≈ padrino m de boda; her b. friend, su mejor amiga; the b. thing would be to phone them, lo mejor sería llamarles; we had to wait the b. part of a year, tuvimos que esperar casi un año; with b. wishes from Mary, (in letter) con mis mejores deseos, Mary. II adv (superl of well) mejor; as b. I can, lo mejor que pueda; I like this one b., éste es el que más me gusta; the world's b. dressed man, el hombre mejor vestido del mundo. III n lo mejor; all the b.!, ¡que te vaya bien!; at b., a lo más; to be at one's b., estar en plena forma; to do one's b., hacer todo lo posible; to make the b. of sth, sacar el mejor partido de algo; to the b. of my knowledge, que yo sepa.

bestiality [bestɪˈælɪtɪ] n bestialidad f.

bestow [bɪˈstəʊ] vtr (favour etc) conceder; (honours, power) otorgar (on, a); (title etc) conferir (on, a).

best-seller [bestˈselər] n best-seller m.

best-selling ['bestˌselɪŋ] adj a b.-s. author, un autor de superventas.

bet [bet] I n apuesta f. II vtr (pt & pp bet or betted) apostar. III vi apostar (on, por); fam you b.!, ¡y tanto!

Bethlehem ['beθlɪhem] n Belén.

betray [bɪˈtreɪ] vtr 1 traicionar. 2 (be unfaithful to) engañar. 3 (reveal) revelar.

betrayal [bɪˈtreɪəl] n traición f.

better ['betər] I adj 1 (comp of good) mejor; that's b.!, ¡así está mejor!; the weather is b. than last week, hace mejor tiempo que la semana pasada; to be no b. than ..., no ser más que ...; to get b., mejorar. 2 (healthier) mejor (de salud). 3 b. off, (better) mejor; (richer) más rico,-a; you'd be b. off going home, lo mejor es que te vayas a casa. 4 the b. part of the day, la mayor parte del día. II adv (comp of well) 1 mejor; all the b., so much the b., tanto mejor; b. and b., cada vez mejor; *prov* b. late than never, más vale tarde que nunca. **2 we had b. leave**, más vale que nos vayamos. **3** to think b. of, (*plan*) cambiar de. **III** *n* mejor; **a change for the b.**, una mejora; **to get the b. of sb**, vencer a algn. **IV** *vtr* **1** (*improve*) mejorar. **2** (*surpass*) superar.

betting ['betɪŋ] *n* apuestas *fpl*; *GB* **b. shop**, quiosco *m* de apuestas.

between [bɪ'twiːn] **I** *prep* entre; **b. you and me**, entre nosotros; closed **b. 1 and 2**, cerrado de 1 a 2. **II** *adv* in **b.**, (*position*) en medio; (*time*) entretanto, mientras (tanto).

beverage ['bevərɪdʒ] *n* bebida *f*.

bevy ['bevɪ] *n* bandada *f*.

beware [bɪ'weəʳ] *vi* tener cuidado (**of**, con); **b. !**, ¡cuidado!; **'b. of the dog'**, (*sign*) 'cuidado con el perro'.

bewildered [bɪ'wɪldəd] *adj* desconcertado,-a.

bewilderment [bɪ'wɪldəmənt] *n* desconcierto *m*.

bewitching [bɪ'wɪtʃɪŋ] *adj* fascinador,- a.

beyond [bɪ'jɒnd] **I** *prep* más allá de; **b. belief**, increíble; **b. doubt**, sin lugar a dudas; **it is b. me why ...,** no comprendo por qué ...; **it's b. a joke**, eso ya no tiene gracia; **she is b. caring**, ya no le importa; **this task is b. me**, no puedo con esta tarea. **II** *adv* más allá, más lejos.

bias ['baɪəs] *n* (*tendency*) tendencia *f* (**to-wards**, hacia); (*prejudice*) prejuicio *m*.

bias(s)ed ['baɪəst] *adj* parcial; **to be b. against sth/sb**, tener prejuicio en contra de algo/algn.

bib [bɪb] *n* (*for baby*) babero *m*; (*of apron*) peto *m*.

Bible ['baɪbəl] *n* Biblia *f*; *sl* **B. basher, B. thumper**, evangelista *mf*.

bibliography [bɪblɪ'ɒgrəfɪ] *n* bibliografía *f*.

bicarbonate [baɪ'kɑːbənɪt] *n* bicarbonato *m*; **b. of soda**, bicarbonato sódico.

biceps ['baɪseps] *n* bíceps *m*.

bicker ['bɪkəʳ] *vi* reñir.

bicycle ['baɪsɪkəl] *n* bicicleta *f*; **b. pump**, bomba *f* (de aire); **to go by b.**, ir en bicicleta.

bid [bɪd] **I** *vtr* (*pt* bid *or* bade; *pp* bid *or* bidden) **1** (*say*) decir; **to b. sb farewell**, despedirse de algn. **2** (*command*) mandar, ordenar; **she bade him be quiet**, le mandó que se callase. **3** (*invite*) invitar; **he bade me sit down**, me invitó a sentarme. **4** (*at auction*) (*pt & pp* bid) pujar. **II** *vi* (*at auction*) pujar (**for**, por). **III** *n* **1** (*offer*) oferta *f*. **2** (*at auction*) puja *f*. **3** (*attempt*) intento *m*, tentativa *f*.

bidder ['bɪdəʳ] *n* **the highest b.**, el mejor postor.

bidding ['bɪdɪŋ] *n* **1** (*at auction*) puja *f*. **2** (*order*) orden *f*; **to do sb's b.**, cumplir la orden de algn.

bide [baɪd] *vtr* (*pt* bided *or* bode; *pp* bided) esperar; **to b. one's time**, esperar el momento oportuno.

bidet ['biːdeɪ] *n* bidé *m*.

bifocal [baɪ'fəʊkəl] **I** *adj* bifocal. **II** *npl* **bifocals** lentes *fpl* bifocales.

big [bɪg] **I** *adj* (bigger, biggest) grande (gran *before sing noun*); **a b. clock**, un reloj grande; **a b. surprise**, una gran sorpresa; **my b. brother**, mi hermano mayor; *fam* iron **b. deal!**, ¿y qué?; **b. business**, los grandes negocios; **b. dipper**, montaña rusa; *Astron US* **B. Dipper**, Osa *f* Mayor; **b. toe**, dedo gordo del pie; *fam* **b. gun, b. shot**, pez gordo; *fam* **to make the b. time**, tener éxito; *fam* **b. top**, carpa *f*. **II** *adv* **1** (*on a grand scale*) a lo grande. **2** (*well*) de manera excepcional.

bigamy ['bɪgəmɪ] *n* bigamia *f*.

bighead ['bɪghed] *n* *fam* creído,-a *m,f*, engreído,-a *m,f*.

bigheaded ['bɪg'hedɪd] *adj* creído,-a, engreído,-a.

bigot ['bɪgət] *n* intolerante *mf*.

bigoted ['bɪgətɪd] *adj* intolerante.

bigotry ['bɪgətrɪ] *n* intolerancia *f*.

bigwig ['bɪgwɪg] *n* *fam* pez gordo.

bike [baɪk] *n* (abbr *of* **bicycle** *or* **motorbike**) *n* (*bicycle*) bici *f*; (*motorcycle*) moto *f*; *sl* **on your b.!**, ¡vete de aquí!

bikini [bɪ'kiːnɪ] *n* bikini *m*.

bilateral [baɪ'lætərəl] *adj* bilateral.

bile [baɪl] *n* bilis *f*.

bilingual [baɪ'lɪŋgwəl] *adj* bilingüe.

bill¹ [bɪl] **I** *n* **1** (*for gas etc*) factura *f*, recibo *m*. **2** *esp GB* (*in restaurant*) cuenta *f*. **3** *Parl* proyecto *m* de ley. **4** *US* (*banknote*) billete *m* de banco. **5** (*poster*) cartel *m*; **on the b.**, en cartel; **'post no bills'**, 'prohibido fijar carteles'; *Theat* **to top the b.**, encabezar el reparto; **b. of exchange**, letra *f* de cambio; *Pol* **B. of Rights**, declaración *f* de derechos. **II** *vtr* **1** (*send bill to*) facturar. **2** *Theat* programar.

bill² [bɪl] *n* (*of bird*) pico *m*.

Bill [bɪl] *n dimin of* **William**; *fam* *GB* **sl the Old B.**, la poli.

billboard ['bɪlbɔːd] *n* *US* (*hoarding*) cartelera *f*.

billet ['bɪlɪt] **I** *n* alojamiento *m*. **II** *vtr* alojar.

billfold ['bɪlfəʊld] *n* *US* cartera *f*, billetero *m*.

billiards ['bɪljədz] *n* billar *m*.

billion ['bɪljən] *n* *US* mil millones *mpl*; *GB* (*former use*) billón *m*.

billionaire [bɪljə'neəʳ] *n* multimillonario,-a *m,f*.

billow ['bɪləʊ] **I** *n* (*of water*) ola *f*; (*of smoke*) nube *f*. **II** *vi* (*sea*) ondear; (*sail*) hincharse.

billy goat ['bɪlɪgəʊt] *n* macho cabrío.

bin [bɪn] *n* (*for storage*) cajón *m*; **bread b.**, panera *f*; (*rubbish*) **b.**, cubo *m* de la

basura.
binary ['baɪnərɪ] *adj* **b. number,** número binario.
bind [baɪnd] *vtr* (*pt & pp* **bound**) 1 (*tie up*) atar. 2 *Med* (*bandage*) vendar. 3 (*book*) encuadernar. 4 (*require*) obligar. 5 (*join etc*) unir. ◆**bind over** *vtr Jur* obligar legalmente.
binder ['baɪndər] *n* (*file*) carpeta *f*.
binding ['baɪndɪŋ] *adj* (*promise*) comprometedor,-a; (*contract*) vinculante.
binge [bɪndʒ] *n fam* borrachera *f*; **to go on a b.,** irse de juerga.
bingo ['bɪŋgəʊ] *n* bingo *m*.
binoculars [bɪ'nɒkjʊləz] *npl* prismáticos *mpl*, gemelos *mpl*.
biochemistry [baɪəʊ'kemɪstrɪ] *n* bioquímica *f*.
biodegradable [baɪəʊdɪ'greɪdəbəl] *adj* biodegradable.
biography [baɪ'ɒgrəfɪ] *n* biografía *f*.
biological [baɪə'lɒdʒɪkəl] *adj* biológico, -a; **b. warfare,** guerra biológica.
biologist [baɪ'ɒlədʒɪst] *n* biólogo,-a *m,f*.
biology [baɪ'ɒlədʒɪ] *n* biología *f*.
biorhythm ['baɪəʊrɪðəm] *n* biorritmo *m*.
biosphere ['baɪəsfɪər] *n* biosfera *f*.
birch [bɜːtʃ] I *n* 1 *Bot* abedul *m*. 2 (*rod*) vara *f* (de abedul). II *vtr* azotar.
bird [bɜːd] *n* 1 pájaro *m*, ave *f*; *fig* **to kill two birds with one stone,** matar dos pájaros de un tiro; **they're birds of a feather,** son tal para cual; **b. of prey,** ave de rapiña. 2 *GB sl* (*girl*) tía *f*, chica *f*.
birdcage ['bɜːdkeɪdʒ] *n* jaula *f*.
birdie ['bɜːdɪ] *n Golf* birdie *m*.
bird's-eye view [bɜːdzaɪ'vjuː] *n* vista *f* de pájaro.
bird-watcher ['bɜːdwɒtʃər] *n* ornitólogo,-a *m,f*.
Biro® ['baɪrəʊ] *n fam* boli *m*.
birth [bɜːθ] *n* 1 nacimiento *m*; (*childbirth*) parto *m*; **by b.,** de nacimiento; **to give b. to a child,** dar a luz a un niño; **b. certificate,** partida *f* de nacimiento; **b. control,** (*family planning*) control *m* de la natalidad; (*contraception*) métodos anticonceptivos; **b. rate,** índice *m* de natalidad. 2 **of noble b.,** (*parentage*) de noble linaje.
birthday ['bɜːθdeɪ] *n* cumpleaños *m inv*.
birthmark ['bɜːθmɑːk] *n* antojo *m*.
birthplace ['bɜːθpleɪs] *n* lugar *m* de nacimiento.
Biscay ['bɪskeɪ] *n* Vizcaya; **the Bay of B.,** el golfo de Vizcaya.
biscuit ['bɪskɪt] *n* galleta *f*; (*muffin*) bollo *m*, bizcocho *m*; *fam* **that really takes the b.!,** ¡eso ya es el colmo!
bisect [baɪ'sekt] *vtr* bisegmentar; *Geom* bisecar.
bisexual [baɪ'seksjʊəl] *adj* bisexual.
bishop ['bɪʃəp] *n* 1 *Rel* obispo *m*. 2 *Chess* alfil *m*.

bison ['baɪsən] *n inv* bisonte *m*.
bit¹ [bɪt] *n* 1 (*small piece*) trozo *m*, pedazo *m*; **to smash sth to bits,** hacer añicos algo; *fig* **thrilled to bits,** muy emocionado,-a; *fig* **to do one's b.,** poner de su parte. 2 (*small quantity*) poco *m*; **a b. of sugar,** un poco de azúcar; **a b. of advice,** un consejo; **a b. of news,** una noticia; **bits and pieces,** trastos *mpl*; *fig* **b. by b.,** poco a poco. 3 **a b.,** (*slightly*) un poco; **a b. longer,** un ratito más; **a b. worried,** un poco preocupado. 4 (*coin*) moneda *f*.
bit² [bɪt] *n* (*of tool*) broca *f*.
bit³ [bɪt] *n Comput* bit *m*.
bit⁴ [bɪt] *pt* → **bite.**
bitch [bɪtʃ] I *n* 1 *Zool* (*female*) hembra *f*; (*dog*) perra *f*. 2 *fam* (*spiteful woman*) bruja *f*. II *vi fam* **to b. (about),** (*criticize*) criticar.
bitchy ['bɪtʃɪ] *adj fam* (*spiteful*) maldiciente; (*malicious*) malicioso,-a; (*malevolent*) malintencionado,-a.
bite [baɪt] I *n* 1 (*act*) mordisco *m*. 2 (*wound*) mordedura *f*; (*insect*) b., picadura *f*. 3 (*mouthful*) bocado *m*. 4 *fam* (*snack*) bocado *m*. II *vtr* (*pt* **bit**; *pp* **bitten**) morder; (*insect*) picar; **to b. one's nails,** morderse las uñas; *fig* **to b. the dust,** (*suffer defeat*) morder el polvo; (*die*) palmarla; *fam* **to b. sb's head off,** echarle una bronca a algn. III *vi* 1 morder; (*insect*) picar. 2 *fig* (*take effect*) surtir efecto. 3 *Fishing* picar.
biting ['baɪtɪŋ] *adj* (*wind*) cortante; *fig* (*criticism*) mordaz.
bitten ['bɪtən] *pp* → **bite.**
bitter ['bɪtər] I *adj* 1 amargo,-a. 2 (*weather*) glacial; (*wind*) cortante. 3 (*person*) amargado,-a. 4 (*struggle*) enconado,-a; (*hatred*) implacable. II *n* 1 (*beer*) cerveza amarga. 2 **bitters,** bíter *m*. ◆**bitterly** *adv* **she was b. disappointed,** sufrió una terrible decepción.
bitterness ['bɪtənɪs] *n* 1 amargura *f*. 2 (*of weather*) crudeza *f*. 3 (*of person*) rencor *m*.
bittersweet [bɪtə'swiːt] *adj* agridulce.
bitumen ['bɪtjʊmɪn] *n* betún *m*.
bizarre [bɪ'zɑː] *adj* (*odd*) extraño,-a; (*eccentric*) estrafalario,-a.
blab [blæb] *vi fam* parlotear; (*let out a secret*) chivarse.
black [blæk] I *adj* 1 (*colour*) negro,-a; **a b. and white television,** un televisor en blanco y negro; *fig* **b. and blue,** amoratado,-a; **to put sth down in black and white,** poner algo por escrito; *Av* **b. box,** caja negra; **b. coffee,** café solo; **b. eye,** ojo morado; **b. hole,** agujero negro; **b. humour,** humor negro; **b. magic,** magia negra; **b. market,** mercado negro; **b. pudding,** morcilla *f*; **B. Sea,** Mar Negro; *Aut* **b. spot,** punto negro; *GB* **the B. Country,** la región de los Midlands; *fig* **b.**

sheep, oveja negra. **2** (*gloomy*) negro,-a; *fig* **a b. day,** un día aciago. **II** *n* **1** (*colour*) negro *m*. **2** (*person*) negro,-a. *fam* **III** *vtr* **1** (*make black*) ennegrecer. **2** (*polish*) lustrar. **3** (*boycott*) boicotear. ◆**black out I** *vtr* **1** (*extinguish lights in*) apagar las luces de. **2** (*censor*) censurar. **II** *vi* (*faint*) desmayarse.

blackberry ['blækbərɪ] *n* zarzamora *f*.

blackbird ['blækbɜːd] *n* mirlo *m*.

blackboard ['blækbɔːd] *n* pizarra *f*, encerado *m*.

blackcurrant [blæk'kʌrənt] *n* grosella negra.

blacken ['blækən] *vtr* **1** (*make black*) ennegrecer. **2** *fig* (*defame*) manchar.

blackhead ['blækhed] *n* espinilla *f*.

blackjack ['blækdʒæk] *n Cards* veintiuna *f*.

blackleg ['blækleg] *n* esquirol *m*.

blacklist ['blæklɪst] *n* lista negra.

blackmail ['blækmeɪl] **I** *n* chantaje *m*. **II** *vtr* chantajear.

blackout ['blækaut] *n* **1** (*of lights*) apagón *m*. **2** *Rad TV* censura *f*. **3** (*fainting*) pérdida *f* de conocimiento.

blacksmith ['blæksmɪθ] *n* herrero *m*.

bladder ['blædər] *n* vejiga *f*; **gall b.,** vesícula *f* biliar.

blade [bleɪd] *n* **1** (*of grass*) brizna *f*. **2** (*of knife etc*) hoja *f*. **3** (*of propeller, oar*) pala *f*.

blame [bleɪm] **I** *n* culpa *f*; **to take the b. for sth,** asumir la responsabilidad de algo. **II** *vtr* echar la culpa a; **he is to b.,** él tiene la culpa.

blameless ['bleɪmlɪs] *adj* (*person*) inocente; (*conduct*) intachable.

blancmange [blə'mɒnʒ] *n* tipo de budín *m* dulce.

bland [blænd] *adj* (*climate*) suave; (*food*) soso,-a.

blank [blæŋk] **I** *adj* **1** (*without writing*) en blanco; *Fin* **b. cheque,** cheque *m* en blanco. **2** (*empty*) vacío,-a; **a b. look,** una mirada inexpresiva. **3** **a b. refusal,** (*absolute*) una negativa rotunda. **II** *n* **1** (*space*) espacio *m* en blanco; **to draw a b.,** no tener éxito. **2** *Mil* cartucho *m* de fogueo. **3** *US* (*form*) impreso *m*.

blanket ['blæŋkɪt] **I** *n* manta *f*; *fig* capa *f*. **II** *adj* general.

blare [bleər] *vi* resonar. ◆**blare out** *vtr* pregonar.

blasé ['blɑːzeɪ] *adj* de vuelta de (todo).

blasphemous ['blæsfɪməs] *adj* blasfemo,-a.

blasphemy ['blæsfɪmɪ] *n* blasfemia *f*.

blast [blɑːst] **I** *n* **1** (*of wind*) ráfaga *f*. **2** (*of horn etc*) toque *m*; **at full b.,** a toda marcha. **3** (*explosion*) explosión *f*; *b.* **furnace,** alto horno. **4** (*shock wave*) onda *f* de choque. **II** *vtr* **1** (*blow up*) volar; *fam* **b. (it)!,** ¡maldito sea! **2** *fig* (*destroy*) arruinar. **3** *fig*

(*criticize*) criticar.

blasted ['blɑːstɪd] *adj* maldito,-a.

blast-off ['blɑːstɒf] *n* despegue *m*.

blatant ['bleɪtənt] *adj* (*very obvious*) evidente; (*shameless*) descarado,-a; **a b. lie,** una mentira patente.

blaze¹ [bleɪz] **I** *n* **1** (*burst of flame*) llamarada *f*. **2** (*fierce fire*) incendio *m*. **3** (*of sun*) resplandor *m*. **4** *fig* (*of anger*) arranque *m*. **II** *vi* **1** (*fire*) arder. **2** (*sun etc*) brillar.

blaze² [bleɪz] *vtr* **to b. a trail,** abrir un camino.

blazer ['bleɪzər] *n* chaqueta *f* sport.

bleach [bliːtʃ] **I** *n* (*household*) lejía *f*. **II** *vtr* **1** (*whiten*) blanquear; (*fade*) descolorir. **2** (*hair*) decolorar.

bleachers ['bliːtʃəz] *npl US Sport* (*seats*) gradas *fpl*.

bleak [bliːk] *adj* **1** (*countryside*) desolado, -a. **2** (*weather*) desapacible. **3** (*future*) poco prometedor,-a.

bleary ['blɪərɪ] *adj* (**blearier, bleariest**) (*eyes*) (*due to tears*) lloroso,-a; (*due to tiredness*) cansado,-a.

bleary-eyed ['blɪərɪaɪd] *adj* con los ojos llorosos or cansados.

bleat [bliːt] **I** *n* balido *m*. **II** *vi* (*animal*) balar.

bled [bled] *pt & pp → **bleed**.

bleed [bliːd] **I** *vi* (*pt & pp* **bled**) sangrar. **II** *vtr Med* sangrar; *fam* **to b. sb dry,** sacarle a algn hasta el último céntimo.

bleeding ['bliːdɪŋ] **I** *n* (*loss of blood*) pérdida *f* de sangre. **II** *adj* **1** *Med* sangrante. **2** *sl offens* puñetero,-a.

bleep [bliːp] **I** *n* bip *m*, pitido *m*. **II** *vi* pitar.

bleeper ['bliːpər] *n fam* busca *m*, buscapersonas *m inv*.

blemish ['blemɪʃ] *n* (*flaw*) defecto *m*; (*on fruit*) maca *f*; *fig* mancha *f*; *fig* **without b.,** sin tacha.

blend [blend] **I** *n* mezcla *f*. **II** *vtr* (*mix*) mezclar; (*colours*) armonizar. **II** *vi* (*mix*) mezclarse; (*colours*) armonizar.

blender ['blendər] *n* licuadora *f*.

bless [bles] *vtr* (*pt & pp* **blessed** or **blest**) **1** bendecir; **b. you!,** (*after a sneeze*) ¡Jesús! **2 blessed with good eyesight,** dotado,-a de buena vista.

blessing ['blesɪŋ] *n* bendición *f*; (*advantage*) ventaja *f*; **a mixed b.,** una ventaja relativa.

blew [bluː] *pt → **blow**.

blight [blaɪt] **I** *n* plaga *f*. **II** *vtr fig* (*spoil*) arruinar; (*frustrate*) frustrar.

blimey ['blaɪmɪ] *interj fam* ¡caramba!, ¡caray!

blind [blaɪnd] **I** *adj* ciego,-a; **a b. man,** un ciego; **a b. woman,** una ciega; *fig* **b. faith,** fe ciega; *fig* **to turn a b. eye,** hacer la vista gorda; **b. alley,** callejón *m* sin salida; *Aut* **b. corner,** curva *f* sin visibilidad; **b. spot,** ángulo muerto; *fam* **b.**

date, cita *f* a ciegas. II *adv* a ciegas; *fam* **to get b. drunk**, agarrar una curda. III *n* 1 (*on window*) persiana *f*. 2 *pl* **the b.**, los ciegos. IV *vtr* 1 cegar, dejar ciego; *fig* **blinded by ambition**, cegado por la ambición. 2 (*dazzle*) deslumbrar.

blinders ['blaɪndəz] *npl* US anteojeras *fpl*.

blindfold ['blaɪndfəʊld] I *n* venda *f*. II *vtr* vendar los ojos a.

blinding ['blaɪndɪŋ] *adj* cegador,-a, deslumbrante.

blindly ['blaɪndlɪ] *adv* a ciegas, ciegamente.

blindness ['blaɪndnɪs] *n* ceguera *f*.

blink [blɪŋk] *vi* (*eyes*) pestañear; (*lights*) parpadear.

blinkered ['blɪŋkəd] *adj fig* de miras estrechas.

blinkers ['blɪŋkəz] *npl* (*on horse*) anteojeras *fpl*.

bliss [blɪs] *n* felicidad *f*; **it was b.!**, ¡fue maravilloso!

blissful ['blɪsfʊl] *adj* (*happy*) feliz; (*marvellous*) maravilloso,-a.

blister ['blɪstə'] I *n* (*on skin*) ampolla *f*; (*on paint*) burbuja *f*. II *vi* ampollarse.

blithe [blaɪð] *adj* alegre. ◆**blithely** *adv* alegremente.

blitz [blɪts] I *n* bombardeo aéreo. II *vtr* bombardear.

blizzard ['blɪzəd] *n* ventisca *f*.

bloated ['bləʊtɪd] *adj* hinchado,-a.

blob [blɒb] *n* (*drop*) gota *f*; (*spot*) mancha *f*.

bloc [blɒk] *n Pol* bloque *m*.

block [blɒk] I *n* 1 bloque *m*; (*of wood*) taco *m*; **in b. capitals**, en mayúsculas. 2 **a b. of flats**, un bloque de pisos. 3 (*group of buildings*) manzana *f*. 4 (*obstruction*) bloqueo *m*. 5 *Fin* **a b. of shares**, un paquete de acciones. 6 *fam* (*head*) coco *m*. II *vtr* 1 (*obstruct*) obstruir; *Aut* **'road blocked'**, 'carretera cortada'; **to b. the way**, cerrar el paso. 2 *Sport* (*player*) obstaculizar. 3 *Fin Parl* bloquear. ◆**block up** *vtr* bloquear, obstruir; **to get blocked up**, (*pipe*) obstruirse.

blockade [blɒ'keɪd] *n* bloqueo *m*.

blockage ['blɒkɪdʒ] *n* bloqueo *m*, obstrucción *f*; (*traffic jam*) atasco *m*.

blockbuster ['blɒkbʌstə'] *n fam* exitazo *m*; *Cin TV* gran éxito *m* de taquilla; (*book*) éxito de ventas.

bloke [bləʊk] *n fam* tío *m*, tipo *m*.

blond [blɒnd] *adj & n* rubio (*m*).

blonde [blɒnd] *adj & n* rubia (*f*).

blood [blʌd] *n* 1 sangre *f*; **b. bank**, banco *m* de sangre; **b. cell**, glóbulo *m*; **b. donor**, donante *mf* de sangre; **b. group**, grupo sanguíneo; **b. pressure**, tensión *f* arterial; **b. test**, análisis *m* de sangre; **b. transfusion**, transfusión *f* de sangre; **b. vessel**, vaso sanguíneo; **blue b.**, sangre

azul; **high/low b. pressure**, hipertensión *f*/hipotensión *f*. 2 (*race*) sangre *f*, raza *f*.

bloodbath ['blʌdbɑːθ] *n fig* baño *m* de sangre.

bloodhound ['blʌdhaʊnd] *n* sabueso *m*.

bloodshed ['blʌdʃed] *n* derramamiento *m* de sangre.

bloodshot ['blʌdʃɒt] *adj* inyectado,-a de sangre.

bloodstream ['blʌdstriːm] *n* corriente *f* sanguínea.

bloodthirsty ['blʌdθɜːstɪ] *adj* sanguinario,-a.

bloody ['blʌdɪ] I *adj* (**bloodier, bloodiest**) 1 (*battle*) sangriento,-a. 2 (*bloodstained*) manchado,-a de sangre. 3 *sl* (*damned*) condenado,-a, puñetero,-a. II *adv sl* **it's b. difficult**, ¡joder, qué difícil!; **not b. likely!**, ¡ni de coña! ◆**bloody-minded** [blʌdɪ'maɪndɪd] *adj fam* terco,-a.

blotchy ['blɒtʃɪ] *adj* (*skin etc*) enrojecido,-a; (*paint etc*) cubierto,-a de manchas.

blotting-paper ['blɒtɪŋpeɪpə'] *n* papel *m* secante.

blouse [blaʊz] *n* blusa *f*.

bloom [bluːm] I *n* 1 (*flower*) flor *f*; **in full b.**, en flor. 2 (*on fruit*) vello *m* (*blossom*) florecer. II *vi* florecer.

blooming ['bluːmɪŋ] *adj* 1 (*blossoming*) floreciente. 2 *fam euph* (*damned*) maldito,-a, condenado,-a.

blossom ['blɒsəm] I *n* (*flower*) flor *f*. II *vi* florecer; *fig* **to b. out**, alcanzar la plenitud.

blot [blɒt] I *n* (*of ink*) borrón *m*; *fig* mancha *f*. II *vtr* 1 (*with ink*) emborronar. 2 (*dry*) secar. III *vi* (*ink*) correrse. ◆**blot out** *vtr* (*memories*) borrar; (*view*) ocultar.

blow[1] [bləʊ] *n* golpe *m*; **to come to blows**, llegar a las manos; **it came as a terrible b.**, fue un duro golpe.

blow[2] [bləʊ] I *vi* (*pt* **blew**, *pp* **blown**) 1 (*wind*) soplar; **to b. shut**, cerrarse de golpe. 2 (*fuse*) fundirse. 3 (*tyre*) reventar. II *vtr* 1 (*kiss*) mandar. 2 (*trumpet etc*) tocar; *fig* **to b. one's own trumpet**, darse bombo. 3 (*one's nose*) sonarse. 4 (*fuse*) fundir. 5 *fam* (*waste*) despilfarrar. 6 *fam* (*chances*) dar al traste con. 7 (*explode*) volar; *fig* **to b. sb's cover**, descubrir la tapadera de algn; *fam* **to b. one's top**, salirse de sus casillas. ◆**blow away** → **blow off.** ◆**blow down** *vtr* derribar. ◆**blow off** I *vtr* (*by wind*) llevarse. II (*hat*) salir volando. ◆**blow out** I *vtr* apagar. II *vi* apagarse. ◆**blow over** *vi* (*storm*) calmarse; (*scandal*) olvidarse. ◆**blow up** I *vtr* 1 (*building*) volar. 2 (*inflate*) inflar. 3 *Phot* ampliar. II (*explode*) explotar.

blowlamp ['bləʊlæmp] *n* soplete *m*.

blown [bləʊn] *pp* → **blow.**

blowout ['bləʊaʊt] n Aut reventón m; sl comilona f.

blowtorch ['bləʊtɔːtʃ] n US soplete m.

blow-up ['bləʊʌp] n Phot ampliación f.

blubber ['blʌbər] I n grasa f de ballena. II vi fam llorar a moco tendido.

bludgeon ['blʌdʒən] vtr aporrear; fig to b. sb into doing sth, forzar a algn a hacer algo.

blue [bluː] I adj 1 (colour) azul; fig once in a b. moon, de higos a brevas; fam to scream b. murder, gritar como un loco; b. jeans, vaqueros mpl, tejanos mpl. 2 (sad) triste; to feel b., sentirse deprimido. 3 (obscene) verde; b. joke, chiste m verde. II n 1 (colour) azul m; fam the boys in b., los maderos. 2 out of the b., (suddenly) de repente; (unexpectedly) como llovido del cielo.

bluebell ['bluːbel] n campanilla f.

blueberry ['bluːbərɪ] n arándano m.

bluebottle ['bluːbɒtl] n moscarda f, mosca f azul.

blue-collar ['bluːkɒlər] adj b.-c. worker, obrero,-a m,f.

blueprint ['bluːprɪnt] n anteproyecto m.

blues [bluːz] n 1 Mus the b., el blues. 2 fam (sadness) tristeza f, melancolía f; to have the b., sentirse deprimido.

bluetit ['bluːtɪt] n herrerillo m común.

bluff [blʌf] I n (trick) farol m; to call sb's b., hacer que algn ponga sus cartas encima de la mesa. II adj (abrupt) brusco,-a; (forthright) francote,-a. III vi tirarse un farol; to b. one's way through sth, hacer colar algo.

blunder ['blʌndər] I n metedura f de pata; fam patinazo m. II vi meter la pata, pegar un patinazo.

blunt [blʌnt] I adj 1 (knife) desafilado,-a; (pencil) despuntado,-a; b. instrument, instrumento m contundente. 2 (frank) directo,-a, francote,-a; (statement) tajante. II vtr (pencil) despuntar; (knife) desafilar. ◆**bluntly** adv francamente.

blur [blɜːr] I n aspecto borroso. II vtr (windows) empañar; (shape) desdibujar; (memory) enturbiar.

blurb [blɜːb] n (in book) resumen m.

blurred [blɜːd] adj borroso,-a.

blurt [blɜːt] vtr to b. out, dejar escapar.

blush [blʌʃ] I n rubor m. II vi ruborizarse.

blusher ['blʌʃər] n colorete m.

blustery ['blʌstərɪ] adj borrascoso,-a.

boar [bɔːr] n verraco m; wild b., jabalí m.

board [bɔːd] I n 1 (plank) tabla f (work surface) mesa f; (blackboard) pizarra f; (for games) tablero m. 3 (meals) comida f; full b., pensión completa; b. and lodging, casa f y comida. 4 (committee) junta f, consejo m; b. of directors, consejo de administración; b. room, sala f del consejo. 5 Naut on b., a bordo. 6 fig above b.,

en regla; **across-the-b.**, general; to let sth go by the b., abandonar algo. II vtr (ship, plane etc) embarcarse en, subir a. III vi 1 (lodge) alojarse. 2 (at school) estar interno,-a. ◆**board up** vtr tapar.

boarder ['bɔːdər] n 1 (in boarding house) huésped m,f. 2 (at school) interno,-a m,f.

boarding ['bɔːdɪŋ] n 1 (embarkation) embarque m; b. card, b. pass, tarjeta f de embarque. 2 (lodging) alojamiento m, pensión f; b. house, pensión f; b. school, internado m.

boast [bəʊst] I n jactancia f, alarde m. II vi jactarse, alardear (about, de). III vtr presumir de, alardear de; the town boasts an Olympic swimming pool, la ciudad disfruta de una piscina olímpica.

boat [bəʊt] n barco m; (small) barca f, bote m; (launch) lancha f; (large) buque m; fig we're all in the same b., todos estamos en el mismo barco; fishing b., barco de pesca.

boater ['bəʊtər] n canotié m, canotier m.

boatswain ['bəʊsən] n contramaestre m.

boatyard ['bəʊtjɑːd] n astillero m.

bob [bɒb] I n 1 (haircut) pelo m a lo chico. 2 fam inv (shilling) chelín m. II vi to b. up and down, subir y bajar.

bobbin ['bɒbɪn] n (of sewing machine) canilla f; (for lace-making) bolillo m.

bobby ['bɒbɪ] n fam (policeman) poli m.

bobsleigh ['bɒbsleɪ] n bobsleigh m.

bode¹ [bəʊd] → **bide**.

bode² [bəʊd] vtr & vi presagiar; to b. well/ill, ser de buen/mal agüero.

bodice ['bɒdɪs] n 1 (sleeveless undergarment) corpiño m. 2 (of dress) cuerpo m.

bodily ['bɒdɪlɪ] I adj físico,-a; b. harm, daños mpl corporales. II adv to carry sb b., llevar a algn en brazos.

body ['bɒdɪ] n 1 cuerpo m; b. language, expresión f corporal; b. odour, olor m corporal. 2 (corpse) cadáver m. 3 (main part) parte f principal. 4 Aut carrocería f; Naut casco m. 5 (organization) organismo m; (profession) cuerpo m; the b. politic, el estado. 6 (group of people) conjunto m, grupo m.

body-blow ['bɒdɪbləʊ] n fig duro golpe m.

body-builder ['bɒdɪbɪldər] n culturista m,f.

body-building ['bɒdɪbɪldɪŋ] n culturismo m.

bodyguard ['bɒdɪgɑːd] n guardaespaldas mf inv.

bodywork ['bɒdɪwɜːk] n Aut carrocería f.

Boer ['bəʊər] adj the B. War, la guerra del Transvaal.

bog [bɒg] n 1 ciénaga f. 2 sl (lavatory) meódromo m. ◆**bog down** vtr to get bogged down, atascarse.

bogey ['bəʊgɪ] n 1 (spectre) espectro m, fantasma m. 2 (bugbear) pesadilla f. 3

Golf bogey *m.* **4** *sl (mucus)* moco *m.*

boggle ['bɒgəl] *vi fam* **the mind boggles,** ¡es alucinante!

bogus ['bəʊgəs] *adj* falso,-a; **b. company,** compañía fantasma.

boil¹ [bɔɪl] **I** *n* **to come to the b.,** empezar a hervir. **II** *vtr (water)* hervir; *(food)* cocer; *(egg)* cocer, pasar por agua. **III** *vi* hervir; *fig* **to b. with rage,** estar furioso.
◆**boil down** *vi* reducirse (**to,** a).
◆**boil over** *vi (milk)* salirse.

boil² [bɔɪl] *n Med* furúnculo *m.*

boiled [bɔɪld] *adj* **b. egg,** huevo cocido *or* pasado por agua.

boiler ['bɔɪlər] *n* caldera *f.*; **b. suit,** mono *m.*

boiling ['bɔɪlɪŋ] *adj* **b. water,** agua hirviendo; **it's b. hot,** *(food)* quema; *(weather)* hace un calor agobiante; **b. point,** punto *m* de ebullición.

boisterous ['bɔɪstərəs] *adj* **1** *(person, party)* bullicioso,-a. **2** *(weather)* borrascoso,-a.

bold [bəʊld] *adj* **1** *(brave)* valiente. **2** *(daring)* audaz. **3** *(features)* marcado,-a; *Typ* **b. type,** negrita *f.* **4** *(impudent)* descarado,-a.

Bolivia [bə'lɪvɪə] *n* Bolivia.

Bolivian [bə'lɪvɪən] *adj & n* boliviano,-a *(m,f).*

bollard ['bɒlɑːd] *n Aut* baliza *f.*

bollocks ['bɒləks] *npl vulg* cojones *mpl*; **b.!,** *(disagreement)* ¡y un huevo!

Bolshevik ['bɒlʃəvɪk] *adj & n* bolchevique *(mf).*

bolster ['bəʊlstər] **I** *n (pillow)* cabezal *m,* travesaño *m.* **II** *vtr (strengthen)* reforzar; *(support)* apoyar.

bolt [bəʊlt] **I** *n* **1** *(on door)* cerrojo *m*; *(small)* pestillo *m.* **2** *Tech* perno *m,* tornillo *m.* **3** *(of lightning)* rayo *m.* **4** *(crossbow)* flecha *f.* **II** *vtr* **1** *(lock)* cerrar con cerrojo. **2** *Tech* sujetar con pernos. **3** *fam (food)* engullir. **III** *vi (person)* largarse; *(horse)* desbocarse. **IV** *adv* **b. upright,** derecho.

bomb [bɒm] **I** *n* bomba *f*; *GB sl* **to cost a b.,** costar un ojo de la cara; **b. disposal squad,** brigada *f* de artificieros; **b. scare,** amenaza *f* de bomba; **car b.,** cochebomba *m*; **letter b.,** carta-bomba *f.* **II** *vtr (city etc)* bombardear; *(by terrorists)* volar. **III** *vi fam* **to b. (along,** *(car)* ir a toda pastilla.

bombard [bɒm'bɑːd] *vtr* bombardear.

bombardment [bɒm'bɑːdmənt] *n* bombardeo *m.*

bombastic [bɒm'bæstɪk] *adj* rimbombante.

bomber ['bɒmər] *n* **1** *Av* bombardero *m*; **b. jacket,** cazadora *f.* **2** terrorista *mf* que coloca bombas.

bombshell ['bɒmʃel] *n* **1** *Mil* obús *m.* **2** *fig (surprise)* bomba *f.* **3** *fam* **a blonde b.,** una rubia explosiva.

bona fide ['bəʊnə'faɪdɪ] *adj* **1** *(genuine)* auténtico,-a. **2** *(in good faith)* bienintencionado,-a.

bond [bɒnd] **I** *n* **1** *(link)* lazo *m,* vínculo *m.* **2** *Fin* bono *m.* **3** *Jur (bail)* fianza *f.* **4** *(binding agreement)* acuerdo *m.* **5** *(warehouse)* depósito *m*; **in b.,** en depósito. **6** *US (guarantee)* garantía *f.* **7 bonds,** *(shackles)* cadenas *fpl.* **II** *vtr* **1** *(join)* pegar. **2** *(merchandise)* poner en depósito.

bondage ['bɒndɪdʒ] *n* esclavitud *f.*

bone [bəʊn] **I** *n* hueso *m*; *(in fish)* espina *f*; *fig* **b. of contention,** manzana *f* de la discordia; *fig* **to make no bones about sth,** no andarse con rodeos en un asunto; **b. china,** porcelana fina. **2 bones,** *(remains)* restos *mpl*; **the bare bones,** lo esencial. **II** *vtr (meat)* deshuesar; *(fish)* quitar las espinas a. ◆**bone up on** *vtr fam* empollar.

bone-dry [bəʊn'draɪ] *adj* completamente seco,-a.

bone-idle [bəʊn'aɪdəl] *adj* gandul,-a.

bonfire ['bɒnfaɪər] *n* hoguera *f,* fogata *f*; **B. Night,** noche *f* del cinco de noviembre.

bonkers ['bɒŋkəz] *adj GB sl* chalado,-a.

bonnet ['bɒnɪt] *n* **1** *(child's)* gorra *f.* **2** *Aut* capó *m.*

bonus ['bəʊnəs] *n* **1** *(on wages)* prima *f.* **2** *Fin (on shares)* dividendo *m* extraordinario. **3** *GB Ins* beneficio *m.*

bony ['bəʊnɪ] *adj (bonier, boniest) (person)* huesudo,-a; *(fish)* lleno,-a de espinas.

boo [buː] **I** *interj* ¡bu!. **II** *n* abucheo *m.* **III** *vtr* abuchear.

boob [buːb] *n GB sl* **1** *(silly mistake)* patinazo *m.* **2 boobs,** *(breasts)* tetas *fpl.*

booby ['buːbɪ] *n* **b. prize,** premio *m* de consolación; **b. trap,** trampa *f*; *Mil* trampa explosiva.

boogie ['buːgɪ] *vi fam* bailar.

book [bʊk] **I** *n* **1** libro *m*; *fig* **in my b.,** según mi punto de vista; *fig* **by the b.,** según las reglas; **b. end,** sujetalibros *m inv*; *GB* **b. token,** vale *m* para comprar libros; **savings b.,** libreta *f* de ahorros. **2** *(of stamps)* carpeta *f*; *(of matches)* cajetilla *f.* **3** *Com* **books,** cuentas *fpl*; **to keep the books,** llevar las cuentas. **II** *vtr* **1** *(reserve)* reservar; *(return flight)* cerrar. **2** *(engage)* contratar. **3** *(by police)* poner una multa a. **4** *Ftb* amonestar. ◆**book into** *vtr (hotel)* reservar una habitación en. ◆**book out** *vi (of hotel)* marcharse. ◆**book up** *vtr* **booked up,** completo.

booking ['bʊkɪŋ] *n esp GB (reservation)* reserva *f*; **b. office,** taquilla *f.*

bookmaker ['bʊkmeɪkər] *n* corredor,-a *m,f* de apuestas.

bookseller ['bʊkselər] *n* librero,-a *m,f.*

bookshelf ['bʊkʃelf] *n* **bookshelves,** estantería *f sing.*

bookshop ['bukʃɒp] n librería f.

bookstall ['bukstɔːl] n quiosco m.

bookstore ['bukstɔːr] n US librería f.

bookworm ['bukwɜːm] n fam ratón m de biblioteca.

boom¹ [buːm] I n 1 (noise) estampido m, trueno m. 2 (sudden prosperity) boom m, auge m. II vi 1 (thunder) retumbar; (cannon) tronar. 2 (prosper) estar en auge.

boom² [buːm] n (of microphone) jirafa f.

boomerang ['buːməræŋ] I n bumerang m, bumerán m.

booming ['buːmɪŋ] adj 1 (voice, thunder) que retumba. 2 (prosperous) en auge.

boon [buːn] n (blessing) bendición f.

boost [buːst] I n estímulo m, empujón m. II vt 1 (increase) aumentar. 2 to b. sb's confidence, subirle la moral a algn. 3 (tourism, exports) fomentar. 4 (voltage) elevar.

booster ['buːstər] n 1 Elec elevador m de voltaje. 2 Rad TV (amplifier) amplificador m. 3 Med b. (shot), revacunación f.

boot¹ [buːt] I n 1 bota f; (short) botín m; fig he's too big for his boots, es muy creído; fam to put the b. in, pisotear; fam she got the b., la echaron (del trabajo); b. polish, betún m. 2 GB Aut maletero m. II vtr fam 1 Ftb (ball) chutar. 2 to b. (out), echar a patadas.

boot² [buːt] n to b., además.

bootblack ['buːtblæk] n esp US limpiabotas mf inv.

booth [buːð, buːθ] n 1 (in language lab etc) cabina f; **telephone b.**, cabina telefónica. 2 (at fair) puesto m.

bootleg ['buːtleg] adj de contrabando.

bootlegger ['buːtlegər] n contrabandista m.

booty ['buːtɪ] n botín m.

booze [buːz] fam I n priva f. II vi privar.

bop [bɒp] I n 1 Mus be-bop m. 2 fam (dance) baile m. II vi fam (dance) bailar.

Bordeaux [bɔːˈdəu] n 1 (city) Burdeos. 2 (wine) burdeos m.

border ['bɔːdər] I n 1 borde m, margen m. 2 Sew ribete m. 3 (frontier) frontera f; **b. town**, pueblo fronterizo. 4 (flower bed) arriate m. III vtr Sew ribetear. ◆**border on** vtr 1 Geog lindar con. 2 fig rayar en.

borderline ['bɔːdəlaɪn] I n 1 (border) frontera f. 2 (dividing line) línea divisoria. II adj 1 (on the border) fronterizo,-a. 2 fig (case etc) dudoso,-a.

bore¹ [bɔːr] I vtr Tech taladrar, perforar. II n 1 Tech (hole) taladro m. 2 (of gun) calibre m.

bore² [bɔːr] I vtr aburrir. II n (person) pesado,-a m,f; pelma mf; (thing) lata f; rollo m; **what a b.!**, ¡qué rollo!

bore³ [bɔːr] pt → **bear¹**.

bored [bɔːd] adj aburrido,-a; **to be b. stiff or to tears**, estar aburrido,-a como una ostra.

boredom ['bɔːdəm] n aburrimiento m.

boring ['bɔːrɪŋ] adj (uninteresting) aburrido,-a; (tedious) pesado,-a, latoso,-a.

born [bɔːn] I pp → **bear¹**; **to be b.**, nacer; **I wasn't b. yesterday**, no nací ayer. II adj (having natural ability) nato,-a; **b. poet**, poeta nato.

born-again ['bɔːnəgen] adj Rel converso,-a.

borne [bɔːn] pp → **bear¹**.

borough ['bʌrə] n 1 (town) ciudad f; US (municipality) municipio m. 2 esp GB (constituency) distrito m electoral.

borrow ['bɒrəu] I vtr pedir o tomar prestado; **can I b. your pen?**, ¿me dejas tu bolígrafo? 2 (ideas etc) apropiarse. II vi pedir or tomar prestado.

borstal ['bɔːstəl] n GB fam reformatorio m.

bosom ['buzəm] n 1 (breast) pecho m; (breasts) pechos mpl; **b. friend**, amigo,-a m,f del alma. 2 fig seno m.

boss [bɒs] I n 1 (head) jefe,-a m,f; (factory owner etc) patrón,-ona m,f. 2 esp US Pol jefe m; pej cacique m. II vtr to b. sb about or around, mandar sobre algn.

bossy ['bɒsɪ] adj (bossier, bossiest) fam mandón,-ona.

bosun ['bəusən] n contramaestre m.

botanic(al) [bəˈtænɪk(əl)] adj botánico,-a; **b. garden**, jardín m botánico.

botany ['bɒtənɪ] n botánica f.

botch [bɒtʃ] I vtr chapucear; **a botched job**, una chapuza. II n chapuza f.

both [bəuθ] I adj ambos,-as, los dos, las dos; **b. men are teachers**, ambos son profesores; **hold it with b. hands**, sujétalo con las dos manos. II pron b. (of them), ambos,-as, los dos, las dos; **b. of you**, vosotros dos. III conj a la vez; b. England and Spain are in Europe, tanto Inglaterra como España están en Europa.

bother ['bɒðər] I vtr 1 (disturb) molestar; (be a nuisance to) dar la lata a. 2 (worry) preocupar; fam **I can't be bothered**, no tengo ganas. II vi 1 molestarse; both b. about me, no te preocupes por mí; **he didn't b. shaving**, no se molestó en afeitarse. III n 1 (disturbance) molestia f; (nuisance) lata f. 2 (trouble) problemas mpl. IV interj GB ¡maldito sea!

bothersome ['bɒðəsəm] adj molesto,-a.

bottle ['bɒtəl] n 1 botella f; (of perfume, ink) frasco m; fam **to hit the b.**, darle a la bebida; **baby's b.**, biberón m; **b. opener**, abrebotellas m inv. 2 GB sl **to have a lot of b.**, (nerve) tener muchas agallas. II vtr (wine) embotellar; (fruit) envasar. ◆**bottle out** vi GB sl encogerse. ◆**bottle up** vtr reprimir.

bottle-bank ['bɒtəlbæŋk] n contenedor m de vidrio.

bottled ['bɒtəld] adj (beer, wine) en botella, embotellado,-a; (fruit) envasado,-a.

bottle-green ['bɒtəlgriːn] *adj* verde botella.

bottleneck ['bɒtlnek] *n Aut* embotellamiento *m*, atasco *m*.

bottom ['bɒtəm] **I** *adj* **1** (*lowest*) más bajo,-a; (*drawer, shelf*) de abayo; *Aut* b. **gear**, primera *f*. **2** (*last*) último,-a; **b. line**, *Fin* saldo *m* final; *fig* resultado *m* final. **II** *n* **1** parte *f* inferior; (*of sea, garden, street, box*) fondo *m*; (*of bottle*) culo *m*; (*of page, hill*) pie *m*; *Educ* to be (**at**) **the b. of the class**, ser el último *or* la última de la clase; **to touch b.**, tocar fondo; *fam* **bottoms up!**, ¡salud! **2 to get to the b. of a matter**, llegar al meollo de una cuestión; **who is at the b. of all this?**, ¿quién está detrás de todo esto? **3** (*buttocks*) trasero *m*. ◆**bottom out** *vi Fin* tocar fondo.

bottomless ['bɒtəmlɪs] *adj* (*pit*) sin fondo; (*mystery*) insondable.

boudoir ['buːdwɑːr] *n* tocador *m*.

bough [baʊ] *n* rama *f*.

bought [bɔːt] *pt & pp* → **buy**.

bouillon ['buːjɒn] *n* caldo *m*.

boulder ['bəʊldər] *n* canto rodado.

boulevard ['buːlvɑːr] *n* bulevar *m*.

bounce [baʊns] **I** *vi* **1** (*ball*) rebotar. **2** (*jump*) saltar. **3** *sl* (*cheque*) ser rechazado (por el banco). **II** *vtr* (*ball*) botar. **III** *n* **1** (*of ball*) bote *m*. **2** (*jump*) salto *m*. **3** (*energy*) vitalidad *f*. ◆**bounce back** *vi* (*recover health*) recuperarse, recobrarse.

bouncer ['baʊnsər] *n sl* gorila *m*.

bound[1] [baʊnd] *adj* **1** (*tied up*) atado,-a. **2** (*book*) encuadernado,-a. **3** (*obliged*) obligado,-a. **4 b.** (**up**), (*linked*) vinculado,-a (**with**, a). **5 it's b. to happen**, sucederá con toda seguridad; **it was b. to fail**, estaba prevista el fracaso.

bound[2] [baʊnd] **I** *vi* saltar. **II** *n* salto *m*.

bound[3] [baʊnd] *adj* **b. for**, con destino a, rumbo a; **to be b. for**, dirigirse a.

boundary ['baʊndərɪ] *n* límite *m*.

boundless ['baʊndlɪs] *adj* ilimitado,-a, sin límites.

bounds [baʊndz] *npl* **beyond the b.** of reality, más allá de la realidad; **her ambition knows no b.**, su ambición no conoce límites; **the river is out of b.**, está prohibido bajar al río.

bounty ['baʊntɪ] *n* prima *f*, gratificación *f*.

bouquet [buːˈkeɪ, bəʊˈkeɪ] *n* **1** (*of flowers*) ramillete *m*. **2** [buːˈkeɪ] (*of wine*) aroma *m*, buqué *m*.

bourbon ['bɜːbən] *n* bourbon *m*.

bourgeois ['bʊəʒwɑː] *adj & n* burgués, -esa (*m,f*).

bourgeoisie [bʊəʒwɑːˈziː] *n* burguesía *f*.

bout [baʊt] *n* **1** (*of work*) turno *m*, tanda *f*. **2** (*of illness*) ataque *m*. **2** *Box* combate *m*.

boutique [buːˈtiːk] *n* boutique *f*, tienda *f*.

bow[1] [baʊ] **I** *vi* **1** hacer una reverencia. **2** (*give in*) ceder. **II** *n* (*with head, body*) reverencia *f*. ◆**bow out** *vi* retirarse (**of**, de).

bow[2] [bəʊ] **I** *n Sport & Mus* arco *m*; *fig* **to have more than one string to one's b.**, ser una persona de recursos. **2** (*knot*) lazo *m*; **b. tie**, pajarita *f*.

bow[3] [baʊ] *n esp Naut* proa *f*.

bowel ['baʊəl] *n* **1** intestino *m*. **2 bowels**, entrañas *fpl*.

bowl[1] [bəʊl] *n* **1** (*dish*) cuenco *m*; (*for soup*) tazón *m*; (*for washing hands*) palangana *f*; (*for washing clothes, dishes*) barreño *m*; (*of toilet*) taza *f*. **2** *Geol* cuenca *f*.

bowl[2] [bəʊl] **I** *n* bola *f*. **II** *vtr* (*in cricket*) lanzar. **III** *vi* **1** (*play bowls*) jugar a los bolos. **2** (*in cricket*) lanzar la pelota. ◆**bowl along** *vi fam* (*car*) ir volando. ◆**bowl out** *vtr* (*in cricket*) eliminar. ◆**bowl over** *vtr* **1** (*knock down*) derribar. **2** *fig* (*astonish*) desconcertar.

bow-legged ['bəʊleg(ɪ)d] *adj* patizambo,-a.

bowler[1] ['bəʊlər] *n* (*in cricket*) lanzador,-a *m,f*.

bowler[2] ['bəʊlər] *n* (*hat*) bombín *m*.

bowling ['bəʊlɪŋ] *n* (*game*) bolos *mpl*; **b. alley**, bolera *f*; **b. green**, campo de bolos.

bowls [bəʊlz] *npl Sport* bolos *mpl*.

box[1] [bɒks] **I** *n* **1** caja *f*; (*large*) cajón *m*; (*of matches*) cajetilla *f*; **jewellery b.**, joyero *m*; *Theat* **b. office**, taquilla *f*; **b. office success**, éxito taquillero. **2** *Press* recuadro *m*. **3** *Jur* (*witness*) b., barra *f* de los testigos. **4** *Theat* palco *m*. **5** *GB fam* (*television*) caja tonta. **II** *vtr* (*pack*) embalar.

box[2] [bɒks] *Sport* **I** *vi* boxear. **II** *vtr* (*hit*) pegar; **to b. sb's ears**, dar un cachete a algn.

boxer ['bɒksər] *n* **1** *Box* boxeador *m*. **2** (*dog*) bóxer *m*.

boxing ['bɒksɪŋ] *n* boxeo *m*; **b. ring**, cuadrilátero *m*.

Boxing Day ['bɒksɪŋdeɪ] *n GB* el día de San Esteban (26 de diciembre).

boxroom ['bɒksruːm] *n* trastero *m*.

boy [bɔɪ] *n* **1** (*child*) niño *m*, chico *m*; (*youth*) joven *m*; *fam* **oh b.!**, ¡vaya! **2** (*son*) hijo *m*.

boycott ['bɔɪkɒt] **I** *n* boicot *m*. **II** *vtr* boicotear.

boyfriend ['bɔɪfrend] *n* novio *m*; (*live-in*) compañero *m*.

boyhood ['bɔɪhʊd] *n* niñez *f*, juventud *f*.

boyish ['bɔɪɪʃ] *adj* juvenil, de muchacho.

bra [brɑː] *n abbr of* **brassiere**.

brace [breɪs] **I** *n* **1** (*clamp*) abrazadera *f*; (*of drill*) berbiquí *m*; (*for teeth*) aparato *m*. **2** (*of wood*) puntal *m*. **3** (*pair*) par *m*. **4** *GB* **braces**, tirantes *mpl*. **II** *vtr* **1** (*wall*) apuntalar. **2** (*strengthen*) reforzar. **3 to b. oneself**, prepararse (**for**, para). ◆**brace**

up *vi* cobrar ánimo.

bracelet ['breislit] *n* pulsera *f*.

bracing ['breisiŋ] *adj (wind)* fresco,-a; *(stimulating)* tonificante.

bracken ['brækən] *n* helecho *m*.

bracket ['brækit] **I** *n* 1 *Typ (round)* paréntesis *m*; *(square)* corchete *m*; *(curly)* llave *f*; **in brackets**, entre paréntesis. 2 *(support)* soporte *m*; *(for lamp)* brazo *m*; *(shelf)* repisa *f*. 3 *(for tax)* sector *m*. **II** *vtr* 1 *Ling (phrase etc)* poner entre paréntesis. 2 *(group together)* agrupar, juntar.

brag [bræg] *vi* jactarse **(about,** de).

braggart ['brægət] *n* fanfarrón,-ona *m,f*.

braid [breid] **I** *vtr* trenzar. **II** *n* 1 *Sew* galón *m*. 2 *esp US (plait)* trenza *f*.

Braille [breil] *n* Braille *m*.

brain [brein] *n* 1 cerebro *m*; **she's got cars on the b.,** está obsesionada por los coches; *Med* **b. death,** muerte *f* cerebral; *fig* **b. drain,** fuga *f* de cerebros; **b. wave,** idea *f* genial. 2 *fam* **brains,** inteligencia *f*; **to have brains,** ser inteligente; **b. trust,** grupo *m* de expertos. 3 *Culin* **brains,** sesos *mpl*.

brainchild ['breintʃaild] *n* invento *m*, idea *f* genial.

brainpower ['breinpauər] *n* capacidad *f* intelectual.

brainstorm ['breinstɔ:m] *n* 1 *(outburst)* arranque *m*. 2 *(brain wave)* genialidad *f*, lluvia *f* de ideas.

brainwash ['breinwɒʃ] *vtr* lavar el cerebro a.

brainy ['breini] *adj* **(brainier, brainiest)** *fam* listo,-a.

braise [breiz] *vtr* cocer a fuego lento.

brake [breik] **I** *n Aut (also pl)* freno *m*; **b. drum,** tambor *m* del freno; **b. fluid,** líquido *m* de frenos; **b. light,** luz *f* de freno. **II** *vi* frenar, echar el freno.

bramble ['bræmbl] *n* zarza *f*, zarzamora *f*.

bran [bræn] *n* salvado *m*.

branch [brɑ:ntʃ] **I** *n (of tree)* rama *f*; *(of road)* bifurcación *f*; *(of science etc)* ramo *m*; *Com* **b. (office),** sucursal *f*. **II** *vi (road)* bifurcarse. ◆**branch off** *vi* desviarse. ◆**branch out** *vi* diversificarse.

brand [brænd] **I** *n* 1 *Com* marca *f*; **b. name,** marca *f* de fábrica. 2 *(type)* clase *f*. 3 *(on cattle)* hierro *m*. **II** *vtr* 1 *(animal)* marcar con hierro candente. 2 *(label)* tildar.

brandish ['brændiʃ] *vtr* blandir.

brand-new [brænd'nju:] *adj* flamante.

brandy ['brændi] *n* coñac *m*, brandy *m*.

brash [bræʃ] *adj* 1 *(impudent)* descarado, -a. 2 *(reckless)* temerario,-a. 3 *(loud, showy)* chillón,-ona.

brass [brɑ:s] *n* 1 latón *m*; *sl (money)* pasta *f*; *Mus* instrumentos *mpl* de metal; **b. band,** banda *f* de metal.

brassiere ['bræsiər] *n* sostén *m*, sujetador

m.

brat [bræt] *n fam* mocoso,-a *m,f*.

bravado [brə'vɑ:dəu] *n* bravuconería *f*.

brave [breiv] **I** *adj* valiente, valeroso,-a. **II** *US* **(Indian) b.,** guerrero *m* indio. **III** *vtr* 1 *(face)* hacer frente a. 2 *(defy)* desafiar. ◆**bravely** *adv* valientemente.

bravery ['breivəri] *n* valentía *f*, valor *m*.

bravo [brɑ:'vəu] *interj* ¡bravo!

brawl [brɔ:l] **I** *n* reyerta *f*. **II** *vi* pelearse.

brawn [brɔ:n] *n* 1 *(strength)* fuerza física. 2 *Culin GB* carne *f* de cerdo adobada.

bray [brei] **I** *n (of donkey)* rebuzno *m*. **II** *vi* rebuznar.

brazen ['breizən] *adj* descarado,-a.

brazil [brə'zil] *n* **b. nut,** nuez *f* del Brasil.

Brazil [brə'zil] *n* (el) Brasil.

Brazilian [brə'ziliən] *adj* & *n* brasileño,-a *(m,f)*.

breach [bri:tʃ] *n* 1 *(in wall)* brecha *f*. 2 *(violation)* incumplimiento *m*; **b. of confidence,** abuso *m* de confianza; **b. of contract,** incumplimiento de contrato; **b. of the law,** violación *f* de la ley; **b. of the peace,** alteración *f* del orden público. 3 *(in relations)* ruptura *f*. **II** *vtr* violar.

bread [bred] *n* 1 pan *m*; **b. and butter,** pan con mantequilla; *fig* **our daily b.,** el pan nuestro de cada día. 2 *sl (money)* pasta *f*, *Am* plata *f*.

breadboard ['bredbɔ:d] *n* tabla *f* (para cortar el pan).

breadcrumb ['bredkrʌm] *n* miga *f* de pan; **breadcrumbs,** pan *m sing* rallado.

breadline ['bredlain] *n fam* miseria *f*; **to be on the b.,** vivir en la miseria.

breadth [bredθ] *n* 1 *(width)* anchura *f*; **it is two metres in b.,** tiene dos metros de ancho. 2 *(extent)* amplitud *f*.

breadwinner ['bredwinər] *n* cabeza *mf* de familia.

break [breik] **I** *vtr* (*pt* **broke;** *pp* **broken**) 1 romper; **to b. a leg,** romperse la pierna; **to b. a record,** batir un récord; **to b. even,** no tener ni ganancias ni pérdidas; *fig* **to b. one's back,** matarse a trabajar; *fig* **to b. sb's heart,** partirle el corazón a algn; *fig* **to b. the ice,** romper el hielo. 2 *(fail to keep)* faltar a; **to b. a contract,** romper un contrato; **to b. the law,** violar la ley. 3 *(destroy)* destrozar; *Fin* arruinar. 4 *(interrupt)* interrumpir. 5 *(code)* descifrar. 6 *(fall)* amortiguar. 7 **she broke the news to him,** le comunicó la noticia.

II *vi* 1 romperse; *(clouds)* dispersarse; *(waves)* romper. 2 *(storm)* estallar. 3 *(voice)* cambiar. 4 *(health)* resentirse. 5 **when day breaks,** al rayar el alba. 6 *(story)* divulgarse.

III *n* 1 *(fracture)* rotura *f*; *(crack)* grieta *f*; *(opening)* abertura *f*. 2 *(in relationship)* ruptura *f*. 3 *(pause)* pausa *f*, descanso *m*; *(at school)* recreo *m*; **to take a b.,** descansar un rato; *(holiday)* tomar unos días libres; **without a b.,** sin parar. **4** *fam (chance)* oportunidad *f*; **a lucky b.,** un golpe de suerte.

◆**break away** *vi* **1** *(become separate)* desprenderse **(from,** de). **2** *(escape)* escaparse. ◆**break down** *vt* **1** *(door)* derribar. **2** *(resistance)* acabar con. **3** *(costs)* desglosar. **II** *vi* **1** *Aut* tener una avería. **2** *(resistance)* ceder. **3** *(health)* debilitarse. **4** *(weep)* ponerse a llorar. ◆**break in** *vt* acostumbrar; **to b. in a pair of shoes,** cogerle la forma a los zapatos. **II** *vi (burglar)* entrar por la fuerza. ◆**break into** *vt* **1** *(burgle)* *(house)* allanar; *(safe)* forzar. **2** **to b. into song,** empezar a cantar. ◆**break off** *vt* partir. **II** *vi* **1** *(become detached)* desprenderse. **2** *(talks)* interrumpirse. **3** *(stop)* pararse. ◆**break out** *vi* **1** *(prisoners)* escaparse. **2** *(war etc)* estallar; **to b. out in a rash,** salirle a uno una erupción. ◆**break through** *vt* **1** *(crowd)* abrirse paso por; *(cordon)* romper. **2** *(clouds)* atravesar. **II** *vi* **1** *(crowd)* abrirse paso. **2** *(sun)* salir. ◆**break up** *vt* *(object)* romper; *(car)* desguazar; *(crowd)* disolver. **II** *vi* **1** *(object)* romperse. **2** *(crowd)* disolverse; *(meeting)* levantarse. **3** *(relationship)* fracasar; *(couple)* separarse. **4** *Educ* terminar. ◆**break with** *vt (past)* romper con.

breakable ['breɪkəbəl] *adj* frágil.
breakage ['breɪkɪdʒ] *n (breaking)* rotura *f*.
breakaway ['breɪkəweɪ] *adj* disidente.
breakdown ['breɪkdaʊn] *n* **1** *Aut* avería *f*; **b. truck,** grúa *f*. **2** *(nervous)* **b.,** crisis *f* nerviosa. **3** *(in communications)* ruptura *f*. **4** *(analysis)* análisis *m*; *Fin* desglose *m*.
breaker ['breɪkə'] *n* **1** *(wave)* ola *f* grande. **2** *Tech* trituradora *f*. **3** *(switch)* interruptor automático.
breakfast ['brekfəst] *n* desayuno *m*; **to have b.,** desayunar. **II** *vi* desayunar.
break-in ['breɪkɪn] *n* robo *m* (con allanamiento de morada).
breaking ['breɪkɪŋ] *n* rotura *f*; **b. point,** punto *m* de ruptura. **2** *Jur* **b. and entering,** allanamiento *m* de morada.
breakthrough ['breɪkθru:] *n* paso *m* adelante, avance *m*.
breakwater ['breɪkwɔ:tə'] *n* rompeolas *m inv*.
breast [brest] *n (chest)* pecho *m*; *(of woman)* pecho, seno *m*; *(of chicken etc)* pechuga *f*; *fig* **to make a clean b. of it,** dar la cara.
breast-feed ['brestfi:d] *vtr* dar el pecho a, amamantar a.
breaststroke ['breststrəʊk] *n* braza *f*.
breath [breθ] *n* **1** aliento *m*; *(breathing)* respiración *f*; **in the same b.,** al mismo tiempo; **out of b.,** sin aliento; **to catch one's b.,** recobrar el aliento; **to draw b.,**

respirar; **under one's b.,** en voz baja; *fig* **to take sb's b. away,** dejar pasmado a algn; *Aut* **b. test,** alcoholemia *f*. **2 to go out for a b. of fresh air,** salir a tomar el aire.
Breathalyzer® ['breθəlaɪzə'] *n GB* alcoholímetro *m*.
breathe [bri:ð] *vtr* respirar; **to b. a sigh of relief,** dar un suspiro de alivio. **II** *vi* respirar; **to b. in,** aspirar; **to b. out,** espirar; **to b. heavily,** resoplar.
breather ['bri:ðə'] *n fam (rest)* descanso *m*.
breathing ['bri:ðɪŋ] *n* respiración *f*; **b. space,** pausa *f*, respiro *m*.
breathless ['breθlɪs] *adj* sin aliento, jadeante.
breathtaking ['breθteɪkɪŋ] *adj* impresionante.
breeches ['brɪtʃɪz, 'brɪtʃɪz] *npl* bombachos *mpl*; **knee b., riding b.,** pantalones *mpl* de montar.
breed [bri:d] *n (of animal)* raza *f*; *fig (class)* clase *f*. **II** *vtr (pt & pp bred) (animals)* criar; *fig (ideas)* engendrar. **III** *vi (animals)* reproducirse.
breeder ['bri:də'] *n* **1** *(person)* criador,-a *m,f*. **2** *(fast)* **b. reactor,** reactor *m* generador.
breeding ['bri:dɪŋ] *n* **1** *(of animals)* cría *f*; *fig* **b. ground,** caldo *m* de cultivo. **2** *(of person)* educación *f*.
breeze [bri:z] *n* brisa *f*; *Constr* **b. block,** bloque *m* de cemento. **II** *vi* **to b. in/out,** entrar/salir despreocupadamente.
breezy ['bri:zɪ] *adj (breezier, breeziest)* **1** *(weather)* ventoso,-a. **2** *(person)* despreocupado,-a.
brevity ['brevɪtɪ] *n* brevedad *f*.
brew [bru:] **I** *vtr (beer)* elaborar; *(hot drink)* preparar. **II** *vi (tea)* reposar; *fig* **a storm is brewing,** se prepara una tormenta; *fam* **something's brewing,** algo se está cociendo. **III** *n* **1** *(of tea)* infusión *f*; *fam (of beer)* birra *f*. **2** *(magic potion)* brebaje *m*.
brewer ['bru:ə'] *n* cervecero,-a *m,f*.
brewery ['bruərɪ] *n* cervecería *f*.
brewing ['bru:ɪŋ] **I** *adj* cervecero,-a. **II** *n (of beer)* elaboración *f* de la cerveza.
briar ['braɪə'] *n* brezo *m*.
bribe [braɪb] **I** *vtr* sobornar. **II** *n* soborno *m*.
bribery ['braɪbərɪ] *n* soborno *m*.
bric-a-brac ['brɪkəbræk] *n* baratijas *fpl*.
brick [brɪk] *n* ladrillo *m*; *fam (reliable person)* persona *f* de confianza.
bricklayer ['brɪkleɪə'] *n* albañil *m*.
brickwork ['brɪkwɜ:k] *n* ladrillos *mpl*.
bridal ['braɪdəl] *adj* nupcial.
bride [braɪd] *n* novia *f*; **the b. and groom,** los novios.
bridegroom ['braɪdgru:m] *n* novio *m*.
bridesmaid ['braɪdzmeɪd] *n* dama *f* de

honor.

bridge¹ [brɪdʒ] **I** n puente m; (of nose) caballete m; (of ship) puente de mando. **II** vtr (river) tender un puente sobre. **2** (gap) llenar; Fin **bridging loan**, crédito m a corto plazo.

bridge² [brɪdʒ] n Cards bridge m.

bridle ['braɪdəl] **I** n brida f; (bit) freno m; **b. path**, camino m de herradura. **II** vtr (horse) embridar.

brief [briːf] **I** adj **1** (short) breve. **2** (concise) conciso,-a. **II** n **1** (report) informe m; **in b.**, en resumen. **2** Jur expediente m. **3** Mil instrucciones fpl. **4** briefs, (for men) calzoncillos mpl; (for women) bragas fpl. **III** vtr **1** (inform) informar. **2** (instruct) dar instrucciones a. **◆briefly** adv brevemente; **as b. as possible**, con la mayor brevedad (posible).

briefcase ['briːfkeɪs] n cartera f, portafolios mpl.

briefing ['briːfɪŋ] n (meeting) reunión informativa.

brigade [brɪ'geɪd] n brigada f.

brigadier [brɪgə'dɪər] n general m de brigada.

bright [braɪt] adj **1** (light, sun, eyes) brillante; (colour) vivo,-a; (day) claro,-a. **2** (cheerful) alegre; **to look on the b. side**, mirar el lado bueno. **3** (clever) listo,-a, espabilado,-a. **4** (promising) prometedor,-a. **◆brightly** adv brillantemente.

brighten ['braɪtən] **I** vtr (prospects) mejorarse; (face) iluminarse. **◆brighten up I** vtr (room etc) alegrar. **II** vi (weather) despejarse; (person) animarse.

brightness ['braɪtnɪs] n **1** (of sun) resplandor m; (of day) claridad f; (of colour) viveza f. **2** (cleverness) inteligencia f.

brilliance ['brɪljəns] n **1** (of light) brillo m; (of colour) viveza f. **2** (of person) brillantez f.

brilliant ['brɪljənt] **I** adj brillante; (idea) genial; fam (very good) estupendo,-a. **II** n brillante m.

brim [brɪm] **I** n borde m; (of hat) ala f; **full to the b.**, lleno hasta el borde. **II** vi rebosar (with, de). **◆brim over** rebosar.

brine [braɪn] n salmuera f.

bring [brɪŋ] vtr (pt & pp **brought**) **1** (carry sth to sb, take sth or sb with you; could you b. that book?, ¿podrías traerme el libro? **2** (take to a different position) llevar; **the war brought hunger to many homes**, la guerra llevó el hambre a muchos hogares. **3** (cause) provocar; **he brought it upon himself**, se lo buscó. **4** (persuade) convencer; **how did they b. themselves to do it?**, ¿cómo llegaron a hacerlo? **5** (lead) llevar. **6 to b. an action against**, acusar.
◆bring about vtr provocar. **◆bring along** vtr traer. **◆bring back** vtr **1** (re-

turn) devolver. **2** (reintroduce) volver a introducir. **3** (make one remember) traerle a la memoria. **◆bring down** vtr **1** (from upstairs) bajar. **2** (government) derribar; **Theat to b. the house down**, echar el teatro abajo con los aplausos. **3** (reduce) rebajar. **◆bring forward** vtr **1** (meeting etc) adelantar. **2** (present) presentar. **3** Fin **brought forward**, suma y sigue. **◆bring in** vtr **1** (yield) dar. **2** (show in) hacer entrar. **3** (law etc) introducir; (fashion) lanzar. **◆bring off** vtr lograr, conseguir. **◆bring on** vtr provocar. **◆bring out** vtr **1** (publish) publicar. **2** (reveal) recalcar; **he brings out the worst in me**, despierta lo peor que hay en mí. **◆bring round** vtr **1** (revive) hacer volver en sí. **2** (persuade) convencer. **◆bring to** vtr reanimar. **◆bring up** vtr **1** (educate) criar, educar. **2** (subject) plantear. **3** (vomit) devolver.

brink [brɪŋk] n (edge) borde m; fig **on the b. of ruin**, al borde de la ruina; **on the b. of tears**, a punto de llorar.

brisk [brɪsk] adj enérgico,-a; (pace) rápido,-a; (trade) activo,-a; (weather) fresco,-a.

bristle ['brɪsəl] **I** n cerda f. **II** vi **1** erizarse. **2** (show anger) enfurecer (at, con). **◆bristle with** vtr (be full of) estar lleno,-a de.

Brit [brɪt] n fam británico,-a m,f.

Britain ['brɪtən] n (Great) B., Gran Bretaña.

British ['brɪtɪʃ] **I** adj británico,-a; **the B. Isles**, las Islas Británicas. **II** npl **the B.**, los británicos.

brittle ['brɪtəl] adj quebradizo,-a, frágil.

broach [brəʊtʃ] vtr (subject) abordar.

broad [brɔːd] adj **1** (wide) ancho,-a; (large) extenso,-a. **2 a b. hint**, (clear) una indirecta clara. **3** (daylight) pleno,-a. **4** (not detailed) general. **5** (accent) marcado,-a, cerrado,-a. **II** n US sl (woman) tía f. **◆broadly** adv en términos generales.

broadcast ['brɔːdkɑːst] Rad TV **I** n emisión f. **II** vtr (pt & pp **broadcast**) emitir, transmitir.

broadcaster ['brɔːdkɑːstər] n locutor,-a m,f.

broadcasting ['brɔːdkɑːstɪŋ] n Rad radiodifusión f; TV transmisión f; Rad **b. station**, emisora f.

broaden ['brɔːdən] vtr ensanchar.

broad-minded [brɔːd'maɪndɪd] adj liberal, tolerante.

broadsheet ['brɔːdʃiːt] n folleto m.

broccoli ['brɒkəlɪ] n brécol m.

brochure ['brəʊʃʊər, brə'ʃʊər] n folleto m.

broil [brɔɪl] vtr US asar a la parrilla.

broke [brəʊk] adj fam **to be (flat) b.**, estar sin blanca.

broken ['brəʊkən] *adj* **1** roto,-a; (*machinery*) averiado,-a; (*leg*) fracturado,-a. **2** (*home*) deshecho,-a; (*person*) destrozado, -a; (*ground*) accidentado,-a; **to speak b. English**, chapurrear el inglés.

broken-hearted [brəʊkən'hɑːtɪd] *adj fig* con el corazón destrozado.

broker ['brəʊkəʳ] *n* corredor *m*, agente *mf* de Bolsa.

brolly ['brɒlɪ] *n fam* paraguas *m inv*.

bronchitis [brɒŋ'kaɪtɪs] *n* bronquitis *f*.

bronze [brɒnz] **I** *n* bronce *m*. **II** *adj* (*material*) de bronce; (*colour*) bronceado,-a.

bronzed [brɒnzd] *adj* (*suntanned*) bronceado,-a.

brooch [brəʊtʃ] *n* broche *m*.

brood [bruːd] **I** *n* (*birds*) cría *f*; *hum* (*children*) prole *m*. **II** *vi* (*hen*) empollar; *fig* (*ponder*) rumiar; *fig* **to b. over a problem**, darle vueltas a un problema.

broody ['bruːdɪ] *adj* **1** *fam* (*woman*) con ganas de tener hijos. **2** (*pensive*) pensativo,-a. **3** (*moody*) melancólico,-a.

brook[1] [brʊk] *n* arroyo *m*.

brook[2] [brʊk] *vtr* (*usu in negative*) soportar, aguantar.

broom [bruːm] *n* **1** escoba *f*. **2** *Bot* retama *f*.

broomstick ['bruːmstɪk] *n* palo *m* de escoba.

Bros *Com abbr of* **Brothers**, Hermanos *mpl*, Hnos.

broth [brɒθ] *n* caldo *m*.

brothel ['brɒθəl] *n* burdel *m*.

brother ['brʌðəʳ] *n* hermano *m*; **brothers and sisters**, hermanos.

brotherhood ['brʌðəhʊd] *n* hermandad *f*.

brother-in-law ['brʌðərɪnlɔː] *n* cuñado *m*.

brotherly ['brʌðəlɪ] *adj* fraternal.

brought [brɔːt] *pt & pp* → **bring**.

brow [braʊ] *n* **1** (*forehead*) frente *f*. **2** (*eyebrow*) ceja *f*. **3** (*of hill*) cima *f*.

brown [braʊn] **I** *adj* **1** marrón *m*; (*hair, eyes*) castaño,-a; **b. bread**, pan *m* integral; **b. paper**, papel *m* de estraza; **b. sugar**, azúcar moreno. **2** (*tanned*) moreno,-a. **II** *n* marrón *m*. **III** *vtr Culin* dorar; (*tan*) broncear.

Brownie ['braʊnɪ] *n* niña exploradora.

brownish ['braʊnɪʃ] *adj* pardusco,-a.

browse [braʊz] **I** *vi* (*person in shop*) mirar; (*through book*) hojear. **II** *n* **to have a b.**, dar un vistazo (**in**, a).

bruise [bruːz] **I** *n* morado *m*, cardenal *m*. **II** *vtr* (*body*) contusionar; (*fruit*) estropear. **III** *vi* (*body*) magullarse; (*fruit*) estropearse.

brunch [brʌntʃ] *n* combinación *f* de desayuno y almuerzo.

brunette [bruː'net] *adj & n* morena (*f*).

brunt [brʌnt] *n* lo peor; **to bear the b.**, llevar el peso.

brush[1] [brʌʃ] **I** *n* **1** (*for hair, teeth*) cepillo

m; *Art* pincel *m*; (*for house-painting*) brocha *f*. **2** (*with the law*) roce *m*. **II** *vtr* **1** cepillar; **to b. one's hair**, cepillarse el pelo; **to b. one's teeth**, cepillarse los dientes. **2** (*touch lightly*) rozar. **III** *vi* **b. against**, rozar al pasar. ◆**brush aside** *vtr* dejar de lado. ◆**brush off** *vtr* ignorar. ◆**brush up** *vtr* repasar.

brush[2] [brʌʃ] *n* (*undergrowth*) broza *f*, maleza *f*.

brushwood ['brʌʃwʊd] *n* maleza *f*.

brusque [bruːsk, brʌsk] *adj* brusco,-a; (*words*) áspero,-a.

Brussels ['brʌsəlz] *n* Bruselas.

brutal ['bruːtəl] *adj* brutal, cruel.

brute [bruːt] **I** *adj* bruto,-a; **b. force**, fuerza bruta. **II** *n* (*animal*) bruto *m*; (*person*) bestia *f*.

BSc [biːes'siː] *abbr of* **Bachelor of Science**.

bubble ['bʌbl] **I** *n* burbuja *f*; **b. bath**, espuma *f* de baño; **b. gum**, chicle *m*; **soap b.**, pompa *f* de jabón. **II** *vi* burbujear; *Culin* borbotear.

bubbly ['bʌblɪ] **I** *adj* (*bubblier, bubbliest*) efervescente. **II** *n fam* champán *m*, cava *m*.

buck[1] [bʌk] **I** *n* **1** *Zool* macho *m*; (*male deer*) ciervo *m*; (*male goat*) macho cabrío; *fam* **to pass the b. to sb**, echarle el muerto a algn. **II** *vi* (*horse*) corcovear. ◆**buck up I** *vtr fam* **b. your ideas up!**, ¡espabílate!. **II** *vi* (*cheer up*) animarse.

buck[2] [bʌk] *n US fam* dólar *m*.

bucket ['bʌkɪt] **I** *n* cubo *m*; *fam* **it rained buckets**, llovía a cántaros. **II** *vi fam* (*rain*) llover a cántaros.

buckle ['bʌkl] **I** *n* hebilla *f*. **II** *vtr* abrochar con hebilla. **III** *vi* **1** (*wall, metal*) combarse. **2** (*knees*) doblarse.

bud [bʌd] **I** *n* (*shoot*) brote *m*; (*flower*) capullo *m*. **II** *vi* brotar; *fig* florecer.

Buddhism ['bʊdɪzəm] *n* budismo *m*.

budding ['bʌdɪŋ] *adj* en ciernes.

buddy ['bʌdɪ] *n US fam* amigote *m*, compinche *m*.

budge [bʌdʒ] *vi* **1** (*move*) moverse. **2** (*yield*) ceder.

budgerigar ['bʌdʒərɪgɑːʳ] *n* periquito *m*.

budget ['bʌdʒɪt] **I** *n* presupuesto *m*; *Pol* **the B.**, los presupuestos del Estado. **II** *vi* hacer un presupuesto (**for**, para).

budgie ['bʌdʒɪ] *n fam* → **budgerigar**.

buff[1] [bʌf] **I** *adj & n* (*colour*) color (*m*) de ante. **II** *vtr* dar brillo a.

buff[2] [bʌf] *n fam* (*enthusiast*) aficionado,-a *m,f*.

buffalo ['bʌfələʊ] *n* (*pl* **buffaloes** *or* **buffalo**) búfalo *m*.

buffer ['bʌfəʳ] **I** *n* **1** (*device*) amortiguador *m*; *Rail* tope *m*; **b. zone**, zona *f* de seguridad. **2** *Comput* memoria intermedia. **II** *vtr* amortiguar.

buffet[1] ['bʊfeɪ] *n* **1** (*snack bar*) bar *m*; (*at* *railway station*) cantina f; *Rail* **b. car**, coche m restaurante. **2** (*self-service meal*) bufet m libre. **3** (*item of furniture*) aparador m.

buffet² ['bʌfɪt] *vtr* golpear.

buffoon [bə'fu:n] *n* bufón m, payaso m.

bug [bʌg] **I** *n* **1** (*insect*) bicho m. **2** *fam* (*microbe*) microbio m; **the flu b.**, el virus de la gripe. **3** (*hidden microphone*) micrófono oculto. **4** *Comput* error m. **II** *vtr fam* **1** to **b. a room**, ocultar micrófonos en una habitación; to **b. a phone**, pinchar un teléfono. **2** (*annoy*) fastidiar, molestar.

bugger ['bʌgər] **I** *n* **1** sodomita m. **2** *sl offens* (*person*) gilipollas mf inv; (*thing*) coñazo m; **poor b.!**, ¡el pobre! **II** *interj sl offens* ¡joder!. **III** *vtr* sodomizar. ◆**bugger about** *vi vulg* **1** *vi* hacer chorradas. **II** *vtr* **they really buggered him about**, se las hicieron pasar canutas. ◆**bugger off** *vi sl offens* pirarse; **b. off!**, ¡vete a la mierda! ◆**bugger up** *vtr sl vulg* jorobar.

buggy ['bʌgɪ] *n* (*baby's pushchair*) cochecito m de niño.

bugle ['bju:gəl] *n* bugle m.

build [bɪld] **I** *vtr* (*pt & pp* **built**) construir. **II** *n* (*physique*) tipo m, físico m. ◆**build up** *vtr* (*accumulate*) acumular; to **b. up a reputation**, labrarse una buena reputación.

builder ['bɪldər] *n* constructor,-a m,f; (*contractor*) contratista mf.

building ['bɪldɪŋ] *n* edificio m, construcción f; **b. site**, obra f; **b. society**, sociedad hipotecaria.

build-up ['bɪldʌp] *n* **1** (*accumulation*) aumento m; (*of gas*) acumulación f. **2** (*publicity*) propaganda f.

built [bɪlt] *pt & pp* → **build**.

built-in [bɪlt'ɪn] *adj* **1** (*cupboard*) empotrado,-a. **2** (*incorporated*) incorporado,-a.

built-up [bɪlt'ʌp] *adj* urbanizado,-a.

bulb [bʌlb] *n* **1** *Bot* bulbo m. **2** (*lightbulb*) bombilla f.

Bulgaria [bʌl'geərɪə] *n* Bulgaria f.

Bulgarian [bʌl'geərɪən] **I** *adj* búlgaro,-a. **II** *n* **1** (*person*) búlgaro,-a m,f. **2** (*language*) búlgaro m.

bulge [bʌldʒ] **I** *n* protuberancia f; (*in pocket*) bulto m. **II** *vi* (*swell*) hincharse; (*be full*) estar repleto,-a.

bulk [bʌlk] *n* **1** (*mass*) masa f, volumen m; *Com* **in b.**, a granel; **to buy in b.**, comprar algo al por mayor. **2** (*greater part*) mayor parte f.

bulky ['bʌlkɪ] *adj* (**bulkier, bulkiest**) **1** (*large*) voluminoso,-a. **2** **this crate is rather b.**, esta caja es un armatoste.

bull [bul] *n* **1** toro m; *fig* **to take the b. by the horns**, coger al toro por los cuernos. **2** *Fin* alcista mf.

bulldog ['buldɒg] *n* buldog m.

bulldoze ['buldəuz] *vtr* (*land*) nivelar; (*building*) derribar.

bulldozer ['buldəuzər] *n* bulldozer m.

bullet ['bulɪt] *n* bala f; **b. wound**, balazo m.

bulletin ['bulɪtɪn] *n* boletín m; *Rad TV* **news b.**, boletín de noticias.

bullet-proof ['bulɪtpru:f] *adj* a prueba de balas; **b.-p. vest**, chaleco m antibalas.

bullfight ['bulfaɪt] *n* corrida f de toros.

bullfighter ['bulfaɪtər] *n* torero,-a m,f.

bullfighting ['bulfaɪtɪŋ] *n* los toros mpl; (*art*) tauromaquia f.

bullion ['buljən] *n* (*gold, silver*) lingote m.

bullish ['bulɪʃ] *adj Fin* (*market*) en alza.

bullock ['bulək] *n* buey m.

bullring ['bulrɪŋ] *n* plaza f de toros.

bull's-eye ['bulzaɪ] *n* (*of target*) blanco m.

bully ['bulɪ] **I** *n* el matón m. **II** *vtr* (*terrorize*) intimidar; (*bulldoze*) tiranizar. **III** *interj* **iron b. for you!**, ¡bravo!

bulwark ['bulwək] *n* baluarte m.

bum¹ [bʌm] *n fam* (*bottom*) culo m.

bum² [bʌm] *fam* **I** *n* **1** *US* (*tramp*) vagabundo m. **2** (*idler*) holgazán,-ana m,f. **II** *vi* gorronear. ◆**bum around** *vi fam* vaguear.

bumblebee ['bʌmbəlbi:] *n* abejorro m.

bumbling ['bʌmblɪŋ] *adj* torpe.

bump [bʌmp] **I** *n* **1** (*swelling*) chichón m; (*lump*) abolladura f; (*on road*) bache m. **2** (*blow*) choque m, golpe m. **3** (*jolt*) sacudida f. **II** *vtr* golpear; to **b. one's head**, darse un golpe en la cabeza. **III** *vi* chocar (*into*, contra). ◆**bump into** *vtr* (*meet*) tropezar con. ◆**bump off** *vtr sl* liquidar.

bumper ['bʌmpər] **I** *adj* abundante; **b. edition**, edición f especial. **II** *n Aut* parachoques m inv.

bumptious ['bʌmpʃəs] *adj* presuntuoso, -a, engreído,-a.

bumpy ['bʌmpɪ] *adj* (**bumpier, bumpiest**) con muchos baches.

bun [bʌn] *n* **1** (*bread*) panecillo m; (*sweet*) bollo m; *fig vulg* **she's got a b. in the oven**, esta preñada. **2** (*of hair*) moño m.

bunch [bʌntʃ] **I** *n* **1** (*of keys*) manojo m; (*of flowers*) ramo m; (*of grapes*) racimo m; (*of people*) grupo m; (*gang*) pandilla f. **II** *vi* to **b. together**, juntarse, agruparse.

bundle ['bʌndəl] **I** *n* (*of clothes*) bulto m, fardo m; (*of papers*) fajo m; (*of wood*) haz m. **II** *vtr* **1** (*make a bundle of*) liar, atar. **2** (*push*) empujar.

bung [bʌŋ] **I** *n* tapón m. **II** *vtr fam* **1** (*throw*) arrojar. **2** (*put*) meter. ◆**bung up** *vtr fam* atascar.

bungalow ['bʌŋgələu] *n* chalé m, bungalow m.

bungle ['bʌŋgəl] *vtr* chapucear.

bunion ['bʌnjən] *n* juanete m.

bunk [bʌŋk] *n* (*bed*) litera f.

bunker [ˈbʌŋkər] n 1 (coal) carbonera. 2 Mil búnker m. 3 Golf bunker m.

bunny [ˈbʌnɪ] n fam (baby talk) b. (rabbit), conejito m.

bunting [ˈbʌntɪŋ] n (material) lanilla f; (flags) banderines mpl; Naut empavesada f.

buoy [bɔɪ] I n boya f. II vtr mantener a flote (up, a). ◆**buoy up** vtr fig alentar, animar.

buoyancy [ˈbɔɪənsɪ] n 1 (of object) flotabilidad f. 2 Fin tendencia f alcista. 3 (optimism) optimismo m.

buoyant [ˈbɔɪənt] adj 1 (object) flotante. 2 Fin con tendencia alcista. 3 (optimistic) optimista.

burble [ˈbɜːbəl] vi 1 (stream) murmurar; (baby) balbucear. 2 (talk quickly) farfullar.

burden [ˈbɜːdən] I n carga f; fig to be a b. to sb, ser una carga para algn. II vtr cargar (with, con).

bureau [ˈbjʊərəʊ] n (pl bureaux) 1 (desk) escritorio m. 2 (office) agencia f, oficina f. 3 US (chest of drawers) cómoda f. 4 US Pol departamento m del Estado.

bureaucracy [bjʊəˈrɒkrəsɪ] n burocracia f.

bureaucrat [ˈbjʊərəkræt] n burócrata mf.

bureaucratic [bjʊərəˈkrætɪk] adj burocrático,-a.

burgeon [ˈbɜːdʒən] vi florecer.

burger [ˈbɜːgər] n fam abbr of hamburger.

burglar [ˈbɜːglər] n ladrón,-ona m,f; b. alarm, alarma f antirrobo.

burglary [ˈbɜːglərɪ] n robo m con allanamiento de morada.

burial [ˈberɪəl] n entierro m.

burly [ˈbɜːlɪ] adj (burlier, burliest) fornido,-a, fuerte.

Burma [ˈbɜːmə] n Birmania.

Burmese [bɜːˈmiːz] I adj birmano,-a. II n 1 (person) birmano,-a m,f. 2 (language) birmano m.

burn [bɜːn] I n quemadura f. II vtr (pt & pp burnt or burned) quemar. III vi 1 (fire) arder; (building, food) quemarse. 2 (lamp) estar encendido,-a. 3 (sore) escocer. ◆**burn down** I vtr incendiar. II vi incendiarse. ◆**burn out** vi (people) quemarse. ◆**burn up** vtr (energy, calories) quemar.

burner [ˈbɜːnər] n quemador m.

burning [ˈbɜːnɪŋ] adj 1 (on fire) incendiado,-a; (hot) abrasador,-a. 2 (passionate) ardiente. 3 a b. question, una cuestión candente.

burnt [bɜːnt] adj quemado,-a; b. almonds, almendras tostadas.

burp [bɜːp] I n eructo m. II vi eructar.

burrow [ˈbʌrəʊ] I n madriguera f; (for rabbits) conejera f. II vi 1 hacer una madriguera. 2 (search) hurgar.

bursar [ˈbɜːsər] n tesorero,-a m,f.

bursary [ˈbɜːsərɪ] n beca f.

burst [bɜːst] I n 1 (explosion) estallido m; (of tyre) reventón m. 2 (of applause) arranque m; (rage) arrebato m; b. of gunfire, ráfaga f de tiros; b. of laughter, carcajadas fpl. II vtr (pt & pp burst) (balloon) reventar; fig the river b. its banks, el río se salió de madre. III vi 1 reventarse; (shell) estallar. 2 (enter suddenly) irrumpir (into, en). ◆**burst into** vi to b. into laughter/tears, echarse a reír/allorar. ◆**burst open** vi abrirse violentamente. ◆**burst out** vi to b. out laughing, echarse a reír.

bursting [ˈbɜːstɪŋ] adj the bar was b. with people, el bar estaba atestado de gente; fam to be b. to do sth, reventar por hacer algo.

bury [ˈberɪ] vtr 1 enterrar; to be buried in thought, estar absorto en pensamientos. 2 (hide) ocultar.

bus [bʌs] n (pl buses, US busses) autobús m; b. conductor, revisor m; b. driver, conductor,-a m,f; b. stop, parada f de autobús.

bush [bʊʃ] n 1 (shrub) arbusto m. 2 Austral the b., el monte; fam b. telegraph, radio f macuto.

bushy [ˈbʊʃɪ] adj espeso,-a, tupido,-a.

business [ˈbɪznɪs] n 1 (commerce) negocios mpl; how's b.?, ¿cómo andan los negocios?; to be away on b., estar en viaje de negocios; b. deal, negocio m; b. hours, horas fpl de oficina; b. trip, viaje m de negocios. 2 (firm) empresa f. 3 (matter) asunto m; I mean b., estoy hablando en serio; it's no b. of mine, no es asunto mío; to make it one's b. to ...., encargarse de ...; to get down to b., ir al grano; to go about one's b., ocuparse de sus asuntos.

businesslike [ˈbɪznɪslaɪk] adj (practical) eficiente; (methodical) metódico,-a, (serious) serio,-a.

businessman [ˈbɪznɪsmæn] n hombre m de negocios.

businesswoman [ˈbɪznɪswʊmən] n mujer f de negocios.

busker [ˈbʌskər] n fam músico,-a m,f callejero,-a.

bust¹ [bʌst] n 1 (of woman) pecho m. 2 Art busto m.

bust² [bʌst] I vtr 1 fam estropear. 2 sl (place) hacer una redada. II adj fam 1 (damaged) estropeado,-a. 2 to go b., (bankrupt) quebrar.

bustle [ˈbʌsəl] I n (activity, noise) bullicio m. II vi to b. about, ir y venir.

bustling [ˈbʌslɪŋ] adj bullicioso,-a.

bust-up [ˈbʌstʌp] n fam riña f, pelea f.

busy [ˈbɪzɪ] I adj 1 ocupado,-a, atareado,-a; (life) ajetreado,-a; (street) concurrido,-a. 2 esp US Tel ocupado,-a;

b. signal, señal f de comunicando. II *vtr* **to b. oneself doing sth,** ocuparse haciendo algo.

busybody ['bɪzɪbɒdɪ] n entrometido,-a m,f.

but [bʌt] I *conj* 1 pero; **b. yet,** a pesar de todo. 2 (after negative) sino; **not two b. three,** no dos sino tres; **she's not Spanish b. Portuguese,** no es española sino portuguesa. II *adv* **had we b. known,** de haberlo sabido; **we can b. try,** al menos podemos intentarlo. **b. for her we would have drowned,** si no hubiera sido por ella, nos habríamos ahogado. III *prep* salvo, menos; **everyone b. her,** todos menos ella; **he's anything b. handsome,** es todo menos guapo. IV *npl* **ifs and buts,** pegas fpl.

butane ['bjuːteɪn] n butano m; **b. gas,** gas butano.

butcher ['bʊtʃər] I n carnicero,-a m,f; **b.'s (shop),** carnicería f. II *vtr* (animals) matar; (people) masacrar.

butler ['bʌtlər] n mayordomo m.

butt[1] [bʌt] n 1 (end) extremo m; (of rifle) culata f; (of cigarette) colilla f. 2 **he was the b. of all the jokes,** era el blanco de todas las bromas. 3 US fam (bottom) culo m.

butt[2] [bʌt] I n (with head) cabezazo m. II *vtr* 1 (strike with head) dar un cabezazo a. 2 **to b. your way through,** (shove) abrirte paso. ◆**butt in** *vi* entrar en la conversación.

butt[3] [bʌt] n (barrel) tonel m.

butter ['bʌtər] I n mantequilla f; **b. dish,** mantequera f. II *vtr* untar con mantequilla.

buttercup ['bʌtəkʌp] n ranúnculo m, botón m de oro.

butterfingers ['bʌtəfɪŋgəz] n fam manazas mf inv.

butterfly ['bʌtəflaɪ] n mariposa f.

buttock ['bʌtək] n nalga f; **buttocks,** nalgas fpl.

button ['bʌtən] I n botón m. II *vtr* **to b. (up),** abrochar(se), abotonar(se).

buttonhole ['bʌtənhəʊl] n ojal m.

buttress ['bʌtrɪs] I n contrafuerte m. 2 (support) apoyo m. II *vtr* apuntalar; fig reforzar, apoyar.

buxom ['bʌksəm] adj (woman) pechugona.

buy [baɪ] I n compra f; **a good b.,** una ganga. II *vtr* (pt & pp bought) 1 comprar; **she bought that car from a neighbour,** compró ese coche a un vecino. 2 sl (believe) tragar. ◆**buy off** *vtr* sobornar. ◆**buy out** *vtr* adquirir la parte de. ◆**buy up** *vtr* comprar en grandes cantidades.

buzz [bʌz] I n 1 (of bee) zumbido m; (of conversation) rumor m. 2 fam (telephone call) telefonazo m. II *vi* zumbar.

buzzer ['bʌzər] n timbre m.

by [baɪ] I *prep* 1 (indicating agent) por; **composed by Bach,** compuesto,-a por Bach; **a film by Almodóvar,** una película de Almodóvar. 2 (via) por; **he left by the back door,** salió por la puerta trasera. 3 (manner) por; **by car/train,** en coche/tren; **by credit card,** con tarjeta de crédito; **by chance,** por casualidad; **by oneself,** solo,-a; **made by hand,** hecho a mano; **you can obtain a ticket by filling in the coupon,** puede conseguir una entrada llenando el cupón. 4 (amount) por; **little by little,** poco a poco; **they are sold by the dozen,** se venden por docenas; **to be paid by the hour,** cobrar por horas. 5 by far, con mucho; **he won by a foot,** ganó por un pie. 6 (beside) al lado de, junto a; **side by side,** juntos. 7 **to walk by a building,** (pass) pasar por delante de un edificio. 8 (time) para; **by now,** ya; **by then,** para entonces; **we have to be there by nine,** tenemos que estar allí para las nueve; **by the time we arrive,** (para) cuando lleguemos; **by this time next year,** el año que viene por estas fechas. 9 (during) de; **by day/night,** de día/noche. 10 (in an oath) por; **by God!,** ¡por Dios! 11 Math por. 12 (according to) según; **is that O.K by you?,** ¿te viene bien? 13 **he had two children by his first wife,** tuvo dos hijos con su primera esposa. 14 (phrases) **bit by bit,** poco a poco; **day by day,** día a día; **what do you mean by that?,** ¿qué quieres decir con eso?; **by the way,** a propósito.
II *adv* 1 **to go by,** (past) pasar; **she just walked by,** pasó de largo. 2 **by and by,** con el tiempo; **by and large,** en conjunto.

bye [baɪ] I n 1 fam ¡hasta luego! 2 **by the b.** por cierto.

bye-bye ['baɪbaɪ] n fam ¡adiós!, ¡hasta luego!

by-election ['baɪɪlekʃən] n elección f parcial.

bygone ['baɪgɒn] I adj pasado,-a. II *npl* **let bygones be bygones,** lo pasado pasado está.

by-law ['baɪlɔː] n ley f municipal.

bypass ['baɪpɑːs] I n 1 (road) carretera f de circunvalación. 2 Med **b. surgery,** cirugía f de by-pass. II *vtr* evitar.

by-product ['baɪprɒdʌkt] n Chem Ind derivado m, subproducto m; fig consecuencia f.

by-road ['baɪrəʊd] n carretera secundaria.

bystander ['baɪstændər] n testigo mf.

byte [baɪt] n Comput byte m, octeto m.

byword ['baɪwɜːd] n **it became a b. for modernity,** se convirtió en sinónimo de modernidad.

C

C, c |si:| n 1 (the letter) C, c f. 2 Mus do m.

C 1 abbr of **Celsius**, C. 2 abbr of **Centigrade**, C.

cab |kæb| n US taxi m; c. driver, taxista mf.

cabaret |ˈkæbəreɪ| n cabaret m.

cabbage |ˈkæbɪdʒ| n col f, berza f; **red c.**, (col) lombarda f.

cabin |ˈkæbɪn| n 1 (hut) choza f; **log c.**, cabaña f. 2 Naut camarote m. 3 (of lorry, plane) cabina f.

cabinet |ˈkæbɪnɪt| n 1 (item of furniture) armario m; (glass-fronted) vitrina f. **c. maker**, ebanista mf. 2 Pol gabinete m, consejo m de ministros.

cable |ˈkeɪbəl| I n cable m; **c. car**, teleférico m; **c. TV**, televisión f por cable. II vtr & vi cablegrafiar, telegrafiar.

cache |kæʃ| n alijo m.

cackle |ˈkækəl| vi cacarear.

cactus |ˈkæktəs| n (pl cacti |ˈkæktaɪ|) cactus m.

CAD |kæd| abbr of **computer-aided** or **assisted design** or **draughting**, diseño m con ayuda de ordenador.

cad |kæd| n GB fam canalla m.

caddie |ˈkædɪ| n Golf cadi m.

cadet |kəˈdet| n Mil cadete m.

cadge |kædʒ| fam vtr & vi gorronear.

Caesarean |si:ˈzeərɪən| n Med **she had a c.**, le hicieron una cesárea; **C. section**, operación f cesárea.

café |ˈkæfeɪ| n, **cafeteria** |kæfɪˈtɪərɪə| n cafetería f.

caffeine |ˈkæfi:n| n cafeína f.

cage |keɪdʒ| I n jaula f. II vtr enjaular.

cagey |ˈkeɪdʒɪ| adj (cagier, cagiest) fam reservado,-a.

cagoule |kəˈguːl| n (garment) canguro m.

Cairo |ˈkaɪrəʊ| n (el) Cairo.

cajole |kəˈdʒəʊl| vtr engatusar.

cake |keɪk| I n 1 pastel m, tarta f; fam fig **it's a piece of c.**, está chupado; **birthday c.**, pastel m de cumpleaños; **c. shop**, pastelería f. 2 (of soap) pastilla f. II vi (mud) endurecerse. II vtr **caked with ...**, cubierto,-a de ....

calamity |kəˈlæmɪtɪ| n calamidad f.

calcium |ˈkælsɪəm| n calcio m.

calculate |ˈkælkjʊleɪt| vtr calcular.

calculated |ˈkælkjʊleɪtɪd| adj intencionado,-a.

calculating |ˈkælkjʊleɪtɪŋ| adj 1 **c. machine**, calculadora f. 2 pej (person) calculador,-a.

calculation |kælkjʊˈleɪʃən| n cálculo m.

calculator |ˈkælkjʊleɪtər| n calculadora f.

calendar |ˈkælɪndər| n calendario m; **c. year**, año m civil.

calf¹ |kɑːf| n (pl **calves** |kɑːvz|) (of cattle) becerro,-a m,f; ternero,-a m,f; (of other animals) cría f.

calf² |kɑːf| n (pl **calves** |kɑːvz|) Anat pantorilla f.

calfskin |ˈkɑːfskɪn| n piel f de becerro.

caliber |ˈkælɪbər|, **calibre** |ˈkælɪbər| n calibre m.

call |kɔːl| I vtr 1 llamar; **to c. sb names**, poner verde a algn; **what's he called?**, ¿cómo se llama? 2 (meeting etc) convocar; **to c. sth to mind**, traer algo a la memoria.
II vi 1 llamar; Tel **who's calling?**, ¿de parte de quién? 2 **to c. at sb's (house)**, pasar por casa de algn; **to c. for sth/sb**, pasar a recoger algo/a algn. 3 (trains) parar. 4 **to c. for**, (require) exigir; **that wasn't called for**, eso no estaba justificado.
III n 1 llamada f, grito m. 2 (visit) visita f; **to pay a c. on sb**, visitar a algn. 3 Tel **(phone) c.**, llamada f; **c. box**, cabina telefónica. 4 Med **to be on c.**, estar de guardia. 5 **there's no c. for you to worry**, no hay motivo para que te preocupes.
◆**call away** vtr **to be called away on business**, tener que ausentarse por motivos de trabajo. ◆**call back** vtr 1 (phone again) llamar otra vez; (visit again) volver. ◆**call in** I vtr (doctor) llamar. II vi 1 **I'll c. in tomorrow**, (visit) mañana me paso. 2 Naut hacer escala (at, en). ◆**call off** vtr suspender. ◆**call on** vtr 1 visitar. 2 **to c. on sb for support**, recurrir a algn en busca de apoyo. ◆**call out** I vtr 1 (shout) gritar. 2 (doctor) hacer venir; (workers) convocar a la huelga. II vi gritar. ◆**call up** vtr 1 Tel llamar (por teléfono). 2 Mil llamar a filas, reclutar.

caller |ˈkɔːlər| n visita mf; Tel persona f que llama.

calling |ˈkɔːlɪŋ| n esp Rel llamada f, vocación f.

callous |ˈkæləs| adj insensible, duro,-a.

call-up |ˈkɔːlʌp| n llamamiento m a filas.

calm |kɑːm| I adj 1 (weather, sea) en calma. 2 (relaxed) tranquilo,-a; **keep c.!**, ¡tranquilo,-a!. II n 1 (of weather, sea) calma f. 2 (tranquility) tranquilidad f. III vtr calmar, tranquilizar. IV vi **to c. (down)**, calmarse, tranquilizarse.

Calor Gas® |ˈkæləgæs| n (gas m) butano m.

calorie, calory |ˈkælərɪ| n caloría f.

calve |kɑːv| vi (cow) parir (un becerro).

calves |kɑːvz| npl → **calf¹**, **calf²**.

Cambodia |kæmˈbəʊdɪə| n Camboya f.

came |keɪm| pt → **come**.

camel ['kæməl] *n* camello,-a *m,f.*

cameo ['kæmɪəʊ] *n* camafeo *m.*

camera ['kæmərə] *n* 1 cámara *f* or máquina *f* fotográfica; *Cin TV* cámara. 2 *Jur* in c., a puerta cerrada.

cameraman ['kæmərəmən] *n* cámara *mf.*

Cameroon [kæmə'ru:n] *n* Camerún.

camomile ['kæməmaɪl] *n* camomila *f*; c. tea, (infusión *f* de) manzanilla *f.*

camouflage ['kæməflɑ:ʒ] I *n* camuflaje *m.* II *vtr* camuflar.

camp¹ [kæmp] I *n* campamento *m*; c. bed, cama *f* plegable; c. site, camping *m.* II *vi* to go camping, ir de camping.

camp² [kæmp] *adj fam* afeminado,-a; *(affected)* amanerado,-a.

campaign [kæm'peɪn] I *n* campaña *f.* II *vi* to c. for sb/sth, hacer una campaña a favor de algn/de algo.

campaigner [kæm'peɪnər] *n* defensor,-a *m,f* (for, de).

camper ['kæmpər] *n* 1 *(person)* campista *mf.* 2 *US (vehicle)* caravana *f.*

camping ['kæmpɪŋ] *n* c. ground, c. site, camping *m.*

campus ['kæmpəs] *n* campus *m*, ciudad *f* universitaria.

can¹ [kæn] *v aux (pt could)* 1 *(be able to)* poder; he could have come, podría haber venido; I'll phone you as soon as I c., te llamaré en cuanto pueda; she can't do it, no puede hacerlo; I cannot understand why, *(fml & emphatic)* no entiendo por qué. 2 *(know how to)* saber; c. you ski?, ¿sabes esquiar?; I can't speak English, no sé hablar inglés. 3 *(be permitted to)* poder; he can't go out tonight, no le dejan salir esta noche. 4 *(be possible)* poder; she could have forgotten, puede (ser) que lo haya olvidado; they can't be very poor, no deben ser muy pobres; what c. it be?, ¿qué será?

can² [kæn] I *n* 1 *(of oil)* bidón *m.* 2 *US (tin)* lata *f*, bote *m.* II *vtr* 1 *(fish, fruit)* envasar, enlatar. 2 *US fam* desestimar.

Canada ['kænədə] *n* Canadá.

Canadian [kə'neɪdɪən] *adj & n* canadiense *(mf).*

canal [kə'næl] *n* canal *m.*

canary [kə'neəri] *n* canario *m.*

Canary Islands [kə'neəraɪləndz] *npl* (Islas *fpl*) Canarias *fpl.*

cancel ['kænsəl] *vtr (train, contract)* cancelar; *(sum annul)* anular; *(permission)* retirar; *(decree)* revocar.

cancellation [kænsɪ'leɪʃən] *n* cancelación *f*; *Com* anulación *f.*

cancer ['kænsər] *n* 1 *Med* cáncer *m*; breast c., cáncer de mama; c. research, cancerología *f.* 2 C., *(in astrology)* Cáncer *m.*

candelabra [kændɪ'lɑ:brə] *n* candelabro *m.*

candid ['kændɪd] *adj* franco,-a, sincero,-a.

candidate ['kændɪdeɪt, 'kændɪdɪt] *n* candidato,-a *m,f*; *(in exam)* opositor,-a *m,f.*

candle ['kændəl] *n* vela *f*; *(in church)* cirio *m.*

candlelight ['kændəllaɪt] *n* luz *f* de vela; by c., a la luz de las velas.

candlestick ['kændəlstɪk] *n* candelero *m*, palmatoria *f*; *(in church)* cirial *m.*

candour, *US* **candor** ['kændər] *n* franqueza *f.*

candy ['kændɪ] *n US* caramelo *m.*

candyfloss ['kændɪflɒs] *n GB* algodón *m* dulce.

cane [keɪn] *n* 1 *Bot* caña *f*; c. sugar, azúcar *m* de caña. 2 *(wicker)* mimbre *m.* 3 *(walking stick)* bastón *m*; *(for punishment)* palmeta *f.* II *vtr* castigar con la palmeta.

canine ['keɪnaɪn] *adj Zool* canino,-a; c. tooth, colmillo *m.*

canister ['kænɪstər] *n* bote *m.*

canned [kænd] *adj* enlatado,-a; c. foods, conservas *fpl.*

cannibal ['kænɪbəl] *adj & n* caníbal *(mf).*

cannon ['kænən] I *n (pl cannons or cannon)* cañón *m*; *fig* c. fodder, carne *f* de cañón. II *vi* chocar (into, contra).

cannonball ['kænənbɔ:l] *n* bala *f* de cañón.

cannot ['kænɒt, kæ'nɒt] *v aux → can¹.*

canoe [kə'nu:] *n* canoa *f*; *Sport* piragua *f.*

canon ['kænən] *n Rel* canon *m.*

canopy ['kænəpɪ] *n* 1 *(on throne)* dosel *m.* 2 *(awning)* toldo *m.*

can't [kɑ:nt] *v aux → can¹.*

Cantabria *n* Cantabria.

cantankerous [kæn'tæŋkərəs] *adj* intratable.

canteen [kæn'ti:n] *n* 1 *(restaurant)* cantina *f.* 2 *(set of cutlery)* juego *m* de cubiertos. 3 *(flask)* cantimplora *f.*

canter ['kæntər] I *n* medio galope. II *vi* ir a medio galope.

canvas ['kænvəs] *n* 1 *Tex* lona *f.* 2 *(painting)* lienzo *m.*

canvass ['kænvəs] *vi* 1 *Pol* hacer propaganda electoral. 2 *Com* hacer promoción, buscar clientes.

canvasser ['kænvəsər] *n* 1 *Pol* persona *f* que hace propaganda electoral de puerta en puerta.

canyon ['kænjən] *n* cañón *m*; the Grand C., el Gran Cañón.

cap [kæp] I *n* 1 gorro *m*; *(soldier's)* gorra *f.* 2 *GB Sport* to win a c. for England, ser seleccionado,-a para el equipo de Inglaterra. 3 *(of pen)* capuchón *m*; *(of bottle)* chapa *f.* II *vtr* 1 *(bottle)* poner la chapa a; *fig* to c. it all, para colmo. 2 *GB Sport* seleccionar.

capability [keɪpə'bɪlɪtɪ] *n* habilidad *f.*

capable ['keɪpəbəl] *adj* 1 *(skilful)* hábil. 2 *(able)* capaz (of, de).

capacity [kə'pæsɪtɪ] *n* 1 capacidad *f.* 2

(position) puesto *m*; **in her c. as manageress**, en calidad de gerente.
cape¹ [keɪp] *n (garment)* capa *f*.
cape² [keɪp] *n Geog* cabo *m*, promontorio *m*; **C. Horn**, Cabo de Hornos; **C. Town**, Ciudad del Cabo; **C. Verde**, Cabo Verde.
caper [ˈkeɪpəʳ] *n (prank)* travesura *f*.
capital [ˈkæpɪtəl] **I** *n* 1 *(town)* capital *f*. 2 Fin capital *m*; **c. expenditure**, inversión *f* de capital. 3 *(letter)* mayúscula *f*. **II** *adj* 1 *(city)* capital. 2 **c. punishment**, pena *f* capital. 3 *(primary)* primordial. 4 **c. letter**, mayúscula *f*.
capitalism [ˈkæpɪtəlɪzəm] *n* capitalismo *m*.
capitalist [ˈkæpɪtəlɪst] *adj & n* capitalista *(mf)*.
capitalize [ˈkæpɪtəlaɪz] *vi* Fin capitalizar; *fig* **to c. on sth**, sacar provecho *or* beneficio de algo.
capitulate [kəˈpɪtjuleɪt] *vi* capitular.
Capricorn [ˈkæprɪkɔːn] *n* Capricornio *m*.
capsicum [ˈkæpsɪkəm] *n* pimiento *m*.
capsize [kæpˈsaɪz] **I** *vtr* hacer zozobrar. **II** *vi* zozobrar.
capsule [ˈkæpsjuːl] *n* cápsula *f*.
captain [ˈkæptɪn] **I** *n* capitán *m*. **II** *vtr* capitanear.
caption [ˈkæpʃən] *n (under picture)* leyenda *f*; Cin subtítulo *m*.
captivating [ˈkæptɪveɪtɪŋ] *adj* seductor, -a.
captive [ˈkæptɪv] **I** *n* cautivo,-a *m,f*. **II** *adj* cautivo,-a.
captivity [kæpˈtɪvɪtɪ] *n* cautiverio *m*.
capture [ˈkæptʃəʳ] **I** *vtr* 1 capturar, apresar; Mil *(town)* tomar. 2 *(market)* acaparar. 3 *fig (mood)* captar. **II** *n (of fugitive)* captura *f*; *(of town)* toma *f*.
car [kɑːʳ] *n* 1 coche *m*, Am carro *m*; **c. ferry**, transbordador *m* para coches; GB **c. park**, parking *m*, aparcamiento *m*; **c. wash**, túnel *m* de lavado. 2 GB Rail coche *m*.
carafe [kəˈræf, kəˈrɑːf] *n* garrafa *f*.
caramel [ˈkærəmel] *n* azúcar *m* quemado; *(sweet)* caramelo *m*.
carat [ˈkærət] *US* **karat** *n* kilate *m*.
caravan [ˈkærəvæn] *n* 1 *(vehicle)* remolque *m*, caravana *f*. 2 *(in the desert)* caravana *f*.
carbohydrate [kɑːbəʊˈhaɪdreɪt] *n* hidrato *m* de carbono, carbohidrato *m*.
carbon [ˈkɑːbən] *n* carbono *m*; **c. copy**, copia *f* al papel carbón; *fig* copia exacta; **c. dioxide**, dióxido *m* de carbono; **c. paper**, papel *m* carbón.
carburettor [kɑːbjʊˈretəʳ], *US* **carburetor** [ˈkɑːbjʊreɪtəʳ] *n* carburador *m*.
carcass [ˈkɑːkəs] *n* res *f* muerta.
card [kɑːd] *n* 1 tarjeta *f*; **birthday/visiting c.**, tarjeta de cumpleaños/de visita. 2 *(in file)* ficha *f*; *(identity)* carnet *m*; **c. index**, fichero *m*. 3 **pack of cards**, baraja *f*, cartas *fpl*; *(play-*

ing) **c.**, naipe *m*, carta *f*; *fig* **on the cards**, previsto.
cardboard [ˈkɑːdbɔːd] *n* cartón *m*; **c. box**, caja *f* de cartón; **c. cutout**, recortable *m*.
cardiac [ˈkɑːdɪæk] *adj* cardíaco,-a; **c. arrest**, paro cardíaco.
cardigan [ˈkɑːdɪgən] *n* rebeca *f*.
cardinal [ˈkɑːdɪnəl] **I** *n* Rel cardenal *m*. **II** *adj* cardinal; **c. numbers**, números *mpl* cardinales.
care [keəʳ] **I** *vi (be concerned)* preocuparse *(about, por)*; **I don't c.**, no me importa; *fam* **for all I c.**, me trae sin cuidado; *fam* **he couldn't c. less**, le importa un bledo. **II** *n* 1 *(attention, protection)* cuidado *m*, atención *f*; **'c. of...'**, *(on letter)* 'al cuidado de...'; **medical c.**, asistencia *f* médica; **to take c. of**, cuidar; *(business)* ocuparse de. 2 *(carefulness)* cuidado *m*; **take c.**, *(be careful)* ten cuidado; *(as farewell)* ¡cuídate! 3 *(worry)* preocupación *f*. ◆**care for** *vtr* 1 *(look after)* cuidar. 2 *(like)* gustar, interesar; **would you c. for a coffee?**, ¿te apetece un café?
career [kəˈrɪəʳ] **I** *n* carrera *f*. **II** *vi* correr a toda velocidad.
carefree [ˈkeəfriː] *adj* despreocupado,-a.
careful [ˈkeəful] *adj* cuidadoso,-a; *(cautious)* prudente; **be c.!**, ¡ojo!; ¡ojo!; **to be c.**, tener cuidado. ◆**carefully** *adv (painstakingly)* cuidadosamente; *(cautiously)* con cuidado.
careless [ˈkeəlɪs] *adj* descuidado,-a; *(about clothes)* desaliñado,-a; *(driving)* negligente; **a c. mistake**, un descuido. ◆**carelessly** *adv* descuidadamente, a la ligera.
carelessness [ˈkeəlɪsnɪs] *n* descuido *m*.
caress [kəˈres] **I** *n* caricia *f*. **II** *vtr* acariciar.
caretaker [ˈkeəteɪkəʳ] *n (in school etc)* bedel *mf*; *(in block of flats)* portero,-a *m,f*.
cargo [ˈkɑːgəʊ] *n (pl cargoes or cargos)* carga *f*, cargamento *m*; Naut **c. boat**, buque *m* de carga, carguero *m*.
Caribbean [kærɪˈbiːən, *US* kəˈrɪbɪən] *adj* caribe, caribeño,-a; **the C. (Sea)**, el *(Mar)* Caribe.
caricature [ˈkærɪkətjʊəʳ] *n* caricatura *f*.
caring [ˈkeərɪŋ] *adj* solidario,-a.
carnage [ˈkɑːnɪdʒ] *n fig* carnicería *f*.
carnal [ˈkɑːnəl] *adj* carnal.
carnation [kɑːˈneɪʃən] *n* clavel *m*.
carnival [ˈkɑːnɪvəl] *n* carnaval *m*.
carnivorous [kɑːˈnɪvərəs] *adj* carnívoro, -a.
carol [ˈkærəl] *n* villancico *m*.
carp¹ [kɑːp] *n (fish)* carpa *f*.
carp² [kɑːp] *vi* refunfuñar.
carpenter [ˈkɑːpɪntəʳ] *n* carpintero,-a *m,f*.
carpentry [ˈkɑːpɪntrɪ] *n* carpintería *f*.
carpet [ˈkɑːpɪt] **I** *n* moqueta *f*. **II** *vtr fig* **carpeted with**, cubierto,-a de.

carriage |ˈkærɪdʒ| n 1 (horse-drawn) carruaje m; Rail vagón m, coche m; (of gun) cureña f; (of typewriter) carro m. 2 (of goods) porte m, transporte m.

carriageway |ˈkærɪdʒweɪ| n GB carril m, autovía f; **dual c.**, autovía f.

carrier |ˈkærɪər| n 1 (company) transportista mf; GB **c. bag**, bolsa f de plástico; **c. pigeon**, paloma mensajera. 2 Med portador,-a m,f.

carrot |ˈkærət| n zanahoria f.

carry |ˈkærɪ| I vtr 1 llevar; (goods) transportar. 2 (stock) tener; (responsibility, penalty) conllevar, implicar. 3 **the motion was carried**, se aprobó la moción. 4 (disease) ser portador,-a de. II vi (sound) oírse. ◆**carry away** vtr llevarse; **to get carried away**, entusiasmarse. ◆**carry forward** vtr Fin carried forward, suma y sigue. ◆**carry off** vtr (prize) llevarse; **fam to c. it off**, salir airoso,-a. ◆**carry on** I vtr continuar; (conversation) mantener. II vi 1 continuar, seguir adelante; **c. on!**, ¡adelante! 2 fam (make a fuss) hacer una escena; **don't c. on about it**, ¡no te enrolles! 3 fam **to c. on with sb**, estar liado,-a con algn. ◆**carry out** vtr (plan) llevar a cabo, realizar; (test) verificar.

carrycot |ˈkærɪkɒt| n cuna f portátil.

carsick |ˈkɑːsɪk| adj mareado,-a (en el coche).

cart |kɑːt| I n (horse-drawn) carro m; (handcart) carretilla f. II vtr carretear.

cartel |kɑːˈtel| n cártel m.

carton |ˈkɑːtən| n (of cream etc) caja f.

cartoon |kɑːˈtuːn| n (strip) tira cómica, historieta f; Art cartón m; (animated) dibujos mpl animados.

cartoonist |kɑːˈtuːnɪst| n caricaturista mf.

cartridge |ˈkɑːtrɪdʒ| n 1 cartucho m. 2 (for pen) recambio m; **c. paper**, papel guarro m.

carve |kɑːv| vtr 1 (wood) tallar; (stone, metal) cincelar, esculpir. 2 (meat) trinchar.

cascade |kæˈskeɪd| n cascada f.

case¹ |keɪs| n 1 (aso m; **a c. in point**, un buen ejemplo; **in any c.**, en cualquier caso, de todas formas; **in c. of doubt**, en caso de duda; **just in c.**, por si acaso. 2 Med caso m; **c. history**, historial clínico. 3 Jur causa f.

case² |keɪs| I n 1 (suitcase) maleta f; (small) estuche m; (soft) funda f. 2 **a c. of wine**, una caja de botellas de vino. 3 Typ **lower c.**, minúscula f; **upper c.**, mayúscula f.

cash |kæʃ| I n dinero efectivo; **to pay c.**, pagar al contado or en efectivo; **c. desk**, caja f; **c. on delivery**, entrega f contra reembolso; **c. dispenser**, cajero automático; **c. register**, caja registradora. II vtr (cheque) cobrar. ◆**cash in** I vi fam **to c. in on sth**, sacar provecho de algo. II vtr hacer efectivo,-a.

cash-and-carry |kæʃənˈkærɪ| adj & adv de venta al por mayor y pago al contado.

cashew |ˈkæʃuː| n **c. (nut)**, anacardo m.

cashier |kæˈʃɪər| n cajero,-a m,f.

cashmere |ˈkæʃmɪər| n cachemira f.

casino |kəˈsiːnəʊ| n casino m.

cask |kɑːsk| n tonel m, barril m.

casket |ˈkɑːskɪt| n (box) cofre m; (coffin) ataúd m.

casserole |ˈkæsərəʊl| n 1 (container) cacerola f. 2 Culin guisado m.

cassette |kæˈset| n casete f; **c. recorder**, casette m.

cast |kɑːst| I vtr (pt & pp cast) 1 (net, fishing line) echar, arrojar; (light) proyectar; (glance) lanzar; (anchor) echar; (vote) emitir; (skin) mudar. 2 fig **to c. doubts on sth**, poner algo en duda; **to c. suspicion on sb**, levantar sospechas sobre algn. 3 (metal) moldear; **c. iron**, hierro fundido. 4 Theat (play) hacer el reparto de. II n 1 (mould) molde m; (product) pieza f. 2 Med (plaster) c., escayola f. 3 Theat reparto m. ◆**cast off** vi Naut soltar (las) amarras.

castanets |kæstəˈnets| npl castañuelas fpl.

castaway |ˈkɑːstəweɪ| n náufrago,-a m,f.

caste |kɑːst| n casta f.

caster |ˈkɑːstər| n **c. sugar**, azúcar molido muy fino.

Castile |kæˈstiːl| n Castilla f.

Castilian |kæˈstɪljən| I adj castellano,-a. II n C. (Spanish), (language) castellano m.

casting |ˈkɑːstɪŋ| n **c. vote**, voto m de calidad.

cast-iron |kɑːstˈaɪən| adj de hierro fundido.

castle |ˈkɑːsəl| I n 1 castillo m. 2 Chess torre f. II vi Chess enrocar.

castor¹ |ˈkɑːstər| n **c. oil**, aceite m de ricino.

castor² |ˈkɑːstər| n (on furniture) ruedecilla f.

castrate |kæˈstreɪt| vtr castrar.

casual |ˈkæʒjʊəl| adj 1 (meeting etc) fortuito,-a. 2 (worker) eventual. 3 (clothes) (de) sport. 4 (visit) de paso. 5 (person, attitude) despreocupado,-a, informal.

casualty |ˈkæʒjʊəltɪ| n 1 Mil baja f; **casualties**, pérdidas fpl. 2 (injured) herido,-a m,f.

cat |kæt| n gato,-a m,f; fig **to let the c. out of the bag**, descubrir el pastel.

Catalan |ˈkætələn| I adj catalán,-ana; C. **flag**, senyera f. II n 1 (person) catalán,-ana m,f. 2 (language) catalán m.

catalogue, US catalog |ˈkætəlɒg| I n catálogo m. II vtr catalogar.

Catalonia |kætəˈləʊnɪə| n Cataluña f.

catalyst |ˈkætəlɪst| n catalizador m.

catapult |ˈkætəpʌlt| n tirachinas m inv.

catarrh |kəˈtɑː| n catarro m.

catastrophe |kəˈtæstrəfɪ| n catástrofe f.

catastrophic |kætəˈstrɒfɪk| adj

catastrófico,-a.

catch [kætʃ] I *vtr* (*pt & pp* **caught**) 1 (*ball, thief*) coger; (*fish*) pescar; (*mouse etc*) atrapar; (*train, bus*) coger, *Am* agarrar; **to c. a cold**, coger un resfriado; **to c. fire**, (*log*) prenderse; (*building*) incendiarse; **to c. hold of**, agarrar; **to c. sb's eye**, captar la atención de algn; **to c. sight of**, entrever. 2 (*surprise*) pillar, sorprender. 3 (*hear*) entender. 4 **to c. one's breath**, (*hold*) sostener la respiración; (*recover*) recuperar el aliento. II *vi* (*sleeve etc*) engancharse (**on**, en); (*fire*) encenderse. III *n* 1 (*of ball*) parada *f*; (*of fish*) presa *f*. 2 (*on door*) pestillo *m*. 3 (*drawback*) pega *f*; **c. question**, pregunta *f* con pega. 4 **c. phrase**, slogan *m*.
◆**catch on** *vi fam* 1 (*become popular*) ganar popularidad. 2 (*understand*) caer en la cuenta. ◆**catch out** *vtr fam* **to c. sb out**, pillar a algn cometiendo una falta.
◆**catch up** *vi* 1 **to c. up with sb**, (*reach*) alcanzar a algn. 2 (*with news*) ponerse al corriente (**on**, de); **to c. up on sleep**, recuperar el sueño perdido; **to c. up with work**, ponerse al día de trabajo.

catching [ˈkætʃɪŋ] *adj* (*disease*) contagioso,-a.

catchment [ˈkætʃmənt] *n* **c. area**, zona *f* de captación.

catchword [ˈkætʃwɜːd] *n* lema *m*.

catchy [ˈkætʃɪ] *adj* (**catchier, catchiest** *fam* (*tune*) pegadizo,-a.

categoric(al) [kætɪˈgɒrɪk(əl)] *adj* categórico,-a.

categorize [ˈkætɪgəraɪz] *vtr* clasificar.

category [ˈkætɪgərɪ] *n* categoría *f*.

cater [ˈkeɪtər] *vi* 1 **to c. for**, (*wedding etc*) proveer comida para. 2 **to c. for**, (*taste*) atender a.

caterer [ˈkeɪtərər] *n* proveedor,-a *m,f*.

catering [ˈkeɪtərɪŋ] *n* abastecimiento *m* (de comidas por encargo).

caterpillar [ˈkætəpɪlər] *n* 1 oruga *f*. 2 **c.** (**tractor**), tractor *m* de oruga.

cathedral [kəˈθiːdrəl] *n* catedral *f*.

Catholic [ˈkæθəlɪk] *adj & n* católico,-a (*m,f*).

catholic [ˈkæθəlɪk] *adj* católico,-a.

Catholicism [kəˈθɒlɪsɪzəm] *n* catolicismo *m*.

Catseye® [ˈkætsaɪ] *n GB* catafaro *m*.

cattle [ˈkætəl] *npl* ganado *m* (vacuno).

catty [ˈkætɪ] *adj* (**cattier, cattiest** *fam* (*remark*) malintencionado,-a; (*person*) malicioso,-a.

catwalk [ˈkætwɔːk] *n* pasarela *f*.

Caucasian [kɔːˈkeɪzɪən] *adj & n* caucásico,-a (*m,f*), blanco,-a (*m,f*).

caucus [ˈkɔːkəs] *n* comité *m* central, ejecutiva *f*.

caught [kɔːt] *pt & pp* → **catch**.

cauliflower [ˈkɒlɪflaʊər] *n* coliflor *f*.

cause [kɔːz] I *n* 1 (*origin*) causa *f*. 2

(*reason*) motivo *m*. 3 **for a good c.**, por una buena causa. II *vtr* causar; **to c. sb to do sth**, hacer que algn haga algo.

caustic [ˈkɔːstɪk] *adj* cáustico,-a; *fig* mordaz.

caution [ˈkɔːʃən] I *n* 1 (*care*) cautela *f*, prudencia *f*. 2 (*warning*) aviso *m*, advertencia *f*. 3 *GB Jur* reprensión *f*. II *vtr* advertir, amonestar.

cautious [ˈkɔːʃəs] *adj* cauteloso,-a, prudente.

cavalcade [kævəlˈkeɪd] *n* cabalgata *f*.

cavalier [kævəˈlɪər] I *adj* arrogante. II *n* caballero *m*.

cavalry [ˈkævəlrɪ] *n* caballería *f*.

cave [keɪv] *n* cueva *f*. ◆**cave in** *vi* (*roof etc*) derrumbarse, hundirse.

caveman [ˈkeɪvmæn] *n* hombre *m* de las cavernas.

cavern [ˈkævən] *n* caverna *f*.

caviar(e) [ˈkævɪɑːr] *n* caviar *m*.

cavity [ˈkævɪtɪ] *n* 1 (*hole*) cavidad *f*. 2 (*in tooth*) caries *f inv*.

cavort [kəˈvɔːt] *vi* retozar, brincar.

CB [siːˈbiː] *abbr* **Citizens' Band**, banda ciudadana, CB.

CBI [siːbiːˈaɪ] *GB abbr of* **Confederation of British Industry**, ≈ CEOE *f*.

cc [siːˈsiː] *abbr of* **cubic centimetre(s)**, cc.

CD [siːˈdiː] *abbr of* **compact disc**, CD *m*; **CD player**, tocadiscos *m* digital *o* compacto.

cease [siːs] I *vtr* cesar; **to c. doing** *or* **to do sth**, dejar de hacer algo. II *vi* terminar.

cease-fire [siːsˈfaɪər] *n* alto *m* el fuego.

ceaseless [ˈsiːslɪs] *adj* incesante.

cedar [ˈsiːdər] *n* cedro *m*.

cede [siːd] *vtr* ceder.

ceiling [ˈsiːlɪŋ] *n* techo *m*.

celebrate [ˈselɪbreɪt] I *vtr* (*occasion*) celebrar. II *vi* divertirse.

celebrated [ˈselɪbreɪtɪd] *adj* célebre.

celebration [selɪˈbreɪʃən] *n* 1 celebración *f*. 2 **celebrations**, festividades *fpl*.

celebrity [sɪˈlebrɪtɪ] *n* celebridad *f*.

celery [ˈselərɪ] *n* apio *m*.

celibate [ˈselɪbət] *adj & n* célibe (*mf*).

cell [sel] *n* 1 (*in prison*) celda *f*. 2 *Biol Pol* célula *f*. 3 *Elec* pila *f*.

cellar [ˈselər] *n* sótano *m*; (*for wine*) bodega *f*.

cello [ˈtʃeləʊ] *n* violoncelo *m*.

cellophane [ˈseləfeɪn] *n* celofán *m*.

celluloid [ˈseljʊlɔɪd] *n* celuloide *m*.

cellulose [ˈseljʊləʊs] *n* celulosa *f*.

Celsius [ˈselsɪəs] *adj* Celsio.

Celt [kelt, selt] *n* celta *mf*.

Celtic [ˈkeltɪk, ˈseltɪk] I *n* (*language*) celta *m*. II *adj* celta.

cement [sɪˈment] I *n* cemento *m*; **c. mixer**, hormigonera *f*. II *vtr Constr* unir con cemento; *fig* (*friendship*) cimentar.

cemetery [ˈsemɪtrɪ] *n* cementerio *m*.

censor ['sensər] **I** n censor,-a m,f. **II** vtr censurar.

censorship ['sensəʃɪp] n censura f.

censure ['senʃər] **I** n censura f. **II** vtr censurar.

census ['sensəs] n censo m.

cent [sent] n **1** centavo m, céntimo m. **2** **per** c., por ciento.

centenary [sen'ti:nərɪ] n centenario m.

center ['sentər] n & vtr US → **centre**.

centigrade ['sentɪgreɪd] adj centígrado, -a.

centilitre, US **centiliter** ['sentɪli:tər] n centílitro m.

centimetre, US **centimeter** ['sentɪmi:tər] n centímetro m.

centipede ['sentɪpi:d] n ciempiés m inv.

central ['sentrəl] adj central; **c. heating**, calefacción f central; **C. America**, Centroamérica; **C. American**, centroamericano,-a m,f. ◆**centrally** adv **c. heated**, con calefacción central; **c. situated**, céntrico,-a.

centralize ['sentrəlaɪz] vtr centralizar.

centre ['sentər] **I** n centro m; **town c.**, centro de la ciudad; Ftb **c. forward**, delantero centro; Ftb **c. half**, medio centro; Pol **c. party**, partido m centrista; **sports c.**, centro deportivo. **II** vtr (attention etc) centrar (**on**, en).

century ['sentʃərɪ] n siglo m; **the nineteenth c.**, el siglo diecinueve.

ceramic [sɪ'ræmɪk] n **1** cerámica f. **II** adj de cerámica.

ceramics [sɪ'ræmɪks] n sing cerámica f.

cereal ['stərɪəl] n cereal m.

cerebral ['serɪbrəl, sɪ'ri:brəl] adj cerebral; **c. palsy**, parálisis f cerebral.

ceremony ['serɪmənɪ] n ceremonia f.

certain ['sɜːtən] **I** adj **1** (sure) seguro,-a; **to be c.**, estar seguro,-a; **to make c. of sth**, asegurarse de algo. **2** (to a c. extent**, hasta cierto punto. **3** (not known) cierto, -a; **a c. Miss Ward**, una tal señorita Ward. **4** (true) cierto,-a. **II** adv **for c.**, a ciencia cierta. ◆**certainly** adv desde luego; **c. not**, de ninguna manera.

certainty ['sɜːtəntɪ] n certeza f; (assurance) seguridad f.

certificate [sə'tɪfɪkɪt] n certificado m; Educ diploma m.

certified ['sɜːtɪfaɪd] adj certificado,-a; (copy) compulsado,-a.

certify ['sɜːtɪfaɪ] vtr certificar.

cervical ['sɜːvɪkəl, sə'vaɪkəl] adj **c. cancer**, cáncer m del útero; **c. smear**, frotis m cervical.

cervix ['sɜːvɪks] n **1** (uterus) cuello m del útero. **2** (neck) cerviz f, cuello m.

cessation [se'seɪʃən] n cese m.

cesspit ['sespɪt] n pozo negro.

Ceuta n Ceuta.

Ceylon ['sɪ'lɒn] n Ceilán.

cf abbr of **confer**, (compare) compárese,

cfr.

chafe [tʃeɪf] **I** vtr (make sore) rozar. **II** vi (skin) irritarse; (item of clothing) rozar.

chaffinch ['tʃæfɪntʃ] n pinzón m vulgar.

chagrin ['ʃægrɪn] n disgusto m, desilusión f.

chain [tʃeɪn] **I** n cadena f; fig (of events) serie f; **c. of mountains**, cordillera f; **c. reaction**, reacción f en cadena; **c. saw**, sierra mecánica. **II** vtr **to c. (up)**, encadenar.

chain-smoke ['tʃeɪnsməʊk] vi fumar un pitillo tras otro.

chair [tʃeər] **I** n **1** silla f; (with arms) sillón m; **c. lift**, telesilla m. **2** (position) presidencia f; Univ cátedra f. **II** vtr presidir.

chairman ['tʃeəmən] n presidente m.

chairperson ['tʃeəpɜːsən] n presidente,-a m,f.

chalet ['ʃæleɪ] n chalet m, chalé m.

chalk [tʃɔːk] **I** n (for writing) tiza f. **II** ◆**chalk up** vtr fam (victory etc) apuntarse.

challenge ['tʃælɪndʒ] **I** vtr **1** retar, desafiar; **to c. sb to do sth**, retar a algn a que haga algo. **2** (authority etc) poner a prueba; (statement) poner en duda. **3** Mil dar el alto a. **II** n **1** reto m, desafío m. **2** Mil quién vive m.

challenging ['tʃælɪndʒɪŋ] adj (idea) desafiante; (task) que presenta un desafío.

chamber ['tʃeɪmbər] n **1** (hall) cámara f; **C. of Commerce**, Cámara de Comercio. **2** Mus **c. music**, música f de cámara. **3** GB Jur **chambers**, gabinete m sing.

chambermaid ['tʃeɪmbəmeɪd] n camarera f.

chameleon [kə'mi:lɪən] n camaleón m.

champagne [ʃæm'peɪn] n (French) champán m; (from Catalonia) cava m.

champion ['tʃæmpɪən] n campeón,-ona m,f; fig **c. of human rights**, defensor,-a de los derechos humanos.

championship ['tʃæmpɪənʃɪp] n campeonato m.

chance [tʃɑːns] **I** n **1** (fortune) casualidad f, azar m; **by c.**, por casualidad; **to take a c.**, arriesgarse; **c. meeting**, encuentro m casual. **2** (likelihood) posibilidad f; **(the) chances are that ...**, lo más posible es que .... **3** (opportunity) oportunidad f. **II** vtr **to c. upon**, encontrar por casualidad. **III** vtr arriesgar.

chancellor ['tʃɑːnsələr] n **1** (head of state, in embassy) canciller m. **2** GB Univ rector,-a m,f. **3** GB **C. of the Exchequer**, ministro,-a m,f de Hacienda.

chandelier [ʃændɪ'lɪər] n araña f (de luces).

change [tʃeɪndʒ] **I** vtr cambiar; **to c. gear**, cambiar de marcha; **to c. one's mind/the subject**, cambiar de opinión/de tema; **to c. trains**, hacer trasbordo; **to get changed**, cambiarse de ropa; fig **to c.**

hands, cambiar de dueño,-a. II *vi* cambiar, cambiarse; **to c. for the better/ worse,** mejorar/empeorar; **to c. into,** convertirse en. III *n* 1 cambio *m*; **for a c.,** para variar; **c. of heart,** cambio de parecer; **c.** of **scene,** cambio de aires. 2 (*money*) cambio *m*; (*after purchase*) vuelta *f*; **small c.,** suelto *m*. ◆**change over** *vi* cambiarse.

changeable ['tʃeɪndʒəbəl] *adj* (*weather*) variable; (*person*) inconstante.

changeover ['tʃeɪndʒəʊvə'] *n* conversión *f*.

changing ['tʃeɪndʒɪŋ] *n* 1 **c. room,** vestuario *m*. 2 *Mil* relevo *m* (de la guardia). II *adj* cambiante.

channel ['tʃænəl] I *n* 1 *Geog* canal *m*; (*of river*) cauce *m*; **the C. Islands,** las Islas Anglonormandas; **the English C.,** el Canal de la Mancha. 2 (*administrative*) vía *f*. 3 *TV Rad* canal *m*, cadena *f*. II *vtr* fig (*ideas etc*) canalizar, encauzar.

chant [tʃɑːnt] I *n Rel* cántico *m*; (*of demonstrators*) slogan *m*. II *vtr & vi Rel* cantar; (*demonstrators*) corear.

chaos ['keɪɒs] *n* caos *m*.

chaotic [keɪˈɒtɪk] *adj* caótico,-a.

chap [tʃæp] *n fam* chico *m*, tío *m*.

chapel ['tʃæpəl] *n* capilla *f*.

chaperon(e) ['ʃæpərəʊn] *n* carabina *f*.

chaplain ['tʃæplɪn] *n* capellán *m*.

chapter ['tʃæptə'] *n* 1 capítulo *m*. 2 *Rel* cabildo *m*.

char [tʃɑː'] *vtr* chamuscar, carbonizar.

character ['kærɪktə'] *n* 1 carácter *m*. 2 *fam* (*person*) tipo *m*. 3 *Theat* personaje *m*.

characteristic [kærɪktəˈrɪstɪk] I *n* característica *f*. II *adj* característico,-a.

characterize ['kærɪktəraɪz] *vtr* caracterizar.

charcoal ['tʃɑːkəʊl] *n Min* carbón *m* vegetal; *Art* **c. drawing,** carboncillo *m*; **c. grey,** gris marengo *o* oscuro.

charge [tʃɑːdʒ] I *vtr* 1 cobrar; **c. it to my account,** cárguelo en mi cuenta. 2 **to c. sb with a crime,** acusar a algn de un crimen. 3 *Mil* cargar contra. 4 *Elec* cargar. II *vi Elec Mil* cargar; **to c. about,** andar a lo loco. III *n* 1 (*cost*) precio *m*; **bank charges,** comisión *f*; **free of c.,** gratis; **service c.,** servicio *m*; **c. account,** cuenta *f* corriente. 2 **to be in c. of,** estar a cargo de; **to take c. of,** hacerse cargo de. 3 *Jur* cargo *m*, acusación *f*. 4 (*explosive*) carga explosiva. 5 *Elec* carga *f*.

charged [tʃɑːdʒd] *adj* fig emotivo,-a.

charismatic [kærɪzˈmætɪk] *adj* carismático,-a.

charitable ['tʃærɪtəbəl] *adj* (*person*) caritativo,-a; (*organization*) benéfico,-a.

charity ['tʃærɪtɪ] *n* caridad *f*; (*organization*) institución benéfica.

charlady ['tʃɑːleɪdɪ] *n GB* mujer *f* de la limpieza.

charlatan ['ʃɑːlətən] *n* (*doctor*) curandero,-a *m,f*.

charm [tʃɑːm] I *n* 1 (*quality*) encanto *m*. 2 (*spell*) hechizo *m*; **lucky c.,** amuleto *m*. II *vtr* encantar.

charming ['tʃɑːmɪŋ] *adj* encantador,-a.

chart [tʃɑːt] I *n* 1 (*giving information*) tabla *f*; (*graph*) gráfico *m*. 2 (*map*) carta *f* de navegación. 3 *Mus* **the charts,** la lista de éxitos. II *vtr Av Naut* (*on map*) trazar.

charter ['tʃɑːtə'] I *n* 1 (*of institution*) estatutos *mpl*; (*of rights*) carta *f*. 2 **c. flight,** vuelo *m* chárter. II *vtr* (*plane, boat*) fletar.

chartered accountant [tʃɑːtəd əˈkaʊntənt] *n GB* contable *mf* diplomado,-a.

charwoman ['tʃɑːwʊmən] *n GB* → **charlady.**

chase [tʃeɪs] I *vtr* perseguir; (*hunt*) cazar. II *n* persecución *f*; (*hunt*) caza *f*.

chasm ['kæzəm] *n Geog* sima *f*; fig abismo *m*.

chassis ['ʃæsɪ] *n* chasis *m inv*.

chastise [tʃæsˈtaɪz] *vtr* castigar.

chastity ['tʃæstɪtɪ] *n* castidad *f*.

chat [tʃæt] I *n* charla *f*; *GB* **c. show,** coloquio *m*. II *vi* charlar. ◆**chat up** *vtr fam* (intentar) ligar con algn.

chatter ['tʃætə'] I *vi* (*person*) parlotear; (*bird*) piar; (*teeth*) castañetear. II *n* (*of person*) parloteo *m*; (*of birds*) gorjeo *m*; (*of teeth*) castañeteo *m*.

chatterbox ['tʃætəbɒks] *n fam* parlanchín,-ina *m,f*.

chatty ['tʃætɪ] *adj* (*chattier, chattiest*) hablador,-a.

chauffeur ['ʃəʊfə', ʃəʊˈfɜː'] *n* chófer *mf*.

chauvinism ['ʃəʊvɪnɪzəm] *n* chovinismo *m*; **male c.,** machismo *m*.

chauvinist ['ʃəʊvɪnɪst] *adj & n* chovinista (*mf*); **male c.,** machista *m*.

cheap [tʃiːp] I *adj* barato,-a; (*fare*) económico,-a; (*joke*) de mal gusto; (*contemptible*) bajo,-a; **feel dirt c.,** tirado,-a. II *n GB fam* **on the c.,** en plan barato. III *adv* barato. ◆**cheaply** *adv* barato, en plan económico.

cheapen ['tʃiːpən] *vtr* fig degradar.

cheat [tʃiːt] I *vtr* engañar; **to c. sb out of sth,** estafar algo a algn. II *vi* 1 (*at games*) hacer trampa; (*in exam etc*) copiar(se). 2 *fam* (*husband, wife*) poner cuernos (**on,** a). III *n* (*trickster*) tramposo,-a.

check [tʃek] I *vtr* repasar; (*facts*) comprobar; (*tickets*) controlar; (*tyres, oil*) revisar. 2 (*impulse*) refrenar; (*growth*) retardar. 3 (*stop*) detener. 4 *Chess* dar jaque a. II *vi* comprobar. II *n* 1 (*of documents etc*) revisión *f*; (*of facts*) comprobación *f*. 2 *Chess* jaque *m*. 3 (*pattern*) cuadro *m*. 4 **to keep in c.,** (*feelings*) contener; (*enemy*) mantener a raya. 5 *US* → **cheque.** ◆**check in** *vi* (*at airport*) facturar; (*at hotel*) registrarse (**at,** en). ◆**check out** *vi* (*of ho-*

tel) dejar el hotel. **II** *vtr (facts)* verificar.
◆**check up** *vi* to c. up on sb, hacer averiguaciones sobre algn; **to c. up on sth,** comprobar algo.

checked ['tʃekt] *adj* a cuadros.

checker ['tʃekər] *n US (cashier)* cajero,-a *m,f.*

checkered ['tʃekəd] *adj US* → **chequered.**

checkers ['tʃekəz] *n US (game)* damas *fpl.*

check-in ['tʃekın] *n* **c.-in desk,** *(at airport)* mostrador *m* de facturación.

checkmate ['tʃekmeıt] **I** *n Chess* jaque mate *m.* **II** *vtr Chess* dar (jaque) mate a; *fig* poner en un callejón sin salida.

checkout ['tʃekaʊt] *n (counter)* caja *f.*

checkpoint ['tʃekpɔınt] *n* control *m.*

checkup ['tʃekʌp] *n Med* chequeo *m,* examen médico.

cheek [tʃi:k] *n* 1 mejilla *f.* 2 *fam (nerve)* cara *f;* **what c.!,** ¡vaya jeta!

cheekbone ['tʃi:kbəʊn] *n* pómulo *m.*

cheeky ['tʃi:kı] *adj (cheekier, cheekiest) fam* fresco,-a, descarado,-a.

cheep [tʃi:p] **I** *n (of bird)* pío *m.* **II** *vi* piar.

cheer [tʃıər] **I** *vi* aplaudir, aclamar. **II** *vtr* 1 *(applaud)* vitorear, aclamar. 2 *(make hopeful)* animar. **III** *n* viva *m;* **cheers,** aplausos *mpl; fam* **cheers!,** *(thank you)* gracias; *(before drinking)* ¡salud! ◆**cheer up** *vi* animarse. II *vtr* to c. sb up, alegrar *or* animar a algn.

cheerful ['tʃıəfʊl] *adj* alegre.

cheerio ['tʃıərı'əʊ] *interj GB fam* ¡hasta luego!

cheese [tʃi:z] *n* queso *m.*

cheesecake ['tʃi:zkeık] *n* tarta *f* de queso.

cheetah ['tʃi:tə] *n* guepardo *m.*

chef [ʃef] *n* chef *m.*

chemical ['kemıkəl] **I** *n* sustancia química, producto químico. **II** *adj* químico,-a.

chemist ['kemıst] *n* 1 químico,-a *m,f.* 2 *GB* **c.'s (shop),** farmacia *f;* **dispensing c.,** farmacéutico,-a *m,f.*

chemistry ['kemıstrı] *n* química *f.*

cheque [tʃek] *n* cheque *m;* **to pay by c.,** pagar con (un) cheque; **c. book,** talonario *m* (de cheques); **c. card,** tarjeta *f* de identificación bancaria.

chequered ['tʃekəd] *adj* a cuadros; *fig* **a c. career,** una carrera con altibajos.

cherish ['tʃerıʃ] *vtr* 1 *(person)* tenerle mucho cariño a. 2 *fig (hopes etc)* abrigar.

cherry ['tʃerı] *n* cereza *f.*

chess [tʃes] *n* ajedrez *m.*

chessboard ['tʃesbɔ:d] *n* tablero *m* de ajedrez.

chesspiece ['tʃespi:s] *n* pieza *f* de ajedrez.

chest [tʃest] *n* 1 *Anat* pecho *m.* 2 *(for linen)* arca *f; (for valuables)* cofre *m;* **c. of**

drawers, cómoda *f.*

chestnut ['tʃesnʌt] *n (tree, colour)* castaño *m; (nut)* castaña *f.*

chew [tʃu:] *vtr* masticar, mascar.

chewing gum ['tʃu:ıŋgʌm] *n* chicle *m.*

chic [ʃi:k] *adj* elegante.

chick [tʃık] *n* pollito *m.*

chicken ['tʃıkın] **I** *n* 1 pollo *m.* 2 *sl (coward)* gallina *f.* **II** *vi fam* to c. out, rajarse (por miedo).

chickenpox ['tʃıkınpɒks] *n* varicela *f.*

chickpea ['tʃıkpi:] *n* garbanzo *m.*

chicory ['tʃıkərı] *n* achicoria *f.*

chief [tʃi:f] **I** *n* jefe *m.* **II** *adj* principal. ◆**chiefly** *adv (above all)* sobre todo; *(mainly)* principalmente.

chiffon [ʃı'fɒn, 'ʃıfɒn] *n* gasa *f.*

chilblain ['tʃılbleın] *n* sabañón *m.*

child [tʃaıld] *n (pl children)* niño,-a *m,f; (son)* hijo *m; (daughter)* hija *f;* **c. minder,** persona *f* que cuida niños en su propia casa.

childbirth ['tʃaıldbɜ:θ] *n* parto *m.*

childhood ['tʃaıldhʊd] *n* infancia *f,* niñez *f.*

childish ['tʃaıldıʃ] *adj* pueril, aniñado.

childlike ['tʃaıldlaık] *adj* infantil.

children ['tʃıldrən] *npl* → **child.**

Chile ['tʃılı] *n* Chile.

Chilean ['tʃılıən] *adj y n* chileno,-a *(m,f).*

chill [tʃıl] **I** *n* 1 *Med* resfriado *m.* 2 *(coldness)* fresco *m.* **II** *adj* frío,-a. **III** *vtr (meat)* refrigerar; *(wine)* enfriar.

chil(l)i ['tʃılı] *n* chile *m.*

chilly ['tʃılı] *adj (chillier, chilliest)* frío,-a.

chime [tʃaım] **I** *n (peal)* campanada *f.* **II** *vtr* to c. five o'clock, *(of clock)* dar las cinco. **III** *vi* sonar. ◆**chime in** *vi fam* intervenir.

chimney ['tʃımnı] *n* chimenea *f;* **c. sweep,** deshollinador *m.*

chimpanzee [tʃımpæn'zi:] *n* chimpancé *m.*

chin [tʃın] *n* barbilla *f,* mentón *m;* **double c.,** papada *f.*

china ['tʃaınə] *n* loza *f.*

China ['tʃaınə] *n* China *f.*

Chinese [tʃaı'ni:z] **I** *adj* chino,-a. **II** *n* 1 *(person)* chino,-a *m,f.* 2 *(language)* chino *m.*

chink[1] [tʃıŋk] *n (opening)* resquicio *m; (crack)* grieta *f.*

chink[2] [tʃıŋk] **I** *vi* tintinear. **II** *n* tintineo *m.*

chip [tʃıp] **I** *n* 1 *(of wood)* astilla *f; (of stone)* lasca *f; (in cup)* mella *f.* 2 *GB Culin* **chips,** patatas fritas. 3 *Comput* chip *m.* 4 *(in gambling)* ficha *f.* **II** *vtr (wood)* astillar; *(stone)* resquebrajar; *(china, glass)* mellar. **III** *vi (wood)* astillarse; *(china, glass)* mellarse; *(paint)* desconcharse. ◆**chip in** *vi fam* 1 meterse. 2 *(with money)* poner algo (de dinero).

chiropodist [kɪ'rɒpədɪst] n pedicuro,-a m,f.

chirp [tʃɜːp] vi (birds) gorjear.

chisel ['tʃɪzəl] n cincel m.

chit [tʃɪt] n nota f; (small invoice) vale m.

chitchat [tʃɪttʃæt] n fam palique m.

chivalry ['ʃɪvəlrɪ] n caballerosidad f.

chives [tʃaɪvz] npl cebolleta f sing.

chlorine ['klɔːriːn] n cloro m.

chock-a-block [tʃɒkə'blɒk], **chock-full** [tʃɒk'fʊl] adj fam (lleno,-a) hasta los topes.

chocolate ['tʃɒkəlɪt] I n chocolate m; **chocolates**, bombones mpl. II adj de chocolate.

choice [tʃɔɪs] I n elección f; **a wide c.**, un gran surtido; **by c.**, por gusto. II adj selecto,-a.

choir ['kwaɪər] n coro m, coral f.

choirboy ['kwaɪəbɔɪ] n niño m de coro.

choke [tʃəʊk] I vtr 1 (person) ahogar. 2 (obstruct) obstruir. II vi ahogarse; **to c. on food**, atragantarse con la comida. III n Aut estárter m. ◆**choke back** vtr (emotions) tragarse.

cholera ['kɒlərə] n cólera m.

cholesterol [kə'lestərɒl] n colesterol m.

choose [tʃuːz] I vtr (pt **chose**; pp **chosen**) escoger, elegir; (decide on) optar por. II vi escoger, elegir.

choos(e)y ['tʃuːzɪ] adj (**choosier**, **choosiest**) fam exigente.

chop [tʃɒp] I vtr 1 (wood) cortar; (tree) talar. 2 Culin cortar a pedacitos. II n 1 (blow) tajo m; (with axe) hachazo m. 2 Culin chuleta f.

chopper ['tʃɒpər] n fam helicóptero m.

choppy ['tʃɒpɪ] adj (**choppier**, **choppiest**) (sea) picado,-a.

chopsticks ['tʃɒpstɪks] npl palillos mpl.

chord [kɔːd] n Mus acorde m; **fig it strikes a c.**, (me) suena.

chore [tʃɔːr] n quehacer m, tarea f.

chortle ['tʃɔːtəl] vi reír con ganas.

chorus ['kɔːrəs] n Mus Theat coro m; (in a song) estribillo m; **c. girl**, corista f.

chose [tʃəʊz] pt → **choose**.

chosen ['tʃəʊzən] pp → **choose**.

Christ [kraɪst] n Cristo m, Jesucristo m.

christen ['krɪsən] vtr bautizar.

christening ['krɪsənɪŋ] n bautizo m.

Christian ['krɪstʃən] I adj cristiano,-a; **c. name**, nombre m de pila. II n cristiano,-a m,f.

Christianity [krɪstɪ'ænɪtɪ] n cristianismo m.

Christmas ['krɪsməs] n Navidad f; **merry C.**, feliz Navidad; **C. card**, tarjeta f de Navidad; **C. carol**, villancico m; **C. Day**, día m de Navidad; **C. Eve**, Nochebuena f.

chrome [krəʊm] n cromo m.

chromium ['krəʊmɪəm] n cromo m; **c. plating**, cromado m.

chromosome ['krəʊməsəʊm] n cromosoma m.

chronic ['krɒnɪk] adj crónico,-a.

chronicle ['krɒnɪkəl] I n crónica f. II vtr hacer la crónica de.

chronological [krɒnə'lɒdʒɪkəl] adj cronológico,-a.

chrysanthemum [krɪ'sænθəməm] n crisantemo m.

chubby ['tʃʌbɪ] adj (**chubbier**, **chubbiest**) rellenito,-a.

chuck [tʃʌk] vtr fam tirar; **to c. one's job in or up**, dejar el trabajo; **to c. sb out**, echar a algn; **to c. sth away or out**, tirar algo.

chuckle ['tʃʌkəl] I vi reír entre dientes. II n sonrisita f.

chug [tʃʌg] vi traquetear.

chum [tʃʌm] n compinche mf, compañero,-a m,f fam.

chunk [tʃʌŋk] n fam cacho m, pedazo m.

church [tʃɜːtʃ] n iglesia f; **to go to c.**, ir a misa; **C. of England**, Iglesia Anglicana.

churchyard ['tʃɜːtʃjɑːd] n cementerio m, campo santo.

churlish ['tʃɜːlɪʃ] adj grosero,-a.

churn [tʃɜːn] I n (for butter) mantequera f; GB (for milk) lechera f. II vtr (butter) hacer. III vi revolverse, agitarse. ◆**churn out** vtr fam producir en serie.

chute [ʃuːt] n (channel) conducto m; (slide) tobogán m.

chutney ['tʃʌtnɪ] n conserva f (de frutas) picante.

CIA [siːaɪ'eɪ] US abbr of **Central Intelligence Agency**, Agencia f Central de Información, CIA f.

CID [siːaɪ'diː] GB abbr of **Criminal Investigation Department**, ≈ Brigada f de Investigación Criminal, BIC.

cider ['saɪdər] n sidra f.

cigar [sɪ'gɑːr] n puro m.

cigarette [sɪgə'ret] n cigarrillo m; **c. case**, pitillera f; **c. end**, colilla f; **c. holder**, boquilla f; **c. lighter**, mechero m.

Cinderella [sɪndə'relə] n Cenicienta f.

cine camera ['sɪnɪkæmərə] n GB cámara cinematográfica.

cinema ['sɪnɪmə] n cine m.

cinnamon ['sɪnəmən] n canela f.

cipher ['saɪfər] n (numeral) cifra f.

circle ['sɜːkəl] I n 1 círculo m; (of people) corro m; **in business circles**, en el mundo de los negocios. 2 Theat anfiteatro m. II vtr (surround) rodear; (move round) dar la vuelta a. III vi dar vueltas.

circuit ['sɜːkɪt] n 1 (journey) recorrido m. 2 Elec circuito m. 3 Sport (events) liga f; GB (track) circuito m. 4 GB Jur **c. judge**, juez mf de distrito.

circular ['sɜːkjʊlər] adj & n circular (f).

circulate ['sɜːkjʊleɪt] I vtr (news) hacer circular. II vi circular.

circulation [sɜːkjʊ'leɪʃən] n 1 (of blood)

circulación f. 2 (of newspaper) tirada f.
circumcise ['sɜːkəmsaɪz] vtr circuncidar.
circumference [səˈkʌmfərəns] n circunferencia f.
circumspect ['sɜːkəmspekt] adj prudente.
circumstance ['sɜːkəmstəns] n (usu pl) circunstancia f; **under no circumstances**, en ningún caso; **economic circumstances**, situación económica.
circumvent [sɜːkəmˈvent] vtr fig burlar.
circus ['sɜːkəs] n circo m.
cirrhosis [sɪˈrəʊsɪs] n cirrosis f.
CIS [siːaɪˈes] n abbr of **Commonwealth of Independent States**, CEI.
cistern ['sɪstən] n cisterna f.
cite [saɪt] vtr (quote) citar.
citizen ['sɪtɪzən] n ciudadano,-a m,f.
citizenship ['sɪtɪzənʃɪp] n ciudadanía f.
citr(o)us ['sɪtrəs] adj c. **fruit**, agrios mpl.
city ['sɪtɪ] n 1 ciudad f. 2 **Fin the C.**, el centro financiero de Londres.
civic ['sɪvɪk] adj cívico,-a; GB c. **centre**, centro cívico; c. **duties**, obligaciones cívicas.
civil ['sɪvəl] adj 1 civil; c. **defence**, defensa f civil; c. **rights**, derechos mpl civiles; c. **servant**, funcionario,-a m,f; Pol c. **service**, administración pública. 2 (polite) cortés, educado,-a.
civilian [sɪˈvɪljən] adj & n civil (mf); c. **clothing** traje m de paisano.
civilization [sɪvɪlaɪˈzeɪʃən] n civilización f.
civilized ['sɪvɪlaɪzd] adj civilizado,-a.
clad [klæd] adj lit vestido,-a.
claim [kleɪm] I vtr 1 (benefits, rights) reclamar; Jur (compensation) exigir. 2 (assert) afirmar. II n 1 (demand) reclamación f; Jur demanda f; **to put in a c.**, reclamar una indemnización f. 2 (right) derecho m. 3 (assertion) pretensión f.
claimant ['kleɪmənt] n Jur demandante mf.
clairvoyant [kleəˈvɔɪənt] n clarividente mf.
clam [klæm] n almeja f. ◆**clam up** n fam callarse.
clamber ['klæmbər] vi trepar (over, por).
clammy ['klæmɪ] adj (clammier, clammiest) (weather) bochornoso,-a; (hand) pegajoso,-a.
clamour ['klæmər] n US → **clamour**.
clamour ['klæmər] I n clamor m. II vi clamar; **to c. for**, pedir a gritos.
clamp [klæmp] I n (for carpentry) tornillo m de banco; Tech abrazadera f; wheel c., cepo m. II vtr sujetar con abrazaderas. ◆**clamp down on** vtr aumentar los esfuerzos contra.
clan [klæn] n clan m.
clandestine [klænˈdestɪn] adj
clang [klæŋ] I vi sonar. II n sonido metálico.

clap [klæp] I vi aplaudir. II n 1 palmada f. 2 a c. **of thunder**, un trueno.
clapping ['klæpɪŋ] n aplausos mpl.
claret ['klærət] n GB (wine) clarete m; (colour) burdeos m.
clarify ['klærɪfaɪ] vtr aclarar.
clarinet [klærɪˈnet] n clarinete m.
clarity ['klærɪtɪ] n claridad f.
clash [klæʃ] I vi 1 (cymbals) sonar; (swords) chocar; fig (disagree) estar en desacuerdo. 2 (colours) desentonar. 3 (dates) coincidir. II n 1 (sound) sonido m. 2 (fight) choque m; fig (conflict) conflicto m.
clasp [klɑːsp] I n 1 (on belt) cierre m; (on necklace) broche m. 2 (grasp) apretón m; c. **knife**, navaja f. II vtr (object) agarrar; **to c. hands**, juntar las manos.
class [klɑːs] I n 1 clase f; c. **struggle**, lucha f de clases; Educ c. **of '84**, promoción f de 1984; Rail **second c. ticket**, billete m de segunda (clase). II vtr clasificar.
classic ['klæsɪk] I adj clásico,-a. II n 1 (author) autor clásico; (work) obra clásica. 2 **the classics**, (literature) las obras clásicas; (languages) clásicas fpl.
classical ['klæsɪkəl] adj clásico,-a.
classified ['klæsɪfaɪd] adj (information) secreto,-a; c. **advertisements**, anuncios mpl por palabras.
classify ['klæsɪfaɪ] vtr clasificar.
classless ['klɑːslɪs] adj sin clases.
classmate ['klɑːsmeɪt] n compañero,-a m,f de clase.
classroom ['klɑːsruːm] n aula f, clase f.
clatter ['klætər] I vi hacer ruido; (things falling) hacer estrépito. II n ruido m, estrépito m.
clause [klɔːz] n 1 Jur cláusula f. 2 Ling oración f.
claw [klɔː] I n 1 (of bird, lion) garra f; (of cat) uña f; (of crab) pinza f. II vtr agarrar, arañar; (tear) desgarrar. ◆**claw at** vtr agarrar, arañar.
clay [kleɪ] n arcilla f; c. **pigeon shooting**, tiro m al plato.
clean [kliːn] I adj 1 limpio,-a. 2 (unmarked, pure) sin defecto; a c. **copy**, una copia en limpio; **to have a c. record**, no tener antecedentes (penales). 3 (not obscene) decente. 4 fig **to make a c. sweep of it**, arrasar. II adv 1 **to play c.**, jugar limpio; fam **to come c.**, confesarlo todo. 2 fam por completo; **it went c. through the middle**, pasó justo por el medio. III vtr (room) limpiar; **to c. one's teeth**, lavarse los dientes. ◆**clean out** vtr (room) limpiar a fondo. ◆**clean up** vtr & vi limpiar.
clean-cut ['kliːnkʌt] adj (person) limpio,-a, pulcro,-a.
cleaner ['kliːnər] n limpiador,-a m,f.
cleaning ['kliːnɪŋ] n limpieza f.
cleanliness ['klenlɪnɪs] n limpieza f.

cleanse [klenz] *vtr* limpiar.

cleansing ['klenzıŋ] *n* c. lotion, leche limpiadora.

clear [klıə*r*] I *adj* 1 claro,-a; *(road, day)* despejado,-a; **c. conscience,** conciencia tranquila. 2 *(obvious)* claro,-a; **to make sth c.,** aclarar algo. 3 *(majority)* absoluto; *(profit)* neto; **three c. days,** tres días completos. 4 *(free)* libre. II *adv* 1 *fig* **loud and c.,** claramente. 2 **stand c.!,** ¡apártese!; **to stay c. of,** evitar. III *adv* 1 *(room)* vaciar; *Com* liquidar; **to c. one's throat,** aclararse la garganta; **to c. the table,** quitar la mesa. 2 *(authorize)* autorizar. 3 *(hurdle)* salvar. **4 to c. sb of a charge,** exculpar a algn de un delito. IV *vi (sky)* despejarse. ◆**clear away** *vtr* quitar. ◆**clear off** *vi fam* largarse; **c. off!,** ¡largo! ◆**clear out** *vtr (room)* limpiar a fondo; *(cupboard)* vaciar. ◆**clear up** I *vtr* 1 *(tidy)* recoger; *(arrange)* ordenar. 2 *(mystery)* resolver; *(misunderstanding)* aclarar. II *vi (weather)* despejarse; *(problem)* desaparecer. ◆**clearly** *adv* 1 claramente. 2 *(at start of sentence)* evidentemente.

clearance ['klıərəns] *n* 1 *(of area)* despeje *m*; *Com* **c. sale,** liquidación *f* (de existencias). 2 *(space)* espacio *m* libre. 3 *(authorization)* autorización *f*.

clear-cut [klıə'kʌt] *adj* claro,-a.

clearing ['klıərıŋ] *n* 1 *(in wood)* claro *m*. 2 *(of rubbish)* limpieza *f*. 3 *(of cheque)* compensación *f*.

clearway ['klıəweı] *n GB* carretera *f* donde está prohibido parar.

cleaver ['kli:və*r*] *n* cuchillo *f* de carnicero.

clef [klef] *n* clave *f*; **bass/treble c.,** clave de fa/de sol.

cleft [kleft] *n* hendidura *f*, grieta *f*.

clementine ['kleməntaın] *n* clementina *f*.

clench [klentʃ] *vtr (teeth, fist)* apretar.

clergy ['klɜ:dʒı] *n* clero *m*.

clergyman ['klɜ:dʒımən] *n* clérigo *m*.

clerical ['klerıkəl] *adj* 1 *Rel* clerical. 2 *(staff, work)* de oficina.

clerk [klɑ:k, *US* klɜ:rk] *n* 1 *(office worker)* oficinista *mf*; *(civil servant)* funcionario,-a *m,f*. 2 *US Com* dependiente,-a *m,f*, vendedor,-a *m,f*.

clever ['klevə*r*] *adj* 1 *(person)* inteligente, listo,-a; **to be c. at sth,** tener aptitud para algo; *fam* **c. Dick,** sabiondo,-a *m,f*. 2 *(argument)* ingenioso,-a.

cliché ['kli:ʃeı] *n* cliché *m*.

click [klık] I *n (sound)* clic *m*. II *vtr (tongue)* chasquear. III *vi* **it didn't c.,** *(I didn't realize)* no me di cuenta.

client ['klaıənt] *n* cliente *mf*.

clientele [kli:ən'tel] *n* clientela *f*.

cliff [klıf] *n* acantilado *m*.

climate ['klaımıt] *n* clima *m*.

climax ['klaımæks] *n* 1 *(peak)* clímax *m*, punto *m* culminante. 2 *(sexual)* orgasmo *m*.

climb [klaım] I *vtr (ladder)* subir a; *(mountain)* escalar; *(tree)* trepar a. II *vi (plants)* trepar; *Av* subir; *fig (socially)* ascender. III *n* subida *f*, ascensión *f*. ◆**climb down** *vi* bajar; *fig* volverse atrás.

climber ['klaımə*r*] *n* alpinista *mf*, *Am* andinista *mf*.

climbing ['klaımıŋ] *n Sport* montañismo *m*, alpinismo *m*, *Am* andinismo *m*.

clinch [klıntʃ] I *vtr* resolver; *(deal)* cerrar. II *n sl* abrazo apasionado.

cling [klıŋ] *vi (pt & pp* **clung)** *(hang on)* agarrarse; *(clothes)* ajustarse; *(smell)* pegarse; **to c. together,** unirse.

clinic ['klınık] *n (in state hospital)* ambulatorio *m*; *(specialized)* clínica *f*.

clinical ['klınıkəl] *adj* 1 *Med* clínico,-a. 2 *(detached)* frío,-a.

clink [klıŋk] I *vi* tintinear. II *n* tintineo *m*.

clip¹ [klıp] I *vtr (cut)* cortar; *(ticket)* picar. II *n* 1 *(of film)* extracto *m*. 2 *(with scissors)* tijeretada *f*.

clip² [klıp] I *n (for hair)* pasador *m*; *(for paper)* clip *m*, sujetapapeles *m inv*; *(brooch)* clip *m*. II *vtr* sujetar.

clippers ['klıpəz] *npl (for hair)* maquinilla *f* para rapar; *(for nails)* cortaúñas *m inv*; *(for hedge)* tijeras *fpl* de podar.

clipping ['klıpıŋ] *n* recorte *m*.

clique [kli:k, klık] *n* peq camarilla *f*.

cloak [kləʊk] I *n (garment)* capa *f*. II *vtr* encubrir.

cloakroom ['kləʊkru:m] *n* guardarropa *m*; *euph (toilets)* servicios *mpl*.

clock [klɒk] I *n* reloj *m*. II *vtr (race)* cronometrar. ◆**clock in, clock on** *vi* fichar. ◆**clock off, clock out** *vi* fichar a la salida. ◆**clock up** *vtr (mileage)* hacer.

clockwise ['klɒkwaız] *adj & adv* en el sentido de las agujas del reloj.

clockwork ['klɒkwɜ:k] *n* mecanismo *m*; **c. toy,** juguete *m* de cuerda.

clog [klɒg] I *vtr* obstruir; *(pipe)* atascar; **to get clogged up,** atascarse. II *n (footwear)* zueco *m*.

cloister ['klɔıstə*r*] *n* claustro *m*.

close¹ [kləʊs] I *adj* 1 *(in space, time)* cercano,-a; *(print, weave)* compacto,-a; *(encounter)* cara a cara; *(contact)* directo, -a; **c. to,** cerca de; **c. together,** juntos; *fig* **we had a c. shave,** nos libramos por los pelos. 2 *(relationship)* estrecho,-a; *(friend)* íntimo. 3 *(inspection)* detallado,-a; *(watch)* atento,-a. 4 *(contest)* reñido,-a; **a c. resemblance,** un gran parecido. 5 *(air)* cargado,-a; *(weather)* bochornoso,-a. 6 *(secretive)* reservado,-a. 7 *Sport, (in hunting)* veda *f*. II *adv* cerca; **they live c. by** or **c. at hand,** viven cerca; **to stand c. together,** estar apretados,-as. ◆**closely** *adv* 1 *(tightly)* estrechamente, muy; **c.**

contested, muy reñido,-a; **they are c. related**, (people) son parientes próximos. 2 (attentively) con atención; **to follow (events) c.**, seguir de cerca (los acontecimientos).

close² [kləʊz] I vtr 1 cerrar; **closing time**, hora f de cierre. 2 (end) concluir, terminar; (meeting) levantar. II vi 1 (shut) cerrar, cerrarse. 2 (end) concluirse, terminarse. III n fin m, final m. ◆**close down** vi (business) cerrar para siempre; Rad TV cerrar. ◆**close in** vi to c. in on sb, rodear a algn.

closed [kləʊzd] adj cerrado,-a; Ind **c. shop**, empresa f que emplea solamente a miembros de un sindicato.

close-knit [kləʊs'nɪt] adj fig unido,-a.

closet [ˈklɒzɪt] n US armario m.

close-up [ˈkləʊsʌp] n primer plano m.

closure [ˈkləʊʒər] n cierre m.

clot [klɒt] I n 1 (of blood) coágulo m; Med **c. on the brain**, embolia f cerebral. 2 fam tonto,-a m,f. II vi coagularse.

cloth [klɒθ] n tela f, paño m; (rag) trapo m; (tablecloth) mantel m.

clothe [kləʊð] vtr (pt & pp **clothed** or **clad**) vestir (**in**, **with**, de); fig revestir, cubrir (**in**, **with**, de).

clothes [kləʊðz] npl ropa f sing, vestidos mpl; **c. brush**, cepillo m de la ropa; **c. hanger**, percha f; **c. horse**, tendedero m plegable; **c. line**, tendedero m; **c. peg**, pinza f.

clothing [ˈkləʊðɪŋ] n ropa f.

cloud [klaʊd] I n nube f. II vtr nublar; fig **to c. the issue**, complicar el asunto. III vi to c. over, nublarse.

cloudy [ˈklaʊdɪ] adj (**cloudier**, **cloudiest**) 1 (sky) nublado,-a. 2 (liquid) turbio,-a.

clout [klaʊt] fam I n 1 (blow) tortazo m. 2 (influence) influencia f. II vtr dar un tortazo a.

clove¹ [kləʊv] n (spice) clavo m.

clove² [kləʊv] n (of garlic) diente m.

clover [ˈkləʊvər] n trébol m.

clown [klaʊn] I n payaso m. II vi to c. (**about** or **around**), hacer el payaso.

cloying [ˈklɔɪɪŋ] adj empalagoso,-a.

club [klʌb] I n 1 (society) club m; sports **c.**, club deportivo. 2 (heavy stick) garrote m, porra f; Golf palo m. 3 Cards trébol m. 4 Culin **c. sandwich**, sándwich m doble. II vtr aporrear. III vi to c. **together**, pagar entre varios.

clubhouse [ˈklʌbhaʊs] n sede f de un club.

cluck [klʌk] I n cloqueo m. II vi cloquear.

clue [kluː] n (sign) indicio m; (to mystery) pista f; (in crossword) clave f; fam **I haven't a c.**, no tengo ni idea.

clump [klʌmp] n (of trees) grupo m; (of plants) mata f.

clumsy [ˈklʌmzɪ] adj (**clumsier**, **clumsiest**) torpe; (awkward)

tosco,-a.

clung [klʌŋ] pt & pp → **cling**.

cluster [ˈklʌstər] I n grupo m; (of grapes) racimo m. II vi agruparse.

clutch [klʌtʃ] I vtr agarrar. II vi fig to c. **at straws**, aferrarse a cualquier cosa. III n 1 Aut embrague m. 2 fig **to fall into sb's clutches**, caer en las garras de algn.

clutter [ˈklʌtər] vtr to c. (**up**), llenar, atestar.

cm abbr of **centimetre(s)**, centímetro(s), cm.

CND [siːen'diː] GB abbr of **Campaign for Nuclear Disarmament**, campaña f para el desarme nuclear.

Co I Com abbr of **Company**, Cí, Cª, Cía. 2 abbr of **County**.

c/o [siː'əʊ] abbr of **care of**, en casa de, c/ d.

coach [kəʊtʃ] I n 1 Aut autocar m; (carriage) carruaje m; **c. tour**, excursión f en autocar. 2 Rail coche m, vagón m. 3 Sport entrenador,-a m,f. II vtr Sport entrenar; Educ dar clases particulares a.

coagulate [kəʊˈægjʊleɪt] vi coagularse.

coal [kəʊl] n carbón m, hulla f; **c. bunker**, carbonera f; **c. merchant**, carbonero m; **c. mine**, mina f de carbón.

coalfield [ˈkəʊlfiːld] n yacimiento m de carbón.

coalition [kəʊəˈlɪʃən] n coalición f.

coarse [kɔːs] adj (material) basto,-a; (skin) áspero,-a; (language) grosero,-a, ordinario,-a.

coast [kəʊst] I n costa f, litoral m; fam fig **the c. is clear**, no hay moros en la costa. II vi Aut ir en punto muerto.

coastal [ˈkəʊstəl] adj costero,-a.

coaster [ˈkəʊstər] n (mat) salvamanteles m inv.

coastguard [ˈkəʊstgɑːd] n guardacostas m inv.

coastline [ˈkəʊstlaɪn] n litoral m, costa f.

coat [kəʊt] I n 1 (overcoat) abrigo m; (short) chaquetón m; **c. hanger**, percha f 2 (of animal) pelo m. 3 (of paint) mano f, capa f. 4 **c. of arms**, escudo m de armas. II vtr cubrir (**with**, de); (with liquid) bañar (**with**, en).

coating [ˈkəʊtɪŋ] n capa f, baño m.

coax [kəʊks] vtr engatusar.

cob [kɒb] n mazorca f.

cobble [ˈkɒbəl] n adoquín m.

cobbler [ˈkɒblər] n zapatero m.

cobweb [ˈkɒbweb] n telaraña f.

cocaine [kəˈkeɪn] n cocaína f.

cock [kɒk] I n 1 Orn gallo m; (male bird) macho m. 2 (on gun) percutor m. 3 sl vulg (penis) polla f. II vtr (ears) erguir. ◆**cock up** vtr GB sl chapucear.

cocker [ˈkɒkər] n **c. spaniel**, cocker m.

cockerel [ˈkɒkərəl] n gallo m joven.

cockeyed [ˈkɒkaɪd] adj fam (lopsided)

torcido,-a; (scheme) disparatado,-a.
cockle ['kɒkəl] n berberecho m.
cockney ['kɒknɪ] I adj del East End
londinense. II n persona f del East End
londinense.
cockpit ['kɒkpɪt] n cabina f del piloto.
cockroach ['kɒkrəʊtʃ] n cucaracha f.
cocktail ['kɒkteɪl] n cóctel m; **c. lounge,**
bar m; **c. party,** cóctel; **prawn c.,** cóctel
de gambas; **Molotov c.,** cóctel Molotov.
cocky ['kɒkɪ] adj (**cockier, cockiest**) fam
creído,-a.
cocoa ['kəʊkəʊ] n cacao m.
coconut ['kəʊkənʌt] n coco m.
cocoon [kə'kuːn] n capullo m.
COD [siːəʊ'diː] GB abbr of **cash on delivery, CAE.**
cod [kɒd] n bacalao m; **c. liver oil,** aceite
m de hígado de bacalao.
code [kəʊd] I n código m; (symbol) clave
f; Tel prefijo m. II vtr (message) cifrar,
poner en clave.
co-ed [kəʊ'ed] fam I adj mixto,-a. II n
colegio mixto.
coerce [kəʊ'ɜːs] vtr coaccionar.
coercion [kəʊ'ɜːʃən] n coacción f.
coexist [kəʊɪg'zɪst] vi coexistir.
coffee ['kɒfɪ] n café m; **c. bar/shop,** cafetería f; **c. break,** descanso m; **c. table,**
mesita f de café.
coffeepot ['kɒfɪpɒt] n cafetera f.
coffer ['kɒfər] n arca f.
coffin ['kɒfɪn] n ataúd m.
cog [kɒg] n diente m.
cognac ['kɒnjæk] n coñac m.
coherent [kəʊ'hɪərənt] adj coherente.
coil [kɔɪl] I vtr to c. (up), enrollar. II vi
enroscarse. III n 1 (loop) vuelta f; (of
rope) rollo m; (of hair) rizo m. 2 (contraceptive) espiral f. 3 Elec carrete m, bobina f.
coin [kɔɪn] I n moneda f. II vtr 1 (money)
acuñar. 2 fig to c. a phrase, por así decirlo.
coinage ['kɔɪnɪdʒ] n moneda f, sistema m
monetario.
coincide [kəʊɪn'saɪd] vi coincidir (with,
con).
coincidence [kəʊ'ɪnsɪdəns] n coincidencia
f.
coincidental [kəʊɪnsɪ'dentəl] adj casual.
◆**coincidentally** adv por casualidad or
coincidencia.
Coke® [kəʊk] n (abbr of **Coca-Cola®**) fam
coca-cola f.
coke [kəʊk] n (coal) coque m.
colander ['kɒləndər] n colador m.
cold [kəʊld] I adj frío,-a; **I'm c.,** tengo
frío; **it's c.,** (weather) hace frío; (thing)
está frío,-a; fig **to get c. feet** (about
doing sth), entrarle miedo a algn (de hacer algo); **c. cream,** crema f hidratante;
fig **it leaves me c.,** no me dice nada; **c.
war,** guerra fría. II n 1 frío m. 2 Med res-

friado m; **to catch a c.,** resfriarse, acatarrarse; **to have a c.,** estar resfriado,-a; **c.
sore,** herpes m (en el labio).
cold-blooded [kəʊld'blʌdɪd] adj 1 (animal) de sangre fría. 2 fig (person) frío,-a;
(crime) a sangre fría.
coleslaw ['kəʊlslɔː] n ensalada f de col.
collaborate [kə'læbəreɪt] vi colaborar
(with, con).
collaborator [kə'læbəreɪtər] n Pol colabo-
racionista mf.
collapse [kə'læps] I vi (break down) derrumbarse; (cave in) hundirse; fig (prices)
caer en picado; Med sufrir un colapso. II
vtr (table) plegar. III n (breaking down)
derrumbamiento m; (caving in) hundimiento m; Med colapso m.
collapsible [kə'læpsəbəl] adj plegable.
collar ['kɒlər] I n (of garment) cuello m;
(for dog) collar m. II vtr fam pescar, agarrar.
collarbone ['kɒləbəʊn] n clavícula f.
collateral [kɒ'lætərəl] I n Fin garantía
subsidiaria. II adj colateral.
colleague ['kɒliːg] n colega mf.
collect [kə'lekt] I vtr 1 (gather) recoger. 2
(stamps etc) coleccionar. 3 (taxes) recaudar. II vi 1 (people) reunirse. 2 (for charity) hacer una colecta (for, para). III adv
US Tel **to call c.,** llamar a cobro revertido.
collection [kə'lekʃən] n 1 (of mail) recogida f; (of money) colecta f. 2 (of stamps)
colección f. 3 (of taxes) recaudación f. 4
(of people) grupo m.
collective [kə'lektɪv] I adj colectivo,-a; **c.
bargaining,** negociación colectiva. II n
colectivo m.
collector [kə'lektər] n 1 (of stamps) coleccionista mf. 2 **tax c.,** recaudador,-a
m,f (de impuestos).
college ['kɒlɪdʒ] n colegio m; (of university) colegio mayor.
collide [kə'laɪd] vi chocar, colisionar.
collie ['kɒlɪ] n perro m pastor escocés.
colliery ['kɒljərɪ] n GB mina f de carbón.
collision [kə'lɪʒən] n choque m.
colloquial [kə'ləʊkwɪəl] adj coloquial.
collusion [kə'luːʒən] n conspiración f.
cologne [kə'ləʊn] n (agua f de) colonia f.
Colombia [kə'lɒmbɪə] n Colombia.
Colombian [kə'lɒmbɪən] adj & n
colombiano,-a (m,f).
colon[1] ['kəʊlən] n Typ dos puntos mpl.
colon[2] ['kəʊlən] n Anat colon m.
colonel ['kɜːnəl] n coronel m.
colonial [kə'ləʊnɪəl] adj colonial.
colonize ['kɒlənaɪz] vtr colonizar.
colony ['kɒlənɪ] n colonia f.
color ['kʌlər] n & vtr & vi US → **colour.**
colossal [kə'lɒsəl] adj colosal.
colour ['kʌlər] I n 1 color m; **what c. is
it?,** ¿de qué color es?; **c. film/television,**
película ftelevisión f en color; **c.**

scheme, combinación f de colores. **2** (race) color m; **c. bar**, discriminación f racial. **3 colours**, GB Sport colores mpl; Mil (flag) bandera f sing. II vtr colorear. III vi to c. (**up**), ruborizarse.

colour-blind ['kʌləblaɪnd] adj daltónico, -a.

Coloured ['kʌləd] adj de color.

coloured ['kʌləd] adj (photograph) en color.

colourful ['kʌləful] adj **1** con muchos colores; fig lleno,-a de color; (person) pintoresco,-a.

colouring ['kʌlərɪŋ] n (colour) colorido m.

colourless ['kʌləlɪs] adj incoloro,-a; fig soso,-a.

colt [kəʊlt] n potro m.

column ['kɒləm] n columna f.

columnist ['kɒləmnɪst] n columnista mf.

coma ['kəʊmə] n coma m; **to go into a c.**, entrar en coma.

comb [kəʊm] I n peine m. II vtr **1** peinar; **to c. one's hair**, peinarse.

combat ['kɒmbæt] I n combate m. II vtr (enemy, disease) combatir. III vi combatir (**against**, contra).

combination [kɒmbɪ'neɪʃən] n combinación f.

combine [kəm'baɪn] I vtr combinar. II vi combinarse; (companies) asociarse. III ['kɒmbaɪn] n **1** Com asociación f. **2 c. harvester**, cosechadora f.

combustion [kəm'bʌstʃən] n combustión f.

come [kʌm] vi (pt **came**; pp **come**) **1** venir; (arrive) llegar; **coming!**, ¡voy!; **to c. and go**, ir y venir; fig **in years to c.**, en el futuro. **2** to c. **apart/undone**, desatarse / soltarse. **3** (happen) suceder; **that's what comes of being too impatient**, es lo que pasa por ser demasiado impaciente; fam **how c.?**, ¿y eso? **4 I came to believe that ...**, llegué a creer que ... **5** fig **c. what may**, pase lo que pase. **6** sl (have orgasm) correrse.
◆**come about** vi ocurrir, suceder.
◆**come across** I vtr (thing) encontrar por casualidad; **to c. across sb**, tropezar con algn. II vi fig **to c. across well**, causar buena impresión.
◆**come along** vi **1** (arrive) venir; **c. along!**, ¡venga! **2** (make progress) progresar.
◆**come away** vi (leave) salir; (part) desprenderse (**from**, de).
◆**come back** vi (return) volver.
◆**come before** vtr **1** preceder a. **2** (court) comparecer ante.
◆**come by** vtr adquirir.
◆**come down** vi bajar; (rain) caer; (building) ser derribado; **to c. down with the flu**, coger la gripe.
◆**come forward** vi (advance) avanzar; (volunteer) ofrecerse.
◆**come in** vi **1** (enter) entrar; **c. in!**, ¡pase! **2** (arrive) (train) llegar; (tide) subir; fam fig **where do I c. in?**, y yo ¿qué pinto? **3** **to c. in handy**, venir

bien. **4** **to c. in for**, ser objeto de.
◆**come into** vtr **1** (enter) entrar en. **2** (inherit) heredar.
◆**come off** I vtr (fall from) caerse de; fam **c. off it!**, ¡venga ya!. II vi **1** (fall) caerse; (stain) quitarse; (button) caerse. **2** fam (take place) pasar; (succeed) salir bien. III vi fig **to c. off badly**, salir mal.
◆**come on** vi **1 c. on!**, (hurry) ¡venga! **2** (make progress) progresar. **3** (rain, illness) comenzar.
◆**come out** vi **1** salir (**of**, de); (book) aparecer; (product) estrenarse; (facts) revelarse. **2** (stain) quitarse; (colour) desteñir. **3** **to c. out against/in favour of sth**, declararse en contra/a favor de algn; GB Ind **to c. out (on strike)**, declararse en huelga. **4** (turn out) salir.
◆**come over** I vi venir. II vtr fig **1** (hill) aparecer en lo alto de ?. fam **what's c. over you?**, ¿qué te pasa?
◆**come round** I vtr (corner) dar la vuelta a. II vi **1** (visit) venir. **2** (regain consciousness) volver en sí. **3** **to c. round to sb's way of thinking**, dejarse convencer por algn.
◆**come through** I vtr **1** (cross) cruzar. **2** (illness) recuperarse de; (accident) sobrevivir. II vi (message) llegar.
◆**come to** I vi (regain consciousness) volver en sí. **2** **to c. to one's senses**, fig recobrar la razón. **2** (amount to) costar. **3** (arrive at) llegar a; **to c. to an end**, terminar; fam **c. to that**, a propósito.
◆**come under** vtr fig **to c. under fire from sb**, ser criticado,-a por algn.
◆**come up** vi **1** (rise) subir; (approach) acercarse (**to**, a). **2** (difficulty, question) surgir; **to c. up with a solution**, encontrar una solución; **to c. up against problems**, encontrarse con problemas. **3** (sun) salir. **4** **to c. up to**, igualar; **to c. up to sb's expectations**, satisfacer a algn. **5** fam **three chips, coming up!**, ¡van tres de patatas fritas! ◆**come upon** vtr → **come across**.

comeback ['kʌmbæk] n fam **1** (of person) reaparición f; **to make a c.**, reaparecer. **2** (answer) réplica f.

comedian [kə'miːdɪən] n cómico m.

comedienne [kəmiːdɪ'en] n cómica f.

comedown ['kʌmdaʊn] n fam desilusión f, revés m.

comedy ['kɒmɪdɪ] n comedia f.

comet ['kɒmɪt] n cometa m.

comeuppance [kʌm'ʌpəns] n fam **to get one's c.**, llevarse su merecido.

comfort ['kʌmfət] n **1** comodidad f; US **c. station**, servicios mpl. **2** (consolation) consuelo m; **to take c. in or from sth**, consolarse con algo. II vtr consolar.

comfortable ['kʌmfətəbəl] adj (chair, person, margin) cómodo,-a; (temperature) agradable. ◆**comfortably** adv (win) con facilidad; **to be c. off**, vivir cómodamente.

comforter ['kʌmfətəʳ] n **1** GB (scarf) bufanda *f*. 2 *(for baby)* chupete *m*. 3 *US* edredón *m*.

comforting ['kʌmfətɪŋ] *adj* consolador,-a.

comic ['kɒmɪk] I *adj* cómico,-a; c. strip, tira cómica, historieta *f*. II *n* 1 *(person)* cómico,-a *m,f*. 2 *Press* tebeo *m*, comic *m*.

coming ['kʌmɪŋ] I *adj* (year) próximo,-a; (generation) futuro,-a. II *n* venida *f*, llegada *f*; comings and goings, idas y venidas; *fig* c. and going, ajetreo *m*.

comma ['kɒmə] *n* coma *f*.

command [kə'mɑ:nd] I *vtr* 1 mandar. 2 *(respect)* infundir; *(sympathy)* merecer; *(money etc)* disponer de. II *n* 1 *(order)* orden *f*; *(authority)* mando *m*; to be at sb's c., estar a las órdenes de algn. 2 *(of language)* dominio *m*. 3 *(disposal)* disposición *f*.

commandeer [kɒmən'dɪər] *vtr* requisar.

commander [kə'mɑ:ndər] *n* comandante *m*.

commanding [kə'mɑ:ndɪŋ] *adj* dominante; *Mil* c. officer, comandante *m*.

commandment [kə'mɑ:ndmənt] *n* mandamiento *m*.

commando [kə'mɑ:ndəʊ] *n* comando *m*.

commemorate [kə'meməreɪt] *vtr* conmemorar.

commence [kə'mens] *vtr & vi fml* comenzar.

commend [kə'mend] *vtr* 1 *(praise)* alabar, elogiar. 2 *(entrust)* encomendar. 3 *(recommend)* recomendar.

commensurate [kə'menʃərɪt] *adj* proporcional; c. to *or* with, en proporción con.

comment ['kɒment] I *n* comentario *m*; no c., sin comentario. II *vi* hacer comentarios.

commentary ['kɒməntərɪ] *n* comentario *m*.

commentator ['kɒmənteɪtər] *n* comentarista *mf*.

commerce ['kɒmɜ:s] *n* comercio *m*.

commercial [kə'mɜ:ʃəl] I *adj* comercial; *TV* c. break, corte publicitario. II *n* *TV* anuncio *m*.

commiserate [kə'mɪzəreɪt] *vi* compadecerse (with, de).

commission [kə'mɪʃən] I *n* 1 *Mil* despacho *m* (de oficial); out of c., fuera de servicio. 2 *(of enquiry)* comisión *f*; *(job)* encargo *m*. 3 *(payment)* comisión *f*. II *vtr* 1 *Mil* nombrar. 2 *(order)* encargar. 3 *Naut* poner en servicio.

commissionaire [kəmɪʃə'neər] *n* GB portero *m*.

commissioner [kə'mɪʃənər] *n* *(official)* comisario *m*; c. of police, comisario de policía.

commit [kə'mɪt] *vtr* 1 *(crime)* cometer; to c. suicide, suicidarse. 2 to c. oneself (to do sth), comprometerse (a hacer algo). 3

to c. sth to sb's care, confiar algo a algn.

commitment [kə'mɪtmənt] *n* compromiso *m*.

committee [kə'mɪtɪ] *n* comisión *f*, comité *m*.

commode [kə'məʊd] *n* (chair) silla *f* con orinal; *(chest of drawers)* cómoda *f*.

commodity [kə'mɒdɪtɪ] *n* artículo *m*.

common ['kɒmən] I *adj* 1 común; that's c. knowledge, eso lo sabe todo el mundo; c. law, derecho consuetudinario; C. Market, Mercado *m* Común; GB c. room, sala *f* de profesores *or* de estudiantes. 2 *(ordinary)* corriente. 3 *(vulgar)* ordinario,-a, maleducado,-a. II *n* *(land)* campo *m* *or* terreno *m* comunal.

commonplace ['kɒmənpleɪs] *adj* corriente.

Commons ['kɒmənz] *npl* GB the (House of) C., (la Cámara de) los Comunes.

Commonwealth ['kɒmənwelθ] *n* GB the C., la Commonwealth; C. of Independent States, Comunidad *f* de Estados Independientes.

commotion [kə'məʊʃən] *n* alboroto *m*.

commune¹ [kə'mju:n] *vi* *(converse)* conversar íntimamente; *(with nature)* estar en comunión (with, con).

commune² ['kɒmju:n] *n* comuna *f*.

communicate [kə'mju:nɪkeɪt] I *vi* comunicarse (with, con). II *vtr* comunicar.

communication [kəmju:nɪ'keɪʃən] *n* 1 comunicación *f*. 2 GB *Rail* c. cord, timbre *m* de alarma.

communion [kə'mju:njən] *n* comunión *f*; to take c., comulgar.

communiqué [kə'mju:nɪkeɪ] *n* comunicado *m* oficial.

communism ['kɒmjʊnɪzəm] *n* comunismo *m*.

communist ['kɒmjʊnɪst] *adj & n* comunista (*mf*).

community [kə'mju:nɪtɪ] *n* comunidad *f*; *(people)* colectividad *f*; c. centre, centro *m* social.

commute [kə'mju:t] I *vi* viajar diariamente al lugar de trabajo. II *vtr Jur* conmutar.

commuter [kə'mju:tər] *n* persona *f* que viaja diariamente al lugar de trabajo.

compact¹ [kəm'pækt] I *adj* 1 compacto,-a; *(style)* conciso,-a; c. disc, disco compacto. II ['kɒmpækt] *n* *(for powder)* polvera *f*.

compact² ['kɒmpækt] *n Pol* pacto *m*.

companion [kəm'pænjən] *n* compañero, -a *m,f*.

companionship [kəm'pænjənʃɪp] *n* compañerismo *m*.

company ['kʌmpənɪ] *n* 1 compañía *f*; to keep sb c., hacer compañía a algn. 2 *Com* empresa *f*, compañía *f*.

comparable ['kɒmpərəbəl] *adj* compara-

comparative [kəm'pærətɪv] **I** *adj* comparativo,-a; *(relative)* relativo,-a. **II** *n Ling* comparativo *m*. ◆**comparatively** *adv* relativamente.

compare [kəm'peəʳ] **I** *vtr* comparar (**to**, **with**, con); **(as) compared with**, en comparación con. **II** *vi* compararse.

comparison [kəm'pærɪsən] *n* comparación *f*; **by c.**, en comparación; **there's no c.**, no se puede comparar.

compartment [kəm'pɑːtmənt] *n (section)* compartimiento *m*; *Rail* departamento *m*.

compass ['kʌmpəs] *n* **1** brújula *f*. **2** *(pair of)* **compasses**, compás *m*. **3** *fig (range)* límites *mpl*.

compassion [kəm'pæʃən] *n* compasión *f*.

compassionate [kəm'pæʃənət] *adj* compasivo,-a.

compatible [kəm'pætəbəl] *adj* compatible.

compel [kəm'pel] *vtr* **1** *(oblige)* obligar; **to c. sb to do sth**, obligar a algn a hacer algo. **2** *(admiration)* despertar.

compelling [kəm'pelɪŋ] *adj* irresistible.

compensate ['kɒmpenseɪt] **I** *vtr* compensar; **to c. sb for sth**, indemnizar a algn de algo. **II** *vi* compensar.

compensation [kɒmpen'seɪʃən] *n* compensación *f*; *(for loss)* indemnización *f*.

compere ['kɒmpeəʳ] *GB n* animador,-a *m,f*.

compete [kəm'piːt] *vi* competir.

competence ['kɒmpɪtəns] *n* **1** *(ability)* aptitud *f*. **2** *(of court etc)* competencia *f*.

competent ['kɒmpɪtənt] *adj* competente.

competition [kɒmpɪ'tɪʃən] *n* **1** *(contest)* concurso *m*. **2** *Com* competencia *f*.

competitive [kəm'petɪtɪv] *adj* competitivo,-a.

competitor [kəm'petɪtəʳ] *n* competidor,-a *m,f*.

compilation [kɒmpɪ'leɪʃən] *n* recopilación *f*.

compile [kəm'paɪl] *vtr* compilar, recopilar.

complacency [kəm'pleɪsənsɪ] *n* complacencia *f*.

complacent [kəm'pleɪsənt] *adj* autocomplaciente.

complain [kəm'pleɪn] *vi* quejarse (**of**, **about**, de).

complaint [kəm'pleɪnt] *n* **1** queja *f*; *Com* reclamación *f*. **2** *Jur* demanda *f*. **3** *Med* enfermedad *f*.

complement ['kɒmplɪmənt] **I** *n* **1** complemento *m*. **2** *Naut* dotación *f*. **II** *vtr* complementar.

complementary [kɒmplɪ'mentərɪ] *adj* complementario,-a.

complete [kəm'pliːt] **I** *adj* **1** *(entire)* completo,-a. **2** *(absolute)* total. **II** *vtr* completar; **to c. a form**, rellenar un formulario. ◆**completely** *adv* completamente,

por completo.

completion [kəm'pliːʃən] *n* terminación *f*; **near c.**, casi terminado,-a; **on c.**, en cuanto se termine.

complex ['kɒmpleks] **I** *adj* complejo,-a. **II** *n* complejo *m*; **inferiority c.**, complejo de inferioridad.

complexion [kəm'plekʃən] *n* tez *f*; *fig* aspecto *m*.

compliance [kəm'plaɪəns] *n* conformidad *f*; **in c. with**, de acuerdo con.

complicate ['kɒmplɪkeɪt] *vtr* complicar.

complicated ['kɒmplɪkeɪtɪd] *adj* complicado,-a.

complication [kɒmplɪ'keɪʃən] *n* complicación *f*.

complicity [kəm'plɪsɪtɪ] *n* complicidad *f*.

compliment ['kɒmplɪmənt] **I** *n* **1** cumplido *m*; **to pay sb a c.**, hacerle un cumplido a algn. **2 compliments**, saludos *mpl*. **II** ['kɒmplɪment] *vtr* felicitar; **to c. sb on sth**, felicitar a algn por algo.

complimentary [kɒmplɪ'mentərɪ] *adj* **1** *(praising)* elogioso,-a. **2** *(free)* gratis.

comply [kəm'plaɪ] *vi* obedecer; **to c. with**, *(order)* cumplir con; *(request)* acceder a.

component [kəm'pəʊnənt] **I** *n* componente *m*. **II** *adj* componente; **c. part**, parte *f*.

compose [kəm'pəʊz] *vtr* & *vi* **1** componer; **to be composed of**, componerse de. **2 to c. oneself**, calmarse.

composed [kəm'pəʊzd] *adj (calm)* sereno,-a.

composer [kəm'pəʊzəʳ] *n* compositor,-a *m,f*.

composite ['kɒmpəzɪt] *adj* compuesto,-a.

composition [kɒmpə'zɪʃən] *n* composición *f*; *(essay)* redacción *f*.

compost ['kɒmpɒst] *n* abono *m*.

composure [kəm'pəʊʒəʳ] *n* calma *f*, serenidad *f*.

compound¹ ['kɒmpaʊnd] **I** *n* compuesto *m*. **II** *adj* compuesto,-a. **III** [kəm'paʊnd] *vtr (problem)* agravar.

compound² ['kɒmpaʊnd] *n (enclosure)* recinto *m*.

comprehend [kɒmprɪ'hend] *vtr* comprender.

comprehensible [kɒmprɪ'hensəbəl] *adj* comprensible.

comprehension [kɒmprɪ'henʃən] *n* comprensión *f*.

comprehensive [kɒmprɪ'hensɪv] *adj* **1** *(knowledge)* amplio,-a; *(study)* detallado,-a. **2** *Ins* a todo riesgo. **3** *GB* **c. school**, ≈ instituto *m* de segunda enseñanza.

compress [kəm'pres] *vtr* comprimir. **II** ['kɒmpres] *n* compresa *f*.

comprise [kəm'praɪz] *vtr* comprender; *(consist of)* constar de.

compromise ['kɒmprəmaɪz] **I** *n* término

medio; **to reach a c.,** llegar a un acuerdo. **II** *vi (two people)* llegar a un acuerdo; *(individual)* transigir. **III** *vtr (person)* comprometer.

compulsion [kəmˈpʌlʃən] *n* obligación *f*.

compulsive [kəmˈpʌlsɪv] *adj* compulsivo,-a.

compulsory [kəmˈpʌlsərɪ] *adj* obligatorio,-a.

computer [kəmˈpjuːtə^r] *n* ordenador *m*, computadora *f*; **c. programmer**, programador,-a *m,f*; **de ordenadores**; **c. science**, informática *f*; **personal c.**, ordenador personal.

computerize [kəmˈpjuːtəraɪz] *vtr* informatizar.

computing [kəmˈpjuːtɪŋ] *n* informática *f*.

comrade [ˈkɒmreɪd] *n* **1** *(companion)* compañero,-a *m,f*. **2** *Pol* camarada *mf*.

comradeship [ˈkɒmreɪdʃɪp] *n* camaradería *f*.

con [kɒn] *sl* **I** *vtr* estafar, timar. **II** *n* estafa *f*, camelo *m*; **c. man**, estafador *m*.

concave [ˈkɒnkeɪv] *adj* cóncavo,-a.

conceal [kənˈsiːl] *vtr* ocultar; *(emotions)* disimular.

concede [kənˈsiːd] *vtr* conceder.

conceit [kənˈsiːt] *n* presunción *f*, vanidad *f*.

conceited [kənˈsiːtɪd] *adj* presuntuoso,-a.

conceivable [kənˈsiːvəbl] *adj* concebible.

conceive [kənˈsiːv] *vtr & vi* concebir.

concentrate [ˈkɒnsəntreɪt] **I** *vtr* concentrar. **II** *vi* **to c. on sth,** concentrarse en algo.

concentration [kɒnsənˈtreɪʃən] *n* concentración *f*; **c. camp,** campo *m* de concentración.

concept [ˈkɒnsept] *n* concepto *m*.

conception [kənˈsepʃən] *n* *Med* concepción *f*; *(understanding)* concepto *m*, idea *f*.

concern [kənˈsɜːn] **I** *vtr* **1** concernir, afectar; **as far as I'm concerned,** por lo que a mí se refiere. **2** *(worry)* preocupar. **II** *n* **1** *(worry)* **it's no c. of mine,** no es asunto mío. **2** *(worry)* preocupación *f*. **3** *Com* negocio *m*.

concerned [kənˈsɜːnd] *adj* **1** *(affected)* afectado,-a. **2** *(worried)* preocupado,-a *(about,* por).

concerning [kənˈsɜːnɪŋ] *prep* con respecto a, en cuanto a.

concert [ˈkɒnsət, ˈkɒnsɜːt] *n* *Mus* concierto *m*; **c. hall,** sala *f* de conciertos.

concerted [kənˈsɜːtɪd] *adj* concertado,-a.

concertina [kɒnsəˈtiːnə] *n* concertina *f*.

concerto [kənˈtʃeətəʊ] *n* concierto *m*.

concession [kənˈseʃən] *n* **1** concesión *f*; **tax c.,** privilegio *m* fiscal. **2** *Com* reducción *f*.

concise [kənˈsaɪs] *adj* conciso,-a.

conclude [kənˈkluːd] *vtr & vi* concluir.

conclusion [kənˈkluːʒən] *n* conclusión *f*; **to reach a c.,** llegar a una conclusión.

conclusive [kənˈkluːsɪv] *adj* concluyente.

concoct [kənˈkɒkt] *vtr (dish)* confeccionar; *fig (plan)* fraguar; *(excuse)* inventar.

concoction [kənˈkɒkʃən] *n* *(mixture)* mezcolanza *f*; *pej (drink)* brebaje *m*.

concourse [ˈkɒŋkɔːs] *n* explanada *f*.

concrete [ˈkɒnkriːt] **I** *n* hormigón *m*; **c. mixer,** hormigonera *f*. **II** *adj* **1** *(definite)* concreto,-a. **2** *(made of concrete)* de hormigón.

concur [kənˈkɜː] *vi* **1** **to c. with,** *(agree)* estar de acuerdo con. **2** *(coincide)* coincidir.

concurrent [kənˈkʌrənt] *adj* simultáneo,-a.

concussion [kənˈkʌʃən] *n* conmoción *f* cerebral.

condemn [kənˈdem] *vtr* condenar.

condemnation [kɒndemˈneɪʃən] *n* condena *f*.

condensation [kɒndenˈseɪʃən] *n* condensación *f*.

condense [kənˈdens] **I** *vtr* condensar. **II** *vi* condensarse.

condensed [kənˈdenst] *adj* **c. milk,** leche condensada.

condescending [kɒndɪˈsendɪŋ] *adj* condescendiente.

condition [kənˈdɪʃən] **I** *n* condición *f*; **to be in good c.,** estar en buen estado; **on c. that ...,** a condición de que ...; **on one c.,** con una condición; **heart c.,** enfermedad cardíaca; **conditions,** *(circumstances)* circunstancias *fpl*. **II** *vtr* condicionar.

conditional [kənˈdɪʃənəl] *adj* condicional.

conditioner [kənˈdɪʃənə^r] *n* acondicionador *m*.

condolences [kənˈdəʊlənsɪz] *npl* pésame *m sing*; **please accept my c.,** le acompaño en el sentimiento.

condom [ˈkɒndəm] *n* preservativo *m*.

condone [kənˈdəʊn] *vtr* perdonar, consentir.

condor [ˈkɒndɔː^r] *n* cóndor *m*.

conducive [kənˈdjuːsɪv] *adj* conducente.

conduct [ˈkɒndʌkt] **I** *n* *(behaviour)* conducta *f*, comportamiento *m*. **II** [kənˈdʌkt] *vtr* *(lead)* guiar; *(business, orchestra)* dirigir; **conducted tour,** visita acompañada; **to c. oneself,** comportarse. **III** *vi* *Mus* dirigir.

conductor [kənˈdʌktə^r] *n* **1** *(on bus)* cobrador *m*. **2** *US Rail* revisor,-a *m,f*. **3** *Mus* director,-a *m,f*. **4** *Phys* conductor *m*.

conductress [kənˈdʌktrɪs] *n* *(on bus)* cobradora *f*.

cone [kəʊn] *n* **1** cono *m*; **ice-cream c.,** cucurucho *m*. **2** *Bot* piña *f*.

confectioner [kənˈfekʃənə^r] *n* confitero,-a *m,f*; **c.'s (shop),** confitería *f*.

confectionery [kənˈfekʃənərɪ] *n* dulces

mpl.
confederate [kən'fedərit] **I** adj confederado,-a. **II** n confederado,-a m,f; Jur cómplice mf.
confer [kən'fɜːr] **I** vtr to c. a title on sb, conferir un título a algn. **II** vi consultar.
conference ['kɒnfərəns] n conferencia f.
confess [kən'fes] **I** vi confesar; Rel confesarse. **II** vtr confesar.
confession [kən'feʃən] n confesión f.
confessional [kən'feʃənəl] n confesionario m.
confetti [kən'feti] n confeti m.
confide [kən'faid] vi to c. in sb, confiar en algn.
confidence ['kɒnfidəns] n 1 confianza f; **vote of c./no c.**, voto m de confianza/de censura; **c. trick**, camelo m. 2 (secret) confidencia f; **in c.**, en confianza.
confident ['kɒnfidənt] adj seguro,-a.
confidential [kɒnfi'denʃəl] adj (secret) confidencial; (entrusted) de confianza.
confine [kən'fain] vtr encerrar; fig limitar.
confinement [kən'fainmənt] n 1 (prison) prisión f; **to be in solitary c.**, estar incomunicado,-a. 2 Med parto m.
confirm [kən'fɜːm] vtr confirmar.
confirmation [kɒnfə'meiʃən] n confirmación f.
confirmed [kən'fɜːmd] adj empedernido,-a.
confiscate ['kɒnfiskeit] vtr confiscar.
conflict ['kɒnflikt] **I** n conflicto m. **II** [kən'flikt] vi chocar (with, con).
conflicting [kən'fliktiŋ] adj contradictorio,-a.
conform [kən'fɔːm] vi conformarse; **to c. to or with**, (customs) amoldarse a; (rules) someterse a.
confound [kən'faund] vtr confundir, desconcertar.
confront [kən'frʌnt] vtr hacer frente a.
confrontation [kɒnfrʌn'teiʃən] n confrontación f.
confuse [kən'fjuːz] vtr (person) despistar; (thing) confundir (with, con); **to get confused**, confundirse.
confused [kən'fjuːzd] adj (person) confundido,-a; (mind, ideas) confuso,-a.
confusing [kən'fjuːziŋ] adj confuso,-a.
confusion [kən'fjuːʒən] n confusión f.
congeal [kən'dʒiːl] vi coagularse.
congenial [kən'dʒiːniəl] adj agradable.
congenital [kən'dʒenitəl] adj congénito, -a.
congested [kən'dʒestid] adj 1 (street) repleto,-a de gente; (city) superpoblado, -a. 2 Med congestionado,-a.
congestion [kən'dʒestʃən] n congestión f.
conglomeration [kənglɒmə'reiʃən] n conglomeración f.
congratulate [kən'grætjuleit] vtr felicitar.
congratulations [kəngrætju'leiʃənz] npl

felicitaciones fpl; **c.!**, ¡enhorabuena!
congregate ['kɒngrigeit] vi congregarse.
congregation [kɒngri'geiʃən] n (group) congregación f; Rel fieles mpl.
congress ['kɒngres] n congreso m.
Congressman ['kɒngresmən] n congresista m.
conifer ['kɒnifər] n conífera f.
conjecture [kən'dʒektʃər] **I** n conjetura f. **II** vtr conjeturar. **III** vi hacer conjeturas.
conjugal ['kɒndʒugəl] adj conyugal.
conjugate ['kɒndʒugeit] vtr conjugar.
conjunction [kən'dʒʌŋkʃən] n conjunción f; fig **in c. with**, conjuntamente con.
conjunctivitis [kəndʒʌŋkti'vaitis] n conjuntivitis f.
conjure ['kʌndʒər] **I** vtr to c. (up), (magician) hacer aparecer; (memories) evocar. **II** vi hacer juegos de manos.
conjurer ['kʌndʒərər] n prestidigitador,-a m,f.
conker ['kɒŋkər] n fam castaña f.
connect [kə'nekt] **I** vtr (join) juntar, unir; (wires) empalmar; fig **to be connected by marriage**, estar emparentado,-a por matrimonio. 2 (instal) instalar; Elec conectar. 3 Tel (person) poner. 4 fig (associate) asociar. **II** vi unirse; (rooms) comunicarse; (train, flight) enlazar or empalmar (with, con).
connected [kə'nektid] adj unido,-a; (events) relacionado,-a; fig **to be well c.**, (person) fam tener enchufe.
connection [kə'nekʃən] n 1 (joint) juntura f, unión f; Elec conexión f; Tel instalación f. 2 Rail correspondencia f. 3 fig (of ideas) relación f; **in c. with**, (regarding) con respecto a. 4 (person) contacto m.
connive [kə'naiv] vi to c. at, hacer la vista gorda con.
connoisseur [kɒni'sɜːr] n conocedor,-a m,f.
connotation [kɒnə'teiʃən] n connotación f.
conquer ['kɒŋkər] vtr (enemy, bad habit) vencer; (country) conquistar.
conqueror ['kɒŋkərər] n conquistador m.
conquest ['kɒŋkwest] n conquista f.
conscience ['kɒnʃəns] n conciencia f; **to have a clear c.**, tener la conciencia tranquila; **to have a guilty c.**, sentirse culpable.
conscientious [kɒnʃi'enʃəs] adj concienzudo,-a; **c. objector**, objetor,-a m,f de conciencia.
conscious ['kɒnʃəs] adj (aware) consciente; (choice etc) deliberado,-a.
consciousness ['kɒnʃəsnis] n Med conocimiento m; (awareness) consciencia f.
conscript ['kɒnskript] n recluta m.
conscription [kən'skripʃən] n servicio m militar obligatorio.
consecrate ['kɒnsikreit] vtr consagrar.

consecutive [kən'sekjʊtɪv] *adj* consecutivo,-a.

consensus [kən'sensəs] *n* consenso *m*.

consent [kən'sent] **I** *n* consentimiento *m*; **by common c.**, de común acuerdo. **II** *vi* consentir (to, en).

consequence ['kɒnsɪkwəns] *n* consecuencia *f*.

consequent ['kɒnsɪkwənt] *adj* consiguiente. ◆**consequently** *adv* por consiguiente.

conservation [kɒnsə'veɪʃən] *n* conservación *f*.

conservative [kən'sɜːvətɪv] **I** *adj* cauteloso,-a. **II** *adj & n* Pol **C.**, conservador,-a (*m,f*).

conservatory [kən'sɜːvətrɪ] *n* 1 (*greenhouse*) invernadero *m*. 2 *Mus* conservatorio *m*.

conserve [kən'sɜːv] **I** *vtr* conservar. **II** ['kɒnsɜːv] *n* conserva *f*.

consider [kən'sɪdər] *vtr* 1 (*ponder on, regard*) considerar; **to c. doing sth,** pensar hacer algo. 2 (*keep in mind*) tener en cuenta.

considerable [kən'sɪdərəbəl] *adj* considerable. ◆**considerably** *adv* bastante.

considerate [kən'sɪdərɪt] *adj* considerado,-a.

consideration [kənsɪdə'reɪʃən] *n* consideración *f*; **without due c.,** sin reflexión.

considering [kən'sɪdərɪŋ] *prep* teniendo en cuenta.

consign [kən'saɪn] *vtr* Com consignar; *fig* entregar.

consignment [kən'saɪnmənt] *n* envío *m*.

consist [kən'sɪst] *vi* **to c. of,** consistir en.

consistency [kən'sɪstənsɪ] *n* 1 (*of actions*) consecuencia *f*. 2 (*of mixture*) consistencia *f*.

consistent [kən'sɪstənt] *adj* consecuente; **c. with,** de acuerdo con.

consolation [kɒnsə'leɪʃən] *n* consuelo *m*; **c. prize,** premio *m* de consolación.

console[1] [kən'səʊl] *vtr* consolar.

console[2] ['kɒnsəʊl] *n* consola *f*.

consolidate [kən'sɒlɪdeɪt] **I** *vtr* consolidar. **II** *vi* consolidarse.

consonant ['kɒnsənənt] *n* consonante *f*.

consortium [kən'sɔːtɪəm] *n* consorcio *m*.

conspicuous [kən'spɪkjʊəs] *adj* (*striking*) llamativo,-a; (*easily seen*) visible; (*mistake*) evidente.

conspiracy [kən'spɪrəsɪ] *n* conjura *f*.

conspire [kən'spaɪər] *vi* conspirar.

constable ['kʌnstəbəl] *n* policía *m*, guardia *m*; **chief c.,** jefe *m* de policía.

constabulary [kən'stæbjʊlərɪ] *n* GB comisaría *f*.

constant ['kɒnstənt] **I** *adj* constante; (*continuous*) incesante; (*loyal*) fiel, leal. **II** *n* constante *f*.

constellation [kɒnstɪ'leɪʃən] *n* constelación *f*.

consternation [kɒnstə'neɪʃən] *n* consternación *f*.

constipated ['kɒnstɪpeɪtɪd] *adj* **to be c.,** estar estreñido,-a.

constipation [kɒnstɪ'peɪʃən] *n* estreñimiento *m*.

constituency [kən'stɪtjʊənsɪ] *n* circunscripción *f* electoral.

constituent [kən'stɪtjʊənt] **I** *adj* (*component*) constituyente. **II** *n* 1 (*part*) componente *m*. 2 *Pol* votante *mf*.

constitute ['kɒnstɪtjuːt] *vtr* constituir.

constitution [kɒnstɪ'tjuːʃən] *n* constitución *f*.

constitutional [kɒnstɪ'tjuːʃənəl] *adj* constitucional.

constrained [kən'streɪnd] *adj* **to feel c. to do sth,** sentirse obligado,-a a hacer algo.

constraint [kən'streɪnt] *n* coacción *f*; **to feel c. in sb's presence,** sentirse cohibido,-a ante algn.

construct [kən'strʌkt] *vtr* construir.

construction [kən'strʌkʃən] *n* construcción *f*.

constructive [kən'strʌktɪv] *adj* constructivo,-a.

construe [kən'struː] *vtr* interpretar.

consul ['kɒnsəl] *n* cónsul *mf*.

consulate ['kɒnsjʊlɪt] *n* consulado *m*.

consult [kən'sʌlt] *vtr & vi* consultar (about, sobre).

consultant [kən'sʌltənt] *n* Med especialista *mf*; Com Ind asesor,-a *m,f*.

consultation [kɒnsəl'teɪʃən] *n* consulta *f*.

consulting [kən'sʌltɪŋ] *adj* **c. room,** consulta *f*.

consume [kən'sjuːm] *vtr* consumir.

consumer [kən'sjuːmər] *n* consumidor,-a *m,f*; **c. goods,** bienes *mpl* de consumo.

consummate I ['kɒnsəmeɪt] *vtr* consumar. II ['kɒnsəmɪt] *adj* consumado,-a.

consumption [kən'sʌmpʃən] *n* 1 (*of food*) consumo *m*; **fit for c.,** apto,-a para el consumo. 2 *Med* tisis *f*.

cont. *abbr of* **continued,** sigue.

contact ['kɒntækt] **I** *n* contacto *m*; **c. lenses,** lentes *fpl* de contacto. **II** *vtr* ponerse en contacto con.

contagious [kən'teɪdʒəs] *adj* contagioso,-a.

contain [kən'teɪn] *vtr* contener; **to c. oneself,** contenerse.

container [kən'teɪnər] *n* 1 (*box, package*) recipiente *m*; (*bottle*) envase *m*. 2 *Naut* contenedor *m*.

contaminate [kən'tæmɪneɪt] *vtr* contaminar.

contamination [kəntæmɪ'neɪʃən] *n* contaminación *f*.

contd. *abbr of* **continued,** sigue.

contemplate ['kɒntempleɪt] *vtr* 1 (*consider*) considerar, pensar en. 2 (*look at*) contemplar.

contemporary [kənˈtempərəri] *adj & n* contemporáneo,-a (*m,f*).

contempt [kənˈtempt] *n* desprecio *m*; **to hold in c.**, despreciar; **c. of court**, desacato *m* a los tribunales.

contemptible [kənˈtemptəbəl] *adj* despreciable.

contemptuous [kənˈtemptjuəs] *adj* despectivo,-a.

contend [kənˈtend] **I** *vi* competir; *fig* **there are many problems to c. with**, se han planteado muchos problemas. **II** *vtr* afirmar.

contender [kənˈtendər] *n* contendiente *mf*.

content¹ [ˈkɒntent] *n* contenido *m*; **table of contents**, índice *m* de materias.

content² [kənˈtent] **I** *adj* contento,-a. **II** *vtr* contentar. **III** *n* contento *m*; **to one's heart's c.**, todo lo que uno quiera.

contented [kənˈtentid] *adj* contento,-a, satisfecho,-a.

contention [kənˈtenʃən] *n* 1 (*dispute*) controversia *f*. 2 (*point*) punto *m* de vista.

contentment [kənˈtentmənt] *n* contento *m*.

contest [ˈkɒntest] **I** *n* concurso *m*; *Sport* prueba *f*. **II** [kənˈtest] *vtr* 1 (*matter*) rebatir; (*verdict*) impugnar; *fig* (*will*) disputar. 2 *Pol* (*seat*) luchar por.

contestant [kənˈtestənt] *n* concursante *mf*.

context [ˈkɒntekst] *n* contexto *m*.

continent [ˈkɒntinənt] *n* continente *m*; **(on) the C.**, (en) Europa.

continental [kɒntiˈnentəl] *adj* 1 continental; **c. shelf**, plataforma *m* continental. 2 *GB* **C.**, europeo,-a; **c. quilt**, edredón *m* de pluma.

contingency [kənˈtindʒənsi] *n* contingencia *f*; **c. plans**, planes *mpl* para casos de emergencia.

contingent [kənˈtindʒənt] *adj & n* contingente (*m*).

continual [kənˈtinjuəl] *adj* continuo,-a, constante.

continuation [kəntinjuˈeiʃən] *n* (*sequel etc*) continuación *f*; (*extension*) prolongación *f*.

continue [kənˈtinju:] *vtr & vi* continuar, seguir; **to c. to do sth**, seguir *or* continuar haciendo algo.

continuous [kənˈtinjuəs] *adj* continuo,-a.

contort [kənˈtɔ:t] *vtr* retorcer.

contortion [kənˈtɔ:ʃən] *n* contorsión *f*.

contour [ˈkɒntuər] *n* contorno *m*; **c. line**, línea *f* de nivel.

contraband [ˈkɒntrəbænd] *n* contrabando *m*.

contraception [kɒntrəˈsepʃən] *n* anticoncepción *f*.

contraceptive [kɒntrəˈseptiv] *adj & n* anticonceptivo (*m,f*).

contract [kənˈtrækt] **I** *vi* *Phys* contraerse.

II *vtr* 1 contraer. **2 to c. to do sth**, (*make agreement*) comprometerse por contrato a hacer algo. **III** [ˈkɒntrækt] *n* contrato *m*; **to enter into a c.**, hacer un contrato.

contraction [kənˈtrækʃən] *n* contracción *f*.

contractor [kənˈtræktər] *n* contratista *mf*.

contradict [kɒntrəˈdikt] *vtr* contradecir.

contradiction [kɒntrəˈdikʃən] *n* contradicción *f*; **it's a c. in terms**, no tiene lógica.

contradictory [kɒntrəˈdiktəri] *adj* contradictorio,-a.

contraption [kənˈtræpʃən] *n* *fam* cacharro *m*.

contrary [ˈkɒntrəri] **I** *adj* 1 contrario,-a. 2 [kənˈtreəri] terco,-a. **II** *n* **on the c.**, todo lo contrario; **unless I tell you to the c.**, a menos que te diga lo contrario. **III** *adv* **c. to**, en contra de.

contrast [kənˈtrɑ:st] **I** *vi* contrastar. **II** [ˈkɒntrɑ:st] *n* contraste *m*.

contrasting [kənˈtrɑ:stiŋ] *adj* opuesto,-a.

contravene [kɒntrəˈvi:n] *vtr* contravenir.

contribute [kənˈtribju:t] **I** *vtr* (*money*) contribuir con; (*ideas, information*) aportar. **II** *vi* 1 contribuir; (*in discussion*) participar. 2 *Press* colaborar (**to**, en).

contribution [kɒntriˈbju:ʃən] *n* 1 (*of money*) contribución *f*; (*of ideas etc*) aportación *f*. 2 *Press* colaboración *f*.

contributor [kənˈtribjutər] *n* (*to newspaper*) colaborador,-a *mf*.

contrive [kənˈtraiv] *vtr* inventar, idear; **to c. to do sth**, buscar la forma de hacer algo.

contrived [kənˈtraivd] *adj* artificial, forzado,-a.

control [kənˈtrəʊl] **I** *vtr* controlar; (*person, animal*) dominar; (*vehicle*) manejar; **to c. one's temper**, controlarse. **II** *n* 1 (*power*) control *m*, dominio *m*; (*authority*) autoridad *f*; **out of c.**, fuera de control; **to be in c.**, estar al mando; **to be under c.**, (*situation*) estar bajo control; **to go out of c.**, descontrolarse; **to lose c.**, perder los estribos. 2 *Aut Av* (*device*) mando *m*; *Rad TV* botón *m* de control; **c. panel**, tablero *m* de instrumentos; **c. room**, sala *f* de control; *Av* **c. tower**, torre *f* de control.

controversial [kɒntrəˈvɜ:ʃəl] *adj* controvertido,-a, polémico,-a.

controversy [ˈkɒntrəvɜ:si, kənˈtrɒvəsi] *n* polémica *f*.

conurbation [kɒnɜːˈbeiʃən] *n* conurbación *f*.

convalesce [kɒnvəˈles] *vi* convalecer.

convalescence [kɒnvəˈlesəns] *n* convalecencia *f*.

convalescent [kɒnvəˈlesənt] *adj* convaleciente; **c. home**, clínica *f* de reposo.

convene [kənˈvi:n] **I** *vtr* convocar. **II** *vi* reunirse.

convenience [kənˈvi:niəns] *n* conveniencia f, comodidad f; **all modern conveniences,** todas las comodidades; **at your c.,** cuando le convenga; **c. food,** comida precocinada; *GB euph* **public conveniences,** aseos públicos.

convenient [kənˈviːnɪənt] *adj* (*time, arrangement*) conveniente, oportuno,-a; (*place*) bien situado,-a.

convent [ˈkɒnvənt] *n* convento *m*.

convention [kənˈvenʃən] *n* convención *f*.

conventional [kənˈvenʃənəl] *adj* clásico,-a; (*behaviour*) convencional.

converge [kənˈvɜːdʒ] *vi* converger.

conversant [kənˈvɜːsənt] *adj fml* **to be c. with a subject,** ser versado,-a en una materia.

conversation [kɒnvəˈseɪʃən] *n* conversación *f*.

conversational [kɒnvəˈseɪʃənəl] *adj* coloquial.

converse¹ [kənˈvɜːs] *vi* conversar.

converse² [ˈkɒnvɜːs] *n* **the c.,** lo opuesto. ◆**conversely** *adv* a la inversa.

conversion [kənˈvɜːʃən] *n* Math Rel conversión *f* (**to,** a; **into,** en).

convert [kənˈvɜːt] I *vtr* convertir. II [ˈkɒnvɜːt] *n* converso,-a *m,f*.

convertible [kənˈvɜːtəbəl] I *adj* convertible. II *n* Aut descapotable *m*.

convex [ˈkɒnveks, kɒnˈveks] *adj* convexo,-a.

convey [kənˈveɪ] *vtr* 1 (*carry*) transportar. 2 (*sound*) transmitir; (*idea*) comunicar.

conveyor [kənˈveɪər] *n* **c. belt,** cinta transportadora.

convict [kənˈvɪkt] I *vtr* declarar culpable a, condenar. II [ˈkɒnvɪkt] *n* presidiario,-a *m,f*.

conviction [kənˈvɪkʃən] *n* 1 (*belief*) creencia *f*, convicción *f*. 2 *Jur* condena *f*.

convince [kənˈvɪns] *vtr* convencer.

convincing [kənˈvɪnsɪŋ] *adj* convincente.

convoluted [ˈkɒnvəluːtɪd] *adj* intrincado,-a.

convoy [ˈkɒnvɔɪ] *n* convoy *m*.

convulse [kənˈvʌls] *vtr* convulsionar; *fam* **to be convulsed with laughter,** troncharse de risa.

convulsion [kənˈvʌlʃən] *n* convulsión *f*.

coo [kuː] *vi* (*pigeon*) arrullar.

cook [kʊk] I *vtr* cocinar, guisar; (*dinner*) preparar; *sl* **to c. the books,** falsificar las cuentas. II *vi* (*person*) cocinar, guisar; (*food*) cocerse. III *n* cocinero,-a *m,f*.

cookbook [ˈkʊkbʊk] *n US* libro *m* de cocina.

cooker [ˈkʊkər] *n* cocina *f*.

cookery [ˈkʊkərɪ] *n* cocina *f*; **c. book,** libro *m* de cocina.

cookie [ˈkʊkɪ] *n US* galleta *f*.

cooking [ˈkʊkɪŋ] *n* cocina *f*.

cool [kuːl] I *adj* 1 fresco,-a; **it's c.,** (*weather*) hace fresquito. 2 *fig* (*calm*) tranquilo,-a; (*reserved*) frío,-a. II *n* 1

(*coolness*) fresco *m*. 2 *sl* **to lose one's c.,** perder la calma. III *vtr* (*air*) refrescar; (*drink*) enfriar. IV *adv fam* **to play it c.,** hacer como si nada. ◆**cool down, cool off** *vi fig* calmarse; (*feelings*) enfriarse.

coolness [ˈkuːlnɪs] *n* 1 *fig* (*calmness*) calma *f*; (*composure*) aplomo *m*. 2 *fam* (*nerve, cheek*) frescura *f*.

coop [kuːp] I *n* gallinero *m*. II *vtr* **to c. (up),** encerrar.

co-operate [kəʊˈɒpəreɪt] *vi* cooperar.

co-operation [kəʊɒpəˈreɪʃən] *n* cooperación *f*.

co-operative [kəʊˈɒpərətɪv] I *adj* (*helpful*) cooperador,-a. II *n* cooperativa *f*.

co-ordinate [kəʊˈɔːdɪneɪt] I *vtr* coordinar. II [kəʊˈɔːdɪnɪt] *n* Math coordenada *f*. 2 **co-ordinates,** (*clothes*) conjunto *m sing*.

co-ordination [kəʊɔːdɪˈneɪʃən] *n* coordinación *f*.

cop [kɒp] *sl* I *n* (*policeman*) poli *m*. II *vtr* **you'll c. it,** te vas a ganar una buena. ◆**cop out** *vi* rajarse.

cope [kəʊp] *vi* arreglárselas; **to c. with,** (*person, work*) poder con; (*problem*) hacer frente a.

Copenhagen [kəʊpənˈheɪgən] *n* Copenhague.

copious [ˈkəʊpɪəs] *adj* copioso,-a, abundante.

copper¹ [ˈkɒpər] I *n* Min cobre *m*. II *adj* (*colour*) cobrizo,-a.

copper² [ˈkɒpər] *n sl* poli *mf*.

coppice [ˈkɒpɪs], **copse** [kɒps] *n* arboleda *f*, bosquecillo *m*.

copulate [ˈkɒpjʊleɪt] *vi* copular.

copy [ˈkɒpɪ] I *n* 1 copia *f*. 2 (*of book*) ejemplar *m*. 3 *Print* manuscrito *m*. 4 *Press fam* asunto *m*. II *vtr & vi* copiar.

copycat [ˈkɒpɪkæt] *n fam* copión,-ona *m,f*.

copyright [ˈkɒpɪraɪt] *n* derechos *mpl* de autor.

coral [ˈkɒrəl] *n* coral *m*; **c. reef,** arrecife *m* de coral.

cord [kɔːd] *n* 1 (*string*) cuerda *f*; *Elec* cordón *m*. 2 *Tex* (*corduroy*) pana *f*; **cords,** pantalones *mpl* de pana.

cordial [ˈkɔːdɪəl] I *adj* cordial. II *n* licor *m*.

cordon [ˈkɔːdən] I *n* cordón *m*. II *vtr* **to c. off a street,** acordonar una calle.

corduroy [ˈkɔːdərɔɪ] *n* pana *f*.

core [kɔːr] I *n* (*of fruit*) corazón *m*; *Elec* núcleo *m*; *fig* **hard c.,** los incondicionales. II *vtr* quitarle el corazón a.

coriander [kɒrɪˈændər] *n* culantro *m*.

cork [kɔːk] *n* corcho *m*; **c. oak,** alcornoque *m*.

corkscrew [ˈkɔːkskruː] *n* sacacorchos *m inv*.

corn¹ [kɔːn] *n* cereal *m*; (*grain*) granos *mpl*; (*maize*) maíz *m*; **c. on the cob,** ma-

zorca f de maíz.
corn² [kɔːn] n Med callo m.
cornea ['kɔːnɪə] n córnea f.
corner ['kɔːnər] I n 1 (of street) esquina f; (bend in road) curva f; **round the c.**, a la vuelta de la esquina; Ftb **c. kick**, córner m; **c. shop**, tienda pequeña de barrio. 2 (of room) rincón m. II vtr 1 (enemy) arrinconar. 2 Com acaparar. III vi Aut tomar una curva.
cornerstone ['kɔːnəstəʊn] n piedra f angular.
cornet ['kɔːnɪt] n 1 Mus corneta f. 2 GB (for ice cream) cucurucho m.
cornflakes ['kɔːnfleɪks] npl copos mpl de maíz, cornflakes mpl.
cornflour ['kɔːnflaʊər] n harina f de maíz.
cornstarch ['kɔːnstɑːtʃ] n US → cornflour.
Cornwall ['kɔːnwəl] n Cornualles.
corny ['kɔːnɪ] adj (cornier, corniest) fam gastado,-a.
corollary [kə'rɒlərɪ] n corolario m.
coronary ['kɒrənərɪ] adj coronario,-a; **c. thrombosis**, trombosis coronaria.
coronation [kɒrə'neɪʃən] n coronación f.
coroner ['kɒrənər] n juez mf de instrucción.
corporal¹ ['kɔːpərəl] adj corporal; **c. punishment**, castigo m corporal.
corporal² ['kɔːpərəl] n Mil cabo m.
corporate ['kɔːpərɪt] adj corporativo,-a.
corporation [kɔːpə'reɪʃən] n 1 (business) sociedad anónima. 2 (of city) ayuntamiento m.
corps [kɔː] n (pl corps [kɔːz]) cuerpo m.
corpse [kɔːps] n cadáver m.
corpulent ['kɔːpjʊlənt] adj corpulento,-a.
corpuscle ['kɔːpʌsəl] n corpúsculo m.
corral [kə'rɑːl] n US corral m.
correct [kə'rekt] I vtr 1 (mistake) corregir. 2 (child) reprender. II adj correcto,-a, exacto,-a; (behaviour) formal.
correction [kə'rekʃən] n corrección f.
correlation [kɒrɪ'leɪʃən] n correlación f.
correspond [kɒrɪ'spɒnd] vi 1 corresponder; **to c. to**, equivaler a. 2 (by letter) escribirse.
correspondence [kɒrɪ'spɒndəns] n correspondencia f; **c. course**, curso m por correspondencia.
correspondent [kɒrɪ'spɒndənt] n Press corresponsal mf; **special c.**, enviado,-a m,f especial.
corridor ['kɒrɪdɔːr] n pasillo m.
corroborate [kə'rɒbəreɪt] vtr corroborar.
corrode [kə'rəʊd] I vtr corroer. II vi corroerse.
corrosion [kə'rəʊʒən] n corrosión f.
corrugated ['kɒrʊgeɪtɪd] adj **c. iron**, hierro ondulado.
corrupt [kə'rʌpt] I adj (person) corrompido,-a, corrupto,-a; (actions) deshonesto,-a. II vtr & vi corromper.

corruption [kə'rʌpʃən] n corrupción f.
corset ['kɔːsɪt] n (garment) faja f.
Corsica ['kɔːsɪkə] n Córcega.
cortège [kɔː'teɪʒ] n cortejo m, comitiva f.
cosh [kɒʃ] n GB porra f.
cosmetic [kɒz'metɪk] I n cosmético m. II adj cosmético,-a; **c. surgery**, cirugía plástica.
cosmic ['kɒzmɪk] adj cósmico,-a.
cosmonaut ['kɒzmənɔːt] n cosmonauta mf.
cosmopolitan [kɒzmə'pɒlɪtən] adj cosmopolita.
cosset ['kɒsɪt] vtr mimar.
cost [kɒst] I n (price) precio m, coste m; **c. of living**, coste de la vida; **to count the c.**, considerar las consecuencias; **at all costs**, a toda costa. II vtr & vi (pt & pp cost) costar, valer; **how much does it c.?**, ¿cuánto cuesta?; **whatever it costs**, cueste lo que cueste. III vtr (pt & pp costed) Com find calcular el coste de.
co-star ['kəʊstɑːr] n Cin Theat coprotagonista mf.
Costa Rica [kɒstə'riːkə] n Costa Rica.
Costa Rican [kɒstə'riːkən] adj & n costarricense (mf).
cost-effective [kɒstɪ'fektɪv] adj rentable.
costly ['kɒstlɪ] adj (costlier, costliest) costoso,-a.
costume ['kɒstjuːm] n traje m; **swimming c.**, bañador m; **c. jewellery**, bisutería f.
cosy ['kəʊzɪ] adj (cosier, cosiest) (atmosphere) acogedor,-a; (bed) calentito,-a; **it's c. in here**, aquí se está bien.
cot [kɒt] n cuna f.
cottage ['kɒtɪdʒ] n casa f de campo; **c. cheese**, requesón m; **c. industry**, industria casera; GB **c. pie**, pastel m de carne picada con puré de patatas.
cotton ['kɒtən] n 1 Bot algodonero m; Tex algodón m; **c. wool**, algodón hidrófilo. 2 (thread) hilo m. ◆**cotton on** vi fam **to c. on to sth**, caer en la cuenta de algo.
couch [kaʊtʃ] n sofá m; (in surgery) camilla f.
couchette [kuː'ʃet] n Rail litera f.
cough [kɒf] I vi toser. II n tos f; **c. drop**, pastilla f para la tos; **c. mixture**, jarabe m para la tos. ◆**cough up** vtr fam **to c. up the money**, soltar la pasta.
could [kʊd] v aux → **can¹**.
council ['kaʊnsəl] n (body) consejo m; GB **c. house**, vivienda f de protección oficial; **town c.**, consejo m municipal, ayuntamiento m.
councillor, US **councilor** ['kaʊnsələr] n concejal mf.
counsel ['kaʊnsəl] I n 1 (advice) consejo m. 2 Jur abogado,-a m,f. II vtr aconsejar.
counsellor, US **counselor** ['kaʊnsələr] n 1 (adviser) asesor,-a m,f. 2 US Jur abogado,-a m,f.

count¹ [kaʊnt] I *vtr* 1 contar. 2 *fig* to c. oneself lucky, considerarse afortunado, -a. II *vi* contar; **that doesn't c.**, eso no vale; **to c. ten**, contar hasta diez. III *n* 1 cuenta *f*; (*total*) recuento *m*. 2 *Jur* cargo *m*. ◆**count on** *vtr* contar con.

count² [kaʊnt] *n* (*nobleman*) conde *m*.

countdown ['kaʊntdaʊn] *n* cuenta *f* atrás.

countenance ['kaʊntɪnəns] I *n* semblante *m*, rostro *m*. II *vtr* aprobar.

counter¹ ['kaʊntəʳ] *n* 1 (*in shop*) mostrador *m*; (*in bank*) ventanilla *f*. 2 (*in board games*) ficha *f*.

counter² ['kaʊntəʳ] *n* contador *m*.

counter³ ['kaʊntəʳ] I *adv* c. to, en contra de. II *vtr* (*attack*) contestar a; (*trend*) contrarrestar. III *vi* contestar.

counteract [kaʊntər'ækt] *vtr* contrarrestar.

counterattack ['kaʊntərətæk] *n* contraataque *m*.

counterfeit ['kaʊntəfɪt] I *adj* falsificado, -a; **c. coin**, moneda falsa. II *n* falsificación *f*. III *vtr* falsificar.

counterfoil ['kaʊntəfɔɪl] *n* GB (*of cheque*) matriz *f*.

countermand [kaʊntə'mɑːnd] *vtr* (*command*) revocar; *Com* (*order*) anular.

counterpart ['kaʊntəpɑːt] *n* homólogo,-a *m,f*.

counterproductive [kaʊntəprə'dʌktɪv] *adj* contraproducente.

countersign ['kaʊntəsaɪn] *vtr* refrendar.

countess ['kaʊntɪs] *n* condesa *f*.

countless ['kaʊntlɪs] *adj* innumerable, incontable.

country ['kʌntrɪ] *n* 1 (*state*) país *m*; **native c.**, patria *f*. 2 (*rural area*) campo *m*; **c. dancing**, baile *m* popular.

countryman ['kʌntrɪmən] *n* 1 (*rural*) hombre *m* del campo. 2 (*compatriot*) compatriota *m*.

countryside ['kʌntrɪsaɪd] *n* (*area*) campo *m*; (*scenery*) paisaje *m*.

county ['kaʊntɪ] *n* condado *m*.

coup [kuː] *n* golpe *m*; **c. d'état**, golpe de estado.

couple ['kʌpəl] I *n* 1 (*of people*) pareja *f*; **a married c.**, un matrimonio. 2 (*of things*) par *m*; **fam a c. of times**, un par de veces. II *vtr* (*wagons*) enganchar.

coupling ['kʌplɪŋ] *n* Rail enganche *m*.

coupon ['kuːpɒn] *n* 1 cupón *m*. 2 GB Ftb quiniela *f*.

courage ['kʌrɪdʒ] *n* coraje *m*, valentía *f*.

courageous [kə'reɪdʒəs] *adj* valeroso,-a, valiente.

courgette [kʊə'ʒet] *n* calabacín *m*.

courier ['kʊərɪəʳ] *n* 1 (*messenger*) mensajero,-a *m,f*. 2 (*guide*) guía *mf* turístico,-a.

course [kɔːs] *n* 1 (*of river*) curso *m*; *Naut Av* rumbo *m*. 2 *fig* desarrollo *m*; **in the c.**

of construction, en vías de construcción; **in the c. of time**, con el tiempo. 3 (*series*) ciclo *m*; **a c. of treatment**, un tratamiento. 4 *Educ* curso *m*; *Univ* asignatura *f*. 5 (*for golf*) campo *m*; (*for horse-racing*) hipódromo *m*. 6 *Culin* plato *m*. 7 **of c.**, claro, por supuesto; **of c. not!**, ¡claro que no!.

court [kɔːt] I *n* 1 *Jur* tribunal *m*; **c. martial**, consejo *m* de guerra; **c. order**, orden *f* judicial. 2 (*royal*) corte *f*. 3 *Sport* pista *f*, cancha *f*. II *vtr* (*woman*) hacer la corte a; *fig* to c. **danger**, buscar el peligro; *fig* to c. **disaster**, exponerse al desastre. III *vi* (*couple*) tener relaciones.

courteous ['kɜːtɪəs] *adj* cortés.

courtesy ['kɜːtɪsɪ] *n* 1 cortesía *f*, educación *f*. 2 **by c. of**, por cortesía de.

courthouse ['kɔːthaʊs] *n* palacio *m* de justicia.

courtier ['kɔːtɪəʳ] *n* cortesano,-a *m,f*.

court-martial ['kɔːtmɑːʃəl] *vtr* someter a consejo de guerra.

courtroom ['kɔːtruːm] *n* sala *f* de justicia.

courtyard ['kɔːtjɑːd] *n* patio *m*.

cousin ['kʌzən] *n* primo,-a *m,f*; **first c.**, primo,-a hermano,-a.

cove [kəʊv] *n* cala *f*, ensenada *f*.

covenant ['kʌvənənt] *n* convenio *m*, pacto *m*.

cover ['kʌvəʳ] I *vtr* 1 cubrir (**with**, de); (*furniture*) revestir (**with**, de); (*with lid*) tapar. 2 (*hide*) disimular. 3 (*protect*) abrigar. 4 (*distance*) recorrer. 5 *Journ* investigar. 6 (*deal with*) abarcar. 7 (*include*) incluir. 8 *Sport* marcar. II *vi* to c. **for sb**, sustituir a algn. III *n* 1 cubierta *f*; (*lid*) tapa *f*; (*on bed*) manta *f*; (*of chair etc*) funda *f*. 2 (*of book*) tapa *f*; (*of magazine*) portada *f*; **c. girl**, modelo *f* de revista. 3 (*in restaurant*) cubierto *m*. 4 **under separate c.**, por separado. 5 *Ins* **full c.**, cobertura completa; *GB* **c. note**, seguro *m* provisional. 6 (*protection*) abrigo *m*; **to take c.**, abrigarse; **under c.**, al abrigo; (*indoors*) bajo techo. ◆**cover up** I *vtr* 1 cubrir. 2 (*crime*) encubrir. II *vi* 1 (*person*) abrigarse. 2 **to c. up for sb**, encubrir a algn.

coverage ['kʌvərɪdʒ] *n* cobertura *f*.

coveralls ['kʌvərɔːlz] *npl* US mono *m sing*.

covering ['kʌvərɪŋ] I *n* cubierta *f*, envoltura *f*. II *adj* (*letter*) explicatorio,-a.

covert ['kʌvət] *adj* disimulado,-a, secreto,-a.

cover-up ['kʌvərʌp] *n* encubrimiento *m*.

covet ['kʌvɪt] *vtr* codiciar.

cow¹ [kaʊ] *n* vaca *f*; *pej* (*woman*) arpía *f*, bruja *f*.

cow² [kaʊ] *vtr* intimidar.

coward ['kaʊəd] *n* cobarde *mf*.

cowardice ['kaʊədɪs] *n* cobardía *f*.

cowardly ['kauədlɪ] adj cobarde.

cowboy ['kaubɔɪ] n vaquero m.

cower ['kauə'] vi (with fear) encogerse.

cox [kɒks] n timonel m.

coy [kɔɪ] adj (shy) tímido,-a; (demure) coquetón,-ona.

cozy ['kəuzɪ] adj US → **cosy**.

crab [kræb] n 1 cangrejo m. 2 **c. apple**, manzana f silvestre.

crack [kræk] I vtr 1 (cup) partir; (bone) fracturar; (nut) cascar; (safe) forzar. 2 (whip) hacer restallar. 3 fig (problem) dar con la solución de; (joke) contar. II vi 1 (glass) partirse; (wall) agrietarse. 2 (whip) restallar. 3 **fam to get cracking on sth**, ponerse a hacer algo. III n 1 (in cup) raja f; (in wall, ground) grieta f. 2 (of whip) restallido m; (of gun) detonación f. 3 fam (blow) golpetazo m. 4 **fam to have a c. at sth**, (attempt) intentar hacer algo. 5 sl (wisecrack) réplica aguda. 6 sl (drug) crack m. IV adj sl de primera. ◆**crack down on** vtr atajar con mano dura. ◆**crack up** vi fam fig (go mad) desquiciarse; (with laughter) partirse de risa.

cracker ['krækə'] n 1 (biscuit) galleta salada. 2 (firework) petardo m.

crackle ['krækəl] vi crujir; (fire) crepitar.

cradle ['kreɪdəl] n (baby's) cuna f.

craft [krɑːft] n 1 (occupation) oficio m; (art) arte m; (skill) destreza f. 2 (cunning) maña f. 3 Naut embarcación f.

craftsman ['krɑːftsmən] n artesano m.

craftsmanship ['krɑːftsmənʃɪp] n arte f.

crafty ['krɑːftɪ] adj (craftier, craftiest) astuto,-a.

crag [kræg] n peña f, peñasco m.

cram [kræm] I vtr atiborrar; **crammed with**, atestado,-a, de. II vi Educ fam empollar.

cramp¹ [kræmp] n Med calambre m; **cramps**, retortijones mpl.

cramp² [kræmp] vtr (development etc) poner trabas a.

cramped [kræmpt] adj atestado,-a; (writing) apretado,-a.

cranberry ['krænbərɪ] n arándano m.

crane [kreɪn] n 1 Zool grulla f común. 2 (device) grúa f. II vtr estirar.

crank [kræŋk] n 1 Tech manivela f. 2 fam (eccentric) tío raro.

crankshaft ['kræŋkʃɑːft] n árbol m del cigüeñal.

cranny ['krænɪ] n fig **in every nook and c.**, en todos los rincones.

crap [kræp] n fam mierda f.

crash [kræʃ] I vtr **to c. one's car**, tener un accidente con el coche. II vi 1 (car, plane) estrellarse; (collide) chocar; **to c. into**, estrellarse contra. 2 Com quebrar. III n 1 (noise) estrépito m. 2 (collision) choque m; **car/plane c.**, accidente m de coche/avión; **c. course**, curso intensivo; **c. helmet**, casco m protector. 3 Com

quiebra f.

crash-land [kræʃ'lænd] vi hacer un aterrizaje forzoso.

crass [kræs] adj (person) grosero,-a; (error) garrafal.

crate [kreɪt] n caja f, cajón m (para embalaje).

crater ['kreɪtə'] n cráter m.

cravat [krə'væt] n pañuelo m (de hombre).

crave [kreɪv] vi **to c. for sth**, ansiar algo.

craving ['kreɪvɪŋ] n ansia f; (in pregnancy) antojo m.

crawfish ['krɔːfɪʃ] n langosta f.

crawl [krɔːl] I vi (baby) gatear; (vehicle) avanzar lentamente; fig **to c. to sb**, arrastrarse a los pies de algn. II n (swimming) crol m.

crayfish ['kreɪfɪʃ] n cangrejo m de río.

crayon ['kreɪɒn] n cera f.

craze [kreɪz] n manía f; (fashion) moda f; **it's the latest c.**, es el último grito.

crazy ['kreɪzɪ] adj (crazier, craziest) fam loco,-a, chalado,-a; GB **c. paving**, pavimento m en mosaico.

creak [kriːk] vi (floor) crujir; (hinge) chirriar.

cream [kriːm] I n 1 (of milk) nata f; **c. coloured**, color crema; fig **the c.**, la flor y nata; **c. cheese**, queso m crema. 2 (cosmetic) crema f. II vtr 1 (milk) desnatar. 2 Culin batir; **creamed potatoes**, puré m de patatas.

creamy ['kriːmɪ] adj (creamier, creamiest) cremoso,-a.

crease [kriːs] I n (wrinkle) arruga f; (fold) pliegue m; (on trousers) raya f. II vtr (clothes) arrugar. III vi arrugarse.

create [kriː'eɪt] vtr crear.

creation [kriː'eɪʃən] n creación f.

creative [kriː'eɪtɪv] adj (person) creativo,-a.

creativity [kriːeɪ'tɪvɪtɪ] n creatividad f.

creator [kriː'eɪtə'] n creador,-a m,f.

creature ['kriːtʃə'] n (animal) criatura f.

crèche [kreʃ] n guardería f.

credence ['kriːdəns] n **to give c. to**, dar crédito a.

credentials [krɪ'denʃəlz] npl credenciales fpl.

credible ['kredɪbəl] adj creíble.

credit ['kredɪt] I n 1 Com crédito m; **on c.**, a crédito; **c. card**, tarjeta f de crédito. 2 **to give c. to sb for sth**, reconocer algo a algn. 3 (benefit) honor m; **to be a c. to**, hacer honor a. 4 Cin TV **credits**, créditos mpl. II vtr 1 Com abonar. 2 (believe) creer. 3 fig atribuir; **he is credited with having ...**, se le atribuye haber ....

creditor ['kredɪtə'] n acreedor,-a m,f.

creed [kriːd] n credo m.

creek [kriːk] n 1 GB cala f. 2 US Austral riachuelo m.

creep [kriːp] I vi (pt & pp **crept**) andar si-

lenciosamente; (*insect*) arrastrarse; (*plant*) trepar; **to c. up on sb**, sorprender a algn. II *n fam* (*person*) pelotillero,-a *m,f*.
creeper ['kri:pə^r] *n Bot* trepadora *f*.
creepy ['kri:pɪ] *adj* (**creepier, creepiest**) *fam* espeluznante.
cremate [krɪ'meɪt] *vtr* incinerar.
crematorium [kremə'tɔ:rɪəm] *n* crematorio *m*.
crepe [kreɪp] *n* **1** *Tex* crepé *m*. **2 c. paper**, papel *m* crespón.
crept [krept] *pt & pp* → **creep**.
crescendo [krɪ'ʃendəʊ] *n* crescendo *m*.
crescent ['kresənt] **I** *n* (*shape*) medialuna *f*; *GB* (*street*) calle *f* en medialuna. **II** *adj* creciente.
cress [kres] *n* berro *m*.
crest [krest] *n* **1** (*of cock, wave*) cresta *f*; (*on helmet*) penacho *m*; (*of hill*) cima *f*. **2** (*heraldic*) blasón *m*.
crestfallen ['krestfɔ:lən] *adj* abatido,-a.
Crete [kri:t] *n* Creta.
cretin ['kretɪn] *n* cretino,-a *m,f*.
crevasse [krɪ'væs] *n* grieta *f*, fisura *f*.
crevice ['krevɪs] *n* grieta *f*, hendedura *f*.
crew [kru:] *n Av Naut* tripulación *f*; **c. cut**, corte *m* al rape; **c.-neck sweater**, jersey *m* con cuello redondo.
crib [krɪb] **I** *n* (*manger*) pesebre *m*; (*for baby*) cuna *f*. **II** *vtr fam* **1** (*copy*) copiar. **2** (*steal*) quitar.
crick [krɪk] *n fam* **a c. in the neck**, una tortícolis.
cricket¹ ['krɪkɪt] *n Ent* grillo *m*.
cricket² ['krɪkɪt] *n Sport* cricket *m*.
crime [kraɪm] *n* delincuencia *f*; (*offence*) delito *m*.
criminal ['krɪmɪnəl] *adj & n* criminal (*mf*); **c. law**, derecho *m* penal; **c. record**, antecedentes *mpl* penales.
crimson ['krɪmzən] *adj & n* carmesí (*m*).
cringe [krɪndʒ] *vi* abatirse, encogerse.
crinkle ['krɪŋkəl] *vtr* fruncir, arrugar.
cripple ['krɪpəl] **I** *n* lisiado,-a *m,f*, mutilado,-a *m,f*. **II** *vtr* mutilar, dejar cojo,-a; *fig* paralizar.
crisis ['kraɪsɪs] *n* (*pl* **crises** ['kraɪsi:z]) crisis *f inv*.
crisp [krɪsp] **I** *adj* crujiente; (*lettuce*) fresco,-a; (*banknote*) nuevo,-a; (*weather*) frío,-a y seco,-a; *fig* (*style*) directo,-a. **II** *n GB* (*potato*) c., patata *f* frita.
crisscross ['krɪskrɒs] *n* líneas *fpl* entrecruzadas.
criterion [kraɪ'tɪərɪən] *n* (*pl* **criteria** [kraɪ'tɪərɪə]) criterio *m*.
critic ['krɪtɪk] *n Art Theat* crítico,-a *m,f*.
critical ['krɪtɪkəl] *adj* crítico,-a. ◆**critically** *adv* críticamente; **c. ill**, gravemente enfermo,-a.
criticism ['krɪtɪsɪzəm] *n* crítica *f*.
criticize ['krɪtɪsaɪz] *vtr* criticar.
croak [krəʊk] *vi* (*frog*) croar; (*raven*) graznar; (*person*) hablar con voz ronca.

crochet ['krəʊʃeɪ] *n* ganchillo *m*.
crockery ['krɒkərɪ] *n* loza *f*.
crocodile ['krɒkədaɪl] *n* cocodrilo *m*.
crocus ['krəʊkəs] *n* azafrán *m*.
crony ['krəʊnɪ] *n* compinche *mf*.
crook [krʊk] **I** *n* **1** (*of shepherd*) cayado *m*. **2** *fam* caco *m*. **II** *vtr* (*arm*) doblar.
crooked ['krʊkɪd] *adj* **1** (*stick, picture*) torcido,-a; (*path*) tortuoso,-a. **2** *fam* (*dishonest*) deshonesto,-a.
crop [krɒp] **I** *n* **1** cultivo *m*; (*harvest*) cosecha *f*; (*of hair*) mata *f*. **2** (*whip*) fusta *f*. **II** *vtr* (*hair*) rapar; (*grass*) cortar. ◆**crop up** *vi fam* surgir, presentarse.
croquet ['krəʊkeɪ] *n* croquet *m*.
cross [krɒs] **I** *n* **1** cruz *f*. **2** (*breeds*) cruce *m*. **3 c. section**, sección *f* transversal. **II** *vtr* **1** cruzar. **2** *Rel* **to c. oneself**, hacer la señal de la cruz; *fam* **c. my heart!**, ¡te lo juro! **3** (*thwart*) contrariar. **III** *vi* cruzar; (*roads*) cruzarse; **to c. over**, cruzar. **IV** *adj* **1** *fig* **they are at c. purposes**, hay un malentendido entre ellos. **2** (*angry*) enfadado,-a. ◆**cross off**, **cross out** *vtr* tachar, rayar.
crossbar ['krɒsbɑ:^r] *n* travesaño *m*.
cross-country ['krɒskʌntrɪ] **I** *n* **c.-c. race**, cros *m*. **II** [krɒs'kʌntrɪ] *adv* campo través.
cross-examine [krɒsɪg'zæmɪn] *vtr* interrogar.
cross-eyed ['krɒsaɪd] *adj* bizco,-a.
crossfire ['krɒsfaɪə^r] *n* fuego cruzado.
crossing ['krɒsɪŋ] *n* cruce *m*; **pedestrian c.**, paso *m* de peatones; **sea c.**, travesía *f*.
cross-legged [krɒs'legɪd] *adj* con las piernas cruzadas.
cross-reference [krɒs'refərəns] *n* remisión *f*.
crossroads ['krɒsrəʊdz] *n* cruce *m*; *fig* encrucijada *f*.
crosswind ['krɒswɪnd] *n* viento *m* lateral.
crossword ['krɒswɜ:d] *n* **c.** (**puzzle**), crucigrama *m*.
crotch [krɒtʃ] *n* entrepierna *f*.
crotchet ['krɒtʃɪt] *n Mus* negra *f*.
crotchety ['krɒtʃɪtɪ] *adj fam* gruñón,-ona.
crouch [kraʊtʃ] *vi* **c.** (**down**), agacharse.
crow¹ [krəʊ] *n* cuervo *m*; *fig* **as the c. flies**, en línea recta; **c.'s-feet**, patas *fpl* de gallo.
crow² [krəʊ] **I** *vi* (*cock*) cantar; *fig* **to c. over sth**, jactarse de algo. **2** (*baby*) balbucir. **II** *n* (*of cock*) canto *m*.
crowbar ['krəʊbɑ:^r] *n* palanca *f*.
crowd [kraʊd] **I** *n* muchedumbre *f*; **the c.**, el populacho; *fam* (*gang*) pandilla *f*. **II** *vtr* (*streets*) llenar. **III** *vi* apiñarse; **to c. in/out**, entrar/salir en tropel.
crowded ['kraʊdɪd] *adj* atestado,-a, lleno,-a.
crown [kraʊn] **I** *n* **1** corona *f*; (*garland*) guirnalda *f*; **the c. jewels**, las joyas de la

corona; **GB** *Jur* c. **court**, tribunal *m* superior; **C. Prince**, príncipe heredero. 2 *Anat* coronilla *f*; *(of hat, tree)* copa *f*. II *vtr* coronar; *fam fig* **to c. it all**, y para más inri.

crucial ['kru:ʃəl] *adj* decisivo,-a.

crucifix ['kru:sɪfɪks] *n* crucifijo *m*.

crucifixion [kru:sɪ'fɪkʃən] *n* crucifixión *f*.

crucify ['kru:sɪfaɪ] *vtr* crucificar.

crude [kru:d] *adj* 1 *(manners, style)* tosco,-a, grosero,-a; *(tool)* primitivo,-a. 2 **c. oil**, crudo *m*.

cruel ['kru:əl] *adj* cruel (**to**, con).

cruelty ['kru:əltɪ] *n* crueldad *f* (**to**, hacia).

cruet ['kru:ɪt] *n* **c. set**, vinagreras *fpl*.

cruise [kru:z] I *vi* 1 *Naut* hacer un crucero. 2 *Aut* viajar a velocidad constante; *Av* viajar a velocidad de crucero. II *n* Naut crucero *m*. 2 **c. missile**, misil teledirigido.

cruiser ['kru:zər] *n* (barco de) crucero *m*.

crumb [krʌm] *n* miga *f*, migaja *f*.

crumble ['krʌmbəl] I *vtr* desmigar. II *vi* *(wall)* desmoronarse; *fig (hopes)* desvanecerse.

crumbly ['krʌmblɪ] *adj* (**crumblier**, **crumbliest**) que se desmigaja.

crumpet ['krʌmpɪt] *n* **GB** clase *f* de crepe grueso que se puede tostar.

crumple ['krʌmpəl] *vtr* arrugar.

crunch [krʌntʃ] I *vtr (food)* ronchar; *(with feet)* hacer crujir. II *n fam* **when it comes to the c.**, a la hora de la verdad.

crunchy ['krʌntʃɪ] *adj* (**crunchier**, **crunchiest**) crujiente.

crusade [kru:'seɪd] *n* cruzada *f*.

crush [krʌʃ] I *vtr* aplastar; *(wrinkle)* arrugar; *(grind)* moler; *(squeeze)* exprimir. II *n* 1 *(of people)* gentío *m*. 2 **orange c.**, naranjada *f*.

crushing ['krʌʃɪŋ] *adj fig (defeat, reply)* aplastante.

crust [krʌst] *n* corteza *f*.

crutch [krʌtʃ] *n* Med muleta *f*; *fig* apoyo *m*.

crux [krʌks] *n* **the c. of the matter**, el quid de la cuestión.

cry [kraɪ] I *vi* (*pt* & *pp* **cried**) 1 gritar. 2 *(weep)* llorar. II *vtr* gritar; *fig* **to c. wolf**, dar una falsa alarma. III *n* 1 grito *m*. 2 *(weep)* llanto *m*. ◆**cry off** *vi fam* rajarse. ◆**cry out** *vi* gritar; **to c. out for sth**, pedir algo a gritos.

crying ['kraɪɪŋ] *adj* **it's a c. shame**, es una vergüenza.

cryptic ['krɪptɪk] *adj* enigmático,-a.

crystal ['krɪstəl] *n* cristal *m*.

crystal-clear [krɪstəl'klɪər] *adj* claro,-a como el agua.

crystallize ['krɪstəlaɪz] I *vtr* cristalizar. II *vi* cristalizarse.

cub [kʌb] *n* 1 *(animal)* cachorro *m*. 2 *(junior scout)* niño *m* explorador.

Cuba ['kju:bə] *n* Cuba.

Cuban ['kju:bən] *adj* & *n* cubano,-a (*m*,*f*).

cubbyhole ['kʌbɪhəʊl] *n* cuchitril *m*.

cube [kju:b] I *n* cubo *m*; *(of sugar)* terrón *m*; **c. root**, raíz cúbica. II *vtr* Math elevar al cubo.

cubic ['kju:bɪk] *adj* cúbico,-a.

cubicle ['kju:bɪkəl] *n* cubículo *m*; *(at swimming pool)* caseta *f*.

cuckoo ['kuku:] I *n* cuco *m*; **c. clock**, reloj *m* de cuco. II *adj fam* lelo,-a.

cucumber ['kju:kʌmbər] *n* pepino *m*.

cuddle ['kʌdəl] I *vtr* abrazar. II *vi* abrazarse.

cuddly ['kʌdlɪ] *adj* **c. toy**, muñeco *m* de peluche.

cue¹ [kju:] *n* Theat pie *m*.

cue² [kju:] *n (in billiards)* taco *m*; **c. ball**, bola blanca.

cuff¹ [kʌf] *n (of sleeve)* puño *m*; **US** *(of trousers)* dobladillo *m*; *fig* **to do sth off the c.**, improvisar algo.

cuff² [kʌf] I *vtr* abofetear. II *n* bofetada *f*.

cufflinks ['kʌflɪŋks] *npl* gemelos *mpl*.

cul-de-sac ['kʌldəsæk] *n* callejón *m* sin salida.

cull [kʌl] *vtr* 1 *(choose)* escoger. 2 *(animals)* eliminar.

culminate ['kʌlmɪneɪt] *vi* **to c. in**, terminar en.

culmination [kʌlmɪ'neɪʃən] *n* culminación *f*, punto *m* culminante.

culottes [kju:'lɒts] *npl* falda-pantalón *f sing*.

culprit ['kʌlprɪt] *n* culpable *mf*.

cult [kʌlt] *n* culto *m*; **c. figure**, ídolo *m*.

cultivate ['kʌltɪveɪt] *vtr* cultivar.

cultivated ['kʌltɪveɪtɪd] *adj (person)* culto,-a.

cultivation [kʌltɪ'veɪʃən] *n* cultivo *m* (de la tierra).

cultural ['kʌltʃərəl] *adj* cultural.

culture ['kʌltʃər] *n* cultura *f*.

cultured ['kʌltʃəd] *adj* → **cultivated**.

cumbersome ['kʌmbəsəm] *adj (awkward)* incómodo,-a; *(bulky)* voluminoso,-a.

cum(m)in ['kʌmɪn] *n* comino *m*.

cumulative ['kju:mjʊlətɪv] *adj* acumulativo,-a.

cunning ['kʌnɪŋ] I *adj* astuto,-a. II *n* astucia *f*.

cup [kʌp] I *n* taza *f*; *Sport* copa *f*; **C. Final**, final *f* de copa; **c. tie**, partido *m* de copa. II *vtr (hands)* ahuecar.

cupboard ['kʌbəd] *n* armario *m*; *(on wall)* alacena *f*.

curate ['kjʊərɪt] *n* cura *m* coadjutor.

curator [kjʊə'reɪtər] *n* conservador,-a *m*,*f*.

curb [kɜ:b] I *n (kerb)* bordillo *m*. II *vtr (horse)* refrenar; *fig (public spending)* contener.

curd [kɜ:d] *n* cuajada *f*.

curdle ['kɜ:dəl] *vi* cuajarse.

cure ['kjuər] I *vtr* curar. II *n* (*remedy*) cura *f*, remedio *m*.

curfew ['kɜːfjuː] *n* toque *m* de queda.

curiosity [ˌkjuərɪ'ɒsɪtɪ] *n* curiosidad *f*.

curious ['kjuərɪəs] *adj* 1 (*inquisitive*) curioso,-a. 2 (*odd*) extraño,-a.

curl [kɜːl] I *vtr* (*hair*) rizar; (*lip*) fruncir. II *vi* rizarse. III *n* (*of hair*) rizo *m*; (*of smoke*) espiral *f*. ◆**curl up** *vi* enroscarse.

curly ['kɜːlɪ] *adj* (**curlier**, **curliest**) rizado,-a.

currant ['kʌrənt] *n* pasa *f* (de Corinto).

currency ['kʌrənsɪ] *n* 1 moneda *f*; **foreign c.**, divisa *f*. 2 **to gain c.**, cobrar fuerza.

current ['kʌrənt] I *adj* 1 (*opinion*) general; (*word*) en uso; (*year*) en curso; **c. account**, cuenta *f* corriente; **c. affairs**, actualidad *f sing* (política); **Fin c. assets**, activo *m sing* disponible. 2 **the c. issue**, (*of magazine*, *newspaper*) el último número. II *n* corriente *f*. ◆**currently** *adv* actualmente.

curriculum [kə'rɪkjələm] *n* (*pl* **curricula** [kə'rɪkjələ]) plan *m* de estudios; **c. vitae**, curriculum *m* (vitae).

curry[1] ['kʌrɪ] *n* curry *m*; **chicken c.**, pollo *m* al curry.

curry[2] ['kʌrɪ] *vtr* **to c. favour with**, congraciarse con.

curse [kɜːs] I *n* maldición *f*; (*oath*) palabrota *f*; *fig* azote *m*. II *vtr* maldecir. III *vi* blasfemar.

cursor ['kɜːsər] *n* cursor *m*.

cursory ['kɜːsərɪ] *adj* rápido,-a.

curt [kɜːt] *adj* brusco,-a, seco,-a.

curtail [kɜː'teɪl] *vtr* (*expenses*) reducir; (*text*) acortar.

curtain ['kɜːtən] *n* cortina *f*; *Theat* telón *m*; *fig* velo *m*.

curts(e)y ['kɜːtsɪ] I *n* reverencia *f*. II *vi* hacer una reverencia (**to**, a).

curve [kɜːv] I *n* curva *f*. II *vtr* encorvar. III *vi* torcerse, describir una curva.

cushion ['kuʃən] I *n* cojín *m*, (*large*) almohadón *m*; (*of billiard table*) banda *f*. II *vtr* *fig* amortiguar; (*person*) proteger.

cushy ['kuʃɪ] *adj* (**cushier**, **cushiest**) *fam* cómodo,-a.

custard ['kʌstəd] *n* natillas *fpl*; **c. powder**, polvos *mpl* para natillas.

custodian [kʌs'təudɪən] *n* conserje *mf*, guarda *mf*.

custody ['kʌstədɪ] *n* custodia *f*; **to take into c.**, detener.

custom ['kʌstəm] *n* 1 (*habit*) costumbre *f*. 2 *Com* clientela *f*.

customary ['kʌstəmərɪ] *adj* habitual.

customer ['kʌstəmər] *n* cliente *mf*.

customize ['kʌstəmaɪz] *vtr* hacer por encargo.

custom-made [ˌkʌstəm'meɪd] *adj* hecho,-a a la medida.

customs ['kʌstəmz] *n sing* or *pl* aduana *f*;

c. duty, derechos *mpl* de aduana; **c. officer**, **agente** *mf* de aduana.

cut [kʌt] I *vtr* (*pt* & *pp* **cut**) 1 cortar; (*stone*) tallar; (*record*) grabar; **he's cutting a tooth**, le está saliendo un diente; **to c. one's finger**, cortarse el dedo; *fig* **to c. a long story short**, en resumidas cuentas; *fig* **to c. corners**, recortar presupuestos. 2 (*reduce*) reducir. 3 (*divide up*) dividir (**into**, en). II *n* 1 corte *m*; (*in skin*) corte *m*; (*wound*) herida *f*; (*with knife*) cuchillada *f*. 2 (*of meat*) clase *f* de carne. 3 (*reduction*) reducción *f*. 4 *fig* **to be a c. above sb**, estar por encima de algn. III *adj* cortado,-a; (*price*) reducido,-a; *fig* **c. and dried**, convenido,-a de antemano; **c. glass**, cristal tallado. IV *vi* 1 cortar; *fam* *fig* **to c. loose**, romper con todo. 2 **Cin c. !**, ¡corten! ◆**cut back** *vtr* (*expenses*) reducir; (*production*) disminuir. ◆**cut down** *vtr* (*tree*) talar; **to c. down on**, reducir. ◆**cut in** *vi* (*driver*) adelantar bruscamente. ◆**cut off** *vtr* (*water* etc) cortar; (*place*) aislar; (*heir*) excluir; *Tel* **I've been c. off**, me han cortado (la comunicación). ◆**cut out** I *vtr* 1 (*from newspaper*) recortar; (*person*) **to be c. out for sth**, estar hecho,-a para algo. 2 (*delete*) suprimir. II *vi* (*engine*) calarse. ◆**cut up** *vtr* cortar en pedazos.

cutback ['kʌtbæk] *n* reducción *f* (**in**, de).

cute [kjuːt] *adj* mono,-a, lindo,-a; *US fam pej* listillo,-a.

cuticle ['kjuːtɪkəl] *n* cutícula *f*.

cutlery ['kʌtlərɪ] *n* cubiertos *mpl*.

cutlet ['kʌtlɪt] *n* chuleta *f*.

cut-price [ˌkʌt'praɪs] *adj* (*article*) a precio rebajado.

cutthroat ['kʌtθrəut] I *n* asesino,-a *m,f*, matón *m*. II *adj* (*cruel*) cruel; (*competition*) feroz.

cutting ['kʌtɪŋ] I *n* (*from newspaper*) recorte *m*; *Rail* tajo *m*. II *adj* cortante; (*remark*) mordaz.

CV, cv [siː'viː] *abbr of* **curriculum vitae**.

cwt. *abbr of* **hundredweight**, quintal *m*.

cyanide ['saɪənaɪd] *n* cianuro *m*.

cycle ['saɪkəl] I *n* 1 ciclo *m*. 2 (*bicycle*) bicicleta *f*; (*motorcycle*) moto *f*. II *vi* ir en bicicleta.

cycling ['saɪklɪŋ] *n* ciclismo *m*.

cyclist ['saɪklɪst] *n* ciclista *mf*.

cyclone ['saɪkləun] *n* ciclón *m*.

cygnet ['sɪgnɪt] *n* pollo *m* de cisne.

cylinder ['sɪlɪndər] *n* 1 cilindro *m*. 2 (*for gas*) bombona *f*.

cymbal ['sɪmbəl] *n* címbalo *m*, platillo *m*.

cynic ['sɪnɪk] *n* cínico,-a *m,f*.

cynical ['sɪnɪkəl] *adj* cínico,-a.

cynicism ['sɪnɪsɪzəm] *n* cinismo *m*.

cypress ['saɪprəs] *n* ciprés *m*.

Cypriot ['sɪprɪət] *adj & n* chipriota (*mf*).
Cyprus ['saɪprəs] *n* Chipre.
cyst [sɪst] *n* quiste *m*.
cystitis [sɪ'staɪtɪs] *n* cistitis *f*.
czar [zɑːr] *n* zar *m*.

Czech [tʃek] **I** *adj* checo,-a. **II** *n* 1 (*person*) checo,-a *m,f*. 2 (*language*) checo *m*.
Czechoslovakia [tʃekəʊsləʊ'vækɪə] *n* Checoslovaquia.

D

D, d [diː] *n* 1 (*the letter*) D, d *f*. 2 *Mus* re *m*.
D.A. [diː'eɪ] *US abbr of* **District Attorney**.
dab [dæb] **I** *n* (*small quantity*) toque *m*. **II** *vtr* 1 (*apply*) aplicar. 2 (*touch lightly*) tocar ligeramente.
dabble ['dæbəl] *vi* to d. in politics, meterse en política.
dachshund ['dækshʊnd] *n* perro *m* salchicha.
dad [dæd], **daddy** ['dædɪ] *n fam* papá *m*, papi *m*.
daddy-longlegs [dædɪ'lɒŋlegz] *n inv GB fam* típula *f*.
daffodil ['dæfədɪl] *n* narciso *m*.
daft [dɑːft] *adj GB fam* chalado,-a; (*idea*) tonto,-a.
dagger ['dægər] *n* puñal *m*, daga *f*.
dahlia ['deɪljə] *n* dalia *f*.
daily ['deɪlɪ] **I** *adj* diario,-a, cotidiano,-a. **II** *adv* diariamente; **three times d.**, tres veces al día. **III** *n* 1 (*newspaper*) diario *m*. 2 *GB fam* (*cleaning lady*) asistenta *f*.
dainty ['deɪntɪ] *adj* (**daintier, daintiest**) (*flower*) delicado,-a; (*child*) precioso,-a; (*food*) exquisito,-a.
dairy ['deərɪ] *n* (*on farm*) vaquería *f*; (*shop*) lechería *f*; **d. farming**, industria lechera; **d. produce**, productos lácteos.
dais ['deɪɪs] *n* (*in hall*) tarima *f*; (*in ceremony*) estrado *m*.
daisy ['deɪzɪ] *n* margarita *f*.
daisywheel ['deɪzɪwiːl] *n* (*printer*) margarita *f*.
dale [deɪl] *n* valle *m*, hondonada *f*.
Dalmatian [dæl'meɪʃən] *n* (*perro m*) dálmata *m*.
dam [dæm] **I** *n* (*barrier*) dique *m*; (*lake*) presa *f*. **II** *vtr* (*water*) represar. ◆**dam up** *vtr fig* (*emotion*) contener.
damage ['dæmɪdʒ] **I** *n* 1 daño *m*; (*to health, reputation*) perjuicio *m*; (*to relationship*) deterioro *m*. 2 *Jur* **damages**, daños *mpl* y perjuicios *mpl*. **II** *vtr* (*harm*) dañar, hacer daño a; (*spoil*) estropear; (*undermine*) perjudicar.
damaging ['dæmɪdʒɪŋ] *adj* perjudicial.
damn [dæm] **I** *vtr* condenar. **II** *interj fam* **d.** (**it**)!, ¡maldito,-a sea!; **well, I'll be damned!**, ¡vaya por Dios!. **III** *n fam* **I don't give a d.**, me importa un bledo. **IV** *adj fam* maldito,-a. **V** *adv fam* muy, sumamente.

damned [dæmd] **I** *adj* → **damn IV**. **II** *adv* → **damn V**.
damnedest ['dæmdɪst] *n fam* **to do one's d. to ...**, hacer todo lo posible para ....
damning ['dæmɪŋ] *adj* (*evidence*) irrefutable; (*criticism*) mordaz.
damp [dæmp] **I** *adj* húmedo,-a; (*wet*) mojado,-a. **II** *n* humedad *f*. **III** *vtr* 1 (*for ironing*) humedecer. 2 **to d. (down)**, (*fire*) sofocar; *fig* (*violence*) frenar.
dampen ['dæmpən] *vtr* humedecer; *fig* frenar.
damper ['dæmpər] *n fig* **to put a d. on sth**, poner freno a algo.
damsel ['dæmzəl] *n lit* doncella *f*.
damson ['dæmzən] *n* ciruela damascena.
dance [dɑːns] **I** *n* baile *m*; (*classical, tribal*) danza *f*; **d. band**, orquesta *f* de baile; **d. floor**, pista *f* de baile; **d. hall**, salón *m* de baile. **II** *vi & vtr* bailar.
dancer ['dɑːnsər] *n* (*by profession*) bailarín,-ina *m,f*.
dandelion ['dændɪlaɪən] *n* diente *m* de león.
dandruff ['dændrəf] *n* caspa *f*.
Dane [deɪn] *n* danés,-esa *m,f*.
danger ['deɪndʒər] *n* 1 (*risk*) riesgo *m*; (*of war etc*) amenaza *f*. 2 (*peril*) peligro *m*; **'d.'**, 'peligro'; **out of d.**, fuera de peligro.
dangerous ['deɪndʒərəs] *adj* peligroso,-a; (*risky*) arriesgado,-a; (*harmful*) nocivo,-a; (*illness*) grave. ◆**dangerously** *adv* peligrosamente.
dangle ['dæŋgəl] **I** *vi* (*hang*) colgar; (*swing*) balancearse. **II** *vtr* (*legs*) colgar; (*bait*) dejar colgado,-a; (*swing*) balancear en el aire.
Danish ['deɪnɪʃ] **I** *adj* danés,-esa; **D. pastry**, pastel *m* de hojaldre. **II** *n* (*language*) danés *m*.
dapper ['dæpər] *adj* pulcro,-a.
dappled ['dæpəld] *adj* (*shade*) moteado,-a.
dare [deər] **I** *vi* atreverse, osar; **he doesn't d. be late**, no se atreve a llegar tarde; **how d. you!**, ¿cómo te atreves?; *esp GB* **I d. say**, quizás, (*I'll believe you*) ya (lo creo). **II** *vtr* (*challenge*) desafiar. **III** *n* desafío *m*.
daredevil ['deədevəl] *adj & n* atrevido,-a (*m,f*), temerario,-a (*m,f*).
daring ['deərɪŋ] **I** *adj* 1 (*bold*) audaz, osado,-a. 2 (*clothes*) atrevido,-a **II** *n* atrevimiento *m*, osadía *f*.
dark [dɑːk] *adj* 1 (*room, colour*) oscuro,-a; (*hair, complexion*) moreno,-a; (*eyes, fu-*

ture) negro,-a. 2 *fig* (*gloomy*) triste. 3 *fig* **to be a d. horse**, ser una incógnita; (*discreet*) ser una caja de sorpresas. 4 *fig* (*sinister*) siniestro,-a. II *n* 1 (*darkness*) oscuridad *f*, tinieblas *fpl*; **after d.**, después del anochecer. 2 *fig* **to be in the d.** (*about*), estar a oscuras (sobre).

darken ['dɑːkən] I *vtr* (*sky*) oscurecer; (*colour*) hacer más oscuro,-a. II *vi* oscurecerse; (*sky*) nublarse; *fig* (*face*) ensombrecerse.

darkness ['dɑːknɪs] *n* oscuridad *f*, tinieblas *fpl*.

darkroom ['dɑːkruːm] *n* cuarto oscuro.

darling ['dɑːlɪŋ] *adj* & *n* querido,-a (*m,f*).

darn [dɑːn] I *vtr* zurcir. II *n* zurcido *m*.

dart [dɑːt] I *n* 1 (*missile*) dardo *m*. 2 **darts**, *sing* dardos *mpl*. II *vi* (*fly about*) revolotear; **to d. in/out**, entrar/salir corriendo.

dartboard ['dɑːtbɔːd] *n* diana *f*.

dash [dæʃ] I *n* 1 (*rush*) carrera *f*. 2 *esp US* (*race*) sprint *m*. 3 (*small amount*) poquito *m*; (*of salt*) pizca *f*; (*of liquid*) gota *f*. 4 *Typ* guión largo; (*hyphen*) guión. 5 (*vitality*) brío *m*. II *vtr* 1 (*throw*) arrojar. 2 (*smash*) estrellar; *fig* **to d. sb's hopes**, desvanecer las esperanzas de algn. III *vi* (*rush*) correr; **to d. around**, correr de un lado a otro; **to d. out**, salir corriendo; *fam* **I must d.!**, ¡me voy pitando! ◆**dash off** *vi* salir corriendo.

dashboard ['dæʃbɔːd] *n* *Aut* salpicadero *m*.

dashing ['dæʃɪŋ] *adj* (*appearance*) garboso,-a.

data ['deɪtə, 'dɑːtə] *npl* datos *mpl*; **d. bank** *or* **base**, banco *m* de datos; **d. processing**, (*act*) proceso *m* de datos; (*science*) informática *f*; **d. protection act**, ley *f* de informática.

date¹ [deɪt] I *n* 1 fecha *f*; **what's the d. today?** ¿qué día es hoy?; **out of d.**, (*ideas*) anticuado,-a; (*expression*) desusado,-a; (*invalid*) caducado,-a; **to d.**, hasta la fecha; *fig* **to be up to d.**, estar al día; **d. of birth**, fecha de nacimiento. 2 (*social event*) compromiso *m*; *fam* (*with girl, boy*) cita *f*. 3 *US fam* (*person dated*) ligue *m*. II *vtr* (*ruins*) datar. III *vi* (*ideas*) quedar anticuado,-a. ◆**d. back to**, **date from** *vtr* remontar a, datar de.

date² [deɪt] *n* (*fruit*) dátil *m*; **d. palm**, datilera *f*.

dated ['deɪtɪd] *adj* (*idea*) anticuado,-a; (*fashion*) pasado,-a de moda; (*expression*) desusado,-a.

daub [dɔːb] *vtr* embadurnar; (*with oil, grease*) untar.

daughter ['dɔːtə] *n* hija *f*.

daughter-in-law ['dɔːtərɪnlɔː] *n* nuera *f*, hija política.

daunting ['dɔːntɪŋ] *adj* desalentador,-a.

dawdle ['dɔːdəl] *vi* *fam* (*walk slowly*)

andar despacio; (*waste time*) perder el tiempo.

dawn [dɔːn] I *n* alba *f*, amanecer *m*. II *vi* 1 (*day*) amanecer. 2 *fig* (*age, hope*) comenzar. 3 *fig* **suddenly it dawned on him that ...**, de repente cayó en la cuenta de que ....

day [deɪ] *n* 1 día *m*; **d. in, d. out**, día tras día; **d. by d.**, diariamente; **good d.!**, ¡buenos días!; **once a d.**, una vez al día; **one of these days**, un día de éstos; **(on) the next** *or* **following d.**, el *or* al día siguiente; **the d. after tomorrow**, pasado mañana; **the d. before yesterday**, anteayer; **the other d.**, el otro día; *fig* **to live from d. to d.**, vivir al día; *fig* **to win the d.**, llevarse la palma; *fam* **to call it a d.**, (*finish*) dar por acabado un trabajo; (*give up*) darse por vencido,-a; *fam* **to make sb's d.**, alegrarle a algn el día; *GB Rail* **d. return (ticket)**, billete *m* de ida y vuelta para el mismo día; **d. trip**, excursión *f* de un día. 2 (*daylight*) día *m*; **by d.**, de día; **d. and night**, de día y de noche; *GB* **d. shift**, turno *m* de día. 3 (*period of work*) jornada *f*; **an eight-hour d.**, una jornada de ocho horas; **paid by the d.**, pagado,-a a jornal; **d. off**, día de fiesta; **I'll take a d. off tomorrow**, mañana me tomaré el día libre. 4 (*era*) época *f*; **in those days**, en aquellos tiempos; **these days, in this d. and age**, hoy (en) día.

daybreak ['deɪbreɪk] *n* amanecer *m*.

daydream ['deɪdriːm] I *n* ensueño *m*; (*vain hope*) fantasía *f*. II *vi* soñar despierto,-a; (*hope vainly*) hacerse ilusiones.

daylight ['deɪlaɪt] *n* luz *f* del día; **in broad d.**, en pleno día; **to scare the (living) daylights out of sb**, pegarle a algn un susto de muerte.

daytime ['deɪtaɪm] *n* día *m*; **in the d.**, de día.

day-to-day ['deɪtədeɪ] *adj* cotidiano,-a, diario,-a.

daze [deɪz] *n* aturdimiento *m*; **in a d.**, aturdido,-a.

dazed [deɪzd] *adj* aturdido,-a, atontado, -a.

dazzle ['dæzəl] *vtr* deslumbrar.

D-day ['diːdeɪ] *n* día *m* D.

deacon ['diːkən] *n* diácono *m*.

dead [ded] I *adj* 1 muerto,-a; **he was shot d.**, le mataron a tiros; **to be d.**, estar muerto,-a; *fam* **d. over my d. body!**, ¡sobre mi cadáver!; **d. man**, muerto *m*. 2 (*machine*) averiado,-a; (*phone*) cortado,-a. 3 (*numb*) entumecido,-a; (*limb*) adormecido,-a; **my leg's gone d.**, se me ha dormido la pierna. 4 (*silence, secrecy*) total; **d. end**, callejón *m* sin salida; *Sport* **d. heat**, empate *m*; *fam* **d. loss**, inútil *m*, birria *f*. II *adv* 1 (*exactly*) justo; **d. on time**, a la hora en punto. 2 **to stop d.**, pararse en seco. **3** (very) muy; *fam* **d. beat, d. tired,** rendido,-a; *fam* **it's d. easy!,** ¡esto es chupado,-a!; *Aut* **'d. slow',** 'al paso'; *fam* **you're d. right,** tienes toda la razón. **III** *n* **1 the d.,** (pl) los muertos. **2** at **d. of night,** a altas horas de la noche.

deaden ['dedən] *vtr* (impact, noise) amortiguar; *fig* (pain, feeling) calmar, aliviar.

deadline ['dedlaɪn] *n* (date) fecha *f* tope; (time) hora *f* tope; **we have to meet the d.,** tenemos que hacerlo dentro del plazo.

deadlock ['dedlɒk] *n* punto muerto.

deadly ['dedlɪ] **I** *adj* (**deadlier, deadliest**) mortal; (weapon) mortífero,-a; (aim) certero,-a. **II** *adv* (extremely) terriblemente, sumamente.

deadpan ['dedpæn] *adj fam* (face) sin expresión; (humour) guasón,-ona.

deaf [def] **I** *adj* sordo,-a; *fig* **to turn a d. ear,** hacerse el sordo; **d. mute,** sordomudo,-a *m,f*. **II** *npl* **the d.,** los sordos; **the d. and dumb,** los sordomudos.

deafen ['defən] *vtr* ensordecer.

deafening ['defənɪŋ] *adj* ensordecedor,-a.

deafness ['defnɪs] *n* sordera *f*.

deal [di:l] **I** *n* **1** *Com Pol* trato *m*, pacto *m*; **business d.,** negocio *m*, transacción *f*; **to do a d. with sb,** (transaction) cerrar un trato con algn; (agreement) hacer algo con algn; *fam* **it's a d.!,** ¡trato hecho! **2** (amount) cantidad *f*; **a good d. of criticism,** muchas críticas; **a good d. slower,** mucho más despacio. **3** *Cards* reparto *m*. **II** *vtr* (pt & pp **dealt**) **1** *Cards* dar (**to,** a). **2 to d. sb a blow,** asestarle un golpe a algn. ◆**deal in** *vtr* (goods) comerciar en, tratar en; (drugs) traficar con. ◆**deal out** *vtr* repartir. ◆**deal with** *vtr* (firm, person) tratar con; (subject, problem) abordar, ocuparse de; (in book etc) tratar de.

dealer ['di:lər] *n* **1** *Com* (in goods) comerciante *mf*; (in drugs) traficante *mf*. **2** *Cards* repartidor,-a *m,f*.

dealings ['di:lɪŋz] *npl* **1** (relations) trato *m sing*. **2** *Com* negocios *mpl*.

dealt [delt] *pt & pp* → **deal**.

dean [di:n] *n* **1** *Rel* deán *m*. **2** *Univ* decano *m*.

dear [dɪər] **I** *adj* **1** (loved) querido,-a; **to hold sth/sb d.,** apreciar mucho algo/a algn. **2** (in letter) Querido,-a; *fml* **D. Andrew,** Querido Andrew; *fml* **D. Madam,** Estimada señora; *fml* **D. Sir(s),** Muy señor(es) mío(s). **3 it is very d. to me,** (precious) le tengo un gran cariño. **4** *GB* (expensive) caro,-a. **II** *n* querido,-a; **my d.,** mi vida. **III** *interj* oh d.!, **d. me!,** (surprise) ¡caramba!; (disappointment) ¡qué pena! ◆**dearly** *adv* muchísimo; *fig* **he paid d. for his mistake,** su error le costó

caro.

dearth [dɜːθ] *n fml* escasez *f*.

death [deθ] *n* **1** muerte *f*; **to put sb to d.,** dar muerte a algn; *fam* **to be bored to d.,** aburrirse como una ostra; *fam* **to be scared to d.,** estar muerto,-a de miedo; *fam fig* **to be sick to d. of,** estar hasta la coronilla de; **d. certificate,** certificado *m* de defunción; **d. penalty, d. sentence,** pena *f* de muerte; **d. rate,** índice *m* de mortalidad; **d. squad,** escuadrón *m* de la muerte. **2** *fig* **(end) fin** *m*.

deathbed [deθbed] *n* **to be on one's d.,** estar en el lecho de muerte.

deathly ['deθlɪ] *adj* (**deathlier, deathliest**) (silence) sepulcral; **d. pale,** pálido,-a como un muerto.

debacle [deɪˈbɑːkəl] *n* debacle *f*.

debar [dɪˈbɑːr] *vtr fml* excluir, prohibir.

debase [dɪˈbeɪs] *vtr fig* envilecer; **to d. oneself,** humillarse.

debate [dɪˈbeɪt] **I** *n* debate *m*; **a heated d.,** una discusión acalorada. **II** *vtr* **1** (discuss) discutir. **2** (wonder about) dar vueltas a. **II** *vi* discutir.

debat(e)able [dɪˈbeɪtəbəl] *adj* discutible.

debauchery [dɪˈbɔːtʃərɪ] *n* libertinaje *m*.

debilitating [dɪˈbɪlɪteɪtɪŋ] *adj* debilitante; (heat, climate) agotador,-a.

debit ['debɪt] **I** *n* débito *m*; **d. balance,** saldo negativo. **II** *vtr* **d. Mr Jones with £20,** cargar la suma de veinte libras en la cuenta del Sr. Jones.

debris ['debri:, 'deɪbri:] *n sing* escombros *mpl*.

debt [det] *n* deuda *f*; **to be deeply in d.,** estar cargado,-a de deudas; *fig* **to be in sb's d.,** estar en deuda con algn.

debtor ['detər] *n* deudor,-a *m,f*.

debug [di:ˈbʌg] *vtr Comput* eliminar fallos de.

debunk [di:ˈbʌŋk] *vtr fam* desacreditar, desprestigiar.

debut ['debju:, 'deɪbju:] *n* debut *m*; **to make one's d.,** debutar.

debutante ['debjutɑ:nt] *n* debutante *f*.

decade [de'keɪd, 'dekeɪd] *n* decenio *m*, década *f*.

decadence ['dekədəns] *n* decadencia *f*.

decadent ['dekədənt] *adj* decadente.

decaffeinated [di:ˈkæfɪneɪtɪd] *adj* descafeinado,-a.

decanter [dɪˈkæntər] *n* jarra *f*, jarro *m*.

decapitate [dɪˈkæpɪteɪt] *vtr* decapitar.

decay [dɪˈkeɪ] **I** *n* **1** (of food, body) descomposición *f*; (of teeth) caries *f inv*; (of buildings) desmoronamiento *m*; *fig* decadencia *f*. **II** *vi* descomponerse; (teeth) cariarse; (building) deteriorarse; *fig* corromperse.

deceased [dɪˈsiːst] *fml adj* difunto,-a, fallecido,-a.

deceit [dɪˈsiːt] *n* **1** (dishonesty) falta *f* de

honradez, falsedad *f.* 2 *(trick)* engaño *m*, mentira *f.*

deceitful [dɪˈsiːtful] *adj* falso,-a.

deceive [dɪˈsiːv] *vtr (mislead)* engañar; *(lie to)* mentir.

December [dɪˈsembər] *n* diciembre *m.*

decency [ˈdiːsənsɪ] *n* decencia *f*; *(modesty)* pudor *m*; *(morality)* moralidad *f.*

decent [ˈdiːsənt] *adj* decente; *(person)* honrado,-a; *fam (kind)* simpático,-a.

decentralize [diːˈsentrəlaɪz] *vtr* descentralizar.

deception [dɪˈsepʃən] *n* engaño *m.*

deceptive [dɪˈseptɪv] *adj* engañoso,-a. ◆**deceptively** *adv* **it looks d.** simple, parece engañosamente sencillo,-a.

decibel [ˈdesɪbel] *n* decibelio *m.*

decide [dɪˈsaɪd] I *vtr* 1 decidir; **to d. to do sth**, decidir hacer algo. 2 *(matter, question)* resolver, determinar. II *vi (reach decision)* decidirse; **to d. against sth**, decidirse en contra de algo. ◆**decide on** *vtr (choose)* optar por.

decided [dɪˈsaɪdɪd] *adj* 1 *(noticeable)* marcado,-a. 2 *(resolute)* decidido,-a; *(views)* categórico,-a. ◆**decidedly** *adv fml* 1 *(clearly)* indudablemente. 2 *(resolutely)* decididamente.

deciding [dɪˈsaɪdɪŋ] *adj* decisivo,-a.

deciduous [dɪˈsɪdjuːəs] *adj* de hoja caduca.

decimal [ˈdesɪməl] I *adj* decimal; **d. point**, coma *f* (de fracción decimal). II *n* decimal *m.*

decimate [ˈdesɪmeɪt] *vtr* diezmar.

decipher [dɪˈsaɪfər] *vtr* descifrar.

decision [dɪˈsɪʒən] *n* 1 decisión *f*; *Jur* fallo *m*; **to come to a d.**, llegar a una decisión; **to make a d.**, tomar una decisión. 2 *(resolution)* resolución *f.*

decisive [dɪˈsaɪsɪv] *adj* 1 *(resolute)* decidido,-a, resuelto,-a. 2 *(conclusive)* decisivo,-a.

deck [dek] I *n* 1 *(of ship)* cubierta *f*; **on/ below d.**, en/bajo cubierta; **d. chair**, tumbona *f.* 2 *(of bus)* piso *m*; **top d.**, piso de arriba. 3 *esp US (of cards)* baraja *f.* 4 *(of record player)* plato *m.* II *vtr* **to d. out**, adornar.

declaration [dekləˈreɪʃən] *n* declaración *f.*

declare [dɪˈkleər] *vtr* declarar; *(winner, innocence)* proclamar; *(decision)* manifestar.

declared [dɪˈkleəd] *adj (opponent)* declarado,-a; *(intention)* manifiesto,-a.

decline [dɪˈklaɪn] I *n* 1 *(decrease)* disminución *f.* 2 *(deterioration)* deterioro *m*; *(of health)* empeoramiento *m*; **to fall into d.**, empezar a decaer. II *vi* 1 *(decrease)* disminuir; *(amount)* bajar; *(business)* decaer. 2 *(deteriorate)* deteriorarse; *(health)* empeorar. 3 *(refuse)* negarse. III *vtr* 1 *(refuse)* rechazar. 2 *Ling* declinar.

declutch [dɪˈklʌtʃ] *vi* soltar el embrague.

decode [diːˈkəʊd] *vtr* descifrar.

decompose [diːkəmˈpəʊz] *vi* descomponerse.

décor [ˈdeɪkɔːr] *n* decoración *f*; *Theat* decorado *m.*

decorate [ˈdekəreɪt] *vtr* 1 *(adorn)* decorar, adornar (**with**, con). 2 *(paint)* pintar; *(wallpaper)* empapelar. 3 *(honour)* condecorar.

decoration [dekəˈreɪʃən] *n* 1 *(decor)* decoración *f*; **Christmas decorations**, adornos navideños. 2 *(medal)* condecoración *f.*

decorative [ˈdekərətɪv] *adj* decorativo,-a.

decorator [ˈdekəreɪtər] *n* decorador,-a *m,f*; *(painter)* pintor,-a *m,f*; *(paperhanger)* empapelador,-a *m,f.*

decorum [dɪˈkɔːrəm] *n* decoro *m.*

decoy [ˈdiːkɔɪ] *n fig* señuelo *m.*

decrease [ˈdiːkriːs] I *n* disminución *f*; *(in speed, size, price)* reducción *f.* II [dɪˈkriːs] *vi* disminuir; *(strength)* menguar; *(price, temperature)* bajar; *(speed, size)* reducir. III *vtr* disminuir, reducir; *(price, temperature)* bajar.

decree [dɪˈkriː] I *n* 1 *Pol Rel* decreto *m.* 2 *esp US Jur* sentencia *f*; **d. absolute**, sentencia definitiva de divorcio; **d. nisi**, sentencia provisional de divorcio. II *vtr* *Pol Rel* decretar, pronunciar.

decrepit [dɪˈkrepɪt] *adj* decrépito,-a.

dedicate [ˈdedɪkeɪt] *vtr* consagrar, dedicar.

dedicated [ˈdedɪkeɪtɪd] *adj* ardiente; **d. to**, entregado,-a.

dedication [dedɪˈkeɪʃən] *n (act)* dedicación *f*; *(commitment)* entrega *f*; *(in book)* dedicatoria *f.*

deduce [dɪˈdjuːs] *vtr* deducir (**from**, de).

deduct [dɪˈdʌkt] *vtr* descontar (**from**, de).

deduction [dɪˈdʌkʃən] *n* 1 *(conclusion)* conclusión *f.* 2 *(subtraction)* descuento *m.*

deed [diːd] *n* 1 *(act)* acto *m*; *(feat)* hazaña *f.* 2 *Jur* escritura *f*; **title deeds**, título *m sing* de propiedad.

deem [diːm] *vtr fml* estimar.

deep [diːp] I *adj* 1 profundo,-a; *(breath, sigh)* hondo,-a; **it's ten metres d.**, tiene diez metros de profundidad. 2 *(voice)* grave; *(shame)* grande; *(interest)* vivo,-a. 3 *(colour)* oscuro,-a. 4 *(serious)* grave. II *adv* **to dig d.**, cavar hondo; **to be d. in thought**, estar absorto,-a; **to look d. into sb's eyes**, penetrar a algn con la mirada; *fig* **nine d.**, de nueve en fondo. ◆**deeply** *adv* profundamente; *(breathe)* hondo; **to be d. in debt**, estar cargado,-a de deudas.

deepen [ˈdiːpən] I *vtr (well)* profundizar, ahondar; *fig (knowledge)* aumentar. II *vi (river etc)* hacerse más hondo or profundo; *fig* *(emotion)* intensificarse; *(sound, voice)* hacerse más grave.

deep-freeze [diːpˈfriːz] I n congelador m. II vtr congelar.

deep-fry [diːpˈfraɪ] vtr freír en mucho aceite.

deep-rooted [diːpˈruːtɪd] adj fig arraigado,-a.

deep-seated [diːpˈsiːtɪd] adj fig arraigado,-a.

deep-set [diːpˈset] adj (eyes) hundido,-a.

deer [dɪər] n inv ciervo m.

deface [dɪˈfeɪs] vtr (book, poster) garabatear.

de facto [deɪˈfæktəu] adj & adv fml de hecho.

defamation [defəˈmeɪʃən] n difamación f.

default [dɪˈfɔːlt] I vi 1 (not act) faltar a sus compromisos. 2 Jur estar en rebeldía. 3 (not pay) suspender pagos. II n 1 (failure to act) omisión f. 2 (failure to pay) incumplimiento m de pago. 3 Jur rebeldía f; **in d. of**, a falta de; **to win by d.**, ganar por incomparecencia del adversario.

defaulter [dɪˈfɔːltər] n (on loan) moroso,-a mf; Jur Mil rebelde mf.

defeat [dɪˈfiːt] I vtr 1 derrotar, vencer; (motion) rechazar. II n 1 (of army, team) derrota f; (of motion) rechazo m. 2 fig fracaso m.

defeatist [dɪˈfiːtɪst] adj & n derrotista (mf).

defect [ˈdiːfekt] I n defecto m; (flaw) desperfecto m. II [dɪˈfekt] vi desertar (**from**, de); (from country) huir.

defective [dɪˈfektɪv] adj (faulty) defectuoso,-a; (flawed) con desperfectos; (lacking) incompleto,-a.

defector [dɪˈfektər] n Pol tránsfuga mf, tránsfuga mf.

defence [dɪˈfens] n 1 defensa f; **the Ministry of D.**, el Ministerio de Defensa; **to come to sb's d.**, salir en defensa de algn. 2 usu sing Jur defensa f. 3 Sport GB [dɪˈfens], US [ˈdiːfens] **the d.**, la defensa.

defenceless [dɪˈfensləs] adj indefenso,-a.

defend [dɪˈfend] vtr defender.

defendant [dɪˈfendənt] n Jur acusado,-a m,f.

defender [dɪˈfendər] n defensor,-a m,f; Sport defensa mf.

defending [dɪˈfendɪŋ] adj Sport defensor,-a; **d. champion**, campeón,-ona m,f titular.

defense [dɪˈfens, ˈdiːfens] n US → **defence**.

defensive [dɪˈfensɪv] I adj defensivo,-a. II n **to be on the d.**, estar a la defensiva.

defer[1] [dɪˈfɜː] vtr aplazar, retrasar.

defer[2] [dɪˈfɜː] vi **to d. to**, deferir a.

deference [ˈdefərəns] n fml deferencia f, respeto m; **out of** or **in d. to**, por respeto o por deferencia a.

defiance [dɪˈfaɪəns] n 1 (challenge) desafío m; **in d. of**, a despecho de. 2 (resistance) resistencia f.

defiant [dɪˈfaɪənt] adj (challenging) desafiante; (bold) insolente.

deficiency [dɪˈfɪʃənsɪ] n 1 (lack) falta f, carencia f. 2 (shortcoming) defecto m.

deficient [dɪˈfɪʃənt] adj deficiente; **to be d. in sth**, carecer de algo.

deficit [ˈdefɪsɪt] n déficit m.

defile [dɪˈfaɪl] vtr fml 1 (mind) corromper; (honour) manchar; (woman) deshonrar. 2 (desecrate) profanar.

define [dɪˈfaɪn] vtr definir; (duties, powers) delimitar.

definite [ˈdefɪnɪt] adj 1 (clear) claro,-a; (progress) notable. 2 (date, place) determinado,-a; **is it d.?**, ¿es seguro? ◆**definitely** I adv sin duda; **he was d. drunk**, no cabe duda de que estaba borracho. II interj ¡desde luego!

definition [defɪˈnɪʃən] n definición f; **by d.**, por definición.

definitive [dɪˈfɪnɪtɪv] adj definitivo,-a.

deflate [dɪˈfleɪt] vtr 1 (tyre etc) desinflar. 2 fig rebajar; **to d. sb**, hacer bajar los humos a algn. 3 **to d. the economy**, tomar medidas deflacionistas.

deflationary [dɪˈfleɪʃənərɪ] adj Econ deflacionista.

deflect [dɪˈflekt] vtr desviar.

deflection [dɪˈflekʃən] n desviación f.

deforestation [diːfɒrɪsˈteɪʃən] n deforestación f.

deformed [dɪˈfɔːmd] adj deforme.

deformity [dɪˈfɔːmɪtɪ] n deformidad f.

defraud [dɪˈfrɔːd] vtr estafar.

defrost [diːˈfrɒst] vtr 1 (frozen food) descongelar. 2 US (windscreen) desempañar.

deft [deft] adj hábil, diestro,-a.

defunct [dɪˈfʌŋkt] adj (person) difunto,-a; (thing) en desuso.

defuse [diːˈfjuːz] vtr (bomb) desactivar; fig **to d. a situation**, reducir la tensión de una situación.

defy [dɪˈfaɪ] vtr 1 (person) desafiar; (law, order) contravenir. 2 (challenge) retar, desafiar.

degenerate [dɪˈdʒenəreɪt] I vi degenerar (into, en). II [dɪˈdʒenərɪt] adj & n degenerado,-a (m,f).

degrading [dɪˈɡreɪdɪŋ] adj degradante.

degree [dɪˈɡriː] n 1 grado m; **to some d.**, hasta cierto punto. 2 (stage) etapa f; **by degrees**, poco a poco. 3 (qualification) título m; (doctorate) doctorado m; **to have a d. in science**, ser licenciado en ciencias.

dehydrated [diːhaɪˈdreɪtɪd] adj (person) deshidratado,-a; (vegetables) seco,-a.

de-ice [diːˈaɪs] vtr quitar el hielo a, deshelar.

de-icer [diːˈaɪsər] n anticongelante m.

deign [deɪn] vi dignarse.

deity [ˈdeɪɪtɪ] n deidad f.

dejected [dɪ'dʒektɪd] adj desalentado,-a, abatido,-a.

delay [dɪ'leɪ] **I** vtr **1** (flight, train) retrasar; (person) entretener; **delayed action,** acción retardada. **2** (postpone) aplazar. **II** vi **don't d.,** no lo deje para más tarde. **III** n retraso m.

delectable [dɪ'lektəbəl] adj delicioso,-a.

delegate [n 'delɪgət] n delegado,-a m,f. **II** ['delɪgeɪt] vtr delegar (to, en); **to d. sb to do sth,** encargar a algn que haga algo.

delegation [delɪ'geɪʃən] n delegación f.

delete [dɪ'li:t] vtr tachar, suprimir.

deliberate [I dɪ'lɪbərɪt] **I** adj (intentional) deliberado,-a, intencionado,-a; (studied) premeditado,-a; (careful) prudente; (unhurried) pausado,-a. **II** vtr [dɪ'lɪbəreɪt] deliberar (on, about, sobre). **◆deliberately** adv (intentionally) a propósito; (unhurriedly) pausadamente.

deliberation [dɪlɪbə'reɪʃən] n **1** esp pl (consideration) deliberación f. **2** (care) cuidado m; (unhurriedness) pausa f.

delicacy ['delɪkəsɪ] n **1** delicadeza f. **2** (food) manjar m (exquisito).

delicate ['delɪkɪt] adj delicado,-a; (handiwork) fino,-a; (instrument) sensible; (flavour) sutil.

delicious [dɪ'lɪʃəs] adj delicioso,-a.

delight [dɪ'laɪt] **I** n **1** (pleasure) placer m; **he took d. in it,** le encantó. **2** (source of pleasure) encanto m, delicia f. **II** vtr encantar.

delighted [dɪ'laɪtɪd] adj encantado,-a; (smile) de alegría; **I'm d. to see you,** me alegro mucho de verte.

delightful [dɪ'laɪtfʊl] adj encantador,-a; (view, person) muy agradable; (meal, weather) delicioso,-a.

delinquency [dɪ'lɪŋkwənsɪ] n delincuencia f; **juvenile d.,** delincuencia juvenil.

delinquent [dɪ'lɪŋkwənt] adj & n delincuente (mf).

delirious [dɪ'lɪrɪəs] adj delirante.

deliver [dɪ'lɪvər] vtr **1** (goods) repartir, entregar; (message) dar; (order) despachar; **fig to d. the goods,** cumplir con la obligación. **2** (blow) asestar; (speech, verdict) pronunciar. **3** Med ayudar en el nacimiento de. **4** fml (rescue) liberar.

delivery [dɪ'lɪvərɪ] n **1** (of goods) reparto m, entrega f; **to take d. of an order,** recibir un pedido; **d. note,** albarán m de entrega; **GB d. van,** furgoneta f de reparto. **2** (of speech) declamación f. **3** (of baby) parto m.

delta ['deltə] n Geog delta m.

delude [dɪ'lu:d] vtr engañar; **don't d. yourself,** no te hagas ilusiones.

deluge ['delju:dʒ] **I** n **1** (flood) inundación f; (rain) diluvio m; fig (of letters etc) avalancha f. **II** vtr fml inundar.

delusion [dɪ'lu:ʒən] n **1** (state, act) enga-

ño m. **2** (false belief) ilusión f (vana); **delusions of grandeur,** delirios mpl de grandeza.

de luxe [də'lʌks, də'lʊks] adj de lujo inv.

delve [delv] vi **to d. into,** (pocket) hurgar en; (subject) profundizar en.

demand [dɪ'mɑ:nd] **I** n **1** solicitud f; (for pay rise, rights) reclamación f; (need) necesidad f; **on d.,** a petición. **2** (claim) exigencia f; **to be in d.,** ser solicitado,-a. **3** Econ demanda f. **II** vtr **1** exigir; (rights) reclamar; **to d. that ...,** insistir en que ... (+ subj). **2** (need) requerir.

demanding [dɪ'mɑ:ndɪŋ] adj **1** (person) exigente. **2** (job) agotador,-a.

demean [dɪ'mi:n] vtr fml **to d. oneself,** rebajarse.

demeaning [dɪ'mi:nɪŋ] adj fml humillante.

demeanour, US **demeanor** [dɪ'mi:nər] n fml **1** (behaviour) comportamiento m, conducta f. **2** (bearing) porte m.

demented [dɪ'mentɪd] adj Med demente; fam loco,-a.

demise [dɪ'maɪz] n (death) fml fallecimiento m; fig (of institution) desaparición f; (of ambition etc) fracaso m.

demist [di:'mɪst] vtr Aut desempañar.

demo ['deməʊ] n fam manifestación f; **d. tape,** maqueta f.

demobilize [di:'məʊbɪlaɪz] vtr desmovilizar.

democracy [dɪ'mɒkrəsɪ] n democracia f.

democrat ['deməkræt] n demócrata mf; Pol **Christian D.,** democratacristiano,-a m,f; **Social D.,** socialdemócrata mf.

democratic [demə'krætɪk] adj democrático,-a; US Pol **D. party,** partido m demócrata.

demographic [deməʊ'græfɪk] adj demográfico,-a.

demolish [dɪ'mɒlɪʃ] vtr (building) derribar, demoler; fig (theory, proposal) echar por tierra.

demolition [demə'lɪʃən] n demolición f.

demon ['di:mən] n demonio m.

demonstrate ['demənstreɪt] **I** vtr demostrar. **II** vi Pol manifestarse.

demonstration [demən'streɪʃən] n **1** (proof) demostración f, prueba f. **2** (explanation) explicación f. **3** Pol manifestación f.

demonstrative [dɪ'mɒnstrətɪv] adj expresivo,-a.

demonstrator ['demənstreɪtər] n manifestante mf.

demoralize [dɪ'mɒrəlaɪz] vtr desmoralizar.

demoralizing [dɪ'mɒrəlaɪzɪŋ] adj desmoralizador,-a, desmoralizante.

demote [dɪ'məʊt] vtr rebajar de graduación a.

demure [dɪ'mjʊər] adj (person) recatado, -a.

den [den] n 1 (of animal) guarida f. 2 fam (study) estudio m.

denial [dɪ'naɪəl] n 1 (of charge) desmentido m. 2 (of rights) denegación f; (of request) negativa f.

denim ['denɪm] n dril m; **d. skirt**, falda tejana; **denims**, tejanos mpl, vaqueros mpl.

Denmark ['denmɑːk] n Dinamarca.

denomination [dɪnɒmɪ'neɪʃən] n 1 Rel confesión f. 2 Fin (of coins) valor m.

denominator [dɪ'nɒmɪneɪtər] n denominador m.

denote [dɪ'nəʊt] vtr (show) indicar; (mean) significar.

denounce [dɪ'naʊns] vtr denunciar; (criticize) censurar.

dense [dens] adj 1 denso,-a; (crowd) numeroso,-a. 2 fam (stupid) torpe. ◆**densely** adv densamente.

density ['densɪtɪ] n densidad f.

dent [dent] I n abolladura f. II vtr (car) abollar.

dental ['dentəl] adj dental; **d. floss**, hilo m dental; **d. surgeon**, odontólogo,-a m,f; **d. surgery**, (place) clínica f dental; (treatment) cirugía f dental.

dentist ['dentɪst] n dentista mf.

dentistry ['dentɪstrɪ] n odontología f.

denture ['dentʃər] n (usu pl) dentadura postiza.

denunciation [dɪnʌnsɪ'eɪʃən] n denuncia f, condena f.

deny [dɪ'naɪ] vtr 1 (repudiate) negar; (rumour, report) desmentir; (charge) rechazar. 2 (refuse) negar.

deodorant [diː'əʊdərənt] n desodorante m.

depart [dɪ'pɑːt] vi marcharse, irse; fig (from subject) desviarse (**from**, de).

department [dɪ'pɑːtmənt] n sección f; (in university) departamento m; (in government) ministerio m; **d. store**, grandes almacenes mpl .

departure [dɪ'pɑːtʃər] n partida f; Av Rail salida f; Av **d. lounge**, sala f de embarque.

depend [dɪ'pend] I vi (rely) fiarse (**on, upon**, de). II v impers (be determined by) depender (**on, upon**, de); **it depends on the weather**, según el tiempo que haga; **that depends**, según.

dependable [dɪ'pendəbəl] adj (person) responsable, fiable; (income) seguro,-a; (machine) fiable.

dependant, US **dependent** [dɪ'pendənt] n dependiente mf.

dependence [dɪ'pendəns] n dependencia f.

dependent [dɪ'pendənt] I adj dependiente; **to be d. on sth**, depender de algo. II n US → **dependant**.

depict [dɪ'pɪkt] vtr Art representar; fig describir.

deplete [dɪ'pliːt] vtr reducir.

deplorable [dɪ'plɔːrəbəl] adj lamentable.

deplore [dɪ'plɔːr] vtr deplorar.

deploy [dɪ'plɔɪ] vtr Mil desplegar; fig utilizar.

depopulate [diː'pɒpjuleɪt] vtr despoblar.

deport [dɪ'pɔːt] vtr expulsar (**from**, de; **to**, a).

deportation [diːpɔː'teɪʃən] n expulsión f.

deportment [dɪ'pɔːtmənt] n fml porte m.

depose [dɪ'pəʊz] vtr deponer.

deposit [dɪ'pɒzɪt] I n 1 sedimento m; Min yacimiento m; (in wine) poso m. 2 (in bank) depósito m; **d. account**, cuenta f de ahorros. 3 Com (on purchase) señal f; (on rented car, flat) aepósito m; (on house) entrada f. II vtr depositar; (into account) ingresar.

deposition [depə'zɪʃən] n 1 (of leader) destitución f. 2 Jur (of witness) declaración f.

depositor [dɪ'pɒzɪtər] n depositante mf.

depot ['depəʊ] n almacén m; Mil depósito m; (bus garage) garaje m (de autobuses).

depraved [dɪ'preɪvd] adj (person) depravado,-a.

deprecate ['deprɪkeɪt] vtr desaprobar, censurar.

depreciate [dɪ'priːʃɪeɪt] vi depreciarse.

depreciation [dɪpriːʃɪ'eɪʃən] n depreciación f.

depress [dɪ'pres] vtr 1 (person) deprimir. 2 Econ (profits) reducir; (trade) dificultar. 3 fml (switch, lever etc) presionar; (clutch, piano pedal) pisar.

depressed [dɪ'prest] adj 1 (person) deprimido,-a; **to get d.**, deprimirse. 2 (market) en crisis. 3 (surface) hundido,-a.

depressing [dɪ'presɪŋ] adj deprimente.

depression [dɪ'preʃən] n depresión f.

deprivation [deprɪ'veɪʃən] n (hardship) privación f; (loss) pérdida f.

deprive [dɪ'praɪv] vtr privar (**of**, de).

deprived [dɪ'praɪvd] adj necesitado,-a.

Dept abbr of **Department**, dpt, dpto; (in store) sección f.

depth [depθ] n 1 profundidad f. 2 fig (of emotion) intensidad f; (of thought) complejidad f; **to be in the depths of despair**, estar completamente desesperado,-a; **in d.**, a fondo.

deputation [depju'teɪʃən] n delegación f.

deputy ['depjutɪ] n 1 (substitute) suplente mf; **d. chairman**, vicepresidente m,f; **d. head**, subdirector,-a m,f. 2 Pol diputado,-a m,f.

derail [dɪ'reɪl] vtr hacer descarrilar.

deranged [dɪ'reɪndʒd] adj trastornado,-a.

derby ['dɑːbɪ] n 1 Sport prueba f. 2 ['dɜːrbɪ] US sombrero hongo.

derelict ['derɪlɪkt] adj abandonado,-a, en ruinas.

deride [dɪ'raɪd] vtr ridiculizar, burlarse de.

derisive [dɪ'raɪsɪv] *adj* burlón,-ona.

derisory [dɪ'raɪsərɪ] *adj* irrisorio,-a.

derivative [dɪ'rɪvətɪv] I *adj (art, writing)* sin originalidad. II *n (of word, substance)* derivado *m*.

derive [dɪ'raɪv] I *vtr* sacar. II *vi (word)* derivarse **(from**, de); *(skill)* provenir **(from**, de).

derogatory [dɪ'rɒgətərɪ] *adj (remark, article)* despectivo,-a; *(meaning)* peyorativo,-a.

derrick ['derɪk] *n* Petrol torre *f* de perforación.

descend [dɪ'send] I *vi* 1 descender; **to d. from**, *(be related to)* descender de. II *vtr (stairs)* bajar.

descendant [dɪ'sendənt] *n* descendiente *mf*.

descent [dɪ'sent] *n* 1 descenso *m*. 2 fig *(into madness, poverty)* caída *f*. 3 *(slope)* declive *m*. 4 *(ancestry)* ascendencia *f*.

describe [dɪ'skraɪb] *vtr* 1 describir. 2 *(circle)* trazar.

description [dɪ'skrɪpʃən] *n* 1 descripción *f*; **to defy d.**, superar la descripción. 2 *(type)* clase *f*.

desecrate ['desɪkreɪt] *vtr* profanar.

desert[1] ['dezət] *n* desierto *m*.

desert[2] [dɪ'zɜːt] I *vtr (place, family)* abandonar. II *vi* Mil desertar **(from**, de).

deserter [dɪ'zɜːtər] *n* desertor,-a *m,f*.

desertion [dɪ'zɜːʃən] *n* abandono *m*; Pol defección *f*; Mil deserción *f*.

deserts [dɪ'zɜːts] *npl* **to get one's just d.**, llevarse su merecido.

deserve [dɪ'zɜːv] *vtr (rest, punishment)* merecer; *(prize, praise)* ser digno,-a de.

deservedly [dɪ'zɜːvɪdlɪ] *adv* con (toda) razón.

deserving [dɪ'zɜːvɪŋ] *adj (person)* de valía; *(cause)* meritorio,-a.

design [dɪ'zaɪn] I *n* 1 diseño *m*. 2 *(drawing, blueprint)* plano *m*. 3 *(layout)* disposición *f*. 4 *(pattern)* dibujo *m*. 5 fig *(scheme)* intención *f*; **by d.**, a propósito; fam **to have designs on**, tener puestas las miras en. II *vtr* diseñar.

designate ['dezɪgneɪt] I *vtr* 1 *(appoint)* designar, nombrar. 2 fml *(boundary)* señalar. II ['dezɪgnɪt] *adj* designado,-a.

designer [dɪ'zaɪnər] *n* Art diseñador,-a *m,f*; **d. jeans**, pantalones *mpl* de marca.

desirable [dɪ'zaɪərəbəl] *adj* deseable; *(asset, offer)* atractivo,-a.

desire [dɪ'zaɪər] I *n* deseo *m*; **I haven't the slightest d. to go**, no me apetece nada ir. II *vtr* desear.

desist [dɪ'zɪst] *vi* fml desistir **(from**, de).

desk [desk] *n (in school)* pupitre *m*; *(in office)* escritorio *m*; US Sl **d. clerk**, recepcionista *mf*; **d. job**, trabajo *m* de oficina; **news d.**, redacción *f*; **reception d.**, recepción *f*.

desktop ['desktɒp] *n* **d. computer**, orde-

nador *m* de sobremesa; **d. publishing**, autoedición *f*.

desolate ['desəlɪt] *adj* 1 *(uninhabited)* desierto,-a; *(barren)* yermo,-a. 2 *(person)* desconsolado,-a.

desolation [desə'leɪʃən] *n* 1 *(of place)* desolación *f*; *(by destruction)* asolamiento *m*. 2 *(of person)* desconsuelo *m*.

despair [dɪs'peər] I *n* desesperación *f*; **to drive sb to d.**, desesperar a algn. II *vi* desesperar(se) **(of**, de).

despairing [dɪs'peərɪŋ] *adj* desesperado,-a.

despatch [dɪs'pætʃ] *n & vtr →* **dispatch.**

desperate ['despərɪt] *adj* 1 desesperado, -a; *(struggle)* encarnizado,-a. 2 *(need)* apremiante. ◆**desperately** *adv (recklessly)* desesperadamente; *(struggle)* encarnizadamente; *(ill)* gravemente; *(in love)* locamente; *(difficult)* sumamente.

desperation [despə'reɪʃən] *n* desesperación *f*; **in d.**, a la desesperada.

despicable [dɪs'pɪkəbəl] *adj* despreciable; *(behaviour)* indigno,-a.

despise [dɪs'paɪz] *vtr* despreciar, menospreciar.

despite [dɪs'paɪt] *prep* fml a pesar de.

despondent [dɪs'pɒndənt] *adj* abatido,-a.

despot ['despɒt] *n* déspota *mf*.

dessert [dɪ'zɜːt] *n* postre *m*; **d. wine**, vino *m* dulce.

dessertspoon [dɪ'zɜːtspuːn] *n* 1 cuchara *f* de postre. 2 **d.(ful)**, *(measure)* cucharada *f* de postre.

destination [destɪ'neɪʃən] *n* destino *m*.

destined ['destɪnd] *adj* 1 **d. to fail**, condenado,-a al fracaso. 2 *(bound)* con destino **(for**, a).

destiny ['destɪnɪ] *n* destino *m*.

destitute ['destɪtjuːt] *adj* indigente.

destroy [dɪ'strɔɪ] *vtr* destruir; *(vehicle, old furniture)* destrozar.

destroyer [dɪ'strɔɪər] *n* Naut destructor *m*.

destruction [dɪ'strʌkʃən] *n* destrucción *f*; fig ruina *f*.

destructive [dɪ'strʌktɪv] *adj (gale etc)* destructor,-a; *(tendency, criticism)* destructivo,-a.

detach [dɪ'tætʃ] *vtr (remove)* separar.

detachable [dɪ'tætʃəbəl] *adj* separable **(from**, de).

detached [dɪ'tætʃt] *adj* 1 *(separated)* separado,-a; **d. house**, casa *f* independiente. 2 *(impartial)* objetivo,-a.

detachment [dɪ'tætʃmənt] *n* 1 *(impartiality)* objetividad *f*; *(aloofness)* despego *m*. 2 Mil destacamento *m*.

detail ['diːteɪl] I *n* 1 detalle *m*, pormenor *m*; **without going into detail(s)**, sin entrar en detalles; **details**, *(information)* información *f sing*. 2 Mil destacamento *m*. II *vtr* 1 *(list)* detallar, enumerar. 2 Mil *(appoint)* destacar.

detailed ['diːteɪld] *adj* detallado,-a,

minucioso,-a.

detain [dɪ'teɪn] vtr 1 Jur detener. 2 (delay) retener.

detainee [di:teɪ'ni:] n Pol preso,-a m,f.

detect [dɪ'tekt] vtr 1 (error, movement) advertir; (difference) notar; (smell, sound) percibir. 2 (discover) descubrir; (enemy ship) detectar; (position) localizar.

detection [dɪ'tekʃən] n 1 descubrimiento m; (of smell, sound) percepción f. 2 (discovery) (of enemy ship) detección f.

detective [dɪ'tektɪv] n detective mf; **d. story**, novela policíaca.

detector [dɪ'tektəʳ] n aparato m detector.

detention [dɪ'tenʃən] n (of suspect etc) detención f, arresto m; Educ **to get d.**, quedarse castigado,-a.

deter [dɪ'tɜːʳ] vtr (dissuade) disuadir (from, de); (stop) impedir.

detergent [dɪ'tɜːdʒənt] n detergente m.

deteriorate [dɪ'tɪərɪəreɪt] vi deteriorarse.

deterioration [dɪtɪərɪə'reɪʃən] n empeoramiento m; (of substance, friendship) deterioro m.

determination [dɪtɜːmɪ'neɪʃən] n (resolution) resolución f.

determine [dɪ'tɜːmɪn] vtr determinar.

determined [dɪ'tɜːmɪnd] adj (person) decidido,-a; (effort) enérgico,-a.

deterrent [dɪ'terənt] I adj disuasivo,-a. II n fuerza disuasoria.

detest [dɪ'test] vtr detestar, odiar.

detonate ['detəneɪt] vtr & vi detonar.

detonation [detə'neɪʃən] n detonación f.

detour ['di:tʊəʳ] n desvío m.

detract [dɪ'trækt] vi quitar mérito (from, a).

detractor [dɪ'træktəʳ] n detractor,-a m,f.

detriment ['detrɪmənt] n perjuicio m (to, de).

detrimental [detrɪ'mentəl] adj perjudicial (to, para).

deuce [dju:s] n Ten cuarenta iguales mpl.

devaluation [di:væljʊ'eɪʃən] n devaluación f.

devastate ['devəsteɪt] vtr (city, area) asolar; fig (person) desolar.

devastating ['devəsteɪtɪŋ] adj (fire) devastador,-a; (wind, flood) arrollador,-a.

devastation [devə'steɪʃən] n asolación f.

develop [dɪ'veləp] I vtr 1 desarrollar; (trade) fomentar; (skill) perfeccionar; (plan) elaborar; (habit) contraer; (interest) mostrar. 2 (natural resources) aprovechar; Constr (site) urbanizar. 3 Phot revelar. II vi 1 (body, industry) desarrollarse; (system) perfeccionarse; (interest) crecer. 2 (appear) crearse; (evolve) evolucionar.

developer [dɪ'veləpəʳ] n (property) d., inmobiliaria f.

development [dɪ'veləpmənt] n 1 desarrollo m; (of trade) fomento m; (of skill) perfección f; (of character) formación f. 2 (advance) avance m. 3 **there are no new**

developments, no hay ninguna novedad. 4 (exploitation) explotación f. 5 Constr urbanización f.

deviate ['di:vɪeɪt] vi desviarse (from, de).

deviation [di:vɪ'eɪʃən] n (from norm, route) desviación f (from, de); (from truth) alejamiento m.

device [dɪ'vaɪs] n 1 aparato m; (mechanism) mecanismo m. 2 (trick, scheme) ardid m.

devil ['devəl] n diablo m, demonio m; **d.'s advocate**, abogado,-a m,f del diablo; fam **where the d. did you put it?**, ¿dónde demonios lo pusiste?; **you lucky d.!**, ¡vaya suerte que tienes!

devious ['di:vɪəs] adj 1 (winding) tortuoso,-a. 2 esp pej (person) taimado,-a.

devise [dɪ'vaɪz] vtr idear, concebir.

devoid [dɪ'vɔɪd] adj desprovisto,-a (of, de).

devolution [di:və'lu:ʃən] n Pol transmisión f de poderes a las regiones.

devote [dɪ'vəʊt] vtr dedicar; **she devoted her life to helping the poor**, consagró su vida a la ayuda de los pobres.

devoted [dɪ'vəʊtɪd] adj fiel, leal (to, a).

devotee [devə'ti:] n (of religion) devoto,-a m,f; (of theatre, sport) aficionado,-a m,f; Pol partidario,-a mf.

devotion [dɪ'vəʊʃən] n devoción f; (to cause) dedicación f.

devour [dɪ'vaʊəʳ] vtr devorar.

devout [dɪ'vaʊt] adj devoto,-a.

dew [dju:] n rocío m.

dexterity [dek'sterɪtɪ] n destreza f.

dext(e)rous ['dekstrəs] adj diestro,-a.

diabetes [daɪə'bi:ti:z, daɪə'bi:tɪs] n diabetes f.

diabetic [daɪə'betɪk] adj & n diabético,-a (m,f).

diabolical [daɪə'bɒlɪkəl] adj 1 (evil) diabólico,-a. 2 fam (unbearable) espantoso,-a.

diagnose [daɪəg'nəʊz] vtr diagnosticar.

diagnosis [daɪəg'nəʊsɪs] n (pl diagnoses [daɪəg'nəʊsi:z]) diagnóstico m.

diagonal [daɪ'ægənəl] adj & n diagonal (f). ◆**diagonally** adv en diagonal, diagonalmente.

diagram ['daɪəgræm] n diagrama m; (of process, system) esquema m; (of workings) gráfico m.

dial ['daɪəl, daɪl] I n (of clock) esfera f; (of radio) cuadrante m; (of telephone) disco m; (of machine) botón m selector. II vi & vtr Tel marcar; **dialling code**, prefijo m; **dialling tone**, señal f de marcar.

dialect ['daɪəlekt] n dialecto m.

dialogue, US **dialog** ['daɪəlɒg] n diálogo m.

diameter [daɪ'æmɪtəʳ] n diámetro m.

diametrically [daɪə'metrɪkəlɪ] adv diametralmente.

diamond ['daɪəmənd] n 1 diamante m. 2

(shape) rombo *m*.
diaper ['daɪəpəʳ] *n US* pañal *m*.
diaphragm ['daɪəfræm] *n* diafragma *m*.
diarrhoea, *US* **diarrhea** [daɪə'rɪə] *n* diarrea *f*.
diary ['daɪərɪ] *n* **1** diario *m*; **to keep a d.**, llevar un diario. **2** *GB (for appointments)* agenda *f*.
dice [daɪs] **I** *npl* dados *mpl*. **II** *vtr* Culin cortar en cuadritos.
dichotomy [daɪ'kɒtəmɪ] *n* dicotomía *f*.
dictate [dɪk'teɪt] **I** *vtr (letter, order)* dictar. **II** *vi* **to d. to sb**, dar órdenes a algn. **III** ['dɪkteɪt] *n fig* the dictates of conscience, los dictados de la conciencia.
dictation [dɪk'teɪʃən] *n* dictado *m*.
dictator [dɪk'teɪtəʳ] *n* dictador,-a *m,f*.
dictatorship [dɪk'teɪtəʃɪp] *n* dictadura *f*.
diction ['dɪkʃən] *n* dicción *f*.
dictionary ['dɪkʃənərɪ] *n* diccionario *m*.
did [dɪd] *pt* → **do**.
die [daɪ] *vi* **1** morir, morirse; *fam* fig **to be dying for sth/to do sth**, morirse por algo/de ganas de hacer algo. **2** *fig (flame)* extinguirse; *fig* **to d. hard**, *(habit)* tardar en desaparecer. **3** *(engine)* calarse; *(battery)* agotarse. ◆**die away** *vi* desvanecerse. ◆**die down** *vi (fire)* extinguirse; *(wind)* amainar; *(noise, excitement)* disminuir. ◆**die off** *vi* morir uno por uno. ◆**die out** *vi* extinguirse.
die-hard ['daɪhɑːd] *n* reaccionario,-a *m,f*.
diesel ['diːzəl] *n* **1** *(oil)* gasoil *m*. **2** **d. engine**, motor *m* diesel. **2** *fam (vehicle)* vehículo *m* diesel.
diet ['daɪət] **I** *n (normal food)* dieta *f*; *(selected food)* régimen *m*; **to be on a d.**, estar a régimen. **II** *vi* estar a régimen.
dietician [daɪə'tɪʃən] *n* especialista *mf* en dietética.
differ ['dɪfəʳ] *vi (be unlike)* ser distinto,-a; *(disagree)* discrepar.
difference ['dɪfərəns] *n* **1** *(dissimilarity)* diferencia *f*; **it makes no d. (to me)**, (me) da igual; **what d. does it make?**, ¿qué más da? **2** *(disagreement)* desacuerdo *m*.
different,-a ['dɪfərənt] *adj* diferente, distinto,-a; **you look d.**, pareces otro,-a. ◆**differently** *adv* de otra manera.
differentiate [dɪfə'renʃɪeɪt] **I** *vtr* distinguir, diferenciar *(from,* de). **II** *vi* distinguir *(between,* entre).
difficult ['dɪfɪkəlt] *adj* difícil.
difficulty ['dɪfɪkəltɪ] *n* dificultad *f*; *(problem)* problema *m*; **to be in difficulties**, estar en un aprieto.
diffident ['dɪfɪdənt] *adj* tímido,-a.
diffuse [dɪ'fjuːs] **I** *adj (light)* difuso,-a; *fig* vago,-a. **II** [dɪ'fjuːz] *vtr* difundir; *(heat)* desprender.
dig [dɪg] **I** *n* **1** *(poke)* codazo *m*. **2** *fam (gibe)* pulla *f*. **3** *(archeological)* excavación

f. **3** *GB* **digs**, *(lodgings)* alojamiento *m* *sing*; *(room)* habitación *f sing* alquilada. **II** *vtr (pt & pp* **dug) 1** *(earth)* cavar; *(tunnel)* excavar. **2** *fam fig* **to d. one's heels in**, mantenerse en sus trece. **III** *vi (person)* cavar; *(animal)* escarbar; *(excavate)* excavar. ◆**dig in** *vi Mil* atrincherarse. ◆**dig out** *vtr fig (old suit)* sacar; *(information)* descubrir. ◆**dig up** *vtr (weeds)* arrancar; *(buried object)* desenterrar; *(road)* levantar; *fig* sacar a relucir.
digest [daɪdʒest] **I** *n (summary)* resumen *m*. **II** [dɪ'dʒest] *vtr (food)* digerir; *fig (facts)* asimilar.
digestion [dɪ'dʒestʃən] *n* digestión *f*.
digestive [dɪ'dʒestɪv] *adj* digestivo,-a; *GB* **d. biscuit**, galleta *f* integral.
digger ['dɪgəʳ] *n* excavadora *f*.
digit ['dɪdʒɪt] *n* **1** *Math* dígito *m*. **2** *fml Anat* dedo *m*.
digital ['dɪdʒɪtəl] *adj* digital.
dignified ['dɪgnɪfaɪd] *adj (manner)* solemne, serio,-a; *(appearance)* majestuoso,-a.
dignitary ['dɪgnɪtərɪ] *n* dignatario *m*.
dignity ['dɪgnɪtɪ] *n* dignidad *f*.
digress [daɪ'gres] *vi* apartarse del tema.
dike [daɪk] *n US* → **dyke**.
dilapidated [dɪ'læpɪdeɪtɪd] *adj* en mal estado.
dilemma [dɪ'lemə, daɪ'lemə] *n* dilema *m*.
diligent ['dɪlɪdʒənt] *adj (worker)* diligente; *(inquiries, search)* esmerado,-a.
dilute [daɪ'luːt] **I** *vtr* diluir; *(wine, milk)* aguar; *fig (effect, influence)* atenuar. **II** *vi* diluirse.
dim [dɪm] **I** *adj (dimmer, dimmest)* **1** *(light)* débil, tenue; *(room)* oscuro,-a; *(outline)* borroso,-a; *(eyesight)* defectuoso,-a; *fig (memory)* vago,-a; *fig (future)* sombrío,-a. **2** *fam (stupid)* torpe. **II** *vtr (light)* bajar. **III** *vi (light)* bajarse; *(sight)* nublarse; *fig (joy)* extinguirse. ◆**dimly** *adv* vagamente.
dime [daɪm] *n US* moneda *f* de diez centavos.
dimension [daɪ'menʃən] *n* dimensión *f*.
diminish [dɪ'mɪnɪʃ] *vtr & vi* disminuir.
diminutive [dɪ'mɪnjʊtɪv] **I** *adj* diminuto,-a. **II** *n Ling* diminutivo *m*.
dimmer ['dɪməʳ] *n* **d. (switch)**, regulador *m* de voltaje.
dimple ['dɪmpəl] *n* hoyuelo *m*.
din [dɪn] *n (of crowd)* alboroto *m*; *(of machinery)* estruendo *m*.
dine [daɪn] *vi fml* cenar; **to d. out**, cenar fuera.
diner ['daɪnəʳ] *n* **1** *(person)* comensal *mf*. **2** *US (restaurant)* restaurante barato.
dinghy ['dɪŋɪ] *n* bote *m*; **(rubber) d.**, bote *m* neumático.
dingy ['dɪndʒɪ] *adj (dingier, dingiest)* **1** *(dark)* oscuro,-a. **2** *(dirty)* sucio,-a. **3** *(colour)* desteñido,-a.

dining car ['daɪnɪŋkɑ:r] n vagón m restaurante.

dining room ['daɪnɪŋruːm] n comedor m.

dinner ['dɪnər] n (at midday) comida f; (in evening) cena f; **d. jacket**, smoking m; **d. service**, vajilla f; **d. table**, mesa f de comedor.

dinosaur ['daɪnəsɔːr] n dinosaurio m.

dint [dɪnt] n **by d. of**, a fuerza de.

diocese ['daɪəsɪs] n diócesis f inv.

dioxide [daɪ'ɒksaɪd] n bióxido m.

dip [dɪp] **I** n 1 fam (bathe) chapuzón m. 2 (of road) pendiente f; (in ground) depresión f. 3 Culin salsa f. **II** vt 1 bañar; (spoon, hand) meter. 2 GB Aut to **d. one's lights**, poner luces de cruce. **III** vi (road) bajar. **◆dip into** vtr 1 (savings) echar mano de. 2 (book) hojear.

diphthong ['dɪfθɒŋ] n diptongo m.

diploma [dɪ'pləʊmə] n diploma m.

diplomacy [dɪ'pləʊməsɪ] n diplomacia f.

diplomat ['dɪpləmæt] n diplomático,-a m,f.

diplomatic [dɪplə'mætɪk] adj diplomático,-a.

dipstick ['dɪpstɪk] n indicador m de nivel del aceite.

dire [daɪər] adj (urgent) extremo,-a; (serious) grave.

direct [dɪ'rekt, 'daɪrekt] **I** adj 1 directo, -a; **d. current**, corriente continua. 2 the **d. opposite**, todo lo contrario. **II** adv directamente. **III** vtr 1 dirigir; **can you d. me to a bank?**, ¿me puede indicar dónde hay un banco? 2 fml (order) mandar.

direction [dɪ'rekʃən, daɪ'rekʃən] n 1 dirección f; **sense of d.**, sentido m de la orientación. 2 **directions**, (to place) señas fpl; **d. for use**, modo m de empleo. 1 Theat puesta f en escena.

directive [dɪ'rektɪv, daɪ'rektɪv] n directiva f.

directly [dɪ'rektlɪ, daɪ'rektlɪ] **I** adv 1 (above etc) exactamente, justo. 2 (speak) francamente. 3 (descend) directamente. 4 (come) en seguida. **II** conj fam en cuanto.

director [dɪ'rektər, daɪ'rektər] n director,-a m,f.

directory [dɪ'rektərɪ, daɪ'rektərɪ] n Tel guía telefónica; **d. enquiries**, (servicio m de) información f.

dirt [dɜːt] n suciedad f.

dirt-cheap [dɜːt'tʃiːp] adv & adj fam tirado,-a.

dirty ['dɜːtɪ] **I** adj (dirtier, dirtiest) 1 sucio,-a. 2 **to give sb a d. look**, fulminar a algn con la mirada. 3 (joke) verde; (mind) pervertido,-a; **d. word**, palabrota f; **d. old man**, viejo m verde. **II** vtr ensuciar.

disability [dɪsə'bɪlɪtɪ] n incapacidad f, discapacidad f; **d. pension**, pensión f por invalidez.

disabled [dɪ'seɪbəld] **I** adj minusválido,

-a. **II** npl the **d.**, los minusválidos.

disadvantage [dɪsəd'vɑːntɪdʒ] n desventaja f; (obstacle) inconveniente m.

disaffection [dɪsə'fekʃən] n descontento m.

disagree [dɪsə'griː] vi 1 (differ) no estar de acuerdo (with, con), (on or over sth, sobre algo). 2 (not match) discrepar (with, de, con). 3 **garlic disagrees with me**, el ajo no me sienta bien.

disagreeable [dɪsə'grɪəbəl] adj desagradable.

disagreement [dɪsə'griːmənt] n 1 desacuerdo m; (argument) riña f. 2 (noncorrespondence) discrepancia f.

disallow [dɪsə'laʊ] vtr (goal) anular; (objection) rechazar.

disappear [dɪsə'pɪər] vi desaparecer.

disappearance [dɪsə'pɪərəns] n desaparición f.

disappoint [dɪsə'pɔɪnt] vtr (person) decepcionar, defraudar; (hope, ambition) frustrar.

disappointed [dɪsə'pɔɪntɪd] adj decepcionado,-a.

disappointing [dɪsə'pɔɪntɪŋ] adj decepcionante.

disappointment [dɪsə'pɔɪntmənt] n decepción f.

disapproval [dɪsə'pruːvəl] n desaprobación f.

disapprove [dɪsə'pruːv] vi **to d. of**, desaprobar.

disarm [dɪs'ɑːm] **I** vtr desarmar. **II** vi desarmarse.

disarmament [dɪs'ɑːməmənt] n desarme m.

disarray [dɪsə'reɪ] n fml **in d.**, (room, papers) en desorden; (hair) desarreglado,-a; (thoughts) confuso,-a.

disaster [dɪ'zɑːstər] n desastre m.

disastrous [dɪ'zɑːstrəs] adj desastroso,-a.

disband [dɪs'bænd] **I** vtr disolver. **II** vi disolverse.

disbelief [dɪsbɪ'liːf] n incredulidad f.

disc [dɪsk] n disco m; Comput disquete m; **d. jockey**, disc-jockey mf, pinchadiscos mf inv.

discard [dɪs'kɑːd] vtr (old things) deshacerse de; (plan) descartar.

discern [dɪ'sɜːn] vtr (shape, difference) percibir; (truth) darse cuenta de.

discerning [dɪ'sɜːnɪŋ] adj (person) perspicaz; (taste) refinado,-a.

discharge [dɪs'tʃɑːdʒ] fml **I** vtr 1 (smoke) emitir; (liquid) echar; (cargo) descargar. 2 (prisoner) soltar; (patient) dar de alta a; (soldier) licenciar; (employee) despedir. 3 (debt) saldar. 4 (fulfil) cumplir. **II** ['dɪstʃɑːdʒ] n 1 (of current, load) descarga f; (of gases) escape m. 2 (of prisoner) liberación f; (of patient) alta f; (of soldier) licencia f. 3 (of debt) descargo m. 4 (of duty) cumplimiento m.

disciple [dɪˈsaɪpəl] n discípulo,-a m,f.
discipline [ˈdɪsɪplɪn] I n disciplina f. II vtr (child) castigar; (worker) sancionar; (official) expedientar.
disclaim [dɪsˈkleɪm] vtr fml negar tener.
disclose [dɪsˈkləʊz] vtr revelar.
disclosure [dɪsˈkləʊʒər] n revelación f.
disco [ˈdɪskəʊ] n (abbr of discotheque) fam disco f.
discolour, US **discolor** [dɪsˈkʌlər] vtr descolorir.
discomfort [dɪsˈkʌmfət] n 1 (lack of comfort) incomodidad f. 2 (pain) malestar m. 3 (unease) inquietud f.
disconcert [dɪskənˈsɜːt] vtr desconcertar.
disconcerting [dɪskənˈsɜːtɪŋ] adj desconcertante.
disconnect [dɪskəˈnekt] vtr desconectar (from, de); (gas, electricity) cortar.
disconnected [dɪskəˈnektɪd] adj inconexo,-a.
disconsolate [dɪsˈkɒnsəlɪt] adj desconsolado,-a.
discontent [dɪskənˈtent] n descontento m.
discontented [dɪskənˈtentɪd] adj descontento,-a.
discontinue [dɪskənˈtɪnjuː] vtr fml abandonar; (work) interrumpir.
discord [ˈdɪskɔːd] n 1 fml discordia f. 2 Mus disonancia f.
discordant [dɪsˈkɔːdənt] adj discordante.
discotheque [ˈdɪskətek] n discoteca f.
discount [ˈdɪskaʊnt] I n descuento m. II [dɪsˈkaʊnt] vtr 1 (price) rebajar. 2 (view, suggestion) descartar.
discourage [dɪsˈkʌrɪdʒ] vtr (dishearten) desanimar; (advances) rechazar.
discouraging [dɪsˈkʌrɪdʒɪŋ] adj desalentador,-a.
discover [dɪsˈkʌvər] vtr descubrir; (missing person, object) encontrar.
discovery [dɪsˈkʌvərɪ] n descubrimiento m.
discredit [dɪsˈkredɪt] I n descrédito m. II vtr (person, régime) desacreditar; (theory) poner en duda.
discreet [dɪsˈkriːt] adj discreto,-a; (distance, silence) prudente; (hat, house) modesto,-a.
discrepancy [dɪsˈkrepənsɪ] n diferencia f.
discretion [dɪsˈkreʃən] n discreción f; (prudence) prudencia f; at the d. of ..., a juicio de ....
discriminate [dɪsˈkrɪmɪneɪt] vi discriminar (between, entre); to d. against sth/sb, discriminar algo/a algn.
discriminating [dɪsˈkrɪmɪneɪtɪŋ] adj (person) entendido,-a; (taste) refinado,-a.
discrimination [dɪskrɪmɪˈneɪʃən] n 1 (bias) discriminación f. 2 (distinction) diferenciación f.
discuss [dɪsˈkʌs] vtr discutir; (in writing) tratar de.
discussion [dɪsˈkʌʃən] n discusión f.

disdain [dɪsˈdeɪn] fml I n desdén m. II vtr desdeñar.
disdainful [dɪsˈdeɪnful] adj fml desdeñoso,-a.
disease [dɪˈziːz] n enfermedad f; fig mal m.
disembark [dɪsɪmˈbɑːk] vtr & vi desembarcar.
disenchanted [dɪsɪnˈtʃɑːntɪd] adj desencantado,-a, desilusionado,-a.
disengage [dɪsɪnˈgeɪdʒ] vtr soltar; Aut to d. the clutch, soltar el embrague, desembragar.
disentangle [dɪsɪnˈtæŋgəl] vtr desenredar.
disfigure [dɪsˈfɪgər] vtr desfigurar.
disgrace [dɪsˈgreɪs] I n 1 desgracia f; to be in d., estar desacreditado,-a; to fall into d., caer en desgracia. 2 (shame) vergüenza f, escándalo m. II vtr deshonrar, desacreditar.
disgraceful [dɪsˈgreɪsful] adj vergonzoso,-a.
disgruntled [dɪsˈgrʌntəld] adj contrariado,-a, disgustado,-a.
disguise [dɪsˈgaɪz] I n disfraz m; in d., disfrazado,-a. II vtr 1 (person) disfrazar (as, de). 2 (feelings) disimular.
disgust [dɪsˈgʌst] I n 1 (loathing) repugnancia f, asco m. 2 (strong disapproval) indignación f. II vtr 1 (revolt) repugnar, dar asco a. 2 (offend) indignar.
disgusting [dɪsˈgʌstɪŋ] adj asqueroso,-a, repugnante; (behaviour, state of affairs) intolerable.
dish [dɪʃ] n (for serving) fuente f; (course) plato m; to wash or do the dishes, fregar los platos. ◆**dish out** vtr fam (food) servir; (books, advice) repartir; to d. it out (to sb), (criticize) criticar (a algn). ◆**dish up** vtr (meal) servir.
dishcloth [ˈdɪʃklɒθ] n trapo m de fregar.
dishearten [dɪsˈhɑːtən] vtr desanimar.
dishevelled, US **disheveled** [dɪˈʃevəld] adj (hair) despeinado,-a; (appearance) desaliñado,-a.
dishonest [dɪsˈɒnɪst] adj (person) poco honrado,-a; (means) fraudulento,-a.
dishonesty [dɪsˈɒnɪstɪ] n (of person) falta f de honradez.
dishonour, US **dishonor** [dɪsˈɒnər] I n fml deshonra f. II vtr (name) deshonrar.
dishonourable [dɪsˈɒnərəbəl] adj deshonroso,-a.
dishtowel [ˈdɪʃtaʊəl] n US trapo m de cocina.
dishwasher [ˈdɪʃwɒʃər] n lavaplatos m inv; (person) lavaplatos mf inv.
disillusion [dɪsɪˈluːʒən] vtr desilusionar.
disincentive [dɪsɪnˈsentɪv] n freno m.
disinfect [dɪsɪnˈfekt] vtr desinfectar.
disinfectant [dɪsɪnˈfektənt] n desinfectante m.
disinherit [dɪsɪnˈherɪt] vtr desheredar.

disintegrate [dɪsˈɪntɪgreɪt] vi desintegrarse.

disintegration [dɪsɪntɪˈgreɪʃən] n desintegración f.

disinterested [dɪsˈɪntrɪstɪd] adj desinteresado,-a.

disjointed [dɪsˈdʒɔɪntɪd] adj inconexo,-a.

disk [dɪsk] n US disco m; Comput disquete m; **d. drive**, disquetera f, disketera f.

diskette [dɪsˈket] n Comput disquete m.

dislike [dɪsˈlaɪk] I n antipatía f, aversión f (**for**, **of**, **a**, hacia). II vtr tener antipatía o aversión a o hacia.

dislocate [ˈdɪsləkeɪt] vtr (joint) dislocar.

dislodge [dɪsˈlɒdʒ] vtr sacar.

disloyal [dɪsˈlɔɪəl] adj desleal.

dismal [ˈdɪzməl] adj 1 (prospect) sombrío,-a; (place, weather) deprimente; (person) triste. 2 (failure) lamentable.

dismantle [dɪsˈmæntəl] vtr desmontar.

dismay [dɪsˈmeɪ] I n consternación f. II vtr consternar.

dismiss [dɪsˈmɪs] vtr 1 (idea) descartar. 2 (employee) despedir; (official) destituir. 3 **to d. sb**, (from room, presence) dar permiso a algn para retirarse. 4 (reject) rechazar; Jur desestimar; (case) sobreseer.

dismissal [dɪsˈmɪsəl] n 1 (of employee) despido m; (of official) destitución f. 2 (of claim) rechazo m; Jur desestimación f.

dismount [dɪsˈmaʊnt] vi fml apearse (**from**, de).

disobedience [dɪsəˈbiːdɪəns] n desobediencia f.

disobedient [dɪsəˈbiːdɪənt] adj desobediente.

disobey [dɪsəˈbeɪ] vtr & vi desobedecer; (law) violar.

disorder [dɪsˈɔːdər] n 1 (untidiness) desorden m. 2 (riot) disturbio m. 3 (of organ, mind) trastorno m; (of speech) defecto m.

disorderly [dɪsˈɔːdəlɪ] adj 1 (untidy) desordenado,-a; (meeting) alborotado,-a; (conduct) escandaloso,-a.

disorganized [dɪsˈɔːgənaɪzd] adj desorganizado,-a.

disorient [dɪsˈɔːrɪənt], **disorientate** [dɪsˈɔːrɪənteɪt] vtr desorientar.

disown [dɪsˈəʊn] vtr desconocer.

disparaging [dɪsˈpærɪdʒɪŋ] adj despectivo,-a.

disparity [dɪsˈpærɪtɪ] n fml disparidad f.

dispassionate [dɪsˈpæʃənɪt] adj desapasionado,-a.

dispatch [dɪsˈpætʃ] I n 1 (official message) despacho m; (journalist's report) reportaje m; (military message) parte m. 2 (of mail) envío m; (of goods) consignación f. II vtr 1 (mail) enviar; (goods) expedir. 2 fam (food) zamparse; (job) despachar.

dispel [dɪsˈpel] vtr disipar.

dispensary [dɪsˈpensərɪ] n dispensario m.

dispense [dɪsˈpens] vtr (supplies) repartir; (justice) administrar. ◆**dispense with** vtr (do without) prescindir de.

dispenser [dɪsˈpensər] n máquina expendedora; **cash d.**, cajero automático; **soap d.**, dosificador m de jabón.

dispensing chemist [dɪsˈpensɪŋˈkemɪst] n GB farmacéutico,-a m,f.

dispersal [dɪsˈpɜːsəl] n dispersión f.

disperse [dɪsˈpɜːs] I vtr dispersar. II vi dispersarse; (fog) disiparse.

dispirited [dɪsˈpɪrɪtɪd] adj abatido,-a.

displace [dɪsˈpleɪs] vtr 1 desplazar; **displaced person**, desterrado,-a m,f. 2 (supplant) sustituir.

display [dɪsˈpleɪ] I n (exhibition) exposición f; Comput visualización f; (of feelings, skills) demostración f; (of force) despliegue m; **d. window**, escaparate m; **military d.**, desfile m militar. II vtr 1 mostrar; (goods) exponer; Comput visualizar. 2 (feelings) manifestar.

displease [dɪsˈpliːz] vtr disgustar; (offend) ofender.

displeasure [dɪsˈpleʒər] n disgusto m.

disposable [dɪsˈpəʊzəbəl] adj 1 (throwaway) desechable. 2 (available) disponible.

disposal [dɪsˈpəʊzəl] n 1 (removal) eliminación f. 2 (availability) disponibilidad f; **at my d.**, a mi disposición. 3 fml (arrangement) disposición f. 4 (sale) venta f; (of property) traspaso m.

dispose [dɪsˈpəʊz] I vi **to d. of**, (remove) eliminar; (rubbish) tirar; (unwanted object) deshacerse de; (matter) resolver; (sell) vender; (property) traspasar. II vtr fml (arrange) disponer.

disposed [dɪsˈpəʊzd] adj (inclined) dispuesto,-a.

disposition [dɪspəˈzɪʃən] n 1 (temperament) genio m. 2 fml (arrangement) disposición f.

disproportionate [dɪsprəˈpɔːʃənɪt] adj desproporcionado,-a (**to**, a).

disprove [dɪsˈpruːv] vtr refutar.

dispute [dɪsˈpjuːt] I n (disagreement) discusión f; (quarrel) disputa f; **industrial d.**, conflicto m laboral. II [dɪsˈpjuːt] vtr (claim) refutar; (territory) disputar; (matter) discutir. III vi discutir (**about**, **over**, de, sobre).

disqualify [dɪsˈkwɒlɪfaɪ] vtr 1 Sport descalificar. 2 (make ineligible) incapacitar.

disquiet [dɪsˈkwaɪət] n preocupación f, inquietud f.

disregard [dɪsrɪˈgɑːd] I n indiferencia f, (for safety) despreocupación f. II vtr descuidar; (ignore) ignorar.

disrepair [dɪsrɪˈpeər] n mal estado m; **in (a state of) d.**, en mal estado; **to fall into d.**, deteriorarse.

disreputable [dɪsˈrepjʊtəbəl] adj (person, area) de mala fama; (behaviour) vergonzoso,-a.

disrepute |dɪsrɪ'pjuːt| n mala fama f, oprobio m.

disrespectful |dɪsrɪ'spektful| adj irrespetuoso,-a.

disrupt |dɪs'rʌpt| vtr (meeting, traffic) interrumpir; (schedule etc) desbaratar.

disruption |dɪs'rʌpʃən| n (of meeting, traffic) interrupción f; (of schedule etc) desbaratamiento m.

dissatisfaction |dɪssætɪs'fækʃən| n descontento m, insatisfacción f.

dissatisfied |dɪs'sætɪsfaɪd| adj descontento,-a.

dissect |dɪ'sekt. daɪ'sekt| vtr disecar.

disseminate |dɪ'semɪneɪt| vtr fml diseminar, difundir.

dissent |dɪ'sent| I n disentimiento m. II vi disentir.

dissertation |dɪsə'teɪʃən| n disertación f; Univ tesina f (on, sobre).

disservice |dɪs'sɜːvɪs| n perjuicio m; to do sth/sb a d., perjudicar algo/a algn.

dissident |'dɪsɪdənt| adj & n disidente (mf).

dissimilar |dɪ'sɪmɪlə| adj distinto,-a.

dissipate |'dɪsɪpeɪt| I vtr 1 disipar. 2 (waste) derrochar. II vi disiparse.

dissociate |dɪ'səʊʃɪeɪt| vtr to d. oneself, distanciarse.

dissolute |'dɪsəluːt| adj disoluto,-a.

dissolution |dɪsə'luːʃən| n disolución f; (of agreement) rescisión f.

dissolve |dɪ'zɒlv| I vtr disolver. II vi disolverse.

dissuade |dɪ'sweɪd| vtr disuadir (from, de).

distance |'dɪstəns| I n distancia f; in the d., a lo lejos; fam to stay the d., completar la prueba. II vtr distanciarse.

distant |'dɪstənt| adj 1 (place, time) lejano,-a. 2 (look) distraído,-a. 2 (aloof) distante, frío,-a.

distaste |dɪs'teɪst| n aversión f.

distasteful |dɪs'teɪstful| adj desagradable.

distend |dɪ'stend| fml vtr dilatar. II vi dilatarse.

distil, US **distill** |dɪs'tɪl| vtr destilar.

distillery |dɪs'tɪlərɪ| n destilería f.

distinct |dɪs'tɪŋkt| adj 1 (different) diferente; as d. from, a diferencia de. 2 (smell, change) marcado,-a; (idea, intention) claro,-a.

distinction |dɪs'tɪŋkʃən| n 1 (difference) diferencia f. 2 (excellence) distinción f. 3 Educ sobresaliente m.

distinctive |dɪs'tɪŋktɪv| adj distintivo,-a.

distinguish |dɪs'tɪŋgwɪʃ| vtr distinguir.

distinguished |dɪs'tɪŋgwɪʃt| adj distinguido,-a.

distinguishing |dɪs'tɪŋgwɪʃɪŋ| adj distintivo,-a, característico,-a.

distort |dɪs'tɔːt| vtr (misrepresent) deformar; (words) tergiversar.

distortion |dɪs'tɔːʃən| n deformación f;

(of sound, image) distorsión f.

distract |dɪ'strækt| vtr distraer.

distracted |dɪ'stræktɪd| adj distraído,-a.

distraction |dɪ'strækʃən| n (interruption) distracción f; (confusion) confusión f; to drive sb to d., sacar a algn de quicio.

distraught |dɪ'strɔːt| adj (anguished) afligido,-a.

distress |dɪ'stres| I n (mental) angustia f; (physical) dolor m; d. signal, señal f de socorro. II vtr (upset) angustiar.

distressing |dɪ'stresɪŋ| adj penoso,-a.

distribute |dɪ'strɪbjuːt| vtr distribuir, repartir.

distribution |dɪstrɪ'bjuːʃən| n distribución f.

distributor |dɪ'strɪbjʊtə| n 1 Com distribuidor,-a m,f. 2 Aut delco m.

district |'dɪstrɪkt| n (of country) región f; (of town) barrio m; US d. attorney, fiscal m; d. council, corporación f local; d. nurse, practicante mf.

distrust |dɪs'trʌst| I n recelo m. II vtr desconfiar de.

disturb |dɪ'stɜːb| vtr 1 (inconvenience) molestar. 2 (silence) romper; (sleep) interrumpir. 3 (worry) perturbar. 4 (papers) desordenar.

disturbance |dɪ'stɜːbəns| n 1 (of routine) alteración f. 2 (commotion) disturbio m, alboroto m.

disturbed |dɪ'stɜːbd| adj (mentally) inestable.

disturbing |dɪ'stɜːbɪŋ| adj inquietante.

disuse |dɪs'juːs| n desuso m.

disused |dɪs'juːzd| adj abandonado,-a.

ditch |dɪtʃ| I n zanja f; (at roadside) cuneta f; (for irrigation) acequia f. II vtr fam (plan, friend) abandonar.

dither |'dɪðə| vi GB fam vacilar, titubear.

ditto |'dɪtəʊ| n ídem, lo mismo.

dive |daɪv| I n 1 (into water) salto m de cabeza; (of submarine) inmersión f; (of plane) picado m; Sport salto m. 2 fam (bar) antro m. II vi tirarse de cabeza; (submarine) sumergirse; (plane) bajar en picado; Sport saltar. 3 he dived for the phone, se precipitó hacia el teléfono.

diver |'daɪvə| n (person) buceador,-a m,f; (professional) buzo m; Sport saltador,-a m,f .

diverge |daɪ'vɜːdʒ| vi divergir.

diverse |daɪ'vɜːs| adj (varied) diverso,-a, variado,-a; (different) distinto,-a, diferente.

diversion |daɪ'vɜːʃən| n 1 (distraction) distracción f. 2 GB (detour) desvío m.

divert |daɪ'vɜːt| vtr desviar.

divide |dɪ'vaɪd| I vtr dividir. II vi (road, stream) bifurcarse. III n división f, diferencia f.

dividend |'dɪvɪdend| n Com dividendo m;

fig beneficio *m*.

divine [dɪˈvaɪn] *adj* divino,-a.

diving board [ˈdaɪvɪŋbɔːd] *n* trampolín *m*.

divinity [dɪˈvɪnɪtɪ] *n* 1 divinidad *f*. 2 (*subject*) teología *f*.

division [dɪˈvɪʒən] *n* 1 división *f*. 2 (*maths*) división *f*. 2 (*sharing*) reparto *m*. 3 (*of organization*) sección *f*.

divorce [dɪˈvɔːs] I *n* divorcio *m*. II *vtr* **she divorced him**, se divorció de él. III *vi* divorciarse.

divorcé [dɪˈvɔːseɪ], **divorcée** [dɪvɔːˈsiː] *n* divorciado,-a *m,f*.

divulge [daɪˈvʌldʒ] *vtr fml* divulgar, revelar.

DIY [diːaɪˈwaɪ] *n GB abbr of* do-it-yourself, bricolaje *m*.

dizziness [ˈdɪzɪnɪs] *n* vértigo *m*.

dizzy [ˈdɪzɪ] *adj* (**dizzier**, **dizziest**) 1 (*person*) (*unwell*) mareado,-a. 2 (*height*, *pace*) vertiginoso,-a.

DJ [ˈdiːdʒeɪ] *n fam abbr of* disc jockey.

DNA [diːenˈeɪ] *n abbr of* deoxyribonucleic acid, ácido *m* desoxirribonucleico, ADN *m*.

do [duː, *unstressed* dʊ, də] I *v aux* (3rd person sing pres **does**; *pt* **did**; *pp* **done**) 1 (*in negatives and questions*) (*not translated in Span*) **do you want some coffee?** ¿quieres café?; **do you drive?**, ¿tienes carnet de conducir?; **don't you want to come?**, ¿no quieres venir?; **he doesn't smoke**, no fuma. 2 (*emphatic*) (*not translated in Span*) **do come with us!**, ¡ánimo, vente con nosotros!; **I do like your bag**, me encanta tu bolso. 3 (*substituting main verb*) (*in sentence*) (*not translated in Span*) **I don't believe him** – **neither do I**, no le creo - yo tampoco; **I'll go if you do**, si vas tú, voy yo; **I think it's dear, but he doesn't**, a mí me parece caro pero a él no; **who went?** – **I did**, ¿quién asistió? - yo. 4 (*in question tags*) **you refused, didn't he?**, dijo que no, ¿verdad?; **I don't like it, do you?**, a mí no me gusta, ¿y a ti?

II *vtr* 1 hacer; (*task*) realizar; (*duty*) cumplir con; **to do one's best**, hacer todo lo posible; **to do sth again**, volver a hacer algo; **to do sth for sb**, hacer algo por algn; **to do the cooking/cleaning**, cocinar/limpiar; **to do the dishes**, lavar los platos; **what can I do for you?**, ¿en qué puedo servirle?; **what do you do (for a living)?**, ¿a qué te dedicas?; **what's to be done?**, ¿qué se puede hacer?; *fam* **he's done it!**, ¡lo ha conseguido! 2 **do you do sportswear?**, (*make*, *offer*) ¿aquí tienen ropa de deporte? 3 (*distance*) recorrer; (*speed*) **we were doing eighty**, íbamos a ochenta; **this car can do a hundred and twenty**, este coche puede alcanzar los ciento veinte.

III *vi* 1 (*act*) hacer; **do as I tell you**, haz lo que te digo; **you did right**, hiciste bien. 2 **he did badly in the exams**, los exámenes le salieron mal; **how are you doing?**, ¿qué tal?; **how do you do?**, (*greeting*) ¿cómo está usted?; (*answer*) mucho gusto; **to do well**, (*person*) tener éxito; (*business*) ir bien. 3 **five pounds will do**, (*suffice*) con cinco libras será suficiente; *fam* **that will do!**, ¡basta ya! 4 **this cushion will do as a pillow**, (*be suitable*) este cojín servirá de almohada; **this won't do**, esto no puede ser.

IV *n fam* 1 *GB* (*party*) fiesta *f*; (*event*) ceremonia *f*. 2 **do's and don'ts**, reglas *fpl* de conducta.

◆**do away with** *vtr* 1 (*abolish*) abolir; (*discard*) deshacerse de. 2 (*kill*) asesinar. ◆**do down** *vtr fam* (*humiliate*) hacer quedar mal. ◆**do for** *fam* *vtr* (*destroy*, *ruin*) arruinar; **fig I'm done for if I don't finish this**, estoy perdido,-a si no acabo esto. ◆**do in** *vtr sl* 1 (*kill*) cargarse. 2 **I'm done in**, (*exhausted*) estoy hecho,-a polvo. ◆**do over** *vtr fam* 1 *US* (*repeat*) repetir. 2 *GB* (*thrash*) dar una paliza a. ◆**do up** *vtr* 1 (*wrap*) envolver. 2 (*belt etc*) abrochar; (*laces*) atar. 3 (*dress up*) arreglar. 4 *fam* (*redecorate*) renovar. ◆**do with** *vtr* 1 **I could do with a rest**, (*need*) un descanso no me vendría nada mal. 2 **to have or be to do with**, (*concern*) tener que ver con. ◆**do without** *vtr* pasar sin, prescindir de.

docile [ˈdəʊsaɪl] *adj* dócil; (*animal*) manso,-a.

dock¹ [dɒk] I *n Naut* **the docks**, el muelle. II *vi* 1 (*ship*) atracar. 2 (*spacecraft*) acoplarse.

dock² [dɒk] *vtr* (*reduce*) descontar.

dock³ [dɒk] *n Jur* banquillo *m* (de los acusados).

docker [ˈdɒkər] *n* estibador *m*.

dockland [ˈdɒklænd] *n* zona *f* del puerto.

dockyard [ˈdɒkjɑːd] *n* astillero *m*.

doctor [ˈdɒktər] I *n* 1 *Med* médico,-a *m,f*. 2 *Univ* doctor,-a *m,f*; **D. of Law**, doctor en derecho. II *vtr pej* (*figures*) falsificar; (*text*) arreglar; (*drink etc*) adulterar.

doctorate [ˈdɒktərɪt] *n* doctorado *m*.

doctrine [ˈdɒktrɪn] *n* doctrina *f*.

document [ˈdɒkjʊmənt] I *n* documento *m*; **documents**, documentación *f*. II *vtr* documentar.

documentary [dɒkjʊˈmentərɪ] *adj* & *n* documental (*m*).

dodge [dɒdʒ] *vtr* 1 (*blow*) esquivar; (*pursuer*) despistar; *fig* eludir. 2 **to do one's taxes**, engañar a Hacienda. II *vi* (*move aside*) echarse a un lado. III *n* 1 (*movement*) regate *m*. 2 *fam* (*trick*) truco *m*.

dodgem® [ˈdɒdʒəm] *n fam* **d.** (**car**), coche *m* de choque.

dodgy ['dɒdʒɪ] *adj* (**dodgier, dodgiest**) *GB fam* (*risky*) arriesgado,-a; (*tricky*) difícil; (*dishonest, not working properly*) chungo,-a.

doe [dəʊ] *n inv* (*of deer*) gama *f*; (*of rabbit*) coneja *f*.

does [dʌz] *3rd person sing pres* → **do**.

doesn't ['dʌzənt] = **does not**.

dog [dɒg] **I** *n* **1** perro,-a *m,f*; *fam fig* **a d.'s life**, una vida de perros; **d. collar**, (*of dog*) collar *m* de perro; *Rel fam* alzacuello *m*. **2** (*male canine*) macho *m*; (*fox*) zorro *m*; (*wolf*) lobo *m*. **3** *fam* **dirty d.**, canalla *m*. **4** *US fam* (*disappointment*) desastre *m*. **II** *vtr* acosar; **to d. sb's footsteps**, seguir los pasos de algn; *fig* **dogged by bad luck**, perseguido,-a por la mala suerte.

dog-eared ['dɒgɪəd] *adj* (*book*) con los bordes de las páginas doblados; (*shabby*) sobado,-a.

dogged ['dɒgɪd] *adj* obstinado,-a, tenaz.

doghouse ['dɒghaʊs] *n GB fam* perrera *f*; *fig* **to be in the d.**, estar castigado,-a.

dogma ['dɒgmə] *n* dogma *m*.

dogmatic [dɒg'mætɪk] *adj* dogmático,-a.

dogsbody ['dɒgzbɒdɪ] *n GB fam* (*drudge*) burro *m* de carga.

doh [dəʊ] *n* Mus do *m*.

doing ['duːɪŋ] *n* **1** (*action*) obra *f*; **it was none of my d.**, yo no tuve nada que ver; *fig* **it took some d.**, costó trabajo hacerlo. **2 doings**, (*activities*) actividades *fpl*.

do-it-yourself [duːɪtjʊ'self] *n* bricolaje *m*.

doldrums ['dɒldrəmz] *npl fam fig* **to be in the d.**, (*person*) estar abatido,-a; (*trade*) estar estancado,-a.

dole [dəʊl] **I** *n GB fam* **the d.**, el paro; **to be** *or* **go on the d.**, estar en el paro; *fig* **d. queue**, los parados. **II** *vtr* **to d. (out)**, repartir.

doleful ['dəʊlfʊl] *adj* triste, afligido,-a.

doll [dɒl] **I** *n* **1** (*toy*) muñeca *f*. **2** *US fam* (*girl*) muñeca *f*. **II** *vtr fam* **to d. oneself up**, ponerse guapa.

dollar ['dɒlər] *n* dólar *m*.

dolphin ['dɒlfɪn] *n* delfín *m*.

domain [də'meɪn] *n* **1** (*sphere*) campo *m*, esfera *f*; **that's not my d.**, no es de mi competencia. **2** (*territory*) dominio *m*.

dome [dəʊm] *n* (*roof*) cúpula *f*; (*ceiling*) bóveda *f*.

domestic [də'mestɪk] *adj* **1** (*appliance, pet*) doméstico,-a; **d. science**, economía doméstica. **2** (*home-loving*) casero,-a. **3** (*flight, news*) nacional; (*trade, policy*) interior.

domesticate [də'mestɪkeɪt] *vtr* (*make home-loving*) volver hogareño,-a *or* casero,-a.

domicile ['dɒmɪsaɪl] *n* domicilio *m*.

dominant ['dɒmɪnənt] *adj* dominante.

dominate ['dɒmɪneɪt] *vtr & vi* dominar.

domineering [dɒmɪ'nɪərɪŋ] *adj* domi-

nante.

Dominican [də'mɪnɪkən] *adj & n* (*of Dominica*) dominicano,-a (*m,f*); **D. Republic**, República Dominicana.

dominion [də'mɪnjən] *n* dominio *m*.

domino ['dɒmɪnəʊ] *n* (*pl* **dominoes**) (*piece*) ficha *f* de dominó; **dominoes**, (*game*) dominó *m sing*.

don [dɒn] *n GB Univ* catedrático,-a *m,f*.

donate [dəʊ'neɪt] *vtr* donar.

donation [dəʊ'neɪʃən] *n* donativo *m*.

done [dʌn] *adj* **1** (*finished*) terminado,-a; **it's over and d. with**, se acabó. **2** *fam* (*tired*) rendido,-a. **3** (*meat*) hecho,-a; (*vegetables*) cocido,-a.

donkey ['dɒŋkɪ] *n* burro,-a *m,f*.

donor ['dəʊnər] *n* donante *m*.

don't [dəʊnt] = **do not**.

doodle ['duːdəl] *vi fam* (*write*) garabatear; (*draw*) hacer dibujos.

doom [duːm] **I** *n* (*fate*) destino *m* (*funesto*); (*ruin*) perdición *f*; (*death*) muerte *f*. **II** *vtr usu pass* (*destine*) destinar; **doomed to failure**, condenado,-a al fracaso.

doomsday ['duːmzdeɪ] *n* día *m* del juicio final.

door [dɔːr] *n* puerta *f*; **front/back d.**, puerta principal/trasera; *fig* **behind closed doors**, a puerta cerrada; **d. handle, manilla** *f* (de la puerta); **d. knocker**, picaporte *m*; **next d. (to)**, (en) la casa de al lado (de).

doorbell ['dɔːbel] *n* timbre *m* (de la puerta).

doorknob ['dɔːnɒb] *n* pomo *m*.

doorman ['dɔːmən] *n* portero *m*.

doormat ['dɔːmæt] *n* felpudo *m*, esterilla *f*; *fam fig* (*person*) trapo *m*.

doorstep ['dɔːstep] *n* peldaño *m*; *fig* **on one's d.**, a la vuelta de la esquina.

door-to-door [dɔːtə'dɔːr] *adj* a domicilio.

doorway ['dɔːweɪ] *n* portal *m*, entrada *f*.

dope [dəʊp] **I** *n* **1** *sl* (*drug*) chocolate *m*. **2** *fam* (*person*) imbécil *mf*. **II** *vtr* (*food, drink*) adulterar con drogas; *Sport* dopar.

dop(e)y ['dəʊpɪ] *adj* (**dopier, dopiest**) *fam* **1** (*sleepy*) medio dormido,-a; (*fuddled*) atontado,-a. **2** *sl* (*silly*) torpe.

dormant ['dɔːmənt] *adj* inactivo,-a; *fig* (*rivalry*) latente.

dormitory ['dɔːmɪtərɪ] *n* **1** (*in school*) dormitorio *m*. **2** *US* (*in university*) colegio *m* mayor.

dosage ['dəʊsɪdʒ] *n fml* (*amount*) dosis *f inv*.

dose [dəʊs] **I** *n* dosis *f inv*. **II** *vtr* (*patient*) medicar.

doss [dɒs] *vi GB sl* sobar.

dosshouse ['dɒshaʊs] *n GB sl* pensión *f* de mala muerte.

dossier ['dɒsɪeɪ] *n* expediente *m*.

dot [dɒt] **I** *n* punto *m*; **on the d.**, en punto. **II** *vtr* **1** *fam* **to d. one's i's and

cross one's t's, poner los puntos sobre las íes. **2** (*scatter*) esparcir, salpicar.

dote [dəʊt] *vi* to d. on sb, chochear con algn.

double [ˈdʌbəl] **I** *adj* doble; **it's d. the price**, cuesta dos veces más; **d. bass**, contrabajo *m*; **d. bed**, cama *f* de matrimonio; **d. bill**, programa *m* doble; *GB* **d. cream**, nata *f* para montar; **d. glazing**, ventana *f* doble. **II** *adv* doble; **folded d.**, doblado,-a por la mitad. **III** *n* **1** vivo retrato *m*; *Cin Theat* doble *m*. **2** to earn **d.**, ganar el doble; *fam* **at** or **on the d.**, corriendo. **3** *Ten* **doubles**, (partido *m* sing de) dobles *mpl.* **IV** *vtr* doblar; *fig* (*efforts*) redoblar. **V** *vi* **1** (*increase*) doblarse. **2** to **d. as**, (*serve*) hacer las veces de.
◆**double back** *vi* to d. back on one's tracks, volver sobre sus pasos.
◆**double up I** *vtr* (*bend*) doblar. **II** *vi* **1** (*bend*) doblarse. **2** (*share room*) compartir la habitación (**with**, con).

double-barrelled [ˈdʌbəlbærəld] *adj* **1** (*gun*) de dos cañones. **2** *GB* (*surname*) compuesto,-a.

double-breasted [ˈdʌbəlbrestɪd] *adj* cruzado,-a.

double-check [dʌbəlˈtʃek] *vtr & vi* repasar dos veces.

double-cross [dʌbəlˈkrɒs] *fam* **I** *vtr* engañar, traicionar. **II** *n* engaño *m*, traición *f.*

double-decker [dʌbəlˈdekəʳ] *n GB* **d.-d.** (*bus*), autobús *m* de dos pisos.

double-edged [ˈdʌbəlˈedʒd] *adj* de doble filo.

doubt [daʊt] **I** *n* duda *f*; **beyond** (**all**) **d.**, sin duda alguna; **no d.**, sin duda; **there's no d. about it**, no cabe la menor duda; **to be in d. about sth**, dudar algo; **to be open to d.**, (*fact*) ser dudoso,-a; (*outcome*) ser incierto,-a. **II** *vtr* **1** (*distrust*) desconfiar de. **2** (*not be sure of*) dudar; **I d. if** or **whether he'll come**, dudo que venga.

doubtful [ˈdaʊtfʊl] *adj* **1** (*future*) dudoso,-a, (*look*) dubitativo,-a; **I'm a bit d. about it**, no me convence del todo; **it's d. whether ...**, no se sabe seguro si ... **2** (*questionable*) sospechoso,-a.

doubtless [ˈdaʊtlɪs] *adv* sin duda, seguramente.

dough [dəʊ] *n* **1** (*for bread*) masa *f*; (*for pastries*) pasta *f.* **2** *sl* (*money*) pasta *f.*

doughnut [ˈdəʊnʌt] *n* rosquilla *f*, dónut® *m.*

douse [daʊs] *vtr* **1** (*soak*) mojar. **2** (*extinguish*) apagar.

dove [dʌv] *n* paloma *f.*

dovetail [ˈdʌvteɪl] *vtr fig* (*plans*) sincronizar.

dowdy [ˈdaʊdɪ] *adj* (*dowdier, dowdiest*) poco elegante.

down¹ [daʊn] **I** *prep* **1** (*to or at a lower level*) **d. the river**, río abajo; **to go d. the road**, bajar la calle. **2** (*along*) por. **3**

1 (*to lower level*) (hacia) abajo; (*to floor*) al suelo; (*to ground*) a tierra; **to fall d.**, caerse; **to go d.**, (*price, person*) bajar; (*sun*) ponerse. **2** (*at lower level*) abajo; **d. there**, allí abajo; **face d.**, boca abajo; *fig* **to be d. with a cold**, estar resfriado,-a; *fam fig* **to feel d.**, estar deprimido,-a; *fam fig* **d. under**, Australia *f*, Nueva Zelanda *f.* **3 I'm d. to my last stamp**, no me queda más que un solo sello; **sales are d. by five percent**, las ventas han bajado en cinco por ciento. **4** to take sth **d.**, (*in writing*) apuntar algo. **5 d. through the ages**, a través de los siglos. **III** *adj* (*payment*) al contado; (*on property*) de entrada. **IV** *vtr fam* (*drink*) tomarse de un trago; (*food*) zamparse. **V** *n* **ups and downs**, altibajos *mpl.* **VI** *interj* **d. with taxes!**, ¡abajo los impuestos!

down² [daʊn] *n* **1** (*on bird*) plumón *m*. **2** (*on cheek, peach*) pelusa *f*; (*on body*) vello *m.*

down-and-out [ˈdaʊnənaʊt] **I** *adj* en las últimas. **II** *n* vagabundo,-a *m,f.*

downbeat [ˈdaʊnbiːt] *adj fam* (*gloomy*) deprimido,-a.

downcast [ˈdaʊnkɑːst] *adj* abatido,-a.

downfall [ˈdaʊnfɔːl] *n* (*of régime*) caída *f*; (*of person*) perdición *f.*

downgrade [daʊnˈgreɪd] *vtr* degradar.

downhearted [daʊnˈhɑːtɪd] *adj* desalentado,-a.

downhill [daʊnˈhɪl] **I** *adj* (*skiing*) de descenso; *fam* **after his first exam, the rest were all d.**, después del primer examen, los demás le fueron sobre ruedas. **II** *adv* **to go d.**, ir cuesta abajo; *fig* (*standards*) deteriorarse.

down-market [daʊnˈmɑːkɪt] **I** *adj* barato,-a. **II** *adv* **to move d.**, (*of company*) producir artículos más asequibles.

downpour [ˈdaʊnpɔːʳ] *n* chaparrón *m.*

downright [ˈdaʊnraɪt] *fam* **I** *adj* (*blunt*) tajante; (*categorical*) categórico,-a; **it's a d. lie**, es una mentira y gorda. **II** *adv* (*totally*) completamente.

downstairs [daʊnˈsteəz] **I** *adv* abajo; (*to ground floor*) a la planta baja; **to go d.**, bajar la escalera. **II** *adj* (*on ground floor*) de la planta baja.

downstream [daʊnˈstriːm] *adv* río abajo.

down-to-earth [daʊntəˈɜːθ] *adj* realista.

downtown [daʊnˈtaʊn] *adv US* en el centro (de la ciudad).

downturn [ˈdaʊntɜːn] *n* baja *f.*

downward [ˈdaʊnwəd] *adj* (*slope*) descendente; (*look*) hacia abajo; *Fin* (*tendency*) a la baja.

downward(s) [ˈdaʊnwəd(z)] *adv* hacia abajo.

dowry [ˈdaʊərɪ] *n* dote *f.*

doz *abbr of* **dozen**, docena *f*, doc.

doze [dəʊz] **I** *vi* dormitar. **II** *n* cabezada *f*; **to have a d.**, echar una cabezada.

◆**doze off** *vi* quedarse dormido,-a.

dozen ['dʌzən] *n* docena *f*; **half a d./a d. eggs,** media docena/una docena de huevos; *fam* **dozens of,** un montón de.

Dr *abbr of* Doctor, Doctor,-a *m,f*, Dr., Dra.

drab [dræb] *adj* (**drabber, drabbest**) 1 (*ugly*) feo,-a; (*dreary*) monótono,-a, gris. 2 (*colour*) pardo,-a.

draft [drɑːft] I *n* 1 borrador *m*. 2 (*bill of exchange*) giro *m*. 3 US servicio militar obligatorio. 4 US → **draught.** II *vtr* 1 hacer un borrador de. 2 US Mil reclutar.

draftsman ['drɑːftsmən] *n* US → **draughtsman.**

drag [dræg] I *vtr* 1 (*pull*) arrastrar; *fig* **to d. one's heels (over sth),** dar largas a (algo). 2 (*lake*) rastrear. II *vi* 1 (*trail*) arrastrarse. 2 (*person*) rezagarse. III *n* 1 Tech resistencia *f* (aerodinámica). 2 *fam* (*nuisance*) lata *f*. 3 *fam* (*on cigarette*) calada *f*. 4 *sl* **to be in d.,** ir vestido de mujer. ◆**drag off** *vtr* llevarse arrastrando. ◆**drag on** *vi* (*of war, strike*) hacerse interminable. ◆**drag out** *vtr* (*speech etc*) alargar.

dragon ['drægən] *n* dragón *m*.

dragonfly ['drægənflaɪ] *n* libélula *f*.

drain [dreɪn] I *n* 1 (*for water*) desagüe *m*; (*for sewage*) alcantarilla *f*. 2 (*grating*) sumidero *m*. 3 *fig* **the boys are a d. on her strength,** los niños la dejan agotada. II *vtr* 1 (*marsh etc*) avenar; (*reservoir*) desecar. 2 (*crockery*) escurrir. 3 (*empty*) (*glass*) apurar; *fig* (*capital etc*) agotar. III *vi* 1 (*liquid*) escurrirse. 2 **to d. (away),** (*liquid*) irse.

drainage ['dreɪnɪdʒ] *n* (*of marsh*) avenamiento *m*; (*of reservoir, building*) desagüe *m*; (*of town*) alcantarillado *m*.

drainpipe ['dreɪnpaɪp] *n* tubo *m* de desagüe.

dram [dræm] *n fam* trago *m* (de whisky).

drama ['drɑːmə] *n* 1 (*play*) obra *f* de teatro; *fig* drama. 2 Lit (*subject*) teatro *m*.

dramatic [drə'mætɪk] *adj* 1 (*change*) impresionante, (*moment*) emocionante. 2 Theat dramático,-a, teatral.

dramatist ['dræmətɪst] *n* dramaturgo,-a *m,f*.

dramatization [dræmətaɪ'zeɪʃən] *n* adaptación *f* teatral.

dramatize ['dræmətaɪz] *vtr* 1 (*adapt*) hacer una adaptación teatral de. 2 (*exaggerate*) dramatizar.

drank [dræŋk] *pt* → **drink.**

drape [dreɪp] I *vtr* **to d. sth over sth,** colgar algo sobre algo; **draped with,** cubierto,-a de. II *n* 1 (*of cloth*) caída *f*. 2 US cortina *f*.

draper ['dreɪpər] *n GB* pañero,-a *m,f*.

drastic ['dræstɪk] *adj* 1 (*measures*) drástico,-a, severo,-a. 2 (*change*) radical.

draught [drɑːft] I *n* 1 (*of cold air*) co-

rriente *f* (de aire). 2 (*of liquid*) trago *m*. 3 **d. (beer),** cerveza *f* de barril. 4 *GB* **draughts,** (*game*) damas *fpl*. 5 Naut calado *m*. II *adj* (*animal*) de tiro.

draughtboard ['drɑːftbɔːd] *n GB* tablero *m* de damas.

draughtsman ['drɑːftsmən] *n* delineante *mf*.

draw [drɔː] I *vtr* 1 (*picture*) dibujar; (*line*) trazar. 2 (*pull*) tirar de; (*train, carriage*) arrastrar; (*curtains*) (*open*) descorrer; (*close*) correr; (*blinds*) bajar. 3 (*remove*) sacar; (*salary*) cobrar; (*cheque*) librar. 4 (*attract*) atraer; (*attention*) llamar. 5 *fig* (*strength*) sacar. **6 to d. breath,** respirar. **7 to d. lots,** echar a suertes. 8 (*comparison*) hacer; (*conclusion*) sacar. II *vi* 1 (*sketch*) dibujar. 2 (*move*) **the train drew into/out of the station,** el tren entró en/salió de la estación; **to d. apart (from),** separarse (de); **to d. to an end,** acabarse. 3 Sport **they drew two all,** empataron a dos. III *n* 1 (*raffle*) sorteo *m*. 2 Sport empate *m*. 3 *fig* (*attraction*) atracción *f*. ◆**draw in** *vi* (*days*) acortarse. ◆**draw on** *vtr* (*savings*) recurrir a; (*experience*) aprovecharse de. ◆**draw out** *vtr* 1 (*make long*) alargar. 2 (*encourage to speak*) desatar la lengua a. 3 (*from pocket, drawer etc*) sacar. ◆**draw up** *vtr* (*contract*) preparar; (*plan*) esbozar.

drawback ['drɔːbæk] *n* desventaja *f*, inconveniente *m*.

drawbridge ['drɔːbrɪdʒ] *n* puente levadizo.

drawer ['drɔːər] *n* cajón *m*.

drawing ['drɔːɪŋ] *n* dibujo *m*; *fam fig* **to go back to the d. board,** volver a empezar; *GB* **d. pin,** chincheta *f*; *fml* **d. room,** sala *f* de estar.

drawl [drɔːl] I *vi* hablar arrastrando las palabras. II *n* voz cansina; US **a Southern d.,** un acento sureño.

drawn [drɔːn] *adj* (*tired*) ojeroso,-a.

dread [dred] I *vtr* temer, tener pavor a. II *n* temor *m*.

dreadful ['dredful] *adj* 1 (*shocking*) espantoso,-a. 2 *fam* (*awful*) fatal; **how d.!,** ¡qué horror! ◆**dreadfully** *adv fam* (*horribly*) terriblemente; (*very*) muy, sumamente.

dream [driːm] I *n* 1 sueño *m*. 2 (*daydream*) ensueño *m*. 3 *fam* (*marvel*) maravilla *f*. II *vtr* (*pt & pp* **dreamed** *or* **dreamt**) soñar. III *vi* soñar (**of, about,** con).

dreamer ['driːmər] *n* soñador,-a *m,f*.

dreamy ['driːmɪ] *adj* (**dreamier, dreamiest**) (*absent-minded*) distraído,-a; (*wonderful*) de ensueño.

dreary ['drɪərɪ] *adj* (**drearier, dreariest**) (*gloomy*) triste. 2 *fam* (*boring*) aburrido,-a, pesado,-a.

dredge [dredʒ] *vtr & vi* dragar, rastrear. ◆**dredge up** *vtr* 1 (*body*) sacar del agua. **2** *fam fig* sacar a relucir.

dregs [dregz] *npl* poso *m sing*.

drench [drentʃ] *vtr* empapar.

dress [dres] **I** *n* **1** (*frock*) vestido *m*. **2** (*clothing*) ropa *f*; **d. rehearsal**, ensayo *m* general; **d. shirt**, camisa *f* de etiqueta. **II** *vtr* **1** (*person*) vestir; **he was dressed in a grey suit**, llevaba (puesto) un traje gris. **2** (*salad*) aliñar. **3** (*wound*) vendar. **III** *vi* vestirse. ◆**dress up I** *vi* **1** (*in disguise*) disfrazarse (**as**, de). **2** (*in best clothes*) vestirse elegante. **II** *vtr fig* disfrazar.

dresser [dresər] *n* **1** *GB* (*in kitchen*) aparador *m*. **2** *US* (*in bedroom*) tocador *m*. **3** *Theat* ayudante *mf* de camerino.

dressing [dresɪŋ] *n* **1** (*bandage*) vendaje *m*. **2** (**salad**) **d.**, aliño *m*. **3 d. gown**, bata *f*; **d. room**, *Theat* camerino *m*; *Sport* vestuario *m*; **d. table**, tocador *m*.

dressmaker [dresmeɪkər] *n* modista *mf*.

dressy [dresɪ] *adj* (**dressier**, **dressiest**) vistoso,-a.

drew [druː] *pt* → **draw**.

dribble [drɪbəl] **I** *vi* **1** (*baby*) babear. **2** (*liquid*) gotear. **II** *vtr Sport* (*ball*) driblar. **III** *n* (*saliva*) saliva *f*; (*of water, blood*) gotas *fpl*.

dried [draɪd] *adj* (*fruit*) seco,-a; (*milk*) en polvo.

drier [draɪər] *n* → **dryer**.

drift [drɪft] **I** *vi* **1** (*boat*) ir a la deriva; *fig* (*person*) ir sin rumbo, vagar; **they drifted away**, se marcharon poco a poco. **2** (*snow*) amontonarse. **II** *n* **1** (*flow*) flujo *m*. **2** (*of snow*) ventisquero *m*; (*of sand*) montón *m*. **3** *fig* (*meaning*) idea *f*.

driftwood [drɪftwʊd] *n* madera *f* flotante.

drill [drɪl] **I** *n* **1** (*handtool*) taladro *m*; *Min* barrena *f*; **dentist's d.**, fresa *f*; **pneumatic d.**, martillo neumático *m*. **2** *esp Mil* instrucción *f*. **II** *vtr* **1** (*wood etc*) taladrar. **2** (*soldiers, children*) instruir. **III** *vi* (*by hand*) taladrar; (*for oil, coal*) perforar, sondar.

drink [drɪŋk] **I** *vtr* (*pt* **drank**; *pp* **drunk**) beber. **II** *vi* beber; **to have sth to d.**, tomarse algo; **to d. to sth/sb**, brindar por algo/algn. **III** *n* bebida *f*; (*alcoholic*) copa *f*.

drinker [drɪŋkər] *n* bebedor,-a *m,f*.

drinking [drɪŋkɪŋ] *n* **d. water**, agua *f* potable.

drip [drɪp] **I** *n* goteo *m*. **2** *Med* gota a gota *m inv*. **3** *fam* (*person*) necio,-a *m,f*. **II** *vi* gotear; **he was dripping with sweat**, el sudor le caía a gotas.

drip-dry [drɪpdraɪ] *adj* que no necesita planchado.

dripping [drɪpɪŋ] *n Culin* pringue *f*.

drive [draɪv] **I** *vtr* (*pt* **drove**; *pp* **driven**) **1** (*vehicle*) manejar, *Am* manejar; (*person*) llevar. **2** (*power*) impulsar. **3** (*enemy*) acosar; (*ball*) mandar. **4** (*stake*) hincar; (*nail*)

clavar. **5** (*compel*) forzar, obligar; **to d. sb mad**, volver loco,-a a algn. **6 to d. (off)**, rechazar. **II** *vi Aut* conducir, *Am* manejar. **III** *n* **1** (*trip*) paseo *m* en coche; **to go for a d.**, dar una vuelta en coche. **2** (*to house*) camino *m* de entrada. **3** (*transmission*) transmisión *f*; *Aut* tracción *f*; *Aut* **left-hand d.**, conducción *f* por la izquierda. **4** *Golf* golpe *m* inicial. **5** (*campaign*) campaña *f*. **6** (*need*) necesidad *f*; (*energy*) energía *f*, vigor *m*; **sex d.**, instinto *m* sexual.

drive-in [draɪvɪn] *n US* (*cinema*) autocine *m*.

driven [drɪvən] *pp* → **drive**.

driver [draɪvər] *n* (*of car, bus*) conductor,-a *m,f*; (*of train*) maquinista *mf*; (*of lorry*) camionero,-a *m,f*; (*of racing car*) piloto *mf*; *US* **d.'s license**, carnet *m* de conducir.

driveway [draɪvweɪ] *n* (*to house*) camino *m* de entrada.

driving [draɪvɪŋ] **I** *n* **1 d. licence**, carnet *m* de conducir. **2 d. school**, autoescuela *f*; **d. test**, examen *m* de conducir. **II** *adj* **1** (*rain*) intenso,-a. **2 d. force**, fuerza *f* motriz.

drizzle [drɪzəl] **I** *n* llovizna *f*. **II** *vi* lloviznar.

droll [drəʊl] *adj* gracioso,-a.

dromedary [drɒmədərɪ] *n* dromedario *m*.

drone [drəʊn] *vi* (*bee etc*) zumbar.

droop [druːp] *vi* (*flower*) marchitarse; (*eyelids*) caerse.

drop [drɒp] **I** *n* **1** (*of liquid*) gota *f*; **eye drops**, colirio *m sing*. **2** (*sweet*) pastilla *f*. **3** (*descent*) desnivel *m*. **4** (*in price*) bajada *f*; (*in temperature*) descenso *m*. **II** *vtr* **1** (*let fall*) dejar caer; (*lower*) bajar; (*reduce*) disminuir; **to d. a hint**, soltar una indirecta. **2** (*abandon*) (*subject, change etc*) abandonar, dejar; *Sport* **he was dropped from the team**, le echaron del equipo. **3** (*omit*) (*spoken syllable*) comerse. **III** *vi* **1** (*object*) caerse; (*person*) tirarse; (*voice, price, temperature*) bajar; (*wind*) amainar; (*speed*) disminuir. ◆**drop by**, **drop in**, **drop round** *vi fam* (*visit*) pasarse (**at**, por). ◆**drop off I** *vi fam* (*fall asleep*) quedarse dormido,-a. **II** *vtr* (*deliver*) dejar. ◆**drop out** *vi* (*from college*) dejar los estudios; (*from society*) marginarse; (*from competition*) retirarse.

dropout [drɒpaʊt] *n fam pej* automarginado,-a *m,f*.

dropper [drɒpər] *n* cuentagotas *m inv*.

droppings [drɒpɪŋz] *npl* excrementos *mpl*.

drought [draʊt] *n* sequía *f*.

drove [drəʊv] *n* (*of cattle*) manada *f*.

drown [draʊn] **I** *vtr* **1** ahogar. **2** (*place*) inundar. **II** *vi* ahogarse; **he** (**was**) **drowned**, murió ahogado.

drowsy ['draʊzɪ] *adj* (**drowsier, drowsiest**) soñoliento,-a; **to feel d.**, tener sueño.

drudgery ['drʌdʒərɪ] *n* trabajo duro y pesado.

drug [drʌg] **I** *n* **1** (*medicine*) medicamento *m*. **2** (*narcotic*) droga *f*, estupefaciente *m*; **to be on drugs**, drogarse; **d. addict**, drogadicto,-a *m,f*; **d. addiction**, drogadicción *f*; **d. squad**, brigada *f* antidroga. **II** *vtr* drogar; (*food, drink*) adulterar con drogas.

druggist ['drʌgɪst] *n US* farmacéutico,-a *m,f*.

drugstore ['drʌgstɔːʳ] *n US* establecimiento *m* donde se compran medicamentos, periódicos etc.

drum [drʌm] **I** *n* **1** tambor *m*; **to play the drums**, tocar la batería. **2** (*container*) bidón *m*. **II** *vi* fig (*with fingers*) tabalear. **III** *vtr* fig **to d. sth into sb**, enseñar algo a algn a machamartillo. ◆**drum up** *vtr fam* solicitar.

drummer ['drʌməʳ] *n* (*in band*) tambor *mf*; (*in pop group*) batería *mf*.

drumstick ['drʌmstɪk] *n Mus* baqueta *f*, *fam* palillo *m*.

drunk [drʌŋk] **I** *adj* borracho,-a; **to get d.**, emborracharse. **II** *n* borracho,-a *m,f*.

drunkard ['drʌŋkəd] *n* borracho,-a *m,f*.

dry [draɪ] **I** *adj* (**drier, driest** *or* **dryer, dryest**) **1** seco,-a. **2** (*wry*) socarrón,-ona. **II** *vtr* (*pt & pp* **dried**) secar. **III** *vi* **to d.** (**off**), secar.

dry-clean [draɪ'kliːn] *vtr* limpiar *or* lavar en seco.

dryer ['draɪəʳ] *n* secadora *f*.

dub[1] [dʌb] *vtr* (*subtitle*) doblar (**into**, a).

dub[2] [dʌb] *vtr* **1** (*give nickname to*) apodar. **2** (*knight*) armar.

dubious ['djuːbɪəs] *adj* **1** (*morals etc*) dudoso,-a; (*compliment*) equívoco,-a. **2** (*doubting*) indeciso,-a.

Dublin ['dʌblɪn] *n* Dublín *m*.

duchess ['dʌtʃɪs] *n* duquesa *f*.

duck[1] [dʌk] *n* pato,-a *m,f*; *Culin* pato *m*.

duck[2] [dʌk] **I** *vtr* **1** (*submerge*) dar una ahogadilla a. **2** (*evade*) esquivar. **II** *vi* **1** (*evade blow*) esquivar. **2** *fam* **to d.** (**out**), rajarse.

duckling ['dʌklɪŋ] *n* patito *m*.

duct [dʌkt] *n* (*for fuel etc*) conducto *m*; *Anat* canal *m*.

dud [dʌd] *fam* **I** *adj* **1** (*useless*) inútil; (*defective*) estropeado,-a. **2** (*banknote*) falso,-a; (*cheque*) sin fondos. **II** *n* (*useless thing*) engañifa *f*; (*person*) desastre *m*.

due [djuː] **I** *adj* **1** (*expected*) esperado,-a; **the train is d.** (**to arrive**) **at ten**, el tren debe llegar a las diez. **2** *fml* (*proper*) debido,-a; **in d. course**, a su debido tiempo. **3** (*owing*) pagadero,-a; **how much are you d.?**, (*owed*) ¿cuánto te deben? **4 to be d. to**, (*caused by*) deberse a; **d. to**, (*because of*) debido de. **II** *adv* (*north etc*) derecho hacia. **III** *n* **1 to give sb their d.**, dar a algn su merecido. **2 dues**, (*fee*) cuota *f sing*.

duel ['djuːəl] *n* duelo *m*.

duet [dju'et] *n* dúo *m*.

duffel ['dʌfəl] *n* **d. bag**, petate *m*; **d. coat**, trenca *f*.

dug [dʌg] *pt & pp* → **dig**.

duke [djuːk] *n* duque *m*.

dull [dʌl] **I** *adj* **1** (*boring*) pesado,-a; (*place*) sin interés. **2** (*light*) apagado,-a; (*weather*) gris. **3** (*sound, ache*) sordo,-a. **4** *fig* (*slow-witted*) torpe. **II** *vtr* (*pain*) aliviar. **2** *fig* (*faculty*) embotar.

duly ['djuːlɪ] *adv fml* (*properly*) debidamente; (*as expected*) como era de esperar; (*in due course*) a su debido tiempo.

dumb [dʌm] **I** *adj* **1** *Med* mudo,-a. **2** *fam* (*stupid*) tonto,-a. **II** *npl* **the d.**, los mudos.

dumbbell ['dʌmbel] *n Sport* pesa *f*.

dumbfounded [dʌm'faʊndɪd], **dumbstruck** ['dʌmstrʌk] *adj* pasmado,-a.

dummy ['dʌmɪ] *n* **1** (*sham*) imitación *f*. **2** (*in shop window*) maniquí *m*; (*of ventriloquist*) muñeco *m*. **3** *GB* (*for baby*) chupete *m*.

dump [dʌmp] **I** *n* **1** (*tip*) vertedero *m*; (*for old cars*) cementerio *m* de (de coches). **2** *fam pej* (*place*) estercolero *m*; (*town*) poblacho *m*; (*dwelling*) tugurio *m*. **3** *Mil* depósito *m*. **II** *vtr* **1** (*rubbish*) verter; (*truck contents*) descargar. **2** (*person*) dejar; *Com* inundar el mercado con. **3** *Comput* (*transfer*) copiar de memoria interna.

dumping ['dʌmpɪŋ] *n* vertido *m*.

dumpling ['dʌmplɪŋ] *n Culin* bola *f* de masa hervida.

dumpy ['dʌmpɪ] *adj* (**dumpier, dumpiest**) *fam* rechoncho,-a.

dunce [dʌns] *n fam* tonto,-a *m,f*.

dune [djuːn] *n* (**sand**) **d.**, duna *f*.

dung [dʌŋ] *n* estiércol *m*.

dungarees [dʌŋgə'riːz] *npl* mono *m sing*.

dungeon ['dʌndʒən] *n* calabozo *m*, mazmorra *f*.

duo ['djuːəʊ] *n Mus* dúo *m*; *fam* pareja *f*.

dupe [djuːp] **I** *vtr* engañar. **II** *n* ingenuo,-a *m,f*.

duplex ['djuːpleks] *n US* (*house*) casa adosada; *US* **d. apartment**, dúplex *m inv*.

duplicate ['djuːplɪkeɪt] **I** *vtr* **1** (*copy*) duplicar; (*film, tape*) reproducir. **2** (*repeat*) repetir. **II** ['djuːplɪkɪt] *n* duplicado *m*; **in d.**, por duplicado.

durable ['djʊərəbəl] *adj* duradero,-a.

duration [djʊ'reɪʃən] *n fml* duración *f*.

duress [djʊ'res] *n fml* coacción *f*.

during ['djʊərɪŋ] *prep* durante.

dusk [dʌsk] *n fml* crepúsculo *m*; **at d.**, al anochecer.

dust [dʌst] **I** *n* polvo *m*; **d. cloud**, polvareda *f*; **d. jacket**, sobrecubierta *f*. **II** *vtr* **1**

(*furniture*) quitar el polvo *a*. 2 (*cake*) espolvorear.

dustbin ['dʌstbin] *n GB* cubo *m* de la basura.

duster ['dʌstəʳ] *n* (*for housework*) trapo *m* or paño *m* (del polvo); **feather d.**, plumero *m*.

dustman ['dʌstmən] *n GB* basurero *m*.

dustpan ['dʌstpæn] *n* recogedor *m*.

dusty ['dʌsti] *adj* (**dustier, dustiest**) polvoriento,-a.

Dutch [dʌtʃ] I *adj* holandés,-esa; *fig* D. **cap**, diafragma *m*. II *n* 1 *pl* **the D.**, los holandeses. 2 (*language*) holandés *m*; **it's double D. to me**, me suena a chino. III *adv fig* **to go D. (with sb)**, pagar cada uno lo suyo.

Dutchman ['dʌtʃmən] *n* holandés *m*.

Dutchwoman ['dʌtʃwumən] *n* holandesa *f*.

duty ['dju:ti] *n* 1 deber *m*; **to do one's d.**, cumplir con su deber. 2 (*task*) función *f*. 3 **to be on d.**, estar de servicio; *Med Mil* estar de guardia; **d. chemist**, farmacia *f* de guardia. 4 (*tax*) impuesto *m*; **customs d.**, derechos *mpl* de aduana.

duty-free ['dju:tɪfri:] I *adj* libre de impuestos. II *adv* sin pagar impuestos. III *n* duty-free *m*.

duvet ['du:veɪ] *n* edredón *m*.

dwarf [dwɔ:f] I *n* (*pl* **dwarves** [dwɔ:vz]) (*person*) enano,-a *m,f*. II *vtr* hacer parecer pequeño,-a.

dwell [dwel] *vi* (*pt & pp* **dwelt**) *fml* morar. ◆**dwell on** *vtr* hablar extensamente de; **let's not d. on it**, olvidémoslo.

dwelling ['dwelɪŋ] *n fml & hum* morada *f*, vivienda *f*.

dwindle ['dwindəl] *vi* menguar, disminuir.

dye [daɪ] I *n* tinte *m*. II *vtr* (*pres p* **dyeing**; *pt & pp* **dyed**) teñir; **to d. one's hair black**, teñirse el pelo de negro.

dying ['daɪɪŋ] *adj* (*person*) moribundo,-a *m,f*, agonizante *mf*; *fig* (*custom*) en vías de desaparición.

dyke [daɪk] *n* 1 (*bank*) dique *m*; (*causeway*) terraplén *m*. 2 *offens sl* tortillera *f*.

dynamic [daɪ'næmɪk] *adj* dinámico,-a.

dynamics [daɪ'næmɪks] *n* dinámica *f*.

dynamism ['daɪnəmɪzəm] *n fig* dinamismo *m*.

dynamite ['daɪnəmaɪt] *n* dinamita *f*.

dynamo ['daɪnəməu] *n* dínamo *f*.

dynasty ['dɪnəsti] *n* dinastía *f*.

dysentery ['dɪsəntri] *n* disentería *f*.

dyslexia [dɪs'leksɪə] *n* dislexia *f*.

E

E, e [i:] *n* 1 (*the letter*) E, e *f*. 2 *Mus* mi *m*.

E *abbr* of **East**, Este, E.

each [i:tʃ] I *adj* cada; **e. day/month**, todos los días/meses; **e. person**, cada cual; **e. time I see him**, cada vez que lo veo. II *pron* 1 cada uno,-a; **two pounds e.**, dos libras cada uno; **we bought one e.**, nos compramos uno cada uno. 2 **e. other**, el uno al otro; **they hate e. other**, se odian.

eager ['i:gəʳ] *adj* (*anxious*) impaciente; (*desirous*) deseoso,-a; **to be e. for success**, codiciar el éxito. ◆**eagerly** *adv* (*anxiously*) con impaciencia; (*keenly*) con ilusión.

eagle ['i:gəl] *n* águila *f*.

ear [ɪəʳ] *n* 1 oreja *f*; (*sense of hearing*) oído *m*. 2 (*of corn etc*) espiga *f*.

earache ['ɪəreɪk] *n* dolor *m* de oídos.

eardrum ['ɪədrʌm] *n* tímpano *m*.

earl [ɜ:l] *n* conde *m*.

earlobe ['ɪələub] *n* lóbulo *m*.

early ['ɜ:li] I *adj* 1 (*before the usual time*) temprano,-a; **to have an e. night**, acostarse pronto; **you're e.!**, ¡qué pronto has venido! 2 (*at first stage, period*) **at an e. age**, siendo joven; **e. on**, al principio; **e. work**, obra de juventud; **in her e. forties**, a los cuarenta y pocos;

it's still e. days, aún es pronto. 3 (*in the near future*) **an e. reply**, una respuesta pronta; **at the earliest**, cuanto antes. II *adv* 1 (*before the expected time*) temprano; pronto; **earlier on**, antes; **five minutes e.**, con cinco minutos de adelanto; **to leave e.**, irse pronto. 2 (*near the beginning*) **as e. as 1914**, ya en 1914; **as e. as possible**, tan pronto como sea posible; **to book e.**, reservar con tiempo; **in e. July**, a principios de julio.

earmark ['ɪəmɑ:k] *vtr* destinar (**for**, para, a).

earn [ɜ:n] *vtr* 1 (*money*) ganar; **to e. one's living**, ganarse la vida. 2 (*reputation*) ganarse. 3 **to e. interest**, cobrar interés or intereses.

earnest ['ɜ:nɪst] I *adj* serio,-a, formal. II *n* **in e.**, de veras, en serio.

earnings ['ɜ:nɪŋz] *npl* ingresos *mpl*.

earring ['ɪərɪŋ] *n* pendiente *m*.

earshot ['ɪəʃɒt] *n* **out of e.**, fuera del alcance del oído; **within e.**, al alcance del oído.

earth [ɜ:θ] *n* 1 tierra *f*; *fig* **to be down to e.**, ser práctico; **where/why on e. ...?**, ¿pero dónde/por qué demonios ...? 2 *Elec* toma *f* de tierra. II *vtr Elec* conectar a tierra.

earthenware ['ɜ:θənweəʳ] I *n* loza *f*. II

adj de barro.
earthquake ['ɜ:θkweɪk] *n* terremoto *m*.
earthshattering ['ɜ:θʃætərɪŋ] *adj* trascendental; **e. news**, noticia bomba.
earthworm ['ɜ:θwɜ:m] *n* lombriz *f* de tierra.
earthy ['ɜ:θɪ] *adj* (**earthier, earthiest**) 1 (*taste*) terroso,-a. 2 (*bawdy*) tosco,-a.
earwig ['ɪəwɪg] *n* tijereta *f*.
ease [i:z] I *n* 1 (*freedom from discomfort*) tranquilidad *f*; *Mil* posición *f* de descanso; **at e.**, relajado,-a. 2 (*lack of difficulty*) facilidad *f*. 3 (*affluence*) comodidad *f*. 4 **e. of manner**, naturalidad *f*. II *vtr* 1 (*pain*) aliviar. 2 (*move gently*) deslizar con cuidado. ◆**ease off, ease up** *vi* 1 (*decrease*) disminuir. 2 (*slow down*) ir más despacio.
easel ['i:zəl] *n* caballete *m*.
east [i:st] I *n* este *m*; **the Middle E.**, el Oriente Medio. II *adj* del este, oriental; **E. Germany**, Alemania Oriental. III *adv* al *or* hacia al este.
Easter ['i:stər] *n* Semana Santa, Pascua *f*; **E. egg**, huevo *m* de Pascua; **E. Sunday**, Domingo *m* de Resurrección.
easterly ['i:stəlɪ] *adj* (*from the east*) del este; (*to the east*) hacia al este.
eastern ['i:stən] *adj* oriental.
eastward(s) ['i:stwəd(z)] *adv* hacia el este.
easy ['i:zɪ] (**easier, easiest**) I *adj* 1 (*simple*) fácil, sencillo,-a. 2 (*unworried, comfortable*) cómodo,-a, tranquilo,-a; *fam* **I'm e.!**, me da lo mismo; **e. chair**, butacón *m*. II *adv* **go e. on the wine**, no te pases con el vino; *fam* **to take things e.**, tomarse las cosas con calma; *fam* **take it e.!**, ¡tranquilo! ◆**easily** *adv* fácilmente; **e. the best**, con mucho el mejor.
easy-going [i:zɪ'gəʊɪŋ] *adj* (*calm*) tranquilo,-a; (*lax*) despreocupado,-a; (*undemanding*) poco exigente.
eat [i:t] (*pt* **ate** [et, eɪt], *pp* **eaten**) *vtr* comer. ◆**eat away** *vtr* desgastar; (*metal*) corroer. ◆**eat into** *vtr* 1 (*wood*) roer. 2 *fig* (*savings*) consumir. ◆**eat out** *vi* comer fuera. ◆**eat up** *vtr* 1 (*meal*) terminar. 2 *fig* (*petrol*) consumir; (*miles*) recorrer rápidamente.
eatable ['i:təbəl] *adj* comestible.
eaten ['i:tən] *pp* → **eat**.
eau de Cologne [əʊdəkə'ləʊn] *n* colonia *f*.
eaves [i:vz] *npl* alero *m sing*.
eavesdrop ['i:vzdrɒp] *vi* escuchar disimuladamente.
ebb [eb] I *n* reflujo *m*; **e. and flow**, flujo y reflujo; *fig* **to be at a low e.**, estar decaído. II *vi* 1 (*tide*) bajar; **to e. and flow**, subir y bajar. 2 *fig* **to e. away**, decaer.
ebony ['ebənɪ] I *n* ébano *m*. II *adj* de ébano.
eccentric [ɪk'sentrɪk] *adj & nm,f*

excéntrico,-a.
ecclesiastic [ɪkli:zɪ'æstɪk] *adj & nm,f* eclesiástico,-a.
echelon ['eʃəlɒn] *n* escalafón *m*.
echo ['ekəʊ] I *n* (*pl* **echoes**) eco *m*. II *vtr* (*repeat*) repetir. III *vi* resonar, hacer eco.
eclectic [ɪ'klektɪk] *adj* ecléctico,-a.
eclipse [ɪ'klɪps] I *n* eclipse *m*. II *vtr* eclipsar.
ecological [i:kə'lɒdʒɪkəl] *adj* ecológico, -a.
ecology [ɪ'kɒlədʒɪ] *n* ecología *f*.
economic [i:kə'nɒmɪk] *adj* económico,-a; (*profitable*) rentable.
economical [i:kə'nɒmɪkəl] *adj* económico,-a.
economics [i:kə'nɒmɪks] *n sing* (*science*) economía *f*; *Educ* (ciencias *fpl*) económicas *fpl*.
economist [ɪ'kɒnəmɪst] *n* economista *mf*.
economize [ɪ'kɒnəmaɪz] *vi* economizar.
economy [ɪ'kɒnəmɪ] *n* 1 *Pol* **the e.**, la economía. 2 (*saving*) ahorro *m*; **e. class**, clase *f* turista.
ecosystem ['i:kəʊsɪstəm] *n* ecosistema *m*.
ecstasy ['ekstəsɪ] *n* éxtasis *m*.
ecstatic [ek'stætɪk] *adj* extático,-a.
Ecuador ['ekwədɔ:r] *n* Ecuador.
eczema ['eksɪmə] *n* eczema *m*.
eddy ['edɪ] I *n* remolino *m*. II *vi* arremolinarse.
edge [edʒ] I *n* borde *m*; (*of knife*) filo *m*; (*of coin*) canto *m*; (*of water*) orilla *f*; **on the e. of town**, en las afueras de la ciudad; **to have the e. on sb**, llevar ventaja a algn; *fig* **to be on e.**, tener los nervios de punta. II *vtr Sew* ribetear. III *vi* **to e. closer**, acercarse lentamente; **to e. forward**, avanzar poco a poco.
edgeways ['edʒweɪz] *adv* de lado; *fig* **I couldn't get a word in e.**, no pude decir ni pío.
edging ['edʒɪŋ] *n* borde *m*; *Sew* ribete *m*.
edgy ['edʒɪ] *adj* (**edgier, edgiest**) nervioso,-a.
edible ['edɪbəl] *adj* comestible.
edict ['i:dɪkt] *n Hist* edicto *m*; *Jur* decreto *m*.
Edinburgh ['edɪnbrə] *n* Edimburgo.
edit ['edɪt] *vtr* 1 (*prepare for printing*) preparar para la imprenta. 2 (*rewrite*) corregir; **to e. sth out**, suprimir algo. 3 *Press* ser redactor,-a de. 4 *Cin Rad TV* montar; (*cut*) cortar.
edition [ɪ'dɪʃən] *n* edición *f*.
editor ['edɪtər] *n* (*of book*) editor,-a *m,f*; *Press* redactor, -a *m,f*; *Cin TV* montador,-a *m,f*.
editorial [edɪ'tɔ:rɪəl] I *adj* editorial; **e. staff**, redacción *f*. II *n* editorial *m*.
educate ['edjʊkeɪt] *vtr* educar.
educated ['edjʊkeɪtɪd] *adj* culto,-a.
education [edjʊ'keɪʃən] *n* 1 (*schooling*) enseñanza *f*; **adult e.**, educación *f* de

adultos; **Ministry of E.,** Ministerio *m* de Educación. **2** *(training)* formación *f.* **3** *(studies)* estudios *mpl.* **4** *(culture)* cultura *f.*

educational [edju'keɪʃənəl] *adj* educativo,-a, educacional.

eel [iːl] *n* anguila *f.*

eerie ['ɪərɪ] *adj* **(eerier, eeriest)** siniestro,-a.

efface [ɪ'feɪs] *vtr* borrar.

effect [ɪ'fekt] **I** *n* **1** efecto *m*; **in e.,** efectivamente; **to come into e.,** entrar en vigor; **to have an e. on,** afectar a; **to no e.,** sin resultado alguno; **to take e.,** *(drug)* surtir efecto; *(law)* entrar en vigor. **2** *(impression)* impresión *f.* **3** **effects,** *(possessions)* efectos *mpl.* **II** *vtr fml* provocar.

effective [ɪ'fektɪv] *adj* **1** *(successful)* eficaz. **2** *(real)* efectivo,-a. **3** *(impressive)* impresionante. ◆**effectively** *adv* **1** *(successfully)* eficazmente. **2** *(in fact)* en efecto.

effeminate [ɪ'femɪnɪt] *adj* afeminado,-a.

effervescent [efə'vesənt] *adj* efervescente.

efficiency [ɪ'fɪʃənsɪ] *n* *(of person)* eficacia *f*; *(of machine)* rendimiento *m.*

efficient [ɪ'fɪʃənt] *adj* eficaz, eficiente; *(machine)* de buen rendimiento.

effigy ['efɪdʒɪ] *n* efigie *f.*

effluent ['efluənt] *n* vertidos *mpl.*

effort ['efət] *n* **1** esfuerzo *m*; **to make an e.,** hacer un esfuerzo, esforzarse. **2** *(attempt)* intento *m.*

effortless ['efətlɪs] *adj* sin esfuerzo.

effrontery [ɪ'frʌntərɪ] *n* desfachatez *f.*

effusive [ɪ'fjuːsɪv] *adj* efusivo,-a.

eg [iː'dʒiː] *abbr* of **exempli gratia,** p. ej.

egalitarian [ɪgælɪ'teərɪən] *adj* igualitario,-a.

egg [eg] **I** *n* huevo *m*; *fam fig* **to put all one's eggs in one basket,** jugárselo todo a una carta; **e. cup,** huevera *f*; **e. timer,** reloj *m* de arena; **e. white,** clara *f* de huevo. **II** *vtr* **to e. sb on (to do sth),** empujar a algn *(a hacer algo).*

eggplant ['egplɑːnt] *n US* berenjena *f.*

eggshell ['egʃel] *n* cáscara *f* de huevo.

ego ['iːgəʊ, 'egəʊ] *n* **1** ego *m*; *fam* **e. trip,** autobombo *m.* **2** *fam* amor propio.

egocentric(al) [iːgəʊ'sentrɪk(əl)] *adj* egocéntrico,-a.

egoism ['iːgəʊɪzəm] *n* egoísmo *m.*

egoist ['iːgəʊɪst] *n* egoísta *mf.*

egotistic(al) [iːgəʊ'tɪstɪk(əl)] *adj* egotista.

Egypt ['iːdʒɪpt] *n* Egipto.

Egyptian [ɪ'dʒɪpʃən] *adj & n* egipcio,-a *(m,f).*

eiderdown ['aɪdədaʊn] *n* edredón *m.*

eight [eɪt] *adj & n* ocho *(m) inv.*

eighteen [eɪ'tiːn] *adj & n* dieciocho *(m) inv.*

eighteenth [eɪ'tiːnθ] **I** *adj & n* decimoctavo *(m,f).* **II** *n* *(fraction)* decimoctavo

m.

eighth [eɪtθ] **I** *adj & n* octavo,-a *(m,f).* **II** *n* *(fraction)* octavo *m.*

eighty ['eɪtɪ] *adj & n* ochenta *(m) inv.*

Eire ['eərə] *n* Eire.

either ['aɪðər, 'iːðər] **I** *pron* **1** *(affirmative)* cualquiera; **e. of them,** cualquiera de los dos; **e. of us,** cualquiera de nosotros dos. **2** *(negative)* ninguno, ninguna, ni el uno ni el otro, ni la una ni la otra; **I don't want e. of them,** no quiero ninguno de los dos. **II** *adj* *(both)* cada, los dos, las dos; **on e. side,** en ambos lados; **in e. case,** en cualquier de los dos casos. **III** *conj* **o; e. ... or ...,** o ... o ...; **e. Friday or Saturday,** o (bien) el viernes o el sábado. **IV** *adv* *(after negative)* tampoco; **I don't want to do it e.,** yo tampoco quiero hacerlo.

ejaculate [ɪ'dʒækjʊleɪt] *vi* *(man)* eyacular.

eject [ɪ'dʒekt] **I** *vtr* expulsar. **II** *vi* Av eyectarse.

eke [iːk] *vtr* **to e. out a living,** ganarse la vida a duras penas.

elaborate [ɪ'læbəreɪt] **I** *vtr* **1** *(devise)* elaborar. **2** *(explain)* explicar detalladamente. **II** *vi* explicarse; **to e. on sth,** explicar algo con más detalles. **III** [ɪ'læbərɪt] *adj* **1** *(complicated)* complicado,-a. **2** *(detailed)* detallado,-a; *(style)* esmerado,-a.

elapse [ɪ'læps] *vi* transcurrir, pasar.

elastic [ɪ'læstɪk] **I** *adj* elástico,-a; *fig* flexible; **e. band,** goma elástica. **II** *n* elástico *m.*

Elastoplast® [ɪ'læstəplɑːst] *n* tirita *f.*

elated [ɪ'leɪtɪd] *adj* eufórico,-a.

elation [ɪ'leɪʃən] *n* regocijo *m.*

elbow ['elbəʊ] **I** *n* **1** codo *m*; *fig* **e. room,** espacio *m.* **2** *(bend)* recodo *m.* **II** *vtr* **to e. sb,** dar un codazo a algn.

elder¹ ['eldər] **I** *adj* mayor. **II** *n* **the elders,** los ancianos.

elder² ['eldər] *n Bot* saúco *m.*

elderly ['eldəlɪ] **I** *adj* anciano,-a. **II** *npl* **the e.,** los ancianos.

eldest ['eldɪst] **I** *adj* mayor. **II** *n* el or la mayor.

elect [ɪ'lekt] **I** *vtr* **1** *Pol* elegir. **2 to e. to do sth,** *(choose)* decidir hacer algo. **II** *adj* **the president e.,** el presidente electo.

election [ɪ'lekʃən] **I** *n* elección *f*; **general e.,** elecciones *fpl* generales. **II** *adj* electoral.

electioneering [ɪlekʃə'nɪərɪŋ] *n* electoralismo *m.*

elector [ɪ'lektər] *n* elector,-a *m,f.*

electoral [ɪ'lektərəl] *adj* electoral.

electorate [ɪ'lektərɪt] *n* electorado *m.*

electric [ɪ'lektrɪk] *adj* **1** eléctrico,-a; **e. blanket,** manta eléctrica; **e. chair,** silla eléctrica; **e. shock,** electrochoque *m.* **2** *fig* electrizante.

electrical [ɪ'lektrɪkəl] *adj* eléctrico,-a.

electrician [ɪlek'trɪʃən] *n* electricista *mf*.

electricity [ɪlek'trɪsɪtɪ] *n* electricidad *f*; **e. bill**, recibo *m* de la luz.

electrify [ɪ'lektrɪfaɪ] *vtr* 1 (*railway line*) electrificar. 2 *fig* (*excite*) electrizar.

electrocute [ɪ'lektrəkjuːt] *vtr* electrocutar.

electron [ɪ'lektrɒn] *n* electrón *m*.

electronic [ɪlek'trɒnɪk] *adj* electrónico,-a.

electronics [ɪlek'trɒnɪks] *n* 1 (*science*) electrónica *f*. 2 (*of machine*) componentes *mpl* electrónicos.

elegant ['elɪgənt] *adj* elegante.

element ['elɪmənt] *n* 1 elemento *m*. 2 (*part*) parte *f*. 3 (*electrical*) resistencia *f*. 4 *fam fig* **to be in one's e.**, estar en su salsa.

elementary [elɪ'mentərɪ] *adj* (*basic*) elemental; (*not developed*) rudimentario,-a; (*easy*) fácil; **e. school**, escuela primaria.

elephant ['elɪfənt] *n* elefante *m*.

elevate ['elɪveɪt] *vtr* elevar; (*in rank*) ascender.

elevation [elɪ'veɪʃən] *n* 1 elevación *f*. 2 *Archit* alzado *m*. 3 (*above sea level*) altitud *f*.

elevator ['elɪveɪtər] *n* US ascensor *m*.

eleven [ɪ'levən] *adj & n* once (*m*) *inv*.

elevenses [ɪ'levənzɪz] *npl fam* bocadillo *m* de las once.

eleventh [ɪ'levənθ] I *adj & nm,f* undécimo,-a. II *n* (*fraction*) undécimo *m*.

elicit [ɪ'lɪsɪt] *vtr* obtener.

eligible ['elɪdʒəbəl] *adj* apto,-a; **he isn't e. to vote**, no tiene derecho al voto.

eliminate [ɪ'lɪmɪneɪt] *vtr* eliminar.

elite [ɪ'liːt] *n* elite *f*.

elitist [ɪ'liːtɪst] *adj* elitista.

elm [elm] *n* olmo *m*.

elocution [elə'kjuːʃən] *n* elocución *f*.

elongate ['iːlɒŋgeɪt] *vtr* alargar.

elope [ɪ'ləʊp] *vi* fugarse para casarse.

eloquent ['eləkwənt] *adj* elocuente.

else [els] *adv* 1 **anyone e.**, alguien más; **anything e.?**, ¿algo más?; **everything e.**, todo lo demás; **no-one e.**, nadie más; **someone e.**, otro,-a; **something e.**, otra cosa, algo más; **somewhere e.**, en otra parte; **what e.?**, ¿qué más?; **where e.?**, ¿en qué otro sitio? 2 **or e.**, (*otherwise*) si no.

elsewhere [els'weər] *adv* en otra parte.

elucidate [ɪ'luːsɪdeɪt] *vtr* aclarar.

elude [ɪ'luːd] *vtr* 1 (*escape*) eludir; **his name eludes me**, no consigo acordarme de su nombre. 2 (*avoid*) esquivar.

elusive [ɪ'luːsɪv] *adj* esquivo,-a; (*evasive*) evasivo,-a.

emaciated [ɪ'meɪsɪeɪtɪd] *adj* demacrado,-a.

emanate ['eməneɪt] *vi* provenir (**from**, de).

emancipate [ɪ'mænsɪpeɪt] *vtr* emancipar.

emancipation [ɪmænsɪ'peɪʃən] *n* emancipación *f*.

embankment [ɪm'bæŋkmənt] *n* 1 (*made of earth*) terraplén *m*. 2 (*of river*) dique *m*.

embargo [em'bɑːgəʊ] *n* (*pl* **embargoes**) embargo *m*.

embark [em'bɑːk] I *vtr* (*merchandise*) embarcar. II *vi* embarcar, embarcarse; *fig* **to e. upon**, emprender; (*sth difficult*) embarcarse en.

embarkation [embɑː'keɪʃən] *n* embarque *m*.

embarrass [ɪm'bærəs] *vtr* avergonzar.

embarrassed [ɪm'bærəst] *adj* avergonzado,-a.

embarrassing [ɪm'bærəsɪŋ] *adj* embarazoso,-a.

embarrassment [ɪm'bærəsmənt] *n* vergüenza *f*.

embassy ['embəsɪ] *n* embajada *f*.

embed [ɪm'bed] *vtr* (*jewels*) incrustar; *fig* grabar.

embellish [ɪm'belɪʃ] *vtr* embellecer; (*story*) exagerar.

ember ['embər] *n* ascua *f*, rescoldo *m*.

embezzle [ɪm'bezəl] *vtr* desfalcar, malversar.

embezzlement [ɪm'bezəlmənt] *n* malversación *f*.

embitter [ɪm'bɪtər] *vtr* amargar.

embittered [ɪm'bɪtəd] *adj* amargado,-a, resentido,-a.

emblem ['embləm] *n* emblema *m*.

embody [ɪm'bɒdɪ] *vtr* 1 (*include*) abarcar. 2 (*personify*) encarnar.

embossed [ɪm'bɒst] *adj* en relieve.

embrace [ɪm'breɪs] I *vtr* 1 abrazar. 2 (*accept*) adoptar. 3 (*include*) abarcar. II *vi* abrazarse. III *n* abrazo *m*.

embroider [ɪm'brɔɪdər] *vtr* 1 *Sew* bordar. 2 *fig* (*story, truth*) adornar, embellecer.

embroidery [ɪm'brɔɪdərɪ] *n* bordado *m*.

embryo ['embrɪəʊ] *n* embrión *m*.

emerald ['emərəld] *n* esmeralda *f*.

emerge [ɪ'mɜːdʒ] *vi* salir; (*problem*) surgir; **it emerged that ...**, resultó que ....

emergence [ɪ'mɜːdʒəns] *n* aparición *f*.

emergency [ɪ'mɜːdʒənsɪ] *n* emergencia *f*; *Med* urgencia *f*; **in an e.**, en caso de emergencia; **e. exit**, salida *f* de emergencia; **e. landing**, aterrizaje forzoso; **e. measures**, medidas *fpl* de urgencia; **e. stop**, frenazo *m* en seco; *Pol* **state of e.**, estado *m* de excepción.

emery ['emərɪ] *n* **e. board**, lima *f* de uñas.

emigrant ['emɪgrənt] *n* emigrante *mf*.

emigrate ['emɪgreɪt] *vi* emigrar.

emigration [emɪ'greɪʃən] *n* emigración *f*.

eminent ['emɪnənt] *adj* eminente.

emission [ɪ'mɪʃən] *n* emisión *f*.

emit [ɪ'mɪt] *vtr* (*signals*) emitir; (*smells*) despedir; (*sound*) producir.

emotion [ɪ'məʊʃən] n emoción f.

emotional [ɪ'məʊʃənəl] adj 1 emocional. 2 (moving) conmovedor,-a.

emotive [ɪ'məʊtɪv] adj emotivo,-a.

emperor ['empərəʳ] n emperador m.

emphasis ['emfəsɪs] n (pl **emphases** ['emfəsiːz]) énfasis m; **to place e. on sth**, hacer hincapié en algo.

emphasize ['emfəsaɪz] vtr subrayar, hacer hincapié en; (insist) insistir; (highlight) hacer resaltar.

emphatic [em'fætɪk] adj (forceful) enfático,-a; (convinced) categórico,-a.
◆**emphatically** adv categóricamente.

empire ['empaɪəʳ] n imperio m.

employ [ɪm'plɔɪ] vtr emplear; (time) ocupar.

employee [emplɔɪˈiː, emplɔɪˈəʳ] n empleado,-a m, f.

employer [ɪm'plɔɪəʳ] n patrón,-ona m, f.

employment [ɪm'plɔɪmənt] n empleo m; **e. agency**, agencia f de colocaciones; **full e.**, pleno empleo.

empower [ɪm'paʊəʳ] vtr autorizar.

empress ['emprɪs] n emperatriz f.

emptiness ['emptɪnɪs] n vacío m.

empty ['emptɪ] I adj (**emptier**, **emptiest**) vacío,-a; **an e. house**, una casa deshabitada; **e. promises**, promesas fpl vanas. II vtr vaciar. III vi 1 vaciarse. 2 (river) desembocar (**into**, en). IV npl **empties**, envases vacíos.

empty-handed [emptɪ'hændɪd] adj con las manos vacías.

emulate ['emjʊleɪt] vtr emular.

emulsion [ɪ'mʌlʃən] n emulsión f; **e. paint**, pintura f mate.

enable [ɪ'neɪbəl] vtr permitir.

enact [ɪn'ækt] vtr (play) representar; (law) promulgar.

enamel [ɪ'næməl] n esmalte m.

enamoured, US **enamored** [ɪ'næməd] adj enamorado,-a; **to be e. of or by sth**, encantarle algo a algn.

encase [ɪn'keɪs] vtr **encased in**, revestido de.

enchant [ɪn'tʃɑːnt] vtr encantar.

enchanting [ɪn'tʃɑːntɪŋ] adj encantador,-a.

encircle [ɪn'sɜːkəl] vtr rodear.

enclave ['enkleɪv] n enclave m.

enclose [ɪn'kləʊz] vtr 1 (surround) rodear. 2 (fence in) cercar. 3 (in envelope) adjuntar; **please find enclosed**, le enviamos adjunto.

enclosure [ɪn'kləʊʒəʳ] n 1 (fenced area) cercado m. 2 (in envelope) documento adjunto. 3 (of racecourse) recinto m.

encompass [ɪn'kʌmpəs] vtr abarcar.

encore ['ɒŋkɔː] I interj ¡otra!, ¡bis! II n repetición f, bis m.

encounter [ɪn'kaʊntəʳ] I n (meeting) encuentro m. II vtr encontrar, encontrarse con; (problems) tropezar con.

encourage [ɪn'kʌrɪdʒ] vtr 1 (person) animar. 2 (tourism, trade) fomentar.

encouragement [ɪn'kʌrɪdʒmənt] n estímulo m.

encroach [ɪn'krəʊtʃ] vi **to e. on**, (territory) invadir; (rights) usurpar; (time, freedom) quitar.

encrusted [ɪn'krʌstɪd] adj incrustado,-a (**with**, de).

encumber [ɪn'kʌmbəʳ] vtr estorbar; (with debts) gravar.

encyclop(a)edia [ensaɪkləʊ'piːdɪə] n enciclopedia f.

end [end] I n 1 (of stick) punta f; (of street) final m; (of table) extremo m; **to make ends meet**, llegar a final de mes; **fig it makes my hair stand on e.**, me pone el pelo de punta. 2 (conclusion) fin m, final m; (of period) fin m; **for hours on e.**, hora tras hora; **no e. of**, un sinfín de; **to bring an e. to sth**, poner fin a algo; **to put an e. to**, acabar con. 3 (aim) objetivo m, fin m; **to no e.**, en vano. II vtr acabar, terminar. III vi acabarse, terminarse. ◆**end up** vi terminar; **it ended up in the dustbin**, fue a parar al cubo de la basura; **to e. up doing sth**, terminar por hacer algo.

endanger [ɪn'deɪndʒəʳ] vtr poner en peligro.

endangered [ɪn'deɪndʒəd] adj en peligro.

endearing [ɪn'dɪərɪŋ] adj simpático,-a.

endeavour, US **endeavor** [ɪn'devəʳ] I n esfuerzo m. II vtr intentar, procurar.

ending ['endɪŋ] n final m.

endive ['endaɪv] n Bot 1 endibia f. 2 US escarola f.

endless ['endlɪs] adj interminable.

endorse [ɪn'dɔːs] vtr 1 Fin endosar. 2 (approve) aprobar; (support) apoyar.

endorsement [ɪn'dɔːsmənt] n 1 Fin endoso m. 2 Aut nota f de sanción. 3 (approval) aprobación f.

endow [ɪn'daʊ] vtr dotar; **to be endowed with**, estar dotado,-a de.

endurance [ɪn'djʊərəns] n resistencia f.

endure [ɪn'djʊəʳ] I vtr (bear) aguantar, soportar. II vi perdurar.

enemy ['enəmɪ] adj & n enemigo,-a (m,f).

energetic [enə'dʒetɪk] adj enérgico,-a.

energy ['enədʒɪ] n energía f.

enforce [ɪn'fɔːs] vtr (law) hacer cumplir.

enforcement [ɪn'fɔːsmənt] n aplicación f.

engage [ɪn'geɪdʒ] vtr 1 (hire) contratar. 2 (attention) llamar. 3 (in conversation) entablar. 4 Tech engranar; Aut **to e. the clutch**, pisar el embrague.

engaged [ɪn'geɪdʒd] adj 1 (betrothed) prometido,-a; **to get e.**, prometerse. 2 (busy) ocupado,-a; Tel **it's e.**, está comunicando.

engagement [ɪn'geɪdʒmənt] n 1 (betrothal) petición f de mano; (period) noviazgo *m*; **e. ring**, anillo *m* de compromiso. **2** (*appointment*) cita *f*. **3** *Mil* combate *m*.

engaging [ɪnˈgeɪdʒɪŋ] *adj* simpático,-a, agradable.

engender [ɪnˈdʒendər] *vtr* engendrar.

engine [ˈendʒɪn] *n* motor *m*; *Rail* locomotora *f*; **e. room**, sala *f* de máquinas; **e. driver**, maquinista *mf*.

engineer [endʒɪˈnɪər] **I** *n* **1** ingeniero,-a *m*, *f*; **civil e.**, ingeniero de caminos. **2** *US Rail* maquinista *mf*. **II** *vtr fig* (*contrive*) maquinar.

engineering [endʒɪˈnɪərɪŋ] *n* ingeniería *f*; **electrical e.**, electrotecnia *f*; **civil e.**, ingeniería civil.

England [ˈɪŋglənd] *n* Inglaterra.

English [ˈɪŋglɪʃ] **I** *adj* inglés,-esa. **II** *n* **1** (*language*) inglés *m*. **2** *pl* **the E.**, los ingleses.

Englishman [ˈɪŋglɪʃmən] *n* inglés *m*.

English-speaking [ˈɪŋglɪʃspiːkɪŋ] *adj* de habla inglesa.

Englishwoman [ˈɪŋglɪʃwʊmən] *n* inglesa *f*.

engraving [ɪnˈgreɪvɪŋ] *n* grabado *m*.

engrossed [ɪnˈgrəʊst] *adj* absorto,-a (**in**, en).

engulf [ɪnˈgʌlf] *vtr* tragarse.

enhance [ɪnˈhɑːns] *vtr* (*beauty*) realzar; (*power, chances*) aumentar.

enigma [ɪˈnɪgmə] *n* enigma *m*.

enjoy [ɪnˈdʒɔɪ] **I** *vtr* **1** disfrutar de; **to e. oneself**, pasarlo bien. **2** (*benefit from*) gozar de.

enjoyable [ɪnˈdʒɔɪəbəl] *adj* agradable; (*amusing*) divertido,-a.

enjoyment [ɪnˈdʒɔɪmənt] *n* placer *m*, gusto *m*.

enlarge [ɪnˈlɑːdʒ] **I** *vtr* extender, ampliar; *Phot* ampliar. **II** *vi* **to e. upon a subject**, extenderse sobre un tema.

enlargement [ɪnˈlɑːdʒmənt] *n* *Phot* ampliación *f*.

enlighten [ɪnˈlaɪtən] *vtr* iluminar.

enlightened [ɪnˈlaɪtənd] *adj* **1** (*learned*) culto,-a; (*informed*) bien informado,-a **2** *Hist* ilustrado,-a.

enlightenment [ɪnˈlaɪtənmənt] *n* **the Age of E.**, el Siglo de las Luces.

enlist [ɪnˈlɪst] **I** *vtr Mil* reclutar; **to e. sb's help**, conseguir ayuda de algn. **II** *vi Mil* alistarse.

enmity [ˈenmɪtɪ] *n* enemistad *f*, hostilidad *f*.

enormous [ɪˈnɔːməs] *adj* enorme. ◆**enormously** *adv* enormemente; **I enjoyed myself e.**, lo pasé genial.

enough [ɪˈnʌf] **I** *adj* bastante, suficiente; **e. books**, bastantes libros; **e. money**, bastante dinero; **have we got e. petrol?**, ¿tenemos suficiente gasolina? **II** *adv* bastante; **oddly e. ...**, lo curioso es que ...; **sure e.**, en efecto. **III** *n* lo bastante,

lo suficiente; **e. to live on**, lo suficiente para vivir; **it isn't e.**, no basta; **more than e.**, más que suficiente; **fam e. is e.**, ¡ya está!; *fam* **I've had e.!**, ¡estoy harto!

enquire [ɪnˈkwaɪər] *vi* preguntar.

enquiry [ɪnˈkwaɪərɪ] *n* **1** (*question*) pregunta *f*; **to make an e.**, preguntar; **enquiries**, información *f*. **2** (*investigation*) investigación *f*.

enrage [ɪnˈreɪdʒ] *vtr* enfurecer.

enrich [ɪnˈrɪtʃ] *vtr* enriquecer.

enrol, *US* **enroll** [ɪnˈrəʊl] **I** *vtr* matricular. **II** *vi* matricularse, inscribirse.

enrolment [ɪnˈrəʊlmənt] *n* matrícula *f*.

en route [ɒnˈruːt] *adv* en or por el camino.

ensign [ˈensaɪn] *n* (*flag*) bandera *f*; *Naut* pabellón *m*.

enslave [ɪnˈsleɪv] *vtr* esclavizar.

ensue [ɪnˈsjuː] *vi* **1** (*follow*) seguir. **2** (*result*) resultar (**from**, de).

ensure [ɪnˈʃʊər] *vtr* asegurar.

entail [ɪnˈteɪl] *vtr* (*involve*) suponer.

entangle [ɪnˈtæŋgəl] *vtr* enredar.

enter [ˈentər] **I** *vtr* **1** (*go into*) entrar en; *fig* (*join*) ingresar en. **2** (*write down*) apuntar, anotar. **3** **to e. one's name for a course**, (*register*) matricularse en un curso. **4** *Comput* dar entrada a. **II** *vi* entrar. ◆**enter into** *vtr* **1** (*agreement*) firmar; (*negotiations*) iniciar; (*bargain*) cerrar. **2** (*relations*) establecer; (*conversation*) entablar.

enterprise [ˈentəpraɪz] *n* empresa *f*; **free e.**, libre empresa; **private e.**, iniciativa privada; (*as a whole*) el sector privado; **public e.**, el sector público.

enterprising [ˈentəpraɪzɪŋ] *adj* emprendedor,-a.

entertain [entəˈteɪn] **I** *vtr* **1** (*amuse*) divertir. **2** (*consider*) considerar; **to e. an idea**, abrigar una idea. **II** *vi* tener invitados.

entertainer [entəˈteɪnər] *n* artista *mf*.

entertaining [entəˈteɪnɪŋ] *adj* divertido, -a.

entertainment [entəˈteɪnmənt] *n* **1** diversión *f*. **2** *Theat* espectáculo *m*.

enthralling [ɪnˈθrɔːlɪŋ] *adj* fascinante.

enthuse [ɪnˈθjuːz] *vi* entusiasmarse (**over**, por).

enthusiasm [ɪnˈθjuːzɪæzəm] *n* entusiasmo *m*.

enthusiast [ɪnˈθjuːzɪæst] *n* entusiasta *mf*.

enthusiastic [ɪnθjuːzɪˈæstɪk] *adj* entusiasta; (*praise*) caluroso,-a; **to be e. about sth**, entusiasmarse por algo.

entice [ɪnˈtaɪs] *vtr* seducir, atraer.

enticing [ɪnˈtaɪsɪŋ] *adj* atractivo,-a, tentador,-a.

entire [ɪnˈtaɪər] *adj* entero,-a, todo,-a. ◆**entirely** *adv* **1** (*completely*) totalmente. **2** (*solely*) exclusivamente.

entirety [ɪnˈtaɪərɪtɪ] *n* **in its e.**, en su totalidad.

entitle |ın'taıtəl| *vtr* **1** dar derecho a; **to be entitled to**, tener derecho a. **2** (*book etc*) titular.

entity |'entıtı| *n* entidad *f*.

entourage |ɒntʊ'rɑːʒ| *n* séquito *m*.

entrails |'entreılz| *npl* tripas *fpl*; *fig* entrañas *fpl*.

entrance¹ |'entrəns| *n* **1** entrada *f*; **e. fee**, (*to museum etc*) entrada; (*to organization*) cuota *f*. **2** (*admission*) ingreso *m*; **e. examination**, examen *m* de ingreso.

entrance² |ın'trɑːns| *vtr* encantar.

entrant |'entrənt| *n* (*in competition*) participante *mf*; (*applicant*) aspirante *mf*.

entreat |ın'triːt| *vtr fml* suplicar, rogar.

entrenched |ın'trentʃt| *adj* firmemente enraizado,-a.

entrepreneur |ɒntrəprə'nɜːr| *n* empresario, -a *m,f*.

entrust |ın'trʌst| *vtr* encargar (**with**, de); **to e. sth to sb**, dejar algo al cuidado de algn.

entry |'entrı| *n* **1** (*entrance*) entrada *f*; **no e.**, dirección prohibida. **2** (*in competition*) participante *mf*.

enumerate |ı'njuːməreıt| *vtr* enumerar.

enunciate |ı'nʌnsıeıt| *vtr* (*words*) articular; (*ideas*) formular.

envelop |ın'veləp| *vtr* envolver.

envelope |'envələʊp| *n* sobre *m*.

envious |'envıəs| *adj* envidioso,-a; **to feel e.**, tener envidia.

environment |ın'vaıərənmənt| *n* medio *m* ambiente.

environmental |ınvaıərən'mentəl| *adj* medioambiental.

envisage |ın'vızıdʒ| *vtr* (*imagine*) imaginarse; (*foresee*) prever.

envoy |'envɔı| *n* enviado *n m,f*.

envy |'envı| **I** *n* envidia *f*. **II** *vtr* envidiar, tener envidia de.

enzyme |'enzaım| *n* enzima *m*.

ephemeral |ı'femərəl| *adj* efímero,-a.

epic |'epık| **I** *n* epopeya *f*. **II** *adj* épico,-a.

epidemic |epı'demık| *n* epidemia *f*; *fig* (*of crime etc*) ola *f*.

epilepsy |'epılepsı| *n* epilepsia *f*.

epilogue, *US* **epilog** |'epılɒg| *n* epílogo *m*.

episode |'epısəʊd| *n* episodio *m*.

epistle |ı'pısəl| *n* epístola *f*.

epitaph |'epıtɑːf| *n* epitafio *m*.

epitome |ı'pıtəmı| *n fml* personificación *f*.

epitomize |ı'pıtəmaız| *vtr fml* personificar.

epoch |'iːpɒk| *n* época *f*.

equable |'ekwəbəl| *adj* **1** (*person*) ecuánime. **2** (*climate*) uniforme.

equal |'iːkwəl| **I** *adj* igual; **to be e. to the occasion**, estar a la altura de las circunstancias; **e. pay**, igualdad *f* de salarios. **II** *n* igual *mf*; **to treat sb as an e.**,

tratar a algn de igual a igual. **III** *vtr* **1** *Math* equivaler. **2** (*match*) igualar.

◆**equally** *adv* igualmente; **e. pretty**, igual de bonito; **to share sth e.**, dividir algo en partes iguales.

equality |iː'kwɒlıtı| *n* igualdad *f*.

equalize |'iːkwəlaız| **I** *vi Ftb* empatar. **II** *vtr* igualar.

equalizer |'iːkwəlaızər| *n Ftb* gol *m* del empate; (*of sound*) ecualizador *m*.

equanimity |ekwə'nımıtı| *n* ecuanimidad *f*.

equate |ı'kweıt| *vtr* equiparar, comparar (**to**, a con).

equation |ı'kweıʒən, ı'kweıʃən| *n Math* ecuación *f*.

equator |ı'kweıtər| *n* ecuador *m*.

equatorial |ekwə'tɔːrıəl| *adj* ecuatorial.

equestrian |ı'kwestrıən| *adj* ecuestre.

equilibrium |iːkwı'lıbrıəm| *n* equilibrio *m*.

equinox |'iːkwınɒks| *n* equinoccio *f*.

equip |ı'kwıp| *vtr* (*with tools, machines*) equipar; (*with food*) proveer.

equipment |ı'kwıpmənt| *n* (*materials*) equipo *m*; **office e.**, material *m* de oficina.

equipped |ı'kwıpt| *adj* (*with tools, machines*) equipado,-a; (*with skills*) dotado,-a.

equitable |'ekwıtəbəl| *adj* equitativo,-a.

equities |'ekwıtız| *npl* acciones ordinarias.

equivalent |ı'kwıvələnt| *adj & n* equivalente (*m*); **to be e. to**, equivaler a, ser equivalente a.

equivocal |ı'kwıvəkəl| *adj* equívoco,-a.

era |'ıərə| *n* era *f*.

eradicate |ı'rædıkeıt| *vtr* erradicar.

erase |ı'reız| *vtr* borrar.

eraser |ı'reızər| *n* goma *f* de borrar.

erect |ı'rekt| **I** *adj* **1** (*upright*) erguido,-a. **2** (*penis*) erecto,-a. **II** *vtr* (*monument*) levantar, erigir.

erection |ı'rekʃən| *n* **1** (*of building*) construcción *f*. **2** (*penis*) erección *f*.

ermine |'ɜːmın| *n* armiño *m*.

erode |ı'rəʊd| *vtr* **1** (*rock, soil*) erosionar. **2** (*metal*) corroer, desgastar; *fig* (*power, confidence*) hacer perder.

erosion |ı'rəʊʒən| *n Geol* erosión *f*.

erotic |ı'rɒtık| *adj* erótico,-a.

err |ɜːr| *vi* errar; **to e. on the side of ...**, pecar por exceso de ....

errand |'erənd| *n* recado *m*; **e. boy**, recadero *m*.

erratic |ı'rætık| *adj* (*performance, behaviour*) irregular; (*weather*) muy variable; (*person*) caprichoso,-a.

erroneous |ı'rəʊnıəs| *adj* erróneo,-a.

error |'erər| *n* error *m*, equivocación *f*.

erupt |ı'rʌpt| *vi* **1** (*volcano*) entrar en erupción; (*violence*) estallar. **2** **his skin erupted in a rash**, le salió una erupción.

eruption [ɪ'rʌpʃən] n erupción f.

escalate ['eskəleɪt] vi (war) intensificarse; (prices) aumentar; (change) convertirse (into, en).

escalation [eskə'leɪʃən] n (of war) intensificación f, escalada f; (of prices) subida f.

escalator ['eskəleɪtər] n escalera mecánica.

escalope ['eskəlɒp] n escalope m.

escapade ['eskəpeɪd] n aventura f.

escape [ɪs'keɪp] I n huida f, fuga f; (of gas) escape m; **e. route**, vía f de escape. II vi escaparse. III vtr 1 (avoid) evitar, huir de; **to e. punishment**, librarse del castigo. 2 fig **his name escapes me**, no recuerdo su nombre.

escapism [ɪs'keɪpɪzəm] n evasión f.

escort ['eskɔːt] I n 1 (companion) acompañante mf. 2 Mil escolta f. II [ɪs'kɔːt] vtr 1 (accompany) acompañar. 2 (protect) escoltar.

Eskimo ['eskɪməʊ] adj & n esquimal (mf).

esoteric [esəʊ'terɪk] adj esotérico,-a.

especial [ɪs'peʃəl] adj especial. ◆**especially** adv especialmente, sobre todo.

espionage ['espɪənɑːʒ] n espionaje m.

esplanade [esplə'neɪd] n paseo marítimo.

espouse [ɪs'paʊz] vtr fml (cause) abrazar, adoptar.

espresso [e'spresəʊ] n **e.** (coffee), café m exprés.

esquire [ɪs'kwaɪər] n GB señor m; **Timothy Whiteman E.**, Sr. Don Timothy Whiteman.

essay ['eseɪ] n Educ redacción f.

essence ['esəns] n esencia f; **in e.**, esencialmente.

essential [ɪ'senʃəl] I adj esencial, imprescindible. II n necesidad básica; **the essentials**, lo fundamental. ◆**essentially** adv esencialmente.

establish [ɪs'tæblɪʃ] vtr 1 (found) establecer; (business) montar. 2 Jur **to e. a fact**, probar un hecho; **to e. the truth**, demostrar la verdad.

established [ɪs'tæblɪʃt] adj (person) establecido,-a; (fact) conocido,-a.

establishment [ɪs'tæblɪʃmənt] n establecimiento m; **the E.**, el sistema.

estate [ɪs'teɪt] n 1 (land) finca f; GB **e. agent**, agente mf inmobiliario,-a; GB **e. car**, coche m modelo familiar. 2 (housing) **e.**, zona urbanizada. 3 (property) bienes mpl. 4 (inheritance) herencia f.

esteem [ɪs'stiːm] I n **to hold sb in great e.**, apreciar mucho a algn. II vtr estimar.

esthetic [es'θetɪk] adj US estético,-a.

estimate ['estɪmɪt] I n (calculation) cálculo m; (likely cost of work) presupuesto m; **rough e.**, cálculo aproximado. II ['estɪmeɪt] vtr calcular; fig pensar, creer.

estimation [estɪ'meɪʃən] n 1 (opinion) juicio m, opinión f. 2 (esteem) estima f.

estrange [ɪs'streɪndʒ] vtr **to become estranged**, alejarse (from, de).

Estremadura [estreɪmə'dʊrə] n Extremadura.

estuary ['estjʊərɪ] n estuario m.

etching ['etʃɪŋ] n aguafuerte m.

eternal [ɪ'tɜːnəl] adj eterno,-a, incesante; **e. triangle**, triángulo amoroso.

eternity [ɪ'tɜːnɪtɪ] n eternidad f.

ether ['iːθər] n éter m.

ethereal [ɪ'θɪərɪəl] adj etéreo,-a.

ethical ['eθɪkəl] adj ético,-a.

ethics ['eθɪks] n ética f.

Ethiopia [iːθɪ'əʊpɪə] n Etiopía.

ethnic ['eθnɪk] adj étnico,-a.

ethos ['iːθɒs] n carácter distintivo.

etiquette ['etɪket] n protocolo m, etiqueta f.

etymology [etɪ'mɒledʒɪ] n etimología f.

eucalyptus [juːkə'lɪptəs] n eucalipto m.

euphemism ['juːfɪmɪzəm] n eufemismo m.

euphoria [juː'fɔːrɪə] n euforia f.

Eurocheque ['jʊərəʊtʃek] n eurocheque m.

Eurocrat ['jʊərəkræt] n eurócrata mf.

Euro-MP ['jʊərəʊempiː] n eurodiputado, -a m,f.

Europe ['jʊərəp] n Europa.

European [jʊərə'pɪən] adj & n europeo,-a (m,f); **E. Economic Community**, Comunidad Económica Europea.

euthanasia [juːθə'neɪzɪə] n eutanasia f.

evacuate [ɪ'vækjʊeɪt] vtr evacuar.

evacuation [ɪvækjʊ'eɪʃən] n evacuación f.

evade [ɪ'veɪd] vtr evadir.

evaluate [ɪ'væljʊeɪt] vtr evaluar.

evaluation [ɪvæljʊ'eɪʃən] n evaluación f.

evangelical [iːvæn'dʒelɪkəl] adj evangélico,-a.

evangelist [ɪ'vændʒɪlɪst] n evangelista mf.

evaporate [ɪ'væpəreɪt] I vtr evaporar; **evaporated milk**, leche condensada sin endulzar. II vi evaporarse; fig desvanecerse.

evasion [ɪ'veɪʒən] n 1 evasión f. 2 (evasive answer) evasiva f.

evasive [ɪ'veɪsɪv] adj evasivo,-a.

eve [iːv] n víspera f; **on the e. of**, en vísperas de.

even ['iːvən] I adj 1 (smooth) liso,-a; (level) llano,-a. 2 (regular) uniforme. 3 (equally balanced) igual; Sport **to be e.**, ir empatados,-as; **to get e. with sb**, desquitarse con algn. 4 (number) par. 5 (at the same level) a nivel. 6 (quantity) exacto,-a. II adv incluso, hasta, aun; **e. now**, incluso ahora; **e. so**, aun así; **e. the children knew**, hasta los niños lo sabían. 7 (negative) ni siquiera; **she can't e. write her name**, ni siquiera sabe escribir su nombre; **without e. speaking**, sin hablar siquiera. **3** (*before comparative*) aun, todavía; **e. worse,** aun peor. **4 e. as,** mientras; **e. if,** incluso si; **e. though,** aunque. **III** *vtr* igualar.

evening ['i:vnɪŋ] *n* **1** (*early*) tarde *f*; (*late*) noche *f*; **in the e.,** por la tarde; **tomorrow e.,** mañana por la tarde; **e. class,** clase nocturna; **e. dress,** (*man*) traje *m* de etiqueta; (*woman*) traje de noche; **e. paper,** periódico vespertino. **2** (*greeting*) **good e.!,** (*early*) ¡buenas tardes!; (*late*) ¡buenas noches!

event [ɪ'vent] *n* **1** (*happening*) suceso *m*, acontecimiento *m*. **2** (*case*) caso *m*; **at all events,** en todo caso; **in the e. of fire,** en caso de incendio. **3** *Sport* prueba *f*.

eventful [ɪ'ventful] *adj* (*busy*) un día agitado; (*memorable*) un día memorable.

eventual [ɪ'ventʃuəl] *adj* (*ultimate*) final; (*resulting*) consiguiente. ◆**eventually** *adv* finalmente.

eventuality [ɪventʃu'ælɪtɪ] *n* eventualidad *f*.

ever ['evər] *adv* **1** nunca, jamás; **stronger than e.,** más fuerte que nunca. **2** (*interrogative*) alguna vez; **have you e. been there?,** ¿has estado allí alguna vez? **3** (*always*) siempre; **for e.,** para siempre; **for e. and e.,** para siempre jamás. **4** (*emphasis*) **how e. did you manage it?,** ¿cómo diablos lo conseguiste?; **why e. not?,** ¿por qué no?; **fam e. so, e. such,** muy; **thank you e. so much,** muchísimas gracias.

evergreen ['evəgri:n] **I** *adj* de hoja perenne. **II** *n* árbol *m* o planta *f* de hoja perenne.

everlasting [evə'lɑ:stɪŋ] *adj* eterno,-a.

evermore [evə'mɔ:r] *adv* **for e.,** para siempre jamás.

every ['evrɪ] *adj* **1** (*each*) cada; **e. now and then,** de vez en cuando; **e. day,** todos los días; **e. other day,** cada dos días; **e. one of you,** todos,-as vosotros,-as; **e. citizen,** todo ciudadano. **2** **you had e. right to be angry,** tenías toda la razón para estar enfadado.

everybody ['evrɪbɒdɪ] *pron* todo el mundo, todos,-as.

everyday ['evrɪdeɪ] *adj* diario,-a, de todos los días; **an e. occurrence,** un suceso cotidiano.

everyone ['evrɪwʌn] *pron* todo el mundo, todos,-as.

everything ['evrɪθɪŋ] *pron* todo; **he eats e.,** come de todo; **she means e. to me,** ella lo es todo para mí.

everywhere ['evrɪweər] *adv* en todas partes, por todas partes.

evict [ɪ'vɪkt] *vtr* desahuciar.

evidence ['evɪdəns] **I** *n* **1** (*proof*) evidencia *f*. **2** *Jur* testimonio *m*; **to give e.,** prestar declaración. **3** (*sign*) indicio *m*, señal *f*; **to be in e.,** dejarse notar.

evident ['evɪdənt] *adj* evidente, manifiesto,-a. ◆**evidently** *adv* evidentemente, al parecer.

evil ['i:vəl] **I** *adj* (*wicked*) malo,-a, malvado,-a; (*harmful*) nocivo,-a; (*unfortunate*) aciago,-a. **II** *n* mal *m*.

evocative [ɪ'vɒkətɪv] *adj* evocador,-a.

evoke [ɪ'vəʊk] *vtr* evocar.

evolution [i:və'lu:ʃən] *n* evolución *f*; *Biol* desarrollo *m*.

evolve [ɪ'vɒlv] **I** *vi* (*species*) evolucionar; (*ideas*) desarrollarse. **II** *vtr* desarrollar.

ewe [ju:] *n* oveja *f*.

ex [eks] *n* **her e.,** su ex marido; **his e.,** su ex mujer.

ex- [eks] *pref* ex, antiguo,-a; **ex-minister,** ex ministro *m*.

exacerbate [ɪg'zæsəbeɪt] *vtr* exacerbar.

exact [ɪg'zækt] **I** *adj* (*accurate*) exacto,-a; (*definition*) preciso,-a; **this e. spot,** ese mismo lugar. **II** *vtr* exigir. ◆**exactly** *adv* exactamente; precisamente; **e.!,** ¡exacto!

exacting [ɪg'zæktɪŋ] *adj* exigente.

exaggerate [ɪg'zædʒəreɪt] *vi & vtr* exagerar.

exaggeration [ɪgzædʒə'reɪʃən] *n* exageración *f*.

exalt [ɪg'zɔ:lt] *vtr fml* exaltar.

exam [ɪg'zæm] *n fam* examen *m*.

examination [ɪgzæmɪ'neɪʃən] *n* **1** *Educ* examen *m*; **to sit an e.,** hacer un examen. **2** *Med* reconocimiento *m*. **3** *Jur* interrogatorio *m*.

examine [ɪg'zæmɪn] *vtr Educ* examinar; (*customs*) registrar; *Med* hacer un reconocimiento médico a; *Jur* interrogar.

examiner [ɪg'zæmɪnər] *n* examinador,-a *m,f*.

example [ɪg'zɑ:mpəl] *n* ejemplo *m*; (*specimen*) ejemplar *m*; **for e.,** por ejemplo.

exasperate [ɪg'zɑ:spəreɪt] *vtr* exasperar.

exasperation [ɪgzɑ:spə'reɪʃən] *n* exasperación *f*.

excavate ['ekskəveɪt] *vtr* excavar.

excavation [ekskə'veɪʃən] *n* excavación *f*.

exceed [ek'si:d] *vtr* exceder, sobrepasar. ◆**exceedingly** *adv* extremadamente, sumamente.

excel [ɪk'sel] **I** *vi* sobresalir. **II** *vtr* superar.

excellency ['eksələnsɪ] *n* **His E.,** Su Excelencia.

excellent ['eksələnt] *adj* excelente.

except [ɪk'sept] **I** *prep* excepto, salvo; **e. for the little ones,** excepto los pequeños; **e. that ...,** salvo que .... **II** *vtr* exceptuar.

exception [ɪk'sepʃən] *n* **1** excepción *f*; **with the e. of,** a excepción de; **without e.,** sin excepción. **2** (*objection*) objeción *f*; **to take e. to sth,** ofenderse por algo.

exceptional [ɪk'sepʃənəl] *adj* excepcional.

excerpt [ek'sɜːpt] *n* extracto *m*.
excess [ɪk'ses] **I** *n* exceso *m*. **II** *adj* ['ekses] excedente; **e. baggage,** exceso *m* de equipaje; **e. fare,** suplemento *m*.
excessive [ɪk'sesɪv] *adj* excesivo,-a. ◆**excessively** *adv* excesivamente, en exceso.
exchange [ɪks'tʃeɪndʒ] **I** *n* **1** cambio *m*; **e. of ideas,** intercambio *m* de ideas; **in e. for,** a cambio de. **2** Fin **e. rate,** tipo *m* de cambio. **3** (telephone) **e.,** central telefónica. **II** *vtr* intercambiar; **to e. blows,** golpearse. **2** (*prisoners*) canjear.
exchequer [ɪks'tʃekər] *n GB* the E., Hacienda *f*; **Chancellor of the E.,** Ministro *m* de Hacienda.
excise ['eksaɪz] *n* impuesto *m* sobre el consumo; **e. duty,** derechos *mpl* de aduana.
excitable [ɪk'saɪtəbəl] *adj* excitable.
excite [ɪk'saɪt] *vtr* (*stimulate*) excitar; (*move*) emocionar; (*enthuse*) entusiasmar; (*arouse*) provocar.
excitement [ɪk'saɪtmənt] *n* (*stimulation*) excitación *f*; (*emotion*) emoción *f*; (*commotion*) agitación *f*.
exciting [ɪk'saɪtɪŋ] *adj* apasionante, emocionante.
exclaim [ɪk'skleɪm] *vi* exclamar. **II** *vtr* gritar.
exclamation [eksklə'meɪʃən] *n* exclamación *f*; **e. mark,** *US* **e. point,** signo *m* de admiración.
exclude [ɪk'skluːd] *vtr* excluir; (*from club*) no admitir.
excluding [ɪk'skluːdɪŋ] *prep* excepto.
exclusion [ɪk'skluːʒən] *n* exclusión *f*.
exclusive [ɪk'skluːsɪv] **I** *adj* exclusivo,-a; (*neighbourhood*) selecto,-a; (*club*) cerrado, -a. **II** *n Press* exclusiva *f*. ◆**exclusively** *adv* exclusivamente.
excommunicate [ekskə'mjuːnɪkeɪt] *vtr* excomulgar.
excrement ['ekskrɪmənt] *n* excremento *m*.
excruciating [ɪk'skruːʃɪeɪtɪŋ] *adj* insoportable. ◆**excruciatingly** *adv* horriblemente.
excursion [ɪk'skɜːʃən] *n* excursión *f*.
excusable [ɪk'skjuːzəbəl] *adj* perdonable.
excuse [ɪk'skjuːz] **I** *vtr* **1** perdonar, disculpar; **e. me!,** con permiso; **may I be excused for a moment?,** ¿puedo salir un momento? **2** (*exempt*) dispensar. **3** (*justify*) justificar. **II** [ɪk'skjuːs] *n* excusa *f*; **to make an e.,** dar excusas.
ex-directory [eksdɪ'rektərɪ] *adj Tel* que no se encuentra en la guía telefónica.
execute ['eksɪkjuːt] *vtr* **1** (*order*) cumplir; (*task*) realizar. **2** Jur cumplir. **3** (*person*) ejecutar.
execution [eksɪ'kjuːʃən] *n* **1** (*of order*) cumplimiento *m*; (*of task*) realización *f*. **2**

Jur cumplimiento *m*. **3** (*of person*) ejecución *f*.
executioner [eksɪ'kjuːʃənər] *n* verdugo *m*.
executive [ɪg'zekjutɪv] **I** *adj* ejecutivo,-a. **II** *n* ejecutivo,-a *m,f*.
executor [ɪg'zekjutər] *n* albacea *m*.
exemplary [ɪg'zemplərɪ] *adj* ejemplar.
exemplify [ɪg'zemplɪfaɪ] *vtr* ejemplificar.
exempt [ɪg'zempt] **I** *vtr* eximir (**from,** de). **II** *adj* exento,-a; **e. from tax,** libre de impuesto.
exemption [ɪg'zempʃən] *n* exención *f*.
exercise ['eksəsaɪz] **I** *n* ejercicio *m*; **e. book,** cuaderno *m*. **II** *vtr* **1** (*rights, duties*) ejercer. **2** (*dog*) sacar de paseo. **III** *vi* hacer ejercicio.
exert [ɪg'zɜːt] *vtr* (*influence*) ejercer; **to e. oneself,** esforzarse.
exertion [ɪg'zɜːʃən] *n* esfuerzo *m*.
exhale [eks'heɪl] **I** *vtr* (*breathe*) exhalar. **II** *vi* espirar.
exhaust [ɪg'zɔːst] **I** *vtr* agotar. **II** *n* (*gas*) gases *mpl* de combustión; **e. pipe,** tubo *m* de escape.
exhausted [ɪg'zɔːstɪd] *adj* agotado,-a.
exhaustion [ɪg'zɔːstʃən] *n* agotamiento *m*.
exhaustive [ɪg'zɔːstɪv] *adj* exhaustivo,-a.
exhibit [ɪg'zɪbɪt] **I** *n* Art objeto expuesto; Jur prueba *f* instrumental. **II** *vtr* Art exponer; (*surprise etc*) mostrar.
exhibition [eksɪ'bɪʃən] *n* exposición *f*.
exhibitionist [eksɪ'bɪʃənɪst] *adj & n* exhibicionista (*mf*).
exhilarating [ɪg'zɪləreɪtɪŋ] *adj* estimulante.
exhilaration [ɪgzɪlə'reɪʃən] *n* regocijo *m*.
exhume [eks'hjuːm] *vtr* exhumar.
exile ['eksaɪl] **I** *n* **1** (*banishment*) exilio *m*. **2** (*person*) exiliado,-a *m,f*. **II** *vtr* exiliar.
exist [ɪg'zɪst] *vi* existir; (*have little money*) malvivir.
existence [ɪg'zɪstəns] *n* existencia *f*.
existing [ɪg'zɪstɪŋ] *adj* existente, actual.
exit ['eksɪt] **I** *n* **1** salida *f*. **2** Theat mutis *m*. **II** *vi* Theat hacer mutis.
exodus ['eksədəs] *n* éxodo *m*.
exonerate [ɪg'zɒnəreɪt] *vtr fml* exonerar (**from,** de).
exorbitant [ɪg'zɔːbɪtənt] *adj* exorbitante, desorbitado,-a.
exotic [ɪg'zɒtɪk] *adj* exótico,-a.
expand [ɪk'spænd] **I** *vtr* (*enlarge*) ampliar; (*gas, metal*) dilatar. **II** *vi* (*grow*) ampliarse; (*metal*) dilatarse; (*become more friendly*) abrirse. ◆**expand on** *vtr* ampliar.
expanse [ɪk'spæns] *n* extensión *f*.
expansion [ɪk'spænʃən] *n* (*in size*) expansión *f*; (*of gas, metal*) dilatación *f*.
expatriate [eks'pætrɪɪt] **I** *adj & n* expatriado,-a (*m,f*). **II** [eks'pætrɪeɪt] *vtr* expatriar.

expect [ɪk'spekt] I *vtr* 1 *(anticipate)* esperar; **I half-expected that to happen**, suponía que iba a ocurrir. 2 *(demand)* contar con. 3 *(suppose)* suponer. II *vi fam* **to be expecting**, estar embarazada.

expectancy [ɪk'spektənsɪ] *n* expectación *f.*

expectant [ɪk'spektənt] *adj* ilusionado,-a; **e. mother**, mujer embarazada.

expectation [ekspek'teɪʃən] *n* esperanza *f;* **contrary to e.**, contrariamente a lo que se esperaba.

expedient [ɪk'spiːdɪənt] I *adj* conveniente, oportuno,-a. II *n* expediente *m*, recurso *m.*

expedition [ekspɪ'dɪʃən] *n* expedición *f.*

expel [ɪk'spel] *vtr* expulsar.

expend [ɪk'spend] *vtr* gastar.

expendable [ɪk'spendəbəl] *adj* prescindible.

expenditure [ɪk'spendɪtʃər] *n* desembolso *m.*

expense [ɪk'spens] *n* gasto *m*; **all expenses paid**, con todos los gastos pagados; **to spare no e.**, no escatimar gastos; *fig* **at the e. of**, a costa de; **e. account**, cuenta *f* de gastos de representación.

expensive [ɪk'spensɪv] *adj* caro,-a, costoso,-a.

experience [ɪk'spɪərɪəns] I *n* experiencia *f.* II *vtr (sensation)* experimentar; *(difficulty, loss)* sufrir.

experienced [ɪk'spɪərɪənst] *adj* experimentado,-a.

experiment [ɪk'sperɪmənt] I *n* experimento *m.* II *vi* experimentar, hacer experimentos **(on, with**, con).

experimental [ɪksperɪ'mentəl] *adj* experimental.

expert ['eksp3ːt] I *adj* experto,-a. II *n* experto,-a *m,f*, especialista *mf.*

expertise [eksp3ː'tiːz] *n* pericia *f.*

expire [ɪk'spaɪər] *vi* 1 *(die)* expirar; *(mandate)* terminar. 2 *Com Ins* vencer; *(ticket)* caducar.

expiry [ɪk'spaɪərɪ] *n* vencimiento *m*; **e. date**, fecha *f* de caducidad.

explain [ɪk'spleɪn] I *vtr* explicar; *(clarify)* aclarar; **to e. oneself**, justificarse. II *vi* explicarse.

explanation [eksplə'neɪʃən] *n* explicación *f*; *(clarification)* aclaración *f.*

explanatory [ɪk'splænətərɪ] *adj* explicativo,-a, aclaratorio,-a.

explicit [ɪk'splɪsɪt] *adj* explícito,-a.

explode [ɪk'spləʊd] I *vtr* 1 *(bomb)* hacer explotar. 2 *fig (theory)* echar por tierra. II *vi* 1 *(bomb)* estallar, explotar; *fig* **to e. with** *or* **in anger**, montar en cólera.

exploit ['eksplɔɪt] I *n* proeza *f*, hazaña *f.* II [ɪk'splɔɪt] *vtr* explotar.

exploitation [eksplɔɪ'teɪʃən] *n* explotación *f.*

exploratory [ek'splɒrətərɪ] *adj*

exploratorio,-a.

explore [ɪk'splɔːr] *vtr* explorar.

explorer [ɪk'splɔːrər] *n* explorador,-a *m,f.*

explosion [ɪk'spləʊʒən] *n* explosión *f.*

explosive [ɪk'spləʊsɪv] I *adj* explosivo,-a; **e. issue**, asunto delicado. II *n* explosivo *m.*

exponent [ɪk'spəʊnənt] *n* exponente *m*; *(supporter)* defensor *m,f.*

export [ɪk'spɔːt] I *vtr* exportar. II ['ekspɔːt] *n* 1 *(trade)* exportación *f.* 2 *(commodity)* artículo *m* de exportación.

exporter [eks'pɔːtər] *n* exportador,-a *m,f.*

expose [ɪk'spəʊz] *vtr (uncover)* exponer; *(secret)* revelar; *(plot)* descubrir; **to e. oneself**, exhibirse desnudo.

exposed [ɪk'spəʊzd] *adj* expuesto,-a.

exposure [ɪk'spəʊʒər] *n* 1 *(to light, cold, heat)* exposición *f*; **to die of e.**, morir de frío. 2 *Phot* fotografía *f*; **e. meter**, fotómetro *m.* 3 *(of criminal)* descubrimiento *m.*

expound [ɪk'spaʊnd] *vtr* exponer.

express [ɪk'spres] I *adj* 1 *(explicit)* expreso,-a. 2 *GB (letter)* urgente; **e. train**, expreso *m.* II *n Rail* expreso *m.* III *vtr* expresar. IV *adv* **send it e.**, mándalo urgente. ◆**expressly** *adv fml* expresamente.

expression [ɪk'spreʃən] *n* expresión *f.*

expulsion [ɪk'spʌlʃən] *n* expulsión *f.*

exquisite [ɪk'skwɪzɪt] *adj* exquisito,-a.

extend [ɪk'stend] I *vtr* 1 *(enlarge)* ampliar; *(lengthen)* alargar; *(increase)* aumentar; *fig* **the prohibition was extended to cover cigarettes**, extendieron la prohibición a los cigarrillos. 2 *(give)* rendir, dar; **to e. a welcome to sb**, recibir a algn. 3 *(prolong)* prolongar. II *vi* 1 *(stretch)* extenderse. 2 *(last)* prolongarse.

extension [ɪk'stenʃən] *n* 1 extensión *f*; *(of time)* prórroga *f.* 2 *Constr* anexo *m.*

extensive [ɪk'stensɪv] *adj* extenso,-a.

extent [ɪk'stent] *n* 1 *(area)* extensión *f.* 2 **to some e.**, hasta cierto punto; **to a large e.**, en gran parte; **to a lesser e.**, en menor grado; **to such an e.**, hasta tal punto.

extenuating [ɪk'stenjʊeɪtɪŋ] *adj* atenuante.

exterior [ɪk'stɪərɪər] I *adj* exterior, externo,-a. II *n* exterior *m.*

exterminate [ɪk'stɜːmɪneɪt] *vtr* exterminar.

extermination [ɪkstɜːmɪ'neɪʃən] *n* exterminación *f*, exterminio *m.*

external [ɪk'stɜːnəl] *adj* externo,-a, exterior.

extinct [ɪk'stɪŋkt] *adj* extinguido,-a.

extinction [ɪk'stɪŋkʃən] *n* extinción *f.*

extinguish [ɪk'stɪŋgwɪʃ] *vtr* extinguir, apagar.

extinguisher [ɪk'stɪŋgwɪʃər] *n* extintor *m.*

extol, *US* **extoll** [ɪk'stəʊl] *vtr* ensalzar,

alabar.

extort [ɪk'stɔːt] *vtr* arrancar; *(money)* sacar.

extortion [ɪk'stɔːʃən] *n* extorsión *f*.

extortionate [ɪk'stɔːʃənɪt] *adj* desorbitado,-a.

extra ['ekstrə] I *adj* extra; *(spare)* de sobra. II *adv* extra; **e. fine**, extra fino. III *n* *(additional charge)* suplemento *m*; *Cin* extra *mf*; *(newspaper)* edición *f* especial.

extract ['ekstrækt] I *n* extracto *m*. II [ɪk'strækt] *vtr (tooth, information)* extraer; *(confession)* arrancar.

extraction [ɪk'strækʃən] *n* extracción *f*.

extracurricular [ekstrəkə'rɪkjʊləʳ] *adj* extracurricular.

extradite ['ekstrədaɪt] *vtr* extraditar.

extramarital [ekstrə'mærɪtəl] *adj* extramatrimonial.

extramural [ekstrə'mjʊərəl] *adj* **e. course**, curso *m* para estudiantes libres.

extraordinary [ɪk'strɔːdənərɪ] *adj (meeting)* extraordinario,-a; *(behaviour etc)* extraño,-a.

extravagance [ɪk'strævɪgəns] *n (with money)* derroche *m*; *(of behaviour)* extravagancia *f*.

extravagant [ɪk'strævɪgənt] *adj (wasteful)* derrochador,-a; *(excessive)* exagerado,-a; *(luxurious)* lujoso,-a.

extreme [ɪk'striːm] I *adj* extremo,-a; **an e. case**, un caso excepcional; **to hold e. views**, tener opiniones radicales. II *n* extremo *m*; **in the e.**, en sumo grado. ◆**extremely** *adv* extremadamente; **I'm e. sorry**, lo siento de veras.

extremist [ɪk'striːmɪst] *n* extremista *mf*.

extremity [ɪk'stremɪtɪ] *n* extremidad *f*.

extricate ['ekstrɪkeɪt] *vtr* sacar; **to e. one-self**, lograr salir *(from,* de).

extrovert ['ekstrəvɜːt] *adj & n* extrovertido,-a *(m,f)*.

exuberant [ɪg'zjuːbərənt] *adj* exuberante.

exude [ɪg'zjuːd] *vtr & vi (moisture, sap)* exudar; *fig* rebosar.

exultant [ɪg'zʌltənt] *adj* jubiloso,-a.

eye [aɪ] I *n* ojo *m*; *fig* **I couldn't believe my eyes**, no podía creerlo; **in the eyes of**, según; *fig* **not to take one's eyes off sb/sth**, no quitar la vista de encima a algn/algo; *fig* **to catch sb's e.**, llamar la atención a algn; *fig* **to have an e. for**, tener buen ojo para; *fig* **to make eyes at sb**, echar miraditas a algn; *fig* **to see e. to e. with sb**, estar de acuerdo con algn; *fig* **to turn a blind e.**, hacer la vista gorda (to, a); *fig* **with an e. to**, con miras a; **to keep an e. on sb/sth**, vigilar a algn/algo; **to keep an e. out for**, estar pendiente de; **black e.**, ojo morado. II *vtr* observar.

eyeball ['aɪbɔːl] *n* globo *m* ocular.

eyebrow ['aɪbraʊ] *n* ceja *f*.

eyecatching ['aɪkætʃɪŋ] *adj* llamativo,-a.

eyelash ['aɪlæʃ] *n* pestaña *f*.

eyelid ['aɪlɪd] *n* párpado *m*.

eyeliner ['aɪlaɪnəʳ] *n* lápiz *m* de ojos.

eye-opener ['aɪəʊpənəʳ] *n* revelación *f*, gran sorpresa *f*.

eyeshadow ['aɪʃædəʊ] *n* sombra *f* de ojos.

eyesight ['aɪsaɪt] *n* vista *f*.

eyesore ['aɪsɔːʳ] *n* monstruosidad *f*.

eyestrain ['aɪstreɪn] *n* vista cansada.

eyewash ['aɪwɒʃ] *n* colirio *m*; *fig* **it's all e.**, eso son disparates.

eyewitness ['aɪwɪtnɪs] *n* testigo *mf* ocular.

F

F, f [ef] *n* 1 *(the letter)* F, f *f*. 2 *Mus* fa *m*.

F [ef] *abbr of* **Fahrenheit**, Fahrenheit, F.

fable ['feɪbəl] *n* fábula *f*.

fabric ['fæbrɪk] *n* 1 *Tex* tela *f*, tejido *m*. 2 *Constr* estructura *f*.

fabricate ['fæbrɪkeɪt] *vtr* fabricar.

fabrication [fæbrɪ'keɪʃən] *n fig* fabricación *f*.

fabulous ['fæbjʊləs] *adj* fabuloso,-a.

façade [fə'sɑːd, fæ'sɑːd] *n* fachada *f*.

face [feɪs] I *n* 1 cara *f*, rostro *m*; **f. to f.**, cara a cara; **I told him to his f.**, se lo dije en la cara; **she slammed the door in my f.**, me dió con la puerta en las narices; **to look sb in the f.**, mirarle a algn a la cara; **f. cloth**, paño *m*; **f. cream**, crema *f* facial; **f. pack**, mascarilla *f* facial. 2 *(expression)* cara *f*, expresión *f*; **to pull a long f.**, poner cara larga; **to pull faces**, hacer muecas. 3 *(surface)* superficie *f*; *(of*

card, coin) cara *f*; *(of watch)* esfera *f*; **f. down/up**, boca abajo/arriba; *fig* **in the f. of danger**, ante el peligro; **f. value**, valor *m* nominal; **to take sth at f. value**, entender algo sólo en su sentido literal. 4 *(appearance)* aspecto *m*; **on the f. of it**, a primera vista; **to lose f.**, desprestigiarse; **to save f.**, salvar las apariencias. II *vtr* 1 *(look onto)* dar a; *(be opposite)* estar enfrente de. 2 **to f. the wall/window**, *(of person)* estar de cara a la pared/ventana. 3 *(problem)* hacer frente a; **let's f. it**, hay que reconocerlo. 4 **to f. up to**, hacer cara a. 4 *(tolerate)* soportar, aguantar.

III *vi* **to f. on to**, dar a; **to f. towards**, mirar hacia; **f. this way**, vuélvase de este lado.

facelift ['feɪslɪft] *n Med* lifting *m*; *fig* renovación *f*.

facet ['fæsɪt] n faceta f.

facetious [fə'si:ʃəs] adj bromista.

facial ['feɪʃəl] adj facial.

facile ['fæsaɪl] adj superficial.

facilitate [fə'sɪlɪteɪt] vtr facilitar.

facility [fə'sɪlɪtɪ] n 1 (ease) facilidad f. 2 **facilities**, (means) facilidades fpl; **credit f.**, facilidades de crédito. 3 **facilities**, (rooms, equipment) instalaciones fpl; **cooking f.**, derecho m a cocina.

facing ['feɪsɪŋ] adj de enfrente.

facsimile [fæk'sɪmɪlɪ] n 1 (copy) facsímil m. 2 (message) telefax m. 3 (machine) facsímil m.

fact [fækt] n 1 hecho m; **as a matter of f.**, de hecho; **the f. that he confessed**, el hecho de que confesara; **in f.**, en realidad.

fact-finding ['fæktfaɪndɪŋ] adj investigador,-a.

faction ['fækʃən] n (group) facción f.

factor ['fæktər] n factor m.

factory ['fæktərɪ] n fábrica f.

factual ['fæktʃʊəl] adj a **f. error**, un error de hecho.

faculty ['fækəltɪ] n 1 facultad f. 2 US Univ profesorado m, cuerpo m docente.

fad [fæd] n fam (craze) moda pasajera; (whim) capricho m.

fade [feɪd] vi (colour) desteñirse; (flower) marchitarse; (light) apagarse. ◆**fade away** vi desvanecerse. ◆**fade in, fade out** vtr Cin TV fundir.

faded ['feɪdɪd] adj (colour) desteñido,-a; (flower) marchito,-a.

fag [fæg] n sl 1 GB fam (cigarette) pitillo m. 2 US sl (homosexual) marica m.

fail [feɪl] I n 1 Educ suspenso m. 1 **without f.**, sin falta. II vtr 1 **don't f. me, no me falles; words f. me**, no encuentro palabras. 2 (exam) suspender. 3 (to be unable) no lograr; **he failed to score**, no logró marcar. 4 (neglect) dejar de; **don't f. to come**, no deje de venir. 5 (of health) deteriorar. III vi 1 (show, film) fracasar; (brakes) fallar. 2 (business) quebrar; Educ suspender.

failing ['feɪlɪŋ] I n 1 (shortcoming) defecto m. 2 (weakness) punto m débil. II prep a falta de.

failure ['feɪljər] n 1 fracaso m. 2 Com quiebra f. 3 Educ suspenso m. 4 (person) fracasado,-a m,f. 5 (breakdown) avería f; **brake f.**, fallo m de los frenos; **power f.**, apagón m; Med **heart f.**, paro cardíaco. 6 **her f. to answer**, (neglect) el hecho de que no contestara.

faint [feɪnt] I adj 1 (sound) débil; (colour) pálido,-a; (outline) borroso,-a; (recollection) vago,-a; **I haven't the faintest idea**, no tengo ni la más mínima idea. 2 (giddy) mareado,-a. II n desmayo m. III vi desmayarse.

faint-hearted [feɪnt'hɑ:tɪd] adj

temeroso,-a.

fair¹ [feər] I adj 1 (impartial) imparcial; (just) justo,-a; **it's not f.**, no hay derecho; fam **f. enough!**, ¡vale! 2 (hair) rubio,-a. 3 (weather) bueno,-a. 4 (beautiful) bello,-a. 5 a **f. number**, un buen número; **he has a f. chance**, tiene bastantes probabilidades. II adv **to play f.**, jugar limpio. ◆**fairly** adv 1 (justly) justamente. 2 (moderately) bastante.

fair² [feər] n feria f; **trade f.**, feria de muestras.

fairground ['feəgraʊnd] n real m de la feria.

fairness ['feənɪs] n justicia f, equidad f; **in all f.**, para ser justo,-a.

fairy ['feərɪ] n hada f; **f. godmother**, hada madrina; **f. tale**, cuento m de hadas. ◆**f. offers marica m.**

fait accompli [feɪtə'kɒmplɪ] n fml hecho consumado.

faith [feɪθ] n 1 Rel fe f. 2 (trust) confianza f; **in good f.**, de buena fe.

faithful ['feɪθfʊl] I adj fiel. II npl **the f.**, los fieles. ◆**faithfully** adv fielmente; **yours f.**, (in letter) le saluda atentamente.

fake [feɪk] I adj falso,-a. II n 1 (object) falsificación f. 2 (person) impostor,-a m,f. III vtr 1 (forge) falsificar. 2 (feign) fingir. IV vi (pretend) fingir.

falcon ['fɔ:lkən] n halcón m.

Falklands ['fɔ:klændz] npl **the F.**, las (Islas) Malvinas.

fall [fɔ:l] I n 1 caída f. 2 (of rock) desprendimiento m; **f. of snow**, nevada f. 3 (decrease) baja f. 4 US otoño m. 5 (usu pl) cascada f; **Niagara Falls**, las cataratas del Niágara. II vi (pt **fell**; pp **fallen**) 1 caer, caerse; **they f. into two categories**, se dividen en dos categorías; fig **night was falling**, anochecía; fig **to f. into line**, aceptar las reglas; fig **to f. short**, no alcanzar (of, -). 2 (in battle) caer. 3 (temperature, prices) bajar. 4 **to f. asleep**, dormirse; **to f. ill**, caer enfermo,-a; **to f. in love**, enamorarse. ◆**fall back** vi replegarse. ◆**fall back on** vtr echar mano a, recurrir a. ◆**fall behind** vi (in race) quedarse atrás; **to f. behind with one's work**, retrasarse en el trabajo. ◆**fall down** vi 1 (picture etc) caerse. 2 (building) derrumbarse. 3 (argument) fallar. ◆**fall for** vtr 1 (person) enamorarse de. 2 (trick) dejarse engañar por. ◆**fall in** vi 1 (roof) desplomarse. 2 Mil formar filas. ◆**fall off** I vi 1 (drop off) caerse. II vtr **to f. off sth**, caerse de algo. 2 (part) desprenderse. 3 (diminish) disminuir. ◆**fall out** vi 1 (hair) caerse. 2 Mil romper filas. 3 (quarrel) pelearse. ◆**fall over** vi caerse. ◆**fall through** vi (plan) fracasar.

fallacy ['fæləsɪ] n falacia f.

fallen ['fɔ:lən] pp → **fall**.

fallible ['fælɪbəl] *adj* falible.

fall-out ['fɔːlaʊt] *n* (**radioactive**) f., lluvia radioactiva; f. **shelter**, refugio antiatómico.

fallow ['fæləʊ] *adj Agr* en barbecho.

false [fɔːls] *adj* falso,-a; f. **step**, paso m en falso; f. **start**, salida nula; f. **teeth**, dentadura postiza; f. **alarm**, falsa alarma.

falsehood ['fɔːlshʊd] *n* falsedad *f*.

falsify ['fɔːlsɪfaɪ] *vt* (**records**, **accounts**) falsificar; (**story**) falsear.

falter ['fɔːltə'] *vi* vacilar; (**voice**) fallar.

faltering ['fɔːltərɪŋ] *adj* vacilante.

fame [feɪm] *n* fama *f*.

familiar [fə'mɪljə'] *adj* 1 (**common**) familiar, conocido,-a; **his face is** f., su cara me suena. 2 (**aware**, **knowledgeable**) enterado,-a, al corriente (**with**, de). 3 **to be on** f. **terms with sb**, (**know well**) tener confianza con algn.

familiarity [fəmɪlɪ'ærɪtɪ] *n* 1 (**awareness**, **knowledge**) familiaridad (**with**, con). 2 (**intimacy**) confianza *f*.

familiarize [fə'mɪljəraɪz] *vtr* 1 (**become acquainted**) familiarizarse (**with**, con). 2 (**make understandable**) popularizar.

family ['fæmɪlɪ] *n* familia *f*; f. **allowance**, subsidio m familiar; f. **doctor**, médico m de cabecera; f. **man**, hombre hogareño; f. **planning**, planificación *f* familiar; f. **tree**, árbol genealógico.

famine ['fæmɪn] *n* hambre *f*, escasez *f* de alimentos.

famished ['fæmɪʃt] *adj fam* muerto,-a de hambre.

famous ['feɪməs] *adj* célebre, famoso,-a (**for**, por). ◆**famously** *adv fam* estupendamente.

fan [fæn] **I** *n* 1 abanico m; *Elec* ventilador m. 2 (**person**) aficionado,-a m,f; (**of pop star etc**) fan m,f; f. **club**, club m de fans; **football** f., hincha m,f. **II** *vtr* 1 abanicar. 2 (**fire**, **passions**) avivar. ◆**fan out** *vi* (**troops**) desplegarse en abanico.

fanatic [fə'nætɪk] *adj & n* fanático,-a (m,f).

fanatical [fə'nætɪkəl] *adj* fanático,-a.

fanciful ['fænsɪfʊl] *adj* 1 (**person**) caprichoso,-a. 2 (**idea**) fantástico,-a.

fancy ['fænsɪ] **I** *adj* (**fancier**, **fanciest**) de fantasía; f. **dress**, disfraz m; f. **dress ball**, baile m de disfraces; f. **prices**, precios *mpl* exorbitantes. **II** *n* 1 (**imagination**) fantasía *f*. 2 (**whim**) capricho m, antojo m; **to take a** f. **to sb**, cogerle cariño a algn; **to take a** f. **to sth**, encapricharse con algo; **what takes your** f.?, ¿qué se le antoja? **III** *vtr* 1 (**image**) imaginarse; *fam* f. **that!**, ¡fíjate!; *fam* f. **seeing you here!**, ¡qué casualidad verte por aquí! 2 (**like**, **want**) apetecer; **do you** f. **a drink?**, ¿te apetece una copa?; *fam* **I** f. **her**, ella me gusta; *fam* **to** f. **oneself**, ser creído,-a *or* presumido,-a.

fanfare ['fænfeə'] *n* fanfarria *f*.

fang [fæŋ] *n* colmillo m.

fantasize ['fæntəsaɪz] *vi* fantasear.

fantastic [fæn'tæstɪk] *adj* fantástico,-a.

fantasy ['fæntəsɪ] *n* fantasía *f*.

far [fɑː'] (**farther** *or* **further**, **farthest** *or* **furthest**) **I** *adj* 1 (**distant**) lejano,-a; **the** F. **East**, el Lejano Oriente. 2 **at the** f. **end**, en el otro extremo. 3 **the** f. **left**, la extrema izquierda. **II** *adv* 1 (**distant**) lejos; f. **and wide**, por todas partes; f. **off**, a lo lejos; **farther back**, más atrás; **farther north**, más al norte; **how** f. **is it to Cardiff?**, ¿cuánto hay de aquí a Cardiff?; *fig* **as** f. **as I can**, en lo que puedo; **as** f. **as I know**, que yo sepa; **as** f. **as possible**, en lo posible; *fig* f. **from complaining**, **he seemed pleased**, lejos de quejarse, parecía contento; *fig* **he went so** f. **as to swear**, llegó a jurar; *fig* **I'm** f. **from satisfied**, no estoy satisfecho,-a ni mucho menos; *fig* **in so** f. **as ...**, en la medida en que ...; *fam* **to go too** f., pasarse de la raya. 2 (**in time**) f. **back as the fifties**, ya en los años cincuenta; f. **into the night**, hasta muy entrada la noche; **so** f., hasta ahora. 3 (**much**) mucho; **by** f., con mucho; f. **cleverer**, mucho más listo,-a; f. **too much**, demasiado; **you're not** f. **wrong**, casi aciertas.

faraway ['fɑːrəweɪ] *adj* lejano,-a, remoto,-a.

farce [fɑːs] *n* farsa *f*.

farcical ['fɑːsɪkəl] *adj* absurdo,-a.

fare [feə'] **I** *n* 1 (**ticket price**) tarifa *f*, precio m del billete; (**for boat**) pasaje m; **half** f., media tarifa. 2 (**passenger**) pasajero,-a m,f. 3 (**food**) comida *f*. **II** *vi* **how did you** f.?, ¿qué tal te fue?

farewell [feə'wel] **I** *interj arch* ¡adiós! **II** *n* despedida *f*.

far-fetched [fɑː'fetʃt] *adj* rebuscado,-a.

farm [fɑːm] **I** *n* granja *f*, *Am* hacienda *f*. **II** *vtr* cultivar, labrar. ◆**farm out** *vtr* encargar fuera.

farmer ['fɑːmə'] *n* granjero,-a m,f, *Am* hacendado,-a m,f.

farmhand ['fɑːmhænd] *n* peón m, labriego,-a m,f.

farmhouse ['fɑːmhaʊs] *n* granja *f*, *Am* hacienda *f*.

farming ['fɑːmɪŋ] **I** *n* 1 (**agriculture**) agricultura *f*. 2 (**of land**) cultivo m, labranza *f*. **II** *adj* agrícola.

farmyard ['fɑːmjɑːd] *n* corral m.

far-reaching [fɑː'riːtʃɪŋ] *adj* de gran alcance.

far-sighted [fɑː'saɪtɪd] *adj* 1 (**person**) con visión de futuro. 2 (**plan**) con miras al futuro.

fart [fɑːt] *vulg* **I** *n* pedo m. **II** *vi* echarse un pedo.

farther ['fɑːðə'] *adj & adv comp* → **far**.

farthest ['fɑːðɪst] *adj & adv superl* → **far**.

fascinate ['fæsɪneɪt] *vtr* fascinar.

fascinating ['fæsɪneɪtɪŋ] *adj* fascinante.

fascination [fæsɪ'neɪʃən] *n* fascinación *f*.

fascism ['fæʃɪzəm] *n* fascismo *m*.

fascist ['fæʃɪst] *adj & n* fascista (*mf*).

fashion ['fæʃən] **I** *n* 1 (*manner*) manera *f*, modo *m*; **after a f.**, más o menos. 2 (*latest style*) moda *f*; **to go/be out of f.**, pasar/no estar de moda; **f. designer**, diseñador,-a *m,f* de modas; **f. parade**, desfile *m* de modelos. **II** *vtr* (*metal*) labrar; (*clay*) formar.

fashionable ['fæʃənəbəl] *adj* 1 de moda. 2 (*area, hotel*) elegante.

fast¹ [fɑːst] **I** *adj* 1 (*quick*) rápido,-a. 2 **hard and f. rules**, reglas estrictas. 3 (*clock*) adelantado,-a. **II** *adv* 1 rápidamente, deprisa; **how f.?**, ¿a qué velocidad? 2 (*securely*) firmemente; **f. asleep**, profundamente dormido,-a.

fast² [fɑːst] **I** *n* ayuno *m*. **II** *vi* ayunar.

fasten ['fɑːsən] **I** *vtr* 1 (*attach*) sujetar; (*fix*) fijar. 2 (*belt*) abrochar; (*bag*) asegurar; (*shoe laces*) atar. **II** *vi* (*dress*) abrocharse.

fastener ['fɑːsənər] *n* cierre *m*.

fastidious [fæ'stɪdɪəs] *adj* quisquilloso,-a.

fat [fæt] **I** *adj* (*fatter, fattest*) 1 gordo,-a. 2 (*book, file*) grueso,-a. 3 (*meat*) que tiene mucha grasa. **II** *n* grasa *f*; **cooking f.**, manteca *f* de cerdo.

fatal ['feɪtəl] *adj* 1 (*accident, illness*) mortal. 2 (*ill-fated*) fatal, funesto,-a. 3 (*fateful*) fatídico,-a. ◆**fatally** *adv* **f. wounded**, mortalmente herido,-a.

fatalistic [feɪtə'lɪstɪk] *adj* fatalista.

fatality [fə'tælɪtɪ] *n* víctima *f* mortal.

fate [feɪt] *n* destino *m*, suerte *f*.

fateful ['feɪtful] *adj* fatídico,-a, aciago,-a.

father ['fɑːðər] *n* 1 padre *m*; **my f. and mother**, mis padres; **F. Christmas**, Papá *m* Noel. 2 *Rel* padre *m*.

father-in-law ['fɑːðərɪnlɔː] *n* suegro *m*.

fatherland ['fɑːðəlænd] *n* patria *f*.

fatherly ['fɑːðəlɪ] *adj* paternal.

fathom ['fæðəm] **I** *n* Naut braza *f*. **II** *vtr* comprender. ◆**fathom out** *vtr* comprobar; **I can't f. it out**, no me lo explico.

fatigue [fə'tiːg] *n* 1 (*tiredness*) fatiga *f*. 2 *Mil* faena *f*; **f. dress**, traje *m* de faena.

fatten ['fætən] *vtr* engordar.

fattening ['fætənɪŋ] *adj* que engorda.

fatty ['fætɪ] **I** *adj* (*food*) graso,-a; *Anat* (*tissue*) adiposo,-a. **II** *n* fam (*person*) gordinflón,-ona *m,f*.

fatuous ['fætjuəs] *adj* necio,-a.

faucet ['fɔːsɪt] *n* US grifo *m*.

fault [fɔːlt] *n* 1 (*defect*) defecto *m*. 2 (*in merchandise*) desperfecto *m*; **to find f. with**, poner reparos a. 3 (*blame*) culpa *f*; **to be at f.**, tener la culpa. 4 (*mistake*) error *m*. 5 *Geol* falla *f*. 6 *Ten* falta *f*. **II** *vtr* criticar.

faultless ['fɔːltlɪs] *adj* intachable.

faulty ['fɔːltɪ] *adj* defectuoso,-a.

fauna ['fɔːnə] *n* fauna *f*.

faux pas [fəu'pɑː] *n inv* fml (*mistake*) paso *m* en falso; (*blunder*) metedura *f* de pata.

favour, US **favor** ['feɪvər] **I** *n* 1 favor *m*; **in f. of**, a favor de; **to be in f. with sb**, gozar del favor de algn; **to ask sb a f.**, pedirle un favor a algn. 2 **1-0 in our f.**, (*advantage*)1-0 a favor nuestro. **II** *vtr* 1 (*person*) favorecer a. 2 (*approve*) estar a favor de.

favourable ['feɪvərəbəl] *adj* favorable.

favourite ['feɪvərɪt] *adj & n* favorito,-a, *m,f*.

favouritism ['feɪvərɪtɪzəm] *n* favoritismo *m*.

fawn¹ [fɔːn] **I** *adj* (de) color café claro. **II** *n* 1 *Zool* cervato *m*. 2 color *m* café claro.

fawn² [fɔːn] *vi* adular (**on**, a).

fax [fæks] **I** *n* (*machine, message*) fax *m*. **II** *vtr* mandar por fax.

fear [fɪər] **I** *n* miedo *m*, temor *m*; **for f. of**, por temor a; **fam no f.!**, ¡ni pensarlo! **II** *vtr* temer; **I fear it's too late**, me temo que ya es tarde. **III** *vi* temer (**for**, por).

fearful ['fɪəful] *adj* 1 (*person*) temeroso,-a. 2 (*frightening*) espantoso,-a.

fearless ['fɪəlɪs] *adj* intrépido,-a.

feasible ['fiːzəbəl] *adj* (*practicable*) factible; (*possible*) viable.

feasibility [fiːzə'bɪlɪtɪ] *n* viabilidad *f*.

feast [fiːst] *n* 1 banquete *m*; *fam* comilona *f*. 2 *Rel* **f. day**, fiesta *f* de guardar.

feat [fiːt] *n* hazaña *f*.

feather ['feðər] **I** *n* pluma *f*; **f. duster**, plumero *m*. **II** *vtr* *fam* **to f. one's nest**, hacer su agosto.

feature ['fiːtʃər] **I** *n* 1 (*of face*) rasgo *m*, facción *f*. 2 (*characteristic*) característica *f*. 3 **f. film**, largometraje *m*. 4 *Press* crónica *f* especial. **II** *vtr* poner de relieve. 2 *Cin* tener como protagonista a. **III** *vi* figurar.

February ['februərɪ] *n* febrero *m*.

fed [fed] *adj fam* **f. up**, harto,-a (**with**, de).

federal ['fedərəl] *adj* federal.

federation [fedə'reɪʃən] *n* federación *f*.

fee [fiː] *n* (*of lawyer, doctor*) honorarios *mpl*; *Ftb* **transfer f.**, prima *f* de traslado; *Univ* **tuition fees**, derechos *mpl* de matrícula.

feeble ['fiːbəl] *adj* débil.

feed [fiːd] **I** *vtr* (*pt & pp* **fed**) 1 (*give food to*) dar de comer a; (*fig* (*fire*) alimentar; **to f. a baby**, (*breast-feed*) amamantar a un bebé; (*with bottle*) dar el biberón a un bebé. 2 *Elec* alimentar. 3 (*insert*) introducir. **II** *vi* comer (**on**, -); (*cows, sheep*) pacer. **III** *n* 1 (*food*) comida *f*; **cattle f.**, pienso *m*. 2 *Tech* alimentación *f*. ◆**feed up** *vtr* cebar.

feedback ['fiːdbæk] *n* 1 *Tech* feedback *m*. 2 *fig* reacción *f*.

feeder ['fiːdər] *n* *Tech* alimentador *m*.

feeding ['fiːdɪŋ] n f. bottle, biberón m.

feel [fiːl] I vi (pt & pp felt) 1 (emotion, sensation) sentir; **how do you f.?**, ¿qué tal te encuentras?; **I f. bad about it**, me da pena; **I f.** (sorry) **for him**, le compadezco; **to f. happy/uncomfortable**, sentirse feliz/incómodo; **to f. cold/sleepy**, tener frío/sueño; ◆**m to f. up to sth**, sentirse con ánimos para hacer algo. 2 (seem) **your hand feels cold**, tienes la mano fría; **it feels like summer**, parece verano. 3 (opinion) opinar; **I f. sure that ...**, estoy seguro,-a de que ... 4 **I f. like an ice cream**, me apetece un helado; **to f. like doing sth**, tener ganas de hacer algo. II vtr 1 (touch) tocar. 2 **she feels a failure**, se siente inútil. III n 1 (touch, sensation) tacto m; **fig to get the f. for sth**, cogerle el truco a algo. 2 (atmosphere) ambiente m. ◆**feel for** vtr 1 (search for) buscar. 2 (have sympathy for) compadecer.

feeler ['fiːlə'] n Ent antena f; **fig to put out one's feelers**, tantear el terreno.

feeling ['fiːlɪŋ] n 1 (emotion) sentimiento m; **ill f.**, rencor m. 2 (compassion) compasión f. 3 **I had the f. that ...**, (impression) tuve la impresión de que ... 4 (sensitivity) sensibilidad f. 5 (opinion) opinión f; **to express one's feelings**, expresar sus opiniones. II adj sensible, compasivo,-a.

feet [fiːt] npl → **foot**.

feign [feɪn] vtr fingir.

feint [feɪnt] Sport I n finta f. II vi fintar.

fell[1] [fel] pt → **fall**.

fell[2] [fel] vtr (trees) talar; fig (enemy) derribar.

fellow ['feləʊ] n 1 (companion) compañero,-a m,f; (citizen, concaudadano,-a m,f; **f. countryman/ countrywoman**, compatriota m,f; **f. men**, prójimos mpl; **f. passenger/student**, compañero,-a m,f; de viaje/estudios. 2 fam (chap) tipo m, tío m. 3 (of society) socio,-a m,f.

fellowship ['feləʊʃɪp] n 1 (comradeship) camaradería f. 2 Univ beca f de investigación.

felony ['felənɪ] n crimen m, delito m mayor.

felt[1] [felt] pt & pp → **feel**.

felt[2] [felt] n Tex fieltro m.

felt-tip(ped) ['felttɪp(t)] adj **f.-t. pen**, rotulador m.

female ['fiːmeɪl] I adj 1 Zool hembra f. 2 femenino,-a. II n 1 Zool hembra f. 2 (woman) mujer f; (girl) chica f.

feminine ['femɪnɪn] adj femenino,-a.

feminism ['femɪnɪzəm] n feminismo m.

feminist ['femɪnɪst] adj & n feminista (m,f).

fence [fens] I n 1 cerca f, valla f; fig **to sit on the f.**, ver los toros desde la barrera. II vi Sport practicar la esgrima. ◆**fence**

in vtr meter en un cercado.

fencing ['fensɪŋ] n Sport esgrima f.

fend [fend] vi **to f. for oneself**, valerse por sí mismo. ◆**fend off** vtr (blow) parar; (question) rehuir; (attack) rechazar.

fender ['fendə'] n 1 (fireplace) pantalla f. 2 US Aut parachoques m inv. 3 Naut defensa f.

ferment I ['fɜːment] n fig **in a state of f.**, agitado,-a. II [fə'ment] vtr & vi fermentar.

fern [fɜːn] n helecho m.

ferocious [fə'rəʊʃəs] adj feroz.

ferocity [fə'rɒsɪtɪ] n ferocidad f.

ferret ['ferɪt] I n hurón m. II vi huronear, husmear. ◆**ferret out** vtr descubrir.

ferry ['ferɪ] I n 1 (small) barca f de pasaje. 2 (large, for cars) transbordador m, ferry m. II vtr transportar.

fertile ['fɜːtaɪl] adj fértil.

fertility [fə'tɪlɪtɪ] n (of soil) fertilidad f.

fertilize ['fɜːtɪlaɪz] vtr 1 (soil) abonar. 2 (egg) fecundar.

fertilizer ['fɜːtɪlaɪzə'] n abono m.

fervent ['fɜːvənt] adj ferviente.

fervour, US **fervor** ['fɜːvə'] n fervor m.

fester ['festə'] vi supurar.

festival ['festɪvəl] n (event) festival m; (celebration) fiesta f.

festive ['festɪv] adj festivo,-a; **the f. season**, las fiestas de Navidad.

festivity [fe'stɪvɪtɪ] n **the festivities**, las fiestas.

festoon [fe'stuːn] vtr adornar.

fetch [fetʃ] vtr 1 (go for) ir a buscar. 2 (bring) traer. 3 **how much did it f.?**, (sell for) ¿por cuánto se vendió?

fetching ['fetʃɪŋ] adj atractivo,-a.

fete [feɪt] I n fiesta f. II vtr festejar.

fetish ['fetɪʃ, 'fiːtɪʃ] n fetiche m.

fetus ['fiːtəs] n US → **foetus**.

feud [fjuːd] I n enemistad duradera. II vi pelear.

feudal ['fjuːdəl] adj feudal.

fever ['fiːvə'] n fiebre f.

feverish ['fiːvərɪʃ] adj febril.

few [fjuː] adj 1 (not many) pocos,-as; **f. as**, solamente. 2 (some) algunos,-as, unos,-as cuantos,-as; **a f. books**, unos o algunos libros; **she has fewer books than I thought**, tiene menos libros de lo que pensaba; **for the past f. years**, durante estos últimos años; **in the next f. days**, dentro de unos días; **quite a f.**, bastantes. II pron 1 (not many) pocos,-as; **there are too f.**, no hay suficientes; **the fewer the better**, cuantos menos mejor. 2 **a f.**, (some) algunos,-as, unos,-as cuantos,-as; **the chosen f.**, los elegidos; **who has the fewest?**, ¿quién tiene menos?

fiancé [fɪ'ɒnseɪ] n prometido m.

fiancée [fɪ'ɒnseɪ] n prometida f.

fiasco [fɪ'æskəʊ] n fiasco m.

fib [fɪb] *fam* **I** *n* trola *f*. **II** *vi* contar trolas.

fibre, *US* **fiber** ['faɪbər] *n* fibra *f*.

fibreglass, *US* **fiberglass** ['faɪbəglɑːs] *n* fibra *f* de vidrio.

fickle ['fɪkəl] *adj* inconstante, voluble.

fiction ['fɪkʃən] *n* ficción *f*.

fictional ['fɪkʃənəl] *adj* **1** *Lit* novelesco,-a. **2** *(imaginary)* ficticio,-a.

fictitious [fɪk'tɪʃəs] *adj* ficticio,-a.

fiddle ['fɪdəl] *fam* **I** *n* **1** *Mus* violín *m*. **2** *(shady deal)* trampa *f*. **II** *vtr* estafar; *(accounts)* falsificar. **III** *vi* juguetear (**with**, con). ◆**fiddle about** *vi* perder tiempo.

fiddly ['fɪdlɪ] *adj* laborioso,-a.

fidelity [fɪ'delɪtɪ] *n* fidelidad *f*.

fidget ['fɪdʒɪt] *vi* **1** moverse; **stop fidgeting!**, ¡estáte quieto! **2** jugar (**with**, con).

field [fiːld] *n* **1** campo *m*; **f. glasses**, gemelos *mpl*; **f. marshal**, mariscal *m* de campo. **2** *Geol Min* yacimiento *m*. **3** **f. trip**, viaje *m* de estudios; **f. work**, trabajo *m* de campo. **II** *vtr Sport* **1** *(ball)* parar y devolver. **2** *(team)* presentar.

fiend [fiːnd] *n* demonio *m*; *fam (fanatic)* fanático,-a *m,f*.

fiendish ['fiːndɪʃ] *adj fam* diabólico,-a.

fierce [fɪəs] *adj (animal)* feroz; *(argument)* acalorado,-a; *(heat, competition)* intenso, -a; *(wind)* violento,-a.

fiery ['faɪərɪ] *adj (temper)* fogoso,-a; *(speech)* acalorado,-a; *(colour)* encendido,-a.

fifteen [fɪf'tiːn] *adj & n* quince (*m*) *inv*.

fifteenth [fɪf'tiːnθ] **I** *adj & n* decimoquinto,-a (*m,f*). **II** *n (fraction)* quinzavo *m*.

fifth [fɪfθ] **I** *adj & n* quinto,-a (*m,f*). **II** *n (fraction)* quinto *m*.

fifty ['fɪftɪ] **I** *adj & n* cincuenta *inv*; *fam* **a f.-f. chance**, una probabilidad del cincuenta por ciento; *fam* **to go f.-f.**, ir a medias. **II** *n* cincuenta *m inv*.

fig¹ [fɪg] *n (fruit)* higo *m*, fig.

fig² [fɪg] *abbr of* **figure**, fig.

fight [faɪt] **I** *vtr (pt & pp* **fought**) **1** pelear(se) con, luchar con; *(of boxer)* enfrentarse a, luchar con; *Taur* lidiar; *fig (corruption)* combatir (**against**, contra). **2** *(battle)* librar; *(war)* hacer. **3** *(decision)* recurrir contra. **II** *vi* **1** pelear(se), luchar. **2** *(quarrel)* reñir; **to f. over sth**, disputarse la posesión de algo. **3** *fig (struggle)* luchar (**for/against**, por/contra). **II** *n* **1** pelea *f*, lucha *f*; *Box* combate *m*. **2** *(quarrel)* riña *f*. **3** *fig (struggle)* lucha *f*. **4** *(spirit)* combatividad *f*. ◆**fight back I** *vtr (tears)* contener. **II** *vi* contraatacar. ◆**fight off** *vtr* **1** *(attack)* rechazar. **2** *(illness)* cortar. ◆**fight out** *vtr* discutir.

fighter ['faɪtər] *n* **1** *(person)* combatiente *mf*; *Box* púgil *m*. **2** *fig* luchador,-a *m,f*; **f. (plane)**, (avión *m* de) caza *m*; **f. bomber**, cazabombardero *m*.

fighting ['faɪtɪŋ] **I** *adj* **he's got a f.**

chance, tiene verdaderas posibilidades. **II** *n* lucha *f*.

figment ['fɪgmənt] *n* **it's a f. of your imagination**, es un producto de tu imaginación.

figurative ['fɪgərətɪv] *adj* figurado,-a.

figure ['fɪgər, *US* 'fɪgjər] **I** *n* **1** *(form, outline)* forma *f*, silueta *f*. **2** *(shape, statue, character)* figura *f*; **she has a good f.**, tiene buen tipo. **3** *(in book)* dibujo *m*. **4** **f. of speech**, figura retórica. **5** *Math* cifra *f*. **II** *vtr US* imaginarse. **III** *vi* **1** *(appear)* figurar. **2** *US fam* **that figures**, eso tiene sentido. ◆**figure out** *vtr fam* comprender; **I can't f. it out**, no me lo explico.

figurehead ['fɪgəhed] *n fig* figura decorativa.

filament ['fɪləmənt] *n* filamento *m*.

filch [fɪltʃ] *vtr sl* mangar, birlar.

file [faɪl] **I** *n* **1** *(tool)* lima *f*. **2** *(folder)* carpeta *f*. **3** *(archive, of computer)* archivo *m*; on f., archivado,-a. **4** *(line)* fila *m*; **in single f.**, en fila india. **II** *vtr* **1** *(smooth)* limar. **2** *(put away)* archivar. **III** *vi* **to f. past**, desfilar.

filing ['faɪlɪŋ] *n* clasificación *f*; **f. cabinet**, archivador *m*; *(for cards)* fichero *m*.

Filipino [fɪlɪ'piːnəʊ] *n* filipino,-a *m,f*.

fill [fɪl] **I** *vtr* **1** *(space, time)* llenar (**with**, de). **2** *(post, requirements)* cubrir. **3** *Culin* rellenar. **II** *vi* llenarse (**with**, de). **III** *n* **to eat one's f.**, comer hasta hartarse. ◆**fill in I** *vtr* **1** *(space, form)* rellenar. **2** *(inform)* *fam* poner al corriente (**on**, de). **3** *(time)* pasar. **II** *vi* **to f. in for sb**, sustituir a algn. ◆**fill out I** *vtr US (form)* llenar. **II** *vi fam* engordar. ◆**fill up I** *vtr* llenar hasta arriba; *Aut* **f. her up!**, ¡lléne-la! **II** *vi* llenarse.

fillet ['fɪlɪt] *n* filete *m*; **f. steak**, filete.

filling ['fɪlɪŋ] **I** *adj* que llena mucho. **II** *n* **1** *(stuffing)* relleno *m*. **2** *(in tooth)* empaste *m*. **3** *GB* **f. station**, gasolinera *f*.

fillip ['fɪlɪp] *n fam* estímulo *m*.

film [fɪlm] **I** *n* **1** *Cin*, *Phot* película *f*; **f. star**, estrella *f* de cine. **2** *(layer)* capa *f*. **II** *vtr Cin* filmar. **III** *vi Cin* rodar.

film-strip ['fɪlmstrɪp] *n* cortometraje *m*.

filter ['fɪltər] **I** *n* filtro *m*; *Aut* **f. lane**, carril *m* de acceso. **II** *vtr* filtrar. **III** *vi Aut* **to f. to the right**, girar a la derecha. ◆**filter through** *vi fig* filtrarse (**to**, a).

filter-tip ['fɪltətɪp] *n (cigarette)* cigarrillo *m* con filtro.

filth [fɪlθ] *n (dirt)* basura *f*; *fig* porquerías *fpl*.

filthy ['fɪlθɪ] *adj (filthier, filthiest)* **1** *(dirty)* asqueroso,-a. **2** *(obscene)* obsceno, -a.

fin [fɪn] *n Zool Av* aleta *f*.

final ['faɪnəl] **I** *adj* **1** *(last)* último,-a, final. **2** *(definitive)* definitivo,-a. **II** *n* **1** *Sport* final *f*. **2** *Univ* **finals**, exámenes *mpl* de fin de carrera. ◆**finally** adv (lastly) por último; (at last) por fin.

finale [fɪˈnɑːlɪ] n final m.

finalist [ˈfaɪnəlɪst] n finalista mf.

finalize [ˈfaɪnəlaɪz] vtr ultimar; (date) fijar.

finance [ˈfaɪnæns, fɪˈnæns] I n 1 finanzas fpl. 2 **finances**, fondos mpl. II vtr financiar.

financial [faɪˈnænʃəl, fɪˈnænʃəl] adj financiero,-a; f. **crisis**, crisis económica; f. **year**, año económico.

financier [faɪˈnænsɪəʳ, fɪˈnænsɪəʳ] n financiero,-a m,f.

finch [fɪntʃ] n pinzón m.

find [faɪnd] I vtr (pt & pp found) 1 (locate) encontrar. 2 (think) encontrar. 3 **this found its way into my bag**, esto vino a parar a mi bolso. 4 (discover) descubrir; **it has been found that ...**, se ha comprobado que ... 5 Jur **to f. sb guilty/not guilty**, declarar culpable/inocente a algn. 6 **I can't f. the courage to tell him**, no tengo valor para decírselo; **I found it impossible to get away**, me resultó imposible irme. II n hallazgo m. ◆**find out** I vtr 1 (enquire) averiguar. 2 (discover) descubrir. II vi 1 **to f. out about sth**, informarse sobre algo. 2 (discover) enterarse.

findings [ˈfaɪndɪŋz] npl conclusiones fpl.

fine¹ [faɪn] I n multa f. II vtr multar.

fine² [faɪn] I adj 1 (delicate etc) fino,-a. 2 (subtle) sutil. 3 (excellent) excelente. 4 (weather) bueno; **it was f.**, hacía buen tiempo. 5 **the f. arts**, las bellas artes. 6 (all right) bien. II adv fam muy bien. III interj ¡vale! ◆**finely** adv 1 finamente; f. **chopped**, picado fino. 2 f. **tuned**, a punto.

finery [ˈfaɪnərɪ] n galas fpl.

finesse [fɪˈnes] n (delicacy) finura f; (cunning) astucia f; (tact) sutileza f.

finger [ˈfɪŋgəʳ] I n dedo m (de la mano); fam **to keep one's fingers crossed**, esperar que todo salga bien; fam **you've put your f. on it**, has dado en el clavo; **middle f.**, dedo corazón. II vtr tocar; pej manosear.

fingernail [ˈfɪŋgəneɪl] n uña f.

fingerprint [ˈfɪŋgəprɪnt] n huella f dactilar.

fingertip [ˈfɪŋgətɪp] n punta f or yema f del dedo.

finicky [ˈfɪnɪkɪ] adj (person) quisquilloso, -a.

finish [ˈfɪnɪʃ] I n 1 fin m; (of race) llegada f. 2 (surface) acabado m. II vtr 1 (complete) acabar, terminar; **to f. doing sth**, terminar de hacer algo. 2 (use up) agotar. III vi acabar, terminar; **to f. second**, quedar el segundo. ◆**finish off** vtr 1 (complete) terminar completamente. 2 (kill) fam rematar. ◆**finish up** I vtr aca-

bar, agotar. II vi **to f. up in jail**, ir a parar a la cárcel.

finished [ˈfɪnɪʃt] adj 1 (product) acabado, -a. 2 fam (exhausted) rendido,-a.

finishing [ˈfɪnɪʃɪŋ] adj **to put the f. touch(es) to sth**, darle los últimos toques a algo; f. **line**, (línea f de) meta f; f. **school**, escuela privada de modales para señoritas.

finite [ˈfaɪnaɪt] adj finito,-a; (verb) conjugable.

Finland [ˈfɪnlənd] n Finlandia.

Finn [fɪn] n finlandés,-esa m,f.

Finnish [ˈfɪnɪʃ] I adj finlandés,-esa. II n (language) finlandés m.

fir [fɜː] n abeto m.

fire [ˈfaɪəʳ] I n 1 fuego m. 2 (accident etc) incendio m; **to be on f.**, estar en llamas; **to catch f.**, incendiarse; f. **alarm**, alarma f de incendios; f. **brigade**, (cuerpo m de) bomberos mpl; f. **engine**, coche m de bomberos; f. **escape**, escalera f de incendios; f. **exit**, salida f de emergencia; f. **extinguisher**, extintor m; f. **fighting**, extinción f de incendios; f. **station**, parque m de bomberos. 3 (heater) estufa f. 4 Mil fuego m; **to open f.**, abrir fuego; fig **to come under f.**, ser el blanco de las críticas. II vtr 1 (gun) disparar (at, a); (rocket) lanzar; fig **to f. questions at sb**, bombardear a algn a preguntas. 2 fam (dismiss) despedir. III vi (shoot) disparar (at, sobre).

firearm [ˈfaɪərɑːm] n arma f de fuego.

fire-fighter [ˈfaɪəfaɪtəʳ] n US bombero m.

fireman [ˈfaɪəmən] n bombero m.

fireplace [ˈfaɪəpleɪs] n chimenea f; (hearth) hogar m.

fireside [ˈfaɪəsaɪd] n hogar m; **by the f.**, al calor de la lumbre.

firewood [ˈfaɪəwʊd] n leña f.

fireworks [ˈfaɪəwɜːks] npl fuegos mpl artificiales.

firing [ˈfaɪərɪŋ] n Mil tiroteo m; f. **line**, línea f de fuego; f. **squad**, pelotón m de fusilamiento.

firm [fɜːm] I adj firme; **to be f. with sb**, (strict) tratar a algn con firmeza. II n empresa f, firma f. ◆**firmly** adv firmemente.

firmness [ˈfɜːmnɪs] n firmeza f.

first [fɜːst] I adj primero,-a; (before masculine singular noun) primer; **Charles the F.**, Carlos Primero; **for the f. time**, por primera vez; **in the f. place**, en primer lugar; f. **floor**, primer piso m, US planta baja; f. **name**, nombre m de pila. II adv (before anything else) primero; f. **and foremost**, ante todo; f. **of all**, en primer lugar. III n 1 **the f.**, el primero; la primera; **the f. of April**, el uno or el primero de abril; f. **aid**, primeros auxilios; f. **aid box**, botiquín m. 2 **at f.**, al principio; **from the (very) f.**, desde el principio. 3

Aut primera f. **4** *Univ* to get a f., sacar un sobresaliente. ◆**firstly** *adv* en primer lugar.

first-class [ˈfɜːstklɑːs] **I** *adj* de primera clase. **II first class** *adv* to travel f. c., viajar en primera.

first-hand [ˈfɜːsthænd] *adv & adj* de primera mano.

first-rate [ˈfɜːstreɪt] *adj* de primera.

fiscal [ˈfɪskəl] *adj* fiscal.

fish [fɪʃ] **I** *n* (*pl* **fish**) **1** pez *m*; f. shop, pescadería f. **2** *Culin* pescado *m*; f. and chips, pescado frito con patatas fritas; *US* f. stick, palito *m* de pescado. **II** *vi* pescar; *fig* to f. in one's pocket for sth, buscar algo en el bolsillo.

fishbone [ˈfɪʃbəʊn] *n* espina f, raspa f.

fisherman [ˈfɪʃəmən] *n* pescador *m*.

fishfinger [fɪʃˈfɪŋgəʳ] *n* palito *m* de pescado.

fishing [ˈfɪʃɪŋ] *n* pesca f; to go f., ir de pesca; f. net, red f de pesca; f. rod, caña f de pescar; f. tackle, aparejo *m* de pesca.

fishmonger [ˈfɪʃmʌŋgəʳ] *n* *GB* pescadero,-a *m,f*; **fishmonger's** (**shop**), pescadería f.

fishy [ˈfɪʃɪ] *adj* (**fishier, fishiest**) de pescado; *fam fig* there's something f. going on, aquí hay gato encerrado.

fist [fɪst] *n* puño *m*.

fit¹ [fɪt] **I** *vtr* **1** ir bien a; that suit doesn't f. you, ese traje no te entalla. **2** *Sew* probar. **3** the key doesn't f. the lock, la llave no es de esta cerradura. **4** (*install*) colocar; a car fitted with a radio, un coche provisto de radio. **5** *fig* she doesn't f. the description, no responde a la descripción. **II** *vi* **1** (*be of right size*) caber. **2** (*facts etc*) cuadrar. **III** *adj* **1** (*suitable*) apto,-a, adecuado,-a (*for*, para); are you f. to drive?, ¿estás en condiciones de conducir? **2** (*healthy*) en (plena) forma; to keep f., mantenerse en forma. **IV** *n* ajuste *m*; *Sew* corte *m*; to be a good f., encajar bien. ◆**fit in I** *vi* he didn't f. in with his colleagues, no encajó con sus compañeros de trabajo. **2** (*tally*) cuadrar (**with**, con). **II** *vtr* (*find time for*) encontrar un hueco para. ◆**fit out** *vtr* equipar.

fit² [fɪt] *n* **1** *Med* ataque *m*; *fig* arrebato *m*; f. of anger, arranque *m* de cólera; *fig* by fits and starts, a trompicones.

fitful [ˈfɪtfʊl] *adj* discontinuo,-a.

fitness [ˈfɪtnɪs] *n* **1** (*aptitude*) aptitud f, capacidad f. **2** (*health*) (buen) estado físico.

fitted [ˈfɪtɪd] *adj* empotrado,-a; f. carpet, moqueta f. f. cupboard, armario empotrado.

fitter [ˈfɪtəʳ] *n* ajustador,-a *m,f*.

fitting [ˈfɪtɪŋ] **I** *adj* apropiado,-a. **II** *n* **1** (*of dress*) prueba f. f. room, probador *m*. **2** (*usu pl*) accesorio *m*; light fittings, apli-

ques eléctricos.

five [faɪv] *adj & n* cinco (*m*) *inv*.

fiver [ˈfaɪvəʳ] *n fam* billete *m* de cinco libras *or* dólares.

fix [fɪks] **I** *n* **1** *fam* to be in a f., estar en un apuro. **2** (*drugs*) *sl* chute *m*. **II** *vtr* **1** (*fasten*) fijar, asegurar. **2** (*date, price*) fijar; (*limit*) señalar. **3** he'll f. it with the boss, (*arrange*) se las arreglará con el jefe. **4** (*repair*) arreglar. **5** *US* (*food, drink*) preparar. ◆**fix up** *vtr* (*arrange*) arreglar; to f. sb up with sth, proveer a algn de algo.

fixation [fɪkˈseɪʃən] *n* idea fija.

fixed [fɪkst] *adj* **1** fijo,-a. **2** *fam* (*match etc*) amañado,-a.

fixture [ˈfɪkstʃəʳ] *n* **1** *Sport* encuentro *m*. **2** fixtures, (*in building*) accesorios *mpl*.

fizz [fɪz] **I** *n* burbujeo *m*. **II** *vi* burbujear. ◆**fizzle out** [ˈfɪzlaʊt] *vi* quedar en nada.

fizzy [ˈfɪzɪ] *adj* (**fizzier, fizziest**) (*water*) con gas.

flabbergasted [ˈflæbəgɑːstɪd] *adj* pasmado,-a.

flabby [ˈflæbɪ] *adj* (**flabbier, flabbiest**) fofo,-a.

flag [flæg] **I** *n* **1** bandera f; *Naut* pabellón *m*. **II** *vtr fig* to f. down a car, hacer señales a un coche para que pare. **III** *vi* (*interest*) decaer; (*conversation*) languidecer.

flagpole [ˈflægpəʊl] *n* asta f de bandera.

flagrant [ˈfleɪgrənt] *adj* flagrante.

flagship [ˈflægʃɪp] *n* buque insignia *m*.

flagstone [ˈflægstəʊn] *n* losa f.

flair [fleəʳ] *n* facilidad f.

flak [flæk] *n* **1** *Mil* fuego antiaéreo. **2** *fam* críticas *fpl*.

flake [fleɪk] **I** *n* (*of snow*) copo *m*; (*of skin, soap*) escama f; (*of paint*) desconchón *m*. **II** *vi* (*skin*) descamarse; (*paint*) desconcharse.

flamboyant [flæmˈbɔɪənt] *adj* extravagante.

flame [fleɪm] *n* llama f; to go up in flames, incendiarse.

flameproof [ˈfleɪmpruːf] *adj* ininflamable.

flamingo [fləˈmɪŋgəʊ] *n* flamenco *m*.

flammable [ˈflæməbəl] *adj* inflamable.

flan [flæn] *n* tarta rellena; fruit f., tarta de fruta.

flank [flæŋk] **I** *n* **1** (*of animal*) ijada f. **2** *Mil* flanco *m*. **II** *vtr* flanquear.

flannel [ˈflænəl] *n* **1** *Tex* franela f. **2** *GB* (*face cloth*) toallita f.

flap [flæp] **I** *n* **1** (*of envelope, pocket*) solapa f; (*of tent*) faldón *m*. **2** (*of wings, arms*) aleteo *m*. **3** *fam* to get into a f., ponerse nervioso,-a. **II** *vtr* (*wings*) batir. **II** *vi* (*wings*) aletear; (*flag*) ondear. **III** *n* **1** (*of tent*) faldón *m*.

flare [fleəʳ] **I** *n* **1** (*flame*) llamarada f. **2** *Mil Naut* bengala f. **II** *vi* to f. (**up**), (*fire*) llamear; *fig* (*person*) encolerizarse; (*trouble*) estallar.

flared [fleəd] *adj* (*trousers* etc)

acampanado,-a.

flash [flæʃ] **I** n **1** (of light) destello m; (of lightning) relámpago m; fig in a f., en un santiamén; fig a f. in the pan, un éxito fugaz. **2** news f., noticia f de última hora. **3** Phot flash m. **II** adj sl chulo,-a. **III** vtr **1** (torch) dirigir. **2** Rad TV transmitir. **3** he flashed his card, enseñó rápidamente su carnet. **IV** vi **1** (light) destellar. **2** a car flashed past, un coche pasó como un rayo.

flashback ['flæʃbæk] n flashback m.

flashcube ['flæʃkjuːb] n cubo m flash.

flashlight ['flæʃlaɪt] n US linterna f.

flashy ['flæʃɪ] adj (flashier, flashiest) fam chillón,-a.

flask [flɑːsk, flæsk] n frasco m; (thermos) f., termo m.

flat [flæt] **I** adj (flatter, flattest) **1** (surface) llano,-a. **2** (beer) sin gas. **3** (battery) descargado,-a; (tyre) desinflado,-a. **4** (rate) fijo,-a. **5** (categorical) rotundo,-a. **6** (dull) soso,-a. **7** Mus **B** f., si m bemol. **II** adv **1** to fall f. on one's face, caerse de bruces. **2** in ten seconds f., en diez segundos justos. **3** fam to go f. out, ir a toda gas. **III** n **1** (appartment) piso m. **2** US Aut pinchazo m. **3** mud flats, marismas fpl. **♦flatly** adv rotundamente.

flatmate ['flætmeɪt] n GB compañero,-a m,f de piso.

flatten ['flætən] vtr **1** (make level) allanar. **2** (crush) aplastar.

flatter ['flætə'] vtr **1** adular, halagar. **2** (clothes, portrait) favorecer. **3** to f. oneself, hacerse ilusiones.

flattering ['flætərɪŋ] adj **1** (words) halagador,-a. **2** (dress, portrait) favorecedor,-a.

flattery ['flætərɪ] n adulación f, halago m.

flaunt [flɔːnt] vtr hacer alarde de.

flavour, US **flavor** ['fleɪvə'] **I** n **1** sabor m. **II** vtr Culin sazonar (**with**, con).

flavoured, US **flavored** ['fleɪvəd] adj **strawberry f.**, con sabor a fresa.

flavouring, US **flavoring** ['fleɪvərɪŋ] n condimento m; **artificial f.**, aroma m artificial.

flaw [flɔː] n (failing) defecto m; (fault) desperfecto m.

flawless ['flɔːlɪs] adj perfecto,-a.

flax [flæks] n lino m.

flaxen ['flæksən] adj (hair) rubio pajizo.

flea [fliː] n pulga f; **f. market**, rastro m.

fleck [flek] n (speck) mota f, punto m.

fledg(e)ling ['fledʒlɪŋ] adj fig novato,-a.

flee [fliː] **I** vtr (pt & pp **fled**) huir de. **II** vi huir (**from**, de).

fleece [fliːs] **I** n **1** (sheep's coat) lana f. **2** (sheared) vellón m. **II** vtr fam (cheat) sangrar.

fleet [fliːt] n flota f.

fleeting ['fliːtɪŋ] adj fugaz.

Flemish ['flemɪʃ] **I** adj flamenco,-a. **II** n

(language) flamenco m.

flesh [fleʃ] n **1** carne f; fig **in the f.**, en persona; fig **to be of f. and blood**, ser de carne y hueso; f. **wound**, herida f superficial. **2** (of fruit) pulpa f.

flew [fluː] pt → **fly**.

flex [fleks] **I** n GB Elec cable m. **II** vtr (muscles) flexionar.

flexible ['fleksɪbəl] adj flexible.

flexibility [fleksɪ'bɪlɪtɪ] n flexibilidad f.

flick [flɪk] **I** n movimiento rápido; (of finger) capirotazo m. **II** vtr (with finger) dar un capirotazo a. **♦flick through** vtr (book) hojear.

flicker ['flɪkə'] **I** n **1** parpadeo m; (of light) titileo m. **2** fig a f. of hope, un destello de esperanza. **II** vi (eyes) parpadear; (flame) vacilar.

flier ['flaɪə'] n aviador,-a m,f.

flight [flaɪt] n **1** vuelo m; **f. path**, trayectoria f de vuelo; **f. recorder**, registrador m de vuelo. **2** (of ball) trayectoria f. **3** (escape) huida f, fuga f; **to take f.**, darse a la fuga. **4** (of stairs) tramo m.

flight-deck ['flaɪtdek] n (cockpit) cabina f del piloto.

flimsy ['flɪmzɪ] adj (flimsier, flimsiest) (cloth) ligero,-a; (paper) fino,-a; (structure) poco sólido,-a; (excuse) poco convincente.

flinch [flɪntʃ] vi (wince) estremecerse.

fling [flɪŋ] **I** vtr (pt & pp **flung**) arrojar. **II** n fam **to have a f.**, echar una cana al aire.

flint [flɪnt] n **1** (stone) pedernal m. **2** (in lighter) piedra f de mechero.

flip [flɪp] **I** n (flick) capirotazo m. **II** vtr (toss) tirar (al aire); **to f. a coin**, echar a cara o cruz.

flip-flop ['flɪpflɒp] n **1** Comput báscula f biestable. **2** (footwear) chancleta f.

flippant ['flɪpənt] adj frívolo,-a.

flipper ['flɪpə'] n aleta f.

flirt [flɜːt] **I** n coqueto,-a m,f. **II** vi flirtear, coquetear; **to f. with death**, jugar con la muerte.

flirtation [flɜː'teɪʃən] n flirteo m, coqueteo m.

flit [flɪt] vi revolotear.

float [fləʊt] **I** n **1** flotador m. **2** (money) cambio m. **3** (in procession) carroza f. **II** vtr **1** poner a flote. **2** (shares) emitir; (currency, business) hacer flotar. **III** vi flotar.

floating ['fləʊtɪŋ] adj flotante; (population) indeciso,-a.

flock [flɒk] **I** n Zool rebaño m; Orn bandada f; Rel grey f; (crowd) multitud f. **II** vi acudir en masa.

flog [flɒg] vtr **1** azotar; fam fig **flogged to death**, (idea) trillado. **2** sl (sell) vender.

flood [flʌd] **I** n inundación f; (of river) riada f; fig torrente m. **II** vtr inundar. **III** vi (river) desbordarse; fig **to f. in**, entrar a raudales.

flooding |'flʌdɪŋ| n inundaciones fpl.

floodlight |'flʌdlaɪt| n foco m.

floor |flɔːr| I n 1 (of room) suelo m; **dance f.**, pista f de baile. 2 (of ocean, forest) fondo m. 3 (storey) piso m; **first f.**, GB primer piso m, US planta baja; GB **ground f.**, planta baja. II vtr fig dejar perplejo,-a.

floorboard |'flɔːbɔːd| n tabla f (del suelo).

flop |flɒp| I n fam fracaso m. II vi 1 **to f. down on the bed**, tumbarse en la cama. 2 fam fracasar.

floppy |'flɒpɪ| adj (**floppier, floppiest**) flojo,-a; Comput f. disk, disco m flexible.

flora |'flɔːrə| n flora f.

florid |'flɒrɪd| adj (style) florido,-a.

florist |'flɒrɪst| n florista mf; **f.'s**, floristería f.

flounce¹ |flaʊns| vi to f. in/out, entrar/salir airadamente.

flounce² |flaʊns| n Sew volante m.

flounder¹ |'flaʊndər| n (fish) platija f.

flounder² |'flaʊndər| vi 1 (struggle) forcejear; fig enredarse. 2 (be at a loss) no saber que decir o hacer.

flour |'flaʊər| n harina f.

flourish |'flʌrɪʃ| I n 1 (gesture) ademán m (teatral). 2 (under signature) rúbrica f. II vtr (brandish) agitar. III vi (thrive) florecer; (plant) crecer.

flourishing |'flʌrɪʃɪŋ| adj floreciente.

flout |flaʊt| vtr Jur desacatar.

flow |fləʊ| I n flujo m; (of river) corriente f; (of traffic) circulación f; (of capital) movimiento m; (of people, goods) afluencia f; **f. chart**, diagrama m de flujo; Comput organigrama m. II vi (blood, river) fluir; (sea) subir; (traffic) circular.

flower |'flaʊər| I n flor f; **f. bed**, arriate m. II vi florecer.

flowerpot |'flaʊəpɒt| n maceta f.

flowery |'flaʊrɪ| adj fig florido,-a.

flowing |'flaʊɪŋ| adj (hair) suelto,-a; (dress) de mucho vuelo; (style) fluido,-a; (shape, movement) natural.

flown |fləʊn| pp → **fly**.

flu |fluː| n (abbr of influenza) gripe f.

fluctuate |'flʌktjʊeɪt| vi fluctuar.

fluctuation |flʌktjʊ'eɪʃən| n fluctuación f.

flue |fluː| n conducto m de humos; (chimney) cañón m.

fluent |'fluːənt| adj 1 he speaks f. German, habla el alemán con soltura. 2 (eloquent) fluido,-a.

fluff |flʌf| I n (down) pelusa f. II vtr fam to f. sth, hacer algo mal.

fluffy |'flʌfɪ| adj (**fluffier, fluffiest**) (pillow) mullido,-a; (toy) de peluche; (cake) esponjoso,-a.

fluid |'fluːɪd| I adj (movement) natural; (style, prose) fluido,-a; (situation) incierto,-a. II n fluido m, líquido m.

fluke |fluːk| n fam chiripa f; **by a f.**, por

chiripa.

flummox |'flʌməks| vtr fam desconcertar.

flung |flʌŋ| pt & pp → **fling**.

fluorescent |flʊə'resənt| adj fluorescente.

fluoride |'flʊəraɪd| n fluoruro m.

flurry |'flʌrɪ| n 1 (of wind) ráfaga f; (of snow) nevasca f. 2 fig (bustle) agitación f.

flush |flʌʃ| I adj 1 f. with, (level) a ras de. II n (blush) rubor m. III vtr to f. the lavatory, tirar de la cadena. IV vi 1 the loo won't f., la cisterna del wáter no funciona. 2 (blush) ruborizarse.

flushed |flʌʃt| adj (cheeks) rojo,-a, encendido,-a; **f. with success**, emocionado,-a ante el éxito.

fluster |'flʌstər| vtr to get flustered, ponerse nervioso,-a.

flute |fluːt| n flauta f.

flutter |'flʌtər| I vi (leaves, birds) revolotear; (flag) ondear. II n fam (bet, gambling) apuesta pequeña.

flux |flʌks| n (flow) flujo m; (instability) inestabilidad f; fig to be in a state of f., estar continuamente cambiando.

fly¹ |flaɪ| I vtr (pt flew; pp flown) 1 Av pilotar. 2 (merchandize, troops) transportar. 3 (distance) recorrer. 4 (kite) hacer volar. II vi 1 (bird, plane) volar. 2 (go by plane) ir en avión. 3 (flag) ondear. **4 to f. into a rage**, montar en cólera. 5 the train **flew past**, el tren pasó volando. 6 fam to **go flying**, (fall) caerse. III n flies, bragueta f sing.

fly² |flaɪ| n (insect) mosca f; **f. spray**, spray m matamoscas.

flying |'flaɪɪŋ| adj (rapid) rápido,-a; **a f. visit**, una visita relámpago; fig to come out of an affair with f. colours, salir airoso,-a de un asunto; fig to get off to a f. start, empezar con buen pie; **f. picket**, piquete m (informativo); **f. saucer**, platillo m volante. II n 1 (action) vuelo m. 2 (aviation) aviación f.

flyleaf |'flaɪliːf| n (of book) guarda f.

flyover |'flaɪəʊvər| n paso elevado.

flypast |'flaɪpɑːst| n GB Av desfile aéreo.

flyweight |'flaɪweɪt| n Box peso m mosca.

foal |fəʊl| n potro,-a m,f.

foam |fəʊm| I n espuma f; **f. bath**, espuma de baño; **f. rubber**, goma espuma. II vi hacer espuma.

fob |fɒb| vtr fam to f. sb off with excuses, darle largas a algn. ◆fob off vtr fam **he fobbed off his old radio on a stranger**, le colocó su radio vieja a un desconocido.

focus |'fəʊkəs| I vtr centrarse (on, en). II vi enfocar; to f. on sth, Phot enfocar algo; fig centrarse en algo. III n (pl focuses) foco m; to be in f./out of f., estar enfocado,-a/desenfocado,-a.

fodder |'fɒdər| n pienso m.

foe |fəʊ| n fml enemigo,-a m,f.

foetus |'fiːtəs| n feto m.

fog [fɒg] *n* niebla *f*; *(at sea)* bruma *f*.

fogey ['fəʊgɪ] *n fam* old f., cascarrabias *mf inv*.

foggy ['fɒgɪ] *adj* **(foggier, foggiest)** it is f., hay niebla; *fam* I haven't the foggiest (idea), no tengo la más mínima idea.

foghorn ['fɒghɔːn] *n* sirena *f* (de niebla).

foglamp ['fɒglæmp], *US* **foglight** ['fɒglaɪt] *n* faro *m* antiniebla.

foil [fɔɪl] I *n* 1 aluminium f., papel *m* de aluminio. 2 *(in fencing)* florete *m*. II *vtr (plot)* desbaratar.

fold [fəʊld] I *n (crease)* pliegue *m*. II *vtr* plegar, doblar; to f. one's arms, cruzar los brazos. III *vi* to f. (up), *(chair etc)* plegarse; *Com* quebrar.

folder ['fəʊldər] *n* carpeta *f*.

folding ['fəʊldɪŋ] *adj (chair etc)* plegable.

foliage ['fəʊlɪɪdʒ] *n* follaje *m*.

folk [fəʊk] I *npl* 1 *(people)* gente *f*. 2 *fam* folks, *(family)* padres *mpl*; one's f., la familia. II *adj* popular; f. music, música *f* folk; f. song, canción *f* popular.

folklore ['fəʊklɔːr] *n* folclore *m*.

follow ['fɒləʊ] I *vtr* seguir; *(pursue)* perseguir; *(understand)* comprender; *(way of life)* llevar. II *vi* 1 *(come after)* seguir; as follows, como sigue. 2 *(result)* resultar; that doesn't f., eso no es lógico. 3 *(understand)* entender. ◆**follow through, follow up** *vtr (idea)* llevar a cabo; *(clue)* investigar.

follower ['fɒləʊər] *n* seguidor,-a *m,f*.

following ['fɒləʊɪŋ] I *adj* siguiente. II *n* seguidores *mpl*.

folly ['fɒlɪ] *n* locura *f*, desatino *m*.

fond [fɒnd] *adj (loving)* cariñoso,-a; to be f. of sb, tenerle mucho cariño a algn; to be f. of doing sth, ser aficionado,-a a hacer algo.

fondness ['fɒndnɪs] *n (love)* cariño *m* (for, a); *(liking)* afición *f* (for, a).

fondle ['fɒndəl] *vtr* acariciar.

font [fɒnt] *n Rel* pila *f*.

food [fuːd] *n* comida *f*; f. chain, cadena trófica; f. poisoning, intoxicación alimenticia.

foodstuffs ['fuːdstʌfs] *npl* productos alimenticios.

fool [fuːl] I *n* 1 tonto,-a *m,f*, imbécil *mf*; to make a f. of sb, poner a algn en ridículo; to play the f., hacer el tonto. 2 *Culin* ≈ mousse *f* de fruta. II *vtr (deceive)* engañar. III *vi (joke)* bromear; to f. about or around, hacer el tonto.

foolhardy ['fuːlhɑːdɪ] *adj* **(foolhardier, foolhardiest)** temerario,-a; *(person)* intrépido,-a.

foolish ['fuːlɪʃ] *adj* estúpido,-a.

foolproof ['fuːlpruːf] *adj* infalible.

foot [fʊt] I *n (pl feet* [fiːt]) pie *m*; *Zool* pata *f*; on f., a pie, andando; to find one's feet, acostumbrarse; *fam fig* to put one's f. down, *(control)* imponerse; *(in*

**car)* pisar a fondo; *fam fig* to put one's f. in it, meter la pata; *fam fig* to put one's feet up, descansar. II *vtr* to f. the bill, *(pay)* pagar la cuenta.

footage ['fʊtɪdʒ] *n Cin* metraje *m*.

football ['fʊtbɔːl] *n* 1 *(soccer)* fútbol *m*; bar f., futbolín *m*; f. ground, campo *m* de fútbol; f. match, partido *m* de fútbol; f. pools, quinielas *fpl*. 2 *(ball)* balón *m*.

footballer ['fʊtbɔːlər] *n* futbolista *mf*.

footbridge ['fʊtbrɪdʒ] *n* puente *m* para peatones.

foothills ['fʊthɪlz] *npl* estribaciones *fpl*.

foothold ['fʊthəʊld] *n fig* to gain a f., afianzarse en una posición.

footing ['fʊtɪŋ] *n* to lose one's f., perder el equilibrio; on a friendly f., en plan amistoso; on an equal f., en pie de igualdad.

footlights ['fʊtlaɪts] *npl* candilejas *fpl*.

footman ['fʊtmən] *n* lacayo *m*.

footnote ['fʊtnəʊt] *n* nota *f* a pie de página.

footpath ['fʊtpɑːθ] *n (track)* sendero *m*.

footprint ['fʊtprɪnt] *n* pisada *f*.

footsore ['fʊtsɔːr] *adj* con los pies doloridos.

footstep ['fʊtstep] *n* paso *m*.

footwear ['fʊtweər] *n* calzado *m*.

for [fɔːr] I *prep* 1 *(intended)* para; curtains f. the bedroom, cortinas para el dormitorio; f. sale, en venta; it's time f. bed, es hora de acostarse. 2 *(representing)* por; a cheque f. ten pounds, un cheque de diez libras; J f. John, J de Juan; what's the Spanish f. 'rivet'?, ¿cómo se dice 'rivet' en español? 3 *(purpose)* para; it's good f. the digestion, es bueno para la digestión; what's this f.?, ¿para qué sirve esto? 4 *(because of)* por; famous f. its cuisine, famoso,-a por su cocina; to jump f. joy, saltar de alegría. 5 *(on behalf of)* por; the campaign f. peace, la campaña por la paz; will you do it f. me?, ¿lo harás por mí? 6 *(during)* por, durante; I lent it to her f. a year, se lo presté por un año; I shall stay f. two weeks, me quedaré dos semanas; I was ill f. a month, estuve enfermo,-a durante un mes; I've been here f. three months, hace tres meses que estoy aquí. 7 *(distance)* por; I walked f. ten kilometres, caminé diez kilómetros. 8 *(at a point in time)* para; I can do it f. next Monday, puedo hacerlo para el lunes que viene; f. the last time, por última vez. 9 *(destination)* para. 10 *(amount of money)* por; I got the car f. five hundred pounds, conseguí el coche por quinientas libras. 11 *(in favour of)* a favor de; are you f. or against?, ¿estás a favor o en contra?; to vote f. sb, votar a algn. 12 *(to obtain)* para; to run f. the bus, correr para coger el autobús; to send sb f. water, mandar a algn a por agua. 13

(with respect to) en cuanto a; **as f. him,** en cuanto a él; **f. all I care,** por mí; **f. all I know,** que yo sepa; **f. one thing,** para empezar. **14** *(despite)* a pesar de; **f. all that,** aún así; **he's tall f. his age,** está muy alto para su edad. **15** *(instead of)* por; **can you go f. me?,** puede ir por mí? **16** *(towards)* hacia, por; **affection f. sb,** cariño hacia algn; **his love f. you,** su amor por ti. **17** *(as)* por; **to leave sb f. dead,** dar a algn por muerto,-a; **what do you use f. fuel?,** ¿qué utilizan como combustible? **18** *(in exchange)* por; **to exchange one thing f. another,** cambiar una cosa por otra; **how much did you sell it f.?,** ¿por cuánto lo vendiste? **19** (+ *object* + *infin*) **there's no reason f. us to quarrel,** no hay motivo para que riñamos; **it's time f. you to go,** es hora de que os marchéis; **it's easy f. him to say that,** le es fácil decir eso.
  II *conj (since, as)* ya que, puesto que.

forage ['fɒrɪdʒ] **I** *n* forraje *m*. **II** *vi* hurgar.

foray ['fɒreɪ] *n* incursión *f*.

forbearance [fɔː'beərəns] *n* paciencia *f*.

forbid [fə'bɪd] *vtr (pt* **forbade,** *pp* **forbidden** [fə'bɪdən]*)* prohibir; **to f. sb to do sth,** prohibir a algn hacer algo.

forbidding [fə'bɪdɪŋ] *adj (stern)* severo,-a; *(bleak)* inhóspito,-a.

force [fɔːs] **I** *n* **1** fuerza *f*; **by f.,** por la fuerza; **to come into f.,** entrar en vigor. **2** *Mil* cuerpo *m*; **the (armed) forces,** las fuerzas armadas; **the police f.,** la policía. **II** *vtr* forzar; **to f. sb to do sth,** forzar a algn a hacer algo.

forced [fɔːst] *adj* forzado,-a; **f. landing,** aterrizaje forzoso.

force-feed ['fɔːsfiːd] *vtr* alimentar a la fuerza.

forceful ['fɔːsfʊl] *adj* **1** *(person)* enérgico, -a. **2** *(argument)* convincente.

forcible ['fɔːsəbəl] *adj* **1** **f. entry,** allanamiento *m* de morada. ◆**forcibly** *adv* a or por la fuerza.

forceps ['fɔːseps] *npl* fórceps *m sing.*

ford [fɔːd] **I** *n* vado *m*. **II** *vtr* vadear.

fore [fɔː] *fig* **to come to the f.,** empezar a destacar.

forearm ['fɔːrɑːm] *n* antebrazo *m*.

foreboding [fɔː'bəʊdɪŋ] *n* presentimiento *m*.

forecast ['fɔːkɑːst] **I** *n* pronóstico *m*. **II** *vtr (pt & pp* **forecast** *or* **forecasted)** pronosticar.

forecourt ['fɔːkɔːt] *n (of garage)* área *f* de servicio.

forefathers ['fɔːfɑːðəz] *npl* antepasados *mpl.*

forefinger ['fɔːfɪŋgər] *n* índice *m.*

forefront ['fɔːfrʌnt] *n* **in the f.,** a la vanguardia.

forego [fɔː'gəʊ] *vtr fml (pt* **forewent;** *pp* **foregone)** sacrificar.

foregone ['fɔːgɒn] *adj* **a f. conclusion,** un resultado inevitable.

foreground ['fɔːgraʊnd] *n* primer plano *m.*

forehead ['fɒrɪd, 'fɔːhed] *n* frente *f.*

foreign ['fɒrɪn] *adj* extranjero,-a; *(trade, policy)* exterior; **f. exchange,** divisas *fpl;* **the F. Office,** el Ministerio de Asuntos Exteriores; **f. body,** cuerpo extraño.

foreigner ['fɒrɪnər] *n* extranjero,-a *m,f.*

foreman ['fɔːmən] *n* **1** *Ind* capataz *m.* **2** *Jur* presidente *m* del jurado.

foremost ['fɔːməʊst] *adj* principal; **first and f.,** ante todo.

forename ['fɔːneɪm] *n* nombre *m* de pila.

forensic [fə'rensɪk] *adj* forense.

forerunner ['fɔːrʌnər] *n* precursor,-a *m,f.*

foresee [fɔː'siː] *vtr (pt* **foresaw** *pp* **foreseen)** prever.

foreseeable [fɔː'siːəbəl] *adj* previsible; **in the f. future,** en un futuro próximo.

foreshadow [fɔː'ʃædəʊ] *vtr* presagiar.

foresight ['fɔːsaɪt] *n* previsión *f.*

forest ['fɒrɪst] *n* bosque *m.*

forestall [fɔː'stɔːl] *vtr (plan)* anticiparse a; *(danger)* prevenir.

forestry ['fɒrɪstrɪ] *n* silvicultura *f.*

foretaste ['fɔːteɪst] *n* anticipo *m* (**of,** de).

foretell [fɔː'tel] *vtr (pt & pp* **foretold)** presagiar.

forever [fə'revər] *adv* **1** *(eternally)* siempre. **2** *(for good)* para siempre. **3** *fam (ages)* siglos *mpl.*

foreword ['fɔːwɜːd] *n* prefacio *m.*

forfeit ['fɔːfɪt] **I** *n (penalty)* pena *f;* *(in games)* prenda *f.* **II** *vtr* perder.

forgave [fə'geɪv] *pt* → **forgive.**

forge [fɔːdʒ] **I** *n* **1** *(furnace)* fragua *f.* **2** *(blacksmith's)* herrería *f.* **II** *vtr* **1** *(counterfeit)* falsificar. **2** *(metal)* forjar. **III** *vi* **to f. ahead,** hacer grandes progresos.

forger ['fɔːdʒər] *n* falsificador,-a *m,f.*

forgery ['fɔːdʒərɪ] *n* falsificación *f.*

forget [fə'get] **I** *vtr (pt* **forgot;** *pp* **forgotten)** olvidar, olvidarse de; **I forgot to close the window,** se me olvidó cerrar or me olvidé de cerrar la ventana; **I've forgotten my key,** he olvidado la llave. **II** *vi* olvidarse.

forgetful [fə'getfʊl] *adj* olvidadizo,-a.

forget-me-not [fə'getmɪnɒt] *n* nomeolvides *f inv.*

forgive [fə'gɪv] *vtr (pt* **forgave** *pp* **forgiven** [fə'gɪvən]*)* perdonar; **to f. sb for sth,** perdonar algo a algn.

forgiveness [fə'gɪvnəs] *n* perdón *m.*

forgo [fɔː'gəʊ] *vtr* → **forego.**

forgot [fə'gɒt] *pt,* **forgotten** [fə'gɒtən] *pp* → **forget.**

fork [fɔːk] **I** *n* **1** *Agr* horca *f.* **2** *(cutlery)* tenedor *m.* **3** *(in road)* bifurcación *f.* **II** *vi (roads)* bifurcarse. ◆**fork out** *vtr fam (money)* soltar.

fork-lift truck [fɔːklɪft'trʌk] *n* carretilla *f*

elevadora de horquilla.

forlorn [fə'lɔːn] *adj (forsaken)* abandonado,-a; *(desolate)* triste; *(without hope)* desesperado,-a.

form [fɔːm] I *n* 1 *(shape)* forma *f* 2 *(type)* clase *f.* 3 **for f.'s sake,** para guardar las formas. 4 *(document)* formulario *m.* 5 **on/on top/off f.,** en/en plena/en baja forma. 6 *Educ* clase *f;* **the first f.,** el primer curso. II *vtr* formar; **to f. an impression,** formarse una impresión. III *vi* formarse.

formal ['fɔːməl] *adj* 1 *(official)* oficial; **a f. application,** una solicitud en forma. 2 *(party, dress)* de etiqueta. 3 *(ordered)* formal. 4 *(person)* formalista. ◆**formally** *adv* oficialmente.

formality [fɔː'mælɪtɪ] *n* formalidad *f.*

format ['fɔːmæt] I *n* formato *m.* II *vtr Comput* formatear.

formation [fɔː'meɪʃən] *n* formación *f.*

formative ['fɔːmətɪv] *adj* formativo,-a.

former ['fɔːmər] *adj* 1 *(time)* anterior. 2 *(one-time)* antiguo,-a; *(person)* ex; **the f. champion,** el excampeón. 3 *(first)* aquél, aquélla; **Peter and Lisa came, the f. wearing a hat,** vinieron Peter y Lisa, aquél llevaba sombrero. ◆**formerly** *adv* antiguamente.

formidable ['fɔːmɪdəbəl] *adj (prodigious)* formidable; *(daunting)* terrible.

formula ['fɔːmjʊlə] *n* fórmula *f.*

forsake [fə'seɪk] *vtr (pt **forsook** [fə'sʊk] pp **forsaken** [fə'seɪkən]) Lit* 1 *(abandon, desert)* abandonar. 2 *(give up)* renunciar a.

fort [fɔːt] *n* fortaleza *f.*

forte ['fɔːteɪ] *n* fuerte *m.*

forth [fɔːθ] *adv fml* **and so f.,** y así sucesivamente; **to go back and f.,** ir de acá para allá.

forthcoming [fɔːθ'kʌmɪŋ] *adj* 1 *(event)* próximo,-a. 2 **no money was f.,** no hubo oferta de dinero. 3 *(communicative)* comunicativo,-a.

forthright ['fɔːθraɪt] *adj* franco,-a.

fortify ['fɔːtɪfaɪ] *vtr* fortificar.

fortitude ['fɔːtɪtjuːd] *n* fortaleza *f,* fuerza *f.*

fortnight ['fɔːtnaɪt] *n GB* quincena *f.*

fortnightly ['fɔːtnaɪtlɪ] *GB* I *adj* quincenal. II *adv* cada quince días.

fortress ['fɔːtrɪs] *n* fortaleza *f.*

fortunate ['fɔːtʃənɪt] *adj* afortunado,-a; **it was f. that he came,** fue una suerte que viniera. ◆**fortunately** *adv* afortunadamente.

fortune ['fɔːtʃuːn] *n* 1 *(luck, fate)* suerte *f;* **to tell sb's f.,** echar la buenaventura a algn. 2 *(money)* fortuna *f.*

fortune-teller ['fɔːtʃəntelər] *n* adivino,-a *m,f.*

forty ['fɔːtɪ] *adj & n* cuarenta *(m) inv.*

forum ['fɔːrəm] *n* foro *m.*

forward ['fɔːwəd] I *adv* 1 *(also **forwards**) (direction and movement)* hacia adelante. 2

fig **to come f.,** ofrecerse. 3 **from this day f.,** de ahora en adelante. II *adj* 1 *(movement)* hacia adelante; *(position)* delantero,-a. 2 *(person)* fresco,-a. III *n Sport* delantero,-a *m,f.* IV *vtr* 1 *(send on)* remitir. 2 *fml (send goods)* expedir. 3 *fml (further)* fomentar.

forwent [fɔː'went] *pt →* **forego.**

fossil ['fɒsɪl] *n* fósil *m;* **f. fuel,** combustible *m* fósil.

foster ['fɒstər] I *vtr* 1 *(child)* criar. 2 *fml (hopes)* abrigar; *(relations)* fomentar. II *adj* **f. child,** hijo,-a adoptivo,-a; **f. father** padre adoptivo; **f. mother,** madre adoptiva; **f. parents,** padres adoptivos.

fought [fɔːt] *pt & pp →* **fight.**

foul [faʊl] I *adj* 1 *(smell)* fétido,-a; *(taste)* asqueroso,-a. 2 *(deed)* atroz; *(weather)* de perros. 3 *(language)* grosero,-a. **4** to **fall f. of,** tener problemas con; *Sport* **f. play,** juego sucio; *Jur* **f. play is suspected,** se sospecha que se haya cometido un acto criminal. II *n Sport* falta *f.* III *vtr* 1 *(dirty)* ensuciar; *(air)* contaminar. 2 *Sport* cometer una falta contra.

found¹ [faʊnd] *pt & pp →* **find.**

found² [faʊnd] *vtr (establish)* fundar.

foundation [faʊn'deɪʃən] *n* 1 *(establishment)* fundación *f.* 2 *(basis)* fundamento *m.* 3 **f.** *(cream),* maquillaje *m* de fondo. 2 *Constr* **foundations,** cimientos *mpl.*

founder¹ ['faʊndər] *n* fundador,-a *m,f.*

founder² ['faʊndər] *vi fml (sink)* hundirse. 2 *fig (plan, hopes)* fracasar.

foundry ['faʊndrɪ] *n* fundición *f.*

fountain ['faʊntɪn] *n (structure)* fuente *f;* *(jet)* surtidor *m;* **f. pen,** pluma estilográfica.

four [fɔː] *adj & n* cuatro *(m) inv;* **on all fours,** a gatas.

four-door ['fɔːdɔː] *adj Aut* de cuatro puertas.

four-poster [fɔː'pəʊstər] *n* **f.-p.** *(bed),* cama *f* con dosel.

foursome ['fɔːsəm] *n* grupo *m* de cuatro personas.

fourteen [fɔː'tiːn] *adj & n* catorce *(m) inv.*

fourteenth [fɔː'tiːnθ] I *adj & n* decimocuarto,-a *(m,f).* II *n (fraction)* catorceavo *m.*

fourth [fɔːθ] I *adj & n* cuarto,-a *(m,f).* II *n* 1 *(fraction)* cuarto *m.* 2 *Aut* cuarta *f (velocidad).*

fowl [faʊl] *n* aves *fpl* de corral.

fox [fɒks] I *n* zorro,-a *m,f.* II *vtr* 1 *(perplex)* dejar perplejo,-a. 2 *(deceive)* engañar.

foyer ['fɔɪeɪ, 'fɔɪə] *n* vestíbulo *m.*

fracas ['fræka:] *n* gresca *f,* reyerta *f.*

fraction ['frækʃən] *n* fracción *f.*

fracture ['fræktʃər] I *n* fractura *f.* II *vtr* fracturar.

fragile ['frædʒaɪl] *adj* frágil.

fragment ['frægmənt] n fragmento m.

fragrance ['freigrəns] n fragancia f, perfume m.

fragrant ['freigrənt] adj fragante, aromático,-a.

frail [freil] adj frágil, delicado,-a.

frame [freim] I n 1 (of window, door, picture) marco m; (of machine) armazón m; (of bicycle) cuadro m; (of spectacles) montura f; fig f. of mind, estado m de ánimo. 2 Cin TV fotograma m. II vtr 1 (picture) enmarcar. 2 (question) formular. 3 fam (innocent person) incriminar.

framework ['freimwɜ:k] n fig within the f. of ..., dentro del marco de ...

franc [fræŋk] n franco m.

France [frɑːns] n Francia f.

franchise ['fræntʃaiz] n 1 Pol derecho m al voto. 2 Com concesión f, licencia f.

frank [fræŋk] I adj franco,-a. II vtr (mail) franquear. ◆**frankly** adv francamente.

frankness ['fræŋknis] n franqueza f.

frantic ['fræntik] adj (anxious) desesperado,-a; (hectic) frenético,-a.

fraternal [frə'tɜːnəl] adj fraterno,-a.

fraternity [frə'tɜːniti] n (society) asociación f; Rel cofradía f; US Univ club m de estudiantes.

fraud [frɔːd] n 1 fraude m. 2 (person) impostor,-a m,f.

fraught [frɔːt] adj 1 (full) cargado,-a (with, de). 2 (tense) nervioso,-a.

fray¹ [frei] vi 1 (cloth) deshilacharse. 2 (nerves) crisparse; his temper frequently frayed, se irritaba a menudo.

fray² [frei] n combate m.

freak [friːk] I n 1 (monster) monstruo m. 2 fam (eccentric) estrafalario,-a m,f. 3 fam (fan) fanático,-a m,f. II adj 1 (unexpected) inesperado,-a. 2 (unusual) insólito,-a.

freckle ['frekəl] n peca f.

free [friː] I adj 1 libre; to set sb f., poner en libertad a algn; f. kick, tiro m libre; f. speech, libertad f de expresión; f. will, libre albedrío m; f. trade, libre cambio m; f. time, tiempo m libre. 2 f. (of charge), (gratis) gratuito,-a; f. gift, obsequio m. 3 (generous) generoso,-a. II adv 1 (for) f., gratis. 2 (loose) suelto,-a. III vtr 1 (liberate) poner en libertad a. 2 (loose) soltar. 3 (untie) desatar. 4 (exempt) eximir (from, de). ◆**freely** adv 1 libremente. 2 (openly) abiertamente.

freedom ['friːdəm] n 1 (liberty) libertad f; f. of the press, libertad de prensa. 2 (exemption) exención f.

free-for-all ['friːfərɔːl] n pelea f.

freehold ['friːhəuld] adj en propiedad absoluta.

freelance ['friːlɑːns] adj independiente.

freemason ['friːmeisən] n francmasón, -ona m,f.

free-range ['friːreindʒ] adj GB de granja.

free-style ['friːstail] n Swimming estilo m

libre.

freeway ['friːwei] n US autopista f.

freewheel [friː'wiːl] vi ir en punto muerto.

freeze [friːz] I vtr (pt froze; pp frozen) congelar. II n Meteor helada f; price f., congelación f de precios; TV Cin f. frame, imagen congelada. III vi (liquid) helarse; (food) congelarse.

freeze-dried ['friːzdraid] adj liofilizado,-a.

freezer ['friːzər] n congelador m.

freezing ['friːziŋ] adj 1 glacial. 2 f. point, punto m de congelación; above/below f. point, sobre/bajo cero.

freight [freit] n 1 (transport) transporte m. 2 (goods, price) flete m; f. train, tren m de mercancías.

French [frentʃ] I adj francés,-esa; F. bean, judía f verde; F. dressing, vinagreta f; US F. fries, patatas fpl fritas; F. window, puerta f vidriera. II n 1 (language) francés m. 2 pl the F., los franceses.

Frenchman ['frentʃmən] n francés m.

Frenchwoman ['frentʃwumən] n francesa f.

frenetic [fri'netik] adj frenético,-a.

frenzy ['frenzi] n frenesí m.

frequency ['friːkwənsi] n frecuencia f.

frequent [adj 'friːkwənt] I adj frecuente. II [fri'kwent] vtr frecuentar. ◆**frequently** adv frecuentemente, a menudo.

fresh [freʃ] adj 1 fresco,-a; f. water, agua f dulce; f. bread, pan del día. 2 (new) nuevo,-a; open a f. packet, abre otro paquete. 3 (air) puro,-a; in the f. air, al aire libre. ◆**freshly** adv recién, recientemente.

freshen ['freʃən] vi (wind) refrescar. ◆**freshen up** vi asearse.

fresher ['freʃər], **freshman** ['freʃmən] n Univ estudiante mf de primer año, novato,-a m,f.

freshness ['freʃnis] n frescura f.

freshwater ['freʃwɔːtər] adj de agua dulce.

fret [fret] vi preocuparse (about, por).

FRG [efɑː'dʒiː] n Hist abbr of Federal Republic of Germany, República Federal de Alemania, RFA.

friar ['fraiər] n fraile m.

friction ['frikʃən] n fricción f.

Friday ['fraidi] n viernes m.

fridge [fridʒ] n fam nevera f, frigorífico m.

friend [frend] n amigo,-a m,f; a f. of mine, un,-a amigo,-a mío,-a; to make friends with sb, hacerse amigo,-a de algn; to make friends again, hacer las paces.

friendliness ['frendlinis] n amabilidad f, simpatía f.

friendly ['frendli] adj (friendlier, friendliest) (person) simpático,-a; (at-

mosphere) acogedor,-a; f. **advice**, consejo *m* de amigo; f. **nation**, nación amiga.

friendship ['frendʃɪp] *n* amistad *f*.

frieze [friːz] *n* friso *m*.

frigate ['frɪgɪt] *n* fragata *f*.

fright [fraɪt] *n* 1 (*fear*) miedo *m*; **to take f.**, asustarse. 2 (*shock*) susto *m*; **to get a f.**, pegarse un susto.

frighten ['fraɪtən] *vtr* asustar. ◆**frighten away**, **frighten off** *vtr* ahuyentar.

frightened ['fraɪtənd] *adj* asustado,-a; **to be f. of sb**, tenerle miedo a algn.

frightening ['fraɪtənɪŋ] *adj* espantoso,-a.

frightful ['fraɪtful] *adj* espantoso,-a, horroroso,-a. ◆**frightfully** *adv* tremendamente, terriblemente.

frigid ['frɪdʒɪd] *adj* frígido,-a.

frill [frɪl] *n* (*on dress*) volante *m*; *fig* **frills**, (*decorations*) adornos *mpl*.

fringe [frɪndʒ] *n* 1 (*of hair*) flequillo *m*. 2 (*edge*) borde *m*; *fig* **on the f. of society**, al margen de la sociedad; **f. theatre**, teatro *m* experimental; **f. benefits**, extras *mpl*.

Frisbee® ['frɪzbɪ] *n* platillo *m*.

frisk [frɪsk] *vtr* *fam* (*search*) registrar.

frisky ['frɪskɪ] *adj* (**friskier, friskiest**) 1 (*children, animals*) juguetón,-a. 2 (*adult*) vivo,-a.

fritter ['frɪtəʳ] *n* buñuelo *m*. ◆**fritter away** *vtr* malgastar.

frivolous ['frɪvələs] *adj* frívolo,-a.

frizzy ['frɪzɪ] *adj* (**frizzier, frizziest**) crespo,-a.

frock [frɒk] *n* vestido *m*; **f. coat**, levita *f*.

frog [frɒg] *n* rana *f*; **frogs' legs**, ancas *fpl* de rana; *fig* **to have a f. in one's throat**, tener carraspera.

frogman ['frɒgmən] *n* hombre *m* rana.

frolic ['frɒlɪk] *vi* retozar, juguetear.

from [frɒm, *unstressed* frəm] *prep* 1 (*time*) desde, a partir de; **f. now on**, a partir de ahora; **f. Monday to Friday**, de lunes a viernes; **f. the eighth to the seventeenth**, desde el ocho hasta el diecisiete; **f. time to time**, de vez en cuando. 2 (*price, number*) desde, de; **dresses f. five pounds**, vestidos desde cinco libras; **a number f. one to ten**, un número del uno a diez. 3 (*origin*) de; **a letter f. her father**, una carta de su padre; **f. English into Spanish**, del inglés al español; **he's f. Malaga**, es de Málaga; **the train f. Bilbao**, el tren procedente de Bilbao; **to go f. door to door**, ir de puerta en puerta; **her eyes were red f. crying**, tenía los ojos rojos de llorar. 4 (*distance*) de; **the town is four miles f. the coast**, el pueblo está a cuatro millas de la costa. 5 (*out of*) de; **bread is made f. flour**, el pan se hace con harina. 6 (*remove, subtract*) a; **he took the book f. the child**, le quitó el libro al niño; **take three f. five**, restar tres a cinco. 7 (*according to*) según,

por; **f. what the author said**, según lo que dijo el autor; **speaking f. my own experience**, hablando por experiencia propia. 8 (*position*) desde, de; **f. here**, desde aquí. 9 **can you tell margarine f. butter?**, ¿puedes distinguir entre la margarina y la mantequilla?

front [frʌnt] **I** *n* 1 parte delantera; **in f.** (**of**), delante (de). 2 (*of building*) fachada *f*. 3 *Mil Pol Meteor* frente *m*. 4 (*seaside*) paseo marítimo. 5 *fig* **she put on a brave f.**, hizo de tripas corazón. **II** *adj* delantero,-a, de delante; **f. bench**, primera fila de escaños donde se sientan los ministros del Gobierno o de la Oposición; **f. door**, puerta *f* principal; **f. room**, salón *m*; **f. seat**, asiento *m* de delante.

frontier ['frʌntɪəʳ] *n* frontera *f*.

front-page ['frʌntpeɪdʒ] *adj* de primera página.

frost [frɒst] **I** *n* 1 (*covering*) escarcha *f*. 2 (*freezing*) helada *f*. **II** *vt* *US Culin* recubrir con azúcar glas. ◆**frost over** *vi* escarchar.

frostbite ['frɒstbaɪt] *n* congelación *f*.

frosted ['frɒstɪd] *adj* 1 (*glass*) esmerilado,-a. 2 *US Culin* recubierto,-a de azúcar glas.

frosty ['frɒstɪ] *adj* (**frostier, frostiest**) 1 **it will be a f. night tonight**, esta noche habrá helada. 2 *fig* glacial.

froth [frɒθ] **I** *n* espuma *f*; (*from mouth*) espumarajos *mpl*. **II** *vi* espumar.

frothy ['frɒθɪ] *adj* (**frothier, frothiest**) espumoso,-a.

frown [fraʊn] *vi* fruncir el ceño. ◆**frown upon** *vtr* desaprobar.

froze [frəʊz] *pt* → **freeze**.

frozen ['frəʊzən] *adj* (*liquid, feet etc*) helado,-a; (*food*) congelado,-a.

frugal ['fruːgəl] *adj* frugal.

fruit [fruːt] *n* 1 *Bot* fruto *m*. 2 (*apple, orange etc*) fruta *f*; **f. cake**, pastel *m* con fruto seco; **f. machine**, máquina *f* tragaperras; **f. salad**, macedonia *f* de frutas. 3 **fruits**, (*rewards*) frutos *mpl*.

fruitful ['fruːtful] *adj* *fig* provechoso,-a.

fruition [fruːˈɪʃən] *n* *fml* **to come to f.**, realizarse.

frustrate [frʌˈstreɪt] *vtr* frustrar.

frustrated [frʌˈstreɪtɪd] *adj* frustrado,-a.

frustration [frʌˈstreɪʃən] *n* frustración *f*.

fry¹ [fraɪ] **I** *vtr* (*pt & pp* fried) freír. **II** *vi* *fig* asarse.

fry² [fraɪ] *npl* **small f.**, gente *f* de poca monta.

frying pan ['fraɪɪŋpæn], *US* **fry-pan** ['fraɪpæn] *n* sartén *f*.

ft *abbr of* **foot**, pie *m*; *abbr of* **feet**, pies *mpl*.

fuck [fʌk] *vulg offens* *vtr & vi* joder; **f.** (**it**)!, ¡joder! ◆**fuck off** *vi* f. off!, ¡vete a la mierda! ◆**fuck up** *vtr* joder.

fucking ['fʌkɪŋ] *vulg* **I** *adj* f. idiot!, ¡gilipollas!; **where are my f. keys?**, ¿dónde coño están las llaves? II *adv* a **f. good film**, una película de puta madre.

fuddy-duddy ['fʌdɪdʌdɪ] *n* persona chapada a la antigua.

fudge [fʌdʒ] I *n Culin* dulce *m* hecho con azúcar, leche y mantequilla. II *vtr* (*figures*) amañar.

fuel ['fjʊəl] I *n* 1 combustible *m*; (*for engines*) carburante *m*; **f. tank**, depósito *m* de combustible. II *vtr fig* (*ambition*) estimular; (*difficult situation*) empeorar.

fugitive ['fjuːdʒɪtɪv] *n fml* fugitivo,-a *m,f*.

fulfil, US fulfill [fʊl'fɪl] *vtr* 1 (*task, ambition*) realizar; (*promise*) cumplir; (*role*) desempeñar. 2 (*wishes*) satisfacer.

fulfilment, US fulfillment [fʊl'fɪlmənt] *n* 1 (*of ambition*) realización *f*. 2 (*of duty, promise*) cumplimiento *m*.

full [fʊl] I *adj* 1 lleno,-a; **f. of**, lleno,-a de; **I'm f. (up)**, no puedo más. 2 (*complete*) completo,-a; **at f. speed**, a toda velocidad; **f. text**, texto íntegro; *fam* **in f. swing**, en plena marcha; **f. board**, pensión completa; **f. employment**, pleno empleo *m*; **f. house**, lleno total; **f. moon**, luna llena; **f. stop**, punto *m*. II *n* **in f.**, en su totalidad; **name in f.**, nombre *m* y apellidos completos. III *adv* **f. well**, perfectamente. ◆**fully** *adv* completamente.

full-blown ['fʊlbləʊn] *adj* auténtico,-a.

fullness ['fʊlnɪs] *n* **in the f. of time**, con el tiempo.

full-scale [fʊlskeɪl] *adj* 1 (*model*) de tamaño natural. 2 **f.-s. search**, registro *m* a fondo; **f.-s. war**, guerra generalizada *or* total.

full-time [fʊltaɪm] I *adj* de jornada completa. II *adv* **to work f. t.**, trabajar a tiempo completo.

fully-fledged [fʊlɪfledʒd] *adj* hecho,-a y derecho,-a.

fulsome ['fʊlsəm] *adj* excesivo,-a, exagerado,-a.

fumble ['fʌmbəl] *vi* hurgar; **to f. for sth**, buscar algo a tientas; **to f. with sth**, manejar algo con torpeza.

fume [fjuːm] I *n* (*usu pl*) humo *m*. II *vi* echar humo.

fun [fʌn] I *n* (*amusement*) diversión *f*; **in** *or* **for f.**, en broma; **to have f.**, divertirse, pasarlo bien; **to make f. of sb**, reírse de algn. II *adj* divertido,-a.

function ['fʌŋkʃən] I *n* 1 función *f*. 2 (*ceremony*) acto *m*; (*party*) recepción *f*. II *vi* funcionar.

functional ['fʌŋkʃənəl] *adj* funcional.

fund [fʌnd] I *n* 1 *Com* fondo *m*. 2 **funds**, fondos *mpl*. II *vtr* (*finance*) patrocinar.

fundamental [fʌndə'mentəl] I *adj* fundamental. II *npl* **fundamentals**, los fundamentos *m*.

funeral ['fjuːnərəl] *n* funeral *m*; **f. march**, marcha *f* fúnebre; *US* **f. parlor**, funeraria

f; **f. service**, misa *f* de cuerpo presente.

funfair ['fʌnfeə^r] *n GB* parque *m* de atracciones.

fungus ['fʌŋɡəs] *n* (*pl* **fungi** ['fʌŋɡaɪ]) 1 *Bot* hongo *m*. 2 *Med* fungo *m*.

funnel ['fʌnəl] I *n* 1 (*for liquids*) embudo *m*. 2 *Naut* chimenea *f*. II *vtr fig* (*funds, energy*) encauzar.

funny ['fʌnɪ] *adj* (**funnier, funniest**) 1 (*peculiar*) raro,-a, extraño,-a; **that's f.!**, ¡qué raro! 2 (*amusing*) divertido,-a, gracioso,-a; **I found it very f.**, me hizo mucha gracia. 3 *fam* (*ill*) mal. 4 *fam* (*dishonest*) dudoso,-a. ◆**funnily** *adv fam* **f. enough**, aunque parezca extraño.

fur [fɜː^r] I *n* 1 (*of living animal*) pelo *m*. 2 (*of dead animal*) piel *f*. 3 (*in kettle, on tongue*) sarro *m*. II *adj* de piel; **f. coat**, abrigo *m* de pieles.

furious ['fjʊərɪəs] *adj* 1 (*angry*) furioso,-a. 2 (*vigorous*) violento,-a.

furlong ['fɜːlɒŋ] *n* (*measurement*) = aprox 201 metros.

furnace ['fɜːnɪs] *n* horno *m*.

furnish ['fɜːnɪʃ] *vtr* 1 (*house*) amueblar. 2 *fml* (*food*) suministrar; (*details*) facilitar.

furnishings ['fɜːnɪʃɪŋz] *npl* muebles *mpl*. 2 (*fittings*) accesorios *mpl*.

furniture ['fɜːnɪtʃə^r] *n* muebles *mpl*; **a piece of f.**, un mueble.

furrow ['fʌrəʊ] *n Agr* surco *m*; (*on forehead*) arruga *f*.

furry ['fɜːrɪ] *adj* (**furrier, furriest**) 1 (*hairy*) peludo,-a. 2 (*tongue, kettle*) sarroso,-a.

further ['fɜːðə^r] I *adj* → **far**. 1 (*new*) nuevo,-a; **until f. notice**, hasta nuevo aviso. 2 (*additional*) otro,-a, adicional. 3 (*later*) posterior; **f. education**, estudios *mpl* superiores. II *adv* 1 (*more*) más; **f. back**, más atrás; **f. along**, más adelante; **she heard nothing f.**, no volvió a saber nada más. 2 *fml* **f. to your letter of the 9th**, con referencia a su carta del 9 del corriente. 3 *fml* (*besides*) además. II *vtr* fomentar.

furthermore ['fɜːðəmɔː^r] *adv fml* además.

furthest ['fɜːðɪst] *adj* → **far**; más lejano,-a.

furtive ['fɜːtɪv] *adj* furtivo,-a.

fury ['fjʊərɪ] *n* furia *f*, furor *m*.

fuse [fjuːz] I *n* 1 *Elec* fusible *m*; **f. box**, caja *f* de fusibles. 2 (*of bomb*) mecha *f*. II *vi* 1 *Elec* **the lights fused**, se fundieron los plomos. 2 *fig* (*merge*) fusionarse. II *vtr* 1 *Elec* fundir; **to f. the lights**, fundir los plomos de. 2 *fig* (*merge*) fusionar. 3 (*melt*) fundir.

fuselage ['fjuːzɪlɑːʒ] *n* fuselaje *m*.

fuss [fʌs] I *n* (*commotion*) jaleo *m*; **to kick up a f.**, armar un escándalo; **stop making a f.**, (*complaining*) deja de quejarte; **to make a f. of**, (*pay attention to*) mimar a. II *vi* preocuparse (**about**, por).

fussy ['fʌsɪ] *adj* (*fussier, fussiest*) exigente; (*nitpicking*) quisquilloso,-a.

futile ['fjuːtaɪl] *adj* inútil, vano,-a.

futility [fjuːˈtɪlɪtɪ] *n* inutilidad *f*.

future ['fjuːtʃər] I *n* futuro *m*, porvenir *m*; in the near f., en un futuro próximo; in f., de aquí en adelante. II *adj* futuro,-a.

futuristic [fjuːtʃəˈrɪstɪk] *adj* futurista.

fuzzy ['fʌzɪ] *adj* (*fuzzier, fuzziest*) 1 (*hair*) muy rizado,-a. 2 (*blurred*) borroso,-a.

G

G, g [dʒiː] *n* 1 (*the letter*) G, g *f*. 2 *Mus* G, sol *m*.

g [dʒiː] *abbr of* gram(s), gramme(s), g.

gabble ['gæbəl] I *n* chapurreo *m*. II *vi* hablar atropelladamente.

gable ['geɪbəl] *n* aguilón *m*.

gadget ['gædʒɪt] *n* artilugio *m*, aparato *m*.

Gaelic ['geɪlɪk] I *adj* gaélico,-a. II *n* (*language*) gaélico *m*.

gaffe [gæf] *n* metedura *f* de pata, plancha *f*; to make a g., meter la pata, patinar.

gag [gæg] I *n* 1 mordaza *f*. 2 *fam* (*joke*) chiste *m*. II *vtr* amordazar.

gage [geɪdʒ] *n* & *vtr US* → gauge.

gaiety ['geɪətɪ] *n* regocijo *m*.

gaily ['geɪlɪ] *adv* alegremente.

gain [geɪn] I *n* ganancia *f*, beneficio *m*; (*increase*) aumento *m*. II *vtr* ganar; *fig* to g. ground, ganar terreno; to g. speed, ganar velocidad, acelerar; to g. weight, aumentar de peso.

gait [geɪt] *n* (*manera f de*) andar *m*.

gal (*pl gal or* gals) *abbr of* gallon *m*.

gala ['gɑːlə, 'geɪlə] *n* gala *f*, fiesta *f*.

galaxy ['gæləksɪ] *n* galaxia *f*.

gale [geɪl] *n* vendaval *m*.

Galicia [gəˈlɪʃə] *n* Galicia.

Galician [gəˈlɪʃɪən, gəˈlɪʃən] I *adj* gallego,-a. II *n* 1 (*person*) gallego,-a *m,f*. 2 (*language*) gallego *m*.

gall [gɔːl] I *n* *fam* descaro *m*. II *vtr* molestar, irritar.

gallant ['gælənt] *adj* (*brave*) valiente; (*also* [gəˈlænt]) (*chivalrous*) galante.

gallantry ['gæləntrɪ] *n* (*bravery*) gallardía *f*; (*politeness*) galantería *f*.

galleon ['gælɪən] *n* galeón *m*.

gallery ['gælərɪ] *n* 1 galería *f*. 2 *Theat* gallinero *m*. 3 (*court*) tribuna *f*.

galley ['gælɪ] *n* 1 (*ship*) galera *f*; **g. slave**, galeote *m*. 2 (*kitchen*) cocina *f*.

Gallicism ['gælɪsɪzəm] *n* galicismo *m*.

gallivant ['gælɪvænt] *vi fam* callejear.

gallon ['gælən] *n* galón *m* (≈ 4,55 litros; *US* 3,79 litros).

gallop ['gæləp] I *n* galope *m*. II *vi* galopar.

gallows ['gæləʊz] *npl* horca *f sing*, patíbulo *m sing*.

gallstone ['gɔːlstəʊn] *n* cálculo *m* biliar.

galore [gəˈlɔːr] *adv fam* en cantidad, en abundancia.

galvanize ['gælvənaɪz] *vtr* (*metal*) galvanizar; *fig* to g. sb into action, galvanizar a algn.

galvanized ['gælvənaɪzd] *adj* galvanizado,-a.

gambit ['gæmbɪt] *n Chess* gambito *m*; *fig* táctica *f*.

gamble ['gæmbəl] I *n* (*risk*) riesgo *m*; (*risky undertaking*) empresa arriesgada; (*bet*) apuesta *f*. II *vi* (*bet*) jugar; (*take a risk*) arriesgarse.

gambler ['gæmblər] *n* jugador,-a *m,f*.

gambling ['gæmblɪŋ] *n* juego *m*.

gambol ['gæmbəl] *vi* brincar.

game [geɪm] I *n* 1 juego *m*; **g. of chance**, juego de azar. 2 (*match*) partido *m*; (*of bridge*) partida *f*. 3 **games**, *Sport* juegos *mpl*; *GB Educ* educación física. 4 (*hunting*) caza *f*; *fig* presa *f*; **g. reserve**, coto *m* de caza. II *adj* **g. for anything**, dispuesto,-a a todo. ◆**gamely** *adv* resueltamente.

gamekeeper ['geɪmkiːpər] *n* guardabosque *mf*.

gammon ['gæmən] *n GB* jamón ahumado *or* curado.

gamut ['gæmət] *n* gama *f*; to run the g. of ..., experimentar todas las posibilidades de ....

gang [gæŋ] *n* (*of criminals*) banda *f*; (*of youths*) pandilla *f*; (*of workers*) cuadrilla *f*. ◆**gang up** *vi fam* confabularse (**on**, contra).

gangplank ['gæŋplæŋk] *n* plancha *f*.

gangrene ['gæŋgriːn] *n* gangrena *f*.

gangster ['gæŋstər] *n* gángster *m*.

gangway ['gæŋweɪ] *n Naut* pasarela *f*; *Theat* pasillo *m*.

gantry ['gæntrɪ] *n* puente *m* transversal.

gaol [dʒeɪl] *n* & *vtr GB* → jail.

gap [gæp] *n* 1 abertura *f*, hueco *m*; (*blank space*) blanco *m*; (*in traffic*) claro *m*; to bridge a g., rellenar un hueco. 2 (*in time*) intervalo *m*; (*emptiness*) vacío *m*. 3 (*gulf*) diferencia *f*. 4 (*deficiency*) laguna *f*.

gape [geɪp] *vi* (*person*) quedarse boquiabierto,-a, mirar boquiabierto,-a; (*thing*) estar abierto,-a.

gaping ['geɪpɪŋ] *adj fig* profundo,-a.

garage ['gærɑːʒ, 'gærɪdʒ] *n* garaje *m*; (*for repairs*) taller mecánico; (*filling station*) gasolinera *f*.

garbage ['gɑːbɪdʒ] *n US* basura *f*; *fig* tonterías *fpl*; **g. can**, cubo *m* de la basura; **g. truck**, camión *m* de la basura.

garbled ['gɑːbəld] *adj* embrollado,-a; **g.**

account, relato confuso.

garden ['gɑ:dən] n jardín m; **g. centre,** centro m de jardinería; **g. party,** recepción f al aire libre.

gardener ['gɑ:dənəʳ] n jardinero,-a m,f.

gardening ['gɑ:dənɪŋ] n jardinería f; **his mother does the g.,** su madre es la que cuida el jardín.

gardenia [gɑ:'di:nɪə] n gardenia f.

gargle ['gɑ:gəl] vi hacer gárgaras.

gargoyle ['gɑ:gɔɪl] n gárgola f.

garish ['geərɪʃ] adj chillón,-ona.

garland ['gɑ:lənd] n guirnalda f.

garlic ['gɑ:lɪk] n ajo m.

garment ['gɑ:mənt] n prenda f.

garnish ['gɑ:nɪʃ] vtr guarnecer.

garrison ['gærɪsən] n guarnición f.

garrulous ['gærʊləs] adj locuaz.

garter ['gɑ:təʳ] n liga f.

gas [gæs] I n 1 gas m; **g. chamber,** cámara f de gas; **g. cooker,** cocina f de gas; **g. fire,** estufa f de gas; **g. mask,** careta f antigás; **g. ring,** hornillo m de gas; **g. station,** gasolinera f. II vtr (asphyxiate) asfixiar con gas. III n fam (talk) charlotear.

gash [gæʃ] I n herida profunda. II vtr hacer un corte en; **he gashed his forehead,** se hizo una herida en la frente.

gasket ['gæskɪt] n junta f.

gasoline ['gæsəli:n] n US gasolina f.

gasp [gɑ:sp] I n (cry) grito sordo; (breath) bocanada f; fig **to be at one's last g.,** estar en las últimas. II vi (in surprise) quedar boquiabierto,-a; (breathe) jadear.

gassy ['gæsɪ] adj (gassier, gassiest) gaseoso,-a.

gastric ['gæstrɪk] adj gástrico,-a.

gastronomic [gæstrə'nɒmɪk] adj gastronómico,-a.

gate [geɪt] n 1 puerta f. 2 (at football ground) entrada f. **g. (money),** taquilla f. 3 (attendance) entrada f.

gateau ['gætəʊ] n pastel m con nata.

gatecrash ['geɪtkræʃ] I vtr colarse en. II vi colarse.

gateway ['geɪtweɪ] n puerta f; fig pasaporte m.

gather ['gæðəʳ] I vtr 1 (collect) juntar; (pick) coger; (pick up) recoger. 2 (bring together) reunir. 3 (harvest) cosechar. **4 to g. speed,** ir ganando velocidad; **to g. strength,** cobrar fuerzas. 5 (understand) suponer; **I g. that ...,** tengo entendido que .... 6 Sew fruncir. II vi 1 (come together) reunirse. 2 (form) formarse. ◆**gather round** vi agruparse.

gathering ['gæðərɪŋ] I adj creciente. II n reunión f.

gauche [gəʊʃ] adj (clumsy) torpe; (tactless) sin tacto.

gaudy ['gɔ:dɪ] adj (gaudier, gaudiest) chillón,-ona.

gauge [geɪdʒ] I n 1 medida f estándar. 2 (of

gun, wire) calibre m. 2 Rail ancho m de vía. 3 (calibrator) indicador m. 4 fig (indication) indicación f. II vtr 1 (measure) medir, calibrar. 2 fig (judge) juzgar.

gaunt [gɔ:nt] adj (lean) demacrado,-a; (desolate) lúgubre.

gauntlet ['gɔ:ntlɪt] n guantelete m; fig **to run the g. of ...,** estar sometido,-a a ...; fig **to throw down the g.,** arrojar el guante.

gauze [gɔ:z] n gasa f.

gave [geɪv] pt → **give.**

gawky ['gɔ:kɪ] adj (gawkier, gawkiest) desgarbado,-a.

gay [geɪ] adj 1 (homosexual) gay. 2 (happy) alegre.

gaze [geɪz] I n mirada fija. II vi mirar fijamente.

gazelle [gə'zel] n gacela f.

gazette [gə'zet] n gaceta f; US periódico m.

gazump [gə'zʌmp] vi GB fam romper un compromiso de venta para vender a un precio más alto.

GB [dʒi:'bi:] abbr of **Great Britain.**

GCE [dʒi:si:'i:] abbr of **General Certificate of Education (A-Level),** ≈ COU m.

GCSE [dʒi:si:es'i:] abbr of **General Certificate of Secondary Education,** BUP m.

GDP [dʒi:di:'pi:] abbr of **gross domestic product,** producto m interior bruto, PIB m.

GDR [dʒi:di:'ɑ:ʳ] n Hist abbr of **German Democratic Republic,** RDA.

gear [gɪəʳ] I n 1 (equipment) equipo m. 2 fam (belongings) bártulos mpl. 3 fam (clothing) ropa f. 4 Tech engranaje m. 5 Aut velocidad f, marcha f; **first g.,** primera f (velocidad f); **g. lever,** palanca f de cambio. II vtr ajustar, adaptar.

gearbox ['gɪəbɒks] n caja f de cambios.

gearstick ['gɪəstɪk], US **gearshift** ['gɪəʃɪft] n palanca f de cambio.

geese [gi:s] npl → **goose.**

gel [dʒel] I n gel m; (for hair) gomina f. II vi fig (ideas etc) cuajar. III vtr (hair) engominar.

gelatin ['dʒelətɪn] n gelatina f.

gelignite ['dʒelɪgnaɪt] n gelignita f.

gem [dʒem] n piedra preciosa; fig (person) joya f.

Gemini ['dʒemɪnaɪ] n Géminis m sing.

gen [dʒen] n fam **to get the g. on sth,** informarse sobre algo.

gender ['dʒendəʳ] n género m.

gene [dʒi:n] n gene m, gen m.

general ['dʒenərəl] I adj general; **g. knowledge,** conocimientos generales; **in g.,** en general; **the g. public,** el público; **g. practitioner (GP),** médico m de cabecera. II n Mil general m. ◆**generally** adv generalmente, en general.

generalization [dʒenərəlaɪˈzeɪʃən] *n* generalización *f*.

generalize [ˈdʒenərəlaɪz] *vtr & vi* generalizar.

generate [ˈdʒenəreɪt] *vtr* generar.

generation [dʒenəˈreɪʃən] *n* generación *f*; **g. gap**, abismo *m* or conflicto *m* generacional.

generator [ˈdʒenəreɪtə*] *n* generador *m*.

generosity [dʒenəˈrɒsɪtɪ] *n* generosidad *f*.

generous [ˈdʒenərəs] *adj* generoso,-a; (*plentiful*) copioso,-a.

genetic [dʒɪˈnetɪk] *adj* genético,-a; **g. engineering**, ingeniería genética.

genetics [dʒɪˈnetɪks] *n* genética *f*.

Geneva [dʒɪˈniːvə] *n* Ginebra.

genial [ˈdʒiːnɪəl, ˈdʒiːnjəl] *adj* cordial.

genie [ˈdʒiːnɪ] *n* duende *m*, genio *m*.

genitals [ˈdʒenɪtəlz] *npl* órganos *mpl* genitales.

genius [ˈdʒiːnjəs, ˈdʒiːnɪəs] *n* 1 (*person*) genio *m*. 2 (*gift*) don *m*.

genre [ˈʒɒnrə] *n* género *m*.

gent [dʒent] *n* (*abbr of* **gentleman**) *fam* señor *m*, caballero *m*; **the gents**, los servicios (de caballeros).

genteel [dʒenˈtiːl] *adj* fino,-a, distinguido,-a.

gentle [ˈdʒentəl] *adj* dulce, tierno,-a; (*breeze*) suave. ◆**gently** con cuidado.

gentleman [ˈdʒentəlmən] *n* caballero *m*; **g.'s agreement**, pacto *m* de caballeros.

gentry [ˈdʒentrɪ] *n* pequeña nobleza, alta burguesía.

genuine [ˈdʒenjuɪn] *adj* auténtico,-a, genuino,-a; (*sincere*) sincero,-a. ◆**genuinely** *adv* auténticamente.

geographic(al) [dʒɪəˈɡræfɪk(əl)] *adj* geográfico,-a.

geography [dʒɪˈɒɡrəfɪ, ˈdʒɒɡrəfɪ] *n* geografía *f*.

geologic(al) [dʒɪəˈlɒdʒɪk(əl)] *adj* geológico,-a.

geology [dʒɪˈɒlədʒɪ] *n* geología *f*.

geometric(al) [dʒɪəˈmetrɪk(əl)] *adj* geométrico,-a.

geometry [dʒɪˈɒmɪtrɪ] *n* geometría *f*.

geopolitical [dʒiːəʊpəˈlɪtɪkəl] *adj* geopolítico,-a.

geranium [dʒɪˈreɪnɪəm] *n* geranio *m*.

geriatric [dʒerɪˈætrɪk] *adj* geriátrico,-a.

germ [dʒɜːm] *n* 1 *Biol & fig* germen *m*. 2 *Med* microbio *m*.

German [ˈdʒɜːmən] I *adj* alemán,-ana; **G. measles**, rubeola *f*. II *n* 1 alemán,-ana *m,f*. 2 (*language*) alemán *m*.

Germany [ˈdʒɜːmənɪ] *n* Alemania.

germinate [ˈdʒɜːmɪneɪt] *vi* germinar.

gestation [dʒeˈsteɪʃən] *n* gestación *f*.

gesticulate [dʒeˈstɪkjʊleɪt] *vi* gesticular.

gesture [ˈdʒestʃə*] I *n* gesto *m*, ademán *m*; **it's an empty g.**, es pura formalidad. II *vi* gesticular, hacer gestos.

get [get] I *vtr* (*pt & pp* got, pp US *also*

gotten) 1 (*obtain*) obtener, conseguir; to **g. one's own way**, salirse con la suya. 2 (*earn*) ganar. 3 (*fetch*) (*something*) traer; (*somebody*) ir a por; **g. the police!**, ¡llama a la policía! *Tel* **g. me Mr Brown**, póngame con el Sr. Brown. 4 (*receive*) recibir; *fam* **he got the sack**, le despidieron. 5 (*bus, train, thief etc*) *Span* coger; *Am* agarrar. 6 (*prepare*) preparar; **can I g. you something to eat?**, ¿quieres comer algo? 7 (*ask*) pedir; **g. him to call me**, dile que me llame. 8 to **g. sb to agree to sth**, conseguir que algn acepte algo. 9 **when did you g. the house painted?**, ¿cuándo os pintaron la casa?; to **g. one's hair cut**, cortarse el pelo. 10 **they got him in the chest**, le dieron en el pecho. 11 **have got, have got to → have**. 12 *fam* (*understand*) entender. 13 (*record*) (*in writing*) apuntar; (*on tape*) grabar.

II *vi* 1 (*become*) ponerse; to **g. dark**, anochecer; to **g. dressed**, vestirse; to **g. drunk**, emborracharse; to **g. late**, hacerse tarde; to **g. married**, casarse; to **g. used to doing sth**, acostumbrarse a hacer algo; to **get paid**, cobrar. 2 *fig* **we are not getting anywhere**, así no vamos a ninguna parte. 3 (*arrive*) llegar. 4 to **g. to**, (*come to*) llegar a; to **g. to know sb**, llegar a conocer a algn.

◆**get about** *vi* (*person*) salir; (*news*) difundirse. ◆**get across** *vi* (*idea etc*) hacer comprender. ◆**get ahead** *vi* progresar. ◆**get along** *vi* 1 (*leave*) marcharse. 2 (*manage*) arreglárselas. 3 (*two people*) llevarse bien. ◆**get around** *vi* (*person*) salir; (*travel*) viajar; (*news*) difundirse. ◆**get at** *vtr* 1 (*reach*) alcanzar. 2 (*ascertain*) descubrir. 3 (*insinuate*) insinuar; **what are you getting at?**, ¿a dónde quieres llegar? 4 (*criticize*) criticar. ◆**get away** *vi* escaparse. ◆**get away with** *vtr* salir impune de. ◆**get back** I *vi* 1 (*return*) regresar, volver. 2 **g. back!**, (*move backwards*) ¡atrás!. II *vtr* (*recover*) recuperar; *fam* to **g. one's own back on sb**, vengarse de algn. ◆**get by** *vi* 1 (*manage*) arreglárselas; **she can g. by in French**, sabe defenderse en francés. 2 (*pass*) pasar. ◆**get down** I *vtr* (*depress*) deprimir. II *vi* (*descend*) bajar. ◆**get down to** *vi* ponerse a; to **g. down to the facts**, ir al grano. ◆**get in** *vi* 1 (*arrive*) llegar. 2 *Pol* ser elegido,-a. II *vtr* 1 (*buy*) comprar. 2 (*collect*) recoger; *fam* **he couldn't g. a word in edgeways**, no pudo decir ni pío. ◆**get into** *vtr fig* to **g. into bad habits**, adquirir malas costumbres; to **g. into trouble**, meterse en un lío. ◆**get off** I *vtr* 1 (*bus etc*) bajarse de. 2 (*remove*) quitarse. II *vi* 1 bajarse; *fam* **g. off!**, ¡fuera! 2 to **g. off to a good start**, (*begin*) empezar bien. 3 (*escape*) escaparse; to **g. off lightly**, salir bien librado,-a. ◆get off with vtr fam ligar. ◆get on I vtr (board) subir a. II vi 1 (board) subirse. 2 (make progress) hacer progresos; how are you getting on?, ¿cómo te van las cosas? 3 to g. on (well with sb), llevarse bien (con algn). 4 (continue) seguir; to g. on with one's work, seguir trabajando. 5 it's getting on for eleven, son casi las once; time's getting on, se está haciendo tarde. ◆get on to vtr 1 (find a person) localizar; (find out) descubrir. 2 (continue) pasar a. ◆get out I vtr (object) sacar. II vi 1 (room etc) salir (of, de); (train) bajar (of, de). 2 (escape) escaparse (of, de); to g. out of an obligation, librarse de un compromiso. 3 (news) difundirse; (secret) hacerse público. ◆get over vti 1 (illness) reponerse; I can't g. over him, no le puedo olvidar. 2 (difficulty) vencer. 3 (convey) hacer comprender. ◆get round vtr 1 (problem) salvar; (difficulty) vencer. 2 (rule) soslayar. 3 (win over) persuadir. ◆get round to vi if I g. round to it, si tengo tiempo. ◆get through I vi 1 (message) llegar. 2 Educ aprobar. 3 Tel to g. through to sb, conseguir comunicar con algn. II vtr 1 to g. through a lot of work, trabajar mucho. 2 (consume) consumir. 3 Educ aprobar. ◆get together I vi (people) juntarse, reunirse. II vtr (people) juntar, reunir. ◆get up I vi (rise) levantarse. II vtr 1 (wake) despertar. 2 (disguise) to g. oneself up as ..., disfrazarse de .... ◆get up to vtr 1 hacer; to g. up to mischief, hacer de las suyas.

getaway ['getəweı] n fuga f; to make one's g., fugarse.

get-together ['getəgeðər] n reunión f.

geyser ['gi:zə, US 'gaɪzər] n 1 Geog géiser m. 2 (water heater) calentador m de agua.

ghastly ['gɑ:stlı] adj (ghastlier, ghastliest) horrible, espantoso,-a.

gherkin ['gɜ:kın] n pepinillo m.

ghetto ['getəʊ] n gueto m.

ghost [gəʊst] n fantasma m; g. story, cuento m de fantasmas; g. town, pueblo m fantasma.

ghost-writer ['gəʊstraɪtər] n negro,-a, m,f.

ghoulish ['gu:lıʃ] adj macabro,-a.

giant ['dʒaɪənt] adj & n gigante m.

gibberish ['dʒıbərıʃ] n galimatías m inv.

gibe [dʒaɪb] I n mofa f. II vi mofarse (at, de).

giblets ['dʒıblıts] npl menudillos mpl.

Gibraltar [dʒı'brɔ:ltər] n Gibraltar.

Gibraltarian [dʒıbrɔ:l'teərıən] adj & n gibraltareño,-a (m,f).

giddiness ['gıdınıs] n mareo m; (vertigo) vértigo m.

giddy ['gıdı] adj (giddier, giddiest) mareado,-a; it makes me g., me da vérti-

go; to feel g., sentirse mareado,-a.

gift [gıft] n 1 regalo m; Com obsequio m; g. token, vale m. 2 (talent) don m; to have a g. for music, estar muy dotado,-a para la música.

gifted ['gıftıd] adj dotado,-a.

gig [gıg] n sl Mus actuación f.

gigantic [dʒaɪ'gæntık] adj gigantesco,-a.

giggle ['gıgəl] I n 1 risita f. 2 (lark) broma f, diversión f. II vi reírse tontamente.

gild [gıld] vtr dorar.

gill¹ [dʒıl] n (measurement) medida f de líquidos (= 0,142 litro).

gill² [gıl] n (of fish) branquia f, agalla f.

gilt [gılt] I adj dorado,-a. II n (colour) dorado m.

gilt-edged ['gılted3d] adj g.-e. securities, valores mpl de máxima garantía.

gimmick ['gımık] n truco m; (in advertising) reclamo m.

gin [dʒın] n ginebra f; g. and tonic, gin tonic m.

ginger ['dʒındʒər] I n jengibre m; g. ale, ginger ale m. II adj 1 de jengibre. 2 (hair) pelirrojo,-a.

gingerbread ['dʒındʒəbred] n pan m de jengibre.

gingerly ['dʒındʒəlı] adv cautelosamente.

gipsy ['dʒıpsı] adj & n gitano,-a (m,f).

giraffe [dʒı'rɑ:f] n jirafa f.

girder ['gɜ:dər] n viga f.

girdle ['gɜ:dəl] n faja f.

girl [gɜ:l] n 1 chica f, joven f; (child) niña f; g. guide, US g. scout, exploradora f. 2 (daughter) hija f. 3 (sweetheart) novia f.

girlfriend ['gɜ:lfrend] n 1 (lover) novia f. 2 (female friend) amiga f.

girlhood ['gɜ:lhʊd] n niñez f.

girlish ['gɜ:lıʃ] adj 1 de niña. 2 (effeminate) afeminado,-a.

giro ['dʒaɪrəʊ] n GB giro m (postal); g. (cheque), cheque m de giros postales.

gist [dʒıst] n esencia f, lo esencial; did you get the g. of what he was saying?, ¿cogiste la idea de lo que decía?

give [gıv] n (elasticity) elasticidad f. II vtr (pt gave; pp given) 1 dar; to g. sth to sb, dar algo a algn; to g. a start, pegar un salto; to g. sb a present, regalar algo a algn. 2 (provide) suministrar; to g. sb sth to eat, dar de comer a algn. 3 (pay) pagar. 4 (concert) dar; (speech) pronunciar. 5 (dedicate) dedicar. 6 (grant) otorgar; to g. sb one's attention, prestar atención a algn. 7 to g. sb to understand that ..., dar a entender a algn que .... 8 (yield) ceder; to g. way, Aut ceder el paso; fig ceder; (of legs) flaquear. III vi 1 to g. as good as one gets, devolver golpe por golpe. 2 (yield) ceder; (fabric) dar de sí.

◆give away vtr 1 repartir; (present) regalar. 2 (disclose) revelar; to g. the game away, descubrir el pastel. 3 (betray) trai-

cionar. ◆**give back** vtr devolver.
◆**give in** vi 1 (admit defeat) darse por vencido,-a; (surrender) rendirse. 2 **g. in to**, ceder ante. II vtr (hand in) entregar.
◆**give off** vtr (smell etc) despedir.
◆**give out** vtr distribuir, repartir.
◆**give over** I vtr (hand over) entregar; (devote) dedicar. II vi fam **g. over!**, ¡basta ya! ◆**give up** I vtr 1 (idea) abandonar; **to g. up smoking**, dejar de fumar. 2 (betray) traicionar. 3 (hand over) entregar; **to g. oneself up**, entregarse. II vi (admit defeat) darse por vencido,-a, rendirse. ◆**give up on** vtr darse por vencido con.

given ['gɪvən] I adj 1 (particular) dado,-a; **at a g. time**, en un momento dado. 2 **g. to**, dado,-a a. II conj 1 (considering) dado,-a. 2 (if) si.

glacial ['gleɪsɪəl] adj 1 Geol glaciar. 2 (icy) glacial; fig **g. look**, mirada f glacial.

glacier ['glæsɪər] n glaciar m.

glad [glæd] adj (gladder, gladdest) contento,-a; (happy) alegre; **he'll be only too g. to help you**, tendrá mucho gusto en ayudarle; **to be g.**, alegrarse. ◆**gladly** adv con mucho gusto.

gladiator ['glædɪeɪtər] n Hist gladiador m.

glamor ['glæmər] n US → **glamour**.

glamorous ['glæmərəs] adj atractivo,-a, encantador,-a.

glamour ['glæmər] n atractivo m; (charm) encanto m; **a g. girl**, una belleza.

glance [glɑːns] I n mirada f, vistazo m; **at a g.**, de un vistazo; **at first g.**, a primera vista. II vi echar un vistazo (at, a). ◆**glance off** vtr (ball etc) rebotar de.

glancing ['glɑːnsɪŋ] adj (blow) oblicuo,-a.

gland [glænd] n glándula f.

glandular ['glændjʊlər] adj glandular; **g. fever**, mononucleosis infecciosa.

glare [gleər] I n (light) luz f deslumbrante; (dazzle) deslumbramiento m; (look) mirada f feroz. II vi (dazzle) deslumbrar; (look) lanzar una mirada furiosa (at, a).

glaring ['gleərɪŋ] adj (light) deslumbrante; (colour) chillón,-ona; (obvious) evidente.

glass [glɑːs] n 1 (material) vidrio m; **pane of g.**, cristal m. 2 (drinking vessel) vaso m; **wine g.**, copa f (para vino). 3 **glasses**, gafas fpl; **to wear g.**, llevar gafas.

glasshouse ['glɑːshaʊs] n invernadero m.

glassware ['glɑːsweər] n cristalería f.

glassy ['glɑːsɪ] adj (glassier, glassiest) (water) cristalino,-a; (eyes) vidrioso,-a.

glaze [gleɪz] I n (varnish) barniz m; (for pottery) vidriado m. II vtr 1 (windows) acristalar; 2 (varnish) barnizar; (ceramics) vidriar. 3 Culin glasear.

glazed [gleɪzd] adj (eyes) de mirada ausente.

glazier ['gleɪzɪər] n vidriero,-a m,f.

gleam [gliːm] I n 1 destello m. 2 fig (glimmer) rayo m. II vi brillar, relucir.

gleaming ['gliːmɪŋ] adj brillante, relu-

ciente.

glean [gliːn] vtr fig recoger, cosechar.

glee [gliː] n gozo m.

gleeful ['gliːfʊl] adj gozoso,-a.

glen [glen] n cañada f.

glib [glɪb] adj (glibber, glibbest) pej de mucha labia.

glide [glaɪd] vi 1 (slip, slide) deslizarse. 2 Av planear.

glider ['glaɪdər] n planeador m.

gliding ['glaɪdɪŋ] n vuelo m sin motor.

glimmer ['glɪmər] n 1 (light) luz f tenue. 2 fig (trace) destello m.

glimpse [glɪmps] I n atisbo m. II vtr atisbar.

glint [glɪnt] I n destello m, centelleo m; **he had a g. in his eye**, le brillaban los ojos. II vi destellar, centellear.

glisten ['glɪsən] vi relucir, brillar.

glitter ['glɪtər] I n brillo m. II vi relucir.

gloat [gləʊt] vi jactarse; **to g. over another's misfortune**, recrearse con la desgracia de otro.

global ['gləʊbəl] adj 1 (of the world) mundial. 2 (overall) global.

globe [gləʊb] n globo m, esfera f.

gloom [gluːm] n (obscurity) penumbra f; (melancholy) melancolía f; (despair) desolación f.

gloomy ['gluːmɪ] adj (gloomier, gloomiest) (dark) oscuro,-a; (weather) gris; (dismal) deprimente; (despairing) pesimista; (sad) triste.

glorify ['glɔːrɪfaɪ] vtr glorificar.

glorious ['glɔːrɪəs] adj (momentous) glorioso,-a; (splendid) magnífico,-a, espléndido,-a.

glory ['glɔːrɪ] n gloria f; fig (splendour) esplendor m; fig (triumph) triunfo m.

gloss [glɒs] I n 1 (explanation) glosa f. 2 (sheen) brillo m; **g.** (paint), pintura f brillante. II vi glosar. ◆**gloss over** vtr fig encubrir.

glossary ['glɒsərɪ] n glosario m.

glossy ['glɒsɪ] adj (glossier, glossiest) lustroso,-a; **g. magazine**, revista f de lujo.

glove [glʌv] n guante m; Aut **g. compartment**, guantera f.

glow [gləʊ] I n brillo m; (of fire) incandescencia f; (of sun) arrebol m; (heat) calor m; (light) luz f; (in cheeks) rubor m. II vi brillar; (fire) arder; fig rebosar de.

glower ['glaʊər] vi poner cara de enfadado,-a.

glowing ['gləʊɪŋ] adj 1 (fire) incandescente; (colour) vivo,-a; (light) brillante. 2 (cheeks) encendido,-a. 3 fig (report) entusiasta.

glucose ['gluːkəʊz] n glucosa f.

glue [gluː] I n pegamento m, cola f. II vtr pegar (to, a).

glum [glʌm] adj (glummer, glummest)

alicaído,-a.

glut |glʌt| n superabundancia f, exceso m.

glutton |'glʌtən| n glotón,-ona f,m; fam fig a g. for punishment, masoquista m,f.

GMT |dʒi:em'ti:| abbr of **Greenwich Mean Time,** Hora media de Greenwich, GMT.

gnarled |nɑːld| adj nudoso,-a.

gnash |næʃ| vtr rechinar.

gnat |næt| n mosquito m.

gnaw |nɔː| vtr & vi (chew) roer.

GNP |dʒien'pi:| abbr of **gross national product,** producto nacional bruto, PNB m.

gnome |nəʊm| n gnomo m.

go |gəʊ| **I** vi (3rd person sing pres **goes;** pt **went;** pp **gone**) **1** ir; **to go by car/on foot,** ir en coche/a pie; **to go for a walk,** (ir a) dar un paseo; **to g. on a journey,** ir de viaje; **to go shopping,** ir de compras; fig **to go too far,** pasarse (de la raya). **2** (depart) irse, marcharse; (bus) salir. **3** (disappear) desaparecer. **4** (function) funcionar; fig **to get things going,** poner las cosas en marcha. **5** (sell) venderse; **shoes going cheap,** zapatos a precios de rebaja. **6** (become) quedarse, volverse; **to go blind,** quedarse ciego,-a; **to go mad,** volverse loco,-a. **7** (progress) ir; **everything went well,** todo salió bien; **how's it going?,** qué tal (te van las cosas)? **8 to be going to,** (in the future) ir a; (on the point of) estar a punto de. **9** (fit) caber. **10** (be kept) guardarse. **11** (be available) quedar; **I'll take whatever's going,** me conformo con lo que hay. **12** (be acceptable) valer; **anything goes,** todo vale. **13** (break) romperse; (yield) ceder. **14 how does that song go?,** ¿cómo es aquella canción? **15** (time) pasar; **there are only two weeks to go,** sólo quedan dos semanas. **16** (be inherited) pasar (**to,** a). **17** (say) decir; **as the saying goes,** según el dicho. **18 to let sth go,** soltar algo.

II vtr **1** (travel) hacer, recorrer. **2 to go it alone,** apañárselas solo.

III n **1** (energy) energía f, dinamismo m. **2** (try) intento m; **to have a go at sth,** probar suerte con algo. **3** (turn) turno m; **it's your go,** te toca a ti. **4 to make a go of sth,** tener éxito en algo. **5 I knew from the word go,** lo sabía desde el principio. **6 to have a go at sb,** criticar a algn.

◆**go about I** vtr **1** (task) emprender; **how do you go about it?,** ¿cómo hay que hacerlo? **2 to go about one's business,** ocuparse de sus asuntos. **II** vi (rumour) correr. ◆**go after** vtr (pursue) andar tras. ◆**go against** vtr (oppose) ir en contra de; (verdict) ser desfavorable a. ◆**go ahead** vi **1** (proceed) proceder. **2 we'll go on ahead,** iremos delante. ◆**go along I** vtr (street) pasar por. **II** vi

(progress) progresar. ◆**go along with** vtr **1** (agree with) estar de acuerdo con. **2** (accompany) acompañar. ◆**go around** vi **1** (rumour) correr. **2 there's enough to go around,** hay para todos. **3 go away** vi marcharse. ◆**go back** vi **1** (return) volver, regresar. **2** fig **to go back to,** (date from) datar de. ◆**go back on** vtr **to go back on one's word,** faltar a su palabra. ◆**go back to** vtr volver a. ◆**go by** vi pasar; **as time goes by,** con el tiempo. ◆**go down** vi **1** (descend) bajar; (sun) ponerse; (ship) hundirse. **2** (diminish) disminuir; (temperature) bajar. **3** (be received) ser acogido,-a. ◆**go down with** vtr (contract) coger. ◆**go for** vtr **1** (attack) lanzarse sobre; fam **go for it!,** ja por ello! **2** (fetch) ir por. **3** fam (like) gustar. ◆**go in** vi entrar. ◆**go in for** vtr (exam) presentarse a; (hobby) dedicarse a. ◆**go into** vtr **1** (enter) entrar en; **to go into journalism,** dedicarse al periodismo. **2** (study) examinar; (matter) investigar. **3** (energy, money) invertir en. ◆**go off I** vi **1** (leave) irse, marcharse. **2** (bomb) explotar; (gun) dispararse; (alarm) sonar. **3** (food) pasarse. **4** (event) resultar. **II** vtr fam **to go off sth,** perder el gusto or el interés por algo. ◆**go on** vi **1** (continue) seguir, continuar; **to go on talking,** seguir hablando; **to go on and on about sth,** no parar de hablar sobre algo; (complain) quejarse constantemente de algo. **2** (happen) pasar, ocurrir. **3** (time) transcurrir, pasar. **4** (light) encenderse. ◆**go out** vi **1** (leave) salir; **to go out for a meal,** comer or cenar fuera. **2** (boy and girl) salir juntos. **3** (fire, light) apagarse. **4** (tide) bajar. **5** TV Rad transmitirse. **6 to go (all) out,** ir a por todas. **7** (in competition) perder la eliminatoria. ◆**go over** vtr (revise) repasar. ◆**go over to** vtr acercarse a; **to go over to the enemy,** pasarse al enemigo. **2** (switch to) pasar a. ◆**go round** vi **1** (revolve) dar vueltas. **2 to go round to sb's house,** pasar por casa de algn. ◆**go through I** vi **1** (bill) ser aprobado,-a. **II** vtr **1** (examine) examinar; (search) registrar. **2** (rehearse) ensayar. **3** (spend) gastar. **4** (list etc) explicar. **5** (endure) sufrir. ◆**go through with** vtr llevar a cabo. ◆**go under** vi **1** (ship) hundirse. **2** (business) fracasar. ◆**go up** vi **1** (price etc) subir. **2 to go up to sb,** acercarse a algn. **3** (in a lift) subir. **4 to go up in flames,** quemarse. **5** Sport (be promoted) subir. ◆**go with** vtr **1** (accompany) ir con. **2** (colours) hacer juego con. ◆**go without I** vtr **1** pasarse sin, prescindir de. **2 fam that goes without saying,** eso es evidente. **II** vi (not have) aguantarse sin nada.

goad |gəʊd| vtr aguijonear.

go-ahead |'gəʊəhed| fam n **to give sb the**

go-a., dar luz verde a algn.

goal [gəʊl] *n* 1 *Sport* gol *m*; **g. kick**, saque *m* de puerta; **(g.) post**, poste *m*; **g. scorer**, goleador,-a *m,f*. 2 *(aim, objective)* meta *f*, objetivo *m*.

goalkeeper [ˈgəʊlkiːpəʳ] *n* portero,-a *m,f*.

goat [gəʊt] *n (female)* cabra *f*; *(male)* macho cabrío.

gob [gɒb] *n GB sl* boca *f*.

gobble [ˈgɒbəl] *vtr* engullir.

go-between [ˈgəʊbɪtwiːn] *n* intermediario,-a *m,f*.

goblet [ˈgɒblɪt] *n* copa *f*.

god [gɒd] *n* dios *m*; **for G.'s sake!**, ¡por Dios!; **G.**, Dios; **(my) G.!**, ¡Dios mío!; **G. forbid**, ¡Dios no lo quiera!; **G. only knows**, sabe Dios.

godchild [ˈgɒdtʃaɪld] *n* ahijado,-a *m,f*.

goddaughter [ˈgɒdɔːtəʳ] *n* ahijada *f*.

goddess [ˈgɒdɪs] *n* diosa *f*.

godfather [ˈgɒdfɑːðəʳ] *n* padrino *m*.

godforsaken [ˈgɒdfəseɪkən] *adj (place)* remoto,-a.

godmother [ˈgɒdmʌðəʳ] *n* madrina *f*.

godparents [ˈgɒdpeərənts] *npl* padrinos *mpl*.

godsend [ˈgɒdsend] *n* regalo inesperado.

godson [ˈgɒdsʌn] *n* ahijado *m*.

goggles [ˈgɒgəlz] *npl* gafas protectoras.

going [ˈgəʊɪŋ] **I** *adj (price)* corriente; **the g. rate**, el precio medio. 2 **a g. concern**, un negocio que marcha bien. 3 **to get** *or* **be g.**, marcharse. 4 **to keep g.**, resistir. **II** *n* 1 **that was good g.!**, ¡qué rápido! 2 *fig* **to get out while the g. is good**, retirarse antes que sea demasiado tarde.

goings-on [ˈgəʊɪŋzˈɒn] *npl fam* tejemanejes *mpl*.

go-kart [ˈgəʊkɑːt] *n Sport* kart *m*.

gold [gəʊld] **I** *n* oro *m*; **g. leaf**, pan *m* de oro; **g. medal**, medalla *f* de oro; **g. mine**, mina *f* de oro. **II** *adj* de oro; *(colour)* oro, dorado,-a.

golden [ˈgəʊldən] *adj* de oro; *(colour)* dorado,-a; *fig* **a g. opportunity**, una excelente oportunidad; *Orn* **g. eagle**, águila *f* real; *fig* **g. handshake**, indemnización *f* por despido; **g. wedding**, bodas *fpl* de oro.

goldfish [ˈgəʊldfɪʃ] *n* pez *m* de colores.

gold-plated [ˈgəʊldˈpleɪtɪd] *adj* chapado,-a en oro.

goldsmith [ˈgəʊldsmɪθ] *n* orfebre *m*.

golf [gɒlf] *n* golf *m*; **g. ball**, pelota *f* de golf; **g. club**, *(stick)* palo *m* de golf; *(place)* club *m* de golf; **g. course**, campo *m* de golf.

golfer [ˈgɒlfəʳ] *n* golfista *mf*.

golly [ˈgɒlɪ] *interj* ¡vaya!

gone [gɒn] *adj* desaparecido,-a.

gong [gɒŋ] *n* gong *m*.

good [gʊd] **I** *adj (better, best)* 1 *(before noun)* buen,-a; *(after noun)* bueno,-a; **a g.**

book, un buen libro; **g. afternoon**, **g. evening**, buenas tardes; **g. morning**, buenos días; **g. night**, buenas noches; **it looks g.**, tiene buena pinta; **to be as g. as new**, estar como nuevo,-a; **to feel g.**, sentirse bien; **to have a g. time**, pasarlo bien; **to smell g.**, oler bien; **G. Friday**, Viernes *m* Santo. 2 *(kind)* amable; *(generous)* generoso,-a. 3 *(healthy)* sano,-a. 4 *(morally correct)* correcto,-a; **be g.!**, ¡pórtate bien! 5 **he's g. at languages**, tiene facilidad para los idiomas. 6 *(attractive)* bonito,-a; **red looks g. on you**, el rojo te favorece mucho; **g. looks**, atractivo *m sing*, belleza *f sing*. 7 **it's as g. as an offer**, equivale a una oferta; **it's g. as a way as any**, es una manera como otra cualquiera. 8 *(at least)* como mínimo. 9 *(sufficient)* bastante. 10 **to make g.**, *(injustice)* reparar; *(loss)* compensar; *(succeed in life)* triunfar. 11 *(reliable)* de confianza. 12 *(propitious)* propicio,-a. 13 **she comes from a g. family**, es de buena familia. 14 *(character)* agradable; **he's in a g. mood**, está de buen humor.

II *n* 1 bien *m*; **g. and evil**, el bien y el mal; **to do g.**, hacer el bien. 2 *(advantage)* bien *m*, provecho *m*; **for your own g.**, para tu propio bien; **it's no g. waiting**, no sirve de nada esperar; **it will do you g.**, te hará bien. 3 **goods**, *(possessions)* bienes *mpl*. 4 *Com* **goods**, artículos *mpl*, géneros *mpl*; **g. train**, tren *m* de mercancías.

III *adv* **she's gone for g.**, se ha ido para siempre.

IV *interj* **g.!**, ¡muy bien!

goodbye [gʊdˈbaɪ] **I** *interj* ¡adiós!. **II** *n* adiós *m*, despedida *f*; **to say g. to sb**, despedirse de algn.

good-for-nothing [ˈgʊdfənʌθɪŋ] *adj & n* inútil *(mf)*.

good-hearted [gʊdˈhɑːtɪd] *adj* de buen corazón.

good-looking [gʊdˈlʊkɪŋ] *adj* guapo,-a.

good-natured [gʊdˈneɪtʃəd] *adj* amable, bondadoso,-a.

goodness [ˈgʊdnɪs] *n* bondad *f*; **my g.!**, ¡Dios mío!; **thank g.!**, ¡gracias a Dios!; **for g. sake!**, ¡por Dios!

good-tempered [gʊdˈtempəd] *adj* apacible.

goodwill [gʊdˈwɪl] *n* 1 buena voluntad *f*. 2 *Com (reputation)* buen nombre *m*.

goose [guːs] *n (pl* geese [giːs]) ganso *m*, oca *f*.

gooseberry [ˈgʊzbərɪ, ˈguːsbərɪ] *n* uva espina, grosella espinosa; *fam* **to play g.**, hacer de carabina.

gooseflesh [ˈguːsfleʃ] *n*, **goosepimples** [ˈguːspɪmpəlz] *npl* carne *f* de gallina.

goose-step [ˈguːsstep] *vi* ir a paso de la oca.

gore¹ [gɔːʳ] *n* sangre derramada.

gore² [gɔːr] vtr Taur cornear, dar cornadas a.

gorge [gɔːdʒ] I n desfiladero m. II vtr & vi to g. (oneself), atiborrarse (on, de).

gorgeous [ˈgɔːdʒəs] adj magnífico,-a, estupendo,-a; (person) atractivo,-a, guapo,-a.

gorilla [gəˈrɪlə] n gorila m.

gorse [gɔːs] n aulaga f.

gory [ˈgɔːrɪ] adj (gorier, goriest) sangriento,-a.

gosh [gɒʃ] interj fam ¡cielos!, ¡caray!

go-slow [gəʊˈsləʊ] n huelga f de celo.

gospel [ˈgɒspəl] n the G., el Evangelio; fam it's the g. truth, es la pura verdad.

gossip [ˈgɒsɪp] I n 1 (rumour) cotilleo m; g. column, ecos mpl de sociedad. 2 (person) chismoso,-a m,f, cotilla mf. II vi (natter) cotillear, chismorrear.

got [gɒt] pt & pp → get.

Gothic [ˈgɒθɪk] adj gótico,-a.

gotten [ˈgɒtən] pp US → get.

gourmet [ˈgʊəmeɪ] n gourmet mf.

gout [gaʊt] n gota f.

govern [ˈgʌvən] vtr 1 gobernar. 2 (determine) determinar.

governess [ˈgʌvənɪs] n institutriz f.

governing [ˈgʌvənɪŋ] adj gobernante; g. body, consejo m de administración.

government [ˈgʌvənmənt] n gobierno m.

governmental [gʌvənˈmentəl] adj gubernamental.

governor [ˈgʌvənər] n (ruler) gobernador,-a m,f; (of prison) director,-a m,f; (of school) administrador,-a m,f.

gown [gaʊn] n (dress) vestido largo; Jur Univ toga f.

GP [dʒiːˈpiː] abbr of general practioner.

GPO [dʒiːpiːˈəʊ] GB abbr of General Post Office.

grab [græb] I n agarrón m; fam to be up for grabs, estar disponible. II vtr 1 agarrar; to g. hold of sb, agarrarse a algn. 2 fig a. a bottle of wine, píllate una botella de vino. 3 fig how does that g. you?, ¿qué te parece?

grace [greɪs] I n 1 gracia f; fig to fall from g., caer en desgracia. 2 to say g., bendecir la mesa. 3 to do sth with good g., hacer algo de buena gana. 4 five days' g., (reprieve) un plazo de cinco días. 5 (elegance) elegancia f. 6 Your G., (Su) Excelencia. II vtr 1 (adorn) adornar. 2 (honour) honrar.

graceful [ˈgreɪsfʊl] adj elegante; (movement) garboso,-a. ◆**gracefully** adv 1 (beautifully) con gracia, con elegancia. 2 (accept) con cortesía.

gracious [ˈgreɪʃəs] adj 1 (elegant) elegante. 2 (courteous) cortés. 3 (kind) amable. II interj good g. (me)!, goodness g.!, ¡santo cielo!

grade [greɪd] I n 1 (quality) grado m; (rank) categoría f; Mil rango m. 2 Educ

(mark) nota f. 3 US Educ (class) clase f; US g. school, escuela primaria. 4 (level) nivel m; to make the g., llegar al nivel deseado. 5 US (slope) pendiente f. 6 US g. crossing, paso m a nivel. II vtr clasificar.

gradient [ˈgreɪdɪənt] n (graph) declive m; (hill) cuesta f, pendiente f.

gradual [ˈgrædjʊəl] adj gradual, progresivo,-a. ◆**gradually** adv poco a poco.

graduate [ˈgrædjʊɪt] I n Educ titulado,-a m,f; Univ licenciado,-a m,f; US g. school, escuela f para graduados. II [ˈgrædjʊeɪt] vi 1 Educ sacarse el título; Univ licenciarse (in, en). 2 to g. to, pasar a.

graduation [grædjʊˈeɪʃən] n graduación f; Univ g. ceremony, ceremonia f de entrega de los títulos.

graffiti [grəˈfiːtiː] n grafiti mpl.

graft [grɑːft] I n 1 Med injerto m. 2 fam (work) trabajo m. 3 US (bribery) soborno m. II vtr Med injertar (on to, en). III vi fam trabajar duro.

grain [greɪn] n 1 (cereals) cereales mpl. 2 (particle) grano m; fig there's not a g. of truth in it, no tiene ni pizca de verdad. 3 (in wood) fibra f; (in stone) veta f; (in leather) flor f; fig to go against the g., ir a contrapelo.

gram [græm] n gramo m.

grammar [ˈgræmər] n gramática f; g. (book), libro m de gramática; g. school, instituto estatal de segunda enseñanza al que se ingresa por examen selectivo.

grammatical [grəˈmætɪkəl] adj gramatical.

gramme [græm] n gramo m.

gramophone [ˈgræməfəʊn] n gramófono m.

granary [ˈgrænərɪ] n granero m.

grand [grænd] I adj 1 grande; (before sing noun) gran; g. piano, piano m de cola; G. Prix, Gran Premio m. 2 (splendid) grandioso,-a, magnífico,-a; (impressive) impresionante. 3 g. total, total m. 4 fam (wonderful) estupendo,-a. II n sl mil libras fpl, US mil dólares mpl.

grandchild [ˈgræntʃaɪld] n nieto,-a m,f.

granddad [ˈgrændæd] n fam abuelo m.

granddaughter [ˈgrændɔːtər] n nieta f.

grandeur [ˈgrændʒər] n grandeza f, grandiosidad f.

grandfather [ˈgrænfɑːðər] n abuelo m; g. clock, reloj m de caja.

grandiose [ˈgrændɪəʊs] adj grandioso,-a.

grandma [ˈgrænmɑː] n fam abuelita f.

grandmother [ˈgrænmʌðər] n abuela f.

grandpa [ˈgrænpɑː] n fam abuelito m.

grandparents [ˈgrænpeərənts] npl abuelos mpl.

grandson [ˈgrænsʌn] n nieto m.

grandstand [ˈgrænstænd] n tribuna f.

granite ['grænɪt] n granito m.

granny ['grænɪ] n fam abuelita f.

grant [grɑːnt] I vtr 1 (allow) conceder, otorgar. 2 (admit) admitir; **to take sb for granted**, no apreciar a algn en lo que vale; **to take sth for granted**, dar algo por sentado. II n Educ beca f; (subsidy) subvención f.

granulated ['grænjʊleɪtɪd] adj granulado,-a.

granule ['grænjuːl] n gránulo m.

grape [greɪp] n uva f; **g. juice**, mosto m.

grapefruit ['greɪpfruːt] n pomelo m.

grapevine ['greɪpvaɪn] n Bot vid f; (against wall) parra f; fam **I heard it on** or **through the g.**, me enteré por ahí.

graph [grɑːf, græf] n gráfica f.

graphic ['græfɪk] adj gráfico,-a; **g. arts**, artes fpl gráficas; **g. designer**, grafista mf.

graphics ['græfɪks] n 1 (study) grafismo m. 2 pl Comput gráficas fpl.

grapple ['græpəl] I vi (struggle) luchar cuerpo a cuerpo (with, con); fig **to g. with a problem**, intentar resolver un problema. II n (hook) garfio m.

grasp [grɑːsp] I vtr 1 agarrar. 2 (understand) comprender. II n 1 (grip) agarrón m. 2 (understanding) comprensión f; **within sb's g.**, al alcance de algn.

grasping ['grɑːspɪŋ] adj avaro,-a.

grass [grɑːs] n 1 hierba f; (lawn) césped m; (pasture) pasto m; **keep off the g.**, 'prohibido pisar el césped'; **g. court**, pista f de hierba; **g. roots**, base f; **g. snake**, culebra f. 2 sl (drug) hierba f. II vi GB sl chivarse (on, a). ◆**grass over** vi cubrirse de hierba.

grasshopper ['grɑːshɒpə'] n saltamontes m inv.

grassland ['grɑːslænd] n pradera f.

grass-roots ['grɑːsruːts] adj de base; **at g.-r. level**, a nivel popular.

grassy ['grɑːsɪ] adj (grassier, grassiest) cubierto,-a de hierba.

grate¹ [greɪt] I vtr Culin rallar. II vi chirriar.

grate² [greɪt] n 1 (in fireplace) rejilla f. 2 (fireplace) chimenea f. 3 Constr rejilla f, reja f.

grateful ['greɪtfʊl] adj agradecido,-a; **to be g. for**, agradecer.

grater ['greɪtə'] n Culin rallador m.

gratification [grætɪfɪ'keɪʃən] n (pleasure) placer m, satisfacción f.

gratify ['grætɪfaɪ] vtr 1 (please) complacer. 2 (yield to) sucumbir a.

gratifying ['grætɪfaɪɪŋ] adj grato,-a.

grating¹ ['greɪtɪŋ] n rejilla f, reja f.

grating² ['greɪtɪŋ] adj chirriante; (tone) áspero,-a.

gratis ['greɪtɪs, 'grætɪs] adv gratis.

gratitude ['grætɪtjuːd] n agradecimiento m.

gratuitous [grə'tjuːɪtəs] adj gratuito,-a.

gratuity [grə'tjuːɪtɪ] n gratificación f.

grave¹ [greɪv] n sepultura f, tumba f.

grave² [greɪv] adj (look etc) serio,-a; (situation) grave.

gravel ['grævəl] n grava f, gravilla f.

gravestone ['greɪvstəʊn] n lápida f sepulcral.

graveyard ['greɪvjɑːd] n cementerio m.

gravity ['grævɪtɪ] n gravedad f.

gravy ['greɪvɪ] n salsa f, jugo m (de la carne).

gray [greɪ] adj & n US → **grey**.

graze¹ [greɪz] vi pacer, pastar.

graze² [greɪz] I vtr (scratch) rasguñar; (brush against) rozar. II n rasguño m.

grease [griːs, griːz] I n grasa f. II vtr engrasar.

greaseproof ['griːspruːf] adj **g. paper**, papel graso.

greasy ['griːsɪ, 'griːzɪ] adj (greasier, greasiest) 1 (oily) grasiento,-a; (hair, food) graso,-a. 2 (slippery) resbaladizo,-a. 3 fam (ingratiating) pelotillero,-a.

great [greɪt] I adj 1 grande; (before sing noun) gran; (pain, heat) fuerte; **a g. many**, muchos,-as; **G. Britain**, Gran Bretaña. 2 fam (excellent) estupendo,-a, magnífico,-a; **to have a g. time**, pasarlo en grande. II adv fam muy bien, estupendamente. ◆**greatly** adv muy, mucho.

great-aunt [greɪt'ɑːnt] n tía abuela.

great-grandchild [greɪt'grænʃaɪld] n bisnieto,-a m f.

great-grandfather [greɪt'grænfɑːðə'] n bisabuelo m.

great-grandmother [greɪt'grænmʌðə'] n bisabuela f.

greatness ['greɪtnɪs] n grandeza f.

great-uncle [greɪt'ʌŋkəl] n tío abuelo.

Greece [griːs] n Grecia f.

greed [griːd], **greediness** ['griːdɪnɪs] n (for food) gula f; (for money) codicia f, avaricia f.

greedy ['griːdɪ] adj (greedier, greediest) (for food) glotón,-ona; (for money) codicioso,-a (for, de).

Greek [griːk] I adj griego,-a. II n 1 (person) griego,-a m,f. 2 (language) griego m.

green [griːn] I n 1 (colour) verde m. 2 Golf campo m; (village) **g.**, plaza f (del pueblo). 3 **greens**, verdura f sing, verduras fpl. II adj 1 verde; **g. bean**, judía f verde; **g. belt**, zona f verde; **g. pepper**, pimiento m verde; **she was g. with envy**, se la comía la envidia. 2 (inexperienced) verde, novato,-a; (gullible) crédulo,-a. 3 Pol **G. Party**, Partido m Verde.

greenery ['griːnərɪ] n follaje m.

greenfly ['griːnflaɪ] n pulgón m.

greengage ['griːngeɪdʒ] n ciruela claudia.

greengrocer ['griːngrəʊsə'] n GB verdulero,-a m,f.

greenhouse ['gri:nhaʊs] n invernadero m;
g. effect, efecto invernadero.

greenish ['gri:nɪʃ] adj verdoso,-a.

Greenland ['gri:nlənd] n Groenlandia.

greet [gri:t] vtr (wave at) saludar; (receive)
recibir; (welcome) dar la bienvenida a.

greeting ['gri:tɪŋ] n 1 saludo m; **greetings
card**, tarjeta f de felicitación. 2 (reception)
recibimiento m; (welcome) bienvenida f.

gregarious [grɪ'geərɪəs] adj gregario,-a,
sociable.

Grenada [grɪ'neɪdə] n Granada.

grenade [grɪ'neɪd] n granada f.

grew [gru:] pt → **grow**.

grey [greɪ] I adj 1 (colour) gris; (hair)
cano,-a; (sky) nublado,-a; **g. matter**, materia f gris. II n 1 (colour) gris m. 2
(horse) caballo tordo.

grey-haired ['greɪheəd] adj canoso,-a.

greyhound ['greɪhaʊnd] n galgo m.

greyish ['greɪɪʃ] adj grisáceo,-a.

grid [grɪd] n 1 (on map) cuadrícula f. 2
(of electricity etc) red f nacional. 3 → **gridiron**.

gridiron ['grɪdaɪən] n Culin parrilla f.

grief [gri:f] n dolor m, pena f; fam **to
come to g.**, (car, driver) sufrir un accidente; (plans) irse al traste.

grievance ['gri:vəns] n (wrong) agravio m;
(resentment) queja f.

grieve [gri:v] I vtr apenar, dar pena a. II
vi apenarse, afligirse; **to g. for sb**, llorar
la muerte de algn.

grievous ['gri:vəs] adj (offence) grave; **g.
bodily harm**, lesiones fpl corporales graves.

grill [grɪl] I vtr 1 Culin asar a la parrilla. 2
fam (interrogate) interrogar duramente. II
n parrilla f. 2 (dish) parrillada f

grill(e) [grɪl] n (grating) reja f.

grim [grɪm] adj (grimmer, grimmest) 1
(sinister) macabro,-a; (landscape) lúgubre;
(smile) sardónico,-a. 2 (manner) severo,-a;
(person) ceñudo,-a. 3 (resolute) inexorable.
4 fam (unpleasant) desagradable; **g. reality**, la dura realidad.

grimace ['grɪmeɪs] I n mueca f. II vi hacer una mueca.

grimy ['graɪmɪ] adj (grimier, grimiest)
mugriento,-a.

grin [grɪn] I vi sonreír abiertamente. II n
sonrisa abierta f.

grind [graɪnd] I vtr (pt & pp ground)
(mill) moler; (crush) triturar; (sharpen)
afilar; **to g. one's teeth**, hacer rechinar
los dientes. II vi rechinar; fig **to g. to a
halt**, (vehicle) pararse lentamente; (production etc) pararse poco a poco. III n fam
the daily g., la rutina cotidiana; **what a
g.!**, ¡qué rollo! ◆**grind down** vtr fig **to
g. down the opposition**, acabar con la
oposición.

grip [grɪp] I n 1 (hold) agarrón m; (handshake) apretón m; (of tyre) adherencia f;

get a g. on yourself!, ¡tranquilízate!; **to
get to grips with a problem**, superar un
problema. 2 (handle) asidero m. 3 (travel
bag) maletín m. 4 (hairgrip) pasador m.
II vtr 1 agarrar, asir; (hand) apretar. 2 fig
(of film, story) captar la atención de; **to be
gripped by fear**, ser presa del miedo.

gripe [graɪp] I vi fam (complain) quejarse.
II n 1 Med (pain) retortijón m. 2 fam
(complaint) queja f.

gripping ['grɪpɪŋ] adj (film, story) apasionante.

grisly ['grɪzlɪ] adj (grislier, grisliest) espeluznante.

gristle ['grɪsəl] n cartílago m, ternilla f.

grit [grɪt] I n 1 (gravel) grava f. 2 fam
(courage) valor m. II vtr fig **to g. one's
teeth**, apretar los dientes.

gritty ['grɪtɪ] adj (grittier, grittiest) valiente.

grizzly ['grɪzlɪ] adj **g. bear**, oso pardo.

groan [grəʊn] I n 1 (of pain) gemido m. 2
fam (of disapproval) gruñido m. II vi 1 (in
pain) gemir. 2 (complain) quejarse
(about, de).

grocer ['grəʊsə'] n tendero, oso m,f.

groceries ['grəʊsərɪz] npl comestibles
mpl.

grocery ['grəʊsərɪ] n (shop) tienda f de ultramarinos; US **g. store**, supermercado
m.

groggy ['grɒgɪ] adj (groggier, groggiest)
fam Box grogui; fig (unsteady) atontado,
-a; (weak) débil.

groin [grɔɪn] n 1 ingle f. 2 US → **groyne**.

groom [gru:m] I n 1 mozo m de cuadra. 2
(bridegroom) novio m. II vtr (horse) almohazar; (clothes, appearance) cuidar.

groove [gru:v] n (furrow etc) ranura f; (of
record) surco m.

grope [grəʊp] vi 1 (search about) andar a
tientas; **to g. for sth**, buscar algo a
tientas. 2 sl (fondle) meter mano.

gross [grəʊs] I adj 1 grosero,-a; (joke)
verde. 2 (fat) obeso,-a. 3 (flagrant) flagrante; (ignorance) craso,-a. 4 Com Econ
bruto,-a. II n gruesa f. III vtr Com
(earn) ganar en bruto; **g. national product**,
producto nacional bruto. II vtr Com recaudar (en
bruto). ◆**grossly** adv enormemente.

grotesque [grəʊ'tesk] adj grotesco,-a.

grotto ['grɒtəʊ] n gruta f.

ground[1] [graʊnd] I n 1 suelo m, tierra f;
at g. level, al nivel del suelo; Av **to get
off the g.**, despegar; Av **g. control**, control m de tierra; **g. floor**, planta baja; Av
g. staff, personal m de tierra; fig **g. swell**,
marejada f. 2 (terrain) terreno m; **to
gain/lose g.**, ganar/perder terreno; fig **to
stand one's g.**, mantenerse firme; football **g.**, campo m de fútbol. 3 US Elec
tierra f. 4 **grounds**, (gardens) jardines
mpl. 5 **grounds**, (reason) motivo m sing.
6 **grounds**, (sediment) poso m sing. II vtr 1
Av obligar a quedarse en tierra; Naut va-

rar. 2 *US Elec* conectar con tierra.

ground² [graund] *adj (coffee)* molido,-a; *US (meat)* picado,-a.

grounding ['graundɪŋ] *n* base *f*; **to have a good g. in,** tener buenos conocimientos de.

groundless ['graundlɪs] *adj* infundado,-a.

groundsheet ['graundʃi:t] *n* tela *f* impermeable.

groundsman ['graundzmən] *n* encargado *m* de campo.

groundwork ['graundwɜ:k] *n* trabajo preparatorio.

group [gru:p] I *n* grupo *m*, conjunto *m*. II *vtr* agrupar, juntar (**into,** en). III *vi* to g. (**together**), agruparse, juntarse.

grouse¹ [graus] *n Orn* urogallo *m*.

grouse² [graus] *fam* I *vi* quejarse (**about,** de). II *n* queja *f*.

grove [grəuv] *n* arboleda *f*.

grovel ['grɒvəl] *vi* humillarse (**to,** ante); *(crawl)* arrastrarse (**to,** ante).

grow [grəu] I *vtr (pt* **grew;** *pp* **grown)** *(cultivate)* cultivar; **to g. a beard,** dejarse *(crecer)* la barba. II *vi* 1 crecer; *(increase)* aumentar. 2 *(become)* hacerse, volverse; **to g. accustomed to,** acostumbrarse a; **to g. dark,** oscurecer; **to g. old,** envejecer. ◆**grow out of** *vtr* 1 he's grown out of his shirt, se le ha quedado pequeña la camisa. 2 *fig (phase etc)* superar. ◆**grow up** *vi* crecer, hacerse mayor.

grower ['grəuər] *n* cultivador,-a *m,f*.

growing ['grəuɪŋ] *adj (child)* que crece; *(problem etc)* creciente; **he's a g. boy,** está dando el estirón.

growl [graul] I *vi* gruñir. II *n* gruñido *m*.

grown [grəun] *adj* crecido,-a, adulto,-a.

grown-up ['grəunʌp] *adj & n* adulto,-a *(m,f)*; **the g.-ups,** los mayores.

growth [grəuθ] *n* 1 crecimiento *m*; *(increase)* aumento *m*; *(development)* desarrollo *m*. 2 *Med* bulto *m*.

groyne [grɔɪn] *n* espigón *m*.

grub [grʌb] *n* 1 *(larva)* gusano *m*. 2 *sl (food)* papeo *m*.

grubby ['grʌbɪ] *adj (grubbier, grubbiest)* sucio,-a.

grudge [grʌdʒ] I *n* rencor *m*; **to bear sb a g.,** guardar rencor a algn. II *vtr (give unwillingly)* dar a regañadientes; **he grudges me my success,** me envidia el éxito.

grudgingly ['grʌdʒɪŋlɪ] *adv* a regañadientes.

gruelling, *US* **grueling** ['gru:əlɪŋ] *adj* penoso,-a.

gruesome ['gru:səm] *adj* espantoso,-a, horrible.

gruff [grʌf] *adj (manner)* brusco,-a; *(voice)* áspero,-a.

grumble ['grʌmbəl] I *vi* refunfuñar. II *n* queja *f*.

grumpy ['grʌmpɪ] *adj (grumpier, grumpiest)* gruñón,-ona.

grunt [grʌnt] I *vi* gruñir. II *n* gruñido *m*.

guarantee [gærən'ti:] I *n* garantía *f*; *(certificate)* certificado *m* de garantía. II *vtr* garantizar; *(assure)* asegurar.

guard [gɑ:d] I *vtr* 1 *(protect)* defender, proteger; *(keep watch over)* vigilar. 2 *(control)* guardar. II *vi* protegerse (**against,** de, contra). III *n* 1 **to be on one's g.,** estar en guardia; **to catch sb off his g.,** coger desprevenido a algn. 2 *(sentry)* guardia *m/f*; **g. of honour,** guardia de honor; **to stand g.,** montar la guardia; **g. dog,** perro *m* guardián. 3 *GB Rail* jefe *m* de tren; **g.'s van,** furgón *m* de cola. 4 *(on machine)* dispositivo *m* de seguridad; **fire g.,** pantalla *f*.

guarded ['gɑ:dɪd] *adj* cauteloso,-a, precavido,-a.

guardhouse ['gɑ:dhaus] *n Mil* 1 *(headquarters)* cuerpo *m* de guardia. 2 *(prison)* prisión *f* militar.

guardian ['gɑ:dɪən] *n* 1 guardián,-ana *m,f*; **g. angel,** ángel *m* de la guarda. 2 *Jur (of minor)* tutor,-a *m,f*.

Guatemala [gwɑːtɪ'mɑːlə] *n* Guatemala.

Guatemalan [gwɑːtɪ'mɑːlən] *adj & n* guatemalteco,-a *(m,f)*.

guava ['gwɑːvə] *n Bot* guayaba *f*; **g. tree,** guayabo *m*.

guer/rilla [gə'rɪlə] *n* guerrillero,-a *m,f*; **g. warfare,** guerra *f* de guerrillas.

guess [ges] I *vtr & vi* 1 adivinar; **I guessed as much,** me lo imaginaba; **to g. right/wrong,** acertar/no acertar. 2 *US fam* pensar, suponer; **I g. so,** supongo que sí. II *n* conjetura *f*, *(estimate)* cálculo *m*; **at a rough g.,** a ojo de buen cubero; **to have** *or* **make a g.,** intentar adivinar.

guesswork ['geswɜːk] *n* conjetura *f*.

guest [gest] *n (at home)* invitado,-a *m,f*; *(in hotel)* cliente,-a *m,f*, huésped,-a *m,f*; **g. artist,** artista *mf* invitado,-a; **g. room,** cuarto *m* de los invitados.

guesthouse ['gesthaus] *n* casa *f* de huéspedes.

guffaw [gʌ'fɔ:] *vi* reírse a carcajadas.

guidance ['gaɪdəns] *n* orientación *f*, consejos *mpl*; **for your g.,** a título de información.

guide [gaɪd] I *vtr* guiar, dirigir. II *n (person)* guía *mf*; *GB* **girl g.,** exploradora *f*; **g. dog,** perro lazarillo. 2 *(guidebook)* guía *f*.

guidebook ['gaɪdbuk] *n* guía *f*.

guided ['gaɪdɪd] *adj* dirigido,-a; **g. tour,** visita con guía; **g. missile,** misil teledirigido.

guideline ['gaɪdlaɪn] *n* pauta *f*.

guild [gɪld] *n* gremio *m*.

guile [gaɪl] *n* astucia *f*.

guillotine ['gɪlətiːn] *n* guillotina *f*.

guilt [gɪlt] *n* 1 culpa *f*. 2 *Jur* culpabilidad *f*.

guilty ['gɪltɪ] *adj (guiltier, guiltiest)*

culpable (**of**, de); **to have a g. con-science**, remorderle a uno la conciencia.

guinea[1] ['gɪnɪ] n **g. pig**, conejillo m de Indias, cobayo m; fig **to act as a g. pig**, servir de conejillo de Indias.

guinea[2] ['gɪnɪ] n (coin) guinea f (approx 21 chelines).

guise [gaɪz] n **under the g. of**, so pretexto de.

guitar [gɪ'tɑːr] n guitarra f.

guitarist [gɪ'tɑːrɪst] n guitarrista mf.

gulf [gʌlf] n **1** golfo m; **G. of Mexico**, Golfo de Méjico; **G. Stream**, corriente f del Golfo de Méjico. **2** fig abismo m.

gull[1] [gʌl] n gaviota f.

gull(e)y ['gʌlɪ] n barranco m, hondonada f.

gullible ['gʌləbəl] adj crédulo,-a.

gulp [gʌlp] I n trago m. II vtr tragar; **to g. sth down**, (drink) tomarse algo de un trago; (food) engullir algo. III vi **1** (swallow air) tragar aire. **2** fig (with fear) tragar saliva.

gum[1] [gʌm] I n goma f. II vtr pegar con goma.

gum[2] [gʌm] n Anat encía f.

gumboots ['gʌmbuːts] npl botas fpl de agua.

gun [gʌn] n arma f de fuego; (handgun) pistola f, revólver m; (rifle) fusil m, escopeta f; (cannon) cañón m; fam **the big guns**, los peces gordos. ◆**gun down** vtr matar a tiros.

gunboat ['gʌnbəʊt] n cañonero m.

gunfire ['gʌnfaɪər] n tiros mpl.

gunman ['gʌnmən] n pistolero m, gángster m.

gunpoint ['gʌnpɔɪnt] n **at g.**, a punta de pistola.

gunpowder ['gʌnpaʊdər] n pólvora f.

gunrunner ['gʌnrʌnər] n traficante mf de armas.

gunshot ['gʌnʃɒt] n disparo m, tiro m.

gunsmith ['gʌnsmɪθ] n armero m.

gurgle ['gɜːgəl] vi (baby) gorjear; (liquid) gorgotear; (stream) murmurar.

guru ['guːruː, 'gʊruː] n gurú m.

gush [gʌʃ] I vi **1** brotar. **2** fig **to g. over sb**, enjabonar a algn. II n (of water) chorro m; (of words) torrente m.

gushing ['gʌʃɪŋ] adj fig (person) efusivo,-a.

gusset ['gʌsɪt] n escudete m.

gust [gʌst] n (of wind) ráfaga f, racha f.

gusto ['gʌstəʊ] n entusiasmo m.

gut [gʌt] I n **1** Anat intestino m. **2** (catgut) cuerda f de tripa. **3** guts, (entrails) tripas fpl; sl **to have g.**, tener agallas. II vtr **1** (fish) destripar. **2** (destroy) destruir por dentro. III adj fam **g. reaction**, reacción f visceral.

gutter ['gʌtər] n (in street) arroyo m; (on roof) canalón m; fig **g. press**, prensa amarilla.

guttural ['gʌtərəl] adj gutural.

guy[1] [gaɪ] n fam tipo m, tío m.

guy[2] [gaɪ] n (rope) viento m, cuerda f.

guzzle ['gʌzəl] vtr & vi fam (food etc) zamparse; (car) tragar mucho.

gym [dʒɪm] fam **1** (gymnasium) gimnasio m. **2** (gymnastics) gimnasia f; **g. shoes**, zapatillas fpl de deporte.

gymnasium [dʒɪm'neɪzɪəm] n gimnasio m.

gymnast ['dʒɪmnæst] n gimnasta mf.

gymnastics [dʒɪm'næstɪks] n gimnasia f.

gynaecologist, US **gynecologist** [gaɪnɪ'kɒlədʒɪst] n ginecólogo,-a m,f.

gypsy ['dʒɪpsɪ] adj & n gitano,-a (m,f).

gyrate [dʒaɪ'reɪt] vi girar.

H

H, h [eɪtʃ] n (the letter) H, h f.

haberdashery ['hæbə'dæʃərɪ] n **1** GB artículos mpl de mercería. **2** US ropa masculina.

habit ['hæbɪt] n **1** costumbre f. **2** (garment) hábito m.

habitable ['hæbɪtəbəl] adj habitable.

habitat ['hæbɪtæt] n hábitat m.

habitual [hə'bɪtjʊəl] adj habitual; (drinker, liar) empedernido,-a. ◆**habitually** adv por costumbre.

hack[1] [hæk] I n (cut) corte m; (with an axe) hachazo m. II vtr (with knife, axe) cortar; (kick) dar un puntapié a.

hack[2] [hæk] n fam (writer) escritorzuelo,-a m,f; (journalist) gacetillero,-a m,f.

hackneyed ['hæknɪd] adj trillado,-a.

hacksaw ['hæksɔː] n sierra f para meta-

les.

had [hæd] pt & pp → **have**.

haddock ['hædək] n abadejo m.

haemophilia [hiːmə'fɪlɪə] n hemofilia f.

haemophiliac [hiːmə'fɪlɪæk] adj & n hemofílico,-a (m,f).

haemorrhage ['hemərɪdʒ] n hemorragia f.

haemorrhoids ['hemərɔɪdz] npl hemorroides fpl.

hag [hæg] n pej bruja f, arpía f.

haggard ['hægəd] adj ojeroso,-a.

haggle ['hægəl] vi regatear.

Hague [heɪg] n **The H.**, La Haya.

hail[1] [heɪl] I n granizo m; fig **a h. of bullets/insults**, una lluvia de balas/insultos. II vi granizar.

hail[2] [heɪl] I vtr **1** (taxi etc) parar. **2** (acclaim) aclamar. II vi **to h. from**, (origi-

nate) ser nativo,-a de.

hailstone ['heɪlstəʊn] *n* granizo *m*.

hailstorm ['heɪlstɔːm] *n* granizada *f*.

hair [heə^r] *n* (*strand*) pelo *m*, cabello *m*; (*mass*) pelo *m*, cabellos *mpl*; (*on arm, leg*) vello *m*; **to have long h.**, tener el pelo largo.

hairbrush ['heəbrʌʃ] *n* cepillo *m* (para el pelo).

haircut ['heəkʌt] *n* corte *m* de pelo; **to have a h.**, cortarse el pelo.

hairdo ['heəduː] *n fam* peinado *m*.

hairdresser ['heədresə^r] *n* peluquero,-a *m,f*; **h.'s** (*shop*), peluquería *f*.

hairdryer, hairdrier ['heədraɪə^r] *n* secador *m* (de pelo).

hair-grip ['heəgrɪp] *n* horquilla *f*, pasador *m*.

hairline ['heəlaɪn] **I** *adj* muy fino,-a. **II** *n* nacimiento *m* del pelo; **receding h.**, entradas *fpl*.

hairnet ['heənet] *n* redecilla *f*.

hairpiece ['heəpiːs] *n* postizo *m*.

hairpin ['heəpɪn] *n* horquilla *f*; **h. bend**, curva muy cerrada.

hair-raising ['heəreɪzɪŋ] *adj* espeluznante.

hair-remover ['heərɪmuːvə^r] *n* depilatorio *m*.

hairspray ['heəspreɪ] *n* laca *f* (para el pelo).

hairstyle ['heəstaɪl] *n* peinado *m*, corte *m* de pelo.

hairy ['heərɪ] *adj* (**hairier, hairiest**) **1** (*with hair*) peludo,-a. **2** *fig* (*frightening*) enervante, espantoso,-a.

hake [heɪk] *n* merluza *f*; (*young*) pescadilla *f*.

half [hɑːf] **I** *n* (*pl* **halves**) mitad *f*; *Sport* (*period*) tiempo *m*; **he's four and a h.**, tiene cuatro años y medio; **to cut in h.**, cortar por la mitad. **II** *adj* medio,-a; **h. a dozen/an hour**, media docena/hora; **h. board**, media pensión; **h. fare**, media tarifa; **h. term**, medio trimestre; **h. year**, semestre *m*. **III** *adv* medio, a medias; **h. asleep**, medio dormido,-a.

half-caste ['hɑːfkɑːst] *adj & n* mestizo,-a (*m,f*).

half-day [hɑːf'deɪ] *n* media jornada.

half-hearted [hɑːf'hɑːtɪd] *adj* poco entusiasta.

half-hour [hɑːf'aʊə^r] *n* media hora.

half-life ['hɑːflaɪf] *n* media vida.

half-mast [hɑːf'mɑːst] *n* **at h.**, a media asta.

half-price [hɑːf'praɪs] *adv* a mitad de precio.

half-time [hɑːf'taɪm] *n* descanso *m*.

half-way [hɑːf'weɪ] **I** *adj* intermedio,-a. **II** *adv* **halfway** [hɑːf'weɪ] a medio camino, a mitad de camino.

half-yearly [hɑːf'jɪəlɪ] *adj* semestral.

halibut ['hælɪbət] *n* mero *m*.

hall [hɔːl] *n* **1** (*lobby*) vestíbulo *m*. **2**

(*building*) sala *f*; *Univ* **h. of residence**, colegio *m* mayor.

hallmark ['hɔːlmɑːk] *n* **1** (*on gold, silver*) contraste *m*. **2** *fig* sello *m*.

hallo [hə'ləʊ] *interj* ¡hola!

hallowed ['hæləʊd] *adj* santificado,-a.

Hallowe(')en [hæləʊ'iːn] *n* víspera *f* de Todos los Santos.

hallucinate [hə'luːsɪneɪt] *vi* alucinar.

hallucination [həluːsɪ'neɪʃən] *n* alucinación *f*.

hallucinogenic [həluːsɪnəʊ'dʒenɪk] *adj* alucinógeno,-a.

hallway ['hɔːlweɪ] *n* vestíbulo *m*.

halo ['heɪləʊ] *n* **1** *Rel* aureola *f*. **2** *Astron* halo *m*.

halt [hɔːlt] **I** *n* (*stop*) alto *m*, parada *f*; **to call a h. to sth**, poner fin a algo. **II** *vtr* parar. **III** *vi* pararse.

halting ['hɔːltɪŋ] *adj* vacilante.

halve [hɑːv] *vtr* **1** partir por la mitad; (*reduce by half*) reducir a la mitad. **2** (*share*) compartir.

halves [hɑːvz] *pl* → **half**.

ham [hæm] *n* jamón *m*; **boiled h.**, jamón de York; **Parma** *or* **cured h.**, jamón serrano.

hamburger ['hæmbɜːgə^r] *n* hamburguesa *f*.

hamlet ['hæmlɪt] *n* aldea *f*.

hammer ['hæmə^r] **I** *n* **1** martillo *m*; **the h. and sickle**, la hoz y el martillo. **2** (*of gun*) percursor *m*. **3** *Sport* lanzamiento *m* de martillo. **II** *vtr* **1** martillar; (*nail*) clavar; *fig* **to h. home**, insistir sobre. **2** *fam* (*defeat*) dar una paliza a. **III** *vi* martillar, dar golpes.

hammering ['hæmərɪŋ] *n fam* paliza *f*.

hammock ['hæmək] *n* hamaca *f*; *Naut* coy *m*.

hamper¹ ['hæmpə^r] *n* cesta *f*.

hamper² ['hæmpə^r] *vtr* estorbar, dificultar.

hamster ['hæmstə^r] *n* hámster *m*.

hamstring ['hæmstrɪŋ] *n* tendón *m* de la corva.

hand [hænd] **I** *n* **1** mano *f*; **by h.**, a mano; (*close*) **at h.**, a mano; **hands up!**, ¡manos arriba!; **on the one/other h.**, por una/otra parte; *fig* **to get out of h.**, descontrolarse; *fig* **to be on h.**, estar a mano; *fig* **to have a h. in**, intervenir en; *fig* **to have time in h.**, sobrarle a uno tiempo; *fig* **to wash one's hands of sth**, lavarse las manos de algo; *fig* **to give sb a h.**, echarle una mano a algn; **h. grenade**, granada *f* de mano. **2** (*worker*) trabajador,-a *m,f*; *Naut* tripulante *m*. **3** (*of clock*) aguja *f*. **4** **to give sb a big h.**, (*applause*) dedicar a algn una gran ovación. **5** (*handwriting*) letra *f*.

II *vtr* (*give*) dar, entregar; *fam fig* **I have to h. it to you**, tengo que reconocerlo.

◆**hand back** *vtr* devolver. ◆**hand**

down *vtr* dejar en herencia. ◆**hand in** *vtr* (*homework*) entregar; (*resignation*) presentar. ◆**hand out** *vtr* repartir. ◆**hand over** *vtr* entregar. ◆**hand round** *vtr* repartir.

handbag ['hændbæg] *n* bolso *m*.

handball ['hændbɔːl] *n* Sport balonmano *m*.

handbook ['hændbʊk] *n* manual *m*.

handbrake ['hændbreɪk] *n* freno *m* de mano.

handcuff ['hændkʌf] I *vtr* esposar. II *npl* **handcuffs**, esposas *fpl*.

handful ['hændfʊl] *n* puñado *m*.

handicap ['hændɪkæp] *n* I *n* 1 Med minusvalía *f*. 2 (*Sport*) hándicap *m*, desventaja *f*. II *vtr* impedir.

handicapped ['hændɪkæpt] *adj* 1 (*physically*) minusválido,-a; (*mentally*) retrasado,-a. 2 Sport en desventaja. 3 *fig* desfavorecido,-a.

handicraft ['hændɪkrɑːft] *n* artesanía *f*.

handiwork ['hændɪwɜːk] *n* (*work*) obra *f*; (*craft*) artesanía *f*.

handkerchief ['hæŋkətʃiːf] *n* pañuelo *m*.

handle ['hændl] I *n* (*of knife*) mango *m*; (*of cup*) asa *f*; (*of door*) pomo *m*; (*of lever*) palanca *f*; (*of drawer*) tirador *m*. II *vtr* 1 manejar; '**h. with care**', 'frágil'. 2 (*problem*) encargarse de; (*people*) tratar; *fam* (*put up with*) soportar. III *vi* (*car*) comportarse.

handlebar ['hændlbɑːr] *n* manillar *m*.

handmade [hænd'meɪd] *adj* hecho,-a a mano.

hand-out ['hændaʊt] *n* 1 (*leaflet*) folleto *m*; Press nota *f* de prensa. 2 (*charity*) limosna *f*.

hand-picked [hænd'pɪkt] *adj* selecto,-a.

handrail ['hændreɪl] *n* pasamanos *m sing inv*.

handshake ['hændʃeɪk] *n* apretón *m* de manos.

handsome ['hænsəm] *adj* 1 (*person*) guapo,-a. 2 (*substantial*) considerable.

handwriting ['hændraɪtɪŋ] *n* letra *f*.

handy ['hændɪ] *adj* (**handier, handiest**) 1 (*useful*) útil, práctico,-a; (*nearby*) a mano. 2 (*dextrous*) diestro,-a.

hang [hæŋ] I *vtr* (*pt & pp* **hung**) 1 colgar. 2 (*head*) bajar. 3 (*pt & pp* **hanged**) ahorcar. II *vi* 1 colgar (*from*, de); (*in air*) flotar. 2 (*criminal*) ser ahorcado,-a; **to h. oneself**, ahorcarse. ◆**hang about**, **hang round** *vi fam* 1 perder el tiempo. 2 *fam* (*wait*) esperar. ◆**hang around** *vi fam* 1 esperar. 2 *fam* frecuentar; **where does he h. around?**, ¿a qué lugares suele ir? ◆**hang on** *vi* 1 agarrarse. 2 (*wait*) esperar. ◆**hang on to** *vtr* (*washing*) tender. II *vi fam* (*frequent*) frecuentar. ◆**hang together** *vi* (*ideas*) ser coherente. ◆**hang up** *vtr* (*picture, telephone*) colgar.

hangar ['hæŋər] *n* hangar *m*.

hanger ['hæŋər] *n* percha *f*.

hang-glider ['hæŋglaɪdər] *n* ala delta.

hang-gliding ['hæŋglaɪdɪŋ] *n* vuelo *m* libre.

hangman ['hæŋmən] *n* verdugo *m*.

hangover ['hæŋəʊvər] *n* resaca *f*.

hang-up ['hæŋʌp] *n fam* (*complex*) complejo *m*.

hanker ['hæŋkər] *vi* **to h. after** sth, anhelar algo.

hankie, hanky ['hæŋkɪ] *n fam* pañuelo *m*.

haphazard [hæp'hæzəd] *adj* caótico,-a, desordenado,-a.

happen ['hæpən] *vi* suceder, ocurrir; **if so happens that**, lo que pasa es que; **if you h. to see my friend**, si por casualidad ves a mi amigo.

happening ['hæpənɪŋ] *n* acontecimiento *m*.

happiness ['hæpɪnɪs] *n* felicidad *f*.

happy ['hæpɪ] *adj* (**happier, happiest**) (*cheerful*) feliz, contento,-a; (*fortunate*) afortunado,-a; **h. birthday!**, ¡feliz cumpleaños! ◆**happily** *adv* (*with pleasure*) felizmente; (*fortunately*) afortunadamente.

happy-go-lucky [hæpɪgəʊ'lʌkɪ] *adj* despreocupado,-a; **a h.-go-l. fellow**, un viva la virgen.

harangue [hə'ræŋ] I *vtr* arengar. II *n* arenga *f*.

harass ['hærəs] *vtr* acosar.

harassment ['hærəsmənt, hə'ræsmənt] *n* hostigamiento *m*, acoso *m*.

harbour, US **harbor** ['hɑːbər] I *n* puerto *m*. II *vtr* 1 (*criminal*) encubrir. 2 (*doubts*) abrigar.

hard [hɑːd] I *adj* 1 duro,-a; (*solid*) sólido,-a; **h. court**, pista (de tenis) rápida; *Comput* **h. disk**, disco duro; **h. shoulder**, arcén *m*. 2 (*difficult*) difícil; **h. of hearing**, duro,-a de oído; *fam* **fig to be h. up**, estar sin blanca. 3 (*harsh*) severo,-a; (*strict*) estricto,-a; **to take a h. line**, tomar medidas severas; **h. drugs**, droga dura; *Pol* **h. left**, extrema izquierda *f*. **h. porn**, pornografía dura; **h. sell**, promoción *f* de venta agresiva. **a h. drinker**, un bebedor inveterado; **a h. worker**, un trabajador concienzudo. 5 **h. luck!**, ¡mala suerte! 6 **h. evidence**, pruebas definitivas; *Com* **h. cash**, dinero *m* en metálico; **h. currency**, divisa *f* fuerte. II *adv* 1 (*hit*) fuerte. 2 (*work*) mucho, concienzudamente; *fig* **to be h. on sb's heels**, pisar los talones a algn. 3 **to be h. done by**, ser tratado,-a injustamente.

hardback ['hɑːdbæk] *n* edición *f* de tapas duras.

hard-boiled ['hɑːdbɔɪld] *adj* duro,-a.

hard-core ['hɑːdkɔːr] *adj* irreductible.

harden ['hɑːdən] I *vtr* endurecer. II *vi* endurecerse.

hardened ['hɑːdənd] *adj fig* habitual.

hard-headed |ˈhɑːdhedɪd| adj realista.
hard-hearted |ˈhɑːdˈhɑːtɪd| adj insensible.
hardliner |ˈhɑːdlaɪnəʳ| n duro,-a m,f.
hardly |ˈhɑːdlɪ| adv apenas; **h. anyone/ ever,** casi nadie/nunca; **he had h. begun when ...,** apenas había comenzado cuando ...; **I can h. believe it,** apenas lo puedo creer.
hardship |ˈhɑːdʃɪp| n privación f, apuro m.
hardware |ˈhɑːdweəʳ| n 1 (goods) ferretería f; **h. shop,** ferretería. 2 Comput hardware m.
hardwearing |hɑːdˈweərɪŋ| adj duradero,-a.
hardworking |ˈhɑːdwɜːkɪŋ| adj muy trabajador,-a.
hardy |ˈhɑːdɪ| adj (hardier, hardiest) (person) robusto,-a, fuerte; (plant) resistente.
hare |heəʳ| I n liebre f. II vi correr muy de prisa.
haricot |ˈhærɪkəʊ| n h. (bean), alubia f.
harm |hɑːm| I n daño m, perjuicio m; **to be out of h.'s way,** estar a salvo. II vtr hacer daño a, perjudicar.
harmful |ˈhɑːmful| adj perjudicial (to, para).
harmless |ˈhɑːmlɪs| adj inofensivo,-a.
harmonica |hɑːˈmɒnɪkə| n armónica f.
harmonize |ˈhɑːmənaɪz| vtr & vi armonizar.
harmony |ˈhɑːmənɪ| n armonía f.
harness |ˈhɑːnɪs| I n 1 (for horse) arreos mpl. II vtr 1 (horse) enjaezar. 2 fig (resources etc) aprovechar.
harp |hɑːp| n arpa f. ◆**harp on** vi fam hablar sin parar.
harpoon |hɑːˈpuːn| I n arpón m. II vtr arponear.
harrowing |ˈhærəʊɪŋ| adj angustioso,-a.
harsh |hɑːʃ| adj severo,-a; (voice) áspero,-a; (sound) discordante.
harvest |ˈhɑːvɪst| I n cosecha f, (of grapes) vendimia f. II vtr cosechar, recoger.
harvester |ˈhɑːvɪstəʳ| n 1 (person) segador,-a m,f. 2 (machine) cosechadora f.
has |hæz| 3rd person sing pres → **have.**
hash¹ |hæʃ| n Culin sofrito m de carne; fam fig **to make a h. of sth,** estropear algo.
hash² |hæʃ| n sl fam hachís m.
hashish |ˈhæʃiːʃ| n hachís m.
hassle |ˈhæsəl| fam I n 1 (nuisance) rollo m. 2 (problem) lío m. 3 (wrangle) bronca f. II vtr fastidiar.
haste |heɪst| n fml prisa f; **to make h.,** darse prisa.
hasten |ˈheɪsən| vi apresurarse.
hasty |ˈheɪstɪ| adj (hastier, hastiest) apresurado,-a; (rash) precipitado,-a. ◆**hastily** adv (quickly) de prisa.
hat |hæt| n sombrero m.
hatch¹ |hætʃ| n escotilla f; serving **h.,**

ventanilla f.
hatch² |hætʃ| vtr 1 (eggs) empollar. 2 fig (plan) tramar. ◆**hatch out** vi salirse del huevo.
hatchback |ˈhætʃbæk| n coche m de 3 or 5 puertas.
hatchet |ˈhætʃɪt| n hacha f; fam **h. man,** matón m.
hate |heɪt| I n odio m. II vtr odiar.
hateful |ˈheɪtful| adj odioso,-a.
hatred |ˈheɪtrɪd| n odio m.
haughty |ˈhɔːtɪ| adj (haughtier, haughtiest) altanero,-a, arrogante.
haul |hɔːl| I n 1 (journey) trayecto m. 2 Fishing redada f. 3 (loot) botín m. II vtr 1 tirar; (drag) arrastrar. 2 (transport) acarrear. ◆**haul up** vtr fam (to court) llevar.
haulage |ˈhɔːlɪdʒ| n transporte m.
haulier |ˈhɔːljəʳ| n transportista mf.
haunch |hɔːntʃ| n cadera f; Culin pernil m.
haunt |hɔːnt| I n guarida f. II vtr 1 (of ghost) aparecerse en. 2 fig atormentar. 3 (frequent) frecuentar.
haunted |ˈhɔːntɪd| adj encantado,-a, embrujado,-a.
Havana |həˈvænə| n La Habana; **H. cigar,** habano m.
have |hæv| I vtr (3rd person sing pres **has**) (pt & pp **had**) 1 (possess) tener, **have you got a car?** ¿tienes coche? 2 (get, experience, suffer) tener; **to h. a holiday,** tomarse unas vacaciones. 3 (partake of) tomar; **to h. a cigarette,** fumarse un cigarrillo; **to h. breakfast/lunch/tea/dinner,** desayunar/comer/merendar/cenar. 4 **to h. a bath/shave,** bañarse/afeitarse; **to h. a nap,** echar la siesta. 5 **to h.** (*obligation*) tener que, deber. 6 (make happen) hacer que; **I'll h. someone come round,** haré que venga alguien. 7 (receive) recibir; **to h. people round,** invitar a gente. 8 **can I h. your pen a moment?,** (borrow) ¿me dejas tu bolígrafo un momento? 9 (party, meeting) hacer, celebrar. 10 **to h. a baby,** tener un niño. 11 **we won't h. it,** (allow) no lo consentiríamos. 12 (hold) tener; fig **to h. sth against sb,** tener algo en contra de algn. 13 legend **has it that ...,** según la leyenda ... 14 fam (deceive) engañar. 15 **you'd better stay,** más vale que te quedes.
II v aux 1 (compound) haber; **I had been waiting for half an hour,** hacía media hora que esperaba; **he hasn't eaten yet,** no ha comido aún; **she had broken the window,** había roto el cristal; **we h. lived here for ten years,** hace diez años que vivimos aquí; **so I h.!,** (emphatic) ¡ay, sí!, es verdad; **yes I h.!,** ¡que sí! 2 (tag questions) **you haven't seen my book, h. you?,** no has visto mis gafas, ¿verdad?; **he's been to France, hasn't he?,** ha estado en Francia, ¿verdad? o ¿no? 3 (have

+ *just*) acabar de.
◆**have on** vtr 1 (*wear*) vestir. 2 *fam* to **h. sb on**, tomarle el pelo a algn. ◆**have out** vtr *fam* to **h. it out with sb**, ajustar cuentas con algn. ◆**have over** vtr (*invite*) invitar.

haven ['heɪvən] *n* puerto *m*; *fig* refugio *m*.

haversack ['hævəsæk] *n* mochila *f*.

havoc ['hævək] *n* to **play h. with**, hacer estragos en.

hawk [hɔːk] *n* Orn Pol halcón *m*.

hawker ['hɔːkə^r] *n* vendedor,-a *m,f* ambulante.

hawthorn ['hɔːθɔːn] *n* espino *m* albar.

hay [heɪ] *n* heno *m*; **h. fever**, fiebre *f* del heno.

haystack ['heɪstæk] *n* almiar *m*.

haywire ['heɪwaɪə^r] *adj fam* **to go h.**, (*machine etc*) estropearse; (*person*) volverse loco,-a.

hazard ['hæzəd] *n* peligro *m*, riesgo *m*; *Golf* obstáculo *m*. II *vtr fml* arriesgar; **to h. a guess**, intentar adivinar.

hazardous ['hæzədəs] *adj* arriesgado,-a, peligroso,-a.

haze [heɪz] *n* (*mist*) neblina *f*; *fig* (*blur*) confusión *f*.

hazel ['heɪzəl] *adj* (de color) avellana.

hazelnut ['heɪzəlnʌt] *n* avellana *f*.

hazy ['heɪzɪ] *adj* (**hazier, haziest**) nebuloso,-a.

he [hiː] *pers pron* él; **he did it**, ha sido él; **he who**, el que.

head [hed] I *n* 1 cabeza *f*; (*mind*) mente *f*; *fig* **three pounds a h.**, tres libras por cabeza; *fig* **to be h. over heels in love**, estar locamente enamorado,-a; *fig* **to keep one's h.**, mantener la calma; *fig* **to lose one's h.**, perder la cabeza; **success went to his h.**, se le subió el éxito a la cabeza; **h. start**, ventaja *f*. 2 (*of nail*) cabeza *f*; (*of beer*) espuma *f*; (*of tape recorder*) cabezal *m*; (*of steam*) presión *f*; *fig* **to come to a h.**, llegar a un momento decisivo. 3 (*boss*) cabeza *m*; (*of company*) director,-a *m,f*; **h. teacher**, director,-a *m,f*. 4 (*of coin*) cara *f*; **heads or tails**, cara o cruz. II *adj* principal; **h. office**, oficina *f* central. III *vtr* 1 (*list etc*) encabezar. 2 *Ftb* cabecear. ◆**head for** *vtr* dirigirse hacia. ◆**head off** I *vi* irse. II *vtr* (*avert*) evitar.

headache ['hedeɪk] *n* dolor *m* de cabeza; *fig* quebradero *m* de cabeza.

header ['hedə^r] *n* Ftb cabezazo *m*.

head-first [hed'fɜːst] *adv* de cabeza.

head-hunter ['hedhʌntə^r] *n fig* cazatalentos *mf inv*.

heading ['hedɪŋ] *n* título *m*; (*of letter*) membrete *m*.

headlamp ['hedlæmp] *n* faro *m*.

headland ['hedlənd] *n* punta *f*, cabo *m*.

headlight ['hedlaɪt] *n* faro *m*.

headline ['hedlaɪn] *n* titular *m*.

headlong ['hedlɒŋ] *adj & adv* de cabeza;

to rush h. into sth, lanzarse a hacer algo sin pensar.

headmaster [hed'mɑːstə^r] *n* director *m*.

headmistress [hed'mɪstrɪs] *n* directora *f*.

head-on ['hedɒn] *adj* a **h.-on collision**, un choque frontal.

headphones ['hedfəʊnz] *npl* auriculares *mpl*.

headquarters ['hedkwɔːtəz] *npl* 1 oficina *f* central, sede *f*. 2 *Mil* cuartel *m* general.

headrest ['hedrest] *n* Aut apoyacabezas *m*.

headroom ['hedruːm] *n* altura *f* libre.

headscarf ['hedskɑːf] *n* pañuelo *m*.

headstrong ['hedstrɒŋ] *adj* testarudo,-a.

headway ['hedweɪ] *n* to **make h.**, avanzar, progresar.

headwind ['hedwɪnd] *n* viento *m* de proa.

heady ['hedɪ] *adj* (**headier, headiest**) embriagador,-a.

heal [hiːl] I *vi* cicatrizar. II *vtr* (*illness*) curar.

health [helθ] *n* salud *f*; *fig* prosperidad *f*; **to be in good/bad h.**, estar bien/mal de salud; **your good h.!**, ¡salud!; **h. foods**, alimentos *mpl* naturales; **h. food shop**, tienda *f* de alimentos naturales; **h. service**, ≈ Insalud *m*.

healthy ['helθɪ] *adj* (**healthier, healthiest**) sano,-a; (*good for health*) saludable; (*thriving*) próspero,-a.

heap [hiːp] I *n* montón *m*. II *vtr* amontonar; *fig* (*praises*) colmar de; **a heaped spoonful**, una cucharada colmada.

hear [hɪə^r] I *vtr* (*pt & pp* **heard** [hɜːd]) 1 oír. 2 (*listen to*) escuchar. 3 **I won't h. of it!**, ¡ni hablar! 4 (*find out*) enterarse de. II *vi* (*law*) ver; (*evidence*) oír. II *vi* **to h. from sb**, tener noticias de algn.

hearing ['hɪərɪŋ] *n* 1 oído *m*; **h. aid**, audífono *m*. 2 *Jur* audiencia *f*; *fig* **to give sb a fair h.**, escuchar a algn.

hearsay ['hɪəseɪ] *n* rumores *mpl*.

hearse [hɜːs] *n* coche *m* fúnebre.

heart [hɑːt] *n* 1 corazón *m*; **h. attack**, infarto *m* de miocardio; **h. transplant**, trasplante *m* de corazón; **a broken h.**, un corazón roto; **at h.**, en el fondo; **to take sth to h.**, tomarse algo a pecho; **to have a good h.**, (*be kind*) tener buen corazón. 2 (*courage*) valor *m*; **his h. wasn't in it**, no ponía interés en ello; **to lose h.**, desanimarse. 3 (*core*) meollo *m*; (*of lettuce*) cogollo *m*.

heartbeat ['hɑːtbiːt] *n* latido *m* del corazón.

heart-breaking ['hɑːtbreɪkɪŋ] *adj* desgarrador,-a.

heart-broken ['hɑːtbrəʊkən] *adj* hundido,-a; **he's h.-b.**, tiene el corazón destrozado.

heartburn ['hɑːtbɜːn] *n* acedía *f*.

heartening ['hɑːtənɪŋ] *adj* alentador,-a.

heartfelt ['hɑːtfelt] *adj* sincero,-a.

hearth [hɑːθ] n 1 (*fireplace*) chimenea f. 2 *fml* (*home*) hogar m.

heartless ['hɑːtlɪs] adj cruel, insensible.

heart-throb ['hɑːtθrɒb] n ídolo m.

hearty ['hɑːtɪ] adj (*heartier, heartiest*) (*person*) francote; (*meal*) abundante; (*welcome*) cordial; **to have a h. appetite**, ser de buen comer.

heat [hiːt] I n 1 calor m. 2 *Sport* eliminatoria f. 3 *Zool* **on h.**, en celo. II vtr calentar. ◆**heat up** vt i (*warm up*) calentarse. 2 (*increase excitement*) acalorarse.

heated ['hiːtɪd] adj *fig* (*argument*) acalorado,-a.

heater ['hiːtəʳ] n calentador m.

heath [hiːθ] n (*land*) brezal m.

heathen ['hiːðən] adj & n pagano,-a (m,f).

heather ['heðəʳ] n brezo m.

heating ['hiːtɪŋ] n calefacción f.

heatwave ['hiːtweɪv] n ola f de calor.

heave [hiːv] I n (*pull*) tirón m; (*push*) empujón m. II vtr 1 (*lift*) levantar; (*haul*) tirar; (*push*) empujar. 2 (*throw*) arrojar. III vi subir y bajar.

heaven ['hevən] I n 1 cielo m; **for heaven's sake!**, ¡por Dios!. 2 **h. on earth**, un paraíso en la tierra. II *interj* **good heavens!**, ¡por Dios!

heavenly ['hevənlɪ] adj celestial.

heavy ['hevɪ] I adj (*heavier, heaviest*) pesado,-a; (*rain, meal*) fuerte; (*traffic*) denso,-a; (*loss*) grande; **h. going**, duro,-a, **is it h.?**, ¿pesa mucho?; **a h. drinker/smoker**, un,-a bebedor,-a/fumador,-a empedernido,-a; *Mus* **h. metal**, heavy metal m. II n sl gorila m. ◆**heavily** adv **it rained h.**, llovió mucho; **to sleep h.**, dormir profundamente.

heavyweight ['hevɪweɪt] n *Box* peso pesado.

Hebrew ['hiːbruː] I adj hebreo,-a m,f. II n (*language*) hebreo m.

Hebrides ['hebrɪdiːz] npl **the H.**, las (Islas) Hébridas.

heckle ['hekəl] vtr interrumpir.

heckler ['hekləʳ] n altercador,-a m,f.

hectare ['hektɑː] n hectárea f.

hectic ['hektɪk] adj agitado,-a.

hedge [hedʒ] I n seto m. II vtr cercar con un seto; *fig* **to h. one's bets**, cubrirse.

hedgehog ['hedʒhɒg] n erizo m.

hedgerow ['hedʒrəʊ] n seto vivo.

heed [hiːd] vtr **to take h. of**, hacer caso de.

heedless ['hiːdlɪs] adj desatento,-a.

heel [hiːl] n talón m; (*of shoe*) tacón m; (*of palm*) pulpejo m; *fig* **to be on sb's heels**, pisarle los talones a algn; **high heels**, zapatos mpl de tacón alto.

heeled [hiːld] adj *fam* **fig well-h.**, adinerado,-a.

hefty ['heftɪ] adj (*heftier, heftiest*) 1 (*person*) fornido,-a. 2 (*package*) pesado,-a. 2 (*large*) grande.

height [haɪt] n 1 altura f; (*of person*) estatura f; *Av* **to gain/lose h.**, subir/bajar; **what h. are you?**, ¿cuánto mides?; *fig* **the h. of ignorance**, el colmo de la ignorancia. 2 *Geog* cumbre f.

heighten ['haɪtən] vtr (*intensify*) realzar; (*increase*) aumentar.

heir [eəʳ] n heredero m.

heiress ['eərɪs] n heredera f.

heirloom ['eəluːm] n reliquia f or joya f de familia.

held [held] pt & pp → **hold**.

helicopter ['helɪkɒptəʳ] n helicóptero m.

helium ['hiːlɪəm] n helio m.

hell [hel] n infierno m; *fam* **what the h. are you doing?**, ¿qué diablos estás haciendo?; *offens* **go to h.!**, ¡vete a hacer puñetas!; *fam* **a h. of a party**, una fiesta estupenda; *fam* **she's had a h. of a day**, ha tenido un día fatal.

hellish ['helɪʃ] adj *fam* infernal.

hello [hə'ləʊ, 'heləʊ] *interj* ¡hola!; *Tel* ¡diga!; (*showing surprise*) ¡hala!

helm [helm] n timón m; **to be at the h.**, llevar el timón.

helmet ['helmɪt] n casco m.

help [help] I n 1 ayuda f; **h.!**, ¡socorro! 2 (*daily*) n,-a, asistenta f. II vtr 1 ayudar; **can I h. you?**, (*in shop*) ¿qué desea? 2 (*alleviate*) aliviar. 3 **h. yourself!**, (*to food etc*) ¡sírvete! 4 (*avoid*) evitar; **I can't h. it**, no lo puedo remediar. ◆**help out** vtr **to h. sb out**, echarle una mano a algn.

helper ['helpəʳ] n ayudante,-a m,f.

helpful ['helpfʊl] adj (*person*) amable; (*thing*) útil.

helping ['helpɪŋ] n ración f; **who wants a second h.?**, ¿quién quiere repetir?

helpless ['helplɪs] adj (*defenceless*) desamparado,-a; (*powerless*) incapaz. ◆**helplessly** adv inútilmente, en vano.

helter-skelter [heltə'skeltəʳ] I n tobogán m. II adj atropellado,-a. III adv atropelladamente.

hem [hem] I n *Sew* dobladillo m. II vtr *Sew* hacer un dobladillo a. ◆**hem in** vtr cercar, rodear.

hemisphere ['hemɪsfɪəʳ] n hemisferio m.

hemophilia [hiːmə'fɪlɪə] n *US* → **haemophilia**.

hemorrhage ['hemərɪdʒ] n *US* → **haemorrhage**.

hen [hen] n gallina f; *fam* **h. party**, reunión f de mujeres.

hence [hens] adv *fml* 1 **six months h.**, (*from now*) de aquí a seis meses. 2 (*consequently*) por lo tanto.

henceforth [hens'fɔːθ] adv *fml* de ahora en adelante.

henchman ['hentʃmən] n *pej* secuaz m.

henna ['henə] n *Bot* alheña f 2. (*dye*) henna f.

henpecked ['henpekt] adj *fam* **a h. husband**, un calzonazos.

hepatitis [hepə'taɪtɪs] n hepatitis f.

her [hɜːr, unstressed hə] I poss adj (one thing) su; (more than one) sus; (to distinguish) de ella; **are they h. books or his?**, ¿los libros son de ella o de él?; **she has cut h. finger**, se ha cortado el dedo. II object pron 1 (direct object) la; **I saw h. recently**, la vi hace poco. 2 (indirect object) le; (with other third person pronouns) se; **he gave h. money**, le dio dinero; **they handed it to h.**, se lo entregaron. 3 (after prep) ella; **for h.**, para ella. 4 (as subject) fam ella; **look, it's h.!**, ¡mira, es ella!

herald ['herəld] I n heraldo m. II vtr anunciar.

heraldry ['herəldrɪ] n heráldica f.

herb [hɜːb] n hierba f; **h. tea**, infusión f.

herbal ['hɜːbəl] adj herbario,-a; **h. remedies**, curas fpl de hierbas.

herd [hɜːd] n (of cattle) manada f; (of goats) rebaño m; fig (large group) multitud f.

here [hɪər] I adv aquí; **come h.**, ven aquí; **h.!**, ¡presente!; **h. goes!**, ¡vamos a ver!; **here's to success!**, ¡brindemos por el éxito!; **h. you are!**, ¡toma! II interj look **h., you can't do that!**, ¡oiga, que no se permite hacer eso!

hereafter [hɪər'ɑːftər] fml I adv de ahora en adelante. II n **the h.**, la otra vida, el más allá.

hereby [hɪə'baɪ] adv fml por la presente.

hereditary [hɪ'redɪtərɪ] adj hereditario,-a.

heresy ['herəsɪ] n herejía f.

heretic ['herətɪk] n hereje mf.

heritage ['herɪtɪdʒ] n patrimonio m; Jur herencia f.

hermetically [hɜː'metɪklɪ] adv **h. sealed**, herméticamente cerrado.

hermit ['hɜːmɪt] n ermitaño,-a m,f.

hermitage ['hɜːmɪtɪdʒ] n ermita f.

hernia ['hɜːnɪə] n hernia f.

hero ['hɪərəʊ] n (pl heroes) héroe m; (in novel) protagonista m; **h. worship**, idolatría f.

heroic [hɪ'rəʊɪk] adj heroico,-a.

heroin ['herəʊɪn] n heroína f.

heroine ['herəʊɪn] n heroína f; (in novel) protagonista f.

heron ['herən] n garza f.

herring ['herɪŋ] n arenque m.

hers [hɜːz] poss pron 1 (attribute) (one thing) suyo,-a; (more than one) suyos,-as; (to distinguish) de ella; **they are h. not his**, son de ella, no de él. 2 (noun reference) (one thing) el suyo, la suya; (more than one) los suyos, las suyas; **my car is blue and h. is red**, mi coche es azul y el suyo es rojo.

herself [hɜː'self] pers pron 1 (reflexive); **she dressed h.**, se vistió. 2 (alone) ella misma; **she was by h.**, estaba sola. 3 (emphatic) **she told me so h.**, eso dijo ella.

hesitant ['hezɪtənt] adj vacilante.

hesitate ['hezɪteɪt] vi vacilar.

hesitation [hezɪ'teɪʃən] n indecisión f.

heterogeneous [hetərəʊ'dʒiːnɪəs] adj heterogéneo,-a.

heterosexual [hetərəʊ'seksjʊəl] adj & n heterosexual (mf).

hey [heɪ] interj ¡oye!, ¡oiga!

heyday ['heɪdeɪ] n auge m, apogeo m.

HGV [eɪtʃdʒiː'viː] GB abbr of **heavy goods vehicle**, vehículo m de carga pesada.

hi [haɪ] interj fam ¡hola!

hiatus [haɪ'eɪtəs] n fml laguna f.

hibernate ['haɪbəneɪt] vi hibernar.

hibernation [haɪbə'neɪʃən] n hibernación f.

hibiscus [haɪ'bɪskəs] n hibisco m.

hiccough ['hɪkʌp] n & vi = **hiccup**.

hiccup ['hɪkʌp] n hipo m; fam (minor problem) problemilla m; **to have hiccups**, tener hipo.

hide¹ [haɪd] I vtr (pt hid [hɪd] pp hidden ['hɪdən]) (conceal) esconder; (obscure) ocultar. II vi esconderse, ocultarse. III n puesto m.

hide² [haɪd] n (of animal) piel f.

hide-and-seek [haɪdən'siːk] n escondite m.

hideous ['hɪdɪəs] adj (horrific) horroroso,-a; (extremely ugly) espantoso,-a.

hide-out ['haɪdaʊt] n escondrijo m, guarida f.

hiding¹ ['haɪdɪŋ] n **to go into h.**, esconderse.

hiding² ['haɪdɪŋ] n fam paliza f.

hierarchy ['haɪərɑːkɪ] n jerarquía f.

hi-fi ['haɪfaɪ] n hifi m; **hi-fi equipment**, equipo m de alta fidelidad.

high [haɪ] I adj 1 alto,-a; **how h. is that wall?**, ¿qué altura tiene esa pared?; **it's three feet h.**, tiene tres pies de alto; **h. chair**, silla alta para niños; **h. jump**, salto m de altura. 2 (elevated) elevado,-a; **h. blood pressure**, tensión alta; **h. prices**, precios elevados; **to be in h. spirits**, estar de buen humor. 3 (important) importante; **h. wind**, viento m fuerte; **to have a h. opinion of sb**, tener muy buena opinión de algn; **H. Court**, Tribunal Supremo; **h. fidelity**, alta fidelidad f; **h. road**, carretera f principal; **h. school**, instituto m de enseñanza media; **the H. Street**, la Calle Mayor. 4 sl (drugged) colocado,-a. II adv alto; **to fly h.**, volar a gran altura. III n (high point) punto m máximo.

highbrow ['haɪbraʊ] adj & n intelectual (mf).

high-class ['haɪkluːs] adj de alta categoría.

higher ['haɪər] adj superior; **h. education**, enseñanza f superior.

high-flier, high-flyer [haɪˈflaɪəʳ] n fig persona dotada y ambiciosa.

high-handed [haɪˈhændɪd] adj despótico,-a.

high-heeled [haɪˈhiːld] adj de tacón alto.

highlands [ˈhaɪləndz] npl tierras altas.

highlight [ˈhaɪlaɪt] I n 1 (in hair) reflejo m. 2 (of event) atracción f principal. II vtr 1 hacer resaltar. 2 (a text) marcar con un rotulador fosforescente.

highly [ˈhaɪlɪ] adv (very) sumamente; to **speak h. of sb,** hablar muy bien de algn.

highly-strung [haɪlɪˈstrʌŋ] adj muy nervioso,-a.

Highness [ˈhaɪnɪs] n alteza mf; **Your H.,** Su Alteza.

high-pitched [ˈhaɪpɪtʃt] adj estridente.

high-powered [ˈhaɪpaʊəd] adj (person) dinámico,-a.

high-ranking [ˈhaɪrænkɪŋ] adj **h. official,** alto funcionario.

high-rise [ˈhaɪraɪz] adj **h.-r. building,** rascacielos m inv.

high-speed [ˈhaɪspiːd] adj & adv **h.-s. lens,** objetivo ultrarrápido; **h.-s. train,** tren m de alta velocidad.

highway [ˈhaɪweɪ] n US carretera f, autopista f; GB **H. Code,** código m de la circulación.

highwayman [ˈhaɪweɪmən] n salteador m de caminos.

hijack [ˈhaɪdʒæk] I vtr secuestrar. II n secuestro m.

hijacker [ˈhaɪdʒækəʳ] n secuestrador,-a m,f; (of planes) pirata mf del aire.

hike [haɪk] I n 1 (walk) excursión f. 2 **price h.,** aumento m de precio. II vi de excursión.

hiker [ˈhaɪkəʳ] n excursionista mf.

hilarious [hɪˈleərɪəs] adj graciosísimo,-a.

hill [hɪl] n colina f; (slope) cuesta f.

hillside [ˈhɪlsaɪd] n ladera f.

hilltop [ˈhɪltɒp] n cima f de una colina.

hilly [ˈhɪlɪ] adj (**hillier, hilliest**) accidentado,-a.

hilt [hɪlt] n puño m, empuñadura f; **I'll support you up to the h.,** te daré mi apoyo total.

him [hɪm] object pron 1 (direct object) lo, le; **hit h.!,** ¡pégale!; **she loves h.,** lo quiere. 2 (indirect object) le; (with other third person pronouns) se; **give h. the money,** dale el dinero; **give it to h.,** dáselo. 3 (after prep) él; **it's not like h. to say that,** no es propio de él decir eso. 4 (as subject) fam él; **it's h.,** es él.

himself [hɪmˈself] pers pron 1 (reflexive) se; **he hurt h.,** se hizo daño. 2 (alone) solo, por sí mismo; **by h.,** solo. 3 (emphatic) él mismo.

hind¹ [haɪnd] adj trasero,-a; **h. legs,** patas traseras.

hind² [haɪnd] n Zool cierva f.

hinder [ˈhɪndəʳ] vtr dificultar, estorbar; to

h. sb from doing sth, impedir a algn hacer algo.

hindrance [ˈhɪndrəns] n estorbo m.

hindsight [ˈhaɪndsaɪt] n retrospectiva f.

Hindu [hɪnˈduː, ˈhɪndu:] adj & n hindú (mf).

Hinduism [ˈhɪnduːɪzəm] n hinduismo m.

hinge [hɪndʒ] I n bisagra f; fig eje m. II vtr engoznar. ◆**hinge on** vtr depender de.

hint [hɪnt] I n 1 indirecta f; **to take the h.,** coger la indirecta. 2 (clue) pista f. 3 (trace) pizca f. 4 (advice) consejo m. II vi 1 lanzar indirectas. 2 (imply) insinuar algo.

hip¹ [hɪp] n cadera f; **h. flask,** petaca f.

hip² [hɪp] adj sl en la onda.

hippie [ˈhɪpɪ] adj & n fam hippy (mf).

hippopotamus [hɪpəˈpɒtəməs] n hipopótamo m.

hire [haɪəʳ] I n alquiler m; **bicycles for h.,** se alquilan bicicletas; **taxi for h.,** taxi m libre; **h. purchase,** compra f a plazos. II vtr 1 (rent) alquilar. 2 (employ) contratar. ◆**hire out** vtr (car) alquilar; (people) contratar.

his [hɪz] I poss adj (one thing) su; (more than one) sus; (to distinguish) de él; **he washed h. face,** se lavó la cara; **is it h. dog or hers?,** ¿el perro es de él o de ella? II poss pron 1 (one thing) suyo, -a; (more than one) suyos,-as; (to distinguish) de él. 2 (noun reference) (one thing) el suyo, la suya; (more than one) los suyos, las suyas; **my car is blue and h. is red,** mi coche es azul y el suyo es rojo.

Hispanic [hɪˈspænɪk] I adj hispánico,-a. II n US hispano,-a m,f, latino,-a m,f.

hiss [hɪs] I n siseo m; Theat silbido m. II vtr & vi silbar.

historian [hɪˈstɔːrɪən] n historiador,-a m,f.

historic [hɪˈstɒrɪk] adj histórico,-a.

historical [hɪˈstɒrɪkəl] adj histórico,-a; **h. novel,** novela histórica.

history [ˈhɪstərɪ] n historia f.

hit [hɪt] I n 1 (blow) golpe m; **direct h.,** impacto directo; fam **h. list,** lista negra; fam **h. man,** asesino m a sueldo. 2 (success) éxito m; **h. parade,** lista f de éxitos. II vtr (pt & pp hit) 1 (strike) golpear, pegar; **he was h. in the leg,** le dieron en la pierna; **the car h. the kerb,** el coche chocó contra el bordillo; fam fig **to h. the roof,** poner el grito en el cielo. 2 (affect) afectar. 3 **to h. the headlines,** ser noticia. ◆**hit back** vi (reply to criticism) replicar. ◆**hit on, hit upon** vtr dar con; **we h. on the idea of ...,** se nos ocurrió la idea de .... ◆**hit out** vi to **h. out at sb,** atacar a algn.

hit-and-run [hɪtənˈrʌn] adj **h.-and-r. driver,** conductor que atropella a algn y no para.

hitch [hɪtʃ] **I** n dificultad f. **II** vtr (fasten) atar. **III** vi fam (hitch-hike) hacer autostop.
◆**hitch up** vtr remangarse.

hitch-hike ['hɪtʃhaɪk] vi hacer autostop or dedo.

hitch-hiker ['hɪtʃhaɪkə'] n autostopista mf.

hitherto [hɪðə'tuː] adv fml hasta la fecha.

HIV [eɪtʃaɪ'viː] abbr of **human immuno-deficiency virus**, virus m de immuno-deficiencia humano, VIH; **to be diagnosed HIV positive/negative**, dar seropositivo,-a/seronegativo,-a en la prueba del SIDA.

hive [haɪv] n colmena f; fig lugar muy activo.

HM abbr of **His or Her Majesty**, Su Majestad mf, SM.

hoard [hɔːd] **I** n (provisions) reservas fpl; (money etc) tesoro m. **II** vtr (objects) acumular; (money) atesorar.

hoarding ['hɔːdɪŋ] n (billboard) valla publicitaria; (temporary fence) valla.

hoarfrost ['hɔːfrɒst] n escarcha f.

hoarse [hɔːs] adj ronco,-a; **to be h.**, tener la voz ronca.

hoax [həʊks] n (joke) broma pesada; (trick) engaño m.

hob [hɒb] n (of cooker) encimera f.

hobble ['hɒbəl] vi cojear.

hobby ['hɒbɪ] n pasatiempo m, afición f.

hobbyhorse ['hɒbɪhɔːs] n (toy) caballito m de juguete; fig (fixed idea) idea fija, manía f.

hobo ['həʊbəʊ] n US vagabundo,-a m,f.

hockey ['hɒkɪ] n hockey m.

hog [hɒg] **I** n cerdo m, puerco m; fam **to go the whole h.**, liarse la manta a la cabeza. **II** vtr fam acaparar.

hoist [hɔɪst] **I** n (crane) grúa f; (lift) montacargas m inv. **II** vtr levantar, subir; **to h. the flag**, izar la bandera.

hold [həʊld] **I** vtr (pt & pp **held**) 1 (keep in hand) aguantar, tener (en la mano); (grip) agarrar; (support) (weight) soportar; (opinion) sostener; **to h. sb**, abrazar a algn; **to h. sb's hand**, cogerle la mano a algn; fig **she can h. her own in French**, se defiende en francés. 2 (contain) dar cabida a; **the jug holds a litre**, en la jarra cabe un litro. 3 (meeting) celebrar; (conversation) mantener. 4 (reserve) guardar. 5 **to h. office**, ocupar un puesto. 6 (consider) considerar. 7 **he was held for two hours at the police station**, estuvo detenido durante dos horas en la comisaría; **to h. one's breath**, contener la respiración; **to h. sb hostage**, retener a algn como rehén. 8 Tel **to h. the line**, no colgar.

II vi 1 (rope) aguantar. 2 fig (offer) ser válido,-a.

III n 1 **to get h. of**, (grip) coger, agarrar; fig localizar; **can you get h. of a newspa-**per?, ¿puedes conseguir un periódico? 2 (control) control m. 3 Naut bodega f. 4 (in wrestling) llave f.
◆**hold back I** vtr (crowd) contener; (feelings) reprimir; (truth) ocultar; **I don't want to h. you back**, (delay) no quiero entretenerle. **II** vi (hesitate) vacilar.
◆**hold down** vtr 1 (control) dominar. 2 fam (job) desempeñar; **to h. sb at arm's length**, mantener a distancia. ◆**hold on** vi 1 (keep a firm grasp) agarrarse bien. 2 (wait) esperar; Tel **h. on!**, ¡no cuelgue! ◆**hold out I** vtr (hand) tender. **II** vi 1 (last) (things) durar; (person) resistir. 2 **to h. out for**, insistir en. ◆**hold up** vtr 1 (rob) (train) asaltar; (bank) atracar. 2 (delay) retrasar; **we were held up for half an hour**, sufrimos media hora de retraso. 3 (raise) levantar. 4 (support) apuntalar.

holdall ['həʊldɔːl] n GB bolsa f de viaje.

holder ['həʊldə'] n 1 (receptacle) recipiente m. 2 (owner) poseedor,-a m,f; (bearer) portador,-a m,f; (of passport) titular m; **record h.**, plusmarquista mf.

holding ['həʊldɪŋ] n 1 (property) propiedad f. 2 Fin valor m en cartera; **h. company**, holding m.

hold-up ['həʊldʌp] n 1 (robbery) atraco m. 2 (delay) retraso m; (in traffic) atasco m.

hole [həʊl] n 1 agujero m; (large) hoyo m; (in the road) bache m. 2 Golf hoyo m. 3 sl (of place) antro m.

holiday ['hɒlɪdeɪ] **I** n (one day) día m de fiesta; GB (several days) vacaciones fpl; **to be/go on h.**, estar/ir de vacaciones; **h. resort**, lugar turístico. **II** vi GB pasar las vacaciones; (in summer) veranear.

holiday-maker ['hɒlɪdeɪmeɪkə'] n GB turista mf; (in summer) veraneante mf.

holiness ['həʊlɪnɪs] n santidad f.

Holland ['hɒlənd] n Holanda.

hollow ['hɒləʊ] **I** adj 1 hueco,-a. 2 (cheeks, eyes) hundido,-a. 3 fig (insincere) falso,-a; (empty) vacío,-a. **II** n hueco m; Geog hondonada f. **III** vtr **to h.** (out), hacer un hueco en.

holly ['hɒlɪ] n acebo m.

holocaust ['hɒləkɔːst] n holocausto m.

holster ['həʊlstə'] n pistolera f.

holy ['həʊlɪ] adj sagrado,-a, santo,-a; (blessed) bendito,-a; **H. Ghost**, Espíritu Santo; **H. Land**, Tierra Santa; **H. See**, Santa Sede.

homage ['hɒmɪdʒ] n homenaje m; **to pay h. to sb**, rendir homenaje a algn.

home [həʊm] **I** n 1 casa f, hogar m; **at h.**, en casa; fig **make yourself at h.!**, ¡estás en tu casa!; fig **to feel at h.**, estar a gusto. 2 (institution) asilo m; **old people's h.**, asilo de ancianos. 3 (country) patria f. 4 Sport **to play at h.**, jugar en casa; US **h. base**, (in baseball) base f del bateador; **h. run**, carrera completa. **II** adj 1 (domestic) del hogar; GB **h. help**, asistenta f. 2

Pol interior; **h. affairs,** asuntos *mpl* interiores; *GB* **H. Office,** Ministerio *m* del Interior; *GB* **H. Secretary,** Ministro,-a *m,f* del Interior. 3 *(native)* natal. **III** *adv* en casa; **to go h.,** ir a casa; **to leave h.,** irse de casa.

homeland ['həʊmlænd] *n* patria *f*; *(birthplace)* tierra *f* natal.

homeless ['həʊmlɪs] **I** *adj* sin techo. **II** *npl* **the h.,** los sin techo.

homely ['həʊmlɪ] *adj* (**homelier, homeliest**) **1** *GB (person)* casero,-a; *(atmosphere)* familiar. **2** *US (unattractive)* sin atractivo.

home-made ['həʊmmeɪd] *adj* casero,-a.

homeopathy [həʊmɪ'ɒpəθɪ] *n US* → **homoeopathy.**

homesick ['həʊmsɪk] *adj* **to be h.,** tener morriña.

homeward(s) ['həʊmwəd(z)] *adv* hacia casa.

homework ['həʊmwɜːk] *n* deberes *mpl*.

homicide ['hɒmɪsaɪd] *n* homicidio *m*.

homing ['həʊmɪŋ] *adj* **1 h. device,** cabeza buscadora. **2 h. pigeon,** paloma mensajera.

homoeopathy [həʊmɪ'ɒpəθɪ] *n* homeopatía *f*.

homogeneous [hɒmə'dʒiːnɪəs] *adj* homogéneo,-a.

homosexual [həʊməʊ'seksjʊəl] *adj & n* homosexual *(mf)*.

Honduran [hɒn'djʊərən] *adj & n* hondureño,-a *(m,f)*.

Honduras [hɒn'djʊərəs] *n* Honduras *f*.

honest ['ɒnɪst] *adj* honrado,-a; *(sincere)* sincero,-a, franco,-a; *(fair)* justo,-a; **the h. truth,** la pura verdad; ◆**honestly** *adv* honradamente; *(question)* ¿de verdad?; *(exclamation)* ¡hay que ver!; **h., it doesn't matter,** de verdad, no tiene importancia.

honesty ['ɒnɪstɪ] *n* honradez *f*.

honey ['hʌnɪ] *n* miel *f*; *US fam (endearment)* cariño *m*.

honeycomb ['hʌnɪkəʊm] *n* panal *m*.

honeymoon ['hʌnɪmuːn] *n* luna *f* de miel.

honeysuckle ['hʌnɪsʌkəl] *n* madreselva *f*.

honk ['hɒŋk] *vi Aut* tocar la bocina.

honor ['ɒnər] *n & vtr US* → **honour.**

honorary ['ɒnərərɪ] *adj (member)* honorario,-a; *(duties)* honorífico,-a.

honour ['ɒnər] **I** *n* **1** honor *m*. **2** *US Jur* **Her H., His H., Your H.,** Su Señoría *f*. **3** *Mil* **honours,** honores *mpl*. **4 Honours degree,** licenciatura *f* superior. **II** *vtr* **1** *(respect)* honrar. **2** *(obligation)* cumplir con.

honourable ['ɒnərəbəl] *adj (person)* honrado,-a; *(action)* honroso,-a.

hood [hʊd] *n* **1** *(of garment)* capucha *f*. **2** *(of car)* capota *f*; *US (bonnet)* capó *m*.

hoodlum ['huːdləm] *n* matón *m*.

hoodwink ['hʊdwɪŋk] *vtr* engañar.

hoof [huːf] *n (pl* **hoofs** *or* **hooves** [huːvz]) *(of horse)* casco *m*; *(of cow, sheep)* pezuña *f*.

hook [hʊk] **I** *n* **1** gancho *m*; *Fishing* anzuelo *m*; *Sew* **hooks and eyes,** corchetes *mpl*; **to take the phone off the h.,** descolgar el teléfono. **2** *Box* gancho *m*. **II** *vtr* **1** enganchar. **2** *Box* hacer un gancho a. ◆**hook up** *vtr & vi Rad TV Comput* conectar **(with,** con).

hooked [hʊkt] *adj* **1** *(nose)* aguileño,-a. **2** *sl (addicted)* enganchado,-a **(on,** a); **to get h.,** engancharse.

hook-up ['hʊkʌp] *n* **1** *Comput* conexión *f*. **2** *Rad TV* emisión *f* múltiple.

hooligan ['huːlɪgən] *n sl* gamberro,-a *m,f*.

hoop [huːp] *n* aro *m*; *(of barrel)* fleje *m*.

hooray [huː'reɪ] *interj* ¡hurra!

hoot [huːt] **I** *n* **1** ululato *m*; *fam* **hoots of laughter,** carcajadas *fpl*; *fam* **I don't care a h.,** me importa un pepino. **2** *(of car horn)* bocinazo *m*. **II** *vi* **1** *(owl)* ulular. **2** *(car)* dar un bocinazo; *(train)* silbar; *(siren)* pitar.

hooter ['huːtər] *n esp GB (of car)* bocina *f*; *(siren)* sirena *f*.

Hoover® ['huːvər] *GB* **I** *n* aspiradora *f*. **II** *vtr* **to h.,** pasar la aspiradora por.

hop¹ [hɒp] **I** *vi* saltar; **to h. on one leg,** andar a la pata coja. **II** *n (small jump)* brinco *m*.

hop² [hɒp] *n Bot* lúpulo *m*.

hope [həʊp] **I** *n* esperanza *f*; *(false)* ilusión *f*; **to have little h. of doing sth,** tener pocas posibilidades de hacer algo. **II** *vtr & vi* esperar; **I h. so/not,** espero que sí/no; **we h. you're well,** esperamos que estés bien.

hopeful ['həʊpfʊl] *adj (confident)* optimista; *(promising)* prometedor,-a. ◆**hopefully** *adv* **1** *(confidently)* con optimismo. **2 h. the weather will be fine,** *(it is hoped)* esperemos que haga buen tiempo.

hopeless ['həʊpləs] *adj* desesperado,-a; *fam* **to be h. at sports,** ser negado,-a para los deportes. ◆**hopelessly** *adv* desesperadamente; **h. lost,** completamente perdido,-a.

horde [hɔːd] *n* multitud *f*.

horizon [hə'raɪzən] *n* horizonte *m*.

horizontal [hɒrɪ'zɒntəl] *adj* horizontal.

hormone ['hɔːməʊn] *n* hormona *f*.

horn [hɔːn] *n* **1** cuerno *m*. **2** *Mus fam* trompeta *f*; *French* **h.,** trompa *f*; **hunting h.,** cuerno *m* de caza. **3** *Aut* bocina *f*.

hornet ['hɔːnɪt] *n* avispón *m*.

horny ['hɔːnɪ] *adj* (**hornier, horniest**) **1** *(hands)* calloso,-a. **2** *sl (sexually aroused)* caliente, cachondo,-a.

horoscope ['hɒrəskəʊp] *n* horóscopo *m*.

horrendous [hɒ'rendəs] *adj* horrendo,-a.

horrible ['hɒrəbəl] *adj* horrible.

horrid ['hɒrɪd] adj horrible.

horrific [hə'rɪfɪk] adj horrendo,-a.

horrify ['hɒrɪfaɪ] vtr horrorizar.

horror ['hɒrər] n horror m; fam a little h., un diablillo; **h. film**, película f de miedo or de terror.

hors d'oeuvre [ɔː'dɜːvr] n entremés m.

horse [hɔːs] n 1 caballo m; **h. race**, carrera f de caballos. 2 Gymn potro m. 3 Tech caballete m. 4 **h. chestnut**, (tree) castaño m de Indias.

horseback ['hɔːsbæk] n **on h.**, a caballo.

horseman ['hɔːsmən] n jinete m.

horseplay ['hɔːspleɪ] n payasadas fpl.

horsepower ['hɔːspaʊər] n caballo m (de vapor).

horseradish ['hɔːsrædɪʃ] n rábano rusticano.

horseshoe ['hɔːsʃuː] n herradura f.

horsewoman ['hɔːswʊmən] n amazona f.

horticulture ['hɔːtɪkʌltʃər] n horticultura f.

hose [həʊz] n (pipe) manguera f.

hosiery ['həʊzɪərɪ] n medias fpl y calcetines mpl.

hospice ['hɒspɪs] n residencia f para enfermos terminales.

hospitable ['hɒspɪtəbəl, hɒ'spɪtəbəl] adj hospitalario,-a; **h. atmosphere**, ambiente acogedor.

hospital ['hɒspɪtəl] n hospital m.

hospitality [hɒspɪ'tælɪtɪ] n hospitalidad f.

host¹ [həʊst] n 1 (at home) anfitrión m. 2 Theat TV presentador m. 3 Biol huésped m. II vtr Theat TV presentar.

host² [həʊst] n (large number) montón m.

Host [həʊst] n Rel hostia f.

hostage ['hɒstɪdʒ] n rehén m.

hostel ['hɒstəl] n hostal m.

hostess ['həʊstɪs] n 1 (at home etc) anfitriona f. 2 Theat TV presentadora f. 3 (air) **h.**, azafata f.

hostile ['hɒstaɪl] adj hostil.

hostility [hɒ'stɪlɪtɪ] n hostilidad f.

hot [hɒt] adj (hotter, hottest) 1 caliente; fig **h. line**, teléfono rojo; **h. spot**, (nightclub) club nocturno. 2 (weather) caluroso,-a; **it's very h.**, hace mucho calor; **to feel h.**, tener calor. 3 (spicy) picante; **h. dog**, perrito m caliente. 4 (temper) fuerte. 5 fam (fresh) de última hora. 6 fam (good) bueno,-a; **it's not so h.**, no es nada del otro mundo. 7 (popular) popular. 8 (dangerous) peligroso,-a; fig **to get oneself into h. water**, meterse en un lío; fam **h. seat**, primera fila. ◆**hot up** vi fam things are hotting up, la cosa se está poniendo al rojo vivo.

hotbed ['hɒtbed] n fig hervidero m.

hotel [həʊ'tel] n hotel m.

hotelier [həʊ'telɪər] n hotelero,-a m,f.

hot-headed [hɒt'hedɪd] adj impetuoso,-a.

hothouse ['hɒthaʊs] n invernadero m.

hotplate ['hɒtpleɪt] n (cooker) placa f de cocina; (to keep food warm) calientaplatos m inv.

hotshot ['hɒtʃɒt] n fam as m.

hot-water ['hɒtwɔːtər] adj **h.-w. bottle**, bolsa f de agua caliente.

hound [haʊnd] I n perro m de caza. II vtr acosar.

hour [aʊər] n hora f; **60 miles an h.**, 60 millas por hora; **by the h.**, por horas; **h. hand**, manecilla f.

hourly ['aʊəlɪ] I adj cada hora. II adv por horas.

house [haʊs] I n 1 casa f; **at my h.**, en mi casa; fig **on the h.**, cortesía de la casa; **h. arrest**, arresto domiciliario; **h. plant**, planta f de interior. 2 Pol H. of Commons, Cámara f de los Comunes; **H. of Lords**, Cámara de los Lores; US H. of Representatives, Cámara de Representantes; **Houses of Parliament**, Parlamento m. 3 (company) empresa f; **publishing h.**, editorial f. 4 Theat sala f. II [haʊz] vtr alojar; (store) guardar.

houseboat ['haʊsbəʊt] n casa f flotante.

housebreaking ['haʊsbreɪkɪŋ] n allanamiento m de morada.

housecoat ['haʊskəʊt] n bata f.

household ['haʊshəʊld] n hogar m; **h. products**, productos domésticos.

housekeeper ['haʊskiːpər] n ama f de llaves.

housekeeping ['haʊskiːpɪŋ] n administración doméstica; **h. money**, dinero m para los gastos domésticos.

house-train ['haʊstreɪn] vtr (pet) educar.

house-warming ['haʊswɔːmɪŋ] n **h.-w. (party)**, fiesta f que se da al estrenar casa.

housewife ['haʊswaɪf] n ama f de casa.

housework ['haʊswɜːk] n trabajo m doméstico.

housing ['haʊzɪŋ] n vivienda f; **h. estate**, urbanización f.

hovel ['hʌvəl, 'hɒvəl] n casucha f.

hover ['hɒvər] vi (bird) cernerse; (aircraft) permanecer inmóvil (en el aire).

hovercraft ['hɒvəkrɑːft] n aerodeslizador m.

how [haʊ] adv 1 (direct question) ¿cómo?; **h. are you?**, ¿cómo estás?; fam **h. come?**, ¿por qué? 2 (indirect question) cómo; **I don't know h. to tell you**, no sé cómo decírtelo. 3 (very) qué; **h. funny!**, ¡qué divertido! 4 **h. about going to the cinema?**, (suggestion) ¿te apetece ir al cine?; **h. about a stroll?**, ¿qué te parece un paseo? 5 (quantity) cuánto; **h. old is she?**, ¿cuántos años tiene?; **h. tall are you?**, ¿cuánto mides? 6 **h. many?**, ¿cuántos,-as?; **h. much?**, ¿cuánto,-a?; **I don't know h. many people there were**, no sé cuánta gente había.

however [haʊ'evər] adv 1 (nevertheless) no obstante, sin embargo. 2 (with adjective)

h. difficult it may be, por difícil que sea; h. much, por mucho que (+ subj).

howl [haʊl] I n aullido m. II vi aullar.

howler ['haʊlər] n fam despiste m.

HP, hp [eɪtʃ'piː] 1 GB abbr of **hire purchase**. 2 abbr of **horsepower**, cv mpl.

HQ [eɪtʃ'kjuː] interj GB abbr of **headquarters**.

hub [hʌb] n Aut cubo m; fig eje m.

hubbub ['hʌbʌb] n alboroto m.

hubcap ['hʌbkæp] n Aut tapacubos m inv.

huddle ['hʌdəl] I n grupo m. II vi to h. (up or together), acurrucarse.

hue¹ [hjuː] n (colour) tinte m; (shade) matiz m.

hue² [hjuː] n h. and cry, fuerte protesta f.

huff [hʌf] n to be in a h., estar de mala uva.

hug [hʌɡ] I vtr abrazar. II n abrazo m.

huge [hjuːdʒ] adj enorme. ◆**hugely** adv enormemente.

hulk [hʌlk] n 1 Naut casco m. 2 (thing, person) armatoste m.

hull [hʌl] n Naut casco m.

hullaba(ll)oo [hʌləbə'luː] n fam follón m.

hullo [hʌ'ləʊ] interj GB ¡hola!

hum [hʌm] I vtr (tune) tararear. II vi (bees, engine) zumbar; (sing) tararear. III n (of bees) zumbido m.

human ['hjuːmən] I adj humano,-a; h. race, raza humana; h. being, ser humano. II n ser humano.

humane [hjuː'meɪn] adj humano,-a.

humanitarian [hjuːmænɪ'teərɪən] adj humanitario,-a.

humanity [hjuː'mænɪtɪ] n 1 humanidad f. 2 Univ the humanities, las humanidades.

humble ['hʌmbəl] I adj humilde. II vtr humillar.

humbug ['hʌmbʌɡ] n 1 fam tonterías fpl. 2 GB (mint) h., caramelo m de menta.

humdrum ['hʌmdrʌm] adj monótono,-a, aburrido,-a.

humid ['hjuːmɪd] adj húmedo,-a.

humidity [hjuː'mɪdɪtɪ] n humedad f.

humiliate [hjuː'mɪlɪeɪt] vtr humillar.

humiliation [hjuːmɪlɪ'eɪʃən] n humillación f.

humility [hjuː'mɪlɪtɪ] n humildad f.

humor ['hjuːmər] n US → **humour**.

humorous ['hjuːmərəs] adj (writer) humorístico,-a; (person, story) gracioso,-a, divertido,-a.

humour ['hjuːmər] I n humor m. II vtr seguir la corriente a.

hump [hʌmp] I n 1 (on back) joroba f. 2 (small hill) montículo m. II vtr GB sl cargar (a la espalda).

humus ['hjuːmas] n mantillo m, humus m.

hunch [hʌntʃ] n fam corazonada f.

hunchback ['hʌntʃbæk] n jorobado,-a, m,f.

hundred ['hʌndrəd] I n cien m, ciento m;

(rough number) centenar m; a h. and twenty-five, ciento veinticinco; five h., quinientos. II adj cien; a h. people, cien personas; a h. per cent, cien por cien; two h. chairs, doscientas sillas.

hundredth ['hʌndrədθ] adj & n centésimo,-a (m).

hundredweight ['hʌndrədweɪt] n ciento doce libras fpl (≈ quintal m).

hung [hʌŋ] adj 1 fam h. over, con resaca. 2 fam h. up, acomplejado,-a.

Hungarian [hʌŋ'ɡeərɪən] adj & n húngaro,-a (m,f).

Hungary ['hʌŋɡərɪ] n Hungría.

hunger ['hʌŋɡər] I n hambre f; h. strike, huelga f de hambre. II vi fig tener hambre (for, de).

hungry ['hʌŋɡrɪ] adj (hungrier, hungriest) hambriento,-a; to be h., tener hambre; to go h., pasar hambre.

hunk [hʌŋk] n 1 (piece) buen pedazo m. 2 sl (man) machote m.

hunt [hʌnt] I vtr cazar. II vi (for game) cazar; (search) buscar. III n caza f; (search) búsqueda f. ◆**hunt down** vtr perseguir.

hunter ['hʌntər] n cazador,-a m,f.

hunting ['hʌntɪŋ] n caza f; (expedition) cacería f.

hurdle ['hɜːdəl] n Sport valla f; fig obstáculo m.

hurl [hɜːl] vtr arrojar, lanzar.

hurrah [hʊ'rɑː], **hurray** [hʊ'reɪ] interj ¡hurra!; h. for John!, ¡viva John!

hurricane ['hʌrɪkən, 'hʌrɪkeɪn] n huracán m.

hurried ['hʌrɪd] adj apresurado,-a; (action etc) hecho,-a de prisa. ◆**hurriedly** adv deprisa, apresuradamente.

hurry ['hʌrɪ] I vi darse prisa. II vtr meter prisa a. III n to be in a h., tener prisa.

hurt [hɜːt] I vtr (pt & pp **hurt**) hacer daño a; (wound) herir; (feelings) ofender. II vi doler; **my arm hurts**, me duele el brazo; fam it doesn't h. to go out once in a while, no viene mal salir de vez en cuando. III adj (physically) herido,-a; (mentally) dolido,-a.

hurtful ['hɜːtfʊl] adj hiriente.

hurtle ['hɜːtəl] vi lanzarse; to h. down, desplomarse.

husband ['hʌzbənd] n marido m, esposo m.

hush [hʌʃ] I vtr callar; to h. sth up, echar tierra a un asunto. II n silencio m. III interj ¡silencio!

hush-hush [hʌʃ'hʌʃ] adj fam confidencial.

husky¹ ['hʌskɪ] adj (huskier, huskiest) ronco,-a.

husky² ['hʌskɪ] n (dog) perro m esquimal.

hustings ['hʌstɪŋz] npl Pol 1 (platform) tribuna f sing electoral. 2 (election) elecciones fpl.

hustle ['hʌsəl] **I** vtr **1** (jostle) empujar. **2** fam meter prisa a. **II** n bullicio m; **h. and bustle,** ajetreo m.

hut [hʌt] n cabaña f; (shed) cobertizo m; Mil barraca f.

hutch [hʌtʃ] n jaula f; **rabbit h.,** conejera f.

hyacinth ['haɪəsɪnθ] n jacinto m.

hybrid ['haɪbrɪd] adj & n híbrido,-a (m,f).

hydrant ['haɪdrənt] n **fire h.,** boca f de incendio.

hydraulic [haɪ'drɔlɪk] adj hidráulico,-a.

hydrocarbon [haɪdrəʊ'kɑːbən] n hidrocarburo m.

hydrochloric [haɪdrəʊ'klɒrɪk] adj **h. acid,** ácido clorhídrico.

hydroelectric [haɪdrəʊ'lektrɪk] adj hidroeléctrico,-a.

hydrofoil ['haɪdrəfɔɪl] n hidroala f.

hydrogen ['haɪdrɪdʒən] n hidrógeno m.

hyena [haɪ'iːnə] n hiena f.

hygiene ['haɪdʒiːn] n higiene f.

hygienic [haɪ'dʒiːnɪk] adj higiénico,-a.

hymn [hɪm] n himno m; **h. book,** cantoral m.

hype [haɪp] n fam campaña publicitaria, movida f.

hyper- ['haɪpər] pref hiper-; **hyperactive,**

hiperactivo,-a.

hypermarket ['haɪpəmɑːkɪt] n GB hipermercado m.

hypersensitive [haɪpə'sensɪtɪv] adj hipersensible f.

hyphen ['haɪfən] n guión m.

hypnosis [hɪp'nəʊsɪs] n hipnosis f.

hypnotist ['hɪpnətɪst] n hipnotizador,-a m,f.

hypnotize ['hɪpnətaɪz] vtr hipnotizar.

hypochondriac [haɪpə'kɒndræk] adj & n hipocondríaco,-a (m,f).

hypocrisy [hɪ'pɒkrəsɪ] n hipocresía f.

hypocrite ['hɪpəkrɪt] n hipócrita mf.

hypocritical [hɪpə'krɪtɪkəl] adj hipócrita.

hypodermic [haɪpə'dɜːmɪk] adj Med hipodérmico,-a; **h. needle,** aguja hipodérmica.

hypothesis [haɪ'pɒθɪsɪs] n (pl **hypotheses** [haɪ'pɒθɪsiːz]) hipótesis f.

hypothetic(al) [haɪpə'θetɪk(əl)] adj hipotético,-a.

hysteria [hɪ'stɪərɪə] n histeria f.

hysterical [hɪ'sterɪkəl] adj histérico,-a.

hysterics [hɪ'sterɪks] n or npl **1** ataque m de histeria. **2** fam (of laughter) ataque m de risa.

I

I, i [aɪ] n (the letter) I, i f.

I [aɪ] pers pron yo; **I know her,** (yo) la conozco.

ICBM [aɪsiːbiː'em] abbr of **intercontinental ballistic missile,** MBI m.

ice [aɪs] **I** n hielo m; **i. axe,** pico m (de alpinista); **i. cream,** helado m; **i. cube,** cubito m de hielo; **i. hockey,** hockey m sobre hielo; **i. lolly,** polo m; **i. rink,** pista f de patinaje; **i. skate,** patín m de cuchilla. **II** vtr (cake) alcorzar. ◆**ice over, ice up** vi (pond etc) helarse; (windscreen, plane wings) cubrirse de hielo.

iceberg ['aɪsbɜːg] n iceberg m.

icebox ['aɪsbɒks] n **1** (compartment of fridge) congelador m. **2** US (fridge) nevera f, frigorífico m.

icecap ['aɪskæp] n casquete m glaciar.

Iceland ['aɪslənd] n Islandia.

ice-skating ['aɪsskeɪtɪŋ] n patinaje m sobre hielo.

icicle ['aɪsɪkəl] n carámbano m.

icing ['aɪsɪŋ] n alcorza f; **i. sugar,** azúcar m glas.

icon ['aɪkɒn] n icono m.

icy ['aɪsɪ] adj (icier, iciest) (road etc) helado,-a; fig (smile) glacial.

ID [aɪ'diː] US abbr of **identification, identity; ID card,** documento m nacional de identidad, DNI m.

I'd [aɪd] = **I would; I had.**

idea [aɪ'dɪə] n **1** idea f. **2** (aim) intención f. **3** (impression) impresión f.

ideal [aɪ'dɪəl] adj & n ideal (m). ◆**ideally** adv **1** (perfectly) perfectamente. **2** (in the best conditions) de ser posible.

idealist [aɪ'dɪəlɪst] n idealista mf.

idealistic [aɪdɪə'lɪstɪk] adj idealista.

idealize [aɪ'dɪəlaɪz] vtr idealizar.

identical [aɪ'dentɪkəl] adj idéntico,-a.

identification [aɪdentɪfɪ'keɪʃən] n **1** identificación f. **2** (papers) documentación f.

identify [aɪ'dentɪfaɪ] **I** vtr (body) identificar; (cause) descubrir. **II** vi identificarse (with, con).

Identikit® [aɪ'dentɪkɪt] n **I.** picture, retrato m robot.

identity [aɪ'dentɪtɪ] n identidad f; **i. card,** carné m de identidad; **proof of i.,** prueba f de identidad.

ideological [aɪdɪə'lɒdʒɪkəl] adj ideológico,-a.

ideology [aɪdɪ'ɒlədʒɪ] n ideología f.

idiom ['ɪdɪəm] n modismo m; fig (style) lenguaje m.

idiomatic [ɪdɪə'mætɪk] adj idiomático,-a.

idiosyncrasy [ɪdɪəʊ'sɪŋkrəsɪ] n idiosincrasia f.

idiot ['ɪdɪət] n idiota mf, tonto,-a m,f.

idiotic [ɪdɪ'ɒtɪk] adj (behaviour) idiota,

tonto,-a; *(joke, plan)* estúpido,-a.

idle ['aɪdəl] **I** *adj* holgazán,-ana; *(not working)* *(person)* desempleado,-a; *(machinery)* parado,-a; *(gossip)* frívolo,-a; *(threat)* vano,-a. **II** *vi (engine)* funcionar en vacío. ◆**idle away** *vtr (time)* desperdiciar.

idleness ['aɪdəlnɪs] *n (laziness)* holgazanería *f*; *(unemployment)* desempleo *m*; *(stoppage)* paro *m*.

idol ['aɪdəl] *n* ídolo *m*.

idolize ['aɪdəlaɪz] *vtr* idolatrar.

idyllic [ɪ'dɪlɪk] *adj* idílico,-a.

i.e. *abbr of* **id est** (that is to say), esto es, a saber, i.e.

if [ɪf] **I** *conj* 1 si; **if at all**, si acaso; **rarely, if ever**, raras veces; **if I were rich**, si fuera rico,-a; **if necessary**, (en) caso de que sea necesario; **if not**, si no; **if so**, de ser así; **if I were you**, yo en tu lugar. 2 *(whenever)* si; **if you need help, ask**, siempre que necesites ayuda, pídela. 3 *(although)* aunque, si bien. 4 *(exclamations)* **if only I'd known!**, ¡de haberlo sabido!; **if only she were here!**, ¡ojalá estuviera aquí!. **II** *n* **ifs and buts**, pegas *fpl*.

igloo ['ɪɡluː] *n* iglú *m*.

ignite [ɪɡ'naɪt] **I** *vtr* encender. **II** *vi* encenderse.

ignition [ɪɡ'nɪʃən] *n* ignición *f*; *Aut* encendido *m*; **i. key**, llave *f* de contacto.

ignorance ['ɪɡnərəns] *n* ignorancia *f*.

ignorant ['ɪɡnərənt] *adj* ignorante *(of, de)*; **to be i. of the facts**, ignorar *or* desconocer los hechos.

ignore [ɪɡ'nɔːr] *vtr (warning, remark)* no hacer caso de; *(behaviour, fact)* pasar por alto.

ill [ɪl] **I** *adj* 1 enfermo,-a; **to be taken i.**, caer enfermo,-a; **to feel i.**, encontrarse mal. 2 *(bad)* malo,-a; **i. feeling**, resentimiento *m*; **i. will**, mala voluntad. **II** *n* mal *m*. **III** *adv* difícilmente.

I'll [aɪl] = **I shall; I will**.

ill-advised [ɪlǝd'vaɪzd] *adj (person)* imprudente; *(act)* desatinado,-a; **you'd be i.-a. to go**, harías mal en ir.

ill-disposed [ɪldɪs'pǝʊzd] *adj* poco dispuesto,-a.

illegal [ɪ'liːɡǝl] *adj* ilegal.

illegible [ɪ'ledʒɪbǝl] *adj* ilegible.

illegitimate [ɪlɪ'dʒɪtɪmɪt] *adj* ilegítimo,-a.

ill-fated [ɪl'feɪtɪd] *adj* abocado,-a al fracaso.

ill-founded [ɪl'faʊndɪd] *adj* infundado,-a.

illicit [ɪ'lɪsɪt] *adj* ilícito,-a.

illiteracy [ɪ'lɪtǝrǝsɪ] *n* analfabetismo *m*.

illiterate [ɪ'lɪtǝrɪt] *adj (person)* analfabeto,-a; *fam (uneducated)* inculto,-a.

illness ['ɪlnɪs] *n* enfermedad *f*.

illogical [ɪ'lɒdʒɪkǝl] *adj* ilógico,-a.

ill-treat [ɪl'triːt] *vtr* maltratar.

illuminate [ɪ'luːmɪneɪt] *vtr* 1 *(light up)* iluminar, alumbrar; *fig (clarify)* aclarar. 2

(manuscript) iluminar.

illuminating [ɪ'luːmɪneɪtɪŋ] *adj (experience, book)* instructivo,-a; *(remark)* revelador,-a.

illumination [ɪluːmɪ'neɪʃǝn] *n* 1 iluminación *f*; *fig (clarification)* aclaración *f*. 2 *GB* **illuminations**, iluminación *f*.

illusion [ɪ'luːʒǝn] *n* ilusión *f*; **to be under the i. that ...**, engañarse pensando que ....

illusory [ɪ'luːsǝrɪ] *adj* ilusorio,-a.

illustrate ['ɪlǝstreɪt] *vtr* ilustrar.

illustration [ɪlǝ'streɪʃǝn] *n* ilustración *f*; *(example)* ejemplo *m*.

illustrious [ɪ'lʌstrɪǝs] *adj* ilustre.

I'm [aɪm] = **I am**.

image ['ɪmɪdʒ] *n* imagen *f*.

imagery ['ɪmɪdʒǝrɪ] *n Lit* imágenes *fpl*.

imaginary [ɪ'mædʒɪnǝrɪ] *adj* imaginario, -a.

imagination [ɪmædʒɪ'neɪʃǝn] *n* imaginación *f*; *(inventiveness)* inventiva *f*.

imaginative [ɪ'mædʒɪnǝtɪv] *adj* imaginativo,-a.

imagine [ɪ'mædʒɪn] *vtr (visualize)* imaginar; *(think)* suponer, imaginarse; **just i.!**, ¡imagínate!

imbalance [ɪm'bælǝns] *n* desequilibrio *m*.

imbecile ['ɪmbɪsiːl] *n* imbécil *mf*.

imitate ['ɪmɪteɪt] *vtr* imitar.

imitation [ɪmɪ'teɪʃǝn] **I** *n* imitación *f*, copia *f*; *pej* remedo *m*. **II** *adj* de imitación.

immaculate [ɪ'mækjʊlɪt] *adj (clean)* inmaculado,-a; *(tidy)* perfectamente ordenado,-a; *(clothes)* impecable; *(work)* perfecto,-a; **the I. Conception**, la Inmaculada Concepción.

immaterial [ɪmǝ'tɪǝrɪǝl] *adj* irrelevante; **it's i. to me whether ...**, me trae sin cuidado si ....

immature [ɪmǝ'tjʊǝr] *adj* inmaduro,-a.

immediate [ɪ'miːdɪǝt] *adj* 1 inmediato,-a; *(urgent)* urgente. 2 *(close)* cercano,-a; *(danger)* inminente. 3 *(cause)* primero,-a. ◆**immediately I** *adv* 1 inmediatamente. 2 *(directly)* directamente. **II** *conj* en cuanto.

immense [ɪ'mens] *adj* inmenso,-a, enorme. ◆**immensely** *adv (rich)* enormemente; *(interesting, difficult)* sumamente.

immerse [ɪ'mɜːs] *vtr* sumergir **(in**, en); *fig* **to be immersed in sth**, estar absorto,-a en algo.

immersion [ɪ'mɜːʃǝn] *n* inmersión *f*; *GB* **i. heater**, calentador *m* de inmersión; **i. course**, cursillo intensivo.

immigrant ['ɪmɪɡrǝnt] *adj & n* inmigrante *(mf)*.

immigration [ɪmɪ'ɡreɪʃǝn] *n* inmigración *f*.

imminent ['ɪmɪnǝnt] *adj* inminente.

immobile [ɪ'mǝʊbaɪl] *adj* inmóvil.

immobilize [ɪ'mǝʊbɪlaɪz] *vtr* inmovilizar.

immodest [ɪˈmɒdɪst] *adj* indecente.

immoral [ɪˈmɒrəl] *adj* inmoral.

immortal [ɪˈmɔːtəl] *adj* inmortal.

immortality [ɪmɔːˈtælɪtɪ] *n* inmortalidad *f*.

immortalize [ɪˈmɔːtəlaɪz] *vtr* inmortalizar.

immune [ɪˈmjuːn] *adj* inmune; *(exempt)* exento,-a.

immunity [ɪˈmjuːnɪtɪ] *n* inmunidad *f*.

immunize [ˈɪmjunaɪz] *vtr* inmunizar *(against*, contra*).

impact [ˈɪmpækt] *n* impacto *m*; *(crash)* choque *m*.

impair [ɪmˈpeər] *vtr* perjudicar; *(sight etc)* dañar.

impart [ɪmˈpɑːt] *vtr fml* *(news)* comunicar; *(knowledge)* transmitir.

impartial [ɪmˈpɑːʃəl] *adj* imparcial.

impassable [ɪmˈpɑːsəbəl] *adj* *(road, ground)* intransitable; *(barrier)* infranqueable.

impasse [æmˈpɑːs] *n* punto muerto.

impassive [ɪmˈpæsɪv] *adj* impasible.

impatience [ɪmˈpeɪʃəns] *n* impaciencia *f*.

impatient [ɪmˈpeɪʃənt] *adj* impaciente; *(fretful)* irritable; **to get i.**, perder la paciencia.

impeccable [ɪmˈpekəbəl] *adj* impecable.

impede [ɪmˈpiːd] *vtr* *(prevent)* impedir; *(hinder)* estorbar; *(obstruct)* poner trabas a.

impediment [ɪmˈpedɪmənt] *n* impedimento *m*; *(obstacle)* estorbo *m*; **speech i.**, defecto *m* del habla.

impending [ɪmˈpendɪŋ] *adj fml* inminente.

impenetrable [ɪmˈpenɪtrəbəl] *adj* impenetrable; *fig* *(mystery, thoughts)* insondable.

imperative [ɪmˈperətɪv] **I** *adj fml* imperativo,-a; *(tone)* imperioso,-a; *(urgent)* urgente. **II** *n* Ling imperativo *m*.

imperceptible [ɪmpəˈseptəbəl] *adj* imperceptible.

imperfect [ɪmˈpɜːfɪkt] **I** *adj* imperfecto, -a; *(goods)* defectuoso,-a. **II** *n* Ling imperfecto *m*.

imperfection [ɪmpəˈfekʃən] *n* defecto *m*.

imperial [ɪmˈpɪərɪəl] *adj* **1** imperial. **2** *(measure)* **i. gallon**, galón británico *(approx* 4,543 litres*).

imperialism [ɪmˈpɪərɪəlɪzəm] *n* imperialismo *m*.

imperialist [ɪmˈpɪərɪəlɪst] *adj & n* imperialista *(mf)*.

imperious [ɪmˈpɪərɪəs] *adj* imperioso,-a.

impersonal [ɪmˈpɜːsənəl] *adj* impersonal.

impersonate [ɪmˈpɜːsəneɪt] *vtr* hacerse pasar por; *(famous people)* imitar.

impersonation [ɪmpɜːsəˈneɪʃən] *n* imitación *f*.

impertinent [ɪmˈpɜːtɪnənt] *adj* impertinente.

impervious [ɪmˈpɜːvɪəs] *adj* *(rock)* impermeable; *fig* **to be i.** *(reason)*, no atender a razones.

impetuous [ɪmˈpetjuəs] *adj* impetuoso,-a.

impetus [ˈɪmpɪtəs] *n* ímpetu *m*; *fig* impulso *m*.

impinge [ɪmˈpɪndʒ] *vi fml* afectar *(on*, a*).

implant [ɪmˈplɑːnt] Med **I** *vtr* implantar. **II** [ˈɪmplɑːnt] *n* implantación *f*.

implement [ˈɪmplɪmənt] **I** *n* *(tool)* herramienta *f*; *(instrument)* instrumento *m*; **farm implements**, aperos *mpl* de labranza. **II** [ˈɪmplɪment] *vtr* *(decision, plan)* llevar a cabo; *(law, policy)* aplicar.

implicate [ˈɪmplɪkeɪt] *vtr* implicar *(in*, en*).

implication [ɪmplɪˈkeɪʃən] *n* implicación *f*; *(consequence)* consecuencia *f*.

implicit [ɪmˈplɪsɪt] *adj* *(implied)* implícito,-a; *(trust)* absoluto,-a; *(faith)* incondicional.

implore [ɪmˈplɔːr] *vtr* implorar, suplicar.

imply [ɪmˈplaɪ] *vtr* **1** *(involve)* implicar. **2** *(hint)* dar a entender; *(mean)* significar.

impolite [ɪmpəˈlaɪt] *adj* maleducado,-a.

import [ˈɪmpɔːt] **I** *n* **1** Com *(usu pl)* importación *f*; **i. duty**, derechos *mpl* de importación. **2** *fml* *(meaning)* sentido *m*. **II** [ɪmˈpɔːt] *vtr* Com importar.

importance [ɪmˈpɔːtəns] *n* importancia *f*; *(standing)* envergadura *f*; **of little i.**, de poca monta.

important [ɪmˈpɔːtənt] *adj* importante; **it's not i.**, no importa.

importer [ɪmˈpɔːtər] *n* Com importador,-a *m,f*.

impose [ɪmˈpəʊz] **I** *vtr* imponer *(on, upon*, a*). **II** *vi* **to i. on** *or* **upon**, *(take advantage of)* abusar de.

imposing [ɪmˈpəʊzɪŋ] *adj* imponente, impresionante.

imposition [ɪmpəˈzɪʃən] *n* *(of tax etc)* imposición *f*; *(unfair demand)* abuso *m*; **would it be an i. if ...?**, ¿le molestaría si ...?

impossibility [ɪmpɒsəˈbɪlɪtɪ] *n* imposibilidad *f*.

impossible [ɪmˈpɒsəbəl] **I** *adj* imposible; *(person)* insoportable. **II** *n* **to do the i.**, hacer lo imposible. ◆**impossibly** *adv* de manera insoportable; **i. difficult**, de una dificultad insuperable.

impostor [ɪmˈpɒstər] *n* impostor,-a *m,f*.

impotent [ˈɪmpətənt] *adj* impotente.

impound [ɪmˈpaʊnd] *vtr* incautarse de.

impoverished [ɪmˈpɒvərɪʃt] *adj* *(person, country)* empobrecido,-a; *(soil)* agotado,-a.

impracticable [ɪmˈpræktɪkəbəl] *adj* impracticable, irrealizable.

impractical [ɪmˈpræktɪkəl] *adj* *(person)* poco práctico,-a; *(project, solution etc)* poco viable.

imprecise [ɪmprɪˈsaɪs] *adj* impreciso,-a.

impregnable [ɪmˈpregnəbəl] *adj*

inexpugnable.

impregnate ['impregneit] *vtr* **1** (*soak*) impregnar (**with**, de). **2** *fml* (*fertilize*) fecundar.

impress [im'pres] *vtr* **1** impresionar; **to i: sb favourably/unfavourably**, dar a algn buena/mala impresión. **2** (*mark*) imprimir (**on**, en); (*pattern*) estampar (**on**, en); *fig* **to i: sth on sb**, convencer a algn de la importancia de algo.

impression [im'preʃən] *n* **1** impresión *f*; **to be under the i: that ...**, tener la impresión de que ...; **to give the i: of ...**, dar la impresión de .... **2** (*imprint*) marca *f*; (*in snow*) huella *f*. **3** (*imitation*) imitación *f*. **4** *Print* (*number of copies*) edición *f*.

impressionist [im'preʃənist] *adj & n* impresionista (*mf*).

impressive [im'presiv] *adj* impresionante.

imprint [im'print] **I** *vtr* (*mark*) dejar huella (**on**, en). **II** ['imprint] *n* **1** (*mark*) marca *f*; (*left by foot etc*) huella *f*. **2** (*publisher's name*) pie *m* de imprenta.

imprison [im'prizən] *vtr* encarcelar.

imprisonment [im'prizənmənt] *n* encarcelamiento *m*.

improbable [im'probəbl] *adj* (*event*) improbable; (*story*) inverosímil.

impromptu [im'promptju:] **I** *adj* (*speech*) improvisado,-a; (*visit*) imprevisto,-a. **II** *adv* de improviso.

improper [im'propər] *adj* **1** impropio,-a; (*method*) inadecuado,-a. **2** (*indecent*) indecente; (*behaviour*) deshonesto,-a. **3** (*wrong*) incorrecto,-a.

improve [im'pru:v] **I** *vtr* mejorar; (*knowledge*) perfeccionar; (*mind*) cultivar; (*increase*) aumentar. **II** *vi* mejorarse; (*increase*) aumentar. ◆**improve on** *vtr* superar; (*offer, bid*) sobrepujar.

improvement [im'pru:vmənt] *n* mejora *f*; (*in skill*) perfeccionamiento *m*; (*increase*) aumento *m*.

improvise ['imprəvaiz] *vtr & vi* improvisar.

imprudent [im'pru:dənt] *adj* imprudente.

impudence ['impjudəns] *n* insolencia *f*.

impudent ['impjudənt] *adj* insolente.

impulse ['impʌls] *n* impulso *m*; **to act on (an) i.**, dejarse llevar por un impulso.

impulsive [im'pʌlsiv] *adj* irreflexivo,-a.

impunity [im'pju:niti] *n* impunidad *f*.

impure [im'pjuər] *adj* **1** (*act*) impuro,-a; (*thought*) impúdico,-a. **2** (*air*) contaminado,-a.

impurity [im'pjuəriti] *n* **1** (*of act*) deshonestidad *f*. **2** (*usu pl*) (*in air, substance*) impureza *f*.

in [in] **I** *prep* **1** (*place*) en; (*within*) dentro de; **in bed**, en la cama; **in England/Brazil/China**, en Inglaterra/Brasil/China; **in prison**, en la cárcel; **in the distance**, a

lo lejos. **2** (*motion*) en; **I threw it in the fire**, lo eché al fuego; **she arrived in Paris**, llegó a París. **3** (*time*) (*during*) en, durante; **I haven't seen her in years**, hace años que no la veo; **in May/1945**, en mayo/1945; **in spring**, en primavera; **in the daytime**, durante el día; **in the morning**, por la mañana; **at ten in the morning**, a las diez de la mañana. **4** (*time*) (*within*) dentro de; **I arrived in time**, llegué a tiempo. **5** (*time*) (*after*) al cabo de. **6** (*manner*) en; **in alphabetical order**, en orden alfabético; **in a loud/quiet voice**, en voz alta/baja; **in fashion**, de moda; **in French**, en francés; **in an odd way**, de una manera rara; **in writing**, por escrito; **write in pencil**, escribe con lápiz. **7** (*wearing*) en; **dressed in blue**, vestido,-a de azul; **in uniform**, de uniforme. **8** (*weather etc*) a, en; **in the rain**, bajo la lluvia; **in the sun**, al sol; **in darkness**, en la oscuridad; **in daylight**, a la luz del día; **in the shade**, a la sombra. **9** (*state, emotion*) en; **carved in wood**, tallado,-a en madera; **in bloom/danger/public/silence**, en flor/peligro/público/silencio; **in love**, enamorado,-a; **in tears**, llorando. **10** (*ratio, numbers*) de; **cut in half**, cortado,-a por la mitad; **in threes**, de tres en tres; **one in six**, uno de cada seis; **two metres in length**, dos metros de largo. **11** (*profession*) en; **to be in insurance**, trabajar en seguros. **12** (*person*) en; **he has it in him to win**, es capaz de ganar. **13** (*after superlative*) de; **the smallest car in the world**, el coche más pequeño del mundo. **14** (*before present participle*) in **behaving this way**, con su comportamiento; **in so doing**, con ello. **15** (*phrases*) **in all**, en total; **in itself/himself/herself**, en sí; **in that ...**, dado que ....
II *adv* **in here/there**, aquí/allí dentro; **let's go in**, vamos adentro; **to be in**, (*at home*) estar (en casa); (*at work*) estar; (*tide*) estar alta; *fam* (*in fashion*) estar de moda; **the bus is in**, el autobús ha llegado; **to invite sb in**, invitar a algn a entrar; *fam* **to be in on sth**, estar enterado,-a de algo; *fam* **we're in for a storm**, vamos a tener tormenta.
III *adj fam* **1** (*fashionable*) (*place*) de moda; (*clothes*) del último grito. **2 an i**, joke, una broma privada.
IV *n fam* **ins and outs**, detalles *mpl*.

inability [inə'biliti] *n* incapacidad *f*.

inaccessible [inæk'sesəbəl] *adj* inaccesible.

inaccurate [in'ækjurit] *adj* inexacto,-a; (*statement*) erróneo,-a; (*figures, total*) incorrecto,-a.

inactivity [inæk'tiviti] *n* inactividad *f*.

inadequate [in'ædikwit] *adj* **1** (*lacking*) insuficiente. **2** (*not capable*) incapaz; (*un-*

suitable) inadecuado,-a. 3 (*defective*) defectuoso,-a.

inadvertent [ɪnəd'vɜːtənt] *adj* involuntario,-a. ◆**inadvertently** *adv* involuntariamente.

inadvisable [ɪnəd'vaɪzəbəl] *adj* imprudente.

inane [ɪ'neɪn] *adj* necio,-a, fatuo,-a.

inanimate [ɪn'ænɪmɪt] *adj* inanimado,-a.

inappropriate [ɪnə'prəʊprɪɪt] *adj* inoportuno,-a; (*behaviour*) poco apropiado,-a.

inarticulate [ɪnɑː'tɪkjʊlɪt] *adj* (*cry, sound*) inarticulado,-a; (*words*) mal pronunciado,-a.

inasmuch as [ɪnəz'mʌtʃəz] *conj fml* 1 (*since*) puesto que, ya que. 2 (*in so far as*) en la medida en que.

inattentive [ɪnə'tentɪv] *adj* desatento,-a.

inaudible [ɪn'ɔːdəbəl] *adj* inaudible.

inaugural [ɪn'ɔːgjʊrəl] *adj* inaugural.

inaugurate [ɪn'ɔːgjʊreɪt] *vtr* (*building*) inaugurar; (*president*) investir.

inauguration [ɪnɔːgjʊ'reɪʃən] *n* (*of building*) inauguración *f*; (*of president*) investidura *f*.

inauspicious [ɪnɔː'spɪʃəs] *adj* (*start*) poco prometedor,-a; (*circumstances*) desfavorable.

inborn [ɪn'bɔːn] *adj* innato,-a.

inbred ['ɪnbred] *adj* 1 (*quality*) innato,-a. 2 (*family*) endogámico,-a.

Inc, inc *US Com abbr of* **Incorporated**, ≈ S.A.

incalculable [ɪn'kælkjʊləbəl] *adj* incalculable.

incapable [ɪn'keɪpəbəl] *adj* incapaz.

incapacitate [ɪnkə'pæsɪteɪt] *vtr fml* incapacitar.

incapacity [ɪnkə'pæsɪtɪ] *n* incapacidad *f*.

incarcerate [ɪn'kɑːsəreɪt] *vtr fml* encarcelar.

incarnation [ɪnkɑː'neɪʃən] *n* encarnación *f*.

incendiary [ɪn'sendɪərɪ] **I** *adj* incendiario,-a. **II** *n* bomba incendiaria.

incense[1] ['ɪnsens] *n* incienso *m*.

incense[2] [ɪn'sens] *vtr* enfurecer, sacar de quicio.

incentive [ɪn'sentɪv] *n* incentivo *m*.

incessant [ɪn'sesənt] *adj* incesante; (*demands*) constante. ◆**incessantly** *adv* sin cesar.

incest ['ɪnsest] *n* incesto *m*.

inch [ɪntʃ] *n* pulgada *f* (*approx* 2,54 cm); *fig* **i. by i.**, poco a poco; *fig* **she wouldn't give an i.**, no quería ceder ni un ápice. ◆**inch forward** *vtr & vi* avanzar poco a poco.

incidence ['ɪnsɪdəns] *n* frecuencia *f*.

incident ['ɪnsɪdənt] *n* incidente *m*.

incidental [ɪnsɪ'dentəl] *adj* (*accessory*) incidental, accesorio,-a; (*risk*) inherente (**to**, a); **i. music**, música *f* de fondo.

◆**incidentally** *adv* a propósito.

incinerator [ɪn'sɪnəreɪtər] *n* incinerador *m*.

incipient [ɪn'sɪpɪənt] *adj fml* incipiente.

incision [ɪn'sɪʒən] *n* incisión *f*.

incisive [ɪn'saɪsɪv] *adj* (*comment*) incisivo,-a; (*reply*) tajante; (*mind*) penetrante.

incite [ɪn'saɪt] *vtr* incitar; **to i. sb to do sth**, incitar a algn a hacer algo.

inclination [ɪnklɪ'neɪʃən] *n* inclinación *f*; **my i. is to stay**, yo prefiero quedarme.

incline [ɪn'klaɪn] **I** *vtr* 1 **I'm inclined to believe him**, me inclino a creerlo; **if you feel so inclined**, si quieres; **she's inclined to be aggressive**, tiende a ser agresiva. 2 (*head etc*) inclinar. **II** *vi* (*slope*) inclinarse. **III** [ɪn'klaɪn, 'ɪnklaɪn] *n* (*slope*) pendiente *f*; **steep i.**, cuesta empinada.

include [ɪn'kluːd] *vtr* incluir (**in**, en); (*in price*) comprender (**in**, en); (*in list*) figurar (**in**, en).

including [ɪn'kluːdɪŋ] *prep* incluso, inclusive.

inclusion [ɪn'kluːʒən] *n* inclusión *f*.

inclusive [ɪn'kluːsɪv] *adj* inclusivo,-a; **pages six to ten i.**, de la página seis a la diez, ambas inclusive; **the rent is i. of bills**, el alquiler incluye las facturas.

incognito [ɪnkɒg'niːtəʊ] *adv* de incógnito.

incoherent [ɪnkəʊ'hɪərənt] *adj* incoherente.

income ['ɪnkʌm] *n* ingresos *mpl*; (*from investment*) réditos *mpl*; **i. tax**, impuesto *m* sobre la renta; **i. tax return**, declaración *f* de la renta.

incoming ['ɪnkʌmɪŋ] *adj* (*flight, train*) de llegada; (*tide*) ascendente; (*mail, message, call*) recibido,-a.

incomparable [ɪn'kɒmpərəbəl] *adj* incomparable, sin par.

incompatible [ɪnkəm'pætəbəl] *adj* incompatible (**with**, con).

incompetence [ɪn'kɒmpɪtəns] *n* incompetencia *f*.

incompetent [ɪn'kɒmpɪtənt] *adj* incompetente.

incomplete [ɪnkəm'pliːt] *adj* incompleto,-a.

incomprehensible [ɪnkɒmprɪ'hensəbəl] *adj* incomprensible.

inconceivable [ɪnkən'siːvəbəl] *adj* inconcebible.

inconclusive [ɪnkən'kluːsɪv] *adj* (*vote*) no decisivo,-a; (*proof*) no concluyente.

incongruous [ɪn'kɒŋgrʊəs] *adj* incongruente.

inconsiderate [ɪnkən'sɪdərɪt] *adj* desconsiderado,-a; **how i. of you!**, ¡qué falta de consideración por tu parte!

inconsistency [ɪnkən'sɪstənsɪ] *n* inconsecuencia *f*; (*contradiction*) contradicción *f*.

inconsistent [ɪnkən'sɪstənt] *adj* inconsecuente; *(contradictory)* contradictorio,-a; **your evidence is i. with the facts,** su testimonio no concuerda con los hechos.

inconspicuous [ɪnkən'spɪkjuəs] *adj* que pasa desapercibido,-a; *(discrete)* discreto, -a.

incontrovertible [ɪnkɒntrə'vɜːtəbəl] *adj fml* incontrovertible.

inconvenience [ɪnkən'viːnɪəns] **I** *n* inconveniente *f*; *(annoyance)* molestia *f*. **II** *vtr (annoy)* molestar; *(cause difficulty to)* incomodar.

inconvenient [ɪnkən'viːnɪənt] *adj* molesto,-a; *(time)* inoportuno,-a; *(design)* poco práctico,-a.

incorporate [ɪn'kɔːpəreɪt] *vtr* incorporar **(in, into,** a); *(include)* incluir; *(contain)* contener.

incorporated [ɪn'kɔːpəreɪtɪd] *adj US Com* **i. company,** sociedad anónima.

incorrect [ɪnkə'rekt] *adj* incorrecto,-a.

incorrigible [ɪn'kɒrɪdʒəbəl] *adj* incorregible.

increase ['ɪnkriːs] **I** *n* aumento *m*; *(in number)* incremento *m*; *(in price etc)* subida *f*. **II** [ɪn'kriːs] *vtr* aumentar; *(price etc)* subir. **III** *vi* aumentar.

increasing [ɪn'kriːsɪŋ] *adj* creciente. ◆**increasingly** *adv* cada vez más.

incredible [ɪn'kredəbəl] *adj* increíble.

incredulous [ɪn'kredjʊləs] *adj* incrédulo,-a.

increment ['ɪnkrɪmənt] *n* incremento *m*.

incriminate [ɪn'krɪmɪneɪt] *vtr* incriminar.

incriminating [ɪn'krɪmɪneɪtɪŋ] *adj* incriminatorio,-a.

incubation [ɪnkjʊ'beɪʃən] *n* incubación *f*.

incubator ['ɪnkjʊbeɪtə'] *n* incubadora *f*.

incumbent [ɪn'kʌmbənt] **I** *n* titular *mf*. **II** *adj fml* **to be i. on sb to do sth,** ser la obligación de algn hacer algo.

incur [ɪn'kɜː'] *vtr (blame)* incurrir en; *(risk)* correr; *(debt)* contraer; *(loss)* sufrir.

incurable [ɪn'kjʊərəbəl] *adj* incurable.

indebted [ɪn'detɪd] *adj* endeudado,-a; *fig (grateful)* agradecido,-a; *fig* **to be i. to sb,** estar en deuda con algn.

indecent [ɪn'diːsənt] *adj* indecente; **i. assault,** atentado *m* contra el pudor; **i. exposure,** exhibicionismo *m*.

indecision [ɪndɪ'sʒən] *n* indecisión *f*.

indecisive [ɪndɪ'saɪsɪv] *adj (person)* indeciso,-a; *(evidence)* poco concluyente; *(victory)* no decisivo,-a.

indeed [ɪn'diːd] *adv* **1** *fml (in fact)* efectivamente, en realidad. **2 I'm very sorry i.,** lo siento de veras; **it's very hard i.,** es verdaderamente difícil; **thank you very much i.,** muchísimas gracias.

indefinite [ɪn'defɪnɪt] *adj* indefinido,-a.

indelible [ɪn'deləbəl] *adj* indeleble.

indemnify [ɪn'demnɪfaɪ] *vtr* indemnizar **(for,** por).

indemnity [ɪn'demnɪtɪ] *n* **1** *(insurance)* indemnidad *f*. **2** *(compensation)* indemnización *f*.

indentation [ɪnden'teɪʃən] *n* **1** *Typ* sangría *f*. **2** *(of edge)* muesca *f*; *(of surface)* depresión *f*.

independence [ɪndɪ'pendəns] *n* independencia *f*; *US* **I. Day,** día *m* de la Independencia *(4 julio)*.

independent [ɪndɪ'pendənt] *adj* independiente; *GB* **i. school,** colegio *m* no subvencionado por el estado; **to become i.,** independizarse.

in-depth ['ɪndepθ] *adj* minucioso,-a, exhaustivo,-a.

indestructible [ɪndɪ'strʌktəbəl] *adj* indestructible.

indeterminate [ɪndɪ'tɜːmɪnɪt] *adj* indeterminado,-a.

index ['ɪndeks] **I** *n (pl* **indexes** or **indices)** **1** *(in book)* índice *m*; *(in library)* catálogo *m*; **i. card,** ficha *f*. **2** *Math* exponente *m*; *Econ* índice *m*. **3 i. finger,** dedo *m* índice. **II** *vtr* catalogar.

index-linked ['ɪndekslɪŋkt] *adj* sujeto,-a al aumento de la inflación.

India ['ɪndɪə] *n* (la) India.

Indian ['ɪndɪən] *adj & n (of America)* indio,-a *(m,f)*; *(of India)* hindú *(m,f)*; **I. Ocean,** Océano Indico; **I. Summer,** veranillo *m* de San Martín.

indicate ['ɪndɪkeɪt] **I** *vtr* indicar. **II** *vi Aut* poner el intermitente.

indication [ɪndɪ'keɪʃən] *n* indicio *m*.

indicative [ɪn'dɪkətɪv] **I** *adj* indicativo,-a. **II** *n Ling* indicativo *m*.

indicator ['ɪndɪkeɪtə'] *n* indicador *m*; *Aut* intermitente *m*.

indices ['ɪndɪsiːz] *npl* → **index.**

indict [ɪn'daɪt] *vtr* acusar **(for,** de).

indictment [ɪn'daɪtmənt] *n* **1** *Jur* acusación *f*; *fig* **a damning i. of his books,** una crítica feroz de sus libros.

indifference [ɪn'dɪfərəns] *n* indiferencia *f*.

indifferent [ɪn'dɪfərənt] *adj* **1** *(uninterested)* indiferente. **2** *(mediocre)* regular.

indigenous [ɪn'dɪdʒɪnəs] *adj* indígena.

indigestion [ɪndɪ'dʒestʃən] *n* indigestión *f*; **to suffer from i.,** tener un empacho.

indignant [ɪn'dɪgnənt] *adj* indignado,-a; *(look)* de indignación; **to get i. about sth,** indignarse por algo.

indignity [ɪn'dɪgnɪtɪ] *n* indignidad *f*.

indigo ['ɪndɪgəʊ] **I** *n* añil *m*. **II** *adj* (de color) añil.

indirect [ɪndɪ'rekt, ɪndaɪ'rekt] *adj* indirecto,-a.

indiscreet [ɪndɪ'skriːt] *adj* indiscreto,-a.

indiscretion [ɪndɪ'skreʃən] *n* indiscreción *f*.

indiscriminate [ɪndɪ'skrɪmɪnɪt] *adj (punishment, shooting)* indiscriminado,-a; *(praise, reading)* sin criterio.

indispensable [ɪndɪ'spensəbəl] *adj*

indispensable, imprescindible.

indisposed [ˌɪndɪˈspəʊzd] *adj fml* indispuesto,-a.

indisputable [ˌɪndɪˈspjuːtəbəl] *adj* indiscutible, incontestable.

indistinct [ˌɪndɪˈstɪŋkt] *adj* indistinto,-a; *(memory)* confuso,-a, vago,-a; *(shape etc)* borroso,-a.

indistinguishable [ˌɪndɪˈstɪŋgwɪʃəbəl] *adj* indistinguible.

individual [ˌɪndɪˈvɪdjuəl] **I** *adj* **1** *(separate)* individual; *(for one)* particular; *(personal)* personal. **2** *(characteristic)* particular; *(original)* original. **II** *n (person)* individuo *m*; *private* i., particular *m*.

individualist [ˌɪndɪˈvɪdjuəlɪst] *n* individualista *mf*.

indoctrinate [ɪnˈdɒktrɪneɪt] *vtr* adoctrinar.

indoctrination [ɪnˌdɒktrɪˈneɪʃən] *n* adoctrinamiento *m*.

indolent [ˈɪndələnt] *adj fml* indolente.

Indonesia [ˌɪndəʊˈniːzɪə] *n* Indonesia.

Indonesian [ˌɪndəʊˈniːzɪən] **I** *adj* indonesio,-a. **II** *n* **1** *(person)* indonesio,-a *m,f.* **2** *(language)* indonesio *m*.

indoor [ˈɪndɔːr] *adj (plant)* de interior; i. **football**, fútbol *m* sala; i. **pool**, piscina cubierta.

indoors [ɪnˈdɔːz] *adv (inside)* dentro (de casa); *(at home)* en casa; **let's go i.**, vamos adentro.

induce [ɪnˈdjuːs] *vtr* **1** *(persuade)* inducir, persuadir. **2** *(cause)* producir; *Med (labour)* provocar.

inducement [ɪnˈdjuːsmənt] *n* incentivo *m*, aliciente *m*.

induction [ɪnˈdʌkʃən] *n* **1** *Med (of labour)* provocación *f*. **2** *Elec* inducción *f*. **3** *Educ* introducción *f*.

indulge [ɪnˈdʌldʒ] **I** *vtr* **1** *(child)* consentir; *(person)* complacer; **to i. oneself**, darse gusto. **2** *(whim)* ceder a, satisfacer. **II** *vi* darse el gusto (**in**, de).

indulgence [ɪnˈdʌldʒəns] *n* **1** *(of child)* mimo *m*; *(of attitude)* indulgencia *f*; *(of whim)* satisfacción *f*.

indulgent [ɪnˈdʌldʒənt] *adj* indulgente.

industrial [ɪnˈdʌstrɪəl] *adj* industrial; *(accident)* laboral; *(disease)* profesional; *GB* **to take i. action**, declararse en huelga; *GB* i. **dispute**, conflicto *m* laboral; i. **estate**, polígono *m* industrial; i. **relations**, relaciones *fpl* laborales.

industrialist [ɪnˈdʌstrɪəlɪst] *n* industrial *mf*.

industrialize [ɪnˈdʌstrɪəlaɪz] *vtr* industrializar; **to become industrialized**, industrializarse.

industrious [ɪnˈdʌstrɪəs] *adj* trabajador, -a.

industry [ˈɪndəstrɪ] *n* **1** industria *f*. **2** *(diligence)* aplicación *f*.

inebriated [ɪnˈiːbrɪeɪtɪd] *adj* embriagado,-a.

inedible [ɪnˈedəbəl] *adj* incomible.

ineffective [ˌɪnɪˈfektɪv] *adj* ineficaz.

ineffectual [ˌɪnɪˈfektʃuəl] *adj (aim, protest)* ineficaz; *(person)* incompetente.

inefficiency [ˌɪnɪˈfɪʃənsɪ] *n* ineficacia *f*; *(of person)* incompetencia *f*.

inefficient [ˌɪnɪˈfɪʃənt] *adj* ineficaz; *(person)* inepto,-a.

ineligible [ɪnˈelɪdʒəbəl] *adj* no apto **(for**, para).

inept [ɪnˈept] *adj (person)* inepto,-a; *(remark)* estúpido,-a.

inequality [ˌɪnɪˈkwɒlɪtɪ] *n* desigualdad *f*.

inert [ɪnˈɜːt] *adj* inerte.

inertia [ɪnˈɜːʃə] *n* inercia *f*.

inescapable [ˌɪnɪˈskeɪpəbəl] *adj* ineludible.

inevitability [ɪnˌevɪtəˈbɪlɪtɪ] *n* inevitabilidad *f*.

inevitable [ɪnˈevɪtəbəl] *adj* inevitable.

inexcusable [ˌɪnɪkˈskjuːzəbəl] *adj* inexcusable, imperdonable.

inexhaustible [ˌɪnɪɡˈzɔːstəbəl] *adj* inagotable.

inexorable [ɪnˈeksərəbəl] *adj fml* inexorable.

inexpensive [ˌɪnɪkˈspensɪv] *adj* económico,-a.

inexperience [ˌɪnɪkˈspɪərɪəns] *n* inexperiencia *f*.

inexperienced [ˌɪnɪkˈspɪərɪənst] *adj* inexperto,-a.

inexplicable [ˌɪnɪkˈsplɪkəbəl] *adj* inexplicable.

infallible [ɪnˈfæləbəl] *adj* infalible.

infamous [ˈɪnfəməs] *adj* infame.

infancy [ˈɪnfənsɪ] *n* infancia *f*.

infant [ˈɪnfənt] *n* niño,-a *m,f*; *GB* i. **school**, parvulario *m*.

infantile [ˈɪnfəntaɪl] *adj* infantil.

infantry [ˈɪnfəntrɪ] *n* infantería *f*.

infatuated [ɪnˈfætjueɪtɪd] *adj* encaprichado,-a.

infatuation [ɪnˌfætjuˈeɪʃən] *n* encaprichamiento *m*.

infect [ɪnˈfekt] *vtr (cut)* infectar; *(water)* contaminar; *(person)* contagiar.

infection [ɪnˈfekʃən] *n (of cut)* infección *f*; *(of water)* contaminación *f*; *(with illness)* contagio *m*.

infectious [ɪnˈfekʃəs] *adj (disease)* infeccioso,-a; *fig* contagioso,-a.

infer [ɪnˈfɜːr] *vtr* inferir **(from**, de).

inference [ˈɪnfərəns] *n* inferencia *f*.

inferior [ɪnˈfɪərɪər] **I** *adj* inferior **(to**, a). **II** *n pej* inferior *mf*.

inferiority [ɪnˌfɪərɪˈɒrɪtɪ] *n* inferioridad *f*.

inferno [ɪnˈfɜːnəʊ] *n lit* infierno *m*; *fig* **the house was a raging i.**, la casa ardía en llamas.

infertile [ɪnˈfɜːtaɪl] *adj* estéril.

infertility [ˌɪnfəˈtɪlɪtɪ] *n* esterilidad *f*.

infest [ɪnˈfest] *vtr* infestar, plagar **(with**,

de).

infighting ['ɪnfaɪtɪŋ] *n fig* luchas *fpl* internas.

infiltrate ['ɪnfɪltreɪt] *vtr* infiltrarse (**into**, en).

infinite ['ɪnfɪnɪt] *adj* infinito,-a.

infinitive [ɪn'fɪnɪtɪv] *n* infinitivo *m*.

infinity [ɪn'fɪnɪtɪ] *n* infinidad *f*; *Math* infinito *m*.

infirm [ɪn'fɜːm] I *adj* (*ailing*) enfermizo,-a; (*weak*) débil. II *npl* **the i.**, los inválidos.

infirmary [ɪn'fɜːmərɪ] *n* hospital *m*.

infirmity [ɪn'fɜːmɪtɪ] *n fml* (*ailment*) enfermedad *f*; (*weakness*) debilidad *f*.

inflame [ɪn'fleɪm] *vtr* (*passion*) encender; (*curiosity*) avivar; (*crowd*) excitar; **to be inflamed with rage**, rabiar.

inflamed [ɪn'fleɪmd] *adj* inflamado,-a; **to become i.**, inflamarse.

inflammable [ɪn'flæməbəl] *adj* (*material*) inflamable; *fig* (*situation*) explosivo,-a.

inflammation [ɪnflə'meɪʃən] *n* inflamación *f*.

inflatable [ɪn'fleɪtəbəl] *adj* inflable.

inflate [ɪn'fleɪt] I *vtr* inflar. II *vi* inflarse.

inflated [ɪn'fleɪtɪd] *adj* 1 *fig* (*prices*) inflacionista. 2 *pej* (*view, idea*) exagerado,-a.

inflation [ɪn'fleɪʃən] *n* inflación *f*.

inflexible [ɪn'fleksəbəl] *adj* inflexible.

inflict [ɪn'flɪkt] *vtr* (*blow*) asestar (**on**, a); (*damage*) causar (**on**, a); (*defeat*) infligir (**on**, a).

in-flight ['ɪnflaɪt] *adj* durante el vuelo.

influence ['ɪnfluəns] I *n* influencia *f*; *fam* **to be under the i.**, llevar una copa de más. II *vtr* influir en.

influential [ɪnflu'enʃəl] *adj* influyente.

influenza [ɪnflu'enzə] *n* gripe *f*.

influx ['ɪnflʌks] *n* afluencia *f*.

inform [ɪn'fɔːm] I *vtr* informar (**of, about**, de, sobre); (*police*) avisar (**of, about**, de). II *vi* **to i. against** *or* **on**, denunciar.

informal [ɪn'fɔːməl] *adj* 1 (*occasion, behaviour*) informal; (*language, treatment*) familiar. 2 (*unofficial*) no oficial.

informality [ɪnfɔː'mælɪtɪ] *n* (*of occasion, behaviour*) sencillez *f*; (*of treatment*) familiaridad *f*.

informant [ɪn'fɔːmənt] *n* informante *mf*.

information [ɪnfə'meɪʃən] *n* información *f*; (*details*) detalles *mpl*; (*facts*) datos *mpl*; (*knowledge*) conocimientos *mpl*; (*news*) noticias *fpl*; **a piece of i.**, un dato; **i. bureau**, centro *m* de información; **i. technology**, informática *f*.

informative [ɪn'fɔːmətɪv] *adj* informativo,-a.

informed [ɪn'fɔːmd] *adj* enterado,-a; **keep me i.**, téngame al corriente.

informer [ɪn'fɔːmər] *n* delator,-a *m,f*; (*to the police*) soplón,-ona *m,f*.

infrared [ɪnfrə'red] *adj* infrarrojo,-a.

infrastructure ['ɪnfrəstrʌktʃər] *n* infraes-

tructura *f*.

infringe [ɪn'frɪndʒ] I *vtr* (*law, rule*) infringir; (*copyright*) no respetar. II *vi* **to i. on** *or* **upon**, (*rights*) violar; (*privacy*) invadir.

infringement [ɪn'frɪndʒmənt] *n* (*of law, rule*) infracción *f*; (*of rights*) violación *f*.

infuriate [ɪn'fjʊərɪeɪt] *vtr* poner furioso, -a.

infuriating [ɪn'fjʊərɪeɪtɪŋ] *adj* exasperante.

infusion [ɪn'fjuːʒən] *n* infusión *f*.

ingenious [ɪn'dʒiːnɪəs] *adj* ingenioso,-a.

ingenuity [ɪndʒɪ'njuːɪtɪ] *n* ingenio *m*.

ingenuous [ɪn'dʒenjʊəs] *adj* ingenuo,-a.

ingot ['ɪŋɡət] *n* lingote *m*.

ingrained [ɪn'ɡreɪnd] *adj fig* arraigado,-a.

ingratiate [ɪn'ɡreɪʃɪeɪt] *vtr pej* **to i. oneself with sb**, congraciarse con.

ingratiating [ɪn'ɡreɪʃɪeɪtɪŋ] *adj* zalamero,-a.

ingratitude [ɪn'ɡrætɪtjuːd] *n* ingratitud *f*.

ingredient [ɪn'ɡriːdɪənt] *n* ingrediente *m*.

inhabit [ɪn'hæbɪt] *vtr* vivir en, ocupar.

inhabitant [ɪn'hæbɪtənt] *n* habitante *mf*.

inhale [ɪn'heɪl] I *vtr* (*gas*) inhalar; (*air*) aspirar. II *vi* aspirar; (*smoker*) tragar el humo.

inherent [ɪn'hɪərənt] *adj* inherente.

inherit [ɪn'herɪt] *vtr* heredar (**from**, de).

inheritance [ɪn'herɪtəns] *n* herencia *f*.

inhibit [ɪn'hɪbɪt] *vtr* (*freedom*) limitar; (*person*) cohibir; **to i. sb from doing sth**, impedir a algn hacer algo.

inhibited [ɪn'hɪbɪtɪd] *adj* cohibido,-a.

inhibition [ɪnhɪ'bɪʃən] *n* cohibición *f*.

inhospitable [ɪnhɒ'spɪtəbəl] *adj* inhospitalario,-a; (*climate, place*) inhóspito,-a.

inhuman [ɪn'hjuːmən] *adj* inhumano,-a.

iniquity [ɪ'nɪkwɪtɪ] *n fml* iniquidad *f*.

initial [ɪ'nɪʃəl] I *adj* inicial, primero,-a. II *n* 1 inicial *f*. 2 **initials**, (*of name*) iniciales *fpl*; (*of abbreviation*) siglas *fpl*. III *vtr* firmar con las iniciales. **◆initially** *adv* al principio.

initiate [ɪ'nɪʃɪeɪt] *vtr* 1 iniciar; (*reform*) promover; (*lawsuit*) entablar. 2 (*into society*) admitir (**into**, en); (*into knowledge*) iniciar (**into**, en).

initiation [ɪnɪʃɪ'eɪʃən] *n* 1 (*start*) principio *m*. 2 (*admission*) iniciación *f*.

initiative [ɪ'nɪʃɪtɪv] *n* iniciativa *f*.

inject [ɪn'dʒekt] *vtr* 1 (*drug etc*) inyectar. 2 *fig* (*capital*) invertir; (*life, hope*) infundir.

injection [ɪn'dʒekʃən] *n* 1 inyección *f*. 2 *fig* (*of capital*) inversión *f*.

injunction [ɪn'dʒʌŋkʃən] *n* interdicto *m*.

injure ['ɪndʒər] *vtr* herir; **to i. oneself**, hacerse daño; *fig* (*health, reputation*) perjudicar.

injured ['ɪndʒəd] I *adj* herido,-a; *fig* (*look, tone*) ofendido,-a. II *npl* **the i.**, los heridos.

injury ['ɪndʒərɪ] n (hurt) herida f; fig (harm) daño m; Sport i. time, (tiempo m de) descuento m.

injustice [ɪn'dʒʌstɪs] n injusticia f.

ink [ɪŋk] n tinta f; **invisible i.**, tinta simpática.

inkling ['ɪŋklɪŋ] n (idea) idea f; (suspicion) sospecha f; (sign) señal f.

inkwell ['ɪŋkwel] n tintero m.

inlaid [ɪn'leɪd] adj (wood) taraceado,-a; (ivory, gems) incrustado,-a.

inland ['ɪnlənd] I adj (del) interior; GB I. **Revenue**, Hacienda f. II [ɪn'lænd] adv (travel) tierra adentro.

in-laws ['ɪnlɔːz] npl fam familia f sing política.

inlet ['ɪnlet] n 1 (in coastline) ensenada f, cala f. 2 (in pipe, machine) entrada f, admisión f.

inmate ['ɪnmeɪt] n (of prison) preso,-a m,f; (of hospital) enfermo,-a m,f; (of asylum, camp) internado,-a m,f.

inn [ɪn] n (with lodging) posada f, mesón m.

innate [ɪ'neɪt] adj innato,-a.

inner ['ɪnər] adj 1 (region) interior; (structure) interno,-a; **i. city**, zona urbana desfavorecida; **i. tube**, cámara f de aire. 2 fig (thoughts) íntimo,-a; (peace etc) interior.

innermost ['ɪnəməʊst] adj (room) más interior; fig (thoughts) más íntimo,-a.

innings ['ɪnɪŋz] n (in cricket) entrada f, turno m.

innocence ['ɪnəsəns] n inocencia f.

innocent ['ɪnəsənt] adj & n inocente (mf).

innocuous [ɪ'nɒkjʊəs] adj inocuo,-a.

innovation [ɪnə'veɪʃən] n novedad f.

innuendo [ɪnjʊ'endəʊ] n indirecta f.

inoculate [ɪ'nɒkjʊleɪt] vtr inocular.

inoculation [ɪnɒkjʊ'leɪʃən] n inoculación f.

inoffensive [ɪnə'fensɪv] adj inofensivo,-a.

inopportune [ɪn'ɒpətjuːn, ɪnɒpə'tjuːn] adj inoportuno,-a.

inordinate [ɪn'ɔːdɪnɪt] adj desmesurado,-a.

inpatient ['ɪnpeɪʃənt] n interno-a m,f.

input ['ɪnpʊt] n (of resources) inversión f; (of power) entrada f; Comput (of data) input m, entrada f.

inquest ['ɪnkwest] n investigación f judicial.

inquire [ɪn'kwaɪər] I vtr preguntar; (find out) averiguar. II vi preguntar (about, por); (find out) informarse (about, de). ◆**inquire after** vtr preguntar por. ◆**inquire into** vtr investigar, indagar.

inquiry [ɪn'kwaɪərɪ] n 1 pregunta f; '**inquiries**', 'información'. 2 (investigation) investigación f.

inquisitive [ɪn'kwɪzɪtɪv] adj (curious) curioso,-a; (questioning) preguntón,-ona.

inroads ['ɪnrəʊdz] npl the firm is making **i. into the market**, la empresa está ganando terreno en el mercado; **to make i. into one's capital**, reducir su capital.

insane [ɪn'seɪn] adj loco,-a; (act) insensato,-a; fig **to drive sb i.**, volver loco,-a a algn.

insanity [ɪn'sænɪtɪ] n demencia f, locura f.

insatiable [ɪn'seɪʃəbəl] adj insaciable.

inscribe [ɪn'skraɪb] vtr fml inscribir; (book) dedicar.

inscription [ɪn'skrɪpʃən] n (on stone, coin) inscripción f; (in book, on photo) dedicatoria f.

inscrutable [ɪn'skruːtəbəl] adj inescrutable, insondable.

insect ['ɪnsekt] n insecto m; **i. bite**, picadura f.

insecticide [ɪn'sektɪsaɪd] n insecticida m.

insecure [ɪnsɪ'kjʊər] adj inseguro,-a.

insecurity [ɪnsɪ'kjʊərɪtɪ] n inseguridad f.

insemination [ɪnsemɪ'neɪʃən] n inseminación f.

insensible [ɪn'sensəbəl] adj fml inconsciente.

insensitive [ɪn'sensɪtɪv] adj insensible.

inseparable [ɪn'sepərəbəl] adj inseparable.

insert ['ɪnsɜːt] I n encarte m. II [ɪn'sɜːt] vtr introducir.

insertion [ɪn'sɜːʃən] n introducción f; (of clause, text) inserción f.

inshore [ɪn'ʃɔːr] I adj (fishing) de bajura. II [ɪn'ʃɔːr] adv cerca de la costa.

inside [ɪn'saɪd] I n 1 interior m; **on the i.**, por dentro; **to turn sth i. out**, volver algo al revés. 2 fam **insides**, tripas fpl. II ['ɪnsaɪd] adj interior; Sport **i. forward**, interior mf; **i. lane**, carril m interior. III [ɪn'saɪd] adv (be) dentro, adentro; (run etc) (hacia) adentro; **to come i.**, entrar; GB fam **he spent a year i.**, pasó un año en chirona. IV prep 1 (place) dentro de. 2 fam **i. (of)**, (time) en menos de.

insider [ɪn'saɪdər] n **i. dealing**, uso indebido de información privilegiada y confidencial para operaciones comerciales.

insidious [ɪn'sɪdɪəs] adj insidioso,-a.

insight ['ɪnsaɪt] n perspicacia f.

insignia [ɪn'sɪgnɪə] n inv insignia f.

insignificant [ɪnsɪg'nɪfɪkənt] adj insignificante.

insincere [ɪnsɪn'sɪər] adj poco sincero,-a.

insinuate [ɪn'sɪnjʊeɪt] vtr insinuar.

insipid [ɪn'sɪpɪd] adj soso,-a, insulso,-a.

insist [ɪn'sɪst] I vi insistir (**on**, en); (argue) obstinarse (**on**, en). II vtr **to i. that ...**, insistir en que ...

insistence [ɪn'sɪstəns] n insistencia f.

insistent [ɪn'sɪstənt] adj insistente.

in so far as [ɪnsəʊ'fɑːrəz] adv en tanto que.

insole [ɪnˈsəʊl] n (of shoe) plantilla f.
insolent [ˈɪnsələnt] adj insolente.
insoluble [ɪnˈsɒljʊbəl] adj insoluble.
insomnia [ɪnˈsɒmnɪə] n insomnio m.
insomniac [ɪnˈsɒmnɪæk] n insomne mf.
inspect [ɪnˈspekt] vtr inspeccionar, examinar; (troops) pasar revista a.
inspection [ɪnˈspekʃən] n inspección f; (of troops) revista f.
inspector [ɪnˈspektər] n inspector,-a m,f; (on bus, train) revisor,-a m,f.
inspiration [ɪnspɪˈreɪʃən] n inspiración f; to get i. from sb/sth, inspirarse en algn/ algo.
inspire [ɪnˈspaɪər] vtr 1 inspirar; to i. respect in sb, infundir respeto a algn. 2 to i. sb to do sth, animar a algn a hacer algo.
inspired [ɪnˈspaɪəd] adj inspirado,-a.
instability [ɪnstəˈbɪlɪtɪ] n inestabilidad f.
install, US instal [ɪnˈstɔːl] vtr instalar.
installation [ɪnstəˈleɪʃən] n instalación f.
instalment, US installment [ɪnˈstɔːlmənt] n 1 (of payment) plazo m; to pay by instalments, pagar a plazos; US i. plan, venta f or compra f a plazos. 2 (of novel, programme) entrega f; (of journal) fascículo m.
instance [ˈɪnstəns] n ejemplo m, caso m; for i., por ejemplo; in the first i., en primer lugar.
instant [ˈɪnstənt] I n (moment) instante m, momento m; in an i., en un instante. II adj inmediato,-a; (coffee, meal) instantáneo,-a. ◆**instantly** adv inmediatamente.
instead [ɪnˈsted] I adv en cambio. II prep i. of, en vez de, en lugar de.
instep [ˈɪnstep] n empeine m.
instigation [ɪnstɪˈɡeɪʃən] n instigación f.
instil, US instill [ɪnˈstɪl] vtr (idea, habit) inculcar (in, a, en); (courage, respect) infundir (in, a).
instinct [ˈɪnstɪŋkt] n instinto m.
instinctive [ɪnˈstɪŋktɪv] adj instintivo,-a.
institute [ˈɪnstɪtjuːt] I n instituto m; (centre) centro m; (professional body) colegio m. II vtr fml 1 (system) establecer. 2 (start) iniciar; (proceedings) entablar.
institution [ɪnstɪˈtjuːʃən] n 1 institución f. 2 (home) asilo m; (asylum) manicomio m.
instruct [ɪnˈstrʌkt] vtr instruir; (order) mandar; I am instructed to say that ..., me han encargado decir que ....
instruction [ɪnˈstrʌkʃən] n 1 instrucción f. 2 instructions, instrucciones fpl; 'instructions for use', 'modo de empleo'.
instructive [ɪnˈstrʌktɪv] adj instructivo,-a.
instructor [ɪnˈstrʌktər] n instructor,-a m,f; (of driving) profesor,-a m,f.
instrument [ˈɪnstrəmənt] n instrumento m; i. panel, tablero m de mandos.
instrumental [ɪnstrəˈmentəl] adj 1 Mus instrumental. 2 to be i. in sth, contribuir decisivamente a algo.
insubordinate [ɪnsəˈbɔːdɪnɪt] adj insubordinado,-a.
insubstantial [ɪnsəbˈstænʃəl] adj insubstancial; (structure) poco sólido,-a.
insufferable [ɪnˈsʌfərəbəl] adj insoportable.
insufficient [ɪnsəˈfɪʃənt] adj insuficiente.
insular [ˈɪnsjʊlər] adj 1 Geog insular. 2 fig pej estrecho,-a de miras.
insulate [ˈɪnsjʊleɪt] vtr aislar (against, from, de).
insulating tape [ˈɪnsjʊleɪtɪŋteɪp] n cinta f aislante.
insulation [ɪnsjʊˈleɪʃən] n aislamiento m.
insulin [ˈɪnsjʊlɪn] n insulina f.
insult [ˈɪnsʌlt] I n (words) insulto m; (action) afrenta f, ofensa f. II [ɪnˈsʌlt] vtr insultar, ofender.
insulting [ɪnˈsʌltɪŋ] adj insultante, ofensivo,-a.
insuperable [ɪnˈsuːpərəbəl] adj insuperable.
insurance [ɪnˈʃʊərəns] n seguro m; fire i., seguro contra incendios; i. broker, agente mf de seguros; i. company, compañía f de seguros; i. policy, póliza f (de seguros); private health i., seguro médico privado.
insure [ɪnˈʃʊər] vtr asegurar (against, contra).
insurgent [ɪnˈsɜːdʒənt] adj & n insurrecto,-a, (m,f).
insurmountable [ɪnsəˈmaʊntəbəl] adj (problem etc) insuperable; (barrier) infranqueable.
intact [ɪnˈtækt] adj intacto,-a.
intake [ˈɪnteɪk] n 1 (of air, water) entrada f; (of electricity etc) toma f. 2 (of food, calories) consumo m. 3 (of students, recruits) número m de admitidos.
integral [ˈɪntɪɡrəl] I adj 1 (intrinsic) integrante. 2 (whole) íntegro,-a. 3 Math integral. II n Math integral f.
integrate [ˈɪntɪɡreɪt] I vtr integrar. II vi integrarse.
integration [ɪntɪˈɡreɪʃən] n integración f.
integrity [ɪnˈteɡrɪtɪ] n integridad f, honradez f.
intellect [ˈɪntɪlekt] n intelecto m.
intellectual [ɪntɪˈlektjʊəl] adj & n intelectual (mf).
intelligence [ɪnˈtelɪdʒəns] n 1 inteligencia f. 2 (information) información f.
intelligent [ɪnˈtelɪdʒənt] adj inteligente.
intelligentsia [ɪntelɪˈdʒentsɪə] n intelectualidad f.
intelligible [ɪnˈtelɪdʒəbəl] adj inteligible.
intend [ɪnˈtend] vtr 1 (mean) tener la intención de. 2 to i. sth for sb, destinar algo a algn.
intended [ɪnˈtendɪd] adj (planned) previsto,-a.

intense [ɪn'tens] *adj* intenso,-a; *(person)* muy serio,-a. ◆**intensely** *adv (extremely)* enormemente, sumamente.

intensify [ɪn'tensɪfaɪ] *vtr (search)* intensificar; *(effort)* redoblar; *(production, pollution)* aumentar.

intensity [ɪn'tensɪtɪ] *n* intensidad *f*.

intensive [ɪn'tensɪv] *adj* intensivo,-a; *Med* **i. care unit**, unidad *f* de vigilancia intensiva.

intent [ɪn'tent] **I** *adj (absorbed)* absorto,-a; *(gaze etc)* atento,-a; **to be i. on doing sth**, estar resuelto,-a a hacer algo. **II** *n fml* intención *f*, propósito *m*; **to all intents and purposes**, a todos los efectos.

intention [ɪn'tenʃən] *n* intención *f*.

intentional [ɪn'tenʃənəl] *adj* deliberado, -a. ◆**intentionally** *adv* a propósito.

interact [ɪntər'ækt] *vi (people)* interrelacionarse.

interaction [ɪntər'ækʃən] *n* interacción *f*.

interactive [ɪntər'æktɪv] *adj* interactivo, -a.

intercede [ɪntə'siːd] *vi* interceder (with, ante).

intercept [ɪntə'sept] *vtr* interceptar.

interchange ['ɪntətʃeɪndʒ] **I** *n* **1** *(exchange)* intercambio *m*. **2** *(on motorway)* cruce *m*. **II** [ɪntə'tʃeɪndʒ] *vtr* intercambiar (with, con).

interchangeable [ɪntə'tʃeɪndʒəbl] *adj* intercambiable.

intercity [ɪntə'sɪtɪ] *adj* Rail de largo recorrido.

intercom ['ɪntəkɒm] *n* portero automático.

intercontinental [ɪntəkɒntɪ'nentəl] *adj.* **i. ballistic missile**, misil balístico intercontinental.

intercourse ['ɪntəkɔːs] *n* **1** *(dealings)* trato *m*. **2** *(sexual)* relaciones *fpl* sexuales.

interest ['ɪntrɪst] **I** *n* **1** interés *m*. **2** *(advantage)* provecho *m*; **in the i. of**, en pro de. **3** *Com (share)* participación *f*. **4** *Fin* interés *m*; **i. rate**, tipo *m* de interés. **II** *vtr* interesar; **he's interested in politics**, le interesa la política.

interesting ['ɪntrɪstɪŋ] *adj* interesante.

interface ['ɪntəfeɪs] *n* interface *f*.

interfere [ɪntə'fɪər] *vi* **1** *(meddle)* entrometerse (**in**, en); **to i. with**, *(hinder)* dificultar; *(spoil)* estropear; *(prevent)* impedir. **2** *Rad TV* interferir (with, con).

interference [ɪntə'fɪərəns] *n (meddling)* intromisión *f*; *(hindrance)* estorbo *m*; *Rad TV* interferencia *f*.

interim ['ɪntərɪm] **I** *n fml* **in the i.**, en el ínterin. **II** *adj* interino,-a, provisional.

interior [ɪn'tɪərɪər] **I** *adj* interior. **II** *n* interior *m*; **i. design**, diseño *m* de interiores.

interlock [ɪntə'lɒk] *vi* encajarse; *(fingers)* entrelazarse; *(cogs)* engranarse.

interloper ['ɪntələʊpər] *n* intruso,-a *m,f*.

interlude ['ɪntəluːd] *n (break)* intervalo *m*; *Cin Theat* intermedio *m*; *Mus* interludio *m*.

intermediary [ɪntə'miːdɪərɪ] *n* intermediario,-a *m,f*.

intermediate [ɪntə'miːdɪɪt] *adj* intermedio,-a.

interminable [ɪn'tɜːmɪnəbl] *adj* interminable.

intermission [ɪntə'mɪʃən] *n Cin Theat* intermedio *m*.

intermittent [ɪntə'mɪtənt] *adj* intermitente.

intern [ɪn'tɜːn] **I** *vtr* internar. **II** ['ɪntɜːn] *n US Med* interno,-a *m,f*.

internal [ɪn'tɜːnəl] *adj* interior; *(dispute, injury)* interno,-a; *US* **I. Revenue**, ≈ Hacienda *f*. ◆**internally** *adv* interiormente; **'not to be taken i.'**, 'uso externo'.

international [ɪntə'næʃənəl] **I** *adj* internacional. **II** *n Sport (player)* internacional *mf*; *(match)* partido *m* internacional.

interplay ['ɪntəpleɪ] *n* interacción *f*.

interpret [ɪn'tɜːprɪt] **I** *vtr* interpretar. **II** *vi* actuar de intérprete.

interpretation [ɪntɜːprɪ'teɪʃən] *n* interpretación *f*.

interpreter [ɪn'tɜːprɪtər] *n* intérprete *mf*.

interrelated [ɪntərɪ'leɪtɪd] *adj* estrechamente relacionado,-a.

interrogate [ɪn'terəgeɪt] *vtr* interrogar.

interrogation [ɪnterə'geɪʃən] *n* interrogatorio *m*.

interrogative [ɪntə'rɒgətɪv] *Ling* **I** *adj* interrogativo,-a. **II** *n (word)* palabra interrogativa.

interrupt [ɪntə'rʌpt] *vtr & vi* interrumpir.

interruption [ɪntə'rʌpʃən] *n* interrupción *f*.

intersect [ɪntə'sekt] **I** *vtr* cruzar. **II** *vi* cruzarse.

intersection [ɪntə'sekʃən] *n* **1** *(crossroads)* cruce *m*. **2** *(of two lines)* intersección *f*.

intersperse [ɪntə'spɜːs] *vtr* esparcir.

intertwine [ɪntə'twaɪn] **I** *vtr* entrelazar (with, con). **II** *vi* entrelazarse (with, con).

interval ['ɪntəvəl] *n* **1** *(of time, space)* intervalo *m*; **at intervals**, *(time, space)* a intervalos; *(time)* de vez en cuando. **2** *GB Cin Theat* intermedio *m*.

intervene [ɪntə'viːn] *vi* **1** *(person)* intervenir (**in**, en). **2** *(event)* sobrevenir. **3** *(time)* transcurrir.

intervention [ɪntə'venʃən] *n* intervención *f*.

interview ['ɪntəvjuː] **I** *n* entrevista *f*; **to give an i.**, conceder una entrevista. **II** *vtr* entrevistar.

interviewer ['ɪntəvjuːər] *n* entrevistador,-a *m,f*.

intestine [ɪn'testɪn] *n (usu pl)* intestino *m*; **large/small i.**, intestino grueso/delgado.

intimacy ['ɪntɪməsɪ] *n (closeness)* intimi-

dad *f*; *euph* (*sex*) relación íntima; **intimacies**, intimidades *fpl*.
intimate¹ ['ɪntɪmɪt] *adj* íntimo,-a; (*knowledge*) profundo,-a.
intimate² ['ɪntɪmeɪt] *vtr fml* dar a entender.
intimidate [ɪn'tɪmɪdeɪt] *vtr* intimidar.
intimidating [ɪn'tɪmɪdeɪtɪŋ] *adj* atemorizante.
into ['ɪntuː, *unstressed* 'ɪntə] *prep* 1 (*motion*) en, a, con; **he fell i. the water**, se cayó al agua; **I bumped i. a friend**, me topé con un amigo; **to get i. a car**, subir a un coche; **to go i. a house**, entrar en una casa. 2 (*state*) en, a; **he grew i. a man**, se hizo un hombre; **to burst i. tears**, echarse a llorar; **to change pounds i. pesetas**, cambiar libras en *or* por pesetas; **to translate sth i. French**, traducir algo al francés. 3 **to work i. the night**, trabajar hasta muy avanzada la noche. 4 **to divide sth i. three**, dividir algo en tres. 5 *fam* **to be i. sth**, ser aficionado,-a a algo.
intolerable [ɪn'tɒlərəbəl] *adj* intolerable.
intolerant [ɪn'tɒlərənt] *adj* intolerante.
intonation [ɪntəʊ'neɪʃən] *n* entonación *f*.
intoxicated [ɪn'tɒksɪkeɪtɪd] *adj* borracho,-a.
intoxicating [ɪn'tɒksɪkeɪtɪŋ] *adj* embriagador,-a; **i. liquor**, bebida alcohólica.
intoxication [ɪntɒksɪ'keɪʃən] *n* embriaguez *f*.
intractable [ɪn'træktəbəl] *adj fml* (*person*) intratable; (*problem*) insoluble.
intransigent [ɪn'trænsɪdʒənt] *adj fml* intransigente, intolerante.
intransitive [ɪn'trænsɪtɪv] *adj* intransitivo,-a.
intravenous [ɪntrə'viːnəs] *adj* intravenoso,-a.
in-tray ['ɪntreɪ] *n* bandeja *f* de asuntos pendientes.
intrepid [ɪn'trepɪd] *adj* intrépido,-a, audaz.
intricate ['ɪntrɪkɪt] *adj* intrincado,-a.
intrigue [ɪn'triːg, 'ɪntriːg] I *n* intriga *f*. II [ɪn'triːg] *vtr* intrigar. III *vi* intrigar, conspirar.
intriguing [ɪn'triːgɪŋ] *adj* intrigante.
intrinsic [ɪn'trɪnsɪk] *adj fml* intrínseco,-a.
introduce [ɪntrə'djuːs] *vtr* 1 (*person, programme*) presentar (**to**, a). 2 (*bring in*) introducir (**into**, **to**, en); *Com* lanzar (**into**, **to**, a); (*topic*) proponer.
introduction [ɪntrə'dʌkʃən] *n* 1 (*of person, programme*) presentación *f*; (*in book*) introducción *f*. 2 (*bringing in*) introducción *f*; *Com* (*of product*) lanzamiento *m*.
introductory [ɪntrə'dʌktərɪ] *adj* introductorio,-a; (*remarks*) preliminar; *Com* de lanzamiento.

introspective [ɪntrə'spektɪv] *adj* introspectivo,-a.
introvert ['ɪntrəvɜːt] *n* introvertido,-a *m,f*.
intrude [ɪn'truːd] *vi* entrometerse (**into**, **on**, en); (*disturb*) molestar.
intruder [ɪn'truːdər] *n* intruso,-a *m,f*.
intrusion [ɪn'truːʒən] *n* incursión *f*.
intuition [ɪntjʊ'ɪʃən] *n* intuición *f*.
inundate ['ɪnʌndeɪt] *vtr* inundar (**with**, de).
invade [ɪn'veɪd] *vtr* invadir.
invader [ɪn'veɪdər] *n* invasor,-a *m,f*.
invalid¹ ['ɪnvəlɪd] *n* (*disabled person*) minusválido,-a *m,f*; (*sick person*) enfermo,-a *m,f*.
invalid² [ɪn'vælɪd] *adj* inválido,-a, nulo,-a.
invalidate [ɪn'vælɪdeɪt] *vtr* invalidar.
invaluable [ɪn'væljʊəbəl] *adj* inestimable.
invariable [ɪn'veərɪəbəl] *adj* invariable.
invasion [ɪn'veɪʒən] *n* invasión *f*.
invent [ɪn'vent] *vtr* inventar.
invention [ɪn'venʃən] *n* invento *m*; (*creativity*) inventiva *f*; (*lie*) mentira *f*.
inventive [ɪn'ventɪv] *adj* inventivo,-a.
inventor [ɪn'ventər] *n* inventor,-a *m,f*.
inventory ['ɪnvəntərɪ] *n* inventario *m*.
invert [ɪn'vɜːt] *vtr* invertir.
invertebrate [ɪn'vɜːtɪbrɪt] I *adj* invertebrado,-a. II *n* invertebrado *m*.
inverted [ɪn'vɜːtɪd] *adj* (**in**) **i. commas**, (entre) comillas *fpl*.
invest [ɪn'vest] I *vtr* invertir (**in**, en); **to i. sb with sth**, conferir algo a algn. II *vi* invertir (**in**, en).
investigate [ɪn'vestɪgeɪt] *vtr* (*crime, subject*) investigar; (*cause, possibility*) estudiar.
investigation [ɪnvestɪ'geɪʃən] *n* (*of crime*) investigación *f*; (*of cause*) examen *m*.
investigator [ɪn'vestɪgeɪtər] *n* investigador,-a *m,f*; **private i.**, detective privado.
investment [ɪn'vestmənt] *n* inversión *f*.
investor [ɪn'vestər] *n* inversor,-a *m,f*.
inveterate [ɪn'vetərɪt] *adj* empedernido,-a.
invidious [ɪn'vɪdɪəs] *adj* (*task*) ingrato,-a; (*comparison*) injusto,-a.
invigilator [ɪn'vɪdʒɪleɪtər] *n GB* vigilante *mf*.
invigorating [ɪn'vɪgəreɪtɪŋ] *adj* vigorizante.
invincible [ɪn'vɪnsəbəl] *adj* invencible.
invisible [ɪn'vɪzəbəl] *adj* invisible.
invitation [ɪnvɪ'teɪʃən] *n* invitación *f*.
invite [ɪn'vaɪt] *vtr* 1 invitar (**to**, a). 2 (*comments etc*) solicitar; (*criticism*) provocar; **to i. trouble**, buscarse problemas.
inviting [ɪn'vaɪtɪŋ] *adj* (*attractive*) atractivo,-a; (*food*) apetitoso,-a.
invoice ['ɪnvɔɪs] I *n* factura *f*. II *vtr* facturar.

invoke [ɪn'vəʊk] vtr fml invocar.
involuntary [ɪn'vɒləntərɪ] adj involuntario,-a.
involve [ɪn'vɒlv] vtr 1 (concern) implicar (in, en); **the issues involved**, las cuestiones en juego; **to be involved in an accident**, sufrir un accidente. 2 (entail) suponer, implicar; (trouble, risk) acarrear.
involved [ɪn'vɒlvd] adj (complicated) complicado,-a; (romantically attached) enredado,-a, liado,-a.
involvement [ɪn'vɒlvmənt] n (participation) participación f; (in crime) implicación f.
inward ['ɪnwəd] I adj interior. II adv → **inwards.** ◆**inwardly** adv interiormente, por dentro.
inwards ['ɪnwədz] adv hacia dentro.
iodine ['aɪədiːn] n yodo m.
iota [aɪ'əʊtə] n pizca f, ápice m.
IOU [aɪəʊ'juː] abbr of **I owe you**, pagaré m.
IQ [aɪ'kjuː] abbr of **intelligence quotient**, coeficiente m intelectual, CI m.
IRA [aɪɑː'reɪ] abbr of **Irish Republican Army**, Ejército m Republicano irlandés, IRA m.
Iran [ɪ'rɑːn] n Irán.
Iranian [ɪ'reɪnɪən] adj & n iraní (mf).
Iraq [ɪ'rɑːk] n Irak.
Iraqi [ɪ'rɑːkɪ] adj & n iraquí (mf).
irascible [ɪ'ræsɪbəl] adj fml irascible.
irate [aɪ'reɪt] adj airado,-a, furioso,-a.
Ireland ['aɪələnd] n Irlanda; **Republic of I.**, República de Irlanda.
iris ['aɪərɪs] n 1 Anat iris m inv. 2 Bot lirio m.
Irish ['aɪrɪʃ] I adj irlandés,-esa; **I. coffee**, café m irlandés; **I. Sea**, Mar m de Irlanda. II n 1 (language) irlandés m. 2 pl the I., los irlandeses.
Irishman ['aɪrɪʃmən] n irlandés m.
Irishwoman ['aɪrɪʃwʊmən] n irlandesa f.
irksome ['ɜːksəm] adj fastidioso,-a.
iron ['aɪən] I n 1 hierro m; **the i. and steel industry**, la industria siderúrgica; **I. Curtain**, Telón m de Acero; **i. ore**, mineral m de hierro. 2 (for clothes) plancha f. 3 (for golf) hierro m. 4 **irons**, (chains) grillos mpl. II vtr (clothes) planchar. ◆**iron out** vtr 1 (crease) planchar. 2 fam fig (problem) resolver.
ironic(al) [aɪ'rɒnɪk(əl)] adj irónico,-a.
ironing ['aɪənɪŋ] n 1 to do the i., planchar; **i. board**, mesa f de la plancha. 2 (clothes to be ironed) ropa f para planchar; (clothes ironed) ropa planchada.
ironmonger ['aɪənmʌŋɡər] n GB ferretero,-a m,f; **i.'s (shop)**, ferretería f.
irony ['aɪrənɪ] n ironía f.
irrational [ɪ'ræʃənəl] adj irracional.
irreconcilable [ɪrekən'saɪləbəl] irreconciliable.
irrefutable [ɪrɪ'fjuːtəbəl] adj fml irrefuta-

ble.
irregular [ɪ'reɡjʊlər] adj 1 irregular; (abnormal) anormal. 2 (uneven) desigual.
irrelevant [ɪ'reləvənt] adj no pertinente.
irreparable [ɪ'repərəbəl] adj irreparable.
irreplaceable [ɪrɪ'pleɪsəbəl] adj irremplazable.
irrepressible [ɪrɪ'presəbəl] adj incontenible.
irresistible [ɪrɪ'zɪstəbəl] adj irresistible.
irresolute [ɪ'rezəljuːt] adj fml indeciso,-a.
irrespective [ɪrɪ'spektɪv] adj **i. of**, sin tener en cuenta.
irresponsible [ɪrɪ'spɒnsəbəl] adj irresponsable.
irreverent [ɪ'revərənt] adj irreverente.
irrevocable [ɪ'revəkəbəl] adj irrevocable.
irrigate ['ɪrɪɡeɪt] vtr regar.
irrigation [ɪrɪ'ɡeɪʃən] n riego m; **i. channel**, acequia f; **i. system**, sistema m de regadío.
irritable ['ɪrɪtəbəl] adj irritable.
irritate ['ɪrɪteɪt] vtr (annoy) fastidiar; Med irritar.
irritating ['ɪrɪteɪtɪŋ] adj irritante.
irritation [ɪrɪ'teɪʃən] n 1 (annoyance) fastidio m; (ill humour) mal humor m. 2 Med irritación f.
is [ɪz] 3rd person sing pres → **be**.
Islam ['ɪzlɑːm] n Islam m.
Islamic [ɪz'læmɪk] adj islámico,-a.
island ['aɪlənd] n isla f; (traffic) isleta f.
islander ['aɪləndər] n isleño,-a m,f.
isle [aɪl] n isla f.
isn't ['ɪzənt] = **is not**.
isolate ['aɪsəleɪt] vtr aislar (from, de).
isolated ['aɪsəleɪtɪd] adj aislado,-a.
isolation [aɪsə'leɪʃən] n aislamiento m.
Israel ['ɪzreɪəl] n Israel.
Israeli [ɪz'reɪlɪ] I adj israelí. II n israelí mf.
issue ['ɪʃjuː] I n 1 (matter) cuestión f; **to take i. with sb (over sth)**, manifestar su desacuerdo con algn (en algo). 2 (of banknotes etc) emisión f; (of passport) expedición f. 3 (of journal etc) ejemplar m. 4 (of supplies) reparto m. 5 fml (outcome) resultado m. 6 Jur (offspring) descendencia f. II vtr 1 (book) publicar; (banknotes etc) emitir; (passport) expedir. 2 (supplies) repartir. 3 (order, instructions) dar; (warrant) dictar. III vi fml (blood) brotar (from, de); (smoke) salir (from, de).
isthmus ['ɪsməs] n istmo m.

it [ɪt] pers pron 1 (subject) él, ella, ello (often omitted); **it's here**, está aquí. 2 (direct object) lo, la; **I don't believe it**, no me lo creo; **I liked the house and bought it**, me gustó la casa y la compré. 3 (indirect object) le; **give it a kick**, dale una patada. 4 (after prep) él, ella, ello; **I saw the beach and ran towards it**, vi la playa y fui corriendo hacia ella; **we'll talk about

it later, ya hablaremos de ello. 5 (*abstract*) ello; **let's get down to it!,** ¡vamos a ello! 6 (*impersonal*) **it's late,** es tarde; **it's me,** soy yo; **it's raining,** está lloviendo; **it's said that ...,** se dice que ...; **it's two miles to town,** hay dos millas de aquí al pueblo; **that's it!,** (*agreeing*) ¡precisamente!; (*finishing*) ¡se acabó!; **this is it!,** ¡ha llegado la hora!; **who is it?,** ¿quién es?
Italian [ɪ'tæljən] **I** *adj* italiano,-a. **II** *n* 1 (*person*) italiano,-a *m,f*. 2 (*language*) italiano *m*.
italic [ɪ'tælɪk] *n* cursiva *f*.
Italy ['ɪtəlɪ] *n* Italia.
itch [ɪtʃ] **I** *n* picor *m*; *fig* **an i. to travel,** unas ganas locas de viajar. **II** *vi* 1 (*skin*) picar. 2 *fig* anhelar; *fam* **to be itching to do sth,** tener muchas ganas de hacer algo.
itchy ['ɪtʃɪ] *adj* (**itchier, itchiest**) que pica.

item ['aɪtəm] *n* 1 (*in list*) artículo *m*; (*in collection*) pieza *f*; **i. of clothing,** prenda *f* de vestir. 2 (*on agenda*) asunto *m*; (*in show*) número *m*; **news i.,** noticia *f*.
itemize ['aɪtəmaɪz] *vtr* detallar.
itinerant [ɪ'tɪnərənt] *adj fml* itinerante.
itinerary [aɪ'tɪnərərɪ] *n* itinerario *m*.
it'll ['ɪtl] = **it will.**
its [ɪts] *poss adj* (*one thing*) su; (*more than one*) sus.
itself [ɪt'self] *pers pron* 1 (*reflexive*) se; **the cat scratched i.,** el gato se arañó. 2 (*emphatic*) él *or* ella *or* ello mismo,-a; (*after prep*) sí (mismo,-a); **in i.,** en sí.
ITV [aɪtiː'viː] *GB abbr of* **Independent Television,** televisión *f* independiente, ITV *f*.
IUD [aɪjuː'diː] *abbr of* **intrauterine** (**contraceptive**) **device,** dispositivo intrauterino, DIU *m*.
ivory ['aɪvərɪ] *n* marfil *m*.
ivy ['aɪvɪ] *n* hiedra *f*.

J

J, j [dʒeɪ] *n* (*the letter*) J, j *f*.
jab [dʒæb] **I** *n* pinchazo *m*; (*poke*) golpe seco. **II** *vtr* pinchar; (*with fist*) dar un puñetazo a.
jabber ['dʒæbər] *fam vi* (*chatter*) charlotear; (*speak quickly*) hablar atropelladamente.
jack [dʒæk] *n* 1 *Aut* gato *m*. 2 *Cards* sota *f*. 3 (*bowls*) boliche *m*. ◆**jack in** *vtr GB fam* dejar. ◆**jack up** *vtr Aut* levantar (con el gato); *fig* (*prices*) aumentar.
jackal ['dʒækɔːl] *n* chacal *m*.
jackdaw ['dʒækdɔː] *n Orn* grajilla *f*.
jacket ['dʒækɪt] *n* 1 chaqueta *f*; (*of suit*) americana *f*; (*bomber jacket*) cazadora *f*. 2 (*of book*) sobrecubierta *f*; *US* (*of record*) funda *f*. 3 **j. potatoes,** patatas *fpl* al horno.
jack-knife ['dʒæknaɪf] **I** *n* navaja *f*. **II** *vi* colear.
jack-of-all-trades [dʒækəv'ɔːltreɪdz] *n* persona *f* mañosa *or* de muchos oficios.
jackpot ['dʒækpɒt] *n* (*premio m*) gordo *m*.
Jacuzzi® [dʒə'kuːzɪ] *n* jacuzzi® *m*.
jade [dʒeɪd] *n* jade *m*.
jaded ['dʒeɪdɪd] *adj* (*tired*) agotado,-a; (*palate*) hastiado,-a.
jagged ['dʒægɪd] *adj* dentado,-a.
jaguar ['dʒægjʊər] *n* jaguar *m*.
jail [dʒeɪl] **I** *n* cárcel *f*, prisión *f*. **II** *vtr* encarcelar.
jailbreak ['dʒeɪlbreɪk] *n* fuga *f*, evasión *f*.
jailer ['dʒeɪlər] *n* carcelero,-a *m,f*.
jam¹ [dʒæm] *n Culin* mermelada *f*.
jam² [dʒæm] **I** *n* 1 (*blockage*) atasco *m*; *fam* (*fix*) apuro *m*. 2 *Mus* improvisación *f*. **II** *vtr* 1 (*cram*) meter a la fuerza. 2 (*block*)

atascar; *Rad* interferir. **III** *vi* (*door*) atrancarse; (*brakes*) agarrotarse.
Jamaica [dʒə'meɪkə] *n* Jamaica.
jam-packed [dʒæm'pækt] *adj fam* (*with people*) atestado,-a; (*with things*) atiborrado,-a.
jangle ['dʒæŋgəl] *vi* tintinear.
janitor ['dʒænɪtər] *n* portero *m*, conserje *m*.
January ['dʒænjʊərɪ] *n* enero *m*.
Japan [dʒə'pæn] *n* (el) Japón.
Japanese [dʒæpə'niːz] **I** *adj* japonés,-esa. **II** *n* (*person*) japonés,-esa *m,f*; (*language*) japonés *m*.
jar¹ [dʒɑːr] *n* (*glass*) tarro *m*; (*earthenware*) tinaja *f*; (*jug*) jarra *f*; *GB fam* **to have a j.,** tomar una copa.
jar² [dʒɑːr] *vi* (*sounds*) chirriar; (*appearance*) chocar; (*colours*) desentonar; *fig* **to j. on one's nerves,** ponerle a uno los nervios de punta.
jargon ['dʒɑːgən] *n* jerga *f*, argot *m*.
jasmin(e) ['dʒæzmɪn] *n* jazmín *m*.
jaundice ['dʒɔːndɪs] *n* ictericia *f*.
jaundiced ['dʒɔːndɪst] *adj Med* ictérico, -a; *fig* (*bitter*) amargado,-a.
jaunt [dʒɔːnt] *n* (*walk*) paseo *m*; (*trip*) excursión *f*.
jaunty ['dʒɔːntɪ] *adj* (**jauntier, jauntiest**) (*sprightly*) garboso,-a; (*lively*) vivaz.
javelin ['dʒævəlɪn] *n* jabalina *f*.
jaw [dʒɔː] **I** *n* mandíbula *f*. **II** *vi fam* estar de palique.
jay [dʒeɪ] *n Orn* arrendajo *m* (común).
jaywalker ['dʒeɪwɔːkər] *n* peatón *m* imprudente.
jazz [dʒæz] *n* jazz *m*. ◆**jazz up** *vtr* ale-

grar; (premises) arreglar.

jazzy ['dʒæzɪ] adj (jazzier, jazziest) fam (showy) llamativo,-a; (brightly coloured) de colores chillones.

jealous ['dʒeləs] adj celoso,-a; (envious) envidioso,-a; **to be j. of ...**, tener celos de ....

jealousy ['dʒeləsɪ] n celos mpl; (envy) envidia f.

jeans [dʒiːnz] npl vaqueros mpl, tejanos mpl.

jeep [dʒiːp] n jeep m, todo terreno m inv.

jeer [dʒɪər] I n (boo) abucheo m; (mocking) mofa f. II vi (boo) abuchear; (mock) burlarse.

jeering ['dʒɪərɪŋ] adj burlón,-ona.

Jehovah [dʒɪ'həʊvə] n J.'s Witness, testigo mf de Jehová.

jelly ['dʒelɪ] n gelatina f.

jellyfish ['dʒelɪfɪʃ] n medusa f.

jeopardize ['dʒepədaɪz] vtr poner en peligro; (agreement etc) comprometer.

jeopardy ['dʒepədɪ] n riesgo m, peligro m.

jerk [dʒɜːk] I n 1 (jolt) sacudida f; (pull) tirón m. 2 pej (idiot) imbécil mf. II vtr (shake) sacudir; (pull) dar un tirón a. III vi (move suddenly) dar una sacudida; **the car jerked forward**, el coche avanzaba a tirones.

jerkin ['dʒɜːkɪn] n chaleco m.

jersey ['dʒɜːzɪ] n jersey m, suéter m.

jest [dʒest] I n broma f. II vi bromear.

Jesuit ['dʒezjʊɪt] adj & n jesuita (m).

Jesus ['dʒiːzəs] n Jesús m; **J. Christ**, Jesucristo m.

jet¹ [dʒet] I n 1 (stream of water) chorro m. 2 (spout) surtidor m. 3 Av reactor m; **j. engine**, reactor m; **j. lag**, cansancio debido al desfase horario. II vi fam volar.

jet² [dʒet] n **j. black**, negro,-a como el azabache.

jet-set ['dʒetset] n **the j.-s.**, la alta sociedad, la jet.

jettison ['dʒetɪsən] vtr echar al mar; fig deshacerse de; (project etc) abandonar.

jetty ['dʒetɪ] n muelle m, malecón m.

Jew [dʒuː] n judío,-a m,f.

jewel ['dʒuːəl] n joya f; (stone) piedra preciosa; (in watch) rubí m; fig (person) joya f.

jeweller, jeweler ['dʒuːələr] n joyero,-a m,f; **j.'s (shop)**, joyería f.

jewellery, jewelry ['dʒuːəlrɪ] n joyas fpl, alhajas fpl.

Jewess ['dʒuːɪs] n judía f.

Jewish ['dʒuːɪʃ] adj judío,-a.

jibe [dʒaɪb] n & vi = **gibe**.

jiffy ['dʒɪfɪ] n fam momento m; **in a j.**, en un santiamén; **just a j.!**, ¡un momento!

jig [dʒɪg] n Mus giga f.

jigsaw ['dʒɪgsɔː] n (puzzle) rompecabezas m inv.

jilt [dʒɪlt] vtr fam dejar plantado,-a.

jingle ['dʒɪŋgəl] I n Rad TV canción f que acompaña un anuncio. II vi tintinear.

jingoistic [dʒɪŋgəʊ'ɪstɪk] adj patriotero, -a.

jinx [dʒɪŋks] I n (person) gafe mf. II vtr gafar.

jitters ['dʒɪtəz] npl fam **to get the j.**, tener canguelo.

jive [dʒaɪv] I n swing m. II vi bailar el swing.

job [dʒɒb] n 1 trabajo m; (task) tarea f; **to give sth up as a bad j.**, darse por vencido,-a; **jam just the j.!**, ¡me viene de perlas! 2 (occupation) (puesto m de) trabajo m, empleo m; (trade) oficio m; GB fam **jobs for the boys**, enchufismo m; **j. centre**, oficina f de empleo; **j. hunting**, búsqueda f de empleo; **j. sharing**, trabajo compartido a tiempo parcial. 3 fam **we had a j. to ...**, nos costó (trabajo) .... 4 (duty) deber m. 5 fam **it's a good j. that ...**, menos mal que ....

jobless ['dʒɒbləs] adj parado,-a.

jockey ['dʒɒkɪ] I n jinete m, jockey m. II vi **to j. for position**, luchar para conseguir una posición aventajada.

jocular ['dʒɒkjʊlər] adj jocoso,-a.

jog [dʒɒg] I n trote m. II vtr empujar; fig (memory) refrescar. III vi Sport hacer footing; fig **to j. along**, (progress slowly) avanzar poco a poco; (manage) ir tirando.

jogging ['dʒɒgɪŋ] n footing m.

join [dʒɔɪn] I vtr 1 juntar; **to j. forces with sb**, unir fuerzas con algn. 2 (road) empalmar con; (river) desembocar en. 3 (meet) reunirse con. 4 (group) unirse a; (institution) entrar; (army) alistarse a. 5 (party) afiliarse a; (club) hacerse socio,-a de. II vi 1 unirse. 2 (roads) empalmar; (rivers) confluir. 3 (become a member of political party) afiliarse; (become member of club) hacerse socio,-a. III n juntura f. ◆**join in** I vi participar, tomar parte; (debate) intervenir. II vtr participar en, tomar parte en. ◆**join up** I vtr juntar. II vi (of roads) unirse; Mil alistarse.

joiner ['dʒɔɪnər] n GB carpintero,-a m,f.

joinery ['dʒɔɪnərɪ] n carpintería f.

joint [dʒɔɪnt] I n 1 juntura f, unión f; Tech Anat articulación f; **out of j.**, dislocado,-a. 2 Culin corte m de carne para asar; (once roasted) asado m. 3 sl (nightclub etc) garito m. 4 sl (drug) porro m. II adj colectivo,-a; **j. (bank) account**, cuenta conjunta; **j. venture**, empresa conjunta. ◆**jointly** adv conjuntamente, en común.

joist [dʒɔɪst] n vigueta f.

joke [dʒəʊk] I n chiste m; (prank) broma f; **to play a j. on sb**, gastarle una broma a algn; **to tell a j.**, contar un chiste; fam (person, thing) hazmerreír m, payaso,-a m,f. II vi estar de broma; **you must be joking!**, ¡no hablarás en serio!

joker ['dʒəʊkər] n 1 bromista mf. 2 Cards comodín m.

jolly ['dʒɒlɪ] I adj (jollier, jolliest) alegre. II adv fam (very) muy; **she played j. well,** jugó muy bien.

jolt [dʒəʊlt] I n 1 sacudida f; (pull) tirón m. 2 fig (fright) susto m. II vi moverse a sacudidas. III vtr sacudir.

Jordan ['dʒɔːdən] n 1 (river) Jordán m. 2 (country) Jordania.

joss-stick ['dʒɒstɪk] n varita f de incienso.

jostle ['dʒɒsəl] I vi dar empujones. II vtr dar empujones a.

jot [dʒɒt] n jota f, pizca f; **not a j.,** ni jota. ◆**jot down** vtr apuntar.

jotter ['dʒɒtər] n GB bloc m.

journal ['dʒɜːnəl] n 1 revista f. 2 (diary) diario m. 3 (newspaper) periódico m.

journalism ['dʒɜːnəlɪzəm] n periodismo m.

journalist ['dʒɜːnəlɪst] n periodista mf.

journey ['dʒɜːnɪ] I n viaje m; (distance) trayecto m. II vi fml viajar.

jovial ['dʒəʊvɪəl] adj jovial.

jowl [dʒaʊl] n quijada f.

joy [dʒɔɪ] n alegría f; (pleasure) placer m.

joyful ['dʒɔɪfʊl] adj alegre, contento,-a.

joyous ['dʒɔɪəs] adj lit alegre.

joyride ['dʒɔɪraɪd] n fam paseo m en un coche robado.

joystick ['dʒɔɪstɪk] n Av palanca f de mando; (of video game) joystick m.

JP [dʒeɪ'piː] abbr of Justice of the Peace.

Jr abbr of **junior**.

jubilant ['dʒuːbɪlənt] adj jubiloso,-a.

jubilation [dʒuːbɪ'leɪʃən] n júbilo m.

jubilee ['dʒuːbɪliː] n festejos mpl; **golden j.,** quincuagésimo aniversario.

judge [dʒʌdʒ] I n juez mf, jueza f; (in competition) jurado m. II vtr 1 Jur juzgar. 2 (estimate) considerar. 3 (competition) actuar de juez de. 4 (assess) juzgar. III vi juzgar; **judging from what you say,** a juzgar por lo que dices.

judg(e)ment ['dʒʌdʒmənt] n 1 Jur sentencia f, fallo m; **to pass j.,** dictar sentencia. 2 (opinion) juicio m; **to pass j.,** opinar (on, sobre); **to reserve j.,** no opinar (on, sobre). 3 (ability) buen juicio m. 4 (trial) juicio m.

judicial [dʒuː'dɪʃəl] adj judicial.

judiciary [dʒuː'dɪʃɪərɪ] n magistratura f.

judicious [dʒuː'dɪʃəs] adj fml juicioso,-a.

judo ['dʒuːdəʊ] n judo m.

jug [dʒʌg] n GB jarra f; **milk j.,** jarra de leche.

juggernaut ['dʒʌgənɔːt] n GB camión pesado.

juggle ['dʒʌgəl] vi (perform) hacer juegos malabares (with, con); fig (responsibilities) ajustar.

juggler ['dʒʌglər] n malabarista mf.

juice [dʒuːs] n jugo m; (of citrus fruits) zumo m.

juicy ['dʒuːsɪ] adj (juicier, juiciest) 1 jugoso,-a. 2 fam fig picante.

jukebox ['dʒuːkbɒks] n rocola f.

July [dʒuː'laɪ, dʒə'laɪ] n julio m.

jumble ['dʒʌmbəl] I n revoltijo m; **j. sale,** mercadillo m de caridad. II vtr revolver.

jumbo ['dʒʌmbəʊ] n j. (jet), jumbo m.

jump [dʒʌmp] I n 1 salto m; (sudden increase) subida repentina; **j. leads,** cables mpl de arranque; **j. suit,** mono m. II vi 1 saltar, dar un salto; fig **to j. to conclusions,** sacar conclusiones precipitadas. 2 fig (start) sobresaltarse. 3 (increase) aumentar de golpe. III vtr saltar; fam fig **to j. the gun,** precipitarse; GB **to j. the queue,** colarse; **to j. the lights,** saltarse el semáforo. ◆**jump at** vtr aceptar sin pensarlo.

jumper ['dʒʌmpər] n 1 GB (sweater) jersey m. 2 US (dress) pichi m, falda f con peto. 3 US Aut **j. cables,** cables mpl de emergencia.

jumpy ['dʒʌmpɪ] adj (jumpier, jumpiest) fam nervioso,-a.

junction ['dʒʌŋkʃən] n (of roads) cruce m; Rail Elec empalme m.

juncture ['dʒʌŋktʃər] n fml **at this j.,** en esta coyuntura.

June [dʒuːn] n junio m.

jungle ['dʒʌŋgəl] n jungla f, selva f; fig laberinto m; **the concrete j.,** la jungla de asfalto.

junior ['dʒuːnjər] I adj 1 (son of) hijo; **David Hughes j.,** David Hughes hijo. 2 **j. school,** escuela f de EGB (Enseñanza General Básica); **j. team,** equipo m juvenil. 3 (lower in rank) subalterno,-a. II n 1 (person of lower rank) subalterno,-a m,f. 2 (younger person) menor mf.

junk [dʒʌŋk] n 1 fam trastos mpl; **j. food,** comida basura; **j. mail,** propaganda f (por correo); **j. shop,** tienda f de segunda mano. 2 (boat) junco m.

junkie ['dʒʌŋkɪ] n sl yonqui mf.

junta ['dʒʌntə, 'dʒʊntə, US 'hʊntə] n junta f militar.

jurisdiction [dʒʊərɪs'dɪkʃən] n fml jurisdicción f.

juror ['dʒʊərər] n jurado,-a m,f.

jury ['dʒʊərɪ] n jurado m.

just [dʒʌst] I adj 1 (fair) justo,-a; fml (well-founded) justificado,-a. II adv 1 **he had j. arrived,** acababa de llegar. 2 (at this very moment) ahora mismo, en este momento; **he was j. leaving when Rosa arrived,** estaba a punto de salir cuando llegó Rosa; **I'm j. coming!,** ¡ya voy!; **j. as ...,** cuando ..., justo al...; **j. as I thought,** me lo figuraba. 3 (only) solamente; **j. in case,** por si acaso; **j. a minute!,** ¡un minuto! 4 (barely) por poco; **I only j. caught the bus,** cogí el autobús por los pelos; **j. about,** casi; **j. enough,** justo lo suficiente. **5** (*emphatic*) **it's j. fantastic!**, ¡es sencillamente fantástico!; **you'll j. have to wait**, tendrás que esperar. **6** (*exactly*) exactamente, justo; **that's j. it!**, ¡precisamente! **7** (*equally*) **j. as fast as**, tan rápido como.

justice ['dʒʌstɪs] *n* **1** justicia *f*; **he was brought to j.**, lo llevaron ante los tribunales; **you didn't do yourself j.**, no diste lo mejor de ti. **2** *US* (*judge*) juez *mf*; *GB* **J. of the Peace**, juez de paz.

justifiable ['dʒʌstɪfaɪəbəl] *adj* justificable.

justification [dʒʌstɪfɪ'keɪʃən] *n* justifica-

ción *f*.

justified ['dʒʌstɪfaɪd] *adj* **to be j. in doing sth**, tener razón en hacer algo.

justify ['dʒʌstɪfaɪ] *vtr* justificar.

jut [dʒʌt] *vi* sobresalir; **to j. out over**, proyectarse sobre.

juvenile ['dʒuːvənaɪl] **I** *adj* **1** juvenil; **j. court**, tribunal *m* de menores; **j. delinquent**, delincuente *mf* juvenil. **2** (*immature*) infantil. **II** *n* menor *mf*, joven *mf*.

juxtapose [dʒʌkstə'pəʊz] *vtr* yuxtaponer.

K

K, k [keɪ] *n* (*the letter*) K, k *f*.

kaleidoscope [kə'laɪdəskəʊp] *n* caleidoscopio *m*.

Kampuchea [kæmpʊ'tʃɪə] *n* Kampuchea.

kangaroo [kæŋgə'ruː] *n* canguro *m*.

karat ['kærət] *n US* quilate *m*.

karate [kə'rɑːtɪ] *n* kárate *m*.

kebab [kə'bæb] *n Culin* pincho moruno, brocheta *f*.

keel [kiːl] *n* quilla *f*; *fig* **to be on an even k.**, estar en calma. ◆**keel over** *vi fam* desmayarse.

keen [kiːn] *adj* **1** (*eager*) entusiasta. **2** (*intense*) profundo,-a. **3** (*mind, senses*) agudo,-a; (*look*) penetrante; (*blade*) afilado,-a; (*competition*) fuerte.

keep [kiːp] **I** *n* **1 to earn one's k.**, ganarse el pan. **2** (*tower*) torreón *m*. **3** *fam* **for keeps**, para siempre.
II *vtr* (*pt & pp* **kept**) **1** guardar; **to k. one's room tidy**, mantener su cuarto limpio; **to k. sb informed**, tener a algn al corriente; **to k. sth in mind**, tener algo en cuenta. **2** (*not give back*) quedarse con. **3** (*detain*) detener; **to k. sb waiting**, hacer esperar a algn. **4** (*maintain*) mantener; (*animals*) criar. **5** (*the law*) observar; (*a promise*) cumplir. **6** (*a secret*) guardar. **7** (*diary, accounts*) llevar. **8** (*prevent*) **to k. sb from doing sth**, impedir a algn hacer algo. **9** (*own, manage*) tener; (*shop, hotel*) llevar. **10** (*stock*) tener.
III *vi* **1** (*remain*) seguir; **k. still!**, ¡estáte quieto,-a!; **to k. fit**, mantenerse en forma; **to k. going**, seguir adelante; **to k. in touch**, no perder el contacto. **2** (*do frequently*) no dejar de; **she keeps forgetting her keys**, siempre se olvida las llaves. **3** (*food*) conservarse.
◆**keep at** *vi* perseverar en. ◆**keep away I** *vtr* mantener a distancia. **II** *vi* mantenerse a distancia. ◆**keep back** *vtr* (*information*) ocultar, callar; (*money etc*) retener. ◆**keep down** *vtr* **to k. prices down**, mantener los precios bajos. ◆**keep off** *vtr* **k. off the grass**, prohibi-

do pisar la hierba. ◆**keep on I** *vtr* **1** (*clothes etc*) no quitarse; **to k. an eye on sth/sb**, vigilar algo/a algn. **2** (*continue to employ*) no despedir a. **II** *vi* (*continue to do*) seguir. ◆**keep out I** *vtr* no dejar pasar. **II** *vi* no entrar; **k. out!**, ¡prohibida la entrada! ◆**keep to** *vtr* (*subject*) limitarse a; **to k. to one's room**, quedarse en el cuarto; **k. to the point!**, ¡ciñete a la cuestión!; **to k. to the left**, circular por la izquierda. ◆**keep up** *vtr* **1** mantener; **to k. up appearances**, guardar las apariencias. **2 k. it up!**, ¡sigue así! **3** (*prevent from sleeping*) mantener despierto,-a. ◆**keep up with** *vtr* **to k. up with the times**, estar al día.

keeper ['kiːpər] *n* (*in zoo*) guarda *mf*; (*in record office*) archivero,-a *m,f*; (*in museum*) conservador,-a *m,f*.

keeping ['kiːpɪŋ] *n* **1** (*care*) cuidado *m*. **2 in k. with**, en armonía con; **out of k. with**, en desacuerdo con.

keepsake ['kiːpseɪk] *n* recuerdo *m*.

keg [keg] *n* barril *m*.

kennel ['kenəl] *n* caseta *f* para perros; **kennels**, hotel *m* sing de perros.

Kenya ['kenjə, 'kiːnjə] *n* Kenia.

Kenyan ['kenjən, 'kiːnjən] *adj & n* keniano,-a (*m,f*).

kept [kept] *pt & pp* → **keep**.

kerb [kɜːb] *n* bordillo *m*.

kernel ['kɜːnəl] *n* (*of fruit, nut*) pepita *f*; (*of wheat*) grano *m*; *fig* meollo *m*.

kerosene, kerosine ['kerəsiːn] *n US* queroseno *m*.

ketchup ['ketʃəp] *n* ketchup *m*, salsa *f* de tomate.

kettle ['ketəl] *n* hervidor *m*; **that's a different k. of fish**, eso es harina de otro costal.

key [kiː] **I** *n* **1** (*for lock*) llave *f*; **k. ring**, llavero *m*. **2** (*to code*) clave *f*. **3** (*of piano, typewriter*) tecla *f*. **4** *Mus* tono *m*. **II** *adj* clave. **III** *n Comput* teclear. ◆**key in** *vtr Comput* introducir.

keyboard ['kiːbɔːd] *n* teclado *m*.

keyed up [ki:d'ʌp] adj nervioso,-a.

keyhole ['ki:həʊl] n ojo m de la cerradura.

keynote ['ki:nəʊt] n Mus tónica f; fig nota f dominante.

kg abbr of **kilogram(s)**, kilogramo(s) m (pl), kg.

khaki ['ka:kɪ] adj & n caqui (m).

kick [kɪk] I n 1 (from person) patada f, puntapié m; (from horse etc) coz f; (from gun) culatazo m. 2 fam I get a k. out of it, eso me encanta; to do sth for kicks, hacer algo por gusto. II vi (animal) cocear; (person) dar patadas; (gun) dar un culatazo. III vtr dar un puntapié a. ◆**kick off** vi fam empezar; Ftb sacar. ◆**kick out** vtr echar a patadas. ◆**kick up** vtr fam (fuss) armar.

kick-off ['kɪkɒf] n Ftb saque m inicial.

kid¹ [kɪd] n 1 Zool cabrito m; fig to handle sb with k. gloves, tratar a algn con guante blanco. 2 fam niño,-a m,f, chiquillo,-a m,f; the kids, los críos.

kid² [kɪd] I vi fam tomar el pelo; **no kidding!**, ¡va en serio!. II vtr tomar el pelo a; **to k. oneself**, (fool) hacerse ilusiones.

kidnap ['kɪdnæp] vtr secuestrar.

kidnapper ['kɪdnæpər] n secuestrador,-a m,f.

kidnapping ['kɪdnæpɪŋ] n secuestro m.

kidney ['kɪdnɪ] n riñón m.

kill [kɪl] vtr matar; fig **to k. time**, pasar el rato; fam **my feet are killing me**, ¡cómo me duelen los pies!. ◆**kill off** vtr exterminar.

killer ['kɪlər] n asesino,-a m,f; **k. whale**, orca f.

killing ['kɪlɪŋ] n asesinato m; fig **to make a k.**, forrarse de dinero.

killjoy ['kɪldʒɔɪ] n aguafiestas mf inv.

kiln [kɪln] n horno m.

kilo ['ki:ləʊ] n kilo m.

kilogram(me) ['kɪləʊgræm] n kilogramo m.

kilometre, US **kilometer** [kɪ'lɒmɪtər] n kilómetro m.

kilowatt ['kɪləʊwɒt] n kilovatio m.

kilt [kɪlt] n falda escocesa, kilt m.

kin [kɪn] n familiares mpl, parientes mpl.

kind¹ [kaɪnd] I n tipo m, clase f; **they are two of a k.**, son tal para cual; **in k.**, (payment) en especie; (treatment) con la misma moneda. II adv fam **k. of**, en cierta manera.

kind² [kaɪnd] adj amable, simpático,-a; fml **would you be so k. as to ...?**, ¿me haría usted el favor de ...?

kindergarten ['kɪndəga:tən] n jardín m de infancia.

kind-hearted [kaɪnd'hɑ:tɪd] adj bondadoso,-a.

kindle ['kɪndəl] vtr encender.

kindly ['kaɪndlɪ] I adj (kindlier, kindliest)

amable, bondadoso,-a. II adv fml (please) por favor; **k. remit a cheque**, sírvase enviar cheque; **to look k. on**, aprobar.

kindness ['kaɪndnɪs] n bondad f, amabilidad f.

kindred ['kɪndrɪd] adj **k. spirits**, almas gemelas.

kinetic [kɪ'netɪk] adj cinético,-a.

king [kɪŋ] n rey m; (draughts) dama f.

kingdom ['kɪŋdəm] n reino m.

kingfisher ['kɪŋfɪʃər] n Orn martín m pescador.

king-size ['kɪŋsaɪz] adj extralargo,-a.

kink [kɪŋk] n (in rope) coca f; (in hair) rizo m.

kinky ['kɪŋkɪ] adj (kinkier, kinkiest) fam raro,-a; (sexually) pervertido,-a.

kiosk ['ki:ɒsk] n quiosco m.

kiss [kɪs] I n beso m. II vtr besar. III vi besarse.

kit [kɪt] n 1 (gear) equipo m; Mil avíos mpl. 2 (clothing) ropa f. 3 (toy model) maqueta f. ◆**kit out** vtr equipar.

kitchen ['kɪtʃɪn] n cocina f; **k. sink**, fregadero m.

kite [kaɪt] n 1 (toy) cometa f. 2 Orn milano m.

kitten ['kɪtən] n gatito,-a m,f.

kitty ['kɪtɪ] n (money) fondo m común; Cards bote m.

kiwi ['ki:wi:] n Bot Orn kiwi m.

km (pl **km** or **kms**) abbr of **kilometre(s)**, km.

knack [næk] n **to get the k. of doing sth**, cogerle el truquillo a algo.

knapsack ['næpsæk] n mochila f.

knead [ni:d] vtr dar masaje a; (bread etc) amasar.

knee [ni:] I n rodilla f. II vtr dar un rodillazo a.

kneecap ['ni:kæp] I n rótula f. II vtr romper la rótula a.

kneel [ni:l] vi (pt & pp **knelt**) **to k. (down)**, arrodillarse.

knell [nel] n lit toque m de difuntos.

knelt [nelt] pt & pp → **kneel**.

knew [nju:] pt → **know**.

knickers ['nɪkəz] npl bragas fpl.

knife [naɪf] I n (pl **knives** [naɪvz]) cuchillo m. II vtr apuñalar, dar una puñalada a.

knight [naɪt] I n Hist caballero m; Chess caballo m. II vtr armar caballero.

knighthood ['naɪthʊd] n (rank) título m de caballero.

knit [nɪt] I vtr (pt & pp **knit**) 1 tejer. 2 (join) juntar (together, -); fig **to k. one's brow**, fruncir el ceño. II vi 1 tejer, hacer punto. 2 (bone) soldarse.

knitting ['nɪtɪŋ] n punto m; **k. machine**, máquina f de tejer; **k. needle**, aguja f de tejer.

knit-wear ['nɪtweər] n géneros mpl de punto.

knob [nɒb] n 1 (of stick) puño m; (of

drawer) tirador m; (*button*) botón m. 2 (*small portion*) trozo m.

knock [nɒk] I n golpe m; fig revés m. II vtr 1 golpear. 2 fam (*criticize*) criticar. III vi chocar (**against, into,** contra); (*at door*) llamar (**at,** a). ◆**knock down** vtr 1 (*demolish*) derribar. 2 *Aut* atropellar. 3 (*price*) rebajar. ◆**knock off** I vtr 1 tirar. 2 fam (*steal*) birlar. 3 sl (*kill*) liquidar. II vi **they k. off at five,** se piran a las cinco. ◆**knock out** vtr 1 (*make unconscious*) dejar sin conocimiento; Box poner fuera de combate, derrotar por K.O. 2 (*surprise*) dejar pasmado,-a. ◆**knock over** vtr (*cup*) volcar; (*with car*) atropellar.

knocker ['nɒkər] n (*on door*) aldaba f.

knock-kneed [nɒk'ni:d] adj patizambo,-a.

knockout ['nɒkaut] n 1 Box K.O. m, knock-out m. 2 fam maravilla f.

knot [nɒt] I n nudo m; (*group*) grupo m. II vtr anudar.

knotty ['nɒtɪ] adj (**knottier, knottiest**) nudoso,-a; fig a **k. problem,** un problema espinoso.

know [nəu] vtr & vi (pt **knew;** pp **known**) I saber; **as far as I k.,** que yo sepa; **to get to k. sth,** enterarse de algo; **to let sb k.,**

avisar al algn. 2 (*be acquainted with*) conocer; **we got to k. each other at the party,** nos conocimos en la fiesta.

know-all ['nəuɔːl] n fam sabelotodo mf.

know-how ['nəuhau] n fam conocimiento práctico.

knowing ['nəuɪŋ] adj (*deliberate*) deliberado,-a; **a k. smile,** una sonrisa de complicidad. ◆**knowingly** adv (*shrewd*) a sabiendas; (*deliberately*) deliberadamente.

knowledge ['nɒlɪdʒ] n 1 conocimiento m; **without my k.,** sin saberlo yo. 2 (*learning*) conocimientos mpl.

knowledgeable ['nɒlɪdʒəbəl] adj erudito,-a; **k. about,** muy entendido,-a en.

known [nəun] adj conocido,-a.

knuckle ['nʌkəl] n Anat nudillo m; Culin hueso m. ◆**knuckle down** vi fam ponerse a trabajar en serio.

KO [keɪ'əu] fam abbr of **knockout,** K.O. m.

Koran [kɔː'rɑːn] n Corán m.

Korea [kə'rɪə] n Corea.

Korean [kə'rɪən] adj & n coreano,-a (m,f).

Kurd [kɜːd] n curdo,-a m,f.

Kuwait [ku'weɪt] n Kuwait.

L

L, l [el] n (*the letter*) L, l f.

lab [læb] n fam abbr of **laboratory.**

label ['leɪbəl] I n etiqueta f; **record l.,** ≈ casa discográfica. II vtr poner etiqueta a.

labor ['leɪbər] n & vi US → **labour.**

laboratory [lə'bɒrətərɪ, US 'læbrətɔːrɪ] n laboratorio m.

laborious [lə'bɔːrɪəs] adj penoso,-a.

labour ['leɪbər] I n 1 (*work*) trabajo m; (*task*) tarea f. 2 (*workforce*) mano f de obra. 3 labours, esfuerzos mpl. 4 L. (Party), el Partido Laborista. 5 (*childbirth*) parto m; **to be in l.,** estar de parto. II adj laboral. III vi 1 (*work*) trabajar (duro). 2 (*move with difficulty*) avanzar penosamente. IV vtr (*stress, linger on*) machacar; (*a point*) insistir en.

laboured ['leɪbəd] adj (*breathing*) fatigoso,-a; (*style*) forzado,-a.

labourer ['leɪbərər] n peón m; **farm l.,** peón m agrícola.

labour-saving ['leɪbəseɪvɪŋ] adj **l.-s. devices,** electrodomésticos mpl.

labyrinth ['læbərɪnθ] n laberinto m.

lace [leɪs] I n 1 (*fabric*) encaje m. 2 laces, cordones mpl. II vtr 1 (*shoes*) atarse los cordones. 2 (*add spirits to*) echar licor (**with,** a). ◆**lace up** vtr atar con cordones.

lacerate ['læsəreɪt] vtr lacerar.

lack [læk] I n falta f, escasez f; **for l. of,** por falta de. II vtr carecer de. III vi carecer (**in,** de).

lackadaisical [lækə'deɪzɪkəl] adj (*lazy*) perezoso,-a; (*indifferent*) indiferente.

lacklustre, US **lackluster** ['læklʌstər] adj (*eyes*) apagado,-a; (*performance*) anodino,-a.

laconic [lə'kɒnɪk] adj lacónico,-a.

lacquer ['lækər] I n laca f. II vtr (*hair*) poner laca en.

lad [læd] n fam chaval m, muchacho m; fam **the lads,** los amigotes; (*stable*) l., mozo m de cuadra.

ladder ['lædər] I n 1 escalera f (de mano); fig escala f. 2 (*in stocking*) carrera f. II vtr **I've laddered my stocking,** me he hecho una carrera en las medias.

laden ['leɪdən] adj cargado,-a (**with,** de).

ladle ['leɪdəl] n cucharón m.

lady ['leɪdɪ] n señora f; Pol **First L.,** primera dama; (WC) '**Ladies',** 'Señoras'; **ladies and gentlemen!,** ¡señoras y señores!; **L. Brown,** Lady Brown.

ladybird ['leɪdɪbɜːd], US Canada **ladybug** ['leɪdɪbʌg] n mariquita f.

lady-in-waiting [leɪdɪɪn'weɪtɪŋ] n dama f de honor.

ladylike ['leɪdɪlaɪk] adj elegante.

ladyship ['leɪdɪʃɪp] n **Her L., Your L.,**

su señoría.

lag [læg] I *n* time l., demora *f*. II *vi* to l. (behind), quedarse atrás, retrasarse. III *vtr Tech* revestir.

lager ['lɑːgər] *n* cerveza rubia.

lagoon [lə'guːn] *n* laguna *f*.

laid [leɪd] *pt & pp* **lay**.

laid-back [leɪd'bæk] *adj fam* tranquilo,-a.

lain [leɪn] *pp* of **lie**.

lair [leər] *n* guarida *f*.

lake [leɪk] *n* lago *m*.

lamb [læm] *n* cordero *m*; (*meat*) carne *f* de cordero; l. chop, chuleta *f* de cordero; **l.'s wool**, lana *f* de cordero.

lame [leɪm] *adj* 1 cojo,-a. 2 *fig* (*excuse*) poco convincente; (*argument*) flojo,-a.

lament [lə'ment] I *n Mus* elegía *f*. II *vtr* (*death*) llorar, lamentar. III *vi* llorar (**for**, a), lamentarse (**over**, de).

lamentable ['læməntəbəl] *adj* lamentable.

laminated ['læmɪneɪtɪd] *adj* (*metal*) laminado,-a; (*glass*) instalable; (*paper*) plastificado,-a.

lamp [læmp] *n* lámpara *f*; *Aut* faro *m*.

lampoon [læm'puːn] I *n* sátira *f*. II *vtr* satirizar.

lamp-post ['læmppəʊst] *n* farola *f*.

lampshade ['læmpʃeɪd] *n* pantalla *f*.

lance [lɑːns] I *n* lanza *f*; *GB Mil* l. corporal, cabo interino; *Med* lanceta *f*. II *vtr Med* abrir con lanceta.

land [lænd] I *n* 1 tierra *f*; (*soil*) suelo *m*; by l., por tierra; **farm** l., tierras *fpl* de cultivo. 2 (*country*) país *m*. 3 (*property*) tierras *fpl*; (*estate*) finca *f*; **piece** of l., terreno *m*. II *vtr* 1 (*plane*) hacer aterrizar. 2 (*disembark*) desembarcar. 3 *Fishing* pescar. 4 *fam* (*obtain*) conseguir; (*contract*) ganar. 5 *fam* **she got landed** (**with the responsibility**), tuvo que cargar con la responsabilidad. 6 (*blow*) asestar. III *vi* (*plane*) aterrizar. 2 (*disembark*) desembarcar. 3 (*after falling*) caer (**in**, sobre). ◆**land up** *vi fam* ir a parar.

landing ['lændɪŋ] *n* 1 (*of staircase*) rellano *m*. 2 (*of plane*) aterrizaje *m*; l. **strip**, pista *f* de aterrizaje. 3 (*of passengers*) desembarco *m*; l. **stage**, desembarcadero *m*.

landlady ['lændleɪdɪ] *n* (*of flat*) dueña *f*, propietaria *f*; (*of boarding house*) patrona *f*; (*of pub*) dueña.

landlord ['lændlɔːd] *n* (*of flat*) dueño *m*, propietario *m*; (*of pub*) patrón *m*, dueño.

landmark ['lændmɑːk] *n* 1 señal *f*, marca *f*; (*well-known place*) lugar muy conocido. 2 *fig* hito *m*.

landowner ['lændəʊnər] *n* terrateniente *mf*.

landscape ['lændskeɪp] I *n* paisaje *m*. II *vtr* ajardinar.

landslide ['lændslaɪd] *n* desprendimiento *m* de tierras; l. **victory**, victoria arrolladora.

lane [leɪn] *n* (*in country*) camino *m*; (*in town*) callejón *m*; (*of motorway*) carril *m*; *Sport* calle *f*; *Naut* ruta *f*.

language ['læŋgwɪdʒ] *n* 1 lenguaje *m*; **bad** l., palabrotas *fpl*. 2 (*of a country*) idioma *m*, lengua *f*; l. **laboratory**, laboratorio *m* de idiomas.

languid ['læŋgwɪd] *adj* lánguido,-a.

languish ['læŋgwɪʃ] *vi* languidecer; (*project, plan etc*) quedar abandonado,-a; (*in prison*) pudrirse.

lank [læŋk] *adj* (*hair*) lacio,-a.

lanky ['læŋkɪ] *adj* (**lankier, lankiest**) larguirucho,-a.

lantern ['læntən] *n* farol *m*.

lap¹ [læp] *n Anat* regazo *m*.

lap² [læp] *n* (*circuit*) vuelta *f*; *fig* etapa *f*. II *vtr* (*overtake*) doblar.

lap³ [læp] I *vtr* (*pt & pp* **lapped**) (*cat*) beber a lengüetadas. II *vi* (*waves*) lamer, besar. ◆**lap up** *vtr* 1 (*cat*) beber a lengüetadas. 2 *fig* (*wallow in*) disfrutar con; (*flattery*) recibir con estusiasmo. 3 *fig* (*believe*) tragar.

lapel [lə'pel] *n* solapa *f*.

Lapland ['læplænd] *n* Laponia.

lapse [læps] I *n* 1 (*of time*) lapso *m*. 2 (*error*) error *m*, desliz *m*; (*of memory*) fallo *m*. II *vi* 1 (*time*) pasar, transcurrir. 2 (*expire*) caducar. 3 (*err*) cometer un error; (*fall back*) caer (**into**, en). 4 *Rel* perder la fe.

larceny ['lɑːsənɪ] *n GB* latrocinio *m*; *US* hurto *m*.

larch [lɑːtʃ] *n* alerce *m*.

lard [lɑːd] *n* manteca *f* de cerdo.

larder ['lɑːdər] *n* despensa *f*.

large [lɑːdʒ] I *adj* grande; (*amount*) importante; (*extensive*) amplio,-a; **by and l.**, por lo general. II *n* to **be at l.**, andar suelto,-a; **the public at l.**, el público en general. ◆**largely** *adv* (*mainly*) en gran parte; (*chiefly*) principalmente.

large-scale ['lɑːdʒskeɪl] *adj* (*project, problem etc*) de gran envergadura; (*map*) a gran escala.

lark¹ [lɑːk] *n Orn* alondra *f*.

lark² [lɑːk] *n* (*joke*) broma *f*; **what a l.!**, qué risa! ◆**lark about, lark around** *vi fam* hacer el tonto.

larva ['lɑːvə] *n* larva *f*.

laryngitis [lærɪn'dʒaɪtɪs] *n* laringitis *f*.

larynx ['lærɪŋks] *n Anat* laringe *f*.

laser ['leɪzər] *n* láser *m*; l. **printer**, impresora *f* láser.

lash [læʃ] I *n* 1 (*eyelash*) pestaña *f*. 2 (*blow with whip*) latigazo *m*. II *vtr* 1 (*beat*) azotar. 2 (*rain*) caer con fuerza. 3 (*tie*) atar. ◆**lash out** *vi* 1 (*with fists*) repartir golpes a diestro y siniestro; (*verbally*) criticar (**at**, a). 2 *fam* (*spend money*) tirar la casa por la ventana.

lass [læs] *n fam* chavala *f*, muchacha *f*.

lasso [læ'suː] I *n* lazo *m*. II *vtr* coger con el lazo.

last [lɑːst] I adj 1 (final) último,-a, final; fam the l. straw, el colmo. 2 (most recent) último,-a. 3 (past) pasado,-a; (previous) anterior; l. but one, penúltimo,-a; l. month, el mes pasado; l. night, anoche; the night before l., anteanoche. II adv 1 when I l. saw her, la última vez que la vi. 2 (at the end) en último lugar; (in race etc) último; at (long) l., por fin; l. but not least, el último en orden pero no en importancia. III n el último, la última. IV vi 1 (time) durar; (hold out) aguantar. 2 (be enough for) llegar, alcanzar. ◆lastly adv por último, finalmente.

last-ditch [ˈlɑːstdɪtʃ] adj (effort, attempt) último,-a y desesperado,-a.

lasting [ˈlɑːstɪŋ] adj duradero,-a.

last-minute [ˈlɑːstmɪnɪt] adj de última hora.

latch [lætʃ] n picaporte m, pestillo m.

late [leɪt] I adj 1 (not on time) tardío,-a; (hour) avanzado,-a; to be five minutes l., llegar con cinco minutos de retraso. 2 (far on in time) tarde; in l. autumn, a finales del otoño; in the l. afternoon, a última hora de la tarde; she's in her twenties, ronda los treinta. 3 (dead) difunto,-a. II adv 1 (not on time) tarde; to arrive l., llegar tarde. 2 (far on in time) tarde; l. at night, a altas horas de la noche; l. in life, a una edad avanzada. 3 as l. as 1950, todavía en 1950; of l., últimamente. ◆lately adv últimamente, recientemente.

latecomer [ˈleɪtkʌmər] n tardón,-ona m,f.

latent [ˈleɪtənt] adj 1 latente. 2 (desire) oculto,-a.

later [ˈleɪtər] I adj (comp of late) 1 (subsequent) más tarde; in her l. novels, en sus novelas posteriores. 2 (more recent) más reciente. II adv (comp of late) más tarde, después; l. on, más adelante, más tarde.

lateral [ˈlætərəl] adj lateral.

latest [ˈleɪtɪst] I adj (superl of late) (most recent) último,-a, más reciente. II n lo último; have you heard the l.?, ¿te enteraste de lo último?; Friday at the l., el viernes a más tardar.

lathe [leɪð] n Tech torno m.

lather [ˈlɑːðər] I n (of soap) espuma f; (horse's sweat) sudor m. II vtr (with soap) enjabonar.

Latin [ˈlætɪn] I adj & n latino,-a (m,f); L. America, América Latina, Latinoamérica f; L. American, latinoamericano,-a (m,f). II n (language) latín m.

latitude [ˈlætɪtjuːd] n latitud f.

latrine [ləˈtriːn] n letrina f.

latter [ˈlætər] I adj 1 (last) último,-a. 2 (second of two) segundo,-a. II pron éste,-a; the former ... the l., aquél ... éste, aquél ... ésta.

lattice [ˈlætɪs] n enrejado m, rejilla f.

laudable [ˈlɔːdəbəl] adj loable.

laugh [lɑːf] I n risa f; (guffaw) carcajada f; for a l., para divertirse. II vi reír, reírse. ◆laugh at vi to at sb/sth, reírse de algn/algo. ◆laugh about vi to l. about sb/sth, reírse de algn/algo. ◆laugh off vtr tomar a risa.

laughable [ˈlɑːfəbəl] adj (situation, suggestion) ridículo,-a; (amount, offer) irrisorio,-a.

laughing-stock [ˈlɑːfɪŋstɒk] n hazmerreír m inv.

laughter [ˈlɑːftər] n risa f.

launch [lɔːntʃ] I n 1 (vessel) lancha f. 2 → launching. II vtr (attack, rocket, new product) lanzar. 2 (ship) botar. 3 (film, play) estrenar. 4 (company) fundar. 5 fig (scheme) iniciar.

launching [ˈlɔːntʃɪŋ] n 1 (of rocket, new product) lanzamiento m. 2 (of ship) botadura f. 3 (of film, play) estreno m. 4 (of new company) fundación f.

launchpad [ˈlɔːntʃpæd] n plataforma f de lanzamiento.

launder [ˈlɔːndər] vtr lavar y planchar; fig (money) blanquear.

launderette [lɔːndəˈret], US **Laundromat®** [ˈlɔːndrəmæt] n lavandería automática.

laundry [ˈlɔːndrɪ] n 1 (place) lavandería f. 2 (dirty clothes) ropa sucia; to do the l., lavar la ropa.

laurel [ˈlɒrəl] n laurel m; fam fig to rest on one's laurels, dormirse en los laureles.

lava [ˈlɑːvə] n lava f.

lavatory [ˈlævətərɪ] n 1 excusado m, retrete m. 2 (room) baño m; public l., servicios mpl, aseos mpl.

lavender [ˈlævəndər] n lavanda f.

lavish [ˈlævɪʃ] I adj 1 (generous) pródigo,-a. 2 (abundant) abundante. 3 (luxurious) lujoso,-a. II vtr (money) colmar de (on, a); (care, attention) prodigarse en (on, con).

law [lɔː] n 1 ley f; by l., según la ley; l. and order, el orden público; to lay down the l., dictar la ley. 2 (as subject) derecho m; l. court, tribunal m de justicia. 3 fam the l., los maderos.

law-abiding [ˈlɔːəbaɪdɪŋ] adj respetuoso,-a de la ley.

lawful [ˈlɔːfʊl] adj legal; (permitted by law) lícito,-a; (legitimate) legítimo,-a.

lawn [lɔːn] n césped m; l. tennis, tenis m sobre hierba.

lawnmower [ˈlɔːnməʊər] n cortacésped m.

lawsuit [ˈlɔːsjuːt] n pleito m.

lawyer [ˈlɔːjər] n abogado,-a m,f; l.'s office, bufete m de abogados.

lax [læks] adj (not strict) relajado,-a; (not demanding) poco exigente; (careless) descuidado,-a.

laxative [ˈlæksətɪv] adj & n laxante (m).

laxity [ˈlæksɪtɪ] n relajamiento m; (careless-

ness) descuido *m; (negligence)* negligencia *f.*

lay¹ [leɪ] *adj* **1** *Rel* laico,-a. **2** *(nonspecialist)* lego,-a.

lay² [leɪ] *vtr (pt & pp* **laid)** **1** *(place)* poner, colocar; *(cable, trap)* tender; *(foundations)* echar. **2** *(fire)* preparar; *(table)* poner. **3** *(leave)* dejar. **4** *(eggs)* poner. **5** *vulg* follar. **6** *(set down)* asentar; *(blame)* echar. ◆**lay aside** *vtr* dejar a un lado. ◆**lay by** *vtr (save)* guardar; *(money)* ahorrar. ◆**lay down** *vtr (put down)* poner; *(let go)* dejar; **to l. down one's arms,** rendir las armas. **2** *(plan)* formular. **3** *(establish)* fijar, imponer; *(principles)* sentar. ◆**lay into** *vtr fam (physically)* dar una paliza a; *(verbally)* arremeter contra. ◆**lay off** *vtr* **1** *(dismiss)* despedir. **2** *fam* dejar en paz. **II** *vi* **l. off!,** ¡para ya! ◆**lay on** *vtr* **1** *(provide)* proveer de; *(food)* preparar. **2** *(spread)* aplicar; *fam* **to l. it on thick,** cargar las tintas. ◆**lay out** *vtr* **1** *(open out)* extender. **2** *(arrange)* disponer. **3** *(ideas)* exponer. **4** *(plan)* trazar. **5** *fam (spend)* gastar. **6** *fam (knock out)* derribar. ◆**lay up** *vtr* **1** *(store)* guardar. **2** *(accumulate)* almacenar. **3** *fam* **to be laid up,** tener que guardar cama.

lay³ [leɪ] *pt of* **lie².**

layabout ['leɪəbaʊt] *n fam* vago,-a *m,f.*

lay-by ['leɪbaɪ] *n* área *f* de descanso.

layer ['leɪər] *n* capa *f.*

layman ['leɪmən] *n* lego,-a *m,f.*

layout ['leɪaʊt] *n (arrangement)* disposición *f; (presentation)* presentación *f; Typ* composición *f; (plan)* diseño *m,* trazado *m.*

laze [leɪz] *vi* holgazanear, gandulear.

laziness ['leɪzɪnɪs] *n* pereza *f,* holgazanería *f.*

lazy ['leɪzɪ] *adj (lazier, laziest)* perezoso, -a, holgazán,-ana; **at a l. pace,** a paso lento.

lb *abbr of* **pound,** libra *f.*

lead¹ [led] *n* **1** *(metal)* plomo *m.* **2** *(in pencil)* mina *f.*

lead² [liːd] **I** *n* **1** *(front position)* delantera *f; (advantage)* ventaja *f;* **to take the l.,** *(in race)* tomar la delantera; *(score)* adelantarse. **2** *(clue)* pista *f.* **3** *Theat* primer papel *m;* **l. singer,** cantante *mf* principal. **4** *(leash)* correa *f.* **5** *Elec* cable *m.* **II** *vtr (pt & pp* **led)** **1** *(conduct)* llevar, conducir. **2** *(be the leader of)* dirigir, encabezar. **3** *(influence)* llevar a; **this leads me to believe that,** esto me lleva a creer que; **she's easily led,** se deja llevar fácilmente. **4** *(life)* llevar. **III** *vi* **1** *(road)* llevar, conducir (to, a). **2** *(go first)* ir delante; *(in race)* llevar la delantera. **3** **to l. to,** llevar a. ◆**lead away** *vtr* llevar. ◆**lead on** *vtr* **1** *vi (go ahead)* ir adelante. **II** *vtr (deceive)* engañar, timar. ◆**lead up to** *vtr* llevar a.

leaden ['ledən] *adj (sky)* plomizo,-a; *(food)* pesado,-a.

leader ['liːdər] *n* **1** jefe,-a *m,f,* líder *mf; (in race)* líder. **2** *Press* editorial *m,* artículo *m* de fondo.

leadership ['liːdəʃɪp] *n* **1** *(command)* dirección *f,* mando *m; Pol* liderazgo *m.* **2** *(leaders)* dirigentes *mpl,* cúpula *f.*

lead-free ['ledfriː] *adj* sin plomo.

leading ['liːdɪŋ] *adj* **1** *(main)* principal. **2** *(outstanding)* destacado,-a.

leaf [liːf] *n (pl* **leaves** [liːvz]) hoja *f;* **to turn over a new l.,** hacer borrón y cuenta nueva. ◆**leaf through** *vtr* hojear.

leaflet ['liːflɪt] *n* folleto *m.*

league [liːg] *n* **1** *(alliance)* alianza *f; (association)* sociedad *f; fam* **to be in l. with sb,** estar conchabado,-a con algn. **2** *Sport* liga *f.*

leak [liːk] **I** *n* **1** *(hole)* agujero *m; (in roof)* gotera *f; (of gas, liquid)* fuga *f,* escape *m; (of information)* filtración *f.* **II** *vi* **1** *(container)* tener un agujero; *(pipe)* tener un escape; *(roof)* gotear; *(boat)* hacer agua. **2** *(gas, liquid)* salirse. **3** *(information)* filtrarse; *(news)* trascender. **III** *vtr (information)* filtrar (to, a).

leaky ['liːkɪ] *adj (leakier, leakiest) (container)* agujereado,-a; *(roof)* que tiene goteras; *(ship)* que hace agua.

lean¹ [liːn] *adj (meat)* magro,-a; *(person)* flaco,-a; *(harvest)* escaso,-a.

lean² [liːn] *vi (pt & pp* **leaned** or **leant) 1** inclinarse. **2** **to l. on/against,** apoyarse en/contra; *fig* **to l. on sb,** *(pressurize)* presionar a algn; *(depend)* depender de algn. **II** *vtr* apoyar (on, en). ◆**lean back** *vi* reclinarse. ◆**lean forward** *vi* inclinarse hacia delante. ◆**lean out** *vi* asomarse. ◆**lean over** *vi* inclinarse.

leaning ['liːnɪŋ] **I** *adj* inclinado,-a. **II** *n fig (tendency)* inclinación *f,* tendencia *f.*

leant [lent] *pt & pp →* **lean².**

lean-to ['liːntuː] *n (hut)* cobertizo *m.*

leap [liːp] **I** *n (jump)* salto *m;* **l. year,** año bisiesto. **II** *vi (pt & pp* **leaped** or **leapt)** saltar; *fig* **her heart leapt,** su corazón dio un vuelco. ◆**leap at** *vtr fig (chance)* no dejar escapar.

leapfrog ['liːpfrɒg] *n* pídola *f.*

leapt [lept] *pt & pp →* **leap.**

learn [lɜːn] **I** *vtr (pt & pp* **learned** or **learnt) 1** aprender; **to l. (how) to ski,** aprender a esquiar. **2** **to l. that,** enterarse de que. **II** *vi* **1** aprender. **2** **to l. about** o **of,** *(find out)* enterarse de.

learned ['lɜːnɪd] *adj* erudito,-a.

learner ['lɜːnər] *n (beginner)* principiante *mf;* **l. driver,** aprendiz,-a *m,f* de conductor.

learning ['lɜːnɪŋ] *n (knowledge)* conocimientos *mpl; (erudition)* saber *m.*

learnt [lɜːnt] *pt & pp →* **learn.**

lease [li:s] **I** *n* contrato *m* de arrendamiento; *fig* **to give sb a new l. of life,** dar nueva vida a algn. **II** *vtr* arrendar.

leasehold ['li:shəʊld] **I** *n* derechos *mpl* de arrendamiento. **II** *adj* (*property*) arrendado,-a.

leash [li:ʃ] *n* correa *f*.

least [li:st] (*superl of* **little**) **I** *adj* menor, mínimo,-a; **he has the l. time,** él es quien menos tiempo tiene. **II** *adv* menos; **l. of all him,** él menos que nadie. **III** *n* lo menos; **at l.,** por lo menos, al menos; **not in the l.!,** ¡en absoluto!; **to say the l.,** por no decir más.

leather ['leðər] **I** *n* piel *f*, cuero *m*. **II** *adj* de piel.

leave¹ [li:v] **I** *vtr* (*pt & pp* **left**) **1** dejar; (*go away from*) abandonar; (*go out of*) salir de. **2 l. him alone!,** ¡déjale en paz!; *fam* **l. it to me,** yo me encargo. **3** (*bequeath*) legar. **4** (*forget*) dejarse, olvidarse. **5 I have two biscuits left,** me quedan dos galletas. **6 to be left over,** sobrar. **II** *vi* (*go away*) irse, marcharse; (*go out*) salir; **the train leaves in five minutes,** el tren sale dentro de cinco minutos. ◆**leave behind** *vtr* **1** dejar atrás. **2** (*forget*) olvidarse. ◆**leave on** *vtr* **1** (*clothes*) dejar puesto,-a. **2** (*lights, radio*) dejar encendido,-a. ◆**leave out** *vtr* (*omit*) omitir; *fig* **to feel left out,** sentirse excluido,-a.

leave² [li:v] *n* **1** (*permission*) permiso *m*. **2** (*time off*) vacaciones *fpl*; **Mil on l.,** de permiso; **l. of absence,** excedencia *f*. **3 to take one's l. of sb,** despedirse de algn.

leaves [li:vz] *npl* → **leaf**.

Lebanon ['lebənən] *n* (**the**) **L.,** (el) Líbano.

lecherous ['letʃərəs] *adj* lascivo,-a.

lecture ['lektʃər] **I** *n* **1** conferencia *f*; *Univ* clase *f*; **to give a l.,** dar una conferencia (**on,** sobre); **l. hall, l. room, l. theatre,** sala *f* de conferencias; *Univ* aula *f*. **2** (*rebuke*) sermón *m*. **II** *vi* dar una conferencia; *Univ* dar clases. **III** *vtr* (*reproach*) sermonear.

lecturer ['lektʃərər] *n* conferenciante *mf*; *Univ* profesor,-a *m,f*.

led [led] *pt & pp* → **lead²**.

ledge [ledʒ] *n* **1** (*shelf*) repisa *f*; (*of window*) alféizar *m*. **2** (*on mountain*) saliente *m*.

ledger ['ledʒər] *n* libro *m* mayor.

lee [li:] *n* **1** *Naut* sotavento *m*. **2** *fig* abrigo *m*.

leech [li:tʃ] *n* sanguijuela *f*.

leek [li:k] *n* puerro *m*.

leer [liər] *vi* mirar con lascivia.

leeway ['li:wei] *n* libertad *f*; **this gives me a certain amount of l.,** esto me da cierto margen de libertad.

left¹ [left] **I** *adj* izquierdo,-a; *Pol* **l. wing,**

izquierda *f*. **II** *adv* a la izquierda. **III** *n* **1** izquierda *f*; **on the l.,** a mano izquierda. **2** *Pol* **to be on the L.,** ser de izquierdas.

left² [left] *pt & pp* → **leave¹**.

left-hand ['lefthænd] *adj* **l.-h. drive,** con el volante a la izquierda; **on the l.-h. side,** a mano izquierda.

left-handed [left'hændɪd] *adj* zurdo,-a.

left-luggage [left'lʌgɪdʒ] *n* GB **l.-l. office,** consigna *f*.

leftovers ['leftəʊvəz] *npl* sobras *fpl*.

left-wing [left'wɪŋ] *adj* de izquierdas, izquierdista.

leg [leg] *n* **1** (*of person*) pierna *f*; (*of animal, table*) pata *f*; *Culin* (*of lamb*) pierna; (*of trousers*) pernera *f*. **2** (*stage*) etapa *f*.

legacy ['legəsi] *n* herencia *f*, legado *m*.

legal ['li:gəl] *adj* **1** legal; (*permitted by law*) lícito,-a; **l. tender,** moneda *f* de curso legal. **2** (*relating to the law*) jurídico,-a; **l. aid,** asesoramiento jurídico gratuito; **l. dispute,** contencioso *m*; *US* **l. holiday,** fiesta *f* nacional. ◆**legally** *adv* legalmente.

legalize ['li:gəlaɪz] *vtr* legalizar.

legend ['ledʒənd] *n* leyenda *f*.

legendary ['ledʒəndərɪ] *adj* legendario,-a.

leggings ['legɪŋz] *npl* polainas *fpl*.

legible ['ledʒəbəl] *adj* legible.

legion ['li:dʒən] *n* legión *f*.

legislation [ledʒɪs'leɪʃən] *n* legislación *f*.

legislative ['ledʒɪslətɪv] *adj* legislativo,-a.

legislator ['ledʒɪsleɪtər] *n* legislador,-a *m,f*.

legislature ['ledʒɪsleɪtʃər] *n* asamblea legislativa.

legitimate [lɪ'dʒɪtɪmɪt] *adj* legítimo,-a.

legroom ['legrʊm] *n* espacio *m* para las piernas.

leisure ['leʒər, *US* 'li:ʒər] *n* ocio *m*, tiempo *m* libre; **at l.,** con calma; **do it at your l.,** hazlo cuando tengas tiempo; **l. activities,** pasatiempos *mpl*; **l. centre,** centro recreativo.

leisurely ['leʒəlɪ, *US* 'li:ʒəlɪ] *adj* (*unhurried*) tranquilo,-a; (*slow*) lento,-a.

lemon ['lemən] *n* limón *m*; **l. curd,** crema *f* de limón; **l. juice,** zumo *m* de limón; **l. tea,** té *m* con limón.

lemonade [lemə'neɪd] *n* limonada *f*.

lend [lend] *vtr* (*pt & pp* **lent**) prestar; **to l. oneself** *or* **itself to sth,** prestarse a *or* para algo.

lending ['lendɪŋ] *n* **l. library,** biblioteca *f* pública.

length [leŋθ] *n* **1** longitud *f*, largo *m*; **it is five metres in l.,** tiene cinco metros de largo. **2** (*duration*) duración *f*. **3** (*of string*) trozo *m*; (*of cloth*) retal *m*. **4** (*of swimming pool*) largo *m*; *fig* **to go to any lengths to achieve sth,** hacer lo que sea para conseguir algo. **5 at l.,** (*finally*) finalmente; (*in depth*) a fondo.

lengthen ['leŋkθən, 'leŋθən] *vtr* alargar;

(lifetime) prolongar. **II** *vi* alargarse; *(lifetime)* prolongarse.

lengthways ['leŋθweiz] *adv* a lo largo.

lengthy ['leŋθɪ, 'leŋθi] *adj* (**lengthier, lengthiest**) largo,-a; *(film, illness)* de larga duración; *(meeting, discussion)* prolongado,-a.

lenient ['li:nɪənt] *adj* indulgente.

lens [lenz] *n (of eye)* cristalino *m*; *(of spectacles)* lente *f*; *Phot* objetivo *m*.

Lent [lent] *n* Cuaresma *f*.

lent [lent] *pt & pp* → **lend**.

lentil ['lentɪl] *n* lenteja *f*.

Leo ['li:əʊ] *n* Leo *m*.

leopard ['lepəd] *n* leopardo *m*.

leotard ['li:ətɑ:d] *n* leotardo *m*.

leper ['lepər] *n* leproso,-a *m,f*.

leprosy ['leprəsɪ] *n* lepra *f*.

lesbian ['lezbɪən] *adj & n* lesbiana *(f)*.

less [les] **I** *adj (comp of* **little**) menos. **II** *pron* menos; **the l. said about it, the better,** cuanto menos se hable de eso mejor. **III** *adv* menos; **l. and l.,** cada vez menos; **still l.,** menos aún. **IV** *prep* menos; **a year l. two days,** un año menos dos días.

lessen ['lesən] *vtr & vi* disminuir.

lesser ['lesər] *adj* menor; **to a l. extent,** en menor grado.

lesson ['lesən] *n* 1 clase *f*; *(in book)* lección *f*; **Spanish lessons,** clases de español. 2 *Rel* lectura *f*.

lest [lest] *conj fml* 1 para (que) no; **l. we forget,** para que no lo olvidemos. 2 *(for fear that)* por miedo a que.

let [let] **I** *vtr (pt & pp* **let**) 1 dejar, permitir; **to l. go of sth,** soltar algo; **to l. sb know,** avisar a algn; *fig* **to l. oneself go,** dejarse ir. 2 *(rent out)* alquilar; **'to l.',** se alquila'. 3 **l. alone,** ni mucho menos. **II** *v aux* **l. him wait,** que espere; **l. me go!,** ¡suéltame!; **l.'s go!,** ¡vamos!; ¡vámonos!; **l.'s see,** a ver. ◆**let down** *vtr* 1 *(lower)* bajar; *(lengthen)* alargar; *fam fig* **to l. one's hair down,** desmelenarse. 2 *(deflate)* desinflar. 3 *(fail)* fallar, defraudar. ◆**let in** *vtr* 1 *(admit)* dejar entrar; **to l. oneself in for,** meterse en. ◆**let off** *vtr* 1 *(bomb)* hacer explotar; *(fireworks)* hacer estallar. 2 *(liquid, air)* soltar. 3 *fam* **to l. sb off,** *(pardon)* perdonar. ◆**let on** *vi fam* **don't l. on,** *(reveal information)* no se lo digas. ◆**let out** *vtr* 1 *(release)* soltar; *(news)* divulgar; *(secret)* revelar. 2 *(air, water)* dejar salir. 3 *(cry)* soltar. 4 *Sew* ensanchar. ◆**let up** *vi* cesar, parar.

letdown ['letdaʊn] *n* decepción *f*.

lethal ['li:θəl] *adj* letal.

lethargic [lɪ'θɑ:dʒɪk] *adj* aletargado,-a.

letter ['letər] *n* 1 *(of alphabet)* letra *f*; **to the l.,** al pie de la letra. 2 *(written message)* carta *f*; **l. box,** buzón *m*; *Com* **l. of credit,** carta de crédito.

letterhead ['letəhed] *n* membrete *m*.

lettering ['letərɪŋ] *n* rótulo *m*.

lettuce ['letɪs] *n* lechuga *f*.

let-up ['letʌp] *n fam* descanso *m*, respiro *m*.

leukaemia, *US* **leukemia** [lu:'ki:mɪə] *n* leucemia *f*.

level ['levəl] **I** *adj* 1 *(flat)* llano,-a; *(even)* nivelado,-a; *(equal)* igual, parejo,-a; **a l. spoonful of,** una cucharada rasa de; **to be l. with,** estar a nivel de; *GB* **l. crossing,** paso *m* a nivel. 2 *(steady)* estable; *(tone)* uniforme. **II** *vtr* 1 nivelar, allanar. 2 *(building)* arrasar. 3 *(stare, criticism)* dirigir. **III** *n* nivel *m*; **to be on a l. with,** estar al mismo nivel que; *fam* **to be on the l.,** *(be honest)* ser de fiar; *(be truthful)* decir la verdad. ◆**level off, level out** *vi* estabilizarse. ◆**level with** *vtr fam* ser franco,-a con.

level-headed [levəl'hedɪd] *adj* sensato,-a.

lever ['li:vər] **I** *n* palanca *f*. **II** *vtr* apalancar; **to l. sth out,** sacar algo con palanca.

leverage ['li:vərɪdʒ] *n fig* influencia *f*.

levy ['levɪ] **I** *vtr (tax)* recaudar; *(fine)* imponer. **II** *n (of tax)* recaudación *f*; *(of fine)* imposición *f*.

lewd [lu:d] *adj (person)* lascivo,-a; *(story)* obsceno,-a.

liability [laɪə'bɪlɪtɪ] *n* 1 *Jur* responsabilidad *f*. 2 *(handicap)* estorbo *m*. 3 *Fin* **liabilities,** pasivo *m sing*.

liable ['laɪəbəl] *adj* 1 *Jur* responsable; *(susceptible)* sujeto,-a; **to be l. for,** ser responsable de. 2 **to be l. to do sth,** ser propenso,-a a hacer algo; **it's l. to happen,** es muy probable que (así) suceda.

liaise [lɪ'eɪz] *vi* comunicarse (**with,** con).

liaison [lɪ'eɪzɒn] *n* 1 enlace *m*; **l. officer,** oficial *mf* de enlace. 2 *(love affair)* amorío *m*.

liar ['laɪər] *n* mentiroso,-a *m,f*, embustero,-a *m,f*.

libel ['laɪbəl] **I** *n* libelo *m*. **II** *vtr* difamar, calumniar.

liberal ['lɪbərəl] **I** *adj* 1 liberal; **L. Party,** Partido *m* Liberal. 2 *(abundant)* abundante. **II** *n Pol* **L.,** liberal *mf*.

liberate ['lɪbəreɪt] *vtr* liberar; *(prisoner etc)* poner en libertad; **liberated woman,** mujer liberada.

liberation [lɪbə'reɪʃən] *n* liberación *f*.

liberty ['lɪbətɪ] *n* libertad *f*; **to be at l. to say sth,** ser libre de decir algo; **to take liberties,** tomarse libertades.

Libra ['li:brə] *n* Libra *f*.

librarian [laɪ'breərɪən] *n* bibliotecario,-a *m,f*.

library ['laɪbrərɪ] *n* biblioteca *f*.

Libya ['lɪbɪə] *n* Libia.

Libyan ['lɪbɪən] *adj & n* libio,-a *(m,f)*.

lice [laɪs] *npl* → **louse**.

licence ['laɪsəns] *n* 1 *(permit)* licencia *f*, permiso *m*; *Aut* **l. number,** matrícula *f*. 2

(*freedom*) libertad *f*; (*excessive freedom*) libertinaje *m*.

license ['laɪsəns] **I** *vtr* dar licencia a, autorizar. **II** *n US* → **licence**.

licensed ['laɪsənst] *adj* autorizado,-a; **l. premises**, local autorizado para la venta de bebidas alcohólicas.

licentious [laɪ'senʃəs] *adj* licencioso,-a.

lichen ['laɪkən, 'lɪtʃən] *n* liquen *m*.

lick [lɪk] **I** *vtr* lamer; **to l. one's lips**, relamerse. **II** *n* lamedura *f*; *fam* **a l. of paint**, una mano de pintura.

licorice ['lɪkərɪs, 'lɪkərɪʃ] *n US* → **liquorice**.

lid [lɪd] *n* **1** (*cover*) tapa *f*. **2** (*of eye*) párpado *m*.

lie¹ [laɪ] **I** *vi* mentir. **II** *n* mentira *f*.

lie² [laɪ] **I** *vi* (*pt* **lay**; *pp* **lain**) **1** (*act*) echarse, acostarse; (*state*) estar echado,-a, estar acostado,-a; (*be buried*) yacer. **2** (*be situated*) encontrarse, hallarse; **the valley lay before us**, el valle se extendía ante nosotros. **3** (*remain*) quedarse. **II** *n* (*position*) situación *f*; (*direction*) orientación *f*. ◆**lie about, lie around** *vi* (*person*) estar tumbado,-a; (*things*) estar tirado,-a. ◆**lie down** *vi* acostarse, echarse.

lie-in ['laɪɪn] *n fam* **to have a l.-in**, levantarse tarde.

lieu [ljuː, luː] *in* **in l. of**, en lugar de.

lieutenant [lef'tenənt, *US* luː'tenənt] *n* **1** *Mil* teniente *m*. **2** (*non-military*) lugarteniente *m*.

life [laɪf] *n* (*pl* **lives** [laɪvz]) **1** vida *f*; **to come to l.**, cobrar vida; **to take one's own l.**, suicidarse; *fam* **how's l.?**, ¿qué tal?; **l. belt**, cinturón *m* salvavidas; **l. imprisonment**, cadena perpetua; **l. insurance**, seguro *m* de vida; **l. jacket**, chaleco *m* salvavidas; **l. style**, estilo *m* de vida; **l. story**, biografía *f*. **2** (*liveliness*) vitalidad *f*; *fam* **to be the l.** (**and soul**) **of the party**, ser el alma de la fiesta.

lifeboat ['laɪfbəʊt] *n* (*on ship*) bote *m* salvavidas; (*on shore*) lancha *f* de socorro.

lifeguard ['laɪfɡɑːd] *n* socorrista *mf*.

lifeless ['laɪflɪs] *adj* sin vida.

lifelike ['laɪflaɪk] *adj* natural; (*portrait*) fiel.

lifeline ['laɪflaɪn] *n fig* cordón *m* umbilical.

lifelong ['laɪflɒŋ] *adj* de toda la vida.

life-size(d) ['laɪfsaɪz(d)] *adj* (de) tamaño natural.

lifetime ['laɪftaɪm] *n* vida *f*; **in his l.**, durante su vida; **it's the chance of a l.**, es una ocasión única.

lift [lɪft] **I** *vtr* **1** levantar; (*head etc*) alzar; (*pick up*) coger. **2** (*troops*) transportar. **3** *fam* (*steal*) birlar; (*plagiarize*) plagiar. **II** *vi* (*clouds, mist*) disiparse. **III** *n* **1** *GB* (*elevator*) ascensor *m*. **2** **to give sb a l.**, llevar a algn en coche. **3** *fig* (*boost*) estímulo *m*. ◆**lift up** *vtr* levantar, alzar.

lift-off ['lɪftɒf] *n* despegue *m*.

light¹ [laɪt] **I** *n* **1** luz *f*; *fig* **in the l. of**, en vista de; *fig* **to bring sth to l.**, sacar algo a la luz; *fig* **to come to l.**, salir a la luz; **l. bulb**, bombilla *f*; **l. meter**, fotómetro *m*; **l. pen**, lápiz óptico; **l. year**, año *m* luz. **2** (*lamp*) luz *f*, lámpara *f*; (*traffic light*) semáforo *m*; (*headlight*) faro *m*. **3** (*flame*) lumbre *f*; **to set l. to sth**, prender fuego a algo; *fam* **have you got a l.?**, ¿tiene fuego? **II** *vtr* (*pt* & *pp* **lighted** *or* **lit**) **1** (*illuminate*) iluminar, alumbrar. **2** (*ignite*) encender. **III** *adj* claro,-a; (*hair*) rubio,-a. ◆**light up I** *vtr* iluminar, alumbrar. **II** *vi* iluminarse. **2** *fam* encender un cigarrillo.

light² [laɪt] **I** *adj* ligero,-a; (*rain*) fino,-a; (*breeze*) suave; *fig* (*sentence etc*) leve; *fig* **to make l. of sth**, dar poca importancia a algo. **II** *adv* to travel l., ir ligero,-a de equipaje. ◆**lightly** *adv* **1** ligeramente. **2** **to get off l.**, salir casi indemne.

lighten¹ ['laɪtən] **I** *vtr* **1** (*colour*) aclarar. **2** (*illuminate*) iluminar. **II** *vi* aclararse.

lighten² ['laɪtən] *vtr* **1** (*weight*) aligerar. **2** *fig* (*mitigate*) aliviar; (*heart*) alegrar.

lighter ['laɪtər] *n* (*cigarette*) **l.**, encendedor *m*, mechero *m*.

light-headed [laɪt'hedɪd] *adj* **1** (*dizzy*) mareado,-a. **2** (*frivolous*) frívolo,-a.

light-hearted [laɪt'hɑːtɪd] *adj* alegre.

lighthouse ['laɪthaʊs] *n* faro *m*.

lighting ['laɪtɪŋ] *n* **1** (*act*) iluminación *f*. **2** (*system*) alumbrado *m*.

lightness¹ ['laɪtnɪs] *n* luminosidad *f*, claridad *f*.

lightness² ['laɪtnɪs] *n* (*of weight*) ligereza *f*.

lightning ['laɪtnɪŋ] *n* (*flash*) relámpago *m*; (*stroke*) rayo *m*; **l. conductor**, **l. rod**, pararrayos *m inv*; **l. strike**, huelga *f* relámpago.

lightweight ['laɪtweɪt] *adj* (*suit etc*) ligero,-a; *Box* de peso ligero; *fig* (*person*) light.

like¹ [laɪk] **I** *adj* parecido,-a, semejante. **2** (*equal*) igual. **II** *adv* (*as*) **l. as not**, a lo mejor. **III** *prep* **1** (*similar to*) como, parecido,-a a; (*the same as*) igual que; **it's not l. her to do that**, no es propio de ella hacer eso; **I've never seen anything l. it**, nunca he visto cosa igual; **l. that**, así; **people l. that**, ese tipo de gente; **what's he l.?**, ¿cómo es?; *fam* **that's more l. it!**, ¡así se hace! **2** **to feel l.**, (*want*) tener ganas de; **I feel l. a change**, me apetece un cambio. **IV** *n* **brushes, combs and the l.**, cepillos, peines y cosas por el estilo.

like² [laɪk] **I** *vtr* **1 do you l. chocolate?**, ¿te gusta el chocolate?; **he likes dancing**, le gusta bailar; **she likes children**, le gustan los niños. **2** (*want*) querer; **whether you l. it or not**, quieras o no (quieras); **would you l. a drink?**, ¿te apetece tomar algo? **II** vi querer, gustar; **as you l.**, como quieras; **whenever you l.**, cuando quieras. **III** n gusto m.

likeable ['laɪkəbəl] adj simpático,-a.

likelihood ['laɪklɪhʊd] n probabilidad f.

likely ['laɪklɪ] I adj (**likelier, likeliest**) probable; **he's l. to cause trouble**, es probable que cause problemas; **where are you l. to be this afternoon?**, ¿dónde piensas estar esta tarde? **II** adv probablemente; **not l.!**, ¡ni hablar!

likeness ['laɪknɪs] n 1 semejanza f, parecido m. 2 (portrait) retrato m.

likewise ['laɪkwaɪz] adv 1 (also) también, asimismo. 2 (the same) lo mismo, igual.

liking ['laɪkɪŋ] n (for thing) afición f; (for person) simpatía f; (for friend) cariño m; **to take a l. to sth**, cogerle el gusto a algo; **to take a l. to sb**, coger cariño a algn.

lilac ['laɪlək] I n 1 Bot lila f. 2 (colour) lila m. II adj lila, de color lila.

lilt [lɪlt] n melodía f.

lily ['lɪlɪ] n lirio m, azucena f; **l. of the valley**, lirio de los valles.

limb [lɪm] n miembro m; fig **to be out on a l.**, (in danger) estar en peligro; GB (isolated) estar aislado,-a.

limber ['lɪmbə'] vi Sport entrar en calor; fig prepararse (**for**, para).

limbo ['lɪmbəʊ] n limbo m; fig olvido m; **to be in l.**, caer en el olvido.

lime¹ [laɪm] n Chem cal f.

lime² [laɪm] n (fruit) lima f; (tree) limero m.

limelight ['laɪmlaɪt] n fig **to be in the l.**, estar en el candelero.

limerick ['lɪmərɪk] n quintilla humorística.

limestone ['laɪmstəʊn] n piedra caliza.

limit ['lɪmɪt] I n límite m; (maximum) máximo m; (minimum) mínimo m. II vtr (restrict) limitar.

limitation [lɪmɪ'teɪʃən] n limitación f.

limited ['lɪmɪtɪd] adj limitado,-a; **l. edition**, edición limitada; GB **l. (liability) company**, sociedad anónima.

limitless ['lɪmɪtlɪs] adj ilimitado,-a.

limousine ['lɪməzi:n, lɪmə'zi:n] n limusina f.

limp¹ [lɪmp] I vi cojear. II n cojera f.

limp² [lɪmp] adj 1 (floppy) flojo,-a. 2 (weak) débil.

limpet ['lɪmpɪt] n lapa f.

linchpin ['lɪntʃpɪn] n Tech pezonera f; fig eje m.

line¹ [laɪn] n 1 línea f; (straight) raya f; **to be on the right lines**, ir por buen camino; US **State l.**, límite m de un Estado. 2 (of writing) renglón m; (of poetry) verso m; **Theat to learn one's lines**, aprenderse el papel. 3 (row) fila f; (of trees) hilera f; US (queue) cola f; Mil **l. of fire**, línea f

de fuego; Mil **to be in the front l.**, estar en primera línea; fig **to be in l.**, coincidir (**with**, con); fam **to bring sb into l.**, pararle los pies a algn; fam **to step out of l.**, salirse de las reglas; fig **sth along these lines**, algo por el estilo. 4 (rope) cuerda f; (wire) cable m; fishing **l.**, sedal m. 5 Tel línea f; **hold the l.!**, ¡no cuelgue! 6 GB Rail vía f. 7 (range of goods) surtido m; **a new l.**, una nueva línea. 8 (of descent) linaje m.

line² [laɪn] I vtr (pipe etc) revestir; Sew forrar; fam **to l. one's pockets**, forrarse.
◆**line up** I vtr 1 (arrange in rows) poner en fila. 2 **he has something lined up for this evening**, tiene algo organizado para esta noche. II vi (people) ponerse en fila; (troops) formar; (in queue) hacer cola.

linear ['lɪnɪə'] adj lineal.

lined [laɪnd] adj 1 (paper) rayado,-a; (face) arrugado,-a. 2 (garment) forrado,-a.

linen ['lɪnɪn] n 1 (cloth) lino m. 2 (clothes) ropa f; (sheets etc) ropa blanca.

liner ['laɪnə'] n transatlántico m.

linesman ['laɪnzmən] n Sport juez m de línea.

line-up ['laɪnʌp] n Sport alineación f.

linger ['lɪŋgə'] vi tardar; (dawdle) rezagarse; (smell, doubt) persistir; fig (memory) perdurar.

lingerie ['lænʒəri:] n fml ropa f interior (de mujer).

lingering ['lɪŋgərɪŋ] adj (doubt) persistente; (look) lánguido,-a.

lingo ['lɪŋgəʊ] n (pl **lingoes**) fam 1 (language) lengua f, idioma m. 2 (jargon) jerga f.

linguist ['lɪŋgwɪst] n lingüista mf; **he's a good l.**, se le dan bien los idiomas.

linguistic [lɪŋ'gwɪstɪk] adj lingüístico,-a.

linguistics [lɪŋ'gwɪstɪks] n lingüística f.

lining ['laɪnɪŋ] n forro m.

link [lɪŋk] I n 1 (of chain) eslabón m. 2 (connection) conexión f; fig vínculo m; rail **l.**, enlace ferroviario; **5 links**, campo m sing de golf. II vtr unir. ◆**link up** vi unirse; (meet) encontrarse; (spaceships) acoplarse.

link-up ['lɪŋkʌp] n Tel TV conexión f; (meeting) encuentro m; (of spaceships) acoplamiento m.

lino ['laɪnəʊ] n fam linóleo m.

linoleum [lɪ'nəʊlɪəm] n linóleo m, linóleum m.

lion ['laɪən] n león m.

lioness ['laɪənɪs] n leona f.

lip [lɪp] n 1 labio m. 2 (of jug) pico m.

lip-read ['lɪpri:d] vtr & vi leer en los labios.

lip-service ['lɪpsɜ:vɪs] n palabrería f.

lipstick ['lɪpstɪk] n lápiz m de labios.

liqueur [lɪ'kjʊə'] n licor m.

liquid ['lɪkwɪd] adj & n líquido,-a (m).

liquidate ['lɪkwɪdeɪt] vtr liquidar.

liquidation [lɪkwɪ'deɪʃən] n liquidación f. **to go into l.**, entrar en liquidación.

liquidize ['lɪkwɪdaɪz] vtr licuar.

liquidizer ['lɪkwɪdaɪzər] n licuadora f.

liquor ['lɪkər] n US alcohol m, bebidas alcohólicas.

liquorice ['lɪkərɪs, 'lɪkərɪʃ] n regaliz m.

Lisbon ['lɪzbən] n Lisboa.

lisp [lɪsp] I n ceceo m. II vi cecear.

list¹ [lɪst] I n lista f; (catalogue) catálogo m. II vtr (make a list of) hacer una lista de; (put on a list) poner en una lista; **it is not listed**, no figura en la lista.

list² [lɪst] Naut I n escora f. II vi escorar.

listen ['lɪsən] vi escuchar; (pay attention) prestar atención. **listen out for** vtr estar atento,-a a.

listener ['lɪsənər] n oyente mf.

listless ['lɪstlɪs] adj apático,-a.

lit [lɪt] pt & pp → **light**¹.

liter ['liːtər] n US → **litre**.

literacy ['lɪtərəsɪ] n alfabetización f.

literal ['lɪtərəl] adj literal. **literally** adv literalmente.

literary ['lɪtərərɪ] adj literario,-a.

literate ['lɪtərɪt] adj alfabetizado,-a.

literature ['lɪtərɪtʃər] n 1 literatura f. 2 fam (documentation) folleto informativo.

lithe [laɪð] adj fml ágil.

Lithuania [lɪθjʊ'eɪnɪə] n Lituania.

Lithuanian [lɪθjʊ'eɪnɪən] I adj lituano,-a. II n (person) lituano,-a m,f; (language) lituano m.

litigation [lɪtɪ'geɪʃən] n litigio m.

litmus ['lɪtməs] n fig l. **test**, prueba f contundente.

litre ['liːtər] n litro m.

litter ['lɪtər] I n 1 (rubbish) basura f; (papers) papeles mpl; **l. bin**, papelera f. 2 (offspring) camada f. 3 arch (stretcher) camilla f. II vtr ensuciar.

littered ['lɪtəd] adj cubierto,-a (with, de).

little ['lɪtəl] I adj 1 pequeño,-a; **a l. dog**, un perrito; **a l. house**, una casita; **l. finger**, dedo m meñique. 2 (not much) poco,-a; **a l. cheese**, un poco de queso. II pron poco m; **save me a l.**, guárdame un poco. III adv poco; **l. by l.**, poco a poco; **as l. as possible**, lo menos posible; **they were a l. surprised**, se quedaron algo sorprendidos.

live¹ [lɪv] I vi vivir; **long l. the King!**, ¡viva el Rey! II vtr vivir; **to l. an interesting life**, vivir una vida interesante. **live down** vtr conseguir que se olvide. **live for** vtr vivir para. **live off** vtr vivir de. **live on** I vtr (food, money) vivir de. II vi (memory) persistir. **live through** vtr (durante). **live together** vi vivir juntos. **live up** vtr fam **l. it up**, pegarse la gran vida. **live up to** vtr (promises) cumplir con; **it didn't l. up to expectations**, no fue lo que se esperaba. **live with** vtr 1 vivir con. 2 fig (accept) aceptar.

live² [laɪv] adj 1 (living) vivo,-a. 2 TV Rad en directo, en vivo. 3 (ammunition) real; (bomb) sin explotar; Elec con corriente; fam **he's a real l. wire!**, ¡éste no para nunca!

livelihood ['laɪvlɪhʊd] n sustento m.

lively ['laɪvlɪ] adj (livelier, liveliest) (person) vivo,-a; (place) animado,-a; fig (interest) entusiástico,-a.

liven ['laɪvən] vtr to l. (up), animar.

liver ['lɪvər] n hígado m.

livery ['lɪvərɪ] n librea f.

livestock ['laɪvstɒk] n ganado m.

livid ['lɪvɪd] adj lívido,-a; fam (angry) furioso,-a.

living ['lɪvɪŋ] I adj vivo,-a. II n vida f; **l. conditions**, condiciones fpl de vida; **l. expenses**, dietas fpl; **to earn or make one's l.**, ganarse la vida; **l. room**, sala f de estar; **l. standards**, nivel m de vida; **l. wage**, sueldo mínimo.

lizard ['lɪzəd] n (large) lagarto m; (small) lagartija f.

llama ['lɑːmə] n llama f.

load [ləʊd] I n 1 (cargo) carga f; (weight) peso m; Elec Tech carga f; fam **loads (of)**, montones de; fam **that's a l. of rubbish!**, ¡no son más que tonterías! II vtr cargar. **load up** vi & vtr cargar.

loaded ['ləʊdɪd] adj cargado,-a (with, de); fig **a l. question**, una pregunta intencionada. 2 fam **to be l.**, (rich) estar forrado,-a. 3 (dice) trucado,-a.

loading ['ləʊdɪŋ] n carga f; **l. bay**, cargadero m.

loaf¹ [ləʊf] n (pl loaves) pan m; (French stick) barra f de pan; (sliced) pan de molde.

loaf² [ləʊf] vi to l. (about or around), holgazanear.

loan [ləʊn] I n préstamo m; Fin empréstito m; **on l.**, prestado,-a; (footballer) cedido,-a. II vtr prestar.

loath [ləʊθ] adj to be l. to do sth, ser reacio,-a a hacer algo.

loathe [ləʊð] vtr aborrecer, odiar.

loathing ['ləʊðɪŋ] n aborrecimiento m, odio m.

loathsome ['ləʊðsəm] adj odioso,-a, repugnante.

loaves [ləʊvz] npl → **loaf**.

lob [lɒb] n Ten hacer un lob.

lobby ['lɒbɪ] I n 1 (hall) vestíbulo m. 2 (pressure group) grupo m de presión, lobby m. II vtr presionar. III vi ejercer presiones.

lobe [ləʊb] n lóbulo m.

lobster ['lɒbstər] n langosta f.

local ['ləʊkəl] I adj local; (person) del pueblo; Med l. **anaesthetic**, anestesia f local; Tel l. **call**, llamada urbana; l. **government**, gobierno m municipal. II n fam 1

the locals, los vecinos. 2 *GB* (*pub*) bar *m* del barrio. ◆**locally** *adv* en *or* de la localidad.

locality [ləʊˈkælɪtɪ] *n* localidad *f*.

locate [ləʊˈkeɪt] *vtr* (*situate*) situar, ubicar; (*find*) localizar.

location [ləʊˈkeɪʃən] *n* 1 lugar *m*, situación *f*. 2 *Cin* l. shots, exteriores *mpl*; **they're on l. in Australia,** están rodando en Australia.

loch [lɒx, lɒk] *n Scot* lago *m*.

lock[1] [lɒk] **I** *n* 1 (*on door etc*) cerradura *f*; (*bolt*) cerrojo *m*; (*padlock*) candado *m*. 2 (*on canal*) esclusa *f*. **II** *vtr* cerrar con llave *or* cerrojo *or* candado. **III** *vi* (*door etc*) cerrarse; (*wheels*) trabarse. ◆**lock up** *vtr* (*house*) cerrar; (*jail*) meter en la cárcel.

lock[2] [lɒk] *n lit* (*of hair*) mechón *m*.

locker [ˈlɒkəʳ] *n* (*cupboard*) armario ropero; l. room, vestuario *m* con armarios roperos.

locket [ˈlɒkɪt] *n* medallón *m*.

lockout [ˈlɒkaʊt] *n* cierre *m* patronal.

locksmith [ˈlɒksmɪθ] *n* cerrajero *m*.

lockup [ˈlɒkʌp] *n* (*garage*) garaje alejado de la casa; *US* (*prison*) cárcel *f*.

locomotive [ləʊkəˈməʊtɪv] *n* locomotora *f*.

locust [ˈləʊkəst] *n* langosta *f*.

lodge [lɒdʒ] **I** *n* 1 (*gamekeeper's*) casa *f* del guarda; (*porter's*) portería *f*; (*hunter's*) refugio *m*. 2 (*masonic*) logia *f*. 3 (*beaver's den*) madriguera *f*. **II** *vtr* 1 (*accommodate*) alojar. 2 (*complaint*) presentar. **III** *vi* 1 (*live*) alojarse. 2 (*get stuck*) meterse (**in,** en).

lodger [ˈlɒdʒəʳ] *n* huésped,-a *m,f*.

lodging [ˈlɒdʒɪŋ] *n* alojamiento *m*; l. **house,** casa *f* de huéspedes.

loft [lɒft] *n* desván *m*.

lofty [ˈlɒftɪ] *adj* (*loftier, loftiest*) *lit* (*high*) alto,-a; *pej* (*haughty*) altivo,-a.

log[1] [lɒg] **I** *n* 1 tronco *m*; (*for fuel*) leño *m*; l. **cabin,** cabaña *f* de troncos. 2 *Naut* diario *m* de a bordo. **II** *vtr* (*record*) registrar. ◆**log in, log on** *vi Comput* entrar (en sistema). ◆**log out, log off** *vi Comput* salir (del sistema).

logarithm [ˈlɒgərɪðəm] *n* logaritmo *m*.

log-book [ˈlɒgbʊk] *n Naut* diario de a bordo; *Av* diario de vuelo; *Aut* documentación *f* (del coche).

loggerheads [ˈlɒgəhedz] *npl* **to be at l. with sb,** estar a mal con algn.

logic [ˈlɒdʒɪk] *n* lógica *f*.

logical [ˈlɒdʒɪkəl] *adj* lógico,-a.

logistics [ləˈdʒɪstɪks] *npl* logística *f*.

logo [ˈləʊgəʊ] *n* logotipo *m*.

loin [lɔɪn] *n* (*of animal*) ijada *f*; *Culin* (*of pork*) lomo *m*; (*of beef*) solomillo *m*.

loiter [ˈlɔɪtəʳ] *vi* (*hang about*) holgazanear; (*lag behind*) rezagarse; (*prowl*) merodear.

loll [lɒl] *vi* (*tongue, head*) colgar. ◆**loll about, loll around** *vi* repantigarse.

lollipop [ˈlɒlɪpɒp] *n* pirulí *m*, chupachup® *m*; **ice(d) l.,** polo *m*; *GB fam* l. **lady** *or* **man,** guardia *mf* (que para el tráfico para que crucen los colegiales).

lolly [ˈlɒlɪ] *n fam* 1 (*sweet*) pirulí *m*, chupachup® *m*; **ice(d) l.,** polo *m*. 2 *fam* (*money*) pasta *f*.

London [ˈlʌndən] *n* Londres.

Londoner [ˈlʌndənəʳ] *n* londinense *mf*.

lone [ləʊn] *adj* (*solitary*) solitario,-a; (*single*) solo,-a.

loneliness [ˈləʊnlɪnɪs] *n* soledad *f*.

lonely [ˈləʊnlɪ] *adj* (*lonelier, loneliest*) solo,-a, solitario,-a.

long[1] [lɒŋ] **I** *adj* 1 (*size*) largo,-a; **how l. is the table?,** ¿cuánto tiene de largo la mesa?; **it's three metres l.,** tiene tres metros de largo; l. **jump,** salto *m* de longitud. 2 (*time*) mucho,-a; **at l. last,** por fin; **how l. is the film?,** ¿cuánto tiempo dura la película? 3 *adv* mucho, mucho tiempo; **all day l.,** todo el día; **as l. as the exhibition lasts,** mientras dure la exposición; **as l. as** *or* **so l. as you don't mind,** con tal de que no te importe; **before l.,** dentro de poco; **how l. have you been here?,** ¿cuánto tiempo llevas aquí?

long[2] [lɒŋ] *vi* añorar; **to l. for,** anhelar.

long-distance [lɒŋˈdɪstəns] *adj* de larga distancia; l.-d. **call,** conferencia interurbana; l.-d. **runner,** corredor,-a *m,f* de fondo.

longhand [ˈlɒŋhænd] *n* escritura *f* a mano.

longing [ˈlɒŋɪŋ] *n* (*desire*) anhelo *m*; (*nostalgia*) nostalgia *f*.

longitude [ˈlɒndʒɪtjuːd] *n* longitud *f*.

long-playing [ˈlɒŋpleɪɪŋ] *adj* de larga duración; l.-p. **record,** elepé *m*.

long-range [lɒŋˈreɪndʒ] *adj* (*missile etc*) de largo alcance; (*weather forecast*) de largo plazo.

long-sighted [lɒŋˈsaɪtɪd] *adj* 1 *Med* présbita. 2 *fig* previsor,-a.

long-standing [lɒŋˈstændɪŋ] *adj* antiguo,-a, de mucho tiempo.

long-suffering [lɒŋˈsʌfrɪŋ] *adj* sufrido,-a.

long-term [lɒŋˈtɜːm] *adj* a largo plazo.

long-winded [lɒŋˈwɪndɪd] *adj* prolijo,-a.

loo [luː] *n GB fam* váter *m*.

look [lʊk] **I** *n* 1 (*glance*) mirada *f*; **to take a l. at,** (*peep*) echar un vistazo a; (*examine*) examinar. 2 (*appearance*) aspecto *m*, apariencia *f*; **I don't like the l. of it,** me da mala espina. 3 (*fashion*) moda *f*. 4 (*good*) **looks,** belleza *f*. **II** *vi* 1 mirar. 2 (*seem*) parecer; **he looks well,** tiene buena cara; **it looks delicious,** tiene un aspecto buenísimo; **she looks like her father,** (*resembles*) se parece a su padre. **III** *vtr* mirar. ◆**look after** *vtr* cuidar a, ocuparse de.

◆**look at** vtr mirar; fig whichever way you l. at it, desde cualquier punto de vista. ◆**look away** vi apartar la mirada.

◆**look back** vi 1 mirar hacia atrás; fig since then he has never looked back, desde entonces ha ido prosperando. 2 (remember) recordar. ◆**look down** vi fig to l. down on sth/sb, despreciar algo/a algn.

◆**look for** vtr buscar. ◆**look forward to** vtr esperar con ansia; I l. forward to hearing from you, (in letter) espero noticias suyas. ◆**look into** vtr examinar, investigar. ◆**look on** I vtr (consider) considerar. II vi quedarse mirando. ◆**look onto** vtr dar a. ◆**look out** vi 1 the bedroom looks out onto the garden, el dormitorio da al jardín. 2 l. out!, ¡cuidado!, ¡ojo! ◆**look over** vtr (examine) revisar; (place) inspeccionar. II vi quedarse mirando. ◆**look round** I vi mirar alrededor; (turn head) volver la cabeza. II vtr (house, shop) ver. ◆**look through** vtr 1 (window) mirar por. 2 (leaf through) hojear; (examine) revisar; (check) registrar. ◆**look to** vtr 1 (take care of) velar por. 2 (turn to) recurrir a. ◆**look up** I vi 1 (glance upwards) alzar la vista. 2 fam (improve) mejorar. II vtr 1 (look for) buscar. 2 (visit) ir a visitar. ◆**look upon** vtr considerar. ◆**look up to** vtr (person) respetar.

lookout ['lukaut] n 1 (person) centinela mf; (place) mirador m; to be on the l. for, estar al acecho de algn; fam that's his l.!, ¡eso es asunto suyo!

loom[1] [luːm] n telar m.

loom[2] [luːm] vi alzarse; fig (threaten) amenazar.

loony ['luːnɪ] adj (loonier, looniest) fam loco,-a.

loop [luːp] I n 1 lazo m. 2 Comput bucle m. II vtr 1 encordar. 2 Av to l. the loop, rizar el rizo.

loophole ['luːphəʊl] n fig escapatoria f.

loose [luːs] adj 1 (not secure) flojo,-a; (papers, hair, clothes) suelto,-a; (tongue) desatado,-a; (baggy) holgado,-a; to set sb l., soltar a algn; fam to be at a l. end, no saber qué hacer. 2 (not packaged) a granel; l. tobacco, tabaco m en hebras; l. change, suelto m. 3 (not exact) vago,-a; (translation) libre. 4 (lax) relajado,-a; a l. woman, una mujer fácil. ◆**loosely** adv 1 (approximately) aproximadamente. 2 (vaguely) vagamente.

loosen ['luːsən] I vtr aflojar; (belt) desabrochar; fig (restrictions) flexibilizar. II vi (slacken) aflojarse.

loot [luːt] I n botín m. II vtr saquear.

lop [lɒp] vtr podar. ◆**lop off** vtr cortar.

lope [ləʊp] vi andar a zancadas.

lopsided [lɒp'saɪdɪd] adj ladeado,-a.

lord [lɔːd] n 1 (British peer) lord m; the House of Lords, la Cámara de los Lores; the L. Mayor, el señor alcalde. 2

Rel the L., El Señor; good L.!, ¡Dios mío!; the L.'s Prayer, el Padrenuestro. 3 (judge) señoría m.

lordship ['lɔːdʃɪp] n GB His L., Your L., su señoría.

lorry ['lɒrɪ] n GB camión m; l. driver, camionero,-a m,f; l. load, carga f.

lose [luːz] I vtr (pt & pp lost) perder; to l. time, (of clock) atrasarse. II vi perder; to l. to sb, perder contra algn; to l. out, salir perdiendo.

loser ['luːzər] n perdedor,-a m,f.

loss [lɒs] n pérdida f; to make a l., perder; fig to be at a l. for words, quedarse de una pieza; to be at a l. what to do, no saber qué hacer.

lost [lɒst] adj 1 perdido,-a; to get l., perderse; fam get l.!, ¡vete a la porra!; l. property office, US l. and found department, oficina f de objetos perdidos. 2 (disoriented) desorientado,-a; (distracted) distraído,-a; l. in thought, ensimismado,-a.

lot [lɒt] n 1 (fate) suerte f. 2 to cast lots for sth, echar algo a suertes. 3 US (of land) parcela f. 4 (in an auction) lote m. 5 (everything) todo m; he ate the l., se lo comió todo. 6 a l. of, (much) mucho, -a; (many) muchos,-as; he feels a l. better, se encuentra mucho mejor; she reads a l., lee mucho; fam lots of, montones de, cantidad de.

lotion ['ləʊʃən] n loción f.

lottery ['lɒtərɪ] n lotería f; l. ticket, ≈ décimo m de lotería.

loud [laʊd] I adj 1 (voice) alto,-a; (noise) fuerte; (laugh) estrepitoso,-a; (applause) clamoroso,-a; (protests, party) ruidoso,-a. 2 (flashy) chillón,-ona. 3 (vulgar) hortera. II adv to read/think out l., leer/pensar en voz alta.

loud-hailer [laʊd'heɪlər] n megáfono m.

loudspeaker [laʊd'spiːkər] n altavoz m.

lounge [laʊndʒ] I n GB salón m, sala f de estar. II vi hacer el vago.

louse [laʊs] n (pl lice [laɪs]) piojo m.

lousy ['laʊzɪ] adj (lousier, lousiest) fam fatal; a l. trick, una cochinada.

lout [laʊt] n gamberro m.

lovable ['lʌvəbl] adj adorable.

love [lʌv] I n 1 amor m (for, por); (passion) pasión f (for, por); to be in l. with sb, estar enamorado,-a de algn; to fall in l., enamorarse; to make l., hacer el amor; (with) l. (from) Mary, (in letter) un abrazo, Mary; l. affair, amorío m; l. letter/story, carta f/historia f de amor; l. life, vida f sentimental. 2 (person) amor m, cariño m; fam chato,-a m,f; my l., mi amor. 3 Ten forty l., cuarenta a cero. II vtr (person) querer a, amar a; he loves cooking/football, le encanta cocinar/el fútbol.

lovely ['lʌvlɪ] adj (lovelier, loveliest)

lover ['lʌvə^r] n 1 (*sexual partner*) amante mf. 2 (*enthusiast*) aficionado,-a mf, amigo,-a m,f.

loving ['lʌvɪŋ] adj cariñoso,-a.

low¹ [ləʊ] I adj 1 bajo,-a; (*neckline*) escotado,-a; the L. Countries, los Países Bajos. 2 (*in quantity*) bajo,-a. 3 (*poor*) pobre. 4 (*battery*) gastado,-a; l. frequency, baja frecuencia. 5 to feel l., sentirse deprimido,-a. 6 (*reprehensible*) malo,-a. II adv bajo. III n 1 Meteor área f de baja presión. 2 (*low point*) punto más bajo; to reach an all-time l., tocar fondo.

low² [ləʊ] vi (*cow*) mugir.

lowdown ['ləʊdaʊn] n fam pormenores mpl.

lower ['ləʊə^r] I adj (*comp of low*) inferior; Typ l. case, minúscula f; l. class, clase baja. II adv comp → low. III vtr bajar; (*flag*) arriar; (*reduce*) reducir; (*price*) rebajar.

lower-class ['ləʊəklɑːs] adj de clase baja.

lowest ['ləʊɪst] adj (*superl of low*) más bajo,-a; (*price, speed*) mínimo,-a. II n at the l., como mínimo.

low-key [ləʊ'kiː] adj sin ceremonia.

lowlands ['ləʊləndz] npl tierras bajas.

lowly ['ləʊlɪ] adj (*lowlier, lowliest*) humilde.

low-necked [ləʊ'nekt] adj escotado,-a.

loyal ['lɔɪəl] adj leal, fiel.

loyalty ['lɔɪəltɪ] n lealtad f, fidelidad f.

lozenge ['lɒzɪndʒ] n pastilla f.

LP [el'piː] abbr of long-playing record, LP m.

L-plate ['elpleɪt] n GB (placa f de la ele.

LSD [eles'diː] abbr of lysergic acid diethylamide, dietilamida f del ácido lisérgico, LSD m.

Ltd GB Com abbr of Limited (Liability), Sociedad Anónima, S.A..

lubricant ['luːbrɪkənt] n lubricante m.

lubricate ['luːbrɪkeɪt] vtr lubricar; (*engine*) engrasar.

lubrication [luːbrɪ'keɪʃən] n engrase m.

lucid ['luːsɪd] adj lúcido,-a.

luck [lʌk] n suerte f; bad l.!, ¡mala suerte!; good l.!, ¡(buena) suerte!; to be in l., estar de suerte; to be out of l., no tener suerte; fig to push one's l., tentar la suerte; fig to try one's l., probar fortuna.

lucky ['lʌkɪ] adj (*luckier, luckiest*) (*person*) afortunado,-a; (*day*) de suerte; (*move*) oportuno,-a; (*charm*) de la suerte; a l. break, una oportunidad. ◆**luckily** adv por suerte, afortunadamente.

lucrative ['luːkrətɪv] adj lucrativo,-a.

ludicrous ['luːdɪkrəs] adj absurdo,-a, ridículo,-a.

lug [lʌg] vtr fam arrastrar.

luggage ['lʌgɪdʒ] n equipaje m; l. rack, Aut baca f; Rail portaequipajes m inv.

lukewarm ['luːkwɔːm] adj (*water etc*) tibio,-a; fig (*reception etc*) poco entusiasta.

lull [lʌl] I n (*in storm*) calma chicha; (*in fighting*) tregua f. II vtr (*cause to sleep*) adormecer; to l. sb into a false sense of security, infundir una falsa seguridad a algn.

lullaby ['lʌləbaɪ] n canción f de cuna, nana f.

lumbago [lʌm'beɪgəʊ] n lumbago m.

lumber ['lʌmbə^r] I n 1 GB (*junk*) trastos viejos. 2 US (*timber*) maderos mpl. II vtr fam cargar (with, de).

lumberjack ['lʌmbədʒæk] n leñador m.

luminous ['luːmɪnəs] adj luminoso,-a.

lump [lʌmp] I n (*of coal etc*) trozo m; (*of sugar, earth*) terrón m; (*in sauce*) grumo m; (*swelling*) bulto m; fam fig (*in throat*) nudo m; l. sum, cantidad f global. II vtr fam (*endure*) aguantar. ◆**lump together** vtr apelotonar.

lumpy ['lʌmpɪ] adj (*lumpier, lumpiest*) (*bed*) lleno,-a de bultos; (*sauce*) grumoso,-a.

lunacy ['luːnəsɪ] n locura f.

lunar ['luːnə^r] adj lunar.

lunatic ['luːnətɪk] adj & n loco,-a (m,f); l. asylum, manicomio m.

lunch [lʌntʃ] I n comida f, almuerzo m; l. hour, hora f de comer. II vi comer, almorzar.

luncheon ['lʌntʃən] n arch fml almuerzo m; l. voucher, vale m de comida; (*pork*) l. meat, carne f de cerdo troceada, chopped m.

lunchtime ['lʌntʃtaɪm] n hora f de comer.

lung [lʌŋ] n pulmón m.

lunge [lʌndʒ] I n arremetida f. II vi (*also l. forward*) arremeter; to l. (out) at sb, arremeter contra algn.

lurch [lɜːtʃ] I n 1 (*of vehicle*) sacudida f; (*of person*) tambaleo m. 2 fam to leave sb in the l., dejar a algn en la cuneta. II vi (*vehicle*) dar sacudidas; (*person*) tambalearse.

lure [lʊə^r] I n (*decoy*) señuelo m; (*bait*) cebo m; fig (*charm*) aliciente m. II vtr atraer con engaños.

lurid ['lʊərɪd] adj 1 (*gruesome*) espeluznante; (*sensational*) sensacionalista. 2 (*gaudy*) chillón,-ona.

lurk [lɜːk] vi (*lie in wait*) estar al acecho; (*hide*) esconderse.

luscious ['lʌʃəs] adj (*food*) delicioso,-a.

lush [lʌʃ] adj (*vegetation*) exuberante.

lust [lʌst] I n (*sexual desire*) lujuria f; (*craving*) ansia f; (*greed*) codicia f. II vi to l. after sth/sb, codiciar algo/desear a algn.

luster ['lʌstə^r] n US → lustre.

lustre ['lʌstə^r] n lustre m.

lusty ['lʌstɪ] adj (**lustier**, **lustiest**) robusto,-a.

lute [luːt] n laúd m.

Luxembourg ['lʌksəmbɜːg] n Luxemburgo.

luxuriant [lʌg'zjʊərɪənt] adj (plants) exuberante; (hair etc) abundante.

luxurious [lʌg'zjʊərɪəs] adj lujoso,-a.

luxury ['lʌkʃərɪ] n lujo m; **l. flat**, piso m de lujo.

lychee ['laɪtʃiː] n lichi m.

lying ['laɪɪŋ] **I** adj mentiroso,-a. **II** n mentiras fpl.

lynch [lɪntʃ] vtr linchar.

lyre [laɪə] n Mus lira f.

lyric ['lɪrɪk] **I** adj lírico,-a. **II** n **1** (poem) poema m lírico. **2 lyrics**, (words of song) letra f sing.

lyrical ['lɪrɪkəl] adj lírico,-a.

M

M, m [em] n (the letter) M, m f.

m 1 abbr of **metre(s)**, m. **2** abbr of **million(s)**, m.

macabre [mə'kɑːbrə] adj macabro,-a.

mac(c)aroni [mækə'rəʊnɪ] n macarrones mpl.

mace¹ [meɪs] n (club, ceremonial staff) maza f.

mace² [meɪs] n (spice) macis f inv.

machine [mə'ʃiːn] **I** n máquina f; **m. gun**, ametralladora f; **m. language**, lenguaje m máquina. **II** vtr trabajar a máquina.

machine-gun [mə'ʃiːngʌn] vtr ametrallar.

machine-readable [mə'ʃiːnriːdəbəl] adj Comput para ser leído,-a por ordenador.

machinery [mə'ʃiːnərɪ] n (machines) maquinaria f; (workings of machine) mecanismo m; fig **the bureaucratic m.**, la maquinaria burocrática.

mac [mæk] n GB fam abbr of **mackintosh**.

mackerel ['mækrəl] n (pl **mackerel**) caballa f.

mac(k)intosh ['mækɪntɒʃ] n impermeable m.

macroeconomics [mækrəʊiːkə'nɒmɪks] n macroeconomía f.

mad [mæd] adj (**madder**, **maddest**) **1** loco,-a; (animal) furioso,-a; (dog) rabioso,-a; **to be m.**, estar loco,-a; **to drive sb m.**, volver loco,-a a algn; **to go m.**, volverse loco,-a; **you must be m.!**, ¿estás loco? **2** (idea, plan) disparatado,-a. **3** fam **to be m. about sth/sb**, estar loco, -a por algo/algn. **4** fam **to be m. at sb**, estar enfadado,-a con algn. **5** (gallop, race etc) desenfrenado,-a. ◆**madly** adv fam (extremely) terriblemente; **to be m. in love with sb**, estar locamente enamorado,-a de algn.

madam ['mædəm] n **1** señora f; **Dear M.**, (in letter) Muy señora mía, Estimada señora. **2** (brothelkeeper) madam f.

madden ['mædən] vtr enloquecer.

maddening ['mædənɪŋ] adv exasperante.

made [meɪd] pt & pp → **make**.

Madeira [mə'dɪərə] n **1** (island) Madeira. **2** (wine) madeira m; **M. cake**, bizcocho m.

made-to-measure [meɪdtə'meʒər] adj hecho,-a a (la) medida.

made-up ['meɪdʌp] adj **1** (face, person) maquillado,-a; (eyes, lips) pintado,-a. **2** (story, excuse) inventado,-a.

madman ['mædmən] n loco m.

madness ['mædnɪs] n locura f.

Madrid [mə'drɪd] n Madrid.

Mafia ['mæfɪə] n mafia f.

magazine [mægə'ziːn] n **1** (periodical) revista f. **2** (in rifle) recámara f. **3** Mil (storehouse) almacén m; (for explosives) polvorín m.

maggot ['mægət] n larva f, gusano m.

magic ['mædʒɪk] **I** n magia f. **II** adj **1** mágico,-a; **m. wand**, varita mágica. **2** fam (wonderful) estupendo,-a.

magical ['mædʒɪkəl] adj mágico,-a.

magician [mə'dʒɪʃən] n **1** (wizard) mago,-a m,f. **2** (conjuror) prestidigitador,-a m,f.

magistrate ['mædʒɪstreɪt] n juez mf de paz; **magistrates' court**, juzgado m de paz.

magnanimous [mæg'nænɪməs] adj magnánimo,-a.

magnet ['mægnɪt] n imán m.

magnetic [mæg'netɪk] adj magnético,-a; fig (personality) carismático,-a; **m. tape**, cinta magnetofónica.

magnetism ['mægnɪtɪzəm] n magnetismo m.

magnificence [mæg'nɪfɪsəns] n magnificencia f.

magnificent [mæg'nɪfɪsənt] adj magnífico,-a.

magnify ['mægnɪfaɪ] vtr **1** (enlarge) aumentar. **2** fig (exaggerate) exagerar.

magnifying glass ['mægnɪfaɪɪŋglɑːs] n lupa f.

magnitude ['mægnɪtjuːd] n magnitud f.

magpie ['mægpaɪ] n urraca f.

mahogany [mə'hɒgənɪ] **I** n caoba f. **II** adj de caoba.

maid [meɪd] n **1** criada f, Am mucama f. **2** pej **old m.**, solterona f.

maiden ['meɪdən] **I** n lit doncella f. **II** adj **1** (unmarried) soltera; **m. aunt**, tía soltera,

m. name, apellido m de soltera. 2 (*voyage, flight*) inaugural.

mail [meɪl] I n correo m; **by m.**, por correo; **m. order**, venta f por correo; **m. train**, (tren m) correo. II vtr (*post*) echar al buzón; (*send*) enviar por correo.

mailbox ['meɪlbɒks] n US buzón m.

mailing list ['meɪlɪŋlɪst] n lista f de direcciones.

mailman ['meɪlmæn] n US cartero m.

maim [meɪm] vtr lisiar.

main [meɪn] I adj (*problem, door* etc) principal; (*square, mast, sail*) mayor; (*office*) central; **the m. thing is to keep calm**, lo esencial es mantener la calma; *Culin* **m. course**, plato m principal; **m. road**, carretera f principal. II n 1 (*pipe, wire*) conducto m principal; **the mains**, (*water* or *gas system*) la cañería maestra; *Elec* la red eléctrica; **a radio that works on battery or mains**, una radio que funciona con pilas o con corriente. 2 **in the m.**, por regla general. II **mainly** adv principalmente, sobre todo; (*for the most part*) en su mayoría.

mainframe ['meɪnfreɪm] n **m. computer**, unidad f, central f.

mainland ['meɪnlənd] n continente m.

mainstay ['meɪnsteɪ] n fig sustento m, sostén m.

mainstream ['meɪnstriːm] n corriente f principal.

maintain [meɪn'teɪn] vtr mantener; (*conversation*) sostener; (*silence, appearances*) guardar; (*road, machine*) conservar en buen estado.

maintenance ['meɪntənəns] n 1 mantenimiento m. 2 (*divorce allowance*) pensión f.

maisonette [meɪzə'net] n dúplex m.

maize [meɪz] n maíz m.

majestic [mə'dʒestɪk] adj majestuoso,-a.

majesty ['mædʒɪstɪ] n majestad f.

major ['meɪdʒər] I adj 1 principal, mayor; (*contribution, operation*) importante. 2 *Mus* mayor. II n 1 *Mil* comandante m. 2 US Univ especialidad f. III vi US Univ **to m. in**, especializarse en.

Majorca [mə'jɔːkə] n Mallorca.

Majorcan [mə'jɔːkən] adj & n mallorquín,-ina (m,f).

majority [mə'dʒɒrɪtɪ] n mayoría f; **to be in the m.**, ser (la) mayoría.

make [meɪk] (pt & pp **made**) I vtr 1 hacer; (*manufacture*) fabricar; (*create*) crear; (*clothes, curtains*) confeccionar; (*meal*) preparar; (*payment*) efectuar; (*speech*) pronunciar; (*decision*) tomar; (*mistake*) cometer; **to be made of**, ser de; **to m. a noise**, hacer ruido. 2 (*render*) poner, volver; (*convert*) convertir (**into**, en); (*appoint*) nombrar; **he made it clear that ...**, dejó claro que .... 3 (*force, compel*) obligar; (*cause*) causar; **to m. do with sth**, arreglárselas con algo. 4 (*earn*) ga-

nar; **to m. a living**, ganarse la vida; **to m. a name for oneself**, hacerse famoso, -a; *fig* **to m. the best of sth**, sacar partido de algo. 5 **7 and 5 m. 12**, 7 y 5 son 12. 6 (*calculate, reckon*) calcular; **what time do you m. it?**, ¿qué hora tienes? 7 (*think*) opinar; **I don't know what to m. of it**, no sé qué pensar de eso; **it doesn't m. sense**, no tiene sentido. 8 (*achieve*) alcanzar, conseguir. 9 **it will m. or break her**, será su consagración o su ruina. 10 **to m. a fresh start**, volver a empezar. II vi 1 hacer; **to m. sure of sth**, asegurarse de algo. 2 **she made as if to leave**, hizo como si quisiera marcharse. III n 1 (*brand*) marca f. 2 *fam* **to be on the m.**, andar tras el dinero.

◆**make for** vtr 1 (*move towards*) dirigirse hacia; (*attack*) atacar. 2 **this makes for less work**, esto ahorra trabajo.

◆**make out** I vtr 1 (*list, receipt*) hacer; (*cheque*) extender. 2 (*perceive*) distinguir; (*writing*) descifrar. 3 (*understand*) entender. 4 (*claim*) pretender. 5 **to m. out a case for doing sth**, exponer los argumentos para hacer algo. II vi **how did you m. out?**, ¿qué tal te fue?

◆**make up** I vtr 1 (*parcel, list*) hacer; (*prescription*) preparar; (*assemble*) montar. 2 (*story*) inventar. 3 (*apply cosmetics to*) maquillar; (*one's face*) maquillarse. 4 (*loss*) compensar; (*lost time*) recuperar. 5 (*constitute*) componer. 6 **to m. it up with sb**, hacer las paces (con algn). 7 **to m. up one's mind**, decidirse. II vi maquillarse. ◆**make up to** vtr 1 **to m. up to sb**, congraciarse con algn. 2 **to m. it up to sb for sth**, compensar a algn por algo.

make-believe ['meɪkbɪliːv] n (*fantasy*) fantasía f; (*pretence*) fingimiento m; **to live in a world of m.-b.**, vivir en un mundo de ensueño.

maker ['meɪkər] n fabricante m.

makeshift ['meɪkʃɪft] adj (*improvised*) improvisado,-a; (*temporary*) provisional.

make-up ['meɪkʌp] n 1 (*cosmetics*) maquillaje m; **m.-up remover**, desmaquillador m. 2 (*composition*) composición f; (*character*) carácter m.

making ['meɪkɪŋ] n 1 (*manufacture*) fabricación f; (*preparation*) preparación f. 2 **he has the makings of a politician**, tiene madera de político.

malaise [mæ'leɪz] n malestar m.

malaria [mə'leərɪə] n malaria f.

Malay [mə'leɪ] I adj malayo,-a. II n 1 (*person*) malayo,-a m.f. 2 (*language*) malayo m.

Malaysia [mə'leɪzɪə] n Malasia.

male [meɪl] I adj (*animal, plant*) macho; (*person*) varón; (*sex*) masculino; *pej* **m. chauvinism**, machismo m. II n (*person*) varón m; (*animal, plant*) macho m.

malevolent [mə'levələnt] adj malévo-

-a.

malfunction [mæl'fʌŋkʃən] I n mal funcionamiento m. II vi funcionar mal.

malice ['mælɪs] n malicia f; *Jur* with m. aforethought, con premeditación.

malicious [mə'lɪʃəs] adj malévolo,-a.

malign [mə'laɪn] I adj maligno,-a; *(influence)* perjudicial. II vtr calumniar, difamar.

malignant [mə'lɪgnənt] adj 1 *(person)* malvado,-a. 2 *Med* maligno,-a.

mall [mɔːl, mæl] n US centro m comercial.

malleable ['mælɪəbəl] adj maleable.

mallet ['mælɪt] n mazo m.

malnutrition [mælnju:'trɪʃən] n desnutrición f.

malpractice [mæl'præktɪs] n procedimiento m ilegal; *Med* negligencia f.

malt [mɔːlt] n malta f.

Malta ['mɔːltə] n Malta.

mammal ['mæməl] n mamífero m.

mammary ['mæmərɪ] adj **m. gland,** mama f.

mammoth ['mæməθ] I n *Zool* mamut m. II adj gigantesco,-a.

man [mæn] I n (pl **men**) 1 hombre m; **old m.,** viejo m; **young m.,** joven m; *fig* **he's a m. of his word,** es hombre de palabra; *fig* **the m. in the street,** el hombre de la calle; **m. Friday,** factótum m; *fam* **dirty old m.,** viejo verde. 2 *(humanity)* el hombre; *(human being)* el humano. 3 *(husband)* marido m; *(partner)* pareja f. 4 **our m. in Madrid,** nuestro representante en Madrid. 5 *Chess* pieza f. II vtr *(boat, plane)* tripular; *(post)* servir; **manned flight,** vuelo tripulado.

manage ['mænɪdʒ] I vtr 1 *(company, household)* llevar; *(money, affairs, person)* manejar. 2 *(succeed)* conseguir; **to m. to do sth,** lograr hacer algo. II vi *(cope physically)* poder; *(esp financially)* arreglárselas; **we're managing,** vamos tirando.

manageable ['mænɪdʒəbəl] adj manejable.

management ['mænɪdʒmənt] n dirección f.

manager ['mænɪdʒər] n 1 *(of company, bank)* director,-a m,f; *(head of department)* jefe,-a m,f. 2 *(of pop group etc)* mánager m. 3 *Sport* entrenador m.

manageress [mænɪdʒə'res] n *(of shop, restaurant)* encargada f; *(of company)* directora f.

managerial [mænɪ'dʒɪərɪəl] adj directivo,-a.

managing ['mænɪdʒɪŋ] adj directivo,-a; **m. director,** director,-a m,f, gerente.

mandarin ['mændərɪn] I n **m.** *(orange)*, mandarina f.

mandate ['mændeɪt] n mandato m.

mandatory ['mændətərɪ] adj *fml* obligatorio,-a.

mane [meɪn] n *(of horse)* crin f; *(of lion)* melena f.

maneuver [mə'nu:vər] n & vtr US → **manoeuvre.**

manfully ['mænfʊlɪ] adv valientemente.

manger ['meɪndʒər] n pesebre m.

mangle¹ ['mæŋgəl] n *(for wringing)* rodillo m.

mangle² ['mæŋgəl] vtr *(crush)* aplastar; *(destroy by cutting)* despedazar.

mango ['mæŋgəʊ] n *(pl* **mangoes***)* mango m.

mangy ['meɪndʒɪ] adj *(mangier, mangiest)* *(animal)* sarnoso,-a; *fam (carpet)* raído,-a.

manhandle ['mænhændəl] vtr maltratar.

manhole ['mænhəʊl] n boca f de acceso.

manhood ['mænhʊd] n 1 *(age)* mayoría f de edad; **to reach m.,** llegar a la edad viril. 2 *(manly qualities)* virilidad f.

mania ['meɪnɪə] n manía f.

maniac ['meɪnɪæk] n maníaco,-a m,f; *fam* loco,-a m,f.

manic ['mænɪk] adj maníaco,-a.

manic-depressive ['mænɪkdɪ'presɪv] adj & n maníaco,-a *(m,f)* depresivo,-a.

manicure ['mænɪkjʊər] I n manicura f. II vtr **to m. one's nails,** hacerse la manicura.

manifest ['mænɪfest] *fml* I adj manifiesto,-a. II vtr manifestar.

manifesto [mænɪ'festəʊ] n programa m electoral.

manifold ['mænɪfəʊld] adj *fml (many)* múltiples; *(varied)* diversos,-as.

manipulate [mə'nɪpjʊleɪt] vtr 1 manipular. 2 *fig (accounts etc)* falsificar.

mankind [mæn'kaɪnd] n la humanidad, el género humano.

manly ['mænlɪ] adj *(manlier, manliest)* varonil, viril.

man-made ['mænmeɪd] adj *(lake)* artificial; *(fibres, fabric)* sintético,-a.

manner ['mænər] n 1 *(way, method)* manera f, modo m; **in this m.,** de esta manera. 2 *(way of behaving)* forma f de ser. 3 *fml (type, class)* clase f. 4 *(good)* **manners,** buenos modales; **bad manners,** falta f *sing* de educación.

mannerism ['mænərɪzəm] n *(gesture)* gesto m; *(affectation)* amaneramiento m.

manoeuvre [mə'nu:vər] I n maniobra f. II vtr maniobrar; *(person)* manejar. III vi maniobrar.

manor ['mænər] n **m. house,** casa solariega.

manpower ['mænpaʊər] n mano f de obra.

mansion ['mænʃən] n casa f grande; *(in country)* casa solariega.

manslaughter ['mænslɔːtər] n homicidio involuntario.

mantelpiece ['mæntəlpi:s] n *(shelf)* repisa f de chimenea; *(fireplace)* chimenea f.

mantle ['mæntəl] *n fig (of snow)* manto *m*, capa *f*.

manual ['mænjʊəl] *adj & n* manual *(m)*.

manufacture [mænjʊ'fæktʃər] I *vtr* fabricar. II *n* fabricación *f*.

manufacturer [mænjʊ'fæktʃərər] *n* fabricante *mf*.

manure [mə'njʊər] *n* abono *m*, estiércol *m*.

manuscript ['mænjʊskrɪpt] *n* manuscrito *m*.

many ['menɪ] I *adj (more, most)* mucho,-a, muchos,-as; **a great m.**, muchísimos,-as; **as m. ... as ...**, tantos, -as ... como ...; **how m. days?**, ¿cuántos días?; **m. a time**, muchas veces; **so m. flowers!**, ¡cuántas flores!; **too m.**, demasiados,-as. II *pron* muchos,-as.

map [mæp] I *n (of country)* mapa *m*; *(of town, bus route)* plano *m*. II *vtr* trazar un mapa de. ◆**map out** *vtr (route)* trazar en un mapa; *fig (future etc)* planear.

maple ['meɪpəl] *n* arce *m*.

mar [mɑːr] *vtr* estropear; **to m. sb's enjoyment**, aguarle la fiesta a algn.

marathon ['mærəθən] *n* maratón *m*.

marble ['mɑːbəl] I *n (stone)* mármol *m*. 2 *(glass ball)* canica *f*. II *adj* de mármol.

March [mɑːtʃ] *n* marzo *m*.

march [mɑːtʃ] I *n* 1 *Mil* marcha *f*; *fig* **to steal a m. on sb**, tomar la delantera a algn. 2 *(demonstration)* manifestación *f*. II *vi* 1 marchar. 2 *(demonstrate)* manifestarse. III *vtr Mil* hacer marchar.

march past ['mɑːtʃpɑːst] *n* desfile *m*.

mare [meər] *n* yegua *f*.

margarine [mɑːdʒə'riːn] *n* margarina *f*.

margin ['mɑːdʒɪn] *n* margen *m*; *fig* **to win by a narrow m.**, ganar por escaso margen; **m. of error**, *(in statistics)* error muestral.

marginal ['mɑːdʒɪnəl] *adj* marginal; *Pol* **m. seat**, escaño *m* pendiente. ◆**marginally** *adv* ligeramente.

marigold ['mærɪɡəʊld] *n* caléndula *f*.

marijuana, marihuana [mærɪ'hwɑːnə] *n* marihuana *f*, marijuana *f*.

marinate ['mærɪneɪt] *vtr* adobar.

marine [mə'riːn] I *adj* marino,-a. II *n* soldado *m* de infantería de marina; *GB* **the Marines**, *US* **the M. Corps**, la infantería de marina.

marital ['mærɪtəl] *adj* matrimonial; **m. status**, estado *m* civil.

maritime ['mærɪtaɪm] *adj* marítimo,-a.

marjoram ['mɑːdʒərəm] *n* mejorana *f*.

mark¹ [mɑːk] I *n* 1 *(left by blow etc)* señal *f*; *(stain)* mancha *f*; *fig* **to make one's m.**, distinguirse. 2 *(sign, token)* señal *f*; *(indication)* indicio *m*. 3 *(in exam etc)* nota *f*; **to get high marks**, sacar buenas notas. 4 *fig* **to hit the m.**, dar en el clavo; *fig* **to be wide of the m.**, estar lejos de la verdad. II *vtr* 1 *(stain)* manchar. 2 *(with*

tick, cross) señalar. 3 *(exam)* corregir; *(student)* dar notas a. 4 **'10% off marked price'**, 'descuento del 10% sobre el precio indicado'. 5 **m. my words**, fíjate en lo que te digo. 6 *Sport* marcar. 7 **to m. time**, *Mil* marcar el paso; *fig* hacer tiempo. ◆**mark out** *vtr* 1 *(area)* delimitar. 2 **to m. sb out for**, destinar a algn a.

mark² [mɑːk] *n (unit of currency)* marco *m*.

marked [mɑːkt] *adj (noticeable)* marcado,-a, acusado,-a.

marker ['mɑːkər] *n* 1 *(bookmark)* registro *m*. 2 *Sport* marcador,-a *m,f*. 3 *(pen)* rotulador *m* fluorescente.

market ['mɑːkɪt] I *n* 1 mercado *m*; **m. garden**, *(small)* huerto *m*; *(large)* huerta *f*; **on the m.**, en venta; **m. forces**, tendencias *fpl* del mercado; **m. price**, precio *m* de mercado; **m. research**, estudio *m* de mercado. II *vtr (sell)* poner en venta; *(promote)* promocionar.

marketable ['mɑːkɪtəbəl] *adj* comerciable.

marketing ['mɑːkɪtɪŋ] *n* marketing *m*, mercadotecnia *f*.

marketplace ['mɑːkɪtpleɪs] *n* mercado *m*.

marksman ['mɑːksmən] *n* tirador *m*.

marmalade ['mɑːməleɪd] *n* mermelada *f* *(de cítricos)*.

maroon [mə'ruːn] *adj (colour)* granate.

marooned [mə'ruːnd] *adj* bloqueado,-a.

marquee [mɑː'kiː] *n* carpa *f*, entoldado *m*.

marquess, marquis ['mɑːkwɪs] *n* marqués *m*.

marriage ['mærɪdʒ] *n (state)* matrimonio *m*; *(wedding)* boda *f*; **m. bureau**, agencia *f* matrimonial; **m. certificate**, certificado *m* de matrimonio.

married ['mærɪd] *adj* casado,-a; **m. life**, vida *f* conyugal.

marrow ['mærəʊ] *n* 1 *(bone)* **m.**, médula *f*. 2 *Bot* calabacín *m*.

marry ['mærɪ] *vtr (take in marriage)* casarse con; *(give in marriage)* casar *(to, con)*; *(unite in marriage)* casar; **to get married**, casarse.

Mars [mɑːz] *n* Marte *m*.

marsh [mɑːʃ] *n* pantano *m*; **salt m.**, marisma *f*.

marshal ['mɑːʃəl] I *n* 1 *Mil* mariscal *m*. 2 *GB (at sports event etc)* oficial *m*. 3 *US (sheriff)* alguacil *m*. 4 *US (of police or fire department)* jefe *m*. II *vtr* 1 *Mil* formar. 2 *(facts etc)* ordenar.

marshy ['mɑːʃɪ] *adj (marshier, marshiest)* pantanoso,-a.

martial ['mɑːʃəl] *adj* marcial; **m. arts**, artes *fpl* marciales; **m. law**, ley *f* marcial.

martyr ['mɑːtər] I *n* mártir *mf*. II *vtr* martirizar.

martyrdom ['mɑːtədəm] *n* martirio *m*.

marvel ['mɑːvəl] I *n* maravilla *f*. II *vi* **to**

m. at, maravillarse de.

marvellous, US **marvelous** [ˈmɑːvələs] adj maravilloso,-a.

Marxism [ˈmɑːksɪzəm] n marxismo m.

Marxist [ˈmɑːksɪst] adj & n marxista (mf).

marzipan [ˈmɑːzɪpæn] n mazapán m.

mascara [mæˈskɑːrə] n rímel m.

mascot [ˈmæskət] n mascota f.

masculine [ˈmæskjʊlɪn] adj masculino,-a; (woman) hombruna.

mash [mæʃ] I n (for animals) afrecho m. II vtr to m. (up), machacar; mashed potatoes, puré m de patatas.

mask [mɑːsk] I n máscara f; (of doctor, dentist etc) mascarilla f. II vtr enmascarar; fig (conceal) ocultar (from, de).

masochist [ˈmæsəkɪst] adj & n masoquista (mf).

mason [ˈmeɪsən] n 1 (builder) albañil m. 2 (freemason) masón m, francmasón m.

masonic [məˈsɒnɪk] adj masónico,-a.

masonry [ˈmeɪsənrɪ] n (stonework) albañilería f.

masquerade [mæskəˈreɪd] I n (pretence) farsa f. II vi to m. as, hacerse pasar por.

mass¹ [mæs] n Rel misa f; to say m., decir misa.

mass² [mæs] I n 1 masa f. 2 (large quantity) montón m; (of people) multitud f. 3 the masses, las masas. II adj masivo,-a; m. media, medios mpl de comunicación (de masas); m. production, fabricación f en serie. III vi (people) congregarse; Mil concentrarse.

massacre [ˈmæsəkər] I n masacre f. II vtr masacrar.

massage [ˈmæsɑːʒ, mæˈsɑːdʒ] I n masaje m. II vtr dar masajes a. 2 fig (figures) amañar.

masseur [mæˈsɜːr] n masajista m.

masseuse [mæˈsɜːz] n masajista f.

massive [ˈmæsɪv] adj enorme; (heart attack) grave.

mast [mɑːst] n 1 Naut mástil m. 2 Rad TV torre f.

master [ˈmɑːstər] I n 1 (of dog, servant) amo m; (of household) señor m. 2 GB (teacher) profesor m. 3 Univ m.'s degree, ≈ máster m. 4 (expert) maestro m. 5 (boy) M. James Brown, el señor James Brown. II adj 1 m. copy, original m; m. key, llave f maestra. 2 (expert) maestro,-a. III vtr 1 (person, situation) dominar. 2 (subject, skill) llegar a dominar.

masterful [ˈmɑːstəful] adj autoritario,-a; (imperious) imperioso,-a; (personality) dominante.

masterly [ˈmɑːstəlɪ] adj magistral.

mastermind [ˈmɑːstəmaɪnd] I n (person) cerebro m. II vtr ser el cerebro de.

masterpiece [ˈmɑːstəpiːs] n obra f maestra.

mastery [ˈmɑːstərɪ] n 1 (control) dominio m (of, de). 2 (skill, expertise) maestría f.

masturbate [ˈmæstəbeɪt] vi masturbarse.

mat¹ [mæt] n (rug) alfombrilla f; (doormat) felpudo m; (rush mat) estera f; Sport colchoneta f.

mat² [mæt] adj mate.

match¹ [mætʃ] n cerilla f, fósforo m.

match² [mætʃ] I n 1 Sport partido m; Box combate m. 2 fig to meet one's m., (equal) encontrar uno la horma de su zapato. II vtr 1 (equal, be the equal of) igualar. 2 (be in harmony with) armonizar; they are well matched, (teams) van iguales; (couple) hacen buena pareja. 3 (colours, clothes) hacer juego con; (pair of socks, gloves) ser el compañero de. III vi (harmonize) hacer juego.

matchbox [ˈmætʃbɒks] n caja f de cerillas.

matching [ˈmætʃɪŋ] adj que hace juego.

mate [meɪt] I n 1 (at school, work) compañero,-a m,f, colega m,f; GB fam (friend) amigo,-a m,f. 2 Zool (male) macho m; (female) hembra f. 3 (assistant) ayudante mf. 4 Naut first/second m., primer/segundo oficial. II vtr Zool aparear. III vi Zool aparearse.

material [məˈtɪərɪəl] I n 1 (substance) materia f. 2 (cloth) tejido m, tela f. 3 (information) material m. 4 materials, (ingredients, equipment) materiales mpl. II adj 1 substancial. 2 (not spiritual) material.

materialistic [mətɪərɪəˈlɪstɪk] adj materialista.

materialize [məˈtɪərɪəlaɪz] vi 1 (hopes) realizarse; (plan, idea) concretarse. 2 (show up) presentarse.

maternal [məˈtɜːnəl] adj maternal; (uncle etc) materno,-a.

maternity [məˈtɜːnɪtɪ] n maternidad f; m. dress, vestido m premamá; m. hospital, maternidad f.

math [mæθ] n US → maths.

mathematical [mæθəˈmætɪkəl] adj matemático,-a.

mathematician [mæθəməˈtɪʃən] n matemático,-a m,f.

mathematics [mæθəˈmætɪks] n matemáticas fpl.

maths [mæθs] n fam matemáticas fpl.

matinée [ˈmætɪneɪ] n Cin sesión f de tarde; Theat función f de tarde.

mating [ˈmeɪtɪŋ] n apareamiento m; m. call, reclamo m; m. season, época f de celo.

matriculation [mətrɪkjʊˈleɪʃən] n Univ matriculación f.

matrimonial [mætrɪˈməʊnɪəl] adj matrimonial.

matrimony [ˈmætrɪmənɪ] n matrimonio m; (married life) vida f conyugal.

matrix [ˈmeɪtrɪks] n (pl matrices [ˈmeɪtrɪsiːz]) matriz f.

matron [ˈmeɪtrən] n (in hospital) enfermera f jefe.

matronly ['meɪtrənlɪ] adj madura y recia.
matt [mæt] adj mate.
matted ['mætɪd] adj enmarañado,-a.
matter ['mætər] n 1 (affair, question) asunto m; as a m. of course, por rutina; as a m. of fact, en realidad; that's another m., eso es otra cosa. 2 (problem) what's the m.?, ¿qué pasa? 3 no m. what he does, haga lo que haga; no m. when, no importa cuando; no m. where you go, dondequiera que vayas; no m. how clever he is, por muy inteligente que sea; no m. how, como sea. 4 (substance) materia f, sustancia f. 5 (content) contenido m; (subject) tema m. 6 Med (pus) pus m. II vi importar; it doesn't m., no importa, da igual.
matter-of-fact ['mætərəvfækt] adj (person) práctico,-a; (account) realista; (style) prosaico,-a.
mattress ['mætrɪs] n colchón m.
mature [mə'tʃuər] I adj maduro,-a; Fin vencido,-a. II vi madurar; Fin vencer. III vtr madurar.
maturity [mə'tʃuərɪtɪ] n madurez f.
maul [mɔːl] vtr 1 (wound) agredir. 2 (handle roughly) maltratar. 3 (touch in unpleasant way) sobar.
mauve [məʊv] adj & n malva (m).
max [mæks] abbr of **maximum**, máximo m, max.
maxim ['mæksɪm] n máxima f.
maximize ['mæksɪmaɪz] vtr maximizar.
maximum ['mæksɪməm] I n (pl maxima ['mæksɪmə]) máximo m. II adj máximo, -a.
may [meɪ] v aux (pt might) 1 (possibility, probability) poder, ser posible; be that as it m., sea como sea; come what m., pase lo que pase; he m. or might come, puede que venga; you m. or might as well stay, más vale que te quedes. 2 (permission) poder; m. I?, ¿me permite?; you m. smoke, pueden fumar. 3 (wish) ojalá (+ subj); m. you always be happy!, ¡ojalá seas siempre feliz!
May [meɪ] n mayo m; M. Day, el Primero or el Uno de Mayo.
maybe ['meɪbɪ] adv quizá(s), tal vez.
mayhem ['meɪhem] n (disturbance) alboroto m; (havoc) estragos mpl.
mayonnaise [meɪə'neɪz] n mayonesa f, mahonesa f.
mayor [meər] n (man) alcalde m; (woman) alcaldesa f.
mayoress ['meərɪs] n alcaldesa f.
maze [meɪz] n laberinto m.
MD [em'diː] 1 abbr of **Doctor of Medicine**, Dr. en Medicina. 2 fam abbr of **Managing Director**.
me [miː] pron 1 (as object) me; he gave it to me, me lo dio; listen to me, escúchame; she knows me, me conoce. 2 (after prep) mí; it's for me, es para mí; with

me, conmigo. 3 (emphatic) yo; it's me, soy yo; what about me?, ¿y yo, qué?
meadow ['medəʊ] n prado m, pradera f.
meagre, US **meager** ['miːgər] adj exiguo,-a.
meal¹ [miːl] n (flour) harina f.
meal² [miːl] n (food) comida f.
mealtime ['miːltaɪm] n hora f de comer.
mean¹ [miːn] vtr (pt & pp **meant**) 1 (signify) significar, querer decir; what do you m. by that?, ¿qué quieres decir con eso? 2 (intend) pensar, tener la intención de; I m. it, (te) lo digo en serio; she was meant to arrive on the 7th, tenía que or debía llegar el día 7; they m. well, tienen buenas intenciones; she didn't m. to do it, lo hizo sin querer. 3 (entail) suponer. 4 (refer to) referirse a. 5 (destine) destinar (for, a, para).
mean² [miːn] adj (meaner, meanest) 1 (miserly) tacaño,-a. 2 (unkind) malo,-a; (petty) mezquino,-a; US (bad-tempered) malhumorado,-a; to be m. to sb, tratar mal a algn. 3 (inferior) mediocre; (origins) humilde. 4 it was no m. feat, fue toda una hazaña.
mean³ [miːn] I adj (average) medio,-a. II n (average) promedio m; Math media f.
meander [mɪ'ændər] vi 1 (river) serpentear; (person) vagar; fig (digress) divagar.
meaning ['miːnɪŋ] n sentido m, significado m.
meaningful ['miːnɪŋfʊl] adj significativo,-a.
meaningless ['miːnɪŋlɪs] adj sin sentido.
meanness ['miːnnɪs] n 1 (miserliness) tacañería f. 2 (nastiness) maldad f.
means [miːnz] n 1 sing or pl (method) medio m, manera f; by m. of, por medio de, mediante. 2 pl (resources, wealth) medios mpl (de vida), recursos mpl (económicos); to live beyond one's m., vivir por encima de sus posibilidades. 3 by all m.!, ¡por supuesto!; by no m., de ninguna manera.
meant [ment] pt & pp → **mean¹**.
meantime ['miːntaɪm] I adv mientras tanto. II n in the m., mientras tanto.
meanwhile ['miːnwaɪl] adv mientras tanto.
measles ['miːzəlz] n sarampión m.
measure ['meʒər] I n 1 (action, step) medida f. 2 (ruler) regla f. 3 in some m., hasta cierto punto. 4 Mus compás m. II vtr (object, area) medir; (person) tomar las medidas de. ◆**measure up** vi to m. (up) (to sth), estar a la altura de (algo).
measurement ['meʒəmənt] n medida f.
meat [miːt] n carne f; Culin m. pie, empanada f de carne.
meatball ['miːtbɔːl] n albóndiga f.
meaty ['miːtɪ] adj (meatier, meatiest) 1 carnoso,-a. 2 fig (story) jugoso,-a.

Mecca ['mekə] n la Meca.
mechanic [mɪ'kænɪk] n (person) mecánico,-a m,f.
mechanical [mɪ'kænɪkəl] adj mecánico, -a.
mechanics [mɪ'kænɪks] n 1 sing (science) mecánica f. 2 pl (technical aspects) mecanismo m sing.
mechanism ['mekənɪzəm] n mecanismo m.
medal ['medəl] n medalla f.
medallion [mɪ'dæljən] n medallón m.
medallist, US medalist ['medəlɪst] n medalla f.
meddle ['medəl] vi entrometerse (in, en); **to m. with sth,** manosear algo.
media ['miːdɪə] npl medios mpl de comunicación m. coverage, cobertura periodística.
median ['miːdɪən] I adj mediano,-a. II n Geom mediana f; Math valor mediano.
mediate ['miːdɪeɪt] vi mediar.
mediator ['miːdɪeɪtər] n mediador,-a m,f.
medical ['medɪkəl] I adj (treatment) médico,-a; (book) de medicina. II n fam reconocimiento médico.
medicated ['medɪkeɪtɪd] adj medicinal.
medicine ['medsɪn, 'medɪsɪn] n (science) medicina f; (drugs etc) medicamento m.
medieval [medɪ'iːvəl] adj medieval.
mediocre [miːdɪ'əʊkər] adj mediocre.
meditate ['medɪteɪt] vi meditar (on, sobre).
meditation [medɪ'teɪʃən] n meditación f.
Mediterranean [medɪtə'reɪnɪən] I adj mediterráneo,-a. II n **the M.,** el Mediterráneo.
medium ['miːdɪəm] I adj (average) mediano,-a; Rad **m. wave,** onda media. II n 1 (pl **media**) (means) medio m. 2 (pl **mediums**) (spiritualist) médium mf.
medley ['medlɪ] n (mixture) mezcla f; Mus popurrí m.
meek [miːk] adj manso,-a, sumiso,-a; (humble) humilde.
meet [miːt] I vtr (pt & pp **met**) 1 (by chance) encontrar, encontrarse con; (by arrangement) reunirse con; (in formal meeting) entrevistarse con. 2 (get to know) conocer; **I'd like you to m. my mother,** quiero presentarle a mi madre; **the first time I met him,** cuando lo conocí; **pleased to m. you!,** ¡mucho gusto! 3 (await arrival of) esperar; (collect) ir a buscar. 4 (danger) encontrar; (opponent) enfrentarse con. 5 (satisfy) satisfacer; (obligations) cumplir con; (expenses) hacer frente a. II vi (by chance) encontrarse; (by arrangement) reunirse; (formal meeting) entrevistarse; (get to know each other) conocerse; Sport enfrentarse; (join) unirse; (rivers) confluir; **their eyes met,** cruzaron las miradas. III n (hunting) partida f de caza. ◆**meet with** vtr (difficulty) trope-

zar con; (loss) sufrir; (success) tener; esp US (person) reunirse con.
meeting ['miːtɪŋ] n (chance encounter) encuentro m; (prearranged) cita f; (formal) entrevista f; (of committee etc) reunión f; (of assembly) sesión f; (of shareholders) junta f; (rally) mitin m; Sport encuentro m; (of rivers) confluencia f.
megabyte ['megəbaɪt] n Comput megabyte m.
megaphone ['megəfəʊn] n megáfono m.
melancholy ['melənkəlɪ] I n melancolía f. II adj melancólico,-a.
Melilla [me'liːjə] n Melilla.
mellow ['meləʊ] I adj maduro,-a; (wine) añejo,-a; (colour, voice) suave; (person) apacible. II vi (fruit) madurar; (colour, voice) suavizarse.
melodramatic [melədrə'mætɪk] adj melodramático,-a.
melody ['melədɪ] n melodía f.
melon ['melən] n melón m.
melt [melt] I vtr (metal) fundir; fig (sb's heart) ablandar. II vi (snow) derretirse; (metal) fundirse; fig ablandarse. ◆**melt away** vi (snow) derretirse; fig (money) desaparecer; fig (confidence) desvanecerse. ◆**melt down** vtr (metal) fundir.
melting ['meltɪŋ] n fundición f; **m. point,** punto m de fusión; **m. pot,** crisol m.
member ['membər] n miembro mf; (of a society) socio,-a m,f; (of a party, union) afiliado,-a m,f; **M. of Parliament,** diputado,-a m,f.
membership ['membəʃɪp] n (state) calidad f de socio; (entry) ingreso m; Pol afiliación f; (number of members) número m de socios; **m. card,** carnet m de socio.
memento [mə'mentəʊ] n recuerdo m.
memo ['meməʊ] n (official note) memorándum m; (personal note) nota f, apunte m.
memoirs ['memwɑːz] npl memorias fpl.
memorable ['memərəbəl] adj memorable.
memorandum [memə'rændəm] n (pl **memoranda** (official note) memorándum m; (personal note) nota f, apunte m.
memorial [mɪ'mɔːrɪəl] I adj (plaque etc) conmemorativo,-a. II n monumento conmemorativo.
memorize ['meməraɪz] vtr memorizar, aprender de memoria.
memory ['memərɪ] n memoria f; (recollection) recuerdo m.
men [men] npl → man.
menace ['menɪs] I n (threat) amenaza f; (danger) peligro m; fam (person) pesado,-a m,f. II vtr amenazar.
menacing ['menɪsɪŋ] adj amenazador,-a.
menagerie [mɪ'nædʒərɪ] n casa f de fieras.
mend [mend] I vtr reparar, arreglar; (clothes) remendar; (socks etc) zurcir. II vi

(ill person) reponerse. **III** n *(patch)* remiendo m; *(darn)* zurcido m; *fig* **to be on the m.,** ir mejorando.

mending ['mendɪŋ] n *(repair)* reparación f; *(darning)* zurcido m; *(clothes for mending)* ropa f para remendar.

menial ['miːnɪəl] adj *(task)* servil, bajo,-a.

menopause ['menəpɔːz] n menopausia f.

menstrual ['menstruəl] adj menstrual.

menstruation [menstru'eɪʃən] n menstruación f.

mental ['mentəl] adj **1** mental; **m. home, m. hospital,** hospital psiquiátrico; **m. illness,** enfermedad f mental. **2** fam *(crazy)* chalado,-a. ◆**mentally** adv **m.** ill, enfermo,-a mental; **to be m. handicapped,** ser un,-a disminuido,-a psíquico,-a.

mentality [men'tælɪtɪ] n mentalidad f.

mention ['menʃən] **I** n mención f. **II** vtr mencionar; **don't m. it!,** ¡de nada!

mentor ['mentɔːr] n mentor m.

menu ['menjuː] n **1** *(card)* carta f; *(fixed meal)* menú m; **today's m.,** menú del día. **2** Comput menú m.

MEP [emi'piː] abbr of **Member of the European Parliament,** eurodiputado,-a mf.

mercenary ['mɜːsɪnərɪ] adj & n mercenario,-a *(m,f)*.

merchandise ['mɜːtʃəndaɪz] n mercancías fpl, géneros mpl.

merchant ['mɜːtʃənt] n Com Fin comerciante mf; *(retailer)* detallista mf; **m. bank,** banco m comercial; **m. navy,** marina f mercante.

merciful ['mɜːsɪfʊl] adj clemente, compasivo,-a *(towards, con)*.

merciless ['mɜːsɪlɪs] adj despiadado,-a.

mercury ['mɜːkjʊrɪ] n mercurio m.

Mercury ['mɜːkjʊrɪ] n Mercurio m.

mercy ['mɜːsɪ] n misericordia f, compasión f; **at the m. of,** a la merced de; **to have m. on,** tener compasión de.

mere [mɪər] adj mero,-a, simple. ◆**merely** adv simplemente.

merge [mɜːdʒ] **I** vtr *(blend)* unir *(with, con)*; Com fusionar. **II** vi unirse; *(roads)* empalmar; Com fusionarse.

merger ['mɜːdʒər] n Com fusión f.

meringue [mə'ræŋ] n merengue m.

merit ['merɪt] **I** n *(of person)* mérito m; *(of plan etc)* ventaja f. **II** vtr merecer.

mermaid ['mɜːmeɪd] n sirena f.

merry ['merɪ] adj *(merrier, merriest)* alegre; fam *(tipsy)* achispado,-a; **m. Christmas!,** ¡felices Navidades!

merry-go-round ['merɪɡəʊraʊnd] n tiovivo m.

mesh [meʃ] **I** n Tex malla f; Tech engranaje m; fig red f. **II** vtr Tech engranar.

mesmerize ['mezməraɪz] vtr hipnotizar.

mess [mes] **I** n **1** *(confusion)* confusión f; *(disorder)* desorden m; **to be in a m.,** *(of*

room etc) estar desordenado,-a. **2** *(in life, affairs)* lío m; **to get into a m.,** meterse en un lío. **3** *(dirt)* suciedad f. **4** Mil *(food)* rancho m. **5** Mil *(room)* comedor m. ◆**mess about, mess around** fam **I** vtr fastidiar. **II** vi *(act the fool)* hacer el primo; *(idle)* gandulear; *(kill time)* pasar el rato. ◆**mess about with** vtr fam *(fiddle with)* manosear; **to m. about with sb,** tener un lío con algn. ◆**mess up** vtr fam *(make untidy)* desordenar; *(dirty)* ensuciar; *(spoil)* estropear.

message ['mesɪdʒ] n *(communication)* recado m; *(of story etc)* mensaje m; fam **to get the m.,** comprender.

messenger ['mesɪndʒər] n mensajero,-a m,f.

Messrs ['mesəz] Com abbr of pl of **Mr,** Sres.

messy ['mesɪ] adj *(messier, messiest)* *(untidy)* desordenado,-a; *(confused)* enredado,-a; *(dirty)* sucio,-a.

met [met] pt & pp → **meet.**

metabolism [me'tæbəlɪzəm] n metabolismo m.

metal ['metəl] **I** n metal m. **II** adj metálico,-a.

metallic [mɪ'tælɪk] adj metálico,-a; **m. blue,** azul metalizado.

metallurgy [me'tælədʒɪ] n metalurgia f.

metalwork ['metəlwɜːk] n *(craft)* metalistería f; *(objects)* objetos mpl de metal.

metaphor ['metəfɔːr, 'metəfər] n metáfora f.

mete [miːt] vtr **to m. out,** imponer.

meteor ['miːtɪər] n bólido m.

meteoric [miːtɪ'ɒrɪk] adj meteórico,-a.

meteorite ['miːtɪəraɪt] n meteorito m.

meteorology [miːtɪə'rɒlədʒɪ] n meteorología f.

meter[1] ['miːtər] n contador m.

meter[2] ['miːtər] n US → **metre.**

method ['meθəd] n método m.

methodical [mɪ'θɒdɪkəl] adj metódico,-a.

Methodist ['meθədɪst] adj & n metodista *(mf)*.

meths [meθs] n fam abbr of **methylated spirits.**

methylated spirits [meθɪleɪtɪd'spɪrɪts] n alcohol metilado or desnaturalizado.

meticulous [mə'tɪkjʊləs] adj meticuloso,-a.

metre ['miːtər] n metro m.

metric ['metrɪk] adj métrico,-a.

metropolis [mɪ'trɒpəlɪs] n metrópoli f.

metropolitan [metrə'pɒlɪtən] adj metropolitano,-a.

mettle ['metəl] n valor m.

mew [mjuː] vi *(cat)* maullar.

mews [mjuːz] n *(street)* callejuela f; **m. flat,** apartamento m de lujo en unas caballerizas reconvertidas.

Mexican ['meksɪkən] adj & n mejicano,-a *(m,f)*, mexicano,-a *(m,f)*.

Mexico ['meksikəu] n Méjico, México.

miaow [mi:'au] I vi maullar. II n maullido m.

mice [mais] npl → **mouse**.

mickey ['miki] n fam **to take the m. (out of sb)**, tomar el pelo (a algn).

microbe ['maikrəub] n microbio m.

microchip ['maikrəutʃip] n microplaqueta f, microchip m.

microcomputer [maikrəukəm'pju:tər] n microordenador m.

microcosm ['maikrəukɒzəm] n microcosmo m.

microfilm ['maikrəufilm] n microfilm m.

microphone ['maikrəfəun] n micrófono m.

microprocessor [maikrəu'prəusesər] n microprocesador m.

microscope ['maikrəskəup] n microscopio m.

microwave ['maikrəuweiv] n microonda f; **m. (oven)**, (horno m) microondas m inv.

mid [mid] adj (in) **m. afternoon**, a media tarde; (in) **m. April**, a mediados de abril; **to be in one's m. thirties**, tener unos treinta y cinco años.

midair [mid'eər] I adj (collision, explosion) en el aire. II n fig **to leave sth in m.**, dejar algo en el aire.

midday [mid'dei] I n mediodía m. II adj de mediodía.

middle ['midəl] I adj de en medio; **m. age**, mediana edad f; **the M. Ages**, la Edad Media; **the m. class**, la clase media. II n 1 centro m, medio m; **in the m. of**, en medio de; **in the m. of winter**, en pleno invierno; fam **in the m. of nowhere**, en el quinto pino. 2 fam (waist) cintura f.

middle-aged [midəl'eidʒd] adj de mediana edad.

middle-class [midəl'klɑ:s] adj de clase media.

middleman ['midəlmæn] n intermediario m.

middleweight ['midəlweit] n peso medio.

middling ['midliŋ] adj mediano,-a.

midfielder [mid'fi:ldər] n Sport centrocampista mf.

midge [midʒ] n mosca enana.

midget ['midʒit] n enano,-a m,f.

Midlands ['midlændz] npl **the M.**, la región central de Inglaterra.

midnight ['midnait] n medianoche f.

midst [midst] prep **in the m. of**, en medio de.

midsummer [mid'sʌmər] n pleno verano; **M.'s Day**, Día m de San Juan (24 de junio).

midway ['midwei] adv a medio camino.

midweek ['midwi:k] I adv entre semana. II adj de entre semana.

midwife ['midwaif] n comadrona f, partera f.

midwifery ['midwifəri] n obstetricia f.

midwinter [mid'wintər] n pleno invierno m.

might¹ [mait] v aux → **may**.

might² [mait] n fml fuerza f, poder m.

mighty ['maiti] I adj (**mightier, mightiest**) (strong) fuerte; (powerful) poderoso, -a; (great) enorme.

migraine ['mi:grein, 'maigrein] n jaqueca f.

migrant ['maigrənt] I adj migratorio,-a. II n (person) emigrante mf; (bird) ave migratoria.

migrate [mai'greit] vi emigrar.

migration [mai'greiʃən] n migración f.

mike [maik] n fam (abbr of **microphone**) micro m.

mild [maild] adj (person, character) apacible; (climate) templado,-a; (punishment) leve; (tobacco, taste) suave. ◆**mildly** adv (softly, gently) suavemente; (slightly) ligeramente; **and that's putting it m.**, y esto es decir poco.

mildew ['mildju:] n moho m; (on plants) añublo m.

mildness ['maildnis] n (of character) apacibilidad f; (of climate, taste) suavidad f; (of punishment) levedad f.

mile [mail] n milla f; fam **miles better**, muchísimo mejor.

mileage ['mailidʒ] n kilometraje m.

milestone ['mailstəun] n hito m.

milieu ['mi:ljɜ:] n medio m ambiente.

militant ['militənt] adj & n militante (mf).

military ['militəri] adj militar; **to do one's m. service**, hacer el servicio militar.

militia [mi'liʃə] n milicia f.

milk [milk] I n leche f; **m. chocolate**, chocolate m con leche; **m. shake**, batido m. II vtr 1 (cow, goat) ordeñar. 2 fam **they milked him of all his money**, le sangraron hasta la última peseta.

milkman ['milkmən] n lechero m.

milky ['milki] adj (**milkier, milkiest**) lechoso,-a; (colour) pálido,-a; **M. Way**, Vía Láctea.

mill [mil] I n (grinder) molino m; (for coffee) molinillo m; (factory) fábrica f; **cotton m.**, hilandería f. II vtr moler. ◆**mill about, mill around** vi arremolinarse.

millennium [mi'leniəm] n (pl **millenniums** or **milenia** [mi'leniə]) milenio m.

miller ['milər] n molinero,-a m,f.

millet ['milit] n mijo m.

milligram(me) ['miligræm] n miligramo m.

millilitre, US **milliliter** ['mili:li:tər] n mililitro m.

millimetre, US **millimeter** ['mili:mi:tər]

n milímetro *m*.

milliner ['mɪlɪnər] *n* sombrerero,-a *m,f*.

millinery ['mɪlɪnərɪ] *n* sombreros *mpl* de señora.

million ['mɪljən] *n* millón *m*.

millionaire [mɪljə'neər] *n* millonario,-a *m,f*.

millstone ['mɪlstəʊn] *n* muela *f*; *fig* carga *f*.

mime [maɪm] **I** *n* (*art*) mímica *f*; (*play*) pantomima *f*. **II** *vtr* representar con gestos.

mimic ['mɪmɪk] **I** *adj & n* mímico,-a (*m,f*). **II** *vtr* imitar.

mimicry ['mɪmɪkrɪ] *n* imitación *f*.

minaret ['mɪnəret] *n* alminar *m*, minarete *m*.

mince [mɪns] **I** *n* *GB* (*meat*) carne picada; **m. pie**, pastel *m* de picadillo de fruta. **II** *vtr* picar; *fig* **he doesn't m. his words**, no tiene pelos en la lengua. **III** *vi* (*walk*) **to m. (along)**, andar con pasos menuditos.

mincemeat ['mɪnsmiːt] *n* (*dried fruit*) conserva *f* de picadillo de fruta; (*meat*) carne picada.

mincer ['mɪnsər] *n* picadora *f* de carne.

mind [maɪnd] **I** *n* **1** (*intellect*) mente *f*; (*brain*) cabeza *f*; **what kind of car do you have in m.?**, ¿en qué clase de coche estás pensando?; **to lose one's m.**, perder el juicio; **it slipped my m.**, lo olvidé por completo; **to call sth to m.**, recordar algo. **2** (*opinion*) **to be in two minds about sth**, estar indeciso,-a; **to my m.**, a mi parecer. **II** *vtr* **1** (*child*) cuidar; (*house*) vigilar; (*be careful of*) tener cuidado con; **m. the step!**, ¡ojo con el escalón!; **m. your own business!**, ¡no te metas donde no te llaman! **2** (*object to*) tener inconveniente en; **I wouldn't m. a cup of coffee**, me vendría bien un café; **never m.**, no importa. **III** *vi* **1 I you, he is fifty**, ten en cuenta que tiene cincuenta años. **2** (*object*) importar; **do you m. if I open the window?**, ¿le importa que abra la ventana?

minder ['maɪndər] *n* *fam* (*bodyguard*) guardaespaldas *m inv*; (*for child*) niñera *f*; (*babysitter*) canguro *mf*.

mindful ['maɪndfʊl] *adj* consciente.

mindless ['maɪndlɪs] *adj* (*task*) de autómata; (*violence*) injustificable.

mine¹ [maɪn] *poss pron* (el) mío, (la) mía, (los) míos, (las) mías, lo mío; **a friend of m.**, un amigo mío; **these gloves are m.**, estos guantes son míos; **which is m.?**, ¿cuál es el mío?

mine² [maɪn] **I** *n* mina *f*; *fig* **a m. of information**, un pozo de información. **II** *vtr* (*coal etc*) extraer; *Mil* minar.

minefield ['maɪnfiːld] *n* campo *m* de minas.

miner ['maɪnər] *n* minero,-a *m,f*.

mineral ['mɪnərəl] **I** *adj* mineral; **m.**

water, agua *f* mineral. **II** *n* mineral *m*.

minesweeper ['maɪnswiːpər] *n* dragaminas *m inv*.

mingle ['mɪŋgəl] *vi* mezclarse.

miniature ['mɪnɪtʃər] **I** *n* miniatura *f*. **II** *adj* (*railway*) en miniatura; (*camera, garden*) diminuto,-a.

minibus ['mɪnɪbʌs] *n* microbús *m*.

minim ['mɪnɪm] *n* *Mus* blanca *f*.

minimal ['mɪnɪməl] *adj* mínimo,-a.

minimum ['mɪnɪməm] **I** *adj* mínimo,-a; **m. wage**, salario mínimo. **II** *n* mínimo *m*.

mining ['maɪnɪŋ] **I** *n* minería *f*, explotación *f* de minas; *Mil Naut* minado *m*. **II** *adj* minero,-a.

miniskirt ['mɪnɪskɜːt] *n* minifalda *f*.

minister ['mɪnɪstər] **I** *n* *Pol* ministro,-a *m,f*; *Rel* pastor,-a *m,f*. **II** *vi* **to m. to sb**, atender a algn.

ministerial [mɪnɪ'stɪərɪəl] *adj* *Pol* ministerial.

ministry ['mɪnɪstrɪ] *n* *Pol* ministerio *m*; *Rel* sacerdocio *m*.

mink [mɪŋk] *n* visón *m*; **m. coat**, abrigo *m* de visón.

minnow ['mɪnəʊ] *n* piscardo *m*.

minor ['maɪnər] **I** *adj* (*lesser*) menor; (*unimportant*) sin importancia; (*role*) secundario,-a; *Mus* menor. **II** *n* *Jur* menor *mf* de edad.

Minorca [mɪ'nɔːkə] *n* Menorca *f*.

minority [maɪ'nɒrɪtɪ] *n* minoría *f*; **to be in the m.**, ser (la) minoría; *Pol* **m. party**, partido minoritario.

mint¹ [mɪnt] **I** *n* *Fin* **the M.**, la Casa de la Moneda; **in m. condition**, en perfecto estado. **II** *vtr* (*coin, words*) acuñar.

mint² [mɪnt] *n* *Bot* menta *f*; (*sweet*) pastilla *f* de menta.

minus ['maɪnəs] **I** *prep* **5 m. 3**, 5 menos 3; **m. 10 degrees**, 10 grados bajo cero. **II** *adj* negativo,-a. **III** *n* **m. (sign)**, signo *m* (de) menos.

minute¹ ['mɪnɪt] *n* **1** minuto *m*; **at the last m.**, a última hora; **just a m.**, (espera) un momento; **this very m.**, ahora mismo. **2 minutes**, (*notes*) el acta.

minute² [maɪ'njuːt] *adj* (*tiny*) diminuto, -a; (*examination*) minucioso,-a.

miracle ['mɪrəkəl] *n* milagro *m*.

miraculous [mɪ'rækjʊləs] *adj* milagroso, -a.

mirage [mɪ'rɑːʒ] *n* espejismo *m*.

mire [maɪər] *n* fango *m*, lodo *m*; (*muddy place*) lodazal *m*.

mirror ['mɪrər] **I** *n* espejo *m*; *fig* reflejo *m*; **rear-view m.**, retrovisor *m*; **m. image**, réplica *f*. **II** *vtr* reflejar.

mirth [mɜːθ] *n* alegría *f*; (*laughter*) risas *fpl*.

misadventure [mɪsəd'ventʃər] *n* desgracia *f*; **death by m.**, muerte *f* accidental.

misanthropist [mɪ'zænθrəpɪst] *n* misántropo,-a *m,f*.

misapprehension [ˌmɪsæprɪ'henʃən] n malentendido m.

misbehave [ˌmɪsbɪ'heɪv] vi portarse mal.

miscalculate [mɪs'kælkjʊleɪt] vtr & vi calcular mal.

miscarriage [ˌmɪs'kærɪdʒ] n Med aborto m (espontáneo); **m. of justice**, error m judicial.

miscellaneous [ˌmɪsɪ'leɪnɪəs] adj variado,-a; **m. expenses**, gastos diversos.

mischief ['mɪstʃɪf] n (naughtiness) travesura f; fml (evil) malicia f; fam (harm) daño m; **to get up to m.**, hacer travesuras.

mischievous ['mɪstʃɪvəs] adj (naughty) travieso,-a; (playful) juguetón,-ona; fml (wicked) malicioso,-a.

misconception [ˌmɪskən'sepʃən] n concepto erróneo.

misconduct [mɪs'kɒndʌkt] n mala conducta; **professional m.**, error m profesional.

misconstrue [ˌmɪskən'struː] vtr interpretar mal.

miscount [mɪs'kaʊnt] vtr (votes etc) contar mal.

misdeed [mɪs'diːd] n fechoría f.

misdemeanour, US **misdemeanor** [ˌmɪsdɪ'miːnər] n (misdeed) fechoría f; Jur delito m menor.

miser ['maɪzər] n avaro,-a m,f.

miserable ['mɪzərəbəl] adj (sad) triste; (unfortunate) desgraciado,-a; (wretched) miserable.

miserly ['maɪzəlɪ] adj avaro,-a, tacaño,-a.

misery ['mɪzərɪ] n (sadness) tristeza f; (wretchedness) desgracia f; (suffering) sufrimiento m; (poverty) miseria f; fam (person) aguafiestas mf.

misfire [mɪs'faɪər] vi (engine, plan etc) fallar.

misfit ['mɪsfɪt] n (person) inadaptado,-a m,f.

misfortune [mɪs'fɔːtʃən] n desgracia f.

misgiving [mɪs'gɪvɪŋ] n (doubt) recelo m; (fear) temor m.

misguided [mɪs'gaɪdɪd] adj equivocado,-a.

mishandle [mɪs'hændl] vtr llevar or manejar mal.

mishap ['mɪshæp] n contratiempo m.

misinform [ˌmɪsɪn'fɔːm] vtr informar mal.

misinterpret [ˌmɪsɪn'tɜːprɪt] vtr interpretar mal.

misjudge [mɪs'dʒʌdʒ] vtr juzgar mal.

mislay [mɪs'leɪ] vtr extraviar.

mislead [mɪs'liːd] vtr despistar; (deliberately) engañar.

misleading [mɪs'liːdɪŋ] adj (erroneous) erróneo,-a; (deliberately) engañoso,-a.

mismanagement [mɪs'mænɪdʒmənt] n mala administración f.

misnomer [mɪs'nəʊmər] n nombre equivocado.

misogynist [mɪ'sɒdʒɪnɪst] n misógino,-a

m,f.

misplace [mɪs'pleɪs] vtr (trust) encauzar mal; (book, spectacles etc) extraviar.

misprint ['mɪsprɪnt] n errata f, error m de imprenta.

misrepresent [ˌmɪsreprɪ'zent] vtr (facts) desvirtuar; (words) tergiversar.

miss¹ [mɪs] n señorita f.

miss² [mɪs] **I** n (throw etc) fallo m; fam **to give sth a m.**, pasar de algo. **II** vtr 1 (when throwing) fallar; (when shooting) errar. 2 (train etc) perder; (opportunity) dejar pasar; **you have missed the point**, no has captado la idea; fig **to m. the boat**, perder el tren. 3 (omit) saltarse. 4 **I m. you**, te echo de menos. **III** vi (when throwing) fallar; (when shooting) errar; **is anything missing?**, ¿falta algo? ◆**miss out I** vtr (omit) saltarse; (on purpose) pasar por alto. **II** vtr **to m. out on**, perderse.

misshapen [mɪs'ʃeɪpən] adj deforme.

missile ['mɪsaɪl] US ['mɪsəl] n Mil misil m; (object thrown) proyectil m.

missing ['mɪsɪŋ] adj (object) perdido,-a; (person) desaparecido,-a; (from meeting etc) ausente; **m. person**, desaparecido,-a m,f; **three cups are m.**, faltan tres tazas.

mission ['mɪʃən] n misión f.

missionary ['mɪʃənərɪ] n misionero,-a m,f.

misspent ['mɪsspent] adj (youth) malgastado,-a.

mist [mɪst] **I** n neblina f; (thick) niebla f; (at sea) bruma f. **II** vi **to m. over or up**, (countryside) cubrirse de neblina; (window etc) empañarse.

mistake [mɪs'teɪk] **I** n error m; **by m.**, por equivocación; **I hurt him by m.**, le golpeé sin querer; **to make a m.**, equivocarse, cometer un error. **II** vtr (pt mistook; pp mistaken) (meaning) malentender; **to m. Jack for Bill**, confundir a Jack con Bill.

mistaken [mɪs'teɪkən] adj equivocado,-a, erróneo,-a; **you are m.**, estás equivocado,-a.

mister ['mɪstər] n señor m.

mistletoe ['mɪsltəʊ] n muérdago m.

mistook [mɪs'tʊk] pt → **mistake**.

mistreat [mɪs'triːt] vtr tratar mal.

mistress ['mɪstrɪs] n (of house) señora f, ama f; (lover) amante f; Educ (primary school) maestra f; (secondary school) profesora f.

mistrust [mɪs'trʌst] **I** n recelo m. **II** vtr desconfiar de.

misty ['mɪstɪ] adj (mistier, mistiest) (day) de niebla; (window etc) empañado,-a.

misunderstand [ˌmɪsʌndə'stænd] vtr & vi malentender.

misunderstanding [ˌmɪsʌndə'stændɪŋ] n malentendido m; (disagreement) desavenencia f.

misuse [mɪs'juːs] I *n* mal uso *m*; *(of funds)* malversación *f*; *(of power)* abuso *m*. II [mɪs'juːz] *vtr* emplear mal; *(funds)* malversar; *(power)* abusar de.

miter ['maɪtər] *n US → mitre*.

mitigate ['mɪtɪgeɪt] *vtr* atenuar.

mitigating ['mɪtɪgeɪtɪŋ] *adj* **m. circumstances**, circunstancias *fpl* atenuantes.

mitre ['maɪtər] *n* mitra *f*.

mitten ['mɪtən] *n* manopla *f*; *(fingerless)* mitón *m*.

mix [mɪks] I *n* mezcla *f*. II *vtr* mezclar. III *vi (blend)* mezclarse (**with**, con); *(go well together)* ir bien juntos. ◆**mix up** *vtr (confuse)* confundir (**with**, con); *(papers)* revolver; **to be mixed up in sth**, estar involucrado,-a en algo.

mixed [mɪkst] *adj (assorted)* surtido,-a; *(varied)* variado,-a; *(school)* mixto,-a; *(feelings)* contradictorio,-a.

mixed-up [mɪkst'ʌp] *adj (objects, papers etc)* revuelto,-a; *(person)* confuso,-a.

mixer ['mɪksər] *n* **1** *Culin* batidora *f*. **2 to be a good m.**, *(person)* tener don de gentes.

mixture ['mɪkstʃər] *n* mezcla *f*.

mix-up [mɪksʌp] *n fam* confusión *f*, lío *m*.

mm *abbr of* **millimetre(s)**, mm.

moan [məʊn] I *n (groan)* gemido *m*, quejido *m*. II *vi (groan)* gemir; *(complain)* quejarse (**about**, de).

moat [məʊt] *n* foso *m*.

mob [mɒb] I *n* multitud *f*; *(riff-raff)* gentuza *f*; **the m.**, el populacho. II *vtr* acosar.

mobile ['məʊbaɪl, US 'məʊbəl] I *adj* móvil; **m. home**, caravana *f*. II *n (hanging ornament)* móvil *m*.

nobility [məʊ'bɪlɪtɪ] *n* movilidad *f*.

mobilize ['məʊbɪlaɪz] *vtr* movilizar.

mock [mɒk] I *adj (sympathy etc)* fingido,-a; *(objects)* de imitación. II *vtr (make fun of)* burlarse de. III *vi* burlarse (**at**, de).

mockery ['mɒkərɪ] *n* burla *f*.

mode [məʊd] *n (manner)* modo *m*, estilo *m*; *(fashion)* moda *f*.

model ['mɒdəl] I *n* modelo *m*; *(fashion model)* modelo *mf*; *(scale)* **m.**, maqueta *f*. II *adj (railway)* en miniatura; *(pupil)* ejemplar; *(school)* modelo. III *vtr (clay etc)* modelar; *(clothes)* presentar. IV *vi (make models)* modelar; *(work as model)* trabajar de modelo.

modem ['məʊdem] *n Comput* modem *m*.

moderate¹ ['mɒdərɪt] I *adj* moderado,-a; *(reasonable)* razonable; *(average)* regular; *(ability)* mediocre. II *n Pol* moderado,-a *m,f*. ◆**moderately** *adv* medianamente.

moderate² ['mɒdəreɪt] I *vtr* moderar. II *vi* moderarse; *(wind)* calmarse; *(in debate)* arbitrar.

moderation [mɒdə'reɪʃən] *n* moderación *f*; **in m.**, con moderación.

modern ['mɒdən] *adj* moderno,-a; *(history)* contemporáneo,-a; **m. languages**, lenguas modernas.

modernize ['mɒdənaɪz] *vtr* modernizar.

modest ['mɒdɪst] *adj* modesto,-a; *(chaste)* púdico,-a; *(price)* módico,-a; *(success)* discreto,-a.

modesty ['mɒdɪstɪ] *n (humility)* modestia *f*; *(chastity)* pudor *m*.

modification [mɒdɪfɪ'keɪʃən] *n* modificación *f*.

modify ['mɒdɪfaɪ] *vtr* modificar.

module ['mɒdjuːl] *n* módulo *m*.

mogul ['məʊgʌl] *n* magnate *m*.

mohair ['məʊheər] I *n* mohair *m*. II *adj* de mohair.

moist [mɔɪst] *adj* húmedo,-a.

moisten ['mɔɪsən] *vtr* humedecer.

moisture ['mɔɪstʃər] *n* humedad *f*.

moisturizer ['mɔɪstʃəraɪzər] *n* crema *f* or leche *f* hidratante.

molar ['məʊlər] *n* muela *f*.

molasses [mə'læsɪz] *n* melaza *f*.

mold [məʊld] *n US → mould*.

mole¹ [məʊl] *n (beauty spot)* lunar *m*.

mole² [məʊl] *n (animal)* topo *m*.

molecule ['mɒlɪkjuːl] *n* molécula *f*.

molest [mə'lest] *vtr* importunar; *(sexually assault)* acosar (sexualmente).

mollycoddle ['mɒlɪkɒdəl] *vtr fam* mimar, consentir.

molt [məʊlt] *vi US → moult*.

molten ['məʊltən] *adj* fundido,-a; *(lava)* líquido,-a.

mom [mɒm] *n US fam* mamá *f*.

moment ['məʊmənt] *n* momento *m*; **at the m.**, en este momento; **for the m.**, de momento; **in a m.**, dentro de un momento; **at any m.**, dentro de un momento a otro.

momentary ['məʊməntərɪ] *adj* momentáneo,-a. ◆**momentarily** *adv* momentáneamente; *US (soon)* dentro de poco.

momentous [məʊ'mentəs] *adj* trascendental.

momentum [məʊ'mentəm] *n Phys* momento *m*; *(speed)* velocidad *f*; *fig* **to gather m.**, cobrar velocidad.

mommy ['mɒmɪ] *n US fam* mamá *f*.

Monaco ['mɒnəkəʊ] *n* Mónaco *m*.

monarch ['mɒnək] *n* monarca *m*.

monarchy ['mɒnəkɪ] *n* monarquía *f*.

monastery ['mɒnəstərɪ] *n* monasterio *m*.

Monday ['mʌndɪ] *n* lunes *m*.

monetarism ['mʌnɪtərɪzəm] *n* monetarismo *m*.

monetary ['mʌnɪtərɪ] *adj* monetario,-a.

money ['mʌnɪ] *n* dinero *m*; *(currency)* moneda *f*; **to make m.**, ganar dinero; **to put m. on**, apostar por.

moneylender ['mʌnɪlendər] *n* prestamista *mf*.

money-spinner ['mʌnɪspɪnər] *n fam* negocio m rentable.

Mongolia [mɒŋˈɡəʊlɪə] n Mongolia.

mongolism [ˈmɒŋɡəlɪzəm] n mongolismo m.

mongrel [ˈmʌŋɡrəl] n perro mestizo.

monitor [ˈmɒnɪtə[r]] I n (screen) monitor m; Educ delegado,-a m,f. II vtr (check) controlar; (progress, events) seguir de cerca.

monk [mʌŋk] n monje m.

monkey [ˈmʌŋkɪ] n mono m; **m. nut**, cacahuete m; **m. wrench**, llave inglesa.

monochrome [ˈmɒnəkrəʊm] adj monocromo,-a; (television, photo) en blanco y negro.

monocle [ˈmɒnəkəl] n monóculo m.

monologue US **monolog** [ˈmɒnəlɒɡ] n monólogo m.

monopolize [məˈnɒpəlaɪz] vtr Fin monopolizar; (attention etc) acaparar.

monopoly [məˈnɒpəlɪ] n monopolio m.

monotone [ˈmɒnətəʊn] n in a m., con una voz monótona.

monotonous [məˈnɒtənəs] adj monótono,-a.

monotony [məˈnɒtənɪ] n monotonía f.

monsoon [mɒnˈsuːn] n monzón m.

monster [ˈmɒnstə[r]] n monstruo m.

monstrosity [mɒnˈstrɒsɪtɪ] n monstruosidad f.

monstrous [ˈmɒnstrəs] adj (huge) enorme; (hideous) monstruoso,-a; (outrageous) escandaloso,-a.

montage [ˈmɒntɑːʒ] n montaje m.

month [mʌnθ] n mes m.

monthly [ˈmʌnθlɪ] I adj mensual; **m. instalment**, mensualidad f. II n (periodical) revista f mensual. III adv mensualmente, cada mes.

monument [ˈmɒnjʊmənt] n monumento m.

monumental [mɒnjʊˈmentəl] adj monumental; fam (huge) enorme.

moo [muː] I n mugido m. II vi mugir.

mood [muːd] n humor m; **to be in a good/bad m.**, estar de buen/mal humor; **to be in the m. for (doing) sth**, estar de humor para (hacer) algo.

moody [ˈmuːdɪ] adj (moodier, moodiest) (changeable) de humor variable; (badtempered) malhumorado,-a.

moon [muːn] n luna f; fam **over the m.**, en el séptimo cielo.

moonlight [ˈmuːnlaɪt] n luz f de la luna.

moonlighting [ˈmuːnlaɪtɪŋ] n fam pluriempleo m.

moonlit [ˈmuːnlɪt] adj (night) de luna.

moor[1] [mʊə[r]] n (heath) páramo m.

moor[2] [mʊə[r], mɔː[r]] vtr Naut amarrar.

Moor [mʊə[r]] n moro,-a m,f.

Moorish [ˈmʊərɪʃ] adj moro,-a.

moorland [ˈmʊələnd] n páramo m.

moose [muːs] n inv alce m.

moot [muːt] adj **it's a m. point**, es discutible.

mop [mɒp] I n (for floor) fregona f; fam **m. of hair**, melena f. II vtr fregar. ◆**mop up** vtr (liquids) enjugar; (enemy forces) acabar con.

mope [məʊp] vi estar alicaído,-a. ◆**mope about, mope around** vi andar abatido,-a.

moped [ˈməʊped] n ciclomotor m, vespa f.

moral [ˈmɒrəl] I adj moral. II n moraleja f; **morals**, moral f sing, moralidad f sing.

morale [məˈrɑːl] n moral f, estado m de ánimo.

morality [məˈrælɪtɪ] n moralidad f.

morass [məˈræs] n pantano m; fig lío m.

morbid [ˈmɔːbɪd] adj Med mórbido,-a; (mind) morboso,-a.

more [mɔː[r]] I adj más; **and what is m.**, y lo que es más; **is there any m. tea?**, ¿queda más té?; **I've no m. money**, no me queda más dinero; **m. tourists**, más turistas. II pron más; **how many m.?**, ¿cuántos más?; **I need some m.**, necesito más; **it's m. than enough**, es más que suficiente; **many/much m.**, muchos,-as/ mucho más; **m. than a hundred**, más de cien; **the m. he has, the m. he wants**, cuanto más tiene más quiere. III adv más; **I won't do it any m.**, no lo volveré a hacer; **she doesn't live here any m.**, ya no vive aquí; **m. and m. difficult**, cada vez más difícil; **m. or less**, más o menos; **once m.**, una vez más.

moreover [mɔːˈrəʊvə[r]] adv además.

morgue [mɔːɡ] n depósito m de cadáveres.

morning [ˈmɔːnɪŋ] I n mañana f; (before dawn) madrugada f; **in the m.**, por la mañana; **on Monday mornings**, los lunes por la mañana; **tomorrow m.**, mañana por la mañana. II adj matutino,-a.

Moroccan [məˈrɒkən] adj & n marroquí (mf).

Morocco [məˈrɒkəʊ] n Marruecos m.

moron [ˈmɔːrɒn] n fam imbécil mf.

morose [məˈrəʊs] adj malhumorado,-a, hosco,-a.

morphine [ˈmɔːfiːn] n morfina f.

Morse [mɔːs] n **M. (code)**, (alfabeto m) Morse m.

morsel [ˈmɔːsəl] n (of food) bocado m; fig trozo m.

mortal [ˈmɔːtəl] I adj mortal. II n mortal mf. ◆**mortally** adv mortalmente; **m. wounded**, herido,-a de muerte.

mortality [mɔːˈtælɪtɪ] n mortalidad f.

mortar [ˈmɔːtə[r]] n mortero m.

mortgage [ˈmɔːɡɪdʒ] I n hipoteca f. II vtr hipotecar.

mortify [ˈmɔːtɪfaɪ] vtr mortificar; fam **I was mortified**, me sentí avergonzado,-a.

mortuary [ˈmɔːtjʊərɪ] n depósito m de cadáveres.

mosaic [məˈzeɪɪk] n mosaico m.

Moscow ['mɒskəʊ, US 'mɒskaʊ] n Moscú.

Moslem ['mɒzləm] adj & n musulmán, -ana (m,f).

mosque [mɒsk] n mezquita f.

mosquito [mɒsˈkiːtəʊ] n (pl **mosquitoes**) mosquito m; **m. net**, mosquitero m.

moss [mɒs] n musgo m.

most [məʊst] I adj (superl of **much**, **many**) 1 (greatest in quantity etc) más; **this house suffered (the) m. damage**, esta casa fue la más afectada; **who made (the) m. mistakes?**, ¿quién cometió más errores? 2 (the majority of) la mayoría de, la mayor parte de; **for the m. part**, por lo general; **the m. of the time**, la mayor parte del tiempo; **m. people**, la mayoría de la gente.
II pron (greatest part) la mayor parte; (greatest number) lo máximo, lo más; (the majority of people) la mayoría; **at the (very) m.**, como máximo; **to make the m. of sth**, aprovechar algo al máximo.
III adv (superl of **much**) 1 más; **the m. intelligent student**, el estudiante más inteligente; **what I like m.**, lo que más me gusta. 2 (very) muy; **m. likely**, muy probablemente; **m. of all**, sobre todo.
◆**mostly** adv (chiefly) en su mayor parte; (generally) generalmente; (usually) normalmente.

MOT [eməʊˈtiː] GB abbr of Ministry of Transport; **MOT test**, inspección técnica de vehículos, ITV.

motel [məʊˈtel] n motel m.

moth [mɒθ] n mariposa nocturna; **clothes m.**, polilla f.

mother ['mʌðər] I n madre f; **unmarried m.**, madre soltera; **M.'s Day**, Día m de la Madre; **m. tongue**, lengua materna. II vtr cuidar maternalmente.

motherhood ['mʌðəhʊd] n maternidad f.

mother-in-law ['mʌðərɪnlɔː] n suegra f.

motherly ['mʌðəlɪ] adj maternal.

mother-of-pearl [mʌðərəvˈpɜːl] n madreperla f, nácar m.

mother-to-be [mʌðətəˈbiː] n futura madre.

motif [məʊˈtiːf] n Art Mus motivo m; (embroidered etc) adorno m; fig (main subject) tema m.

motion ['məʊʃən] I n (movement) movimiento m; (gesture) además m; (proposal) moción f. II vtr & vi hacer señas; **to m. (to) sb to do sth**, hacer señas a algn para que haga algo.

motionless ['məʊʃənlɪs] adj inmóvil.

motivate ['məʊtɪveɪt] vtr motivar.

motivation [məʊtɪˈveɪʃən] n motivación f.

motive ['məʊtɪv] I adj (force) motriz. II n (reason) motivo m; Jur móvil m; **with the best of motives**, con la mejor intención.

motley ['mɒtlɪ] adj (motlier, motliest)

(multicoloured) abigarrado,-a; (varied) variado,-a.

motor ['məʊtər] n (engine) motor m; fam (car) máquina f; **m. racing**, carreras fpl de coches.

motorbike ['məʊtəbaɪk] n fam motocicleta f, moto f.

motorboat ['məʊtəbəʊt] n (lancha) motora f.

motorcar ['məʊtəkaːr] n coche m, automóvil m.

motorcycle ['məʊtəsaɪkəl] n motocicleta f.

motorcyclist ['məʊtəsaɪklɪst] n motociclista mf.

motoring ['məʊtərɪŋ] n automovilismo m.

motorist ['məʊtərɪst] n automovilista mf.

motorway ['məʊtəweɪ] n GB autopista f.

mottled ['mɒtəld] adj (skin, animal) con manchas; (surface) moteado,-a.

motto ['mɒtəʊ] n lema m.

mould[1], US **mold** [məʊld] n (fungus) moho m.

mould[2], US **mold** [məʊld] I n molde m. II vtr moldear; (clay) modelar.

moulder, US **molder** ['məʊldər] vi **to m. (away)**, desmoronarse.

moulding, US **molding** ['məʊldɪŋ] n moldura f.

mouldy, US **moldy** ['məʊldɪ] adj (mouldier, mouldiest) mohoso,-a; **to go m.**, enmohecerse.

moult [məʊlt] vi mudar.

mound [maʊnd] n montón m; (small hill) montículo m.

mount[1] [maʊnt] n monte m; **M. Everest**, (Monte) Everest m.

mount[2] [maʊnt] I n (horse) montura f; (support) soporte m, base f; (for photograph) marco m; (for jewel) engaste m. II vtr (horse) subirse or montar a; (campaign) organizar; (photograph) enmarcar; (jewel) engastar. III vi (go up) subir; (get on horse, bike) montar; (increase) subir. ◆**mount up** vi (accumulate) acumularse.

mountain ['maʊntɪn] I n montaña f; fig (pile) montón m. II adj de montaña, montañés,-esa; **m. bike**, bicicleta f de montaña; **m. range**, sierra f, cordillera f.

mountaineer [maʊntɪˈnɪər] n alpinista mf, Am andinista mf.

mountaineering [maʊntɪˈnɪərɪŋ] n alpinismo m, Am andinismo m.

mountainous ['maʊntɪnəs] adj montañoso,-a.

mourn [mɔːn] vtr & vi **to m. (for) sb**, llorar la muerte de algn.

mourner ['mɔːnər] n doliente mf.

mournful ['mɔːnfʊl] adj triste; (voice) lúgubre.

mourning ['mɔːnɪŋ] n luto m; **in m.**, de luto.

mouse [maʊs] n (pl **mice**) also Comput ratón m.

mousetrap ['maʊstræp] n ratonera f.

mousse [muːs] n Culin mousse f; (for hair) (styling) m., espuma f (moldeadora).

moustache [məˈstɑːʃ] n bigote(s) m(pl).

mousy ['maʊsɪ] adj (mousier, mousiest) (colour) pardusco,-a; (hair) castaño claro; (shy) tímido,-a.

mouth [maʊθ] I n (pl mouths [maʊðz]) 1 boca f; fam down in the m., deprimido, -a. 2 (of cave etc) entrada f; (of river) desembocadura f. II vtr [maʊð] pronunciar; (insults) proferir.

mouthful ['maʊθfʊl] n (of food) bocado m; (of drink) sorbo m; to be a bit of a m., ser difícil de pronunciar.

mouth organ [maʊθɔːgən] n armónica f.

mouthpiece ['maʊθpiːs] n Mus boquilla f; (of telephone) micrófono m; fig (spokesman) portavoz m.

mouthwash ['maʊθwɒʃ] n elixir m, enjuague m bucal.

mouthwatering ['maʊθwɔːtərɪŋ] adj muy apetitoso,-a, que le hace a uno la boca agua.

movable ['muːvəbəl] adj movible, móvil.

move [muːv] I n 1 (movement) movimiento m; to be on the m., estar en marcha; **we must make a m.,** debemos irnos ya; fam **get a m. on!,** ¡date prisa! 2 (in game) jugada f; (turn) turno m. 3 (course of action) medida f; **to make the first m.,** dar el primer paso. 4 (to new home) mudanza f; (to new job) traslado m.

II vtr 1 mover; (furniture etc) cambiar de sitio; (transfer) trasladar; **to m. house,** mudarse (de casa). 2 (in game) mover. 3 (motivate) inducir; (persuade) persuadir; I won't be moved, no me harán cambiar de parecer. 4 (affect emotionally) conmover. 5 (resolution etc) proponer.

III vi 1 (change position) moverse, desplazarse; (change house) mudarse (de casa); (change post) trasladarse; **m. out of the way!,** ¡quítate de en medio! 2 (train etc) estar en marcha; **to start moving,** ponerse en marcha. 3 (travel) ir. 4 (leave) irse, marcharse. 5 (in game) hacer una jugada. 6 (take action) tomar medidas. ◆**move about, move around** I vtr cambiar de sitio. II vi (be restless) ir y venir; (travel) viajar de un lugar a otro. ◆**move along** I vtr (move forward) hacer avanzar; (keep moving) hacer circular. II vi (move forward) avanzar; (keep moving) circular; **m. along!,** (to person on bench) ¡haz sitio! ◆**move away** I vtr alejar, apartar (**from,** de). II vi (move aside) apartarse; (leave) irse; (change house) mudarse (de casa). ◆**move back** I vtr (to original place) volver. II vi (withdraw) retirarse; (to original place) volver. ◆**move forward** I

vtr avanzar; (clock) adelantar. II vi avanzar, adelantarse. ◆**move in** vi (into new home) instalarse. ◆**move off** vi (go away) irse, marcharse; (train) salir. ◆**move on** vi (keep moving) circular; (go forward) avanzar; (time) transcurrir. ◆**move out** vi (leave) irse, marcharse; (leave house) mudarse. ◆**move over** vi correrse. ◆**move up** vi (go up) subir; fig (be promoted) ser ascendido,-a, ascender; (move along) correrse, hacer sitio.

movement ['muːvmənt] n 1 movimiento m; (gesture) gesto m, además m. 2 (of goods) transporte m; (of employees) traslado m. 3 (trend) corriente f. 4 (of machine) mecanismo m. 5 (of goods, capital) circulación f.

movie ['muːvɪ] n US película f; **to go to the movies,** ir al cine; **m. star,** estrella f de cine.

moving ['muːvɪŋ] adj (that moves) móvil; (car etc) en marcha; fig (touching) conmovedor,-a.

mow [maʊ] vtr (pt mowed; pp mown o mowed) (lawn) cortar; (corn, wheat) segar; fig to m. down, segar.

mower ['maʊər] n cortacésped m & f.

MP [em'piː] abbr of Member of Parliament.

mph [empiːˈeɪtʃ] abbr of miles per hour, millas fpl por hora.

MPhil [em'fɪl] abbr of Master of Philosophy.

Mr ['mɪstər] abbr of mister, señor m, Sr.

Mrs ['mɪsɪz] abbr señora f, Sra.

Ms [maz] abbr señora f, Sra, señorita f, Srta.

MSc [emes'siː] abbr of Master of Science.

much [mʌtʃ] I adj mucho,-a; **as m. ... as,** tanto,-a ... como; **how m. chocolate?,** ¿cuánto chocolate?; **m. admiration,** mucha admiración; **so m.,** tanto,-a. II adv mucho; **as m. as,** tanto como; **as m. as possible,** todo lo posible; **how m.?,** ¿cuánto?; **how m. is it?,** ¿cuánto es?, ¿cuánto vale?; **m. better,** mucho mejor; **m. more,** mucho más; **so m. the better,** ¡tanto mejor!; **thank you very m.,** muchísimas gracias; **they are m. the same,** son más o menos iguales; **too m.,** demasiado; **without so m. as,** sin siquiera. III pron mucho; **I thought as m.,** lo suponía; **m. of the town was destroyed,** gran parte de la ciudad quedó destruida; **m. remains to be done,** queda mucho por hacer.

muck [mʌk] n (dirt) suciedad f; (mud) lodo m; fig porquería f. ◆**muck about, muck around** fam I vi (idle) perder el tiempo; (play the fool) hacer el tonto. II vtr to m. sb about, fastidiar a algn. ◆**muck up** vtr (dirty) ensuciar; fig (spoil) echar a perder.

mucky ['mʌkɪ] *adj (muckier, muckiest)* sucio,-a.

mucus ['mjuːkəs] *n* moco *m*, mucosidad *f*.

mud [mʌd] *n* lodo *m*, barro *m*; *(thick)* fango *m*; **to sling m. at sb**, poner a algn por los suelos; **m. flat**, marisma *f*.

muddle ['mʌdəl] **I** *n* desorden *m*; *fig (mix-up)* embrollo *m*, lío *m*; **to get into a m.**, hacerse un lío. **II** *vtr* **to m. (up)**, confundir. ◆**muddle through** *vi* arreglárselas, ingeniárselas.

muddy ['mʌdɪ] *adj (muddier, muddiest) (lane)* cubierto,-a de lodo; *(liquid)* turbio,-a.

mudguard ['mʌdɡɑːd] *n* guardabarros *m inv*.

muff¹ [mʌf] *n* manguito *m*; **ear muffs**, orejeras *fpl*.

muff² [mʌf] *vtr fam* pifiar; **to m. it (up)**, estropearlo.

muffin ['mʌfɪn] *n* panecillo *m*.

muffle ['mʌfəl] *vtr (sound)* amortiguar; **to m. (up)**, *(person)* abrigar.

muffler ['mʌflər] *n US Aut* silenciador *m*.

mug¹ [mʌɡ] *n (large cup)* tazón *m*; *(beer tankard)* jarra *f*.

mug² [mʌɡ] **I** *n fam (fool)* tonto,-a *m,f*; *(face)* jeta *f*. **II** *vtr* atracar, asaltar.

mugging ['mʌɡɪŋ] *n* asalto *m*.

muggy ['mʌɡɪ] *adj (muggier, muggiest)* bochornoso,-a.

mule [mjuːl] *n* mulo,-a *m,f*.

mull [mʌl] *vtr* **mulled wine**, vino *m* caliente con especias. ◆**mull over** *vtr* **to m. over sth**, reflexionar sobre algo.

multicoloured, US **multicolored** ['mʌltɪkʌləd] *adj* multicolor.

multinational [mʌltɪ'næʃənəl] *adj & nf* multinacional.

multiple ['mʌltɪpəl] **I** *adj* múltiple; **m. sclerosis**, esclerosis *f* múltiple. **II** *n* múltiplo *m*.

multiplication [mʌltɪplɪ'keɪʃən] *n* multiplicación *f*; **m. sign**, signo *m* de multiplicar.

multiply ['mʌltɪplaɪ] **I** *vtr* multiplicar (**by**, por). **II** *vi* multiplicarse.

multipurpose [mʌltɪ'pɜːpəs] *adj* multiuso *inv*.

multistorey, US **multistory** [mʌltɪ'stɔːrɪ] *adj (building)* de varios pisos; **m. car park**, parking *m* de varias plantas.

multitude [mʌltɪtjuːd] *n* multitud *f*, muchedumbre *f*.

mum¹ [mʌm] *n fam* mamá *f*.

mum² [mʌm] *adj* **to keep m.**, no decir ni pío.

mumble ['mʌmbəl] **I** *vi* hablar entre dientes. **II** *vtr* decir entre dientes.

mummy¹ ['mʌmɪ] *n fam (mother)* mamá *f*, mami *f*.

mummy² ['mʌmɪ] *n (body)* momia *f*.

mumps [mʌmps] *n* paperas *fpl*.

munch [mʌntʃ] *vtr & vi* mascar.

mundane [mʌn'deɪn] *adj pej (ordinary)* banal; *(job, life)* rutinario,-a.

municipal [mjuː'nɪsɪpəl] *adj* municipal.

municipality [mjuːnɪsɪ'pælɪtɪ] *n* municipio *m*.

mural ['mjʊərəl] *adj & nm* mural.

Murcia [muː'siːə] *n* Murcia.

murder ['mɜːdər] **I** *n* asesinato *m*, homicidio *m*. **II** *vtr* asesinar.

murderer ['mɜːdərər] *n* asesino *m*.

murderess ['mɜːdərɪs] *n* asesina *f*.

murderous ['mɜːdərəs] *adj* homicida.

murky ['mɜːkɪ] *adj (murkier, murkiest)* oscuro,-a; *(water)* turbio,-a.

murmur ['mɜːmər] **I** *n* murmullo *m*; *(of traffic)* ruido *m*; *(complaint)* queja *f*. **II** *vtr & vi* murmurar.

muscle ['mʌsəl] **I** *n* músculo *m*. **II** *vi fam* **to m. in on sth**, entrometerse en asuntos ajenos.

muscular ['mʌskjʊlər] *adj (pain, tissue)* muscular; *(person)* musculoso,-a.

muse [mjuːz] *vi* **to m. on** *or* **about sth**, meditar algo.

Muse [mjuːz] *n (in mythology)* musa *f*.

museum [mjuː'zɪəm] *n* museo *m*.

mushroom ['mʌʃruːm] **I** *n* seta *f*, hongo *m*; *Culin* champiñón *m*. **II** *vi fig* crecer de la noche a la mañana.

music ['mjuːzɪk] *n* música *f*; **m. hall**, teatro *m* de variedades.

musical ['mjuːzɪkəl] **I** *adj* musical; **to be m.**, estar dotado,-a para la música. **II** *n* musical *m*.

musician [mjuː'zɪʃən] *n* músico,-a *m,f*.

Muslim ['mʊzlɪm] *adj & n* musulmán, -ana *(m,f)*.

muslin ['mʌzlɪn] *n* muselina *f*.

mussel ['mʌsəl] *n* mejillón *m*.

must [mʌst] **I** *v aux* **1** *(obligation)* deber, tener que; **you m. arrive on time**, tienes que *or* debes llegar a la hora. **2** *(probability)* deber de; **he m. be ill**, debe de estar enfermo. **II** *n fam* necesidad *f*.

mustard ['mʌstəd] *n* mostaza *f*.

muster ['mʌstər] **I** *vtr fig* **to m. (up) courage**, cobrar fuerzas. **II** *vi* reunirse, juntarse.

mustn't ['mʌsənt] = **must not**.

musty ['mʌstɪ] *adj (mustier, mustiest)* que huele a cerrado *or* a humedad.

mute [mjuːt] **I** *adj* mudo,-a. **II** *n (person)* mudo,-a *m,f*; *Mus* sordina *f*.

muted ['mjuːtɪd] *adj (sound)* sordo,-a; *(colour)* suave.

mutilate ['mjuːtɪleɪt] *vtr* mutilar.

mutiny ['mjuːtɪnɪ] **I** *n* motín *m*. **II** *vi* amotinarse.

mutter ['mʌtər] **I** *n (mumble)* murmullo *m*. **II** *vtr* murmurar, decir entre dientes. **III** *vi (angrily)* refunfuñar.

mutton ['mʌtən] *n (carne f de)* cordero *m*.

mutual ['mjuːtʃʊəl] *adj* mutuo,-a; *(shared)* común.

muzzle ['mʌzl] **I** *n (snout)* hocico *m; (for dog)* bozal *m; (of gun)* boca *f*. **II** *vtr (dog)* abozalar; *fig* amordazar.

my [maɪ] *poss adj* mi; **my cousins,** mis primos; **my father,** mi padre; **one of my friends,** un amigo mío; **I washed my hair,** me lavé el pelo; **I twisted my ankle,** me torcí el tobillo.

myriad ['mɪrɪəd] *n lit* miríada *f*.

myself [maɪ'self] *pers pron* **1** *(emphatic)* yo mismo,-a; **my husband and m.,** mi marido y yo. **2** *(reflexive)* me; **I hurt m.,** me hice daño. **3** *(after prep)* mí (mismo,-a).

mysterious [mɪ'stɪərɪəs] *adj* misterioso, -a.

mystery ['mɪstərɪ] *n* misterio *m*.

mystical ['mɪstɪkəl] *adj* místico,-a.

mystify ['mɪstɪfaɪ] *vtr* dejar perplejo,-a.

mystique [mɪ'stiːk] *n* misterio *m*.

myth [mɪθ] *n* mito *m; it's a complete m.,** es pura fantasía.

mythology [mɪ'θɒlədʒɪ] *n* mitología *f*.

N

N, n [en] *n (the letter)* N, n *f*.

N *abbr of* **North,** Norte, N.

nab [næb] *vtr fam* pillar.

nag [næg] **I** *vtr* dar la tabarra a; **to n. sb to do sth,** dar la tabarra a algn para que haga algo. **II** *vi* quejarse.

nagging ['nægɪŋ] *adj (persistent)* continuo,-a.

nail [neɪl] **I** *n* **1** *(of finger, toe)* uña *f; (metal)* clavo *m; (for wood)* clavo *m;* **clippers,** cortaúñas *m inv;* **n. polish, n. varnish,** esmalte *m* or laca *f* de uñas. **2** *(metal)* clavo *m; fig* **to hit the n. on the head,** dar en el clavo. **II** *vtr* **1** clavar. **2** *fam (catch, trap)* pillar, coger.

nailbrush ['neɪlbrʌʃ] *n* cepillo *m* de uñas.

nailfile ['neɪlfaɪl] *n* lima *f* de uñas.

nail-scissors ['neɪlsɪzəz] *npl* tijeras *fpl* de uñas.

naïve [naɪ'iːv] *adj* ingenuo,-a.

naked ['neɪkɪd] *adj* desnudo,-a; *(flame)* sin protección; **the n. truth,** la pura verdad.

name [neɪm] **I** *n* **1** nombre *m; (surname)* apellido *m;* **what's your n.?,** ¿cómo te llamas?; **to call sb names,** poner verde a algn. **2** *(reputation)* reputación *f;* **to have a bad/good n.,** tener mala/buena reputación; **to make a n. for oneself,** hacerse famoso,-a. **II** *vtr* **1** llamar. **2** *(appoint)* nombrar. **3** *(refer to)* mencionar.

nameless ['neɪmlɪs] *adj* anónimo,-a; **to remain n.,** permanecer en el anonimato.

namely ['neɪmlɪ] *adv* a saber.

namesake ['neɪmseɪk] *n* tocayo,-a *m,f*.

nanny ['nænɪ] *n* niñera *f*.

nap [næp] *n (sleep)* siesta *f;* **to have a n.,** echar la *or* una siesta. **II** *vi fig* **to catch sb napping,** coger a algn desprevenido.

napalm ['neɪpɑːm] *n* napalm *m*.

nape [neɪp] *n* nuca *f;* coger *m*.

napkin ['næpkɪn] *n (table)* **n.,** servilleta *f*.

Naples ['neɪpəlz] *n* Nápoles *f*.

nappy ['næpɪ] *n GB* pañal *m*.

narcissus [nɑː'sɪsəs] *n Bot* narciso *m*.

narcotic [nɑː'kɒtɪk] **I** *adj* narcótico,-a. **II** *n (usu pl)* narcótico *m,* estupefaciente *m*.

narrate [nə'reɪt] *vtr* narrar, relatar.

narration [nə'reɪʃən] *n* narración *f,* relato *m*.

narrative ['nærətɪv] **I** *n Lit* narrativa *f; (story)* narración *f*. **II** *adj* narrativo,-a.

narrator [nə'reɪtər] *n* narrador,-a *m,f*.

narrow ['nærəʊ] **I** *adj* **1** *(passage, road etc)* estrecho,-a, angosto,-a. **2** *(restricted)* reducido,-a, *(sense)* estricto,-a; **to have a n. escape,** librarse por los pelos. **II** *vi* estrecharse. ◆**narrowly** *adv* **1** *(closely)* de cerca. **2** *(by a small margin)* por poco. ◆**narrow down** **I** *vtr* reducir, limitar. **II** *to* **n. down to,** reducirse a.

narrow-minded [nærəʊ'maɪndɪd] *adj* de miras estrechas.

nasal ['neɪzəl] *adj* nasal; *(voice)* gangoso, -a.

nastiness ['nɑːstɪnɪs] *n* **1** *(unpleasantness)* carácter *m* desagradable. **2** *(maliciousness)* mala intención.

nasty ['nɑːstɪ] *adj (nastier, nastiest)* **1** *(person)* desagradable; **a n. business,** un asunto feo; **a n. trick,** una mala jugada *or* pasada; **cheap and n.,** hortera; **to turn n.,** *(of weather, situation)* ponerse feo. **2** *(unfriendly)* antipático,-a; *(malicious)* mal intencionado,-a; *fam* **he's a n. piece of work,** es un saco de tío. **3** *(dirty)* sucio,-a, asqueroso,-a. **4** *(illness, accident)* grave.

nation ['neɪʃən] *n* nación *f*.

national ['næʃnəl] **I** *adj* nacional; **n. anthem,** himno *m* nacional; **n. insurance,** seguridad *f* social; *GB Mil* **n. service,** servicio *m* militar. **II** *n* súbdito, -a *m,f*.

nationalism ['næʃnəlɪzəm] *n* nacionalismo *m*.

nationalist ['næʃnəlɪst] *adj & n* nacionalista *(mf)*.

nationality [næʃə'nælɪtɪ] *n* nacionalidad *f*.

nationalization [næʃnəlaɪ'zeɪʃən] *n* nacionalización *f*.

nationalize ['næʃnəlaɪz] *vtr* nacionalizar.

nationwide ['neɪʃənwaɪd] *adj* de ámbito nacional.

native ['neɪtɪv] I *adj* 1 *(place)* natal; **n. land**, patria *f*; **n. language**, lengua materna. 2 *(innate)* innato,-a. 3 *(plant, animal)* originario,-a (**to**, de). II *n* nativo,-a *m,f*, natural *mf*; *(original inhabitant)* indígena *mf*.

NATO, Nato ['neɪtəʊ] *abbr of* **North Atlantic Treaty Organization**, Organización *f* del Tratado del Atlántico Norte, OTAN *f*.

natter ['nætə'] *fam* I *vi* charlar. II *n* charla *f*.

natural ['nætʃərəl] I *adj* 1 natural. 2 *(normal)* normal; **it's only n. that ...**, es lógico que ... . 3 *(born)* nato,-a. II *n* 1 **she's a n. for the job**, es la persona ideal para el trabajo. 2 *Mus* becuadro *m*. ◆**naturally** *adv* 1 *(of course)* naturalmente. 2 *(by nature)* por naturaleza. 3 *(in a relaxed manner)* con naturalidad.

naturalize ['nætʃərəlaɪz] *vtr* **to become naturalized**, naturalizarse.

nature ['neɪtʃə'] *n* 1 naturaleza *f*. 2 *(character)* naturaleza *f*, carácter *m*; **by n.**, por naturaleza; **human n.**, la naturaleza humana. 3 *(sort, kind)* índole *f*, clase *f*.

naught [nɔːt] *n arch* nada *f*; **to come to n.**, fracasar.

naughty ['nɔːtɪ] *adj* (**naughtier, naughtiest**) 1 *(child)* travieso,-a. 2 *(joke, story)* atrevido,-a, picante. ◆**naughtily** *adv* **to behave n.**, portarse mal.

nausea ['nɔːzɪə] *n Med (sickness)* náusea *f*.

nauseate ['nɔːzɪeɪt] *vtr (disgust)* dar asco a.

nauseating ['nɔːzɪeɪtɪŋ] *adj* nauseabundo,-a.

nautical ['nɔːtɪkəl] *adj* náutico,-a; **n. mile**, milla marítima.

naval ['neɪvəl] *adj* naval; **n. officer**, oficial *mf* de marina; **n. power**, potencia marítima *or* naval.

Navarre [nə'vɑː'] *n* Navarra.

nave [neɪv] *n Arch* nave *f*.

navel ['neɪvəl] *n Anat* ombligo *m*.

navigate ['nævɪgeɪt] I *vtr (river)* navegar por; *Naut (ship)* gobernar. II *vi* navegar; *(in driving)* indicar la dirección.

navigation [nævɪ'geɪʃən] *n Naut* navegación *f*.

navigator ['nævɪgeɪtə'] *n* 1 *Naut* navegante *mf*, oficial *mf* de derrota. 2 *Aut Av* copiloto *mf*.

navvy ['nævɪ] *n GB fam* peón *m*.

navy ['neɪvɪ] *n* marina *f*; **n. blue**, azul marino.

Nazi ['nɑːtsɪ] *adj & n* nazi *(mf)*.

Nazism ['nɑːtsɪzəm] *n* nazismo *m*.

NB, nb [en'biː] *abbr of* **nota bene** (note well), N.B.

neap [niːp] *n* **n. (tide)**, marea muerta.

near [nɪə'] I *adj* 1 *(in space)* cercano,-a; *(in time)* próximo,-a; **in the n. future**, en un futuro próximo; **it was a n. thing**, poco faltó. II *adv (in space)* cerca; **n. and far**, por todas partes; **that's n. enough**, (ya) vale, está bien. III *prep* cerca de; **n. the end of the film**, hacia el final de la película. IV *vtr* acercarse a. ◆**nearly** *adv* casi; **very n.**, casi, casi; **we haven't n. enough**, no alcanza ni con mucho.

nearby [nɪə'baɪ] I *adj* cercano,-a. II *adv* cerca.

nearside ['nɪəsaɪd] *n Aut (with left-hand drive)* lado izquierdo; *(with right-hand drive)* lado derecho.

near-sighted [nɪə'saɪtɪd] *adj* miope.

neat [niːt] *adj* 1 *(room, habits etc)* ordenado,-a; *(handwriting)* claro,-a; *(appearance)* pulcro,-a. 2 *(idea)* ingenioso,-a. 3 *(whisky etc)* solo,-a. 4 *US fam (fine)* chulísimo,-a. ◆**neatly** *adv* 1 *(carefully)* cuidadosamente. 2 *(cleverly)* hábilmente.

necessary ['nesɪsərɪ] I *adj* 1 *(essential)* necesario,-a; **to do what is n.**, hacer lo que haga falta; **if n.**, si es preciso. 2 *(unavoidable)* inevitable. II *n* **lo necesario**. ◆**necessarily** [nesɪ'serɪlɪ] *adv* necesariamente, por fuerza.

necessitate [nɪ'sesɪteɪt] *vtr* necesitar, exigir.

necessity [nɪ'sesɪtɪ] *n* 1 necesidad *f*; **out of n.**, por necesidad. 2 *(article)* requisito *m* indispensable; **necessities**, artículos *mpl* de primera necesidad.

neck [nek] I *n* cuello *m*; *(of animal)* pescuezo *m*; **to be n. and n.**, ir parejos; **to be up to one's n. in debt**, estar hasta el cuello de deudas; **to risk one's n.**, jugarse el tipo; **to stick one's n. out**, arriesgarse; **to win/lose by a n.**, *(in horse racing)* ganar/perder por una cabeza; **low n.**, escote bajo. II *vi fam* magrearse.

necklace ['neklɪs] *n* collar *m*.

neckline ['neklaɪn] *n (of dress)* escote *m*.

necktie ['nektaɪ] *n* corbata *f*.

nectar ['nektə'] *n* néctar *m*.

nectarine ['nektəriːn] *n* nectarina *f*.

née [neɪ] *adj* **n. Brown**, de soltera Brown.

need [niːd] I *n* 1 necesidad *f*; **if so, fuera necesario**; **there's no n. for you to do that**, no hace falta que hagas eso. 2 *(poverty)* indigencia *f*; **to be in n.**, estar necesitado; **to help a friend in n.**, sacar a un amigo de un apuro. II *vtr* 1 necesitar; **I n. to see him**, tengo que verle; *iron* **that's all I n.**, sólo me faltaba eso. 3 *(action, solution etc)* requerir, exigir; **aux** *v* tener que, deber; **n. he go?**, ¿tiene que ir?; **you needn't wait**, no hace falta que esperes.

needle ['niːdəl] I *n* 1 *(for sewing, knitting)* aguja *f*. 2 *Bot* hoja *f*. 3 *GB fam* **to get the n.**, picarse. II *vtr fam* pinchar.

needless ['niːdlɪs] *adj* innecesario,-a; **n. to say**, huelga decir. ◆**needlessly** *adv* innecesariamente.

needlework ['niːdəlwɜːk] n (sewing) costura f; (embroidery) bordado m.

needy ['niːdɪ] adj (needier, neediest) necesitado,-a.

negate [nɪ'geɪt] vtr 1 (deny) negar. 2 (nullify) anular.

negative ['negətɪv] I adj negativo,-a. II n 1 Ling negación f. 2 Phot negativo m.

neglect [nɪ'glekt] I vtr 1 (child, duty etc) descuidar, desatender. 2 to n. to do sth, (omit to do) no hacer algo. II n dejadez f; n. of duty, incumplimiento m del deber.

neglectful [nɪ'glektful] adj descuidado,-a, negligente.

negligée ['neglɪʒeɪ] n salto m de cama.

negligence ['neglɪdʒəns] n negligencia f, descuido m.

negligent ['neglɪdʒənt] adj negligente, descuidado,-a.

negligible ['neglɪdʒɪbəl] adj insignificante.

negotiate [nɪ'gəʊʃɪeɪt] I vtr 1 (contract) negociar. 2 fig (obstacle) salvar, franquear. II vi negociar.

negotiation [nɪgəʊʃɪ'eɪʃən] n negociación f.

negro ['niːgrəʊ] n (pl **negroes**) negro,-a m,f.

neigh [neɪ] I n relincho m. II vi relinchar.

neighbour, US **neighbor** ['neɪbər] n vecino,-a m,f; Rel prójimo m.

neighbourhood, US **neighborhood** ['neɪbəhʊd] n (district) vecindad f, barrio m; (people) vecindario m.

neighbouring, US **neighboring** ['neɪbərɪŋ] adj vecino,-a.

neither ['naɪðər, 'niːðər] I adj & pron ninguno de los dos, ninguna de las dos. II adv & conj 1 ni ... ni ... nor, ni ... II adv & conj 1 ni ... ni ... nor, ni ... tampoco; she was not there and n. was her sister, ella no estaba, ni su hermana tampoco.

neon ['niːɒn] n neón m; n. light, luz f de neón.

nephew ['nevjuː, 'nefjuː] n sobrino m.

nerve [nɜːv] n 1 Anat nervio m; to get on sb's nerves, poner los nervios de punta a algn; n. gas, gas nervioso. 2 (courage) valor m. 3 fam (cheek) cara f, descaro m; what a n.!, ¡qué cara!

nerve-racking ['nɜːvrækɪŋ] adj crispante, exasperante.

nervous ['nɜːvəs] adj 1 nervioso,-a; n. breakdown, depresión nerviosa. 2 (afraid) miedoso,-a. 3 (timid) tímido,-a.

nest [nest] n 1 Orn nido m; (hen's) nidal m; (animal's) madriguera f; n. egg, ahorros mpl. II vi (birds) anidar.

nestle ['nesəl] I vtr recostar. II vi (settle comfortably) acomodarse.

net¹ [net] n red f; GB n. curtains, visillos mpl.

net² [net] I adj neto,-a; n. weight, peso neto. II vtr (earn) ganar neto.

netball ['netbɔːl] n Sport baloncesto femenino.

Netherlands ['neðələndz] npl the N., los Países Bajos.

netting ['netɪŋ] n redes fpl, malla f.

nettle ['netəl] I n Bot ortiga f. II vtr fam irritar.

network ['netwɜːk] n red f.

neurosis [njʊ'rəʊsɪs] n neurosis f.

neurotic [njʊ'rɒtɪk] adj & n neurótico,-a (m,f).

neuter ['njuːtər] I adj neutro,-a. II n Ling neutro m. III vtr (geld) castrar.

neutral ['njuːtrəl] I adj neutro,-a; Pol to remain n., permanecer neutral. II n Aut punto muerto.

neutrality [njuː'trælɪtɪ] n neutralidad f.

neutralize ['njuːtrəlaɪz] vtr neutralizar.

neutron ['njuːtrɒn] n Phys neutrón m; n. bomb, bomba f de neutrones.

never ['nevər] adv nunca, jamás; he n. complains, nunca se queja, no se queja nunca; n. again, nunca (ja)más; n. in all my life, jamás en la vida; fam n. mind, da igual, no importa; fam well, I n. (did)!, ¡no me digas!

never-ending [nevər'endɪŋ] adj sin fin, interminable.

nevertheless [nevəðə'les] adv sin embargo, no obstante.

new [njuː] adj nuevo,-a; as good as n., como nuevo; n. baby, recién nacido m; n. moon, luna nueva; N. Year, Año nuevo; N. Year's Eve, Nochevieja f; N. York, Nueva York; N. Zealand, Nueva Zelanda. ◆**newly** adv recién, recientemente.

newborn ['njuːbɔːn] adj recién nacido,-a.

newcomer ['njuːkʌmər] n recién llegado,-a m,f; (to job etc) nuevo,-a m,f.

newfangled ['njuːfæŋgəld] adj novedoso,-a.

newlywed ['njuːlɪwed] n recién casado,-a m,f.

news [njuːz] n noticias fpl; a piece of n., una noticia; fam it's n. to me, ahora me entero; n. agency, agencia f de información; n. bulletin, boletín informativo; n. clipping, recorte m de periódico.

newsagent ['njuːzeɪdʒənt] n vendedor,-a m,f de periódicos.

newsflash ['njuːzflæʃ] n noticia f de última hora.

newsletter ['njuːzletər] n hoja informativa.

newspaper ['njuːzpeɪpər] n periódico m, diario m.

newsprint ['njuːzprɪnt] n papel m de periódico.

newsreader ['njuːzriːdər] n TV Rad presentador,-a m,f de los informativos.

newsreel ['njuːzriːl] n noticiario m.

news-stand ['njuːzstænd] n quiosco m de periódicos.

newt [njuːt] n Zool tritón m.

next [nekst] I adj 1 (in place) de al lado. 2 (in time) próximo,-a; **the n. day**, el día siguiente; **n. Friday**, el viernes que viene; **the week after n.**, dentro de dos semanas. 3 (in order) siguiente, próximo,-a; **of kin**, pariente m más cercano. II adv 1 después, luego; **what shall we do n.?**, ¿qué hacemos ahora? 2 (next time) la próxima vez. III prep **n. to**, al lado de, junto a; **n. to nothing**, casi nada.

next door I adj & adv de al lado; **our n.-d. neighbour**, el vecino or la vecina de al lado.

NHS [enetʃ'es] GB abbr of **National Health Service**, ≈ Seguridad f Social, SS f.

nib [nɪb] n plumilla f.

nibble ['nɪbəl] vtr & vi mordisquear.

nice [naɪs] adj 1 (person) simpático,-a; (thing) agradable; **n. and cool**, fresquito,-a; **to smell/taste n.**, oler/saber bien. 2 (nice-looking) bonito,-a, Am lindo,-a. 3 iron menudo,-a; **a n. mess you've made!**, ¡menudo lío has hecho! 4 fml (subtle) sutil. ◆**nicely** adv muy bien.

niche [niːtʃ] n 1 hornacina f, nicho m. 2 fig hueco m.

nick [nɪk] I n 1 (notch) muesca f; (cut) herida pequeña; fam **in the n. of time**, en el momento preciso. 2 GB sl **the n.**, (prison) chirona f. II vtr GB sl 1 (steal) birlar. 2 (arrest) pillar.

nickel ['nɪkəl] n 1 níquel m; **n. silver**, alpaca f. 2 US moneda f de cinco centavos.

nickname ['nɪkneɪm] I n apodo m. II vtr apodar.

nicotine ['nɪkətiːn] n nicotina f.

niece [niːs] n sobrina f.

nifty ['nɪftɪ] adj (niftier, niftiest) 1 (quick) rápido,-a. 2 (agile) ágil. 3 (ingenious) ingenioso,-a.

Nigeria [naɪ'dʒɪərɪə] n Nigeria.

nigger ['nɪgər] n offens negro,-a m,f.

niggling ['nɪglɪŋ] adj (trifling) insignificante; (irritating) molesto,-a.

night [naɪt] n noche f; **at n.**, de noche; **at twelve o'clock at n.**, a las doce de la noche; **last n.**, anoche; **to have a n. out**, salir por la noche; **n. life**, vida nocturna; fam **n. owl**, trasnochador,-a m,f; **n. school**, escuela nocturna; **n. shift**, turno m de noche.

nightclub ['naɪtklʌb] n sala f de fiestas; (disco) discoteca f.

nightdress ['naɪtdres] n camisón m.

nightfall ['naɪtfɔːl] n anochecer m.

nightgown ['naɪtgaʊn] n camisón m.

nightingale ['naɪtɪŋgeɪl] n ruiseñor m.

nightly ['naɪtlɪ] I adj de cada noche. II

adv todas las noches.

nightmare ['naɪtmeər] n pesadilla f.

nightshade ['naɪtʃeɪd] n Bot **deadly n.**, belladona f.

night-time ['naɪttaɪm] n noche f; **at n.**, por la noche.

nil [nɪl] n nada f; Sport cero m; **two n.**, dos a cero.

Nile [naɪl] n **the N.**, el Nilo.

nimble ['nɪmbəl] adj ágil, rápido,-a.

nine [naɪn] adj & n nueve (m) inv; fam **dressed up to the nines**, de punta en blanco.

nineteen [naɪn'tiːn] adj & n diecinueve (m) inv.

nineteenth [naɪn'tiːnθ] adj decimonoveno,-a.

ninety ['naɪntɪ] adj & n noventa (m) inv.

ninth [naɪnθ] I adj & n noveno,-a (m,f). II n (fraction) noveno m.

nip [nɪp] I vtr 1 (pinch) pellizcar. 2 (bite) morder; **to n. sth in the bud**, cortar algo de raíz. II n 1 (pinch) pellizco m. 2 (bite) mordisco m.

nipple ['nɪpəl] n Anat (female) pezón m; (male) tetilla f.

nippy ['nɪpɪ] adj (nippier, nippiest) fam 1 GB (quick) rápido,-a. 2 (cold) fresquito, -a.

nit [nɪt] n liendre f.

nitrogen ['naɪtrədʒən] n Chem nitrógeno m.

nitroglycerin(e) [naɪtrəʊ'glɪsərɪn] n Chem nitroglicerina f.

nitty-gritty [nɪtɪ'grɪtɪ] n fam **to get down to the n.g.**, ir al grano.

nitwit ['nɪtwɪt] n fam imbécil mf.

no [nəʊ] I adv no; **come here! - no!**, ¡ven aquí! - ¡no!; **no longer**, ya no; **no less than**, no menos de; II adj ninguno,-a; **she has no children**, no tiene hijos; **I have no idea**, no tengo (ni) idea; **it's no good** or **use**, no vale la pena; Aut **'no parking'**, 'prohibido aparcar'; **no sensible person**, ninguna persona razonable; fam **no way!**, ¡ni hablar!; **he's a no**, no m; **she won't take no for an answer**, no se dará por vencida; **to say no**, decir que no.

no. (pl **nos.**) abbr of **number**, número m, nº, núm.

nobility [nəʊ'bɪlɪtɪ] n nobleza f.

noble ['nəʊbəl] adj noble.

nobleman ['nəʊbəlmən] n noble m.

noblewoman ['nəʊbəlwʊmən] n noble f.

nobody ['nəʊbədɪ] I pron nadie; **there was n. there**, no había nadie; **n. else**, nadie más. II n nadie m, **he's a n.**, es un don nadie.

nocturnal [nɒk'tɜːnəl] adj nocturno,-a.

nod [nɒd] I n (of greeting) saludo m con la cabeza; (of agreement) señal f de asentimiento. II vi (greet) saludar con la cabeza; (agree) asentir con la cabeza. III vtr **to n. one's head**, inclinar la cabeza. ◆**nod**

off vi dormirse.

no-go ['nəʊ'gəʊ] adj **no-go area**, zona prohibida.

noise [nɔɪz] n ruido m; **to make a n.**, hacer ruido.

noiseless ['nɔɪzlɪs] adj silencioso,-a, sin ruido.

noisy ['nɔɪzɪ] adj (**noisier, noisiest**) ruidoso,-a.

nomad ['nəʊmæd] n nómada mf.

no-man's-land ['nəʊmænzlænd] n tierra f de nadie.

nominal ['nɒmɪnəl] adj nominal; (payment, rent) simbólico,-a.

nominate ['nɒmɪneɪt] vtr 1 (propose) designar, proponer. 2 (appoint) nombrar.

nomination [nɒmɪ'neɪʃən] n 1 (proposal) propuesta f. 2 (appointment) nombramiento m.

nominative ['nɒmɪnətɪv] n nominativo m.

nominee [nɒmɪ'niː] n persona propuesta.

non- [nɒn] pref no.

non-aggression [nɒnə'greʃən] n Pol no agresión f; **n.-a. pact**, pacto m de no agresión.

non-alcoholic [nɒnælkə'hɒlɪk] adj sin alcohol.

non-aligned [nɒnə'laɪnd] adj Pol no alineado,-a.

nonchalant ['nɒnʃələnt] adj (indifferent) indiferente; (calm) imperturbable, impasible.

noncommittal [nɒnkə'mɪtəl] adj (person) evasivo,-a; (answer) que no compromete (a nada).

nonconformist [nɒnkən'fɔːmɪst] n inconformista mf.

nondescript ['nɒndɪskrɪpt] adj indescriptible; (uninteresting) soso,-a.

none [nʌn] I pron ninguno,-a; **I know n. of them**, no conozco a ninguno de ellos; **n. at all**, nada en absoluto; **n. other than ...**, nada menos que ...; II adv de ningún modo; **she's n. the worse for it**, no se ha visto afectada or perjudicada por ello; **n. too soon**, a buena hora.

nonentity [nɒn'entɪtɪ] n (person) cero m a la izquierda.

nonetheless [nʌnðə'les] adv no obstante, sin embargo.

nonevent [nɒnɪ'vent] n fracaso m.

nonexistent [nɒnɪg'zɪstənt] adj inexistente.

nonfiction [nɒn'fɪkʃən] n literatura f no novelesca.

no-nonsense [nəʊ'nɒnsens] adj (person) recto,-a, serio,-a.

nonplussed [nɒn'plʌst] adj perplejo,-a.

non-profit(-making) [nɒn'prɒfɪt(meɪkɪŋ)] adj sin fin lucrativo.

nonreturnable [nɒnrɪ'tɜːnəbəl] adj no retornable.

nonsense ['nɒnsəns] n tonterías fpl, disparates mpl; **that's n.**, eso es absurdo.

nonsmoker [nɒn'sməʊkər] n no fumador,-a m,f, persona f que no fuma.

nonstarter [nɒn'stɑːtər] n fig **to be a n.**, (person) estar destinado a fracasar; (plan) ser irrealizable.

nonstick [nɒn'stɪk] adj antiadherente.

nonstop [nɒn'stɒp] I adj sin parar; (train) directo,-a. II adv sin parar.

noodles ['nuːdəlz] npl Culin fideos mpl.

nook [nʊk] n recoveco m, rincón m.

noon [nuːn] n mediodía m; **at n.**, a mediodía.

no-one ['nəʊwʌn] pron nadie; **n. came**, no vino nadie.

noose [nuːs] n lazo m; (hangman's) soga f.

nor [nɔːr] conj ni, ni tampoco; **neither ... n.**, ni ... ni; **neither you n. I**, ni tú ni yo; **n. do I**, (ni) yo tampoco.

norm [nɔːm] n norma f.

normal ['nɔːməl] adj normal.

normality [nɔː'mælɪtɪ] n normalidad f.

normally ['nɔːməlɪ] adv normalmente.

Normandy ['nɔːməndɪ] n Normandía f.

north [nɔːθ] I n norte m; **the N.**, el norte; **N. America**, América del Norte, Norteamérica; **N. Pole**, Polo m Norte; **N. Sea**, Mar m del Norte. II adv hacia el norte, al norte. III adj del norte; **n. wind**, viento m del norte.

northeast [nɔːθ'iːst] n nor(d)este m.

northerly ['nɔːðəlɪ] adj norte, del norte.

northern ['nɔːðən] adj norte, septentrional; **n. hemisphere**, hemisferio m norte; **N. Ireland**, Irlanda del Norte.

northerner ['nɔːðənər] n norteño,-a, mf.

northward ['nɔːθwəd] adj & adv hacia el norte.

northwest [nɔːθ'west] n noroeste m.

Norway ['nɔːweɪ] n Noruega f.

Norwegian [nɔː'wiːdʒən] I adj noruego,-a. II n 1 (person) noruego,-a m,f. 2 (language) noruego m.

nose [nəʊz] n 1 nariz f; fig (right) under sb's n., delante de las propias narices de algn; GB fam **to get up sb's n.**, hincharle a algn las narices. 2 (sense of smell) olfato m. 3 (of car, plane) morro m. ◆**nose about, nose around** vi curiosear.

nosebleed ['nəʊzbliːd] n hemorragia f nasal.

nosedive ['nəʊzdaɪv] Av I n picado m. II vi descender en picado.

nostalgia [nɒs'tældʒə] n nostalgia f.

nostalgic [nɒs'tældʒɪk] adj nostálgico,-a.

nostril ['nɒstrɪl] n Anat orificio m nasal.

nosy ['nəʊzɪ] adj (nosier, nosiest) fam entrometido,-a.

not [nɒt] adv no; **he's n. in today**, hoy no está; **I'm n. sorry to leave**, no siento nada irme; **n. at all**, en absoluto; **thank you - n. at all**, gracias - no hay de qué; **n. one (of them)** thanked me, nadie me dio las gracias; **n. that I don't want to**

come, no es que no quiera ir; **n. too well**, bastante mal; **n. without reason**, no sin razón; *fam* **n. likely!**, ¡ni hablar!
notable ['nəʊtəbəl] *adj* notable.
◆**notably** *adv* notablemente.
notary ['nəʊtərɪ] *n* notario *m*.
notch [nɒtʃ] *n* muesca *f*; (*cut*) corte *m*.
◆**notch up** *vtr fig* to n. up a victory, apuntarse una victoria.
note [nəʊt] **I** *n* **1** *Mus* nota *f*; *fig* to strike the right n., acertar. **2** (*on paper*) nota *f*. **3** to take n. of, (*notice*) prestar atención a. **4** *Fin* billete *m* (de banco). **5** notes, apuntes *mpl*; to take n., tomar apuntes. **II** *vtr* **1** (*write down*) apuntar, anotar. **2** (*notice*) notar, fijarse en.
notebook ['nəʊtbuk] *n* cuaderno *m*, libreta *f*.
noted ['nəʊtɪd] *adj* notable, célebre.
notepad ['nəʊtpæd] *n* bloc *m* de notas.
notepaper ['nəʊtpeɪpər] *n* papel *m* de carta.
noteworthy ['nəʊtwɜːðɪ] *adj* digno,-a de mención.
nothing ['nʌθɪŋ] **I** *n* nada; **I saw n.**, no vi nada; **for n.**, (*free of charge*) gratis; **it's n.**, no es nada; **it's n. to do with you**, no tiene nada que ver contigo; **n. else**, nada más; **there's n. in it**, no es cierto; *fam* **n. much**, poca cosa; *fam* **there's n. to it**, es facilísimo. **II** *adv* **she looks n. like her sister**, no se parece en nada a su hermana.
notice ['nəʊtɪs] **I** *n* **1** (*warning*) aviso *m*; **he gave a month's n.**, presentó la dimisión con un mes de antelación; **at short n.**, con poca antelación; **until further n.**, hasta nuevo aviso; **without n.**, sin previo aviso. **2** (*attention*) atención *f*; **to take no n. of sth**, no hacer caso de algo; **to take n. of sth**, prestar atención a algo; **it escaped my n.**, se me escapó; **to come to one's n.**, llegar al conocimiento de uno. **3** *(in newspaper etc)* anuncio *m*. **4** (*sign*) letrero *m*, aviso *m*. **II** *vtr* darse cuenta de, notar.
noticeable ['nəʊtɪsəbəl] *adj* que se nota, evidente.
noticeboard ['nəʊtɪsbɔːd] *n* tablón *m* de anuncios.
notification [nəʊtɪfɪ'keɪʃən] *n* aviso *m*.
notify ['nəʊtɪfaɪ] *vtr* avisar.
notion ['nəʊʃən] *n* **1** idea *f*, concepto *m*. **2** (*whim*) capricho *m*. **3** *US Sew* notions, artículos *mpl* de mercería.
notorious [nəʊ'tɔːrɪəs] *adj* muy conocido,-a.
notwithstanding [nɒtwɪθ'stændɪŋ] **I** *prep* a pesar de. **II** *adv* sin embargo, no obstante.
nougat ['nuːgɑː] *n* turrón blando.
nought [nɔːt] *n* cero *m*.
noun [naʊn] *n* nombre *m*, sustantivo *m*.
nourish ['nʌrɪʃ] *vtr* nutrir; *fig* (*hopes*)

abrigar.
nourishing ['nʌrɪʃɪŋ] *adj* nutritivo,-a.
nourishment ['nʌrɪʃmənt] *n* alimentación *f*, nutrición *f*.
novel[1] ['nɒvəl] *n* novela *f*.
novel[2] ['nɒvəl] *adj* original, novedoso,-a.
novelist ['nɒvəlɪst] *n* novelista *mf*.
novelty ['nɒvəltɪ] *n* novedad *f*.
November [nəʊ'vembər] *n* noviembre *m*.
novice ['nɒvɪs] *n* **1** (*beginner*) novato,-a *m,f*, principiante *mf*. **2** *Rel* novicio,-a *m,f*.
now [naʊ] **I** *adv* **1** (*at this moment*) ahora; **just n.**, right n., ahora mismo; **from n. on**, de ahora en adelante; **n. and then**, **n. and again**, de vez en cuando. **2** (*for events in past*) entonces. **3** (*at present, these days*) actualmente, hoy (en) día. **4** (*not related to time*) **n.** (**then**), ahora bien; **n., n.!**, ¡vamos!, ¡ya está bien!. **II** *conj* **n.** (**that**), ahora que, ya que. **III** *n* **until n.**, hasta ahora; **he'll be home by n.**, ya habrá llegado a casa.
nowadays ['naʊədeɪz] *adv* hoy (en) día, actualmente.
nowhere ['nəʊweər] *adv* en ninguna parte; **that will get you n.**, eso no te servirá de nada; **it's n. near ready**, no está preparado, ni mucho menos.
noxious ['nɒkʃəs] *adj* nocivo,-a.
nozzle ['nɒzəl] *n* boca *f*, boquilla *f*.
nuance [njuː'ɑːns] *n* matiz *m*.
nub [nʌb] *n* **the n. of the matter**, el quid de la cuestión.
nuclear ['njuːklɪər] *adj* nuclear; **n. arms**, armas *fpl* nucleares; **n. disarmament**, desarme *m* nuclear; **n. power**, energía *f* nuclear; **n. power station**, central *f* nuclear.
nucleus ['njuːklɪəs] *n* núcleo *m*.
nude [njuːd] **I** *adj* desnudo,-a. **II** *n* *Art Phot* desnudo *m*; **in the n.**, al desnudo.
nudge [nʌdʒ] **I** *vtr* dar un codazo a. **II** *n* codazo *m*.
nudist ['njuːdɪst] *adj & n* nudista (*mf*).
nudity ['njuːdɪtɪ] *n* desnudez *f*.
nugget ['nʌgɪt] *n* *Min* pepita *f*; **gold n.**, pepita de oro.
nuisance ['njuːsəns] *n* **1** molestia *f*, pesadez *f*; **what a n.!**, ¡qué lata! **2** (*person*) pesado,-a *m,f*.
nuke [njuːk] *sl* **I** *n* (*bomb*) bomba *f* nuclear o atómica. **II** *vtr* atacar con armas nucleares.
null [nʌl] *adj* nulo,-a; **n. and void**, nulo y sin valor.
nullify ['nʌlɪfaɪ] *vtr* (*pt & pp* nullified) anular.
numb [nʌm] **I** *adj* (*without feeling*) entumecido,-a; *fig* paralizado,-a; **n. with fear**, paralizado de miedo. **II** *vtr* (*with cold*) entumecer (de frío); (*with anaesthetic*) adormecer.
number ['nʌmbər] **I** *n* **1** número *m*; *Tel*

have you got my n.?, ¿tienes mi (número de) teléfono?; *fam* **to look after n. one,** barrer para adentro. 2 *(quantity)* **a n.** of people, varias personas. II *vtr* 1 *(put a number on)* numerar. 2 *(count)* contar; **his days are numbered,** tiene los días contados.

numberplate ['nʌmbəpleɪt] *n* GB Aut matrícula *f*.

numeral ['njuːmərəl] *n* número *m*, cifra *f*.

numerate ['njuːmərət] *adj* **to be n.,** tener un conocimiento básico de matemáticas.

numerical [njuː'merɪkəl] *adj* numérico,-a.
◆ **numerically** *adv* numéricamente.

numerous ['njuːmərəs] *adj* numeroso,-a.

numismatics [njuːmɪz'mætɪks] *n* numismática *f*.

nun [nʌn] *n* monja *f*.

nuptial ['nʌpʃəl] *adj* nupcial.

nurse [nɜːs] I *n* enfermera *f*; *(male)* enfermero *m*; **children's n.,** niñera *f*. II *vtr* 1 *(look after)* cuidar, atender. 2 *(baby)* acunar. 3 *(suckle)* amamantar. 4 *fig (grudge etc)* guardar.

nursery ['nɜːsərɪ] *n* 1 *(institution)* guardería *f*; **n. school,** jardín de infancia. 2 *(in house)* cuarto *m* de los niños; **n.**

rhyme, poema *m* infantil. 3 *(garden centre)* vivero *m*.

nursing ['nɜːsɪŋ] *n* **n. home,** clínica *f*.

nurture ['nɜːtʃər] *vtr (animal)* alimentar; *(feelings)* abrigar.

nut [nʌt] *n* 1 *(fruit)* fruto seco; *fig* **a tough n. to crack,** un hueso duro de roer. 2 *sl (head)* coco *m*. 3 *sl (mad person)* loco,-a *m,f*. 4 Tech tuerca *f*.

nutcracker ['nʌtkrækər] *n* cascanueces *m inv*.

nutmeg ['nʌtmeg] *n* nuez moscada *f*.

nutrition [njuː'trɪʃən] *n* nutrición *f*.

nutritious [njuː'trɪʃəs] *adj* nutritivo,-a, alimenticio,-a.

nutshell ['nʌtʃel] *n* cáscara *f*; *fig* **in a n.,** en pocas palabras.

nylon ['naɪlɒn] I *n* 1 nilón *m*, nailon *m*. 2 **nylons,** medias *fpl* de nilón. II *adj* de nilón.

nymph [nɪmf] *n* ninfa *f*.

nymphomaniac [nɪmfə'meɪnɪæk] *n* ninfómana *f*.

O

O, o [əʊ] *n* 1 *(the letter)* O, o *f*. 2 Math Tel cero *m*.

oak [əʊk] *n* roble *m*.

OAP [əʊeɪ'piː] GB *fam abbr of* **old-age pensioner**.

oar [ɔːr] *n* remo *m*.

oarsman ['ɔːzmən] *n* remero *m*.

oasis [əʊ'eɪsɪs] *n (pl* **oases** [əʊ'eɪsiːz]) oasis *m inv*.

oat [əʊt] *n* avena *f*; **rolled oats,** copos *mpl* de avena.

oath [əʊθ] *n (pl* **oaths** [əʊðz]) 1 *Jur* juramento *m*; **to take an o.,** prestar juramento; **(an oath) on my o.,** palabra de honor. 2 *(swearword)* palabrota *f*.

oatmeal ['əʊtmiːl] *n* harina *f* de avena.

obedience [ə'biːdɪəns] *n* obediencia *f*.

obedient [ə'biːdɪənt] *adj* obediente.

obese [əʊ'biːs] *adj* obeso,-a.

obey [ə'beɪ] *vtr* obedecer; *(law)* cumplir con.

obituary [ə'bɪtjʊərɪ] *n* necrología *f*.

object¹ ['ɒbdʒɪkt] *n* 1 *(thing)* objeto *m*. 2 *(aim, purpose)* fin *m*, objetivo *m*. 3 **the o. of criticism,** el blanco de las críticas. 4 *(obstacle)* inconveniente *m*. 5 *Ling* complemento *m*.

object² [əb'dʒekt] *vi* oponerse (**to,** a); **do you o. to my smoking?,** ¿le molesta que fume?

objection [əb'dʒekʃən] *n* 1 objeción *f*. 2 *(drawback)* inconveniente *m*; **provided**

there's no o., si no hay inconveniente.

objectionable [əb'dʒekʃənəbəl] *adj (unacceptable)* inaceptable; *(unpleasant)* ofensivo,-a.

objective [əb'dʒektɪv] I *adj* objetivo,-a. II *n* objetivo *m*.

objector [əb'dʒektər] *n* objetor,-a *m,f*.

obligation [ɒblɪ'geɪʃən] *n* obligación *f*; **to be under an o. to sb,** estarle muy agradecido,-a a algn.

obligatory [ə'blɪgətərɪ] *adj* obligatorio,-a.

oblige [ə'blaɪdʒ] *vtr* 1 *(compel)* obligar; **I'm obliged to do it,** me veo obligado,-a a hacerlo. 2 *(do a favour for)* hacer un favor a. 3 **to be obliged,** *(grateful)* estar agradecido,-a.

obliging [ə'blaɪdʒɪŋ] *adj* solícito,-a.

oblique [ə'bliːk] *adj* oblicuo,-a, inclinado,-a; *fig* **an o. reference,** una alusión indirecta.

obliterate [ə'blɪtəreɪt] *vtr* 1 *(memory)* borrar. 2 *(species, race)* eliminar; *(village)* arrasar.

oblivion [ə'blɪvɪən] *n* olvido *m*; **to sink into o.,** caer en el olvido.

oblivious [ə'blɪvɪəs] *adj* inconsciente.

oblong ['ɒblɒŋ] I *adj* oblongo,-a. II *n* rectángulo *m*.

obnoxious [əb'nɒkʃəs] *adj* repugnante.

oboe ['əʊbəʊ] *n* oboe *m*.

obscene [əb'siːn] *adj* obsceno,-a.

obscure [əb'skjʊər] I *adj* 1 oscuro,-a;

(vague) vago,-a. **2** *(author, poet etc)* desconocido,-a. **II** *vtr (truth)* ocultar.

obsequious [əb'si:kwɪəs] *adj* servil.

observance [əb'zɜːvəns] *n* **1** observancia *f*. **2** *Rel* **observances**, prácticas religiosas.

observant [əb'zɜːvənt] *adj* observador,-a.

observation [ɒbzə'veɪʃən] *n* observación *f*; *(surveillance)* vigilancia *f*.

observatory [əb'zɜːvətərɪ] *n* observatorio *m*.

observe [əb'zɜːv] *vtr* **1** observar; *(in surveillance)* vigilar. **2** *(remark)* advertir. **3** *(obey)* respetar.

observer [əb'zɜːvəʳ] *n* observador,-a *m,f*.

obsess [əb'ses] *vtr* obsesionar; **to be obsessed**, estar obsesionado,-a *(with, by, con)*.

obsession [əb'seʃən] *n* obsesión *f*.

obsessive [əb'sesɪv] *adj* obsesivo,-a.

obsolete ['ɒbsəliːt, ɒbsə'liːt] *adj* obsoleto,-a.

obstacle ['ɒbstəkəl] *n* obstáculo *m*; *fig* impedimento *m*; **o. race**, carrera *f* de obstáculos.

obstinate ['ɒbstɪnɪt] *adj* **1** *(person)* obstinado,-a, terco,-a. **2** *(pain)* persistente.

obstruct [əb'strʌkt] *vtr* **1** obstruir; *(pipe etc)* atascar; *(view)* tapar. **2** *(hinder)* estorbar; *(progress)* dificultar.

obstruction [əb'strʌkʃən] *n* **1** obstrucción *f*. **2** *(hindrance)* obstáculo *m*.

obtain [əb'teɪn] *vtr* obtener, conseguir.

obtainable [əb'teɪnəbəl] *adj* obtenible.

obtrusive [əb'truːsɪv] *adj* **1** *(interfering)* entrometido,-a. **2** *(noticeable)* llamativo, -a.

obtuse [əb'tjuːs] *adj* obtuso,-a.

obviate ['ɒbvɪeɪt] *vtr fml* obviar.

obvious ['ɒbvɪəs] *adj* obvio,-a, evidente. ◆**obviously** *adv* evidentemente; **o.!**, ¡claro!, ¡por supuesto!

occasion [ə'keɪʒən] **I** *n* **1** ocasión *f*, en **o.**, de vez en cuando; **on the o.**, con motivo de. **2** *(event)* acontecimiento *m*. **3** *(cause)* motivo *m*. **II** *vtr fml* ocasionar.

occasional [ə'keɪʒənəl] *adj* **1** esporádico,-a, eventual. ◆**occasionally** *adv* de vez en cuando.

occupant ['ɒkjʊpənt] *n* ocupante *mf*; *(tenant)* inquilino,-a *m,f*.

occupation [ɒkjʊ'peɪʃən] *n* **1** *(job, profession)* profesión *f*, ocupación *f*. **2** *(pastime)* pasatiempo *m*. **3** *(of building, house, country)* ocupación *f*.

occupational [ɒkjʊ'peɪʃənəl] *adj* profesional, laboral; **o. hazards**, gajes *mpl* del oficio.

occupied ['ɒkjʊpaɪd] *adj* ocupado,-a.

occupier ['ɒkjʊpaɪəʳ] *n GB* ocupante *mf*; *(tenant)* inquilino,-a *m,f*.

occupy ['ɒkjʊpaɪ] *vtr* **1** *(live in)* ocupar, habitar. **2** *(time)* pasar; **to o. one's time**

in doing sth, dedicar su tiempo a hacer algo. **3** *(building, factory etc in protest)* tomar posesión de.

occur [ə'kɜːʳ] *vi* **1** *(event)* suceder, acaecer; *(change)* producirse. **2** *(be found)* encontrarse. **3 it occurred to me that ...**, se me ocurrió que ....

occurrence [ə'kʌrəns] *n* acontecimiento *m*.

ocean ['əʊʃən] *n* océano *m*.

ocean-going ['əʊʃəngəʊɪŋ] *adj* de alta mar.

ochre, *US* **ocher** ['əʊkəʳ] **I** *n* ocre *m*; **red o.**, almagre *m*; **yellow o.**, ocre amarillo. **II** *adj* (de color) ocre.

o'clock [ə'klɒk] *adv* **(it's) one o'c.**, (es) la una; **(it's) two o'c.**, (son) las dos.

octave ['ɒktɪv] *n* octava *f*.

October [ɒk'təʊbəʳ] *n* octubre *m*.

octogenarian [ɒktəʊdʒɪ'neərɪən] *adj & n* octogenario,-a *(m,f)*.

octopus ['ɒktəpəs] *n* pulpo *m*.

odd [ɒd] **I** *adj* **1** *(strange)* raro,-a, extraño,-a. **2** *(occasional)* esporádico,-a; **at o. times**, de vez en cuando; **the o. customer**, algún que otro cliente; **o. job**, trabajillo *m*. **3 an o. number**, *(not even)* un impar. **4** *(unpaired)* desparejado,-a; **a o. sock**, un calcetín suelto; *fig* **to be the o. man out**, estar de más. **II** *adv y* poco; **twenty o. people**, veinte y pico *or y* tantas personas. ◆**oddly** *adv* extrañamente; **o. enough**, por extraño que parezca.

oddity ['ɒdɪtɪ] *n* **1** *(thing)* curiosidad *f*; *(person)* estrafalario,-a *m,f*. **2** *(quality)* rareza *f*.

odds [ɒdz] *npl* **1** *(chances)* probabilidades *fpl*; **he's fighting against the o.**, lleva las de perder; **the o. are that ...**, lo más probable es que ... *(+ subj)*. **2** *(in betting)* puntos *mpl* de ventaja; **the o. are five to one**, las apuestas están cinco a uno. **3** *GB* **it makes no o.**, da lo mismo; *fig* **at o. with sb**, reñido,-a con algn. **4 o. and ends**, *(small things)* cositas *fpl*; *(trinkets)* chucherías *fpl*.

odds-on ['ɒdzɒn] *adj* seguro,-a; **o.-on favourite**, *(horse)* caballo favorito.

ode [əʊd] *n* oda *f*.

odious ['əʊdɪəs] *adj* repugnante.

odour, *US* **odor** ['əʊdəʳ] *n* olor *m*; *(fragrance)* perfume *m*.

OECD [əʊiːsiː'diː] *abbr of* **Organization for Economic Co-operation and Development**, ≈ Organización *f* para la Cooperación y el Desarrollo Económico, OCDE *f*.

of [ɒv, *unstressed* əv] *prep* **1** *(belonging to, part of)* de; **a friend of mine**, un amigo mío; **the end of the novel**, el final de la novela. **2** *(containing)* de; **a bottle of wine**, una botella de vino. **3** *(origin)* de; **of good family**, de buena familia. **4** *(by)* de, por; **beloved of all,** amado,-a por todos. 5 *(quantity)* de; **there are four of us,** somos cuatro; **two of them,** dos de ellos. 6 *(from)* de. 7 *(material)* de; **a dress (made) of silk,** un vestido de seda. 8 *(apposition)* de; **the city of Lisbon,** la ciudad de Lisboa. 9 *(characteristic)* de; **that's typical of her,** es muy propio de ella; **that's very kind of you,** es usted muy amable. 10 *(with adj)* de; **hard of hearing,** duro,-a de oído. 11 *(after superlative)* de; **the thing she wanted most of all,** lo que más quería. 12 *(cause)* por; **because of,** a causa de; **of necessity,** por necesidad. 13 *(concerning, about)* de, sobre; **to dream of sth/sb,** soñar con algo/algn; **to think of sb,** pensar en algn. 14 *(with dates)* de; **the seventh of November,** el siete de noviembre.

off [ɒf] **I** *prep* 1 *(movement)* de; **she fell o. her horse,** se cayó del caballo. 2 *(removal)* de; **I'll take sth o. the price for you,** se lo rebajaré un poco. 3 *(distance, situation)* de; **a few kilometres o. the coast,** a unos kilómetros de la costa; **a house o. the road,** una casa apartada de la carretera. 4 **the ship went o. course,** el barco se desvió; **to be o. form,** no estar en forma. 5 **I'm o. wine,** he perdido el gusto al vino.

II *adv* 1 **he turned o. the radio,** apagó la radio. 2 *(absent)* fuera; **I have a day o.,** tengo un día libre; **to be o. sick,** estar de baja por enfermedad. 3 *(completely)* completamente; **this will kill o. any germs,** esto rematará cualquier germen. 4 **my arrival is three days o.,** faltan tres días para su llegada; **six miles o.,** a seis millas. 5 **I'm o. to London,** me voy a Londres; **she ran o.,** se fue corriendo. 6 **ten per cent o.,** un descuento del diez por ciento; **to take one's shoes o.,** quitarse los zapatos. 7 **o. and on,** de vez en cuando.

III *adj* 1 *(gas etc)* apagado,-a; *(water)* cortado,-a. 2 *(cancelled)* cancelado,-a. 3 *(low)* bajo,-a; *(unsatisfactory)* malo,-a; **on the o. chance,** por si acaso; **the o. season,** la temporada baja. 4 **to be better o. like that,** así estás mejor. 5 *(gone bad)* *(meat, fish)* malo,-a, pasado,-a; *(milk)* agrio,-a.

offal [ˈɒfəl] *n (of chicken etc)* menudillos *mpl;* *(of cattle, pigs)* asaduras *fpl.*

off-colour, US **off-color** [ˈɒfkʌləʳ] *adj* 1 GB *(ill)* indispuesto,-a. 2 *(joke, story)* indecente.

offence [əˈfens] *n* 1 *Jur* delito *m.* 2 *(insult)* ofensa *f;* **to give o.,** ofender; **to take o. at sth,** ofenderse por algo. 3 *Mil (attack)* ofensiva *f.*

offend [əˈfend] *vtr* ofender.

offender [əˈfendəʳ] *n (criminal)* delincuente *mf.*

offense [əˈfens] *n* US → **offence.**

offensive [əˈfensɪv] **I** *adj* 1 *(insulting)* ofensivo,-a. 2 *(repulsive)* repugnante. **II** *n* *Mil* ofensiva *f;* **to be on the o.,** estar a la ofensiva.

offer [ˈɒfəʳ] **I** *vtr* 1 ofrecer; **to o. to do a job,** ofrecerse para hacer un trabajo. 2 *(propose)* proponer. **II** *n* 1 oferta *f;* *(proposal)* propuesta *f;* **o. of marriage,** proposición *f* de matrimonio. 2 *Com* **on o.,** de oferta.

offering [ˈɒfərɪŋ] *n* 1 ofrecimiento *m.* 2 *Rel* ofrenda *f.*

offhand [ɒfˈhænd] **I** *adj (abrupt)* brusco, -a; *(inconsiderate)* descortés. **II** *adv* **I don't know o.,** así sin pensarlo, no lo sé.

office [ˈɒfɪs] *n* 1 *(room)* despacho *m;* *(building)* oficina *f;* **o. hours,** horas *fpl* de oficina. 2 GB *Pol* ministerio *m.* 3 US *(federal agency)* agencia *f* gubernamental. 4 *(position)* cargo *m;* **to hold o.,** ocupar un cargo. 5 *Pol* **to be in o.,** estar en el poder.

officer [ˈɒfɪsəʳ] *n* 1 *Mil* oficial *mf.* 2 *(police)* o., agente *mf* de policía. 3 *(government official)* funcionario,-a *m,f.* 4 *(of company, society)* director,-a *m,f.*

official [əˈfɪʃəl] **I** *adj* oficial. **II** *n* funcionario,-a *m,f.*

officiate [əˈfɪʃɪeɪt] *vi* 1 ejercer; **to o. as,** ejercer de. 2 *Rel* oficiar.

officious [əˈfɪʃəs] *adj pej* entrometido,-a.

off-line [ˈɒflaɪn] *adj* Comput desconectado,-a.

off-licence [ˈɒflaɪsəns] *n* GB tienda *f* de bebidas alcohólicas.

off-peak [ɒfˈpiːk] *adj (flight)* de temporada baja; *(rate)* de fuera de las horas punta.

off-putting [ˈɒfpʊtɪŋ] *adj* GB *fam* desconcertante.

offset [ˈɒfset] *vtr (pt & pp* **offset)** *(balance out)* compensar.

offshoot [ˈɒfʃuːt] *n* 1 *Bot* renuevo *m.* 2 *fig (of organization)* ramificación *f.*

offshore [ˈɒfʃɔːʳ] *adj* 1 *(breeze etc)* terral. 2 *(oil rig)* costa afuera. 3 *(overseas)* en el extranjero; **o. investment,** inversión *f* en el extranjero.

offside [ɒfˈsaɪd] **I** *adv* Ftb fuera de juego. **II** *n* Aut *(with left-hand drive)* lado derecho; *(with right-hand drive)* lado izquierdo.

offspring [ˈɒfsprɪŋ] *n inv (child)* vástago *m;* *(children)* progenitura *f.*

offstage [ɒfˈsteɪdʒ] *adj & adv* entre bastidores.

often [ˈɒfən, ˈɒftən] *adv* a menudo, con frecuencia; **every so o.,** de vez en cuando.

ogle [ˈəʊgəl] *vtr & vi* **to o. (at) sb,** comerse a algn con los ojos.

oh [əʊ] *interj* ¡oh!, ¡ay!; **oh, my God!,**

¡Dios mío!

oil [ɔɪl] I n 1 aceite m; **o. lamp**, lámpara f de aceite, quinqué m; **o. rig**, plataforma petrolera; **o. tanker**, petrolero m. 3 (painting) pintura f al óleo; **o. colour**, **o. paint**, óleo m. II vtr engrasar.

oilcan ['ɔɪlkæn] n aceitera f.

oilfield ['ɔɪlfiːld] n yacimiento petrolífero.

oilskin ['ɔɪlskɪn] n 1 hule m. 2 **oilskins**, chubasquero m sing, impermeable m sing de hule.

oily ['ɔɪlɪ] adj (oilier, oiliest) aceitoso,-a, grasiento,-a; (hair, skin) graso,-a.

ointment ['ɔɪntmənt] n ungüento m, pomada f.

O.K., okay [əʊˈkeɪ] fam I interj ¡vale!, ¡de acuerdo!! II adj bien; **is it O.K. if ...?**, ¿está bien si ...? III vtr dar el visto bueno a.

old [əʊld] I adj 1 viejo,-a; **an o. man**, un anciano; **o. age**, vejez f; **o. age pensioner**, pensionista mf; GB **o. boy**, antiguo alumno; **o. hand**, veterano,-a m,f; **good o. John!**, ¡el bueno de John! 2 **how o. are you?**, ¿cuántos años tienes?; **she's five years o.**, tiene cinco años. 3 (previous) antiguo,-a. II n of o., de antaño.

old-fashioned [əʊldˈfæʃənd] adj (outdated) a la antigua; (unfashionable) anticuado,-a, pasado,-a de moda.

olive ['ɒlɪv] n 1 (tree) olivo m; **o. grove**, olivar m. 2 (fruit) aceituna f, oliva f. 3 (wood) olivo m. 4 o. (green), (colour) verde m oliva.

Olympic [əˈlɪmpɪk] I adj olímpico,-a; **O. Games**, Juegos Olímpicos. II npl **the Olympics**, las Olimpíadas.

omelette ['ɒmlɪt] n tortilla f; Spanish **o.**, tortilla española o de patatas.

omen ['əʊmen] n presagio m.

ominous ['ɒmɪnəs] adj de mal agüero.

omission [əʊˈmɪʃən] n omisión f; fig olvido m.

omit [əʊˈmɪt] vtr omitir; (accidentally) pasar por alto; (forget) olvidarse (to, de).

omnipotent [ɒmˈnɪpətənt] I adj omnipotente. II n the O., el Todopoderoso.

on [ɒn] I prep 1 (location) sobre, encima de, en; **I hit him on the head**, le di un golpe en la cabeza; **it's on the desk**, está encima de o sobre el escritorio; **hanging on the wall**, colgado de la pared; **on page four**, en la página cuatro; **have you got any money on you?**, ¿llevas dinero?; **the drinks are on me/the house**, invito yo/invita la casa. 2 (alongside) en; **a town on the coast**, un pueblo en la costa. 3 (direction) en, a; **on the right**, a la derecha; **on the way**, en el camino. 4 (time) **on April 3rd**, el tres de abril; **on a sunny day**, un día de sol; **on Monday**, el lunes;

on Mondays, los lunes; **on that occasion**, en aquella ocasión; **on the following day**, al día siguiente; **on time**, a tiempo. 5 en; **on TV/the radio**, en la tele/radio; **to play with on the piano**, tocar algo al piano; **on the phone**, al teléfono. 6 (at the time of) a; **on his arrival**, a su llegada; **on second thoughts**, pensándolo bien; **on learning of this**, al conocer este hecho. 7 **she lives on bread**, vive de pan; **to depend on**, depender de. 8 (transport) en, a; **on foot**, a pie; **on the train/plane/bus**, en el tren/avión/autobús; (travel by) en tren/avión/autobús. 9 (state, process) en, de; **on holiday**, de vacaciones; **she is here on business**, está aquí de negocios. 10 (regarding) sobre; **a lecture on numismatics**, una conferencia sobre numismática; **they congratulated him on his success**, le felicitaron por su éxito. 11 **on condition that**, (subject to) bajo la condición de que. 12 (against) contra; **an attack on**, un ataque contra. 13 **he's on the Times**, (working for) trabaja para el Times.

II adj 1 (covering) encima, puesto; **she had a coat on**, llevaba puesto un abrigo. 2 fam **have you anything on tonight?**, ¿tienes algún plan para esta noche? 3 **and so on**, y así sucesivamente; **go on!**, ¡sigue!; **he talks on and on**, habla sin parar; **to work on**, seguir trabajando. 4 **from that day on**, a partir de aquel día; **later on**, más tarde.

III adj fam 1 to be on, (TV, radio, light) estar encendido,-a; (engine) estar en marcha; (film, play) en cartelera; **that film was on last week**, pusieron esa película la semana pasada. 2 Theat TV **you're on!**, ¡a escena! 3 (definitely planned) previsto,-a; **you're on!**, ¡trato hecho! 4 **that isn't on**, eso no vale.

once [wʌns] I adv 1 (one time) una vez; **o. a week**, una vez por semana; **o. in a while**, de vez en cuando; **o. more**, una vez más; **o. or twice**, un par de veces; fig **o. and for all**, de una vez por todas. 2 (formerly) en otro tiempo; **o. (upon a time) there was**, érase una vez. 3 **at o.**, en seguida, inmediatamente; **don't all speak at o.**, no habléis todos a la vez. II conj una vez que (+ subj), en cuanto (+ subj).

oncoming ['ɒnkʌmɪŋ] adj (car, traffic) que viene en dirección contraria.

one [wʌn] I adj 1 un, una; **for o. thing**, primero; **you're the o. person who knows**, tú eres el único que lo sabe; **the o. and only**, el único, la única; **o. and the same**, el mismo, la misma. 2 (indefinite) un, una; **he'll come back o. day**, un día volverá. II dem pron any o., cualquiera; **that o.**, ése, ésa; **this o.**, éste, ésta; (distant)

aquél, aquélla; **the blue ones**, los azules, las azules; **the o. on the table**, el o. la que está encima de la mesa; **the ones that, the ones who**, los *or* las que.
III *indef pron* **1** uno,-a *m,f;* **I**, for o., am against it, yo, por lo menos, estoy en contra; **I'm not o. to complain**, no soy de los que se quejan; **o. at a time**, de uno en uno; **o. by o.**, uno tras otro; *fig* **o. and all**, todo el mundo. **2** *(indefinite person)* uno,-a *m,f;* **o. has to fight**, hay que luchar; **o. hopes that will never happen**, esperemos que no ocurra; **to break o.'s leg/arm**, romperse la pierna/el brazo. **3** o. another, el uno al otro; **they love o. another**, se aman.
IV *n (digit)* uno *m;* **o. hundred/thousand**, cien/mil.

one-armed [ˈwɑnɑːmd] *adj fig* **o.-a. bandit**, máquina *f* tragaperras.

one-man [ˈwɑnmæn] *adj* **o.-m. show**, un espectáculo con un solo artista.

one-man band [wɑnmænˈbænd] *n* hombre *m* orquesta *(inv)*.

one-off [ˈwɑnɒf] *adj GB fam* único,-a, fuera de serie.

oneself [wɑnˈself] *pron* **1** *(reflexive)* uno,-a mismo,-a *m,f*, sí mismo,-a *m,f;* **to talk to o.**, hablar para sí. **2** *(alone)* uno,-a mismo,-a *m,f;* **by o.**, solo,-a. **3** *(one's usual self)* el *or* la de siempre.

one-sided [wɑnsaɪdɪd] *adj (bargain)* desigual; *(judgement)* parcial; *(decision)* unilateral.

one-to-one [ˈwɑntəwɑn] *adj* **o.-to-o. tuition**, clase *f* individual.

one-way [ˈwɑnweɪ] *adj* **1** *(ticket)* de ida. **2** *(street)* de dirección única.

ongoing [ˈɒngəʊɪŋ] *adj* **1** *(in progress)* en curso, actual. **2** *(developing)* en desarrollo.

onion [ˈʌnjən] *n* cebolla *f.*

on-line [ɒnˈlaɪn] *adj Comput* conectado,-a.

onlooker [ˈɒnlʊkə^r] *n* espectador,-a *m,f.*

only [ˈəʊnlɪ] **I** *adj* único,-a; **o. son**, hijo único. **II** *adv* **1** solamente, sólo; '**staff o.**', 'reservado al personal'. **2** *(not earlier than)* apenas; **he has just left**, acaba de marcharse hace un momento; **o. yesterday**, ayer mismo. **3** o. **too glad!**, ¡con mucho gusto!. **III** *conj* pero.

onset [ˈɒnset] *n (start)* comienzo *m.*

onslaught [ˈɒnslɔːt] *n* embestida *f.*

onto [ˈɒntʊ, *unstressed* ˈɒntə] *prep* → **on**.

onus [ˈəʊnəs] *n* responsabilidad *f.*

onward [ˈɒnwəd] *adj* hacia adelante.

onward(s) [ˈɒnwəd(z)] *adv* a partir de, en adelante; **from this time o.**, de ahora en adelante.

ooze [uːz] **I** *vi* rezumar. **II** *vtr* rebosar.

opaque [əʊˈpeɪk] *adj* opaco,-a.

OPEC [ˈəʊpek] *abbr* of **Organization of Petroleum Exporting Countries**, Organización *f* de los Países Exportadores de Petróleo, OPEP *f.*

open [ˈəʊpən] **I** *adj* **1** abierto,-a; **half o.**, entreabierto; **wide o.**, abierto de par en par; **in the o. air**, al aire libre; **to be o. with sb**, ser sincero,-a con algn; *fig* **with o. arms**, con los brazos abiertos; **to keep an o. mind**, no tener prejuicios; **I am o. to suggestions**, acepto cualquier sugerencia; **o. to criticism**, susceptible a la crítica; **o. admiration**, franca admiración; *US* **o. house**, fiesta *f* de inauguración de residencia; **an o. question**, una cuestión sin resolver; **o. season**, *(in hunting)* temporada *f* de caza; *Av Rail* **o. ticket**, billete abierto; *GB* **O. University**, Universidad *f* a Distancia; *Jur* **o. verdict**, veredicto inconcluso. **2** *(car etc)* descubierto,-a. **3** *(opposition)* manifiesto,-a.
II *vtr* **1** abrir; **to o. fire**, abrir fuego; *fig* **to o. one's heart to sb**, sincerarse con algn. **2** *(exhibition etc)* inaugurar; *(negotiations, conversation)* entablar.
III *vi* **1** abrir, abrirse; **to o. onto**, *(of door, window)* dar a. **2** *(start)* empezar; *Theat Cin* estrenarse.
IV *n* **1** **in the o.**, al aire libre; *fig* **to bring into the o.**, hacer público. **2** *Sport* open *m.*
◆ **open out I** *vtr* abrir, desplegar. **II** *vi (flowers)* abrirse; *(view)* extenderse.
◆ **open up I** *vtr (market etc)* abrir; *(possibilities)* crear. **II** *vi* **1** abrirse; *fam* **o. up!**, ¡abre la puerta! **2** *(start)* empezar.
◆ **openly** *adv* abiertamente.

opener [ˈəʊpənə^r] *n* tin o., *US* can o., abrelatas *m inv.*

opening [ˈəʊpənɪŋ] *n* **1** *(act)* apertura *f;* **o. night**, noche *f* de estreno; *GB* **o. time**, hora *f* de apertura de los bares. **2** *(beginning)* comienzo *m.* **3** *(aperture)* abertura *f; (gap)* brecha *f.* **4** *Com* oportunidad *f. (vacancy)* vacante *f.*

open-minded [əʊpənˈmaɪndɪd] *adj* sin prejuicios.

openness [ˈəʊpənnɪs] *n* franqueza *f.*

open-plan [ˈəʊpənplæn] *adj (office)* abierto,-a.

opera [ˈɒpərə] *n* ópera *f;* **o. house**, ópera, teatro *m* de la ópera.

operate [ˈɒpəreɪt] **I** *vi* **1** *(function)* funcionar. **2** *Med* operar; **to o. on sb for appendicitis**, operar a algn de apendicitis. **II** *vtr* **1** *(control)* manejar. **2** *(business)* dirigir.

operatic [ɒpəˈrætɪk] *adj* de ópera.

operating [ˈɒpəreɪtɪŋ] *n* **1** **o. costs**, gastos *mpl* de funcionamiento. **2** *Med* **o. table**, mesa *f* de operaciones. **2** **o. theatre**, *US* **o. theater**, quirófano *m.*

operation [ɒpəˈreɪʃən] *n* **1** *(of machine)* funcionamiento *m; (by person)* manejo *m.* **2** *Mil* maniobra *f.* **3** *Med* operación *f*, intervención quirúrgica; **to undergo an o. for**, ser operado,-a de

operational [ˌɒpəˈreɪʃənəl] *adj* 1 (*ready for use*) operativo,-a. 2 *Mil* operacional.

operative [ˈɒpərətɪv] *adj* 1 *Jur* (*in force*) vigente; **to become o.**, entrar en vigor. 2 (*significant*) clave, significativo,-a; **the o. word**, la palabra clave.

operator [ˈɒpəreɪtə^r] *n* 1 *Ind* operario,-a *m,f*. 2 *Tel* operador,-a *m,f*. 3 (*dealer*) negociante *mf*, agente *mf*; **tour o.**, agente de viajes.

opinion [əˈpɪnjən] *n* opinión *f*; **in my o.**, en mi opinión, a mi juicio; **it's a matter of o.**, es cuestión de opiniones; **to have a high o. of sb**, tener buen concepto de algn; **o. poll**, encuesta *f*, sondeo *m*.

opinionated [əˈpɪnjəneɪtɪd] *adj* dogmático,-a.

opium [ˈəʊpɪəm] *n* opio *m*.

opponent [əˈpəʊnənt] *n* adversario,-a *m,f*.

opportune [ˈɒpətjuːn] *adj* oportuno,-a.

opportunist [ˌɒpəˈtjuːnɪst] *adj & n* oportunista (*mf*).

opportunity [ˌɒpəˈtjuːnɪtɪ] *n* 1 oportunidad *f*, ocasión *f*. 2 (*prospect*) perspectiva *f*.

oppose [əˈpəʊz] *vtr* oponerse a.

opposed [əˈpəʊzd] *adj* opuesto,-a; **to be o. to sth**, estar en contra de algo; **as o. to**, comparado,-a con.

opposing [əˈpəʊzɪŋ] *adj* adversario,-a.

opposite [ˈɒpəzɪt, ˈɒpəsɪt] I *adj* 1 (*facing*) de enfrente; (*page*) contiguo,-a. 2 (*contrary*) opuesto,-a, contrario,-a; **in the o. direction**, en dirección contraria. II *n* lo contrario *m*; **quite the o.!**, ¡al contrario! III *prep* enfrente de, frente a. IV *adv* enfrente.

opposition [ˌɒpəˈzɪʃən] *n* 1 oposición *f*; **in o. to**, en contra de. 2 *Pol* **the o.**, la oposición.

oppress [əˈpres] *vtr* oprimir.

oppression [əˈpreʃən] *n* opresión *f*.

oppressive [əˈpresɪv] *adj* opresivo,-a; (*atmosphere*) agobiante; (*heat*) sofocante.

opt [ɒpt] *vi* optar; **to o. for**, optar por; **to o. to do sth**, optar por hacer algo. ◆**opt out** *vi* retirarse; **to o. out of doing sth**, decidir no hacer algo.

optical [ˈɒptɪkəl] *adj* óptico,-a.

optician [ɒpˈtɪʃən] *n* óptico,-a *m,f*.

optics [ˈɒptɪks] *n* óptica *f*.

optimist [ˈɒptɪmɪst] *n* optimista *mf*.

optimistic [ˌɒptɪˈmɪstɪk] *adj* optimista. ◆**optimistically** *adv* con optimismo.

optimum [ˈɒptɪməm] I *n* grado óptimo. II *adj* óptimo,-a.

option [ˈɒpʃən] *n* opción *f*; **I have no o.**, no tengo más remedio; **to keep one's options open**, no comprometerse; **with the o. of**, con opción a.

optional [ˈɒpʃənəl] *adj* optativo,-a, facultativo,-a; *Educ* **o. subject**, (asignatura *f*) optativa *f*.

opulence [ˈɒpjʊləns] *n* opulencia *f*.

or [ɔː^r, *unstressed* ə] *conj* 1 o; (*before a word beginning with* o *or* ho) u; (*before else*, si no, o bien; **whether you like it or not**, tanto si te gusta como si no; **either a bun or a piece of cake**, (o) una magdalena o un trozo de pastel. 2 (*with negative*) ni; **he can't read or write**, no sabe leer ni escribir; → **nor**.

oral [ˈɔːrəl, ˈɒrəl] I *adj* oral. II *n* examen *m* oral. ◆**orally** *adv* **to be taken o.**, por vía oral.

orange [ˈɒrɪndʒ] I *n* naranja *f*; **o. juice**, zumo *m* de naranja. II *adj* de color naranja.

orator [ˈɒrətə^r] *n* orador,-a *m,f*.

oratory [ˈɒrətərɪ] *n* oratoria *f*.

orbit [ˈɔːbɪt] I *n* *Astron* órbita *f*. II *vtr* girar alrededor de. III *vi* girar.

orchard [ˈɔːtʃəd] *n* huerto *m*.

orchestra [ˈɔːkɪstrə] *n* orquesta *f*.

orchestral [ɔːˈkestrəl] *adj* orquestal.

orchid [ˈɔːkɪd] *n* orquídea *f*.

ordain [ɔːˈdeɪn] *vtr* 1 *Rel* ordenar; **to be ordained**, ordenarse. 2 (*decree*) decretar.

ordeal [ɔːˈdiːl] *n* mala experiencia *f*.

order [ˈɔːdə^r] I *n* 1 (*sequence*) orden *m*; **in alphabetical o.**, por orden alfabético; **to put in o.**, ordenar. 2 (*condition*) estado *m*; **is your passport in o.?**, ¿tienes el pasaporte en regla?; **'out of o.'**, averiado,-a. 3 (*peace*) orden *m*; **to restore o.**, reestablecer el orden público. 4 (*command*) orden *f*. 5 *Com* pedido *m*, encargo *m*; **to be on o.**, estar pedido; **to o.**, a la medida; **o. form**, hoja *f* de pedido. 6 *Rel* orden *f*. 7 (*of the highest o.*, (*quality*) de primera calidad. 8 (*kind*) índole *f*, tipo *m*; *Biol* orden *m*. 9 **in the o. of**, del orden de. 10 **in o. that**, para que (+ *subj*), a fin de que (+ *subj*); **in o. to** (+ *infin*), para, a fin de (+ *infin*). II *vtr* 1 (*command*) ordenar, mandar; **to o. sb to do sth**, mandar a algn hacer algo. 2 *Com* pedir, encargar; **to o. a dish**, pedir un plato.

orderly [ˈɔːdəlɪ] I *adj* usual, normal; (*average*) corriente, común; **the o. citizen**, el ciudadano de a pie. II *n* 1 *Med* enfermero *m*. 2 *Mil* ordenanza *m*.

ordinary [ˈɔːdənrɪ] I *adj* usual, normal; (*average*) corriente, común; **the o. citizen**, el ciudadano de a pie. II *n* **the o.**, lo corriente, lo normal; **out of the o.**, fuera de lo común.

ordnance [ˈɔːdnəns] *n* *GB* **O. Survey**, servicio *m* oficial de topografía y cartografía.

ore [ɔː^r] *n* mineral *m*.

organ [ˈɔːgən] *n* *Mus Anat etc* órgano *m*.

organic [ɔːˈgænɪk] *adj* orgánico,-a.

organism [ˈɔːgənɪzəm] *n* organismo *m*.

organization [ˌɔːgənaɪˈzeɪʃən] *n* organización *f*.

organize [ˈɔːgənaɪz] *vtr* organizar.

organizer [ˈɔːgənaɪzə^r] *n* organizador,-a

orgasm ['ɔ:gæzəm] n orgasmo m.

orgy ['ɔ:dʒɪ] n orgía f.

Orient ['ɔ:rɪənt] n the O., el Oriente.

Oriental [ɔ:rɪ'entəl] adj & n oriental (mf).

origin ['ɒrɪdʒɪn] n origen m; country of o., país m natal or de origen.

original [ə'rɪdʒɪnəl] I adj 1 original; (first) primero,-a. 2 (imaginative) original. II n original m. ◆**originally** adv 1 (at first) en un principio. 2 (with imagination) con originalidad.

originality [ərɪdʒɪ'nælɪtɪ] n originalidad f.

originate [ə'rɪdʒɪneɪt] I vt originar. II vi to o. from or in, tener su origen en.

Orkneys ['ɔ:knɪz] npl (Islas) Órcadas.

ornament ['ɔ:nəmənt] n ornamento m, adorno m.

ornamental [ɔ:nə'mentəl] adj decorativo,-a.

ornate [ɔ:'neɪt] adj vistoso,-a.

ornithology [ɔ:nɪ'θɒlədʒɪ] n ornitología f.

orphan ['ɔ:fən] I n huérfano,-a m,f. II vtr she was orphaned, quedó huérfana.

orphanage ['ɔ:fənɪdʒ] n orfanato m.

orthodox ['ɔ:θədɒks] adj ortodoxo,-a.

orthodoxy ['ɔ:θədɒksɪ] n ortodoxia f.

orthopaedic, US **orthopedic** [ɔ:θəʊ'pi:dɪk] adj ortopédico,-a.

oscillate ['ɒsɪleɪt] vi oscilar.

ostensible [ɒ'stensɪbəl] adj 1 (apparent) ostensible. 2 (pretended) aparente.

ostentatious [ɒsten'teɪʃəs] adj ostentoso,-a.

osteopath ['ɒstɪəpæθ] n osteópata mf.

ostracize ['ɒstrəsaɪz] vtr (from society) condenar al ostracismo; (from group) aislar, excluir.

ostrich ['ɒstrɪtʃ] n avestruz f.

other ['ʌðəʳ] I adj otro,-a; every o. day, cada dos días; on the o. hand, por otra parte; o. people have seen it, otros lo han visto; the o. four, los otros cuatro; the o. one, el otro, la otra; the o. thing, lo otro. 2 he must be somewhere or o., debe de estar en alguna parte. II pron otro,-a m,f; many others, otros muchos; the others, los otros, los demás; we see each o. quite often, nos vemos con bastante frecuencia.

otherwise ['ʌðəwaɪz] I adv 1 (if not) si no. 2 (differently) de otra manera. 3 (in other respects) por lo demás. II adj distinto,-a.

otter ['ɒtəʳ] n nutria f.

ought [ɔ:t] v aux 1 (obligation) deber; I thought I o. to tell you, creí que debía decírtelo; **she o. to do it,** debería hacerlo. 2 (vague desirability) tener que, deber; **you o. to see the exhibition,** deberías ver la exposición. 3 (expectation) deber; **he o. to pass the exam,** seguramente aprobará el examen; **that o. to do,** con eso bastará.

ounce [aʊns] n onza f.

our [aʊəʳ] poss adj nuestro,-a.

ours [aʊəz] poss pron 1 (el) nuestro, (la) nuestra. 2 of o., nuestro,-a; **a friend of o.,** un amigo nuestro.

ourselves [aʊə'selvz] pers pron pl 1 (reflexive) nos. 2 (emphatic) nosotros mismos, nosotras mismas. 3 by o., a solas.

oust [aʊst] vtr 1 (from a post) desbancar. 2 (from property etc) desalojar.

out [aʊt] I adv 1 (outside, away) fuera; o. there, ahí fuera; to go o., salir. 2 I told him straight o., se lo dije muy claramente; **o. loud,** en voz alta. 3 hear me o., escúcheme hasta el final. 4 o. of, (place) fuera de; **move o. of the way!,** ¡quítate de en medio!; **o. of danger,** fuera de peligro; **to go o. of the room,** salir de la habitación; **o. of control,** fuera de control; **o. of date,** (expired) caducado,-a; (old-fashioned) pasado,-a de moda. 5 o. of, (cause, motive) por. 6 o. of, (made from) de. 7 o. of, (short of, without) sin; **I'm o. of money,** se me ha acabado el dinero; **o. of breath,** sin aliento. 8 o. of, (among) entre; **forty o. of fifty,** cuarenta de cada cincuenta; (in exam etc) cuarenta sobre cincuenta.
II adj 1 the sun is o., ha salido el sol. 2 (unfashionable) pasado,-a de moda. 3 (fire) apagado,-a. 4 (not working) estropeado,-a. 5 she's o., (not in) ha salido, no está. 6 to be o. for sth/to do sth, buscar algo. 7 the book is just o., el libro acaba de salir. 8 (inaccurate) equivocado,-a; **to be o. in one's calculations,** equivocarse en los cálculos. 9 before the week is o., antes de que acabe la semana.
III prep (out of) por; **he jumped o. the window,** saltó por la ventana.

out-and-out ['aʊtənaʊt] adj redomado,-a.

outboard ['aʊtbɔ:d] adj o. motor, fueraborda m.

outbreak ['aʊtbreɪk] n (of war) comienzo m; (of spots) erupción f; (of disease) brote m; (of violence) ola f; (of anger) arrebato m; **at the o. of war,** cuando estalló la guerra.

outbuilding ['aʊtbɪldɪŋ] n dependencia f.

outburst ['aʊtbɜ:st] n (of anger) arrebato m; (of generosity) arranque m.

outcast ['aʊtkɑ:st] n marginado,-a m,f.

outcome ['aʊtkʌm] n resultado m.

outcrop ['aʊtkrɒp] n Geol afloramiento m.

outcry ['aʊtkraɪ] n there was an o., hubo fuertes protestas.

outdated [aʊt'deɪtɪd] adj anticuado,-a, obsoleto,-a.

outdo [aʊt'du:] vtr to o. sb, superar a algn.

outdoor ['aʊtdɔ:ʳ] adj 1 al aire libre 2 (clothes) de calle.

outdoors [aʊt'dɔ:z] adv fuera, al aire libre.

outer ['autə^r] *adj* exterior, externo,-a.

outfit ['autfit] *n* **1** (*kit, equipment*) equipo *m*. **2** (*set of clothes*) conjunto *m*. **3** *fam* (*group*) grupo *m*.

outgoing ['autgəuiŋ] **I** *adj* **1** (*departing*) saliente. **2** (*sociable*) extrovertido,-a. **II** *npl* outgoings, gastos *mpl*.

outgrow [aut'grəu] *vtr* **he's outgrowing all his clothes**, toda la ropa se le está quedando pequeña; **she'll o. it**, se le pasará con la edad.

outhouse ['authaus] *n* → **outbuilding**.

outing ['autiŋ] *n* excursión *f*.

outlandish [aut'lændiʃ] *adj* estrafalario, -a.

outlast [aut'lɑːst] *vtr* durar más que.

outlaw ['autlɔː] **I** *n* proscrito,-a *m,f*. **II** *vtr* prohibir.

outlet ['autlet, 'autlit] *n* **1** (*opening*) salida *f*. **2** (*for emotions*) válvula *f* de escape. **3** *Com* mercado *m*. **4** (*for water*) desagüe *m*.

outline ['autlain] **I** *n* **1** (*draft*) bosquejo *m*. **2** (*outer line*) contorno *m*; (*silhouette*) perfil *m*. **II** *vtr* **1** (*draw lines of*) perfilar. **2** (*summarize*) resumir. **3** (*describe roughly*) trazar las líneas generales de.

outlive [aut'liv] *vtr* sobrevivir a.

outlook ['autluk] *n* **1** (*point of view*) punto *m* de vista. **2** (*prospect*) perspectiva *f*; *Meteor* previsión *f*.

outlying ['autlaiiŋ] *adj* (*remote*) aislado,-a.

outmoded [aut'məudid] *adj* anticuado,-a.

outnumber [aut'nʌmbə^r] *vtr* exceder en número.

out-of-the-way [autənðə'wei] *adj* **1** (*distant*) apartado,-a, aislado,-a. **2** (*uncommon*) poco corriente.

outpatient ['autpeiʃənt] *n* paciente externo,-a; **outpatients' department**, departamento *m* de consulta externa.

outpost ['autpəust] *n* avanzada *f*.

output ['autput] *n* **1** producción *f*; (*of machine*) rendimiento *m*. **2** *Elec* potencia *f*. **3** *Comput* salida *f*.

outrage ['autreidʒ] **I** *n* ultraje *m*; **it's an o.!**, ¡es un escándalo!. **II** *vtr* **to be outraged by sth**, indignarse por algo.

outrageous [aut'reidʒəs] *adj* (*behaviour*) escandaloso,-a; (*clothes*) extravagante; (*price*) exhorbitante.

outright ['autrait] **I** *adj* (*absolute*) absoluto,-a. **II** [aut'rait] *adv* **1** (*completely*) por completo. **2** (*directly*) directamente, sin reserva. **3** (*immediately*) en el acto.

outset ['autset] *n* comienzo *m*, principio *m*.

outside [aut'said] **I** *prep* **1** fuera de. **2** (*beyond*) más allá de. **3** (*other than*) aparte de. **II** ['autsaid] *adj* **1** (*exterior*) exterior, externo,-a. **2** (*remote*) remoto,-a. **III** [aut'said] *adv* fuera, afuera. **IV** *n* exterior *m*; **on the o.**, por fuera; *fam* **at the o.**,

como mucho.

outsider [aut'saidə^r] *n* **1** (*stranger*) extraño,-a *m,f*, forastero,-a *m,f*. **2** *Pol* candidato,-a *m,f* con pocas posibilidades de ganar.

outsize(d) ['autsaiz(d)] *adj* (*clothes*) de talla muy grande.

outskirts ['autskɜːts] *npl* afueras *fpl*.

outspoken [aut'spəukən] *adj* directo,-a, abierto,-a.

outstanding [aut'stændiŋ] *adj* **1** (*exceptional*) destacado,-a. **2** (*unpaid, unresolved*) pendiente.

outstretched [aut'stretʃt] *adj* extendido,-a.

outward ['autwəd] *adj* **1** (*external*) exterior, externo,-a. **2** **the o. journey**, el viaje de ida. ◆**outwardly** *adv* aparentemente.

outward(s) ['autwəd(z)] *adv* hacia (a)fuera.

outweigh [aut'wei] *vtr* **1** (*prevail over*) prevalecer sobre. **2** (*weigh more than*) pesar más que.

oval ['əuvəl] **I** *adj* oval, ovalado,-a. **II** *n* óvalo *m*.

ovary ['əuvəri] *n* ovario *m*.

ovation [əu'veiʃən] *n* ovación *f*.

oven ['ʌvən] *n* horno *m*.

ovenproof ['ʌvənpruːf] *adj* refractario,-a.

over ['əuvə^r] **I** *prep* **1** (*above*) encima de. **2** (*on top of*) sobre, encima de. **3** (*across*) al otro lado de; **the bridge o. the river**, el puente que cruza el río. **4** (*during*) durante. **5** (*throughout*) por. **6** **all o.**, por todo,-a; **famous all o. the world**, famoso en el mundo entero. **7** (*by the agency of*) por; **o. the phone**, por teléfono. **8** (*more than*) más que; **men o. twenty-five**, hombres mayores de veinticinco años; **o. and above**, además de. **9** (*recovered from*) recuperado,-a de. **II** *adv* **1** **o. there**, allá; **why don't you come o. tomorrow?**, ¿por qué no vienes a casa mañana? **2** (*throughout*) por; **all o.**, por todas partes. **3** (*more*) más. **4** (*again*) otra vez; **o. and o.** (**again**), una y otra vez; **twice o.**, dos veces seguidas. **5** (*in excess*) de más. **III** *adj* (*finished*) acabado,-a; **it's** (**all**) **o.**, se acabó; **the danger is o.**, ha pasado el peligro.

overall ['əuvərɔːl] **I** *adj* total, global. **II** [əuvə'rɔːl] *adv* (*on the whole*) por lo general, en conjunto. **III** ['əuvərɔːl] *n* **1** *GB* guardapolvo *m*. **2** overalls, mono *m sing*.

overawe [əuvə'rɔː] *vtr* **to be overawed**, sobrecogerse.

overbearing [əuvə'beəriŋ] *adj* (*domineering*) dominante; (*important*) significativo, -a.

overboard ['əuvəbɔːd] *adv* por la borda; **man o.!**, ¡hombre al agua!; *fam* **to go o.**, pasarse.

overcast ['əuvəkɑːst] *adj* nublado,-a.

overcharge |əuvə'tʃɑːdʒ| vtr 1 (charge too much) cobrar demasiado. 2 (overload) sobrecargar.

overcoat |'əuvəkəut| n abrigo m.

overcome |əuvə'kʌm| vtr 1 (conquer) vencer; o. by grief, deshecho por el dolor. 2 (obstacle) superar.

overconfident |əuvə'kɒnfɪdənt| adj presumido,-a, creído,-a.

overcrowded |əuvə'kraudɪd| adj (room) atestado,-a (de gente); (country) superpoblado,-a.

overcrowding |əuvə'kraudɪŋ| n (of prisons etc) hacinamiento m; (of country) superpoblación f.

overdo |əuvə'duː| vtr 1 (carry too far) exagerar; don't o. it, no te pases. 2 Culin cocer o asar demasiado.

overdose |'əuvədəus| n sobredosis f.

overdraft |'əuvədrɑːft| n giro m en descubierto; (amount) saldo m deudor.

overdraw |əuvə'drɔː| vtr to be overdrawn, tener la cuenta en descubierto.

overdue |əuvə'djuː| adj (rent, train etc) atrasado,-a; (reform) largamente esperado,-a.

overestimate |əuvər'estɪmeɪt| vtr sobreestimar.

overflow |əuvə'fləu| I vi (river) desbordarse; (cup etc) derramarse. II |'əuvəfləu| n (of river etc) desbordamiento m; o. pipe, cañería f de desagüe.

overgrown |əuvə'grəun| adj 1 (with grass) cubierto,-a (de hierba). 2 (in size) demasiado grande.

overhaul |əuvə'hɔːl| I vtr revisar. II |'əuvəhɔːl| n revisión f y reparación f.

overhead |'əuvəhed| I adj (por) encima de la cabeza; o. cable, cable aéreo. II |əuvə'hed| adv arriba, por encima de la cabeza.

overheads |'əuvəhedz| npl gastos mpl generales.

overhear |əuvə'hɪər| vtr oír por casualidad.

overheat |əuvə'hiːt| vi recalentarse.

overjoyed |əuvə'dʒɔɪd| adj rebosante de alegría.

overlap |əuvə'læp| vi superponerse; fig our plans o., nuestros planes coinciden parcialmente.

overleaf |əuvə'liːf| adv al dorso.

overload |əuvə'ləud| I vtr sobrecargar. II n sobrecarga f.

overlook |əuvə'luk| vtr 1 (fail to notice) saltarse. 2 (ignore) no hacer caso de; we'll o. it this time, esta vez haremos la vista gorda. 3 (have a view of) dar a, tener vista a.

overnight |əuvə'naɪt| I adv 1 (during the night) por la noche; we stayed there o., pasamos la noche allí. 2 (suddenly) de la noche a la mañana. II adj |'əuvənaɪt| (sudden) repentino,-a.

overpay |əuvə'peɪ| vtr pagar demasiado.

overpower |əuvə'pauər| vtr 1 (subdue) dominar. 2 (affect strongly) abrumar.

overrate |əuvə'reɪt| vtr sobreestimar, supervalorar.

override |əuvə'raɪd| vtr 1 (disregard) hacer caso omiso de. 2 (annul, cancel out) anular. 3 (be more important than) contar más que.

overriding |əuvə'raɪdɪŋ| adj principal; (importance) primordial; (need) imperioso,-a.

overrule |əuvə'ruːl| vtr invalidar; Jur denegar.

overrun |əuvə'rʌn| vtr 1 (country) invadir. 2 (allotted time) excederse de.

overseas |əuvə'siːz| I adv en ultramar; to live o., vivir en el extranjero. II |'əuvəsiːz| adj de ultramar; (person) extranjero,-a; (trade) exterior.

oversee |əuvə'siː| vtr supervisar.

overseer |'əuvəsɪər| n supervisor,-a m,f; (foreman) capataz m.

overshadow |əuvə'ʃædəu| vtr fig eclipsar.

overshoot |əuvə'ʃuːt| vtr to o. a turning, pasarse un cruce; fig to o. the mark, pasarse de la raya.

oversight |'əuvəsaɪt| n descuido m.

oversleep |əuvə'sliːp| vi quedarse dormido,-a.

overspill |'əuvəspɪl| n exceso m de población.

overstate |əuvə'steɪt| vtr exagerar.

overstep |əuvə'step| vtr fig to o. the mark, pasarse de la raya.

overt |'əuvɜːt, əu'vɜːt| adj patente.

overtake |əuvə'teɪk| vtr 1 GB Aut adelantar. 2 (surpass) superar a. 3 (of night) sorprender.

overthrow |əuvə'θrəu| vtr (government) derribar.

overtime |'əuvətaɪm| n horas fpl extra.

overtone |'əuvətəun| n matiz m.

overture |'əuvətjuər| n 1 Mus obertura f; fig (introduction) introducción f. 2 (proposal) propuesta f.

overturn |əuvə'tɜːn| vtr & vi volcar.

overweight |əuvə'weɪt| adj demasiado pesado,-a.

overwhelm |əuvə'welm| vtr 1 (defeat) aplastar; (overpower) abrumar; I'm overwhelmed, estoy abrumado,-a. 2 (with letters, work etc) inundar.

overwhelming |əuvə'welmɪŋ| adj (defeat) aplastante; (desire etc) irresistible.

overwork |əuvə'wɜːk| I vi trabajar demasiado. II vtr (person) forzar; (excuse etc) abusar de.

overwrought |əuvə'rɔːt| adj 1 (tense) muy nervioso,-a. 2 lit (too elaborate) forzado,-a.

owe |əu| vtr deber.

owing |'əuɪŋ| adj o. to, debido a, a causa

de.

owl [aʊl] *n* lechuza *f*, búho *m*.

own [əʊn] I *adj* propio,-a; **it's his o. fault**, es culpa suya. II *pron* 1 **my o., your o., his o.** etc, lo mío, lo tuyo, lo suyo, etc; *fig* **to come into one's o.**, realizarse; *fam* **to get one's o. back**, tomarse la revancha. 2 **on one's o.**, (*without help*) uno,-a mismo,-a; (*alone*) solo,-a. III *vtr* poseer, ser dueño,-a de. ◆**own up** *vtr* to o. **up** (**to**), confesar.

owner ['əʊnər] *n* propietario,-a *m,f*,

dueño,-a *m,f*.

ownership ['əʊnəʃɪp] *n* propiedad *f*, posesión *f*.

ox [ɒks] *n* (*pl* **oxen**) buey *m*.

oxide ['ɒksaɪd] *n Chem* óxido *m*.

oxtail ['ɒksteɪl] *n* rabo *m* de buey.

oxygen ['ɒksɪdʒən] *n* oxígeno *m*; **o. mask**, máscara *f* de oxígeno.

oyster ['ɔɪstər] *n* ostra *f*.

ozone ['əʊzəʊn] *n* ozono *m*; **o. layer**, capa *f* de ozono.

P

P, p [piː] *n* (*the letter*) P, p *f*.

p 1 (*pl* **pp**) *abbr of* **page**, pág., p. 2 [piː] *GB fam abbr of* **penny, pence**, penique(s) *m(pl)*.

PA [piːˈeɪ] *fam* **1** *abbr of* **personal assistant**, ayudante *mf* personal. **2** *abbr of* **public-address** (**system**).

pa *abbr of* **per annum** (*per year*), al año.

pace [peɪs] I *n* (*step*) paso *m*; (*speed*) ritmo *m*; **to keep p. with**, seguir a; *fig* avanzar al mismo ritmo que; **to set the p.**, marcar el paso a; *fig* marcar la pauta. II *vi* **to p. up and down**, ir de un lado a otro.

pacemaker ['peɪsmeɪkər] *n Sport* liebre *f*; *Med* marcapasos *m inv*.

Pacific [pəˈsɪfɪk] *adj* **the P.** (**Ocean**), el (océano) Pacífico.

pacifist ['pæsɪfɪst] *adj & n* pacifista (*mf*).

pacify ['pæsɪfaɪ] *vtr* (*person*) calmar; (*country*) pacificar.

pack1 [pæk] I *n* (*parcel*) paquete *m*; (*bundle*) bulto *m*; *US* (*of cigarettes*) paquete *m*; *GB* (*of cards*) baraja *f*; (*of hounds*) jauría *f*. II *vtr* 1 (*goods*) embalar, envasar; (*in suitcase*) poner; **to p. one's bags**, hacer las maletas; *fig* marcharse. 2 (*fill*) atestar. 3 (*press down*) (*snow*) apretar. III *vi* 1 hacer las maletas; *fam* **to send sb packing**, mandar a paseo a algn. 2 (*of people*) apiñarse (**into**, en). ◆**pack in** *vtr GB fam* (*give up*) dejar. ◆**pack off** *vtr fam* mandar. ◆**pack up** *fam* I *vtr* 1 (*give up*) dejar. II *vi* 1 (*stop working*) terminar; (*machine etc*) estropearse.

pack2 [pæk] *vtr* (*meeting*) llenar de partidarios.

package ['pækɪdʒ] I *n* 1 (*parcel*) paquete *m*; (*bundle*) bulto *m*; **p. tour**, viaje *m* todo incluido. 2 (*of proposals etc*) paquete *m*; (*agreement*) acuerdo *m*; **p. deal**, convenio *m* general. II *vtr* (*goods*) envasar, embalar.

packet ['pækɪt] *n* paquete *m*; *fam* (*fortune*) dineral *m*.

packing ['pækɪŋ] *n* embalaje *m*; **p. case**, caja *f* de embalar; **to do one's p.**, hacer

las maletas.

pact [pækt] *n* pacto *m*.

pad1 [pæd] I *n* 1 almohadilla *f*; (*of paper*) bloc *m*, taco *m*. 2 **launch p.**, plataforma *f* de lanzamiento. 3 *fam* (*flat*) piso *m*. II *vtr* (*chair*) acolchar. ◆**pad out** *vtr fig* meter paja en.

pad2 [pæd] *vi* **to p. about** *or* **around**, andar silenciosamente.

padding ['pædɪŋ] *n* (*material*) relleno *m*; *fig* (*in speech etc*) paja *f*.

paddle1 ['pædəl] I *n* (*oar*) pala *f*; (*boat or steamer*) vapor *m* de ruedas. II *vtr* (*boat*) remar con pala en. III *vi* (*in boat*) remar con pala.

paddle2 ['pædəl] *vi* chapotear.

paddling pool ['pædəlɪŋpuːl] *n* piscina *f* para niños.

paddock ['pædək] *n* potrero *m*; (*in race course*) paddock *m*.

paddy ['pædɪ] *n* arrozal *m*.

padlock ['pædlɒk] I *n* candado *m*. II *vtr* cerrar con candado.

paediatrician [piːdɪəˈtrɪʃən] *n* pediatra *mf*.

pagan ['peɪgən] *adj & n* pagano,-a (*m,f*).

page1 [peɪdʒ] *n* página *f*.

page2 [peɪdʒ] I *n* (*servant*) paje *m*; (*of knight*) escudero *m*; (*at club*) botones *m inv*. II *vtr* (*call*) llamar por altavoz.

pageant ['pædʒənt] *n* (*show*) espectáculo *m*; (*procession*) desfile *m*; (*on horses*) cabalgata *f*.

pageantry ['pædʒəntrɪ] *n* pompa *f*, boato *m*.

paid [peɪd] *adj* pagado,-a; *fig* **to put p. to sth**, acabar con algo.

pail [peɪl] *n* cubo *m*; (*child's*) cubito *m*.

pain [peɪn] I *n* 1 dolor *m*; (*grief*) sufrimiento *m*; *fam* **he's a p.** (**in the neck**), es un pelmazo; **on p. of death**, so pena de muerte. 2 **to take pains over sth**, esmerarse en algo. II *vtr* (*grieve*) dar pena a.

pained [peɪnd] *adj* de reproche.

painful ['peɪnfʊl] *adj* doloroso,-a; *fam* (*very bad*) malísimo,-a. ◆**painfully** *adv* **1 p. shy**, lastimosamente tímido,-a. **2**

fam terriblemente.

painkiller ['peɪnkɪlər] n analgésico m.

painless ['peɪnlɪs] adj sin dolor; fig sin dificultades.

painstaking ['peɪnzteɪkɪŋ] adj (person) concienzudo,-a; (care, research) esmerado,-a.

paint [peɪnt] I n pintura f. II vtr pintar; **to p. sth white**, pintar algo de blanco. III vi pintar.

paintbrush ['peɪntbrʌʃ] n Art pincel m; (for walls) brocha f.

painter ['peɪntər] n pintor,-a m,f.

painting ['peɪntɪŋ] n cuadro m; (activity) pintura f.

paintwork ['peɪntwɜːk] n pintura f.

pair [peər] n (of gloves, shoes) par m; (of people, cards) pareja f; **a p. of scissors**, unas tijeras; **a p. of trousers**, un pantalón, unos pantalones.

pajamas [pəˈdʒæməz] npl US → **pyjamas**.

Pakistan [pɑːkɪˈstɑːn] n Paquistán.

Pakistani [pɑːkɪˈstɑːnɪ] adj & n paquistaní (m,f).

pal [pæl] n fam amigo,-a m,f, colega mf.

palace ['pælɪs] n palacio m.

palatable ['pælətəbəl] adj (tasty) sabroso,-a; fig aceptable.

palate ['pælɪt] n paladar m.

palatial [pəˈleɪʃəl] adj magnífico,-a, suntuoso,-a.

palaver [pəˈlɑːvər] n fam lío m, follón m.

pale¹ [peɪl] I adj (skin) pálido,-a; (colour) claro,-a; (light) tenue; **to turn p.**, palidecer. II vi palidecer.

pale² [peɪl] n fig **to be beyond the p.**, ser inaceptable.

Palestine ['pælɪstaɪn] n Palestina.

Palestinian [pælɪˈstɪnɪən] adj & n palestino,-a (m,f).

palette ['pælɪt] n paleta f; **p. knife**, espátula f.

paling ['peɪlɪŋ] n valla f.

palisade [pælɪˈseɪd] n palizada f, estacada f.

pall¹ [pɔːl] n fig manto m; (of smoke) cortina f.

pall² [pɔːl] vi aburrir; **it never palls**, nunca cansa.

pallet ['pælɪt] n plataforma f de carga.

pallid ['pælɪd] adj pálido,-a.

pallor ['pælər] n palidez f.

palm¹ [pɑːm] n (tree) palmera f; (leaf) palma f; **date p.**, palma datilera; **P. Sunday**, domingo m de Ramos.

palm² [pɑːm] n Anat palma f. ◆**palm off** vtr **to p. sth off on sb**, colocar or endosar algo a algn.

palmistry ['pɑːmɪstrɪ] n quiromancia f.

palpable ['pælpəbəl] adj palpable.

palpitate ['pælpɪteɪt] vi palpitar.

palpitation [pælpɪˈteɪʃən] n palpitación f.

paltry ['pɔːltrɪ] adj (paltrier, paltriest)

insignificante.

pamper ['pæmpər] vtr mimar, consentir.

pamphlet ['pæmflɪt] n folleto m.

pan¹ [pæn] I n 1 (saucepan) cazuela f, cacerola f. 2 (of scales) platillo m. 3 (of lavatory) taza f. II vtr fam (critize) dejar por los suelos.

pan² [pæn] vi Cin tomar vistas panorámicas.

panacea [pænəˈsɪə] n panacea f.

panache [pəˈnæʃ] n garbo m, salero m.

Panama ['pænəmɑː] n Panamá; **P. Canal**, Canal m de Panamá.

pancake ['pænkeɪk] n crepe f.

panda ['pændə] n panda m; GB **p. car**, coche m patrulla.

pandemonium [pændɪˈməʊnɪəm] n alboroto m.

pander ['pændər] vi **to p. to**, (person) complacer a; (wishes) acceder a.

pane [peɪn] n cristal m, vidrio m.

panel ['pænəl] n 1 (of wall) panel m; (flat surface) tabla f; (of instruments) tablero m; (of ceiling) artesón m. 2 (jury) jurado m; Rad TV concursantes mpl.

panelling, US **paneling** ['pænəlɪŋ] n paneles mpl.

pang [pæŋ] n (of pain, hunger) punzada f; (of childbirth) dolores mpl; fig (of conscience) remordimiento m.

panic ['pænɪk] I n pánico m; **to get into a p.**, ponerse histérico,-a. II vi aterrarse.

panicky ['pænɪkɪ] adj asustadizo,-a.

panic-stricken ['pænɪkstrɪkən] adj aterrado,-a.

panorama [pænəˈrɑːmə] n panorama m.

pansy ['pænzɪ] n Bot pensamiento m; fam pej mariquita m.

pant [pænt] I n jadeo m. II vi jadear.

panther ['pænθər] n pantera f.

panties ['pæntɪz] npl bragas fpl.

pantomime ['pæntəmaɪm] n Theat (play) función f musical navideña; (mime) pantomima f.

pantry ['pæntrɪ] n despensa f.

pants [pænts] npl (underpants) (ladies') bragas fpl; (men's) calzoncillos mpl; US (trousers) pantalones mpl, pantalón m.

papal ['peɪpəl] adj papal.

paper ['peɪpər] I n 1 papel m; **fig on p.**, en teoría; **p. money**, papel moneda; **writing p.**, papel de escribir. 2 (exam) examen m; (essay) trabajo m (escrito). 3 Pol libro m. 4 (newspaper) periódico m; **the papers**, la prensa. 5 **papers**, (documents) documentos mpl. II vtr empapelar.

paperback ['peɪpəbæk] n libro m en rústica.

paperclip ['peɪpəklɪp] n clip m, sujetapapeles m inv.

paperweight ['peɪpəweɪt] n pisapapeles m inv.

paperwork ['peɪpəwɜːk] n papeleo m.

papier-mâché [pæpjeɪˈmæʃeɪ] n cartón m

piedra.

paprika ['pæprɪkə] n pimentón molido.

par [pɑːʳ] n (parity) igualdad f; Golf par m; fig it's p. for the course, es lo normal en estos casos; fig to feel below p., estar en baja forma.

parable ['pærəbəl] n parábola f.

parachute ['pærəʃuːt] I n paracaídas m inv. II vi to p. (down), saltar or lanzarse en paracaídas.

parade [pə'reɪd] I n desfile m; Mil to be on p., pasar revista. II vtr Mil hacer desfilar; fig (flaunt) hacer alarde de. III vi (troops) pasar revista; (procession) desfilar.

paradise ['pærədaɪs] n paraíso m.

paradox ['pærədɒks] n paradoja f.

paradoxical [pærə'dɒksɪkəl] adj paradójico,-a.

paraffin ['pærəfɪn] n parafina f; liquid p., aceite m de parafina; p. lamp, lámpara f de petróleo.

paragon ['pærəgɒn] n modelo m.

paragraph ['pærəgrɑːf] n párrafo m.

Paraguay ['pærəgwaɪ] n Paraguay.

Paraguayan [pærə'gwaɪən] adj & n paraguayo,-a (m,f).

parallel ['pærəlel] I adj paralelo,-a (to, with, a); fig comparable (to, with, a). II n Geog paralelo m; Geom paralela f; fig paralelo. III vtr fig ser paralelo,-a a.

paralysis [pə'rælɪsɪs] n parálisis f.

paralyse, US **paralyze** ['pærəlaɪz] vtr paralizar.

parameter [pə'ræmɪtəʳ] n parámetro m.

paramilitary [pærə'mɪlɪtərɪ] adj paramilitar.

paramount ['pærəmaʊnt] adj of p. importance, de suma importancia.

paranoid ['pærənɔɪd] adj & n paranoico,-a (m,f).

paraphernalia [pærəfə'neɪlɪə] n parafernalia f.

paraphrase ['pærəfreɪz] vtr parafrasear.

parasite ['pærəsaɪt] n parásito m.

parasol ['pærəsɒl] n sombrilla f.

paratrooper ['pærətruːpəʳ] n paracaidista mf.

parcel ['pɑːsəl] I n paquete m; p. bomb, paquete m bomba. II vtr to p. up, envolver, empaquetar.

parched [pɑːtʃt] adj (land) reseco,-a; (lips, mouth) seco,-a; fig to be p., estar muerto,-a de sed.

parchment ['pɑːtʃmənt] n pergamino m.

pardon ['pɑːdən] I n perdón m; Jur indulto m; I beg your p., (Usted) perdone; (I beg your) p.?, ¿cómo (dice)? II vtr perdonar; Jur indultar; p. me!, ¡Usted perdone!

parent ['peərənt] n parents, padres mpl.

parental [pə'rentəl] adj paternal; p. guidance, consejos mpl paternales.

parenthesis [pə'renθɪsɪs] n (pl parentheses [pə'renθɪsiːz]) paréntesis m inv; in

p., entre paréntesis.

pariah [pə'raɪə] n paria mf.

Paris ['pærɪs] n París.

parish ['pærɪʃ] n parroquia f.

Parisian [pə'rɪzɪən] adj & n parisino,-a (m,f).

parity ['pærɪtɪ] n igualdad f; (of shares) paridad f.

park [pɑːk] I n parque m. II vtr (car) aparcar, Am parquear.

parking ['pɑːkɪŋ] n aparcamiento m, estacionamiento m; 'no p.', 'prohibido aparcar'; US p. lot, aparcamiento; p. meter, parquímetro m; p. space, aparcamiento.

parliament ['pɑːləmənt] n parlamento m.

parliamentary [pɑːlə'mentərɪ] adj parlamentario,-a.

parlour, US **parlor** ['pɑːləʳ] n salón m.

parochial [pə'rəʊkɪəl] adj parroquial; pej (narrow-minded) de miras estrechas.

parody ['pærədɪ] n parodia f.

parole [pə'rəʊl] n Jur libertad f condicional; on p., en libertad bajo palabra.

parquet ['pɑːkeɪ] n p. floor, suelo m de parqué.

parrot ['pærət] n loro m, papagayo m.

parry ['pærɪ] vtr parar.

parsimonious [pɑːsɪ'məʊnɪəs] adj tacaño,-a.

parsley ['pɑːslɪ] n perejil m.

parsnip ['pɑːsnɪp] n chirivía f.

parson ['pɑːsən] n cura m.

part [pɑːt] I n 1 parte f; (piece) trozo m; (episode) capítulo m; Tech pieza f; for the most p., en la mayor parte. 2 Cin Theat papel m; to play a p. in sth, desempeñar un papel en algo; to take p. in sth, participar en algo. 3 (place) lugar m; in these parts, por estos lugares. 4 for my p., por mi parte; to take sb's p., tomar partido por algn; to take sth in good p., tomarse bien algo. II adj (partial) parcial; in p. exchange, como parte del pago. III adv (partly) en parte. IV vtr (separate) separar; to p. company with sb, separarse de algn; to p. one's hair, hacerse la raya (en el pelo). V vi separarse; (say goodbye) despedirse. ◆**part with** vtr separarse de. ◆**partly** adv en parte.

partial ['pɑːʃəl] adj parcial; to be p. to sth, ser aficionado,-a a algo.

participant [pɑː'tɪsɪpənt] n participante mf; (in competition) concursante mf.

participate [pɑː'tɪsɪpeɪt] vi participar (in, en).

participation [pɑːtɪsɪ'peɪʃən] n participación f.

participle ['pɑːtɪsɪpəl] n participio m.

particle ['pɑːtɪkəl] n partícula f.

particular [pə'tɪkjʊləʳ] I adj 1 (special) particular, especial; in this p. case, en este caso concreto; that p. person, esa persona en particular. 2 (fussy) exigente,

II *npl* **particulars**, pormenores *mpl*; **to take down sb's particulars**, anotar los datos personales de algn. ◆**particularly** *adv* particularmente, especialmente.

parting ['pɑːtɪŋ] I *n* (*separation*) separación *f*; (*farewell*) despedida *f*; (*in hair*) raya *f*. II *adj* de despedida.

partisan [pɑːtɪ'zæn, 'pɑːtɪzæn] I *n* Mil guerrillero,-a *m,f*; (*supporter*) partidario,-a *m,f*. II *adj* (*supporter*) a ultranza; (*of party*) partidista.

partition [pɑː'tɪʃən] I *n* (*wall*) tabique *m*; (*of country*) partición *f*. II *vtr* dividir.

partner ['pɑːtnəʳ] I *n* compañero,-a *m,f*; (*in dancing, tennis*) pareja *f*; (*husband*) marido *m*; (*wife*) mujer *f*; Com socio,-a *m,f*. II *vtr* acompañar.

partnership ['pɑːtnəʃɪp] *n* (*relationship*) vida *f* en común; Com sociedad *f*.

partridge ['pɑːtrɪdʒ] *n* perdiz *f*; (*young*) perdiz pardilla.

part-time [pɑːt'taɪm] I *adj* (*work etc*) de tiempo parcial. II *adv* a tiempo parcial.

party ['pɑːtɪ] I *n* 1 (*celebration*) fiesta *f*. 2 (*group*) grupo *m*. 3 Pol partido *m*; **p. political broadcast**, espacio *m* electoral. 4 Jur parte *f*. II *adj* de fiesta; Tel **p. line**, línea compartida.

pass [pɑːs] I *n* 1 (*of mountain*) desfiladero *m*. 2 (*permit*) permiso *m*; **bus p.**, abono *m* de autobús. 3 Sport pase *m*. 4 *fam* **to make a p. at sb**, intentar ligar con algn. II *vtr* 1 pasar; (*overtake*) adelantar. 2 (*exam, law*) aprobar; Jur **to p. sentence**, dictar sentencia.
III *vi* 1 pasar; (*procession*) desfilar; (*car*) adelantar; (*people*) cruzarse; Sport hacer un pase; **we passed on the stairs**, nos cruzamos en la escalera. 2 (*pain*) remitir; (*opportunity*) perderse; (*time*) pasar. 3 (*happen*) ocurrir, pasar. 4 (*in exam*) aprobar.
◆**pass away** *vi euph* pasar a mejor vida. ◆**pass by** I *vtr* pasar de largo. II *vi* pasar cerca (de). ◆**pass for** *vtr* pasar por. ◆**pass off** I *vtr* hacer pasar; **to p. oneself off as sth**, hacerse pasar por algo. II *vi* (*happen*) transcurrir. ◆**pass on** I *vtr* (*hand on*) transmitir. II *vi euph* pasar a mejor vida. ◆**pass out** *vi* (*faint*) desmayarse; Mil graduarse. ◆**pass over** *vtr* 1 (*aircraft*) volar por. 2 (*disregard*) pasar por alto. ◆**pass up** *vtr fam* (*opportunity*) renunciar; (*offer*) rechazar.

passable ['pɑːsəbəl] *adj* (*road*) transitable; (*acceptable*) pasable.

passage ['pæsɪdʒ] *n* 1 (*alleyway*) callejón *m*; (*hallway*) pasillo *m*. 2 (*movement*) tránsito *m*; Naut travesía *f*; Mus Lit pasaje *m*.

passageway ['pæsɪdʒweɪ] *n* (*interior*) pasillo *m*; (*exterior*) pasaje *m*.

passbook ['pɑːsbʊk] *n* libreta *f* de banco.

passenger ['pæsɪndʒəʳ] *n* pasajero,-a *m,f*.

passer-by [pɑːsə'baɪ] *n* transeúnte *mf*.

passing ['pɑːsɪŋ] I *n* 1 (*of time*) transcurso *m*; **in p.**, de pasada. 2 (*of law*) aprobación *f*. II *adj* que pasa; (*glance*) rápido,-a; (*thought*) pasajero,-a.

passion ['pæʃən] *n* pasión *f*; **p. fruit**, granadilla *f*.

passionate ['pæʃənɪt] *adj* apasionado,-a.

passive ['pæsɪv] *adj* pasivo,-a.

Passover ['pɑːsəʊvəʳ] *n* Pascua *f* de los judíos.

passport ['pɑːspɔːt] *n* pasaporte *m*.

password ['pɑːswɜːd] *n* contraseña *f*.

past [pɑːst] I *n* pasado *m*; **in the p.**, en el pasado; **to have a p.**, tener antecedentes. II *adj* pasado,-a; (*former*) anterior; **in the p. weeks**, en las últimas semanas. III *adv* por delante; **to run p.**, pasar corriendo. IV *prep* (*beyond*) más allá de; (*more than*) más de; **he's p. forty**, pasa de los cuarenta (años); **it's five p. ten**, son las diez y cinco; *fam* **to be p. it**, estar muy carroza.

pasta ['pæstə] *n* pasta *f*, pastas *fpl*.

paste [peɪst] I *n* pasta *f*; (*glue*) engrudo *m*. II *vtr* (*stick*) pegar; (*put paste on*) engomar.

pastel ['pæstəl] *adj* & *n* pastel (*m*).

pasteurized ['pæstjʊəraɪzd] *adj* pasteurizado,-a.

pastille ['pæstɪl] *n* pastilla *f*.

pastime ['pɑːstaɪm] *n* pasatiempo *m*.

pastor ['pɑːstəʳ] *n* pastor *m*.

pastoral ['pɑːstərəl] *adj* pastoral.

pastry ['peɪstrɪ] *n* (*dough*) pasta *f*; (*cake*) pastel *m*.

pasture ['pɑːstʃəʳ] *n* pasto *m*.

pasty[1] ['pæstɪ] *n* Culin empanada *f*, pastel *m* de carne.

pasty[2] ['peɪstɪ] *adj* (**pastier, pastiest**) (*complexion*) pálido,-a.

pat [pæt] I *n* (*caress*) caricia *f*; (*tap*) palmadita *f*; *fig* **to give sb a p. on the back**, felicitar a algn. II *vtr* acariciar; **to p. sb on the back**, dar a algn una palmadita en la espalda.

patch [pætʃ] *n* (*of material*) parche *m*; (*of land*) terreno *m*; (*of colour*) mancha *f*; *fig* **to go through a bad p.**, pasar por una mala racha. ◆**patch up** (*garment*) poner un parche en; **to p. things up**, (*after argument*) limar asperezas.

patchwork ['pætʃwɜːk] I *n* labor *f* de retales. II *adj* (*quilt etc*) hecho,-a con retales distintos.

patchy ['pætʃɪ] *adj* (**patchier, patchiest**) (*colour, performance*) desigual; (*knowledge*) incompleto,-a.

pâté ['pæteɪ] *n* paté *m*.

patent[1] ['peɪtənt] I *n* Com patente *f*. II *adj* (*obvious*) patente, evidente; Med **p. medicine**, específico *m*. III *vtr* Com patentar. ◆**patently** *adv* **it is p. obvious**, está clarísimo.

patent[2] ['peɪtənt] *n* **p. (leather)**, charol

m.

paternal [pə'tɜːnəl] *adj* paternal; *(grandmother etc)* paterno,-a.

paternity [pə'tɜːnɪtɪ] *n* paternidad *f*.

path [pɑːθ] *n* camino *m*, sendero *m*; *(route)* ruta *f*; *(of missile)* trayectoria *f*.

pathetic [pə'θetɪk] *adj (pitiful)* patético, -a; *fam (hopeless)* malísimo,-a; **she was a p. sight**, daba lástima verla.

pathological [pæθə'lɒdʒɪkəl] *adj* patológico,-a.

pathologist [pə'θɒlədʒɪst] *n* patólogo,-a *m,f*.

pathology [pə'θɒlədʒɪ] *n* patología *f*.

pathos ['peɪθɒs] *n* patetismo *m*.

pathway ['pɑːθweɪ] *n* camino *m*, sendero *m*.

patience ['peɪʃəns] *n* 1 paciencia *f*; **to lose one's p. with sb**, perder la paciencia con algn. 2 *GB* Cards solitario *m*.

patient ['peɪʃənt] I *adj* paciente; **to be p. with sb**, tener paciencia con algn. II *n* Med paciente *mf*.

patio ['pætɪəʊ] *n* patio *m*.

patriotic [pætrɪ'ɒtɪk] *adj (person)* patriota; *(speech, act)* patriótico,-a.

patrol [pə'trəʊl] I *n* patrulla *f*; **p. car**, coche *m* patrulla. II *vtr* patrullar por.

patrolman [pə'trəʊlmən] *n US* policía *m*.

patron ['peɪtrən] *n* 1 *(of charity)* patrocinador,-a *m,f*; *(of arts)* mecenas *m* *inv*; **p. saint**, (santo,-a *m,f*) patrón,-ona *m,f*. 2 *(customer)* cliente,-a *m,f* habitual.

patronize ['pætrənaɪz] *vtr* 1 *(arts)* fomentar; *(shop)* ser cliente,-a *m,f* habitual de; *(club etc)* frecuentar. 2 *pej (person)* tratar con condescendencia.

patronizing ['pætrənaɪzɪŋ] *adj* *pej* condescendiente.

patter¹ ['pætər] I *n (of rain)* repiqueteo *m*; *(of feet)* pasito *m*. II *vi (rain)* repiquetear; *(feet)* hacer ruido sordo.

patter² ['pætər] *n fam* labia *f*; *(of salesman)* discursillo preparado.

pattern ['pætən] *n Sew* patrón *m*; *(design)* dibujo *m*; *(on material)* estampado *m*; *fig (of behaviour)* modelo *m*.

paunch [pɔːntʃ] *n* panza *f*.

pauper ['pɔːpər] *n* pobre *mf*.

pause [pɔːz] I *n* pausa *f*; *(silence)* silencio *m*. II *vi* hacer una pausa; *(be silent)* callarse.

pave [peɪv] *vtr* pavimentar; *(with stones)* empedrar; *fig* **to p. the way for sb/sth**, preparar el terreno para algn/algo.

pavement ['peɪvmənt] *n* acera *f*; *US (road surface)* calzada *f*, pavimento *m*.

pavilion [pə'vɪljən] *n* pabellón *m*; *GB Sport (changing rooms)* vestuarios *mpl*.

paving ['peɪvɪŋ] *n (on road)* pavimento *m*; *(on floor)* enlosado *m*; *(with stones)* empedrado *m*; **p. stone**, losa *f*.

paw [pɔː] I *n (foot)* pata *f*; *(of cat)* garra *f*; *(of lion)* zarpa *f*. II *vtr (of lion)* dar zarpazos a; *pej (of person)* manosear, sobar.

pawn¹ [pɔːn] *n Chess* peón *m*; *fig* **to be sb's p.**, ser el juguete de algn.

pawn² [pɔːn] *vtr* empeñar.

pawnbroker ['pɔːnbrəʊkər] *n* prestamista *mf*.

pawnshop ['pɔːnʃɒp] *n* casa *f* de empeños.

pay [peɪ] I *n (wages)* paga *f*, sueldo *m*; **p. packet**, sobre *m* de la paga; **p. rise**, aumento *m* del sueldo; **p. slip**, nómina *f*. II *vtr (pt & pp paid)* 1 pagar; **to be or get paid**, cobrar. 2 *(attention)* prestar; *(homage)* rendir; *(visit)* hacer; **to p. sb a compliment**, halagar a algn. 3 *(be profitable for)* compensar. III *vi* 1 pagar; **to p. for sth**, pagar *(por)* algo. 2 *(be profitable)* ser rentable. ◆**pay back** *vtr* reembolsar; *fig* **to p. sb back**, vengarse de algn. ◆**pay in** *vtr (money)* ingresar. ◆**pay off** I *vtr (debt)* liquidar; *(mortgage)* cancelar. II *vi (be successful)* dar resultado. ◆**pay out** *vtr (spend)* gastar (**on**, en). ◆**pay up** *vi* pagar.

payable ['peɪəbəl] *adj* pagadero,-a.

payday ['peɪdeɪ] *n* día *m* de pago.

payee [peɪ'iː] *n* portador,-a *m,f*.

payment ['peɪmənt] *n* pago *m*; *(of cheque)* cobro *m*; **advance p.**, anticipo *m*; **down p.**, entrada *f*; **monthly p.**, mensualidad *f*.

payoff ['peɪɒf] *n (reward)* recompensa *f*; *fam (bribe)* soborno *m*.

payroll ['peɪrəʊl] *n* nómina *f*.

pc *abbr of* **per cent**, p.c.; *abbr of* **personal computer**, PC.

PE [piː'iː] *abbr of* **physical education**.

pea [piː] *n* guisante *m*.

peace [piːs] *n* paz *f*; *(calm)* tranquilidad *f*; **at** *or* **in p.**, en paz; **p. and quiet**, tranquilidad; **to make p.**, hacer las paces; *(of countries)* firmar la paz.

peaceable ['piːsəbəl] *adj* pacífico,-a.

peaceful ['piːsfʊl] *adj (demonstration)* pacífico,-a; *(place)* tranquilo,-a.

peace-keeping ['piːskiːpɪŋ] *adj* pacificador,-a; **p.-k. forces**, fuerzas *fpl* de pacificación.

peach [piːtʃ] *n* melocotón *m*.

peacock ['piːkɒk] *n* pavo *m* real.

peak [piːk] *n (of cap)* visera *f*; *(of mountain)* pico *m*; *(summit)* cima *f*; *fig* cumbre *f*; **p. hours**, horas *fpl* punta; **p. period**, horas de mayor consumo; **p. season**, temporada alta.

peal [piːl] *n (of bells)* repique *m*; **p. of thunder**, trueno *m*; **peals of laughter**, carcajadas *fpl*.

peanut ['piːnʌt] *n* cacahuete *m*; **p. butter**, mantequilla *f* or manteca *f* de cacahuete.

pear [peər] *n* pera *f*.

pearl [pɜːl] *n* perla *f*.

peasant ['pezənt] *adj & n* campesino,-a *(m,f)*.

peat [piːt] *n* turba *f*; **p. bog**, turbera *f*.

pebble ['pebəl] n guijarro m; (small) china f.

pecan [pɪ'kæn] n (nut) pacana f.

peck [pek] I n (of bird) picotazo m; fam (kiss) besito m. II vtr (bird) picotear; fam (kiss) dar un besito a. III vi to p. at one's food, picar la comida.

pecking order ['pekɪŋ'ɔːdər] n fig jerarquía f.

peckish ['pekɪʃ] adj fam to feel p., empezar a tener hambre.

peculiar [pɪ'kjuːlɪər] adj (odd) extraño,-a; (particular) característico,-a.

peculiarity [pɪkjuːlɪ'ærɪtɪ] n (oddity) rareza f; (characteristic) característica f, peculiaridad f.

pedal ['pedəl] I n pedal m. II vi pedalear.

pedantic [pɪ'dæntɪk] adj pedante.

peddle ['pedəl] vtr & vi Com vender de puerta en puerta; to p. drugs, traficar con drogas.

peddler ['pedlər] n (of drugs) traficante mf; US → pedlar.

pedestal ['pedɪstəl] n pedestal m; fig to put sb on a p., poner a algn sobre un pedestal.

pedestrian [pɪ'destrɪən] I n peatón,-ona m,f; p. crossing, paso m de peatones. II adj pey prosaico,-a.

pediatrician [piːdɪə'trɪʃən] n US → paediatrician.

pedigree ['pedɪgriː] I n linaje m; (family tree) árbol genealógico; (of animal) pedigrí m. II adj (animal) de raza.

pedlar ['pedlər] n vendedor,-a m,f ambulante.

pee [piː] fam I n pis m. II vi hacer pis.

peek [piːk] I n ojeada f. II vi to p. at sth, mirar algo a hurtadillas.

peel [piːl] I n piel f; (of orange, lemon) cáscara f. II vtr (fruit) pelar. III vi (paint) desconcharse; (wallpaper) despegarse; (skin) pelarse.

peeler ['piːlər] n potato p., pelapatatas m inv.

peelings ['piːlɪŋz] npl peladuras fpl, mondaduras fpl.

peep¹ [piːp] n (sound) pío m.

peep² [piːp] I n (glance) ojeada f; (furtive look) mirada furtiva. II vi to p. at sth, echar una ojeada a algo; to p. out from behind sth, dejarse ver detrás de algo.

peephole ['piːphəʊl] n mirilla f.

peer¹ [pɪər] n (noble) par m; (equal) igual mf; p. group, grupo parejo.

peer² [pɪər] vi mirar detenidamente; (shortsightedly) mirar con ojos de miope.

peerage ['pɪərɪdʒ] n título m de nobleza.

peeved [piːvd] adj fam fastidiado,-a, de mal humor.

peevish ['piːvɪʃ] adj malhumorado,-a.

peg [peg] I n clavija f; (for coat, hat) percha f. II vtr (clothes) tender; (prices) fijar.

pejorative [pɪ'dʒɒrətɪv] adj peyorativo,-a.

Pekinese [piːkə'niːz] adj & n pequinés, -esa (m,f).

Peking [piː'kɪŋ] n Pekín.

pelican ['pelɪkən] n pelícano m; GB p. crossing, paso m de peatones.

pellet ['pelɪt] n bolita f; (for gun) perdigón m.

pelt¹ [pelt] n (skin) pellejo m.

pelt² [pelt] I vtr to p. sb with sth, tirar algo a algn. II vi fam 1 it's pelting (down), (raining) llueve a cántaros. 2 to p. along, (rush) correr a toda prisa.

pelvis ['pelvɪs] n pelvis f.

pen¹ [pen] I n pluma f. II vtr escribir.

pen² [pen] I n (enclosure) corral m; (for sheep) redil m; (for children) corralito m. II vtr to p. in, acorralar.

penal ['piːnəl] adj castigar; Sport penalizar.

penalize ['piːnəlaɪz] vtr castigar; Sport penalizar.

penalty ['penəltɪ] n (punishment) pena f; Sport castigo; Ftb penalti m; to pay the p. for sth, cargar con las consecuencias de algo; p. area, área f de castigo.

penance ['penəns] n penitencia f.

pence [pens] npl → penny.

pencil ['pensəl] n lápiz m; p. case, estuche m de lápices; p. sharpener, sacapuntas m inv.

pendant ['pendənt] n colgante m.

pending ['pendɪŋ] I adj pendiente. II prep (while) mientras; p. a decision, (until) hasta que se tome una decisión.

pendulum ['pendjʊləm] n péndulo m.

penetrate ['penɪtreɪt] I vtr penetrar; fig adentrarse en. II vi atravesar; (get inside) penetrar.

penetrating ['penɪtreɪtɪŋ] adj (look) penetrante; (mind) perspicaz; (sound) agudo, -a.

penfriend ['penfrend] n amigo,-a m,f por carta.

penguin ['peŋgwɪn] n pingüino m.

penicillin [penɪ'sɪlɪn] n penicilina f.

peninsula [pɪ'nɪnsjʊlə] n península f.

penis ['piːnɪs] n pene m.

penitent ['penɪtənt] adj Rel penitente; (repentant) arrepentido,-a.

penitentiary [penɪ'tenʃərɪ] n US cárcel f, penal m.

penknife ['pennaɪf] n navaja f, cortaplumas m inv.

penniless ['penɪlɪs] adj sin dinero.

penny ['penɪ] n (pl pennies, pence [pens]) penique m.

penpal ['penpæl] n US → penfriend.

pension ['penʃən] n pensión f; retirement p., jubilación f.

pensioner ['penʃənər] n jubilado,-a m,f.

pensive ['pensɪv] adj pensativo,-a.

pentagon ['pentəgən] n US Pol the P., el Pentágono m.

Pentecost ['pentɪkɒst] n Pentecostés m.

penthouse ['penthaʊs] *n* ático *m*.

pent-up ['pent'ʌp] *adj* reprimido,-a.

penultimate [pɪ'nʌltɪmɪt] *adj* penúltimo,-a.

people ['piːpəl] *npl* **1** gente *f sing*; (*individuals*) personas *fpl*; **many p.**, mucha gente; **old p.'s home**, asilo *m* de ancianos; **p. say that ...**, se dice que ...; **some p.**, algunas personas. **2** (*citizens*) ciudadanos *mpl*; (*inhabitants*) habitantes *mpl*; **the p.**, el pueblo. **3** (*nation*) pueblo *m*, nación *f*.

pep [pep] *n fam* ánimo *m*, energía *f*; **p. talk**, discurso *m* enardecedor. ◆**pep up** *vtr fam* animar.

pepper ['pepər] **I** *n* (*spice*) pimienta *f*; (*fruit*) pimiento *m*; **black p.**, pimienta negra; **p. pot**, pimentero *m*; **red/green p.**, pimiento rojo/verde; **p. mill**, molinillo *m* de pimienta. **II** *vtr fig* **peppered with**, salpicado,-a de.

peppermint ['pepəmɪnt] *n* menta *f*; (*sweet*) pastilla *f* de menta.

per [pɜːr] *prep* por; **5 times p. week**, 5 veces a la semana; **p. cent**, por ciento; **p. day/annum**, al or por día/año; **p. capita**, per cápita.

perceive [pə'siːv] *vtr* (*see*) percibir.

percentage [pə'sentɪdʒ] *n* porcentaje *m*.

perceptible [pə'septəbəl] *adj* (*visible*) perceptible; (*sound*) audible; (*improvement*) sensible.

perception [pə'sepʃən] *n* percepción *f*.

perceptive [pə'septɪv] *adj* perspicaz.

perch¹ [pɜːtʃ] *n* (*fish*) perca *f*.

perch² [pɜːtʃ] **I** *n* (*for bird*) percha *f*. **II** *vi* (*bird*) posarse (**on**, en).

percolate ['pɜːkəleɪt] **I** *vtr* filtrar; **percolated coffee**, café *m* filtro. **II** *vi* filtrarse.

percolator ['pɜːkəleɪtər] *n* cafetera *f* de filtro.

percussion [pə'kʌʃən] *n* percusión *f*.

perennial [pə'renɪəl] *adj* perenne.

perfect ['pɜːfɪkt] **I** *adj* perfecto,-a; **he's a p. stranger to us**, nos es totalmente desconocido; **p. tense**, tiempo perfecto. **II** [pə'fekt] *vtr* perfeccionar. ◆**perfectly** *adv* perfectamente; (*absolutely*) completamente.

perfection [pə'fekʃən] *n* perfección *f*.

perforate ['pɜːfəreɪt] *vtr* perforar.

perforation [pɜːfə'reɪʃən] *n* perforación *f*; (*on stamps etc*) perforado *m*.

perform [pə'fɔːm] **I** *vtr* (*task*) ejecutar, realizar; (*piece of music*) interpretar; *Theat* representar. **II** *vi* (*machine*) funcionar; *Mus* interpretar; *Theat* actuar.

performance [pə'fɔːməns] *n* (*of task*) ejecución *f*, realización *f*; *Mus* interpretación *f*; *Theat* representación *f*; *Sport* actuación *f*; (*of machine etc*) rendimiento *m*.

performer [pə'fɔːmər] *n Mus* intérprete *mf*; *Theat* actor *m*, actriz *f*.

perfume ['pɜːfjuːm] *n* perfume *m*.

perfunctory [pə'fʌŋktərɪ] *adj* superficial.

perhaps [pə'hæps, præps] *adv* tal vez, quizá(s).

peril ['perɪl] *n* (*risk*) riesgo *m*; (*danger*) peligro *m*.

perilous ['perɪləs] *adj* (*risky*) arriesgado,-a; (*dangerous*) peligroso,-a. ◆**perilously** *adv* peligrosamente.

perimeter [pə'rɪmɪtər] *n* perímetro *m*.

period ['pɪərɪəd] **I** *n* **1** período *m*; (*stage*) etapa *f*. **2** *Educ* clase *f*. **3** (*full stop*) punto *m*. **4** (*menstruation*) regla *f*. **II** *adj* (*dress, furniture*) de época.

periodic [pɪərɪ'ɒdɪk] *adj* periódico,-a. ◆**periodically** *adv* de vez en cuando.

periodical [pɪərɪ'ɒdɪkəl] **I** *adj* periódico,-a. **II** *n* revista *f*.

peripheral [pə'rɪfərəl] **I** *adj* periférico,-a. **II** *n Comput* unidad periférica.

perish ['perɪʃ] *vi* perecer; (*material*) echarse a perder.

perishable ['perɪʃəbəl] *adj* perecedero,-a.

perjury ['pɜːdʒərɪ] *n* perjurio *m*.

perk [pɜːk] *n fam* extra *m*. ◆**perk up** *vi* (*person*) animarse; (*after illness*) reponerse.

perky ['pɜːkɪ] *adj* (*perkier, perkiest*) animado,-a, alegre.

perm [pɜːm] **I** *n* permanente *f*. **II** *vtr* **to have one's hair permed**, hacerse la permanente.

permanent ['pɜːmənənt] *adj* permanente; (*address, job*) fijo,-a.

permeate ['pɜːmɪeɪt] *vtr & vi* penetrar; *fig* extenderse por.

permissible [pə'mɪsəbəl] *adj* admisible.

permission [pə'mɪʃən] *n* permiso *m*.

permissive [pə'mɪsɪv] *adj* permisivo,-a.

permit ['pɜːmɪt] **I** *n* permiso *m*; *Com* licencia *f*. **II** [pə'mɪt] *vtr* **to p. sb to do sth**, permitir a algn hacer algo.

pernicious [pə'nɪʃəs] *adj* pernicioso,-a.

perpendicular [pɜːpən'dɪkjʊlər] **I** *adj* perpendicular; (*cliff*) vertical. **II** *n* perpendicular *f*.

perpetrate ['pɜːpɪtreɪt] *vtr* cometer.

perpetual [pə'petʃʊəl] *adj* (*noise*) continuo,-a; (*arguing*) interminable; (*snow*) perpetuo,-a.

perplex [pə'pleks] *vtr* dejar perplejo,-a.

perplexing [pə'pleksɪŋ] *adj* desconcertante.

persecute ['pɜːsɪkjuːt] *vtr* perseguir; (*harass*) acosar.

persecution [pɜːsɪ'kjuːʃən] *n* persecución *f*; (*harassment*) acoso *m*.

perseverance [pɜːsɪ'vɪərəns] *n* perseverancia *f*.

persevere [pɜːsɪ'vɪər] *vi* perseverar.

Persian ['pɜːʃən] *adj* persa; **P. Gulf**, golfo Pérsico.

persist [pə'sɪst] *vi* empeñarse (**in**, en).

persistence [pə'sɪstəns] *n* empeño *m*.

persistent [pə'sɪstənt] *adj (person)* perseverante; *(smell etc)* persistente; *(continual)* constante.

person ['pɜːsən] *n (pl* **people** ['piːpəl]*)* persona *f; (individual)* individuo *m;* **in p.**, en persona.

personable ['pɜːsənəbəl] *adj (handsome)* bien parecido,-a; *(pleasant)* amable.

personal ['pɜːsənəl] **I** *adj (private)* personal; *(friend)* íntimo,-a. **p. computer**, ordenador *m* personal; **p. column**, anuncios *mpl* personales; **p. pronoun**, pronombre *m* personal. **2** *(in person)* en persona; **he will make a p. appearance**, estará aquí en persona. **3** *pej (comment etc)* indiscreto,-a. ◆**personally** *adv (for my part)* personalmente; *(in person)* en persona.

personality [pɜːsə'nælɪtɪ] *n* personalidad *f.*

personify [pə'sɒnɪfaɪ] *vtr* personificar, encarnar.

personnel [pɜːsə'nel] *n* personal *m.*

perspective [pə'spektɪv] *n* perspectiva *f.*

Perspex® ['pɜːspeks] *n* plexiglás® *m.*

perspiration [pɜːspə'reɪʃən] *n* transpiración *f.*

perspire [pə'spaɪər] *vi* transpirar.

persuade [pə'sweɪd] *vtr* persuadir; **to p. sb to do sth**, persuadir a algn para que haga algo.

persuasion [pə'sweɪʒən] *n* persuasión *f; (opinion, belief)* credo *m.*

persuasive [pə'sweɪsɪv] *adj* persuasivo,-a.

pert [pɜːt] *adj* pizpireta, coqueto,-a.

pertain [pə'teɪn] *vi* estar relacionado,-a **(to**, con).

pertinent ['pɜːtɪnənt] *adj (relevant)* pertinente; **p. to**, relacionado,-a con, a propósito de.

perturbing [pə'tɜːbɪŋ] *adj* inquietante.

Peru [pə'ruː] *n* Perú.

peruse [pə'ruːz] *vtr fml* leer.

Peruvian [pə'ruːvɪən] *adj & n* peruano,-a *(m,f).*

pervade [pə'veɪd] *vtr (of smell)* penetrar. *(of light)* difundirse por; *fig (of influence)* extenderse por.

pervasive [pə'veɪsɪv] *adj (smell)* penetrante; *(influence)* extendido,-a.

perverse [pə'vɜːs] *adj (wicked)* perverso, -a; *(contrary)* contrario,-a a todo.

perversion [pə'vɜːʃən] *n Med Psych* perversión *f; (of justice, truth)* desvirtuación *f.*

pervert ['pɜːvɜːt] **I** *n Med* pervertido,-a *m,f (sexual).* **II** [pə'vɜːt] *vtr* pervertir; *(justice, truth)* desvirtuar.

pessimist ['pesɪmɪst] *n* pesimista *mf.*

pessimistic [pesɪ'mɪstɪk] *adj* pesimista.

pest [pest] *n* **1** *Zool* animal nocivo; *Bot* planta nociva. **2** *fam (person)* pelma *mf; (thing)* lata *f.*

pester ['pestər] *vtr* molestar, fastidiar.

pet [pet] **I** *n* **1** animal doméstico. **2** *(favourite)* preferido,-a *m,f; fam* cariño *m.* **II** *adj (favourite)* preferido,-a. **III** *vtr* acariciar. **IV** *vi (sexually)* besuquearse.

petal ['petəl] *n* pétalo *m.*

peter ['piːtər] *vi* **to p. out**, agotarse.

petite [pə'tiːt] *adj* menuda, chiquita.

petition [pɪ'tɪʃən] *n* petición *f.*

petrify ['petrɪfaɪ] *vtr lit* petrificar; *fig* **they were petrified**, se quedaron de piedra.

petrol ['petrəl] *n* gasolina *f;* **p. can**, bidón *m* de gasolina; **p. pump**, surtidor *m* de gasolina; **p. station**, gasolinera *f;* **p. tank**, depósito *m* de gasolina.

petroleum [pə'trəʊlɪəm] *n* petróleo *m.*

petticoat ['petɪkəʊt] *n* enaguas *fpl.*

petty ['petɪ] *adj (pettier, pettiest) (trivial)* insignificante; *(small-minded)* mezquino, -a; **p. cash**, dinero *m* para gastos pequeños; *Naut* **p. officer**, sargento *m* de marina.

petulant ['petjʊlənt] *adj* malhumorado,-a.

pew [pjuː] *n* banco *m* de iglesia; *fam* **take a p.!**, ¡siéntate!

pewter ['pjuːtər] *n* peltre *m.*

phantom ['fæntəm] *adj & n* fantasma *(m).*

pharmaceutical [fɑːmə'sjuːtɪkəl] *adj* farmacéutico,-a.

pharmacist ['fɑːməsɪst] *n* farmacéutico,-a *m,f.*

pharmacy ['fɑːməsɪ] *n* farmacia *f.*

phase [feɪz] **I** *n* fase *f.* **II** *vtr* **to p. sth in/ out**, introducir/retirar algo progresivamente.

PhD [piːeɪtʃ'diː] *abbr of* **Doctor of Philosophy**, Doctor,-a *m,f* en Filosofía.

pheasant ['fezənt] *n* faisán *m (vulgar).*

phenomenal [fɪ'nɒmɪnəl] *adj* fenomenal.

phenomenon [fɪ'nɒmɪnən] *n (pl* **phenomena** [fɪ'nɒmɪnə]*)* fenómeno *m.*

phial [faɪəl] *n* frasco *m.*

philanthropist [fɪ'lænθrəpɪst] *n* filántropo,-a *m,f.*

philately [fɪ'lætəlɪ] *n* filatelia *f.*

Philippines ['fɪlɪpiːnz] *n* **the P.**, las (Islas) Filipinas.

philosopher [fɪ'lɒsəfər] *n* filósofo,-a *m,f.*

philosophical [fɪlə'sɒfɪkəl] *adj* filosófico,-a.

philosophy [fɪ'lɒsəfɪ] *n* filosofía *f.*

phlegm [flem] *n* flema *f.*

phlegmatic [fleg'mætɪk] *adj* flemático,-a.

phobia ['fəʊbɪə] *n* fobia *f.*

phone [fəʊn] *n* → **telephone**.

phone-in ['fəʊnɪn] *n fam* programa *m* de radio *or* televisión con línea telefónica abierta.

phonetic [fə'netɪk] **I** *adj* fonético,-a. **II** *n* **phonetics**, fonética *f sing.*

phoney ['fəʊnɪ] **I** *adj (phonier, phoniest) (thing)* falso,-a; *(person)* farsante. **II** *n (person)* farsante *mf.*

phonograph ['fəʊnəgrɑːf] *n US* toca-

discos m inv.
phosphate ['fɒsfeɪt] n fosfato m.
photo ['fəʊtəʊ] n (abbr of **photograph**) foto f.
photocopier ['fəʊtəʊkɒpɪər] n fotocopiadora f.
photocopy ['fəʊtəʊkɒpɪ] I n fotocopia f. II vtr fotocopiar.
photogenic [fəʊtəʊ'dʒenɪk] adj fotogénico,-a.
photograph ['fəʊtəɡræf, 'fəʊtəɡrɑːf] I n fotografía f; **black and white/colour p.**, fotografía en blanco y negro/en color. II vtr fotografiar.
photographer [fə'tɒɡrəfər] n fotógrafo,-a m,f.
photography [fə'tɒɡrəfɪ] n fotografía f.
phrase [freɪz] I n frase f; **p. book**, libro m de frases. II vtr expresar.
physical ['fɪzɪkəl] adj físico,-a; **p. education**, educación física. ◆**physically** adv físicamente; **p. handicapped**, minusválido,-a; **to be p. fit**, estar en forma.
physician [fɪ'zɪʃən] n médico,-a m,f.
physicist ['fɪzɪsɪst] n físico,-a m,f.
physics ['fɪzɪks] n física f.
physiological [fɪzɪəʊ'lɒdʒɪkəl] adj fisiológico,-a.
physiotherapist [fɪzɪəʊ'θerəpɪst] n fisioterapeuta mf.
physique [fɪ'ziːk] n físico m.
pianist ['pɪənɪst] n pianista mf.
piano [pɪ'ænəʊ] n piano m.
piccolo ['pɪkələʊ] n flautín m.
pick [pɪk] I n 1 (tool) pico m, piqueta f. 2 **take your p.**, (choice) elige el que quieras. II vtr 1 (choose) escoger; (team) seleccionar. 2 (flowers, fruit) coger, recoger. 3 (scratch) hurgar; **to p. one's nose**, hurgarse la nariz; **to p. one's teeth**, mondarse los dientes. 4 **to p. sb's pocket**, robar algo del bolsillo de algn. 5 (lock) forzar. III vi **to p. at one's food**, comer sin ganas. ◆**pick off** vtr 1 (remove) quitar. 2 (shoot) matar uno a uno. ◆**pick on** vtr (persecute) meterse con. ◆**pick out** vtr (choose) elegir; (distinguish) distinguir; (identify) identificar. ◆**pick up** vtr 1 (object on floor) recoger; (telephone) descolgar; **to p. oneself up**, levantarse; fig reponerse. 2 (collect) recoger; (shopping, person) buscar; **to p. up speed**, ganar velocidad. 3 (acquire) conseguir; (learn) aprender. II vi (improve) mejorarse, ir mejorando; (prices) subir.
pickaxe, US **pickax** ['pɪkæks] n piqueta f.
picket ['pɪkɪt] I n piquete m; **p. line**, piquete m. II vtr piquetear. III vi hacer piquete.
pickle ['pɪkəl] I n 1 Culin salsa f picante. 2 fam (mess) lío m, apuro m. II vtr Culin

conservar en adobo or escabeche; **pickled onions**, cebollas fpl en vinagre.
pickpocket ['pɪkpɒkɪt] n carterista mf.
pick-up ['pɪkʌp] n **p.-up (arm)**, (on record player) brazo m; **p.-up (truck)**, furgoneta f.
picnic ['pɪknɪk] I n comida f de campo, picnic m. II vi hacer una comida de campo.
pictorial [pɪk'tɔːrɪəl] adj ilustrado,- a.
picture ['pɪktʃər] I n 1 (painting) cuadro m; (drawing) dibujo m; (portrait) retrato m; (photo) foto f; (illustration) ilustración f; **p. book**, libro ilustrado; **p. postcard**, tarjeta f postal. 2 TV imagen f; Cin película f; **to go to the pictures**, ir al cine. II vtr (imagine) imaginarse.
picturesque [pɪktʃə'resk] adj pintoresco, -ca.
pie [paɪ] n (of fruit) tarta f, pastel m; (of meat etc) pastel, empanada f; (pasty) empanadilla f.
piece [piːs] n 1 (of food) pedazo m, trozo m; (of paper) trozo; (part) pieza f; **a p. of advice**, un consejo; **a p. of furniture**, un mueble; **a p. of land**, una parcela; **a p. of news**, una noticia; **to break sth into pieces**, hacer algo pedazos; fig **to go to pieces**, perder el control (de sí mismo). 2 Lit Mus obra f, pieza f. 3 (coin) moneda f. 4 (in chess) pieza f; (in draughts) ficha f. ◆**piece together** vtr (facts) reconstruir; (jigsaw) hacer.
piecemeal ['piːsmiːl] adv (by degrees) poco a poco, a etapas; (unsystematically) desordenadamente.
piecework ['piːswɜːk] n trabajo a destajo; **to be on p.**, trabajar a destajo.
pier [pɪər] n embarcadero m, muelle m; (promenade) paseo m de madera que entra en el mar.
pierce [pɪəs] vtr perforar; (penetrate) penetrar en.
piercing ['pɪəsɪŋ] adj (sound etc) penetrante.
piety ['paɪɪtɪ] n piedad f.
pig [pɪɡ] n cerdo m; fam (person) cochino m; (glutton) tragón,-ona m,f; sl offens (policeman) madero m.
pigeon ['pɪdʒɪn] n paloma f; Culin Sport pichón m.
pigeonhole ['pɪdʒɪnhəʊl] n casilla f.
piggy ['pɪɡɪ] n **p. bank**, hucha f en forma de cerdito.
pigheaded [pɪɡ'hedɪd] adj terco,-a, cabezota.
piglet ['pɪɡlɪt] n cerdito m, lechón m.
pigment ['pɪɡmənt] n pigmento m.
pigskin ['pɪɡskɪn] n piel f de cerdo.
pigsty ['pɪɡstaɪ] n pocilga f.
pigtail ['pɪɡteɪl] n trenza f; (bullfighter's) coleta f.
pike [paɪk] n (fish) lucio m.
pilchard ['pɪltʃəd] n sardina f.

pile¹ ['paɪl] I n montón m. II vtr amontonar. III vi to p. into, apiñarse en; to p. on/off a bus, subir a/bajar de un autobús en tropel. ◆pile up I vtr (things) amontonar; (riches, debts) acumular. II vi amontonarse.

pile² ['paɪl] n (on carpet) pelo m; thick p., pelo largo.

piles ['paɪlz] npl Med almorranas fpl, hemorroides fpl.

pile-up ['paɪlʌp] n Aut choque m en cadena.

pilfer ['pɪlfəʳ] vtr & vi hurtar.

pilgrim ['pɪlgrɪm] n peregrino,-a m,f.

pilgrimage ['pɪlgrɪmɪdʒ] n peregrinación f.

pill [pɪl] n píldora f, pastilla f; to be on the p., estar tomando la píldora (anticonceptiva).

pillage ['pɪlɪdʒ] vtr & vi pillar, saquear.

pillar ['pɪləʳ] n pilar m, columna f; GB p. box, buzón m.

pillion ['pɪljən] n asiento trasero (de una moto).

pillow ['pɪləʊ] n almohada f.

pillowcase ['pɪləʊkeɪs] n funda f de almohada.

pilot ['paɪlət] I n piloto m. II adj (trial) piloto inv; p. light, piloto m; p. scheme, proyecto piloto. III vtr pilotar.

pimp [pɪmp] n chulo m.

pimple ['pɪmpəl] n grano m, espinilla f.

pin [pɪn] I n alfiler m; Tech clavija f; (wooden) espiga f; (in plug) polo m; Bowling bolo m; US (brooch) broche m; pins and needles, hormigueo m. II vtr (on board) clavar con chinchetas; (garment etc) sujetar con alfileres; to p. sb against a wall, tener a algn contra una pared; fig to p. one's hopes on sth, poner sus esperanzas en algo; fam to p. a crime on sb, endosar un delito a algn. ◆pin down vtr fig to p. sb down, hacer que algn se comprometa.

pinafore ['pɪnəfɔːʳ] n (apron) delantal m; p. dress, pichi m.

pinball ['pɪnbɔːl] n flipper m, máquina f de petacos.

pincers ['pɪnsəz] npl (on crab) pinzas fpl; (tool) tenazas fpl.

pinch [pɪntʃ] I n (nip) pellizco m; fig at a p., en caso de apuro; a p. of salt, una pizca de sal. II vtr pellizcar; fam (steal) birlar. III vi (shoes) apretar.

pincushion ['pɪnkʊʃən] n acerico m.

pine¹ [paɪn] n (tree) pino m; p. cone, piña f.

pine² [paɪn] vi to p. (away), consumirse, morirse de pena; to p. for sth/sb, añorar algo/a algn.

pineapple ['paɪnæpəl] n piña f.

ping [pɪŋ] n sonido metálico; (of bullet) silbido m.

ping-pong ['pɪŋpɒŋ] n ping-pong m.

pink [pɪŋk] I n (colour) rosa m; Bot clavel m. II adj (colour) rosa inv; Pol fam rojillo,-a.

pinnacle ['pɪnəkəl] n (of building) pináculo m; (of mountain) cima f, pico m; fig (of success) cumbre f.

pinpoint ['pɪnpɔɪnt] vtr señalar.

pinstripe ['pɪnstraɪp] adj a rayas.

pint [paɪnt] n pinta f; GB fam a p. (of beer), una pinta (de cerveza).

pioneer [paɪə'nɪəʳ] I n (settler) pionero,-a m,f; (forerunner) precursor,-a m,f. II vtr ser pionero,-a en.

pious ['paɪəs] adj piadoso,-a, devoto,-a; pej beato,-a.

pip¹ [pɪp] n (seed) pepita f.

pip² [pɪp] n (sound) señal f (corta); (on dice) punto m.

pipe [paɪp] I n conducto m, tubería f; (of organ) caramillo m; fam the pipes, (bagpipes) la gaita. 2 (for smoking) pipa f; p. cleaner, limpiapipas m inv; fig p. dream, sueño m imposible. II vtr (water) llevar por tubería; (oil) transportar por oleoducto; piped music, hilo m musical. ◆pipe down vi fam callarse. ◆pipe up vi fam hacerse oír.

pipeline ['paɪplaɪn] n tubería f, cañería f; (for gas) gasoducto m; (for oil) oleoducto m.

piper ['paɪpəʳ] n gaitero,-a m,f.

piping ['paɪpɪŋ] I n (for water, gas etc) tubería f, cañería f. II adj p. hot, bien caliente.

piquant ['piːkənt] adj picante; (fig) intrigante.

pique [piːk] I n enojo m. II vtr herir.

pirate ['paɪrɪt] n pirata m; p. edition, edición pirata; p. radio, emisora pirata; p. ship, barco m pirata.

pirouette [pɪrʊ'et] I n pirueta f. II vi hacer piruetas.

Pisces ['paɪsiːz] n Piscis m.

piss [pɪs] sl I vi mear. II n meada f.

pissed [pɪst] adj GB sl (drunk) borracho, -a.

pistachio [pɪs'tɑːʃɪəʊ] n (nut) pistacho m.

pistol ['pɪstəl] n pistola f.

piston ['pɪstən] n pistón m.

pit [pɪt] I n mano m; (large) hoya f; (coal mine) mina f de carbón; Theat platea f; (in motor racing) foso m, box m. II vtr to p. one's wits against sb, medirse con algn.

pitch¹ [pɪtʃ] I vtr 1 Mus (sound) entonar. 2 (throw) lanzar, arrojar. 3 (tent) armar. II vi (ship) cabecear; to p. forward, caerse hacia adelante. III n 1 Mus (of sound) tono m 2 Sport campo m, cancha f. 3 (in market area) puesto m. 4 (throw) lanzamiento m.

pitch² [pɪtʃ] n (tar) brea f, pez f.

pitch-black [pɪtʃ'blæk], **pitch-dark** [pɪtʃ'dɑːk] adj negro,-a como la boca del lobo.

pitched [pɪtʃt] *adj* p. battle, batalla *f* campal.

pitcher ['pɪtʃər] *n* (*container*) cántaro *m*, jarro *m*.

pitchfork ['pɪtʃfɔːk] *n* horca *f*.

piteous ['pɪtɪəs] *adj* lastimoso,-a.

pitfall ['pɪtfɔːl] *n* dificultad *f*, obstáculo *m*.

pith [pɪθ] *n* (*of orange*) piel blanca; *fig* meollo *m*.

pithy ['pɪθɪ] *adj* (**pithier, pithiest**) *fig* contundente.

pitiful ['pɪtɪfʊl] *adj* (*producing pity*) lastimoso,-a, (*terrible*) lamentable.

pitiless ['pɪtɪlɪs] *adj* despiadado,-a, implacable.

pittance ['pɪtəns] *n* miseria *f*.

pity ['pɪtɪ] **I** *n* 1 (*compassion*) compasión *f*, piedad *f*; **to take p. on sb**, compadecerse de algn. 2 (*shame*) lástima *f*, pena *f*; **what a p.!**, ¡qué pena!, ¡qué lástima! **II** *vtr* compadecerse de; **I p. them**, me dan pena.

pivot ['pɪvət] **I** *n* pivote *m*. **II** *vi* girar sobre su eje.

pizza ['piːtsə] *n* pizza *f*; **p. parlour**, pizzería *f*.

placard ['plækɑːd] *n* pancarta *f*.

placate [plə'keɪt] *vtr* aplacar, apaciguar.

place [pleɪs] **I** *n* 1 sitio *m*, lugar *m*; **to be in/out of p.**, estar en/fuera de su sitio; **to take p.**, tener lugar. 2 (*seat*) sitio *m*; (*on bus*) asiento *m*; (*at university*) plaza *m*; **to change places with sb**, intercambiar el sitio con algn; **to feel out of p.**, encontrarse fuera de lugar; **to take sb's p.**, sustituir a algn. 3 (*position on scale*) posición *f*; (*social position*) rango *m*; **in the first p.**, en primer lugar; **to take first p.**, ganar el primer lugar. 4 (*house*) casa *f*; (*building*) lugar *m*; **we're going to his p.**, vamos a su casa. **II** *vtr* 1 poner, colocar; **to p. a bet**, hacer una apuesta; **to p. an order with sb**, hacer un pedido a algn. 2 (*face, person*) recordar; (*in job*) colocar en un empleo.

placid ['plæsɪd] *adj* apacible.

plagiarize ['pleɪdʒəraɪz] *vtr* plagiar.

plague [pleɪɡ] **I** *n* (*of insects*) plaga *f*; *Med* peste *f*. **II** *vtr* **to p. sb with requests**, acosar a algn a peticiones.

plaice [pleɪs] *n inv* (*fish*) platija *f*.

plaid [plæd, pleɪd] *n* (*cloth*) tejido *m* escocés.

plain [pleɪn] **I** *adj* 1 (*clear*) claro,-a, evidente; *fig* **he likes p. speaking**, le gusta hablar con franqueza. 2 (*simple*) sencillo,-a; (*chocolate*) amargo,-a; (*flour*) sin levadura; **in p. clothes**, vestido,-a de paisano; **the p. truth**, la verdad lisa y llana. 3 (*unattractive*) poco atractivo,-a. **II** *n Geog* llanura *f*, llano *m*. ◆**plainly** *adv* claramente; (*simply*) sencillamente; **to**

speak p., hablar con franqueza.

plaintiff ['pleɪntɪf] *n* demandante *mf*.

plaintive ['pleɪntɪv] *adj* lastimero,-a.

plait [plæt] **I** *n* trenza *f*. **II** *vtr* trenzar.

plan [plæn] **I** *n* (*scheme*) plan *m*, proyecto *m*; (*drawing*) plano *m*. **II** *vtr* 1 (*for future*) planear, proyectar; (*economy*) planificar. 2 (*intend*) pensar, tener la intención de; **it wasn't planned**, no estaba previsto. **III** *vi* hacer planes; **to p. on doing sth**, tener la intención de hacer algo.

plane¹ [pleɪn] **I** *n* 1 *Math* plano *m*; *fig* nivel *m*. 2 *Av fam* avión *m*. **II** *adj Geom* plano,-a. **III** *vi* (*glide*) planear.

plane² [pleɪn] **I** *n* (*tool*) cepillo *m*. **II** *vtr* cepillar.

plane³ [pleɪn] *n Bot* p. (tree), plátano *m*.

planet ['plænɪt] *n* planeta *m*.

plank [plæŋk] *n* tabla *f*, tablón *m*.

planner ['plænər] *n* planificador,-a *m,f*.

planning ['plænɪŋ] *n* planificación *f*; **family p.**, planificación familiar; **p. permission**, permiso *m* de obras.

plant¹ [plɑːnt] **I** *n* planta *f*. **II** *vtr* (*flowers*) plantar; (*seeds*) sembrar; (*bomb*) colocar.

plant² [plɑːnt] *n* (*factory*) planta *f*, fábrica *f*; (*machinery*) maquinaria *f*.

plantation [plæn'teɪʃən] *n* plantación *f*.

plaque [plæk] *n* placa *f*; (*on teeth*) sarro *m*.

plaster ['plɑːstər] **I** *n Constr* yeso *m*; *Med* escayola *f*; *GB* **sticking p.**, esparadrapo *m*, tirita *f*; **p. of Paris**, yeso mate. **II** *vtr Constr* enyesar; *fig* (*cover*) cubrir de.

plastered ['plɑːstəd] *adj sl* borracho,-a, trompa.

plasterer ['plɑːstərər] *n* yesero,-a *m,f*.

plastic ['plæstɪk, 'plɑːstɪk] **I** *n* plástico *m*. **II** *adj* (*cup, bag*) de plástico; **p. surgery**, cirugía plástica.

Plasticine® ['plæstɪsiːn] *n* plastilina *f*.

plate [pleɪt] **I** *n* 1 plato *m*. 2 (*sheet*) placa *f*; **gold p.**, chapa *f* de oro; **p. glass**, vidrio cilindrado. 3 *Print* grabado *m*, lámina *f*. **II** *vtr* chapar.

plateau ['plætəʊ] *n* meseta *f*.

platform ['plætfɔːm] *n* 1 plataforma *f*; (*stage*) estrado *m*; (*at meeting*) tribuna *f*. 2 *Rail* andén *m*; **p. ticket**, billete *m* de andén. 3 *Pol* (*programme*) programa *m*.

platinum ['plætɪnəm] *n* platino *m*.

platitude ['plætɪtjuːd] *n* lugar común, tópico *m*.

platoon [plə'tuːn] *n Mil* pelotón *m*.

platter ['plætər] *n* fuente *f*.

plausible ['plɔːzəbəl] *adj* plausible.

play [pleɪ] **I** *vtr* 1 (*game*) jugar a. 2 *Sport* (*position*) jugar de; (*team*) jugar contra; **to p. a shot**, (*in golf, tennis*) golpear. 3 (*instrument, tune*) tocar; **to p. a record**, poner un disco. 4 *Theat* (*part*) hacer (el papel de); (*play*) representar; *fig* **to p. a part in sth**, participar en algo; *fig* **to p.**

the fool, hacer el tonto. II *vi* 1 *(children)* jugar (**with,** con); *(animals)* juguetear. 2 *Sport* jugar; **to p. fair,** jugar limpio; **to p. for time,** tratar de ganar tiempo. 3 *(joke)* bromear. 4 *Mus* tocar; *(instrument)* sonar. III *n* 1 *Theat* obra *f* de teatro. 2 *Sport* juego *m*; **fair/foul p.,** juego limpio/sucio. 3 *Tech & fig (movement)* juego *m*; *fig* **to bring sth into p.,** poner algo en juego; **a p. on words,** un juego de palabras. ◆**play around** *vi (waste time)* gandulear; *(be unfaithful)* tener líos. ◆**play down** *vtr* minimizar, quitar importancia a. ◆**play on** *vtr (take advantage of)* aprovecharse de; *(nerves etc)* exacerbar. ◆**play up I** *vtr (annoy)* dar la lata, fastidiar. II *vi (child etc)* dar guerra.

playboy ['pleɪbɔɪ] *n* playboy *m*.

player ['pleɪə'] *n* *Sport* jugador,-a *m,f*; *Mus* músico,-a *m,f*; *Theat (man)* actor *m*; *(woman)* actriz *f*.

playful ['pleɪfʊl] *adj* juguetón,-ona.

playground ['pleɪgraʊnd] *n* patio *m* de recreo.

playgroup ['pleɪgruːp] *n* jardín *m* de infancia.

playing ['pleɪɪŋ] *n* juego *m*; **p. card,** carta *f*, naipe *m*; **p. field,** campo *m* de deportes.

playmate ['pleɪmeɪt] *n* compañero,-a *m,f* de juego.

play-off ['pleɪɒf] *n* *Sport* partido *m* de desempate.

playpen ['pleɪpen] *n* corralito *m* or parque *m* (de niños).

playschool ['pleɪskuːl] *n* jardín *m* de infancia.

plaything ['pleɪθɪŋ] *n* juguete *m*.

playwright ['pleɪraɪt] *n* dramaturgo,-a *m,f*.

PLC, plc [piːel'siː] *GB abbr of* **Public Limited Company,** Sociedad *f* Anónima, S.A.

plea [pliː] *n* 1 *(request)* petición *f*, súplica *f*; *(excuse)* pretexto *m*, disculpa *f*. 2 *Jur* alegato *m*.

plead [pliːd] I *vtr* 1 *Jur fig* **to p. sb's cause,** defender la causa de algn. 2 **to p. ignorance,** *(give as excuse)* alegar ignorancia. II *vi* 1 *(beg)* rogar, suplicar; **to p. with sb to do sth,** suplicar a algn que haga algo. 2 *Jur* **to p. guilty/not guilty,** declararse culpable/inocente.

pleasant ['plezənt] *adj* agradable.

pleasantry ['plezəntrɪ] *n* cumplido *m*.

please [pliːz] I *vtr (give pleasure to)* agradar, complacer; *(satisfy)* satisfacer; *fam* **p. yourself,** como quieras. II *vi* complacer; *(give satisfaction)* satisfacer; **easy/hard to p.,** poco/muy exigente. III *adv* por favor; **may I? - p. do,** ¿me permite? - desde luego; **'p. do not smoke',** 'se ruega no fumar'; **yes, p.,** sí, por favor.

pleased [pliːzd] *adj (happy)* contento,-a;

(satisfied) satisfecho,-a; **p. to meet you!,** ¡encantado,-a!, ¡mucho gusto!; **to be p. about sth,** alegrarse de algo.

pleasing ['pliːzɪŋ] *adj (pleasant)* agradable, grato,-a; *(satisfactory)* satisfactorio,-a.

pleasure ['pleʒə'] *n* placer *m*; **it's a p. to talk to him,** da gusto hablar con él; **to take great p. in doing sth,** disfrutar mucho haciendo algo; **with p.,** con mucho gusto.

pleat [pliːt] I *n* pliegue *m*. II *vtr* hacer pliegues en.

pledge [pledʒ] I *n* promesa *f*; *(token of love etc)* señal *f*; *(guarantee)* prenda *f*. II *vtr (promise)* prometer; *(pawn)* empeñar.

plentiful ['plentɪfʊl] *adj* abundante.

plenty ['plentɪ] *n* abundancia *f*; **p. of potatoes,** muchas patatas; **p. of time,** tiempo de sobra; **we've got p.,** tenemos de sobra.

pliable ['plaɪəbəl] *adj* flexible.

pliers ['plaɪəz] *npl* alicates *mpl*, tenazas *fpl*.

plight [plaɪt] *n* situación *f* grave.

plimsolls ['plɪmsəlz] *npl* *GB* zapatos *mpl* de tenis.

plinth [plɪnθ] *n* plinto *m*.

plod [plɒd] *vi* andar con paso pesado; *fig* **to p. on,** perseverar; *fig* **to p. through a report,** estudiar laboriosamente un informe.

plodder ['plɒdə'] *n* trabajador,-a *m,f* or estudiante *mf* tenaz.

plonk¹ [plɒŋk] *vtr fam* dejar caer.

plonk² [plɒŋk] *n* *GB fam (wine)* vinazo *m*.

plot¹ [plɒt] I *n* 1 *(conspiracy)* complot *m*. 2 *Theat Lit (story)* argumento *m*, trama *f*. II *vtr* 1 *(course, route)* trazar. 2 *(scheme)* fraguar. III *vi* conspirar, tramar.

plot² [plɒt] *n* *Agr* terreno *m*; *(for building)* solar *m*; **vegetable p.,** campo *m* de hortalizas.

plough [plaʊ] I *n* arado *m*. II *vtr* arar. III *vi* *fig* **the car ploughed through the fencing,** el coche atravesó la valla; **to p. into sth,** chocar contra algo; *fig* **to p. through a book,** leer un libro con dificultad. ◆**plough back** *vtr (profits)* reinvertir.

plow [plaʊ] *n* *US* → **plough.**

ploy [plɔɪ] *n* estratagema *f*.

pluck [plʌk] I *vtr* 1 arrancar (**out of,** de). 2 *(flowers)* coger. 3 *(chicken)* desplumar. 4 *(guitar)* puntear. II *n* *(courage)* valor *m*, ánimo *m*. ◆**pluck up** *vtr* **to p. up courage,** armarse de valor.

plucky ['plʌkɪ] *adj (pluckier, pluckiest)* valiente.

plug [plʌg] I *n* 1 *(in bath etc)* tapón *m*. 2 *Elec* enchufe *m*, clavija *f*; **2/3 pin p.,** clavija bipolar/tripolar. 3 *Aut* 1 *(hole)* tapar. 2 *fam (publicize)* dar publicidad a; *(idea etc)* hacer hincapié en. ◆**plug in** *vtr &*

vi enchufar.

plum [plʌm] *n (fruit)* ciruela *f; fig* **a p. job**, un chollo.

plumage ['pluːmɪdʒ] *n* plumaje *m.*

plumb [plʌm] I *n* plomo *m;* **p. line**, plomada *f.* II *adj* vertical. III *adv US fam* **p. in the middle**, justo en medio. IV *vtr fig* **to p. the depths**, tocar fondo.

plumber ['plʌmə'] *n* fontanero,-a *m,f.*

plumbing ['plʌmɪŋ] *n (occupation)* fontanería *f; (system)* tuberías *fpl*, cañerías *fpl.*

plume [pluːm] *n* penacho *m.*

plummet ['plʌmɪt] *vi (bird, plane)* caer en picado; *fig (prices)* bajar vertiginosamente; *(morale)* caer a plomo.

plump[1] [plʌmp] *adj (person)* relleno,-a; *(baby)* rechoncho,-a.

plump[2] [plʌmp] *vi* **to p. for sth**, optar por algo. ◆**plump down** *vtr* dejar caer. ◆**plump up** *vtr (cushions)* ahuecar.

plunder ['plʌndə'] I *vtr* saquear. II *n (action)* saqueo *m*, pillaje *m; (loot)* botín *m.*

plunge [plʌndʒ] I *vtr (immerse)* sumergir; *(thrust)* arrojar. II *vi (dive)* lanzarse, zambullirse; *fig (fall)* caer, hundirse; *(prices)* desplomarse. III *n (dive)* zambullida *f; fig (fall)* desplome *m; fig* **to take the p.**, dar el paso decisivo.

plunger ['plʌndʒə'] *n Tech* émbolo *m; (for pipes)* desatascador *m.*

pluperfect [pluː'pɜːfɪkt] *n* pluscuamperfecto *m.*

plural ['plʊərəl] *adj* & *n* plural *(m).*

plus [plʌs] I *prep* más; **three p. four makes seven**, tres más cuatro hacen siete. II *n Math* signo *m* más; *fig (advantage)* ventaja *f.*

plush [plʌʃ] I *n* felpa *f.* II *adj fam* lujoso,-a.

plutonium [pluː'təʊnɪəm] *n* plutonio *m.*

ply [plaɪ] I *vtr* to p. one's trade, ejercer su oficio; **to p. sb with drinks**, no parar de ofrecer copas a algn. II *vi (ship)* ir y venir; **to p. for hire**, ir en busca de clientes.

plywood ['plaɪwʊd] *n* madera contrachapada.

p.m. [piː'em] *abbr of* **post meridiem** (after noon), después del mediodía; **at 2 p.m.**, a las dos de la tarde.

PM [piː'em] *GB fam abbr of* **Prime Minister.**

PMT [piːem'tiː] *fam abbr of* **premenstrual tension.**

pneumatic [njuː'mætɪk] *adj* neumático,-a.

pneumonia [njuː'məʊnɪə] *n* pulmonía *f.*

PO [piː'əʊ] *abbr of* **Post Office.**

poach[1] [pəʊtʃ] *vtr* 1 *vtr* **to p. fish/game**, pescar/cazar furtivamente. 2 *fig fam (steal)* birlar.

poach[2] [pəʊtʃ] *vtr Culin (egg)* escalfar; *(fish)* hervir.

poacher ['pəʊtʃə'] *n* pescador/cazador furtivo.

pocket ['pɒkɪt] I *n* 1 bolsillo *m; fig* **to be £10 in/out of p.**, salir ganando/perdiendo 10 libras; **p. money**, dinero *m* de bolsillo. 2 *(of air)* bolsa *f.* 3 *(of resistance)* foco *m.* II *vtr (money)* embolsar.

pocketbook ['pɒkɪtbʊk] *n US* bolso *m.*

pocketknife ['pɒkɪtnaɪf] *n* navaja *f.*

pod [pɒd] *n* vaina *f.*

podgy ['pɒdʒɪ] *adj (podgier, podgiest)* gordinflón,-ona, regordete.

podium ['pəʊdɪəm] *n* podio *m.*

poem ['pəʊɪm] *n* poema *m.*

poet ['pəʊɪt] *n* poeta *mf.*

poetic [pəʊ'etɪk] *adj* poético,-a.

poetry ['pəʊɪtrɪ] *n* poesía *f.*

poignant ['pɔɪnjənt] *adj* conmovedor,-a.

point [pɔɪnt] I *n* 1 *(sharp end)* punta *f.* 2 *(place)* punto *m; fig* **p. of no return**, punto sin retorno. 3 *(quality)* **good/bad p.**, cualidad buena/mala; **weak/strong p.**, punto débil/fuerte. 4 *(moment)* **at that p.**, en aquel momento; **from that p. onwards**, desde entonces; **to be on the p. of doing sth**, estar a punto de hacer algo. 5 *(score)* punto *m*, tanto *m;* **to win on points**, ganar por puntos; **match p.**, *(in tennis)* pelota *f* de match. 6 *(in argument)* punto *m;* **to make one's p.**, insistir en el argumento; **I take your p.**, entiendo lo que quieres decir. 7 *(purpose)* propósito *m;* **I don't see the p.**, no veo el sentido; **that isn't the p.**, **it's beside the p.**, eso no viene al caso; **there's no p. in going**, no merece la pena ir; **to come to the p.**, llegar al meollo de la cuestión. 8 *(on scale)* punto *m; (in share index)* entero *m;* **six p. three**, seis coma tres; *fig* **up to a p.**, hasta cierto punto. 9 *Geog* punta *f.* 10 **power p.**, toma *f* de corriente. 11 **points**, *Aut* platinos *mpl; Rail* agujas *fpl.* II *vtr (way etc)* señalar, indicar; **to p. a gun at sb**, apuntar a algn con una pistola. III *vi* señalar, indicar; **to p. at sth/sb**, señalar algo/a algn con el dedo. ◆**point out** *vtr* indicar, señalar; *(mention)* hacer resaltar.

point-blank [pɔɪnt'blæŋk] I *adj* a quemarropa; *(refusal)* rotundo,-a. II *adv (shoot)* a quemarropa; *(refuse)* rotundamente.

pointed ['pɔɪntɪd] *adj (sharp)* puntiagudo,-a; *fig (comment)* intencionado,-a; *(cutting)* mordaz. ◆**pointedly** *adv fig (significantly)* con intención; *(cuttingly)* con mordacidad.

pointer ['pɔɪntə'] *n* 1 *(indicator)* indicador *m*, aguja *f; (for map)* puntero *m.* 2 *(dog)* perro *m* de muestra.

pointless ['pɔɪntlɪs] *adj* sin sentido.

poise [pɔɪz] I *n (bearing)* porte *m; (self-assurance)* aplomo *m.* II *vtr fig* **to be poised to do sth**, estar listo,-a para hacer algo.

poison ['pɔɪzən] I *n* veneno *m.* II *vtr* envenenar.

poisoning ['pɔɪzənɪŋ] n envenenamiento m; (by food etc) intoxicación f.

poisonous ['pɔɪzənəs] adj (plant, snake) venenoso,-a; (gas) tóxico,-a; fig (rumour) pernicioso,-a.

poke [pəʊk] vtr (with finger or stick) dar con la punta del dedo or del bastón a; **to p. one's head out**, asomar la cabeza; **to p. the fire**, atizar el fuego. ◆**poke about, poke around** vi fisgonear, hurgar en. ◆**poke out** vtr (eye) sacar.

poker¹ ['pəʊkər] n (for fire) atizador m.

poker² ['pəʊkər] n Cards póquer m.

poker-faced ['pəʊkəfeɪst] adj fam de cara impasible.

poky ['pəʊkɪ] adj (pokier, pokiest) US fam pej minúsculo,-a; **a p. little room**, un cuartucho.

Poland ['pəʊlənd] n Polonia.

polar ['pəʊlər] adj polar; **p. bear**, oso m polar.

Pole [pəʊl] n polaco,-a m,f.

pole¹ [pəʊl] n palo m; **p. vault**, salto m con pértiga.

pole² [pəʊl] n Geog polo m; fig **to be poles apart**, ser polos opuestos.

police [pə'liːs] I npl policía f sing; **p. car**, coche m patrulla; **p. constable**, policía m; **p. force**, cuerpo m de policía; **p. record**, antecedentes mpl penales; **p. state**, estado m policial; **p. station**, comisaría f. II vtr vigilar.

policeman [pə'liːsmən] n policía m.

policewoman [pə'liːswʊmən] n (mujer f) policía f.

policy ['pɒlɪsɪ] n Pol política f; (of company) norma f, principio m; Ins póliza f (de seguros).

polio ['pəʊlɪəʊ] n poliomielitis f.

polish ['pɒlɪʃ] I vtr pulir; (furniture) encerar; (shoes) limpiar; (silver) sacar brillo a. II n 1 (for furniture) cera f; (for shoes) betún m; (for nails) esmalte m. 2 (shine) brillo m; fig (refinement) refinamiento m. ◆**polish off** vtr fam (work) despachar; (food) zamparse. ◆**polish up** vtr fig perfeccionar.

Polish ['pəʊlɪʃ] I adj polaco,-a. II n the P., pl los polacos. 2 (language) polaco m.

polished ['pɒlɪʃt] adj fig (manners) refinado,-a; (style) pulido,-a; (performance) impecable.

polite [pə'laɪt] adj educado,-a.

politeness [pə'laɪtnɪs] n educación f.

politic ['pɒlɪtɪk] adj prudente.

political [pə'lɪtɪkəl] adj político,-a.

politician [pɒlɪ'tɪʃən] n político,-a m,f.

politics ['pɒlɪtɪks] n sing política f.

polka ['pɒlkə] n (dance) polca f; **p. dot**, lunar m.

poll [pəʊl] I n 1 votación f; **the polls**, las elecciones; **to go to the polls**, acudir a las urnas. 2 (survey) encuesta f; GB **p. tax**, contribución urbana. II vtr (votes)

obtener.

pollen ['pɒlən] n polen m.

polling ['pəʊlɪŋ] n votación f; **p. booth**, cabina f electoral; **p. station**, colegio m electoral.

pollute [pə'luːt] vtr contaminar.

pollution [pə'luːʃən] n contaminación f, polución f; **environmental p.**, contaminación ambiental.

polo ['pəʊləʊ] n Sport polo m; **p. neck** (sweater), jersey m de cuello vuelto.

polyester [pɒlɪ'estər] n poliéster m.

polymer ['pɒlɪmər] n Chem polímero m.

Polynesia [pɒlɪ'niːʒɪə] n Polinesia.

polystyrene [pɒlɪ'staɪriːn] n poliestireno m.

polytechnic [pɒlɪ'teknɪk] n escuela politécnica, politécnico m.

polythene ['pɒlɪθiːn] n polietileno m.

pomegranate ['pɒmɪɡrænɪt] n granada f.

pomp [pɒmp] n pompa f.

pompom ['pɒmpɒm], **pompon** ['pɒmpɒn] n borla f, pompón m.

pompous ['pɒmpəs] adj (person) presumido,-a; (speech) rimbombante.

pond [pɒnd] n estanque m.

ponder ['pɒndər] I vtr considerar. II vi **to p. over sth**, meditar sobre algo.

ponderous ['pɒndərəs] adj pesado,-a.

pong [pɒŋ] n GB fam hedor m.

pontoon¹ [pɒn'tuːn] n Constr pontón m.

pontoon² [pɒn'tuːn] n Cards veintiuna f.

pony ['pəʊnɪ] n poney m.

ponytail ['pəʊnɪteɪl] n cola f de caballo.

poodle ['puːdəl] n caniche m.

poof [pʊf] n GB sl offens marica m.

pool¹ [puːl] n (of water, oil etc) charco m; (pond) estanque m; (in river) pozo m; **swimming p.**, piscina f.

pool² [puːl] I n 1 (common fund) fondo m común. 2 **typing p.**, servicio m de mecanografía. 3 US (snooker) billar americano. 4 GB football pools, quinielas fpl. II vtr (funds) reunir; (ideas, resources) juntar.

poor [pʊər, pɔːr] I adj pobre; (quality) malo,-a; fam **you p. thing!**, ¡pobrecito!. II npl **the p.**, los pobres.

poorly ['pʊəlɪ, 'pɔːlɪ] I adv (badly) mal. II adj (poorlier, poorliest) (ill) mal, malo,-a.

pop [pɒp] I vtr (burst) hacer reventar; (cork) hacer saltar. II vi (burst) reventar; (cork) saltar; fam **I'm just popping over to Ian's**, voy un momento a casa de Ian. III n 1 (noise) pequeña explosión. 2 fam (drink) gaseosa f. 3 fam (father) papá m. 4 Mus fam música f pop; **p. singer**, cantante mf pop. ◆**pop in** vi fam entrar un momento, pasar.

popcorn ['pɒpkɔːn] n palomitas fpl.

Pope [pəʊp] n the P., el Papa.

poplar ['pɒplər] n álamo m.

poppy ['pɒpɪ] n amapola f.

populace ['pɒpjʊləs] n (people) pueblo m.

popular ['pɒpjʊləʳ] adj popular; *(fashionable)* de moda; *(common)* corriente.

popularity [pɒpjʊ'lærɪtɪ] n popularidad f.

popularize ['pɒpjʊləraɪz] vtr popularizar.

populate ['pɒpjʊleɪt] vtr poblar.

population [pɒpjʊ'leɪʃən] n población f; **the p. explosion,** la explosión demográfica.

porcelain ['pɔːslɪn] n porcelana f.

porch [pɔːtʃ] n *(of church)* pórtico m; *(of house)* porche m, entrada f; US *(veranda)* terraza f.

porcupine ['pɔːkjʊpaɪn] n puerco m espín.

pore¹ [pɔːʳ] vi **to p. over sth,** leer or estudiar algo detenidamente.

pore² [pɔːʳ] n Anat poro m.

pork [pɔːk] n carne f de cerdo.

pornography [pɔː'nɒgrəfɪ] n pornografía f.

porous ['pɔːrəs] adj poroso,-a.

porpoise ['pɔːpəs] n marsopa f.

porridge ['pɒrɪdʒ] n gachas fpl de avena.

port¹ [pɔːt] n *(harbour)* puerto m; **p. of call,** puerto de escala.

port² [pɔːt] n Naut Av *(larboard)* babor m.

port³ [pɔːt] n *(wine)* vino m de Oporto, oporto m.

portable ['pɔːtəbəl] adj portátil.

portent ['pɔːtent] n fml augurio m, presagio m.

porter ['pɔːtəʳ] n *(in hotel etc)* portero,-a m,f; Rail mozo m de estación; US mozo de los coches-cama.

portfolio [pɔːt'fəʊlɪəʊ] n *(file)* carpeta f; *(of artist, politician)* cartera f.

porthole ['pɔːthəʊl] n portilla f.

portion ['pɔːʃən] n *(part, piece)* parte f, porción f; *(of food)* ración f. **♦portion out** vtr repartir.

portly ['pɔːtlɪ] adj *(portlier, portliest)* corpulento,-a.

portrait ['pɔːtrɪt, 'pɔːtreɪt] n retrato m.

portray [pɔː'treɪ] vtr *(paint portrait of)* retratar; *(describe)* describir; Theat representar.

Portugal ['pɔːtjʊgəl] n Portugal.

Portuguese [pɔːtjʊ'giːz] I adj portugués,-esa. II n *(person)* portugués, -esa m,f; *(language)* portugués m.

pose [pəʊz] I vtr *(problem)* plantear; *(threat)* representar. II vi *(for painting)* posar; pej *(behave affectedly)* hacer pose; **to p. as,** hacerse pasar por. III n *(stance)* postura f; pej *(affectation)* pose f.

posh [pɒʃ] GB fam I adj elegante, de lujo; *(person)* presumido,-a; *(accent)* de clase alta.

position [pə'zɪʃən] I n 1 posición f; *(location)* situación f; *(rank)* rango m; **to be in a p. to do sth,** estar en condiciones de hacer algo. 2 *(opinion)* postura f. 3 *(job)* puesto m. II vtr colocar.

positive ['pɒzɪtɪv] adj positivo,-a; *(sign)* favorable; *(proof)* incontrovertible; *(sure)* seguro,-a; fam *(absolute)* auténtico,-a.

possess [pə'zes] vtr poseer; *(of fear)* apoderarse de.

possessed [pə'zest] adj poseído,-a.

possession [pə'zeʃən] n posesión f; **possessions,** bienes mpl.

possessive [pə'zesɪv] adj posesivo,-a.

possibility [pɒsɪ'bɪlɪtɪ] n posibilidad f; **possibilities,** *(potential)* potencial m sing.

possible ['pɒsɪbəl] adj posible; **as much as p.,** todo lo posible; **as often as p.,** cuanto más mejor; **as soon as p.,** cuanto antes. **♦possibly** adv posiblemente; *(perhaps)* tal vez, quizás; **I can't p. come,** no puedo venir de ninguna manera.

post¹ [pəʊst] I n *(of wood)* poste m. II vtr *(fix)* fijar.

post² [pəʊst] n *(job)* puesto m; US **trading p.,** factoría f. II vtr enviar.

post³ [pəʊst] GB I n *(mail)* correo m; **by p.,** por correo; **p. office,** oficina f de correos; **P. Office Box,** apartado m de correos. II vtr *(letter)* echar al correo; **to p. sth to sb,** mandar algo por correo a algn.

postage ['pəʊstɪdʒ] n franqueo m.

postal ['pəʊstəl] adj postal, de correos; **p. order,** giro m postal; **p. vote,** voto m por correo.

postbox ['pəʊstbɒks] n GB buzón m.

postcard ['pəʊstkɑːd] n *(tarjeta f)* postal f.

postcode ['pəʊstkəʊd] n GB código m postal.

postdate [pəʊst'deɪt] vtr poner fecha adelantada a.

poster ['pəʊstəʳ] n póster m; *(advertising)* cartel m.

posterior [pɒs'tɪərɪəʳ] I n hum trasero m, pompis m. II adj posterior.

posterity [pɒ'sterɪtɪ] n posteridad f.

postgraduate [pəʊst'grædjʊɪt] I n posgraduado,-a m,f. II adj de posgraduado.

posthumous ['pɒstjʊməs] adj póstumo, -a.

postman ['pəʊstmən] n GB cartero m.

postmark ['pəʊstmɑːk] n matasellos m inv.

postmaster ['pəʊstmɑːstəʳ] n administrador m de correos; **p. general,** director m general de correos.

postmortem [pəʊst'mɔːtəm] n autopsia f.

postpone [pəʊst'pəʊn, pə'spəʊn] vtr aplazar.

postscript ['pəʊsskrɪpt] n posdata f.

posture ['pɒstʃəʳ] I n postura f; *(affected)* pose f. II vi adoptar una pose.

postwar ['pəʊstwɔːt] adj de la posguerra.

posy ['pəʊzɪ] n ramillete m.

pot [pɒt] I n *(container)* tarro m, pote m; *(for cooking)* olla f; *(for flowers)* maceta f;

fam **to go to p.**, irse al traste; **p. shot**, tiro *m* al azar. II *vtr* (*plant*) poner en una maceta.

potassium [pə'tæsɪəm] *n* potasio *m*.

potato [pə'teɪtəʊ] *n* (*pl* **potatoes**) patata *f*.

potent ['pəʊtənt] *adj* potente.

potential [pə'tenʃəl] I *adj* potencial, posible. II *n* potencial *m*. ◆**potentially** *adv* en potencia.

pothole ['pɒthəʊl] *n Geol* cueva *f*; (*in road*) bache *m*.

potholing ['pɒthəʊlɪŋ] *n GB* espeleología *f*.

potion ['pəʊʃən] *n* poción *f*, pócima *f*.

potluck [pɒt'lʌk] *n fam* **to take p.**, conformarse con lo que haya.

potted ['pɒtɪd] *adj* (*food*) en conserva; (*plant*) en maceta o tiesto.

potter¹ ['pɒtər] *n* alfarero, -a *m,f*.

potter² ['pɒtər] *vi GB* **to p. about** *or* **around**, entretenerse.

pottery ['pɒtərɪ] *n* (*craft, place*) alfarería *f*; (*objects*) cerámica *f*.

potty¹ ['pɒtɪ] *adj* (**pottier**, **pottiest**) *GB fam* chiflado, -a.

potty² ['pɒtɪ] *n fam* orinal *m*.

pouch [paʊtʃ] *n* 1 bolsa pequeña; (*for ammunition*) morral *m*; (*for tobacco*) petaca *f*. 2 *Zool* bolsa *f* abdominal.

poultry ['pəʊltrɪ] *n* (*live*) aves *fpl* de corral; (*food*) pollos *mpl*.

pounce [paʊns] *vi* **to p. on**, abalanzarse encima de.

pound¹ [paʊnd] I *vtr* (*strike*) aporrear. II *vi* (*heart*) palpitar; (*walk heavily*) andar con paso pesado.

pound² [paʊnd] *n* (*money, weight*) libra *f*.

pound³ [paʊnd] *n* (*for dogs*) perrera *f*; (*for cars*) depósito *m* de coches.

pour [pɔːr] I *vtr* echar, verter; **to p. sb a drink**, servirle una copa a algn. II *vi* correr, fluir; **it's pouring with rain**, está lloviendo a cántaros. ◆**pour out** *vtr* echar, verter; *fig* **to p. one's heart out to sb**, desahogarse con algn.

pouring ['pɔːrɪŋ] *adj* (*rain*) torrencial.

pout [paʊt] I *vi* hacer pucheros. II *n* puchero *m*.

poverty ['pɒvətɪ] *n* pobreza *f*.

poverty-stricken ['pɒvətɪstrɪkən] *adj* necesitado, -a; **to be p.-s.**, vivir en la miseria.

powder ['paʊdər] I *n* polvo *m*; **p. compact**, polvera *f*; **p. keg**, polvorín *m*; **p. puff**, borla *f*; **p. room**, servicios *mpl* de señoras. II *vtr* **to p. one's nose**, ponerse polvos en la cara; *euph* ir a los servicios o al tocador.

powdered ['paʊdəd] *adj* (*milk*) en polvo.

power ['paʊər] I *n* 1 fuerza *f*; (*energy*) energía *f*; *Elec* corriente *f*; **to cut la corriente**, cortar la corriente; **p. point**, enchufe *m*; **p. station**, central eléctrica. 2 (*ability*) poder

m. 3 (*authority*) poder *m*; (*nation*) potencia *f*; (*influence*) influencia *f*; **to be in p.**, estar en el poder; *Pol* **to come into p.**, subir al poder; **the p. of veto**, el derecho de veto. 4 *Tech* potencia *f*; (*output*) rendimiento *m*. II *vtr* propulsar, impulsar.

powerboat ['paʊəbəʊt] *n* lancha *f* (motora).

powerful ['paʊəful] *adj* (*strong*) fuerte; (*influential*) poderoso, -a; (*remedy*) eficaz; (*engine, machine*) potente; (*emotion*) fuerte; (*speech*) conmovedor, -a.

powerless ['paʊələs] *adj* impotente, ineficaz.

pp *abbr* **of pages**, págs., pp.

PR [piː'ɑːr] *abbr* **of public relations**.

practicable ['præktɪkəbəl] *adj* factible.

practical ['præktɪkəl] *adj* práctico, -a; (*useful*) útil; (*sensible*) adecuado, -a. ◆**practically** *adv* (*almost*) casi.

practicality [præktɪ'kælɪtɪ] *n* (*of suggestion, plan*) factibilidad *f*; **practicalities**, detalles prácticos.

practice ['præktɪs] I *n* 1 (*habit*) costumbre *f*. 2 (*exercise*) práctica *f*; *Sport* entrenamiento *m*; *Mus* ensayo *m*; **to be out of p.**, no estar en forma. 3 (*way of doing sth*) práctica *f*; **in p.**, en la práctica; **to put sth into p.**, poner algo en práctica. 4 (*of profession*) ejercicio *m*. 5 (*place*) (*of doctors*) consultorio *m*; (*of lawyers*) bufete *m*. 6 (*clients*) (*of doctors*) pacientes *mpl*; (*of lawyers*) clientela *f*. II *vtr* & *vi US* → **practise**.

practise ['præktɪs] I *vtr* practicar; (*method*) seguir; (*principle*) poner en práctica; *Mus* ensayar; (*profession*) ejercer. II *vi* practicar; *Sport* entrenar; *Mus* ensayar; (*doctor*) practicar; (*lawyer*) ejercer.

practising, *US* **practicing** ['præktɪsɪŋ] *adj* (*doctor etc*) en ejercicio; (*Christian etc*) practicante.

practitioner [præk'tɪʃənər] *n GB Med* **general p.**, médico, -a *m,f* de cabecera; **medical p.**, médico, -a *m,f*.

pragmatic [præg'mætɪk] *adj* pragmático, -a.

prairie ['preərɪ] *n* pradera *f*; *US* llanura *f*.

praise [preɪz] I *n* alabanza *f*. II *vtr* alabar, elogiar.

praiseworthy ['preɪzwɜːðɪ] *adj* loable.

pram [præm] *n GB* cochecito *m* de niño.

prance [prɑːns] *vi* (*horse*) encabritarse; **to p. about**, (*person*) pegar brincos.

prank [præŋk] *n* broma *f*; (*of child*) travesura *f*.

prawn [prɔːn] *n* gamba *f*.

pray [preɪ] *vi* rezar, orar.

prayer [preər] *n* rezo *m*, oración *f*; (*entreaty*) súplica *f*; **p. book**, misal *m*.

preach [priːtʃ] *vi* predicar.

preacher ['priːtʃər] *n* predicador, -a *m,f*.

precarious [prɪˈkeərɪəs] *adj* precario,-a.

precaution [prɪˈkɔːʃən] *n* precaución *f*.

precede [prɪˈsiːd] *vtr* preceder.

precedence [ˈpresɪdəns] *n* preferencia *f*, prioridad *f*; **to take p. over sth/sb**, tener prioridad sobre algo/algn.

precedent [ˈpresɪdənt] *n* precedente *m*.

preceding [prɪˈsiːdɪŋ] *adj* precedente.

precinct [ˈpriːsɪŋkt] *n* recinto *m*; *US (district)* distrito *m*; **pedestrian/shopping p.**, zona *f* peatonal/comercial.

precious [ˈpreʃəs] **I** *adj* precioso,-a; **p. stones**, piedras preciosas. **II** *adv* fam **p. little/few**, muy poco/pocos.

precipice [ˈpresɪpɪs] *n* precipicio *m*.

precipitate [prɪˈsɪpɪteɪt] **I** *vtr* precipitar; *fig* arrojar. **II** *adj* precipitado,-a.

precise [prɪˈsaɪs] *adj* preciso,-a, exacto,-a; *(meticulous)* meticuloso,-a. ◆**precisely** *adv (exactly)* precisamente, exactamente; **p.!**, ¡eso es!, ¡exacto!

precision [prɪˈsɪʒən] *n* precisión *f*.

preclude [prɪˈkluːd] *vtr* excluir; *(misunderstanding)* evitar.

precocious [prɪˈkəʊʃəs] *adj* precoz.

preconceived [ˈpriːkənˈsiːvd] *adj* preconcebido,-a.

precondition [priːkənˈdɪʃən] *n* condición previa.

precursor [prɪˈkɜːsər] *n* precursor,-a *m,f.*

predator [ˈpredətər] *n* depredador *m*.

predecessor [ˈpriːdɪsesər] *n* antecesor,-a *m,f.*

predetermine [priːdɪˈtɜːmɪn] *vtr* predeterminar.

predicament [prɪˈdɪkəmənt] *n* apuro *m*, aprieto *m*.

predict [prɪˈdɪkt] *vtr* predecir, pronosticar.

predictable [prɪˈdɪktəbəl] *adj* previsible.

prediction [prɪˈdɪkʃən] *n* pronóstico *m*.

predispose [priːdɪˈspəʊz] *vtr* **to be predisposed to doing sth**, estar predispuesto,-a a hacer algo.

predominant [prɪˈdɒmɪnənt] *adj* predominante. ◆**predominantly** *adv* en su mayoría.

predominate [prɪˈdɒmɪneɪt] *vi* predominar.

pre-empt [prɪˈempt] *vtr* adelantarse a.

preen [priːn] *vtr* **to p. oneself**, *(of bird)* arreglarse las plumas; *fig (of person)* pavonearse.

prefab [ˈpriːfæb] *n* GB fam *(house)* casa prefabricada.

prefabricated [priːˈfæbrɪkeɪtɪd] *adj* prefabricado,-a.

preface [ˈprefɪs] **I** *n* prefacio *m*. **II** *vtr* prologar.

prefect [ˈpriːfekt] *n* GB Educ monitor,-a *m,f.*

prefer [prɪˈfɜːr] *vtr* preferir; **I p. coffee to tea**, prefiero el café al té.

preferable [ˈprefərəbəl] *adj* preferible

(to, a). ◆**preferably** *adv* preferentemente.

preference [ˈprefərəns] *n* preferencia *f*; *(priority)* prioridad *f*; **to give p. to sth**, dar prioridad a algo.

preferential [prefəˈrenʃəl] *adj* preferente.

prefix [ˈpriːfɪks] *n* prefijo *m*.

pregnancy [ˈpregnənsɪ] *n* embarazo *m*.

pregnant [ˈpregnənt] *adj (woman)* embarazada; *(animal)* preñada; *fig* **a p. pause**, una pausa cargada de significado.

prehistoric(al) [priːhɪˈstɒrɪk(əl)] *adj* prehistórico,-a.

prejudice [ˈpredʒʊdɪs] **I** *n (bias)* prejuicio *m*; *(harm)* perjuicio *m*. **II** *vtr (bias)* predisponer; *(harm)* perjudicar.

prejudiced [ˈpredʒʊdɪst] *adj* parcial; **to be p. against/in favour of**, estar predispuesto,-a en contra/a favor de.

preliminary [prɪˈlɪmɪnərɪ] **I** *adj* preliminar; *Sport (round)* eliminatorio,-a. **II** *n* **preliminaries**, preliminares *mpl.*

prelude [ˈpreljuːd] *n* preludio *m*.

premarital [priːˈmærɪtəl] *adj* prematrimonial.

premature [preməˈtjʊər, ˈpremətjʊər] *adj* prematuro,-a. ◆**prematurely** *adv* antes de tiempo.

premeditate [prɪˈmedɪteɪt] *vtr (crime)* premeditar.

premenstrual [priːˈmenstrʊəl] *adj* **p. tension**, tensión *f* premenstrual.

premier [ˈpremjər] **I** *n* Pol primer,-a ministro,-a *m,f.* **II** *adj* primer, primero, -a.

premiere [ˈpremɪeər] *n* Cin estreno *m*.

premise [ˈpremɪs] *n* premisa *f*.

premises [ˈpremɪsɪz] *npl* local *m sing*; **on the p.**, en el local.

premium [ˈpriːmɪəm] *n* Com Fin Ind prima *f*; **to be at a p.**, tener sobreprecio; *fig* estar muy solicitado,-a; GB **p. bonds**, bonos cotizados sobre la par.

premonition [preməˈnɪʃən] *n* presentimiento *m*.

preoccupied [priːˈɒkjʊpaɪd] *adj* preocupado,-a; **to be p. with sth**, preocuparse por algo.

prep [prep] **1** *fam abbr of* **preparation**, deberes *mpl*. **2** *abbr of* **preparatory school**.

prepaid [priːˈpeɪd] *adj* con el porte pagado.

preparation [prepəˈreɪʃən] *n* preparación *f*; *(plan)* preparativo *m*; GB Educ *(homework)* deberes *mpl.*

preparatory [prɪˈpærətərɪ] *adj* preparatorio,-a, preliminar; **p. school**, escuela primaria privada.

prepare [prɪˈpeər] **I** *vtr* preparar; **to p. to do sth**, prepararse para hacer algo. **II** *vi* prepararse *(for, para).*

prepared [prɪˈpeəd] *adj (ready)* preparado,-a; **to be p. to do sth**, *(willing)* estar dispuesto,-a a hacer algo.

preponderance [prɪ'pɒndərəns] n preponderancia f.

preposition [prepə'zɪʃən] n preposición f.

preposterous [prɪ'pɒstərəs] adj absurdo,-a, ridículo,-a.

prerequisite [priː'rekwɪzɪt] n condición f previa.

prerogative [prɪ'rɒgətɪv] n prerrogativa f.

preschool [priː'skuːl] adj preescolar.

prescribe [prɪ'skraɪb] vtr (set down) prescribir; Med recetar; fig (recommend) recomendar.

prescription [prɪ'skrɪpʃən] n Med receta f.

presence ['prezəns] n presencia f; (attendance) asistencia f; fig p. of mind, presencia de ánimo.

present¹ ['prezənt] I adj 1 (in attendance) presente; Ling p. tense, (tiempo m) presente m; to be p. at, estar presente en 2 (current) actual. II n (time) presente m, actualidad f; at p., actualmente; for the p., de momento; up to the p., hasta ahora. ◆**presently** adv (soon) dentro de poco; US (now) ahora.

present² [prɪ'zent] I vtr 1 (give as gift) regalar; (medals, prizes etc) entregar; to p. sb with sth, obsequiar a algn con algo. 2 (report etc) presentar; (opportunity) ofrecer; (problems) plantear. 3 (introduce) (person, programme) presentar. II ['prezənt] n (gift) regalo m; (formal) obsequio m.

presentable [prɪ'zentəbəl] adj presentable; to make oneself p., arreglarse.

presentation [prezən'teɪʃən] n 1 presentación f; p. ceremony, ceremonia f de entrega. 2 Rad TV representación f.

present-day ['prezəntdeɪ] adj actual, de hoy en día.

presenter [prɪ'zentər] n Rad locutor,-a m,f; TV presentador,-a m,f.

preservation [prezə'veɪʃən] n conservación f.

preservative [prɪ'zɜːvətɪv] n conservante m.

preserve [prɪ'zɜːv] I vtr 1 (keep) mantener. 2 Culin conservar. II n 1 (hunting) coto m. 2 Culin conserva f.

preside [prɪ'zaɪd] vi presidir.

president ['prezɪdənt] n Pol presidente,-a m,f; US Com director,-a m,f, gerente mf.

presidential [prezɪ'denʃəl] adj presidencial.

press [pres] I vtr 1 apretar; (button) pulsar; (grapes) pisar; (trousers etc) planchar. 2 (urge) presionar; to p. sb to do sth, acosar a algn para que haga algo. II vi 1 (push) apretar; to p. against sb/sth, apretarse contra algn o algo; to p. on sth, hacer presión sobre algo. 2 (urge) apremiar; time presses, el tiempo apre-

mia. III n 1 p. stud, botón m de presión. 2 (machine) prensa f; to go to p., entrar en prensa. 3 Press prensa f; the p., la prensa; to get a good/bad p., tener buena/mala prensa; p. agency, agencia f de prensa; p. conference, rueda f de prensa; p. cutting, recorte m de prensa. ◆**press on** vi seguir adelante.

pressed [prest] adj to be (hard) p. for, andar escaso,-a de; I'd be hard p. to do it, me costaría mucho hacerlo.

pressing ['presɪŋ] adj apremiante, urgente.

pressure ['preʃər] n presión f; Med Meteor high/low p., altas/bajas presiones; p. cooker, olla f a presión; p. gauge, manómetro m; fig to bring p. (to bear) on sb, ejercer presión sobre algn.

pressurize ['preʃəraɪz] vtr fig presionar; pressurized cabin, cabina presurizada.

prestige [pre'stiːʒ] n prestigio m.

presumably [prɪ'zjuːməblɪ] adv es de suponer que.

presume [prɪ'zjuːm] I vtr suponer, presumir. II vi (suppose) suponer; we p. so/not, suponemos que sí/no.

presumption [prɪ'zʌmpʃən] n 1 (supposition) suposición f. 2 (boldness) osadía f. (conceit) presunción f.

presumptuous [prɪ'zʌmptjʊəs] adj presuntuoso,-a.

presuppose [priːsə'pəʊz] vtr presuponer.

pretence, US pretense [prɪ'tens] n 1 (deception) fingimiento m; false pretences, estafa f sing; under the p. of, so pretexto de. 2 (claim) pretensión f.

pretend [prɪ'tend] I vtr (feign) fingir, aparentar; (claim) pretender. II vi (feign) fingir.

pretense [prɪ'tens] n US → pretence.

pretension [prɪ'tenʃən] n pretensión f.

pretentious [prɪ'tenʃəs] adj presuntuoso,-a, pretencioso,-a.

pretext ['priːtekst] n pretexto m; on the p. of, so pretexto de.

pretty ['prɪtɪ] I adj (prettier, prettiest) bonito,-a, guapo,-a. II adv fam bastante; p. much the same, más o menos lo mismo.

prevail [prɪ'veɪl] vi 1 predominar. 2 (win through) prevalecer. 3 to p. upon o on sb to do sth, (persuade) persuadir o convencer a algn para que haga algo.

prevailing [prɪ'veɪlɪŋ] adj (wind) predominante; (opinion) general; (condition, fashion) actual.

prevalent ['prevələnt] adj predominante; (illness) extendido,-a.

prevaricate [prɪ'værɪkeɪt] vi andar con ambages.

prevent [prɪ'vent] vtr impedir; (accident) evitar; (illness) prevenir; to p. sb from doing sth, impedir a algn hacer algo; to p. sth from happening, evitar que pase algo.

prevention |prɪ'venʃən| n prevención f.

preventive |prɪ'ventɪv| adj preventivo,-a.

preview |'priːvjuː| n (of film etc) preestreno m.

previous |'priːvɪəs| **I** adj anterior, previo,-a; **p. conviction**, antecedente m penal. **II** adv **p. to going**, antes de ir.
◆**previously** adv anteriormente, previamente.

prewar |'priːwɔːr| adj de antes de la guerra.

prey |preɪ| **I** n presa f; fig víctima f. **II** vi **to p. on**, alimentarse de.

price |praɪs| **I** n precio m; **what p. is that coat?**, ¿cuánto cuesta el abrigo?; **p. list**, lista f de precios; **p. tag**, etiqueta f. **II** vtr (put price on) poner un precio a; (value) valorar.

priceless |'praɪsləs| adj que no tiene precio.

prick |prɪk| **I** vtr picar; **to p. one's finger**, pincharse el dedo; fig **to p. up one's ears**, aguzar el oído. **II** n **1** (with pin) pinchazo m. **2** sl (penis) polla f. **3** sl offens (person) gilipollas mf inv.

prickle |'prɪkl| **I** n espina f; (spike) pincho m; (sensation) picor m. **II** vtr & vi pinchar, picar.

prickly |'prɪklɪ| adj (pricklier, prickliest) espinoso,-a; fig (touchy) enojadizo,-a; **p. heat**, sarpullido m por causa del calor; **p. pear**, higo chumbo.

pride |praɪd| **I** n orgullo m; (arrogance) soberbia f; **to take p. in sth**, enorgullecerse de algo. **II** vtr **to p. oneself on**, enorgullecerse de.

priest |priːst| n sacerdote m, cura m.

priestess |'priːstɪs| n sacerdotisa f.

priesthood |'priːsthud| n (clergy) clero m; (office) sacerdocio m.

prig |prɪg| n gazmoño,-a m,f, mojigato,-a m,f.

prim |prɪm| adj (primmer, primmest) **p. (and proper)**, remilgado,-a.

prim(a)eval |praɪ'miːvəl| adj primitivo,-a.

primary |'praɪmərɪ| **I** adj fundamental, principal; **of p. importance**, primordial; **p. colour**, color primario; **p. education/school**, enseñanza/escuela primaria. **II** n US Pol (elección f) primaria f.
◆**primarily** adv ante todo.

primate¹ |'praɪmeɪt| n Rel primado m.

primate² |'praɪmeɪt| n Zool primate m.

prime |praɪm| **I** adj **1** principal; (major) primordial; **P. Minister**, primer,-a ministro,-a m,f. **2** (first-rate) de primera; **p. number**, número primo. **II** n **in the p. of life** en la flor de la vida. **III** vtr (pump, engine) cebar; (surface) imprimar; fig (prepare) preparar.

primer¹ |'praɪmər| n (textbook) cartilla f.

primer² |'praɪmər| n (paint) imprimación f.

primitive |'prɪmɪtɪv| adj primitivo,-a; (method, tool) rudimentario,-a.

primrose |'prɪmrəʊz| n primavera f.

Primus® |'praɪməs| n hornillo m de camping.

prince |prɪns| n príncipe m; **P. Charming**, Príncipe Azul.

princess |prɪn'ses| n princesa f.

principal |'prɪnsɪpəl| **I** adj principal. **II** n Educ director,-a m,f; Theat (in play) protagonista mf principal.

principle |'prɪnsɪpəl| n principio m; **in p.**, en principio; **on p.**, por principio.

print |prɪnt| **I** vtr **1** imprimir; (publish) publicar; fig grabar; **printed matter**, impresos mpl. **2** (write) escribir con letra de imprenta. **II** n **1** (of hand, foot) huella f; Print letra f; **out of p.**, agotado,-a. **2** Tex estampado m; **p. skirt**, falda estampada. **3** Art grabado m; Phot copia f. ◆**print out** vtr Comput imprimir.

printer |'prɪntər| n (person) impresor,-a m,f; (machine) impresora f.

printing |'prɪntɪŋ| n (industry) imprenta f; (process) impresión f; (print run) tirada f; **p. press**, prensa f.

print-out |'prɪntaʊt| n Comput impresión f; (copy) copia impresa.

prior |'praɪər| adj previo,-a, anterior; **p. to leaving**, antes de salir.

priority |praɪ'ɒrɪtɪ| n prioridad f.

prise |praɪz| vtr **to p. sth open/off**, abrir algo con palanca.

prism |'prɪzəm| n prisma f.

prison |'prɪzən| n cárcel f, prisión f.

prisoner |'prɪzənər| n preso,-a m,f; **to hold sb p.**, detener a algn; **p. of war**, prisionero,-a m,f de guerra.

privacy |'praɪvəsɪ, 'prɪvəsɪ| n intimidad f.

private |'praɪvɪt| **I** adj privado,-a; (secretary) particular; (matter) personal; (letter) confidencial; **one's p. life**, la vida privada de uno; **'P.'**, (notice) (on road) 'carretera privada'; (on gate) 'propiedad privada'; (on envelope) 'confidencial'; **p. detective**, **fam p. eye**, detective mf privado,-a; **p. school**, escuela privada. **II** n Mil soldado raso. ◆**privately** adv en privado; (personally) personalmente.

privet |'prɪvɪt| n alheña f.

privilege |'prɪvɪlɪdʒ| n privilegio m.

privileged |'prɪvɪlɪdʒd| adj privilegiado,-a.

privy |'prɪvɪ| **I** adj GB **P. Council**, Consejo Privado; **to be p. to sth**, estar enterado,-a de algo. **II** n (lavatory) retrete m.

prize |praɪz| **I** n premio m. **II** adj (first-class) de primera (categoría o clase). **III** vtr (value) apreciar, valorar.

prize-giving |'praɪzgɪvɪŋ| n distribución f de premios.

prizewinner |'praɪzwɪnər| n premiado,-a m,f.

pro¹ [prəʊ] *n* pro *m*; **the pros and cons of an issue,** los pros y los contras de una cuestión.

pro² [prəʊ] *n* (*abbr of* **professional**) *fam* profesional *mf*.

pro-³ [prəʊ] *pref* (*in favour of*) pro-.

probability [prɒbəˈbɪlɪtɪ] *n* probabilidad *f*.

probable [ˈprɒbəbəl] *adj* probable. ◆**probably** *adv* probablemente.

probation [prəˈbeɪʃən] *n* *Jur* to be on p., estar en libertad condicional; **to be on two months' p.,** (*at work*) trabajar dos meses de prueba.

probe [prəʊb] **I** *n* *Med* Astronaut sonda *f*; (*investigation*) sondeo *m*. **II** *vtr* *Med* sondar; (*investigate*) investigar. ◆**probe into** *vtr* investigar.

problem [ˈprɒbləm] *n* problema *m*.

problematic(al) [prɒbləˈmætɪk(əl)] *adj* problemático,-a; **it's p.,** tiene sus problemas.

procedure [prəˈsiːdʒər] *n* procedimiento *m*; (*legal, business*) gestión *f*, trámite *m*.

proceed [prəˈsiːd] *vi* seguir, proceder; **to p. to do sth,** ponerse a hacer algo; **to p. to the next matter,** pasar a la siguiente cuestión.

proceedings [prəˈsiːdɪŋz] *npl* (*of meetings*) actas *fpl*; (*measures*) medidas *fpl*; *Jur* proceso *m sing*.

proceeds [ˈprəʊsiːdz] *npl* ganancias *fpl*.

process [ˈprəʊses] **I** *n* proceso *m*; (*method*) método *m*, sistema *m*; **in the p. of,** en vías de. **II** *vtr* (*information*) tramitar; (*food*) tratar; *Comput* procesar.

processing [ˈprəʊsesɪŋ] *n* (*of information*) evaluación *f*; *Comput* tratamiento *m*.

procession [prəˈseʃən] *n* desfile *m*; *Rel* procesión *f*.

proclaim [prəˈkleɪm] *vtr* proclamar, declarar.

proclamation [prɒkləˈmeɪʃən] *n* proclamación *f*.

procrastinate [prəʊˈkræstɪneɪt] *vi* dejar las cosas para después.

procure [prəˈkjʊər] *vtr* conseguir, procurarse.

prod [prɒd] *vtr* (*with stick etc*) golpear; (*push*) empujar.

prodigal [ˈprɒdɪgəl] *adj* pródigo,-a.

prodigious [prəˈdɪdʒəs] *adj* prodigioso,-a.

prodigy [ˈprɒdɪdʒɪ] *n* prodigio *m*.

produce [prəˈdjuːs] **I** *vtr* **1** producir; *Ind* fabricar. **2** *Theat* dirigir; *Rad* TV realizar; *Cin* producir. **3** (*give birth to*) dar a luz a. **4** (*document*) enseñar; (*bring out*) sacar. **II** [ˈprɒdjuːs] *n* productos *mpl*; **p. of Spain,** producto *m* de España.

producer [prəˈdjuːsər] *n* **1** productor,-a *m,f*; *Ind* fabricante *mf*. **2** *Theat* director, -a *m,f* de escena; *Rad* TV realizador,-a *m,f*; *Cin* productor,-a *m,f*.

product [ˈprɒdʌkt] *n* producto *m*.

production [prəˈdʌkʃən] *n* **1** producción *f*; *Ind* fabricación *f*. **2** *Theat* representación *f*; *Rad* TV realización *f*; *Cin* producción *f*; **p. line,** cadena *f* de montaje.

productive [prəˈdʌktɪv] *adj* productivo, -a.

productivity [prɒdʌkˈtɪvɪtɪ] *n* productividad *f*.

profane [prəˈfeɪn] *adj* (*secular*) profano,-a; (*language*) blasfemo,-a.

profess [prəˈfes] *vtr* (*faith*) profesar; (*opinion*) expresar; (*claim*) pretender.

profession [prəˈfeʃən] *n* profesión *f*.

professional [prəˈfeʃənəl] **I** *adj* profesional; (*soldier*) de profesión; (*polished*) de gran calidad. **II** *n* profesional *mf*.

professor [prəˈfesər] *n* catedrático,-a *m,f*.

proficiency [prəˈfɪʃənsɪ] *n* (*in language*) capacidad *f*; (*in skill*) pericia *f*.

proficient [prəˈfɪʃənt] *adj* (*in language*) experto,-a; (*in skill*) hábil.

profile [ˈprəʊfaɪl] *n* perfil *m*; **in p.,** de perfil.

profit [ˈprɒfɪt] **I** *n* **1** beneficio *m*, ganancia *f*; **to make a p. on,** sacar beneficios de. **2** *fml* (*benefit*) provecho *m*. **II** *vi* *fig* sacar provecho; **to p. from,** aprovecharse de.

profitability [prɒfɪtəˈbɪlɪtɪ] *n* rentabilidad *f*.

profitable [ˈprɒfɪtəbəl] *adj* Com rentable; *fig* (*worthwhile*) provechoso,-a.

profiteer [prɒfɪˈtɪər] **I** *n* especulador,-a *m,f*. **II** *vi* obtener beneficios excesivos.

profound [prəˈfaʊnd] *adj* profundo,-a.

profuse [prəˈfjuːs] *adj* profuso,-a, abundante. ◆**profusely** *adv* con profusión; **to sweat p.,** sudar mucho.

profusion [prəˈfjuːʒən] *n* profusión *f*, abundancia *f*.

prognosis [prɒgˈnəʊsɪs] *n* *Med* pronóstico *m*; *fig* (*prediction*) augurio *m*.

program [ˈprəʊgræm] *Comput* **I** *n* programa *m*. **II** *vi & vtr* programar.

programme, *US* **program** [ˈprəʊgræm] **I** *n* programa *m*; (*plan*) plan *m*. **II** *vtr* **1** (*plan*) planear, planificar. **2** (*computer*) programar.

programmer,   *US*   **programer** [ˈprəʊgræmər] *n* programador,-a *m,f*.

progress [ˈprəʊgres] **I** *n* progreso *m*; (*development*) desarrollo *m*; *Med* mejora *f*; **to make p.,** hacer progresos; **in p.,** en curso. **II** [prəˈgres] *vi* avanzar; (*develop*) desarrollar; (*improve*) hacer progresos; *Med* mejorar.

progressive [prəˈgresɪv] *adj* (*increasing*) progresivo,-a; *Pol* progresista. ◆**progressively** *adv* progresivamente.

prohibit [prəˈhɪbɪt] *vtr* prohibir; **to p. sb from doing sth,** prohibir a algn hacer algo.

prohibitive [prəˈhɪbɪtɪv] *adj* prohibitivo, -a.

project [ˈprɒdʒekt] **I** *n* proyecto *m*; (*plan*)

plan *m*; *Educ* trabajo *m*. II [prə'dʒekt] *vtr* proyectar, planear. III *vi* (*stick out*) sobresalir.

projectile [prə'dʒektaɪl] *n fml* proyectil *m*.

projection [prə'dʒekʃən] *n* 1 (*overhang*) saliente *m*. 2 *Cin* proyección *f*. 3 (*forecast*) proyección *f*.

projector [prə'dʒektər] *n Cin* proyector *m*.

proletariat [prəʊlɪ'eərɪət] *n* proletariado *m*.

prolific [prə'lɪfɪk] *adj* prolífico,-a.

prologue ['prəʊlɒg] *n* prólogo *m*.

prolong [prə'lɒŋ] *vtr* prolongar.

prom [prɒm] *n* (*abbr of* promenade) *GB fam* (*seafront*) paseo marítimo; (*concert*) concierto sinfónico en que parte del público está de pie.

promenade [prɒmə'nɑːd] I *n* (*at seaside*) paseo marítimo. II *vi* pasearse.

prominence ['prɒmɪnəns] *n* prominencia *f*; *fig* (*importance*) importancia *f*.

prominent ['prɒmɪnənt] *adj* (*standing out*) saliente; *fig* (*important*) importante; (*famous*) eminente.

promiscuous [prə'mɪskjʊəs] *adj* promiscuo,-a.

promise ['prɒmɪs] I *n* promesa *f*; **to show p.**, ser prometedor,-a. II *vtr* & *vi* prometer.

promising ['prɒmɪsɪŋ] *adj* prometedor,-a.

promontory ['prɒməntərɪ] *n* promontorio *m*.

promote [prə'məʊt] *vtr* ascender; (*product*) promocionar; (*ideas*) fomentar; *Ftb* **they've been promoted**, han subido.

promoter [prə'məʊtər] *n* promotor,-a *m,f*.

promotion [prə'məʊʃən] *n* (*in rank*) promoción *f*, ascenso *m*; (*of product*) promoción *f*; (*of arts etc*) fomento *m*.

prompt [prɒmpt] I *adj* (*quick*) rápido,-a; (*punctual*) puntual. II *adv* **at 2 o'clock p.**, a las 2 en punto. III *vtr* 1 (*motivate*) incitar; **to p. sb to do sth**, instar a algn a hacer algo. 2 (*actor*) apuntar. ◆**promptly** *adv* (*quickly*) rápidamente; (*punctually*) puntualmente.

prone [prəʊn] *adj* 1 **to be p. to do sth**, ser propenso,-a a hacer algo. 2 *fml* (*face down*) prono,-a.

prong [prɒŋ] *n* punta *f*, diente *m*.

pronoun ['prəʊnaʊn] *n* pronombre *m*.

pronounce [prə'naʊns] I *vtr* pronunciar; *fml* (*declare*) declarar. II *vi* *fml* **to p. on sth**, opinar sobre algo.

pronounced [prə'naʊnst] *adj* pronunciado,-a.

pronouncement [prə'naʊnsmənt] *n fml* declaración *f*.

pronunciation [prənʌnsɪ'eɪʃən] *n* pronunciación *f*.

proof [pruːf] I *n* prueba *f*. II *adj* 1 (*secure*)

a prueba de. 2 **this rum is 70% p.**, este ron tiene 70 grados. III *vtr* impermeabilizar.

prop[1] [prɒp] I *n* (*support*) puntal *m*; *fig* sostén *m*. II *vtr* (*support*) apoyar; *fig* sostener. ◆**prop up** *vtr* apoyar.

prop[2] [prɒp] *n Theat fam* accesorio *m*.

propaganda [prɒpə'gændə] *n* propaganda *f*.

propel [prə'pel] *vtr* propulsar.

propeller [prə'pelər] *n* hélice *f*.

propelling pencil [prəpelɪŋ'pensəl] *n* portaminas *m inv*.

propensity [prə'pensɪtɪ] *n fml* propensión *f*.

proper ['prɒpər] *adj* 1 adecuado,-a, correcto,-a; **the p. time**, el momento oportuno. 2 (*real*) real, auténtico,-a; (*actual, exact*) propiamente dicho,-a. 3 (*characteristic*) propio,-a; *Ling* **p. noun**, nombre propio. ◆**properly** *adv* (*suitably, correctly, decently*) correctamente; **it wasn't p. closed**, no estaba bien cerrado,-a; **she refused, quite p.**, se negó, y con razón.

property ['prɒpətɪ] *n* 1 (*quality*) propiedad *f*. 2 (*possession*) propiedad *f*, posesión *f*; **personal p.**, bienes *mpl*; **public p.**, dominio público. 3 (*estate*) finca *f*.

prophecy ['prɒfɪsɪ] *n* profecía *f*.

prophesy ['prɒfɪsaɪ] *vtr* (*predict*) predecir; *Rel* profetizar.

prophet ['prɒfɪt] *n* profeta *mf*.

proportion [prə'pɔːʃən] *n* proporción *f*; (*part, quantity*) parte *f*; **in p. to** *or* **with**, en proporción a.

proportional [prə'pɔːʃənəl] *adj* proporcional (**to**, a); *Pol* **p. representation**, representación *f* proporcional.

proportionate [prə'pɔːʃənɪt] *adj* proporcional.

proposal [prə'pəʊzəl] *n* propuesta *f*; (*suggestion*) sugerencia *f*; **p. of marriage**, propuesta de matrimonio.

propose [prə'pəʊz] I *vtr* proponer; (*suggest*) sugerir; *fml* (*intend*) tener la intención de. II *vi* declararse.

proposition [prɒpə'zɪʃən] *n* propuesta *f*; *Math* proposición *f*.

proprietor [prə'praɪətər] *n* propietario,-a *m,f*.

propriety [prə'praɪətɪ] *n* (*decency*) decoro *m*.

propulsion [prə'pʌlʃən] *n* propulsión *f*.

prosaic [prəʊ'zeɪɪk] *adj* prosaico,-a.

prose [prəʊz] *n Lit* prosa *f*; *Educ* texto *m* para traducir.

prosecute ['prɒsɪkjuːt] *vtr* procesar.

prosecution [prɒsɪ'kjuːʃən] *n* (*action*) proceso *m*, juicio *m*; **the p.**, la acusación.

prosecutor ['prɒsɪkjuːtər] *n* acusador,-a *m,f*.

prospect ['prɒspekt] I *n* (*outlook*) perspectiva *f*; (*hope*) esperanza *f*; **the job has**

prospects, es un trabajo con porvenir. II [prə'spekt] *vtr* explorar. III *vi* to **p. for gold/oil**, buscar oro/petróleo.

prospective [prə'spektɪv] *adj (future)* futuro,-a; *(possible)* eventual, probable.

prospector [prə'spektər] *n* gold p., buscador,-a *m,f* del oro.

prospectus [prə'spektəs] *n* prospecto *m*.

prosper ['prɒspər] *vi* prosperar.

prosperity [prɒ'sperɪtɪ] *n* prosperidad *f*.

prosperous ['prɒspərəs] *adj* próspero,-a.

prostitute ['prɒstɪtjuːt] *n* prostituta *f*.

prostitution [prɒstɪ'tjuːʃən] *n* prostitución *f*.

prostrate ['prɒstreɪt] *adj (face down)* boca abajo; **p. with grief**, deshecho de dolor.

protagonist [prəʊ'tægənɪst] *n* protagonista *mf*.

protect [prə'tekt] *vtr* proteger; *(interests etc)* salvaguardar; **to p. sb from sth**, proteger a algn de algo.

protection [prə'tekʃən] *n* protección *f*.

protective [prə'tektɪv] *adj* protector,-a.

protégé(e) ['prəʊteʒeɪ] *n* protegido,-a *m,f*.

protein ['prəʊtiːn] *n* proteína *f*.

protest ['prəʊtest] I *n* protesta *f*; *(complaint)* queja *f*. II [prə'test] *vtr* protestar de. III *vi GB* protestar.

Protestant ['prɒtɪstənt] *adj & n* protestante *(mf)*.

protester [prə'testər] *n* manifestante *mf*.

protocol ['prəʊtəkɒl] *n* protocolo *m*.

prototype ['prəʊtətaɪp] *n* prototipo *m*.

protracted [prə'træktɪd] *adj* prolongado,-a.

protrude [prə'truːd] *vi fml* sobresalir.

protuberance [prə'tjuːbərəns] *n fml* protuberancia *f*.

proud [praʊd] *adj* orgulloso,-a; *(arrogant)* soberbio,-a.

prove [pruːv] I *vtr* 1 probar, demostrar; *Math* comprobar; **to p. oneself**, dar pruebas de valor. **2 it proved to be disastrous**, *(turned out)* resultó ser desastroso,-a.

proverb ['prɒvɜːb] *n* refrán *m*, proverbio *m*.

provide [prə'vaɪd] I *vtr* proporcionar; *(supplies)* suministrar, proveer. II *vi* to **p. for sb**, mantener a algn.

provided [prə'vaɪdɪd] *conj* **p. (that)**, con tal de que.

providing [prə'vaɪdɪŋ] *conj* → **provided**.

province ['prɒvɪns] *n* provincia *f*; *fig (field of knowledge)* campo *m*.

provincial [prə'vɪnʃəl] I *adj* provincial; *pej* provinciano,-a. II *n pej* provinciano,-a *m,f*.

provision [prə'vɪʒən] *n* provisión *f*; *(supply)* suministro *m*; **provisions**, *(food)* provisiones *fpl*, víveres *mpl*.

provisional [prə'vɪʒənəl] *adj* provisional.

proviso [prə'vaɪzəʊ] *n* **with the p. that**, a

condición de que.

provocation [prɒvə'keɪʃən] *n* provocación *f*.

provocative [prə'vɒkətɪv] *adj* provocador,-a; *(flirtatious)* provocativo,-a.

provoke [prə'vəʊk] *vtr* provocar.

prow [praʊ] *n* proa *f*.

prowess ['praʊɪs] *n* destreza *f*.

prowl [praʊl] I *n* merodeo *m*; **to be on the p.**, merodear, rondar. II *vi* merodear; *fam* to **p. about or around**, rondar.

prowler ['praʊlər] *n fam* merodeador *m*.

proximity [prɒk'sɪmɪtɪ] *n* proximidad *f*; **in p. to**, **in the p. of**, cerca de.

proxy ['prɒksɪ] *n* poderes *mpl*; *(person)* apoderado,-a *m,f*; **by p.**, por poderes.

prudence ['pruːdəns] *n* prudencia *f*.

prudent ['pruːdənt] *adj* prudente.

prudish ['pruːdɪʃ] *adj* remilgado,-a.

prune[1] [pruːn] *n* ciruela pasa.

prune[2] [pruːn] *vtr (roses etc)* podar; *fig* acortar.

pry [praɪ] *vi* curiosear, husmear; **to p. into sb's affairs**, meterse en asuntos ajenos.

PS, ps [piː'es] *abbr of (postscript)*, P.S., P.D.

psalm [sɑːm] *n* salmo *m*.

pseudo- ['sjuːdəʊ] *pref* pseudo-, seudo-.

pseudonym ['sjuːdənɪm] *n* (p)seudónimo *m*.

psyche ['saɪkɪ] *n* psique *f*.

psychiatric [saɪkɪ'ætrɪk] *adj* psiquiátrico,-a.

psychiatrist [saɪ'kaɪətrɪst] *n* psiquiatra *mf*.

psychiatry [saɪ'kaɪətrɪ] *n* psiquiatría *f*.

psychic ['saɪkɪk] I *adj* psíquico,-a. II *n* médium *m*.

psychoanalysis [saɪkəʊə'nælɪsɪs] *n* psicoanálisis *f*.

psychoanalyst [saɪkəʊ'ænəlɪst] *n* psicoanalista *mf*.

psychological [saɪkə'lɒdʒɪkəl] *adj* psicológico,-a.

psychologist [saɪ'kɒlədʒɪst] *n* psicólogo,-a *m,f*.

psychology [saɪ'kɒlədʒɪ] *n* psicología *f*.

psychopath ['saɪkəʊpæθ] *n* psicópata *mf*.

PTO, pto [piːtiː'əʊ] *abbr of* **please turn over**, sigue.

pub [pʌb] *n GB fam* bar *m*, pub *m*.

puberty ['pjuːbətɪ] *n* pubertad *f*.

pubic ['pjuːbɪk] *adj* púbico,-a.

public ['pʌblɪk] I *adj* público,-a; **to make sth p.**, hacer público algo; **p. company**, empresa pública; **p. convenience**, servicios *mpl*, aseos *mpl*; **p. holiday**, fiesta *f* nacional; **p. house**, pub *m*, taberna *f*; **p. opinion**, opinión pública; **p. relations**, relaciones públicas; *GB* **p. school**, colegio privado; **p. transport**, transporte público. II *n* **the p.**, el público; **in p.**, en público.

public-address system [pʌblɪkə'dres sɪstəm] n megafonía f.

publican ['pʌblɪkən] n tabernero,-a m,f.

publication [pʌblɪ'keɪʃən] n publicación f.

publicity [pʌ'blɪsɪtɪ] n publicidad f.

publicize ['pʌblɪsaɪz] vtr (make public) hacer público,-a; (advertise) hacer publicidad a.

public-spirited [pʌblɪk'spɪrɪtɪd] adj de espíritu cívico.

publish ['pʌblɪʃ] vtr publicar, editar.

publisher ['pʌblɪʃər] n (person) editor,-a m,f; (firm) (casa f) editorial f.

publishing ['pʌblɪʃɪŋ] n (business) industria f editorial; **p. company** or **house**, casa f editorial.

pucker ['pʌkər] vtr (lips, brow) fruncir, arrugar.

pudding ['pʊdɪŋ] n Culin pudín m; (dessert) postre m; **Christmas p.**, pudín a base de frutos secos típico de Navidad; **p. basin**, cuenco m; **steamed p.**, budín m.

puddle ['pʌdəl] n charco m.

puff [pʌf] I n (of wind) racha f; (of smoke) bocanada f; **p. pastry**, pasta f de hojaldre. II vi (person) jadear, resoplar; (train) echar humo; **to p. on one's pipe**, chupar la pipa. III vtr (cigarette) dar una calada a. ◆**puff up** vi hincharse.

puffy ['pʌfɪ] adj (puffier, puffiest) hinchado,-a.

pugnacious [pʌg'neɪʃəs] adj belicoso,-a.

pull [pʊl] I n 1 **to give sth a p.**, (tug) dar un tirón a algo. 2 (of engine) tracción f; fig (attraction) atracción f; (influence) enchufe m. II vtr 1 (tug) dar un tirón a; **to p. a muscle**, sufrir un tirón en un músculo; **to p. the trigger**, apretar el gatillo; **to p. to pieces**, hacer pedazos; fig poner algo por los suelos; fig **to p. sb's leg**, tomar el pelo a algn. 2 (draw) tirar, arrastrar; fig **to p. one's weight**, hacer su parte del trabajo. 3 (draw out) sacar. 4 fam (people) atraer. III vi 1 (drag) tirar; **to p. alongside sb**, acercarse a algn. ◆**pull apart** vtr desmontar; fig (criticise) poner por los suelos. ◆**pull down** vtr (building) derribar. ◆**pull in I** vtr (crowds) atraer. II vi (train) entrar en la estación; (stop) parar. ◆**pull off I** vtr fam (carry out) llevar a cabo. II vi (vehicle) arrancar. ◆**pull out I** vtr (withdraw) retirar. II vi Aut **to p. out to overtake**, salir para adelantar. ◆**pull over** vi hacerse a un lado. ◆**pull through** vi reponerse, restablecerse. ◆**pull together** vtr **to p. oneself together**, calmarse. ◆**pull up I** vtr 1 (uproot) desarraigar; **to p. up one's socks**, subirse los calcetines; fig espabilarse. 2 (chair) acercar. II vi (stop) pararse.

pulley ['pʊlɪ] n polea f.

pullover ['pʊləʊvər] n jersey m.

pulp [pʌlp] I n (of paper, wood) pasta f; (of fruit) pulpa f; fam fig (book etc) basura f. II vtr reducir a pulpa.

pulpit ['pʊlpɪt] n púlpito m.

pulsate [pʌl'seɪt] vi vibrar, palpitar.

pulse[1] [pʌls] n Anat pulso m.

pulse[2] [pʌls] n Bot Culin legumbre f.

pumice (stone) ['pʌmɪs(stəʊn)] n piedra f pómez.

pummel ['pʌməl] vtr aporrear.

pump[1] [pʌmp] I n bomba f. II vtr bombear; **to p. sth in/out**, meter/sacar algo con una bomba; fam fig **to p. sb for information**, sonsacar información a algn. ◆**pump out** vtr (empty) vaciar. ◆**pump up** vtr (tyre) inflar.

pump[2] [pʌmp] n (shoe) zapatilla f.

pumpkin ['pʌmpkɪn] n calabaza f.

pun [pʌn] n juego m de palabras.

punch[1] [pʌntʃ] I n (for making holes) perforadora f; (for tickets) taladradora f; (in leather etc) punzón m. II vtr (make hole in) perforar; (in ticket) picar; (in leather) punzar.

punch[2] [pʌntʃ] I n (blow) puñetazo m; (in boxing) pegada f; fig **it lacks p.**, le falta fuerza; **p. line**, remate m (de un chiste). II vtr (with fist) dar un puñetazo a.

punch[3] [pʌntʃ] n (drink) ponche m.

punch-up ['pʌntʃʌp] n fam pelea f.

punctual ['pʌŋktjʊəl] adj puntual.

punctuate ['pʌŋktjʊeɪt] vtr puntuar; fig salpicar.

punctuation [pʌŋktjʊ'eɪʃən] n puntuación f.

puncture ['pʌŋktʃər] I n pinchazo m. II vtr (tyre) pinchar.

pundit ['pʌndɪt] n fam experto,-a m,f.

pungent ['pʌndʒənt] adj (smell) acre; (taste) fuerte.

punish ['pʌnɪʃ] vtr castigar.

punishable ['pʌnɪʃəbəl] adj castigable, punible.

punishment ['pʌnɪʃmənt] n castigo m.

punk [pʌŋk] n fam 1 punk mf; **p. music**, música f punk. 2 US mamón m.

punt [pʌnt] I n (boat) batea f. II vi ir en batea.

punter ['pʌntər] n GB (gambler) jugador,-a m,f; (customer) cliente,-a m,f.

puny ['pjuːnɪ] adj (punier, puniest) enclenque, endeble.

pup [pʌp] n cachorro,-a m,f.

pupil[1] ['pjuːpɪl] n Educ alumno,-a m,f.

pupil[2] ['pjuːpɪl] n Anat pupila f.

puppet ['pʌpɪt] n títere m.

puppy ['pʌpɪ] n cachorro,-a m,f, perrito m.

purchase ['pɜːtʃɪs] I n compra f. II vtr comprar; **purchasing power**, poder adquisitivo.

purchaser [ˈpɜːtʃɪsəʳ] n comprador,-a m,f.

pure [pjʊəʳ] adj puro,-a. ◆**purely** adv simplemente.

purée [ˈpjʊəreɪ] n puré m.

purge [pɜːdʒ] I n purga f. II vtr purgar.

purify [ˈpjʊərɪfaɪ] vtr purificar.

purl [pɜːl] vtr (in knitting) hacer punto del revés.

purple [ˈpɜːpəl] adj morado,-a, purpúreo,-a; **to go p. (in the face)**, ponerse morado,-a.

purport [pɜːˈpɔːt] vi fml pretender; **to p. to be sth**, pretender ser algo.

purpose [ˈpɜːpəs] n 1 propósito m, intención f; **on p.**, a propósito. 2 (use) utilidad f.

purposeful [ˈpɜːpəsfʊl] adj (resolute) decidido,-a, resoluto,-a.

purr [pɜːʳ] vi (cat) ronronear; (engine) zumbar.

purse [pɜːs] I n GB monedero m; US (bag) bolso m; (prize money) premio m en metálico f. II vtr **to p. one's lips**, apretarse los labios.

purser [ˈpɜːsəʳ] n contador,-a m,f.

pursue [pəˈsjuː] vtr (criminal) perseguir; (person) seguir; (pleasure) buscar; (career) ejercer.

pursuer [pəˈsjuːəʳ] n fml perseguidor,-a m,f.

pursuit [pəˈsjuːt] n (of criminal) persecución f; (of animal) caza f; (of pleasure) búsqueda f; (pastime) pasatiempo m.

purveyor [pəˈveɪəʳ] n fml proveedor,-a m,f.

pus [pʌs] n pus m.

push [pʊʃ] I n empujón m; fig (drive) brío m, dinamismo m. II vtr 1 empujar; (button) pulsar, apretar; **to p. one's finger into a hole**, meter el dedo en un agujero. 2 fig (pressurize) instar; (harass) acosar; fam **to be (hard) pushed for time**, andar justo,-a de tiempo. 3 fam (product) promover; **to p. drugs**, pasar droga. III vi empujar. ◆**push aside** vtr (object) apartar. ◆**push in** vi colarse. ◆**push off** vi (in boat) desatracar; fam **p. off!**, ¡lárgate! ◆**push on** vi (continue) seguir adelante. ◆**push through** vtr abrirse paso entre.

pushchair [ˈpʊʃtʃeəʳ] n GB sillita f (de ruedas).

pusher [ˈpʊʃəʳ] n sl (of drugs) camello m.

pushover [ˈpʊʃəʊvəʳ] n fam **it's a p.**, está chupado; **she's a p.**, es un ligue fácil.

push-up [ˈpʊʃʌp] n Gymn flexión f (de brazos).

pushy [ˈpʊʃɪ] adj (pushier, pushiest) fam agresivo,-a.

puss [pʊs], **pussy** [ˈpʊsɪ] n fam minino m.

put [pʊt] I vtr (pt & pp **put**) 1 poner; (place) colocar; (insert) meter; **to p. to**

bed, acostar a; **to p. a picture up on the wall**, colgar un cuadro en la pared; **to p. a stop to sth**, poner término a algo; fig **to p. one's foot in it**, meter la pata. 2 (present) presentar, exponer; **to p. a question to sb**, hacer una pregunta a algn. 3 (express) expresar, decir; **to p. it mildly**, y me quedo corto; **to p. sth simply**, explicar algo de manera sencilla. 4 (estimate) calcular. 5 (money) ingresar; (invest) invertir.
II vi Naut **to p. to sea**, zarpar.
III adv **to stay p.**, quedarse quieto,-a.
◆**put about** vtr (rumour) hacer correr.
◆**put across** vtr (idea etc) comunicar.
◆**put aside** vtr (money) ahorrar; (time) reservar. ◆**put away** vtr (tidy away) recoger; fam (eat) zamparse; (save money) ahorrar. ◆**put back** vtr (postpone) aplazar; **to p. the clock back**, retrasar la hora. ◆**put by** vtr (money) ahorrar.
◆**put down** vtr (set down) dejar; (suppress) sofocar; (humiliate) humillar; (criticize) criticar; (animal) provocar la muerte de; (write down) apuntar. ◆**put down to** vtr achacar a. ◆**put forward** vtr (theory) exponer; (proposal) hacer; **to p. one's name forward for sth**, presentarse como candidato,-a para algo.
◆**put in** I vtr (install) instalar; (complaint, request) presentar; (time) pasar. II vi Naut hacer escala (at, en). ◆**put off** vtr (postpone) aplazar; **to p. sb off (doing) sth**, (dissuade) disuadir a algn de (hacer) algo. ◆**put on** vtr (clothes) poner,-nerse; (show) montar; (concert) dar; (switch on) (radio) poner; (light) encender; (water, gas) abrir; **to p. on weight**, aumentar de peso; **to p. on the brakes**, frenar; fig **to p. on a straight face**, poner cara de serio,-a. ◆**put out** vtr (light, fire) apagar; (place outside) sacar; (extend) (arm) extender; (tongue) sacar; (hand) tender; (spread) (rumour) hacer correr; (annoy) molestar; (inconvenience) incordiar; (anger) **to be p. out by sth**, enojarse por algo. ◆**put through** vtr Tel **p. me through to Pat, please**, póngame con Pat, por favor. ◆**put together** vtr (join) unir, reunir; (assemble) armar, montar. ◆**put up** vtr (raise) levantar, subir; (picture) colocar; (curtains) colgar; (building) construir; (tent) armar; (prices) subir, aumentar; (accommodate) alojar, hospedar; **to p. up a fight**, ofrecer resistencia. ◆**put up to** vtr **to p. sb up to sth**, incitar a algn a hacer algo. ◆**put up with** vtr aguantar, soportar.

putrid [ˈpjuːtrɪd] adj fml putrefacto,-a.

putt [pʌt] I n tiro m al hoyo. II vtr & vi tirar al hoyo.

putting [ˈpʌtɪŋ] n **p. green**, minigolf m.

putty [ˈpʌtɪ] n masilla f.

puzzle [ˈpʌzəl] I n rompecabezas m inv;

(crossword) crucigrama *m*; *fig (mystery)* misterio *m*. II *vtr* dejar perplejo,-a; **to be puzzled about sth**, no entender algo. ◆**puzzle over** *vtr* **to p. over sth**, dar vueltas a algo (en la cabeza).

puzzling ['pʌzlɪŋ] *adj* extraño,-a, curioso,-a.

pygmy ['pɪgmɪ] *n* pigmeo,-a *m,f*; *fig* enano,-a *m,f*.

pyjamas [pə'dʒɑːməz] *npl* pijama *m sing*.

pylon ['paɪlən] *n* torre *f* (de conducción eléctrica).

pyramid ['pɪrəmɪd] *n* pirámide *f*.

Pyrenees [pɪrə'niːz] *npl* **the P.**, los Pirineos.

Pyrex® ['paɪreks] *n* pírex® *m*.

python ['paɪθən] *n* pitón *m*.

Q

Q, q [kjuː] *n (the letter)* Q, q *f*.

quack [kwæk] I *n* 1 *(of duck)* graznido *m*. 2 *fam (doctor)* curandero,-a *m,f*. II *vi* graznar.

quad [kwɒd] *n fam* 1 *GB (of school, university)* patio *m* interior. 2 *(quadruplet)* cuatrillizo,-a *m,f*.

quadrangle ['kwɒdræŋgəl] *n* 1 *Geom* cuadrángulo *m*. 2 *(courtyard)* patio *m* interior.

quadruple ['kwɒdrupəl, kwɒ'druːpəl] I *n* cuádruplo *m*. II *adj* cuádruple. III *vtr* cuadruplicar. IV *vi* cuadruplicarse.

quadruplet ['kwɒdruplɪt, kwɒ'druːplɪt] *n* cuatrillizo,-a *m,f*.

quagmire ['kwægmaɪər, 'kwɒgmaɪər] *n (land)* cenagal *m*.

quail¹ [kweɪl] *n Orn* codorniz *f*.

quail² [kweɪl] *vi fig* encogerse.

quaint [kweɪnt] *adj (picturesque)* pintoresco,-a; *(original)* singular.

quake [kweɪk] I *vi* temblar. II *n fam* temblor *m* de tierra.

Quaker ['kweɪkər] *n* cuáquero,-a *m,f*.

qualification [kwɒlɪfɪ'keɪʃən] *n* 1 *(ability)* aptitud *f*. 2 *(requirement)* requisito *m*. 3 *(diploma etc)* título *m*. 4 *(reservation)* reserva *f*.

qualified ['kwɒlɪfaɪd] *adj* 1 capacitado,-a; **q. teacher**, profesor titulado. 2 **q. approval**, *(modified)* aprobación condicional.

qualify ['kwɒlɪfaɪ] I *vtr* 1 *(entitle)* capacitar. 2 *(modify)* modificar; *(statement)* matizar; *Ling* calificar. II *vi* 1 **to q. as**, *(doctor etc)* sacar el título de; **when did you q.?**, ¿cuándo terminaste la carrera? 2 *(in competition)* quedar clasificado,-a.

qualifying ['kwɒlɪfaɪɪŋ] *adj (round, exam)* eliminatorio,-a.

quality ['kwɒlɪtɪ] *n* 1 *(excellence)* calidad *f*; **q. control**, control *m* de calidad; **q. newspapers**, prensa *f* no sensacionalista. 2 *(attribute)* cualidad *f*.

qualm [kwɑːm] *n* 1 *(scruple)* escrúpulo *m*. 2 *(doubt)* duda *f*.

quandary ['kwɒndərɪ, 'kwɒndrɪ] *n* **to be in a q.**, estar en un dilema.

quango ['kwæŋgəʊ] *n* organización semiautónoma paralela.

quantity ['kwɒntɪtɪ] *n* cantidad *f*.

quarantine ['kwɒrəntiːn] *n* cuarentena *f*.

quarrel ['kwɒrəl] I *n (argument)* riña *f*, pelea *f*; *(disagreement)* desacuerdo *m*. II *vi (argue)* pelearse, reñir; **to q. with sth**, discrepar de algo.

quarrelsome ['kwɒrəlsəm] *adj* camorrista.

quarry¹ ['kwɒrɪ] *Min* I *n* cantera *f*. II *vtr* extraer.

quarry² ['kwɒrɪ] *n* presa *f*.

quart [kwɔːt] *n (measurement)* cuarto *m* de galón *(GB approx* 1,13 litros; *US approx* 0,94 litros).

quarter ['kwɔːtər] I *n* 1 cuarto *m*, cuarta parte; **a q. of an hour**, un cuarto de hora; **a q. of a cake**, la cuarta parte de un pastel. 2 **it's a q. to three**, *US* **it's a q. of three**, son las tres menos cuarto. 3 *(three months)* trimestre *m*. 4 *GB (weight)* cuarto *m* de libra. 5 *US (coin)* cuarto *m* (de dólar). 6 *(district)* barrio *m*. 7 **there was criticism from all quarters**, *(areas, people)* todos lo criticaron. 8 *(of moon)* cuarto *m*. 9 **quarters**, *(lodgings)* alojamiento *m sing*; *Mil* **officers' q.**, residencia *f sing* de oficiales; **at close quarters**, muy cerca. II *vtr* 1 *(cut into quarters)* dividir en cuartos. 2 *(accommodate)* alojar.

quarterfinal ['kwɔːtəfaɪnəl] *n Sport* cuarto *m* de final.

quarterly ['kwɔːtəlɪ] I *adj* trimestral. II *n* publicación *f* trimestral. III *adv* trimestralmente.

quartermaster ['kwɔːtəmɑːstər] *n* 1 *Mil* oficial *m* de intendencia. 2 *Naut* cabo *m* de la Marina.

quartet(te) [kwɔː'tet] *n* cuarteto *m*.

quartz [kwɔːts] *n* cuarzo *m*; **q. watch**, reloj *m* de cuarzo.

quash [kwɒʃ] *vtr Jur* anular; *(uprising)* aplastar.

quasi ['kwɑːzɪ, 'kweɪzaɪ, 'kweɪsaɪ] *pref* cuasi.

quaver ['kweɪvər] I *n* 1 *Mus* corchea *f*. 2 *(in voice)* temblor *m*. II *vi (voice)* temblar.

quay(side) ['kiː(saɪd)] *n* muelle *m*.

queasy ['kwiːzɪ] *adj (queasier, queasiest)*

to feel q., *(ill)* tener náuseas.
queen [kwiːn] *n* 1 reina *f.* 2 offens loca *f*, marica *m*.
queer [kwɪəʳ] I *adj* 1 *(strange)* extraño,-a, raro,-a. 2 *fam (mad)* loco,-a. 3 *fam (unwell)* mareado,-a. 4 offens maricón. II *n sl* offens marica *m*, maricón *m*.
quell [kwel] *vtr* reprimir.
quench [kwentʃ] *vtr* apagar.
querulous ['kwerʊləs, 'kwerjʊləs] *adj fml* quejumbroso,-a.
query ['kwɪəri] I *n (question)* pregunta *f.* II *vtr (ask question about)* preguntar acerca de; *(have doubts about)* poner en duda.
quest [kwest] *n lit* búsqueda *f*, busca *f.*
question ['kwestʃən] I *n* 1 *(interrogative)* pregunta *f*; **to ask sb a q.**, hacer una pregunta a algn; **he did it without q.**, lo hizo sin rechistar; **q. mark**, signo *m* de interrogación; *fig* interrogante *m.* 2 *(problem, issue)* asunto *m*, cuestión *f*; **it's a q. of two hours**, es cuestión de dos horas. 3 *(doubt)* duda *f*; **beyond q.**, fuera de duda; **in q.**, en duda; **to call sth into q.**, poner algo en duda. 4 **out of the q.**, imposible; **that's out of the q.**, ¡ni hablar! 5 *Educ* problema *m.* II *vtr (ask questions of)* hacer preguntas a; *(interrogate)* interrogar; *(query)* poner en duda.
questionable ['kwestʃənəbəl] *adj (doubtful)* dudoso,-a; *(debatable)* discutible.
questionnaire [kwestʃə'neəʳ] *n* cuestionario *m.*
queue [kjuː] *GB* I *n* cola *f.* II *vi* **to q. (up)**, hacer cola.
quibble ['kwɪbəl] I *n* pega *f.* II *vi* poner pegas *(with, a)*; *fam* buscarle tres pies al gato.
quick [kwɪk] *adj* 1 *(fast)* rápido,-a; **a q. look**, un vistazo; **a q. snack**, un bocado; **be q.!**, ¡date prisa! 2 *(wit)* agudo,-a; *(tv)* agudo,-a. 3 **she has a q. temper**, se enfada con nada. ◆**quickly** *adv* rápidamente, de prisa.
quicken ['kwɪkən] I *vtr* acelerar; **to q. one's pace**, acelerar el paso. II *vi (speed up)* acelerarse.
quickness ['kwɪknɪs] *n* 1 *(speed)* rapidez *f.* 2 *(of wit)* agudeza *f*, viveza *f.*
quicksand ['kwɪksænd] *n* arenas movedizas.
quicksilver ['kwɪksɪlvəʳ] *n* mercurio *m.*
quick-witted [kwɪk'wɪtɪd] *adj* agudo,-a.
quid [kwɪd] *n GB sl* libra *f* (esterlina).
quiet ['kwaɪət] I *n* 1 *(silence)* silencio *m.* 2 *(calm)* tranquilidad *f.* II *adj* 1 *(silent)* silencioso,-a; *(street)* tranquilo,-a; **a q. voice**, una voz suave; **keep q.!**, ¡silencio! 2 *(calm)* tranquilo,-a. 3 *Com Fin* **business is q. today**, hoy hay poco negocio. 4 *(person)* reservado,-a. 5 *(secret)* confidencial. 6 *(not showy) (clothes)*

sobrio,-a; *(colours)* apagado,-a. 7 *(ceremony, dinner)* íntimo,-a. II *vtr US* calmar. III *vi US* calmarse. ◆**quietly** *adv* 1 *(silently)* silenciosamente; **he spoke q.**, habló en voz baja. 2 *(calmly)* tranquilamente. 3 *(discreetly)* discretamente.
quieten ['kwaɪətən] I *vtr (silence)* callar; *(calm)* calmar. II *vi (silence)* callarse; *(calm)* calmarse. ◆**quieten down** *GB* I *vtr* calmar. II *vi* calmarse.
quietness ['kwaɪətnɪs] *n* 1 *(silence)* silencio *m.* 2 *(calm)* tranquilidad *f.*
quill [kwɪl] *n (feather, pen)* pluma *f*; *(of porcupine)* púa *f.*
quilt [kwɪlt] I *n* edredón *m.* II *vtr* acolchar.
quin [kwɪn] *n* quintillizo,-a *m,f.*
quinine [kwɪ'niːn, *US* 'kwaɪnaɪn] *n* quinina *f.*
quintessential [kwɪntɪ'senʃəl] *adj* fundamental.
quintet(te) [kwɪn'tet] *n* quinteto *m.*
quintuple ['kwɪntjʊpəl, kwɪn'tjuːpəl] I *adj* quíntuplo,-a. II *n* quíntuplo *m.* III *vtr* quintuplicar.
quintuplet ['kwɪntjʊplɪt, kwɪn'tjuːplɪt] *n* quintillizo,-a *m,f.*
quip [kwɪp] I *n* salida *f*; *(joke)* chiste *m.* II *vi* bromear.
quirk [kwɜːk] *n* 1 *(peculiarity)* manía *f.* 2 *(of fate)* arbitrariedad *f.*
quit [kwɪt] I *vtr (pt & pp quitted or esp US quit)* 1 *(leave)* dejar, abandonar. 2 **q. making that noise!**, ¡deja de hacer ese ruido!. II *vi* 1 *(go)* irse; *(give up)* dimitir. 2 *(cease)* dejar de hacer algo. III *adj* **let's call it quits**, dejémoslo estar.
quite [kwaɪt] *adv* 1 *(entirely)* totalmente; **she's q. right**, tiene toda la razón. 2 *(rather)* bastante; **q. a few**, bastantes; **q. a while**, un buen rato; **q. often**, con bastante frecuencia; **that's q. enough!**, ¡ya está bien! 3 **he's q. a character**, es un tipo original; **to be q. sth**, ser increíble. 4 *(exactly)* exactamente; **q. (so)!**, ¡en efecto!; ¡exacto!
quiver¹ ['kwɪvəʳ] *vi* temblar.
quiver² ['kwɪvəʳ] *n (for arrows)* aljaba *f*, carcaj *m.*
quiz [kwɪz] I *n Rad TV* **q. show**, concurso *m.* II *vtr* hacer preguntas a.
quizzical ['kwɪzɪkəl] *adj* 1 *(bemused)* burlón,-ona. 2 *(enquiring)* curioso,-a.
quota ['kwəʊtə] *n* 1 *(proportional share)* cuota *f*, parte *f.* 2 *(prescribed amount, number)* cupo *m.*
quotation [kwəʊ'teɪʃən] *n* 1 *Lit* cita *f.* 2 **q. marks**, comillas *fpl.* 2 *Fin* cotización *f.*
quote [kwəʊt] I *vtr* 1 *(cite)* citar. 2 *Com* **to q. a price**, dar un presupuesto. 3 *Fin* cotizar. II *n* 1 *Lit* cita *f.* 2 *Com* presupuesto *m.*
quotient ['kwəʊʃənt] *n* cociente *m.*

R

R, r [ɑ:ʳ] *n (the letter)* R, r *f.*

rabbi ['ræbaɪ] *n* rabí *m,* rabino *m.*

rabbit ['ræbɪt] I *n* conejo,-a *m,f;* r. hutch, conejera *f.* II *vi fam* to r. (on), enrollarse.

rabble ['ræbəl] *n pej* the r., el populacho.

rabies ['reɪbiz] *n* rabia *f.*

RAC [ɑːreɪ'siː] *GB abbr of* **Royal Automobile Club,** ≈ Real Automóvil Club *m* de España, RACE.

race¹ [reɪs] I *n Sport* carrera *f.* 2 *GB* the races, las carreras (de caballos). II *vtr* 1 I'll r. you!, ¡te echo una carrera! 2 *(car, horse)* hacer correr. 3 *(engine)* acelerar. III *vi (go quickly)* correr; *(pulse)* acelerarse.

race² [reɪs] *n (people)* raza *f.*

racecourse ['reɪskɔːs] *n GB* hipódromo *m.*

racehorse ['reɪshɔːs] *n* caballo *m* de carreras.

racer ['reɪsəʳ] *n Sport* 1 *(person)* corredor,-a *m,f.* 2 *(bicycle)* bicicleta *f* de carreras; *(car)* coche *m* de carreras.

racetrack ['reɪstræk] *n (for cars, people, bikes)* pista *f; US (for horses)* hipódromo *m.*

racial ['reɪʃəl] *adj* racial.

racing ['reɪsɪŋ] I *n* carreras *fpl.* II *adj* de carreras; r. car/bike, coche *m*/moto *f* de carreras.

racism ['reɪsɪzəm] *n* racismo *m.*

racist ['reɪsɪst] *adj & n* racista *(mf).*

rack [ræk] I *n* 1 *(shelf)* estante *m; (for clothes)* percha *f; (luggage)* r., portaequipajes *m inv;* **roof r.,** baca *f.* 2 *(for torture)* potro *m.* II *vtr* lit *(torment)* atormentar; *fam* **fig** to r. **one's brains,** devanarse los sesos.

racket¹ ['rækɪt] *n* 1 *(din)* ruido *m,* jaleo *m.* 2 *(swindle)* timo *m; (shady business)* chanchullo *m.*

racket² ['rækɪt] *n Sport* raqueta *f.*

racquet ['rækɪt] *n →* **racket.**

racy ['reɪsɪ] *adj (racier, raciest) (lively)* vivo,-a; *(risqué)* atrevido,-a.

radar ['reɪdɑːʳ] *n* radar *m.*

radiance ['reɪdɪəns] *n* resplandor *m.*

radiant ['reɪdɪənt] *adj* radiante, resplandeciente.

radiate ['reɪdɪeɪt] *vtr* irradiar; *fig* she radiated happiness, rebosaba de alegría.

radiation [reɪdɪ'eɪʃən] *n* radiación *f.*

radiator ['reɪdɪeɪtəʳ] *n* radiador *m.*

radical ['rædɪkəl] *adj* radical.

radio ['reɪdɪəʊ] *n* radio *f;* on the r., en or por la radio; r. station, emisora *f* (de radio).

radioactive [reɪdɪəʊ'æktɪv] *adj* radiactivo,-a.

radio-controlled [reɪdɪəʊkən'trəʊld] *adj* teledirigido,-a.

radiography [reɪdɪ'ɒɡrəfɪ] *n* radiografía *f.*

radiology [reɪdɪ'ɒlədʒɪ] *n* radiología *f.*

radiotherapy [reɪdɪəʊ'θerəpɪ] *n* radioterapia *f.*

radish ['rædɪʃ] *n* rábano *m.*

radius ['reɪdɪəs] *n* radio *m;* within a r. of, en un radio de.

RAF [ɑːreɪ'ef] *GB abbr of* **Royal Air Force,** fuerzas aéreas británicas.

raffle ['ræfəl] I *n* rifa *f.* II *vtr* rifar.

raft [rɑːft] *n* balsa *f.*

rafter ['rɑːftəʳ] *n* viga *f* de madera.

rag¹ [ræɡ] I *n* 1 *(torn piece)* harapo *m;* r. doll, muñeca *f* de trapo. 2 *(for cleaning)* trapo *m.* 3 *fam* rags, *(clothes)* trapos *mpl.* 4 *Press pej* periodicucho *m.*

rag² [ræɡ] I *n GB Univ* función benéfica. II *vtr* gastar bromas a.

rag-and-bone [ræɡən'bəʊn] *adj GB* r.-and-b. man, trapero *m.*

rage [reɪdʒ] I *n* 1 *(fury)* cólera *f.* 2 *fam* it's all the r., hace furor. II *vi* 1 *(person)* rabiar, estar furioso,-a. 2 *fig (storm, sea)* rugir; *(wind)* bramar.

ragged ['ræɡɪd] *adj* 1 *(clothes)* hecho,-a jirones. 2 *(person)* harapiento,-a. 3 *(edge)* mellado,-a. 4 *fig (uneven)* desigual.

raging ['reɪdʒɪŋ] *adj* 1 *(angry)* furioso,-a. 2 *fig (sea)* embravecido,-a. 3 *(intense)* feroz; *(storm)* violento,-a.

raid [reɪd] I *n Mil* incursión *f; (by police)* redada *f; (robbery etc)* atraco *m.* II *vtr Mil* hacer una incursión en; *(police)* hacer una redada en; *(rob)* asaltar; *fam* to r. the larder, vaciar la despensa.

raider ['reɪdəʳ] *n (invader)* invasor,-a *m,f.*

rail [reɪl] *n* 1 barra *f.* 2 *(railing)* barandilla *f.* 3 Rail carril *f;* **by r.,** *(send sth)* por ferrocarril; *(travel)* en tren.

railcard ['reɪlkɑːd] *n GB* abono *m.*

railing ['reɪlɪŋ] *n (usu pl)* verja *f.*

railroad ['reɪlrəʊd] *n US* ferrocarril *m.*

railway ['reɪlweɪ] *n GB* ferrocarril *m;* r. line, r. track, vía férrea; r. station, estación *f* de ferrocarril.

railwayman ['reɪlweɪmən] *n GB* ferroviario *m.*

rain [reɪn] I *n* lluvia *f;* in the r., bajo la lluvia. II *vi* llover; it's raining, llueve.

rainbow ['reɪnbəʊ] *n* arco *m* iris.

raincoat ['reɪnkəʊt] *n* impermeable *m.*

raindrop ['reɪndrɒp] *n* gota *f* de lluvia.

rainfall ['reɪnfɔːl] *n (falling of rain)* precipitación *f; (amount)* pluviosidad *f.*

rainforest ['reɪnfɒrɪst] *n* selva *f* tropical.

rainy ['reɪnɪ] *adj (rainier, rainiest)* lluvioso,-a.

raise [reɪz] I *n US* aumento *m* (de

sueldo). **II** *vtr* **1** levantar; *(glass)* brindar; *(voice)* subir; *(building)* erigir. **2** *(prices)* aumentar. **3** *(money, help)* reunir. **4** *(issue)* plantear. **5** *(crops, children)* criar. **6** *Rad* comunicar con. **7** *(standards)* mejorar. **8** *(laugh)* provocar.

raisin ['reɪzən] *n* pasa *f*.

rake¹ [reɪk] **I** *n* *(garden tool)* rastrillo *m*; *(for fire)* hurgón *m*. **II** *vtr* *(leaves)* rastrillar; *(fire)* hurgar; *(with machine gun)* barrer.

rake² [reɪk] *n (dissolute man)* calavera *m*, libertino *m*.

rally ['rælɪ] **I** *n* **1** *(gathering)* reunión *f*; *Pol* mitin *m*. **2** *Aut* rallye *m*. **3** *Ten* jugada *f*. **II** *vtr (support)* reunir. **III** *vi* recuperarse.
♦**rally round** *vi* formar una piña.

RAM [ræm] *Comput abbr of* **random access memory**, RAM.

ram [ræm] *n* **1** *Zool* carnero *m*. **2** *Tech* maza *f*. **II** *vtr* **1** *(drive into place)* hincar; *(cram)* embutir; *fam* **to r. sth home,** hacer algo patente. **2** *(crash into)* chocar con.

ramble ['ræmbəl] **I** *n (walk)* caminata *f*. **II** *vi* **1** *(walk)* hacer una excursión a pie. **2** *fig (digress)* divagar.

rambler ['ræmblər] *n* **1** *(person)* excursionista *mf*. **2** *Bot* rosal *m* trepador.

rambling ['ræmblɪŋ] *adj* **1** *(incoherent)* incoherente. **2** *(house)* laberíntico,-a. **3** *Bot* trepador,-a.

ramp [ræmp] *n* **1** rampa *f*. **2** *Av (movable stairway)* escalerilla *f*.

rampage [ræm'peɪdʒ] **I** *n* **to be on the r.,** desmandarse. **II** *vi* **to r. about,** comportarse como un loco.

rampant ['ræmpənt] *adj* incontrolado,-a; **corruption is r.,** la corrupción está muy extendida.

rampart ['ræmpɑːt] *n* muralla *f*.

ramshackle ['ræmʃækəl] *adj* destartalado,-a.

ran [ræn] *pt* → **run.**

ranch [rɑːntʃ] *n US* rancho *m*, hacienda *f*.

rancher [rɑːntʃər] *n US* ranchero,-a *m,f*.

rancid ['rænsɪd] *adj* rancio,-a.

rancour, *US* **rancor** ['ræŋkər] *n fml* rencor *m*.

R&D [ɑːrən'diː] *n abbr of* **Research and Development,** I+D.

random ['rændəm] **I** *n* **at r.,** al azar. **II** *adj* fortuito,-a; **r. selection,** selección hecha al azar.

randy ['rændɪ] *adj (randier, randiest) GB fam* cachondo,-a, caliente.

rang [ræŋ] *pt* → **ring.**

range [reɪndʒ] **I** *n* **1** *(of mountains)* cordillera *f*, sierra *f*. **2** *US (open land)* pradera *f*. **3** *(choice)* surtido *m*, *(of products)* gama *f*. **4** *Mus* registro *m*. **5** *firing r.,* campo *m* de tiro. **6** *(of missile)* alcance *m*; **at close r.,** de cerca; **long-/short-r. missiles,** misiles *mpl* de largo/corto alcance. **7** **r. of vision,** campo *m* de visión. **8** *Culin* coci-

na *f* de carbón. **II** *vi (extend)* extenderse *(to,* hasta); **prices r. from five to twenty pounds,** los precios oscilan entre cinco y veinte libras. **III** *vtr lit (wander)* vagar por.

ranger ['reɪndʒər] *n* **1** *(forest)* guardabosques *mf inv*. **2** *US (mounted policeman)* policía *m* montado.

rank¹ [ræŋk] **I** *n* **1** *Mil (row)* fila *f*; **the ranks,** los soldados rasos; **the r. and file,** la base. **2** *(position in army)* graduación *f*; *(in society)* rango *m*. **3** *(taxi)* r., parada *f* de taxis. **II** *vtr (classify)* clasificar. **III** *vi (figure)* figurar; **to r. above/below sb,** figurar por encima/debajo de algn; **to r. with,** estar al mismo nivel que.

rank² [ræŋk] *adj fml* **1** *(vegetation)* exuberante. **2** *(foul-smelling)* fétido,-a. **3** *(thorough)* total, absoluto,-a.

ransack ['rænsæk] *vtr (plunder)* saquear; *(rummage in)* registrar.

ransom ['rænsəm] *n* rescate *m*; **to hold sb to r.,** pedir rescate por algn; *fig* poner a algn entre la espada y la pared.

rant [rænt] *vi* vociferar; *fam* **to r. and rave,** pegar gritos.

rap [ræp] **I** *n* **1** *(blow)* golpe *m* seco; *(on door)* golpecito *m*. **2** *Mus* rap *m*. **II** *vtr & vi (knock)* golpear.

rape¹ [reɪp] *Jur* **I** *n* violación *f*. **II** *vtr* violar.

rape² [reɪp] *n Bot* colza *f*.

rapeseed ['reɪpsiːd] *n* **r. oil,** aceite *m* de colza.

rapid ['ræpɪd] **I** *adj* rápido,-a. **II** *npl* **rapids,** *(in river)* rápidos *mpl*.

rapidity [rə'pɪdɪtɪ] *n* rapidez *f*.

rapist ['reɪpɪst] *n* violador,-a *m,f*.

rapport [ræ'pɔːt] *n* compenetración *f*.

rapture ['ræptʃər] *n* éxtasis *m*.

rapturous ['ræptʃərəs] *adj* muy entusiasta.

rare¹ [reər] *adj* raro,-a, poco común.
♦**rarely** *adv* raras veces.

rare² [reər] *adj (steak)* poco hecho,-a.

rarefied ['reərɪfaɪd] *adj* enrarecido,-a.

raring ['reərɪŋ] *adj fam* **to be r. to do sth,** morirse de ganas de hacer algo.

rarity ['reərɪtɪ] *n* rareza *f*.

rascal ['rɑːskəl] *n* granuja *mf*.

rash¹ [ræʃ] *n* **1** *Med* erupción *f*, sarpullido *m*. **2** *fig (of robberies etc)* racha *f*.

rash² [ræʃ] *adj (reckless)* impetuoso,-a; *(words, actions)* precipitado,-a, imprudente.

rasher ['ræʃər] *n* loncha *f*.

rasping ['rɑːspɪŋ] *adj* áspero,-a.

raspberry ['rɑːzbərɪ] *n* frambuesa *f*.

rat [ræt] *n* rata *f*; **r. poison,** raticida *m*.

rate [reɪt] **I** *n* **1** *(ratio)* índice *m*, tasa *f*; **at any r.,** *(at least)* al menos; *(anyway)* en cualquier caso. **2** *(cost)* precio *m*; *Fin (of interest, exchange)* tipo *m*. **3** **at the r. of,** *(speed)* a la velocidad de; *(quantity)* a razón de. **4 first r.**, de primera categoría. **5 GB rates**, impuestos *mpl* municipales. **II** *vtr* **1** (*estimate*) estimar. **2** (*evaluate*) tasar. **3** (*consider*) considerar.

rateable ['reɪtəbəl] *adj* GB **r. value**, valor *m* catastral.

ratepayer ['reɪtpeɪəʳ] *n* GB contribuyente *mf*.

rather ['rɑːðəʳ] *adv* **1** (*quite*) más bien, bastante; (*very much so*) muy. **2** (*more accurately*) mejor dicho; **r. than**, (*instead of*) en vez de; (*more than*) más que. **3 she would r. stay here**, (*prefer to*) prefiere quedarse aquí.

ratify ['rætɪfaɪ] *vtr* ratificar.

rating ['reɪtɪŋ] *n* **1** (*valuation*) tasación *f*; (*score*) valoración *f*. **2** TV (**programme**) **ratings**, índice *m sing* de audiencia. **3** Naut marinero *m* sin graduación.

ratio ['reɪʃɪəʊ] *n* razón *f*; **in the r. of**, a razón de.

ration ['ræʃən] **I** *n* **1** (*allowance*) ración *f*. **2 rations**, víveres *mpl*. **II** *vtr* racionar.

rational ['ræʃənəl] *adj* racional.

rationale [ræʃə'nɑːl] *n* base *f*.

rationalize ['ræʃənəlaɪz] *vtr* racionalizar.

rattle ['rætəl] **I** *n* **1** (*of train, cart*) traqueteo *m*; (*of metal*) repiqueteo *m*; (*of glass*) tintineo *m*. **2** (*toy*) sonajero *m*; (*instrument*) carraca *f*. **II** *vtr* **1** (*keys etc*) hacer sonar. **2** *fam* (*unsettle*) poner nervioso,-a. **III** *vi* sonar; (*metal*) repiquetear; (*glass*) tintinear.

rattlesnake ['rætəlsneɪk] *n* serpiente *f* de cascabel.

raucous ['rɔːkəs] *adj* estridente.

ravage ['rævɪdʒ] *fml* **I** *n* (*usu pl*) estragos *mpl*. **II** *vtr* asolar, devastar.

rave [reɪv] **I** *vi* **1** (*be delirious*) delirar. **2** (*be angry*) enfurecerse (**at**, con). **3** *fam* (*show enthusiasm*) entusiasmarse (**about**, por). **II** *n fam* **r. review**, crítica *f* muy favorable.

raven ['reɪvən] *n* cuervo *m*.

ravenous ['rævənəs] *adj* **I'm r.**, tengo un hambre que no veo.

ravine [rə'viːn] *n* barranco *m*.

raving ['reɪvɪŋ] *n fam* **r. mad**, loco,-a de atar.

ravishing ['rævɪʃɪŋ] *adj* (*person*) encantador,-a.

raw [rɔː] **I** *adj* **1** (*uncooked*) crudo,-a. **2** (*not processed*) bruto,-a; (*alcohol*) puro,-a; **r. material**, materia prima. **3** (*emotion*) instintivo,-a. **4** (*weather*) crudo,-a. **5 r. deal**, trato injusto. **6** (*wound*) abierto,-a; **r. flesh**, carne viva. **7** US (*inexperienced*) novato,-a. **8** (*frank*) franco,-a.

ray[1] [reɪ] *n* rayo *m*; *fig* **r. of hope**, rayo de esperanza.

ray[2] [reɪ] *n* (*fish*) raya *f*.

rayon ['reɪɒn] *n* rayón *m*.

raze [reɪz] *vtr* arrasar.

razor ['reɪzəʳ] *n* (*for shaving*) maquinilla *f*

de afeitar; **r. blade**, hoja *f* de afeitar.

Rd *abbr of* Road, calle *f*, c/.

re [riː] *prep* respecto a, con referencia a.

reach [riːtʃ] **I** *vtr* **1** (*arrive at*) llegar a. **2** (*contact*) localizar. **II** *vi* alcanzar; **to r. for sth**, intentar coger algo; **to r. out**, extender la mano. **III** *n* **1** (*range*) alcance *m*; **out of r.**, fuera del alcance; **within r.**, al alcance. **2** Box extensión *f* del brazo. **3 reaches**, (*on a river*) recta *f sing*.

react [rɪ'ækt] *vi* reaccionar.

reaction [rɪ'ækʃən] *n* reacción *f*.

reactor [rɪ'æktəʳ] *n* reactor *m*.

read [riːd] **I** *vtr* (*pt & pp* **read** [red]) **1** leer. **2** (*decipher*) descifrar. **3** (*understand*) entender; (*interpret*) interpretar. **4** Univ estudiar. **II** *vi* **1** (*dial*) marcar. **2** (*signpost, text*) decir. ◆**read out** *vtr* leer en voz alta.

readable ['riːdəbəl] *adj* **1** (*interesting*) interesante. **2** (*legible*) legible.

reader ['riːdəʳ] *n* **1** lector,-a *m,f*. **2** (*book*) libro *m* de lectura. **3** GB Univ profesor,-a adjunto,-a.

readership ['riːdəʃɪp] *n* Press lectores *mpl*.

readiness ['redɪnɪs] *n* **1** (*preparedness*) preparación *f*. **2** (*willingness*) buena disposición.

reading ['riːdɪŋ] *n* **1** lectura *f*. **2** *fig* interpretación *f*. **3** (*of laws, bill*) presentación *f*.

readjust [riːə'dʒʌst] **I** *vtr* reajustar. **II** *vi* (*adapt oneself*) adaptarse.

ready ['redɪ] *adj* **1** (*prepared*) listo,-a, preparado,-a; **r., steady, go!**, ¡preparados, listos, ya! **2 r. to**, (*about to*) a punto de. **3** (*to hand*) a mano; **r. cash**, dinero *m* en efectivo. **4** (*willing*) dispuesto,-a. ◆**readily** *adv* **1** (*easily*) fácilmente; **r. available**, disponible en el acto. **2** (*willingly*) de buena gana.

ready-cooked [redɪ'kʊkt] *adj* precocinado,-a.

ready-made [redɪ'meɪd] *adj* confeccionado,-a; (*food*) preparado,-a.

real [rɪəl] *adj* **1** real, verdadero,-a; *fam* **for r.**, de veras. **2** (*genuine*) auténtico,-a; **r. leather**, piel legítima. **3** US Com **r. estate**, bienes *mpl* inmuebles; **r. estate agent**, agente inmobiliario. ◆**really** *adv* verdaderamente, realmente; **r. don't know**, no lo sé de verdad; **r.?**, ¿de veras?

realism ['rɪəlɪzəm] *n* realismo *m*.

realistic ['rɪəlɪstɪk] *adj* realista.

reality [rɪ'ælɪtɪ] *n* realidad *f*; **in r.**, en realidad.

realize ['rɪəlaɪz] *vtr* **1** (*become aware of*) darse cuenta de. **2** (*assets, plan*) realizar.

realization [rɪəlaɪ'zeɪʃən] *n* **1** (*understanding*) comprensión *f*. **2** (*of plan, assets*) realización *f*.

realm [relm] *n* (*kingdom*) reino *m*; *fig* (*field*) terreno *m*.

ream [ri:m] n (of paper) resma f.
reap [ri:p] vtr Agr cosechar; fig to r. the benefits, llevarse los beneficios.
reappear [ri:ə'pɪər] vi reaparecer.
reappraisal [ri:ə'preɪzəl] n revaluación f.
rear¹ [rɪər] I n 1 (back part) parte f de atrás. 2 fam (buttocks) trasero m. II adj trasero,-a; r. entrance, puerta f de atrás.
rear² [rɪər] I vtr 1 (breed, raise) criar. 2 (lift up) levantar. II vi to r. up, (horse) encabritarse.
rearguard ['rɪəgɑːd] n retaguardia f.
rearmament [ri:'ɑːməmənt] n rearme m.
rearrange [ri:ə'reɪndʒ] vtr 1 (furniture) colocar de otra manera. 2 (appointment) fijar otra fecha para.
rear-view ['rɪəvju:] adj r.-v. mirror, (espejo m) retrovisor m.
reason ['ri:zən] I n 1 motivo m, razón f; for no r., sin razón; for some r., por algún motivo. 2 (good sense) razón f; it stands to r., es lógico; to listen to r., atender a razones. II vi 1 to r. with sb, convencer a algn. 2 (argue, work out) razonar.
reasonable ['ri:zənəbəl] adj 1 (fair) razonable. 2 (sensible) sensato,-a. 3 (average) regular. ◆**reasonably** adv (fairly) bastante.
reasoning ['ri:zənɪŋ] n razonamiento m.
reassurance [ri:ə'ʃʊərəns] n consuelo m.
reassure [ri:ə'ʃʊər] vtr 1 (comfort) tranquilizar. 2 (restore confidence) dar confianza a.
reassuring [ri:ə'ʃʊərɪŋ] adj consolador, a.
rebate ['ri:beɪt] n devolución f; tax r., devolución fiscal.
rebel ['rebəl] I adj & n rebelde (mf). II [rɪ'bel] vi rebelarse, sublevarse (against, contra).
rebellion [rɪ'beljən] n rebelión f.
rebellious [rɪ'beljəs] adj rebelde.
rebound ['ri:baʊnd] I n (of ball) rebote m; fig on the r., de rebote. II [rɪ'baʊnd] vi (ball) rebotar.
rebuff [rɪ'bʌf] I n desaire m. II vtr desairar.
rebuild [ri:'bɪld] vtr reconstruir.
rebuke [rɪ'bju:k] I n reproche m. II vtr reprochar.
rebut [rɪ'bʌt] vtr refutar.
recalcitrant [rɪ'kælsɪtrənt] adj fml recalcitrante.
recall [rɪ'kɔ:l] vtr 1 (soldiers, products) hacer volver; (ambassador) retirar. 2 (remember) recordar.
recant [rɪ'kænt] vi fml retractarse.
recap [rɪ'kæp] I vtr & vi resumir; to r., en resumen. II ['ri:kæp] n recapitulación f.
recapitulate [ri:kə'pɪtjʊleɪt] vtr & vi fml recapitular.
recapture [ri:'kæptʃər] vtr fig recuperar.
recd Com abbr of **received**, recibido, -a.

recede [rɪ'si:d] vi retroceder; (fade) desvanecerse.
receipt [rɪ'si:t] n 1 (act) recepción f; to acknowledge r. of sth, acusar recibo de algo. 2 Com (paper) recibo m. 3 receipts, (takings) recaudación f sing.
receive [rɪ'si:v] vtr 1 recibir. 2 Jur (stolen goods) ocultar. 3 (welcome) acoger. 4 TV Rad captar.
receiver [rɪ'si:vər] n 1 (person) receptor,-a m,f. 2 Jur (of stolen goods) perista mf. 3 GB Jur official r., síndico m. 4 Tel auricular m. 5 Rad receptor m.
recent ['ri:sənt] adj reciente; in r. years, en los últimos años. ◆**recently** adv hace poco, recientemente.
receptacle [rɪ'septəkəl] n receptáculo m.
reception [rɪ'sepʃən] n 1 (welcome) acogida f. 2 (party) recepción f; wedding r., banquete m de bodas. 3 r. (desk), recepción f. 4 Rad TV recepción f.
receptionist [rɪ'sepʃənɪst] n recepcionista mf.
recess [rɪ'ses, rɪ'ses] n 1 (in a wall) hueco m. 2 (secret place) escondrijo m. 3 US Educ recreo m; Parl período m de vacaciones.
recession [rɪ'seʃən] n recesión f.
recharge [rɪ'tʃɑːdʒ] vtr (battery) recargar.
rechargeable [ri:'tʃɑːdʒəbəl] adj recargable.
recipe ['resɪpɪ] n Culin receta f; fig fórmula f.
recipient [rɪ'sɪpɪənt] n receptor,-a m,f; (of letter) destinatario,-a m,f.
reciprocate [rɪ'sɪprəkeɪt] I vtr (favour etc) devolver. II vi hacer lo mismo.
recital [rɪ'saɪtəl] n recital m.
recite [rɪ'saɪt] vtr & vi recitar.
reckless ['rekləs] adj (unwise) imprudente; (fearless) temerario,-a.
reckon ['rekən] vtr & vi 1 (calculate) calcular; (count) contar. 2 fam (think) creer; (consider) considerar. ◆**reckon on** vtr contar con.
reckoner ['rekənər] n ready r., tabla f de cálculo.
reckoning ['rekənɪŋ] n cálculo m; by my r. ..., según mis cálculos ...; fig day of r., día m del juicio final.
reclaim [rɪ'kleɪm] vtr 1 (recover) recuperar; (demand back) reclamar. 2 (marshland etc) convertir.
recline [rɪ'klaɪn] vi recostarse, reclinarse.
reclining [rɪ'klaɪnɪŋ] adj recostado,-a; r. seat, asiento m abatible.
recluse [rɪ'klu:s] n recluso,-a m,f.
recognition [rekəg'nɪʃən] n reconocimiento m; (appreciation) apreciación f; changed beyond all r., irreconocible.
recognizable [rekəg'naɪzəbəl] adj reconocible.
recognize ['rekəgnaɪz] vtr reconocer.

recoil [rɪˈkɔɪl] **I** n (of gun) culatazo m; (of spring) aflojamiento m. **II** [rɪˈkɔɪl] vi **1** (gun) dar un culatazo; (spring) aflojarse. **2** (in fear) espantarse.

recollect [rekəˈlekt] vtr recordar.

recollection [rekəˈlekʃən] n recuerdo m.

recommend [rekəˈmend] vtr recomendar.

recommendation [rekəmenˈdeɪʃən] n recomendación f.

recompense [ˈrekəmpens] **I** n recompensa f; Jur indemnización f. **II** vtr recompensar; Jur indemnizar.

reconcile [ˈrekənsaɪl] vtr (two people) reconciliar; (two ideas) conciliar; to r. oneself to, resignarse a.

recondition [riːkənˈdɪʃən] vtr (engine) revisar.

reconnaissance [rɪˈkɒnɪsəns] n Mil reconocimiento m.

reconnoitre, US **reconnoiter** [rekəˈnɔɪtər] vtr Mil reconocer.

reconsider [riːkənˈsɪdər] vtr reconsiderar.

reconstruct [riːkənˈstrʌkt] vtr reconstruir.

reconstruction [riːkənˈstrʌkʃən] n reconstrucción f.

record [ˈrekɔːd] **I** n **1** (account) relación f; (of meeting) actas fpl; off the r., confidencialmente. **2** (document) documento m; r. of attendance, registro m de asistencia; **public records**, archivos mpl. **3** Med historial médico. **4** Mus disco m; r. player, tocadiscos m inv. **5** Sport récord m. **II** [rɪˈkɔːd] vtr **1** (relate) hacer constar; (note down) apuntar. **2** (record, voice) grabar. **3** (of thermometer etc) marcar.

redcurrant [ˈredkʌrənt] n grosella roja.

redden [ˈredən] **I** vi (blush) enrojecerse; ponerse colorado,-a. **II** vtr (make red) teñir de rojo.

reddish [ˈredɪʃ] adj rojizo,-a.

redeem [rɪˈdiːm] vtr **1** (regain) recobrar; (from pawn) desempeñar; (voucher) canjear. **2** (debt) amortizar. **3** (film, novel etc) salvar. **4** Rel redimir; fig to r. oneself, redimirse.

redeeming [rɪˈdiːmɪŋ] adj compensatorio,-a; his only r. feature, lo único que le salva.

redemption [rɪˈdempʃən] n fml **1** (of debt) amortización f. **2** Rel redención f; beyond r., sin remedio.

redeploy [riːdɪˈplɔɪ] vtr transferir.

red-handed [redˈhændɪd] adj to catch sb r.-h., coger a algn con las manos en la masa.

redhead [ˈredhed] n pelirrojo,-a m,f.

red-hot [redˈhɒt] adj **1** candente; r.-h. news, noticia(s) f(pl) de última hora. **2** fam (passionate) ardiente.

redial [riːˈdaɪəl] n Tel (facility) rellamada f.

redirect [riːdɪˈrekt] vtr **1** (funds) redistribuir. **2** (letter) remitir a la nueva dirección.

red-light [redˈlaɪt] adj fam r.-l. district, barrio chino.

redouble [riːˈdʌbəl] vtr redoblar.

redress [rɪ'dres] *fml* I *n* reparación *f*. II *vtr* reparar.

redskin ['redskɪn] *n offens* piel roja *mf*.

reduce [rɪ'djuːs] *vtr* 1 reducir. 2 (*in rank*) degradar. 3 *Culin* (*sauce*) espesar. 4 *Med* recomponer.

reduction [rɪ'dʌkʃən] *n* reducción *f*; *Com* (*in purchase price*) descuento *m*, rebaja *f*.

redundancy [rɪ'dʌndənsɪ] *n* despido *m*.

redundant [rɪ'dʌndənt] *adj* 1 (*superfluous*) redundante. 2 *Ind* **to be made r.**, perder el empleo; **to make sb r.**, despedir a algn.

reed [riːd] *n* 1 *Bot* caña *f*. 2 *Mus* caramillo *m*.

reef [riːf] *n* arrecife *m*.

reek [riːk] I *n* tufo *m*. II *vi* apestar.

reel [riːl] I *n* 1 (*spool*) bobina *f*, carrete *m*. 2 *Scot Mus* danza *f* tradicional. II *vi* (*stagger*) tambalearse.

re-elect [riːɪ'lekt] *vtr* reelegir.

ref [ref] *n* 1 *Sport fam abbr of* referee. 2 *Com abbr of* **reference**, ref.

refectory [rɪ'fektərɪ] *n* refectorio *m*.

refer [rɪ'fɜːr] I *vtr* mandar, enviar; **to r. a matter to a tribunal**, remitir un asunto a un tribunal. II *vi* 1 (*allude*) referirse, aludir (**to, a**). 2 (*consult*) consultar (**to, -**).

referee [refə'riː] I *n* 1 *Sport* árbitro,-a *m,f*. 2 (*for job application*) garante *mf*. II *vtr Sport* arbitrar.

reference ['refərəns] *n* 1 referencia *f*; **with r. to**, referente a, con referencia a; **r. book**, libro *m* de consulta; **r. library**, biblioteca *f* de consulta. 2 (*character report*) informe *m*, referencia *f*.

referendum [refə'rendəm] *n* referéndum *m*.

refill ['riːfɪl] I *n* 1 (*replacement*) recambio *m*, carga *f*. 2 *fam* (*drink*) otra copa. II [riː'fɪl] *vtr* rellenar.

refine [rɪ'faɪn] *vtr* refinar.

refined [rɪ'faɪnd] *adj* refinado,-a.

refinement [rɪ'faɪnmənt] *n* refinamiento *m*.

refinery [rɪ'faɪnərɪ] *n* refinería *f*.

reflect [rɪ'flekt] I *vtr* (*light, attitude*) reflejar. II *vi* (*think*) reflexionar; **to r. on sth**, meditar sobre algo.

reflection [rɪ'flekʃən] *n* 1 (*indication, mirror image*) reflejo *m*. 2 (*thought*) reflexión *f*; **on r.**, pensándolo bien. 3 (*criticism*) crítica *f*.

reflector [rɪ'flektər] *n* 1 *Astron* reflector *m*. 2 (*of vehicle*) catafaro *m*.

reflex ['riːfleks] *n* reflejo *m*.

reflexive [rɪ'fleksɪv] *adj* reflexivo,-a.

reform [rɪ'fɔːm] I *n* reforma *f*. II *vtr* reformar.

reformation [refə'meɪʃən] *n* reforma *f*.

reformatory [rɪ'fɔːmətərɪ] *n* reformatorio *m*.

reformer [rɪ'fɔːmər] *n* reformador,-a *m,f*.

refrain [rɪ'freɪn] I *n* *Mus* estribillo *m*; *fig*

refresh [rɪ'freʃ] *vtr* refrescar.

refresher [rɪ'freʃər] *n* **r. course**, cursillo *m* de reciclaje.

refreshing [rɪ'freʃɪŋ] *adj* refrescante; **a r. change**, un cambio muy agradable.

refreshment [rɪ'freʃmənt] *n* refresco *m*.

refrigerator [rɪ'frɪdʒəreɪtər] *n* nevera *f*, frigorífico *m*.

refuel [riː'fjuːəl] *vi* repostar combustible.

refuge ['refjuːdʒ] *n* refugio *m*, cobijo *m*; **to take r.**, refugiarse.

refugee [refjuː'dʒiː] *n* refugiado,-a *m,f*.

refund ['riːfʌnd] I *n* reembolso *m*. II [rɪ'fʌnd] *vtr* reembolsar, devolver.

regain [rɪ'geɪn] *vtr* recuperar; (*consciousness*) recobrar.

regal ['riːgəl] *adj* regio,-a.

regard [rɪ'gɑːd] I *n* 1 (*concern*) consideración *f*, respeto *m*; **with r. to**, respecto a. 2 (*esteem*) estima *f*. 3 **regards**, (*good wishes*) recuerdos *mpl*; **give him my regards**, dale recuerdos de mi parte. II *vtr* 1 (*consider*) considerar. 2 **as regards**, (*regarding*) respecto a.

regarding [rɪ'gɑːdɪŋ] *prep* respecto a.

regardless [rɪ'gɑːdlɪs] I *prep* a pesar de; **r. of the outcome**, pase lo que pase. II *adv* a toda costa.

regime [reɪ'ʒiːm] *n* régimen *m*.

regiment ['redʒɪmənt] I *n* regimiento *m*. II *vtr* regimentar.

regimental [redʒɪ'mentəl] *adj* del regimiento.

region ['riːdʒən] *n* 1 región *f*. 2 **in the r. of**, aproximadamente.

regional ['riːdʒənəl] *adj* regional.

regionalism ['riːdʒənəlɪzəm] *n* regionalismo *m*.

register ['redʒɪstər] *n* 1 registro *m*. II *vtr* 1 (*record*) registrar. 2 (*letter*) certificar. 3 (*show*) mostrar; **his face registered fear**, en su rostro se reflejaba el miedo. III *vi* (*for course*) inscribirse; *Univ* matricularse.

registered ['redʒɪstəd] *adj* certificado,-a; **r. letter**, carta certificada; **r. trademark**, marca registrada.

registrar [redʒɪ'strɑːr, 'redʒɪstrɑːr] *n* 1 (*record keeper*) registrador,-a *m,f*. 2 *GB Med* interno,-a *m,f*. 3 *Univ* secretario,-a *m,f* general.

registration [redʒɪ'streɪʃən] *n* inscripción *f*; *Univ* matrícula *f*; *GB Aut* **r. number**, matrícula *f*.

registry ['redʒɪstrɪ] *n* registro *m*; **to get**

married in a r. office, casarse por lo civil; r. office, registro civil.

regret [rɪ'gret] I n (*remorse*) remordimiento m; (*sadness*) pesar m; **regrets**, (*excuses*) excusas fpl; **to have no regrets**, no arrepentirse de nada. II vtr arrepentirse de, lamentar.

regretful [rɪ'gretful] adj arrepentido,-a.

regrettable [rɪ'gretəbəl] adj lamentable.

regroup [riː'gruːp] I vtr reagrupar. II vi reagruparse.

regular ['regjʊlər] I adj 1 regular. 2 (*usual*) normal. 3 (*staff*) permanente. 4 (*frequent*) frecuente. 5 r. **army**, tropas fpl regulares. II n 1 (*customer*) cliente mf habitual. 2 Mil militar m de carrera. ◆**regularly** adv con regularidad.

regularity [regjʊ'lærɪtɪ] n regularidad f.

regulate ['regjʊleɪt] vtr regular.

regulation [regjʊ'leɪʃən] I n 1 (*control*) regulación f. 2 (*rule*) regla f. II adj reglamentario,-a.

rehabilitation [riːəbɪlɪ'teɪʃən] n rehabilitación f; r. **centre**, centro m de reinserción.

rehearsal [rɪ'hɜːsəl] n ensayo m.

rehearse [rɪ'hɜːs] vtr & vi ensayar.

reign [reɪn] I n reinado m. II vi reinar.

reigning ['reɪnɪŋ] adj r. **champion**, campeón m actual.

reimburse [riːɪm'bɜːs] vtr reembolsar.

rein [reɪn] n (*for horse*) rienda f; fig **he gave free r. to his emotions**, dio rienda suelta a sus emociones.

reindeer ['reɪndɪər] n reno m.

reinforce [riːɪn'fɔːs] vtr (*strengthen*) reforzar; (*support*) apoyar; **reinforced concrete**, hormigón armado.

reinforcement [riːɪn'fɔːsmənt] n 1 refuerzo m; Constr armazón m. 2 Mil **reinforcements**, refuerzos mpl.

reinstate [riːɪn'steɪt] vtr (*to job*) reincorporar.

reiterate [riː'ɪtəreɪt] vtr & vi reiterar.

reject ['riːdʒekt] I n 1 desecho m. 2 Com **rejects**, artículos defectuosos. II [rɪ'dʒekt] vtr rechazar.

rejection [rɪ'dʒekʃən] n rechazo m.

rejoice [rɪ'dʒɔɪs] vi regocijarse (**at**, **over**, de).

rejuvenate [rɪ'dʒuːvɪneɪt] vtr rejuvenecer; fig revitalizar.

relapse [rɪ'læps] I n 1 Med recaída f; **to have a r.**, sufrir una recaída. 2 (*into crime, alcoholism*) reincidencia f. II vi recaer.

relate [rɪ'leɪt] I vtr 1 (*connect*) relacionar. 2 (*tell*) relatar. II vi relacionarse.

related [rɪ'leɪtɪd] adj 1 (*linked*) relacionado,-a (**to**, con). 2 **to be r. to sb**, ser pariente de algn.

relation [rɪ'leɪʃən] n 1 (*link*) relación f; **in** or **with r. to**, respecto a; **it bears no r. to what we said**, no tiene nada que ver con

lo que dijimos. 2 (*member of family*) pariente,-a m,f.

relationship [rɪ'leɪʃənʃɪp] n 1 (*link*) relación f. 2 (*between people*) relaciones fpl; **to have a good/bad r. with sb**, llevarse bien/mal con algn.

relative [rɪ'leɪtɪv] I n pariente mf. II adj 1 relativo,-a. ◆**relatively** adv relativamente.

relax [rɪ'læks] I vtr (*muscles, rules*) relajar. II vi relajarse.

relaxation [riːlæk'seɪʃən] n 1 (*rest*) descanso m, relajación f. 2 (*of rules*) relajación f. 3 (*pastime*) distracción f.

relaxed [rɪ'lækst] adj relajado,-a; (*peaceful*) tranquilo,-a.

relaxing [rɪ'læksɪŋ] adj relajante.

relay [rɪ'leɪ] I n 1 relevo m; r. **race**), carrera f de relevos. 2 Rad TV retransmisión f. II [rɪ'leɪ] vtr 1 (*pass on*) difundir. 2 Rad TV retransmitir.

release [rɪ'liːs] I n 1 (*of prisoner*) liberación f, puesta f en libertad; (*of gas*) escape m. 2 Com puesta f en venta. 3 Cin estreno m. 4 (*record*) disco m. 5 Press comunicado m. II vtr 1 (*let go*) soltar; (*prisoner*) poner en libertad; (*gas*) despedir. 2 Com poner en venta. 3 Cin estrenar. 4 (*record*) editar. 5 (*publish*) publicar.

relegate ['relɪgeɪt] vtr 1 relegar. 2 Ftb **to be relegated**, bajar a una división inferior.

relent [rɪ'lent] vi ceder; (*storm*) aplacarse.

relentless [rɪ'lentlɪs] adj implacable.

relevant ['relɪvənt] adj pertinente (**to**, a); **it is not r.**, no viene al caso.

reliable [rɪ'laɪəbəl] adj (*person*) de fiar; a r. **car**, un coche seguro; a r. **source**, una fuente fidedigna. ◆**reliably** adv **to be r. informed that**, saber de buena tinta que.

reliability [rɪlaɪə'bɪlɪtɪ] n 1 (*of person*) formalidad f. 2 (*of car, machine*) fiabilidad f.

reliant [rɪ'laɪənt] adj **to be r. on**, depender de.

relic ['relɪk] n 1 Rel reliquia f. 2 (*reminder of past*) vestigio m. 3 **relics**, (*human remains*) restos mpl mortales.

relief [rɪ'liːf] n 1 alivio m. 2 (*help*) auxilio m, ayuda f. 3 Art Geog relieve m.

relieve [rɪ'liːv] vtr 1 aliviar; (*monotony*) romper. 2 (*take over from*) relevar. 3 euph **to r. oneself**, hacer sus necesidades. 4 **to r. sb of sth**, coger algo a algn.

relieved [rɪ'liːvd] adj aliviado,-a, tranquilizado,-a.

religion [rɪ'lɪdʒən] n religión f.

religious [rɪ'lɪdʒəs] adj religioso,-a.

relinquish [rɪ'lɪŋkwɪʃ] vtr renunciar a; **to r. one's hold on sth**, soltar algo.

relish ['relɪʃ] I n 1 (*enjoyment*) deleite m. 2 Culin condimento m. II vtr agradar.

relocate [riːləʊ'keɪt] vtr trasladar.

reluctance [rɪ'lʌktəns] n desgana f.

reluctant [rɪ'lʌktənt] adj reacio,-a; to be r. to do sth, estar poco dispuesto,-a a hacer algo. ◆**reluctantly** adv de mala gana, a regañadientes.

rely [rɪ'laɪ] vi contar (**on**, con), confiar (**on**, en).

remain [rɪ'meɪn] I vi (stay) permanecer, quedarse. 2 (be left) quedar; **it remains to be seen**, está por ver. II npl **remains**, restos mpl.

remainder [rɪ'meɪndər] n resto m.

remaining [rɪ'meɪnɪŋ] adj restante.

remand [rɪ'mɑ:nd] Jur I vtr remitir; **remanded in custody**, en prevención. II n detención f, prisión f; **on r.**, detenido,-a.

remark [rɪ'mɑ:k] I n comentario m. II vtr comentar.

remarkable [rɪ'mɑ:kəbəl] adj extraordinario,-a; (strange) curioso,-a.

remedial [rɪ'mi:dɪəl] adj reparador,-a; r. classes, clases fpl para niños atrasados en los estudios.

remedy ['remɪdɪ] I n remedio m. II vtr remediar.

remember [rɪ'membər] I vtr 1 acordarse de, recordar. 2 r. me to your mother, dale recuerdos a tu madre. II vi acordarse, recordar; **I don't r.**, no me acuerdo.

remembrance [rɪ'membrəns] n in r. of, en recuerdo de; **R. Day**, día m en que se conmemora el armisticio de 1918.

remind [rɪ'maɪnd] vtr recordar; **r. me to do it**, recuérdame que lo haga; **she reminds me of your sister**, me recuerda a tu hermana; **that reminds me**, ahora que me acuerdo.

reminder [rɪ'maɪndər] n recordatorio m, aviso m.

reminisce [remɪ'nɪs] vi rememorar.

reminiscent [remɪ'nɪsənt] adj fml nostálgico,-a; **to be r. of**, recordar.

remiss [rɪ'mɪs] adj (negligent) descuidado,-a.

remission [rɪ'mɪʃən] n 1 Med remisión f. 2 Jur perdón m.

remit [rɪ'mɪt] vtr 1 (send) remitir. 2 Jur referir a otro tribunal.

remittance [rɪ'mɪtəns] n 1 (sending) envío m. 2 (payment) giro m, pago m.

remnant ['remnənt] n resto m; **remnants**, (of cloth) retales mpl.

remorse [rɪ'mɔ:s] n remordimiento m.

remorseful [rɪ'mɔ:sfʊl] adj lleno,-a de remordimiento.

remorseless [rɪ'mɔ:slɪs] adj despiadado,-a.

remote [rɪ'məʊt] adj 1 (far away) remoto,-a; **r. control**, mando m a distancia. 2 (isolated) aislado,-a. 3 **r. person**, persona reservada. 4 (possibility) remoto,-a; **I haven't the remotest idea**, no tengo la más mínima idea.

◆**remotely** adv 1 (vaguely) vagamente. 2 (distantly) en lugar aislado.

remote-controlled [rɪməʊtkən'trəʊld] adj teledirigido,-a.

remould, US **remold** ['ri:məʊld] n Aut neumático recauchutado.

removable [rɪ'mu:vəbəl] adj (detachable) que se puede quitar.

removal [rɪ'mu:vəl] n 1 (moving house) mudanza f, US van, camión m de mudanzas. 2 (of stain etc) eliminación f.

remove [rɪ'mu:v] vtr 1 (move) quitar; **to r. one's make-up**, desmaquillarse; **to r. one's name from a list**, tachar su nombre de una lista. 2 (from office) despedir.

removed [rɪ'mu:vd] adj far r. from, muy diferente de.

remover [rɪ'mu:vər] n make-up r., desmaquillador m; **nail varnish r.**, quitaesmalte m; **stain r.**, quitamanchas m inv.

remuneration [rɪmju:nə'reɪʃən] n fml remuneración f.

renaissance [rə'neɪsəns] I n renacimiento m; **the R.**, el Renacimiento. II adj renacentista.

rend [rend] vtr (pt & pp rent) fml rasgar.

render ['rendər] vtr fml 1 (give) dar. 2 (make) hacer. 3 Com presentar. 4 (translate) traducir.

rendering ['rendərɪŋ] n 1 (of song, piece of music) interpretación f. 2 (translation) traducción f.

rendezvous ['rɒndɪvu:] I n 1 (meeting) cita f. 2 (place) lugar m de reunión. II vi reunirse.

renegade ['renɪgeɪd] n renegado,-a m,f.

renew [rɪ'nju:] vtr (contract etc) renovar; (talks etc) reanudar; **with renewed vigour**, con renovadas fuerzas.

renewal [rɪ'nju:əl] n (of contract etc) renovación f; (of talks etc) reanudación f.

renounce [rɪ'naʊns] vtr fml renunciar.

renovate ['renəveɪt] vtr renovar, hacer reformas en.

renown [rɪ'naʊn] n renombre m.

renowned [rɪ'naʊnd] adj renombrado,-a.

rent [rent] I n 1 (for building, car, TV) alquiler m. 2 (for land) arriendo m. II vtr 1 (building, car, TV) alquilar. 2 (land) arrendar.

rental ['rentəl] n (of house etc) alquiler m.

renunciation [rɪnʌnsɪ'eɪʃən] n fml renuncia f.

reorganize [ri:'ɔ:gənaɪz] vtr reorganizar.

rep [rep] fam 1 Com representante mf. 2 Theat teatro m de repertorio.

repair [rɪ'peər] I n reparación f, arreglo m; **in good/bad r.**, en buen/mal estado. II vtr 1 arreglar; (car) reparar; (clothes) remendar. 2 (make amends for) reparar.

repartee [repɑ:'ti:] n réplica aguda.

repatriate [ri:'pætrieɪt] vtr repatriar.

repay [ri:'peɪ] vtr (pt & pp repaid) devolver; **to r. a debt,** liquidar una deuda; **to r. a kindness,** devolver un favor.

repayment [riː'peɪmənt] *n* pago *m*.

repeal [rɪ'piːl] *fur* I *n* revocación *f*. II *vtr* revocar.

repeat [rɪ'piːt] I *vtr* repetir; **to r. oneself,** repetirse. II *n* (*repetition*) repetición *f*; *TV* reposición *f*.

repeated [rɪ'piːtɪd] *adj* repetido,-a. ◆**repeatedly** *adv* repetidas veces.

repel [rɪ'pel] *vtr* 1 (*fight off*) repeler. 2 (*disgust*) repugnar.

repellent [rɪ'pelənt] I *adj* repelente. II *n* (*insect*) -r., loción *f* or spray *m* antiinsectos; **water-r.,** impermeable *m*.

repent [rɪ'pent] *vtr & vi* arrepentirse (de).

repentance [rɪ'pentəns] *n* arrepentimiento *m*.

repercussion [riːpə'kʌʃən] *n* (*usu pl*) repercusión *f*.

repertoire ['repətwɑːr] *n* repertorio *m*.

repertory ['repətəri] *n Theat* teatro *m* de repertorio.

repetition [repɪ'tɪʃən] *n* repetición *f*.

repetitive [rɪ'petɪtɪv] *adj* repetitivo,-a.

replace [rɪ'pleɪs] *vtr* 1 (*put back*) volver a poner en su sitio. 2 (*substitute for*) sustituir, reemplazar.

replacement [rɪ'pleɪsmənt] *n* 1 (*returning*) reemplazo *m*. 2 (*person*) sustituto,-a *m,f*. 3 (*part*) pieza *f* de recambio.

replay ['riːpleɪ] *n* repetición *f*.

replenish [rɪ'plenɪʃ] *vtr* 1 (*fill up*) rellenar. 2 **to r. stocks,** reponer las existencias.

replete [rɪ'pliːt] *adj fml* repleto,-a.

replica ['replɪkə] *n* réplica *f*.

reply [rɪ'plaɪ] I *n* respuesta *f*, contestación *f*. II *vi* responder, contestar.

report [rɪ'pɔːt] I *n* 1 informe *m*; **medical r.,** parte médico; *GB* **school r.,** informe escolar. 2 (*piece of news*) noticia *f*. 3 *Press Rad TV* reportaje *m*. 4 (*rumour*) rumor *m*. 5 *fml* (*of gun*) estampido *m*. II *vtr* 1 **it is reported that** ..., se dice que .... 2 (*tell authorities about*) denunciar. 3 *Press* hacer un reportaje sobre. III *vi* (*of committee member etc*) 1 hacer un informe. 2 *Press* hacer un reportaje. 3 (*for duty etc*) presentarse; *Mil* **to r. sick,** coger la baja por enfermedad.

reported [rɪ'pɔːtɪd] *adj* **r. speech,** estilo indirecto. ◆**reportedly** *adv fml* según se dice.

reporter [rɪ'pɔːtər] *n* periodista *mf*.

repose [rɪ'pəʊz] *fml* I *n* reposo *m*. II *vtr & vi* reposar.

repossess [riːpə'zes] *vtr* volver a tomar posesión.

reprehensible [reprɪ'hensəbəl] *adj* reprensible, censurable.

represent [reprɪ'zent] *vtr* representar.

representation [reprɪzen'teɪʃən] *n* 1 representación *f*. 2 *fml* (*statement*)

queja *f sing*.

representative [reprɪ'zentətɪv] I *adj* representativo,-a. II *n* 1 representante *mf*. 2 *US Pol* diputado,-a *m,f*; **House of Representatives,** Cámara *f* de Representantes.

repress [rɪ'pres] *vtr* reprimir, contener.

repression [rɪ'preʃən] *n* represión *f*.

repressive [rɪ'presɪv] *adj* represivo,-a.

reprieve [rɪ'priːv] I *n* 1 *fur* indulto *m*. 2 *fig* alivio *m*. II *vtr* 1 *fur* indultar. 2 (*give temporary relief to*) aliviar temporalmente.

reprimand ['reprɪmɑːnd] I *n* reprimenda *f*. II *vtr* reprender.

reprisal [rɪ'praɪzəl] *n* represalia *f*.

reproach [rɪ'prəʊtʃ] I *n* reproche *m*; **beyond r.,** intachable. II *vtr* reprochar.

reproachful [rɪ'prəʊtʃful] *adj* reprobador,-a.

reproduce [riːprə'djuːs] I *vtr* reproducir. II *vi* reproducirse.

reproduction [riːprə'dʌkʃən] *n* reproducción *f*.

reproof [rɪ'pruːf] *n fml* reprobación *f*, censura *f*.

reprove [rɪ'pruːv] *vtr fml* reprobar, censurar.

reptile ['reptaɪl] *n* reptil *m*.

republic [rɪ'pʌblɪk] *n* república *f*.

republican [rɪ'pʌblɪkən] *adj & n* republicano,-a (*m,f*); *US Pol* **R. Party,** Partido Republicano.

repudiate [rɪ'pjuːdɪeɪt] *vtr fml* 1 (*reject*) rechazar. 2 (*not acknowledge*) negarse a reconocer.

repugnant [rɪ'pʌgnənt] *adj* repugnante.

repulse [rɪ'pʌls] *vtr* rechazar.

repulsive [rɪ'pʌlsɪv] *adj* repulsivo,-a.

reputable ['repjʊtəbəl] *adj* (*company etc*) acreditado,-a; (*person, products*) de toda confianza.

reputation [repjʊ'teɪʃən] *n* reputación *f*.

repute [rɪ'pjuːt] *n fml* reputación *f*.

reputed [rɪ'pjuːtɪd] *adj* supuesto,-a; **to be r. to be,** ser considerado,-a como. ◆**reputedly** *adv* según se dice.

request [rɪ'kwest] I *n* petición *f*, solicitud *f*; **available on r.,** disponible a petición de los interesados; *GB* **r. stop,** (*for bus*) parada *f* discrecional. II *vtr* pedir, solicitar.

require [rɪ'kwaɪər] *vtr* 1 (*need*) necesitar, requerir. 2 (*demand*) exigir.

requirement [rɪ'kwaɪəmənt] *n* 1 (*need*) necesidad *f*. 2 (*demand*) requisito *m*.

requisite ['rekwɪzɪt] *fml* I *adj* requerido, -a. II *n* requisito *m*.

requisition [rekwɪ'zɪʃən] I *n* requisición *f*. II *vtr* requisar.

rescind [rɪ'sɪnd] *vtr fml* (*contract*) rescindir; (*law*) abrogar.

rescue ['reskjuː] I *n* rescate *m*; **r. team,** equipo *m* de rescate. II *vtr* rescatar.

rescuer ['reskjʊər] *n* rescatador,-a *m,f*.

research [rɪ'sɜːtʃ] I n investigación f; **R. and Development,** Investigación más Desarrollo. II vtr & vi investigar.

researcher [rɪ'sɜːtʃər] n investigador,-a m,f.

resemblance [rɪ'zembləns] n semejanza f.

resemble [rɪ'zembəl] vtr parecerse a.

resent [rɪ'zent] vtr ofenderse por.

resentful [rɪ'zentful] adj ofendido,-a.

resentment [rɪ'zentmənt] n resentimiento m.

reservation [rezə'veɪʃən] n reserva f.

reserve [rɪ'zɜːv] I n 1 reserva f; **to keep sth in r.,** guardar algo de reserva. 2 Sport suplente mf. 3 Mil reserves, reservas fpl. II vtr reservar.

reserved [rɪ'zɜːvd] adj reservado,-a.

reservoir ['rezəvwɑːr] n embalse m, pantano m; fig reserva f.

reshape [riː'ʃeɪp] vtr rehacer; fig reorganizar.

reshuffle [riː'ʃʌfəl] n Pol remodelación f.

reside [rɪ'zaɪd] vi fml residir.

residence ['rezɪdəns] n fml (home) residencia f; (address) domicilio m; (period of time) permanencia f.

resident ['rezɪdənt] adj & n residente (mf); **to be r. in,** estar domiciliado,-a en.

residential [rezɪ'denʃəl] adj residencial.

residue ['rezɪdjuː] n residuo m.

resign [rɪ'zaɪn] I vtr 1 (give up) dimitir. 2 **to r. oneself to sth,** resignarse a algo. II vi (from job) dimitir.

resignation [rezɪg'neɪʃən] n 1 (from a job) dimisión f. 2 (acceptance) resignación f.

resigned [rɪ'zaɪnd] adj resignado,-a.

resilience [rɪ'zɪlɪəns] n resistencia f.

resilient [rɪ'zɪlɪənt] adj (strong) resistente.

resin ['rezɪn] n resina f.

resist [rɪ'zɪst] vtr 1 (not yield to) resistir. 2 (oppose) oponerse a.

resistance [rɪ'zɪstəns] n resistencia f.

resit [riː'sɪt] vtr (exam) volver a presentarse a.

resolute ['rezəluːt] adj resuelto,-a, decidido,-a.

resolution [rezə'luːʃən] n resolución f.

resolve [rɪ'zɒlv] I n resolución f. II vtr resolver; **to r. to do,** resolverse a hacer. III vi resolverse.

resonant ['rezənənt] adj resonante.

resort [rɪ'zɔːt] I n 1 (place) lugar m de vacaciones; **tourist r.,** centro turístico. 2 (recourse) recurso m; **as a last r.,** como último recurso. II vi recurrir (to, a).

resound [rɪ'zaʊnd] vi resonar; fig tener resonancia.

resounding [rɪ'zaʊndɪŋ] adj **a r. failure,** un fracaso total; **a r. success,** un éxito rotundo.

resource [rɪ'sɔːs] n recurso m.

resourceful [rɪ'sɔːsful] adj ingenioso,-a.

respect [rɪ'spekt] I n 1 (deference) respeto m; **to pay one's respects to sb,** presentar sus respetos a algn. 2 (relation, reference) respecto m; **in that r.,** a ese respecto; **with r. to,** con referencia a. II vtr respetar.

respectable [rɪ'spektəbəl] adj respetable; (clothes) decente.

respectful [rɪ'spektful] adj respetuoso,-a.

respective [rɪ'spektɪv] adj respectivo,-a. ◆**respectively** adv respectivamente.

respite ['respaɪt] n fml respiro m.

resplendent [rɪ'splendənt] adj resplandeciente.

respond [rɪ'spɒnd] vi responder.

response [rɪ'spɒns] n 1 (reply) respuesta f. 2 (reaction) reacción f.

responsibility [rɪspɒnsə'bɪlɪtɪ] n responsabilidad f.

responsible [rɪ'spɒnsəbəl] adj responsable (for, de); **to be r. to sb,** tener que dar cuentas a algn.

responsive [rɪ'spɒnsɪv] adj sensible.

rest[1] [rest] I n 1 (break) descanso m; (cure, peace) tranquilidad f; US **r. room,** aseos mpl. 2 (peace) tranquilidad f; **at r.,** (object) inmóvil. 3 (support) apoyo m. 4 Mus pausa f. II vtr 1 descansar. 2 (lean) apoyar; **to r. a ladder against a wall,** apoyar una escalera contra una pared. III vi 1 descansar. 2 (be calm) quedarse tranquilo,-a. 3 **it doesn't r. with me,** no depende de mí; **we'll let the matter r.,** dejémoslo estar.

rest[2] [rest] n **the r.,** (remainder) el resto, lo demás; **the r. of the day,** el resto del día; **the r. of the girls,** las demás chicas; **the r. of us,** los demás.

restaurant ['restərɒnt] n restaurante m; Rail **r. car,** coche m restaurante.

restful ['restful] adj relajante.

restitution [restɪ'tjuːʃən] n fml restitución f; **to make r.,** restituir.

restive ['restɪv] adj inquieto,-a, nervioso,-a.

restless ['restlɪs] adj agitado,-a, inquieto,-a.

restoration [restə'reɪʃən] n 1 (giving back) devolución f. 2 GB Hist **the R.,** la Restauración. 3 (of building, piece of furniture) restauración f.

restore [rɪ'stɔːr] vtr 1 (give back) devolver. 2 (re-establish) restablecer. 3 (building etc) restaurar.

restrain [rɪ'streɪn] vtr contener; **to r. one's anger,** reprimir la cólera; **to r. oneself,** contenerse.

restrained [rɪ'streɪnd] adj (person) moderado,-a; (emotion) contenido,-a.

restraint [rɪ'streɪnt] n 1 (restriction) restricción f; (hindrance) traba f. 2 (moderation) moderación f.

restrict [rɪ'strɪkt] vtr restringir, limitar.

restriction [rɪ'strɪkʃən] n restricción f, limitación f.

restrictive [rɪ'strɪktɪv] adj restrictivo,-a.

result [rɪ'zʌlt] **I** n 1 resultado m. 2 (consequence) consecuencia f; **as a r. of**, como consecuencia de. **II** vi 1 resultar; **to r. from**, resultar de. 2 **to r. in**, causar.

resume [rɪ'zjuːm] **I** vtr 1 (journey, work, conversation) reanudar; (control) reasumir. **II** vi recomenzar.

résumé ['rezjuːmeɪ] n resumen m.

resumption [rɪ'zʌmpʃən] n (of journey, work, conversation) reanudación f.

resurface [riː'sɜːfɪs] **I** vtr (road) rehacer el firme de. **II** vi fig resurgir.

resurgence [rɪ'sɜːdʒəns] n resurgimiento m.

resurrection [rezə'rekʃən] n resurrección f.

resuscitate [rɪ'sʌsɪteɪt] vtr Med reanimar.

retail ['riːteɪl] **I** n venta f al por menor; **r. outlet**, punto m de venta; **r. price**, precio m de venta al público; **R. Price Index**, Índice m de Precios al Consumo. **II** vtr vender al por menor. **III** vi venderse al por menor. **IV** adv al por menor.

retailer ['riːteɪlə*] n detallista mf.

retain [rɪ'teɪn] vtr 1 (heat) conservar; (personal effects) guardar. 2 (water) retener. 3 (facts, information) recordar. 4 **to r. the services of a lawyer**, contratar a un abogado.

retainer [rɪ'teɪnə*] n 1 (payment) anticipo m sobre los honorarios. 2 (servant) criado,-a m,f.

retaliate [rɪ'tælɪeɪt] vi tomar represalias (against, contra).

retaliation [rɪtælɪ'eɪʃən] n represalias fpl; **in r.**, en represalia.

retarded [rɪ'tɑːdɪd] adj retrasado,-a.

retch [retʃ] vi tener náuseas.

retentive [rɪ'tentɪv] adj retentivo,-a.

rethink ['riːθɪŋk] n fam **to have a r. about sth**, volver a reflexionar sobre algo.

reticent ['retɪsənt] adj reticente.

retina ['retɪnə] n retina f.

retinue ['retɪnjuː] n séquito m.

retire [rɪ'taɪə*] **I** vi 1 jubilar. **II** vi 1 (stop working) jubilarse. 2 (from race) retirarse; **to r. for the night**, irse a la cama, acostarse.

retired [rɪ'taɪəd] adj jubilado,-a.

retirement [rɪ'taɪəmənt] n jubilación f.

retiring [rɪ'taɪərɪŋ] adj 1 (reserved) reservado,-a. 2 (official) saliente.

retort [rɪ'tɔːt] **I** n réplica f. **II** vi replicar.

retrace [rɪ'treɪs] vtr (recall) reconstruir; **to r. one's steps**, volver sobre sus pasos.

retract [rɪ'trækt] **I** vtr 1 (claws) retraer; (landing gear) replegar. 2 (statement) retirar. **II** vi 1 (claws) retraerse; (landing gear) replegarse. 2 fml retractarse.

retread ['riːtred] n Aut neumático recauchutado.

retreat [rɪ'triːt] **I** n 1 Mil retirada f. 2 (shelter) refugio m. 3 Rel retiro m. **II** vi retirarse (from, de).

retribution [retrɪ'bjuːʃən] n merecido m.

retrieval [rɪ'triːvəl] n recuperación f; Comput information r. system, sistema m de recuperación de datos.

retrieve [rɪ'triːv] vtr 1 (recover) recuperar; (of dog) cobrar; Comput recoger. 2 (rescue) salvar. 3 Ten devolver.

retriever [rɪ'triːvə*] n perro m cazador.

retrograde ['retrəʊgreɪd] adj retrógrado,-a.

retrospect ['retrəʊspekt] n **in r.**, retrospectivamente.

retrospective [retrəʊ'spektɪv] **I** adj retrospectivo,-a. **II** n Art (exposición f) retrospectiva f.

return [rɪ'tɜːn] **I** n 1 (of person) regreso m, vuelta f; **by r. of post**, a vuelta de correo; **in r. for**, a cambio de; **many happy returns!**, ¡felicidades!; r. match, partido m de vuelta; **r. ticket**, billete m de ida y vuelta. 2 (of sth borrowed, stolen) devolución f. 3 (profit) beneficio m, ganancia f. 4 (interest) interés m. **II** vtr 1 (give back) devolver; '**r. to sender**', 'devuélvase al remitente'; **to r. a favour/sb's love**, corresponder a un favor/al amor de algn. 2 Pol reelegir. 3 Jur (verdict) pronunciar. **III** vi 1 (come or go back) volver, regresar. 2 (reappear) reaparecer.

returnable [rɪ'tɜːnəbl] adj (bottle) retornable.

reunion [riː'juːnjən] n reunión f.

reunite [riːjuː'naɪt] vtr **to be reunited with**, (after separation) reunirse con.

rev [rev] fam **I** n Aut revolución f. **II** vi **to r. (up)**, acelerar el motor.

revamp [riː'væmp] vtr modernizar, renovar.

reveal [rɪ'viːl] vtr (make known) revelar; (show) dejar ver.

revealing [rɪ'viːlɪŋ] adj revelador,-a.

reveille [rɪ'vælɪ] n diana f.

revel ['revəl] vi disfrutar (in, con); **to r. in doing sth**, gozar muchísimo haciendo algo.

revelation [revə'leɪʃən] n revelación f.

revelry ['revəlrɪ] n jarana f, juerga f.

revenge [rɪ'vendʒ] n venganza f; **to take r. on sb for sth**, vengarse de algo en algn.

revenue ['revɪnjuː] n renta f.

reverberate [rɪ'vɜːbəreɪt] vi 1 (sound) reverberar. 2 (ideas, news) resonar.

reverberation [rɪvɜːbə'reɪʃən] n resonancia f.

revere [rɪ'vɪə*] vtr reverenciar.

reverence ['revərəns] n reverencia f.

reverend ['revərənd] Rel **I** adj reverendo,-a; **R. Mother**, reverenda madre. **II** n (Protestant) pastor m; (Catholic) padre m.

reverie ['revərɪ] n ensueño m.

reversal [rɪ'vɜːsəl] n 1 (of order) inversión f. 2 (of attitude, policy) cambio m total. 3 Jur revocación f.

reverse [rɪ'vɜːs] I adj inverso,-a. II n 1 quite the r., todo lo contrario. 2 (other side) (of cloth) revés m; (of coin) cruz f; (of page) dorso m. 3 Aut r. gear, marcha f atrás. III vtr 1 (order) invertir. 2 (turn round) volver del revés. 3 (change) cambiar totalmente. 4 Jur revocar. 5 GB Tel to r. the charges, poner una conferencia a cobro revertido. IV vi Aut dar marcha atrás.

revert [rɪ'vɜːt] vi volver (to, a).

review [rɪ'vjuː] I n 1 (examination) examen m. 2 Mil revista f. 3 Press crítica f, reseña f. 4 (magazine) revista f. II vtr 1 (examine) examinar. 2 Mil to r. the troops, pasar revista a las tropas. 3 (book etc) hacer una crítica de.

reviewer [rɪ'vjuːər] n crítico,-a m,f.

revile [rɪ'vaɪl] vtr fml injuriar.

revise [rɪ'vaɪz] vtr 1 (look over) revisar; (at school) repasar. 2 (change) modificar. 3 (proofs) corregir.

revision [rɪ'vɪʒən] n 1 revisión f; (at school) repaso m. 2 (change) modificación f. 3. (of proofs) corrección f.

revitalize [riː'vaɪtəlaɪz] vtr revivificar.

revival [rɪ'vaɪvəl] n 1 (of interest) renacimiento m; (of the economy) reactivación f; (of a country) resurgimiento m. 2 Theat reestreno m. 3 Med reanimación f.

revive [rɪ'vaɪv] I vtr 1 (interest) renovar; (a law) restablecer; (hopes) reactivar; (hopes) despertar. 2 Theat reestrenar. 3 Med reanimar. II vi 1 (interest, hopes) renacer. 2 Med volver en sí.

revoke [rɪ'vəʊk] vtr revocar; (permission) suspender.

revolt [rɪ'vəʊlt] I n rebelión f, sublevación f. II vi rebelarse, sublevarse. III vtr repugnar, dar asco a.

revolting [rɪ'vəʊltɪŋ] adj repugnante.

revolution [revə'luːʃən] n revolución f.

revolutionary [revə'luːʃənərɪ] adj & n revolucionario,-a (m,f).

revolve [rɪ'vɒlv] I vi girar; fig to r. around, girar en torno a. II vtr hacer girar.

revolver [rɪ'vɒlvər] n revólver m.

revolving [rɪ'vɒlvɪŋ] adj giratorio,-a.

revue [rɪ'vjuː] n revista f.

revulsion [rɪ'vʌlʃən] n repulsión f.

reward [rɪ'wɔːd] I n recompensa f. II vtr recompensar.

rewarding [rɪ'wɔːdɪŋ] adj provechoso,-a.

rewire [riː'waɪər] vtr Elec to r. a house, poner nueva instalación eléctrica a una casa.

reword [riː'wɜːd] vtr expresar con otras palabras.

rewrite [riː'raɪt] vtr (pt rewrote [riː'rəʊt] pp rewritten [riː'rɪtən]) escribir de nuevo.

rhapsody ['ræpsədɪ] n Mus rapsodia f.

rhetoric ['retərɪk] n retórica f.

rhetorical [rɪ'tɒrɪkəl] adj retórico,-a.

rheumatism ['ruːmətɪzəm] n reuma m.

rheumatoid ['ruːmətɔɪd] adj r. arthritis, reuma m articular.

Rhine [raɪn] n the R., el Rin.

rhinoceros [raɪ'nɒsərəs] n rinoceronte m.

rhododendron [rəʊdə'dendrən] n rododendro m.

Rhone [rəʊn] n the R., el Ródano.

rhubarb ['ruːbɑːb] n ruibarbo m.

rhyme [raɪm] I n rima f; (poem) poema m. II vi rimar.

rhythm ['rɪðəm] n ritmo m.

rib¹ [rɪb] n 1 Anat costilla f. 2 Knit canalé m. 3 (of umbrella) varilla f. 4 Bot (of leaf) nervio m.

rib² [rɪb] vtr fam burlarse de.

ribald ['rɪbəld] adj (humour) verde.

ribbon ['rɪbən] n cinta f; (in hair etc) lazo m; torn to ribbons, hecho,-a jirones.

rice [raɪs] n arroz m; brown r., arroz integral; r. paper, papel de arroz; r. pudding, arroz con leche.

rich [rɪtʃ] I adj (person, food) rico,-a; (soil) fértil; (voice) sonoro,-a; (colour) vivo,-a. II npl the r., los ricos. ◆**richly** adv ricamente; r. deserved, bien merecido,-a.

riches ['rɪtʃɪz] npl riquezas fpl.

richness ['rɪtʃnɪs] n riqueza f; (of soil) fertilidad f; (of voice) sonoridad f; (of colour) viveza f.

rickets ['rɪkɪts] n Med raquitismo m.

rickety ['rɪkɪtɪ] adj (chair etc) cojo,-a; (car) desvencijado,-a.

ricochet ['rɪkəʃeɪ, 'rɪkəʃet] I n rebote m. II vi rebotar.

rid [rɪd] vtr (pt & pp rid) librar; to get r. of sth, deshacerse de algo; to r. oneself of, librarse de.

riddance ['rɪdəns] n fam good r.!, ¡ya era hora!

ridden ['rɪdən] pp → ride.

riddle¹ ['rɪdəl] n 1 (puzzle) acertijo m, adivinanza f. 2 (mystery) enigma m.

riddle² ['rɪdəl] vtr (with bullets) acribillar.

ride [raɪd] I n paseo m, vuelta f; a short bus r., un corto trayecto en autobús; fam to take sb for a r., tomar el pelo a algn; horse r., paseo a caballo. II vtr (pt rode; pp ridden) (bicycle, horse) montar en; can you r. a bike?, ¿sabes montar en bici? III vi 1 (on horse) montar a caballo. 2 (travel) (in bus, train etc) viajar. 3 Naut to r. at anchor, estar anclado,-a. ◆**ride out** vtr sobrevivir; to r. out the storm, capear el temporal.

rider ['raɪdər] n (of horse) (man) jinete m, (woman) amazona f; (of bicycle) ciclista mf; (of motorbike) motociclista mf.

ridge [rɪdʒ] n (crest of a hill) cresta f; (hillock) loma f; (of roof) caballete m; Meteor área *m*.

ridicule ['rɪdɪkju:l] I *n* burla *f*. II *vtr* burlarse de.

ridiculous [rɪ'dɪkjuləs] *adj* ridículo,-a.

riding ['raɪdɪŋ] *n* equitación *f*; **r. breeches**, pantalones *mpl* de montar; **r. school**, escuela hípica.

rife [raɪf] *adj* abundante; **rumour is r. that ...**, corre la voz de que ...; **to be r. with**, abundar en.

riffraff ['rɪfræf] *n fam* chusma *f*, gentuza *f*.

rifle¹ ['raɪfəl] *n* fusil *m*, rifle *m*; **r. range**, campo *m* de tiro.

rifle² ['raɪfəl] *vtr* desvalijar.

rift [rɪft] *n* 1 *Geol* falla *f*. 2 *fig (in friendship)* ruptura *f*; *Pol (in party)* escisión *f*; *(quarrel)* desavenencia *f*.

rig [rɪg] I *n* 1 *Naut* aparejo *m*. 2 *(oil)* r., *(onshore)* torre *f* de perforación; *(offshore)* plataforma petrolífera. II *vtr pej* amañar. ◆**rig out** *vtr fam* ataviar. ◆**rig up** *vtr* improvisar.

rigging ['rɪgɪŋ] *n* aparejo *m*, jarcia *f*.

right [raɪt] I *adj* 1 *(not left)* derecho,-a; **the r. hand**, la mano derecha. 2 *(correct)* correcto,-a; *(time)* exacto,-a.; **to be r.**, tener razón; **all r.**, de acuerdo; **r.?**, ¿vale?; **that's r.**, eso es; **the r. word**, la palabra justa. 3 *(true)* cierto,-a. 4 *(suitable)* adecuado,-a; **the r. time**, el momento oportuno. 5 *(proper)* apropiado,-a. 6 *fam (healthy)* bien. 7 *fam (complete)* auténtico,-a. 8 *(in order)* en orden. 9 **r. angle**, ángulo recto.
II *n* 1 *(right side)* derecha *f*. 2 *(right hand)* mano derecha. 3 *Pol* **the R.**, la derecha. 4 *(lawful claim)* derecho *m*; **in one's own r.**, por derecho propio; **r. of way**, *(across land)* derecho de paso; *(on roads)* prioridad *f*; **civil rights**, derechos civiles. 5 **r. and wrong**, el bien y el mal.
III *adv* 1 *(correctly)* bien; **it's just r.**, es justo lo que hace falta. 2 **r. away**, *(immediately)* en seguida. 3 *(to the right)* a la derecha; **r. and left**, a diestro y siniestro; **to turn r.**, girar a la derecha. 4 *(directly)* directamente; **go r. on**, sigue recto; **r. at the top**, en todo lo alto; **r. in the middle**, justo en medio; **r. to the end**, hasta el final.
IV *vtr* 1 *(correct)* corregir. 2 *(put straight)* enderezar.

righteous ['raɪtʃəs] *adj (upright)* recto,-a.

rightful ['raɪtful] *adj* legítimo,-a.

right-hand [raɪt'hænd] *adj* derecho,-a; **r.-h. drive**, conducción *f* por la derecha; **r.-h. side**, lado derecho; *fam* **r.-h. man**, brazo derecho.

right-handed [raɪt'hændɪd] *adj (person)* que usa la mano derecha; *(tool)* para la mano derecha.

rightly ['raɪtlɪ] *adv* debidamente; **and r. so**, y con razón.

right-wing ['raɪtwɪŋ] *adj* de derechas, de-

rechista.

right-winger [raɪt'wɪŋər] *n* derechista *mf*.

rigid ['rɪdʒɪd] *adj* rígido,-a, inflexible.

rigidity [rɪ'dʒɪdɪtɪ] *n* rigidez *f*, inflexibilidad *f*.

rigmarole ['rɪgmərəʊl] *n fam* galimatías *f inv*.

rigorous ['rɪgərəs] *adj* riguroso,-a.

rigour, *US* **rigor** ['rɪgər] *n* rigor *m*, severidad *f*.

rile [raɪl] *vtr fam* irritar, sacar de quicio.

rim [rɪm] *n (edge)* borde *m*; *(of wheel)* llanta *f*; *(of spectacles)* montura *f*.

rind [raɪnd] *n (of fruit, cheese)* corteza *f*.

ring¹ [rɪŋ] I *n* 1 *(sound of bell)* toque *m*; *(of doorbell, alarm clock)* timbre *m*. 2 *Tel* llamada *f*. II *vtr (pt* **rang**; *pp* **rung**) 1 *(bell)* tocar; *fig* **it rings a bell**, me suena. 2 *GB Tel* llamar por teléfono. III *vi* 1 *(bell, phone etc)* sonar. 2 **my ears are ringing**, tengo un pitido en los oídos. 3 *Tel* llamar. ◆**ring back** *vtr GB Tel* volver a llamar. ◆**ring off** *vi GB Tel* colgar. ◆**ring out** *vi* resonar. ◆**ring up** *vtr GB Tel* llamar por teléfono a.

ring² [rɪŋ] I *n* 1 *(metal hoop)* aro *m*; *(curtain r.)*, anilla *f*; **3 r. binder**, carpeta *f* de anillas. 2 *(for finger)* anillo *m*, sortija *f*; **r. finger**, dedo *m* anular. 3 *(circle)* círculo *m*; **r. road**, carretera *f* de circunvalación. 4 *Gymn* **rings**, anillas *fpl*. 5 *(group of people)* corro *m*; *(of spies)* red *f*; *(of thieves)* banda *f*. 6 *(arena)* pista *f*; *Box* cuadrilátero *m*; *(for bullfights)* ruedo *m*; **circus r.**, pista de circo. II *vtr* 1 *(bird, animal)* anillar. 2 *(surround)* rodear.

ringing ['rɪŋɪŋ] *n (of bell)* toque *m*, repique *m*; *(in ears)* pitido *m*.

ringleader ['rɪŋli:dər] *n* cabecilla *mf*.

ringlet ['rɪŋlɪt] *n* tirabuzón *m*.

rink [rɪŋk] *n* pista *f*; **ice r.**, pista de hielo.

rinse [rɪns] I *n* 1 *(of clothes, hair)* aclarado *m*; *(of dishes)* enjuagado *m*. 2 *(tint for hair)* reflejo *m*. II *vtr* 1 aclarar; *(dishes)* enjuagar. 2 **to r. one's hair**, *(tint)* darse reflejos en el pelo.

Rioja [rɪ'ɒxə] *n* Rioja.

riot ['raɪət] I *n* 1 disturbio *m*, motín *m*; **to run r.**, desmandarse; **r. police**, policía *f* antidisturbios. 2 *fig (of colour)* profusión *f*. II *vi* amotinarse.

rioter ['raɪətər] *n* amotinado,-a *m,f*.

riotous ['raɪətəs] *adj* 1 amotinado,-a. 2 *(noisy)* bullicioso,-a. 3 *(unrestrained)* desenfrenado,-a.

rip [rɪp] I *n (tear)* rasgón *m*. II *vtr* rasgar, rajar; **to r. one's trousers**, rajarse los pantalones. III *vi* rasgarse, rajarse. ◆**rip off** *vtr fam* **to r. sb off**, timar a algn. ◆**rip up** *vtr* hacer pedacitos.

ripcord ['rɪpkɔːd] *n* cuerda *f* de apertura.

ripe [raɪp] *adj* 1 maduro,-a. 2 *(ready)* listo,-a; **the time is r.**, es el momento oportuno.

ripen ['raɪpən] *vtr & vi* madurar.

rip-off ['rɪpɒf] *n fam* timo *m*.

ripple ['rɪpəl] I *n* 1 (*on water, fabric*) onda *f*. 2 (*sound*) murmullo *m*. II *vtr* (*water*) ondular. III *vi* 1 (*water*) ondularse. 2 (*applause*) extenderse.

rise [raɪz] I *n* 1 (*of slope, hill*) cuesta *f*. 2 (*of waters*) crecida *f*. 3 (*in status*) ascenso *m*. 4 (*in prices, temperature*) subida *f*; (*in wages*) aumento *m*. 5 (*in sound*) aumento *m*. 6 to give r. to, ocasionar. II *vi* (*pt* rose; *pp* risen ['rɪzən]) 1 (*land etc*) elevarse. 2 (*waters*) crecer; (*river*) nacer; (*tide*) subir; (*wind*) levantarse. 3 (*sun, moon*) salir. 4 (*voice*) alzarse. 5 (*in rank*) ascender. 6 (*prices, temperature*) subir; (*wages*) aumentar. 7 (*curtain*) subir. 8 (*from bed*) levantarse. 9 (*stand up*) levantarse; *fig* (*city, building*) erguirse. 10 to r. to a challenge, aceptar un reto; to r. to the occasion, ponerse a la altura de las circunstancias. ◆**rise above** *vtr* estar por encima de. ◆**rise up** *vi* (*rebel*) sublevarse.

rising ['raɪzɪŋ] I *adj* (*sun*) naciente; (*tide*) creciente; (*prices*) en aumento; r. damp, humedad *f*. II *n* 1 (*of sun*) salida *f*. 2 (*rebellion*) levantamiento *m*.

risk [rɪsk] I *n* riesgo *m*; at r., en peligro; at your own r., por su cuenta y riesgo; to take risks, arriesgarse. II *vtr* arriesgar; I'll r. it, correré el riesgo.

risky ['rɪskɪ] *adj* (riskier, riskiest) arriesgado,-a.

risqué ['rɪskeɪ] *adj* atrevido,-a; (*joke*) picante.

rite [raɪt] *n* rito *m*; the last rites, la extremaunción *f*.

ritual ['rɪtjʊəl] *adj & n* ritual (*m*).

rival ['raɪvəl] I *adj & n* rival (*m,f*). II *vtr* rivalizar con.

rivalry ['raɪvəlrɪ] *n* rivalidad *f*.

river ['rɪvə] *n* río *m*; down/up r., río abajo/arriba.

river-bank ['rɪvəbæŋk] *n* orilla *f*, ribera *f*.

river-bed ['rɪvəbed] *n* lecho *m*.

rivet ['rɪvɪt] I *n* Tech remache *m*, roblón *m*. II *vtr* Tech remachar; *fig* cautivar.

riveting ['rɪvɪtɪŋ] *adj fig* fascinante.

road [rəʊd] *n* 1 carretera *f*; GB A/B r., carretera nacional/secundaria; main r., carretera principal; r. accident, accidente *m* de tráfico; r. safety, seguridad *f* vial; r. sign, señal *f* de tráfico; r. works, obras *fpl*. 2 (*street*) calle *f*. 3 (*way*) camino *m*.

roadblock ['rəʊdblɒk] *n* control *m* policial.

roadhog ['rəʊdhɒg] *n fam* loco,-a *m,f* del volante, dominguero,-a *m,f*.

roadside ['rəʊdsaɪd] *n* borde *m* de la carretera; r. restaurant/café, restaurante *m*/cafetería *f* de carretera.

roadway ['rəʊdweɪ] *n* calzada *f*.

roadworthy ['rəʊdwɜːðɪ] *adj* (*vehicle*) en

buen estado.

roam [rəʊm] I *vtr* vagar por, rondar. II *vi* vagar.

roar [rɔː] I *n* (*of lion*) rugido *m*; (*of bull, sea, wind*) bramido *m*; (*of crowd*) clamor *m*. II *vi* (*lion, crowd*) rugir; (*bull, sea, wind*) bramar; (*crowd*) clamar; *fig* to r. with laughter, reírse a carcajadas.

roaring ['rɔːrɪŋ] *adj fam fig* a r. success, un éxito clamoroso; to do a r. trade, hacer un negocio redondo.

roast [rəʊst] I *adj* (*meat*) asado,-a; r. beef, rosbif *m*. II *n* Culin asado *m*. III *vtr* (*meat*) asar; (*coffee, nuts*) tostar. IV *vi* asarse; *fig* I'm roasting, me aso de calor.

rob [rɒb] *vtr* robar; (*bank*) atracar.

robber ['rɒbə] *n* ladrón,-a *m,f*; bank r., atracador,-a *m,f*.

robbery ['rɒbərɪ] *n* robo *m*.

robe [rəʊb] *n* (*ceremonial*) toga *f*; (*dressing gown*) bata *f*.

robin ['rɒbɪn] *n* petirrojo *m*.

robot ['rəʊbɒt] *n* robot *m*.

robust [rəʊ'bʌst] *adj* (*sturdy*) robusto,-a.

rock [rɒk] I *n* 1 roca *f*; *fig* to be on the rocks, (*of marriage*) estar a punto de fracasar; *fig* whisky on the rocks, whisky *m* con hielo. 2 US (*stone*) piedra *f*. 3 GB (*sweet*) stick of r., barra *f* de caramelo. 4 Mus música *f* rock; r. and roll, rock and roll *m*. II *vtr* 1 (*chair*) mecer; (*baby*) acunar. 2 (*shake*) hacer temblar; *fig* (*shock*) conmover. III *vi* 1 (*move to and fro*) mecerse. 2 (*shake*) vibrar.

rock-bottom [rɒk'bɒtəm] *adj* bajísimo,-a; r.-b. prices, precios regalados.

rockery ['rɒkərɪ] *n* jardín *m* de rocas.

rocket ['rɒkɪt] I *n* cohete *m*; r. launcher, lanzacohetes *m inv*. II *vi* fam (*prices*) dispararse.

rocking-chair ['rɒkɪŋtʃeə] *n* mecedora *f*.

rocking-horse ['rɒkɪŋhɔːs] *n* caballito *m* de balancín.

rocky ['rɒkɪ] *adj* (rockier, rockiest) rocoso,-a; *fam fig* (*unsteady*) inseguro,-a; the R. Mountains, las Montañas Rocosas.

rod [rɒd] *n* (*of metal*) barra *f*; (*stick*) vara *f*; fishing r., caña *f* de pescar.

rode [rəʊd] *pt* → ride.

rodent ['rəʊdənt] *n* roedor *m*.

roe[1] [rəʊ] *n Zool* r. (deer), corzo,-a *m,f*.

roe[2] [rəʊ] *n* (*fish eggs*) hueva *f*.

rogue [rəʊg] *n* granuja *m*.

role *n*, **rôle** [rəʊl] *n* papel *m*; to play a r., desempeñar un papel.

roll [rəʊl] I *n* 1 rollo *m*; r. of banknotes, fajo *m* de billetes; *fam* big rolls of fat, michelines *mpl*. 2 (*bread*) r., bollo *m*. 3 (*list of names*) lista *f*, nómina *f*; to call the r., pasar lista. 4 (*of ship*) balanceo *m*. 5 (*of drum*) redoble *m*; (*of thunder*) fragor *m*. II *vtr* 1 (*ball*) hacer rodar. 2 (*cigarette*) liar.

3 *(move)* mover. 4 *(push)* empujar. 5 *(lawn, road)* allanar. **III** *vi* 1 *(ball)* rodar; *fam* **to be rolling in money**, estar forrado,-a. 2 *(animal)* revolcarse. 3 *(ship)* balancearse. 4 *(drum)* redoblar; *(thunder)* retumbar. ◆**roll about, roll around** *vi* rodar (de acá para allá). ◆**roll by** *vi* *(years)* pasar. ◆**roll in** *vi* *(arrive)* llegar. 2 *(money)* llegar a raudales. ◆**roll over** *vi* dar una vuelta. ◆**roll up I** *vtr* enrollar; *(blinds)* subir; **to r. up one's sleeves**, (ar)remangarse. **II** *vi* *fam* *(arrive)* llegar.

roll-call ['rəʊlkɔːl] *n* to have a r., pasar lista.

roller ['rəʊlər] *n* 1 *Tech* rodillo *m*; **r. coaster**, montaña rusa; **r. skate**, patín *m* de ruedas. 2 *(large wave)* ola *f* grande. 3 *usu pl (for hair)* rulo *m*.

rolling ['rəʊlɪŋ] **I** *adj* 1 *Rail* **r. stock**, material *m* rodante. 2 *(countryside)* ondulado,-a. **II** *n* rodamiento *m*; *(of ground)* apisonamiento *m*; **r. pin**, rodillo *m* (de cocina).

ROM [rɒm] *Comput abbr of* **read only memory**, memoria *f* sólo de lectura, ROM *f*.

Roman ['rəʊmən] *adj & n* romano,-a *(m,f)*; **R. Catholic**, católico,-a *m,f* (romano,-a); **R. law**, derecho romano; **R. numerals**, números romanos.

Romance [rəʊ'mæns] *adj Ling* románico,-a, romance; **R. languages**, lenguas románicas.

romance [rəʊ'mæns] **I** *n* 1 *(tale)* novela romántica. 2 *(love affair)* aventura amorosa. 3 *(romantic quality)* lo romántico. **II** *vi* fantasear.

Romania [rəʊ'meɪnɪə] *n* → **Rumania**.

romantic [rəʊ'mæntɪk] *adj & n* romántico,-a *(m,f)*.

Rome [rəʊm] *n* Roma *f*.

romp [rɒmp] **I** *n* juguetón *m*. **II** *vi* juguetear.

rompers ['rɒmpəz] *npl* pelele *m sing*.

roof [ruːf] **I** *n (pl* **roofs** [ruːfs, ruːvz]) 1 tejado *m*; *fam fig* **to go through the r.**, *(of prices)* subir por las nubes; *(with anger)* subirse por las paredes. 2 *Aut* techo *m*; **r. rack**, baca *f*. 3 *(of mouth)* cielo *m*. **II** *vtr* techar.

roofing ['ruːfɪŋ] *n* materiales *mpl* usados para techar.

rook [rʊk] *n* 1 *Orn* grajo *m*. 2 *Chess* torre *f*.

rookie ['rʊkɪ] *n US fam (novice)* novato,-a *m,f*.

room [ruːm] *n* 1 habitación *f*, cuarto *m*; **single r.**, habitación individual; **r. service**, servicio *m* de habitación. 2 *(space)* sitio *m*, espacio *m*; **make r. for me**, hazme sitio.

rooming-house ['ruːmɪŋhaʊs] *n US* pensión *f*.

roommate ['ruːmmeɪt] *n* compañero,-a *m,f* de habitación.

roomy ['ruːmɪ] *adj* (**roomier, roomiest**) amplio,-a.

roost [ruːst] **I** *n* palo *m*, percha *f*; *(hen)* **r.**, gallinero *m*; *fig* **to rule the r.**, llevar la batuta. **II** *vi* posarse.

rooster ['ruːstər] *n esp US* gallo *m*.

root[1] [ruːt] **I** *n* raíz *f*; **to take r.**, echar raíces. **II** *vtr* arraigar. **III** *vi* arraigar. ◆**root out, root up** *vtr* arrancar de raíz.

root[2] [ruːt] *vi (search)* buscar; **to r. about** *or* **around for sth**, hurgar en busca de algo.

root[3] [ruːt] *vi fam* **to r. for a team**, animar a un equipo.

rope [rəʊp] **I** *n* 1 *(thin)* cuerda *f*; *(thick)* soga *f*; *Naut* cabo *m*. 2 *fig* **to have sb on the ropes**, tener a algn contra las cuerdas; *fam fig* **to know the ropes**, estar al tanto. **II** *vtr (package)* atar; *(climbers)* encordar. ◆**rope in** *vtr fam* enganchar. ◆**rope off** *vtr* acordonar.

rop(e)y ['rəʊpɪ] *adj (ropier, ropiest) GB fam* chungo,-a.

rosary ['rəʊzərɪ] *n* rosario *m*.

rose[1] [rəʊz] *pt* → **rise**.

rose[2] [rəʊz] *n* 1 *Bot* rosa *f*; **r. bed**, rosaleda *f*; *Naut* cabo *m*. **r. bush**, rosal *m*. 2 *(colour)* rosa *m*. 3 *(of watering can)* alcachofa *f*.

rosé ['rəʊzeɪ] *n (vino)* rosado *m*.

rosebud ['rəʊzbʌd] *n* capullo *m* de rosa.

rosemary ['rəʊzmərɪ] *n* romero *m*.

rosette [rəʊ'zet] *n (of ribbons)* escarapela *f*.

roster ['rɒstər] *n* lista *f*.

rostrum ['rɒstrəm] *n* tribuna *f*.

rosy ['rəʊzɪ] *adj (rosier, rosiest)* 1 *(complexion)* sonrosado,-a. 2 *fig (future)* prometedor,-a.

rot [rɒt] **I** *n* 1 *(decay)* putrefacción *f*; **dry r.**, putrefacción *f* de la madera. 2 *(nonsense)* tonterías *fpl*. **II** *vtr* pudrir. ◆**rot away** *vi* pudrirse.

rota ['rəʊtə] *n usu GB* lista *f*.

rotary ['rəʊtərɪ] *adj* rotatorio,-a, giratorio,-a.

rotate [rəʊ'teɪt] **I** *vtr* 1 *(revolve)* hacer girar. 2 *(jobs, crops)* alternar. **II** *vi (revolve)* girar.

rotating [rəʊ'teɪtɪŋ] *adj* rotativo,-a.

rotation [rəʊ'teɪʃən] *n* rotación *f*.

rote [rəʊt] *n* **by r.**, de memoria.

rotten ['rɒtən] *adj* 1 *(decayed)* podrido,-a; *(tooth)* picado,-a. 2 *fam (very bad)* malísimo,-a; *fam* **I feel r.**, me encuentro fatal.

rouble ['ruːbəl] *n* rublo *m*.

rouge [ruːʒ] **I** *n* colorete *m*. **II** *vtr* poner colorete a.

rough [rʌf] **I** *adj* 1 *(surface, skin)* áspero, -a; *(terrain)* accidentado,-a; *(road)* desigual; *(sea)* agitado,-a; *(weather)* tempestuoso,-a. 2 *(rude)* grosero,-a; *(vio-

lent) violento,-a. **3** (_voice_) bronco,-a. **4** (_wine_) áspero,-a. **5** (_bad_) malo,-a; _fam_ to feel r., encontrarse fatal. **6** (_approximate_) aproximado,-a. **7** (_plan etc_) preliminar; r. draft, borrador _m_; r. sketch, esbozo _m_. **8** (_harsh_) severo,-a. **II** _adv_ duramente; _fam_ fig to sleep r., dormir a la intemperie. **III** _n_ **1** _fam_ (_person_) matón _m_. **2** Golf the r., la hierba alta. **IV** _vtr fam_ to r. it, vivir sin comodidades. ◆**roughly** _adv_ **1** (_crudely_) toscamente. **2** (_clumsily_) torpemente. **3** (_not gently_) bruscamente. **4** (_approximately_) aproximadamente.

roughage ['rʌfɪdʒ] _n_ (_substance_) fibra _f_.
rough-and-ready ['rʌfən'redɪ] _adj_ improvisado,-a.
roughcast ['rʌfkɑːst] _n_ mortero grueso.
roughen ['rʌfən] _vtr_ poner áspero,-a.
roulette [ruː'let] _n_ ruleta _f_.
Roumania [ruː'meɪnɪə] _n_ → **Rumania**.
round [raʊnd] **I** _adj_ redondo,-a; **in r. figures**, en números redondos; r. table, mesa redonda; r. trip, viaje _m_ de ida y vuelta. **II** _n_ **1** (_circle_) círculo _m_. **2** (_series_) serie _f_; r. of talks, ronda _f_ de negociaciones. **3** (_of ammunition_) cartucho _m_; (_salvo_) salva _f_. **4** a r. of toast, unas tostadas. **5** (_of drinks_) ronda _f_. **6** the daily r., (_routine_) la rutina diaria. **7** Golf partido _m_; _Cards_ partida _f_. **8** Box round _m_. **9** (_in a competition_) eliminatoria _f_. **10** rounds, (_doctor's_) visita _f sing_; (_of salesman_) recorrido _m sing_. **III** _adv_ all year r., durante todo el año; to invite sb r., invitar a algn a casa. **IV** _prep_ alrededor de; r. here, por aquí; r. the clock, día y noche; r. the corner, a la vuelta de la esquina. **V** _vtr_ (_turn_) dar la vuelta a. ◆**round off** _vtr_ acabar, concluir. ◆**round on** _vtr_ (_attack_) atacar. ◆**round up** _vtr_ (_cattle_) acorralar, rodear; (_people_) reunir. ◆**roundly** _adv_ completamente, totalmente.

roundabout ['raʊndəbaʊt] **I** _n_ **1** (_merry-go-round_) tiovivo _m_. **2** GB Aut rotonda _f_. **II** _adj_ indirecto,-a.
rounders ['raʊndəz] _n_ GB juego _m_ parecido al béisbol.
round-shouldered [raʊnd'ʃəʊldəd] _adj_ cargado,-a de espaldas.
round-up ['raʊndʌp] _n_ **1** (_of cattle_) rodeo _m_; (_of suspects_) redada _f_. **2** (_summary_) resumen _m_.
rouse [raʊz] _vtr_ despertar; (_stir up_) suscitar.
rousing ['raʊzɪŋ] _adj_ (_cheer_) entusiasta; (_applause_) caluroso,-a; (_speech, song_) conmovedor,-a.
rout [raʊt] **I** _n_ aniquilación _f_. **II** _vtr_ aniquilar.
route [ruːt] **I** _n_ **1** ruta _f_; (_of bus_) línea _f_; _Naut_ derrota _f_; fig camino _m_; r. map, mapa _m_ de carreteras. **2** US R., = carretera _f_ nacional. **II** _vtr_ encaminar.

routine [ruː'tiːn] **I** _n_ **1** rutina _f_. **2** _Theat_ número _m_. **II** _adj_ rutinario,-a.
roving ['rəʊvɪŋ] _adj_ errante; r. reporter, enviado,-a _m,f_ especial.
row¹ [rəʊ] _n_ **1** fila _f_, hilera _f_; fig three times in a r., tres veces seguidas.
row² [rəʊ] _vtr & vi_ (_in a boat_) remar.
row³ [raʊ] **I** _n_ **1** (_quarrel_) pelea _f_, bronca _f_. **2** (_noise_) jaleo _m_; (_protest_) escándalo _m_. **II** _vi_ pelearse.
rowboat ['rəʊbəʊt] _n_ US bote _m_ de remos.
rowdy ['raʊdɪ] **I** _adj_ (**rowdier, rowdiest**) **1** (_noisy_) ruidoso,-a; (_disorderly_) alborotador,-a. **2** (_quarrelsome_) camorrista. **II** _n_ camorrista _mf_.
rowing ['rəʊɪŋ] _n_ remo _m_; r. boat, bote _m_ de remos.
royal ['rɔɪəl] **I** _adj_ real; r. blue, azul marino; the R. Family, la Familia Real. **II** _npl_ the Royals, la familia de la Familia Real. ◆**royally** _adv_ fig magníficamente.
royalty ['rɔɪəltɪ] _n_ **1** (_royal persons_) miembro(s) _m(pl)_ de la Familia Real. **2** royalties, derechos _mpl_ de autor.
RPI [ɑːpiː'aɪ] _n abbr_ of **Retail Price Index**, IPC.
rpm [ɑːpiː'em] _abbr_ **revolutions per minute**, revoluciones _fpl_ por minuto, r.p.m.
RSPCA [ɑːrespiːsiː'eɪ] GB _abbr_ of **Royal Society for the Prevention of Cruelty to Animals**, = Sociedad _f_ Protectora de Animales, SPA.
RSVP [ɑːresviː'piː] _abbr_ of **répondez s'il vous plaît** (please reply), se ruega contestación, S.R.C.
Rt Hon GB _Pol abbr of_ (the) **Right Honourable**, su Señoría.
rub [rʌb] **I** _n_ to give sth a r., frotar algo. **II** _vtr_ frotar; (_hard_) restregar; (_massage_) friccionar. **III** _vi_ rozar (**against**, contra). ◆**rub down** _vtr_ rozar; (_horse_) almohazar; (_surface_) raspar. ◆**rub in** _vtr_ **1** (_cream etc_) frotar con. **2** _fam_ don't r. it in, no me lo refriegues. ◆**rub off** **I** _vtr_ (_erase_) borrar. **II** _vi_ fig to r. off on sb, influir en algn. ◆**rub out** _vtr_ borrar. ◆**rub up** _vtr fam_ fig to r. sb up the wrong way, fastidiar a algn.
rubber¹ ['rʌbə] _n_ **1** (_substance_) caucho _m_, goma _f_; r. band, goma _f_; r. plant, gomero _m_; r. stamp, tampón _m_. **2** GB (_eraser_) goma _f_ (de borrar). **3** _sl_ (_condom_) goma _f_.
rubber² ['rʌbə] _n_ _Bridge_ rubber _m_.
rubbery ['rʌbərɪ] _adj_ (_elastic_) elástico,-a.
rubbish ['rʌbɪʃ] _n_ **1** GB (_refuse_) basura _f_; r. bin, cubo _m_ de la basura; r. dump, vertedero _m_. **2** _fam_ (_worthless thing_) birria _f_. **3** _fam_ (_nonsense_) tonterías _fpl_.
rubble ['rʌbəl] _n_ escombros _mpl_.
rubric ['ruːbrɪk] _n_ rúbrica _f_.
ruby ['ruːbɪ] _n_ rubí _m_.

rucksack ['rʌksæk] n mochila f.

ructions ['rʌkʃənz] npl fam jaleo m sing.

rudder ['rʌdəʳ] n timón m.

ruddy ['rʌdɪ] adj (ruddier, ruddiest) 1 (complexion) rojizo,-a, colorado,-a. 2 GB fam (damned) maldito,-a.

rude [ru:d] adj 1 (impolite) maleducado,-a; (foul-mouthed) grosero,-a; **don't be r. to your mother,** no le faltes al respeto a tu madre. 2 **a r. awakening,** un despertar repentino.

rudimentary [ru:dɪˈmentərɪ] adj rudimentario,-a.

rudiments ['ru:dɪmənts] npl rudimentos mpl.

rue [ru:] vtr arrepentirse de.

rueful ['ru:fʊl] adj (regretful) arrepentido,-a; (sad) triste.

ruff [rʌf] n 1 (on animal) collarín m. 2 (collar) gorguera f.

ruffian ['rʌfɪən] n canalla m.

ruffle ['rʌfl] vtr 1 (water) agitar. 2 (feathers) encrespar; (hair) despeinar. 3 fig (annoy) hacer perder la calma a.

ruffled ['rʌfld] adj 1 (hair) alborotado,-a; (clothes) en desorden. 2 (perturbed) perturbado,-a.

rug [rʌg] n alfombra f, alfombrilla f.

rugby ['rʌgbɪ] n rugby m; **r. league,** rugby a trece; **r. union,** rugby a quince.

rugged ['rʌgɪd] adj 1 (terrain) accidentado,-a; (features) marcado,-a. 2 (character) vigoroso,-a.

rugger ['rʌgəʳ] n fam rugby m.

ruin ['ru:ɪn] I n 1 ruina f. 2 **ruins,** ruinas fpl, restos mpl; **in r.,** en ruinas. II vtr arruinar; (spoil) estropear.

rule [ru:l] I n 1 regla f, norma f; **to work to r.,** hacer una huelga de celo; **as a r.,** por regla general. 2 (government) dominio m; (of monarch) reinado m; **r. of law,** imperio m de la ley. II vtr & vi 1 (govern) gobernar; (of monarch) reinar. 2 (decide) decidir; (decree) decretar. 3 (draw) tirar.
◆**rule out** vtr descartar.

ruled [ru:ld] adj rayado,-a.

ruler ['ru:ləʳ] n 1 dirigente mf; (monarch) soberano,-a m,f. 2 (for measuring) regla f.

ruling ['ru:lɪŋ] I adj (in charge) dirigente; fig (predominant) predominante; **the r. party,** el partido en el poder. II n Jur fallo m.

rum [rʌm] n ron m.

Rumania [ru:ˈmeɪnɪə] n Rumania f.

Rumanian [ru:ˈmeɪnɪən] I adj rumano,-a. II n (person) rumano,-a m,f; (language) rumano m.

rumble ['rʌmbl] I n 1 ruido sordo; (of thunder) estruendo m. 2 (of stomach) ruido m. II vi 1 hacer un ruido sordo; (thunder) retumbar. 2 (stomach etc) hacer ruidos.

ruminate ['ru:mɪneɪt] vi (chew, ponder) rumiar.

rummage ['rʌmɪdʒ] vi revolver (**through,** en).

rumour, US **rumor** ['ru:məʳ] I n rumor m; **r. has it that ...,** se dice que .... II vtr it is rumoured that, se rumorea que.

rump [rʌmp] n (of animal) ancas fpl; fam hum (of person) trasero m; **r. steak,** filete m de lomo.

rumpus ['rʌmpəs] n fam jaleo m.

run [rʌn] I n 1 carrera f; **on the r.,** fugado,-a; **to go for a r.,** hacer footing; fig **in the long r.,** a largo plazo. 2 (trip) paseo m, vuelta f. 3 (sequence) serie f. 4 **ski r.,** pista f de esquí. 5 (demand) gran demanda f; **a r. on,** una gran demanda de. 6 **to give sb the r. of a house,** poner una casa a disposición de algn. 7 Print tirada f. 8 (in stocking) carrera f.
II vtr (pt **ran;** pp **run**) 1 correr; **to r. a race,** correr en una carrera; **to r. errands,** hacer recados. 2 (drive) llevar. 3 (house, business) llevar; (company) dirigir; (organize) organizar. 4 (fingers) pasar. 5 **it's a cheap car to r.,** (operate) es un coche económico; Comput **to r. a program,** pasar un programa. 6 Press publicar.
III vi 1 correr. 2 (colour) desteñirse. 3 (water, river) correr; **to leave the tap running,** dejar el grifo abierto; fam **your nose is running,** se te caen los mocos. 4 (operate) funcionar; **trains r. every two hours,** hay trenes cada dos horas. 5 Naut **to r. aground,** encallar. 6 Pol **to r. for president,** presentarse como candidato a la presidencia. 7 **so the story runs,** según lo que se dice. 8 (range) oscilar (**between,** entre). 9 **we're running low on milk,** nos queda poca leche. 10 **shyness runs in the family,** la timidez le viene de familia. 11 Cin Theat estar en cartel. 12 (last) durar. 13 (stocking) tener una carrera.
◆**run about** vi corretear. ◆**run across** vtr (meet) tropezar con. ◆**run away** vi fugarse; (horse) desbocarse. ◆**run down** I vtr 1 (stairs) bajar corriendo. 2 (in car) atropellar. 3 (criticize) criticar. II vi (battery) agotarse; (clock) pararse. ◆**run in** vtr Aut rodar. ◆**run into** vtr 1 (room) entrar corriendo en. 2 (people, problems) tropezar con. 3 (crash into) chocar contra. ◆**run off** I vtr Print (copies) tirar. II vi escaparse. ◆**run on** I vtr Typ enlazar. II vi (function) funcionar con. ◆**run out** vi 1 (exit) salir corriendo. 2 (come to an end) agotarse; (of contract) vencer; **to r. out of,** quedarse sin. ◆**run over** I vtr 1 (in car) atropellar. 2 (rehearse) ensayar. II vi (overflow) rebosar. ◆**run through** vtr 1 (of river) pasar por. 2 (read quickly) echar una vistazo a. 3 (rehearse) ensayar. ◆**run up** vtr 1 (flag) izar. 2 (debts) acumular. ◆**run up against** vtr tropezar con.

runaway ['rʌnəweɪ] I n fugitivo,-a m,f. II

adj (*person*) huido,-a; (*horse*) desbocado,
-a; (*vehicle*) incontrolado,-a; (*inflation*) galopante; (*success*) clamoroso,-a.

rundown ['rʌndaʊn] *n fam* **to give sb a
r.**, poner a algn al corriente.

run-down [rʌn'daʊn] *adj* **1** (*exhausted*)
agotado,-a. **2** (*dilapidated*) ruinoso,-a.

rung¹ [rʌŋ] *pp* → **ring**.

rung² [rʌŋ] *n* (*of ladder*) escalón *m*,
peldaño *m*.

runner ['rʌnər] *n* **1** corredor,-a *m,f.* **2**
(*horse*) caballo *m* de carreras. **3** (*of skate*)
cuchilla *f.* **4** (*on table*) tapete *m*. **5 r.
bean**, judía escarlata.

runner-up ['rʌnər'ʌp] *n* subcampeón,-ona
m,f.

running ['rʌnɪŋ] **I** *n* **1** he likes running,
le gusta correr; *fig* **to be in the r. for sth**,
tener posibilidades de conseguir algo. **2**
(*of company*) dirección *f.* **3** (*of machine*)
funcionamiento *m*. **II** *adj* **1** direct
commentary, comentario *m* en directo; **r.
costs**, gastos *mpl* de mantenimiento; *Pol*
r. mate, candidato *m* a la vicepresi-
dencia; **r. water**, agua *f* corriente. **2**
three weeks r., tres semanas seguidas.

runny ['rʌnɪ] *adj* (**runnier, runniest**)
blando,-a; (*egg*) crudo,-a; (*butter*)
derretido,-a; (*nose*) que moquea.

run-of-the-mill [rʌnəvðə'mɪl] *adj* corriente y moliente.

runt [rʌnt] *n fam* enano,-a *m,f.*

run-up ['rʌnʌp] *n* (*to elections*) preliminares *mpl.*

runway ['rʌnweɪ] *n Av* pista *f* (de aterrizaje y despegue).

rupee [ruː'piː] *n* rupia *f.*

rupture ['rʌptʃər] **I** *n* **1** *Med* hernia *f.* **2**
fig ruptura *f.* **II** *vtr* **1 to r. oneself**,
herniarse. **2** (*break*) romper.

rural ['rʊərəl] *adj* rural.

ruse [ruːz] *n* ardid *m*, astucia *f.*

rush¹ [rʌʃ] *n Bot* junco *m.*

rush² [rʌʃ] **I** *n* **1** (*hurry*) prisa *f*; (*hustle
and bustle*) ajetreo *m*; **there's no r.**, no
corre prisa; **r. hour**, hora punta. **2** (*demand*) demanda *f.* **3** (*of wind*) ráfaga *f.* **4**
(*of water*) torrente *m.* **5** *Mil* ataque *m.* **II**
vtr **1** (*task*) hacer de prisa; (*person*) meter
prisa a; **to r. sb to hospital**, llevar a algn
urgentemente al hospital. **2** (*attack*) a-
balanzarse sobre; *Mil* tomar por asalto.
III *vi* (*go quickly*) precipitarse. ◆**rush
about** *vi* correr de un lado a otro.
◆**rush into** *vtr fig* **to r. into sth**, hacer
algo sin pensarlo bien. ◆**rush off** *vi* irse
corriendo.

rusk [rʌsk] *n* galleta dura para niños.

Russia ['rʌʃə] *n* Rusia.

Russian ['rʌʃən] **I** *adj* ruso,-a. **II** *n* **1**
(*person*) ruso,-a *m,f.* **2** (*language*) ruso *m.*

rust [rʌst] **I** *n* **1** (*substance*) herrumbre *f.* **2**
(*colour*) pardo rojizo. **II** *vtr* oxidar. **III** *vi*
oxidarse.

rustic ['rʌstɪk] *adj* rústico,-a.

rustle ['rʌsəl] **I** *n* crujido *m.* **II** *vtr* (*papers
etc*) hacer crujir. **III** *vi* (*steal cattle*) robar
ganado.

rustproof ['rʌstpruːf] *adj* inoxidable.

rusty ['rʌstɪ] *adj* (**rustier, rustiest**)
oxidado,-a; *fam* **fig my French is a bit r.**,
tengo el francés un poco oxidado.

rut [rʌt] *n* **1** (*furrow*) surco *m*; (*groove*) ranura *f.* **2** *fig* **to be in a r.**, ser esclavo de
la rutina. **3** *Zool* celo *m.*

ruthless ['ruːθlɪs] *adj* despiadado,-a.

rye [raɪ] *n* centeno *m*; **r. bread**, pan *m* de
centeno; **r. grass**, ballica *f*; *US* **r.
(whiskey)**, whisky *m* de centeno.

S

S, s [es] *n* (*the letter*) S, s *f.*

Sabbath ['sæbəθ] *n* (*Jewish*) sábado *m*;
(*Christian*) domingo *m*.

sabbatical [sə'bætɪkəl] *adj* sabático,-a.

sabotage ['sæbətɑːʒ] **I** *n* sabotaje *m*. **II**
vtr sabotear.

saccharin ['sækərɪn] *n* sacarina *f.*

sachet ['sæʃeɪ] *n* bolsita *f*, sobrecito *m.*

sack [sæk] **I** *n* **1** (*bag*) saco *m*. **2** *fam* **to
get the s.**, ser despedido,-a; *fam* **to give
sb the s.**, despedir a algn. **II** *vtr* **1** *fam*
despedir. **2** *Mil* saquear.

sacking ['sækɪŋ] *n Tex* arpillera *f.*

sacrament ['sækrəmənt] *n* sacramento *m.*

sacred ['seɪkrɪd] *adj* sagrado,-a.

sacrifice ['sækrɪfaɪs] **I** *n* sacrificio *m*. **II**
vtr sacrificar.

sacrificial [sækrɪ'fɪʃəl] *adj* **s. lamb**, chivo
expiatorio.

sacrilege ['sækrɪlɪdʒ] *n* sacrilegio *m.*

sacrosanct ['sækrəʊsæŋkt] *adj*
sacrosanto,-a.

sad [sæd] *adj* (**sadder, saddest**) triste;
how s.!, ¡qué pena!

sadden ['sædən] *vtr* entristecer.

saddle ['sædəl] **I** *n* (*for horse*) silla *f* (de
montar); (*of bicycle etc*) sillín *m.* **II** *vtr*
(*horse*) ensillar; *fam* **to s. sb with sth**,
cargarle a algn con algo.

saddlebag ['sædəlbæg] *n* alforja *f.*

sadist ['seɪdɪst] *n* sádico,-a *m,f.*

sadistic [sə'dɪstɪk] *adj* sádico,-a.

sadness ['sædnɪs] *n* tristeza *f.*

sadomasochism [seɪdəʊ'mæsəkɪzəm] *n*
sadomasoquismo *m.*

sae [eseɪ'iː] *abbr* of **stamped addressed
envelope**, sobre franqueado.

safari [sə'fɑːrɪ] *n* safari *m*; **s. park**, re-

serva f.
safe [seɪf] I *adj* 1 *(unharmed)* ileso,-a; *(out of danger)* a salvo; **s. and sound**, sano,-a y salvo,-a. 2 *(not dangerous)* inocuo,-a. 3 *(secure, sure)* seguro,-a; **to be on the s. side**, para mayor seguridad; **s. house**, *(for spies etc)* piso franco. 4 *(driver)* prudente. II *n (for money etc)* caja f fuerte. ◆**safely** *adv* 1 con toda seguridad. 2 **to arrive s.**, llegar sin incidentes.
safe-conduct [seɪfˈkɒndʌkt] *n* salvoconducto *m*.
safe-deposit [seɪfdɪˈpɒzɪt] *n* **s.-d. (box)**, cámara blindada.
safeguard [ˈseɪfgɑːd] I *n (protection)* salvaguarda f; *(guarantee)* garantía f. II *vtr* proteger, salvaguardar.
safekeeping [seɪfˈkiːpɪŋ] *n* custodia f.
safety [ˈseɪftɪ] *n* seguridad f; **for s. first!**, ¡la seguridad ante todo!; **s. belt**, cinturón *m* de seguridad; **s. net**, red f de protección; **s. pin**, imperdible *m*.
saffron [ˈsæfrən] *n* azafrán *m*.
sag [sæg] *vi* 1 *(roof)* hundirse; *(wall)* pandear; *(wood, iron)* combarse; *(flesh)* colgar. 2 *fig (spirits)* flaquear.
sage¹ [seɪdʒ] I *adj (wise)* sabio,-a. II *n (person)* sabio,-a *m,f*.
sage² [seɪdʒ] *n* salvia f.
Sagittarius [sædʒɪˈteərɪəs] *n* Sagitario *m*.
Sahara [səˈhɑːrə] *n* the S., el Sahara.
Saharan [səˈhɑːrən] *adj* saharaui, sahariano,-a.
said [sed] *adj* dicho,-a.
sail [seɪl] I *n* 1 *(canvas)* vela f; **to set s.**, zarpar. 2 *(trip)* paseo *m* en barco. II *vtr (ship)* gobernar; *lit* navegar. III *vi* 1 ir en barco. 2 *(set sail)* zarpar. ◆**sail through** *vtr fam* **we sailed through university**, en la universidad todo le fue sobre ruedas.
sailing [ˈseɪlɪŋ] *n* navegación f; *(yachting)* vela f; *fam* **it's all plain s.**, es todo coser y cantar; **s. boat** *or* **ship**, velero *m*, barco *m* de vela.
sailor [ˈseɪlə'] *n* marinero *m*.
saint [seɪnt] *n* santo,-a *m,f*; *(before all masculine names except those beginning Do or To)* San; *(before feminine names)* Santa; **S. Dominic**, Santo Domingo; **S. Helen**, Santa Elena; **S. John**, San Juan; **All Saints' Day**, Día *m* de Todos los Santos.
saintly [ˈseɪntlɪ] *adj (saintlier, saintliest)* santo,-a.
sake [seɪk] *n* **for the s. of**, por *(el bien de)*; **for your own s.**, por tu propio bien.
salad [ˈsæləd] *n* ensalada f; **potato s.**, ensaladilla f *(rusa)*; **s. bowl**, ensaladera f; **s. cream**, salsa f tipo mahonesa; **s. dressing**, vinagreta f, aliño *m*.
salami [səˈlɑːmɪ] *n* salchichón *m*, salami *m*.
salary [ˈsælərɪ] *n* salario *m*, sueldo *m*.
sale [seɪl] *n* 1 venta f; **for** *or* **on s.**, en venta; **sales department**, departamento

m comercial; **sales manager**, jefe,-a *m,f* de ventas. 2 *(at low prices)* rebajas *fpl*.
salesclerk [ˈseɪlzklɑːk] *n* dependiente,-a *m,f*.
salesman [ˈseɪlzmən] *n* 1 vendedor *m*; *(in shop)* dependiente *m*. 2 *(commercial traveller)* representante *m*.
salesroom [ˈseɪlzruːm] *n* sala f de subastas.
saleswoman [ˈseɪlzwʊmən] *n* 1 vendedora f; *(in shop)* dependienta f. 2 *(commercial traveller)* representante f.
salient [ˈseɪlɪənt] *adj fig* sobresaliente.
saliva [səˈlaɪvə] *n* saliva f.
sallow [ˈsæləʊ] *adj* cetrino,-a.
salmon [ˈsæmən] I *n* salmón *m*. II *adj (of color)* salmón.
salmonella [sælməˈnelə] *n Biol Med (bacteria)* salmonela f; *(food poisoning)* salmonelosis f.
salon [ˈsælɒn] *n* salón *m*.
saloon [səˈluːn] *n* 1 *(on ship)* cámara f. 2 *US (bar)* taberna f, bar *m*; *GB* **s. (bar)**, bar de lujo. 3 *(car)* turismo *m*.
salt [sɔːlt] I *n* sal f; *fig* **to take sth with a pinch of s.**, creer algo con reservas; **bath salts**, sales de baño; **smelling salts**, sales aromáticas. II *adj* salado,-a. III *vtr* 1 *(cure)* salar. 2 *(add salt to)* echar sal a.
saltcellar [ˈsɔːltselə'] *n* salero *m*.
saltwater [ˈsɔːltwɔːtə'] *adj* de agua salada.
salty [ˈsɔːltɪ] *adj (saltier, saltiest)* salado,-a.
salubrious [səˈluːbrɪəs] *adj* salubre, sano,-a.
salutary [ˈsæljʊtərɪ] *adj (experience)* beneficioso,-a; *(warning)* útil.
salute [səˈluːt] I *n (greeting)* saludo *m*. II *vtr* 1 *Mil* saludar. 2 *fig (achievement etc)* aplaudir. III *vi Mil* saludar.
salvage [ˈsælvɪdʒ] I *n* 1 *(of ship etc)* salvamento *m*, rescate *m*. 2 *(objects recovered)* objetos recuperados. 3 *Jur* derecho *m* de salvamento. II *vtr (from wreck etc)* rescatar.
salvation [sælˈveɪʃən] *n* salvación f; **S. Army**, Ejército *m* de Salvación.
Samaritan [səˈmærɪtən] *n* samaritano,-a *m,f*; **the Samaritans**, ≈ el teléfono de la Esperanza.
same [seɪm] I *adj* mismo,-a; **at that very s. moment**, en ese mismísimo momento; **at the s. time**, *(simultaneously)* al mismo tiempo; *(however)* sin embargo; **in the s. way**, del mismo modo; **the two cars are the s.**, los dos coches son iguales. II *pron* el mismo, la misma, lo mismo; *fam* **the s. here**, lo mismo digo yo; *fam* **the s. to you!**, ¡igualmente!. III *adv* del mismo modo, igual; **all the s., just the s.**, sin embargo, aun así; **it's all the s. to me**, *(a mí)* me da igual *or* lo mismo.
sample [ˈsɑːmpəl] I *n* muestra f. II *vtr (wines)* catar; *(dish)* probar.

sanatorium [sænə'tɔ:rɪəm] n sanatorio m.

sanctimonious [sæŋktɪ'məʊnɪəs] adj beato,-a.

sanction ['sæŋkʃən] I n 1 (authorization) permiso m. 2 (penalty) sanción f. 3 Pol **sanctions**, sanciones fpl. II vtr sancionar.

sanctity ['sæŋktɪtɪ] n (sacredness) santidad f; (of marriage) indisolubilidad f.

sanctuary ['sæŋktjʊərɪ] n 1 Rel santuario m. 2 Pol asilo m. 3 (for birds, animals) reserva f.

sand [sænd] I n arena f; **s. castle**, castillo m de arena; **s. dune**, duna f. II vtr to **s.** (**down**), lijar.

sandal ['sændəl] n sandalia f.

sandalwood ['sændəlwʊd] n sándalo m.

sandbag ['sændbæg] n saco terrero.

sandpaper ['sændpeɪpər] n papel m de lija.

sandpit ['sændpɪt] n (in playground etc) arenal m.

sandstone ['sændstəʊn] n arenisca f.

sandwich ['sænwɪdʒ, 'sænwɪtʃ] I n (bread roll) bocadillo m; (sliced bread) sandwich m; Educ **s. course**, curso teórico-práctico. II vtr intercalar; **it was sandwiched between two lorries**, quedó encajonado entre dos camiones.

sandy ['sændɪ] adj (**sandier, sandiest**) 1 (earth, beach) arenoso,-a. 2 (hair) rubio rojizo.

sane [seɪn] adj (not mad) cuerdo,-a; (sensible) sensato,-a.

sang [sæŋ] pt → **sing**.

sanitarium [sænɪ'teərɪəm] n US sanatorio m.

sanitary ['sænɪtərɪ] adj sanitario,-a; (hygienic) higiénico,-a; **s. towel**, US **s. napkin**, compresa f.

sanitation [sænɪ'teɪʃən] n sanidad f (pública); (plumbing) sistema m de saneamiento.

sanity ['sænɪtɪ] n cordura f, juicio m; (good sense) sensatez f.

sank [sæŋk] pt → **sink**.

Santa Claus [sæntə'klɔ:z] n Papá Noel m, San Nicolás m.

sap[1] [sæp] n Bot savia f.

sap[2] [sæp] vtr (undermine) minar; fig agotar.

sapling ['sæplɪŋ] n Bot árbol m joven.

sapphire ['sæfaɪər] n zafiro m.

sarcasm ['sɑ:kæzəm] n sarcasmo m.

sarcastic [sɑ:'kæstɪk] adj sarcástico,-a.

sardine [sɑ:'di:n] n sardina f.

Sardinia [sɑ:'dɪnɪə] n Cerdeña f.

sardonic [sɑ:'dɒnɪk] adj sardónico,-a.

sash[1] [sæʃ] n faja f.

sash[2] [sæʃ] n **s. window**, ventana f de guillotina.

sat [sæt] pt & pp → **sit**.

Satan ['seɪtən] n Satán m, Satanás m.

satanic [sə'tænɪk] adj satánico,-a.

satchel ['sætʃəl] n cartera f de colegial.

satellite ['sætəlaɪt] n satélite m; **s. dish aerial**, antena parabólica.

satin ['sætɪn] n satén m; **s. finish**, (acabado m) satinado m.

satire ['sætaɪər] n sátira f.

satirical [sə'tɪrɪkəl] adj satírico,-a.

satisfaction [sætɪs'fækʃən] n satisfacción f.

satisfactory [sætɪs'fæktərɪ] adj satisfactorio,-a.

satisfied ['sætɪsfaɪd] adj satisfecho,-a.

satisfy ['sætɪsfaɪ] vtr 1 satisfacer. 2 (fulfil) cumplir con. 3 (convince) convencer.

satisfying ['sætɪsfaɪɪŋ] adj satisfactorio,-a; (pleasing) agradable; (meal) que llena.

saturate ['sætʃəreɪt] vtr saturar (**with**, de).

Saturday ['sætədɪ] n sábado m.

sauce [sɔ:s] n 1 salsa f. 2 fam (impudence) descaro m.

saucepan ['sɔ:spən] n cacerola f; (large) olla f.

saucer ['sɔ:sər] n platillo m.

saucy ['sɔ:sɪ] adj (**saucier, sauciest**) fam fresco,-a.

Saudi Arabia [saʊdɪə'reɪbɪə] n Arabia f Saudita or Saudí.

Saudi Arabian [saʊdɪə'reɪbɪən] adj & n saudita (mf), saudí (mf).

sauna ['sɔ:nə] n sauna f.

saunter ['sɔ:ntər] I n paseo m. II vi pasearse.

sausage ['sɒsɪdʒ] n (frankfurter etc) salchicha f; (cured) salchichón m; (spicy) chorizo m; fam **s. dog**, perro m salchicha; GB **s. roll**, empanada f de carne.

sauté ['səʊteɪ] vtr saltear.

savage ['sævɪdʒ] I adj 1 (ferocious) feroz; (cruel) cruel; (violent) salvaje. 2 (primitive) salvaje. II n salvaje mf, fig (attack) embestir; fig (criticize) criticar despiadadamente.

save [seɪv] I vtr 1 (rescue) salvar, rescatar; fig to **s. face**, salvar las apariencias. 2 (put by) guardar; (money, energy, time) ahorrar; (food) almacenar; **it saved him a lot of trouble**, le evitó muchos problemas. II vi 1 to **s.** (**up**), ahorrar. 2 to **s. on paper**, (economize) ahorrar papel. III n Ftb parada f. IV prep arch salvo, excepto.

saving ['seɪvɪŋ] I n 1 (of time, money) ahorro m. 2 **savings**, ahorros mpl; **s. account**, cuenta f de ahorros; **s. bank**, caja f de ahorros. II adj **it's his only s. grace**, es el único mérito que tiene.

saviour, US **savior** ['seɪvjər] n salvador,-a m,f.

savour, US **savor** ['seɪvər] I n sabor m, gusto m. II vi saborear.

savoury, US **savory** ['seɪvərɪ] adj (tasty) sabroso,-a; (salted) salado,-a; (spicy) picante.

saw[1] [sɔ:] I n (tool) sierra f. II vtr & vi

(pt sawed; pp sawed or sawn) serrar. ◆**saw up** vtr serrar (into, en).

saw² [sɔ:] pt → **see¹**.

sawdust ['sɔ:dʌst] n (a)serrín m.

sawmill ['sɔ:mɪl] n aserradero m, serrería f.

sawn-off ['sɔ:nɒf] adj recortado,-a; **s.-o. shotgun**, escopeta f de cañones recortados.

saxophone ['sæksəfəʊn] n saxofón m.

say [seɪ] I vtr (pt & pp said) 1 decir; **it goes without saying that** ..., huelga decir que ...; **it is said that** ..., se dice que ...; **not to s.** ..., por no decir ...; **that is to s.**, es decir; **to s. yes/no**, decir que sí/no; fam **I s.!**, ¡oiga!; **what does the sign s.?**, ¿qué pone en el letrero? 2 (think) pensar. 3 **shall we s. Friday then**?, ¿quedamos el viernes, pues? II n **I have no s. in the matter**, no tengo ni voz ni voto en el asunto; **to have one's s.**, dar su opinión.

saying ['seɪɪŋ] n refrán m, dicho m.

scab [skæb] n 1 Med costra f. 2 fam pej esquirol mf.

scaffold ['skæfəld] n (for execution) patíbulo m.

scaffolding ['skæfəldɪŋ] n Constr andamio n.

scald [skɔ:ld] I n escaldadura f. II vtr escaldar.

scale¹ [skeɪl] n (of fish, on skin) escama f; (in boiler) incrustaciones fpl.

scale² [skeɪl] I n 1 escala f; **on a large s.**, a gran escala; **to s.**, a escala; **s. model**, maqueta f. 2 (extent) alcance m. 3 Mus escala f. II vtr (climb) escalar. ◆**scale down** vtr (drawing) reducir a escala; (production) reducir.

scales [skeɪlz] npl (pair of) s., (shop, kitchen) balanza f sing; (bathroom) báscula f sing.

scallop ['skɒləp] n 1 (mollusc) vieira f. 2 (shell) venera f.

scalp [skælp] I n cuero cabelludo; (head) cabeza f. II vtr arrancar el cuero cabelludo a.

scalpel ['skælpəl] n bisturí m.

scamper ['skæmpər] vi corretear.

scampi ['skæmpɪ] n gambas empanadas.

scan [skæn] I vtr 1 (scrutinize) escrutar; (horizon) otear. 2 (glance at) ojear. 3 (of radar) explorar. II n Med exploración ultrasónica; (in gynaecology etc) ecografía f.

scandal ['skændəl] n 1 escándalo m; **what a s.!**, ¡qué vergüenza! 2 (gossip) chismes mpl.

Scandinavia [skændɪ'neɪvɪə] n Escandinavia.

Scandinavian [skændɪ'neɪvɪən] adj & n escandinavo,-a (m,f).

scanner ['skænər] n Med escáner m.

scant [skænt] adj escaso,-a.

scanty ['skæntɪ] adj (scantier, scantiest)

escaso,-a; (meal) insuficiente; (clothes) ligero,-a.

scapegoat ['skeɪpgəʊt] n chivo expiatorio.

scar [skɑ:r] n cicatriz f.

scarce [skeəs] adj escaso,-a; fig **to make oneself s.**, largarse. ◆**scarcely** adv apenas.

scarcity ['skeəsɪtɪ] n escasez f; (rarity) rareza f.

scare [skeər] I n (fright) susto m; (widespread alarm) pánico m; **bomb s.**, amenaza f de bomba. II vtr asustar, espantar; fam **to be scared stiff**, estar muerto,-a de miedo. ◆**scare away**, **scare off** vtr ahuyentar.

scarecrow ['skeəkrəʊ] n espantapájaros m inv.

scarf [skɑ:f] n (pl scarfs or scarves [skɑ:vz]) (long, woollen) bufanda f; (square) pañuelo m; (silk) fular m.

scarlet ['skɑ:lɪt] I adj escarlata. II n escarlata f; **s. fever**, escarlatina f.

scarves [skɑ:vz] npl → **scarf**.

scathing ['skeɪðɪŋ] adj mordaz, cáustico,-a.

scatter ['skætər] I vtr 1 (papers etc) esparcir, desparramar. 2 (crowd) dispersar. II vi dispersarse.

scatterbrained ['skætəbreɪnd] adj fam ligero,-a de cascos; (forgetful) despistado,-a.

scattered ['skætəd] adj **s. showers**, chubascos aislados.

scavenger ['skævɪndʒər] n 1 (person) rebuscador,-a m,f; trapero m. 2 (animal) (animal m) carroñero,-a m.

scenario [sɪ'nɑ:rɪəʊ] n Cin guión m.

scene [si:n] n 1 Theat Cin TV escena f; **behind the scenes**, entre bastidores. 2 (place) lugar m, escenario m; **a change of s.**, un cambio de aires. 3 (view) panorama m. 4 **to make a s.**, (fuss) montar un espectáculo.

scenery ['si:nərɪ] n 1 (landscape) paisaje m. 2 Theat decorado m.

scenic ['si:nɪk] adj (picturesque) pintoresco,-a.

scent [sent] I n 1 (smell) olor m; (of food) aroma m; (perfume) perfume m. 3 (in hunting) pista f. II vtr (add perfume to) perfumar; (smell) olfatear; fig presentir.

sceptic ['skeptɪk] n escéptico,-a m,f.

sceptical ['skeptɪkəl] adj escéptico,-a.

scepticism ['skeptɪsɪzəm] n escepticismo m.

sceptre ['septər] n cetro m.

schedule ['ʃedju:l, US 'skedʒʊəl] I n 1 (plan, agenda) programa m; (timetable) horario m; **on s.**, a la hora (prevista); **to be behind s.**, llevar retraso. 2 (list) lista f; (inventory) inventario m. II vtr (plan) programar, fijar.

scheduled ['ʃedju:ld, US 'skedʒʊəld] adj

scheme 247 **scramble**

previsto,-a, fijo,-a; **s. flight,** vuelo regular.

scheme [ski:m] **I** n **1** (plan) plan m; (project) proyecto m; (idea) idea f; **colour s.,** combinación f de colores. **2** (plot) intriga f; (trick) ardid m. **II** vi tramar, intrigar.

scheming ['ski:mɪŋ] adj intrigante, maquinador,-a.

schism ['sɪzəm] n cisma m.

schizophrenic [skɪtsəʊ'frenɪk] adj & n esquizofrénico,-a (m,f).

scholar ['skɒlər] n (learned person) erudito,-a m,f; (pupil) alumno,-a m,f.

scholarship ['skɒləʃɪp] n **1** (learning) erudición f. **2** (grant) beca f; **s. holder,** becario,-a m,f.

school [sku:l] **I** n **1** escuela f, colegio m; **drama s.,** academia f de arte dramático; **of s. age,** en edad escolar; **s. year,** año m escolar. **2** US (university) universidad f. **3** (university department) facultad f. **4** (group of artists) escuela f; **s. of thought,** corriente f de opinión. **II** vtr (teach) enseñar; (train) formar.

schoolbook ['sku:lbʊk] n libro m de texto.

schoolboy ['sku:lbɔɪ] n alumno m.

schoolchild ['sku:ltʃaɪld] n alumno,-a m,f.

schooldays ['sku:ldeɪz] npl años mpl de colegio.

schoolgirl ['sku:lgɜ:l] n alumna f.

schooling ['sku:lɪŋ] n educación f, estudios mpl.

schoolmaster ['sku:lmɑ:stər] n profesor m; (primary school) maestro m.

schoolmistress ['sku:lmɪstrɪs] n profesora f; (primary school) maestra f.

schoolteacher ['sku:ltiːtʃər] n profesor,-a m,f; (primary school) maestro,-a m,f.

schooner ['sku:nər] n Naut goleta f.

sciatica [saɪ'ætɪkə] n ciática f.

science ['saɪəns] n ciencia f; (school subject) ciencias; **s. fiction,** ciencia-ficción f.

scientific [saɪən'tɪfɪk] adj científico,-a.

scientist ['saɪəntɪst] n científico,-a m,f.

scintillating ['sɪntɪleɪtɪŋ] adj brillante.

scissors ['sɪzəz] npl tijeras fpl; **a pair of s.,** unas tijeras.

scoff¹ [skɒf] vi (mock) mofarse (**at,** de).

scoff² [skɒf] vtr fam (eat) zamparse.

scold [skəʊld] vtr regañar, reñir.

scone [skəʊn, skɒn] n bollo m, pastelito m.

scoop [sku:p] n **1** (for flour) pala f; (for ice cream) cucharón m; (amount) palada f, cucharada f. **2** Press exclusiva f. **◆scoop out** vtr (flour etc) sacar con pala; (water) (from boat) achicar. **◆scoop up** vtr recoger.

scooter ['sku:tər] n (child's) patinete m; (adult's) Vespa® f.

scope [skəʊp] n **1** (range) alcance m; (of

undertaking) ámbito m. **2** (freedom) libertad f.

scorch [skɔːtʃ] vtr (singe) chamuscar.

scorching ['skɔːtʃɪŋ] adj fam abrasador,-a.

score [skɔːr] **I** n **1** Sport tanteo m; Cards Golf puntuación f; (result) resultado m. **2** (notch) muesca f. **3 I have a s. to settle with you,** tengo que ajustar las cuentas contigo. **4 on that s.,** a ese respecto. **5** (twenty) veintena f. **6** Mus (of opera) partitura f; (of film) música f. **II** vtr **1** (goal) marcar; (points) conseguir. **2** (wood) hacer una muesca en; (paper) rayar. **III** vi **1** Sport marcar un tanto; Ftb marcar un gol; (keep the score) llevar el tanteo. **2** (have success) tener éxito (**with,** con); sl ligar (**with,** con). **◆score out** vtr (word etc) tachar.

scoreboard ['skɔːbɔːd] n marcador m.

scorer ['skɔːrər] n **1** (goal striker) goleador m. **2** (scorekeeper) encargado,-a m,f del marcador.

scorn [skɔːn] **I** n desprecio m. **II** vtr despreciar.

scornful ['skɔːnfʊl] adj desdeñoso,-a.

Scorpio ['skɔːpɪəʊ] n Escorpión m.

scorpion ['skɔːpɪən] n alacrán m, escorpión m.

Scot [skɒt] n escocés,-esa m,f.

scotch [skɒtʃ] vtr (plot) frustrar; (rumour) negar, desmentir.

Scotch [skɒtʃ] **I** adj escocés,-esa; **S. tape®,** cinta adhesiva, celo® m. **II** n (whisky) whisky m escocés.

scot-free [skɒt'friː] adj impune.

Scotland ['skɒtlənd] n Escocia.

Scots [skɒts] **I** adj escocés,-esa. **II** n **the S.,** pl los escoceses.

Scotsman ['skɒtsmən] n escocés m.

Scotswoman ['skɒtswʊmən] n escocesa f.

Scottish ['skɒtɪʃ] adj escocés,-esa.

scoundrel ['skaʊndrəl] n sinvergüenza mf, canalla m.

scour¹ ['skaʊər] vtr (clean) fregar, restregar.

scour² ['skaʊər] vtr (search) (countryside) rastrear; (building) registrar.

scourge [skɜːdʒ] n fig azote m.

scout [skaʊt] **I** n Mil explorador,-a m,f; Sport Cin cazatalentos m inv; **boy s.,** boy m scout. **II** vi Mil reconocer el terreno; **to s. around for sth,** andar en busca de algo.

scowl [skaʊl] **I** vi fruncir el ceño; **to s. at sb,** mirar a algn con ceño. **II** n ceño m.

scrabble ['skræbəl] **I** vi escarbar; **to s. around for sth,** revolver todo para encontrar algo. **II** n **S.®,** Scrabble® m.

scraggy ['skrægɪ] adj (scraggier, scraggiest) delgado,-a, flacucho,-a.

scramble ['skræmbəl] **I** vi trepar; **to s. for,** pelearse por; **to s. up a tree,** trepar a un árbol. II *vtr* 1 *Culin* **scrambled eggs,** huevos revueltos. 2 *Rad Tel (message)* codificar; *(broadcast)* interferir. III *n (climb)* subida *f;* **fig it's going to be a s.,** *(rush)* va a ser muy apresurado.

scrap¹ [skræp] I *n* 1 *(small piece)* pedazo *m;* **there isn't a s. of truth in it,** no tiene ni un ápice de verdad; **s.** (metal), chatarra *f;* **s. dealer** *or* **merchant,** chatarrero, -a *m,f;* **s. paper,** papel *m* de borrador; **s. yard,** *(for cars)* cementerio *m* de coches. 2 **scraps,** restos *mpl; (of food)* sobras *fpl.* II *vtr (discard)* desechar; *fig (idea)* descartar.

scrap² [skræp] *fam* I *n (fight)* pelea *f.* II *vi* pelearse (**with,** con).

scrapbook ['skræpbʊk] *n* álbum *m* de recortes.

scrape [skreɪp] I *vtr (paint, wood)* raspar; *(knee)* arañarse, hacerse un rasguño en. II *vi (make noise)* chirriar; *(rub)* rozar. III *n fam (trouble)* lío *m.* ◆**scrape through** *vi fam (exam)* aprobar por los pelos. ◆**scrape together** *vtr* reunir a duras penas.

scraper ['skreɪpər] *n* rasqueta *f.*

scrapheap ['skræphi:p] *n (dump)* vertedero *m.*

scratch [skrætʃ] I *n (on skin, paintwork)* arañazo *m; (on record)* raya *f.* 2 *(noise)* chirrido *m.* 3 **fig to be up to s.,** dar la talla; *fig* **to start from s.,** partir de cero. II *adj* **s. team,** equipo improvisado. III *vtr* 1 *(with nail, claw)* arañar, rasguñar; *(paintwork)* rayar. 2 *(to relieve itching)* rascarse.

scrawl [skrɔːl] I *n* garabatos *mpl.* II *vtr (message etc)* garabatear. III *vi* hacer garabatos.

scrawny ['skrɔːnɪ] *adj* **(scrawnier, scrawniest)** flaco,-a.

scream [skriːm] I *n* chillido *m;* **screams of laughter,** carcajadas *fpl.* II *vtr (insults etc)* gritar. III *vi* chillar; **to s. at sb,** chillar a algn.

scree [skriː] *n* pedregal *m.*

screech [skriːtʃ] I *n (of person)* chillido *m; (of tyres, brakes)* chirrido *m.* II *vi (person)* chillar; *(tyres)* chirriar.

screen [skriːn] I *n* 1 *(movable partition)* biombo *m.* 2 *fig* cortina *f.* 3 *Cin TV Comput* pantalla *f;* **s. test,** casting *m.* II *vtr* 1 *(protect)* proteger; *(conceal)* tapar. 2 *(sieve) (coal etc)* tamizar; *fig (candidates)* seleccionar. 3 *(show) (film)* proyectar; *(for first time)* estrenar. 4 *Med* examinar.

screening ['skriːnɪŋ] *n* 1 *(of film)* proyección *f; (for first time)* estreno *m.* 2 *Med* exploración *f.*

screenplay ['skriːnpleɪ] *n* guión *m.*

screw [skruː] I *n* 1 tornillo *m.* 2 *(propeller)* hélice *f.* II *vtr* 1 atornillar; **to s. sth down** *or* **in** *or* **on,** fijar algo con tornillos. 2 *vulg* joder. ◆**screw up** *vtr* 1 *(piece of paper)* arrugar; *(one's face)* torcer. 2 *sl*

(ruin) joder.

screwdriver ['skruːdraɪvər] *n* destornillador *m.*

scribble ['skrɪbəl] I *n* garabatos *mpl.* II *vtr (message etc)* garabatear. III *vi* hacer garabatos.

script [skrɪpt] *n* 1 *(writing)* escritura *f; (handwriting)* letra *f; Typ* letra cursiva. 2 *(in exam)* escrito *m.* 3 *Cin* guión *m.*

Scripture ['skrɪptʃər] *n* **Holy S.,** Sagrada Escritura.

scroll [skrəʊl] *n* rollo *m* de pergamino.

scrounge [skraʊndʒ] *fam* I *vi* gorronear; **to s. (around)** for, buscar; **to s. off sb,** vivir a costa de algn. II *vtr* gorronear.

scrounger ['skraʊndʒər] *n fam* gorrón, -ona *m,f.*

scrub¹ [skrʌb] *n (undergrowth)* maleza *f.*

scrub² [skrʌb] I *vtr* 1 frotar. 2 *fam (cancel)* borrar. II *n (cleaning)* fregado *m.*

scruff [skrʌf] *n* pescuezo *m,* cogote *m.*

scruffy ['skrʌfɪ] *adj* **(scruffier, scruffiest)** *fam* desaliñado,-a.

scrum [skrʌm] *n Rugby* melée *f;* **s. half,** medio *m* melée.

scruple ['skruːpəl] *n* escrúpulo *m.*

scrupulous ['skruːpjʊləs] *adj* escrupuloso,-a. ◆**scrupulously** *adv* **s. honest,** sumamente honrado,-a.

scrutinize ['skruːtɪnaɪz] *vtr* escudriñar.

scrutiny ['skruːtɪnɪ] *n* escrutinio *m.*

scuff [skʌf] *vtr (the floor)* rayar; *(one's feet)* arrastrar.

scuffle ['skʌfəl] I *n* pelea *f.* II *vi* pelearse (**with,** con).

scullery ['skʌlərɪ] *n* cuarto *m* de pila.

sculptor ['skʌlptər] *n* escultor *m.*

sculpture ['skʌlptʃər] *n* escultura *f.*

scum [skʌm] *n* 1 *(on liquid)* espuma *f.* 2 *fig* escoria *f.*

scupper ['skʌpər] *vtr GB fam (plan etc)* desbaratar.

scurrilous ['skʌrɪləs] *adj (abusive)* difamatorio,-a.

scurry ['skʌrɪ] *vi (run)* corretear; *(hurry)* apresurarse; **to s. away** *or* **off,** escabullirse.

scuttle¹ ['skʌtəl] *n* cubo *m;* **coal s.,** cubo del carbón.

scuttle² ['skʌtəl] *vtr (ship)* barrenar.

scuttle³ ['skʌtəl] *vi* **to s. away** *or* **off,** escabullirse.

scythe [saɪð] I *n* guadaña *f.* II *vtr* guadañar.

SDI [esdɪ'aɪ] *abbr of* **Strategic Defence Initiative,** Iniciativa *f* para la Defensa Estratégica.

sea [siː] *n* mar *mf;* **by the s.,** a orillas del mar; **out at s.,** en alta mar; **to go by s.,** ir en barco; **to put to s.,** zarpar; *fig* **to be all at s.,** estar desorientado,-a; **s. breeze,** brisa marina; *fig* **s. change,** metamorfosis *f;* **s. level,** nivel *m* del mar; **s. lion,** león marino; **s. water,** agua *f* de mar.

seabed ['si:bed] *n* fondo *m* del mar.

seaboard ['si:bɔːd] *n US* costa *f*, litoral *m*.

seafood ['si:fuːd] *n* mariscos *mpl*.

seafront ['si:frʌnt] *n* paseo marítimo.

seagull ['si:gʌl] *n* gaviota *f*.

seal¹ [si:l] *n Zool* foca *f*.

seal² [si:l] I *n* 1 *(official stamp)* sello *m*. 2 *(airtight closure)* cierre hermético; *(on bottle)* precinto *m*. II *vtr* 1 *(with official stamp)* sellar; *(with wax)* lacrar. 2 *(close)* cerrar; *(make airtight)* cerrar herméticamente. 3 *(determine)* **this sealed his fate**, esto decidió su destino. ◆**seal off** *(pipe etc)* cerrar; *(area)* acordonar.

seam [si:m] *n* 1 *Sew* costura *f*; *Tech* juntura *f*; *fam* **to be bursting at the seams**, *(room)* rebosar de gente. 2 *Geol Min* veta *f*, filón *m*.

seaman ['si:mən] *n* marinero *m*.

seamy ['si:mɪ] *adj* *(seamier, seamiest)* *fig* sórdido,-a.

séance ['seɪɑːns] *n* sesión *f* de espiritismo.

seaplane ['si:pleɪn] *n* hidroavión *m*.

seaport ['si:pɔːt] *n* puerto marítimo.

search [sɜːtʃ] I *vtr* buscar en; *(building, suitcase)* registrar; *(person)* cachear; *(one's conscience)* examinar. II *vi* buscar; **to s. through**, registrar. III *n* búsqueda *f*; *(of building etc)* registro *m*; *(of person)* cacheo *m*; **in s. of**, en busca de; **s. party**, equipo *m* de salvamento; **s. warrant**, orden *f* de registro.

searching ['sɜːtʃɪŋ] *adj* *(look)* penetrante; *(question)* indagatorio,-a.

searchlight ['sɜːtʃlaɪt] *n* reflector *m*.

seashell ['si:ʃel] *n* concha marina.

seashore ['si:ʃɔːr] *n* *(beach)* playa *f*.

seasick ['si:sɪk] *adj* mareado,-a; **to get s.**, marearse.

seaside ['si:saɪd] *n* playa *f*, costa *f*; **s. resort**, lugar turístico de veraneo; **s. town**, pueblo costero,-a.

season¹ ['si:zən] *n* época *f*; *(of year)* estación *f*; *(for sport etc)* temporada *f*; **the busy s.**, la temporada alta; **the rainy s.**, la estación de lluvias; **in s.**, *(fruit)* en sazón; *(animal)* en celo; *GB* **s. ticket**, abono *m*.

season² ['si:zən] *vtr Culin* sazonar.

seasonal ['si:zənəl] *adj* estacional.

seasoned ['si:zənd] *adj* 1 *Culin* sazonado,-a. 2 *fig* *(campaigner)* curtido,-a, avezado,-a.

seasoning ['si:zənɪŋ] *n* condimento *m*, aderezo *m*.

seat [si:t] I *n* 1 asiento *m*; *(place)* plaza *f*; *Cin Theat* localidad *f*; **to take a s.**, sentarse; *Aut* **s. belt**, cinturón *m* de seguridad. 2 *(of cycle)* sillín *m*; *fam* *(buttocks)* trasero *m*. 3 *(of power, learning)* centro *m*, sede *f*. 4 *Parl* escaño *m*. II *vtr* 1 *(guests etc)* sentar. 2 *(accommodate)* tener cabida para.

seating ['si:tɪŋ] *n* asientos *mpl*; **s. capacity**, cabida *f*, aforo *m*.

seaweed ['si:wiːd] *n* alga *f* (marina).

seaworthy ['si:wɜːðɪ] *adj* en condiciones de navegar.

sec [sek] *n fam* *(abbr of* **second***)* segundo *m*.

secede [sɪ'si:d] *vi* separarse *(from*, de*)*.

secluded [sɪ'klu:dɪd] *adj* retirado,-a, apartado,-a.

second¹ ['sekənd] I *adj* segundo,-a; **every s. day**, cada dos días; **it's the s. highest mountain**, es la segunda montaña más alta; **on s. thought(s)** ..., pensándolo bien ...; **to have s. thoughts about sth**, dudar de algo; **to settle for s. best**, conformarse con lo que hay. II *n* 1 *(in series)* segundo,-a *m,f*; **Charles the S.**, Carlos Segundo; **the s. of October**, el dos de octubre. 2 *Aut* *(gear)* segunda *f*. 3 *Com* **seconds**, artículos defectuosos. III *vtr* *(motion)* apoyar. IV *adv* to **come s.**, terminar en segundo lugar. ◆**secondly** *adv* en segundo lugar.

second² ['sekənd] *n* *(time)* segundo *m*; *fam* **in a s.**, enseguida; *fam* **just a s.!**, ¡un momento!; **s. hand**, *(of watch, clock)* segundero *m*.

secondary ['sekəndərɪ] *adj* secundario,-a; *GB* **s. school**, escuela secundaria.

second-class [sekənd'klɑːs] I *adj* de segunda clase. II *adv* **to travel s.-c.**, viajar en segunda.

second-hand ['sekəndhænd] *adj & adv* de segunda mano.

secondment [sɪ'kɒndmənt] *n GB* traslado *m* temporal.

second-rate ['sekəndreɪt] *adj* de segunda categoría.

secrecy ['si:krəsɪ] *n* secreto *m*; **in s.**, en secreto.

secret ['si:krɪt] I *adj* secreto,-a; **to keep sth s.**, mantener algo en secreto; **s. ballot**, votación secreta. II *n* secreto *m*; *fig* clave *f*; **in s.**, en secreto; **to keep a s.**, guardar un secreto. ◆**secretly** *adv* en secreto.

secretarial [sekrɪ'teərɪəl] *adj* de secretario,-a.

secretary ['sekrətrɪ] *n* secretario,-a *m,f*; **S. of State**, *GB* ministro,-a *m,f* con cartera; *US* ministro,-a *m,f* de Asuntos Exteriores.

secretion [sɪ'kri:ʃən] *n* secreción *f*.

secretive ['si:krɪtɪv] *adj* reservado,-a.

sect [sekt] *n* secta *f*.

sectarian [sek'teərɪən] *adj & n* sectario,-a *(m,f)*.

section ['sekʃən] *n* 1 *(part)* sección *f*, parte *f*; *(of law)* artículo *m*; *(of community)* sector *m*; *(of orchestra, department)* sección *f*. 2 *(cut)* corte *m*.

sector ['sektər] *n* sector *m*.

secular ['sekjʊlər] *adj (school, teaching)* laico,-a; *(music, art)* profano,-a; *(priest)* seglar, secular.

secure [sɪ'kjʊər] I *adj* seguro,-a; *(window, door)* bien cerrado,-a; *(ladder etc)* firme. II *vtr* 1 *(make safe)* asegurar. 2 *(fix) (rope, knot)* sujetar, fijar; *(object to floor)* afianzar; *(window, door)* cerrar bien. 3 *(obtain)* conseguir, obtener. 4 *Fin (guarantee)* avalar.

security [sɪ'kjʊərɪtɪ] *n* 1 seguridad *f*; **national s.**, seguridad nacional; **S. Council**, *(of United Nations)* Consejo *m* de Seguridad. 2 *Fin (guarantee)* fianza *f*; *(guarantor)* fiador,-a *m,f*. 3 *Fin* securities, valores *mpl*.

sedan [sɪ'dæn] *n* 1 *(also s. chair)* silla *f* de manos. 2 *US Aut* turismo *m*.

sedate [sɪ'deɪt] I *adj* sosegado,-a. II *vtr* sedar.

sedation [sɪ'deɪʃən] *n* sedación *f*.

sedative ['sedɪtɪv] *adj & n* sedante *(m)*.

sediment ['sedɪmənt] *n* sedimento *m*; *(of wine)* poso *m*.

seduce [sɪ'djuːs] *vtr* seducir.

seduction [sɪ'dʌkʃən] *n* seducción *f*.

seductive [sɪ'dʌktɪv] *adj* seductor,-a.

see¹ [siː] *vtr & vi (pt saw; pp seen)* 1 ver; **I'll s. what can be done**, veré lo que se puede hacer; **let's s.**, a ver; **that remains to be seen**, eso queda por ver; **s. page 10**, véase la página 10; **s. you (later/soon!)**, ¡hasta luego/pronto! 2 *(meet with)* ver, tener cita con; **they are seeing each other**, *(of couple)* salen juntos. 3 *(visit)* ver; **to s. the world**, recorrer el mundo. 4 *(understand)* entender; **as far as I can s.**, por lo visto; **I s.**, ya veo; **you s.**, he hasn't got a car, es que no tiene coche, ¿sabes? 5 **he sees himself as a second Caruso**, se cree otro Caruso. 6 *(ensure)* asegurarse de. 7 **to s. sb home**, acompañar a algn a casa. ◆**see about** *vtr (deal with)* ocuparse de. ◆**see off** *vtr (say goodbye to)* despedirse de. ◆**see out** *vtr* 1 *(show out)* acompañar hasta la puerta. 2 *(survive)* sobrevivir. ◆**see through** *vtr* 1 *fam* **to s. through sb**, verle el plumero a algn. 2 **I'll s. you through**, puedes contar con mi ayuda; **£20 should s. me through**, con 20 libras me las apaño. 3 **to s. sth through**, *(carry out)* llevar algo a cabo. ◆**see to** *vtr (deal with)* ocuparse de.

see² [siː] *n Rel* sede *f*; **the Holy S.**, la Santa Sede.

seed [siːd] *n* 1 *Bot* semilla *f*; *(of fruit)* pepita *f*; **to go to s.**, *(of plant)* granar; *fig (of person)* descuidarse. 2 *Ten (player)* cabeza *mf* de serie. II *vtr* 1 *(sow with seed)* sembrar. 2 *(grapes)* despepitar. 3 *Ten* preseleccionar.

seedling ['siːdlɪŋ] *n* plantón *m*.

seedy ['siːdɪ] *adj (seedier, seediest) fam*

(bar etc) sórdido,-a; *(clothes)* raído,-a; *(appearance)* desaseado,-a.

seeing ['siːɪŋ] *conj* **s. that**, visto que, dado que.

seek [siːk] I *vtr (pt & pp sought)* 1 *(look for)* buscar. 2 *(advice, help)* solicitar. II *vtr* buscar; **to s. to do sth**, procurar hacer algo. ◆**seek after** *vtr* buscar; **much sought after**, *(person)* muy solicitado,-a; *(thing)* muy cotizado,-a.

seem [siːm] *vi* parecer; **I s. to remember his name was Colin**, creo recordar que su nombre era Colin; **it seems to me that**, me parece que; **so it seems**, eso parece.

seeming ['siːmɪŋ] *adj* aparente. ◆**seemingly** *adv* aparentemente, según parece.

seen [siːn] *pp* → **see¹**.

seep [siːp] *vi* **to s. through/into/out**, filtrarse por/en/de.

seesaw ['siːsɔː] I *n* balancín *m*, subibaja *m*. II *vi* 1 columpiarse, balancearse. 2 *fig* vacilar, oscilar.

seethe [siːð] *vi* bullir, hervir; *fig* **to s. with anger**, rabiar; **to s. with people**, rebosar de gente.

see-through ['siːθruː] *adj* transparente.

segment ['segmənt] *n* segmento *m*; *(of orange)* gajo *m*.

segregate ['segrɪgeɪt] *vtr* segregar *(from, de)*.

segregation [segrɪ'geɪʃən] *n* segregación *f*.

seize [siːz] *vtr (grab)* agarrar, asir; *Jur (property, drugs)* incautar; *(assets)* secuestrar; *(territory)* tomar; *(arrest)* detener; **to s. an opportunity**, aprovechar una ocasión; **to s. power**, hacerse con el poder. ◆**seize on** *vtr (chance)* agarrar; *(idea)* aferrarse a. ◆**seize up** *vi* agarrotarse.

seizure ['siːʒər] *n* 1 *Jur (of property, drugs)* incautación *f*; *(of newspaper)* secuestro *m*; *(arrest)* detención *f*. 2 *Med* ataque *m* (de apoplejía).

seldom ['seldəm] *adv* rara vez, raramente.

select [sɪ'lekt] I *vtr (thing)* escoger, elegir; *(team)* seleccionar. II *adj* selecto,-a.

selected [sɪ'lektɪd] *adj* selecto,-a, escogido,-a; *(team, player)* seleccionado,-a; *Lit* **s. works**, obras escogidas.

selection [sɪ'lekʃən] *n (choosing)* elección *f*; *(people or things chosen)* selección *f*; *(range)* surtido *m*.

selective [sɪ'lektɪv] *adj* selectivo,-a.

self [self] *n (pl* **selves** [selvz]*)* uno,-a mismo,-a, sí mismo,-a; *Psych* **the s.**, el yo.

self- [self] *pref* auto-.

self-adhesive [selfəd'hiːsɪv] *adj* autoadhesivo,-a.

self-assured [selfə'ʃʊəd] *adj* seguro,-a de sí mismo,-a.

self-catering [self'keɪtərɪŋ] *adj* sin servicio de comida.

self-centred, *US* **self-centered** [self'sentəd] *adj* egocéntrico,-a.

self-confessed [selfkən'fest] *adj* confeso,-a.

self-confidence [self'kɒnfɪdəns] *n* confianza f en sí mismo,-a.

self-confident [self'kɒnfɪdənt] *adj* seguro,-a de sí mismo,-a.

self-conscious [self'kɒnʃəs] *adj* cohibido,-a.

self-contained [selfkən'teɪnd] *adj (flat)* con entrada propia; *(person)* independiente.

self-control [selfkən'trəʊl] *n* autocontrol *m*.

self-defence, *US* **self-defense** [selfdɪ'fens] *n* autodefensa f.

self-discipline [self'dɪsɪplɪn] *n* autodisciplina f.

self-employed [selfɪm'plɔɪd] *adj (worker)* autónomo,-a.

self-esteem [selfɪ'stiːm] *n* amor propio, autoestima f.

self-evident [self'evɪdənt] *adj* evidente, patente.

self-governing [self'gʌvənɪŋ] *adj* autónomo,-a.

self-important [selfɪm'pɔːtənt] *adj* engreído,-a, presumido,-a.

self-indulgent [selfɪn'dʌldʒənt] *adj* inmoderado,-a.

self-interest [self'ɪntrɪst] *n* egoísmo *m*.

selfish [selfɪʃ] *adj* egoísta.

selfishness [selfɪʃnɪs] *n* egoísmo *m*.

selfless [selflɪs] *adj* desinteresado,-a.

self-made [selfmeɪd] *adj* **s.-m. man,** hombre m que se ha hecho a sí mismo.

self-pity [self'pɪtɪ] *n* lástima f de sí mismo,-a, autocompasión f.

self-portrait [self'pɔːtreɪt] *n* autorretrato *m*.

self-possessed [selfpə'zest] *adj* sereno, -a, dueño,-a de sí mismo,-a.

self-preservation [selfprezə'veɪʃən] *n (instinct of)* **s.-p.,** instinto *m* de conservación.

self-raising [self'reɪzɪŋ] *adj* GB **s.-r. flour,** harina f con levadura.

self-reliant [selfrɪ'laɪənt] *adj* autosuficiente.

self-respect [selfrɪ'spekt] *n* amor propio, dignidad f.

self-righteous [self'raɪtʃəs] *adj* santurrón,-ona.

self-satisfied [self'sætɪsfaɪd] *adj* satisfecho,-a de sí mismo,-a.

self-service [self'sɜːvɪs] I *n (in shop etc)* autoservicio *m*. II *adj* de autoservicio.

self-sufficient [selfsə'fɪʃənt] *adj* autosuficiente.

self-taught [self'tɔːt] *adj* autodidacta.

sell [sel] I *vtr (pt & pp sold)* vender. II *vi* venderse; **this record is selling well,** este disco se vende bien. III *n* **hard/soft s.,** *(in advertising)* publicidad agresiva/discreta. ◆**sell off** *vtr* vender; *(goods)* liquidar. ◆**sell out** I *vi* to s. out to the enemy, claudicar ante el enemigo. II *vtr* Com **we're sold out of sugar,** se nos ha agotado el azúcar; Theat 'sold out', 'agotadas las localidades'.

seller ['selər] *n* vendedor,-a m,f.

selling ['selɪŋ] *n* venta f; **s. point,** atractivo *m* comercial; **s. price,** precio *m* de venta.

sellotape® ['seləteɪp] I *n* celo® *m*, cinta adhesiva. II *vtr* pegar o fijar con celo®.

sell-out ['selaʊt] *n* **1** Theat éxito m de taquilla. **2** *(act of disloyalty)* claudicación f.

semaphore ['seməfɔːr] *n* semáforo *m*.

semblance ['sembləns] *n* apariencia f; **there was some s. of truth in it,** había algo de verdad en ello.

semen ['siːmen] *n* semen *m*.

semester [sɪ'mestər] *n* semestre *m*.

semi- ['semɪ] *pref* semi-.

semicircle ['semɪsɜːkəl] *n* semicírculo *m*.

semicolon [semɪ'kəʊlən] *n* punto y coma *m*.

semiconductor [semɪkən'dʌktər] *n* semiconductor *m*.

semidetached [semɪdɪ'tætʃt] GB I *adj* adosado,-a. II *n* chalé adosado, casa adosada.

semifinal [semɪ'faɪnəl] *n* semifinal f.

seminar ['semɪnɑːr] *n* seminario *m*.

seminary ['semɪnərɪ] *n* seminario *m*.

semolina [semə'liːnə] *n* sémola f.

senate ['senɪt] *n* **1** Pol senado *m*. **2** Univ claustro *m*.

senator ['senətər] *n* senador,-a m,f.

send [send] I *vtr (pt & pp sent)* **1** *(letter)* enviar, mandar; *(radio signal)* transmitir; *(rocket, ball)* lanzar; **she was sent to prison,** la mandaron a la cárcel; **to s. sth flying,** tirar algo. **2** to **s. sb mad,** *(cause to become)* volver loco,-a a algn; to **s. for sb,** mandar llamar a algn; to **s. for sth,** encargar algo. II *vi* to **s. for sth,** escribir pidiendo algo. ◆**send away** I *vtr (dismiss)* despedir. II *vi* to **s. away for sth,** escribir pidiendo algo. ◆**send back** *vtr (goods etc)* devolver; *(person)* hacer volver. ◆**send in** *vtr (application etc)* mandar; *(troops)* enviar. ◆**send off** *vtr* **1** *(letter etc)* enviar; *(goods)* despachar. **2** Ftb *(player)* expulsar. ◆**send on** *vtr (luggage)(ahead)* facturar; *(later)* mandar (más tarde). ◆**send out** *vtr* **1** *(person)* echar. **2** *(invitations)* enviar. **3** *(emit)* emitir. ◆**send up** *vtr* **1** hacer subir; *(rocket)* lanzar; *(smoke)* echar. **2** GB fam *(make fun of) (person)* burlarse de; *(book etc)* satirizar.

sender ['sendər] *n* remitente mf.

sendoff ['sendɒf] *n* fam despedida f.

senile ['siːnaɪl] *adj* senil.

senior ['si:njər] **I** adj **1** (in age) mayor; William Armstrong S., William Armstrong padre; **s. citizen,** jubilado,-a m,f. **2** (in rank) superior; (with longer service) más antiguo,-a; Mil **s. officer,** oficial mf de alta graduación. **II** n **1** she's three years my s., (in age) me lleva tres años. **2** GB Educ mayor mf; US Educ estudiante mf del último curso.

seniority [si:nɪ'ɒrɪtɪ] n antigüedad f.

sensation [sen'seɪʃən] n sensación f; **to be a s.,** ser un éxito; **to cause a s.,** causar sensación.

sensational [sen'seɪʃənəl] adj (marvellous) sensacional; (exaggerated) sensacionalista.

sense [sens] **I** n **1** (faculty) sentido m; (feeling) sensación f; **s. of direction/humour,** sentido m de la orientación/del humor. **2** (wisdom) sentido m común, juicio m; **common s.,** sentido común. **3** (meaning) sentido m; (of word) significado m; **in a s.,** en cierto sentido; **it doesn't make s.,** no tiene sentido. **4 to come to one's senses,** recobrar el juicio. **II** vtr sentir, percatarse de.

senseless ['senslɪs] adj **1** (absurd) insensato,-a, absurdo,-a. **2** (unconscious) sin conocimiento.

sensibility [sensɪ'bɪlɪtɪ] n **1** (sensitivity) sensibilidad f. **2 sensibilities,** susceptibilidad f sing.

sensible ['sensɪbəl] adj **1** (wise) sensato, -a. **2** (choice) acertado,-a. **3** (clothes, shoes) práctico,-a, cómodo,-a. **4** fml (difference) apreciable.

sensitive ['sensɪtɪv] adj **1** (person) sensible; (touchy) susceptible. **2** (skin) delicado,-a; (document) confidencial.

sensor ['sensər] n sensor m.

sensual ['sensjʊəl] adj sensual.

sensuous ['sensjʊəs] adj sensual.

sent [sent] pt & pp → **send.**

sentence ['sentəns] **I** n **1** frase f; Ling oración f. **2** Jur sentencia f; **to pass s. on sb,** imponer una pena a algn; **life s.,** cadena perpetua. **II** vtr Jur condenar.

sentiment ['sentɪmənt] n **1** (sentimentality) sensiblería f. **2** (feeling) sentimiento m. **3** (opinion) opinión f.

sentimental [sentɪ'mentəl] adj sentimental.

sentry ['sentrɪ] n centinela m.

separate ['sepəreɪt] **I** vtr separar (from, de); (divide) dividir (into, en); (distinguish) distinguir. **II** vi separarse. **III** ['sepərɪt] adj separado,-a; (different) distinto,-a; (entrance) particular. **IV** npl **separates,** (clothes) piezas fpl. ◆**separately** adv por separado.

separation [sepə'reɪʃən] n separación f.

separatist ['sepərətɪst] n separatista mf.

September [sep'tembər] n se(p)tiembre m.

septic ['septɪk] adj séptico,-a; **to become s.,** (of wound) infectarse; **s. tank,** fosa séptica.

sequel ['si:kwəl] n secuela f; (of film etc) continuación f.

sequence ['si:kwəns] n **1** (order) secuencia f, orden m. **2** (series) serie f, sucesión f; Cin film s., secuencia f.

serenade [serɪ'neɪd] n serenata f.

serene [sɪ'ri:n] adj sereno,-a, tranquilo,-a.

sergeant ['sɑ:dʒənt] n Mil sargento m; (of police) cabo m; **s. major,** sargento mayor, brigada m.

serial ['sɪərɪəl] n **1** Rad TV serial m; (soap opera) radionovela f, telenovela f. **2 s. number,** número m de serie.

series ['sɪəri:z] n inv serie f; (of books) colección f; (of concerts, lectures) ciclo m.

serious ['sɪərɪəs] adj **1** (solemn, earnest) serio,-a; **I am s.,** hablo en serio. **2** (causing concern) grave. ◆**seriously** adv **1** (in earnest) en serio. **2** (dangerously, severely) gravemente.

seriousness ['sɪərɪəsnɪs] n gravedad f, seriedad f; **in all s.,** hablando en serio.

sermon ['sɜ:mən] n sermón m.

serpent ['sɜ:pənt] n serpiente f.

serrated [sɪ'reɪtɪd] adj dentado,-a.

serum ['sɪərəm] n suero m.

servant ['sɜ:vənt] n (domestic) criado,-a m,f; fig servidor,-a m,f.

serve [sɜ:v] **I** vtr **1** servir. **2** (customer) atender a. **3** Ten servir. **4 if my memory serves me right,** si mal no recuerdo; **it serves him right,** bien merecido lo tiene. **5 fam to s. time,** cumplir una condena; **to s. one's apprenticeship,** hacer el aprendizaje. **II** vi **1** servir; **to s. on a committee,** ser miembro de una comisión. **2** Ten servir. **3** (be useful) servir (as, de). **III** n Ten servicio m. ◆**serve out, serve up** vtr servir.

service ['sɜ:vɪs] **I** n **1** servicio m; **at your s.!,** a sus órdenes!; **how can I be of s. to you?,** ¿en qué puedo servirle?; **s. (charge) included,** servicio incluido; **s. area,** área m de servicio; **s. industry,** sector m de servicios; **s. station,** estación f de servicio. **2 medical s.,** servicios médicos; Mil **the Services,** las Fuerzas Armadas; **the train s. to Bristol,** la línea de trenes a Bristol. **3** (maintenance) mantenimiento m. **4** Rel oficio m; (mass) misa f. **5** Ten servicio m; **s. line,** línea f de saque. **6** (set of dishes) juego m. **II** vtr (car, machine) revisar.

serviceable ['sɜ:vɪsəbəl] adj **1** (fit for use) útil, servible. **2** (practical) práctico,-a.

serviceman ['sɜ:vɪsmən] n militar m.

serviette [sɜ:vɪ'et] n GB servilleta f.

sesame ['sesəmɪ] n sésamo m.

session ['seʃən] n **1** sesión f; **to be in s.,** estar reunido,-a; (of Parliament, court) celebrar una sesión. **2** Educ (academic year) año académico.

set¹ [set] **I** *vtr* **1** (*put, place*) poner, colocar; (*trap*) poner (**for**, para); **the novel is s. in Moscow**, la novela se desarrolla en Moscú; **to s. fire to sth**, prender fuego a algo. **2** (*time, price*) fijar; (*record*) establecer; (*trend*) imponer. **3** (*mechanism etc*) ajustar; (*bone*) encajar; **to s. one's watch**, poner el reloj en hora. **4** (*arrange*) arreglar; **he s. the words to music**, puso música a la letra; **to s. the table**, poner la mesa. **5** (*exam, homework*) poner; (*example*) dar; (*precedent*) sentar. **6** (*jewel*) engastar; **to s. sth free**, poner en libertad a algn; **to s. sth going**, poner algo en marcha. **7** (*pearl, diamond etc*) engastar. **8** *Print* componer.
II *vi* **1** (*sun, moon*) ponerse. **2** (*jelly, jam*) cuajar; (*cement*) fraguar; (*bone*) encajarse. **3** **to s. to**, (*begin*) ponerse a.
III *vi* **1 shampoo and s.**, lavar y marcar. **2** (*stage*) *Cin* plató *m*; *Theat* escenario *m*; (*scenery*) decorado *m*.
IV *adj* **1** (*task, idea*) fijo,-a; (*date, time*) señalado,-a; (*opinion*) inflexible; (*smile*) rígido,-a; (*gaze*) fijo,-a; **s. phrase**, frase hecha; **to be s. on doing sth**, estar empeñado,-a en hacer algo; **s. square**, cartabón *m*. **2** (*ready*) listo,-a.
◆**set about** *vtr* **1** (*begin*) empezar. **2** (*attack*) agredir. ◆**set aside** *vtr* (*time, money*) reservar; (*differences*) dejar de lado. ◆**set back** *vtr* **1** (*delay*) retrasar; (*hinder*) entorpecer. **2** *fam* (*cost*) costar. ◆**set down** *vtr* (*luggage etc*) dejar (en el suelo); *GB* (*passengers*) dejar. ◆**set in** *vi* (*winter, rain*) comenzar; **panic s. in**, cundió el pánico. ◆**set off I** *vi* (*depart*) salir. **II** *vtr* **1** (*bomb*) hacer estallar; (*burglar alarm*) hacer sonar; (*reaction*) desencadenar. **2** (*enhance*) hacer resaltar. ◆**set out I** *vi* **1** (*depart*) salir; **to s. out for ...**, partir hacia ... **2** **to s. out to do sth**, proponerse hacer algo. **II** *vtr* (*arrange*) disponer; (*present*) presentar. ◆**set up I** *vtr* **1** (*position*) colocar; (*statue, camp*) levantar; (*tent, stall*) montar. **2** (*business etc*) establecer; (*bank*) montar; (*committee*) constituir; *fam* **you've been s. up!**, ¡te han timado! **II** *vi* establecerse.

set² [set] *n* **1** (*series*) serie *f*; **s.** (*of golf clubs etc*) juego *m*; (*of tools*) estuche *m*; (*of turbines etc*) equipo *m*; (*of books, poems*) colección *f*; (*of teeth*) dentadura *f*; **chess s.**, juego de ajedrez; **s. of cutlery**, cubertería *f*; **s. of kitchen utensils**, batería *f* de cocina. **2** (*of people*) grupo *m*; *pej* (*clique*) camarilla *f*. **3** *Math* conjunto *m*. **4** *Ten* set *m*. **5 TV s.**, televisor *m*.

setback ['setbæk] *n* revés *m*, contratiempo *m*.

settee [se'ti:] *n* sofá *m*.

setting ['setɪŋ] *n* **1** (*background*) marco *m*; (*of novel, film*) escenario *m*. **2** (*of jewel*)

engaste *m*.

settle ['setǝl] **I** *vtr* **1** (*put in position*) colocar. **2** (*decide on*) acordar; (*date, price*) fijar; (*problem*) resolver; (*differences*) arreglar. **3** (*debt*) pagar; (*account*) saldar. **4** (*nerves*) calmar; (*stomach*) asentar. **5** *fam* (*put an end to*) acabar con. **6** (*establish*) (*person*) instalar. **7** (*colonize*) asentarse en. **II** *vi* **1** (*bird, insect*) posarse; (*dust*) depositarse; (*snow*) cuajar; (*sediment*) precipitarse; (*liquid*) asentarse; **to s. into an armchair**, acomodarse en un sillón. **2** (*put down roots*) afincarse (**in**, a una colonia) asentarse. **3** (*weather*) serenarse. **4** (*child, nerves*) calmarse. **5** (*pay*) pagar; **to s. out of court**, llegar a un acuerdo amistoso.
◆**settle down** *vi* **1** (*put down roots*) instalarse; (*marry*) casarse. **2** **to s. down to work**, ponerse a trabajar. **3** (*child*) calmarse; (*situation*) normalizarse. ◆**settle for** *vi* conformarse con. ◆**settle in** *vi* (*move in*) instalarse; (*become adapted*) adaptarse. ◆**settle with** *vtr* (*pay debt to*) ajustar cuentas con.

settlement ['setǝlmǝnt] *n* **1** (*agreement*) acuerdo *m*. **2** (*of debt*) pago *m*; (*of account*) liquidación *f*. **3** (*dowry*) dote *m*. **4** (*colonization*) colonización *f*. **5** (*colony*) asentamiento *m*; (*village*) poblado *m*.

settler ['setlǝr] *n* colono *m*.

setup ['setʌp] *n* (*system*) sistema *m*; (*situation*) situación *f*; *sl* montaje *m*.

seven ['sevǝn] *adj* & *n* siete (*m*) *inv*.

seventeen [sevǝn'ti:n] *adj* & *n* diecisiete (*m*), diez y siete (*m*).

seventeenth [sevǝn'ti:nθ] **I** *adj* & *n* decimoséptimo,-a (*m,f*). **II** *n* (*fraction*) decimoséptima parte.

seventh ['sevǝnθ] **I** *adj* & *n* séptimo,-a (*m,f*). **II** *n* séptimo *m*.

seventy ['sevǝntɪ] *adj* & *n* setenta (*m*) *inv*.

sever ['sevǝr] *vtr* (*cut*) cortar; *fig* (*relations*) romper.

several ['sevǝrǝl] **I** *adj* **1** (*more than a few*) varios,-as. **2** (*different*) distintos,-as; *fml* (*separate*) respectivos,-as. **II** *pron* algunos,-as.

severance ['sevǝrǝns] *n* (*of relations etc*) ruptura *f*; **s. pay**, indemnización *f* por despido.

severe [sɪ'vɪǝr] *adj* severo,-a; (*climate, blow*) duro,-a; (*illness, loss*) grave; (*pain*) intenso,-a.

severity [sɪ'verɪtɪ] *n* (*of person, criticism, punishment*) severidad *f*; (*of climate*) rigor *m*; (*of illness*) gravedad *f*; (*of pain*) intensidad *f*; (*of style*) austeridad *f*.

Seville [sǝ'vɪl] *n* Sevilla.

sew [sǝʊ] *vtr* & *vi* (*pt sewed*; *pp sewed* o *sewn*) coser. ◆**sew up** *vtr* (*stitch together*) coser; (*mend*) remendar.

sewage ['su:ɪdʒ] *n* aguas *fpl* residuales.

sewer ['su:ǝr] *n* alcantarilla *f*, cloaca *f*.

sewerage ['su:ərɪdʒ] *n* alcantarillado *m*.

sewing ['səʊɪŋ] *n* costura *f*; **s. machine,** máquina *f* de coser.

sewn [səʊn] *pp* → **sew.**

sex [seks] **I** *n* sexo *m*; **s. education,** educación *f* sexual; **to have s. with sb,** tener relaciones sexuales con algn; **s. appeal,** sex-appeal *m*.

sexist ['seksɪst] *adj & n* sexista (*mf*).

sexual ['seksjʊəl] *adj* sexual.

sexuality [seksjʊ'ælɪtɪ] *n* sexualidad *f*.

sexy ['seksɪ] *adj* (**sexier, sexiest**) *fam* sexi, erótico,-a.

shabby ['ʃæbɪ] *adj* (**shabbier, shabbiest**) 1 (*garment*) raído,-a; (*house*) desvencijado,-a; (*person*) (*in rags*) harapiento,-a; (*unkempt*) desaseado,-a. 2 (*treatment*) mezquino,-a.

shack [ʃæk] *n* choza *f*.

shackles ['ʃækəlz] *npl* grilletes *mpl*, grillos *mpl*; *fig* trabas *fpl*.

shade [ʃeɪd] **I** *n* 1 (*shadow*) sombra *f*; in the s., a la sombra. 2 (*eyeshade*) visera *f*; (*lampshade*) pantalla *f*; *US* (*blind*) persiana *f*. 3 (*of colour*) tono *m*, matiz *m*; *fig* (*of meaning*) matiz *m*. 4 (*small amount*) poquito *m*. 5 *fam* **shades,** gafas *fpl* de sol. **II** *vtr* (*from sun*) proteger contra el sol.

shadow ['ʃædəʊ] **I** *n* 1 (*shade*) sombra *f*; (*darkness*) oscuridad *f*; *fig* without a s. of a doubt, sin lugar a dudas. 2 *GB* the s. cabinet, el gabinete de la oposición. **II** *vtr fig* seguir la pista a.

shadowy ['ʃædəʊɪ] *adj* (*dark*) oscuro,-a; (*hazy*) vago,-a.

shady ['ʃeɪdɪ] *adj* (**shadier, shadiest**) (*place*) a la sombra; (*suspicious*) (*person*) sospechoso,-a; (*deal*) turbio,-a.

shaft [ʃɑːft] *n* 1 (*of tool, golf club*) mango *m*; (*of lance*) asta *f*; (*of arrow*) astil *m*. 2 *Tech* eje *m*. 3 (*of mine*) pozo *m*; (*of lift, elevator*) hueco *m*. 4 (*beam of light*) rayo *m*.

shaggy ['ʃægɪ] *adj* (**shaggier, shaggiest**) (*hairy*) peludo,-a; (*long-haired*) melenudo,-a; (*beard*) desgreñado,-a.

shake [ʃeɪk] **I** *n* sacudida *f*. **II** *vtr* (*pt* **shook;** *pp* **shaken**) (*carpet etc*) sacudir; (*bottle*) agitar; (*dice*) mover; (*building*) hacer temblar; **the news shook him,** la noticia le conmocionó; **to s. hands with sb,** estrechar la mano a algn; **to s. one's head,** negar con la cabeza. **III** *vi* (*person, building*) temblar; **to s. with cold,** tiritar de frío. ◆**shake off** *vtr* 1 (*dust etc*) sacudir. 2 *fig* (*bad habit*) librarse de; (*cough, cold*) quitarse de encima; (*pursuer*) dar esquinazo a. ◆**shake up** *vtr fig* (*shock*) trastornar; (*reorganize*) reorganizar.

shake-up ['ʃeɪkʌp] *n fig* reorganización *f*.

shaken ['ʃeɪkən] *pp* → **shake.**

shaky ['ʃeɪkɪ] *adj* (**shakier, shakiest**) (*hand, voice*) tembloroso,-a; (*step*)

shall [ʃæl, *unstressed* ʃəl] *v aux* 1 (*used to form future tense*) (*first person only*) **I s.** (*or* **I'll**) buy it, lo compraré; **I s. not** (*or* **I shan't**) say anything, no diré nada. 2 (*used to form questions*) (*usu first person*) **s. I close the door?,** ¿cierro la puerta?; **s. I mend it for you?,** ¿quieres que te lo repare?; **s. we go?,** ¿nos vamos? 3 (*emphatic, command, threat*) (*all persons*) **we s. overcome,** venceremos; **you s. leave immediately,** te irás enseguida.

shallow ['ʃæləʊ] *adj* poco profundo,-a; *fig* superficial.

sham [ʃæm] **I** *adj* falso,-a; (*illness etc*) fingido,-a. **II** *n* 1 (*pretence*) engaño *m*, farsa *f*. 2 (*person*) fantoche *m*. **III** *vtr* fingir, simular. **IV** *vi* fingir.

shambles ['ʃæmblz] *n* confusión *f*; **the performance was a s.,** la función fue un desastre.

shame [ʃeɪm] **I** *n* 1 vergüenza *f*; **to put to s.,** (*far outdo*) eclipsar, sobrepasar. 2 (*pity*) pena *f*, lástima *f*; **what a s.!,** ¡qué pena!, ¡qué lástima!. **II** *vtr* avergonzar; (*disgrace*) deshonrar.

shamefaced ['ʃeɪmfeɪst] *adj* avergonzado,-a.

shameful ['ʃeɪmfʊl] *adj* vergonzoso,-a.

shameless ['ʃeɪmlɪs] *adj* descarado,-a.

shampoo [ʃæm'puː] **I** *n* champú *m*. **II** *vtr* lavar con champú; **to s. one's hair,** lavarse el pelo.

shamrock ['ʃæmrɒk] *n* trébol *m*.

shandy ['ʃændɪ] *n GB* clara *f*, cerveza *f* con gaseosa.

shantytown ['ʃæntɪtaʊn] *n* barrio *m* de chabolas.

shape [ʃeɪp] **I** *n* 1 forma *f*; (*shadow*) silueta *m*; **to take s.,** tomar forma. 2 **in good/bad s.,** (*condition*) en buen/ mal estado; **to be in good s.,** (*health*) estar en forma. **II** *vtr* dar forma a; (*clay*) modelar; (*stone*) tallar; (*character*) formar; (*destiny*) determinar; **star-shaped,** con forma de estrella. **III** *vi* (*also* **s. up**) tomar forma; **to s. up well,** (*events*) tomar buen cariz; (*person*) hacer progresos.

shapeless ['ʃeɪplɪs] *adj* amorfo,-a, informe.

shapely ['ʃeɪplɪ] *adj* (**shapelier, shapeliest**) escultural.

share [ʃeəʳ] **I** *n* 1 (*portion*) parte *f*. 2 *Fin* acción *f*; **s. index,** índice *m* de la Bolsa; **s. prices,** cotizaciones *fpl*. **II** *vtr* 1 (*divide*) dividir. 2 (*have in common*) compartir. **III** *vi* compartir. ◆**share out** *vtr* repartir.

shareholder ['ʃeəhəʊldəʳ] *n* accionista *mf*.

shark [ʃɑːk] *n* 1 (*fish*) tiburón *m*. 2 *fam* (*swindler*) estafador,-a *m,f*; **loan s.,** usurero,-a *m,f*.

sharp [ʃɑːp] **I** *adj* 1 (*razor, knife*)

afilado,-a; (needle, pencil) puntiagudo,-a.
2 (angle) agudo,-a; (features) anguloso,-a;
(bend) cerrado,-a. 3 (outline) definido,-a;
(contrast) marcado,-a. 4 (observant) perspicaz; (clever) listo,-a; (quick-witted)
avispado,-a; (cunning) astuto,-a. 5
(sudden) brusco,-a. 6 (pain, cry) agudo,-a;
(wind) penetrante. 7 (sour) acre. 8 (criticism) mordaz; (temper) arisco,-a; (tone)
seco,-a. 9 Mus sostenido,-a; (out of tune)
desafinado,-a. II adv at 2 o'clock s.,
(exactly) a las dos en punto. III n Mus
sostenido m. ◆sharply adv 1 (abruptly)
bruscamente. 2 (clearly) marcadamente.

sharpen ['ʃɑːpən] vtr 1 (knife) afilar;
(pencil) sacar punta a. 2 fig (desire, intelligence) agudizar.

sharpener ['ʃɑːpənər] n (for knife) afilador m; (for pencil) sacapuntas m inv.

sharp-eyed ['ʃɑːpaɪd] adj con ojos de
lince.

shatter ['ʃætər] I vtr hacer añicos; (nerves)
destrozar; (hopes) frustrar. II vi hacerse
añicos.

shave [ʃeɪv] I n afeitado m; to have a s.,
afeitarse; fig to have a close s., escaparse
por los pelos. II vtr (pt shaved; pp
shaved or shaven ['ʃeɪvən]) (person) afeitar; (wood) cepillar. III vi afeitarse.

shaver ['ʃeɪvər] n (electric) s., máquina f
de afeitar.

shaving ['ʃeɪvɪŋ] n 1 (of wood) viruta f. 2
s. brush, brocha f de afeitar; s. cream,
crema f de afeitar; s. foam, espuma f de
afeitar.

shawl [ʃɔːl] n chal m.

she [ʃiː] pers pron ella.

she- [ʃiː] pref (of animal) hembra; s.-cat,
gata f.

sheaf [ʃiːf] n (pl sheaves [ʃiːvz]) Agr gavilla f; (of arrows) haz m; (of papers,
banknotes) fajo m.

shear [ʃɪər] I vtr (pt sheared; pp shorn or
sheared) (sheep) esquilar; to s. off,
cortar. II vi esquilar ovejas.

shears [ʃɪəz] npl tijeras fpl (grandes).

sheath [ʃiːθ] n 1 (for sword) vaina f; (for
knife, scissors) funda f. 2 (contraceptive)
preservativo m.

sheaves [ʃiːvz] npl → sheaf.

shed¹ [ʃed] n (in garden) cobertizo m;
(workmen's hut) barraca f; (for cattle) establo m; (in factory) nave f.

shed² [ʃed] vtr (pt & pp shed) 1 (clothes)
despojarse de; (unwanted thing) deshacerse de; the snake s. its skin, la
serpiente mudó de piel. 2 (blood, tears)
derramar.

sheen [ʃiːn] n brillo m.

sheep [ʃiːp] n inv oveja f.

sheepdog ['ʃiːpdɒg] n perro m pastor.

sheepish ['ʃiːpɪʃ] adj avergonzado,-a.

sheepskin ['ʃiːpskɪn] n piel f de carnero.

sheer [ʃɪər] adj 1 (utter) total, puro,-a. 2

(cliff) escarpado,-a; (drop) vertical. 3
(stockings, cloth) fino,-a.

sheet [ʃiːt] n 1 (on bed) sábana f. 2 (of
paper) hoja f; (of tin, glass, plastic) lámina
f; (of ice) capa f.

sheik(h) [ʃeɪk] n jeque m.

shelf [ʃelf] n (pl shelves [ʃelvz]) (on bookcase) estante m; (in cupboard) tabla f;
shelves, estantería f.

shell [ʃel] I n 1 (of egg, nut) cáscara f; (of
pea) vaina f; (of tortoise etc) caparazón m;
(of snail etc) concha f. 2 (of building)
armazón m. 3 (mortar etc) obús m, proyectil m; (cartridge) cartucho m; s. shock,
neurosis f de guerra. II vtr 1 (peas) desvainar; (nuts) pelar. 2 Mil bombardear.

shellfish ['ʃelfɪʃ] n inv marisco m, mariscos mpl.

shelter ['ʃeltər] I n 1 (protection) abrigo m,
amparo m; to take s., refugiarse (from,
de). 2 (place) refugio m; (for homeless) asilo m; bus s., marquesina f. II vtr 1 (protect) abrigar, proteger. 2 (take into one's
home) ocultar. III vi refugiarse.

sheltered ['ʃeltəd] adj (place) abrigado,-a;
to lead a s. life, vivir apartado,-a del
mundo.

shelve [ʃelv] vtr fig (postpone) dar carpetazo a.

shelves [ʃelvz] npl → shelf.

shepherd ['ʃepəd] I n pastor m; s.'s pie,
pastel m de carne picada con puré de patatas. II vtr fig to s. sb in, hacer entrar a
algn.

sheriff ['ʃerɪf] n GB gobernador m civil;
Scot juez m presidente; US sheriff m.

sherry ['ʃerɪ] n jerez m.

Shetland ['ʃetlənd] n the S. Isles, S., las
Islas Shetland; S. wool, lana f Shetland.

shield [ʃiːld] I n 1 escudo m; (of policeman) placa f. 2 (on machinery) blindaje m.
II vtr proteger (from, de).

shift [ʃɪft] I n 1 (change) cambio m; US
Aut (gear) s., cambio m de velocidades. 2
(period of work, group of workers) turno m;
to be on the day s., hacer el turno de
día. II vtr (change) cambiar; (move)
cambiar de sitio, trasladar. III vi (move)
moverse; (change place) cambiar de sitio;
(opinion) cambiar; (wind) cambiar de dirección.

shiftless ['ʃɪftlɪs] n perezoso,-a, vago,-a.

shiftwork ['ʃɪftwɜːk] n trabajo m por
turnos.

shifty ['ʃɪftɪ] adj (shiftier, shiftiest) (look)
furtivo,-a; (person) sospechoso,-a.

shilling ['ʃɪlɪŋ] n chelín m.

shimmer ['ʃɪmər] I vi relucir; (shine) brillar. II n luz trémula, reflejo trémulo;
(shining) brillo m.

shin [ʃɪn] n espinilla f; s. pad, espinillera
f.

shine [ʃaɪn] I vi (pt & pp shone) 1 (light)
brillar; (metal) relucir. 2 fig (excel) sobre-

salir (at, en). **II** *vtr* **1** *(lamp)* dirigir. **2** *(pt & pp* **shined**) *(polish)* sacar brillo a; *(shoes)* limpiar. **III** *n* brillo *m*, lustre *m*.

shingle ['ʃɪŋgəl] *n* **1** *(pebbles)* guijarros *mpl*. **2** *(roof tile)* tablilla *f*.

shingles ['ʃɪŋgəlz] *npl* Med herpes *m*.

shining ['ʃaɪnɪŋ] *adj fig (outstanding)* ilustre.

shiny ['ʃaɪnɪ] *adj* **(shinier, shiniest)** brillante.

ship [ʃɪp] **I** *n* barco *m*, buque *m*. **II** *vtr* **1** *(take on board)* embarcar. **2** *(transport)* transportar (en barco); *(send)* enviar, mandar.

shipbuilding ['ʃɪpbɪldɪŋ] *n* construcción *f* naval.

shipment ['ʃɪpmənt] *n* **1** *(act)* transporte *m*. **2** *(load)* consignación *f*, envío *m*.

shipper ['ʃɪpə'] *n (person)* cargador,-a *m,f*.

shipping ['ʃɪpɪŋ] *n* **1** *(ships)* barcos *mpl*; **s. lane**, vía *f* de navegación. **2** *(loading)* embarque *m*; *(transporting)* transporte *m* (en barco); **s. company**, compañía naviera.

shipshape ['ʃɪpʃeɪp] *adj & adv* en perfecto orden.

shipwreck ['ʃɪprek] **I** *n* naufragio *m*. **II** *vtr* to be shipwrecked, naufragar.

shipyard ['ʃɪpjɑːd] *n* astillero *m*.

shire [ʃaɪə'] *n GB* condado *m*.

shirk [ʃɜːk] **I** *vtr (duty)* faltar a; *(problem)* eludir. **II** *vi* gandulear.

shirt [ʃɜːt] *n* camisa *f*; **in s. sleeves**, en mangas de camisa; *fam* **keep your s. on!**, ¡no te sulfures!

shit [ʃɪt] *vulg* **I** *n* mierda *f*; **sl in the s.**, jodido,-a. **II** *interj* ¡mierda!. **III** *vi* cagar.

shiver ['ʃɪvə'] **I** *vi (with cold)* tiritar; *(with fear)* temblar, estremecerse. **II** *n (with cold, fear)* escalofrío *m*.

shoal [ʃəʊl] *n (of fish)* banco *m*.

shock [ʃɒk] **I** *n* **1** *(jolt)* choque *m*; **s. absorber**, amortiguador *m*; **s. wave**, onda expansiva. **2** *(upset)* conmoción *f*; *(scare)* susto *m*. **3** Med shock *m*. **II** *vtr* **1** *(upset)* conmover; *(startle)* sobresaltar; *(scandalize)* escandalizar.

shocking ['ʃɒkɪŋ] *adj* **1** *(causing horror)* espantoso,-a; *fam (very bad)* horroroso,-a. **2** *(disgraceful)* escandaloso,-a. **3 s. pink**, rosa chillón.

shod [ʃɒd] *pt & pp → shoe.*

shoddy ['ʃɒdɪ] *adj* **(shoddier, shoddiest)** *(goods)* de mala calidad; *(work)* chapucero,-a.

shoe [ʃuː] **I** *n* **1** zapato *m*; *(for horse)* herradura *f*; **brake s.**, zapata *f*; **s. polish**, betún *m*; **s. repair shop**, remiendo *m* de zapatos; **s. shop**, *US* **s. store**, zapatería *f*. **2** **shoes**, calzado *m* sing. **II** *vtr (pt & pp* **shod**) *(horse)* herrar.

shoebrush ['ʃuːbrʌʃ] *n* cepillo *m* para los zapatos.

shoehorn ['ʃuːhɔːn] *n* calzador *m*.

shoelace ['ʃuːleɪs] *n* cordón *m* (de zapatos).

shoestring ['ʃuːstrɪŋ] *n fig* **to do sth on a s.**, hacer algo con poquísimo dinero.

shone [ʃɒn, *US* ʃəʊn] *pt & pp → shine* **I** & **II**.

shoo [ʃuː] **I** *interj* ¡fuera!. **II** *vtr* to **s.** *(away)*, espantar.

shook [ʃʊk] *pt → shake.*

shoot [ʃuːt] **I** *n Bot* retoño *m*; *(of vine)* sarmiento *m*. **II** *vtr (pt & pp* **shot**) **1** pegar un tiro a; *(kill)* matar; *(execute)* fusilar; *(hunt)* cazar; to **s. dead**, matar a tiros. **2** *(missile, glance)* lanzar; *(bullet, ball)* disparar. **3** *(film)* rodar, filmar; *Phot* fotografiar. **4** *sl* to **s.** *(up)*, *(heroin etc)* chutarse. **III** *vi* **1** *(with gun)* disparar (at **sb**, sobre, a algn); to **s. at a target**, tirar al blanco; *Ftb* to **s. at the goal**, chutar a puerta. **2** to **s. past** *or* **by**, pasar flechado,-a. ◆**shoot down** *vtr (aircraft)* derribar. ◆**shoot out** *vi (person)* salir disparado,-a; *(water)* brotar; *(flames)* salir. ◆**shoot up** *vi (flames)* subir; *(water)* brotar; *(prices)* dispararse.

shooting ['ʃuːtɪŋ] **I** *n* **1** *(shots)* tiros *mpl*; *(murder)* asesinato *m*; *(hunting)* caza *f*; **s. star**, estrella *f* fugaz. **2** *(of film)* rodaje *m*. **II** *adj (pain)* punzante.

shoot-out ['ʃuːtaʊt] *n* tiroteo *m*.

shop [ʃɒp] **I** *n* **1** tienda *f*; *(large store)* almacén *m*; **s. assistant**, dependiente,-a *m,f*; **s. window**, escaparate *m*. **2** *(workshop)* taller *m*; **s. floor**, *(place)* planta *f*; *(workers)* obreros *mpl*; *GB* **s. steward**, enlace *mf* sindical. **II** *vi* hacer compras; **to go shopping**, ir de compras.

shopkeeper ['ʃɒpkiːpə'] *n* tendero,-a *m,f*.

shoplifter ['ʃɒplɪftə'] *n* ladrón,-ona *m,f* (de tiendas).

shopper ['ʃɒpə'] *n* comprador,-a *m,f*.

shopping ['ʃɒpɪŋ] *n (purchases)* compras *fpl*; **s. bag/basket**, bolsa *f*/cesta *f* de la compra; **s. centre** *or* **precinct**, centro *m* comercial.

shopsoiled ['ʃɒpsɔɪld], *US* **shopworn** ['ʃɒpwɔːn] *adj* deteriorado,-a.

shore¹ [ʃɔː'] *n (of sea, lake)* orilla *f*; *US (beach)* playa *f*; *(coast)* costa *f*; **to go on s.**, desembarcar.

shore² [ʃɔː'] *vtr* to **s.** *(up)*, apuntalar.

shorn [ʃɔːn] *pp → shear.*

short [ʃɔːt] **I** *adj* **1** corto,-a; *(not tall)* bajo,-a; **in a s. while**, dentro de un rato; **in the s. term**, a corto plazo; **s. circuit**, cortocircuito *m*; **s. cut**, atajo *m*; *GB* **s. list**, lista *f* de seleccionados; **s. story**, relato corto, cuento *m*; **s. wave**, onda corta. **2** *(brief)* corto,-a, breve; **'Bob' is s. for 'Robert'**, 'Bob' es el diminutivo de 'Robert'; **for s.**, para abreviar; **in s.**, en pocas palabras. **3** **to be s. of breath**, faltarle a uno la respiración; **to be s. of food**, andar escaso,-a de comida. **4** *(curt)* brusco,-a, seco,-a. **II** adv **1 to pull up s.**, pararse en seco. **2 to cut s.**, (holiday) interrumpir; (meeting) suspender; **we're running s. of coffee**, se nos está acabando el café. **3 s. of**, (except) excepto, menos. **III** n **1** Cin cortometraje m. **2** Fam (drink) copa f. **IV** vi **to s. (out)**, tener un cortocircuito. ◆**shortly** adv (soon) dentro de poco; **s. after**, poco después.

shortage ['ʃɔːtɪdʒ] n escasez f.

shortbread ['ʃɔːtbred] n mantecado m.

short-change ['ʃɔːtʃeɪndʒ] vtr **to s.-c. sb**, no devolver el cambio completo a algn; fig timar a algn.

short-circuit [ʃɔːt'sɜːkɪt] **I** vtr provocar un cortocircuito en. **II** vi tener un cortocircuito.

shortcomings ['ʃɔːtkʌmɪŋz] npl defectos mpl.

shortcrust ['ʃɔːtkrʌst] n **s. pastry**, pasta brisa.

shorten ['ʃɔːtən] vtr (skirt, visit) acortar; (word) abreviar; (text) resumir.

shortfall ['ʃɔːtfɔːl] n déficit m.

shorthand ['ʃɔːthænd] n taquigrafía f; GB **s. typing**, taquimecanografía f; GB **s. typist**, taquimecanógrafo,-a m,f.

short-list ['ʃɔːtlɪst] vtr poner en la lista de seleccionados.

short-lived ['ʃɔːtlɪvd] adv efímero,-a.

short-range ['ʃɔːtreɪndʒ] adj de corto alcance.

shorts [ʃɔːts] npl **1** pantalones mpl cortos; **a pair of s.**, un pantalón corto. **2** US (underpants) calzoncillos mpl.

short-sighted [ʃɔːt'saɪtɪd] adj (person) miope; fig (plan etc) sin visión de futuro.

short-staffed [ʃɔːt'stɑːft] adj escaso,-a de personal.

short-tempered [ʃɔːt'tempəd] adj de mal genio.

short-term ['ʃɔːtɜːm] adj a corto plazo.

shot¹ [ʃɒt] **I** n **1** (act, sound) tiro m, disparo m. **2** (projectile) bala f; (pellets) perdigones mpl; fig **he was off like a s.**, salió disparado; Sport **s. put**, lanzamiento m de peso. **3** (person) tirador,-a m,f. **4** Ftb (kick) tiro m (a puerta); (in billiards, cricket, golf) golpe m. **5** (attempt) tentativa f; **to have a s. at sth**, intentar hacer algo. **6** (injection) inyección f; fam pinchazo m. **7** (drink) trago m. **8** Phot foto f; Cin toma f.

shot² [ʃɒt] pt & pp → **shoot**.

shotgun ['ʃɒtgʌn] n escopeta f.

should [ʃʊd, unstressed ʃəd] v aux **1** (duty) deber; **all employees s. wear helmets**, todos los empleados deben llevar casco; **he s. have been an architect**, debería haber sido arquitecto. **2** (probability) deber de; **he s. have finished by now**, ya debe de haber acabado; **this s. be interesting**, esto promete ser interesante. **3** (conditional use) **if anything strange s.**

happen, si pasara algo raro. **4 I s. like to ask a question**, quisiera hacer una pregunta.

shoulder ['ʃəʊldər] **I** n **1** hombro m; **s. blade**, omóplato m; **s. strap**, (of garment) tirante m; (of bag) correa f; Aut **hard s.**, arcén m. **2** Culin paletilla f. **II** vtr fig (responsibilities) cargar con.

shout [ʃaʊt] **I** n grito m. **II** vtr gritar. **III** vi gritar; **to s. at sb**, gritar a algn. ◆**shout down** vtr abuchear.

shouting ['ʃaʊtɪŋ] n gritos mpl, vocerío m.

shove [ʃʌv] **I** n fam empujón m. **II** vtr empujar; **to s. sth into one's pocket**, meterse algo en el bolsillo a empellones. **III** vi empujar; (jostle) dar empellones. ◆**shove off** vi fam largarse. ◆**shove up** vi fam (move along) correrse.

shovel ['ʃʌvəl] **I** n pala f; (mechanical s., excavadora f. **II** vtr mover con pala or a paladas.

show [ʃəʊ] **I** vtr (pt **showed**; pp **shown** or **showed**) **1** (ticket etc) mostrar; (painting etc) exponer; (film) poner; (latest plans etc) presentar. **2** (display) demostrar; **to s. oneself to be**, comportarse como. **3** (teach) enseñar; (explain) explicar. **4** (temperature, way etc) indicar; (profit etc) registrar. **5** (prove) demostrar. **6** (conduct) llevar; **to s. sb in**, hacer pasar a algn; **to s. sb to the door**, acompañar a algn hasta la puerta.

II vi **1** (be visible) notarse. **2** fam (turn up) aparecer. **3** Cin **what's showing?**, ¿qué ponen?

III n **1** (display) demostración f. **2** (outward appearance) apariencia f. **3** (exhibition) exposición f; **on s.**, expuesto,-a; **boat s.**, salón náutico; **motor s.**, salón del automóvil. **4** Theat (entertainment) espectáculo m; (performance) función f; Rad TV programa m; **s. business**, fam **s. biz**, el mundo del espectáculo. ◆**show off I** vtr (highlight) hacer resaltar. **2** fam (flaunt) hacer alarde de. **II** vi fam farolear. ◆**show up I** vtr **1** (reveal) sacar a luz; (highlight) hacer resaltar. **2** fam (embarrass) dejar en evidencia. **II** vi **1** (stand out) destacarse. **2** fam (arrive) aparecer.

showdown ['ʃəʊdaʊn] n enfrentamiento m.

shower ['ʃaʊər] **I** n **1** (rain) chubasco m, chaparrón m. **2** fig (of stones, blows etc) lluvia f. **3** (bath) ducha f; **to have a s.**, ducharse. **II** vtr **1** (spray) rociar. **2** fig **to s. gifts/praise on sb**, colmar a algn de regalos/elogios. **III** vi ducharse.

showerproof ['ʃaʊərpruːf] adj impermeable.

showing ['ʃəʊɪŋ] n (of film) proyección f.

showjumping ['ʃəʊdʒʌmpɪŋ] n hípica f.

shown [ʃəʊn] pp → **show**.

show-off ['ʃəʊɒf] n fam farolero,-a m,f.

showpiece ['ʃəʊpiːs] n (in exhibition etc) obra maestra; fig (at school etc) modelo f.

showroom ['ʃəʊruːm] n Com exposición f; Art galería f.

shrank [ʃræŋk] pt → **shrink**.

shrapnel ['ʃræpnəl] n metralla f.

shred [ʃred] I n triza f; (of cloth) jirón m; (of paper) tira f. II vtr (paper) hacer trizas; (vegetables) rallar.

shredder ['ʃredər] n (for waste paper) trituradora f; (for vegetables) rallador m.

shrew [ʃruː] n 1 Zool musaraña f. 2 fig (woman) arpía f.

shrewd [ʃruːd] adj astuto,-a; (clear-sighted) perspicaz; (wise) sabio,-a; (decision) acertado,-a.

shriek [ʃriːk] I n chillido m; **shrieks** of laughter, carcajadas fpl. II vi chillar.

shrill [ʃrɪl] adj agudo,-a, estridente.

shrimp [ʃrɪmp] I n camarón m. II vi pescar camarones.

shrine [ʃraɪn] n (tomb) sepulcro m; (relic case) relicario m; (chapel) capilla f; (holy place) lugar sagrado.

shrink [ʃrɪŋk] I vtr (pt **shrank**; pp **shrunk**) encoger. II vi 1 (clothes) encoger(se). 2 (savings) disminuir. 3 to s. (back), echarse atrás; to s. from doing sth, no tener valor para hacer algo. II n fam (psychiatrist) psiquiatra m,f.

shrinkage ['ʃrɪŋkɪdʒ] n 1 (of cloth) encogimiento m; (of metal) contracción f. 2 (of savings etc) disminución f.

shrink-wrapped ['ʃrɪŋkræpt] adj envuelto,-a en plástico.

shrivel ['ʃrɪvəl] I vtr to s. (up), encoger; (plant) secar; (skin) arrugar. II vi encogerse; (plant) secarse; (skin) arrugarse.

shroud [ʃraʊd] I n Rel sudario m. II vtr fig envolver.

Shrove Tuesday [ʃrəʊv'tjuːzdɪ] n martes m de carnaval.

shrub [ʃrʌb] n arbusto m.

shrubbery ['ʃrʌbərɪ] n arbustos mpl.

shrug [ʃrʌg] vtr to s. one's shoulders, encogerse de hombros. II vi encogerse de hombros. III n encogimiento m de hombros. ◆**shrug off** vtr no dejarse desanimar por.

shrunk [ʃrʌŋk] pp → **shrink**.

shudder ['ʃʌdər] I n 1 escalofrío m, estremecimiento m. 2 (of machinery) sacudida f. II vi 1 (person) estremecerse. 2 (machinery) dar sacudidas.

shuffle ['ʃʌfəl] I vtr (feet) arrastrar. 2 (papers etc) revolver; (cards) barajar. II vi 1 (walk) andar arrastrando los pies. 2 Cards barajar.

shun [ʃʌn] vtr (person) esquivar; (responsibility) rehuir.

shunt [ʃʌnt] vtr Rail cambiar de vía; Elec derivar.

shut [ʃʌt] I vtr (pt & pp **shut**) cerrar. II vi

cerrarse. III adj cerrado,-a. ◆**shut down** I vtr (factory) cerrar. II vi (factory) cerrar. ◆**shut off** vtr (gas, water etc) cortar. ◆**shut out** vtr 1 (lock out) dejar fuera a. 2 (exclude) excluir. ◆**shut up** I vtr 1 (close) cerrar. 2 (imprison) encerrar. 3 fam (silence) callar. II vi fam (keep quiet) callarse.

shutdown ['ʃʌtdaʊn] n cierre m.

shutter ['ʃʌtər] n 1 (on window) contraventana f, postigo m. 2 Phot obturador m.

shuttle ['ʃʌtəl] I n 1 (in weaving) lanzadera f. 2 Av puente aéreo; (space) s., transbordador m espacial. II vtr y venir.

shuttlecock ['ʃʌtəlkɒk] n volante m.

shy [ʃaɪ] I adj (**shyer**, **shyest** or **shier**, **shiest**) (timid) tímido,-a; (reserved) reservado,-a. II vi (horse) espantarse (at, de); fig to s. away from doing sth, negarse a hacer algo.

shyness ['ʃaɪnɪs] n timidez f.

Siberia [saɪ'bɪərɪə] n Siberia.

sibling ['sɪblɪŋ] n fml (brother) hermano m; (sister) hermana f; **siblings**, hermanos.

Sicily ['sɪsɪlɪ] n Sicilia.

sick [sɪk] adj 1 (ill) enfermo,-a; s. **leave**, baja f por enfermedad; s. **pay**, subsidio m de enfermedad. 2 to feel s., (about to vomit) tener ganas de devolver; to be s., devolver. 3 fam (fed up) harto,-a. 4 fam (mind, joke) morboso,-a; s. **humour**, humor negro.

sickbay ['sɪkbeɪ] n enfermería f.

sicken ['sɪkən] I vtr (make ill) poner enfermo; (revolt) dar asco a. II vi (fall ill) enfermar.

sickening ['sɪkənɪŋ] adj nauseabundo,-a; (revolting) repugnante; (horrifying) escalofriante.

sickle ['sɪkəl] n hoz f.

sickly ['sɪklɪ] adj (**sicklier**, **sickliest**) 1 (person) enfermizo,-a. 2 (taste) empalagoso,-a. 3 (smile) forzado,-a.

sickness ['sɪknɪs] n 1 (illness) enfermedad f. 2 (nausea) náuseas fpl.

side [saɪd] I n 1 lado m; (of coin etc) cara f; (of hill) ladera f; **by the s.** of, junto a. 2 (of body) costado m; (of animal) ijar m; a s. of bacon, una loncha de tocino; by my s., a mi lado; s. by s., juntos. 3 (edge) borde m; (of lake, river) orilla f. 4 fig (aspect) aspecto m. 5 (team) equipo m; Pol partido m; she's on our s., está de nuestro lado; to take sides with sb, ponerse de parte de algn; s. dish, guarnición f; s. effect, efecto secundario; s. entrance, entrada f lateral; s. street, calle f lateral. II vi to s. with sb, ponerse de parte de algn.

sideboard ['saɪdbɔːd] n aparador m.

sideburns ['saɪdbɜːnz] npl patillas fpl.

sidelight ['saɪdlaɪt] n Aut luz f lateral, piloto m.

sideline ['saɪdlaɪn] n 1 *Sport* línea f de banda. 2 *Com (product)* línea suplementaria; *(job)* empleo suplementario.

sidelong ['saɪdlɒŋ] *adj* de reojo.

side-saddle ['saɪdsædəl] I n silla f de amazona. II *adv* to ride s., montar a la inglesa.

sideshow ['saɪdʃəʊ] n atracción secundaria.

sidestep ['saɪdstep] I *vtr (issue)* esquivar. II *vi Box* fintar.

sidetrack ['saɪdtræk] *vtr fig (person)* despistar.

sidewalk ['saɪdwɔ:k] n US acera f.

sideways ['saɪdweɪz] I *adj (movement)* lateral; *(look)* de reojo. II *adv* de lado.

siding ['saɪdɪŋ] n Rail apartadero m, vía muerta.

sidle ['saɪdəl] *vi* to s. up to sb, acercarse furtivamente a algn.

siege [si:dʒ] n sitio m, cerco m; to lay s. to, sitiar.

sieve [sɪv] I n *(fine)* tamiz m; *(coarse)* criba f. II *vtr (fine)* tamizar; *(coarse)* cribar.

sift [sɪft] *vtr (sieve)* tamizar; *fig* to s. through, examinar cuidadosamente.

sigh [saɪ] I *vi* suspirar. II n suspiro m.

sight [saɪt] I n 1 *(faculty)* vista f; at first s., a primera vista; to catch s. of, divisar; to know by s., conocer de vista; to lose s. of sth/sb, perder algo/a algn de vista. 2 *(range of vision)* vista f; within s., a la vista; to come into s., aparecer. 3 *(spectacle)* espectáculo m. 4 *(on gun)* mira f; *fig* to set one's sights on, tener la mira puesta en. 5 **sights**, monumentos *mpl.* II *vtr* ver; *(land)* divisar.

sightseeing ['saɪtsi:ɪŋ] n turismo m; to go s., hacer turismo.

sign [saɪn] I n 1 *(symbol)* signo m. 2 *(gesture)* gesto m, seña f; *(signal)* señal f. 3 *(indication)* señal f; *(trace)* rastro m, huella f; as a s. of, como muestra de. 4 *(notice)* anuncio m; *(board)* letrero m. II *vtr* 1 *(letter etc)* firmar. 2 *Ftb* fichar. III *vi* firmar. ◆**sign on** I *vtr (worker)* contratar. II *vi (worker)* firmar un contrato; *GB fam* apuntarse al paro; *(regularly)* firmar el paro. ◆**sign up** I *vtr (soldier)* reclutar; *(worker)* contratar. II *vi (soldier)* alistarse; *(worker)* firmar un contrato.

signal ['sɪɡnəl] I n señal f; *Rad TV* sintonía f; *Rail* s. **box**, garita f de señales. II *vtr* 1 *(message)* transmitir por señales. 2 *(direction etc)* indicar. III *vi (with hands)* hacer señales; *(in car)* señalar.

signalman ['sɪɡnəlmən] n guardavía m.

signature ['sɪɡnɪtʃər] n *(name)* firma f; *Rad TV* s. **tune**, sintonía f.

signet ['sɪɡnɪt] n s. **ring**, (anillo m de) sello m.

significance [sɪɡ'nɪfɪkəns] n *(meaning)* significado m; *(importance)* importancia f.

significant [sɪɡ'nɪfɪkənt] *adj (meaningful)*

significativo,-a; *(important)* importante. ◆**significantly** *adv (markedly)* sensiblemente.

signify ['sɪɡnɪfaɪ] *vtr* 1 *(mean)* significar. 2 *(show, make known)* indicar.

signpost ['saɪnpəʊst] n poste m indicador.

silence ['saɪləns] I n silencio m. II *vtr* acallar; *(engine)* silenciar.

silencer ['saɪlənsər] n silenciador m.

silent ['saɪlənt] *adj* silencioso,-a; *(not talkative)* callado,-a; *(film)* mudo,-a; be s.!, ¡cállate!; to remain s., guardar silencio. ◆**silently** *adv* silenciosamente.

silhouette [sɪlu:'et] n silueta f.

silicon ['sɪlɪkən] n silicio m; s. **chip**, chip m (de silicio).

silk [sɪlk] I n seda f. II *adj* de seda.

silky ['sɪlkɪ] *adj (silkier, silkiest) (cloth)* sedoso,-a; *(voice etc)* aterciopelado,-a.

sill [sɪl] n *(of window)* alféizar m.

silly ['sɪlɪ] *adj (sillier, silliest)* tonto,-a.

silo ['saɪləʊ] n silo m.

silt [sɪlt] n cieno m. ◆**silt up** *vi* obstruirse con cieno.

silver ['sɪlvər] I n 1 *(metal)* plata f. 2 *(coins)* monedas *fpl* (de plata). 3 *(tableware)* vajilla f de plata. II *adj* de plata; s. **foil**, *(tinfoil)* papel m de aluminio; s. **paper**, papel de plata; s. **wedding**, bodas *fpl* de plata.

silver-plated [sɪlvə'pleɪtɪd] *adj* plateado,-a.

silversmith ['sɪlvəsmɪθ] n platero,-a *m,f.*

silverware ['sɪlvəweər] n vajilla f de plata.

silvery ['sɪlvərɪ] *adj* plateado,-a.

similar ['sɪmɪlər] *adj* parecido,-a, semejante (to, a); to be s., parecerse. ◆**similarly** *adv* 1 *(as well)* igualmente. 2 *(likewise)* del mismo modo, asimismo.

similarity [sɪmɪ'lærɪtɪ] n semejanza f.

simile ['sɪmɪlɪ] n símil m.

simmer ['sɪmər] I *vtr* cocer a fuego lento. II *vi* cocerse a fuego lento. ◆**simmer down** *vi fam* calmarse.

simpering ['sɪmpərɪŋ] *adj* melindroso,-a.

simple ['sɪmpəl] *adj* 1 sencillo,-a; s. **interest**, interés m simple. 2 *(natural)* natural. 3 *(foolish)* simple; *(naïve)* ingenuo,-a; *(dim)* de pocas luces. ◆**simply** *adv* 1 *(plainly)* sencillamente. 2 *(only)* simplemente, sólo.

simplicity [sɪm'plɪsɪtɪ] n 1 sencillez f. 2 *(naïveté)* ingenuidad f.

simplify ['sɪmplɪfaɪ] *vtr* simplificar.

simulate ['sɪmjʊleɪt] *vtr* simular.

simulator ['sɪmjʊleɪtər] n flight s., simulador de vuelo.

simultaneous [sɪməl'teɪnɪəs] *adj* simultáneo,-a. ◆**simultaneously** *adv* simultáneamente.

sin [sɪn] I n pecado m. II *vi* pecar.

since [sɪns] I *adv (ever)* ..., desde

entonces; **long s.,** hace mucho tiempo; **it has s. come out that ...,** desde entonces se ha sabido que .... **II** *prep* desde; **she has been living here s.** 1975, vive aquí desde 1975. **III** *conj* **1** *(time)* desde que; **how long is it s. you last saw him?,** ¿cuánto tiempo hace que lo viste por última vez? **2** *(because, as)* ya que, puesto que.

sincere [sɪn'sɪər] *adj* sincero,-a.
◆**sincerely** *adv* sinceramente; **Yours s.,** *(in letter)* le saluda atentamente.

sincerity [sɪn'serɪtɪ] *n* sinceridad *f*.

sinew ['sɪnjuː] *n (tendon)* tendón *m*; *(in meat)* nervio *m*.

sinful ['sɪnful] *adj (person)* pecador,-a; *(act, thought)* pecaminoso,-a; *fig (waste etc)* escandaloso,-a.

sing [sɪŋ] **I** *vtr (pt* **sang;** *pp* **sung)** cantar. **II** *vi (person, bird)* cantar; *(kettle, bullets)* silbar.

singe [sɪndʒ] *vtr* chamuscar.

singer ['sɪŋər] *n* cantante *mf*.

singing ['sɪŋɪŋ] *n (art)* canto *m*; *(songs)* canciones *fpl*; *(of kettle)* silbido *m*.

single ['sɪŋgəl] **I** *adj* **1** *(solitary)* solo,-a. **2** *(only one)* único,-a. **3** *(not double)* sencillo,-a; **s. bed/room,** cama *f* / habitación *f* individual. **4** *(unmarried)* soltero,-a. **II** *n* **1** *Rail* billete *m* de ida. **2** *(record)* single *m*. **3** *Sport* **singles,** individuales *mpl*. ◆**single out** *vtr (choose)* escoger; *(distinguish)* distinguir. ◆**singly** *adv (individually)* por separado; *(one by one)* uno por uno.

single-breasted [sɪŋgəl'brestɪd] *adj (suit, jacket)* recto,-a.

single-handed [sɪŋgəl'hændɪd] *adj & adv* sin ayuda.

single-minded [sɪŋgəl'maɪndɪd] *adj* resuelto,-a.

singlet ['sɪŋglɪt] *n GB* camiseta *f*.

singular ['sɪŋgjʊlər] **I** *adj* **1** *Ling* singular. **2** *fml (outstanding)* excepcional. **3** *fml (unique)* único,-a. **II** *n Ling* singular *m*. ◆**singularly** *adv* excepcionalmente.

sinister ['sɪnɪstər] *adj* siniestro,-a.

sink¹ [sɪŋk] *n (in kitchen)* fregadero *m*.

sink² [sɪŋk] **I** *vtr (pt* **sank;** *pp* **sunk)** **1** *(ship)* hundir, echar a pique; *fig (hopes)* acabar con. **2** *(hole, well)* cavar; *(post, knife, teeth)* hincar. **II** *vi* **1** *(ship)* hundirse. **2** *fig* **my heart sank,** se me cayó el alma a los pies. **3** *(sun)* ponerse. **4** **to s. to one's knees,** hincarse de rodillas. ◆**sink in** *vi (penetrate)* penetrar; *fig* **it hasn't sunk in yet,** todavía no me he/se ha *etc* hecho a la idea.

sinner ['sɪnər] *n* pecador,-a *m,f*.

sinus ['saɪnəs] *n* seno *m*.

sip [sɪp] **I** *n* sorbo *m*. **II** *vtr* sorber, beber a sorbos.

siphon ['saɪfən] *n* sifón *m*. ◆**siphon off** *vtr (liquid)* sacar con sifón; *fig (funds,*

traffic) desviar.

sir [sɜːr] *n fml* **1** señor *m*; **yes, s.,** sí, señor. **2** *(title)* sir; **S. Walter Raleigh,** Sir Walter Raleigh.

siren ['saɪərən] *n* sirena *f*.

sirloin ['sɜːlɔɪn] *n* solomillo *m*.

sissy ['sɪsɪ] *n fam (coward)* miedica *mf*.

sister ['sɪstər] *n* **1** *(relation)* hermana *f*. **2** *GB Med* enfermera *f* jefe. **3** *Rel* hermana *f*; *(before name)* sor.

sister-in-law ['sɪstərɪnlɔː] *n* cuñada *f*.

sit [sɪt] **I** *vtr (pt & pp* **sat) 1** *(child etc)* sentar *(in, on,* en*)*. **2** *GB (exam)* presentarse a. **II** *vi* **1** *(action)* sentarse. **2** *(be seated)* estar sentado,-a. **3** *(object)* estar; *(be situated)* hallarse; *(person)* quedarse. **4** *(assembly)* reunirse. ◆**sit back** *vi* recostarse. ◆**sit down** *vi* sentarse. ◆**sit in on** *vtr* asistir sin participar a. ◆**sit out** *vtr* aguantar hasta el final. ◆**sit through** *vtr* aguantar. ◆**sit up** *vi* **1** incorporarse. **2** *(stay up late)* quedarse levantado,-a.

site [saɪt] **I** *n* **1** *(area)* lugar *m*; **building s.,** solar *m*; *(under construction)* obra *f*. **2** *(location)* situación *f*; **nuclear testing s.,** zona *f* de pruebas nucleares. **II** *vtr* situar.

sit-in ['sɪtɪn] *n fam (demonstration)* sentada *f*; *(strike)* huelga *f* de brazos caídos.

sitting ['sɪtɪŋ] *n (of committee)* sesión *f*; *(in canteen)* turno *m*. **II** *adj* **s. room,** sala *f* de estar.

situated ['sɪtjʊeɪtɪd] *adj* situado,-a, ubicado,-a.

situation [sɪtjʊ'eɪʃən] *n* **1** situación *f*. **2** *(job)* puesto *m*; *GB* **'situations vacant',** *(in newspaper)* 'ofertas de trabajo'.

six [sɪks] *adj & n* seis *m inv*.

sixteen [sɪks'tiːn] *adj & n* dieciséis *m inv*, diez y seis *m inv*.

sixteenth [sɪks'tiːnθ] **I** *adj & n* decimosexto,-a *(m,f)*. **II** *n (fraction)* dieciseisavo *m*.

sixth [sɪksθ] **I** *adj & n* sexto,-a; *GB Educ* **s. form,** ≈ COU; **s. former,** ≈ estudiante de COU. **II** *n* **1** *(in series)* sexto,-a *m,f*. **2** *(fraction)* sexto *m*, sexta parte *f*.

sixty ['sɪkstɪ] *adj & n* sesenta *m inv*.

size [saɪz] *n (in general)* tamaño *m*; *(of garment)* talla *f*; *(of shoes)* número *m*; *(of person)* estatura *f*; *(scope)* alcance *m*; **what s. do you take?,** *(garment)* ¿qué talla tienes?; *(shoes)* ¿qué número calzas? ◆**size up** *vtr (person)* juzgar; *(situation, problem)* evaluar.

sizeable ['saɪzəbəl] *adj (building etc)* *(bastante)* grande; *(sum)* considerable; *(problem)* importante.

sizzle ['sɪzəl] *vi* chisporrotear.

skate¹ [skeɪt] **I** *n* patín *m*. **II** *vtr* patinar.

skate² [skeɪt] *n (fish)* raya *f*.

skateboard ['skeɪtbɔːd] *n* monopatín *m*.

skater ['skeɪtər] *n* patinador,-a *m,f*.

skating ['skeɪtɪŋ] *n* patinaje *m*; **s. rink,**

pista f de patinaje.

skeleton ['skelɪtən] I n 1 esqueleto m. 2 (of building) armazón m. 3 (outline) esquema m. II adj (staff, service) reducido,-a; **s. key**, llave maestra.

skeptic ['skeptɪk] n US → **sceptic**.

sketch [sketʃ] I n 1 (preliminary drawing) bosquejo m, esbozo m; (drawing) dibujo m; (outline) esquema m; (rough draft) boceto m. 2 Theat TV sketch m. II vtr (draw) dibujar; (preliminary drawing) bosquejar, esbozar.

sketch-book ['sketʃbʊk], **sketch-pad** ['sketʃpæd] n bloc m de dibujo.

sketchy ['sketʃɪ] adj (**sketchier**, **sketchiest**) (incomplete) incompleto,-a; (not detailed) vago,-a.

skewer ['skjʊər] n pincho m, broqueta f.

ski [ski:] I n esquí m. II adj de esquí; **s. boots**, botas fpl de esquiar; **s. jump**, (action) salto m con esquís; **s. lift**, telesquí m; (with seats) telesilla f; **s. pants**, pantalón m sing de esquiar; **s. resort**, estación f de esquí; **s. stick or pole**, bastón m de esquiar. III vi esquiar; **to go skiing**, ir a esquiar.

skid [skɪd] I n patinazo m. II vi patinar.

skier ['ski:ər] n esquiador,-a m,f.

skiing ['ski:ɪŋ] n esquí m.

skilful, US **skillful** ['skɪlfʊl] adj hábil, diestro,-a.

skill [skɪl] n 1 (ability) habilidad f, destreza f; (talent) don m. 2 (technique) técnica f.

skilled [skɪld] adj 1 (dextrous) hábil, diestro,-a; (expert) experto,-a. 2 (worker) cualificado,-a.

skim [skɪm] I vtr 1 (milk) desnatar; **skimmed milk**, leche desnatada. 2 (brush against) rozar; **to s. the ground**, (bird, plane) volar a ras de suelo. II vi fig **to s. through a book**, hojear un libro.

skimp [skɪmp] vtr & vi (food, material) escatimar; (work) chapucear.

skimpy ['skɪmpɪ] adj (**skimpier**, **skimpiest**) (shorts) muy corto,-a; (meal) escaso,-a.

skin [skɪn] I n 1 piel f. (of face) cutis m; (complexion) tez f; **s. cream**, crema f de belleza. 2 (of fruit) piel f; (of lemon) cáscara f; (peeling) mondadura f. 3 (of sausage) pellejo m. 4 (on milk etc) nata f. II vtr 1 (animal) despellejar. 2 (graze) arañar.

skin-deep [skɪn'di:p] adj superficial.

skin-diving ['skɪndaɪvɪŋ] n buceo m, submarinismo m.

skinhead ['skɪnhed] n fam cabeza mf rapada.

skinny ['skɪnɪ] adj (**skinnier**, **skinniest**) fam flaco,-a.

skin-tight ['skɪntaɪt] adj (clothing) muy ajustado,-a.

skip[1] [skɪp] I n (jump) salto m, brinco m.

II vi (jump) saltar, brincar; (with rope) saltar a la comba; fig **to s. over sth**, saltarse algo. III vtr fig saltarse.

skip[2] [skɪp] n (container) contenedor m.

skipper ['skɪpər] n Naut Sport fam capitán,-ana m,f.

skipping ['skɪpɪŋ] n comba f; **s. rope**, comba f.

skirmish ['skɜ:mɪʃ] n escaramuza f.

skirt [skɜ:t] I n falda f. II vtr (town etc) rodear; (coast) bordear; fig (problem) esquivar.

skirting ['skɜ:tɪŋ] GB n s. (**board**), zócalo m.

skit [skɪt] n sátira f, parodia f.

skittle ['skɪtəl] n 1 (pin) bolo m. 2 **skittles**, (game) (juego m de los) bolos mpl, boliche m.

skive [skaɪv] vi GB fam escaquearse.

skulk [skʌlk] vi (hide) esconderse; (prowl) merodear; (lie in wait) estar al acecho.

skull [skʌl] n Anat cráneo m; fam calavera f.

skunk [skʌŋk] n mofeta f.

sky [skaɪ] n cielo m; **s. blue**, azul m celeste.

skylight ['skaɪlaɪt] n tragaluz m, claraboya f.

skyline ['skaɪlaɪn] n (of city) perfil m.

skyscraper ['skaɪskreɪpər] n rascacielos m inv.

slab [slæb] n (of stone) losa f; (of chocolate) tableta f; (of cake) trozo m.

slack [slæk] I adj 1 (not taut) flojo,-a. 2 (lax) descuidado,-a; (lazy) vago,-a. 3 (market) flojo,-a; **business is s.**, hay poco negocio. II n (in rope) parte floja.

slacken ['slækən] I vtr 1 (rope) aflojar. 2 (speed) reducir. II vi 1 (rope) aflojarse; (wind) amainar. 2 (trade) aflojar.
◆**slacken off** vi disminuir.

slacks [slæks] npl dated pantalones mpl, pantalón m.

slag [slæg] n 1 Min escoria f; **s. heap**, escorial m. 2 GB sl (woman) puta f.
◆**slag off** vtr GB poner verde a.

slain [sleɪn] npl the **s.**, los caídos.

slam [slæm] I n (of door) portazo m. II vtr (bang) cerrar de golpe; to **s. sth down on the table**, soltar algo sobre la mesa de un palmetazo; to **s. the door**, dar un portazo; to **s. on the brakes**, dar un frenazo. III vi (door) cerrarse de golpe.

slander ['slɑ:ndər] I n difamación f, calumnia f. II vtr difamar, calumniar.

slang [slæŋ] n argot m, jerga f.

slant [slɑ:nt] I n 1 inclinación f; (slope) pendiente f. 2 fig (point of view) punto m de vista. II vtr fig (problem etc) enfocar subjetivamente. III vi inclinarse.

slanting ['slɑ:ntɪŋ] adj inclinado,-a.

slap [slæp] I n palmada f; (in face) bofetada f. II adv fam **he ran s. into the fence**, se dio de lleno contra la valla; **s. in the**

middle of ...], justo en medio de III
vtr pegar con la mano; *(hit in face)* dar
una bofetada a; **to s. sb on the back,** dar
a algn una palmada en la espalda.

slapdash ['slæp'dæʃ] *adj fam*
descuidado,-a; *(work)* chapucero,-a.

slapstick ['slæpstɪk] *n* bufonadas *fpl*, payasadas *fpl*.

slap-up ['slæpʌp] *adj fam* **s.-up meal,**
comilona *f*.

slash [slæʃ] I *n Typ fam* barra oblicua. II
vtr 1 *(with knife)* acuchillar; *(with sword)*
dar un tajo a. 2 *fig (prices)* rebajar.

slat [slæt] *n* tablilla *f*, listón *m*.

slate [sleɪt] I *n* pizarra *f*; *fig* **to wipe the
s. clean,** hacer borrón y cuenta nueva. II
vtr GB fam criticar duramente.

slaughter ['slɔːtər] I *n (of animals)* matanza *f*; *(of people)* carnicería *f*. II *vtr
(animals)* matar; *(people)* matar bru-
talmente; *(in large numbers)* masacrar.

slaughterhouse ['slɔːtəhaʊs] *n* matadero
m.

Slav [slɑːv] *adj & n* eslavo,-a *(m,f)*.

slave [sleɪv] I *n* esclavo,-a *m,f*; **s. trade,**
trata *f* de esclavos. II *vi* **to s. (away),** dar
el callo.

slavery ['sleɪvərɪ] *n* esclavitud *f*.

Slavonic [slə'vɒnɪk] *adj* eslavo,-a.

slay [sleɪ] *vtr (pt slew; pp slain)* matar.

sleazy ['sliːzɪ] *adj* **(sleazier, sleaziest)**
sórdido,-a.

sled [sled] I *n US* trineo *m*. II *vi* ir en trineo.

sledge [sledʒ] *n GB* trineo *m*.

sledgehammer ['sledʒhæmər] *n* almáde-
na *f*.

sleek [sliːk] *adj (hair)* lustroso,-a; *(appearance)* impecable.

sleep [sliːp] I *n* sueño *m*. II *vi* 1 dormir;
to go to s., dormirse; *fig* **to send to s.,**
(hacer) dormir; *fam* **to s. like a log,**
dormir como un lirón. 2 **my foot has
gone to s.,** se me ha dormido el pie.
◆**sleep in** *vi GB (oversleep)* quedarse
dormido,-a; *(have a lie-in)* quedarse en la
cama. ◆**sleep with** *vtr fam* **to s. with
sb,** acostarse con algn.

sleeper ['sliːpər] *n* 1 *(person)* durmiente
mf; **to be a heavy s.,** tener el sueño pesado. 2 *GB Rail (on track)* traviesa *f*. 3
Rail (coach) coche-cama *m*; *(berth)* litera
f.

sleeping ['sliːpɪŋ] *adj* **s. bag,** saco *m* de
dormir; **S. Beauty,** la Bella durmiente; **s.
car,** coche-cama *m*; *GB Com* **s. partner,**
socio,-a *m,f* comanditario,-a; **s. pill,**
somnífero *m*.

sleepless ['sliːplɪs] *adj* **to have a s. night,**
pasar la noche en blanco.

sleepwalker ['sliːpwɔːkər] *n* sonámbulo,
-a *m,f*.

sleepy ['sliːpɪ] *adj* **(sleepier, sleepiest)**
soñoliento,-a; **to be** *or* **feel s.,** tener sue-

ño.

sleet [sliːt] I *n* aguanieve *f*. II *vi* it's
sleeting, cae aguanieve.

sleeve [sliːv] *n (of garment)* manga *f*; *(of
record)* funda *f*.

sleigh [sleɪ] *n* trineo *m*; **s. bell,** cascabel
m.

sleight [slaɪt] *n* **s. of hand,** juego *m* de
manos.

slender ['slendər] *adj* 1 *(thin)* delgado,-a.
2 *fig (hope, chance)* remoto.

slept [slept] *pt & pp* → **sleep.**

slew [sluː] *pt* → **slay.**

slice [slaɪs] I *n* 1 *(of bread)* rebanada *f*; *(of
ham)* loncha *f*; *(of beef etc)* tajada *f*; *(of
lemon etc)* rodaja *f*; *(of cake)* trozo *m*. 2
(utensil) pala *f*. II *vtr (food)* cortar a re-
banadas *or* tajos *or* rodajas; *(divide)*
partir.

slick [slɪk] I *adj* 1 *(programme, show)*
logrado,-a. 2 *(skilful)* hábil, mañoso,-a. II
n (oil) **s.,** marea negra.

slide [slaɪd] I *n* 1 *(act)* resbalón *m*. 2 *(in
prices etc)* baja *f*. 3 *(in playground)* tobogán *m*. 4 *Phot* diapositiva *f*; **s. projector,**
proyector *m* de diapositivas. 5 **s. rule,** regla *f* de cálculo. 6 *GB (for hair)* pasador
m. II *vtr (pt & pp slid)* deslizar;
(furniture) correr. III *vi (on purpose)* deslizarse; *(slip)* resbalar.

sliding ['slaɪdɪŋ] *adj (door, window)*
corredizo,-a; *Fin* **s. scale,** escala *f* móvil.

slight [slaɪt] I *adj* 1 *(small)* pequeño,-a;
not in the slightest, en absoluto. 2
(build) menudo,-a; *(slim)* delgado,-a;
(frail) delicado,-a. 3 *(trivial)* leve. II *n
(affront)* desaire *m*. III *vtr* 1 *(scorn)* despreciar. 2 *(snub)* desairar. ◆**slightly** *adv
(a little)* ligeramente, algo.

slim [slɪm] I *adj* **(slimmer, slimmest)** 1
(person) delgado,-a. 2 *fig (resources)*
escaso,-a; *(hope, chance)* remoto,-a. II *vi*
adelgazar.

slime [slaɪm] *n (mud)* lodo *m*, cieno *m*; *(of
snail)* baba *f*.

slimming ['slɪmɪŋ] I *adj (diet, pills)* para
adelgazar; *(food)* que no engorda. II *n
(process)* adelgazamiento *m*.

slimy ['slaɪmɪ] *adj* **(slimier, slimiest)**
(muddy) lodoso,-a; *(snail)* baboso,-a. 2 *fig
(person)* zalamero,-a.

sling [slɪŋ] I *n* 1 *(catapult)* honda *f*;
(child's) tirador *m*. 2 *Med* cabestrillo *m*. II
vtr (pt & pp slung) (throw) tirar.

slink [slɪŋk] *vi (pt & pp slunk)* **to s. off,**
escabullirse.

slip [slɪp] I *n* 1 *(slide)* resbalón *m*; *fam fig*
to give sb the s., dar esquinazo a algn. 2
(mistake) error *m*; *(moral)* desliz *m*; **a s.
of the tongue,** un lapsus linguae. 3
(underskirt) combinación *f*. 4 *(of paper)*
trocito *m*. II *n (slide)* resbalar. 2 *Med*
dislocarse; **slipped disc,** vértebra disloca-
da. 3 *(move quickly)* ir de prisa. 4

(standards etc) deteriorarse. **III** *vtr* **1** *(slide)* dar a escondidas. **2 it slipped my memory,** se me fue de la cabeza. ◆**slip away** *vi (person)* escabullirse. ◆**slip off** *vtr (clothes)* quitarse rápidamente. ◆**slip on** *vtr (clothes)* ponerse rápidamente. ◆**slip out** *vi* **1** *(leave)* salir. **2** *fig* **the secret slipped out,** se le escapó el secreto. ◆**slip up** *vi fam (blunder)* cometer un desliz.

slipper ['slɪpəʳ] *n* zapatilla *f*.

slippery ['slɪpərɪ] *adj* resbaladizo,-a.

slip-road ['slɪprəʊd] *n GB* vía *f* de acceso.

slipshod ['slɪpʃɒd] *adj* descuidado,-a; *(work)* chapucero,-a.

slip-up ['slɪpʌp] *n fam (blunder)* desliz *m*.

slipway ['slɪpweɪ] *n* grada *f*.

slit [slɪt] **I** *n (opening)* hendidura *f*; *(cut)* corte *m*, raja *f*. **II** *vtr (pt & pp slit)* cortar, rajar.

slither ['slɪðəʳ] *vi* deslizarse.

sliver ['slɪvəʳ] *n (of wood, glass)* astilla *f*; *(of ham)* loncha *f*.

slob [slɒb] *n fam* dejado,-a *m,f*.

slog [slɒg] **I** *n fam* **it was a hard s.,** costó un montón. **II** *vi* **1** *fam* **to s. away,** currar tinta. **2** *(walk)* caminar trabajosamente. **III** *vtr (hit)* golpear fuerte.

slogan ['sləʊgən] *n* eslogan *m*, lema *m*.

slop [slɒp] **I** *vi* **to s. (over),** derramarse; **to s. about,** chapotear. **II** *vtr* derramar.

slope [sləʊp] **I** *n (incline)* cuesta *f*, pendiente *f*; *(up)* subida *f*; *(down)* bajada *f*; *(of mountain)* ladera *f*; *(of roof)* vertiente *f*. **II** *vi* inclinarse; **to s. up/ down,** subir/bajar en pendiente. ◆**slope off** *vi fam* largarse.

sloping ['sləʊpɪŋ] *adj* inclinado,-a.

sloppy ['slɒpɪ] *adj (sloppier, sloppiest)* *fam* descuidado,-a; *(work)* chapucero,-a; *(appearance)* desaliñado,-a.

slot [slɒt] **I** *n* **1** *(for coin)* ranura *f*; *(opening)* rendija *f*; **s. machine,** *(for gambling)* (máquina *f*) tragaperras *f inv*; *(vending machine)* distribuidor automático. **2** *Rad TV* espacio *m*. **II** *vtr (place)* meter; *(put in)* introducir. **III** *vi* **to s. in** or **together,** encajar.

sloth [sləʊθ] *n fml (laziness)* pereza *f*.

slouch [slaʊtʃ] *vi* andar or sentarse con los hombros caídos.

slovenly ['slʌvənlɪ] *adj* descuidado,-a; *(appearance)* desaliñado,-a; *(work)* chapucero,-a.

slow [sləʊ] **I** *adj* lento,-a; **in s. motion,** a cámara lenta; **to be s. to do sth,** tardar en hacer algo. **2** *(clock)* atrasado,-a. **3** *(stupid)* lento,-a, torpe. **II** *adv* despacio, lentamente. **III** *vtr (car)* reducir la marcha de; *(progress)* retrasar. **IV** *vi* **to s. down** or **up,** ir más despacio; *(in car)* reducir la velocidad. ◆**slowly** *adv* despacio, lentamente.

sludge [slʌdʒ] *n (mud)* fango *m*, lodo *m*.

slug [slʌg] **I** *n* **1** *Zool* babosa *f*. **2** *US fam (bullet)* posta *f*. **3** *fam (blow)* porrazo *m*. **II** *vtr fam (hit)* aporrear.

sluggish ['slʌgɪʃ] *adj* **1** *(river, engine)* lento,-a; *Com* flojo,-a. **2** *(lazy)* perezoso,-a.

sluice [sluːs] *n (waterway)* canal *m*.

sluicegate ['sluːsgeɪt] *n* esclusa *f*.

slum [slʌm] *n (usu pl)* barrios bajos.

slumber ['slʌmbəʳ] *fml* **I** *n (sleep)* sueño *m*. **II** *vi* dormir.

slump [slʌmp] **I** *n* **1** *(drop in sales etc)* bajón *m*. **2** *(economic depression)* crisis económica. **II** *vi* **1** *(sales etc)* caer de repente; *(prices)* desplomarse; *(the economy)* hundirse; *fig (morale)* hundirse. **2** *(fall)* caer.

slung [slʌŋ] *pt & pp* → **sling**.

slur [slɜːʳ] **I** *n (stigma)* mancha *f*; *(slanderous remark)* calumnia *f*. **II** *vtr (word)* tragarse.

slush [slʌʃ] *n* **1** *(melting snow)* nieve medio fundida. **2** *fam* sentimentalismo *m*. **3** *US fam* **s. fund,** fondos *mpl* para sobornos.

slut [slʌt] *n offens* **1** *(untidy woman)* marrana *f*. **2** *(whore)* fulana *f*.

sly [slaɪ] *adj (slyer, slyest* or *slier, sliest)* **1** *(cunning)* astuto,-a. **2** *(secretive)* furtivo,-a. **3** *(mischievous)* travieso,-a. **4** *(underhand)* malicioso,-a.

smack¹ [smæk] **I** *n* **1** *(slap)* bofetada *f*. **2** *(sharp sound)* ruido sonoro. **II** *vtr* **1** *(slap)* dar una bofetada a. **2** *(hit)* golpear; *fig* **to s. one's lips,** relamerse.

smack² [smæk] *vi fig* **to s. of,** oler a.

small [smɔːl] **I** *adj* **1** pequeño,-a; **a s. table,** una mesita; **in s. letters,** en minúsculas; **in the s. hours,** a altas horas de la noche; **s. ads,** anuncios *mpl* por palabras; *fig* **s. print,** letra pequeña. **2** *(in height)* bajo,-a. **3** *(scant)* escaso,-a; **s. change,** cambio *m*, suelto *m*. **4** *(minor)* insignificante; **s. businessmen,** pequeños comerciantes; **s. talk,** charloteo *m*. **5** *(increase)* ligero,-a. **II** *n* **1 s. of the back,** región *f* lumbar. **2** *GB fam* **smalls,** *(underwear)* paños *mpl* menores.

smallholder ['smɔːlhəʊldəʳ] *n* minifundista *mf*.

smallpox ['smɔːlpɒks] *n* viruela *f*.

smarmy ['smɑːmɪ] *adj (smarmier, smarmiest)* *fam* cobista, zalamero,-a.

smart [smɑːt] **I** *adj* **1** *(elegant)* elegante. **2** *(clever)* listo,-a; inteligente; *fam* **s. alec(k),** listillo. **3** *(quick)* rápido,-a; *(pace)* ligero,-a. **II** *vi* **1** *(sting)* picar, escocer. **2** *fig* sufrir.

smarten ['smɑːtən] **I** *vtr* **to s. (up),** arreglar. **II** *vi* **to s. oneself (up),** arreglarse.

smash [smæʃ] **I** *n* **1** *(loud noise)* estrépito *m*; *(collision)* choque violento. **2** *Ten* smash *m*. **II** *vtr* **1** *(break)* romper; *(shatter)* hacer pedazos; (crush) aplastar. 2 (destroy) destrozar; (defeat) aplastar. 3 (record) fulminar. III vi (break) romperse; (shatter) hacerse pedazos; (crash) estrellarse; Ten hacer un mate. ◆smash up vtr fam (car) hacer pedazos; (place) destrozar.

smashing ['smæʃɪŋ] adj GB fam estupendo,-a.

smattering ['smætərɪŋ] n he had a s. of French, hablaba un poquito de francés.

smear [smɪər] I n 1 (smudge) mancha f; (test), citología f. 2 fig (defamation) calumnia f. II vtr 1 (butter etc) untar; (grease) embadurnar. 2 (make dirty) manchar. 3 fig (defame) calumniar, difamar.

smell [smel] I n 1 (sense) olfato m. 2 (odour) olor m. II vtr & vi smelled or smelt) oler; fig olfatear. III vi oler (a); it smells good/like lavender, huele bien/a lavanda; he smelt of whisky, olía a whisky.

smelly ['smelɪ] adj (smellier, smelliest) fam maloliente, apestoso,-a.

smelt [smelt] vtr (ore) fundir.

smile [smaɪl] I n sonrisa f. II vi sonreír; to s. at sb, sonreír a algn; to s. at sth, reírse de algo.

smiling ['smaɪlɪŋ] adj sonriente, risueño,-a.

smirk [smɜːk] I n (conceited) sonrisa satisfecha; (foolish) sonrisa f boba. II vi (conceitedly) sonreír con satisfacción; (foolishly) sonreír bobamente.

smith [smɪθ] n herrero m.

smithy ['smɪðɪ] n herrería f.

smitten ['smɪtən] adj fam to be s. with sb, estar enamorado,-a de algn.

smock [smɒk] n (blouse) blusón m; (worn in pregnancy) blusón de premamá; (overall) bata f.

smog [smɒg] n niebla tóxica, smog m.

smoke [sməuk] I n humo m; s. bomb, bomba f de humo; s. screen, cortina f de humo. II vi fumar; (chimney etc) echar humo. III vtr 1 (tobacco) fumar; to s. a pipe, fumar en pipa. 2 (fish, meat) ahumar.

smoked [sməukt] adj ahumado,-a.

smokeless ['sməuklɪs] adj s. fuel, combustible sin humo; s. zone, zona libre de humos.

smoker ['sməukər] n 1 (person) fumador,-a m,f. 2 Rail vagón m de fumadores.

smoking ['sməukɪŋ] n 'no s.', 'prohibido fumar'.

smoky ['sməukɪ] adj (smokier, smokiest) 1 (chimney) humeante; (room) lleno,-a de humo; (atmosphere) cargado,-a de humo; (food) ahumado,-a. 2 (colour) ahumado,-a.

smolder ['sməuldər] vi US → smoulder.

smooth [smu:ð] I adj 1 (surface) liso,-a; (skin) suave; (road) llano,-a; (sea)

tranquilo,-a. 2 (beer, wine) suave. 3 (flowing) fluido,-a. 4 (flight) tranquilo,-a; (transition) sin problemas. 5 pej (slick) zalamero,-a. II vtr 1 (hair etc) alisar. 2 (plane down) limar. ◆smooth out vtr (creases) alisar; fig (difficulties) allanar; (problems) resolver. ◆smooth over vtr fig to s. things over, limar asperezas. ◆smoothly adv sobre ruedas.

smother ['smʌðər] vtr 1 (asphyxiate) asfixiar; (suffocate) sofocar. 2 fig (cover) cubrir (with, de).

smoulder ['sməuldər] vi (fire) arder sin llama; fig (passions) arder; smouldering hatred, odio latente.

smudge [smʌdʒ] I n (stain) mancha f; (of ink) borrón m. II vtr manchar; (piece of writing) emborronar.

smug [smʌg] adj (smugger, smuggest) engreído,-a.

smuggle ['smʌgəl] vtr pasar de contrabando.

smuggler ['smʌglər] n contrabandista mf.

smuggling ['smʌglɪŋ] n contrabando m.

smutty ['smʌtɪ] adj (smuttier, smuttiest) fam obsceno,-a; (joke) verde; (book, film etc) pornográfico,-a.

snack [snæk] n bocado m; s. bar, cafetería f.

snag [snæg] I n (difficulty) pega f, problemilla m. II vtr (clothing) enganchar.

snail [sneɪl] n caracol m.

snake [sneɪk] n (big) serpiente f; (small) culebra f.

snap [snæp] I n 1 (noise) ruido seco; (of branch, fingers) chasquido m. 2 (bite) mordisco m. 3 Phot (foto f) instantánea f. II adj (sudden) repentino,-a. III vtr 1 (branch etc) partir en dos. 2 (make noise) hacer un ruido seco; to s. one's fingers, chasquear los dedos; to s. sth shut, cerrar algo de golpe. 3 Phot sacar una foto de. IV vi 1 (break) romperse. 2 (whip) chasquear; to s. shut, cerrarse de golpe. 3 (dog) amenazar; fam to s. at sb, regañar a algn. ◆snap off vtr (branch etc) arrancar. II vi (branch etc) separarse. ◆snap up vtr fam to s. up a bargain, llevarse una ganga.

snappy ['snæpɪ] adj (snappier, snappiest) fam 1 (quick) rápido,-a; look s.!, make it s.!, ¡date prisa! 2 (stylish) elegante. 3 (short-tempered) irritable.

snapshot ['snæpʃɒt] n (foto f) instantánea f.

snare [sneər] I n trampa f. II vtr (animal) cazar con trampa; fig (person) hacer caer en la trampa.

snarl¹ [snɑːl] I n gruñido m. II vi gruñir.

snarl² [snɑːl] I n (in wool) maraña f. II vtr to s. (up), (wool) enmarañar; (traffic) atascar; (plans) enredar.

snatch [snætʃ] I n 1 fam (theft) robo m;

bag s., tirón *m*. **2** (*fragment*) fragmentos *mpl*. **II** *vtr* **1** (*grab*) arrebatar. **2** *fam* (*steal*) robar; (*kidnap*) secuestrar. **III** *vi* **1 to s. off**, escabullirse; **to s. in/out**, entrar/salir a hurtadillas. **2 to s. on sb**, (*tell tales*) chivarse de algn.

sneakers ['sni:kəz] *npl US* zapatillas *fpl* de deporte.

sneaky ['sni:kɪ] *adj* (**sneakier, sneakiest**) solapado,-a.

sneer [snɪə^r] *vi* **to s. at**, hacer un gesto de desprecio a.

sneeze [sni:z] **I** *n* estornudo *m*. **II** *vi* estornudar.

sniff [snɪf] **I** *n* (*by person*) aspiración *f*; (*by dog*) husmeo *m*. **II** *vtr* (*flower etc*) oler; (*suspiciously*) husmear; (*snuff etc*) aspirar; (*glue*) esnifar. **III** *vi* aspirar por la nariz.

snigger ['snɪgə^r] **I** *n* risa disimulada. **II** *vi* reír disimuladamente; **to s. at sth**, burlarse de algo.

snip [snɪp] **I** *n* **1** (*cut*) tijeretada *f*; (*small piece*) recorte *m*. **2** *GB fam* (*bargain*) ganga *f*. **II** *vtr* cortar a tijeretazos.

sniper ['snaɪpə^r] *n* francotirador,-a *m,f*.

snippet ['snɪpɪt] *n* (*of cloth, paper*) recorte *m*; (*of conversation*) fragmento *m*.

snivel ['snɪvəl] *vi* lloriquear.

snivelling ['snɪvəlɪŋ] *adj* llorón,-ona.

snob [snɒb] *n* (e)snob *mf*.

snobbery ['snɒbərɪ] *n* (e)snobismo *m*.

snobbish ['snɒbɪʃ] *adj* (e)snob.

snooker ['snu:kə^r] *n* snooker *m*, billar ruso.

snoop [snu:p] *vi* fisgar, fisgonear.

snooty ['snu:tɪ] *adj* (**snootier, snootiest**) *fam* (e)snob.

snooze [snu:z] *fam* **I** *n* cabezada *f*. **II** *vi* echar una cabezada.

snore [snɔ:^r] **I** *n* ronquido *m*. **II** *vi* roncar.

snoring ['snɔ:rɪŋ] *n* ronquidos *mpl*.

snorkel ['snɔ:kəl] *n* (*of swimmer*) tubo *m* de respiración; (*of submarine*) esnórquel *m*.

snort [snɔ:t] **I** *n* resoplido *m*. **II** *vi* resoplar.

snout [snaʊt] *n* (*of animal, gun etc*) morro *m*.

snow [snəʊ] **I** *n* nieve *f*; **s. shower**, nevada *f*. **II** *vi* nevar; **it's snowing**, está nevando. **III** *vtr fig* **to be snowed under with work**, estar agobiado,-a de trabajo.

snowball ['snəʊbɔ:l] **I** *n* bola *f* de nieve. **II** *vi fig* aumentar rápidamente.

snowbound ['snəʊbaʊnd] *adj* aislado,-a por la nieve.

snowdrift ['snəʊdrɪft] *n* ventisquero *m*.

snowdrop ['snəʊdrɒp] *n* campanilla *f* de invierno.

snowfall ['snəʊfɔ:l] *n* nevada *f*.

snowflake ['snəʊfleɪk] *n* copo *m* de nieve.

snowman, ['snəʊmæn] *n* hombre *m* de nieve.

snowplough, *US* **snowplow** ['snəʊplaʊ] *n* quitanieves *m inv*.

snowshoe ['snəʊʃu:] *n* raqueta *f* (de nieve).

snowstorm ['snəʊstɔ:m] *n* nevasca *f*.

snowy ['snəʊɪ] *adj* (**snowier, snowiest**) (*mountain*) nevado,-a; (*climate*) nevoso,-a; (*day*) de nieve.

Snr, snr *esp US abbr of* **senior**.

snub [snʌb] **I** *n* (*of person*) desaire *m*; (*of offer*) rechazo *m*. **II** *vtr* (*person*) desairar; (*offer*) rechazar.

snub-nosed ['snʌbnəʊzd] *adj* de nariz respingona.

snuff [snʌf] *n* rapé *m*.

snug [snʌg] *adj* (**snugger, snuggest**) **1** (*cosy*) cómodo,-a. **2** (*tightfitting*) ajustado, -a. ◆**snugly** *adv* **to fit s.**, (*clothes*) quedar ajustado,-a; (*object in box etc*) encajar.

snuggle ['snʌgəl] *vi* **to s. down in bed**, acurrucarse en la cama; **to s. up to sb**, arrimarse a algn.

so [səʊ] **I** *adv* **1** (*to such an extent*) tanto; **he was so tired that ...**, estaba tan cansado que ...; **it's so long since ...**, hace tanto tiempo que ...; **he isn't so nice as his sister**, no es tan agradable como su hermana; *fam* **so long!**, ¡hasta luego! **2** (*degree*) tanto; **a week or so**, una semana más o menos; **twenty or so**, una veintena; **we loved her so (much)**, la queríamos tanto; **so many books**, tantos libros; *fam* **he's ever so handsome!**, ¡es tan guapo!; *iron* **so much for that**, ¿qué le vamos a hacer? **3** (*thus, in this way*) así, de esta manera; **and so on, and so forth**, y así sucesivamente; **if so**, en este caso; **I think/hope so**, creo/espero que sí; **I told you so**, ya te lo dije; **it so happens that ...**, da la casualidad de que ...; **so be it!**, ¡así sea!; **so far**, hasta ahora *or* allí; **so it seems**, eso parece; **so they say**, eso dicen; **you're late!** — **so I am!**, ¡llegas tarde! — ¡tienes razón! **4** (*also*) **I'm going to Spain** — **so am I**, voy a España - yo también.

II *conj* **1** (*expresses result*) así que; **you like England, do you?**, ¿así que te gusta Inglaterra, pues?; *fam* **so what?**, ¿y qué? **2** (*expresses purpose*) para que; **I'll put the key here so (that) everyone can see it**, pongo la llave aquí para que todos la vean.

so-and-so ['səʊənsəʊ] *n fam* **Mr So-and-so**, Don Fulano de tal; *pej* **an old so-and-so**, un viejo imbécil.

soak [səʊk] **I** *vtr* (*washing, food*) remojar; (*cotton, wool*) empapar (**in**, en). **II** *vi* (*washing, food*) estar en remojo. ◆**soak in** *vi* penetrar. ◆**soak up** *vtr* absorber.

soaking ['səʊkɪŋ] *adj* (*object*) empapado,

-a; (person) calado,-a hasta los huesos.

soap [soup] **I** n 1 jabón m; **s. flakes**, jabón en escamas; **s. powder**, jabón en polvo. 2 TV **s. opera**, culebrón m. **II** vtr enjabonar.

soapy ['soupɪ] adj (soapier, soapiest) jabonoso,-a; (hands) cubierto,-a de jabón.

soar [sɔːr] vi (bird, plane) remontar el vuelo; fig (skyscraper) elevarse; (hopes, prices) aumentar.

sob [sɒb] **I** n sollozo m. **II** vi sollozar.

sober ['soubər] adj (not drunk, moderate) sobrio,-a; (sensible) sensato,-a; (serious) serio,-a; (colour) discreto,-a. ◆**sober up** vi **he sobered up**, se le pasó la borrachera.

so-called ['souˈkɔːld] adj supuesto,-a, llamado,-a.

soccer ['sɒkər] n fútbol m.

sociable ['soufəbəl] adj (gregarious) sociable; (friendly) amistoso,-a.

social ['soufəl] adj social; **s. class**, clase f social; **s. climber**, arribista mf; **S. Democratic**, socialdemócrata; US **s. insurance**, seguro m social; **s. security**, seguridad f social; **the s. services**, los servicios sociales; **s. welfare**, seguro social; **s. work**, asistencia f social; **s. worker**, asistente,-a m,f social. ◆**socially** adv socialmente.

socialist ['soufəlɪst] adj & n socialista (mf).

socialite ['soufəlaɪt] n vividor,-a m,f.

socialize ['soufəlaɪz] **I** vi alternar, mezclarse con la gente. **II** vtr socializar.

society [səˈsaɪətɪ] n 1 sociedad f; **the consumer s.**, la sociedad de consumo; **(high) s.**, la alta sociedad. 2 (club) asociación f. 3 (companionship) compañía f. **II** adj de sociedad; **s. column**, ecos mpl de sociedad.

sociologist [səʊsɪˈɒlədʒɪst] n sociólogo,-a m,f.

sociology [səʊsɪˈɒlədʒɪ] n sociología f.

sock [sɒk] n calcetín m.

socket ['sɒkɪt] n 1 (of eye) cuenca f. 2 Elec enchufe m.

sod¹ [sɒd] n fml (piece of turf) terrón m.

sod² [sɒd] vulg **I** n 1 offens (bastard) cabrón,-ona m,f; **the lazy s.!**, ¡qué tío más vago! 2 (wretch) desgraciado,-a m,f; **the poor s.**, el pobrecito. 3 vulg **I've done s. all today**, hoy no he pegado ni golpe. **II** vtr **s. it!**, ¡maldita sea!

soda ['soudə] n 1 Chem sosa f; **baking s.**, bicarbonato sódico. 2 **s. water**, soda f. 3 US (fizzy drink) gaseosa f.

sodden ['sɒdən] adj empapado,-a.

sodium ['soudɪəm] n sodio m.

sofa ['soufə] n sofá m; **s. bed**, sofá cama.

soft [sɒft] adj 1 (not hard) blando,-a; **s. toy**, muñeco m de peluche. 2 (skin, colour, hair, light, music) suave; (breeze, steps) ligero,-a. 3 (lenient) permisivo,-a. 4

(voice) bajo,-a. 5 (foolish) lelo,-a; **s. touch**, ser fácil de engañar. 6 **to have a s. spot for sb**, tener debilidad por algn. 7 (easy) fácil; **s. job**, chollo m. 8 (drink) no alcohólico,-a; **s. drinks**, refrescos mpl. 9 **s. drugs**, drogas blandas; **s. porn**, pornografía blanda. ◆**softly** adv (gently) suavemente; (quietly) silenciosamente.

soften ['sɒfən] **I** vtr (leather, heart) ablandar; (skin) suavizar; fig (blow) amortiguar. **II** vi (leather, heart) ablandarse; (skin) suavizarse.

softness ['sɒftnɪs] n 1 blandura f. 2 (of hair, skin) suavidad f. 3 (foolishness) estupidez f.

software ['sɒftweər] n Comput software m; **s. package**, paquete m.

soggy ['sɒgɪ] adj (soggier, soggiest) empapado,-a; (bread) pastoso,-a.

soil [sɔɪl] **I** n (earth) tierra f. **II** vtr (dirty) ensuciar; fig (reputation) manchar.

soiled [sɔɪld] adj sucio,-a.

solace ['sɒlɪs] n fml consuelo m.

solar ['soulər] adj solar.

sold [sould] pt & pp → sell.

solder ['sɒldər] **I** n soldadura f. **II** vtr soldar.

soldier ['souldʒər] n soldado m; (military man) militar m; **toy s.**, soldadito m de plomo. ◆**soldier on** vi fig continuar contra viento y marea.

sole¹ [soul] n (of foot) planta f; (of shoe, sock) suela f.

sole² [soul] n (fish) lenguado m.

sole³ [soul] adj (only) único,-a.

solemn ['sɒləm] adj solemne.

solicit [səˈlɪsɪt] **I** vtr (request) solicitar. **II** vi (prostitute) abordar a los clientes.

solicitor [səˈlɪsɪtər] n abogado,-a m,f; (for wills) notario,-a m,f.

solid ['sɒlɪd] **I** adj 1 (not liquid) sólido,-a; (firm) firme. 2 (not hollow, pure) (metal) macizo,-a. 3 (fog etc) espeso,-a; (of strong material) resistente; **a man of s. build**, un hombre fornido. 4 (reliable) formal. 5 (unanimous) unánime. **II** n sólido m. ◆**solidly** adv sólidamente; **s. built**, (house etc) de construcción sólida; **to work s.**, trabajar sin descanso.

solidarity [sɒlɪˈdærɪtɪ] n solidaridad f.

solidify [səˈlɪdɪfaɪ] vi solidificarse.

soliloquy [səˈlɪləkwɪ] n soliloquio m.

solitaire ['sɒlɪteər] n solitario m.

solitary ['sɒlɪtərɪ] adj 1 (alone) solitario, -a; (secluded) apartado,-a. 2 (only) solo,-a.

solitude ['sɒlɪtjuːd] n soledad f.

solo ['soulou] n solo m.

soloist ['soulouɪst] n solista mf.

solstice ['sɒlstɪs] n solsticio m.

solution [səˈluːʃən] n solución f.

solve [sɒlv] vtr resolver, solucionar.

solvent ['sɒlvənt] adj & n solvente (m).

sombre, US **somber** ['sɒmbər] adj (dark)

sombrío,-a; *(gloomy)* lúgubre; *(pessimistic)* pesimista.

some [SʌM] **I** *adj* **1** *(with plural nouns)* unos,-as, algunos,-as; *(several)* varios,-as; *(a few)* unos,-as cuantos,-as; **did she bring s. flowers?**, ¿trajo flores?; **there were s. roses**, había unas rosas; **s. more peas**, más guisantes **2** *(with singular nouns)* algún, alguna; *(a little)* un poco de; **if you need s. help**, si necesitas ayuda; **there's s. wine left**, queda un poco de vino; **would you like s. coffee?**, ¿quiere café? **3** *(certain)* cierto,-a, alguno,-a; **in s. ways**, en cierto modo; **to s. extent**, hasta cierto punto; **s. people say that ...**, algunas personas dicen que .... **4** *(unspecified)* algún, alguna; **for s. reason or other**, por una razón o por otra; **in s. book or other**, en algún libro que otro; **s. day**, algún día; **s. other time**, otro día. **5** *(quite a lot of)* bastante; **it's s. distance away**, queda bastante lejos; **s. years ago**, hace algunos años.
II *pron* **1** *(people)* algunos,-as, unos,-as; **s. go by bus and s. by train**, unos van en autobús y otros en tren. **2** *(objects)* algunos,-as; *(a few)* unos,-as cuantos,-as; *(a little)* algo, un poco; *(certain ones)* algunos,-as.
III *adv* **s. thirty cars**, unos treinta coches.

somebody ['sʌmbədɪ] *pron* alguien; **s. else**, otro,-a.

somehow ['sʌmhaʊ] *adv* **1** *(in some way)* de alguna forma. **2** *(for some reason)* por alguna razón.

someone ['sʌmwʌn] *pron & n* → **somebody**.

someplace ['sʌmpleɪs] *adv US* → **somewhere**.

somersault ['sʌməsɔːlt] **I** *n* *(by acrobat etc)* salto *m* mortal; *(by child)* voltereta *f*; *(by car)* vuelta *f* de campana. **II** *vi* *(acrobat etc)* dar un salto mortal; *(child)* dar volteretas; *(car)* dar una vuelta de campana.

something ['sʌmθɪŋ] *pron & n* algo; **s. to eat/drink**, algo de comer/beber; **are you drunk or s.?**, ¿estás borracho o qué?; **s. must be done**, hay que hacer algo; **she has a certain s.**, tiene un no sé qué; **is s. the matter?**, ¿le pasa algo?; **s. else**, otra cosa; **s. of the kind**, algo por el estilo.

sometime ['sʌmtaɪm] *adv* algún día; **s. last week**, un día de la semana pasada; **s. next year**, durante el año que viene.

sometimes ['sʌmtaɪmz] *adv* a veces, de vez en cuando.

somewhat ['sʌmwɒt] *adv fml* algo, un tanto.

somewhere ['sʌmweəʳ] *adv* **1** *(in some place)* en alguna parte; *(to some place)* a alguna parte; **s. else**, *(in some other place)* en otra parte; *(to some other place)* a otra

parte; **s. or other**, no sé dónde. **2 s. in the region of**, *(approximately)* más o menos.

son [sʌn] *n* hijo *m*; **eldest/youngest s.**, hijo mayor/menor.

song [sɒŋ] *n* canción *f*; *(of bird)* canto *m*.

songwriter ['sɒŋraɪtəʳ] *n* compositor,-a *m,f* *(de canciones)*.

sonic ['sɒnɪk] *adj* sónico,-a.

son-in-law ['sʌnɪnlɔː] *n* yerno *m*.

sonnet ['sɒnɪt] *n* soneto *m*.

sonny ['sʌnɪ] *n fam* hijo *m*, hijito *m*.

soon [suːn] *adv* **1** *(within a short time)* pronto, dentro de poco; *(quickly)* rápidamente; **see you s.!**, ¡hasta pronto!; **s. after midnight**, poco después de medianoche; **s. afterwards**, poco después. **2 as s. as I arrived**, en cuanto llegué; **as s. as possible**, cuanto antes. **3** *(early)* pronto; *fig* **don't speak too s.**, no cantes victoria. **4** *(preference)* **I would just as s. stay at home**, prefiero quedarme en casa. **5** *(indifference)* **I would** *(just)* **as s. read as watch TV**, tanto me da la leer como ver la tele.

sooner ['suːnəʳ] *adv* **1** *(earlier)* más temprano; **s. or later**, tarde o temprano; **the s. the better**, cuanto antes mejor. **2 no s. had he finished than he fainted**, *(immediately after)* nada más acabar se desmayó. **3 I would s. do it alone**, *(rather)* prefiero hacerlo yo solo.

soot [sʊt] *n* hollín *m*.

soothe [suːð] *vtr* *(calm)* tranquilizar; *(pain)* aliviar.

sop [sɒp] *n* **1** *fig* *(concession)* favor *m*; *(bribe)* soborno *m*. **2 sops**, *(food)* sopa *f sing*. ◆**sop up** *vtr* empapar.

sophisticated [sə'fɪstɪkeɪtɪd] *adj* sofisticado,-a.

soporific [sɒpə'rɪfɪk] *adj* soporífero,-a.

sopping ['sɒpɪŋ] *adj fam* **s. (wet)**, como una sopa.

soppy ['sɒpɪ] *adj* *(soppier, soppiest)* *fam* sentimentaloide.

soprano [sə'prɑːnəʊ] *n* soprano *mf*.

sorcerer ['sɔːsərəʳ] *n* brujo *m*.

sorceress ['sɔːsərɪs] *n* bruja *f*.

sordid ['sɔːdɪd] *adj* sórdido,-a.

sore [sɔːʳ] **I** *adj* **1** dolorido,-a; **to have a s. throat**, tener dolor de garganta. **2** *fam* *(angry)* enfadado,-a; **to feel s. about sth**, estar resentido,-a por algo. **II** *n* llaga *f*. ◆**sorely** *adv* *(very)* muy; *(a lot)* mucho; *(deeply)* profundamente.

sorrow ['sɒrəʊ] *n* pena *f*, dolor *m*.

sorrowful ['sɒrəʊfʊl] *adj* afligido,-a.

sorry ['sɒrɪ] **I** *adj* *(sorrier, sorriest)* **1** **I feel very s. for her**, me da mucha pena. **2** *(pitiful)* triste. **3 to be s.** *(about sth)*, sentir *(algo)*; **I'm s. I'm late**, siento llegar tarde. **II** *interj* **1** *(apology)* ¡perdón! **2** *GB* *(for repetition)* ¿cómo?

sort [sɔːt] **I** *n* **1** *(kind)* clase *f*, tipo *m*;

(brand) marca *f*; **it's a s.** of teapot, es una especie de tetera. **2 he is a musician of sorts,** tiene algo de músico; **there's an office of sorts,** hay una especie de despacho. **3 s. of,** en cierto modo. II *vtr (classify)* clasificar. ◆**sort out** *vtr* 1 *(classify)* clasificar; *(put in order)* ordenar. 2 *(problem)* arreglar, solucionar.

sorting ['sɔːtɪŋ] *n* **s. office,** sala *f* de batalla.

SOS [esəʊ'es] *abbr of* **save our souls,** S.O.S. *m*.

so-so ['səʊsəʊ] *adv fam* así así, regular.

soufflé ['suːfleɪ] *n* soufflé *m*, suflé *m*.

sought [sɔːt] *pt & pp* → **seek.**

soul [səʊl] *n* 1 alma *f*. **2 he's a good s.,** *(person)* es muy buena persona. 3 *Mus (música f)* soul *m*.

soul-destroying ['səʊldɪstrɔɪɪŋ] *adj (boring)* monótono,-a; *(demoralizing)* desmoralizador,-a.

soulful ['səʊlfʊl] *adj* conmovedor,-a.

sound¹ [saʊnd] I *n* sonido *m*; *(noise)* ruido *m*; *fig* **I don't like the s. of it,** no me gusta nada la idea; **s. barrier,** barrera *f* del sonido; **s. effects,** efectos sonoros. II *vtr (bell, trumpet)* tocar; **to s. the alarm,** dar la señal de alarma. III *vi* 1 *(trumpet, bell, alarm)* sonar. 2 *(give an impression)* parecer; **how does it to you?,** ¿qué te parece?; **it sounds interesting,** parece interesante.

sound² [saʊnd] I *adj* 1 *(healthy)* sano,-a; *(in good condition)* en buen estado. 2 *(safe, dependable)* seguro,-a; *(correct)* acertado,-a; *(logical)* lógico,-a. 3 *(basis etc)* sólido,-a. 4 *(defeat etc)* rotundo,-a; *(examination etc)* a fondo. 5 *(sleep)* profundo,-a. II *adv* **to be s. asleep,** estar profundamente dormido,-a.

sound³ [saʊnd] *vtr Naut Med* sondar. ◆**sound out** *vtr* sondear.

sound⁴ [saʊnd] *n Geog* estrecho *m*.

sounding ['saʊndɪŋ] *n Naut* sondeo *m*.

soundproof ['saʊndpruːf] *adj* insonorizado,-a.

soundtrack ['saʊndtræk] *n* banda sonora.

soup [suːp] *n* sopa *f*; *(thin, clear)* caldo *m*; *fam* **in the s.,** en un apuro; **s. dish,** plato hondo; **s. spoon,** cuchara *f* sopera.

sour [saʊər] *adj* 1 *(fruit, wine)* agrio,-a; *(milk)* cortado,-a; **to go s.,** *(milk)* cortarse; *(wine)* agriarse; *fig (situation)* empeorar; *fam* **fig s. grapes!,** ¡te aguantas! 2 *fig (person)* amargado,-a.

source [sɔːs] *n* fuente *f*; *(of infection)* foco *m*.

south [saʊθ] I *n* sur *m*; **in the s. of England,** en el sur de Inglaterra; **to the s. of York,** al sur de York. II *adj* del sur; **S. Africa,** Sudáfrica; **S. African,** sudafricano,-a *(m,f)*; **S. Pole,** Polo *m* Sur. III *adv (location)* al sur; *(direction)* hacia el sur.

southeast [saʊθ'iːst] I *n* sudeste *m*. II *adv (location)* al sudeste; *(direction)* hacia el sudeste.

southeasterly [saʊθ'iːstəlɪ] *adj* del sudeste.

southerly ['sʌðəlɪ] *adj (direction)* hacia el sur; *(point)* al sur; *(wind)* del sur.

southern ['sʌðən] *adj* del sur, meridional; **S. Europe,** Europa del Sur; **the s. hemisphere,** el hemisferio sur.

southerner ['sʌðənər] *n* sureño,-a *m,f*.

southward ['saʊθwəd] *adj & adv* hacia el sur.

southwest [saʊθ'west] I *n* suroeste *m*. II *adj* suroeste. III *adv (location)* al suroeste; *(direction)* hacia el suroeste.

souvenir [suːvə'nɪər] *n* recuerdo *m*, souvenir *m*.

sovereign ['sɒvrɪn] I *n* 1 *(monarch)* soberano,-a *m,f*. 2 *arch (coin)* soberano *m*. II *adj* soberano,-a.

soviet ['səʊvɪət] I *n* 1 *(council)* soviet *m*. 2 **the Soviets,** los soviéticos. II *adj* soviético,-a; *Hist* **S. Union,** Unión Soviética.

sow¹ [səʊ] *vtr (pt sowed; pp sowed or sown)* sembrar.

sow² [saʊ] *n Zool* cerda *f*.

soy [sɔɪ] *n US* soja *f*; **s. sauce,** salsa *f* de soja.

soya ['sɔɪə] *n GB* soja *f*.

spa [spɑː] *n* balneario *m*.

space [speɪs] I *n* 1 espacio *m*; *(room)* espacio *f*; **s. shuttle,** transbordador *m* espacial; **s. station,** estación *f* espacial. 2 *(room)* sitio *m*; **in a confined s.,** en un espacio reducido. II *vtr (also s. out)* espaciar, separar.

spacecraft ['speɪskrɑːft] *n inv* nave *f* espacial.

spaceman ['speɪsmən] *n* astronauta *m*, cosmonauta *m*.

spacing ['speɪsɪŋ] *n* **double s.,** doble espacio.

spacious ['speɪʃəs] *adj* espacioso,-a, amplio,-a.

spade¹ [speɪd] *n (for digging)* pala *f*.

spade² [speɪd] *n Cards (international pack)* pica *f*; *(Spanish pack)* espada *f*.

spaghetti [spə'getɪ] *n* espaguetis *mpl*.

Spain [speɪn] *n* España.

span [spæn] I *n (of wing)* envergadura *f*; *(of hand)* palmo *m*; *(of arch)* luz *f*; *(of road)* tramo *m*; *(of time)* lapso *m*; **life s.,** vida *f*. II *vtr (river etc)* extenderse sobre, atravesar; *(period of time etc)* abarcar.

Spaniard ['spænjəd] *n* español,-a *m,f*.

spaniel ['spænjəl] *n* perro *m* de aguas.

Spanish ['spænɪʃ] I *adj* español,-a. II *n* 1 **the S.,** los españoles. 2 *(language)* español *m*, castellano *m*.

Spanish-speaking ['spænɪʃspiːkɪŋ] *adj* de habla española, hispanohablante.

spank [spæŋk] *vtr* zurrar.

spanner ['spænər] n llave f (para tuercas); GB fam **to throw a s. in the works,** estropear los planes.

spar¹ [spɑːr] n Naut palo m, verga f.

spar² [spɑːr] vi **1** Box entrenarse. **2** (argue) discutir.

spare [speər] **I** vtr **1** (do without) prescindir de; **can you s. me 10?,** ¿me puedes dejar 10?; **I can't s. the time,** no tengo tiempo; **there's none to s.,** no sobra nada. **2** (begrudge) escatimar. **3** (show mercy to) perdonar. **4** s. **me the details,** ahórrate los detalles. **II** adj **1** (left over) sobrante; (surplus) de sobra, de más; **a s. moment,** un momento libre; **s. part,** (pieza f de) recambio m; **s. room,** cuarto m de los invitados; **s. tyre,** Aut neumático m de recambio; GB fam (on body) michelines mpl; **s. wheel,** rueda f de recambio. **2** (thin) enjuto,-a. **III** n Aut (pieza f de) recambio m.

sparing ['speərɪŋ] adj **to be s. with praise,** escatimar elogios; **to be s. with words,** ser parco,-a en palabras. ◆**sparingly** adv en poca cantidad.

spark [spɑːk] **I** n chispa f; Aut **s. plug,** bujía f. **II** vi echar chispas. ◆**spark off** vtr desatar.

sparking ['spɑːkɪŋ] adj **s. plug,** bujía f.

sparkle ['spɑːkəl] **I** vi **1** (diamond, glass) centellear, destellar; (eyes) brillar. **II** n **1** (of diamond, glass) centelleo m, destello m; (of eyes) brillo m.

sparkling ['spɑːkɪŋ] adj **1** (diamond, glass) centelleante; (eyes) brillante; **s. wine,** vino espumoso. **2** fig (person, conversation) vivaz.

sparrow ['spærəʊ] n gorrión m.

sparse [spɑːs] adj (thin) escaso,-a; (scattered) esparcido,-a; (hair) ralo,-a.

Spartan ['spɑːtən] adj & n espartano,-a (m,f).

spasm ['spæzəm] n **1** Med espasmo m; (of coughing) acceso m. **2** (of anger, activity) arrebato m.

spasmodic [spæz'mɒdɪk] adj **1** Med espasmódico,-a. **2** (irregular) irregular.

spastic ['spæstɪk] adj & n Med espástico,-a (m,f).

spat [spæt] pt & pp → **spit**¹

spate [speɪt] n **1** (of letters) avalancha f; (of words) torrente m; (of accidents) racha f. **2** GB (river) desbordamiento m; **to be in full s.,** estar crecido,-a.

spatter ['spætər] vtr salpicar (with, de).

spatula ['spætjʊlə] n espátula f.

spawn [spɔːn] **I** n (of fish, frogs) huevas fpl. **II** vi (fish, frogs) frezar. **III** vtr fig pej generar.

speak [spiːk] **I** vtr (pt **spoke,** pp **spoken**) **1** (utter) decir; **s. the truth,** decir la verdad. **2** (language) hablar. **II** vi **1** (in general) hablar; **roughly speaking,** a grandes rasgos; **so to s.,** por así decirlo; **speaking**

of ..., a propósito de ...; **to s. to sb,** hablar con algn. **2** (make a speech) pronunciar un discurso; (take the floor) tomar la palabra. **3** Tel hablar; **speaking!,** ¡al habla!; **who's speaking, please?,** ¿de parte de quién? ◆**speak for** vtr (person, group) hablar en nombre de; **it speaks for itself,** es evidente. ◆**speak out** vi **to s. out against sth,** denunciar algo. ◆**speak up** vi hablar más fuerte; fig **to s. up for sb,** intervenir a favor de algn.

speaker ['spiːkər] n **1** (in dialogue) interlocutor,-a m,f; (lecturer) conferenciante m,f; (public) s., orador,-a m,f. **2** (of language) hablante mf. **3** GB Parl **the S.,** el Presidente de la Cámara de los Comunes; US **the S. of the House,** el Presidente de la Cámara de los Representantes. **4** (loudspeaker) altavoz m.

spear [spɪər] n lanza f; (javelin) jabalina f; (harpoon) arpón m.

spearhead ['spɪəhed] vtr encabezar.

spec [spek] n fam **on s.,** sin garantías.

special ['speʃəl] **I** adj especial; (specific) específico,-a; (exceptional) extraordinario,-a; **s. delivery,** (letter) exprés; (parcel) de entrega inmediata; **s. edition,** número m especial; **s. effects,** efectos mpl especiales. **II** n Rad TV programa m especial. ◆**specially** adv (specifically) especialmente; (on purpose) a propósito.

specialist ['speʃəlɪst] n especialista mf.

speciality [speʃɪ'ælɪtɪ] n especialidad f.

specialize ['speʃəlaɪz] vi especializarse (in, en).

specialty ['speʃəltɪ] n US → **speciality.**

species ['spiːʃiːz] n (pl **species**) especie f.

specific [spɪ'sɪfɪk] adj específico,-a; (definite) concreto,-a; (precise) preciso,-a; **to be s.,** concretar. ◆**specifically** adv (exactly) específicamente; (expressly) expresamente; (namely) en concreto.

specification [spesɪfɪ'keɪʃən] n **specifications,** datos específicos.

specify ['spesɪfaɪ] vtr especificar, precisar.

specimen ['spesɪmɪn] n (sample) muestra f; (example) ejemplar m; **urine/tissue s.,** espécimen m de orina/tejido.

speck [spek] n (of dust) mota f; (stain) manchita f; (small trace) pizca f.

speckled ['spekəld] adj moteado,-a.

specs [speks] npl fam abbr of **spectacles.**

spectacle ['spektəkəl] n **1** (display) espectáculo m. **2** **spectacles,** (glasses) gafas fpl.

spectacular [spek'tækjʊlər] **I** adj espectacular, impresionante. **II** n Cin TV (gran) espectáculo m.

spectator [spek'teɪtər] n espectador,-a m,f.

spectre, US **specter** ['spektər] n espectro m, fantasma m.

spectrum ['spektrəm] n espectro m.

speculate ['spekjʊleɪt] *vi* especular.

speculation [spekjʊ'leɪʃən] *n* especulación *f*.

speech [spiːtʃ] *n* 1 *(faculty)* habla *f*; *(pronunciation)* pronunciación *f*; **freedom of s.**, libertad *f* de expresión. 2 *(address)* discurso *m*; **to give a s.**, pronunciar un discurso. 3 *Ling* part of s., parte *f* de la oración.

speechless ['spiːtʃlɪs] *adj* mudo,-a, boquiabierto,-a.

speed [spiːd] **I** *n* 1 velocidad *f*; *(rapidity)* rapidez *f*; **at top s.**, a toda velocidad; **s. limit**, límite *m* de velocidad. **II** *vi* 1 *(pt & pp sped)* *(go fast)* ir corriendo; *(hurry)* apresurarse; **to s. along**, *(car etc)* ir a toda velocidad; **to s. past**, pasar volando. 2 *(pt & pp speeded)* *(exceed speed limit)* conducir con exceso de velocidad. ◆**speed up** I *vtr* *(pt & pp speeded up)* acelerar; *(person)* meter prisa a. II *vi* *(person)* darse prisa.

speedboat ['spiːdbəʊt] *n* lancha rápida.

speeding ['spiːdɪŋ] *n* exceso *m* de velocidad.

speedometer [spɪ'dɒmɪtər] *n* velocímetro *m*.

speedway ['spiːdweɪ] *n* 1 *(racing)* carreras *fpl* de motos. 2 *(track)* pista *f* de carreras.

speedy ['spiːdɪ] *adj* *(speedier, speediest)* veloz, rápido,-a.

spell¹ [spel] **I** *vtr* *(pt & pp spelt* or *spelled)* *(letter by letter)* deletrear; *fig* *(denote)* significar; **how do you s. your name?**, ¿cómo se escribe su nombre?. **II** *vi* **she can't s.**, comete faltas de ortografía. ◆**spell out** *vtr fig* explicar con detalle.

spell² [spel] *n* *(magical)* hechizo *m*, encanto *m*.

spell³ [spel] *n* 1 *(period)* período *m*; *(short period)* rato *m*; *Meteor* **cold s.**, ola *f* de frío. 2 *(shift)* turno *m*.

spellbound ['spelbaʊnd] *adj* hechizado, -a, embelesado,-a.

spelling ['spelɪŋ] *n* ortografía *f*.

spend [spend] *vtr* *(pt & pp spent)* 1 *(money)* gastar *(on*, en). 2 *(time)* pasar; **to s. time on sth**, dedicar tiempo a algo.

spending ['spendɪŋ] *n* gastos *mpl*; **s. money**, dinero *m* de bolsillo; **s. power**, poder adquisitivo.

spendthrift ['spendθrɪft] *adj & n* derrochador,-a *(m,f)*.

spent [spent] *adj* gastado,-a.

sperm [spɜːm] *n* esperma *m*; **s. bank**, banco *m* de esperma; **s. whale**, cachalote *m*.

spew [spjuː] *vtr* **to s.** *(up)*, vomitar.

sphere [sfɪər] *n* esfera *f*.

spice [spaɪs] *n* 1 especia *f*. 2 *fig* sal *f*. **II** *vtr* 1 *Culin* sazonar. 2 **to s.** *(up)*, *(story etc)* salpimentar.

spic(k)-and-span [spɪkən'spæn] *adj* *(very*

clean) limpísimo,-a; *(well-groomed)* acicalado,-a.

spicy ['spaɪsɪ] *adj* *(spicier, spiciest)* 1 *Culin* sazonado,-a; *(hot)* picante. 2 *fig* *(story etc)* picante.

spider ['spaɪdər] *n* araña *f*; **s.'s web**, telaraña *f*.

spike¹ [spaɪk] *n* *(sharp point)* punta *f*; *(metal rod)* pincho *m*; *(on railing)* barrote *m*; *Sport* *(on shoes)* clavo *m*.

spike² [spaɪk] *n Bot* espiga *f*.

spiky ['spaɪkɪ] *adj* *(spikier, spikiest)* puntiagudo,-a; *(hairstyle)* de punta.

spill [spɪl] **I** *vtr* *(pt & pp spilled* or *spilt)* derramar. **II** *vi* *(liquid)* derramarse. ◆**spill over** *vi* desbordarse.

spin [spɪn] **I** *vtr* *(pt & pp spun)* 1 *(wheel etc)* hacer girar; *(washing)* centrifugar. 2 *(cotton, wool)* hilar; *(spider's web)* tejer. **II** *vi* *(wheel etc)* girar; *Av* caer en barrena; **Aut patinar**. **III** *n* 1 *(turn)* vuelta *f*, giro *m*. 2 *Sport* efecto *m*. 3 *Av* barrena *f*; *Aut* patinazo *m*. 4 *GB* **to go for a s.**, *(ride)* dar una vuelta.

spinach ['spɪnɪtʃ] *n* espinacas *fpl*.

spinal ['spaɪnəl] *adj* espinal, vertebral; **s. column**, columna *f* vertebral; **s. cord**, médula *f* espinal.

spindly ['spɪndlɪ] *adj* *(spindlier, spindliest)* *fam* *(long-bodied)* larguirucho,-a; *(long-legged)* zanquilargo,-a.

spin-dryer [spɪn'draɪər] *n* secador centrífugo.

spine [spaɪn] *n* 1 *Anat* columna *f* vertebral, espinazo *m*; *(of book)* lomo *m*. 2 *Zool* púa *f*; *Bot* espina *f*.

spineless ['spaɪnlɪs] *adj fig* *(weak)* sin carácter.

spinning ['spɪnɪŋ] *n* 1 *(of cotton etc)* *(act)* hilado *m*; *(art)* hilandería *f*; **s. wheel**, rueca *f*. 2 **s. top**, peonza *f*.

spin-off ['spɪnɒf] *n* *(by-product)* derivado *m*; *fig* efecto secundario.

spinster ['spɪnstər] *n* soltera *f*.

spiral ['spaɪərəl] **I** *n* espiral *f*. **II** *adj* en espiral; **s. staircase**, escalera *f* de caracol.

spirit¹ ['spɪrɪt] *n* 1 *(soul)* espíritu *m*, alma *f*; *(ghost)* fantasma *m*. 2 *(attitude)* espíritu *m*; *(mood)* humor *m*; **to take sth in the right s.**, tomar algo a bien; **community s.**, civismo *m*. 3 *(courage)* valor *m*; *(liveliness)* ánimo *m*; *(vitality)* vigor *m*; **to break sb's s.**, quebrar la voluntad de algn. 5 **spirits**, *(mood)* humor *m* sing; **to be in good s.**, estar de buen humor; **to be in high/low s.**, estar muy animado/ desanimado.

spirit² ['spɪrɪt] *n* 1 *Chem* alcohol *m*; **s. level**, nivel *m* de aire. 2 **spirits**, *(alcoholic drinks)* licores *mpl*.

spirited ['spɪrɪtɪd] *adj* *(person, attempt)* valiente; *(horse)* fogoso,-a; *(attack)* enérgico,-a.

spiritual ['spɪrɪtjʊəl] *adj* espiritual.
spit¹ [spɪt] I *vtr* (*pt & pp* **spat**) escupir. II *vi* escupir; *fam* **he's the spitting image of his father**, es el vivo retrato de su padre. III *n* (*saliva*) saliva *f*.
spit² [spɪt] *n* Culin asador *m*.
spite [spaɪt] I *n* 1 (*ill will*) rencor *m*, ojeriza *f*. 2 **in s. of**, a pesar de, pese a; **in s. of the fact that**, a pesar de que, pese a que. II *vtr* (*annoy*) fastidiar.
spiteful ['spaɪtfʊl] *adj* (*person*) rencoroso,-a; (*remark*) malévolo,-a; (*tongue*) viperino,-a.
spittle ['spɪtəl] *n* saliva *f*.
splash [splæʃ] I *vtr* salpicar. II *vi* 1 **to s.** (**about**), (*in water*) chapotear. 2 (*water etc*) salpicar. III *n* 1 (*noise*) chapoteo *m*. 2 (*spray*) salpicadura *f*; *fig* (*of colour*) mancha *f*. ◆**splash out** *vi fam* tirar la casa por la ventana.
spleen [spli:n] *n* Anat bazo *m*.
splendid ['splendɪd] *adj* espléndido,-a.
splendour, *US* **splendor** ['splendər] *n* esplendor *m*.
splint [splɪnt] *n* tablilla *f*.
splinter ['splɪntər] I *n* 1 (*wood*) astilla *f*; (*bone, stone*) esquirla *f*; (*glass*) fragmento *m*; **s. group**, grupo *m* disidente. II *vi* 1 (*wood etc*) astillarse. 2 Pol escindirse.
split [splɪt] I *n* 1 (*crack*) grieta *f*, hendidura *f*; (*tear*) desgarrón *m*; *fig* (*division*) cisma *m*; Pol escisión *f*. 2 Gymn **to do the splits**, abrir las piernas en cruz. II *adj* partido,-a; **in a s. second**, en una fracción de segundo; **s. personality**, desdoblamiento *m* de personalidad. III *vtr* (*pt & pp* **split**) 1 (*crack*) agrietar; (*cut*) partir; (*tear*) rajar; (*atom*) desintegrar; *fig* **to s. hairs**, buscarle tres pies al gato. 2 (*divide*) dividir. 3 (*share out*) repartir. IV *vi* 1 (*crack*) agrietarse; (*into two parts*) partirse; (*garment*) rajarse. 2 (*divide*) dividirse. 3 Pol escindirse. ◆**split up** I *vtr* (*break up*) partir; (*divide up*) dividir; (*share out*) repartir. II *vi* (*couple*) separarse.
splutter ['splʌtər] *vi* (*person*) balbucear; (*candle, fat*) chisporrotear; (*engine*) petardear.
spoil [spɔɪl] I *vtr* (*pt & pp* **spoiled** *or* **spoilt**) 1 (*ruin*) estropear, echar a perder. 2 (*child*) mimar; **to be spoilt for choice**, tener demasiadas cosas para elegir. II *vi* (*food*) estropearse.
spoilsport ['spɔɪlspɔːt] *n fam* aguafiestas *mf inv*.
spoilt [spɔɪlt] *adj* 1 (*food, merchandise*) estropeado,-a. 2 (*child*) mimado,-a.
spoke¹ [spəʊk] *pt* → **speak**.
spoke² [spəʊk] *n* (*of wheel*) radio *m*, rayo *m*.
spoken ['spəʊkən] *pp* → **speak**.
spokesman ['spəʊksmən] *n* portavoz *m*.
spokeswoman ['spəʊkswʊmən] *n* porta-

voz *f*.
sponge [spʌndʒ] I *n* esponja *f*; *fig* **to throw in the s.**, arrojar la toalla; *GB* **s. cake**, bizcocho *m*. II *vtr* (*wash*) lavar con esponja. III *vi fam* vivir de gorra. ◆**sponge off**, **sponge on** *vtr* vivir a costa de.
spongy ['spʌndʒɪ] *adj* (**spongier**, **spongiest**) esponjoso,-a.
sponsor ['spɒnsər] I *vtr* patrocinar; Fin avalar; (*support*) respaldar. II *n* patrocinador,-a *m,f*; Fin avalador,-a *m,f*.
sponsorship ['spɒnsəʃɪp] *n* patrocinio *m*; Fin aval *m*; (*support*) respaldo *m*.
spontaneous [spɒn'teɪnɪəs] *adj* espontáneo,-a.
spoof [spu:f] *n fam* 1 (*parody*) burla *f*. 2 (*hoax*) engaño *m*.
spooky ['spu:kɪ] *adj* (**spookier**, **spookiest**) *fam* espeluznante.
spool [spu:l] *n* bobina *f*, carrete *m*.
spoon [spu:n] I *n* cuchara *f*; (*small*) cucharita *f*. II *vtr* sacar con cuchara; (*serve*) servir con cuchara.
spoon-feed ['spu:nfi:d] *vtr* (*baby*) dar de comer con cuchara a; *fig* (*spoil*) mimar.
spoonful ['spu:nfʊl] *n* cucharada *f*.
sporadic [spə'rædɪk] *adj* esporádico,-a.
sport [spɔːt] I *n* 1 deporte *m*. 2 *fam* **he's a good s.**, es buena persona; **be a s.!**, ¡sé amable! II *vtr* (*display*) lucir.
sporting ['spɔːtɪŋ] *adj* deportivo,-a.
sports [spɔːts] I *npl* deportes *mpl*, deporte *m sing*. II *adj* **s. car**, coche deportivo; **s. jacket**, chaqueta *f* (de) sport.
sportsman ['spɔːtsmən] *n* deportista *m*.
sportsmanlike ['spɔːtsmənlaɪk] *adj* deportivo,-a.
sportsmanship ['spɔːtsmənʃɪp] *n* deportividad *f*.
sportswear ['spɔːtsweər] *n* (*for sport*) ropa *f* de deporte; (*casual clothes*) ropa *f* (de) sport.
sportswoman ['spɔːtswʊmən] *n* deportista *f*.
sporty ['spɔːtɪ] *adj* (**sportier**, **sportiest**) *fam* deportivo,-a.
spot [spɒt] *n* 1 (*dot*) punto *m*; (*on fabric*) lunar *m*. 2 (*stain*) mancha *f*. 3 (*pimple*) grano *m*. 4 (*place*) sitio *m*, lugar *m*; **on the s.**, (*person*) allí, presente; **to decide sth on the s.**, decidir algo en el acto; **s. check**, chequeo rápido; *fig* **weak s.**, punto débil; **to be in a tight s.**, estar en un apuro; **to put sb on the s.**, poner a algn en un aprieto. 5 *fam* (*small amount*) poquito *m*; **a s. of bother**, unos problemillas. 6 Rad TV Theat (*in show*) espacio *m*; (*advertisement*) spot *m*, anuncio *m*. II *vtr* (*notice*) darse cuenta de, notar; (*see*) ver.
spotless ['spɒtlɪs] *adj* (*very clean*) impecable; *fig* (*reputation etc*) intachable.
spotlight ['spɒtlaɪt] *n* foco *m*; Aut faro *m*

auxiliar; *fig* **to be in the s.,** ser objeto de la atención pública.

spot-on ['spɒt'ɒn] *adj fam* exacto,-a.

spotted ['spɒtɪd] *adj* (*with dots*) con puntos; (*fabric*) con lunares; (*speckled*) moteado,-a.

spotty ['spɒtɪ] *adj* (*spottier, spottiest*) *fig* con granos.

spouse [spaʊs] *n* cónyuge *mf.*

spout [spaʊt] I *n* (*of jug*) pico *m;* (*of teapot*) pitorro *m.* II *vtr fam* (*nonsense*) soltar. III *vi* **to s. out/up,** (*liquid*) brotar.

sprain [spreɪn] I *n* esguince *m.* II *vtr* torcer; **to s. one's ankle,** torcerse el tobillo.

sprang [spræŋ] *pt* → **spring²**.

sprawl [sprɔ:l] I *vi* 1 (*sit, lie*) tumbarse. 2 (*city, plant*) extenderse. II *n* (*of city*) extensión *f.*

spray¹ [spreɪ] I *n* 1 (*of water*) rociada *f;* (*from sea*) espuma *f;* (*from aerosol*) pulverización *f.* 2 (*aerosol*) spray *m;* (*for plants*) pulverizador *m;* **s. can,** aerosol *m.* II *vtr* (*water*) rociar; (*insecticide, perfume*) pulverizar.

spray² [spreɪ] *n* (*of flowers*) ramita *f.*

spread [spred] I *n* 1 extensión *f;* (*of ideas*) difusión *f;* (*of disease, fire*) propagación *f;* (*of terrorism*) generalización *f.* 2 (*range*) gama *f.* 3 (*of wings*) envergadura *f.* 4 (*for bread*) pasta *f;* **cheese s.,** queso para untar. 5 *fam* (*large meal*) banquetazo *m.* 6 *Press* **full-page s.,** plana entera; **two-page s.,** doble página *f.* II *vtr* (*pt & pp* **spread**) 1 (*unfold*) desplegar; (*lay out*) extender; *fig* **to s. one's wings,** desplegar las alas. 2 (*butter etc*) untar. 3 (*news*) difundir; (*rumour*) hacer correr; (*disease, fire*) propagar; (*panic*) sembrar. III *vi* 1 (*stretch out*) extenderse; (*unfold*) desplegarse. 2 (*news*) difundirse; (*rumour*) correr; (*disease*) propagarse.

spread-eagled [spred'i:gəld] *adj* despatarrado,-a.

spreadsheet ['spredʃi:t] *n Comput* hoja *f* de cálculo.

spree [spri:] *n* juerga *f;* **to go on a s.,** ir de juerga.

sprig [sprɪg] *n* ramita *f.*

sprightly ['spraɪtlɪ] *adj* (**sprightlier, sprightliest**) (*nimble*) ágil; (*energetic*) enérgico,-a; (*lively*) animado,-a.

spring¹ [sprɪŋ] I *n* (*season*) primavera *f.* II *adj* primaveral; **s. onion,** cebolleta *f;* **s. roll,** rollo *m* de primavera.

spring² [sprɪŋ] I *n* 1 (*of water*) manantial *m,* fuente *f.* 2 (*of watch etc*) resorte *m;* (*of mattress*) muelle *m;* *Aut* ballesta *f.* II *vi* (*pt* **sprang;** *pp* **sprung**) 1 (*jump*) saltar; **the lid sprang open,** la tapa se abrió de golpe. 2 (*appear*) aparecer (de repente). III *vtr* 1 **to s. a leak,** hacer agua. 2 *fig* (*news, surprise*) dar de golpe ◆**spring up** *vi* aparecer; (*plants*) brotar; (*buildings*)

elevarse; (*problems*) surgir.

springboard ['sprɪŋbɔ:d] *n* trampolín *m.*

spring-clean [sprɪŋ'kli:n] *vtr* limpiar a fondo.

springtime ['sprɪŋtaɪm] *n* primavera *f.*

springy ['sprɪŋɪ] *adj* (**springier, springiest**) (*bouncy*) elástico,-a; *fig* (*step*) saltarín.

sprinkle ['sprɪŋkəl] *vtr* (*with water*) rociar (**with,** de); (*with sugar*) espolvorear (**with,** de).

sprint [sprɪnt] I *n* esprint *m.* II *vi* esprintar.

sprinter ['sprɪntə'] *n* esprínter *mf,* velocista *mf.*

sprout [spraʊt] I *vi* (*bud*) brotar; *fig* crecer rápidamente. II *n* (**Brussels**) **sprouts,** coles *fpl* de Bruselas.

spruce¹ [spru:s] *n inv Bot* picea *f.*

spruce² [spru:s] *adj* (*neat*) pulcro,-a; (*smart*) apuesto,-a. ◆**spruce up** *vtr* acicalar.

sprung [sprʌŋ] *pp* → **spring²**.

spry [spraɪ] *adj* (**sprier, spriest**) (*nimble*) ágil; (*active*) activo,-a; (*lively*) vivaz.

spun [spʌn] *pt & pp* → **spin.**

spur [spɜ:'] I *n* 1 espuela *f.* 2 *fig* (*stimulus*) acicate *m;* **on the s. of the moment,** sin pensarlo. II *vtr* 1 (*horse*) espolear. 2 *fig* incitar.

spurious ['spjʊərɪəs] *adj* falso,-a.

spurn [spɜ:n] *vtr fml* desdeñar, rechazar.

spurt [spɜ:t] I *n* 1 (*of liquid*) chorro *m.* 2 *fig* (*of activity etc*) racha *f;* (*effort*) esfuerzo *m.* II *vi* 1 (*liquid*) chorrear. 2 (*make an effort*) hacer un último esfuerzo; (*accelerate*) acelerar.

spy [spaɪ] I *n* espía *mf.* II *vtr fml* (*see*) divisar. III *vi* espiar (**on,** a).

spyhole ['spaɪhəʊl] *n* mirilla *f.*

spying ['spaɪɪŋ] *n* espionaje *m.*

squabble ['skwɒbəl] I *n* riña *f,* pelea *f.* II *vi* reñir, pelearse (**over, about,** por).

squad [skwɒd] *n Mil* pelotón *m;* (*of police*) brigada *f;* *Sport* equipo *m;* **drugs s.,** brigada antidroga.

squadron ['skwɒdrən] *n Mil* escuadrón *m;* *Av* escuadrilla *f;* *Naut* escuadra *f.*

squalid ['skwɒlɪd] *adj* (*very dirty*) asqueroso,-a; (*poor*) miserable; (*motive*) vil.

squall¹ [skwɔ:l] *n* (*wind*) ráfaga *f.*

squall² [skwɔ:l] *vi* chillar, berrear.

squalor ['skwɒlə'] *n* (*dirtiness*) mugre *f;* (*poverty*) miseria *f.*

squander ['skwɒndə'] *vtr* (*money*) derrochar, despilfarrar; (*time*) desperdiciar.

square [skweə'] I *n* 1 cuadro *m;* (*on chessboard, crossword*) casilla *f;* *fig* **we're back to s. one!,** ¡volvemos a partir desde cero! (*in town*) plaza *f.* 3 *Math* cuadrado *m.* II *adj* 1 (*in shape*) cuadrado,-a. 2 *Math* cuadrado,-a; **s. metre,** metro cuadra-

s. **root**, raíz cuadrada. **3** fam (fair) justo,-a; **to be s. with sb**, (honest) ser franco,-a con algn. **4 a s. meal**, una buena comida. **5** (old-fashioned) carroza; (conservative) carca. III vtr **1** (make square) cuadrar; **to s. one's shoulders**, sacar el pecho. **2** Math elevar al cuadrado. **3** (settle) arreglar. IV vi (agree) cuadrar (**with**, con). ◆**squarely** adv (directly) directamente, de lleno.

squash[1] [skwɒʃ] I n GB (drink) concentrado m. II vtr **1** (crush) aplastar. **2** fig (objection) echar por tierra. III vi (crush) aplastarse.

squash[2] [skwɒʃ] n Sport squash m.

squat [skwɒt] I adj (person) rechoncho,-a. II vi **1** (crouch) agacharse, sentarse en cuclillas. **2** (in building) ocupar ilegalmente. III n (building) edificio m ocupado ilegalmente.

squatter ['skwɒtər] n ocupante mf ilegal, okupa m,f.

squawk [skwɔːk] I n graznido m. II vi graznar.

squeak [skwiːk] I n (of mouse) chillido m; (of hinge, wheel) chirrido m; (of shoes) crujido m. II vi (mouse) chillar; (hinge, wheel) chirriar, rechinar; (shoes) crujir.

squeaky ['skwiːki] adj (squeakier, squeakiest) chirriante; (voice) chillón, -ona; (shoes) que crujen.

squeal [skwiːl] I n (of animal, person) chillido m. II vi **1** (animal, person) chillar. **2** fam (inform) chivarse.

squeamish ['skwiːmɪʃ] adj muy sensible.

squeeze [skwiːz] I vtr apretar; (lemon etc) exprimir; (sponge) estrujar; **to s. paste out of a tube**, sacar pasta de un tubo apretando. II vi **to s. in**, apretujarse. III n **1** (pressure) estrujón m; **a s. of lemon**, unas gotas de limón. **2** (of hand) apretón m; (hug) abrazo m; (crush) apiñamiento m; **credit s.**, reducción f de créditos.

squelch [skweltʃ] vi chapotear.

squid [skwɪd] n calamar m; (small) chipirón m.

squiggle ['skwɪgəl] n garabato m.

squint [skwɪnt] I n **1** bizquera f; **to have a s.**, ser bizco,-a. **2** fig (quick look) vistazo m. II vi ser bizco,-a. **2 to s. at sth**, (glance) echar un vistazo a algo; (with eyes half-closed) mirar algo con los ojos entrecerrados.

squirm [skwɜːm] vi retorcerse; fig (feel embarrassed) sentirse incómodo,-a.

squirrel ['skwɪrəl] n ardilla f.

squirt [skwɜːt] I n (of liquid) chorro m. II vtr lanzar a chorro. III vi **to s. out**, salir a chorros.

Sr abbr → **Snr**.

Sri Lanka [sriːˈlæŋkə] n Sri Lanka.

St 1 abbr of **Saint**, San, Sto., Sta. **2** abbr of **Street**, c/.

st GB abbr of **stone**, peso que equivale a

6,350 kilogramos.

stab [stæb] I n (with knife) puñalada f; (of pain) punzada f; **fam to have a s. at doing sth**, intentar hacer algo. II vtr apuñalar.

stabbing ['stæbɪŋ] adj (pain) punzante.

stability [stəˈbɪlɪtɪ] n estabilidad f.

stable[1] ['steɪbəl] adj estable.

stable[2] ['steɪbəl] n cuadra f, caballeriza f.

stack [stæk] I n (pile) montón m; **fam he's got stacks of money**, está forrado. II vtr (pile up) amontonar, apilar; **fig the odds are stacked against us**, todo está en contra nuestra.

stadium ['steɪdɪəm] n estadio m.

staff [stɑːf] n **1** (personnel) personal m; Mil estado m mayor; **s. meeting**, claustro m; GB **s. nurse**, enfermera cualificada. **2** (stick) bastón m; (of shepherd) cayado m. II vtr proveer de personal.

staffroom ['stɑːfruːm] n sala f de profesores.

stag [stæg] n ciervo m, venado m; fam **s. party**, despedida f de soltero.

stage [steɪdʒ] I n **1** (platform) plataforma f. **2** (in theatre) escenario m; **s. door**, entrada f de artistas; **s. fright**, miedo escénico; **s. manager**, director,-a m,f de escena. **3** (phase) of development, journey, rocket) etapa f; (of road, pipeline) tramo m; **at this s. of the negotiations**, a estas alturas de las negociaciones; **in stages**, por etapas. II vtr **1** (play) poner en escena, montar. **2** (arrange) organizar; (carry out) llevar a cabo.

stagecoach ['steɪdʒkəʊtʃ] n diligencia f.

stagger ['stægər] I vi tambalearse. II vtr **1** (amaze) asombrar. **2** (hours, work) escalonar.

staggering ['stægərɪŋ] adj asombroso,-a.

stagnant ['stægnənt] adj estancado,-a.

stagnate [stægˈneɪt] vi estancarse.

staid [steɪd] adj (person) conservador,-a; (manner, clothes) serio,-a, formal.

stain [steɪn] I n **1** mancha f; **s. remover**, quitamanchas m inv. **2** (dye) tinte m. II vtr **1** manchar. **2** (dye) teñir. III vi mancharse.

stained [steɪnd] adj **s. glass window**, vidriera f de colores.

stainless ['steɪnlɪs] adj (steel) inoxidable.

stair [steər] n escalón m, peldaño m; **stairs**, escalera f sing.

staircase ['steəkeɪs] n escalera f.

stake[1] [steɪk] I n (stick) estaca f; (for plant) rodrigón m; (post) poste m. II vtr **to s. (out)**, cercar con estacas.

stake[2] [steɪk] n **1** (bet) apuesta f; **the issue at s.**, el tema en cuestión; **to be at s.**, (at risk) estar en juego. **2** (investment) interés m. II vtr (bet) apostar; (invest) invertir; **to s. a claim to sth**, reivindicar algo.

stale [steɪl] *adj (food)* pasado,-a; *(bread)* duro,-a.

stalemate ['steɪlmeɪt] *n Chess* tablas *fpl*; *fig* **to reach s.**, llegar a un punto muerto.

stalk¹ [stɔːk] *n (of plant)* tallo *m*; *(of fruit)* rabo *m*.

stalk² [stɔːk] I *vtr (of hunter)* cazar al acecho; *(of animal)* acechar. II *vi* **he stalked out**, salió airado.

stall¹ [stɔːl] I *n* 1 *(in market)* puesto *m*; *(at fair)* caseta *f*. 2 *(stable)* establo *m*; *(stable compartment)* casilla *f* de establo. 3 *Theat* **stalls**, platea *f sing*. II *vtr Aut* calar. III *vi Aut* calarse; *Av* perder velocidad.

stall² [stɔːl] *vi* dar largas a un asunto.

stallion ['stæljən] *n* semental *m*.

stalwart ['stɔːlwət] *n* incondicional *m,f*.

stamina ['stæmɪnə] *n* resistencia *f*.

stammer ['stæmə'] I *n* tartamudeo *m*. II *vi* tartamudear.

stamp [stæmp] I *n* 1 *(postage stamp)* sello *m*; **s. album**, álbum *m* de sellos; **s. collector**, filatelista *mf*; *GB* **s. duty**, póliza *f*. 2 *(rubber stamp)* tampón *m*; *(for metals)* cuño *m*. 3 *(with foot)* patada *f*. II *vtr* 1 *(with postage stamp)* poner el sello a; **stamped addressed envelope**, sobre franqueado. 2 *(with rubber stamp)* sellar. 3 **to s. one's feet**, patear; *(in dancing)* zapatear. III *vi* patear. ◆**stamp out** *vtr fig (racism etc)* acabar con; *(rebellion)* sofocar.

stampede [stæm'piːd] I *n* estampida *f*, *(rush)* desbandada *f*. II *vi* desbandarse; *(rush)* precipitarse.

stance [stæns] *n* postura *f*.

stand [stænd] I *n* 1 *(position)* posición *f*, postura *f*; **to make a s.**, resistir. 2 *(of lamp, sculpture)* pie *m*. 3 *(market stall)* puesto *m*; *(at fair)* caseta *f*; *(at exhibition)* stand *m*; **newspaper s.**, quiosco *m*. 4 *(platform)* plataforma *f*; *(in stadium)* tribuna *f*; *US (witness box)* estrado *m*. II *vtr (pt & pp* **stood)** 1 *(place)* poner, colocar. 2 *(tolerate)* aguantar, soportar. 3 **s. one's ground**, mantenerse firme. III *vi* 1 *(be upright)* estar de pie; *(get up)* levantarse; *(remain upright)* quedarse de pie; **s. still!**, ¡estáte quieto,-a! 2 *(measure)* medir. 3 *(be situated)* estar, encontrarse. 4 *(remain unchanged)* permanecer. 5 *(remain valid)* seguir vigente. **6 as things s.**, tal como están las cosas. 7 *Pol* presentarse. ◆**stand back** *vi (allow sb to pass)* abrir paso. ◆**stand by** I *vi* 1 *(do nothing)* quedarse sin hacer nada. 2 *(be ready)* estar listo,-a. II *vtr (person)* apoyar a; *(promise)* cumplir con; *(decision)* atenerse a. ◆**stand down** *vi fig* retirarse. ◆**stand for** *vtr* 1 *(mean)* significar. 2 *(represent)* representar. 3 *(tolerate)* aguantar. ◆**stand in** *vi* sustituir *(for, -)*. ◆**stand out** *vi (mountain etc)* desta-

carse *(against, contra)*; *fig (person)* destacar. ◆**stand up** *vi (get up)* ponerse de pie; *(be standing)* estar de pie; *fig* **s. up to wear and tear**, es muy resistente; *fig* **to s. up for sb**, defender a algn; *fig* **to s. up to sb**, hacer frente a algn.

standard ['stændəd] I *n* 1 *(level)* nivel *m*; **s. of living**, nivel de vida. 2 *(criterion)* criterio *m*. 3 *(norm)* norma *f*, estándar *m*. 4 *(flag)* estandarte *m*. II *adj* normal, estándar; **s. lamp**, lámpara *f* de pie.

standardize ['stændədaɪz] *vtr* normalizar.

standby ['stændbaɪ] *n* 1 *(thing)* recurso *m*. 2 *(person)* suplente *mf*; **to be on s.**, *Mil* estar de retén; *Av* estar en la lista de espera; **s. ticket**, billete *m* sin reserva.

stand-in ['stændɪn] *n* suplente *mf*; *Cin* doble *mf*.

standing ['stændɪŋ] I *adj (not sitting)* de pie; *(upright)* recto,-a; **to give sb a s. ovation**, ovacionar a algn de pie; **there was s. room only**, no quedaban asientos. 2 *(committee)* permanente; *(invitation)* permanente; *GB* **s. order**, pago fijo. II *n* 1 *(social position)* rango *m*. 2 *(duration)* duración *f*; *(in job)* antigüedad *f*.

stand-offish [stænd'ɒfɪʃ] *adj fam* distante.

standpoint ['stændpɔɪnt] *n* punto *m* de vista.

standstill ['stændstɪl] *n* **at a s.**, *(car, traffic)* parado,-a; *(industry)* paralizado,-a; **to come to a s.**, *(car, traffic)* pararse; *(industry)* paralizarse.

stank [stæŋk] *pt* → **stink**.

staple¹ ['steɪpəl] I *n (fastener)* grapa *f*. II *vtr* grapar.

staple² ['steɪpəl] I *adj (food)* básico,-a; *(product)* de primera necesidad. II *n (food)* alimento básico.

stapler ['steɪpələ'] *n* grapadora *f*.

star [stɑː'] I *n* estrella *f*. II *adj* estelar. III *vtr Cin* tener como protagonista a. IV *vi Cin* **to s. in a film**, protagonizar una película.

starboard ['stɑːbəd] *n* estribor *m*.

starch [stɑːtʃ] I *n* almidón *m*. II *vtr* almidonar.

stardom ['stɑːdəm] *n* estrellato *m*.

stare [steə'] I *n* mirada fija. II *vi* mirar fijamente.

starfish ['stɑːfɪʃ] *n* estrella *f* de mar.

stark [stɑːk] *adj (landscape)* desolado,-a; *(décor)* austero,-a; **the s. truth**, la dura realidad; **s. poverty**, la miseria.

stark-naked ['stɑːkneɪkɪd] *adj fam* en cueros.

starling ['stɑːlɪŋ] *n* estornino *m*.

starry ['stɑːrɪ] *adj (starrier, starriest)* estrellado,-a.

starry-eyed [stɑːrɪ'aɪd] *adj (idealistic)* idealista; *(in love)* enamorado,-a.

start [stɑːt] *n* 1 *(beginning)* principio *m*,

comienzo *m*; *(of race)* salida *f*; **at the s.**, al principio; **for a s.**, para empezar; **from the s.**, desde el principio; **to make a fresh s.**, volver a empezar. 2 *(advantage)* ventaja *f*. 3 *(jump)* sobresalto *m*. II *vi* 1 *(begin)* empezar, comenzar; **to s. doing sth**, empezar a hacer algo. 2 *(cause)* causar, provocar. 3 *(found)* fundar; **to s. a business**, montar un negocio. 4 *(set in motion)* arrancar. III *vi* 1 *(begin)* empezar, comenzar; *(engine)* arrancar; **starting from Monday**, a partir del lunes. 2 *(take fright)* asustarse, sobresaltarse. ◆**start off** *vi* 1 *(begin)* empezar, comenzar; **to s. off by/with**, empezar por/con. 2 *(leave)* salir, ponerse en camino. ◆**start up** I *vtr (engine)* arrancar. II *vi* empezar; *(car)* arrancar.

starter ['stɑːtər] *n* 1 *Sport (official)* juez *mf* de salida; *(competitor)* competidor,-a *m,f*. 2 *Aut* motor *m* de arranque. 3 *Culin fam* entrada *f*.

starting ['stɑːtɪŋ] *n* **s. block**, taco *m* de salida; **s. point**, punto *m* de partida; **s. post**, línea *f* de salida.

startle ['stɑːtəl] *vtr* asustar.

startling ['stɑːtlɪŋ] *adj* 1 *(frightening)* alarmante. 2 *(news etc)* asombroso,-a; *(coincidence)* extraordinario,-a.

starvation [stɑː'veɪʃən] *n* hambre *f*.

starve [stɑːv] I *vtr* privar de comida; *fig* **he was starved of affection**, fue privado de cariño. II *vi* pasar hambre; **to s. to death**, morirse de hambre.

starving ['stɑːvɪŋ] *adj* hambriento,-a; *fam* **I'm s.!**, estoy muerto,-a de hambre.

state [steɪt] I *n* 1 estado *m*; **s. of emergency**, estado de emergencia; **s. of mind**, estado de ánimo; **to be in no fit s. to do sth**, no estar en condiciones de hacer algo; **the States**, los Estados Unidos; *US* **the S. Department**, el Ministerio de Asuntos Exteriores. II *adj* 1 *Pol* estatal; **s. education**, enseñanza pública; **s. ownership**, propiedad *f* del Estado. 2 *(ceremonial)* de gala; **s. visit**, visita *f* oficial. III *vtr* declarar, afirmar; *(case)* exponer; *(problem)* plantear.

stated ['steɪtɪd] *adj* indicado,-a.

stately ['steɪtlɪ] *adj (statelier, stateliest)* majestuoso,-a; **s. home**, casa solariega.

statement ['steɪtmənt] *n* 1 declaración *f*; **official s.**, comunicado *m* oficial; *Jur* **to make a s.**, prestar declaración. 2 *Fin* estado *m* de cuenta; **monthly s.**, balance *m* mensual.

statesman ['steɪtsmən] *n* estadista *m*.

static ['stætɪk] I *adj* estático,-a. II *n Rad* ruido.

station ['steɪʃən] I *n* 1 estación *f*. **s. wagon**, camioneta *f*. 2 *(position)* puesto *m*. 3 *(social standing)* rango *m*. II *vtr (place)* colocar; *Mil* apostar.

stationary ['steɪʃənrɪ] *adj (not moving)*

inmóvil; *(unchanging)* estacionario,-a.

stationer ['steɪʃənər] *n* papelero,-a *m,f*; **s.'s (shop)**, papelería *f*.

stationery ['steɪʃənrɪ] *n (paper)* papel *m* de escribir; *(pens, ink etc)* artículos *mpl* de escritorio.

stationmaster ['steɪʃənmɑːstər] *n* jefe *m* de estación.

statistic [stə'tɪstɪk] *n* estadística *f*.

statistical [stə'tɪstɪkəl] *adj* estadístico,-a.

statistics [stə'tɪstɪks] *npl (science)* estadística *f sing*; *(data)* estadísticas *fpl*.

statue ['stætjuː] *n* estatua *f*.

status ['steɪtəs] *n* estado *m*; **social s.**, estatus *m*; **s. symbol**, signo *m* de prestigio; **s. quo**, status quo *m*.

statute ['stætjuːt] *n* estatuto *m*.

statutory ['stætjutrɪ] *adj* reglamentario, -a; *(offence)* contemplado,-a por la ley; *(right)* legal; *(holiday)* oficial.

staunch [stɔːntʃ] *adj* incondicional, acérrimo.

stave [steɪv] *n Mus* pentagrama *m*. ◆**stave off** *vtr (repel)* rechazar; *(avoid)* evitar; *(delay)* aplazar.

stay[1] [steɪ] I *n* estancia *f*. II *vi* 1 *(remain)* quedarse, permanecer. 2 *(reside temporarily)* alojarse; **she's staying with us for a few days**, ha venido a pasar unos días con nosotros. III *vtr fig* **to s. the course**, aguantar hasta el final; **staying power**, resistencia *f*. ◆**stay in** *vi* quedarse en casa. ◆**stay on** *vi* quedarse. ◆**stay out** *vi* **to s. out all night**, no volver a casa en toda la noche. ◆**stay up** *vi* no acostarse.

stay[2] [steɪ] *n (rope)* estay *m*, viento *m*.

stead [sted] *n* **in sb's s.**, en lugar de algn; **to stand sb in good s.**, resultar muy útil a algn.

steadfast ['stedfɑːst, 'stedfɑːst] *adj* firme.

steady ['stedɪ] I *adj (steadier, steadiest)* firme, seguro,-a; *(gaze)* fijo,-a; *(prices)* estable; *(demand, speed)* constante; *(pace)* regular; *(worker)* aplicado,-a; **s. job**, empleo fijo. II *vtr (table etc)* estabilizar; *(nerves)* calmar. III *vi (market)* estabilizarse. ◆**steadily** *adv (improve)* constantemente; *(walk)* con paso seguro; *(gaze)* fijamente; *(rain, work)* sin parar.

steak [steɪk] *n* bistec *m*.

steal [stiːl] *(pt* **stole***; pp* **stolen***)* I *vtr* robar; **to s. a glance at sth**, echar una mirada furtiva a algn; **to s. the show**, llevarse todos los aplausos. II *vi* 1 *(rob)* robar. 2 *(move quietly)* moverse con sigilo; **to s. away**, escabullirse.

stealth [stelθ] *n* sigilo *m*.

stealthy ['stelθɪ] *adj (stealthier, stealthiest)* sigiloso,-a, furtivo,-a. ◆**stealthily** *adv* a hurtadillas.

steam [stiːm] *n* vapor *m*; *fam* **to let off s.**, desahogarse; **s. engine**, máquina *f* de vapor. II *vtr Culin* cocer al vapor. III *vi* (give off steam) echar vapor; (bowl of soup etc) humear. ◆**steam up** vi (window etc) empañarse.

steamer ['sti:mər] n Naut vapor m.

steamroller ['sti:mrəʊlər] n apisonadora f.

steamship ['sti:mʃɪp] n vapor m.

steamy ['sti:mɪ] adj (**steamier, steamiest**) lleno,-a de vapor.

steel [sti:l] I n acero m; **s. industry**, industria siderúrgica. II vtr fig to s. one-self to do sth, armarse de valor para hacer algo.

steelworks ['sti:lwɜ:ks] npl acería f sing.

steep¹ [sti:p] adj (hill etc) empinado,-a; fig (price, increase) excesivo,-a.

steep² [sti:p] vtr (washing) remojar; (food) poner en remojo.

steeple ['sti:pəl] n aguja f.

steeplechase ['sti:pəltʃeɪs] n carrera f de obstáculos.

steer [stɪər] I vtr dirigir; (car) conducir; (ship) gobernar. II vi (car) conducirse; fig to s. clear of sth, evitar algo.

steering ['stɪərɪŋ] n dirección f; **assisted s.**, dirección asistida; **s. wheel**, volante m.

stem [stem] I n 1 (of plant) tallo m; (of glass) pie m; (of pipe) tubo m. 2 (of word) raíz f. II vi to s. from, derivarse de. III vtr (blood) restañar; (flood, attack) contener.

stench [stentʃ] n hedor m.

stencil ['stensəl] n 1 (for artwork etc) plantilla f. 2 (for typing) cliché m.

step [step] I n 1 paso m; (sound) paso, pisada f; **s. by s.**, poco a poco. 2 (measure) medida f; **a s. in the right direction**, un paso acertado. 3 (stair) peldaño m, escalón m. 4 **steps**, escalera f. II vi dar un paso; **s. this way, please**, haga el favor de pasar por aquí; to s. aside, apartarse. ◆**step down** vi dimitir. ◆**step forward** vi (volunteer) ofrecerse. ◆**step in** vi intervenir. ◆**step up** vtr aumentar.

stepbrother ['stepbrʌðər] n hermanastro m.

stepchild ['steptʃaɪld] n hijastro,-a m,f.

stepdaughter ['stepdɔ:tər] n hijastra f.

stepfather ['stepfɑ:ðər] n padrastro m.

stepladder ['steplædər] n escalera f de tijera.

stepmother ['stepmʌðər] n madrastra f.

stepping-stone ['stepɪŋstəʊn] n pasadera f; fig trampolín m.

stepsister ['stepsɪstər] n hermanastra f.

stepson ['stepsʌn] n hijastro m.

stereo ['sterɪəʊ] I n estéreo m. II adj estereo(fónico,-a).

stereotype ['sterɪətaɪp] n estereotipo m.

sterile ['steraɪl] adj (barren) estéril.

sterilize ['sterɪlaɪz] vtr esterilizar.

sterling ['stɜ:lɪŋ] I n libras fpl esterlinas; **s. silver**, plata f de ley; **the pound s.**, la

libra esterlina. II adj (person, quality) excelente.

stern¹ [stɜ:n] adj (severe) severo,-a.

stern² [stɜ:n] n Naut popa f.

steroid ['sterɔɪd] n esteroide m.

stethoscope ['steθəskəʊp] n estetoscopio m.

stew [stju:] I n estofado m, cocido m. II vtr (meat) guisar, estofar; (fruit) cocer.

steward ['stjʊəd] n (on estate) administrador m; (on ship) camarero m; (on plane) auxiliar m de vuelo.

stewardess ['stjʊədɪs] n (on ship) camarera f; (on plane) azafata f.

stick¹ [stɪk] n 1 palo m; (walking stick) bastón m; (of dynamite) cartucho m; fam **to give sb s.**, dar caña a algn. 2 fam **to live in the sticks**, vivir en el quinto pino.

stick² [stɪk] I vtr (pt & pp **stuck**) 1 (push) meter; (knife) clavar; **he stuck his head out of the window**, sacó la cabeza por la ventana. 2 fam (put) meter. 3 (with glue etc) pegar. 4 fam (tolerate) soportar, aguantar. II vi 1 (become attached) pegarse. 2 (window, drawer) atrancarse; (machine part) encasquillarse. ◆**stick at** vtr perseverar en. ◆**stick by** vtr (friend) ser fiel a; (promise) cumplir con. ◆**stick out** I vi (project) sobresalir; (be noticeable) resaltar. II vtr (tongue) sacar; fig to s. one's neck out, jugarse el tipo. ◆**stick to** vtr (principles) atenerse a. ◆**stick up** I vi (project) sobresalir; (hair) ponerse de punta. II vtr 1 (poster) fijar. 2 (hand etc) levantar. ◆**stick up for** vtr defender.

sticker ['stɪkər] n (label) etiqueta adhesiva; (with slogan) pegatina f.

stickler ['stɪklər] n meticuloso,-a; **to be a s. for detail**, ser muy detallista.

stick-up ['stɪkʌp] n US fam atraco m, asalto m.

sticky ['stɪkɪ] adj (**stickier, stickiest**) pegajoso,-a; (label) engomado,-a; (weather) bochornoso,-a; fam (situation) difícil.

stiff [stɪf] I adj 1 rígido,-a, tieso,-a; (collar, lock) duro,-a; (joint) entumecido,-a; (machine part) atascado,-a; **to have a s. neck**, tener tortícolis. 2 fig (test) difícil; (punishment) severo,-a; (price) excesivo,-a; (drink) fuerte; (person) (unnatural) estirado,-a. II n fam (corpse) fiambre m.

stiffen ['stɪfən] I vtr (fabric) reforzar; (collar) almidonar; fig (resistance) fortalecer. II vi (person) ponerse tieso,-a; (joints) entumecerse; fig (resistance) fortalecerse.

stiffness ['stɪfnɪs] n rigidez f.

stifle ['staɪfəl] I vtr (person) sofocar; (yawn) reprimir. II vi ahogarse, sofocarse.

stifling ['staɪflɪŋ] adj sofocante, agobiante.

stigma ['stɪgmə] n estigma m.

stile [staɪl] n escalones mpl para pasar por encima de una valla.

stiletto [stɪ'letəʊ] n zapato m con tacón

de aguja.

still¹ [stɪl] **I** *adv* **1** (*up to this time*) todavía, aún. **2** (*with comp adj & adv*) (*even*) aún; **s. colder**, aún más frío. **3** (*nonetheless*) no obstante, con todo. **4** (*however*) sin embargo. **5** (*motionless*) quieto; **to stand s.**, no moverse. **II** *adj* (*calm*) tranquilo,-a; (*peaceful*) sosegado,-a; (*silent*) silencioso,-a; (*motionless*) inmóvil. **III** *n Cin* fotograma *m*; *Art* **s. life**, naturaleza muerta. **IV** *vtr fml* (*fears etc*) calmar.

still² [stɪl] *n* (*apparatus*) alambique *m*.

stillborn ['stɪlbɔːn] *adj* nacido,-a muerto,-a.

stillness ['stɪlnɪs] *n* calma *f*; (*silence*) silencio *m*.

stilt [stɪlt] *n* zanco *m*.

stilted ['stɪltɪd] *adj* afectado,-a.

stimulant ['stɪmjʊlənt] *n* estimulante *m*.

stimulate ['stɪmjʊleɪt] *vtr* estimular.

stimulating ['stɪmjʊleɪtɪŋ] *adj* estimulante.

stimulus ['stɪmjʊləs] *n* (*pl* **stimuli** ['stɪmjʊlaɪ]) estímulo *m*; *fig* incentivo *m*.

sting [stɪŋ] **I** *n* (*part of bee, wasp*) aguijón *m*; (*wound*) picadura *f*; (*burning*) escozor *m*; *fig* (*of remorse*) punzada *f*; *fig* (*of remark*) sarcasmo *m*. **II** *vtr* (*pt & pp* **stung**) picar; (*conscience*) remorder; *fig* (*remark*) herir en lo vivo. **III** *vi* picar.

stingy ['stɪndʒɪ] *adj* (**stingier, stingiest**) *fam* (*person*) tacaño,-a; (*amount*) escaso,-a; **to be s. with**, escatimar.

stink [stɪŋk] **I** *n* peste *m*, hedor *m*. **II** *vi* (*pt* **stank**; *pp* **stunk**) apestar, heder (**of**, a).

stinking ['stɪŋkɪŋ] **I** *adj* (*smelly*) apestoso,-a; *fam* **to have a s. cold**, tener un catarro bestial. **II** *adv fam* **he's very rich**, está podrido de dinero.

stint [stɪnt] **I** *n* (*period*) período *m*, temporada *f*; (*shift*) turno *m*; **he did a two-year s. in the navy**, sirvió durante dos años en la Marina. **II** *vtr* escatimar.

stipulate ['stɪpjʊleɪt] *vtr* estipular.

stipulation [stɪpjʊ'leɪʃən] *n* estipulación *f*.

stir [stɜː*ʳ*] **I** *n fig* revuelo *m*. **II** *vtr* **1** (*liquid*) remover. **2** (*move*) agitar. **3** *fig* (*curiosity, interest*) despertar; (*anger*) provocar. **III** *vi* (*move*) rebullirse. ◆**stir up** *vtr fig* (*memories, curiosity*) despertar; (*anger*) provocar; (*revolt*) fomentar.

stirring ['stɜːrɪŋ] *adj* conmovedor,-a.

stirrup ['stɪrəp] *n* estribo *m*.

stitch [stɪtʃ] **I** *n Sew* puntada *f*; (*in knitting*) punto *m*; *Med* punto (de sutura); *fam* **we were in stitches**, nos tronchábamos de risa. **II** *vtr* (*pin*) punzada *f*. **II** *vtr* *Sew* coser; *Med* suturar, dar puntos a.

stoat [stəʊt] *n* armiño *m*.

stock [stɒk] *n* **1** (*supply*) reserva *f*; *Com* (*goods*) existencias *fpl*, stock *m*; (*selection*) surtido *m*; **out of s.**, agotado,-a; **to have sth in s.**, tener existencias de algo; *fig* **to take s. of**, evaluar. **2** *Fin* capital *m* social; **stocks and shares**, acciones *fpl*, valores *mpl*; **S. Exchange**, Bolsa *f* (de valores); **s. market**, bolsa. **3** *Agr* ganado *m*; **s. farming**, ganadería *f*. **4** *Culin* caldo *m*; **s. cube**, cubito *m* de caldo. **5** (*descent*) estirpe *f*. **II** *adj* **1** (*goods*) corriente. **2** (*excuse, response*) de siempre; (*phrase*) gastado,-a. **III** *vtr* **1** (*have in stock*) tener existencias de. **2** (*provide*) abastecer, surtir (**with**, de); (*cupboard*) llenar (**with**, de). ◆**stock up** *vi* abastecerse (**on**, **with**, de).

stockbroker ['stɒkbrəʊkə*ʳ*] *n* corredor,-a *m,f* de Bolsa.

stockholder ['stɒkhəʊldə*ʳ*] *n US* accionista *mf*.

stocking ['stɒkɪŋ] *n* media *f*; **a pair of stockings**, unas medias.

stockist ['stɒkɪst] *n* distribuidor,-a *m,f*.

stockpile ['stɒkpaɪl] **I** *n* reservas *fpl*. **II** *vtr* almacenar; (*accumulate*) acumular.

stocks [stɒks] *npl Hist* cepo *m sing*.

stocktaking ['stɒkteɪkɪŋ] *n Com* inventario *m*.

stocky ['stɒkɪ] *adj* (**stockier, stockiest**) (*squat*) rechoncho,-a; (*heavily built*) fornido,-a.

stodgy ['stɒdʒɪ] *adj* (**stodgier, stodgiest**) (*food*) indigesto,-a; *fig* (*book, person*) pesado,-a.

stoical ['stəʊɪkəl] *adj* estoico,-a.

stoke [stəʊk] *vtr* (*poke*) atizar; **to s. (up)**, (*feed*) alimentar.

stole¹ [stəʊl] *pt* → **steal**.

stole² [stəʊl] *n* estola *f*.

stolen ['stəʊlən] *pp* → **steal**.

stolid ['stɒlɪd] *adj* impasible.

stomach ['stʌmək] **I** *n* estómago *m*; **s. ache**, dolor *m* de estómago; **s. upset**, trastorno gástrico. **II** *vtr fig* aguantar.

stone [stəʊn] **I** *n* **1** piedra *f*; (*on grave*) lápida *f*; *fig* **at a s.'s throw**, a tiro de piedra. **2** *Med* cálculo *m*. **3** (*of fruit*) hueso *m*. **4** (*weight*) *aprox* 6.348 kg. **II** *adj* de piedra; **the S. Age**, la Edad de Piedra. **III** *vtr* (*kill*) lapidar.

stone-cold [stəʊn'kəʊld] *adj* helado,-a.

stoned [stəʊnd] *adj sl* (*drugged*) colocado,-a; (*drunk*) como una cuba.

stone-deaf [stəʊn'def] *adj* sordo,-a como una tapia.

stonework ['stəʊnwɜːk] *n* mampostería *f*.

stony ['stəʊnɪ] *adj* (**stonier, stoniest**) (*ground*) pedregoso,-a; *fig* (*look, silence*) glacial.

stood [stʊd] *pt & pp* → **stand**.

stool [stuːl] *n* **1** (*seat*) taburete *m*. **2** *Med* heces *fpl*.

stoop [stuːp] *vi* **1** (*have a stoop*) andar encorvado,-a. **2** (*bend*) inclinarse, agacharse (**down**, -). **3** *fig* **to s. to**, rebajarse a; **he wouldn't s. so low**, no se rebajaría tanto.

stop [stɒp] **I** *n* **1** (*halt*) parada *f*, alto *m*; **to come to a s.**, pararse; **to put a s. to sth**, poner fin a algo. **2** (*break*) pausa *f*; (*for refuelling etc*) escala *f*. **3** (*for bus, tram*) parada *f*. **4** (*punctuation mark*) punto *m*. **II** *vtr* **1** parar; (*conversation*) interrumpir; (*pain, abuse etc*) poner fin a. **2** (*payments*) suspender; (*cheque*) anular. **3 s. singing**, deja de cantar; **s. it!**, ¡basta ya! **4** (*prevent*) evitar; **to s. sb from doing sth**, impedir a algn hacer algo. **5** (*hole*) tapar; (*gap*) rellenar. **III** *vi* **1** (*person, moving vehicle*) pararse, detenerse; **my watch has stopped**, se me ha parado el reloj; **to s. dead**, pararse en seco. **2** (*cease*) acabarse, terminar. **3** *fam* (*stay*) pararse. ◆**stop by** *vi fam* visitar. ◆**stop off** *vi* pararse un rato. ◆**stop over** *vi* (*spend the night*) pasar la noche; (*for refuelling etc*) hacer escala. ◆**stop up** *vtr* (*hole*) tapar.

stopgap ['stɒpgæp] *n* (*thing*) medida *f* provisional; (*person*) sustituto,-a *m,f*.

stopover ['stɒpəʊvə'] *n* parada *f*; *Av* escala *f*.

stoppage ['stɒpɪdʒ] *n* **1** (*of game, payments*) suspensión *f*; (*of work*) paro *m*; (*strike*) huelga *f*; (*deduction*) deducción *f*; (*blockage*) obstrucción *f*.

stopper ['stɒpə'] *n* tapón *m*.

stop-press [stɒp'pres] *n* noticias *fpl* de última hora.

stopwatch ['stɒpwɒtʃ] *n* cronómetro *m*.

storage ['stɔːrɪdʒ] *n* almacenaje *m*, almacenamiento *m*; **s. battery**, acumulador *m*; **s. heater**, placa acumuladora.

store [stɔː'] **I** *n* **1** (*stock*) provisión *f*; *fig* (*of wisdom*) reserva *f*. **2 stores**, víveres *mpl*. **3** (*warehouse*) almacén *m*. **4** *US* (*shop*) tienda *f*; **department s.**, gran almacén *m*. **II** *vtr* **1** (*furniture, computer data*) almacenar; (*keep*) guardar. **2 to s. (up)**, acumular.

storekeeper ['stɔːkiːpə'] *n US* tendero,-a *m,f*.

storeroom ['stɔːruːm] *n* despensa *f*.

storey ['stɔːrɪ] *n* piso *m*.

stork [stɔːk] *n* cigüeña *f*.

storm [stɔːm] **I** *n* tormenta *f*; (*with wind*) vendaval *m*; *fig* (*uproar*) revuelo *m*; **by s. he has taken New York by s.**, ha cautivado a todo Nueva York. **II** *vtr* tomar por asalto. **III** *vi* (*with rage*) echar pestes.

stormy ['stɔːmɪ] *adj* (*stormier, stormiest*) (*weather*) tormentoso,-a; *fig* (*discussion*) acalorado,-a; (*relationship*) tempestuoso,-a.

story¹ ['stɔːrɪ] *n* historia *f*; (*tale, account*) relato *m*; (*article*) artículo *m*; (*plot*) trama *f*; (*joke*) chiste *m*; (*rumour*) rumor *m*; **it's a long s.**, sería largo de contar; **tall s.**,

cuento chino.

story² ['stɔːrɪ] *n US* → **storey**.

storybook ['stɔːrɪbʊk] *n* libro *m* de cuentos.

storyteller ['stɔːrɪtelə'] *n* cuentista *mf*.

stout [staʊt] **I** *adj* **1** (*fat*) gordo,-a, corpulento,-a. **2** (*strong*) fuerte. **3** (*brave*) valiente; (*determined*) firme. **II** *n* (*beer*) cerveza negra. ◆**stoutly** *adv* resueltamente.

stove¹ [stəʊv] *n* **1** (*for heating*) estufa *f*. **2** (*cooker*) cocina *f*.

stow [stəʊ] *vtr* **1** (*cargo*) estibar. **2** (*put away*) guardar. ◆**stow away** *vi* (*on ship, plane*) viajar de polizón.

stowaway ['stəʊəweɪ] *n* polizón *mf*.

straddle ['strædəl] *vtr* **1** (*horse etc*) sentarse a horcajadas sobre. **2** *fig* (*embrace*) abarcar.

straggle ['strægəl] *vi* **1** (*lag behind*) rezagarse. **2** (*spread untidily*) desparramarse.

straggler ['stræglə'] *n* rezagado,-a *m,f*.

straight [streɪt] **I** *adj* **1** (*not bent*) recto,-a, derecho,-a; (*hair*) liso,-a; **to keep a s. face**, contener la risa. **2 I work eight hours s.**, trabajo ocho horas seguidas. **3** (*honest*) honrado,-a; (*answer*) sincero,-a; (*refusal*) rotundo,-a; **let's get things s.**, pongamos las cosas claras. **4** (*drink*) solo,-a, sin mezcla. **II** *adv* **1** (*in a straight line*) en línea recta. **2** (*directly*) directamente, derecho; **keep s. ahead**, sigue todo recto; **he walked s. in**, entró sin llamar. **3 s. away**, en seguida; **s. off**, en el acto. **4** (*frankly*) francamente. **III** *n GB Sport* **the home s.**, la recta final.

straighten ['streɪtən] *vtr* (*sth bent*) enderezar, poner derecho,-a; (*tie, picture*) poner bien; (*hair*) alisar. ◆**straighten out** *vtr* (*problem*) resolver.

straightforward [streɪt'fɔːwəd] *adj* **1** (*honest*) honrado,-a; (*sincere*) franco,-a. **2** *GB* (*simple*) sencillo,-a.

strain¹ [streɪn] **I** *vtr* **1** (*rope etc*) estirar; *fig* crear tensiones en. **2** *Med* torcer(se); (*eyes, voice*) forzar; (*heart*) cansar. **3** (*liquid*) filtrar; (*vegetables, tea*) colar. **II** *vi* (*pull*) tirar (**at**, de); *fig* **to s. to do sth**, esforzarse por hacer algo. **III** *n* **1** tensión *f*; (*effort*) esfuerzo *m*. **2** (*exhaustion*) agotamiento *m*. **3** *Med* torcedura *f*. **4** *Mus* **strains**, son *m sing*.

strain² [streɪn] *n* **1** (*breed*) raza *f*. **2** (*streak*) vena *f*.

strained [streɪnd] *adj* **1** (*muscle*) torcido,-a; (*eyes*) cansado,-a; (*voice*) forzado,-a. **2** (*atmosphere*) tenso,-a.

strainer ['streɪnə'] *n* colador *m*.

strait [streɪt] *n* **1** (*usu pl*) *Geog* estrecho *m*. **2** (*usu pl*) (*difficulty*) aprieto *m*; **in dire straits**, en un gran aprieto.

straitjacket ['streɪtdʒækɪt] *n* camisa *f* de fuerza.

strait-laced [streɪt'leɪst] *adj* remilgado,-a.

strand¹ [strænd] *vtr fig (person)* abandonar; **to leave stranded,** dejar plantado,-a.

strand² [strænd] *n (of thread)* hebra *f*; *(of hair)* pelo *m*.

strange [streɪndʒ] *adj* 1 *(unknown)* desconocido,-a; *(unfamiliar)* nuevo,-a. 2 *(odd)* raro,-a, extraño,-a.

stranger [streɪndʒər] *n (unknown person)* desconocido,-a *m,f*; *(outsider)* forastero,-a *m,f*.

strangle [stræŋgəl] *vtr* estrangular.

stranglehold [stræŋgəlhəʊld] *n* **to have a s. on sb,** tener a algn agarrado,-a por el cuello.

strangulation [stræŋgjʊˈleɪʃən] *n* estrangulación *f*.

strap [stræp] **I** *n (of leather)* correa *f*; *(on bag)* bandolera *f*; *(on dress)* tirante *m*. **II** *vtr* atar con correa.

strapping [stræpɪŋ] *adj fam* fornido,-a, robusto,-a.

strategic [strəˈtiːdʒɪk] *adj* estratégico,-a.

strategy [strætɪdʒɪ] *n* estrategia *f*.

stratosphere [strætəsfɪər] *n* estratosfera *f*.

stratum [strɑːtəm] *n (pl strata)* estrato *m*.

straw [strɔː] *n* 1 paja *f*; *fig* **to clutch at straws,** agarrarse a un clavo ardiente; *fam* **that's the last s.!,** ¡eso ya es el colmo! 2 *(for drinking)* pajita *f*.

strawberry [strɔːbərɪ] *n* fresa *f*; *(large)* fresón *m*.

stray [streɪ] **I** *vi (from path)* desviarse; *(get lost)* extraviarse. **II** *n animal* extraviado. **III** *adj (bullet)* perdido,-a; *(animal)* callejero,-a.

streak [striːk] **I** *n* 1 *(line)* raya *f*; **s. of lightning,** rayo *m*. 2 *(in hair)* reflejo *m*. 3 *fig (of genius etc)* vena *f*; *(of luck)* racha *f*. **II** *vtr* rayar **(with,** de). **III** *vi* **to s. past,** pasar como un rayo.

stream [striːm] **I** *n* 1 *(brook)* arroyo *m*, riachuelo *m*. 2 *(current)* corriente *f*. 3 *(of water, air)* flujo *m*; *(of tears)* torrente *m*; *(of blood)* chorro *m*; *(of light)* raudal *m*. 4 *fig (of abuse)* sarta *f*; *(of people)* oleada *f*. 3 *GB Educ* clase *f*. **II** *vtr GB Educ* poner en grupos. **III** *vi* 1 *(liquid)* correr. 2 *fig* **to s. in/out/past,** *(people etc)* entrar/salir/pasar en tropel. 3 *(hair, banner)* ondear.

streamer [striːmər] *n (paper ribbon)* serpentina *f*.

streamlined [striːmlaɪnd] *adj* 1 *(car)* aerodinámico,-a. 2 *(system, method)* racionalizado,-a.

street [striːt] *n* calle *f*; **the man in the s.,** el hombre de la calle; **s. map, s. plan,** (plano *m)* callejero *m*.

streetcar [striːtkɑːr] *n US* tranvía *m*.

streetlamp [striːtlæmp] *n* farol *m*.

streetwise [striːtwaɪz] *adj* espabilado,-a.

strength [streŋθ] *n* 1 fuerza *f*; *(of rope etc)* resistencia *f*; *(of emotion, colour)* intensi-

dad *f*; *(of alcohol)* graduación *f*. 2 *(power)* poder *m*; **on the s. of,** a base de. 3 *(ability)* punto *m* fuerte. **4 to be at full s./below s.,** tener/no tener completo el cupo.

strengthen [streŋθən] **I** *vtr* 1 reforzar; *(character)* fortalecer. 2 *(intensify)* intensificar **II** *vi* 1 *(gen)* reforzarse. 2 *(intensify)* intensificarse.

strenuous [strenjʊəs] *adj* 1 *(denial)* enérgico,-a; *(effort, life)* intenso,-a. 2 *(exhausting)* fatigoso,-a, cansado,-a.

stress [stres] **I** *n* 1 Tech tensión *f*. 2 Med estrés *m*. 3 *(emphasis)* hincapié *m*; *(on word)* acento *m*. **II** *vtr* 1 *(emphasize)* subrayar; *(word)* acentuar.

stretch [stretʃ] **I** *vtr* 1 *(elastic)* estirar; *(wings)* desplegar. **II** *vi (elastic)* estirarse; *fig* **my money won't s. to it,** mi dinero no me llegará para eso. **III** *n* 1 *(length)* trecho *m*, tramo *m*. 2 *(of land)* extensión *f*; *(of time)* intervalo *m*. ◆**stretch out I** *vtr (arm, hand)* alargar; *(legs)* estirar. **II** *vi* 1 *(person)* estirarse. 2 *(countryside, years etc)* extenderse.

stretcher [stretʃər] *n* camilla *f*.

strew [struː] *vtr (pt strewed; pp strewed or strewn [struːn])* esparcir.

stricken [strɪkən] *adj (with grief)* afligido,-a; *(with illness)* aquejado,-a; *(by disaster etc)* afectado,-a; *(damaged)* dañado,-a.

strict [strɪkt] *adj* 1 estricto,-a. 2 *(absolute)* absoluto,-a. ◆**strictly** *adv* 1 *(categorically)* terminantemente. 2 *(precisely)* estrictamente; **s. speaking,** en sentido estricto.

stride [straɪd] **I** *n* zancada *f*, tranco *m*; *fig (progress)* progresos *mpl*. **II** *vi (pt strode; pp stridden [strɪdən])* **to s. (along),** andar a zancadas.

strident [straɪdənt] *adj (voice, sound)* estridente; *(protest etc)* enérgico,-a.

strife [straɪf] *n* conflictos *mpl*.

strike [straɪk] **I** *vtr (pt & pp struck)* 1 *(hit)* pegar, golpear. 2 *(collide with)* chocar contra; *(bullet, lightning)* alcanzar. 3 *(match)* encender. 4 *(pose)* adoptar. 5 *(bargain)* cerrar; *(balance)* encontrar. 6 **the clock struck three,** el reloj dio las tres. 7 *(oil, gold)* descubrir; *fam* **to s. it lucky/rich,** tener suerte/hacerse rico,-a. 8 *(impress)* impresionar; **it strikes me …,** me parece …. **II** *vi (pt & pp struck)* 1 *(attack)* atacar; *(disaster)* sobrevenir. 2 *(clock)* dar la hora. 3 *(workers)* declararse en huelga. **III** *n* 1 *(by workers)* huelga *f*; **on s.,** en huelga; **to call a s.,** convocar una huelga. 2 *(of oil, gold)* descubrimiento *m*. 3 *(blow)* golpe *m*. 4 *Mil* ataque *m*. ◆**strike back** *vi* devolver el golpe. ◆**strike down** *vtr* fulminar, abatir. ◆**strike out I** *vtr (cross out)* tachar. **II** *vi* **to s. out at sb,** arremeter contra algn.

◆**strike up** *vtr* **1** *(friendship)* trabar; *(conversation)* entablar. **2** *(tune)* empezar a tocar.

striker ['straɪkər] *n* **1** *(worker)* huelguista *mf*. **2** *fam Ftb* marcador,-a *m,f*.

striking ['straɪkɪŋ] *adj (eye-catching)* llamativo,-a; *(noticeable)* notable; *(impressive)* impresionante.

string [strɪŋ] **I** *n* **1** *(cord)* cuerda *f*; *fig* **to pull strings for sb**, enchufar a algn; **s. bean**, judía *f* verde. **2** *(of events)* cadena *f*; *(of lies)* sarta *f*. **3** *(of racket, guitar)* cuerda *f*; *Mus* **the strings**, los instrumentos de cuerda. **II** *vtr (pt & pp* **strung)** **1** *(beads)* ensartar. **2** *(racket etc)* encordar. **3** *(beans)* quitar la hebra a.

stringent ['strɪndʒənt] *adj* severo,-a, estricto,-a.

strip¹ [strɪp] **I** *vtr* **1** *(person)* desnudar; *(bed)* quitar la ropa de; *(paint)* quitar. **2** *Tech* **to s. (down)**, desmontar. **II** *vi (undress)* desnudarse; *(perform striptease)* hacer un striptease. ◆**strip off I** *vtr* quitar. **II** *vi (undress)* desnudarse.

strip² [strɪp] *n* tira *f*; *(of land)* franja *f*; *(of metal)* fleje *m*; *GB fam (cartoon,* historieta *f*; **s. lighting**, alumbrado *m* fluorescente; **to tear sb off a s.**, echar una bronca a algn.

stripe [straɪp] *n* raya *f*; *Mil* galón *m*.

striped [straɪpt] *adj* rayado,-a, a rayas.

stripper ['strɪpər] *n* persona *f* que hace striptease.

strive [straɪv] *vi (pt* **strove;** *pp* **striven** ['strɪvən])* **to s. to do sth**, esforzarse por hacer algo.

strobe [strəʊb] *n* **s. lighting**, luces estroboscópicas.

strode [strəʊd] *pt* → **stride**.

stroke [strəʊk] **I** *n* **1** **a s. of luck**, un golpe de suerte. **2** *(in golf, cricket)* golpe *m*; *(rowing)* remada *f*; *Swimming* brazada *f*. **3** *(of pen)* trazo *m*; *(of brush)* pincelada *f*. **4** *(caress)* caricia *f*. **5** *Med* apoplejía *f*. **II** *vtr* acariciar.

stroll [strəʊl] **I** *vi* dar un paseo. **II** *n* paseo *m*.

stroller ['strəʊlər] *n US (for baby)* cochecito *m*.

strong [strɒŋ] **I** *adj* **1** fuerte. **2** *(durable)* sólido,-a. **3** *(firm, resolute)* firme. **4** *(colour)* intenso,-a; *(light)* brillante. **5** *(incontestable)* convincente. **6 to be 20 s.**, contar con 20 miembros. **II** *adv* fuerte; **to be going s.**, *(business)* ir fuerte; *(elderly person)* conservarse bien. ◆**strongly** *adv* fuertemente.

strongbox ['strɒŋbɒks] *n* caja *f* fuerte.

stronghold ['strɒŋhəʊld] *n Mil* fortaleza *f*; *fig* baluarte *m*.

strongroom ['strɒŋruːm] *n* cámara acorazada.

stroppy ['strɒpɪ] *adj (stroppier, stroppiest) GB fam* de mala uva.

strove [strəʊv] *pt* → **strive**.

struck [strʌk] *pt & pp* → **strike**.

structural ['strʌktʃərəl] *adj* estructural.

structure ['strʌktʃər] *n* estructura *f*; *(constructed thing)* construcción *f*; *(building)* edificio *m*.

struggle ['strʌgəl] **I** *vi* luchar. **II** *n* lucha *f*; *(physical fight)* pelea *f*.

strum [strʌm] *vtr* rasguear.

strung [strʌŋ] *pt & pp* → **string**.

strut [strʌt] *vi* pavonearse.

stub [stʌb] **I** *n* **1** *(of cigarette)* colilla *f*; *(of pencil)* cabo *m*; *(of cheque)* matriz *f*. **II** *vtr* **1** *(strike)* golpear. **2 to s. (out)**, apagar.

stubble ['stʌbəl] *n* *(in field)* rastrojo *m*; *(on chin)* barba *f* de tres días.

stubborn ['stʌbən] *adj* **1** terco,-a, testarudo,-a. **2** *(stain)* difícil. **3** *(refusal)* rotundo,-a.

stucco ['stʌkəʊ] *n* estuco *m*.

stuck [stʌk] *pt & pp* → **stick²**.

stuck-up [stʌk'ʌp] *adj fam* creído,-a.

stud¹ [stʌd] **I** *n (on clothing)* tachón *m*; *(on football boots)* taco *m*; *(on shirt)* botonadura *f*. **II** *vtr (decorate)* tachonar (**with**, de); *fig (dot, cover)* salpicar (**with**, de).

stud² [stʌd] *n (horse)* semental *m*.

student ['stjuːdənt] *n* estudiante *mf*; **s. teacher**, profesor,-a *m,f* en prácticas.

studio ['stjuːdɪəʊ] *n TV Cin* estudio *m*; *(artist's)* taller *m*; **s. apartment, s. flat**, estudio.

studious ['stjuːdɪəs] *adj* estudioso,-a. ◆**studiously** *adv* cuidadosamente.

study ['stʌdɪ] **I** *vtr* estudiar; *(facts etc)* examinar, investigar; *(behaviour)* observar. **II** *vi* estudiar; **to s. to be a doctor**, estudiar para médico. **III** *n* **1** estudio *m*; **s. group**, grupo *m* de trabajo. **2** *(room)* despacho *m*, estudio *m*.

stuff [stʌf] **I** *vtr* **1** *(container)* llenar (**with**, de); *Culin* rellenar (**with**, con or de); *(animal)* disecar. **2** *(cram)* atiborrar (**with**, de). **II** *n* **1** *fam (material)* material *m*. **2** *fam (things)* cosas *fpl*; *fam* trastos *mpl*.

stuffing ['stʌfɪŋ] *n Culin* relleno *m*.

stuffy ['stʌfɪ] *adj (stuffier, stuffiest)* **1** *(room)* mal ventilado,-a; *(atmosphere)* cargado,-a. **2** *(pompous)* estirado,-a; *(narrow-minded)* de miras estrechas.

stumble ['stʌmbəl] *vi* tropezar, dar un traspié; *fig* **to s. across** or **on** or **upon**, tropezar or dar con.

stumbling ['stʌmblɪŋ] *n* **s. block**, escollo *m*.

stump [stʌmp] **I** *n* **1** *(of pencil)* cabo *m*; *(of tree)* tocón *m*; *(of arm, leg)* muñón *m*. **2** *(in cricket)* estaca *f*. **II** *vtr (puzzle)* confundir; **to be stumped**, estar perplejo,-a.

stun [stʌn] *vtr (of blow)* aturdir; *fig (of news etc)* sorprender.

stung [stʌŋ] *pt & pp* → **sting**.

stunk [stʌŋk] *pt & pp* → **stink**.

stunning ['stʌnɪŋ] *adj (blow)* duro,-a;

(news) sorprendente; *fam (woman, outfit)* fenomenal.

stunt¹ [stʌnt] *vtr (growth)* atrofiar.

stunt² [stʌnt] *n* **1** *Av* acrobacia *f.* **2** *publicity* s., truco publicitario. **3** *Cin* escena peligrosa; **s. man,** doble *m.*

stunted [stʌntɪd] *adj* enano,-a, mal desarrollado,-a.

stupefy [stjuːpɪfaɪ] *vtr (alcohol, drugs)* aturdir; *fig (news etc)* dejar pasmado,-a.

stupendous [stjuːpendəs] *adj (wonderful)* estupendo,-a.

stupid [stjuːpɪd] *adj* estúpido,-a, imbécil.

stupidity [stjuːpɪdɪtɪ] *n* estupidez *f.*

stupor [stjuːpəʳ] *n* estupor *m.*

sturdy [stɜːdɪ] *adj (sturdier, sturdiest)* robusto,-a, fuerte; *(resistance)* enérgico,-a.

stutter [stʌtəʳ] **I** *vi* tartamudear. **II** *n* tartamudeo *m.*

sty [staɪ] *n (pen)* pocilga *f.*

style(e) [staɪ] *n Med* orzuelo *m.*

style [staɪl] **I** *n* **1** estilo *m;* *(of dress)* modelo *m.* **2** *(fashion)* moda *f.* **3** **to live in s.,** *(elegance)* vivir a lo grande. **II** *vtr (hair)* marcar.

stylish [staɪlɪʃ] *adj* con estilo.

stylist [staɪlɪst] *n (hairdresser)* peluquero,-a *mf.*

stylus [staɪləs] *n (of record player)* aguja *f.*

suave [swɑːv] *adj* amable, afable; *pej* zalamero,-a.

sub [sʌb] *n fam* **1** *abbr of* **substitute.** **2** *abbr of* **subscription.**

sub- [sʌb] *pref* sub-.

subconscious [sʌbkɒnʃəs] **I** *adj* subconsciente. **II** *n* **the s.,** el subconsciente.

subcontract [sʌbkəntrækt] *vtr* subcontratar.

subcontractor [sʌbkəntræktəʳ] *n* subcontratista *mf.*

subdivide [sʌbdɪvaɪd] *vtr* subdividir *(into,* en).

subdue [səbdjuː] *vtr* **1** *(nation, people)* sojuzgar. **2** *(feelings)* dominar. **3** *(colour, light)* atenuar.

subdued [səbdjuːd] *adj* **1** *(person, emotion)* callado,-a. **2** *(voice, tone)* bajo,-a. **3** *(light)* tenue; *(colour)* apagado,-a.

subject [sʌbdʒɪkt] **I** *n* **1** *(citizen)* súbdito *m.* **2** *(topic)* tema *m;* **s. matter,** materia *f;* *(contents)* contenido *m.* **3** *Educ* asignatura *f.* **4** *Ling* sujeto *m.* **II** *adj* **s. to,** *(law, tax)* sujeto,-a a; *(charge)* expuesto,-a a; *(changes, delays)* propenso,-a a; *(illness)* propenso,-a a; *(conditional upon)* previo, -a. **III** [səbdʒekt] *vtr* someter.

subjective [səbdʒektɪv] *adj* subjetivo,-a.

subjunctive [səbdʒʌŋktɪv] **I** *adj* subjuntivo,-a. **II** *n* subjuntivo *m.*

sublet [sʌblet] *vtr & vi* subarrendar.

sublime [səblaɪm] *adj* sublime.

sub-machine-gun [sʌbməʃiːŋgʌn] *n* ametralladora *f.*

submarine [sʌbməriːn] *n* submarino *m.*

(news) sorprendente; *fam (woman, outfit)* fenomenal.

submerge [səbmɜːdʒ] *vtr* sumergir; *(flood)* inundar; *fig* **submerged in ...,** sumido,-a en .....

submission [səbmɪʃən] *n* **1** *(yielding)* sumisión *f.* **2** *(of documents)* presentación *f.* **3** *(report)* informe *m.*

submissive [səbmɪsɪv] *adj* sumiso,-a.

submit [səbmɪt] **I** *vtr* **1** *(present)* presentar. **2** *(subject)* someter (to, a). **II** *vi (surrender)* rendirse.

subnormal [sʌbnɔːməl] *adj* subnormal.

subordinate [səbɔːdɪnɪt] *adj & n* subordinado,-a *(m,f).*

subpoena [səbpiːnə] **I** *n* citación *f.* **II** *vtr* citar.

subscribe [səbskraɪb] *vi (magazine)* suscribirse (to, a); *(opinion, theory)* adherirse (to, a).

subscriber [səbskraɪbəʳ] *n* abonado,-a *m,f.*

subscription [səbskrɪpʃən] *n (to magazine)* abono *m;* *(to club)* cuota *f.*

subsequent [sʌbsɪkwənt] *adj* subsiguiente. ◆**subsequently** *adv* posteriormente.

subside [səbsaɪd] *vi (land)* hundirse; *(floodwater)* bajar; *(wind, anger)* amainar.

subsidence [səbsaɪdəns] *n (of land)* hundimiento *m;* *(of floodwater)* bajada *f;* *(of wind)* amaine *m.*

subsidiary [səbsɪdɪərɪ] *adj (role)* secundario,-a. **II** *n Com* sucursal *f,* filial *f.*

subsidize [sʌbsɪdaɪz] *vtr* subvencionar.

subsidy [sʌbsɪdɪ] *n* subvención *f.*

subsistence [səbsɪstəns] *n* subsistencia *f.*

substance [sʌbstəns] *n* **1** sustancia *f.* **2** *(essence)* esencia *f.* **3** **a woman of s.,** *(wealth)* una mujer acaudalada.

substantial [səbstænʃəl] *adj* **1** *(solid)* sólido,-a. **2** *(sum, loss)* importante; *(difference, improvement)* notable; *(meal)* abundante.

substantiate [səbstænʃɪeɪt] *vtr* respaldar.

substitute [sʌbstɪtjuːt] **I** *vtr* sustituir; **to s. X for Y,** sustituir X por Y. **II** *n (person)* suplente *mf;* *(thing)* sucedáneo *m.*

subtitle [sʌbtaɪtəl] *n* subtítulo *m.*

subtle [sʌtəl] *adj* sutil; *(taste)* delicado,-a; *(remark)* ingenioso,-a; *(irony)* fino,-a.

subtlety [sʌtəltɪ] *n* sutileza *f;* *(of remark)* ingeniosidad *f;* *(of irony, joke)* finura *f.*

subtract [səbtrækt] *vtr* restar.

subtraction [səbtrækʃən] *n* resta *f.*

suburb [sʌbɜːb] *n* barrio periférico; **the suburbs,** las afueras.

suburban [səbɜːbən] *adj* suburbano,-a.

suburbia [səbɜːbɪə] *n* barrios residenciales periféricos.

subversive [səbvɜːsɪv] *adj & n* subversivo,-a *(m,f).*

subway [sʌbweɪ] *n* **1** *GB (underpass)* paso subterráneo. **2** *US (underground railway)* metro *m.*

succeed [sək'si:d] I *vi* 1 (*person*) tener éxito; (*plan*) salir bien; **to s. in doing sth**, conseguir hacer algo. 2 (*follow after*) suceder; **to s. to**, (*throne*) suceder a. II *vtr* (*monarch*) suceder a.

succeeding [sək'si:dɪŋ] *adj* sucesivo,-a.

success [sək'ses] *n* éxito m.

successful [sək'sesful] *adj* (*person*) de éxito, exitoso,-a; (*business*) próspero,-a; (*marriage*) feliz; **to be s. in doing sth**, lograr hacer algo. ◆**successfully** *adv* con éxito.

succession [sək'seʃən] *n* sucesión f, serie f; **in s.**, sucesivamente.

successive [sək'sesɪv] *adj* sucesivo,-a, consecutivo,-a.

successor [sək'sesər] *n* sucesor,-a m,f.

succinct [sək'sɪŋkt] *adj* sucinto,-a.

succumb [sə'kʌm] *vi* sucumbir (**to**, a).

such [sʌtʃ] I *adj* 1 (*of that sort*) tal, semejante; **artists s. as Monet**, artistas como Monet; **at s. and s. a time**, a tal hora; **in s. a way that**, de tal manera que. 2 (*so much, so great*) tanto,-a; **he's always in s. a hurry**, siempre anda con tanta prisa; **she was in s. pain**, sufría tanto; **s. a lot of books**, tantos libros. II *adv* (*so very*) tan; **it's s. a long time ago**, hace tanto tiempo; **she's s. a clever woman**, es una mujer tan inteligente; **we had s. good weather**, hizo un tiempo tan bueno.

suchlike ['sʌtʃlaɪk] I *adj* tal. II *n* (*things*) cosas *fpl* por el estilo; (*people*) gente *f* por el estilo.

suck [sʌk] I *vtr* (*by pump*) aspirar; (*liquid*) sorber; (*lollipop, blood*) chupar. II *vi* (*person*) chupar; (*baby*) mamar. ◆**suck in** *vtr* (*of whirlpool*) tragar.

sucker ['sʌkər] *n* 1 *fam* primo,-a *m,f*, bobo,-a *m,f*. 2 *Zool* ventosa *f*; *Bot* chupón *m*.

suckle ['sʌkəl] *vtr* (*mother*) amamantar.

suction ['sʌkʃən] *n* succión *f*.

sudden ['sʌdən] *adj* 1 (*hurried*) súbito,-a, repentino,-a. 2 (*unexpected*) imprevisto,-a. 3 (*abrupt*) brusco,-a; **all of a s.**, de repente. ◆**suddenly** *adv* de repente.

suds [sʌdz] *npl* espuma *f* de jabón, jabonaduras *fpl*.

sue [su:, sju:] *Jur* I *vtr* demandar. II *vi* presentar una demanda; **to s. for divorce**, solicitar el divorcio.

suede [sweɪd] *n* ante *m*, gamuza *f*; (*for gloves*) cabritilla *f*.

suet ['su:ɪt] *n* sebo *m*.

suffer ['sʌfər] I *vtr* 1 sufrir. 2 (*tolerate*) aguantar, soportar. II *vi* sufrir; **to s. from**, sufrir de.

sufferer ['sʌfərər] *n Med* enfermo,-a *m,f*.

suffering ['sʌfərɪŋ] *n* (*affliction*) sufrimiento *m*; (*pain, torment*) dolor *m*.

suffice [sə'faɪs] *vi fml* bastar, ser suficiente.

sufficient [sə'fɪʃənt] *adj* suficiente,

bastante. ◆**sufficiently** *adv* suficientemente, bastante.

suffocate ['sʌfəkeɪt] I *vtr* asfixiar. II *vi* asfixiarse.

suffocating ['sʌfəkeɪtɪŋ] *adj* (*heat*) agobiante, sofocante.

suffrage ['sʌfrɪdʒ] *n* sufragio *m*.

suffuse [sə'fju:z] *vtr lit* bañar, cubrir (**with**, de).

sugar ['ʃugər] I *n* azúcar *m & f*; **s. beet**, remolacha *f* (azucarera); **s. bowl**, azucarero *m*; **s. cane**, caña *f* de azúcar. II *vtr* azucarar, echar azúcar a.

sugary ['ʃugərɪ] *adj* 1 (*like sugar*) azucarado,-a. 2 *fig* (*insincere*) zalamero,-a; (*over-sentimental*) sentimentaloide.

suggest [sə'dʒest] *vtr* 1 (*propose*) sugerir. 2 (*advise*) aconsejar. 3 (*indicate, imply*) indicar.

suggestion [sə'dʒestʃən] *n* 1 (*proposal*) sugerencia *f*. 2 (*trace*) sombra *f*; (*small amount*) toque *m*.

suggestive [sə'dʒestɪv] *adj* (*remark*) indecente.

suicidal [sjuɪ'saɪdəl] *adj* suicida.

suicide ['sjuɪsaɪd] *n* suicidio *m*.

suit [su:t, sju:t] I *n* 1 traje *m* de chaqueta. 2 *Jur* pleito *m*. 3 *Cards* palo *m*; *fig* **to follow s.**, seguir el ejemplo. II *vtr* 1 (*be convenient to*) convenir a, venir bien a. 2 (*be right, appropiate for*) ir bien a; **red really suits you**, el rojo te favorece mucho; **they are well suited**, están hechos el uno para el otro. 3 (*adapt*) adaptar a. 4 (*please*) **s. yourself!**, ¡como quieras!

suitable ['sju:təbəl] *adj* (*convenient*) conveniente; (*appropriate*) adecuado,-a; **the most s. woman for the job**, la mujer más indicada para el puesto. ◆**suitably** *adv* (*correctly*) correctamente; (*properly*) adecuadamente.

suitcase ['su:tkeɪs] *n* maleta *f*.

suite [swi:t] *n* 1 (*of furniture*) juego *m*. 2 (*of hotel rooms, music*) suite *f*.

suitor ['sju:tər] *n Lit* (*wooer*) pretendiente *m*.

sulfur ['sʌlfər] *n US →* **sulphur**.

sulk [sʌlk] *vi* enfurruñarse.

sulky ['sʌlkɪ] *adj* (**sulkier, sulkiest**) malhumorado,-a, enfurruñado,-a.

sullen ['sʌlən] *adj* hosco,-a; (*sky*) plomizo,-a.

sulphur ['sʌlfər] *n* azufre *m*.

sulphuric [sʌl'fjʊərɪk] *adj* sulfúrico,-a.

sultan ['sʌltən] *n* sultán *m*.

sultana [sʌl'tɑːnə] *n* (*raisin*) pasa *f* de Esmirna.

sultry ['sʌltrɪ] *adj* (**sultrier, sultriest**) 1 (*muggy*) bochornoso,-a. 2 (*seductive*) sensual.

sum [sʌm] *n* 1 (*arithmetic problem, amount*) suma *f*. 2 (*total amount*) total *m*; (*of money*) importe *m*. ◆**sum up** *vtr* resumir. II *vi* resumir; **to s. up ...**, en resumidas cuentas ....

summarize ['sʌmǝraɪz] vtr & vi resumir.

summary ['sʌmǝrɪ] **I** n resumen m. **II** adj sumario,-a.

summer ['sʌmǝr] **I** n verano m. **II** adj (holiday etc) de verano; (weather) veraniego,-a; (resort) de veraneo.

summerhouse ['sʌmǝhaʊs] n cenador m, glorieta f.

summertime ['sʌmǝtaɪm] n verano m.

summit ['sʌmɪt] n **1** (of mountain) cima f, cumbre f. **2** Pol s. (meeting), cumbre f.

summon ['sʌmǝn] vtr **1** (meeting, person) convocar. **2** (aid) pedir. **3** Jur citar.
◆**summon up** vtr (resources) reunir; to s. up one's courage, armarse de valor.

summons ['sʌmǝnz] **I** n **1** (call) llamada f, llamamiento m. **2** Jur citación f judicial. **II** vtr Jur citar.

sumptuous ['sʌmptjʊǝs] adj suntuoso,-a.

sun [sʌn] **I** n sol m. **II** vtr to s. oneself, tomar el sol.

sunbathe ['sʌnbeɪð] vi tomar el sol.

sunbed ['sʌnbed] n (in garden) tumbona f; (with sunlamp) solario m.

sunburn ['sʌnbɜːn] n (burn) quemadura f de sol.

sunburnt ['sʌnbɜːnt] adj (burnt) quemado,-a por el sol; (tanned) bronceado,-a.

Sunday ['sʌndɪ] n domingo m inv; S. newspaper, periódico m del domingo; S. school, catequesis f.

sundial ['sʌndaɪǝl] n reloj m de sol.

sundown ['sʌndaʊn] n US anochecer m.

sundry ['sʌndrɪ] **I** adj diversos,-as, varios,-as; fam all and s., todos sin excepción. **II** npl Com sundries, artículos mpl diversos; (expenses) gastos diversos.

sunflower ['sʌnflaʊǝr] n girasol m.

sung [sʌŋ] pp → sing.

sunglasses ['sʌnglɑːsɪz] npl gafas fpl de sol.

sunk [sʌŋk] pp → sink.

sunlamp ['sʌnlæmp] n lámpara f solar.

sunlight ['sʌnlaɪt] n sol m, luz f del sol.

sunlit ['sʌnlɪt] adj iluminado,-a por el sol.

sunny ['sʌnɪ] adj (sunnier, sunniest) **1** (day) de sol; (place) soleado,-a; it is s., hace sol. **2** fig (smile, disposition) alegre; (future) prometedor,-a.

sunrise ['sʌnraɪz] n salida f del sol.

sunroof ['sʌnruːf] n Aut techo corredizo.

sunset ['sʌnset] n puesta f del sol.

sunshade ['sʌnʃeɪd] n sombrilla f.

sunshine ['sʌnʃaɪn] n sol m, luz f del sol.

sunstroke ['sʌnstrǝʊk] n insolación f.

suntan ['sʌntæn] n bronceado m; s. oil or lotion, (aceite m) bronceador m.

super ['suːpǝr] adj fam fenomenal.

super- ['suːpǝr] pref super-, sobre-.

superannuation [suːpǝrænjʊ'eɪʃǝn] n GB jubilación f, pensión f.

superb [suː'pɜːb] adj espléndido,-a.

supercilious [suːpǝ'sɪlɪǝs] adj (condescending) altanero,-a; (disdainful) desdeñoso,-a.

superficial [suːpǝ'fɪʃǝl] adj superficial.

superfluous [suː'pɜːflʊǝs] adj sobrante, superfluo,-a; to be s., sobrar.

superhuman [suːpǝ'hjuːmǝn] adj sobrehumano,-a.

superimpose [suːpǝrɪm'pǝʊz] vtr sobreponer.

superintendent [suːpǝrɪn'tendǝnt] n director,-a m,f; police s., subjefe,-a m,f de policía.

superior [suː'pɪǝrɪǝr] **I** adj **1** superior. **2** (haughty) altivo,-a. **II** n superior,-a m,f.

superiority [suːpɪǝrɪ'ɒrɪtɪ] n superioridad f.

superlative [suː'pɜːlǝtɪv] **I** adj superlativo,-a. **II** n Ling superlativo m.

superman ['suːpǝmæn] n superhombre m, supermán m.

supermarket ['suːpǝmɑːkɪt] n supermercado m.

supernatural [suːpǝ'nætʃǝrǝl] **I** adj sobrenatural. **II** n the s., lo sobrenatural.

superpower ['suːpǝpaʊǝr] n Pol superpotencia f.

supersede [suːpǝ'siːd] vtr fml suplantar.

supersonic [suːpǝ'sɒnɪk] adj supersónico,-a.

superstitious [suːpǝ'stɪʃǝs] adj supersticioso,-a.

supertanker ['suːpǝtæŋkǝr] n superpetrolero m.

supervise ['suːpǝvaɪz] vtr supervisar; (watch over) vigilar.

supervision [suːpǝ'vɪʒǝn] n supervisión f.

supervisor ['suːpǝvaɪzǝr] n supervisor,-a m,f.

supper ['sʌpǝr] n cena f; to have s., cenar.

supplant [sǝ'plɑːnt] vtr suplantar.

supple ['sʌpǝl] adj flexible.

supplement ['sʌplɪmǝnt] **I** n suplemento m. **II** ['sʌplɪment] vtr complementar.

supplementary [sʌplɪ'mentǝrɪ] adj adicional.

supplier [sǝ'plaɪǝr] n suministrador,-a m,f; Com proveedor,-a m,f.

supply [sǝ'plaɪ] **I** n **1** suministro m; Com provisión f; (stock) surtido m; s. and demand, oferta f y demanda. **2** supplies, (food) víveres mpl; Mil pertrechos mpl; office supplies, material m sing para oficina. **II** vtr **1** (provide) suministrar. **2** (with provisions) aprovisionar. **3** (information) facilitar. **4** Com surtir.

support [sǝ'pɔːt] **I** n **1** (moral) apoyo m. **2** (funding) ayuda económica. **II** vtr **1** (weight etc) sostener. **2** fig (back) apoyar; (substantiate) respaldar. **3** Sport ser (hincha) de. **4** (sustain) mantener; (feed) alimentar.

supporter [sǝ'pɔːtǝr] n Pol partidario,-a m,f; Sport hincha mf.

suppose [sə'pəʊz] *vtr* suponer; *(presume)* creer; **I s. not/so**, supongo que no/sí; **you're not supposed to smoke in here**, no está permitido fumar aquí dentro; **you're supposed to be in bed**, deberías estar acostado,-a ya.

supposed [sə'pəʊzd] *adj* supuesto,-a. ◆**supposedly** *adv* teóricamente.

suppress [sə'pres] *vtr* suprimir; *(feelings, laugh etc)* contener; *(news, truth)* callar; *(revolt)* sofocar.

supranational [su:prə'næʃənəl] *adj* supranacional.

supremacy [su'preməsɪ] *n* supremacía *f*.

supreme [su'pri:m] *adj* supremo,-a; **with s. indifference**, con total indiferencia. ◆**supremely** *adv* sumamente.

surcharge ['sɜ:tʃɑ:dʒ] *n* recargo *m*.

sure [ʃʊər] I *adj* 1 seguro,-a; **I'm s. (that) ...**, estoy seguro,-a de que ...; **make s. that it's ready**, asegúrate de que esté listo; **s. of oneself**, seguro,-a de sí mismo,-a. 2 *US fam* **s. thing!**, ¡claro! II *adv* 1 *(of course)* claro. 2 *(certainly)* seguro,-a. 3 **s. enough**, efectivamente. ◆**surely** *adv (without a doubt)* sin duda; **s. not!**, ¡no puede ser!

surety ['ʃʊərtɪ] *n* 1 *(sum)* fianza *f*. 2 *(person)* fiador,-a *m,f*; **to stand s. for sb**, ser fiador de algn.

surf [sɜ:f] I *n* *(waves)* oleaje *m*; *(foam)* espuma *f*. II *vi* *Sport* hacer surf.

surface ['sɜ:fɪs] I *n* superficie *f*; *(of road)* firme *m*. II *adj* superficial; **s. area**, área *f* de la superficie; **by s. mail**, por vía terrestre *or* marítima. III *vtr (road)* revestir. IV *vi (submarine etc)* salir a la superficie; *fam (wake up)* levantarse.

surface-to-air [sɜ:fɪstʊ'eər] *adj* **s.-to-a. missile**, misil *m* tierra-aire.

surfboard ['sɜ:fbɔ:d] *n* tabla *f* de surf.

surfeit ['sɜ:fɪt] *n fml* exceso *m*.

surfer ['sɜ:fər] *n* surfista *mf*.

surfing ['sɜ:fɪŋ] *n* surf *m*, surfing *m*.

surge [sɜ:dʒ] I *n* 1 *(growth)* alza *f*. 2 *(of sea, sympathy)* oleada *f*; *fig (of anger, energy)* arranque *m*. II *vi* **to s. forward**, *(people)* avanzar en tropel.

surgeon ['sɜ:dʒən] *n* cirujano,-a *m,f*.

surgery ['sɜ:dʒərɪ] *n* 1 *(treatment)* cirugía *f*. 2 *GB (consulting room)* consultorio *m*; **s. hours**, horas *fpl* de consulta. 3 *US (operating theatre)* quirófano *m*.

surgical ['sɜ:dʒɪkəl] *adj* quirúrgico,-a; **s. spirit**, alcohol *m* de 90°.

surly ['sɜ:lɪ] *adj* (**surlier**, **surliest**) *(bad-tempered)* hosco,-a, malhumorado,-a; *(rude)* maleducado,-a.

surmount [sɜ:'maʊnt] *vtr* superar, vencer.

surname ['sɜ:neɪm] *n* apellido *m*.

surpass [sɜ:'pɑ:s] *vtr* superar.

surplus ['sɜ:pləs] I *n* *(of goods)* excedente *m*; *(of budget)* superávit *m*. II *adj* exce-

dente.

surprise [sə'praɪz] I *n* sorpresa *f*; **to take sb by s.**, coger desprevenido,-a a algn. II *adj (visit)* inesperado,-a; **s. attack**, ataque *m* sorpresa. III *vtr* sorprender.

surprising [sə'praɪzɪŋ] *adj* sorprendente. ◆**surprisingly** *adv* sorprendentemente, de modo sorprendente.

surrealist [sə'rɪəlɪst] *adj & n* surrealista *(mf)*.

surrender [sə'rendər] I *n* *Mil* rendición *f*; *(of weapons)* entrega *f*; *Ins* rescate *m*. II *vtr* *Mil* rendir; *(right)* renunciar a. III *vi (give in)* rendirse.

surreptitious [sʌrəp'tɪʃəs] *adj* subrepticio,-a.

surrogate ['sʌrəgɪt] *n fml* sustituto,-a *m,f*; **s. mother**, madre *f* de alquiler.

surround [sə'raʊnd] I *n* marco *m*, borde *m*. II *vtr* rodear.

surrounding [sə'raʊndɪŋ] I *adj* circundante. II *npl* **surroundings**, *(of place)* alrededores *mpl*, cercanías *fpl*.

surveillance [sɜ:'veɪləns] *n* vigilancia *f*.

survey ['sɜ:veɪ] I *n* 1 *(of building)* inspección *f*; *(of land)* medición *f*. 2 *(of trends etc)* encuesta *f*. 3 *(overall view)* panorama *m*. II [sɜ:'veɪ] *vtr* 1 *(building)* inspeccionar; *(land)* medir. 2 *(trends etc)* hacer una encuesta sobre. 3 *(look at)* contemplar.

surveyor [sɜ:'veɪər] *n* agrimensor,-a *m,f*; **quantity s.**, aparejador,-a *m,f*.

survival [sə'vaɪvəl] *n* supervivencia *f*.

survive [sə'vaɪv] I *vi* sobrevivir; *(remain)* perdurar. II *vtr* sobrevivir a.

survivor [sə'vaɪvər] *n* superviviente *mf*.

susceptible [sə'septəbəl] *adj* *(to attack)* susceptible *(to, a)*; *(to illness)* propenso,-a *(to, a)*.

suspect ['sʌspekt] I *adj* *(dubious)* sospechoso,-a. II *n* sospechoso,-a *m,f*. III [sə'spekt] *vtr* 1 *(person)* sospechar *(of, de)*; *(plot, motives)* recelar de. 2 *(think likely)* imaginar, creer.

suspend [sə'spend] *vtr* suspender; *(pupil)* expulsar por un tiempo.

suspended [sə'spendɪd] *adj* 1 suspendido,-a; *Jur* **s. sentence**, condena *f* condicional. 2 *Sport* sancionado,-a.

suspender [sə'spendər] *n* 1 *(for stocking)* liga *f*; **s. belt**, liguero *m*. 2 *US* **suspenders**, tirantes *mpl*.

suspense [sə'spens] *n* incertidumbre *f*; *Cin Theat* suspense *m*; **to keep sb in s.**, mantener a algn en la incertidumbre.

suspension [sə'spenʃən] *n* 1 suspensión *f*. 2 *Sport* sanción *f*. 3 *(of pupil, employee)* expulsión *f* temporal. 4 **s. bridge**, puente *m* colgante.

suspicion [sə'spɪʃən] *n* 1 sospecha *f*; *(mistrust)* recelo *m*; *(doubt)* duda *f*. 2 *(trace)* pizca *f*.

suspicious [sə'spɪʃəs] *adj* 1 *(arousing*

suspicion) sospechoso,-a. **2** (*distrustful*) receloso,-a; **to be s. of sb**, desconfiar de algn.

sustain [sə'steɪn] *vtr* **1** sostener. **2** (*nourish*) sustentar. **3** *Jur* (*objection*) admitir. **4** (*injury etc*) sufrir.

sustained [sə'steɪnd] *adj* sostenido,-a.

sustenance ['sʌstɪnəns] *n* sustento *m*.

swab [swɒb] **I** *n* (*cotton wool*) algodón *m*; (*for specimen*) frotis *m*. **II** *vtr* (*wound*) limpiar.

swagger ['swæɡə'] **I** *n* pavoneo *m*. **II** *vi* pavonearse.

swallow[1] ['swɒləʊ] **I** *n* (*of drink, food*) trago *m*. **II** *vtr* **1** (*drink, food*) tragar. **2** *fig* (*believe*) tragarse. **III** *vi* tragar. ◆**swallow up** *vtr fig* **1** (*engulf*) tragar. **2** (*eat up*) consumir.

swallow[2] ['swɒləʊ] *n* *Orn* golondrina *f*.

swam [swæm] *pt* → **swim**.

swamp [swɒmp] **I** *n* ciénaga *f*. **II** *vtr* **1** (*boat*) hundir. **2** *fig* inundar (**with**, de).

swan [swɒn] *n* cisne *m*. **II** *vi* **fam to s. around**, pavonearse; **to s. around doing nothing**, hacer el vago.

swap [swɒp] **I** *n* *fam* intercambio *m*. **II** *vtr* cambiar. ◆**swap round**, **swap over** *vtr* (*switch*) cambiar.

swarm [swɔːm] **I** *n* enjambre *m*. **II** *vi* (*bees*) enjambrar; *fig* **Neath was swarming with tourists**, Neath estaba lleno de turistas.

swarthy ['swɔːðɪ] *adj* (**swarthier**, **swarthiest**) moreno,-a.

swastika ['swɒstɪkə] *n* esvástica *f*, cruz gamada.

swat [swɒt] *vtr* aplastar.

swathe [sweɪð] *vtr* (*bind up*) envolver.

sway [sweɪ] **I** *n* **1** (*movement*) balanceo *m*. **2 to hold s. over sb**, dominar a algn. **II** *vi* **1** (*swing*) balancearse, mecerse. **2** (*totter*) tambalearse. **III** *vtr* *fig* (*persuade*) convencer.

swear [sweə'] **I** *vtr* (*pt* **swore**; *pp* **sworn**) (*vow*) jurar; **to s. an oath**, prestar juramento. **II** *vi* **1** (*formally*) jurar, prestar juramento. **2** (*curse*) soltar tacos, decir palabrotas; (*blaspheme*) jurar; **to s. at sb**, echar pestes contra algn.

swear-word ['sweəwɜːd] *n* palabrota *f*.

sweat [swet] **I** *n* (*perspiration*) sudor *m*; *fam* (*hard work*) trabajo duro. **II** *vi* (*perspire*) sudar; *fig* (*work hard*) sudar la gota gorda. **III** *vtr* *fam* **to s. it out**, aguantar.

sweater ['swetə'] *n* suéter *m*.

sweatshirt ['swetʃɜːt] *n* sudadera *f*.

sweaty ['swetɪ] *adj* (**sweatier**, **sweatiest**) sudoroso,-a.

swede [swiːd] *n* *Bot* nabo sueco.

Swede [swiːd] *n* (*person*) sueco,-a *m,f*.

Sweden ['swiːdən] *n* Suecia *f*.

Swedish ['swiːdɪʃ] **I** *adj* sueco,-a. **II** *n* **1** (*language*) sueco *m*. **2 the S.**, *pl* los suecos.

sweep [swiːp] **I** *n* **1** (*with broom*) barrido *m*; *fig* **to make a clean s. of things**, hacer tabla rasa. **2** (*of arm*) gesto amplio. **3** (*of river, road*) curva *f*. **4** (*chimney s.*), deshollinador,-a *m,f*. **II** *vtr* (*pt & pp* **swept**) **1** (*floor etc*) barrer. **2** (*of search-light*) recorrer; (*minefield*) rastrear. **3** (*spread through*) extenderse por. **III** *vi* **1** (*with broom*) barrer. **2 to s. in/out/past**, entrar/salir/pasar rápidamente. ◆**sweep aside** *vtr* apartar bruscamente; *fig* (*objections*) rechazar. ◆**sweep away** *vtr* **1** (*dust*) barrer. **2** (*of storm*) arrastrar. ◆**sweep up** *vi* barrer.

sweeper ['swiːpə'] *n* **1** (*machine*) barredora *f*. **2** *Ftb* líbero *m*.

sweeping ['swiːpɪŋ] *adj* **1** (*broad*) amplio,-a; **a s. statement**, una declaración demasiado general. **2** (*victory*) aplastante. **3** (*reforms, changes etc*) radical.

sweet [swiːt] **I** *adj* **1** dulce; (*sugary*) azucarado,-a; **to have a s. tooth**, ser goloso,-a; **s. pea**, guisante *m* de olor; **s. shop**, bombonería *f*. **2** (*pleasant*) agradable; (*smell*) fragante; (*sound*) melodioso, -a. **3** (*person, animal*) encantador,-a. **II** *n* **1** *GB* caramelo *m*; (*chocolate*) bombón *m*. **2** (*dessert*) postre *m*.

sweet-and-sour ['swiːtənsaʊə'] *adj* agridulce.

sweetcorn ['swiːtkɔːn] *n* maíz tierno.

sweeten ['swiːtən] *vtr* **1** (*tea etc*) azucarar. **2** *fig* (*temper*) aplacar; **to s. the pill**, suavizar el golpe.

sweetener ['swiːtənə'] *n* (*for tea, coffee*) edulcorante *m*.

sweetheart ['swiːthɑːt] *n* **1** (*boyfriend*) novio *m*; (*girlfriend*) novia *f*. **2** (*dear, love*) cariño *m*, amor *m*.

sweetness ['swiːtnɪs] *n* dulzura *f*; (*of smell*) fragancia *f*; (*of sound*) suavidad *f*.

swell [swel] **I** *n* (*of sea*) marejada *f*, oleaje *m*. **II** *adj* *US fam* fenomenal. **III** *vi* (*pt* **swelled**; *pp* **swollen**) (*part of body*) hincharse; (*river*) subir. ◆**swell up** *vi* hincharse.

swelling ['swelɪŋ] *n* hinchazón *f*; *Med* tumefacción *f*.

sweltering ['sweltərɪŋ] *adj* agobiante.

swept [swept] *pt & pp* → **sweep**.

swerve [swɜːv] **I** *n* **1** (*by car*) viraje *m*. **2** *Sport* (*by player*) regate *m*. **II** *vi* **1** (*car*) dar un viraje brusco. **2** *Sport* (*player*) dar un regate.

swift [swɪft] **I** *adj* rápido,-a, veloz. **II** *n* *Orn* vencejo *m* (común). ◆**swiftly** *adv* rápidamente.

swig [swɪg] *fam* **I** *n* trago *m*. **II** *vtr* beber a tragos.

swill [swɪl] **I** *n* **1** bazofia *f*. **2** (*rinse*) enjuague *m*. **II** *vtr* **1** (*rinse*) enjuagar. **2** *fam* (*drink*) beber a grandes tragos. ◆**swill out** *vtr* enjuagar.

swim [swɪm] I vi (pt **swam**; pp **swum**) nadar; **to go swimming**, ir a nadar; fam **my head is swimming**, la cabeza me da vueltas. II vtr (the Channel) pasar a nado. III n baño m; **to go for a s.**, ir a nadar or bañarse.

swimmer ['swɪmər] n nadador,-a m,f.

swimming ['swɪmɪŋ] n natación f; **s. cap**, gorro m de baño; **s. costume**, traje m de baño, bañador m; **s. pool**, piscina f; **s. trunks**, bañador m.

swimsuit ['swɪmsuːt] n traje m de baño, bañador m.

swindle ['swɪndəl] I n estafa f. II vtr estafar.

swindler ['swɪndlər] n estafador,-a m.

swine [swaɪn] n 1 (pl **swine**) (pig) cerdo m, puerco m. 2 (pl **swines**) fam (person) canalla mf, cochino,-a m,f.

swing [swɪŋ] I n 1 balanceo m, vaivén m; fig (in votes etc) viraje m; **s. bridge**, puente giratorio; **s. door**, puerta giratoria. 2 Box Golf swing m. 3 (plaything) columpio m. 4 (rhythm) ritmo m; (jazz style) swing m; **in full s.**, en plena marcha. II vi (pt & pp **swung**) 1 (move to and fro) balancearse; (arms, legs) menearse; (on swing) columpiarse; **to s. open/shut**, abrirse/cerrarse de golpe. 2 (turn) girar; **he swung round**, dio media vuelta. III vtr 1 (cause to move to and fro) balancear; (arms, legs) menear; (on swing) columpiar. 2 (turn) hacer girar; **she swung the sack onto her back**, se echó el saco a los hombros.

swingeing ['swɪndʒɪŋ] adj drástico,-a.

swipe [swaɪp] I n golpe m. II vtr 1 (hit) dar un tortazo a. 2 fam (steal) birlar.

swirl [swɜːl] I n remolino m; (of cream, smoke) voluta f. II vi arremolinarse.

swish [swɪʃ] I adj fam (smart) elegante. II vtr (tail) menear. III vi (whip) dar un chasquido; (skirt) crujir.

Swiss [swɪs] I adj suizo,-a. II n inv (person) suizo,-a m,f; **the S.**, pl los suizos.

switch [swɪtʃ] I n 1 Elec interruptor m. 2 (changeover) cambio repentino; (exchange) intercambio m. 3 (stick) vara f; (riding whip) fusta f. II vtr 1 (jobs, direction) cambiar de. 2 (allegiance) cambiar (to, por); (attention) desviar (to, hacia). ◆**switch off** vtr apagar. ◆**switch on** vtr encender. ◆**switch over** vi cambiar (to, a).

switchboard ['swɪtʃbɔːd] n centralita f.

Switzerland ['swɪtsələnd] n Suiza.

swivel ['swɪvəl] I n **s. chair**, silla giratoria. II vtr & vi columpiar.

swollen ['swəʊlən] adj (ankle, face) hinchado,-a; (river, lake) crecido,-a.

swoon [swuːn] arch I n desmayo m. II vi desmayarse.

swoop [swuːp] I n 1 (of bird) calada f; (of

plane) descenso m en picado. 2 (by police) redada f. II vi 1 **to s. down**, (bird) abalanzarse (on, sobre); (plane) bajar en picado. 2 (police) hacer una redada.

swop [swɒp] vtr → **swap**.

sword [sɔːd] n espada f.

swordfish ['sɔːdfɪʃ] n pez m espada.

swore [swɔːr] pt → **swear**.

sworn [swɔːn] adj jurado,-a.

swot [swɒt] fam vi empollar.

swum [swʌm] pp → **swim**.

swung [swʌŋ] pt & pp **swing**.

sycamore ['sɪkəmɔːr] n sicomoro m.

syllable ['sɪləbəl] n sílaba f.

syllabus ['sɪləbəs] n programa m de estudios.

symbol ['sɪmbəl] n símbolo m.

symbolic [sɪm'bɒlɪk] adj simbólico,-a.

symbolize ['sɪmbəlaɪz] vtr simbolizar.

symmetry ['sɪmɪtrɪ] n simetría f.

sympathetic [sɪmpə'θetɪk] adj 1 (showing pity) compasivo,-a. 2 (understanding) comprensivo,-a; (kind) amable.

sympathize ['sɪmpəθaɪz] vi 1 (show pity) compadecerse (with, de). 2 (understand) comprender.

sympathizer ['sɪmpəθaɪzər] n simpatizante mf.

sympathy ['sɪmpəθɪ] n 1 (pity) compasión f. 2 (condolences) pésame m; **letter of s.**, pésame; **to express one's s.**, dar el pésame. 3 (understanding) comprensión f.

symphony ['sɪmfənɪ] n sinfonía f.

symposium [sɪm'pəʊzɪəm] n simposio m.

symptom ['sɪmptəm] n síntoma m.

symptomatic [sɪmptə'mætɪk] adj sintomático,-a.

synagogue ['sɪnəgɒg] n sinagoga f.

synchronize ['sɪŋkrənaɪz] vtr sincronizar.

syndicate ['sɪndɪkɪt] n corporación f; **newspaper s.**, sindicato periodístico.

syndrome ['sɪndrəʊm] n síndrome m.

synonym ['sɪnənɪm] n sinónimo m.

synopsis [sɪ'nɒpsɪs] n sinopsis f inv.

syntax ['sɪntæks] n sintaxis f inv.

synthesis ['sɪnθɪsɪs] n (pl **syntheses** ['sɪnθɪsiːz]) síntesis f inv.

synthesizer ['sɪnθɪsaɪzər] n sintetizador m.

synthetic [sɪn'θetɪk] adj sintético,-a.

syphilis ['sɪfɪlɪs] n sífilis f.

syphon ['saɪfən] n → **siphon**.

Syria ['sɪrɪə] n Siria.

Syrian ['sɪrɪən] adj & n sirio,-a (m,f).

syringe [sɪ'rɪndʒ] n jeringa f, jeringuilla f.

syrup ['sɪrəp] n jarabe m, almíbar m.

system ['sɪstəm] n sistema m; fam **the s.**, el orden establecido; Comput **systems analyst**, analista mf de sistemas.

systematic [sɪstɪ'mætɪk] adj sistemático,-a.

T

T, t [ti:] *n (the letter)* T, t *f.*

t *abbr of* **ton(s), tonne(s),** t.

ta [tɑ:] *interj GB fam* gracias.

tab [tæb] *n* 1 *(flap)* lengüeta *f; (label)* etiqueta *f; fam* **to keep tabs on sb,** vigilar a algn. 2 *US fam (bill)* cuenta *f.*

tabby ['tæbɪ] *n* t. (cat), gato,-a *m,f* romano,-a.

table ['teɪbəl] **I** *n* 1 mesa *f;* **to lay** or **set the t.,** poner la mesa; **t. lamp,** lámpara *f* de mesa; **t. mat,** salvamanteles *m inv;* **t. tennis,** ping-pong® *m,* tenis *m* de mesa; **t. wine,** vino *m* de mesa. 2 *(of figures)* tabla *f,* cuadro *m;* **t. of contents,** índice *m* de materias. **II** *vtr* presentar.

tablecloth ['teɪbəlklɒθ] *n* mantel *m.*

tablespoon ['teɪbəlspu:n] *n* cucharón *m.*

tablespoonful ['teɪbəlspu:nfʊl] *n* cucharada *f* grande.

tablet ['tæblɪt] *n* 1 *Med* pastilla *f.* 2 *(of stone)* lápida *f.* 3 *(of soap)* pastilla *f; (of chocolate)* tableta *f.* 4 *US (of writing paper)* bloc *m.*

tableware ['teɪbəlweəʳ] *n* vajilla *f.*

tabloid ['tæblɔɪd] *n* periódico *m* de pequeño formato; **t. press,** prensa sensacionalista.

taboo [tə'bu:] *adj & n* tabú *(m).*

tabulate ['tæbjʊleɪt] *vtr* disponer en listas.

tacit ['tæsɪt] *adj* tácito,-a.

taciturn ['tæsɪtɜ:n] *adj* taciturno,-a.

tack [tæk] **I** *n* 1 *(small nail)* tachuela *f.* 2 *Sew* hilván *m.* 3 *Naut* amura *f; (distance)* bordada *f; fig* **to change t.,** cambiar de rumbo. **II** *vtr* 1 **to t. sth down,** clavar algo con tachuelas. 2 *Sew* hilvanar. **III** *vi Naut* virar de bordo. **◆tack on** *vtr (add)* añadir.

tackle ['tækəl] **I** *n* 1 *(equipment)* aparejos *mpl;* **fishing t.,** aparejos de pescar. 2 *Sport* placaje *m; Ftb* entrada *f.* **II** *vtr* agarrar; *(task)* emprender; *(problem)* abordar; *Sport* placar; *Ftb* entrar a.

tacky¹ ['tækɪ] *adj* **(tackier, tackiest)** pegajoso,-a.

tacky² ['tækɪ] *adj fam (shoddy)* cutre.

tact [tækt] *n* tacto *m,* diplomacia *f.*

tactful ['tæktfʊl] *adj* diplomático,-a.

tactical ['tæktɪkəl] *adj* táctico,-a.

tactic ['tæktɪk] *n* táctica *f;* **tactics,** táctica *f sing.*

tactless ['tæktlɪs] *adj (person)* poco diplomático,-a; *(question)* indiscreto,-a.

tadpole ['tædpəʊl] *n* renacuajo *m.*

tag [tæg] *n (label)* etiqueta *f.* 2 *(saying)* coletilla *f.* **◆tag along** *vi fam* pegarse. **◆tag on** *vtr (add to end)* añadir.

tail [teɪl] **I** *n* 1 cola *f;* **t. end,** cola. 2 *(of shirt)* faldón *m;* **to wear tails,** ir de frac;

t. coat, frac *m.* 3 **tails,** *(of coin)* cruz *f sing.* **II** *vtr sl (follow)* seguir de cerca. **◆tail away, tail off** *vi* desvanecerse.

tailback ['teɪlbæk] *n* caravana *f.*

tail-gate ['teɪlgeɪt] *n Aut* puerta trasera.

tailor ['teɪləʳ] **I** *n* sastre *m;* **t.'s (shop),** sastrería *f.* **II** *vtr (suit)* confeccionar; *fig* adaptar.

tailor-made [teɪlə'meɪd] *adj* hecho,-a a la medida.

tailwind ['teɪlwɪnd] *n* viento *m* de cola.

taint [teɪnt] *vtr* contaminar; *fig* corromper.

tainted ['teɪntɪd] *adj* contaminado,-a; *(reputation)* manchado,-a.

take [teɪk] **I** *vtr (pt* **took;** *pp* **taken)** 1 tomar, coger; **to a. an opportunity,** aprovechar una oportunidad; **to t. hold of sth,** agarrar algo; **to t. sth from one's pocket,** sacarse algo del bolsillo; **t. your time!,** ¡tómate el tiempo que quieras!; **to t. a bath,** bañarse; **to t. care,** cuidar; **his car takes six people,** este coche lleva seis personas en su coche; **is this seat taken?,** ¿está ocupado este asiento?; **to t. a decision,** tomar una decisión; **to t. a liking/dislike to sb,** tomar cariño/antipatía a algn; **to t. a photograph,** sacar una fotografía; **t. the first road on the left,** coja la primera a la izquierda; **to t. the train,** coger el tren. 2 *(accept)* aceptar; *(earn)* **to t. so much per week,** recaudar tanto por semana. 3 *(win)* ganar; *(prize)* llevarse. 4 *(eat, drink)* tomar; **to t. drugs,** drogarse. 5 **she's taking (a degree in) law,** estudia derecho; **to t. an exam (in ...),** examinarse (de ....). 6 *(person to a place)* llevar. 7 *(endure)* aguantar. 8 *(consider)* considerar. 9 **I t. it that ...,** supongo que ...; **what do you t. me for?,** ¿por quién me tomas? 10 *(require)* requerir; **it takes an hour to get there,** se tarda una hora en llegar hasta allí. 11 **to be taken ill,** enfermar. **II** *n Cin* toma *f.*

◆take after *vtr* parecerse a. **◆take apart** *vtr (machine)* desmontar. **◆take away** *vtr* 1 *(carry off)* llevarse. 2 **to t. sth away from sb,** quitarle algo a algn. 3 *Math* restar. **◆take back** *vtr* 1 *(give back)* devolver; *(receive back)* recuperar. 2 *(withdraw)* retractarse. **◆take down** *vtr* 1 *(lower)* bajar. 2 *(demolish)* derribar. 3 *(write)* apuntar. **◆take in** *vtr* 1 *(shelter, lodge)* alojar, acoger. 2 *Sew* meter. 3 *(include)* abarcar. 4 *(understand)* entender. 5 *(deceive)* engañar. **◆take off** *vtr* 1 quitar; **he took off his jacket,** se quitó la chaqueta. 2 *(lead* or *carry away)* llevarse. 3 *(deduct)* descontar. 4 *(imitate)* imitar burlonamente. **II** *vi Av* despegar.

◆**take on** vtr 1 (undertake) encargarse de. 2 (acquire) tomar. 3 (employ) contratar. 4 (compete with) competir con.
◆**take out** vtr sacar, quitar; **he's taking me out to dinner**, me ha invitado a cenar fuera. ◆**take over** I vtr Com Pol tomar posesión de; **the rebels took over the country**, los rebeldes se apoderaron del país. II vi to t. over from sb, relevar a algn. ◆**take to** vtr (become fond of) coger cariño a; **to t. to drink**, darse a la bebida. ◆**take up** vtr 1 Sew acortar. 2 (accept) aceptar; (adopt) adoptar. 3 **I've taken up the piano/French**, he empezado a tocar el piano/a aprender francés. 4 (occupy) ocupar.

takeaway ['teɪkəweɪ] GB I n (food) comida f para llevar; (restaurant) restaurante m que vende comida para llevar. II adj (food) para llevar.

take-home pay ['teɪkhəʊmpeɪ] n sueldo neto.

takeoff ['teɪkɒf] n 1 Av despegue m. 2 (imitation) imitación burlona.

takeover ['teɪkəʊvər] n Com absorción f; military t., golpe m de estado; t. bid, oferta pública de adquisición, OPA f.

takings ['teɪkɪŋz] npl Com recaudación f sing.

talc [tælk] n talco m.

talcum powder ['tælkəmpaʊdər] n (polvos mpl de) talco m.

tale [teɪl] n cuento m; to tell tales, contar chismes.

talent ['tælənt] n talento m.

talented ['tæləntɪd] adj dotado,-a.

talk [tɔːk] I vi hablar; (chat) charlar; (gossip) chismorrear; fam **now you're talking!**, ¡eso sí que me interesa!. II vtr to t. nonsense, decir tonterías; to t. sense, hablar con sentido común; to t. shop, hablar del trabajo. III n 1 (conversation) conversación f. 2 (words) palabras fpl; **he's all t.**, no hace más que hablar. 3 (rumour) rumor m; (gossip) chismes mpl. 4 (lecture) charla f. ◆**talk into** vtr to t. sb into sth, convencer a algn para que haga algo. ◆**talk out of** vtr to t. sb out of sth, disuadir a algn de que haga algo. ◆**talk over** vtr discutir.

talkative ['tɔːkətɪv] adj hablador,-a.

talking-to ['tɔːkɪŋtuː] n fam regañina f.

tall [tɔːl] adj alto,-a; **a tree ten metres t.**, un árbol de diez metros (de alto); **how t. are you?**, ¿cuánto mides?; fig **that's a t. order**, eso es mucho pedir.

tally ['tælɪ] I vi to t. with sth, corresponderse con algo. II n Com apunte m; to keep a t. of, llevar la cuenta de.

talon ['tælən] n garra f.

tambourine [tæmbə'riːn] n pandereta f.

tame [teɪm] I adj 1 (animal) domado,-a; (by nature) manso,-a; (person) dócil. 2 (style) soso,-a. II vtr domar.

tamper ['tæmpər] vi to t. with, (text) adulterar; (records, an entry) falsificar; (lock) intentar forzar.

tampon ['tæmpɒn] n tampón m.

tan [tæn] I n 1 (colour) marrón rojizo. 2 (suntan) bronceado m. II adj (colour) marrón rojizo. III vtr 1 (leather) curtir. 2 (skin) broncear. IV vi ponerse moreno,-a.

tang [tæŋ] n sabor m fuerte.

tangent ['tændʒənt] n tangente f; fig to go off at a t., salirse por la tangente.

tangerine [tændʒə'riːn] n clementina f.

tangible ['tændʒəbəl] adj tangible.

tangle ['tæŋgəl] n (of thread) maraña f; fig lío m; fig to get into a t., hacerse un lío.

tank [tæŋk] n 1 (container) depósito m. 2 Mil tanque m.

tanker ['tæŋkər] n Naut tanque m; (for oil) petrolero m; Aut camión m cisterna.

Tannoy® ['tænɔɪ] n sistema m de megafonía.

tantalize ['tæntəlaɪz] vtr atormentar.

tantalizing ['tæntəlaɪzɪŋ] adj atormentador,-a.

tantamount ['tæntəmaʊnt] adj t. to, equivalente a.

tantrum ['tæntrəm] n rabieta f.

tap¹ [tæp] I vtr golpear suavemente; (with hand) dar una palmadita a. II vi to t. at the door, llamar suavemente a la puerta. III n golpecito m; t. dancing, claqué m.

tap² [tæp] I n (for water) grifo m; fig funds on t., fondos mpl disponibles. II vtr 1 (tree) sangrar; fig to t. new markets, explotar nuevos mercados. 2 (phone) pinchar.

tape [teɪp] I n 1 cinta f; sticky t., cinta adhesiva; t. measure, cinta métrica. 2 (for recording) cinta f (magnetofónica); t. recorder, magnetófono m, cassette m; t. recording, grabación f. II vtr 1 pegar (con cinta adhesiva). 2 (record) grabar (en cinta).

taper ['teɪpər] I vi estrecharse; (to a point) afilarse. II n (candle) vela f. ◆**taper off** vi ir disminuyendo.

tapestry ['tæpɪstrɪ] n tapiz m.

tapping ['tæpɪŋ] n (of tree) sangría f; (of resources) explotación f; Tel intervención f ilegal de un teléfono.

tar [tɑːr] n alquitrán m.

target ['tɑːgɪt] n 1 (object aimed at) blanco m; t. practice, tiro m al blanco. 2 (purpose) meta f.

tariff ['tærɪf] n tarifa f, arancel m.

tarmac® ['tɑːmæk] n 1 (substance) alquitrán m 2 Av pista f de aterrizaje. II vtr alquitranar.

tarnish ['tɑːnɪʃ] vtr deslustrar.

tarpaulin [tɑː'pɔːlɪn] n lona f.

tart¹ [tɑːt] n GB Culin tarta f.

tart² [tɑːt] adj (taste) ácido,-a, agrio,-a.

tart³ [tɑːt] fam I n puta f. II vtr GB to t. oneself up, emperifollarse.

tartan ['tɑːtən] n tartán m.

tartar ['tɑːtər] n 1 Chem tártaro m. 2 Culin t. sauce, salsa tártara.

task [tɑːsk] n tarea f; to take sb to t., reprender a algn; Mil t. force, destacamento m (de fuerzas).

tassel ['tæsəl] n borla f.

taste [teɪst] I n 1 (sense) gusto m; (flavour) sabor m; it has a burnt t., sabe a quemado. 2 (sample) (of food) bocado m; (of drink) trago m; to give sb a t. of his own medicine, pagar a algn con la misma moneda. 3 (liking) afición f; to have a t. for sth, gustarle a uno algo. 4 in bad t., de mal gusto; to have (good) t., tener (buen) gusto. II vtr (sample) probar. III vi to t. of sth, saber a algo.

tasteful ['teɪstfʊl] adj de buen gusto.

tasteless ['teɪstlɪs] adj 1 (food) soso,-a. 2 (in bad taste) de mal gusto.

tasty ['teɪstɪ] adj (tastier, tastiest) sabroso,-a.

tattered ['tætəd] adj hecho,-a jirones.

tatters ['tætəz] npl in t., hecho,-a jirones.

tattoo¹ [tæ'tuː] n Mil retreta f.

tattoo² [tæ'tuː] I vtr tatuar. II n (mark) tatuaje m.

tatty ['tætɪ] adj (tattier, tattiest) GB en mal estado; (material, clothing) raído,-a; (décor) deslustrado,-a.

taught [tɔːt] pt & pp → teach.

taunt [tɔːnt] I vtr to t. sb with sth, echar algo en cara a algn. II n pulla f.

Taurus ['tɔːrəs] n Tauro m.

taut [tɔːt] adj tenso,-a, tirante.

tavern ['tævən] n taberna f.

tawdry ['tɔːdrɪ] adj (tawdrier, tawdriest) hortera.

tawn(e)y ['tɔːnɪ] adj leonado,-a, rojizo,-a.

tax [tæks] I n impuesto m; t. free, exento,-a de impuestos; t. collector, recaudador,-a m,f (de impuestos); t. evasion, evasión f fiscal; t. return, declaración f de renta. II vtr 1 gravar. 2 (patience etc) poner a prueba.

taxable ['tæksəbəl] adj imponible.

taxation [tæk'seɪʃən] n impuestos mpl.

taxi ['tæksɪ] I n taxi m; t. driver, taxista mf; t. rank, parada f de taxis. II vi (aircraft) rodar por la pista.

taxidermy ['tæksɪdɜːmɪ] n taxidermia f.

taxing ['tæksɪŋ] adj exigente.

taxpayer ['tækspeɪər] n contribuyente mf.

TB, tb [tiː'biː] abbr of tuberculosis.

tea [tiː] n 1 té m; t. bag, bolsita f de té; t. break, descanso m; t. cosy, cubretetera f; t. leaf, hoja f de té; t. service or set, juego m de té; t. towel, paño m (de cocina). 2 (snack) merienda f; (high) t., merienda-cena f.

teach [tiːtʃ] I vtr (pt & pp taught) enseñar; (subject) dar clases de; to t. sb (how) to do sth, enseñar a algn a hacer algo. II vi dar clases, ser profesor,-a.

teacher ['tiːtʃər] n profesor,-a m,f; (in primary school) maestro,-a m,f.

teaching ['tiːtʃɪŋ] n enseñanza f.

teacup ['tiːkʌp] n taza f de té.

teak [tiːk] n teca f.

team [tiːm] n equipo m; (of oxen) yunta f.

team-mate ['tiːmmeɪt] n compañero,-a m,f de equipo.

teamwork ['tiːmwɜːk] n trabajo m en equipo.

teapot ['tiːpɒt] n tetera f.

tear¹ [tɪər] n lágrima f; to be in tears, estar llorando; t. gas, gas lacrimógeno.

tear² [teər] I vtr (pt tore; pp torn) 1 rajar, desgarrar. 2 to t. sth out of sb's hands, arrancarle algo de las manos a algn. II vi 1 (cloth) rajarse. 2 to t. along, ir a toda velocidad. 3 (in clothes) rasgón m. ◆**tear down** vtr derribar. ◆**tear off** vtr arrancar. ◆**tear out** vtr arrancar. ◆**tear up** vtr 1 romper, hacer pedazos. 2 (uproot) arrancar de raíz.

tearful ['tɪəfʊl] adj lloroso,-a.

tearoom ['tiːruːm] n GB → teashop.

tease [tiːz] I vtr tomar el pelo a. II n bromista mf.

teashop ['tiːʃɒp] n GB salón m de té.

teaspoon ['tiːspuːn] n cucharilla f.

teaspoonful ['tiːspuːnfʊl] n cucharadita f.

teat [tiːt] n (of animal) teta f; (of bottle) tetina f.

teatime ['tiːtaɪm] n hora f del té.

technical ['teknɪkəl] adj técnico,-a; t. college, instituto m de formación profesional. ◆**technically** adv (theoretically) en teoría.

technicality [teknɪ'kælɪtɪ] n detalle m técnico.

technician [tek'nɪʃən] n técnico,-a m,f.

technique [tek'niːk] n técnica f.

technological [teknə'lɒdʒɪkəl] adj tecnológico,-a.

technology [tek'nɒlədʒɪ] n tecnología f.

teddy bear ['tedɪbeər] n oso m de felpa.

tedious ['tiːdɪəs] adj tedioso,-a, aburrido,-a.

tee [tiː] n Golf tee m m.

teem [tiːm] vi to t. with, rebosar de; fam it was teeming down, llovía a cántaros.

teenage ['tiːneɪdʒ] adj adolescente.

teenager ['tiːneɪdʒər] n adolescente mf.

teens [tiːnz] npl adolescencia f sing.

tee-shirt ['tiːʃɜːt] n camiseta f.

teeter ['tiːtər] vi balancearse.

teeth [tiːθ] npl → tooth.

teethe [tiːð] vi echar los dientes.

teething ['tiːðɪŋ] n t. ring, chupador m; fig t. troubles, dificultades fpl iniciales.

teetotaller [tiː'təʊtələr] n abstemio,-a

m,f.

telecommunications ['telɪkəmjuːnɪ'keɪʃənz] *n* telecomunicaciones *fpl.*

telegram ['telɪgræm] *n* telegrama *m.*

telegraph ['telɪgræf, 'telɪgrɑːf] I *n* telégrafo *m*; t. **pole**, poste telegráfico. II *vtr & vi* telegrafiar.

telepathy [tɪ'lepəθɪ] *n* telepatía *f.*

telephone ['telɪfəʊn] I *n* teléfono *m*; *GB* t. **booth**, t. **box**, cabina *f* (telefónica); t. **call**, llamada telefónica; t. **directory**, guía telefónica; t. **number**, número *m* de teléfono. II *vtr* telefonear, llamar por teléfono.

telephonist [tɪ'lefənɪst] *n GB* telefonista *mf.*

telephoto ['telɪfəʊtəʊ] *adj* t. **lens**, teleobjetivo *m.*

teleprinter ['telɪprɪntər] *n* teletipo *m.*

telescope ['telɪskəʊp] I *n* telescopio *m.* II *vi* plegarse (como un catalejo). III *vtr* plegar.

telescopic [telɪ'skɒpɪk] *adj* (*umbrella*) plegable.

televise ['telɪvaɪz] *vtr* televisar.

television ['telɪvɪʒən] *n* televisión *f*; t. **programme**, programa *m* de televisión; t. (**set**), televisor *m.*

telex ['teleks] I *n* télex *m.* II *vtr* enviar por télex.

tell [tel] I *vtr* (*pt & pp* **told**) 1 (*say*) decir; (*relate*) contar; (*inform*) comunicar; to t. **lies**, mentir; to t. **sb about sth**, contarle algo a algn; **you're telling me!**, ¡a mí me lo vas a contar! 2 (*order*) mandar; to t. **sb to do sth**, decir a algn que haga algo. 3 (*distinguish*) distinguir; to **know how to t. the time**, saber decir la hora. 4 **all told**, en total. II *vi* 1 (*reveal*) reflejar. 2 **who can t.?**, (*know*) ¿quién sabe? 3 (*have effect*) notarse; **the pressure is telling on her**, está acusando la presión. ◆**tell off** *vtr fam* regañar, reñir.

teller ['telər] *n* (*in bank etc*) cajero,-a *m,f.*

telling ['telɪŋ] *adj* (*action*) eficaz; (*blow, argument*) contundente.

telltale ['telteɪl] *n* chivato,-a *m,f*; t. **signs**, señales reveladoras.

telly ['telɪ] *n GB fam* **the t.**, la tele.

temp [temp] *n* (*abbr of* **temporary**) *fam* trabajador,-a eventual *m,f* temporal.

temper ['tempər] I *n* 1 (*mood*) humor *m*; to **keep one's t.**, no perder la calma; to **lose one's t.**, perder los estribos. 2 (*temperament*) to **have a bad t.**, tener (mal) genio. II *vtr* (*in metallurgy*) templar; *fig* suavizar.

temperament ['tempərəmənt] *n* temperamento *m.*

temperamental [tempərə'mentəl] *adj* temperamental.

temperate ['tempərɪt] *adj* 1 mesurado,-a. 2 (*climate*) templado,-a.

temperature ['temprɪtʃər] *n* temperatura *f*; to **have a t.**, tener fiebre.

tempest ['tempɪst] *n* tempestad *f.*

temple¹ ['tempəl] *n Archit* templo *m.*

temple² ['tempəl] *n Anat* sien *f.*

tempo ['tempəʊ] *n* tempo *m.*

temporary ['tempərərɪ] *adj* provisional; (*setback, improvement*) momentáneo,-a; (*staff*) temporal.

tempt [tempt] *vtr* tentar; to t. **providence**, tentar la suerte; to t. **sb to do sth**, incitar a algn a hacer algo.

temptation [temp'teɪʃən] *n* tentación *f.*

tempting ['temptɪŋ] *adj* tentador,-a.

ten [ten] *adj & n* diez (*m*) *inv.*

tenable ['tenəbəl] *adj* (*opinion*) sostenible.

tenacious [tɪ'neɪʃəs] *adj* tenaz.

tenancy ['tenənsɪ] *n* (*of house*) alquiler *m*; (*of land*) arrendamiento *m.*

tenant ['tenənt] *n* (*of house*) inquilino,-a *m,f*; (*of farm*) arrendatario,-a *m,f.*

tend¹ [tend] *vi* (*be inclined*) tender, tener tendencia (to, a).

tend² [tend] *vtr* (*care for*) cuidar.

tendency ['tendənsɪ] *n* tendencia *f.*

tender¹ ['tendər] *adj* (*affectionate*) cariñoso,-a; (*compassionate*) compasivo,-a; (*meat*) tierno,-a.

tender² ['tendər] I *vtr* ofrecer; to t. **one's resignation**, presentar la dimisión. II *vi Com* to t. **for**, sacar a concurso. III *n* 1 *Com* oferta *f.* 2 **legal t.**, moneda *f* de curso legal.

tenderness ['tendənɪs] *n* ternura *f.*

tendon ['tendən] *n* tendón *m.*

tenement ['tenɪmənt] *n* casa *f* de vecindad.

tenet ['tenɪt] *n* principio *m.*

tennis ['tenɪs] *n* tenis *m*; t. **ball**, pelota *f* de tenis; t. **court**, pista *f* de tenis; t. **player**, tenista *mf*; t. **racket** raqueta *f* de tenis; t. **shoe**, zapatilla *f* de tenis.

tenor ['tenər] *n Mus* tenor *m.*

tense¹ [tens] *adj* tenso,-a.

tense² [tens] *n Gram* tiempo *m.*

tension ['tenʃən] *n* tensión *f.*

tent [tent] *n* tienda *f* de campaña; t. **peg**, estaca *f.*

tentacle ['tentəkəl] *n* tentáculo *m.*

tentative ['tentətɪv] *adj* 1 (*not definite*) de prueba. 2 (*hesitant*) indeciso,-a.

tenterhooks ['tentəhʊks] *npl fig* **on t.**, sobre ascuas.

tenth [tenθ] I *adj & n* décimo,-a (*m,f*). II *n* (*fraction*) décimo *m.*

tenuous ['tenjʊəs] *adj* 1 tenue. 2 (*argument*) flojo,-a.

tenure ['tenjʊər] *n* 1 (*of office*) ocupación *f.* 2 (*of property*) arrendamiento *m.*

tepid ['tepɪd] *adj* tibio,-a.

term [tɜːm] I *n* 1 (*period*) período *m*; *Educ* trimestre *m*; t. **of office**, mandato *m*, legislatura *f*; **in the long/short t.**, a largo/corto plazo. 2 (*word*) término *m*; *fig* in

terms of money, en cuanto al dinero. **3 terms,** (conditions) fpl; **to come to terms with,** hacerse a la idea de. **4 to be on good/bad terms with sb,** tener buenas/malas relaciones con algn. II vtr calificar de.

terminal ['tɜːmɪnəl] I adj terminal; **t. cancer,** cáncer incurable. II n terminal f.

terminate ['tɜːmɪneɪt] I vtr terminar; **to t. a pregnancy,** abortar. II vi terminarse.

terminology [tɜːmɪ'nɒlədʒɪ] n terminología f.

terminus ['tɜːmɪnəs] n (pl **termini** ['tɜːmɪnaɪ]) terminal m.

terrace ['terəs] n **1** Agr bancal m. **2** GB (of houses) hilera f de casas. **3** (patio) terraza f. **4** Ftb **the terraces,** las gradas.

terraced ['terəst] adj GB **t. houses,** casas fpl (de estilo uniforme) en hilera.

terrain [tə'reɪn] n terreno m.

terrible ['terəbl] adj terrible; fig **I feel t.,** (ill) me encuentro fatal. ◆**terribly** adv terriblemente.

terrier ['terɪər] n terrier m.

terrific [tə'rɪfɪk] adj **1** fam (excellent) fenomenal. **2** (extreme) tremendo,-a.

terrify ['terɪfaɪ] vtr aterrorizar.

terrifying ['terɪfaɪɪŋ] adj aterrador,-a.

territory ['terɪtərɪ] n territorio m.

terror ['terər] n terror m.

terrorism ['terərɪzəm] n terrorismo m.

terrorist ['terərɪst] adj & n terrorista (mf).

terrorize ['terəraɪz] vtr aterrorizar.

terry ['terɪ] n **t. towel,** toalla f de rizo.

terse [tɜːs] adj (curt) lacónico,-a.

test [test] I vtr probar, someter a una prueba; (analyze) analizar; Med hacer un análisis de. II n prueba f, examen m; **to put to the t.,** poner a prueba; **to stand the t.,** pasar la prueba; **t. match,** partido m internacional; **t. pilot,** piloto m de pruebas; **t. tube,** probeta f; **t.-tube baby,** niño m probeta.

testament ['testəmənt] n testamento m; **Old/New T.,** Antiguo/Nuevo Testamento.

testicle ['testɪkəl] n testículo m.

testify ['testɪfaɪ] I vtr declarar. II vi fig **to t. to sth,** atestiguar algo.

testimonial [testɪ'məunɪəl] n recomendación f.

testimony ['testɪmənɪ] n testimonio m, declaración f.

tetanus ['tetənəs] n tétano(s) m inv.

tether ['teðər] I n ronzal m; fig **to be at the end of one's t.,** estar hasta la coronilla. II vtr (animal) atar.

Texas ['teksəs] n Tejas.

text [tekst] n texto m.

textbook ['tekstbuk] n libro m de texto.

textile ['tekstaɪl] I n tejido m. II adj textil.

texture ['tekstʃər] n textura f.

Thai [taɪ] adj & n tailandés,-esa (m,f).

Thailand ['taɪlænd] n Tailandia.

Thames [temz] n the T., el Támesis.

than [ðæn, unstressed ðən] conj que; (with numbers) de; **he's older t. me,** es mayor que yo; **I have more/less t. you,** tengo más/menos que tú; **more interesting t. we thought,** más interesante de lo que creíamos; **more t. once,** más de una vez; **more t. ten people,** más de diez personas.

thank [θæŋk] vtr agradecer a; **t. you,** gracias.

thankful ['θæŋkful] adj agradecido,-a.

thankless ['θæŋklɪs] adj (task) ingrato,-a.

thanks [θæŋks] npl gracias fpl; **no t.,** no gracias; **many t.,** muchas gracias; **t. for phoning,** gracias por llamar; **t. to,** gracias a.

thanksgiving [θæŋks'gɪvɪŋ] n US **T. Day,** Día m de Acción de Gracias.

that [ðæt, unstressed ðət] I dem pron (pl **those**) **1** ése m, ésa f; (further away) aquél m, aquélla f; **this one is new but t. is old,** éste es nuevo pero ése es viejo. **2** (indefinite) eso; (remote) aquello; **after t.,** después de eso; **like t.,** así; **t.'s right,** eso es; **t.'s where I live,** allí vivo yo; **what's t.?,** ¿qué es eso?; **who's t.?,** ¿quién es? **3** (with relative) **t. which I saw,** lo que vi.

II dem adj (pl **those**) (masculine) ese; (feminine) esa; (further away) (masculine) aquel; (feminine) aquella; **at t. time,** en aquella época; **t. book,** ese o aquel libro; **t. one,** ése, aquél.

III rel pron **1** (subject, direct object) que; **all** (t.) **you said,** todo lo que dijiste; **the letter** (t.) **I sent you,** la carta que te envié. **2** (governed by preposition) que, el/la que, los/las que, el/la cual, los/las cuales; **the car** (t.) **they came in,** el coche en el que vinieron. **3** (when) que, en que; **the moment** (t.) **you arrived,** en el momento en que llegaste.

IV conj que; **come here so t. I can see you,** ven aquí (para) que te vea; **he said** (t.) **he would come,** dijo que vendría.

V adv así de, tanto, tan; **cut off t. much,** córteme un trozo así de grande; **I don't think it can be t. old,** no creo que sea tan viejo; **we haven't got t. much money,** no tenemos tanto dinero.

thatched [θætʃt] adj cubierto,-a con paja; **t. cottage,** casita f con techo de paja; **t. roof,** techo m de paja.

thaw [θɔː] I vtr (snow) derretir; (food, freezer) descongelar. II vi descongelarse; (snow) derretirse. III n deshielo m.

the [ðə, before vowel ðɪ, emphatic ðiː] I def art **1** el, la; pl los, las; al or to t., al, a la; pl a los, a las; of or from t., del, de la; pl de los, de las; **t. Alps,** los Alpes; **t. right time,** la hora exacta; **t. voice of t. people,** la voz del pueblo. **2** (omitted)

George t. Sixth, Jorge Sexto. 3 by t. day, al día; by t. dozen, a docenas. 4 (with adjectives used as nouns) t. elderly, los ancianos. 5 (indicating kind) he's not t. person to do that, no es de los que hacen tales cosas. 6 (enough) he hasn't t. patience to wait, no tiene suficiente paciencia para esperar. II adv t. more t. merrier, cuantos más mejor; t. sooner t. better, cuanto antes mejor.

theatre, US **theater** ['θɪətər] n teatro m.

theatre-goer, US **theater-goer** ['θɪətəgəʊər] n aficionado,-a m,f al teatro.

theatrical [θɪ'ætrɪkəl] adj teatral.

theft [θeft] n robo m; petty t., hurto m.

their [ðeər] poss adj (one thing) su; (various things) sus.

theirs [ðeəz] poss pron (el) suyo, (la) suya; pl (los) suyos, (las) suyas.

them [ðem] pers pron pl 1 (direct object) los, las; (indirect object) les; I know t., los or las conozco; I shall tell t. so, se lo diré (a ellos or ellas); it's t.!, ¡son ellos!; speak to t., hábleles. 2 (with preposition) ellos, ellas; walk in front of t., camine delante de ellos; they took the keys away with t., se llevaron las llaves; both of t., the two of t., los dos; neither of t., ninguno de los dos; none of t., ninguno de ellos.

theme [θiːm] n tema m; t. tune, sintonía f.

themselves [ðəm'selvz] pers pron pl (as subject) ellos mismos, ellas mismas; (as direct or indirect object) se; (after a preposition) sí mismos, sí mismas; they did it by t., lo hicieron ellos solos.

then [ðen] I adv 1 (at that time) entonces; since t., desde entonces; there and t., en el acto; till t., hasta entonces. 2 (next, afterwards) luego. 3 (anyway) de todas formas. 4 (in that case) entonces; go t., pues vete. II conj entonces. III adj the t. president, el entonces presidente.

theology [θɪ'ɒlədʒɪ] n teología f.

theoretic(al) [θɪə'retɪk(əl)] adj teórico,-a. ◆**theoretically** adv teóricamente.

theory ['θɪərɪ] n teoría f.

therapist ['θerəpɪst] n terapeuta mf.

therapy ['θerəpɪ] n terapia f.

there [ðeər] I adv 1 (indicating place) allí, allá; (nearer speaker) ahí; here and t., acá y allá; in t., ahí dentro; is Peter t.?, ¿está Peter? 2 (emphatic) that man t., aquel hombre. 3 (unstressed) t. is..., t. are..., hay...; t. were many cars, había muchos coches; t. were six of us, éramos seis. 4 (in respect) t.'s the difficulty, ahí está la dificultad. II interj so t.!, ¡ea!; t., t., bien, bien.

thereabouts ['ðeərəbaʊts], US **thereabout** ['ðeərəbaʊt] adv in Cambridge or t., en Cambridge o por allí cerca; at four o'clock or t., a las cuatro o así.

thereafter [ðeər'ɑːftər] adv a partir de entonces.

thereby ['ðeəbaɪ] adv por eso o ello.

therefore ['ðeəfɔːr] adv por lo tanto, por eso.

thermal ['θɜːməl] I adj (spring) termal; Phys térmico,-a. II n Meteor corriente térmica.

thermometer [θə'mɒmɪtər] n termómetro m.

Thermos® ['θɜːməs] n T. (flask), termo m.

thermostat ['θɜːməstæt] n termostato m.

thesaurus [θɪ'sɔːrəs] n diccionario m de sinónimos.

these [ðiːz] I dem adj pl estos,-as. II dem pron pl éstos,-as; → **this**.

thesis ['θiːsɪs] n tesis f inv.

they [ðeɪ] pron pl 1 ellos, ellas; t. are dancing, están bailando; t. are rich, son ricos. 2 (stressed) t. alone, ellos solos; t. themselves told me, me lo dijeron ellos mismos. 3 (with relative) los, las. 4 (indefinite) that's what t. say, eso es lo que se dice; t. say that ..., se dice que ....

thick [θɪk] I adj 1 (book etc) grueso,-a; a wall two metres t., un muro de dos metros de espesor. 2 (dense) espeso,-a. 3 fam (stupid) tonto,-a. II adv densamente. III n to be in the t. of it, estar metido,-a de lleno.

thicken ['θɪkən] I vtr espesar. II vi espesarse; fig (plot) complicarse.

thickness ['θɪknɪs] n (of wall etc) espesor m; (of wire, lips) grueso m; (of layer, woodland) espesura f.

thickset [θɪk'set] adj (person) rechoncho, -a.

thick-skinned [θɪk'skɪnd] adj fig poco sensible.

thief [θiːf] n (pl **thieves** [θiːvz]) ladrón, -ona m,f.

thigh [θaɪ] n muslo m.

thimble ['θɪmbəl] n dedal m.

thin [θɪn] I adj (thinner, thinnest) 1 delgado,-a; a t. slice, una loncha fina. 2 (hair, vegetation) ralo,-a; (colour) claro,-a; (population) escaso,-a. 3 fig (voice) débil; a t. excuse, una pobre pretexto. II vtr to t. (down), (paint) diluir. ◆**thinly** adv poco, ligeramente.

thing [θɪŋ] n 1 cosa f; my things, (clothing) mi ropa f sing; (possessions) mis cosas fpl; for one t., en primer lugar; the t. is ..., resulta que ...; what with one t. and another, entre unas cosas y otras; as things are, tal como están las cosas. 2 poor little t.!, ¡pobrecito,-a!

think [θɪŋk] I vtr (pt & pp **thought**) 1 (believe) pensar, creer; I t. so/not, creo que sí/no. 2 I thought as much, yo me lo imaginaba. II vi 1 pensar (of, about, en); give me time to t., dame tiempo para reflexionar; to t. ahead, prevenir. 2 (have

as opinion) opinar, pensar; **to t. highly of sb**, apreciar a algn; **what do you t.?**, ¿a ti qué te parece? **3 just t.!**, ¡imagínate!
◆**think out** *vtr* meditar. **a carefully thought-out answer**, una respuesta razonada. ◆**think over** *vtr* reflexionar; **we'll have to t. it over**, lo tendremos que pensar. ◆**think up** *vtr* imaginar, idear.

thinking ['θɪŋkɪŋ] *adj* racional.

think-tank ['θɪŋktæŋk] *n fam* grupo *m* de expertos.

third [θɜːd] I *adj* tercero,-a; *(before masculine singular noun)* tercer; **(on) the t. of March**, el tres de marzo; **the T. World**, el Tercer Mundo; **t. party insurance**, seguro *m* a terceros. II *n* **1** *(in series)* tercero,-a *m,f.* **2** *(fraction)* tercio *m*, tercera parte. ◆**thirdly** *adv* en tercer lugar.

third-rate ['θɜːdreɪt] *adj* de calidad inferior.

thirst [θɜːst] *n* sed *f*.

thirsty ['θɜːstɪ] *adj* **(thirstier, thirstiest)** sediento,-a; **to be t.**, tener sed.

thirteen [θɜː'tiːn] *adj & n* trece *(m)* inv.

thirteenth [θɜː'tiːnθ] I *adj & n* decimotercero,-a *(m,f).* II *n (fraction)* decimotercera parte.

thirtieth ['θɜːtɪɪθ] I *adj & n* trigésimo,-a *(m,f).* II *n (fraction)* trigésima parte.

thirty ['θɜːtɪ] *adj & n* treinta *(m)* inv.

this [ðɪs] I *dem adj (pl* **these)** *(masculine)* este; *(feminine)* esta; **t. book/these books**, este libro/estos libros; **t. one**, éste, ésta. II *(pl* **these)** *dem pron* **1** *(indefinite)* esto; **it was like t.**, fue así. **2** *(place)* **t. is where we met**, fue aquí donde nos conocimos. **3** *(time)* **it should have come before t.**, debería haber llegado ya. **4** *(specific person or thing)* éste *m*, ésta *f*; **I prefer these to those**, me gustan más éstos que aquéllos; *(introduction)* **t. is Mr Álvarez**, le presento al Sr. Álvarez; *Tel* **t. is Julia (speaking)**, soy Julia. III *adv* **he got t. far**, llegó hasta aquí; **t. small/big**, así de pequeño/grande.

thistle ['θɪsəl] *n* cardo *m*.

thong [θɒŋ] *n* correa *f*.

thorax ['θɔːræks] *n* tórax *m*.

thorn [θɔːn] *n* espina *f*.

thorough ['θʌrə] *adj (careful)* minucioso,-a; *(work)* concienzudo,-a; *(knowledge)* profundo,-a; **to carry out a t. enquiry into a matter**, investigar a fondo un asunto. ◆**thoroughly** *adv (carefully)* a fondo; *(wholly)* completamente.

thoroughbred ['θʌrəbred] I *adj (horse)* de pura sangre. II *n (horse)* pura sangre *mf*.

thoroughfare ['θʌrəfeə] *n (road)* carretera *f*; *(street)* calle *f*.

those [ðəʊz] I *dem pron* **1** ésos,-as; *(remote)* aquéllos,-as; **t. who**, los que, las que; *(remote)* aquéllos,-as; → **that** I & II.

though [ðəʊ] I *conj* **1** aunque; **strange t.**

it may seem, por (muy) extraño que parezca. **2 as t.**, como si; **it looks as t. he's gone**, parece que se ha ido. II *adv* sin embargo.

thought [θɔːt] *n* **1** *(act of thinking)* pensamiento *m*; **what a tempting t.!**, ¡qué idea más tentadora! **2** *(reflection)* reflexión *f*. **3 it's the t. that counts**, *(intention)* lo que cuenta es la intención.

thoughtful ['θɔːtfʊl] *adj (pensive)* pensativo,-a; *(considerate)* atento,-a.

thoughtless ['θɔːtlɪs] *adj (person)* desconsiderado,-a; *(action)* irreflexivo,-a.

thousand ['θaʊzənd] *adj & n* mil *(m)* inv; **thousands of people**, miles de personas.

thousandth ['θaʊzənθ] I *adj* milésimo,-a. II *n* **1** *(in series)* milésimo,-a *m,f.* **2** *(fraction)* milésima parte.

thrash [θræʃ] I *vtr* dar una paliza a. II *vi* **to t. about** *or* **around**, agitarse. ◆**thrash out** *vtr* discutir a fondo.

thread [θred] I *n* **1** hilo *m*; **length of t.**, hebra *f*. **2** *(of screw)* rosca *f*. II *vtr* **1** *(needle)* enhebrar. **2 to t. one's way**, colarse *(through*, por).

threadbare ['θredbeə] *adj* raído,-a.

threat [θret] *n* amenaza *f*.

threaten ['θretən] *vtr* amenazar; **to t. to do sth**, amenazar con hacer algo.

threatening ['θretənɪŋ] *adj* amenazador,-a. ◆**threateningly** *adv* de modo amenazador.

three [θriː] *adj & n* tres *(m).*

three-dimensional [θriːdɪ'menʃənəl] *adj* tridimensional.

threefold ['θriːfəʊld] I *adj* triple. II *adv* tres veces; **to increase t.**, triplicarse.

three-piece ['θriːpiːs] *adj* **t. suit**, traje *m* de tres piezas; **t.-p. suite**, tresillo *m*.

three-ply ['θriːplaɪ] *adj* de tres hebras.

three-wheeler [θriː'wiːlə] *n Aut* coche *m* de tres ruedas; *(tricycle)* triciclo *m*.

thresh [θreʃ] *vtr* trillar.

threshold ['θreʃəʊld] *n* umbral *m*; *fig* **to be on the t. of**, estar a las puertas *o* en los umbrales de.

threw [θruː] *pt* → **throw**.

thrifty ['θrɪftɪ] *adj* **(thriftier, thriftiest)** económico,-a, ahorrador,-a.

thrill [θrɪl] I *n* **1** *(excitement)* emoción *f*. **2** *(quiver)* estremecimiento *m*. II *vtr (excite)* emocionar; *(audience)* entusiasmar.

thriller ['θrɪlə] *n* novela *f*/película *f* de suspense.

thrilling ['θrɪlɪŋ] *adj* emocionante.

thrive [θraɪv] *vi (pt* **thrived** *or* **throve;** *pp* **thrived** *or* **thriven** ['θrɪvən]) **1** *(person)* rebosar de salud. **2** *fig (business)* prosperar; **he thrives on it**, le viene de maravilla.

thriving ['θraɪvɪŋ] *adj fig* próspero,-a.

throat [θrəʊt] *n* garganta *f*.

throb [θrɒb] I *n* *(of heart)* latido *m*; *(of machine)* zumbido *m*. II *vi (heart)* latir; *(machine)* zumbar; **my head is throbbing,**

me va a estallar la cabeza.

throes [θrəuz] *npl* to be in one's death t., estar agonizando; *fig* in the t. of ..., en pleno,-a ....

throne [θrəun] *I n* trono *m*.

throng [θrɒŋ] **I** *n* multitud *f*, gentío *m*. **II** *vi* apiñarse. **III** *vtr* atestar.

throttle [θrɒtəl] **I** *n* (valve), (of engine) válvula reguladora. **II** *vtr* (person) estrangular. ◆**throttle back** *vtr* (engine) desacelerar.

through [θru:] **I** *prep* **1** (place) a través de, por; **to look** t. **the window**, mirar por la ventana. **2** (time) a lo largo de; **all** t. **his life**, durante toda su vida. **3** (by means of) por, mediante; **I learnt of it** t. **Jack**, me enteré por Jack. **4** (because of) a or por causa de; t. **ignorance**, por ignorancia. **II** *adj* a t. **train**, un tren directo; t. **traffic**, tránsito *m*. **III** *adv* **1** (from one side to the other) de un lado a otro; **to let** sb t., dejar pasar a algn; *fig* **socialist/ French** t. **and** t., socialista/francés por los cuatro costados. **2** I'm t. **with him**, he terminado con él. **3** Tel **to get** t. **to sb**, comunicar con algn; **you're** t., ¡hablen!

throughout [θru:'aut] **I** *prep* por todo,-a; t. **the year**, durante todo el año. **II** *adv* (place) en todas partes; (time) todo el tiempo.

throve [θrəuv] *pt* → **thrive**.

throw [θrəu] **I** *vtr* (pt **threw**; pp **thrown**) **1** tirar, arrojar; (to the ground) derribar; (rider) desmontar; *fig* **he threw a fit**, le dio un ataque; *fig* **to** t. **a party**, dar una fiesta. **2** (disconcert) desconcertar. **II** *n* tiro *m*, lanzamiento *m*; (in wrestling) presa *m*. ◆**throw away** *vtr* (rubbish) tirar; (money) malgastar; (opportunity) perder. ◆**throw in** *vtr* tirar; Sport sacar de banda; *fig* **to** t. **in the towel**, arrojar la toalla. **3** (include) añadir; (in deal) incluir (gratis). ◆**throw off** *vtr* (person, thing) deshacerse de; (clothes) quitarse. ◆**throw out** *vtr* (rubbish) tirar; (person) echar. ◆**throw up** **I** *vtr* **1** lanzar al aire. **2** Constr construir rápidamente. **II** *vi* fam vomitar, devolver.

throwaway ['θrəuəwei] *adj* desechable.

throw-in ['θrəuin] *n* Sport saque *m* de banda.

thrown [θrəun] pp → **throw**.

thru [θru:] *prep US* → **through**.

thrush [θrʌʃ] *n* Orn tordo *m*, zorzal *m*.

thrust [θrʌst] **I** *vtr* (pt & pp **thrust**) empujar con fuerza; **he** t. **a letter into my hand**, me puso una carta violentamente en la mano. **II** *n* (push) empujón *m*; Av Phys empuje *m*.

thud [θʌd] *n* ruido sordo.

thug [θʌg] *n* (lout) gamberro *m*; (criminal) criminal *m*.

thumb [θʌm] **I** *n* pulgar *m*. **II** *vtr* **1** manosear. **2** **to** t. **a lift**, hacer autostop.

◆**thumb through** *vtr* (book) hojear.

thumbtack ['θʌmtæk] *n* US chincheta *f*.

thump [θʌmp] **I** *n* **1** (sound) ruido sordo. **2** (blow) golpazo *m*; fam torta *f*. **II** *vtr* golpear. **III** *vi* **1** **to** t. **on the table**, golpear la mesa. **2** (heart) latir ruidosamente.

thunder ['θʌndər] **I** *n* trueno *m*; t. **of applause**, estruendo *m* de aplausos. **II** *vi* tronar.

thunderbolt ['θʌndəbəult] *n* (lighting) rayo *m*; fig (news) bomba *f*.

thunderclap ['θʌndəklæp] *n* trueno *m*.

thunderous ['θʌndərəs] *adj* fig ensordecedor,-a.

thunderstorm ['θʌndəstɔːm] *n* tormenta *f*.

thundery ['θʌndəri] *adj* (weather) tormentoso,-a.

Thursday ['θɜːzdi] *n* jueves *m*.

thus [ðʌs] *adv* así, de esta manera; **and** t. ..., así que ....

thwart [θwɔːt] *vtr* frustrar, desbaratar.

thyme [taim] *n* tomillo *m*.

thyroid ['θairɔid] *n* tiroides *f inv*.

tiara [ti'ɑːrə] *n* diadema *f*; Rel tiara *f*.

tic [tik] *n* tic *m*.

tick[1] [tik] **I** *n* **1** (sound) tic-tac *m*. **2** GB fam I'll **do it in a** t., ahora mismo lo hago. **II** *n* (mark) marca *f* de visto bueno. **II** *vi* hacer tic-tac. **III** *vtr* marcar. ◆**tick off** *vtr* **1** (mark) marcar. **2** GB fam (reprimand) regañar. ◆**tick over** *vi* Aut funcionar al ralentí.

tick[2] [tik] *n* Ent garrapata *f*.

ticket ['tikit] *n* **1** (for bus etc) billete *m*; Theat entrada *f*; (for lottery) décimo *m*. **2** collector, revisor,-a *m,f*; t. **office**, taquilla *f*. **2** (receipt) recibo *m*. **3** (label) etiqueta *f*. **4** Aut multa *f*.

tickle ['tikəl] **I** *vtr* hacer cosquillas a. **II** *vi* hacer cosquillas. **III** *n* cosquillas *fpl*.

ticklish ['tikliʃ] *adj* to **be** t., tener cosquillas.

tidal ['taidəl] *adj* de la marea; t. **wave**, ola *f* gigante.

tidbit ['tidbit] *n* US → **titbit**.

tiddlywinks ['tidliwiŋks] *n* (game) pulga *f*.

tide [taid] *n* **1** marea *f*; **high/low** t., marea alta/baja. **2** fig (of events) curso *m*; **the** t. **has turned**, han cambiado las cosas; **to go against the** t., ir contra corriente.

tidings ['taidiŋz] *npl fml* noticias *fpl*.

tidy ['taidi] **I** *adj* (tidier, tidiest) **1** (room, habits) ordenado,-a. **2** (appearance) arreglado,-a. **II** *vtr* arreglar; **to** t. **away**, poner en su sitio. **III** *vi* **to** t. **(up)**, ordenar las cosas.

tie [tai] **I** *vtr* (shoelaces etc) atar; **to** t. **a knot**, hacer un nudo. **II** *vi* Sport empatar (with, con). **III** *n* **1** (bond) lazo *m*, vínculo *m*. **2** fig (hindrance) atadura *f*. **3** (clothing) corbata *f*. **4** Sport (match) partido *m*;

(draw) empate *m*. ◆**tie down** *vtr* sujetar; *fig* **to be tied down**, estar atado,-a; *fig* **to s. sb down to a promise**, obligar a algn a cumplir una promesa. ◆**tie up** *vtr* 1 (*parcel, dog*) atar. 2 (*deal*) concluir. 3 (*capital*) inmovilizar; *fig* **I'm tied up just now**, de momento estoy muy ocupado,-a.

tiebreaker ['taɪbreɪkər] *n* tie-break *m*.

tiepin ['taɪpɪn] *n* alfiler *m* de corbata.

tier [tɪər] *n* (*of seats*) fila *f*; (*in stadium*) grada *f*; **four-t. cake**, pastel *m* de cuatro pisos.

tiger ['taɪgər] *n* tigre *m*.

tight [taɪt] **I** *adj* 1 apretado,-a; (*clothing*) ajustado,-a; (*seal*) hermético,-a; **my shoes are too t.**, me aprietan los zapatos, *fig* **to be in a t. corner**, estar en un apuro. 2 (*scarce*) escaso,-a; (*money*) **s's a bit t.**, estamos escasos de dinero. 3 (*mean*) agarrado,-a. 4 *fam* (*drunk*) borracho,-a. **II** *adv* estrechamente; (*seal*) herméticamente; **hold t.**, agárrate fuerte; **shut t.**, bien cerrado,-a; **to sit t.**, no moverse de su sitio.

tighten ['taɪtən] **I** *vtr* (*screw*) apretar, (*rope*) tensar; *fig* **to t. (up) restrictions**, intensificar las restricciones. **II** *vi* apretarse; (*cable*) tensarse.

tightfisted [taɪt'fɪstɪd] *adj* tacaño,-a.

tightrope ['taɪtrəʊp] *n* cuerda floja; **t. walker**, funámbulo,-a *m,f*.

tights [taɪts] *npl* (*thin*) medias *fpl*, panties *mpl*; (*thick*) leotardos *mpl*; (*of dancer*) mallas *fpl*.

tile [taɪl] **I** *n* (*of roof*) teja *f*, (*glazed*) azulejo *m*; (*for floor*) baldosa *f*. **II** *vtr* (*roof*) tejar; (*wall*) azulejar; (*floor*) embaldosar.

tiled [taɪld] *adj* (*roof*) de or con tejas; (*wall*) revestido,-a de azulejos; (*floor*) embaldosado,-a.

till¹ [tɪl] *n* (*for cash*) caja *f*.

till² [tɪl] *vtr* (*field*) labrar, cultivar.

till³ [tɪl] **I** *prep* hasta; **from morning t. night**, de la mañana a la noche; **t. then**, hasta entonces. **II** *conj* hasta que.

tiller ['tɪlər] *n Naut* caña *f* del timón.

tilt [tɪlt] **I** *n* 1 (*angle*) inclinación *f*. 2 (*at*) **full t.**, (*speed*) a toda velocidad. **II** *vi* **to t. over**, volcarse; **to t. (up)**, inclinarse. **III** *vtr* inclinar.

timber ['tɪmbər] *n* (*wood*) madera *f* (de construcción); (*trees*) árboles *mpl*; (*piece of*) **t.**, viga *f*.

time [taɪm] **I** *n* 1 tiempo *m*; **all the t.**, todo el tiempo; **for some t. (past)**, desde hace algún tiempo; **I haven't seen him for a long t.**, hace mucho (tiempo) que no lo veo; **in a short t.**, en poco tiempo; **in no t.**, en un abrir y cerrar de ojos; **in t.**, a tiempo; **in three weeks' t.**, dentro de tres semanas; **to take one's t. over sth**, hacer algo con calma; *fam* **to do t.**, cumplir una condena; **t. bomb**, bomba *f*

de relojería; **t. limit**, límite *m* de tiempo; (*for payment etc*) plazo *m*; **t. switch**, interruptor *m* electrónico automático; **t. zone**, huso horario. 2 (*era*) época *f*, tiempos *mpl*; **a sign of the times**, un signo de los tiempos; **to be behind the times**, tener ideas anticuadas. 3 (*point in time*) momento *m*; **(at) any t. (you like)**, cuando quieras; **at no t.**, en ningún momento; **at that t.**, (*en aquel*) entonces; **at the same t.**, al mismo tiempo; **at times**, a veces; **from t. to t.**, de vez en cuando; **he may turn up at any t.**, puede llegar en cualquier momento. 4 (*time of day*) hora *f*, **and about t. too!**, ¡ya era hora!; **in good t.**, con anticipación; **on t.**, puntualmente; **what's the t.?**, ¿qué hora es? 5 **t. of year** época *f* del año. 6 **to have a good/bad t.**, pasarlo bien/mal. 7 (*occasion*) vez *f*; **four at a t.**, cuatro a la vez; **next t.**, la próxima vez; **several times over**, varias veces; **three times running**, tres veces seguidas; **t. after t.**, una y otra vez. 8 (*in multiplication*) **three times four**, tres (multiplicado) por cuatro; **four times as big**, cuatro veces más grande. 9 *Mus* compás *m*; **in t.**, al compás.
II *vtr* 1 (*speech*) calcular la duración de; *Sport* (*race*) cronometrar. 2 (*choose the time of*) escoger el momento oportuno para.

time-consuming ['taɪmkənsjuːmɪŋ] *adj* que ocupa mucho tiempo.

time-lag ['taɪmlæg] *n* intervalo *m*.

timeless ['taɪmlɪs] *adj* eterno,-a.

timely ['taɪmlɪ] *adj* (**timelier, timeliest**) oportuno,-a.

timer ['taɪmər] *n* (*device*) temporizador *m*.

timetable ['taɪmteɪbəl] *n* horario *m*.

timid ['tɪmɪd] *adj* tímido,-a.

timing ['taɪmɪŋ] *n* 1 (*timeliness*) oportunidad *f*; (*coordination*) coordinación *f*; **your t. was wrong**, no calculaste bien. 2 *Sport* cronometraje *m*.

tin [tɪn] **I** *n* 1 (*metal*) estaño *m*; **t. plate**, hojalata *f*. 2 (*container*) lata *f*. **II** *vtr* (*tins*) enlatar; **tinned food**, conservas *fpl*.

tinfoil ['tɪnfɔɪl] *n* papel *m* de estaño.

tinge [tɪndʒ] **I** *n* tinte *m*, matiz *m*. **II** *vtr* teñir.

tingle ['tɪŋgəl] *vi* **my feet are tingling**, siento un hormigueo en los pies.

tinker ['tɪŋkər] **I** *n pej* calderero,-a *m,f*. **II** *vi* **stop tinkering with the radio**, deja de toquetear la radio.

tinkle ['tɪŋkəl] *vi* tintinear.

tin-opener ['tɪnəʊpənər] *n* abrelatas *m inv*.

tinsel ['tɪnsəl] *n* oropel *m*.

tint [tɪnt] **I** *n* tinte *m*, matiz *m*. **II** *vtr* teñir; **to t. one's hair**, teñirse el pelo.

tiny ['taɪnɪ] *adj* (**tinier, tiniest**) pequeñito,-a; **t. bit**, un poquitín.

tip[1] [tɪp] **I** *n* (*end*) punta *f*; (*of cigarette*) colilla *f*; **it's on the t. of my tongue**, lo tengo en la punta de la lengua. **II** *vtr* poner cantera a; **tipped with steel**, con punta de acero.

tip[2] [tɪp] **I** *n* **1** (*gratuity*) propina *f*. **2** (*advice*) consejo *m*. **3** *Sport* (*racing*) pronóstico *m*. **II** *vtr* **1** dar una propina a. **2** *Sport* pronosticar. ◆**tip off** *vtr* (*police*) dar el chivatazo a.

tip[3] [tɪp] **I** *n GB* (*rubbish*) t., vertedero *m*. **II** *vtr* inclinar; *GB* (*rubbish*) verter. **III** *vi* to t. (up), ladearse; (*cart*) bascular. ◆**tip over I** *vtr* volcar. **II** *vi* volcarse.

tipple ['tɪpəl] *fam* **I** *vi* empinar el codo. **II** *n* bebida alcohólica; **what's your t.?**, ¿qué te gusta beber?

tipsy ['tɪpsɪ] *adj* (*tipsier, tipsiest*) contentillo,-a.

tiptoe ['tɪptəʊ] **I** *vi* andar de puntillas; **to t. in/out**, entrar/salir de puntillas. **II** *n* **on t.**, de puntillas.

tiptop ['tɪptɒp] *adj fam* de primera.

tire[1] ['taɪər] *n US →* **tyre**.

tire[2] ['taɪər] **I** *vtr* cansar; **to t. sb out**, agotar a algn. **II** *vi* cansarse; **to t. of doing sth**, cansarse de hacer algo.

tired ['taɪəd] *adj* cansado,-a; **t. out**, rendido,-a; **to be t.**, estar cansado,-a; **to be t. of sth**, estar harto,-a de algo.

tireless ['taɪəlɪs] *adj* incansable.

tiresome ['taɪəsəm] *adj* pesado,-a.

tiring ['taɪərɪŋ] *adj* agotador,-a.

tissue ['tɪʃu:, 'tɪsju:] *n* **1** *Biol* tejido *m*. **2** *Tex* tisú *m*; **t. paper**, papel *m* de seda. **3** (*handkerchief*) pañuelo *m* de papel, kleenex® *m*.

tit[1] [tɪt] *n* **to give t. for tat**, devolver la pelota.

tit[2] [tɪt] *n sl* (*breast*) teta *f*.

titbit ['tɪtbɪt] *n* golosina *f*.

titillate ['tɪtɪleɪt] *vtr* excitar.

tit(t)ivate ['tɪtɪveɪt] *vtr* emperifollar.

title ['taɪtəl] *n* **1** título *m*; *Cin* **credit titles**, ficha técnica; **t. page**, portada *f*; **t. role**, papel *m* principal. **2** *Jur* título *m*.

titter ['tɪtər] **I** *vi* reírse nerviosamente; (*foolishly*) reírse tontamente. **II** *n* risa ahogada; (*foolish*) risilla tonta.

titular ['tɪtjʊlər] *adj* titular.

TM *abbr of* **trademark**, marca *f* (de fábrica).

to [tu:; *unstressed before vowels* tʊ, *before consonants* tə] **I** *prep* **1** (*with place*) a; (*expressing direction*) hacia; **from town to town**, de ciudad en ciudad; **he went to France/Japan**, fue a Francia/Japón; **I'm going to Mary's**, voy a casa de Mary; **it is thirty miles to London**, Londres está a treinta millas; **the train to Madrid**, el tren de Madrid; **to the east**, hacia el este; **to the right**, a la derecha; **what school do you go to?**, ¿a qué escuela vas? **2** (*time*) a; **from day to day**, de día en día; **from two to four**, de dos a cuatro; **ten (minutes) to six**, las seis menos diez. **3** (*as far as*) hasta; **accurate to a millimetre**, exacto,-a hasta el milímetro. **4** (*with indirect object*) **he gave it to his cousin**, se lo dio a su primo; **what's that to you?**, ¿qué te importa a ti? **5** (*towards a person*) **he was very kind to me**, se portó muy bien conmigo. **6** (*of*) de; **heir to an estate**, heredero *m* de una propiedad; **adviser to the president**, consejero *m* del presidente. **7** (*to come to sb's assistance*), acudir en ayuda de algn; **to everyone's surprise**, para sorpresa de todos; **to this end**, con este fin. **8** **to the best of my knowledge**, que yo sepa. **9** (*compared to*) **that's nothing to what I've seen**, eso no es nada en comparación con lo que he visto yo. **10** (*in proportion*) **one house to the square kilometre**, una casa por kilómetro cuadrado; **six votes to four**, seis votos contra cuatro. **11** (*about*) **what did he say to my suggestion?**, ¿qué contestó a mi sugerencia?

II *with infin* **1** *with simple infinitives* to *is not translated but is shown by the verb endings*; **to buy**, comprar; **to come**, venir. **2** (*in order to*) para; (*with verbs of motion or purpose*) a, por; **he did it to help me**, lo hizo para ayudarme; **he stopped to talk**, se detuvo a hablar; **he fought to convince them**, luchó por convencerles. **3** *various verbs followed by dependent infinitives take particular prepositions* (a, de, en, por, con, para etc) *and others take no preposition*; → *the entry of the verb in question*. **4** (*with adj and infin*) a, de; **difficult to do**, difícil de hacer; **ready to listen**, dispuesto,-a a escuchar; **too hot to drink**, demasiado caliente para bebérselo. **5** (*with noun and infin*) **the first to complain**, el primero en quejarse; **this is the time to do it**, éste es el momento de hacerlo; **to have a great deal to do**, tener mucho que hacer. **6** (*expressing following action*) **he awoke to find the light still on**, al despertarse encontró la lámpara todavía encendida. **7** (*with verbs of ordering, wishing etc*) **he asked me to do it**, me pidió que lo hiciera. **8** (*expressing obligation*) **fifty employees are to go**, cincuenta empleados deben ser despedidos; **to have to do sth**, tener que hacer algo. **9** (*replacing infin*) **go if you want to**, váyase si quiere.

III *adv* to go to and fro, ir y venir; **to push the door to**, encajar la puerta.

toad [təʊd] *n* sapo *m*.

toadstool ['təʊdstu:l] *n* hongo *m* (venenoso).

toast[1] [təʊst] *Culin* **I** *n* pan tostado; **a slice of t.**, una tostada. **II** *vtr* tostar.

toast[2] [təʊst] **I** *n* (*drink*) brindis *m inv*; **to drink a t. to**, brindar por. **II** *vtr* brindar por.

toaster ['təʊstər] n tostador m (de pan).

tobacco [tə'bækəʊ] n tabaco m.

tobacconist [tə'bækənɪst] n GB estanquero,-a m,f; **t.'s (shop)**, estanco m.

toboggan [tə'bɒgən] n tobogán m.

today [tə'deɪ] I n hoy m. II adv hoy; (nowadays) hoy en día; **a week t.**, justo dentro de una semana.

toddler ['tɒdlər] n niño,-a m,f que empieza a andar; **the toddlers**, los pequeñitos.

toddy ['tɒdɪ] n (drink) ponche m.

to-do [tə'duː] n lío m, jaleo m.

toe [təʊ] I n dedo m del pie; **big t.**, dedo gordo. II vtr to **t. the line**, conformarse.

toenail ['təʊneɪl] n uña f del dedo del pie.

toffee ['tɒfɪ] n caramelo m.

together [tə'geðər] adv junto, juntos,-as; **all t.**, todos juntos; **t. with**, junto con; **to bring t.**, reunir.

toil [tɔɪl] I n trabajo duro. II vi afanarse, trabajar (duro); **to t. up a hill**, subir penosamente una cuesta.

toilet ['tɔɪlɪt] n 1 wáter m, retrete m; (for public) servicios mpl. 2 **t. paper** or **tissue**, papel higiénico; **t. roll**, rollo m de papel higiénico. 2 (washing etc) aseo m (personal); **t. bag**, neceser m; **t. soap**, jabón m de tocador.

toiletries ['tɔɪlɪtrɪz] npl artículos mpl de aseo.

token ['təʊkən] I n 1 (sign) señal f; **as a t. of respect**, en señal de respeto. 2 Com vale m; **book t.**, vale para comprar libros. II adj simbólico,-a.

told [təʊld] pt & pp → tell.

tolerable ['tɒlərəbəl] adj tolerable.

tolerance ['tɒlərəns] n tolerancia f.

tolerant ['tɒlərənt] adj tolerante.

tolerate ['tɒləreɪt] vtr tolerar.

toll[1] [təʊl] I vtr tocar. II vi doblar.

toll[2] [təʊl] n 1 Aut peaje m. 2 (loss) pérdidas fpl; **the death t.**, el número de víctimas mortales.

tomato [tə'mɑːtəʊ, US tə'meɪtəʊ] n (pl tomatoes) tomate m; **t. sauce**, salsa f de tomate.

tomb [tuːm] n tumba f, sepulcro m.

tomboy ['tɒmbɔɪ] n marimacho f.

tombstone ['tuːmstəʊn] n lápida f sepulcral.

tomcat ['tɒmkæt] n gato m (macho).

tomorrow [tə'mɒrəʊ] I n mañana m; **the day after t.**, pasado mañana; **t. night**, mañana por la noche. II adv mañana; **see you t.!**, ¡hasta mañana!; **t. week**, dentro de ocho días a partir de mañana.

ton [tʌn] n tonelada f; fam **tons of**, montones de.

tone [təʊn] I n tono m. II vi to **t. with sth**, armonizar con algo. ◆**tone down** vtr atenuar.

tone-deaf ['təʊndef] adj to be **t.-d.**, no

tener oído.

tongs [tɒŋz] npl (for sugar, hair) tenacillas fpl; (fire) t., tenazas fpl.

tongue [tʌŋ] n 1 lengua f; fig **to say sth t. in cheek**, decir algo con la boca pequeña; fig **t. twister**, trabalenguas m inv. 2 (of shoe) lengüeta f; (of bell) badajo m.

tongue-tied ['tʌŋtaɪd] adj mudo,-a (por la timidez).

tonic ['tɒnɪk] I n 1 Med tónico m. 2 (drink) tónica f. II adj tónico,-a; Mus **t. sol-fa**, solfeo m.

tonight [tə'naɪt] adv & n esta noche.

tonnage ['tʌnɪdʒ] n (of ship) tonelaje m.

tonne ['tʌn] n → ton.

tonsil ['tɒnsəl] n amígdala f; **to have one's tonsils out**, ser operado,-a de las amígdalas.

tonsillitis [tɒnsɪ'laɪtɪs] n amigdalitis f.

too [tuː] adv 1 (besides) además. 2 (also) también. 3 (excessively) demasiado; **t. much money**, demasiado dinero; **ten pounds t. much**, diez libras de más; **t. frequently**, con demasiada frecuencia; **t. old**, demasiado viejo.

took [tʊk] pt → take.

tool [tuːl] n (utensil) herramienta f.

toolbox ['tuːlbɒks] n caja f de herramientas.

toot [tuːt] n Aut I vtr tocar. II vi tocar la bocina.

tooth [tuːθ] n (pl teeth [tiːθ]) 1 diente m; (molar) muela f; fig **to fight t. and nail**, luchar a brazo partido. 2 (of saw) diente m; (of comb) púa f.

toothache ['tuːθeɪk] n dolor m de muelas.

toothbrush ['tuːθbrʌʃ] n cepillo m de dientes.

toothpaste ['tuːθpeɪst] n pasta dentífrica f.

toothpick ['tuːθpɪk] n mondadientes m inv.

top[1] [tɒp] I n 1 (upper part) parte f de arriba; (of hill) cumbre f, cima f; (of tree) copa f; **from t. to bottom**, de arriba a abajo; **on t. of**, encima de; fig **on t. of it all** ..., para colmo ...; **t. hat**, sombrero m de copa. 2 (surface) superficie f. 3 (of list etc) cabeza f. 4 (of bottle etc) tapa f, tapón m. 5 (garment) camiseta f. 6 (best) lo mejor. 7 fig **at the t. of one's voice**, a voz en grito. II adj 1 (part) superior, de arriba; **the t. floor**, el último piso; **t. coat**, (of paint) última mano. 2 (highest) más alto,-a; Aut **t. gear**, directa f. 3 (best) mejor. III vtr 1 (place on top of) coronar. 2 Theat **to t. the bill**, encabezar el reparto. ◆**top up** vtr llenar hasta el tope; **to t. up the petrol tank**, llenar el depósito; fig and **to t. it all**, y para colmo.

top[2] [tɒp] n (toy) peonza f.

topic ['tɒpɪk] n tema m.

topical ['tɒpɪkəl] adj de actualidad.

top-level ['tɒplevəl] adj de alto nivel.

topmost ['tɒpməʊst] adj (el) más alto, (la) más alta.

topple ['tɒpl] I vi (building) venirse abajo; (over), volcarse. II vtr volcar; fig (government) derrocar.

top-secret [tɒp'si:krɪt] adj de alto secreto.

topsy-turvy [tɒpsɪ'tɜːvɪ] adj & adv al revés; (in confusion) en desorden, patas arriba.

torch [tɔːtʃ] n (electric) linterna f.

tore [tɔːr] pt → **tear²**.

torment ['tɔːment] I vtr atormentar. II n ['tɔːment] tormento m, suplicio m.

torn [tɔːn] pp → **tear²**.

tornado [tɔː'neɪdəʊ] n tornado m.

torpedo [tɔː'piːdəʊ] n torpedo m.

torrent ['tɒrənt] n torrente m.

torrential [tɒ'renʃəl] adj torrencial.

torrid ['tɒrɪd] adj tórrido,-a.

torso ['tɔːsəʊ] n torso m.

tortoise ['tɔːtəs] n tortuga f de tierra.

tortoiseshell ['tɔːtəsʃel] adj de carey.

torture ['tɔːtʃər] I vtr torturar; fig atormentar. II n tortura f; fig tormento m.

Tory ['tɔːrɪ] adj & n GB Pol conservador,-a (m,f).

toss [tɒs] I vtr 1 (ball) tirar; **to t. a coin**, echar a cara o cruz. 2 (throw about) sacudir. II vi 1 **to t. about**, agitarse; **to t. and turn**, dar vueltas en la cama. 2 Sport **to t. (up)**, sortear. III n 1 (of ball) lanzamiento m; (of coin) sorteo m (a cara o cruz). 2 (of head) sacudida f.

tot¹ [tɒt] n 1 (tiny) n 1, (child) nene, a m,f. 2 (of whisky etc) trago m.

tot² [tɒt] GB vtr **to t. up**, sumar.

total ['təʊtəl] I n total m; (in bill) importe m; grand t., suma f total. II adj total. III vtr sumar. IV vi **to t. up to**, ascender a. ◆**totally** adv totalmente.

totalitarian [təʊtælɪ'teərɪən] adj totalitario,-a.

tote [təʊt] n fam Sport totalizador m.

tote bag ['təʊtbæg] n petate m.

totem ['təʊtəm] n tótem m.

totter ['tɒtər] vi tambalearse.

touch [tʌtʃ] I vtr 1 tocar; fig **to t. on a subject**, tocar un tema. 2 (equal) igualar. 3 (move) conmover. II vi tocarse; **fig it was t. and go whether we caught the train**, estuvimos a punto de perder el tren. III n 1 toque m. 2 (sense of touch) tacto m. 3 **it was a nice t. of his**, fue un detalle de su parte; **to put the finishing touches to sth**, dar los últimos toques a algo. 4 (ability) habilidad f. 5 (contact) contacto m; **to be/get/keep in t. with sb**, estar/ponerse/mantenerse en contacto con algn; **to be out of t. with sth**, no estar al tanto de algo. 6 (small amount) pizca f. 7 Sport **in t.**, fuera de banda. ◆**touch down** vi (plane) aterrizar. ◆**touch off**

vtr desencadenar. ◆**touch up** vtr (picture) retocar.

touchdown ['tʌtʃdaʊn] n 1 (of plane) aterrizaje m; (of space capsule) amerizaje m. 2 Rugby ensayo m.

touched [tʌtʃt] adj 1 (moved) emocionado,-a. 2 fam (crazy) tocado,-a.

touching ['tʌtʃɪŋ] adj conmovedor,-a.

touchline ['tʌtʃlaɪn] n línea f de banda.

touchy ['tʌtʃɪ] adj (touchier, touchiest) fam (person) susceptible; (subject) delicado,-a.

tough [tʌf] I adj (material, competitor etc) fuerte, resistente; (test, criminal, meat) duro,-a; (punishment) severo,-a; (problem) difícil. II n (person) matón m.

toughen ['tʌfən] vtr endurecer.

toupee ['tuːpeɪ] n tupé m.

tour [tʊər] I n 1 (journey) viaje m; package t., viaje organizado. 2 (of monument etc) visita f; (of city) recorrido turístico. 3 Sport Theat gira f; **on t.**, de gira. II vtr 1 (country) viajar por. 2 (building) visitar. 3 Theat estar de gira en. III vi estar de viaje.

tourism ['tʊərɪzəm] n turismo m.

tourist ['tʊərɪst] n turista mf; t. centre, centro m de información turística; Av t. class, clase f turista.

tournament ['tʊənəmənt] n torneo m.

tousled ['taʊzəld] adj (hair) despeinado, -a.

tout [taʊt] I vtr Com tratar de vender; (tickets) revender. II vi salir a la caza y captura de compradores. III n Com gancho m; ticket t., revendedor m de entradas.

tow [təʊ] I n **to take a car in t.**, remolcar un coche. II vtr remolcar.

towards [tə'wɔːdz, tɔːdz] prep 1 (direction, time) hacia. 2 (with regard to) hacia, (para) con; **our duty t. others**, nuestro deber para con los demás; **what is your attitude t. religion?**, ¿cuál es su actitud respecto a la religión?

towel ['taʊəl] I n toalla f; hand t., toallita f; t. rail, toallero m. II vtr **to t. dry**, secar con una toalla.

towelling ['taʊəlɪŋ] n felpa f.

tower ['taʊər] I n torre f. II vi **to t. over or above sth**, dominar algo.

towering ['taʊərɪŋ] adj impresionante, enorme.

town [taʊn] n ciudad f; (small) pueblo m; **to go into t.**, ir al centro; fam **to go to t.**, tirar la casa por la ventana; t. council, ayuntamiento m; t. councillor, concejal,-a m,f; t. hall, ayuntamiento m; t. planning, urbanismo m.

townspeople ['taʊnzpiːpəl] npl ciudadanos mpl.

towpath ['təʊpɑːθ] n sendero m a lo largo de un canal.

towrope ['təʊrəʊp] n cable m de remolque.

toxic ['toksɪk] adj tóxico,-a.

toy [tɔɪ] I n juguete m. II vi to t. with an idea, acariciar una idea; **to t. with one's food**, comer sin gana.

toyshop ['tɔɪʃɒp] n juguetería f.

trace [treɪs] I n 1 (sign) indicio m, vestigio m. 2 (tracks) huella(s) f(pl). II vtr 1 (drawing) calcar. 2 (plan) bosquejar. 3 (locate) seguir la pista de.

tracing ['treɪsɪŋ] n **t. paper**, papel m de calco.

track [træk] I n 1 (trail) huellas fpl, pista f; **to keep/lose t. of sb**, no perder/perder de vista a algn. 2 (pathway) camino m; **to be on the right/wrong t.**, ir por el buen/mal camino. 3 Sport pista f; (for motor racing) circuito m; fig **t. record**, historial m. 4 Rail vía f; fig **he has a one-t. mind**, tiene una única obsesión. 5 (on record) canción f. II vtr seguir la pista de; (with radar) seguir la trayectoria de. ◆**track down** vtr (locate) localizar.

tracksuit ['træksuːt] n chándal m.

tract¹ [trækt] n (expanse) extensión f.

tract² [trækt] n (treatise) tratado m; (pamphlet) folleto m.

traction ['trækʃən] n tracción f.

tractor ['træktər] n tractor m.

trade [treɪd] I n 1 (profession) oficio m; **by t.**, de oficio. 2 Com comercio m; **it's good for t.**, es bueno para los negocios; **the building t.**, (la industria de la construcción); **t. name**, nombre m comercial; **t. union**, sindicato m; **t. unionist**, sindicalista mf. II vi comerciar (**in**, en). III vtr **to t. sth for sth**, trocar algo por algo. ◆**trade in** vtr dar como entrada.

trademark ['treɪdmɑːk] n marca f (de fábrica); **registered t.**, marca registrada.

trader ['treɪdər] n comerciante mf.

tradesman ['treɪdzmən] n (shopkeeper) tendero m.

trading ['treɪdɪŋ] n comercio m; GB **t. estate**, polígono m industrial.

tradition [trə'dɪʃən] n tradición f.

traditional [trə'dɪʃənəl] adj tradicional.

traffic ['træfɪk] I n 1 tráfico m, circulación f; **t. island**, isleta f; **t. jam**, atasco m; **t. lights**, semáforo m sing; **t. warden**, ≈ guardia mf urbano,-a. 2 (trade) tráfico m. II vi (pt & pp **trafficked**) **to t. in drugs**, traficar con droga.

trafficker ['træfɪkər] n traficante mf.

tragedy ['trædʒɪdɪ] n tragedia f.

tragic ['trædʒɪk] adj trágico,-a.

trail [treɪl] I vtr 1 (drag) arrastrar. 2 (follow) rastrear. II vi 1 (drag) arrastrar. 2 **to t. behind**, rezagarse. III n 1 (track) pista f, rastro m. 2 (path) senda f, camino m. 3 (of smoke) estela f.

trailer ['treɪlər] n 1 Aut remolque m. 2 US Aut (caravan) caravana f. 3 Cin tráiler m, avance m.

train [treɪn] I n 1 Rail tren m. 2 (of vehicles) convoy m; (of followers) séquito m; (of events) serie f. 3 (of dress) cola f. II vtr 1 (teach) formar; Sport entrenar; (animal) amaestrar; (voice etc) educar. 2 (gun) apuntar (**on**, a); (camera) enfocar (**on**, a). III vi prepararse; Sport entrenarse.

trainee [treɪ'niː] n aprendiz,-a m,f.

trainer ['treɪnər] n 1 Sport entrenador,-a m,f; (of dogs) amaestrador,-a m,f; (of lions) domador,-a m,f. 2 **trainers**, (shoes) zapatillas fpl de deporte.

training ['treɪnɪŋ] n (instruction) formación f; Sport entrenamiento m; (of animals) amaestramiento m; (of lions) doma f; **to go into t.**, empezar el entrenamiento; **vocational t.**, formación profesional.

traipse [treɪps] vi fam vagar.

trait [treɪt] n rasgo m.

traitor ['treɪtər] n traidor,-a m,f.

trajectory [trə'dʒektərɪ] n trayectoria f.

tram [træm], **tramcar** ['træmkɑː] n GB tranvía m.

tramp [træmp] I vi 1 (travel on foot) caminar. 2 (walk heavily) andar con pasos pesados. II n (person) vagabundo,-a m,f; pej **she's a t.**, es una fulana.

trample ['træmpəl] vtr **to t. down the grass**, pisotear la hierba; **to t. sth underfoot**, pisotear algo.

trampoline ['træmpəliːn] n cama elástica.

trance [trɑːns] n trance m.

tranquil ['træŋkwɪl] adj tranquilo,-a.

tranquillity [træŋ'kwɪlɪtɪ] n tranquilidad f.

tranquillizer ['træŋkwɪlaɪzər] n tranquilizante m.

transact [træn'zækt] vtr negociar.

transaction [træn'zækʃən] n (procedure) tramitación f; (deal) transacción f.

transatlantic [trænzət'læntɪk] adj transatlántico,-a.

transcend [træn'send] vtr trascender.

transcribe [træn'skraɪb] vtr transcribir.

transcript ['trænskrɪpt] n transcripción f.

transcription [træn'skrɪpʃən] n transcripción f.

transfer [træns'fɜːr] I vtr trasladar; (funds) trasferir; Jur ceder; Ftb traspasar; Tel **to t. the charges**, hacer una llamada a cobro revertido. II ['trænsfɜːr] n 1 traslado m; (of funds) transferencia f; Jur cesión f; Ftb traspaso m. 2 (picture, design) calcomanía f.

transform [træns'fɔːm] vtr transformar.

transformation [trænsfə'meɪʃən] n transformación f.

transfusion [træns'fjuːʒən] n Med transfusión f (de sangre).

transgress [trænz'gres] vi fml transgredir.

transient ['trænzɪənt] adj transitorio,-a.

transistor [træn'zɪstər] n transistor m.

transit ['trænzɪt] n tránsito m; **in t.**, de

tránsito.

transition [træn'zɪʃən] *n* transición *f*.

transitive ['trænzɪtɪv] *adj* transitivo,-a.

transitory ['trænzɪtərɪ] *adj* transitorio,-a.

translate [træns'leɪt] *vtr* traducir.

translation [træns'leɪʃən] *n* traducción *f*.

translator [træns'leɪtər] *n* traductor,-a *m,f*.

translucent [trænz'luːsənt] *adj* translúcido,-a.

transmission [trænz'mɪʃən] *n* transmisión *f*.

transmit [trænz'mɪt] *vtr* transmitir.

transmitter [trænz'mɪtər] *n* Rad (set) transmisor *m*; Rad TV (station) emisora *f*.

transparency [træns'pærənsɪ] *n* Phot diapositiva *f*.

transparent [træns'pærənt] *adj* transparente.

transpire [træn'spaɪər] *vi (happen)* ocurrir; **it transpired that ...,** ocurrió que ....

transplant [træns'plɑːnt] I *vtr* trasplantar. II ['trænsplɑːnt] *n* trasplante *m*.

transport [træns'pɔːt] I *vtr* transportar. II ['trænspɔːt] *n* transporte *m*; **t. aircraft/ship,** avión *m*/buque *m* de transporte; GB **t. café,** bar *m* de carretera.

transportation [trænspɔː'teɪʃən] *n* transporte *m*.

transvestite [trænz'vestaɪt] *n fam* travesti *mf*.

trap [træp] I *n* trampa *f*; **t. door,** trampilla *f*; Theat escotillón *m*. II *vtr* atrapar.

trapeze [trə'piːz] *n* trapecio *m*.

trappings ['træpɪŋz] *npl* parafernalia *f sing*.

trash [træʃ] *n (inferior goods)* bazofia *f*; US *(rubbish)* basura *f*; *fig* **to talk a lot of t.,** decir tonterías; US **t. can,** cubo *m* de la basura.

trashy ['træʃɪ] *adj (trashier, trashiest)* de ínfima calidad.

trauma ['trɔːmə] *n* trauma *m*.

traumatic [trɔː'mætɪk] *adj* traumático,-a.

travel ['trævəl] I *vi* 1 viajar; **to t. through,** recorrer. 2 *(vehicle, electric current)* ir; *fig (news)* propagarse. II *vtr* recorrer. III *n* viajar *m*; **t. agency,** agencia *f* de viajes.

traveller, US **traveler** ['trævələr] *n* viajero,-a *m,f*; **t.'s cheque,** cheque *m* de viaje.

travelling, US **traveling** ['trævəlɪŋ] I *adj (salesman)* ambulante. II *n* viajes *mpl*, (el) viajar *m*; **I'm fond of t.,** me gusta viajar; **t. expenses,** gastos *mpl* de viaje.

travel-sick ['trævəlsɪk] *adj* **to be t.,** estar mareado,-a.

travesty ['trævɪstɪ] *n* parodia *f*.

trawler ['trɔːlər] *n* barco *m* de arrastre.

tray [treɪ] *n (for food)* bandeja *f*; *(for letters)* cesta *f* (para la correspondencia).

treacherous ['tretʃərəs] *adj* 1 *(person)* traidor,-a; *(action)* traicionero,-a. 2

(dangerous) peligroso,-a.

treachery ['tretʃərɪ] *n* traición *f*.

treacle ['triːkəl] *n GB* melaza *f*.

tread [tred] I *vi (pt* **trod;** *pp* **trod** *or* **trodden)** pisar; **to t. on,** pisar. II *vi* 1 *(step on)* pisar. 2 **to t. water,** mantenerse a flote verticalmente. III *n* 1 *(step)* paso *m*; *(sound)* ruido *m* de pasos. 2 *(of tyre)* banda *f* de rodadura.

treadmill ['tredmɪl] *n fig* rutina *f*.

treason ['triːzən] *n* traición *f*.

treasure ['treʒər] I *n* tesoro *m*. II *vtr (keep)* guardar como oro en paño; *(value)* apreciar muchísimo.

treasurer ['treʒərər] *n* tesorero,-a *m,f*.

treasury ['treʒərɪ] *n Pol* **the T.,** ≈ Ministerio *m* de Hacienda; T. **bill,** bono *m* del Tesoro.

treat [triːt] I *n* 1 *(present)* regalo *m*. 2 *(pleasure)* placer *m*. II *vtr* 1 tratar; **to t. badly,** maltratar. 2 *(regard)* considerar. 3 **he treated them to dinner,** les invitó a cenar.

treatise ['triːtɪz] *n* tratado *m*.

treatment ['triːtmənt] *n* 1 *(of person)* trato *m*. 2 *(of subject, of patient)* tratamiento *m*.

treaty ['triːtɪ] *n* tratado *m*.

treble ['trebəl] I *adj* 1 *(triple)* triple; Mus **t. clef,** clave *f* de sol; Mus **t. voice,** voz *f* tiple. II *vtr* triplicar. III *vi* triplicarse.

tree [triː] *n* árbol *m*; **apple/cherry t.,** manzano *m*/cerezo *m*.

treetop ['triːtɒp] *n* copa *f*.

trek [trek] I *n (journey)* viaje *m* (largo *y* difícil); *fam (walk)* caminata *f*. II *vi (pt & pp* **trekked)** hacer un viaje largo *y* difícil; *fam (walk)* ir caminando.

trellis ['trelɪswɜːk] *n* enrejado *m*.

tremble ['trembəl] *vi* temblar, estremecerse.

trembling ['tremblɪŋ] *adj* tembloroso,-a.

tremendous [trɪ'mendəs] *adj (huge)* enorme; *(success)* arrollador,-a; *(shock etc)* tremendo,-a; *fam (marvellous)* estupendo,-a.

tremor ['tremər] *n* temblor *m*.

trench [trentʃ] *n* 1 *(ditch)* zanja *f*; Mil trinchera *f*. 2 **t. coat,** trinchera *f*.

trend [trend] I *n (tendency)* tendencia *f*; *(fashion)* moda *f*. II *vi* tender **(to, towards,** hacia).

trendy ['trendɪ] *adj (trendier, trendiest) fam (person)* moderno,-a; *(clothes)* a la última.

trepidation [trepɪ'deɪʃən] *n* turbación *f*.

trespass ['trespəs] *vi* entrar sin autorización.

trespasser ['trespəsər] *n* intruso,-a *m,f*.

trestle ['tresəl] *n* caballete *m*.

trial ['traɪəl] *n* 1 Jur proceso *m*, juicio *m*. 2 *(test)* prueba *f*; **on t.,** a prueba; **by t. and error,** a fuerza de equivocarse. 3 **trials,** *(competition)* concurso *m sing*. 4 **trials,** *(suffering)* sufrimiento *m sing*; **t.**

and tribulations, tribulaciones *fpl*.
triangle ['traɪæŋgəl] *n* triángulo *m*.
tribe [traɪb] *n* tribu *f*.
tribunal [traɪ'bjuːnəl] *n* tribunal *m*.
tributary ['trɪbjʊtərɪ] *n (river)* afluente *m*.
tribute ['trɪbjuːt] *n* 1 *(payment)* tributo *m*. 2 *(mark of respect)* homenaje *m*; **to pay t. to**, rendir homenaje a.
trice [traɪs] *n fam* **in a t.**, en un abrir y cerrar de ojos.
trick [trɪk] I *n* 1 *(ruse)* ardid *m*; *(dishonest)* engaño *m*; *(in question)* trampa *f*. 2 *(practical joke)* broma *f*; **to play a t. on sb**, gastarle una broma a algn; *(malicious)* jugar una mala pasada a algn. 3 *(of magic, knack)* truco *m*; **that'll do the t.!**, ¡eso es exactamente lo que hace falta! 4 *Cards* baza *f*. II *vtr* engañar; **to t. sb out of sth**, estafar algo a algn.
trickery ['trɪkərɪ] *n* engaños *mpl*, trampas *fpl*.
trickle ['trɪkəl] I *vi* discurrir; *(water)* gotear. II *n* hilo *m*.
tricky ['trɪkɪ] *adj* **(trickier, trickiest)** *(person)* astuto,-a; *(situation, mechanism)* delicado,-a.
tricycle ['traɪsɪkəl] *n* triciclo *m*.
tried [traɪd] *pt & pp →* **try**.
trifle ['traɪfəl] I *n* 1 *(insignificant thing)* bagatela *f*; **he's a t. optimistic**, es ligeramente optimista. 2 *GB Culin* postre *m* (de bizcocho, jerez, gelatina, frutas y nata). II *vi* **to t. with**, tomar a la ligera.
trifling ['traɪflɪŋ] *adj* insignificante, trivial.
trigger ['trɪgəʳ] I *n (of gun)* gatillo *m*; *(of mechanism)* disparador *m*. II *vtr* **to t. (off)**, desencadenar.
trill [trɪl] *n (of music, bird)* trino *m*; *Ling* vibración *f*.
trilogy ['trɪlədʒɪ] *n* trilogía *f*.
trim [trɪm] I *adj* **(trimmer, trimmest)** *(neat)* aseado,-a; **to have a t. figure**, tener buen tipo. II *vtr* 1 *(cut)* recortar; *(expenses)* disminuir. 2 *(decorate)* adornar. III *n* 1 *(condition)* estado *m*; *Naut* asiento *m*. 2 *(cut)* recorte *m*.
trimming ['trɪmɪŋ] *n* 1 *(cut)* recorte *m*. 2 *(on clothes)* adorno *m*. 3 *Culin* **trimmings**, guarnición *f sing*.
trinket ['trɪŋkɪt] *n* baratija *f*.
trio ['triːəʊ] *n* trío *m*.
trip [trɪp] I *n* 1 *(journey)* viaje *m*; *(excursion)* excursión *f*; **to go on a t.**, ir de excursión. 2 *sl* **to be on a t.**, *(on drugs)* estar colocado,-a. II *vi* 1 **to t. (up)**, *(stumble)* tropezar **(over, con)**; *fig (err)* equivocarse. 2 **to t. along**, ir con paso ligero. III *vtr* **to t. sb (up)**, poner la zancadilla a algn; *fig* coger o pillar a algn.
tripe [traɪp] *n* 1 *Culin* callos *mpl*. 2 *fam* bobadas *fpl*.
triple ['trɪpəl] I *adj* triple. II *vtr* triplicar. III *vi* triplicarse.
triplet ['trɪplɪt] *n* trillizo,-a *m,f*.

triplicate ['trɪplɪkɪt] *adj* **in t.**, por triplicado.
tripod ['traɪpɒd] *n* trípode *m*.
trite [traɪt] *adj (sentiment)* banal; *(subject)* trillado,-a.
triumph ['traɪəmf] I *n* triunfo *m*. II *vi* triunfar.
triumphant [traɪ'ʌmfənt] *adj* triunfante.
trivia ['trɪvɪə] *npl* trivialidades *fpl*.
trivial ['trɪvɪəl] *adj* trivial, banal.
trod [trɒd] *pt & pp →* **tread**.
trodden ['trɒdən] *pp →* **tread**.
trolley ['trɒlɪ] *n GB* carro *m*.
trombone [trɒm'bəʊn] *n* trombón *m*.
troop [truːp] I *n* 1 *(of people)* grupo *m*. 2 *Mil* **troops**, tropas *fpl*. II *vi* **to t. in/out/off**, entrar/salir/marcharse en tropel.
trooper ['truːpəʳ] *n* soldado *m* de caballería.
trooping ['truːpɪŋ] *n GB* **t. the colour**, ceremonia *f* de homenaje a la bandera de un regimiento.
trophy ['trəʊfɪ] *n* trofeo *m*.
tropic ['trɒpɪk] *n* trópico *m*.
tropical ['trɒpɪkəl] *adj* tropical.
trot [trɒt] I *vi* trotar. II *n* trote *m*; **to go at a t.**, ir al trote; *fam* **on the t.**, *(in succession)* seguidos,-as.
trouble ['trʌbəl] I *n* 1 *(misfortune)* desgracia *f*. 2 *(problems)* problemas *mpl*; **to be in t.**, estar en un lío; **to cause sb t.**, ocasionar problemas a algn; **to get sb out of t.**, sacar a algn de un apuro; **the t. is that ...**, lo que pasa es que .... 3 *(effort)* esfuerzo *m*; **it's no t.**, no es ninguna molestia; **it's not worth the t.**, no merece la pena; **to take the t. to do sth**, molestarse en hacer algo. 4 *(conflict)* conflicto *m*. 5 *Med* enfermedad *f*; **to have liver t.**, tener problemas de hígado. II *vtr* 1 *(affect)* afligir; *(worry)* preocupar; **that doesn't t. him at all**, eso le tiene sin cuidado. 2 *(bother)* molestar. III *vi* molestarse.
troubled ['trʌbəld] *adj* agitado,-a.
troublemaker ['trʌbəlmeɪkəʳ] *n* alborotador,-a *m,f*.
troubleshooter ['trʌbəlʃuːtəʳ] *n Ind* persona encargada de solucionar problemas.
troublesome ['trʌbəlsəm] *adj* molesto,-a.
trough [trɒf] *n* 1 *(drinking)* t., abrevadero *m*; *(feeding)* t., pesebre *m*. 2 *(of wave)* seno *m*. 3 *Geog Meteor* depresión *f*.
trounce [traʊns] *vtr* dar una paliza a.
troupe [truːp] *n Theat* compañía *f*.
trousers ['traʊzəz] *npl* pantalón *m sing*, pantalones *mpl*.
trousseau ['truːsəʊ] *n* ajuar *m*.
trout [traʊt] *n* trucha *f*.
trowel ['traʊəl] *n* 1 *(builder's)* palustre *m*. 2 *(for gardening)* desplantador *m*.
truant ['truːənt] *n* **to play t.**, hacer novillos.
truce [truːs] *n* tregua *f*.
truck[1] [trʌk] *n* 1 *GB Rail* vagón *m*. 2

US *Aut* camión *m*; t. **driver**, camionero,-a *m,f*.

truck² [trʌk] *n* 1 to have no t. with, no estar dispuesto a toerar. 2 *US* verduras *fpl*; t. **farming**, cultivo *m* hortalizas.

truculent ['trʌkjulənt] *adj* truculento,-a.

trudge [trʌdʒ] *vi* caminar con dificultad.

true [tru:] *adj* (**truer, truest**) 1 verdadero,-a; **it's t. that** ..., es verdad que ...; **to come t.**, cumplirse, hacerse realidad. 2 (**faithful**) fiel. 3 (**aim**) acertado,-a. ◆**truly** *adv* 1 de verdad; **really and t.?**, ¿de veras? 2 (**faithfully**) fielmente; **yours t.**, atentamente.

truffle ['trʌfəl] *n* trufa *f*.

trump [trʌmp] *Cards* I *n* triunfo *m*. II *vtr* fallar.

trumped-up ['trʌmptʌp] *adj* inventado, -a.

trumpet ['trʌmpit] *n* trompeta *f*.

trumpeting ['trʌmpitiŋ] *n* (*of elephant*) berrido *m*.

truncheon ['trʌntʃən] *n* GB porra *f* (de policía).

trundle ['trʌndəl] *vi* rodar.

trunk [trʌŋk] *n* 1 (*of tree, body*) tronco *m*. 2 (*of elephant*) trompa *f*. 3 (*luggage*) baúl *m*. 4 GB *Tel* t. **call**, conferencia interurbana; GB t. **road**, carretera *f* principal.

trunks [trʌŋks] *npl* (**bathing**) t., bañador *m sing*.

truss [trʌs] I *vtr* (*tie*) atar. II *n* 1 *Constr* cuchillo *m* de armadura. 2 *Med* braguero *m*.

trust [trʌst] I *n* 1 confianza *f*; **breach of t.**, abuso *m* de confianza. 2 *Jur* fideicomiso *m*. 3 *Fin* trust *m*. II *vtr* 1 (*hope*) esperar. 2 (*rely upon*) fiarse de; **to t. sb with sth**, confiar algo a algn. III *vi* confiar (**in**, en).

trusted ['trʌstid] *adj* de fiar.

trustee [trʌs'ti:] *n* *Jur* fideicomisario,-a *m,f*; (*in bankruptcy*) síndico *m*.

trustful ['trʌstful], **trusting** ['trʌstiŋ] *adj* confiado,-a.

trustworthy ['trʌstwɜːði] *adj* (*person*) de confianza; (*information*) fidedigno,-a.

trusty ['trʌsti] *adj* (**trustier, trustiest**) fiel, leal.

truth [tru:θ] *n* verdad *f*; **to tell the t.**, decir la verdad.

truthful ['tru:θful] *adj* (*person*) veraz, sincero,-a; (*testimony*) verídico,-a. ◆**truthfully** *adv* sinceramente.

try [trai] I *vtr* (*pt & pp* **tried**) 1 (*attempt*) intentar; **to t. do sth**, tratar de *or* intentar hacer algo. 2 (*test*) probar, ensayar; **to t. sb's patience**, poner a prueba la paciencia de algn. 3 *Jur* juzgar. II *vi* intenta. III *n* 1 (*attempt*) tentativa *f*, intento *m*. 2 *Sport* ensayo *m*. ◆**try on** *vtr* (*dress*) probarse. ◆**try out** *vtr* probar.

trying ['traiiŋ] *adj* (*person*) molesto,-a, pesado,-a; **to have a t. time**, pasar un mal rato.

tsar [zɑːʳ] *n* zar *m*.

T-shirt ['ti:ʃɜːt] *n* camiseta *f*.

tub [tʌb] *n* 1 (*container*) tina *f*, cuba *f*. 2 (*bath*) bañera *f*.

tuba ['tju:bə] *n* tuba *f*.

tubby ['tʌbi] *adj* (**tubbier, tubbiest**) rechoncho,-a.

tube [tju:b] *n* 1 tubo *m*; *Anat* conducto *m*; (*of bicycle*) cámara *f* (de aire). 2 GB *fam* **the t.**, (*underground*) el metro.

tuberculosis [tjubɜːkju'ləusis] *n* tuberculosis *f*.

tubing ['tju:biŋ] *n* tubería *f*; (*piece of*) t., (*trozo m de*) tubo *m*.

tubular ['tju:bjuləʳ] *adj* tubular.

tuck [tʌk] I *vtr* to **t. in** the bedclothes, remeter la ropa de la cama; **to t. sb in**, arropar a algn; **to t. one's shirt into one's trousers**, meterse la camisa por dentro (de los pantalones). II *n* *Sew* pliegue *m*. ◆**tuck in** *vi* *fam* devorar.

Tuesday ['tju:zdi] *n* martes *m*.

tuft [tʌft] *n* (*of hair*) mechón *m*.

tug [tʌg] I *vtr* (*pull at*) tirar de; (*haul along*) arrastrar; *Naut* remolcar. II *n* 1 (*pull*) tirón *m*; **t. of war**, (*game*) lucha *f* de la cuerda; *fig* lucha encarnizada. 2 *Naut* remolcador *m*.

tugboat ['tʌgbəut] *n* remolcador *m*.

tuition [tju:'iʃən] *n* instrucción *f*; **private t.**, clases *fpl* particulares; **t. fees**, honorarios *mpl*.

tulip ['tju:lip] *n* tulipán *m*.

tumble ['tʌmbəl] I *vi* (*person*) caerse; (*acrobat*) dar volteretas; (*building*) venirse abajo. II *vtr* volcar. III *n* 1 caída *f*. 2 **t. dryer**, secadora *f*.

tumbledown ['tʌmbəldaun] *adj* en ruinas.

tumbler ['tʌmbləʳ] *n* vaso *m*.

tummy ['tʌmi] *n* *fam* estómago *m*, barriga *f*.

tumour, *US* **tumor** ['tju:məʳ] *n* tumor *m*.

tumult ['tju:mʌlt] *n* tumulto *m*.

tuna ['tju:nə] *n* atún *m*, bonito *m*.

tune [tju:n] I *n* 1 (*melody*) melodía *f*; *fig* **to change one's t.**, cambiar de tono. 2 *Mus* tono *m*; **in/out of t.**, afinado/ desafinado; **to sing out of t.**, desafinar. II *vtr* *Mus* afinar. III *vi* *Rad TV* **to t. in to a station**, sintonizar una emisora. ◆**tune up** *vi* afinar los instrumentos.

tuneful ['tju:nful] *adj* melodioso,-a.

tuner ['tju:nəʳ] 1 (*of pianos*) afinador,-a *m,f*. 2 *Rad TV* (*knob*) sintonizador *m*.

tunic ['tju:nik] *n* túnica *f*.

tuning ['tju:niŋ] *n* 1 *Mus* afinación *f*; **t. fork**, diapasón *m*. 2 *Rad TV* **t. in**, sintonización *f*.

Tunisia [tju:'niziə] *n* Túnez *m*.

Tunisian [tju:'niziən] *adj & n* tunecino,-a

(m,f).

tunnel ['tʌnəl] **I** n túnel m; Min galería f. **II** vtr to t. through, abrir un túnel a través de.

turban ['tɜːbən] n turbante m.

turbine ['tɜːbaɪn] n turbina f.

turbulent ['tɜːbjulənt] adj turbulento,-a.

tureen [tə'riːn] n sopera f.

turf [tɜːf] n 1 (grass) césped m; (peat) turba f. 2 GB t. accountant, (in horse racing) corredor,-a m,f de apuestas. ◆**turf out** vtr GB fam to t. sb out, poner a algn de patitas en la calle.

Turk [tɜːk] n turco,-a m,f.

Turkey ['tɜːkɪ] n Turquía.

turkey ['tɜːkɪ] n pavo m.

Turkish ['tɜːkɪʃ] **I** adj turco,-a. **II** n (language) turco m.

turmoil ['tɜːmɔɪl] n confusión f.

turn [tɜːn] **I** vtr 1 volver; (rotate) girar, hacer girar; to t. sth inside out, volver algo del revés; to t. a page, volver una hoja; to t. one's head/gaze, volver la cabeza/mirada (towards, hacia); to t. the corner, doblar la esquina; fig he's turned forty, ha cumplido los cuarenta. 2 (change) transformar (into, en). 3 (on lathe) tornear.

II vi 1 (rotate) girar. 2 (turn round) volverse, dar la vuelta; to t. to sb, volverse hacia algn; fig (for help) acudir a algn; to t. upside down, volcarse; fig to t. on sb, volverse contra algn. 3 (become) volverse; the milk has turned sour, la leche se ha cortado.

III n 1 (of wheel) vuelta f; meat done to a t., carne en su punto. 2 (change of direction) cambio m de dirección; (in road) curva f; to take a t. for the better, empezar a mejorar; left/right t., giro m al izquierdo/a la derecha. 3 to do sb a good t., hacer un favor a algn. 4 Med ataque m. 5 (in game, queue) turno m, vez f; it's your t., te toca a ti; to take it in turns to do sth, turnarse para hacer algo. 6 Theat número m. 7 t. of phrase, giro m. ◆**turn aside I** vtr desviar. **II** vi desviarse. ◆**turn away I** vtr (person) rechazar. **II** vi volver la cabeza. ◆**turn back I** vtr (person) hacer retroceder; (clock) retrasar. **II** vi volverse. ◆**turn down vtr** 1 (gas, radio etc) bajar. 2 (reject) rechazar. 3 (fold) doblar. ◆**turn in fam I** vtr (person) entregar a la policía. **II** vi acostarse. ◆**turn off I** vtr (electricity) desconectar; (gas, light) apagar; (water) cerrar. **II** vi desviarse. ◆**turn on I** vtr (electricity) encender; (tap, gas) abrir; (machine) poner en marcha; fam it turns me on, me encanta. ◆**turn out I** vtr 1 (extinguish) apagar. 2 (eject) echar; (empty) vaciar. 3 (produce) producir. **II** vi 1 (attend) asistir. 2 it turns out that ..., resulta que ...; things have turned well, las cosas

han salido bien. ◆**turn over I** vtr (turn upside down) poner al revés; (page) dar la vuelta a. **II** vi volverse. ◆**turn round I** vtr volver. **II** vi (rotate) girar, dar vueltas. ◆**turn up I** vtr 1 (collar) levantar; to t. up one's shirt sleeves, arremangarse; turned-up nose, nariz respingona. 2 Rad TV subir. **II** vi 1 fig something is sure to t. up, algo saldrá. 2 (arrive) llegar, presentarse; nobody turned up, nadie se presentó. 3 (attend) asistir.

turning ['tɜːnɪŋ] n 1 fig t. point, punto decisivo. 2 (in road) salida f.

turnip ['tɜːnɪp] n nabo m.

turnout ['tɜːnaut] n asistencia f.

turnover ['tɜːnəuvə] n Com (sales) facturación f; (of goods) movimiento m.

turnpike ['tɜːnpaɪk] n US autopista f de peaje.

turnstile ['tɜːnstaɪl] n torniquete m.

turntable ['tɜːnteɪbl] n (for record) plato m (giratorio).

turn-up ['tɜːnʌp] n GB 1 (of trousers) vuelta f. 2 fam fig what a t.-up for the books!, ¡vaya sorpresa!

turpentine ['tɜːpəntaɪn] n (esencia f de) trementina f.

turquoise ['tɜːkwɔɪz] I n (colour, stone) turquesa f. II adj t. (blue), azul turquesa.

turret ['tʌrɪt] n torrecilla f.

turtle ['tɜːtl] n tortuga f.

turtledove ['tɜːtldʌv] n tórtola f.

turtleneck ['tɜːtlnek] n a t. (sweater), un jersey de cuello alto.

tusk [tʌsk] n colmillo m.

tussle ['tʌsl] n pelea f, lucha f.

tutor ['tjuːtə] n Univ tutor,-a m,f; private t., profesor,-a m,f particular.

tutorial [tjuː'tɔːrɪəl] n Univ tutoría f, seminario m.

tuxedo [tʌk'siːdəu] n US smoking m.

TV [tiː'viː] abbr of television, TV.

twang [twæŋ] I n 1 (of instrument) sonido m vibrante. 2 nasal t., gangueo m. II vtr puntear. III vi (string) vibrar.

tweak [twiːk] vtr pellizcar.

tweed [twiːd] n cheviot m.

tweezers ['twiːzəz] npl pinzas fpl.

twelfth [twelfθ] I adj & n duodécimo,-a (m,f). II n (fraction) duodécimo m.

twelve [twelv] adj & n doce (m) inv.

twentieth ['twentɪθ] I adj & n vigésimo,-a (m,f). II n (fraction) vigésimo m.

twenty ['twentɪ] adj & n veinte (m) inv.

twice [twaɪs] adv dos veces; he's t. as old as I am, tiene el doble de años que yo.

twiddle ['twɪdl] I vtr dar vueltas a; to t. one's moustache, mesarse el bigote; to t. one's thumbs, estar mano sobre mano. II vi to t. with sth, juguetear con algo.

twig¹ [twɪg] n ramilla f.

twig² [twɪg] vi GB fam caer en la cuenta.

twilight ['twaɪlaɪt] n crepúsculo m.

twin [twɪn] **I** n mellizo,-a m,f; **identical twins**, gemelos (idénticos); **t. brother/ sister**, hermano gemelo/hermana gemela; **t. beds**, camas fpl gemelas. **II** vtr hermanar.

twine [twaɪn] **I** n bramante m. **II** vtr entretejer. **III** vi **to t. round sth**, enroscarse alrededor de algo.

twinge [twɪndʒ] n (of pain) punzada f; fig **t. of conscience**, remordimiento m.

twinkle ['twɪŋkəl] vi (stars) centellear; (eyes) brillar.

twinkling ['twɪŋklɪŋ] n (of stars) centelleo m; fig **in the t. of an eye**, en un abrir y cerrar de ojos.

twirl [twɜːl] **I** vtr girar rápidamente. **II** vi (spin) girar rápidamente; (dancer) piruetear. **III** n (movement) giro rápido; (of dancer) pirueta f.

twist [twɪst] **I** vtr torcer; (sense) tergiversar; **to t. one's ankle**, torcerse el tobillo. **II** vi (smoke) formar volutas; (path) serpentear. **III** n 1 (of yarn) torzal m. 2 (movement) torsión f; Med torcedura f; fig **to give a new t. to sth**, dar un nuevo enfoque a algo. 3 (in road) vuelta f. 4 (dance) twist m.

twit [twɪt] n GB fam jilipollas mf inv.

twitch [twɪtʃ] **I** vtr dar un tirón a. **II** vi crisparse; **his face twitches**, tiene un tic en la cara.

twitter ['twɪtər] **I** vi gorjear. **II** n gorjeo m.

two [tuː] **I** adj dos inv; fig **to be in or of t. minds about sth**, estar indeciso,-a respecto a algo. **II** n dos m inv; fig **to put t. and t. together**, atar cabos.

two-faced ['tuːfeɪst] adj hipócrita.

two-party ['tuːpɑːtɪ] adj **t-p. system**, bi-

partidismo m.

twopence ['tʌpəns] n GB dos peniques.

two-piece ['tuːpiːs] **I** adj de dos piezas. **II** n (suit) traje m de dos piezas.

two-seater ['tuːsiːtər] adj & n biplaza (f).

twosome ['tuːsəm] n pareja f.

two-time ['tuːtaɪm] vtr fam poner los cuernos a.

two-way ['tuːweɪ] adj 1 (street) de dos direcciones. 2 **t.-w. radio**, aparato m emisor y receptor.

tycoon [taɪˈkuːn] n magnate m.

type [taɪp] **I** n 1 (kind) tipo m, clase f; (brand) marca f; (of car) modelo m. 2 Typ carácter m; (print) caracteres mpl. **II** vtr & vi escribir a máquina.

typecast ['taɪpkɑːst] vtr encasillar.

typescript ['taɪpskrɪpt] n texto m escrito a máquina.

typeset ['taɪpset] vtr componer.

typesetter ['taɪpsetər] n 1 (person) cajista mf. 2 (machine) máquina f para componer tipos.

typewriter ['taɪpraɪtər] n máquina f de escribir.

typewritten ['taɪprɪtən] adj escrito,-a a máquina.

typhoid ['taɪfɔɪd] n **t. (fever)**, fiebre tifoidea.

typhoon [taɪˈfuːn] n tifón m.

typical ['tɪpɪkəl] adj típico,-a.

typify ['tɪpɪfaɪ] vtr tipificar.

typing ['taɪpɪŋ] n mecanografía f.

typist ['taɪpɪst] n mecanógrafo,-a m,f.

tyrannical [tɪˈrænɪkəl] adj tiránico,-a.

tyrannize ['tɪrənaɪz] vtr tiranizar.

tyranny ['tɪrənɪ] n tiranía f.

tyrant ['taɪrənt] n tirano,-a m,f.

tyre [taɪər] n neumático m; **t. pressure**, presión f de los neumáticos.

U

U, u [juː] n (the letter) U, u f.

ubiquity [juːˈbɪkwɪtɪ] n ubicuidad f.

udder ['ʌdər] n ubre f.

UFO, ufo ['juːefəʊ, 'juːfəʊ] abbr of unidentified flying object, OVNI m, ovni m.

ugh [ʊx, ʊh, ʌh] interj ¡uf!, ¡puf!

ugly ['ʌglɪ] adj (uglier, ugliest) feo,-a; (situation) desagradable; fig u. **duckling**, patito feo.

UK [juːˈkeɪ] abbr of United Kingdom, R.U.

Ukraine ['juːkreɪn] n the U., Ucrania.

ulcer ['ʌlsər] n (sore) llaga f; (internal) úlcera f.

ulterior [ʌlˈtɪərɪər] adj (motive) oculto,-a.

ultimate ['ʌltɪmɪt] adj 1 (final) último,-a; (aim) final. 2 (basic) esencial. ◆**ultimately** adv 1 (finally) finalmente. 2 (basically) en el fondo.

ultimatum [ʌltɪˈmeɪtəm] n ultimátum m.

ultrasound ['ʌltrəsaʊnd] n ultrasonido m.

ultraviolet [ʌltrəˈvaɪəlɪt] adj ultravioleta.

umbilical [ʌmˈbɪlɪkəl, ʌmbɪˈlaɪkəl] adj u. **cord**, cordón m umbilical.

umbrella [ʌmˈbrelə] n paraguas m inv.

umpire ['ʌmpaɪər] **I** n árbitro m. **II** vtr arbitrar.

umpteen [ʌmpˈtiːn] adj fam muchísimos,-as, la tira de.

umpteenth [ʌmpˈtiːnθ] adj enésimo,-a.

UN [juːˈen] abbr of United Nations (Organization), ONU f sing.

unabashed [ʌnəˈbæʃt] adj 1 (unperturbed) inmutable, imperturbable. 2 (shameless) desvergonzado,-a, descarado,-a.

unable [ʌnˈeɪbəl] adj incapaz; **to be u. to do sth/anything**, no poder hacer algo/ nada.

unacceptable [ʌnək'septəbəl] *adj* inaceptable.

unaccompanied [ʌnə'kʌmpənɪd] *adj* solo,-a.

unaccountable [ʌnə'kauntəbəl] *adj* inexplicable.

unaccustomed-for [ʌnə'kauntɪdfɔːr] *adj* to be u.-f., faltar.

unaccustomed [ʌnə'kʌstəmd] *adj* **he's u. to this climate**, no está muy acostumbrado a este clima.

unaffected [ʌnə'fektɪd] *adj* **1** no afectado,-a (**by**, por). **2** (*indifferent*) indiferente (**by**, a). **3** (*natural*) (*person*) natural; (*style*) llano,-a.

unaided [ʌn'eɪdɪd] *adj* sin ayuda, solo,-a.

unanimous [juː'nænɪməs] *adj* unánime.

unannounced [ʌnə'naunst] *adj* sin avisar.

unanswered [ʌn'ɑːnsəd] *adj* sin contestar.

unapproachable [ʌnə'prəʊtʃəbəl] *adj* inabordable, inaccesible.

unarmed [ʌn'ɑːmd] *adj* desarmado,-a.

unashamed [ʌnə'ʃeɪmd] *adj* desvergonzado,-a.

unasked [ʌn'ɑːskt] *adv* **u.** (**for**), (*unrequested*) no solicitado,-a; (*spontaneous*) espontáneo,-a.

unassuming [ʌnə'sjuːmɪŋ] *adj* sin pretensiones.

unattached [ʌnə'tætʃt] *adj* **1** (*independent*) libre; (*loose*) suelto,-a. **2** (*person*) soltero,-a y sin compromiso.

unattended [ʌnə'tendɪd] *adj* (*counter etc*) desatendido,-a; **to leave a child u.**, dejar a un niño solo.

unauthorized [ʌn'ɔːθəraɪzd] *adj* **1** (*person*) no autorizado,-a. **2** (*trade etc*) ilícito,-a, ilegal.

unavoidable [ʌnə'vɔɪdəbəl] *adj* inevitable; (*accident*) imprevisible.

unaware [ʌnə'weər] *adj* to be u. of sth, ignorar algo.

unawares [ʌnə'weəz] *adv* **1** (*unexpectedly*) desprevenido,-a. **2** (*without knowing*) inconscientemente.

unbalanced [ʌn'bælənst] *adj* desequilibrado,-a.

unbearable [ʌn'beərəbəl] *adj* insoportable.

unbeatable [ʌn'biːtəbəl] *adj* (*team*) invencible; (*price, quality*) inmejorable.

unbelievable [ʌnbɪ'liːvəbəl] *adj* increíble.

unbend [ʌn'bend] *vi fam fig* relajarse.

unbia(s)sed [ʌn'baɪəst] *adj* imparcial.

unborn [ʌn'bɔːn] *adj* sin nacer, nonato,-a.

unbreakable [ʌn'breɪkəbəl] *adj* irrompible; *fig* inquebrantable.

unbroken [ʌn'brəʊkən] *adj* **1** (*whole*) intacto,-a. **2** (*uninterrupted*) continuo,-a. **3** (*record*) imbatido,-a.

unbutton [ʌn'bʌtən] *vtr* desabrochar.

uncalled-for [ʌn'kɔːldfɔːr] *adj* (*inappropriate*) insensato,-a; (*unjustified*) inmerecido,-a.

uncanny [ʌn'kænɪ] *adj* misterioso,-a, extraño,-a.

unceasing [ʌn'siːsɪŋ] *adj* incesante.

uncertain [ʌn'sɜːtən] *adj* **1** (*not certain*) incierto,-a; (*doubtful*) dudoso,-a; **in no u. terms**, claramente. **2** (*hesitant*) indeciso,-a.

uncertainty [ʌn'sɜːtəntɪ] *n* incertidumbre *f*.

unchanged [ʌn'tʃeɪndʒd] *adj* igual.

unchecked [ʌn'tʃekt] *adj* **1** (*unrestrained*) desenfrenado,-a. **2** (*not examined*) no comprobado,-a.

uncivilized [ʌn'sɪvɪlaɪzd] *adj* (*tribe*) incivilizado,-a, salvaje; (*not cultured*) inculto,-a.

uncle ['ʌŋkəl] *n* tío *m*.

uncomfortable [ʌn'kʌmftəbəl] *adj* incómodo,-a; **to make things u. for**, complicarle la vida a.

uncommon [ʌn'kɒmən] *adj* **1** (*rare*) poco común; (*unusual*) extraordinario,-a. **2** (*excessive*) excesivo,-a. ◆**uncommonly** *adv* not u., con cierta frecuencia.

uncompromising [ʌn'kɒmprəmaɪzɪŋ] *adj* intransigente; **u. honesty**, sinceridad absoluta.

unconcerned [ʌnkən'sɜːnd] *adj* indiferente (**about**, a).

unconditional [ʌnkən'dɪʃənəl] *adj* incondicional; **u. refusal**, negativa rotunda.

unconnected [ʌnkə'nektɪd] *adj* no relacionado,-a.

unconscious [ʌn'kɒnʃəs] **I** *adj* **1** inconsciente (**of**, de). **2** (*unintentional*) involuntario,-a. **II** *n* the u., el inconsciente.

unconsciousness [ʌn'kɒnʃəsnɪs] *n Med* pérdida *f* del conocimiento.

uncontested [ʌnkən'testɪd] *adj Pol* u. seat, escaño *m* ganado sin oposición.

uncontrollable [ʌnkən'trəʊləbəl] *adj* incontrolable; (*desire*) irresistible.

unconventional [ʌnkən'venʃənəl] *adj* poco convencional, original.

uncooperative [ʌnkəʊ'ɒpərətɪv] *adj* poco cooperativo,-a.

uncouth [ʌn'kuːθ] *adj* (*rude*) grosero,-a.

uncover [ʌn'kʌvər] *vtr* destapar; *fig* descubrir.

undamaged [ʌn'dæmɪdʒd] *adj* (*article etc*) sin desperfectos; (*person*) indemne; (*reputation*) intacto,-a.

undaunted [ʌn'dɔːntɪd] *adj* firme, impávido,-a.

undecided [ʌndɪ'saɪdɪd] *adj* **1** (*person*) indeciso,-a. **2** (*issue*) pendiente; **it's still u.**, está aún por decidir.

undefeated [ʌndɪ'fiːtɪd] *adj* invicto,-a.

undefined [ʌndɪ'faɪnd] *adj*

indeterminado,-a.

undeniable [ʌndɪ'naɪəbəl] adj innegable.

under ['ʌndə'] I prep 1 debajo de; **u. the sun**, bajo el sol. 2 (less than) menos de; **incomes u. £1,000**, ingresos inferiores a 1.000 libras; **u. age**, menor de edad. 3 (of rank) de rango inferior a. 4 **u. Caesar**, bajo César. 5 (subject to) bajo; **u. arrest**, detenido,-a; **u. cover**, a cubierto; **u. obligation to**, en la obligación de; **u. the circumstances**, dadas las circunstancias; fig **I was u. the impression that** ..., tenía la impresión de que .... 6 (according to) según, conforme a. II adv interior.

under- ['ʌndə'] pref (below) sub-, infra-; (insufficiently) insuficientemente.

underarm ['ʌndərɑːm] I adj **u. deodorant**, desodorante m para las axilas. II adv Sport por debajo del hombro.

undercarriage [ʌndə'kærɪdʒ] n tren m de aterrizaje.

undercharge [ʌndə'tʃɑːdʒ] vtr cobrar menos de lo debido.

underclothes ['ʌndəkləʊðz] npl ropa f sing interior.

undercoat ['ʌndəkəʊt] n (of paint) primera mano.

undercover [ʌndə'kʌvə'] adj secreto,-a.

undercurrent [ʌndə'kʌrənt] n 1 (in sea) corriente submarina. 2 fig sentimiento m latente.

undercut [ʌndə'kʌt] vtr Com vender más barato que.

underdeveloped [ʌndədɪ'veləpt] adj subdesarrollado,-a.

underdog ['ʌndədɒg] n desvalido,-a m,f.

underestimate [ʌndər'estɪmeɪt] vtr infravalorar.

underexposure [ʌndərɪk'spəʊʒə'] n Phot subexposición f.

underfed [ʌndə'fed] adj subalimentado,-a.

underfoot [ʌndə'fʊt] adv en el suelo.

undergo [ʌndə'gəʊ] vtr experimentar; (change) sufrir; (test etc) pasar por.

undergraduate [ʌndə'grædjʊɪt] n estudiante mf universitario,-a.

underground ['ʌndəgraʊnd] I adj subterráneo,-a; fig clandestino,-a. II [ʌndə'graʊnd] adv fig **to go u.**, pasar a la clandestinidad. III ['ʌndəgraʊnd] n 1 Pol movimiento clandestino. 2 **the u.**, (subway) el metro.

undergrowth ['ʌndəgrəʊθ] n maleza f.

underhand ['ʌndəhænd] I adj (method) ilícito,-a; (person) solapado,-a. II adv bajo cuerda.

underline [ʌndə'laɪn] vtr subrayar.

underling ['ʌndəlɪŋ] n pej mandado,-a m,f.

underlying [ʌndə'laɪɪŋ] adj (basic) fundamental.

undermine [ʌndə'maɪn] vtr socavar, minar.

underneath [ʌndə'niːθ] I prep debajo de, bajo. II adv abajo, debajo. III adj de abajo. IV n parte f inferior.

undernourished [ʌndə'nʌrɪʃt] adj desnutrido,-a.

underpaid [ʌndə'peɪd] adj mal pagado,-a.

underpass ['ʌndəpɑːs] n paso subterráneo.

underprivileged [ʌndə'prɪvɪlɪdʒd] I adj desfavorecido,-a. II npl **the u.**, los menos favorecidos.

underrate [ʌndə'reɪt] vtr → undervalue.

undershirt ['ʌndəʃɜːt] n US camiseta f.

underskirt ['ʌndəskɜːt] n combinación f.

understand [ʌndə'stænd] vtr & vi (pt & pp understood) 1 (comprehend) entender, comprender; fam **do I make myself understood?**, ¿me explico? 2 (assume, believe) entender; **she gave me to u. that** ..., me dio a entender que .... 3 (hear) tener entendido. 4 **to u. one another**, entenderse.

understandable [ʌndə'stændəbəl] adj comprensible.

understanding [ʌndə'stændɪŋ] I n 1 (intellectual grasp) entendimiento m, comprensión f. 2 (interpretation) intepretación f. 3 (agreement) acuerdo m. 4 **on the u. that** ..., a condición de que .... II adj comprensivo,-a.

understatement [ʌndə'steɪtmənt] n **to make an u.**, minimizar, subestimar; **to say that the boy is rather clever is an u.**, decir que el chico es bastante listo es quedarse corto.

understood [ʌndə'stʊd] adj 1 **I wish it to be u. that** ..., que conste que .... 2 (agreed on) convenido,-a. 3 (implied) sobreentendido,-a.

understudy ['ʌndəstʌdɪ] n suplente mf.

undertake [ʌndə'teɪk] vtr (pt undertook; pp undertaken [ʌndə'teɪkən]) 1 (responsibility) asumir; (task, job) encargarse de. 2 (promise) comprometerse a.

undertaker ['ʌndəteɪkə'] n empresario,-a m,f de pompas fúnebres; **u.'s**, funeraria f.

undertaking [ʌndə'teɪkɪŋ] n 1 (task) empresa f. 2 (guarantee) garantía f.

undertone ['ʌndətəʊn] n **in an u.**, en voz baja.

underwater [ʌndə'wɔːtə'] I adj submarino,-a. II adv bajo el agua.

underwear ['ʌndəweə'] n inv ropa f interior.

underworld ['ʌndəwɜːld] n (criminals) hampa f, bajos fondos.

underwrite [ʌndə'raɪt] vtr (pt underwrote; pp underwritten) 1 (guarantee) garantizar, avalⱶ. 2 (insure) asegurar.

underwriter ['ʌndəraɪtə'] n 1 Fin suscriptor,-a m,f. 2 (insurer) asegurador,-a m,f.

undesirable |ʌndɪ'zaɪrəbəl| *adj & n* indeseable (*mf*).

undeterred |ʌndɪ'tɜːd| *adj* sin inmutarse; **u. by**, sin arredrarse ante.

undies |'ʌndɪz| *npl fam* bragas *fpl*.

undignified |ʌn'dɪgnɪfaɪd| *adj* (*attitude etc*) indecoroso,-a.

undisciplined |ʌn'dɪsɪplɪnd| *adj* indisciplinado,-a.

undisclosed |ʌndɪs'kləʊzd| *adj* sin revelar.

undiscovered |ʌndɪs'kʌvəd| *adj* sin descubrir.

undisguised |ʌndɪs'gaɪzd| *adj fig* no disimulado,-a.

undisputed |ʌndɪ'spjuːtɪd| *adj* (*unchallenged*) incontestable; (*unquestionable*) indiscutible.

undivided |ʌndɪ'vaɪdɪd| *adj* **to give one's u. attention**, prestar toda la atención.

undo |ʌn'duː| *vtr* (*pt* **undid**; *pp* **undone**) 1 deshacer; (*button*) desabrochar. 2 (*put right*) enmendar.

undone[1] |ʌn'dʌn| *adj* (*unfinished*) inacabado,-a.

undone[2] |ʌn'dʌn| *adj* (*knot etc*) deshecho,-a; **to come u.**, (*shoelace*) desatarse; (*button, blouse*) desabrocharse; (*necklace etc*) soltarse.

undoubted |ʌn'daʊtɪd| *adj* indudable.

undress |ʌn'dres| I *vtr* desnudar. II *vi* desnudarse.

undressed |ʌn'drest| *adj* (*naked*) desnudo,-a.

undue |ʌn'djuː| *adj* 1 (*excessive*) excesivo,-a. 2 (*improper*) indebido,-a.

undulate |'ʌndjʊleɪt| *vi* ondular, ondear.

unearth |ʌn'ɜːθ| *vtr* desenterrar.

unearthly |ʌn'ɜːθlɪ| *adj* 1 (*being*) sobrenatural. 2 *fam* (*din*) espantoso,-a; **at an u. hour**, a una hora intempestiva.

uneasy |ʌn'iːzɪ| *adj* 1 (*worried*) preocupado,-a; (*disturbing*) inquietante. 2 (*uncomfortable*) incómodo,-a.

uneconomic(al) |ʌniːkə'nɒmɪk(əl)| *adj* poco económico,-a.

uneducated |ʌn'edjʊkeɪtɪd| *adj* inculto,-a.

unemployed |ʌnɪm'plɔɪd| I *adj* en paro, parado,-a; **to be u.**, estar en paro. II *npl* **the u.**, los parados.

unemployment |ʌnɪm'plɔɪmənt| *n* paro *m*, desempleo *m*; **u. benefit**, *US* **u. compensation**, subsidio *m* de desempleo.

unending |ʌn'endɪŋ| *adj* interminable.

unenviable |ʌn'envɪəbəl| *adj* poco envidiable.

unequal |ʌn'iːkwəl| *adj* desigual.

unequivocal |ʌnɪ'kwɪvəkəl| *adj* inequívoco,-a.

uneven |ʌn'iːvən| *adj* 1 (*not level*) desigual; (*bumpy*) accidentado,-a. 2 (*variable*) irregular.

uneventful |ʌnɪ'ventfʊl| *adj* sin aconteci-

mientos.

unexceptional |ʌnɪk'sepʃənəl| *adj* ordinario,-a.

unexpected |ʌnɪk'spektɪd| *adj* (*unhoped for*) inesperado,-a; (*event*) imprevisto,-a.

unfailing |ʌn'feɪlɪŋ| *adj* indefectible; (*incessant*) constante; (*patience*) inagotable.

unfair |ʌn'feəʳ| *adj* injusto,-a; *Sport* sucio,-a.

unfaithful |ʌn'feɪθfʊl| *adj* (*friend*) desleal; (*husband, wife*) infiel.

unfamiliar |ʌnfə'mɪljəʳ| *adj* (*unknown*) desconocido,-a; (*not conversant*) no familiarizado,-a (**with**, con).

unfashionable |ʌn'fæʃənəbəl| *adj* pasado,-a de moda; (*ideas etc*) poco popular.

unfasten |ʌn'fɑːsən| *vtr* (*knot*) desatar; (*clothing, belt*) desabrochar.

unfavourable *US* **unfavorable** |ʌn'feɪvərəbəl| *adj* desfavorable; (*criticism*) adverso,-a; (*winds*) contrario,-a.

unfeeling |ʌn'fiːlɪŋ| *adj* insensible.

unfinished |ʌn'fɪnɪʃt| *adj* inacabado,-a; **u. business**, un asunto pendiente.

unfit |ʌn'fɪt| *adj* 1 (*thing*) inadecuado,-a; (*person*) no apto,-a (**for**, para). 2 (*incompetent*) incompetente. 3 (*physically*) incapacitado,-a; **to be u.**, no estar en forma.

unflinching |ʌn'flɪntʃɪŋ| *adj* 1 (*determined*) resuelto,-a. 2 (*fearless*) impávido,-a.

unfold |ʌn'fəʊld| I *vtr* 1 (*sheet*) desdoblar; (*newspaper*) abrir. 2 (*plan, secret*) revelar. II *vi* 1 (*open up*) abrirse; (*landscape*) extenderse. 2 (*plot*) desarrollarse. 3 (*secret*) descubrirse.

unforeseen |ʌnfɔː'siːn| *adj* imprevisto,-a.

unforgettable |ʌnfə'getəbəl| *adj* inolvidable.

unforgivable |ʌnfə'gɪvəbəl| *adj* imperdonable.

unfortunate |ʌn'fɔːtʃənɪt| *adj* (*person, event*) desgraciado,-a; (*remark*) desafortunado,-a; **how u.!**, ¡qué mala suerte! ◆**unfortunately** *adv* desgraciadamente, por desgracia.

unfounded |ʌn'faʊndɪd| *adj* infundado,-a.

unfriendly |ʌn'frendlɪ| *adj* (**unfriendlier**, **unfriendliest**) antipático,-a, poco amistoso,-a.

unfurl |ʌn'fɜːl| *vi* desplegarse.

unfurnished |ʌn'fɜːnɪʃt| *adj* sin amueblar.

ungainly |ʌn'geɪnlɪ| *adj* (*gait*) desgarbado,-a.

ungodly |ʌn'gɒdlɪ| *adj* (**ungodlier, ungodliest**) (*behaviour*) impío,-a; *fam fig* **at an u. hour**, a una hora intempestiva.

ungrateful |ʌn'greɪtfʊl| *adj* (*person*) desagradecido,-a; (*task*) ingrato,-a.

unguarded |ʌn'gɑːdɪd| *adj* 1 (*unprotected*)

desatendido,-a; (imprudent) desprevenido,-a. 2 (frank) franco,-a.

unhappiness [ʌn'hæpɪnɪs] n 1 (sadness) tristeza f. 2 (wretchedness) desdicha f.

unhappy [ʌn'hæpɪ] adj (unhappier, unhappiest) 1 (sad) triste. 2 (wretched) desgraciado,-a, infeliz; (unfortunate) desafortunado,-a.

unharmed [ʌn'hɑːmd] adj ileso,-a, indemne.

unhealthy [ʌn'helθɪ] adj (unhealthier, unhealthiest) 1 (ill) enfermizo,-a. 2 (unwholesome) malsano,-a.

unheard [ʌn'hɜːd] adj 1 her request went u., su petición no fue atendida. 2 u. of, (outrageous) inaudito,-a; (without precedent) sin precedente.

unhesitating [ʌn'hezɪteɪtɪŋ] adj resuelto,-a.

unhook [ʌn'hʊk] vtr (from hook) descolgar; (clothing) desabrochar.

unhurt [ʌn'hɜːt] adj ileso,-a, indemne.

unhygienic [ʌnhaɪ'dʒiːnɪk] adj antihigiénico,-a.

unidentified [ʌnaɪ'dentɪfaɪd] adj u. flying object, objeto volador no identificado, ovni m.

unification [juːnɪfɪ'keɪʃən] n unificación f.

uniform ['juːnɪfɔːm] adj & nm uniforme.

uniformity [juːnɪ'fɔːmɪtɪ] n uniformidad f.

unify ['juːnɪfaɪ] vtr unificar.

unilateral [juːnɪ'lætərəl] adj unilateral.

unimportant [ʌnɪm'pɔːtənt] adj poco importante.

uninformed [ʌnɪn'fɔːmd] adj (opinion) sin fundamento.

uninhabited [ʌnɪn'hæbɪtɪd] adj despoblado,-a.

uninhibited [ʌnɪn'hɪbɪtɪd] adj sin inhibición.

uninspired [ʌnɪn'spaɪəd] adj (person) falto,-a de inspiración; (performance) insulso,-a.

uninspiring [ʌnɪn'spaɪərɪŋ] adj que no inspira.

unintelligible [ʌnɪn'telɪdʒəbəl] adj ininteligible, incomprensible.

unintentional [ʌnɪn'tenʃənəl] adj involuntario,-a. ◆**unintentionally** adv sin querer.

uninteresting [ʌn'ɪntrɪstɪŋ] adj poco interesante.

uninterrupted [ʌnɪntə'rʌptɪd] adj ininterrumpido,-a.

union ['juːnjən] I n 1 unión f. 2 (organization) sindicato m. 3 US the U., los Estados Unidos; U. Jack, bandera f del Reino Unido. II adj sindical.

unique [juː'niːk] adj único,-a.

unison ['juːnɪsən] n Mus unisonancia f; fig (harmony) armonía f; in u., al unísono.

unit ['juːnɪt] n 1 unidad f; monetary u.,

unidad monetaria; GB Fin u. trust, sociedad f de inversiones. 2 (piece of furniture) módulo m; kitchen u., mueble m de cocina. 3 Tech grupo m; Comput central processing u., procesador m central; visual display u., pantalla f. 4 (department) servicio m. 5 (team) equipo m.

unite [juː'naɪt] I vtr unir. II vi unirse.

united [juː'naɪtɪd] adj unido,-a; U. Kingdom, Reino Unido; U. States (of America), Estados Unidos (de América); U. Nations, Naciones Unidas.

unity ['juːnɪtɪ] n unidad f; (harmony) armonía f.

universal [juːnɪ'vɜːsəl] adj universal.

universe ['juːnɪvɜːs] n universo m.

university [juːnɪ'vɜːsɪtɪ] I n universidad f. II adj universitario,-a.

unjust [ʌn'dʒʌst] adj injusto,-a.

unkempt [ʌn'kempt] adj descuidado,-a; (hair) despeinado,-a; (appearance) desaliñado,-a.

unkind [ʌn'kaɪnd] adj (not nice) poco amable; (cruel) despiadado,-a.

unknown [ʌn'nəʊn] I adj desconocido,-a; u. quantity, incógnita f. II n the u., lo desconocido.

unlawful [ʌn'lɔːfʊl] adj (not legal) ilegal.

unleash [ʌn'liːʃ] vtr 1 (dog) soltar. 2 fig (release) liberar; (provoke) desencadenar.

unless [ʌn'les] conj a menos que, a no ser que.

unlike [ʌn'laɪk] I adj diferente, distinto, -a. II prep a diferencia de.

unlikely [ʌn'laɪklɪ] adj 1 (improbable) poco probable. 2 (unusual) raro,-a.

unlimited [ʌn'lɪmɪtɪd] adj ilimitado,-a.

unload [ʌn'ləʊd] vtr & vi descargar.

unlock [ʌn'lɒk] vtr abrir (con llave).

unlucky [ʌn'lʌkɪ] adj (unluckier, unluckiest) (unfortunate) desgraciado,-a; to be u., (person) tener mala suerte; (thing) traer mala suerte. ◆**unluckily** adv desafortunadamente, por desgracia.

unmanageable [ʌn'mænɪdʒəbəl] adj (people) ingobernable; (child, hair) incontrolable.

unmanned [ʌn'mænd] adj (spacecraft etc) no tripulado,-a.

unmarried [ʌn'mærɪd] adj soltero,-a.

unmask [ʌn'mɑːsk] vtr fig (plot) descubrir.

unmistak(e)able [ʌnmɪs'teɪkəbəl] adj inconfundible. ◆**unmistak(e)ably** adv sin lugar a dudas.

unmitigated [ʌn'mɪtɪgeɪtɪd] adj 1 (absolute) absoluto,-a; (liar) rematado,-a. 2 (grief) profundo,-a.

unnamed [ʌn'neɪmd] adj (anonymous) anónimo,-a.

unnatural [ʌn'nætʃərəl] adj 1 (against nature) antinatural; (abnormal) anormal. 2 (affected) afectado,-a.

unnecessary [ʌn'nesɪsərɪ] adj

innecesario,-a, inútil; **it's u. to add that ...**, sobra añadir que ....

unnoticed [ʌn'nəʊtɪst] adj desapercibido,-a; **to let sth pass u.**, pasar algo por alto.

unobserved [ʌnəb'zɜ:vd] adj inadvertido,-a.

unobtainable [ʌnəb'teɪnəbəl] adj inasequible, inalcanzable.

unobtrusive [ʌnəb'tru:sɪv] adj discreto, -a.

unoccupied [ʌn'ɒkjʊpaɪd] adj (house) desocupado,-a; (seat) libre.

unofficial [ʌnə'fɪʃəl] adj no oficial.

unorthodox [ʌn'ɔ:θədɒks] adj 1 (behaviour etc) poco ortodoxo,-a. 2 Rel heterodoxo,-a.

unpack [ʌn'pæk] I vtr (boxes) desembalar; (suitcase) deshacer. II vi deshacer la(s) maleta(s).

unpalatable [ʌn'pælətəbəl] adj desagradable.

unparalleled [ʌn'pærəleld] adj 1 (in quality) incomparable. 2 (without precedent) sin precedente.

unpardonable [ʌn'pɑ:dənəbəl] adj imperdonable.

unperturbed [ʌnpə'tɜ:bd] adj impasible.

unpleasant [ʌn'plezənt] adj desagradable (**to**, con).

unpleasantness [ʌn'plezəntnɪs] n disgusto m.

unplug [ʌn'plʌg] vtr desenchufar.

unpopular [ʌn'pɒpjʊlər] adj impopular; **to make oneself u.**, ganarse la antipatía de todos.

unprecedented [ʌn'presidentid] adj sin precedente.

unpredictable [ʌnprɪ'dɪktəbəl] adj imprevisible.

unprepared [ʌnprɪ'peəd] adj (speech etc) improvisado,-a; (person) desprevenido,-a.

unprincipled [ʌn'prɪnsɪpəld] adj sin escrúpulos.

unprintable [ʌn'prɪntəbəl] adj (word, comment) malsonante.

unproductive [ʌnprə'dʌktɪv] adj (inefficient) improductivo,-a; (fruitless) infructuoso,-a.

unprofessional [ʌnprə'feʃənəl] adj (unethical) poco profesional; (substandard) de aficionado,-a.

unprotected [ʌnprə'tektɪd] adj indefenso,-a.

unprovoked [ʌnprə'vəʊkt] adj gratuito, -a.

unpunished [ʌn'pʌnɪʃt] adj impune.

unqualified [ʌn'kwɒlɪfaɪd] adj 1 (without qualification) sin título; (incompetent) incompetente. 2 (unconditional) incondicional; (denial) rotundo,-a; (endorsement) sin reserva; (success) total.

unquestionable [ʌn'kwestʃənəbəl] adj indiscutible.

unquestioning [ʌn'kwestʃənɪŋ] adj incondicional; (obedience) ciego,-a.

unravel [ʌn'rævəl] I vtr desenmarañar. II vi desenmarañarse.

unreadable [ʌn'ri:dəbəl] adj 1 (handwriting) ilegible. 2 (book) imposible de leer.

unreal [ʌn'rɪəl] adj irreal.

unrealistic [ʌnrɪə'lɪstɪk] adj poco realista.

unreasonable [ʌn'ri:zənəbəl] adj poco razonable; (demands) desmedido,-a; (prices) exorbitante; (hour) inoportuno,-a.

unrefined [ʌnrɪ'faɪnd] adj 1 (sugar, oil etc) sin refinar. 2 (person) tosco,-a, basto,-a.

unrelated [ʌnrɪ'leɪtɪd] adj (not connected) no relacionado,-a.

unrelenting [ʌnrɪ'lentɪŋ] adj (behaviour) implacable; (struggle) encarnizado,-a.

unreliable [ʌnrɪ'laɪəbəl] adj 1 (person) de poca confianza. 2 (information) que no es de fiar; (machine) poco fiable.

unrelieved [ʌnrɪ'li:vd] adj (boredom) total.

unremitting [ʌnrɪ'mɪtɪŋ] adj 1 (efforts etc) incesante. 2 (person) incansable.

unrepentant [ʌnrɪ'pentənt] adj impenitente.

unreserved [ʌnrɪ'zɜ:vd] adj (praise, support) sin reserva. ◆**unreservedly** adv sin reserva.

unrest [ʌn'rest] n (social etc) malestar m; **political u.**, agitación política.

unrivalled, US **unrivaled** [ʌn'raɪvəld] adj sin par, sin rival.

unroll [ʌn'rəʊl] vtr desenrollar.

unruffled [ʌn'rʌfəld] adj fig tranquilo,-a.

unruly [ʌn'ru:lɪ] adj (unrulier, unruliest) 1 (child) revoltoso,-a. 2 (hair) rebelde.

unsafe [ʌn'seɪf] adj (dangerous) peligroso,-a; (risky) inseguro,-a; **to feel u.**, sentirse expuesto,-a.

unsaid [ʌn'sed] adj **it's better left u.**, más vale no decir nada; **much was left u.**, quedó mucho por decir.

unsatisfactory [ʌnsætɪs'fæktərɪ] adj insatisfactorio,-a; **it's most u.**, deja mucho que desear.

unsavoury, US **unsavory** [ʌn'seɪvərɪ] adj desagradable.

unscathed [ʌn'skeɪðd] adj ileso,-a, indemne.

unscrew [ʌn'skru:] vtr destornillar.

unscrupulous [ʌn'skru:pjʊləs] adj sin escrúpulos.

unseemly [ʌn'si:mlɪ] adj impropio,-a.

unseen [ʌn'si:n] I adj invisible; (unnoticed) inadvertido,-a. II n GB Educ texto no trabajado en clase.

unselfish [ʌn'selfɪʃ] adj desinteresado,-a.

unsettle [ʌn'setəl] vtr perturbar.

unsettled [ʌn'setəld] adj 1 (person) nervioso,-a. 2 (situation) inestable. 3 (weather) inestable. 4 (matter, debt) pendiente. 4 (land) sin colonizar.

unshaven [ʌnˈʃeɪvən] *adj* sin afeitar.
unsightly [ʌnˈsaɪtlɪ] *adj* feo,-a, desagradable.
unskilled [ʌnˈskɪld] *adj (worker)* no cualificado,-a; *(work)* no especializado,-a.
unsociable [ʌnˈsəʊʃəbəl] *adj* insociable, huraño,-a.
unsophisticated [ʌnsəˈfɪstɪkeɪtɪd] *adj* 1 *(naive)* ingenuo,-a. 2 *(simple)* poco sofisticado,-a.
unsound [ʌnˈsaʊnd] *adj* 1 *(unstable)* inestable; **of u. mind,** demente. 2 *(fallacious)* falso,-a.
unspeakable [ʌnˈspiːkəbəl] *adj* indecible. 2 *fig (evil)* atroz.
unspoken [ʌnˈspəʊkən] *adj* 1 *(tacit)* tácito,-a. 2 *(feeling)* interior, secreto,-a.
unstable [ʌnˈsteɪbəl] *adj* inestable.
unsteady [ʌnˈstedɪ] *adj (not firm)* inestable; *(table, chair)* cojo,-a; *(hand, voice)* tembloroso,-a.
unstinting [ʌnˈstɪntɪŋ] *adj* pródigo,-a (**in,** en, de).
unstuck [ʌnˈstʌk] *adj* **to come u.,** despegarse; *fig* venirse abajo.
unsuccessful [ʌnsəkˈsesfʊl] *adj* 1 *(fruitless)* fracasado,-a; *(useless)* vano,-a. 2 *(businessman etc)* fracasado,-a; *(candidate)* derrotado,-a; **to be u. at sth,** no tener éxito con algo. ◆**unsuccessfully** *adv* sin éxito, en vano.
unsuitable [ʌnˈsuːtəbəl] *adj* 1 *(person)* no apto,-a. 2 *(thing)* inadecuado,-a; *(remark)* inoportuno,-a; *(time)* inconveniente.
unsuited [ʌnˈsuːtɪd] *adj* 1 *(person)* no apto,-a; *(thing)* impropio,-a (**to, para**). 2 *(incompatible)* incompatible.
unsure [ʌnˈʃʊə] *adj* poco seguro,-a.
unsuspecting [ʌnsəˈspektɪŋ] *adj* confiado,-a; **he went in u.,** entró sin sospechar nada.
unswerving [ʌnˈswɜːvɪŋ] *adj* firme.
unsympathetic [ʌnsɪmpəˈθetɪk] *adj (unfeeling)* impasible; *(not understanding)* poco comprensivo,-a.
untapped [ʌnˈtæpt] *adj (mine etc)* sin explotar.
untarnished [ʌnˈtɑːnɪʃt] *adj fig* sin mancha.
untenable [ʌnˈtenəbəl] *adj* insostenible.
unthinkable [ʌnˈθɪŋkəbəl] *adj* impensable, inconcebible.
untidy [ʌnˈtaɪdɪ] *adj (untidier, untidiest) (room, person)* desordenado,-a; *(hair)* despeinado,-a; *(appearance)* desaseado,-a.
untie [ʌnˈtaɪ] *vtr* desatar; *(free)* soltar.
until [ʌnˈtɪl] **I** *conj* hasta que; **she worked u. she collapsed,** trabajó hasta desfallecer; **u. she gets back,** hasta que vuelva. **II** *prep* hasta; **u. now,** hasta ahora; **u. ten o'clock,** hasta las diez; **not u. Monday,** hasta el lunes no.
untimely [ʌnˈtaɪmlɪ] *adj* 1 *(premature)* prematuro,-a. 2 *(inopportune)*

untold [ʌnˈtəʊld] *adj* 1 *(indescribable)* indecible. 2 *fig (loss, wealth)* incalculable. 3 *(not told)* sin contar.
untouchable [ʌnˈtʌtʃəbəl] *adj & n* intocable *(mf)*.
untoward [ʌntəˈwɔːd, ʌnˈtəʊəd] *adj* 1 *(unfortunate)* desafortunado,-a. 2 *(adverse)* adverso,-a.
untrained [ʌnˈtreɪnd] *adj* 1 *(unskilled)* sin preparación profesional. 2 *(inexpert)* inexperto,-a.
untrue [ʌnˈtruː] *adj* 1 *(false)* falso,-a. 2 *(unfaithful)* infiel. 3 *(inexact)* inexacto,-a.
untrustworthy [ʌnˈtrʌstwɜːðɪ] *adj* 1 *(person)* de poca confianza. 2 *(source)* no fidedigno,-a.
unused [ʌnˈjuːzd] *adj* 1 *(car)* sin usar; *(flat etc)* sin estrenar; *(stamp)* sin matar. 2 *(not in use)* que no ya se utiliza. 3 [ʌnˈjuːst] *(unaccustomed)* desacostumbrado,-a (**to, a**).
unusual [ʌnˈjuːʒʊəl] *adj* 1 *(rare)* insólito,-a, poco común; *(original)* original; *(exceptional)* excepcional. ◆**unusually** *adv* excepcionalmente.
unveil [ʌnˈveɪl] *vtr* descubrir.
unwarranted [ʌnˈwɒrəntɪd] *adj* injustificado,-a; *(remark)* gratuito,-a.
unwavering [ʌnˈweɪvərɪŋ] *adj (loyalty)* constante, firme; *(courage)* inquebrantable.
unwelcome [ʌnˈwelkəm] *adj (visitor)* molesto,-a; *(visit)* inoportuno,-a; *fig (news etc)* desagradable.
unwell [ʌnˈwel] *adj* malo,-a, indispuesto,-a.
unwieldy [ʌnˈwiːldɪ] *adj (difficult to handle)* poco manejable; *(clumsy)* torpe.
unwilling [ʌnˈwɪlɪŋ] *adj* **to be u. to do sth,** no estar dispuesto a hacer algo. ◆**unwillingly** *adv* de mala gana.
unwind [ʌnˈwaɪnd] *(pt & pp unwound)* **I** *vtr* desenrollar. **II** *vi* 1 desenrollarse. 2 *(relax)* relajarse.
unwise [ʌnˈwaɪz] *adj* imprudente, desaconsejable.
unwitting [ʌnˈwɪtɪŋ] *adj* involuntario,-a.
unworkable [ʌnˈwɜːkəbəl] *adj (not feasible)* impracticable; *(suggestion)* irrealizable.
unworthy [ʌnˈwɜːðɪ] *adj* indigno,-a.
unwrap [ʌnˈræp] *vtr (gift)* desenvolver; *(package)* deshacer.
unwritten [ʌnˈrɪtən] *adj* no escrito,-a; *(agreement)* verbal.
unyielding [ʌnˈjiːldɪŋ] *adj* inflexible.
up [ʌp] **I** *prep* 1 *(movement)* **to climb up the mountain,** escalar la montaña; **to walk up the street,** ir calle arriba. 2 *(position)* en lo alto de; **further up the street,** más adelante (en la misma calle); **halfway up the ladder,** a mitad de la escalera.

II adv **1** (upwards) arriba, hacia arriba; (position) arriba; **from ten pounds up**, de diez libras para arriba; **halfway up**, a medio camino; **right up** (to the top), hasta arriba (del todo); **to go** or **come up**, subir; **'this side up'**, 'este lado hacia arriba'. **2 the moon is up**, ha salido la luna. **3** (towards) hacia; **to come** or **go up to sb**, acercarse a algn; **to walk up and down**, ir de un lado a otro. **4** (in, to) **he's up in Yorkshire**, está en Yorkshire. **5** (increased) **bread is up**, el pan ha subido. **6 it's up for discussion**, se está discutiendo; **up for sale**, en venta. **7** fam **something's up (with you)?**, ¿qué pasa (contigo)? **8 to be up against sth**, enfrentarse con algo. **9 up to**, (as far as, until) hasta; **I can spend up to £5**, puedo gastar un máximo de cinco libras; **up to here**, hasta aquí; **up to now**, hasta ahora. **10 to be up to**, (depend on) depender de; (be capable of) estar a la altura de; **I don't feel up to doing it today**, hoy no me encuentro con fuerzas para hacerlo; **it's not up to much**, no vale gran cosa. **11 he's up to sth**, está tramando algo. **III** adj **1** (out of bed) levantado,-a. **2** (finished) terminado,-a; **time's up**, (ya) es la hora. **IV** vtr fam aumentar. **V** n fig **ups and downs**, altibajos mpl.

up-and-coming [ʌpənˈkʌmɪŋ] adj prometedor,-a.

upbringing [ˈʌpbrɪŋɪŋ] n educación f.

update [ʌpˈdeɪt] vtr actualizar, poner al día.

upgrade [ʌpˈgreɪd] vtr **1** (promote) ascender. **2** (improve) mejorar la calidad de.

upheaval [ʌpˈhiːvəl] n trastorno m.

uphill [ˈʌphɪl] **I** adj ascendente; fig arduo,-a. **II** adv cuesta arriba.

uphold [ʌpˈhəʊld] vtr (pt & pp upheld) sostener.

upholstery [ʌpˈhəʊlstərɪ] n tapizado m, tapicería f.

upkeep [ˈʌpkiːp] n mantenimiento m.

up-market [ˈʌpmɑːkɪt] adj de categoría.

upon [əˈpɒn] prep fml en, sobre; **once u. a time ...**, érase una vez ...; **u. my word**, (mi) palabra de honor.

upper [ˈʌpə] **I** adj **1** (position) superior; **u. storey**, piso de arriba; fig **to have the u. hand**, llevar la delantera. **2** (in rank) alto,-a; **the u. class**, la clase alta; **the U. House**, la Cámara Alta. **II** n (of shoe) pala f.

upper-class [ˈʌpəklæs] adj de la clase alta.

uppermost [ˈʌpəməʊst] adj más alto,-a; fig **it was u. in my mind**, era lo que me preocupaba más.

upright [ˈʌpraɪt] **I** adj **1** (vertical) vertical.

2 (honest) honrado,-a. **II** adv derecho. **III** n Ftb (post) poste m.

uprising [ʌpˈraɪzɪŋ] n sublevación f.

uproar [ˈʌprɔː] n tumulto m, alboroto m.

uproot [ʌpˈruːt] vtr (plant) arrancar de raíz.

upset [ʌpˈset] **I** vtr (pt & pp upset) **1** (overturn) volcar; (spill) derramar. **2** (shock) trastornar; (worry) preocupar; (displease) disgustar. **3** (spoil) desbaratar. **4** (make ill) sentar mal a. **II** [ˈʌpset] n **1** (reversal) revés m. **2** Sport resultado inesperado. **III** [ʌpˈset] adj (shocked) alterado,-a; (displeased) disgustado,-a; **to have an u. stomach**, sentirse mal del estómago.

upshot [ˈʌpʃɒt] n resultado m.

upside [ˈʌpsaɪd] n **u. down**, al revés.

upstage [ʌpˈsteɪdʒ] vtr fam eclipsar.

upstairs [ʌpˈsteəz] **I** adv al piso de arriba; **she lives u.**, vive en el piso de arriba. **II** n piso m de arriba.

upstart [ˈʌpstɑːt] n advenedizo,-a m,f.

upstream [ʌpˈstriːm] adv río arriba.

uptake [ˈʌpteɪk] n fam **to be quick on the u.**, cogerlas al vuelo.

uptight [ʌpˈtaɪt] adj fam nervioso,-a.

up to date [ʌptəˈdeɪt] adj **1** (current) al día. **2** (modern) moderno,-a.

upturn [ˈʌptɜːn] n mejora f.

upward [ˈʌpwəd] adj ascendente.

upward(s) [ˈʌpwəd(z)] adv hacia arriba; **from ten (years) u.**, a partir de los diez años; fam **u. of**, algo más de.

uranium [jʊˈreɪnɪəm] n uranio m.

urban [ˈɜːbən] adj urbano,-a.

urbane [ɜːˈbeɪn] adj urbano,-a, cortés.

urchin [ˈɜːtʃɪn] n **1** (child) pilluelo,-a m,f. **2 sea u.**, erizo m de mar.

urge [ɜːdʒ] **I** vtr **1** (press) instar; (plead) exhortar. **2** (advocate) preconizar; **to u. that sth should be done**, insistir en que se haga algo. **II** n impulso m. ◆ **urge on** vtr animar a.

urgency [ˈɜːdʒənsɪ] n urgencia f.

urgent [ˈɜːdʒənt] adj urgente; (need, tone) apremiante.

urinal [jʊˈraɪnəl] n (toilet) urinario m; (bowl) orinal m.

urinate [ˈjʊərɪneɪt] vi orinar.

urine [ˈjʊərɪn] n orina f.

urn [ɜːn] n **1** urna f. **2 tea u.**, tetera f grande.

Uruguay [ˈjʊərəgwaɪ] n Uruguay.

Uruguayan [jʊərəˈgwaɪən] adj & n uruguayo,-a (m,f).

us [ʌs] pers pron **1** (as object) nos; **let's forget it**, olvidémoslo. **2** (after prep) nosotros,-as; **both of us**, nosotros dos; **he's one of us**, es de los nuestros. **3** (after v to be) nosotros,-as; **they wouldn't believe it was us**, no creía que fuéramos nosotros. **4** fam me; **give us a kiss!**, ¡dame un beso!

US [juːˈes] abbr of **United States**,

EE.UU. *mpl.*
USA [ju:es'eɪ] *abbr of* **United States of America,** EE.UU. *mpl.*
usage ['ju:sɪdʒ] *n* 1 (*habit, custom*) costumbre *f.* 2 *Ling* uso *m.*
use [ju:z] I *vtr* 1 emplear, utilizar; **what is it used for?,** ¿para qué sirve?; **to u. force,** hacer uso de la fuerza. 2 (*consume*) consumir, gastar. 3 (*take unfair advantage of*) aprovecharse de. 4 *fam* **I could u. a drink,** no me vendría mal un trago. II *v aux* (*past tense only*) soler, acostumbrar; **where did you u. to live?,** ¿dónde vivías (antes)? III [ju:s] *n* 1 uso *m,* empleo *m;* (*handling*) manejo *m;* **directions for u.,** modo de empleo; **in u.,** en uso; **'not in u.',** (*on lift*) 'no funciona'; **ready for u.,** listo para usar; **to make (good) u. of sth,** aprovechar algo; **to put to good u.,** sacar partido de. 2 (*application*) aplicación *f.* 3 (*usefulness*) utilidad *f;* **it's no u.,** es inútil; **what's the u.?,** ¿para qué?; *fam* **it's no u. crying,** no sirve de nada llorar; **of u.,** útil; **to be of u.,** servir. ◆ **use up** *vtr* acabar.
used [ju:zd] *adj* 1 (*second-hand*) usado,-a. 2 [ju:st] **to be u. to,** estar acostumbrado,-a a.
useful ['ju:sfʊl] *adj* útil; (*practical*) práctico,-a; **to come in u.,** venir bien.
usefulness ['ju:sfʊlnɪs] *n* utilidad *f.*
useless ['ju:slɪs] *adj* inútil.
user ['ju:zər] *n* 1 usuario,-a *m,f.* 2 *fam* (*of drugs*) drogadicto,-a *m,f.*
usher ['ʌʃər] I *n Cin Theat* acomodador,-a *m,f.* 2 (*in court etc*) ujier

m. II *vtr* **to u. in,** *Cin Theat* acomodar; (*at home*) hacer pasar; **to u. out,** acompañar hasta la puerta.
USSR [ju:eses'ɑ:r] *Hist abbr of* **Union of Soviet Socialist Republics,** URSS *f.*
usual ['ju:ʒʊəl] I *adj* corriente, normal; **as u.,** como siempre; **at the u. hour,** a la hora habitual; **earlier than u.,** más pronto que de costumbre; **the u. problems,** los problemas de siempre. II *n* lo habitual; **out of the u.,** fuera de lo común. ◆ **usually** *adv* normalmente.
usurpation [ju:zɜ:'peɪʃən] *n* usurpación *f.*
utensil [ju:'tensəl] *n* utensilio *m;* **kitchen utensils,** batería *f sing* de cocina.
uterus ['ju:tərəs] *n* útero *m.*
utilitarian [ju:tɪlɪ'teərɪən] *adj* 1 (*in philosophy*) utilitarista. 2 (*useful*) utilitario,-a.
utility [ju:'tɪlɪtɪ] *n* 1 utilidad *f;* **u. room,** cuarto *m* de planchar; (*for storage*) trascocina *f.* 2 (*public*) **u.,** empresa *f* de servicio público.
utilize ['ju:tɪlaɪz] *vtr* utilizar.
utmost ['ʌtməʊst] I *adj* sumo,-a; **of the u. importance,** de suma importancia. II *n* máximo *m;* **to do** *or* **try one's u.,** hacer todo lo posible; **to the u.,** al máximo, a más no poder.
utopian [ju:'təʊpɪən] *adj* utópico,-a.
utter¹ ['ʌtər] *vtr* (*words*) pronunciar; (*sigh*) dar; (*cry, threat*) lanzar.
utter² ['ʌtər] *adj* total, completo,-a.
utterance ['ʌtərəns] *n* declaración *f.*
U-turn ['ju:tɜ:n] *n* cambio *m* de sentido; *Pol* giro *m* de 180° grados.

V

V, v [vi:] *n* (*the letter*) V, v *f.*
V *abbr of* **volt(s),** V.
v 1 *abbr of* **versus,** v. 2 (*also* **vs**) *abbr of* **versus,** contra.
vacancy ['veɪkənsɪ] *n* 1 (*job*) vacante *f.* 2 (*room*) habitación *f* libre; **'no vacancies',** 'completo'.
vacant ['veɪkənt] *adj* 1 (*empty*) vacío,-a. 2 (*job*) vacante; *GB* **'situations v.',** 'ofertas de trabajo'. 3 (*free, not in use*) libre.
vacate [və'keɪt] *vtr* (*flat*) desalojar.
vacation [və'keɪʃən] I *n* vacaciones *fpl;* **on v.,** de vacaciones. II *vi US* pasar las vacaciones (**in,** at, en).
vacationer [və'keɪʃənər], **vacationist** [və'keɪʃənɪst] *n US* **summer v.,** veraneante *mf.*
vaccinate ['væksɪneɪt] *vtr* vacunar.
vaccine ['væksi:n] *n* vacuna *f.*
vacuum ['vækjʊəm] I *n* vacío *m;* **v. cleaner,** aspiradora *f;* **v. flask,** termo *m.* II *vtr* (*carpet, room*) pasar la aspiradora por.
vacuum-packed ['vækjʊəmpækt] *adj*

envasado,-a al vacío.
vagina [və'dʒaɪnə] *n* vagina *f.*
vagrant ['veɪgrənt] *adj & n* vagabundo,-a (*m,f*).
vague [veɪg] *adj* (*imprecise*) vago,-a, impreciso,-a; (*indistinct*) borroso,-a.
vain [veɪn] *adj* 1 (*proud*) vanidoso,-a, presumido,-a. 2 (*hopeless*) vano,-a; **in v.,** en vano.
valentine ['væləntaɪn] *n* 1 (*card*) tarjeta *f* que se manda el Día de los Enamorados. 2 (*sweetheart*) novio,-a *m,f.*
valet ['væleɪ, 'væleɪ] *n* ayuda *m* de cámara.
valiant ['vælɪənt] *adj* valiente.
valid ['vælɪd] *adj* válido,-a; **no longer v.,** caducado,-a.
valley ['vælɪ] *n* valle *m.*
valour, *US* **valor** ['vælər] *n* valor *m,* valentía *f.*
valuable ['væljʊəbəl] I *adj* valioso,-a, de valor. II *npl* **valuables,** objetos *mpl* de valor.

valuation [ˌvæljʊˈeɪʃən] n 1 (act) valoración f. 2 (price) valor m.

value [ˈvæljuː] I n valor m; **50 pence is good v.**, 50 peniques es un buen precio; **to get good v. for money**, sacarle jugo al dinero; **v. added tax**, impuesto m sobre el valor añadido. II vtr valorar.

valve [vælv] n 1 Anat Tech válvula f. 2 Rad lámpara f.

vampire [ˈvæmpaɪər] n vampiro m.

van [væn] n GB 1 Aut furgoneta f. 2 Rail furgón m.

vandal [ˈvændəl] n vándalo,-a,m,f.

vandalism [ˈvændəlɪzəm] n vandalismo m.

vandalize [ˈvændəlaɪz] vtr destruir, destrozar.

vanguard [ˈvæŋgɑːd] n vanguardia f.

vanilla [vəˈnɪlə] n vainilla f.

vanish [ˈvænɪʃ] vi desaparecer.

vanity [ˈvænɪtɪ] n vanidad f; **v. bag, v. case**, neceser m.

vantage [ˈvɑːntɪdʒ] n ventaja f; **v. point**, posición estratégica.

vaporizer [ˈveɪpəraɪzər] n (device) vaporizador m; (spray) pulverizador m.

vapour, US vapor [ˈveɪpər] n vapor m; (on windowpane) vaho m; **v. trail**, estela f de humo.

variable [ˈveərɪəbəl] adj & n variable (f).

variance [ˈveərɪəns] n **to be at v.**, no concordar; **to be at v. with sb**, estar en desacuerdo con algn.

variation [ˌveərɪˈeɪʃən] n variación f.

varicose [ˈværɪkəʊs] adj **v. veins**, varices fpl.

varied [ˈveərɪd] adj variado,-a, diverso,-a.

variety [vəˈraɪətɪ] n 1 (diversity) variedad f; (assortment) surtido m; **for a v. of reasons**, por razones diversas. **2 v. show**, espectáculo m de variedades.

various [ˈveərɪəs] adj diversos,-as, varios,-as.

varnish [ˈvɑːnɪʃ] I n barniz m; GB **nail v.**, esmalte m de uñas. II vtr barnizar; (nails) esmaltar.

vary [ˈveərɪ] vi variar; **prices v. from £2 to £4**, los precios oscilan entre 2 y 4 libras; **to v. in size**, variar de tamaño.

varying [ˈveərɪɪŋ] adj **with v. degrees of success**, con más o menos éxito.

vase [vɑːz] n florero m, jarrón m.

Vaseline® [ˈvæsɪliːn] n vaselina f.

vast [vɑːst] adj vasto,-a; (majority) inmenso,-a.

VAT, Vat [ˌviːeɪˈtiː, væt] abbr of value added tax, IVA m.

vat [væt] n cuba f, tina f.

Vatican [ˈvætɪkən] n **the V.**, el Vaticano.

vault¹ [vɔːlt] n bóveda f; (for wine) bodega f; (tomb) cripta f; (of bank) cámara acorazada.

vault² [vɔːlt] I vtr & vi saltar. II n Gymn salto m.

vaunt [vɔːnt] vtr fml jactarse de, hacer alarde de.

VCR [ˌviːsiːˈɑːr] abbr of video cassette recorder, (grabador m de) video m.

VD [ˌviːˈdiː] abbr of venereal disease, enfermedad venérea.

VDU [ˌviːdiːˈjuː] abbr of visual display unit, pantalla f.

veal [viːl] n ternera f.

veer [vɪər] vi (ship) virar; (car) girar.

vegetable [ˈvedʒtəbəl] n (food) verdura f, hortaliza f; **v. garden**, huerta f, huerto m.

vegetarian [ˌvedʒɪˈteərɪən] adj & n vegetariano,-a (m,f).

vegetation [ˌvedʒɪˈteɪʃən] n vegetación f.

vehement [ˈviːɪmənt] adj vehemente.

vehicle [ˈviːɪkəl] n vehículo m.

veil [veɪl] I n velo m. II vtr velar.

vein [veɪn] n vena f.

velocity [vɪˈlɒsɪtɪ] n velocidad f.

velvet [ˈvelvɪt] n terciopelo m.

velvety [ˈvelvɪtɪ] adj aterciopelado,-a.

vendetta [venˈdetə] n vendetta f.

vending [ˈvendɪŋ] n **v. machine**, máquina expendedora.

vendor [ˈvendɔːr] n vendedor,-a m,f.

veneer [vɪˈnɪər] n 1 (covering) chapa f. 2 fig apariencia f.

venerable [ˈvenərəbəl] adj venerable.

venereal [vɪˈnɪərɪəl] adj venéreo,-a.

Venetian [vɪˈniːʃən] adj & n veneciano,-a (m,f); **v. blind**, persiana f graduable.

Venezuela [ˌvenɪˈzweɪlə] n Venezuela f.

Venezuelan [ˌvenɪˈzweɪlən] adj & n venezolano,-a (m,f).

vengeance [ˈvendʒəns] n venganza f; fam **it was raining with a v.**, llovía con ganas.

Venice [ˈvenɪs] n Venecia f.

venison [ˈvenzən, ˈvenɪsən] n carne f de venado.

venom [ˈvenəm] n veneno m.

venomous [ˈvenəməs] adj venenoso,-a; fig **v. tongue**, lengua viperina.

vent [vent] I n 1 (opening) abertura f, orificio m; (grille) rejilla f de ventilación; **air v.**, respiradero m 2 (of volcano) chimenea f. II vtr fig (feelings) descargar.

ventilate [ˈventɪleɪt] vtr ventilar.

ventilation [ˌventɪˈleɪʃən] n ventilación f.

ventilator [ˈventɪleɪtər] n ventilador m.

ventriloquist [venˈtrɪləkwɪst] n ventrílocuo,-a m,f.

venture [ˈventʃər] I vtr arriesgar, aventurar; **he didn't v. to ask**, no se atrevió a preguntarlo. II vi arriesgarse; **to v. out of doors**, atreverse a salir. III n empresa arriesgada, aventura f; Com **business/joint v.**, empresa comercial/colectiva.

venue [ˈvenjuː] n 1 (meeting place) lugar m de reunión. 2 (for concert etc) local m.

Venus [ˈviːnəs] n (goddess) Venus f; (planet) Venus m.

veranda(h) [və'rændə] *n* porche *m*, terraza *f*.

verb [vɜːb] *n* verbo *m*.

verbal ['vɜːbəl] *adj* verbal.

verbatim [və'beitim] I *adj* textual. II *adv* textualmente.

verbose [vɜː'bəus] *adj* prodigo,-a en palabras.

verdict ['vɜːdɪkt] *n* 1 *Jur* veredicto *m*, fallo *m*. 2 (*opinion*) opinión *f*, juicio *m*.

verge [vɜːdʒ] I *n* 1 (*margin*) borde *m*; *fig* **on the v. of**, al borde de; *fig* **to be on the v. of doing sth**, estar a punto de hacer algo. 2 *GB* (*of road*) arcén *m*. II *vi* rayar (**on**, en).

verification [verɪfɪ'keɪʃən] *n* verificación *f*, comprobación *f*.

verify ['verɪfaɪ] *vtr* verificar, comprobar.

veritable ['verɪtəbəl] *adj* auténtico,-a.

vermicelli [vɜːmɪ'selɪ] *npl* fideos *mpl*.

vermin ['vɜːmɪn] *npl* 1 (*animals*) bichos *mpl*, sabandijas *fpl*. 2 *fig* gentuza *f sing*.

vermouth ['vɜːməθ] *n* vermú *m*, vermut *m*.

verruca [və'ruːkə] *n* verruga *f*.

versatile ['vɜːsətaɪl] *adj* (*person*) polifacético,-a; (*object*) versátil.

verse [vɜːs] *n* 1 (*stanza*) estrofa *f*. 2 (*poetry*) versos *mpl*, poesía *f*. 3 (*of song*) copla *f*. 4 (*of Bible*) versículo *m*.

versed [vɜːst] *adj* **to be** (**well**) **v. in**, ser (muy) versado en.

version ['vɜːʃən, 'vɜːʒən] *n* 1 versión *f*; **stage v.**, adaptación *f* teatral. 2 *Aut* modelo *m*.

versus ['vɜːsəs] *prep* contra.

vertebra ['vɜːtɪbrə] *n* (*pl* **vertebras** *or* **vertebrae** ['vɜːtɪbriː]) vértebra *f*.

vertical ['vɜːtɪkəl] *adj* & *n* vertical (*f*).

vertigo ['vɜːtɪgəu] *n* vértigo *m*.

verve [vɜːv] *n* vigor *m*, brío *m*.

very ['verɪ] I *adv* 1 (*extremely*) muy; **to be v. hungry**, tener mucha hambre; **v. much**, muchísimo; **v. well**, muy bien. 2 (*emphatic*) **at the v. latest**, como máximo; **at the v. least**, como mínimo; **the v. best**, el mejor de todos; **the v. first/last**, el primero/último de todos; **the v. same day**, el mismo día. 3 *Rel* **at the v. end/beginning**, al final/principio de todo. 2 (*precise*) **at this v. moment**, en este mismo momento; **in her v. words**, sus palabras exactas; **in the v. middle**, justo en medio. 3 (*mere*) **the v. thought of it!**, ¡sólo con pensarlo!

vespers ['vespəz] *npl* vísperas *fpl*.

vessel ['vesəl] *n* 1 (*container*) vasija *f*. 2 *Naut* buque *m*, nave *f*. 3 *Anat Bot* vaso *m*.

vest [vest] *n* 1 (*undershirt*) camiseta *f* de tirantes. 2 *US* chaleco *m*. II *vtr Jur* conferir a (**with**, -).

vested ['vestɪd] *adj Jur Fin* **v. interests**, derechos adquiridos; *fig* intereses *mpl*

personales.

vestibule ['vestɪbjuːl] *n* vestíbulo *m*.

vestige ['vestɪdʒ] *n* vestigio *m*.

vestry ['vestrɪ] *n* sacristía *f*.

vet [vet] I *n fam abbr of* **veterinary surgeon**. II *vtr GB* someter a investigación, examinar.

veteran ['vetərən] *n* 1 veterano,-a *m,f*. 2 *US* (*war*) ex combatiente *mf*.

veterinarian [vetərɪ'neərɪən] *n US* veterinario,-a *m,f*.

veterinary ['vetərɪnərɪ] *adj* veterinario,-a; **v. medicine**, veterinaria *f*; *GB* **v. surgeon**, veterinario,-a *m,f*.

veto ['viːtəu] I *n* (*pl* **vetoes**) veto *m*. II *vtr Pol* vetar; (*suggestion etc*) descartar.

vexed [vekst] *adj* 1 (*annoyed*) disgustado, -a. 2 (*debated*) controvertido, -a.

VHF [viːeɪtʃ'ef] *abbr of* **very high frequency**, frecuencia muy alta, VHF.

via ['vaɪə] *prep* por, vía.

viable ['vaɪəbəl] *adj* viable, factible.

viaduct ['vaɪədʌkt] *n* viaducto *m*.

vibrant ['vaɪbrənt] *adj* 1 (*sound*) vibrante. 2 *fig* (*personality*) vital; (*city*) animado,-a.

vibrate [vaɪ'breɪt] *vi* vibrar (**with**, de).

vibration [vaɪ'breɪʃən] *n* vibración *f*.

vicar ['vɪkər] *n* párroco *m*.

vicarage ['vɪkərɪdʒ] *n* casa *f* del párroco.

vicarious [vɪ'keərɪəs] *adj* experimentado,-a por otro; (*punishment*) sufrido,-a por otro.

vice¹ [vaɪs] *n* vicio *m*.

vice² [vaɪs] *n* (*tool*) torno *m* de banco.

vice³ [vaɪs] *pref* vice-; **v. chancellor**, rector,-a *m,f*; **v. president**, vicepresidente,-a *m,f*.

vice-chairman [vaɪs'tʃeəmən] *n* vicepresidente *m*.

vice versa [vaɪs'vɜːsə] *adv* viceversa.

vicinity [vɪ'sɪnɪtɪ] *n* (*area*) vecindad *f*; **in the v. of**, (*geographic location*) cerca de, en las inmediaciones de; (*amount*) alrededor de.

vicious ['vɪʃəs] *adj* (*violent*) violento,-a; (*malicious*) malintencionado,-a; (*cruel*) cruel; **v. circle**, círculo vicioso.

victim ['vɪktɪm] *n* víctima *f*.

victimize ['vɪktɪmaɪz] *vtr* perseguir, tratar injustamente.

victor ['vɪktər] *n* vencedor,-a *m,f*.

victorious [vɪk'tɔːrɪəs] *adj* victorioso,-a.

victory ['vɪktərɪ] *n* victoria *f*.

video ['vɪdɪəu] *n* vídeo *m*; **v. camera**, videocámara *f*; **v. cassette**, videocasete *m*; **v. club**, videoclub *m*; **v. game**, videojuego *m*; **v.** (**cassette**) **recorder**, vídeo *m*; **v. tape**, cinta *f* de vídeo.

video-tape ['vɪdɪəuteɪp] *vtr* grabar (en vídeo).

vie [vaɪ] *vi* competir (**against, with**, con).

Vienna [vɪ'enə] *n* Viena.

Viennese [vɪə'niːz] *adj* & *n* vienés,-esa

(m,f).

Vietnam [vjet'næm] n Vietnam.

view [vju:] I n 1 (sight) vista f, panorama m; **in full v.**, completamente visible; **on v.**, a la vista; **to come into v.**, aparecer; fig **in v. of the fact that ...**, dado que .... 2 (opinion) opinión f; **point of v.**, punto m de vista; **to take a dim v. of**, ver con malos ojos. 3 (aim) fin m; **with a v. to**, con la intención de. II vtr 1 (look at) mirar; (house etc) visitar. 2 (consider) contemplar; (topic, problem) enfocar.

viewer ['vju:ər] n 1 TV televidente mf. 2 Phot visionador m.

viewfinder ['vju:faɪndər] n visor m.

viewpoint ['vju:pɔɪnt] n punto m de vista.

vigil ['vɪdʒɪl] n vigilia f.

vigilante [vɪdʒɪ'læntɪ] n v. **group**, patrulla ciudadana.

vigorous ['vɪgərəs] adj vigoroso,-a, enérgico,-a.

vigour, US **vigor** ['vɪgər] n vigor m.

vile [vaɪl] adj 1 (evil) vil, infame. 2 (disgusting) repugnante. 3 fam (awful) horrible.

vilify ['vɪlɪfaɪ] vtr denigrar.

villa ['vɪlə] n 1 (in country) casa f de campo. 2 GB chalet m.

village ['vɪlɪdʒ] n (small) aldea f; (larger) pueblo m.

villager ['vɪlɪdʒər] n aldeano,-a m,f.

villain ['vɪlən] n villano,-a m,f; Cin Theat malo,-a m,f.

vinaigrette [vɪneɪ'gret] n vinagreta f.

vindicate ['vɪndɪkeɪt] vtr justificar, vindicar.

vindictive [vɪn'dɪktɪv] adj vengativo,-a.

vine [vaɪn] n vid f; (climbing) parra f.

vinegar ['vɪnɪgər] n vinagre m.

vineyard ['vɪnjəd] n viña f, viñedo m.

vintage ['vɪntɪdʒ] I n 1 (crop, year) cosecha f. 2 (season) vendimia f. 3 (era) era f. II adj 1 (wine) añejo,-a. 2 (classic) clásico,-a; **v. car**, coche m de época.

vinyl ['vaɪnɪl] n vinilo m.

viola [vɪ'əʊlə] n viola f.

violate ['vaɪəleɪt] vtr violar.

violence ['vaɪələns] n violencia f.

violent ['vaɪələnt] adj 1 violento,-a. 2 (intense) intenso,-a.

violet ['vaɪəlɪt] I n 1 Bot violeta f. 2 (colour) violeta m. II adj violeta.

violin [vaɪə'lɪn] n violín m.

violinist [vaɪə'lɪnɪst] n violinista mf.

VIP [vi:aɪ'pi:] fam abbr of **very important person**, personaje m muy importante.

viper ['vaɪpər] n víbora f.

virgin ['vɜːdʒɪn] I n virgen f; **the V. Mary**, la Virgen María; **to be a v.**, ser virgen. II adj virgen.

virginity [və'dʒɪnɪtɪ] n virginidad f.

Virgo ['vɜːgəʊ] n Virgo m.

virile ['vɪraɪl] adj viril.

virtual ['vɜːtjʊəl] adj virtual; Comput **v. reality**, realidad f virtual. ◆**virtually** adv (almost) prácticamente.

virtue ['vɜːtjuː, 'vɜːtʃuː] n virtud f; **by v. of**, en virtud de.

virtuous ['vɜːtʃʊəs] adj virtuoso,-a.

virulent ['vɪrʊlənt] adj virulento,-a.

virus ['vaɪrəs] n virus m inv.

visa ['viːzə] n visado m, Am visa f.

vis-à-vis [viːzɑː'viː] prep 1 (regarding) respecto a. 2 (opposite) frente a.

viscose ['vɪskəʊs] n viscosa f.

viscount ['vaɪkaʊnt] n vizconde m.

visibility [vɪzɪ'bɪlɪtɪ] n visibilidad f.

visible ['vɪzɪbəl] adj visible.

vision ['vɪʒən] n 1 visión f. 2 (eyesight) vista f.

visit ['vɪzɪt] I vtr 1 (person) visitar, hacer una visita a. 2 (place) visitar. II n visita f; **to pay sb a v.**, hacerle una visita a algn.

visiting ['vɪzɪtɪŋ] adj GB **v. card**, tarjeta f de visita; Med **v. hours**, horas fpl de visita; Sport **v. team**, equipo m visitante.

visitor ['vɪzɪtər] n 1 (guest) invitado,-a m,f; **we've got visitors**, tenemos visita. 2 (in hotel) cliente,-a m,f. 3 (tourist) turista mf.

visor ['vaɪzər] n visera f.

vista ['vɪstə] n vista f, panorama m.

visual ['vɪʒʊəl, 'vɪzjʊəl] adj visual; **v. aids**, medios mpl visuales.

visualize ['vɪʒʊəlaɪz, 'vɪzjʊəlaɪz] vtr 1 (imagine) imaginar(se). 2 (foresee) prever.

vital ['vaɪtəl] adj 1 (lively) enérgico,-a. 2 (essential) fundamental. 3 (decisive) decisivo,-a; fam **v. statistics**, medidas fpl del cuerpo de la mujer. 4 Med (function, sign) vital. ◆**vitally** adv **it's v. important**, es de vital importancia.

vitality [vaɪ'tælɪtɪ] n vitalidad f.

vitamin ['vɪtəmɪn, US 'vaɪtəmɪn] n vitamina f.

viva ['vaɪvə] n (abbr of **viva voce**) GB examen m oral.

vivacious [vɪ'veɪʃəs] adj vivaz.

vivacity [vɪ'væsɪtɪ] n viveza f, vivacidad f.

vivid ['vɪvɪd] adj 1 (bright, lively) vivo,-a, intenso,-a. 2 (graphic) gráfico,-a.

vixen ['vɪksən] n zorra f.

V-neck(ed) ['viːnek(t)] adj con el cuello en pico.

vocabulary [və'kæbjʊlərɪ] n vocabulario m.

vocal ['vəʊkəl] adj vocal; **v. cords**, cuerdas fpl vocales.

vocalist ['vəʊkəlɪst] n cantante mf.

vocation [vəʊ'keɪʃən] n vocación f.

vocational [vəʊ'keɪʃənəl] adj profesional; **v. training**, formación f profesional.

vociferous [vəʊ'sɪfərəs] adj 1 (protest) enérgico,-a. 2 (noisy) clamoroso,-a.

vodka ['vɒdkə] n vodka m & f.

vogue [vəʊg] n boga f, moda f; **in v.**, de

moda.

voice [vɔɪs] **I** n voz f; **to lose one's v.**, quedarse afónico; fig **at the top of one's v.**, a voz en grito. **II** vtr **1** (express) manifestar. **2** Ling sonorizar.

void [vɔɪd] **I** adj **1** v. of, sin. **2** Jur nulo, -a, inválido,-a. **II** n vacío m.

volatile ['vɒlətaɪl] adj volátil.

volcanic [vɒl'kænɪk] adj volcánico,-a.

volcano [vɒl'keɪnəʊ] n (pl **volcanoes**) volcán m.

volition [və'lɪʃən] n fml **of one's own v.**, por voluntad propia.

volley ['vɒlɪ] **I** n **1** (of shots) descarga f. **2** fig (of stones, insults) lluvia f. **3** Ten volea f. **II** vtr Ten volear.

volleyball ['vɒlɪbɔːl] n voleibol m.

volt [vəʊlt] n voltio m.

voltage ['vəʊltɪdʒ] n voltaje m.

voluble ['vɒljʊbəl] adj locuaz, hablador,-a.

volume ['vɒljuːm] n **1** volumen m. **2** (book) volumen m, tomo m; fig **to speak volumes**, decirlo todo.

voluntary ['vɒləntərɪ] adj voluntario,-a; **v. organization**, organización benéfica.

volunteer [vɒlən'tɪər] **I** n voluntario,-a m,f. **II** vtr (help etc) ofrecer. **III** vi **1** ofrecerse (**for**, para). **2** Mil alistarse como voluntario.

voluptuous [və'lʌptjʊəs] adj voluptuoso,-a.

vomit ['vɒmɪt] **I** vtr & vi vomitar. **II** n vómito m.

voracious [vɒ'reɪʃəs] adj voraz.

vortex ['vɔːteks] n (pl **vortices** ['vɔːtɪsiːz]) vórtice m; fig vorágine f.

vote [vəʊt] **I** n voto m; (voting) votación f; **v. of confidence**, voto de confianza; **to take a v. on sth**, someter algo a votación; **to have the v.**, tener derecho al voto. **II** vtr **1** votar. **2** (elect) elegir. **3** fam proponer. **III** vi votar; **to v. for sb**, votar a algn.

voter ['vəʊtər] n votante mf.

voting ['vəʊtɪŋ] n votación f.

vouch [vaʊtʃ] vi **to v. for sth/sb**, responder de algo/por algn.

voucher ['vaʊtʃər] n GB vale m.

vow [vaʊ] **I** n voto m. **II** vtr jurar.

vowel ['vaʊəl] n vocal f.

voyage ['vɔɪɪdʒ] n viaje m; (crossing) travesía f; **to go on a v.**, hacer un viaje en (barco).

vulgar ['vʌlɡər] adj (coarse) vulgar, ordinario,-a; (in poor taste) de mal gusto.

vulgarity [vʌl'ɡærɪtɪ] n (coarseness) vulgaridad f, ordinariez f; (poor taste) mal gusto m.

vulnerable ['vʌlnərəbəl] adj vulnerable.

vulture ['vʌltʃər] n buitre m.

vulva ['vʌlvə] n vulva f.

W

W, w ['dʌbəljuː] n (the letter) W, w f.

W 1 abbr of **West**, O. **2** abbr of **Watt(s)**, W.

wad [wɒd] n (of paper) taco m; (of cotton wool) bolita f; (of banknotes) fajo m.

waddle ['wɒdəl] vi andar como los patos.

wade [weɪd] vi caminar por el agua; **to w. across a river**, vadear un río.
◆**wade through** vtr hacer con dificultad; **I'm wading through the book**, me cuesta mucho terminar el libro.

wafer ['weɪfər] n barquillo m; Rel hostia f.

waffle¹ ['wɒfəl] n Culin (tipo m de) barquillo m.

waffle² ['wɒfəl] GB fam **I** vi meter mucha paja; **to w. on**, parlotear. **II** n paja f.

waft [wɑːft, wɒft] **I** vtr llevar por el aire. **II** vi flotar (por or en el aire).

wag [wæɡ] **I** vtr menear. **II** vi (tail) menearse.

wage [weɪdʒ] **I** n (also **wages**) salario m, sueldo m; **w. earner**, asalariado,-a m,f. **II** vtr (campaign) realizar (**against**, contra); **to w. war**, hacer la guerra (**on**, a).

wage-packet ['weɪdʒpækɪt] n sueldo m.

wager ['weɪdʒər] **I** n apuesta f. **II** vtr apostar.

waggle ['wæɡəl] **I** vtr menear. **II** vi menearse.

wa(g)gon ['wæɡən] n (horse-drawn) carro m; GB Rail vagón m.

wail [weɪl] **I** n lamento m, gemido m. **II** vi (person) lamentar, gemir.

waist [weɪst] n Anat cintura f; Sew talle m.

waistcoat ['weɪstkəʊt] n GB chaleco m.

waistline ['weɪstlaɪn] n Anat cintura; Sew talle m.

wait [weɪt] **I** n espera f; (delay) demora f; **to lie in w.**, estar al acecho. **II** vi **1** esperar, aguardar; **I can't w. to see her**, me muero de ganas de verla; **while you w.**, en el acto; **to keep sb waiting**, hacer esperar a algn. **2** **to w. at table**, servir la mesa. ◆**wait about, wait around** vi esperar. ◆**wait on** vtr servir.

waiter ['weɪtər] n camarero m.

waiting ['weɪtɪŋ] n 'No W.', 'Prohibido Aparcar'; **w. list**, lista f de espera; **w. room**, sala f de espera.

waitress ['weɪtrɪs] n camarera f.

waive [weɪv] vtr fml (rule) no aplicar.

wake¹ [weɪk] vtr (pt **woke**; pp **woken**) **to w. sb (up)**, despertar a algn. **II** vi **to w. (up)**, despertar(se). **III** n (for dead) velatorio m.

wake² [weɪk] n (in water) estela f; fig **in the w.** of, tras.

waken ['weɪkən] vtr lit despertar.

Wales [weɪlz] n (el país de) Gales.

walk [wɔːk] **I** n 1 (long) caminata m; (short) paseo m; **it's an hour's w.**, está a una hora de camino; **to go for a w.**, dar un paseo; **to take the dog for a w.**, sacar a pasear al perro. 2 (gait) modo m de andar. 3 **people from all walks of life**, gente f de toda condición. **II** vtr 1 **we walked her home**, la acompañamos a casa. 2 (dog) pasear. **III** vi 1 andar. 2 (go on foot) ir andando. ◆**walk away** vi alejarse; fig **to w. away with a prize**, llevarse un premio. ◆**walk into** vtr 1 (place) entrar en; fig (trap) caer en. 2 (bump into) chocarse contra. ◆**walk out** vi salir; Ind declararse en huelga; **to w. out on sb**, abandonar a algn. ◆**walk up** vi **to w. up to sb**, abordar a algn.

walkabout ['wɔːkəbaʊt] n (by Queen etc) paseo m informal entre la gente.

walker ['wɔːkər] n paseante mf; Sport marchador,-a m,f.

walkie-talkie [wɔːkɪ'tɔːkɪ] n walkie-talkie m.

walking ['wɔːkɪŋ] **I** n andar m; (hiking) excursionismo m. **II** adj **at w. pace**, a paso de marcha; **w. shoes**, zapatos mpl de andar; **w. stick**, bastón m.

Walkman® ['wɔːkmən] n (pl **Walkmans**) walkman® m.

walkout ['wɔːkaʊt] n Ind huelga f.

walkover ['wɔːkəʊvər] n **it was a w.**, fue pan comido.

walkway ['wɔːkweɪ] n esp US paso m de peatones.

wall [wɔːl] **I** n 1 (freestanding, exterior) muro m; fig **to have one's back to the w.**, estar entre la espada y la pared; **city w.**, muralla f; **garden w.**, tapia f. 2 (interior) pared f; **w. map**, mapa m mural. 3 Ftb barrera f. ◆**wall up** vtr (door, fireplace) tabicar.

walled [wɔːld] adj (city) amurallado,-a; (garden) cercado,-a con tapia.

wallet ['wɔlɪt] n cartera f.

wallflower ['wɔːlflaʊər] n 1 Bot alhelí m. 2 fam **to be a w.**, ser un convidado de piedra.

wallop ['wɔləp] fam **I** n golpazo m. **II** vtr 1 (hit) pegar fuerte. 2 (defeat) dar una paliza a.

wallow ['wɔləʊ] vi revolcarse (**en**, in); fig **to w. in self-pity**, sumirse en la autocompasión.

wallpaper ['wɔːlpeɪpər] **I** n papel pintado. **II** vtr empapelar.

wally ['wɔlɪ] n fam idiota mf.

walnut ['wɔːlnʌt] n nuez f; (tree, wood) nogal m.

walrus ['wɔːlrəs] n morsa f.

waltz [wɔːls] **I** n vals m. **II** vi bailar un vals.

wan [wɒn] adj (**wanner**, **wannest**) pálido,-a; (look, smile) apagado,-a.

wand [wɒnd] n (magic) w., varita f (mágica).

wander ['wɒndər] **I** vtr **to w. the streets**, vagar por las calles. **II** vi 1 (aimlessly) vagar, errar; **to w. about**, deambular; **to w. in/out**, entrar/salir sin prisas. 2 (stray) desviarse; (mind) divagar; **his glance wandered round the room**, recorrió el cuarto con la mirada.

wandering ['wɒndərɪŋ] adj errante; (tribe) nómada; (speech) divagador,-a.

wane [weɪn] vi menguar; (interest) decaer.

wangle ['wæŋgəl] vtr fam agenciarse.

wank [wæŋk] sl **I** n paja f. **II** vi hacerse una paja.

wanker ['wæŋkər] n sl mamón,-ona mf inv.

want [wɒnt] **I** n 1 (lack) falta f; **for w. of**, por falta de. 2 (poverty) miseria f. **II** vtr 1 (desire) querer, desear; **to w. to do sth**, querer hacer algo. 2 fam (need) necesitar; **the grass wants cutting**, hace falta cortar el césped. 3 (seek) buscar; **you're wanted on the phone**, te llaman al teléfono. ◆**want for** vtr carecer de; **to w. for nothing**, tenerlo todo.

wanting ['wɒntɪŋ] adj 1 **she is w. in tact**, le falta tacto. 2 **he was found w.**, no daba la talla.

wanton ['wɒntən] adj 1 (motiveless) sin motivo; **w. cruelty**, crueldad gratuita. 2 (unrestrained) desenfrenado,-a; (licentious) lascivo,-a.

war [wɔːr] n guerra f; **to be at w.**, estar en guerra (**with**, con); fig **to declare/wage w. on**, declarar/hacer la guerra a.

warble ['wɔːbəl] vi gorjear.

ward [wɔːd] n 1 (of hospital) sala f. 2 Jur pupilo,-a m,f; **w. of court**, pupilo,-a bajo tutela judicial. 3 GB Pol distrito m electoral. ◆**ward off** vtr (blow) parar, desviar; (attack) rechazar; (danger) evitar; (illness) prevenir.

warden ['wɔːdən] n (of residence) guardián,-ana m,f; **game w.**, guardia m de coto.

warder ['wɔːdər] n GB carcelero,-a m,f.

wardrobe ['wɔːdrəʊb] n 1 armario m, ropero m. 2 (clothes) guardarropa m. 3 Theat vestuario m.

warehouse ['weəhaʊs] n almacén m.

wares [weəz] npl mercancías fpl.

warfare ['wɔːfeər] n guerra f.

warhead ['wɔːhed] n (nuclear) w., ojiva f nuclear.

warm [wɔːm] **I** adj 1 (water) tibio,-a; (hands) caliente; (climate) cálido,-a; **a w. day**, un día de calor; **I am w.**, tengo calor; **it is (very) w. today**, hoy hace (mucho) calor; **w. clothing**, ropa f de abrigo.

2 (welcome, applause) cálido,-a. **II** vtr calentar; fig alegrar. **III** vi calentarse; **to w. to sb**, cogerle simpatía a algn. ◆**warm up I** vtr **1** calentar; (soup) (re)calentar. **2** (audience) animar. **II** vi **1** calentarse; (food) (re)calentarse; (person) entrar en calor. **2** (athlete) hacer ejercicios de calentamiento. **3** fig (audience, party) animarse. ◆**warmly** adv fig calurosamente; (thank) con efusión.

warm-blooded [wɔːm'blʌdid] adj de sangre caliente.

warm-hearted [wɔːm'hɑːtid] adj afectuoso,-a.

warmth [wɔːmθ] n (heat) calor m; fig cordialidad f.

warn [wɔːn] vtr avisar (of, de), advertir (about, sobre; against, contra); **he warned me not to go**, me advirtió que no fuera; **to w. sb that**, advertir a algn que.

warning ['wɔːniŋ] **I** adj **w. light**, piloto m; **w. sign**, señal f de aviso. **II** n **1** (of danger) advertencia f, aviso m. **2** (replacing punishment) amonestación f. **3** (notice) aviso m; **without w.**, sin previo aviso.

warp [wɔːp] **I** vtr **1** (wood) alabear, combar. **2** fig (mind) pervertir. **II** vi alabearse, combarse.

warrant ['wɒrənt] **I** n **1** Jur orden f judicial; **death w.**, sentencia f de muerte. **2** (authorization note) cédula f; Com **bono m. II** vtr **1** (justify) justificar. **2** (guarantee) garantizar.

warranty ['wɒrənti] n Com garantía f.

warren ['wɒrən] n conejera f; fig laberinto m.

Warsaw ['wɔːsɔː] n Varsovia.

warship ['wɔːʃip] n buque m or barco m de guerra.

wart [wɔːt] n verruga f.

wartime ['wɔːtaim] n tiempos mpl de guerra.

wary ['weəri] adj (warier, wariest) cauteloso,-a; **to be w. of doing sth**, dudar en hacer algo; **to be w. of sb/sth**, recelar de algn/algo.

was [wɒz] pt → **be**.

wash [wɒʃ] **I** n **1** lavado m; **to have a w.**, lavarse. **2** (of ship) estela f; (sound) chapoteo m. **II** vtr **1** lavar; (dishes) fregar; **to w. one's hair**, lavarse el pelo. **2** (sea, river) arrastrar. **III** vi **1** (person) lavarse. **2** (do the laundry) hacer la colada. **3** (lap) batir. ◆**wash away** vtr (of sea) llevarse; (traces) borrar. ◆**wash off** vi quitarse lavando. ◆**wash out I** vtr **1** (stain) quitar lavando. **2** (bottle) enjuagar. **II** vi quitarse lavando. ◆**wash up I** vtr GB (dishes) fregar. **II** vi GB fregar los platos. **2** US lavarse rápidamente.

washable ['wɒʃəbəl] adj lavable.

washbasin ['wɒʃbeisən], **washbowl**

['wɒʃbəul] n palangana f.

washcloth ['wɒʃklɒθ] n US manopla f.

washer ['wɒʃər] n (on tap) junta f.

washing ['wɒʃiŋ] n **1** (action) lavado m; (of clothes) colada f; (dirty) w., ropa sucia; **to do the w.**, hacer la colada; **w. line**, tendedero m; **w. machine**, lavadora f; **w. powder**, detergente m.

washing-up [wɒʃiŋ'ʌp] n GB **1** (action) fregado m; **w.-up bowl**, barreño m; **w.-up liquid**, (detergente m) lavavajillas. **2** (dishes) platos mpl (para fregar).

washout ['wɒʃaut] n fam fracaso m.

washroom ['wɒʃruːm] n US servicios mpl.

wasp [wɒsp] n avispa f.

wastage ['weistidʒ] n pérdidas fpl.

waste [weist] **I** adj **1** (unwanted) desechado,-a; **w. food**, restos mpl de comida; **w. products**, productos mpl de desecho. **2** (ground) baldío,-a. **II** n **1** (unnecessary use) desperdicio m; (of resources, effort, money) derroche m; (of time) pérdida f; **to go to w.**, echarse a perder. **2** (left-overs) desperdicios mpl; (rubbish) basura f; **radio-active w.**, desechos radioactivos; **w. disposal unit**, trituradora f (de desperdicios); **w. pipe**, tubo m de desagüe. **III** vtr (squander) desperdiciar, malgastar; (resources) derrochar; (money) despilfarrar; (time) perder. ◆**waste away** vi consumirse.

wasteful ['weistful] adj derrochador,-a.

wasteland ['weistlænd] n baldío m.

wastepaper [weist'peipər] n papeles usados; **w. basket**, papelera f.

watch [wɒtʃ] **I** n **1** (look-out) vigilancia f; **to keep a close w. on sth/sb**, vigilar algo/a algn muy atentamente. **2** Mil (body) guardia f; (individual) centinela m; **to be on w.**, estar de guardia. **3** (timepiece) reloj m. **II** vtr **1** (observe) mirar, observar. **2** (keep an eye on) vigilar; (with suspicion) acechar. **3** (be careful of) tener cuidado con; fig **to w. one's step**, ir con pies de plomo. **III** vi (look) mirar, observar; **w. out!**, ¡cuidado! ◆**watch out for** vtr (be careful of) tener cuidado con.

watchband ['wɒtʃbænd] n US = **watchstrap**.

watchdog ['wɒtʃdɒg] n perro m guardián; fig guardián,-ana m,f.

watchful ['wɒtʃful] adj vigilante.

watchmaker ['wɒtʃmeikər] n relojero,-a m,f.

watchman ['wɒtʃmən] n vigilante m; **night w.**, (of site) vigilante nocturno.

watchstrap ['wɒtʃstræp] n correa f (de reloj).

watchtower ['wɒtʃtauər] n atalaya f.

water ['wɔːtər] **I** n **1** agua f; **w. bottle**, cantimplora f; **w. lily**, nenúfar m; **w. main**, conducción f de aguas; **w. polo**,

water polo m; **w. sports**, deportes acuáti-
cos; **w. tank**, depósito m de agua; **territorial waters**, aguas jurisdiccionales; **fig
it's all w. under the bridge**, ha llovido
mucho desde entonces. 2 **to pass w.**, orinar. II *vtr* (*plants*) regar. III *vi* **my eyes
are watering**, me lloran los ojos; **my
mouth watered**, se me hizo la boca agua.
◆**water down** (*drink*) aguar.

watercolour, *US* **watercolor**
['wɔːtəkʌlə] n acuarela f.

watercress ['wɔːtəkres] n berro m.

waterfall ['wɔːtəfɔːl] n cascada f; (*very
big*) catarata f.

waterfront ['wɔːtəfrʌnt] n (*shore*) orilla f
del agua; (*harbour*) puerto m.

watering ['wɔːtərɪŋ] n (*of plants*) riego m;
w. can, regadera f; **w. place**, abrevadero
m.

waterline ['wɔːtəlaɪn] n línea f de flota-
ción.

waterlogged ['wɔːtəlɒgd] adj anegado,-a.

watermark ['wɔːtəmɑːk] n filigrana f.

watermelon ['wɔːtəmelən] n sandía f.

waterproof ['wɔːtəpruːf] I adj (*material*)
impermeable; (*watch*) sumergible. II n
(*coat*) impermeable m.

watershed ['wɔːtəʃed] n Geog línea divisoria de aguas; fig punto decisivo.

water-skiing ['wɔːtəskiːɪŋ] n esquí acuático.

watertight ['wɔːtətaɪt] adj hermético,-a.

waterway ['wɔːtəweɪ] n vía f fluvial.

waterworks ['wɔːtəwɜːks] npl central f
sing de abastecimiento de agua; fig **to
turn on the w.**, empezar a llorar.

watery ['wɔːtərɪ] adj 1 (*soup*) aguado,-a;
(*coffee*) flojo,-a. 2 (*eyes*) lacrimoso,-a. 3
(*pale*) pálido,-a.

watt [wɒt] n vatio m.

wave [weɪv] I n 1 (*at sea*) ola f. 2 (*in
hair* & Rad) onda f. 3 fig (*of anger, strikes
etc*) oleada f. 4 (*gesture*) saludo m con la
mano. II *vtr* 1 agitar; (*brandish*) blandir.
2 (*hair*) ondular. III *vi* 1 agitar el brazo;
she waved (to me), (*greeting*) me saludó
con la mano; (*goodbye*) se despidió (de
mí) con la mano; (*signal*) me hizo señas
con la mano. 2 (*flag*) ondear; (*corn*) ondular.

wavelength ['weɪvleŋθ] n longitud f de
onda.

waver ['weɪvə] *vi* (*hesitate*) vacilar
(**between**, entre); (*voice*) temblar; (*courage*) flaquear.

wavy ['weɪvɪ] adj (**wavier**, **waviest**)
ondulado,-a.

wax[1] [wæks] I n cera f. II *vtr* encerar.

wax[2] [wæks] *vi* 1 (*moon*) crecer. 2 **to w.
lyrical**, exaltarse.

waxwork ['wækswɜːk] n waxworks, museo m de cera.

way [weɪ] I n 1 (*route*) camino m; (*road*)
vía f, camino; **a letter is on the w.**, una

carta está en camino; **on the w.**, en el camino; **on the w. here**, de camino para
aquí; **out of the w.**, apartado,-a; **to ask
the w.**, preguntar el camino; **to go the
wrong w.**, ir por el camino equivocado;
to lose one's w., perderse; **to make
one's w. through the crowd**, abrirse camino entre la multitud; **which is the w.
to the station?**, ¿por dónde se va a la
estación?; fig **she went out of her w. to
help**, se desvivió por ayudar; **w. in**, entrada f; **w. out**, salida f; fig **the easy w.
out**, la solución fácil; **I can't find my w.
out**, no encuentro la salida; **on the w.
back**, en el viaje de regreso; **on the w.
up/down**, en la subida/bajada; **there's no
w. through**, el paso está cerrado; **you're
in the w.**, estás estorbando; (**get**) **out of
the w.!**, ¡quítate de en medio!; fig **to get
sb/sth out of the w.**, desembarazarse de
algn/algo; **I kept out of the w.**, me
mantuve a distancia; Aut **right of w.**,
prioridad f; **there's a wall in the w.**, hay
un muro en medio; **to give w.**, ceder;
Aut ceder el paso. 2 (*direction*) dirección
f; **come this w.**, venga por aquí; **which
w. did he go?**, ¿por dónde se fue?; **that
w.**, por allá; **the other w. round**, al revés. 3 (*distance*) distancia f; **a long w.
off**, lejos; **he'll go a long w.**, llegará
lejos; fig **we've come a long w.**, hemos
hecho grandes progresos. 4 **to get under
w.**, (*travellers, boat*) ponerse en marcha;
(*meeting, match*) empezar. 5 (*means,
method*) método m, manera f; **do it any
w. you like**, hazlo como quieras; **I'll do
it my w.**, lo haré a mi manera. 6 (*manner*) modo m, manera f; **in a friendly w.**,
de modo amistoso; **one w. or another**,
de un modo o de otro; **the French w. of
life**, el estilo de vida francés; **the w.
things are going**, tal como van las cosas;
to my w. of thinking, a mi modo de ver;
fam **no w.!**, ¡ni hablar!; **she has a w.
with children**, tiene un don para los niños; **by w. of**, a modo de; **either w.**, en
cualquier caso; **in a w.**, en cierto sentido;
in many ways, desde muchos puntos de
vista; **in some ways**, en algunos aspectos;
in no w., de ninguna manera. 7 (*custom*)
hábito m, costumbre f; **to be set in one's
ways**, tener costumbres arraigadas. 8
(*state*) estado m; **leave it the w. it is**, déjalo tal como está; **he is in a bad w.**, está
bastante mal. 9 **by the w.**, a propósito, en
the w. of business, en el curso de los negocios.
II adv fam mucho, muy; **it was w. off
target**, cayó muy desviado del blanco; **w.
back in 1940**, allá en 1940.

waylay [weɪ'leɪ] *vtr* (*pt* & *pp* **waylaid**)
1 (*attack*) atacar por sorpresa. 2 fig (*intercept*) salirle al paso a algn.

wayside ['weɪsaɪd] n fig **to fall by the w.**,

quedarse en el camino.

wayward ['weɪwəd] *adj* rebelde; *(capricious)* caprichoso,-a.

WC [dʌblju:'si:] *abbr* of **water closet**, wáter *m*, WC.

we [wi:] *pers pron* nosotros,-as.

weak [wi:k] *adj* débil; *(argument, excuse)* pobre; *(team, piece of work, tea)* flojo,-a.

weaken ['wi:kən] I *vtr* debilitar; *(argument)* quitar fuerza a. II *vi* 1 debilitarse. 2 *(concede ground)* ceder.

weakling ['wi:klɪŋ] *n* enclenque *mf*.

weakness ['wi:knɪs] *n* debilidad *f*; *(character flaw)* punto flaco.

wealth [welθ] *n* riqueza *f*; *fig* abundancia *f*.

wealthy ['welθɪ] *adj* **(wealthier, wealthiest)** rico,-a.

wean [wi:n] *vtr* **(child)** destetar; *fig* **to w. sb from the habit**, desacostumbrar (gradualmente) a algn de un hábito.

weapon ['wepən] *n* arma *f*.

wear [weəʳ] I *vtr* (*pt* **wore**; *pp* **worn**) 1 *(clothes)* llevar puesto, vestir; *(shoes)* llevar puestos, calzar; **he wears glasses**, lleva gafas; **to w. black**, vestirse de negro. 2 *(erode)* desgastar. II *vi* to w. **(thin/smooth)**, desgastarse (con el roce); *fig* **my patience is wearing thin**, se me está acabando la paciencia. III *n* 1 ropa *f*; **leisure w.**, ropa de sport. 2 *(use) (clothes)* uso *m*. 3 *(deterioration)* desgaste *m*; **normal w. and tear**, desgaste natural. ◆**wear away** I *vtr* erosionar. II *vi (stone etc)* erosionarse; *(inscription)* borrarse. ◆**wear down** I *vtr* **(heels)** desgastar; *fig* **to w. sb down**, vencer la resistencia de algn. II *vi* desgastarse. ◆**wear off** *vi (effect, pain)* pasar, desaparecer. ◆**wear out** I *vtr* gastar; *fig* agotar. II *vi* gastarse.

wearisome ['wɪərɪsəm] *adj* fatigoso,-a.

weary ['wɪərɪ] I *adj* **(wearier, weariest)** 1 *(tired)* cansado,-a. 2 *(fed up)* harto,-a. II *vtr* cansar. III *vi* cansarse (**of**, de). ◆**wearily** *adv* con cansancio.

weasel ['wi:zəl] *n* comadreja *f*.

weather ['weðəʳ] I *n* tiempo *m*; **the w. is fine**, hace buen tiempo; *fig* **to feel under the w.**, no encontrarse bien; **w. chart**, mapa meteorológico; **w. forecast**, parte meteorológico; **w. vane**, veleta *f*. II *vtr* *fig (crisis)* aguantar; **to w. the storm**, capear el temporal.

weather-beaten ['weðəbi:tən] *adj* curtido,-a.

weathercock ['weðəkɒk] *n* veleta *f*.

weatherman ['weðəmæn] *n* hombre *m* del tiempo.

weave [wi:v] I *n* tejido *m*. II *vtr* **(wove**; *pp* **woven)** 1 *Tex* tejer. 2 *(interwine)* entretejer. 3 *(intrigues)* tramar. III *vi (person, road)* zigzaguear.

weaver ['wi:vəʳ] *n* tejedor,-a *m,f*.

web [web] *n* 1 *(of spider)* telaraña *f*. 2 *(of*

lies) sarta *f*.

webbed [webd] *adj* Orn palmeado,-a.

wed [wed] *vtr arch* (*pt* & *pp* **wed** *or* **wedded**) casarse con.

wedding ['wedɪŋ] *n* boda *f*, casamiento *m*; **w. cake**, tarta *f* nupcial; **w. day**, día *m* de la boda; **w. dress**, traje *m* de novia; **w. present**, regalo *m* de boda; **w. ring**, alianza *f*.

wedge [wedʒ] I *n* 1 cuña *f*; *(for table leg)* calce *m*. 2 *(of cake, cheese)* trozo *m* grande. II *vtr* calzar; **to be wedged tight**, *(object)* estar completamente atrancado,-a.

Wednesday ['wenzdɪ] *n* miércoles *m*.

wee¹ [wi:] *adj esp Scot* pequeñito,-a.

wee² [wi:] *fam* I *n* pipí *m*. II *vi* hacer pipí.

weed [wi:d] I *n* 1 *Bot* mala hierba. II *vtr* 1 *(garden)* escardar. 2 *fig* **to w. out**, eliminar. III *vi* escardar.

weedkiller ['wi:dkɪləʳ] *n* herbicida *m*.

weedy ['wi:dɪ] *adj* **(weeedier, weediest)** *pej* debilucho,-a.

week [wi:k] *n* semana *f*; **a w.** (**ago**) **today/yesterday**, hoy hace/ayer hizo una semana; **a w. today**, justo dentro de una semana; **last/next w.**, la semana pasada/que viene; **once a w.**, una vez por semana; **w. in, w. out**, semana tras semana.

weekday ['wi:kdeɪ] *n* día *m* laborable.

weekend [wi:k'end] *n* fin *m* de semana.

weekly ['wi:klɪ] I *adj* semanal. II *adv* semanalmente; **twice w.**, dos veces por semana. III *Press* semanario *m*.

weep [wi:p] I *vi* (*pt* & *pp* **wept**) llorar; **to w. for sb**, llorar la muerte de algn. II *vtr* *(tears)* derramar.

weeping ['wi:pɪŋ] *adj* **w. willow**, sauce *m* llorón.

weigh [weɪ] I *vtr* 1 pesar. 2 *fig (consider)* ponderar. 3 **to w. anchor**, levar anclas. II *vi* 1 pesar. 2 *fig (influence)* influir. ◆**weigh down** *vtr* sobrecargar. ◆**weigh in** *vi* 1 *Sport* pesarse. 2 *fam (join in)* intervenir. ◆**weigh up** *vtr (matter)* evaluar; *(person)* formar una opinión sobre; **to w. up the pros and cons**, sopesar los pros y los contras.

weight [weɪt] I *n* peso *m*; **to lose w.**, adelgazar; **to put on w.**, subir de peso; *fam fig* **to pull one's w.**, poner de su parte. 2 *(of clock, scales)* pesa *f*. 3 *fig* **that's a w. off my mind**, eso me quita un peso de encima.

weighting ['weɪtɪŋ] *n* GB *(on salary)* suplemento *m* de salario.

weightlifter ['weɪtlɪftəʳ] *n* halterófilo,-a *m,f*.

weighty ['weɪtɪ] *adj* **(weightier, weightiest)** pesado,-a; *fig (problem, matter)* importante, grave; *(argument)* de peso.

weir [wɪəʳ] *n* presa *f*.

weird [wɪəd] *adj* raro,-a, extraño,-a.

welcome ['welkəm] I *adj (person)*

bienvenido,-a; (news) grato,-a; (change) oportuno,-a; **to make sb w.**, acoger a algn calurosamente; **you're w.!**, ¡no hay de qué! II *n* (greeting) bienvenida *f*. III *vtr* acoger; (more formally) darle la bienvenida a; (news) acoger con agrado; (decision) aplaudir.

welcoming ['welkəmɪŋ] *adj* (person) acogedor,-a; (smile) de bienvenida.

weld [weld] *vtr* soldar.

welfare ['welfeər] *n* 1 (well-being) bienestar *m*; **animal/child w.**, protección *f* de animales/de menores; **w. work**, asistencia *f* social; **w. worker**, asistente *mf* social. 2 *US* (social security) seguridad *f* social.

well[1] [wel] *n* 1 pozo *m*. 2 (of staircase, lift) hueco *m*. 3 (of court hall) hemiciclo *m*. ◆**well up** *vi* brotar.

well[2] [wel] I *adj* 1 (healthy) bien; **are you keeping w.?**, estás bien de salud?; **to get w.**, reponerse. 2 (satisfactory); **all is w.**, todo va bien; **it's just as w.**, menos mal. 3 **it is as w. to remember this**, conviene recordar eso.

II *adv* (better, best) 1 (properly) bien; **he has done w. (for himself)**, ha prosperado; **the business is doing w.**, el negocio marcha bien; **she did w. in the exam**, el examen le fue bien; **w. done!**, ¡muy bien! **he took it w.**, lo tomó a bien. 2 (thoroughly) bien; **I know it only too w.**, lo sé de sobra; *Culin* **w. done**, muy hecho,-a. 3 **he's w. over thirty**, tiene treinta años bien cumplidos; **w. after six o'clock**, mucho después de las seis. 4 (easily, with good reason) **he couldn't very w. say no**, difícilmente podía decir que no; **I may w. do that**, puede que haga eso. 5 **as w.**, también; **as w. as**, así como; **children as w. as adults**, tanto niños como adultos.

III *interj* 1 (surprise) ¡bueno!, ¡vaya!; **w. I never!**, ¡no me digas! 2 (agreement, interrogation, resignation) bueno; **very w.**, bueno; **w.?**, ¿y bien? 3 (doubt) pues; **w., I don't know**, pues no sé. 4 (resumption) **w., as I was saying**, pues (bien), como iba diciendo.

well-behaved ['welbɪheɪvd] *adj* (child) formal, educado,-a.

well-being ['welbiːɪŋ] *n* bienestar *m*.

well-built ['welbɪlt] *adj* (building etc) de construcción sólida; (person) fornido,-a.

well-earned ['welɜːnd] *adj* merecido,-a.

well-educated [wel'edukeɪtɪd] *adj* culto,-a.

well-heeled ['welhiːld] *adj* *fam* adinerado,-a.

wellingtons ['welɪŋtənz] *npl* botas *fpl* de goma.

well-informed ['welɪnfɔːmd] *adj* bien informado,-a.

well-known ['welnəʊn] *adj* (bien)

conocido,-a.

well-mannered ['welmænəd] *adj* educado,-a.

well-meaning [wel'miːnɪŋ] *adj* bien intencionado,-a.

well-off [wel'ɒf] *adj* (rich) acomodado,-a.

well-read [wel'red] *adj* culto,-a.

well-spoken [wel'spəʊkən] *adj* con acento culto.

well-to-do [weltə'duː] *adj* acomodado,-a.

well-wisher ['welwɪʃər] *n* admirador,-a *m,f*.

Welsh [welʃ] I *adj* galés,-esa; **W. rarebit**, tostada *f* con queso fundido. II *n* 1 (language) galés *m*. 2 **the W.**, *pl* los galeses.

Welshman ['welʃmən] *n* galés *m*.

Welshwoman ['welʃwʊmən] *n* galesa *f*.

welterweight ['weltəweɪt] *n* (peso *m*) wélter *m*.

wench [wentʃ] *n* dated pej moza *f*.

went [went] *pt* → **go**.

wept [wept] *pt & pp* → **weep**.

were [wɜːr, unstressed wər] *pt* → **be**.

west [west] I *n* oeste *m*, occidente *m*; **in** or **to the w.**, al oeste; *Pol* **the W.**, los países occidentales. II *adj* del oeste, occidental; **the W. Indies**, las Antillas; **W. Indian**, antillano,-a. III *adv* al oeste, hacia el oeste.

westerly ['westəlɪ] *adj* (wind) del oeste.

western ['westən] I *adj* del oeste, occidental; **W. Europe**, Europa Occidental. II *n* *Cin* western *m*, película *f* del oeste.

westward ['westwəd] *adj* in a w. direction, hacia el oeste.

westwards ['westwədz] *adv* hacia el oeste.

wet [wet] I *adj* (wetter, wettest) 1 mojado,-a; (slightly) húmedo,-a; '**w. paint**', 'recién pintado'; **w. through**, (person) calado,-a hasta los huesos; (thing) empapado,-a; **w. suit**, traje isotérmico. 2 (rainy) lluvioso,-a. 3 *fam* (person) soso,-a; **w. blanket**, aguafiestas *mf inv*. II *n* *fam* apocado,-a *m,f*. III *vtr* (pt & pp wet) mojar; **to w. oneself**, orinarse.

whack [wæk] I *vtr* (hit hard) golpear fuertemente. II *n* 1 (blow) porrazo *m*. 2 *fam* (share) parte *f*, porción *f*.

whale [weɪl] *n* (pl whale or whales) ballena *f*.

wharf [wɔːf] *n* (pl wharves ['wɔːvz]) muelle *m*.

what [wɒt, unstressed wət] I *adj* 1 (direct question) qué; **w.** (sort of) bird is that?, ¿qué tipo de ave es ésa?; **w. good is that?**, ¿para qué sirve eso? 2 (indirect question) qué; **ask her w. colour she likes**, pregúntale qué color le gusta.

II *pron* 1 (direct question) qué; **w. are you talking about?**, ¿de qué estás hablando?; **w. about your father?**, ¿y tu padre (qué)?; **w. about going tomorrow?**, ¿qué te parece si vamos mañana?; **w. can I do for you?**, ¿en qué puedo servirle?; **w. did it cost?**, ¿cuánto costó?; **w. did you do that for?**, ¿por qué hiciste eso?; **w. (did you say)?**, ¿cómo?; **w. does it sound like?**, ¿cómo suena?; **w. is happening?**, ¿qué pasa?; **w. is it?**, *(definition)* ¿qué es?; *(what's the matter)* ¿qué pasa?; **w.'s it called?**, ¿cómo se llama?; **w.'s this for?**, ¿para qué sirve esto? **2** *(indirect question)* qué, lo que; **he asked me w.** I thought, me preguntó lo que pensaba; **I didn't know w. to say**, no sabía qué decir. **3** *(and)* **w.'s more**, y además; **come w. may**, pase lo que pase; **guess w.!**, ¿sabes qué?; **it's just w. I need**, es exactamente lo que necesito. **4** *exclam (surprise, indignation)* ¡cómo!; **w., no dessert!**, ¿cómo, no hay postre? **III** *interj* **w. a goal!**, ¡qué *or* vaya golazo!; **w. a lovely picture!**, ¡qué cuadro más bonito!

whatever [wɒt'evə^r, *unstressed* wət'evə^r] **I** *adj* **1** *(any)* cualquiera que; **at w. time you like**, a la hora que quieras; **w. colour**, no importa de qué color. **2** *(with negative)* **nothing w.**, nada en absoluto; **with no interest w.**, sin interés alguno. **II** *pron* **1** *(anything, all that)* (todo) lo que; **do w. you like**, haz lo que quieras. **2** *(no matter what)* **don't tell him w. you do**, no se le ocurra decírselo; **w. (else) you find**, cualquier (otra) cosa que encuentres; **he goes out w. the weather**, sale haga el tiempo que haga. **III** *inter* **w. happened?**, ¿qué pasó?

whatsoever [wɒtsəʊ'evə^r] *adj* **anything w.**, cualquier cosa; **nothing w.**, nada en absoluto.

wheat [wiːt] *n* trigo *m*; **w. germ**, germen *m* de trigo.

wheedle ['wiːdəl] *vtr* **to w. sb into doing sth**, engatusar a algn para que haga algo; **to w. sth out of sb**, sonsacar algo a algn halagándole.

wheel [wiːl] **I** *n* rueda *f*. **II** *vtr (bicycle)* empujar. **III** *vi* **1** *(bird)* revolotear. **2** **to w. round**, girar sobre los talones.

wheelbarrow ['wiːlbærəʊ] *n* carretilla *f*.

wheelchair ['wiːltʃeə^r] *n* silla *f* de ruedas.

wheeze [wiːz] *vi* respirar con dificultad, resollar.

when [wen] **I** *adv* **1** *(direct question)* cuándo; **since w.?**, ¿desde cuándo?; **w. did he arrive?**, ¿cuándo llegó? **2** *(indirect question)* cuándo; **tell me w. to go**, dime cuándo debo irme. **3** *(on which)* cuando, en que; **the days w. I work**, los días en que trabajo. **II** *conj* **1** cuando; **I'll tell you w. she comes**, se lo diré cuando llegue; **w. he was a boy ...**, de niño .... **2** *(whenever)* cuando. **3** *(given that, if)* si. **4** *(although)* aunque.

whence [wens] *adv fml lit (from where)* de

dónde.

whenever [wen'evə^r] **I** *conj (when)* cuando; *(every time)* siempre que. **II** *adv* **w. that might be**, sea cuando sea.

where [weə^r] *adv* **1** *(direct question)* dónde; *(direction)* adónde; **w. are you going?**, ¿adónde vas?; **w. did we go wrong?**, ¿en qué nos equivocamos?; **w. do you come from?**, ¿de dónde es usted? **2** *(indirect question)* dónde; *(direction)* adónde; **tell me w. you went**, dime a-dónde fuiste. **3** *(at, in which)* donde; *(direction)* adonde, a donde. **4** *(when)* cuando.

whereabouts [weərə'baʊts] **I** *adv* **w. do you live?**, ¿por dónde vives? **II** ['weərəbaʊts] *n* paradero *m*.

whereas [weər'æz] *conj* **1** *(but, while)* mientras que. **2** *Jur* considerando que.

whereby [weə'baɪ] *adv* por el *or* a lo cual.

whereupon [weərə'pɒn] *conj fml* después de lo cual.

wherever [weər'evə^r] **I** *conj* dondequiera que; **I'll find him w. he is**, le encontraré dondequiera que esté; **sit w. you like**, siéntate donde quieras. **II** *adv (direct question)* adónde.

wherewithal ['weəwɪðɔːl] *n fam* pelas *fpl*.

whet [wet] *vtr* **to w. sb's appetite**, abrir el apetito a algn.

whether ['weðə^r] *conj* **1** *(if)* si; **I don't know w. it is true**, no sé si es verdad; **I doubt w. he'll win**, dudo que gane. **2** **w. he comes or not**, venga o no.

which [wɪtʃ] **I** *adj* **1** *(direct question)* qué; **w. colour do you prefer?**, ¿qué color prefieres?; **w. one?**, ¿cuál?; **w. way?**, ¿por dónde? **2** *(indirect question)* qué; **tell me w. dress you like**, dime qué vestido te gusta. **3 by w. time**, y para entonces; **in w. case**, en cuyo caso.

II *pron* **1** *(direct question)* cuál, cuáles; **w. of you did it?**, ¿quién de vosotros lo hizo? **2** *(indirect question)* cuál, cuáles; **I don't know w. I'd rather have**, no sé cuál prefiero. **3** *(defining relative)* que; *(after preposition)* que, el *or* la cual, los *or* las cuales, el *or* la que, los *or* las que; **here are the books w. I have read**, aquí están los libros que he leído; **the accident (w.) I told you about**, el accidente del que te hablé; **the car in w. he was travelling**, el coche en (el) que viajaba; **this is the one (w.) I like**, éste es el que me gusta. **4** *(non-defining relative)* el *or* la cual, los *or* las cuales; **I played three sets, all of w. I lost**, jugué tres sets, todos los cuales perdí. **5** *(referring to a clause)* lo cual, lo que; **he won, w. made me very happy**, ganó, lo cual *or* lo que me alegró mucho.

whichever [wɪtʃ'evə^r] **I** *adj* el/la que, cualquiera que; **I'll take w. books you**

don't want, tomaré los libros que no quieras; **w. system you choose,** cualquiera que sea el sistema que elijas. II *pron* el que, la que.

whiff [wɪf] *n* 1 *(quick smell)* ráfaga *f*; *(of air, smoke)* bocanada *f*. 2 *fam (bad smell)* tufo *m*.

while [waɪl] I *n* 1 *(length of time)* rato *m*, tiempo *m*; **in a little w.,** dentro de poco; **once in a w.,** de vez en cuando. 2 **it's not worth your w. staying,** no merece la pena que te quedes. II *conj* 1 *(time)* mientras; **he fell asleep w. driving,** se durmió mientras conducía. 2 *(although)* aunque. 3 *(whereas)* mientras que. ◆**while away** *vtr* **to w. away the time,** pasar el rato.

whilst [waɪlst] *conj* → **while** III.

whim [wɪm] *n* capricho *m*, antojo *m*.

whimper ['wɪmpər] I *n* quejido *m*. II *vi* lloriquear.

whine [waɪn] *vi* 1 *(child)* lloriquear; *(with pain)* dar quejidos. 2 *(complain)* quejarse. 3 *(engine)* chirriar.

whip [wɪp] I *n* 1 *(for punishment)* látigo *m*; *(for riding)* fusta *f*. 2 *GB Parl* oficial *mf* encargado,-a de la disciplina de un partido. II *vtr* 1 *(as punishment)* azotar; *(horse)* fustigar. 2 *Culin* batir; **whipped cream,** nata montada. 3 *fam (steal)* mangar. ◆**whip away** *vtr* arrebatar. ◆**whip up** *vtr* *(passions, enthusiasm)* avivar; *(support)* incrementar.

whipping ['wɪpɪŋ] *n* fig **w. boy,** cabeza *f* de turco.

whip-round ['wɪpraʊnd] *n fam* colecta *f*.

whirl [wɜːl] I *n* 1 giro *m*; *fig* torbellino *m*. II *vtr* **to w. sth round,** dar vueltas a *or* hacer girar algo. III *vi* **to w. round,** girar con rapidez; *(leaves etc)* arremolinarse; **my head's whirling,** me está dando vueltas la cabeza.

whirlpool ['wɜːlpuːl] *n* remolino *m*.

whirlwind ['wɜːlwɪnd] *n* torbellino *m*.

whir(r) [wɜːr] *vi* zumbar, runrunear.

whisk [wɪsk] I *n Culin* batidor *m*; *(electric)* batidora *f*. II *vtr Culin* batir. ◆**whisk away, whisk off** *vtr* quitar bruscamente; llevarse de repente.

whisker ['wɪskər] *n* **whiskers,** *(of person)* patillas *fpl*; *(of cat)* bigotes *mpl*.

whisky, *US* **whiskey** ['wɪskɪ] *n* whisky *m*.

whisper ['wɪspər] I *n* 1 *(sound)* susurro *m*. 2 *(rumour)* rumor *m*. II *vtr* decir en voz baja. III *vi* susurrar.

whistle ['wɪsəl] I *n* 1 *(instrument)* pito *m*. 2 *(sound)* silbido *m*, pitido *m*. II *vtr (tune)* silbar. III *vi* 1 *(person, kettle, wind)* silbar; *(train)* pitar.

white [waɪt] I *adj* blanco,-a; **to go w.,** *(face)* palidecer; *(hair)* encanecer; **w. coffee,** café *m* con leche; **w. hair,** pelo cano; **a w. Christmas,** una Navidad con nieve; *fig* **a w. lie,** una mentira piadosa;

US **the W. House,** la Casa Blanca; *Pol* **w. paper,** libro blanco; **w. sauce,** bechamel *f*. II *n* 1 *(colour, person, of eye)* blanco *m*. 2 *(of egg)* clara *f*. 3 **whites,** ropa *f sing* blanca.

white-collar ['waɪtkɒlər] *adj* **w.-c. worker,** empleado *m* de oficina.

whiteness ['waɪtnɪs] *n* blancura *f*.

whitewash ['waɪtwɒʃ] I *n* 1 cal *f*. 2 *fig (cover-up)* encubrimiento *m*. 3 *fig (defeat)* paliza *f*. II *vtr* 1 *(wall)* enjalbegar, blanquear. 2 *fig* encubrir.

whiting ['waɪtɪŋ] *n inv (fish)* pescadilla *f*.

Whitsun(tide) ['wɪtsən(taɪd)] *n* pentecostés *m*.

whittle ['wɪtəl] *vtr* cortar en pedazos; **to w. away at,** roer; *fig* **to w. down,** reducir poco a poco.

whiz(z) [wɪz] *vi* 1 *(sound)* silbar. **2 to w. past,** pasar volando; *fam* **w. kid,** joven *mf* dinámico,-a y emprendedor,-a.

who [huː] *pron* 1 *(direct question)* quién, quiénes; **w. are they?** ¿quiénes son?; **w. is it?** ¿quién es? 2 *(indirect question)* quién; **I don't know w. did it,** no sé quién lo hizo. 3 *rel (defining)* que; **those w. don't know,** los que no saben. 4 *rel (nondefining)* quien, quienes, el *o* la cual, los *or* las cuales; **Elena's mother, w. is very rich ...,** la madre de Elena, la cual es muy rica ....

whodun(n)it [huː'dʌnɪt] *n fam* novela *f or* obra *f* de teatro *or* película *f* de suspense.

whoever [huː'evər] *pron* 1 quienquiera que; **give it to w. you like,** dáselo a quien quieras; **w. said that is a fool,** el que dijo eso es un tonto; **w. you are,** quienquiera que seas. 2 *(direct question)* **w. told you that?** ¿quién te dijo eso?

whole [həʊl] I *adj* 1 *(entire)* entero,-a, íntegro,-a. **a w. week,** una semana entera; **he took the w. lot,** se los llevó todos. 2 *(in one piece)* intacto,-a. II *n* 1 *(single unit)* todo *m*, conjunto *m*; **as a w.,** en su totalidad. 2 *(all)* totalidad *f*; **the w. of London,** todo Londres. 3 **on the w.,** en general.

wholefood ['həʊlfuːd] *n* alimentos *mpl* integrales.

wholehearted [həʊl'hɑːtɪd] *adj (enthusiastic)* entusiasta; *(sincere)* sincero,-a; *(unreserved)* incondicional.

wholemeal ['həʊlmiːl] *adj* integral.

wholesale ['həʊlseɪl] *Com* I *n* venta *f* al por mayor. II *adj* al por mayor; *fig* total. III *adv* al por mayor; *fig* en su totalidad.

wholesaler ['həʊlseɪlər] *n* mayorista *mf*.

wholesome ['həʊlsəm] *adj* sano,-a.

wholly ['həʊlɪ] *adv* enteramente, completamente.

whom [huːm] *pron fml* 1 *(direct question)* *(accusative)* a quién?; **w. did you talk to?,** ¿con quién hablaste?; *(after preposition)* **of/from w.?,** ¿de quién?; **w. are you**

referring?, ¿a quién te refieres? 2 *rel (accusative)* que, a quien, a quienes; **those w. I have seen**, aquéllos a quien he visto. 3 *rel (after preposition)* quien, quienes, el *o* la cual, los *o* las cuales; **my brothers, both of w. are miners**, mis hermanos, que son mineros los dos.

whooping cough ['hu:pɪŋkɒf] *n* tos ferina.

whopping ['wɒpɪŋ] *adj fam* enorme.

whore [hɔːʳ] *n offens* puta *f*.

whose [huːz] I *pron* 1 *(direct question)* de quién, de quiénes; **w. are these gloves?**, ¿de quién son estos guantes?; **w. is this?**, ¿de quién es esto? 2 *(indirect question)* de quién, de quiénes; **I don't know w. these coats are**, no sé de quién son estos abrigos. 3 *rel* cuyo(s), cuya(s); **the man w. children we saw**, el hombre a cuyos hijos vimos. II *adj* **w. car/house is this?**, ¿de quién es este coche/esta casa?

why [waɪ] I *adv* por qué; *(for what purpose)* para qué; **w. did you do that?**, ¿por qué hiciste eso?; **w. not go to bed?**, ¿por qué no te acuestas?; **I don't know w. he did it**, no sé por qué lo hizo; **that is w. I didn't come**, por eso no vine; **there's no reason w. you shouldn't go**, no hay motivo para que no vayas. II *interj* 1 *(fancy that!)* ¡toma!, ¡vaya!; **w., it's David!**, ¡si es David! 2 *(protest, assertion)* sí, vamos.

wick [wɪk] *n* mecha *f*.

wicked ['wɪkɪd] *adj* 1 malvado,-a. 2 *fam* malísimo,-a; *(temper)* de perros.

wicker ['wɪkaʳ] I *n* mimbre. II *adj* de mimbre.

wickerwork ['wɪkəwɜːk] *n (material)* mimbre *m*; *(articles)* artículos *mpl* de mimbre.

wicket ['wɪkɪt] *n Cricket (stumps)* palos *mpl*.

wide [waɪd] I *adj* 1 *(road, trousers)* ancho,-a; *(gap, interval)* grande; **it is ten metres w.**, tiene diez metros de ancho. 2 *(area, knowledge, support, range)* amplio, -a; **w. interests**, intereses muy diversos. 3 *(off target)* desviado,-a. II *adv* **from far and w.**, de todas partes; **to open one's eyes w.**, abrir los ojos de par en par; **w. apart**, muy separados,-as; **w. awake**, completamente despierto,-a; **w. open**, abierto,-a de par en par; **with mouth w. open**, boquiabierto,-a. ◆**widely** *adv (travel etc)* extensamente; *(believed)* generalmente; **he is w. known**, es muy conocido.

wide-angle ['waɪdæŋgəl] *adj Phot* **w.-a. lens**, objetivo *m* gran angular.

widen ['waɪdən] I *vtr* ensanchar; *(interests)* ampliar. II *vi* ensancharse.

wide-ranging ['waɪdreɪndʒɪŋ] *adj (interests)* muy diversos,-as; *(discussion)* amplio,-a; *(study)* de gran alcance.

widespread ['waɪdspred] *adj (unrest, belief)* general; *(damage)* extenso,-a; **to become w.**, generalizarse.

widow ['wɪdəʊ] *n* viuda *f*.

widowed ['wɪdəʊd] *adj* enviudado,-a.

widower ['wɪdəʊəʳ] *n* viudo *m*.

width [wɪdθ] *n* 1 anchura *f*. 2 *(of material, swimming pool)* ancho *m*.

wield [wiːld] *vtr (weapon)* blandir; *fig (power)* ejercer.

wife [waɪf] *n (pl wives)* mujer *f*, esposa *f*.

wig [wɪg] *n* peluca *f*.

wiggle ['wɪgəl] I *vtr (finger etc)* menear; **to w. one's hips**, contonearse. II *vi* menearse.

Wight [waɪt] *n* **Isle of W.**, Isla *f* de Wight.

wild [waɪld] I *adj* 1 *(animal, tribe)* salvaje; **w. beast**, fiera *f*; *fig* **w. goose chase**, búsqueda *f* inútil. 2 *(plant)* silvestre. 3 *(landscape)* agreste; **the W. West**, el Salvaje Oeste. 4 *(temperament, behaviour)* alocado,-a; *(appearance)* desordenado,-a; *(passions etc)* desenfrenado,-a; *(laughter, thoughts)* loco,-a; *(applause)* fervoroso,-a; **to make a w. guess**, adivinar al azar; *fam fig* **she is w. about him/about tennis**, está loca por él/por el tenis. 5 *GB fam fig (angry)* furioso,-a. II *adv fig* **to run w.**, *(children)* desmandarse. III *n* **in the w.**, en el estado salvaje; *fig* **to live out in the wilds**, vivir en el quinto pino. ◆**wildly** *adv* 1 *(rush round etc)* como un,-a loco,-a; *(shoot)* sin apuntar; *(hit out)* a tontas y a locas. 2 **w. enthusiastic**, loco,-a de entusiasmo; **w. inaccurate**, totalmente erróneo,-a.

wildcat ['waɪldkæt] *n* **w. strike**, huelga *f* salvaje.

wilderness ['wɪldənɪs] *n* desierto *m*.

wildfire ['waɪldfaɪəʳ] *n* **to spread like w.**, correr como la pólvora.

wildlife ['waɪldlaɪf] *n* fauna *f*; **w. park**, parque *m* natural.

wilful, *US* **willful** ['wɪlfʊl] *adj 1 (stubborn)* terco,-a. 2 *Jur* premeditado,-a.

will¹ [wɪl] I *n* 1 voluntad *f*; **good/ill w.**, buena/mala voluntad; **of my own free w.**, por mi propia voluntad. 2 *Jur (testament)* testamento *m*; **to make one's w.**, hacer testamento. II *vtr* **fate willed that ...**, el destino quiso que ....

will² [wɪl] *v aux (pt would)* 1 *(future) (esp 2nd & 3rd person)* they'll come, vendrán; **w. he be there? - yes, he w.**, ¿estará allí? - sí, (estará); **you'll tell him, won't you?**, se lo dirás, ¿verdad?; **don't forget, w. you!**, ¡que no se te olvide, vale!; **she won't do it**, no lo hará. 2 *(command)* you **w. be here at eleven!**, ¡debes estar aquí a las once! 3 *(future perfect)* they'll have finished by tomorrow, habrán terminado para mañana. 4 *(willingness)* **be quiet, w. you! - no, I won't!**, ¡quiere callarse? -

no quiero; **I won't have it!**, ¡no lo permito!; **will you have a drink? - yes, I w.**, ¿quiere tomar algo? - sí, por favor; **won't you sit down?**, ¿quiere sentarse? 5 *(custom)* **accidents w. happen**, siempre habrá accidentes. 6 *(persistence)* **if you w. go out without a coat ...**, si te empeñas en salir sin abrigo .... 7 *(probability)* **he'll be on holiday now**, ahora estará de vacaciones. 8 *(ability)* **the lift w. hold ten people**, en el ascensor caben diez personas.

willing ['wılıŋ] *adj (obliging)* complaciente; **I'm quite w. to do it**, lo haré con mucho gusto; **to be w. to do sth**, estar dispuesto,-a a hacer algo. ◆**willingly** *adv* de buena gana.

willingness ['wılıŋnıs] *n* buena voluntad.

willow ['wıləu] *n* **w. (tree)**, sauce *m*.

willpower ['wılpauər] *n* (fuerza *f* de) voluntad *f*.

willy-nilly [wılı'nılı] *adv* por gusto o por fuerza.

wilt [wılt] *vi* marchitarse.

wily ['waılı] *adj (wilier, wiliest)* astuto,-a.

win [wın] **I** *n* victoria *f*. **II** *vtr (pt & pp* **won)** 1 ganar; *(prize)* llevarse; *(victory)* conseguir. 2 *fig (sympathy, friendship)* ganarse; *(praise)* cosechar; **to w. sb's love**, conquistar a algn. **III** *vi* ganar. ◆**win back** *vtr* recuperar. ◆**win over** *vtr (to cause, idea)* atraer **(to,** a hacia); *(voters, support)* ganarse. ◆**win through** *vi* conseguir triunfar.

wince [wıns] *vi* tener un rictus de dolor.

winch [wıntʃ] *n* cigüeña *f*, torno *m*.

wind¹ [wınd] **I** *n* 1 viento *m*; *fig* **to get w. of sth**, olerse algo; **w. tunnel**, túnel aerodinámico. 2 *(breath)* aliento *m*; **to get one's second w.**, recobrar el aliento. 3 *Med* flato *m*, gases *mpl*. 4 **w. instrument**, instrumento *m* de viento. **II** *vtr* **to be winded**, quedarse sin aliento.

wind² [waınd] **I** *vtr (pt & pp* **wound)** 1 *(onto a reel)* enrollar; **to w. a bandage round one's finger**, vendarse el dedo. 2 **to w. on/back**, *(film, tape)* avanzar/rebobinar. 3 *(clock)* dar cuerda a. **II** *vi (road, river)* serpentear. ◆**wind down I** *vtr (window)* bajar. **II** *vi fam (person)* relajarse. ◆**wind up I** *vtr* 1 *(roll up)* enrollar. 2 *(business etc)* cerrar; *(debate)* clausurar. 3 *(clock)* dar cuerda a. **II** *vi (meeting)* terminar.

windfall ['wındfɔːl] *n fig* ganancia inesperada.

winding ['waındıŋ] *adj (road, river)* sinuoso,-a; *(staircase)* de caracol.

windmill ['wındmıl] *n* molino *m* (de viento).

window ['wındəu] *n* ventana *f*; *(of vehicle, ticket office etc)* ventanilla *f*; *(shop)* **w.**, escaparate *m*; **to clean the windows**, limpiar los cristales; **w. box**, jardinera *f*;

w. cleaner, limpiacristales *mf inv*.

windowpane ['wındəupeın] *n* cristal *m*.

window-shopping ['wındəuʃɒpıŋ] *n* **to go w.-s.**, ir a mirar escaparates.

windowsill ['wındəusıl] *n* alféizar *m*.

windpipe ['wındpaıp] *n* tráquea *f*.

windscreen ['wındskriːn], *US* **windshield** ['wındʃiːld] *n* parabrisas *m inv*; **w. washer**, lavaparabrisas *m inv*; **w. wiper**, limpiaparabrisas *m inv*.

windswept ['wındswept] *adj (landscape)* expuesto,-a a los vientos; *(person, hair)* despeinado,-a (por el viento).

windy ['wındı] *adj (windier, windiest)* *(weather)* ventoso,-a; *(place)* desprotegido,-a del viento; **it is very w. today**, hoy hace mucho viento.

wine [waın] *n* vino *m*; **w. cellar**, bodega *f*; **w. list**, lista *f* de vinos; **w. merchant**, vinatero,-a *m,f*; **w. tasting**, cata *f* de vinos; **w. vinegar**, vinagre *m* de vino.

wineglass ['waınglɑːs] *n* copa *f* (para vino).

wing [wıŋ] *n* 1 *Orn Av* ala *f*. 2 *(of building)* ala *f*. 3 *Aut* aleta *f*; **w. mirror**, retrovisor *m* externo. 4 *Theat* **(in the) wings**, *(entre)* bastidores *mpl*. 5 *Ftb* banda *f*. 6 *Pol* ala *f*; **the left w.**, la izquierda.

winger ['wıŋər] *n Ftb* extremo *m*.

wink [wıŋk] **I** *n* guiño *m*; *fam fig* **I didn't get a w. (of sleep)**, no pegué ojo. **II** *vi* 1 *(person)* guiñar (el ojo). 2 *(light)* parpadear.

winner ['wınər] *n* ganador,-a *m,f*.

winning ['wınıŋ] *adj (person, team)* ganador,-a; *(number)* premiado,-a; *(goal)* decisivo,-a; **w. post**, meta *f*.

winnings ['wınıŋz] *npl* ganancias *fpl*.

winter ['wıntər] **I** *n* invierno *m*. **II** *adj* de invierno; **w. sports**, deportes *mpl* de invierno. **III** *vi* invernar.

wintry ['wıntrı] *adj (wintrier, wintriest)* invernal.

wipe [waıp] **I** *vtr* limpiar; **to w. one's brow**, enjugarse la frente; **to w. one's feet/nose**, limpiarse los pies/las narices. ◆**wipe away** *vtr (tear)* enjugar. ◆**wipe off** *vtr* quitar frotando; **to w. sth off the blackboard/the tape**, borrar algo de la pizarra/de la cinta. ◆**wipe out** *vtr* 1 *(erase)* borrar. 2 *(army)* aniquilar; *(species etc)* exterminar. ◆**wipe up** *vtr* limpiar.

wire [waıər] **I** *n* 1 alambre *m*; *Elec* cable *m*; *Tel* hilo; **w. cutters**, cizalla *f sing*. 2 *(telegram)* telegrama *m*. **II** *vtr* 1 **to w. (up) a house**, poner la instalación eléctrica de una casa; **to w. (up) an appliance to the mains**, conectar un aparato a la toma eléctrica. 2 *(information)* enviar por telegrama.

wireless ['waıəlıs] *n* radio *f*.

wiring ['waıərıŋ] *n (network)* cableado *m*; *(action)* instalación *f* del cableado.

wiry ['waɪərɪ] adj (wirier, wiriest) (hair) estropajoso,-a; (person) nervudo,-a.

wisdom ['wɪzdəm] n 1 (learning) sabiduría f, saber m. 2 (good sense) (of person) cordura f; (of action) sensatez f. 3 w. tooth, muela f del juicio.

wise [waɪz] adj 1 sabio,-a; a w. man, un sabio; the Three W. Men, los Reyes Magos. 2 (remark) juicioso,-a; (decision) acertado,-a; it would be w. to keep quiet, sería prudente callarse. ◆wisely adv (with prudence) prudentemente.

wisecrack ['waɪzkræk] n fam salida f, ocurrencia f.

wish [wɪʃ] I n 1 (desire) deseo m (for, de); to make a w., pedir un deseo. 2 best wishes, felicitaciones fpl; give your mother my best wishes, salude a su madre de mi parte; with best wishes, Peter, (at end of letter) saludos cordiales, Peter. II vtr 1 (want) querer, desear; I w. I could stay longer, me gustaría poder quedarme más tiempo; I w. you had told me!, ¡ojalá me lo hubieras dicho!; to w. to do sth, querer hacer algo. 2 to w. sb goodnight, darle las buenas noches a algn; to w. sb well, desearle a algn mucha suerte. III vi (want) desear; as you w., como quieras; do as you w., haga lo que quiera; to w. for sth, desear algo.

wishful ['wɪʃful] adj it's w. thinking, es hacerse ilusiones.

wishy-washy ['wɪʃɪwɒʃɪ] adj fam (person) soso,-a; (ideas) poco definido,-a.

wisp [wɪsp] n (of wool, hair) mechón m; (of smoke) voluta f.

wistful ['wɪstful] adj melancólico,-a.

wit [wɪt] n 1 (intelligence) (often pl) inteligencia f; fig to be at one's wits' end, estar para volverse loco,-a; fam fig to have one's wits about one, ser despabilado,-a. 2 (humour) ingenio m. 3 (person) ingenioso,-a m,f.

witch [wɪtʃ] n bruja f; fig w. hunt, caza f de brujas.

witchcraft ['wɪtʃkrɑːft] n brujería f.

with [wɪð, wɪθ] prep con; a room w. a bath, un cuarto con baño; do you have any money w. you?, ¿traes dinero?; the man w. the glasses, el hombre de las gafas; he went w. me/you, fue conmigo/contigo; fam w. (sugar) or without (sugar)?, ¿con o sin azúcar?; I have six w. this one, con éste tengo seis; w. all his faults, I admire him, le admiro con todos sus defectos; w. your permission, con su permiso; we're all w. you, (support) todos estamos contigo; you're not w. me, are you? (understand) no me entiendes, ¿verdad?; he's w. Lloyds, trabaja para Lloyds; she is popular w. her colleagues, todos sus colegas la estiman mucho; to fill a vase w. water, llenar un jarrón de agua; it is made w.

butter, está hecho con mantequilla; she put on weight w. so much eating, engordó de tanto comer; to be paralysed w. fear, estar paralizado,-a de miedo; w. experience, con la experiencia.

withdraw [wɪð'drɔː] I vtr (pt withdrew; pp withdrawn) 1 retirar, sacar; to w. money from the bank, sacar dinero del banco. 2 (go back on) retirar; (statement) retractarse de; (plan, claim) renunciar a. II vi 1 retirarse. 2 (drop out) renunciar.

withdrawal [wɪð'drɔːəl] n retirada f; (of statement) retractación f; (of complaint, plan) renuncia f; w. symptoms, síndrome m de abstinencia.

withdrawn [wɪð'drɔːn] adj (person) introvertido,-a.

wither ['wɪðər] vi marchitarse.

withering ['wɪðərɪŋ] adj (look) fulminante; (criticism) mordaz.

withhold [wɪð'həuld] vtr (pt & pp withheld [wɪð'held]) (money) retener; (decision) aplazar; (consent) negar; (information) ocultar.

within [wɪ'ðɪn] I prep 1 (inside) dentro de. 2 (range) the house is w. walking distance, se puede ir andando a la casa; situated w. five kilometres of the town, situado,-a a menos de cinco kilómetros de la ciudad; w. sight of the sea, con vistas al mar; fig w. an inch of death, a dos dedos de la muerte. 3 (time) they arrived w. a few days of each other, llegaron con pocos días de diferencia; w. the hour, dentro de una hora; w. the next five years, durante los cinco próximos años. II adv dentro; from w., desde dentro.

with-it ['wɪðɪt] adj fam she is very w. it, tiene ideas muy modernas; to get w. it, ponerse de moda.

without [wɪ'ðaut] prep sin; he did it w. my knowing, lo hizo sin que lo supiera yo; fig to do or go w. sth, (voluntarily) prescindir de algo; (forcibly) pasar(se) sin algo.

withstand [wɪð'stænd] vtr (pt & pp withstood) resistir a; (pain) aguantar.

witness ['wɪtnɪs] I n 1 (person) testigo mf; w. box, US w. stand, barra f de los testigos. 2 (evidence) to bear w. to sth, dar fe de algo. II vtr 1 (see) presenciar, ser testigo de. 2 fig (notice) notar. 3 jur to w. a document, firmar un documento como testigo.

witticism ['wɪtɪsɪzəm] n ocurrencia f, salida f.

witty ['wɪtɪ] adj (wittier, wittiest) ingenioso,-a, agudo,-a.

wives [waɪvz] npl → wife.

wizard ['wɪzəd] n hechicero m, mago m.

wizened ['wɪzənd] adj (face) arrugado,-a.

wobble ['wɒbəl] vi (table, chair etc) tambalearse; (jelly) temblar.

woe [wəʊ] *n lit* infortunio *m*; **w. betide you if I catch you!**, ¡ay de ti si te cojo!

woeful ['wəʊfʊl] *adj* **1** (*person*) afligido,-a. **2** (*sight*) penoso,-a; **w. ignorance**, una ignorancia lamentable.

woke [wəʊk] *pt* → **wake**[1].

woken ['wəʊkən] *pp* → **wake**[1].

wolf [wʊlf] *n* (*pl* **wolves**) lobo *m*; *fig* **a w. in sheep's clothing**, un lobo con piel de cordero.

woman ['wʊmən] *n* (*pl* **women**) mujer *f*; **old w.**, vieja *f*; **women's libber**, feminista *mf*; *fam* **women's lib**, movimiento *m* feminista; **women's rights**, derechos *mpl* de la mujer.

womanhood ['wʊmənhʊd] *n* (*adult*) edad adulta de la mujer.

womanizer ['wʊmənaɪzəʳ] *n* mujeriego *m*.

womanly ['wʊmənlɪ] *adj* femenino,-a.

womb [wuːm] *n* matriz *f*, útero *m*.

women ['wɪmɪn] *npl* → **woman**.

won [wʌn] *pt & pp* → **win**.

wonder ['wʌndəʳ] **I** *n* **1** (*miracle*) milagro *m*; **no w. he hasn't come**, no es de extrañar que no haya venido. **2** (*amazement*) admiración *f*, asombro *m*. **II** *vtr* **1** (*be surprised*) sorprenderse. **2** (*ask oneself*) preguntarse; **I w. why**, ¿por qué será? **III** *vi* **1** (*marvel*) maravillarse; **to w. at sth**, admirarse de algo. **2** **it makes you w.**, (*reflect*) te da qué pensar.

wonderful ['wʌndəfʊl] *adj* maravilloso,-a.
◆**wonderfully** *adv* maravillosamente.

wont [wəʊnt] *fml* **I** *adj* **to be w. to**, soler. **II** *n* costumbre; **it is his w. to ...**, tiene la costumbre de ....

woo [wuː] *vtr lit* (*court*) cortejar; *fig* intentar congraciarse con.

wood [wʊd] *n* **1** (*forest*) bosque *m*. **2** (*material*) madera *f*; (*for fire*) leña *f*; *fam fig* **touch w.!**, ¡toca madera! **3** *Golf* palo *m* de madera. **4** (*bowling*) bola *f*.

woodcarving ['wʊdkɑːvɪŋ] *n* **1** (*craft*) tallado *m* en madera. **2** (*object*) talla *f* en madera.

woodcutter ['wʊdkʌtəʳ] *n* leñador,-a *m,f*.

wooded ['wʊdɪd] *adj* arbolado,-a.

wooden ['wʊdən] *adj* **1** de madera; **w. spoon/leg**, cuchara *f*/pata *f* de palo. **2** *fig* rígido,-a; (*acting*) sin expresión.

woodlouse ['wʊdlaʊs] *n* cochinilla *f*.

woodpecker ['wʊdpekəʳ] *n* pájaro carpintero.

woodwind ['wʊdwɪnd] *n* **w.** (**instruments**), instrumentos *mpl* de viento de madera.

woodwork ['wʊdwɜːk] *n* **1** (*craft*) carpintería *f*. **2** (*of building*) maderaje *m*.

woodworm ['wʊdwɜːm] *n* carcoma *f*.

wool [wʊl] **I** *n* lana *f*; *fig* **to pull the w. over sb's eyes**, dar gato por liebre a algn. **II** *adj* de lana.

woollen, *US* **woolen** ['wʊlən] **I** *adj* **1** de

lana. **2** (*industry*) lanero,-a. **II** *npl* **woollens**, géneros *mpl* de lana *or* de punto.

woolly, *US* **wooly** ['wʊlɪ] *adj* (**woollier, woolliest**, *US* **woolier, wooliest**) **1** (*made of wool*) de lana. **2** *fig* (*unclear*) confuso, -a.

word [wɜːd] **I** *n* **1** (*spoken, written*) palabra *f*; **in other words ...**, es decir ..., o sea ...; **words failed me**, me quedé sin habla; *fig* **a w. of advice**, un consejo; *fig* **I'd like a w. with you**, quiero hablar contigo un momento; *fig* **she didn't say it in so many words**, no lo dijo de modo tan explícito; **in the words of the poet ...**, como dice el poeta ...; *fig* **w. for w.**, palabra por palabra; **w. processing**, procesamiento *m* de textos; **w. processor**, procesador *m* de textos. **2** *fig* (*message*) mensaje *m*; **by w. of mouth**, de palabra; **is there any w. from him?**, ¿hay noticias de él?; **to send w.**, mandar recado. **3** *fig* (*rumour*) voz *f*, rumor *m*. **4** *fig* (*promise*) palabra *f*; **he's a man of his w.**, es hombre de palabra. **II** *vtr* (*express*) formular; **a badly worded letter**, una carta mal redactada.

wording ['wɜːdɪŋ] *n* expresión *f*; **I changed the w. slightly**, cambié algunas palabras.

word-perfect [wɜːd'pɜːfekt] *adj* **to be w.-p.**, saberse el papel perfectamente.

wore [wɔːʳ] *pt* → **wear**.

work [wɜːk] **I** *n* **1** trabajo *m*; **his w. in the field of physics**, su labor en el campo de la física; **it's hard w.**, cuesta trabajo. **2** (*employment*) trabajo *m*, empleo *m*; **out of w.**, parado,-a. **3** (*action*) obra *f*, acción *f*; **keep up the good w.!**, ¡que siga así! **4 a piece of w.**, un trabajo; **a w. of art**, una obra de arte. **5 works**, obras *fpl*; **public works**, obras (públicas). **6 works**, (*machinery*) mecanismo *m sing*. **7** *GB* **works**, (*factory*) fábrica *f*.
II *vtr* **1** (*drive*) hacer trabajar; **to w. one's way up/down**, subir/bajar a duras penas; *fig* **to w. one's way up in a firm**, trabajarse el ascenso en una empresa. **2** (*machine*) manejar; (*mechanism*) accionar. **3** (*miracles, changes*) operar, hacer. **4** (*land*) cultivar; (*mine*) explotar. **5** (*wood, metal etc*) trabajar.
III *vi* **1** trabajar (**on, at**; en); **to w. as a gardener**, trabajar de jardinero. **2** (*machine*) funcionar; **it works on gas**, funciona con gas. **3** (*drug*) surtir efecto; (*system*) funcionar bien; (*plan, trick*) salir bien. **4** (*operate*) obrar; **to w. loose**, soltarse; **we have no data to w. on**, no tenemos datos en que basarnos.
◆**work off** *vtr* (*fat*) eliminar trabajando; (*anger*) desahogar. ◆**work out I** *vtr* **1** (*plan*) idear; (*itinerary*) planear; (*details*) desarrollar. **2** (*problem*) solucionar; (*solu-*

tion) encontrar; *(amount)* calcular; **I can't w. out how he did it**, no me explico cómo lo hizo. **II** *vi* **1 things didn't w. out for her**, las cosas no le salieron bien. **2 it works out at 5 each**, sale a 5 cada uno. **3** *Sport* hacer ejercicio. ◆**work through** *vi* penetrar (**to**, hasta). ◆**work up** *vtr* (*excite*) aclarar; **to get worked up**, excitarse; **to w. up enthusiasm**, entusiasmarse (**for**, con).

workable ['wɜːkəbəl] *adj* factible.

workaholic [wɜːkə'hɒlɪk] *n* *fam* trabajoadicto,-a.

workbench ['wɜːkbentʃ] *n* obrador *m*.

worker ['wɜːkər] *n* trabajador,-a *m,f*; *(manual)* obrero,-a *m,f*.

workforce ['wɜːkfɔːs] *n* mano *f* de obra.

working ['wɜːkɪŋ] **I** *adj* **1** *(population, capital)* activo,-a; **w. class**, clase obrera; **w. man**, obrero *m*. **2** *(clothes, conditions, hours)* de trabajo; **w. day**, día *m* laborable; *(number of hours)* jornada *f* laboral. **3 it is in w. order**, funciona. **4** *(majority)* suficiente; **w. knowledge**, conocimientos básicos. **II** *n* **workings**, *(mechanics)* funcionamiento *m sing*; *Min* explotación *f sing*.

workman ['wɜːkmən] *n* (manuel) obrero *m*.

workmanship ['wɜːkmənʃɪp] *n* *(appearance)* acabado *m*; *(skill)* habilidad *f*, arte *m* **a fine piece of w.**, un trabajo excelente.

workmate ['wɜːkmeɪt] *n* compañero,-a *m,f* de trabajo.

work-out ['wɜːkaʊt] *n* entrenamiento *m*.

worksheet ['wɜːkʃiːt] *n* plan *m* de trabajo.

workshop ['wɜːkʃɒp] *n* taller *m*.

worktop ['wɜːktɒp] *n* encimera *f*.

work-to-rule [wɜːktə'ruːl] *n* huelga *f* de celo.

world [wɜːld] *n* mundo *m*; **all over the w.**, en todo el mundo; **the best in the w.**, el mejor del mundo; *fig* **there is a w. of difference between A and B**, hay un mundo de diferencia entre A y B; *fig* **to feel on top of the w.**, sentirse fenomenal; *fig* **to think the w. of sb**, adorar a algn; *fam* **fig it is out of this w.**, es una maravilla; **the W. Bank**, el Banco Mundial; *Ftb* **the W. Cup**, los Mundiales; **w. record**, récord *m* mundial; **w. war**, guerra *f* mundial.

world-class ['wɜːldklɑːs] *adj* de categoría mundial.

world-famous ['wɜːldfeɪməs] *adj* de fama mundial.

worldly ['wɜːldlɪ] *adj* mundano,-a.

worldwide ['wɜːldwaɪd] *adj* mundial.

worm [wɜːm] **I** *n* **1** gusano *m*; *(earth)* **w.**, lombriz *f*. **2** *Med* **worms**, lombrices *fpl*. **II** *vtr* **to w. a secret out of sb**, sonsacarle un secreto a algn.

worn [wɔːn] *adj* gastado,-a, usado,-a.

worn-out ['wɔːnaʊt] *adj* *(thing)* gastado, -a; *(person)* rendido,-a, agotado,-a.

worried ['wʌrɪd] *adj* inquieto,-a, preocupado,-a.

worry ['wʌrɪ] **I** *vtr* **1** preocupar, inquietar; **it doesn't w. me**, me trae sin cuidado. **2** *(pester)* molestar. **II** *vi* preocuparse *(about, por)*; **don't w.**, no te preocupes. **III** *n* *(state)* inquietud *f*; *(cause)* preocupación *f*.

worrying ['wʌrɪɪŋ] *adj* inquietante, preocupante.

worse [wɜːs] **I** *adj* *(comp of bad)* peor; **he gets w. and w.**, va de mal en peor; **to get w.**, empeorar; *fam* **w. luck!**, ¡mala suerte! **II** *n* **a change for the w.**, un empeoramiento; *fig* **to take a turn for the w.**, empeorar. **III** *adv* *(comp of badly)* peor; **w. than ever**, peor que nunca.

worship ['wɜːʃɪp] **I** *vtr* adorar. **II** *n* **1** adoración *f*. **2** *(ceremony)* culto *m*. **3** *GB* **his W. the Mayor**, el señor alcalde; *Jur* **your W.**, señoría.

worshipper ['wɜːʃɪpər] *n* devoto,-a *m,f*.

worst [wɜːst] **I** *adj* *(superl of bad)* peor; **the w. part about it is that ...**, lo peor es que .... **II** *n* **1** *(person)* el *o* la peor, los *o* las peores. **2 the w. of the storm is over**, ya ha pasado lo peor de la tormenta. **III** *adv* *(superl of badly)* peor; *fig* **to come off w.**, salir perdiendo.

worth [wɜːθ] **I** *adj* **1 to be w. £3**, valer 3 libras; **a house w. £50,000**, una casa que vale 50.000 libras. **2** *(deserving of)* merecedor,-a de; **a book w. reading**, un libro que merece la pena leer; **for what it's w.**, por si sirve de algo; **it's w. your while**, it's w. it, vale *o* merece la pena; **it's w. mentioning**, es digno de mención. **II** *n* **1** *(in money)* valor *m*; **five pounds' w. of petrol**, gasolina por valor de 5 libras. **2** *(of person)* valía *f*.

worthless ['wɜːθlɪs] *adj* sin valor; *(person)* despreciable.

worthwhile [wɜːθ'waɪl] *adj* valioso,-a, que vale la pena.

worthy ['wɜːðɪ] *adj* **(worthier, worthiest) 1** *(deserving)* digno,-a *(of, de)*; *(winner, cause)* justo,-a. **2** *(citizen)* respetable; *(effort, motives, action)* loable.

would [wʊd, *unstressed* wəd] *v aux* **1** *(conditional)* **I w. go if I had time**, iría si tuviera tiempo; **he w. have won but for that**, habría ganado si no hubiera sido por eso; **we w. if we could**, lo haríamos si pudiéramos; **you would have to choose me!**, ¡tenías que elegirme precisamente a mí! **2** *(reported speech)* **he said that he w. come**, dijo que vendría. **3** *(willingness)* **the car wouldn't start**, el coche no arrancaba; **they asked him to come but he wouldn't**, le invitaron a venir pero no quiso; **w. you do me a fa-**

vour?, ¿quiere hacerme un favor? **4** (wishing) **we w. like to know why**, quisiera saber por qué; **I'd rather go home**, preferiría ir a casa; **w. you take a cigarette?**, ¿quiere un cigarrillo? **5** (custom) **we w. go for walks**, solíamos dar un paseo. **6 try as I w.**, por mucho que lo intentara. **7** (conjecture) **it w. have been about three weeks ago**, debe haber sido hace unas tres semanas; **w. this be your cousin?**, ¿será éste tu primo? **8** (expectation) **so it w. appear**, según parece.

would-be ['wʊdbiː] adj en potencia; a w.-be **politician**, un aspirante a político; pej a w.-be **poet**, un supuesto poeta.

wound¹ [waʊnd] pt & pp → **wind²**.

wound² [wuːnd] **I** n herida f. **II** vtr herir.

wove [wəʊv] pt → **weave**.

woven ['wəʊvən] pp → **weave**.

wow [waʊ] fam **I** vtr encandilar. **II** interj ¡caramba!

WP 1 abbr of **word processing. 2** abbr of **word processor**.

wrangle ['ræŋgəl] **I** n disputa f. **II** vi disputar (**over**, acerca de, por).

wrap [ræp] **I** vtr **1 to w. (up)**, envolver; **he wrapped his arms around her**, la estrechó entre sus brazos; fam **we wrapped up the deal**, concluimos el negocio. **II** vi fam **w. up well**, abrígate. **III** n (shawl) chal m; (cape) capa f.

wrapper ['ræpə'] n (of sweet) envoltorio m; (of book) sobrecubierta f.

wrapping ['ræpiŋ] n **w. paper**, papel m de envolver.

wreath [riːθ] n (pl **wreaths** [riːðz, riːθs]) (of flowers) corona f; **laurel w.**, corona de laurel.

wreck [rek] **I** n **1** Naut naufragio m; (ship) barco naufragado. **2** (of car, plane) restos mpl; (of building) ruinas fpl. **3** fig (person) ruina f. **II** vtr **1** (ship) hacer naufragar. **2** (car, machine) destrozar. **3** fig (health, life) arruinar; (plans, hopes) desbaratar; (chances) echar a perder.

wreckage ['rekidʒ] n (of ship, car, plane) restos mpl; (of building) ruinas fpl.

wren [ren] n chochín m.

wrench [rentʃ] **I** n **1** (pull) tirón m. **2** Med torcedura f. **3** (tool) GB llave inglesa; US llave. **II** vtr **to w. oneself free**, soltarse de un tirón; **to w. sth off sb**, arrebatarle algo a algn; **to w. sth off/open**, quitar/abrir algo de un tirón.

wrestle ['resəl] vi luchar.

wrestler ['reslə'] n luchador,-a m,f.

wrestling ['reslɪŋ] n lucha f.

wretch [retʃ] n (poor) **w.**, desgraciado,-a m,f.

wretched ['retʃɪd] adj **1** desdichado,-a; (conditions) deplorable; fam (bad, poor) horrible. **2 I feel w.**, (ill) me siento fatal. **3** (contemptible) despreciable. **4** fam

(damned) maldito,-a, condenado,-a.

wriggle ['rɪgəl] **I** vtr menear. **II** vi **to w.** (**about**), (worm) serpentear; (restless child) moverse nerviosamente; **to w. free**, escapar deslizándose.

wring [rɪŋ] vtr (pt & pp **wrung**) **1** (clothes) escurrir; (hands) retorcer. **2** fig (extract) arrancar, sacar.

wringing ['rɪŋɪŋ] adj **to be w. wet**, estar empapado,-a.

wrinkle ['rɪŋkəl] **I** n arruga f. **II** vtr arrugar. **III** vi arrugarse.

wrist [rɪst] n muñeca f.

wristwatch ['rɪstwɒtʃ] n reloj m de pulsera.

writ [rɪt] n orden f judicial.

write [raɪt] **I** vtr (pt **wrote**; pp **written**) escribir; (article) redactar; (cheque) extender. **II** vi escribir (**about**, sobre); **to w. for a paper**, colaborar en un periódico. ◆**write back** vi contestar. ◆**write down** vtr poner por escrito; (note) apuntar. ◆**write in** vi escribir. ◆**write off** **I** vtr (debt) condonar; (car) destrozar. **II** vi **to w. off for sth**, pedir algo por escrito. ◆**write out** vtr (cheque, recipe) extender. ◆**write up** vtr (notes) redactar; (diary, journal) poner al día.

write-off ['raɪtɒf] n **the car's a w.-o.**, el coche está hecho una ruina.

writer ['raɪtə'] n (by profession) escritor,-a m,f; (of book, article) autor,-a m,f.

writhe [raɪð] vi retorcerse.

writing ['raɪtɪŋ] n **1** (script) escritura f; (handwriting) letra f; **in w.**, por escrito. **2** writings, escritos mpl. **3** (action) escritura f; **w. desk**, escritorio m.

written ['rɪtən] pp → **write**.

wrong [rɒŋ] **I** adj **1** (person) equivocado,-a; **I was w. about that boy**, me equivoqué con ese chico; **to be w.**, no tener razón; **you're w. in thinking that ...**, te equivocas si piensas que .... **2** (answer, way) incorrecto,-a, equivocado,-a; **my watch is w.**, mi reloj anda mal; **to drive on the w. side of the road**, conducir por el lado contrario de la carretera; **to go the w. way**, equivocarse de camino; Tel **I've got the w. number**, me he confundido de número. **3** (unsuitable) impropio,-a inadecuado,-a; (time) inoportuno,-a; **to say the w. thing**, decir algo inoportuno. **4** (immoral etc) malo,-a; **there's nothing w. in that**, no hay nada malo en ello; **what's w. with smoking?**, ¿qué tiene de malo fumar? **5 is anything w.?**, ¿pasa algo?; **something's w.**, hay algo que no está bien; **what's w.?**, ¿qué pasa?; **what's w. with you?**, ¿qué te pasa? **II** adv mal, incorrectamente; **to get it w.**, equivocarse; Tel **to go w.**, (plan) fallar, salir mal. **III** n **1** (evil, bad action) mal m; **you did w. to hit him**, hiciste mal en pegarle. **2**

(injustice) injusticia *f; (offence)* agravio *m;* **the rights and wrongs of a matter,** lo justo y lo injusto de un asunto. **3 to be in the w.,** *(to blame)* tener la culpa. **IV** *vtr (treat unfairly)* ser injusto,-a con; *(offend)* agraviar.
◆**wrongly** *adv* 1 *(incorrectly)* incorrectamente. 2 *(mistakenly)* equivocadamente. 3

(unjustly) injustamente.
wrongdoing ['rɒŋduːɪŋ] *n* maldad *f.*
wrongful ['rɒŋful] *adj* injusto,-a.
wrote [rəʊt] *pt* → **write.**
wrung [rʌŋ] *pt & pp* → **wring.**
wry [raɪ] *adj (wrier, wriest or wryer, wryest)* sardónico,-a.

X

X, x [eks] *n (the letter)* X, x *f.*
xenophobia [zenə'fəʊbɪə] *n* xenofobia *f.*
xenophobic [zenə'fəʊbɪk] *adj* xenófobo, -a.
Xerox® ['zɪərɒks] **I** *n* xerocopia *f.* **II** *vtr* xerocopiar.
Xmas ['eksməs, 'krɪsməs] *n abbr of*

Christmas.
X-ray [eks'reɪ] **I** *n (beam)* rayo *m* X; **X-r. therapy,** radioterapia *f.* **2** *(picture)* radiografía *f;* **to have an X-r.,** hacerse una radiografía. **II** *vtr* radiografiar.
xylophone ['zaɪləfəʊn] *n* xilófono *m.*

Y

Y, y [waɪ] *n (the letter)* Y, y *f.*
yacht [jɒt] *n* yate *m;* **y. club,** club náutico.
yachting ['jɒtɪŋ] *n Sport* navegación *f* a vela; *(competition)* regatas *fpl.*
yachtsman ['jɒtsmən] *n* balandrista *m.*
yachtswoman ['jɒtswʊmən] *n* balandrista *f.*
yam [jæm] *n* 1 ñame *m.* 2 *US (sweet potato)* boniato *m.*
yank [jæŋk] *fam vtr* tirar; *(tooth)* arrancar.
Yank [jæŋk] *n GB pej* yanqui *mf.*
Yankee ['jæŋkɪ] *adj & n pej* yanqui *mf.*
yap [jæp] *vi (dog)* aullar; *fam (person)* darle al pico.
yard¹ [jɑːd] *n (measure)* yarda *f (aprox* 0.914 metros).
yard² [jɑːd] *n* 1 patio *m;* US jardín *m.*
yardstick ['jɑːdstɪk] *n fig* criterio *m,* norma *f.*
yarn [jɑːn] *n* 1 *Sew* hilo *m.* 2 *(story)* historia *f,* cuento *m;* **to spin a y.,** *(lie)* inventarse una historia.
yawn [jɔːn] **I** *vi* bostezar. **II** *n* bostezo *m.*
yawning ['jɔːnɪŋ] *adj (gap)* profundo,-a.
yd *(pl yds) abbr of* yard.
yeah [jeə] *adv fam* sí.
year [jɪər] *n* 1 año *m;* **all y. round,** durante todo el año; **last y.,** el año pasado; **next y.,** el año que viene; **y. in, y. out,** año tras año; **I'm ten years old,** tengo diez años. 2 *Educ* curso *m;* **first-y. student,** estudiante *mf* de primero.
yearly ['jɪəlɪ] **I** *adj* anual. **II** *adv* anualmente, cada año.
yearn [jɜːn] *vi* **to y. for sth,** anhelar algo.
yearning ['jɜːnɪŋ] *n* anhelo *m* (**for,** de).
yeast [jiːst] *n* levadura *f.*
yell [jel] **I** *vi* gritar. **II** *n* grito *m,* alarido

m.
yellow ['jeləʊ] **I** *adj* amarillo,-a; *fam fig (cowardly)* cobarde; *Tel* **y. pages,** páginas amarillas. **II** *n* amarillo *m.*
yelp [jelp] **I** *vi* aullar. **II** *n* aullido *m.*
yen [jen] *n* 1 *(currency)* yen *m.* 2 **to have a y. for sth,** tener ganas de algo.
yeoman ['jəʊmən] *n GB* **Y. of the Guard,** alabardero *m* de la Casa Real británica.
yes [jes] **I** *adv* sí; **you said y.,** dijiste que sí. **II** *n* sí *m.*
yesterday ['jestədeɪ] *adv & n* ayer *m;* **the day before y.,** anteayer; **y. morning,** ayer por la mañana.
yet [jet] **I** *adv* 1 **not y.,** aún no, todavía no; **as y.,** hasta ahora; **I haven't eaten y.,** no he comido todavía. 2 *(in questions)* ya; **has he arrived y.?,** ¿ha venido ya? 3 *(even)* más; **y. again,** otra vez; **y. more,** todavía más. 4 *(eventually)* todavía, aún; **he'll win y.,** todavía puede ganar. **II** *conj* sin embargo.
yew [juː] *n* tejo *m.*
yield [jiːld] **I** *n* 1 rendimiento *m.* 2 *Agr* cosecha *f.* 3 *Fin* beneficio *m.* **II** *vtr* producir; *Agr* dar; *(money)* producir. **III** *vi* 1 *(surrender, break)* ceder. 2 *Aut* ceder el paso.
YMCA [waɪemsiː'eɪ] *abbr of* Young Men's Christian Association, albergue *m* para hombres jóvenes.
yob(bo) ['jɒb(əʊ)] *n fam* gamberro,-a *m,f.*
yoga ['jəʊɡə] *n* yoga *m.*
yog(h)urt ['jɒɡət] *n* yogur *m.*
yoke [jəʊk] **I** *n* yugo *m.* **II** *vtr (oxen)* uncir; *fig* unir.
yokel ['jəʊkəl] *n pej* paleto,-a *m,f.*
yolk [jəʊk] *n* yema *f.*

yonder ['jɒndəʳ] *adv* más allá.

you [juː, *unstressed* ju] *pers pron* 1 *(subject)* *(familiar use)* *(sing)* tú; *(pl)* vosotros,-as; **how are y?**, ¿cómo estás?, ¿cómo estáis? 2 *(subject)* *(polite use)* *(sing)* usted; *(pl)* ustedes; **how are y?**, ¿cómo está?, ¿cómo están? 3 *(subject)* *(impers use)* y. **never know**, nunca se sabe. 4 *(object)* *(familiar use)* *(sing)* *(before verb)* te; *(after preposition)* ti; *(pl)* *(before verb)* os; *(after preposition)* vosotros,-as; **I saw y.**, te vi, os vi; **it's for y.**, es para ti, es para vosotros,-as; **with you**, contigo, con vosotros,-as. 5 *(object)* *(polite use)* *(sing)* *(before verb)* le; *(after preposition)* usted; *(pl)* *(before verb)* les; *(after preposition)* ustedes; **I saw y.**, le vi, les vi; **it's for y.**, es para usted, es para ustedes; **with you**, con usted, con ustedes. 6 *(object)* *(impers use)* **alcohol makes you drunk**, el alcohol emborracha.

young [jʌŋ] I *adj* 1 *(age)* joven; *(brother etc)* pequeño,-a; **y. lady**, señorita *f*; **y. man**, joven *m*. II *n* 1 *(people)* **the y.**, los jóvenes, la juventud. 2 *(animals)* crías *fpl*.

youngster ['jʌŋstəʳ] *n* muchacho,-a *m,f*.

your [jɔːʳ, *unstressed* jə] *poss adj* 1 *(familiar use)* *(sing)* tu, tus; *(pl)* vuestro,-a, vuestros,-as. 2 *(polite use)* su, sus. 3 *(impers use)* **the house is on y. right**, la casa queda a la derecha; **they clean y. shoes for you**, te limpian los zapatos. 4 *(formal address)* Su; **Y. Majesty**, Su Majestad.

yours [jɔːz] *poss pron* 1 *(familiar use)* *(sing)* el tuyo, la tuya, los tuyos, las tuyas; *(pl)* el vuestro, la vuestra, los vuestros, las vuestras; **the house is y.**, la casa es tuya. 2 *(polite use)* *(sing)* el suyo, la suya; *(pl)* los suyos, las suyas; **the house is y.**, la casa es suya. 3 *(in letters)* **yours faithfully**, le(s) saluda atentamente; **y. sincerely**, reciba un cordial saludo de.

yourself [jɔː'self, *unstressed* jə'self] *(pl* **yourselves** [jɔː'selvz] *) pers pron* 1 *(familiar use)* *(sing)* tú mismo,-a; *(pl)* vosotros,-as mismos,-as; **by y.**, *(tú)* solo,-a; **by yourselves**, vosotros,-as solos,-as. 2 *(polite use)* *(sing)* usted mismo,-a; *(pl)* ustedes mismos,-as; **by y.**, *(usted)* solo,-a; **by yourselves**, *(ustedes)* solos,-as. 3 *reflexive pron* 1 *(familiar use)* *(sing)* te; *pl (familiar use)* os; **enjoy y.**, ¡diviértete!; **enjoy yourselves**, ¡divertíos! 2 *(polite use)* se; **enjoy y.**, ¡diviértase!; **enjoy yourselves**, ¡diviértanse!

youth [juːθ] *n* 1 juventud *f*. 2 *(young man)* joven *m*; **y. club**, club *m* juvenil; **y. hostel**, albergue *m* juvenil.

youthful ['juːθfʊl] *adj* juvenil, joven.

Yugoslav ['juːgəʊslɑːv] *adj & n* yugoslavo,-a *(m,f)*.

Yugoslavia [juːgəʊ'slɑːvɪə] *n* Yugoslavia.

Yugoslavian [juːgəʊ'slɑːvɪən] *adj & n* yugoslavo,-a *(m,f)*.

YWCA [waɪdʌbəljuːsiː'eɪ] *abbr of* **Young Women's Christian Association**, albergue *m* para mujeres jóvenes.

Z

Z, z [zed, *US* ziː] *n (the letter)* Z, z *f*.

zany ['zeɪnɪ] *adj* **(zanier, zaniest)** *fam* 1 *(mad)* chiflado,-a. 2 *(eccentric)* estrafalario,-a.

zap [zæp] I *interj* ¡zas! II *vtr sl* 1 *(hit)* pegar. 2 *fam (kill)* cargarse a. III *vi* TV hacer zapping.

zeal [ziːl] *n (enthusiasm)* entusiasmo *m*.

zealous ['zeləs] *adj (enthusiasm)* entusiasta.

zebra ['ziːbrə, 'zebrə] *n* cebra *f*; GB **z. crossing**, paso *m* de peatones.

zenith ['zenɪθ] *n Astron* cenit *m*; *fig* apogeo *m*.

zero ['zɪərəʊ] *n* cero *m*; **z. hour**, hora *f* cero.

zest [zest] *n (eagerness)* entusiasmo *m*.

zigzag ['zɪgzæg] I *n* zigzag *m*. II *vi* zigzaguear.

Zimbabwe [zɪm'bɑːbweɪ] *n* Zimbabue.

zinc [zɪŋk] *n* cinc *m*, zinc *m*.

zip [zɪp] I *n* 1 **z. (fastener)**, cremallera *f*. 2 *fam* brío *m*; *US* **z. code**, código *m* postal. II *vi* cerrarse con cremallera. ◆**zip by** *vi* pasar como un rayo. ◆**zip up** *vtr* cerrar con cremallera; **to z. sb up**, cerrar la cremallera a algn.

zipper ['zɪpəʳ] *n US* cremallera *f*.

zodiac ['zəʊdɪæk] *n* zodiaco *m*, zodíaco *m*.

zombie ['zɒmbɪ] *n* zombie *mf*.

zone [zəʊn] I *n* zona *f*. II *vtr* dividir en zonas.

zoo [zuː] *n* zoo *m*.

zoological [zəʊə'lɒdʒɪkəl] *adj* zoológico,-a.

zoologist [zəʊ'ɒlədʒɪst] *n* zoólogo,-a *m,f*.

zoology [zəʊ'ɒlədʒɪ] *n* zoología *f*.

zoom [zuːm] I *n* 1 *(buzz)* zumbido *m*. 2 **z. lens**, zoom *m*, teleobjetivo *m*. II *vi* 1 *(buzz)* zumbar. 2 **to z. past**, pasar volando. ◆**zoom in** *vi (camera)* acercarse rápidamente.

zucchini [zuː'kiːnɪ] *n US* calabacín *m*.

Zulu ['zuːluː] *adj & n* zulú *(mf)*.